Peterson's
Two-Year
Colleges
2006

THOMSON

PETERSON'S

Australia • Canada • Mexico • Singapore • Spain • United Kingdom • United States

About Thomson Peterson's

Thomson Peterson's (www.petersons.com) is a leading provider of education information and advice, with books and online resources focusing on education search, test preparation, and financial aid. Its Web site offers searchable databases and interactive tools for contacting educational institutions, online practice tests and instruction, and planning tools for securing financial aid. Thomson Peterson's serves 110 million education consumers annually.

For more information, contact Thomson Peterson's, 2000 Lenox Drive, Lawrenceville, NJ 08648; 800-338-3282; or find us on the World Wide Web at www.petersons.com/about.

Editor: Fern A. Oram; Production Editor: Bernadette Webster; Copy Editors: Bret Bollmann, Jim Colbert, Michael Haines, Sally Ross, Jill C. Schwartz, Mark D. Snider, Pam Sullivan, and Valerie Bolus Vaughan; Research Project Manager: Daniel Margolin; Research Associates: Mary Meyer-Penniston and Amy L. Weber; Programmers: Phyllis Johnson and Alex Lin; Manufacturing Manager: Ivona Skibicki; Composition Manager: Linda M. Williams; Client Relations Representatives: Mimi Kaufman, Karen Mount, Mary Ann Murphy, Jim Swinarski, and Eric Wallace; Contributing Editors: Kitty M. Villa and Richard Woodland.

ISSN 0894-9328
ISBN 0-7689-1750-6

Printed in the United States of America

10 9 8 7 6 5 4 3 2 1   07 06 05

Thirty-sixth Edition

Contents

APPENDIX

A Note from the Peterson's Editors

For more than 35 years, Thomson Peterson's has given students and parents the most comprehensive, up-to-date information on undergraduate institutions in the United States. Thomson Peterson's researches the data published in *Peterson's Two-Year Colleges* each year. The information is furnished by the colleges and is accurate at the time of publishing.

This guide also features advice and tips on the college search and selection process, such as how to decide if a two-year college is right for you, how to approach transferring between colleges, and what's in store for adults returning to college. If you seem to be getting more, not less, anxious about choosing and getting into the right college, *Peterson's Two-Year Colleges* provides just the right help, giving you the information you need to make important college decisions and ace the admission process.

Opportunities abound for students, and this guide can help you find what you want in a number of ways:

- In "What You Need to Know About Two-Year Colleges," David R. Pierce, former President of the American Association of Community Colleges, outlines the basic features and advantages of two-year colleges. "Surviving Standardized Tests" gives an overview of the common examinations students take prior to attending college. "Who's Paying for This? Financial Aid Basics" provides guidelines for financing your college education. "Frequently Asked Questions About Transferring" takes a look at the two-year college scene from the perspective of a student who is looking toward the day when he or she may pursue additional education at a four-year institution. "Returning to School: Advice for Adult Students" is an analysis of the pros and cons (mostly pros) of returning to college after already having begun a professional career. "What International Students Need to Know About Admission to U.S. Colleges" is an article written particularly for students overseas who are considering a U.S. college education. "Searching for Two-Year Colleges Online" outlines why you'll want to visit Petersons.com for even more college search and selection resources. Finally, "How to Use This Guide" gives details on the data in this guide: what terms mean and why they're here.

- If you already have specifics in mind, such as a particular institution or major, turn to the easy-to-use **Quick-Reference Chart** or **Indexes.** You can look up a particular feature—location and programs offered—or use the alphabetical index and immediately find the colleges that meet your criteria.

- For information about particular colleges, turn to the **Profiles of Two-Year Colleges** section. Here, our comprehensive college descriptions are arranged alphabetically by state. They provide a complete picture of need-to-know information about every accredited two-year college—from admission to graduation, including expenses, financial aid, majors, and campus safety. All the information you need to apply is placed together at the conclusion of each college profile. In addition, for nearly 100 colleges, two-page narrative descriptions appear in the **In-Depth Descriptions of Two-Year Colleges** section, in the back of the book. These descriptions are paid for and written by college officials and offer great detail about each college. They are edited to provide a consistent format across entries for your ease of comparison.

Thomson Peterson's publishes a full line of resources to help you and your family with any information you need to guide you through the admissions process. Peterson's publications can be found at your local bookstore, library, and high school guidance office—or visit us on the Web at www.petersons.com.

Colleges will be pleased to know that Thomson Peterson's helped you in your selection. Admissions staff members are more than happy to answer questions, address specific problems and help in any way they can. The editors at Thomson Peterson's wish you great success in your college search.

The College Admissions Process:

An overview

What You Need to Know About Two-Year Colleges

David R. Pierce

Two-year colleges—better known as community colleges—are often called "the people's colleges." With their open-door policies (admission is open to individuals with a high school diploma or its equivalent), community colleges provide access to higher education for millions of Americans who might otherwise be excluded from higher education. Community college students are diverse, of all ages, races, and economic backgrounds. While many community college students enroll full-time, an equally large number attend on a part-time basis so they can fulfill employment and family commitments as they advance their education.

Community colleges can also be referred to as either technical or junior colleges, and they may either be under public or independent control. What unites these two-year colleges is that they are regionally accredited, postsecondary institutions, whose highest credential awarded is the associate degree. With few exceptions, community colleges offer a comprehensive curriculum, which includes transfer, technical, and continuing education programs.

IMPORTANT FACTORS IN A COMMUNITY COLLEGE EDUCATION

The student who attends a community college can count on receiving high-quality instruction in a supportive learning community. This setting frees the student to pursue his or her own goals, nurture special talents, explore new fields of learning, and develop the capacity for lifelong learning.

From the student's perspective, four characteristics capture the essence of community colleges:

- They are community-based institutions that work in close partnership with high schools, community groups, and employers in extending high-quality programs at convenient times and places.
- Community colleges are cost effective. Annual tuition and fees at public community colleges average approximately half those at public four-year colleges and less than 15 percent of private four-year institutions. In addition, since most community colleges are generally close to their students' homes, these students can also save a

significant amount of money on the room, board, and transportation expenses traditionally associated with a college education.

- They provide a caring environment, with faculty members who are expert instructors, known for excellent teaching and for meeting students at the point of their individual needs, regardless of age, sex, race, current job status, or previous academic preparation. Community colleges join a strong curriculum with a broad range of counseling and career services that are intended to assist students in making the most of their educational opportunities.
- Many offer comprehensive programs, including transfer curricula in such liberal arts programs as chemistry, psychology, and business management, that lead directly to a baccalaureate degree and career programs that prepare students for employment or assist those already employed in upgrading their skills. For those students who need to strengthen their academic skills, community colleges also offer a wide range of developmental programs in mathematics, languages, and learning skills, designed to prepare the student for success in college studies.

GETTING TO KNOW YOUR TWO-YEAR COLLEGE

The first step in determining the quality of a community college is to check the status of its accreditation. Once you have established that a community college is appropriately accredited, find out as much as you can about the programs and services it has to offer. Much of that information can be found in materials the college provides. However, the best way to learn about a college is to visit in person.

During a campus visit, be prepared to ask a lot of questions. Talk to students, faculty members, administrators, and counselors about the college and its programs, particularly those in which you have a special interest. Ask about available certificates and associate degrees. Don't be shy. Do what you can to dig below the surface. Ask college officials about the transfer rate to four-year colleges. If a college emphasizes student services, find out what particular assistance is offered, such as educational or career guidance. Colleges are eager to provide you with the information you need to make informed decisions.

COMMUNITY COLLEGES CAN SAVE YOU MONEY

If you are able to live at home while you attend college, you will certainly save money on room and board, but it does cost something to commute. Many two-year colleges offer you instruction in your own home through cable television or public broadcast stations or through home study courses that can save both time and money. Look into all the options, and be sure to add up all the costs of attending various colleges before deciding which is best for you.

FINANCIAL AID

Many students who attend community colleges are eligible for a range of financial aid programs, including Federal Pell Grants, Perkins and Stafford Loans, state aid, and on-campus jobs. Your high school counselor or the financial aid officer at a community college will also be able to help you. It is in your interest to apply for financial aid months in advance of the date you intend to start your college program, so find out early what assistance is available to you. While many community colleges are able to help students who make a last-minute decision to attend college, either through short-term loans or emergency grants, if you are considering entering college and think you might need financial aid, it is best to find out as much as you can as early as you can.

WORKING AND GOING TO SCHOOL

Many two-year college students maintain full-time or part-time employment while they earn their degrees. Over the years, a steadily growing number of students have chosen to attend community colleges while they fulfill family and employment responsibilities. To enable these students to balance the demands of home, work, and school, most community colleges offer classes at night and on weekends.

For the full-time student, the usual length of time it takes to obtain an associate degree is two years. However, your length of study will depend on the course load you take: the fewer credits you earn each term, the longer it will take you to earn a degree. To assist you in moving more quickly to your degree, many community colleges now award credit through examination or for equivalent knowledge gained through relevant life experiences. Be certain to find out the credit options that are available to

you at the college in which you are interested. You may discover that it will take less time to earn a degree than you first thought.

PREPARATION FOR TRANSFER

Studies have repeatedly shown that students who first attend a community college and then transfer to a four-year college or university do at least as well academically as the students who entered the four-year institutions as freshmen. Most community colleges have agreements with nearby four-year institutions to make transfer of credits easier. If you are thinking of transferring, be sure to meet with a counselor or faculty adviser before choosing your courses. You will want to map out a course of study with transfer in mind. Make sure you also find out the credit-transfer requirements of the four-year institution you might want to attend.

ATTENDING A TWO-YEAR COLLEGE IN ANOTHER REGION

Although many community colleges serve a specific county or district, they are committed (to the extent of their ability) to the goal of equal educational opportunity without regard to economic status, race, creed, color, sex, or national origin. Independent two-year colleges recruit from a much broader geographical area—throughout the United States and, increasingly, around the world.

Although some community colleges do provide on-campus housing for their students, most do not. However, even if on-campus housing is not available, most colleges do have housing referral services.

NEW CAREER OPPORTUNITIES

Community colleges realize that many entering students are not sure about the field in which they want to focus their studies or the career they would like to pursue. Often, students discover fields and careers they never knew existed. Community colleges have the resources to help students identify areas of career interest and to set challenging occupational goals.

Once a career goal is set, you can be confident that a community college will provide job-relevant, technical education. About half of the students who take courses for credit at community colleges do so to prepare for employment or to acquire or upgrade skills for their current job. Especially helpful in charting a career path is the assistance of a counselor or a faculty adviser, who can discuss job opportunities in your chosen field and help you map out your course of study.

In addition, since community colleges have close ties to their communities, they are in constant contact with leaders in business, industry, organized labor, and public life. Community colleges work with these individuals and their organizations to prepare students for direct entry into the world of work. For example, some community colleges have established partnerships with local businesses and industries to provide specialized training programs. Some also provide the academic portion of apprenticeship training, while others offer extensive job-shadowing and cooperative education opportunities.

Be sure to examine all of the career-preparation opportunities offered by the community colleges in which you are interested.

David R. Pierce is the former President of the American Association of Community Colleges.

Surviving Standardized Tests

WHAT ARE STANDARDIZED TESTS?

Colleges and universities in the United States use tests to help evaluate applicants' readiness for admission or to place them in appropriate courses. The tests that are most frequently used by colleges are the ACT Assessment of American College Testing, Inc., and the College Board's SAT. In addition, the Educational Testing Service (ETS) offers the TOEFL test, which evaluates the English-language proficiency of nonnative speakers. The tests are offered at designated testing centers located at high schools and colleges throughout the United States and U.S. territories and at testing centers in various countries throughout the world. The ACT Assessment test and the SAT tests are each taken by more than a million students each year. The TOEFL test is taken by more than 800,000 students each year.

Upon request, special accommodations for students with documented visual, hearing, physical, or learning disabilities are available. Examples of special accommodations include tests in Braille or large print and such aids as a reader, recorder, magnifying glass, or sign language interpreter. Additional testing time may be allowed in some instances. Contact the appropriate testing program or your guidance counselor for details on how to request special accommodations.

College Board SAT Program

Currently, the SAT Program consists of the SAT and the SAT Subject Tests. The SAT is a 3-hour 45-minute test made up of ten sections, primarily multiple-choice, that focuses on college success skills of writing, critical reading, and mathematics. The writing component measures grammar and usage and includes a short, student-written essay. The critical reading sections test verbal reasoning and critical reading skills. Emphasis is placed on reading passages, which are 400–850 words in length. Some reading passages are paired; the second opposes, supports, or in some way complements the point of view expressed in the first. The three mathematics sections test a student's ability to solve problems involving arithmetic, Algebra I and II, and geometry. They include questions that require students to produce their own responses, in addition to questions that students can choose from four or five answer choices. Calculators may be used on the SAT mathematics sections.

The SAT Subject Tests are 1-hour tests, primarily multiple-choice, in specific subjects that measure students' knowledge of these subjects and their ability to apply that knowledge. Some colleges may require or recommend these tests for placement, or even admission. The Subject Tests measure a student's academic achievement in high school and may indicate readiness for cer-

tain college programs. Tests offered include Literature, U.S. History, World History, Mathematics Level IC, Mathematics Level IIC, Biology E/M (Ecological/Molecular), Chemistry, Physics, French, German, Modern Hebrew, Italian, Latin, and Spanish, as well as Foreign Language Tests with Listening in Chinese, French, German, Japanese, Korean, Spanish, and English Language Proficiency (ELPT). The Mathematics Level IC and IIC tests require the use of a scientific calculator.

SAT scores are automatically sent to each student who has taken the test. On average, they are mailed about three weeks after the test. Students may request that the scores be reported to their high schools or to the colleges to which they are applying.

ACT Assessment Program

The ACT Assessment Program is a comprehensive data collection, processing, and reporting service designed to assist in educational and career planning. The ACT Assessment instrument consists of four academic tests, taken under timed conditions, and a Student Profile Section and Interest Inventory, completed when students register for the ACT Assessment.

The academic tests cover four areas—English, mathematics, reading, and science reasoning. The ACT Assessment consists of 215 multiple-choice questions and takes approximately 3 hours and 30 minutes to complete with breaks (testing time is actually 2 hours and 55 minutes). They are designed to assess the student's educational development and readiness to handle college-level work. The minimum standard score is 1, the maximum is 36, and the national average is 21. Students should note that beginning in February 2005, an optional writing test was offered.

DON'T FORGET TO . . .

- Take the SAT or ACT Assessment before application deadlines.
- Note that test registration deadlines precede test dates by about six weeks.
- Register to take the TOEFL test if English is not your native language and you are planning on studying at a North American college.
- Practice your test-taking skills with **Peterson's Ultimate SAT Tool Kit, Peterson's Ultimate ACT Tool Kit, The Real ACT Prep Guide** (published by Peterson's), and **Peterson's TOEFL Success** (some available with software).
- Contact the College Board or American College Testing, Inc., in advance if you need special accommodations when taking tests.

The Student Profile Section requests information about each student's admission and enrollment plans, academic and out-of-class high school achievements and aspirations, and high school course work. The student is also asked to supply biographical data and self-reported high school grades in the four subject-matter areas covered by the academic tests.

The ACT Assessment has a number of career planning services, including the ACT Assessment Interest Inventory, which is designed to measure six major dimensions of student interests–business contact, business operations, technical, science, arts, and social service. Results are used to compare the student's interests with those of college-bound students who later majored in each of a wide variety of areas. Inventory results are also used to help students compare their work-activity preferences with work activities that characterize twenty-three "job families."

Because the information resulting from the ACT Assessment Program is used in a variety of educational settings, American College Testing, Inc., prepares three reports for each student: the Student Report, the High School Report, and the College Report. The Student Report normally is sent to the student's high school, except after the June test date, when it is sent directly to the student's home address. The College Report is sent to the colleges the student designates.

Early in the school year, American College Testing, Inc., sends registration packets to high schools across the country that contain all the information a student needs to register for the ACT Assessment. High school guidance offices also receive a supply of *Preparing for the ACT Assessment*, a booklet that contains a complete practice test, an answer key, and general information about preparing for the test.

Test of English as a Foreign Language (TOEFL)

The TOEFL is used by various organizations, such as colleges and universities, to determine English proficiency. Beginning in September, the new TOEFL (TOEFL iBT) will be offered in the United States and in the rest of the world in 2006. The test will be offered in an Internet-based format. The TOEFL iBT tests students in the areas of speaking, listening, reading, and writing.

The current TOEFL tests students in the areas of listening, structure, reading comprehension, and writing. Score requirements are set by individual institutions. For more information on TOEFL, and to obtain a copy of the Information Bulletin, contact the Educational Testing Service.

Peterson's *TOEFL CBT Success* can help you prepare for the current exam. The CD version of the book includes a TOEFL practice test and adaptive English skill building exercise. An online CBT test can also be taken for a small fee at petersons.com.

Contact your secondary school counselor for full information about the SAT and ACT Assessment programs and the TOEFL test.

2005–06 ACT ASSESSMENT AND SAT TEST DATES

ACT Assessment
September 24, 2005*
October 22, 2005
December 10, 2005
February 11, 2006**
April 8, 2006
June 10, 2006

All test dates fall on a Saturday. Tests are also given on the Sundays following the Saturday test dates for students who cannot take the test on Saturday because of religious reasons. The basic ACT Assessment registration fee for 2004–05 was $28 ($45 outside of the U.S.). The optional writing test is $14 and is refundable for students who are absent on test day.

*The September test is available only in Arizona, California, Florida, Georgia, Illinois, Indiana, Maryland, Nevada, North Carolina, Pennsylvania, South Carolina, Texas, and Washington.

**The February test date is not available in New York.

SAT
October 8, 2005 (SAT and SAT Subject Tests)
November 5, 2005 (SAT, SAT Subject Tests, and Language Tests with Listening, including ELPT*)
December 3, 2005 (SAT and SAT Subject Tests)
January 28, 2006 (SAT, SAT Subject Tests, and ELPT)
April 1, 2006 (SAT only)**
May 6, 2006 (SAT and SAT Subject Tests)
June 3, 2006 (SAT and SAT Subject Tests)

For the 2004–05 academic year, the basic fee for the SAT was $41.50. The basic fee for the SAT Subject Tests was $17, $18 for the Language Tests with Listening, and $8 each for all other Subject Tests. Students can take up to three SAT Subject Tests on a single date, and a $17 basic registration and reporting fee should be added for each test date. Tests are also given on the Sundays following the Saturday test dates for students who cannot take the test on Saturday because of religious reasons. Fee waivers are available to juniors and seniors who cannot afford test fees.

*Language Tests with Listening (including the English Language Proficiency Test, or ELPT) are only offered on November 5; the ELPT is offered on November 5 and January 28 at some test centers. See the Registration Bulletin for details.

**The April 1 test date is only available in the U.S. and its territories.

Who's Paying for This?
Financial Aid Basics

A college education can be expensive—costing more than $150,000 for four years at some of the higher priced private colleges and universities. Even at the lower cost state colleges and universities, the cost of a four-year education can approach $50,000. Determining how you and your family will come up with the necessary funds to pay for your education requires planning, perseverance, and learning as much as you can about the options that are available to you.

Paying for college should not be looked at as a four-year financial commitment. For most families, paying the total cost of a student's college education out of current savings is usually not realistic. For families that have planned ahead and have financial savings established for higher education, the burden is a lot easier. But for most, meeting the cost of college requires the pooling of current income and assets and investing in longer-term loan options. These family resources, together with possible financial assistance from state, federal, and institutional sources, enable millions of students each year to attend the institution of their choice.

FINANCIAL AID PROGRAMS

There are three types of financial aid:

1. Gift-aid—Scholarships and grants are funds that do not have to be repaid.
2. Loans—Loans must be repaid, usually after graduation; the amount you have to pay back is the total you've borrowed plus any accrued interest. This is considered a source of self-help aid.
3. Student employment—Student employment is a job arranged for you by the financial aid office. This is another source of self-help aid.

The federal government has two major grant programs—the Federal Pell Grant and the Federal Supplemental Educational Opportunity Grant. These grants are targeted to low-to-moderate income families with significant financial need. The federal government also sponsors a student employment program called Federal Work-Study, which offers jobs both on and off campus; and several loan programs, including those for students and for parents of undergraduate students.

There are two types of student loan programs, subsidized and unsubsidized. The Subsidized Stafford Loan and the Federal Perkins Loan are need-based, government-subsidized loans. Students who borrow through these programs do not have to pay interest on the loan until after they graduate or leave school. The Unsubsidized Stafford Loan and the Parent Loan Program are not based on need, and borrowers are responsible for the interest while the student is in school. There are different methods on how these loans are administered. Once you choose your college, the financial aid office will guide you through this process.

After you've submitted your financial aid application and you've been accepted for admission, each college will send you a letter describing your financial aid award. Most award letters show estimated college costs, how much you and your family are expected to contribute, and the amount and types of aid you have been awarded. Most students are awarded aid from a combination of sources and programs. Hence, your award is often called a financial aid "package."

SOURCES OF FINANCIAL AID

More than 14 million people apply for financial aid each year. The largest single source of aid is the federal government, which awarded almost $81.5 billion during 2003–04.

The next largest source of financial aid is found in the college and university community. Institutions award an estimated $23 billion to students each year. Most of this aid is awarded to students who have a demonstrated need based on the Federal Methodology. Some institutions use a different formula, the Institutional Methodology (IM), to award their own funds in conjunction with other forms of aid. Institutional aid may be either need-based or non-need based. Aid that is not based on need is usually awarded for a student's academic performance (merit awards), specific talents or abilities, or to attract the type of students a college seeks to enroll.

Another source of financial aid is from state government, awarding more than $6 billion per year. All states offer grant and/or scholarship aid, most of which is need-based. However, more and more states are offering substantial merit-based aid programs. Most state programs award aid only to students attending college in their home state.

9

Other sources of financial aid include:

- Private agencies
- Foundations
- Corporations
- Clubs
- Fraternal and service organizations
- Civic associations
- Unions
- Religious groups that award grants, scholarships, and low-interest loans
- Employers that provide tuition reimbursement benefits for employees and their children

More information about these different sources of aid is available from high school guidance offices, public libraries, college financial aid offices, directly from the sponsoring organizations, and on the Web at www.finaid. org.

HOW NEED-BASED FINANCIAL AID IS AWARDED

When you apply for aid, your family's financial situation is analyzed using a government-approved formula called the Federal Methodology. This formula looks at five items:

1. Demographic information of the family.
2. Income of the parents.
3. Assets of the parents.
4. Income of the student.
5. Assets of the student.

This analysis determines the amount you and your family are expected to contribute toward your college expenses, called your Expected Family Contribution or EFC. If the EFC is equal to or more than the cost of attendance at a particular college, then you do not demonstrate financial need. However, even if you don't have financial need, you may still qualify for aid, as there are grants, scholarships, and loan programs that are not need-based.

If the cost of your education is greater than your EFC, then you do demonstrate financial need and qualify for assistance. The amount of your financial need that can be met varies from school to school. Some are able to meet your full need, while others can only cover a certain percentage of need. Here's the formula:

Cost of Attendance
– Expected Family Contribution
= Financial Need

The EFC remains constant, but your need will vary according to the costs of attendance at a particular college. In general, the higher the tuition and fees at a particular college, the higher the cost of attendance will be. Expenses for books and supplies, room and board, transportation, and other miscellaneous costs are included

in the overall cost of attendance. It is important to remember that you do not have to be "needy" to qualify for financial aid. Many middle and upper-middle income families qualify for need-based financial aid.

APPLYING FOR FINANCIAL AID

Every student must complete the Free Application for Federal Student Aid (FAFSA) to be considered for financial aid. The FAFSA is available from your high school guidance office, many public libraries, colleges in your area, or directly from the U.S. Department of Education.

Students are encouraged to apply for federal student aid on the Web. The electronic version of the FAFSA can be accessed at http://www.fafsa.ed.gov. Both the student and at least one parent must apply for a federal pin number at http://www.pin.ed.gov. The pin number serves as your electronic signature when applying for aid on the Web.

To award their own funds, some colleges require an additional application, the Financial Aid PROFILE® form. The PROFILE asks supplemental questions that some colleges and awarding agencies feel provide a more accurate assessment of the family's ability to pay for college. It is up to the college to decide whether it will use only the FAFSA or both the FAFSA and the PROFILE. PROFILE applications are available from the high school guidance office and on the Web. Both the paper application and the Web site list those colleges and programs that require the PROFILE application.

If Every College You're Applying to for Fall 2006 Requires Just the FAFSA

. . . then it's pretty simple: Complete the FAFSA after January 1, 2006, being certain to send it in before any college-imposed deadlines. (You are not permitted to send in the 2006-07 FAFSA before January 1, 2006.) Most college FAFSA application deadlines are in February or early March. It is easier if you have all your financial records for the previous year available, but if that is not possible, you are strongly encouraged to use estimated figures.

After you send in your FAFSA, either with the paper application or electronically, you'll receive a Student Aid Report (SAR) that includes all of the information you reported and shows your EFC. If you provided an e-mail address, the SAR is sent to you electronically; otherwise, you will receive a paper copy in the mail. Be sure to review the SAR, checking to see if the information you reported is accurate. If you used estimated numbers to complete the FAFSA, you may have to resubmit the SAR with any corrections to the data. The college(s) you have designated on the FAFSA will receive the information you reported and will use that data to make their decision. In many instances, the colleges you've applied to will ask you to send copies of your and your parents' federal income tax returns for 2005, plus any other documents needed to verify the information you reported.

If a College Requires the PROFILE

Step 1: Register for the Financial Aid PROFILE in the fall of your senior year in high school.

You can apply for the PROFILE online at http://profileonline.collegeboard.com/index.jsp. Registration information with a list of the colleges that require the PROFILE are available in most high school guidance offices. There is a fee for using the Financial Aid PROFILE application ($23 for the first college and $18 for each additional college). You must pay for the service by credit card when you register. If you do not have a credit card, you will be billed.

Step 2: Fill out your customized Financial Aid PROFILE.

Once you register, your application will be immediately available online and will have questions which all students must complete, questions which must be completed by the student's parents (unless the student is independent and the colleges or programs selected do not require parent information), and *may* have supplemental questions needed by one or more of your schools or programs. If required, those will be found in Section Q of the application.

In addition to the PROFILE Application you complete online, you may also be required to complete a Business/Farm Supplement via traditional paper format. Completion of this form is not a part of the online process. If this form is required, instructions on how to download and print the supplemental form are provided. If your biological or adoptive parents are separated or divorced and your colleges and programs require it, your noncustodial parent may be asked to complete the Noncustodial POFILE.

Once you complete and submit your PROFILE Application, it will be processed and sent directly to your requested colleges and programs.

IF YOU DON'T QUALIFY FOR NEED-BASED AID

If you are not eligible for need-based aid, you can still find ways to lessen the burden on your parents.

Here are some suggestions:

- Search for merit scholarships. You can start at the initial stages of your application process. College merit awards are becoming increasingly important as more and more colleges award these grants to students they especially want to attract. As a result, applying to a college at which your qualifications put you at the top of the entering class may give you a larger merit award. Another source of aid to look for is private scholarships that are given for special skills and talents. Additional information can be found at Petersons.com and at www.finaid.org.

- Seek employment during the summer and the academic year. The student employment office at your college can help you locate a school-year job. Many colleges and local businesses have vacancies remaining after they have hired students who are receiving Federal Work-Study financial aid.

- Borrow through the Unsubsidized Stafford Loan programs. These are open to all students. The terms and conditions are similar to the subsidized loans. The biggest difference is that the borrower is responsible for the interest while still in college, although most lenders permit students to delay paying the interest right away and add the accrued interest to the total amount owed. You must file the FAFSA to be considered.

- After you've secured what you can through scholarships, working, and borrowing, your parents will be expected to meet their share of the college bill (the Expected Family Contribution). Many colleges offer monthly payment plans that spread the cost over the academic year. If the monthly payments are too high, parents can borrow through the Federal Parent Loan for Undergraduate Students (PLUS program), through one of the many private education loan programs available, or through home equity loans and lines of credit. Families seeking assistance in financing college expenses should inquire at the financial aid office about what programs are available at the college. Some families seek the advice of professional financial advisers and tax consultants.

HOW IS YOUR EXPECTED FAMILY CONTRIBUTION CALCULATED?

The chart on the next page makes the following assumptions:

- two parent family where age of older parent is 45
- lower income families (under $30,000) will file the 1040A or 1040EZ tax form
- student income is less than $2300
- there are no student assets
- there is only one family member attending college

All figures are estimates and may vary when the complete FAFSA or PROFILE application is submitted.

Approximate Expected Family Contribution

ASSETS		INCOME BEFORE TAXES								
	FAMILY SIZE	$20,000	30,000	40,000	50,000	60,000	70,000	80,000	90,000	100,000
$ 20,000										
	3	$ 0	1,180	2,850	5,000	8,100	10,000	13,350	16,700	20,300
	4	0	300	1,950	3,750	6,300	8,100	11,500	14,800	18,400
	5	0	0	1,100	2,750	4,900	6,400	9,600	13,000	16,600
	6	0	0	150	1,800	3,600	4,800	7,600	11,000	14,600
$ 30,000										
	3	$ 0	1,180	2,850	5,000	8,100	10,000	13,350	16,700	20,300
	4	0	300	1,950	3,750	6,300	8,100	11,500	14,800	18,400
	5	0	0	1,100	2,750	4,900	6,400	9,600	13,000	16,600
	6	0	0	150	1,800	3,600	4,800	7,600	11,000	14,600
$ 40,000										
	3	$ 0	1,180	2,850	5,000	8,600	10,500	13,850	17,200	20,800
	4	0	300	1,950	3,750	6,800	8,500	1,200	15,300	18,900
	5	0	0	1,100	2,750	5,400	6,900	10,100	13,500	17,100
	6	0	0	150	1,800	4,100	5,300	8,100	11,500	15,100
$ 50,000										
	3	$ 0	1,180	3,200	5,000	9,100	11,000	14,350	17,700	21,300
	4	0	300	2,260	3,750	7,300	9,100	12,500	15,800	19,400
	5	0	0	1,400	2,750	5,900	7,400	10,600	14,000	17,600
	6	0	0	480	1,800	4,600	5,800	8,600	12,000	15,600
$ 60,000										
	3	$ 0	1,180	3,500	6,500	9,600	11,500	14,850	18,200	21,800
	4	0	300	2,500	5,250	7,800	9,600	13,000	15,300	19,900
	5	0	0	1,700	4,250	6,400	7,900	11,100	14,500	18,100
	6	0	0	750	3,300	5,100	6,300	9,200	12,500	16,100
$ 80,000										
	3	$ 0	1,180	4,200	7,500	10,600	12,500	15,850	19,200	22,800
	4	0	300	3,100	6,250	8,800	10,600	14,000	17,300	20,900
	5	0	0	2,200	5,250	7,400	8,900	12,100	15,500	19,100
	6	0	0	1,250	4,300	6,100	7,300	10,200	13,500	17,100
$ 100,000										
	3	$ 0	1,180	5,000	8,500	11,600	13,500	16,850	20,200	23,800
	4	0	300	3,700	7,250	9,800	11,600	15,000	18,300	21,900
	5	0	0	2,700	6,250	8,400	9,900	13,100	16,500	20,100
	6	0	0	1,800	5,300	7,100	8,300	11,200	14,500	18,100
$ 120,000										
	3	$ 0	1,180	5,850	9,500	12,600	14,500	17,850	21,200	24,800
	4	0	300	4,400	8,250	10,800	12,600	16,000	19,300	22,900
	5	0	0	3,350	7,250	9,400	10,900	14,100	17,500	21,100
	6	0	0	2,300	6,300	8,100	9,300	12,200	15,500	19,100
$ 140,000										
	3	$ 0	1,180	6,800	10,500	13,600	15,500	18,850	22,200	24,800
	4	0	300	5,200	9,250	11,800	13,600	17,000	20,300	23,900
	5	0	0	4,000	8,250	10,400	11,900	15,100	18,500	22,100
	6	0	0	2,875	7,300	9,100	10,300	13,200	16,500	20,100

Frequently Asked Questions About Transferring

Muriel M. Shishkoff

Among the students attending two-year colleges are a large number who began their higher education knowing they would eventually transfer to a four-year school to obtain their bachelor's degree. There are many reasons why students are going this route. Upon graduating from high school, some simply do not have definite career goals. Although they don't want to put their education on hold, they prefer not to pay exorbitant amounts in tuition while trying to "find themselves." As the cost of a university education escalates—even in public institutions—the option of spending the freshman and sophomore years at a two-year college looks attractive to many students. Others attend a two-year college because they are unable to meet the initial entrance standards—a specified grade point average (GPA), standardized test scores, or knowledge of specific academic subjects—required by the four-year school of their choice. Many such students praise the community college system for giving them the chance to be, academically speaking, "born again." In addition, students from other countries often find that they can adapt more easily to language and cultural changes at a two-year school before transferring to a larger, more diverse four-year college.

If your plan is to attend a two-year college with the ultimate goal of transferring to a four-year school, you will be pleased to know that the increased importance of the community college route to a bachelor's degree is recognized by all segments of higher education. As a result, many two-year schools have revised their course outlines and established new courses in order to comply with the programs and curricular offerings of the universities. Institutional improvements to make transferring easier have also proliferated at both the two- and four-year levels. The generous transfer policies of the Pennsylvania, New York, and Florida state university systems, among others, reflect this attitude; these systems accept *all* credits from students who have graduated from accredited community colleges.

If you are interested in moving from a two-year college to a four-year school, the sooner you make up your mind that you are going to make the switch, the better position you will be in to transfer successfully (that is, without having wasted valuable time and credits). The ideal point at which to make such a decision is *before* you register for classes at your two-year school; a counselor can help you plan your course work with an eye toward fulfilling the requirements needed for your major course of study.

Naturally, it is not always possible to plan your transferring strategy that far in advance, but keep in mind that the key to a successful transfer is *preparation,* and preparation takes time—time to think through your objectives and time to plan the right classes to take at that school.

As students face the prospect of transferring from a two-year to a four-year school, many thoughts and concerns about this complicated and often frustrating process race through their minds. Here are answers to the questions that are most frequently asked by transferring students.

Q Does every college and university accept transfer students?

A Most four-year institutions accept transfer students, but some do so more enthusiastically than others. Graduating from a community college is an advantage at, for example, Arizona State University and the University of Massachusetts Boston; both accept more community college transfer students than traditional freshmen. At the State University of New York at Albany, graduates of two-year transfer programs within the State University of New York System are given priority for upper-division (i.e., junior- and senior-level) vacancies.

Schools offering undergraduate work at the upper division only, such as Metropolitan State University in St. Paul, Minnesota, are especially receptive to transfer applications. On the other hand, some schools accept only a few transfer students; others refuse entrance to sophomores or those in their final year. Princeton University requires an "excellent academic record and particularly compelling reasons to transfer." Check the catalogs of several colleges for their transfer requirements before you make your final choice.

Q Do students who go directly from high school to a four-year college do better academically than transfer students from community colleges?

A On the contrary: some institutions report that transfers from two-year schools who persevere until graduation do *better* than those who started as freshmen.

Q Why is it so important that my two-year college be accredited?

A Four-year colleges and universities accept transfer credit only from schools formally recognized by a regional, national, or professional educational agency. This accreditation signifies that an institution or program of study meets or exceeds a minimum level of educational quality necessary for meeting stated educational objectives.

Q After enrolling at a four-year school, may I still make up necessary courses at a community college?

A Some institutions restrict credit after transfer to their own facilities. Others allow students to take a limited number of transfer courses after matriculation, depending on the subject matter. A few provide opportunities for cross-registration or dual enrollment, which means taking classes on more than one campus.

Q What do I need to do to transfer?

A First, send for your high school and college transcripts. Having chosen the school you wish to transfer to, check its admission requirements against your transcripts. If you find that you are admissible, file an application as early as possible before the deadline. Part of the process will be asking your former schools to send *official transcripts* to the admission office, i.e., not the copies you used in determining your admissibility.

Plan your transfer program with the head of your new department as soon as you have decided to transfer. Determine the recommended general education pattern and necessary preparation for your major. At your present school, take the courses you will need to meet transfer requirements for the new one.

Q What qualifies me for admission as a transfer student?

A Admission requirements for most four-year institutions vary. Depending on the reputation or popularity of the school and program you wish to enter, requirements may be quite selective and competitive. Usually, you will need to show satisfactory test scores, an academic record up to a certain standard, and completion of specific subject matter.

Transfer students can be eligible to enter a four-year school in a number of ways: by having been eligible for admission directly upon graduation from high school, by making up shortcomings in grades (or in subject matter not covered in high school) at a community college, or by satisfactory completion of necessary courses or credit hours at another postsecondary institution. Ordinarily, students coming from a community college or from another four-year institution must meet or exceed the receiving institution's standards for freshmen and show appropriate college-level course work taken since high school. Students who did not graduate from high school can present proof of proficiency through results on the General Educational Development (GED) test.

Q Are exceptions ever made for students who don't meet all the requirements for transfer?

A Extenuating circumstances, such as disability, low family income, refugee or veteran status, or athletic talent, may permit the special enrollment of students who would not otherwise be eligible but who demonstrate the potential for academic success. Consult the appropriate office—the Educational Opportunity Program, the disabled students' office, the athletic department, or the academic dean—to see whether an exception can be made in your case.

Q How far in advance do I need to apply for transfer?

A Some schools have a rolling admission policy, which means that they process transfer applications as they are received, all year long. With other schools, you must apply during the priority filing period, which can be up to a year before you wish to enter. Check the date with the admission office at your prospective campus.

Q Is it possible to transfer courses from several different institutions?

A Institutions ordinarily accept the courses that they consider transferable, regardless of the number of accredited schools involved. However, there is the danger of exceeding the maximum number of credit hours that can be transferred from all other schools or earned through credit by examination, extension courses, or correspondence courses. The limit placed on transfer credits varies from school to school, so read the catalog carefully to avoid taking courses you won't be able to use. To avoid duplicating courses, keep attendance at different campuses to a minimum.

Q What is involved in transferring from a semester system to a quarter or trimester system?

A In the semester system, the academic calendar is divided into two equal parts. The quarter system is more aptly named trimester, since the academic calendar is divided into three equal terms (not counting a summer session). To convert semester units into quarter units or credit hours, simply multiply the semester units by one and a half. Conversely, multiply quarter units by two thirds to come up with semester units. If you are used to a semester system of fifteen- to sixteen-week courses, the ten-week courses of the quarter system may seem to fly by.

Q Why might a course be approved for transfer credit by one four-year school but not by another?

A The beauty of postsecondary education in the United States lies in its variety. Entrance policies and graduation requirements are designed to reflect and serve each institution's mission. Because institutional policies vary so widely, schools may interpret the subject matter of a course from quite different points of view. Given that the granting of transfer credit indicates that a course is viewed as being, in effect, parallel to one offered by the receiving institution, it is easy to see how this might be the case at one university and not another.

Q Must I take a foreign language to transfer?

A Foreign language proficiency is often required for admission to a four-year institution; such proficiency also often figures in certain majors or in the general education pattern. At Princeton University, for example, where foreign language proficiency is a

graduation requirement, all students must demonstrate it by the end of their junior year.

However, at the University of Southern California and other schools, the foreign language competence necessary for admission can be certified before entrance. Often, two or three years of a single language in high school will do the trick. Find out if scores received on Advanced Placement examinations, placement examinations given by the foreign language department, or SAT Subject Tests will be accepted in lieu of college course work.

Q Will the school to which I'm transferring accept pass/no pass, pass/fail, or credit/no credit grades in lieu of letter grades?

A Usually, a limit is placed on the number of these courses you can transfer, and there may be other restrictions as well. If you want to use other-than-letter grades for the fulfillment of general education requirements or lower-division (freshman and sophomore) preparation for the major, check with the receiving institution.

Q Which is more important for transfer—my grade point average or my course completion pattern?

A Some schools believe that your past grades indicate academic potential and overshadow prior preparation for a specific degree program. Others require completion of certain introductory courses before transfer to prepare you for upper-division work in your major. In any case, appropriate course selection will cut down the time to graduation and increase your chances of making a successful transfer.

Q What happens to my credits if I change majors?

A If you change majors after admission, your transferable course credit should remain fairly intact. However, because you may need extra or different preparation for your new major, some of the courses you've taken may now be useful only as electives. The need for additional lower-level preparation may mean you're staying longer at your new school than you originally planned. On the other hand, you may already have taken courses that count toward your new major as part of the university's general education pattern.

Excerpted from *Transferring Made Easy: A Guide to Changing Colleges Successfully,* by Muriel M. Shishkoff, © 1991 by Muriel M. Shishkoff (published by Peterson's).

Returning to School: Advice for Adult Students

Sandra Cook, Ph.D.
Director, University Advising Center, San Diego State University

Many adults think for a long time about returning to school without taking any action. One purpose of this article is to help the "thinkers" finally make some decisions by examining what is keeping them from action. Another purpose is to describe not only some of the difficulties and obstacles that adult students may face when returning to school but also tactics for coping with them.

If you have been thinking about going back to college, and believing that you are the only person your age contemplating college, you should know that approximately 7 million adult students are currently enrolled in higher education institutions. This number represents 50 percent of total higher education enrollments. The majority of adult students are enrolled at two-year colleges.

There are many reasons why adult students choose to attend a two-year college. Studies have shown that the three most important criteria that adult students consider when choosing a college are location, cost, and availability of the major or program desired. Most two-year colleges are public institutions that serve a geographic district, making them readily accessible to the community. Costs at most two-year colleges are far less than at other types of higher education institutions. For many students who plan to pursue a bachelor's degree, completing their first two years of college at a community college is an affordable means to that end. If you are interested in an academic program that will transfer to a four-year institution, most two-year colleges offer the "general education" courses that comprise most freshman and sophomore years. If you are interested in a vocational or technical program, two-year colleges excel in providing this type of training.

UNCERTAINTY, CHOICE, AND SUPPORT

There are three different "stages" in the process of adults returning to school. The first stage is uncertainty. Do I really want to go back to school? What will my friends or family think? Can I compete with those 18-year-old whiz kids? Am I too old? The second stage is choice. Once the decision to return has been made, you must choose where you will attend. There are many criteria to use in making this decision. The third stage is support. You have just added another role to your already-too-busy life. There are, however, strategies that will help you accomplish your goals—perhaps not without struggle, but with grace and humor nonetheless. Let's look at each of these stages.

UNCERTAINTY

Why are you thinking about returning to school? Is it to:

- fulfill a dream that had to be delayed?
- become more educationally well-rounded?
- fill an intellectual void in your life?

These reasons focus on *personal growth*.

If you are returning to school to:

- meet people and make friends
- attain and enjoy higher social status and prestige among friends, relatives, and associates
- understand/study a cultural heritage, or
- have a medium in which to exchange ideas,

you are interested in *social and cultural opportunities*.

If you are like most adult students, you want to:

- qualify for a new occupation
- enter or reenter the job market
- increase earnings potential, or
- qualify for a more challenging position in the same field of work.

You are seeking *career growth*.

Understanding the reasons why you want to go back to school is an important step in setting your educational goals and will help you to establish some criteria for selecting a college. However, don't delay your decision because you have not been able to clearly define your motives. Many times, these aren't clear until you have already begun the process, and they may change as you move through your college experience.

Assuming you agree that additional education will benefit you, what is it that keeps you from returning to school? You may have a litany of excuses running through your mind:

- I don't have time.
- I can't afford it.
- I'm too old to learn.
- My friends will think I'm crazy.
- The teachers will be younger than I.
- My family can't survive without me to take care of them every minute.
- I'll be X years old when I finish.
- I'm afraid.
- I don't know what to expect.

And that is just what these are—excuses. You can make school, like anything else in your life, a priority or not. If you really want to return, you can. The more you understand your motivation for returning to school and the more you understand what excuses are keeping you from taking action, the easier your task will be.

If you think you don't have time: The best way to decide how attending class and studying can fit into your schedule is to keep track of what you do with your time each day for several weeks. Completing a standard time-management grid (each day is plotted out by the half hour) is helpful for visualizing how your time is spent. For each 3-credit-hour class you take, you will need to find 3 hours for class plus 6 to 9 hours for reading-studying-library time. This study time should be spaced evenly throughout the week, not loaded up on one day. It is not possible to learn or retain the material that way. When you examine your grid, see where there are activities that could be replaced with school and study time. You may decide to give up your bowling league or some time in front of the TV. Try not to give up sleeping, and don't cut out every moment of free time. Here are some suggestions that have come from adults who have returned to school:

- Enroll in a time-management workshop. It helps you rethink how you use your time.
- Don't think you have to take more than one course at a time. You may eventually want to work up to taking more, but consider starting with one. (It is more than you are taking now!)
- If you have a family, start assigning to them those household chores that you usually do—and don't redo what they do.
- Use your lunch hour or commuting time for reading.

If you think you cannot afford it: As mentioned earlier, two-year colleges are extremely affordable. If you cannot afford the tuition, look into the various financial aid options. Most federal and state funds are available to full- and part-time students. Loans are also available. While many people prefer not to accumulate a debt for school, these same people will think nothing of taking out a loan

to buy a car. After five or six years, which is the better investment? Adult students who work should look into whether their company has a tuition-reimbursement policy. There are also private scholarships, available through foundations, service organizations, and clubs, that are focused on adult learners. Your public library and a college financial aid adviser are two excellent sources for reference materials regarding financial aid.

If you think you are too old to learn: This is pure myth. A number of studies have shown that adult learners perform as well as or better than traditional-age students.

If you are afraid your friends will think you're crazy: Who cares? Maybe they will, maybe they won't. Usually, they will admire your courage and be just a little jealous of your ambition (although they'll never tell you that). Follow your dreams, not theirs.

If you are concerned because the teachers or students will be younger than you: Don't be. The age differences that may be apparent in other settings evaporate in the classroom. If anything, an adult in the classroom strikes fear into the hearts of some 18-year-olds because adults have been known to be prepared, ask questions, be truly motivated, and be there to learn!

If you think your family will have a difficult time surviving while you are in school: If you have done everything for them up to now, they might struggle. Consider this an opportunity to help them become independent and self-sufficient. Your family can only make you feel guilty if you let them. You are not abandoning them; you are becoming an educational role model. When you are happy and working toward your goals, everyone benefits. Admittedly, it sometimes takes time for them to realize this. For single parents, there are schools that offer support groups, child care, and cooperative babysitting.

If you're appalled at the thought of being X years old when you graduate in Y years: How old will you be in Y years if you don't go back to school?

If you are afraid or don't know what to expect: Know that these are natural feelings when one encounters any new situation. Adult students find that their fears usually dissipate once they begin classes. Fear of trying is usually the biggest roadblock to the reentry process.

No doubt you have dreamed up a few more reasons for not making the decision to return to school. Keep in mind that what you are doing is making up excuses, and you are using these excuses to release you from the obligation to make a decision about your life. The thought of returning to college can be scary. Anytime anyone ventures into unknown territory, there is a risk, but taking risks is a necessary component of personal and professional growth. It is your life, and you alone are responsible for making the decisions that determine its course. Education is an investment in your future.

CHOICE

Once you have decided to go back to school, your next task is to decide where to go. If your educational goals are well defined (e.g., you want to pursue a degree in order to change careers), then your task is a bit easier. But even if your educational goals are still evolving, do not defer your return. Many students who enter higher education with a specific major in mind change that major at least once.

Most students who attend a public two-year college choose the community college in the district in which they live. This is generally the closest and least expensive option if the school offers the programs you want. If you are planning to begin your education at a two-year college and then transfer to a four-year school, there are distinct advantages to choosing your four-year school early. Many community and four-year colleges have "articulation" agreements that designate what credits from the two-year school will transfer to the four-year college and how. Some four-year institutions accept an associate degree as equivalent to the freshman and sophomore years, regardless of the courses you have taken. Some four-year schools accept two-year college work only on a course-by-course basis. If you can identify which school you will transfer to, you can know in advance exactly how your two-year credits will apply, preventing an unexpected loss of credit or time.

Each institution of higher education is distinctive. Your goal in choosing a college is to come up with the best student-institution fit—matching your needs with the offerings and characteristics of the school. The first step in choosing a college is to determine what criteria are most important to you in attaining your educational goals. Location, cost, and program availability are the three main factors that influence an adult student's college choice. In considering location, don't forget that some colleges have conveniently located branch campuses. In considering cost, remember to explore your financial aid options before ruling out an institution because of its tuition. Program availability should include not only the major in which you are interested, but also whether or not classes in that major are available when you can take them.

Some additional considerations beyond location, cost, and programs are:

- Does the school have a commitment to adult students and offer appropriate services, such as child care, tutoring, and advising?
- Are classes offered at times when you can take them?
- Are there academic options for adults, such as credit for life or work experience, credit by examination (including CLEP and PEP), credit for military service, or accelerated programs?
- Is the faculty sensitive to the needs of adult learners?

Once you determine which criteria are vital in your choice of an institution, you can begin to narrow your choices. There are myriad ways for you to locate the information you desire. Many urban newspapers publish a "School Guide" several times a year in which colleges and universities advertise to an adult student market. In addition, schools themselves publish catalogs, class schedules, and promotional materials that contain much of the information you need, and they are yours for the asking. Many colleges sponsor information sessions and open houses that allow you to visit the campus and ask questions. An appointment with an adviser is a good way to assess the fit between you and the institution. Be sure to bring your questions with you to your interview.

SUPPORT

Once you have made the decision to return to school and have chosen the institution that best meets your needs, take some additional steps to ensure your success during your crucial first semester. Take advantage of institutional support and build some social support systems of your own. Here are some ways of doing just that:

- Plan to participate in any orientation programs. These serve the threefold purpose of providing you with a great deal of important information, familiarizing you with the campus and its facilities, and giving you the opportunity to meet and begin networking with other students.
- Take steps to deal with any academic weaknesses. Take mathematics and writing placement tests if you have reason to believe you may need some extra help in these areas. It is not uncommon for adult students to need a math refresher course or a program to help alleviate math anxiety. Ignoring a weakness won't make it go away.
- Look into adult reentry programs. Many institutions offer adults workshops focusing on ways to improve study skills, textbook reading, test-taking, and time-management skills.
- Build new support networks by joining an adult student organization, making a point of meeting other adult students through workshops, or actively seeking out a "study buddy" in each class—that invaluable friend who shares and understands your experience.
- You can incorporate your new status as "student" into your family life. Doing your homework with your children at a designated "homework time" is a valuable family activity and reinforces the importance of education.
- Make sure you take a reasonable course load in your first semester. It is far better to have some extra time on your hands and to succeed magnificently than to spend the entire semester on the brink of a breakdown. Also, whenever possible, try to focus your first courses not only on requirements, but also on areas of personal interest.

■ Faculty members, advisers, and student affairs personnel are there to help you during difficult times—let them assist you as often as necessary.

After completing your first semester, you will probably look back in wonder at why you thought going back to school was so imposing. Certainly, it's not without its occasional exasperations. But, as with life, keeping things in perspective and maintaining your sense of humor make the difference between just coping and succeeding brilliantly.

What International Students Need to Know About Admission to U.S. Colleges

Kitty M. Villa

Assistant Director, International Office, University of Texas at Austin

Selecting an institution and securing admission require a significant investment of time and effort.

There are two principles to remember about admission to a college in the United States. First, applying is almost never a one-time request for admission but an ongoing process that may involve several exchanges of information between applicant and institution. "Admission process" or "application process" means that a "yes" or "no" is usually not immediate, and requests for additional information are to be expected. To successfully manage this process, you must be prepared to send additional information when requested and then wait for replies. You need a thoughtful balance of persistence to communicate regularly and effectively with your selected colleges and patience to endure what can be a very long process.

The second principle involves a marketplace analogy. The most successful applicants are alert to opportunities to create a positive impression that sets them apart from other applicants. They are able to market themselves to their target institution. Institutions are also trying to attract the highest-quality student that they can. The admissions process presents you with the opportunity to analyze your strengths and weaknesses as a student and to look for ways to present yourself in the most marketable manner.

FIRST STEP—SELECTING INSTITUTIONS

With thousands of institutions of higher education in the United States, how do you begin to narrow your choices down to the institutions that are best for you? There are many factors to consider, and you must ultimately decide which factors are most important to you.

Location

You may spend several years studying in the United States. Do you prefer an urban or rural campus? Large or small metropolitan area? If you need to live on campus, will you be unhappy at a college where most students commute from off-campus housing? How do you feel about extremely hot summers or cold winters? Eliminating institutions that do not match your preferences in terms of location will narrow your choices.

Recommendations from Friends, Professors, or Others

There are valid academic reasons to consider the recommendations of people who know you well and have first-hand knowledge about particular institutions. Friends and contacts may be able to provide you with "inside information" about the campus or its academic programs to which published sources have no access. You should carefully balance anecdotal information with your own research and your own impressions. However, current and former students, professors, and others may provide excellent information during the application process.

Your Own Academic and Career Goals

Consideration of your academic goals is more complex than it may seem at first glance. All institutions do not offer the same academic programs. The application form usually provides a definitive listing of the academic programs offered by an institution. A course catalog describes the degree program and all the courses offered. In addition to printed sources, there is a tremendous amount of institutional information available through the Internet. Program descriptions, even course descriptions and course syllabi, are often available to peruse online.

You may be interested in the rankings of either the college or of a program of study. Keep in mind, however, that rankings usually assume that quality is quantifiable. Rankings are usually based on presumptions about how data relate to quality that are likely to be unproven. It is important to carefully consider the source and the criteria of any ranking information before believing and acting upon it.

Your Own Educational Background

You may be concerned about the interpretation of your educational credentials, since your country's degree nomenclature and the grading scale may differ from those in the United States. Colleges use reference books about the educational systems of other countries to help them understand specific educational credentials. Generally, these credentials are interpreted by each institution; there is not a single interpretation that applies to every institution. The lack of uniformity is good news for most students, since it means that students from a wide variety of educational backgrounds can find a U.S. college that is appropriate to their needs.

To choose an appropriate institution, you can and should do an informal self-evaluation of your educational background. This self-analysis involves three important questions:

How Many Years of Study Have You Completed?

Completion of secondary school with at least twelve total years of education usually qualifies students to apply for undergraduate degree programs. Completion of a college degree program that involves at least sixteen years of total education qualifies one to apply for admission to graduate (master's) degree programs in the United States.

Does the Education That You Have Completed in Your Country Provide Access to Further Study in the United States?

Consider the kind of institution where you completed your previous studies. If educational opportunities in your country are limited, it may be necessary to investigate many U.S. institutions and programs in order to find a match.

Are Your Previous Marks or Grades Excellent, Average, or Poor?

Your educational record influences your choice of U.S. institutions. If your grades are average or poor, it may be advisable to apply to several institutions with minimally difficult or noncompetitive entrance levels.

YOU are one of the best sources of information about the level and quality of your previous studies. Awareness of your educational assets and liabilities will serve you well throughout the application process.

SECOND STEP—PLANNING AND ASSEMBLING THE APPLICATION

Planning and assembling a college application can be compared to the construction of a building. First, you must start with a solid foundation, which is the application form itself. The application, often available online as well as in paper form, usually contains a wealth of useful information, such as deadlines, fees, and degree programs available at that institution. To build a solid application, it is best to begin well in advance of the application deadline.

How to Obtain the Application Form

Application forms and links to institutional Web sites may also be available at a U.S. educational advising center associated with the American Embassy or Consulate in your country. These centers are excellent resources for international students and provide information about standardized test administration, scholarships, and other matters important to students who are interested in studying in the United States. Your local U.S. Embassy or Consulate can guide you to the nearest educational advising center.

Completing the Application Form

Whether sent by mail or electronically, the application form must be thoroughly filled out. Parts of the application may not seem to apply to you or your situation. Do your best to answer all the questions.

Remember that this is a process. You provide information, and your proposed college then requests clarification and further information. If you have questions, it is better to initiate the entire process by submitting the application form rather than asking questions before you apply. The college will be better able to respond to you after it has your application. Always complete as much as you can. Do not permit uncertainty about the completion of the application form to cause unnecessary delays.

What Are the Key Components of a Complete Application?

Institutional requirements vary, but the standard components of a complete application include:

- Transcript
- Required standardized examination scores
- Evidence of financial support
- Letters of recommendation
- Application fee

Transcript

A complete academic record or transcript includes all courses completed, grades earned, and degrees awarded. Most colleges require an official transcript to be sent directly from the school or university. In many other countries, however, the practice is to issue official transcripts and degree certificates directly to the student. If you have only one official copy of your transcript, it may be a challenge to get additional certified copies that are acceptable to U.S. colleges. Some institutions will issue additional official copies for application purposes.

If your institution does not provide this service, you may have to seek an alternate source of certification. As a last resort, you may send a photocopy of your official transcript, explain that you have only one original, and ask the college for advice on how to deal with this situation.

Required Standardized Examination Scores

Arranging to take standardized examinations and earning the required scores seem to cause the most anxiety for international students.

The college application form usually indicates which examinations are required. The standardized examination required most often for undergraduate admission is the Test of English as a Foreign Language (TOEFL). In most countries, TOEFL has changed from a paper-and-pencil test to a computer-based test. Institutions may also require the SAT of undergraduate applicants. Some institutions also require the Test of Spoken English (TSE). These standardized examinations are administered by the Educational Testing Service (ETS).

These examinations are offered in almost every country of the world. It is advisable to begin planning for standardized examinations at least six months prior to the application deadline of your desired institutions. Test centers fill up quickly, so it is important to register as soon as possible. Information about the examinations is available at U.S. educational advising centers associated with embassies or consulates.

FOR MORE INFORMATION

Questions about test formats, locations, dates, and registration may be addressed to:

TOEFL/TSE Services
P.O. Box 6151
Princeton, New Jersey 08541-6151
Web sites: http://www.ets.org
          http://www.toefl.org
E-mail: toefl@ets.org
Telephone: 609-771-7100

Most universities require that the original test scores, not a student copy, be sent directly by the testing service. When you register for the test, be sure to indicate that the testing service should send the test scores directly to your proposed colleges.

You should usually begin your application process before you receive your test scores. Delaying submission of your application until the test scores arrive may cause you to miss deadlines and negatively effect the outcome of your application. If you want to know your scores in order to assess your chances of admission to an institution with rigorous admission standards, you should take the tests early.

Many colleges in the United States set minimum required scores on the TOEFL or on other standardized examinations. Test scores are an important factor, but most institutions also look at a number of other factors in their consideration of a candidate for admission.

Evidence of Financial Support

Evidence of financial support is required to issue immigration documents to admitted students. This is part of a complete application package but usually plays no role in determining admission. Most institutions make admissions decisions without regard to the source and amount of financial support.

Letters of Recommendation

Most institutions require one or more letters of recommendation. The best letters are written by former professors, employers, or others who can comment on your academic achievements or professional potential.

Some colleges provide a special form for the letters of recommendation. If possible, use the forms provided. If you are applying to a large number of colleges, however, or if your recommenders are not available to complete several forms, it may be necessary for you to duplicate a general recommendation letter.

Application Fee

Most colleges require an application fee, which must be paid to initiate consideration of the application.

THIRD STEP—DISTINGUISH YOUR APPLICATION

To distinguish your application—to market yourself successfully—is ultimately the most important part of the application process. As you select your prospective colleges, you begin to analyze your strengths and weaknesses as a prospective student. As you complete your application, you should strive to create a positive impression and set yourself apart from other applicants, to highlight your assets and bring these qualities to the attention of the appropriate college administrators and professors. Applying early is a very easy way to distinguish your application.

Deadline or Guideline?

The application deadline is the last date that an application for a given semester will be accepted. Often, the application will specify that all required documents and information be submitted before the deadline date. To meet the deadlines, start the application process early. This also gives you more time to take—and perhaps retake and improve on—the required standardized tests.

Admissions deliberations may take several weeks or months. In the meantime, most institutions accept additional information, including improved test scores, after the posted deadline.

Even if your application is initially rejected, you may be able to provide additional information to change the decision. You can request reconsideration based on additional information, such as improved test scores, strong letters of recommendation, or information about your class rank. Applying early allows more time to improve your application. Also, some students may decide not to accept their offers of admission, leaving room for offers to students on a waiting list. Reconsideration of the admission decisions can occur well beyond the application deadline.

Think of the deadline as a guideline rather than an impermeable barrier. Many factors—the strength of the application, your research interests, the number of spaces available at the proposed institution—can override the enforcement of an application deadline. So, if you lack a test score or transcript by the official deadline, you may still be able to apply and be accepted.

Statement of Purpose

The statement of purpose is your first and perhaps best opportunity to present yourself as an excellent candidate for admission. Whether or not a personal history essay or statement of purpose is required, always include a carefully written statement of purpose with your applications. A compelling statement of purpose does not have to be lengthy, but it should include some basic components:

- Part One—Introduce yourself and describe your educational background. This is your opportunity to describe any facet of your educational experience that you wish to emphasize. Perhaps you attended a highly ranked secondary school or college in your home country. Mention the name and any noteworthy characteristics of the secondary school or college from which you graduated. Explain the grading scale used at your school. Do not forget to mention your rank in your graduating class and any honors you may have received. This is not the time to be modest.
- Part Two—Describe your current academic interests and goals. It is very important to describe in some detail your specific study or career interests. Think about how these will fit into those of the institution to which you are applying, and mention the reasons why you have selected that institution.
- Part Three—Describe your long-term goals. When you finish your program of study, what do you plan to do next? If you already have a job offer or a career plan, describe it. Give some thought to how you'll demonstrate that studying in the United States will ultimately benefit others.

Use Personal Contacts When Possible

Appropriate and judicious use of your own network of contacts can be very helpful. Friends, former professors, former students of your selected institutions, and others may be willing to advise you during the application process and provide you with introductions to key administrators or professors. If suggested, you may wish to contact certain professors or administrators by mail, telephone, or e-mail. A personal visit to discuss your interest in the institution may be appropriate. Whatever your choice of communication, try to make the encounter pleasant and personal. Your goal is to make a positive impression, not to rush the admission decision.

There is no single right way to be admitted to U.S. colleges. The same characteristics that make the educational choice in the United States so difficult—the number of institutions and the variety of programs of study—are the same attributes that allow so many international students to find the institution that's right for them.

Searching for Two-Year Colleges Online

The Internet can be a great tool for gathering information about two-year colleges. There are many worthwhile sites that are ready to help guide you through the various aspects of the selection process, including Peterson's College Bound Channel at www.petersons.com/ugchannel.

HOW PETERSON'S COLLEGE BOUND CHANNEL CAN HELP

Choosing a college involves a serious commitment of time and resources. Therefore, it is important to have the most up-to-date information about prospective schools at your fingertips. That is why Peterson's College Bound Channel is a great place to start your college search and selection process.

Find a College

Peterson's College Bound Channel is a comprehensive information resource that will help you make sense of the college admissions process. Peterson's College Bound Channel offers visitors enhanced search criteria and an easily navigable interface. The Channel is organized into various sections that make finding a program easy and fun. You can search for colleges based on name or location for starters, or do a detailed search on the following criteria:

- *Location*
- *Major*
- *Tuition*
- *Size*
- *Student/faculty ratio*
- *Average GPA*
- *Type of college*
- *Sports*
- *Religion*

Once you have found the school of your choice, simply click on it to get information about the institution, including majors, off-campus programs, costs, faculty, admission requirements, location, academic programs, academic facilities, athletics, student life, financial aid, student government, and application information and contacts.

E-mail the School

If, after looking at the information provided on Peterson's College Bound Channel, you still have questions, you can send an e-mail directly to the admissions department of the school. Just click on the "E-mail the School" button and send your message. In most instances, if you keep your questions short and to the point, you will receive an answer in no time at all.

School Web Site

For institutions that have provided information about their Web sites, simply click on the "School Web Site" button and you will be taken directly to that institution's Web page. Once you arrive at the school's Web site, look around and get a feel for the place. Often, schools offer virtual tours of the campus, complete with photos and commentary. If you have specific questions about the school, a visit to a school's Web site will often yield an answer.

Detailed Description

If the schools you are interested in have provided Peterson's with an **In-Depth Description,** you can do a keyword search on that description. Here, schools are given the opportunity to communicate unique features of their programs to prospective students.

Microsite

Several educational institutions provide students access to microsites, where more information about the types of resources and services offered can be found. In addition, students can take campus tours, apply for admissions, and explore academic majors.

Apply

The Apply link gives you the ability to directly apply to the school online.

Add to My List

The My List feature is designed to help you with your college planning. Here you can save the list of schools you're interested in, which you can then revisit at any time, access all the features of the site, and be reminded of important dates. You'll also be notified when new features are added to the site.

Get Recruited

Here's your chance to stop looking for colleges and let them find you with CollegesWantYou[SM] (www. collegeswantyou.com), the new approach to the search and selection process. Unlike other college search and selection tools, CollegesWantYou[SM] allows you to enter information on your preferences, test scores, and extracurricular activities into the online form, and before you know it, colleges that meet your specifications will be in touch with you. Registration is free, and all you need to do is complete a short profile indicating your preferences and then sit back and wait as colleges contact you directly!

Write Admissions Essays

This year, 500,000 college applicants will write 500,000 different admissions essays. Half will be rejected by their first-choice school, while only 11 percent will gain admission to the nation's most selective colleges. With acceptance rates at all-time lows, setting yourself apart requires more than just blockbuster SAT scores and impeccable transcripts-it requires the perfect application essay. Named "the world's premier application essay editing service" by the New York Times Learning Network and "one of the best essay services on the Internet" by the *Washington Post,* EssayEdge (www.essayedge.com) has helped more

applicants write successful personal statements than any other company in the world. Learn more about EssayEdge and how it can give you an edge over hundreds of applicants with comparable academic credentials.

Practice for Your Test

At Thomson Peterson's, we understand that the college admissions process can be very stressful. With the stakes so high and the competition getting tighter every year, it's easy to feel like the process is out of your control. Fortunately, preparing for college admissions tests, like the SAT, ACT, and PSAT, helps you exert some control over the options you will have available to you. You can visit Peterson's Test Prep Channel (www.petersonstestprep. com) to learn more about how Thomson Peterson's can help you maximize your scores—and your options.

Use the Tools to Your Advantage

Choosing a college is an involved and complicated process. The tools available to you on www.petersons.com/ ugchannel can help you to be more productive in this process. So, what are you waiting for? Fire up your computer; your future alma mater may be just a click away!

How to Use This Guide

Peterson's Two-Year Colleges 2006 contains a wealth of information for anyone interested in colleges offering associate degrees. This section details the criteria that institutions must meet to be included in this guide and provides information about research procedures used by Thomson Peterson's.

QUICK-REFERENCE CHART

The **Two-Year Colleges At-a-Glance** chart is a geographically arranged table that lists colleges by name and city within the state, territory, or country in which they are located. Areas are listed in the following order: United States, U.S. territories, and other countries; the institutions in these countries are included because they are accredited by recognized U.S. accrediting bodies (see **Criteria for Inclusion** section).

The At-a-Glance chart contains basic information that enables you to compare institutions quickly according to broad characteristics such as enrollment, application requirements, types of financial aid available, and numbers of sports and majors offered. An asterisk (*) after an institution's name denotes that a **Special Message** is included in the college's profile, and a dagger (†) indicates that an institution has one or more entries in the **In-Depth Descriptions of Two-Year Colleges** section.

Column 1: Degrees Awarded

C = *college transfer associate degree:* the degree awarded after a "university-parallel" program, equivalent to the first two years of a bachelor's degree.

T = *terminal associate degree:* the degree resulting from a one- to three-year program providing training for a specific occupation.

B = *bachelor's degree (baccalaureate):* the degree resulting from a liberal arts, science, professional, or preprofessional program normally lasting four years, although in some cases an accelerated program can be completed in three years.

M = *master's degree:* the first graduate (postbaccalaureate) degree in the liberal arts and sciences and certain professional fields, usually requiring one to two years of full-time study.

D = *doctoral degree (doctorate):* the highest degree awarded in research-oriented academic disciplines, usually requiring from three to six years of full-time study beyond the baccalaureate and intended as preparation for university-level teaching and research.

F = *first professional degree:* the degree required to be academically qualified to practice in certain professions, such as law and medicine, having as a prerequisite at least two years of college credit and usually requiring a total of at least six years of study including prior college-level work.

Column 2: Institutional Control

Private institutions are designated as one of the following:

Ind = *independent* (nonprofit)

I-R = *independent-religious:* nonprofit; sponsored by or affiliated with a particular religious group or having a nondenominational or interdenominational religious orientation.

Prop = *proprietary* (profit-making)

Public institutions are designated by the source of funding, as follows:

Fed = *federal*

St = *state*

Comm = *commonwealth* (Puerto Rico)

Terr = *territory* (U.S. territories)

Cou = *county*

Dist = *district:* an administrative unit of public education, often having boundaries different from units of local government.

City = *city*

St-L = *state and local:* "local" may refer to county, district, or city.

St-R = *state-related:* funded primarily by the state but administratively autonomous.

Column 3: Student Body

M = *men only* (100% of student body)

PM = *coed, primarily men*

W = *women only* (100% of student body)

PW = *coed, primarily women*

M/W = *coeducational*

Column 4: Undergraduate Enrollment

The figure shown represents the number of full-time and part-time students enrolled in undergraduate degree programs as of fall 2004.

Columns 5–7: Enrollment Percentages

Figures are shown for the percentages of the fall 2004 undergraduate enrollment made up of students attending part-time (column 5) and students 25 years of age or older (column 6). Also listed is the percentage of students in the last graduating class who completed a college-transfer associate program and went directly on to four-year colleges (column 7).

For columns 8 through 15, the following letter codes are used: Y = yes; N = no; R = recommended; S = for some.

Columns 8–10: Admission Policies

The information in these columns shows whether the college has an open admission policy (column 8) whereby virtually all applicants are accepted without regard to standardized test scores, grade average, or class rank; whether a high school equivalency certificate is accepted in place of a high school diploma for admission consideration (column 9); and whether a high school transcript (column 10) is required as part of the application process. In column 10, the combination of the codes R and S indicates that a high school transcript is recommended for all applicants and required for some.

Columns 11–12: Financial Aid

These columns show which colleges offer the following types of financial aid: need-based aid (column 11) and part-time jobs (column 12), including those offered through the federal government's Federal Work-Study program.

Columns 13–15: Services and Facilities

These columns show which colleges offer the following: career counseling (column 13) on either an individual or group basis, job placement services (column 14) for individual students, and college-owned or -operated housing facilities (column 16) for noncommuting students.

Column 16: Sports

This figure indicates the number of sports that a college offers at the intramural and/or intercollegiate levels.

Column 17: Majors

This figure indicates the number of major fields of study in which a college offers degree programs.

PROFILES OF TWO-YEAR COLLEGES AND SPECIAL MESSAGES

The **Profiles of Two-Year Colleges** contain basic data in capsule form for quick review and comparison. The following outline of the profile format shows the section headings and the items that each section covers. Any item that does not apply to a particular college or for which no information was supplied is omitted from that college's profile. **Special Messages,** which appear in the profiles just below the bulleted highlights, have been written by those colleges that wished to supplement the profile data with additional information.

Bulleted Highlights

The bulleted highlights feature important information for quick reference and comparison. The number of *possible* bulleted highlights that an ideal profile would have if all questions were answered in a timely manner are represented below. However, not every institution provides all of the information necessary to fill out every bulleted line. In such instances, the line will not appear.

First bullet

Institutional control: Private institutions are designated as *independent* (nonprofit), *proprietary* (profit-making), or independent, with a specific religious denomination or affiliation. Nondenominational or interdenominational religious orientation is possible and would be indicated. Public institutions are designated by the source of funding. Designations include *federal, state, province, commonwealth* (Puerto Rico), *territory* (U.S. territories), *county, district* (an educational administrative unit often having boundaries different from units of local government), *city, state and local* (local may refer to county, district, or city), or *state-related* (funded primarily by the state but administratively autonomous).

Religious affiliation is also noted here.

Institutional type: Each institution is classified as one of the following:

Two-year college: Awards baccalaureate degrees, but the vast majority of students are enrolled in two-year programs.

Four-year college: Awards baccalaureate degrees; may also award associate degrees; does not award graduate (postbaccalaureate) degrees.

Five-year college: Awards a five-year baccalaureate in a professional field such as architecture or pharmacy; does not award graduate degrees.

Upper-level institution: Awards baccalaureate degrees, but entering students must have at least two years of previous college-level credit; may also offer graduate degrees.

Comprehensive institution: Awards baccalaureate degrees; may also award associate degrees; offers graduate degree programs, primarily at the master's, specialist's, or professional level, although one or two doctoral programs may be offered.

University: Offers four years of undergraduate work plus graduate degrees through the doctorate in more than two academic or professional fields.

Founding date: If the year an institution was chartered differs from the year when instruction actually began, the earlier date is given.

System or administrative affiliation: Any coordinate institutions or system affiliations are indicated. An institution that has separate colleges or campuses for men and women but shares facilities and courses it is termed a coordinate institution. A formal administrative grouping of institutions, either private or public, of which the college is a part, or the name of a single institution with which the college is administratively affiliated is a system.

Second bullet

Calendar: Most colleges indicate one of the following: *4-1-4, 4-4-1,* or a similar arrangement (two terms of equal length plus an abbreviated winter or spring term, with the numbers referring to months); *semesters; trimesters; quarters; 3-3* (three courses for each of three terms); *modular* (the academic year is divided into small blocks of time; course of varying lengths are assembled according to individual programs); or *standard year* (for most Canadian institutions).

Third bullet

Degree: This names the full range of levels of certificates, diplomas, and degrees, including prebaccalaureate, graduate, and professional, that are offered by this institution.

Associate degree: Normally requires at least two but fewer than four years of full-time college work or its equivalent.

Bachelor's degree (baccalaureate): Requires at least four years but not more than five years of full-time college-level work or its equivalent. This includes all bachelor's degrees in which the normal four years of work are completed in three years and bachelor's degrees conferred in a five-year cooperative (work-study plan) program. A cooperative plan provides for alternate class attendance and employment in business, industry, or government. This allows students to combine actual work experience with their college studies.

Master's degree: Requires the successful completion of a program of study of at least the full-time equivalent of one but not more than two years of work beyond the bachelor's degree.

Doctoral degree (doctorate): The highest degree in graduate study. The doctoral degree classification includes

Doctor of Education, Doctor of Juridical Science, Doctor of Public Health, and the Doctor of Philosophy in any nonprofessional field.

First professional degree: The first postbaccalaureate degree in one of the following fields: chiropractic (DC, DCM), dentistry (DDS, DMD), medicine (MD), optometry (OD), osteopathic medicine (DO), rabbinical and Talmudic studies (MHL, Rav), pharmacy (BPharm, PharmD), podiatry (PodD, DP, DPM), veterinary medicine (DVM), law (JD), or divinity/ministry (BD, MDiv).

First professional certificate (postdegree): Requires completion of an organized program of study after completion of the first professional degree. Examples are refresher courses or additional units of study in a specialty or subspecialty.

Post-master's certificate: Requires completion of an organized program of study of 24 credit hours beyond the master's degree but does not meet the requirements of academic degrees at the doctoral level.

Fourth bullet

Setting: Schools are designated as *urban* (located within a major city), *suburban* (a residential area within commuting distance of a major city), *small-town* (a small but compactly settled area not within commuting distance of a major city), or *rural* (a remote and sparsely populated area). The phrase *easy access to . . .* indicates that the campus is within an hour's drive of the nearest major metropolitan area that has a population greater than 500,000.

Fifth bullet

Endowment: The total dollar value of donations, investments, and other monies to the institution or the multicampus educational system of which the institution is a part.

Sixth bullet

Student body: An institution is *coed* (coeducational—admits men and women), *primarily* (80 percent or more) *women, primarily men, women only,* or *men only.*

Undergraduate students: Represents the number of full-time and part-time students enrolled in undergraduate degree programs as of fall 2004. The percentage of full-time undergraduates and the percentages of men and women are given.

Special Messages

These messages have been written by those colleges that wished to supplement the profile data with additional timely and important information.

Category Overviews

Undergraduates

For fall 2004, the number of full- and part-time undergraduate students is listed. This list provides the number of states and U.S. territories, including the District of Columbia and Puerto Rico and other countries, from which undergraduates come. Percentages are given of undergraduates who are from out of state; Native American, African American, and Asian American or Pacific Islander; international students; transfer students; and living on campus

Retention: The percentage of 2003 freshmen who returned for the fall 2004 term.

Freshmen

Admission: Figures are given for the number of students who applied for fall 2004 admission, the number of those who were admitted, and the number who enrolled. Freshman statistics include the average high school GPA; the percentage of freshmen who took the SAT and received verbal and math scores above 500, above 600, and above 700, as well as the percentage of freshmen taking the ACT Assessment who received a composite score of 18 or higher.

Faculty

Total: The total number of faculty members; the percentage of full-time faculty members as of fall 2004; and the percentage of full-time faculty members who hold doctoral/first professional/terminal degrees.

Student-faculty ratio: The school's estimate of the ratio of matriculated undergraduate students to faculty members teaching undergraduate courses.

Majors

This section lists the major fields of study offered by the college.

Academic Programs

Details are given here on study options available at each college.

Accelerated degree program: Students may earn a bachelor's degree in three academic years.

Academic remediation for entering students: Instructional courses designed for students deficient in the general competencies necessary for a regular postsecondary curriculum and educational setting.

Adult/continuing education programs: Courses offered for nontraditional students who are currently working or are returning to formal education.

Advanced placement: Credit toward a degree awarded for acceptable scores on College Board Advanced Placement tests.

Cooperative (co-op) education programs: Formal arrangements with off-campus employers allowing students to combine work and study in order to gain degree-related experience, usually extending the time required to complete a degree.

Distance learning: For-credit courses that can be accessed off campus via cable television, the Internet, satellite, videotapes, correspondence course, or other media.

Double major: A program of study in which a student concurrently completes the requirements of two majors.

English as a second language (ESL): A course of study designed specifically for students whose native language is not English.

External degree programs: A program of study in which students earn credits toward a degree through a combination of independent study, college courses, proficiency examinations, and personal experience. External degree programs require minimal or no classroom attendance.

Freshmen honors college: A separate academic program for talented freshmen.

Honors programs: Any special program for very able students offering the opportunity for educational enrichment, independent study, acceleration, or some combination of these.

Independent study: Academic work, usually undertaken outside the regular classroom structure, chosen or designed by the student with departmental approval and instructor supervision.

Internships: Any short-term, supervised work experience usually related to a student's major field for which the student earns academic credit. The work can be full- or part-time, on or off campus, paid or unpaid.

Off-campus study: A formal arrangement with one or more domestic institutions under which students may take courses at the other institution(s) for credit.

Part-time degree program: Students may earn a degree through part-time enrollment in regular session (daytime) classes or evening, weekend, or summer classes.

Self-designed major: Program of study based on individual interests, designed by the student with the assistance of an adviser.

Services for LD students: Special help for learning-disabled students with resolvable difficulties, such as dyslexia.

Study abroad: An arrangement by which a student completes part of the academic program studying in another country. A college may operate a campus abroad or it may have a cooperative agreement with other U.S. institutions or institutions in other countries.

Summer session for credit: Summer courses through which students may make up degree work or accelerate their program.

Tutorials: Undergraduates can arrange for special in-depth academic assignments (not for remediation) working with faculty one-on-one or in small groups.

ROTC: Army, Navy, or Air Force Reserve Officers' Training Corps programs offered either on campus or at a cooperating host institution [designated by (C)].

Unusual degree programs: Nontraditional programs such as a 3-2 degree program, in which 3 years of liberal arts study is followed by two years of study in a professional field at another institution (or in a professional division of the same institution), resulting in two bachelor's degrees or a bachelor's and a master's degree.

Library

This section lists the name of the main library; the number of other libraries on campus; numbers of books, microform titles, serials, commercial online services, and audiovisual materials.

Computers on Campus

This paragraph includes the number of on-campus computer terminals and PCs available for general student use and their locations; computer purchase or lease plans; PC requirements for entering students; and campuswide computer network, e-mail, and access to computer labs, the Internet, and software.

Student Life

Housing options: The institution's policy about whether students are permitted to live off campus or are required to live on campus for a specified period; whether freshmen-only, coed, single-sex, cooperative, and disabled student housing options are available; whether campus housing is leased by the school and/or provided by a third party; whether freshman applicants are given priority for college housing. The phrase *college housing not available* indicates that no college-owned or -operated housing facilities are provided for undergraduates and that noncommuting students must arrange for their own accommodations. However, housing may be offered by a third party.

Activities and organizations: Lists information on drama-theater groups, choral groups, marching bands, student-run campus newspapers, student-run radio stations, and social organizations (sororities, fraternities, eating clubs, etc.) and how many are represented on campus.

Campus security: Campus safety measures including 24-hour emergency response devices (telephones and alarms) and patrols by trained security personnel, student patrols, late-night transport-escort service, and controlled dormitory access (key, security card, etc.).

Student services: Information provided indicates services offered to students by the college, such as legal services, health clinics, personal-psychological counseling, and women's centers.

Athletics

Membership in one or more of the following athletic associations is indicated by initials.

NCAA: National Collegiate Athletic Association
NAIA: National Association of Intercollegiate Athletics
NCCAA: National Christian College Athletic Association
NSCAA: National Small College Athletic Association
NJCAA: National Junior College Athletic Association
CIAU: Canadian Interuniversity Athletic Union

The overall NCAA division in which all or most intercollegiate teams compete is designated by a roman numeral I, II, or III. All teams that do not compete in this division are listed as exceptions.

Sports offered by the college are divided into two groups: *intercollegiate* (**M** or **W** following the name of each sport indicates that it is offered for men or women) and *intramural*. An **s** in parentheses following an **M** or **W** for an intercollegiate sport indicates that athletic scholarships (or grants-in-aid) are offered for men or women in that sport, and a **c** indicates a club team as opposed to a varsity team.

Standardized Tests

The most commonly required standardized tests are ACT Assessment, SAT, and SAT Subject Tests. These and other standardized tests may be used for selective admission, as a basis for counseling or course placement, or for both purposes. This section notes if a test is used for admission or placement and whether it is required, required for some, or recommended.

In addition to the ACT Assessment and SAT, the following standardized entrance and placement examinations are referred to by their initials:

ABLE: Adult Basic Learning Examination
ACT ASSET: ACT Assessment of Skills for Successful Entry and Transfer
ACT PEP: ACT Proficiency Examination Program
CAT: California Achievement Tests
CELT: Comprehensive English Language Test
CPAt: Career Programs Assessment
CPT: Computerized Placement Test
DAT: Differential Aptitude Test
LSAT: Law School Admission Test
MAPS: Multiple Assessment Program Service
MCAT: Medical College Admission Test
MMPI: Minnesota Multiphasic Personality Inventory

OAT: Optometry Admission Test

PAA: Prueba de Aptitude Académica (Spanish-language version of the SAT I)

PCAT: Pharmacy College Admission Test

PSAT: Preliminary SAT

SCAT: Scholastic College Aptitude Test

SRA: Scientific Research Association (administers verbal, arithmetical, and achievement tests)

TABE: Test of Adult Basic Education

TASP: Texas Academic Skills Program

TOEFL: Test of English as a Foreign Language (for international students whose native language is not English)

WPCT: Washington Pre-College Test

Costs

Costs are given for the 2005–06 academic year or for the 2004–05 academic year if 2005–06 figures were not yet available. Annual expenses may be expressed as a comprehensive fee (including full-time tuition, mandatory fees, and college room and board) or as separate figures for full-time tuition, fees, room and board, or room only. For public institutions where tuition differs according to residence, separate figures are given for area or state residents and for nonresidents. Part-time tuition is expressed in terms of a per-unit rate (per credit, per semester hour, etc.) as specified by the institution.

The tuition structure at some institutions is complex in that freshmen and sophomores may be charged a different rate from that for juniors and seniors, a professional or vocational division may have a different fee structure from the liberal arts division of the same institution, or part-time tuition may be prorated on a sliding scale according to the number of credit hours taken. Tuition and fees may vary according to academic program, campus/location, class time (day, evening, weekend), course/credit load, course level, degree level, reciprocity agreements, and student level. Room and board charges are reported as an average for one academic year and may vary according to the board plan selected, campus/location, type of housing facility, or student level. If no college-owned or -operated housing facilities are offered, the phrase *college housing not available* will appear in the Housing section of the Student Life paragraph.

Tuition payment plans that may be offered to undergraduates include *tuition prepayment, installment payments,* and *deferred payment.* A tuition prepayment plan gives a student the option of locking in the current tuition rate for the entire term of enrollment by paying the full amount in advance rather than year by year. Colleges that offer such a prepayment plan may also help the student to arrange financing.

The availability of full or partial undergraduate tuition waivers to minority students, children of alumni, employees or their children, adult students, and senior citizens may be listed.

Financial Aid

Financial aid information presented represents aid awarded to undergraduates for the 2004–05 academic year. Figures are given for the number of undergraduates who applied for aid, the number who were judged to have need, and the number who had their need met. The number of Federal Work-Study and/or part-time jobs and average earnings are listed, as well as the number of non-need based awards that were made. Non-need based awards are college-administered scholarships for which the college determines the recipient and amount of each award. These scholarships are awarded to full-time undergraduates on the basis of merit or personal attributes without regard to need, although they many certainly be given to students who also happen to need aid. The average percent of need met, the average financial aid package awarded to undergraduates (the amount of scholarships, grants, Work-Study payments, or loans in the institutionally administered financial aid package divided by the number of students who received any financial aid—amounts used to pay the officially designated Expected Family Contribution (EFC), such as PLUS or other alternative loans, are excluded from the amounts reported), the average amount of need-based gift aid, and the average amount of non-need based aid are given. Average indebtedness, which is the average per-borrower indebtedness of the last graduating undergraduate class from amounts borrowed at this institution through any loan programs, excluding parent loans, is listed last.

Applying

Application and admission options include the following:

Early admission: Highly qualified students may matriculate before graduating from high school.

Early action plan: An admission plan that allows students to apply and be notified of an admission decision well in advance of the regular notification dates. If accepted, the candidate is not committed to enroll; students may reply to the offer under the college's regular reply policy.

Early decision plan: A plan that permits students to apply and be notified of an admission decision (and financial aid offer, if applicable) well in advance of the regular notification date. Applicants agree to accept an offer of admission and to withdraw their applications from other colleges. Candidates who are not accepted under early decision are automatically considered with the regular applicant pool, without prejudice.

Deferred entrance: The practice of permitting accepted students to postpone enrollment, usually for a period of one academic term or year.

Application fee: The fee required with an application is noted. This is typically nonrefundable, although under certain specified conditions it may be waived or returned.

Requirements: Other application requirements are grouped into three categories: *required for all, required for some,* and *recommended.* They may include an essay, standardized test scores, a high school transcript, a minimum high school grade point average (expressed as a number on a scale of 0 to 4.0, where 4.0 equals A, 3.0 equals B, etc.), letters of recommendation, an interview on campus or with local alumni, and, for certain types of schools or programs, special requirements such as a musical audition or an art portfolio.

Application deadlines and notification dates: Admission application deadlines and dates for notification of acceptance or rejection are given either as specific dates or as *rolling* and *continuous.* Rolling means that applications are processed as they are received, and qualified students are accepted as long as there are openings. Continuous means that applicants are notified of acceptance or rejection as applications are processed up until the date indicated or the actual beginning of classes. The application deadline and the notification date for transfers are given if they differ from the dates for freshmen. Early decision and early action application deadlines and notification dates are also indicated when relevant.

Freshmen Application Contact

The name, title, and telephone number of the person to contact for application information are given at the end of the profile. The admission office address is listed. Toll-free telephone numbers may also be included. The admission office fax number and e-mail address, if available, are listed, provided the school wanted them printed for use by prospective students.

Additional Information

Each college that has an **In-Depth Description** in the guide will have a cross-reference appended to the profile, referring you directly to that **In-Depth Description.**

IN-DEPTH DESCRIPTIONS OF TWO-YEAR COLLEGES

Nearly 100 two-page narrative descriptions appear here. This section shifts the focus to a variety of other factors, some of them intangible, which should also be considered in the college decision-making equation. The descriptions are prepared exclusively by college officials and are designed to help give students a better sense of the individuality of each institution, in terms that include campus environment, student activities, and lifestyle. Such quality-of-life intangibles can be the deciding factors in the college selection process. The absence from this section of any college does not constitute an editorial decision on the part of Thomson Peterson's. In essence, this section is an open forum for colleges, on a voluntary basis, to commu-

nicate their particular messages to prospective students. The colleges included have paid a fee to Thomson Peterson's to provide this information to you. The descriptions are arranged alphabetically by the official name of the institution and are edited to provide a consistent format across entries for your ease of comparison.

INDEXES

Associate Degree Programs at Two- and Four-Year Colleges

These indexes present hundreds of undergraduate fields of study that are currently offered most widely according to the colleges' responses on *Thomson Peterson's Annual Survey of Undergraduate Institutions.* The majors appear in alphabetical order, each followed by an alphabetical list of the schools that offer an associate-level program in that field. Liberal Arts and Studies indicates a general program with no specified major. The terms used for the majors are those of the U.S. Department of Education Classification of Instructional Programs (CIPs). Many institutions, however, use different terms. Readers should visit www.petersons.com in order to contact a college and ask for its catalog or refer to the **In-Depth Description** in this book for the school's exact terminology. In addition, although the term "major" is used in this guide, some colleges may use other terms, such as "concentration," "program of study," or "field."

DATA COLLECTION PROCEDURES

The data contained in the **Profiles of Two-Year Colleges** and **Indexes** were researched between fall 2004 and spring 2005 through *Thomson Peterson's Annual Survey of Undergraduate Institutions.* Questionnaires were sent to the more than 1,700 colleges that meet the outlined inclusion criteria. All data included in this edition have been submitted by officials (usually admission and financial aid officers, registrars, or institutional research personnel) at the colleges themselves. In addition, the great majority of institutions that submitted data were contacted directly by Thomson Peterson's research staff to verify unusual figures, resolve discrepancies, and obtain additional data. All usable information received in time for publication has been included. The omission of any particular item from the **Profiles of Two-Year Colleges** and **Indexes** listing signifies either that the item is not applicable to that institution or that data were not available. Because of the comprehensive editorial review that takes place in our offices and because all material comes directly from college officials, Thomson Peterson's has every reason to believe that the information presented in this guide is accurate at the time of printing. However, students should check with a specific college or university at the time of application to verify such figures as tuition and fees, which may have changed since the publication of this volume.

CRITERIA FOR INCLUSION IN THIS BOOK

Peterson's Two-Year Colleges 2006 covers accredited institutions in the United States, U.S. territories, and other countries that award the associate degree as their most popular undergraduate offering (a few also offer bachelor's, master's, or doctoral degrees). The term two-year college is the commonly used designation for institutions that grant the associate degree, since two years is the normal duration of the traditional associate degree program. However, some programs may be completed in one year, others require three years, and, of course, part-time programs may take a considerably longer period. Therefore, "two-year college" should be understood as a conventional term that accurately describes most of the institutions included in this guide but which should not be taken literally in all cases. Also included are some non-degree-granting institutions, usually branch campuses of a multicampus system, which offer the equivalent of the first two years of a bachelor's degree, transferable to a bachelor's degree–granting institution.

To be included in this guide, an institution must have full accreditation or be a candidate for accreditation (preaccreditation) status by an institutional or specialized accrediting body recognized by the U.S. Department of Education or the Council for Higher Education Accreditation (CHEA). Institutional accrediting bodies, which review each institution as a whole, include the six regional associations of schools and colleges (Middle States, New England, North Central, Northwest, Southern, and Western), each of which is responsible for a specified portion of the United States and its territories. Other institutional accrediting bodies are national in scope and accredit specific kinds of institutions (e.g., Bible colleges, independent colleges, and rabbinical and Talmudic schools). Program registration by the New York State Board of Regents is considered to be the equivalent of institutional accreditation, since the board requires that all programs offered by an institution meet its standards before recognition is granted. This guide also includes institutions outside the United States that are accredited by these U.S. accrediting bodies. There are recognized specialized or professional accrediting bodies in more than forty different fields, each of which is authorized to accredit institutions or specific programs in its particular field. For specialized institutions that offer programs in one field only, we designate this to be the equivalent of institutional accreditation. A full explanation of the accrediting process and complete information on recognized, institutional (regional and national) and specialized accrediting bodies can be found online at www.chea.org or at www.ed.gov//admins/finaid/accred/index.html.

Quick-Reference
CHART

Two-Year Colleges At-a-Glance

This chart includes the names and locations of accredited two-year colleges in the United States and U.S. territories and shows institutions' responses to the *Thomson Peterson's Survey of Undergraduate Institutions*. If an institution submitted incomplete data, one or more columns opposite the institution's name is blank. An asterisk after the school name denotes a *Special Message* following the college's profile, and a dagger indicates that the institution has one or more entries in the *In-Depth Descriptions of Two-Year Colleges* section. If a school does not appear, it did not report any of the information.

Degrees Awarded: College Transfer Associate (C); Terminal Associate (T); Bachelor's (B); Master's (M); Doctoral (D); First Professional (F)
Institutional Control: County, District, City, State and Local, State-Related; Independent, Independent-Religious, Proprietary; Federal, State, Commonwealth, Territory
Student Body: Men, Primarily Men, Women, Primarily Women, Coed

Y—Yes; N—No; R—Recommended; S—For Some

Institution	Location	Degrees Awarded	Institutional Control	Student Body	Undergraduate Enrollment Fall 2004	Percent Attending Part-Time	Percent 25 Years of Age or Older	Percent of Grads Going on to Four-Year Colleges	Open Admissions	High School Equivalency Certificate Accepted	High School Transcript Required	Need-Based Aid Required	Part-Time Jobs Available	Career Counseling Available	Job Placement Services Available	College Housing Available	Number of Sports Offered	Number of Majors Offered
UNITED STATES																		
Alabama																		
Alabama Southern Community College	Monroeville	C,T	St	M/W	1,500		36		Y	Y	Y	Y	Y	Y	Y	N	3	35
Bessemer State Technical College	Bessemer	T	St	M/W	2,087		51		N	Y	Y	Y	Y	Y	Y	N		10
Bevill State Community College	Sumiton	C,T	St	M/W	4,327	43	33		Y	Y	Y	Y	Y	Y	Y		9	12
Bishop State Community College	Mobile	C,T	St	M/W	4,439	44	51		Y	Y	Y	Y	Y			N	3	16
Calhoun Community College	Decatur	C,T	St	M/W	8,879		38		Y	Y	Y	S				N		46
Central Alabama Community College	Alexander City	C,T	St	M/W	1,790	52	33		Y	Y	Y	Y	Y	Y	Y	N	5	11
Chattahoochee Valley Community College	Phenix City	C,T	St	M/W	613	18	45	18	Y	Y	Y	Y	Y	Y	Y	N	2	24
Community College of the Air Force	Maxwell Air Force Base	T	Fed	PM	364,934	85	63		Y		Y			Y		Y	15	51
Enterprise-Ozark Community College	Enterprise	C,T	St	M/W	1,590	46	21		Y	Y	Y	Y	Y	Y	Y	N	6	28
Gadsden State Community College	Gadsden	C,T	St	M/W	5,549		34		Y	Y	Y	Y	Y	Y	Y	Y	7	21
Gadsden State Community College-Ayers Campus	Anniston	C,T	St	M/W	1,137	40	39		Y	Y	Y	Y	Y	Y	Y	Y		11
George Corley Wallace State Community College	Selma	C,T	St	M/W	1,758		35	25	Y	Y		Y	Y	Y	Y	N	4	22
George C. Wallace Community College	Dothan	C,T	St	M/W	3,083		43		Y	Y		Y	Y	Y	Y	N	3	21
H. Councill Trenholm State Technical College	Montgomery	T	St	M/W	1,615	46												
ITT Technical Institute	Birmingham	T,B	Prop	M/W	415													
James H. Faulkner State Community College*	Bay Minette	C,T	St	M/W	3,067	37	39		Y	Y	Y	Y	Y	Y	Y	Y	6	16
Jefferson Davis Community College	Brewton	C,T	St	M/W	1,442	37												
Jefferson State Community College	Birmingham	C,T	St	M/W	7,007	58	36		Y	Y	S	Y	Y	Y	Y	N	8	22
J. F. Drake State Technical College	Huntsville	C	St	M/W	786	38	55		Y		Y		Y	Y	Y	N		7
Lawson State Community College	Birmingham	C,T	St	M/W	2,168	35												
Lurleen B. Wallace Community College	Andalusia	C,T	St	M/W	1,490													
Northeast Alabama Community College	Rainsville	C,T	St	M/W	2,015	51	32	30	Y	Y			Y	Y	Y	N		18
Northwest-Shoals Community College	Muscle Shoals	C	St	M/W	4,338	45	40		Y	Y	Y	Y	Y	Y	Y	Y	9	35
Prince Institute of Professional Studies	Montgomery	T	Ind	PW	94	40												
Reid State Technical College	Evergreen	T	St	M/W	620	37	55		Y		Y		Y	Y	Y	N		2
Remington College–Mobile Campus	Mobile	C,T,B	Prop	M/W	454													
Shelton State Community College	Tuscaloosa	C,T	St	M/W	5,778	39	32		Y	Y	Y	Y	Y	Y	Y	N	6	32
Snead State Community College	Boaz	C,T	St	M/W	1,787	37												
Southern Union State Community College	Wadley	C,T	St	M/W			33		Y	Y	Y	Y	Y	Y	Y	N	6	6
Alaska																		
U of Alaska Anchorage, Kenai Peninsula College	Soldotna	C,T	St	M/W	1,923													
U of Alaska Anchorage, Matanuska-Susitna College	Palmer	C,T	St	M/W	1,313	72	82		Y	Y	Y	Y	Y	Y		N		8
U of Alaska Southeast, Ketchikan Campus	Ketchikan	C,T	St-L	M/W	692													
American Samoa																		
American Samoa Community College	Pago Pago	C,T	Terr	M/W	1,537					Y	Y		Y	Y	Y	N	8	16
Arizona																		
Arizona Western College	Yuma	C,T	St-L	M/W	6,450	72			Y	Y			Y	Y	Y	Y	9	43
Central Arizona College	Coolidge	C,T	Cou	M/W	6,525		71		Y				Y	Y	Y	Y	7	26
Chandler-Gilbert Community College	Chandler	C,T	St-L	M/W	8,663		31	95	Y				Y	Y	Y			7
Chaparral College	Tucson	C,T,B	Prop	M/W	400													
Cochise College	Douglas	C,T	St-L	M/W	4,270	52	33		Y			R	Y	Y	Y	Y	3	37
Coconino Community College	Flagstaff	C,T	St	M/W	3,689		38		Y	Y	S	Y	Y			N		7
Eastern Arizona College	Thatcher	C,T	St-L	M/W	3,732	61	19		Y			R	Y	Y	Y	Y	10	49
Estrella Mountain Community College	Avondale	C,T	St-L	M/W	5,947	77			Y					Y	Y			2
Everest College	Phoenix	C,T	Prop	M/W	650	39	95	2	N	Y	Y	Y		Y	Y	N		4
GateWay Community College	Phoenix	C,T	St-L	M/W	9,377	90	31		Y			S	Y	Y	Y	N	3	39
Glendale Community College	Glendale	C,T	St-L	M/W	20,649	70	44		Y			S	Y	Y	Y	N	11	28
High-Tech Institute	Phoenix	T,B	Prop	M/W	1,544													
International Institute of the Americas	Phoenix	C,T,B	Ind	M/W	1,386													
ITT Technical Institute	Tucson	T,B	Prop	M/W	375													
Mohave Community College	Kingman	C,T	St	M/W	6,187	80	69		Y			S		Y		N		23
Northland Pioneer College	Holbrook	C,T	St-L	M/W	4,928	80			Y									
Paradise Valley Community College	Phoenix	C,T	St-L	M/W	8,237				Y				Y	Y	Y	N	6	7
Phoenix College	Phoenix	C,T	St-L	M/W	13,150													
Pima Community College	Tucson	C,T	St-L	M/W	31,555	70	42	15	Y			Y	Y	Y	Y	N	16	59

This chart includes the names and locations of accredited two-year colleges in the United States and U.S. territories and shows institutions' responses to the *Thomson Peterson's Survey of Undergraduate Institutions*. If an institution submitted incomplete data, one or more columns opposite the institution's name is blank.

An asterisk after the school name denotes a *Special Message* following the college's profile, and a dagger indicates that the institution has one or more entries in the *In-Depth Descriptions of Two-Year Colleges* section. If a school does not appear, it did not report any of the information.

Legend: Y—Yes; N—No; R—Recommended; S—For Some

Column headers (left to right): Degrees Awarded [College Transfer Associate (C), Terminal Associate (T), Bachelor's (B), Master's (M), Doctoral (D), First Professional (F)]; Institutional Control [County, District, City, State and Local, State-Related, Proprietary, Federal, Independent, Independent-Religious]; Student Body [Men, Primarily Men, Women, Primarily Women, Coed]; Undergraduate Enrollment Fall 2004; Percent Attending Part-Time; Percent 25 Years of Age or Older; Percent of Grade Going on to Four-Year Colleges; High School Equivalency Certificate Accepted; Open Admissions; High School Transcript Required; Need-Based Aid Available; Part-Time Jobs Available; Career Counseling Available; Job Placement Services Available; College Housing Available; Number of Sports Offered; Number of Majors Offered.

Institution	Location	Degrees	Control	Student Body	Enroll. Fall 2004	% Part-Time	% 25+	% to 4-Yr	HS Equiv	Open Adm	HS Transcript	Need-Based Aid	Part-Time Jobs	Career Counsel	Job Placement	College Housing	Sports	Majors
Pima Medical Institute	Mesa	T	Prop	M/W	592				N					S		N		2
Pima Medical Institute	Tucson	T	Prop	M/W	711				N		Y			S	Y	N	N	3
The Refrigeration School	Phoenix	T	Prop	M/W	350													
Scottsdale Community College	Scottsdale	C,T	St-L	M/W	11,465													
South Mountain Community College	Phoenix	C,T	St-L	M/W	3,933		42	18	Y			Y	Y	Y	Y	N	8	19
Tohono O'odham Community College	Sells	C,T	Ind	M/W	171													
Universal Technical Institute	Avondale	T	Priv								Y			Y				
Yavapai College	Prescott	C,T	St-L	M/W	7,375	81	70	80	Y	Y	Y	Y	Y	Y	Y	Y	5	25
Arkansas																		
Arkansas Northeastern College	Blytheville	C,T	St	M/W	2,018	45	40	5	Y	Y	R	Y	Y	Y	Y	N		14
Arkansas State University–Beebe	Beebe	C,T	St	M/W	3,192	44												
Arkansas State University–Mountain Home	Mountain Home	C,T	St	M/W	1,313	46	44		Y	Y	Y	Y		Y		N		11
Black River Technical College	Pocahontas	C,T	St	M/W	1,243	48	53	4	Y	Y	S	Y		Y	Y	N		10
Cossatot Community College of the University of Arkansas	De Queen	C,T	St	M/W	1,067				Y	Y	R	Y	Y	Y	Y	N		12
Crowley's Ridge College	Paragould	C,T	I-R	M/W	183													
East Arkansas Community College	Forrest City	C,T	St	M/W	1,415		47		Y	Y	Y	Y		Y	Y	N		7
ITT Technical Institute	Little Rock	T,B	Prop	M/W	352													
Mid-South Community College	West Memphis	C,T	St	M/W	1,265	67	48		Y	Y	Y	Y	Y	Y	Y	N		5
North Arkansas College	Harrison	C,T	St-L	M/W	2,120	43												
Ouachita Technical College	Malvern	C,T	St	M/W	1,381	61	45		Y	Y	Y	Y	Y	Y	Y	N		16
Ozarka College	Melbourne	C,T	St	M/W	756	25												
Phillips Comm Coll of the U of Arkansas	Helena	C,T	St-L	M/W	2,322		45	80	Y	Y		Y	Y	Y	Y	N	4	31
Pulaski Technical College	North Little Rock	C,T	St	M/W	7,222	50	54		Y	Y	Y	Y	Y	Y	Y	N		6
Rich Mountain Community College	Mena	C,T	St-L	M/W	973			75	Y	Y	Y	Y	Y	Y	Y	N		2
South Arkansas Community College	El Dorado	C,T	St	M/W	1,087	64												
Southeast Arkansas College	Pine Bluff	C,T	St	M/W	2,197	54												
Southern Arkansas University Tech	Camden	C,T	St	M/W	1,223	62												
University of Arkansas Community College at Batesville	Batesville	C,T	St	M/W	1,317	40	40		Y	Y		Y	Y		Y			13
University of Arkansas Community College at Hope	Hope	C,T	St	M/W	1,213	44	38		Y			Y	Y	Y	Y	N		10
University of Arkansas Community College at Morrilton	Morrilton	C,T	St	M/W	1,514		44		Y	Y	Y	Y	Y	Y		N		17
California																		
American Academy of Dramatic Arts/Hollywood†	Hollywood	C	Ind	M/W	177													
American River College	Sacramento	C,T	Dist	M/W	30,000													
Butte College	Oroville	C,T	Dist	M/W	14,251													
Cabrillo College	Aptos	C,T	Dist	M/W	13,905													
California Culinary Academy	San Francisco	T	Prop	M/W	822													
Cañada College	Redwood City	C,T	St-L	M/W	6,421													
Cerro Coso Community College	Ridgecrest	C,T	St	M/W	5,020	76	55		Y		R	Y	Y	Y	Y	N	2	31
Chabot College	Hayward	C,T	St	M/W	15,075													
Citrus College	Glendora	C,T	St-L	M/W	11,790		25		Y	Y	Y	Y	Y	Y	Y	N	12	43
Coastline Community College	Fountain Valley	C	St-L	M/W	8,559	94												
Coleman College	San Marcos	T	Ind	M/W	203													
College of the Canyons	Santa Clarita	C,T	St-L	M/W	14,190	70	35		Y		R	Y	Y	Y	Y	N	11	46
College of the Desert	Palm Desert	C,T	St-L	M/W	9,946													
College of the Sequoias	Visalia	C,T	St-L	M/W	11,169	60												
Columbia College	Sonora	C,T	St-L	M/W	3,572	74	68	91	Y	Y	S	Y	Y	Y	Y	Y	3	32
Compton Community College	Compton	C,T	St-L	M/W	7,900		69	25	Y			Y	Y	Y	Y	N	6	76
Contra Costa College	San Pablo	C,T	St-L	M/W	8,834	55	54		Y			Y	Y	Y	Y	N	7	46
Copper Mountain College	Joshua Tree	C,T	St	M/W	1,800													
Cuesta College	San Luis Obispo	C,T	Dist	M/W	10,771													
Cuyamaca College	El Cajon	C,T	St	M/W	7,690													
De Anza College	Cupertino	C,T	St-L	M/W	23,344	62	52	13	Y			Y	Y	Y	Y	N	13	65
Diablo Valley College	Pleasant Hill	C,T	St-L	M/W	21,097													
East Los Angeles College	Monterey Park	C,T	St-L	M/W	24,015	76												
El Camino College	Torrance	C	St	M/W	27,039													
Fashion Careers of California College	San Diego	C,T	Prop	PW	104		9	0	N	Y	Y	Y	Y	Y	Y	N		2
Feather River College	Quincy	C,T	St-L	M/W	1,635	76	31		Y			Y	Y	Y	Y	Y	8	19
Fashion Inst of Design & Merchandising, LA Campus†	Los Angeles	C	Prop	M/W	3,191	20	18		N	Y	Y	Y	Y	Y	Y	N		8
Fashion Inst of Design & Merchandising, SD Campus	San Diego	C	Prop	M/W	259	11	10	18	N	Y	Y		Y	Y	Y	N		7
Fashion Inst of Design & Merchandising, SF Campus	San Francisco	C	Prop	PW	806	19	25		N	Y	Y		Y	Y	Y	N		8
Foothill College	Los Altos Hills	C,T	St-L	M/W	17,406		57	31	Y		R	Y	Y	Y	Y	N	9	66
Foundation College	San Diego	C,T	Ind	M/W	106				N	Y				Y		N		6
Gavilan College	Gilroy	C,T	St-L	M/W	5,060													
Glendale Community College	Glendale	C,T	St-L	M/W	15,767	70	42		Y		R	Y	Y	Y	Y	N	9	61
ITT Technical Institute	Anaheim	T,B	Prop	M/W	642													
ITT Technical Institute	Rancho Cordova	T,B	Prop	M/W	518													
ITT Technical Institute	San Bernardino	T,B	Prop	M/W	920													
ITT Technical Institute	San Diego	T,B	Prop	M/W	990													

This chart includes the names and locations of accredited two-year colleges in the United States and U.S. territories and shows institutions' responses to the *Thomson Peterson's Survey of Undergraduate Institutions*. If an institution submitted incomplete data, one or more columns opposite the institution's name is blank.
An asterisk after the school name denotes a *Special Message* following the college's profile, and a dagger indicates that the institution has one or more entries in the *In-Depth Descriptions of Two-Year Colleges* section. If a school does not appear, it did not report any of the information.

Y—Yes; N—No; R—Recommended; S—For Some

Name	Location	Degrees Awarded	Institutional Control	Student Body	Undergrad Enroll. Fall 2004	% Attending Part-Time	% 25 or Older	% Grads to Four-Year	Open Admissions	HS Equiv. Cert. Accepted	HS Transcript Required	Need-Based Aid Required	Part-Time Jobs Available	Career Counseling Available	Job Placement Services	College Housing Available	No. of Sports	No. of Majors
ITT Technical Institute	Sylmar	T,B	Prop	M/W	755													
ITT Technical Institute	Torrance	T,B	Prop	M/W	708													
ITT Technical Institute	West Covina	T,B	Prop	M/W	816													
Long Beach City College	Long Beach	C,T	St	M/W	28,069	54	23		Y		R	Y	Y	Y	Y	N	18	69
Los Angeles Harbor College	Wilmington	C,T	St-L	M/W	9,469	76												
Los Angeles Pierce College	Woodland Hills	C,T	St-L	M/W	16,255													
Los Angeles Trade-Technical College	Los Angeles	C,T	St-L	M/W	13,194	68												
Los Angeles Valley College	Van Nuys	C,T	St-L	M/W	18,761	73												
Maric College	Salida	T	Prop	PW	289													
Maric College	San Diego	C,T	Prop	M/W	298													
Merritt College	Oakland	C,T	St-L	M/W	7,984	85												
MiraCosta College*	Oceanside	C,T	St	M/W	10,166													
Modesto Junior College	Modesto	C,T	St-L	M/W	17,535	53			Y		R	Y	Y	Y	Y	N	15	87
Mt. San Antonio College	Walnut	C,T	Dist	M/W	26,440	70												
Mt. San Jacinto College	San Jacinto	C,T	St-L	M/W	12,592													
Napa Valley College	Napa	C,T	St-L	M/W	6,908	72			Y		S	Y	Y	Y	Y	N	20	37
National Polytechnic College of Engineering and Oceaneering	Wilmington	C	Prop	PM	272													
Orange Coast College	Costa Mesa	C,T	St-L	M/W	22,520	60		34	Y				Y	Y	Y	N	14	102
Oxnard College	Oxnard	C	St	M/W	7,233													
Palomar College	San Marcos	C	St-L	M/W	28,597													
Pasadena City College	Pasadena	C,T	St-L	M/W	29,688	42			Y				Y	Y	Y	N	11	104
Pima Medical Institute	Chula Vista	T	Prop	M/W	447						Y	Y		Y	Y	N		2
Platt College†	Newport Beach	C,B	Ind	M/W	270													
Platt College San Diego*	San Diego	C,B	Prop	M/W	335	70	90		N	Y	Y					N		22
Professional Golfers Career College	Temecula	T	Ind	PM	318	50				Y	Y			Y	Y	Y		
Riverside Community College District	Riverside	T	St-L	M/W	32,228	73	40		Y		Y	Y	Y	Y	Y	N	16	65
The Salvation Army College for Officer Training at Crestmont	Rancho Palos Verdes	C,T	I-R	M/W	33	100			N	Y	Y	Y				Y		1
San Diego City College	San Diego	C	St-L	M/W	13,625	63			Y		S	Y	Y	Y	Y	N	16	68
San Diego Miramar College	San Diego	C	St-L	M/W	8,080	47	55		Y				Y	Y	Y	N	2	35
San Joaquin Delta College	Stockton	C,T	Dist	M/W	17,131	61	40		Y				Y	Y	Y	N	18	82
San Joaquin Valley College	Visalia	T	Ind	M/W	2,924					Y	Y	Y		Y	Y	Y		19
San Jose City College	San Jose	C,T	Dist	M/W	9,819													
Santa Barbara City College	Santa Barbara	T	St-L	M/W	15,456	59	25		Y	Y	R	Y	Y	Y	Y	N	10	79
Santa Monica College†	Santa Monica	C,T	St-L	M/W	24,497	64												
Santa Rosa Junior College	Santa Rosa	C,T	St-L	M/W	32,567	56			Y				Y	Y	Y	N	15	70
Sierra College	Rocklin	C,T	St	M/W	19,416	72												
Silicon Valley College	Walnut Creek	T,B	Prop	M/W	472													
Solano Community College	Suisun City	C,T	St-L	M/W	12,027	46			Y	Y		Y	Y	Y	Y	N	7	48
Southwestern College	Chula Vista	C,T	St-L	M/W	18,799	70												
Taft College	Taft	C	St-L	M/W	7,024	92	55		Y		S	Y	Y	Y	Y	Y	5	24
Ventura College	Ventura	C,T	St-L	M/W	12,096	66												
Victor Valley College	Victorville	C,T	St	M/W	10,580	65												
Vista Community College	Berkeley	C,T	St-L	M/W	4,500													
West Hills Community College	Coalinga	C,T	St	M/W	4,344	58												
Westwood College–Anaheim†	Anaheim	T,B	Prop	M/W	674	15												
Westwood College–Inland Empire†	Upland	T,B	Prop	M/W	803	19												
Westwood College–Long Beach†	Long Beach	T,B	Prop	M/W	265	50			Y	Y	Y	Y	Y	Y	Y	N	2	4
Westwood College–Los Angeles†	Los Angeles	T,B	Prop	M/W	679	15												
Yuba College	Marysville	C	St-L	M/W	9,165	48			Y	Y	Y	Y	Y	Y	Y		9	58
Colorado																		
Arapahoe Community College	Littleton	C,T	St	M/W	8,000				Y				Y	Y	Y	N	6	50
CollegeAmerica–Fort Collins	Fort Collins	T,B	Prop	M/W	232													
Colorado Mountn Coll, Alpine Cmps	Steamboat Springs	C,T	Dist	M/W	1,104	21			Y	Y	Y	Y	Y	Y	Y	Y	6	20
Colorado Mountn Coll*†	Glenwood Springs	C,T	Dist	M/W	493	23			Y	Y	Y	Y	Y	Y	Y	Y	7	25
Colorado Mountn Coll, Timberline Cmps	Leadville	C,T	Dist	M/W	407	33			Y	Y	Y	Y	Y	Y	Y	Y	6	24
Colorado Northwestern Community College*	Rangely	C,T	St	M/W	2,242	78		12	Y	Y	Y	Y	Y	Y	Y	Y	12	40
Colorado School of Trades	Lakewood	T	Prop	M/W	115													
Community College of Aurora	Aurora	C,T	St	M/W	5,525	73	59	20	Y				Y	Y	Y	Y		17
Community College of Denver	Denver	C,T	St	M/W	9,274	76	47		Y				Y	Y	Y	N	23	29
Front Range Community College	Westminster	C,T	St	M/W	15,669	66	19		Y				Y	Y	Y	N		30
Institute of Business & Medical Careers	Fort Collins	T	Priv	PW	302													
IntelliTec College	Colorado Springs	T	Prop	M/W	427													
IntelliTec College	Grand Junction	C	Prop	M/W	255													
ITT Technical Institute	Thornton	T,B	Prop	M/W	491													
Morgan Community College	Fort Morgan	C,T	St	M/W	1,564	78												
Otero Junior College	La Junta	C,T	St	M/W	1,676	52	49	36	Y	Y	R	Y	Y	Y	Y	Y	5	27
Pikes Peak Community College	Colorado Springs	C,T	St	M/W	10,581	65												
Pima Medical Institute	Denver	T	Prop	M/W	724				N		S	Y			Y	N		4
Red Rocks Community College	Lakewood	C,T	St	M/W	7,693	71												

This chart includes the names and locations of accredited two-year colleges in the United States and U.S. territories and shows institutions' responses to the *Thomson Peterson's Survey of Undergraduate Institutions*. If an institution submitted incomplete data, one or more columns opposite the institution's name is blank.
An asterisk after the school name denotes a *Special Message* following the college's profile, and a dagger indicates that the institution has one or more entries in the *In-Depth Descriptions of Two-Year Colleges* section. If a school does not appear, it did not report any of the information.

Y—Yes; N—No; R—Recommended; S—For Some

Institution	Location	Degrees Awarded	Institutional Control	Student Body	Undergrad Enrollment Fall 2004	Percent Attending Part-Time	Percent 25 Years or Older	Percent of Grads Going on to Four-Year Colleges	HS Equivalency Cert Accepted	HS Transcript Required	Open Admissions	Need-Based Aid Required	Part-Time Jobs Available	Career Counseling Available	Job Placement Services Available	College Housing Available	Number of Sports Offered	Number of Majors Offered
Trinidad State Junior College	Trinidad	C,T	St	M/W	2,106		59							Y	Y	Y	Y	13	50
Westwood College–Denver†	Broomfield	T	Prop	M/W	951														
Westwood College–Denver North†	Denver	T,B	Prop	M/W	1,423	24	32		N	Y	Y	Y	Y	Y	Y	N		23
Westwood College–Denver South†	Denver	T,B	Prop	M/W	429	31													
Connecticut																		
Asnuntuck Community College	Enfield	T	St	M/W	1,476	69	50		Y	Y	Y	Y	Y	Y	Y	N		15
Briarwood College†	Southington	C,T,B	Prop	M/W	637	38	38	7	N	Y	Y	Y	Y	Y	Y	Y	3	22
Capital Community College	Hartford	C,T	St	M/W	3,436	74	56		Y	Y	R	Y	Y	Y	Y	N		20
Gateway Community College	New Haven	C,T	St	M/W	5,326	71	53	40	Y	Y	Y	Y	Y	Y	Y	N	4	34
Goodwin College	East Hartford	C,T	Prop	M/W	940	85	59		Y	Y	Y		Y	Y	Y	N		12
International College of Hospitality Management, *César Ritz**†	Suffield	C,T	Prop	M/W	116		14	35	N	Y	Y	Y	Y	Y	Y	Y	3	1
Manchester Community College	Manchester	C,T	St	M/W	5,906	57	35		Y	Y	Y	Y	Y	Y	Y	N	4	31
Middlesex Community College	Middletown	C,T	St	M/W	2,400	69													
Naugatuck Valley Community College	Waterbury	C,T	St	M/W	5,155														
Northwestern Connecticut Community-Technical Coll	Winsted	C,T	St	M/W	1,516	66	36	30	Y	Y		Y	Y	Y	Y	N		35
Quinebaug Valley Community College	Danielson	C,T	St	M/W	1,721	67	60		Y	Y	R,S	Y	Y	Y	Y	N		18
St. Vincent's College	Bridgeport	C	I-R	M/W	413														
Three Rivers Community College	Norwich	C,T	St	M/W	3,624		63		Y	Y	R	Y	Y	Y	Y	N	1	41
Tunxis Community College	Farmington	C,T	St	M/W	4,035	69	47		Y	Y	Y		Y	Y	Y	N		23
Delaware																		
Delaware College of Art and Design	Wilmington	C,T	Ind	M/W	194	24	13		N		Y		Y	Y	Y	Y		6
Delaware Tech & Comm Coll, Jack F Owens Cmps	Georgetown	T	St	M/W	3,565	58	48		Y			Y	Y	Y	Y	N	2	36
Delaware Tech & Comm Coll, Stanton/ Wilmington Cmps	Newark	T	St	M/W	6,892	60	49		Y		Y	Y	Y	Y	Y	N	5	43
Delaware Tech & Comm Coll, Terry Cmps	Dover	T	St	M/W	2,304		57		Y		Y	Y	Y	Y	Y	N		25
Florida																		
Brevard Community College	Cocoa	C,T	St	M/W	14,616	64	38	42	Y	Y	Y	Y	Y	Y	Y	N	5	37
Broward Community College	Fort Lauderdale	C,T	St	M/W	33,141	70	29	39	Y	Y		Y	Y	Y	Y	N	8	48
Central Florida Community College	Ocala	C,T	St-L	M/W	5,999	59	41	33	Y	Y	Y	Y	Y	Y	Y	N	4	31
Central Florida Institute	Palm Harbor	T	Prop	M/W	346														
Chipola College	Marianna	C,T,B	St	M/W	2,249	54	27	45	Y	Y		Y		Y	Y	N	3	19
College of Business and Technology†	Miami	C	Prop	M/W	1,000		70		Y	Y	Y			Y	Y			
Daytona Beach Community College	Daytona Beach	C,T	St	M/W	11,945	60	42		Y	Y	Y	Y	Y	Y	Y	N	11	95
Edison College	Fort Myers	C,T	St-L	M/W	10,642														
Florida Career College	Miami	T	Prop	M/W	2,131	19													
Florida Community College at Jacksonville	Jacksonville	C,T	St	M/W	23,425	70	47	81	Y	Y	Y					N	11	90
Florida Culinary Institute	West Palm Beach	T	Prop	M/W	600														
Florida Hospital College of Health Sciences	Orlando	T,B	Ind	M/W	1,403	57			Y	Y	S		Y	Y	Y	N		6
Florida Keys Community College	Key West	C,T	St	M/W	1,551		55		Y	Y	S	Y	Y	Y	Y	N		8
Florida National College	Hialeah	C,T	Prop	M/W	1,977	9	60		Y	Y	Y	Y	Y	Y	Y	N		34
The Florida School of Midwifery	Gainesville	T	Ind	W	25														
Full Sail Real World Education	Winter Park	T,B	Prop	PM	4,227		19		Y	Y	Y	Y	Y	Y	Y	N		6
Gulf Coast Community College	Panama City	C,T	St	M/W	6,058	63	41	60	Y	Y	Y	Y	Y	Y	Y	N	5	45
Hillsborough Community College	Tampa	C,T	St	M/W	22,149	68	37		Y	Y		Y	Y	Y	Y	N	5	63
Indian River Community College	Fort Pierce	C,T	St	M/W	38,464		48	78	Y	Y	Y	Y	Y	Y	Y	N	7	85
ITT Technical Institute	Fort Lauderdale	T,B	Prop	M/W	588														
ITT Technical Institute	Jacksonville	T,B	Prop	M/W	568														
ITT Technical Institute	Miami	T,B	Prop	M/W	450														
ITT Technical Institute	Tampa	T,B	Prop	M/W	573														
Keiser College	Fort Lauderdale	C,T,B	Prop	M/W	6,121	18	70		N	Y	Y	Y		Y	Y	N		22
Keiser College	Miami	C,T	Prop	M/W	393		55	12			Y					N		9
Keiser College	Pembroke Pines	C,T,B	Prop	M/W															
Keiser College	Port St. Lucie	C,T	Prop	M/W															
Keiser College	West Palm Beach	C,T,B	Prop	M/W															
Lake City Community College	Lake City	C,T	St	M/W	2,695														
Lake-Sumter Community College	Leesburg	C,T	St-L	M/W	3,576	67	39		Y	Y	Y	Y	Y	Y	Y	N	4	14
Manatee Community College	Bradenton	C,T	St	M/W	9,172	62													
Miami Dade College*†	Miami	C,T,B	St-L	M/W	57,026	65	41	78	Y	Y		Y	Y	Y	Y	N	10	142
National School of Technology, Inc.	North Miami Beach	T	Prop	M/W	608														
New England Inst of Tech & Florida Culinary Inst	West Palm Beach	C,T	Prop	M/W	1,200														
North Florida Community College	Madison	C,T	St	M/W	1,297	54													
Palm Beach Community College	Lake Worth	C,T	St	M/W	24,024	69	37	90	Y	Y		Y		Y	Y	N	9	67
Pasco-Hernando Community College	New Port Richey	C,T	St	M/W	7,213	66	42		Y	Y	Y	Y	Y	Y	Y	N	5	17
Pensacola Junior College	Pensacola	C,T	St	M/W	11,000														
Polk Community College	Winter Haven	C,T	St	M/W	7,047	72	38		Y	Y	Y	Y	Y	Y	Y	N	5	22
St. Johns River Community College	Palatka	C,T	St	M/W	3,459														
St. Petersburg College	St. Petersburg	C,T,B	St-L	M/W	24,102	67	46		Y	Y	Y	Y		Y	Y	N	5	46
Santa Fe Community College	Gainesville	C,T	St-L	M/W	13,806	52	28	59	Y	Y	Y	Y	Y	Y	Y	N	10	38

This chart includes the names and locations of accredited two-year colleges in the United States and U.S. territories and shows institutions' responses to the *Thomson Peterson's Survey of Undergraduate Institutions.* If an institution submitted incomplete data, one or more columns opposite the institution's name is blank.

An asterisk after the school name denotes a *Special Message* following the college's profile, and a dagger indicates that the institution has one or more entries in the *In-Depth Descriptions of Two-Year Colleges* section. If a school does not appear, it did not report any of the information.

Y—Yes; N—No; R—Recommended; S—For Some

College	Location	Degrees Awarded	Institutional Control	Student Body	Undergrad Enrollment Fall 2004	% Part-Time	% 25 or Older	% Grads to 4-Yr	Open Admissions	HS Equiv. Cert. Accepted	HS Transcript Required	Need-Based Aid Available	Part-Time Jobs Available	Career Counseling Available	Job Placement Services Available	College Housing Available	Number of Sports Offered	Number of Majors Offered
Seminole Community College	Sanford	C,T	St-L	M/W	12,202	63	45			Y	Y	Y	Y	Y	Y	N	6	50
South University	West Palm Beach	T,B,M	Prop	M/W	502	31	38	3	N	Y	Y	Y	Y	Y	Y			14
Valencia Community College	Orlando	C,T	St	M/W	29,447		31	75	Y	Y	Y	Y	Y	Y	Y	N		41
Georgia																		
Abraham Baldwin Agricultural College	Tifton	C,T	St	M/W	3,407	42												
Albany Technical College	Albany	T	St	M/W	2,783	51				Y		Y			Y	Y	N		11
Altamaha Technical College	Jesup	T	St	M/W	1,061	54				Y		Y					N		
Andrew College†	Cuthbert	C	I-R	M/W	331	1	2	96	N	Y	Y			Y			Y	20	39
Appalachian Technical College	Jasper	T	St	M/W	976	60											N		
Athens Technical College	Athens	T	St	M/W	2,815	59	40			Y		Y	Y	Y	Y	Y	N		33
Atlanta Metropolitan College	Atlanta	C,T	St	M/W	1,802	53	43		N	Y	Y	Y		Y			N	2	32
Atlanta Technical College	Atlanta	T	St	M/W	3,274	54				Y		Y					N		
Augusta Technical College	Augusta	T	St	M/W	4,343	52	49		Y		Y	Y	Y	Y	Y	N	1	10
Bainbridge College	Bainbridge	C,T	St	M/W	2,610		47	30		Y	S	Y	Y	Y	Y	N	2	34
Central Georgia Technical College	Macon	T	St	M/W	5,464	53	59			Y		Y	Y	Y	Y	Y	N		10
Chattahoochee Technical College	Marietta	T	St	M/W	5,116	60	52			Y		Y	Y	Y	Y	Y	N		14
Coastal Georgia Community College	Brunswick	C,T	St	M/W	2,210		50			Y		Y	Y	Y	Y		N	6	35
Columbus Technical College	Columbus	T	St	M/W	3,726	55						Y	Y	Y	Y	Y	N		5
Coosa Valley Technical College	Rome	T	St	M/W	2,755	60				Y		Y					N		
Darton College	Albany	C,T	St	M/W	4,126	54	38	75	N	Y		Y	Y	Y	Y	Y	N	10	60
DeKalb Technical College	Clarkston	T	St	M/W	4,576	61	64			Y		Y	Y	Y	Y	Y	N		19
East Central Technical College	Fitzgerald	T	St	M/W	1,272	49				Y		Y					N		
Flint River Technical College	Thomaston	T	St	M/W	894	44				Y		Y					N		
Gainesville College	Oakwood	C,T	St	M/W	5,781		11	80	N	Y		Y	Y	Y	Y	Y	N	10	46
Georgia Aviation & Technical College	Eastman	T	St	M/W	203	33				Y		Y					N		
Georgia Perimeter College	Decatur	C,T	St	M/W	18,986	55												
Gordon College	Barnesville	C,T	St	M/W	3,449	33		50	Y	Y		Y	Y	Y	Y		Y	13	25
Griffin Technical College	Griffin	T	St	M/W	3,383	58	49			Y		Y	Y		Y	Y	N		6
Gupton-Jones College of Funeral Service	Decatur	T	Ind	M/W	198													
Gwinnett Technical College	Lawrenceville	T	St	M/W	4,466	59	80			Y		Y					N		25
Heart of Georgia Technical College	Dublin	T	St	M/W	1,367	61				Y		Y					N		4
ITT Technical Institute	Duluth	T,B	Prop	M/W	101													
Lanier Technical College	Oakwood	T	St	M/W	3,019	62				Y		Y					N		16
Middle Georgia College*	Cochran	C,T	St	M/W	2,628	36	26		N	Y	Y	Y	Y	Y	Y	Y	Y	9	15
Middle Georgia Technical College	Warner Robbins	T	St	M/W	2,446	47				Y		Y	Y	Y			N		
Moultrie Technical College	Moultrie	T	St	M/W	1,826	50				Y		Y					N		
North Georgia Technical College	Clarkesville	T	St	M/W	1,934	48				Y		Y					Y		
North Metro Technical College	Acworth	T	St	M/W	1,827	63				Y		Y					N		
Northwestern Technical College	Rock Springs	T	St	M/W	1,663	56	60			Y		Y	Y	Y	Y	Y	N		10
Ogeechee Technical College	Statesboro	T	St	M/W	2,084	48	39			Y		Y					N		9
Okefenokee Technical College	Waycross	T	St	M/W	1,843	59				Y		Y					N		9
Sandersville Technical College	Sandersville	T	St	M/W	705	63				Y		Y					N		
Savannah Technical College	Savannah	T	St	M/W	3,714	57	59			Y		Y			Y	Y	N		11
Southeastern Technical College	Vidalia	T	St	M/W	1,048	53				Y		Y					N		9
South Georgia Technical College	Americus	T	St	M/W	1,693	46				Y		Y					Y	1	
Southwest Georgia Technical College	Thomasville	T	St	M/W	1,598	55	74			Y		Y	Y	Y	Y	Y	N		11
Swainsboro Technical College	Swainsboro	T	St	M/W	666	50				Y		Y					N		
Truett-McConnell College	Cleveland	C,T,B	I-R	M/W	359	9	4		N	Y	Y	Y					Y	6	6
Valdosta Technical College	Valdosta	T	St	M/W	2,303	54	29			Y		Y		Y	Y	Y	N		
Waycross College	Waycross	C,T	St	M/W	1,026	68											N		
West Central Technical College	Waco	T	St	M/W	2,634	68	13					Y	Y	Y	Y	Y	N		13
West Georgia Technical College	LaGrange	T	St	M/W	1,862	58	60			Y		Y	Y	Y			N		6
Westwood College–Atlanta Campus†	Atlanta	T,B	Prop	M/W														
Guam																		
Guam Community College	Barrigada	T	Terr	M/W	1,754	78	47		Y	Y	Y	Y	Y	Y			N		29
Hawaii																		
Hawaii Business College	Honolulu	C,T	Ind	M/W	303					Y	Y	Y	Y	Y	Y		N		6
Hawaii Community College	Hilo	C,T	St	M/W	2,409	57												
Hawaii Tokai International College	Honolulu	C	Ind	M/W	50													
Honolulu Community College	Honolulu	C,T	St	M/W	4,238	61												
Kapiolani Community College	Honolulu	C,T	St	M/W	7,174	61	40			Y			Y	Y	Y	Y	N	2	17
Kauai Community College	Lihue	C	St	M/W	1,210					Y	R,S	Y	Y	Y	Y	Y	N	3	11
Windward Community College	Kaneohe	C,T	St	M/W	1,761		32			Y		Y	Y	Y	Y	Y	N		2
Idaho																		
Apollo College	Boise	C,T	Prop	M/W	469	5	65			Y	Y	Y	Y		Y	Y	N		3
College of Southern Idaho	Twin Falls	C,T	St-L	M/W	7,105	55	49			Y	Y	Y	Y	Y	Y		Y	13	73

Two-Year Colleges At-a-Glance

This chart includes the names and locations of accredited two-year colleges in the United States and U.S. territories and shows institutions' responses to the *Thomson Peterson's Survey of Undergraduate Institutions*. If an institution submitted incomplete data, one or more columns opposite the institution's name is blank. An asterisk after the school name denotes a *Special Message* following the college's profile, and a dagger indicates that the institution has one or more entries in the *In-Depth Descriptions of Two-Year Colleges* section. If a school does not appear, it did not report any of the information.

Y—Yes; N—No; R—Recommended; S—For Some

Column headers (left to right): Degrees Awarded [College Transfer Associate (C); Terminal Associate (T); Bachelor's (B); Master's (M); Doctoral (D); First Professional (F)] · Institutional Control [County, District, City, State and Local, State Related; Federal, State, Commonwealth, Proprietary, Independent-Religious, Independent] · Student Body [Men, Primarily Men; Women, Primarily Women; Coed] · Undergraduate Enrollment Fall 2004 · Percent Attending Part-Time · Percent 25 Years of Age or Older · Percent of Grads Going on to Four-Year Colleges · High School Equivalency Certificate Accepted · Open Admissions · High School Transcript Required · Need-Based Aid Available · Part-Time Jobs Available · Career Counseling Available · Job Placement Services Available · College Housing Available · Number of Sports Available · Number of Majors Offered

Institution	City	Deg	Ctrl	Body	Enroll	%PT	%25+	%Grads	HSEq	OpnAd	HSTr	Need	PTJob	Career	JobPl	Hsng	Sports	Majors
Eastern Idaho Technical College	Idaho Falls	T	St	M/W	788	36	47		Y	Y	Y	Y		Y	Y	N		11
ITT Technical Institute	Boise	T,B	Prop	M/W	389													
North Idaho College	Coeur d'Alene	C,T	St-L	M/W	4,519	39	36		N	Y	S	Y	Y	Y	Y	Y	18	68
Illinois																		
Black Hawk College	Moline	C,T	St-L	M/W	6,600	52	43		Y		Y	Y	Y	Y	Y	N	6	70
Career Colleges of Chicago	Chicago	T	Prop	PW	144	76	71		Y	Y	Y	Y		Y	Y	N		4
Carl Sandburg College	Galesburg	C,T	St-L	M/W	5,000													
City Colls of Chicago, Malcolm X Coll	Chicago	C,T	St-L	M/W	8,024	49												
City Colls of Chicago, Wilbur Wright Coll	Chicago	C,T	St-L	M/W	6,896		43	33	Y	Y		Y	Y	Y	Y	N	6	30
College of DuPage	Glen Ellyn	C,T	St-L	M/W	29,854	64	34	76	Y			Y	Y	Y	Y	N	16	85
College of Lake County	Grayslake	C,T	Dist	M/W	15,866		41		Y		S	Y	Y	Y	Y	N	9	40
The Cooking and Hospitality Institute of Chicago†	Chicago	C,T	Prop	M/W	950													
Danville Area Community College	Danville	C,T	St-L	M/W	3,000		41		Y	Y	Y	Y		Y	Y	N	7	52
Elgin Community College	Elgin	C,T	St-L	M/W	10,851	69	51	72	Y		S		Y	Y	Y	N	7	49
Fox College	Oak Lawn		Prop	M/W	251													
Gem City College	Quincy	T	Prop	M/W	150													
Heartland Community College	Normal	C,T	St-L	M/W	4,566	60	38	94	Y	Y	R	Y		Y	Y	N		37
Highland Community College	Freeport	C,T	St-L	M/W	2,462	53	58	80	Y	Y	S	Y	Y	Y	Y	N	6	42
Illinois Eastern Comm Colls, Frontier Comm Coll	Fairfield	C,T	St-L	M/W	1,960	88	56		Y	Y	Y	Y	Y	Y	Y	N		8
Illinois Eastern Comm Colls, Lincoln Trail Coll	Robinson	C,T	St-L	M/W	1,496	73	54		Y	Y	Y	Y	Y	Y	Y	N	4	14
Illinois Eastern Comm Colls, Olney Central Coll	Olney	C,T	St-L	M/W	1,670	51	64		Y	Y	Y	Y	Y	Y	Y	N	4	19
Illinois Eastern Comm Colls, Wabash Valley Coll	Mount Carmel	C,T	St-L	M/W	5,191	88	53		Y	Y	Y	Y	Y	Y	Y	N	6	18
Illinois Valley Community College	Oglesby	C,T	Dist	M/W	4,315		6		Y			Y	Y	Y	Y	N	4	26
ITT Technical Institute	Burr Ridge	T	Prop	M/W	355													
ITT Technical Institute	Matteson	T	Prop	M/W	430													
ITT Technical Institute	Mount Prospect	T,B	Prop	M/W	590													
John A. Logan College	Carterville	C	St-L	M/W	5,501		54		Y	Y	Y		Y	Y	Y	N	5	49
John Wood Community College	Quincy	C,T	Dist	M/W	2,411	49	32		Y	Y	Y	Y	Y	Y		N	5	35
Kaskaskia College	Centralia	C,T	St-L	M/W	4,601	57	42		Y	Y	Y	Y	Y			N	6	21
Kishwaukee College	Malta	C,T	St-L	M/W	4,076	86												
Lake Land College	Mattoon	C,T	St-L	M/W	7,196		36		Y		R	Y	Y	Y	Y	N	8	37
Lewis and Clark Community College	Godfrey	C,T	Dist	M/W	7,446		30		Y		R	Y	Y	Y	Y	N	7	25
Lincoln College†	Lincoln	C	Ind	M/W	758	8												
Lincoln Land Community College	Springfield	C,T	Dist	M/W	6,942	60	39		Y		R	Y	Y	Y	Y	N	6	29
MacCormac College	Chicago	C,T	Ind	PW	377	58												
McHenry County College	Crystal Lake	C,T	St-L	M/W	5,940	66												
Moraine Valley Community College	Palos Hills	C,T	St-L	M/W	16,077	59	36	85	Y	Y	Y	Y	Y	Y	Y	Y	9	28
Morrison Institute of Technology†	Morrison	C,T	Ind	PM	125	3	8	20	Y		Y	Y	Y		Y		5	6
Morton College	Cicero	C,T	St-L	M/W	5,244													
Oakton Community College	Des Plaines	C,T	Dist	M/W	9,893													
Parkland College	Champaign	C,T	Dist	M/W	9,536	52	31		Y	Y	R	Y	Y	Y	Y		7	53
Prairie State College	Chicago Heights	C,T	St-L	M/W	5,342	67	50		Y		Y	Y	Y	Y	Y		9	24
Rend Lake College	Ina	C,T	St	M/W	5,142													
Richland Community College	Decatur	C,T	Dist	M/W	3,568		40	37	Y	Y	Y	Y	Y	Y	Y	N		27
Rock Valley College	Rockford	C,T	Dist	M/W	9,475	62	43		Y		Y	Y	Y	Y	Y	N	8	22
Sauk Valley Community College	Dixon	C,T	Dist	M/W	3,161		50		Y		R	Y	Y	Y	Y	N	5	52
Shawnee Community College	Ullin	C,T	St-L	M/W	3,191	70	54		Y	Y	Y	Y	Y	Y	Y	N	8	25
South Suburban College	South Holland	C,T	St-L	M/W	6,672													
Southwestern Illinois College	Belleville	C,T	Dist	M/W	16,425													
Spoon River College	Canton	C,T	St	M/W	2,927													
Triton College	River Grove	C,T	St	M/W	10,464													
Waubonsee Community College	Sugar Grove	C,T	Dist	M/W	8,682	70	21	85	Y			Y	Y			N	11	42
Westwood College–Chicago Du Page†	Woodridge	T,B	Prop	M/W	470	11												
Westwood College–Chicago Loop Campus†	Chicago	T,B	Prop	M/W	106	1												
Westwood College–Chicago O'Hare Airport†	Schiller Park	T,B	Prop	M/W	425	26												
Westwood College–Chicago River Oaks†	Calumet City	T,B	Prop	M/W	650	9												
Worsham College of Mortuary Science	Wheeling	T	Ind	M/W	115													
Indiana																		
Ancilla College	Donaldson	C,T	I-R	M/W	631	36	40	59	Y	Y	Y	Y	Y	Y	Y	N	5	15
Brown Mackie College, Merrillville Campus	Merrillville	T	Prop	M/W	450													
Brown Mackie College, Michigan City Campus	Michigan City	C,T	Prop	M/W	427		44		N	Y	Y	Y	Y	Y	Y	N		7
Brown Mackie College, South Bend Campus	South Bend	C,T	Prop	PW	513													
Davenport University	Granger	C,T,B	Ind	M/W					Y	Y		Y						
Davenport University	Hammond	C,T	Ind	M/W					Y	Y		Y						
Davenport University	Merrillville	C,T,B	Ind	M/W					Y	Y		Y						
Holy Cross College	Notre Dame	C,B	I-R	M/W	492	4	2	85	N	Y	Y		Y	Y		Y	16	1
Indiana Business College	Anderson	T	Prop	M/W	230				N	Y	Y		Y	Y	Y			6
Indiana Business College	Columbus	T	Prop	M/W	250				N	Y	Y	Y	Y	Y	Y			9

This chart includes the names and locations of accredited two-year colleges in the United States and U.S. territories and shows institutions' responses to the *Thomson Peterson's Survey of Undergraduate Institutions*. If an institution submitted incomplete data, one or more columns opposite the institution's name is blank.

An asterisk after the school name denotes a *Special Message* following the college's profile, and a dagger indicates that the institution has one or more entries in the *In-Depth Descriptions of Two-Year Colleges* section. If a school does not appear, it did not report any of the information.

Y—Yes; N—No; R—Recommended; S—For Some

Column key (diagonal headers): Degrees Awarded — College Transfer Associate (C); County, District City, State and Local; Bachelor's (B), Master's (M), Doctoral (D), First Professional (F), Terminal Associate (T) · Institutional Control (Independent, Independent-Religious, Proprietary; Federal, State, Commonwealth, State-Related) · Student Body (Men, Primarily Men, Women, Primarily Women, Coed)

Institution	Location	Degrees Awarded	Institutional Control	Student Body	Undergraduate Enrollment Fall 2004	Percent Attending Part-Time	Percent of Grads Going on to Four-Year Colleges	Percent 25 Years of Age or Older	Open Admissions	High School Equivalency Certificate Accepted	High School Transcript Required	Need-Based Aid Available	Part-Time Jobs Available	Career Counseling Available	Job Placement Services Available	College Housing Available	Number of Sports Offered	Number of Majors Offered
Indiana Business College	Evansville	T	Prop	M/W	237				N	Y	Y	Y	Y	Y				7
Indiana Business College	Fort Wayne	T	Prop	M/W	268				N	Y	Y	Y	Y	Y				5
Indiana Business College†	Indianapolis	T	Prop	M/W	643				N	Y	Y	Y	Y	Y	Y	N		12
Indiana Business College	Lafayette	T	Prop	M/W	185				N	Y	Y	Y	Y	Y				7
Indiana Business College	Marion	T	Prop	M/W	140				N	Y	Y	Y	Y					4
Indiana Business College	Muncie	T	Prop	M/W	313		0		N	Y	Y	Y	Y	Y	Y	N		10
Indiana Business College	Terre Haute	T	Prop	M/W	227				N	Y	Y			Y	Y			10
Indiana Business College–Medical	Indianapolis	T	Prop	M/W	550				N	Y	Y			Y	Y			4
International Business College	Indianapolis	T	Prop	M/W	315		1		Y	Y	Y	Y		Y	Y	Y		
ITT Technical Institute	Fort Wayne	T,B	Prop	M/W	468													
ITT Technical Institute	Indianapolis	T,B	Prop	M/W	899													
ITT Technical Institute	Newburgh	T,B	Prop	M/W	400													
Ivy Tech State College–Bloomington	Bloomington	C,T	St	M/W	3,169	55	47		Y			Y	Y	Y	Y			21
Ivy Tech State College–Central Indiana	Indianapolis	C,T	St	M/W	10,832	66	57		Y			Y	Y	Y	Y	N	6	35
Ivy Tech State College–Columbus	Columbus	C,T	St	M/W	1,855	63	58		Y			Y	Y	Y	Y	N		26
Ivy Tech State College–Eastcentral	Muncie	C,T	St	M/W	5,472	53	57		Y			Y	Y	Y	Y	N		31
Ivy Tech State College–Kokomo	Kokomo	C,T	St	M/W	2,762	61	59		Y			Y	Y	Y	Y	N		24
Ivy Tech State College–Lafayette	Lafayette	C,T	St	M/W	5,274	57	50		Y			Y	Y	Y	Y	N		32
Ivy Tech State College–North Central	South Bend	C,T	St	M/W	4,654	72	61		Y			Y	Y	Y	Y	N		33
Ivy Tech State College–Northeast	Fort Wayne	C,T	St	M/W	5,554	63	60		Y			Y	Y	Y	Y	N		29
Ivy Tech State College–Northwest	Gary	C,T	St	M/W	4,684	64	64		Y			Y	Y	Y	Y	N		30
Ivy Tech State College–Southcentral	Sellersburg	C,T	St	M/W	3,050	72	61		Y			Y	Y	Y	Y	N		26
Ivy Tech State College–Southeast	Madison	C,T	St	M/W	1,711	63	56		Y			Y	Y	Y	Y	N		12
Ivy Tech State College–Southwest	Evansville	C,T	St	M/W	4,378	66	51		Y			Y	Y	Y	Y	N		35
Ivy Tech State College–Wabash Valley	Terre Haute	C,T	St	M/W	4,684	59	55		Y			Y	Y	Y	Y	N	2	37
Ivy Tech State College–Whitewater	Richmond	C,T	St	M/W	1,605	71	62		Y			Y	Y	Y	Y	N	1	23
Sawyer College	Hammond	C,T	Prop	M/W	261													
Vincennes University	Vincennes	C,T	St	M/W	5,175													
Iowa																		
AIB College of Business	Des Moines	T	Ind	M/W	938	20												
Clinton Community College	Clinton	C,T	St-L	M/W	1,298	55	36	59	Y		Y	Y	Y	Y	Y	N	11	14
Des Moines Area Community College	Ankeny	C,T	St-L	M/W	13,719	56	30	72	Y	Y	S	Y	Y	Y	Y	N	7	52
Ellsworth Community College	Iowa Falls	C,T	St-L	M/W	930		18	60	Y	Y	Y	Y	Y	Y	Y	Y	14	47
Hawkeye Community College	Waterloo	C,T	St-L	M/W	5,374	38	27	62	Y	Y	Y	Y	Y	Y	Y	N	5	60
Indian Hills Community College	Ottumwa	C,T	St-L	M/W	2,867	29	40	45	Y	Y	S	Y	Y	Y	Y	Y	10	25
Iowa Central Community College	Fort Dodge	C,T	St-L	M/W	4,567		26	45	Y	Y	Y	Y	Y	Y	Y	Y	12	35
Iowa Lakes Community College	Estherville	C,T	St-L	M/W	2,993	54	35	60	Y	Y	Y	Y	Y	Y	Y	Y	16	195
Iowa Western Community College	Council Bluffs	C,T	Dist	M/W	4,299		34	67	Y	Y	Y	Y	Y	Y	Y	Y	7	55
Kaplan College	Davenport	C,T,B	Prop	M/W	9,194	82												
Kirkwood Community College	Cedar Rapids	C,T	St-L	M/W	15,032	45												
Marshalltown Community College	Marshalltown	C,T	Dist	M/W	1,421	36												
Muscatine Community College	Muscatine	C,T	St	M/W	1,280	57	43	45	Y		Y	Y	Y	Y	Y	Y	6	15
Northeast Iowa Community College	Calmar	C,T	St-L	M/W	4,724													
North Iowa Area Community College	Mason City	C,T	St-L	M/W	3,004	41	22	70	Y	Y	R,S	Y	Y	Y	Y	Y	15	29
Northwest Iowa Community College	Sheldon	C,T	St	M/W	1,079	51												
St. Luke's College	Sioux City	T	Ind	M/W	134	30	45	61	N	Y	Y	Y				Y		3
Scott Community College	Bettendorf	C,T	St-L	M/W	4,697	53	44	55	Y		Y	Y	Y	Y	Y	N	2	30
Southwestern Community College	Creston	C,T	St	M/W	1,254	47	30		Y	Y	Y	Y	Y	Y	Y	Y	7	16
Vatterott College	Des Moines		Prop	M/W	131													
Western Iowa Tech Community College	Sioux City	C,T	St	M/W	5,370		30		Y	Y	Y	Y	Y	Y	Y	Y	8	26
Kansas																		
Allen County Community College	Iola	C,T	St-L	M/W	2,256	63	35	60	Y	Y		Y	Y	Y	Y	Y	11	69
Barton County Community College	Great Bend	C,T	St-L	M/W	3,976	72	47		Y	Y	R	Y	Y	Y	Y	Y	14	83
Brown Mackie College, Lenexa Campus	Lenexa	T	Prop	M/W	230													
Butler County Community College	El Dorado	C,T	St-L	M/W	8,793	60	42	95	Y	Y		Y	Y	Y	Y	Y	12	41
Cloud County Community College	Concordia	C,T	St-L	M/W	3,521		12	77	Y	Y		Y	Y	Y	Y	Y	8	29
Coffeyville Community College	Coffeyville	C,T	St-L	M/W	1,766	62	43	70	Y		Y	Y	Y	Y	Y	Y	13	69
Colby Community College*	Colby	C,T	St-L	M/W	1,761	41	22	60	Y		Y	Y	Y	Y	Y	Y	10	58
Cowley County Comm Coll and Voc-Tech School	Arkansas City	C,T	St-L	M/W	4,523	49	19		Y	Y	Y	Y	Y	Y	Y	Y	8	41
Dodge City Community College	Dodge City	C,T	St-L	M/W	1,956		67	92	Y					Y	Y	Y	11	71
Donnelly College	Kansas City	C,T	I-R	M/W	398	50												
Fort Scott Community College	Fort Scott	C,T	St-L	M/W	1,923				Y		Y	Y	Y	Y	Y	Y	10	36
Garden City Community College	Garden City	C,T	Cou	M/W	2,174	57	39	60	Y	Y		Y	Y	Y	Y	Y	15	64
Hesston College	Hesston	C,T	I-R	M/W	465	12	50		Y	Y	Y	Y	Y	Y	Y		7	7
Highland Community College	Highland	C,T	St-L	M/W	3,040		31		Y	Y	Y	Y	Y	Y	Y	Y	8	69
Hutchinson Comm Coll and Area Vocational School	Hutchinson	C,T	St-L	M/W	4,526	54	32	70	Y	Y	R	Y	Y	Y	Y	Y	14	40
Independence Community College	Independence	C,T	St	M/W	1,100		44		Y	Y	Y	Y	Y	Y	Y	Y	8	40
Johnson County Community College	Overland Park	C,T	St-L	M/W	18,612	66	43		Y	Y	S	Y	Y	Y	Y	N	8	36

This chart includes the names and locations of accredited two-year colleges in the United States and U.S. territories and shows institutions' responses to the *Thomson Peterson's Survey of Undergraduate Institutions*. If an institution submitted incomplete data, one or more columns opposite the institution's name is blank. An asterisk after the school name denotes a *Special Message* following the college's profile, and a dagger indicates that the institution has one or more entries in the *In-Depth Descriptions of Two-Year Colleges* section. If a school does not appear, it did not report any of the information.

Y—Yes; N—No; R—Recommended; S—For Some

College	Location	Degrees Awarded	Institutional Control	Student Body	Undergrad Enrollment Fall 2004	Percent Attending Part-Time	Percent 25 Years of Age or Older	Percent of Grads Going on to Four-Year Colleges	High School Equivalency Certificate Accepted	Open Admissions	High School Transcript Required	Need-Based Aid Available	Part-Time Jobs Available	Career Counseling Available	Job Placement Services Available	College Housing Available	Number of Sports Offered	Number of Majors Offered
Kansas City Kansas Community College	Kansas City	C,T	St-L	M/W	5,573	67	49		Y	Y	Y		Y	Y		N	8	22
Manhattan Area Technical College	Manhattan	T	St-L	M/W	350	5	32			Y				Y		N		12
Northeast Kansas Technical College	Atchison		St	M/W														
Pratt Comm Coll and Area Vocational School	Pratt	C,T	St-L	M/W	1,451	57			Y	Y	Y	Y	Y			Y	10	65
Seward County Community College	Liberal	C,T	St-L	M/W	2,325		67	67	Y	Y	Y	Y	Y	Y	Y	Y	4	45
Wichita Area Technical College	Wichita	C,T	Dist	M/W	2,052	73												
Kentucky																		
Ashland Community and Technical College	Ashland	C,T	St	M/W	2,565		41	40	Y	Y	Y	Y	Y	Y		N	2	12
Beckfield College	Florence	T	Prop	M/W	480													
Big Sandy Community and Technical College	Prestonsburg	C,T	St	M/W	4,406		44	36	Y	Y	Y	Y	Y	Y		N	5	12
Bowling Green Technical College	Bowling Green		St	M/W														
Brown Mackie College, Hopkinsville Campus	Hopkinsville	C	Prop	PW	130													
Brown Mackie College, Northern Kentucky Campus	Fort Mitchell	C,T	Prop	M/W	400		59		Y	Y		Y	Y	Y	Y	N		5
Daymar College	Louisville	T	Prop	M/W	227													
Draughons Junior College	Bowling Green	C	Prop	PW	368	53												
Elizabethtown Community and Technical College	Elizabethtown	C,T	St	M/W	3,615	54	50		Y	Y	Y	Y	Y	Y		N	7	12
Gateway Community and Technical College	Covington	C	St	M/W	2,597					Y						N		
Hazard Community and Technical College	Hazard	C,T	St	M/W	3,500		35		Y	Y	Y							13
Henderson Community College	Henderson	C,T	St	M/W	2,241		57		Y	Y	Y	Y	Y	Y		N	5	19
Hopkinsville Community College	Hopkinsville	C,T	St	M/W	3,104	54	52		Y	Y	S	Y	Y	Y	Y	N	5	18
ITT Technical Institute	Louisville	T,B	Prop	M/W	476													
Jefferson Community College	Louisville	C,T	St	M/W	10,024	61	41		Y			Y	Y	Y	Y	N		17
Jefferson Technical College	Louisville	T	St	M/W	3,778	84	38		Y					Y	Y	N		
Lexington Community College	Lexington	C,T	St	M/W	8,639	38												
Louisville Technical Institute	Louisville	T	Prop	M/W	667	6												
Maysville Community and Technical College	Maysville	C,T	St	M/W	1,917	60												
National College of Business & Technology	Danville	T	Prop	M/W	326				Y	Y	Y	Y	Y	Y	Y	N		5
National College of Business & Technology	Florence	T	Prop	M/W	189				Y	Y	S	Y	Y	Y	Y	N		5
National College of Business & Technology	Lexington	T	Prop	M/W	378				Y	Y	Y	Y	Y	Y	Y	N		5
National College of Business & Technology	Louisville	T	Prop	M/W	678				Y	Y	S	Y	Y	Y	Y	N		6
National College of Business & Technology	Pikeville	T	Prop	M/W	219				Y	Y	S	Y	Y	Y	Y	N		5
National College of Business & Technology	Richmond	T	Prop	M/W	363				Y	Y	S	Y	Y	Y	Y	N		5
Owensboro Community and Technical College	Owensboro	C,T	St	M/W	3,664	50	28	26	Y	Y	Y	Y	Y	Y		N	2	17
Rowan Technical College	Morehead	T	St	M/W	842	65												
Somerset Community College	Somerset	C,T	St	M/W	5,850		50		Y	Y	Y	Y	Y	Y		N	4	27
Southeast Kentucky Community and Technical College	Cumberland	C,T	St	M/W	4,519				Y	Y	Y	Y	Y	Y		N	5	14
Spencerian College	Louisville	C,T	Prop	M/W	1,326		50		Y	Y	Y	Y	Y	Y	Y			3
Spencerian College–Lexington	Lexington	T	Prop	M/W	376		31			Y	Y	Y	Y	Y	Y			4
West Kentucky Community and Technical College	Paducah	C,T	St	M/W	3,545		41		Y	Y	S	Y	Y	Y		N	4	10
Louisiana																		
Baton Rouge Community College	Baton Rouge	C,T	St	M/W	5,761													
Bossier Parish Community College	Bossier City	C,T	St	M/W	4,121				Y	Y	Y	Y	Y	Y	Y	N	10	12
Delgado Community College	New Orleans	C,T	St	M/W	16,501	55												
Delta College of Arts and Technology	Baton Rouge	T	Prop	PW	434													
Elaine P. Nunez Community College	Chalmette	C,T	St	M/W	2,363	49												
ITI Technical College	Baton Rouge	T	Prop	M/W	361													
ITT Technical Institute	St. Rose	T,B	Prop	M/W	541													
Louisiana Technical College	Baton Rouge	C	St	M/W	15,481	46										N		
Remington College–Lafayette Campus	Lafayette	T	Prop	M/W	452													
River Parishes Community College	Sorrento	C	St	M/W	724													3
Maine																		
Andover College*	Portland	T	Prop	M/W	502		70		Y	Y	Y	Y	Y	Y	Y	N		16
Central Maine Medical Center School of Nursing	Lewiston	T	Ind	PW	114	81	84		N	Y	Y	Y				Y		1
Eastern Maine Community College	Bangor	C,T	St	M/W	1,790	58	26		N	Y	Y	Y	Y	Y	Y	Y	10	19
Kennebec Valley Community College	Fairfield	C,T	St	M/W	1,772	68	66		Y	Y	Y	Y	Y	Y	Y	N	4	36
Northern Maine Community College	Presque Isle	T	St-R	M/W	1,013	37												
Southern Maine Community College	South Portland	C,T	St	M/W	4,103	48	48		N	Y	Y	Y	Y	Y	Y	Y	7	46
York County Community College	Wells	C,T	St	M/W	990													
Maryland																		
Allegany College of Maryland	Cumberland	C,T	St-L	M/W	3,705	43	35	80	Y	Y	Y	Y	Y	Y		N	6	26
Anne Arundel Community College	Arnold	C,T	St-L	M/W	14,290	67	43		Y			Y	Y	Y	Y	N	8	69
Baltimore City Community College	Baltimore	C,T	St	M/W	7,095		57		Y	Y	Y	Y	Y	Y		N	3	35
Baltimore International College†	Baltimore	C,T,B	Ind	M/W	556	5	24		N	Y	Y	Y	Y	Y	Y			4
Carroll Community College	Westminster	C,T	St-L	M/W	3,073	56	31		Y		Y	Y	Y	Y		N		15
Cecil Community College	North East	C	Cou	M/W	1,781	65	31		Y	Y	R	Y	Y	Y	Y	N	6	34
Chesapeake College	Wye Mills	C,T	St-L	M/W	2,354	69												

This chart includes the names and locations of accredited two-year colleges in the United States and U.S. territories and shows institutions' responses to the *Thomson Peterson's Survey of Undergraduate Institutions*. If an institution submitted incomplete data, one or more columns opposite the institution's name is blank. An asterisk after the school name denotes a *Special Message* following the college's profile, and a dagger indicates that the institution has one or more entries in the *In-Depth Descriptions of Two-Year Colleges* section. If a school does not appear, it did not report any of the information.

Y—Yes; N—No; R—Recommended; S—For Some

		Degrees Awarded	Institutional Control	Student Body	Undergraduate Enrollment Fall 2004	Percent Attending Part-Time	Percent 25 Years of Age or Older	Percent of Grads Going on to Four-Year Colleges	High School Equivalency Certificate Accepted	High School Transcript Required	Open Admissions	Need-Based Aid Required	Part-Time Jobs Available	Career Counseling Available	Job Placement Services Available	College Housing Available	Number of Sports Offered	Number of Majors Offered
College of Southern Maryland	La Plata	C,T	St-L	M/W	7,423	66	37		Y			R	Y	Y	Y	Y	N	7	14
The Community College of Baltimore County	Baltimore	C,T	Cou	M/W	20,025														
Frederick Community College	Frederick	C,T	St-L	M/W	4,736		60		Y				Y	Y	Y	Y	N	6	41
Garrett College	McHenry	C,T	St-L	M/W	613	41	22		Y			Y	Y	Y	Y	Y	Y	6	24
Hagerstown Business College	Hagerstown	T	Prop	M/W	932		55		Y	Y	Y	Y	Y	Y	Y	Y			13
Hagerstown Community College	Hagerstown	C,T	St-L	M/W	3,528	67	37		Y		S	Y	Y	Y	Y	N	12	19
Harford Community College	Bel Air	C,T	St-L	M/W	5,492	61	33	23	Y			Y	Y	Y	Y	N	8	29
Howard Community College	Columbia	C,T	St-L	M/W	6,711		43	76	Y		S	Y	Y	Y	Y	N	9	55
Montgomery College	Rockville	C,T	St-L	M/W	21,805	64													
Prince George's Community College	Largo	C,T	Cou	M/W	12,564	73													
TESST College of Technology	Towson	T	Prop	M/W															
Wor-Wic Community College	Salisbury	C,T	St-L	M/W	3,110	71	47		Y			R		Y	Y	Y	N		18
Massachusetts																			
Bay State College†	Boston	C,T,B	Ind	M/W	757		12		N	Y	Y	Y	Y	Y	Y	Y			18
Berkshire Community College	Pittsfield	C,T	St	M/W	2,364	59	40	47	Y	Y	Y	Y	Y	Y	Y	N		18
Bristol Community College	Fall River	C,T	St	M/W	6,639	56	35	43	Y	Y	Y	Y	Y	Y	Y	N		71
Bunker Hill Community College†	Boston	C,T	St	M/W	7,821	67	52	35	Y	Y	Y	Y	Y	Y	Y	N	7	40
Cape Cod Community College	West Barnstable	C,T	St	M/W	4,243	65	58	67	Y	Y	Y	Y	Y	Y	Y	N	12	41
Dean College	Franklin	C,T,B	Ind	M/W	1,303														
Fisher College†	Boston	C,B	Ind	M/W	556														
Greenfield Community College	Greenfield	C,T	St	M/W	2,353	56	46		Y	Y	S	Y	Y	Y	Y	N		29
Holyoke Community College	Holyoke	C,T	St	M/W	6,298	49	31		Y	Y	Y	Y	Y	Y	Y	N	8	40
ITT Technical Institute	Norwood	T	Prop	M/W	272														
ITT Technical Institute	Woburn	T	Prop	M/W	285														
Labouré College	Boston	C,T	I-R	M/W	432														
Massachusetts Bay Community College†	Wellesley Hills	C,T	St	M/W	5,132	56	42		Y	Y			Y	Y	Y	N	7	36
Massasoit Community College	Brockton	C,T	St	M/W	6,808	53													
Middlesex Community College	Bedford	C,T	St	M/W	8,016														
Mount Wachusett Community College*	Gardner	C,T	St	M/W	4,165	56	42	61	Y	Y	Y	Y	Y	Y	Y	N		28
New England College of Finance	Boston	T	Ind	PW	812		22	50	Y	Y	Y					N		6
Northern Essex Community College*	Haverhill	C,T	St	M/W	7,194		51	40	Y		Y	Y	Y	Y	Y	N	11	59
North Shore Community College	Danvers	C,T	St	M/W	6,690	59	45	57	Y	Y	S	Y	Y	Y	Y	N		42
Quinsigamond Community College	Worcester	C,T	St	M/W	6,591	57													
Springfield Technical Community College	Springfield	C,T	St	M/W	6,114	55	42		Y	Y	Y	Y	Y	Y	Y	N	9	57
Urban College of Boston	Boston	T	Ind	PW	609	98													
Michigan																			
Alpena Community College	Alpena	C,T	St-L	M/W	1,937	49	40	42	Y		Y	Y	Y	Y	Y	Y	7	29
Bay de Noc Community College	Escanaba	C,T	Cou	M/W	2,549		36	60	Y	Y	Y	Y	Y	Y		Y	5	27
Bay Mills Community College	Brimley	C	Dist	M/W	489		75		Y	Y	Y	Y	Y	Y			Y		12
Davenport University	Alma	C,T,B	Ind	M/W						Y	Y		Y						
Davenport University	Bad Axe	C,T,B	Ind	M/W						Y	Y		Y						
Davenport University	Bay City	C,T,B	Ind	M/W						Y	Y		Y						
Davenport University	Caro	C,T,B	Ind	M/W						Y	Y		Y						
Davenport University	Midland	C,T,B	Ind	M/W				6		Y	Y		Y	Y	Y	Y	N		18
Davenport University	Romeo	C,T,B	Ind	M/W						Y	Y		Y						
Davenport University	Saginaw	C,T,B	Ind	M/W						Y	Y		Y						
Delta College	University Center	C,T	Dist	M/W	10,343	62	34		Y		R	Y	Y	Y	Y	N	8	115
Glen Oaks Community College	Centreville	C,T	St-L	M/W	1,710	61	53		Y		Y	Y	Y	Y	Y	N	7	5
Gogebic Community College	Ironwood	C,T	St-L	M/W	981	47			Y	Y	Y	Y	Y	Y	Y	N	11	43
Grand Rapids Community College	Grand Rapids	C,T	Dist	M/W	14,144	55	28	78	Y	Y	Y	Y	Y	Y	Y	N	14	30
Henry Ford Community College	Dearborn	C,T	Dist	M/W	12,123		44		Y	Y	R	Y	Y	Y	Y	N	12	53
ITT Technical Institute	Canton	T	Prop	M/W	327														
ITT Technical Institute	Grand Rapids	T	Prop	M/W	616														
ITT Technical Institute	Troy	T	Prop	M/W	658														
Jackson Community College	Jackson	C,T	Cou	M/W	5,837	63	44		Y	Y		Y	Y			N		26
Kalamazoo Valley Community College	Kalamazoo	C,T	St-L	M/W	10,634	63	50		Y			Y	Y	Y	Y	N	6	29
Kellogg Community College	Battle Creek	C,T	St-L	M/W	5,523	67													
Kirtland Community College	Roscommon	C,T	Dist	M/W	1,918	68													
Lansing Community College	Lansing	C,T	St-L	M/W	19,471	68	18		Y		S	Y	Y	Y	Y	N	9	104
Macomb Community College	Warren	C,T	Dist	M/W	20,471	66	45		Y			Y	Y	Y	Y	N	11	73
Mid Michigan Community College	Harrison	C,T	St-L	M/W	3,232	55	32	15	Y	Y	R	Y	Y	Y	Y	N		52
Monroe County Community College	Monroe	C,T	Cou	M/W	3,943	62													
Montcalm Community College	Sidney	C,T	St-L	M/W	2,080	68	45		Y		R	Y	Y	Y	Y	N	1	22
Mott Community College	Flint	C,T	Dist	M/W	10,328	66	46		Y		Y	Y	Y	Y	Y	N	6	51
Muskegon Community College	Muskegon	C,T	St-L	M/W	5,000		52		Y	Y		Y	Y	Y	Y	N	8	45
Northwestern Michigan College	Traverse City	C,T	St-L	M/W	4,609	56	37		Y	Y	S	Y	Y	Y	Y	Y	7	44
Oakland Community College	Bloomfield Hills	C,T	St-L	M/W	24,296	71	47		Y		R	Y	Y	Y	Y	N	8	90
St. Clair County Community College	Port Huron	C,T	St-L	M/W	4,523														

This chart includes the names and locations of accredited two-year colleges in the United States and U.S. territories and shows institutions' responses to the *Thomson Peterson's Survey of Undergraduate Institutions*. If an institution submitted incomplete data, one or more columns opposite the institution's name is blank. An asterisk after the school name denotes a *Special Message* following the college's profile, and a dagger indicates that institution has one or more entries in the *In-Depth Descriptions of Two-Year Colleges* section. If a school does not appear, it did not report any of the information.

Y—Yes; N—No; R—Recommended; S—For Some

Institution	Location	Degrees Awarded	Institutional Control	Student Body	Undergrad Enrollment Fall 2004	% 25 Years or Older	% Attending Part-Time	% Going on to 4-Yr Colleges	HS Equivalency Cert. Accepted	Open Admissions	HS Transcript Required	Need-Based Aid Available	Part-Time Jobs Available	Career Counseling Available	Job Placement Services Available	College Housing Available	No. of Sports	No. of Majors
Schoolcraft College	Livonia	C,T	Dist	M/W	10,213	67	38		Y	Y	R,S	Y	Y	Y	Y	N	5	36
Southwestern Michigan College	Dowagiac	C,T	St-L	M/W	2,777	63	40		Y	Y	Y	Y	Y	Y	Y	N	14	27
Washtenaw Community College	Ann Arbor	C,T	St-L	M/W	12,070	72												
Wayne County Community College District†	Detroit	C,T	St-L	M/W	11,673		62	70	Y			Y	Y	Y	Y	N	3	34
Minnesota																		
Academy College	Minneapolis	C,T,B	Prop	M/W	320				Y	Y	Y	Y	Y	Y	Y	N		25
Alexandria Technical College	Alexandria	C,T	St	M/W	2,028		23		Y	Y	Y	Y	Y	Y	Y	N	5	52
Anoka-Ramsey Community College	Coon Rapids	C,T	St	M/W	5,606		34		Y	Y	S	Y	Y			N	10	14
Anoka-Ramsey Community College, Cambridge Campus	Cambridge	C,T	St	M/W	1,777		45		Y	Y	S	Y	Y			N	5	12
Anoka Technical College	Anoka	C,T	St	M/W	2,371	55												
Central Lakes College	Brainerd	C,T	St	M/W	2,947													
Century College	White Bear Lake	C,T	St	M/W	8,650	52	33		Y		Y	Y	Y	Y		N	5	36
Dakota County Technical College	Rosemount	C,T	St	M/W	6,069	51												
Duluth Business University	Duluth	T	Prop	PW	325													
Dunwoody College of Technology	Minneapolis	T	Ind	PM	1,611	23												
Globe College	Oakdale	T,B	Priv	M/W	997		48		Y	Y	Y			Y	Y			20
Herzing College	Minneapolis	T,B	Prop	PW	346	41	43		Y	Y	Y			Y	Y	N		8
Hibbing Community College	Hibbing	C,T	St	M/W	1,832		55		Y	Y	Y	Y	Y	Y	Y	Y	11	19
Itasca Community College	Grand Rapids	C,T	St	M/W	1,117	23	20	75	Y	Y	Y	Y	Y			Y	9	29
ITT Technical Institute	Eden Prairie		Prop	M/W														
Lake Superior College	Duluth	C,T	St	M/W	4,281		33		Y		S	Y	Y	Y	Y	N	3	34
McNally Smith College of Music	Saint Paul	C,T	Prop	M/W	454	13	10		Y	Y	Y			Y	Y	N		2
Mesabi Range Community and Technical College	Virginia	C,T	St	M/W	1,509		32	80	Y			Y	Y	Y	Y	Y	13	16
Minneapolis Business College	Roseville	C,T	Prop	PW	300													
Minneapolis Community and Technical College	Minneapolis	C,T	St	M/W	7,091		44		Y			Y	Y	Y	Y	N	3	25
Minnesota School of Business–Brooklyn Center	Brooklyn Center	T,B	Prop	M/W	809				Y	Y	Y					N		19
Minnesota School of Business–Plymouth	Minneapolis	T,B	Prop	M/W	500				Y	Y	Y			Y	Y	N		20
Minnesota School of Business–Richfield	Richfield	T,B	Prop	M/W	944		40		Y	Y	Y	Y		Y	Y	N		20
Minnesota School of Business–St. Cloud	Waite Park	T,B	Prop	M/W	226				Y	Y	Y			Y	Y	N		20
Minnesota School of Business–Shakopee	Shakopee	T,B	Prop	M/W	500				Y	Y	Y			Y	Y	N		
Minnesota State College–Southeast Technical	Winona	C,T	St	M/W	1,817	42	46		Y	Y	Y	Y	Y	Y	Y	N		28
Minnesota State Community and Technical College–Detroit Lakes	Detroit Lakes	C,T	St	M/W	650							Y				N		
Minnesota State Community and Technical College–Fergus Falls	Fergus Falls	C,T	St	M/W	1,739	46												
Minnesota State Community and Technical College–Moorhead	Moorhead	C	St	M/W	2,300							Y				N		
Minnesota State Community and Technical College–Wadena	Wadena	C,T	St	M/W	635							Y				N		
Minnesota West Comm & Tech Coll-Pipestone Cmps	Pipestone	C,T	St	M/W	2,917	24	43		Y	Y	Y	Y	Y	Y	Y	N	7	5
Normandale Community College	Bloomington	C,T	St	M/W	7,811													
North Hennepin Community College	Brooklyn Park	C,T	St	M/W	6,602	63	35		Y		R	Y	Y	Y	Y	N	7	26
Northland Community and Technical College–East Grand Forks	East Grand Forks	C,T	St	M/W	1,442													
Northland Community and Technical College–Thief River Falls	Thief River Falls	C,T	St	M/W	3,109		26	76	Y	Y	Y	Y	Y	Y	Y	N	8	46
Northwest Technical College	Bemidji	T	St	M/W	4,500				Y			Y	Y	Y	Y	N		41
Northwest Technical Institute	Eden Prairie	C,T	Prop	M/W	108													
Rainy River Community College	International Falls	C,T	St	M/W	384		54	62	Y	Y	Y	Y	Y	Y	Y	Y	11	6
Rasmussen College Mankato	Mankato	T	Prop	PW	330													
Rasmussen College Minnetonka	Minnetonka	T	Prop	M/W	325	42												
Rasmussen College St. Cloud	St. Cloud	C,T	Prop	PW	533	53	43		N	Y	Y	Y	Y	Y	Y	N		9
Riverland Community College	Austin	C,T	St	M/W	4,000		42	68	Y	Y	Y	Y	Y	Y	Y	Y	5	28
Rochester Community and Technical College	Rochester	C,T,B	St	M/W	5,862		34		Y	Y	Y	Y	Y	Y	Y	N	10	25
St. Cloud Technical College	St. Cloud	T	St	M/W	3,329	33	25		Y	Y	Y	Y	Y	Y	Y	N	4	56
Saint Paul College–A Community & Technical College	St. Paul	C,T	St-R	M/W	5,442	71			Y	Y	S	Y	Y	Y	Y	N		13
South Central Technical College	North Mankato	C,T	St	M/W	2,350		30		Y	Y	Y		Y	Y	Y	N		17
Vermilion Community College	Ely	C,T	St	M/W	1,191													
Mississippi																		
Coahoma Community College	Clarksdale	C,T	St-L	M/W	1,400		10		Y	Y	Y	Y	Y	Y	Y	Y	3	17
Copiah-Lincoln Community College	Wesson	C,T	St-L	M/W	2,161	34	22		Y	Y	Y	Y	Y	Y	Y	Y	8	45
Copiah-Lincoln Community College–Natchez Campus	Natchez	C,T	St-L	M/W	900	38	50		Y	Y	Y	Y	Y	Y	Y	Y		11
East Central Community College	Decatur	C,T	St-L	M/W	2,382		32		Y	Y	Y	Y	Y	Y	Y	Y	8	41
East Mississippi Community College	Scooba	C,T	St-L	M/W	3,417		30		Y	Y	Y	Y	Y	Y	Y	Y	9	36
Hinds Community College	Raymond	C,T	St-L	M/W	9,961	28	40		Y	Y	Y	Y	Y	Y	Y	Y	10	75
Holmes Community College	Goodman	C,T	St-L	M/W	4,494	28	26	80	Y	Y	Y	Y	Y	Y	Y	Y	8	29
Itawamba Community College	Fulton	C,T	St-L	M/W	4,000		8		Y	Y	Y	Y	Y	Y	Y	Y	7	56
Meridian Community College	Meridian	C,T	St-L	M/W	3,572		30	75	Y	Y	Y	Y	Y	Y	Y	Y	11	21
Mississippi Gulf Coast Community College	Perkinston	C,T	Dist	M/W	10,231													
Northeast Mississippi Community College	Booneville	C,T	St	M/W	3,224	14												
Southwest Mississippi Community College	Summit	C,T	St-L	M/W	2,268													

This chart includes the names and locations of accredited two-year colleges in the United States and U.S. territories and shows institutions' responses to the *Thomson Peterson's Survey of Undergraduate Institutions*. If an institution submitted incomplete data, one or more columns opposite the institution's name is blank. An asterisk after the school name denotes a *Special Message* following the college's profile, and a dagger indicates that the institution has one or more entries in the *In-Depth Descriptions of Two-Year Colleges* section. If a school does not appear, it did not report any of the information.

Y—Yes; N—No; R—Recommended; S—For Some

Name	Location	Degrees Awarded	Institutional Control	Student Body	Undergraduate Enrollment Fall 2004	Percent Attending Part-Time	Percent 25 Years or Older	Percent Going to Four-Year Colleges	HS Equivalency Certificate Accepted	HS Transcript Required	Open Admissions	Need-Based Aid Required	Part-Time Jobs Available	Career Counseling Available	Job Placement Services Available	College Housing Available	Number of Sports Offered	Number of Majors Offered
Virginia College at Jackson	Jackson	T	Prop	M/W	1,108													
Missouri																		
Blue River Community College	Independence	C,T	St-L	M/W	2,290	57	32			Y	Y			Y	Y	Y	N		9
Crowder College	Neosho	C,T	St-L	M/W	2,611	46	23		Y	Y	Y	Y	Y	Y	Y	Y	3	35
East Central College	Union	C,T	Dist	M/W	3,337	55	25	65	Y	Y	Y	Y	Y	Y		N	2	76
Hickey College*	St. Louis	T,B	Prop	M/W	500													
IHM Health Studies Center	St. Louis	T	Ind	M/W	136													
ITT Technical Institute	Arnold	T,B	Prop	M/W	483													
ITT Technical Institute	Earth City	T,B	Prop	M/W	603													
Jefferson College	Hillsboro	C,T	St	M/W	4,065	46												
Linn State Technical College	Linn	T	St	PM	868	10	13			Y		Y	Y	Y	Y	Y	8	20
Longview Community College	Lee's Summit	C,T	St-L	M/W	5,603	56	29		Y	Y			Y	Y	Y	N	4	28
Maple Woods Community College	Kansas City	C,T	St-L	M/W	4,461	57	26		Y	Y			Y	Y	Y	N	3	24
Metropolitan Community College-Business & Technology College	Kansas City	C,T	St-L	PM	357	75	64									N		43
Mineral Area College	Park Hills	C,T	Dist	M/W	2,820	43	36		Y		Y		Y	Y	Y	Y	3	34
Moberly Area Community College	Moberly	C,T	St-L	M/W	3,696	51	24		Y	Y	Y	Y	Y	Y	Y	Y	3	14
North Central Missouri College	Trenton	C,T	Dist	M/W	1,406	49	25		Y	Y	Y	Y	Y	Y	Y	Y	3	17
Patricia Stevens College	St. Louis	C,T	Prop	PW	212													
Penn Valley Community College	Kansas City	C,T	St-L	M/W	4,839	66	54		Y	Y	Y		Y	Y	Y	N	1	38
Ranken Technical College	St. Louis	C,T,B	Ind	PM	1,423	48	40	5	N	Y	Y	Y	Y	Y	Y	Y		11
Saint Charles Community College	St. Peters	C,T	St	M/W	6,772	51	52		Y	Y R,S			Y	Y	Y	N	6	22
St. Louis Community College at Florissant Valley	St. Louis	C,T	Dist	M/W														
St. Louis Community College at Forest Park	St. Louis	C,T	Dist	M/W	7,610		60	75	Y	Y	Y		Y	Y	Y	N	4	51
St. Louis Community College at Meramec	Kirkwood	C,T	Dist	M/W	12,607		42	43	Y	Y	S	Y	Y	Y	Y	N	7	45
Sanford-Brown College	Hazelwood	C,T	Prop	M/W	600													
Southwest Missouri State University–West Plains	West Plains	C,T	St	M/W	1,701													
Three Rivers Community College	Poplar Bluff	C,T	St-L	M/W	3,273	47	38	40	Y	Y	Y		Y	Y	Y	Y	5	24
Vatterott College	Springfield	T	Prop	M/W					N	Y	Y			Y	Y	N		5
Vatterott College	St. Ann	T,B	Prop	M/W	580													
Vatterott College	St. Joseph	T	Prop	M/W														4
Montana																		
Blackfeet Community College	Browning	C,T	Ind	M/W	503	16	61		Y	Y	Y		Y	Y	Y	N	1	16
Dawson Community College	Glendive	C,T	St-L	M/W	539	27	31		Y	Y	Y	Y	Y	Y	Y	Y	10	10
Flathead Valley Community College	Kalispell	C,T	St-L	M/W	2,100	54	50		Y	Y	Y	Y	Y	Y	Y	N	8	22
Fort Peck Community College	Poplar	C,T	Dist	M/W	428		80		Y			Y			N		14
Miles Community College	Miles City	C,T	St-L	M/W	474	24												
Montana State U Coll of Tech-Great Falls	Great Falls	C,T	St	M/W	1,463	51												
Nebraska																		
Central Community College–Columbus Campus	Columbus	C,T	St-L	M/W	1,995	74	50		Y	Y	Y	Y	Y	Y	Y	Y	5	22
Central Community College–Grand Island Campus	Grand Island	C,T	St-L	M/W	2,756	82	57		Y	Y	Y	Y	Y	Y	Y	Y	3	22
Central Community College–Hastings Campus	Hastings	C,T	St-L	M/W	2,545	60	44		Y	Y	Y	Y	Y	Y	Y	Y	6	36
The Creative Center	Omaha	T	Prop	M/W														3
Hamilton College-Omaha	Omaha	T,B	Prop	M/W	700													
ITT Technical Institute	Omaha	T,B	Prop	M/W	382													
Little Priest Tribal College	Winnebago	C,T	Ind	M/W	130	48												
Metropolitan Community College*	Omaha	C,T	St-L	M/W	12,461	61	47		Y		R	Y	Y	Y	Y			33
Mid-Plains Community College	North Platte	C,T	Dist	M/W	3,084	65												
Nebraska Indian Community College	Macy	C,T	Fed	M/W	190	49	66		Y	Y	Y	Y	Y	Y				12
Northeast Community College	Norfolk	C,T	St-L	M/W	4,858	61												
Southeast Community College, Beatrice Campus	Beatrice	C,T	Dist	M/W	1,220													
Southeast Community College, Lincoln Campus	Lincoln	C,T	Dist	M/W	7,917	48	35		Y	Y	Y		Y	Y	Y	N	5	20
Southeast Community College, Milford Campus	Milford	T	Dist	PM	922	3	20		Y	Y	Y	Y	Y	Y	Y	Y	13	29
Vatterott College	Omaha	C	Prop	M/W	414													
Vatterott College	Omaha		Prop	M/W														
Nevada																		
Career College of Northern Nevada	Reno	T	Prop	M/W	389													
Community College of Southern Nevada	North Las Vegas	C	St	M/W	34,204	77	60		Y			Y	Y	Y	Y	N	6	82
Great Basin College	Elko	C,T,B	St	M/W	2,731		60		Y		Y	Y	Y	Y	Y	Y	4	25
ITT Technical Institute	Henderson	T,B	Prop	M/W	536													
Pima Medical Institute	Las Vegas	T	Prop	M/W	329				N	Y	S			Y	N		2	
Truckee Meadows Community College	Reno	C,T	St	M/W	9,697	80	54		Y			Y	Y	Y	Y			49
Western Nevada Community College	Carson City	C,T	St	M/W	4,897		68		Y	Y	S	Y	Y	Y	Y	N	3	42
New Hampshire																		
Hesser College†	Manchester	C,T,B	Prop	M/W	3,398	38	25	65	N	Y	Y	Y	Y	Y	Y	Y	8	33

This chart includes the names and locations of accredited two-year colleges in the United States and U.S. territories and shows institutions' responses to the *Thomson Peterson's Survey of Undergraduate Institutions*. If an institution submitted incomplete data, one or more columns opposite the institution's name is blank.

An asterisk after the school name denotes a *Special Message* following the college's profile, and a dagger indicates that the institution has one or more entries in the *In-Depth Descriptions of Two-Year Colleges* section. If a school does not appear, it did not report any of the information.

Y—Yes; N—No; R—Recommended; S—For Some

College	Location	Degrees Awarded	Institutional Control	Student Body	Undergraduate Enrollment Fall 2004	Percent Attending Part-Time	Percent of Grads Going on to Four-Year Colleges	Percent 25 Years of Age or Older	High School Equivalency Certificate Accepted	Open Admissions	High School Transcript Required	Need-Based Aid Required	Part-Time Jobs Available	Career Counseling Available	Job Placement Services Available	College Housing Available	Number of Sports Offered	Number of Majors Offered
McIntosh College†	Dover	C,T	Prop	M/W	750	65			Y	Y	Y	Y	Y	Y	Y	Y		19
New Hampshire Comm Tech Coll, Berlin/Laconia	Berlin	C,T	St	M/W	2,080	66												
New Hampshire Comm Tech Coll, Manchester/Stratham	Manchester	C,T	St	M/W	4,644	79		9	N	Y	Y	Y		Y	Y	Y	N	8	23
New Hampshire Technical Institute	Concord	C	St	M/W	3,650													
New Jersey																		
Assumption College for Sisters	Mendham	C	I-R	W	33	36	86	100	N	Y	Y	Y				N		2
Atlantic Cape Community College†	Mays Landing	C,T	Cou	M/W	6,515	54	68	14	Y		R	Y	Y	Y	Y	N	10	34
Bergen Community College	Paramus	C,T	Cou	M/W	14,325	49	31	80	Y		Y	Y	Y	Y	Y	N	10	56
Berkeley College†	West Paterson	C,T,B	Prop	M/W	2,313	15	26		N	Y	Y	Y	Y	Y	Y	Y	5	11
Brookdale Community College	Lincroft	C,T	Cou	M/W	12,724	48	28		Y	Y	Y	Y	Y	Y	Y	N	8	57
Burlington County College	Pemberton	C,T	Cou	M/W	7,519	55												
Camden County College*	Blackwood	C,T	St-L	M/W	14,829													
County College of Morris	Randolph	C,T	Cou	M/W	8,496													
Cumberland County College	Vineland	C,T	St-L	M/W	3,176		50		Y	Y	Y	Y	Y	Y	Y	N	6	39
Essex County College	Newark	C,T	Cou	M/W	11,268	46	50	65	Y		Y	Y	Y	Y	Y	N	6	51
Gloucester County College	Sewell	C,T	Cou	M/W	5,610	47												
Hudson County Community College	Jersey City	C,T	St-L	M/W	6,489	34	42	13	Y		Y	Y	Y	Y	Y	N		16
Middlesex County College†	Edison	C,T	Cou	M/W	11,276													
Ocean County College	Toms River	C,T	Cou	M/W	8,436													
Raritan Valley Community College	Somerville	C,T	Cou	M/W	6,451	61	40		Y	Y	Y	Y	Y	Y	Y	N	4	46
Salem Community College	Carneys Point	C,T	Cou	M/W	301	31												
Sussex County Community College	Newton	C,T	St-L	M/W	3,153	54	41		Y		Y	Y	Y	Y		N	6	20
Union County College	Cranford	C,T	St-L	M/W	11,058	52	50		Y		Y	Y	Y	Y	Y	N	6	35
New Mexico																		
Albuquerque Technical Vocational Institute	Albuquerque	C,T	St	M/W	22,927	70	54		Y		R	Y	Y	Y	Y	N		35
Clovis Community College	Clovis	C,T	St	M/W	3,093	64	52		Y	Y	Y	Y	Y	Y	Y	N	5	39
Doña Ana Branch Community College	Las Cruces	C,T	St-L	M/W	6,347	43			Y	Y	Y	Y	Y	Y	Y			22
Institute of American Indian Arts	Santa Fe	C,B	Fed	M/W	183	15	51		N	Y	Y	Y	Y	Y	Y	Y	11	11
International Institute of the Americas	Albuquerque	T,B	Ind	M/W	163													
ITT Technical Institute	Albuquerque	T,B	Prop	M/W	487													
Luna Community College	Las Vegas	C,T	St	M/W	2,041	75	25		Y		Y	Y	Y	Y	Y	N		13
Mesalands Community College	Tucumcari	C,T	St	M/W	563													
New Mexico Military Institute*†	Roswell	C	St	PM	423		0	89	N	Y	Y	Y	Y	Y		Y	17	28
New Mexico State University–Carlsbad	Carlsbad	C,T	St	M/W	1,228													
New Mexico State University–Grants	Grants	C,T	St	M/W	636	63												
Pima Medical Institute	Albuquerque	T	Prop	M/W	576				N	Y	S	Y	Y			N		1
San Juan College	Farmington	C,T	St	M/W	5,224	49	37		Y	Y	Y	Y	Y	Y	Y	N	16	52
Santa Fe Community College	Santa Fe	C,T	St-L	M/W	5,452	83												
New York																		
Adirondack Community College	Queensbury	C,T	St-L	M/W	3,200		46	81	Y	Y	Y	Y	Y	Y	Y	N	13	54
American Academy of Dramatic Arts†	New York	T	Ind	M/W	224													
The Art Institute of New York City†	New York	C,T	Prop	M/W	1,716	41	40	1	Y	Y	Y	Y	Y	Y	Y	N		5
Berkeley College–New York City Campus†	New York	C,T,B	Prop	M/W	2,012	8	31		N	Y	Y	Y	Y	Y	Y	N		8
Berkeley College–Westchester Campus†	White Plains	C,T,B	Prop	M/W	658	8	20		N	Y	Y	Y	Y	Y	Y	Y		8
Borough of Manhattan Comm Coll of City U of NY	New York	C,T	St-L	M/W	17,629	37	42	57	Y	Y	Y	Y	Y	Y	Y	N	4	17
Bronx Comm Coll of City U of NY	Bronx	C,T	St-L	M/W	7,952	41	48		Y	Y	Y	Y	Y	Y	Y	N	6	27
Broome Community College	Binghamton	C,T	St-L	M/W	6,590	37	10	56	Y	Y	Y	Y	Y	Y	Y	N	10	35
Bryant & Stratton Business Inst	Albany	T	Prop	M/W	391	18	51		N	Y	Y	Y	Y	Y	Y	N		7
Bryant & Stratton Business Inst	Syracuse	T	Prop	M/W	570	17												
Bryant & Stratton Business Inst, Amherst Cmps	Clarence	T,B	Prop	M/W	341	41	56		N		Y	Y	Y	Y	N		7
Bryant & Stratton Business Inst	Buffalo	T	Prop	M/W	625	14	46		N		Y	Y	Y	Y	N		5
Bryant & Stratton Business Inst	Lackawanna	T	Prop	M/W	256	20	49	4	N		Y	Y	Y	Y	N		5
Cayuga County Community College	Auburn	C,T	St-L	M/W	3,896	43	35	61	Y	Y	Y	Y	Y	Y	Y	Y	10	26
Clinton Community College	Plattsburgh	C,T	St-L	M/W	2,192	43	31		Y	Y	Y	Y	Y	Y	Y	Y	6	17
Cochran School of Nursing	Yonkers	T	Ind	PW	157	36												
The College of Westchester†	White Plains	C,T	Prop	M/W	973	6												
Columbia-Greene Community College	Hudson	C,T	St-L	M/W	1,715	45	41		Y		Y	Y	Y	Y	Y	N	11	23
Corning Community College	Corning	C,T	St-L	M/W	4,443	47	41	74	Y	Y	Y	Y	Y	Y	Y	N	11	44
Crouse Hospital School of Nursing	Syracuse	T	Ind	M/W	252	44	64		N	Y	Y	Y	Y	Y		Y		1
Dutchess Community College	Poughkeepsie	C,T	St-L	M/W	7,810		48	56	Y	Y	Y	Y	Y	Y	Y	N	10	44
Elmira Business Institute	Elmira	C,T	Priv	PW	340													
Erie Community College	Buffalo	C,T	St-L	M/W	2,870	26	44	29	Y	Y	Y	Y	Y	Y	Y	N	13	17
Erie Community College, North Campus	Williamsville	C,T	St-L	M/W	6,170	38	29	35	Y	Y	Y	Y	Y	Y	Y	N	13	26
Erie Community College, South Campus	Orchard Park	C,T	St-L	M/W	3,793	35	20	39	Y	Y	Y	Y	Y	Y	Y	N	13	18
Eugenio María de Hostos Comm Coll of City U of NY	Bronx	C,T	St-L	M/W	4,340	33	54	25	Y	Y	Y	Y	Y	Y	Y	N	4	17
Finger Lakes Community College	Canandaigua	C,T	St-L	M/W	4,884		32		Y	Y	Y	Y	Y	Y	Y	N	8	49
Fiorello H LaGuardia Comm Coll of City U of NY*	Long Island City	C,T	St-L	M/W	12,875	52												

This chart includes the names and locations of accredited two-year colleges in the United States and U.S. territories and shows institutions' responses to the *Thomson Peterson's Survey of Undergraduate Institutions*. If an institution submitted incomplete data, one or more columns opposite the institution's name is blank. An asterisk after the school name denotes a *Special Message* following the college's profile, and a dagger indicates that that institution has one or more entries in the *In-Depth Descriptions of Two-Year Colleges* section. If a school does not appear, it did not report any of the information.

Y—Yes; N—No; R—Recommended; S—For Some

Degrees Awarded: College Transfer Associate (C); Terminal Associate (T); Bachelor's (B); Master's (M); Doctoral (D); First Professional (P)

College	Location	Degrees Awarded	Institutional Control	Student Body	Undergraduate Enrollment Fall 2004	Percent Attending Part-Time	Percent 25 Years of Age or Older	Percent of Grads Going on to Four-Year Colleges	High School Equivalency Certificate Accepted	Open Admissions	High School Transcript Required	Need-Based Aid Available	Part-Time Jobs Available	Career Counseling Available	Job Placement Services Available	College Housing Available	Number of Sports Offered	Number of Majors Offered
Fulton-Montgomery Community College	Johnstown	C,T	St-L	M/W	2,071	32	27		Y		Y	Y	Y	Y	Y	N	7	44
Genesee Community College	Batavia	C,T	St-L	M/W	5,204	52	19	64	Y	Y	Y	Y	Y	Y	Y	Y	15	37
Herkimer County Community College	Herkimer	C,T	St-L	M/W	3,477		23		Y	Y	Y	Y	Y	Y	Y	Y	10	36
Hudson Valley Community College	Troy	C,T	St-L	M/W	11,405	35	37		Y	Y	Y	Y	Y	Y	Y	N	16	40
Island Drafting and Technical Institute	Amityville	C,T	Prop	PM	222													
ITT Technical Institute	Albany	T	Prop	M/W	390													
ITT Technical Institute	Getzville	T	Prop	M/W	643													
ITT Technical Institute	Liverpool	T	Prop	M/W	334													
Jamestown Business College	Jamestown	T	Prop	M/W	327													
Jamestown Community College	Jamestown	C,T	St-L	M/W	3,274	25	32		Y	Y	Y	Y	Y	Y	Y	N	10	24
Jefferson Community College	Watertown	C,T	St-L	M/W	3,481	46	37	61	N	Y	Y	Y	Y	Y	Y	N	9	29
Kingsborough Comm Coll of City U of NY	Brooklyn	C,T	St-L	M/W	15,357	48	31	75	Y	Y	Y	Y	Y	Y	Y	N	7	38
Long Island Business Institute	Commack	C	Prop	PW	261	60	95	0	Y	Y	Y			Y	Y	N		4
Maria College*†	Albany	C,T	Ind	M/W	788	65	75	18	N	Y	Y	Y	Y	Y	Y	N		12
Mildred Elley	Latham	C,T	Priv		394													
Mohawk Valley Community College†	Utica	C,T	St-L	M/W	6,068	37	26	71	Y	Y	Y	Y	Y	Y	Y	Y	17	53
Monroe College*	Bronx	C,T,B	Prop	M/W	4,284	11	46	26	N		Y	Y	Y	Y	Y	Y	6	8
Monroe College	New Rochelle	C,T,B	Prop	M/W	1,570	15	31	26	N		Y	Y	Y	Y	Y	Y	7	7
Nassau Community College	Garden City	C,T	St-L	M/W	21,446	36	20	65		Y	Y	Y	Y	Y	Y	N	19	55
New York Col Health Professions†	Syosset	T,B,M	Ind	M/W														
Niagara County Community College	Sanborn	C,T	St-L	M/W	5,546	37	31	62	Y	Y	Y	Y	Y	Y	Y	N	10	35
North Country Community College	Saranac Lake	C,T	St-L	M/W	1,407	30	33	34	Y	Y	Y	Y	Y	Y	Y	Y	12	14
Orange County Community College	Middletown	C,T	St-L	M/W	6,269	49	29	62	Y	Y	Y	Y	Y	Y	Y	N	10	41
Phillips Beth Israel School of Nursing	New York	C,T	Ind	PW	175	79	65	10	N	Y	Y	Y	Y			N		1
Queensborough Comm Coll of City U of NY	Bayside	C,T	St-L	M/W	12,798	52	32		Y	Y	Y	Y	Y	Y	Y	N	14	21
Rochester Business Institute	Rochester	T	Prop	M/W	1,223	16												
Rockland Community College	Suffern	C,T	St-L	M/W	6,549	44	39	67	Y		Y	Y	Y	Y	Y	N	11	41
Saint Joseph's Hospital Health Center School of Nursing	Syracuse	T	Ind	PW	293	39												
Cath Med Ctr of Brooklyn & Queens Sch of Nursing	Fresh Meadows	T	Ind	M/W	93													
Schenectady County Community College	Schenectady	C,T	St-L	M/W	4,140	50												
State U of NY Coll of A&T at Morrisville	Morrisville	C,T,B	St	M/W	3,269	14												
State U of NY Coll of Environ Sci & For Ranger Sch†	Wanakena	C,T	St	PM	43													
State U of NY Coll of Technology at Alfred	Alfred	C,T,B	St	M/W	3,500		23	83	N	Y	Y	Y	Y	Y	Y	Y	22	59
State U of NY Coll of Technology at Canton	Canton	C,T,B	St	M/W	2,518	18	21		N	Y	Y	Y	Y	Y	Y	Y	11	36
State U of NY Coll of Technology at Delhi	Delhi	C,T,B	St	M/W	2,170	10	19	81	N	Y	Y	Y	Y	Y	Y	Y	17	40
Sullivan County Community College	Loch Sheldrake	C,T	St-L	M/W	1,902	38												
Tompkins Cortland Community College	Dryden	C,T	St-L	M/W	3,201	33	37		Y		Y	Y	Y	Y	Y	16	45
Villa Maria College of Buffalo	Buffalo	C,T	I-R	M/W	504	24	40	59	N	Y	Y	Y	Y	Y	N		13
Westchester Community College	Valhalla	C,T	St-L	M/W	11,935	54	40			Y	Y	Y	Y	Y	N	11	52

North Carolina

College	Location	Degrees Awarded	Institutional Control	Student Body	Undergraduate Enrollment Fall 2004	Percent Attending Part-Time	Percent 25 Years of Age or Older	Percent of Grads Going on to Four-Year Colleges	High School Equivalency Certificate Accepted	Open Admissions	High School Transcript Required	Need-Based Aid Available	Part-Time Jobs Available	Career Counseling Available	Job Placement Services Available	College Housing Available	Number of Sports Offered	Number of Majors Offered
Alamance Community College	Graham	C,T	St	M/W	4,627	66	47	1	Y		Y	Y		Y	Y	N	4	33
The Art Institute of Charlotte†	Charlotte	T,B	Prop	M/W	716	30			N	Y	Y		Y	Y	Y			
Asheville-Buncombe Technical Community College	Asheville	C,T	St	M/W	5,627	64	47		Y	Y	Y	Y		Y	Y	N	3	27
Beaufort County Community College	Washington	C,T	St	M/W	1,669		58	75	Y	Y	Y	Y	Y	Y	N		21
Bladen Community College	Dublin	C,T	St-L	M/W	1,407	40	62	81	Y	Y	Y	Y	Y	Y	N		15
Blue Ridge Community College	Flat Rock	C	St-L	M/W	1,959	60	69		Y	Y	Y	Y	Y	Y	N	1	22
Brunswick Community College	Supply	C,T	St	M/W	1,003	51	46		Y	Y	Y		Y	Y	N	4	17
Caldwell Comm Coll and Tech Inst	Hudson	C,T	St	M/W	3,613	67	44		Y	Y	Y	Y	Y	Y	N	3	25
Cape Fear Community College	Wilmington	C,T	St	M/W	7,073	52	11	85	Y	Y	Y	Y	Y	Y	N	7	31
Carolinas College of Health Sciences	Charlotte	T	Ind	PW	458	68	46	5	N	Y	Y	Y	Y	Y	Y		3
Carteret Community College	Morehead City	C,T	St	M/W	1,732		53		Y	Y	Y	Y	Y	Y	N	2	18
Catawba Valley Community College	Hickory	C,T	St-L	M/W	3,943	61	46		Y	Y	Y	Y	Y	Y	N	2	42
Central Carolina Community College	Sanford	C,T	St-L	M/W	4,857	62	50		Y	Y	Y	Y	Y	Y	N	5	29
Central Piedmont Community College	Charlotte	C,T	St-L	M/W	16,400	64	50	46	Y	Y	S	Y	Y	Y	N	1	69
Cleveland Community College	Shelby	C,T	St	M/W	2,943	57	47	50	Y	Y	Y	Y	Y	Y	N		31
Coastal Carolina Community College	Jacksonville	C,T	St-L	M/W	4,158	48	45		Y	Y	Y	Y	Y	N		19
Craven Community College	New Bern	C,T	St	M/W	2,555		50		Y	Y	Y	Y	Y	Y	N	2	19
Davidson County Community College	Lexington	C,T	St-L	M/W	2,303	64	55	79	Y		Y	Y	Y	Y	N		20
Durham Technical Community College	Durham	C,T	St	M/W	5,642	74	63	45	Y	Y	Y	Y	Y	Y	N		37
Edgecombe Community College	Tarboro	C,T	St-L	M/W	2,553	63	47	90	Y	Y	Y	Y	Y	Y	N	1	25
Fayetteville Technical Community College	Fayetteville	C,T	St	M/W	10,175	56	59		Y	Y	S	Y	Y	Y	N	3	79
Forsyth Technical Community College	Winston-Salem	C,T	St	M/W	7,157		51		Y	Y	Y	Y	S	Y	Y	N	4	38
Gaston College	Dallas	C,T	St-L	M/W	5,025	67												
Guilford Technical Community College	Jamestown	C,T	St-L	M/W	8,491	65	44		Y	Y	Y	Y	Y	Y	N		52
Halifax Community College	Weldon	C,T	St-L	M/W	1,580				Y	Y	Y	Y	Y	Y	N		16
Haywood Community College	Clyde	C,T	St-L	M/W	1,988	56	43		Y	Y	Y	Y	Y	Y	N	6	21
Isothermal Community College	Spindale	C,T	St	M/W	2,005	51	49		Y	Y	Y	Y	Y	Y	N	3	34
James Sprunt Community College	Kenansville	C,T	St	M/W	1,324	51	51	68	Y	Y	Y	Y	Y	Y	N	2	13
Johnston Community College	Smithfield	C,T	St	M/W	3,758	59	43		Y	Y	Y	Y	Y	Y	N	4	19

This chart includes the names and locations of accredited two-year colleges in the United States and U.S. territories and shows institutions' responses to the *Thomson Peterson's Survey of Undergraduate Institutions.* If an institution submitted incomplete data, one or more columns opposite the institution's name is blank. An asterisk after the school name denotes a *Special Message* following the college's profile, and a dagger indicates that the institution has one or more entries in the *In-Depth Descriptions of Two-Year Colleges* section. If a school does not appear, it did not report any of the information.

Y—Yes; N—No; R—Recommended; S—For Some

Columns: Degrees Awarded · Institutional Control · Student Body · Undergraduate Enrollment Fall 2004 · Percent Attending Part-Time · Percent 25 Years of Age or Older · Percent of Grads Going on to Four-Year Colleges · High School Equivalency Certificate Accepted · High School Transcript Required · Open Admissions · Need-Based Aid Available · Part-Time Jobs Available · Career Counseling Available · Job Placement Services Available · College Housing Available · Number of Sports Offered · Number of Majors Offered

Institution	City	Deg	Ctrl	Body	Enroll	%PT	%25+	%4yr	HSEq	HSTr	Open	Need	PTJob	Career	JobPl	Hous	Sports	Majors
Lenoir Community College	Kinston	C,T	St	M/W	2,607													
Mayland Community College	Spruce Pine	C,T	St-L	M/W	1,019	52	48		Y	Y	Y	Y	Y	Y	Y	N	1	18
McDowell Technical Community College	Marion	C,T	St	M/W	1,078		50	60	Y	Y	S	Y	Y	Y	Y	N	4	19
Mitchell Community College	Statesville	C,T	St	M/W	2,243	56												
Montgomery Community College	Troy	C,T	St	M/W	827	60	57		Y	Y	Y	Y	Y	Y	Y	N		13
Nash Community College	Rocky Mount	C,T	St	M/W	2,567	65												
Piedmont Community College	Roxboro	C,T	St	M/W	2,189	62	47	100	Y	Y	S	Y	Y	Y	Y	N	1	10
Pitt Community College	Greenville	C,T	St-L	M/W	5,980	46												
Randolph Community College	Asheboro	C,T	St	M/W	2,291		41		Y	Y	Y	Y	Y	Y	Y	N		23
Richmond Community College	Hamlet	C,T	St	M/W	1,690	47	57		Y	Y	Y	Y	Y	Y	Y	N		16
Roanoke-Chowan Community College	Ahoskie	C,T	St	M/W	1,014	52	48		Y	Y		Y	Y	Y	Y	N	2	16
Rockingham Community College	Wentworth	C,T	St	M/W	2,141	52					Y	Y	Y	Y	Y	N	8	32
Rowan-Cabarrus Community College	Salisbury	C,T	St	M/W	5,200	57	55	95	Y	Y	Y	Y	Y	Y	Y	N	1	16
Sandhills Community College	Pinehurst	C,T	St-L	M/W	3,502		44		Y	Y	Y	Y	Y	Y	Y	N		48
South College-Asheville	Asheville	T	Prop	M/W	112	21												
Southeastern Community College	Whiteville	C,T	St	M/W	2,460													
Southwestern Community College	Sylva	C,T	St	M/W	2,014	55	36	75	Y	Y	Y	Y	Y	Y	Y	N		32
Stanly Community College	Albemarle	C,T	St	M/W	2,000		48		Y	Y	Y	Y	Y	Y	Y	N		31
Surry Community College	Dobson	C,T	St	M/W	3,600		42	81	Y	Y	Y	Y	Y	Y	Y	N	4	29
Tri-County Community College	Murphy	C,T	St	M/W	1,155		65	40	Y	Y	Y	Y	Y	Y	Y	N		11
Vance-Granville Community College	Henderson	C,T	St	M/W	4,315	55												
Wake Technical Community College	Raleigh	C,T	St-L	M/W	11,372	66	56		Y	Y	Y	Y	Y	Y	Y	N		47
Wilkes Community College	Wilkesboro	C,T	St	M/W	2,532	48	44	70	Y	Y	Y	Y	Y	Y	Y	N	4	23
Wilson Technical Community College	Wilson	C,T	St	M/W	2,077	49	61	80	Y	Y	Y	Y	Y	Y	Y	N		19
North Dakota																		
Bismarck State College	Bismarck	C,T	St	M/W	3,541	34	32		Y	Y	Y	Y	Y	Y	Y	Y	6	23
Lake Region State College	Devils Lake	C,T	St	M/W	1,464	71	21		Y	Y	Y	Y	Y	Y	Y	Y	8	35
Minot State University–Bottineau Campus	Bottineau	C,T	St	M/W	620	38												
North Dakota State College of Science	Wahpeton	C,T	St	M/W	2,468	21	18	81	Y	Y		Y	Y	Y	Y	Y	8	31
United Tribes Technical College	Bismarck	C,T	Fed	M/W	678													
Williston State College	Williston	C,T	St	M/W	937	40	28	80	Y	Y	Y	Y	Y	Y		Y	3	15
Ohio																		
Antonelli College	Cincinnati	T	Prop	M/W	387													
The Art Institute of Cincinnati†	Cincinnati	C	Prop	M/W	74		5	0		Y				Y	Y	N		
The Art Institute of Ohio–Cincinnati	Cincinnati	C,T	Prop	M/W	108		62		Y	Y	Y				Y	Y		17
Belmont Technical College	St. Clairsville	T	St	M/W	1,740	32	55		Y	Y			Y	Y	Y	N		17
Bowling Green State University-Firelands Coll	Huron	C,T	St	M/W	1,918	46	42	33	Y	Y		Y	Y	Y	Y	N	6	28
Bradford School	Columbus	C,T	Prop	M/W	312													
Brown Mackie College, Findlay Campus	Findlay	T	Prop	M/W	526	15	80		Y			Y						8
Brown Mackie College, North Canton Campus	North Canton	T	Prop	M/W	700													
Bryant and Stratton Coll	Parma	T	Prop	M/W	252	44	51	2	N	Y	Y	Y	Y	Y	Y	N		6
Chatfield College	St. Martin	C,T	I-R	PW	230													
Cincinnati College of Mortuary Science	Cincinnati	T,B	Ind	M/W	121													
Cincinnati State Technical and Community College	Cincinnati	C,T	St	M/W	8,472		45	31	Y	Y	Y	Y	Y	Y	Y	N	4	65
Clark State Community College	Springfield	C,T	St	M/W	3,510	57			Y		Y	Y	Y	Y	Y	N	4	37
Cleveland Institute of Electronics	Cleveland	T	Prop	PM	2,612													
Columbus State Community College	Columbus	C,T	St	M/W	21,872	61	57	31	Y		R	Y	Y	Y	Y	N	9	75
Cuyahoga Community College	Cleveland	C,T	St-L	M/W	25,214	60	42		Y		R	S	Y	Y	Y	N	8	32
Davis College	Toledo	T	Prop	M/W	417	55												
Edison State Community College	Piqua	C,T	St	M/W	3,000	66	49		Y	Y	Y			Y	Y	N	2	38
Gallipolis Career College	Gallipolis	T	Ind	PW	161	4												
International College of Broadcasting	Dayton	C,T	Priv	M/W	87									Y				2
ITT Technical Institute	Dayton	T	Prop	M/W	483													
ITT Technical Institute	Hilliard	T	Prop	M/W	26													
ITT Technical Institute	Norwood	C	Prop	M/W	593													
ITT Technical Institute	Strongsville	T	Prop	M/W	709													
ITT Technical Institute	Youngstown	T	Prop	M/W	518													
James A. Rhodes State College	Lima	C,T	St	M/W	2,842	50												
Jefferson Community College	Steubenville	C,T	St-L	M/W	1,260	47	43		Y	Y	S	Y	Y	Y	Y	N	6	25
Kent State University, Salem Campus	Salem	C,T,B	St	M/W	1,320													
Kent State University, Stark Campus	Canton	C,B	St	M/W	3,736													
Kent State University, Trumbull Campus	Warren	C,T	St	M/W	2,270													
Kent State University, Tuscarawas Campus	New Philadelphia	C,T,B,M	St	M/W	1,802		29		Y	Y	Y	Y	Y	Y	Y	N	3	16
Kettering College of Medical Arts	Kettering	C,T,B	I-R	PW	653													
Lakeland Community College	Kirtland	C,T	St-L	M/W	8,635	64												
Lorain County Community College	Elyria	C,T	St-L	M/W	9,409	64												
Marion Technical College	Marion	C,T	St	M/W	2,121	54												
Mercy College of Northwest Ohio	Toledo	C,T,B	I-R	PW	688	47	51		N	Y	Y	Y	Y	Y	Y			6

This chart includes the names and locations of accredited two-year colleges in the United States and U.S. territories and shows institutions' responses to the *Thomson Peterson's Survey of Undergraduate Institutions*. If an institution submitted incomplete data, one or more columns opposite the institution's name is blank. An asterisk after the school name denotes a *Special Message* following the college's profile, and a dagger indicates that the institution has one or more entries in the *In-Depth Descriptions of Two-Year Colleges* section. If a school does not appear, it did not report any of the information.

Legend: **Y—Yes; N—No; R—Recommended; S—For Some**

Column key (slanted headers, left to right): College Transfer Associate (C), Bachelor's (B), Master's (M), Doctoral (D), First Professional (P), Terminal Associate (T) — **Degrees Awarded**; County District City, Federal, State and Local, State-related, Territory, Independent, Independent-Religious, Proprietary — **Institutional Control**; Men, Primarily Men, Women, Primarily Women, Coed — **Student Body**; Undergraduate Enrollment Fall 2004; Percent Attending Part-Time; Percent 25 Years of Age or Older; Percent of Grads Going on to Four-Year Colleges; Open Admissions; High School Equivalency Certificate Accepted; High School Transcript Required; Need-Based Aid Available; Part-Time Jobs Available; Career Counseling Available; Job Placement Services Available; College Housing Available; Number of Sports Offered; Number of Majors Offered.

Institution	Location	Degrees	Control	Student Body	Enroll. Fall 2004	% Part-Time	% 25+	% Grads to 4-Yr	Open Adm.	HS Equiv. Cert.	HS Transcript	Need-Based Aid	Part-Time Jobs	Career Counsel.	Job Placement	College Housing	Sports	Majors
Miami University Hamilton	Hamilton	C,T,B,M	St	M/W	3,330	27	25		Y	Y	Y	Y	Y	Y	Y	N	11	99
North Central State College	Mansfield	T	St	M/W	3,333		49		Y	Y	S	Y	Y	Y	Y	N	7	26
Northwest State Community College	Archbold	C,T	St	M/W	3,145	65	50		Y	Y	S	Y	Y	Y	Y	N	5	32
Ohio Business College	Sandusky	C	Prop	M/W	198													
Ohio Institute of Photography and Technology	Dayton	T	Prop	M/W	581	33	5		N	Y	Y	Y	Y	Y	Y	N		4
Ohio State U Agricultural Technical Institute	Wooster	C,T	St	M/W	791	14	10		Y	Y	Y		Y	Y	Y	Y	5	37
Ohio Valley College of Technology	East Liverpool	T	Prop	PW	126	4												
Owens Community College	Findlay	C,T	St	M/W	2,163	56	47		Y	Y	Y	Y	Y	Y	Y	N	11	19
Owens Community College	Toledo	C,T	St	M/W	17,917	64	50		Y	Y	Y	Y	Y	Y	Y	N	11	24
Remington College–Cleveland Campus	Cleveland	C	Prop	M/W	676							Y		Y	Y	N		
Remington College–Cleveland West Campus	North Olmstead	T	Prop	M/W	407													
RETS Tech Center	Centerville	C,T	Prop	M/W	556		55	0	N	Y	Y		Y		Y	N		6
School of Advertising Art	Kettering	C,T	Prop	M/W	121		3	1						S		N		1
Sinclair Community College	Dayton	C,T	St-L	M/W	19,563	61	47	53	Y		S	Y	Y	Y	Y	N	5	89
Southern State Community College	Hillsboro	C,T	St	M/W	2,356				Y	Y	R	Y	Y	Y	Y	N	5	14
Stark State College of Technology	Canton	C,T	St-L	M/W	5,667	67												
Stautzenberger College	Toledo	T	Prop	M/W	792													
Terra State Community College	Fremont	C,T	St	M/W	2,549	58												
Trumbull Business College	Warren	T	Prop	PW	411	16												
The University of Akron–Wayne College	Orrville	C,T	St	M/W	1,798	43	41	75	Y	Y	S	Y	Y	Y	Y	N	4	21
University of Cincinnati Raymond Walters College	Cincinnati	C,T	St	M/W	4,421	51	41	90	Y	Y	Y	Y	Y	Y	Y	N	18	37
University of Northwestern Ohio*	Lima	C,B	Ind	M/W	2,971	10	18	40	Y	Y	Y	Y	Y	Y	Y	Y	3	16
Oklahoma																		
Community Care College	Tulsa	T	Prop	M/W										Y				
Connors State College	Warner	C,T	St	M/W	2,335													
Eastern Oklahoma State College	Wilburton	C,T	St	M/W	2,639													
Northeastern Oklahoma A&M College	Miami	C,T	St	M/W	2,102	30												
Oklahoma City Community College	Oklahoma City	C,T	St	M/W	12,048	60												
Oklahoma State U, Oklahoma City	Oklahoma City	C,T	St	M/W	5,654													
Seminole State College	Seminole	C,T	St	M/W	2,482	12	47		Y			Y	Y	Y	Y	Y	7	18
Southwestern Oklahoma State University at Sayre	Sayre	C,T	St-L	M/W	585	42	50	75	Y	Y	Y	Y	Y	Y	Y	N		10
Tulsa Welding School	Tulsa	C,T	Prop	PM	362	37								Y	Y	N		1
Vatterott College	Oklahoma City	T,F	Prop	M/W	249									Y				5
Vatterott College	Tulsa	T	Prop	PW	267													
Western Oklahoma State College	Altus	C,T	St	M/W	1,919	65	25		Y	Y	Y	Y	Y	Y		Y	7	51
Oregon																		
Blue Mountain Community College	Pendleton	C,T	St-L	M/W	1,878	54	16		Y			Y	Y	Y		N	4	22
Central Oregon Community College*	Bend	C,T	Dist	M/W	4,048	62	41	50	N				Y	Y	Y	Y	13	38
Chemeketa Community College	Salem	C,T	St-L	M/W	14,454	75	45		Y						S	N	5	48
Clackamas Community College	Oregon City	C,T	Dist	M/W	6,866	58	47	77	Y		R	R		Y	Y	N	10	15
Clatsop Community College	Astoria	C,T	Cou	M/W	1,824	76	50	30	Y		R		Y	Y	Y			12
Columbia Gorge Community College	The Dalles	C,T	St	M/W														
ITT Technical Institute	Portland	T,B	Prop	M/W	525													
Lane Community College	Eugene	C,T	St-L	M/W	11,834		42		Y				Y	Y	Y	N	15	36
Linn-Benton Community College	Albany	C,T	St-L	M/W	5,398	46	43		Y		S		Y	Y	Y	N	5	61
Oregon Coast Community College	Newport	C	Pub	M/W	504	80	58		Y					Y		N		
Pioneer Pacific College	Wilsonville	C,B	Prop	M/W	1,015		64		Y	Y	Y	Y				N		10
Portland Community College	Portland	C,T	St-L	M/W	96,764													
Rogue Community College	Grants Pass	C,T	St-L	M/W	4,211	59	55		Y				Y	Y	Y	N	4	25
Southwestern Oregon Community College	Coos Bay	C,T	St-L	M/W	2,114	57	45		Y		S			Y	Y	Y	10	26
Tillamook Bay Community College	Tillamook	C,T	Dist	M/W	250	88	46									N		14
Umpqua Community College	Roseburg	C,T	St-L	M/W	2,141	60	35		Y		R		Y	Y	Y	Y	1	53
Pennsylvania																		
Academy of Medical Arts and Business	Harrisburg	C,T	Prop	PW	491													
Antonelli Institute	Erdenheim	T	Prop	M/W	147		8	0	Y	Y	Y	Y	Y	Y	Y			2
The Art Institute of Philadelphia	Philadelphia	T,B	Prop	M/W	3,271		20		N	Y	Y	Y	Y	Y	Y	Y	2	15
Berean Institute	Philadelphia	C,T	Ind	M/W	208	18												
Bucks County Community College	Newtown	C,T	Cou	M/W	9,947	59	37		Y					Y	Y	N	8	57
Business Institute of Pennsylvania	Meadville	T	Prop	M/W	76											N		
Business Institute of Pennsylvania	Sharon	T	Prop	M/W	106	8				Y	Y	Y				N		9
Butler County Community College	Butler	C,T	Cou	M/W	3,731		40		Y				Y	Y	Y	N	11	49
Cambria-Rowe Business College	Indiana	C,T	Prop	PW	118	6												
Cambria-Rowe Business College	Johnstown	C,T	Prop	PW	230													
CHI Institute	Southampton	C,T	Prop	M/W	700													
Commonwealth Technical Institute	Johnstown	T	St	M/W	231									Y	Y	Y		7
Community College of Allegheny County†	Pittsburgh	C,T	Cou	M/W	18,964	59	48	39	Y		R	Y	Y	Y	Y	N	15	116
Community College of Beaver County	Monaca	C,T	St	M/W	2,500		56		Y		R		Y	Y	Y	Y	6	30

This chart includes the names and locations of accredited two-year colleges in the United States and U.S. territories and shows institutions' responses to the *Thomson Peterson's Survey of Undergraduate Institutions*. If an institution submitted incomplete data, one or more columns opposite the institution's name is blank. An asterisk after the school name denotes a *Special Message* following the college's profile, and a dagger indicates that that institution has one or more entries in the *In-Depth Descriptions of Two-Year Colleges* section. If a school does not appear, it did not report any of the information.

Y—Yes; N—No; R—Recommended; S—For Some

Institution	Location	Degrees Awarded	Institutional Control	Student Body	Undergraduate Enrollment Fall 2004	Percent Attending Part-Time	Percent 25 Years of Age or Older	Percent of Grads Going on to Four-Year Colleges	High School Equivalency Certificate Accepted	Open Admissions	High School Transcript Required	Need-Based Aid Required	Part-Time Jobs Available	Career Counseling Available	Job Placement Services Available	College Housing Available	Number of Sports Offered	Number of Majors Offered
Community College of Philadelphia	Philadelphia	C,T	St-L	M/W	22,671		53		Y	Y	S		Y	Y	Y	N	8	54
Consolidated School of Business	York	T	Prop	PW	202													
Dean Institute of Technology	Pittsburgh	T	Prop	M/W	228													
Delaware County Community College	Media	C,T	St-L	M/W	10,608	60	42	69	Y	Y	Y	Y	Y	Y	Y	N	8	49
Education Direct Center for Degree Studies	Scranton		Prop	M/W	18,058	100												
Erie Business Center, Main	Erie	T	Prop	M/W	480	40	38		N	Y	Y	Y	Y	Y	Y	Y		14
Erie Business Center South	New Castle	C,T	Prop	PW	100				N	Y	Y	Y	Y	Y	N		4	10
Erie Institute of Technology	Erie	T	Prop	M/W	173													
Harcum College†	Bryn Mawr	C,T	Ind	PW	573	33	40		Y	Y	Y	Y	Y	Y	Y		6	21
Harrisburg Area Community College	Harrisburg	C,T	St-L	M/W	16,109	60	48	67	Y		Y	Y	Y	Y	Y	N	11	86
ICM School of Business & Medical Careers	Pittsburgh	C,T	Prop	M/W	1,095	3	45		N	Y	Y	Y	Y	Y	N			14
Keystone College†	La Plume	C,T,B	Ind	M/W	1,658	26	28	71	Y		Y	Y	Y	Y	Y	Y	16	71
Lackawanna College	Scranton	C,T	Ind	M/W	1,197	37	33	57	Y	Y	Y	Y	Y	Y	Y	Y	7	23
Laurel Business Institute	Uniontown	C,T	Prop	M/W	378	3			Y	Y	Y	Y	Y	Y	Y	N		28
Lehigh Carbon Community College	Schnecksville	C,T	St-L	M/W	6,674	61	33	57	Y		S	Y	Y	Y	Y	N	18	71
Lehigh Valley College†	Center Valley	T	Prop	M/W	1,511	11												
Luzerne County Community College	Nanticoke	C,T	Cou	M/W	6,170	52												
Montgomery County Community College	Blue Bell	C,T	Cou	M/W	10,842	57	27	74	Y	Y	S	Y	Y	Y		N	12	53
New Castle School of Trades	Pulaski	C	Ind	PM	451													
Newport Business Institute	Lower Burrell	T	Prop	M/W	89													
Newport Business Institute	Williamsport	T	Prop	PW	107	1	48	0	N	Y	Y	Y	Y	Y	N			4
Northampton County Area Community College	Bethlehem	C,T	St-L	M/W	8,246	57	41	68	Y	Y	Y	Y	Y	Y	Y	Y	12	50
Oakbridge Academy of Arts	Lower Burrell	C,T	Prop	M/W	103	1												
Orleans Technical Institute-Center City Campus	Philadelphia	C,T	Prop	PW	135	36	73		Y	Y	Y	Y	Y	Y	N			
Pennsylvania Culinary Institute	Pittsburgh	T	Prop	M/W	1,040		32		N	Y	Y		Y	Y	Y			2
Pennsylvania Highland Community College	Johnstown	C,T	St-L	M/W	1,327	55	66		Y		R	Y	Y	Y				22
Pennsylvania Institute of Technology	Media	C,T	Ind	M/W	215	42	51		Y	Y	Y	Y	Y	Y	N	2	9
Penn State U Beaver Campus of the Commonwealth Coll	Monaca	C,T,B	St-R	M/W	655	14	11		N	Y	Y	Y	Y	Y	Y	10	120
Penn State U Delaware County Campus of the Commonwealth Coll	Media	T,B	St-R	M/W	1,636	16	10		N	Y		Y	Y	Y	Y	10	118
Penn State U DuBois Campus of the Commonwealth Coll	DuBois	C,T,B	St-R	M/W	842	27	34		N	Y	Y	Y	Y	Y	N	7	127
Penn State U Fayette Campus of the Commonwealth Coll	Uniontown	C,T,B	St-R	M/W	1,066	26	39		N	Y	Y	Y	Y	Y	Y	11	125
Penn State U Hazleton Campus of the Commonwealth Coll	Hazleton	C,T,B	St-R	M/W	1,108	6	6		N	Y	Y	Y	Y	Y	Y	8	126
Penn State U McKeesport Campus of the Commonwealth Coll	McKeesport	T,B	St-R	M/W	798	11	8		N	Y	Y	Y	Y	Y	Y	12	118
Penn State U Mont Alto Campus of the Commonwealth Coll	Mont Alto	T,B	St-R	M/W	1,018	31	26		N	Y	Y	Y	Y	Y	Y	10	121
Penn State U New Kensington Campus of the Commonwealth Coll	New Kensington	C,T,B	St-R	M/W	977	30	23		N	Y	Y	Y	Y	Y	N	13	125
Penn State U Shenango Campus of the Commonwealth Coll	Sharon	C,T,B	St-R	M/W	958	41	50		N	Y	Y	Y	Y	Y	N	7	123
Penn State U Wilkes-Barre Campus of the Commonwealth Coll	Lehman	C,T,B	St-R	M/W	735	21	14		N	Y	Y	Y	Y	Y	Y	11	123
Penn State U Worthington Scranton Cmps Commonwealth Coll	Dunmore	T,B	St-R	M/W	1,303	23	26		N	Y	Y	Y	Y	Y	N	10	120
Penn State U York Campus of the Commonwealth Coll	York	C,T,B	St-R	M/W	1,571	41	31		N	Y	Y	Y	Y	Y	N	10	124
Pittsburgh Technical Institute	Oakdale		Prop	M/W	1,975													
Reading Area Community College	Reading	C,T	Cou	M/W	4,158	62												
The Restaurant School at Walnut Hill College†	Philadelphia	T,B	Prop	M/W	585													
Rosedale Technical Institute	Pittsburgh	T	Ind	PW	205													
Schuylkill Institute of Business and Technology	Pottsville	T	Prop	M/W	153		45		Y	Y	Y		Y	Y	N			8
South Hills School of Business & Technology	State College	C,T	Prop	M/W	686	8	39	2	N	Y	Y		Y	Y	N			12
Thaddeus Stevens College of Technology	Lancaster	C,T	St	M/W	660		6	10	N	Y	Y	Y		Y	Y	Y	15	19
Thompson Institute	Harrisburg	T,B	Prop	M/W	485		60		Y	Y	Y	Y		Y	Y	Y		9
Triangle Tech, Inc.–DuBois School	DuBois	T	Prop	PM	291													
Triangle Tech, Inc.–Greensburg School	Greensburg	T	Prop	PM	255		49		N	Y	Y	Y		Y	Y	N		8
Triangle Tech, Inc.–Pittsburgh School	Pittsburgh	C,T	Prop	PM	377		35		N	Y	Y	Y		Y	Y	N		6
University of Pittsburgh at Titusville	Titusville	C,T	St-R	M/W	565	25		100	N	Y	Y	Y		Y	Y	Y	11	5
Valley Forge Military College*†	Wayne	C	Ind	M	240													
Westmoreland County Community College	Youngwood	C,T	Cou	M/W	6,194	57	45		Y	Y		Y	Y	Y	N	12	53
The Williamson Free School of Mechanical Trades	Media	T	Ind	M	253													
York Technical Institute	York	T	Priv	M/W	1,296													
Puerto Rico																		
Instituto Comercial de Puerto Rico Junior College	San Juan	T	Prop	M/W	1,270	14			Y	Y	Y	Y	Y	Y	Y			5
Rhode Island																		
Community College of Rhode Island	Warwick	C,T	St	M/W	16,293	65			Y	Y		Y	Y	Y	N	10	43
South Carolina																		
Central Carolina Technical College	Sumter	C,T	St	M/W	3,259	69	46	11	Y	Y	Y	Y	Y	Y	N		17
Forrest Junior College	Anderson	C,T	Prop	PW	165		20	2		Y	Y	Y	Y	Y	N		1
ITT Technical Institute	Greenville	T,B	Prop	M/W	338													
Midlands Technical College	Columbia	C,T	St-L	M/W	10,710	55	40		Y		R	Y	Y	Y	N	4	38

This chart includes the names and locations of accredited two-year colleges in the United States and U.S. territories and shows institutions' responses to the *Thomson Peterson's Survey of Undergraduate Institutions.* If an institution submitted incomplete data, one or more columns opposite the institution's name is blank. An asterisk after the school name denotes a *Special Message* following the college's profile, and a dagger indicates that the institution has one or more entries in the *In-Depth Descriptions of Two-Year Colleges* section. If a school does not appear, it did not report any of the information.

Y—Yes; N—No; R—Recommended; S—For Some

College	Location	Degrees Awarded	Institutional Control	Student Body	Undergrad Enroll Fall 2004	% Part-Time	% 25+	% Grads to 4-Yr	HS Equiv Accepted	HS Transcript Req	Open Admissions	Need-Based Aid	Part-Time Jobs	Career Counseling	Job Placement	College Housing	# Sports	# Majors
Miller-Motte Technical College	Charleston		Prop	M/W														
Northeastern Technical College	Cheraw	C,T	St-L	M/W	1,115		45		Y	Y	Y	Y	Y	Y	Y	N		11
Orangeburg-Calhoun Technical College	Orangeburg	C,T	St-L	M/W	2,491	45												
South University	Columbia	T,B	Prop	M/W	361	41	71		N	Y	Y	Y	Y	Y	Y	N		6
Spartanburg Methodist College*†	Spartanburg	C,T	I-R	M/W	784	8	6	93	Y	N	Y	Y	Y	Y	Y	Y	13	4
Spartanburg Technical College	Spartanburg	C,T	St	M/W	4,095		43		Y	Y	Y	Y	Y	Y	Y	N		24
Technical College of the Lowcountry	Beaufort	C,T	St	M/W	1,765		75		Y	Y		Y	Y	Y	Y	N	1	24
Tri-County Technical College	Pendleton	C,T	St	M/W	4,100		38		Y	Y		Y	Y	Y	Y	N		20
Trident Technical College	Charleston	C,T	St-L	M/W	11,795	55	47		Y	Y	S	Y	Y	Y	Y	N		40
U of South Carolina Salkehatchie	Allendale	C	St	M/W	777													
U of South Carolina at Sumter	Sumter	C	St	M/W	1,042	47	30		N	Y	Y	Y	Y	Y		N	10	2
U of South Carolina at Union	Union	C	St	M/W	406		35		N	Y	Y	Y	Y			N		2
Williamsburg Technical College	Kingstree	C,T	St	PW	595													
York Technical College	Rock Hill	C,T	St	M/W	4,171	51												
South Dakota																		
Kilian Community College	Sioux Falls	C,T	Ind	M/W	444													
Lake Area Technical Institute	Watertown	T	St	M/W	1,057													
Mitchell Technical Institute	Mitchell	C,T	Dist	M/W	832													
Sisseton-Wahpeton Community College	Sisseton	C,T	Fed	M/W	274	46	69		Y	Y	Y		Y	Y	Y	N		12
Southeast Technical Institute	Sioux Falls	T	St	M/W	2,363	19	28		N	Y	Y	Y	Y	Y	Y	Y	2	50
Western Dakota Technical Institute	Rapid City	T	St	M/W	1,057	29												
Tennessee																		
American Academy of Nutrition, Coll of Nutrition	Knoxville	C,T	Prop	M/W	241													
Chattanooga State Technical Community College	Chattanooga	C,T	St	M/W	8,121	53	44		Y	Y	Y	Y	Y	Y	Y	N	3	63
Cleveland State Community College	Cleveland	C,T	St	M/W	2,962	45	43	40	Y	Y	Y	Y	Y	Y	Y	N	10	11
Columbia State Community College	Columbia	C,T	St	M/W	4,613	47	28		Y	Y	Y	Y	Y	Y	Y	N	5	33
Dyersburg State Community College	Dyersburg	C,T	St	M/W	2,477	42	42		Y	Y	Y		Y	Y	Y	N	4	8
Fountainhead College of Technology	Knoxville	C,T,B	Prop	M/W	120													
ITT Technical Institute	Knoxville	T,B	Prop	M/W	575													
ITT Technical Institute	Memphis	T,B	Prop	M/W	520													
ITT Technical Institute	Nashville	T,B	Prop	M/W	713													
Jackson State Community College	Jackson	C,T	St	M/W	3,970	44	43	67	Y	Y	S	Y	Y	Y	Y	N	8	15
Mid-America Baptist Theological Seminary	Germantown	T,M,D,F	I-R	PM	49	37			Y	Y	Y	Y		Y	Y	Y		1
Motlow State Community College	Tullahoma	C,T	St	M/W	3,540	42	31	69	Y	Y	Y	Y		Y	Y	N	9	5
Nashville Auto Diesel College	Nashville	T	Prop	PM	1,306													
Nashville State Technical Community College	Nashville	C,T	St	M/W	7,021	66	55		Y	Y	Y	Y	Y	Y	Y	N		19
National College of Business & Technology	Bristol	T	Prop	M/W	319				Y	Y		Y	Y	Y	Y	N		5
National College of Business & Technology	Knoxville	T	Prop	M/W	209													
National College of Business & Technology	Nashville	T	Prop	M/W	466				Y	Y			Y	Y	Y	N		4
North Central Institute	Clarksville	T	Prop	PM	107	51	50		Y	Y		Y		Y	Y	N		2
Northeast State Technical Community College	Blountville	C,T	St	M/W	5,084	45	47	90	Y	Y	Y	Y	Y	Y	Y	N	3	22
Pellissippi State Technical Community College	Knoxville	C,T	St	M/W	7,563													
Roane State Community College	Harriman	C,T	St	M/W	5,385	45												
South College	Knoxville	T,B	Prop	PW	443													
Volunteer State Community College	Gallatin	C,T	St	M/W	7,044	51	39		Y	Y	Y	Y	Y	Y	Y	N	3	11
Walters State Community College	Morristown	C,T	St	M/W	5,964	48	26		Y	Y	Y	Y	Y	Y	Y	N	4	20
Texas																		
Alvin Community College	Alvin	C,T	St-L	M/W	3,932	59	38		Y	Y	S	Y	Y	Y	Y	N	4	33
Amarillo College	Amarillo	C,T	St-L	M/W	10,196		43	52	Y		Y	Y	Y	Y	Y	N	3	83
Austin Community College	Austin	C,T	Dist	M/W	35,576		39		Y	Y			Y	Y	Y	N	6	75
Border Institute of Technology	El Paso	C,T	Prop	PM	250													
Brazosport College	Lake Jackson	C,T	St-L	M/W	3,389	72	42	35	Y	Y	S	Y		Y	Y	N	11	76
Cedar Valley College	Lancaster	C,T	St	M/W	4,290	66	42		Y	Y	R	Y		Y	Y	N	5	16
Central Texas College†	Killeen	C,T	St-L	M/W	18,351	84	55		Y	Y	Y	Y		Y	Y	Y	10	48
Clarendon College	Clarendon	C,T	St-L	M/W	1,021	61			Y	Y	Y	Y		Y	Y	Y	6	36
Coastal Bend College	Beeville	C,T	Cou	M/W	4,013	55	42		Y	Y	Y	Y		Y	Y	Y	13	67
College of the Mainland	Texas City	C,T	St-L	M/W	3,948	63	41		Y	Y	S	Y		Y	Y	N	11	16
Collin County Community College District	Plano	C,T	St-L	M/W	17,702	60	37		Y	Y		Y		Y	Y	N	3	31
Commonwealth Institute of Funeral Service	Houston	T	Ind	M/W	164	4	48		N	Y	Y		Y		Y	N		1
Court Reporting Institute of Dallas	Dallas	C,T	Prop	PW	526													
Cy-Fair College	Houston	C,T	St-L	M/W	8,540	78			Y	Y				Y	Y	N		
Dallas Institute of Funeral Service	Dallas	C,T	Ind	M/W	234		52		Y	Y	Y					N		1
Del Mar College	Corpus Christi	C,T	St-L	M/W	11,338													
Eastfield College	Mesquite	C,T	St-L	M/W	11,666	81	35	60	Y	Y	R	Y		Y	Y	N	8	29
El Centro College	Dallas	C,T	Cou	M/W	5,884	73												
El Paso Community College	El Paso	C,T	Cou	M/W	19,953		45	39	Y	Y			Y	Y	Y	N	9	77
Frank Phillips College	Borger	C,T	St-L	M/W	1,100		26		Y	Y	Y	Y	Y	Y	Y	Y	4	63

This chart includes the names and locations of accredited two-year colleges in the United States and U.S. territories and shows institutions' responses to the *Thomson Peterson's Survey of Undergraduate Institutions*. If an institution submitted incomplete data, one or more columns opposite the institution's name is blank.

An asterisk after the school name denotes a *Special Message* following the college's profile, and a dagger indicates that the institution has one or more entries in the *In-Depth Descriptions of Two-Year Colleges* section. If a school does not appear, it did not report any of the information.

Y—Yes; N—No; R—Recommended; S—For Some

Column legend:
- **Degrees Awarded:** College Transfer Associate (C), Terminal Associate (T), Bachelor's (B), Master's (M), Doctoral (D), First Professional (F)
- **Institutional Control:** Independent, Independent-Religious, Proprietary; Federal, State, Commonwealth, Territory; State and Local, State-Related; County, District, City
- **Student Body:** Men, Primarily Men, Women, Primarily Women, Coed

Institution	Location	Degrees Awarded	Institutional Control	Student Body	Undergraduate Enrollment Fall 2004	Percent Attending Part-Time	Percent 25 Years of Age or Older	Percent of Grads Going on to Four-Year Colleges	High School Equivalency Certificate Accepted	High School Transcript Required	Open Admissions	Need-Based Aid Available	Part-Time Jobs Available	Career Counseling Available	Job Placement Services Available	College Housing Available	Number of Sports Offered	Number of Majors Offered
Galveston College	Galveston	C,T	St-L	M/W	2,214	63												
Hill College of the Hill Junior College District	Hillsboro	C,T	Dist	M/W	3,236	52												
Houston Community College System	Houston	C,T	St-L	M/W	39,838			25	Y		S	Y	Y	Y	Y	N		65
Howard College	Big Spring	C,T	St-L	M/W	2,728	64	58		Y	Y		Y	Y	Y	Y	Y	8	31
ITT Technical Institute	Arlington	T	Prop	M/W	458													
ITT Technical Institute	Austin	T	Prop	M/W	725													
ITT Technical Institute	Houston	T	Prop	M/W	612													
ITT Technical Institute	Houston	T	Prop	M/W	585													
ITT Technical Institute	Houston	T	Prop	M/W	478													
ITT Technical Institute	Richardson	T	Prop	M/W	715													
ITT Technical Institute	San Antonio	T	Prop	M/W	788													
Jacksonville College	Jacksonville	C,T	I-R	M/W	323	26												
KD Studio	Dallas	T	Prop	M/W	129													
Kilgore College	Kilgore	C,T	St-L	M/W	4,957	45	30		Y	Y	Y	Y	Y	Y	Y	Y	8	65
Kingwood College	Kingwood	C,T	St-L	M/W	6,403	79	35		Y	Y	Y	Y	Y	Y		N	1	17
Lamar State College–Orange	Orange	C,T	St	M/W	1,853	50												
Lamar State College–Port Arthur	Port Arthur	C,T	St	M/W	2,429													
Laredo Community College	Laredo	C,T	St-L	M/W	9,032	67	35		Y			Y	Y	Y	Y	Y	7	29
Lon Morris College	Jacksonville	C,T	I-R	M/W	432	9						Y	Y	Y		N	7	26
McLennan Community College	Waco	C,T	Cou	M/W	7,562	56	42		Y			Y	Y	Y	Y	N	7	26
Midland College	Midland	C,T,B	St-L	M/W	5,531	63	16		Y			Y	Y	Y	Y	Y	11	58
Mountain View College	Dallas	C,T	St-L	M/W	6,410													
MTI College of Business and Technology	Houston	T	Prop	M/W	217		55		N	Y	Y			Y	Y		N		4
MTI College of Business and Technology	Houston	T	Prop	M/W	718		59							Y	Y		N		6
Northeast Texas Community College	Mount Pleasant	C,T	St-L	M/W	2,512	46												
North Harris College	Houston	C,T	St-L	M/W	10,591													
North Lake College	Irving	C,T	Cou	M/W	8,779	67	51		Y	Y	R		Y	Y	Y		N	4	15
Odessa College	Odessa	C,T	St-L	M/W	4,569	61	40	42	Y	Y			Y	Y	Y	Y	Y	10	60
Palo Alto College	San Antonio	C,T	St-L	M/W	7,727													
Panola College	Carthage	C,T	St-L	M/W	1,780	47	30		Y	Y	R,S	Y	Y	Y		Y	7	5
Paris Junior College	Paris	C,T	St-L	M/W	3,862	63												
St. Philip's College	San Antonio	C,T	Dist	M/W	10,164	55	48		Y	Y	Y		Y	Y	Y		N	6	72
San Antonio College	San Antonio	C,T	St-L	M/W	22,226	61	40		Y	Y	R,S		Y	Y	Y		N	5	45
South Plains College	Levelland	C,T	St-L	M/W	9,636	53												
South Texas College	McAllen	C,T,B	Dist	M/W	15,334	54	35		Y	Y	Y		Y	Y	Y		N	10	26
Southwest Institute of Technology	Austin	C,T	Prop	PM	63													
Temple College	Temple	C,T	Dist	M/W	4,068	62	31		Y	Y	S	Y	Y	Y	Y	Y	8	20
Texas Culinary Academy	Austin	C,T	Ind	M/W	200													
Texas State Tech Coll–Harlingen	Harlingen	C,T	St	M/W	4,028	57												
Texas State Tech Coll–Waco/Marshall Campus	Waco	C,T	St	M/W	4,417	32	18		Y	Y	Y		Y	Y	Y	Y	Y	7	44
Trinity Valley Community College	Athens	C,T	St-L	M/W	5,821	58	48		Y	Y			Y		Y	Y	Y	6	54
Weatherford College	Weatherford	C,T	St-L	M/W	3,999													
Western Technical College	El Paso	C,T	Priv		825				Y	Y				Y	Y	N		3
Westwood College–Dallas†	Dallas	T	Prop	M/W	404	2												
Westwood College–Fort Worth†	Euless	T	Prop	M/W	472	21												
Westwood College–Houston South Campus†	Houston	T	Prop	M/W	16													

Utah

Institution	Location	Degrees Awarded	Institutional Control	Student Body	Undergraduate Enrollment Fall 2004	Percent Attending Part-Time	Percent 25 Years of Age or Older	Percent of Grads Going on to Four-Year Colleges	High School Equivalency Certificate Accepted	High School Transcript Required	Open Admissions	Need-Based Aid Available	Part-Time Jobs Available	Career Counseling Available	Job Placement Services Available	College Housing Available	Number of Sports Offered	Number of Majors Offered
College of Eastern Utah	Price	C,T	St	M/W	2,692	46												
Dixie State College of Utah	St. George	C,T,B	St	M/W	8,373	58	21		Y	Y	Y		Y	Y	Y	Y	Y	9	78
ITT Technical Institute	Murray	T,B	Prop	M/W	494													
LDS Business College	Salt Lake City	C,T	I-R	M/W	1,282	25												
Mountain West College	West Valley City	C,T	Prop	M/W	773													
Salt Lake Community College	Salt Lake City	C,T	St	M/W	24,725	66	37		Y				Y	Y	Y		N	6	78
Snow College	Ephraim	C,T	St	M/W	2,975	17	14		Y	Y	Y		Y	Y			Y	12	66
Utah Career College	West Jordan	C	Prop	M/W	482													

Vermont

Institution	Location	Degrees Awarded	Institutional Control	Student Body	Undergraduate Enrollment Fall 2004	Percent Attending Part-Time	Percent 25 Years of Age or Older	Percent of Grads Going on to Four-Year Colleges	High School Equivalency Certificate Accepted	High School Transcript Required	Open Admissions	Need-Based Aid Available	Part-Time Jobs Available	Career Counseling Available	Job Placement Services Available	College Housing Available	Number of Sports Offered	Number of Majors Offered
Community College of Vermont	Waterbury	C,T	St	M/W	5,801		60		Y	Y			Y	Y	Y		N		15
Landmark College†	Putney	C,T	Ind	M/W	334	33	7	90	N	Y	Y	Y		Y			Y	13	1
New England Culinary Institute	Montpelier	T,B	Prop	M/W	606													

Virginia

Institution	Location	Degrees Awarded	Institutional Control	Student Body	Undergraduate Enrollment Fall 2004	Percent Attending Part-Time	Percent 25 Years of Age or Older	Percent of Grads Going on to Four-Year Colleges	High School Equivalency Certificate Accepted	High School Transcript Required	Open Admissions	Need-Based Aid Available	Part-Time Jobs Available	Career Counseling Available	Job Placement Services Available	College Housing Available	Number of Sports Offered	Number of Majors Offered
Blue Ridge Community College	Weyers Cave	C,T	St	M/W	3,942	63	36		Y	Y	S	Y	Y	Y	Y	N	1	12
Dabney S. Lancaster Community College	Clifton Forge	C,T	St	M/W	1,443	59	60		Y	Y			Y	Y	Y	Y	N	9	17
Danville Community College	Danville	C,T	St	M/W	4,089	67	58		Y	Y	Y		Y	Y	Y	Y	N	6	9
Eastern Shore Community College	Melfa	C,T	St	M/W	807	45	50		Y	Y	Y		Y	Y	Y	Y	N		9
ECPI College of Technology	Newport News	T	Prop	M/W	576		64		N	Y	Y		Y	Y	Y	Y	N		17
ECPI College of Technology	Virginia Beach	T,B	Prop	M/W	4,391	2	50		N	Y	Y		Y	Y	Y	Y	Y		20
ECPI Technical College	Glen Allen	T,B	Prop	M/W	427		48						Y				N		6

This chart includes the names and locations of accredited two-year colleges in the United States and U.S. territories and shows institutions' responses to the *Thomson Peterson's Survey of Undergraduate Institutions*. If an institution submitted incomplete data, one or more columns opposite the institution's name is blank.

An asterisk after the school name denotes a *Special Message* following the college's profile, and a dagger indicates that the institution has one or more entries in the *In-Depth Descriptions of Two-Year Colleges* section. If a school does not appear, it did not report any of the information.

Y—Yes; N—No; R—Recommended; S—For Some

Institution	Location	Degrees Awarded	Institutional Control	Student Body	Undergrad Enrollment Fall 2004	% Attending Part-Time	% 25 or Older	% Grads to 4-Yr	Open Admissions	HS Equivalency Accepted	HS Transcript Accepted	Need-Based Aid Required	Part-Time Jobs	Career Counseling	Job Placement	College Housing	Sports Offered	Majors Offered
ECPI Technical College	Richmond	T,B	Prop	M/W	512		46		N	Y	Y	Y	Y	Y	Y	N		25
ECPI Technical College	Roanoke	T,B	Prop	M/W	340		47		N	N	Y	Y	Y	Y	Y	N		21
Germanna Community College	Locust Grove	C,T	St	M/W	4,799	72	53		Y			S	Y	Y	Y	N	7	11
ITT Technical Institute	Chantilly	T	Prop	M/W	147													
ITT Technical Institute	Norfolk	T,B	Prop	M/W	443													
ITT Technical Institute	Richmond	T,B	Prop	M/W	297													
ITT Technical Institute	Springfield	T,B	Prop	M/W	339													
John Tyler Community College	Chester	C,T	St	M/W	6,054	76	51		Y		R	Y	Y	Y		N	4	14
J. Sargeant Reynolds Community College	Richmond	C,T	St	M/W	11,678	75		32	Y	Y	Y	Y	Y	Y	Y	N		39
Lord Fairfax Community College	Middletown	C,T	St	M/W	5,500													
Mountain Empire Community College	Big Stone Gap	C,T	St	M/W	2,885													
National College of Business & Technology	Bluefield	T	Prop	M/W	203					Y	Y		Y	Y	Y	N		5
National College of Business & Technology	Charlottesville	T	Prop	M/W	163					Y	Y	S	Y	Y	Y	N		5
National College of Business & Technology	Harrisonburg	T	Prop	M/W	233					Y	Y	S	Y	Y	Y	N		5
National College of Business & Technology	Lynchburg	T	Prop	M/W	383			24		Y	Y	S	Y	Y	Y	N		5
National College of Business & Technology	Martinsville	T	Prop	M/W	383					Y	Y	S	Y	Y	Y	N		4
National College of Business & Technology	Salem	C,T,B,M	Prop	M/W	756					Y	Y	Y	Y	Y	Y	N		12
New River Community College	Dublin	C,T	St	M/W	4,345	54												
Northern Virginia Community College	Annandale	C,T	St	M/W	39,353		57		Y		Y	S	Y	Y	Y	N	4	55
Parks College	Arlington	T	Prop	M/W														
Patrick Henry Community College	Martinsville	C,T	St	M/W	3,456		58		Y		Y	Y	Y	Y	Y	N	7	15
Paul D. Camp Community College	Franklin	C,T	St	M/W	1,636	76												
Piedmont Virginia Community College	Charlottesville	C,T	St	M/W	4,358	75	44	23	Y	Y		S	Y	Y	Y	N	11	18
Richard Bland Coll of the Coll of William and Mary	Petersburg	C	St	M/W	1,409	45	18	68	N	Y	Y	Y	Y	Y		N	5	1
Southside Virginia Community College	Alberta	C,T	St	M/W	4,686	71	46		Y	Y	Y	Y	Y	Y	Y	N	5	14
Thomas Nelson Community College	Hampton	C,T	St	M/W	7,889	64												
Tidewater Community College	Norfolk	C,T	St	M/W	23,029													
Virginia Western Community College	Roanoke	C,T	St	M/W	8,124	74												

Washington

Institution	Location	Degrees Awarded	Institutional Control	Student Body	Undergrad Enrollment Fall 2004	% Attending Part-Time	% 25 or Older	% Grads to 4-Yr	Open Admissions	HS Equivalency Accepted	HS Transcript Accepted	Need-Based Aid Required	Part-Time Jobs	Career Counseling	Job Placement	College Housing	Sports Offered	Majors Offered
Bates Technical College	Tacoma	T	St	M/W	16,162													
Bellevue Community College	Bellevue	C,T	St	M/W	13,716													
Big Bend Community College	Moses Lake	C,T	St	M/W	2,102	39	30		Y			S	Y	Y	Y	Y	4	14
Cascadia Community College	Bothell	C,T	St	M/W	1,889	50			Y					Y	Y	N		3
Centralia College	Centralia	C,T	St	M/W	3,685		55		Y		Y	Y	Y	Y	Y	N	5	66
Clark College	Vancouver	C,T	St	M/W	9,946	57	36	67	Y	Y	Y	S	Y	Y	Y	N	9	28
Clover Park Technical College	Lakewood	T	St	M/W	8,488	78	61		Y	Y	S	Y	Y	Y	Y	N		30
Crown College	Tacoma	T,B	Prop	M/W	316													
Edmonds Community College	Lynnwood	C,T	St-L	M/W	8,385		11	25	Y				Y	Y	Y	N	10	31
Everett Community College	Everett	C,T	St	M/W	7,188	55	46		Y		R	Y	Y	Y		N	12	71
Green River Community College	Auburn	C,T	St	M/W	6,621	41	31		Y	Y	Y	Y	Y	Y	Y	N	10	24
Highline Community College*	Des Moines	C,T	St	M/W	6,372	49	52		Y				Y	Y	Y	N	7	48
ITT Technical Institute	Bothell	T,B	Prop	M/W	263													
ITT Technical Institute	Seattle	T,B	Prop	M/W	422													
ITT Technical Institute	Spokane	T,B	Prop	M/W	455													
Lake Washington Technical College	Kirkland	C,T	Dist	M/W	4,860	58												
Lower Columbia College	Longview	C,T	St	M/W	3,223	45	36		Y		R	Y	Y	Y		N	5	79
North Seattle Community College	Seattle	C,T	St	M/W	6,125	52	55	40	Y		R	Y	Y	Y	Y	N	1	26
Olympic College	Bremerton	C,T	St	M/W	6,390	49	49	31	Y			S	Y	Y	Y	N	5	46
Peninsula College	Port Angeles	C,T	St	M/W	4,132	64	66		Y			S	Y	Y	Y	Y	11	19
Pima Medical Institute	Seattle	T	Prop	M/W	289				N			S				N		1
Seattle Central Community College	Seattle	C,T	St	M/W	10,721		63		Y				Y	Y	Y	N	6	25
Shoreline Community College	Shoreline	C	St	M/W	8,591		45		Y		Y	Y	Y	Y	Y	N	15	42
South Puget Sound Community College	Olympia	C,T	St	M/W	6,351													
Spokane Community College	Spokane	C,T	St	M/W	7,258													
Spokane Falls Community College	Spokane	C,T	St	M/W	5,734													
Tacoma Community College	Tacoma	C,T	St	M/W	6,056		46		Y				Y	Y	Y	N	11	75
Walla Walla Community College	Walla Walla	C,T	St	M/W	4,440	51	57		Y		R	Y	Y	Y	Y	N	12	31
Whatcom Community College	Bellingham	C,T	St	M/W	4,173		30		Y				Y	Y	Y	N	7	14
Yakima Valley Community College	Yakima	C,T	St	M/W	6,770		46		Y		R,S	Y	Y	Y		N	5	38

West Virginia

Institution	Location	Degrees Awarded	Institutional Control	Student Body	Undergrad Enrollment Fall 2004	% Attending Part-Time	% 25 or Older	% Grads to 4-Yr	Open Admissions	HS Equivalency Accepted	HS Transcript Accepted	Need-Based Aid Required	Part-Time Jobs	Career Counseling	Job Placement	College Housing	Sports Offered	Majors Offered
Community & Technical College at West Virginia University Institute of Technology	Montgomery	T	Cou	M/W														20
Community and Technical College of Shepherd	Martinsburg	C,T	Cou	M/W	1,520													15
Eastern West Virginia Community and Technical College	Moorefield	C,T	St	M/W	694	89												
Fairmont State Community & Technical College†	Fairmont	C,T	St	M/W	3,355	44	15		Y	Y	R				N	Y		18
Marshall Community and Technical College	Huntington	T	Cou	M/W	2,400	43	55		Y	Y	Y				Y	Y	Y	23
Mountain State College	Parkersburg	T	Prop	PW	150													
National Institute of Technology	Cross Lanes	C	Prop	M/W	520													

Two-Year Colleges At-a-Glance

This chart includes the names and locations of accredited two-year colleges in the United States and U.S. territories and shows institutions' responses to the *Thomson Peterson's Survey of Undergraduate Institutions*. If an institution submitted incomplete data, one or more columns opposite the institution's name is blank. An asterisk after the school name denotes a *Special Message* following the college's profile, and a dagger indicates that the institution has one or more entries in the *In-Depth Descriptions of Two-Year Colleges* section. If a school does not appear, it did not report any of the information.

Y—Yes; N—No; R—Recommended; S—For Some

Institution	Location	Degrees Awarded	Institutional Control	Student Body	Undergrad Enrollment Fall 2004	Percent Attending Part-Time	Percent of Grads Going on to Four-Year Colleges	Percent 25 Years of Age or Older	High School Equivalency Certificate Accepted	Open Admissions	High School Transcript Required	Need-Based Aid Available	Part-Time Jobs Available	Career Counseling Available	Job Placement Services Available	College Housing Available	Number of Sports Offered	Number of Majors Offered
New River Community and Technical College	Beckley	C,T	Cou	M/W														15
Southern West Virginia Comm and Tech Coll	Mount Gay	C,T	St	M/W	2,042	34												
Valley College of Technology	Martinsburg	T	Prop	PW	47													
West Virginia Business College	Wheeling	T	Prop	PW	56	7												
West Virginia Northern Community College	Wheeling	C,T	St	M/W	2,879	57												20
West Virginia State Community and Technical College	Institute	C,T	Cou	M/W														22
West Virginia University at Parkersburg	Parkersburg	C,T,B	St	M/W	3,722	42	44	20	Y	Y	S		Y	Y		N	10	22
Wisconsin																		
Blackhawk Technical College	Janesville	C,T	Dist	M/W	2,627	61												
Bryant and Stratton College	Milwaukee	T,B	Prop	M/W	656													
Fox Valley Technical College	Appleton	C,T	St-L	M/W	7,523	70	51	10	Y	Y	Y	Y	Y	Y	Y	N	7	35
Herzing College	Madison	C,T,B	Prop	PM	650			20	Y	Y	Y	Y	Y	Y	Y	N		5
ITT Technical Institute	Green Bay	T,B	Prop	M/W	419													
ITT Technical Institute	Greenfield	T,B	Prop	M/W	548													
Lac Courte Oreilles Ojibwa Community College	Hayward	C,T	Fed	M/W	460	40	75	15	Y	Y	Y	Y	Y	Y	Y	N	4	9
Lakeshore Technical College	Cleveland	C,T	St-L	M/W	3,069	74												
Milwaukee Area Technical College	Milwaukee	C,T	Dist	M/W	55,992				Y	Y	Y	Y	Y	Y	Y	N	12	98
Moraine Park Technical College	Fond du Lac	C,T	St-L	M/W	7,277	81												
Northcentral Technical College	Wausau	C,T	Dist	M/W	3,734	66												
Northeast Wisconsin Technical College	Green Bay	T	St-L	M/W	8,760	66												
Southwest Wisconsin Technical College	Fennimore	T	St-L	M/W	1,861	58	29	4	Y		Y	Y	Y	Y	Y	Y	4	31
U of Wisconsin Center–Baraboo/Sauk County	Baraboo	C,T	St	M/W	561		19	80	N	Y	Y	Y	Y	Y		N	9	1
U of Wisconsin Center–Barron County	Rice Lake	C	St	M/W	616		20		N	Y	Y	Y	Y	Y		N	5	1
U of Wisconsin Center–Manitowoc	Manitowoc	C	St	M/W	635													
U of Wisconsin Center–Marathon County	Wausau	C	St	M/W	1,303	32	21	96	N	Y		Y	Y	Y		Y	19	1
U of Wisconsin Center–Marinette	Marinette	C	St	M/W	486		31	90	Y	Y	Y	Y	Y	Y		N	10	2
U of Wisconsin Center–Richland	Richland Center	C	St	M/W	516	21	16		N	Y	Y	Y	Y	Y		N	10	1
U of Wisconsin Center–Rock County	Janesville	C	St	M/W	880	15	34		N	Y	Y	Y	Y	Y		N	5	1
U of Wisconsin Center–Sheboygan County	Sheboygan	C	St	M/W	731		24		Y	Y	Y	Y	Y	Y	Y	N	7	1
U of Wisconsin Center–Washington County	West Bend	C	St	M/W	942	28	16		N	Y	Y	Y	Y	Y		N	7	1
U of Wisconsin Center–Waukesha County	Waukesha	C	St	M/W	2,214													
Western Wisconsin Technical College	La Crosse	T	Dist	M/W	5,286	61												
Wisconsin Indianhead Technical College	Shell Lake	T	Dist	M/W	3,606													
Wyoming																		
Casper College	Casper	C,T	Dist	M/W	4,023	53	45		Y	Y	Y	Y	Y	Y	Y	Y	11	85
Central Wyoming College	Riverton	C,T	St-L	M/W	1,732	58	41		Y	Y	R	Y	Y	Y	Y	Y	12	37
Eastern Wyoming College	Torrington	C,T	St-L	M/W	1,448	64												
Laramie County Community College	Cheyenne	C,T	St	M/W	4,522	62	45	46	Y	Y	Y	Y	Y	Y	Y	Y	10	79
Northwest College	Powell	C,T	St-L	M/W	1,711	34												
Sheridan College	Sheridan	C,T	St-L	M/W	2,761	63	38		Y	Y	R,S	Y	Y	Y	Y	Y	8	42
Western Wyoming Community College*	Rock Springs	C,T	St-L	M/W	2,654	59	47	35	Y	Y	Y	Y	Y	Y	Y	Y	15	86
INTERNATIONAL																		
Switzerland																		
Schiller International University	Engelberg	C,T	Ind	M/W		58												

Profiles of Two-Year
COLLEGES

U.S. AND U.S. TERRITORIES

ALABAMA

ALABAMA SOUTHERN COMMUNITY COLLEGE
Monroeville, Alabama

- **State-supported** 2-year, founded 1965, part of Alabama College System
- **Calendar** semesters
- **Degree** certificates and associate
- **Rural** 80-acre campus
- **Coed,** 1,500 undergraduate students

Undergraduates Students come from 5 states and territories.
Faculty *Total:* 107, 38% full-time.
Majors Accounting; administrative assistant and secretarial science; art; biology/biological sciences; biomedical technology; business administration and management; business teacher education; chemistry; clinical/medical laboratory technology; computer engineering technology; computer programming; computer science; economics; education; elementary education; engineering; English; finance; fine/studio arts; fire science; forestry technology; health information/medical records administration; history; insurance; kindergarten/preschool education; liberal arts and sciences/liberal studies; mathematics; nursing (registered nurse training); occupational therapy; physical education teaching and coaching; physical therapy; pre-engineering; psychology; respiratory care therapy; social sciences.
Academic Programs *Special study options:* academic remediation for entering students, adult/continuing education programs, advanced placement credit, honors programs, part-time degree program, summer session for credit.
Library Dennis Stone Forte Library plus 1 other with 43,000 titles, 670 serial subscriptions.
Computers on Campus 51 computers available on campus for general student use.
Student Life *Housing:* college housing not available. *Activities and Organizations:* drama/theater group, choral group, Student Government Association, Ambassadors, Circle K, Phi Theta Kappa, Ethnic Student Society. *Campus security:* 24-hour patrols. *Student services:* personal/psychological counseling.
Athletics Member NJCAA. *Intercollegiate sports:* baseball M(s), basketball M(s)/W(s), softball W(s).
Standardized Tests *Required:* ACT COMPASS (for placement). *Recommended:* ACT (for placement).
Costs (2004–05) *Tuition:* state resident $1704 full-time, $71 per credit hour part-time; nonresident $3408 full-time, $142 per credit hour part-time. Full-time tuition and fees vary according to course load. Part-time tuition and fees vary according to course load. *Required fees:* $456 full-time, $19 per credit hour part-time.
Applying *Options:* early admission. *Required:* high school transcript. *Application deadlines:* 9/10 (freshmen), 9/10 (transfers).
Admissions Contact Ms. Jana S. Horton, Registrar, Alabama Southern Community College, PO Box 2000, Monroeville, AL 36461. *Phone:* 251-575-3156 Ext. 252. *E-mail:* jhorton@ascc.edu.

BESSEMER STATE TECHNICAL COLLEGE
Bessemer, Alabama

- **State-supported** 2-year, founded 1966, part of Alabama College System
- **Calendar** semesters
- **Degree** certificates, diplomas, and associate
- **Small-town** 60-acre campus with easy access to Birmingham
- **Endowment** $43,950
- **Coed,** 2,087 undergraduate students

Undergraduates 39% African American, 0.3% Asian American or Pacific Islander, 0.3% Hispanic American, 0.1% Native American.
Freshmen *Admission:* 1,955 applied, 1,136 admitted.
Faculty *Total:* 200, 50% full-time.
Majors Accounting; administrative assistant and secretarial science; automobile/automotive mechanics technology; computer science; construction engineering technology; consumer merchandising/retailing management; drafting and design technology; electrical, electronic and communications engineering technology; nursing (licensed practical/vocational nurse training); ornamental horticulture.
Academic Programs *Special study options:* academic remediation for entering students, advanced placement credit, internships, part-time degree program, services for LD students.
Computers on Campus 180 computers available on campus for general student use. Internet access available.

Student Life *Housing:* college housing not available. *Campus security:* 24-hour patrols, student patrols.
Standardized Tests *Required:* ACT ASSET (for admission).
Costs (2004–05) *Tuition:* state resident $1728 full-time, $72 per credit hour part-time; nonresident $3456 full-time, $144 per credit hour part-time. *Required fees:* $432 full-time, $18 per credit hour part-time.
Financial Aid Of all full-time matriculated undergraduates who enrolled in 2003, 65 Federal Work-Study jobs (averaging $3000). 5 state and other part-time jobs.
Applying *Required:* high school transcript. *Application deadlines:* 8/4 (freshmen), 8/4 (transfers). *Notification:* continuous until 8/4 (freshmen).
Admissions Contact Director of Admissions, Bessemer State Technical College, PO Box 308, Bessemer, AL 35021-0308. *Phone:* 205-428-6391. *Toll-free phone:* 800-235-5368.

BEVILL STATE COMMUNITY COLLEGE
Sumiton, Alabama

- **State-supported** 2-year, founded 1969, part of Alabama College System
- **Calendar** semesters
- **Degree** certificates and associate
- **Rural** 23-acre campus with easy access to Birmingham
- **Coed,** 4,327 undergraduate students, 57% full-time, 63% women, 37% men

Undergraduates 2,465 full-time, 1,862 part-time. Students come from 4 states and territories, 12% African American, 0.4% Asian American or Pacific Islander, 0.3% Hispanic American, 0.2% Native American. *Retention:* 64% of 2002 full-time freshmen returned.
Freshmen *Admission:* 1,004 enrolled.
Faculty *Total:* 335, 36% full-time. *Student/faculty ratio:* 16:1.
Majors Administrative assistant and secretarial science; business administration and management; clinical/medical laboratory technology; computer and information sciences; drafting and design technology; emergency medical technology (EMT paramedic); general studies; heating, air conditioning and refrigeration technology; liberal arts and sciences/liberal studies; nursing (registered nurse training); tool and die technology; welding technology.
Academic Programs *Special study options:* academic remediation for entering students, adult/continuing education programs, advanced placement credit, cooperative education, honors programs, off-campus study, part-time degree program, services for LD students, summer session for credit.
Library 31,690 titles, 192 serial subscriptions.
Computers on Campus 65 computers available on campus for general student use.
Student Life *Activities and Organizations:* choral group, Student LPN Club, Phi Beta Lambda, campus ministries. *Student services:* personal/psychological counseling.
Athletics Member NJCAA. *Intercollegiate sports:* baseball M(s), basketball M(s)/W(s), softball W(s), volleyball W(s). *Intramural sports:* basketball M/W, football M, golf M, softball M/W, swimming and diving M/W, table tennis M/W, tennis M/W, volleyball M/W.
Standardized Tests *Required:* ACT ASSET (for placement). *Required for some:* ACT (for placement).
Costs (2004–05) *Tuition:* state resident $2304 full-time, $72 per credit hour part-time; nonresident $4608 full-time, $144 per credit hour part-time. *Required fees:* $606 full-time, $18 per credit hour part-time, $15 per term part-time.
Financial Aid Of all full-time matriculated undergraduates who enrolled in 2003, 91 Federal Work-Study jobs (averaging $1618).
Applying *Options:* early admission, deferred entrance. *Required:* high school transcript. *Application deadline:* rolling (freshmen), rolling (transfers).
Admissions Contact Ms. Melissa Stowe, Enrollment Supervisor, Bevill State Community College, PO Box 800, Sumiton, AL 35148. *Phone:* 205-932-3221 Ext. 5101.

BISHOP STATE COMMUNITY COLLEGE
Mobile, Alabama

- **State-supported** 2-year, founded 1965, part of Alabama College System
- **Calendar** semesters
- **Degree** certificates and associate
- **Urban** 9-acre campus
- **Coed,** 4,439 undergraduate students, 56% full-time, 67% women, 33% men

Undergraduates 2,497 full-time, 1,942 part-time. Students come from 9 states and territories, 4% are from out of state, 62% African American, 1% Asian American or Pacific Islander, 0.4% Hispanic American, 1% Native American, 14% transferred in.
Freshmen *Admission:* 952 applied, 952 admitted, 832 enrolled.
Faculty *Total:* 176, 66% full-time, 84% with terminal degrees. *Student/faculty ratio:* 14:1.

Majors Accounting technology and bookkeeping; administrative assistant and secretarial science; civil engineering technology; computer and information sciences; drafting and design technology; electrical, electronic and communications engineering technology; engineering technology; funeral service and mortuary science; general studies; graphic and printing equipment operation/ production; health information/medical records technology; instrumentation technology; liberal arts and sciences/liberal studies; nursing (registered nurse training); physical therapist assistant; special education (hearing impaired).

Academic Programs *Special study options:* academic remediation for entering students, adult/continuing education programs, cooperative education, internships, part-time degree program, services for LD students, summer session for credit.

Library Minnie Slade Bishop Library with 56,687 titles, 265 serial subscriptions, 8,607 audiovisual materials.

Computers on Campus 96 computers available on campus for general student use. Internet access, at least one staffed computer lab available.

Student Life *Housing:* college housing not available. *Activities and Organizations:* drama/theater group, student-run radio station, choral group, Student Government Association, Health Occupations Students of America, Phi Beta Lambda, Phi Theta Kappa, Vocational Industrial Clubs of America. *Campus security:* 24-hour emergency response devices and patrols. *Student services:* health clinic.

Athletics Member NJCAA. *Intercollegiate sports:* baseball M, basketball M(s)/W(s), softball W(s).

Standardized Tests *Required for some:* ACT ASSET.

Costs (2004–05) *Tuition:* state resident $2160 full-time, $72 per credit hour part-time; nonresident $4320 full-time, $144 per credit hour part-time. *Required fees:* $540 full-time, $18 per credit hour part-time.

Financial Aid Of all full-time matriculated undergraduates who enrolled in 2003, 299 Federal Work-Study jobs (averaging $2400).

Applying *Options:* common application, early admission, deferred entrance. *Required:* high school transcript. *Application deadline:* rolling (freshmen), rolling (transfers). *Notification:* continuous until 9/17 (freshmen).

Admissions Contact Dr. Terry Hazzard, Dean of Students, Bishop State Community College, 351 North Broad Street, Mobile, AL 36603-5898. *Phone:* 251-690-6419. *Fax:* 251-438-5403. *E-mail:* info@bishop.edu.

CALHOUN COMMUNITY COLLEGE
Decatur, Alabama

- **State-supported** 2-year, founded 1965, part of Alabama College System
- **Calendar** semesters
- **Degree** certificates and associate
- **Suburban** campus
- **Coed,** 8,879 undergraduate students

Undergraduates Students come from 9 states and territories, 16 other countries, 1% are from out of state, 19% African American, 1% Asian American or Pacific Islander, 2% Hispanic American, 2% Native American, 0.2% international.

Freshmen *Admission:* 5,088 applied, 3,952 admitted. *Test scores:* SAT verbal scores over 500: 22%; SAT math scores over 500: 28%; ACT scores over 18: 63%; SAT math scores over 600: 6%; ACT scores over 24: 12%; ACT scores over 30: 1%.

Faculty *Total:* 424, 28% full-time, 13% with terminal degrees. *Student/faculty ratio:* 21:1.

Majors Accounting; aeronautical/aerospace engineering technology; agriculture; biology/biological sciences; business administration and management; child care and support services management; computer and information sciences; computer graphics; criminal justice/police science; dental assisting; drafting and design technology; dramatic/theatre arts; education; electrical and power transmission installation related; electrical, electronic and communications engineering technology; electromechanical and instrumentation and maintenance technologies related; elementary education; emergency medical technology (EMT paramedic); English; entrepreneurship; family resource management; fire services administration; general studies; graphic design; heating, air conditioning and refrigeration technology; heating, air conditioning, ventilation and refrigeration maintenance technology; industrial mechanics and maintenance technology; legal assistant/paralegal; liberal arts and sciences/liberal studies; machine tool technology; mathematics; military technologies; music; nursing (registered nurse training); office management; photographic and film/video technology; pre-dentistry studies; pre-law studies; pre-medical studies; pre-pharmacy studies; pre-veterinary studies; real estate; secondary education; special education (early childhood); transportation management; visual and performing arts.

Academic Programs *Special study options:* academic remediation for entering students, accelerated degree program, adult/continuing education programs, advanced placement credit, cooperative education, distance learning, English as a second language, independent study, part-time degree program, services for LD students, summer session for credit.

Library Brewer Library plus 2 others with 36,699 titles, 202 serial subscriptions, 23,948 audiovisual materials, an OPAC, a Web page.

Computers on Campus 182 computers available on campus for general student use. A campuswide network can be accessed.

Student Life *Housing:* college housing not available. *Activities and Organizations:* drama/theater group, student-run newspaper, television station, choral group, Student Government Association, Black Students Alliance, Phi Theta Kappa, BACCHUS/SADD, VICA. *Campus security:* 24-hour patrols. *Student services:* personal/psychological counseling.

Standardized Tests *Required for some:* SAT or ACT (for admission).

Costs (2005–06) *Tuition:* state resident $3040 full-time, $71 per semester hour part-time; nonresident $5312 full-time, $142 per semester hour part-time. *Required fees:* $768 full-time, $24 per semester hour part-time. *Waivers:* senior citizens and employees or children of employees.

Financial Aid Of all full-time matriculated undergraduates who enrolled in 2003, 50 Federal Work-Study jobs (averaging $3000).

Applying *Required for some:* high school transcript. *Application deadline:* rolling (freshmen), rolling (transfers). *Notification:* continuous (freshmen).

Admissions Contact Ms. Patricia Landers, Admissions Receptionist, Calhoun Community College, PO Box 2216, 6250 Highway 31 North, Decatur, AL 35609-2216. *Phone:* 256-306-2593. *Toll-free phone:* 800-626-3628 Ext. 2594. *Fax:* 256-306-2941. *E-mail:* pml@calhoun.edu.

CENTRAL ALABAMA COMMUNITY COLLEGE
Alexander City, Alabama

- **State-supported** 2-year, founded 1965, part of Alabama College System
- **Calendar** semesters
- **Degree** certificates and associate
- **Small-town** 100-acre campus
- **Coed,** 1,790 undergraduate students

Undergraduates Students come from 6 states and territories, 25% African American, 0.4% Asian American or Pacific Islander, 0.7% Hispanic American, 0.2% Native American.

Faculty *Total:* 193, 27% full-time. *Student/faculty ratio:* 15:1.

Majors Administrative assistant and secretarial science; business administration and management; clothing/textiles; computer programming; computer science; drafting and design technology; electrical, electronic and communications engineering technology; environmental engineering technology; information science/studies; liberal arts and sciences/liberal studies; nursing (registered nurse training).

Academic Programs *Special study options:* academic remediation for entering students, adult/continuing education programs, advanced placement credit, cooperative education, distance learning, internships, part-time degree program, services for LD students, summer session for credit.

Library Thomas D. Russell Library with 35,000 titles, 455 serial subscriptions.

Computers on Campus 70 computers available on campus for general student use. A campuswide network can be accessed from off campus. Internet access, at least one staffed computer lab available.

Student Life *Housing:* college housing not available. *Activities and Organizations:* drama/theater group, student-run radio station, choral group, Cultural Unity, Baptist Campus Ministry, Student Government Association, Phi Theta Kappa. *Campus security:* evening security. *Student services:* personal/psychological counseling.

Athletics Member NJCAA. *Intercollegiate sports:* baseball M(s), golf M(s), softball W(s), tennis M(s)/W(s), volleyball W(s).

Standardized Tests *Required for some:* SAT or ACT (for admission).

Costs (2004–05) *Tuition:* state resident $2700 full-time, $72 per hour part-time; nonresident $4830 full-time, $144 per hour part-time. *Required fees:* $540 full-time, $18 per hour part-time. *Waivers:* senior citizens and employees or children of employees.

Applying *Options:* common application, early admission. *Required:* high school transcript. *Required for some:* 3 letters of recommendation, interview. *Application deadlines:* 9/9 (freshmen), 9/9 (transfers).

Admissions Contact Ms. Bettie Macmillan, Admission, Central Alabama Community College, PO Box 699, Alexander City, AL 35011-0699. *Phone:* 256-234-6346 Ext. 6232. *Toll-free phone:* 800-643-2657 Ext. 6232. *Fax:* 256-234-0384.

CHATTAHOOCHEE VALLEY COMMUNITY COLLEGE
Phenix City, Alabama

- **State-supported** 2-year, founded 1974
- **Calendar** semesters
- **Degree** certificates and associate
- **Small-town** 103-acre campus

Chattahoochee Valley Community College (continued)
- **Endowment** $42,791
- **Coed,** 1,986 undergraduate students, 25% full-time, 19% women, 12% men

Undergraduates 500 full-time, 113 part-time. Students come from 6 states and territories, 10 other countries, 0.3% are from out of state, 39% African American, 1% Asian American or Pacific Islander, 3% Hispanic American, 0.5% Native American, 16% transferred in. *Retention:* 66% of 2002 full-time freshmen returned.

Freshmen *Admission:* 613 enrolled.

Faculty *Total:* 88, 32% full-time. *Student/faculty ratio:* 18:1.

Majors Administrative assistant and secretarial science; agriculture; biology/biological sciences; business administration and management; chemistry; clinical laboratory science/medical technology; criminal justice/law enforcement administration; data processing and data processing technology; dramatic/theatre arts; elementary education; fire science; forestry; industrial radiologic technology; information science/studies; legal administrative assistant/secretary; liberal arts and sciences/liberal studies; mathematics; music; music teacher education; nursing (licensed practical/vocational nurse training); nursing (registered nurse training); physical education teaching and coaching; physics; pre-engineering.

Academic Programs *Special study options:* academic remediation for entering students, adult/continuing education programs, advanced placement credit, distance learning, honors programs, off-campus study, part-time degree program, services for LD students, student-designed majors, summer session for credit.

Library Estelle Bain Owens Learning Resource Center and Library with 54,129 titles, 90 serial subscriptions, 853 audiovisual materials, a Web page.

Computers on Campus 55 computers available on campus for general student use. A campuswide network can be accessed from off campus. Internet access, at least one staffed computer lab available.

Student Life *Housing:* college housing not available. *Activities and Organizations:* drama/theater group, choral group. *Campus security:* 24-hour emergency response devices and patrols. *Student services:* personal/psychological counseling.

Athletics Member NJCAA. *Intercollegiate sports:* baseball M(s), softball W(s).

Standardized Tests *Required for some:* SAT or ACT (for placement).

Costs (2004–05) *Tuition:* state resident $2700 full-time, $90 per semester hour part-time; nonresident $4830 full-time, $161 per semester hour part-time.

Financial Aid Of all full-time matriculated undergraduates who enrolled in 2003, 40 Federal Work-Study jobs (averaging $2000). 10 state and other part-time jobs (averaging $2000).

Applying *Options:* common application, early admission. *Required:* high school transcript. *Application deadline:* rolling (freshmen), rolling (transfers). *Notification:* continuous (freshmen).

Admissions Contact Ms. Rita Cherry, Admissions Clerk, Chattahoochee Valley Community College, PO Box 1000, Phenix City, AL 36869. *Phone:* 334-291-4995. *Toll-free phone:* 800-842-2822. *Fax:* 334-291-4994. *E-mail:* information@cv.edu.

COMMUNITY COLLEGE OF THE AIR FORCE
Maxwell Air Force Base, Alabama

- **Federally supported** 2-year, founded 1972
- **Calendar** continuous
- **Degrees** certificates and associate (courses conducted at 125 branch locations worldwide for members of the U.S. Air Force)
- **Suburban** campus
- **Coed, primarily men,** 364,934 undergraduate students, 15% full-time, 19% women, 81% men

Undergraduates 53,388 full-time, 311,546 part-time. 16% African American, 3% Asian American or Pacific Islander, 0.9% Native American.

Freshmen *Admission:* 30,218 applied, 30,218 admitted, 30,218 enrolled.

Faculty *Total:* 5,609, 100% full-time. *Student/faculty ratio:* 28:1.

Majors Aeronautics/aviation/aerospace science and technology; airframe mechanics and aircraft maintenance technology; air traffic control; apparel and textile marketing management; atmospheric sciences and meteorology; automobile/automotive mechanics technology; avionics maintenance technology; biomedical technology; cardiovascular technology; clinical/medical laboratory technology; commercial and advertising art; communications technology; construction engineering technology; criminal justice/law enforcement administration; dental assisting; dental laboratory technology; dietetics; educational/instructional media design; educational leadership and administration; electrical, electronic and communications engineering technology; environmental health; environmental studies; finance; fire science; health/health care administration; hematology technology; hotel/motel administration; human resources management; industrial technology; legal assistant/paralegal; logistics and materials management; management information systems; medical physiology; medical radiologic technology; mental health/rehabilitation; metallurgical technology; military technologies; music performance; nuclear medical technology; occupational safety and health technology; office management; ophthalmic laboratory technology; parks, recreation and leisure; pharmacy technician; physical therapist assistant; public relations/image management; purchasing, procurement/acquisitions and contracts management; security and loss prevention; social work; surgical technology; vehicle/equipment operation.

Academic Programs *Special study options:* academic remediation for entering students, adult/continuing education programs, advanced placement credit, distance learning, independent study, internships.

Library Air Force Library Service with 5.0 million titles, 56,654 serial subscriptions, an OPAC, a Web page.

Computers on Campus Internet access available.

Student Life *Housing:* on-campus residence required for freshman year. *Options:* coed. Campus housing is university owned, leased by the school and is provided by a third party. Freshman applicants given priority for college housing. *Campus security:* 24-hour emergency response devices and patrols. *Student services:* health clinic, personal/psychological counseling, legal services.

Athletics *Intramural sports:* badminton M/W, baseball M, basketball M/W, bowling M/W, cross-country running M/W, football M, golf M/W, racquetball M/W, softball M/W, squash M/W, table tennis M/W, tennis M/W, track and field M/W, volleyball M/W, weight lifting M/W.

Standardized Tests *Required:* Armed Services Vocational Aptitude Battery (for admission).

Costs (2004–05) *Tuition:* Tuition, room and board, and medical and dental care are provided by the U.S. government. Each student receives a salary from which to pay for uniforms, supplies, and personal expenses. *Waivers:* minority students and adult students.

Applying *Options:* electronic application. *Required:* high school transcript, interview. *Application deadline:* rolling (freshmen), rolling (transfers). *Notification:* continuous (freshmen).

Admissions Contact C.M. Sgt. Robert McAlexander, Director of Admissions/Registrar, Community College of the Air Force, 130 West Maxwell Boulevard, Building 836, Maxwell Air Force Base, Maxwell AFB, AL 36112-6613. *Phone:* 334-953-6436. *E-mail:* ronald.hall@maxwell.af.mil.

ENTERPRISE-OZARK COMMUNITY COLLEGE
Enterprise, Alabama

- **State-supported** 2-year, founded 1965, part of Alabama College System
- **Calendar** semesters
- **Degree** certificates and associate
- **Small-town** 100-acre campus
- **Coed,** 1,590 undergraduate students, 54% full-time, 64% women, 36% men

Undergraduates 866 full-time, 724 part-time. 21% African American, 3% Asian American or Pacific Islander, 4% Hispanic American, 1% Native American.

Freshmen *Admission:* 369 enrolled.

Faculty *Total:* 97, 39% full-time.

Majors Administrative assistant and secretarial science; agricultural business and management; airframe mechanics and aircraft maintenance technology; automobile/automotive mechanics technology; avionics maintenance technology; biological and physical sciences; business administration and management; child development; computer science; consumer merchandising/retailing management; criminal justice/law enforcement administration; criminal justice/police science; education; finance; health information/medical records administration; insurance; journalism; kindergarten/preschool education; legal administrative assistant/secretary; liberal arts and sciences/liberal studies; marketing/marketing management; mass communication/media; medical administrative assistant and medical secretary; parks, recreation and leisure; pre-engineering; real estate; social sciences; special products marketing.

Academic Programs *Special study options:* academic remediation for entering students, adult/continuing education programs, advanced placement credit, English as a second language, honors programs, internships, part-time degree program, services for LD students, summer session for credit.

Library Snuggs Hall with 45,076 titles, 349 serial subscriptions.

Computers on Campus 100 computers available on campus for general student use. A campuswide network can be accessed. Internet access, online (class) registration, at least one staffed computer lab available.

Student Life *Housing:* college housing not available. *Activities and Organizations:* student-run newspaper, choral group. *Campus security:* security personnel. *Student services:* personal/psychological counseling, women's center.

Athletics Member NJCAA. *Intercollegiate sports:* baseball M, basketball M(s)/W(s), cheerleading M(s)/W(s), softball W(s). *Intramural sports:* basketball M/W, football M, volleyball M/W.

Standardized Tests *Recommended:* SAT or ACT (for placement).

Costs (2004–05) *Tuition:* state resident $2700 full-time, $90 per semester hour part-time; nonresident $4860 full-time, $162 per semester hour part-time. *Required fees:* $540 full-time, $18 per semester hour part-time.
Financial Aid Of all full-time matriculated undergraduates who enrolled in 2003, 99 Federal Work-Study jobs (averaging $2000).
Applying *Options:* early admission, deferred entrance. *Required:* high school transcript. *Application deadline:* rolling (freshmen), rolling (transfers). *Notification:* continuous (freshmen).
Admissions Contact Mr. Gary Deas, Associate Dean of Students/Registrar, Enterprise-Ozark Community College, PO Box 1300, Enterprise, AL 36331. *Phone:* 334-347-2623 Ext. 2233.

GADSDEN STATE COMMUNITY COLLEGE
Gadsden, Alabama

- **State-supported** 2-year, founded 1965, part of Alabama College System
- **Calendar** semesters
- **Degree** certificates and associate
- **Small-town** 275-acre campus with easy access to Birmingham
- **Endowment** $1.3 million
- **Coed,** 5,549 undergraduate students, 54% full-time, 61% women, 39% men

Undergraduates 3,016 full-time, 2,533 part-time. Students come from 4 states and territories, 32 other countries, 4% are from out of state, 19% African American, 0.2% Asian American or Pacific Islander, 0.8% Hispanic American, 0.5% Native American, 3% international.
Freshmen *Admission:* 1,726 applied, 1,726 admitted, 1,386 enrolled.
Faculty *Total:* 333, 51% full-time, 3% with terminal degrees.
Majors Administrative assistant and secretarial science; child care and support services management; civil engineering technology; clinical/medical laboratory technology; computer and information sciences; court reporting; criminal justice/police science; emergency medical technology (EMT paramedic); general retailing/wholesaling; general studies; heating, air conditioning and refrigeration technology; legal assistant/paralegal; liberal arts and sciences/liberal studies; mechanical engineering/mechanical technology; medical radiologic technology; nursing (registered nurse training); physical education teaching and coaching; radio and television broadcasting technology; substance abuse/addiction counseling; telecommunications; tool and die technology.
Academic Programs *Special study options:* academic remediation for entering students, adult/continuing education programs, advanced placement credit, cooperative education, English as a second language, external degree program, part-time degree program, services for LD students, summer session for credit.
Library Meadows Library with 72,915 titles, 303 serial subscriptions.
Computers on Campus 200 computers available on campus for general student use. A campuswide network can be accessed. Internet access, at least one staffed computer lab available.
Student Life *Housing Options:* coed. *Activities and Organizations:* drama/theater group, student-run newspaper, radio station, choral group, Science, Math, and Engineering Club, Student Government Association, Circle K, Phi Beta Lambda, VICA. *Campus security:* 24-hour patrols. *Student services:* women's center.
Athletics Member NJCAA. *Intercollegiate sports:* baseball M(s), basketball M(s)/W(s), cross-country running W(s), golf M(s), softball W(s), tennis M(s), volleyball W(s). *Intramural sports:* basketball M/W, volleyball M/W.
Costs (2004–05) *Tuition:* state resident $2160 full-time, $90 per credit hour part-time; nonresident $3864 full-time, $161 per credit hour part-time. *Room and board:* $2800. *Waivers:* minority students, adult students, senior citizens, and employees or children of employees.
Financial Aid Of all full-time matriculated undergraduates who enrolled in 2003, 95 Federal Work-Study jobs (averaging $1364).
Applying *Options:* early admission, deferred entrance. *Required:* high school transcript. *Application deadline:* rolling (freshmen), rolling (transfers).
Admissions Contact Dr. Teresa Rhea, Admissions and Records, Gadsden State Community College, Admissions, Allen Hall, PO Box 227, Gadsden, AL 35902-0227. *Phone:* 256-549-8263. *Toll-free phone:* 800-226-5563. *Fax:* 256-549-8205. *E-mail:* info@gadsdenstate.edu.

GADSDEN STATE COMMUNITY COLLEGE-AYERS CAMPUS
Anniston, Alabama

- **State-supported** 2-year, founded 1966
- **Calendar** semesters
- **Degree** certificates and associate
- **Small-town** 25-acre campus with easy access to Birmingham
- **Coed,** 1,137 undergraduate students, 60% full-time, 57% women, 43% men

Undergraduates 686 full-time, 451 part-time. Students come from 2 states and territories, 31% African American, 0.5% Hispanic American, 0.6% Native American.
Freshmen *Admission:* 278 admitted, 259 enrolled.
Faculty *Total:* 94, 29% full-time, 6% with terminal degrees. *Student/faculty ratio:* 18:1.
Majors Accounting; child care provision; computer science; drafting and design technology; electrical, electronic and communications engineering technology; electrical/electronics equipment installation and repair; heating, air conditioning, ventilation and refrigeration maintenance technology; machine shop technology; machine tool technology; office management; system administration.
Academic Programs *Special study options:* advanced placement credit, part-time degree program, services for LD students.
Library Cain Learning Resource Center with 4,645 titles, 120 serial subscriptions.
Computers on Campus Internet access, online (class) registration, at least one staffed computer lab available.
Student Life *Campus security:* late-night transport/escort service. *Student services:* personal/psychological counseling.
Standardized Tests *Required:* ACT ASSET (for placement).
Costs (2004–05) *Tuition:* state resident $2160 full-time, $72 per credit hour part-time; nonresident $4320 full-time, $144 per credit hour part-time. *Required fees:* $540 full-time, $18 per credit hour part-time. *Room and board:* $2800.
Financial Aid Of all full-time matriculated undergraduates who enrolled in 2003, 25 Federal Work-Study jobs (averaging $2500).
Applying *Options:* deferred entrance. *Required:* high school transcript. *Application deadline:* rolling (freshmen), rolling (transfers). *Notification:* continuous (freshmen).
Admissions Contact Mrs. Michele Conger, Director of Admissions and Records, Gadsden State Community College-Ayers Campus, 1801 Coleman Road, Anniston, AL 36207. *Phone:* 256-835-5400. *Fax:* 256-835-5479. *E-mail:* mlonger@ayers.cc.al.us.

GEORGE CORLEY WALLACE STATE COMMUNITY COLLEGE
Selma, Alabama

- **State-supported** 2-year, founded 1966, part of Alabama College System
- **Calendar** semesters
- **Degree** certificates, diplomas, and associate
- **Small-town** campus
- **Coed,** 1,758 undergraduate students

Freshmen *Admission:* 650 applied, 650 admitted.
Faculty *Total:* 95, 47% full-time. *Student/faculty ratio:* 17:1.
Majors Accounting; biomedical technology; business administration and management; business teacher education; clinical/medical laboratory technology; computer programming; computer science; criminal justice/law enforcement administration; criminal justice/police science; drafting and design technology; electrical, electronic and communications engineering technology; fire science; health information/medical records administration; industrial radiologic technology; machine tool technology; medical/clinical assistant; nursing (licensed practical/vocational nurse training); nursing (registered nurse training); occupational therapy; physical therapy; respiratory care therapy; welding technology.
Academic Programs *Special study options:* academic remediation for entering students, adult/continuing education programs, advanced placement credit, independent study, part-time degree program, services for LD students, summer session for credit.
Library George Corley Wallace Library with 16,598 titles, 2,240 serial subscriptions, 913 audiovisual materials, an OPAC, a Web page.
Computers on Campus 160 computers available on campus for general student use. Internet access, at least one staffed computer lab available.
Student Life *Housing:* college housing not available. *Activities and Organizations:* choral group. *Campus security:* 24-hour patrols.
Athletics Member NJCAA. *Intercollegiate sports:* baseball M(s), basketball M(s), softball W(s), tennis M(s)/W(s). *Intramural sports:* basketball M/W, softball W, tennis M/W.
Standardized Tests *Required:* ACT ASSET (for placement).
Costs (2005–06) *Tuition:* state resident $2160 full-time, $90 per credit hour part-time; nonresident $4320 full-time, $180 per credit hour part-time.
Financial Aid Of all full-time matriculated undergraduates who enrolled in 2003, 50 Federal Work-Study jobs (averaging $3000).
Applying *Options:* common application, early admission, deferred entrance. *Application deadline:* rolling (freshmen), rolling (transfers).
Admissions Contact Ms. Sunette Newman, Registrar, George Corley Wallace State Community College, 3000 Earl Goodwin Parkway, Selma, AL 36702-2530. *Phone:* 334-876-9305. *Fax:* 334-876-9300.

GEORGE C. WALLACE COMMUNITY COLLEGE
Dothan, Alabama

- **State-supported** 2-year, founded 1949
- **Calendar** semesters
- **Degree** certificates and associate
- **Rural** 200-acre campus
- **Coed**, 3,083 undergraduate students

Undergraduates Students come from 31 states and territories, 4 other countries.

Faculty *Total:* 180.

Majors Accounting; administrative assistant and secretarial science; automobile/automotive mechanics technology; business administration and management; carpentry; clinical/medical laboratory technology; commercial and advertising art; computer science; criminal justice/police science; data processing and data processing technology; drafting and design technology; electrical, electronic and communications engineering technology; emergency medical technology (EMT paramedic); heating, air conditioning, ventilation and refrigeration maintenance technology; laser and optical technology; liberal arts and sciences/liberal studies; machine tool technology; medical administrative assistant and medical secretary; nursing (registered nurse training); respiratory care therapy; welding technology.

Academic Programs *Special study options:* academic remediation for entering students, adult/continuing education programs, advanced placement credit, cooperative education, internships, off-campus study, part-time degree program, summer session for credit.

Library 45,353 titles, 399 serial subscriptions.

Computers on Campus 75 computers available on campus for general student use. At least one staffed computer lab available.

Student Life *Housing:* college housing not available. *Activities and Organizations:* drama/theater group, student-run newspaper. *Student services:* personal/psychological counseling, women's center.

Athletics Member NJCAA. *Intercollegiate sports:* basketball M(s)/W(s), tennis M(s)/W(s). *Intramural sports:* basketball M/W, tennis M/W, volleyball M/W.

Standardized Tests *Required for some:* CAT (for LPN program).

Costs (2004–05) *Tuition:* state resident $2160 full-time, $72 per semester hour part-time; nonresident $4320 full-time, $144 per semester hour part-time. *Required fees:* $540 full-time, $18 per semester hour part-time.

Financial Aid Of all full-time matriculated undergraduates who enrolled in 2003, 83 Federal Work-Study jobs (averaging $2217).

Applying *Options:* early admission. *Application deadline:* rolling (freshmen), rolling (transfers).

Admissions Contact Dr. Brenda Barnes, Assistant Dean of Student Affairs, George C. Wallace Community College, 1141 Wallace Drive, Dothan, AL 36303-9234. *Phone:* 334-983-3521 Ext. 283. *Toll-free phone:* 800-543-2426.

H. COUNCILL TRENHOLM STATE TECHNICAL COLLEGE
Montgomery, Alabama

- **State-supported** 2-year, founded 1962, part of Alabama Department of Post Secondary Education
- **Calendar** semesters
- **Degree** certificates, diplomas, and associate
- **Urban** 78-acre campus
- **Coed**

Faculty *Student/faculty ratio:* 14:1.

Student Life *Campus security:* 24-hour emergency response devices and patrols.

Standardized Tests *Required for some:* ACT COMPASS. *Recommended:* ACT (for placement).

Costs (2004–05) *Tuition:* state resident $2160 full-time, $72 per credit hour part-time; nonresident $4320 full-time, $144 per credit hour part-time. *Required fees:* $540 full-time, $18 per credit hour part-time.

Applying *Options:* early admission. *Required:* high school transcript.

Admissions Contact Ms. Tennie McBryde, Registrar, H. Councill Trenholm State Technical College, 1225 Air Base Boulevard, Montgomery, AL 36108. *Phone:* 334-420-4306. *Fax:* 334-420-4201. *E-mail:* tmcbryde@trenholmtech.cc.al.us.

HERZING COLLEGE
Birmingham, Alabama

Admissions Contact Ms. Tess Anderson, Admissions Coordinator, Herzing College, 280 West Valley Avenue, Birmingham, AL 35209. *Phone:* 205-916-2800. *Fax:* 205-916-2807.

ITT TECHNICAL INSTITUTE
Birmingham, Alabama

- **Proprietary** primarily 2-year, founded 1994, part of ITT Educational Services, Inc
- **Calendar** quarters
- **Degrees** associate and bachelor's
- **Suburban** campus
- **Coed**

Student Life *Campus security:* 24-hour emergency response devices.

Standardized Tests *Required:* Wonderlic aptitude test (for admission).

Costs (2004–05) *Tuition:* Please see school catalog for specific information.

Applying *Options:* deferred entrance. *Application fee:* $100. *Required:* high school transcript, interview. *Recommended:* letters of recommendation.

Admissions Contact Jesse L. Johnson, Director of Recruitment, ITT Technical Institute, 500 Riverhills Business Park, Birmingham, AL 35242. *Phone:* 205-991-5410. *Toll-free phone:* 800-488-7033. *Fax:* 205-991-5025.

JAMES H. FAULKNER STATE COMMUNITY COLLEGE
Bay Minette, Alabama

- **State-supported** 2-year, founded 1965, part of Alabama College System
- **Calendar** semesters
- **Degree** certificates and associate
- **Small-town** 105-acre campus
- **Coed**, 3,067 undergraduate students, 63% full-time, 61% women, 39% men

Faulkner State Community College (FSCC), accredited by the Southern Association of Colleges and Schools, offers both transfer and certificate programs. The main campus is located in Bay Minette, Alabama, with branches in Fairhope and Gulf Shores, Alabama. FSCC serves the entire Gulf Coast area. For information, call 800-231-3752 (toll-free).

Undergraduates 1,925 full-time, 1,142 part-time. 3% are from out of state, 13% African American, 0.5% Asian American or Pacific Islander, 0.6% Hispanic American, 1% Native American, 9% live on campus.

Freshmen *Admission:* 853 enrolled.

Faculty *Total:* 158, 39% full-time. *Student/faculty ratio:* 15:1.

Majors Administrative assistant and secretarial science; business administration and management; commercial and advertising art; computer and information sciences; court reporting; dental assisting; environmental engineering technology; general studies; hospitality administration; landscaping and groundskeeping; legal assistant/paralegal; liberal arts and sciences/liberal studies; nursing (licensed practical/vocational nurse training); nursing (registered nurse training); parks, recreation and leisure facilities management; surgical technology.

Academic Programs *Special study options:* academic remediation for entering students, adult/continuing education programs, advanced placement credit, cooperative education, honors programs, internships, part-time degree program, services for LD students.

Library Austin R. Meadows Library with 53,100 titles, 200 serial subscriptions, 2,513 audiovisual materials, an OPAC.

Computers on Campus 208 computers available on campus for general student use. A campuswide network can be accessed. Internet access, at least one staffed computer lab available.

Student Life *Housing Options:* men-only, women-only. *Activities and Organizations:* drama/theater group, student-run newspaper, choral group, Student Government Association, Pow-Wow Leadership Society, Phi Theta Kappa, Association of Computational Machinery, Phi Beta Lambda, national fraternities. *Campus security:* 24-hour patrols, controlled dormitory access. *Student services:* personal/psychological counseling.

Athletics Member NJCAA. *Intercollegiate sports:* baseball M(s), basketball M(s)/W(s), golf M(s), softball W(s), tennis M(s)/W(s), volleyball W(s). *Intramural sports:* basketball M, tennis M/W, volleyball M/W.

Standardized Tests *Required for some:* ACT ASSET, ACT COMPASS. *Recommended:* ACT ASSET, ACT COMPASS.

Costs (2004–05) *Tuition:* state resident $2790 full-time, $93 per credit hour part-time; nonresident $4920 full-time, $164 per credit hour part-time. *Room and board:* $2931. *Waivers:* employees or children of employees.

Applying *Options:* early admission, deferred entrance. *Required:* high school transcript. *Application deadline:* rolling (freshmen), rolling (transfers). *Notification:* continuous until 8/18 (freshmen).

Admissions Contact Ms. Peggy Duck, Director of High School Relations/Student Activities, James H. Faulkner State Community College, 1900 Highway 31 South, Bay Minette, AL 36507. *Phone:* 251-580-2152. *Toll-free phone:* 800-231-3752 Ext. 2111. *Fax:* 251-580-2285.

JEFFERSON DAVIS COMMUNITY COLLEGE
Brewton, Alabama

- **State-supported** 2-year, founded 1965
- **Calendar** semesters
- **Degree** certificates and associate
- **Small-town** 100-acre campus
- **Coed**

Faculty *Student/faculty ratio:* 11:1.

Athletics Member NJCAA.

Standardized Tests *Required:* ACT COMPASS (for placement).

Costs (2004–05) *Tuition:* state resident $1728 full-time, $72 per credit hour part-time; nonresident $3432 full-time, $143 per credit hour part-time. *Required fees:* $440 full-time, $18 per credit hour part-time, $4 per term part-time. *Room and board:* Room and board charges vary according to housing facility.

Financial Aid Of all full-time matriculated undergraduates who enrolled in 2003, 50 Federal Work-Study jobs (averaging $2700).

Applying *Options:* early admission. *Required:* high school transcript.

Admissions Contact Ms. Robin Sessions, Coordinator of Admissions and Records, Jefferson Davis Community College, PO Box 958, Brewton, AL 36427. *Phone:* 251-867-4832. *Fax:* 251-809-1596.

JEFFERSON STATE COMMUNITY COLLEGE
Birmingham, Alabama

- **State-supported** 2-year, founded 1965, part of Alabama College System
- **Calendar** semesters
- **Degree** certificates and associate
- **Suburban** 234-acre campus
- **Coed**, 7,007 undergraduate students, 42% full-time, 61% women, 39% men

Undergraduates 2,946 full-time, 4,061 part-time. Students come from 28 states and territories, 61 other countries, 1% are from out of state, 20% African American, 1% Asian American or Pacific Islander, 1% Hispanic American, 0.3% Native American, 2% international, 8% transferred in.

Freshmen *Admission:* 1,170 enrolled. *Average high school GPA:* 2.65.

Faculty *Total:* 382, 29% full-time, 14% with terminal degrees. *Student/faculty ratio:* 22:1.

Majors Accounting technology and bookkeeping; administrative assistant and secretarial science; agricultural business and management; banking and financial support services; biomedical technology; business/commerce; child care and support services management; clinical/medical laboratory technology; computer and information sciences; construction engineering technology; criminal justice/police science; fire services administration; funeral service and mortuary science; general studies; home furnishings and equipment installation; hospitality administration; liberal arts and sciences/liberal studies; medical radiologic technology; nursing (registered nurse training); physical therapist assistant; radio and television broadcasting technology; robotics technology.

Academic Programs *Special study options:* academic remediation for entering students, adult/continuing education programs, advanced placement credit, distance learning, honors programs, independent study, internships, part-time degree program, services for LD students, summer session for credit. *ROTC:* Army (c), Air Force (c).

Library James B. Allen Library plus 1 other with 77,015 titles, 242 serial subscriptions, 3,349 audiovisual materials, an OPAC.

Computers on Campus A campuswide network can be accessed from off campus. Internet access, online (class) registration, at least one staffed computer lab available.

Student Life *Housing:* college housing not available. *Activities and Organizations:* drama/theater group, student-run newspaper, radio station, choral group, Student Government Association, Phi Theta Kappa, Baptist Campus Ministries, Jefferson State Ambassadors, Students in Free Enterprise (SIFE). *Campus security:* 24-hour patrols. *Student services:* women's center.

Athletics Member NJCAA. *Intercollegiate sports:* baseball M(s), softball W(s). *Intramural sports:* badminton M/W, basketball M/W, bowling M/W, soccer M/W, softball M/W, tennis M/W, volleyball M/W.

Standardized Tests *Required for some:* ACT ASSET, ACT COMPASS. *Recommended:* SAT or ACT (for placement).

Costs (2004–05) *Tuition:* state resident $3060 full-time, $102 per semester hour part-time; nonresident $5190 full-time, $173 per semester hour part-time. *Required fees:* $930 full-time, $30 per semester hour part-time. *Waivers:* senior citizens and employees or children of employees.

Financial Aid Of all full-time matriculated undergraduates who enrolled in 2003, 189 Federal Work-Study jobs (averaging $1926).

Applying *Options:* electronic application, early admission, deferred entrance. *Required for some:* high school transcript. *Application deadline:* rolling (freshmen). *Notification:* continuous (freshmen).

Admissions Contact Mr. Michael Hobbs, Director of Enrollment Services, Jefferson State Community College, 2601 Carson Road, Birmingham, AL 35215-3098. *Phone:* 205-853-1200 Ext. 7991. *Toll-free phone:* 800-239-5900. *Fax:* 205-856-6070.

J. F. DRAKE STATE TECHNICAL COLLEGE
Huntsville, Alabama

- **State-supported** 2-year, founded 1961, part of State of Alabama Department of Postsecondary Education
- **Calendar** semesters
- **Degree** certificates, diplomas, and associate
- **Urban** 6-acre campus with easy access to Huntsville
- **Coed**, 786 undergraduate students, 62% full-time, 52% women, 48% men

Undergraduates 486 full-time, 300 part-time. Students come from 1 other state, 4% are from out of state, 56% African American, 0.8% Asian American or Pacific Islander, 1% Hispanic American, 0.3% Native American.

Freshmen *Admission:* 659 applied, 363 admitted, 197 enrolled.

Faculty *Total:* 71, 35% full-time, 6% with terminal degrees. *Student/faculty ratio:* 20:1.

Majors Accounting; administrative assistant and secretarial science; commercial and advertising art; drafting and design technology; electrical, electronic and communications engineering technology; information science/studies; machine tool technology.

Academic Programs *Special study options:* academic remediation for entering students, cooperative education, internships, part-time degree program, services for LD students.

Computers on Campus 380 computers available on campus for general student use. At least one staffed computer lab available.

Student Life *Housing:* college housing not available. *Activities and Organizations:* student-run newspaper, Phi Beta Lambda, Vocational Industrial Clubs of America. *Campus security:* 24-hour patrols.

Standardized Tests *Required:* ACT COMPASS (for placement).

Costs (2004–05) *Tuition:* state resident $2160 full-time, $72 per semester hour part-time; nonresident $4320 full-time, $144 per semester hour part-time. *Required fees:* $540 full-time, $18 per semester hour part-time. *Waivers:* employees or children of employees.

Applying *Options:* deferred entrance. *Required:* high school transcript. *Application deadline:* rolling (freshmen).

Admissions Contact Mrs. Shirley Clemons, Registrar, J. F. Drake State Technical College, 3421 Meridian Street, Huntsville, AL 35811. *Phone:* 256-551-3109 Ext. 109. *Toll-free phone:* 888-413-7253. *Fax:* 256-551-3142. *E-mail:* clemons@drakestate.edu.

LAWSON STATE COMMUNITY COLLEGE
Birmingham, Alabama

- **State-supported** 2-year, founded 1949, part of Alabama College System
- **Calendar** semesters
- **Degree** certificates and associate
- **Urban** 30-acre campus
- **Coed**

Faculty *Student/faculty ratio:* 16:1.

Student Life *Campus security:* 24-hour emergency response devices and patrols, student patrols.

Athletics Member NJCAA.

Standardized Tests *Recommended:* ACT (for placement).

Costs (2004–05) *One-time required fee:* $10. *Tuition:* state resident $2160 full-time, $72 per credit part-time; nonresident $4320 full-time, $144 per credit part-time. *Required fees:* $540 full-time, $9 per credit part-time, $10 per term part-time.

Financial Aid Of all full-time matriculated undergraduates who enrolled in 2003, 91 Federal Work-Study jobs (averaging $3000).

Applying *Options:* common application, early admission, deferred entrance. *Required:* high school transcript.

Admissions Contact Mr. Darren C. Allen, Director of Admissions and Records, Lawson State Community College, 3060 Wilson Road, SW, Birmingham, AL 35221-1798. *Phone:* 205-929-6361. *Fax:* 205-923-7106. *E-mail:* dallen@lawsonstate.edu.

LURLEEN B. WALLACE COMMUNITY COLLEGE

Andalusia, Alabama

- **State-supported** 2-year, founded 1969, part of Alabama College System
- **Calendar** semesters
- **Degree** certificates and associate
- **Small-town** 200-acre campus
- **Coed**

Student Life *Campus security:* 24-hour emergency response devices.
Athletics Member NJCAA.
Standardized Tests *Recommended:* ACT (for placement).
Costs (2004–05) *Tuition:* state resident $2160 full-time.
Applying *Options:* early admission, deferred entrance. *Required:* high school transcript.
Admissions Contact Mrs. Judy Hall, Director of Student Services, Lurleen B. Wallace Community College, PO Box 1418, Andalusia, AL 36420. *Phone:* 334-222-6591 Ext. 271.

MARION MILITARY INSTITUTE

Marion, Alabama

Admissions Contact Dan Sumlin, Director of Admissions, Marion Military Institute, 1101 Washington Street, Marion, AL 36756. *Phone:* 800-664-1842 Ext. 306. *Toll-free phone:* 800-664-1842 Ext. 307. *Fax:* 334-683-2383. *E-mail:* marionmilitary@zebra.net.

NORTHEAST ALABAMA COMMUNITY COLLEGE

Rainsville, Alabama

- **State-supported** 2-year, founded 1963, part of Alabama College System
- **Calendar** quarters
- **Degree** certificates and associate
- **Rural** 100-acre campus
- **Coed,** 2,015 undergraduate students, 49% full-time, 65% women, 35% men

Undergraduates 978 full-time, 1,037 part-time. Students come from 3 states and territories, 2% are from out of state, 2% African American, 0.2% Asian American or Pacific Islander, 1% Hispanic American, 5% Native American. *Retention:* 62% of 2002 full-time freshmen returned.
Freshmen *Admission:* 456 applied, 456 admitted, 455 enrolled.
Faculty *Total:* 136, 22% full-time, 10% with terminal degrees. *Student/faculty ratio:* 32:1.
Majors Administrative assistant and secretarial science; biological and physical sciences; business administration and management; computer graphics; computer science; computer typography and composition equipment operation; electrical, electronic and communications engineering technology; emergency medical technology (EMT paramedic); finance; hydrology and water resources science; information science/studies; legal administrative assistant/secretary; legal assistant/paralegal; liberal arts and sciences/liberal studies; medical administrative assistant and medical secretary; nursing (registered nurse training); pre-engineering; real estate.
Academic Programs *Special study options:* academic remediation for entering students, accelerated degree program, adult/continuing education programs, advanced placement credit, honors programs, part-time degree program, services for LD students, summer session for credit.
Library 45,000 titles, 142 serial subscriptions, an OPAC.
Computers on Campus 50 computers available on campus for general student use. At least one staffed computer lab available.
Student Life *Housing:* college housing not available. *Activities and Organizations:* drama/theater group, choral group, Baptist Campus Ministry, theater, SGA, Spectrum Art Club, choral group. *Campus security:* 24-hour emergency response devices and patrols, late-night transport/escort service. *Student services:* personal/psychological counseling.
Standardized Tests *Required:* ACT ASSET, ACT COMPASS (for placement).
Costs (2004–05) *Tuition:* state resident $2700 full-time, $90 per credit hour part-time; nonresident $4860 full-time, $161 per credit hour part-time. Full-time tuition and fees vary according to location. Part-time tuition and fees vary according to location. *Waivers:* senior citizens and employees or children of employees.
Financial Aid Of all full-time matriculated undergraduates who enrolled in 2003, 40 Federal Work-Study jobs (averaging $2500).
Applying *Options:* early admission, deferred entrance. *Application deadline:* rolling (freshmen), rolling (transfers). *Notification:* continuous (freshmen).

Admissions Contact Dr. Joe Burke, Director of Admissions, Northeast Alabama Community College, PO Box 159, Rainsville, AL 35986. *Phone:* 256-228-6001.

NORTHWEST-SHOALS COMMUNITY COLLEGE

Muscle Shoals, Alabama

- **State-supported** 2-year, founded 1963, part of State of Alabama Department of Postsecondary Education
- **Calendar** semesters
- **Degree** certificates, diplomas, and associate
- **Small-town** 205-acre campus
- **Coed,** 4,338 undergraduate students, 55% full-time, 59% women, 41% men

Undergraduates 2,371 full-time, 1,967 part-time. Students come from 8 states and territories, 5 other countries, 2% are from out of state, 12% African American, 0.1% Asian American or Pacific Islander, 0.9% Hispanic American, 2% Native American, 0.5% international, 2% live on campus.
Freshmen *Admission:* 940 admitted, 940 enrolled.
Faculty *Total:* 246, 30% full-time, 6% with terminal degrees. *Student/faculty ratio:* 22:1.
Majors Accounting; administrative assistant and secretarial science; agricultural teacher education; art; business administration and management; child development; clinical laboratory science/medical technology; computer and information sciences; computer engineering technology; computer programming; computer science; computer typography and composition equipment operation; criminal justice/law enforcement administration; criminal justice/police science; drafting and design technology; education; electrical, electronic and communications engineering technology; elementary education; fire science; forestry; general studies; industrial electronics technology; industrial mechanics and maintenance technology; information science/studies; liberal arts and sciences/liberal studies; medical laboratory technology; multi-/interdisciplinary studies related; music; nursing (licensed practical/vocational nurse training); nursing (registered nurse training); pharmacy; pre-engineering; secondary education; veterinary sciences; water quality and wastewater treatment management and recycling technology.
Academic Programs *Special study options:* academic remediation for entering students, accelerated degree program, adult/continuing education programs, advanced placement credit, cooperative education, honors programs, internships, part-time degree program, summer session for credit. *ROTC:* Army (b).
Library Larry W. McCoy Learning Resource Center and James Glasgow Library with 57,827 titles, 268 serial subscriptions, 1,428 audiovisual materials.
Computers on Campus 620 computers available on campus for general student use. A campuswide network can be accessed from off campus. Internet access, at least one staffed computer lab available.
Student Life *Housing Options:* coed. Campus housing is university owned. *Activities and Organizations:* choral group, Student Government Association, Science Club, Phi Theta Kappa, Baptist Campus Ministry, Northwest-Shoals Singers. *Campus security:* 24-hour emergency response devices and patrols. *Student services:* personal/psychological counseling.
Athletics Member NJCAA. *Intercollegiate sports:* baseball M(s), basketball M(s)/W(s), cheerleading M(s)/W(s), cross-country running M(s), golf M(s), softball W(s), tennis W(s), volleyball W(s). *Intramural sports:* basketball M/W, softball M/W, table tennis M/W, tennis M/W, volleyball M/W.
Standardized Tests *Required:* ACT, ACT ASSET, or ACT COMPASS (for placement).
Costs (2005–06) *Tuition:* state resident $2304 full-time, $72 per credit hour part-time; nonresident $4608 full-time, $144 per credit hour part-time. *Required fees:* $576 full-time, $16 per credit hour part-time. *Room and board:* room only: $1675. *Waivers:* senior citizens and employees or children of employees.
Financial Aid *Financial aid deadline:* 6/1.
Applying *Options:* common application. *Required:* high school transcript. *Application deadline:* rolling (freshmen), rolling (transfers).
Admissions Contact Dr. Karen Berryhill, Vice President of Student Development Services, Northwest-Shoals Community College, PO Box 2545, Muscle Shoals, AL 35662. *Phone:* 256-331-5261. *Toll-free phone:* 800-645-8967. *Fax:* 256-331-5366.

PRINCE INSTITUTE OF PROFESSIONAL STUDIES

Montgomery, Alabama

- **Independent** 2-year
- **Calendar** quarters
- **Degree** certificates and associate
- **Suburban** campus
- **Endowment** $6040

■ **Coed, primarily women**

Faculty *Student/faculty ratio:* 15:1.

Costs (2004–05) *Tuition:* $5976 full-time, $1992 per term part-time. *Required fees:* $150 full-time, $50 per term part-time.

Applying *Application fee:* $90. *Required:* high school transcript, interview.

Admissions Contact Ms. Patricia L. Hill, President/Director of Admissions, Prince Institute of Professional Studies, 7735 Atlanta Highway, Montgomery, AL 36117. *Phone:* 334-271-1670. *Toll-free phone:* 877-853-5569. *Fax:* 334-271-1671. *E-mail:* admissions@princeinstitute.edu.

REID STATE TECHNICAL COLLEGE
Evergreen, Alabama

■ **State-supported** 2-year, founded 1966, part of Alabama College System
■ **Calendar** semesters
■ **Degree** certificates, diplomas, and associate
■ **Rural** 26-acre campus
■ **Coed,** 620 undergraduate students, 63% full-time, 68% women, 32% men

Undergraduates 390 full-time, 230 part-time. Students come from 2 states and territories, 1% are from out of state, 54% African American, 0.6% Hispanic American, 1% Native American.

Freshmen *Admission:* 100 applied, 100 admitted, 100 enrolled.

Faculty *Total:* 44, 55% full-time, 59% with terminal degrees. *Student/faculty ratio:* 16:1.

Majors Administrative assistant and secretarial science; electrical, electronic and communications engineering technology.

Academic Programs *Special study options:* academic remediation for entering students, adult/continuing education programs, double majors, independent study, internships, part-time degree program, services for LD students, summer session for credit.

Library an OPAC, a Web page.

Computers on Campus 70 computers available on campus for general student use. A campuswide network can be accessed from off campus. Internet access, at least one staffed computer lab available.

Student Life *Housing:* college housing not available. *Activities and Organizations:* student-run newspaper, Student Government Association. *Campus security:* 24-hour emergency response devices, day and evening security guard. *Student services:* personal/psychological counseling.

Standardized Tests *Required:* ACT ASSET, Ability-To-Benefit Admissions Test (for placement).

Costs (2004–05) *Tuition:* state resident $3240 full-time, $72 per credit part-time; nonresident $6480 full-time, $144 per credit part-time. *Required fees:* $648 full-time.

Financial Aid Of all full-time matriculated undergraduates who enrolled in 2003, 35 Federal Work-Study jobs (averaging $1500).

Applying *Options:* common application, early admission. *Required:* high school transcript. *Application deadline:* rolling (freshmen), rolling (transfers).

Admissions Contact Ms. Alesia Stuart, Public Relations/Marketing, Reid State Technical College, PO Box 588, Intersection of I-95 and Highway 83, Evergreen, AL 36401-0588. *Phone:* 251-578-1313 Ext. 108. *Fax:* 251-578-5355.

REMINGTON COLLEGE-MOBILE CAMPUS
Mobile, Alabama

■ **Proprietary** primarily 2-year, part of Education America
■ **Calendar** quarters
■ **Degrees** diplomas, associate, and bachelor's
■ **Suburban** 5-acre campus
■ **Coed**

Faculty *Student/faculty ratio:* 16:1.

Standardized Tests *Required:* Wonderlic aptitude test (for admission).

Costs (2004–05) *Tuition:* $11,430 full-time, $318 per credit hour part-time. Full-time tuition and fees vary according to class time, course level, course load, degree level, location, program, reciprocity agreements, and student level. No tuition increase for student's term of enrollment. *Required fees:* $50 full-time.

Financial Aid Of all full-time matriculated undergraduates who enrolled in 2003, 500 applied for aid, 500 were judged to have need. 15 Federal Work-Study jobs (averaging $5500). *Average percent of need met:* 45. *Average financial aid package:* $7043. *Average need-based loan:* $3000. *Average need-based gift aid:* $7043. *Average indebtedness upon graduation:* $14,000.

Applying *Application fee:* $50. *Required:* high school transcript, interview.

Admissions Contact Mr. Chris Jones, Director of Recruitment, Remington College-Mobile Campus, 828 Downtowner Loop West, Mobile, AL 36609. *Phone:* 251-343-8200 Ext. 208. *Toll-free phone:* 800-866-0850. *Fax:* 251-343-0577.

SHELTON STATE COMMUNITY COLLEGE
Tuscaloosa, Alabama

■ **State-supported** 2-year, founded 1979, part of Alabama College System
■ **Calendar** semesters
■ **Degree** certificates, diplomas, and associate
■ **Small-town** 30-acre campus with easy access to Birmingham
■ **Coed,** 5,778 undergraduate students, 61% full-time, 58% women, 42% men

Undergraduates 3,533 full-time, 2,245 part-time. Students come from 11 states and territories, 2% are from out of state, 32% African American, 1% Asian American or Pacific Islander, 0.9% Hispanic American, 0.2% Native American, 35% transferred in.

Freshmen *Admission:* 3,081 applied, 3,081 admitted, 2,039 enrolled.

Faculty *Total:* 185, 46% full-time, 8% with terminal degrees. *Student/faculty ratio:* 19:1.

Majors Administrative assistant and secretarial science; art teacher education; automobile/automotive mechanics technology; biology/biological sciences; business administration and management; business teacher education; chemistry; clinical/medical laboratory technology; computer science; cosmetology; data processing and data processing technology; drafting and design technology; education; electrical, electronic and communications engineering technology; elementary education; emergency medical technology (EMT paramedic); family and consumer sciences/human sciences; health information/medical records administration; heating, air conditioning, ventilation and refrigeration maintenance technology; kindergarten/preschool education; liberal arts and sciences/liberal studies; medical administrative assistant and medical secretary; medical/clinical assistant; music; music teacher education; nursing (licensed practical/vocational nurse training); nursing (registered nurse training); pharmacy; physical education teaching and coaching; respiratory care therapy; tourism and travel services management; welding technology.

Academic Programs *Special study options:* academic remediation for entering students, accelerated degree program, adult/continuing education programs, advanced placement credit, distance learning, honors programs, part-time degree program, services for LD students, summer session for credit. *ROTC:* Army (c), Air Force (c).

Library Brooks-Cork Library plus 1 other with 50,123 titles, 361 serial subscriptions, 3,247 audiovisual materials, an OPAC, a Web page.

Computers on Campus 150 computers available on campus for general student use. A campuswide network can be accessed from off campus. Internet access, online (class) registration, at least one staffed computer lab available.

Student Life *Housing:* college housing not available. *Activities and Organizations:* drama/theater group, student-run newspaper, choral group, PTK, Student Government Association, African American Cultural Association. *Campus security:* 24-hour emergency response devices and patrols.

Athletics Member NJCAA. *Intercollegiate sports:* baseball M(s), basketball M(s)/W(s), cheerleading M(s)/W(s), soccer W(s), softball W(s). *Intramural sports:* fencing M/W.

Standardized Tests *Required:* ACT COMPASS (for placement).

Costs (2005–06) *Tuition:* state resident $2130 full-time, $71 per credit hour part-time; nonresident $4260 full-time, $142 per credit hour part-time. *Required fees:* $570 full-time, $18 per credit hour part-time. *Payment plan:* deferred payment. *Waivers:* senior citizens and employees or children of employees.

Financial Aid Of all full-time matriculated undergraduates who enrolled in 2003, 97 Federal Work-Study jobs.

Applying *Options:* electronic application. *Required:* high school transcript. *Application deadline:* rolling (freshmen), rolling (transfers).

Admissions Contact Ms. Loretta Jones, Assistant to the Dean of Students, Shelton State Community College, Shelton State Community College, 9500 Old Greensboro Road, Tuscaloosa, AL 35405. *Phone:* 205-391-2236. *Fax:* 205-391-3910.

SNEAD STATE COMMUNITY COLLEGE
Boaz, Alabama

■ **State-supported** 2-year, founded 1898, part of Alabama College System
■ **Calendar** semesters
■ **Degree** certificates and associate
■ **Small-town** 42-acre campus with easy access to Birmingham
■ **Endowment** $1.6 million
■ **Coed**

Faculty *Student/faculty ratio:* 28:1.

Student Life *Campus security:* 24-hour patrols, student patrols.

Athletics Member NJCAA.

Standardized Tests *Required for some:* SAT or ACT (for placement), ACT ASSET, ACT COMPASS.

Snead State Community College (continued)

Costs (2004–05) *Tuition:* state resident $2304 full-time, $72 per semester hour part-time; nonresident $4608 full-time, $144 per semester hour part-time. *Required fees:* $576 full-time, $18 per semester hour part-time. *Room and board:* $1724; room only: $600.

Financial Aid Of all full-time matriculated undergraduates who enrolled in 2003, 41 Federal Work-Study jobs.

Applying *Options:* early admission, deferred entrance. *Required:* high school transcript. *Required for some:* interview.

Admissions Contact Ms. Martha Buchanan, Director of Admissions and Records, Snead State Community College, PO Box 734, Boaz, AL 35957-0734. *Phone:* 256-593-5120 Ext. 207. *Fax:* 256-593-7180. *E-mail:* mbuchanan@snead.edu.

SOUTHERN UNION STATE COMMUNITY COLLEGE
Wadley, Alabama

- **State-supported** 2-year, founded 1922, part of Alabama College System
- **Calendar** quarters
- **Degree** certificates, diplomas, and associate
- **Rural** campus
- **Coed**

Undergraduates 6% live on campus.

Faculty *Total:* 217, 37% full-time. *Student/faculty ratio:* 19:1.

Majors Administrative assistant and secretarial science; business administration and management; finance; information science/studies; liberal arts and sciences/liberal studies; nursing (registered nurse training).

Academic Programs *Special study options:* academic remediation for entering students, adult/continuing education programs, advanced placement credit, cooperative education, internships, part-time degree program, services for LD students, summer session for credit. *ROTC:* Air Force (c).

Library McClintock-Ensminger Library plus 2 others with 90,791 titles, 877 serial subscriptions.

Computers on Campus 225 computers available on campus for general student use. At least one staffed computer lab available.

Student Life *Housing Options:* coed. *Activities and Organizations:* drama/theater group, student-run newspaper, choral group, Student Government Association, Phi Theta Kappa, Music Club, National Student Nurses Association, Global Environmental Organization of Students. *Campus security:* 24-hour patrols, controlled dormitory access. *Student services:* personal/psychological counseling.

Athletics Member NSCAA, NJCAA. *Intercollegiate sports:* baseball M(s), basketball M(s)/W(s), cross-country running M(s)/W(s), softball W(s), volleyball W(s). *Intramural sports:* basketball M/W, bowling M/W.

Costs (2004–05) *Tuition:* state resident $2700 full-time, $90 per credit hour part-time; nonresident $4830 full-time, $161 per credit hour part-time.

Financial Aid Of all full-time matriculated undergraduates who enrolled in 2003, 150 Federal Work-Study jobs (averaging $1000). 35 state and other part-time jobs (averaging $1000).

Applying *Options:* common application, early admission, deferred entrance. *Required:* high school transcript. *Application deadline:* rolling (freshmen), rolling (transfers). *Notification:* continuous (freshmen).

Admissions Contact Mrs. Susan Salatto, Director of Student Development, Southern Union State Community College, PO Box 1000, Roberts Street, Wadley, AL 36276. *Phone:* 256-395-2211. *Fax:* 256-395-2215.

VC TECH
Pelham, Alabama

Admissions Contact 2790 Pelham Parkway, Pelham, AL 35124. *Toll-free phone:* 877-5-VCTECH.

VIRGINIA COLLEGE AT HUNTSVILLE
Huntsville, Alabama

Admissions Contact Ms. Pat Foster, Director of Admissions, Virginia College at Huntsville, 2800-A Bob Wallace Avenue, Huntsville, AL 35805. *Phone:* 205-533-7387.

WALLACE STATE COMMUNITY COLLEGE
Hanceville, Alabama

Admissions Contact Ms. Linda Sperling, Director of Admissions, Wallace State Community College, PO Box 2000, Hanceville, AL 35077-2000. *Phone:* 256-352-8278. *Fax:* 256-352-8228.

ALASKA

CHARTER COLLEGE
Anchorage, Alaska

Admissions Contact Ms. Lily Sirianni, Vice President, Charter College, 2221 East Northern Lights Boulevard, Suite 120, Anchorage, AK 99508-4157. *Phone:* 907-277-1000. *Toll-free phone:* 800-279-1008. *Fax:* 907-274-3342. *E-mail:* contact@chartercollege.org.

ILISAGVIK COLLEGE
Barrow, Alaska

Admissions Contact Dr. Edna Ahgeak MacLean, President, Ilisagvik College, UIC/Narl, Barrow, AK 99723. *Phone:* 907-852-1820. *Toll-free phone:* 800-478-7337.

UNIVERSITY OF ALASKA ANCHORAGE, KENAI PENINSULA COLLEGE
Soldotna, Alaska

- **State-supported** 2-year, founded 1964, part of University of Alaska System
- **Calendar** semesters
- **Degree** certificates and associate
- **Rural** 360-acre campus
- **Endowment** $950,000
- **Coed**

Faculty *Student/faculty ratio:* 15:1.

Student Life *Campus security:* 24-hour emergency response devices.

Standardized Tests *Required:* ACT ASSET (for placement).

Costs (2004–05) *Tuition:* state resident $2970 full-time, $99 per credit hour part-time; nonresident $10,290 full-time, $343 per credit hour part-time. Part-time tuition and fees vary according to course level and course load. *Required fees:* $44 full-time, $4 per credit hour part-time. *Payment plans:* tuition prepayment, installment, deferred payment.

Financial Aid Of all full-time matriculated undergraduates who enrolled in 2003, 50 Federal Work-Study jobs (averaging $3000). 50 state and other part-time jobs (averaging $3000).

Applying *Options:* common application. *Application fee:* $40. *Required:* high school transcript. *Required for some:* interview.

Admissions Contact Ms. Shelly Love, Admission and Registration Coordinator, University of Alaska Anchorage, Kenai Peninsula College, 34820 College Drive, Soldotna, AK 99669-9798. *Phone:* 907-262-0311.

UNIVERSITY OF ALASKA ANCHORAGE, KODIAK COLLEGE
Kodiak, Alaska

Admissions Contact Ms. Karen Hamer, Registrar, University of Alaska Anchorage, Kodiak College, 117 Benny Benson Drive, Kodiak, AK 99615. *Phone:* 907-486-1235. *Fax:* 907-486-1264.

UNIVERSITY OF ALASKA ANCHORAGE, MATANUSKA-SUSITNA COLLEGE
Palmer, Alaska

- **State-supported** 2-year, founded 1958, part of University of Alaska System
- **Calendar** semesters
- **Degree** certificates and associate
- **Small-town** 950-acre campus with easy access to Anchorage
- **Coed**, 1,313 undergraduate students, 28% full-time, 66% women, 34% men

Undergraduates 371 full-time, 942 part-time. Students come from 51 states and territories, 18 other countries, 2% African American, 1% Asian American or Pacific Islander, 1% Hispanic American, 5% Native American. *Retention:* 67% of 2002 full-time freshmen returned.

Freshmen *Admission:* 113 applied, 86 admitted, 67 enrolled.

Faculty *Total:* 110, 17% full-time, 8% with terminal degrees. *Student/faculty ratio:* 14:1.

Majors Accounting; administrative assistant and secretarial science; business administration and management; electrical, electronic and communications engineering technology; fire science; heating, air conditioning, ventilation and refrigeration maintenance technology; human services; liberal arts and sciences/liberal studies.

Academic Programs *Special study options:* academic remediation for entering students, adult/continuing education programs, advanced placement credit, cooperative education, distance learning, double majors, independent study, internships, off-campus study, part-time degree program, summer session for credit.
Library Al Okeson Library with 50,000 titles, 280 serial subscriptions, 1,840 audiovisual materials, an OPAC, a Web page.
Computers on Campus 207 computers available on campus for general student use. A campuswide network can be accessed from off campus. Internet access, online (class) registration, at least one staffed computer lab available. Computer purchase or lease plan available.
Student Life *Housing:* college housing not available. *Activities and Organizations:* student-run newspaper, choral group, student government, Math Club. *Campus security:* 24-hour patrols.
Standardized Tests *Recommended:* SAT or ACT (for placement), ACT COMPASS.
Costs (2005–06) *Tuition:* state resident $2616 full-time, $109 per credit part-time; nonresident $8712 full-time, $363 per credit part-time. Full-time tuition and fees vary according to course level and course load. Part-time tuition and fees vary according to course level and course load. *Required fees:* $200 full-time, $5 per credit part-time, $40 per term part-time. *Payment plan:* installment. *Waivers:* children of alumni, senior citizens, and employees or children of employees.
Financial Aid Of all full-time matriculated undergraduates who enrolled in 2003, 8 Federal Work-Study jobs (averaging $3000).
Applying *Application fee:* $40. *Required:* high school transcript. *Recommended:* minimum 2.0 GPA.
Admissions Contact Ms. Sandra Gravley, Student Services Manager, University of Alaska Anchorage, Matanuska-Susitna College, PO Box 2889, Palmer, AK 99645-2889. *Phone:* 907-745-9712. *Fax:* 907-745-9747. *E-mail:* info@matsu.alaska.edu.

UNIVERSITY OF ALASKA, PRINCE WILLIAM SOUND COMMUNITY COLLEGE
Valdez, Alaska

Admissions Contact Mr. Nathan J. Platt, Director of Student Services, University of Alaska, Prince William Sound Community College, PO Box 97, Valdez, AK 99686-0097. *Phone:* 907-834-1631. *Toll-free phone:* 800-478-8800 Ext. 1600. *Fax:* 907-834-1627. *E-mail:* vnnjp@uaa.alaska.edu.

UNIVERSITY OF ALASKA SOUTHEAST, KETCHIKAN CAMPUS
Ketchikan, Alaska

- **State and locally supported** 2-year, founded 1954, part of University of Alaska System
- **Calendar** semesters
- **Degree** associate
- **Small-town** 51-acre campus
- **Endowment** $2.6 million
- **Coed**

Faculty *Student/faculty ratio:* 15:1.
Student Life *Campus security:* 24-hour emergency response devices.
Standardized Tests *Required for some:* ACT ASSET. *Recommended:* SAT or ACT (for placement).
Costs (2004–05) *Tuition:* state resident $2376 full-time, $99 per credit part-time; nonresident $99 per credit part-time. Full-time tuition and fees vary according to course level and course load. Part-time tuition and fees vary according to course level and course load. *Required fees:* $166 full-time. *Room and board:* $8370; room only: $5940.
Applying *Options:* early admission. *Application fee:* $35. *Required:* high school transcript. *Required for some:* essay or personal statement.
Admissions Contact Mrs. Gail Klein, Student Services Coordinator, University of Alaska Southeast, Ketchikan Campus, 2600 7th Avenue, Ketchikan, AK 99901-5798. *Phone:* 907-228-4508. *Fax:* 907-225-3624. *E-mail:* gail.klein@uas.alaska.edu.

UNIVERSITY OF ALASKA SOUTHEAST, SITKA CAMPUS
Sitka, Alaska

Admissions Contact Mr. Tim Schroeder, Coordinator of Admissions, University of Alaska Southeast, Sitka Campus, 1332 Seward Avenue, Sitka, AK 99835-9418. *Phone:* 907-747-7703. *Toll-free phone:* 800-478-6653. *Fax:* 907-747-7747. *E-mail:* tnkmn@acadl.alaska.edu.

AMERICAN SAMOA

AMERICAN SAMOA COMMUNITY COLLEGE
Pago Pago, American Samoa

- **Territory-supported** 2-year, founded 1969
- **Calendar** semesters
- **Degree** certificates and associate
- **Rural** 20-acre campus
- **Coed,** 1,537 undergraduate students

Undergraduates Students come from 2 other countries.
Freshmen *Admission:* 471 applied, 471 admitted.
Majors Accounting; administrative assistant and secretarial science; agricultural mechanization; agricultural teacher education; agriculture; agronomy and crop science; automobile/automotive mechanics technology; business administration and management; business teacher education; construction engineering technology; health science; liberal arts and sciences/liberal studies; library science; nursing (licensed practical/vocational nurse training); nursing (registered nurse training); public administration.
Academic Programs *Special study options:* academic remediation for entering students, adult/continuing education programs, off-campus study, part-time degree program, summer session for credit.
Library 18,000 titles, 50 serial subscriptions.
Student Life *Housing:* college housing not available. *Activities and Organizations:* student-run newspaper.
Athletics *Intramural sports:* basketball M/W, football M/W, golf M/W, rugby M, soccer M, tennis M/W, track and field M/W, volleyball M/W.
Standardized Tests *Required:* Michigan Test of English Language Proficiency (for placement). *Recommended:* SAT or ACT (for placement).
Costs (2004–05) *Tuition:* territory resident $1000 full-time, $45 per credit hour part-time; nonresident $1400 full-time, $60 per credit hour part-time. *Required fees:* $60 full-time, $30 per term part-time.
Applying *Options:* deferred entrance. *Application deadline:* 8/1 (freshmen).
Admissions Contact Mrs. Sina P. Ward, Registrar, American Samoa Community College, PO Box 2609, Pago Pago, AS 96799. *Phone:* 684-699-1141. *Fax:* 684-699-2062. *E-mail:* admissions@ascc.as.

ARIZONA

APOLLO COLLEGE-PHOENIX, INC.
Phoenix, Arizona

Admissions Contact Mr. Randy Utley, Campus Director, Apollo College-Phoenix, Inc., 2701 West Bethany Home Road, Phoenix, AZ 85051. *Phone:* 602-864-1571. *Toll-free phone:* 800-36-TRAIN.

APOLLO COLLEGE-TRI-CITY, INC.
Mesa, Arizona

Admissions Contact Mr. James Norris Miller, Campus Director, Apollo College-Tri-City, Inc., 630 West Southern Avenue, Mesa, AZ 85210-5004. *Phone:* 480-831-6585. *Toll-free phone:* 800-36-TRAIN.

APOLLO COLLEGE-TUCSON, INC.
Tucson, Arizona

Admissions Contact Ms. Jenell McKinney, Campus Director, Apollo College-Tucson, Inc., 3870 North Oracle Road, Tucson, AZ 85705-3227. *Phone:* 520-888-5885. *Toll-free phone:* 800-36-TRAIN.

APOLLO COLLEGE-WESTSIDE, INC.
Phoenix, Arizona

Admissions Contact Ms. Cindy Nestor, Vice President, Apollo College-Westside, Inc., 2701 West Bethany Home Road, Phoenix, AZ 85017. *Phone:* 602-433-1222 Ext. 251. *Toll-free phone:* 800-36-TRAIN.

ARIZONA AUTOMOTIVE INSTITUTE
Glendale, Arizona

Admissions Contact Mr. Mark LaCara, Director of Admissions, Arizona Automotive Institute, 6829 North 46th Avenue, Glendale, AZ 85301-3597. *Phone:* 623-934-7273 Ext. 211.

ARIZONA COLLEGE OF ALLIED HEALTH
Glendale, Arizona

Admissions Contact 4425 West Olive Avenue, Suite 300, Glendale, AZ 85302-3843.

ARIZONA WESTERN COLLEGE
Yuma, Arizona

- **State and locally supported** 2-year, founded 1962, part of Arizona State Community College System
- **Calendar** semesters
- **Degree** certificates and associate
- **Rural** 640-acre campus
- **Coed,** 6,450 undergraduate students, 28% full-time, 60% women, 40% men

Undergraduates 1,830 full-time, 4,620 part-time. Students come from 26 states and territories, 7% are from out of state, 3% African American, 1% Asian American or Pacific Islander, 65% Hispanic American, 2% Native American, 0.6% international, 6% live on campus. *Retention:* 50% of 2002 full-time freshmen returned.
Freshmen *Admission:* 1,639 enrolled.
Faculty *Total:* 328, 32% full-time, 7% with terminal degrees. *Student/faculty ratio:* 16:1.
Majors Administrative assistant and secretarial science; agricultural business and management; agriculture; art; automobile/automotive mechanics technology; biological and physical sciences; biology/biological sciences; broadcast journalism; business administration and management; chemistry; computer science; criminal justice/law enforcement administration; criminal justice/police science; developmental and child psychology; drafting and design technology; dramatic/theatre arts; education; electrical, electronic and communications engineering technology; engineering technology; English; environmental studies; family and consumer economics related; finance; fire science; geology/earth science; health science; heating, air conditioning, ventilation and refrigeration maintenance technology; hospitality administration; human services; information science/studies; liberal arts and sciences/liberal studies; mathematics; music; nursing (licensed practical/vocational nurse training); nursing (registered nurse training); oceanography (chemical and physical); personal and culinary services related; physical education teaching and coaching; physics; pre-engineering; social sciences; Spanish; welding technology.
Academic Programs *Special study options:* academic remediation for entering students, adult/continuing education programs, advanced placement credit, cooperative education, distance learning, English as a second language, honors programs, independent study, part-time degree program, summer session for credit.
Library Arizona Western College Library with 698 serial subscriptions, 10,800 audiovisual materials, an OPAC, a Web page.
Computers on Campus 500 computers available on campus for general student use. A campuswide network can be accessed from off campus. Internet access, at least one staffed computer lab available.
Student Life *Housing Options:* coed. Campus housing is university owned. *Activities and Organizations:* drama/theater group, student-run newspaper, radio and television station, choral group, Associated Students Governing Board, MECHA, Umoja, Honors Club, UVU. *Campus security:* 24-hour emergency response devices and patrols, student patrols, late-night transport/escort service. *Student services:* health clinic, personal/psychological counseling.
Athletics Member NJCAA. *Intercollegiate sports:* baseball M(s), basketball M(s), football M(s), soccer M(s), softball W(s), volleyball W(s). *Intramural sports:* badminton M/W, basketball M/W, football M, soccer M, softball M/W, swimming and diving M/W, table tennis M/W, volleyball M/W.
Costs (2005–06) *Tuition:* state resident $1140 full-time, $38 per credit hour part-time; nonresident $5700 full-time, $44 per credit hour part-time. Full-time tuition and fees vary according to course load, location, and reciprocity agreements. Part-time tuition and fees vary according to course load, location, and reciprocity agreements. *Room and board:* room only: $1740. Room and board charges vary according to board plan. *Waivers:* employees or children of employees.
Financial Aid Of all full-time matriculated undergraduates who enrolled in 2003, 350 Federal Work-Study jobs (averaging $1500). 100 state and other part-time jobs (averaging $1800).
Applying *Options:* common application, early admission, deferred entrance. *Required for some:* minimum 3.0 GPA. *Application deadline:* rolling (freshmen), rolling (transfers).

Admissions Contact Mr. Bryan Doak, Registrar, Arizona Western College, PO Box 929, Yuma, AZ 85366. *Phone:* 928-317-7617. *Toll-free phone:* 888-293-0392. *Fax:* 928-344-7730. *E-mail:* bryan.doak@azwestern.edu.

THE BRYMAN SCHOOL
Phoenix, Arizona

Admissions Contact Ms. Vicki Maurer, Admission Manager, The Bryman School, 2250 W. Peoria Avenue, Phoenix, AZ 85029. *Phone:* 602-274-4300. *Toll-free phone:* 800-729-4819. *Fax:* 602-248-9087.

CENTRAL ARIZONA COLLEGE
Coolidge, Arizona

- **County-supported** 2-year, founded 1961
- **Calendar** semesters
- **Degree** certificates and associate
- **Rural** 709-acre campus with easy access to Phoenix
- **Coed,** 6,525 undergraduate students, 35% full-time, 56% women, 44% men

Undergraduates 2,272 full-time, 4,253 part-time. Students come from 6 other countries, 5% African American, 0.9% Asian American or Pacific Islander, 33% Hispanic American, 6% Native American, 0.5% international, 17% live on campus.
Freshmen *Admission:* 2,469 applied, 1,801 admitted.
Faculty *Total:* 330, 28% full-time. *Student/faculty ratio:* 17:1.
Majors Accounting; administrative assistant and secretarial science; agriculture; automobile/automotive mechanics technology; business administration and management; child development; civil engineering technology; computer and information sciences; computer science; corrections; criminal justice/law enforcement administration; dietetics; emergency medical technology (EMT paramedic); engineering; health aide; hotel/motel administration; industrial technology; kindergarten/preschool education; legal administrative assistant/secretary; liberal arts and sciences/liberal studies; marketing/marketing management; materials science; medical administrative assistant and medical secretary; medical transcription; nursing (licensed practical/vocational nurse training); nursing (registered nurse training).
Academic Programs *Special study options:* academic remediation for entering students, adult/continuing education programs, distance learning, honors programs, independent study, part-time degree program, services for LD students, student-designed majors, summer session for credit.
Library Learning Resource Center with 99,480 titles, 494 serial subscriptions.
Computers on Campus Internet access, at least one staffed computer lab available.
Student Life *Housing Options:* Campus housing is university owned. *Activities and Organizations:* drama/theater group, student-run newspaper, choral group. *Campus security:* 24-hour emergency response devices and patrols. *Student services:* personal/psychological counseling.
Athletics Member NJCAA. *Intercollegiate sports:* baseball M(s), basketball M(s)/W(s), cross-country running M(s)/W(s), equestrian sports M(s)/W(s), golf M(s), softball W(s), track and field M(s)/W(s).
Standardized Tests *Required:* ACT ASSET or ACT COMPASS (for placement).
Costs (2005–06) *Tuition:* state resident $1316 full-time, $47 per credit part-time; nonresident $6356 full-time, $94 per credit part-time. *Required fees:* $16 full-time, $8 per term part-time. *Room and board:* $4160.
Financial Aid Of all full-time matriculated undergraduates who enrolled in 2003, 68 Federal Work-Study jobs (averaging $1310).
Applying *Options:* common application, early admission, deferred entrance. *Application deadline:* rolling (freshmen), rolling (transfers). *Notification:* continuous (freshmen).
Admissions Contact Ms. Doris Helmich, Interim Dean of Enrollment and Student Services, Central Arizona College, 8470 North Overfield Road, Coolidge, AZ 85228. *Phone:* 520-426-4406. *Toll-free phone:* 800-237-9814. *Fax:* 520-426-4271. *E-mail:* leonor_verduzco@centralaz.edu.

CHANDLER-GILBERT COMMUNITY COLLEGE
Chandler, Arizona

- **State and locally supported** 2-year, founded 1985, part of Maricopa County Community College District System
- **Calendar** semesters
- **Degree** certificates, diplomas, and associate
- **Rural** 80-acre campus with easy access to Phoenix
- **Endowment** $315,961
- **Coed,** 8,663 undergraduate students

Undergraduates Students come from 38 states and territories, 5 other countries, 4% are from out of state, 4% African American, 3% Asian American or Pacific Islander, 16% Hispanic American, 4% Native American, 1% international.

Faculty *Total:* 412, 22% full-time. *Student/faculty ratio:* 19:1.

Majors Accounting; airframe mechanics and aircraft maintenance technology; avionics maintenance technology; business administration and management; computer engineering technology; liberal arts and sciences/liberal studies; management information systems.

Academic Programs *Special study options:* academic remediation for entering students, advanced placement credit, English as a second language, freshman honors college, honors programs, part-time degree program, summer session for credit.

Library Chandler-Gilbert Community College Library with 26,060 titles, 170 serial subscriptions, 990 audiovisual materials, an OPAC.

Computers on Campus 140 computers available on campus for general student use. A campuswide network can be accessed from off campus. Internet access, online (class) registration, at least one staffed computer lab available.

Student Life *Activities and Organizations:* student-run newspaper, choral group. *Campus security:* 24-hour emergency response devices and patrols, late-night transport/escort service. *Student services:* personal/psychological counseling.

Standardized Tests *Required for some:* ACT ASSET.

Costs (2004–05) *Tuition:* area resident $1660 full-time, $55 per credit hour part-time; state resident $6600 full-time, $220 per credit hour part-time; nonresident $6600 full-time, $220 per credit hour part-time. Full-time tuition and fees vary according to reciprocity agreements. Part-time tuition and fees vary according to reciprocity agreements. *Required fees:* $10 full-time, $5 per term part-time. *Room and board:* Room and board charges vary according to housing facility. *Payment plan:* deferred payment. *Waivers:* employees or children of employees.

Applying *Options:* common application, electronic application.

Admissions Contact Ms. Irene Pearl, Supervisor of Admissions and Records, Chandler-Gilbert Community College, 2626 East Pecos Road, Chandler, AZ 85225-2479. *Phone:* 480-732-7307.

CHAPARRAL COLLEGE
Tucson, Arizona

- **Proprietary** primarily 2-year, founded 1972
- **Calendar** 5 five-week modules
- **Degrees** diplomas, associate, and bachelor's (bachelor's degree in business administration only)
- **Suburban** campus with easy access to Phoenix
- **Coed**

Faculty *Student/faculty ratio:* 20:1.

Student Life *Campus security:* 24-hour emergency response devices.

Standardized Tests *Required:* CPAt (for admission).

Applying *Options:* common application. *Application fee:* $35. *Required:* high school transcript, interview. *Required for some:* letters of recommendation, entrance test.

Admissions Contact Ms. Becki Rossini, Director of Admissions, Chaparral College, 4585 East Speedway No. 204, Tucson, AZ 85712. *Phone:* 520-327-6866. *Fax:* 520-325-0108. *E-mail:* admissions@chap-col.edu.

COCHISE COLLEGE
Douglas, Arizona

- **State and locally supported** 2-year, founded 1962, part of Cochise College
- **Calendar** semesters
- **Degree** certificates and associate
- **Rural** 500-acre campus
- **Coed**, 4,270 undergraduate students, 48% full-time, 60% women, 40% men

Undergraduates 2,038 full-time, 2,232 part-time. Students come from 4 states and territories, 8 other countries, 5% are from out of state, 7% African American, 4% Asian American or Pacific Islander, 33% Hispanic American, 1% Native American, 0.5% international, 0.6% transferred in, 17% live on campus.

Freshmen *Admission:* 743 applied, 743 admitted, 740 enrolled.

Faculty *Total:* 371, 25% full-time. *Student/faculty ratio:* 15:1.

Majors Administrative assistant and secretarial science; agriculture; airframe mechanics and aircraft maintenance technology; airline pilot and flight crew; anthropology; art; avionics maintenance technology; behavioral sciences; biology/biological sciences; business administration and management; chemistry; computer programming; computer science; criminal justice/law enforcement administration; criminal justice/police science; drafting and design technology; education; English; film/cinema studies; fire science; history; information science/studies; international relations and affairs; journalism; legal administrative

assistant/secretary; liberal arts and sciences/liberal studies; mass communication/media; medical administrative assistant and medical secretary; nursing (registered nurse training); physical education teaching and coaching; political science and government; pre-engineering; psychology; social sciences; social work; Spanish; teacher assistant/aide.

Academic Programs *Special study options:* academic remediation for entering students, accelerated degree program, cooperative education, distance learning, English as a second language, independent study, internships, part-time degree program, services for LD students, summer session for credit.

Library 42,876 titles, 182 serial subscriptions, a Web page.

Computers on Campus 84 computers available on campus for general student use. Internet access, at least one staffed computer lab available.

Student Life *Housing Options:* Campus housing is university owned. *Activities and Organizations:* choral group, student government, Phi Theta Kappa. *Campus security:* 24-hour emergency response devices and patrols, controlled dormitory access. *Student services:* health clinic, personal/psychological counseling.

Athletics Member NJCAA. *Intercollegiate sports:* baseball M(s), basketball M(s)/W(s), soccer W(s). *Intramural sports:* basketball M.

Standardized Tests *Recommended:* SAT or ACT (for placement).

Costs (2005–06) *Tuition:* state resident $1290 full-time, $43 per credit hour part-time; nonresident $7320 full-time, $62 per credit hour part-time. *Required fees:* $60 full-time, $60 per term part-time. *Room and board:* $3452.

Financial Aid Of all full-time matriculated undergraduates who enrolled in 2003, 137 Federal Work-Study jobs (averaging $1070).

Applying *Options:* early admission, deferred entrance. *Recommended:* high school transcript. *Application deadline:* rolling (freshmen), rolling (transfers). *Notification:* continuous (freshmen).

Admissions Contact Ms. Pati Mapp, Admissions Counselor, Cochise College, 4190 West Highway 80, Douglas, AZ 85607-9724. *Phone:* 520-364-0336. *Toll-free phone:* 800-966-7946. *Fax:* 520-364-0236. *E-mail:* mappp@cochise.cc.az.us.

COCHISE COLLEGE
Sierra Vista, Arizona

Admissions Contact Ms. Debbie Quick, Admissions Officer, Cochise College, 901 North Columbo, Sierra Vista, AZ 85635-2317. *Phone:* 520-515-5412. *Toll-free phone:* 800-593-9567. *Fax:* 520-515-4006. *E-mail:* quickd@cochise.cc.az.us.

COCONINO COMMUNITY COLLEGE
Flagstaff, Arizona

- **State-supported** 2-year, founded 1991
- **Calendar** semesters
- **Degree** certificates and associate
- **Small-town** 5-acre campus
- **Endowment** $11,275
- **Coed**, 3,689 undergraduate students

Faculty *Total:* 205, 12% full-time.

Majors Accounting; biological and physical sciences; business administration and management; criminal justice/law enforcement administration; fire science; information science/studies; liberal arts and sciences/liberal studies.

Academic Programs *Special study options:* academic remediation for entering students, adult/continuing education programs, advanced placement credit, part-time degree program, services for LD students, summer session for credit.

Computers on Campus 100 computers available on campus for general student use. Internet access, at least one staffed computer lab available.

Student Life *Housing:* college housing not available. *Activities and Organizations:* choral group. *Campus security:* 24-hour patrols.

Costs (2005–06) *Tuition:* state resident $1344 full-time, $56 per credit hour part-time; nonresident $5376 full-time, $224 per credit hour part-time.

Applying *Application fee:* $10. *Required for some:* high school transcript. *Application deadline:* rolling (freshmen), rolling (transfers).

Admissions Contact Mr. Steve Miller, Director of Admissions/Registrar, Coconino Community College, 3000 North Fourth Street, Flagstaff, AZ 86003. *Phone:* 928-527-1222. *Toll-free phone:* 800-350-7122. *Fax:* 520-526-1821. *E-mail:* smiller@coco.cc.az.us.

COLLEGEAMERICA-FLAGSTAFF
Flagstaff, Arizona

Admissions Contact Mr. Pescal Berlioux, Executive Director, CollegeAmerica-Flagstaff, 5200 East Cortland Boulevard, Suite A-19, Flagstaff, AZ 86004. *Phone:* 800-977-5455.

DINE COLLEGE
Tsaile, Arizona

Admissions Contact Mrs. Louise Litzin, Registrar, Dine College, PO Box 67, Tsaile, AZ 86556. *Phone:* 928-724-6633. *Fax:* 928-724-3349. *E-mail:* louise@dinecollege.edu.

EASTERN ARIZONA COLLEGE
Thatcher, Arizona

■ **State and locally supported** 2-year, founded 1888, part of Arizona State Community College System
■ **Calendar** semesters
■ **Degree** certificates and associate
■ **Small-town** campus
■ **Endowment** $612,810
■ **Coed,** 3,732 undergraduate students, 39% full-time, 54% women, 46% men

Undergraduates 1,464 full-time, 2,268 part-time. Students come from 29 states and territories, 5% are from out of state, 4% African American, 0.7% Asian American or Pacific Islander, 19% Hispanic American, 6% Native American, 0.7% international, 5% live on campus. *Retention:* 74% of 2002 full-time freshmen returned.
Freshmen *Admission:* 1,553 applied, 1,553 admitted, 665 enrolled.
Faculty *Total:* 170, 42% full-time. *Student/faculty ratio:* 24:1.
Majors Agribusiness; agriculture; anthropology; art; art teacher education; automobile/automotive mechanics technology; biology/biological sciences; business administration and management; business, management, and marketing related; business operations support and secretarial services related; business teacher education; chemistry; child care provision; civil engineering technology; commercial and advertising art; corrections; criminal justice/law enforcement administration; criminal justice/police science; data entry/microcomputer applications; drafting and design technology; dramatic/theatre arts; elementary education; emergency medical technology (EMT paramedic); English; entrepreneurship; foreign languages and literatures; forestry; geology/earth science; health and physical education; health/medical preparatory programs related; history; information science/studies; liberal arts and sciences/liberal studies; machine shop technology; mathematics; mining technology; music; nursing (registered nurse training); physics; political science and government; pre-law studies; pre-medical studies; pre-pharmacy studies; psychology; secondary education; sociology; technology/industrial arts teacher education; welding technology; wildlife biology.
Academic Programs *Special study options:* academic remediation for entering students, adult/continuing education programs, advanced placement credit, cooperative education, double majors, independent study, part-time degree program, services for LD students, study abroad, summer session for credit.
Library Alumni Library plus 1 other with an OPAC, a Web page.
Computers on Campus 458 computers available on campus for general student use. A campuswide network can be accessed from student residence rooms and from off campus. Internet access, online (class) registration, at least one staffed computer lab available.
Student Life *Housing Options:* men-only, women-only. Campus housing is university owned. *Activities and Organizations:* drama/theater group, choral group, marching band, Latter-Day Saints Student Association, Criminal Justice Student Association, Multicultural Council, Phi Theta Kappa, Mark Allen Dorm Club. *Campus security:* late-night transport/escort service, controlled dormitory access, 20-hour patrols by trained security personnel. *Student services:* personal/psychological counseling.
Athletics Member NJCAA. *Intercollegiate sports:* baseball M(s), basketball M(s)/W(s), football M(s), golf M/W, softball W(s), volleyball W(s). *Intramural sports:* basketball M/W, racquetball M/W, swimming and diving M/W, table tennis M/W, tennis M/W, volleyball M/W.
Standardized Tests *Recommended:* SAT or ACT (for placement).
Costs (2005–06) *Tuition:* state resident $1148 full-time, $47 per credit part-time; nonresident $6128 full-time, $92 per credit part-time. *Room and board:* $3910; room only: $1949.
Financial Aid Of all full-time matriculated undergraduates who enrolled in 2003, 259 Federal Work-Study jobs (averaging $1800).
Applying *Options:* electronic application, early admission, deferred entrance. *Recommended:* high school transcript. *Application deadline:* rolling (freshmen), rolling (transfers). *Notification:* continuous (freshmen).
Admissions Contact Mr. Jeff Savage, Coordinator of Recruitment, Eastern Arizona College, 615 North Stadium Avenue, Thatcher, AZ 85552-0769. *Phone:* 928-428-8247. *Toll-free phone:* 800-678-3808. *Fax:* 928-428-8462. *E-mail:* admissions@eac.edu.

ESTRELLA MOUNTAIN COMMUNITY COLLEGE
Avondale, Arizona

■ **State and locally supported** 2-year, part of Maricopa County Community College District System
■ **Calendar** semesters
■ **Degree** certificates and associate
■ **Urban** campus with easy access to Phoenix
■ **Coed,** 5,947 undergraduate students, 23% full-time, 62% women, 38% men

Undergraduates 1,372 full-time, 4,575 part-time. 7% African American, 3% Asian American or Pacific Islander, 31% Hispanic American, 2% Native American, 0.8% international.
Freshmen *Admission:* 5,947 applied, 5,947 admitted, 404 enrolled.
Faculty *Total:* 285, 19% full-time. *Student/faculty ratio:* 20:1.
Majors General studies; liberal arts and sciences/liberal studies.
Costs (2004–05) *Tuition:* state resident $1320 full-time, $55 per credit hour part-time; nonresident $5040 full-time, $80 per credit hour part-time. *Required fees:* $10 full-time, $5 per term part-time.
Financial Aid Of all full-time matriculated undergraduates who enrolled in 2003, 50 Federal Work-Study jobs (averaging $3000).
Admissions Contact Dr. Ernesto Laura, Dean of Student Services, Estrella Mountain Community College, 3000 North Dysart Road, Avondale, AZ 85323-1000. *Phone:* 623-935-8808.

EVEREST COLLEGE
Phoenix, Arizona

■ **Proprietary** 2-year, founded 1982
■ **Calendar** 6 or 12 week terms
■ **Degree** diplomas and associate
■ **Urban** campus
■ **Coed,** 650 undergraduate students, 61% full-time, 78% women, 22% men

Undergraduates 395 full-time, 255 part-time. Students come from 2 states and territories, 2% are from out of state, 10% African American, 2% Asian American or Pacific Islander, 30% Hispanic American, 7% Native American. *Retention:* 65% of 2002 full-time freshmen returned.
Freshmen *Admission:* 126 applied, 77 admitted, 45 enrolled.
Faculty *Total:* 46, 20% full-time, 28% with terminal degrees. *Student/faculty ratio:* 24:1.
Majors Accounting; administrative assistant and secretarial science; computer engineering technology; legal assistant/paralegal.
Academic Programs *Special study options:* adult/continuing education programs, distance learning, double majors, internships, summer session for credit.
Library Academy of Business College Library with 57 serial subscriptions, a Web page.
Computers on Campus 50 computers available on campus for general student use. Internet access, at least one staffed computer lab available.
Student Life *Housing:* college housing not available. *Activities and Organizations:* Collegiate Secretaries International, Toastmasters. *Campus security:* 24-hour emergency response devices and patrols. *Student services:* personal/psychological counseling.
Standardized Tests *Required:* Wonderlic aptitude test, Nelson Denny Reading Test (for admission).
Costs (2005–06) *Tuition:* $11,952 full-time, $249 per quarter hour part-time. *Required fees:* $100 full-time.
Applying *Options:* deferred entrance. *Application fee:* $25. *Required:* high school transcript, minimum 2.0 GPA, interview. *Required for some:* essay or personal statement. *Application deadline:* rolling (freshmen). *Notification:* continuous (freshmen).
Admissions Contact Melissa Agee, Director of Admissions, Everest College, 10400 North 25th Avenue, Suite 190, Phoenix, AZ 85021. *Phone:* 602-942-4141. *Fax:* 602-943-0960.

GATEWAY COMMUNITY COLLEGE
Phoenix, Arizona

■ **State and locally supported** 2-year, founded 1968, part of Maricopa County Community College District System
■ **Calendar** semesters
■ **Degree** certificates and associate
■ **Urban** 20-acre campus
■ **Coed,** 9,377 undergraduate students, 10% full-time, 47% women, 53% men

Undergraduates 976 full-time, 8,401 part-time. Students come from 50 states and territories, 26 other countries, 5% are from out of state.

Freshmen *Admission:* 1,482 enrolled.

Faculty *Total:* 259, 27% full-time. *Student/faculty ratio:* 25:1.

Majors Accounting; aeronautical/aerospace engineering technology; automobile/automotive mechanics technology; business/commerce; carpentry; computer and information sciences; computer and information sciences related; computer programming (specific applications); computer programming (vendor/product certification); construction engineering technology; court reporting; diagnostic medical sonography and ultrasound technology; economics; education; electromechanical technology; finance; general studies; health/health care administration; heating, air conditioning and refrigeration technology; heating, air conditioning, ventilation and refrigeration maintenance technology; industrial technology; information technology; international business/trade/commerce; liberal arts and sciences/liberal studies; management science; materials science; medical radiologic technology; nuclear medical technology; nursing (registered nurse training); occupational safety and health technology; office occupations and clerical services; physical therapist assistant; pipefitting and sprinkler fitting; psychology; real estate; respiratory care therapy; social work; surgical technology; system administration.

Academic Programs *Special study options:* academic remediation for entering students, accelerated degree program, adult/continuing education programs, advanced placement credit, cooperative education, distance learning, English as a second language, honors programs, independent study, internships, part-time degree program, services for LD students, summer session for credit. *ROTC:* Army (c), Air Force (c).

Library Gateway Library with 50,000 titles, 300 serial subscriptions, an OPAC.

Computers on Campus 300 computers available on campus for general student use. Internet access, online (class) registration, at least one staffed computer lab available.

Student Life *Housing:* college housing not available. *Activities and Organizations:* student-run newspaper, Associated Students, African-American Students Association, MECHA SAMO THRACE, Volunteer Committee, VA Club. *Campus security:* 24-hour emergency response devices and patrols, student patrols, late-night transport/escort service. *Student services:* personal/psychological counseling, women's center.

Athletics Member NJCAA. *Intercollegiate sports:* cross-country running M/W, golf M/W, tennis M/W.

Standardized Tests *Required:* ACT ASSET or ACT COMPASS (for placement).

Costs (2004–05) *Tuition:* area resident $1605 full-time, $54 per credit part-time; state resident $6555 full-time, $219 per credit part-time; nonresident $6555 full-time, $219 per credit part-time. Full-time tuition and fees vary according to course load and reciprocity agreements. Part-time tuition and fees vary according to course load and reciprocity agreements. *Required fees:* $2 per credit part-time. *Payment plans:* installment, deferred payment.

Applying *Options:* common application, electronic application, early admission, deferred entrance. *Required for some:* high school transcript. *Application deadline:* rolling (freshmen), rolling (transfers). *Notification:* continuous (freshmen).

Admissions Contact Ms. Cathy Gibson, Director of Admissions and Records, GateWay Community College, 108 North 40th Street, Phoenix, AZ 85034. *Phone:* 602-286-8052. *Fax:* 602-286-8200. *E-mail:* cathy.gibson@gwmail.maricopa.edu.

GLENDALE COMMUNITY COLLEGE

Glendale, Arizona

- **State and locally supported** 2-year, founded 1965, part of Maricopa County Community College District System
- **Calendar** semesters
- **Degree** certificates and associate
- **Suburban** 160-acre campus with easy access to Phoenix
- **Endowment** $191,151
- **Coed**, 20,649 undergraduate students, 30% full-time, 56% women, 44% men

Undergraduates 6,219 full-time, 14,430 part-time. Students come from 50 states and territories, 2% are from out of state, 7% African American, 4% Asian American or Pacific Islander, 22% Hispanic American, 3% Native American, 0.6% international, 27% transferred in. *Retention:* 60% of 2002 full-time freshmen returned.

Freshmen *Admission:* 813 enrolled.

Faculty *Total:* 838, 31% full-time, 65% with terminal degrees. *Student/faculty ratio:* 24:1.

Majors Accounting technology and bookkeeping; administrative assistant and secretarial science; agribusiness; applied horticulture; architectural drafting and CAD/CADD; automobile/automotive mechanics technology; business administration and management; business/commerce; cinematography and film/video production; commercial and advertising art; computer systems networking and telecommunications; consumer merchandising/retailing management; criminal justice/law enforcement administration; criminal justice/police science; electrical, electronic and communications engineering technology; emergency medical technology (EMT paramedic); engineering technology; fire science; human services; industrial technology; kindergarten/preschool education; landscaping and groundskeeping; liberal arts and sciences/liberal studies; management information systems; nursing assistant/aide and patient care assistant; nursing (registered nurse training); public relations/image management; real estate.

Academic Programs *Special study options:* academic remediation for entering students, adult/continuing education programs, advanced placement credit, cooperative education, distance learning, double majors, English as a second language, freshman honors college, honors programs, internships, off-campus study, part-time degree program, services for LD students, summer session for credit. *ROTC:* Army (c), Air Force (c).

Library Library/Media Center plus 1 other with 79,006 titles, 406 serial subscriptions, 3,807 audiovisual materials, an OPAC, a Web page.

Computers on Campus 1500 computers available on campus for general student use. A campuswide network can be accessed from off campus. Internet access, online (class) registration, at least one staffed computer lab available.

Student Life *Housing:* college housing not available. *Activities and Organizations:* drama/theater group, student-run newspaper, choral group, marching band, LDS Student Association, Phi Theta Kappa International Honor Society, band, Glendale Association of Student Nurses, Inter-Varsity Christian Fellowship. *Campus security:* 24-hour patrols, student patrols, late-night transport/escort service. *Student services:* personal/psychological counseling, legal services.

Athletics Member NJCAA. *Intercollegiate sports:* baseball M(s), basketball M(s)/W(s), cross-country running M(s)/W(s), football M(s), golf M(s), soccer M(s)/W(s), softball W(s), tennis M(s)/W(s), track and field M(s)/W(s), volleyball W(s). *Intramural sports:* golf M, racquetball M/W, softball W, tennis M/W, volleyball W.

Standardized Tests *Required for some:* ACT ASSET.

Costs (2004–05) *Tuition:* area resident $1320 full-time, $55 per credit hour part-time; nonresident $5280 full-time, $220 per credit hour part-time. *Required fees:* $10 full-time, $5 per term part-time. *Waivers:* employees or children of employees.

Financial Aid Of all full-time matriculated undergraduates who enrolled in 2003, 350 Federal Work-Study jobs (averaging $1700).

Applying *Options:* common application, electronic application. *Required for some:* high school transcript. *Application deadlines:* 8/23 (freshmen), 8/23 (transfers). *Notification:* continuous until 8/23 (freshmen).

Admissions Contact Mrs. Mary Lou Massal, Senior Associate Dean of Student Services, Glendale Community College, 6000 West Olive Avenue, Glendale, AZ 85302. *Phone:* 623-435-3305. *Toll-free phone:* 623-845-3000. *Fax:* 623-845-3303. *E-mail:* info@gc.maricopa.edu.

HIGH-TECH INSTITUTE

Phoenix, Arizona

- **Proprietary** primarily 2-year
- **Calendar** semesters
- **Degrees** diplomas, associate, and bachelor's
- **Urban** 4-acre campus
- **Coed**

Faculty *Student/faculty ratio:* 27:1.

Financial Aid Of all full-time matriculated undergraduates who enrolled in 2003, 29 Federal Work-Study jobs (averaging $2500).

Applying *Required:* high school transcript.

Admissions Contact Mr. Glen Husband, Vice President of Admissions, High-Tech Institute, 1515 East Indian School Road, Phoenix, AZ 85014-4901. *Phone:* 602-279-9700. *Fax:* 602-279-2999.

INTERNATIONAL INSTITUTE OF THE AMERICAS

Mesa, Arizona

Admissions Contact 925 South Gilbert Road, Suite 201, Mesa, AZ 85204-4448. *Toll-free phone:* 888-886-2428.

INTERNATIONAL INSTITUTE OF THE AMERICAS

Phoenix, Arizona

Admissions Contact Dr. Lynda K. Angel, Vice President, International Institute of the Americas, 4136 North 75th Avenue, Suite 211, Phoenix, AZ 85033-3196. *Phone:* 602-242-6265. *Toll-free phone:* 888-884-2428.

INTERNATIONAL INSTITUTE OF THE AMERICAS
Phoenix, Arizona

- **Independent** primarily 2-year, founded 1979
- **Calendar** semesters
- **Degrees** certificates, diplomas, associate, and bachelor's
- **Urban** campus
- **Coed**

Faculty *Student/faculty ratio:* 17:1.
Student Life *Campus security:* 24-hour emergency response devices.
Applying *Options:* electronic application, early admission, deferred entrance. *Required:* interview.
Admissions Contact John Pechota, Admissions Director, International Institute of the Americas, 6049 North 43 Avenue, Phoenix, AZ 85019. *Phone:* 800-793-2428. *Toll-free phone:* 800-793-2428. *Fax:* 602-973-2572. *E-mail:* info@aibt.edu.

INTERNATIONAL INSTITUTE OF THE AMERICAS
Tucson, Arizona

Admissions Contact Mrs. Leigh Anne Pechota, Director, International Institute of the Americas, 5441 East 22nd Street, Suite 125, Tucson, AZ 85711-5444. *Phone:* 520-748-9799. *Toll-free phone:* 888-292-2428.

ITT TECHNICAL INSTITUTE
Phoenix, Arizona

Admissions Contact Mr. Gene McWhorter, Director of Recruitment, ITT Technical Institute, 4837 East McDowell Road, Phoenix, AZ 85008. *Phone:* 602-252-2331. *Toll-free phone:* 800-879-4881. *Fax:* 602-267-8727.

ITT TECHNICAL INSTITUTE
Tucson, Arizona

- **Proprietary** primarily 2-year, founded 1984, part of ITT Educational Services, Inc
- **Calendar** quarters
- **Degrees** associate and bachelor's
- **Urban** 3-acre campus
- **Coed**

Standardized Tests *Required:* Wonderlic aptitude test (for admission).
Costs (2004–05) *Tuition:* Please see school catalog for specific information.
Applying *Options:* deferred entrance. *Application fee:* $100. *Required:* high school transcript, interview. *Recommended:* letters of recommendation.
Admissions Contact Ms. Linda Lemken, Director of Recruitment, ITT Technical Institute, 1455 West River Road, Tucson, AZ 85704. *Phone:* 520-408-7488. *Toll-free phone:* 800-870-9730. *Fax:* 520-292-9899.

LAMSON COLLEGE
Tempe, Arizona

Admissions Contact Mr. Chico Chavez, Director of Admissions, Lamson College, 1126 North Scottsdale Road, Suite 17, Tempe, AZ 85281. *Phone:* 480-898-7000. *Toll-free phone:* 800-898-7017.

LONG TECHNICAL COLLEGE
Phoenix, Arizona

Admissions Contact Mr. Michael S. Savely, Executive Director, Long Technical College, 13450 North Black Canyon Highway, Suite 104, Phoenix, AZ 85029. *Phone:* 602-548-1955. *Toll-free phone:* 877-548-1955.

MESA COMMUNITY COLLEGE
Mesa, Arizona

Admissions Contact Ms. Carol Petersen, Director, Admissions and Records, Mesa Community College, 1833 West Southern Avenue, Mesa, AZ 85202-4866. *Phone:* 480-461-7478. *Fax:* 480-461-7805. *E-mail:* admissions@mc.maricopa.edu.

MOHAVE COMMUNITY COLLEGE
Kingman, Arizona

- **State-supported** 2-year, founded 1971
- **Calendar** semesters
- **Degree** certificates and associate
- **Small-town** 160-acre campus
- **Coed**, 6,187 undergraduate students, 20% full-time, 67% women, 33% men

Undergraduates 1,208 full-time, 4,979 part-time. Students come from 8 states and territories, 8% are from out of state, 0.7% African American, 2% Asian American or Pacific Islander, 13% Hispanic American, 2% Native American.
Freshmen *Admission:* 332 applied, 332 admitted, 332 enrolled.
Faculty *Total:* 589, 10% full-time, 5% with terminal degrees. *Student/faculty ratio:* 13:1.
Majors Accounting; art; automobile/automotive mechanics technology; business administration and management; ceramic arts and ceramics; computer and information sciences related; computer programming (specific applications); computer science; criminal justice/police science; English; fire science; health science; history; information technology; liberal arts and sciences/liberal studies; marketing/marketing management; mathematics; metal and jewelry arts; music; nursing (registered nurse training); psychology; sociology; word processing.
Academic Programs *Special study options:* academic remediation for entering students, adult/continuing education programs, distance learning, English as a second language, independent study, part-time degree program, summer session for credit.
Library Mohave Community College Library with 45,849 titles, 476 serial subscriptions.
Computers on Campus 120 computers available on campus for general student use. At least one staffed computer lab available.
Student Life *Housing:* college housing not available. *Activities and Organizations:* drama/theater group, student-run newspaper, choral group, Art Club, Pottery Club, Astronomy Club, Phi Theta Kappa, national fraternities, national sororities. *Campus security:* 24-hour emergency response devices, late-night transport/escort service.
Standardized Tests *Recommended:* SAT and SAT Subject Tests or ACT (for placement).
Costs (2005–06) *Tuition:* state resident $1104 full-time, $46 per credit hour part-time; nonresident $3312 full-time, $138 per credit hour part-time. Part-time tuition and fees vary according to course load. *Waivers:* employees or children of employees.
Applying *Options:* early admission, deferred entrance. *Required for some:* high school transcript, interview. *Recommended:* minimum 2.0 GPA. *Application deadline:* rolling (freshmen), rolling (transfers). *Notification:* continuous (freshmen).
Admissions Contact Mr. John Wilson, Registrar/Director of Enrollment Services, Mohave Community College, 1971 Jagerson Avenue, Kingman, AZ 86401. *Phone:* 928-757-0847. *Toll-free phone:* 888-664-2832. *Fax:* 928-757-0808. *E-mail:* thinkmcc@mohave.edu.

NORTHLAND PIONEER COLLEGE
Holbrook, Arizona

- **State and locally supported** 2-year, founded 1974, part of Arizona State Community College System
- **Calendar** semesters
- **Degree** certificates and associate
- **Rural** 50-acre campus
- **Coed**

Faculty *Student/faculty ratio:* 14:1.
Student Life *Campus security:* evening security.
Costs (2004–05) *Tuition:* state resident $912 full-time, $38 per credit part-time; nonresident $6000 full-time, $65 per credit part-time. *Room and board:* room only: $1500.
Financial Aid Of all full-time matriculated undergraduates who enrolled in 2003, 80 Federal Work-Study jobs (averaging $4000).
Applying *Options:* early admission.
Admissions Contact Ms. Dawn Edgmon, Coordinator of Admissions, Northland Pioneer College, PO Box 610, Holbrook, AZ 86025-0610. *Phone:* 928-536-6257. *Toll-free phone:* 800-266-7845. *Fax:* 928-536-6211.

PARADISE VALLEY COMMUNITY COLLEGE
Phoenix, Arizona

- **State and locally supported** 2-year, founded 1985, part of Maricopa County Community College District System

- **Calendar** semesters
- **Degree** certificates and associate
- **Urban** campus
- **Coed,** 8,237 undergraduate students, 26% full-time, 60% women, 40% men

Undergraduates 2,118 full-time, 6,119 part-time. 3% African American, 3% Asian American or Pacific Islander, 10% Hispanic American, 1% Native American.

Faculty *Total:* 344, 24% full-time.

Majors Accounting; administrative assistant and secretarial science; business administration and management; computer typography and composition equipment operation; international business/trade/commerce; liberal arts and sciences/liberal studies; occupational safety and health technology.

Academic Programs *Special study options:* academic remediation for entering students, adult/continuing education programs, advanced placement credit, cooperative education, distance learning, honors programs, services for LD students, summer session for credit.

Library Paradise Valley Community College Library plus 1 other with an OPAC, a Web page.

Computers on Campus 500 computers available on campus for general student use. Internet access, at least one staffed computer lab available.

Student Life *Housing:* college housing not available. *Activities and Organizations:* drama/theater group, student-run newspaper, choral group, Phi Theta Kappa, International Student Club, Recreational Outing Club, AWARE, Student Christian Association. *Campus security:* 24-hour emergency response devices, late-night transport/escort service. *Student services:* personal/psychological counseling.

Athletics Member NJCAA. *Intercollegiate sports:* cross-country running M/W, golf M/W, soccer M/W, softball W, tennis M/W, track and field M/W.

Costs (2004–05) *Tuition:* area resident $1650 full-time; state resident $55 per hour part-time; nonresident $2400 full-time, $80 per hour part-time.

Financial Aid Of all full-time matriculated undergraduates who enrolled in 2003, 50 Federal Work-Study jobs (averaging $2500).

Applying *Options:* early admission. *Application deadline:* rolling (freshmen), rolling (transfers).

Admissions Contact Dr. Shirley Green, Associate Dean of Student Services, Paradise Valley Community College, 18401 North 32nd Street, Phoenix, AZ 85032. *Phone:* 602-787-7020. *Fax:* 602-787-7025.

THE PARALEGAL INSTITUTE, INC.
Phoenix, Arizona

Admissions Contact Mr. John W. Morrison, President, The Paralegal Institute, Inc., 2933 West Indian School Road, Drawer 11408, Phoenix, AZ 85061-1408. *Phone:* 602-212-6501. *Toll-free phone:* 800-354-1254. *E-mail:* paralegalinst@mindspring.com.

PHOENIX COLLEGE
Phoenix, Arizona

- **State and locally supported** 2-year, founded 1920, part of Maricopa County Community College District System
- **Calendar** semesters
- **Degree** certificates, diplomas, and associate
- **Urban** 52-acre campus
- **Coed**

Student Life *Campus security:* 24-hour emergency response devices, student patrols, late-night transport/escort service.

Athletics Member NJCAA.

Standardized Tests *Required:* ACT ASSET (for placement).

Costs (2004–05) *Tuition:* area resident $1320 full-time, $55 per credit hour part-time; state resident $5280 full-time, $220 per credit hour part-time; nonresident $220 per credit hour part-time. *Required fees:* $10 full-time, $5 per term part-time.

Financial Aid Of all full-time matriculated undergraduates who enrolled in 2003, 350 Federal Work-Study jobs (averaging $2800).

Applying *Options:* common application, electronic application, early admission, deferred entrance.

Admissions Contact Ms. Donna Fischer, Supervisor of Admissions and Records, Phoenix College, Phoenix, AZ 85013. *Phone:* 602-285-7500. *Fax:* 602-285-7813.

PIMA COMMUNITY COLLEGE
Tucson, Arizona

- **State and locally supported** 2-year, founded 1966
- **Calendar** semesters

- **Degrees** certificates, associate, and postbachelor's certificates
- **Urban** 483-acre campus
- **Coed,** 31,555 undergraduate students, 30% full-time, 57% women, 43% men

Undergraduates 9,565 full-time, 21,990 part-time. Students come from 40 states and territories, 64 other countries, 3% are from out of state, 4% African American, 3% Asian American or Pacific Islander, 31% Hispanic American, 4% Native American, 1% international, 9% transferred in.

Freshmen *Admission:* 5,890 applied, 5,890 admitted, 5,890 enrolled. *Test scores:* ACT scores over 18: 52%; ACT scores over 24: 14%; ACT scores over 30: 2%.

Faculty *Total:* 1,367, 22% full-time. *Student/faculty ratio:* 21:1.

Majors Accounting; administrative assistant and secretarial science; aircraft powerplant technology; American Indian/Native American studies; anthropology; archeology; architectural drafting and CAD/CADD; art; Asian studies; automobile/automotive mechanics technology; banking and financial support services; building/construction finishing, management, and inspection related; building/property maintenance and management; business administration and management; child care and support services management; child care provision; commercial and advertising art; computer and information sciences; computer systems analysis; computer systems networking and telecommunications; computer technology/computer systems technology; construction engineering technology; criminal justice/police science; criminal justice/safety; dental hygiene; dental laboratory technology; design and visual communications; dramatic/theatre arts; electrical, electronic and communications engineering technology; emergency medical technology (EMT paramedic); environmental engineering technology; fire science; general studies; gerontology; hospitality administration; hotel/motel administration; industrial engineering; international business/trade/commerce; journalism; legal assistant/paralegal; liberal arts and sciences/liberal studies; machine shop technology; medical administrative assistant and medical secretary; medical radiologic technology; music; nursing (registered nurse training); pharmacy technician; political science and government; radio and television; real estate; respiratory care therapy; restaurant, culinary, and catering management; security and protective services related; sign language interpretation and translation; sociology; speech and rhetoric; tourism and travel services management; veterinary/animal health technology; welding technology.

Academic Programs *Special study options:* academic remediation for entering students, accelerated degree program, adult/continuing education programs, advanced placement credit, cooperative education, distance learning, double majors, English as a second language, freshman honors college, honors programs, independent study, internships, part-time degree program, services for LD students, student-designed majors, summer session for credit. *ROTC:* Army (c), Navy (c), Air Force (c).

Library Pima College Library with 217,049 titles, 984 serial subscriptions, 24,005 audiovisual materials, an OPAC, a Web page.

Computers on Campus 2500 computers available on campus for general student use. A campuswide network can be accessed from off campus. Internet access, online (class) registration, at least one staffed computer lab available.

Student Life *Housing:* college housing not available. *Activities and Organizations:* drama/theater group, student-run newspaper, choral group. *Campus security:* 24-hour emergency response devices and patrols, late-night transport/escort service. *Student services:* personal/psychological counseling, women's center.

Athletics Member NJCAA. *Intercollegiate sports:* baseball M(s), basketball M(s)/W(s), cheerleading W, cross-country running M(s)/W(s), football M(s), golf M(s)/W(s), soccer M(s)/W(s), softball W(s), tennis M(s)/W(s), track and field M(s)/W(s), volleyball W(s). *Intramural sports:* badminton M/W, basketball M/W, cross-country running M/W, equestrian sports M(c)/W(c), football M, golf M/W, ice hockey M(c), racquetball M/W, tennis M/W, track and field M/W, volleyball M/W, wrestling M(c).

Standardized Tests *Recommended:* SAT or ACT (for placement).

Costs (2004–05) *Tuition:* state resident $1008 full-time, $42 per credit part-time; nonresident $5064 full-time, $72 per credit part-time. *Required fees:* $70 full-time, $3 per credit part-time, $5 per term part-time. *Waivers:* employees or children of employees.

Applying *Options:* common application, early admission. *Application fee:* $5. *Application deadline:* rolling (freshmen), rolling (transfers).

Admissions Contact Dr. Wendy Kilgore, Director of Enrollment Services and Registration, Pima Community College, 4905B East Broadway Boulevard, Tucson, AZ 85709-1120. *Phone:* 520-206-4640. *Fax:* 520-206-4790.

PIMA MEDICAL INSTITUTE
Mesa, Arizona

- **Proprietary** 2-year, founded 1985, part of Vocational Training Institutes, Inc
- **Calendar** modular
- **Degree** certificates and associate
- **Urban** campus
- **Coed,** 592 undergraduate students

Faculty *Student/faculty ratio:* 15:1.

Pima Medical Institute (continued)

Majors Radiologic technology/science; respiratory therapy technician.

Student Life *Housing:* college housing not available.

Standardized Tests *Required:* Wonderlic aptitude test (for admission).

Applying *Required:* interview. *Required for some:* high school transcript.

Admissions Contact Admissions Office, Pima Medical Institute, Pima Medical Institute, 957 South Dobson Road, Mesa, AZ 85202. *Phone:* 480-644-0267 Ext. 225. *Toll-free phone:* 888-898-9048.

PIMA MEDICAL INSTITUTE
Tucson, Arizona

- **Proprietary** 2-year, founded 1972, part of Vocational Training Institutes, Inc
- **Calendar** modular
- **Degree** certificates and associate
- **Urban** campus
- **Coed,** 711 undergraduate students, 100% full-time, 81% women, 19% men

Undergraduates 711 full-time.

Freshmen *Admission:* 120 applied, 116 admitted, 116 enrolled.

Faculty *Total:* 36, 17% full-time. *Student/faculty ratio:* 13:1.

Majors Physical therapist assistant; radiologic technology/science; respiratory therapy technician.

Academic Programs *Special study options:* academic remediation for entering students, accelerated degree program, adult/continuing education programs, cooperative education, internships.

Library Resource Center with an OPAC, a Web page.

Computers on Campus 30 computers available on campus for general student use. A campuswide network can be accessed. Internet access, at least one staffed computer lab available.

Student Life *Housing:* college housing not available.

Standardized Tests *Required:* Wonderlic Scholastic Level Exam (for admission).

Applying *Options:* common application, early admission. *Application fee:* $150. *Required:* interview. *Required for some:* high school transcript.

Admissions Contact Admissions Office, Pima Medical Institute, Pima Medical Institute, 3350 East Grant Road, Tucson, AZ 85716-2800. *Phone:* 520-326-1600 Ext. 5112. *Toll-free phone:* 888-898-9048.

THE REFRIGERATION SCHOOL
Phoenix, Arizona

- **Proprietary** 2-year
- **Calendar** continuous
- **Degree** certificates, diplomas, and associate
- **Urban** campus
- **Coed**

Faculty *Student/faculty ratio:* 38:1.

Admissions Contact Ms. Mary Simmons, Admissions Director, The Refrigeration School, 4210 East Washington Street, Phoenix, AZ 85034-1816. *Phone:* 602-275-7133. *Fax:* 602-267-4805. *E-mail:* Admissions@rsiaz.org.

RIO SALADO COLLEGE
Tempe, Arizona

Admissions Contact Ms. Ruby Miller, Supervisor of Admissions and Records, Rio Salado College, 2323 West 14th Street, Tempe, AZ 85281-6950. *Phone:* 480-517-8152. *Toll-free phone:* 800-729-1197. *Fax:* 480-517-8199. *E-mail:* admission@email.rio.maricopa.edu.

SCOTTSDALE COMMUNITY COLLEGE
Scottsdale, Arizona

- **State and locally supported** 2-year, founded 1969, part of Maricopa County Community College District System
- **Calendar** semesters
- **Degree** certificates, diplomas, and associate
- **Urban** 160-acre campus with easy access to Phoenix
- **Coed**

Faculty *Student/faculty ratio:* 20:1.

Student Life *Campus security:* 24-hour emergency response devices and patrols, student patrols, late-night transport/escort service, 24-hour automatic surveillance cameras.

Athletics Member NJCAA.

Standardized Tests *Required for some:* ACT ASSET. *Recommended:* ACT ASSET.

Costs (2004–05) *Tuition:* area resident $1650 full-time, $55 per credit hour part-time; state resident $6600 full-time, $214 per credit hour part-time; nonresident $6600 full-time, $220 per credit hour part-time. *Required fees:* $10 full-time.

Financial Aid Of all full-time matriculated undergraduates who enrolled in 2003, 75 Federal Work-Study jobs (averaging $2000). *Financial aid deadline:* 7/15.

Applying *Options:* early admission.

Admissions Contact Ms. Fran Watkins, Supervisor of Admissions and Records, Scottsdale Community College, 9000 East Chaparral Road, Scottsdale, AZ 85256. *Phone:* 602-423-6128. *Fax:* 480-423-6200. *E-mail:* fran.watkins@sccmail.maricopa.edu.

SCOTTSDALE CULINARY INSTITUTE
Scottsdale, Arizona

Admissions Contact Mr. Jon Alberts, President, Scottsdale Culinary Institute, 8100 East Camelback Road, Suite 1001, Scottsdale, AZ 85251-3940. *Phone:* 800-848-2433. *Toll-free phone:* 800-848-2433.

SOUTH MOUNTAIN COMMUNITY COLLEGE
Phoenix, Arizona

- **State and locally supported** 2-year, founded 1979, part of Maricopa County Community College District System
- **Calendar** semesters
- **Degree** certificates and associate
- **Suburban** 108-acre campus
- **Coed,** 3,933 undergraduate students

Undergraduates 2% are from out of state, 14% African American, 2% Asian American or Pacific Islander, 43% Hispanic American, 4% Native American.

Faculty *Total:* 195, 25% full-time, 100% with terminal degrees.

Majors Administrative assistant and secretarial science; art; biology/biological sciences; business administration and management; chemistry; computer typography and composition equipment operation; family and consumer sciences/human sciences; history; information science/studies; liberal arts and sciences/liberal studies; mass communication/media; mathematics; music; physical education teaching and coaching; physics; political science and government; pre-engineering; psychology; sociology.

Academic Programs *Special study options:* academic remediation for entering students, adult/continuing education programs, advanced placement credit, cooperative education, English as a second language, honors programs, part-time degree program, services for LD students, summer session for credit. *ROTC:* Air Force (c).

Library Learning Resource Center with 35,591 titles, 475 serial subscriptions, an OPAC.

Computers on Campus 150 computers available on campus for general student use. Internet access, at least one staffed computer lab available.

Student Life *Housing:* college housing not available. *Campus security:* late-night transport/escort service, 18-hour patrols, campus lockdown. *Student services:* legal services.

Athletics Member NJCAA. *Intercollegiate sports:* baseball M, basketball M/W, cross-country running M/W, soccer M, softball W, tennis M/W, track and field M/W, volleyball W.

Costs (2005–06) *Tuition:* area resident $1440 full-time; state resident $6192 full-time; nonresident $6192 full-time. *Required fees:* $10 full-time.

Financial Aid Of all full-time matriculated undergraduates who enrolled in 2003, 36 Federal Work-Study jobs (averaging $2000).

Applying *Application deadlines:* 8/22 (freshmen), 8/22 (transfers). *Notification:* continuous until 8/22 (freshmen).

Admissions Contact Mr. Tony Bracamonte, Senior Associate Dean of Enrollment Services, South Mountain Community College, 7050 South 24th Street, Phoenix, AZ 85042. *Phone:* 602-243-8120. *Fax:* 602-243-8329. *E-mail:* bracamonte@smc.maricopa.edu.

SOUTHWEST INSTITUTE OF HEALING ARTS
Tempe, Arizona

Admissions Contact Katie Yearous, Student Advisor, Southwest Institute of Healing Arts, 1100 East Apache Boulevard, Tempe, AZ 85281. *Phone:* 480-994-9244. *Toll-free phone:* 888-504-9106.

TOHONO O'ODHAM COMMUNITY COLLEGE
Sells, Arizona

- **Independent** 2-year, founded 1998
- **Calendar** semesters
- **Degree** certificates, diplomas, and associate
- **Coed,** 171 undergraduate students

Undergraduates Students come from 1 other state, 97% Native American.
Costs (2004–05) *Tuition:* state resident $1260 full-time, $42 per credit hour part-time; nonresident $6330 full-time, $72 per credit hour part-time. Full-time tuition and fees vary according to course load. Part-time tuition and fees vary according to course load. *Required fees:* $10 full-time, $10 per term part-time. *Payment plan:* deferred payment.
Applying *Application fee:* $25 (non-residents).
Admissions Contact Tohono O'odham Community College, PO Box 3129 À, Sells, AZ 85634. *Phone:* 520-383-8401. *Fax:* 520-383-8403.

UNIVERSAL TECHNICAL INSTITUTE
Avondale, Arizona

- **Private** 2-year
- **Degree** associate

Faculty *Total:* 107, 100% full-time. *Student/faculty ratio:* 30:1.
Applying *Required:* interview.
Admissions Contact 10695 W. Pierce Street, Avondale, AZ 85323-7946. *Toll-free phone:* 800-859-1202.

YAVAPAI COLLEGE
Prescott, Arizona

- **State and locally supported** 2-year, founded 1966, part of Arizona State Community College System
- **Calendar** semesters
- **Degree** certificates and associate
- **Small-town** 100-acre campus
- **Coed,** 7,375 undergraduate students, 19% full-time, 62% women, 38% men

Undergraduates 1,369 full-time, 6,006 part-time. Students come from 30 states and territories, 5% are from out of state, 1% African American, 1% Asian American or Pacific Islander, 7% Hispanic American, 5% Native American, 5% live on campus.
Freshmen *Admission:* 700 enrolled.
Faculty *Total:* 451, 20% full-time. *Student/faculty ratio:* 13:1.
Majors Accounting; administrative assistant and secretarial science; agribusiness; agricultural business and management; agriculture; aquaculture; architectural drafting and CAD/CADD; automobile/automotive mechanics technology; business administration and management; commercial and advertising art; construction engineering technology; criminal justice/police science; education related; equestrian studies; film/cinema studies; fine arts related; fire science; graphic design; gunsmithing; horse husbandry/equine science and management; information science/studies; legal administrative assistant/secretary; legal assistant/paralegal; liberal arts and sciences/liberal studies; nursing (registered nurse training).
Academic Programs *Special study options:* academic remediation for entering students, adult/continuing education programs, advanced placement credit, cooperative education, distance learning, English as a second language, honors programs, independent study, internships, off-campus study, part-time degree program, services for LD students, summer session for credit. *ROTC:* Army (c), Air Force (c).
Library Yavapai College Library with 81,144 titles, 1,091 serial subscriptions, an OPAC, a Web page.
Computers on Campus 677 computers available on campus for general student use. A campuswide network can be accessed from student residence rooms and from off campus. Internet access, at least one staffed computer lab available.
Student Life *Housing Options:* coed. Campus housing is university owned. *Activities and Organizations:* drama/theater group, student-run newspaper, choral group, Re-Entry Club, Student Nurses Association, Native American Club, International Club, VICA. *Campus security:* 24-hour emergency response devices and patrols, student patrols, late-night transport/escort service, controlled dormitory access. *Student services:* health clinic, personal/psychological counseling, women's center.
Athletics Member NJCAA. *Intercollegiate sports:* baseball M(s), basketball M(s)/W(s), cross-country running W(s), soccer M(s), volleyball W(s).
Standardized Tests *Recommended:* SAT or ACT (for placement).

Costs (2005–06) *Tuition:* state resident $912 full-time, $38 per credit part-time; nonresident $6312 full-time, $48 per credit part-time. Full-time tuition and fees vary according to program. *Required fees:* $72 full-time, $3 per credit part-time. *Room and board:* $4310. Room and board charges vary according to board plan. *Payment plans:* installment, deferred payment. *Waivers:* employees or children of employees.
Applying *Options:* early admission, deferred entrance. *Required:* high school transcript. *Required for some:* essay or personal statement, letters of recommendation. *Application deadline:* rolling (freshmen), rolling (transfers).
Admissions Contact Mr. David Vanness, Admissions, Registration, and Records Manager, Yavapai College, 1100 East Sheldon Street, Prescott, AZ 86301-3297. *Phone:* 928-776-2188. *Toll-free phone:* 800-922-6787. *Fax:* 520-776-2151. *E-mail:* registration@yc.edu.

ARKANSAS

ARKANSAS NORTHEASTERN COLLEGE
Blytheville, Arkansas

- **State-supported** 2-year, founded 1975
- **Calendar** semesters
- **Degree** certificates and associate
- **Rural** 80-acre campus with easy access to Memphis
- **Endowment** $3681
- **Coed,** 2,018 undergraduate students, 55% full-time, 71% women, 29% men

Undergraduates 1,117 full-time, 901 part-time. Students come from 3 states and territories, 19% are from out of state, 32% African American, 1% Asian American or Pacific Islander, 0.6% Hispanic American, 0.3% Native American, 5% transferred in. *Retention:* 50% of 2002 full-time freshmen returned.
Freshmen *Admission:* 562 applied, 562 admitted, 400 enrolled.
Faculty *Total:* 179, 42% full-time, 4% with terminal degrees. *Student/faculty ratio:* 24:1.
Majors Agriculture; applied horticulture; business/commerce; child care and support services management; criminal justice/police science; drafting; general studies; industrial mechanics and maintenance technology; industrial production technologies related; industrial technology; metallurgical technology; middle school education; nursing (registered nurse training); welding technology.
Academic Programs *Special study options:* academic remediation for entering students, adult/continuing education programs, advanced placement credit, distance learning, double majors, part-time degree program, summer session for credit.
Library Adams/Vines Library with 15,493 titles, 165 serial subscriptions, 682 audiovisual materials, an OPAC.
Computers on Campus 280 computers available on campus for general student use. A campuswide network can be accessed. Internet access, at least one staffed computer lab available.
Student Life *Housing:* college housing not available. *Activities and Organizations:* choral group, Gamma Beta Phi, Association of Childhood Education International, Nursing Club, Cultural Diversity, Adult Student Association. *Campus security:* 24-hour patrols.
Standardized Tests *Required:* ACT ASSET (for placement). *Recommended:* ACT (for placement).
Costs (2004–05) *Tuition:* area resident $1410 full-time, $47 per semester hour part-time; state resident $1710 full-time, $57 per semester hour part-time; nonresident $3210 full-time, $107 per semester hour part-time. *Required fees:* $160 full-time, $4 per semester hour part-time, $20 per term part-time. *Payment plans:* installment, deferred payment. *Waivers:* senior citizens and employees or children of employees.
Financial Aid Of all full-time matriculated undergraduates who enrolled in 2003, 42 Federal Work-Study jobs (averaging $2500).
Applying *Options:* deferred entrance. *Recommended:* high school transcript. *Application deadline:* rolling (freshmen), rolling (transfers). *Notification:* continuous (freshmen).
Admissions Contact Mrs. Leslie Wells, Admissions Counselor, Arkansas Northeastern College, PO Box 1109, Blytheville, AR 72316. *Phone:* 870-762-1020 Ext. 1118. *Fax:* 870-763-1654. *E-mail:* lwells@anc.edu.

ARKANSAS STATE UNIVERSITY-BEEBE
Beebe, Arkansas

- **State-supported** 2-year, founded 1927, part of Arkansas State University System
- **Calendar** semesters
- **Degree** certificates and associate

Arkansas State University-Beebe (continued)
■ **Small-town** 320-acre campus with easy access to Memphis
■ **Coed**

Faculty *Student/faculty ratio:* 30:1.
Student Life *Campus security:* 24-hour emergency response devices and patrols.
Standardized Tests *Recommended:* ACT (for placement).
Costs (2004–05) *Tuition:* state resident $60 per credit hour part-time; nonresident $110 per credit hour part-time. Full-time tuition and fees vary according to course load. *Required fees:* $8 per credit hour part-time.
Financial Aid Of all full-time matriculated undergraduates who enrolled in 2003, 36 Federal Work-Study jobs (averaging $1800). 112 state and other part-time jobs (averaging $750).
Applying *Options:* common application, deferred entrance. *Required:* high school transcript.
Admissions Contact Mr. James Washburn, Director of Admissions, Arkansas State University-Beebe, PO Box 1000, Beebe, AR 72012-1000. *Phone:* 501-882-8280. *Toll-free phone:* 800-632-9985. *Fax:* 501-882-8370. *E-mail:* rahayes@asub.arknet.edu.

ARKANSAS STATE UNIVERSITY-MOUNTAIN HOME
Mountain Home, Arkansas

■ **State-supported** 2-year, part of Arkansas State University
■ **Calendar** semesters
■ **Degree** certificates and associate
■ **Small-town** 136-acre campus
■ **Endowment** $2.5 million
■ **Coed,** 1,313 undergraduate students, 54% full-time, 63% women, 37% men

Undergraduates 707 full-time, 606 part-time. Students come from 11 states and territories, 3 other countries, 0.1% are from out of state, 11% transferred in.
Freshmen *Admission:* 425 applied, 308 admitted, 308 enrolled.
Faculty *Total:* 62, 61% full-time, 24% with terminal degrees. *Student/faculty ratio:* 21:1.
Majors Audiology and hearing sciences; business automation/technology/data entry; criminal justice/law enforcement administration; criminal justice/safety; emergency medical technology (EMT paramedic); forensic science and technology; funeral service and mortuary science; information science/studies; liberal arts and sciences/liberal studies; middle school education; opticianry.
Academic Programs *Special study options:* academic remediation for entering students, advanced placement credit, cooperative education, distance learning, independent study, part-time degree program, services for LD students, summer session for credit.
Library Norma Wood Library with 30,682 titles, 6,634 serial subscriptions, 2,150 audiovisual materials, an OPAC, a Web page.
Computers on Campus 60 computers available on campus for general student use. A campuswide network can be accessed from off campus. Internet access, online (class) registration, at least one staffed computer lab available.
Student Life *Housing:* college housing not available. *Activities and Organizations:* drama/theater group, choral group, Phi Theta Kappa, Circle K, Criminal Justice Club, Mortuary Science Club, Student Ambassadors.
Standardized Tests *Required:* ACT ASSET or ACT COMPASS (for placement). *Recommended:* ACT (for placement).
Costs (2005–06) *Tuition:* state resident $1920 full-time, $64 per credit part-time; nonresident $3300 full-time, $110 per credit part-time. Full-time tuition and fees vary according to course load. Part-time tuition and fees vary according to course load. *Required fees:* $240 full-time, $8 per credit part-time. *Room and board:* Room and board charges vary according to housing facility. *Payment plan:* installment. *Waivers:* children of alumni, senior citizens, and employees or children of employees.
Financial Aid Of all full-time matriculated undergraduates who enrolled in 2003, 14 Federal Work-Study jobs (averaging $3200).
Applying *Required:* high school transcript. *Recommended:* placement scores. *Notification:* continuous (freshmen).
Admissions Contact Ms. Tonya Sexton, Recruiter, Arkansas State University-Mountain Home, 1600 South College Street, Mountain Home, AR 72653. *Phone:* 870-508-6262. *Fax:* 870-508-6287. *E-mail:* tsexton@asumh.edu.

ARKANSAS STATE UNIVERSITY-NEWPORT
Newport, Arkansas

Admissions Contact Ms. Tara Byrd, Registrar, Director of Admissions, Arkansas State University-Newport, 7648 Victory Boulevard, Newport, AR 72112. *Phone:* 870-512-7800. *Toll-free phone:* 800-976-1676. *Fax:* 870-512-7825. *E-mail:* tlbryd@asun.arknet.edu.

BLACK RIVER TECHNICAL COLLEGE
Pocahontas, Arkansas

■ **State-supported** 2-year, founded 1972
■ **Calendar** semesters
■ **Degree** associate
■ **Small-town** 55-acre campus
■ **Coed,** 1,243 undergraduate students, 52% full-time, 56% women, 44% men

Undergraduates 652 full-time, 591 part-time. Students come from 2 states and territories.
Freshmen *Admission:* 151 enrolled. *Test scores:* ACT scores over 18: 25%; ACT scores over 24: 10%.
Faculty *Total:* 70, 43% full-time. *Student/faculty ratio:* 16:1.
Majors Avionics maintenance technology; business administration and management; data processing and data processing technology; dietetics; emergency medical technology (EMT paramedic); fire science; industrial technology; information science/studies; liberal arts and sciences/liberal studies; nursing (registered nurse training).
Academic Programs *Special study options:* academic remediation for entering students, cooperative education, honors programs, internships, part-time degree program, services for LD students, student-designed majors, summer session for credit.
Library Black River Technical College Library with 10,000 titles, 200 serial subscriptions, an OPAC.
Computers on Campus 100 computers available on campus for general student use. At least one staffed computer lab available.
Student Life *Housing:* college housing not available. *Campus security:* night patrol.
Standardized Tests *Required for some:* ACT, ACT ASSET, or SAT I.
Costs (2004–05) *Tuition:* area resident $1560 full-time, $52 per credit hour part-time; state resident $1980 full-time, $66 per credit hour part-time; nonresident $5340 full-time, $178 per credit hour part-time. *Required fees:* $90 full-time, $3 per credit hour part-time.
Applying *Options:* common application. *Required for some:* high school transcript, interview. *Application deadline:* rolling (freshmen), rolling (transfers).
Admissions Contact Mr. Jim Ulmer, Director of Admissions, Black River Technical College, 1410 Highway 304 East, Pocahontas, AR 72455. *Phone:* 870-892-4565. *Toll-free phone:* 800-919-3086. *Fax:* 870-892-3546.

COSSATOT COMMUNITY COLLEGE OF THE UNIVERSITY OF ARKANSAS
De Queen, Arkansas

■ **State-supported** 2-year, founded 1991, part of University of Arkansas System
■ **Calendar** semesters
■ **Degree** certificates and associate
■ **Rural** campus
■ **Coed,** 1,067 undergraduate students

Undergraduates Students come from 6 states and territories, 12% African American, 0.3% Asian American or Pacific Islander, 6% Hispanic American, 2% Native American.
Freshmen *Admission:* 361 applied, 301 admitted.
Faculty *Total:* 74, 46% full-time, 3% with terminal degrees. *Student/faculty ratio:* 12:1.
Majors Automobile/automotive mechanics technology; business administration and management; carpentry; computer management; emergency medical technology (EMT paramedic); environmental studies; industrial technology; liberal arts and sciences/liberal studies; medical/clinical assistant; occupational safety and health technology; welding technology; wood science and wood products/pulp and paper technology.
Academic Programs *Special study options:* academic remediation for entering students, adult/continuing education programs, advanced placement credit, cooperative education, distance learning, double majors, English as a second language, external degree program, independent study, internships, off-campus study, part-time degree program, services for LD students, summer session for credit.
Library Kimbell Library.
Computers on Campus Internet access, online (class) registration available.
Student Life *Housing:* college housing not available.
Standardized Tests *Required for some:* SAT or ACT (for placement).
Costs (2004–05) *Tuition:* area resident $960 full-time, $42 per credit hour part-time; state resident $1410 full-time, $50 per credit hour part-time; nonresident $4500 full-time, $150 per credit hour part-time. *Required fees:* $622 full-time, $15 per course part-time, $68 per term part-time. *Payment plan:* installment. *Waivers:* senior citizens and employees or children of employees.

Financial Aid Of all full-time matriculated undergraduates who enrolled in 2003, 14 Federal Work-Study jobs (averaging $2700).
Applying *Options:* common application, electronic application. *Recommended:* high school transcript.
Admissions Contact Ms. Nancy Cowling, Admissions Advisor, Cossatot Community College of the University of Arkansas, PO Box 960, DeQueen, AR 71832. *Phone:* 870-584-4471. *Toll-free phone:* 800-844-4471. *Fax:* 870-642-8766. *E-mail:* ncowling@cccua.edu.

CROWLEY'S RIDGE COLLEGE
Paragould, Arkansas

- **Independent** 2-year, affiliated with Church of Christ
- **Calendar** semesters
- **Degree** associate
- **Small-town** 112-acre campus
- **Endowment** $1.0 million
- **Coed**

Faculty *Student/faculty ratio:* 16:1.
Athletics Member NSCAA.
Standardized Tests *Required:* ACT, ACT ASSET (for placement).
Costs (2004–05) *Comprehensive fee:* $9270 includes full-time tuition ($5970), mandatory fees ($800), and room and board ($2500). Part-time tuition: $199 per semester hour. *Required fees:* $20 per credit part-time. *Room and board:* college room only: $1500.
Financial Aid Of all full-time matriculated undergraduates who enrolled in 2003, 78 Federal Work-Study jobs (averaging $500).
Applying *Options:* common application, electronic application. *Required:* high school transcript, recommendation form filled out by high school. *Required for some:* interview.
Admissions Contact Mrs. Nancy Joneshill, Director of Admissions, Crowley's Ridge College, 100 College Drive, Paragould, AR 72450. *Phone:* 870-236-6901 Ext. 14. *Toll-free phone:* 800-264-1096. *Fax:* 870-236-7748. *E-mail:* njoneshi@crc.pioneer.paragould.ar.us.

EAST ARKANSAS COMMUNITY COLLEGE
Forrest City, Arkansas

- **State-supported** 2-year, founded 1974
- **Calendar** semesters
- **Degree** certificates and associate
- **Small-town** 40-acre campus with easy access to Memphis
- **Endowment** $28,661
- **Coed,** 1,415 undergraduate students

Undergraduates Students come from 4 states and territories.
Faculty *Total:* 100.
Majors Business administration and management; computer engineering technology; criminal justice/law enforcement administration; criminal justice/police science; drafting and design technology; liberal arts and sciences/liberal studies; nursing (licensed practical/vocational nurse training).
Academic Programs *Special study options:* academic remediation for entering students, adult/continuing education programs, advanced placement credit, honors programs, part-time degree program, services for LD students, summer session for credit.
Library Learning Resource Center plus 1 other with 21,908 titles, 109 serial subscriptions.
Computers on Campus 26 computers available on campus for general student use. At least one staffed computer lab available.
Student Life *Housing:* college housing not available. *Activities and Organizations:* drama/theater group, choral group, Gamma Beta Phi, Baptist Student Union, Student Activities Committee, Lambda Alpha Epsilon. *Campus security:* 24-hour emergency response devices, 16-hour patrols by trained security personnel. *Student services:* personal/psychological counseling.
Standardized Tests *Required:* ACT ASSET (for placement). *Recommended:* ACT (for placement).
Costs (2004–05) *Tuition:* area resident $1380 full-time, $46 per credit hour part-time; state resident $1620 full-time, $54 per credit hour part-time; nonresident $1980 full-time, $66 per credit hour part-time. Full-time tuition and fees vary according to course load. Part-time tuition and fees vary according to course load. *Required fees:* $150 full-time, $5 per credit hour part-time. *Payment plan:* installment. *Waivers:* senior citizens and employees or children of employees.
Financial Aid Of all full-time matriculated undergraduates who enrolled in 2003, 74 Federal Work-Study jobs (averaging $1104).
Applying *Options:* early admission, deferred entrance. *Required:* high school transcript. *Application deadline:* rolling (freshmen), rolling (transfers). *Notification:* continuous (freshmen).

Admissions Contact Mrs. Sarah C. Buford, Director of Enrollment Management/Registrar, East Arkansas Community College, 1700 Newcastle Road, Forrest City, AR 72335-2204. *Phone:* 870-633-4480 Ext. 219. *Toll-free phone:* 877-797-3222.

ITT TECHNICAL INSTITUTE
Little Rock, Arkansas

- **Proprietary** primarily 2-year, founded 1993, part of ITT Educational Services, Inc
- **Calendar** quarters
- **Degrees** associate and bachelor's
- **Urban** campus
- **Coed**

Standardized Tests *Required:* Wonderlic aptitude test (for admission).
Costs (2004–05) *Tuition:* Please see school catalog for specific information.
Applying *Options:* deferred entrance. *Application fee:* $100. *Required:* high school transcript, interview. *Recommended:* letters of recommendation.
Admissions Contact Mr. Reed W. Thompson, Director of Recruitment, ITT Technical Institute, 4520 South University Avenue, Little Rock, AR 72204. *Phone:* 501-565-5550. *Toll-free phone:* 800-359-4429. *Fax:* 501-565-4747.

MID-SOUTH COMMUNITY COLLEGE
West Memphis, Arkansas

- **State-supported** 2-year, founded 1993
- **Calendar** semesters
- **Degree** certificates and associate
- **Suburban** 80-acre campus with easy access to Memphis
- **Endowment** $769,394
- **Coed,** 1,265 undergraduate students, 33% full-time, 66% women, 34% men

Undergraduates 423 full-time, 842 part-time. Students come from 2 other countries, 3% are from out of state, 54% African American, 0.9% Asian American or Pacific Islander, 0.9% Hispanic American, 0.3% Native American, 0.4% international, 5% transferred in. *Retention:* 44% of 2002 full-time freshmen returned.
Freshmen *Admission:* 442 applied, 442 admitted, 235 enrolled. *Test scores:* ACT scores over 18: 60%; ACT scores over 24: 9%.
Faculty *Total:* 96, 31% full-time. *Student/faculty ratio:* 13:1.
Majors Computer and information sciences; liberal arts and sciences/liberal studies; management information systems and services related; multi-/interdisciplinary studies related; web/multimedia management and webmaster.
Academic Programs *Special study options:* academic remediation for entering students, adult/continuing education programs, distance learning, independent study, internships, part-time degree program, summer session for credit.
Library Mid-South Community College Library/Media Center with 14,672 titles, 88 serial subscriptions, 2,151 audiovisual materials, an OPAC, a Web page.
Computers on Campus 280 computers available on campus for general student use. A campuswide network can be accessed from off campus. Internet access, at least one staffed computer lab available.
Student Life *Housing:* college housing not available. *Activities and Organizations:* choral group, Phi Theta Kappa, Baptist Collegiate Ministry, Campus Ministry International, Student Ambassador, Skills-USA-Vica. *Campus security:* 24-hour emergency response devices, security during class hours.
Standardized Tests *Required:* ACT ASSET, ACT COMPASS (for placement). *Recommended:* ACT (for placement).
Costs (2005–06) *Tuition:* area resident $1350 full-time, $45 per credit part-time; state resident $1650 full-time, $55 per credit part-time; nonresident $3000 full-time, $100 per credit part-time. *Required fees:* $150 full-time, $5 per credit part-time.
Financial Aid Of all full-time matriculated undergraduates who enrolled in 2003, 29 Federal Work-Study jobs (averaging $1914).
Applying *Options:* common application, electronic application, early admission. *Required:* high school transcript. *Application deadline:* rolling (freshmen), rolling (transfers). *Notification:* continuous (freshmen).
Admissions Contact Ms. Leslie Anderson, Registrar, Mid-South Community College, 2000 West Broadway, West Memphis, AR 72301. *Phone:* 870-733-6732. *Fax:* 870-733-6719. *E-mail:* landerson@midsouthcc.edu.

NATIONAL PARK COMMUNITY COLLEGE
Hot Springs, Arkansas

Admissions Contact Dr. Allen B. Moody, Director of Institutional Services/Registrar, National Park Community College, 101 College Drive, Hot Springs, AR 71913. *Phone:* 501-760-4222. *Fax:* 501-760-4100. *E-mail:* admissions@gccc.cc.ar.us.

NORTH ARKANSAS COLLEGE
Harrison, Arkansas

- **State and locally supported** 2-year, founded 1974
- **Calendar** semesters
- **Degree** certificates and associate
- **Small-town** 40-acre campus
- **Endowment** $103,275
- **Coed**

Faculty *Student/faculty ratio:* 17:1.
Student Life *Campus security:* 24-hour patrols.
Athletics Member NJCAA.
Standardized Tests *Required:* ACT (for placement), ACT ASSET, ACT COMPASS (for placement).
Costs (2004–05) *Tuition:* area resident $1320 full-time, $44 per credit hour part-time; state resident $1650 full-time, $55 per credit hour part-time; nonresident $3390 full-time, $113 per credit hour part-time. Full-time tuition and fees vary according to location and reciprocity agreements. Part-time tuition and fees vary according to location and reciprocity agreements. *Required fees:* $150 full-time, $5 per credit hour part-time, $75 per term part-time.
Financial Aid Of all full-time matriculated undergraduates who enrolled in 2003, 107 Federal Work-Study jobs (averaging $1103).
Applying *Options:* deferred entrance. *Required for some:* high school transcript.
Admissions Contact Ms. Charla McDonald Jennings, Director of Admissions, North Arkansas College, 1515 Pioneer Drive, Harrison, AR 72601. *Phone:* 870-391-3221. *Toll-free phone:* 800-679-6622. *Fax:* 870-391-3339. *E-mail:* charlam@northark.edu.

NORTHWEST ARKANSAS COMMUNITY COLLEGE
Bentonville, Arkansas

Admissions Contact Dr. Charles Mullins, Director of Admissions, NorthWest Arkansas Community College, One College Drive, Bentonville, AR 72712. *Phone:* 479-636-9222 Ext. 4231. *Toll-free phone:* 800-995-6922. *Fax:* 479-619-4116. *E-mail:* asknewstudentadmissions@nwacc.edu.

OUACHITA TECHNICAL COLLEGE
Malvern, Arkansas

- **State-supported** 2-year, founded 1972
- **Calendar** semesters
- **Degree** certificates and associate
- **Small-town** 11-acre campus
- **Coed,** 1,381 undergraduate students, 39% full-time, 54% women, 46% men

Undergraduates 544 full-time, 837 part-time. Students come from 2 states and territories, 2 other countries, 0.8% are from out of state, 11% African American, 0.8% Asian American or Pacific Islander, 1% Hispanic American, 1% Native American, 0.1% international, 7% transferred in. *Retention:* 54% of 2002 full-time freshmen returned.
Freshmen *Admission:* 221 applied, 221 admitted, 217 enrolled. *Test scores:* ACT scores over 18: 73%; ACT scores over 24: 3%.
Faculty *Total:* 86, 31% full-time, 8% with terminal degrees. *Student/faculty ratio:* 17:1.
Majors Accounting; administrative assistant and secretarial science; automobile/automotive mechanics technology; business administration and management; child care and support services management; computer and information sciences; industrial arts; industrial technology; legal administrative assistant/secretary; legal assistant/paralegal; liberal arts and sciences/liberal studies; machine tool technology; management information systems; marketing/marketing management; medical administrative assistant and medical secretary; nursing (licensed practical/vocational nurse training).
Academic Programs *Special study options:* academic remediation for entering students, accelerated degree program, advanced placement credit, cooperative education, distance learning, double majors, independent study, internships, part-time degree program, services for LD students, summer session for credit.
Library Ouachita Technical College Library/Learning Resource Center with 8,000 titles, 100 serial subscriptions, 1,200 audiovisual materials, an OPAC, a Web page.
Computers on Campus 125 computers available on campus for general student use. A campuswide network can be accessed from off campus. Internet access, at least one staffed computer lab available.
Student Life *Housing:* college housing not available. *Activities and Organizations:* student-run newspaper. *Campus security:* 24-hour patrols. *Student services:* personal/psychological counseling.

Standardized Tests *Required for some:* SAT or ACT (for placement), ACT ASSET, ACT COMPASS.
Costs (2005–06) *Tuition:* state resident $1470 full-time; nonresident $4410 full-time. *Required fees:* $390 full-time.
Financial Aid Of all full-time matriculated undergraduates who enrolled in 2003, 18 Federal Work-Study jobs (averaging $2400).
Applying *Options:* electronic application, early admission, deferred entrance. *Application fee:* $20. *Required:* high school transcript. *Application deadline:* rolling (freshmen), rolling (transfers).
Admissions Contact Mr. Vaughn Kesterson, Counselor, Ouachita Technical College, One College Circle, Malvern, AR 72104. *Phone:* 501-337-5000 Ext. 1117. *Toll-free phone:* 800-337-0266. *Fax:* 501-337-9382. *E-mail:* lindaj@otcweb.edu.

OZARKA COLLEGE
Melbourne, Arkansas

- **State-supported** 2-year, founded 1973
- **Calendar** semesters
- **Degree** certificates and associate
- **Rural** 40-acre campus
- **Coed**

Faculty *Student/faculty ratio:* 20:1.
Student Life *Campus security:* security patrols 7 a.m. to 11 p.m.
Standardized Tests *Required:* ACT (for placement), ACT ASSET (for placement).
Costs (2004–05) *Tuition:* state resident $1800 full-time, $60 per credit hour part-time; nonresident $5040 full-time, $168 per credit hour part-time. *Required fees:* $185 full-time, $5 per credit hour part-time, $15 per term part-time.
Financial Aid Of all full-time matriculated undergraduates who enrolled in 2003, 50 Federal Work-Study jobs, 40 state and other part-time jobs.
Applying *Options:* deferred entrance. *Required:* high school transcript. *Required for some:* essay or personal statement, letters of recommendation, interview. *Recommended:* minimum 2.0 GPA.
Admissions Contact Mr. Randy Scaggs, Counselor and Recruiter, Ozarka College, PO Box 12, 218 College Drive, Melbourne, AR 72556. *Phone:* 870-368-7371 Ext. 2028. *Toll-free phone:* 800-821-4335. *Fax:* 870-368-4733. *E-mail:* rscaggs@ozarka.edu.

PHILLIPS COMMUNITY COLLEGE OF THE UNIVERSITY OF ARKANSAS
Helena, Arkansas

- **State and locally supported** 2-year, founded 1965, part of University of Arkansas System
- **Calendar** semesters
- **Degree** certificates and associate
- **Small-town** 80-acre campus with easy access to Memphis
- **Coed,** 2,322 undergraduate students

Faculty *Total:* 70, 86% full-time.
Majors Administrative assistant and secretarial science; agricultural business and management; art; automobile/automotive mechanics technology; biological and physical sciences; biology/biological sciences; business administration and management; business teacher education; chemistry; clinical/medical laboratory technology; computer programming; cosmetology; data processing and data processing technology; drafting and design technology; dramatic/theatre arts; education; English; graphic and printing equipment operation/production; heating, air conditioning, ventilation and refrigeration maintenance technology; industrial arts; industrial radiologic technology; instrumentation technology; liberal arts and sciences/liberal studies; mathematics; medical administrative assistant and medical secretary; music; nursing (licensed practical/vocational nurse training); nursing (registered nurse training); physics; social sciences; welding technology.
Academic Programs *Special study options:* academic remediation for entering students, adult/continuing education programs, advanced placement credit, part-time degree program, services for LD students, summer session for credit.
Library 39,000 titles, 352 serial subscriptions.
Computers on Campus 200 computers available on campus for general student use.
Student Life *Housing:* college housing not available. *Activities and Organizations:* drama/theater group, student-run newspaper, choral group. *Campus security:* 24-hour patrols. *Student services:* personal/psychological counseling.
Athletics *Intramural sports:* basketball M/W, bowling M/W, tennis M/W, volleyball M/W.
Standardized Tests *Required:* ACT (for placement), ACT ASSET (for placement).

Costs (2005–06) *Tuition:* area resident $750 full-time, $50 per semester hour part-time; state resident $885 full-time, $59 per semester hour part-time; nonresident $1455 full-time, $97 per semester hour part-time.
Applying *Options:* early admission. *Application deadlines:* 8/25 (freshmen), 8/25 (transfers). *Notification:* continuous until 8/25 (freshmen).
Admissions Contact Mr. Lynn Boone, Registrar, Phillips Community College of the University of Arkansas, PO Box 785, Helena, AR 72342-0785. *Phone:* 870-338-6474.

PULASKI TECHNICAL COLLEGE
North Little Rock, Arkansas

- **State-supported** 2-year, founded 1945
- **Calendar** semesters
- **Degree** certificates and associate
- **Urban** 40-acre campus with easy access to Little Rock
- **Coed,** 7,222 undergraduate students, 50% full-time, 67% women, 33% men

Undergraduates 3,590 full-time, 3,632 part-time. Students come from 3 states and territories, 1% are from out of state, 43% African American, 1% Asian American or Pacific Islander, 11% Hispanic American, 0.5% Native American, 0.1% international.
Freshmen *Admission:* 4,410 applied, 4,410 admitted, 1,074 enrolled.
Faculty *Total:* 421, 23% full-time. *Student/faculty ratio:* 24:1.
Majors Administrative assistant and secretarial science; computer engineering technology; drafting and design technology; electromechanical technology; industrial technology; information science/studies.
Academic Programs *Special study options:* academic remediation for entering students, advanced placement credit, distance learning, part-time degree program, services for LD students, summer session for credit.
Library Ottenheimer Library with 16,378 titles, 234 serial subscriptions, 1,520 audiovisual materials, an OPAC, a Web page.
Computers on Campus 75 computers available on campus for general student use. A campuswide network can be accessed. Internet access, online (class) registration, at least one staffed computer lab available.
Student Life *Housing:* college housing not available. *Campus security:* security personnel 7 a.m. to 11 p.m.
Standardized Tests *Required:* ACT or ACT COMPASS (for placement).
Costs (2005–06) *Tuition:* state resident $2040 full-time, $68 per credit hour part-time; nonresident $3360 full-time, $112 per credit hour part-time. Full-time tuition and fees vary according to course load. *Required fees:* $250 full-time, $7 per credit hour part-time, $10 per term part-time. *Payment plan:* deferred payment. *Waivers:* senior citizens and employees or children of employees.
Applying *Options:* common application, electronic application. *Required:* high school transcript. *Application deadline:* rolling (freshmen).
Admissions Contact Ms. Janice Hurd, Director of Admissions and Records, Pulaski Technical College, 3000 West Scenic Drive, North Little Rock, AR 72118. *Phone:* 501-812-2232. *Fax:* 501-812-2316.

REMINGTON COLLEGE-LITTLE ROCK CAMPUS
Little Rock, Arkansas

Admissions Contact Mr. David Caldwell, Campus President, Remington College-Little Rock Campus, 8901 Kanis Road, Little Rock, AR 72205. *Phone:* 501-312-0007.

RICH MOUNTAIN COMMUNITY COLLEGE
Mena, Arkansas

- **State and locally supported** 2-year, founded 1983
- **Calendar** semesters
- **Degree** certificates and associate
- **Small-town** 40-acre campus
- **Endowment** $301,360
- **Coed,** 973 undergraduate students, 36% full-time, 74% women, 26% men

Undergraduates 348 full-time, 625 part-time. Students come from 2 states and territories, 2 other countries, 2% are from out of state, 1% Asian American or Pacific Islander, 0.8% Hispanic American, 2% Native American.
Freshmen *Average high school GPA:* 2.81.
Faculty *Total:* 55, 35% full-time, 4% with terminal degrees. *Student/faculty ratio:* 18:1.
Majors Administrative assistant and secretarial science; liberal arts and sciences/liberal studies.
Academic Programs *Special study options:* academic remediation for entering students, adult/continuing education programs, advanced placement credit,

distance learning, double majors, English as a second language, part-time degree program, services for LD students, summer session for credit.
Library St. John Library with 13,299 titles, 81 serial subscriptions, 674 audiovisual materials, an OPAC.
Computers on Campus 88 computers available on campus for general student use. A campuswide network can be accessed from off campus. Internet access, at least one staffed computer lab available.
Student Life *Housing:* college housing not available. *Activities and Organizations:* student-run television station, SGA, Baptist Student Union, Phi Theta Kappa, Golf Club, TV and Video Club. *Campus security:* administrator on night duty. *Student services:* personal/psychological counseling.
Costs (2005–06) *Tuition:* area resident $960 full-time, $40 per semester hour part-time; state resident $1200 full-time, $50 per semester hour part-time; nonresident $3600 full-time, $150 per semester hour part-time. *Required fees:* $72 full-time, $3 per semester hour part-time.
Financial Aid Of all full-time matriculated undergraduates who enrolled in 2003, 12 Federal Work-Study jobs (averaging $1500).
Applying *Options:* common application, early admission. *Required:* high school transcript. *Application deadlines:* 8/25 (freshmen), 8/25 (transfers). *Notification:* continuous until 8/25 (freshmen).
Admissions Contact Dr. Steve Rook, Dean of Students, Rich Mountain Community College, 1100 College Drive, Mena, AR 71953. *Phone:* 479-394-7622 Ext. 1400.

SOUTH ARKANSAS COMMUNITY COLLEGE
El Dorado, Arkansas

- **State-supported** 2-year, founded 1975, part of Arkansas Department of Higher Education
- **Calendar** semesters
- **Degree** certificates and associate
- **Small-town** 4-acre campus
- **Coed**

Faculty *Student/faculty ratio:* 13:1.
Student Life *Campus security:* security guard.
Standardized Tests *Required:* ACT ASSET (for placement). *Recommended:* SAT or ACT (for placement).
Costs (2004–05) *Tuition:* area resident $1710 full-time, $57 per credit hour part-time; state resident $1950 full-time, $65 per credit hour part-time; nonresident $3600 full-time, $120 per credit hour part-time. Full-time tuition and fees vary according to course load and program. Part-time tuition and fees vary according to course load and program. *Required fees:* $95 full-time.
Financial Aid Of all full-time matriculated undergraduates who enrolled in 2003, 45 Federal Work-Study jobs (averaging $1300).
Applying *Options:* early admission, deferred entrance.
Admissions Contact Mr. Dean Inman, Director of Enrollment Services, South Arkansas Community College, PO Box 7010, El Dorado, AR 71731-7010. *Phone:* 870-864-7142. *Toll-free phone:* 800-955-2289 Ext. 142. *Fax:* 870-864-7109. *E-mail:* dinman@southark.edu.

SOUTHEAST ARKANSAS COLLEGE
Pine Bluff, Arkansas

- **State-supported** 2-year, founded 1991
- **Calendar** semesters
- **Degree** certificates and associate
- **Coed**

Faculty *Student/faculty ratio:* 18:1.
Student Life *Campus security:* student patrols.
Standardized Tests *Required:* SAT or ACT (for placement), ACT ASSET (for placement).
Financial Aid Of all full-time matriculated undergraduates who enrolled in 2003, 60 Federal Work-Study jobs (averaging $3000).
Applying *Options:* common application, early admission. *Required:* high school transcript.
Admissions Contact Ms. Barbara Dunn, Coordinator of Admissions and Enrollment Management, Southeast Arkansas College, 1900 Hazel Street, Pine Bluff, AR 71603. *Phone:* 870-543-5957. *Toll-free phone:* 888-SEARK TC. *E-mail:* main@seark.edu.

SOUTHERN ARKANSAS UNIVERSITY TECH
Camden, Arkansas

- **State-supported** 2-year, founded 1967, part of Arkansas Department of Higher Education
- **Calendar** semesters
- **Degree** certificates and associate
- **Rural** 96-acre campus
- **Coed**

Faculty *Student/faculty ratio:* 20:1.

Student Life *Campus security:* 24-hour emergency response devices, patrols by trained security personnel.

Standardized Tests *Required:* SAT or ACT (for placement), ACT ASSET (for placement).

Costs (2004–05) *Tuition:* state resident $1440 full-time, $60 per credit hour part-time; nonresident $1920 full-time, $80 per credit hour part-time. Part-time tuition and fees vary according to course level. *Required fees:* $480 full-time, $20 per credit hour part-time. *Room and board:* $3250.

Financial Aid Of all full-time matriculated undergraduates who enrolled in 2003, 26 Federal Work-Study jobs (averaging $1023).

Applying *Options:* deferred entrance. *Required for some:* high school transcript. *Recommended:* high school transcript, minimum 2.0 GPA.

Admissions Contact Mr. Scott Raney, Admissions Director, Southern Arkansas University Tech, PO Box 3499, East Camden, AR 71711. *Phone:* 870-574-4558. *Fax:* 870-574-4478. *E-mail:* sraney@sautech.edu.

UNIVERSITY OF ARKANSAS COMMUNITY COLLEGE AT BATESVILLE
Batesville, Arkansas

- **State-supported** 2-year, part of University of Arkansas System
- **Calendar** semesters
- **Degree** certificates and associate
- **Small-town** campus
- **Coed**, 1,317 undergraduate students, 60% full-time, 69% women, 31% men

Undergraduates 784 full-time, 533 part-time. 3% African American, 0.5% Asian American or Pacific Islander, 1% Hispanic American, 0.5% Native American, 0.1% international, 9% transferred in. *Retention:* 57% of 2002 full-time freshmen returned.

Freshmen *Admission:* 225 enrolled.

Faculty *Total:* 96, 40% full-time. *Student/faculty ratio:* 13:1.

Majors Business/commerce; computer systems networking and telecommunications; criminal justice/safety; data entry/microcomputer applications; education; emergency medical technology (EMT paramedic); industrial technology; information technology; kindergarten/preschool education; medical office management; nursing (registered nurse training); system administration; web page, digital/multimedia and information resources design.

Academic Programs *Special study options:* academic remediation for entering students, adult/continuing education programs, advanced placement credit, cooperative education, distance learning, double majors, English as a second language, external degree program, independent study, internships, off-campus study, part-time degree program, services for LD students, student-designed majors, summer session for credit.

Library University of Arkansas Community College at Batesville Library with 8,000 titles, 149 serial subscriptions, 1,500 audiovisual materials, an OPAC.

Computers on Campus 25 computers available on campus for general student use. A campuswide network can be accessed. Internet access, at least one staffed computer lab available.

Student Life *Campus security:* security cameras. *Student services:* personal/psychological counseling.

Standardized Tests *Required:* SAT and SAT Subject Tests or ACT (for placement).

Costs (2004–05) *Tuition:* area resident $1080 full-time, $45 per credit hour part-time; state resident $1368 full-time, $57 per credit hour part-time; nonresident $2736 full-time, $114 per credit hour part-time. *Required fees:* $317 full-time, $13 per credit hour part-time, $5 per term part-time.

Financial Aid Of all full-time matriculated undergraduates who enrolled in 2003, 49 Federal Work-Study jobs (averaging $1311).

Applying *Options:* common application. *Application deadline:* rolling (freshmen). *Notification:* continuous (freshmen).

Admissions Contact Mr. Andy Thomas, Director of Admissions, University of Arkansas Community College at Batesville, PO Box 3350, Batesville, AR 72503. *Phone:* 870-612-2010. *Toll-free phone:* 800-508-7878. *Fax:* 870-612-2129. *E-mail:* athomas@uaccb.edu.

UNIVERSITY OF ARKANSAS COMMUNITY COLLEGE AT HOPE
Hope, Arkansas

- **State-supported** 2-year, founded 1966, part of University of Arkansas System
- **Calendar** semesters
- **Degree** certificates, diplomas, and associate
- **Rural** 60-acre campus
- **Coed**, 1,213 undergraduate students, 56% full-time, 70% women, 30% men

Undergraduates 676 full-time, 537 part-time. Students come from 4 states and territories, 30% African American, 0.7% Asian American or Pacific Islander, 1% Hispanic American, 0.7% Native American, 0.2% international.

Freshmen *Admission:* 463 applied, 463 admitted, 299 enrolled.

Faculty *Total:* 62, 60% full-time, 11% with terminal degrees. *Student/faculty ratio:* 19:1.

Majors Business administration and management; child care provision; criminal justice/law enforcement administration; funeral service and mortuary science; human services; industrial mechanics and maintenance technology; liberal arts and sciences/liberal studies; machine shop technology; respiratory care therapy; trade and industrial teacher education.

Academic Programs *Special study options:* academic remediation for entering students, accelerated degree program, distance learning, English as a second language, independent study, internships, part-time degree program, summer session for credit.

Library University of Arkansas Community College at Hope Library with 8,023 titles, 111 serial subscriptions, 614 audiovisual materials, an OPAC, a Web page.

Computers on Campus Internet access, at least one staffed computer lab available.

Student Life *Housing:* college housing not available. *Activities and Organizations:* Student Government Association, Phi Theta Kappa, Phi Beta Lambda, Circle K. *Campus security:* on-campus security during class hours.

Standardized Tests *Required for some:* ACT ASSET. *Recommended:* ACT (for placement), ACT ASSET.

Costs (2004–05) *Tuition:* area resident $1248 full-time, $52 per credit hour part-time; state resident $1368 full-time, $57 per credit hour part-time; nonresident $2664 full-time, $111 per credit hour part-time. Part-time tuition and fees vary according to course load. *Required fees:* $150 full-time, $5 per credit hour part-time. *Payment plan:* installment. *Waivers:* senior citizens and employees or children of employees.

Financial Aid Of all full-time matriculated undergraduates who enrolled in 2003, 26 Federal Work-Study jobs (averaging $2472).

Applying *Options:* early admission. *Required:* high school transcript. *Application deadline:* rolling (freshmen), rolling (transfers).

Admissions Contact Ms. Danita Ormand, Director of Enrollment Services, University of Arkansas Community College at Hope, 71802-0140. *Phone:* 870-777-5722 Ext. 1267. *Fax:* 870-722-6630.

UNIVERSITY OF ARKANSAS COMMUNITY COLLEGE AT MORRILTON
Morrilton, Arkansas

- **State-supported** 2-year, founded 1961, part of University of Arkansas System
- **Calendar** semesters
- **Degree** certificates and associate
- **Rural** 63-acre campus
- **Coed**, 1,514 undergraduate students

Undergraduates Students come from 1 other state, 8% African American, 0.5% Asian American or Pacific Islander, 2% Hispanic American, 0.4% Native American.

Freshmen *Admission:* 595 applied, 595 admitted. *Average high school GPA:* 2.45. *Test scores:* ACT scores over 18: 65%; ACT scores over 24: 15%.

Faculty *Total:* 80, 50% full-time, 3% with terminal degrees. *Student/faculty ratio:* 19:1.

Majors Administrative assistant and secretarial science; automobile/automotive mechanics technology; child development; commercial and advertising art; computer systems networking and telecommunications; computer typography and composition equipment operation; drafting and design technology; heating, air conditioning, ventilation and refrigeration maintenance technology; horticultural science; information science/studies; liberal arts and sciences/liberal studies; machine tool technology; marketing/marketing management; nursing (licensed practical/vocational nurse training); ornamental horticulture; survey technology; welding technology.

Academic Programs *Special study options:* academic remediation for entering students, advanced placement credit, distance learning, double majors, internships, off-campus study, part-time degree program, services for LD students, student-designed majors, summer session for credit.

Library Gordon Library with 6,600 titles, 76 serial subscriptions.

Computers on Campus 200 computers available on campus for general student use. Internet access, at least one staffed computer lab available.

Student Life *Housing:* college housing not available. *Activities and Organizations:* Business Students' Organization, Student Activity Board, Early Childhood Development Organization, Graphic Design Club, Student Practical Nurses Organization. *Campus security:* 24-hour emergency response devices. *Student services:* personal/psychological counseling.

Standardized Tests *Required:* ACT (for placement), ACT ASSET or ACT COMPASS (for placement).

Costs (2005–06) *Tuition:* area resident $1920 full-time, $64 per credit hour part-time; state resident $2100 full-time, $70 per credit hour part-time; nonresident $3060 full-time, $102 per credit hour part-time. Full-time tuition and fees vary according to course load. Part-time tuition and fees vary according to course load. *Required fees:* $210 full-time, $7 per hour part-time. *Payment plan:* installment. *Waivers:* senior citizens and employees or children of employees.

Financial Aid Of all full-time matriculated undergraduates who enrolled in 2003, 20 Federal Work-Study jobs (averaging $1000). *Financial aid deadline:* 7/23.

Applying *Options:* early admission, deferred entrance. *Required:* high school transcript. *Required for some:* immunization records. *Application deadline:* rolling (freshmen), rolling (transfers). *Notification:* continuous (freshmen).

Admissions Contact Dr. Gary Gaston, Vice Chancellor for Student Services, University of Arkansas Community College at Morrilton, One Bruce Street, Morrilton, AR 72110. *Phone:* 501-977-2014. *Toll-free phone:* 800-264-1094. *Fax:* 501-977-2123.

CALIFORNIA

ALLAN HANCOCK COLLEGE
Santa Maria, California

Admissions Contact Ms. Norma Razo, Director of Admissions and Records, Allan Hancock College, 800 South College Drive, Santa Maria, CA 93454-6399. *Phone:* 805-922-6966 Ext. 3272. *Toll-free phone:* 866-342-5242. *Fax:* 805-922-3477. *E-mail:* nrazo@ahc.sbceo.k12.ca.us.

AMERICAN ACADEMY OF DRAMATIC ARTS/HOLLYWOOD
Hollywood, California

- **Independent** 2-year, founded 1974
- **Calendar** continuous
- **Degree** certificates, diplomas, and associate
- **Suburban** 4-acre campus with easy access to Los Angeles
- **Coed**

Faculty *Student/faculty ratio:* 15:1.

Student Life *Campus security:* 24-hour emergency response devices, 8-hour patrols by trained security personnel.

Costs (2004–05) *Tuition:* $14,900 full-time. Full-time tuition and fees vary according to program. *Required fees:* $450 full-time.

Financial Aid Of all full-time matriculated undergraduates who enrolled in 2003, 15 Federal Work-Study jobs (averaging $2000).

Applying *Options:* deferred entrance. *Application fee:* $50. *Required:* essay or personal statement, high school transcript, 2 letters of recommendation, interview, audition. *Recommended:* minimum 2.0 GPA.

Admissions Contact Mr. Dan Justin, Director of Admissions, American Academy of Dramatic Arts/Hollywood, 1336 North LaBrea Avenue, Hollywood, CA 90028. *Phone:* 800-222-2867 Ext. 103. *Toll-free phone:* 800-222-2867. *E-mail:* admissions-ca@aada.org.

► See page 446 for a narrative description.

AMERICAN RIVER COLLEGE
Sacramento, California

- **District-supported** 2-year, founded 1955, part of Los Rios Community College District System
- **Calendar** semesters
- **Degree** certificates and associate
- **Suburban** 153-acre campus
- **Coed**

Faculty *Student/faculty ratio:* 34:1.

Student Life *Campus security:* 24-hour emergency response devices and patrols, student patrols, late-night transport/escort service.

Standardized Tests *Required for some:* nursing exam. *Recommended:* SAT or ACT (for placement).

Financial Aid Of all full-time matriculated undergraduates who enrolled in 2003, 300 Federal Work-Study jobs (averaging $1500). 100 state and other part-time jobs (averaging $2000).

Applying *Options:* common application, early admission, deferred entrance.

Admissions Contact Ms. Robin Neal, Dean of Enrollment Services, American River College, 4700 College Oak Drive, Sacramento, CA 95841-4286. *Phone:* 916-484-8171. *E-mail:* recadmiss@mail.arc.losrios.cc.ca.us.

ANTELOPE VALLEY COLLEGE
Lancaster, California

Admissions Contact Office of Admissions, Antelope Valley College, 3041 West Avenue K, Lancaster, CA 93536-5426. *Phone:* 661-722-6300. *E-mail:* info@avc.edu.

AVIATION & ELECTRONIC SCHOOLS OF AMERICA
Colfax, California

Admissions Contact 210 South Railroad Street, PO Box 1810, Colfax, CA 95713-1810. *Toll-free phone:* 800-345-2742.

BAKERSFIELD COLLEGE
Bakersfield, California

Admissions Contact Ms. Sue Vaughn, Director of Enrollment Services, Bakersfield College, 1801 Panorama Drive, Bakersfield, CA 93305-1299. *Phone:* 661-395-4301. *E-mail:* svaughn@bc.cc.ca.us.

BARSTOW COLLEGE
Barstow, California

Admissions Contact Mr. Don Low, Interim Vice President, Barstow College, 2700 Barstow Road, Barstow, CA 92311-6699. *Fax:* 760-252-1875.

BROOKS COLLEGE
Long Beach, California

Admissions Contact Ms. Christina Varon, Director of Admissions, Brooks College, 4825 East Pacific Coast Highway, Long Beach, CA 90804-3291. *Phone:* 562-498-2441 Ext. 265. *Toll-free phone:* 800-421-3775. *Fax:* 562-597-7412. *E-mail:* info@brookscollege.edu.

BROOKS COLLEGE
Sunnyvale, California

Admissions Contact 1120 Kifer Road, Sunnyvale, CA 94086.

BRYMAN COLLEGE
City of Industry, California

Admissions Contact 12801 Crossroads Parkway South, City of Industry, CA 91746.

BRYMAN COLLEGE
Ontario, California

Admissions Contact 1460 South Milliken Avenue, Ontario, CA 91761.

BUTTE COLLEGE
Oroville, California

- **District-supported** 2-year, founded 1966, part of California Community College System
- **Calendar** semesters
- **Degree** certificates and associate
- **Rural** 900-acre campus
- **Coed**

Butte College (continued)
Faculty *Student/faculty ratio:* 24:1.
Student Life *Campus security:* 24-hour emergency response devices and patrols, student patrols.
Costs (2004–05) *Tuition:* state resident $0 full-time; nonresident $4200 full-time, $175 per unit part-time. Part-time tuition and fees vary according to course load. *Required fees:* $596 full-time, $18 per unit part-time.
Applying *Options:* early admission, deferred entrance. *Required for some:* high school transcript.
Admissions Contact Ms. Nancy Jenson, Registrar, Butte College, 3536 Butte Campus Drive, Oroville, CA 95965. *Phone:* 530-895-2361. *E-mail:* admissions@butte.cc.ca.us.

CABRILLO COLLEGE

Aptos, California

- **District-supported** 2-year, founded 1959, part of California Community College System
- **Calendar** semesters
- **Degree** certificates and associate
- **Small-town** 120-acre campus with easy access to San Jose
- **Coed**

Financial Aid Of all full-time matriculated undergraduates who enrolled in 2003, 50 Federal Work-Study jobs (averaging $4000).
Applying *Options:* early admission. *Required for some:* high school transcript.
Admissions Contact Ms. Gloria Garing, Director of Admissions and Records, Cabrillo College, 6500 Soquel Drive, Aptos, CA 95003. *Phone:* 831-479-6201. *Fax:* 831-479-5782. *E-mail:* ar-mail@cabrillo.edu.

CALIFORNIA CULINARY ACADEMY

San Francisco, California

- **Proprietary** 2-year, founded 1977
- **Calendar** continuous
- **Degree** certificates and associate
- **Urban** campus
- **Coed**

Faculty *Student/faculty ratio:* 16:1.
Student Life *Campus security:* 24-hour emergency response devices and patrols, controlled dormitory access.
Financial Aid Of all full-time matriculated undergraduates who enrolled in 2003, 45 Federal Work-Study jobs (averaging $3000).
Applying *Options:* common application, electronic application. *Application fee:* $65. *Required:* high school transcript, interview.
Admissions Contact Ms. Nancy Seyfert, Vice President of Admissions, California Culinary Academy, 625 Polk Street, San Francisco, CA 94102-3368. *Phone:* 800-229-2433 Ext. 275. *Toll-free phone:* 800-229-2433 (in-state); 800-BAYCHEF (out-of-state). *Fax:* 415-771-2194. *E-mail:* admissions@baychef.com.

CANADA COLLEGE

Redwood City, California

- **State and locally supported** 2-year, founded 1968, part of San Mateo County Community College District System
- **Calendar** semesters
- **Degree** certificates and associate
- **Suburban** 131-acre campus with easy access to San Francisco and San Jose
- **Coed**

Student Life *Campus security:* 12-hour patrols by trained security personnel.
Costs (2004–05) *Tuition:* state resident $0 full-time; nonresident $4008 full-time, $167 per unit part-time. *Required fees:* $624 full-time, $26 per unit part-time, $13 per term part-time.
Financial Aid Of all full-time matriculated undergraduates who enrolled in 2003, 25 Federal Work-Study jobs (averaging $4000).
Applying *Options:* early admission.
Admissions Contact Mr. Jose Romero, Lead Records Clerk, Canada College, 4200 Farm Hill Boulevard, Redwood City, CA 94061. *Phone:* 650-306-3395. *Fax:* 650-306-3113.

CERRITOS COLLEGE

Norwalk, California

Admissions Contact Ms. Stephanie Murguia, Director of Admissions and Records, Cerritos College, 11110 Alondra Boulevard, Norwalk, CA 90650-6298. *Phone:* 562-860-2451. *E-mail:* rbell@cerritos.edu.

CERRO COSO COMMUNITY COLLEGE

Ridgecrest, California

- **State-supported** 2-year, founded 1973, part of Kern Community College District System
- **Calendar** semesters
- **Degree** certificates and associate
- **Small-town** 320-acre campus
- **Coed**, 5,020 undergraduate students, 24% full-time, 61% women, 39% men

Undergraduates 1,218 full-time, 3,802 part-time. Students come from 30 states and territories, 2% are from out of state, 6% African American, 6% Asian American or Pacific Islander, 12% Hispanic American, 3% Native American, 0.4% international, 4% transferred in. *Retention:* 51% of 2002 full-time freshmen returned.
Freshmen *Admission:* 375 applied, 375 admitted, 375 enrolled.
Faculty *Total:* 214, 28% full-time. *Student/faculty ratio:* 14:1.
Majors Art; automobile/automotive mechanics technology; business administration and management; child care and support services management; child care provision; computer and information sciences; computer engineering technology; computer graphics; computer software and media applications related; criminal justice/law enforcement administration; data processing and data processing technology; drafting and design technology; early childhood education; emergency medical technology (EMT paramedic); engineering technology; fine/studio arts; fire science; health and physical education; history; humanities; kindergarten/preschool education; liberal arts and sciences/liberal studies; machine tool technology; natural resources management and policy; nursing (licensed practical/vocational nurse training); parks, recreation and leisure facilities management; physical sciences; pre-engineering; web page, digital/multimedia and information resources design; welding technology.
Academic Programs *Special study options:* academic remediation for entering students, adult/continuing education programs, cooperative education, distance learning, English as a second language, honors programs, part-time degree program, services for LD students, summer session for credit.
Library Walter Stiern Memorial Library with 25,000 titles, 800 serial subscriptions, an OPAC, a Web page.
Computers on Campus 100 computers available on campus for general student use. A campuswide network can be accessed from off campus. At least one staffed computer lab available.
Student Life *Housing:* college housing not available. *Activities and Organizations:* Special Services Club, Art Club, LVN Club, Athletic Club, Drama Club. *Campus security:* patrols by trained security personnel. *Student services:* personal/psychological counseling.
Athletics *Intercollegiate sports:* baseball M, basketball W.
Standardized Tests *Required for some:* ACT ASSET.
Costs (2005–06) *Tuition:* state resident $0 full-time; nonresident $5010 full-time, $162 per unit part-time. *Required fees:* $780 full-time, $26 per unit part-time.
Financial Aid Of all full-time matriculated undergraduates who enrolled in 2003, 150 Federal Work-Study jobs (averaging $2000).
Applying *Options:* early admission. *Recommended:* high school transcript. *Application deadline:* rolling (freshmen), rolling (transfers).
Admissions Contact Mr. Robert Weisenthal, Associate Dean for Student Life, Cerro Coso Community College, 3000 College Heights Boulevard, Ridgecrest, CA 93555. *Phone:* 760-384-6291. *Fax:* 760-375-4776. *E-mail:* lbozarth@cerrocoso.edu.

CHABOT COLLEGE

Hayward, California

- **State-supported** 2-year, founded 1961, part of California Community College System
- **Calendar** semesters
- **Degree** certificates and associate
- **Suburban** 245-acre campus with easy access to San Francisco
- **Coed**

Faculty *Student/faculty ratio:* 24:1.
Student Life *Campus security:* 24-hour emergency response devices, late-night transport/escort service.
Financial Aid Of all full-time matriculated undergraduates who enrolled in 2003, 75 Federal Work-Study jobs (averaging $3000).
Applying *Options:* electronic application. *Required:* high school transcript.
Admissions Contact Ms. Judy Young, Director of Admissions and Records, Chabot College, 25555 Hesperian Boulevard, Hayward, CA 94545. *Phone:* 510-723-6700. *Fax:* 510-723-7510.

CHAFFEY COLLEGE
Rancho Cucamonga, California

Admissions Contact Ms. Cecilia Carerra, Director of Admissions, Registration, and Records, Chaffey College, 5885 Haven Avenue, Rancho Cucamonga, CA 91737-3002. *Phone:* 909-941-2631.

CITRUS COLLEGE
Glendora, California

- **State and locally supported** 2-year, founded 1915, part of California Community College System
- **Calendar** semesters
- **Degree** certificates, diplomas, and associate
- **Small-town** 104-acre campus with easy access to Los Angeles
- **Coed,** 11,790 undergraduate students, 34% full-time, 56% women, 44% men

Undergraduates 3,959 full-time, 7,831 part-time. 6% African American, 10% Asian American or Pacific Islander, 45% Hispanic American, 0.8% Native American.
Faculty *Total:* 506, 33% full-time, 19% with terminal degrees.
Majors Administrative assistant and secretarial science; art; automobile/automotive mechanics technology; behavioral sciences; biology/biological sciences; business administration and management; computer and information sciences related; computer science; cosmetology; criminal justice/law enforcement administration; criminal justice/police science; dance; data processing and data processing technology; dental assisting; drafting and design technology; dramatic/theatre arts; electrical, electronic and communications engineering technology; engineering; engineering technology; English; French; German; health and physical education; hydrology and water resources science; Japanese; journalism; liberal arts and sciences/liberal studies; library assistant; library science; mathematics; mechanical engineering/mechanical technology; modern languages; music; natural sciences; nursing (licensed practical/vocational nurse training); photography; physical education teaching and coaching; physical sciences; public administration; real estate; social sciences; Spanish; visual and performing arts.
Academic Programs *Special study options:* academic remediation for entering students, advanced placement credit, cooperative education, distance learning, English as a second language, honors programs, part-time degree program, services for LD students, study abroad, summer session for credit.
Library Hayden Library with 45,091 titles, 133 serial subscriptions, 4,752 audiovisual materials, an OPAC, a Web page.
Computers on Campus 1100 computers available on campus for general student use. A campuswide network can be accessed. Internet access, online (class) registration, at least one staffed computer lab available.
Student Life *Housing:* college housing not available. *Activities and Organizations:* drama/theater group, student-run newspaper, choral group, Student Government, AGS Honor Society, International Student Association, Cosmetology Club. *Campus security:* 24-hour patrols, student patrols, late-night transport/escort service. *Student services:* health clinic, personal/psychological counseling, legal services.
Athletics *Intercollegiate sports:* baseball M, basketball M/W, cross-country running M/W, football M, golf M/W, soccer M/W, softball W, swimming and diving M/W, tennis M/W, track and field M/W, volleyball W, water polo M/W.
Standardized Tests *Required for some:* Accuplacer.
Costs (2005–06) *Tuition:* state resident $0 full-time; nonresident $4954 full-time, $150 per unit part-time. Full-time tuition and fees vary according to course load. Part-time tuition and fees vary according to course load. *Required fees:* $754 full-time, $26 per unit part-time.
Financial Aid Of all full-time matriculated undergraduates who enrolled in 2003, 141 Federal Work-Study jobs (averaging $5500).
Applying *Required:* high school transcript.
Admissions Contact Admissions and Records, Citrus College, 1000 West Foothill Boulevard, Glendora, CA 91741-1899. *Phone:* 626-914-8511. *Fax:* 626-914-8613. *E-mail:* admissions@citruscollege.edu.

CITY COLLEGE OF SAN FRANCISCO
San Francisco, California

Admissions Contact Mr. Robert Balesteri, Dean of Admissions and Records, City College of San Francisco, 50 Phelan Avenue, San Francisco, CA 94112-1821. *Phone:* 415-239-3291. *Fax:* 415-239-3936.

COASTLINE COMMUNITY COLLEGE
Fountain Valley, California

- **State and locally supported** 2-year, founded 1976, part of Coast Community College District System
- **Calendar** semesters
- **Degree** certificates and associate
- **Urban** campus with easy access to Los Angeles
- **Coed**

Faculty *Student/faculty ratio:* 24:1.
Student Life *Campus security:* 24-hour emergency response devices.
Costs (2004–05) *Tuition:* state resident $0 full-time; nonresident $4470 full-time, $149 per unit part-time. *Required fees:* $806 full-time, $26 per unit part-time.
Financial Aid Of all full-time matriculated undergraduates who enrolled in 2003, 20 Federal Work-Study jobs (averaging $4500).
Applying *Options:* common application, early admission. *Recommended:* high school transcript.
Admissions Contact Jennifer McDonald, Director of Admissions and Records, Coastline Community College, 11460 Warner Avenue, Fountain Valley, CA 92708. *Phone:* 714-241-6163. *Fax:* 714-241-6288.

COLEMAN COLLEGE
San Marcos, California

- **Independent** 2-year, founded 1967
- **Calendar** quarters
- **Degree** certificates and associate
- **Suburban** campus
- **Coed**

Admissions Contact Mr. James Warner, Senior Admissions Officer, Coleman College, 1284 West San Marcos Boulevard, San Marcos, CA 92069. *Phone:* 760-747-3990.

COLLEGE OF ALAMEDA
Alameda, California

Admissions Contact Ms. Barbara Simmons, District Admissions Officer, College of Alameda, 555 Atlantic Avenue, Alameda, CA 94501-2109. *Phone:* 510-466-7370. *E-mail:* hperdue@peralta.cc.ca.us.

COLLEGE OF MARIN
Kentfield, California

Admissions Contact Ms. Gina Longo, Secretary to the Dean of Enrollment Services, College of Marin, 835 College Avenue, Kentfield, CA 94904. *Phone:* 415-485-9417.

COLLEGE OF SAN MATEO
San Mateo, California

Admissions Contact Mr. Henry Villareal, Dean of Admissions and Records, College of San Mateo, 1700 West Hillsdale Boulevard, San Mateo, CA 94402-3784. *Phone:* 650-574-6594. *E-mail:* csmadmission@smccd.cc.ca.us.

COLLEGE OF THE CANYONS
Santa Clarita, California

- **State and locally supported** 2-year, founded 1969, part of California Community College System
- **Calendar** semesters
- **Degree** certificates and associate
- **Suburban** 158-acre campus with easy access to Los Angeles
- **Coed,** 14,190 undergraduate students, 30% full-time, 47% women, 53% men

Undergraduates 4,234 full-time, 9,956 part-time. Students come from 15 states and territories, 3% are from out of state, 4% African American, 9% Asian American or Pacific Islander, 21% Hispanic American, 0.7% Native American, 4% transferred in. *Retention:* 51% of 2002 full-time freshmen returned.
Freshmen *Admission:* 1,913 enrolled.
Faculty *Total:* 564, 29% full-time. *Student/faculty ratio:* 28:1.
Majors Accounting; administrative assistant and secretarial science; art; biological and physical sciences; biology/biological sciences; business administration and management; chemistry; child development; cinematography and film/video production; computer and information sciences related; computer engineering related; computer science; criminal justice/law enforcement administration; criminal justice/police science; developmental and child psychology; drafting and design technology; electrical, electronic and communications engineering technology; English; French; geography; geology/earth science; German; health science; history; hotel/motel administration; humanities; hydrology and water resources science; information science/studies; interior design; jour-

College of the Canyons (continued)

nalism; kindergarten/preschool education; liberal arts and sciences/liberal studies; mathematics; natural sciences; nursing (licensed practical/vocational nurse training); nursing (registered nurse training); physical education teaching and coaching; physical sciences; political science and government; pre-engineering; psychology; quality control technology; real estate; social sciences; Spanish; welding technology.

Academic Programs *Special study options:* academic remediation for entering students, adult/continuing education programs, advanced placement credit, cooperative education, distance learning, double majors, English as a second language, honors programs, independent study, internships, off-campus study, part-time degree program, services for LD students, study abroad, summer session for credit.

Library College of the Canyons Library with 40,646 titles, 233 serial subscriptions, 29,955 audiovisual materials, an OPAC, a Web page.

Computers on Campus 650 computers available on campus for general student use. A campuswide network can be accessed. Internet access, at least one staffed computer lab available.

Student Life *Housing:* college housing not available. *Activities and Organizations:* drama/theater group, student-run newspaper, choral group, HITE, Phi Theta Kappa, Alpha Gamma Sigma, MECHA, Biology Club. *Campus security:* student patrols, late-night transport/escort service. *Student services:* health clinic, personal/psychological counseling.

Athletics *Intercollegiate sports:* baseball M, basketball M/W, cross-country running M/W, football M, golf M, soccer W, softball W, swimming and diving M/W, track and field M/W, volleyball W, water polo M.

Standardized Tests *Recommended:* SAT or ACT (for placement).

Costs (2004–05) *Tuition:* state resident $0 full-time; nonresident $4320 full-time, $145 per unit part-time. *Required fees:* $766 full-time, $26 per unit part-time, $23 per term part-time.

Applying *Options:* electronic application, early admission. *Recommended:* high school transcript. *Application deadlines:* 8/22 (freshmen), 8/22 (transfers). *Notification:* continuous until 8/22 (freshmen).

Admissions Contact Ms. Deborah Rio, Director, Admissions and Records and Online Services, College of the Canyons, 26455 Rockwell Canyon Road, Santa Clara, CA 91355. *Phone:* 661-362-3280. *Toll-free phone:* 888-206-7827. *Fax:* 661-254-7996.

COLLEGE OF THE DESERT

Palm Desert, California

- **State and locally supported** 2-year, founded 1959, part of California Community College System
- **Calendar** semesters
- **Degree** certificates, diplomas, and associate
- **Small-town** 160-acre campus
- **Coed**

Student Life *Campus security:* 24-hour emergency response devices, late-night transport/escort service.

Financial Aid Of all full-time matriculated undergraduates who enrolled in 2003, 125 Federal Work-Study jobs (averaging $750). 50 state and other part-time jobs (averaging $750).

Applying *Options:* early admission.

Admissions Contact Ms. Kathi Westerfield, Registrar, College of the Desert, 43-500 Monterey Avenue, Palm Desert, CA 92260-9305. *Phone:* 760-773-2519. *Toll-free phone:* 760-773-2516.

COLLEGE OF THE REDWOODS

Eureka, California

Admissions Contact Ms. Sue Bailey, Director of Enrollment Management, College of the Redwoods, 7351 Tompkins Hill Road, Eureka, CA 95501-9300. *Phone:* 707-476-4168. *Toll-free phone:* 800-641-0400. *Fax:* 707-476-4406. *E-mail:* admissions@redwoods.edu.

COLLEGE OF THE SEQUOIAS

Visalia, California

- **State and locally supported** 2-year, founded 1925, part of California Community College System
- **Calendar** semesters
- **Degree** certificates and associate
- **Suburban** 215-acre campus
- **Endowment** $1.2 million
- **Coed**

Faculty *Student/faculty ratio:* 26:1.

Student Life *Campus security:* 24-hour emergency response devices and patrols, student patrols, late-night transport/escort service, 18 hour patrols by trained security personnel.

Athletics Member NJCAA.

Costs (2004–05) *Tuition:* state resident $0 full-time; nonresident $4890 full-time, $163 per unit part-time. Part-time tuition and fees vary according to course load. *Required fees:* $806 full-time, $26 per unit part-time, $13 per term part-time.

Applying *Options:* early admission. *Required:* high school transcript.

Admissions Contact Mr. Don Mast, Associate Dean of Admissions/Registrar, College of the Sequoias, 915 South Mooney Boulevard, Visalia, CA 93277-2234. *Phone:* 559-737-4844. *Fax:* 559-737-4820.

COLLEGE OF THE SISKIYOUS

Weed, California

COS is located at the base of Mt. Shasta in northern California, 60 miles south of the Oregon border, and provides many recreational opportunities. COS offers excellent transfer and vocational programs, support services, on-campus residence halls, and athletic programs. Small class sizes and individualized instruction provide a supportive environment that encourages learning.

Admissions Contact Ms. Christina Bruck, Recruitment and Outreach Coordinator, College of the Siskiyous, 800 College Avenue, Weed, CA 96094. *Phone:* 530-938-5847. *Toll-free phone:* 888-397-4339 Ext. 5847. *Fax:* 530-938-5367. *E-mail:* info@siskiyous.edu.

COLUMBIA COLLEGE

Sonora, California

- **State and locally supported** 2-year, founded 1968, part of Yosemite Community College District System
- **Calendar** semesters
- **Degree** certificates and associate
- **Rural** 200-acre campus
- **Coed**, 3,572 undergraduate students, 26% full-time, 54% women, 46% men

Undergraduates 914 full-time, 2,658 part-time. Students come from 7 states and territories, 5% are from out of state, 0.8% African American, 2% Asian American or Pacific Islander, 7% Hispanic American, 2% Native American, 0.1% international.

Freshmen *Admission:* 312 applied, 312 admitted, 312 enrolled.

Faculty *Total:* 150, 41% full-time. *Student/faculty ratio:* 12:1.

Majors Administrative assistant and secretarial science; anthropology; art; automobile/automotive mechanics technology; biology/biological sciences; business administration and management; chemistry; computer science; culinary arts; developmental and child psychology; dramatic/theatre arts; English; environmental studies; fire science; food services technology; forestry technology; geology/earth science; health teacher education; history; hotel/motel administration; humanities; liberal arts and sciences/liberal studies; mathematics; music; natural resources management and policy; photography; physical education teaching and coaching; physical sciences; physics; psychology; sociology; special products marketing.

Academic Programs *Special study options:* academic remediation for entering students, adult/continuing education programs, advanced placement credit, cooperative education, distance learning, double majors, English as a second language, independent study, internships, part-time degree program, services for LD students, summer session for credit.

Library Columbia College Library with 34,892 titles, 320 serial subscriptions, 4,852 audiovisual materials, an OPAC, a Web page.

Computers on Campus 85 computers available on campus for general student use. Internet access, at least one staffed computer lab available.

Student Life *Housing Options:* Campus housing is provided by a third party. *Activities and Organizations:* drama/theater group, choral group, International Club, Jazz Club, Ecology Action Club, Christian Club. *Campus security:* 24-hour emergency response devices and patrols, late-night transport/escort service. *Student services:* health clinic.

Athletics Member NJCAA. *Intercollegiate sports:* basketball M, tennis M/W, volleyball W.

Standardized Tests *Required:* CPT, ACCUPLACER (for placement).

Costs (2005–06) *Tuition:* state resident $0 full-time; nonresident $4200 full-time, $167 per unit part-time. *Required fees:* $624 full-time, $26 per unit part-time. *Room and board:* room only: $4615.

Financial Aid Of all full-time matriculated undergraduates who enrolled in 2003, 42 Federal Work-Study jobs (averaging $2350).

Applying *Options:* common application, electronic application, early admission. *Required for some:* high school transcript. *Application deadline:* rolling (freshmen), rolling (transfers). *Notification:* continuous (freshmen).

Admissions Contact Dr. Kathleen Smith, Director Student Success/Matriculation, Columbia College, Columbia College, 11600 Columbia College Drive, Sonora, CA 95370. *Phone:* 209-588-5231. *Fax:* 209-588-5337. *E-mail:* chavezc@yosemite.cc.ca.us.

COMPTON COMMUNITY COLLEGE
Compton, California

- **State and locally supported** 2-year, founded 1927, part of California Community College System
- **Calendar** semesters
- **Degree** associate
- **Urban** 83-acre campus with easy access to Los Angeles
- **Coed,** 7,900 undergraduate students

Undergraduates Students come from 4 states and territories, 25 other countries.
Freshmen *Admission:* 1,650 applied, 1,650 admitted.
Faculty *Total:* 347, 29% full-time.
Majors Accounting; administrative assistant and secretarial science; African-American/Black studies; airline pilot and flight crew; art; art teacher education; automobile/automotive mechanics technology; behavioral sciences; biological and physical sciences; biology/biological sciences; business administration and management; chemistry; child development; civil engineering technology; commercial and advertising art; computer engineering technology; computer programming; construction engineering technology; criminal justice/law enforcement administration; criminal justice/police science; cultural studies; dance; data processing and data processing technology; developmental and child psychology; drafting and design technology; dramatic/theatre arts; economics; electrical, electronic and communications engineering technology; emergency medical technology (EMT paramedic); engineering; English; family and consumer sciences/human sciences; fiber, textile and weaving arts; fire science; foods, nutrition, and wellness; French; German; graphic and printing equipment operation/production; health science; Hispanic-American, Puerto Rican, and Mexican-American/Chicano studies; history; human services; industrial radiologic technology; information science/studies; jazz/jazz studies; journalism; kindergarten/preschool education; legal assistant/paralegal; liberal arts and sciences/liberal studies; literature; machine tool technology; mathematics; mechanical engineering/mechanical technology; music; nuclear medical technology; nursing (registered nurse training); parks, recreation and leisure; parks, recreation and leisure facilities management; philosophy; photography; physical education teaching and coaching; physical sciences; physics; pre-engineering; psychology; real estate; respiratory care therapy; social sciences; social work; sociology; Spanish; speech and rhetoric; teacher assistant/aide; telecommunications; trade and industrial teacher education; welding technology.
Academic Programs *Special study options:* academic remediation for entering students, adult/continuing education programs, advanced placement credit, English as a second language, honors programs, part-time degree program, services for LD students, summer session for credit.
Library Compton Community College Library with 45,000 titles, 400 serial subscriptions.
Computers on Campus 30 computers available on campus for general student use.
Student Life *Housing:* college housing not available. *Activities and Organizations:* drama/theater group. *Campus security:* 24-hour patrols. *Student services:* personal/psychological counseling.
Athletics *Intercollegiate sports:* baseball M, basketball M/W, cross-country running M/W, football M, golf M, track and field M/W. *Intramural sports:* basketball M/W.
Costs (2004–05) *Tuition:* state resident $0 full-time; nonresident $3576 full-time, $149 per unit part-time. *Required fees:* $624 full-time, $26 per unit part-time.
Financial Aid Of all full-time matriculated undergraduates who enrolled in 2003, 300 Federal Work-Study jobs (averaging $3000).
Applying *Options:* early admission. *Application deadline:* rolling (freshmen), rolling (transfers). *Notification:* continuous (freshmen).
Admissions Contact Mr. Phillip Glezer, Interim Associate Dean, Admissions and Records, Compton Community College, 1111 East Artesia Boulevard, Compton, CA 91221. *Phone:* 310-900-1600 Ext. 2047.

CONCORDE CAREER INSTITUTE
North Hollywood, California

Admissions Contact 12412 Victory Boulevard, North Hollywood, CA 91606.

CONTRA COSTA COLLEGE
San Pablo, California

- **State and locally supported** 2-year, founded 1948, part of Contra Costa Community College District and California Community College System

- **Calendar** semesters
- **Degree** certificates and associate
- **Small-town** 83-acre campus with easy access to San Francisco
- **Coed,** 8,834 undergraduate students, 45% full-time, 62% women, 38% men

Undergraduates 3,973 full-time, 4,861 part-time. Students come from 5 states and territories, 16 other countries, 28% African American, 15% Asian American or Pacific Islander, 28% Hispanic American, 0.6% Native American, 2% international.
Freshmen *Admission:* 5,794 applied, 4,126 enrolled.
Faculty *Total:* 415, 28% full-time, 22% with terminal degrees.
Majors Administrative assistant and secretarial science; African-American/Black studies; anthropology; art; automobile/automotive mechanics technology; biology/biological sciences; biology/biotechnology laboratory technician; business administration and management; chemistry; computer programming; computer science; criminal justice/law enforcement administration; criminal justice/police science; culinary arts; dental hygiene; drafting and design technology; electrical, electronic and communications engineering technology; emergency medical technology (EMT paramedic); engineering; English; family and consumer sciences/human sciences; French; geography; geology/earth science; German; Hispanic-American, Puerto Rican, and Mexican-American/Chicano studies; history; humanities; industrial arts; Italian; journalism; kindergarten/preschool education; liberal arts and sciences/liberal studies; materials science; mathematics; music; nursing (licensed practical/vocational nurse training); nursing (registered nurse training); philosophy; physics; political science and government; quality control technology; real estate; sociology; Spanish; welding technology.
Academic Programs *Special study options:* academic remediation for entering students, adult/continuing education programs, cooperative education, English as a second language, honors programs, off-campus study, part-time degree program, services for LD students, study abroad, summer session for credit. *ROTC:* Army (c), Air Force (c).
Library Contra Costa College Library with 57,017 titles, 333 serial subscriptions, 1,860 audiovisual materials, a Web page.
Computers on Campus 180 computers available on campus for general student use. Online (class) registration, at least one staffed computer lab available.
Student Life *Housing:* college housing not available. *Activities and Organizations:* drama/theater group, student-run newspaper. *Campus security:* 24-hour patrols. *Student services:* personal/psychological counseling, women's center.
Athletics *Intercollegiate sports:* baseball M, basketball M/W, cross-country running M/W, football M, softball W, track and field M/W, volleyball W.
Standardized Tests *Recommended:* SAT or ACT (for placement).
Costs (2004–05) *Tuition:* state resident $0 full-time; nonresident $4410 full-time, $147 per unit part-time. *Required fees:* $780 full-time, $26 per unit part-time.
Financial Aid Of all full-time matriculated undergraduates who enrolled in 2003, 100 Federal Work-Study jobs (averaging $3000).
Applying *Options:* common application, early admission. *Application deadline:* rolling (freshmen).
Admissions Contact Mrs. Linda Ames, Admissions and Records Supervisor, Contra Costa College, 2600 Mission Bell Drive, San Pablo, CA 94806-3195. *Phone:* 510-235-7800 Ext. 4211.

COPPER MOUNTAIN COLLEGE
Joshua Tree, California

- **State-supported** 2-year, founded 1966
- **Calendar** semesters
- **Degree** certificates and associate
- **Coed**
- 100% of applicants were admitted

Admissions Contact Dr. Laraine Turk, Associate Dean of Student Services, Copper Mountain College, 6162 Rotary Way, Joshua Tree, CA 92252. *Phone:* 760-366-5290.

COSUMNES RIVER COLLEGE
Sacramento, California

Admissions Contact Ms. Dianna L. Moore, Supervisor of Admissions Records, Cosumnes River College, 8401 Center Parkway, Sacramento, CA 95823-5799. *Phone:* 916-688-7423. *Fax:* 916-688-7467.

CRAFTON HILLS COLLEGE
Yucaipa, California

Admissions Contact Mr. Marco Cota, Interim Director of Admissions, Crafton Hills College, 11711 Sand Canyon Road, Yucaipa, CA 92399. *Phone:* 909-389-3355. *Fax:* 909-389-9141. *E-mail:* admissions@craftonhills.edu.

CUESTA COLLEGE
San Luis Obispo, California

- **District-supported** 2-year, founded 1964
- **Calendar** semesters
- **Degree** certificates and associate
- **Rural** 129-acre campus
- **Coed**

Student Life *Campus security:* 24-hour emergency response devices and patrols, late-night transport/escort service.
Standardized Tests *Recommended:* Assessment and Placement Services for Community Colleges.
Costs (2004–05) *Tuition:* state resident $0 full-time; nonresident $4704 full-time, $186 per unit part-time. *Required fees:* $826 full-time, $26 per unit part-time.
Applying *Options:* common application, electronic application, early admission, deferred entrance. *Required:* high school transcript. *Recommended:* essay or personal statement.
Admissions Contact Ms. Juileta Siu, Admissions Clerk, Cuesta College, PO Box 8106, Highway 1, San Luis Obispo, CA 93403-8106. *Phone:* 805-546-3140. *Fax:* 805-546-3975. *E-mail:* admit@cuesta.edu.

CUYAMACA COLLEGE
El Cajon, California

- **State-supported** 2-year, founded 1978, part of Grossmont-Cuyamaca Community College District
- **Calendar** semesters
- **Degree** certificates, diplomas, and associate
- **Suburban** 165-acre campus with easy access to San Diego
- **Coed**

Standardized Tests *Required:* ACT ASSET (for placement).
Costs (2004–05) *Tuition:* state resident $0 full-time; nonresident $5205 full-time. Full-time tuition and fees vary according to course load. Part-time tuition and fees vary according to course load. *Required fees:* $825 full-time.
Financial Aid Of all full-time matriculated undergraduates who enrolled in 2003, 81 Federal Work-Study jobs (averaging $1600). 39 state and other part-time jobs (averaging $900).
Applying *Options:* common application, electronic application, early admission.
Admissions Contact Dr. Beth Appenzeller, Dean of Admissions and Records, Cuyamaca College, 900 Rancho San Diego Parkway, El Cajon, CA 92019-4304. *Phone:* 619-660-4302. *Fax:* 610-660-4575.

CYPRESS COLLEGE
Cypress, California

Admissions Contact Mr. David Wassenaar, Dean of Admissions and Records, Cypress College, 9200 Valley View, Cypress, CA 90630. *Phone:* 714-484-7435. *Fax:* 714-484-7446. *E-mail:* info@cypress.cc.ca.us.

DE ANZA COLLEGE
Cupertino, California

- **State and locally supported** 2-year, founded 1967, part of California Community College System
- **Calendar** quarters
- **Degree** certificates, diplomas, and associate
- **Small-town** 112-acre campus with easy access to San Francisco and San Jose
- **Coed**, 23,344 undergraduate students, 38% full-time, 53% women, 47% men

Undergraduates 8,860 full-time, 14,484 part-time. Students come from 48 states and territories, 79 other countries, 6% African American, 33% Asian American or Pacific Islander, 15% Hispanic American, 0.5% Native American, 6% international.
Freshmen *Admission:* 2,411 enrolled. *Average high school GPA:* 2.86.
Faculty *Total:* 812, 63% full-time.
Majors Accounting; administrative assistant and secretarial science; art; art history, criticism and conservation; automobile/automotive mechanics technology; behavioral sciences; biology/biological sciences; business administration and management; business machine repair; ceramic arts and ceramics; child development; commercial and advertising art; computer graphics; computer management; computer programming; computer science; construction engineering technology; corrections; criminal justice/law enforcement administration; criminal justice/police science; cultural studies; developmental and child psychology; dramatic/theatre arts; drawing; economics; engineering; engineering technology; English; environmental studies; film/cinema studies; history; humani-

ties; industrial technology; information science/studies; international relations and affairs; journalism; legal assistant/paralegal; liberal arts and sciences/liberal studies; machine tool technology; marketing/marketing management; mass communication/media; mathematics; mechanical design technology; medical/clinical assistant; music; nursing (licensed practical/vocational nurse training); nursing (registered nurse training); philosophy; photography; physical education teaching and coaching; physical therapy; physics; political science and government; pre-engineering; printmaking; psychology; purchasing, procurement/acquisitions and contracts management; radio and television; real estate; sculpture; social sciences; sociology; Spanish; speech and rhetoric; technical and business writing.
Academic Programs *Special study options:* academic remediation for entering students, adult/continuing education programs, advanced placement credit, cooperative education, English as a second language, external degree program, honors programs, internships, part-time degree program, services for LD students, study abroad, summer session for credit. *ROTC:* Army (c), Air Force (c).
Library A. Robert DeHart Learning Center with 80,000 titles, 927 serial subscriptions.
Computers on Campus 800 computers available on campus for general student use. A campuswide network can be accessed from off campus. At least one staffed computer lab available.
Student Life *Housing:* college housing not available. *Activities and Organizations:* drama/theater group, student-run newspaper, choral group, Student Nurses Association, Phi Theta Kappa, Automotive Club, Vietnamese Club, Filipino Club. *Campus security:* 24-hour emergency response devices, student patrols, late-night transport/escort service. *Student services:* health clinic, personal/psychological counseling, legal services.
Athletics *Intercollegiate sports:* baseball M, basketball M/W, cross-country running M/W, football M, golf M/W, soccer M/W, softball W, swimming and diving M/W, tennis M/W, track and field M/W, volleyball M/W, water polo M. *Intramural sports:* badminton M/W, basketball M, soccer M/W, swimming and diving M/W, volleyball M/W.
Standardized Tests *Required for some:* SAT (for placement), CPT, DTLS, DTMS.
Costs (2004–05) *Tuition:* state resident $0 full-time; nonresident $3600 full-time, $100 per unit part-time. *Required fees:* $612 full-time, $17 per unit part-time.
Applying *Options:* common application, early admission. *Application fee:* $22. *Application deadline:* rolling (freshmen), rolling (transfers). *Notification:* continuous (freshmen).
Admissions Contact Ms. Kathleen Kayne, Director of Records and Admissions, De Anza College, 21250 Stevens Creek Boulevard, Cupertino, CA 95014. *Phone:* 408-864-8292. *Fax:* 408-864-8329. *E-mail:* webregda@fhda.edu.

DEEP SPRINGS COLLEGE
Deep Springs, California

Admissions Contact Dr. L. Jackson Newell, President, Deep Springs College, HC 72, Box 45001, Dyer, NV 89010-9803. *Phone:* 760-872-2000. *E-mail:* apcom@deepsprings.edu.

DIABLO VALLEY COLLEGE
Pleasant Hill, California

- **State and locally supported** 2-year, founded 1949, part of Contra Costa Community College District, part of California Community Colleges
- **Calendar** semesters
- **Degree** certificates and associate
- **Suburban** 100-acre campus with easy access to San Francisco
- **Coed**

Student Life *Campus security:* 24-hour emergency response devices and patrols, student patrols.
Costs (2004–05) *Tuition:* nonresident $4250 full-time, $165 per credit part-time. *Required fees:* $780 full-time, $26 per credit part-time.
Financial Aid Of all full-time matriculated undergraduates who enrolled in 2003, 67 Federal Work-Study jobs (averaging $3000). *Financial aid deadline:* 5/23.
Applying *Options:* early admission. *Recommended:* high school transcript.
Admissions Contact Catherine Fites-Chavis, Supervisor of Admissions and Records, Diablo Valley College, 321 Golf Club Road, Pleasant Hill, CA 94523-1529. *Phone:* 925-685-1230 Ext. 2330.

DON BOSCO TECHNICAL INSTITUTE
Rosemead, California

Admissions Contact Mr. Tom Bauman, Director of College Admissions, Don Bosco Technical Institute, 1151 San Gabriel Boulevard, Rosemead, CA 91770-4299. *Phone:* 626-940-2036.

EAST LOS ANGELES COLLEGE
Monterey Park, California

- **State and locally supported** 2-year, founded 1945, part of Los Angeles Community College District
- **Calendar** semesters
- **Degree** certificates and associate
- **Urban** 84-acre campus with easy access to Los Angeles
- **Coed**

Faculty *Student/faculty ratio:* 34:1.

Student Life *Campus security:* 24-hour emergency response devices and patrols, late-night transport/escort service.

Costs (2004–05) *Tuition:* state resident $0 full-time; nonresident $4200 full-time, $177 per unit part-time. *Required fees:* $660 full-time, $26 per unit part-time.

Financial Aid Of all full-time matriculated undergraduates who enrolled in 2003, 189 Federal Work-Study jobs (averaging $3000).

Applying *Options:* common application, early admission. *Recommended:* high school transcript, English and mathematics placement test.

Admissions Contact Mr. Jeremy Allred, Associate Dean of Admissions, East Los Angeles College, 1301 Avenida Cesar Chavez, Monterey Park, CA 91754-6001. *Phone:* 323-265-8801. *Fax:* 323-265-8688.

EL CAMINO COLLEGE
Torrance, California

- **State-supported** 2-year, founded 1947, part of California Community College System
- **Calendar** semesters
- **Degree** certificates, diplomas, and associate
- **Urban** 115-acre campus with easy access to Los Angeles
- **Coed**

Applying *Options:* early admission. *Required:* high school transcript.

Admissions Contact Mr. William Robinson, Director of Admissions, El Camino College, 16007 Crenshaw Boulevard, Torrance, CA 90506. *Phone:* 310-660-3418. *Toll-free phone:* 866-ELCAMINO. *Fax:* 310-660-3818.

EMPIRE COLLEGE
Santa Rosa, California

Admissions Contact Ms. Dahnja Barker, Admissions Officer, Empire College, 3035 Cleveland Avenue, Santa Rosa, CA 95403. *Phone:* 707-546-4000. *Fax:* 707-546-4058. *E-mail:* rhurd@empcol.com.

EVEREST COLLEGE
Rancho Cucamonga, California

Admissions Contact 9616 Archibald Avenue, Suite 100, Rancho Cucamonga, CA 91730.

EVERGREEN VALLEY COLLEGE
San Jose, California

Admissions Contact Ms. Kathleen Moberg, Director of Admissions and Records, Evergreen Valley College, 3095 Yerba Buena Road, San Jose, CA 95135-1598. *Phone:* 408-270-6423. *Fax:* 408-223-9351.

FASHION CAREERS OF CALIFORNIA COLLEGE
San Diego, California

- **Proprietary** 2-year, founded 1979
- **Calendar** quarters
- **Degree** certificates and associate
- **Urban** campus
- **Coed, primarily women,** 104 undergraduate students, 100% full-time, 89% women, 11% men

Undergraduates 104 full-time. Students come from 18 states and territories, 3 other countries, 27% are from out of state, 13% African American, 11% Asian American or Pacific Islander, 23% Hispanic American, 2% international. *Retention:* 75% of 2002 full-time freshmen returned.

Freshmen *Admission:* 72 enrolled.

Faculty *Total:* 10. *Student/faculty ratio:* 32:1.

Majors Fashion/apparel design; fashion merchandising.

Academic Programs *Special study options:* adult/continuing education programs, cooperative education, double majors, internships.

Library Fashion Careers of California Library with 800 titles, 14 serial subscriptions, 175 audiovisual materials.

Computers on Campus 36 computers available on campus for general student use. Internet access, at least one staffed computer lab available.

Student Life *Housing:* college housing not available. *Campus security:* 24-hour emergency response devices.

Standardized Tests *Required:* Wonderlic aptitude test (for admission).

Costs (2005–06) *Tuition:* $15,900 full-time, $400 per credit part-time. *Required fees:* $325 full-time.

Financial Aid Of all full-time matriculated undergraduates who enrolled in 2003, 10 Federal Work-Study jobs (averaging $1200).

Applying *Options:* common application, electronic application. *Application fee:* $25. *Required:* essay or personal statement, high school transcript, interview. *Application deadline:* rolling (freshmen), rolling (transfers).

Admissions Contact Ms. Leslie Phillips, Admissions Representative, Fashion Careers of California College, 1923 Morena Boulevard, San Diego, CA 92110. *Phone:* 619-275-4700 Ext. 309. *Toll-free phone:* 888-FCCC999. *Fax:* 619-275-0635. *E-mail:* leslie@fashioncollege.com.

FEATHER RIVER COLLEGE
Quincy, California

- **State and locally supported** 2-year, founded 1968, part of California Community College System
- **Calendar** semesters
- **Degree** certificates, diplomas, and associate
- **Rural** 150-acre campus
- **Coed,** 1,635 undergraduate students, 24% full-time, 58% women, 42% men

Undergraduates 387 full-time, 1,248 part-time. Students come from 24 states and territories, 6 other countries, 23% are from out of state, 10% African American, 2% Asian American or Pacific Islander, 8% Hispanic American, 3% Native American, 1% international, 4% transferred in, 24% live on campus. *Retention:* 62% of 2002 full-time freshmen returned.

Freshmen *Admission:* 155 applied, 155 admitted, 155 enrolled.

Faculty *Total:* 82, 32% full-time. *Student/faculty ratio:* 18:1.

Majors Administrative assistant and secretarial science; animal/livestock husbandry and production; biology/biological sciences; business/commerce; child care and support services management; child care/guidance; construction engineering technology; criminal justice/law enforcement administration; English; forestry; history; liberal arts and sciences/liberal studies; mathematics; natural resources management; nursing (licensed practical/vocational nurse training); parks, recreation and leisure facilities management; parks, recreation, and leisure related; physical sciences; social sciences.

Academic Programs *Special study options:* academic remediation for entering students, adult/continuing education programs, advanced placement credit, cooperative education, distance learning, double majors, honors programs, independent study, part-time degree program, services for LD students, summer session for credit.

Library Feather River Library with 20,782 titles, 4,122 serial subscriptions, 1,762 audiovisual materials, an OPAC.

Computers on Campus 146 computers available on campus for general student use. A campuswide network can be accessed. Internet access, at least one staffed computer lab available.

Student Life *Housing Options:* coed. Campus housing is university owned. *Activities and Organizations:* drama/theater group, choral group, Mountain Ultimate Disc (MUD), Varsity Club, Feather River Outings Group, SIFE, Chess Club. *Campus security:* student patrols.

Athletics *Intercollegiate sports:* baseball M, basketball M/W, equestrian sports M/W, football M, soccer M/W, softball W. *Intramural sports:* cheerleading W(c), ultimate Frisbee M(c)/W(c).

Costs (2004–05) *Tuition:* state resident $0 full-time; nonresident $5250 full-time, $175 per unit part-time. *Required fees:* $806 full-time, $26 per unit part-time. *Room and board:* room only: $3753. Room and board charges vary according to housing facility. *Payment plan:* deferred payment.

Financial Aid Of all full-time matriculated undergraduates who enrolled in 2003, 22 Federal Work-Study jobs (averaging $750). 103 state and other part-time jobs (averaging $1504).

Applying *Options:* electronic application.

Admissions Contact Ms. Karen Hayden, Registrar, Feather River College, 570 Golden Eagle Avenue, Quincy, CA 95971. *Phone:* 530-283-0202 Ext. 285. *Toll-free phone:* 800-442-9799 Ext. 286. *Fax:* 530-283-9961. *E-mail:* info@frc.edu.

FIDM/The Fashion Institute of Design & Merchandising, Los Angeles Campus

Los Angeles, California

- **Proprietary** 2-year, founded 1969, part of Fashion Institute of Design and Merchandising
- **Calendar** quarters
- **Degrees** associate (also includes Orange County Campus)
- **Urban** campus
- **Coed**, 3,191 undergraduate students, 80% full-time, 90% women, 10% men

Undergraduates 2,549 full-time, 642 part-time. Students come from 40 states and territories, 30 other countries, 29% are from out of state.

Freshmen *Admission:* 916 admitted, 916 enrolled.

Faculty *Total:* 214, 24% full-time. *Student/faculty ratio:* 26:1.

Majors Apparel and accessories marketing; apparel and textiles; commercial and advertising art; consumer merchandising/retailing management; design and visual communications; fashion/apparel design; fashion merchandising; interior design.

Academic Programs *Special study options:* academic remediation for entering students, adult/continuing education programs, advanced placement credit, cooperative education, distance learning, English as a second language, independent study, internships, part-time degree program, services for LD students, study abroad, summer session for credit.

Library Resource and Research Center with 19,099 titles, 369 serial subscriptions, 3,607 audiovisual materials, an OPAC.

Computers on Campus 322 computers available on campus for general student use. A campuswide network can be accessed from student residence rooms and from off campus. Internet access, online (class) registration, at least one staffed computer lab available.

Student Life *Housing:* college housing not available. *Options:* Campus housing is provided by a third party. *Activities and Organizations:* student-run newspaper, ASID (student chapter), International Club, DECA, Association of Manufacturing Students, Honor Society. *Campus security:* 24-hour emergency response devices and patrols, late-night transport/escort service. *Student services:* personal/psychological counseling.

Standardized Tests *Required:* Wonderlic Aptitude Test (for admission).

Costs (2005–06) *Tuition:* $16,275 full-time. Full-time tuition and fees vary according to program. Part-time tuition and fees vary according to program. No tuition increase for student's term of enrollment. *Required fees:* $500 full-time. *Payment plan:* tuition prepayment. *Waivers:* employees or children of employees.

Financial Aid Of all full-time matriculated undergraduates who enrolled in 2003, 88 Federal Work-Study jobs (averaging $2935).

Applying *Options:* common application, electronic application, deferred entrance. *Application fee:* $225. *Required:* essay or personal statement, high school transcript, 3 letters of recommendation. *Required for some:* interview, major-determined project. *Recommended:* minimum 2.0 GPA. *Application deadline:* rolling (freshmen), rolling (transfers).

Admissions Contact Ms. Susan Aronson, Director of Admissions FIDM/The Fashion Institute of Design and Merchandise, FIDM/The Fashion Institute of Design & Merchandising, Los Angeles Campus, FIDM LA, 919 South Grand Avenue, Los Angeles, CA 90015. *Phone:* 213-624-1200 Ext. 5400. *Toll-free phone:* 800-624-1200. *Fax:* 213-624-4799. *E-mail:* info@fidm.com.

► **See page 494 for a narrative description.**

FIDM/The Fashion Institute of Design & Merchandising, Orange County Campus

Irvine, California

Admissions Contact Admissions, FIDM/The Fashion Institute of Design & Merchandising, Orange County Campus, 17590 Gillette Avenue, Irvine, CA 92614-5610. *Phone:* 949-851-6200. *Toll-free phone:* 888-974-3436. *Fax:* 949-851-6808.

FIDM/The Fashion Institute of Design & Merchandising, San Diego Campus

San Diego, California

- **Proprietary** 2-year, founded 1985, part of Fashion Institute of Design and Merchandising
- **Calendar** quarters
- **Degree** associate
- **Urban** campus
- **Coed**, 259 undergraduate students, 89% full-time, 92% women, 8% men

Undergraduates 231 full-time, 28 part-time. Students come from 15 states and territories, 1 other country, 19% are from out of state, 7% African American, 13% Asian American or Pacific Islander, 24% Hispanic American, 1% Native American, 0.4% international.

Freshmen *Admission:* 160 admitted, 160 enrolled.

Faculty *Total:* 35, 9% full-time. *Student/faculty ratio:* 20:1.

Majors Apparel and accessories marketing; commercial and advertising art; consumer merchandising/retailing management; design and visual communications; fashion/apparel design; fashion merchandising; interior design.

Academic Programs *Special study options:* academic remediation for entering students, adult/continuing education programs, advanced placement credit, cooperative education, distance learning, English as a second language, independent study, internships, part-time degree program, services for LD students, study abroad, summer session for credit.

Library Resource and Research Center with 2,642 titles, 100 serial subscriptions, 915 audiovisual materials, an OPAC.

Computers on Campus 32 computers available on campus for general student use. A campuswide network can be accessed from student residence rooms and from off campus. Internet access, online (class) registration, at least one staffed computer lab available.

Student Life *Housing:* college housing not available. *Options:* Campus housing is provided by a third party. *Activities and Organizations:* ASID (student chapter), DECA, Honor Society, Phi Theta Kappa. *Campus security:* 24-hour emergency response devices and patrols. *Student services:* personal/psychological counseling.

Costs (2005–06) *Tuition:* $16,275 full-time. Full-time tuition and fees vary according to program. Part-time tuition and fees vary according to program. No tuition increase for student's term of enrollment. *Required fees:* $500 full-time. *Payment plan:* tuition prepayment. *Waivers:* employees or children of employees.

Applying *Options:* common application, electronic application, deferred entrance. *Application fee:* $225. *Required:* essay or personal statement, high school transcript, 3 letters of recommendation. *Required for some:* interview, major-determined project. *Recommended:* minimum 2.5 GPA. *Application deadline:* rolling (freshmen), rolling (transfers).

Admissions Contact Ms. Susan Aronson, Director of Admissions, FIDM/The Fashion Institute of Design & Merchandising, San Diego Campus, FIDM San Diego, 1010 2nd Avenue, San Diego, CA 92101. *Phone:* 213-624-1200 Ext. 5400. *Toll-free phone:* 800-243-3436. *Fax:* 619-232-4322. *E-mail:* info@fidm.com.

FIDM/The Fashion Institute of Design & Merchandising, San Francisco Campus

San Francisco, California

- **Proprietary** 2-year, founded 1973, part of Fashion Institute of Design and Merchandising
- **Calendar** quarters
- **Degree** associate
- **Urban** campus
- **Coed, primarily women,** 806 undergraduate students, 81% full-time, 93% women, 7% men

Undergraduates 653 full-time, 153 part-time. Students come from 15 states and territories, 20 other countries, 6% are from out of state, 7% African American, 16% Asian American or Pacific Islander, 17% Hispanic American, 0.6% Native American, 2% international.

Freshmen *Admission:* 292 admitted, 292 enrolled.

Faculty *Total:* 70, 19% full-time. *Student/faculty ratio:* 22:1.

Majors Apparel and accessories marketing; apparel and textiles; commercial and advertising art; consumer merchandising/retailing management; design and visual communications; fashion/apparel design; fashion merchandising; interior design.

Academic Programs *Special study options:* academic remediation for entering students, adult/continuing education programs, advanced placement credit, cooperative education, distance learning, English as a second language, honors programs, independent study, internships, part-time degree program, services for LD students, study abroad, summer session for credit.

Library Resource and Research Center with 5,073 titles, 173 serial subscriptions, 616 audiovisual materials, an OPAC.

Computers on Campus 81 computers available on campus for general student use. A campuswide network can be accessed from student residence rooms and from off campus. Internet access, online (class) registration, at least one staffed computer lab available.

Student Life *Housing:* college housing not available. *Options:* Campus housing is provided by a third party. *Activities and Organizations:* ASID (student chapter), DECA, Visual Design Form, Honor Society. *Campus security:* 24-hour emergency response devices and patrols. *Student services:* personal/psychological counseling.

Standardized Tests *Required:* Wonderlic aptitude test (for admission).

Costs (2005–06) *Tuition:* $16,275 full-time. Full-time tuition and fees vary according to program. Part-time tuition and fees vary according to program. No tuition increase for student's term of enrollment. *Required fees:* $500 full-time. *Payment plan:* tuition prepayment. *Waivers:* employees or children of employees.

Applying *Options:* common application, electronic application, deferred entrance. *Application fee:* $225. *Required:* essay or personal statement, high school transcript, 3 letters of recommendation. *Required for some:* interview, major-determined project. *Recommended:* minimum 2.0 GPA. *Application deadline:* rolling (freshmen), rolling (transfers).

Admissions Contact Ms. Susan Aronson, Director of Admissions/FIDM, FIDM/The Fashion Institute of Design & Merchandising, San Francisco Campus, 55 Stockton Street, San Francisco, CA 94108. *Phone:* 213-624-1200 Ext. 5400. *Toll-free phone:* 800-711-7175. *Fax:* 415-296-7299. *E-mail:* info@fidm.com.

FOOTHILL COLLEGE
Los Altos Hills, California

- **State and locally supported** 2-year, founded 1958, part of Foothill-DeAnza Community College District
- **Calendar** quarters
- **Degree** certificates and associate
- **Suburban** 122-acre campus with easy access to San Jose
- **Coed,** 17,406 undergraduate students, 22% full-time, 51% women, 49% men

Undergraduates 3,852 full-time, 13,554 part-time. Students come from 51 states and territories, 101 other countries, 2% are from out of state, 2% African American, 26% Asian American or Pacific Islander, 12% Hispanic American, 0.4% Native American, 4% international.

Freshmen *Admission:* 5,284 applied, 5,284 admitted.

Faculty *Total:* 608, 26% full-time. *Student/faculty ratio:* 38:1.

Majors Accounting; American studies; anthropology; art; art history, criticism and conservation; athletic training; avionics maintenance technology; biology/biological sciences; biology/biotechnology laboratory technician; business administration and management; chemistry; child development; classics and languages, literatures and linguistics; commercial and advertising art; communication/speech communication and rhetoric; computer engineering technology; computer science; creative writing; cultural studies; dental assisting; dental hygiene; diagnostic medical sonography and ultrasound technology; dramatic/theatre arts; economics; electrical, electronic and communications engineering technology; emergency medical technology (EMT paramedic); engineering; English; fine/studio arts; French; geography; geology/earth science; German; history; humanities; international business/trade/commerce; Japanese; landscape architecture; legal studies; liberal arts and sciences/liberal studies; library science; linguistics; literature; mathematics; medical radiologic technology; music; ornamental horticulture; philosophy; photography; physical education teaching and coaching; physician assistant; physics; plant nursery management; political science and government; psychology; radio and television; radiologic technology/science; real estate; respiratory care therapy; social sciences; sociology; Spanish; speech and rhetoric; tourism and travel services management; veterinary technology; women's studies.

Academic Programs *Special study options:* academic remediation for entering students, accelerated degree program, adult/continuing education programs, advanced placement credit, cooperative education, distance learning, English as a second language, honors programs, independent study, internships, off-campus study, part-time degree program, services for LD students, student-designed majors, study abroad, summer session for credit. *ROTC:* Army (c), Air Force (c).

Library Hubert H. Semans Library with 70,000 titles, 450 serial subscriptions, an OPAC, a Web page.

Computers on Campus 400 computers available on campus for general student use. A campuswide network can be accessed from off campus. Internet access, online (class) registration, at least one staffed computer lab available.

Student Life *Housing:* college housing not available. *Activities and Organizations:* drama/theater group, student-run newspaper, radio station, choral group, Alpha Gamma Sigma, student government. *Campus security:* 24-hour emergency response devices and patrols, late-night transport/escort service. *Student services:* health clinic, personal/psychological counseling, legal services.

Athletics Member NJCAA. *Intercollegiate sports:* basketball M/W, football M, golf M/W, soccer M/W, softball W, swimming and diving M/W, tennis M, volleyball W, water polo M/W.

Costs (2004–05) *Tuition:* state resident $0 full-time; nonresident $4500 full-time, $100 per unit part-time. *Required fees:* $833 full-time, $17 per unit part-time, $23 per term part-time.

Financial Aid Of all full-time matriculated undergraduates who enrolled in 2003, 80 Federal Work-Study jobs (averaging $1300). 210 state and other part-time jobs.

Applying *Options:* electronic application. *Recommended:* high school transcript. *Application deadline:* 9/15 (freshmen), rolling (transfers). *Notification:* continuous (freshmen).

Admissions Contact Ms. Penny Johnson, Dean, Counseling and Student Services, Foothill College, Admissions and Records, 12345 El Monte Road, Los Altos Hills, CA 94022. *Phone:* 650-949-7326. *Fax:* 650-949-7375.

FOUNDATION COLLEGE
San Diego, California

- **Independent** 2-year
- **Calendar** continuous
- **Degree** certificates and associate
- **Urban** campus
- **Coed,** 106 undergraduate students, 100% full-time, 22% women, 78% men

Undergraduates 106 full-time. 18% African American, 18% Asian American or Pacific Islander, 20% Hispanic American, 3% Native American.

Freshmen *Admission:* 221 applied, 109 admitted, 16 enrolled.

Faculty *Total:* 13, 77% full-time. *Student/faculty ratio:* 8:1.

Majors Computer engineering technology; computer programming; computer science; computer systems networking and telecommunications; computer technology/computer systems technology; data processing and data processing technology.

Student Life *Housing:* college housing not available.

Costs (2005–06) *Tuition:* $17,940 full-time, $260 per credit part-time. *Required fees:* $1200 full-time, $120 per course part-time.

Applying *Application deadline:* rolling (freshmen), rolling (transfers). *Notification:* continuous (freshmen).

Admissions Contact Peggy Aplin, Admissions Manager, Foundation College, 5353 Mission Center Road, Suite 100, San Diego, CA 92108-1306. *Phone:* 619-683-3273 Ext. 105. *Toll-free phone:* 888-707-3273. *E-mail:* jdurb@foundationcollege.com.

FRESNO CITY COLLEGE
Fresno, California

Admissions Contact Ms. Stephanie Pauhi, Office Assistant, Fresno City College, 1101 East University Avenue, Fresno, CA 93741. *Phone:* 559-442-8225. *Fax:* 559-237-4232.

FULLERTON COLLEGE
Fullerton, California

Admissions Contact Mr. Peter Fong, Dean of Admissions and Records, Fullerton College, 321 East Chapman Avenue, Fullerton, CA 92832-2095. *Phone:* 714-992-7582. *E-mail:* pfong@fullcoll.edu.

GAVILAN COLLEGE
Gilroy, California

- **State and locally supported** 2-year, founded 1919, part of California Community College System
- **Calendar** semesters
- **Degree** certificates, diplomas, and associate
- **Rural** 150-acre campus with easy access to San Jose
- **Coed**

Student Life *Campus security:* 24-hour emergency response devices and patrols, late-night transport/escort service.

Standardized Tests *Required for some:* ACT ASSET.

Costs (2004–05) *Tuition:* state resident $0 full-time; nonresident $3816 full-time, $159 per unit part-time. *Required fees:* $624 full-time, $26 per unit part-time.

Financial Aid Of all full-time matriculated undergraduates who enrolled in 2003, 50 Federal Work-Study jobs (averaging $2000). *Financial aid deadline:* 6/30.

Admissions Contact Ms. Joy Parker, Director of Admissions, Gavilan College, 5055 Santa Teresa Boulevard, Gilroy, CA 95020. *Phone:* 408-848-4735. *Fax:* 408-846-4910.

GLENDALE COMMUNITY COLLEGE
Glendale, California

- **State and locally supported** 2-year, founded 1927, part of California Community College System
- **Calendar** semesters
- **Degree** certificates and associate
- **Urban** 119-acre campus with easy access to Los Angeles
- **Endowment** $5.3 million
- **Coed,** 15,767 undergraduate students, 30% full-time, 59% women, 41% men

Undergraduates 4,712 full-time, 11,055 part-time. Students come from 59 states and territories, 121 other countries, 1% are from out of state, 3% African American, 9% Asian American or Pacific Islander, 22% Hispanic American, 0.5% Native American, 27% international, 5% transferred in.

Freshmen *Admission:* 5,313 applied, 2,770 admitted, 2,125 enrolled.

Faculty *Total:* 705, 34% full-time.

Majors Accounting; administrative assistant and secretarial science; airframe mechanics and aircraft maintenance technology; airline pilot and flight crew; applied art; art; art history, criticism and conservation; aviation/airway management; avionics maintenance technology; biological and physical sciences; business administration and management; ceramic arts and ceramics; child development; commercial and advertising art; computer and information sciences related; computer engineering related; computer engineering technology; computer programming related; computer programming (specific applications); computer science; computer software and media applications related; computer/technical support; cosmetology; criminal justice/police science; culinary arts; dance; data entry/microcomputer applications; data entry/microcomputer applications related; data processing and data processing technology; desktop publishing and digital imaging design; drafting and design technology; dramatic/theatre arts; education; electromechanical technology; English; fashion/apparel design; finance; fire science; foreign languages and literatures; health information/medical records administration; hotel/motel administration; humanities; industrial technology; journalism; legal administrative assistant/secretary; liberal arts and sciences/liberal studies; machine tool technology; mass communication/media; mathematics; medical administrative assistant and medical secretary; medical/clinical assistant; mental health/rehabilitation; music; nursing (licensed practical/vocational nurse training); nursing (registered nurse training); parks, recreation and leisure; photography; real estate; social sciences; speech and rhetoric; welding technology.

Academic Programs *Special study options:* academic remediation for entering students, adult/continuing education programs, advanced placement credit, cooperative education, distance learning, English as a second language, honors programs, independent study, internships, part-time degree program, services for LD students, study abroad, summer session for credit.

Library Glendale Community College Library with 91,371 titles, 312 serial subscriptions, 1,893 audiovisual materials, an OPAC, a Web page.

Computers on Campus 534 computers available on campus for general student use. A campuswide network can be accessed from off campus. Internet access, online (class) registration, at least one staffed computer lab available.

Student Life *Housing:* college housing not available. *Activities and Organizations:* drama/theater group, student-run newspaper, choral group, Alpha Gamma Sigma, Armenian Student Association, Korean Christian Fellowship, Theatre Guild, International Student Association. *Campus security:* student patrols, late-night transport/escort service. *Student services:* health clinic, personal/psychological counseling.

Athletics *Intercollegiate sports:* baseball M, basketball M/W, cross-country running M/W, football M, soccer M/W, softball W, tennis M/W, track and field M/W, volleyball W.

Standardized Tests *Recommended:* CPT.

Costs (2005–06) *Tuition:* state resident $0 full-time; nonresident $3600 full-time, $150 per unit part-time. Full-time tuition and fees vary according to course load. Part-time tuition and fees vary according to course load. *Required fees:* $740 full-time, $26 per unit part-time. *Payment plan:* deferred payment.

Financial Aid Of all full-time matriculated undergraduates who enrolled in 2003, 300 Federal Work-Study jobs (averaging $2500).

Applying *Options:* common application, electronic application, early admission, deferred entrance. *Recommended:* high school transcript. *Application deadline:* rolling (freshmen), rolling (transfers).

Admissions Contact Ms. Sharon Combs, Dean, Admissions and Records, Glendale Community College, 1500 North Verdugo Road, Glendale, CA 91208. *Phone:* 818-551-5115. *Fax:* 818-551-5255. *E-mail:* info@glendale.edu.

GOLDEN WEST COLLEGE
Huntington Beach, California

Admissions Contact Ms. Shirley Donnelly, Director of Enrollment Services, Golden West College, 15744 Golden West Street, Huntington Beach, CA 92647. *Phone:* 714-892-7711 Ext. 58196.

GROSSMONT COLLEGE
El Cajon, California

Admissions Contact Ms. Sharon Clark, Registrar, Grossmont College, El Cajon, CA 92020-1799. *Phone:* 619-644-7170. *Fax:* 619-644-7922.

HARTNELL COLLEGE
Salinas, California

Admissions Contact Ms. Mary Dominguez, Director of Admissions, Hartnell College, 156 Homestead Avenue, Salinas, CA 93901-1697. *Phone:* 831-755-6711. *Fax:* 331-759-6014.

HEALD COLLEGE-CONCORD
Concord, California

Admissions Contact Director of Admissions, Heald College-Concord, 5130 Commercial Circle, Concord, CA 94520. *Phone:* 925-288-5800. *Toll-free phone:* 800-755-3550. *E-mail:* info@heald.edu.

HEALD COLLEGE-FRESNO
Fresno, California

Admissions Contact Director of Admissions, Heald College-Fresno, 255 West Bullard Avenue, Fresno, CA 93704-1706. *Phone:* 559-438-4222. *Toll-free phone:* 800-755-3550. *E-mail:* info@heald.edu.

HEALD COLLEGE-HAYWARD
Hayward, California

Admissions Contact Director of Admissions, Heald College-Hayward, 25500 Industrial Boulevard, Hayward, CA 94545. *Phone:* 510-783-2100. *Toll-free phone:* 800-755-3550. *E-mail:* info@heald.edu.

HEALD COLLEGE-RANCHO CORDOVA
Rancho Cordova, California

Admissions Contact Director of Admissions, Heald College-Rancho Cordova, 2910 Prospect Park Drive, Rancho Cordova, CA 95670-6005. *Phone:* 916-638-1616. *Toll-free phone:* 800-755-3550. *E-mail:* info@heald.edu.

HEALD COLLEGE-ROSEVILLE
Roseville, California

Admissions Contact Director of Admissions, Heald College-Roseville, 7 Sierra Gate Plaza, Roseville, CA 95678. *Phone:* 916-789-8600. *Toll-free phone:* 800-755-3550. *E-mail:* info@heald.edu.

HEALD COLLEGE-SALINAS
Salinas, California

Admissions Contact Director of Admissions, Heald College-Salinas, 1450 North Main Street, Salinas, CA 93906. *Phone:* 831-443-1700. *Toll-free phone:* 800-755-3550. *E-mail:* info@heald.edu.

HEALD COLLEGE-SAN FRANCISCO
San Francisco, California

Admissions Contact Director of Admissions, Heald College-San Francisco, 350 Mission Street, San Francisco, CA 94105. *Phone:* 415-808-3000. *Toll-free phone:* 800-755-3550. *E-mail:* info@heald.edu.

HEALD COLLEGE-SAN JOSE
Milpitas, California

Admissions Contact Director of Admissions, Heald College-San Jose, 341 Great Mall Parkway, Milpitas, CA 95035. *Phone:* 408-934-4900. *Toll-free phone:* 800-755-3550. *E-mail:* info@heald.edu.

HEALD COLLEGE-STOCKTON
Stockton, California

Admissions Contact Director of Admissions, Heald College-Stockton, 1605 East March Lane, Stockton, CA 95210. *Phone:* 209-473-5200. *Toll-free phone:* 800-755-3550. *E-mail:* info@heald.edu.

HIGH-TECH INSTITUTE
Sacramento, California

Admissions Contact Mr. Richard Dyer, School Director, High-Tech Institute, 1111 Howe Avenue, #250, Sacramento, CA 95825. *Phone:* 916-929-9700. *Toll-free phone:* 800-987-0110.

IMPERIAL VALLEY COLLEGE
Imperial, California

Admissions Contact Mrs. Sandra Standiford, Dean of Admissions, Imperial Valley College, PO Box 158, Imperial, CA 92251. *Phone:* 760-352-8320 Ext. 200.

IRVINE VALLEY COLLEGE
Irvine, California

Admissions Contact Mr. Jess Craig, Dean of Students, Irvine Valley College, 5500 Irvine Center Drive, Irvine, CA 92618. *Phone:* 949-451-5410.

ITT TECHNICAL INSTITUTE
Anaheim, California

- **Proprietary** primarily 2-year, founded 1982, part of ITT Educational Services, Inc
- **Calendar** quarters
- **Degrees** associate and bachelor's
- **Suburban** 5-acre campus with easy access to Los Angeles
- **Coed**

Standardized Tests *Required:* Wonderlic aptitude test (for admission).
Costs (2004–05) *Tuition:* Please see school catalog for specific information.
Financial Aid Of all full-time matriculated undergraduates who enrolled in 2003, 20 Federal Work-Study jobs (averaging $5000).
Applying *Options:* deferred entrance. *Application fee:* $100. *Required:* high school transcript, interview. *Recommended:* letters of recommendation.
Admissions Contact Mr. Albert A. Naranjo, Director of Recruitment, ITT Technical Institute, 525 North Muller Avenue, Anaheim, CA 92801. *Phone:* 714-535-3700. *Fax:* 714-535-1802.

ITT TECHNICAL INSTITUTE
Lathrop, California

Admissions Contact Mr. Donald Fraser, Director of Recruitment, ITT Technical Institute, 16916 South Harlan Road, Lathrop, CA 95330. *Phone:* 209-858-0077. *Toll-free phone:* 800-346-1786. *Fax:* 209-858-0277.

ITT TECHNICAL INSTITUTE
Oxnard, California

Admissions Contact Mr. Dean K. Dunbar, Director of Recruitment, ITT Technical Institute, 2051 Solar Drive, Building B, Oxnard, CA 93036. *Phone:* 805-988-0143. *Toll-free phone:* 800-530-1582. *Fax:* 805-988-1813.

ITT TECHNICAL INSTITUTE
Rancho Cordova, California

- **Proprietary** primarily 2-year, founded 1954, part of ITT Educational Services, Inc
- **Calendar** quarters
- **Degrees** associate and bachelor's
- **Urban** 5-acre campus
- **Coed**

Standardized Tests *Required:* Wonderlic aptitude test (for admission).
Costs (2004–05) *Tuition:* Please see school catalog for specific information.
Applying *Options:* deferred entrance. *Application fee:* $100. *Required:* high school transcript, interview. *Recommended:* letters of recommendation.
Admissions Contact Mr. Robert Menszer, Director of Recruitment, ITT Technical Institute, 10863 Gold Center Drive, Rancho Cordova, CA 95670. *Phone:* 916-851-3900. *Toll-free phone:* 800-488-8466. *Fax:* 916-851-9225.

ITT TECHNICAL INSTITUTE
San Bernardino, California

- **Proprietary** primarily 2-year, founded 1987, part of ITT Educational Services, Inc
- **Calendar** quarters
- **Degrees** associate and bachelor's
- **Urban** campus with easy access to Los Angeles
- **Coed**

Standardized Tests *Required:* Wonderlic aptitude test (for admission).
Costs (2004–05) *Tuition:* Please see school catalog for specific information.
Applying *Options:* deferred entrance. *Application fee:* $100. *Required:* high school transcript, interview. *Recommended:* letters of recommendation.
Admissions Contact Ms. Maria Alamat, Director of Recruitment, ITT Technical Institute, 630 East Brier Drive, Suite 150, San Bernardino, CA 92408. *Phone:* 909-889-3800 Ext. 11. *Toll-free phone:* 800-888-3801. *Fax:* 909-888-6970.

ITT TECHNICAL INSTITUTE
San Diego, California

- **Proprietary** primarily 2-year, founded 1981, part of ITT Educational Services, Inc
- **Calendar** quarters
- **Degrees** associate and bachelor's
- **Suburban** campus
- **Coed**

Standardized Tests *Required:* Wonderlic aptitude test (for admission).
Costs (2004–05) *Tuition:* Please see school catalog for specific information.
Applying *Options:* deferred entrance. *Application fee:* $100. *Required:* high school transcript, interview. *Recommended:* letters of recommendation.
Admissions Contact Ms. Sheryl Schulgen, Director of Recruitment, ITT Technical Institute, 9680 Granite Ridge Drive, San Diego, CA 92123. *Phone:* 858-571-8500. *Toll-free phone:* 800-883-0380. *Fax:* 858-571-1277.

ITT TECHNICAL INSTITUTE
Sylmar, California

- **Proprietary** primarily 2-year, founded 1982, part of ITT Educational Services, Inc
- **Calendar** quarters
- **Degrees** associate and bachelor's
- **Urban** campus with easy access to Los Angeles
- **Coed**

Standardized Tests *Required:* Wonderlic aptitude test (for admission).
Costs (2004–05) *Tuition:* Please see school catalog for specific information.
Applying *Options:* deferred entrance. *Application fee:* $100. *Required:* high school transcript, interview. *Recommended:* letters of recommendation.
Admissions Contact Mr. Dominick Miciotta, Director of Recruitment, ITT Technical Institute, 12669 Encinitas Avenue, Sylmar, CA 91342. *Phone:* 818-364-5151. *Toll-free phone:* 800-363-2086. *Fax:* 818-364-5150.

ITT TECHNICAL INSTITUTE
Torrance, California

- **Proprietary** primarily 2-year, founded 1987, part of ITT Educational Services, Inc
- **Calendar** quarters
- **Degrees** associate and bachelor's
- **Urban** campus with easy access to Los Angeles
- **Coed**

Standardized Tests *Required:* Wonderlic aptitude test (for admission).
Costs (2004–05) *Tuition:* Please see school catalog for specific information.
Financial Aid Of all full-time matriculated undergraduates who enrolled in 2003, 6 Federal Work-Study jobs (averaging $4000).
Applying *Options:* deferred entrance. *Application fee:* $100. *Required:* high school transcript, interview. *Recommended:* letters of recommendation.
Admissions Contact Mr. Freddie Polk, Director of Recruitment, ITT Technical Institute, 20050 South Vermont Avenue, Torrance, CA 90502. *Phone:* 310-380-1555. *Fax:* 310-380-1557.

ITT TECHNICAL INSTITUTE
West Covina, California

- **Proprietary** primarily 2-year, founded 1982, part of ITT Educational Services, Inc
- **Calendar** quarters
- **Degrees** associate and bachelor's
- **Suburban** 4-acre campus with easy access to Los Angeles
- **Coed**

ITT Technical Institute (continued)
Standardized Tests *Required:* Wonderlic aptitude test (for admission).
Costs (2004–05) *Tuition:* Please see school catalog for specific information.
Financial Aid Of all full-time matriculated undergraduates who enrolled in 2003, 20 Federal Work-Study jobs (averaging $4500).
Applying *Options:* deferred entrance. *Application fee:* $100. *Required:* high school transcript, interview. *Recommended:* letters of recommendation.
Admissions Contact Mr. Michael Snyder, Director of Recruitment, ITT Technical Institute, 1530 West Cameron Avenue, West Covina, CA 91790. *Phone:* 626-960-8681. *Toll-free phone:* 800-414-6522. *Fax:* 626-337-5271.

LAKE TAHOE COMMUNITY COLLEGE
South Lake Tahoe, California

Admissions Contact Ms. Linda M. Stevenson, Director of Admissions and Records, Lake Tahoe Community College, One College Drive, South Lake Tahoe, CA 96150-4524. *Phone:* 530-541-4660 Ext. 282. *Fax:* 530-541-7852.

LANEY COLLEGE
Oakland, California

Admissions Contact Mrs. Barbara Simmons, District Admissions Officer, Laney College, 900 Fallon Street, Oakland, CA 94607-4893. *Phone:* 510-466-7369.

LAS POSITAS COLLEGE
Livermore, California

Admissions Contact Mrs. Sylvia R. Rodriguez, Director of Admissions and Records, Las Positas College, 3033 Collier Canyon Road, Livermore, CA 94551-7650. *Phone:* 925-373-4942.

LASSEN COMMUNITY COLLEGE DISTRICT
Susanville, California

Admissions Contact Mr. Chris J. Alberico, Registrar, Lassen Community College District, Highway 139, PO Box 3000, Susanville, CA 96130. *Phone:* 530-257-6181 Ext. 132.

LONG BEACH CITY COLLEGE
Long Beach, California

- **State-supported** 2-year, founded 1927, part of California Community College System
- **Calendar** semesters
- **Degree** certificates and associate
- **Urban** 40-acre campus with easy access to Los Angeles
- **Coed**, 28,069 undergraduate students

Undergraduates 1% are from out of state.
Faculty *Total:* 1,096, 30% full-time. *Student/faculty ratio:* 33:1.
Majors Accounting; administrative assistant and secretarial science; advertising; airline pilot and flight crew; architectural engineering technology; art; automobile/automotive mechanics technology; aviation/airway management; avionics maintenance technology; biology/biological sciences; business administration and management; carpentry; computer programming; computer typography and composition equipment operation; consumer merchandising/retailing management; criminal justice/law enforcement administration; culinary arts; dance; data processing and data processing technology; developmental and child psychology; dietetics; drafting and design technology; dramatic/theatre arts; electrical, electronic and communications engineering technology; engineering; English; family and consumer economics related; family and consumer sciences/human sciences; fashion/apparel design; fashion merchandising; film/cinema studies; fire science; food services technology; French; German; heating, air conditioning, ventilation and refrigeration maintenance technology; heavy equipment maintenance technology; horticultural science; hotel/motel administration; human services; industrial arts; industrial radiologic technology; industrial technology; interior design; international business/trade/commerce; journalism; kindergarten/preschool education; legal administrative assistant/secretary; liberal arts and sciences/liberal studies; machine tool technology; marketing/marketing management; mathematics; medical administrative assistant and medical secretary; medical/clinical assistant; music; nursing (registered nurse training); ornamental horticulture; photography; physical education teaching and coaching; physical sciences; pre-engineering; radio and television; real estate; social sciences; Spanish; special products marketing; speech and rhetoric; tourism and travel services management; welding technology.

Academic Programs *Special study options:* academic remediation for entering students, adult/continuing education programs, advanced placement credit, distance learning, English as a second language, honors programs, internships, part-time degree program, services for LD students, summer session for credit.
Library Long Beach City College Library plus 1 other with 151,367 titles, 471 serial subscriptions, 3,150 audiovisual materials, an OPAC, a Web page.
Computers on Campus 200 computers available on campus for general student use. Internet access, online (class) registration, at least one staffed computer lab available.
Student Life *Housing:* college housing not available. *Activities and Organizations:* drama/theater group, student-run newspaper, radio and television station, choral group, American Criminal Justice Association, AGS Scholarship Organization, American Association of Future Firefighters, Vietnamese Club, Network Christian Fellowship. *Campus security:* 24-hour emergency response devices and patrols, student patrols, late-night transport/escort service. *Student services:* health clinic, personal/psychological counseling, women's center, legal services.
Athletics Member NJCAA. *Intercollegiate sports:* badminton M/W, baseball M, basketball M/W, cross-country running M/W, football M, golf M/W, soccer M/W, softball W, swimming and diving M/W, tennis M/W, track and field M/W, volleyball M/W, water polo M/W. *Intramural sports:* archery M/W, basketball M/W, bowling M/W, football M/W, golf M/W, racquetball M/W, soccer M/W, softball M/W, swimming and diving M/W, tennis M/W, track and field M/W, volleyball M/W, weight lifting M, wrestling M.
Costs (2004–05) *Tuition:* nonresident $144 per unit part-time.
Financial Aid Of all full-time matriculated undergraduates who enrolled in 2003, 275 Federal Work-Study jobs (averaging $4400). 225 state and other part-time jobs (averaging $4400).
Applying *Options:* early admission. *Recommended:* high school transcript. *Application deadline:* rolling (freshmen).
Admissions Contact Mr. Ross Miyashiro, Dean of Admissions and Records, Long Beach City College, 4901 East Carson Boulevard, Long Beach, CA 90808. *Phone:* 562-938-4130. *Fax:* 562-938-4858.

LOS ANGELES CITY COLLEGE
Los Angeles, California

Admissions Contact Elaine Geismar, Director of Student Assistance Center, Los Angeles City College, 855 North Vermont Avenue, Los Angeles, CA 90029. *Phone:* 323-953-4340. *Fax:* 323-953-4536.

LOS ANGELES COUNTY COLLEGE OF NURSING AND ALLIED HEALTH
Los Angeles, California

Admissions Contact Ms. Maria Caballero, Manager, Admissions, Los Angeles County College of Nursing and Allied Health, 1237 North Mission Road, Los Angeles, CA 90033. *Phone:* 323-226-4911. *Fax:* 323-226-6343.

LOS ANGELES HARBOR COLLEGE
Wilmington, California

- **State and locally supported** 2-year, founded 1949, part of Los Angeles Community College District System
- **Calendar** semesters
- **Degree** certificates and associate
- **Suburban** 80-acre campus
- **Coed**

Faculty *Student/faculty ratio:* 40:1.
Student Life *Campus security:* 24-hour emergency response devices and patrols.
Costs (2004–05) *Tuition:* state resident $0 full-time; nonresident $4320 full-time, $180 per unit part-time. *Required fees:* $624 full-time.
Financial Aid Of all full-time matriculated undergraduates who enrolled in 2003, 122 Federal Work-Study jobs (averaging $1800).
Applying *Options:* early admission, deferred entrance. *Required for some:* essay or personal statement, high school transcript.
Admissions Contact Mr. David Ching, Dean of Admissions and Records, Los Angeles Harbor College, 1111 Figueroa Place, Wilmington, CA 90744-2397. *Phone:* 310-233-4091. *Fax:* 310-834-1882.

LOS ANGELES MISSION COLLEGE
Sylmar, California

Admissions Contact Ms. Angela Merrill, Admissions Supervisor, Los Angeles Mission College, 13356 Eldridge Avenue, Sylmar, CA 91342-3245. *Phone:* 818-364-7658.

LOS ANGELES PIERCE COLLEGE
Woodland Hills, California

- **State and locally supported** 2-year, founded 1947, part of Los Angeles Community College District System
- **Calendar** semesters
- **Degree** certificates and associate
- **Suburban** 425-acre campus with easy access to Los Angeles
- **Coed**

Student Life *Campus security:* 24-hour patrols, late-night transport/escort service.
Athletics Member NJCAA.
Costs (2004–05) *Tuition:* state resident $0 full-time; nonresident $3696 full-time, $154 per unit part-time. *Required fees:* $624 full-time, $26 per unit part-time, $12 per term part-time.
Financial Aid Of all full-time matriculated undergraduates who enrolled in 2003, 124 Federal Work-Study jobs (averaging $3000). 28 state and other part-time jobs (averaging $3000).
Applying *Options:* common application, electronic application, early admission.
Admissions Contact Ms. Shelley L. Gerstl, Dean of Admissions and Records, Los Angeles Pierce College, 6201 Winnetka Avenue, Woodland Hills, CA 91371-0001. *Phone:* 818-719-6448.

LOS ANGELES SOUTHWEST COLLEGE
Los Angeles, California

Admissions Contact Dr. Lawrence Jarmon, Vice President of Student Services, Los Angeles Southwest College, 1600 West Imperial Highway, Los Angeles, CA 90047-4810. *Phone:* 323-241-5279.

LOS ANGELES TRADE-TECHNICAL COLLEGE
Los Angeles, California

- **State and locally supported** 2-year, founded 1925, part of Los Angeles Community College District System
- **Calendar** semesters
- **Degree** certificates, diplomas, and associate
- **Urban** 25-acre campus
- **Coed**

Student Life *Campus security:* 24-hour patrols, student patrols, late-night transport/escort service.
Costs (2004–05) *Tuition:* state resident $0 full-time; nonresident $4152 full-time, $154 per unit part-time. *Required fees:* $456 full-time, $18 per unit part-time.
Applying *Options:* early admission, deferred entrance. *Recommended:* high school transcript.
Admissions Contact Mrs. Rosemary Royal, Dean of Enrollment Management, Los Angeles Trade-Technical College, 400 West Washington Boulevard, Los Angeles, CA 90015. *Phone:* 213-763-5301.

LOS ANGELES VALLEY COLLEGE
Van Nuys, California

- **State and locally supported** 2-year, founded 1949, part of Los Angeles Community College District System
- **Calendar** semesters
- **Degree** certificates and associate
- **Suburban** 105-acre campus
- **Endowment** $120,000
- **Coed**

Student Life *Campus security:* 24-hour emergency response devices and patrols, student patrols, late-night transport/escort service.
Athletics Member NJCAA.
Standardized Tests *Required:* ACT (for placement).

Costs (2004–05) *Tuition:* state resident $0 full-time; nonresident $3696 full-time, $154 per unit part-time. *Required fees:* $450 full-time, $18 per unit part-time.
Financial Aid Of all full-time matriculated undergraduates who enrolled in 2003, 100 Federal Work-Study jobs (averaging $4000).
Applying *Options:* common application, electronic application, early admission. *Recommended:* high school transcript.
Admissions Contact Mr. Florentino Manzano, Associate Dean, Los Angeles Valley College, 5800 Fulton Avenue, Valley Glen, CA 91401. *Phone:* 818-947-2353. *Fax:* 818-947-2501.

LOS MEDANOS COLLEGE
Pittsburg, California

Admissions Contact Ms. Gail Newman, Director of Admissions and Records, Los Medanos College, 2700 East Leland Road, Pittsburg, CA 94565-5197. *Phone:* 925-439-2181 Ext. 7500.

MARIC COLLEGE
Anaheim, California

Admissions Contact 1360 South Anaheim Boulevard, Anaheim, CA 92805. *Toll-free phone:* 800-206-0095.

MARIC COLLEGE
North Hollywood, California

Admissions Contact Mr. Mark Newman, Executive Director, Maric College, 6180 Laurel Canyon Boulevard, Suite 101, North Hollywood, CA 91606. *Phone:* 818-763-2563 Ext. 240. *Toll-free phone:* 800-404-9729.

MARIC COLLEGE
Panorama City, California

Admissions Contact 14355 Roscoe Boulevard, Panorama City, CA 91402. *Toll-free phone:* 800-206-0095.

MARIC COLLEGE
Sacramento, California

Admissions Contact Mr. Charles Reese, Director of Admissions, Maric College, 4330 Watt Avenue, Suite 400, Sacramento, CA 95821. *Phone:* 916-649-8168. *Toll-free phone:* 800-955-8168.

MARIC COLLEGE
Salida, California

- **Proprietary** 2-year
- **Calendar** semesters
- **Degree** diplomas and associate
- **Coed, primarily women**

Faculty *Student/faculty ratio:* 8:1.
Costs (2004–05) *Tuition:* $9995 full-time. Full-time tuition and fees vary according to degree level and program. No tuition increase for student's term of enrollment. *Required fees:* $98 full-time.
Admissions Contact Mrs. Linda Stovall, Chief Admission Officer, Maric College, 5172 Kiernan Court, Salida, CA 95368. *Phone:* 209-543-7000.

MARIC COLLEGE
San Diego, California

- **Proprietary** 2-year, founded 1976
- **Calendar** semesters
- **Degrees** certificates and associate (also includes Vista campus)
- **Urban** 4-acre campus
- **Coed**

Student Life *Campus security:* 24-hour patrols.
Applying *Options:* common application. *Required:* essay or personal statement, high school transcript, interview.
Admissions Contact Admissions, Maric College, 3666 Kearny Villa Road, Suite 100, San Diego, CA 92123-1995. *Phone:* 858-654-3601. *Toll-free phone:* 800-400-8232.

MARYMOUNT COLLEGE, PALOS VERDES, CALIFORNIA
Rancho Palos Verdes, California

Admissions Contact Ms. Nina Lococo, Dean of Admission and School Relations, Marymount College, Palos Verdes, California, 30800 Palos Verdes Drive East, Rancho Palos Verdes, CA 90815. *Phone:* 310-377-5501 Ext. 182. *Fax:* 310-265-0962. *E-mail:* admissions@marymountpv.edu.

MENDOCINO COLLEGE
Ukiah, California

Admissions Contact Ms. Kristie A. Taylor, Director of Admissions and Records, Mendocino College, 1000 Hensley Creek Road, Ukiah, CA 95482-0300. *Phone:* 707-468-3103. *Fax:* 707-468-3430. *E-mail:* ktaylor@mendocino.cc.ca.us.

MERCED COLLEGE
Merced, California

Admissions Contact Ms. Helen Torres, Admissions Clerk, Merced College, 3600 M Street, Merced, CA 95348-2898. *Phone:* 209-384-6187.

MERRITT COLLEGE
Oakland, California

- **State and locally supported** 2-year, founded 1953, part of Peralta Community College District System
- **Calendar** semesters
- **Degree** certificates and associate
- **Urban** 130-acre campus with easy access to San Francisco
- **Coed**

Standardized Tests *Recommended:* SAT or ACT (for placement).
Applying *Options:* early admission, deferred entrance.
Admissions Contact Ms. Barbara Simmons, District Admissions Officer, Merritt College, 12500 Campus Drive, Oakland, CA 94619-3196. *Phone:* 510-466-7369. *E-mail:* hperdue@peralta.cc.ca.us.

MIRACOSTA COLLEGE
Oceanside, California

- **State-supported** 2-year, founded 1934, part of California Community College System
- **Calendar** semesters
- **Degree** certificates, diplomas, and associate
- **Suburban** 131-acre campus with easy access to San Diego
- **Endowment** $894,495
- **Coed**

MiraCosta's campuses in Oceanside and Cardiff are minutes from the beach. MiraCosta offers a strong university transfer program, including transfer admission guarantees. Courses of special interest include music technology, multimedia, horticulture, and computer science. Facilities include technology hubs at both campuses and a wellness center at the Oceanside campus.

Faculty *Student/faculty ratio:* 23:1.
Student Life *Campus security:* 24-hour emergency response devices, student patrols, late-night transport/escort service, trained security personnel during class hours.
Athletics Member NJCAA.
Costs (2004–05) *Tuition:* state resident $0 full-time; nonresident $5344 full-time, $151 per unit part-time. Part-time tuition and fees vary according to course load. *Required fees:* $814 full-time, $26 per unit part-time.
Financial Aid Of all full-time matriculated undergraduates who enrolled in 2003, 83 Federal Work-Study jobs (averaging $1315).
Applying *Options:* early admission, deferred entrance.
Admissions Contact Admissions and Records Assistant, MiraCosta College, One Barnard Drive, Oceanside, CA 92056. *Phone:* 760-795-6620. *Toll-free phone:* 888-201-8480. *Fax:* 760-795-6626.

MISSION COLLEGE
Santa Clara, California

Admissions Contact Dr. Sam Bersolo, Interim Vice President of Student Services, Mission College, 3000 Mission College Boulevard, Santa Clara, CA 95054-1897. *Phone:* 408-855-5195. *Fax:* 408-855-5467.

MODESTO JUNIOR COLLEGE
Modesto, California

- **State and locally supported** 2-year, founded 1921, part of Yosemite Community College District System
- **Calendar** semesters
- **Degree** certificates and associate
- **Urban** 229-acre campus
- **Endowment** $817,811
- **Coed,** 17,535 undergraduate students

Freshmen *Admission:* 10,451 applied, 10,451 admitted.
Faculty *Student/faculty ratio:* 40:1.
Majors Accounting; administrative assistant and secretarial science; agricultural business and management; agricultural mechanization; agricultural production; agriculture; agronomy and crop science; animal sciences; apparel and textiles; architectural engineering technology; art; autobody/collision and repair technology; automobile/automotive mechanics technology; banking and financial support services; behavioral sciences; biology/biological sciences; building/home/construction inspection; business administration and management; child care and support services management; child care provision; child development; commercial and advertising art; communications systems installation and repair technology; computer graphics; computer/information technology services administration related; computer installation and repair technology; computer science; construction management; corrections; criminal justice/law enforcement administration; criminal justice/police science; dairy science; data entry/microcomputer applications; dental assisting; drafting and design technology; dramatic/theatre arts; electrical, electronic and communications engineering technology; electrical/electronics equipment installation and repair; emergency medical technology (EMT paramedic); engineering; English; family and consumer economics related; fashion merchandising; finance; fire science; food science; food services technology; foreign languages and literatures; forestry; forestry technology; general studies; graphic and printing equipment operation/production; heating, air conditioning, ventilation and refrigeration maintenance technology; housing and human environments; humanities; human services; industrial arts; industrial electronics technology; interior design; kindergarten/preschool education; landscape architecture; machine shop technology; machine tool technology; management information systems; marketing/marketing management; mass communication/media; mathematics; medical/clinical assistant; music; nursing assistant/aide and patient care assistant; nursing (registered nurse training); office management; office occupations and clerical services; ornamental horticulture; parks, recreation and leisure facilities management; photography; physical education teaching and coaching; plant nursery management; poultry science; radio and television; real estate; respiratory care therapy; social sciences; special products marketing; speech and rhetoric; welding technology; word processing.
Academic Programs *Special study options:* academic remediation for entering students, adult/continuing education programs, advanced placement credit, cooperative education, distance learning, English as a second language, honors programs, independent study, part-time degree program, services for LD students, study abroad, summer session for credit.
Library Modesto Junior College Library with 69,865 titles, 4,161 audiovisual materials, an OPAC, a Web page.
Computers on Campus 95 computers available on campus for general student use. A campuswide network can be accessed from off campus. Internet access, at least one staffed computer lab available.
Student Life *Housing:* college housing not available. *Activities and Organizations:* drama/theater group, student-run newspaper, radio and television station, choral group, Young Farmers, Red Nations, Psychology Club, Alpha Gamma Sigma, MECHA. *Campus security:* 24-hour emergency response devices and patrols, late-night transport/escort service. *Student services:* health clinic, personal/psychological counseling.
Athletics *Intercollegiate sports:* baseball M, basketball M/W, cross-country running M/W, football M, golf M, gymnastics W, soccer M/W, softball W, swimming and diving M/W, tennis M/W, track and field M/W, volleyball W, water polo M/W, wrestling M. *Intramural sports:* basketball M/W, football M, softball W, table tennis M/W, tennis M/W, volleyball M/W.
Costs (2005–06) *Tuition:* state resident $0 full-time; nonresident $3624 full-time, $151 per unit part-time. *Required fees:* $662 full-time, $26 per unit part-time, $36 per year part-time.
Financial Aid Of all full-time matriculated undergraduates who enrolled in 2003, 152 Federal Work-Study jobs (averaging $2732). 62 state and other part-time jobs (averaging $1655).
Applying *Options:* electronic application. *Recommended:* high school transcript, interview. *Application deadline:* rolling (freshmen), rolling (transfers). *Notification:* continuous (freshmen).
Admissions Contact Ms. Susie Agostini, Dean of Matriculation, Admissions, and Records, Modesto Junior College, 435 College Avenue, Modesto, CA 95350. *Phone:* 209-575-6470. *Fax:* 209-575-6859. *E-mail:* mjcadmissions@mail.yosemite.cc.ca.us.

MONTEREY PENINSULA COLLEGE
Monterey, California

Admissions Contact Dr. Elizabeth L. Cipres, Dean of Enrollment Services, Monterey Peninsula College, 980 Fremont Street, Monterey, CA 93940. *Phone:* 831-645-1372. *Fax:* 831-646-4015. *E-mail:* rmontori@mpc.edu.

MOORPARK COLLEGE
Moorpark, California

Admissions Contact Ms. Kathy Colborn, Registrar, Moorpark College, 7075 Campus Road, Moorpark, CA 93021-2899. *Phone:* 805-378-1415. *Fax:* 805-378-1583. *E-mail:* mcadmissions@vcccd.net.

MT. SAN ANTONIO COLLEGE
Walnut, California

- **District-supported** 2-year, founded 1946, part of California Community College System
- **Calendar** semesters
- **Degree** certificates, diplomas, and associate
- **Suburban** 421-acre campus with easy access to Los Angeles
- **Coed**

Student Life *Campus security:* 24-hour emergency response devices and patrols, late-night transport/escort service.
Costs (2004–05) *Tuition:* state resident $0 full-time; nonresident $3386 full-time, $165 per unit part-time. *Required fees:* $672 full-time, $26 per unit part-time, $48 per term part-time.
Financial Aid Of all full-time matriculated undergraduates who enrolled in 2003, 250 Federal Work-Study jobs (averaging $2898).
Applying *Options:* early admission, deferred entrance. *Required for some:* high school transcript.
Admissions Contact Ms. Patricia Montoya, Acting Director of Admissions and Records, Mt. San Antonio College, 1100 North Grand Avenue, Walnut, CA 91789. *Phone:* 909-594-5611 Ext. 4415. *Toll-free phone:* 800-672-2463 Ext. 4415. *E-mail:* admissions@mtsac.edu.

MT. SAN JACINTO COLLEGE
San Jacinto, California

- **State and locally supported** 2-year, founded 1963, part of California Community College System
- **Calendar** semesters
- **Degree** certificates, diplomas, and associate
- **Suburban** 180-acre campus with easy access to San Diego
- **Endowment** $2.0 million
- **Coed**

Faculty *Student/faculty ratio:* 24:1.
Student Life *Campus security:* part-time trained security personnel.
Standardized Tests *Required:* Assessment and Placement Services for Community Colleges (for placement).
Costs (2004–05) *Tuition:* state resident $0 full-time; nonresident $5086 full-time, $167 per unit part-time. *Required fees:* $5010 full-time, $18 per unit part-time.
Financial Aid Of all full-time matriculated undergraduates who enrolled in 2003, 109 Federal Work-Study jobs (averaging $1114). 125 state and other part-time jobs (averaging $1000).
Applying *Options:* early admission. *Recommended:* high school transcript.
Admissions Contact Ms. Susan Loomis, Supervisor, Enrollment Services, Mt. San Jacinto College, 1499 North State Street, San Jacinto, CA 92583-2399. *Phone:* 909-672-6752 Ext. 2401. *Toll-free phone:* 800-624-5561 Ext. 1410. *Fax:* 909-654-6738. *E-mail:* egonzale@msjc.edu.

MTI COLLEGE OF BUSINESS AND TECHNOLOGY
Sacramento, California

Admissions Contact Ms. Monica Burden, Director of Admissions, MTI College of Business and Technology, 5221 Madison Avenue, Sacramento, CA 95841. *Phone:* 916-339-1500.

NAPA VALLEY COLLEGE
Napa, California

- **State and locally supported** 2-year, founded 1942, part of California Community College System
- **Calendar** semesters
- **Degree** certificates and associate
- **Suburban** 188-acre campus with easy access to San Francisco
- **Coed**, 6,908 undergraduate students, 28% full-time, 61% women, 39% men

Undergraduates 1,909 full-time, 4,999 part-time. 8% African American, 18% Asian American or Pacific Islander, 20% Hispanic American, 1% Native American. *Retention:* 66% of 2002 full-time freshmen returned.
Freshmen *Admission:* 2,000 applied, 2,000 admitted, 525 enrolled.
Faculty *Total:* 311, 32% full-time. *Student/faculty ratio:* 22:1.
Majors Accounting; administrative assistant and secretarial science; agriculture; art; behavioral sciences; biological and physical sciences; biomedical technology; business administration and management; child development; communications technology; computer science; corrections; cosmetology; criminal justice/law enforcement administration; criminal justice/police science; data processing and data processing technology; drafting and design technology; electrical, electronic and communications engineering technology; emergency medical technology (EMT paramedic); engineering; environmental engineering technology; environmental studies; humanities; kindergarten/preschool education; legal administrative assistant/secretary; legal assistant/paralegal; machine tool technology; management information systems; marketing/marketing management; music; nursing (registered nurse training); photography; radio and television; real estate; respiratory care therapy; telecommunications; welding technology.
Academic Programs *Special study options:* academic remediation for entering students, advanced placement credit, cooperative education, distance learning, English as a second language, part-time degree program, services for LD students, study abroad, summer session for credit.
Library Napa Valley College Library plus 1 other with 42,000 titles, 250 serial subscriptions, an OPAC.
Computers on Campus 90 computers available on campus for general student use. Internet access, at least one staffed computer lab available.
Student Life *Housing:* college housing not available. *Activities and Organizations:* drama/theater group, student-run newspaper, choral group, Hispano-Americano Club, African-American Club, Environmental Action Coalition, International Student Club, Phi Theta Kappa. *Campus security:* late-night transport/escort service. *Student services:* personal/psychological counseling, women's center.
Athletics Member NJCAA. *Intercollegiate sports:* baseball M, basketball M/W, cross-country running M/W, soccer M, softball W, swimming and diving M/W, tennis M/W, volleyball W, wrestling M. *Intramural sports:* archery M/W, badminton M/W, basketball M/W, bowling M/W, fencing M/W, gymnastics M/W, racquetball M/W, rugby M, skiing (cross-country) M/W, skiing (downhill) M/W, soccer M/W, swimming and diving M/W, tennis M/W, volleyball M/W, water polo M/W, weight lifting M/W, wrestling M.
Standardized Tests *Required for some:* SAT or ACT (for placement).
Costs (2005–06) *Tuition:* state resident $0 full-time; nonresident $3624 full-time, $151 per unit part-time. Full-time tuition and fees vary according to course load. Part-time tuition and fees vary according to course load. *Required fees:* $648 full-time, $26 per unit part-time, $12 per term part-time. *Payment plan:* deferred payment.
Financial Aid *Financial aid deadline:* 3/2.
Applying *Required for some:* high school transcript. *Application deadline:* rolling (freshmen), rolling (out-of-state freshmen), rolling (transfers).
Admissions Contact Dr. Edward Shenk, Vice President of Student Services, Napa Valley College, 2277 Napa-Vallejo Highway, Napa, CA 94558-6236. *Phone:* 707-253-3000. *Fax:* 707-253-3064. *E-mail:* snelson@admin.nvc.cc.ca.us.

NATIONAL POLYTECHNIC COLLEGE OF ENGINEERING AND OCEANEERING
Wilmington, California

- **Proprietary** 2-year
- **Calendar** continuous
- **Degree** certificates and associate
- **Suburban** 5-acre campus with easy access to Los Angeles
- **Coed, primarily men**

Faculty *Student/faculty ratio:* 15:1.
Student Life *Campus security:* 24-hour emergency response devices.
Costs (2004–05) *Tuition:* $16,100 full-time.
Financial Aid Of all full-time matriculated undergraduates who enrolled in 2003, 22 Federal Work-Study jobs (averaging $4000).
Applying *Options:* common application, electronic application, deferred entrance. *Application fee:* $50. *Required:* essay or personal statement, high school transcript, interview, physical examination.
Admissions Contact Ms. Deborah Montgomery, Director of Admissions, National Polytechnic College of Engineering and Oceaneering, 272 South Fries

National Polytechnic College of Engineering and Oceaneering (continued)
Avenue, Wilmington, CA 90744-6399. *Phone:* 310-834-2501 Ext. 237. *Toll-free phone:* 800-432-DIVE Ext. 237. *Fax:* 310-834-7132. *E-mail:* sestep@diveco.com.

NORTHROP RICE AVIATION INSTITUTE OF TECHNOLOGY
Inglewood, California

Admissions Contact Mr. James Michael Rice, Chief Administrative Officer, Northrop Rice Aviation Institute of Technology, 1155 West Arbor Vitae Street, Suite 115, Inglewood, CA 90301-2904. *Phone:* 310-568-8541.

NORTHWESTERN TECHNICAL COLLEGE
Sacramento, California

Admissions Contact Mr. Robert Naylor, Director of Admissions, Northwestern Technical College, 1825 Bell Street, #100, Sacramento, CA 95825. *Phone:* 916-649-2400. *Toll-free phone:* 866-649-2400.

OHLONE COLLEGE
Fremont, California

Admissions Contact Ms. Allison Hill, Director, Admissions and Records, Ohlone College, 43600 Mission Boulevard, Fremont, CA 94539-5884. *Phone:* 510-659-6108.

ORANGE COAST COLLEGE
Costa Mesa, California

- **State and locally supported** 2-year, founded 1947, part of Coast Community College District System
- **Calendar** semesters plus summer session
- **Degree** certificates and associate
- **Suburban** 200-acre campus with easy access to Los Angeles
- **Endowment** $5.1 million
- **Coed,** 22,520 undergraduate students, 40% full-time, 51% women, 49% men

Undergraduates 9,046 full-time, 13,474 part-time. Students come from 52 states and territories, 76 other countries, 2% are from out of state, 2% African American, 25% Asian American or Pacific Islander, 17% Hispanic American, 0.8% Native American, 3% international, 9% transferred in. *Retention:* 79% of 2002 full-time freshmen returned.

Freshmen *Admission:* 2,915 enrolled.

Faculty *Total:* 940, 32% full-time. *Student/faculty ratio:* 20:1.

Majors Accounting; administrative assistant and secretarial science; aeronautics/aviation/aerospace science and technology; airline pilot and flight crew; anthropology; architectural engineering technology; art; athletic training; avionics maintenance technology; behavioral sciences; biology/biological sciences; building/home/construction inspection; business administration and management; cardiovascular technology; chemistry; child care and support services management; child care provision; cinematography and film/video production; clinical laboratory science/medical technology; commercial and advertising art; communications technology; computer engineering technology; computer graphics; computer programming; computer programming (specific applications); computer typography and composition equipment operation; construction engineering technology; culinary arts; cultural studies; dance; data entry/microcomputer applications related; data processing and data processing technology; dental hygiene; dietetics; drafting and design technology; dramatic/theatre arts; economics; electrical and power transmission installation; electrical, electronic and communications engineering technology; electrical/electronics equipment installation and repair; emergency medical technology (EMT paramedic); engineering; English; family and consumer economics related; family and consumer sciences/human sciences; fashion merchandising; film/cinema studies; food science; food services technology; foods, nutrition, and wellness; French; general retailing/wholesaling; geography; geology/earth science; German; health science; heating, air conditioning, ventilation and refrigeration maintenance technology; history; horticultural science; hotel/motel administration; housing and human environments; human development and family studies; humanities; industrial design; industrial radiologic technology; information science/studies; interior design; journalism; kindergarten/preschool education; kinesiology and exercise science; legal administrative assistant/secretary; liberal arts and sciences/liberal studies; machine shop technology; machine tool technology; marine technology; marketing/marketing management; mass communication/media; mathematics; medical administrative assistant and medical secretary; medical/clinical assistant; music; musical instrument fabrication and repair; music management and merchandising; natural sciences; nuclear medical technology; ornamental horticulture; philosophy; photography; physical education

teaching and coaching; physics; political science and government; religious studies; respiratory care therapy; restaurant, culinary, and catering management; retailing; selling skills and sales; social sciences; sociology; Spanish; special products marketing; welding technology; word processing.

Academic Programs *Special study options:* academic remediation for entering students, adult/continuing education programs, advanced placement credit, cooperative education, distance learning, double majors, English as a second language, external degree program, freshman honors college, honors programs, internships, off-campus study, part-time degree program, services for LD students, student-designed majors, study abroad, summer session for credit. *ROTC:* Army (c), Air Force (c).

Library Norman E. Watson Library with 84,447 titles, 420 serial subscriptions, 2,510 audiovisual materials, an OPAC, a Web page.

Computers on Campus 1515 computers available on campus for general student use. A campuswide network can be accessed from off campus. Internet access, at least one staffed computer lab available.

Student Life *Housing:* college housing not available. *Activities and Organizations:* drama/theater group, student-run newspaper, choral group, Vietnamese Student Association, International Club, Adventurist Souls, Muslim Student Association. *Campus security:* 24-hour emergency response devices and patrols, student patrols, late-night transport/escort service. *Student services:* health clinic, personal/psychological counseling, legal services.

Athletics *Intercollegiate sports:* baseball M, basketball M/W, bowling M(c)/W(c), crew M/W, cross-country running M/W, football M, golf M/W, soccer M/W, softball W, swimming and diving M/W, tennis M/W, track and field M/W, volleyball M/W, water polo M/W.

Costs (2004–05) *Tuition:* state resident $0 full-time; nonresident $5215 full-time, $146 per unit part-time. *Required fees:* $728 full-time, $26 per unit part-time.

Financial Aid Of all full-time matriculated undergraduates who enrolled in 2003, 108 Federal Work-Study jobs (averaging $3000). *Financial aid deadline:* 5/28.

Applying *Options:* common application. *Application deadline:* rolling (freshmen), rolling (transfers). *Notification:* continuous (freshmen).

Admissions Contact Ms. Nancy Kidder, Administrative Dean of Admissions and Records, Orange Coast College, 2701 Fairview Road, Costa Mesa, CA 92626. *Phone:* 714-432-5788. *Fax:* 714-432-5072. *E-mail:* nkidder@cccd.edu.

OXNARD COLLEGE
Oxnard, California

- **State-supported** 2-year, founded 1975, part of Ventura County Community College District System
- **Calendar** semesters
- **Degree** certificates, diplomas, and associate
- **Urban** 119-acre campus
- **Coed**

Faculty *Student/faculty ratio:* 25:1.

Student Life *Campus security:* 24-hour patrols.

Costs (2004–05) *Tuition:* state resident $0 full-time; nonresident $3912 full-time, $163 per unit part-time. Full-time tuition and fees vary according to course load. Part-time tuition and fees vary according to course load. *Required fees:* $624 full-time, $26 per unit part-time, $13 per term part-time.

Financial Aid Of all full-time matriculated undergraduates who enrolled in 2003, 80 Federal Work-Study jobs (averaging $3000).

Applying *Options:* common application, electronic application, early admission.

Admissions Contact Ms. Susan O. Brent, Registrar, Oxnard College, 4000 South Rose Avenue, Oxnard, CA 93033-6699. *Phone:* 805-986-5843. *Fax:* 805-986-5943.

PALOMAR COLLEGE
San Marcos, California

- **State and locally supported** 2-year, founded 1946, part of California Community College System
- **Calendar** semesters
- **Degree** certificates and associate
- **Suburban** 156-acre campus with easy access to San Diego
- **Coed**

Faculty *Student/faculty ratio:* 24:1.

Student Life *Campus security:* 24-hour patrols, student patrols, late-night transport/escort service.

Standardized Tests *Required for some:* ACT ASSET.

Applying *Options:* electronic application.

Admissions Contact Mr. Herman Lee, Director of Enrollment Services, Palomar College, 1140 West Mission Road, San Marcos, CA 92069-1487. *Phone:* 760-744-1150 Ext. 2171. *Fax:* 760-744-2932. *E-mail:* admissions@palomar.edu.

PALO VERDE COLLEGE
Blythe, California

Admissions Contact Ms. Sally Rivera, Vice President of Student Services, Palo Verde College, 1 College Drive, Blythe, CA 92225. *Phone:* 760-921-5409. *Fax:* 760-921-3608.

PASADENA CITY COLLEGE
Pasadena, California

- **State and locally supported** 2-year, founded 1924, part of California Community College System
- **Calendar** semesters
- **Degree** certificates and associate
- **Urban** 55-acre campus with easy access to Los Angeles
- **Coed,** 29,688 undergraduate students, 100% full-time, 56% women, 44% men

Undergraduates 29,688 full-time. Students come from 15 states and territories, 6% African American, 29% Asian American or Pacific Islander, 34% Hispanic American, 0.7% Native American.
Faculty *Total:* 1,296, 29% full-time. *Student/faculty ratio:* 20:1.
Majors Accounting; administrative assistant and secretarial science; advertising; African-American/Black studies; African studies; airline pilot and flight crew; anthropology; architectural engineering technology; art; art history, criticism and conservation; astronomy; automobile/automotive mechanics technology; aviation/airway management; avionics maintenance technology; biological and physical sciences; biology/biological sciences; broadcast journalism; business administration and management; business teacher education; carpentry; ceramic arts and ceramics; ceramic sciences and engineering; chemistry; civil engineering technology; communications technology; computer engineering technology; computer programming; computer science; computer typography and composition equipment operation; construction engineering technology; cosmetology; criminal justice/law enforcement administration; cultural studies; data processing and data processing technology; dental hygiene; developmental and child psychology; drafting and design technology; dramatic/theatre arts; drawing; economics; electrical, electronic and communications engineering technology; engineering; engineering technology; English; fashion merchandising; fiber, textile and weaving arts; finance; fire science; forestry technology; French; geography; geology/earth science; German; Hispanic-American, Puerto Rican, and Mexican-American/Chicano studies; history; human services; industrial radiologic technology; information science/studies; interdisciplinary studies; interior design; journalism; kindergarten/preschool education; landscape architecture; Latin American studies; legal administrative assistant/secretary; legal studies; liberal arts and sciences/liberal studies; library science; machine tool technology; marketing/marketing management; mass communication/media; mathematics; mechanical engineering/mechanical technology; medical/clinical assistant; metal and jewelry arts; modern languages; music; music therapy; nursing (licensed practical/vocational nurse training); nursing (registered nurse training); occupational therapy; parks, recreation and leisure; pharmacy; philosophy; photography; physical education teaching and coaching; physical sciences; physics; political science and government; psychology; radio and television; real estate; religious studies; sign language interpretation and translation; social sciences; sociology; Spanish; speech and rhetoric; statistics; teacher assistant/aide; telecommunications; tourism and travel services management; veterinary sciences; welding technology.
Academic Programs *Special study options:* academic remediation for entering students, adult/continuing education programs, advanced placement credit, English as a second language, honors programs, part-time degree program, services for LD students, student-designed majors, study abroad, summer session for credit.
Library Pasadena City College Library plus 1 other with 120,000 titles, 350 serial subscriptions, an OPAC.
Computers on Campus 300 computers available on campus for general student use. At least one staffed computer lab available.
Student Life *Housing:* college housing not available. *Activities and Organizations:* drama/theater group, student-run newspaper, radio station, choral group, marching band. *Campus security:* 24-hour emergency response devices and patrols, late-night transport/escort service, cadet patrols. *Student services:* health clinic, personal/psychological counseling, women's center.
Athletics *Intercollegiate sports:* baseball M, basketball M/W, cross-country running M/W, football M, soccer M/W, softball W, swimming and diving M/W, tennis M/W, track and field M/W, volleyball W, water polo M.
Costs (2004–05) *Tuition:* state resident $0 full-time; nonresident $4470 full-time, $149 per unit part-time. *Required fees:* $806 full-time, $26 per unit part-time, $13 per term part-time.

Applying *Options:* early admission, deferred entrance. *Application deadline:* rolling (freshmen), rolling (transfers). *Notification:* continuous (freshmen).
Admissions Contact Ms. Carol Kaser, Supervisor of Admissions and Records, Pasadena City College, 1570 East. Colorado Boulevard, Pasadena, CA 91106. *Phone:* 626-585-7397. *Fax:* 626-585-7915.

PIMA MEDICAL INSTITUTE
Chula Vista, California

- **Proprietary** 2-year, administratively affiliated with Vocational Training Institutes, Inc
- **Calendar** modular
- **Degree** certificates and associate
- **Urban** campus
- **Coed,** 447 undergraduate students, 100% full-time, 79% women, 21% men

Undergraduates 447 full-time. Students come from 1 other state.
Freshmen *Admission:* 53 applied, 45 admitted, 45 enrolled.
Faculty *Total:* 7, 86% full-time. *Student/faculty ratio:* 14:1.
Majors Radiologic technology/science; respiratory therapy technician.
Academic Programs *Special study options:* cooperative education, internships.
Student Life *Housing:* college housing not available.
Standardized Tests *Required:* Wonderlic Scholastic Level Exam (for admission).
Costs (2005–06) *Tuition:* No tuition increase for student's term of enrollment. Programs costs vary from $21,693 to $22,827. *Required fees:* $100 full-time. *Payment plans:* tuition prepayment, installment.
Applying *Options:* common application. *Application fee:* $100. *Required:* high school transcript, interview.
Admissions Contact Admissions Office, Pima Medical Institute, Pima Medical Institute, 780 Bay Boulevard, Suite 101, Chula Vista, CA 91910. *Phone:* 619-425-3200. *Toll-free phone:* 888-898-9048.

PLATT COLLEGE
Cerritos, California

Admissions Contact Ms. Ilene Holt, Dean of Student Services, Platt College, 10900 East 183rd Street, Suite 290, Cerritos, CA 90703-5342. *Phone:* 562-809-5100. *Toll-free phone:* 800-807-5288.

PLATT COLLEGE
Newport Beach, California

- **Independent** primarily 2-year, founded 1985
- **Calendar** continuous
- **Degrees** certificates, diplomas, associate, and bachelor's
- **Urban** campus
- **Coed**

Faculty *Student/faculty ratio:* 16:1.
Student Life *Campus security:* 24-hour emergency response devices.
Standardized Tests *Required:* CPAt (for admission).
Applying *Application fee:* $75. *Required:* essay or personal statement, high school transcript, interview.
Admissions Contact Ms. Lisa Rhodes, President, Platt College, 3901 MacArthur Boulevard, Suite 101, Newport Beach, CA 92660. *Phone:* 949-833-2300 Ext. 222. *Toll-free phone:* 888-866-6697 Ext. 230. *Fax:* 949-833-0269. *E-mail:* lrhodes@plattcollege.edu.

▶ See page 544 for a narrative description.

PLATT COLLEGE
Ontario, California

Admissions Contact Ms. Jennifer Abandonato, Director of Admissions, Platt College, 3700 Inland Empire Boulevard, Ontario, CA 91764. *Phone:* 909-941-9410. *Toll-free phone:* 888-866-6697.

▶ See page 546 for a narrative description.

PLATT COLLEGE-LOS ANGELES, INC
Alhambra, California

Admissions Contact Mr. Detroit Whiteside, Director of Admissions, Platt College-Los Angeles, Inc, 7470 North Figueroa Street, Los Angeles, CA 90041-1717. *Phone:* 323-258-8050. *Toll-free phone:* 888-866-6697. *Fax:* 323-258-8532. *E-mail:* ademitroff@plattcollege.edu.

▶ See page 542 for a narrative description.

PLATT COLLEGE SAN DIEGO
San Diego, California

- **Proprietary** primarily 2-year, founded 1879
- **Calendar** continuous
- **Degrees** certificates, diplomas, associate, and bachelor's
- **Suburban** campus with easy access to San Diego
- **Coed,** 335 undergraduate students, 100% full-time, 27% women, 73% men

Students' investment in themselves should not take a lifetime to repay. Platt offers the BS degree in media arts (2½ years); AAS degrees in multimedia design and graphic design (15 months); specialized diplomas in DV production, 3-D animation, and Web design; and diplomas in multimedia and graphic design. For further information, students should call 866-PLATT-COLLEGE (toll-free) or visit the College's Web site (http://www.platt.edu).

Undergraduates 335 full-time. Students come from 4 states and territories, 2 other countries, 5% are from out of state, 8% African American, 13% Asian American or Pacific Islander, 21% Hispanic American, 1% Native American. *Retention:* 42% of 2002 full-time freshmen returned.
Freshmen *Admission:* 259 admitted, 109 enrolled.
Faculty *Total:* 21, 33% full-time, 5% with terminal degrees. *Student/faculty ratio:* 20:1.
Majors Animation, interactive technology, video graphics and special effects; art; cinematography and film/video production; commercial and advertising art; communication and media related; computer graphics; computer software and media applications related; computer typography and composition equipment operation; design and applied arts related; design and visual communications; desktop publishing and digital imaging design; digital communication and media/multimedia; general studies; graphic communications; graphic communications related; graphic design; intermedia/multimedia; liberal arts and sciences and humanities related; mathematics; photographic and film/video technology; web/multimedia management and webmaster; web page, digital/multimedia and information resources design.
Student Life *Housing:* college housing not available. *Campus security:* 24-hour emergency response devices, video camera. *Student services:* personal/psychological counseling.
Costs (2005–06) *Tuition:* $17,226 full-time. Full-time tuition and fees vary according to program. No tuition increase for student's term of enrollment. *Required fees:* $100 full-time. *Payment plans:* tuition prepayment, installment. *Waivers:* employees or children of employees.
Applying *Required:* high school transcript, interview.
Admissions Contact Carly Westerfield, Coordinator, Platt College San Diego, 6250 El Cajon Boulevard, San Diego, CA 92115-3919. *Phone:* 619-265-0107. *Toll-free phone:* 866-752-8826. *Fax:* 619-265-8655. *E-mail:* info@platt.edu.

PORTERVILLE COLLEGE
Porterville, California

Admissions Contact Ms. Judy Pope, Director of Admissions and Records/Registrar, Porterville College, 100 East College Avenue, Porterville, CA 93257-6058. *Phone:* 559-791-2222. *Fax:* 559-791-2349.

PROFESSIONAL GOLFERS CAREER COLLEGE
Temecula, California

- **Independent** 2-year
- **Calendar** semesters
- **Degree** associate
- **Coed, primarily men,** 318 undergraduate students, 100% full-time, 4% women, 96% men
- 100% of applicants were admitted

Undergraduates 318 full-time. Students come from 50 states and territories, 13 other countries, 75% are from out of state, 1% African American, 26% Asian American or Pacific Islander, 4% Hispanic American, 2% Native American.
Freshmen *Admission:* 40 applied, 40 admitted. *Average high school GPA:* 2.5.
Faculty *Total:* 23, 22% full-time. *Student/faculty ratio:* 15:1.
Academic Programs *Special study options:* English as a second language.
Library Professional Golfers Career College with 2,291 titles, 45 serial subscriptions, 115 audiovisual materials, a Web page.
Computers on Campus 20 computers available on campus for general student use. Internet access, at least one staffed computer lab available.
Student Life *Housing Options:* coed. Campus housing is leased by the school.
Costs (2005–06) *Tuition:* $4,790.00 per semester for students who are citizens of the United States or are permanent residents. $5,090.00 per semester for international students. $360 mandatory fee per semester. $2500 per semester for room only.

Applying *Options:* early admission, deferred entrance. *Application fee:* $75. *Required:* high school transcript, 4 letters of recommendation.
Admissions Contact Mr. David Ober, Director of Admissions, Professional Golfers Career College, PO Box 892319, 261 Ynez Road, Temecula, CA 92589-2319. *Phone:* 951-693-2963 Ext. 19. *Toll-free phone:* 800-877-4380. *E-mail:* david.ober@golfcollege.edu.

QUEEN OF THE HOLY ROSARY COLLEGE
Mission San Jose, California

Admissions Contact Sr. Mary Paul Mehegan, Dean of the College, Queen of the Holy Rosary College, 43326 Mission Boulevard, PO Box 3908, Mission San Jose, CA 94539. *Phone:* 510-657-2468 Ext. 322. *Fax:* 510-657-1734.

REEDLEY COLLEGE
Reedley, California

Admissions Contact Ms. Leticia Alvarez, Admissions and Records Manager, Reedley College, 995 North Reed Avenue, Reedley, CA 93654. *Phone:* 559-638-0323 Ext. 3624.

RIO HONDO COLLEGE
Whittier, California

Admissions Contact Ms. Mary Becerril, Supervisor, Records/Admissions, Rio Hondo College, 3600 Workman Mill Road, Whittier, CA 90601-1699. *Phone:* 562-692-0921 Ext. 3153. *Fax:* 562-692-9318.

RIVERSIDE COMMUNITY COLLEGE DISTRICT
Riverside, California

- **State and locally supported** 2-year, founded 1916, part of California Community College System
- **Calendar** semesters
- **Degree** certificates and associate
- **Suburban** 108-acre campus with easy access to Los Angeles
- **Coed,** 32,228 undergraduate students, 27% full-time, 57% women, 43% men

Undergraduates 8,817 full-time, 23,411 part-time. Students come from 23 states and territories, 60 other countries, 14% African American, 10% Asian American or Pacific Islander, 34% Hispanic American, 0.6% Native American, 2% transferred in.
Freshmen *Admission:* 1,574 applied, 1,574 admitted, 1,574 enrolled.
Faculty *Total:* 1,376, 17% full-time. *Student/faculty ratio:* 24:1.
Majors Accounting; agricultural business and management; anatomy; anthropology; architecture; art; astronomy; biological and physical sciences; botany/plant biology; business administration and management; chemistry; child development; clinical/medical laboratory assistant; computer and information sciences; computer graphics; computer programming; computer programming related; computer systems networking and telecommunications; computer/technical support; criminal justice/law enforcement administration; culinary arts; cultural studies; dental hygiene; dietetics; dramatic/theatre arts; economics; education; engineering; English; environmental studies; family and consumer sciences/human sciences; forestry; French; geography; geology/earth science; German; health and physical education; health science; history; humanities; journalism; kindergarten/preschool education; landscape architecture; liberal arts and sciences/liberal studies; library science; marketing research; mathematics; medical microbiology and bacteriology; music; nursing (registered nurse training); oceanography (chemical and physical); pharmacy; philosophy; physical sciences; physical therapy; political science and government; pre-law studies; psychology; sign language interpretation and translation; social sciences; Spanish; speech and rhetoric; theology; urban studies/affairs; word processing.
Academic Programs *Special study options:* academic remediation for entering students, adult/continuing education programs, advanced placement credit, distance learning, double majors, English as a second language, internships, part-time degree program, services for LD students, study abroad, summer session for credit. *ROTC:* Army (c), Air Force (c).
Library Digital Library Learning Resource Center with 101,243 titles, 911 serial subscriptions, 5,417 audiovisual materials, an OPAC, a Web page.
Computers on Campus 200 computers available on campus for general student use. A campuswide network can be accessed from off campus. Internet access, at least one staffed computer lab available.
Student Life *Housing:* college housing not available. *Activities and Organizations:* drama/theater group, student-run newspaper, radio station, choral group, marching band, Marching Tigers Band, Wind Ensemble, Student Nurses Orga-

nization, Gospel Singers, Alpha Gamma Sigma. *Campus security:* 24-hour patrols, late-night transport/escort service. *Student services:* health clinic, personal/psychological counseling.
Athletics *Intercollegiate sports:* baseball M, basketball M/W, cross-country running M/W, football M, golf M, soccer M/W, softball W, swimming and diving M/W, tennis M/W, track and field M/W, volleyball W, water polo M/W. *Intramural sports:* badminton M/W, basketball M/W, bowling M/W, football M, golf M/W, racquetball M/W, soccer M/W, tennis M/W, volleyball M/W, weight lifting M/W.
Standardized Tests *Required:* Assessment and Placement Services for Community Colleges (for placement).
Costs (2005–06) *Tuition:* state resident $0 full-time; nonresident $5250 full-time, $175 per unit part-time. *Required fees:* $820 full-time, $26 per unit part-time, $20 per term part-time.
Applying *Required:* high school transcript. *Application deadline:* rolling (freshmen), rolling (transfers). *Notification:* continuous (freshmen).
Admissions Contact Ms. Lorraine Anderson, District Dean of Admissions and Records, Riverside Community College District, 4800 Magnolia Avenue, Riverside, CA 92506. *Phone:* 951-222-8600. *Fax:* 951-222-8037.

SACRAMENTO CITY COLLEGE
Sacramento, California

Admissions Contact Mr. Sam T. Sandusky, Dean, Student Services, Sacramento City College, 3835 Freeport Boulevard, Sacramento, CA 95822-1386. *Phone:* 916-558-2438. *Fax:* 916-558-2190.

SADDLEBACK COLLEGE
Mission Viejo, California

Admissions Contact Admissions Office, Saddleback College, 28000 Marguerite Parkway, Mission Viejo, CA 92692-3635. *Phone:* 949-582-4555. *E-mail:* earaiza@saddleback.cc.ca.us.

SAGE COLLEGE
Moreno Valley, California

Admissions Contact 12125 Day Street, Building L, Moreno Valley, CA 92557-6720.

THE SALVATION ARMY COLLEGE FOR OFFICER TRAINING AT CRESTMONT
Rancho Palos Verdes, California

- **Independent religious** 2-year, founded 1878, administratively affiliated with The Salvation Army
- **Calendar** quarters
- **Degree** associate
- **Suburban** 44-acre campus with easy access to Los Angeles
- **Endowment** $81.0 million
- **Coed,** 33 undergraduate students, 100% full-time, 58% women, 42% men

Undergraduates 33 full-time. Students come from 14 states and territories, 1 other country, 49% are from out of state, 4% African American, 7% Asian American or Pacific Islander, 15% Hispanic American, 0.5% Native American, 2% international, 100% live on campus. *Retention:* 98% of 2002 full-time freshmen returned.
Freshmen *Admission:* 23 applied, 18 admitted, 14 enrolled.
Faculty *Total:* 34, 59% full-time, 32% with terminal degrees. *Student/faculty ratio:* 2:1.
Majors Divinity/ministry.
Academic Programs *Special study options:* academic remediation for entering students, accelerated degree program, cooperative education, distance learning, English as a second language, external degree program, independent study, internships, off-campus study, student-designed majors.
Library The Salvation Army Elfman Memorial Library with 35,700 titles, 125 serial subscriptions, an OPAC.
Computers on Campus 65 computers available on campus for general student use. A campuswide network can be accessed from student residence rooms and from off campus. Internet access, at least one staffed computer lab available. Computer purchase or lease plan available.
Student Life *Housing:* on-campus residence required through sophomore year. *Options:* Campus housing is university owned. *Activities and Organizations:* drama/theater group, choral group. *Campus security:* 24-hour emergency response devices and patrols. *Student services:* health clinic, personal/psychological counseling.

Costs (2005–06) *Comprehensive fee:* $10,600 includes full-time tuition ($1500), mandatory fees ($850), and room and board ($8250).
Applying *Application fee:* $15. *Required:* essay or personal statement, high school transcript, letters of recommendation, interview. *Application deadline:* 6/1 (freshmen).
Admissions Contact Maj. Donna Ames, Director of Curriculum, The Salvation Army College for Officer Training at Crestmont, 30840 Hawthorne Boulevard, Rancho Palos Verdes, CA 90275. *Phone:* 310-544-6419. *Toll-free phone:* 310-544-6440. *Fax:* 310-265-6520.

SAN BERNARDINO VALLEY COLLEGE
San Bernardino, California

Admissions Contact Mr. Joe Cobrales, Director of Admissions and Records, San Bernardino Valley College, 701 South Mt Vernon Avenue, San Bernardino, CA 92410-2748. *Phone:* 909-888-6511.

SAN DIEGO CITY COLLEGE
San Diego, California

- **State and locally supported** 2-year, founded 1914, part of San Diego Community College District System
- **Calendar** semesters
- **Degree** certificates and associate
- **Urban** 56-acre campus
- **Coed,** 13,625 undergraduate students

Undergraduates 13% African American, 11% Asian American or Pacific Islander, 29% Hispanic American, 1% Native American.
Freshmen *Admission:* 4,678 admitted.
Faculty *Total:* 485, 33% full-time, 26% with terminal degrees. *Student/faculty ratio:* 35:1.
Majors Accounting; administrative assistant and secretarial science; African-American/Black studies; anthropology; art; artificial intelligence and robotics; automobile/automotive mechanics technology; behavioral sciences; biology/biological sciences; business administration and management; carpentry; commercial and advertising art; computer engineering technology; consumer services and advocacy; cosmetology; court reporting; data processing and data processing technology; developmental and child psychology; drafting and design technology; dramatic/theatre arts; electrical, electronic and communications engineering technology; emergency medical technology (EMT paramedic); engineering technology; English; environmental engineering technology; fashion merchandising; finance; graphic and printing equipment operation/production; Hispanic-American, Puerto Rican, and Mexican-American/Chicano studies; hospitality administration; industrial arts; industrial technology; insurance; interior design; journalism; labor and industrial relations; Latin American studies; legal administrative assistant/secretary; legal assistant/paralegal; liberal arts and sciences/liberal studies; machine tool technology; marketing/marketing management; mathematics; modern languages; music; nursing (licensed practical/vocational nurse training); nursing (registered nurse training); occupational safety and health technology; parks, recreation and leisure; photography; physical education teaching and coaching; physical sciences; political science and government; postal management; pre-engineering; psychology; radio and television; real estate; social sciences; social work; sociology; special products marketing; speech and rhetoric; teacher assistant/aide; telecommunications; tourism and travel services management; transportation technology; welding technology.
Academic Programs *Special study options:* academic remediation for entering students, adult/continuing education programs, cooperative education, distance learning, English as a second language, external degree program, honors programs, independent study, off-campus study, part-time degree program, services for LD students, student-designed majors, summer session for credit. *ROTC:* Air Force (c).
Library San Diego City College Library with 73,000 titles, 337 serial subscriptions, an OPAC.
Computers on Campus 121 computers available on campus for general student use. A campuswide network can be accessed from student residence rooms and from off campus. Internet access, online (class) registration, at least one staffed computer lab available.
Student Life *Housing:* college housing not available. *Activities and Organizations:* drama/theater group, student-run newspaper, radio station, choral group, Alpha Gamma Sigma, Association of United Latin American Students, MECHA, Afrikan Student Union, Student Nurses Association. *Campus security:* 24-hour emergency response devices and patrols, late-night transport/escort service. *Student services:* health clinic, personal/psychological counseling.
Athletics Member NJCAA. *Intercollegiate sports:* baseball M, basketball M/W, cross-country running M/W, football M, golf M/W, soccer M/W, softball W, tennis M/W, track and field M/W, volleyball M/W. *Intramural sports:* archery M/W, badminton M/W, baseball M, basketball M/W, bowling M/W, racquetball M/W, soccer M/W, softball W, swimming and diving M/W, tennis M/W, track and field M/W, volleyball M/W, weight lifting M/W.

San Diego City College (continued)

Costs (2005–06) *One-time required fee:* $36. *Tuition:* state resident $0 full-time; nonresident $3840 full-time, $160 per unit part-time. Full-time tuition and fees vary according to course load. Part-time tuition and fees vary according to course load. *Required fees:* $650 full-time, $26 per unit part-time, $13 per term part-time.

Financial Aid Of all full-time matriculated undergraduates who enrolled in 2003, 100 Federal Work-Study jobs (averaging $4000).

Applying *Options:* electronic application. *Required for some:* high school transcript. *Application deadline:* rolling (freshmen), rolling (transfers).

Admissions Contact Ms. Lou Humphries, Supervisor of Admissions and Records, San Diego City College, 1313 Twelfth Avenue, San Diego, CA 92101-4787. *Phone:* 619-388-3474. *Fax:* 619-388-3135. *E-mail:* lhumphr@sdccd.edu.

SAN DIEGO GOLF ACADEMY
Vista, California

Admissions Contact Ms. Deborah Wells, Admissions Coordinator, San Diego Golf Academy, 1910 Shadowridge Drive, Suite 111, Vista, CA 92083. *Phone:* 760-414-1501. *Toll-free phone:* 800-342-7342. *Fax:* 760-918-8949. *E-mail:* sdga@sdgagolf.com.

SAN DIEGO MESA COLLEGE
San Diego, California

Admissions Contact Ms. Ivonne Alvarez, Director of Admissions and Records, San Diego Mesa College, 7250 Mesa College Drive, San Diego, CA 92111. *Phone:* 619-388-2689. *Fax:* 619-388-3960. *E-mail:* ialvarez@sdccd.cc.ca.us.

SAN DIEGO MIRAMAR COLLEGE
San Diego, California

- **State and locally supported** 2-year, founded 1969, part of San Diego Community College District System
- **Calendar** semesters
- **Degree** associate
- **Suburban** 120-acre campus
- **Coed,** 8,080 undergraduate students

Undergraduates 6% African American, 20% Asian American or Pacific Islander, 16% Hispanic American, 1% Native American.

Faculty *Total:* 284, 25% full-time.

Majors Accounting; administrative assistant and secretarial science; airframe mechanics and aircraft maintenance technology; anthropology; applied mathematics; art; automobile/automotive mechanics technology; avionics maintenance technology; biology/biological sciences; business administration and management; chemistry; corrections; criminal justice/law enforcement administration; criminal justice/police science; developmental and child psychology; emergency medical technology (EMT paramedic); English; fine/studio arts; fire science; geography; humanities; information science/studies; legal assistant/paralegal; liberal arts and sciences/liberal studies; mathematics; occupational safety and health technology; philosophy; physical education teaching and coaching; physical sciences; physics; psychology; social sciences; sociology; Spanish; transportation technology.

Academic Programs *Special study options:* academic remediation for entering students, accelerated degree program, adult/continuing education programs, advanced placement credit, cooperative education, distance learning, double majors, English as a second language, honors programs, independent study, part-time degree program, services for LD students, student-designed majors, study abroad, summer session for credit.

Library Miramar College Library with 19,301 titles, 135 serial subscriptions, 901 audiovisual materials, an OPAC.

Computers on Campus 130 computers available on campus for general student use. A campuswide network can be accessed. Internet access, online (class) registration, at least one staffed computer lab available.

Student Life *Housing:* college housing not available. *Activities and Organizations:* student-run newspaper, Science Club, International Club, Parent Student Advisory Board, Filipino-American Student Union, Miramar-U. S. Tennis Association. *Campus security:* 24-hour emergency response devices and patrols. *Student services:* health clinic, personal/psychological counseling.

Athletics *Intercollegiate sports:* water polo M/W. *Intramural sports:* tennis M/W.

Costs (2005–06) *Tuition:* state resident $0 full-time; nonresident $4492 full-time, $186 per unit part-time. *Required fees:* $652 full-time, $26 per unit part-time.

Financial Aid Of all full-time matriculated undergraduates who enrolled in 2003, 39 Federal Work-Study jobs (averaging $1500).

Applying *Options:* electronic application.

Admissions Contact Ms. Dana Andras, Admissions Supervisor, San Diego Miramar College, 10440 Black Mountain Road, San Diego, CA 92126-2999. *Phone:* 619-536-7854. *Toll-free phone:* 619-388-7844. *Fax:* 619-388-7915. *E-mail:* dandras@sdccd.edu.

SAN JOAQUIN DELTA COLLEGE
Stockton, California

- **District-supported** 2-year, founded 1935, part of California Community College System
- **Calendar** semesters
- **Degree** certificates and associate
- **Urban** 165-acre campus with easy access to Sacramento
- **Coed,** 17,131 undergraduate students, 39% full-time, 59% women, 41% men

Undergraduates 6,668 full-time, 10,463 part-time. Students come from 15 states and territories, 9% African American, 19% Asian American or Pacific Islander, 25% Hispanic American, 1% Native American, 0.5% international. *Retention:* 25% of 2002 full-time freshmen returned.

Freshmen *Admission:* 22,118 applied, 22,118 admitted, 1,762 enrolled.

Faculty *Total:* 565, 38% full-time. *Student/faculty ratio:* 33:1.

Majors Accounting; agricultural business and management; agricultural mechanization; agriculture; animal sciences; anthropology; art; automobile/automotive mechanics technology; behavioral sciences; biology/biological sciences; botany/plant biology; broadcast journalism; business administration and management; business/managerial economics; carpentry; chemistry; child development; civil engineering technology; commercial and advertising art; computer engineering technology; computer programming; computer science; construction engineering technology; corrections; criminal justice/police science; culinary arts; dance; developmental and child psychology; drafting and design technology; dramatic/theatre arts; drawing; economics; electrical, electronic and communications engineering technology; emergency medical technology (EMT paramedic); engineering; engineering related; engineering technology; English; family and consumer sciences/human sciences; fashion merchandising; fire science; food services technology; French; geology/earth science; German; graphic and printing equipment operation/production; health science; heating, air conditioning, ventilation and refrigeration maintenance technology; history; humanities; industrial radiologic technology; interior design; Italian; Japanese; journalism; kindergarten/preschool education; liberal arts and sciences/liberal studies; literature; machine tool technology; marketing/marketing management; mathematics; mechanical engineering/mechanical technology; music; natural resources management and policy; natural sciences; nursing (licensed practical/vocational nurse training); nursing (registered nurse training); ornamental horticulture; philosophy; photography; physical education teaching and coaching; physical sciences; political science and government; psychiatric/mental health services technology; psychology; public administration; religious studies; social sciences; sociology; Spanish; special products marketing; speech and rhetoric.

Academic Programs *Special study options:* academic remediation for entering students, adult/continuing education programs, advanced placement credit, cooperative education, distance learning, English as a second language, honors programs, independent study, part-time degree program, services for LD students, summer session for credit.

Library Goleman Library plus 1 other with 92,398 titles, 605 serial subscriptions, an OPAC, a Web page.

Computers on Campus 400 computers available on campus for general student use. A campuswide network can be accessed from off campus. Internet access, online (class) registration, at least one staffed computer lab available.

Student Life *Housing:* college housing not available. *Activities and Organizations:* drama/theater group, student-run newspaper, radio station, choral group, Alpha Gamma Sigma, Fashion Club, International Club, Badminton Club. *Campus security:* 24-hour emergency response devices and patrols, late-night transport/escort service. *Student services:* personal/psychological counseling, legal services.

Athletics Member NJCAA. *Intercollegiate sports:* baseball M, basketball M/W, cross-country running M/W, fencing M/W, football M, golf M/W, soccer M/W, softball W, swimming and diving M/W, tennis M/W, track and field M/W, volleyball W, water polo M/W, wrestling M. *Intramural sports:* badminton M/W, basketball M/W, bowling M/W, soccer M/W, swimming and diving M/W, tennis M/W, ultimate Frisbee M/W, volleyball M/W, weight lifting M/W.

Standardized Tests *Recommended:* Michigan Test of English Language Proficiency.

Costs (2004–05) *Tuition:* state resident $0 full-time; nonresident $5250 full-time, $175 per unit part-time. *Required fees:* $780 full-time, $26 per unit part-time. *Payment plan:* installment. *Waivers:* employees or children of employees.

Financial Aid Of all full-time matriculated undergraduates who enrolled in 2003, 315 Federal Work-Study jobs (averaging $3100). 210 state and other part-time jobs (averaging $1172).

Applying *Options:* common application, electronic application, early admission. *Application deadline:* rolling (freshmen), rolling (transfers). *Notification:* continuous (freshmen).

Admissions Contact Ms. Catherine Mooney, Registrar, San Joaquin Delta College, 5151 Pacific Avenue, Stockton, CA 95207. *Phone:* 209-954-5635. *Fax:* 209-954-5769. *E-mail:* admissions@deltacollege.edu.

SAN JOAQUIN VALLEY COLLEGE
Visalia, California

- **Independent** 2-year, founded 1977
- **Calendar** semesters
- **Degree** certificates and associate
- **Small-town** campus
- **Coed,** 2,924 undergraduate students, 100% full-time, 72% women, 28% men

Undergraduates 2,924 full-time. 7% African American, 6% Asian American or Pacific Islander, 45% Hispanic American, 1% Native American.

Freshmen *Admission:* 2,924 applied, 2,924 admitted.

Faculty *Total:* 345, 65% full-time, 79% with terminal degrees. *Student/faculty ratio:* 14:1.

Majors Aircraft powerplant technology; airframe mechanics and aircraft maintenance technology; business/commerce; computer systems networking and telecommunications; computer/technical support; corrections; dental assisting; dental hygiene; electrical, electronic and communications engineering technology; heating, air conditioning, ventilation and refrigeration maintenance technology; medical administrative assistant and medical secretary; medical/clinical assistant; nursing (licensed practical/vocational nurse training); pharmacy technician; respiratory care therapy; security and loss prevention; surgical technology; tourism and travel services management; veterinary technology.

Academic Programs *Special study options:* academic remediation for entering students.

Library SJVC Visalia Campus Library with 4,720 titles, 53 serial subscriptions, 125 audiovisual materials.

Computers on Campus 740 computers available on campus for general student use. A campuswide network can be accessed. At least one staffed computer lab available.

Student Life *Housing:* college housing not available. *Activities and Organizations:* Associated Student Body, Students in Free Enterprise, American Medical Technologists. *Campus security:* late-night transport/escort service, full-time security personnel.

Costs (2005–06) *Tuition:* $11,220 full-time.

Applying *Required:* high school transcript. *Required for some:* essay or personal statement, interview.

Admissions Contact Mr. Joseph Holt, Director of Marketing and Admissions, San Joaquin Valley College, 8400 West Mineral King Avenue, Visalia, CA 93291. *Phone:* 559-651-2500.

SAN JOSE CITY COLLEGE
San Jose, California

- **District-supported** 2-year, founded 1921, part of San Jose/Evergreen Community College District System
- **Calendar** semesters
- **Degree** associate
- **Urban** 58-acre campus
- **Coed**

Financial Aid Of all full-time matriculated undergraduates who enrolled in 2003, 105 Federal Work-Study jobs (averaging $2500).

Applying *Options:* early admission, deferred entrance.

Admissions Contact Mr. Carlo Santos, Director of Admissions/Registrar, San Jose City College, 2100 Moorpark Avenue, San Jose, CA 95128-2799. *Phone:* 408-288-3707.

SANTA ANA COLLEGE
Santa Ana, California

Admissions Contact Mrs. Christie Steward, Admissions Clerk, Santa Ana College, 1530 West 17th Street, Santa Ana, CA 92704. *Phone:* 714-564-6053. *Fax:* 714-564-4379.

SANTA BARBARA CITY COLLEGE
Santa Barbara, California

- **State and locally supported** 2-year, founded 1908, part of California Community College System
- **Calendar** semesters
- **Degree** certificates and associate
- **Small-town** 65-acre campus
- **Coed,** 15,456 undergraduate students, 41% full-time, 52% women, 48% men

Undergraduates 6,267 full-time, 9,189 part-time. Students come from 49 states and territories, 59 other countries, 6% are from out of state, 3% African American, 5% Asian American or Pacific Islander, 23% Hispanic American, 1% Native American, 5% international, 5% transferred in.

Freshmen *Admission:* 2,610 applied, 2,610 admitted, 1,701 enrolled.

Faculty *Total:* 633, 36% full-time. *Student/faculty ratio:* 29:1.

Majors Accounting; acting; administrative assistant and secretarial science; African-American/Black studies; American Indian/Native American studies; anthropology; applied horticulture; art history, criticism and conservation; athletic training; automobile/automotive mechanics technology; biology/biological sciences; biomedical technology; biotechnology; business administration and management; chemistry; child care and support services management; commercial and advertising art; communication/speech communication and rhetoric; computer engineering; computer science; cosmetology; criminal justice/law enforcement administration; culinary arts related; cultural studies; drafting and design technology; dramatic/theatre arts; economics; electrical, electronic and communications engineering technology; electrical/electronics equipment installation and repair; engineering; engineering technology; English; environmental/environmental health engineering; environmental studies; film/cinema studies; finance; fine/studio arts; foodservice systems administration; French; geography; geology/earth science; health information/medical records technology; Hispanic-American, Puerto Rican, and Mexican-American/Chicano studies; history; hotel/motel administration; industrial engineering; industrial technology; information science/studies; information technology; institutional food workers; interior design; international relations and affairs; kindergarten/preschool education; kinesiology and exercise science; landscaping and groundskeeping; legal studies; liberal arts and sciences/liberal studies; marine technology; marketing/marketing management; mathematics; medical radiologic technology; music; nursing (licensed practical/vocational nurse training); nursing (registered nurse training); ornamental horticulture; parks, recreation and leisure; philosophy; physical education teaching and coaching; physics; political science and government; psychology; real estate; sales, distribution and marketing; selling skills and sales; sociology; Spanish; system administration; theatre design and technology; therapeutic recreation.

Academic Programs *Special study options:* academic remediation for entering students, adult/continuing education programs, advanced placement credit, cooperative education, distance learning, double majors, English as a second language, honors programs, independent study, internships, part-time degree program, services for LD students, study abroad, summer session for credit. *ROTC:* Army (c).

Library Eli Luria Library with 121,622 titles, 3,325 serial subscriptions, 9,230 audiovisual materials, an OPAC, a Web page.

Computers on Campus 1465 computers available on campus for general student use. A campuswide network can be accessed from off campus. Internet access, at least one staffed computer lab available.

Student Life *Housing:* college housing not available. *Activities and Organizations:* drama/theater group, student-run newspaper, choral group, MECHA, International-Cultural Exchange Club, Geology Club, Computer Club, Future Teachers Club. *Campus security:* 24-hour emergency response devices and patrols, late-night transport/escort service. *Student services:* health clinic, personal/psychological counseling.

Athletics *Intercollegiate sports:* baseball M, basketball M/W, cross-country running M/W, football M, golf M/W, soccer M/W, softball W, tennis M/W, track and field M/W, volleyball M/W.

Standardized Tests *Recommended:* SAT (for placement), SAT Subject Tests (for placement), SAT II: Writing Test (for placement), California State University EPT, UC Subject A Exam.

Costs (2005–06) *Tuition:* state resident $0 full-time; nonresident $4530 full-time, $151 per unit part-time. Full-time tuition and fees vary according to course load. Part-time tuition and fees vary according to course load. *Required fees:* $842 full-time, $26 per unit part-time, $62 per year part-time. *Waivers:* employees or children of employees.

Applying *Options:* early admission. *Recommended:* high school transcript. *Application deadlines:* 8/27 (freshmen), 8/27 (transfers). *Notification:* continuous (freshmen).

Admissions Contact Ms. Allison Curtis, Director of Admissions and Records, Santa Barbara City College, 721 Cliff Drive, Santa Barbara, CA 93109. *Phone:* 805-965-0581 Ext. 2352. *Fax:* 805-962-0497 Ext. 2200. *E-mail:* admissions@sbcc.edu.

SANTA MONICA COLLEGE
Santa Monica, California

- **State and locally supported** 2-year, founded 1929, part of California Community College System
- **Calendar** semester plus optional winter and summer terms
- **Degree** certificates and associate

Santa Monica College (continued)
- **Urban** 40-acre campus with easy access to Los Angeles
- **Endowment** $4.6 million
- **Coed**

Faculty *Student/faculty ratio:* 26:1.
Student Life *Campus security:* 24-hour emergency response devices and patrols, student patrols, late-night transport/escort service.
Athletics Member NJCAA.
Standardized Tests *Required for some:* ACT, ACT COMPASS, ACCUPLACER.
Costs (2004–05) *Tuition:* state resident $0 full-time; nonresident $4470 full-time, $149 per unit part-time. *Required fees:* $570 full-time, $18 per unit part-time, $30 per term part-time.
Financial Aid Of all full-time matriculated undergraduates who enrolled in 2003, 450 Federal Work-Study jobs (averaging $3000).
Applying *Options:* early admission. *Required:* high school transcript.
Admissions Contact Ms. Teresita Rodriguez, Dean of Enrollment Services, Santa Monica College, 1900 Pico Boulevard, Santa Monica, CA 90405-1628. *Phone:* 310-434-4880 Ext. 4774.

▶ See page 550 for a narrative description.

SANTA ROSA JUNIOR COLLEGE
Santa Rosa, California

- **State and locally supported** 2-year, founded 1918, part of California Community College System
- **Calendar** semesters
- **Degree** certificates and associate
- **Urban** 93-acre campus with easy access to San Francisco
- **Endowment** $14.0 million
- **Coed**, 32,567 undergraduate students

Undergraduates Students come from 29 states and territories, 39 other countries, 1% are from out of state, 2% African American, 5% Asian American or Pacific Islander, 16% Hispanic American, 1% Native American.
Freshmen *Admission:* 4,820 applied, 4,820 admitted.
Faculty *Total:* 1,426, 22% full-time, 11% with terminal degrees. *Student/faculty ratio:* 23:1.
Majors Advertising; aeronautical/aerospace engineering technology; agricultural business and management; agricultural mechanization; agriculture; animal health; animal physiology; anthropology; art; astronomy; athletic training; atmospheric sciences and meteorology; behavioral sciences; biology/biological sciences; botany/plant biology; business administration and management; chemistry; child guidance; communication/speech communication and rhetoric; computer science; construction management; criminal justice/law enforcement administration; cultural studies; dental hygiene; dietetics; dramatic/theatre arts; economics; education; engineering; engineering technology; English; environmental studies; family and consumer sciences/human sciences; film/cinema studies; fishing and fisheries sciences and management; forestry; French; geography; geology/earth science; German; history; hotel/motel administration; industrial design; Italian; journalism; landscape architecture; Latin; liberal arts and sciences/liberal studies; mathematics; music; natural resources management and policy; nursing (registered nurse training); occupational therapy; oceanography (chemical and physical); ophthalmic laboratory technology; philosophy; physical education teaching and coaching; physical sciences; physical therapy; physician assistant; physics; political science and government; pre-pharmacy studies; psychology; range science and management; social sciences; sociology; Spanish; speech-language pathology; wildlife and wildlands science and management.
Academic Programs *Special study options:* academic remediation for entering students, adult/continuing education programs, advanced placement credit, cooperative education, distance learning, English as a second language, independent study, internships, off-campus study, part-time degree program, services for LD students, study abroad, summer session for credit. *ROTC:* Army (c).
Library Plover Library plus 1 other with 119,803 titles, 393 serial subscriptions, 9,430 audiovisual materials, an OPAC, a Web page.
Computers on Campus 1325 computers available on campus for general student use. A campuswide network can be accessed from off campus that provide access to library databases. Internet access, online (class) registration, at least one staffed computer lab available.
Student Life *Housing:* college housing not available. *Activities and Organizations:* drama/theater group, student-run newspaper, choral group, International Club, MECHA, Alpha Gamma Sigma, Asian/Pacific Island Association, Phi Theta Kappa. *Campus security:* 24-hour emergency response devices and patrols. *Student services:* health clinic, personal/psychological counseling, women's center.
Athletics Member NJCAA. *Intercollegiate sports:* baseball M, basketball M/W, cross-country running M/W, football M, golf M, ice hockey M(c), rugby M(c), soccer M/W, softball W, swimming and diving M/W, tennis M/W, track and field M/W, volleyball W, water polo M/W, wrestling M.

Standardized Tests *Required for some:* Assessment and Placement Services for Community Colleges.
Costs (2005–06) *Tuition:* state resident $0 full-time; nonresident $5630 full-time, $203 per unit part-time. *Required fees:* $746 full-time, $26 per unit part-time.
Financial Aid Of all full-time matriculated undergraduates who enrolled in 2003, 228 Federal Work-Study jobs (averaging $3500).
Applying *Options:* electronic application, early admission. *Application deadline:* rolling (freshmen), rolling (transfers). *Notification:* continuous (freshmen).
Admissions Contact Diane Traversi, Co-Administrator, Admissions and Records, Santa Rosa Junior College, 1501 Mendocino Avenue, Santa Rosa, CA 95401. *Phone:* 707-527-4685. *Fax:* 707-527-4798. *E-mail:* admininfo@santarosa.edu.

SANTIAGO CANYON COLLEGE
Orange, California

Admissions Contact Denise Pennock, Admissions and Records, Santiago Canyon College, 8045 East Chapman, Orange, CA 92669. *Phone:* 714-564-4000. *Fax:* 714-564-4379.

SHASTA COLLEGE
Redding, California

Admissions Contact Ms. Cassandra Ryan, Admissions and Records Office Director, Shasta College, PO Box 496006, Redding, CA 96049-6006. *Phone:* 530-225-4841.

SIERRA COLLEGE
Rocklin, California

- **State-supported** 2-year, founded 1936, part of California Community College System
- **Calendar** semesters
- **Degree** certificates and associate
- **Suburban** 327-acre campus with easy access to Sacramento
- **Coed**

Faculty *Student/faculty ratio:* 25:1.
Student Life *Campus security:* 24-hour emergency response devices and patrols, late-night transport/escort service.
Standardized Tests *Required:* APS (for placement). *Recommended:* ACT (for placement).
Financial Aid Of all full-time matriculated undergraduates who enrolled in 2003, 150 Federal Work-Study jobs (averaging $2340).
Applying *Options:* common application, electronic application, early admission.
Admissions Contact Ms. Carla Epting-Davis, Associate Dean of Student Services, Sierra College, 5000 Rocklin Road, Rocklin, CA 93677-3397. *Phone:* 916-789-2939. *E-mail:* jradford-harris@sierracollege.edu.

SILICON VALLEY COLLEGE
Emeryville, California

Admissions Contact Ms. Marianne Dulay, Admissions Representative, Silicon Valley College, 1400 65th Street, Suite 200, Emeryville, CA 94608. *Phone:* 510-601-0133 Ext. 14. *Toll-free phone:* 800-750-5627. *E-mail:* mdulay@svcollege.com.

SILICON VALLEY COLLEGE
Fremont, California

Admissions Contact Mr. Anton Croos, Admissions Director, Silicon Valley College, 41350 Christy Street, Fremont, CA 94538. *Phone:* 510-623-9966 Ext. 212. *Toll-free phone:* 800-750-5627. *Fax:* 510-623-9822. *E-mail:* acroos@svcollege.com.

SILICON VALLEY COLLEGE
San Jose, California

Admissions Contact Ms. Patricia Fraser, Admissions Director, Silicon Valley College, 6201 San Ignacio Avenue, San Jose, CA 95119. *Phone:* 408-360-0840 Ext. 247. *Toll-free phone:* 800-750-5627. *E-mail:* pfraser@svcollege.com.

SILICON VALLEY COLLEGE
Walnut Creek, California

- **Proprietary** primarily 2-year, founded 1997
- **Calendar** continuous
- **Degrees** certificates, diplomas, associate, and bachelor's
- **Coed**

Student Life *Campus security:* 24-hour emergency response devices.

Standardized Tests *Required:* CPAt (for admission).

Costs (2004–05) *Tuition:* $14,000 full-time. Full-time tuition and fees vary according to degree level and program. No tuition increase for student's term of enrollment. *Payment plans:* tuition prepayment, installment, deferred payment.

Applying *Application fee:* $125. *Required:* high school transcript, interview, entrance exam. *Required for some:* essay or personal statement.

Admissions Contact Mr. Mark Millen, Admissions Director, Silicon Valley College, 2800 Mitchell Drive, Walnut Creek, CA 94598. *Phone:* 925-280-0235 Ext. 37. *Toll-free phone:* 800-750-5627. *E-mail:* mmillen@svcollege.com.

SKYLINE COLLEGE
San Bruno, California

Admissions Contact Supervisor, Admissions Office, Skyline College, 3300 College Drive, San Bruno, CA 94066-1698. *Phone:* 650-738-4251. *E-mail:* skyadmissions@smccd.net.

SOLANO COMMUNITY COLLEGE
Suisun City, California

- **State and locally supported** 2-year, founded 1945, part of California Community College System
- **Calendar** semesters
- **Degree** certificates, diplomas, and associate
- **Rural** 192-acre campus with easy access to Sacramento and San Francisco
- **Coed**, 12,027 undergraduate students

Undergraduates Students come from 43 states and territories, 6 other countries, 1% are from out of state, 15% African American, 18% Asian American or Pacific Islander, 14% Hispanic American, 1% Native American, 0.2% international.

Faculty *Total:* 374, 39% full-time. *Student/faculty ratio:* 27:1.

Majors Accounting; African-American/Black studies; African studies; airframe mechanics and aircraft maintenance technology; art; automobile/automotive mechanics technology; avionics maintenance technology; biological and physical sciences; biology/biological sciences; business administration and management; business machine repair; chemistry; commercial and advertising art; computer programming; cosmetology; criminal justice/law enforcement administration; cultural studies; drafting and design technology; electrical, electronic and communications engineering technology; English; family and consumer sciences/human sciences; fashion merchandising; finance; fire science; French; German; Hispanic-American, Puerto Rican, and Mexican-American/Chicano studies; history; journalism; kindergarten/preschool education; legal administrative assistant/secretary; liberal arts and sciences/liberal studies; machine tool technology; marketing/marketing management; mathematics; music; nursing (registered nurse training); ornamental horticulture; photography; physical education teaching and coaching; physics; political science and government; psychology; public administration; social sciences; Spanish; telecommunications; welding technology.

Academic Programs *Special study options:* academic remediation for entering students, adult/continuing education programs, advanced placement credit, cooperative education, distance learning, double majors, English as a second language, honors programs, independent study, off-campus study, part-time degree program, services for LD students, study abroad, summer session for credit.

Library Solano Community College Library with 32,000 titles.

Computers on Campus 300 computers available on campus for general student use. A campuswide network can be accessed from off campus. Internet access, online (class) registration, at least one staffed computer lab available.

Student Life *Housing:* college housing not available. *Activities and Organizations:* drama/theater group, student-run newspaper, choral group, national fraternities. *Campus security:* 24-hour patrols, student patrols, late-night transport/escort service. *Student services:* personal/psychological counseling.

Athletics *Intercollegiate sports:* baseball M, basketball M/W, football M, softball W, swimming and diving M/W, volleyball W, water polo M/W.

Standardized Tests *Recommended:* SAT and SAT Subject Tests or ACT (for placement).

Costs (2004–05) *Tuition:* state resident $0 full-time; nonresident $4530 full-time. *Required fees:* $819 full-time.

Financial Aid Of all full-time matriculated undergraduates who enrolled in 2003, 125 Federal Work-Study jobs (averaging $2000). 30 state and other part-time jobs (averaging $2000).

Applying *Options:* electronic application, early admission, deferred entrance. *Application deadline:* rolling (freshmen), rolling (transfers).

Admissions Contact Mr. Gerald Fisher, Dean of Admissions and Records, Solano Community College, 4000 Suisun Valley Road, Fairfield, CA 94534. *Phone:* 707-864-7113. *Fax:* 707-864-7175. *E-mail:* admissions@solano.cc.ca.us.

SONOMA COLLEGE
Petaluma, California

Admissions Contact Ms. Delores Ford, Chief Operating Officer/Campus Director, Sonoma College, 130 Avram Avenue, Rhonert Park, CA 94928. *Phone:* 707-664-9267 Ext. 12. *Toll-free phone:* 800-437-9474. *E-mail:* info@westerni.org.

SONOMA COLLEGE
San Francisco, California

Admissions Contact 78 First Street, San Francisco, CA 94105. *Toll-free phone:* 888-649-7801.

SOUTH COAST COLLEGE
Orange, California

Admissions Contact 2011 West Chapman Avenue, Orange, CA 92868. *Toll-free phone:* 800-337-8366.

SOUTHERN CALIFORNIA INSTITUTE OF TECHNOLOGY
Anaheim, California

Admissions Contact Director of Admissions, Southern California Institute of Technology, 1900 West Crescent Avenue, Building B, Anaheim, CA 92801. *Phone:* 714-520-5552.

SOUTHWESTERN COLLEGE
Chula Vista, California

- **State and locally supported** 2-year, founded 1961, part of California Community College System
- **Calendar** semesters
- **Degree** certificates and associate
- **Suburban** 158-acre campus with easy access to San Diego
- **Endowment** $320,596
- **Coed**

Faculty *Student/faculty ratio:* 22:1.

Student Life *Campus security:* 24-hour emergency response devices, student patrols, late-night transport/escort service.

Costs (2004–05) *Tuition:* state resident $0 full-time; nonresident $4008 full-time; $167 per unit part-time. Full-time tuition and fees vary according to course load. *Required fees:* $502 full-time, $18 per unit part-time, $35 per term part-time.

Applying *Options:* early admission. *Required for some:* high school transcript.

Admissions Contact Ms. Georgia A. Copeland, Director of Admissions and Records, Southwestern College, 900 Otay Lakes Road, Chula Vista, CA 91910. *Phone:* 619-482-6550.

TAFT COLLEGE
Taft, California

- **State and locally supported** 2-year, founded 1922, part of California Community College System
- **Calendar** semesters
- **Degree** certificates and associate
- **Small-town** 15-acre campus
- **Endowment** $14,405
- **Coed**, 7,024 undergraduate students, 8% full-time, 26% women, 74% men

Undergraduates 561 full-time, 6,463 part-time. Students come from 16 states and territories, 5% are from out of state, 14% African American, 4% Asian American or Pacific Islander, 24% Hispanic American, 2% Native American, 11% transferred in, 6% live on campus.

Freshmen *Admission:* 1,249 applied, 1,249 admitted, 262 enrolled.

Taft College (continued)

Faculty *Total:* 91, 41% full-time, 9% with terminal degrees. *Student/faculty ratio:* 18:1.

Majors Accounting; administrative assistant and secretarial science; art; automobile/automotive mechanics technology; biology/biological sciences; business administration and management; computer science; criminal justice/law enforcement administration; data processing and data processing technology; dental hygiene; drafting and design technology; electrical, electronic and communications engineering technology; English; general studies; industrial arts; journalism; kindergarten/preschool education; liberal arts and sciences/liberal studies; mathematics; parks, recreation and leisure; physical education teaching and coaching; physical sciences; pre-engineering; social sciences.

Academic Programs *Special study options:* academic remediation for entering students, adult/continuing education programs, advanced placement credit, distance learning, English as a second language, honors programs, independent study, part-time degree program, services for LD students, summer session for credit.

Library Taft College Library with 28,500 titles, 150 serial subscriptions, 25 audiovisual materials, an OPAC, a Web page.

Computers on Campus 91 computers available on campus for general student use. A campuswide network can be accessed. Internet access, online (class) registration, at least one staffed computer lab available.

Student Life *Housing Options:* coed, disabled students. Campus housing is university owned. *Activities and Organizations:* student-run newspaper, International Club, Alpha Gamma Sigma, Rotoract Club, ASB Club. *Campus security:* controlled dormitory access, parking lot security. *Student services:* personal/psychological counseling.

Athletics *Intercollegiate sports:* baseball M, basketball W, soccer M, softball W, volleyball W.

Costs (2005–06) *Tuition:* state resident $0 full-time; nonresident $4530 full-time, $151 per unit part-time. Full-time tuition and fees vary according to course load. Part-time tuition and fees vary according to course load. *Required fees:* $780 full-time, $26 per unit part-time. *Room and board:* $3146; room only: $1294. *Payment plan:* installment.

Financial Aid Of all full-time matriculated undergraduates who enrolled in 2003, 370 Federal Work-Study jobs (averaging $2295).

Applying *Options:* electronic application. *Required for some:* high school transcript. *Application deadlines:* rolling (freshmen), 8/1 (transfers).

Admissions Contact Ms. Gayle Roberts, Director of Financial Aid and Admissions, Taft College, 29 Emmons Park Drive, Taft, CA 93268. *Phone:* 661-763-7763. *Fax:* 661-763-7758. *E-mail:* lporter@taft.org.

VENTURA COLLEGE
Ventura, California

- **State and locally supported** 2-year, founded 1925, part of California Community College System
- **Calendar** semesters
- **Degree** certificates, diplomas, and associate
- **Suburban** 103-acre campus with easy access to Los Angeles
- **Coed**

Faculty *Student/faculty ratio:* 22:1.

Student Life *Campus security:* 24-hour emergency response devices and patrols, student patrols.

Costs (2004–05) *Tuition:* state resident $0 full-time; nonresident $4890 full-time, $163 per unit part-time. *Required fees:* $576 full-time, $26 per unit part-time, $23 per term part-time.

Financial Aid Of all full-time matriculated undergraduates who enrolled in 2003, 70 Federal Work-Study jobs.

Applying *Required:* high school transcript.

Admissions Contact Ms. Susan Bricker, Registrar, Ventura College, 4667 Telegraph Road, Ventura, CA 93003-3899. *Phone:* 805-654-6456. *Fax:* 805-654-6466. *E-mail:* sbricker@server.vcccd.cc.ca.us.

VICTOR VALLEY COLLEGE
Victorville, California

- **State-supported** 2-year, founded 1961, part of California Community College System
- **Calendar** semesters
- **Degree** certificates and associate
- **Small-town** 253-acre campus with easy access to Los Angeles
- **Coed**

Student Life *Campus security:* 24-hour emergency response devices and patrols, late-night transport/escort service, part-time trained security personnel.

Athletics Member NCAA, NJCAA.

Standardized Tests *Recommended:* ACCUPLACER.

Costs (2004–05) *Tuition:* state resident $0 full-time; nonresident $3576 full-time, $149 per unit part-time. *Required fees:* $624 full-time, $26 per unit part-time.

Financial Aid Of all full-time matriculated undergraduates who enrolled in 2003, 300 Federal Work-Study jobs (averaging $5000). 50 state and other part-time jobs (averaging $5000).

Applying *Options:* early admission.

Admissions Contact Ms. Becky Millen, Director of Admissions and Records, Victor Valley College, 18422 Bear Valley Road, Victorville, CA 92392. *Phone:* 760-245-4271 Ext. 2668. *Fax:* 760-245-9745. *E-mail:* millenb@vvc.edu.

VISTA COMMUNITY COLLEGE
Berkeley, California

- **State and locally supported** 2-year, founded 1974
- **Calendar** semesters
- **Degree** certificates and associate
- **Urban** campus with easy access to San Francisco
- **Coed**

Faculty *Student/faculty ratio:* 25:1.

Costs (2004–05) *Tuition:* nonresident $4632 full-time, $193 per unit part-time. Full-time tuition and fees vary according to course load and program. Part-time tuition and fees vary according to course load and program. *Required fees:* $432 full-time, $18 per unit part-time.

Financial Aid Of all full-time matriculated undergraduates who enrolled in 2003, 50 Federal Work-Study jobs (averaging $3000). 20 state and other part-time jobs (averaging $2000).

Applying *Options:* common application, electronic application, early admission, deferred entrance. *Recommended:* high school transcript.

Admissions Contact Dr. Mario Rivas, Vice President of Student Services, Vista Community College, 2020 Milvia Street, Berkeley, CA 94704. *Phone:* 510-981-2820. *Fax:* 510-841-7333. *E-mail:* sfogarino@peralta.cc.ca.us.

WESTERN CAREER COLLEGE
Pleasant Hill, California

Admissions Contact 380 Civic Drive, Pleasant Hill, CA 94523. *Toll-free phone:* 800-584-4520.

WESTERN CAREER COLLEGE
Sacramento, California

Admissions Contact 8909 Folsom Boulevard, Sacramento, CA 95826. *Toll-free phone:* 800-321-2386.

WESTERN CAREER COLLEGE
San Leandro, California

Admissions Contact 170 Bay Fair Mall, San Leandro, CA 94578. *Toll-free phone:* 800-584-4553.

WEST HILLS COMMUNITY COLLEGE
Coalinga, California

- **State-supported** 2-year, founded 1932, part of California Community College System
- **Calendar** semesters
- **Degree** certificates, diplomas, and associate
- **Small-town** 193-acre campus
- **Coed**

Faculty *Student/faculty ratio:* 20:1.

Standardized Tests *Recommended:* SAT or ACT (for placement).

Financial Aid Of all full-time matriculated undergraduates who enrolled in 2003, 253 Federal Work-Study jobs (averaging $1351). 42 state and other part-time jobs (averaging $1669).

Applying *Options:* early admission. *Recommended:* high school transcript.

Admissions Contact Mrs. Darlene Georgatos, Director of Admissions and Records, West Hills Community College, 300 Cherry Lane, Coalinga, CA 93210-1399. *Phone:* 559-934-3204. *Toll-free phone:* 800-266-1114. *E-mail:* darlenegeorgatos@westhillcollege.com.

WEST LOS ANGELES COLLEGE
Culver City, California

Admissions Contact Mr. Len Isaksen, Director of Admissions, West Los Angeles College, 4800 Freshman Drive, Culver City, CA 90230-3519. *Phone:* 310-287-4255.

WEST VALLEY COLLEGE
Saratoga, California

Admissions Contact Mr. Albert Moore, Admissions and Records Supervisor, West Valley College, 14000 Fruitvale Avenue, Saratoga, CA 95070-5698. *Phone:* 408-741-2533.

WESTWOOD COLLEGE-ANAHEIM
Anaheim, California

- **Proprietary** primarily 2-year
- **Calendar** continuous
- **Degrees** associate and bachelor's
- **Suburban** campus with easy access to Los Angeles
- **Coed**
- 37% of applicants were admitted

Applying *Required:* interview, HS diploma or GED and passing scores on SAT/ACT or Accuplacer test.
Admissions Contact Mr. Paul Sallenbach, Director of Admissions, Westwood College-Anaheim, 2461 West La Palma Avenue, Anaheim, CA 92801-2610. *Phone:* 714-226-9990. *Toll-free phone:* 877-650-6050. *Fax:* 714-826-7398. *E-mail:* info@westwood.edu.

▶ **See page 564 for a narrative description.**

WESTWOOD COLLEGE-INLAND EMPIRE
Upland, California

- **Proprietary** primarily 2-year
- **Calendar** continuous
- **Degrees** associate and bachelor's
- **Suburban** campus with easy access to Los Angeles
- **Coed**

Applying *Required:* interview, H.S. diploma or GED, pass entrance exam (or provide acceptable SAT/ACT scores).
Admissions Contact Mr. Lyle Seavers, Director of Admissions, Westwood College-Inland Empire, 20 West 7th Street, Upland, CA 91786-7148. *Phone:* 909-931-7550. *Toll-free phone:* 866-288-9488. *Fax:* 909-931-9195. *E-mail:* info@westwood.edu.

▶ **See page 586 for a narrative description.**

WESTWOOD COLLEGE-LONG BEACH
Long Beach, California

- **Proprietary** primarily 2-year, founded 2002, part of AITU Colleges
- **Calendar** continuous
- **Degrees** associate and bachelor's
- **Urban** 1-acre campus with easy access to Los Angeles
- **Coed,** 265 undergraduate students, 100% full-time, 34% women, 66% men

Undergraduates 265 full-time. Students come from 4 states and territories, 2% are from out of state, 14% African American, 8% Asian American or Pacific Islander, 48% Hispanic American, 0.4% Native American, 0.4% international.
Freshmen *Admission:* 204 applied, 102 admitted, 102 enrolled.
Faculty *Total:* 19, 11% full-time, 11% with terminal degrees. *Student/faculty ratio:* 15:1.
Majors CAD/CADD drafting/design technology; computer hardware engineering; design and visual communications; graphic design.
Academic Programs *Special study options:* accelerated degree program, adult/continuing education programs, advanced placement credit, cooperative education, external degree program, freshman honors college, honors programs, independent study, internships, off-campus study, part-time degree program, services for LD students, student-designed majors.
Library Westwood College Library plus 1 other with an OPAC.
Computers on Campus A campuswide network can be accessed from off campus. Internet access, online (class) registration, at least one staffed computer lab available. Computer purchase or lease plan available.
Student Life *Housing:* college housing not available. *Activities and Organizations:* Westwood Expo, Mentorship Program, Director's Advisory Board. *Campus security:* 24-hour emergency response devices and patrols, late-night transport/escort service. *Student services:* personal/psychological counseling.
Athletics *Intramural sports:* basketball M/W, soccer M/W.
Standardized Tests *Required:* ACCUPLACER (for admission). *Recommended:* SAT or ACT (for admission).
Costs (2004–05) *Tuition:* $18,645 full-time. Full-time tuition and fees vary according to course load and program. Part-time tuition and fees vary according to course load, degree level, and program. *Required fees:* $2726 full-time. *Payment plans:* tuition prepayment, installment. *Waivers:* employees or children of employees.
Applying *Options:* common application, electronic application. *Application fee:* $100. *Required:* high school transcript, interview. *Application deadlines:* 8/2 (freshmen), 10/4 (transfers). *Notification:* continuous (freshmen).
Admissions Contact Jesse Kamekona, Director of Admissions, Westwood College-Long Beach, 3901 Via Oro Avenue, Suite 103, Long Beach, CA 90810. *Phone:* 310-522-2088 Ext. 100. *Toll-free phone:* 888-403-3308. *Fax:* 310-522-2098. *E-mail:* cmcvey@westwood.edu.

▶ **See page 588 for a narrative description.**

WESTWOOD COLLEGE-LOS ANGELES
Inglewood, California

Admissions Contact Mr. Keith Watson, Director of Admissions, Westwood College-Los Angeles, 8911 Aviation Boulevard, Inglewood, CA 90301-2904. *Phone:* 310-337-4444. *Toll-free phone:* 800-597-8690. *Fax:* 310-337-1176. *E-mail:* info@westwood.edu.

▶ **See page 594 for a narrative description.**

WESTWOOD COLLEGE-LOS ANGELES
Los Angeles, California

- **Proprietary** primarily 2-year
- **Calendar** continuous
- **Degrees** associate and bachelor's
- **Urban** campus with easy access to Los Angeles
- **Coed**

Applying *Application fee:* $100. *Required:* interview, HS diploma/GED and passing scores on ACT/SAT or Accuplacer.
Admissions Contact Mr. Ron Milman, Director of Admissions, Westwood College-Los Angeles, 3460 Wilshire Boulevard, Suite 700, Los Angeles, CA 90010-2210. *Phone:* 213-739-9999. *Toll-free phone:* 877-377-4600. *Fax:* 213-382-2468. *E-mail:* info@westwood.edu.

▶ **See page 590 for a narrative description.**

WYOTECH
Fremont, California

Admissions Contact Mr. Joseph Files, Vice President of Marketing and Admissions, WyoTech, 200 Whitney Place, Fremont, CA 94539-7663. *Phone:* 510-580-5440. *Toll-free phone:* 800-248-8585.

WYOTECH
West Sacramento, California

Admissions Contact 980 Riverside Parkway, West Sacramento, CA 95605-1507.

YUBA COLLEGE
Marysville, California

- **State and locally supported** 2-year, founded 1927, part of California Community College System
- **Calendar** semesters
- **Degree** certificates and associate
- **Rural** 160-acre campus with easy access to Sacramento
- **Endowment** $3.7 million
- **Coed,** 9,165 undergraduate students, 35% full-time, 66% women, 34% men

Undergraduates 3,216 full-time, 5,949 part-time. 4% African American, 11% Asian American or Pacific Islander, 28% Hispanic American, 2% Native American.
Faculty *Total:* 830, 14% full-time, 5% with terminal degrees.
Majors Accounting; administrative assistant and secretarial science; advertising; African-American/Black studies; agricultural business and management; agricultural mechanization; agriculture; agronomy and crop science; animal sciences; art; automobile/automotive mechanics technology; biological and physical sciences; biology/biological sciences; business administration and management; chemistry; child development; communication/speech communication and rhetoric; computer and information sciences related; computer science; corrections; cosmetology; criminal justice/law enforcement administration; criminal justice/police science; cultural studies; dramatic/theatre arts; education; electrical, electronic and communications engineering technology; elementary education; English; family and consumer economics related; family and con-

Yuba College (continued)

sumer sciences/human sciences; fire science; health teacher education; Hispanic-American, Puerto Rican, and Mexican-American/Chicano studies; history; human services; industrial radiologic technology; industrial technology; kindergarten/preschool education; machine tool technology; mass communication/media; mathematics; music; nursing (licensed practical/vocational nurse training); nursing (registered nurse training); philosophy; photography; physical education teaching and coaching; pre-engineering; psychiatric/mental health services technology; psychology; robotics technology; social sciences; substance abuse/addiction counseling; veterinary technology; welding technology; women's studies; word processing.

Academic Programs *Special study options:* academic remediation for entering students, advanced placement credit, distance learning, double majors, English as a second language, part-time degree program, services for LD students, summer session for credit.

Library Learning Resource Center and Library plus 1 other with 65,000 titles, 1,300 serial subscriptions, 9,419 audiovisual materials, an OPAC.

Computers on Campus 200 computers available on campus for general student use. A campuswide network can be accessed from student residence rooms and from off campus. Internet access, online (class) registration, at least one staffed computer lab available.

Student Life *Activities and Organizations:* drama/theater group, choral group. *Campus security:* 24-hour patrols, student patrols. *Student services:* health clinic, personal/psychological counseling, women's center.

Athletics Member NCAA. *Intercollegiate sports:* baseball M(s), basketball M/W, cross-country running M/W, football M, soccer M/W, softball W, tennis M/W, track and field M/W, volleyball W.

Costs (2005–06) *Tuition:* state resident $0 full-time. *Required fees:* $26 per unit part-time.

Financial Aid Of all full-time matriculated undergraduates who enrolled in 2003, 290 Federal Work-Study jobs (averaging $2400). 50 state and other part-time jobs (averaging $1000).

Applying *Options:* common application, electronic application. *Required:* high school transcript.

Admissions Contact Dr. David Farrell, Dean of Student Development, Yuba College, 2088 North Beale Road, Marysville, CA 95901. *Phone:* 530-741-6705.

COLORADO

AIMS COMMUNITY COLLEGE
Greeley, Colorado

Admissions Contact Ms. Susie Gallardo, Admissions Technician, Aims Community College, Box 69, Greeley, CO 80632-0069. *Phone:* 970-330-8008 Ext. 6624. *Fax:* 970-339-6682. *E-mail:* wgreen@aims.edu.

ARAPAHOE COMMUNITY COLLEGE
Littleton, Colorado

- **State-supported** 2-year, founded 1965, part of Community Colleges of Colorado
- **Calendar** semesters
- **Degree** certificates, diplomas, and associate
- **Suburban** 52-acre campus with easy access to Denver
- **Coed**, 8,000 undergraduate students, 100% full-time, 56% women, 44% men

Undergraduates 8,000 full-time. Students come from 35 other countries.
Freshmen *Average high school GPA:* 2.0.
Faculty *Total:* 414, 28% full-time. *Student/faculty ratio:* 19:1.
Majors Accounting; administrative assistant and secretarial science; architectural engineering technology; automobile/automotive mechanics technology; biological and physical sciences; building/home/construction inspection; business administration and management; child care and support services management; child care provision; clinical laboratory science/medical technology; clinical/medical laboratory technology; commercial and advertising art; communications systems installation and repair technology; communications technology; computer graphics; computer/information technology services administration related; computer programming; computer programming related; computer programming (specific applications); computer science; computer software and media applications related; computer systems networking and telecommunications; computer/technical support; construction management; consumer merchandising/retailing management; criminal justice/law enforcement administration; criminal justice/police science; data modeling/warehousing and database administration; drafting and design technology; electrical, electronic and communications engineering technology; emergency medical technology (EMT paramedic); engineering; environmental engineering technology; finance; food services technology;

funeral service and mortuary science; health information/medical records administration; information science/studies; legal administrative assistant/secretary; legal assistant/paralegal; liberal arts and sciences/liberal studies; management information systems; marketing/marketing management; mechanical design technology; medical/clinical assistant; nursing (registered nurse training); pharmacy; physical therapy; tourism and travel services management; web page, digital/multimedia and information resources design.

Academic Programs *Special study options:* academic remediation for entering students, accelerated degree program, adult/continuing education programs, advanced placement credit, cooperative education, distance learning, double majors, English as a second language, honors programs, independent study, internships, off-campus study, part-time degree program, services for LD students, student-designed majors, study abroad, summer session for credit. *ROTC:* Army (c), Air Force (c).

Library Weber Center for Learning Resources plus 1 other with 45,000 titles, 441 serial subscriptions, an OPAC, a Web page.

Computers on Campus 200 computers available on campus for general student use. A campuswide network can be accessed from off campus. Internet access, at least one staffed computer lab available.

Student Life *Housing:* college housing not available. *Activities and Organizations:* drama/theater group, student-run newspaper, choral group. *Campus security:* 24-hour emergency response devices and patrols, late-night transport/escort service. *Student services:* personal/psychological counseling.

Athletics Member NJCAA. *Intramural sports:* skiing (cross-country) M/W, skiing (downhill) M/W, soccer M/W, swimming and diving M/W, tennis M/W, volleyball M/W.

Standardized Tests *Required:* CPT (for placement). *Recommended:* SAT II: Writing Test (for placement).

Financial Aid Of all full-time matriculated undergraduates who enrolled in 2003, 100 Federal Work-Study jobs (averaging $4200). 200 state and other part-time jobs (averaging $4200).

Applying *Options:* common application, electronic application, early admission, deferred entrance. *Application deadline:* rolling (freshmen), rolling (transfers).

Admissions Contact Mr. Howard Fukaye, Admissions Specialist, Arapahoe Community College, 5900 South Santa Fe Drive, PO Box 9002, Littleton, CO 80160-9002. *Phone:* 303-797-5622. *Fax:* 303-797-5970. *E-mail:* hfukaye@arapahoe.edu.

BEL-REA INSTITUTE OF ANIMAL TECHNOLOGY
Denver, Colorado

Admissions Contact Ms. Paulette Kaufman, Director, Bel-Rea Institute of Animal Technology, 1681 South Dayton Street, Denver, CO 80247. *Phone:* 303-751-8700. *Toll-free phone:* 800-950-8001.

BLAIR COLLEGE
Colorado Springs, Colorado

Admissions Contact Ms. Dawn Collins, Director of Admissions, Blair College, 1815 Jet Wing Drive, Colorado Springs, CO 80916. *Phone:* 719-630-6580. *Toll-free phone:* 888-741-4271.

BOULDER COLLEGE OF MASSAGE THERAPY
Boulder, Colorado

Admissions Contact 6255 Longbow Drive, Boulder, CO 80301. *Toll-free phone:* 800-442-5131.

CAMBRIDGE COLLEGE
Aurora, Colorado

Admissions Contact 12500 East Iliff Avenue, # 100, Aurora, CO 80014.

COLLEGEAMERICA-COLORADO SPRINGS
Colorado Spring, Colorado

Admissions Contact 3645 Citadel Drive South, Colorado Spring, CO 80909.

COLLEGEAMERICA-DENVER
Denver, Colorado

Admissions Contact Barbara W. Thomas, President, CollegeAmerica-Denver, 1385 South Colorado Boulevard, Denver, CO 80222-1912. *Phone:* 303-691-9756. *Toll-free phone:* 800-97-SKILLS.

COLLEGEAMERICA-FORT COLLINS
Fort Collins, Colorado

- **Proprietary** primarily 2-year, founded 1962
- **Calendar** continuous
- **Degrees** associate and bachelor's
- **Suburban** campus
- **Coed**

Faculty *Student/faculty ratio:* 22:1.

Costs (2004–05) *Comprehensive fee:* $14,325. Full-time tuition and fees vary according to program. Part-time tuition: $275 per credit. No tuition increase for student's term of enrollment. *Payment plans:* tuition prepayment, installment, deferred payment.

Applying *Required:* essay or personal statement, high school transcript, interview. *Required for some:* letters of recommendation. *Recommended:* minimum 2.0 GPA.

Admissions Contact Ms. Anna DiTorrice-Mull, Director of Admissions, CollegeAmerica-Fort Collins, 4601 South Mason Street, Fort Collins, CO 80525. *Phone:* 970-223-6060 Ext. 8002. *Toll-free phone:* 800-97-SKILLS. *Fax:* 970-225-6059. *E-mail:* anna@collegeamerica.edu.

COLORADO MOUNTAIN COLLEGE, ALPINE CAMPUS
Steamboat Springs, Colorado

- **District-supported** 2-year, founded 1965, part of Colorado Mountain College District System
- **Calendar** semesters
- **Degree** certificates and associate
- **Rural** 10-acre campus
- **Coed,** 1,104 undergraduate students, 41% full-time, 47% women, 53% men

Undergraduates 454 full-time, 650 part-time. Students come from 49 states and territories, 40% are from out of state, 44% live on campus.

Freshmen *Admission:* 579 applied, 579 admitted. *Average high school GPA:* 2.40.

Faculty *Total:* 19.

Majors Accounting; behavioral sciences; biological and physical sciences; biology/biological sciences; business administration and management; computer engineering technology; consumer merchandising/retailing management; data entry/microcomputer applications related; English; fine/studio arts; geology/earth science; hospitality administration; hotel/motel administration; humanities; liberal arts and sciences/liberal studies; marketing/marketing management; mathematics; parks, recreation and leisure facilities management; physical sciences; social sciences.

Academic Programs *Special study options:* academic remediation for entering students, adult/continuing education programs, advanced placement credit, cooperative education, distance learning, honors programs, independent study, internships, part-time degree program, services for LD students, study abroad, summer session for credit.

Library 17,000 titles, 192 serial subscriptions, an OPAC, a Web page.

Computers on Campus 60 computers available on campus for general student use. A campuswide network can be accessed from student residence rooms. Internet access, at least one staffed computer lab available.

Student Life *Housing:* on-campus residence required for freshman year. *Options:* coed. Campus housing is university owned. *Activities and Organizations:* student-run newspaper, student government, Forensics Team, Ski Club, International Club, Phi Theta Kappa. *Campus security:* 24-hour emergency response devices, controlled dormitory access. *Student services:* health clinic, personal/psychological counseling.

Athletics *Intercollegiate sports:* skiing (downhill) M/W. *Intramural sports:* basketball M/W, skiing (cross-country) M/W, skiing (downhill) M/W, soccer M/W, ultimate Frisbee M/W, volleyball M/W.

Standardized Tests *Recommended:* SAT or ACT (for placement).

Costs (2005–06) *Tuition:* area resident $1290 full-time, $43 per credit part-time; state resident $2160 full-time, $72 per credit part-time; nonresident $6930 full-time, $231 per credit part-time. Full-time tuition and fees vary according to course load. Part-time tuition and fees vary according to course load. *Required fees:* $180 full-time. *Room and board:* $6392; room only: $3288. Room and board charges vary according to board plan and location. *Waivers:* employees or children of employees.

Applying *Options:* early admission, deferred entrance. *Required:* high school transcript. *Application deadline:* rolling (freshmen), rolling (transfers).

Admissions Contact Ms. Janice Bell, Admissions Assistant, Colorado Mountain College, Alpine Campus, PO Box 10001, Department PG, Glenwood Springs, CO 81602. *Phone:* 970-870-4417 Ext. 4417. *Toll-free phone:* 800-621-8559. *E-mail:* joinus@coloradomtn.edu.

COLORADO MOUNTAIN COLLEGE, SPRING VALLEY CAMPUS
Glenwood Springs, Colorado

- **District-supported** 2-year, founded 1965, part of Colorado Mountain College District System
- **Calendar** semesters
- **Degree** certificates and associate
- **Rural** 680-acre campus
- **Coed,** 493 undergraduate students, 67% full-time, 61% women, 39% men

Colorado Mountain College (CMC) offers high-quality education programs in a variety of occupational and transfer-degree options. CMC's Associate of Arts and Associate of Science degrees are part of the State Transfer Guarantee to any 4-year public college/university in Colorado. CMC also offers specialized occupational programs in the ski industry, natural resources, culinary, outdoor leadership, photography, graphic design, and veterinary technology.

Undergraduates 332 full-time, 161 part-time. Students come from 38 states and territories, 45% are from out of state, 44% live on campus.

Freshmen *Admission:* 579 applied, 579 admitted. *Average high school GPA:* 2.40.

Faculty *Total:* 22. *Student/faculty ratio:* 17:1.

Majors Accounting; art; behavioral sciences; biological and physical sciences; biology/biological sciences; business administration and management; commercial and advertising art; computer engineering technology; computer systems networking and telecommunications; computer/technical support; criminal justice/law enforcement administration; data entry/microcomputer applications related; dramatic/theatre arts; English; humanities; liberal arts and sciences/liberal studies; mathematics; natural sciences; nursing (licensed practical/vocational nurse training); nursing (registered nurse training); photography; psychology; social sciences; therapeutic recreation; veterinary technology.

Academic Programs *Special study options:* academic remediation for entering students, adult/continuing education programs, advanced placement credit, cooperative education, distance learning, honors programs, independent study, internships, part-time degree program, services for LD students, study abroad, summer session for credit.

Library Quigley Library with 36,000 titles, 186 serial subscriptions, an OPAC, a Web page.

Computers on Campus 65 computers available on campus for general student use. A campuswide network can be accessed from student residence rooms. Internet access, at least one staffed computer lab available.

Student Life *Housing:* on-campus residence required for freshman year. *Options:* coed. Campus housing is university owned. Freshman applicants given priority for college housing. *Activities and Organizations:* drama/theater group, student-run newspaper, student government, outdoor activities, World Awareness Society, Peer Mentors, Student Activities Board. *Campus security:* 24-hour emergency response devices, controlled dormitory access. *Student services:* personal/psychological counseling.

Athletics Member NJCAA. *Intercollegiate sports:* soccer M/W. *Intramural sports:* basketball M/W, rock climbing M/W, skiing (cross-country) M/W, skiing (downhill) M/W, ultimate Frisbee M/W, volleyball M/W.

Standardized Tests *Recommended:* SAT or ACT (for placement).

Costs (2005–06) *Tuition:* area resident $1290 full-time, $43 per credit part-time; state resident $2160 full-time, $72 per credit part-time; nonresident $6930 full-time, $231 per credit part-time. Full-time tuition and fees vary according to course load. Part-time tuition and fees vary according to course load. *Required fees:* $180 full-time. *Room and board:* $6392; room only: $3288. Room and board charges vary according to board plan and location. *Payment plan:* installment. *Waivers:* senior citizens and employees or children of employees.

Applying *Options:* early admission, deferred entrance. *Required:* high school transcript. *Application deadline:* rolling (freshmen), rolling (transfers).

Admissions Contact Ms. Deb Markiecki, Admissions Assistant, Colorado Mountain College, Spring Valley Campus, PO Box 10001, Department PG, Glenwood Springs, CO 81601. *Phone:* 970-947-8276 Ext. 8276. *Toll-free phone:* 800-621-8559. *E-mail:* joinus@coloradomtn.edu.

► **See page 484 for a narrative description.**

COLORADO MOUNTAIN COLLEGE, TIMBERLINE CAMPUS
Leadville, Colorado

- **District-supported** 2-year, founded 1965, part of Colorado Mountain College District System
- **Calendar** semesters
- **Degree** certificates and associate

Colorado Mountain College, Timberline Campus (continued)
- **Rural** 200-acre campus
- **Coed,** 407 undergraduate students, 48% full-time, 43% women, 57% men

Undergraduates 194 full-time, 213 part-time. Students come from 48 states and territories, 76% are from out of state, 30% live on campus.
Freshmen *Admission:* 242 applied, 242 admitted. *Average high school GPA:* 2.40.
Faculty *Total:* 14. *Student/faculty ratio:* 15:1.
Majors Accounting; art; behavioral sciences; biological and physical sciences; biology/biological sciences; business administration and management; child development; computer engineering technology; data entry/microcomputer applications; data entry/microcomputer applications related; ecology; English; environmental education; environmental studies; humanities; hydrology and water resources science; kindergarten/preschool education; land use planning and management; liberal arts and sciences/liberal studies; mathematics; parks, recreation and leisure; parks, recreation and leisure facilities management; psychology; social sciences.
Academic Programs *Special study options:* academic remediation for entering students, adult/continuing education programs, advanced placement credit, cooperative education, distance learning, English as a second language, honors programs, independent study, internships, part-time degree program, services for LD students, study abroad, summer session for credit.
Library 25,000 titles, 185 serial subscriptions.
Computers on Campus 30 computers available on campus for general student use. A campuswide network can be accessed from student residence rooms. Internet access, at least one staffed computer lab available.
Student Life *Housing:* on-campus residence required for freshman year. *Options:* coed. Freshman applicants given priority for college housing. *Activities and Organizations:* Environmental Club, Outdoor Club, Student Activities Board. *Campus security:* 24-hour emergency response devices, controlled dormitory access. *Student services:* personal/psychological counseling.
Athletics *Intramural sports:* basketball M, rock climbing M/W, skiing (cross-country) M/W, skiing (downhill) M/W, soccer M/W, volleyball M/W.
Standardized Tests *Recommended:* SAT or ACT (for placement).
Costs (2005–06) *Tuition:* area resident $1290 full-time, $43 per credit part-time; state resident $2160 full-time, $72 per credit part-time; nonresident $6930 full-time, $231 per credit part-time. Full-time tuition and fees vary according to course load. Part-time tuition and fees vary according to course load. *Required fees:* $180 full-time. *Room and board:* $6332; room only: $3288. Room and board charges vary according to board plan and housing facility. *Payment plans:* installment, deferred payment. *Waivers:* senior citizens and employees or children of employees.
Applying *Options:* early admission, deferred entrance. *Required:* high school transcript. *Application deadline:* rolling (freshmen), rolling (transfers).
Admissions Contact Ms. Virginia Espinoza, Admissions Assistant, Colorado Mountain College, Timberline Campus, PO Box 10001, Department PG, Glenwood Springs, CO 81602. *Phone:* 719-486-4291. *Toll-free phone:* 800-621-8559. *E-mail:* joinus@coloradomtn.edu.

COLORADO NORTHWESTERN COMMUNITY COLLEGE
Rangely, Colorado

- **State-supported** 2-year, founded 1962, part of Colorado Community College and Occupational Education System
- **Calendar** semesters
- **Degree** certificates and associate
- **Rural** 150-acre campus
- **Endowment** $27,000
- **Coed,** 2,242 undergraduate students, 22% full-time, 51% women, 49% men

Colorado Northwestern Community College provides a residential campus in Rangely, with athletics and outdoor recreation opportunities. The Rangely and Craig campuses offer AA and AS degrees and vocational programs, such as aviation, construction technology, criminal justice, dental hygiene, and nursing. Students should visit http://www.cncc.edu or call 800-562-1105 (toll-free) for more information.

Undergraduates 499 full-time, 1,743 part-time. Students come from 28 states and territories, 3 other countries, 5% are from out of state, 0.8% African American, 0.6% Asian American or Pacific Islander, 5% Hispanic American, 1% Native American, 0.3% international, 7% transferred in, 62% live on campus. *Retention:* 55% of 2002 full-time freshmen returned.
Freshmen *Admission:* 171 applied, 171 admitted, 171 enrolled.
Faculty *Total:* 277, 15% full-time, 6% with terminal degrees. *Student/faculty ratio:* 9:1.
Majors Accounting; aesthetician/esthetician and skin care; aircraft powerplant technology; airframe mechanics and aircraft maintenance technology; airline pilot and flight crew; art; business administration and management; child care and support services management; criminal justice/law enforcement administra-

tion; dental hygiene; early childhood education; e-commerce; education; emergency medical technology (EMT paramedic); English; entrepreneurship; environmental science; fine arts related; fire science; general studies; geology/earth science; hair styling and hair design; health services/allied health/health sciences; history; human services; instrumentation technology; legal assistant/paralegal; liberal arts and sciences/liberal studies; marine biology and biological oceanography; music; nail technician and manicurist; natural resources/conservation; nursing assistant/aide and patient care assistant; nursing (registered nurse training); parks, recreation and leisure; physical sciences; political science and government; psychology; teacher assistant/aide; wildlife biology.
Academic Programs *Special study options:* academic remediation for entering students, adult/continuing education programs, advanced placement credit, distance learning, double majors, independent study, internships, part-time degree program, services for LD students, student-designed majors, summer session for credit.
Library Colorado Northwestern Community College Library plus 1 other with 20,063 titles, 230 serial subscriptions, 3,559 audiovisual materials, an OPAC.
Computers on Campus 83 computers available on campus for general student use. A campuswide network can be accessed from student residence rooms and from off campus. Internet access, online (class) registration, at least one staffed computer lab available.
Student Life *Housing:* on-campus residence required for freshman year. *Options:* coed. Campus housing is university owned. Freshman applicants given priority for college housing. *Activities and Organizations:* drama/theater group, student-run newspaper, choral group, Campus Activities Board, SADHA, Aero Club, Criminal Justice Club, Spartan Times Newspaper Club. *Campus security:* student patrols, late-night transport/escort service. *Student services:* personal/psychological counseling.
Athletics Member NJCAA. *Intercollegiate sports:* baseball M(s), basketball M(s)/W(s), cross-country running W, softball W(s). *Intramural sports:* basketball M/W, football M/W, golf M/W, racquetball M/W, skiing (cross-country) M/W, skiing (downhill) M/W, softball M/W, table tennis M/W, tennis M/W, volleyball M/W.
Standardized Tests *Recommended:* ACT (for placement).
Costs (2004–05) *Tuition:* state resident $2004 full-time, $67 per credit hour part-time; nonresident $8283 full-time, $276 per credit hour part-time. *Required fees:* $181 full-time, $7 per credit hour part-time, $10 per term part-time. *Room and board:* $5320; room only: $2100.
Financial Aid Of all full-time matriculated undergraduates who enrolled in 2003, 35 Federal Work-Study jobs (averaging $1000). 80 state and other part-time jobs (averaging $1600).
Applying *Options:* early admission, deferred entrance. *Required:* high school transcript. *Required for some:* essay or personal statement, 3 letters of recommendation, interview. *Application deadline:* rolling (freshmen), rolling (transfers).
Admissions Contact Mr. Gene Bilodeau, Registrar, Colorado Northwestern Community College, 500 Kennedy Drive, Rangely, CO 81648. *Phone:* 970-824-1103. *Toll-free phone:* 970-675-3221 Ext. 218 (in-state); 800-562-1105 Ext. 218 (out-of-state). *Fax:* 970-675-3343.

COLORADO SCHOOL OF HEALING ARTS
Lakewood, Colorado

Admissions Contact Victoria Steere, Director, Colorado School of Healing Arts, 7655 West Mississippi Avenue, Suite 100, Lakewood, CO 80226. *Phone:* 303-986-2320.

COLORADO SCHOOL OF TRADES
Lakewood, Colorado

- **Proprietary** 2-year
- **Degree** associate
- **Coed**

Costs (2004–05) *Tuition:* $8100 full-time. Full-time tuition and fees vary according to program. No tuition increase for student's term of enrollment.
Admissions Contact Mr. Robert Martin, Director, Colorado School of Trades, 1575 Hoyt Street, Lakewood, CO 80215-2996. *Phone:* 800-234-4594. *Toll-free phone:* 800-234-4594.

COMMUNITY COLLEGE OF AURORA
Aurora, Colorado

- **State-supported** 2-year, founded 1983
- **Calendar** semesters
- **Degree** certificates and associate
- **Suburban** campus with easy access to Denver
- **Coed,** 5,525 undergraduate students, 27% full-time, 61% women, 39% men

Undergraduates 1,502 full-time, 4,023 part-time. 20% African American, 7% Asian American or Pacific Islander, 11% Hispanic American, 1% Native American, 1% transferred in.

Freshmen *Admission:* 2,726 enrolled.

Faculty *Total:* 325, 10% full-time, 11% with terminal degrees. *Student/faculty ratio:* 16:1.

Majors Accounting; administrative assistant and secretarial science; automobile/automotive mechanics technology; biological and physical sciences; business administration and management; carpentry; commercial and advertising art; criminal justice/law enforcement administration; finance; information science/studies; kindergarten/preschool education; legal assistant/paralegal; liberal arts and sciences/liberal studies; marketing/marketing management; medical administrative assistant and medical secretary; medical/clinical assistant; ophthalmic laboratory technology.

Academic Programs *Special study options:* academic remediation for entering students, adult/continuing education programs, distance learning, English as a second language, external degree program, independent study, internships, off-campus study, part-time degree program, services for LD students, summer session for credit.

Library 7,440 titles, 126 serial subscriptions, an OPAC, a Web page.

Computers on Campus 160 computers available on campus for general student use. A campuswide network can be accessed. Internet access, at least one staffed computer lab available.

Student Life *Housing Options:* Campus housing is leased by the school. *Activities and Organizations:* drama/theater group, student-run newspaper. *Campus security:* late-night transport/escort service. *Student services:* women's center.

Standardized Tests *Recommended:* SAT or ACT (for placement).

Costs (2005–06) *Tuition:* state resident $2184 full-time, $73 per credit hour part-time; nonresident $11,286 full-time, $376 per credit hour part-time. *Required fees:* $128 full-time, $3 per credit hour part-time, $22 per term part-time.

Financial Aid Of all full-time matriculated undergraduates who enrolled in 2003, 61 Federal Work-Study jobs (averaging $2357). 91 state and other part-time jobs (averaging $2431).

Applying *Options:* early admission. *Application deadline:* rolling (freshmen), rolling (transfers). *Notification:* continuous (freshmen).

Admissions Contact Ms. Connie Simpson, Director of Registrations, Records, and Admission, Community College of Aurora, 16000 East CentreTech Parkway, Aurora, CO 80011-9036. *Phone:* 303-360-4700. *Fax:* 303-361-7432. *E-mail:* connie.simpson@ccaurora.edu.

COMMUNITY COLLEGE OF DENVER
Denver, Colorado

- **State-supported** 2-year, founded 1970, part of Community Colleges of Colorado
- **Calendar** semesters
- **Degree** certificates and associate
- **Urban** 171-acre campus
- **Endowment** $857,252
- **Coed,** 9,274 undergraduate students, 24% full-time, 64% women, 36% men

Undergraduates 2,232 full-time, 7,042 part-time. Students come from 35 states and territories, 1% are from out of state, 18% African American, 6% Asian American or Pacific Islander, 26% Hispanic American, 2% Native American, 6% international, 2% transferred in.

Freshmen *Admission:* 1,141 enrolled. *Test scores:* SAT verbal scores over 500: 68%; SAT math scores over 500: 74%; ACT scores over 18: 39%; SAT verbal scores over 600: 37%; SAT math scores over 600: 42%; ACT scores over 24: 9%; SAT verbal scores over 700: 5%; SAT math scores over 700: 11%.

Faculty *Total:* 420, 20% full-time.

Majors Accounting; administrative assistant and secretarial science; business administration and management; commercial and advertising art; computer programming; computer typography and composition equipment operation; construction trades related; dental hygiene; drafting and design technology; electrical, electronic and communications engineering technology; environmental engineering technology; graphic and printing equipment operation/production; heating, air conditioning, ventilation and refrigeration maintenance technology; human services; industrial radiologic technology; information science/studies; intermedia/multimedia; kindergarten/preschool education; legal administrative assistant/secretary; legal assistant/paralegal; liberal arts and sciences/liberal studies; medical administrative assistant and medical secretary; nursing (registered nurse training); parks, recreation and leisure; photography; postal management; radiologic technology/science; tourism and travel services management; veterinary technology.

Academic Programs *Special study options:* academic remediation for entering students, accelerated degree program, adult/continuing education programs, advanced placement credit, cooperative education, distance learning, double majors, English as a second language, freshman honors college, honors pro-

grams, independent study, internships, off-campus study, part-time degree program, services for LD students, study abroad, summer session for credit. *ROTC:* Army (c).

Library Auraria Library plus 1 other with 683,045 titles, 3,233 serial subscriptions, 16,821 audiovisual materials, an OPAC, a Web page.

Computers on Campus 1142 computers available on campus for general student use. A campuswide network can be accessed from off campus. Internet access, at least one staffed computer lab available.

Student Life *Housing:* college housing not available. *Activities and Organizations:* student-run newspaper, Trio Advocates for Multicultural Students, Student Alliance for Human Services, Ad Hoc Nursing, Black Men on Campus, Auraria Fine Arts, national fraternities. *Campus security:* 24-hour emergency response devices and patrols, late-night transport/escort service. *Student services:* health clinic, personal/psychological counseling, women's center, legal services.

Athletics *Intramural sports:* archery M/W, badminton M/W, basketball M/W, bowling M/W, cross-country running M/W, equestrian sports M/W, fencing M/W, field hockey M/W, football M/W, golf M/W, gymnastics M/W, racquetball M/W, riflery M/W, rugby M/W, skiing (cross-country) M/W, skiing (downhill) M/W, soccer M/W, swimming and diving M/W, table tennis M/W, tennis M/W, track and field M/W, volleyball M/W, weight lifting M/W.

Standardized Tests *Recommended:* SAT or ACT (for placement).

Costs (2005–06) *Tuition:* state resident $2183 full-time, $73 per credit part-time; nonresident $10,355 full-time, $345 per credit part-time. Full-time tuition and fees vary according to location and program. Part-time tuition and fees vary according to location and program. *Required fees:* $612 full-time, $28 per credit part-time. *Payment plan:* installment. *Waivers:* senior citizens.

Financial Aid Of all full-time matriculated undergraduates who enrolled in 2003, 95 Federal Work-Study jobs (averaging $2442). 305 state and other part-time jobs (averaging $2156).

Applying *Options:* common application, electronic application, early admission, deferred entrance. *Recommended:* interview. *Application deadline:* rolling (freshmen), rolling (transfers).

Admissions Contact Ms. Emita Samuels, Dean of Enrollment Services, Community College of Denver, PO Box 173363, 1111 West Colfax Avenue, Denver, CO 80217-3363. *Phone:* 303-556-6325. *E-mail:* enrollment_services@ccd.edu.

DENVER ACADEMY OF COURT REPORTING
Westminster, Colorado

Admissions Contact Mr. Howard Brookner, Director of Admissions, Denver Academy of Court Reporting, 7290 Samuel Drive, Suite 200, Denver, CO 80221-2792. *Phone:* 303-427-5292 Ext. 14. *Toll-free phone:* 800-574-2087. *Fax:* 303-427-5383.

DENVER AUTOMOTIVE AND DIESEL COLLEGE
Denver, Colorado

Admissions Contact Mr. John Chalupa, Director of Admissions, Denver Automotive and Diesel College, 460 South Lipan Street, Denver, CO 80223-2025. *Phone:* 303-722-5724. *Toll-free phone:* 800-347-3232. *Fax:* 303-778-8264. *E-mail:* dad@mho.net.

FRONT RANGE COMMUNITY COLLEGE
Westminster, Colorado

- **State-supported** 2-year, founded 1968, part of Community Colleges of Colorado System
- **Calendar** semesters
- **Degree** certificates and associate
- **Suburban** 90-acre campus with easy access to Denver
- **Coed,** 15,669 undergraduate students, 34% full-time, 60% women, 40% men

Undergraduates 5,323 full-time, 10,346 part-time. Students come from 40 states and territories, 104 other countries, 0.7% are from out of state, 1% African American, 4% Asian American or Pacific Islander, 10% Hispanic American, 1% Native American, 0.9% international.

Freshmen *Admission:* 4,933 applied, 4,933 admitted, 3,763 enrolled. *Test scores:* SAT verbal scores over 500: 70%; SAT math scores over 500: 72%; ACT scores over 18: 75%; SAT verbal scores over 600: 25%; SAT math scores over 600: 24%; ACT scores over 24: 20%; SAT verbal scores over 700: 3%; SAT math scores over 700: 3%; ACT scores over 30: 2%.

Faculty *Total:* 1,001, 17% full-time. *Student/faculty ratio:* 17:1.

Majors Accounting technology and bookkeeping; administrative assistant and secretarial science; animal sciences related; applied horticulture; architectural

Front Range Community College (continued)

engineering technology; athletic training; automobile/automotive mechanics technology; business administration and management; business automation/technology/data entry; child care and support services management; design and visual communications; dietitian assistant; drafting and design technology; electrical, electronic and communications engineering technology; entrepreneurship; environmental engineering technology; foods and nutrition related; general studies; heating, air conditioning and refrigeration technology; industrial technology; laser and optical technology; liberal arts and sciences/liberal studies; machine shop technology; management information systems; nursing (registered nurse training); respiratory care therapy; science technologies related; sign language interpretation and translation; welding technology; wildlife and wildlands science and management.

Academic Programs *Special study options:* academic remediation for entering students, adult/continuing education programs, advanced placement credit, cooperative education, distance learning, double majors, English as a second language, external degree program, freshman honors college, honors programs, internships, off-campus study, part-time degree program, services for LD students, student-designed majors, study abroad, summer session for credit. *ROTC:* Army (c), Air Force (c).

Library College Hill Library with an OPAC, a Web page.

Computers on Campus 62 computers available on campus for general student use. A campuswide network can be accessed from off campus that provide access to online courses. Internet access, online (class) registration, at least one staffed computer lab available.

Student Life *Housing:* college housing not available. *Activities and Organizations:* drama/theater group, student-run newspaper, Student Government Association, Student Colorado Registry of Interpreters for the Deaf, Alpha Mu Psi, Alpha Tau Kappa, Hispanic Club. *Campus security:* 24-hour patrols, late-night transport/escort service. *Student services:* personal/psychological counseling, women's center.

Costs (2005–06) *Tuition:* state resident $4578 full-time, $153 per credit part-time; nonresident $10,355 full-time, $345 per credit part-time. *Required fees:* $312 full-time.

Financial Aid Of all full-time matriculated undergraduates who enrolled in 2003, 165 Federal Work-Study jobs (averaging $1316). 277 state and other part-time jobs (averaging $1635).

Applying *Options:* common application, electronic application, early admission, deferred entrance. *Application deadline:* rolling (freshmen), rolling (transfers).

Admissions Contact Ms. Darcy Clodio, Director of Enrollment Services, Front Range Community College, 3645 West 112th Avenue, Westminster, CO 80031. *Phone:* 303-404-5471. *Fax:* 303-439-2614. *E-mail:* darcy.clodio@frontrange.edu.

HERITAGE COLLEGE
Denver, Colorado

Admissions Contact 12 Lakeside Lane, Denver, CO 80212-7413.

INSTITUTE OF BUSINESS & MEDICAL CAREERS
Fort Collins, Colorado

- **Private** 2-year, founded 1987
- **Calendar** continuous
- **Degree** certificates, diplomas, and associate
- **Suburban** campus with easy access to Denver
- **Coed, primarily women**
- 100% of applicants were admitted

Faculty *Student/faculty ratio:* 14:1.

Costs (2004–05) *Tuition:* $13,800 full-time. No tuition increase for student's term of enrollment. *Required fees:* $75 full-time.

Applying *Application fee:* $75. *Required:* high school transcript.

Admissions Contact Mr. Steve Steele, Vice President of Operations, Institute of Business & Medical Careers, 1609 Oakridge Drive, Fort Collins, CO 80525. *Phone:* 970-223-2669 Ext. 102. *Toll-free phone:* 800-495-2669. *Fax:* 970-223-2796. *E-mail:* info@ibmcedu.com.

INTELLITEC COLLEGE
Colorado Springs, Colorado

- **Proprietary** 2-year, founded 1965, part of Technical Trades Institute, Inc
- **Calendar** 6-week terms
- **Degree** certificates, diplomas, and associate
- **Urban** 2-acre campus with easy access to Denver
- **Coed**

Faculty *Student/faculty ratio:* 18:1.

Student Life *Campus security:* 24-hour emergency response devices.

Financial Aid Of all full-time matriculated undergraduates who enrolled in 2003, 10 Federal Work-Study jobs (averaging $6500).

Applying *Options:* common application. *Required:* high school transcript, interview.

Admissions Contact Ms. Ellen Pitrone, Director of Admissions, IntelliTec College, 2315 East Pikes Peak Avenue, Colorado Springs, CO 80909-6030. *Phone:* 719-632-7626. *Toll-free phone:* 800-748-2282. *Fax:* 719-632-7451.

INTELLITEC COLLEGE
Grand Junction, Colorado

- **Proprietary** 2-year
- **Calendar** continuous
- **Degree** certificates, diplomas, and associate
- **Small-town** campus
- **Coed**
- 100% of applicants were admitted

Costs (2004–05) *Tuition:* $155 per credit hour part-time.

Admissions Contact Ms. Lisa Watson, Director of Admissions, IntelliTec College, 772 Horizon Drive, Grand Junction, CO 81506. *Phone:* 970-245-8101.

INTELLITEC MEDICAL INSTITUTE
Colorado Springs, Colorado

Admissions Contact Michelle Squibb, Admissions Representative, IntelliTec Medical Institute, 2345 North Academy Boulevard, Colorado Springs, CO 80909. *Phone:* 719-596-7400. *E-mail:* adm@intellitecmedicalinstitute.com.

ITT TECHNICAL INSTITUTE
Thornton, Colorado

- **Proprietary** primarily 2-year, founded 1984, part of ITT Educational Services, Inc
- **Calendar** quarters
- **Degrees** associate and bachelor's
- **Suburban** 2-acre campus with easy access to Denver
- **Coed**

Standardized Tests *Required:* Wonderlic aptitude test (for admission).

Costs (2004–05) *Tuition:* Please see school catalog for specific information.

Applying *Options:* deferred entrance. *Application fee:* $100. *Required:* high school transcript, interview. *Recommended:* letters of recommendation.

Admissions Contact Niki Donahue, Director of Recruitment, ITT Technical Institute, 500 East 84th Avenue, Suite B12, Thornton, CO 80229. *Phone:* 303-288-4488. *Toll-free phone:* 800-395-4488. *Fax:* 303-288-8166.

LAMAR COMMUNITY COLLEGE
Lamar, Colorado

Admissions Contact Director of Admissions, Lamar Community College, 2401 South Main Street, Lamar, CO 81052-3999. *Phone:* 719-336-1590. *Toll-free phone:* 800-968-6920. *Fax:* 719-336-2400. *E-mail:* admissions@lamarcc.edu.

MORGAN COMMUNITY COLLEGE
Fort Morgan, Colorado

- **State-supported** 2-year, founded 1967, part of Colorado Community College and Occupational Education System
- **Calendar** semesters
- **Degree** certificates and associate
- **Rural** 20-acre campus with easy access to Denver
- **Coed**

Faculty *Student/faculty ratio:* 10:1.

Standardized Tests *Required for some:* ACT (for placement).

Costs (2004–05) *Tuition:* state resident $2004 full-time, $67 per credit hour part-time; nonresident $349 per credit hour part-time. *Required fees:* $160 full-time.

Financial Aid Of all full-time matriculated undergraduates who enrolled in 2003, 20 Federal Work-Study jobs (averaging $1700). 50 state and other part-time jobs (averaging $2000).

Applying *Options:* early admission, deferred entrance. *Required:* high school transcript.

Admissions Contact Ms. Jody Brown, Student Services, Morgan Community College, Student Services, 17800 Road 20, Fort Morgan, CO 80701. *Phone:* 970-542-3156. *Toll-free phone:* 800-622-0216. *Fax:* 970-867-6608. *E-mail:* jody.brown@mcc.cccoes.edu.

NORTHEASTERN JUNIOR COLLEGE
Sterling, Colorado

Admissions Contact Ms. Tina Joyce, Director of Admissions, Northeastern Junior College, 100 College Avenue, Sterling, CO 80751. *Phone:* 970-521-7000. *Toll-free phone:* 800-626-4637. *Fax:* 970-521-6801. *E-mail:* tina.joyce@njc.edu.

OTERO JUNIOR COLLEGE
La Junta, Colorado

- **State-supported** 2-year, founded 1941, part of Colorado Community College and Occupational Education System
- **Calendar** semesters
- **Degree** certificates and associate
- **Rural** 50-acre campus
- **Coed,** 1,676 undergraduate students, 48% full-time, 61% women, 39% men

Undergraduates 805 full-time, 871 part-time. Students come from 12 states and territories, 2% are from out of state, 2% African American, 0.5% Asian American or Pacific Islander, 31% Hispanic American, 1% Native American, 14% transferred in, 14% live on campus.
Freshmen *Admission:* 423 enrolled.
Faculty *Total:* 78, 46% full-time.
Majors Administrative assistant and secretarial science; agricultural business and management; automobile/automotive mechanics technology; biological and physical sciences; biology/biological sciences; business administration and management; child development; computer management; data processing and data processing technology; dramatic/theatre arts; education; elementary education; history; humanities; kindergarten/preschool education; legal administrative assistant/secretary; liberal arts and sciences/liberal studies; literature; mathematics; medical administrative assistant and medical secretary; modern languages; nursing (registered nurse training); physical sciences; political science and government; pre-engineering; psychology; social sciences.
Academic Programs *Special study options:* academic remediation for entering students, adult/continuing education programs, advanced placement credit, distance learning, external degree program, internships, part-time degree program, summer session for credit.
Library Wheeler Library with 36,701 titles, 183 serial subscriptions, an OPAC.
Computers on Campus 100 computers available on campus for general student use. A campuswide network can be accessed from student residence rooms. Internet access, at least one staffed computer lab available.
Student Life *Housing:* on-campus residence required for freshman year. *Options:* coed. Campus housing is university owned. *Activities and Organizations:* drama/theater group, student-run newspaper, choral group. *Campus security:* 24-hour patrols, late-night transport/escort service. *Student services:* personal/psychological counseling.
Athletics Member NJCAA. *Intercollegiate sports:* baseball M(s), basketball M(s)/W(s), golf M(s)/W(s), softball W(s), volleyball W(s). *Intramural sports:* basketball M, volleyball M/W.
Standardized Tests *Recommended:* SAT or ACT (for placement).
Costs (2005–06) *Tuition:* state resident $1746 full-time, $73 per credit part-time; nonresident $6626 full-time, $276 per credit part-time. Full-time tuition and fees vary according to reciprocity agreements. Part-time tuition and fees vary according to reciprocity agreements. *Required fees:* $184 full-time. *Room and board:* $4300. Room and board charges vary according to board plan. *Payment plan:* installment.
Financial Aid Of all full-time matriculated undergraduates who enrolled in 2003, 30 Federal Work-Study jobs (averaging $2000). 100 state and other part-time jobs (averaging $2000).
Applying *Options:* electronic application, early admission. *Recommended:* high school transcript. *Application deadlines:* 8/30 (freshmen), 8/30 (transfers). *Notification:* continuous (freshmen).
Admissions Contact Mr. Brad Franz, Vice President for Student Services, Otero Junior College, 1802 Colorado Avenue, La Junta, CO 81050-3415. *Phone:* 719-384-6833. *Fax:* 719-384-6933. *E-mail:* j_schiro@ojc.cccoes.edu.

PARKS COLLEGE
Aurora, Colorado

Admissions Contact Mr. Rick Harding, Director of Admissions, Parks College, 14280 East Jewell Avenue, Suite 100, Aurora, CO 80014. *Phone:* 303-745-6244.

PARKS COLLEGE
Denver, Colorado

Admissions Contact Ms. JoAnn Q. Navarro, Director of Admissions, Parks College, 9065 Grant Street, Denver, CO 80229-4339. *Phone:* 303-457-2757.

PIKES PEAK COMMUNITY COLLEGE
Colorado Springs, Colorado

- **State-supported** 2-year, founded 1968, part of Colorado Community College System
- **Calendar** semesters
- **Degree** certificates and associate
- **Urban** 287-acre campus with easy access to Denver
- **Endowment** $1.4 million
- **Coed**

Faculty *Student/faculty ratio:* 18:1.
Student Life *Campus security:* 24-hour emergency response devices and patrols, late-night transport/escort service.
Standardized Tests *Recommended:* SAT or ACT (for placement).
Costs (2004–05) *Tuition:* state resident $2004 full-time, $67 per credit hour part-time; nonresident $10,355 full-time, $345 per credit hour part-time. Full-time tuition and fees vary according to course load and reciprocity agreements. Part-time tuition and fees vary according to course load and reciprocity agreements. *Required fees:* $151 full-time, $39 per term part-time.
Financial Aid Of all full-time matriculated undergraduates who enrolled in 2003, 168 Federal Work-Study jobs (averaging $1960). 327 state and other part-time jobs (averaging $1791).
Applying *Required for some:* high school transcript.
Admissions Contact Mr. Troy Nelson, Associate Director, Enrollment Services, Admissions, Pikes Peak Community College, 5675 South Academy Boulevard, Colorado Springs, CO 80906-5498. *Phone:* 719-540-7041. *Toll-free phone:* 866-411-7722. *Fax:* 719-540-7092. *E-mail:* admissions@ppcc.edu.

PIMA MEDICAL INSTITUTE
Denver, Colorado

- **Proprietary** 2-year, founded 1988, part of Vocational Training Institutes, Inc
- **Calendar** modular
- **Degree** certificates and associate
- **Urban** campus
- **Coed,** 724 undergraduate students

Faculty *Student/faculty ratio:* 15:1.
Majors Ophthalmic technology; physical therapist assistant; radiologic technology/science; respiratory therapy technician.
Academic Programs *Special study options:* academic remediation for entering students, cooperative education, internships.
Computers on Campus A campuswide network can be accessed. At least one staffed computer lab available.
Student Life *Housing:* college housing not available.
Standardized Tests *Required:* Wonderlic Scholastic Level Exam (for admission).
Applying *Required:* interview. *Required for some:* high school transcript.
Admissions Contact Admissions Office, Pima Medical Institute, Pima Medical Institute, 1701 West 72nd Avenue, Suite 130, Denver, CO 80221. *Phone:* 303-426-1800. *Toll-free phone:* 888-898-9048.

PLATT COLLEGE
Aurora, Colorado

Admissions Contact Admissions Office, Platt College, 3100 South Parker Road, Suite 200, Aurora, CO 80014-3141. *Phone:* 303-369-5151. *E-mail:* admissions@plattcolo.com.

PUEBLO COMMUNITY COLLEGE
Pueblo, Colorado

Admissions Contact Ms. Mary Santoro, Director of Admissions and Records, Pueblo Community College, 900 West Orman Avenue, Pueblo, CO 81004. *Phone:* 719-549-3010. *Fax:* 719-549-3012. *E-mail:* mary.santoro@pueblocc.edu.

RED ROCKS COMMUNITY COLLEGE
Lakewood, Colorado

- **State-supported** 2-year, founded 1969, part of Colorado Community College and Occupational Education System

Red Rocks Community College *(continued)*
■ **Calendar** semesters
■ **Degree** certificates and associate
■ **Urban** 120-acre campus with easy access to Denver
■ **Coed**

Faculty *Student/faculty ratio:* 9:1.
Student Life *Campus security:* 24-hour emergency response devices and patrols.
Costs (2004–05) *Tuition:* state resident $2004 full-time; nonresident $10,355 full-time. *Required fees:* $218 full-time.
Financial Aid Of all full-time matriculated undergraduates who enrolled in 2003, 21 Federal Work-Study jobs (averaging $2600). 65 state and other part-time jobs (averaging $3600).
Applying *Options:* early admission.
Admissions Contact Ms. Judy Beckmann, Director of Student Recruitment, Red Rocks Community College, 13300 West 6th Avenue Box 5, Lakewood, CO 80228-1255. *Phone:* 303-914-6234. *Fax:* 303-969-6919.

TRINIDAD STATE JUNIOR COLLEGE

Trinidad, Colorado

■ **State-supported** 2-year, founded 1925, part of Colorado Community College and Occupational Education System
■ **Calendar** semesters
■ **Degree** certificates, diplomas, and associate
■ **Small-town** 17-acre campus
■ **Endowment** $4.5 million
■ **Coed**, 2,106 undergraduate students

Undergraduates Students come from 33 states and territories, 5 other countries, 3% African American, 0.5% Asian American or Pacific Islander, 42% Hispanic American, 3% Native American, 0.5% international, 30% live on campus. *Retention:* 60% of 2002 full-time freshmen returned.
Freshmen *Admission:* 1,017 applied, 1,017 admitted.
Faculty *Total:* 112, 36% full-time, 100% with terminal degrees. *Student/faculty ratio:* 20:1.
Majors Accounting; administrative assistant and secretarial science; art teacher education; automobile/automotive mechanics technology; biological and physical sciences; biology/biological sciences; business administration and management; carpentry; chemistry; civil engineering technology; commercial and advertising art; computer and information sciences related; computer science; computer systems networking and telecommunications; construction engineering technology; corrections; cosmetology; criminal justice/police science; data processing and data processing technology; design and visual communications; drafting and design technology; dramatic/theatre arts; education; electrical, electronic and communications engineering technology; engineering; English; farm and ranch management; forestry; heavy equipment maintenance technology; industrial technology; information science/studies; information technology; journalism; kindergarten/preschool education; landscape architecture; liberal arts and sciences/liberal studies; management information systems; marketing/marketing management; mining technology; music; natural resources management and policy; nursing assistant/aide and patient care assistant; nursing (licensed practical/vocational nurse training); nursing (registered nurse training); occupational safety and health technology; physical education teaching and coaching; pre-engineering; psychology; soil conservation; water quality and wastewater treatment management and recycling technology.
Academic Programs *Special study options:* academic remediation for entering students, accelerated degree program, adult/continuing education programs, advanced placement credit, cooperative education, distance learning, double majors, English as a second language, honors programs, independent study, internships, part-time degree program, services for LD students, student-designed majors, summer session for credit.
Library Frendenthal Library plus 1 other with 54,255 titles, 105 serial subscriptions, 1,574 audiovisual materials, an OPAC.
Computers on Campus 125 computers available on campus for general student use. A campuswide network can be accessed from student residence rooms and from off campus. Internet access, online (class) registration, at least one staffed computer lab available.
Student Life *Housing Options:* coed, men-only, women-only. Campus housing is university owned. *Activities and Organizations:* drama/theater group, student-run newspaper, choral group, student association, International Club, Gunsmithing Club, Nursing Club, Cosmetology Club. *Campus security:* 24-hour emergency response devices and patrols, late-night transport/escort service.
Athletics Member NJCAA. *Intercollegiate sports:* baseball M(s), basketball M(s), softball W, volleyball W(s). *Intramural sports:* badminton M/W, basketball M, bowling M/W, football M/W, riflery M/W, skiing (cross-country) M/W, skiing (downhill) M/W, softball M/W, table tennis M/W, tennis M/W, volleyball M/W, weight lifting M/W.

Standardized Tests *Required for some:* ACT (for placement), ACT ASSET, ACCUPLACER. *Recommended:* SAT and SAT Subject Tests or ACT (for placement).
Costs (2004–05) *Tuition:* state resident $2004 full-time, $67 per credit part-time; nonresident $8283 full-time, $276 per credit part-time. *Required fees:* $265 full-time, $14 per credit part-time. *Room and board:* $4458; room only: $1047. Room and board charges vary according to board plan. *Payment plan:* installment. *Waivers:* senior citizens and employees or children of employees.
Financial Aid Of all full-time matriculated undergraduates who enrolled in 2003, 30 Federal Work-Study jobs (averaging $2040). 40 state and other part-time jobs (averaging $2040).
Applying *Options:* common application, electronic application, deferred entrance. *Required:* high school transcript. *Application deadline:* rolling (freshmen), rolling (transfers). *Notification:* continuous (freshmen).
Admissions Contact Maria de la Cruz, Director, Trinidad State Junior College, 600 Prospect, Trinidad, CO 81082-2396. *Phone:* 719-846-5623. *Toll-free phone:* 800-621-8752. *Fax:* 719-846-5620.

WESTWOOD COLLEGE-DENVER

Broomfield, Colorado

■ **Proprietary** 2-year, founded 1965
■ **Calendar** continuous
■ **Degree** certificates and associate
■ **Suburban** 4-acre campus with easy access to Denver
■ **Coed**

Financial Aid Of all full-time matriculated undergraduates who enrolled in 2003, 20 Federal Work-Study jobs.
Applying *Options:* electronic application. *Required:* interview, references, student profile.
Admissions Contact Mr. Robert Lee, Director of Admissions, Westwood College-Denver, 10851 West 120th Avenue, Broomfield, CO 80021. *Phone:* 303-466-1714. *Toll-free phone:* 800-888-3995. *Fax:* 303-469-3797. *E-mail:* info@westwood.edu.

► **See page 592 for a narrative description.**

WESTWOOD COLLEGE-DENVER NORTH

Denver, Colorado

■ **Proprietary** primarily 2-year, founded 1953
■ **Calendar** 5 terms
■ **Degrees** diplomas, associate, and bachelor's
■ **Suburban** 11-acre campus
■ **Coed**, 1,423 undergraduate students, 76% full-time, 32% women, 68% men

Undergraduates 1,086 full-time, 337 part-time. Students come from 38 states and territories, 2 other countries, 16% are from out of state, 3% African American, 3% Asian American or Pacific Islander, 16% Hispanic American, 2% Native American, 0.1% international, 0.2% transferred in. *Retention:* 28% of 2002 full-time freshmen returned.
Freshmen *Admission:* 2,332 applied, 1,048 admitted, 224 enrolled.
Faculty *Total:* 97, 35% full-time, 5% with terminal degrees. *Student/faculty ratio:* 13:1.
Majors Accounting and business/management; animation, interactive technology, video graphics and special effects; architectural drafting and CAD/CADD; automobile/automotive mechanics technology; business/commerce; computer and information systems security; computer engineering technology; computer/information technology services administration related; computer programming; computer software technology; computer systems networking and telecommunications; design and visual communications; electrical, electronic and communications engineering technology; graphic design; heating, air conditioning, ventilation and refrigeration maintenance technology; interior architecture; interior design; marketing/marketing management; mechanical drafting and CAD/CADD; medical/clinical assistant; medical transcription; survey technology; web page, digital/multimedia and information resources design.
Academic Programs *Special study options:* academic remediation for entering students, accelerated degree program, advanced placement credit, distance learning, independent study, internships, part-time degree program, services for LD students, summer session for credit.
Library Westwood DNN Library with 2,000 titles, 90 serial subscriptions, 120 audiovisual materials, an OPAC, a Web page.
Computers on Campus 30 computers available on campus for general student use. A campuswide network can be accessed. Internet access available.
Student Life *Housing:* college housing not available. *Activities and Organizations:* American Institute of Graphic Arts, Social Club, Gaming Club. *Campus security:* 24-hour emergency response devices.
Standardized Tests *Required for some:* ACCUPLACER. *Recommended:* SAT or ACT (for admission), SAT and SAT Subject Tests or ACT (for admission), SAT II: Writing Test (for admission).

Costs (2005–06) *Tuition:* $2796 per term part-time. Full-time tuition and fees vary according to course load and program. Part-time tuition and fees vary according to course load and program. *Required fees:* $425 per credit part-time, $120 per term part-time. *Payment plan:* installment. *Waivers:* employees or children of employees.

Applying *Options:* common application, deferred entrance. *Application fee:* $100. *Required:* high school transcript, interview. *Required for some:* ACCUPLACER. *Application deadline:* rolling (freshmen), rolling (transfers). *Notification:* continuous (freshmen).

Admissions Contact Ms. Dianne Hopkins, New Student Coordinator, Westwood College-Denver North, 7350 North Broadway, Denver, CO 80221-3653. *Phone:* 303-650-5050 Ext. 325. *Toll-free phone:* 800-992-5050.

▶ **See page 578 for a narrative description.**

WESTWOOD COLLEGE-DENVER SOUTH

Denver, Colorado

- **Proprietary** primarily 2-year
- **Calendar** continuous
- **Degrees** associate and bachelor's
- **Urban** campus with easy access to Denver, CO
- **Coed**
- 58% of applicants were admitted

Applying *Required:* interview, HS diploma or GED and entrance exam (SAT/ACT or Accuplacer).

Admissions Contact Mr. Ron DeJong, Director of Admissions, Westwood College-Denver South, 3150 South Sheridan Boulevard, Denver, CO 80227-5548. *Phone:* 303-934-2790. *Fax:* 303-934-2583. *E-mail:* info@westwood.edu.

▶ **See page 580 for a narrative description.**

CONNECTICUT

ASNUNTUCK COMMUNITY COLLEGE

Enfield, Connecticut

- **State-supported** 2-year, founded 1972, part of Connecticut Community College System
- **Calendar** semesters
- **Degree** certificates and associate
- **Suburban** 4-acre campus
- **Coed,** 1,476 undergraduate students, 31% full-time, 59% women, 41% men

Undergraduates 456 full-time, 1,020 part-time. Students come from 3 states and territories, 3% are from out of state, 6% African American, 2% Asian American or Pacific Islander, 3% Hispanic American, 0.1% Native American, 3% transferred in. *Retention:* 54% of 2002 full-time freshmen returned.

Freshmen *Admission:* 521 applied, 521 admitted, 188 enrolled.

Faculty *Total:* 122, 18% full-time. *Student/faculty ratio:* 9:1.

Majors Accounting; administrative assistant and secretarial science; art; business administration and management; commercial and advertising art; computer science; criminal justice/safety; engineering science; general studies; human services; kindergarten/preschool education; liberal arts and sciences/liberal studies; mass communication/media; special products marketing; substance abuse/addiction counseling.

Academic Programs *Special study options:* academic remediation for entering students, adult/continuing education programs, advanced placement credit, distance learning, double majors, English as a second language, independent study, internships, part-time degree program, services for LD students, student-designed majors, study abroad, summer session for credit.

Library ACTC Learning Resource Center with 31,700 titles, 257 serial subscriptions, 2,570 audiovisual materials, an OPAC.

Computers on Campus 90 computers available on campus for general student use. A campuswide network can be accessed from off campus. Internet access, at least one staffed computer lab available.

Student Life *Housing:* college housing not available. *Activities and Organizations:* drama/theater group, student-run newspaper, Phi Theta Kappa, Drama Club, Outdoor Club, Poetry Club, Ski Club. *Campus security:* 24-hour patrols, late-night transport/escort service. *Student services:* women's center.

Standardized Tests *Required for some:* SAT (for placement).

Costs (2004–05) *Tuition:* state resident $2112 full-time, $88 per credit part-time; nonresident $6610 full-time, $264 per credit part-time. Full-time tuition and fees vary according to course load. Part-time tuition and fees vary according to course load. *Required fees:* $294 full-time, $53 per credit part-time. *Payment plan:* installment. *Waivers:* senior citizens and employees or children of employees.

Financial Aid Of all full-time matriculated undergraduates who enrolled in 2003, 20 Federal Work-Study jobs (averaging $3000). 5 state and other part-time jobs (averaging $3000).

Applying *Options:* deferred entrance. *Application fee:* $20. *Required:* high school transcript. *Application deadline:* rolling (freshmen), rolling (transfers). *Notification:* continuous (freshmen).

Admissions Contact Ms. Donna Shaw, Director of Admissions and Marketing, Asnuntuck Community College, 170 Elm Street, Enfield, CT 06082-3800. *Phone:* 860-253-3018. *Toll-free phone:* 800-501-3967. *Fax:* 860-253-3014.

BRIARWOOD COLLEGE

Southington, Connecticut

- **Proprietary** primarily 2-year, founded 1966
- **Calendar** semesters
- **Degrees** certificates, diplomas, associate, and bachelor's
- **Small-town** 32-acre campus with easy access to Boston and Hartford
- **Endowment** $27,595
- **Coed,** 637 undergraduate students, 62% full-time, 76% women, 24% men

Undergraduates 393 full-time, 244 part-time. Students come from 11 states and territories, 2 other countries, 7% are from out of state, 19% African American, 1% Asian American or Pacific Islander, 10% Hispanic American, 0.3% Native American, 0.8% international, 13% transferred in, 21% live on campus.

Freshmen *Admission:* 473 applied, 377 admitted, 164 enrolled. *Test scores:* SAT verbal scores over 500: 16%; SAT math scores over 500: 19%; SAT verbal scores over 600: 3%; SAT math scores over 600: 16%; SAT verbal scores over 700: 3%; SAT math scores over 700: 16%.

Faculty *Total:* 91, 27% full-time. *Student/faculty ratio:* 9:1.

Majors Accounting; administrative assistant and secretarial science; biotechnology; business administration and management; child development; communication/speech communication and rhetoric; criminal justice/law enforcement administration; dental assisting; dietetics; fashion merchandising; funeral service and mortuary science; general studies; health information/medical records administration; hotel/motel administration; legal administrative assistant/secretary; legal assistant/paralegal; medical administrative assistant and medical secretary; medical/clinical assistant; medical office management; occupational therapist assistant; radio and television broadcasting technology; tourism and travel services management.

Academic Programs *Special study options:* academic remediation for entering students, accelerated degree program, adult/continuing education programs, advanced placement credit, double majors, English as a second language, independent study, internships, part-time degree program, services for LD students, summer session for credit.

Library Pupillo Library with 11,500 titles, 154 serial subscriptions, 130 audiovisual materials, a Web page.

Computers on Campus 54 computers available on campus for general student use. Internet access, online (class) registration, at least one staffed computer lab available.

Student Life *Housing Options:* coed. Freshman applicants given priority for college housing. *Activities and Organizations:* student-run radio station, student government, Yearbook Committee, Student Ambassador Club, F.A.M.E. (Fashion Merchandising Club). *Campus security:* 24-hour patrols, late-night transport/escort service. *Student services:* personal/psychological counseling.

Athletics *Intramural sports:* basketball M, soccer W, softball M/W.

Standardized Tests *Required:* College Board Diagnostic Tests (for placement).

Costs (2005–06) *Tuition:* $15,200 full-time, $500 per credit part-time. Full-time tuition and fees vary according to program. Part-time tuition and fees vary according to course load and program. No tuition increase for student's term of enrollment. *Required fees:* $220 full-time, $125 per term part-time. *Room only:* $3320. *Payment plan:* installment. *Waivers:* employees or children of employees.

Financial Aid Of all full-time matriculated undergraduates who enrolled in 2003, 33 Federal Work-Study jobs (averaging $600). 30 state and other part-time jobs.

Applying *Options:* common application, electronic application. *Application fee:* $25. *Required:* high school transcript. *Required for some:* essay or personal statement, letters of recommendation, interview. *Application deadline:* rolling (freshmen), rolling (transfers).

Admissions Contact Ms. Donna Yamanis, Director of Enrollment Management, Briarwood College, 2279 Mount Vernon Road, Southington, CT 06489. *Phone:* 860-628-4751 Ext. 133. *Toll-free phone:* 800-952-2444. *Fax:* 860-628-6444.

▶ **See page 474 for a narrative description.**

CAPITAL COMMUNITY COLLEGE
Hartford, Connecticut

- **State-supported** 2-year, founded 1946, part of Connecticut Community College System
- **Calendar** semesters
- **Degree** certificates and associate
- **Urban** 10-acre campus
- **Coed,** 3,436 undergraduate students, 26% full-time, 73% women, 27% men

Undergraduates 896 full-time, 2,540 part-time. Students come from 3 states and territories, 39% African American, 3% Asian American or Pacific Islander, 26% Hispanic American, 0.3% Native American, 0.3% international.

Freshmen *Admission:* 555 enrolled.

Faculty *Total:* 60.

Majors Accounting; administrative assistant and secretarial science; business administration and management; computer and information sciences; computer and information sciences related; computer engineering technology; data entry/microcomputer applications related; electrical, electronic and communications engineering technology; emergency medical technology (EMT paramedic); fire protection and safety technology; fire services administration; information technology; kindergarten/preschool education; liberal arts and sciences/liberal studies; medical/clinical assistant; medical radiologic technology; nursing (registered nurse training); physical therapist assistant; social work; web page, digital/multimedia and information resources design.

Academic Programs *Special study options:* academic remediation for entering students, accelerated degree program, adult/continuing education programs, advanced placement credit, distance learning, double majors, English as a second language, independent study, internships, part-time degree program, services for LD students, summer session for credit.

Library Arthur C. Banks, Jr. Library plus 1 other with 46,760 titles, 359 serial subscriptions, 2,409 audiovisual materials, an OPAC, a Web page.

Computers on Campus 180 computers available on campus for general student use. A campuswide network can be accessed from off campus. Internet access, at least one staffed computer lab available.

Student Life *Housing:* college housing not available. *Activities and Organizations:* drama/theater group, choral group, Latin American Student Association, Student Senate, Senior Renewal Club, Early Childhood Club, Pre-Professional Club. *Campus security:* late-night transport/escort service, security staff during hours of operation, emergency telephones 7 a.m.—11 p.m. *Student services:* personal/psychological counseling.

Standardized Tests *Required for some:* SAT (for placement).

Costs (2005–06) *Tuition:* state resident $2232 full-time, $93 per credit hour part-time; nonresident $6696 full-time, $279 per credit hour part-time. *Required fees:* $304 full-time.

Financial Aid Of all full-time matriculated undergraduates who enrolled in 2003, 87 Federal Work-Study jobs (averaging $3000). 160 state and other part-time jobs (averaging $3000).

Applying *Application fee:* $20. *Recommended:* high school transcript. *Application deadline:* rolling (freshmen), rolling (transfers). *Notification:* continuous until 9/1 (freshmen).

Admissions Contact Ms. Jackie Phillips, Director of the Welcome and Advising Center, Capital Community College, 950 Main Street, Hartford, CT 06103. *Phone:* 860-906-5078. *Toll-free phone:* 800-894-6126. *E-mail:* mball-davis@ccc.commnet.edu.

GATEWAY COMMUNITY COLLEGE
New Haven, Connecticut

- **State-supported** 2-year, founded 1992, part of Connecticut Community College System
- **Calendar** semesters
- **Degree** certificates and associate
- **Urban** 5-acre campus with easy access to New York City
- **Coed,** 5,326 undergraduate students, 29% full-time, 62% women, 38% men

Undergraduates 1,520 full-time, 3,806 part-time. Students come from 8 states and territories, 60 other countries, 0.6% are from out of state, 27% African American, 3% Asian American or Pacific Islander, 13% Hispanic American, 0.5% Native American, 2% international, 8% transferred in.

Freshmen *Admission:* 1,454 enrolled.

Faculty *Total:* 229, 44% full-time, 7% with terminal degrees. *Student/faculty ratio:* 20:1.

Majors Accounting; automobile/automotive mechanics technology; avionics maintenance technology; biomedical technology; business administration and management; computer and information sciences related; computer engineering related; computer engineering technology; computer graphics; computer typography and composition equipment operation; consumer merchandising/retailing management; data entry/microcomputer applications; data processing and data processing technology; dietetics; electrical, electronic and communications

engineering technology; engineering technology; fashion merchandising; fire science; gerontology; hotel/motel administration; human services; industrial radiologic technology; industrial technology; kindergarten/preschool education; legal administrative assistant/secretary; liberal arts and sciences/liberal studies; mechanical engineering/mechanical technology; medical administrative assistant and medical secretary; mental health/rehabilitation; nuclear medical technology; pharmacy; special products marketing; substance abuse/addiction counseling; word processing.

Academic Programs *Special study options:* academic remediation for entering students, adult/continuing education programs, advanced placement credit, distance learning, English as a second language, external degree program, independent study, internships, off-campus study, part-time degree program, services for LD students, summer session for credit.

Library 54,802 titles, 532 serial subscriptions, 9,902 audiovisual materials, an OPAC.

Computers on Campus 385 computers available on campus for general student use. A campuswide network can be accessed from off campus. Internet access, online (class) registration, at least one staffed computer lab available.

Student Life *Housing:* college housing not available. *Campus security:* late-night transport/escort service.

Athletics Member NJCAA. *Intercollegiate sports:* baseball M, basketball M/W, soccer M, softball W.

Costs (2005–06) *Tuition:* state resident $2232 full-time; nonresident $7264 full-time. *Required fees:* $304 full-time.

Financial Aid Of all full-time matriculated undergraduates who enrolled in 2003, 60 Federal Work-Study jobs (averaging $6000).

Applying *Options:* early admission, deferred entrance. *Application fee:* $20. *Required:* high school transcript. *Required for some:* essay or personal statement, interview. *Application deadlines:* 9/1 (freshmen), 9/1 (transfers). *Notification:* continuous until 9/1 (freshmen).

Admissions Contact Ms. Catherine Surface, Director of Admissions, Gateway Community College, 60 Sargent Drive, New Haven, CT 06511. *Phone:* 203-789-7043. *Toll-free phone:* 800-390-7723. *Fax:* 203-285-2018. *E-mail:* gateway_ctc@commnet.edu.

GIBBS COLLEGE
Norwalk, Connecticut

Admissions Contact Mr. Ted Havelka, Vice President of Admissions/Marketing, Gibbs College, 148 East Avenue, Norwalk, CT 06851. *Phone:* 203-633-2311. *Toll-free phone:* 800-845-5333. *Fax:* 203-899-0788. *E-mail:* norwalkadmissions@gibbsnorwalk.com.

GOODWIN COLLEGE
East Hartford, Connecticut

- **Proprietary** 2-year
- **Calendar** semesters
- **Degree** certificates, diplomas, and associate
- **Urban** campus with easy access to Hartford
- **Endowment** $1.0 million
- **Coed,** 940 undergraduate students, 15% full-time, 86% women, 14% men

Undergraduates 145 full-time, 795 part-time. Students come from 1 other state, 28% African American, 2% Asian American or Pacific Islander, 15% Hispanic American, 0.6% Native American, 12% transferred in.

Freshmen *Admission:* 360 applied, 302 admitted, 302 enrolled. *Average high school GPA:* 2.8.

Faculty *Total:* 74, 28% full-time, 5% with terminal degrees. *Student/faculty ratio:* 10:1.

Majors Accounting technology and bookkeeping; administrative assistant and secretarial science; business/commerce; computer and information sciences; computer/technical support; entrepreneurship; medical administrative assistant and medical secretary; medical/clinical assistant; medical insurance coding; non-profit management; nursing (registered nurse training); operations management.

Academic Programs *Special study options:* academic remediation for entering students, accelerated degree program, adult/continuing education programs, advanced placement credit, cooperative education, distance learning, double majors, English as a second language, external degree program, honors programs, independent study, internships, off-campus study, part-time degree program, services for LD students, summer session for credit.

Library Goodwin College Library with 6,000 titles, 1,300 serial subscriptions, 506 audiovisual materials, an OPAC.

Computers on Campus 220 computers available on campus for general student use. A campuswide network can be accessed from off campus. Internet access, at least one staffed computer lab available.

Student Life *Housing:* college housing not available. *Campus security:* evening security patrolman.

Standardized Tests *Required:* ACCUPLACER (for placement). *Recommended:* SAT and SAT Subject Tests or ACT (for placement), SAT II: Writing Test (for placement).

Costs (2005–06) *Tuition:* $12,800 full-time, $400 per credit part-time. *Required fees:* $250 full-time.

Applying *Options:* common application, electronic application, deferred entrance. *Application fee:* $25. *Required:* essay or personal statement, high school transcript, minimum 2.0 GPA, medical exam. *Recommended:* 2 letters of recommendation, interview. *Notification:* continuous until 8/1 (freshmen).

Admissions Contact Mr. Daniel P. Noonan, Director of Enrollment and Student Services, Goodwin College, 745 Burnside Avenue, East Hartford, CT 06108. *Phone:* 860-528-4111 Ext. 230. *Toll-free phone:* 800-889-3282. *Fax:* 860-291-9550. *E-mail:* dnoonan@goodwin.edu.

HOUSATONIC COMMUNITY COLLEGE
Bridgeport, Connecticut

Admissions Contact Ms. Delores Y. Curtis, Director of Admissions, Housatonic Community College, 900 Lafayette Boulevard, Bridgeport, CT 06604-4704. *Phone:* 203-332-5102.

INTERNATIONAL COLLEGE OF HOSPITALITY MANAGEMENT, CESAR RITZ
Suffield, Connecticut

- **Proprietary** *2-year, founded 1992*
- **Calendar** *continuous*
- **Degree** *certificates and associate*
- **Small-town** *56-acre campus with easy access to New York City or Boston, MA*
- **Coed,** *116 undergraduate students, 100% full-time, 59% women, 41% men*

The International College of Hospitality Management, César Ritz, is the only Swiss college of hospitality management in the United States. The Swiss tradition of hôtellerie, combined with practical experience obtained on paid internships in the best American hospitality properties, prepares students for managerial positions in the fastest-growing industry in the world.

Undergraduates 116 full-time. Students come from 6 states and territories, 34 other countries, 50% are from out of state, 6% African American, 16% Asian American or Pacific Islander, 7% Hispanic American, 51% international, 16% transferred in, 90% live on campus.

Freshmen *Admission:* 35 applied, 27 admitted, 27 enrolled.

Faculty *Total:* 13, 54% full-time, 8% with terminal degrees. *Student/faculty ratio:* 6:1.

Majors Hospitality administration.

Academic Programs *Special study options:* academic remediation for entering students, accelerated degree program, adult/continuing education programs, advanced placement credit, cooperative education, distance learning, English as a second language, independent study, internships, part-time degree program, services for LD students, study abroad.

Library International College of Hospitality Management Library with 10,000 titles, 50 serial subscriptions, an OPAC.

Computers on Campus 23 computers available on campus for general student use. A campuswide network can be accessed from off campus. Internet access, at least one staffed computer lab available.

Student Life *Housing Options:* coed. *Activities and Organizations:* student-run newspaper, student committee, student newsletter, yearbook committee, Ritz Guild, Student Ambassadors. *Campus security:* 24-hour emergency response devices, student patrols, late-night transport/escort service, controlled dormitory access, weekend patrols by trained security personnel. *Student services:* health clinic, personal/psychological counseling.

Athletics *Intramural sports:* basketball M/W, soccer M/W, volleyball M/W.

Standardized Tests *Recommended:* SAT (for admission).

Costs (2005–06) *Comprehensive fee:* $20,878 includes full-time tuition ($15,900) and room and board ($4978).

Applying *Options:* common application, electronic application, deferred entrance. *Application fee:* $100. *Required:* high school transcript, 2 letters of recommendation. *Required for some:* essay or personal statement, interview. *Recommended:* interview. *Application deadline:* rolling (freshmen), rolling (transfers). *Notification:* continuous (freshmen).

Admissions Contact Mrs. Tina Merullo, Admissions, International College of Hospitality Management, *Cesar Ritz,* 1760 Mapleton Avenue, Suffield, CT 06078. *Phone:* 860-668-3515 Ext. 126. *Toll-free phone:* 800-955-0809. *Fax:* 860-668-7369. *E-mail:* admissions@ichm.edu.

▶ **See page 504 for a narrative description.**

MANCHESTER COMMUNITY COLLEGE
Manchester, Connecticut

- **State-supported** 2-year, founded 1963, part of Connecticut Community College System
- **Calendar** semesters
- **Degree** certificates and associate
- **Small-town** 160-acre campus with easy access to Hartford
- **Coed,** 5,906 undergraduate students, 43% full-time, 58% women, 42% men

Undergraduates 2,512 full-time, 3,394 part-time. Students come from 5 states and territories, 14% African American, 4% Asian American or Pacific Islander, 10% Hispanic American, 0.3% Native American, 0.7% international, 11% transferred in.

Freshmen *Admission:* 1,964 applied, 1,964 admitted, 1,231 enrolled.

Faculty *Total:* 294, 33% full-time. *Student/faculty ratio:* 22:1.

Majors Accounting; administrative assistant and secretarial science; business administration and management; clinical/medical laboratory technology; commercial and advertising art; communication/speech communication and rhetoric; criminal justice/law enforcement administration; dramatic/theatre arts; engineering science; fine/studio arts; general studies; hotel/motel administration; human services; industrial engineering; industrial technology; information science/studies; journalism; kindergarten/preschool education; legal administrative assistant/secretary; legal assistant/paralegal; liberal arts and sciences/liberal studies; management information systems; marketing/marketing management; medical administrative assistant and medical secretary; music; occupational therapist assistant; physical therapist assistant; respiratory care therapy; social work; surgical technology; teacher assistant/aide.

Academic Programs *Special study options:* academic remediation for entering students, adult/continuing education programs, cooperative education, distance learning, double majors, English as a second language, independent study, internships, off-campus study, part-time degree program, services for LD students, student-designed majors, summer session for credit.

Library 45,265 titles, 493 serial subscriptions, 2,481 audiovisual materials.

Student Life *Housing:* college housing not available. *Activities and Organizations:* drama/theater group, student-run newspaper, choral group. *Student services:* women's center.

Athletics Member NJCAA. *Intercollegiate sports:* baseball M, basketball M/W, soccer M/W, softball W.

Costs (2004–05) *Tuition:* state resident $2112 full-time, $88 per credit hour part-time; nonresident $6336 full-time, $264 per credit hour part-time. *Required fees:* $294 full-time.

Financial Aid Of all full-time matriculated undergraduates who enrolled in 2003, 100 Federal Work-Study jobs (averaging $2000). 25 state and other part-time jobs (averaging $2000).

Applying *Options:* electronic application, deferred entrance. *Application fee:* $20. *Required:* high school transcript. *Application deadline:* rolling (freshmen), rolling (transfers). *Notification:* continuous (freshmen).

Admissions Contact Mr. Peter Harris, Director of Admissions, Manchester Community College, PO Box 1046, MS #12, Manchester, CT 06045-1046. *Phone:* 860-512-3210. *Fax:* 860-512-3221.

MIDDLESEX COMMUNITY COLLEGE
Middletown, Connecticut

- **State-supported** 2-year, founded 1966, part of Connecticut Community College System
- **Calendar** semesters
- **Degree** certificates and associate
- **Suburban** 38-acre campus with easy access to Hartford
- **Coed**

Student Life *Campus security:* 24-hour patrols.

Standardized Tests *Required:* ACCUPLACER (for placement).

Costs (2004–05) *Tuition:* state resident $2115 full-time, $88 per semester hour part-time; nonresident $6336 full-time, $264 per semester hour part-time. Full-time tuition and fees vary according to course load. Part-time tuition and fees vary according to course load. *Required fees:* $294 full-time, $49 per semester part-time.

Financial Aid Of all full-time matriculated undergraduates who enrolled in 2003, 50 Federal Work-Study jobs (averaging $5000). 2 state and other part-time jobs (averaging $5000).

Applying *Options:* early admission, deferred entrance. *Application fee:* $20. *Required:* high school transcript, CPT.

Admissions Contact Dr. Walter Clark, Director of Admissions, Middlesex Community College, 100 Training Hill Road, Middletown, CT 06457-4889. *Phone:* 860-343-5897. *Fax:* 860-344-7488.

NAUGATUCK VALLEY COMMUNITY COLLEGE

Waterbury, Connecticut

- **State-supported** 2-year, founded 1992, part of Connecticut Community-Technical College System
- **Calendar** semesters
- **Degree** certificates and associate
- **Urban** 110-acre campus
- **Coed**

Faculty *Student/faculty ratio:* 5:1.

Student Life *Campus security:* 24-hour emergency response devices and patrols, late-night transport/escort service, security escort service.

Athletics Member NJCAA.

Standardized Tests *Required:* ACCUPLACER (for placement). *Required for some:* SAT (for placement).

Costs (2004–05) *Tuition:* state resident $2406 full-time; nonresident $7178 full-time. Full-time tuition and fees vary according to course level.

Financial Aid Of all full-time matriculated undergraduates who enrolled in 2003, 70 Federal Work-Study jobs (averaging $1942). 16 state and other part-time jobs (averaging $1660).

Applying *Options:* deferred entrance. *Application fee:* $20. *Required:* high school transcript. *Required for some:* interview.

Admissions Contact Ms. Lucretia Sveda, Director of Enrollment Services, Naugatuck Valley Community College, Waterbury, CT 06708. *Phone:* 203-575-8016. *Fax:* 203-596-8766. *E-mail:* nv_admissions@commnet.edu.

NORTHWESTERN CONNECTICUT COMMUNITY COLLEGE

Winsted, Connecticut

- **State-supported** 2-year, founded 1965, part of Connecticut Community-Technical College System
- **Calendar** semesters
- **Degree** certificates and associate
- **Small-town** 5-acre campus with easy access to Hartford
- **Coed,** 1,516 undergraduate students, 34% full-time, 65% women, 35% men

Undergraduates 513 full-time, 1,003 part-time. Students come from 6 states and territories, 1% are from out of state, 2% African American, 2% Asian American or Pacific Islander, 3% Hispanic American, 0.2% Native American, 0.1% international, 7% transferred in. *Retention:* 60% of 2002 full-time freshmen returned.

Freshmen *Admission:* 328 applied, 328 admitted, 268 enrolled.

Faculty *Total:* 95, 29% full-time. *Student/faculty ratio:* 17:1.

Majors Accounting; administrative assistant and secretarial science; art; behavioral sciences; biology/biological sciences; business administration and management; child development; commercial and advertising art; communications technology; computer engineering technology; computer graphics; computer programming; computer science; criminal justice/law enforcement administration; criminal justice/police science; electrical, electronic and communications engineering technology; engineering; English; health science; human services; information science/studies; kindergarten/preschool education; legal assistant/paralegal; liberal arts and sciences/liberal studies; mathematics; medical/clinical assistant; parks, recreation and leisure; parks, recreation and leisure facilities management; physical sciences; pre-engineering; sign language interpretation and translation; social sciences; substance abuse/addiction counseling; therapeutic recreation; veterinary technology.

Academic Programs *Special study options:* academic remediation for entering students, adult/continuing education programs, advanced placement credit, cooperative education, distance learning, double majors, English as a second language, independent study, internships, part-time degree program, services for LD students, summer session for credit.

Library Northwestern Connecticut Community-Technical College Learning Center with 37,666 titles, 267 serial subscriptions, 1,599 audiovisual materials, an OPAC.

Computers on Campus 90 computers available on campus for general student use. A campuswide network can be accessed from off campus. Internet access, at least one staffed computer lab available.

Student Life *Housing:* college housing not available. *Activities and Organizations:* student-run newspaper, Ski Club, Student Senate, Deaf Club, Recreation Club, Early Childhood Educational Club. *Campus security:* evening security patrols.

Costs (2005–06) *Tuition:* state resident $2406 full-time, $141 per semester hour part-time; nonresident $7178 full-time, $414 per semester hour part-time.

Applying *Options:* deferred entrance. *Application fee:* $20. *Application deadline:* rolling (freshmen), rolling (transfers). *Notification:* continuous (freshmen).

Admissions Contact Ms. Beverly Chrzan, Director of Admissions, Northwestern Connecticut Community College, Park Place East, Winsted, CT 06098. *Phone:* 860-738-6329. *Fax:* 860-738-6437. *E-mail:* bschott@nwcc.commnet.edu.

NORWALK COMMUNITY COLLEGE

Norwalk, Connecticut

Admissions Contact Ms. Danita Brown, Admissions Counselor, Norwalk Community College, 188 Richards Avenue, Norwalk, CT 06854-1655. *Phone:* 203-857-7060. *Toll-free phone:* 888-462-6282. *Fax:* 203-857-3335. *E-mail:* nccadmit@commnet.edu.

QUINEBAUG VALLEY COMMUNITY COLLEGE

Danielson, Connecticut

- **State-supported** 2-year, founded 1971, part of Connecticut Community College System
- **Calendar** semesters
- **Degree** certificates and associate
- **Rural** 60-acre campus
- **Coed,** 1,721 undergraduate students, 33% full-time, 69% women, 31% men

Undergraduates 571 full-time, 1,150 part-time. Students come from 3 states and territories, 1% are from out of state, 2% African American, 1% Asian American or Pacific Islander, 9% Hispanic American, 1% Native American, 0.1% international, 9% transferred in.

Freshmen *Admission:* 582 applied, 580 admitted, 356 enrolled.

Faculty *Total:* 127, 13% full-time. *Student/faculty ratio:* 18:1.

Majors Accounting; administrative assistant and secretarial science; art; avionics maintenance technology; business administration and management; computer and information sciences related; computer graphics; computer systems networking and telecommunications; data entry/microcomputer applications; engineering technology; human services; liberal arts and sciences/liberal studies; medical/clinical assistant; plastics engineering technology; pre-engineering; substance abuse/addiction counseling; system administration; word processing.

Academic Programs *Special study options:* academic remediation for entering students, adult/continuing education programs, advanced placement credit, distance learning, English as a second language, external degree program, internships, part-time degree program, services for LD students, summer session for credit.

Library Audrey Beck Library with 31,000 titles, 130 serial subscriptions, an OPAC.

Computers on Campus 80 computers available on campus for general student use. A campuswide network can be accessed. Internet access, at least one staffed computer lab available.

Student Life *Housing:* college housing not available. *Activities and Organizations:* student-run newspaper. *Campus security:* evening security guard.

Costs (2005–06) *Tuition:* state resident $2112 full-time; nonresident $6336 full-time. Full-time tuition and fees vary according to reciprocity agreements. Part-time tuition and fees vary according to reciprocity agreements. *Required fees:* $294 full-time. *Payment plans:* installment, deferred payment. *Waivers:* employees or children of employees.

Financial Aid Of all full-time matriculated undergraduates who enrolled in 2003, 38 Federal Work-Study jobs (averaging $1400). 24 state and other part-time jobs (averaging $1350).

Applying *Options:* common application, electronic application, early admission, deferred entrance. *Application fee:* $20. *Required for some:* high school transcript. *Recommended:* high school transcript. *Application deadlines:* 9/1 (freshmen), 9/1 (transfers). *Notification:* continuous until 9/1 (freshmen).

Admissions Contact Dr. Toni Moumouris, Director of Admissions, Quinebaug Valley Community College, 742 Upper Maple Street, Danielson, CT 06239. *Phone:* 860-774-1130 Ext. 318. *Fax:* 860-774-7768. *E-mail:* qu_lsd@commnet.edu.

ST. VINCENT'S COLLEGE

Bridgeport, Connecticut

- **Independent** 2-year, founded 1991, affiliated with Roman Catholic Church
- **Calendar** semesters
- **Degree** certificates and associate
- **Urban** campus with easy access to New York City
- **Coed**

Faculty *Student/faculty ratio:* 23:1.

Student Life *Campus security:* 24-hour patrols, late-night transport/escort service.

Standardized Tests *Required for some:* SAT or ACT (for placement).

Financial Aid Of all full-time matriculated undergraduates who enrolled in 2003, 15 Federal Work-Study jobs (averaging $1000).

Applying *Options:* deferred entrance. *Application fee:* $30. *Required:* essay or personal statement, high school transcript, letters of recommendation. *Required for some:* interview. *Recommended:* minimum 3.0 GPA.

Admissions Contact Mr. Joseph Marrone, Director of Admissions and Recruitment Marketing, St. Vincent's College, 2800 Main Street, Bridgeport, CT 06606-4292. *Phone:* 203-576-5515.

THREE RIVERS COMMUNITY COLLEGE
Norwich, Connecticut

- **State-supported** 2-year, founded 1963, part of Connecticut Community-Technical College System
- **Calendar** semesters
- **Degrees** certificates and associate (engineering technology programs are offered on the Thames Valley Campus; liberal arts, transfer and career programs are offered on the Mohegan Campus)
- **Small-town** 40-acre campus with easy access to Hartford
- **Coed,** 3,624 undergraduate students

Undergraduates Students come from 6 states and territories, 1% are from out of state, 7% African American, 2% Asian American or Pacific Islander, 5% Hispanic American, 2% Native American, 0.4% international.

Faculty *Total:* 222, 32% full-time.

Majors Accounting; administrative assistant and secretarial science; architectural engineering technology; avionics maintenance technology; business administration and management; civil engineering technology; computer engineering technology; computer programming; computer typography and composition equipment operation; consumer merchandising/retailing management; corrections; criminal justice/law enforcement administration; data processing and data processing technology; drafting and design technology; dramatic/theatre arts; electrical, electronic and communications engineering technology; engineering; engineering science; engineering technology; environmental engineering technology; fire science; hospitality administration; hotel/motel administration; human services; hydrology and water resources science; industrial technology; kindergarten/preschool education; laser and optical technology; legal administrative assistant/secretary; liberal arts and sciences/liberal studies; marketing/marketing management; mechanical engineering/mechanical technology; medical administrative assistant and medical secretary; nuclear/nuclear power technology; nursing (registered nurse training); pre-engineering; public administration; special products marketing; substance abuse/addiction counseling; technical and business writing; tourism and travel services management.

Academic Programs *Special study options:* academic remediation for entering students, adult/continuing education programs, advanced placement credit, cooperative education, double majors, English as a second language, external degree program, independent study, internships, part-time degree program, services for LD students, student-designed majors, study abroad, summer session for credit.

Library Three Rivers Community College Learning Resource Center plus 2 others with 53,768 titles, 549 serial subscriptions, an OPAC.

Computers on Campus 350 computers available on campus for general student use. A campuswide network can be accessed. Internet access, at least one staffed computer lab available.

Student Life *Housing:* college housing not available. *Activities and Organizations:* drama/theater group, student-run newspaper, Student Senate/Student Government Association, Theater Guild, Phi Theta Kappa, Student Nurses Association, African-American Organization, national fraternities. *Campus security:* late-night transport/escort service, 14 hour patrols by trained security personnel. *Student services:* personal/psychological counseling.

Athletics *Intramural sports:* bowling M/W.

Standardized Tests *Required:* ACCUPLACER (for placement).

Costs (2005–06) *Tuition:* state resident $2232 full-time, $93 per semester hour part-time; nonresident $7264 full-time, $279 per semester hour part-time. *Required fees:* $304 full-time.

Financial Aid Of all full-time matriculated undergraduates who enrolled in 2003, 40 Federal Work-Study jobs (averaging $3000). 80 state and other part-time jobs (averaging $3000).

Applying *Options:* early admission, deferred entrance. *Application fee:* $20. *Required for some:* minimum 3.0 GPA. *Recommended:* high school transcript. *Application deadline:* rolling (freshmen), rolling (transfers). *Notification:* continuous (freshmen).

Admissions Contact Ms. Aida Garcia, Admissions and Recruitment Counselor, Mohegan Campus, Three Rivers Community College, Mahan Drive, Norwich, CT 06360. *Phone:* 860-892-5762. *Fax:* 860-886-0691. *E-mail:* info3rivers@trcc.commnet.edu.

TUNXIS COMMUNITY COLLEGE
Farmington, Connecticut

- **State-supported** 2-year, founded 1969, part of Connecticut Community College System
- **Calendar** semesters
- **Degree** certificates and associate
- **Suburban** 12-acre campus with easy access to Hartford
- **Coed,** 4,035 undergraduate students, 31% full-time, 63% women, 37% men

Undergraduates 1,245 full-time, 2,790 part-time. Students come from 6 states and territories, 5% African American, 3% Asian American or Pacific Islander, 8% Hispanic American, 0.5% Native American, 0.9% international.

Freshmen *Admission:* 569 enrolled.

Faculty *Total:* 214, 27% full-time, 14% with terminal degrees. *Student/faculty ratio:* 20:1.

Majors Accounting; administrative assistant and secretarial science; applied art; art; business administration and management; commercial and advertising art; corrections; criminal justice/law enforcement administration; data processing and data processing technology; dental hygiene; engineering; engineering technology; fashion merchandising; forensic science and technology; human services; information science/studies; kindergarten/preschool education; legal administrative assistant/secretary; liberal arts and sciences/liberal studies; marketing/marketing management; medical administrative assistant and medical secretary; physical therapy; substance abuse/addiction counseling.

Academic Programs *Special study options:* academic remediation for entering students, adult/continuing education programs, English as a second language, part-time degree program, summer session for credit.

Library Tunxis Community College Library with 33,866 titles, 285 serial subscriptions, 3,571 audiovisual materials, an OPAC.

Computers on Campus 274 computers available on campus for general student use. A campuswide network can be accessed from off campus. Internet access, at least one staffed computer lab available.

Student Life *Housing:* college housing not available. *Activities and Organizations:* Phi Theta Kappa, Student American Dental Hygiene Association (SADHA), Human Services Club, student newspaper, Bible Club. *Campus security:* 24-hour patrols. *Student services:* health clinic.

Costs (2004–05) *Tuition:* state resident $2112 full-time, $88 per semester hour part-time; nonresident $6884 full-time, $264 per semester hour part-time. Part-time tuition and fees vary according to course load. *Required fees:* $294 full-time. *Waivers:* employees or children of employees.

Applying *Options:* common application, deferred entrance. *Application fee:* $20. *Required:* high school transcript. *Application deadline:* rolling (freshmen), rolling (transfers).

Admissions Contact Mr. Peter McCloskey, Director of Admissions, Tunxis Community College, 271 Scott Swamp Road, Farmington, CT 06032. *Phone:* 860-677-7701 Ext. 152. *Fax:* 860-676-8906.

DELAWARE

DELAWARE COLLEGE OF ART AND DESIGN
Wilmington, Delaware

- **Independent** 2-year, founded 1997, administratively affiliated with Corcoran College of Art and Design
- **Calendar** semesters
- **Degree** associate
- **Urban** 1-acre campus
- **Endowment** $65,295
- **Coed,** 194 undergraduate students, 76% full-time, 51% women, 49% men

Undergraduates 148 full-time, 46 part-time. Students come from 9 states and territories, 45% are from out of state, 9% African American, 1% Asian American or Pacific Islander, 4% Hispanic American, 0.5% Native American, 1% international, 11% transferred in, 50% live on campus.

Freshmen *Admission:* 322 applied, 186 admitted, 108 enrolled. *Average high school GPA:* 2.5.

Faculty *Total:* 20, 25% full-time, 80% with terminal degrees. *Student/faculty ratio:* 5:1.

Majors Animation, interactive technology, video graphics and special effects; fine/studio arts; graphic design; illustration; interior design; photography.

Academic Programs *Special study options:* academic remediation for entering students, adult/continuing education programs, advanced placement credit, double majors, off-campus study, part-time degree program, services for LD students, study abroad, summer session for credit.

Delaware College of Art and Design (continued)

Library Information Resource Center plus 1 other with 8,000 titles, 76 serial subscriptions, 500 audiovisual materials, an OPAC.

Computers on Campus 68 computers available on campus for general student use. A campuswide network can be accessed from student residence rooms and from off campus that provide access to access to email, student Web space. Internet access, at least one staffed computer lab available. Computer purchase or lease plan available.

Student Life *Housing Options:* coed. Campus housing is leased by the school. Freshman applicants given priority for college housing.

Standardized Tests *Recommended:* SAT or ACT (for placement).

Costs (2005–06) *Tuition:* $13,400 full-time, $560 per credit part-time. *Required fees:* $380 full-time, $240 per term part-time. *Room only:* $5230. Room and board charges vary according to housing facility. *Payment plan:* installment. *Waivers:* employees or children of employees.

Applying *Options:* common application, electronic application, deferred entrance. *Application fee:* $25. *Required:* essay or personal statement, high school transcript, minimum 2 GPA, interview, portfolio. *Required for some:* letters of recommendation. *Application deadline:* rolling (freshmen), rolling (transfers). *Notification:* continuous until 8/15 (freshmen).

Admissions Contact Krista Rothwell, Admissions Recruiter, Delaware College of Art and Design, 600 North Market Street, Wilmington, DE 19801. *Phone:* 302-622-8000 Ext. 111. *Toll-free phone:* 302-622-8000 Ext. 118. *Fax:* 302-622-8870. *E-mail:* info@dcad.edu.

DELAWARE TECHNICAL & COMMUNITY COLLEGE, JACK F. OWENS CAMPUS
Georgetown, Delaware

■ **State-supported** 2-year, founded 1967, part of Delaware Technical and Community College System
■ **Calendar** semesters
■ **Degree** certificates, diplomas, and associate
■ **Small-town** 120-acre campus
■ **Coed**, 3,565 undergraduate students, 42% full-time, 65% women, 35% men

Undergraduates 1,492 full-time, 2,073 part-time. Students come from 3 states and territories, 9 other countries, 4% are from out of state, 15% African American, 1% Asian American or Pacific Islander, 3% Hispanic American, 0.7% Native American, 2% international.

Freshmen *Admission:* 1,472 applied, 1,131 admitted, 727 enrolled.

Faculty *Total:* 240, 38% full-time.

Majors Accounting; administrative assistant and secretarial science; agricultural business and management; architectural engineering technology; automobile/automotive mechanics technology; business administration and management; carpentry; chemical engineering; child development; civil engineering technology; clinical/medical laboratory technology; computer programming; construction management; consumer merchandising/retailing management; criminal justice/law enforcement administration; data processing and data processing technology; drafting and design technology; electrical, electronic and communications engineering technology; emergency medical technology (EMT paramedic); engineering; engineering technology; environmental engineering technology; heavy equipment maintenance technology; hospitality administration; hotel/motel administration; human services; journalism; legal administrative assistant/secretary; marketing/marketing management; medical administrative assistant and medical secretary; medical/clinical assistant; medical laboratory technology; nursing (licensed practical/vocational nurse training); nursing (registered nurse training); veterinary technology; welding technology.

Academic Programs *Special study options:* academic remediation for entering students, adult/continuing education programs, cooperative education, distance learning, English as a second language, external degree program, internships, part-time degree program, services for LD students, student-designed majors, summer session for credit.

Library Stephen J. Betze Library plus 1 other with 72,657 titles, 514 serial subscriptions, an OPAC.

Computers on Campus 400 computers available on campus for general student use. A campuswide network can be accessed. Online (class) registration, at least one staffed computer lab available.

Student Life *Housing:* college housing not available. *Activities and Organizations:* student-run radio station, Student Government Association, Student Nursing Association, Phi Beta Kappa, Occupational Therapy Assistant Club, Physical Therapy Assistant Club. *Campus security:* 24-hour patrols, late-night transport/escort service.

Athletics Member NJCAA. *Intercollegiate sports:* baseball M(s), softball W.

Standardized Tests *Required:* CPT (for placement). *Recommended:* SAT or ACT (for placement).

Costs (2004–05) *Tuition:* state resident $1848 full-time, $77 per credit hour part-time; nonresident $4620 full-time, $193 per credit hour part-time. *Required fees:* $180 full-time, $5 per credit hour part-time, $21 per term part-time.

Financial Aid Of all full-time matriculated undergraduates who enrolled in 2003, 250 Federal Work-Study jobs (averaging $2000).

Applying *Options:* early admission. *Application fee:* $10. *Required:* high school transcript. *Application deadline:* rolling (freshmen), rolling (transfers). *Notification:* continuous (freshmen).

Admissions Contact Ms. Claire McDonald, Admissions Counselor, Delaware Technical & Community College, Jack F. Owens Campus, PO Box 610, Georgetown, DE 19947. *Phone:* 302-856-5400.

DELAWARE TECHNICAL & COMMUNITY COLLEGE, STANTON/WILMINGTON CAMPUS
Newark, Delaware

■ **State-supported** 2-year, founded 1968, part of Delaware Technical and Community College System
■ **Calendar** semesters
■ **Degree** certificates, diplomas, and associate
■ **Coed**, 6,892 undergraduate students, 40% full-time, 62% women, 38% men

Undergraduates 2,724 full-time, 4,168 part-time. Students come from 13 states and territories, 45 other countries, 11% are from out of state, 22% African American, 3% Asian American or Pacific Islander, 4% Hispanic American, 0.6% Native American, 2% international.

Freshmen *Admission:* 3,561 applied, 2,686 admitted, 1,778 enrolled.

Faculty *Total:* 471, 33% full-time. *Student/faculty ratio:* 16:1.

Majors Accounting; administrative assistant and secretarial science; architectural engineering technology; banking and financial support services; biomedical technology; business administration and management; chemical engineering; civil engineering technology; corrections; criminal justice/law enforcement administration; criminal justice/police science; culinary arts; data processing and data processing technology; dental hygiene; diagnostic medical sonography and ultrasound technology; drafting and design technology; electrical, electronic and communications engineering technology; emergency medical technology (EMT paramedic); engineering; fire science; food services technology; gerontology; hotel/motel administration; human services; industrial radiologic technology; industrial technology; information science/studies; instrumentation technology; kindergarten/preschool education; kinesiology and exercise science; management information systems; marketing/marketing management; mechanical engineering/mechanical technology; medical administrative assistant and medical secretary; nuclear medical technology; nursing (registered nurse training); occupational safety and health technology; occupational therapist assistant; physical therapist assistant; respiratory care therapy; sign language interpretation and translation; substance abuse/addiction counseling; transportation technology.

Academic Programs *Special study options:* academic remediation for entering students, adult/continuing education programs, cooperative education, English as a second language, external degree program, part-time degree program, services for LD students, summer session for credit.

Library 60,066 titles, 793 serial subscriptions, an OPAC.

Computers on Campus 200 computers available on campus for general student use. A campuswide network can be accessed. At least one staffed computer lab available.

Student Life *Housing:* college housing not available. *Campus security:* 24-hour patrols, late-night transport/escort service.

Athletics Member NJCAA. *Intercollegiate sports:* basketball M, soccer M, softball W, tennis M/W, volleyball M/W. *Intramural sports:* basketball M, tennis M/W.

Standardized Tests *Required:* CPT (for placement).

Costs (2004–05) *Tuition:* state resident $1848 full-time, $77 per credit hour part-time; nonresident $4620 full-time, $193 per credit hour part-time. *Required fees:* $180 full-time, $5 per credit hour part-time, $21 per term part-time.

Applying *Options:* early admission. *Application fee:* $10. *Required:* high school transcript. *Application deadline:* rolling (freshmen), rolling (transfers). *Notification:* continuous (freshmen).

Admissions Contact Ms. Rebecca Bailey, Admissions Coordinator, Wilmington, Delaware Technical & Community College, Stanton/Wilmington Campus, 333 Shipley Street, Wilmington, DE 19713. *Phone:* 302-571-5366.

DELAWARE TECHNICAL & COMMUNITY COLLEGE, TERRY CAMPUS
Dover, Delaware

■ **State-supported** 2-year, founded 1972, part of Delaware Technical and Community College System
■ **Calendar** semesters
■ **Degree** certificates, diplomas, and associate

- **Small-town** 70-acre campus with easy access to Philadelphia
- **Coed,** 2,304 undergraduate students

Undergraduates Students come from 10 states and territories, 10 other countries, 3% are from out of state, 23% African American, 3% Asian American or Pacific Islander, 3% Hispanic American, 0.7% Native American, 2% international.

Freshmen *Admission:* 977 applied, 782 admitted.

Faculty *Total:* 158, 37% full-time. *Student/faculty ratio:* 14:1.

Majors Accounting; administrative assistant and secretarial science; aeronautics/aviation/aerospace science and technology; architectural engineering technology; aviation/airway management; avionics maintenance technology; business administration and management; civil engineering technology; computer engineering technology; computer programming; construction engineering technology; construction management; corrections; criminal justice/law enforcement administration; data processing and data processing technology; drafting and design technology; electrical, electronic and communications engineering technology; electromechanical technology; engineering technology; human services; industrial technology; kindergarten/preschool education; nursing (licensed practical/vocational nurse training); nursing (registered nurse training); survey technology.

Academic Programs *Special study options:* academic remediation for entering students, adult/continuing education programs, cooperative education, English as a second language, internships, part-time degree program, services for LD students, summer session for credit.

Library 9,663 titles, 245 serial subscriptions, an OPAC.

Computers on Campus 125 computers available on campus for general student use. A campuswide network can be accessed. At least one staffed computer lab available.

Student Life *Housing:* college housing not available. *Activities and Organizations:* Students of Kolor, Human Services Organization, Phi Theta Kappa, Alpha Beta Gamma. *Campus security:* late-night transport/escort service.

Standardized Tests *Required:* CPT (for placement).

Costs (2004–05) *Tuition:* state resident $1848 full-time, $77 per credit hour part-time; nonresident $4620 full-time, $193 per credit hour part-time. *Required fees:* $180 full-time, $5 per credit hour part-time, $21 per term part-time.

Financial Aid Of all full-time matriculated undergraduates who enrolled in 2003, 50 Federal Work-Study jobs (averaging $1500).

Applying *Options:* early admission. *Application fee:* $10. *Required:* high school transcript. *Application deadline:* rolling (freshmen), rolling (transfers). *Notification:* continuous (freshmen).

Admissions Contact Mrs. Maria Harris, Admissions Officer, Delaware Technical & Community College, Terry Campus, 100 Campus Drive, Dover, DE 19904. *Phone:* 302-857-1020. *Fax:* 302-857-1020. *E-mail:* mharris@outland.dtcc.edu.

FLORIDA

ATI CAREER TRAINING CENTER
Fort Lauderdale, Florida

Admissions Contact Ms. Wendy Hopkins Goffinet, Director of Admissions, ATI Career Training Center, 2880 NW 62nd Street, Fort Lauderdale, FL 33309-9731. *Phone:* 954-973-4760. *Fax:* 954-973-6422.

ATI CAREER TRAINING CENTER
Miami, Florida

Admissions Contact Ms. Mary Fernandez, Director of Admissions, ATI Career Training Center, 1 NE 19th Street, Miami, FL 33132. *Phone:* 305-573-1600.

ATI CAREER TRAINING CENTER
Oakland Park, Florida

Admissions Contact 3501 NW 9th Avenue, Oakland Park, FL 33309-9612.

ATI HEALTH EDUCATION CENTER
Miami, Florida

Admissions Contact Mrs. Barbara Woosley, Director, ATI Health Education Center, 1395 NW 167th Street, Suite 200, Miami, FL 33169-5742. *Phone:* 305-628-1000.

BREVARD COMMUNITY COLLEGE
Cocoa, Florida

- **State-supported** 2-year, founded 1960, part of Florida Community College System
- **Calendar** semesters
- **Degree** certificates and associate
- **Suburban** 100-acre campus with easy access to Orlando
- **Endowment** $8.1 million
- **Coed,** 14,616 undergraduate students, 36% full-time, 59% women, 41% men

Undergraduates 5,332 full-time, 9,284 part-time. Students come from 34 states and territories, 72 other countries, 4% are from out of state, 9% African American, 3% Asian American or Pacific Islander, 6% Hispanic American, 0.6% Native American, 0.9% international. *Retention:* 65% of 2002 full-time freshmen returned.

Freshmen *Admission:* 4,709 applied, 4,709 admitted, 2,665 enrolled.

Faculty *Total:* 1,061, 19% full-time. *Student/faculty ratio:* 18:1.

Majors Accounting; business administration and management; chemical engineering; clinical/medical laboratory technology; computer engineering technology; computer/information technology services administration related; computer programming; computer programming (specific applications); computer software and media applications related; computer systems analysis; computer systems networking and telecommunications; corrections; criminal justice/law enforcement administration; criminal justice/police science; culinary arts; dental hygiene; digital communication and media/multimedia; drafting and design technology; early childhood education; electrical, electronic and communications engineering technology; electrical/electronics drafting and CAD/CADD; emergency medical technology (EMT paramedic); fire science; international business/trade/commerce; legal assistant/paralegal; liberal arts and sciences/liberal studies; manufacturing technology; medical administrative assistant and medical secretary; medical/clinical assistant; nursing (registered nurse training); radio and television; radiologic technology/science; surgical technology; system administration; system, networking, and LAN/WAN management; veterinary technology; web page, digital/multimedia and information resources design.

Academic Programs *Special study options:* academic remediation for entering students, accelerated degree program, adult/continuing education programs, advanced placement credit, cooperative education, distance learning, double majors, English as a second language, external degree program, honors programs, independent study, internships, part-time degree program, services for LD students, study abroad, summer session for credit. *ROTC:* Army (b), Air Force (b).

Library UCF Library with 213,873 titles, 904 serial subscriptions, 17,904 audiovisual materials, an OPAC, a Web page.

Computers on Campus 125 computers available on campus for general student use. A campuswide network can be accessed from off campus. Online (class) registration, at least one staffed computer lab available.

Student Life *Housing:* college housing not available. *Activities and Organizations:* drama/theater group, student-run newspaper, television station, choral group, Phi Theta Kappa, ROTORACT, African-American Student Union, Student Government Association, Psi Beta. *Campus security:* 24-hour emergency response devices and patrols, late-night transport/escort service. *Student services:* women's center.

Athletics Member NJCAA. *Intercollegiate sports:* baseball M(s), basketball M(s)/W(s), golf M(s), softball W(s), volleyball W(s).

Standardized Tests *Required:* SAT Reasoning, ACT, or CPT (for placement).

Costs (2004–05) *Tuition:* state resident $1428 full-time, $60 per credit hour part-time; nonresident $5400 full-time, $225 per credit hour part-time. *Waivers:* senior citizens and employees or children of employees.

Financial Aid Of all full-time matriculated undergraduates who enrolled in 2003, 200 Federal Work-Study jobs (averaging $2244). 200 state and other part-time jobs (averaging $2000).

Applying *Options:* common application, electronic application. *Application fee:* $20. *Required:* high school transcript. *Application deadline:* rolling (freshmen), rolling (transfers). *Notification:* continuous (freshmen).

Admissions Contact Ms. Stephanie Burnette, Registrar, Brevard Community College, 1519 Clearlake Road, Cocoa, FL 32922-6597. *Phone:* 321-433-7271. *Fax:* 321-433-7172.

BROWARD COMMUNITY COLLEGE
Fort Lauderdale, Florida

- **State-supported** 2-year, founded 1960, part of Florida Community College System
- **Calendar** trimesters
- **Degree** associate
- **Urban** campus with easy access to Miami
- **Coed,** 33,141 undergraduate students, 30% full-time, 62% women, 38% men

Broward Community College (continued)

Undergraduates 10,029 full-time, 23,112 part-time. Students come from 100 other countries, 28% African American, 3% Asian American or Pacific Islander, 22% Hispanic American, 0.2% Native American, 9% international.

Freshmen *Admission:* 7,321 applied, 7,321 admitted, 4,428 enrolled. *Test scores:* SAT verbal scores over 500: 23%; SAT math scores over 500: 25%; SAT verbal scores over 600: 3%; SAT math scores over 600: 4%; SAT math scores over 700: 1%.

Faculty *Total:* 1,428, 26% full-time, 19% with terminal degrees.

Majors Accounting; administrative assistant and secretarial science; airline pilot and flight crew; architectural engineering technology; automobile/automotive mechanics technology; aviation/airway management; avionics maintenance technology; business administration and management; child development; civil engineering technology; clinical laboratory science/medical technology; clinical/medical laboratory technology; computer engineering technology; computer programming; computer science; construction management; corrections; criminal justice/law enforcement administration; criminal justice/police science; data processing and data processing technology; dental hygiene; electrical, electronic and communications engineering technology; elementary education; emergency medical technology (EMT paramedic); engineering science; environmental engineering technology; finance; fire science; hotel/motel administration; industrial radiologic technology; information science/studies; insurance; interior design; kindergarten/preschool education; legal administrative assistant/secretary; legal assistant/paralegal; liberal arts and sciences/liberal studies; marketing/marketing management; mechanical engineering/mechanical technology; medical administrative assistant and medical secretary; medical/clinical assistant; nuclear medical technology; nursing (registered nurse training); physical therapy; pre-engineering; respiratory care therapy; special products marketing; tourism and travel services management.

Academic Programs *Special study options:* academic remediation for entering students, adult/continuing education programs, advanced placement credit, cooperative education, English as a second language, honors programs, part-time degree program, services for LD students, student-designed majors, study abroad, summer session for credit. *ROTC:* Army (b).

Library South Regional/Broward Community College Library with 200,000 titles, 600 serial subscriptions, an OPAC.

Computers on Campus Online (class) registration available.

Student Life *Housing:* college housing not available. *Activities and Organizations:* drama/theater group, student-run newspaper, choral group. *Campus security:* 24-hour emergency response devices and patrols, late-night transport/escort service. *Student services:* personal/psychological counseling, women's center.

Athletics Member NJCAA. *Intercollegiate sports:* baseball M(s), basketball M(s)/W(s), soccer W, softball W(s), swimming and diving M(s)/W(s), tennis W(s), volleyball W(s), wrestling M(s). *Intramural sports:* baseball M, basketball M/W, tennis W.

Standardized Tests *Required:* SAT I, ACT, or CPT (for placement).

Costs (2005–06) *Tuition:* state resident $1500 full-time, $59 per credit hour part-time; nonresident $6001 full-time, $219 per credit hour part-time. *Required fees:* $255 full-time. *Payment plan:* tuition prepayment.

Financial Aid *Financial aid deadline:* 7/1.

Applying *Options:* common application, early admission, deferred entrance. *Application fee:* $25.

Admissions Contact Ms. Barbara Bryan, Associate Vice President for Student Affairs/College Registrar, Broward Community College, 225 East Las Olas Boulevard, Fort Lauderdale, FL 33301-2298. *Phone:* 954-761-7465.

CENTRAL FLORIDA COLLEGE
Winter Park, Florida

Admissions Contact 1573 West Fairbanks Avenue, Suite 1-A, Winter Park, FL 32789.

CENTRAL FLORIDA COMMUNITY COLLEGE
Ocala, Florida

- **State and locally supported** 2-year, founded 1957, part of Florida Community College System
- **Calendar** semesters
- **Degree** certificates and associate
- **Small-town** 139-acre campus
- **Endowment** $12.0 million
- **Coed,** 5,999 undergraduate students, 41% full-time, 65% women, 35% men

Undergraduates 2,436 full-time, 3,563 part-time. Students come from 20 states and territories, 11% African American, 2% Asian American or Pacific Islander, 7% Hispanic American, 0.5% Native American, 0.4% international.

Freshmen *Admission:* 737 applied, 737 admitted, 737 enrolled.

Faculty *Total:* 643, 17% full-time. *Student/faculty ratio:* 17:1.

Majors Accounting technology and bookkeeping; airline pilot and flight crew; applied horticulture/horticultural business services related; automotive engineering technology; business administration and management; child care and support services management; child care provision; computer hardware technology; computer programming; computer systems analysis; criminal justice/law enforcement administration; electrical, electronic and communications engineering technology; emergency medical technology (EMT paramedic); environmental control technologies related; executive assistant/executive secretary; fire protection and safety technology; health information/medical records administration; hospitality administration; industrial radiologic technology; legal administrative assistant/secretary; legal assistant/paralegal; liberal arts and sciences/liberal studies; management information systems and services related; marketing/marketing management; nuclear/nuclear power technology; nursing (registered nurse training); ornamental horticulture; physical therapist assistant; psychiatric/mental health services technology; restaurant, culinary, and catering management; veterinary/animal health technology.

Academic Programs *Special study options:* academic remediation for entering students, adult/continuing education programs, advanced placement credit, cooperative education, distance learning, English as a second language, freshman honors college, honors programs, independent study, internships, part-time degree program, services for LD students, summer session for credit.

Library Learning Resources Center plus 1 other with 54,491 titles, 367 serial subscriptions, an OPAC.

Computers on Campus 737 computers available on campus for general student use. A campuswide network can be accessed from off campus. Internet access, online (class) registration, at least one staffed computer lab available.

Student Life *Housing:* college housing not available. *Options:* Campus housing is provided by a third party. *Activities and Organizations:* drama/theater group, student-run newspaper, choral group, Student Activities Board, African-American Student Union, ROC (Realizing Our Cause), Gay Straight Alliance, Musagettas. *Campus security:* 24-hour emergency response devices and patrols, student patrols, late-night transport/escort service. *Student services:* personal/psychological counseling, women's center.

Athletics Member NJCAA. *Intercollegiate sports:* baseball M(s), basketball M(s)/W(s), softball W(s), tennis W(s).

Standardized Tests *Required:* SAT Reasoning Test or ACT or CPT (for placement).

Costs (2004–05) *Tuition:* state resident $1550 full-time, $52 per credit hour part-time; nonresident $6521 full-time, $217 per credit hour part-time. *Required fees:* $263 full-time, $9 per credit hour part-time. *Waivers:* employees or children of employees.

Financial Aid Of all full-time matriculated undergraduates who enrolled in 2003, 103 Federal Work-Study jobs (averaging $1500).

Applying *Options:* common application, early admission. *Application fee:* $20. *Required:* high school transcript. *Application deadlines:* 8/3 (freshmen), 8/3 (transfers). *Notification:* continuous (freshmen).

Admissions Contact Ms. Sheryl Graham, Executive Director, Student Records and Financial Aid, Central Florida Community College, PO Box 1388, 3001 SW College Road, Ocala, FL 34474-1388. *Phone:* 352-237-2111 Ext. 1340. *Fax:* 352-873-5882. *E-mail:* grahams@cf.edu.

CENTRAL FLORIDA INSTITUTE
Palm Harbor, Florida

- **Proprietary** 2-year
- **Calendar** continuous
- **Degree** certificates, diplomas, and associate
- **Urban** campus
- **Coed**

Faculty *Student/faculty ratio:* 7:1.

Costs (2004–05) *Tuition:* $8479 full-time.

Admissions Contact Carol Bruno, Director of Admissions, Central Florida Institute, 60522 US Highway 19 North, Suite 200, Palm Harbor, FL 34684. *Phone:* 727-786-4707.

CHIPOLA COLLEGE
Marianna, Florida

- **State-supported** primarily 2-year, founded 1947
- **Calendar** semesters
- **Degrees** certificates, associate, and bachelor's
- **Rural** 105-acre campus
- **Coed,** 2,249 undergraduate students, 46% full-time, 62% women, 38% men

Undergraduates 1,030 full-time, 1,219 part-time. Students come from 13 states and territories, 7 other countries, 3% are from out of state, 19% African

American, 0.9% Asian American or Pacific Islander, 2% Hispanic American, 0.7% Native American, 4% transferred in.
Freshmen *Admission:* 798 applied, 755 admitted, 285 enrolled. *Average high school GPA:* 2.5. *Test scores:* SAT verbal scores over 500: 16%; SAT math scores over 500: 36%; ACT scores over 18: 81%; SAT verbal scores over 600: 4%; SAT math scores over 600: 12%; ACT scores over 24: 25%; ACT scores over 30: 3%.
Faculty *Total:* 69, 78% full-time, 12% with terminal degrees. *Student/faculty ratio:* 24:1.
Majors Accounting; agriculture; agronomy and crop science; art; biological and physical sciences; business administration and management; clinical laboratory science/medical technology; computer and information sciences related; computer science; education; finance; liberal arts and sciences/liberal studies; mass communication/media; mathematics teacher education; nursing (registered nurse training); pre-engineering; science teacher education; secondary education; social work.
Academic Programs *Special study options:* academic remediation for entering students, adult/continuing education programs, advanced placement credit, distance learning, honors programs, independent study, part-time degree program, services for LD students, summer session for credit.
Library Chipola Library with 37,740 titles, 226 serial subscriptions.
Computers on Campus 80 computers available on campus for general student use. A campuswide network can be accessed from off campus. Internet access, at least one staffed computer lab available.
Student Life *Housing:* college housing not available. *Activities and Organizations:* drama/theater group, student-run newspaper, choral group, Drama/Theater Group. *Campus security:* night security personnel.
Athletics Member NJCAA. *Intercollegiate sports:* baseball M(s), basketball M(s)/W(s), softball W(s).
Standardized Tests *Required:* SAT or ACT (for placement).
Costs (2004–05) *Tuition:* state resident $1830 full-time, $59 per semester hour part-time; nonresident $5490 full-time, $181 per semester hour part-time. Full-time tuition and fees vary according to course level and degree level. Part-time tuition and fees vary according to course level and degree level.
Applying *Options:* early admission. *Required:* high school transcript. *Application deadline:* rolling (freshmen), rolling (transfers). *Notification:* continuous (freshmen).
Admissions Contact Dr. Jayne Roberts, Dean of Enrollment Services and Register, Chipola College, Marianna, FL 32446. *Phone:* 850-718-2209 Ext. 2209. *Fax:* 850-718-2287.

CITY COLLEGE
Casselberry, Florida

Admissions Contact Ms. Yvonne C. Hunter, Director of Admissions, City College, 853 Semoran Boulevard, Suite 200, Casselberry, FL 32707-5342. *Phone:* 407-831-9816.

CITY COLLEGE
Fort Lauderdale, Florida

Admissions Contact Mr. Michael Beauregard, Vice President, City College, 1401 West Cypress Creek Road, Fort Lauderdale, FL 33309. *Phone:* 954-492-5353. *Fax:* 954-491-1695. *E-mail:* info@citycollege.edu.

CITY COLLEGE
Gainesville, Florida

Admissions Contact 2400 Southwest 13th Street, Gainesville, FL 32608.

CITY COLLEGE
Miami, Florida

Admissions Contact Admissions, City College, 9300 South Dadeland Boulevard, Miami, FL 33156. *Fax:* 305-491-9243.

COLLEGE OF BUSINESS AND TECHNOLOGY
Miami, Florida

- **Proprietary** 2-year, founded 1988
- **Calendar** semesters
- **Degree** certificates, diplomas, and associate
- **Endowment** $3.5 million
- **Coed,** 1,000 undergraduate students, 100% full-time, 65% women, 35% men
- 81% of applicants were admitted

Undergraduates 1,000 full-time. Students come from 7 states and territories, 5% are from out of state.
Freshmen *Admission:* 1,385 applied, 1,125 admitted. *Average high school GPA:* 2.80.
Faculty *Total:* 163, 83% full-time, 39% with terminal degrees. *Student/faculty ratio:* 10:1.
Academic Programs *Special study options:* academic remediation for entering students, accelerated degree program, adult/continuing education programs, advanced placement credit, cooperative education, distance learning, double majors, English as a second language, honors programs, independent study, internships, off-campus study, part-time degree program, services for LD students, summer session for credit.
Library The Bill Clinton Library plus 1 other with 700,000 titles, 200,000 serial subscriptions, 1,200 audiovisual materials, an OPAC, a Web page.
Computers on Campus 560 computers available on campus for general student use. A campuswide network can be accessed from student residence rooms and from off campus. Internet access, online (class) registration, at least one staffed computer lab available. Computer purchase or lease plan available.
Student Life *Housing Options:* Campus housing is provided by a third party.
Costs (2005–06) *Tuition:* $8840 full-time, $260 per credit part-time. Full-time tuition and fees vary according to course load and program. *Payment plans:* installment, deferred payment.
Applying *Options:* common application, electronic application. *Required:* essay or personal statement, high school transcript, minimum 2.6 GPA, 2 letters of recommendation, interview. *Application deadline:* 6/15 (freshmen).
Admissions Contact Ms. Stacy Ortiz, Admissions High School, College of Business and Technology, 8991 Southwest 107 Avenue, Suite 200, Miami, FL 33176. *Phone:* 305-273-4499. *E-mail:* admissions@cbt.edu.

▶ **See page 480 for a narrative description.**

DAYTONA BEACH COMMUNITY COLLEGE
Daytona Beach, Florida

- **State-supported** 2-year, founded 1958, part of Florida Community College System
- **Calendar** semesters
- **Degree** certificates and associate
- **Suburban** 100-acre campus with easy access to Orlando
- **Endowment** $3.1 million
- **Coed,** 11,945 undergraduate students, 40% full-time, 62% women, 38% men

Undergraduates 4,776 full-time, 7,169 part-time. Students come from 51 states and territories, 52 other countries, 5% are from out of state, 12% African American, 2% Asian American or Pacific Islander, 7% Hispanic American, 0.5% Native American, 1% international, 6% transferred in.
Freshmen *Admission:* 3,235 applied, 3,235 admitted, 2,053 enrolled.
Faculty *Total:* 775, 33% full-time, 13% with terminal degrees. *Student/faculty ratio:* 17:1.
Majors Accounting; administrative assistant and secretarial science; advertising; agriculture; anthropology; architectural engineering technology; art; astronomy; atmospheric sciences and meteorology; automobile/automotive mechanics technology; behavioral sciences; biological and physical sciences; biology/biological sciences; business administration and management; chemistry; child development; cinematography and film/video production; civil engineering technology; commercial and advertising art; computer and information sciences related; computer engineering related; computer graphics; computer/information technology services administration related; computer programming; computer programming (specific applications); computer science; computer systems networking and telecommunications; computer typography and composition equipment operation; construction engineering technology; corrections; cosmetology; court reporting; criminal justice/law enforcement administration; criminal justice/police science; criminology; culinary arts; dance; drafting and design technology; dramatic/theatre arts; economics; education; electrical, electronic and communications engineering technology; emergency medical technology (EMT paramedic); engineering; English; fashion/apparel design; finance; fire science; foods, nutrition, and wellness; forestry; geology/earth science; health information/medical records administration; health science; health teacher education; heating, air conditioning, ventilation and refrigeration maintenance technology; history; hospitality administration; hotel/motel administration; humanities; human services; industrial radiologic technology; information science/studies; information technology; insurance; interior design; journalism; kindergarten/preschool education; legal administrative assistant/secretary; legal assistant/paralegal; liberal arts and sciences/liberal studies; marine biology and biological oceanography; marketing/marketing management; mass communication/media; mathematics; medical administrative assistant and medical secretary; music; nursing (licensed practical/vocational nurse training); nursing (registered nurse training); occupational therapy; philosophy; photography; physical education teaching and coaching; physical therapy; physics; postal management; psychology; radio and television; respiratory care therapy; social sciences; sociology;

Daytona Beach Community College (continued)

special products marketing; statistics; telecommunications; tourism and travel services management; zoology/animal biology.

Academic Programs *Special study options:* academic remediation for entering students, adult/continuing education programs, advanced placement credit, cooperative education, English as a second language, honors programs, internships, part-time degree program, services for LD students, study abroad, summer session for credit. *ROTC:* Army (c), Air Force (c).

Library Mary Karl Memorial Library with 66,312 titles, 745 serial subscriptions, 4,503 audiovisual materials, an OPAC, a Web page.

Computers on Campus 752 computers available on campus for general student use. A campuswide network can be accessed. Internet access, online (class) registration, at least one staffed computer lab available. Computer purchase or lease plan available.

Student Life *Housing:* college housing not available. *Activities and Organizations:* drama/theater group, student-run newspaper, choral group, Florida Student Nursing Association, International Club, SGA, History Club, Drama Club. *Campus security:* 24-hour patrols, late-night transport/escort service. *Student services:* personal/psychological counseling, women's center.

Athletics Member NJCAA. *Intercollegiate sports:* basketball M(s), softball W(s). *Intramural sports:* basketball M/W, bowling M/W, fencing M/W, football M, golf M, racquetball M/W, soccer M/W, table tennis M/W, tennis M/W, volleyball M/W.

Standardized Tests *Required:* ACT ASSET, CPT (for placement). *Recommended:* SAT and SAT Subject Tests or ACT (for placement).

Costs (2004–05) *Tuition:* state resident $1825 full-time, $61 per credit hour part-time; nonresident $6850 full-time, $228 per credit hour part-time. Full-time tuition and fees vary according to course load. Part-time tuition and fees vary according to course load. *Required fees:* $40 full-time. *Waivers:* employees or children of employees.

Financial Aid Of all full-time matriculated undergraduates who enrolled in 2003, 193 Federal Work-Study jobs (averaging $1542).

Applying *Options:* common application, early admission, deferred entrance. *Required:* high school transcript. *Application deadline:* rolling (freshmen), rolling (transfers).

Admissions Contact Mr. Thomas LoBasso, Dean of Enrollment Development, Daytona Beach Community College, PO Box 2811, Daytona Beach, FL 32120-2811. *Phone:* 386-506-3732. *Fax:* 386-254-4489. *E-mail:* admissions@dbcc.edu.

EDISON COLLEGE
Fort Myers, Florida

- **State and locally supported** 2-year, founded 1962, part of Florida Community College System
- **Calendar** semesters
- **Degree** certificates and associate
- **Urban** 80-acre campus
- **Coed**

Student Life *Campus security:* 24-hour emergency response devices and patrols, student patrols, late-night transport/escort service.

Standardized Tests *Required:* SAT I, ACT, or CPT (for placement).

Applying *Options:* early admission, deferred entrance. *Application fee:* $20. *Required:* high school transcript.

Admissions Contact Ms. Pat Armstrong, Admissions Specialist, Edison College, PO Box 60210, Fort Myers, FL 33906-6210. *Phone:* 941-489-9121. *Toll-free phone:* 800-749-2ECC. *Fax:* 941-489-9094.

FLORIDA CAREER COLLEGE
Miami, Florida

- **Proprietary** 2-year, founded 1982
- **Calendar** quarters
- **Degree** certificates, diplomas, and associate
- **Urban** campus
- **Coed**

Faculty *Student/faculty ratio:* 15:1.

Student Life *Campus security:* 24-hour emergency response devices.

Costs (2004–05) *Tuition:* $11,160 full-time, $310 per credit part-time. Full-time tuition and fees vary according to course load. Part-time tuition and fees vary according to course load. No tuition increase for student's term of enrollment. *Required fees:* $200 full-time, $100 per term part-time. *Payment plans:* tuition prepayment, installment.

Applying *Options:* common application, deferred entrance. *Application fee:* $100. *Required:* high school transcript, interview.

Admissions Contact Mr. David Knobel, President, Florida Career College, 1321 Southwest 107 Avenue, Miami, FL 33174. *Phone:* 305-553-6065. *Fax:* 305-225-0128.

FLORIDA COLLEGE OF NATURAL HEALTH
Bradenton, Florida

Admissions Contact Ms. Karen Curry, Director, Florida College of Natural Health, 616 67th Street Circle East, Bradenton, FL 34208. *Phone:* 941-954-8999. *Toll-free phone:* 800-966-7117.

FLORIDA COLLEGE OF NATURAL HEALTH
Maitland, Florida

Admissions Contact Mr. Steve Richards, Campus Director, Florida College of Natural Health, 2600 Lake Lucien Drive, Suite 140, Maitland, FL 32751. *Phone:* 407-261-0319. *Toll-free phone:* 800-393-7337.

FLORIDA COLLEGE OF NATURAL HEALTH
Miami, Florida

Admissions Contact Ms. Lissette Vidal, Admissions Coordinator, Florida College of Natural Health, 7925 Northwest 12th Street, Suite 201, Miami, FL 33126. *Phone:* 305-597-9599. *Toll-free phone:* 800-599-9599.

FLORIDA COLLEGE OF NATURAL HEALTH
Pompano Beach, Florida

Admissions Contact Mr. Darren Teigue, Campus Director, Florida College of Natural Health, 2001 West Sample Road, Suite 100, Pompano Beach, FL 33064. *Phone:* 954-975-6400. *Toll-free phone:* 800-541-9299.

FLORIDA COMMUNITY COLLEGE AT JACKSONVILLE
Jacksonville, Florida

- **State-supported** 2-year, founded 1963, part of Florida Community College System
- **Calendar** semesters
- **Degree** certificates, diplomas, and associate
- **Urban** 656-acre campus
- **Endowment** $3.9 million
- **Coed,** 23,425 undergraduate students, 30% full-time, 59% women, 41% men

Undergraduates 7,120 full-time, 16,305 part-time. Students come from 19 states and territories, 108 other countries, 23% are from out of state, 25% transferred in.

Freshmen *Admission:* 2,658 applied, 2,658 admitted, 2,658 enrolled. *Test scores:* SAT verbal scores over 500: 52%; SAT math scores over 500: 46%; ACT scores over 18: 92%; SAT verbal scores over 600: 9%; SAT math scores over 600: 6%; ACT scores over 24: 26%; SAT verbal scores over 700: 1%; ACT scores over 30: 3%.

Faculty *Total:* 1,134, 32% full-time, 10% with terminal degrees. *Student/faculty ratio:* 21:1.

Majors Accounting; administrative assistant and secretarial science; aircraft powerplant technology; airframe mechanics and aircraft maintenance technology; airline pilot and flight crew; architectural drafting and CAD/CADD; architectural engineering technology; autobody/collision and repair technology; automobile/automotive mechanics technology; aviation/airway management; banking and financial support services; biomedical technology; business administration and management; child care and support services management; child care provision; civil engineering technology; commercial and advertising art; computer and information sciences; computer and information sciences related; computer and information systems security; computer engineering technology; computer graphics; computer hardware engineering; computer/information technology services administration related; computer programming; computer programming related; computer programming (specific applications); computer programming (vendor/product certification); computer software and media applications related; computer software engineering; computer systems analysis; computer systems networking and telecommunications; computer/technical support; construction engineering technology; criminal justice/law enforcement administration; criminal justice/police science; culinary arts; data entry/microcomputer applications; data entry/microcomputer applications related; data modeling/warehousing and database administration; dental hygiene; design and visual communications; diagnostic medical sonography and ultrasound technology; dietetics; dietitian assistant; drafting and design technology; electrical, electronic and communications engineering technology; emergency medical technology (EMT paramedic); engineering technology; fashion merchandising; fire protection and safety technology; fire science; foodservice systems administration; health information/medical records administration; hospitality administration; hospitality and recreation marketing; hotel/motel administration; human services; information science/studies; information technology; instrumentation technology; insurance; interior design; legal assistant/paralegal; liberal arts and sciences/liberal studies; machine shop technology; marketing/marketing management; masonry; medical laboratory technology; medical office management; medical radiologic technology; nuclear/nuclear power technology; nursing (registered nurse training); office management; office occupations and clerical services; physical therapist assistant; printmaking; real estate; respiratory care therapy; retailing; sign language interpretation and translation; substance abuse/addiction counseling; system administration; theatre design and technology; tourism and travel services marketing; visual and performing arts related; water quality and wastewater treatment management and recycling technology; web/multimedia management and webmaster; web page, digital/multimedia and information resources design; word processing.

Academic Programs *Special study options:* academic remediation for entering students, accelerated degree program, adult/continuing education programs, advanced placement credit, cooperative education, distance learning, double majors, English as a second language, honors programs, independent study, internships, off-campus study, part-time degree program, services for LD students, study abroad, summer session for credit. *ROTC:* Navy (c).

Library Main Library plus 6 others with 412,856 titles, 4,137 serial subscriptions, 15,286 audiovisual materials, an OPAC, a Web page.

Computers on Campus 2500 computers available on campus for general student use. A campuswide network can be accessed from off campus. Internet access, online (class) registration, at least one staffed computer lab available.

Student Life *Housing:* college housing not available. *Activities and Organizations:* drama/theater group, student-run newspaper, radio and television station, choral group, Phi Theta Kappa, Troupe de Kent, Forensic Team, Brain Bowl Team, International Student Association. *Campus security:* 24-hour emergency response devices and patrols, student patrols, late-night transport/escort service. *Student services:* personal/psychological counseling, women's center.

Athletics Member NJCAA. *Intercollegiate sports:* baseball M(s), basketball M(s)/W(s), softball W(s), tennis W(s), volleyball W(s). *Intramural sports:* badminton M/W, basketball M/W, bowling M/W, football M/W, golf M/W, soccer M/W, softball M/W, table tennis M/W, tennis M/W, volleyball M/W.

Standardized Tests *Required:* (for placement).

Costs (2004–05) *Tuition:* state resident $1808 full-time, $60 per credit part-time; nonresident $6800 full-time, $227 per credit part-time.

Applying *Options:* common application, early admission, deferred entrance. *Application fee:* $15. *Required:* high school transcript. *Application deadline:* rolling (freshmen), rolling (transfers).

Admissions Contact Mr. Peter J. Biegel, District Director of Enrollment Services and Registrar, Florida Community College at Jacksonville, 501 West State Street, Jacksonville, FL 32202. *Phone:* 904-632-3131. *Fax:* 904-632-5105. *E-mail:* admissions@fccj.edu.

FLORIDA CULINARY INSTITUTE
West Palm Beach, Florida

- **Proprietary** 2-year
- **Degrees** associate (degree in science only (18 or 24 month program))
- 600 undergraduate students, 100% full-time

Financial Aid Of all full-time matriculated undergraduates who enrolled in 2003, 28 Federal Work-Study jobs (averaging $4160).

Admissions Contact Mr. David Conway, Associate Director of Admissions, Florida Culinary Institute, 2400 Metrocentre Boulevard, West Palm Beach, FL 33407. *Phone:* 561-842-8324 Ext. 202. *Toll-free phone:* 800-826-9986. *E-mail:* info@floridaculinary.com.

FLORIDA HOSPITAL COLLEGE OF HEALTH SCIENCES
Orlando, Florida

- **Independent** primarily 2-year
- **Calendar** semesters
- **Degrees** certificates, associate, and bachelor's
- **Urban** 9-acre campus
- **Endowment** $1.0 million
- **Coed,** 1,403 undergraduate students, 43% full-time, 75% women, 25% men

Undergraduates 609 full-time, 794 part-time. Students come from 8 states and territories, 23 other countries, 14% African American, 9% Asian American or Pacific Islander, 15% Hispanic American, 0.7% Native American, 8% live on campus.

Freshmen *Admission:* 463 applied, 446 admitted, 138 enrolled. *Average high school GPA:* 2.60. *Test scores:* ACT scores over 18: 68%; ACT scores over 24: 12%.

Faculty *Total:* 84, 52% full-time, 33% with terminal degrees.

Majors Diagnostic medical sonography and ultrasound technology; general studies; nuclear medical technology; nursing (registered nurse training); occupational therapist assistant; radiologic technology/science.

Academic Programs *Special study options:* academic remediation for entering students, advanced placement credit, distance learning, independent study, services for LD students. *ROTC:* Air Force (c).

Library Robert Arthur Williams Library with 74,581 titles, 158 serial subscriptions, 1,627 audiovisual materials, an OPAC.

Computers on Campus 45 computers available on campus for general student use. A campuswide network can be accessed. Internet access, online (class) registration, at least one staffed computer lab available. Computer purchase or lease plan available.

Student Life *Housing Options:* coed. Campus housing is leased by the school. *Activities and Organizations:* drama/theater group, student-run newspaper. *Campus security:* 24-hour emergency response devices and patrols, late-night transport/escort service, controlled dormitory access. *Student services:* personal/psychological counseling.

Standardized Tests *Required for some:* SAT or ACT (for admission).

Costs (2004–05) *Tuition:* $6600 full-time, $220 per credit part-time. *Required fees:* $250 full-time, $125 per term part-time. *Room only:* $1680. Room and board charges vary according to housing facility. *Payment plan:* installment. *Waivers:* employees or children of employees.

Financial Aid *Financial aid deadline:* 7/18.

Applying *Options:* common application, electronic application. *Application fee:* $20. *Required:* minimum 2.7 GPA. *Required for some:* essay or personal statement, high school transcript, 3 letters of recommendation. *Application deadlines:* 7/18 (freshmen), 7/18 (out-of-state freshmen), 7/18 (transfers). *Notification:* continuous until 8/30 (freshmen), continuous until 8/30 (out-of-state freshmen).

Admissions Contact Ms. Fiona Ghosn, Director of Admissions, Florida Hospital College of Health Sciences, 800 Lake Estelle Drive, Orlando, FL 32803. *Phone:* 407-303-9798 Ext. 9624. *Toll-free phone:* 800-500-7747. *Fax:* 407-303-9408. *E-mail:* fiona.ghosn@fhchs.edu.

FLORIDA KEYS COMMUNITY COLLEGE
Key West, Florida

- **State-supported** 2-year, founded 1965, part of Florida Community College System
- **Calendar** trimesters
- **Degree** certificates and associate
- **Small-town** 20-acre campus
- **Endowment** $658,235
- **Coed,** 1,551 undergraduate students

Undergraduates 1% are from out of state.

Freshmen *Admission:* 717 applied, 555 admitted.

Faculty *Total:* 138, 24% full-time, 17% with terminal degrees. *Student/faculty ratio:* 11:1.

Majors Business administration and management; commercial and advertising art; computer programming; liberal arts and sciences/liberal studies; marine biology and biological oceanography; marine technology; nursing (registered nurse training); parks, recreation and leisure.

Academic Programs *Special study options:* academic remediation for entering students, adult/continuing education programs, advanced placement credit, cooperative education, distance learning, double majors, English as a second language, independent study, internships, part-time degree program, services for LD students, student-designed majors, summer session for credit.

Library Florida Keys Community College Library with 29,402 titles, 330 serial subscriptions, 1,001 audiovisual materials, an OPAC.

Computers on Campus Internet access available.

Student Life *Housing:* college housing not available. *Activities and Organizations:* choral group, Florida Student Nursing Association, Nurses Pinning Club, Phi Theta Kappa, Keys Chorale, Ceramics Club. *Campus security:* 24-hour patrols. *Student services:* personal/psychological counseling.

Standardized Tests *Required for some:* SAT or ACT (for placement).

Costs (2004–05) *Tuition:* state resident $1412 full-time, $59 per credit hour part-time; nonresident $5289 full-time, $220 per credit hour part-time. *Required fees:* $141 full-time.

Financial Aid Of all full-time matriculated undergraduates who enrolled in 2003, 30 Federal Work-Study jobs (averaging $2000).

Applying *Options:* early admission, deferred entrance. *Application fee:* $20. *Required for some:* high school transcript. *Application deadline:* rolling (freshmen), rolling (transfers). *Notification:* continuous (freshmen).

Florida Keys Community College (continued)

Admissions Contact Ms. Cheryl A. Malsheimer, Director of Admissions and Records, Florida Keys Community College, 5901 College Road, Key West, FL 33040. *Phone:* 305-296-9081 Ext. 201. *Fax:* 305-292-5163. *E-mail:* dubois_d@firn.edu.

FLORIDA METROPOLITAN UNIVERSITY-ORANGE PARK CAMPUS
Orange Park, Florida

Admissions Contact 805 Wells Road, Orange Park, FL 32073.

FLORIDA NATIONAL COLLEGE
Hialeah, Florida

- **Proprietary** 2-year, founded 1982
- **Calendar** semesters
- **Degree** certificates, diplomas, and associate
- **Urban** campus with easy access to Miami
- **Coed,** 1,977 undergraduate students, 91% full-time, 65% women, 35% men

Undergraduates 1,792 full-time, 185 part-time. Students come from 1 other state, 6% African American, 0.9% Asian American or Pacific Islander, 88% Hispanic American, 0.4% Native American, 3% international.
Freshmen *Admission:* 678 applied, 523 admitted, 523 enrolled.
Faculty *Total:* 45, 51% full-time, 38% with terminal degrees. *Student/faculty ratio:* 18:1.
Majors Accounting; administrative assistant and secretarial science; allied health and medical assisting services related; business administration and management; computer and information systems security; computer graphics; computer programming; computer programming related; computer programming (specific applications); computer science; computer systems networking and telecommunications; computer/technical support; data entry/microcomputer applications; data entry/microcomputer applications related; data processing and data processing technology; dental hygiene; diagnostic medical sonography and ultrasound technology; education; health services/allied health/health sciences; hospitality administration; legal administrative assistant/secretary; legal assistant/paralegal; legal professions and studies related; legal studies; liberal arts and sciences/liberal studies; medical administrative assistant and medical secretary; medical/clinical assistant; radiologic technology/science; system administration; technical and business writing; tourism and travel services management; tourism promotion; web page, digital/multimedia and information resources design; word processing.
Academic Programs *Special study options:* academic remediation for entering students, adult/continuing education programs, cooperative education, English as a second language, services for LD students, student-designed majors, summer session for credit.
Library Hialeah Campus Library with 23,507 titles, 87 serial subscriptions, 3,337 audiovisual materials, an OPAC, a Web page.
Computers on Campus 152 computers available on campus for general student use. A campuswide network can be accessed from off campus. Internet access available.
Student Life *Housing:* college housing not available. *Activities and Organizations:* Student Government Association. *Campus security:* 24-hour emergency response devices.
Standardized Tests *Required:* TABE (for placement).
Costs (2004–05) *Tuition:* $9600 full-time, $290 per credit part-time. Full-time tuition and fees vary according to program. Part-time tuition and fees vary according to program. No tuition increase for student's term of enrollment. *Required fees:* $420 full-time. *Payment plans:* tuition prepayment, deferred payment. *Waivers:* employees or children of employees.
Financial Aid Of all full-time matriculated undergraduates who enrolled in 2003, 20 Federal Work-Study jobs (averaging $8050).
Applying *Options:* common application, deferred entrance. *Required:* high school transcript. *Application deadline:* rolling (freshmen), rolling (transfers). *Notification:* continuous (freshmen).
Admissions Contact Ms. Maria C. Reguerio, Vice President, Florida National College, 4425 West 20 Avenue, Hialeah, FL 33012. *Phone:* 305-821-3333 Ext. 1002. *Fax:* 305-362-0595. *E-mail:* admissions@fnc.edu.

THE FLORIDA SCHOOL OF MIDWIFERY
Gainseville, Florida

- **Independent** 2-year, founded 1993
- **Calendar** quarters
- **Degree** associate
- **Women only**

Faculty *Student/faculty ratio:* 10:1.
Admissions Contact Ms. Gloria Huffman, Director of Finance, The Florida School of Midwifery, PO Box 5505, Gainseville, FL 32627-5505. *Phone:* 352-338-0766.

FLORIDA TECHNICAL COLLEGE
Auburndale, Florida

Admissions Contact Mr. Charles Owens, Admissions Office, Florida Technical College, 298 Havendale Boulevard, Auburndale, FL 33823. *Phone:* 863-967-8822.

FLORIDA TECHNICAL COLLEGE
DeLand, Florida

Admissions Contact Mr. Bill Atkinson, Director, Florida Technical College, 1450 South Woodland Boulevard, 3rd Floor, DeLand, FL 32720. *Phone:* 386-734-3303.

FLORIDA TECHNICAL COLLEGE
Jacksonville, Florida

Admissions Contact Mr. Bryan Gulebiam, Director of Admissions, Florida Technical College, 8711 Lone Star Road, Jacksonville, FL 32211. *Phone:* 407-678-5600.

FLORIDA TECHNICAL COLLEGE
Orlando, Florida

Admissions Contact Ms. Jeanette E. Muschlitz, Director of Admissions, Florida Technical College, 1819 North Semoran Boulevard, Orlando, FL 32807-3546. *Phone:* 407-678-5600. *Fax:* 407-678-1149.

FULL SAIL REAL WORLD EDUCATION
Winter Park, Florida

- **Proprietary** primarily 2-year, founded 1979
- **Calendar** modular
- **Degrees** associate and bachelor's
- **Suburban** campus with easy access to Orlando
- **Coed, primarily men,** 4,227 undergraduate students, 100% full-time, 10% women, 90% men

Undergraduates 4,227 full-time. Students come from 44 states and territories, 9 other countries, 11% African American, 3% Asian American or Pacific Islander, 11% Hispanic American, 0.5% Native American, 2% international.
Freshmen *Admission:* 2,954 applied, 2,025 admitted.
Faculty *Total:* 448, 93% full-time. *Student/faculty ratio:* 6:1.
Majors Audio engineering; cinematography and film/video production; commercial and advertising art; computer graphics; intermedia/multimedia; music management and merchandising.
Academic Programs *Special study options:* academic remediation for entering students, cooperative education, internships, services for LD students, summer session for credit.
Library Full Sail Library with 1,621 titles, 79 serial subscriptions, 628 audiovisual materials, an OPAC.
Computers on Campus 33 computers available on campus for general student use. A campuswide network can be accessed from off campus. Internet access, at least one staffed computer lab available.
Student Life *Housing:* college housing not available. *Options:* Campus housing is provided by a third party. *Activities and Organizations:* Student Chapter of Audio Engineering Society. *Campus security:* 24-hour patrols. *Student services:* personal/psychological counseling.
Costs (2004–05) *Tuition:* Tuition costs ranges from $40,005 to $69,460. Contact school for details.
Financial Aid Of all full-time matriculated undergraduates who enrolled in 2003, 212 Federal Work-Study jobs (averaging $561).
Applying *Options:* common application, electronic application. *Application fee:* $150. *Required:* high school transcript. *Required for some:* minimum "A" average in Algebra II. *Application deadline:* rolling (freshmen).
Admissions Contact Ms. Mary Beth Plank, Director of Admissions, Full Sail Real World Education, 3300 University Boulevard, Winter Park, FL 32792. *Phone:* 407-679-6333 Ext. 2122. *Toll-free phone:* 800-226-7625. *E-mail:* admissions@fullsail.com.

GULF COAST COLLEGE
Tampa, Florida

Admissions Contact Mr. Todd A. Matthews Sr., Regional Vice President, Gulf Coast College, 3910 US Hwy 301 North, Suite 200, Tampa, FL 33619. *Phone:* 813-620-1446. *Toll-free phone:* 888-729-7247. *E-mail:* admissions@websterinstitute.com.

GULF COAST COMMUNITY COLLEGE
Panama City, Florida

- **State-supported** 2-year, founded 1957
- **Calendar** semesters
- **Degree** certificates and associate
- **Suburban** 80-acre campus
- **Endowment** $13.9 million
- **Coed,** 6,058 undergraduate students, 37% full-time, 60% women, 40% men

Undergraduates 2,248 full-time, 3,810 part-time. Students come from 28 states and territories, 8 other countries, 12% African American, 2% Asian American or Pacific Islander, 3% Hispanic American, 0.7% Native American, 0.7% international.

Freshmen *Admission:* 553 enrolled.

Faculty *Total:* 494, 25% full-time. *Student/faculty ratio:* 14:1.

Majors Accounting; administrative assistant and secretarial science; anthropology; art; biology/biological sciences; business administration and management; child care provision; child guidance; civil engineering technology; computer engineering technology; computer programming; computer programming (specific applications); construction engineering technology; criminal justice/law enforcement administration; culinary arts; dental hygiene; drafting and design technology; economics; electrical, electronic and communications engineering technology; electromechanical and instrumentation and maintenance technologies related; elementary education; emergency medical technology (EMT paramedic); engineering technology; English; fire science; foreign languages and literatures; history; hospitality administration; human services; industrial radiologic technology; legal assistant/paralegal; liberal arts and sciences/liberal studies; mathematics; music; nursing (registered nurse training); physical therapist assistant; political science and government; pre-law studies; psychology; radio and television; respiratory care therapy; secondary education; sociology; theatre/theatre arts management.

Academic Programs *Special study options:* academic remediation for entering students, accelerated degree program, adult/continuing education programs, advanced placement credit, cooperative education, distance learning, double majors, English as a second language, external degree program, honors programs, independent study, off-campus study, part-time degree program, services for LD students, summer session for credit.

Library Gulf Coast Community College Library with 80,000 titles, 521 serial subscriptions, 32,041 audiovisual materials, an OPAC, a Web page.

Computers on Campus 850 computers available on campus for general student use. A campuswide network can be accessed from off campus. Internet access, at least one staffed computer lab available.

Student Life *Housing:* college housing not available. *Activities and Organizations:* drama/theater group, student-run newspaper, radio station, choral group, Student Activities Board, Baptist Campus Ministry, Theater Club, Phi Theta Kappa, Muslim Student Association. *Campus security:* patrols by trained security personnel during campus hours. *Student services:* personal/psychological counseling.

Athletics Member NJCAA. *Intercollegiate sports:* baseball M(s), basketball M(s)/W(s), cheerleading M(s)/W(s), softball W(s), volleyball W(s). *Intramural sports:* basketball M/W, volleyball M/W.

Standardized Tests *Required:* CPT (for placement). *Recommended:* SAT and SAT Subject Tests or ACT (for placement).

Costs (2005–06) *Tuition:* state resident $1446 full-time, $48 per credit part-time; nonresident $6232 full-time, $208 per credit part-time. Full-time tuition and fees vary according to course load. Part-time tuition and fees vary according to course load. *Required fees:* $309 full-time, $10 per credit part-time.

Financial Aid Of all full-time matriculated undergraduates who enrolled in 2003, 145 Federal Work-Study jobs (averaging $3200). 60 state and other part-time jobs (averaging $2600).

Applying *Options:* electronic application, early admission, deferred entrance. *Required:* high school transcript. *Application deadline:* rolling (freshmen), rolling (transfers). *Notification:* continuous (freshmen).

Admissions Contact Mrs. Jackie Kuczenski, Administrative Secretary of Admissions, Gulf Coast Community College, 5230 West Highway 98, Panama City, FL 32401. *Phone:* 850-769-1551 Ext. 4892. *Toll-free phone:* 800-311-3628. *Fax:* 850-913-3308.

HERZING COLLEGE
Winter Park, Florida

Admissions Contact Ms. Karen Mohamad, Director of Admissions, Herzing College, 1595 South Semoran Boulevard, Suite 1501, Winter Park, FL 32792-5509. *Phone:* 407-478-0500.

HILLSBOROUGH COMMUNITY COLLEGE
Tampa, Florida

- **State-supported** 2-year, founded 1968, part of Florida Community College System
- **Calendar** semesters
- **Degree** certificates and associate
- **Urban** campus
- **Endowment** $1.6 million
- **Coed,** 22,149 undergraduate students, 32% full-time, 59% women, 41% men

Undergraduates 7,009 full-time, 15,140 part-time. Students come from 40 states and territories, 100 other countries, 4% are from out of state, 19% African American, 4% Asian American or Pacific Islander, 19% Hispanic American, 0.4% Native American, 0.8% international, 19% transferred in. *Retention:* 57% of 2002 full-time freshmen returned.

Freshmen *Admission:* 4,223 applied, 4,223 admitted, 3,791 enrolled.

Faculty *Total:* 774, 30% full-time, 10% with terminal degrees. *Student/faculty ratio:* 28:1.

Majors Accounting; administrative assistant and secretarial science; agricultural production; aquaculture; architectural engineering technology; art; biomedical technology; business administration and management; business operations support and secretarial services related; child development; commercial and advertising art; computer engineering technology; computer programming; computer systems networking and telecommunications; construction engineering technology; corrections; criminal justice/law enforcement administration; criminal justice/police science; culinary arts; culinary arts related; dance; dental hygiene; diagnostic medical sonography and ultrasound technology; digital communication and media/multimedia; dramatic/theatre arts; education; electrical, electronic and communications engineering technology; elementary education; emergency medical technology (EMT paramedic); engineering; environmental studies; finance; fire science; hospitality administration; hotel/motel administration; human services; industrial radiologic technology; information science/studies; interior design; intermedia/multimedia; legal administrative assistant/secretary; legal studies; liberal arts and sciences/liberal studies; marketing/marketing management; mass communication/media; medical administrative assistant and medical secretary; music; nuclear medical technology; nursing (registered nurse training); occupational therapy; office occupations and clerical services; ophthalmic laboratory technology; ornamental horticulture; pharmacy technician; physical education teaching and coaching; physical therapy; radio and television; radio and television broadcasting technology; radiologic technology/science; radio, television, and digital communication related; respiratory care therapy; restaurant, culinary, and catering management; sign language interpretation and translation.

Academic Programs *Special study options:* academic remediation for entering students, adult/continuing education programs, advanced placement credit, cooperative education, distance learning, English as a second language, honors programs, off-campus study, part-time degree program, services for LD students, summer session for credit. *ROTC:* Army (c), Air Force (c).

Library Main Library plus 4 others with 170,615 titles, 1,283 serial subscriptions, 50,000 audiovisual materials, an OPAC, a Web page.

Computers on Campus 600 computers available on campus for general student use. Internet access, online (class) registration, at least one staffed computer lab available.

Student Life *Housing:* college housing not available. *Activities and Organizations:* drama/theater group, student-run newspaper, radio station, Student Government Association, Student Nursing Association, Phi Theta Kappa, Disabled Students Association, Radiography Club, national fraternities. *Campus security:* 24-hour emergency response devices and patrols. *Student services:* personal/psychological counseling.

Athletics Member NJCAA. *Intercollegiate sports:* baseball M(s), basketball M(s)/W(s), softball W(s), tennis W(s), volleyball W(s).

Standardized Tests *Required for some:* CPT.

Costs (2004–05) *Tuition:* state resident $1833 full-time, $61 per credit hour part-time; nonresident $6835 full-time, $228 per credit hour part-time.

Applying *Options:* common application, early admission. *Application fee:* $20. *Required:* high school transcript. *Application deadline:* rolling (freshmen), rolling (transfers).

Admissions Contact Ms. Kathy G. Cecil, Admissions, Registration, and Records Officer, Hillsborough Community College, PO Box 31127, Tampa, FL 33631-3127. *Phone:* 813-253-7027.

INDIAN RIVER COMMUNITY COLLEGE
Fort Pierce, Florida

- **State-supported** 2-year, founded 1960, part of Florida Community College System
- **Calendar** semesters
- **Degree** certificates, diplomas, and associate
- **Small-town** 133-acre campus
- **Coed,** 38,464 undergraduate students

Undergraduates Students come from 33 states and territories, 2% are from out of state, 17% African American, 1% Asian American or Pacific Islander, 12% Hispanic American, 0.4% Native American.

Freshmen *Test scores:* SAT verbal scores over 500: 47%; SAT math scores over 500: 43%; SAT math scores over 600: 5%; SAT math scores over 700: 5%.

Faculty *Total:* 1,562, 10% full-time.

Majors Accounting; administrative assistant and secretarial science; agricultural business and management; airline pilot and flight crew; anthropology; architectural drafting and CAD/CADD; art teacher education; automobile/automotive mechanics technology; banking and financial support services; biology/biological sciences; business administration and management; carpentry; chemistry; child development; civil engineering technology; clinical/medical laboratory technology; clothing/textiles; computer engineering technology; computer programming; computer science; computer typography and composition equipment operation; consumer merchandising/retailing management; corrections; cosmetology; criminal justice/law enforcement administration; criminal justice/police science; culinary arts; dental hygiene; drafting and design technology; dramatic/theatre arts; economics; education; electrical, electronic and communications engineering technology; emergency medical technology (EMT paramedic); engineering; engineering technology; English; family and consumer sciences/human sciences; fashion merchandising; finance; fire science; food/nutrition; forestry; French; health information/medical records administration; heating, air conditioning, ventilation and refrigeration maintenance technology; history; hotel/motel administration; humanities; human services; hydrology and water resources science; industrial radiologic technology; information science/studies; interior design; journalism; kindergarten/preschool education; language interpretation and translation; legal assistant/paralegal; liberal arts and sciences/liberal studies; library science; marine science/merchant marine officer; marketing/marketing management; mathematics; medical administrative assistant and medical secretary; music; nursing (licensed practical/vocational nurse training); nursing (registered nurse training); pharmacy; philosophy; physical education teaching and coaching; physical therapist assistant; physical therapy; physics; political science and government; pre-engineering; psychology; respiratory care therapy; social sciences; social work; sociology; Spanish; special products marketing; speech and rhetoric; survey technology; teacher assistant/aide.

Academic Programs *Special study options:* academic remediation for entering students, adult/continuing education programs, advanced placement credit, distance learning, English as a second language, independent study, part-time degree program, services for LD students, summer session for credit.

Library Charles S. Miley Learning Resource Center with 58,657 titles, 554 serial subscriptions, an OPAC.

Computers on Campus 500 computers available on campus for general student use. A campuswide network can be accessed. Internet access, at least one staffed computer lab available.

Student Life *Housing:* college housing not available. *Activities and Organizations:* drama/theater group, choral group, Phi Beta Lambda, Distributive Education Club of America, International Club, Cultural Exchange, Human Services Club. *Campus security:* 24-hour patrols. *Student services:* health clinic, personal/psychological counseling, women's center.

Athletics Member NJCAA. *Intercollegiate sports:* baseball M(s), basketball M(s)/W(s), softball W(s), swimming and diving M(s)/W(s), volleyball W(s). *Intramural sports:* basketball M/W, racquetball M/W, soccer M, volleyball M/W.

Standardized Tests *Required:* SAT I, ACT, or CPT (for placement).

Costs (2004–05) *Tuition:* state resident $1740 full-time, $58 per credit part-time; nonresident $6570 full-time, $219 per credit part-time.

Financial Aid Of all full-time matriculated undergraduates who enrolled in 2003, 130 Federal Work-Study jobs (averaging $1500).

Applying *Options:* early admission, deferred entrance. *Required:* high school transcript. *Application deadline:* rolling (freshmen), rolling (transfers). *Notification:* continuous (freshmen).

Admissions Contact Mrs. Linda Hays, Dean of Educational Services, Indian River Community College, 3209 Virginia Avenue, Fort Pierce, FL 34981-5596. *Phone:* 772-462-4740.

ITT TECHNICAL INSTITUTE
Fort Lauderdale, Florida

- **Proprietary** primarily 2-year, founded 1991, part of ITT Educational Services, Inc

- **Calendar** quarters
- **Degrees** associate and bachelor's
- **Suburban** campus with easy access to Miami
- **Coed**

Standardized Tests *Required:* Wonderlic aptitude test (for admission).

Costs (2004–05) *Tuition:* Please see school catalog for specific information.

Applying *Options:* deferred entrance. *Application fee:* $100. *Required:* high school transcript, interview. *Recommended:* letters of recommendation.

Admissions Contact Mr. Bob Bixler, Director of Recruitment, ITT Technical Institute, 3401 South University Drive, Fort Lauderdale, FL 33328. *Phone:* 954-476-9300. *Toll-free phone:* 800-488-7797. *Fax:* 954-476-6889.

ITT TECHNICAL INSTITUTE
Jacksonville, Florida

- **Proprietary** primarily 2-year, founded 1991, part of ITT Educational Services, Inc
- **Calendar** quarters
- **Degrees** associate and bachelor's
- **Urban** 1-acre campus
- **Coed**

Standardized Tests *Required:* Wonderlic aptitude test (for admission).

Costs (2004–05) *Tuition:* Please see school catalog for specific information.

Financial Aid Of all full-time matriculated undergraduates who enrolled in 2003, 5 Federal Work-Study jobs.

Applying *Options:* deferred entrance. *Application fee:* $100. *Required:* high school transcript, interview. *Recommended:* letters of recommendation.

Admissions Contact Mr. Jorge Torres, Director of Recruitment, ITT Technical Institute, 6600-10 Youngerman Circle, Jacksonville, FL 32244. *Phone:* 904-573-9100. *Toll-free phone:* 800-318-1264. *Fax:* 904-573-0512.

ITT TECHNICAL INSTITUTE
Lake Mary, Florida

Admissions Contact Mr. Larry Johnson, Director of Recruitment, ITT Technical Institute, 2600 Lake Lucien Drive, Suite 140, Maitland, FL 32751. *Phone:* 407-660-2900. *Fax:* 407-660-2566.

ITT TECHNICAL INSTITUTE
Miami, Florida

- **Proprietary** primarily 2-year, founded 1996, part of ITT Educational Services, Inc
- **Calendar** quarters
- **Degrees** associate and bachelor's
- **Coed**

Standardized Tests *Required:* Wonderlic aptitude test (for admission).

Costs (2004–05) *Tuition:* Please see school catalog for specific information.

Applying *Options:* deferred entrance. *Application fee:* $100. *Required:* high school transcript, interview. *Recommended:* letters of recommendation.

Admissions Contact Mrs. Rosa Sacarello Daratany, Director of Recruitment, ITT Technical Institute, 7955 NW 12th Street, Suite 119, Miami, FL 33126. *Phone:* 305-477-3080. *Fax:* 305-477-7561.

ITT TECHNICAL INSTITUTE
Tampa, Florida

- **Proprietary** primarily 2-year, founded 1981, part of ITT Educational Services, Inc
- **Calendar** quarters
- **Degrees** associate and bachelor's
- **Suburban** campus with easy access to St. Petersburg
- **Coed**

Standardized Tests *Required:* Wonderlic aptitude test (for admission).

Costs (2004–05) *Tuition:* Please see school catalog for specific information.

Applying *Options:* deferred entrance. *Application fee:* $100. *Required:* high school transcript, interview. *Recommended:* letters of recommendation.

Admissions Contact Mr. Joseph E. Rostkowski, Director of Recruitment, ITT Technical Institute, 4809 Memorial Highway, Tampa, FL 33634. *Phone:* 813-885-2244. *Toll-free phone:* 800-825-2831. *Fax:* 813-888-8451.

KEISER COLLEGE
Daytona Beach, Florida

Admissions Contact Mr. Jim Wallis, Director of Admissions, Keiser College, 1800 West International Speedway, Building 3, Daytona Beach, FL 32114. *Phone:* 904-255-1707. *Toll-free phone:* 800-749-4456. *Fax:* 904-239-0955.

KEISER COLLEGE
Fort Lauderdale, Florida

- **Proprietary** primarily 2-year, founded 1977
- **Calendar** 3 semesters per year
- **Degrees** diplomas, associate, and bachelor's (profile includes data from Daytona Beach, Melbourne, Sarasota, Tallahassee, and Lakeland campuses)
- **Suburban** 4-acre campus with easy access to Miami
- **Coed,** 6,121 undergraduate students, 82% full-time, 71% women, 29% men

Undergraduates 5,043 full-time, 1,078 part-time. Students come from 25 other countries, 26% African American, 1% Asian American or Pacific Islander, 17% Hispanic American, 0.5% Native American, 1% international.
Freshmen *Admission:* 2,658 enrolled.
Faculty *Total:* 495, 36% full-time.
Majors Accounting; business administration and management; clinical/medical laboratory technology; computer engineering technology; computer graphics; computer programming; corrections and criminal justice related; culinary arts; emergency medical technology (EMT paramedic); engineering technology; fire science; health/health care administration; hospitality administration; industrial radiologic technology; legal assistant/paralegal; management information systems; medical/clinical assistant; medical radiologic technology; nursing related; occupational therapy; physical therapist assistant; public administration; system administration.
Academic Programs *Special study options:* adult/continuing education programs, distance learning, independent study, internships.
Library Jim Bishop Memorial Library with an OPAC, a Web page.
Computers on Campus A campuswide network can be accessed. Internet access, at least one staffed computer lab available.
Student Life *Housing:* college housing not available. *Campus security:* security guard after 8 p.m.
Standardized Tests *Required:* SAT I, ACT, or Otis-Lennon School Ability Test (for admission).
Costs (2005–06) *Tuition:* Tuition varies by program. Contact institution.
Applying *Options:* deferred entrance. *Application fee:* $55. *Required:* high school transcript, minimum 2.0 GPA, interview. *Application deadline:* rolling (freshmen), rolling (transfers). *Notification:* continuous (freshmen).
Admissions Contact Mr. Brian Woods, Vice President of Enrollment Management, Keiser College, 1500 NW 49th Street, Fort Lauderdale, FL 33309. *Phone:* 954-776-4476. *Toll-free phone:* 800-749-4456. *Fax:* 954-771-4894. *E-mail:* admissions-ftl@keisercollege.edu.

KEISER COLLEGE
Lakeland, Florida

Admissions Contact Mr. Walter Bequette, Director of Admissions, Keiser College, 3515 Aviation Drive, Lakeland, FL 33811. *Phone:* 863-701-7789.

KEISER COLLEGE
Melbourne, Florida

Admissions Contact Ms. Susan Zeigelhofer, Director of Admissions, Keiser College, 900 South Babcock Street, Melbourne, FL 32901-1461. *Phone:* 954-776-4456. *Toll-free phone:* 800-749-4456. *E-mail:* susanz@keisercollege.cc.fl.us.

KEISER COLLEGE
Miami, Florida

- **Proprietary** 2-year
- **Calendar** 3 semesters per year
- **Degree** associate
- **Coed,** 393 undergraduate students, 100% full-time, 71% women, 29% men

Undergraduates 393 full-time. Students come from 3 states and territories, 24% African American, 3% Asian American or Pacific Islander, 65% Hispanic American, 0.3% Native American, 0.5% international.
Faculty *Total:* 18, 28% full-time, 22% with terminal degrees. *Student/faculty ratio:* 18:1.
Majors Business administration and management; computer systems networking and telecommunications; criminal justice/law enforcement administration;

health and medical administrative services related; health services/allied health/health sciences; legal assistant/paralegal; medical office assistant; nursing (registered nurse training); radiologic technology/science.
Student Life *Housing:* college housing not available. *Activities and Organizations:* student-run newspaper, Student Ambassador Program. *Campus security:* 24-hour patrols.
Standardized Tests *Recommended:* SAT or ACT (for admission).
Costs (2004–05) *Tuition:* $10,608 full-time. *Required fees:* $400 full-time. *Payment plan:* installment.
Applying *Required:* high school transcript, interview.
Admissions Contact Mr. Ted Weiner, Director of Admissions, Keiser College, 8505 Mills Drive, Miami, FL 33183. *Phone:* 305-596-2226. *E-mail:* tedw@keisercollege.edu.

KEISER COLLEGE
Orlando, Florida

Admissions Contact 5600 Lake Underhill Road, Orlando, FL 32807.

KEISER COLLEGE
Pembroke Pines, Florida

- **Proprietary** primarily 2-year, founded 1998
- **Calendar** semesters
- **Degrees** diplomas, associate, and bachelor's
- **Coed**

Admissions Contact 12520 Pines Boulevard, Pembroke Pines, FL 33027. *Toll-free phone:* 954-431-4300. *Fax:* 954-431-2929. *E-mail:* admissions-pp@keisercollege.edu.

KEISER COLLEGE
Port St. Lucie, Florida

- **Proprietary** 2-year, founded 1999
- **Calendar** semesters
- **Degree** diplomas and associate
- **Coed**

Admissions Contact 9468 South US 1, Port St. Lucie, FL 34952. *Toll-free phone:* 772-398-9990. *Fax:* 772-335-9619. *E-mail:* admissions-psl@keisercollege.edu.

KEISER COLLEGE
Sarasota, Florida

Admissions Contact Mr. Roger Buck, Executive Director, Keiser College, 332 Sarasota Quay, Sarasota, FL 34236. *Phone:* 941-954-0954.

KEISER COLLEGE
Tallahassee, Florida

Admissions Contact Guy Peirce, Director of Admissions, Keiser College, 1700 Halstead Boulevard, Tallahassee, FL 32308. *Phone:* 850-906-9494. *Toll-free phone:* 800-749-4456. *Fax:* 850-906-9497.

KEISER COLLEGE
West Palm Beach, Florida

- **Proprietary** primarily 2-year, founded 1988
- **Calendar** semesters
- **Degrees** diplomas, associate, and bachelor's
- **Coed**

Admissions Contact 2085 Vista Parkway, West Palm Beach, FL 33411. *Toll-free phone:* 561-471-6000. *Fax:* 561-471-7899. *E-mail:* admissions-wpb@keisercollege.edu.

KEY COLLEGE
Fort Lauderdale, Florida

Admissions Contact Mr. Ronald H. Dooley, President and Director of Admissions, Key College, 5225 West Broward Boulevard, Ft. Lauderdale, FL 33317. *Phone:* 954-581-2223 Ext. 23. *Toll-free phone:* 800-581-8292. *Fax:* 954-583-9458. *E-mail:* rhd114@aol.com.

LAKE CITY COMMUNITY COLLEGE
Lake City, Florida

- **State-supported** 2-year, founded 1962, part of Florida Community College System
- **Calendar** semesters
- **Degree** certificates and associate
- **Small-town** 132-acre campus with easy access to Jacksonville
- **Endowment** $3.3 million
- **Coed**

Faculty *Student/faculty ratio:* 19:1.
Student Life *Campus security:* 24-hour patrols.
Athletics Member NJCAA.
Standardized Tests *Required:* SAT I, ACT, or CPT (for placement). *Recommended:* SAT or ACT (for placement).
Costs (2004–05) *Tuition:* $56 per semester hour part-time; state resident $65 per semester hour part-time; nonresident $211 per semester hour part-time. Full-time tuition and fees vary according to program. Part-time tuition and fees vary according to program. *Room and board:* Room and board charges vary according to board plan.
Financial Aid Of all full-time matriculated undergraduates who enrolled in 2003, 58 Federal Work-Study jobs (averaging $975).
Applying *Options:* early admission, deferred entrance. *Application fee:* $15. *Required for some:* high school transcript.
Admissions Contact Vince C. Rice, Director of Postsecondary Transition, Lake City Community College, Route 19, Box 1030, Lake City, FL 32025-8703. *Phone:* 386-754-4288. *Fax:* 386-755-1521. *E-mail:* admissions@mail.lakecity.cc.fl.us.

LAKE-SUMTER COMMUNITY COLLEGE
Leesburg, Florida

- **State and locally supported** 2-year, founded 1962, part of Florida Department of Education
- **Calendar** semesters
- **Degree** certificates, diplomas, and associate
- **Suburban** 110-acre campus with easy access to Orlando
- **Endowment** $2.8 million
- **Coed**, 3,576 undergraduate students, 33% full-time, 69% women, 31% men

Undergraduates 1,186 full-time, 2,390 part-time. Students come from 8 states and territories, 6 other countries, 1% are from out of state, 11% African American, 2% Asian American or Pacific Islander, 8% Hispanic American, 0.6% Native American, 0.6% international, 27% transferred in.
Freshmen *Admission:* 770 applied, 770 admitted, 691 enrolled. *Average high school GPA:* 3.07.
Faculty *Total:* 175, 29% full-time, 7% with terminal degrees. *Student/faculty ratio:* 20:1.
Majors Business administration and management; commercial and advertising art; computer and information sciences related; computer science; criminal justice/law enforcement administration; emergency medical technology (EMT paramedic); fire science; health information/medical records administration; legal assistant/paralegal; liberal arts and sciences/liberal studies; nursing (registered nurse training); office management; sport and fitness administration; theatre design and technology.
Academic Programs *Special study options:* academic remediation for entering students, adult/continuing education programs, advanced placement credit, cooperative education, distance learning, double majors, independent study, off-campus study, part-time degree program, services for LD students, summer session for credit.
Library Lake-Sumter Community College Library with 69,465 titles, 528 serial subscriptions, 1,262 audiovisual materials, an OPAC, a Web page.
Computers on Campus 537 computers available on campus for general student use. A campuswide network can be accessed from off campus. Internet access, online (class) registration, at least one staffed computer lab available.
Student Life *Housing:* college housing not available. *Activities and Organizations:* drama/theater group, student-run newspaper, television station, choral group, Phi Theta Kappa, Baptist Collegiate Ministry, Environmental Society, Nursing Students' Association. *Campus security:* 24-hour emergency response devices. *Student services:* women's center.
Athletics Member NJCAA. *Intercollegiate sports:* baseball M(s), softball W(s), volleyball W(s). *Intramural sports:* basketball M/W, softball W, volleyball W.
Standardized Tests *Required:* SAT Reasoning Test, ACT, or CPT (for placement).
Costs (2005–06) *Tuition:* state resident $1815 full-time, $61 per credit hour part-time; nonresident $6691 full-time, $223 per credit hour part-time. Full-time tuition and fees vary according to course load. Part-time tuition and fees vary according to course load. *Required fees:* $30 full-time, $1 per credit hour part-time. *Waivers:* employees or children of employees.

Applying *Application fee:* $25. *Required:* high school transcript. *Application deadline:* rolling (freshmen), rolling (transfers). *Notification:* continuous (freshmen).
Admissions Contact Ms. Amy Whitely, Enrollment Specialist, Lake-Sumter Community College, 9501 US Highway 441, Leesburg, FL 34788-8751. *Phone:* 352-365-3561. *Fax:* 352-365-3553. *E-mail:* admissinquiry@lscc.edu.

MANATEE COMMUNITY COLLEGE
Bradenton, Florida

- **State-supported** 2-year, founded 1957, part of Florida Community College System
- **Calendar** semesters
- **Degree** certificates and associate
- **Suburban** 100-acre campus with easy access to Tampa-St. Petersburg
- **Coed**

Faculty *Student/faculty ratio:* 23:1.
Student Life *Campus security:* 24-hour emergency response devices and patrols, late-night transport/escort service.
Athletics Member NJCAA.
Standardized Tests *Required:* SAT or ACT (for placement), Florida College Entry-Level Placement Test (for placement).
Costs (2004–05) *Tuition:* state resident $1833 full-time, $61 per credit part-time; nonresident $6852 full-time, $228 per credit part-time.
Financial Aid Of all full-time matriculated undergraduates who enrolled in 2003, 82 Federal Work-Study jobs (averaging $2800). *Financial aid deadline:* 8/15.
Applying *Options:* early admission. *Application fee:* $20. *Required:* high school transcript.
Admissions Contact Ms. MariLynn Paro, Registrar, Manatee Community College, PO Box 1849, Bradenton, FL 34206. *Phone:* 941-752-5031. *Fax:* 941-727-6380.

MEDVANCE INSTITUTE
Atlantis, Florida

Admissions Contact Ms. Brenda Cortez, Campus Director, MedVance Institute, 170 JFK Drive, Atlantis, FL 33462. *Phone:* 561-304-3466. *Toll-free phone:* 888-86-GO-MED.

MIAMI DADE COLLEGE
Miami, Florida

- **State and locally supported** primarily 2-year, founded 1960, part of Florida Community College System
- **Calendar** 16-16-6-6
- **Degrees** certificates, associate, and bachelor's
- **Urban** campus
- **Endowment** $109.2 million
- **Coed**, 57,026 undergraduate students, 35% full-time, 62% women, 38% men

Miami Dade College offers undergraduate study in more than 200 academic areas and professions. The College is internationally recognized as an educational leader in undergraduate programs that are innovative and diverse within a multicultural, multiethnic environment. Annually, more than 155,000 credit- and noncredit-seeking students are enrolled at 6 major campuses and numerous outreach centers.

Undergraduates 20,115 full-time, 36,911 part-time. Students come from 43 states and territories, 160 other countries, 1% are from out of state, 22% African American, 1% Asian American or Pacific Islander, 65% Hispanic American, 3% international, 2% transferred in.
Freshmen *Admission:* 15,045 applied, 15,045 admitted, 10,345 enrolled. *Test scores:* SAT verbal scores over 500: 20%; SAT math scores over 500: 17%; ACT scores over 18: 38%; SAT verbal scores over 600: 2%; SAT math scores over 600: 1%; ACT scores over 24: 2%.
Faculty *Total:* 2,098, 34% full-time, 16% with terminal degrees. *Student/faculty ratio:* 28:1.
Majors Accounting technology and bookkeeping; administrative assistant and secretarial science; aeronautics/aviation/aerospace science and technology; agriculture; airline pilot and flight crew; air traffic control; American studies; anthropology; architectural drafting and CAD/CADD; architectural engineering technology; art; art teacher education; Asian studies; aviation/airway management; behavioral sciences; biology/biological sciences; biology teacher education; biomedical technology; business administration and management; chemistry; chemistry teacher education; child development; cinematography and film/video production; civil engineering technology; clinical/medical laboratory technology; commercial and advertising art; computer engineering technology; computer graphics; computer programming; computer science; computer software

technology; computer technology/computer systems technology; construction engineering technology; court reporting; criminal justice/law enforcement administration; criminal justice/police science; dance; data processing and data processing technology; dental hygiene; diagnostic medical sonography and ultrasound technology; dietetics; dietetic technician; drafting and design technology; dramatic/theatre arts; economics; education; education (specific subject areas) related; electrical and electronic engineering technologies related; electrical, electronic and communications engineering technology; elementary education; emergency medical technology (EMT paramedic); engineering; engineering related; engineering technology; English; environmental engineering technology; finance; fire science; food science; forestry; French; funeral service and mortuary science; general studies; geology/earth science; German; health information/medical records administration; heating, air conditioning and refrigeration technology; heating, air conditioning, ventilation and refrigeration maintenance technology; histologic technician; history; horticultural science; hospitality administration; humanities; human services; industrial technology; information science/studies; interior design; international relations and affairs; Italian; journalism; kindergarten/preschool education; landscaping and groundskeeping; Latin American studies; legal administrative assistant/secretary; legal assistant/paralegal; literature; management information systems; marketing/marketing management; mass communication/media; mathematics; mathematics teacher education; medical/clinical assistant; middle school education; music; music performance; music teacher education; natural sciences; non-profit management; nuclear medical technology; nursing midwifery; nursing (registered nurse training); ophthalmic technology; ornamental horticulture; parks, recreation and leisure; philosophy; photographic and film/video technology; photography; physical education teaching and coaching; physical sciences; physical therapist assistant; physical therapy; physics; physics teacher education; plant nursery management; political science and government; Portuguese; pre-dentistry studies; pre-engineering; pre-medical studies; pre-nursing studies; pre-pharmacy studies; pre-veterinary studies; psychology; public administration; radio and television; radio and television broadcasting technology; radiologic technology/science; recording arts technology; respiratory care therapy; respiratory therapy technician; science teacher education; sign language interpretation and translation; social sciences; social work; sociology; Spanish; special education; substance abuse/addiction counseling; teacher assistant/aide; telecommunications technology; tourism and travel services management; veterinary sciences.

Academic Programs *Special study options:* academic remediation for entering students, adult/continuing education programs, advanced placement credit, cooperative education, distance learning, English as a second language, freshman honors college, honors programs, independent study, internships, part-time degree program, services for LD students, study abroad, summer session for credit. *ROTC:* Army (c), Air Force (c).

Library Main Library plus 8 others with 327,417 titles, 4,916 serial subscriptions, 17,186 audiovisual materials, an OPAC, a Web page.

Computers on Campus 6750 computers available on campus for general student use. A campuswide network can be accessed from off campus that provide access to Admissions; grades; student feedback of faculty; financial aid. Internet access, online (class) registration, at least one staffed computer lab available. Computer purchase or lease plan available.

Student Life *Housing:* college housing not available. *Activities and Organizations:* drama/theater group, student-run newspaper, radio station, choral group, Welcome Back, Hispanic Heritage Month, Black History Month, Paella Festival. *Campus security:* 24-hour patrols. *Student services:* personal/psychological counseling, women's center.

Athletics Member NJCAA. *Intercollegiate sports:* baseball M(s), basketball M(s)/W(s), softball W(s), volleyball W(s). *Intramural sports:* basketball M/W, racquetball M/W, soccer M/W, softball M/W, swimming and diving M/W, tennis M/W, track and field M/W, volleyball M/W, weight lifting M/W.

Standardized Tests *Recommended:* SAT or ACT (for placement), SAT II: Writing Test (for placement), CPT.

Costs (2004–05) *Tuition:* state resident $1490 full-time, $50 per credit part-time; nonresident $5550 full-time, $185 per credit part-time. Full-time tuition and fees vary according to degree level. Part-time tuition and fees vary according to degree level. *Required fees:* $285 full-time, $10 per credit part-time. *Waivers:* employees or children of employees.

Financial Aid Of all full-time matriculated undergraduates who enrolled in 2003, 800 Federal Work-Study jobs (averaging $5000). 125 state and other part-time jobs (averaging $5000).

Applying *Options:* electronic application, early admission. *Application fee:* $20. *Required:* high school transcript. *Application deadline:* rolling (freshmen). *Notification:* continuous (freshmen).

Admissions Contact Mr. Steven Kelly, College Registrar, Miami Dade College, 11011 SW 104th Street, Miami, FL 33176. *Phone:* 305-237-0633. *Fax:* 305-237-2964. *E-mail:* SKelly@mdc.edu.

▶ **See page 526 for a narrative description.**

NATIONAL SCHOOL OF TECHNOLOGY, INC.
Fort Lauderdale, Florida

Admissions Contact Ashly Miller, Director of Admissions, National School of Technology, Inc., 1040 Bayview Drive, Fort Lauderdale, FL 33304. *Phone:* 954-630-0066.

NATIONAL SCHOOL OF TECHNOLOGY, INC.
Hialeah, Florida

Admissions Contact Mr. Daniel Alonso, Director of Admissions, National School of Technology, Inc., 4410 West 16th Avenue, Suite 52, Hialeah, FL 33012. *Phone:* 305-558-9500.

NATIONAL SCHOOL OF TECHNOLOGY, INC.
Miami, Florida

Admissions Contact Ms. Amber Stenbeck, Director of Admissions, National School of Technology, Inc., 111 Northwest 183rd Street, 2nd Floor, Miami, FL 33169. *Phone:* 305-386-9900.

NATIONAL SCHOOL OF TECHNOLOGY, INC.
North Miami Beach, Florida

- **Proprietary** 2-year, founded 1977
- **Calendar** continuous
- **Degree** diplomas and associate
- **Urban** campus
- **Coed**

Faculty *Student/faculty ratio:* 12:1.
Costs (2004–05) *Tuition:* $10,200 full-time.
Admissions Contact Mr. Walter McQuade, Director of Admissions, National School of Technology, Inc., 16150 Northeast 17th Avenue, North Miami Beach, FL 33162-4744. *Phone:* 305-949-9500.

NEW ENGLAND INSTITUTE OF TECHNOLOGY AT PALM BEACH
West Palm Beach, Florida

- **Proprietary** 2-year, founded 1983
- **Calendar** quarters
- **Degree** certificates, diplomas, and associate
- **Urban** 7-acre campus with easy access to Miami
- **Coed**

Faculty *Student/faculty ratio:* 25:1.
Applying *Options:* early admission. *Application fee:* $150. *Required:* high school transcript.
Admissions Contact Mr. Kevin Cassidy, Director of Admissions, New England Institute of Technology at Palm Beach, 1126 53rd Court, West Palm Beach, FL 33407-2384. *Phone:* 561-842-8324 Ext. 117. *Toll-free phone:* 800-826-9986.

NORTH FLORIDA COMMUNITY COLLEGE
Madison, Florida

- **State-supported** 2-year, founded 1958
- **Calendar** semesters
- **Degree** certificates and associate
- **Small-town** 109-acre campus
- **Coed**

Faculty *Student/faculty ratio:* 18:1.
Student Life *Campus security:* 24-hour emergency response devices.
Athletics Member NJCAA.
Standardized Tests *Required for some:* SAT or ACT (for placement).
Costs (2004–05) *Tuition:* state resident $1671 full-time; nonresident $6141 full-time.

North Florida Community College (continued)

Applying *Options:* common application, early admission. *Application fee:* $20. *Required:* high school transcript, minimum 2.0 GPA.

Admissions Contact Mrs. Betty Starling, Admissions Assistant, North Florida Community College, 1000 Turner Davis Drive, Madison, FL 32340-1602. *Phone:* 850-973-1622. *Fax:* 850-973-1697.

OKALOOSA-WALTON COLLEGE
Niceville, Florida

Admissions Contact Ms. Christine Bishop, Registrar/Division Director Enrollment Services, Okaloosa-Walton College, 100 College Boulevard, Niceville, FL 32578. *Phone:* 850-729-5373. *Toll-free phone:* 850-729-5373. *Fax:* 850-729-5323. *E-mail:* registrar@owcc.net.

ORLANDO CULINARY ACADEMY
Orlando, Florida

Admissions Contact 8511 Commodity Circle, Suite 100, Orlando, FL 32819. *Toll-free phone:* 866-OCA-CHEF.

PALM BEACH COMMUNITY COLLEGE
Lake Worth, Florida

- **State-supported** 2-year, founded 1933, part of Florida Community College System
- **Calendar** semesters
- **Degree** certificates and associate
- **Urban** 150-acre campus with easy access to West Palm Beach
- **Endowment** $11.4 million
- **Coed,** 24,024 undergraduate students, 31% full-time, 59% women, 41% men

Undergraduates 7,403 full-time, 16,621 part-time. Students come from 49 states and territories, 138 other countries, 5% are from out of state, 10% transferred in.

Freshmen *Admission:* 2,469 applied, 2,469 admitted, 2,469 enrolled.

Faculty *Total:* 1,164, 21% full-time, 13% with terminal degrees. *Student/faculty ratio:* 22:1.

Majors Accounting; administrative assistant and secretarial science; airline pilot and flight crew; art; art history, criticism and conservation; biology/biological sciences; botany/plant biology; business administration and management; ceramic arts and ceramics; chemistry; clothing/textiles; commercial and advertising art; computer programming; computer programming (specific applications); computer science; computer/technical support; construction management; criminal justice/law enforcement administration; criminal justice/police science; data processing and data processing technology; dental hygiene; drafting and design technology; dramatic/theatre arts; economics; education; electrical, electronic and communications engineering technology; elementary education; English; family and consumer sciences/human sciences; fashion/apparel design; fashion merchandising; finance; fire science; foods, nutrition, and wellness; health teacher education; history; hotel/motel administration; industrial radiologic technology; interior design; journalism; kindergarten/preschool education; legal administrative assistant/secretary; liberal arts and sciences/liberal studies; literature; marketing/marketing management; mass communication/media; mathematics; music; nursing (registered nurse training); occupational therapy; philosophy; photography; physical education teaching and coaching; physical sciences; physical therapy; political science and government; pre-engineering; psychology; religious studies; social sciences; social work; special products marketing; survey technology; system administration; web page, digital/multimedia and information resources design; word processing; zoology/animal biology.

Academic Programs *Special study options:* academic remediation for entering students, adult/continuing education programs, advanced placement credit, cooperative education, distance learning, double majors, English as a second language, freshman honors college, honors programs, independent study, internships, off-campus study, part-time degree program, services for LD students, student-designed majors, study abroad, summer session for credit.

Library Harold C. Manor Library plus 3 others with 151,000 titles, 1,474 serial subscriptions, 9,700 audiovisual materials, an OPAC, a Web page.

Computers on Campus 2300 computers available on campus for general student use. A campuswide network can be accessed from off campus. Internet access, online (class) registration, at least one staffed computer lab available.

Student Life *Activities and Organizations:* drama/theater group, student-run newspaper, choral group, student government, Phi Theta Kappa, Students for International Understanding, Black Student Union, Drama Club, national fraternities. *Campus security:* 24-hour emergency response devices and patrols. *Student services:* health clinic, women's center.

Athletics Member NJCAA. *Intercollegiate sports:* baseball M(s), basketball M(s)/W(s), softball W(s), volleyball M(s)/W(s). *Intramural sports:* basketball M/W, bowling M/W, football M/W, racquetball M/W, soccer M, tennis M/W, volleyball M/W.

Standardized Tests *Required:* SAT, ACT, or CPT (for placement).

Costs (2004–05) *Tuition:* state resident $1740 full-time, $58 per credit part-time; nonresident $6540 full-time, $215 per credit part-time. *Required fees:* $300 full-time, $10 per term part-time. *Room and board:* room only: $6000. *Payment plan:* tuition prepayment. *Waivers:* minority students, senior citizens, and employees or children of employees.

Applying *Options:* electronic application, early admission, deferred entrance. *Application fee:* $20. *Application deadlines:* 8/20 (freshmen), 8/20 (transfers). *Notification:* continuous until 8/20 (freshmen).

Admissions Contact Ms. Annaleah Morrow, College Registrar, Palm Beach Community College, 4200 Congress Avenue, Lake Worth, FL 33461. *Phone:* 561-868-3032. *Fax:* 561-868-3584.

PASCO-HERNANDO COMMUNITY COLLEGE
New Port Richey, Florida

- **State-supported** 2-year, founded 1972, part of Florida Community College System
- **Calendar** semesters
- **Degree** certificates, diplomas, and associate
- **Small-town** 142-acre campus with easy access to Tampa
- **Endowment** $20.3 million
- **Coed,** 7,213 undergraduate students, 34% full-time, 68% women, 32% men

Undergraduates 2,431 full-time, 4,782 part-time. Students come from 11 states and territories, 10 other countries, 1% are from out of state, 4% African American, 2% Asian American or Pacific Islander, 7% Hispanic American, 0.8% Native American, 0.7% international, 5% transferred in.

Freshmen *Admission:* 2,568 applied, 2,541 admitted, 1,586 enrolled.

Faculty *Total:* 300, 32% full-time, 13% with terminal degrees. *Student/faculty ratio:* 25:1.

Majors Business administration and management; computer programming related; computer programming (specific applications); computer systems networking and telecommunications; criminal justice/law enforcement administration; dental hygiene; drafting and design technology; emergency medical technology (EMT paramedic); human services; information technology; legal assistant/paralegal; liberal arts and sciences/liberal studies; marketing/marketing management; nursing (registered nurse training); physical therapist assistant; radiologic technology/science; web page, digital/multimedia and information resources design.

Academic Programs *Special study options:* academic remediation for entering students, accelerated degree program, adult/continuing education programs, advanced placement credit, cooperative education, distance learning, double majors, honors programs, independent study, internships, off-campus study, part-time degree program, services for LD students, summer session for credit. *ROTC:* Army (c).

Library Pottberg Library plus 2 others with 67,852 titles, 351 serial subscriptions, 4,357 audiovisual materials, an OPAC, a Web page.

Computers on Campus 974 computers available on campus for general student use. A campuswide network can be accessed. Online (class) registration, at least one staffed computer lab available. Computer purchase or lease plan available.

Student Life *Housing:* college housing not available. *Activities and Organizations:* drama/theater group, choral group, Student Government Association, Phi Theta Kappa, Phi Beta Lambda, Human Services, PHCC Cares. *Campus security:* 24-hour patrols.

Athletics Member NJCAA. *Intercollegiate sports:* baseball M(s), basketball M(s), softball W(s), tennis W(s), volleyball W(s).

Standardized Tests *Required:* CPT (preferred), SAT I, or ACT (for placement).

Costs (2004–05) *Tuition:* state resident $1772 full-time, $57 per credit part-time; nonresident $6378 full-time, $213 per credit part-time. *Waivers:* senior citizens.

Financial Aid Of all full-time matriculated undergraduates who enrolled in 2003, 45 Federal Work-Study jobs (averaging $2133).

Applying *Options:* electronic application. *Application fee:* $20. *Required:* high school transcript. *Application deadline:* rolling (freshmen), rolling (transfers). *Notification:* continuous (freshmen).

Admissions Contact Ms. Debra Bullard, Director of Admissions and Student Records, Pasco-Hernando Community College, 10230 Ridge Road, New Port Richey, FL 34654-5199. *Phone:* 727-816-3261. *Fax:* 727-816-3389. *E-mail:* malizim@phcc.edu.

PENSACOLA JUNIOR COLLEGE
Pensacola, Florida

- **State-supported** 2-year, founded 1948, part of Florida Community College System

- **Calendar** semesters
- **Degree** certificates, diplomas, and associate
- **Urban** 160-acre campus
- **Coed**

Student Life *Campus security:* 24-hour emergency response devices and patrols, student patrols, late-night transport/escort service.

Athletics Member NJCAA.

Standardized Tests *Required:* SAT I, ACT, or CPT (for placement).

Costs (2004–05) *Tuition:* state resident $1500 full-time, $50 per credit hour part-time; nonresident $6500 full-time, $200 per credit hour part-time. *Required fees:* $255 full-time.

Financial Aid Of all full-time matriculated undergraduates who enrolled in 2003, 120 Federal Work-Study jobs (averaging $3000).

Applying *Options:* early admission. *Application fee:* $30. *Required:* high school transcript.

Admissions Contact Ms. Martha Caughey, Registrar, Pensacola Junior College, 1000 College Boulevard, Pensacola, FL 32504-8998. *Phone:* 850-484-1600. *Fax:* 850-484-1829.

POLK COMMUNITY COLLEGE
Winter Haven, Florida

- **State-supported** 2-year, founded 1964, part of Florida Community College System
- **Calendar** semesters 16-16-6-6
- **Degree** certificates and associate
- **Suburban** 98-acre campus with easy access to Orlando and Tampa
- **Endowment** $5.9 million
- **Coed,** 7,047 undergraduate students, 28% full-time, 65% women, 35% men

Undergraduates 1,987 full-time, 5,060 part-time. Students come from 25 states and territories, 73 other countries, 10% are from out of state, 14% African American, 2% Asian American or Pacific Islander, 7% Hispanic American, 0.4% Native American, 4% international.

Freshmen *Admission:* 1,080 applied, 1,080 admitted, 1,080 enrolled.

Faculty *Total:* 443, 27% full-time, 10% with terminal degrees. *Student/faculty ratio:* 14:1.

Majors Accounting technology and bookkeeping; business administration and management; child development; corrections; criminal justice/law enforcement administration; criminal justice/police science; data processing and data processing technology; emergency medical technology (EMT paramedic); finance; fire science; health information/medical records administration; information science/studies; legal administrative assistant/secretary; liberal arts and sciences/liberal studies; marketing/marketing management; medical administrative assistant and medical secretary; nursing (registered nurse training); occupational therapist assistant; physical therapist assistant; pre-engineering; radiologic technology/science; surgical technology.

Academic Programs *Special study options:* academic remediation for entering students, accelerated degree program, adult/continuing education programs, advanced placement credit, cooperative education, distance learning, double majors, English as a second language, independent study, part-time degree program, services for LD students, student-designed majors, summer session for credit. *ROTC:* Army (c).

Library Polk Community College Library with 181,000 titles, 325 serial subscriptions, 4,527 audiovisual materials, an OPAC, a Web page.

Computers on Campus 171 computers available on campus for general student use. A campuswide network can be accessed. Internet access, online (class) registration, at least one staffed computer lab available.

Student Life *Housing:* college housing not available. *Activities and Organizations:* drama/theater group, student-run newspaper, choral group. *Campus security:* 24-hour emergency response devices and patrols.

Athletics Member NJCAA. *Intercollegiate sports:* baseball M(s), basketball M(s), soccer W(s), softball W(s), volleyball W(s).

Standardized Tests *Required:* CPT (for placement).

Costs (2004–05) *Tuition:* state resident $1755 full-time, $59 per credit hour part-time; nonresident $6541 full-time, $218 per credit hour part-time. *Required fees:* $255 full-time. *Waivers:* employees or children of employees.

Financial Aid Of all full-time matriculated undergraduates who enrolled in 2003, 16 Federal Work-Study jobs (averaging $400).

Applying *Options:* early admission, deferred entrance. *Application fee:* $20. *Required:* high school transcript. *Application deadline:* rolling (freshmen), rolling (transfers). *Notification:* continuous (freshmen).

Admissions Contact Ms. Barbara Guthrie, Registrar, Polk Community College, 999 Avenue H North East, Winter Haven, FL 33881. *Phone:* 863-297-1010 Ext. 5016. *Toll-free phone:* 863-297-1000 Ext. 5016. *Fax:* 863-297-1010.

REMINGTON COLLEGE-JACKSONVILLE CAMPUS
Jacksonville, Florida

Admissions Contact Mr. Tony Galang, Campus President, Remington College-Jacksonville Campus, 7011 A.C. Skinner Parkway, Jacksonville, FL 32256. *Phone:* 904-296-3435 Ext. 218.

REMINGTON COLLEGE-PINELLAS CAMPUS
Largo, Florida

Admissions Contact Ms. Edna Higgins, Campus President, Remington College-Pinellas Campus, 8550 Ulmerton Road, Largo, FL 33771. *Phone:* 727-532-1999. *Toll-free phone:* 888-900-2343.

REMINGTON COLLEGE-TAMPA CAMPUS
Tampa, Florida

Admissions Contact Ms. Kathy Miller, Director of Admissions, Remington College-Tampa Campus, 2410 East Busch Boulevard, Tampa, FL 33612. *Phone:* 813-935-5700 Ext. 211. *Toll-free phone:* 800-992-4850.

ST. JOHNS RIVER COMMUNITY COLLEGE
Palatka, Florida

- **State-supported** 2-year, founded 1958
- **Calendar** semesters
- **Degree** certificates, diplomas, and associate
- **Small-town** 105-acre campus with easy access to Jacksonville
- **Coed**

Student Life *Campus security:* 24-hour patrols.

Athletics Member NJCAA.

Standardized Tests *Recommended:* SAT and SAT Subject Tests or ACT (for placement).

Costs (2004–05) *Tuition:* state resident $1732 full-time, $62 per semester hour part-time; nonresident $6348 full-time, $232 per semester hour part-time.

Financial Aid Of all full-time matriculated undergraduates who enrolled in 2003, 38 Federal Work-Study jobs (averaging $1070). 33 state and other part-time jobs (averaging $1250).

Applying *Options:* common application, early admission. *Required:* high school transcript.

Admissions Contact Mr. O'Neal Williams, Dean of Admissions and Records, St. Johns River Community College, 5001 Saint Johns Avenue, Palatka, FL 32177-3897. *Phone:* 386-312-4032.

ST. PETERSBURG COLLEGE
St. Petersburg, Florida

- **State and locally supported** primarily 2-year, founded 1927
- **Calendar** semesters
- **Degrees** certificates, diplomas, associate, and bachelor's
- **Suburban** campus
- **Endowment** $13.4 million
- **Coed,** 24,102 undergraduate students, 33% full-time, 63% women, 37% men

Undergraduates 8,012 full-time, 16,090 part-time. Students come from 45 states and territories, 30 other countries, 4% are from out of state, 11% African American, 3% Asian American or Pacific Islander, 6% Hispanic American, 0.7% Native American, 1% international.

Freshmen *Admission:* 3,485 applied, 3,485 admitted, 3,485 enrolled. *Test scores:* SAT verbal scores over 500: 77%; SAT math scores over 500: 84%; ACT scores over 18: 80%; SAT verbal scores over 600: 37%; SAT math scores over 600: 45%; ACT scores over 24: 22%; SAT verbal scores over 700: 8%; SAT math scores over 700: 11%; ACT scores over 30: 3%.

Faculty *Total:* 1,895, 16% full-time.

Majors Accounting technology and bookkeeping; architectural engineering technology; business administration and management; clinical/medical laboratory technology; commercial and advertising art; computer engineering technology; computer programming; computer systems networking and telecommunications; construction engineering technology; corrections; criminal justice/police science; dental hygiene; drafting and design technology; education; electrical, electronic and communications engineering technology; emergency medical technology (EMT paramedic); engineering/industrial management; fire

St. Petersburg College (continued)

science; funeral service and mortuary science; health/health care administration; health information/medical records administration; hospitality administration; human services; hydrology and water resources science; industrial radiologic technology; industrial technology; information science/studies; kindergarten/preschool education; landscaping and groundskeeping; legal administrative assistant/secretary; legal assistant/paralegal; liberal arts and sciences/liberal studies; marketing/marketing management; natural resources management; nursing (registered nurse training); physical therapist assistant; plastics engineering technology; quality control technology; radiologic technology/science; respiratory care therapy; sign language interpretation and translation; substance abuse/addiction counseling; telecommunications; tourism and travel services management; veterinary technology; web/multimedia management and webmaster.

Academic Programs *Special study options:* academic remediation for entering students, adult/continuing education programs, advanced placement credit, cooperative education, distance learning, English as a second language, freshman honors college, honors programs, internships, part-time degree program, services for LD students, summer session for credit.

Library M. M. Bennett Library plus 5 others with 222,990 titles, 1,393 serial subscriptions, 16,543 audiovisual materials, an OPAC, a Web page.

Computers on Campus 2951 computers available on campus for general student use. A campuswide network can be accessed from off campus. Internet access, online (class) registration, at least one staffed computer lab available. Computer purchase or lease plan available.

Student Life *Housing:* college housing not available. *Activities and Organizations:* drama/theater group, student-run newspaper. *Campus security:* late-night transport/escort service. *Student services:* women's center.

Athletics Member NJCAA. *Intercollegiate sports:* baseball M(s), basketball M(s)/W(s), softball W(s), volleyball W(s). *Intramural sports:* basketball M, bowling M/W, volleyball M/W.

Standardized Tests *Required for some:* SAT II: Writing Test (for placement), CPT.

Costs (2004–05) *Tuition:* state resident $1568 full-time, $52 per credit part-time; nonresident $6273 full-time, $209 per credit part-time. Full-time tuition and fees vary according to degree level and program. Part-time tuition and fees vary according to degree level and program. *Required fees:* $265 full-time, $9 per credit part-time. *Payment plan:* deferred payment. *Waivers:* senior citizens and employees or children of employees.

Financial Aid Of all full-time matriculated undergraduates who enrolled in 2003, 350 Federal Work-Study jobs (averaging $2500).

Applying *Options:* common application, electronic application, early admission, deferred entrance. *Application fee:* $35. *Required:* high school transcript. *Application deadline:* rolling (freshmen). *Notification:* continuous (freshmen).

Admissions Contact Mr. Martyn Clay, Admissions Director/Registrar, St. Petersburg College, PO Box 13489, St. Petersburg, FL 33733-3489. *Phone:* 727-712-5892. *Fax:* 727-712-5872. *E-mail:* information@spcollege.edu.

SANFORD-BROWN INSTITUTE
Jacksonville, Florida

Admissions Contact 10255 Fortune Parkway, Suite 501, Jacksonville, FL 32256.

SANFORD-BROWN INSTITUTE
Lauderdale Lakes, Florida

Admissions Contact 4780 N. State Road, 7 Building E, Suite 100, Lauderdale Lakes, FL 33319.

SANFORD-BROWN INSTITUTE
Tampa, Florida

Admissions Contact 5701 E. Hillsborough Avenue, Tampa, FL 33610.

SANTA FE COMMUNITY COLLEGE
Gainesville, Florida

■ **State and locally supported** 2-year, founded 1966, part of Florida Community College System
■ **Calendar** semesters
■ **Degrees** certificates and associate (offers bachelor's degrees in conjunction with Saint Leo College)
■ **Suburban** 175-acre campus with easy access to Jacksonville
■ **Coed,** 13,806 undergraduate students, 48% full-time, 53% women, 47% men

Undergraduates 6,560 full-time, 7,246 part-time. Students come from 46 states and territories, 80 other countries, 3% are from out of state, 12% African American, 3% Asian American or Pacific Islander, 8% Hispanic American, 0.7%

Native American, 3% international, 11% transferred in. *Retention:* 61% of 2002 full-time freshmen returned.

Freshmen *Admission:* 1,796 applied, 1,796 admitted, 1,796 enrolled.

Faculty *Total:* 782, 40% full-time.

Majors Accounting; automobile/automotive mechanics technology; biomedical technology; business administration and management; child development; commercial and advertising art; communications technology; computer engineering technology; computer programming; construction engineering technology; corrections; criminal justice/law enforcement administration; criminal justice/police science; data processing and data processing technology; dental hygiene; drafting and design technology; education; electrical, electronic and communications engineering technology; emergency medical technology (EMT paramedic); engineering; environmental studies; fashion merchandising; finance; fire science; health information/medical records administration; industrial radiologic technology; information science/studies; kindergarten/preschool education; legal administrative assistant/secretary; legal studies; liberal arts and sciences/liberal studies; marketing/marketing management; medical administrative assistant and medical secretary; nuclear medical technology; nursing (registered nurse training); ornamental horticulture; parks, recreation and leisure facilities management; respiratory care therapy.

Academic Programs *Special study options:* academic remediation for entering students, adult/continuing education programs, advanced placement credit, cooperative education, distance learning, English as a second language, honors programs, independent study, part-time degree program, services for LD students, student-designed majors, summer session for credit. *ROTC:* Army (c), Air Force (c).

Library Lawrence W. Tyree Library with 81,832 titles, 624 serial subscriptions, an OPAC, a Web page.

Computers on Campus 400 computers available on campus for general student use. A campuswide network can be accessed from off campus. Internet access, at least one staffed computer lab available.

Student Life *Housing:* college housing not available. *Activities and Organizations:* drama/theater group, choral group, Black Student Union, student government. *Campus security:* 24-hour emergency response devices and patrols. *Student services:* personal/psychological counseling.

Athletics Member NJCAA. *Intercollegiate sports:* baseball M(s), basketball M(s)/W(s), softball W(s). *Intramural sports:* basketball M/W, football M, golf M/W, racquetball M/W, soccer M/W, softball M/W, tennis M/W, volleyball M/W, weight lifting M/W.

Standardized Tests *Required:* SAT I, ACT, or CPT (for placement).

Costs (2005–06) *Tuition:* state resident $1755 full-time, $59 per credit hour part-time; nonresident $6540 full-time, $218 per credit hour part-time.

Financial Aid Of all full-time matriculated undergraduates who enrolled in 2003, 190 Federal Work-Study jobs.

Applying *Options:* early admission. *Application fee:* $30. *Required:* high school transcript. *Application deadline:* rolling (freshmen), rolling (transfers). *Notification:* continuous (freshmen).

Admissions Contact Ms. Margaret Karrh, Registrar, Santa Fe Community College, 3000 Northwest 83rd Street, Gainesville, FL 32606-6200. *Phone:* 352-395-5857. *Fax:* 352-395-4118. *E-mail:* information@sfcc.edu.

SEMINOLE COMMUNITY COLLEGE
Sanford, Florida

■ **State and locally supported** 2-year, founded 1966
■ **Calendar** semesters
■ **Degree** certificates, diplomas, and associate
■ **Small-town** 200-acre campus with easy access to Orlando
■ **Endowment** $3.5 million
■ **Coed,** 12,202 undergraduate students, 37% full-time, 58% women, 42% men

Undergraduates 4,461 full-time, 7,741 part-time. Students come from 18 states and territories, 123 other countries, 3% are from out of state, 14% African American, 4% Asian American or Pacific Islander, 14% Hispanic American, 0.4% Native American, 0.1% international, 19% transferred in.

Freshmen *Admission:* 2,792 enrolled.

Faculty *Total:* 850, 24% full-time, 12% with terminal degrees. *Student/faculty ratio:* 23:1.

Majors Accounting; administrative assistant and secretarial science; architectural engineering technology; automobile/automotive mechanics technology; banking and financial support services; business administration and management; child development; civil engineering technology; computer and information sciences related; computer and information systems security; computer engineering related; computer engineering technology; computer graphics; computer hardware engineering; computer/information technology services administration related; computer programming; computer programming related; computer programming (specific applications); computer programming (vendor/product certification); computer software and media applications related; computer software engineering; computer systems networking and telecommunications; computer/technical support; construction engineering technology; construction management; criminal justice/law enforcement administration; data entry/microcomputer applications; data entry/microcomputer applications related; data modeling/warehousing and database administration; data processing and data processing technology; drafting and design technology; electrical, electronic and communications engineering technology; emergency medical technology (EMT paramedic); finance; fire science; industrial technology; information science/studies; information technology; interior design; legal assistant/paralegal; liberal arts and sciences/liberal studies; marketing/marketing management; nursing (registered nurse training); physical therapy; respiratory care therapy; system administration; telecommunications; web/multimedia management and webmaster; web page, digital/multimedia and information resources design; word processing.

Academic Programs *Special study options:* academic remediation for entering students, accelerated degree program, adult/continuing education programs, advanced placement credit, cooperative education, distance learning, double majors, English as a second language, external degree program, honors programs, independent study, internships, part-time degree program, services for LD students, study abroad, summer session for credit. *ROTC:* Army (b).

Library Seminole Community College Library plus 2 others with 102,744 titles, 353 serial subscriptions, 8,913 audiovisual materials, an OPAC, a Web page.

Computers on Campus 56 computers available on campus for general student use. A campuswide network can be accessed from off campus. Internet access, online (class) registration, at least one staffed computer lab available.

Student Life *Housing:* college housing not available. *Activities and Organizations:* drama/theater group, student-run newspaper, choral group, Phi Beta Lambda, Phi Theta Kappa, Student Government Association, International Student Organization. *Campus security:* 24-hour emergency response devices and patrols. *Student services:* personal/psychological counseling.

Athletics Member NJCAA. *Intercollegiate sports:* baseball M(s), basketball M(s)/W(s), softball W(s). *Intramural sports:* basketball M/W, golf M, tennis M/W, volleyball M/W.

Standardized Tests *Required:* SAT Reasoning Test, ACT, CPT, New MAPS (for placement).

Costs (2004–05) *Tuition:* state resident $1514 full-time, $50 per credit hour part-time; nonresident $5813 full-time, $194 per credit hour part-time. Full-time tuition and fees vary according to course load. Part-time tuition and fees vary according to course load. *Required fees:* $417 full-time, $14 per credit hour part-time. *Payment plan:* deferred payment. *Waivers:* senior citizens and employees or children of employees.

Applying *Options:* early admission, deferred entrance. *Required:* high school transcript, minimum 2.0 GPA. *Application deadline:* rolling (freshmen), rolling (transfers). *Notification:* continuous (freshmen).

Admissions Contact Ms. Pamela Palaez, Director of Admissions, Seminole Community College, 100 Weldon Boulevard, Sanford, FL 32773-6199. *Phone:* 407-328-2041. *Fax:* 407-328-2395. *E-mail:* admissions@scc-fl.edu.

SOUTH FLORIDA COMMUNITY COLLEGE
Avon Park, Florida

Admissions Contact Ms. Annie Alexander-Harvey, Dean of Student Services, South Florida Community College, 600 West College Drive, Avon Park, FL 33825-9356. *Phone:* 863-453-6661 Ext. 7107.

SOUTH UNIVERSITY
West Palm Beach, Florida

- **Proprietary** primarily 2-year, founded 1899, part of Education Management Corporation
- **Calendar** quarters
- **Degrees** associate, bachelor's, and master's
- **Suburban** 1-acre campus with easy access to Miami
- **Coed,** 502 undergraduate students, 69% full-time, 86% women, 14% men

Undergraduates 347 full-time, 155 part-time. Students come from 1 other state, 4 other countries, 51% African American, 0.8% Asian American or Pacific Islander, 9% Hispanic American, 0.2% Native American, 1% international.

Freshmen *Admission:* 53 admitted, 53 enrolled.

Faculty *Total:* 60. *Student/faculty ratio:* 8:1.

Majors Accounting; administrative assistant and secretarial science; business administration and management; health services/allied health/health sciences; information science/studies; information technology; legal administrative assistant/secretary; legal assistant/paralegal; legal studies; medical/clinical assistant; nursing (registered nurse training); physical therapist assistant; pre-nursing studies.

Academic Programs *Special study options:* academic remediation for entering students, adult/continuing education programs, advanced placement credit, double majors, internships, part-time degree program.

Library South University Library plus 3 others with 8,400 titles, 67 serial subscriptions.

Computers on Campus 53 computers available on campus for general student use. A campuswide network can be accessed. Internet access, at least one staffed computer lab available.

Student Life *Housing:* college housing not available. *Activities and Organizations:* student-run newspaper, Pro Bono Club. *Campus security:* evening security personnel. *Student services:* personal/psychological counseling.

Standardized Tests *Required:* SAT or ACT (for admission).

Costs (2004–05) *Tuition:* $11,085 full-time. *Waivers:* employees or children of employees.

Financial Aid Of all full-time matriculated undergraduates who enrolled in 2003, 14 Federal Work-Study jobs (averaging $1530).

Applying *Options:* common application, electronic application, early admission, deferred entrance. *Application fee:* $25. *Required:* high school transcript. *Required for some:* letters of recommendation, interview. *Application deadline:* rolling (freshmen), rolling (transfers).

Admissions Contact Mr. Joe Rogalski, Director of Admissions, South University, 1760 North Congress Avenue, West Palm Beach, FL 33409-5178. *Phone:* 866-629-9200. *Toll-free phone:* 866-629-2902 (in-state); 866-629-9200 (out-of-state). *Fax:* 561-697-9944. *E-mail:* wpbadmiss@southuniversity.edu.

SOUTHWEST FLORIDA COLLEGE
Fort Myers, Florida

Admissions Contact Ms. Carmen King, Director of Admissions, Southwest Florida College, 1685 Medical Lane, Fort Myers, FL 33907. *Phone:* 239-939-4766. *Toll-free phone:* 866-SWFC-NOW.

SOUTHWEST FLORIDA COLLEGE
Tampa, Florida

Admissions Contact Admissions, Southwest Florida College, 3910 Riga Boulevard, Tampa, FL 33619. *Phone:* 813-630-4401. *Toll-free phone:* 877-907-2456.

SUMMIT INSTITUTE
West Palm Beach, Florida

Admissions Contact Mr. Mark Proefrock, Vice President, Summit Institute, 1750 45th Street, West Palm Beach, FL 33407-2192. *Phone:* 561-881-0220.

TALLAHASSEE COMMUNITY COLLEGE
Tallahassee, Florida

Admissions Contact Ms. Sharon Jefferson, Director of Enrollment Services, Tallahassee Community College, 444 Appleyard Drive, Tallahassee, FL 32304-2895. *Phone:* 850-201-8555. *Fax:* 850-201-8474. *E-mail:* enroll@tcc.fl.edu.

VALENCIA COMMUNITY COLLEGE
Orlando, Florida

- **State-supported** 2-year, founded 1967, part of Florida Community College System
- **Calendar** semesters
- **Degree** certificates and associate
- **Urban** campus
- **Endowment** $14.4 million
- **Coed,** 29,447 undergraduate students

Undergraduates Students come from 40 states and territories, 92 other countries, 4% are from out of state.

Freshmen *Test scores:* SAT verbal scores over 500: 70%; SAT math scores over 500: 58%; SAT verbal scores over 600: 13%; SAT math scores over 600: 5%; SAT verbal scores over 700: 1%; SAT math scores over 700: 1%.

Faculty *Total:* 934, 36% full-time, 14% with terminal degrees. *Student/faculty ratio:* 21:1.

Majors Accounting; administrative assistant and secretarial science; business administration and management; cardiovascular technology; cinematography and film/video production; civil engineering technology; commercial and advertising art; computer programming; computer programming related; computer programming (specific applications); construction engineering technology; criminal justice/law enforcement administration; culinary arts; data entry/microcomputer applications; dental hygiene; diagnostic medical sonography and ultrasound technology; drafting and design technology; dramatic/theatre arts; electrical, electronic and communications engineering technology; emergency medical technology (EMT paramedic); environmental engineering technology; fire science; hospitality administration; human resources management; industrial technology; information technology; legal administrative assistant/secretary;

Valencia Community College (continued)

legal assistant/paralegal; liberal arts and sciences/liberal studies; marketing/ marketing management; medical administrative assistant and medical secretary; medical radiologic technology; nursing (registered nurse training); office management; ornamental horticulture; physical education teaching and coaching; pre-engineering; respiratory care therapy; survey technology; tourism and travel services management; word processing.

Academic Programs *Special study options:* academic remediation for entering students, accelerated degree program, adult/continuing education programs, advanced placement credit, cooperative education, distance learning, double majors, English as a second language, honors programs, independent study, internships, part-time degree program, services for LD students, student-designed majors, summer session for credit. *ROTC:* Army (c).

Library Learning Resources Center plus 3 others with 101,000 titles, 650 serial subscriptions, 15,500 audiovisual materials, an OPAC, a Web page.

Computers on Campus 1927 computers available on campus for general student use. A campuswide network can be accessed. At least one staffed computer lab available.

Student Life *Housing:* college housing not available. *Activities and Organizations:* drama/theater group, student-run newspaper, choral group, Phi Theta Kappa, Valencia Intercultural Student Association, Student Government Association, Latin American Student Association, Valencia Student Nurses Association. *Campus security:* 24-hour emergency response devices and patrols, student patrols, late-night transport/escort service. *Student services:* personal/ psychological counseling.

Standardized Tests *Required:* SAT I, ACT, or CPT (for placement).

Costs (2004–05) *Tuition:* state resident $1451 full-time, $60 per credit hour part-time; nonresident $5452 full-time, $227 per credit hour part-time.

Financial Aid Of all full-time matriculated undergraduates who enrolled in 2003, 238 Federal Work-Study jobs (averaging $2400).

Applying *Options:* early admission. *Application fee:* $25. *Required:* high school transcript. *Application deadlines:* 8/5 (freshmen), 8/5 (transfers).

Admissions Contact Dr. Renee K. Simpson, Director of Admissions and Records, Valencia Community College, PO Box 3028, Orlando, FL 32802-3028. *Phone:* 407-582-1511.

WEBSTER COLLEGE
Holiday, Florida

Admissions Contact Ms. Claire L. Walker, Senior Admissions Representative, Webster College, 2127 Grand Boulevard, Holiday, FL 34690. *Phone:* 727-942-0069. *Toll-free phone:* 888-729-7247. *Fax:* 813-938-5709.

WEBSTER COLLEGE
Ocala, Florida

Admissions Contact Admissions Office, Webster College, 1530 SW Third Avenue, Ocala, FL 34474. *Phone:* 352-629-1941.

GEORGIA

ABRAHAM BALDWIN AGRICULTURAL COLLEGE
Tifton, Georgia

- **State-supported** 2-year, founded 1933, part of University System of Georgia
- **Calendar** semesters
- **Degree** certificates and associate
- **Small-town** 390-acre campus
- **Coed**

Faculty *Student/faculty ratio:* 25:1.

Student Life *Campus security:* 24-hour emergency response devices and patrols, late-night transport/escort service.

Athletics Member NJCAA.

Standardized Tests *Required:* SAT or ACT (for placement).

Costs (2004–05) *Tuition:* state resident $1468 full-time, $59 per credit hour part-time; nonresident $5872 full-time, $233 per credit hour part-time. Part-time tuition and fees vary according to course load. *Required fees:* $454 full-time, $27 per credit hour part-time. *Room and board:* room only: $4140. Room and board charges vary according to board plan and housing facility.

Financial Aid Of all full-time matriculated undergraduates who enrolled in 2003, 158 Federal Work-Study jobs (averaging $1675).

Applying *Options:* common application, early admission, deferred entrance. *Application fee:* $5. *Required:* high school transcript.

Admissions Contact Dr. Donna E. Miller, Director of Institutional Research, Abraham Baldwin Agricultural College, 2802 Moore Highway, Tifton, GA 31793. *Phone:* 229-386-7231. *Toll-free phone:* 800-733-3653. *Fax:* 912-386-7006.

ALBANY TECHNICAL COLLEGE
Albany, Georgia

- **State-supported** 2-year, founded 1961
- **Calendar** quarters
- **Degree** certificates, diplomas, and associate
- **Coed,** 2,783 undergraduate students, 49% full-time, 64% women, 36% men

Undergraduates 1,371 full-time, 1,412 part-time. 68% African American, 0.2% Asian American or Pacific Islander, 0.7% Hispanic American, 0.5% Native American.

Freshmen *Admission:* 2,169 applied, 795 admitted, 591 enrolled.

Faculty *Total:* 193, 47% full-time, 2% with terminal degrees. *Student/faculty ratio:* 15:1.

Majors Child care and guidance related; computer and information sciences; corrections and criminal justice related; culinary arts; drafting and design technology; early childhood education; electrical and electronic engineering technologies related; forestry technology; industrial technology; manufacturing technology; pharmacy technician.

Academic Programs *Special study options:* academic remediation for entering students, adult/continuing education programs, advanced placement credit, distance learning, internships, part-time degree program, services for LD students.

Library Albany Technical College Library and Media Center plus 1 other with 42,000 titles, 40 serial subscriptions, 520 audiovisual materials, an OPAC, a Web page.

Computers on Campus 500 computers available on campus for general student use. A campuswide network can be accessed from off campus. Online (class) registration, at least one staffed computer lab available. Computer purchase or lease plan available.

Student Life *Housing:* college housing not available.

Standardized Tests *Required:* ACT COMPASS or ASSET (for placement).

Costs (2004–05) *Tuition:* state resident $1008 full-time, $28 per credit hour part-time; nonresident $2016 full-time, $56 per credit hour part-time. *Required fees:* $138 full-time, $46 per term part-time. *Waivers:* senior citizens.

Applying *Options:* common application, electronic application, deferred entrance. *Application fee:* $15. *Required:* high school transcript. *Recommended:* interview.

Admissions Contact Dr. Patricia Wilson, Director of Admissions, Albany Technical College, 1704 South Slappey Boulevard, Albany, GA 31701. *Phone:* 229-430-3520. *Fax:* 229-430-6180. *E-mail:* pwilson@albanytech.edu.

ALTAMAHA TECHNICAL COLLEGE
Jesup, Georgia

- **State-supported** 2-year
- **Calendar** quarters
- **Degree** certificates, diplomas, and associate
- **Coed,** 1,061 undergraduate students, 46% full-time, 46% women, 54% men

Undergraduates 487 full-time, 574 part-time. 34% African American, 0.3% Asian American or Pacific Islander, 3% Hispanic American, 0.7% Native American.

Freshmen *Admission:* 328 enrolled.

Academic Programs *Special study options:* academic remediation for entering students, advanced placement credit, distance learning, internships, services for LD students.

Library 4,435 titles, 90 serial subscriptions, 292 audiovisual materials.

Student Life *Housing:* college housing not available.

Standardized Tests *Required:* ACT COMPASS or ASSET (for placement).

Costs (2004–05) *Tuition:* state resident $1008 full-time, $28 per credit hour part-time; nonresident $2016 full-time, $56 per credit hour part-time. *Required fees:* $46 per term part-time. *Waivers:* senior citizens.

Applying *Options:* deferred entrance. *Application fee:* $15. *Required:* high school transcript.

Admissions Contact Lillian Burns, Admissions Director, Altamaha Technical College, 1777 West Cherry Street, Jesup, GA 31545. *Phone:* 912-427-5817.

ANDREW COLLEGE
Cuthbert, Georgia

- **Independent United Methodist** 2-year, founded 1854
- **Calendar** semesters
- **Degree** certificates and associate
- **Small-town** 40-acre campus
- **Endowment** $7.0 million
- **Coed,** 331 undergraduate students, 99% full-time, 48% women, 52% men

Undergraduates 328 full-time, 3 part-time. Students come from 11 states and territories, 10 other countries, 16% are from out of state, 45% African American, 0.9% Asian American or Pacific Islander, 4% Hispanic American, 6% international, 6% transferred in, 90% live on campus.

Freshmen *Admission:* 578 applied, 554 admitted, 147 enrolled. *Average high school GPA:* 2.60.

Faculty *Total:* 41, 85% full-time. *Student/faculty ratio:* 12:1.

Majors Agriculture; art; athletic training; biological and physical sciences; biology/biological sciences; business administration and management; chemistry; clinical laboratory science/medical technology; computer and information sciences; dental hygiene; divinity/ministry; dramatic/theatre arts; education; English; forestry; history; humanities; journalism; literature; mass communication/media; mathematics; music; natural sciences; nursing (registered nurse training); occupational therapy; parks, recreation and leisure facilities management; philosophy; physical education teaching and coaching; physical therapy; physics; pre-engineering; pre-pharmacy studies; psychology; religious studies; respiratory care therapy; social sciences; social work; sociology; speech and rhetoric.

Academic Programs *Special study options:* academic remediation for entering students, advanced placement credit, English as a second language, honors programs, part-time degree program, services for LD students, summer session for credit.

Library Pitts Library with 40,000 titles, 100 serial subscriptions.

Computers on Campus 50 computers available on campus for general student use. A campuswide network can be accessed from student residence rooms and from off campus. Internet access, online (class) registration, at least one staffed computer lab available.

Student Life *Housing:* on-campus residence required through sophomore year. *Options:* coed, men-only, women-only. Campus housing is university owned. Freshman campus housing is guaranteed. *Activities and Organizations:* drama/theater group, student-run newspaper, choral group, Drama Club, Outdoor Club, International Club, BSU. *Campus security:* 24-hour patrols, controlled dormitory access, night patrols by trained security personnel. *Student services:* health clinic, personal/psychological counseling.

Athletics Member NJCAA. *Intercollegiate sports:* baseball M(s), golf M(s), soccer M(s)/W(s), softball W(s). *Intramural sports:* archery M/W, badminton M/W, basketball M/W, equestrian sports M/W, fencing M/W, football M, golf M, racquetball M/W, rock climbing M/W, skiing (downhill) M/W, soccer M/W, softball M/W, swimming and diving M/W, table tennis M/W, tennis M/W, ultimate Frisbee M/W, volleyball M/W, weight lifting M/W, wrestling M.

Standardized Tests *Required:* SAT or ACT (for admission).

Costs (2005–06) *Comprehensive fee:* $14,922 includes full-time tuition ($9192) and room and board ($5730).

Financial Aid Of all full-time matriculated undergraduates who enrolled in 2003, 72 Federal Work-Study jobs (averaging $772).

Applying *Options:* electronic application, early admission, deferred entrance. *Application fee:* $20. *Required:* high school transcript. *Required for some:* essay or personal statement, 1 letter of recommendation, interview. *Recommended:* minimum 2.0 GPA. *Application deadlines:* 8/6 (freshmen), 8/6 (transfers).

Admissions Contact Mr. Chip Reese, Director of Admission, Andrew College, 413 College Street, Cuthbert, GA 39840. *Phone:* 229-732-5934. *Toll-free phone:* 800-664-9250. *Fax:* 229-732-2176. *E-mail:* admissions@andrewcollege.edu.

► **See page 448 for a narrative description.**

APPALACHIAN TECHNICAL COLLEGE
Jasper, Georgia

- **State-supported** 2-year, founded 1965
- **Calendar** quarters
- **Degree** certificates, diplomas, and associate
- **Coed,** 976 undergraduate students, 40% full-time, 70% women, 30% men

Undergraduates 388 full-time, 588 part-time. 0.7% African American, 0.2% Asian American or Pacific Islander, 0.5% Hispanic American, 0.3% Native American.

Freshmen *Admission:* 310 enrolled.

Academic Programs *Special study options:* academic remediation for entering students, advanced placement credit, distance learning, internships, services for LD students.

Student Life *Housing:* college housing not available.

Standardized Tests *Required:* ACT COMPASS or ASSET (for placement).

Costs (2004–05) *Tuition:* state resident $1008 full-time, $28 per credit hour part-time; nonresident $2016 full-time, $56 per credit hour part-time. *Required fees:* $138 full-time, $46 per term part-time. *Waivers:* senior citizens.

Applying *Options:* deferred entrance. *Application fee:* $15. *Required:* high school transcript.

Admissions Contact Nina Faix, Admissions Officer, Appalachian Technical College, 100 Campus Drive, Jasper, GA 30143. *Phone:* 706-253-4537.

ASHWORTH COLLEGE
Norcross, Georgia

Admissions Contact Mr. John Graves, Dean of Undergraduate Studies, Ashworth College, 430 Technology Parkway, Norcross, GA 30092. *Toll-free phone:* 800-223-4542. *E-mail:* info@ashworthcollege.com.

ATHENS TECHNICAL COLLEGE
Athens, Georgia

- **State-supported** 2-year, founded 1958, part of Georgia Department of Technical and Adult Education
- **Calendar** quarters
- **Degree** certificates, diplomas, and associate
- **Suburban** 41-acre campus with easy access to Atlanta
- **Coed,** 2,815 undergraduate students, 41% full-time, 63% women, 37% men

Undergraduates 1,146 full-time, 1,669 part-time. Students come from 2 states and territories, 20% African American, 4% Asian American or Pacific Islander, 2% Hispanic American, 0.1% Native American.

Freshmen *Admission:* 774 enrolled.

Faculty *Total:* 190, 37% full-time. *Student/faculty ratio:* 20:1.

Majors Accounting; administrative assistant and secretarial science; automobile/automotive mechanics technology; biology/biotechnology laboratory technician; business machine repair; child development; clinical laboratory science/medical technology; communications technology; computer programming; cosmetology; criminal justice/law enforcement administration; dental assisting; dental hygiene; diagnostic medical sonography and ultrasound technology; drafting and design technology; electrical, electronic and communications engineering technology; engineering technology; heating, air conditioning, ventilation and refrigeration maintenance technology; hotel and restaurant management; industrial radiologic technology; legal assistant/paralegal; machine tool technology; marketing/marketing management; medical administrative assistant and medical secretary; medical/clinical assistant; medical laboratory technology; nursing (licensed practical/vocational nurse training); nursing (registered nurse training); physical therapy; respiratory care therapy; surgical technology; teacher assistant/aide; veterinary technology.

Academic Programs *Special study options:* academic remediation for entering students, adult/continuing education programs, advanced placement credit, distance learning, internships, part-time degree program, services for LD students, summer session for credit.

Library 33,891 titles, 538 serial subscriptions, 3,279 audiovisual materials.

Computers on Campus 277 computers available on campus for general student use. A campuswide network can be accessed. Internet access, online (class) registration, at least one staffed computer lab available.

Student Life *Housing:* college housing not available. *Activities and Organizations:* Athens Technical Student Advisory Council, Phi Theta Kappa, Delta Epsilon Chi, Radiological Technology Society, Organized Black Students Encouraging Unity and Excellence. *Campus security:* 24-hour patrols. *Student services:* personal/psychological counseling.

Costs (2004–05) *Tuition:* state resident $1008 full-time, $28 per quarter hour part-time; nonresident $2016 full-time, $56 per quarter hour part-time. *Required fees:* $138 full-time, $46 per term part-time. *Waivers:* senior citizens.

Financial Aid Of all full-time matriculated undergraduates who enrolled in 2003, 34 Federal Work-Study jobs (averaging $3090).

Applying *Options:* deferred entrance. *Application fee:* $15. *Required:* high school transcript. *Application deadline:* rolling (freshmen). *Notification:* continuous (freshmen).

Admissions Contact Mr. Lenzy Reid, Director of Admissions, Athens Technical College, 800 US Highway 29 North, Athens, GA 30601-1500. *Phone:* 706-355-5124. *Fax:* 706-369-5756.

ATLANTA METROPOLITAN COLLEGE
Atlanta, Georgia

- **State-supported** 2-year, founded 1974, part of University System of Georgia
- **Calendar** semesters
- **Degree** certificates and associate
- **Urban** 68-acre campus
- **Coed,** 1,802 undergraduate students, 47% full-time, 65% women, 35% men

Atlanta Metropolitan College (continued)

Undergraduates 854 full-time, 948 part-time. Students come from 33 states and territories, 39 other countries, 8% are from out of state, 95% African American, 0.8% Asian American or Pacific Islander, 0.6% Hispanic American, 3% international, 8% transferred in.

Freshmen *Admission:* 1,965 applied, 1,455 admitted, 343 enrolled.

Faculty *Total:* 78, 60% full-time, 40% with terminal degrees. *Student/faculty ratio:* 23:1.

Majors African-American/Black studies; art; biology/biological sciences; business administration and management; chemistry; child development; communication/speech communication and rhetoric; computer and information sciences; computer/information technology services administration related; computer science; criminal justice/law enforcement administration; education (multiple levels); engineering technology; English; foreign languages and literatures; general studies; health and physical education; health services/allied health/health sciences; history; human services; information science/studies; information technology; mathematics; music; nursing (licensed practical/vocational nurse training); operations management; physics; political science and government; psychology; social work; speech and rhetoric.

Academic Programs *Special study options:* academic remediation for entering students, adult/continuing education programs, cooperative education, part-time degree program, services for LD students, study abroad, summer session for credit.

Library Atlanta Metropolitan College Library plus 1 other with 48,719 titles, 113 serial subscriptions, 3,874 audiovisual materials, an OPAC, a Web page.

Computers on Campus 585 computers available on campus for general student use. A campuswide network can be accessed from off campus. Internet access, at least one staffed computer lab available.

Student Life *Housing:* college housing not available. *Activities and Organizations:* drama/theater group, student-run newspaper, choral group, International Students Organization, Drama Club, choir, Criminal Justice Club, Study Abroad Club. *Campus security:* 24-hour emergency response devices and patrols. *Student services:* personal/psychological counseling.

Athletics Member NJCAA. *Intercollegiate sports:* basketball M(s)/W(s), cheerleading M/W.

Standardized Tests *Required:* SAT or ACT (for admission). *Required for some:* SAT or ACT (for admission).

Costs (2004–05) *Tuition:* state resident $1478 full-time, $67 per credit hour part-time; nonresident $5882 full-time, $250 per credit hour part-time. *Required fees:* $200 full-time, $100 per term part-time.

Applying *Options:* common application, electronic application. *Application fee:* $20. *Required:* high school transcript, meet the University System of Georgia's freshman index. *Application deadlines:* 7/15 (freshmen), 7/15 (transfers). *Notification:* continuous until 8/12 (freshmen).

Admissions Contact Ms. Audrey Reid, Director, Office of Admissions, Atlanta Metropolitan College, 1630 Metropolitan Parkway, SW, Atlanta, GA 30310-4498. *Phone:* 404-756-4004. *Fax:* 404-756-4407. *E-mail:* admissions@atlm.edu.

ATLANTA TECHNICAL COLLEGE
Atlanta, Georgia

- **State-supported** 2-year, founded 1945
- **Calendar** quarters
- **Degree** certificates, diplomas, and associate
- **Coed,** 3,274 undergraduate students, 46% full-time, 57% women, 43% men

Undergraduates 1,517 full-time, 1,757 part-time. 92% African American, 2% Asian American or Pacific Islander, 0.7% Hispanic American, 0.1% Native American.

Freshmen *Admission:* 848 enrolled.

Academic Programs *Special study options:* academic remediation for entering students, advanced placement credit, distance learning, internships, services for LD students.

Student Life *Housing:* college housing not available.

Standardized Tests *Required:* ACT COMPASS or ASSET (for placement).

Costs (2004–05) *Tuition:* state resident $1008 full-time, $28 per credit hour part-time; nonresident $2016 full-time, $56 per credit hour part-time. *Required fees:* $141 full-time, $47 per term part-time. *Waivers:* senior citizens.

Applying *Options:* deferred entrance. *Application fee:* $15. *Required:* high school transcript.

Admissions Contact Jill Triplett, Admissions Officer, Atlanta Technical College, 1560 Metropolitan Parkway SW, Atlanta, GA 30310. *Phone:* 404-225-4446.

AUGUSTA TECHNICAL COLLEGE
Augusta, Georgia

- **State-supported** 2-year, founded 1961, part of Georgia Department of Technical and Adult Education
- **Calendar** quarters
- **Degree** certificates, diplomas, and associate
- **Urban** 70-acre campus
- **Coed,** 4,343 undergraduate students, 48% full-time, 59% women, 41% men

Undergraduates 2,100 full-time, 2,243 part-time. Students come from 2 states and territories, 51% African American, 2% Asian American or Pacific Islander, 2% Hispanic American, 0.4% Native American, 0.2% international.

Freshmen *Admission:* 1,094 enrolled.

Faculty *Total:* 549, 46% full-time.

Majors Accounting; administrative assistant and secretarial science; child development; computer programming; electrical, electronic and communications engineering technology; emergency medical technology (EMT paramedic); information science/studies; marketing/marketing management; mechanical engineering/mechanical technology; respiratory care therapy.

Academic Programs *Special study options:* academic remediation for entering students, advanced placement credit, cooperative education, distance learning, internships, part-time degree program, services for LD students, summer session for credit.

Library Information Technology Center with 70,816 titles, 445 serial subscriptions, 7,733 audiovisual materials, an OPAC, a Web page.

Computers on Campus 339 computers available on campus for general student use. A campuswide network can be accessed from off campus. Internet access, at least one staffed computer lab available.

Student Life *Housing:* college housing not available. *Activities and Organizations:* VICA, professional organizations. *Campus security:* 24-hour emergency response devices, 12-hour patrols by trained security personnel.

Athletics *Intercollegiate sports:* golf M.

Standardized Tests *Required:* ACT ASSET or COMPASS (for placement).

Costs (2004–05) *Tuition:* state resident $1008 full-time, $28 per quarter hour part-time; nonresident $2016 full-time, $56 per quarter hour part-time. Full-time tuition and fees vary according to course load. Part-time tuition and fees vary according to course load. *Required fees:* $150 full-time, $50 per term part-time. *Waivers:* senior citizens and employees or children of employees.

Applying *Options:* deferred entrance. *Application fee:* $15. *Required:* high school transcript. *Application deadline:* rolling (freshmen), rolling (transfers). *Notification:* continuous (freshmen).

Admissions Contact Mr. Brian Roberts, Director of Admissions and Counseling, Augusta Technical College, 3200 Augusta Tech Drive, Augusta, GA 30906. *Phone:* 706-771-4027. *Fax:* 706-771-4034. *E-mail:* bcrobert@augustatech.edu.

BAINBRIDGE COLLEGE
Bainbridge, Georgia

- **State-supported** 2-year, founded 1972, part of University System of Georgia
- **Calendar** semesters
- **Degree** certificates and associate
- **Small-town** 160-acre campus
- **Coed,** 2,610 undergraduate students, 42% full-time, 70% women, 30% men

Undergraduates 1,093 full-time, 1,517 part-time. Students come from 5 states and territories, 1% are from out of state, 50% African American, 0.7% Asian American or Pacific Islander, 0.7% Hispanic American, 0.2% Native American.

Freshmen *Admission:* 1,318 applied, 1,062 admitted.

Faculty *Total:* 124, 47% full-time, 20% with terminal degrees.

Majors Accounting; administrative assistant and secretarial science; agriculture; art; automobile/automotive mechanics technology; biology/biological sciences; business administration and management; business teacher education; chemistry; criminal justice/law enforcement administration; data processing and data processing technology; drafting and design technology; dramatic/theatre arts; education; electrical, electronic and communications engineering technology; elementary education; English; family and consumer sciences/human sciences; forestry; health teacher education; history; information science/studies; journalism; kindergarten/preschool education; liberal arts and sciences/liberal studies; marketing/marketing management; mathematics; nursing (licensed practical/vocational nurse training); nursing (registered nurse training); political science and government; psychology; sociology; speech and rhetoric; welding technology.

Academic Programs *Special study options:* academic remediation for entering students, adult/continuing education programs, advanced placement credit, distance learning, double majors, independent study, part-time degree program, services for LD students, study abroad, summer session for credit.

Library Bainbridge College Library with 37,387 titles, 180 serial subscriptions, 1,795 audiovisual materials, an OPAC.

Computers on Campus 250 computers available on campus for general student use. A campuswide network can be accessed. Internet access, online (class) registration, at least one staffed computer lab available.

Student Life *Housing:* college housing not available. *Activities and Organizations:* drama/theater group, Phi Theta Kappa, Alpha Beta Gamma, Drama Club, Delta Club, Sigma Kappa Delta. *Campus security:* 24-hour patrols.

Athletics *Intramural sports:* table tennis M/W, volleyball M/W.

Standardized Tests *Required for some:* SAT or ACT (for admission), ACT COMPASS.

Costs (2004–05) *Tuition:* state resident $1468 full-time, $62 per credit hour part-time; nonresident $5872 full-time, $248 per credit hour part-time. *Required fees:* $124 full-time. *Waivers:* senior citizens.

Applying *Options:* electronic application, early admission. *Required for some:* high school transcript, minimum 1.8 GPA, 3 letters of recommendation, interview. *Application deadlines:* 8/1 (freshmen), 8/1 (transfers). *Notification:* continuous (freshmen).

Admissions Contact Mrs. Connie Snyder, Director of Admissions and Records, Bainbridge College, 2500 East Shotwell Street, Bainbridge, GA 39819. *Phone:* 229-248-2504. *Fax:* 229-248-2525. *E-mail:* csnyder@bainbridge.edu.

BAUDER COLLEGE
Atlanta, Georgia

Admissions Contact Ms. Lillie Lanier, Admissions Representative, Bauder College, Phipps Plaza, 3500 Peachtree Road NE, Atlanta, GA 30326. *Phone:* 404-237-7573. *Toll-free phone:* 404-237-7573 (in-state); 800-241-3797 (out-of-state). *Fax:* 404-237-1642. *E-mail:* admissions@bauder.edu.

BROWN MACKIE COLLEGE, ATLANTA CAMPUS
Norcross, Georgia

Admissions Contact Mr. Darrell Woodrum, Director, Brown Mackie College, Atlanta Campus, 4975 Jimmy Carter Boulevard, Suite 600, Norcross, GA 30093. *Phone:* 770-638-0121.

CENTRAL GEORGIA TECHNICAL COLLEGE
Macon, Georgia

- **State-supported** 2-year, founded 1966, part of Georgia Department of Technical and Adult Education
- **Calendar** quarters
- **Degree** certificates, diplomas, and associate
- **Suburban** 152-acre campus
- **Coed**, 5,464 undergraduate students, 47% full-time, 68% women, 32% men

Undergraduates 2,592 full-time, 2,872 part-time. Students come from 5 states and territories, 1 other country, 60% African American, 0.5% Asian American or Pacific Islander, 0.7% Hispanic American, 0.3% Native American, 0.1% international, 23% transferred in.

Freshmen *Admission:* 1,906 applied, 1,409 admitted, 1,347 enrolled. *Average high school GPA:* 2.50.

Faculty *Total:* 454, 23% full-time, 1% with terminal degrees. *Student/faculty ratio:* 16:1.

Majors Accounting; accounting technology and bookkeeping; business administration and management; child care and support services management; clinical/medical laboratory technology; computer management; developmental and child psychology; human resources management; industrial technology; information science/studies.

Academic Programs *Special study options:* academic remediation for entering students, advanced placement credit, distance learning, external degree program, internships, part-time degree program, services for LD students.

Library 16,500 titles, 300 serial subscriptions, 1,800 audiovisual materials, an OPAC, a Web page.

Computers on Campus Internet access, at least one staffed computer lab available.

Student Life *Housing:* college housing not available. *Activities and Organizations:* Skills USA-VICA, student government. *Campus security:* 24-hour patrols.

Costs (2004–05) *Tuition:* state resident $1008 full-time, $28 per credit hour part-time; nonresident $2016 full-time, $56 per credit hour part-time. Full-time tuition and fees vary according to program. Part-time tuition and fees vary according to program. *Required fees:* $138 full-time, $46 per term part-time. *Waivers:* senior citizens.

Financial Aid Of all full-time matriculated undergraduates who enrolled in 2003, 175 Federal Work-Study jobs (averaging $2000). *Financial aid deadline:* 9/1.

Applying *Options:* deferred entrance. *Application fee:* $15. *Required:* high school transcript.

Admissions Contact Amy McDonald, Admissions Director, Central Georgia Technical College, 3300 Macon Tech Drive, Macon, GA 31206. *Phone:* 478-757-3408. *Fax:* 478-757-3454. *E-mail:* info@cgtcollege.org.

CHATTAHOOCHEE TECHNICAL COLLEGE
Marietta, Georgia

- **State-supported** 2-year, founded 1961, part of Georgia Department of Technical and Adult Education
- **Calendar** quarters
- **Degree** certificates, diplomas, and associate
- **Suburban** campus with easy access to Atlanta
- **Coed**, 5,116 undergraduate students, 40% full-time, 55% women, 45% men

Undergraduates 2,033 full-time, 3,083 part-time. 35% African American, 3% Asian American or Pacific Islander, 3% Hispanic American, 0.3% Native American, 1% international.

Freshmen *Admission:* 1,680 enrolled.

Faculty *Total:* 191, 32% full-time. *Student/faculty ratio:* 19:1.

Majors Accounting; automobile/automotive mechanics technology; biomedical technology; business administration and management; child development; computer engineering technology; computer programming; computer typography and composition equipment operation; corrections; criminal justice/police science; data processing and data processing technology; electrical, electronic and communications engineering technology; electromechanical technology; marketing/marketing management.

Academic Programs *Special study options:* academic remediation for entering students, advanced placement credit, distance learning, internships, part-time degree program, services for LD students, study abroad.

Library 22,127 titles, 292 serial subscriptions, 1,826 audiovisual materials, a Web page.

Computers on Campus 200 computers available on campus for general student use. At least one staffed computer lab available.

Student Life *Housing:* college housing not available. *Activities and Organizations:* student government, Vocational Industrial Clubs of America, Institute for Electrical and Electronic Engineers, National Technical-Vocational Honor Society, Phi Beta Lambda. *Campus security:* full-time day and evening security. *Student services:* personal/psychological counseling.

Standardized Tests *Required:* ACT ASSET or COMPASS (for placement).

Costs (2004–05) *Tuition:* state resident $1008 full-time, $28 per credit hour part-time; nonresident $2016 full-time, $56 per credit hour part-time. *Required fees:* $159 full-time, $53 per term part-time. *Waivers:* senior citizens.

Financial Aid Of all full-time matriculated undergraduates who enrolled in 2003, 50 Federal Work-Study jobs (averaging $1500).

Applying *Options:* deferred entrance. *Application fee:* $15. *Required:* high school transcript. *Application deadline:* rolling (freshmen), rolling (transfers).

Admissions Contact Ms. Nichole H. Kennedy, Director of the Access Center, Chattahoochee Technical College, 980 South Cobb Drive, Marietta, GA 30060. *Phone:* 770-528-4581. *Fax:* 770-528-4580.

COASTAL GEORGIA COMMUNITY COLLEGE
Brunswick, Georgia

- **State-supported** 2-year, founded 1961, part of University System of Georgia
- **Calendar** semesters
- **Degree** certificates and associate
- **Small-town** 193-acre campus with easy access to Jacksonville
- **Endowment** $78,366
- **Coed**, 2,210 undergraduate students

Undergraduates Students come from 8 states and territories, 14% are from out of state, 23% African American, 1% Asian American or Pacific Islander, 2% Hispanic American, 0.4% Native American.

Freshmen *Admission:* 644 applied, 494 admitted. *Average high school GPA:* 2.30.

Faculty *Total:* 94, 66% full-time.

Majors Agricultural business and management; art; biology/biological sciences; business administration and management; chemistry; clinical/medical laboratory technology; computer science; criminal justice/law enforcement administration; dental hygiene; education (multiple levels); English; foreign languages and literatures; forestry; geology/earth science; health and physical education; history; liberal arts and sciences/liberal studies; mathematics; medical

Coastal Georgia Community College (continued)

radiologic technology; nursing (registered nurse training); occupational therapy; parks, recreation and leisure facilities management; philosophy; physical therapy; physician assistant; physics; political science and government; pre-dentistry studies; pre-engineering; pre-medical studies; pre-pharmacy studies; pre-veterinary studies; psychology; respiratory care therapy; sociology.

Academic Programs *Special study options:* academic remediation for entering students, adult/continuing education programs, advanced placement credit, distance learning, double majors, part-time degree program, services for LD students, study abroad, summer session for credit.

Library Clara Wood Gould Memorial Library with 535 serial subscriptions, 1,151 audiovisual materials, an OPAC.

Computers on Campus 250 computers available on campus for general student use. A campuswide network can be accessed from off campus. Internet access, at least one staffed computer lab available.

Student Life *Housing:* college housing not available. *Activities and Organizations:* student-run newspaper, Association of Nursing Students, Minority Advisement and Social Development Association, Student Government Association, Baptist Student Union, Phi Theta Kappa. *Campus security:* 24-hour patrols, late-night transport/escort service. *Student services:* personal/psychological counseling.

Athletics Member NJCAA. *Intercollegiate sports:* basketball M(s), softball W(s). *Intramural sports:* basketball M/W, soccer M/W, swimming and diving M/W, tennis M/W, volleyball M/W.

Standardized Tests *Required for some:* SAT and SAT Subject Tests or ACT (for admission), SAT II: Writing Test (for admission).

Costs (2004–05) *Tuition:* state resident $1468 full-time, $62 per credit hour part-time; nonresident $5872 full-time, $245 per credit hour part-time. *Required fees:* $212 full-time, $52 per term part-time. *Waivers:* senior citizens.

Financial Aid Of all full-time matriculated undergraduates who enrolled in 2003, 80 Federal Work-Study jobs (averaging $1500).

Applying *Options:* common application, electronic application, deferred entrance. *Application fee:* $20. *Required:* high school transcript, minimum 2.0 GPA, immunization records. *Application deadlines:* 8/19 (freshmen), 8/19 (transfers). *Notification:* continuous (freshmen).

Admissions Contact Dr. Mollie DeHart, Director of Admissions/Registrar, Coastal Georgia Community College, 3700 Altama Avenue, Brunswick, GA 31525. *Phone:* 912-264-7253. *Toll-free phone:* 800-675-7235. *Fax:* 912-262-3072. *E-mail:* admiss@cgcc.edu.

COLUMBUS TECHNICAL COLLEGE
Columbus, Georgia

- **State-supported** 2-year, founded 1961, part of Georgia Department of Technical and Adult Education
- **Calendar** quarters
- **Degree** certificates, diplomas, and associate
- **Urban** campus with easy access to Atlanta
- **Coed,** 3,726 undergraduate students, 45% full-time, 64% women, 36% men

Undergraduates 1,684 full-time, 2,042 part-time. Students come from 9 states and territories, 51% African American, 1% Asian American or Pacific Islander, 3% Hispanic American, 0.5% Native American.

Freshmen *Admission:* 1,238 enrolled.

Faculty *Total:* 68.

Majors Accounting; administrative assistant and secretarial science; computer engineering related; mechanical engineering/mechanical technology; word processing.

Academic Programs *Special study options:* academic remediation for entering students, adult/continuing education programs, advanced placement credit, distance learning, internships, part-time degree program, services for LD students.

Library Columbus Technical College Library with 26,072 titles, 49 serial subscriptions, 533 audiovisual materials.

Computers on Campus 50 computers available on campus for general student use. A campuswide network can be accessed from off campus. Internet access, at least one staffed computer lab available.

Student Life *Housing:* college housing not available. *Campus security:* security patrols during class hours.

Standardized Tests *Required:* ACT COMPASS or ASSET (for placement).

Costs (2004–05) *Tuition:* state resident $1008 full-time, $28 per credit hour part-time; nonresident $2016 full-time, $56 per credit hour part-time. Full-time tuition and fees vary according to course load. Part-time tuition and fees vary according to course load. *Required fees:* $165 full-time, $55 per term part-time. *Waivers:* senior citizens.

Financial Aid Of all full-time matriculated undergraduates who enrolled in 2003, 6 Federal Work-Study jobs (averaging $2000).

Applying *Options:* common application, deferred entrance. *Application fee:* $15. *Required:* high school transcript. *Required for some:* letters of recommendation, interview.

Admissions Contact BJ Vincent, Admissions Director, Columbus Technical College, 928 Manchester Expressway, Columbus, GA 31904-6572. *Phone:* 706-649-0652. *E-mail:* bvincent@COLUMBUSTECH.edu.

COOSA VALLEY TECHNICAL COLLEGE
Rome, Georgia

- **State-supported** 2-year, founded 1962
- **Calendar** quarters
- **Degree** certificates, diplomas, and associate
- **Coed,** 2,755 undergraduate students, 40% full-time, 65% women, 35% men

Undergraduates 1,099 full-time, 1,656 part-time. 11% African American, 0.8% Asian American or Pacific Islander, 1% Hispanic American, 0.5% Native American.

Freshmen *Admission:* 841 enrolled.

Academic Programs *Special study options:* academic remediation for entering students, advanced placement credit, distance learning, internships, services for LD students.

Student Life *Housing:* college housing not available.

Standardized Tests *Required:* ACT COMPASS or ASSET (for placement).

Costs (2004–05) *Tuition:* state resident $1008 full-time, $28 per credit hour part-time; nonresident $2016 full-time, $56 per credit hour part-time. *Required fees:* $138 full-time, $46 per term part-time. *Waivers:* senior citizens.

Applying *Options:* deferred entrance. *Application fee:* $15. *Required:* high school transcript.

Admissions Contact Stuart Phillips, Admissions Director, Coosa Valley Technical College, 1151 Highway 53 Spur SW, Calhoun, GA 30701. *Phone:* 706-624-1117. *Toll-free phone:* 888-331-CVTC.

DARTON COLLEGE
Albany, Georgia

- **State-supported** 2-year, founded 1965, part of University System of Georgia
- **Calendar** semesters
- **Degree** certificates and associate
- **Suburban** 185-acre campus
- **Coed,** 4,126 undergraduate students, 46% full-time, 72% women, 28% men

Undergraduates 1,904 full-time, 2,222 part-time. Students come from 6 other countries, 4% are from out of state, 43% African American, 1% Asian American or Pacific Islander, 0.9% Hispanic American, 0.1% Native American, 0.8% international, 5% transferred in. *Retention:* 63% of 2002 full-time freshmen returned.

Freshmen *Admission:* 2,194 applied, 1,779 admitted, 1,020 enrolled. *Average high school GPA:* 2.73. *Test scores:* SAT verbal scores over 500: 24%; SAT math scores over 500: 21%; ACT scores over 18: 29%; SAT verbal scores over 600: 5%; SAT math scores over 600: 3%; ACT scores over 24: 1%.

Faculty *Total:* 217, 41% full-time. *Student/faculty ratio:* 20:1.

Majors Accounting; administrative assistant and secretarial science; agriculture; anthropology; art; biology/biological sciences; business administration and management; business teacher education; cardiovascular technology; chemistry; clinical laboratory science/medical technology; computer and information sciences; computer management; computer programming; computer science; criminal justice/law enforcement administration; diagnostic medical sonography and ultrasound technology; dramatic/theatre arts; economics; education; engineering technology; English; environmental science; foreign languages and literatures; forensic science and technology; forestry; general studies; geography; health and physical education; health information/medical records administration; health information/medical records technology; histologic technician; history; journalism; mathematics; music; nuclear medical technology; nursing (licensed practical/vocational nurse training); nursing (registered nurse training); occupational therapist assistant; office occupations and clerical services; optometric technician; pharmacy technician; philosophy; physical therapist assistant; physician assistant; physics; political science and government; pre-dentistry studies; pre-engineering; pre-law studies; pre-medical studies; pre-pharmacy studies; pre-veterinary studies; psychiatric/mental health services technology; psychology; respiratory care therapy; social work; sociology; speech and rhetoric.

Academic Programs *Special study options:* academic remediation for entering students, accelerated degree program, adult/continuing education programs, advanced placement credit, cooperative education, distance learning, double majors, English as a second language, honors programs, independent study, part-time degree program, services for LD students, student-designed majors, study abroad, summer session for credit. *ROTC:* Army (c).

Library Weatherbee Learning Resources Center with 67,507 titles, an OPAC, a Web page.

Computers on Campus A campuswide network can be accessed from off campus. Internet access, online (class) registration, at least one staffed computer lab available.

Student Life *Housing:* college housing not available. *Activities and Organizations:* drama/theater group, student-run newspaper, choral group, Students in Free Enterprise (SIFE), Darton Ambassadors, Alpha Beta Gamma, Darton Association of Nursing Students (DANS), Delta Psi Omega. *Campus security:* 24-hour patrols, student patrols, late-night transport/escort service. *Student services:* personal/psychological counseling, women's center.

Athletics Member NJCAA. *Intercollegiate sports:* baseball M, basketball W, golf M, soccer M/W, softball W, swimming and diving M/W. *Intramural sports:* badminton M/W, basketball M/W, bowling M/W, football M, volleyball M/W.

Standardized Tests *Required for some:* SAT or ACT (for admission), SAT Subject Tests (for admission).

Costs (2005–06) *Tuition:* state resident $1542 full-time, $65 per credit hour part-time; nonresident $6166 full-time, $257 per credit hour part-time. *Required fees:* $300 full-time, $150 per term part-time.

Financial Aid Of all full-time matriculated undergraduates who enrolled in 2003, 60 Federal Work-Study jobs.

Applying *Options:* common application, electronic application, early admission. *Application fee:* $20. *Required:* high school transcript, minimum 1.8 GPA, proof of immunization. *Application deadlines:* 7/20 (freshmen), 7/20 (transfers). *Notification:* continuous until 7/27 (freshmen).

Admissions Contact Assistant Director, Admissions, Darton College, 2400 Gillionville Road, Albany, GA 31707. *Phone:* 229-430-6740. *Fax:* 229-430-2926. *E-mail:* darton@mail.dartnet.peachnet.edu.

DeKalb Technical College
Clarkston, Georgia

- **State-supported** 2-year, founded 1961, part of Georgia Department of Technical and Adult Education
- **Calendar** quarters
- **Degree** certificates, diplomas, and associate
- **Suburban** 17-acre campus with easy access to Atlanta
- **Coed,** 4,576 undergraduate students, 39% full-time, 63% women, 37% men

Undergraduates 1,781 full-time, 2,795 part-time. Students come from 2 states and territories, 0.5% are from out of state, 71% African American, 3% Asian American or Pacific Islander, 2% Hispanic American, 0.3% Native American.

Freshmen *Admission:* 1,347 enrolled.

Faculty *Total:* 462, 20% full-time, 0.2% with terminal degrees. *Student/faculty ratio:* 15:1.

Majors Accounting; administrative assistant and secretarial science; automobile/automotive mechanics technology; business/commerce; clinical/medical laboratory technology; computer engineering technology; computer programming; electrical, electronic and communications engineering technology; electromechanical technology; engineering technology; heating, air conditioning and refrigeration technology; instrumentation technology; legal administrative assistant/secretary; marketing/marketing management; medical/clinical assistant; operations management; ophthalmic laboratory technology; surgical technology; telecommunications.

Academic Programs *Special study options:* academic remediation for entering students, adult/continuing education programs, advanced placement credit, distance learning, internships, part-time degree program, services for LD students, summer session for credit.

Library an OPAC, a Web page.

Computers on Campus 500 computers available on campus for general student use. A campuswide network can be accessed. Internet access, online (class) registration, at least one staffed computer lab available.

Student Life *Housing:* college housing not available. *Activities and Organizations:* Student Government Association, Phi Beta Lambda, National Vocational-Technical Honor Society, Collegiate Secretaries International, Epsilon Delta Phi. *Campus security:* security during class hours.

Costs (2004–05) *Tuition:* state resident $4008 full-time, $28 per credit hour part-time; nonresident $2016 full-time, $56 per credit hour part-time. *Required fees:* $186 full-time, $62 per term part-time. *Waivers:* senior citizens.

Financial Aid Of all full-time matriculated undergraduates who enrolled in 2003, 50 Federal Work-Study jobs (averaging $4000).

Applying *Options:* common application, deferred entrance. *Application fee:* $15. *Required:* high school transcript.

Admissions Contact Mr. Terry Richardson, Coordinator of Admissions, DeKalb Technical College, 495 North Indian Creek Road, Clarkston, GA 30021-2397. *Phone:* 404-297-9522 Ext. 1229. *Fax:* 404-294-4234. *E-mail:* admissionsclark@dekalbtech.org.

East Central Technical College
Fitzgerald, Georgia

- **State-supported** 2-year, founded 1968
- **Calendar** quarters
- **Degree** certificates, diplomas, and associate
- **Rural** 30-acre campus
- **Coed,** 1,272 undergraduate students, 51% full-time, 70% women, 30% men

Undergraduates 655 full-time, 617 part-time. 34% African American, 0.3% Asian American or Pacific Islander, 1% Hispanic American, 0.2% Native American.

Freshmen *Admission:* 379 enrolled.

Academic Programs *Special study options:* academic remediation for entering students, cooperative education, distance learning, internships, services for LD students.

Student Life *Housing:* college housing not available.

Standardized Tests *Required:* ACT COMPASS or ASSET (for placement).

Costs (2004–05) *Tuition:* state resident $1008 full-time, $28 per credit hour part-time; nonresident $2016 full-time, $56 per credit hour part-time. *Required fees:* $159 full-time, $53 per term part-time. *Waivers:* senior citizens.

Applying *Options:* deferred entrance. *Application fee:* $15. *Required:* high school transcript.

Admissions Contact Ms. Connie Coffey, Admissions Director, East Central Technical College, 667 Perry House Road, Fitzgerald, GA 31750. *Phone:* 229-468-2033.

East Georgia College
Swainsboro, Georgia

Admissions Contact Ms. Linda Connelly, Admissions Specialist, East Georgia College, 131 College Circle, Swainsboro, GA 30401. *Phone:* 478-289-2019. *Fax:* 478-289-2038.

Emory University, Oxford College
Oxford, Georgia

Admissions Contact Ms. Jennifer B. Taylor, Associate Dean of Admission and Financial Aid, Emory University, Oxford College, 100 Hamill Street, PO Box 1418, Oxford, GA 30054. *Phone:* 770-784-8328. *Toll-free phone:* 800-723-8328. *Fax:* 770-784-8359.

Flint River Technical College
Thomaston, Georgia

- **State-supported** 2-year, founded 1961
- **Calendar** quarters
- **Degree** certificates, diplomas, and associate
- **Coed,** 894 undergraduate students, 56% full-time, 74% women, 26% men

Undergraduates 503 full-time, 391 part-time. 49% African American, 0.1% Asian American or Pacific Islander, 0.7% Hispanic American, 0.2% Native American.

Freshmen *Admission:* 247 enrolled.

Academic Programs *Special study options:* academic remediation for entering students, advanced placement credit, cooperative education, distance learning, internships, services for LD students.

Library 2,653 titles, 82 serial subscriptions, 202 audiovisual materials.

Student Life *Housing:* college housing not available.

Standardized Tests *Required:* ACT COMPASS or ASSET (for placement).

Costs (2004–05) *Tuition:* state resident $1008 full-time, $28 per credit hour part-time; nonresident $2016 full-time, $56 per credit hour part-time. *Required fees:* $138 full-time, $46 per term part-time. *Waivers:* senior citizens.

Applying *Options:* deferred entrance. *Application fee:* $15. *Required:* high school transcript. *Application deadline:* rolling (freshmen).

Admissions Contact Mr. Gary Williams, Admissions Director, Flint River Technical College, 1533 U.S. Highway 19 South, Thomaston, GA 30286-4752. *Phone:* 706-646-6148. *Toll-free phone:* 800-752-9681.

Floyd College
Rome, Georgia

Admissions Contact Todd Jones, Director of Admissions, Floyd College, 3175 Cedartown Highway SE, Rome, GA 30162. *Phone:* 706-295-6339. *Toll-free phone:* 706-295-6339 (in-state); 800-332-2406 Ext. 6339 (out-of-state). *Fax:* 706-295-6610. *E-mail:* tjones@highlands.edu.

GAINESVILLE COLLEGE
Oakwood, Georgia

- **State-supported** 2-year, founded 1964, part of University System of Georgia
- **Calendar** semesters
- **Degree** associate
- **Small-town** 220-acre campus with easy access to Atlanta
- **Coed,** 5,781 undergraduate students

Undergraduates Students come from 22 states and territories, 12 other countries, 4% are from out of state.

Freshmen *Average high school GPA:* 2.9. *Test scores:* SAT verbal scores over 500: 38%; SAT math scores over 500: 34%; SAT verbal scores over 600: 6%; SAT math scores over 600: 6%.

Faculty *Total:* 112, 63% with terminal degrees. *Student/faculty ratio:* 24:1.

Majors Accounting; agriculture; anthropology; art; art teacher education; automobile/automotive mechanics technology; biological and physical sciences; biology/biological sciences; business administration and management; business teacher education; chemistry; child development; clinical/medical laboratory technology; computer science; criminal justice/law enforcement administration; dental hygiene; dramatic/theatre arts; education; electrical, electronic and communications engineering technology; elementary education; engineering; engineering technology; English; forestry; geology/earth science; history; hotel/motel administration; international business/trade/commerce; journalism; kindergarten/preschool education; legal assistant/paralegal; liberal arts and sciences/liberal studies; marketing/marketing management; mathematics; middle school education; music; music teacher education; physical education teaching and coaching; physics; political science and government; poultry science; psychology; social work; sociology; speech and rhetoric; trade and industrial teacher education.

Academic Programs *Special study options:* academic remediation for entering students, adult/continuing education programs, advanced placement credit, distance learning, double majors, English as a second language, honors programs, internships, off-campus study, part-time degree program, services for LD students, summer session for credit.

Library John Harrison Hosch Library with 70,000 titles, 398 serial subscriptions, an OPAC, a Web page.

Computers on Campus 500 computers available on campus for general student use. A campuswide network can be accessed from off campus. Internet access, online (class) registration, at least one staffed computer lab available.

Student Life *Housing:* college housing not available. *Activities and Organizations:* drama/theater group, student-run newspaper, choral group, student newspaper, Baptist Student Union, Student Government Association, Pre-Law/Political Science Club. *Campus security:* 24-hour patrols. *Student services:* personal/psychological counseling.

Athletics *Intramural sports:* badminton M/W, basketball M/W, bowling M/W, football M/W, golf M/W, soccer M, softball M/W, tennis M/W, volleyball M/W, water polo M/W.

Standardized Tests *Required:* SAT or ACT (for admission). *Required for some:* SAT Subject Tests (for admission).

Costs (2004–05) *Tuition:* state resident $1468 full-time, $62 per credit hour part-time; nonresident $5872 full-time, $245 per credit hour part-time. *Required fees:* $60 full-time, $60 per term part-time.

Financial Aid Of all full-time matriculated undergraduates who enrolled in 2003, 40 Federal Work-Study jobs (averaging $2000). *Financial aid deadline:* 6/1.

Applying *Options:* early admission. *Application fee:* $35. *Required:* high school transcript. *Application deadlines:* 7/1 (freshmen), 7/1 (transfers).

Admissions Contact W. Mack Palmour, Director of Admissions, Gainesville College, PO Box 1358, Gainesville, GA 30503. *Phone:* 770-718-3641. *Fax:* 770-718-3859.

GEORGIA AVIATION & TECHNICAL COLLEGE
Eastman, Georgia

- **State-supported** 2-year, founded 1995
- **Calendar** quarters
- **Degree** certificates, diplomas, and associate
- **Coed,** 203 undergraduate students, 67% full-time, 18% women, 82% men

Undergraduates 135 full-time, 68 part-time. 9% African American, 1% Hispanic American, 0.5% Native American.

Freshmen *Admission:* 79 enrolled.

Academic Programs *Special study options:* academic remediation for entering students, advanced placement credit, cooperative education, internships, services for LD students.

Student Life *Housing:* college housing not available.

Standardized Tests *Required:* ACT COMPASS or ASSET (for placement).

Costs (2004–05) *Tuition:* state resident $1008 full-time, $28 per credit hour part-time; nonresident $2016 full-time, $56 per credit hour part-time. *Required fees:* $150 full-time, $50 per term part-time. *Waivers:* senior citizens.

Applying *Options:* deferred entrance. *Application fee:* $15. *Required:* high school transcript.

Admissions Contact Teresa Spires, Georgia Aviation & Technical College, 71 Airport Road, Eastman, GA 31023. *Phone:* 478-374-6980.

GEORGIA MEDICAL INSTITUTE-DeKALB
Atlanta, Georgia

Admissions Contact Ms. Trish Sherwood, Director of Admissions, Georgia Medical Institute-DeKalb, 1706 Northeast Expressway, Atlanta, GA 30329. *Phone:* 404-327-8787.

GEORGIA MILITARY COLLEGE
Milledgeville, Georgia

Admissions Contact Mrs. Donna W. Findley, Director of Admissions, Georgia Military College, 201 East Greene Street, Milledgeville, GA 31061-3398. *Phone:* 478-445-2751. *Toll-free phone:* 800-342-0413.

GEORGIA PERIMETER COLLEGE
Decatur, Georgia

- **State-supported** 2-year, founded 1964, part of University System of Georgia
- **Calendar** semesters
- **Degree** certificates and associate
- **Suburban** 100-acre campus with easy access to Atlanta
- **Endowment** $136,686
- **Coed**

Faculty *Student/faculty ratio:* 21:1.

Student Life *Campus security:* 24-hour emergency response devices and patrols, late-night transport/escort service.

Athletics Member NJCAA.

Standardized Tests *Required:* SAT or ACT (for admission).

Costs (2004–05) *Tuition:* state resident $1468 full-time, $62 per credit hour part-time; nonresident $5872 full-time, $245 per credit hour part-time. *Required fees:* $256 full-time, $128 per term part-time.

Financial Aid Of all full-time matriculated undergraduates who enrolled in 2003, 218 Federal Work-Study jobs (averaging $3000).

Applying *Options:* early admission. *Application fee:* $20. *Required:* high school transcript.

Admissions Contact Ms. Erin Hart, Director of Enrollment Management, Georgia Perimeter College, 555 North Indian Creek Drive, Clarkston, GA 30021-2396. *Phone:* 404-299-4551. *Toll-free phone:* 888-696-2780. *Fax:* 404-299-4574.

GORDON COLLEGE
Barnesville, Georgia

- **State-supported** 2-year, founded 1852, part of University System of Georgia
- **Calendar** semesters
- **Degree** certificates and associate
- **Small-town** 125-acre campus with easy access to Atlanta
- **Endowment** $4.5 million
- **Coed,** 3,449 undergraduate students, 67% full-time, 66% women, 34% men

Undergraduates 2,297 full-time, 1,152 part-time. Students come from 12 other countries, 1% are from out of state, 27% African American, 2% Asian American or Pacific Islander, 1% Hispanic American, 0.1% Native American, 0.6% international, 20% live on campus.

Freshmen *Admission:* 2,899 applied, 1,579 admitted, 1,145 enrolled. *Average high school GPA:* 2.55. *Test scores:* SAT verbal scores over 500: 33%; SAT math scores over 500: 30%; SAT verbal scores over 600: 6%; SAT math scores over 600: 6%; SAT verbal scores over 700: 1%; SAT math scores over 700: 1%.

Faculty *Total:* 144, 58% full-time, 63% with terminal degrees. *Student/faculty ratio:* 25:1.

Majors Administrative assistant and secretarial science; agriculture; art; behavioral sciences; biological and physical sciences; biology/biological sciences; business administration and management; computer and information sciences related; computer science; dramatic/theatre arts; education; English; general studies; history; information technology; journalism; mathematics; nursing (licensed practical/vocational nurse training); nursing (registered nurse training); parks, recreation and leisure; physical sciences; political science and government; psychology; sociology; Spanish.

Academic Programs *Special study options:* academic remediation for entering students, accelerated degree program, adult/continuing education programs, advanced placement credit, cooperative education, honors programs, off-campus study, part-time degree program, services for LD students, summer session for credit.
Library Hightower Library with 118,000 titles, 98 serial subscriptions, an OPAC, a Web page.
Computers on Campus 142 computers available on campus for general student use. A campuswide network can be accessed from student residence rooms and from off campus. Internet access, online (class) registration, at least one staffed computer lab available.
Student Life *Housing Options:* coed, men-only, women-only. Campus housing is university owned. *Activities and Organizations:* drama/theater group, student-run newspaper, choral group, Explorers, Minority Advisement Program, Georgia Association of Nursing Students, Baptist Student Union, Phi Beta Lambda. *Campus security:* 24-hour patrols, late-night transport/escort service. *Student services:* personal/psychological counseling.
Athletics Member NJCAA. *Intercollegiate sports:* baseball M(s), soccer M(s)/W(s), softball W(s), tennis W(s). *Intramural sports:* badminton M/W, basketball M/W, cheerleading W, football M/W, golf M/W, racquetball M/W, table tennis M/W, tennis M, volleyball M/W, wrestling M.
Standardized Tests *Required:* SAT or ACT (for admission).
Costs (2004–05) *Tuition:* state resident $1468 full-time, $62 per credit part-time; nonresident $5872 full-time, $245 per credit part-time. *Required fees:* $188 full-time, $94 per semester part-time. *Room and board:* $3480; room only: $1600. Room and board charges vary according to board plan. *Waivers:* employees or children of employees.
Financial Aid Of all full-time matriculated undergraduates who enrolled in 2003, 75 Federal Work-Study jobs (averaging $1850).
Applying *Options:* electronic application, early admission, deferred entrance. *Application fee:* $20. *Required:* high school transcript, minimum 1.8 GPA. *Application deadline:* rolling (freshmen), rolling (transfers).
Admissions Contact Mr. Brian Gipson, Director of Admissions, Gordon College, 419 College Drive, Barnesville, GA 30204. *Phone:* 770-358-5023. *Toll-free phone:* 800-282-6504. *Fax:* 770-358-3031. *E-mail:* gordon@gdn.edu.

GRIFFIN TECHNICAL COLLEGE
Griffin, Georgia

- **State-supported** 2-year, founded 1965, part of Georgia Department of Technical and Adult Education
- **Calendar** quarters
- **Degree** certificates, diplomas, and associate
- **Small-town** 10-acre campus with easy access to Atlanta
- **Coed,** 3,383 undergraduate students, 42% full-time, 64% women, 36% men
- 100% of applicants were admitted

Undergraduates 1,427 full-time, 1,956 part-time. 35% African American, 1% Asian American or Pacific Islander, 2% Hispanic American, 0.2% Native American.
Freshmen *Admission:* 1,027 applied, 1,027 admitted, 1,027 enrolled.
Faculty *Total:* 299, 22% full-time. *Student/faculty ratio:* 28:1.
Majors Accounting; administrative assistant and secretarial science; computer programming; criminal justice/police science; industrial radiologic technology; industrial technology.
Academic Programs *Special study options:* academic remediation for entering students, adult/continuing education programs, advanced placement credit, distance learning, honors programs, internships, part-time degree program, services for LD students.
Library Griffin Technical College Library with 12,493 titles, 188 serial subscriptions, 1,326 audiovisual materials, an OPAC, a Web page.
Computers on Campus 500 computers available on campus for general student use. A campuswide network can be accessed. Internet access, online (class) registration, at least one staffed computer lab available.
Student Life *Housing:* college housing not available. *Activities and Organizations:* student-run newspaper, Phi Beta Lambda, Vocational Industrial Clubs of America, student government.
Standardized Tests *Required:* ACT COMPASS or ASSET (for placement).
Costs (2004–05) *Tuition:* state resident $1008 full-time, $28 per credit hour part-time; nonresident $2016 full-time, $56 per credit hour part-time. Full-time tuition and fees vary according to course load. Part-time tuition and fees vary according to course load. *Required fees:* $138 full-time, $46 per term part-time. *Waivers:* senior citizens.
Applying *Options:* deferred entrance. *Application fee:* $15. *Required:* high school transcript.
Admissions Contact Christine James-Brown, Admissions Officer, Griffin Technical College, 501 Varsity Road, Griffin, GA 30223. *Phone:* 770-228-7371. *Fax:* 770-229-3227.

GUPTON-JONES COLLEGE OF FUNERAL SERVICE
Decatur, Georgia

- **Independent** 2-year, founded 1920, part of Pierce Mortuary Colleges, Inc
- **Calendar** quarters
- **Degree** associate
- **Suburban** 3-acre campus with easy access to Atlanta
- **Coed**

Faculty *Student/faculty ratio:* 25:1.
Costs (2004–05) *Tuition:* $7500 full-time. No tuition increase for student's term of enrollment.
Applying *Options:* common application, electronic application. *Application fee:* $25. *Required:* high school transcript, health certificate. *Recommended:* minimum 3.0 GPA.
Admissions Contact Ms. Beverly Wheaton, Registrar, Gupton-Jones College of Funeral Service, 5141 Snapfinger Woods Drive, Decatur, GA 30035. *Phone:* 770-593-2257. *Toll-free phone:* 800-848-5352. *Fax:* 770-593-1891. *E-mail:* gjcfs@mindspring.com.

GWINNETT TECHNICAL COLLEGE
Lawrenceville, Georgia

- **State-supported** 2-year, founded 1984
- **Calendar** quarters
- **Degree** certificates, diplomas, and associate
- **Suburban** 93-acre campus with easy access to Atlanta
- **Coed,** 4,466 undergraduate students, 41% full-time, 55% women, 45% men

Undergraduates 1,840 full-time, 2,626 part-time. 23% African American, 6% Asian American or Pacific Islander, 5% Hispanic American, 0.2% Native American. *Retention:* 48% of 2002 full-time freshmen returned.
Freshmen *Admission:* 1,348 enrolled. *Average high school GPA:* 3.20. *Test scores:* SAT verbal scores over 500: 28%; SAT math scores over 500: 29%; SAT verbal scores over 600: 4%; SAT math scores over 600: 4%.
Faculty *Total:* 212, 35% full-time, 11% with terminal degrees. *Student/faculty ratio:* 22:1.
Majors Accounting; administrative assistant and secretarial science; automobile/automotive mechanics technology; computer programming; computer science; construction management; dental hygiene; drafting and design technology; electrical, electronic and communications engineering technology; emergency medical technology (EMT paramedic); fashion merchandising; horticultural science; hotel/motel administration; industrial radiologic technology; interior design; machine tool technology; management information systems; marketing/marketing management; medical/clinical assistant; ornamental horticulture; photography; physical therapy; respiratory care therapy; telecommunications; tourism and travel services management.
Academic Programs *Special study options:* academic remediation for entering students, adult/continuing education programs, advanced placement credit, internships, part-time degree program, services for LD students, summer session for credit.
Library Gwinnett Technical Institute Media Center with 19,547 titles, 246 serial subscriptions, 2,289 audiovisual materials.
Computers on Campus 264 computers available on campus for general student use. Internet access, at least one staffed computer lab available.
Student Life *Housing:* college housing not available. *Campus security:* patrols by campus police. *Student services:* personal/psychological counseling.
Standardized Tests *Required:* (for admission), (for placement).
Costs (2004–05) *Tuition:* state resident $1008 full-time, $28 per credit hour part-time; nonresident $2016 full-time, $56 per credit hour part-time. *Required fees:* $204 full-time, $68 per term part-time. *Waivers:* senior citizens.
Financial Aid Of all full-time matriculated undergraduates who enrolled in 2003, 20 Federal Work-Study jobs (averaging $2100).
Applying *Options:* deferred entrance. *Application fee:* $20. *Required:* high school transcript. *Application deadline:* 8/1 (freshmen). *Notification:* continuous (freshmen).
Admissions Contact Michelle McIntire, Admissions Director, Gwinnett Technical College, PO Box 1505, 5150 Sugarloaf Parkway, Lawrenceville, GA 30046-1505. *Phone:* 770-962-7580 Ext. 434.

HEART OF GEORGIA TECHNICAL COLLEGE
Dublin, Georgia

- **State-supported** 2-year, founded 1984
- **Calendar** quarters

Heart of Georgia Technical College (continued)
- **Degree** certificates, diplomas, and associate
- **Small-town** campus with easy access to Atlanta
- **Coed,** 1,367 undergraduate students, 39% full-time, 65% women, 35% men

Undergraduates 534 full-time, 833 part-time. 45% African American, 0.4% Asian American or Pacific Islander, 0.7% Hispanic American, 0.3% Native American.
Freshmen *Admission:* 432 enrolled.
Majors Business, management, and marketing related; corrections and criminal justice related; early childhood education; respiratory therapy technician.
Academic Programs *Special study options:* academic remediation for entering students, advanced placement credit, cooperative education, distance learning, internships, services for LD students.
Student Life *Housing:* college housing not available.
Standardized Tests *Required:* ACT COMPASS or ASSET (for placement).
Costs (2004–05) *Tuition:* state resident $1008 full-time, $28 per credit hour part-time; nonresident $2016 full-time, $56 per credit hour part-time. *Required fees:* $150 full-time, $50 per term part-time. *Waivers:* senior citizens.
Applying *Options:* deferred entrance. *Application fee:* $15. *Required:* high school transcript.
Admissions Contact Ms. Lisa Kelly, Director of Admissions, Heart of Georgia Technical College, 560 Pinehill Road, Dublin, GA 31021. *Phone:* 478-274-7837.

HERZING COLLEGE
Atlanta, Georgia

Admissions Contact Stacy Johnston, Director of Admissions, Herzing College, 3355 Lenox Road, Suite 100, Atlanta, GA 30326. *Phone:* 404-816-4533. *Toll-free phone:* 800-573-4533. *Fax:* 404-816-5576. *E-mail:* leec@atl.herzing.edu.

HIGH-TECH INSTITUTE
Marietta, Georgia

Admissions Contact Frank Webster, Office Manager, High-Tech Institute, 1090 Northchase Parkway, Suite 150, Marietta, GA 30067. *Phone:* 770-988-9877. *Toll-free phone:* 800-987-0110.

INTERACTIVE COLLEGE OF TECHNOLOGY
Chamblee, Georgia

Admissions Contact Ms. Diana Mamas, Associate Dean of Admissions, Interactive College of Technology, 5303 New Peachtree Road, Chamblee, GA 30341. *Phone:* 770-216-2960. *Toll-free phone:* 800-550-3475.

ITT TECHNICAL INSTITUTE
Duluth, Georgia

- **Proprietary** primarily 2-year, founded 2003, part of ITT Educational Services, Inc
- **Calendar** quarters
- **Degrees** associate and bachelor's
- **Coed**

Standardized Tests *Required:* (for admission).
Costs (2004–05) *Tuition:* Please see school catalog for specific information.
Applying *Options:* deferred entrance. *Application fee:* $100. *Required:* high school transcript, interview. *Recommended:* letters of recommendation.
Admissions Contact Mr. Chip Hinton, Director of Recruitment, ITT Technical Institute, 10700 Abbotts Bridge Road, Suite 190, Duluth, GA 30097. *Phone:* 678-957-8510. *Toll-free phone:* 866-489-8818.

LANIER TECHNICAL COLLEGE
Oakwood, Georgia

- **State-supported** 2-year, founded 1964
- **Calendar** quarters
- **Degree** certificates, diplomas, and associate
- **Coed,** 3,019 undergraduate students, 38% full-time, 64% women, 36% men

Undergraduates 1,136 full-time, 1,883 part-time. 11% African American, 2% Asian American or Pacific Islander, 4% Hispanic American, 0.2% Native American.

Freshmen *Admission:* 1,083 enrolled.
Majors Accounting; banking and financial support services; business administration, management and operations related; business, management, and marketing related; computer science; computer systems networking and telecommunications; corrections and criminal justice related; data modeling/warehousing and database administration; early childhood education; electrical, electronic and communications engineering technology; fire science; health professions related; industrial technology; occupational safety and health technology; office occupations and clerical services; surgical technology.
Academic Programs *Special study options:* academic remediation for entering students, advanced placement credit, distance learning, services for LD students.
Library 7,096 titles, 154 serial subscriptions, 570 audiovisual materials.
Student Life *Housing:* college housing not available.
Standardized Tests *Required:* ACT COMPASS or ASSET (for placement).
Costs (2004–05) *Tuition:* state resident $1008 full-time, $28 per credit hour part-time; nonresident $2016 full-time, $56 per credit hour part-time. *Required fees:* $165 full-time, $55 per term part-time. *Waivers:* senior citizens.
Applying *Options:* deferred entrance. *Application fee:* $15. *Required:* high school transcript.
Admissions Contact Mike Marlowe, Admissions Director, Lanier Technical College, 2990 Landrum Education Drive, Oakwood, GA 30566. *Phone:* 770-531-6332.

MIDDLE GEORGIA COLLEGE
Cochran, Georgia

- **State-supported** 2-year, founded 1884, part of University System of Georgia
- **Calendar** semesters
- **Degree** certificates and associate
- **Small-town** 165-acre campus
- **Endowment** $1.0 million
- **Coed,** 2,628 undergraduate students, 64% full-time, 61% women, 39% men

Middle Georgia College is a 2-year, residential public college with a student population of approximately 2,600. Transfer programs are offered in more than 100 academic disciplines, including engineering, nursing, business, and education. Numerous clubs and organizations, as well as intercollegiate athletics for men and women, enrich student life.

Undergraduates 1,686 full-time, 942 part-time. Students come from 37 states and territories, 5% are from out of state, 34% African American, 1% Asian American or Pacific Islander, 1% Hispanic American, 0.2% Native American, 0.4% international, 15% transferred in, 32% live on campus.
Freshmen *Admission:* 1,504 applied, 1,421 admitted, 807 enrolled. *Average high school GPA:* 2.82. *Test scores:* SAT verbal scores over 500: 33%; SAT math scores over 500: 35%; ACT scores over 18: 31%; SAT verbal scores over 600: 11%; SAT math scores over 600: 12%; ACT scores over 24: 5%; SAT verbal scores over 700: 1%; SAT math scores over 700: 1%.
Faculty *Total:* 133, 56% full-time, 25% with terminal degrees. *Student/faculty ratio:* 21:1.
Majors Business administration and management; computer and information sciences related; computer engineering related; computer/information technology services administration related; computer science; criminal justice/police science; data processing and data processing technology; fashion merchandising; information science/studies; liberal arts and sciences/liberal studies; nursing (registered nurse training); occupational therapist assistant; physical therapist assistant; public administration; survey technology.
Academic Programs *Special study options:* academic remediation for entering students, accelerated degree program, adult/continuing education programs, advanced placement credit, cooperative education, distance learning, honors programs, part-time degree program, services for LD students, study abroad, summer session for credit.
Library Roberts Memorial Library with 110,000 titles, 147 serial subscriptions, 5,119 audiovisual materials, an OPAC, a Web page.
Computers on Campus 439 computers available on campus for general student use. A campuswide network can be accessed from student residence rooms and from off campus. Internet access, online (class) registration, at least one staffed computer lab available.
Student Life *Housing:* on-campus residence required through sophomore year. *Options:* men-only, women-only. Campus housing is university owned. Freshman campus housing is guaranteed. *Activities and Organizations:* drama/theater group, student-run newspaper, choral group, marching band, Baptist Student Union, Student Government Association, MGC Ambassadors, Encore Productions, United Voices of Praise. *Campus security:* 24-hour emergency response devices and patrols, student patrols, late-night transport/escort service, controlled dormitory access, patrols by police officers. *Student services:* health clinic, personal/psychological counseling.

Athletics Member NJCAA. *Intercollegiate sports:* baseball M(s), basketball M(s)/W(s), soccer M(s)/W(s), softball W(s). *Intramural sports:* badminton M/W, basketball M/W, football M/W, golf M/W, softball M/W, swimming and diving M/W, tennis M/W.

Standardized Tests *Required:* SAT or ACT (for admission). *Required for some:* SAT Subject Tests (for admission).

Costs (2004–05) *Tuition:* state resident $1468 full-time, $62 per credit hour part-time; nonresident $5872 full-time, $245 per credit hour part-time. Part-time tuition and fees vary according to course load. *Required fees:* $374 full-time, $355 per year part-time. *Room and board:* $4160; room only: $1950. Room and board charges vary according to board plan and housing facility.

Financial Aid Of all full-time matriculated undergraduates who enrolled in 2003, 103 Federal Work-Study jobs (averaging $600).

Applying *Options:* common application, electronic application, early admission, deferred entrance. *Application fee:* $20. *Required:* high school transcript, minimum 2.0 GPA. *Required for some:* essay or personal statement, minimum 3.5 GPA, letters of recommendation, interview. *Application deadline:* rolling (freshmen), rolling (transfers). *Notification:* continuous (freshmen).

Admissions Contact Ms. Jennifer Brannon, Director of Admissions, Middle Georgia College, 1100 2nd Street, SE, Cochran, GA 31014. *Phone:* 478-934-3138. *Fax:* 478-934-3403. *E-mail:* admissions@mgc.edu.

MIDDLE GEORGIA TECHNICAL COLLEGE
Warner Robbins, Georgia

- **State-supported** 2-year, founded 1973
- **Calendar** quarters
- **Degree** certificates, diplomas, and associate
- **Coed,** 2,446 undergraduate students, 53% full-time, 57% women, 43% men

Undergraduates 1,296 full-time, 1,150 part-time. 39% African American, 1% Asian American or Pacific Islander, 2% Hispanic American, 0.4% Native American.

Freshmen *Admission:* 957 enrolled.

Academic Programs *Special study options:* academic remediation for entering students, advanced placement credit, cooperative education, distance learning, internships, services for LD students.

Library 2,124 titles, 69 serial subscriptions, 211 audiovisual materials.

Student Life *Housing:* college housing not available.

Standardized Tests *Required:* ACT COMPASS or ASSET (for placement).

Costs (2004–05) *Tuition:* state resident $1008 full-time, $28 per credit hour part-time; nonresident $2016 full-time, $56 per credit hour part-time. *Required fees:* $138 full-time, $46 per term part-time. *Waivers:* senior citizens.

Applying *Options:* deferred entrance. *Application fee:* $15. *Required:* high school transcript.

Admissions Contact Mr. Howard Gregory, Director of Admissions, Middle Georgia Technical College, 80 Cohen Walker Drive, Warner Robins, GA 31088. *Phone:* 478-988-6843. *Toll-free phone:* 800-474-1031.

MOULTRIE TECHNICAL COLLEGE
Moultrie, Georgia

- **State-supported** 2-year, founded 1964
- **Calendar** quarters
- **Degree** certificates, diplomas, and associate
- **Coed,** 1,826 undergraduate students, 50% full-time, 67% women, 33% men

Undergraduates 904 full-time, 922 part-time. 38% African American, 0.4% Asian American or Pacific Islander, 2% Hispanic American, 0.2% Native American.

Freshmen *Admission:* 598 enrolled.

Academic Programs *Special study options:* academic remediation for entering students, advanced placement credit, distance learning, internships, services for LD students.

Student Life *Housing:* college housing not available.

Standardized Tests *Required:* ACT COMPASS or ASSET (for placement).

Costs (2004–05) *Tuition:* state resident $1008 full-time, $28 per credit hour part-time; nonresident $2016 full-time, $56 per credit hour part-time. *Required fees:* $138 full-time, $46 per term part-time. *Waivers:* senior citizens.

Applying *Options:* deferred entrance. *Required:* high school transcript.

Admissions Contact Leigh Wallace, Admissions Director, Moultrie Technical College, 361 Industrial Drive, Moultrie, GA 31768. *Phone:* 229-891-4144.

NORTH GEORGIA TECHNICAL COLLEGE
Clarkesville, Georgia

- **State-supported** 2-year, founded 1943
- **Calendar** quarters

- **Degree** certificates, diplomas, and associate
- **Coed,** 1,934 undergraduate students, 52% full-time, 55% women, 45% men

Undergraduates 1,001 full-time, 933 part-time. 8% African American, 0.9% Asian American or Pacific Islander, 2% Hispanic American, 0.3% Native American.

Freshmen *Admission:* 765 enrolled.

Academic Programs *Special study options:* academic remediation for entering students, advanced placement credit, distance learning, internships, services for LD students.

Library 15,684 titles, 162 serial subscriptions, 990 audiovisual materials.

Standardized Tests *Required:* ACT COMPASS or ASSET (for placement).

Costs (2004–05) *Tuition:* state resident $1008 full-time, $28 per credit hour part-time; nonresident $2016 full-time, $56 per credit hour part-time. *Required fees:* $165 full-time, $55 per term part-time. *Room and board:* $2775; room only: $645. *Waivers:* senior citizens.

Applying *Options:* deferred entrance. *Application fee:* $15. *Required:* high school transcript.

Admissions Contact Gail Taylor, Admissions Director, North Georgia Technical College, PO Box 65, Clarkesville, GA 30523. *Phone:* 706-754-7724.

NORTH METRO TECHNICAL COLLEGE
Acworth, Georgia

- **State-supported** 2-year, founded 1989
- **Calendar** quarters
- **Degree** certificates, diplomas, and associate
- **Coed,** 1,827 undergraduate students, 37% full-time, 58% women, 42% men

Undergraduates 676 full-time, 1,151 part-time. 14% African American, 2% Asian American or Pacific Islander, 3% Hispanic American, 0.6% Native American.

Freshmen *Admission:* 655 enrolled.

Academic Programs *Special study options:* academic remediation for entering students, advanced placement credit, distance learning, internships, services for LD students.

Student Life *Housing:* college housing not available.

Standardized Tests *Required:* ACT COMPASS or ASSET (for placement).

Costs (2004–05) *Tuition:* state resident $1008 full-time, $28 per credit hour part-time; nonresident $2016 full-time, $56 per credit hour part-time. *Required fees:* $46 per term part-time. *Waivers:* senior citizens.

Applying *Options:* deferred entrance. *Application fee:* $15. *Required:* high school transcript.

Admissions Contact Missy Cusack, Admissions Director, North Metro Technical College, 5198 Ross Road, Acworth 30102. *Phone:* 770-975-4079.

NORTHWESTERN TECHNICAL COLLEGE
Rock Springs, Georgia

- **State-supported** 2-year, founded 1966, part of Georgia Department of Technical and Adult Education
- **Calendar** quarters
- **Degree** certificates, diplomas, and associate
- **Rural** campus
- **Coed,** 1,663 undergraduate students, 44% full-time, 64% women, 36% men

Undergraduates 737 full-time, 926 part-time. Students come from 3 states and territories, 5% are from out of state, 5% African American, 0.3% Asian American or Pacific Islander, 1% Hispanic American, 0.5% Native American.

Freshmen *Admission:* 424 enrolled.

Faculty *Total:* 155, 29% full-time. *Student/faculty ratio:* 15:1.

Majors Accounting technology and bookkeeping; computer management; computer programming (specific applications); drafting and design technology; electromechanical technology; executive assistant/executive secretary; human resources management; kindergarten/preschool education; occupational therapist assistant; quality control technology.

Academic Programs *Special study options:* academic remediation for entering students, adult/continuing education programs, advanced placement credit, distance learning, internships, part-time degree program, services for LD students, summer session for credit.

Library Northwestern Technical Institute Library with 350,000 titles, 180 serial subscriptions, 20,000 audiovisual materials, an OPAC, a Web page.

Computers on Campus 270 computers available on campus for general student use. A campuswide network can be accessed from off campus. Internet access, online (class) registration, at least one staffed computer lab available.

Student Life *Housing:* college housing not available. *Activities and Organizations:* student-run newspaper. *Student services:* personal/psychological counseling, women's center.

Northwestern Technical College (continued)

Standardized Tests *Required:* ACT ASSET or COMPASS (for placement).

Costs (2004–05) *Tuition:* state resident $1008 full-time, $28 per credit hour part-time; nonresident $2016 full-time, $56 per credit hour part-time. *Required fees:* $138 full-time, $46 per term part-time. *Waivers:* senior citizens.

Financial Aid Of all full-time matriculated undergraduates who enrolled in 2003, 30 Federal Work-Study jobs (averaging $4800).

Applying *Options:* deferred entrance. *Application fee:* $15. *Required:* high school transcript. *Required for some:* essay or personal statement, letters of recommendation, interview. *Application deadline:* rolling (freshmen).

Admissions Contact Mrs. Carolyn Solmon, Director of Admissions and Career Planning, Northwestern Technical College, 265 Bicentennial Trail, P. O. Box 569, Rock Springs, GA 30739. *Phone:* 706-764-3511. *Toll-free phone:* 800-735-5726. *E-mail:* csolmon@nwtcollege.org.

OGEECHEE TECHNICAL COLLEGE
Statesboro, Georgia

- **State-supported** 2-year, founded 1989, part of Georgia Department of Technical and Adult Education
- **Calendar** quarters
- **Degree** certificates, diplomas, and associate
- **Small-town** campus
- **Coed,** 2,084 undergraduate students, 52% full-time, 69% women, 31% men

Undergraduates 1,075 full-time, 1,009 part-time. 0.2% are from out of state, 38% African American, 0.3% Asian American or Pacific Islander, 1% Hispanic American, 0.5% Native American.

Freshmen *Admission:* 1,839 applied, 639 enrolled.

Faculty *Total:* 158, 46% full-time, 3% with terminal degrees. *Student/faculty ratio:* 17:1.

Academic Programs *Special study options:* academic remediation for entering students, advanced placement credit, distance learning, internships, services for LD students.

Library 2,477 titles, 109 serial subscriptions, 276 audiovisual materials.

Student Life *Housing:* college housing not available.

Standardized Tests *Required:* ACT COMPASS or ASSET (for placement).

Costs (2004–05) *Tuition:* state resident $1008 full-time, $28 per credit hour part-time; nonresident $2016 full-time, $56 per credit hour part-time. Full-time tuition and fees vary according to course load and program. Part-time tuition and fees vary according to course load and program. *Required fees:* $153 full-time, $51 per term part-time. *Waivers:* senior citizens.

Applying *Options:* deferred entrance. *Application fee:* $15. *Required:* high school transcript.

Admissions Contact Mr. Ryan Foley, Admissions Director, Ogeechee Technical College, 1 Joe Kennedy Boulevard, Statesboro, GA 30458. *Phone:* 912-871-1600. *Toll-free phone:* 800-646-1316. *E-mail:* rfoley@ogeecheetech.edu.

OKEFENOKEE TECHNICAL COLLEGE
Waycross, Georgia

- **State-supported** 2-year
- **Calendar** quarters
- **Degree** certificates, diplomas, and associate
- **Small-town** campus
- **Coed,** 1,843 undergraduate students, 41% full-time, 69% women, 31% men

Undergraduates 752 full-time, 1,091 part-time. 25% African American, 0.2% Asian American or Pacific Islander, 0.8% Hispanic American, 0.7% Native American.

Freshmen *Admission:* 524 enrolled.

Faculty *Total:* 180, 56% full-time. *Student/faculty ratio:* 20:1.

Majors Clinical/medical laboratory technology; computer technology/computer systems technology; criminal justice/police science; early childhood education; forestry technology; occupational safety and health technology; office occupations and clerical services; respiratory therapy technician; surgical technology.

Academic Programs *Special study options:* academic remediation for entering students, advanced placement credit, distance learning, internships, services for LD students.

Library 1,714 titles.

Student Life *Housing:* college housing not available.

Standardized Tests *Required:* ACT COMPASS or ASSET (for placement).

Costs (2004–05) *Tuition:* state resident $1008 full-time, $28 per credit hour part-time; nonresident $2016 full-time, $56 per credit hour part-time. *Required fees:* $138 full-time, $46 per term part-time. *Waivers:* senior citizens.

Applying *Options:* deferred entrance. *Application fee:* $15. *Required:* high school transcript.

Admissions Contact Reba Smith, Director of Admissions, Okefenokee Technical College, 1701 Carswell Avenue, Waycross, GA 31503. *Phone:* 912-287-5806.

SANDERSVILLE TECHNICAL COLLEGE
Sandersville, Georgia

- **State-supported** 2-year
- **Calendar** quarters
- **Degree** certificates, diplomas, and associate
- **Coed,** 705 undergraduate students, 37% full-time, 69% women, 31% men

Undergraduates 262 full-time, 443 part-time. 68% African American, 0.1% Asian American or Pacific Islander, 0.4% Hispanic American, 0.6% Native American.

Freshmen *Admission:* 265 enrolled.

Academic Programs *Special study options:* academic remediation for entering students, advanced placement credit, distance learning, internships, services for LD students.

Student Life *Housing:* college housing not available.

Standardized Tests *Required:* ACT COMPASS or ASSET (for placement).

Costs (2004–05) *Tuition:* state resident $1008 full-time, $28 per credit hour part-time; nonresident $2016 full-time, $56 per credit hour part-time. *Required fees:* $138 full-time, $46 per term part-time. *Waivers:* senior citizens.

Applying *Options:* deferred entrance. *Application fee:* $15. *Required:* high school transcript.

Admissions Contact Patrick Wilson, Admissions Director, Sandersville Technical College, 1189 Deepstep Road, Sandersville, GA 31082. *Phone:* 478-553-2065.

SAVANNAH TECHNICAL COLLEGE
Savannah, Georgia

- **State-supported** 2-year, founded 1929, part of Georgia Department of Technical and Adult Education
- **Calendar** quarters
- **Degree** certificates, diplomas, and associate
- **Urban** 15-acre campus
- **Coed,** 3,714 undergraduate students, 43% full-time, 69% women, 31% men

Undergraduates 1,612 full-time, 2,102 part-time. Students come from 4 states and territories, 5% are from out of state, 62% African American, 2% Asian American or Pacific Islander, 3% Hispanic American, 0.4% Native American, 0.6% international, 3% transferred in. *Retention:* 40% of 2002 full-time freshmen returned.

Freshmen *Admission:* 1,084 enrolled.

Faculty *Total:* 201, 28% full-time. *Student/faculty ratio:* 15:1.

Majors Accounting; administrative assistant and secretarial science; biomedical technology; civil engineering technology; computer programming; electrical, electronic and communications engineering technology; electromechanical technology; fire science; information technology; instrumentation technology; surgical technology.

Academic Programs *Special study options:* academic remediation for entering students, advanced placement credit, distance learning, internships, part-time degree program, services for LD students, summer session for credit.

Library 20,804 titles, 160 serial subscriptions, 3,150 audiovisual materials, an OPAC, a Web page.

Computers on Campus Internet access, at least one staffed computer lab available.

Student Life *Housing:* college housing not available. *Activities and Organizations:* Phi Beta Lambda, Vocational Industrial Clubs of America (VICA).

Standardized Tests *Required:* ACT COMPASS or ASSET (for placement).

Costs (2004–05) *Tuition:* state resident $1008 full-time, $28 per credit hour part-time; nonresident $2016 full-time, $56 per credit hour part-time. *Required fees:* $138 full-time, $46 per term part-time. *Waivers:* senior citizens.

Applying *Options:* deferred entrance. *Application fee:* $15. *Required:* high school transcript. *Notification:* continuous (freshmen).

Admissions Contact Angela Southerland, Admissions Director, Savannah Technical College, 5717 White Bluff Road, Savannah, GA 31405. *Phone:* 912-303-1772. *Toll-free phone:* 800-769-6362. *Fax:* 912-303-1781.

SOUTHEASTERN TECHNICAL COLLEGE
Vidalia, Georgia

- **State-supported** 2-year, founded 1989
- **Calendar** quarters
- **Degree** certificates, diplomas, and associate
- **Coed,** 1,048 undergraduate students, 47% full-time, 76% women, 24% men

Undergraduates 497 full-time, 551 part-time. 32% African American, 0.3% Asian American or Pacific Islander, 2% Hispanic American, 0.3% Native American.

Freshmen *Admission:* 312 enrolled.

Majors Accounting; business administration and management; corrections and criminal justice related; data entry/microcomputer applications; early childhood education; electrical, electronic and communications engineering technology; marketing/marketing management; system, networking, and LAN/WAN management; web page, digital/multimedia and information resources design.

Academic Programs *Special study options:* academic remediation for entering students, advanced placement credit, distance learning, internships, services for LD students.

Student Life *Housing:* college housing not available.

Standardized Tests *Required:* ACT COMPASS or ASSET (for placement).

Costs (2004–05) *Tuition:* state resident $1008 full-time, $28 per credit hour part-time; nonresident $2016 full-time, $56 per credit hour part-time. *Required fees:* $138 full-time, $46 per term part-time. *Waivers:* senior citizens.

Applying *Options:* deferred entrance. *Application fee:* $15. *Required:* high school transcript.

Admissions Contact Christopher P. Carroll, Admissions Director, Southeastern Technical College, 3001 East 1st Street, Vidalia, GA 30474. *Phone:* 912-538-3121.

SOUTH GEORGIA COLLEGE
Douglas, Georgia

Admissions Contact Dr. Randy L. Braswell, Director of Admissions, Records, and Research, South Georgia College, 100 West College Park Drive, Douglas, GA 31533-5098. *Phone:* 912-389-4200. *Toll-free phone:* 800-342-6364. *Fax:* 912-389-4392. *E-mail:* admissions@sga.edu.

SOUTH GEORGIA TECHNICAL COLLEGE
Americus, Georgia

- **State-supported** 2-year, founded 1948
- **Calendar** quarters
- **Degree** certificates, diplomas, and associate
- **Coed,** 1,693 undergraduate students, 54% full-time, 55% women, 45% men

Undergraduates 918 full-time, 775 part-time. 57% African American, 0.3% Asian American or Pacific Islander, 0.8% Hispanic American, 0.2% Native American.

Freshmen *Admission:* 417 enrolled.

Academic Programs *Special study options:* academic remediation for entering students, advanced placement credit, cooperative education, distance learning, internships, services for LD students.

Athletics Member NJCAA. *Intercollegiate sports:* basketball M/W.

Standardized Tests *Required:* ACT COMPASS or ASSET (for placement).

Costs (2004–05) *Tuition:* state resident $1008 full-time, $28 per credit hour part-time; nonresident $2016 full-time, $56 per credit hour part-time. *Required fees:* $165 full-time, $55 per term part-time. *Room and board:* $3000; room only: $700. *Waivers:* senior citizens.

Applying *Options:* deferred entrance. *Application fee:* $15. *Required:* high school transcript.

Admissions Contact Karen Werling, Admissions Director, South Georgia Technical College, 900 South Georgia Tech Parkway, Americus, GA 31709-8104. *Phone:* 229-931-2299.

SOUTHWEST GEORGIA TECHNICAL COLLEGE
Thomasville, Georgia

- **State-supported** 2-year, founded 1963, part of Georgia Department of Technical and Adult Education
- **Calendar** quarters
- **Degree** certificates, diplomas, and associate
- **Coed,** 1,598 undergraduate students, 45% full-time, 74% women, 26% men

Undergraduates 719 full-time, 879 part-time. 45% African American, 0.3% Asian American or Pacific Islander, 0.6% Hispanic American, 0.6% Native American, 0.1% international.

Freshmen *Admission:* 394 enrolled.

Faculty *Total:* 114, 43% full-time, 2% with terminal degrees. *Student/faculty ratio:* 18:1.

Majors Accounting; administrative assistant and secretarial science; agricultural mechanization; clinical/medical laboratory technology; heavy equipment maintenance technology; hospitality administration related; information science/

studies; medical radiologic technology; occupational therapist assistant; physical therapy; respiratory care therapy.

Academic Programs *Special study options:* academic remediation for entering students, advanced placement credit, cooperative education, distance learning, internships, part-time degree program, services for LD students, summer session for credit.

Library 19,767 titles, 113 serial subscriptions, 920 audiovisual materials, an OPAC, a Web page.

Computers on Campus 430 computers available on campus for general student use. A campuswide network can be accessed. Internet access, online (class) registration available.

Student Life *Housing:* college housing not available.

Standardized Tests *Required:* ACT ASSETor COMPASS (for placement).

Costs (2004–05) *Tuition:* state resident $1008 full-time, $28 per credit hour part-time; nonresident $2016 full-time, $56 per credit hour part-time. *Required fees:* $138 full-time, $46 per term part-time. *Waivers:* senior citizens.

Applying *Options:* electronic application, deferred entrance. *Application fee:* $20. *Required:* high school transcript.

Admissions Contact Ms. Lorette M. Hoover, Vice President, Southwest Georgia Technical College, 15689 US Highway 19 N, Thomasville, GA 31792. *Phone:* 229-225-5077. *Fax:* 229-225-4330. *E-mail:* lhoover@southwestgatech.edu.

SWAINSBORO TECHNICAL COLLEGE
Swainsboro, Georgia

- **State-supported** 2-year, founded 1963
- **Calendar** quarters
- **Degree** certificates, diplomas, and associate
- **Coed,** 666 undergraduate students, 50% full-time, 77% women, 23% men

Undergraduates 331 full-time, 335 part-time. 44% African American, 0.2% Asian American or Pacific Islander, 0.5% Hispanic American.

Freshmen *Admission:* 186 enrolled.

Academic Programs *Special study options:* advanced placement credit, cooperative education, distance learning, internships, services for LD students.

Student Life *Housing:* college housing not available.

Standardized Tests *Required:* ACT COMPASS or ASSET (for placement).

Costs (2004–05) *Tuition:* state resident $1008 full-time, $28 per credit hour part-time; nonresident $2016 full-time, $56 per credit hour part-time. *Required fees:* $138 full-time, $46 per term part-time. *Waivers:* senior citizens.

Applying *Options:* deferred entrance. *Application fee:* $15. *Required:* high school transcript.

Admissions Contact Mitchell Fagler, Admissions Director, Swainsboro Technical College, 346 Kite Road, Swainsboro, GA 30401. *Phone:* 478-289-2259.

TRUETT-MCCONNELL COLLEGE
Cleveland, Georgia

- **Independent Baptist** primarily 2-year, founded 1946
- **Calendar** semesters
- **Degrees** certificates, associate, and bachelor's
- **Rural** 310-acre campus with easy access to Atlanta
- **Coed,** 359 undergraduate students, 91% full-time, 44% women, 56% men

Undergraduates 326 full-time, 33 part-time. Students come from 4 states and territories, 4 other countries, 2% are from out of state, 13% African American, 1% Asian American or Pacific Islander, 2% Hispanic American, 0.3% Native American, 6% transferred in, 73% live on campus. *Retention:* 21% of 2002 full-time freshmen returned.

Freshmen *Admission:* 487 applied, 417 admitted, 162 enrolled. *Average high school GPA:* 2.90. *Test scores:* SAT verbal scores over 500: 39%; SAT math scores over 500: 37%; ACT scores over 18: 60%; SAT verbal scores over 600: 8%; SAT math scores over 600: 8%; ACT scores over 24: 6%; SAT verbal scores over 700: 1%; SAT math scores over 700: 1%; ACT scores over 30: 2%.

Faculty *Total:* 45, 51% full-time. *Student/faculty ratio:* 11:1.

Majors Business/commerce; Christian studies; education; general studies; liberal arts and sciences/liberal studies; music.

Academic Programs *Special study options:* academic remediation for entering students, accelerated degree program, advanced placement credit, double majors, honors programs, part-time degree program, services for LD students, study abroad, summer session for credit.

Library Cofer Library with 30,779 titles, 155 serial subscriptions, 2,522 audiovisual materials, an OPAC.

Computers on Campus 38 computers available on campus for general student use. A campuswide network can be accessed from student residence rooms and from off campus. Internet access, at least one staffed computer lab available.

Student Life *Housing Options:* men-only, women-only. Campus housing is university owned. *Activities and Organizations:* choral group, intramurals,

Truett-McConnell College (continued)
Baptist Student Union, College Choir, Student Government Association, Fellowship of Christian Athletes (FCA). *Campus security:* 24-hour weekday patrols, 10-hour weekend patrols by trained security personnel. *Student services:* personal/psychological counseling.

Athletics Member NJCAA. *Intercollegiate sports:* baseball M(s), basketball M(s)/W(s), soccer M(s)/W(s). *Intramural sports:* basketball M/W, football M/W, ultimate Frisbee M/W, volleyball M/W.

Standardized Tests *Required:* SAT or ACT (for admission).

Costs (2004–05) *Comprehensive fee:* $15,186 includes full-time tuition ($10,786) and room and board ($4400). Part-time tuition: $360 per credit hour. *Room and board:* college room only: $2000. *Waivers:* employees or children of employees.

Applying *Options:* early admission, deferred entrance. *Application fee:* $25. *Required:* high school transcript, minimum 2.0 GPA, minimum SAT score of 720 or ACT score of 15. *Required for some:* interview. *Application deadlines:* 8/1 (freshmen), 8/1 (transfers). *Notification:* continuous (freshmen).

Admissions Contact Ms. Penny Loggins, Dean for Admissions, Truett-McConnell College, 100 Alumni Drive, Cleveland, GA 30528-9799. *Phone:* 706-865-2134 Ext. 210. *Toll-free phone:* 800-226-8621. *Fax:* 706-865-7615. *E-mail:* admissions@truett.edu.

VALDOSTA TECHNICAL COLLEGE

Valdosta, Georgia

- **State-supported** 2-year, founded 1963, part of Georgia Department of Technical and Adult Education
- **Calendar** quarters
- **Degree** certificates, diplomas, and associate
- **Suburban** 18-acre campus
- **Coed,** 2,303 undergraduate students, 46% full-time, 65% women, 35% men

Undergraduates 1,058 full-time, 1,245 part-time. Students come from 2 states and territories, 1% are from out of state, 38% African American, 0.9% Asian American or Pacific Islander, 2% Hispanic American, 0.5% Native American, 5% transferred in.

Freshmen *Admission:* 657 enrolled.

Faculty *Total:* 276, 33% full-time, 2% with terminal degrees. *Student/faculty ratio:* 12:1.

Academic Programs *Special study options:* academic remediation for entering students, advanced placement credit, distance learning, external degree program, internships, services for LD students.

Library Valdosta Technical College Library plus 1 other with 3,373 titles, 109 serial subscriptions, 225 audiovisual materials, an OPAC.

Computers on Campus 564 computers available on campus for general student use. A campuswide network can be accessed from off campus. Internet access, online (class) registration, at least one staffed computer lab available.

Student Life *Housing:* college housing not available.

Standardized Tests *Required:* ACT COMPASS or ASSET (for placement).

Costs (2004–05) *Tuition:* state resident $1008 full-time, $28 per credit hour part-time; nonresident $2016 full-time, $56 per credit hour part-time. *Required fees:* $171 full-time, $57 per term part-time. *Waivers:* senior citizens.

Applying *Options:* common application, deferred entrance. *Application fee:* $15. *Required:* high school transcript.

Admissions Contact Student Customer Services, Valdosta Technical College, Student Customer Services, PO Box 928, 4089 Val Tech Road, Valdosta, GA 31603-0928. *Phone:* 229-333-2100.

WAYCROSS COLLEGE

Waycross, Georgia

- **State-supported** 2-year, founded 1976, part of University System of Georgia
- **Calendar** semesters
- **Degree** certificates and associate
- **Small-town** 150-acre campus
- **Endowment** $85,583
- **Coed**

Faculty *Student/faculty ratio:* 22:1.

Student Life *Campus security:* late-night transport/escort service, security guards.

Standardized Tests *Required:* SAT or ACT (for admission).

Costs (2004–05) *Tuition:* state resident $1468 full-time, $62 per semester hour part-time; nonresident $5872 full-time. *Required fees:* $154 full-time.

Financial Aid Of all full-time matriculated undergraduates who enrolled in 2003, 20 Federal Work-Study jobs (averaging $2000).

Applying *Options:* electronic application, early admission, deferred entrance. *Application fee:* $20. *Required:* high school transcript.

Admissions Contact Mrs. Susan Dukes, Assistant Director for Admissions, Waycross College, 2001 South Georgia Parkway, Waycross, GA 31503. *Phone:* 912-285-6133. *Fax:* 912-285-6158. *E-mail:* admiss@waycross.edu.

WEST CENTRAL TECHNICAL COLLEGE

Waco, Georgia

- **State-supported** 2-year, founded 1968, part of Georgia Department of Technical and Adult Education
- **Calendar** quarters
- **Degree** certificates, diplomas, and associate
- **Coed,** 2,634 undergraduate students, 32% full-time, 70% women, 30% men

Undergraduates 847 full-time, 1,787 part-time. 47% are from out of state, 21% African American, 0.6% Asian American or Pacific Islander, 2% Hispanic American, 0.7% Native American.

Freshmen *Admission:* 829 enrolled.

Faculty *Total:* 150, 40% full-time.

Majors Accounting; administrative assistant and secretarial science; business administration and management; computer and information sciences related; computer programming (specific applications); data entry/microcomputer applications; dental hygiene; electrical, electronic and communications engineering technology; heavy equipment maintenance technology; industrial radiologic technology; information science/studies; marketing/marketing management; word processing.

Academic Programs *Special study options:* academic remediation for entering students, adult/continuing education programs, advanced placement credit, distance learning, external degree program, internships, part-time degree program, services for LD students.

Library 18,462 titles, 1,635 audiovisual materials.

Computers on Campus 109 computers available on campus for general student use. At least one staffed computer lab available.

Student Life *Housing:* college housing not available.

Costs (2004–05) *Tuition:* state resident $1008 full-time, $28 per credit hour part-time; nonresident $2016 full-time, $56 per credit hour part-time. *Required fees:* $150 full-time, $50 per term part-time. *Waivers:* senior citizens.

Financial Aid Of all full-time matriculated undergraduates who enrolled in 2003, 45 Federal Work-Study jobs (averaging $1000).

Applying *Options:* electronic application, deferred entrance. *Application fee:* $25. *Required:* high school transcript. *Required for some:* interview. *Application deadline:* rolling (freshmen), rolling (transfers).

Admissions Contact Mrs. Mary Alderhold, Director of Student Services, West Central Technical College, 176 Murphy Campus Boulevard, Waco, GA 30182. *Phone:* 770-537-5712.

WEST GEORGIA TECHNICAL COLLEGE

LaGrange, Georgia

- **State-supported** 2-year, founded 1966, part of Georgia Department of Technical and Adult Education
- **Calendar** quarters
- **Degree** certificates, diplomas, and associate
- **Coed,** 1,862 undergraduate students, 42% full-time, 64% women, 36% men

Undergraduates 778 full-time, 1,084 part-time. Students come from 2 states and territories, 5% are from out of state, 42% African American, 0.4% Asian American or Pacific Islander, 0.4% Hispanic American, 0.1% Native American, 7% transferred in.

Freshmen *Admission:* 554 enrolled.

Faculty *Total:* 75, 48% full-time. *Student/faculty ratio:* 12:1.

Majors Accounting technology and bookkeeping; clinical/medical laboratory technology; computer and information sciences; executive assistant/executive secretary; human resources management; marketing/marketing management.

Academic Programs *Special study options:* academic remediation for entering students, advanced placement credit, distance learning, internships, services for LD students.

Library 19,683 titles, 218 serial subscriptions, 525 audiovisual materials.

Student Life *Housing:* college housing not available. *Activities and Organizations:* Student Government Association, Vocational Industrial Clubs of America, Phi Beta Lambda. *Campus security:* 24-hour emergency response devices. *Student services:* personal/psychological counseling.

Costs (2004–05) *Tuition:* state resident $1008 full-time, $28 per credit hour part-time; nonresident $2016 full-time, $56 per credit hour part-time. *Required fees:* $138 full-time, $46 per term part-time. *Waivers:* senior citizens.

Financial Aid Of all full-time matriculated undergraduates who enrolled in 2003, 68 Federal Work-Study jobs (averaging $800).

Applying *Options:* deferred entrance. *Application fee:* $15. *Required:* high school transcript.

Admissions Contact Lori Basham, Admissions Director, West Georgia Technical College, 303 Fort Drive, LaGrange, GA 30240. *Phone:* 706-837-4244.

WESTWOOD COLLEGE-ATLANTA CAMPUS
Atlanta, Georgia

- **Proprietary** primarily 2-year, founded 2003
- **Calendar** continuous
- **Degrees** associate and bachelor's
- **Coed**

Applying *Application fee:* $100. *Required:* interview, HS diploma or GED, and passing scores on ACT/SAT or Accuplacer exam.
Admissions Contact Rory Laney, Director of Admissions, Westwood College-Atlanta Campus, 1100 Spring Street, Ste. 101A, Atlanta, GA 30309. *Phone:* 404-870-8982. *E-mail:* info@westwood.edu.

▶ **See page 566 for a narrative description.**

WESTWOOD COLLEGE—ATLANTA NORTHLAKE
Atlanta, Georgia

Admissions Contact Bruce Karr, Director of Admissions, Westwood College–Atlanta Northlake, 2220 Parklake Drive, Suite 175, Atlanta, GA 30345. *Phone:* 404-962-2999.

▶ **See page 568 for a narrative description.**

YOUNG HARRIS COLLEGE
Young Harris, Georgia

Admissions Contact Mr. Clinton G. Hobbs, Director of Admissions, Young Harris College, PO Box 116, Young Harris, GA 30582-0098. *Phone:* 706-379-3111 Ext. 5147. *Toll-free phone:* 800-241-3754. *Fax:* 706-379-3108. *E-mail:* admissions@yhc.edu.

GUAM

GUAM COMMUNITY COLLEGE
Barrigada, Guam

- **Territory-supported** 2-year, founded 1977
- **Calendar** semesters
- **Degree** certificates, diplomas, and associate
- **Suburban** 22-acre campus
- **Endowment** $6.4 million
- **Coed,** 1,754 undergraduate students, 22% full-time, 60% women, 40% men

Undergraduates 394 full-time, 1,360 part-time. Students come from 10 other countries, 0.3% African American, 91% Asian American or Pacific Islander, 0.6% Hispanic American, 0.1% Native American, 3% international.
Freshmen *Admission:* 378 applied, 375 admitted, 158 enrolled.
Faculty *Total:* 94.
Majors Accounting; administrative assistant and secretarial science; architectural engineering technology; automobile/automotive mechanics technology; business administration and management; child development; civil engineering technology; computer programming (vendor/product certification); computer science; corrections; criminal justice/law enforcement administration; criminal justice/police science; education; electrical, electronic and communications engineering technology; fire science; hospitality administration; hospitality and recreation marketing; hotel/motel administration; kindergarten/preschool education; marketing/marketing management; marketing research; medical/clinical assistant; operations management; safety/security technology; sign language interpretation and translation; tourism and travel services management; tourism and travel services marketing; tourism promotion; vehicle and vehicle parts and accessories marketing.
Academic Programs *Special study options:* academic remediation for entering students, adult/continuing education programs, cooperative education, double majors, English as a second language, honors programs, independent study, internships, off-campus study, part-time degree program, services for LD students, summer session for credit. *ROTC:* Army (c).
Library 15,806 titles, 375 serial subscriptions, 1,567 audiovisual materials, an OPAC.

Computers on Campus 220 computers available on campus for general student use. A campuswide network can be accessed. Internet access, at least one staffed computer lab available.
Student Life *Housing:* college housing not available. *Activities and Organizations:* Council of Post Secondary Student Association (COPSA), Phi Theta Kappa. *Campus security:* 12-hour patrols by trained security personnel. *Student services:* health clinic, personal/psychological counseling.
Costs (2005–06) *Tuition:* area resident $1500 full-time; territory resident $2250 full-time, $50 per credit hour part-time; nonresident $3000 full-time, $75 per credit hour part-time. *Required fees:* $220 full-time, $110 per term part-time.
Financial Aid Of all full-time matriculated undergraduates who enrolled in 2003, 83 Federal Work-Study jobs (averaging $940).
Applying *Options:* common application, early admission. *Required:* high school transcript. *Application deadline:* rolling (freshmen). *Notification:* continuous (freshmen).
Admissions Contact Ms. Deborah D. Leon Guerrero, Registrar, Guam Community College, PO Box 23069, Sesame Street, Barrigada 96921, Guam. *Phone:* 671-735-5531. *Fax:* 671-734-0540. *E-mail:* deborah@guamcc.net.

HAWAII

HAWAII BUSINESS COLLEGE
Honolulu, Hawaii

- **Independent** 2-year, founded 1973
- **Calendar** quarters
- **Degree** certificates, diplomas, and associate
- **Urban** campus
- **Coed,** 303 undergraduate students, 92% full-time, 80% women, 20% men

Undergraduates 279 full-time, 24 part-time. 7% African American, 78% Asian American or Pacific Islander, 2% Hispanic American, 1% Native American, 1% international.
Faculty *Total:* 17. *Student/faculty ratio:* 15:1.
Majors Accounting; business administration and management; computer science; health and medical administrative services related; tourism and travel services management; web page, digital/multimedia and information resources design.
Academic Programs *Special study options:* academic remediation for entering students, adult/continuing education programs, advanced placement credit, cooperative education, double majors, English as a second language, external degree program, independent study, internships, part-time degree program, summer session for credit.
Library 1,000 titles, 25 serial subscriptions.
Computers on Campus A campuswide network can be accessed. Internet access available.
Student Life *Housing:* college housing not available. *Activities and Organizations:* student-run newspaper, SCA (Student Council Association), Computer Club, Polynesian Club, SIFE. *Student services:* personal/psychological counseling.
Standardized Tests *Required:* Wonderlic Basic Skills Test (for placement).
Applying *Options:* deferred entrance. *Application fee:* $30. *Required:* high school transcript. *Required for some:* essay or personal statement, interview. *Application deadline:* rolling (freshmen).
Admissions Contact Seira Puletasi, Registrar, Hawaii Business College, 33 South King Street, Fourth Floor, Honolulu, HI 96813. *Phone:* 808-524-4014 Ext. 136. *Fax:* 808-524-0284. *E-mail:* admin@hbc.edu.

HAWAII COMMUNITY COLLEGE
Hilo, Hawaii

- **State-supported** 2-year, founded 1954, part of University of Hawaii System
- **Calendar** semesters
- **Degree** certificates, diplomas, and associate
- **Small-town** campus
- **Coed**

Student Life *Campus security:* 24-hour patrols.
Applying *Options:* common application, early admission.
Admissions Contact Mrs. Tammy M. Tanaka, Admissions Specialist, Hawaii Community College, 200 West Kawili Street, Hilo, HI 96720-4091. *Phone:* 808-974-7661. *E-mail:* loeding@hawaii.edu.

HAWAII TOKAI INTERNATIONAL COLLEGE
Honolulu, Hawaii

- **Independent** 2-year, founded 1992, part of Tokai University Educational System (Japan)

Hawaii Tokai International College (continued)
- **Calendar** quarters
- **Degree** certificates and associate
- **Urban** campus
- **Coed**

Faculty *Student/faculty ratio:* 12:1.
Student Life *Campus security:* 24-hour patrols.
Costs (2004–05) *Comprehensive fee:* $13,425 includes full-time tuition ($8700), mandatory fees ($225), and room and board ($4500). Part-time tuition: $375 per credit. Part-time tuition and fees vary according to course load. *Required fees:* $75 per term part-time. *Room and board:* college room only: $3000. Room and board charges vary according to board plan.
Applying *Options:* deferred entrance. *Application fee:* $50. *Required:* essay or personal statement, high school transcript, interview.
Admissions Contact Ms. Terry Lee McCandliss, Admissions Officer, Hawaii Tokai International College, 2241 Kapiolani Boulevard, Honolulu, HI 96826. *Phone:* 808-983-4154. *E-mail:* htic@tokai.edu.

HEALD COLLEGE-HONOLULU
Honolulu, Hawaii

Admissions Contact Director of Admissions, Heald College-Honolulu, 1500 Kapiolani Boulevard, Suite 201, Honolulu, HI 96814. *Phone:* 808-955-1500. *Toll-free phone:* 800-755-3550. *E-mail:* info@heald.edu.

HONOLULU COMMUNITY COLLEGE
Honolulu, Hawaii

- **State-supported** 2-year, founded 1920, part of University of Hawaii System
- **Calendar** semesters
- **Degree** certificates and associate
- **Urban** 20-acre campus
- **Endowment** $472,659
- **Coed**

Faculty *Student/faculty ratio:* 23:1.
Student Life *Campus security:* 24-hour emergency response devices.
Costs (2004–05) *Tuition:* state resident $1440 full-time, $47 per credit part-time; nonresident $7290 full-time, $242 per credit part-time. *Required fees:* $30 full-time.
Financial Aid Of all full-time matriculated undergraduates who enrolled in 2003, 41 Federal Work-Study jobs (averaging $1600).
Applying *Options:* common application, early admission.
Admissions Contact Admissions Office, Honolulu Community College, 874 Dillingham Boulevard, Honolulu, HI 96817. *Phone:* 808-845-9129. *E-mail:* admission@hcc.hawaii.edu.

KAPIOLANI COMMUNITY COLLEGE
Honolulu, Hawaii

- **State-supported** 2-year, founded 1957, part of University of Hawaii System
- **Calendar** semesters
- **Degree** certificates and associate
- **Urban** 52-acre campus
- **Coed**, 7,174 undergraduate students, 39% full-time, 58% women, 42% men

Undergraduates 2,833 full-time, 4,341 part-time. Students come from 27 states and territories, 59 other countries, 0.8% African American, 74% Asian American or Pacific Islander, 2% Hispanic American, 0.2% Native American, 6% international, 18% transferred in.
Freshmen *Admission:* 1,434 applied, 1,366 admitted, 787 enrolled.
Faculty *Total:* 377, 60% full-time.
Majors Accounting; clinical/medical laboratory technology; culinary arts; data processing and data processing technology; hotel/motel administration; industrial radiologic technology; legal administrative assistant/secretary; legal assistant/paralegal; liberal arts and sciences/liberal studies; marketing/marketing management; medical/clinical assistant; nursing (registered nurse training); occupational therapy; physical therapy; respiratory care therapy; special products marketing; tourism and travel services management.
Academic Programs *Special study options:* academic remediation for entering students, adult/continuing education programs, advanced placement credit, cooperative education, distance learning, English as a second language, honors programs, internships, off-campus study, part-time degree program, services for LD students, student-designed majors, summer session for credit. *ROTC:* Army (c), Air Force (c).
Library Lama Library with 50,000 titles, 600 serial subscriptions.

Computers on Campus 175 computers available on campus for general student use. A campuswide network can be accessed from off campus. Internet access, at least one staffed computer lab available.
Student Life *Housing:* college housing not available. *Activities and Organizations:* student-run newspaper, choral group, Hawaiian Club, Phi Theta Kappa, Chinese Club, Hospitality Industry, Bayanihan. *Campus security:* 24-hour patrols.
Athletics *Intramural sports:* bowling M/W, volleyball M/W.
Costs (2004–05) *Tuition:* state resident $1188 full-time; nonresident $5868 full-time. *Required fees:* $60 full-time.
Financial Aid Of all full-time matriculated undergraduates who enrolled in 2003, 30 Federal Work-Study jobs (averaging $2275). 440 state and other part-time jobs (averaging $1762).
Applying *Options:* early admission. *Application deadlines:* 7/1 (freshmen), 7/1 (transfers). *Notification:* continuous until 8/15 (freshmen).
Admissions Contact Ms. Cynthia Suzuki, Chief Admissions Officer, Kapiolani Community College, 4303 Diamond Head Road, Honolulu, HI 96816-4421. *Phone:* 808-734-9897. *E-mail:* cio@leahi.kcc.hawaii.edu.

KAUAI COMMUNITY COLLEGE
Lihue, Hawaii

- **State-supported** 2-year, founded 1965, part of University of Hawaii System
- **Calendar** semesters
- **Degree** certificates and associate
- **Small-town** 100-acre campus
- **Coed**, 1,210 undergraduate students

Majors Accounting; administrative assistant and secretarial science; autobody/collision and repair technology; automobile/automotive mechanics technology; carpentry; culinary arts; electrical, electronic and communications engineering technology; hospitality administration; kindergarten/preschool education; liberal arts and sciences/liberal studies; nursing (registered nurse training).
Academic Programs *Special study options:* accelerated degree program, advanced placement credit, cooperative education, distance learning, English as a second language, internships, part-time degree program, services for LD students, summer session for credit.
Library S. W. Wilcox II Learning Resource Center plus 1 other with 51,875 titles, 165 serial subscriptions, 1,248 audiovisual materials, an OPAC, a Web page.
Computers on Campus 173 computers available on campus for general student use. A campuswide network can be accessed. Internet access, at least one staffed computer lab available.
Student Life *Housing:* college housing not available. *Activities and Organizations:* student-run newspaper, choral group, Food Service Club, Hui O Hana Po'okela (Hoper Club), Nursing Club, Phi Theta Kappa, Pamantasan Club. *Campus security:* student patrols, 6-hour evening patrols by trained security personnel. *Student services:* health clinic, personal/psychological counseling.
Athletics *Intramural sports:* basketball M/W, golf M/W, tennis M/W.
Standardized Tests *Recommended:* ACT COMPASS.
Costs (2005–06) *Tuition:* state resident $1176 full-time, $49 per credit part-time; nonresident $5808 full-time, $242 per credit part-time. Full-time tuition and fees vary according to course load. Part-time tuition and fees vary according to course load. *Required fees:* $15 full-time, $1 per credit part-time. *Waivers:* minority students, senior citizens, and employees or children of employees.
Financial Aid Of all full-time matriculated undergraduates who enrolled in 2003, 10 Federal Work-Study jobs (averaging $3000). 30 state and other part-time jobs (averaging $3000).
Applying *Options:* common application, early admission. *Required for some:* high school transcript. *Recommended:* high school transcript. *Application deadlines:* 8/1 (freshmen), 8/1 (transfers). *Notification:* continuous until 8/1 (freshmen).
Admissions Contact Mr. Leighton Oride, Admissions Officer and Registrar, Kauai Community College, 3-1901 Kaumualii Highway, Lihue, HI 96766. *Phone:* 808-245-8225. *Fax:* 808-245-8297. *E-mail:* arkauai@hawaii.edu.

LEEWARD COMMUNITY COLLEGE
Pearl City, Hawaii

Admissions Contact Ms. Veda Tokashiki, Clerk, Leeward Community College, 96-045 Ala Ike, Pearl City, HI 96782-3393. *Phone:* 808-455-0217. *E-mail:* lccar@hawaii.edu.

MAUI COMMUNITY COLLEGE
Kahului, Hawaii

Admissions Contact Mr. Stephen Kameda, Director of Admissions and Records, Maui Community College, 310 Kaahumanu Avenue, Kahului, HI 96732. *Phone:* 808-984-3267. *Toll-free phone:* 800-479-6692. *Fax:* 808-242-9618.

TransPacific Hawaii College
Honolulu, Hawaii

Admissions Contact Ms. Loreen Toji, Assistant to the President, TransPacific Hawaii College, 5257 Kalanianaole Highway, Honolulu, HI 96821. *Phone:* 808-377-5402 Ext. 309. *Fax:* 808-373-4754. *E-mail:* admissions@transpacific.org.

Windward Community College
Kaneohe, Hawaii

- **State-supported** 2-year, founded 1972, part of University of Hawaii System
- **Calendar** semesters
- **Degree** certificates and associate
- **Small-town** 78-acre campus with easy access to Honolulu
- **Coed,** 1,761 undergraduate students

Undergraduates 6% are from out of state.

Freshmen *Admission:* 467 admitted.

Majors Liberal arts and sciences/liberal studies; professional studies.

Academic Programs *Special study options:* academic remediation for entering students, adult/continuing education programs, advanced placement credit, cooperative education, distance learning, independent study, part-time degree program, services for LD students, summer session for credit. *ROTC:* Army (c), Air Force (c).

Library Library.

Computers on Campus 70 computers available on campus for general student use. At least one staffed computer lab available.

Student Life *Housing:* college housing not available. *Activities and Organizations:* drama/theater group, student-run newspaper. *Student services:* personal/psychological counseling.

Costs (2005–06) *Tuition:* state resident $1176 full-time, $49 per credit part-time; nonresident $5808 full-time, $242 per credit part-time. *Required fees:* $40 full-time.

Applying *Options:* early admission. *Application fee:* $25. *Application deadline:* rolling (freshmen), rolling (transfers). *Notification:* continuous until 8/1 (freshmen).

Admissions Contact Mr. Russell Chan, Registrar, Windward Community College, 45-720 Keaahala Road, Kaneohe, HI 96744. *Phone:* 808-235-7400. *E-mail:* wccinfo@hawaii.edu.

IDAHO

Apollo College
Boise, Idaho

- **Proprietary** 2-year, founded 1980, administratively affiliated with U.S. Education Corporation
- **Calendar** semesters
- **Degree** certificates, diplomas, and associate
- **Coed,** 469 undergraduate students, 95% full-time, 87% women, 13% men

Undergraduates 444 full-time, 25 part-time. Students come from 5 states and territories, 21% are from out of state, 0.9% African American, 2% Asian American or Pacific Islander, 9% Hispanic American, 0.9% Native American, 1% transferred in.

Freshmen *Admission:* 42 enrolled. *Average high school GPA:* 3.0.

Faculty *Total:* 49, 39% full-time, 92% with terminal degrees. *Student/faculty ratio:* 10:1.

Majors Dental hygiene; medical office management; occupational therapist assistant.

Library Apollo College with 20,000 titles, 10,000 serial subscriptions, 109 audiovisual materials, an OPAC.

Computers on Campus 55 computers available on campus for general student use. A campuswide network can be accessed. Internet access, at least one staffed computer lab available.

Student Life *Housing:* college housing not available. *Campus security:* 24-hour patrols.

Standardized Tests *Required:* Wonderlic aptitude test (for admission).

Costs (2004–05) *Tuition:* Full-time tuition and fees vary according to program. Program costs range from $16,680 to $43,530. Contact institution for further information.

Applying *Required:* high school transcript, 3 letters of recommendation, interview. *Required for some:* essay or personal statement. *Application deadline:* 3/1 (freshmen). *Notification:* continuous until 9/1 (freshmen).

Admissions Contact Kevin Price, Director of Admissions, Apollo College, 1200 North Liberty, Boise, ID 83704. *Phone:* 208-377-8080 Ext. 35. *Toll-free phone:* 800-473-4365. *Fax:* 208-322-7658. *E-mail:* receptionist@aiht.com.

Brigham Young University -Idaho
Rexburg, Idaho

Admissions Contact Mr. Steven Davis, Assistant Director of Admissions, Brigham Young University -Idaho, 120 Kimball, Rexburg, ID 83460-1615. *Phone:* 208-356-1026. *Fax:* 208-356-1220. *E-mail:* admissions@byui.edu.

College of Southern Idaho
Twin Falls, Idaho

- **State and locally supported** 2-year, founded 1964
- **Calendar** semesters
- **Degree** certificates, diplomas, and associate
- **Small-town** 287-acre campus
- **Endowment** $15.0 million
- **Coed,** 7,105 undergraduate students, 45% full-time, 64% women, 36% men

Undergraduates 3,175 full-time, 3,930 part-time. Students come from 29 states and territories, 27 other countries, 3% are from out of state, 0.5% African American, 0.9% Asian American or Pacific Islander, 9% Hispanic American, 0.8% Native American, 4% international, 10% live on campus.

Freshmen *Admission:* 1,252 enrolled.

Faculty *Total:* 205, 78% full-time. *Student/faculty ratio:* 26:1.

Majors Accounting; agricultural business and management; agriculture; anthropology; art; autobody/collision and repair technology; automobile/automotive mechanics technology; biology/biological sciences; botany/plant biology; business administration and management; business/commerce; cabinetmaking and millwork; chemistry; child development; clinical laboratory science/medical technology; commercial and advertising art; communication/speech communication and rhetoric; computer science; criminal justice/law enforcement administration; criminal justice/police science; culinary arts; dental assisting; dental hygiene; diesel mechanics technology; dietetics; drafting and design technology; dramatic/theatre arts; education; electrical, electronic and communications engineering technology; elementary education; engineering; English; environmental studies; equestrian studies; finance; fish/game management; foreign languages and literatures; forestry; geography; geology/earth science; health/health care administration; heating, air conditioning, ventilation and refrigeration maintenance technology; history; hotel/motel administration; human services; hydrology and water resources science; liberal arts and sciences/liberal studies; library science; marketing/marketing management; mathematics; medical radiologic technology; music; natural sciences; nursing (registered nurse training); occupational therapy; photography; physical education teaching and coaching; physical therapy; physician assistant; physics; political science and government; prepharmacy studies; psychology; public health education and promotion; range science and management; real estate; respiratory care therapy; sociology; surgical technology; veterinary technology; welding technology; woodworking; zoology/animal biology.

Academic Programs *Special study options:* academic remediation for entering students, adult/continuing education programs, advanced placement credit, cooperative education, distance learning, English as a second language, honors programs, independent study, internships, part-time degree program, services for LD students, summer session for credit.

Library College of Southern Idaho Library with 62,556 titles, 374 serial subscriptions, 4,216 audiovisual materials, an OPAC, a Web page.

Computers on Campus 750 computers available on campus for general student use. A campuswide network can be accessed from student residence rooms and from off campus. Internet access, online (class) registration, at least one staffed computer lab available. Computer purchase or lease plan available.

Student Life *Housing Options:* coed. Campus housing is university owned. *Activities and Organizations:* drama/theater group, student-run newspaper, radio station, choral group, BPA, Dex, Chi Alpha (Christian Group), Vet Tech Club, Equine Club. *Campus security:* 24-hour emergency response devices and patrols, controlled dormitory access. *Student services:* health clinic, personal/psychological counseling, women's center, legal services.

Athletics Member NJCAA. *Intercollegiate sports:* baseball M(s)/W, basketball M(s)/W(s), cheerleading M(s)/W(s), equestrian sports M(s)(c)/W(s)(c), volleyball M/W(s). *Intramural sports:* badminton M/W, basketball M/W, football M/W, racquetball M/W, rock climbing M/W, soccer M/W, softball M/W, tennis M/W, ultimate Frisbee M/W, volleyball M/W.

Standardized Tests *Required:* ACT COMPASS (for admission). *Required for some:* ACT (for admission).

Costs (2004–05) *Tuition:* state resident $1800 full-time, $90 per credit part-time; nonresident $5000 full-time, $250 per credit part-time. *Room and board:* $3860. Room and board charges vary according to board plan. *Payment plan:* installment. *Waivers:* senior citizens and employees or children of employees.

College of Southern Idaho (continued)

Financial Aid Of all full-time matriculated undergraduates who enrolled in 2003, 250 Federal Work-Study jobs (averaging $2000). 100 state and other part-time jobs (averaging $2000).

Applying *Options:* common application. *Required:* high school transcript. *Required for some:* letters of recommendation, interview. *Application deadline:* rolling (freshmen), rolling (transfers).

Admissions Contact Dr. John S. Martin, Director of Admissions, Registration, and Records, College of Southern Idaho, PO Box 1238, 315 Falls Avenue, Twin Falls, ID 83303. *Phone:* 208-732-6232. *Toll-free phone:* 800-680-0274. *Fax:* 208-736-3014.

EASTERN IDAHO TECHNICAL COLLEGE
Idaho Falls, Idaho

- **State-supported** 2-year, founded 1970
- **Calendar** semesters
- **Degree** certificates and associate
- **Small-town** 40-acre campus
- **Endowment** $1.4 million
- **Coed,** 788 undergraduate students, 64% full-time, 71% women, 29% men

Undergraduates 505 full-time, 283 part-time. Students come from 5 states and territories, 0.9% African American, 3% Asian American or Pacific Islander, 6% Hispanic American, 0.5% Native American, 11% transferred in. *Retention:* 50% of 2002 full-time freshmen returned.

Freshmen *Admission:* 134 enrolled.

Faculty *Total:* 91, 44% full-time. *Student/faculty ratio:* 10:1.

Majors Accounting; administrative assistant and secretarial science; automobile/automotive mechanics technology; computer systems networking and telecommunications; diesel mechanics technology; electrical, electronic and communications engineering technology; legal assistant/paralegal; marketing/marketing management; medical/clinical assistant; surgical technology; welding technology.

Academic Programs *Special study options:* academic remediation for entering students, adult/continuing education programs, cooperative education, distance learning, internships, part-time degree program, services for LD students, summer session for credit.

Library Richard and Lila Jordan Library plus 1 other with 18,000 titles, 125 serial subscriptions, 150 audiovisual materials, an OPAC, a Web page.

Computers on Campus 105 computers available on campus for general student use. A campuswide network can be accessed. Internet access, at least one staffed computer lab available.

Student Life *Housing:* college housing not available. *Campus security:* 24-hour patrols. *Student services:* personal/psychological counseling.

Standardized Tests *Required:* ACT COMPASS (for placement).

Costs (2004–05) *Tuition:* state resident $1594 full-time, $74 per credit part-time; nonresident $5484 full-time, $148 per credit part-time. Full-time tuition and fees vary according to course load and reciprocity agreements. Part-time tuition and fees vary according to class time and reciprocity agreements. *Required fees:* $106 full-time. *Waivers:* employees or children of employees.

Financial Aid Of all full-time matriculated undergraduates who enrolled in 2003, 37 Federal Work-Study jobs (averaging $1176). 11 state and other part-time jobs (averaging $1619).

Applying *Options:* deferred entrance. *Application fee:* $10. *Required:* high school transcript, interview. *Required for some:* essay or personal statement. *Application deadline:* 8/19 (freshmen).

Admissions Contact Dr. Steve Albiston, Dean of Students, Eastern Idaho Technical College, 1600 South 25th E., Idaho Falls, ID 83404. *Phone:* 208-524-3000 Ext. 3366. *Toll-free phone:* 800-662-0261 Ext. 3371. *Fax:* 208-525-7026. *E-mail:* salbisto@eitc.edu.

ITT TECHNICAL INSTITUTE
Boise, Idaho

- **Proprietary** primarily 2-year, founded 1906, part of ITT Educational Services, Inc
- **Calendar** quarters
- **Degrees** associate and bachelor's
- **Urban** 1-acre campus
- **Coed**

Standardized Tests *Required:* Wonderlic aptitude test (for admission).

Costs (2004–05) *Tuition:* Please see school catalog for specific information.

Financial Aid Of all full-time matriculated undergraduates who enrolled in 2003, 9 Federal Work-Study jobs (averaging $5500).

Applying *Options:* deferred entrance. *Application fee:* $100. *Required:* high school transcript, interview. *Recommended:* letters of recommendation.

Admissions Contact Terry G. Lowder, Director of Recruitment, ITT Technical Institute, 12302 West Explorer Drive, Boise, ID 83713. *Phone:* 208-322-8844. *Toll-free phone:* 800-666-4888. *Fax:* 208-322-0173.

NORTH IDAHO COLLEGE
Coeur d'Alene, Idaho

- **State and locally supported** 2-year, founded 1933
- **Calendar** semesters
- **Degree** certificates and associate
- **Small-town** 42-acre campus
- **Endowment** $4.9 million
- **Coed,** 4,519 undergraduate students, 61% full-time, 63% women, 37% men

Undergraduates 2,764 full-time, 1,755 part-time. Students come from 27 states and territories, 16 other countries, 8% are from out of state, 0.4% African American, 0.6% Asian American or Pacific Islander, 1% Hispanic American, 2% Native American, 0.4% international, 12% transferred in.

Freshmen *Admission:* 1,855 applied, 1,855 admitted, 1,449 enrolled. *Average high school GPA:* 2.81.

Faculty *Total:* 327, 47% full-time. *Student/faculty ratio:* 17:1.

Majors Administrative assistant and secretarial science; agriculture; American Indian/Native American studies; anthropology; art; astronomy; athletic training; automobile/automotive mechanics technology; biological and physical sciences; biology/biological sciences; botany/plant biology; business administration and management; business teacher education; carpentry; chemistry; clinical laboratory science/medical technology; commercial and advertising art; computer and information sciences related; computer programming; computer science; computer/technical support; criminal justice/law enforcement administration; criminal justice/police science; culinary arts; developmental and child psychology; drafting and design technology; dramatic/theatre arts; education; electrical, electronic and communications engineering technology; elementary education; engineering; English; environmental health; fish/game management; forestry; French; geology/earth science; German; health/health care administration; heating, air conditioning, ventilation and refrigeration maintenance technology; heavy equipment maintenance technology; history; hospitality administration; human services; journalism; legal administrative assistant/secretary; legal assistant/paralegal; liberal arts and sciences/liberal studies; machine tool technology; marine technology; mass communication/media; mathematics; medical administrative assistant and medical secretary; music; music teacher education; nursing (licensed practical/vocational nurse training); nursing (registered nurse training); physical sciences; physics; political science and government; psychology; social sciences; sociology; Spanish; welding technology; wildlife and wildlands science and management; wildlife biology; zoology/animal biology.

Academic Programs *Special study options:* academic remediation for entering students, adult/continuing education programs, advanced placement credit, cooperative education, distance learning, English as a second language, independent study, internships, off-campus study, part-time degree program, services for LD students, summer session for credit.

Library Molstead Library Computer Center with 60,893 titles, 751 serial subscriptions, an OPAC, a Web page.

Computers on Campus 145 computers available on campus for general student use. A campuswide network can be accessed. Internet access, at least one staffed computer lab available.

Student Life *Housing Options:* Campus housing is university owned. *Activities and Organizations:* drama/theater group, student-run newspaper, choral group, Ski Club, Fusion, Baptist student ministries, Journalism Club, Phi Theta Kappa. *Campus security:* 24-hour emergency response devices and patrols, late-night transport/escort service. *Student services:* health clinic, personal/psychological counseling, women's center, legal services.

Athletics Member NJCAA. *Intercollegiate sports:* basketball M(s)/W(s), cheerleading M(s)/W(s), soccer M(s)/W(s), softball W(s), volleyball W(s), wrestling M(s). *Intramural sports:* basketball M/W, bowling M/W, cheerleading M/W, crew M(c)/W(c), cross-country running M(c)/W(c), football M/W, golf M/W, racquetball M/W, sailing M(c)/W(c), skiing (cross-country) M(c)/W(c), skiing (downhill) M(c)/W(c), soccer M(c)/W(c), softball M/W, table tennis M/W, tennis M/W, track and field M(c)/W(c), volleyball M/W.

Standardized Tests *Required for some:* ACT ASSET, ACT COMPASS. *Recommended:* SAT or ACT (for placement), ACT ASSET, ACT COMPASS.

Costs (2005–06) *Tuition:* area resident $1068 full-time, $67 per credit part-time; state resident $2068 full-time, $129 per credit part-time; nonresident $5620 full-time, $351 per credit part-time. *Required fees:* $820 full-time, $820 per year part-time. *Room and board:* $5010; room only: $3210.

Financial Aid Of all full-time matriculated undergraduates who enrolled in 2003, 142 Federal Work-Study jobs (averaging $1425). 106 state and other part-time jobs (averaging $1327).

Applying *Options:* electronic application, early admission, deferred entrance. *Application fee:* $25. *Required for some:* essay or personal statement, high school transcript, minimum 2.0 GPA, county residency certificate. *Application deadlines:* 8/20 (freshmen), 8/20 (transfers).

Admissions Contact Ms. Maxine Gish, Director of Admissions, North Idaho College, 1000 West Garden Avenue, Coeur d'Alene, ID 83814-2199. *Phone:* 208-769-3303. *Toll-free phone:* 877-404-4536 Ext. 3311. *Fax:* 208-769-3399 Ext. 3311. *E-mail:* admit@nic.edu.

ILLINOIS

BLACK HAWK COLLEGE
Moline, Illinois

- **State and locally supported** 2-year, founded 1946, part of Black Hawk College District System
- **Calendar** semesters
- **Degree** certificates and associate
- **Urban** 161-acre campus
- **Coed,** 6,600 undergraduate students, 48% full-time, 61% women, 39% men

Undergraduates 3,138 full-time, 3,462 part-time. Students come from 5 states and territories, 3% are from out of state, 7% African American, 0.8% Asian American or Pacific Islander, 7% Hispanic American, 0.5% Native American, 0.1% transferred in. *Retention:* 62% of 2002 full-time freshmen returned.
Freshmen *Admission:* 944 admitted, 944 enrolled. *Test scores:* ACT scores over 18: 64%; ACT scores over 24: 15%; ACT scores over 30: 1%.
Faculty *Total:* 364, 38% full-time, 13% with terminal degrees. *Student/faculty ratio:* 18:1.
Majors Accounting; administrative assistant and secretarial science; agribusiness; agricultural mechanics and equipment technology; agricultural mechanization; agricultural production related; animal/livestock husbandry and production; animal sciences; autobody/collision and repair technology; banking and financial support services; business administration and management; CAD/CADD drafting/design technology; carpentry; child development; civil engineering technology; communications technology; computer/information technology services administration related; computer installation and repair technology; computer programming; computer systems networking and telecommunications; computer/technical support; criminal justice/law enforcement administration; culinary arts; data processing and data processing technology; dental assisting; design and visual communications; diesel mechanics technology; electrical, electronics and communications engineering; electrician; electromechanical technology; electroneurodiagnostic/electroencephalographic technology; engine machinist; environmental control technologies related; environmental health; equestrian studies; finance; finance and financial management services related; fire services administration; health information/medical records administration; heating, air conditioning, ventilation and refrigeration maintenance technology; horse husbandry/equine science and management; horticultural science; information technology; interior design; international business/trade/commerce; legal administrative assistant/secretary; legal assistant/paralegal; library assistant; machine tool technology; management science; manufacturing technology; marketing related; mechanics and repair; medical transcription; nursing (licensed practical/vocational nurse training); nursing (registered nurse training); physical therapist assistant; radio and television broadcasting technology; radiologic technology/science; retailing; security and protective services related; sheet metal technology; sign language interpretation; small business administration; teacher assistant/aide; tool and die technology; truck and bus driver/commercial vehicle operation; vehicle maintenance and repair technologies related; web/multimedia management and webmaster; welding technology.
Academic Programs *Special study options:* academic remediation for entering students, accelerated degree program, adult/continuing education programs, advanced placement credit, cooperative education, distance learning, English as a second language, independent study, internships, off-campus study, part-time degree program, services for LD students, study abroad, summer session for credit.
Library Quad City Campus Library plus 1 other with 59,840 titles, 612 serial subscriptions, 140 audiovisual materials, an OPAC.
Computers on Campus 822 computers available on campus for general student use. A campuswide network can be accessed from off campus. Internet access, online (class) registration, at least one staffed computer lab available. Computer purchase or lease plan available.
Student Life *Housing:* college housing not available. *Activities and Organizations:* drama/theater group, student-run newspaper, television station, choral group. *Campus security:* 24-hour patrols. *Student services:* personal/psychological counseling.
Athletics Member NJCAA. *Intercollegiate sports:* baseball M(s), basketball M(s)/W(s), golf M(s), softball W(s), volleyball W(s). *Intramural sports:* soccer M.
Standardized Tests *Required for some:* ACT (for placement), COMPASS.
Costs (2005–06) *Tuition:* area resident $1860 full-time, $62 per credit hour part-time; state resident $4200 full-time, $140 per credit hour part-time; nonresi-

dent $7770 full-time, $259 per credit hour part-time. *Required fees:* $210 full-time, $7 per credit hour part-time. *Payment plans:* installment, deferred payment. *Waivers:* senior citizens and employees or children of employees.
Financial Aid Of all full-time matriculated undergraduates who enrolled in 2003, 171 Federal Work-Study jobs (averaging $1464). 183 state and other part-time jobs (averaging $1177).
Applying *Options:* early admission, deferred entrance. *Required:* high school transcript. *Application deadline:* rolling (freshmen). *Notification:* continuous (freshmen).
Admissions Contact Ms. Rose Hernandez, Coordinator of Recruitment, Black Hawk College, 6600 34th Avenue, Moline, IL 61265. *Phone:* 309-796-5342. *Fax:* 309-792-5976.

CAREER COLLEGES OF CHICAGO
Chicago, Illinois

- **Proprietary** 2-year, founded 1950
- **Calendar** quarters
- **Degree** certificates and associate
- **Urban** campus
- **Coed, primarily women,** 144 undergraduate students, 24% full-time, 86% women, 14% men

Undergraduates 35 full-time, 109 part-time. Students come from 1 other state.
Freshmen *Admission:* 26 applied, 26 admitted, 26 enrolled.
Faculty *Total:* 19, 32% with terminal degrees. *Student/faculty ratio:* 11:1.
Majors Computer science; court reporting; legal administrative assistant/secretary; medical administrative assistant and medical secretary.
Academic Programs *Special study options:* advanced placement credit, internships, part-time degree program, summer session for credit.
Library Main Library plus 1 other with 1,000 titles, 10 serial subscriptions.
Computers on Campus 46 computers available on campus for general student use. Internet access, at least one staffed computer lab available.
Student Life *Housing:* college housing not available. *Campus security:* 24-hour emergency response devices, guard on duty during building hours.
Standardized Tests *Recommended:* ACT (for admission).
Financial Aid *Financial aid deadline:* 6/1.
Applying *Options:* deferred entrance. *Application fee:* $40. *Required:* high school transcript, interview. *Application deadline:* rolling (freshmen), rolling (transfers).
Admissions Contact Ms. Rosa Alvarado, Admissions Assistant, Career Colleges of Chicago, 11 East Adams Street, Chicago, IL 60603. *Phone:* 312-895-6306. *Fax:* 312-895-6301. *E-mail:* icoburn@careerchi.com.

CARL SANDBURG COLLEGE
Galesburg, Illinois

- **State and locally supported** 2-year, founded 1967, part of Illinois Community College Board
- **Calendar** semesters
- **Degree** certificates and associate
- **Small-town** 105-acre campus with easy access to Peoria
- **Coed**

Faculty *Student/faculty ratio:* 17:1.
Student Life *Campus security:* 24-hour emergency response devices and patrols.
Athletics Member NJCAA.
Standardized Tests *Required:* ACT ASSET (for placement).
Financial Aid Of all full-time matriculated undergraduates who enrolled in 2003, 80 Federal Work-Study jobs (averaging $3000).
Applying *Options:* early admission, deferred entrance. *Required:* high school transcript.
Admissions Contact Ms. Carol Kreider, Director of Admissions and Records, Carl Sandburg College, 2400 Tom L. Wilson Boulevard, Galesburg, IL 61401-9576. *Phone:* 309-341-5234.

CITY COLLEGES OF CHICAGO, HAROLD WASHINGTON COLLEGE
Chicago, Illinois

Admissions Contact Mr. Terry Pendleton, Admissions Coordinator, City Colleges of Chicago, Harold Washington College, 30 East Lake Street, Chicago, IL 60601-2449. *Phone:* 312-553-6006. *Fax:* 312-553-6077.

CITY COLLEGES OF CHICAGO, HARRY S. TRUMAN COLLEGE
Chicago, Illinois

Admissions Contact Mrs. Kelly O'Malley, Assistant Dean, Student Services, City Colleges of Chicago, Harry S. Truman College, 1145 West Wilson Avenue, Chicago, IL 60640-5616. *Phone:* 773-907-4720. *Fax:* 773-989-6135.

CITY COLLEGES OF CHICAGO, KENNEDY-KING COLLEGE
Chicago, Illinois

Admissions Contact Ms. Joyce Collins, Clerical Supervisor for Admissions and Records, City Colleges of Chicago, Kennedy-King College, 6800 South Wentworth Avenue, Chicago, IL 60621. *Phone:* 773-602-5000 Ext. 5055. *Fax:* 773-602-5247. *E-mail:* w.murphy@ccc.edu.

CITY COLLEGES OF CHICAGO, MALCOLM X COLLEGE
Chicago, Illinois

- **State and locally supported** 2-year, founded 1911, part of City Colleges of Chicago
- **Calendar** semesters
- **Degree** certificates and associate
- **Urban** 20-acre campus
- **Coed**

Faculty *Student/faculty ratio:* 22:1.
Student Life *Campus security:* 24-hour emergency response devices and patrols.
Athletics Member NJCAA.
Costs (2004–05) *Tuition:* area resident $1860 full-time, $62 per credit part-time; state resident $6876 full-time, $229 per credit part-time; nonresident $9449 full-time, $315 per credit part-time. Part-time tuition and fees vary according to course load. *Required fees:* $375 full-time, $75 per term part-time.
Financial Aid Of all full-time matriculated undergraduates who enrolled in 2003, 200 Federal Work-Study jobs (averaging $2500).
Applying *Options:* common application, early admission, deferred entrance. *Required:* high school transcript, minimum 2.0 GPA. *Required for some:* essay or personal statement, interview.
Admissions Contact Mr. Ghingo Brooks, Vice President of Enrollment Management and Student Services, City Colleges of Chicago, Malcolm X College, 1900 West Van Buren Street, Chicago, IL 60612. *Phone:* 312-850-7120. *Fax:* 312-850-7092. *E-mail:* gbrooks@ccc.edu.

CITY COLLEGES OF CHICAGO, OLIVE-HARVEY COLLEGE
Chicago, Illinois

Admissions Contact Ms. Ernestine Taylor, Director of Admissions, City Colleges of Chicago, Olive-Harvey College, 10001 South Woodlawn, Chicago, IL 60628-1696. *Phone:* 773-291-6359. *Fax:* 773-291-6304.

CITY COLLEGES OF CHICAGO, RICHARD J. DALEY COLLEGE
Chicago, Illinois

Admissions Contact Ms. Karla Reynolds, Registrar, City Colleges of Chicago, Richard J. Daley College, 7500 South Pulaski Road, Chicago, IL 60652-1242. *Phone:* 773-838-7599. *E-mail:* kreynolds@ccc.edu.

CITY COLLEGES OF CHICAGO, WILBUR WRIGHT COLLEGE
Chicago, Illinois

- **State and locally supported** 2-year, founded 1934, part of City Colleges of Chicago
- **Calendar** semesters
- **Degree** certificates and associate
- **Urban** 20-acre campus with easy access to Chicago, Illinois
- **Coed**, 6,896 undergraduate students, 29% full-time, 57% women, 43% men

Undergraduates 1,973 full-time, 4,923 part-time. 10% African American, 11% Asian American or Pacific Islander, 37% Hispanic American, 0.7% Native American.
Freshmen *Admission:* 2,740 applied, 2,740 admitted. *Average high school GPA:* 2.5.
Faculty *Total:* 249, 40% full-time, 27% with terminal degrees. *Student/faculty ratio:* 22:1.
Majors Accounting; architectural engineering technology; architectural technology; art; biological and physical sciences; business administration and management; computer and information sciences; computer and information systems security; criminal justice/police science; data processing and data processing technology; elementary education; engineering; English; environmental engineering technology; environmental science; general studies; gerontology; Hispanic-American, Puerto Rican, and Mexican-American/Chicano studies; journalism; liberal arts and sciences/liberal studies; library science; machine tool technology; marketing/marketing management; medical radiologic technology; modern languages; music; occupational therapy; physical sciences; pre-engineering; speech and rhetoric.
Academic Programs *Special study options:* academic remediation for entering students, accelerated degree program, adult/continuing education programs, distance learning, English as a second language, part-time degree program, summer session for credit.
Library Learning Resource Center plus 1 other with 60,000 titles, 350 serial subscriptions.
Computers on Campus 700 computers available on campus for general student use. A campuswide network can be accessed. Internet access, at least one staffed computer lab available.
Student Life *Housing:* college housing not available. *Activities and Organizations:* drama/theater group, student-run newspaper, choral group, student government, Circle K, Phi Theta Kappa, Black Student Union. *Campus security:* 24-hour emergency response devices and patrols, student patrols, late-night transport/escort service. *Student services:* legal services.
Athletics Member NJCAA. *Intercollegiate sports:* basketball M(s)/W(s), wrestling M(s). *Intramural sports:* basketball M, cross-country running M/W, golf M/W, volleyball M/W, weight lifting M/W, wrestling M/W.
Standardized Tests *Required:* ACT (for placement).
Costs (2005–06) *Tuition:* area resident $2170 full-time, $64 per credit hour part-time; state resident $6684 full-time, $187 per credit hour part-time; nonresident $9656 full-time, $264 per credit hour part-time. Full-time tuition and fees vary according to course load. Part-time tuition and fees vary according to course load. *Required fees:* $250 full-time, $75 per term part-time. *Payment plan:* installment. *Waivers:* senior citizens and employees or children of employees.
Financial Aid Of all full-time matriculated undergraduates who enrolled in 2003, 67 Federal Work-Study jobs (averaging $1000).
Applying *Options:* common application, early admission, deferred entrance. *Application deadline:* rolling (freshmen), rolling (transfers). *Notification:* continuous (freshmen).
Admissions Contact Ms. Amy Aiello, Assistant Dean of Student Services, City Colleges of Chicago, Wilbur Wright College, 4300 North Narragansett, Chicago, IL 60634. *Phone:* 773-481-8207.

COLLEGE OF DuPAGE
Glen Ellyn, Illinois

- **State and locally supported** 2-year, founded 1967, part of Illinois Community College Board
- **Calendar** quarters
- **Degree** certificates and associate
- **Suburban** 297-acre campus with easy access to Chicago
- **Endowment** $10.5 million
- **Coed**, 29,854 undergraduate students, 36% full-time, 57% women, 43% men

Undergraduates 10,657 full-time, 19,197 part-time. Students come from 19 states and territories, 6% African American, 12% Asian American or Pacific Islander, 8% Hispanic American, 0.3% Native American, 6% transferred in. *Retention:* 65% of 2002 full-time freshmen returned.
Freshmen *Admission:* 3,088 admitted, 3,088 enrolled.
Faculty *Total:* 1,651, 19% full-time, 13% with terminal degrees. *Student/faculty ratio:* 22:1.
Majors Accounting; administrative assistant and secretarial science; automobile/automotive mechanics technology; baking and pastry arts; biological and physical sciences; building/property maintenance and management; business administration and management; child care and support services management; child care provision; child development; cinematography and film/video production; commercial and advertising art; communications systems installation and repair technology; communications technology; computer installation and repair technology; computer programming (specific applications); computer typography and composition equipment operation; corrections; criminal justice/law enforcement administration; criminal justice/police science; culinary arts; data entry/microcomputer applications related; dental hygiene; design and visual commu-

nications; desktop publishing and digital imaging design; drafting and design technology; electrical, electronic and communications engineering technology; electrical/electronics equipment installation and repair; electromechanical technology; emergency medical technology (EMT paramedic); engineering; fashion and fabric consulting; fashion/apparel design; fashion merchandising; fire science; graphic and printing equipment operation/production; health/health care administration; health information/medical records administration; health information/medical records technology; heating, air conditioning, ventilation and refrigeration maintenance technology; hospital and health care facilities administration; hospitality administration; hotel/motel administration; human services; industrial electronics technology; industrial technology; interior design; landscaping and groundskeeping; legal administrative assistant/secretary; liberal arts and sciences/liberal studies; library assistant; library science; machine tool technology; manufacturing technology; marketing/marketing management; massage therapy; mechanical design technology; medical radiologic technology; merchandising; nuclear medical technology; nursing (registered nurse training); occupational therapist assistant; occupational therapy; office management; ornamental horticulture; photography; physical therapist assistant; plastics engineering technology; precision production trades; real estate; respiratory care therapy; restaurant, culinary, and catering management; retailing; robotics technology; sales, distribution and marketing; selling skills and sales; speech-language pathology; substance abuse/addiction counseling; surgical technology; tourism and travel services management; tourism and travel services marketing; tourism promotion; transportation technology; welding technology.

Academic Programs *Special study options:* academic remediation for entering students, accelerated degree program, adult/continuing education programs, advanced placement credit, cooperative education, distance learning, double majors, English as a second language, external degree program, honors programs, independent study, internships, off-campus study, part-time degree program, services for LD students, student-designed majors, study abroad, summer session for credit.

Library College of DuPage Library with 203,300 titles, 6,005 serial subscriptions, 33,600 audiovisual materials, an OPAC, a Web page.

Computers on Campus 2403 computers available on campus for general student use. A campuswide network can be accessed from off campus. Internet access, online (class) registration, at least one staffed computer lab available. Computer purchase or lease plan available.

Student Life *Housing:* college housing not available. *Activities and Organizations:* drama/theater group, student-run newspaper, choral group, Latino Ethnic Awareness Association, The Christian Group, Phi Theta Kappa, International Students Organization, Muslim Student Association. *Campus security:* 24-hour emergency response devices and patrols, student patrols, late-night transport/escort service. *Student services:* health clinic, personal/psychological counseling.

Athletics Member NJCAA. *Intercollegiate sports:* baseball M, basketball M/W, cheerleading M/W, cross-country running M/W, football M, golf M, soccer M/W, softball W, swimming and diving M/W, tennis M/W, track and field M/W, volleyball W. *Intramural sports:* basketball M/W, bowling M/W, golf M/W, ice hockey M(c), racquetball M/W, soccer M/W, softball M/W, swimming and diving M/W, tennis M/W, volleyball M/W, weight lifting M/W.

Standardized Tests *Recommended:* ACT (for placement).

Costs (2005–06) *Tuition:* area resident $2251 full-time, $87 per semester hour part-time; state resident $7243 full-time, $243 per semester hour part-time; nonresident $8619 full-time, $226 per semester hour part-time. *Required fees:* $533 full-time.

Applying *Options:* early admission, deferred entrance. *Application fee:* $10. *Application deadline:* rolling (freshmen), rolling (transfers). *Notification:* continuous (freshmen).

Admissions Contact Mrs. Christine A. Legner, Coordinator of Admission Services, College of DuPage, SRC 2046, 425 Fawell Boulevard, Glen Ellyn, IL 60137-6599. *Phone:* 630-942-2442. *Fax:* 630-790-2686. *E-mail:* protis@cdnet.cod.edu.

COLLEGE OF LAKE COUNTY
Grayslake, Illinois

- **District-supported** 2-year, founded 1967, part of Illinois Community College Board
- **Calendar** semesters
- **Degree** certificates and associate
- **Suburban** 226-acre campus with easy access to Chicago and Milwaukee
- **Endowment** $2.6 million
- **Coed,** 15,866 undergraduate students

Undergraduates Students come from 22 states and territories, 42 other countries, 1% are from out of state, 10% African American, 5% Asian American or Pacific Islander, 18% Hispanic American, 0.4% Native American, 2% international. *Retention:* 60% of 2002 full-time freshmen returned.

Freshmen *Admission:* 2,508 applied, 2,508 admitted.

Faculty *Total:* 840, 24% full-time, 8% with terminal degrees. *Student/faculty ratio:* 20:1.

Majors Accounting technology and bookkeeping; administrative assistant and secretarial science; architectural drafting; art; automobile/automotive mechanics technology; biological and physical sciences; business administration and management; business automation/technology/data entry; business computer programming; business systems networking/ telecommunications; chemical technology; child care provision; civil engineering technology; computer installation and repair technology; construction engineering technology; criminal justice/police science; dental hygiene; electrical, electronic and communications engineering technology; electrician; engineering; fire protection and safety technology; heating, air conditioning, ventilation and refrigeration maintenance technology; industrial mechanics and maintenance technology; landscaping and groundskeeping; liberal arts and sciences/liberal studies; machine shop technology; mechanical engineering/mechanical technology; medical office management; medical radiologic technology; music; music teacher education; natural resources management and policy; nursing (registered nurse training); ornamental horticulture; restaurant, culinary, and catering management; sales operations; social work; substance abuse/addiction counseling; technical and business writing; turf and turfgrass management.

Academic Programs *Special study options:* academic remediation for entering students, adult/continuing education programs, advanced placement credit, cooperative education, distance learning, double majors, English as a second language, honors programs, independent study, internships, off-campus study, part-time degree program, services for LD students, student-designed majors, study abroad, summer session for credit.

Library College of Lake County Library plus 1 other with 106,842 titles, 766 serial subscriptions, 7,433 audiovisual materials, an OPAC, a Web page.

Computers on Campus 1500 computers available on campus for general student use. A campuswide network can be accessed from off campus. Internet access, online (class) registration, at least one staffed computer lab available.

Student Life *Housing:* college housing not available. *Activities and Organizations:* drama/theater group, student-run newspaper, radio station, choral group, Latino Alliance, Asian Student Alliance, Black Student Union, International Student Council, Phi Theta Kappa. *Campus security:* 24-hour emergency response devices and patrols, late-night transport/escort service. *Student services:* health clinic, personal/psychological counseling, women's center.

Athletics Member NJCAA. *Intercollegiate sports:* baseball M(s), basketball M(s)/W(s), cross-country running M(s)/W(s), golf M(s), soccer M(s)/W(s), softball W(s), tennis M(s)/W(s), volleyball W(s). *Intramural sports:* cheerleading W, golf M/W.

Standardized Tests *Recommended:* SAT or ACT (for placement).

Costs (2005–06) *Tuition:* area resident $1889 full-time, $63 per credit hour part-time; state resident $5639 full-time, $188 per credit hour part-time; nonresident $7769 full-time, $259 per credit hour part-time. *Required fees:* $212 full-time, $7 per credit hour part-time. *Payment plan:* installment. *Waivers:* senior citizens and employees or children of employees.

Financial Aid Of all full-time matriculated undergraduates who enrolled in 2003, 68 Federal Work-Study jobs (averaging $1856). 178 state and other part-time jobs (averaging $1937).

Applying *Options:* common application, electronic application, early admission, deferred entrance. *Required for some:* high school transcript, interview. *Application deadline:* rolling (freshmen), rolling (transfers). *Notification:* continuous (freshmen).

Admissions Contact Mr. Melvin Allen, Director, Student Recruitment, College of Lake County, 19351 West Washington Street, Grayslake, IL 60030-1198. *Phone:* 847-543-2383. *Fax:* 847-543-3061. *E-mail:* mallen@clcillinois.edu.

THE COLLEGE OF OFFICE TECHNOLOGY
Chicago, Illinois

Admissions Contact Mr. William Bolton, Director of Admissions, The College of Office Technology, 1514-20 West Division Street, Second Floor, Chicago, IL 60622. *Phone:* 773-278-0042.

THE COOKING AND HOSPITALITY INSTITUTE OF CHICAGO
Chicago, Illinois

- **Proprietary** 2-year, founded 1983, part of Career Education Corporation
- **Calendar** continuous
- **Degree** associate
- **Urban** campus
- **Endowment** $35,000
- **Coed**

Faculty *Student/faculty ratio:* 16:1.

Standardized Tests *Recommended:* SAT or ACT (for placement).

Financial Aid Of all full-time matriculated undergraduates who enrolled in 2003, 10 Federal Work-Study jobs.

The Cooking and Hospitality Institute of Chicago (continued)

Applying *Options:* common application, electronic application, deferred entrance. *Application fee:* $150. *Recommended:* essay or personal statement, high school transcript, interview.

Admissions Contact Mr. Alan Schultz, Director of Admissions, The Cooking and Hospitality Institute of Chicago, 361 West Chestnut, Chicago, IL 60610. *Phone:* 312-873-2064. *Toll-free phone:* 877-828-7772. *Fax:* 312-944-8557. *E-mail:* chic@chicnet.org.

▶ See page 488 for a narrative description.

DANVILLE AREA COMMUNITY COLLEGE
Danville, Illinois

■ **State and locally supported** 2-year, founded 1946, part of Illinois Community College Board
■ **Calendar** semesters
■ **Degree** certificates and associate
■ **Small-town** 50-acre campus
■ **Endowment** $978,329
■ **Coed,** 3,000 undergraduate students

Undergraduates Students come from 4 states and territories, 1% are from out of state, 10% African American, 0.7% Asian American or Pacific Islander, 3% Hispanic American, 0.1% Native American.
Faculty *Total:* 121, 41% full-time, 5% with terminal degrees. *Student/faculty ratio:* 20:1.
Majors Accounting; agricultural business and management; agriculture; art; automobile/automotive mechanics technology; biological and physical sciences; biology/biological sciences; business administration and management; child development; computer programming; criminal justice/law enforcement administration; criminal justice/police science; data processing and data processing technology; drafting and design technology; education; electrical, electronic and communications engineering technology; elementary education; engineering; English; history; horticultural science; humanities; human services; industrial radiologic technology; industrial technology; information science/studies; journalism; kindergarten/preschool education; landscaping and groundskeeping; legal administrative assistant/secretary; liberal arts and sciences/liberal studies; marketing/marketing management; mathematics; mechanical engineering/mechanical technology; medical administrative assistant and medical secretary; nursing (licensed practical/vocational nurse training); nursing (registered nurse training); occupational therapy; ornamental horticulture; philosophy; physical education teaching and coaching; physical therapy; pre-engineering; psychology; real estate; respiratory care therapy; social sciences; social work; substance abuse/addiction counseling; teacher assistant/aide; tourism and travel services management; welding technology.
Academic Programs *Special study options:* academic remediation for entering students, adult/continuing education programs, advanced placement credit, cooperative education, distance learning, double majors, English as a second language, independent study, internships, part-time degree program, services for LD students, summer session for credit.
Library Learning Resources Center with 50,000 titles, 2,487 audiovisual materials, an OPAC.
Computers on Campus 332 computers available on campus for general student use. A campuswide network can be accessed from off campus. Internet access, at least one staffed computer lab available.
Student Life *Housing:* college housing not available. *Activities and Organizations:* choral group, choral group. *Campus security:* 24-hour patrols. *Student services:* personal/psychological counseling.
Athletics Member NJCAA. *Intercollegiate sports:* baseball M(s), basketball M(s)/W(s), cross-country running M(s), softball W(s), track and field M(s)/W(s), volleyball W(s). *Intramural sports:* basketball M/W, cross-country running M, racquetball M/W.
Standardized Tests *Required for some:* ACT ASSET.
Costs (2005–06) *Tuition:* state resident $1392 full-time, $58 per credit hour part-time; nonresident $3600 full-time, $150 per credit hour part-time. *Required fees:* $144 full-time, $6 per credit hour part-time.
Financial Aid Of all full-time matriculated undergraduates who enrolled in 2003, 119 Federal Work-Study jobs (averaging $4300). 100 state and other part-time jobs (averaging $4000).
Applying *Options:* early admission, deferred entrance. *Required:* high school transcript. *Application deadline:* rolling (freshmen), rolling (transfers).
Admissions Contact Ms. Stacy L. Ehmen, Director of Admissions of Records/Registrar, Danville Area Community College, 2000 East Main Street, Danville, IL 61832-5199. *Phone:* 217-443-8800. *Fax:* 217-443-8560. *E-mail:* sehmen@dacc.cc.il.us.

ELGIN COMMUNITY COLLEGE
Elgin, Illinois

■ **State and locally supported** 2-year, founded 1949, part of Illinois Community College Board
■ **Calendar** semesters
■ **Degree** certificates, diplomas, and associate
■ **Suburban** 145-acre campus with easy access to Chicago
■ **Coed,** 10,851 undergraduate students, 31% full-time, 55% women, 45% men

Undergraduates 3,348 full-time, 7,503 part-time. Students come from 4 states and territories, 22 other countries, 1% are from out of state, 5% African American, 6% Asian American or Pacific Islander, 16% Hispanic American, 0.2% Native American, 0.3% international, 29% transferred in.
Freshmen *Admission:* 1,485 admitted, 1,485 enrolled.
Faculty *Total:* 512, 24% full-time, 11% with terminal degrees. *Student/faculty ratio:* 23:1.
Majors Accounting; accounting technology and bookkeeping; administrative assistant and secretarial science; art; automobile/automotive mechanics technology; biological and physical sciences; business administration and management; clinical/medical laboratory technology; commercial and advertising art; computer graphics; computer programming (specific applications); computer typography and composition equipment operation; consumer merchandising/retailing management; corrections; criminal justice/law enforcement administration; criminal justice/police science; culinary arts; design and visual communications; drafting and design technology; electrical, electronic and communications engineering technology; emergency medical technology (EMT paramedic); executive assistant/executive secretary; fire protection and safety technology; fire science; general retailing/wholesaling; gerontology; health information/medical records administration; heating, air conditioning, ventilation and refrigeration maintenance technology; hotel/motel administration; human services; industrial technology; information science/studies; kindergarten/preschool education; legal administrative assistant/secretary; legal assistant/paralegal; liberal arts and sciences/liberal studies; machine tool technology; marketing/marketing management; medical administrative assistant and medical secretary; medical transcription; mental health/rehabilitation; metallurgical technology; nursing (licensed practical/vocational nurse training); nursing (registered nurse training); pre-engineering; social work; substance abuse/addiction counseling; tourism and travel services management; welding technology.
Academic Programs *Special study options:* academic remediation for entering students, accelerated degree program, adult/continuing education programs, advanced placement credit, cooperative education, distance learning, double majors, English as a second language, honors programs, independent study, internships, off-campus study, part-time degree program, services for LD students, student-designed majors, summer session for credit.
Library Renner Learning Resource Center with 58,413 titles, 458 serial subscriptions, 7,394 audiovisual materials, an OPAC, a Web page.
Computers on Campus 1011 computers available on campus for general student use. A campuswide network can be accessed. Internet access, at least one staffed computer lab available. Computer purchase or lease plan available.
Student Life *Housing:* college housing not available. *Activities and Organizations:* drama/theater group, student-run newspaper, choral group, Phi Theta Kappa, United Students of All Cultures, Organization of Latin American Students, Black Student Association, Office Administration Association. *Campus security:* 24-hour patrols. *Student services:* personal/psychological counseling, legal services.
Athletics Member NJCAA. *Intercollegiate sports:* baseball M(s)/W, basketball M(s)/W(s), cross-country running M/W, golf M(s), softball W, tennis W(s), volleyball W(s).
Standardized Tests *Recommended:* ACT (for placement).
Costs (2005–06) *Tuition:* area resident $2250 full-time, $75 per credit hour part-time; state resident $7666 full-time, $256 per credit hour part-time; nonresident $9947 full-time, $332 per credit hour part-time. *Required fees:* $10 full-time, $5 per term part-time.
Applying *Options:* early admission. *Application fee:* $15. *Required for some:* high school transcript. *Application deadline:* rolling (freshmen), rolling (transfers). *Notification:* continuous (freshmen).
Admissions Contact Ms. Kelly Sinclair, Admissions, Recruitment, and Student Life, Elgin Community College, 1700 Spartan Drive, Elgin, IL 60123. *Phone:* 847-214-7414. *E-mail:* admissions@elgin.edu.

FOX COLLEGE
Oak Lawn, Illinois

■ **Proprietary** 2-year, founded 1932
■ **Coed,** 251 undergraduate students, 100% full-time, 92% women, 8% men

Undergraduates 251 full-time. 8% African American, 0.5% Asian American or Pacific Islander, 54% Hispanic American.
Freshmen *Admission:* 136 enrolled.

Costs (2005–06) *Tuition:* $12,720 full-time.
Admissions Contact Ms. Susan Szala, Director of Admissions, Fox College, 4201 West 93rd Street, Oak Lawn, IL 60453. *Phone:* 708-636-7700. *Toll-free phone:* 866-636-7711.

GEM CITY COLLEGE
Quincy, Illinois

- **Proprietary** 2-year, founded 1870
- **Calendar** quarters
- **Degree** diplomas and associate
- **Small-town** campus
- **Coed**

Applying *Options:* early admission, deferred entrance. *Application fee:* $25.
Admissions Contact Admissions Director, Gem City College, PO Box 179, Quincy, IL 62306-0179. *Phone:* 217-222-0391.

HEARTLAND COMMUNITY COLLEGE
Normal, Illinois

- **State and locally supported** 2-year, founded 1990, part of Illinois Community College Board
- **Calendar** semesters
- **Degree** certificates and associate
- **Urban** campus
- **Coed,** 4,566 undergraduate students, 40% full-time, 56% women, 44% men

Undergraduates 1,811 full-time, 2,755 part-time. Students come from 5 states and territories, 2 other countries, 1% are from out of state, 7% African American, 1% Asian American or Pacific Islander, 2% Hispanic American, 0.4% Native American, 0.1% international, 15% transferred in. *Retention:* 55% of 2002 full-time freshmen returned.
Freshmen *Admission:* 1,051 admitted, 1,051 enrolled.
Faculty *Total:* 263, 27% full-time, 13% with terminal degrees. *Student/faculty ratio:* 21:1.
Majors Administrative assistant and secretarial science; biological and physical sciences; business administration and management; business and personal/financial services marketing; child care provision; child development; computer and information sciences; computer and information sciences related; computer engineering technology; computer programming; computer programming (specific applications); computer programming (vendor/product certification); computer science; computer systems networking and telecommunications; computer/technical support; corrections; data entry/microcomputer applications; data entry/microcomputer applications related; drafting and design technology; electrical, electronic and communications engineering technology; engineering; heating, air conditioning, ventilation and refrigeration maintenance technology; industrial mechanics and maintenance technology; industrial technology; information science/studies; information technology; kindergarten/preschool education; liberal arts and sciences/liberal studies; machine tool technology; management information systems; mechanical design technology; nursing (licensed practical/vocational nurse training); nursing (registered nurse training); quality control technology; system administration; web page, digital/multimedia and information resources design; welding technology.
Academic Programs *Special study options:* academic remediation for entering students, adult/continuing education programs, advanced placement credit, cooperative education, distance learning, double majors, English as a second language, independent study, internships, part-time degree program, services for LD students, study abroad, summer session for credit. *ROTC:* Army (c).
Library Heartland Community College Library with 5,000 titles, 188 serial subscriptions, 4,000 audiovisual materials, an OPAC, a Web page.
Computers on Campus 400 computers available on campus for general student use. A campuswide network can be accessed. Internet access, at least one staffed computer lab available.
Student Life *Housing:* college housing not available. *Activities and Organizations:* drama/theater group, student-run newspaper, choral group, Environmental Club, Early Childhood Club, student government, Nursing Club, Phi Theta Kappa. *Campus security:* 24-hour emergency response devices and patrols. *Student services:* personal/psychological counseling.
Standardized Tests *Required for some:* ACT COMPASS. *Recommended:* SAT (for placement), ACT (for placement).
Costs (2005–06) *Tuition:* area resident $1890 full-time, $63 per semester hour part-time; state resident $3780 full-time, $126 per semester hour part-time; nonresident $5670 full-time, $189 per semester hour part-time.
Financial Aid Of all full-time matriculated undergraduates who enrolled in 2003, 65 Federal Work-Study jobs (averaging $1500).
Applying *Recommended:* high school transcript. *Application deadline:* rolling (freshmen), rolling (transfers). *Notification:* continuous (freshmen).

Admissions Contact Ms. Christine Riley, Director of Advisement and Enrollment Services, Heartland Community College, 1500 West Raab Road, Normal, IL 61761. *Phone:* 309-268-8000. *Fax:* 309-268-7992. *E-mail:* angie.robinson@heartland.edu.

HIGHLAND COMMUNITY COLLEGE
Freeport, Illinois

- **State and locally supported** 2-year, founded 1962, part of Illinois Community College Board
- **Calendar** semesters
- **Degree** certificates and associate
- **Rural** 240-acre campus
- **Endowment** $6.8 million
- **Coed,** 2,462 undergraduate students, 47% full-time, 65% women, 35% men

Undergraduates 1,147 full-time, 1,315 part-time. Students come from 8 states and territories, 2% are from out of state. *Retention:* 65% of 2002 full-time freshmen returned.
Freshmen *Admission:* 462 applied, 462 admitted, 462 enrolled.
Faculty *Total:* 188, 27% full-time, 3% with terminal degrees. *Student/faculty ratio:* 19:1.
Majors Accounting; administrative assistant and secretarial science; agricultural business and management; agricultural mechanization; art; automobile/automotive mechanics technology; biological and physical sciences; business administration and management; chemistry; child care and support services management; child care provision; child development; commercial and advertising art; computer and information sciences related; computer programming (specific applications); computer science; computer/technical support; data processing and data processing technology; drafting and design technology; dramatic/theatre arts; education; electrical, electronic and communications engineering technology; engineering; engineering science; engineering technology; geology/earth science; history; human services; kindergarten/preschool education; liberal arts and sciences/liberal studies; marketing/marketing management; mathematics; mechanical engineering/mechanical technology; music teacher education; nursing (registered nurse training); physical sciences; physics; political science and government; pre-engineering; psychology; sociology; speech/theater education.
Academic Programs *Special study options:* academic remediation for entering students, adult/continuing education programs, advanced placement credit, distance learning, English as a second language, external degree program, independent study, internships, part-time degree program, services for LD students, student-designed majors, summer session for credit.
Library Highland Library plus 1 other with 47,000 titles, 3,980 serial subscriptions, 2,776 audiovisual materials, an OPAC, a Web page.
Computers on Campus 200 computers available on campus for general student use. A campuswide network can be accessed. Internet access, at least one staffed computer lab available.
Student Life *Housing:* college housing not available. *Activities and Organizations:* drama/theater group, student-run newspaper, choral group, Phi Theta Kappa, Royal Scots, Prairie Wind, intramurals, Collegiate Choir. *Campus security:* 24-hour patrols. *Student services:* personal/psychological counseling.
Athletics Member NJCAA. *Intercollegiate sports:* baseball M(s)/W(s), basketball M(s)/W(s), golf M(s)/W(s), softball W(s), volleyball W(s). *Intramural sports:* basketball M/W, racquetball M/W, volleyball M/W.
Standardized Tests *Required for some:* ACT (for placement). *Recommended:* ACT (for placement).
Costs (2005–06) *Tuition:* area resident $1488 full-time, $62 per credit hour part-time; state resident $2664 full-time, $111 per credit hour part-time; nonresident $2664 full-time, $111 per credit hour part-time. *Required fees:* $120 full-time.
Financial Aid Of all full-time matriculated undergraduates who enrolled in 2003, 50 Federal Work-Study jobs (averaging $2000). 50 state and other part-time jobs (averaging $2000).
Applying *Options:* early admission, deferred entrance. *Required for some:* high school transcript. *Application deadline:* rolling (freshmen), rolling (transfers).
Admissions Contact Mr. Karl Richards, Dean of Enrollment Services, Highland Community College, 2998 West Pearl City Road, Freeport, IL 61032. *Phone:* 815-235-6121 Ext. 3486. *Fax:* 815-235-6130.

ILLINOIS CENTRAL COLLEGE
East Peoria, Illinois

Admissions Contact Mr. John Avendano, Vice President of Academic Affairs and Student Development, Illinois Central College, One College Drive, East Peoria, IL 61635-0001. *Phone:* 309-694-5784. *Toll-free phone:* 800-422-2293. *Fax:* 309-694-5450.

ILLINOIS EASTERN COMMUNITY COLLEGES, FRONTIER COMMUNITY COLLEGE
Fairfield, Illinois

- **State and locally supported** 2-year, founded 1976, part of Illinois Eastern Community College System
- **Calendar** semesters
- **Degree** certificates and associate
- **Rural** 8-acre campus
- **Coed,** 1,960 undergraduate students, 12% full-time, 61% women, 39% men

Undergraduates 229 full-time, 1,731 part-time. 0.3% African American, 1% Asian American or Pacific Islander, 0.4% Hispanic American, 0.1% Native American.

Freshmen *Admission:* 27 enrolled.

Faculty *Total:* 150, 3% full-time.

Majors Administrative assistant and secretarial science; biological and physical sciences; business automation/technology/data entry; corrections; general studies; liberal arts and sciences/liberal studies; nursing (registered nurse training); quality control technology.

Academic Programs *Special study options:* academic remediation for entering students, adult/continuing education programs, advanced placement credit, cooperative education, distance learning, double majors, English as a second language, external degree program, independent study, part-time degree program, services for LD students, student-designed majors, summer session for credit.

Library 19,088 titles, 7,664 serial subscriptions, 2,679 audiovisual materials.

Computers on Campus 42 computers available on campus for general student use. At least one staffed computer lab available.

Student Life *Housing:* college housing not available.

Standardized Tests *Required:* SAT or ACT (for placement), ACT ASSET (for placement).

Costs (2004–05) *Tuition:* area resident $1536 full-time, $48 per credit hour part-time; state resident $6192 full-time, $193 per credit hour part-time; nonresident $7659 full-time, $239 per credit hour part-time. *Required fees:* $106 full-time, $3 per credit hour part-time. *Waivers:* senior citizens and employees or children of employees.

Applying *Options:* early admission, deferred entrance. *Application fee:* $10. *Required:* high school transcript. *Application deadline:* rolling (freshmen), rolling (transfers). *Notification:* continuous (freshmen).

Admissions Contact Mrs. Suzanne Brooks, Coordinator of Registration and Records, Illinois Eastern Community Colleges, Frontier Community College, 2 Frontier Drive, Fairfield, IL 62837. *Phone:* 618-842-3711 Ext. 4111.

ILLINOIS EASTERN COMMUNITY COLLEGES, LINCOLN TRAIL COLLEGE
Robinson, Illinois

- **State and locally supported** 2-year, founded 1969, part of Illinois Eastern Community College System
- **Calendar** semesters
- **Degree** certificates and associate
- **Rural** 120-acre campus
- **Coed,** 1,496 undergraduate students, 27% full-time, 48% women, 52% men

Undergraduates 411 full-time, 1,085 part-time. 15% African American, 1% Asian American or Pacific Islander, 4% Hispanic American, 0.3% Native American, 0.2% international.

Freshmen *Admission:* 369 enrolled.

Faculty *Total:* 62, 50% full-time.

Majors Biological and physical sciences; building/property maintenance and management; business automation/technology/data entry; corrections; culinary arts; general studies; heating, air conditioning, ventilation and refrigeration maintenance technology; liberal arts and sciences/liberal studies; mechanical engineering/mechanical technology; music; music teacher education; quality control technology; teacher assistant/aide; telecommunications.

Academic Programs *Special study options:* academic remediation for entering students, adult/continuing education programs, advanced placement credit, cooperative education, distance learning, double majors, English as a second language, external degree program, independent study, internships, part-time degree program, services for LD students, student-designed majors, summer session for credit.

Library Eagleton Learning Resource Center with 16,654 titles, 7,391 serial subscriptions, 2,029 audiovisual materials.

Computers on Campus 96 computers available on campus for general student use. At least one staffed computer lab available.

Student Life *Housing:* college housing not available. *Activities and Organizations:* drama/theater group, choral group, national fraternities. *Student services:* personal/psychological counseling.

Athletics Member NJCAA. *Intercollegiate sports:* baseball M(s), basketball M(s)/W(s), softball W(s), volleyball W(s). *Intramural sports:* baseball M, basketball M, softball W, volleyball M/W.

Standardized Tests *Required:* SAT or ACT (for placement), ACT ASSET (for placement).

Costs (2004–05) *Tuition:* area resident $1536 full-time, $48 per credit hour part-time; state resident $6192 full-time, $193 per credit hour part-time; nonresident $7659 full-time, $239 per credit hour part-time. *Required fees:* $106 full-time, $3 per credit hour part-time. *Waivers:* senior citizens and employees or children of employees.

Applying *Options:* early admission, deferred entrance. *Application fee:* $10. *Required:* high school transcript. *Application deadline:* rolling (freshmen), rolling (transfers). *Notification:* continuous (freshmen).

Admissions Contact Ms. Becky Mikeworth, Director of Admissions, Illinois Eastern Community Colleges, Lincoln Trail College, 11220 State Highway 1, Robinson, IL 62454. *Phone:* 618-544-8657 Ext. 1137.

ILLINOIS EASTERN COMMUNITY COLLEGES, OLNEY CENTRAL COLLEGE
Olney, Illinois

- **State and locally supported** 2-year, founded 1962, part of Illinois Eastern Community College System
- **Calendar** semesters
- **Degree** certificates and associate
- **Rural** 128-acre campus
- **Coed,** 1,670 undergraduate students, 49% full-time, 58% women, 42% men

Undergraduates 813 full-time, 857 part-time. 0.8% African American, 0.9% Asian American or Pacific Islander, 0.3% Hispanic American, 0.1% Native American, 0.1% international.

Freshmen *Admission:* 114 enrolled.

Faculty *Total:* 81, 51% full-time.

Majors Accounting; administrative assistant and secretarial science; autobody/collision and repair technology; automobile/automotive mechanics technology; biological and physical sciences; business automation/technology/data entry; cabinetmaking and millwork; corrections; criminal justice/police science; general studies; heavy equipment maintenance technology; industrial mechanics and maintenance technology; liberal arts and sciences/liberal studies; medical administrative assistant and medical secretary; medical radiologic technology; music; music teacher education; nursing (licensed practical/vocational nurse training); nursing (registered nurse training).

Academic Programs *Special study options:* academic remediation for entering students, adult/continuing education programs, advanced placement credit, cooperative education, distance learning, double majors, English as a second language, external degree program, independent study, internships, part-time degree program, services for LD students, student-designed majors, summer session for credit.

Library Anderson Learning Resources Center with 22,976 titles, 81 serial subscriptions, 693 audiovisual materials.

Computers on Campus 125 computers available on campus for general student use. At least one staffed computer lab available.

Student Life *Housing:* college housing not available. *Activities and Organizations:* drama/theater group, student-run newspaper, choral group. *Student services:* personal/psychological counseling, women's center.

Athletics Member NJCAA. *Intercollegiate sports:* baseball M(s), basketball M(s)/W(s), softball W(s), volleyball W(s). *Intramural sports:* baseball M, basketball M/W, softball W.

Standardized Tests *Required:* SAT or ACT (for placement), ACT ASSET (for placement).

Costs (2004–05) *Tuition:* area resident $1536 full-time, $48 per credit hour part-time; state resident $6192 full-time, $193 per credit hour part-time; nonresident $7659 full-time, $239 per credit hour part-time. *Required fees:* $106 full-time, $3 per credit hour part-time. *Waivers:* senior citizens and employees or children of employees.

Applying *Options:* early admission, deferred entrance. *Application fee:* $10. *Required:* high school transcript. *Application deadline:* rolling (freshmen), rolling (transfers). *Notification:* continuous (freshmen).

Admissions Contact Ms. Chris Webber, Assistant Dean for Student Services, Illinois Eastern Community Colleges, Olney Central College, 305 North West Street, Olney, IL 62450. *Phone:* 618-395-7777 Ext. 2005.

ILLINOIS EASTERN COMMUNITY COLLEGES, WABASH VALLEY COLLEGE
Mount Carmel, Illinois

- **State and locally supported** 2-year, founded 1960, part of Illinois Eastern Community College System
- **Calendar** semesters
- **Degree** certificates and associate
- **Rural** 40-acre campus
- **Coed,** 5,191 undergraduate students, 12% full-time, 48% women, 52% men

Undergraduates 627 full-time, 4,564 part-time. 1% African American, 0.8% Asian American or Pacific Islander, 0.6% Hispanic American, 0.2% Native American.

Freshmen *Admission:* 126 enrolled.

Faculty *Total:* 102, 37% full-time.

Majors Administrative assistant and secretarial science; agricultural business and management; agricultural production; biological and physical sciences; business administration and management; business automation/technology/data entry; child development; corrections; court reporting; diesel mechanics technology; electrical, electronic and communications engineering technology; general studies; industrial technology; liberal arts and sciences/liberal studies; machine shop technology; mining technology; radio and television; social work.

Academic Programs *Special study options:* academic remediation for entering students, adult/continuing education programs, advanced placement credit, cooperative education, distance learning, double majors, English as a second language, external degree program, independent study, internships, part-time degree program, services for LD students, student-designed majors, summer session for credit.

Library Bauer Media Center with 34,589 titles, 7,665 serial subscriptions, 1,629 audiovisual materials.

Computers on Campus 100 computers available on campus for general student use. At least one staffed computer lab available.

Student Life *Housing:* college housing not available. *Activities and Organizations:* drama/theater group, student-run newspaper, radio and television station, choral group.

Athletics Member NJCAA. *Intercollegiate sports:* baseball M(s), basketball M(s)/W(s), softball W(s), tennis M, volleyball W(s). *Intramural sports:* baseball M, basketball M/W, cross-country running M/W, softball W, volleyball M/W.

Standardized Tests *Required:* SAT or ACT (for placement), ACT ASSET (for placement).

Costs (2004–05) *Tuition:* area resident $1536 full-time, $48 per credit hour part-time; state resident $6192 full-time, $193 per credit hour part-time; nonresident $7659 full-time, $239 per credit hour part-time. *Required fees:* $106 full-time, $3 per credit hour part-time. *Waivers:* senior citizens and employees or children of employees.

Applying *Options:* early admission, deferred entrance. *Application fee:* $10. *Required:* high school transcript. *Application deadline:* rolling (freshmen), rolling (transfers). *Notification:* continuous (freshmen).

Admissions Contact Mrs. Diana Spear, Assistant Dean for Student Services, Illinois Eastern Community Colleges, Wabash Valley College, 2200 College Drive, Mt. Carmel, IL 62863. *Phone:* 618-262-8641 Ext. 3101.

ILLINOIS VALLEY COMMUNITY COLLEGE
Oglesby, Illinois

- **District-supported** 2-year, founded 1924, part of Illinois Community College Board
- **Calendar** semesters
- **Degree** associate
- **Rural** 410-acre campus with easy access to Chicago
- **Coed,** 4,315 undergraduate students

Faculty *Total:* 189, 36% full-time.

Majors Accounting; administrative assistant and secretarial science; agricultural business and management; agriculture; automobile/automotive mechanics technology; business administration and management; carpentry; child development; computer programming; computer systems networking and telecommunications; criminal justice/law enforcement administration; criminal justice/police science; data processing and data processing technology; drafting and design technology; education; electrical, electronic and communications engineering technology; elementary education; English; industrial technology; journalism; liberal arts and sciences/liberal studies; marketing/marketing management; mechanical design technology; mechanical engineering/mechanical technology; nursing (registered nurse training); pre-engineering.

Academic Programs *Special study options:* academic remediation for entering students, adult/continuing education programs, advanced placement credit, distance learning, English as a second language, honors programs, independent study, internships, off-campus study, part-time degree program, services for LD students, student-designed majors, study abroad, summer session for credit.

Library Jacobs Library with 58,250 titles, 504 serial subscriptions.

Computers on Campus 420 computers available on campus for general student use.

Student Life *Housing:* college housing not available. *Activities and Organizations:* drama/theater group, student-run newspaper, choral group. *Campus security:* 24-hour patrols. *Student services:* personal/psychological counseling.

Athletics *Intercollegiate sports:* basketball M/W, golf M, tennis M/W. *Intramural sports:* basketball M, volleyball W.

Standardized Tests *Recommended:* ACT (for placement).

Financial Aid Of all full-time matriculated undergraduates who enrolled in 2003, 81 Federal Work-Study jobs (averaging $955).

Applying *Options:* early admission, deferred entrance. *Required:* high school transcript. *Application deadline:* rolling (freshmen), rolling (transfers). *Notification:* continuous (freshmen).

Admissions Contact Ms. Tracy Morris, Director of Admissions and Records, Illinois Valley Community College, 815 North Orlando Smith Avenue, Oglesby, IL 61348. *Phone:* 815-224-0437. *Fax:* 815-224-3033. *E-mail:* kathy-sramek@ivcc.edu.

ITT TECHNICAL INSTITUTE
Burr Ridge, Illinois

- **Proprietary** 2-year, part of ITT Educational Services, Inc
- **Calendar** quarters
- **Degree** associate
- **Coed**

Standardized Tests *Required:* Wonderlic aptitude test (for admission).

Costs (2004–05) *Tuition:* Please see school catalog for specific information.

Applying *Options:* deferred entrance. *Application fee:* $100. *Required:* high school transcript, interview. *Recommended:* letters of recommendation.

Admissions Contact Mr. Leo Rodriguez, Director of Recruitment, ITT Technical Institute, 7040 High Grove Boulevard, Burr Ridge, IL 60527. *Phone:* 630-455-6470. *Toll-free phone:* 877-488-0001. *Fax:* 630-455-6476.

ITT TECHNICAL INSTITUTE
Matteson, Illinois

- **Proprietary** 2-year, founded 1993, part of ITT Educational Services, Inc
- **Calendar** quarters
- **Degree** associate
- **Suburban** campus with easy access to Chicago
- **Coed**

Standardized Tests *Required:* Wonderlic aptitude test (for admission).

Costs (2004–05) *Tuition:* Please see school catalog for specific information.

Financial Aid Of all full-time matriculated undergraduates who enrolled in 2003, 6 Federal Work-Study jobs (averaging $4000).

Applying *Options:* deferred entrance. *Application fee:* $100. *Required:* high school transcript, interview. *Recommended:* letters of recommendation.

Admissions Contact Ms. Lillian Williams-McClain, Director, ITT Technical Institute, 600 Holiday Plaza Drive, Matteson, IL 60443. *Phone:* 708-747-2571. *Fax:* 708-747-0023.

ITT TECHNICAL INSTITUTE
Mount Prospect, Illinois

- **Proprietary** primarily 2-year, founded 1986, part of ITT Educational Services, Inc
- **Calendar** quarters
- **Degrees** associate and bachelor's
- **Suburban** 1-acre campus with easy access to Chicago
- **Coed**

Standardized Tests *Required:* Wonderlic aptitude test (for admission).

Costs (2004–05) *Tuition:* Please see school catalog for specific information.

Applying *Options:* deferred entrance. *Application fee:* $100. *Required:* high school transcript, interview. *Recommended:* letters of recommendation.

Admissions Contact Mr. Ernest Lloyd, Director of Recruitment, ITT Technical Institute, 1401 Feehanville Drive, Mount Prospect, IL 60056. *Phone:* 847-375-8800. *Fax:* 847-375-9022.

JOHN A. LOGAN COLLEGE
Carterville, Illinois

- **State and locally supported** 2-year, founded 1967, part of Illinois Community College Board

John A. Logan College (continued)
- **Calendar** semesters
- **Degree** certificates and associate
- **Rural** 160-acre campus
- **Endowment** $19,000
- **Coed,** 5,501 undergraduate students

Undergraduates Students come from 41 states and territories, 20 other countries.

Faculty *Total:* 43, 53% full-time, 2% with terminal degrees.

Majors Accounting; agriculture; art; art teacher education; automobile/automotive mechanics technology; biology/biological sciences; business administration and management; business teacher education; chemistry; clinical/medical laboratory technology; computer science; consumer merchandising/retailing management; cosmetology; criminal justice/law enforcement administration; data processing and data processing technology; dental hygiene; drafting and design technology; education; electrical, electronic and communications engineering technology; elementary education; emergency medical technology (EMT paramedic); English; fashion merchandising; finance; health information/medical records administration; heating, air conditioning, ventilation and refrigeration maintenance technology; history; humanities; information science/studies; journalism; kindergarten/preschool education; legal administrative assistant/secretary; liberal arts and sciences/liberal studies; machine tool technology; marketing/marketing management; mathematics; nursing (licensed practical/vocational nurse training); nursing (registered nurse training); occupational therapy; physical education teaching and coaching; physics; political science and government; pre-engineering; psychology; sign language interpretation and translation; social work; teacher assistant/aide; tourism and travel services management; welding technology.

Academic Programs *Special study options:* academic remediation for entering students, adult/continuing education programs, advanced placement credit, cooperative education, distance learning, internships, off-campus study, part-time degree program, services for LD students, study abroad, summer session for credit. *ROTC:* Army (c), Air Force (c).

Library Learning Resource Center with 33,306 titles, 298 serial subscriptions, a Web page.

Computers on Campus 150 computers available on campus for general student use. Internet access, at least one staffed computer lab available.

Student Life *Housing:* college housing not available. *Activities and Organizations:* drama/theater group, student-run newspaper, choral group. *Campus security:* 24-hour emergency response devices and patrols.

Athletics Member NJCAA. *Intercollegiate sports:* baseball M, basketball M/W, golf M/W, softball W, volleyball W.

Standardized Tests *Required:* ACT ASSET (for placement). *Recommended:* SAT or ACT (for placement).

Costs (2005–06) *Tuition:* area resident $1900 full-time, $57 per credit hour part-time; state resident $6000 full-time, $169 per credit hour part-time; nonresident $9000 full-time, $255 per credit hour part-time.

Applying *Options:* electronic application, early admission. *Required:* high school transcript. *Application deadlines:* 8/25 (freshmen), 8/25 (transfers). *Notification:* continuous (freshmen).

Admissions Contact Mr. Terry Crain, Dean of Student Services, John A. Logan College, 700 Logan College Road, Carterville, IL 62918-9900. *Phone:* 618-985-3741 Ext. 8382. *Fax:* 618-985-4433. *E-mail:* terrycrain@jalc.edu.

JOHN WOOD COMMUNITY COLLEGE
Quincy, Illinois

- **District-supported** 2-year, founded 1974, part of Illinois Community College Board
- **Calendar** semesters
- **Degree** certificates and associate
- **Small-town** campus
- **Coed,** 2,411 undergraduate students, 51% full-time, 63% women, 37% men

Undergraduates 1,221 full-time, 1,190 part-time. Students come from 4 states and territories, 3 other countries, 9% are from out of state, 3% African American, 1% Asian American or Pacific Islander, 0.6% Hispanic American, 0.3% Native American, 0.3% international, 6% transferred in.

Freshmen *Admission:* 783 applied, 783 admitted, 568 enrolled. *Test scores:* ACT scores over 18: 60%; ACT scores over 24: 11%.

Faculty *Total:* 181, 28% full-time, 9% with terminal degrees. *Student/faculty ratio:* 15:1.

Majors Accounting; accounting technology and bookkeeping; administrative assistant and secretarial science; agricultural business and management; agricultural production; animal/livestock husbandry and production; applied horticulture; biological and physical sciences; business administration and management; business/commerce; child guidance; clinical/medical laboratory technology; computer programming (specific applications); criminal justice/police science; early childhood education; electrical, electronic and communications engineer-

ing technology; electrician; emergency medical technology (EMT paramedic); executive assistant/executive secretary; fire protection and safety technology; general studies; health and physical education; hotel/motel administration; industrial electronics technology; industrial mechanics and maintenance technology; legal administrative assistant/secretary; liberal arts and sciences/liberal studies; mechanical drafting and CAD/CADD; medical administrative assistant and medical secretary; medical radiologic technology; nursing (registered nurse training); psychology; restaurant, culinary, and catering management; sales, distribution and marketing; sociology.

Academic Programs *Special study options:* academic remediation for entering students, adult/continuing education programs, advanced placement credit, cooperative education, distance learning, English as a second language, external degree program, independent study, internships, off-campus study, part-time degree program, services for LD students, student-designed majors, study abroad, summer session for credit.

Library 18,000 titles, 160 serial subscriptions, 2,200 audiovisual materials, an OPAC, a Web page.

Computers on Campus 250 computers available on campus for general student use. A campuswide network can be accessed. Internet access, at least one staffed computer lab available.

Student Life *Housing:* college housing not available. *Activities and Organizations:* choral group. *Campus security:* 24-hour emergency response devices, late-night transport/escort service.

Athletics Member NJCAA. *Intercollegiate sports:* baseball M(s), basketball M(s)/W(s), golf M(s), softball W(s), volleyball W(s). *Intramural sports:* basketball M/W, volleyball M/W.

Standardized Tests *Required:* ACT ASSET, ACT COMPASS (for placement). *Recommended:* SAT or ACT (for placement).

Costs (2005–06) *Tuition:* area resident $2280 full-time, $76 per credit hour part-time; state resident $5280 full-time, $176 per credit hour part-time. *Required fees:* $150 full-time, $5 per credit hour part-time.

Financial Aid Of all full-time matriculated undergraduates who enrolled in 2003, 360 Federal Work-Study jobs (averaging $364).

Applying *Options:* common application, early admission. *Required:* high school transcript. *Application deadline:* rolling (freshmen), rolling (transfers). *Notification:* continuous (freshmen).

Admissions Contact Mr. Mark C. McNett, Director of Admissions, John Wood Community College, 1301 South 48th Street, Quincy, IL 62305-8736. *Phone:* 217-641-4339. *Fax:* 217-224-4208. *E-mail:* admissions@jwcc.edu.

JOLIET JUNIOR COLLEGE
Joliet, Illinois

Admissions Contact Ms. Jennifer Kloberdanz, Vice President of Academic Affairs, Joliet Junior College, 1215 Houbolt Road, Joliet, IL 60431. *Phone:* 815-280-2493.

KANKAKEE COMMUNITY COLLEGE
Kankakee, Illinois

Admissions Contact Ms. Michelle Driscoll, Kankakee Community College, Box 888, Kankakee, IL 60901. *Phone:* 815-802-8520.

KASKASKIA COLLEGE
Centralia, Illinois

- **State and locally supported** 2-year, founded 1966, part of Illinois Community College Board
- **Calendar** semesters
- **Degree** certificates and associate
- **Rural** 195-acre campus with easy access to St. Louis
- **Endowment** $537,157
- **Coed,** 4,601 undergraduate students, 43% full-time, 60% women, 40% men

Undergraduates 1,980 full-time, 2,621 part-time. Students come from 23 states and territories, 2 other countries, 3% are from out of state, 6% African American, 0.6% Asian American or Pacific Islander, 1% Hispanic American, 0.5% Native American, 0.1% international, 21% transferred in.

Freshmen *Admission:* 573 enrolled.

Faculty *Total:* 238, 30% full-time, 6% with terminal degrees. *Student/faculty ratio:* 23:1.

Majors Agricultural business and management; applied horticulture; architectural drafting and CAD/CADD; autobody/collision and repair technology; automobile/automotive mechanics technology; biological and physical sciences; business administration and management; business automation/technology/data entry; carpentry; computer programming (specific applications); criminal justice/police science; culinary arts; electrical, electronic and communications engineering technology; executive assistant/executive secretary; general studies; industrial mechanics and maintenance technology; liberal arts and sciences/liberal studies; medical radiologic technology; nursing (registered nurse training); physical therapist assistant; respiratory care therapy.

Academic Programs *Special study options:* academic remediation for entering students, accelerated degree program, adult/continuing education programs, cooperative education, distance learning, double majors, English as a second language, honors programs, independent study, internships, off-campus study, part-time degree program, services for LD students, study abroad, summer session for credit.

Library Kaskaskia College Library with 23,685 titles, 165 serial subscriptions, 480 audiovisual materials, an OPAC, a Web page.

Computers on Campus 129 computers available on campus for general student use. A campuswide network can be accessed from off campus. Internet access, at least one staffed computer lab available.

Student Life *Housing:* college housing not available. *Activities and Organizations:* drama/theater group, student-run newspaper, choral group, Phi Theta Kappa, Administration of Justice, Student Radiology Club, Cosmetology Club, Vocal Music Club. *Campus security:* 24-hour patrols, late-night transport/escort service. *Student services:* personal/psychological counseling.

Athletics Member NJCAA. *Intercollegiate sports:* baseball M(s), basketball M(s)/W(s), cheerleading M(s)/W(s), golf M(s), softball W(s), volleyball W(s).

Standardized Tests *Recommended:* ACT (for admission), ASSET.

Costs (2005–06) *Tuition:* area resident $1696 full-time, $53 per credit hour part-time; state resident $2510 full-time, $78 per credit hour part-time; nonresident $7507 full-time, $235 per credit hour part-time. Full-time tuition and fees vary according to location. Part-time tuition and fees vary according to location. *Required fees:* $224 full-time, $7 per credit hour part-time. *Payment plan:* installment. *Waivers:* senior citizens and employees or children of employees.

Applying *Options:* common application, early admission, deferred entrance. *Required:* high school transcript. *Required for some:* interview. *Application deadline:* rolling (freshmen), rolling (transfers). *Notification:* continuous (freshmen).

Admissions Contact Daniel Herbst, Dean of Enrollment Services, Kaskaskia College, 27210 College Road, Centralia, IL 62801. *Phone:* 618-545-3066. *Toll-free phone:* 800-642-0859. *Fax:* 618-532-1135.

KISHWAUKEE COLLEGE
Malta, Illinois

- **State and locally supported** 2-year, founded 1967, part of Illinois Community College Board
- **Calendar** semesters
- **Degree** certificates and associate
- **Rural** 120-acre campus with easy access to Chicago
- **Endowment** $1.3 million
- **Coed**

Faculty *Student/faculty ratio:* 15:1.

Student Life *Campus security:* 24-hour patrols.

Athletics Member NJCAA.

Standardized Tests *Required for some:* ACT, SAT I, or in-house placement test.

Financial Aid Of all full-time matriculated undergraduates who enrolled in 2003, 107 Federal Work-Study jobs (averaging $1285). 45 state and other part-time jobs (averaging $1100).

Applying *Options:* common application, early admission, deferred entrance. *Required:* high school transcript, transcripts from all other colleges or universities previously attended. *Required for some:* minimum 2.0 GPA. *Recommended:* minimum 2.0 GPA.

Admissions Contact Ms. Sally Misciasci, Admission Analyst, Kishwaukee College, 21193 Malta Road, Malta, IL 60150-9699. *Phone:* 815-825-2086 Ext. 400. *Fax:* 815-825-2306.

LAKE LAND COLLEGE
Mattoon, Illinois

- **State and locally supported** 2-year, founded 1966, part of Illinois Community College Board
- **Calendar** semesters
- **Degree** certificates and associate
- **Rural** 304-acre campus
- **Endowment** $2.7 million
- **Coed,** 7,196 undergraduate students, 44% full-time, 48% women, 52% men

Undergraduates 3,144 full-time, 4,052 part-time. Students come from 23 other countries, 8% African American, 0.4% Asian American or Pacific Islander, 3% Hispanic American, 0.3% Native American, 0.5% international.

Freshmen *Admission:* 2,159 applied, 2,159 admitted.

Faculty *Total:* 191, 61% full-time, 5% with terminal degrees. *Student/faculty ratio:* 21:1.

Majors Accounting technology and bookkeeping; administrative assistant and secretarial science; agricultural business and management; agricultural mechanization; agricultural production; architectural engineering technology; automobile/automotive mechanics technology; biological and physical sciences; business administration and management; child care and support services management; civil engineering technology; computer programming (specific applications); computer systems networking and telecommunications; corrections; criminal justice/police science; dental hygiene; desktop publishing and digital imaging design; drafting and design technology; electrical, electronic and communications engineering technology; electromechanical technology; executive assistant/executive secretary; general studies; graphic and printing equipment operation/production; human services; industrial technology; information technology; legal administrative assistant/secretary; liberal arts and sciences/liberal studies; marketing/marketing management; medical administrative assistant and medical secretary; nursing (registered nurse training); office management; physical therapist assistant; printing press operation; radio and television; social work; telecommunications.

Academic Programs *Special study options:* academic remediation for entering students, accelerated degree program, adult/continuing education programs, cooperative education, distance learning, English as a second language, external degree program, honors programs, internships, part-time degree program, services for LD students, summer session for credit.

Library Virgil H. Judge Learning Resource Center with 36,912 titles, 193 serial subscriptions, 1,446 audiovisual materials, an OPAC.

Computers on Campus 100 computers available on campus for general student use. A campuswide network can be accessed. Internet access, online (class) registration, at least one staffed computer lab available.

Student Life *Housing:* college housing not available. *Activities and Organizations:* student-run newspaper, radio station, choral group, Agriculture Production and Management Club, Cosmetology Club, Agriculture Transfer Club, Phi Theta Kappa, Civil Engineering Technology Club. *Campus security:* 24-hour patrols. *Student services:* personal/psychological counseling.

Athletics Member NJCAA. *Intercollegiate sports:* baseball M(s), basketball M(s)/W(s), cheerleading W, softball W(s), tennis M(s)/W, volleyball W(s). *Intramural sports:* basketball M/W, bowling M/W, golf M/W, softball M/W, volleyball M/W.

Standardized Tests *Required for some:* ACT (for placement). *Recommended:* ACT (for placement).

Costs (2005–06) *Tuition:* area resident $1545 full-time, $52 per credit hour part-time; state resident $3595 full-time, $120 per credit hour part-time; nonresident $7568 full-time, $252 per credit hour part-time. *Required fees:* $358 full-time, $12 per credit hour part-time. *Payment plan:* deferred payment. *Waivers:* senior citizens.

Financial Aid Of all full-time matriculated undergraduates who enrolled in 2003, 120 Federal Work-Study jobs (averaging $1400).

Applying *Options:* common application, electronic application, early admission. *Required for some:* letters of recommendation. *Recommended:* high school transcript. *Application deadline:* rolling (freshmen), rolling (transfers). *Notification:* continuous (freshmen).

Admissions Contact Mr. Jon VanDyke, Dean of Admission Services, Lake Land College, Mattoon, IL 61938-9366. *Phone:* 217-234-5378. *Toll-free phone:* 800-252-4121.

LEWIS AND CLARK COMMUNITY COLLEGE
Godfrey, Illinois

- **District-supported** 2-year, founded 1970, part of Illinois Community College Board
- **Calendar** semesters
- **Degree** certificates and associate
- **Small-town** 275-acre campus with easy access to St. Louis
- **Coed,** 7,446 undergraduate students, 32% full-time, 59% women, 41% men

Undergraduates 2,377 full-time, 5,069 part-time. Students come from 3 states and territories, 4 other countries, 1% are from out of state, 6% African American, 0.3% Asian American or Pacific Islander, 0.6% Hispanic American, 0.2% Native American, 0.4% international.

Faculty *Total:* 309, 28% full-time.

Majors Accounting; administrative assistant and secretarial science; art; automobile/automotive mechanics technology; biological and physical sciences; biology/biological sciences; business administration and management; child development; computer programming; criminal justice/law enforcement administration; data processing and data processing technology; dental hygiene; drafting and design technology; fire science; kindergarten/preschool education; legal administrative assistant/secretary; liberal arts and sciences/liberal studies; machine tool technology; medical administrative assistant and medical secretary; music; nursing (registered nurse training); occupational therapist assistant; pre-engineering; radio and television; teacher assistant/aide.

Lewis and Clark Community College (continued)

Academic Programs *Special study options:* academic remediation for entering students, adult/continuing education programs, advanced placement credit, cooperative education, distance learning, double majors, English as a second language, independent study, internships, off-campus study, part-time degree program, services for LD students, summer session for credit. *ROTC:* Army (b).

Library Reid Memorial with 47,000 titles, 3,500 serial subscriptions, 1,700 audiovisual materials, an OPAC, a Web page.

Computers on Campus 350 computers available on campus for general student use. Internet access, at least one staffed computer lab available.

Student Life *Housing:* college housing not available. *Activities and Organizations:* student-run newspaper, radio station, choral group, Phi Beta Lambda, Data Processing Club, Nursing Club, Clinical Laboratory Technicians Club, Music Club. *Campus security:* 24-hour emergency response devices and patrols. *Student services:* health clinic, personal/psychological counseling.

Athletics Member NJCAA. *Intercollegiate sports:* baseball M, basketball M/W(s), golf M, soccer M(s)/W, softball W, tennis M(s)/W(s), volleyball W(s).

Costs (2004–05) *Tuition:* area resident $1800 full-time, $60 per credit part-time; state resident $5400 full-time, $180 per credit part-time; nonresident $7200 full-time, $240 per credit part-time. *Required fees:* $210 full-time, $7 per credit part-time. *Payment plans:* installment, deferred payment. *Waivers:* senior citizens and employees or children of employees.

Applying *Options:* early admission, deferred entrance. *Required for some:* interview. *Recommended:* high school transcript. *Application deadline:* rolling (freshmen), rolling (transfers). *Notification:* continuous (freshmen).

Admissions Contact Ms. Peggy Hudson, Director of Enrollment Center for Admissions Services, Lewis and Clark Community College, Enrollment Center, 5800 Godfrey Road, Godfrey, IL 62035. *Phone:* 618-468-5100. *Toll-free phone:* 800-500-LCCC. *Fax:* 618-467-2310.

LINCOLN COLLEGE
Lincoln, Illinois

- **Independent** 2-year, founded 1865
- **Calendar** semesters
- **Degree** associate
- **Small-town** 42-acre campus
- **Endowment** $14.0 million
- **Coed**

Faculty *Student/faculty ratio:* 15:1.

Student Life *Campus security:* 24-hour emergency response devices and patrols, controlled dormitory access.

Athletics Member NJCAA.

Standardized Tests *Required:* SAT or ACT (for admission).

Costs (2004–05) *Comprehensive fee:* $19,960 includes full-time tuition ($13,600), mandatory fees ($960), and room and board ($5400). No tuition increase for student's term of enrollment. *Room and board:* Room and board charges vary according to housing facility. *Payment plans:* installment, deferred payment.

Financial Aid Of all full-time matriculated undergraduates who enrolled in 2003, 200 Federal Work-Study jobs (averaging $900).

Applying *Options:* early admission, deferred entrance. *Application fee:* $25. *Required:* high school transcript. *Required for some:* 1 letter of recommendation. *Recommended:* interview.

Admissions Contact Mr. Tony Schilling, Director of Admissions, Lincoln College, 300 Keokuk Street, Lincoln, IL 62656-1699. *Phone:* 800-569-0556 Ext. 254. *Toll-free phone:* 800-569-0556. *Fax:* 217-732-7715. *E-mail:* information@lincolncollege.com.

▶ **See page 514 for a narrative description.**

LINCOLN COLLEGE
Normal, Illinois

Admissions Contact Mr. Joe Hendrix, Director of Admissions, Lincoln College, 715 West Raab Road, Normal, IL 61761. *Phone:* 309-452-0500. *Toll-free phone:* 800-569-0558. *Fax:* 309-454-5652. *E-mail:* admissions@lincoln.mclean.il.us.

▶ **See page 516 for a narrative description.**

LINCOLN LAND COMMUNITY COLLEGE
Springfield, Illinois

- **District-supported** 2-year, founded 1967, part of Illinois Community College Board
- **Calendar** semesters
- **Degree** certificates and associate

- **Suburban** 441-acre campus with easy access to St. Louis
- **Endowment** $1.7 million
- **Coed,** 6,942 undergraduate students, 40% full-time, 59% women, 41% men

Undergraduates 2,756 full-time, 4,186 part-time. Students come from 4 states and territories, 3 other countries, 0.1% are from out of state, 8% African American, 1% Asian American or Pacific Islander, 1% Hispanic American, 0.4% Native American, 0.3% international, 3% transferred in. *Retention:* 47% of 2002 full-time freshmen returned.

Freshmen *Admission:* 722 applied, 722 admitted, 722 enrolled. *Average high school GPA:* 2.97. *Test scores:* SAT verbal scores over 500: 45%; SAT math scores over 500: 67%; ACT scores over 18: 65%; ACT scores over 24: 17%; ACT scores over 30: 1%.

Faculty *Total:* 361, 34% full-time, 34% with terminal degrees. *Student/faculty ratio:* 19:1.

Majors Administrative assistant and secretarial science; agricultural production; architectural drafting and CAD/CADD; art; automobile/automotive mechanics technology; biological and physical sciences; business administration and management; business automation/technology/data entry; child care provision; child guidance; computer programming (specific applications); computer systems networking and telecommunications; criminal justice/police science; electrical, electronic and communications engineering technology; fire protection and safety technology; general studies; hotel/motel administration; landscaping and groundskeeping; legal administrative assistant/secretary; liberal arts and sciences/liberal studies; literature; medical radiologic technology; music; nursing (registered nurse training); occupational therapist assistant; physical therapist assistant; pre-engineering; respiratory care therapy; selling skills and sales.

Academic Programs *Special study options:* academic remediation for entering students, accelerated degree program, adult/continuing education programs, advanced placement credit, distance learning, English as a second language, external degree program, honors programs, independent study, internships, off-campus study, part-time degree program, services for LD students, study abroad, summer session for credit.

Library Learning Resource Center with 65,000 titles, 10,000 serial subscriptions, 3,300 audiovisual materials, an OPAC, a Web page.

Computers on Campus 130 computers available on campus for general student use. A campuswide network can be accessed from off campus. Internet access, online (class) registration, at least one staffed computer lab available.

Student Life *Housing:* college housing not available. *Activities and Organizations:* drama/theater group, student-run newspaper, choral group, Student Senate, Phi Theta Kappa, Model Illinois Government, student newspaper, Madrigals. *Campus security:* 24-hour emergency response devices and patrols, late-night transport/escort service. *Student services:* health clinic, personal/psychological counseling, women's center.

Athletics Member NJCAA. *Intercollegiate sports:* baseball M(s), basketball M(s)/W(s), soccer M(s), softball W(s), volleyball W(s). *Intramural sports:* basketball M/W, tennis M/W.

Costs (2004–05) *Tuition:* area resident $1620 full-time, $54 per credit hour part-time; state resident $6750 full-time, $225 per credit hour part-time; nonresident $8310 full-time, $277 per credit hour part-time. Full-time tuition and fees vary according to course load. Part-time tuition and fees vary according to course load. *Required fees:* $165 full-time, $6 per credit hour part-time. *Payment plan:* installment. *Waivers:* senior citizens and employees or children of employees.

Applying *Options:* common application, early admission, deferred entrance. *Recommended:* high school transcript. *Application deadline:* rolling (freshmen), rolling (transfers). *Notification:* continuous (freshmen).

Admissions Contact Mr. Ron Gregoire, Executive Director of Admissions and Records, Lincoln Land Community College, 5250 Shepherd Road, PO Box 19256, Springfield, IL 62794-9256. *Phone:* 217-786-2243. *Toll-free phone:* 800-727-4161 Ext. 298. *Fax:* 217-786-2492. *E-mail:* ron.gregoire@llcc.edu.

MACCORMAC COLLEGE
Chicago, Illinois

- **Independent** 2-year, founded 1904
- **Calendar** semesters
- **Degree** certificates, diplomas, and associate
- **Urban** campus
- **Coed, primarily women**

Faculty *Student/faculty ratio:* 15:1.

Student Life *Campus security:* late-night transport/escort service.

Standardized Tests *Required:* ACT (for admission). *Recommended:* SAT (for admission).

Costs (2004–05) *Tuition:* $9960 full-time, $350 per credit part-time. *Required fees:* $200 full-time, $10 per credit part-time.

Financial Aid Of all full-time matriculated undergraduates who enrolled in 2003, 16 Federal Work-Study jobs.

Applying *Options:* common application, deferred entrance. *Application fee:* $20. *Required:* high school transcript. *Recommended:* interview.

Admissions Contact Ms. Rosa Medina, Coordinator of Admissions, Mac-Cormac College, 506 South Wabash Avenue, Chicago, IL 60605-1667. *Phone:* 312-922-1884 Ext. 106. *Fax:* 630-941-0937.

McHenry County College
Crystal Lake, Illinois

- **State and locally supported** 2-year, founded 1967, part of Illinois Community College Board
- **Calendar** semesters
- **Degree** certificates and associate
- **Suburban** 109-acre campus with easy access to Chicago
- **Coed**

Faculty *Student/faculty ratio:* 20:1.
Student Life *Campus security:* 24-hour emergency response devices and patrols, late-night transport/escort service.
Athletics Member NJCAA.
Standardized Tests *Recommended:* ACT (for placement).
Costs (2004–05) *Tuition:* area resident $1740 full-time, $58 per credit part-time; state resident $7333 full-time, $244 per credit part-time; nonresident $8601 full-time, $287 per credit part-time. Full-time tuition and fees vary according to reciprocity agreements. Part-time tuition and fees vary according to reciprocity agreements. *Required fees:* $284 full-time, $9 per credit part-time, $7 per term part-time. *Payment plans:* installment, deferred payment.
Financial Aid Of all full-time matriculated undergraduates who enrolled in 2003, 200 Federal Work-Study jobs (averaging $3700). 130 state and other part-time jobs (averaging $2000).
Applying *Options:* early admission, deferred entrance. *Required:* high school transcript.
Admissions Contact Ms. Sue Grenwis, Admissions Specialist, McHenry County College, 8900 US Highway 14, Crystal Lake, IL 60012. *Phone:* 815-455-8530. *Toll-free phone:* 815-455-8530. *Fax:* 815-455-8530. *E-mail:* admissions@mchenry.edu.

Moraine Valley Community College
Palos Hills, Illinois

- **State and locally supported** 2-year, founded 1967, part of Illinois Community College Board
- **Calendar** semesters
- **Degree** certificates and associate
- **Suburban** 294-acre campus with easy access to Chicago
- **Endowment** $12.0 million
- **Coed**, 16,077 undergraduate students, 41% full-time, 59% women, 41% men

Undergraduates 6,527 full-time, 9,550 part-time. Students come from 10 states and territories, 34 other countries, 9% African American, 2% Asian American or Pacific Islander, 9% Hispanic American, 0.3% Native American, 2% international, 1% transferred in. *Retention:* 73% of 2002 full-time freshmen returned.
Freshmen *Admission:* 3,728 applied, 3,728 admitted, 2,572 enrolled. *Test scores:* ACT scores over 18: 68%; ACT scores over 24: 17%; ACT scores over 30: 1%.
Faculty *Total:* 693, 23% full-time. *Student/faculty ratio:* 29:1.
Majors Administrative assistant and secretarial science; automobile/automotive mechanics technology; biological and physical sciences; business administration and management; business/commerce; child care provision; computer programming (specific applications); computer systems networking and telecommunications; corrections; criminal justice/police science; design and visual communications; entrepreneurship; fire protection and safety technology; health information/medical records technology; human resources management; instrumentation technology; liberal arts and sciences/liberal studies; mechanical engineering/mechanical technology; medical radiologic technology; nursing (registered nurse training); parks, recreation and leisure facilities management; respiratory care therapy; restaurant, culinary, and catering management; retailing; selling skills and sales; therapeutic recreation; tourism and travel services marketing; visual and performing arts.
Academic Programs *Special study options:* academic remediation for entering students, accelerated degree program, adult/continuing education programs, advanced placement credit, cooperative education, distance learning, double majors, English as a second language, external degree program, honors programs, independent study, internships, off-campus study, part-time degree program, services for LD students, study abroad, summer session for credit.
Library Robert E. Turner Learning Resources Center/Library plus 1 other with 77,164 titles, 399 serial subscriptions, 22,092 audiovisual materials, an OPAC, a Web page.

Computers on Campus 1200 computers available on campus for general student use. A campuswide network can be accessed from off campus. Internet access, online (class) registration, at least one staffed computer lab available.
Student Life *Housing:* college housing not available. *Activities and Organizations:* drama/theater group, student-run newspaper, choral group, student newspaper, Speech Team, Alliance of Latin American Students, Phi Theta Kappa, Arab Student Union. *Campus security:* 24-hour emergency response devices and patrols, late-night transport/escort service, safety and security programs. *Student services:* personal/psychological counseling, women's center.
Athletics Member NJCAA. *Intercollegiate sports:* baseball M(s), basketball M(s)/W(s), cross-country running M(s)/W(s), golf M(s), soccer M(s)/W(s), tennis W(s), volleyball W(s). *Intramural sports:* badminton M/W, basketball M/W, softball W, volleyball W.
Standardized Tests *Required:* ACT COMPASS (for placement). *Required for some:* ACT (for placement). *Recommended:* ACT (for placement).
Costs (2004–05) *Tuition:* area resident $1770 full-time, $59 per credit hour part-time; state resident $5970 full-time, $199 per credit hour part-time; nonresident $7260 full-time, $242 per credit hour part-time. *Required fees:* $152 full-time, $5 per credit hour part-time, $1 per term part-time. *Payment plan:* installment. *Waivers:* senior citizens and employees or children of employees.
Financial Aid Of all full-time matriculated undergraduates who enrolled in 2003, 84 Federal Work-Study jobs (averaging $1900). 150 state and other part-time jobs (averaging $800).
Applying *Options:* electronic application, early admission, deferred entrance. *Required:* high school transcript. *Required for some:* minimum 2.0 GPA. *Recommended:* minimum 2.0 GPA. *Application deadline:* rolling (freshmen), rolling (transfers). *Notification:* continuous (freshmen).
Admissions Contact Ms. Claudia Roselli, Director, Admissions and Recruitment, Moraine Valley Community College, 10900 South 88th Avenue, Palos Hills, IL 60465-0937. *Phone:* 708-974-5357. *Fax:* 708-974-0681. *E-mail:* roselli@morainevalley.edu.

Morrison Institute of Technology
Morrison, Illinois

- **Independent** 2-year, founded 1973
- **Calendar** semesters
- **Degree** associate
- **Small-town** 17-acre campus
- **Endowment** $76,000
- **Coed, primarily men**, 125 undergraduate students, 97% full-time, 8% women, 92% men

Undergraduates 121 full-time, 4 part-time. Students come from 4 states and territories, 6% are from out of state, 0.8% African American, 4% Hispanic American, 3% transferred in, 55% live on campus.
Freshmen *Admission:* 48 enrolled. *Average high school GPA:* 2.3. *Test scores:* ACT scores over 18: 72%; ACT scores over 24: 10%; ACT scores over 30: 2%.
Faculty *Total:* 12, 75% full-time. *Student/faculty ratio:* 12:1.
Majors CAD/CADD drafting/design technology; construction engineering technology; drafting and design technology; engineering technology; mechanical drafting and CAD/CADD; survey technology.
Academic Programs *Special study options:* academic remediation for entering students, double majors, internships, part-time degree program.
Library Milikan Library with 7,946 titles, 39 serial subscriptions.
Computers on Campus 60 computers available on campus for general student use. A campuswide network can be accessed from student residence rooms. Internet access, at least one staffed computer lab available. Computer purchase or lease plan available.
Student Life *Housing:* on-campus residence required for freshman year. *Options:* coed. Freshman applicants given priority for college housing. *Campus security:* late-night transport/escort service, controlled dormitory access.
Athletics *Intramural sports:* basketball M, bowling M/W, softball M/W, table tennis M/W, volleyball M/W.
Standardized Tests *Recommended:* SAT or ACT (for admission).
Costs (2005–06) *Tuition:* $11,550 full-time, $481 per credit part-time. *Required fees:* $280 full-time, $125 per term part-time. *Room only:* $2400.
Financial Aid Of all full-time matriculated undergraduates who enrolled in 2003, 25 Federal Work-Study jobs (averaging $2000).
Applying *Options:* common application, deferred entrance. *Application fee:* $100. *Required:* high school transcript, proof of immunization. *Application deadline:* rolling (freshmen). *Notification:* continuous until 9/1 (freshmen).
Admissions Contact Mrs. Tammy Pruis, Admission Secretary, Morrison Institute of Technology, 701 Portland Avenue, Morrison, IL 61270. *Phone:* 815-772-7218. *Fax:* 815-772-7584. *E-mail:* admissions@morrison.tec.il.us.

▶ **See page 532 for a narrative description.**

MORTON COLLEGE
Cicero, Illinois

- **State and locally supported** 2-year, founded 1924, part of Illinois Community College Board
- **Calendar** semesters
- **Degree** certificates and associate
- **Suburban** 25-acre campus with easy access to Chicago
- **Coed**

Student Life *Campus security:* 24-hour patrols, security cameras.

Athletics Member NJCAA.

Financial Aid Of all full-time matriculated undergraduates who enrolled in 2003, 15 Federal Work-Study jobs (averaging $2000).

Applying *Application fee:* $10. *Required:* high school transcript.

Admissions Contact Ms. Jill Caccamo-Beer, Director of Enrollment Management, Morton College, 3801 South Central Avenue, Cicero, IL 60804. *Phone:* 708-656-8000 Ext. 400. *Fax:* 708-656-9592. *E-mail:* enroll@morton.cc.il.us.

NORTHWESTERN BUSINESS COLLEGE
Chicago, Illinois

Admissions Contact Mr. Mark Sliz, Director of Admissions, Northwestern Business College, 4839 North Milwaukee Avenue, Chicago, IL 60630. *Phone:* 773-481-3730. *Toll-free phone:* 800-396-5613. *Fax:* 773-481-3738.

▶ **See page 538 for a narrative description.**

OAKTON COMMUNITY COLLEGE
Des Plaines, Illinois

- **District-supported** 2-year, founded 1969, part of Illinois Community College Board
- **Calendar** semesters
- **Degree** certificates and associate
- **Suburban** 193-acre campus with easy access to Chicago
- **Coed**

Faculty *Student/faculty ratio:* 25:1.

Student Life *Campus security:* 24-hour emergency response devices and patrols, student patrols, late-night transport/escort service.

Athletics Member NJCAA.

Costs (2004–05) *Tuition:* $62 per credit part-time; state resident $183 per credit part-time; nonresident $247 per credit part-time. *Required fees:* $3 per credit part-time, $15 per term part-time.

Financial Aid Of all full-time matriculated undergraduates who enrolled in 2003, 15 Federal Work-Study jobs (averaging $3500). 200 state and other part-time jobs (averaging $3200).

Applying *Application fee:* $25. *Required for some:* letters of recommendation, interview. *Recommended:* high school transcript.

Admissions Contact Mr. Dale Cohen, Admissions Specialist, Oakton Community College, 1600 East Golf Road, Des Plaines, IL 60016. *Phone:* 847-635-1703. *Fax:* 847-635-1890. *E-mail:* admiss@oakton.edu.

PARKLAND COLLEGE
Champaign, Illinois

- **District-supported** 2-year, founded 1967, part of Illinois Community College Board
- **Calendar** semesters
- **Degree** certificates and associate
- **Suburban** 233-acre campus
- **Coed**, 9,536 undergraduate students, 48% full-time, 54% women, 46% men

Undergraduates 4,614 full-time, 4,922 part-time. Students come from 30 states and territories, 14 other countries, 1% are from out of state, 14% African American, 3% Asian American or Pacific Islander, 3% Hispanic American, 0.5% Native American, 3% international, 6% transferred in.

Freshmen *Admission:* 3,370 applied, 3,033 admitted, 1,669 enrolled. *Test scores:* ACT scores over 18: 60%; ACT scores over 24: 15%.

Faculty *Total:* 527, 32% full-time, 12% with terminal degrees. *Student/faculty ratio:* 17:1.

Majors Accounting technology and bookkeeping; administrative assistant and secretarial science; advertising; agricultural business and management; agricultural mechanization; art; art teacher education; autobody/collision and repair technology; automobile/automotive mechanics technology; biological and physical sciences; biomedical technology; business administration and management; business automation/technology/data entry; child care provision; computer and information sciences; computer graphics; computer/information technology ser-

vices administration related; computer programming; computer programming (specific applications); computer programming (vendor/product certification); computer science; computer software and media applications related; computer systems networking and telecommunications; computer/technical support; construction management; consumer merchandising/retailing management; criminal justice/safety; data entry/microcomputer applications; dental hygiene; design and visual communications; desktop publishing and digital imaging design; electroneurodiagnostic/electroencephalographic technology; engineering science; equestrian studies; general studies; human services; industrial technology; information science/studies; landscaping and groundskeeping; liberal arts and sciences/liberal studies; medical radiologic technology; music performance; music teacher education; nursing (registered nurse training); occupational therapist assistant; radio and television; radio and television broadcasting technology; respiratory care therapy; sales and marketing/marketing and distribution teacher education; speech-language pathology; system administration; veterinary/animal health technology; web page, digital/multimedia and information resources design.

Academic Programs *Special study options:* academic remediation for entering students, accelerated degree program, adult/continuing education programs, advanced placement credit, cooperative education, distance learning, double majors, English as a second language, honors programs, independent study, internships, off-campus study, part-time degree program, services for LD students, student-designed majors, study abroad, summer session for credit. *ROTC:* Army (c), Navy (c), Air Force (c).

Library Parkland College Library with 122,676 titles, 300 serial subscriptions, 8,115 audiovisual materials, an OPAC, a Web page.

Computers on Campus 800 computers available on campus for general student use. A campuswide network can be accessed. Internet access, online (class) registration, at least one staffed computer lab available.

Student Life *Housing:* college housing not available. *Activities and Organizations:* drama/theater group, student-run newspaper, radio and television station, choral group. *Campus security:* 24-hour emergency response devices and patrols, late-night transport/escort service. *Student services:* personal/psychological counseling, women's center.

Athletics Member NJCAA. *Intercollegiate sports:* baseball M(s), basketball M(s)/W(s), golf M(s), soccer M(s)/W(s), softball W(s), volleyball W(s). *Intramural sports:* basketball M/W, bowling M/W, softball M/W, volleyball M/W.

Standardized Tests *Required for some:* ACT (for admission).

Costs (2005–06) *Tuition:* area resident $2070 full-time, $69 per credit hour part-time; state resident $6000 full-time, $200 per credit hour part-time; nonresident $8850 full-time, $295 per credit hour part-time. *Payment plan:* installment. *Waivers:* senior citizens and employees or children of employees.

Financial Aid Of all full-time matriculated undergraduates who enrolled in 2003, 100 Federal Work-Study jobs (averaging $2000).

Applying *Options:* deferred entrance. *Recommended:* high school transcript. *Application deadline:* rolling (freshmen), rolling (transfers). *Notification:* continuous (freshmen).

Admissions Contact Admissions Representative, Parkland College, 2400 West Bradley Avenue, Champaign, IL 61821-1899. *Phone:* 217-351-2482. *Toll-free phone:* 800-346-8089. *Fax:* 217-351-2640. *E-mail:* mhenry@parkland.edu.

PRAIRIE STATE COLLEGE
Chicago Heights, Illinois

- **State and locally supported** 2-year, founded 1958, part of Illinois Community College Board
- **Calendar** semesters
- **Degree** certificates and associate
- **Suburban** 68-acre campus with easy access to Chicago
- **Endowment** $750,000
- **Coed**, 5,342 undergraduate students, 33% full-time, 62% women, 38% men

Undergraduates 1,745 full-time, 3,597 part-time. Students come from 4 states and territories, 4% are from out of state, 45% African American, 1% Asian American or Pacific Islander, 12% Hispanic American, 0.7% Native American, 0.2% international, 0.4% transferred in.

Freshmen *Admission:* 712 applied, 712 admitted, 712 enrolled.

Faculty *Total:* 363, 21% full-time. *Student/faculty ratio:* 17:1.

Majors Autobody/collision and repair technology; automobile/automotive mechanics technology; child guidance; computer and information sciences; computer graphics; criminal justice/law enforcement administration; dental hygiene; electrical, electronic and communications engineering technology; executive assistant/executive secretary; finance; fire science; human resources management; industrial technology; interior design; liberal arts and sciences/liberal studies; logistics and materials management; management science; mechanical design technology; mental health/rehabilitation; nursing (registered nurse training); photography; substance abuse/addiction counseling; teacher assistant/aide; tool and die technology.

Academic Programs *Special study options:* academic remediation for entering students, adult/continuing education programs, advanced placement credit,

distance learning, English as a second language, honors programs, internships, part-time degree program, services for LD students, student-designed majors, summer session for credit.

Library Learning Resource Center with 45,000 titles, 515 serial subscriptions, 4,000 audiovisual materials, an OPAC.

Computers on Campus 300 computers available on campus for general student use. A campuswide network can be accessed. Internet access, at least one staffed computer lab available.

Student Life *Activities and Organizations:* drama/theater group, student-run newspaper, choral group, Phi Theta Kappa, Black Student Union, Student Government Association, student newspaper, Mental Health Club. *Campus security:* 24-hour emergency response devices and patrols, student patrols, late-night transport/escort service. *Student services:* personal/psychological counseling.

Athletics Member NJCAA. *Intercollegiate sports:* baseball M(s), basketball M(s)/W(s), football M(s), golf M(s)/W(s), soccer M/W, softball M/W(s), tennis W(s). *Intramural sports:* basketball M/W, soccer M/W, softball W, table tennis M/W, volleyball W.

Standardized Tests *Required for some:* ACT COMPASS.

Costs (2005–06) *Tuition:* area resident $1824 full-time, $67 per credit hour part-time; state resident $5280 full-time, $211 per credit hour part-time; nonresident $7200 full-time, $291 per credit hour part-time. Full-time tuition and fees vary according to course load. Part-time tuition and fees vary according to course load. *Required fees:* $236 full-time, $9 per credit hour part-time, $10 per term part-time. *Room and board:* $4500. Room and board charges vary according to location. *Payment plans:* installment, deferred payment. *Waivers:* senior citizens and employees or children of employees.

Financial Aid Of all full-time matriculated undergraduates who enrolled in 2003, 60 Federal Work-Study jobs (averaging $2500).

Applying *Options:* common application, deferred entrance. *Application fee:* $10. *Required:* high school transcript. *Application deadline:* rolling (freshmen), rolling (transfers).

Admissions Contact Ms. Mary Welsh, Director of Admissions, Records and Registration, Prairie State College, 202 South Halsted Street, Chicago Heights, IL 60411. *Phone:* 708-709-3513. *Toll-free phone:* 708-709-3516. *E-mail:* webmaster@prairiestate.edu.

REND LAKE COLLEGE
Ina, Illinois

- **State-supported** 2-year, founded 1967, part of Illinois Community College Board
- **Calendar** semesters
- **Degree** certificates and associate
- **Rural** 350-acre campus
- **Endowment** $1.7 million
- **Coed**

Student Life *Campus security:* 24-hour emergency response devices and patrols, late-night transport/escort service.

Athletics Member NJCAA.

Standardized Tests *Required:* SAT or ACT (for placement), ACT ASSET, ACT COMPASS (for placement).

Costs (2004–05) *Tuition:* area resident $1824 full-time, $57 per credit hour part-time; state resident $2592 full-time, $81 per credit hour part-time; nonresident $4800 full-time, $150 per credit hour part-time.

Financial Aid Of all full-time matriculated undergraduates who enrolled in 2003, 133 Federal Work-Study jobs (averaging $1000). 174 state and other part-time jobs (averaging $940).

Applying *Options:* electronic application, deferred entrance. *Required:* high school transcript.

Admissions Contact Ms. Lisa Price, Director, Counseling, Rend Lake College, 468 North Ken Gray Parkway, Ina, IL 62846-9801. *Phone:* 618-437-5321 Ext. 205. *Toll-free phone:* 618-437-5321 Ext. 230. *Fax:* 618-437-5677. *E-mail:* admiss@rlc.edu.

RICHLAND COMMUNITY COLLEGE
Decatur, Illinois

- **District-supported** 2-year, founded 1971, part of Illinois Community College Board
- **Calendar** semesters
- **Degree** certificates and associate
- **Small-town** 117-acre campus
- **Endowment** $3.8 million
- **Coed,** 3,568 undergraduate students, 37% full-time, 63% women, 37% men

Undergraduates 1,334 full-time, 2,234 part-time. Students come from 1 other state, 14% African American, 0.5% Asian American or Pacific Islander, 1% Hispanic American, 0.3% Native American. *Retention:* 53% of 2002 full-time freshmen returned.

Freshmen *Admission:* 649 applied, 649 admitted.

Faculty *Total:* 244, 27% full-time, 5% with terminal degrees. *Student/faculty ratio:* 14:1.

Majors Accounting; administrative assistant and secretarial science; agricultural business and management; automobile/automotive mechanics technology; biological and physical sciences; business administration and management; child development; computer and information sciences related; computer graphics; computer programming (specific applications); construction engineering technology; criminal justice/police science; data entry/microcomputer applications; data entry/microcomputer applications related; drafting and design technology; electrical, electronic and communications engineering technology; fire science; food services technology; industrial technology; information science/studies; insurance; legal administrative assistant/secretary; liberal arts and sciences/liberal studies; medical administrative assistant and medical secretary; nursing (registered nurse training); pre-engineering; word processing.

Academic Programs *Special study options:* academic remediation for entering students, adult/continuing education programs, advanced placement credit, distance learning, English as a second language, freshman honors college, honors programs, part-time degree program, services for LD students, student-designed majors, summer session for credit.

Library Kitty Lindsay Library with 39,452 titles, 275 serial subscriptions, 2,910 audiovisual materials, an OPAC, a Web page.

Computers on Campus 150 computers available on campus for general student use. Internet access, online (class) registration, at least one staffed computer lab available.

Student Life *Housing:* college housing not available. *Activities and Organizations:* student-run newspaper, Student Senate, Forensics Club, Drama Club, Black Student Association, Student Activities Board. *Campus security:* 24-hour emergency response devices and patrols.

Standardized Tests *Required for some:* ACT (for placement).

Costs (2004–05) *Tuition:* area resident $1530 full-time, $51 per credit hour part-time; state resident $5800 full-time, $193 per credit hour part-time; nonresident $9712 full-time, $324 per credit hour part-time. *Required fees:* $155 full-time, $5 per credit hour part-time, $10 per term part-time.

Financial Aid Of all full-time matriculated undergraduates who enrolled in 2003, 43 Federal Work-Study jobs (averaging $1339). 129 state and other part-time jobs (averaging $578).

Applying *Options:* early admission. *Required:* high school transcript. *Application deadline:* rolling (freshmen), rolling (transfers).

Admissions Contact Ms. Nancy A. Cooper, Dean of Enrollment Services, Richland Community College, One College Park, Decatur, IL 62521. *Phone:* 217-875-7200 Ext. 246. *Fax:* 217-875-7783.

ROCKFORD BUSINESS COLLEGE
Rockford, Illinois

Admissions Contact Ms. Barbara Holliman, Director of Admissions, Rockford Business College, 730 North Church Street, Rockford, IL 61103. *Phone:* 815-965-8616 Ext. 16. *Fax:* 815-965-0360.

ROCK VALLEY COLLEGE
Rockford, Illinois

- **District-supported** 2-year, founded 1964, part of Illinois Community College Board
- **Calendar** semesters
- **Degree** certificates and associate
- **Suburban** 217-acre campus with easy access to Chicago
- **Coed,** 9,475 undergraduate students, 38% full-time, 58% women, 42% men

Undergraduates 3,611 full-time, 5,864 part-time. Students come from 2 states and territories, 3 other countries, 1% are from out of state, 8% African American, 3% Asian American or Pacific Islander, 9% Hispanic American, 0.5% Native American, 0.3% international.

Freshmen *Admission:* 1,090 enrolled.

Faculty *Total:* 310, 45% full-time, 12% with terminal degrees. *Student/faculty ratio:* 21:1.

Majors Accounting; automobile/automotive mechanics technology; avionics maintenance technology; business administration and management; child development; computer engineering technology; computer science; construction engineering technology; criminal justice/law enforcement administration; dental hygiene; electrical, electronic and communications engineering technology; fire science; human services; industrial design; industrial technology; liberal arts and sciences/liberal studies; marketing/marketing management; mechanical design

Rock Valley College (continued)

technology; nursing (registered nurse training); pre-engineering; quality control technology; respiratory care therapy; welding technology.

Academic Programs *Special study options:* academic remediation for entering students, adult/continuing education programs, advanced placement credit, cooperative education, distance learning, English as a second language, honors programs, independent study, internships, part-time degree program, services for LD students, student-designed majors, study abroad, summer session for credit.

Library Educational Resource Center with 67,168 titles, an OPAC, a Web page.

Computers on Campus 130 computers available on campus for general student use. A campuswide network can be accessed from off campus. Internet access, online (class) registration, at least one staffed computer lab available.

Student Life *Housing:* college housing not available. *Activities and Organizations:* drama/theater group, student-run newspaper, choral group, Black Student Alliance, Phi Theta Kappa, Adults on Campus, Inter-Varsity Club, Christian Fellowship. *Campus security:* 24-hour emergency response devices and patrols, late-night transport/escort service. *Student services:* personal/psychological counseling.

Athletics Member NJCAA. *Intercollegiate sports:* baseball M, basketball M/W, football M, golf M, softball W, tennis M/W, volleyball W. *Intramural sports:* basketball M/W, skiing (downhill) M/W.

Standardized Tests *Required for some:* ACT (for placement). *Recommended:* ACT (for placement).

Costs (2005–06) *Tuition:* area resident $1620 full-time, $54 per credit part-time; state resident $5820 full-time, $194 per credit part-time; nonresident $12,510 full-time, $417 per credit part-time. Full-time tuition and fees vary according to course load. Part-time tuition and fees vary according to course load. *Required fees:* $272 full-time, $9 per credit part-time, $2 per term part-time. *Payment plans:* installment, deferred payment. *Waivers:* employees or children of employees.

Financial Aid Of all full-time matriculated undergraduates who enrolled in 2003, 120 Federal Work-Study jobs (averaging $1800).

Applying *Required:* high school transcript. *Application deadlines:* 8/29 (freshmen), 8/29 (transfers). *Notification:* continuous (freshmen).

Admissions Contact Ms. Lisa Allman, Coordinator of Admissions and Records, Rock Valley College, 3301 North Mulford Road, Rockford, IL 61114-5699. *Phone:* 815-921-4262. *Toll-free phone:* 800-973-7821. *Fax:* 815-921-4267.

SAUK VALLEY COMMUNITY COLLEGE
Dixon, Illinois

- **District-supported** 2-year, founded 1965, part of Illinois Community College Board
- **Calendar** semesters
- **Degree** certificates and associate
- **Rural** 165-acre campus
- **Coed**, 3,161 undergraduate students

Undergraduates 1% African American, 1% Asian American or Pacific Islander, 7% Hispanic American, 0.4% Native American.

Freshmen *Admission:* 1,400 applied, 1,400 admitted.

Faculty *Total:* 152, 39% full-time. *Student/faculty ratio:* 18:1.

Majors Accounting; administrative assistant and secretarial science; architecture; art; athletic training; biology/biological sciences; business administration and management; chemistry; chiropractic assistant; communication/speech communication and rhetoric; computer and information sciences related; corrections; criminal justice/law enforcement administration; criminal justice/police science; dramatic/theatre arts; early childhood education; economics; education; electrical, electronic and communications engineering technology; elementary education; English; French; heating, air conditioning, ventilation and refrigeration maintenance technology; history; human services; industrial radiologic technology; legal administrative assistant/secretary; liberal arts and sciences/liberal studies; marketing/marketing management; mathematics; mechanical engineering/mechanical technology; medical office assistant; music; nursing (registered nurse training); occupational therapy; optometric technician; physical education teaching and coaching; physical therapy; physics; political science and government; pre-dentistry studies; pre-medical studies; pre-pharmacy studies; pre-veterinary studies; psychology; public administration and social service professions related; secondary education; social work; sociology; Spanish; special education; speech and rhetoric.

Academic Programs *Special study options:* academic remediation for entering students, accelerated degree program, adult/continuing education programs, cooperative education, distance learning, English as a second language, honors programs, independent study, internships, off-campus study, part-time degree program, services for LD students, student-designed majors.

Library Learning Resource Center plus 1 other with 55,000 titles, 268 serial subscriptions.

Computers on Campus 100 computers available on campus for general student use. A campuswide network can be accessed. Internet access, at least one staffed computer lab available.

Student Life *Housing:* college housing not available. *Activities and Organizations:* drama/theater group, choral group. *Campus security:* 24-hour emergency response devices and patrols, late-night transport/escort service. *Student services:* personal/psychological counseling.

Athletics Member NJCAA. *Intercollegiate sports:* baseball M(s), basketball M(s)/W(s), softball W, tennis M(s)/W(s), volleyball W(s). *Intramural sports:* basketball M/W.

Standardized Tests *Required:* ACT ASSET, Nelson Denny Reading Test (for placement).

Costs (2005–06) *Tuition:* $74 per credit hour part-time; state resident $259 per credit hour part-time; nonresident $293 per credit hour part-time.

Financial Aid Of all full-time matriculated undergraduates who enrolled in 2003, 150 Federal Work-Study jobs (averaging $3000).

Applying *Options:* early admission, deferred entrance. *Recommended:* high school transcript. *Application deadline:* rolling (freshmen), rolling (transfers). *Notification:* continuous (freshmen).

Admissions Contact Ms. Pamela Clodfelter, Director of Admissions, Records, and Placement, Sauk Valley Community College, 173 Illinois Route 2, Dixon, IL 61021. *Phone:* 815-288-5511 Ext. 310. *Fax:* 815-288-3190. *E-mail:* skyhawk@svcc.edu.

SHAWNEE COMMUNITY COLLEGE
Ullin, Illinois

- **State and locally supported** 2-year, founded 1967, part of Illinois Community College Board
- **Calendar** semesters
- **Degree** certificates and associate
- **Rural** 163-acre campus
- **Coed**, 3,191 undergraduate students, 30% full-time, 56% women, 44% men

Undergraduates 943 full-time, 2,248 part-time. Students come from 3 states and territories, 22% African American, 0.7% Asian American or Pacific Islander, 1% Hispanic American, 0.6% Native American.

Freshmen *Admission:* 325 enrolled.

Faculty *Total:* 180, 22% full-time.

Majors Accounting; administrative assistant and secretarial science; agricultural business and management; agriculture; agronomy and crop science; animal sciences; automobile/automotive mechanics technology; biological and physical sciences; business administration and management; child development; cosmetology; criminal justice/police science; electrical, electronic and communications engineering technology; food services technology; horticultural science; human services; information science/studies; legal administrative assistant/secretary; liberal arts and sciences/liberal studies; machine tool technology; medical administrative assistant and medical secretary; nursing (registered nurse training); social work; welding technology; wildlife and wildlands science and management.

Academic Programs *Special study options:* academic remediation for entering students, accelerated degree program, adult/continuing education programs, English as a second language, internships, part-time degree program, services for LD students, summer session for credit.

Library Shawnee Community College Library with 38,000 titles, 245 serial subscriptions, an OPAC, a Web page.

Computers on Campus 40 computers available on campus for general student use. A campuswide network can be accessed from off campus. Internet access, at least one staffed computer lab available.

Student Life *Housing:* college housing not available. *Activities and Organizations:* drama/theater group, student-run newspaper, choral group. *Campus security:* student patrols.

Athletics Member NJCAA. *Intercollegiate sports:* baseball M(s), basketball M(s)/W(s), softball W, tennis M, volleyball W(s). *Intramural sports:* badminton M/W, baseball M, basketball M/W, softball W, table tennis M/W, tennis M/W, volleyball M/W, weight lifting M/W.

Standardized Tests *Required:* ACT ASSET (for placement). *Required for some:* ACT (for placement). *Recommended:* ACT (for placement).

Costs (2004–05) *Tuition:* area resident $1440 full-time, $48 per credit hour part-time; state resident $2580 full-time, $86 per credit hour part-time; nonresident $86 per credit hour part-time. *Payment plan:* installment. *Waivers:* senior citizens and employees or children of employees.

Financial Aid Of all full-time matriculated undergraduates who enrolled in 2003, 60 Federal Work-Study jobs (averaging $2000). 50 state and other part-time jobs (averaging $2000).

Applying *Options:* common application, early admission, deferred entrance. *Required:* high school transcript. *Application deadline:* rolling (freshmen), rolling (transfers). *Notification:* continuous (freshmen).

Admissions Contact Ms. Dee Blakely, Director of Admissions, Shawnee Community College, 8364 Shawnee College Road, Ullin, IL 62992-2206. *Phone:* 618-634-3200 Ext. 3247. *Toll-free phone:* 800-481-2242. *Fax:* 618-634-9028.

SOUTHEASTERN ILLINOIS COLLEGE
Harrisburg, Illinois

Admissions Contact Ms. Tyra Taylor, Registrar, Southeastern Illinois College, 3575 College Road, Harrisburg, IL 62946-4925. *Phone:* 618-252-5400 Ext. 2440. *Toll-free phone:* 866-338-2742.

SOUTH SUBURBAN COLLEGE
South Holland, Illinois

- **State and locally supported** 2-year, founded 1927, part of Illinois Community College Board
- **Calendar** semesters
- **Degree** certificates and associate
- **Suburban** campus with easy access to Chicago
- **Coed**

Faculty *Student/faculty ratio:* 18:1.
Student Life *Campus security:* 24-hour emergency response devices and patrols.
Athletics Member NJCAA.
Standardized Tests *Required:* ACT ASSET (for placement).
Costs (2004–05) *Tuition:* area resident $1874 full-time, $69 per credit hour part-time. Part-time tuition and fees vary according to course load. *Required fees:* $210 full-time, $9 per credit hour part-time.
Financial Aid Of all full-time matriculated undergraduates who enrolled in 2003, 121 Federal Work-Study jobs (averaging $1750).
Applying *Options:* early admission, deferred entrance. *Application fee:* $20. *Required:* high school transcript. *Required for some:* essay or personal statement, interview. *Recommended:* minimum 2.0 GPA.
Admissions Contact Ms. Jazaer Farrar, Director of New Student Services, South Suburban College, 15800 South State Street, South Holland, IL 60473-1270. *Phone:* 708-596-2000 Ext. 2291.

SOUTHWESTERN ILLINOIS COLLEGE
Belleville, Illinois

- **District-supported** 2-year, founded 1946, part of Illinois Community College Board
- **Calendar** semesters
- **Degree** certificates, diplomas, and associate
- **Suburban** 150-acre campus with easy access to St. Louis
- **Endowment** $3.1 million
- **Coed**

Faculty *Student/faculty ratio:* 16:1.
Student Life *Campus security:* 24-hour emergency response devices and patrols, student patrols, late-night transport/escort service.
Athletics Member NJCAA.
Standardized Tests *Required for some:* ACT ASSET or ACT COMPASS, ACT ASSET or ACT COMPASS.
Costs (2004–05) *Tuition:* area resident $1650 full-time; state resident $4680 full-time; nonresident $7410 full-time.
Financial Aid Of all full-time matriculated undergraduates who enrolled in 2003, 170 Federal Work-Study jobs (averaging $1537). 179 state and other part-time jobs (averaging $1004).
Applying *Options:* early admission, deferred entrance. *Application fee:* $10. *Required:* high school transcript.
Admissions Contact Ms. Michelle Birk, Director of Admission, Southwestern Illinois College, 2500 Carlyle Road, Belleville, IL 62221-5899. *Phone:* 618-235-2700 Ext. 5400. *Toll-free phone:* 800-222-5131. *Fax:* 618-277-0631.

SPOON RIVER COLLEGE
Canton, Illinois

- **State-supported** 2-year, founded 1959, part of Illinois Community College Board
- **Calendar** semesters
- **Degree** certificates and associate
- **Rural** 160-acre campus
- **Endowment** $267,036
- **Coed**

Faculty *Student/faculty ratio:* 14:1.
Student Life *Campus security:* 24-hour emergency response devices.
Athletics Member NJCAA.
Standardized Tests *Required for some:* nursing exam, ACT ASSET. *Recommended:* SAT or ACT (for placement).
Costs (2004–05) *Tuition:* area resident $1710 full-time, $57 per credit hour part-time; state resident $2565 full-time, $86 per credit hour part-time; nonresident $4275 full-time, $143 per credit hour part-time. Full-time tuition and fees vary according to course load. Part-time tuition and fees vary according to course load. *Required fees:* $255 full-time, $9 per credit hour part-time.
Applying *Options:* early admission. *Required:* high school transcript.
Admissions Contact Dr. Sharon Wrenn, Dean of Student Services, Spoon River College, 23235 North County 22, Canton, IL 61520-9801. *Phone:* 309-649-6305. *Toll-free phone:* 800-334-7337. *Fax:* 309-649-6235. *E-mail:* info@src.cc.il.us.

SPRINGFIELD COLLEGE IN ILLINOIS
Springfield, Illinois

Admissions Contact Ms. Kim Fontana, Director of Admissions, Springfield College in Illinois, 1500 North Fifth Street, Springfield, IL 62702-2694. *Phone:* 217-525-1420 Ext. 241. *Toll-free phone:* 800-635-7289. *Fax:* 217-525-1497.

TAYLOR BUSINESS INSTITUTE
Chicago, Illinois

Admissions Contact Mr. Rashed Jahangir, Taylor Business Institute, 200 North Michigan Avenue, Suite 301, Chicago, IL 60601.

TRITON COLLEGE
River Grove, Illinois

- **State-supported** 2-year, founded 1964, part of Illinois Community College Board
- **Calendar** semesters
- **Degree** certificates and associate
- **Suburban** 100-acre campus with easy access to Chicago
- **Coed**

Faculty *Student/faculty ratio:* 20:1.
Student Life *Campus security:* 24-hour emergency response devices and patrols.
Athletics Member NJCAA.
Standardized Tests *Recommended:* SAT or ACT (for placement).
Financial Aid Of all full-time matriculated undergraduates who enrolled in 2003, 250 Federal Work-Study jobs (averaging $2000).
Applying *Options:* deferred entrance. *Required:* high school transcript.
Admissions Contact Mr. Doug Olson, Dean of Student Services, Triton College, 2000 Fifth Avenue, River Grove, IL 60171. *Phone:* 708-456-0300 Ext. 3230. *Toll-free phone:* 800-942-7404. *E-mail:* gfuller@triton.cc.il.us.

WAUBONSEE COMMUNITY COLLEGE
Sugar Grove, Illinois

- **District-supported** 2-year, founded 1966, part of Illinois Community College Board
- **Calendar** semesters
- **Degree** certificates and associate
- **Rural** 243-acre campus with easy access to Chicago
- **Endowment** $2118
- **Coed**, 8,682 undergraduate students, 30% full-time, 58% women, 42% men

Undergraduates 2,569 full-time, 6,113 part-time. Students come from 1 other state, 2 other countries, 7% African American, 2% Asian American or Pacific Islander, 17% Hispanic American, 0.6% Native American, 2% transferred in.
Freshmen *Admission:* 1,091 applied, 1,091 admitted, 909 enrolled.
Faculty *Total:* 935, 9% full-time, 8% with terminal degrees. *Student/faculty ratio:* 17:1.
Majors Accounting technology and bookkeeping; administrative assistant and secretarial science; art; art teacher education; autobody/collision and repair technology; automobile/automotive mechanics technology; banking and financial support services; biological and physical sciences; business administration and management; business automation/technology/data entry; child care provision; communication/speech communication and rhetoric; computer and information sciences; computer programming (specific applications); criminal justice/police science; design and visual communications; electrical, electronic and communications engineering technology; engineering; entrepreneurship; execu-

Waubonsee Community College (continued)
tive assistant/executive secretary; fire protection and safety technology; general studies; heating, air conditioning, ventilation and refrigeration maintenance technology; industrial mechanics and maintenance technology; industrial technology; kindergarten/preschool education; liberal arts and sciences/liberal studies; logistics and materials management; massage therapy; mass communication/media; medical/clinical assistant; music; music teacher education; nursing assistant/aide and patient care assistant; nursing (registered nurse training); operations management; quality control technology; retailing; robotics technology; sign language interpretation and translation; social work; tourism and travel services marketing.

Academic Programs *Special study options:* academic remediation for entering students, accelerated degree program, advanced placement credit, distance learning, honors programs, independent study, internships, part-time degree program, services for LD students, study abroad, summer session for credit. *ROTC:* Army (c).

Library Todd Library with 53,679 titles, 562 serial subscriptions, 6,388 audiovisual materials, an OPAC, a Web page.

Computers on Campus 160 computers available on campus for general student use. A campuswide network can be accessed from off campus. Internet access, online (class) registration, at least one staffed computer lab available.

Student Life *Housing:* college housing not available. *Activities and Organizations:* drama/theater group, student-run newspaper, television station, choral group, Phi Theta Kappa, VICA, Alpha Sigma Lamda, Latinos Unidos, Christian Fellowship. *Campus security:* 24-hour emergency response devices and patrols, late-night transport/escort service.

Athletics Member NJCAA. *Intercollegiate sports:* baseball M, basketball M(s)/W(s), cross-country running M(s)/W(s), golf M(s), soccer M(s), softball W(s), tennis M(s)/W(s), volleyball W(s), wrestling M(s). *Intramural sports:* basketball M/W, bowling M/W, golf M/W, table tennis M/W.

Costs (2005–06) *Tuition:* area resident $1860 full-time, $62 per semester hour part-time; state resident $6360 full-time, $212 per semester hour part-time; nonresident $7290 full-time, $243 per semester hour part-time. Full-time tuition and fees vary according to course load. Part-time tuition and fees vary according to course load. *Required fees:* $2 per credit hour part-time. *Payment plans:* installment, deferred payment. *Waivers:* senior citizens and employees or children of employees.

Financial Aid Of all full-time matriculated undergraduates who enrolled in 2003, 23 Federal Work-Study jobs (averaging $2000).

Applying *Application deadline:* rolling (freshmen), rolling (transfers).

Admissions Contact Ms. Faith Marston, Recruitment and Retention Manager, Waubonsee Community College, Route 47 at Waubonsee Drive, Sugar Grove, IL 60554. *Phone:* 630-466-7900 Ext. 2938. *Fax:* 630-466-4964. *E-mail:* recruitment@waubonsee.edu.

WESTWOOD COLLEGE-CHICAGO DU PAGE
Woodridge, Illinois

- **Proprietary** primarily 2-year
- **Calendar** continuous
- **Degrees** associate and bachelor's
- **Suburban** campus with easy access to Chicago, IL
- **Coed**
- 40% of applicants were admitted

Applying *Required:* interview, entrance exam (SAT, ACT or Accuplacer) and H.S. diploma or GED.

Admissions Contact Mr. Scott Kawall, Director of Admissions, Westwood College-Chicago Du Page, 7155 James Avenue, Woodridge, IL 60517-2321. *Phone:* 630-434-8244. *Toll-free phone:* 888-721-7646. *Fax:* 630-434-8255. *E-mail:* info@westwood.edu.

▶ **See page 596 for a narrative description.**

WESTWOOD COLLEGE-CHICAGO LOOP CAMPUS
Chicago, Illinois

- **Proprietary** primarily 2-year, founded 2002
- **Degrees** associate and bachelor's
- **Coed**
- 68% of applicants were admitted

Applying *Required:* interview, HS diploma or GED, and passing SAT/ACT or Accuplacer scores.

Admissions Contact Gus Pyrolis, Acting Director of Admissions, Westwood College-Chicago Loop Campus, 17 North State Street, Suite 1500, Chicago, IL 60602. *Phone:* 312-739-0850. *E-mail:* info@westwood.edu.

▶ **See page 570 for a narrative description.**

WESTWOOD COLLEGE-CHICAGO O'HARE AIRPORT
Schiller Park, Illinois

- **Proprietary** primarily 2-year
- **Calendar** continuous
- **Degrees** associate and bachelor's
- **Urban** campus with easy access to Chicago
- **Coed**

Applying *Required:* essay or personal statement, interview, entrance exam (SAT, ACT or ACCUPLACER) and H.S. diploma/GED.

Admissions Contact Mr. David Traub, Director of Admissions, Westwood College-Chicago O'Hare Airport, 4825 North Scott Street, Suite 100, Schiller Park, IL 60176-1209. *Phone:* 847-928-0200 Ext. 100. *Toll-free phone:* 877-877-8857. *E-mail:* info@westwood.edu.

▶ **See page 572 for a narrative description.**

WESTWOOD COLLEGE-CHICAGO RIVER OAKS
Calumet City, Illinois

- **Proprietary** primarily 2-year
- **Calendar** continuous
- **Degrees** associate and bachelor's
- **Suburban** campus with easy access to Chicago
- **Coed**
- 55% of applicants were admitted

Applying *Required:* interview, HS diploma or GED and passing scores on entrance exam (ACT/SAT or Accuplacer).

Admissions Contact Tash Uray, Director of Admissions, Westwood College-Chicago River Oaks, 80 River Oaks Drive, Suite D-49, Calumet City, IL 60409-5820. *Phone:* 708-832-1988. *Toll-free phone:* 888-549-6873. *Fax:* 708-832-9617. *E-mail:* info@westwood.edu.

▶ **See page 574 for a narrative description.**

WILLIAM RAINEY HARPER COLLEGE
Palatine, Illinois

Admissions Contact Mr. Michael Held, Director of Outreach, William Rainey Harper College, 1200 West Algonquin Road, Palatine, IL 60067. *Phone:* 847-925-6206. *Fax:* 847-925-6044.

WORSHAM COLLEGE OF MORTUARY SCIENCE
Wheeling, Illinois

- **Independent** 2-year
- **Calendar** quarters
- **Degree** associate
- **Coed**
- 100% of applicants were admitted

Faculty *Student/faculty ratio:* 10:1.

Admissions Contact Ms. Stephanie Kann, President, Worsham College of Mortuary Science, 495 Northgate Parkway, Wheeling, IL 60090-2646. *Phone:* 847-808-8444.

INDIANA

AMERICAN TRANS AIR AVIATION TRAINING ACADEMY
Indianapolis, Indiana

Admissions Contact 7251 West McCarty Street, Indianapolis, IN 46241. *Toll-free phone:* 800-241-9699.

ANCILLA COLLEGE
Donaldson, Indiana

- **Independent Roman Catholic** 2-year, founded 1937
- **Calendar** semesters

- **Degree** certificates and associate
- **Rural** 63-acre campus with easy access to Chicago
- **Endowment** $1.8 million
- **Coed,** 631 undergraduate students, 64% full-time, 72% women, 28% men

Undergraduates 402 full-time, 229 part-time. Students come from 10 states and territories, 1% are from out of state, 3% African American, 3% Asian American or Pacific Islander, 3% Hispanic American, 1% Native American, 0.3% international, 9% transferred in. *Retention:* 55% of 2002 full-time freshmen returned.
Freshmen *Admission:* 396 applied, 274 admitted, 203 enrolled. *Average high school GPA:* 2.50. *Test scores:* SAT verbal scores over 500: 27%; SAT math scores over 500: 23%; ACT scores over 18: 32%; SAT verbal scores over 600: 4%; SAT math scores over 600: 6%; ACT scores over 24: 15%; SAT math scores over 700: 1%.
Faculty *Total:* 62, 26% full-time, 21% with terminal degrees. *Student/faculty ratio:* 15:1.
Majors Biology/biological sciences; business administration and management; business operations support and secretarial services related; chemistry; computer programming; computer software and media applications related; computer systems networking and telecommunications; criminal justice/law enforcement administration; elementary education; fine arts related; health/medical preparatory programs related; humanities; liberal arts and sciences/liberal studies; mathematics; social sciences.
Academic Programs *Special study options:* academic remediation for entering students, accelerated degree program, adult/continuing education programs, advanced placement credit, cooperative education, double majors, independent study, internships, part-time degree program, services for LD students, student-designed majors, summer session for credit.
Library Ball Library with 27,859 titles, 152 serial subscriptions, 1,499 audiovisual materials, an OPAC, a Web page.
Computers on Campus 82 computers available on campus for general student use. A campuswide network can be accessed. Internet access, at least one staffed computer lab available. Computer purchase or lease plan available.
Student Life *Housing:* college housing not available. *Activities and Organizations:* student-run newspaper, Student Senate, Scripta Literary Magazine, Ancilla student ambassadors. *Campus security:* 24-hour patrols, late-night transport/escort service. *Student services:* personal/psychological counseling.
Athletics Member NJCAA. *Intercollegiate sports:* baseball M(s), basketball M(s)/W(s), golf M(s), softball W(s), volleyball W(s).
Standardized Tests *Recommended:* SAT (for admission), SAT or ACT (for admission).
Costs (2005–06) *Tuition:* $9600 full-time, $320 per credit hour part-time. *Required fees:* $230 full-time, $55 per term part-time. *Payment plan:* installment. *Waivers:* employees or children of employees.
Financial Aid Of all full-time matriculated undergraduates who enrolled in 2003, 28 Federal Work-Study jobs (averaging $1820). 16 state and other part-time jobs (averaging $1000). *Financial aid deadline:* 3/1.
Applying *Options:* common application, electronic application. *Application fee:* $25. *Required:* high school transcript. *Recommended:* interview. *Application deadline:* rolling (freshmen), rolling (transfers).
Admissions Contact Mr. Jim Bastis, Executive Director of Enrollment Management, Ancilla College, 9601 Union Road, Donaldson, IN 46513. *Phone:* 574-936-8898 Ext. 350. *Toll-free phone:* 866-262-4552 Ext. 350. *Fax:* 574-935-1773. *E-mail:* admissions@ancilla.edu.

BROWN MACKIE COLLEGE, FORT WAYNE CAMPUS
Fort Wayne, Indiana

Admissions Contact 4422 East State Boulevard, Fort Wayne, IN 46815.

BROWN MACKIE COLLEGE, MERRILLVILLE CAMPUS
Merrillville, Indiana

- **Proprietary** 2-year, founded 1890, part of American Education Centers
- **Calendar** quarters
- **Degree** certificates and associate
- **Small-town** 2-acre campus with easy access to Chicago
- **Coed**

Student Life *Campus security:* 24-hour emergency response devices.
Standardized Tests *Required:* ACT ASSET (for placement).
Costs (2004–05) *Tuition:* $159 per credit hour part-time.
Financial Aid Of all full-time matriculated undergraduates who enrolled in 2003, 2 Federal Work-Study jobs.

Applying *Options:* common application, early admission, deferred entrance. *Application fee:* $20. *Required:* high school transcript.
Admissions Contact Ms. Sheryl Elston, Director of Admissions, Brown Mackie College, Merrillville Campus, 1000 East 80th Place, Suite 101, N, Merrillville, IN 46410. *Phone:* 219-769-3321. *Fax:* 219-738-1076.

BROWN MACKIE COLLEGE, MICHIGAN CITY CAMPUS
Michigan City, Indiana

- **Proprietary** 2-year, founded 1890, part of Commonwealth Business College, Inc
- **Calendar** quarters
- **Degree** diplomas and associate
- **Rural** 2-acre campus with easy access to Chicago
- **Coed,** 427 undergraduate students, 100% full-time, 81% women, 19% men

Undergraduates 427 full-time. Students come from 2 states and territories, 15% African American, 0.7% Asian American or Pacific Islander, 4% Hispanic American, 0.7% Native American.
Freshmen *Admission:* 427 applied, 427 admitted, 345 enrolled. *Average high school GPA:* 2.0.
Faculty *Total:* 15, 20% full-time.
Majors Accounting; administrative assistant and secretarial science; business administration and management; computer typography and composition equipment operation; legal administrative assistant/secretary; medical administrative assistant and medical secretary; medical/clinical assistant.
Academic Programs *Special study options:* adult/continuing education programs, advanced placement credit, internships, part-time degree program, student-designed majors, summer session for credit.
Computers on Campus 24 computers available on campus for general student use. At least one staffed computer lab available.
Student Life *Housing:* college housing not available. *Activities and Organizations:* student-run newspaper. *Campus security:* 24-hour emergency response devices.
Standardized Tests *Required:* ABLE, Wonderlic aptitude test (for placement).
Costs (2005–06) *Tuition:* $6284 full-time. *Required fees:* $1080 full-time.
Applying *Options:* early admission, deferred entrance. *Application fee:* $25. *Required:* high school transcript. *Application deadline:* rolling (freshmen), rolling (transfers). *Notification:* continuous (freshmen).
Admissions Contact Ms. Sheryl Elston, Director of Admissions, Brown Mackie College, Michigan City Campus, 325 East US Highway 20, Michigan City, IN 46360. *Phone:* 219-877-3100 Ext. 20. *Toll-free phone:* 800-519-2416.

BROWN MACKIE COLLEGE, SOUTH BEND CAMPUS
South Bend, Indiana

- **Proprietary** 2-year, founded 1882, part of American Education Centers
- **Calendar** quarters
- **Degree** certificates and associate
- **Urban** 5-acre campus with easy access to Chicago
- **Coed, primarily women**

Faculty *Student/faculty ratio:* 16:1.
Student Life *Campus security:* 24-hour emergency response devices.
Costs (2004–05) *Tuition:* $6084 full-time, $169 per credit hour part-time. Full-time tuition and fees vary according to course load. *Required fees:* $360 full-time, $10 per credit hour part-time.
Applying *Options:* common application, deferred entrance. *Application fee:* $20. *Required:* essay or personal statement, high school transcript, interview. *Required for some:* minimum 2.0 GPA, 2 letters of recommendation.
Admissions Contact Ms. Rita Harvey, Admissions Representative; High School, Brown Mackie College, South Bend Campus, 1030 East Jefferson Boulevard, South Bend, IN 46617-3123. *Phone:* 574-237-0774. *Toll-free phone:* 800-743-2447. *Fax:* 574-237-3585. *E-mail:* mcsb@michianacollege.com.

COLLEGE OF COURT REPORTING
Hobart, Indiana

Admissions Contact Ms. Stacy Drohosky, Director of Admissions, College of Court Reporting, 111 West Tenth Street, Suite 111, Hobart, IN 46342. *Phone:* 219-942-1459 Ext. 226. *Fax:* 219-942-1631. *E-mail:* dmiller@ccredu.com.

DAVENPORT UNIVERSITY
Granger, Indiana

- **Independent** primarily 2-year, founded 1977, part of Davenport Educational System
- **Calendar** semesters
- **Degrees** diplomas, associate, and bachelor's
- **Coed**

Faculty *Student/faculty ratio:* 16:1.
Academic Programs *Special study options:* accelerated degree program, distance learning, English as a second language, independent study, internships, student-designed majors.
Costs (2004–05) *Tuition:* $6696 full-time, $279 per credit hour part-time. *Required fees:* $100 full-time, $50 per term part-time.
Applying *Options:* deferred entrance. *Application fee:* $25. *Application deadline:* rolling (freshmen), rolling (transfers). *Notification:* continuous (freshmen).
Admissions Contact Admissions, Davenport University, 415 East Fulton Street, Grand Rapids, MI 49503. *Toll-free phone:* 800-632-9569. *Fax:* 616-732-1142. *E-mail:* gradmiss@davenport.edu.

DAVENPORT UNIVERSITY
Hammond, Indiana

- **Independent** 2-year, founded 1977, part of Davenport Educational System
- **Calendar** semesters
- **Degree** diplomas and associate
- **Coed**

Faculty *Student/faculty ratio:* 16:1.
Academic Programs *Special study options:* accelerated degree program, distance learning, English as a second language, independent study, internships, student-designed majors.
Costs (2004–05) *Tuition:* $6696 full-time, $279 per credit hour part-time. *Required fees:* $100 full-time, $50 per term part-time.
Applying *Options:* deferred entrance. *Application fee:* $25. *Application deadline:* rolling (freshmen), rolling (transfers). *Notification:* continuous (freshmen).
Admissions Contact Admissions, Davenport University, 415 East Fulton Street, Grand Rapids, MI 49503. *Toll-free phone:* 800-632-9569. *Fax:* 616-732-1142. *E-mail:* gradmiss@davenport.edu.

DAVENPORT UNIVERSITY
Merrillville, Indiana

- **Independent** primarily 2-year, founded 1977, part of Davenport Educational System
- **Calendar** semesters
- **Degrees** diplomas, associate, and bachelor's
- **Coed**

Faculty *Student/faculty ratio:* 16:1.
Academic Programs *Special study options:* accelerated degree program, distance learning, English as a second language, independent study, internships, student-designed majors.
Costs (2004–05) *Tuition:* $6696 full-time, $279 per credit hour part-time. *Required fees:* $100 full-time, $50 per term part-time.
Applying *Options:* deferred entrance. *Application fee:* $25. *Application deadline:* rolling (freshmen), rolling (transfers). *Notification:* continuous (freshmen).
Admissions Contact Admissions, Davenport University, 415 East Fulton Street, Grand Rapids, MI 49503. *Toll-free phone:* 800-632-9569. *Fax:* 616-732-1142. *E-mail:* gradmiss@davenport.edu.

HOLY CROSS COLLEGE
Notre Dame, Indiana

- **Independent Roman Catholic** primarily 2-year, founded 1966
- **Calendar** semesters
- **Degrees** associate and bachelor's
- **Urban** 150-acre campus
- **Coed**, 492 undergraduate students, 96% full-time, 37% women, 63% men

Undergraduates 471 full-time, 21 part-time. Students come from 37 states and territories, 12 other countries, 46% are from out of state, 7% transferred in, 54% live on campus.
Freshmen *Admission:* 459 applied, 238 enrolled. *Average high school GPA:* 3.10.
Faculty *Total:* 38, 68% full-time, 32% with terminal degrees. *Student/faculty ratio:* 12:1.

Majors Liberal arts and sciences/liberal studies.
Academic Programs *Special study options:* academic remediation for entering students, advanced placement credit, English as a second language, freshman honors college, internships, off-campus study, part-time degree program, summer session for credit. *ROTC:* Army (c), Air Force (c).
Library Holy Cross Library with 15,000 titles, 160 serial subscriptions, an OPAC.
Computers on Campus 60 computers available on campus for general student use. A campuswide network can be accessed from student residence rooms and from off campus. Internet access, at least one staffed computer lab available.
Student Life *Housing Options:* coed, men-only, women-only. *Activities and Organizations:* drama/theater group, student-run newspaper, choral group, Student Advisory Committee, Campus Ministry, Volunteers in Support of Admissions, intramural athletics. *Campus security:* 24-hour emergency response devices, 24-hour patrols by trained personnel on certain days. *Student services:* personal/psychological counseling.
Athletics *Intercollegiate sports:* basketball M, crew M/W, equestrian sports M/W, ice hockey W, lacrosse M, water polo M/W. *Intramural sports:* basketball M/W, football M/W, golf M/W, lacrosse M, rugby M, skiing (downhill) M, soccer M, softball M/W, table tennis M/W, tennis M/W, ultimate Frisbee M/W, volleyball M/W.
Standardized Tests *Required:* SAT or ACT (for admission).
Costs (2004–05) *Comprehensive fee:* $18,300 includes full-time tuition ($10,750), mandatory fees ($450), and room and board ($7100). Part-time tuition: $345 per semester hour. *Room and board:* Room and board charges vary according to housing facility. *Payment plan:* installment. *Waivers:* employees or children of employees.
Financial Aid Of all full-time matriculated undergraduates who enrolled in 2003, 54 Federal Work-Study jobs (averaging $857).
Applying *Options:* common application, electronic application, deferred entrance. *Application fee:* $50. *Required:* essay or personal statement, high school transcript, minimum 2.5 GPA. *Required for some:* letters of recommendation. *Recommended:* interview. *Application deadline:* rolling (freshmen), rolling (transfers).
Admissions Contact Office of Admissions, Holy Cross College, PO Box 308, Notre Dame, IN 46556. *Phone:* 574-239-8400. *Fax:* 574-233-7427. *E-mail:* vduke@hcc-nd.edu.

INDIANA BUSINESS COLLEGE
Anderson, Indiana

- **Proprietary** 2-year, founded 1902
- **Calendar** quarters
- **Degree** certificates, diplomas, and associate
- **Coed**, 230 undergraduate students

Faculty *Student/faculty ratio:* 20:1.
Majors Accounting; administrative assistant and secretarial science; business administration and management; business administration, management and operations related; health information/medical records technology; medical/clinical assistant.
Academic Programs *Special study options:* adult/continuing education programs, cooperative education, distance learning, double majors, internships, part-time degree program.
Computers on Campus Internet access available.
Standardized Tests *Required:* Wonderlic Scholastic Level Exam (SLE) (for admission).
Applying *Options:* electronic application, early admission. *Application fee:* $50. *Required:* high school transcript, interview. *Application deadline:* rolling (freshmen), rolling (transfers). *Notification:* continuous (freshmen).
Admissions Contact Ms. Charlene Stacy, Executive Director, Indiana Business College, 140 East 53rd Street, Anderson, IN 46013. *Phone:* 765-644-7514. *Toll-free phone:* 800-IBC-GRAD. *Fax:* 765-644-5724.

INDIANA BUSINESS COLLEGE
Columbus, Indiana

- **Proprietary** 2-year
- **Calendar** quarters
- **Degree** certificates, diplomas, and associate
- **Coed**, 250 undergraduate students

Faculty *Student/faculty ratio:* 20:1.
Majors Accounting; administrative assistant and secretarial science; business administration and management; business administration, management and operations related; computer and information sciences and support services related; health professions related; information technology; management information systems and services related; medical/clinical assistant.

Academic Programs *Special study options:* adult/continuing education programs, cooperative education, distance learning, double majors, internships, part-time degree program.
Computers on Campus Internet access available.
Standardized Tests *Required:* Wonderlic Scholastic Level Exam (SLE) (for admission).
Applying *Options:* electronic application. *Application fee:* $50. *Required:* high school transcript, interview. *Application deadline:* rolling (freshmen), rolling (transfers). *Notification:* continuous (freshmen).
Admissions Contact Ms. Angela Rentmeesters, Executive Director, Indiana Business College, 2222 Poshard Drive, Columbus, IN 47203. *Phone:* 812-379-9000. *Toll-free phone:* 800-IBC-GRAD. *Fax:* 812-375-0414.

INDIANA BUSINESS COLLEGE
Evansville, Indiana

- **Proprietary** 2-year
- **Calendar** quarters
- **Degree** certificates, diplomas, and associate
- **Coed,** 237 undergraduate students

Faculty *Student/faculty ratio:* 20:1.
Majors Accounting; administrative assistant and secretarial science; business administration and management; computer programming (specific applications); health information/medical records administration; information technology; medical/clinical assistant.
Academic Programs *Special study options:* adult/continuing education programs, cooperative education, distance learning, double majors, internships, part-time degree program.
Computers on Campus Internet access available.
Standardized Tests *Required:* Wonderlic Scholastic Level Exam (SLE) (for admission).
Applying *Options:* electronic application. *Application fee:* $50. *Required:* high school transcript, interview. *Application deadline:* rolling (freshmen), rolling (transfers). *Notification:* continuous (freshmen).
Admissions Contact Mr. Steve Hardin, Regional Director, Indiana Business College, 4601 Theater Drive, Evansville, IN 47715. *Phone:* 812-476-6000. *Toll-free phone:* 800-IBC-GRAD. *Fax:* 812-471-8576.

INDIANA BUSINESS COLLEGE
Fort Wayne, Indiana

- **Proprietary** 2-year
- **Calendar** quarters
- **Degree** certificates, diplomas, and associate
- **Coed,** 268 undergraduate students

Faculty *Student/faculty ratio:* 20:1.
Majors Accounting; administrative assistant and secretarial science; business administration and management; health professions related; medical/clinical assistant.
Academic Programs *Special study options:* adult/continuing education programs, cooperative education, distance learning, double majors, internships, part-time degree program.
Computers on Campus Internet access available.
Standardized Tests *Required:* Wonderlic Scholastic Level Exam (SLE) (for admission).
Applying *Options:* electronic application. *Application fee:* $50. *Required:* high school transcript, interview. *Application deadline:* rolling (freshmen), rolling (transfers). *Notification:* continuous (freshmen).
Admissions Contact Ms. Janet Hein, Executive Director, Indiana Business College, 6413 North Clinton Street, Fort Wayne, IN 46825. *Phone:* 260-471-7667. *Toll-free phone:* 260-471-6918. *Fax:* 219-471-6918.

INDIANA BUSINESS COLLEGE
Indianapolis, Indiana

- **Proprietary** 2-year, founded 1902
- **Calendar** quarters
- **Degree** certificates, diplomas, and associate
- **Urban** 1-acre campus
- **Coed,** 643 undergraduate students

Faculty *Student/faculty ratio:* 20:1.
Majors Accounting; administrative assistant and secretarial science; business administration and management; business administration, management and operations related; computer and information sciences; computer and information sciences and support services related; computer programming; computer

programming (specific applications); fashion merchandising; information technology; legal administrative assistant/secretary; management information systems and services related.
Academic Programs *Special study options:* adult/continuing education programs, cooperative education, distance learning, double majors, internships, part-time degree program, summer session for credit.
Computers on Campus Internet access, online (class) registration available.
Student Life *Housing:* college housing not available. *Activities and Organizations:* Student Advisory Board, Student Ambassadors, Phi Beta Lambda. *Campus security:* 24-hour patrols.
Standardized Tests *Required:* Wonderlic Scholastic Level Exam (SLE) (for admission).
Applying *Options:* electronic application. *Application fee:* $50. *Required:* high school transcript, interview. *Application deadline:* rolling (freshmen), rolling (transfers). *Notification:* continuous (freshmen).
Admissions Contact Ms. Patricia Mozley, Regional Director, Indiana Business College, 550 East Washington Street, Indianapolis, IN 46204. *Phone:* 317-264-5656. *Toll-free phone:* 800-IBC-GRAD. *Fax:* 317-264-5650.

▶ **See page 502 for a narrative description.**

INDIANA BUSINESS COLLEGE
Lafayette, Indiana

- **Proprietary** 2-year
- **Calendar** quarters
- **Degree** certificates, diplomas, and associate
- **Coed,** 185 undergraduate students

Faculty *Student/faculty ratio:* 20:1.
Majors Accounting; administrative assistant and secretarial science; business administration and management; business administration, management and operations related; computer and information sciences and support services related; information technology; management information systems and services related.
Academic Programs *Special study options:* adult/continuing education programs, cooperative education, distance learning, double majors, internships, part-time degree program.
Computers on Campus Internet access available.
Standardized Tests *Required:* Wonderlic Scholastic Level Exam (SLE) (for admission).
Applying *Options:* electronic application. *Application fee:* $50. *Required:* high school transcript, interview. *Application deadline:* rolling (freshmen), rolling (transfers). *Notification:* continuous (freshmen).
Admissions Contact Mr. Greg Reger, Executive Director, Indiana Business College, 2 Executive Drive, Lafayette, IN 47905. *Phone:* 765-447-9550. *Toll-free phone:* 800-IBC-GRAD. *Fax:* 765-447-0868.

INDIANA BUSINESS COLLEGE
Marion, Indiana

- **Proprietary** 2-year
- **Calendar** quarters
- **Degree** certificates, diplomas, and associate
- **Coed,** 140 undergraduate students

Faculty *Student/faculty ratio:* 20:1.
Majors Accounting; administrative assistant and secretarial science; business administration and management; health and medical administrative services related.
Academic Programs *Special study options:* adult/continuing education programs, cooperative education, distance learning, double majors, internships, part-time degree program.
Computers on Campus Internet access available.
Standardized Tests *Required:* Wonderlic Scholastic Level Exam (SLE) (for admission).
Applying *Options:* electronic application. *Application fee:* $50. *Required:* high school transcript, interview. *Application deadline:* rolling (freshmen), rolling (transfers). *Notification:* continuous (freshmen).
Admissions Contact Mr. Richard Herman, Executive Director, Indiana Business College, 830 North Miller Avenue, Marion, IN 46952. *Phone:* 765-662-7497. *Toll-free phone:* 800-IBC-GRAD. *Fax:* 765-651-9421.

INDIANA BUSINESS COLLEGE
Muncie, Indiana

- **Proprietary** 2-year
- **Calendar** quarters
- **Degree** certificates, diplomas, and associate

Indiana Business College (continued)
- **Coed,** 313 undergraduate students

Faculty *Student/faculty ratio:* 20:1.
Majors Accounting; administrative assistant and secretarial science; business administration and management; business administration, management and operations related; computer and information sciences and support services related; computer programming (specific applications); health information/medical records technology; information technology; management information systems and services related; medical office assistant.
Academic Programs *Special study options:* cooperative education, distance learning, double majors, internships, part-time degree program.
Computers on Campus Internet access available.
Student Life *Housing:* college housing not available. *Activities and Organizations:* Phi Beta Lambda.
Standardized Tests *Required:* Wonderlic Scholastic Level Exam (SLE) (for admission).
Applying *Options:* electronic application. *Application fee:* $50. *Required:* high school transcript, interview. *Application deadline:* rolling (freshmen), rolling (transfers). *Notification:* continuous (freshmen).
Admissions Contact Mr. Gregory Bond, Regional Director, Indiana Business College, 411 West Riggin Road, Muncie, IN 47303. *Phone:* 765-288-8681. *Toll-free phone:* 800-IBC-GRAD. *Fax:* 765-288-8797.

INDIANA BUSINESS COLLEGE

Terre Haute, Indiana

- **Proprietary** 2-year, founded 1902
- **Calendar** quarters
- **Degree** certificates, diplomas, and associate
- **Coed,** 227 undergraduate students

Faculty *Student/faculty ratio:* 20:1.
Majors Accounting; administrative assistant and secretarial science; business administration and management; business administration, management and operations related; computer and information sciences and support services related; computer programming (specific applications); health professions related; information technology; management information systems and services related; medical/clinical assistant.
Academic Programs *Special study options:* adult/continuing education programs, cooperative education, distance learning, double majors, internships, part-time degree program.
Computers on Campus Internet access available.
Standardized Tests *Required:* Wonderlic Scholastic Level Exam (SLE) (for admission).
Applying *Options:* electronic application. *Application fee:* $50. *Required:* high school transcript, interview. *Application deadline:* rolling (freshmen), rolling (transfers). *Notification:* continuous (freshmen).
Admissions Contact Ms. Laura Hale, Executive Director, Indiana Business College, 3175 South Third Place, Terre Haute, IN 47802. *Phone:* 812-232-4458. *Toll-free phone:* 800-IBC-GRAD. *Fax:* 812-234-2361.

INDIANA BUSINESS COLLEGE-MEDICAL

Indianapolis, Indiana

- **Proprietary** 2-year
- **Calendar** quarters
- **Degree** certificates, diplomas, and associate
- **Coed,** 550 undergraduate students

Faculty *Student/faculty ratio:* 20:1.
Majors Health and physical education related; health professions related; massage therapy; medical/clinical assistant.
Academic Programs *Special study options:* adult/continuing education programs, cooperative education, distance learning, double majors, internships, part-time degree program.
Computers on Campus Internet access available.
Standardized Tests *Required:* Wonderlic Scholastic Level Exam (SLE) (for admission).
Applying *Options:* electronic application. *Application fee:* $50. *Required:* high school transcript, interview. *Application deadline:* rolling (freshmen), rolling (transfers). *Notification:* continuous (freshmen).
Admissions Contact Mr. Gary McGee, Senior Regional Director, Indiana Business College-Medical, 8150 Brookville Road, Indianapolis, IN 46239. *Phone:* 317-375-8000. *Toll-free phone:* 800-IBC-6611. *Fax:* 317-351-1871.

INTERNATIONAL BUSINESS COLLEGE

Fort Wayne, Indiana

Admissions Contact Mr. Steve Kinzer, School Director, International Business College, 5699 Coventry Lane, Fort Wayne, IN 46804. *Phone:* 219-459-4513. *Toll-free phone:* 800-589-6363. *Fax:* 219-436-1896.

INTERNATIONAL BUSINESS COLLEGE

Indianapolis, Indiana

- **Proprietary** 2-year, administratively affiliated with Bradford Schools, Charlotte, NC
- **Calendar** semesters
- **Degree** diplomas and associate
- **Coed,** 315 undergraduate students, 100% full-time, 74% women, 26% men

Undergraduates 315 full-time.
Freshmen *Admission:* 597 applied, 559 admitted, 185 enrolled.
Faculty *Total:* 15, 40% full-time, 40% with terminal degrees. *Student/faculty ratio:* 20:1.
Academic Programs *Special study options:* academic remediation for entering students, internships.
Computers on Campus 125 computers available on campus for general student use. Internet access, at least one staffed computer lab available.
Student Life *Housing Options:* Campus housing is leased by the school. Freshman applicants given priority for college housing.
Costs (2005–06) *Tuition:* $11,380 full-time. No tuition increase for student's term of enrollment. *Room only:* $5900. *Payment plan:* installment. *Waivers:* employees or children of employees.
Applying *Options:* common application, electronic application. *Application fee:* $50. *Required:* high school transcript. *Application deadline:* rolling (freshmen). *Notification:* continuous (freshmen).
Admissions Contact Ms. Kathy Chiudioni, Director of Admissions, International Business College, 7205 Shadeland Station, Indianapolis, IN 46256. *Phone:* 317-213-2320. *E-mail:* info@intlbusinesscollege.com.

ITT TECHNICAL INSTITUTE

Fort Wayne, Indiana

- **Proprietary** primarily 2-year, founded 1967, part of ITT Educational Services, Inc
- **Calendar** quarters
- **Degrees** associate and bachelor's
- **Coed**

Standardized Tests *Required:* Wonderlic aptitude test (for admission).
Costs (2004–05) *Tuition:* Please see school catalog for specific information.
Applying *Options:* deferred entrance. *Application fee:* $100. *Required:* high school transcript, interview. *Recommended:* letters of recommendation.
Admissions Contact Mr. Michael D. Frantom, ITT Technical Institute, 4919 Coldwater Road, Fort Wayne, IN 46825. *Phone:* 260-484-4107. *Toll-free phone:* 800-866-4488. *Fax:* 260-484-0860.

ITT TECHNICAL INSTITUTE

Indianapolis, Indiana

- **Proprietary** founded 1966, part of ITT Educational Services, Inc
- **Calendar** quarters
- **Degrees** diplomas, associate, and bachelor's
- **Suburban** 10-acre campus
- **Coed**

Standardized Tests *Required:* Wonderlic aptitude test (for admission).
Costs (2004–05) *Tuition:* Please see school catalog for specific information.
Applying *Options:* deferred entrance. *Application fee:* $100. *Required:* high school transcript, interview. *Recommended:* letters of recommendation.
Admissions Contact Ms. Martha Watson, ITT Technical Institute, 9511 Angola Court, Indianapolis, IN 46268. *Phone:* 317-875-8640. *Toll-free phone:* 800-937-4488. *Fax:* 317-875-8641.

ITT TECHNICAL INSTITUTE

Newburgh, Indiana

- **Proprietary** primarily 2-year, founded 1966, part of ITT Educational Services, Inc
- **Calendar** quarters
- **Degrees** associate and bachelor's

■ **Coed**

Standardized Tests *Required:* Wonderlic aptitude test (for admission).

Costs (2004–05) *Tuition:* Please see school catalog for specific information.

Applying *Options:* deferred entrance. *Application fee:* $100. *Required:* high school transcript, interview. *Recommended:* letters of recommendation.

Admissions Contact Mr. Jim Smolinski, Director of Recruitment, ITT Technical Institute, 10999 Stahl Road, Newburgh, IN 47630. *Phone:* 812-858-1600. *Toll-free phone:* 800-832-4488. *Fax:* 812-858-0646.

IVY TECH STATE COLLEGE-BLOOMINGTON
Bloomington, Indiana

■ **State-supported** 2-year, founded 2001, part of Ivy Tech State College System
■ **Calendar** semesters
■ **Degree** certificates and associate
■ **Endowment** $14.3 million
■ **Coed**, 3,169 undergraduate students, 45% full-time, 60% women, 40% men

Undergraduates 1,427 full-time, 1,742 part-time. 4% African American, 1% Asian American or Pacific Islander, 1% Hispanic American, 0.5% Native American, 0.3% international, 5% transferred in.

Freshmen *Admission:* 899 applied, 899 admitted, 482 enrolled.

Faculty *Total:* 226, 20% full-time.

Majors Accounting technology and bookkeeping; building/property maintenance and management; business administration and management; cabinetmaking and millwork; child care and support services management; computer and information sciences; criminal justice/safety; electrical, electronic and communications engineering technology; electrician; emergency medical technology (EMT paramedic); executive assistant/executive secretary; heating, air conditioning, ventilation and refrigeration maintenance technology; industrial technology; legal assistant/paralegal; liberal arts and sciences/liberal studies; machine tool technology; mechanics and repair; nursing (registered nurse training); pipefitting and sprinkler fitting; psychiatric/mental health services technology; tool and die technology.

Academic Programs *Special study options:* academic remediation for entering students, adult/continuing education programs, advanced placement credit, distance learning, external degree program, internships, part-time degree program, services for LD students, summer session for credit.

Library 5,516 titles, 97 serial subscriptions, 1,281 audiovisual materials, an OPAC, a Web page.

Computers on Campus 221 computers available on campus for general student use. Internet access, online (class) registration available.

Student Life *Activities and Organizations:* Student Government, Phi Theta Kappa. *Campus security:* late-night transport/escort service.

Standardized Tests *Required:* ACT ASSET (for placement).

Costs (2004–05) *Tuition:* state resident $2409 full-time, $80 per credit part-time; nonresident $4871 full-time, $162 per credit part-time. Full-time tuition and fees vary according to course load and reciprocity agreements. Part-time tuition and fees vary according to course load and reciprocity agreements. *Required fees:* $60 full-time, $30 per term part-time. *Payment plan:* installment. *Waivers:* senior citizens and employees or children of employees.

Financial Aid Of all full-time matriculated undergraduates who enrolled in 2003, 51 Federal Work-Study jobs (averaging $3259).

Applying *Options:* deferred entrance. *Required:* high school transcript. *Required for some:* interview. *Application deadline:* rolling (freshmen), rolling (transfers). *Notification:* continuous (freshmen).

Admissions Contact Mr. Neil Frederick, Assistant Director of Admissions, Ivy Tech State College-Bloomington, 200 Daniels Way, Bloomington, IN 47404-1511. *Phone:* 812-330-6026. *Fax:* 812-330-6200. *E-mail:* nfrederi@ivytech.edu.

IVY TECH STATE COLLEGE-CENTRAL INDIANA
Indianapolis, Indiana

■ **State-supported** 2-year, founded 1963
■ **Calendar** semesters
■ **Degree** certificates and associate
■ **Urban** 10-acre campus
■ **Endowment** $14.3 million
■ **Coed**, 10,832 undergraduate students, 34% full-time, 59% women, 41% men

Undergraduates 3,666 full-time, 7,166 part-time. 23% African American, 1% Asian American or Pacific Islander, 2% Hispanic American, 0.4% Native American, 0.3% international, 6% transferred in.

Freshmen *Admission:* 2,628 applied, 2,628 admitted, 1,451 enrolled.

Faculty *Total:* 676, 19% full-time.

Majors Accounting technology and bookkeeping; automobile/automotive mechanics technology; building/property maintenance and management; business administration and management; cabinetmaking and millwork; carpentry; child care and support services management; child guidance; computer and information sciences; criminal justice/safety; design and visual communications; drafting and design technology; electrical, electronic and communications engineering technology; electrician; executive assistant/executive secretary; heating, air conditioning, ventilation and refrigeration maintenance technology; industrial technology; legal assistant/paralegal; liberal arts and sciences/liberal studies; machine shop technology; machine tool technology; masonry; mechanics and repair; medical/clinical assistant; medical radiologic technology; nursing (registered nurse training); occupational safety and health technology; occupational therapist assistant; painting and wall covering; pipefitting and sprinkler fitting; psychiatric/mental health services technology; respiratory care therapy; sheet metal technology; surgical technology; tool and die technology.

Academic Programs *Special study options:* academic remediation for entering students, adult/continuing education programs, advanced placement credit, cooperative education, distance learning, English as a second language, internships, off-campus study, part-time degree program, services for LD students, summer session for credit.

Library 20,247 titles, 138 serial subscriptions, 2,135 audiovisual materials, an OPAC, a Web page.

Computers on Campus 407 computers available on campus for general student use. Internet access, online (class) registration, at least one staffed computer lab available.

Student Life *Housing:* college housing not available. *Activities and Organizations:* student-run newspaper, Student Government, Phi Theta Kappa, Human Services Club, Administrative Office Assistants Club, Radiology Club. *Campus security:* 24-hour emergency response devices and patrols, late-night transport/escort service. *Student services:* personal/psychological counseling.

Athletics *Intramural sports:* baseball M, basketball M/W, cheerleading W, golf M/W, softball W, volleyball M/W.

Standardized Tests *Required:* ACT ASSET (for placement).

Costs (2004–05) *Tuition:* state resident $2409 full-time, $80 per credit part-time; nonresident $4871 full-time, $162 per credit part-time. Full-time tuition and fees vary according to course load and reciprocity agreements. Part-time tuition and fees vary according to course load and reciprocity agreements. *Required fees:* $60 full-time, $30 per term part-time. *Payment plan:* installment. *Waivers:* senior citizens and employees or children of employees.

Financial Aid Of all full-time matriculated undergraduates who enrolled in 2003, 92 Federal Work-Study jobs (averaging $3766).

Applying *Options:* early admission, deferred entrance. *Required:* high school transcript. *Required for some:* interview. *Application deadline:* rolling (freshmen), rolling (transfers). *Notification:* continuous (freshmen).

Admissions Contact Ms. Velma Wade, Counselor, Ivy Tech State College-Central Indiana, One West 26th Street, Indianapolis, IN 46208-4777. *Phone:* 317-921-4824. *Toll-free phone:* 800-732-1470. *Fax:* 317-921-4753. *E-mail:* vwade@ivytech.edu.

IVY TECH STATE COLLEGE-COLUMBUS
Columbus, Indiana

■ **State-supported** 2-year, founded 1963, part of Ivy Tech State College System
■ **Calendar** semesters
■ **Degree** certificates and associate
■ **Small-town** campus with easy access to Indianapolis
■ **Endowment** $14.3 million
■ **Coed**, 1,855 undergraduate students, 37% full-time, 70% women, 30% men

Undergraduates 695 full-time, 1,160 part-time. 2% African American, 0.7% Asian American or Pacific Islander, 0.7% Hispanic American, 0.4% Native American, 0.1% international, 9% transferred in.

Freshmen *Admission:* 407 applied, 407 admitted, 208 enrolled.

Faculty *Total:* 180, 20% full-time.

Majors Accounting technology and bookkeeping; automobile/automotive mechanics technology; building/property maintenance and management; business administration and management; cabinetmaking and millwork; child care and support services management; computer and information sciences; design and visual communications; drafting and design technology; electrical and power transmission installation; electrical, electronic and communications engineering technology; executive assistant/executive secretary; heating, air conditioning, ventilation and refrigeration maintenance technology; industrial technology; legal assistant/paralegal; liberal arts and sciences/liberal studies; machine tool technology; masonry; mechanics and repair; medical/clinical assistant; medical radiologic technology; pipefitting and sprinkler fitting; psychiatric/mental health services technology; robotics technology; surgical technology; tool and die technology.

Academic Programs *Special study options:* academic remediation for entering students, adult/continuing education programs, advanced placement credit,

Ivy Tech State College-Columbus (continued)

distance learning, internships, part-time degree program, services for LD students, summer session for credit.

Library 7,855 titles, 13,382 serial subscriptions, 989 audiovisual materials, an OPAC, a Web page.

Computers on Campus 185 computers available on campus for general student use. Internet access, online (class) registration, at least one staffed computer lab available.

Student Life *Housing:* college housing not available. *Activities and Organizations:* Student Government, Phi Theta Kappa, LPN Club. *Campus security:* late-night transport/escort service, trained evening security personnel, escort service.

Standardized Tests *Required:* ACT ASSET (for placement).

Costs (2004–05) *Tuition:* state resident $2409 full-time, $80 per credit part-time; nonresident $4871 full-time, $162 per credit part-time. Full-time tuition and fees vary according to course load and reciprocity agreements. Part-time tuition and fees vary according to course load and reciprocity agreements. *Required fees:* $60 full-time, $30 per term part-time. *Payment plan:* installment. *Waivers:* senior citizens and employees or children of employees.

Financial Aid Of all full-time matriculated undergraduates who enrolled in 2003, 26 Federal Work-Study jobs (averaging $1694).

Applying *Options:* early admission, deferred entrance. *Required:* high school transcript. *Required for some:* interview. *Application deadline:* rolling (freshmen), rolling (transfers). *Notification:* continuous (freshmen).

Admissions Contact Mr. Neil Bagadiong, Assistant Director of Student Affairs, Ivy Tech State College-Columbus, 4475 Central Avenue, Columbus, IN 47203-1868. *Phone:* 812-372-9925 Ext. 129. *Toll-free phone:* 800-922-4838. *Fax:* 812-372-0311. *E-mail:* nbagadio@ivytech.edu.

IVY TECH STATE COLLEGE-EASTCENTRAL
Muncie, Indiana

- **State-supported** 2-year, founded 1968, part of Ivy Tech State College System
- **Calendar** semesters
- **Degree** certificates and associate
- **Suburban** 15-acre campus with easy access to Indianapolis
- **Endowment** $14.3 million
- **Coed,** 5,472 undergraduate students, 47% full-time, 65% women, 35% men

Undergraduates 2,556 full-time, 2,916 part-time. 7% African American, 0.2% Asian American or Pacific Islander, 0.9% Hispanic American, 0.3% Native American, 5% transferred in.

Freshmen *Admission:* 1,137 applied, 1,137 admitted, 733 enrolled.

Faculty *Total:* 405, 19% full-time.

Majors Accounting technology and bookkeeping; automobile/automotive mechanics technology; building/property maintenance and management; business administration and management; cabinetmaking and millwork; carpentry; child care and support services management; computer and information sciences; construction trades; criminal justice/safety; drafting and design technology; electrical, electronic and communications engineering technology; electrician; executive assistant/executive secretary; heating, air conditioning, ventilation and refrigeration maintenance technology; hospitality administration; industrial mechanics and maintenance technology; industrial technology; legal assistant/paralegal; liberal arts and sciences/liberal studies; machine tool technology; masonry; medical/clinical assistant; medical radiologic technology; nursing (registered nurse training); painting and wall covering; physical therapist assistant; pipefitting and sprinkler fitting; psychiatric/mental health services technology; surgical technology; tool and die technology.

Academic Programs *Special study options:* academic remediation for entering students, adult/continuing education programs, advanced placement credit, distance learning, internships, part-time degree program, services for LD students.

Library 5,779 titles, 145 serial subscriptions, 6,266 audiovisual materials, an OPAC, a Web page.

Computers on Campus 270 computers available on campus for general student use. A campuswide network can be accessed from off campus. Internet access, online (class) registration, at least one staffed computer lab available.

Student Life *Housing:* college housing not available. *Activities and Organizations:* Business Professionals of America, Skills USA-VICA, Student Government, Phi Theta Kappa, Human Services Club.

Standardized Tests *Required:* ACT ASSET (for placement).

Costs (2004–05) *Tuition:* state resident $2409 full-time, $80 per credit part-time; nonresident $4871 full-time, $162 per credit part-time. Full-time tuition and fees vary according to course load and reciprocity agreements. Part-time tuition and fees vary according to course load and reciprocity agreements. *Required fees:* $60 full-time, $30 per term part-time. *Payment plan:* installment. *Waivers:* senior citizens and employees or children of employees.

Financial Aid Of all full-time matriculated undergraduates who enrolled in 2003, 65 Federal Work-Study jobs (averaging $2666).

Applying *Options:* early admission, deferred entrance. *Required:* high school transcript. *Required for some:* interview. *Application deadline:* rolling (freshmen), rolling (transfers). *Notification:* continuous (freshmen).

Admissions Contact Corey Sharp, Recruitment/Outreach Specialist, Ivy Tech State College-Eastcentral, 4301 South Cowan Road, Muncie, IN 47302-9448. *Phone:* 765-289-2291. *Toll-free phone:* 800-589-8324. *Fax:* 765-289-2292. *E-mail:* csharp@ivytech.edu.

IVY TECH STATE COLLEGE-KOKOMO
Kokomo, Indiana

- **State-supported** 2-year, founded 1968, part of Ivy Tech State College System
- **Calendar** semesters
- **Degree** certificates and associate
- **Small-town** 20-acre campus with easy access to Indianapolis
- **Endowment** $14.3 million
- **Coed,** 2,762 undergraduate students, 39% full-time, 63% women, 37% men

Undergraduates 1,089 full-time, 1,673 part-time. 4% African American, 0.3% Asian American or Pacific Islander, 1% Hispanic American, 0.5% Native American, 0.3% transferred in.

Freshmen *Admission:* 1,041 applied, 1,041 admitted, 533 enrolled.

Faculty *Total:* 246, 24% full-time.

Majors Accounting technology and bookkeeping; automobile/automotive mechanics technology; building/property maintenance and management; business administration and management; cabinetmaking and millwork; child care and support services management; computer and information sciences; criminal justice/safety; drafting and design technology; electrical, electronic and communications engineering technology; electrician; emergency medical technology (EMT paramedic); executive assistant/executive secretary; heating, air conditioning, ventilation and refrigeration maintenance technology; industrial technology; legal assistant/paralegal; liberal arts and sciences/liberal studies; machine tool technology; mechanics and repair; medical/clinical assistant; pipefitting and sprinkler fitting; psychiatric/mental health services technology; surgical technology; tool and die technology.

Academic Programs *Special study options:* academic remediation for entering students, adult/continuing education programs, advanced placement credit, distance learning, internships, part-time degree program, services for LD students, summer session for credit.

Library 5,177 titles, 99 serial subscriptions, 772 audiovisual materials, an OPAC, a Web page.

Computers on Campus 320 computers available on campus for general student use. A campuswide network can be accessed from off campus. Internet access, online (class) registration, at least one staffed computer lab available.

Student Life *Housing:* college housing not available. *Activities and Organizations:* Student Government, Collegiate Secretaries International, Licensed Practical Nursing Club, Phi Theta Kappa. *Campus security:* 24-hour emergency response devices, late-night transport/escort service. *Student services:* personal/psychological counseling.

Standardized Tests *Required:* ACT ASSET (for placement).

Costs (2004–05) *Tuition:* state resident $2409 full-time, $80 per credit part-time; nonresident $4871 full-time, $162 per credit part-time. Full-time tuition and fees vary according to course load and reciprocity agreements. Part-time tuition and fees vary according to course load and reciprocity agreements. *Required fees:* $60 full-time, $30 per term part-time. *Payment plan:* installment. *Waivers:* senior citizens and employees or children of employees.

Financial Aid Of all full-time matriculated undergraduates who enrolled in 2003, 45 Federal Work-Study jobs (averaging $1829).

Applying *Options:* early admission. *Required:* high school transcript. *Required for some:* interview. *Application deadline:* rolling (freshmen), rolling (transfers). *Notification:* continuous (freshmen).

Admissions Contact Alayne Cook, Assistant Director of Admissions, Ivy Tech State College-Kokomo, 1815 E. Morgan Street, Kokomo, IN 46903-1373. *Phone:* 765-459-0561 Ext. 318. *Toll-free phone:* 800-459-0561. *Fax:* 765-454-5111. *E-mail:* acook@ivytech.edu.

IVY TECH STATE COLLEGE-LAFAYETTE
Lafayette, Indiana

- **State-supported** 2-year, founded 1968, part of Ivy Tech State College System
- **Calendar** semesters
- **Degree** certificates and associate
- **Suburban** campus with easy access to Indianapolis
- **Endowment** $14.3 million
- **Coed,** 5,274 undergraduate students, 43% full-time, 53% women, 47% men

Undergraduates 2,259 full-time, 3,015 part-time. 3% African American, 0.9% Asian American or Pacific Islander, 3% Hispanic American, 0.5% Native American, 0.4% international, 4% transferred in.

Freshmen *Admission:* 1,572 applied, 1,572 admitted, 623 enrolled.

Faculty *Total:* 325, 20% full-time.

Majors Accounting; accounting technology and bookkeeping; automobile/automotive mechanics technology; building/property maintenance and management; business administration and management; cabinetmaking and millwork; carpentry; child care and support services management; computer and information sciences; drafting and design technology; electrical, electronic and communications engineering technology; electrician; executive assistant/executive secretary; heating, air conditioning, ventilation and refrigeration maintenance technology; industrial technology; ironworking; legal assistant/paralegal; liberal arts and sciences/liberal studies; lineworker; machine tool technology; masonry; mechanics and repair; medical/clinical assistant; nursing (registered nurse training); painting and wall covering; pipefitting and sprinkler fitting; psychiatric/mental health services technology; quality control technology; respiratory care therapy; sheet metal technology; surgical technology; tool and die technology.

Academic Programs *Special study options:* academic remediation for entering students, advanced placement credit, distance learning, internships, part-time degree program, services for LD students, summer session for credit.

Library 8,043 titles, 200 serial subscriptions, 2,234 audiovisual materials, an OPAC, a Web page.

Computers on Campus 267 computers available on campus for general student use. A campuswide network can be accessed. Internet access, online (class) registration, at least one staffed computer lab available.

Student Life *Housing:* college housing not available. *Activities and Organizations:* student-run newspaper, Student Government, Phi Theta Kappa, LPN Club, Accounting Club, Student Computer Technology Association. *Student services:* personal/psychological counseling.

Standardized Tests *Required:* ACT ASSET (for placement).

Costs (2004–05) *Tuition:* state resident $2409 full-time, $80 per credit part-time; nonresident $4871 full-time, $162 per credit part-time. Full-time tuition and fees vary according to course load and reciprocity agreements. Part-time tuition and fees vary according to course load and reciprocity agreements. *Required fees:* $60 full-time, $30 per term part-time. *Payment plan:* installment. *Waivers:* senior citizens and employees or children of employees.

Financial Aid Of all full-time matriculated undergraduates who enrolled in 2003, 65 Federal Work-Study jobs (averaging $2222). 1 state and other part-time job (averaging $2436).

Applying *Required:* high school transcript. *Required for some:* interview. *Application deadline:* rolling (freshmen), rolling (transfers). *Notification:* continuous (freshmen).

Admissions Contact Ms. Judy Dopplefeld, Director of Admissions, Ivy Tech State College-Lafayette, 3101 South Creagy Lane, PO Box 6299, Lafayette, IN 47903. *Phone:* 765-772-9116. *Toll-free phone:* 800-669-4882. *Fax:* 765-772-9107. *E-mail:* jdopplef@ivytech.edu.

IVY TECH STATE COLLEGE-NORTH CENTRAL
South Bend, Indiana

- **State-supported** 2-year, founded 1968, part of Ivy Tech State College System
- **Calendar** semesters
- **Degree** certificates and associate
- **Suburban** 4-acre campus
- **Endowment** $14.3 million
- **Coed,** 4,654 undergraduate students, 28% full-time, 54% women, 46% men

Undergraduates 1,283 full-time, 3,371 part-time. 2% are from out of state, 14% African American, 0.6% Asian American or Pacific Islander, 5% Hispanic American, 0.5% Native American, 0.4% international, 2% transferred in.

Freshmen *Admission:* 902 applied, 902 admitted, 567 enrolled.

Faculty *Total:* 319, 21% full-time.

Majors Accounting technology and bookkeeping; automobile/automotive mechanics technology; building/property maintenance and management; business administration and management; cabinetmaking and millwork; carpentry; child care and support services management; clinical/medical laboratory technology; computer and information sciences; criminal justice/safety; design and visual communications; drafting and design technology; educational/instructional media design; electrical, electronic and communications engineering technology; electrician; emergency medical technology (EMT paramedic); executive assistant/executive secretary; heating, air conditioning, ventilation and refrigeration maintenance technology; hospitality administration; industrial technology; interior design; ironworking; legal assistant/paralegal; liberal arts and sciences/liberal studies; machine tool technology; masonry; mechanics and repair; medical/clinical assistant; nursing (registered nurse training); painting and wall covering; pipefitting and sprinkler fitting; sheet metal technology; tool and die technology.

Academic Programs *Special study options:* academic remediation for entering students, adult/continuing education programs, advanced placement credit, distance learning, English as a second language, internships, off-campus study, part-time degree program, services for LD students, summer session for credit.

Library 6,246 titles, 90 serial subscriptions, 689 audiovisual materials, an OPAC, a Web page.

Computers on Campus 426 computers available on campus for general student use. Internet access, online (class) registration, at least one staffed computer lab available.

Student Life *Housing:* college housing not available. *Activities and Organizations:* Phi Theta Kappa, Student Government, LPN Club. *Campus security:* 24-hour emergency response devices and patrols, late-night transport/escort service, security during open hours. *Student services:* personal/psychological counseling, women's center.

Standardized Tests *Required:* ACT ASSET (for placement).

Costs (2004–05) *Tuition:* state resident $2409 full-time, $80 per credit part-time; nonresident $4871 full-time, $162 per credit part-time. Full-time tuition and fees vary according to course load and reciprocity agreements. Part-time tuition and fees vary according to course load and reciprocity agreements. *Required fees:* $60 full-time, $30 per term part-time. *Payment plan:* installment. *Waivers:* senior citizens and employees or children of employees.

Financial Aid Of all full-time matriculated undergraduates who enrolled in 2003, 100 Federal Work-Study jobs (averaging $1538).

Applying *Options:* early admission, deferred entrance. *Required:* high school transcript. *Required for some:* interview. *Application deadline:* rolling (freshmen), rolling (transfers). *Notification:* continuous (freshmen).

Admissions Contact Ms. Pam Decker, Director of Admissions, Ivy Tech State College-North Central, 220 Dean Johnson Boulevard, South Bend, IN 46601-3415. *Phone:* 574-289-7001 Ext. 423. *Fax:* 219-236-7177. *E-mail:* pdecker@ivytech.edu.

IVY TECH STATE COLLEGE-NORTHEAST
Fort Wayne, Indiana

- **State-supported** 2-year, founded 1969, part of Ivy Tech State College System
- **Calendar** semesters
- **Degree** certificates and associate
- **Urban** 22-acre campus
- **Endowment** $14.3 million
- **Coed,** 5,554 undergraduate students, 37% full-time, 60% women, 40% men

Undergraduates 2,044 full-time, 3,510 part-time. 1% are from out of state, 13% African American, 1% Asian American or Pacific Islander, 2% Hispanic American, 0.6% Native American, 0.3% international, 3% transferred in.

Freshmen *Admission:* 2,180 applied, 2,180 admitted, 489 enrolled.

Faculty *Total:* 405, 20% full-time.

Majors Accounting technology and bookkeeping; automobile/automotive mechanics technology; building/property maintenance and management; business administration and management; cabinetmaking and millwork; child care and support services management; computer and information sciences; construction trades; drafting and design technology; electrical, electronic and communications engineering technology; electrician; executive assistant/executive secretary; heating, air conditioning, ventilation and refrigeration maintenance technology; hospitality administration; industrial technology; ironworking; legal assistant/paralegal; liberal arts and sciences/liberal studies; machine tool technology; masonry; mechanics and repair; medical/clinical assistant; occupational safety and health technology; painting and wall covering; pipefitting and sprinkler fitting; psychiatric/mental health services technology; respiratory care therapy; sheet metal technology; tool and die technology.

Academic Programs *Special study options:* adult/continuing education programs, advanced placement credit, distance learning, English as a second language, internships, part-time degree program, services for LD students, summer session for credit.

Library 18,389 titles, 110 serial subscriptions, 3,397 audiovisual materials, an OPAC, a Web page.

Computers on Campus 382 computers available on campus for general student use. Internet access, online (class) registration, at least one staffed computer lab available.

Student Life *Housing:* college housing not available. *Activities and Organizations:* Student Government, LPN Club, Phi Theta Kappa. *Campus security:* 24-hour emergency response devices and patrols, late-night transport/escort service.

Standardized Tests *Required:* ACT ASSET (for placement).

Costs (2004–05) *Tuition:* state resident $2409 full-time, $80 per credit part-time; nonresident $4871 full-time, $162 per credit part-time. Full-time tuition and fees vary according to course load and reciprocity agreements. Part-time tuition and fees vary according to course load and reciprocity agreements. *Required fees:* $60 full-time, $30 per term part-time. *Payment plan:* installment. *Waivers:* senior citizens and employees or children of employees.

Ivy Tech State College-Northeast (continued)

Financial Aid Of all full-time matriculated undergraduates who enrolled in 2003, 40 Federal Work-Study jobs (averaging $4041).

Applying *Options:* early admission. *Required:* high school transcript. *Required for some:* interview. *Application deadline:* rolling (freshmen), rolling (transfers). *Notification:* continuous (freshmen).

Admissions Contact Mr. Steve Scheer, Director of Admissions, Ivy Tech State College-Northeast, 3800 N. Anthony Boulevard, Ft. Wayne, IN 46805-1489. *Phone:* 260-480-4221. *Toll-free phone:* 800-859-4882. *Fax:* 260-480-4177. *E-mail:* sscheer@ivytech.edu.

IVY TECH STATE COLLEGE-NORTHWEST
Gary, Indiana

- **State-supported** 2-year, founded 1963, part of Ivy Tech State College System
- **Calendar** semesters
- **Degree** certificates and associate
- **Urban** 13-acre campus with easy access to Chicago
- **Endowment** $14.3 million
- **Coed,** 4,684 undergraduate students, 36% full-time, 64% women, 36% men

Undergraduates 1,681 full-time, 3,003 part-time. 32% African American, 0.5% Asian American or Pacific Islander, 9% Hispanic American, 0.3% Native American, 0.2% international, 5% transferred in.

Freshmen *Admission:* 826 applied, 826 admitted, 534 enrolled.

Faculty *Total:* 443, 21% full-time.

Majors Accounting technology and bookkeeping; automobile/automotive mechanics technology; building/property maintenance and management; business administration and management; cabinetmaking and millwork; carpentry; child care and support services management; computer and information sciences; construction trades; criminal justice/safety; drafting and design technology; electrical, electronic and communications engineering technology; electrician; executive assistant/executive secretary; heating, air conditioning, ventilation and refrigeration maintenance technology; ironworking; legal assistant/paralegal; machine tool technology; masonry; mechanics and repair; medical/clinical assistant; nursing (registered nurse training); occupational safety and health technology; painting and wall covering; pipefitting and sprinkler fitting; psychiatric/mental health services technology; respiratory care therapy; sheet metal technology; surgical technology; tool and die technology.

Academic Programs *Special study options:* academic remediation for entering students, adult/continuing education programs, advanced placement credit, distance learning, internships, part-time degree program, services for LD students, summer session for credit.

Library 13,805 titles, 160 serial subscriptions, 4,295 audiovisual materials, an OPAC, a Web page.

Computers on Campus 267 computers available on campus for general student use. Internet access, online (class) registration, at least one staffed computer lab available.

Student Life *Housing:* college housing not available. *Activities and Organizations:* Phi Theta Kappa, LPN Club, Computer Club, Student Government, Business Club. *Campus security:* 24-hour emergency response devices, late-night transport/escort service.

Standardized Tests *Required:* ACT ASSET (for placement).

Costs (2004–05) *Tuition:* state resident $2409 full-time, $80 per credit part-time; nonresident $4871 full-time, $162 per credit part-time. Full-time tuition and fees vary according to course load and reciprocity agreements. Part-time tuition and fees vary according to course load and reciprocity agreements. *Required fees:* $60 full-time, $30 per term part-time. *Payment plan:* installment. *Waivers:* senior citizens and employees or children of employees.

Financial Aid Of all full-time matriculated undergraduates who enrolled in 2003, 74 Federal Work-Study jobs (averaging $2131).

Applying *Options:* deferred entrance. *Required:* high school transcript. *Required for some:* interview. *Application deadline:* rolling (freshmen), rolling (transfers). *Notification:* continuous (freshmen).

Admissions Contact Ms. Twilla Lewis, Associate Dean of Student Affairs, Ivy Tech State College-Northwest, 1440 East 35th Avenue, Gary, IN 46409-1499. *Phone:* 219-981-1111 Ext. 273. *Toll-free phone:* 800-843-4882. *Fax:* 219-981-4415. *E-mail:* tlewis@ivytech.edu.

IVY TECH STATE COLLEGE-SOUTHCENTRAL
Sellersburg, Indiana

- **State-supported** 2-year, founded 1968, part of Ivy Tech State College System
- **Calendar** semesters
- **Degree** certificates and associate
- **Small-town** 63-acre campus with easy access to Louisville
- **Endowment** $14.3 million
- **Coed,** 3,050 undergraduate students, 28% full-time, 52% women, 48% men

Undergraduates 865 full-time, 2,185 part-time. 25% are from out of state, 4% African American, 0.6% Asian American or Pacific Islander, 0.7% Hispanic American, 0.5% Native American, 5% transferred in.

Freshmen *Admission:* 744 applied, 744 admitted, 379 enrolled.

Faculty *Total:* 154, 29% full-time.

Majors Accounting technology and bookkeeping; automobile/automotive mechanics technology; building/property maintenance and management; business administration and management; cabinetmaking and millwork; carpentry; child care and support services management; computer and information sciences; design and visual communications; electrical, electronic and communications engineering technology; electrician; executive assistant/executive secretary; heating, air conditioning, ventilation and refrigeration maintenance technology; industrial technology; legal assistant/paralegal; liberal arts and sciences/liberal studies; machine tool technology; masonry; mechanics and repair; medical/clinical assistant; nursing (registered nurse training); pipefitting and sprinkler fitting; psychiatric/mental health services technology; respiratory care therapy; sheet metal technology; tool and die technology.

Academic Programs *Special study options:* academic remediation for entering students, adult/continuing education programs, advanced placement credit, cooperative education, distance learning, internships, part-time degree program, services for LD students, summer session for credit.

Library 7,634 titles, 66 serial subscriptions, 648 audiovisual materials, an OPAC, a Web page.

Computers on Campus 187 computers available on campus for general student use. A campuswide network can be accessed. Internet access, online (class) registration, at least one staffed computer lab available.

Student Life *Housing:* college housing not available. *Activities and Organizations:* Phi Theta Kappa, Practical Nursing Club, Medical Assistant Club, Accounting Club, Student Government. *Campus security:* late-night transport/escort service.

Standardized Tests *Required:* ACT ASSET (for placement).

Costs (2004–05) *Tuition:* state resident $2409 full-time, $80 per credit part-time; nonresident $4871 full-time, $162 per credit part-time. Full-time tuition and fees vary according to course load and reciprocity agreements. Part-time tuition and fees vary according to course load and reciprocity agreements. *Required fees:* $60 full-time, $30 per term part-time. *Payment plan:* installment. *Waivers:* senior citizens and employees or children of employees.

Financial Aid Of all full-time matriculated undergraduates who enrolled in 2003, 20 Federal Work-Study jobs (averaging $5007). 1 state and other part-time job (averaging $6080).

Applying *Options:* early admission, deferred entrance. *Required:* high school transcript. *Required for some:* interview. *Application deadline:* rolling (freshmen), rolling (transfers). *Notification:* continuous (freshmen).

Admissions Contact Ms. Mindy Steinberg, Director of Admissions, Ivy Tech State College-Southcentral, 8204 Highway 311, Sellersburg, IN 47172-1897. *Phone:* 812-246-3301. *Toll-free phone:* 800-321-9021. *Fax:* 812-246-9905. *E-mail:* msteinbe@ivytech.edu.

IVY TECH STATE COLLEGE-SOUTHEAST
Madison, Indiana

- **State-supported** 2-year, founded 1963, part of Ivy Tech State College System
- **Calendar** semesters
- **Degree** certificates and associate
- **Small-town** 5-acre campus with easy access to Louisville
- **Endowment** $11.2 million
- **Coed,** 1,711 undergraduate students, 37% full-time, 72% women, 28% men

Undergraduates 629 full-time, 1,082 part-time. 2% are from out of state, 1% African American, 0.4% Asian American or Pacific Islander, 0.3% Hispanic American, 0.3% Native American, 0.1% international, 2% transferred in.

Freshmen *Admission:* 357 applied, 357 admitted, 223 enrolled.

Faculty *Total:* 136, 25% full-time.

Majors Accounting technology and bookkeeping; business administration and management; child care and support services management; computer and information sciences; electrical, electronic and communications engineering technology; executive assistant/executive secretary; industrial technology; legal assistant/paralegal; liberal arts and sciences/liberal studies; medical/clinical assistant; nursing (registered nurse training); psychiatric/mental health services technology.

Academic Programs *Special study options:* academic remediation for entering students, advanced placement credit, distance learning, internships, part-time degree program, services for LD students, summer session for credit.

Library 9,027 titles, 14,299 serial subscriptions, 1,341 audiovisual materials, an OPAC, a Web page.

Computers on Campus 123 computers available on campus for general student use. A campuswide network can be accessed. Internet access, online (class) registration, at least one staffed computer lab available.

Student Life *Housing:* college housing not available. *Activities and Organizations:* Student Government, Phi Theta Kappa, LPN Club. *Campus security:* 24-hour emergency response devices.

Standardized Tests *Required:* ACT ASSET (for placement).

Costs (2004–05) *Tuition:* state resident $2409 full-time, $80 per credit part-time; nonresident $4871 full-time, $162 per credit part-time. Full-time tuition and fees vary according to course load and reciprocity agreements. Part-time tuition and fees vary according to course load and reciprocity agreements. *Required fees:* $60 full-time, $30 per term part-time. *Payment plan:* installment. *Waivers:* senior citizens and employees or children of employees.

Financial Aid Of all full-time matriculated undergraduates who enrolled in 2003, 26 Federal Work-Study jobs (averaging $1696).

Applying *Required:* high school transcript. *Required for some:* interview. *Application deadline:* rolling (freshmen), rolling (transfers). *Notification:* continuous (freshmen).

Admissions Contact Ms. Cindy Hutcherson, Assistant Director of Admission/Career Counselor, Ivy Tech State College-Southeast, 590 Ivy Tech Drive, Madison, IN 47250-1881. *Phone:* 812-265-2580. *Toll-free phone:* 800-403-2190. *Fax:* 812-265-4028. *E-mail:* chutcher@ivytech.edu.

IVY TECH STATE COLLEGE-SOUTHWEST
Evansville, Indiana

- **State-supported** 2-year, founded 1963, part of Ivy Tech State College System
- **Calendar** semesters
- **Degree** certificates and associate
- **Suburban** 15-acre campus
- **Endowment** $14.3 million
- **Coed,** 4,378 undergraduate students, 34% full-time, 53% women, 47% men

Undergraduates 1,498 full-time, 2,880 part-time. 2% are from out of state, 7% African American, 0.3% Asian American or Pacific Islander, 0.7% Hispanic American, 0.3% Native American, 0.1% international, 4% transferred in.

Freshmen *Admission:* 888 applied, 888 admitted, 455 enrolled.

Faculty *Total:* 285, 24% full-time.

Majors Accounting technology and bookkeeping; automobile/automotive mechanics technology; boilermaking; building/property maintenance and management; business administration and management; cabinetmaking and millwork; carpentry; child care and support services management; computer and information sciences; construction/heavy equipment/earthmoving equipment operation; criminal justice/safety; design and visual communications; electrical, electronic and communications engineering technology; electrician; emergency medical technology (EMT paramedic); executive assistant/executive secretary; graphic design; heating, air conditioning, ventilation and refrigeration maintenance technology; industrial technology; interior design; ironworking; legal assistant/paralegal; liberal arts and sciences/liberal studies; machine tool technology; masonry; mechanics and repair; medical/clinical assistant; nursing (registered nurse training); painting and wall covering; pipefitting and sprinkler fitting; psychiatric/mental health services technology; robotics technology; sheet metal technology; surgical technology; tool and die technology.

Academic Programs *Special study options:* academic remediation for entering students, advanced placement credit, cooperative education, distance learning, independent study, internships, part-time degree program, services for LD students, summer session for credit.

Library 7,082 titles, 107 serial subscriptions, 1,755 audiovisual materials, an OPAC, a Web page.

Computers on Campus 362 computers available on campus for general student use. Internet access, online (class) registration, at least one staffed computer lab available.

Student Life *Housing:* college housing not available. *Activities and Organizations:* Student Government, Phi Theta Kappa, LPN Club, National Association of Industrial Technology, Design Club. *Campus security:* late-night transport/escort service.

Standardized Tests *Required:* ACT ASSET (for placement).

Costs (2004–05) *Tuition:* state resident $2409 full-time, $80 per credit part-time; nonresident $4871 full-time, $162 per credit part-time. Full-time tuition and fees vary according to course load and reciprocity agreements. Part-time tuition and fees vary according to course load and reciprocity agreements. *Required fees:* $60 full-time, $30 per term part-time. *Payment plan:* installment. *Waivers:* senior citizens and employees or children of employees.

Financial Aid Of all full-time matriculated undergraduates who enrolled in 2003, 65 Federal Work-Study jobs (averaging $2264).

Applying *Options:* early admission, deferred entrance. *Required:* high school transcript. *Required for some:* interview. *Application deadline:* rolling (freshmen), rolling (transfers). *Notification:* continuous (freshmen).

Admissions Contact Ms. Denise Johnson-Kincaid, Director of Admissions, Ivy Tech State College-Southwest, 3501 First Avenue, Evansville, IN 47710-3398. *Phone:* 812-429-1430. *Fax:* 812-429-1483. *E-mail:* ajohnson@ivytech.edu.

IVY TECH STATE COLLEGE-WABASH VALLEY
Terre Haute, Indiana

- **State-supported** 2-year, founded 1966, part of Ivy Tech State College System
- **Calendar** semesters
- **Degree** certificates and associate
- **Suburban** 55-acre campus with easy access to Indianapolis
- **Endowment** $14.3 million
- **Coed,** 4,684 undergraduate students, 41% full-time, 56% women, 44% men

Undergraduates 1,939 full-time, 2,745 part-time. 2% are from out of state, 3% African American, 0.2% Asian American or Pacific Islander, 0.5% Hispanic American, 0.6% Native American, 0.1% international, 3% transferred in.

Freshmen *Admission:* 1,117 applied, 1,117 admitted, 552 enrolled.

Faculty *Total:* 302, 24% full-time.

Majors Accounting technology and bookkeeping; airframe mechanics and aircraft maintenance technology; automobile/automotive mechanics technology; building/property maintenance and management; business administration and management; cabinetmaking and millwork; carpentry; child care and support services management; clinical/medical laboratory technology; computer and information sciences; construction/heavy equipment/earthmoving equipment operation; criminal justice/safety; design and visual communications; drafting and design technology; electrical, electronic and communications engineering technology; electrician; emergency medical technology (EMT paramedic); executive assistant/executive secretary; heating, air conditioning, ventilation and refrigeration maintenance technology; industrial technology; ironworking; legal assistant/paralegal; liberal arts and sciences/liberal studies; machine tool technology; masonry; mechanics and repair; medical/clinical assistant; medical radiologic technology; nursing (registered nurse training); occupational safety and health technology; painting and wall covering; pipefitting and sprinkler fitting; psychiatric/mental health services technology; robotics technology; sheet metal technology; surgical technology; tool and die technology.

Academic Programs *Special study options:* academic remediation for entering students, adult/continuing education programs, advanced placement credit, distance learning, internships, part-time degree program, services for LD students, summer session for credit.

Library 4,403 titles, 77 serial subscriptions, 406 audiovisual materials, an OPAC, a Web page.

Computers on Campus 305 computers available on campus for general student use. A campuswide network can be accessed. Internet access, online (class) registration, at least one staffed computer lab available.

Student Life *Housing:* college housing not available. *Activities and Organizations:* Student Government, Phi Theta Kappa, LPN Club, National Association of Industrial Technology. *Campus security:* 24-hour emergency response devices. *Student services:* personal/psychological counseling, women's center.

Athletics *Intramural sports:* basketball M/W, volleyball M/W.

Standardized Tests *Required:* ACT ASSET (for placement).

Costs (2004–05) *Comprehensive fee:* $314 includes mandatory fees ($60). Full-time tuition and fees vary according to course load and reciprocity agreements. Part-time tuition and fees vary according to course load and reciprocity agreements. *Required fees:* $30 per term part-time. *Payment plan:* installment. *Waivers:* senior citizens and employees or children of employees.

Financial Aid Of all full-time matriculated undergraduates who enrolled in 2003, 51 Federal Work-Study jobs (averaging $2110). 1 state and other part-time job (averaging $2963).

Applying *Options:* early admission, deferred entrance. *Required:* high school transcript. *Required for some:* interview. *Application deadline:* rolling (freshmen), rolling (transfers). *Notification:* continuous (freshmen).

Admissions Contact Mr. Michael Fisher, Director of Admissions, Ivy Tech State College-Wabash Valley, 7999 U.S. Highway 41 South, Terre Haute, IN 47802-4898. *Phone:* 812-298-2300. *Toll-free phone:* 800-377-4882. *Fax:* 812-299-5723. *E-mail:* mfisher@ivytech.edu.

IVY TECH STATE COLLEGE-WHITEWATER
Richmond, Indiana

- **State-supported** 2-year, founded 1963, part of Ivy Tech State College System
- **Calendar** semesters
- **Degree** certificates and associate
- **Small-town** 23-acre campus with easy access to Indianapolis
- **Endowment** $14.3 million
- **Coed,** 1,605 undergraduate students, 29% full-time, 74% women, 26% men

Undergraduates 468 full-time, 1,137 part-time. 4% are from out of state, 4% African American, 0.3% Asian American or Pacific Islander, 0.8% Hispanic American, 0.4% Native American, 2% transferred in.

Freshmen *Admission:* 280 applied, 280 admitted, 151 enrolled.

Ivy Tech State College-Whitewater (continued)

Faculty *Total:* 157, 17% full-time.

Majors Accounting technology and bookkeeping; automobile/automotive mechanics technology; building/property maintenance and management; business administration and management; cabinetmaking and millwork; child care and support services management; computer and information sciences; construction trades; electrical, electronic and communications engineering technology; electrician; executive assistant/executive secretary; heating, air conditioning, ventilation and refrigeration maintenance technology; industrial technology; legal assistant/paralegal; liberal arts and sciences/liberal studies; machine tool technology; mechanics and repair; medical/clinical assistant; nursing (registered nurse training); pipefitting and sprinkler fitting; psychiatric/mental health services technology; robotics technology; tool and die technology.

Academic Programs *Special study options:* academic remediation for entering students, adult/continuing education programs, advanced placement credit, distance learning, independent study, internships, off-campus study, part-time degree program, services for LD students, summer session for credit.

Computers on Campus 169 computers available on campus for general student use. A campuswide network can be accessed. Internet access, online (class) registration, at least one staffed computer lab available.

Student Life *Housing:* college housing not available. *Activities and Organizations:* Student Government, Phi Theta Kappa, LPN Club, CATS 2000, Business Professionals of America. *Campus security:* 24-hour emergency response devices, late-night transport/escort service. *Student services:* personal/psychological counseling.

Athletics *Intramural sports:* softball M/W.

Standardized Tests *Required:* ACT ASSET (for placement).

Costs (2004–05) *Tuition:* state resident $2409 full-time, $80 per credit part-time; nonresident $4871 full-time, $162 per credit part-time. Full-time tuition and fees vary according to course load and reciprocity agreements. Part-time tuition and fees vary according to course load and reciprocity agreements. *Required fees:* $60 full-time, $30 per term part-time. *Payment plan:* installment. *Waivers:* senior citizens and employees or children of employees.

Financial Aid Of all full-time matriculated undergraduates who enrolled in 2003, 14 Federal Work-Study jobs (averaging $3106). 1 state and other part-time job (averaging $3380).

Applying *Options:* early admission. *Required:* high school transcript. *Required for some:* interview. *Application deadline:* rolling (freshmen), rolling (transfers). *Notification:* continuous (freshmen).

Admissions Contact Mr. Jeff Plasterer, Director of Admissions, Ivy Tech State College-Whitewater, 2325 Chester Boulevard, Richmond, IN 47374-1298. *Phone:* 765-966-2656 Ext. 320. *Toll-free phone:* 800-659-4562. *Fax:* 765-962-8741. *E-mail:* jplaster@ivytech.edu.

LINCOLN TECHNICAL INSTITUTE
Indianapolis, Indiana

Admissions Contact Ms. Cindy Ryan, Director of Admissions, Lincoln Technical Institute, 1201 Stadium Drive, Indianapolis, IN 46202-2194. *Phone:* 317-632-5553. *Toll-free phone:* 800-554-4465.

MID-AMERICA COLLEGE OF FUNERAL SERVICE
Jeffersonville, Indiana

Admissions Contact Mr. Richard Nelson, Dean of Students, Mid-America College of Funeral Service, 3111 Hamburg Pike, Jeffersonville, IN 47130-9630. *Phone:* 812-288-8878. *Toll-free phone:* 800-221-6158. *E-mail:* macfs@mindspring.com.

PROFESSIONAL CAREERS INSTITUTE
Indianapolis, Indiana

Admissions Contact Ms. Paulette M. Clay, Director of Admissions, Professional Careers Institute, 7302 Woodland Drive, Indianapolis, IN 46217. *Phone:* 317-299-6001 Ext. 320. *E-mail:* lilgeneral9@hotmail.com.

SAWYER COLLEGE
Hammond, Indiana

- **Proprietary** 2-year, founded 1962
- **Calendar** quarters
- **Degree** associate
- **Suburban** 3-acre campus
- **Coed**

Standardized Tests *Required:* Wonderlic aptitude test (for admission).

Admissions Contact Director, Sawyer College, 6040 Hohman Avenue, Hammond, IN 46320. *Phone:* 219-844-0100. *E-mail:* info@sawyercollege.com.

SAWYER COLLEGE
Merrillville, Indiana

Admissions Contact 3803 East Lincoln Highway, Merrillville, IN 46410. *E-mail:* info@sawyercollege.com.

VINCENNES UNIVERSITY
Vincennes, Indiana

- **State-supported** 2-year, founded 1801
- **Calendar** semesters
- **Degree** certificates and associate
- **Small-town** 100-acre campus
- **Endowment** $25.6 million
- **Coed**

Faculty *Student/faculty ratio:* 15:1.

Student Life *Campus security:* 24-hour emergency response devices and patrols, student patrols, late-night transport/escort service, controlled dormitory access, surveillance cameras.

Athletics Member NJCAA.

Standardized Tests *Required for some:* SAT or ACT (for admission). *Recommended:* SAT or ACT (for admission).

Costs (2004–05) *Tuition:* state resident $3048 full-time, $101 per credit hour part-time; nonresident $7609 full-time, $254 per credit hour part-time. Full-time tuition and fees vary according to course load. Part-time tuition and fees vary according to course load. *Required fees:* $350 full-time. *Room and board:* $5700. Room and board charges vary according to board plan and housing facility.

Financial Aid Of all full-time matriculated undergraduates who enrolled in 2003, 213 Federal Work-Study jobs (averaging $2400). *Financial aid deadline:* 3/10.

Applying *Options:* common application, electronic application, early admission, deferred entrance. *Application fee:* $20. *Required:* high school transcript. *Required for some:* interview.

Admissions Contact Mr. Chris M. Crews, Director of Admissions, Vincennes University, 1002 North First Street, Vincennes, IN 47591. *Phone:* 812-888-4313. *Toll-free phone:* 800-742-9198. *Fax:* 812-888-5707. *E-mail:* vuadmit@indian.vinu.edu.

VINCENNES UNIVERSITY JASPER CAMPUS
Jasper, Indiana

Admissions Contact Ms. LouAnn Gilbert, Director, Vincennes University Jasper Campus, Jasper, IN 47546. *Phone:* 812-482-3030. *Toll-free phone:* 800-809-VUJC. *Fax:* 812-481-5960. *E-mail:* lgilbert@indian.vinu.edu.

IOWA

AIB COLLEGE OF BUSINESS
Des Moines, Iowa

- **Independent** 2-year, founded 1921
- **Calendar** continuous
- **Degree** diplomas and associate
- **Urban** 20-acre campus
- **Coed**

Faculty *Student/faculty ratio:* 21:1.

Student Life *Campus security:* 24-hour emergency response devices, late-night transport/escort service, controlled dormitory access, video security.

Standardized Tests *Recommended:* ACT (for admission).

Costs (2004–05) *Tuition:* $8820 full-time, $245 per credit hour part-time. *Required fees:* $240 full-time, $240 per year part-time. *Room only:* $2775.

Financial Aid Of all full-time matriculated undergraduates who enrolled in 2003, 104 Federal Work-Study jobs (averaging $1135).

Applying *Options:* electronic application. *Application fee:* $25. *Required:* high school transcript. *Recommended:* interview.

Admissions Contact Ms. Gail Cline, Director of Admissions, AIB College of Business, Keith Fenton Administration Building, 2500 Fleur Drive, Des Moines,

IA 50321-1799. *Phone:* 515-244-4221 Ext. 5634. *Toll-free phone:* 800-444-1921. *Fax:* 515-244-6773. *E-mail:* clineg@aib.edu.

CLINTON COMMUNITY COLLEGE
Clinton, Iowa

- **State and locally supported** 2-year, founded 1946, part of Eastern Iowa Community College District
- **Calendar** semesters
- **Degree** certificates, diplomas, and associate
- **Small-town** 20-acre campus
- **Coed,** 1,298 undergraduate students, 45% full-time, 67% women, 33% men

Undergraduates 590 full-time, 708 part-time. Students come from 9 states and territories, 8% are from out of state, 3% African American, 0.5% Asian American or Pacific Islander, 2% Hispanic American, 0.8% Native American, 0.4% international.
Freshmen *Admission:* 215 applied, 215 admitted, 215 enrolled.
Faculty *Total:* 75, 41% full-time.
Majors Administrative assistant and secretarial science; architectural drafting and CAD/CADD; business administration and management; computer/information technology services administration related; electrical, electronic and communications engineering technology; emergency medical technology (EMT paramedic); environmental engineering technology; graphic and printing equipment operation/production; liberal arts and sciences/liberal studies; machine tool technology; nursing (licensed practical/vocational nurse training); nursing (registered nurse training); occupational safety and health technology; pharmacy technician.
Academic Programs *Special study options:* academic remediation for entering students, adult/continuing education programs, advanced placement credit, cooperative education, distance learning, double majors, English as a second language, independent study, internships, part-time degree program, services for LD students, study abroad, summer session for credit.
Library Clinton Community College Library with 18,701 titles, 155 serial subscriptions, an OPAC.
Computers on Campus 37 computers available on campus for general student use. A campuswide network can be accessed from off campus. Internet access, at least one staffed computer lab available.
Student Life *Housing:* college housing not available. *Activities and Organizations:* drama/theater group. *Student services:* personal/psychological counseling.
Athletics Member NJCAA. *Intercollegiate sports:* basketball M(s), cheerleading M/W, soccer M/W, softball W(s), volleyball W(s). *Intramural sports:* basketball M, bowling M/W, football M/W, racquetball M/W, skiing (downhill) M/W, tennis M/W, volleyball M/W, weight lifting M/W.
Standardized Tests *Required:* DTMS and DTLS or ACT (for placement).
Costs (2004–05) *Tuition:* state resident $2720 full-time, $85 per semester hour part-time; nonresident $4080 full-time, $128 per semester hour part-time. *Payment plan:* installment. *Waivers:* employees or children of employees.
Financial Aid Of all full-time matriculated undergraduates who enrolled in 2003, 54 Federal Work-Study jobs (averaging $3000).
Applying *Options:* early admission, deferred entrance. *Required:* high school transcript. *Application deadline:* rolling (freshmen), rolling (transfers). *Notification:* continuous (freshmen).
Admissions Contact Mr. Neil Mandsager, Executive Director of Enrollment Management and Marketing, Clinton Community College, 1000 Lincoln Boulevard, Clinton, IA 52732-6299. *Phone:* 563-244-7007.

DES MOINES AREA COMMUNITY COLLEGE
Ankeny, Iowa

- **State and locally supported** 2-year, founded 1966, part of Iowa Area Community Colleges System
- **Calendar** semesters
- **Degrees** certificates, diplomas, and associate (profile also includes information from the Boone, Carroll, Des Moines, and Newton campuses)
- **Small-town** 362-acre campus
- **Endowment** $1.8 million
- **Coed,** 13,719 undergraduate students, 44% full-time, 56% women, 44% men

Undergraduates 6,002 full-time, 7,717 part-time. Students come from 31 states and territories, 53 other countries, 1% are from out of state, 4% African American, 3% Asian American or Pacific Islander, 2% Hispanic American, 0.3% Native American, 2% international, 3% transferred in.
Freshmen *Admission:* 4,174 enrolled. *Test scores:* ACT scores over 18: 76%; ACT scores over 24: 17%; ACT scores over 30: 1%.
Faculty *Total:* 272, 98% full-time. *Student/faculty ratio:* 50:1.

Majors Accounting; administrative assistant and secretarial science; agricultural business and management; artificial intelligence and robotics; automobile/automotive mechanics technology; biology/biotechnology laboratory technician; business administration and management; carpentry; child development; civil engineering technology; clinical/medical laboratory technology; commercial and advertising art; computer engineering technology; computer programming; computer programming (specific applications); consumer merchandising/retailing management; corrections; criminal justice/law enforcement administration; criminal justice/police science; culinary arts; data processing and data processing technology; dental hygiene; drafting and design technology; education; electrical, electronic and communications engineering technology; fashion merchandising; fire science; graphic and printing equipment operation/production; health/health care administration; heating, air conditioning, ventilation and refrigeration maintenance technology; heavy equipment maintenance technology; horticultural science; hospitality administration; hotel/motel administration; human services; legal administrative assistant/secretary; legal assistant/paralegal; liberal arts and sciences/liberal studies; machine tool technology; marketing/marketing management; medical administrative assistant and medical secretary; medical/clinical assistant; nursing (licensed practical/vocational nurse training); nursing (registered nurse training); quality control technology; respiratory care therapy; safety/security technology; social work; special products marketing; teacher assistant/aide; telecommunications; welding technology.
Academic Programs *Special study options:* academic remediation for entering students, adult/continuing education programs, advanced placement credit, cooperative education, distance learning, English as a second language, honors programs, off-campus study, part-time degree program, services for LD students, student-designed majors, summer session for credit.
Library DMACC District Library plus 4 others with 62,986 titles, 3,784 serial subscriptions, 7,224 audiovisual materials, an OPAC, a Web page.
Computers on Campus 700 computers available on campus for general student use. A campuswide network can be accessed from off campus. Internet access, online (class) registration, at least one staffed computer lab available. Computer purchase or lease plan available.
Student Life *Housing:* college housing not available. *Activities and Organizations:* drama/theater group, student-run newspaper, choral group, Agri-Business Club, Horticulture Club, Hospitality Arts Club, Iowa Delta Epsilon Chi, Dental Hygienist Club. *Campus security:* 24-hour emergency response devices and patrols, late-night transport/escort service. *Student services:* health clinic, personal/psychological counseling.
Athletics Member NJCAA. *Intercollegiate sports:* basketball M(s)/W(s), golf M/W, softball W. *Intramural sports:* badminton M/W, basketball M/W, football M/W, golf M/W, soccer M/W, volleyball M/W.
Standardized Tests *Required:* ACT COMPASS (for placement). *Recommended:* ACT (for placement).
Costs (2005–06) *Tuition:* state resident $2910 full-time, $97 per credit hour part-time; nonresident $5820 full-time, $194 per credit hour part-time. Full-time tuition and fees vary according to course load. Part-time tuition and fees vary according to course load. *Payment plan:* installment. *Waivers:* senior citizens and employees or children of employees.
Financial Aid Of all full-time matriculated undergraduates who enrolled in 2003, 377 Federal Work-Study jobs (averaging $1055).
Applying *Options:* electronic application, early admission, deferred entrance. *Required for some:* high school transcript, interview. *Application deadline:* rolling (freshmen), rolling (transfers).
Admissions Contact Mr. Keith Knowles, Director of Admissions and Assessment, Des Moines Area Community College, Building 1, 2006 South Ankeny Boulevard, Ankeny, IA 50021. *Phone:* 515-964-6216. *Toll-free phone:* 800-362-2127.

ELLSWORTH COMMUNITY COLLEGE
Iowa Falls, Iowa

- **State and locally supported** 2-year, founded 1890, part of Iowa Valley Community College District System
- **Calendar** semesters
- **Degree** diplomas and associate
- **Small-town** 10-acre campus
- **Endowment** $2.3 million
- **Coed,** 930 undergraduate students, 67% full-time, 55% women, 45% men

Undergraduates 627 full-time, 303 part-time. Students come from 18 states and territories, 4 other countries, 9% are from out of state, 8% African American, 0.3% Asian American or Pacific Islander, 4% Hispanic American, 2% international, 38% live on campus.
Freshmen *Admission:* 610 applied, 570 admitted. *Average high school GPA:* 2.55. *Test scores:* ACT scores over 18: 66%; ACT scores over 24: 15%; ACT scores over 30: 2%.
Faculty *Total:* 63, 52% full-time, 3% with terminal degrees. *Student/faculty ratio:* 17:1.
Majors Accounting; administrative assistant and secretarial science; agricultural business and management; art; art teacher education; biological and

Ellsworth Community College (continued)

physical sciences; biology/biological sciences; biology/biotechnology laboratory technician; business administration and management; child development; clinical laboratory science/medical technology; computer and information sciences related; computer systems networking and telecommunications; consumer merchandising/retailing management; corrections; criminal justice/law enforcement administration; data entry/microcomputer applications; data processing and data processing technology; developmental and child psychology; economics; education; environmental engineering technology; equestrian studies; fashion merchandising; history; human services; interior design; kindergarten/preschool education; legal administrative assistant/secretary; liberal arts and sciences/liberal studies; marketing/marketing management; mathematics; medical administrative assistant and medical secretary; medical laboratory technology; natural resources/conservation; nursing (registered nurse training); physical education teaching and coaching; physical sciences; political science and government; pre-engineering; psychology; retailing; social work; sociology; teacher assistant/aide; trade and industrial teacher education; wildlife biology.

Academic Programs *Special study options:* academic remediation for entering students, adult/continuing education programs, advanced placement credit, cooperative education, distance learning, honors programs, internships, part-time degree program, services for LD students, student-designed majors, summer session for credit.

Library Osgood Learning Resource Center with 25,500 titles, 300 serial subscriptions.

Computers on Campus 80 computers available on campus for general student use. A campuswide network can be accessed from off campus. Internet access, at least one staffed computer lab available.

Student Life *Housing:* on-campus residence required for freshman year. *Options:* men-only, women-only, disabled students. *Activities and Organizations:* drama/theater group, student-run newspaper, choral group, Agriculture-Science Club, Biotechnology Club, International Club, Criminal Justice Club, Rodeo Club. *Campus security:* 24-hour emergency response devices and patrols. *Student services:* personal/psychological counseling.

Athletics Member NJCAA. *Intercollegiate sports:* baseball M(s), basketball M(s)/W(s), football M(s), golf M/W, softball W(s), volleyball W(s), wrestling M(s). *Intramural sports:* baseball M, basketball M/W, bowling M/W, equestrian sports M/W, football M/W, racquetball M/W, rugby M, softball M/W, swimming and diving M/W, volleyball M/W, water polo M/W, weight lifting M/W.

Standardized Tests *Required for some:* ACT (for placement), COMPASS. *Recommended:* ACT (for placement).

Costs (2004–05) *Tuition:* state resident $2280 full-time, $95 per hour part-time; nonresident $2832 full-time, $118 per hour part-time. *Required fees:* $540 full-time, $7 per hour part-time.

Financial Aid Of all full-time matriculated undergraduates who enrolled in 2003, 95 Federal Work-Study jobs (averaging $1200). 40 state and other part-time jobs (averaging $1200).

Applying *Options:* electronic application, early admission, deferred entrance. *Required:* high school transcript. *Application deadlines:* rolling (freshmen), 8/1 (out-of-state freshmen), rolling (transfers). *Notification:* continuous (freshmen).

Admissions Contact Mrs. Nancy Walters, Registrar, Ellsworth Community College, 1100 College Avenue, Iowa Falls, IA 50126-1199. *Phone:* 641-648-4611. *Toll-free phone:* 800-ECC-9235.

HAMILTON COLLEGE
Cedar Rapids, Iowa

Admissions Contact Mr. Brad Knudson, Director of Admissions, Hamilton College, 1924 D Street SW, Cedar Rapids, IA 52404. *Phone:* 319-363-0481. *Toll-free phone:* 800-728-0481. *Fax:* 319-363-3812.

HAWKEYE COMMUNITY COLLEGE
Waterloo, Iowa

- **State and locally supported** 2-year, founded 1966
- **Calendar** semesters
- **Degree** certificates, diplomas, and associate
- **Rural** 320-acre campus
- **Coed,** 5,374 undergraduate students, 62% full-time, 58% women, 42% men

Undergraduates 3,345 full-time, 2,029 part-time. Students come from 18 states and territories, 10 other countries, 1% are from out of state, 8% African American, 1% Asian American or Pacific Islander, 1% Hispanic American, 0.4% Native American, 0.6% international, 10% transferred in.

Freshmen *Admission:* 1,843 enrolled. *Average high school GPA:* 2.5. *Test scores:* ACT scores over 18: 46%; ACT scores over 24: 10%; ACT scores over 30: 1%.

Faculty *Total:* 290, 40% full-time, 6% with terminal degrees. *Student/faculty ratio:* 23:1.

Majors Accounting; administrative assistant and secretarial science; agricultural business and management; agricultural mechanization; agronomy and crop

science; airframe mechanics and aircraft maintenance technology; animal sciences; architectural engineering technology; autobody/collision and repair technology; automobile/automotive mechanics technology; avionics maintenance technology; biology/biological sciences; business administration and management; business/commerce; child development; civil engineering technology; clinical/medical laboratory technology; commercial and advertising art; computer engineering technology; computer/information technology services administration related; computer systems networking and telecommunications; computer/technical support; corrections; criminal justice/law enforcement administration; criminal justice/police science; data entry/microcomputer applications related; dental hygiene; drafting and design technology; education; emergency medical technology (EMT paramedic); engineering technology; farm and ranch management; fire science; food science; heating, air conditioning, ventilation and refrigeration maintenance technology; heavy equipment maintenance technology; horticultural science; information technology; interdisciplinary studies; interior design; liberal arts and sciences/liberal studies; machine tool technology; marketing/marketing management; mechanical design technology; mechanical engineering/mechanical technology; medical administrative assistant and medical secretary; natural resources management and policy; nursing (licensed practical/vocational nurse training); nursing (registered nurse training); ornamental horticulture; parks, recreation and leisure facilities management; photography; respiratory care therapy; survey technology; system administration; tool and die technology; web/multimedia management and webmaster; web page, digital/multimedia and information resources design; welding technology; word processing.

Academic Programs *Special study options:* academic remediation for entering students, adult/continuing education programs, advanced placement credit, cooperative education, distance learning, English as a second language, external degree program, part-time degree program, services for LD students, summer session for credit. *ROTC:* Army (c).

Library Hawkeye Community College Library with 37,155 titles, 482 serial subscriptions, 2,078 audiovisual materials, an OPAC, a Web page.

Computers on Campus 300 computers available on campus for general student use. A campuswide network can be accessed. Internet access, online (class) registration, at least one staffed computer lab available.

Student Life *Housing:* college housing not available. *Options:* Campus housing is provided by a third party. *Activities and Organizations:* Student Senate, Phi Theta Kappa, Environmental Conservation Club/Ag Club, Law Enforcement/Criminal Justice, Fashion Merchandising. *Campus security:* 24-hour patrols. *Student services:* personal/psychological counseling, women's center.

Athletics *Intramural sports:* basketball M/W, bowling M/W, golf M/W, softball M/W, volleyball M/W.

Standardized Tests *Required:* ACT ASSET, ACT COMPASS (for placement). *Required for some:* SAT or ACT (for placement). *Recommended:* SAT or ACT (for placement).

Costs (2004–05) *Tuition:* state resident $2790 full-time, $93 per credit part-time; nonresident $5580 full-time, $186 per credit part-time. Full-time tuition and fees vary according to course load. Part-time tuition and fees vary according to course load. *Required fees:* $300 full-time, $10 per credit part-time. *Payment plan:* installment. *Waivers:* employees or children of employees.

Applying *Options:* electronic application, deferred entrance. *Required:* high school transcript. *Application deadline:* rolling (freshmen), rolling (transfers). *Notification:* continuous (freshmen).

Admissions Contact Holly Grimm, Admissions Coordinator, Hawkeye Community College, PO Box 8015, Waterloo, IA 50704-8015. *Phone:* 319-296-4277. *Toll-free phone:* 800-670-4769. *Fax:* 319-296-2505. *E-mail:* admission@hawkeyecollege.edu.

INDIAN HILLS COMMUNITY COLLEGE
Ottumwa, Iowa

- **State and locally supported** 2-year, founded 1966, part of Iowa Area Community Colleges System
- **Calendar** quarters
- **Degree** certificates, diplomas, and associate
- **Small-town** 400-acre campus
- **Coed,** 2,867 undergraduate students, 71% full-time, 59% women, 41% men

Undergraduates 2,046 full-time, 821 part-time. Students come from 16 states and territories, 7% are from out of state, 0.4% transferred in, 15% live on campus.

Freshmen *Admission:* 2,477 applied, 2,477 admitted, 1,069 enrolled.

Faculty *Total:* 148, 86% full-time.

Majors Agricultural mechanization; airline pilot and flight crew; artificial intelligence and robotics; automobile/automotive mechanics technology; avionics maintenance technology; biology/biotechnology laboratory technician; business administration and management; child development; computer engineering technology; computer programming; criminal justice/law enforcement administration; drafting and design technology; electrical, electronic and communications engineering technology; food services technology; health/health care administration; health information/medical records administration; heavy equipment maintenance technology; horticultural science; industrial radiologic technology; laser and optical technology; liberal arts and sciences/liberal studies; machine tool technology; nursing (licensed practical/vocational nurse training); nursing (registered nurse training); physical therapy.

Academic Programs *Special study options:* academic remediation for entering students, adult/continuing education programs, cooperative education, English as a second language, honors programs, internships, part-time degree program, services for LD students, student-designed majors, summer session for credit.

Library Indian Hills Community College Library plus 2 others with 53,073 titles, 350 serial subscriptions, an OPAC, a Web page.

Computers on Campus 150 computers available on campus for general student use. A campuswide network can be accessed. At least one staffed computer lab available.

Student Life *Housing Options:* coed. Campus housing is university owned. *Activities and Organizations:* drama/theater group, Student Senate, Warriors Club. *Campus security:* 24-hour emergency response devices and patrols. *Student services:* personal/psychological counseling, women's center.

Athletics Member NJCAA. *Intercollegiate sports:* baseball M(s), basketball M(s), golf M(s), softball W(s), volleyball W(s). *Intramural sports:* basketball M/W, fencing M/W, football M/W, racquetball M/W, riflery M/W, tennis M/W, volleyball M/W.

Standardized Tests *Required:* ACT ASSET (for placement). *Required for some:* ACT (for placement).

Costs (2004–05) *Tuition:* state resident $2730 full-time, $91 per credit hour part-time; nonresident $4110 full-time, $137 per credit hour part-time. *Required fees:* $60 full-time.

Financial Aid Of all full-time matriculated undergraduates who enrolled in 2003, 123 Federal Work-Study jobs (averaging $742). 62 state and other part-time jobs (averaging $823).

Applying *Options:* common application, early admission. *Required for some:* high school transcript. *Application deadline:* rolling (freshmen), rolling (transfers).

Admissions Contact Mrs. Jane Sapp, Admissions Officer, Indian Hills Community College, 525 Grandview Avenue, Building #1, Ottumwa, IA 52501-1398. *Phone:* 641-683-5155. *Toll-free phone:* 800-726-2585.

IOWA CENTRAL COMMUNITY COLLEGE
Fort Dodge, Iowa

- **State and locally supported** 2-year, founded 1966, part of Iowa Department of Education Division of Community Colleges
- **Calendar** semesters
- **Degree** certificates, diplomas, and associate
- **Small-town** 110-acre campus
- **Coed,** 4,567 undergraduate students

Undergraduates Students come from 25 states and territories, 18 other countries, 5% are from out of state, 22% live on campus.

Faculty *Total:* 280, 26% full-time. *Student/faculty ratio:* 18:1.

Majors Accounting; administrative assistant and secretarial science; airline pilot and flight crew; automobile/automotive mechanics technology; aviation/airway management; biological and physical sciences; broadcast journalism; business administration and management; business teacher education; carpentry; clinical/medical laboratory technology; community organization and advocacy; computer engineering technology; criminal justice/police science; data processing and data processing technology; drafting and design technology; education; electrical, electronic and communications engineering technology; hospitality and recreation marketing; industrial radiologic technology; journalism; liberal arts and sciences/liberal studies; machine tool technology; mass communication/media; medical/clinical assistant; nursing (licensed practical/vocational nurse training); nursing (registered nurse training); occupational therapy; physical therapy; radio and television; science teacher education; social work; sociology; telecommunications; welding technology.

Academic Programs *Special study options:* academic remediation for entering students, adult/continuing education programs, advanced placement credit, cooperative education, distance learning, independent study, internships, part-time degree program, services for LD students, study abroad, summer session for credit.

Library Iowa Central Community College Library plus 1 other with 55,000 titles, 350 serial subscriptions, an OPAC, a Web page.

Computers on Campus 510 computers available on campus for general student use. A campuswide network can be accessed from off campus. Internet access, at least one staffed computer lab available.

Student Life *Activities and Organizations:* drama/theater group, student-run newspaper, radio station, choral group, Student Senate, HOSA, BPA, Phi Beta Lambda. *Campus security:* 24-hour emergency response devices and patrols, student patrols, late-night transport/escort service, controlled dormitory access. *Student services:* health clinic, personal/psychological counseling.

Athletics Member NJCAA. *Intercollegiate sports:* baseball M(s), basketball M(s)/W(s), cross-country running M/W, football M(s), golf M(s)/W(s), soccer M(s)/W(s), softball W(s), volleyball W(s), wrestling M(s). *Intramural sports:*

basketball M/W, football M, golf M/W, softball W, table tennis M/W, tennis M/W, volleyball M/W, weight lifting M, wrestling M.

Standardized Tests *Required:* SAT or ACT (for placement), ACT ASSET or ACT COMPASS (for placement).

Costs (2005–06) *Tuition:* state resident $2790 full-time, $93 per credit part-time; nonresident $4135 full-time, $140 per credit part-time. *Required fees:* $300 full-time, $10 per credit part-time.

Applying *Options:* early admission, deferred entrance. *Required:* high school transcript. *Application deadline:* rolling (freshmen), rolling (transfers).

Admissions Contact Mr. Brian K. Dioguardi, Director of Admissions, Iowa Central Community College, 330 Avenue M, Ft. Dodge, IA 50501. *Phone:* 515-576-0099 Ext. 2471. *Toll-free phone:* 800-362-2793. *Fax:* 515-576-7724. *E-mail:* admis@duke.iccc.cc.ia.us.

IOWA LAKES COMMUNITY COLLEGE
Estherville, Iowa

- **State and locally supported** 2-year, founded 1967, part of Iowa Area Community Colleges System
- **Calendar** semesters
- **Degree** certificates, diplomas, and associate
- **Small-town** 20-acre campus
- **Endowment** $63,000
- **Coed,** 2,993 undergraduate students, 46% full-time, 55% women, 45% men

Undergraduates 1,371 full-time, 1,622 part-time. Students come from 12 states and territories, 2 other countries, 13% are from out of state, 0.5% African American, 0.3% Asian American or Pacific Islander, 0.7% Hispanic American, 0.3% Native American, 0.4% international, 4% transferred in, 24% live on campus.

Freshmen *Admission:* 1,897 applied, 1,541 admitted, 917 enrolled. *Test scores:* ACT scores over 18: 67%; ACT scores over 24: 12%; ACT scores over 30: 1%.

Faculty *Total:* 153, 53% full-time. *Student/faculty ratio:* 19:1.

Majors Accounting; accounting technology and bookkeeping; administrative assistant and secretarial science; agribusiness; agricultural business and management; agricultural business and management related; agricultural business technology; agricultural economics; agricultural/farm supplies retailing and wholesaling; agricultural mechanics and equipment technology; agricultural mechanization; agricultural power machinery operation; agricultural production; agricultural production related; agricultural teacher education; agriculture; agronomy and crop science; airline pilot and flight crew; animal/livestock husbandry and production; animal sciences; applied art; art; art history, criticism and conservation; art teacher education; astronomy; athletic training; autobody/collision and repair technology; automobile/automotive mechanics technology; aviation/airway management; behavioral sciences; biological and physical sciences; biology/biological sciences; botany/plant biology; broadcast journalism; business administration and management; business automation/technology/data entry; business machine repair; business teacher education; carpentry; ceramic arts and ceramics; chemistry; child care provision; child development; chiropractic assistant; commercial and advertising art; communication and journalism related; computer and information sciences related; computer graphics; computer/information technology services administration related; computer programming; computer science; computer software technology; computer systems networking and telecommunications; construction engineering technology; construction management; construction trades; consumer merchandising/retailing management; cooking and related culinary arts; corrections; criminal justice/law enforcement administration; criminal justice/police science; crop production; culinary arts related; data entry/microcomputer applications; data processing and data processing technology; desktop publishing and digital imaging design; developmental and child psychology; drafting and design technology; drawing; early childhood education; ecology; economics; education; elementary education; emergency care attendant (EMT ambulance); emergency medical technology (EMT paramedic); energy management and systems technology; engineering; English; environmental design/architecture; environmental education; environmental engineering technology; environmental studies; family and consumer sciences/human sciences; farm and ranch management; fashion merchandising; finance; fine/studio arts; fish/game management; fishing and fisheries sciences and management; flight instruction; food preparation; foods and nutrition related; food service and dining room management; foreign languages and literatures; forestry; general studies; geology/earth science; graphic and printing equipment operation/production; graphic communications; graphic design; health and physical education; health/health care administration; history; hospitality administration; hotel/motel administration; humanities; human resources management and services related; hydrology and water resources science; information technology; institutional food workers; jazz/jazz studies; journalism; kindergarten/preschool education; landscaping and groundskeeping; legal administrative assistant/secretary; legal assistant/paralegal; legal studies; liberal arts and sciences and humanities related; liberal arts and sciences/liberal studies; literature; marine maintenance and ship repair technology; marketing/marketing management; massage therapy; mass communication/media; mathematics; medical administrative assistant and medical secretary; medical/clinical assistant; medical labo-

Iowa Lakes Community College (continued)

ratory technology; medical office assistant; medical office computer specialist; medical office reception; medical transcription; merchandising, sales, and marketing operations related (general); motorcycle maintenance and repair technology; music; music teacher education; natural resources/conservation; natural sciences; nursing (registered nurse training); office management; office occupations and clerical services; parks, recreation and leisure; pharmacy; philosophy; photography; physical education teaching and coaching; physical sciences; piano and organ; political science and government; pre-dentistry studies; pre-engineering; pre-law studies; pre-medical studies; pre-nursing studies; pre-pharmacy studies; pre-veterinary studies; printing press operation; psychology; radio and television; radio and television broadcasting technology; real estate; receptionist; rehabilitation therapy; restaurant, culinary, and catering management; restaurant/food services management; retailing; sales, distribution and marketing; science teacher education; selling skills and sales; small business administration; small engine mechanics and repair technology; social sciences; social work; sociology; soil science and agronomy; Spanish; speech and rhetoric; sport and fitness administration; surgical technology; system administration; system, networking, and LAN/WAN management; technology/industrial arts teacher education; tourism and travel services management; tourism and travel services marketing; tourism promotion; trade and industrial teacher education; turf and turfgrass management; voice and opera; water, wetlands, and marine resources management; welding technology; wildlife and wildlands science and management; wildlife biology; wind/percussion instruments; word processing.

Academic Programs *Special study options:* academic remediation for entering students, accelerated degree program, adult/continuing education programs, advanced placement credit, cooperative education, distance learning, honors programs, independent study, internships, part-time degree program, services for LD students, study abroad, summer session for credit.

Library Iowa Lakes Community College Library plus 2 others with 36,881 titles, 353 serial subscriptions, 1,133 audiovisual materials, an OPAC.

Computers on Campus 1000 computers available on campus for general student use. A campuswide network can be accessed. Internet access, online (class) registration, at least one staffed computer lab available.

Student Life *Housing Options:* coed. Campus housing is university owned. Freshman campus housing is guaranteed. *Activities and Organizations:* drama/theater group, student-run newspaper, radio and television station, choral group, Criminal Justice Club, Ecology Club, Nursing Club, Student Senate, BPA. *Campus security:* 24-hour emergency response devices, student patrols. *Student services:* personal/psychological counseling, women's center.

Athletics Member NJCAA. *Intercollegiate sports:* baseball M(s), basketball M(s)/W(s), cross-country running M/W, golf M(s)/W(s), softball W(s), volleyball W(s), weight lifting M/W. *Intramural sports:* basketball M/W, football M/W, golf M/W, racquetball M/W, skiing (cross-country) M/W, skiing (downhill) M/W, soccer M/W, softball M/W, swimming and diving M/W, table tennis M/W, tennis M/W, volleyball M/W, weight lifting M/W, wrestling M.

Standardized Tests *Required for some:* ACT (for placement), ACT ASSET, ACT COMPASS.

Costs (2004–05) *Tuition:* state resident $3072 full-time, $96 per credit hour part-time; nonresident $3136 full-time, $98 per credit hour part-time. Full-time tuition and fees vary according to course load and program. Part-time tuition and fees vary according to course load and program. *Required fees:* $452 full-time, $14 per credit hour part-time. *Room and board:* $3920. *Payment plan:* installment. *Waivers:* employees or children of employees.

Financial Aid Of all full-time matriculated undergraduates who enrolled in 2003, 210 Federal Work-Study jobs (averaging $800).

Applying *Options:* deferred entrance. *Required:* high school transcript. *Required for some:* letters of recommendation, interview. *Application deadline:* rolling (freshmen), rolling (transfers).

Admissions Contact Ms. Anne Stansbury, Assistant Director Admissions, Iowa Lakes Community College, 3200 College Drive, Emmetsburg, IA 50536. *Phone:* 712-852-5254. *Toll-free phone:* 800-521-5054. *Fax:* 712-362-3969. *E-mail:* info@iowalakes.edu.

IOWA WESTERN COMMUNITY COLLEGE
Council Bluffs, Iowa

- **District-supported** 2-year, founded 1966, part of Iowa Department of Education Division of Community Colleges
- **Calendar** semesters
- **Degree** certificates, diplomas, and associate
- **Suburban** 282-acre campus with easy access to Omaha
- **Coed,** 4,299 undergraduate students, 50% full-time, 56% women, 44% men

Undergraduates 2,152 full-time, 2,147 part-time. Students come from 27 states and territories, 10 other countries, 2% African American, 1% Asian American or Pacific Islander, 1% Hispanic American, 0.6% Native American, 2% international, 19% live on campus.

Faculty *Total:* 222, 51% full-time.

Majors Accounting; administrative assistant and secretarial science; agricultural business and management; animal/livestock husbandry and production;

architectural engineering technology; automobile/automotive mechanics technology; avionics maintenance technology; building/home/construction inspection; business administration and management; child care and support services management; child care provision; child development; civil engineering technology; commercial and advertising art; computer programming; computer programming related; computer programming (specific applications); computer/technical support; consumer merchandising/retailing management; criminal justice/law enforcement administration; criminal justice/police science; culinary arts; data entry/microcomputer applications; dental hygiene; electrical, electronic and communications engineering technology; electrical/electronics equipment installation and repair; engineering technology; farm and ranch management; fashion merchandising; fire science; food services technology; hospitality and recreation marketing; hotel/motel administration; human services; industrial design; international business/trade/commerce; journalism; legal administrative assistant/secretary; legal assistant/paralegal; liberal arts and sciences/liberal studies; machine tool technology; marketing/marketing management; mechanical design technology; mechanical engineering/mechanical technology; medical administrative assistant and medical secretary; medical/clinical assistant; nursing (licensed practical/vocational nurse training); nursing (registered nurse training); sales, distribution and marketing; selling skills and sales; sign language interpretation and translation; special products marketing; speech/theater education; substance abuse/addiction counseling; word processing.

Academic Programs *Special study options:* academic remediation for entering students, adult/continuing education programs, cooperative education, distance learning, English as a second language, independent study, internships, part-time degree program, services for LD students, summer session for credit. *ROTC:* Army (c), Air Force (c).

Library 59,200 titles, 207 serial subscriptions, an OPAC.

Computers on Campus 263 computers available on campus for general student use. A campuswide network can be accessed from off campus. Internet access, at least one staffed computer lab available.

Student Life *Housing Options:* coed. *Activities and Organizations:* drama/theater group, student-run newspaper, radio and television station, choral group, Student Senate, Health Occupations Student Association, Volunteer Institute Program, Data Processing Student Association, Phi Theta Kappa. *Campus security:* 24-hour patrols, late-night transport/escort service. *Student services:* personal/psychological counseling.

Athletics Member NJCAA. *Intercollegiate sports:* baseball M(s), basketball M(s)/W(s), softball W(s), volleyball W(s). *Intramural sports:* baseball M, basketball M/W, football M/W, golf M/W, tennis M/W, volleyball M/W.

Standardized Tests *Required:* SAT Reasoning Test or ACT or ACT ASSET or ACT COMPASS (for placement).

Costs (2005–06) *One-time required fee:* $25. *Tuition:* state resident $3200 full-time, $100 per credit part-time; nonresident $4800 full-time, $150 per credit part-time. Full-time tuition and fees vary according to course load and reciprocity agreements. Part-time tuition and fees vary according to course load and reciprocity agreements. *Required fees:* $320 full-time, $10 per credit part-time. *Room and board:* $4350. *Payment plans:* installment, deferred payment. *Waivers:* senior citizens and employees or children of employees.

Applying *Options:* early admission, deferred entrance. *Required:* high school transcript. *Application deadline:* rolling (freshmen), rolling (transfers).

Admissions Contact Mrs. Tammy Young, Director of Admissions, Iowa Western Community College, 2700 College Road, Box 4-C, Council Bluffs, IA 51502. *Phone:* 712-325-3288. *Toll-free phone:* 800-432-5852. *Fax:* 712-325-3720. *E-mail:* admissions@iwcc.edu.

KAPLAN COLLEGE
Davenport, Iowa

- **Proprietary** primarily 2-year, founded 1937, part of Kaplan Higher Education
- **Calendar** quarters
- **Degrees** certificates, diplomas, associate, and bachelor's (profile includes both traditional and on-line students)
- **Suburban** campus
- **Coed**

Faculty *Student/faculty ratio:* 11:1.

Applying *Options:* early admission, deferred entrance. *Application fee:* $25. *Required:* high school transcript, interview.

Admissions Contact Mr. Robert Hoffmann, Director of Admissions, Kaplan College, 1801 East Kimberly Road, Suite 1, Davenport, IA 52807. *Phone:* 563-441-2496. *Toll-free phone:* 800-747-1035. *Fax:* 563-355-1320. *E-mail:* infoke@kaplancollege.edu.

KIRKWOOD COMMUNITY COLLEGE
Cedar Rapids, Iowa

- **State and locally supported** 2-year, founded 1966, part of Iowa Department of Education Division of Community Colleges
- **Calendar** semesters

- **Degree** certificates, diplomas, and associate
- **Suburban** 630-acre campus
- **Endowment** $4.4 million
- **Coed**

Faculty *Student/faculty ratio:* 23:1.
Student Life *Campus security:* 24-hour patrols.
Athletics Member NJCAA.
Standardized Tests *Required:* ACT (for placement), ACT COMPASS (for placement).
Costs (2004–05) *Tuition:* $88 per credit hour part-time; state resident $2640 full-time; nonresident $5280 full-time, $176 per credit hour part-time.
Applying *Options:* electronic application, early admission. *Required:* high school transcript.
Admissions Contact Mr. Doug Bannon, Director of Admissions, Kirkwood Community College, PO Box 2068, Cedar Rapids, IA 52406-2068. *Phone:* 319-398-5517. *Toll-free phone:* 800-332-2055. *E-mail:* dbannon@ kirkwood.cc.ia.us.

MARSHALLTOWN COMMUNITY COLLEGE
Marshalltown, Iowa

- **District-supported** 2-year, founded 1927, part of Iowa Valley Community College District System
- **Calendar** semesters
- **Degree** certificates, diplomas, and associate
- **Small-town** 200-acre campus
- **Endowment** $1.7 million
- **Coed**

Faculty *Student/faculty ratio:* 29:1.
Athletics Member NJCAA.
Standardized Tests *Required:* ACT COMPASS (for admission). *Recommended:* ACT (for admission).
Costs (2004–05) *Tuition:* state resident $2850 full-time, $95 per credit part-time; nonresident $3540 full-time, $118 per credit part-time. Full-time tuition and fees vary according to course load and program. Part-time tuition and fees vary according to course load and program. *Required fees:* $660 full-time, $22 per credit part-time. *Room and board:* $4400; room only: $2600.
Financial Aid Of all full-time matriculated undergraduates who enrolled in 2003, 28 Federal Work-Study jobs (averaging $1800).
Applying *Options:* common application, electronic application, early admission. *Required:* high school transcript. *Required for some:* letters of recommendation, interview.
Admissions Contact Ms. Deana Trawny, Director of Admissions, Marshalltown Community College, 3700 South Center Street, Marshalltown, IA 50158. *Phone:* 641-752-7106 Ext. 391. *Toll-free phone:* 866-622-4748. *Fax:* 641-752-8149.

MUSCATINE COMMUNITY COLLEGE
Muscatine, Iowa

- **State-supported** 2-year, founded 1929, part of Eastern Iowa Community College District
- **Calendar** semesters
- **Degree** certificates, diplomas, and associate
- **Small-town** 25-acre campus
- **Coed**, 1,280 undergraduate students, 43% full-time, 61% women, 39% men

Undergraduates 552 full-time, 728 part-time. Students come from 6 states and territories, 4% are from out of state, 1% African American, 0.5% Asian American or Pacific Islander, 10% Hispanic American, 0.5% Native American, 0.6% international.
Freshmen *Admission:* 312 applied, 312 admitted, 312 enrolled. *Test scores:* ACT scores over 18: 80%; ACT scores over 24: 24%; ACT scores over 30: 1%.
Faculty *Total:* 95, 38% full-time.
Majors Accounting; administrative assistant and secretarial science; agricultural/ farm supplies retailing and wholesaling; agricultural production; business administration and management; child care and support services management; computer/ information technology services administration related; emergency medical technology (EMT paramedic); environmental engineering technology; liberal arts and sciences/liberal studies; machine tool technology; natural resources/ conservation; nursing (licensed practical/vocational nurse training); occupational safety and health technology; pharmacy technician.
Academic Programs *Special study options:* academic remediation for entering students, adult/continuing education programs, advanced placement credit, cooperative education, distance learning, double majors, English as a second language, honors programs, independent study, internships, part-time degree program, services for LD students, study abroad, summer session for credit.
Library Muscatine Community College Library with 19,588 titles, 176 serial subscriptions, an OPAC.

Computers on Campus 57 computers available on campus for general student use. A campuswide network can be accessed from off campus. At least one staffed computer lab available.
Student Life *Housing Options:* Campus housing is university owned. *Activities and Organizations:* drama/theater group, student-run newspaper, choral group. *Student services:* personal/psychological counseling.
Athletics Member NJCAA. *Intercollegiate sports:* baseball M(s), softball W(s). *Intramural sports:* golf M/W, skiing (downhill) M/W, softball M/W, table tennis M/W, tennis M/W.
Standardized Tests *Required:* ACT or DTLS, DTMS (for placement).
Costs (2004–05) *Tuition:* area resident $2720 full-time; state resident $85 per semester hour part-time; nonresident $4080 full-time, $128 per semester hour part-time. *Room and board:* room only: $3330. *Payment plan:* installment.
Financial Aid Of all full-time matriculated undergraduates who enrolled in 2003, 52 Federal Work-Study jobs (averaging $3000).
Applying *Options:* early admission, deferred entrance. *Required:* high school transcript. *Application deadline:* rolling (freshmen), rolling (transfers). *Notification:* continuous (freshmen).
Admissions Contact Neil Mandsager, Executive Director of Enrollment Management and Marketing, Muscatine Community College, 152 Colorado Street, Muscatine, IA 52761-5396. *Phone:* 563-288-6012. *Toll-free phone:* 800-351-4669.

NORTHEAST IOWA COMMUNITY COLLEGE
Calmar, Iowa

- **State and locally supported** 2-year, founded 1966, part of Iowa Area Community Colleges System
- **Calendar** semesters
- **Degree** certificates, diplomas, and associate
- **Small-town** 210-acre campus
- **Coed**

Faculty *Student/faculty ratio:* 16:1.
Student Life *Campus security:* security personnel on week nights.
Standardized Tests *Required:* ACT ASSET (for placement). *Required for some:* ACT (for placement).
Financial Aid Of all full-time matriculated undergraduates who enrolled in 2003, 154 Federal Work-Study jobs (averaging $1248). 45 state and other part-time jobs (averaging $980).
Applying *Recommended:* high school transcript.
Admissions Contact Ms. Martha Keune, Admissions Representative, Northeast Iowa Community College, PO Box 400, Calmar, IA 52132. *Phone:* 563-562-3263 Ext. 307. *Toll-free phone:* 800-728-CALMAR. *E-mail:* keunem@ nicc.edu.

NORTH IOWA AREA COMMUNITY COLLEGE
Mason City, Iowa

- **State and locally supported** 2-year, founded 1918, part of Iowa Community Colleges System
- **Calendar** semesters
- **Degree** certificates, diplomas, and associate
- **Rural** 320-acre campus
- **Coed**, 3,004 undergraduate students, 59% full-time, 56% women, 44% men

Undergraduates 1,760 full-time, 1,244 part-time. Students come from 25 states and territories, 7 other countries, 3% are from out of state, 3% African American, 1% Asian American or Pacific Islander, 3% Hispanic American, 0.3% Native American, 0.4% international, 60% transferred in, 15% live on campus. *Retention:* 58% of 2002 full-time freshmen returned.
Freshmen *Admission:* 3,304 applied, 3,304 admitted, 855 enrolled. *Average high school GPA:* 2.68. *Test scores:* ACT scores over 18: 74%; ACT scores over 24: 22%; ACT scores over 30: 6%.
Faculty *Total:* 162, 50% full-time, 6% with terminal degrees. *Student/faculty ratio:* 13:1.
Majors Accounting; accounting technology and bookkeeping; administrative assistant and secretarial science; agricultural business technology; agricultural economics; agricultural production; automobile/automotive mechanics technology; business administration and management; carpentry; clinical/medical laboratory technology; computer and information sciences; criminal justice/police science; electrical, electronic and communications engineering technology; emergency medical technology (EMT paramedic); entrepreneurship; fire services administration; heating, air conditioning, ventilation and refrigeration maintenance technology; industrial electronics technology; liberal arts and sciences/liberal studies; machine shop technology; machine tool technology;

North Iowa Area Community College (continued)

medical/clinical assistant; nursing assistant/aide and patient care assistant; nursing (licensed practical/vocational nurse training); nursing (registered nurse training); physical therapist assistant; sport and fitness administration; tool and die technology; welding technology.

Academic Programs *Special study options:* academic remediation for entering students, advanced placement credit, cooperative education, distance learning, double majors, English as a second language, external degree program, honors programs, independent study, internships, off-campus study, part-time degree program, services for LD students, student-designed majors, summer session for credit.

Library North Iowa Area Community College Library with 29,540 titles, 413 serial subscriptions, 7,773 audiovisual materials, an OPAC, a Web page.

Computers on Campus 365 computers available on campus for general student use. A campuswide network can be accessed from off campus. Internet access, at least one staffed computer lab available.

Student Life *Housing:* on-campus residence required for freshman year. *Options:* coed. Campus housing is provided by a third party. Freshman applicants given priority for college housing. *Activities and Organizations:* student-run newspaper, choral group, Student Senate, school newspaper, intramurals, choral groups, band/orchestra. *Campus security:* 24-hour emergency response devices, controlled dormitory access. *Student services:* health clinic, personal/psychological counseling.

Athletics Member NJCAA. *Intercollegiate sports:* baseball M(s), basketball M(s)/W(s), cross-country running W(s), football M(s), golf M(s)/W(s), soccer M(s)/W(s), softball W(s), track and field M(s)/W(s), volleyball W(s). *Intramural sports:* basketball M/W, bowling M/W, cheerleading W, football M, skiing (downhill) M/W, soccer M/W, softball W, table tennis M/W, tennis M/W, volleyball M/W, weight lifting M/W.

Standardized Tests *Required for some:* ACT (for placement). *Recommended:* ACT (for placement), ACT COMPASS.

Costs (2004–05) *Tuition:* state resident $2655 full-time, $89 per semester hour part-time; nonresident $3983 full-time, $133 per semester hour part-time. *Required fees:* $330 full-time, $11 per semester hour part-time. *Room and board:* $3770. *Payment plan:* installment. *Waivers:* senior citizens and employees or children of employees.

Financial Aid Of all full-time matriculated undergraduates who enrolled in 2003, 125 Federal Work-Study jobs (averaging $2000).

Applying *Options:* common application, electronic application. *Required for some:* high school transcript. *Recommended:* high school transcript. *Application deadline:* rolling (freshmen), rolling (transfers). *Notification:* continuous (freshmen).

Admissions Contact Ms. Rachel McGuire, Director of Admissions, North Iowa Area Community College, 500 College Drive, Mason City, IA 50401. *Phone:* 641-422-4104. *Toll-free phone:* 888-GO NIACC Ext. 4245. *Fax:* 641-422-4385. *E-mail:* request@niacc.edu.

NORTHWEST IOWA COMMUNITY COLLEGE
Sheldon, Iowa

- **State-supported** 2-year, founded 1966, part of Iowa Department of Education Division of Community Colleges
- **Calendar** semesters
- **Degree** certificates, diplomas, and associate
- **Small-town** 263-acre campus with easy access to Sioux City, IA; Sioux Falls, SD
- **Coed**

Faculty *Student/faculty ratio:* 15:1.

Student Life *Campus security:* 24-hour emergency response devices.

Standardized Tests *Required:* ACT COMPASS (for placement). *Required for some:* ACT COMPASS.

Costs (2004–05) *Tuition:* state resident $3496 full-time, $92 per credit part-time; nonresident $4788 full-time, $126 per credit part-time. Full-time tuition and fees vary according to course load. Part-time tuition and fees vary according to course load. *Required fees:* $700 full-time, $15 per credit part-time. *Room and board:* room only: $1900.

Financial Aid Of all full-time matriculated undergraduates who enrolled in 2003, 60 Federal Work-Study jobs (averaging $900).

Applying *Options:* common application, electronic application. *Application fee:* $10. *Required:* high school transcript. *Required for some:* minimum 2.0 GPA.

Admissions Contact Ms. Lisa Story, Director of Enrollment Management, Northwest Iowa Community College, 603 West Park Street, Sheldon, IA 51201-1046. *Phone:* 712-324-5061 Ext. 115. *Toll-free phone:* 800-352-4907. *Fax:* 712-324-4136.

ST. LUKE'S COLLEGE
Sioux City, Iowa

- **Independent** 2-year, part of St. Luke's Regional Medical Center
- **Calendar** semesters
- **Degree** certificates and associate
- **Rural** campus
- **Endowment** $971,786
- **Coed,** 134 undergraduate students, 70% full-time, 84% women, 16% men

Undergraduates 94 full-time, 40 part-time. Students come from 8 states and territories, 29% are from out of state, 1% Asian American or Pacific Islander, 1% Hispanic American, 8% transferred in, 15% live on campus. *Retention:* 82% of 2002 full-time freshmen returned.

Freshmen *Admission:* 52 applied, 40 admitted, 18 enrolled. *Average high school GPA:* 3.12. *Test scores:* ACT scores over 18: 100%; ACT scores over 24: 13%.

Faculty *Total:* 16, 63% full-time, 31% with terminal degrees. *Student/faculty ratio:* 7:1.

Majors Nursing (registered nurse training); radiologic technology/science; respiratory care therapy.

Academic Programs *Special study options:* advanced placement credit, cooperative education, part-time degree program, summer session for credit.

Library St. Luke's Library plus 1 other with 2,038 titles, 119 serial subscriptions, 324 audiovisual materials, an OPAC, a Web page.

Computers on Campus 10 computers available on campus for general student use. A campuswide network can be accessed. Internet access, at least one staffed computer lab available.

Student Life *Housing Options:* coed. Campus housing is university owned. *Campus security:* 24-hour emergency response devices and patrols, late-night transport/escort service. *Student services:* health clinic, personal/psychological counseling.

Standardized Tests *Required:* ACT (for admission).

Costs (2005–06) *Tuition:* $11,700 full-time, $325 per credit part-time. Full-time tuition and fees vary according to course load and program. Part-time tuition and fees vary according to course load and program. *Required fees:* $600 full-time. *Room only:* Room and board charges vary according to board plan. *Payment plan:* installment. *Waivers:* employees or children of employees.

Financial Aid Of all full-time matriculated undergraduates who enrolled in 2003, 12 Federal Work-Study jobs (averaging $1050).

Applying *Options:* electronic application, early admission, early action. *Application fee:* $25. *Required:* essay or personal statement, high school transcript, minimum 2.50 GPA, minimum ACT score of 19. *Required for some:* interview. *Application deadline:* 8/1 (freshmen). *Notification:* 8/1 (freshmen), 12/1 (early action).

Admissions Contact Ms. Sherry McCarthy, Admissions Coordinator, St. Luke's College, 2720 Stone Park Boulevard, Sioux City, IA 51104. *Phone:* 712-279-3149. *Toll-free phone:* 800-352-4660 Ext. 3149. *Fax:* 712-233-8017. *E-mail:* mccartsj@stlukes.org.

SCOTT COMMUNITY COLLEGE
Bettendorf, Iowa

- **State and locally supported** 2-year, founded 1966, part of Eastern Iowa Community College District
- **Calendar** semesters
- **Degree** certificates, diplomas, and associate
- **Urban** campus
- **Coed,** 4,697 undergraduate students, 47% full-time, 61% women, 39% men

Undergraduates 2,212 full-time, 2,485 part-time. Students come from 36 states and territories, 8% are from out of state, 8% African American, 2% Asian American or Pacific Islander, 4% Hispanic American, 0.6% Native American, 1% international.

Freshmen *Admission:* 1,422 applied, 1,422 admitted, 895 enrolled.

Faculty *Total:* 322, 25% full-time. *Student/faculty ratio:* 20:1.

Majors Accounting; administrative assistant and secretarial science; airline pilot and flight crew; autobody/collision and repair technology; automobile/automotive mechanics technology; business administration and management; child care and support services management; clinical/medical laboratory technology; computer and information sciences; criminal justice/police science; culinary arts; diesel mechanics technology; electroneurodiagnostic/electroencephalographic technology; emergency medical technology (EMT paramedic); environmental engineering technology; equestrian studies; heating, air conditioning, ventilation and refrigeration maintenance technology; interior design; liberal arts and sciences/liberal studies; machine tool technology; medical radiologic technology; nursing (licensed practical/vocational nurse training); nursing (registered nurse training); occupational safety and health technology; occupational therapist assistant; pharmacy technician; physical therapy; radio and television broadcasting technology; respiratory care therapy; sign language interpretation and translation.

Academic Programs *Special study options:* academic remediation for entering students, adult/continuing education programs, advanced placement credit, cooperative education, distance learning, double majors, English as a second language, honors programs, independent study, internships, off-campus study, part-time degree program, services for LD students, study abroad, summer session for credit.

Library Scott Community College Library with 22,700 titles, 183 serial subscriptions, an OPAC.

Computers on Campus 200 computers available on campus for general student use. A campuswide network can be accessed from off campus. At least one staffed computer lab available.

Student Life *Housing:* college housing not available. *Activities and Organizations:* drama/theater group, student government, Campus Activities Board. *Campus security:* 24-hour emergency response devices. *Student services:* personal/psychological counseling.

Athletics Member NJCAA. *Intercollegiate sports:* golf M(s)/W(s), soccer M(s)/W(s).

Standardized Tests *Required:* ACT (for placement), College Board Diagnostic Tests (for placement).

Costs (2004–05) *Tuition:* state resident $2720 full-time, $85 per semester hour part-time; nonresident $4080 full-time, $128 per semester hour part-time. *Waivers:* employees or children of employees.

Financial Aid Of all full-time matriculated undergraduates who enrolled in 2003, 72 Federal Work-Study jobs (averaging $3000).

Applying *Options:* early admission, deferred entrance. *Required:* high school transcript. *Application deadline:* rolling (freshmen), rolling (transfers). *Notification:* continuous (freshmen).

Admissions Contact Mr. Neil Mandsager, Executive Director of Enrollment Management and Marketing, Scott Community College, 500 Belmont Road, Bettendorf, IA 52722-6804. *Phone:* 563-441-4007. *Toll-free phone:* 800-895-0811.

SOUTHEASTERN COMMUNITY COLLEGE, NORTH CAMPUS
West Burlington, Iowa

Admissions Contact Ms. Stacy White, Admissions, Southeastern Community College, North Campus, 1015 South Gear Avenue, PO Box 180, West Burlington, IA 52655-0180. *Phone:* 319-752-2731 Ext. 8137. *Toll-free phone:* 866-722-4692. *E-mail:* admoff@secc.cc.ia.us.

SOUTHEASTERN COMMUNITY COLLEGE, SOUTH CAMPUS
Keokuk, Iowa

Admissions Contact Ms. Kari Bevans, Admissions Coordinator, Southeastern Community College, South Campus, PO Box 6007, 335 Messenger Road, Keokuk, IA 52632. *Phone:* 319-752-2731. *Toll-free phone:* 866-722-4692 Ext. 8416. *Fax:* 319-524-8621. *E-mail:* kbevans@secc.cc.ia.us.

SOUTHWESTERN COMMUNITY COLLEGE
Creston, Iowa

- **State-supported** 2-year, founded 1966, part of Iowa Department of Education Division of Community Colleges
- **Calendar** semesters
- **Degree** diplomas and associate
- **Rural** 420-acre campus
- **Endowment** $691,031
- **Coed,** 1,254 undergraduate students, 53% full-time, 57% women, 43% men

Undergraduates 666 full-time, 588 part-time. Students come from 11 states and territories, 4 other countries, 4% are from out of state, 2% African American, 0.2% Asian American or Pacific Islander, 1% Hispanic American, 0.5% international, 5% transferred in, 5% live on campus.

Freshmen *Admission:* 660 applied, 281 admitted, 268 enrolled. *Average high school GPA:* 2.76.

Faculty *Total:* 96, 48% full-time. *Student/faculty ratio:* 14:1.

Majors Accounting; administrative assistant and secretarial science; agricultural business and management; autobody/collision and repair technology; automobile/automotive mechanics technology; business administration and management; carpentry; computer programming; consumer merchandising/retailing management; drafting and design technology; electromechanical technology; liberal arts and sciences/liberal studies; marketing/marketing management; music; nursing (licensed practical/vocational nurse training); nursing (registered nurse training).

Academic Programs *Special study options:* academic remediation for entering students, adult/continuing education programs, advanced placement credit, cooperative education, independent study, internships, part-time degree program, services for LD students, student-designed majors, summer session for credit.

Library Learning Resources Center with 14,742 titles, 170 serial subscriptions, 1,174 audiovisual materials, an OPAC, a Web page.

Computers on Campus 115 computers available on campus for general student use. A campuswide network can be accessed from off campus. Internet access, at least one staffed computer lab available.

Student Life *Housing Options:* men-only, women-only. Campus housing is university owned. *Activities and Organizations:* student-run newspaper, choral group. *Campus security:* 24-hour emergency response devices and patrols, controlled dormitory access. *Student services:* personal/psychological counseling.

Athletics Member NJCAA. *Intercollegiate sports:* baseball M(s), basketball M(s)/W(s), golf M(s), softball W(s), volleyball W(s). *Intramural sports:* basketball M/W, bowling M/W, table tennis M/W, volleyball M/W.

Standardized Tests *Required for some:* SAT or ACT (for admission), ACT COMPASS.

Costs (2004–05) *Tuition:* state resident $2912 full-time, $91 per credit hour part-time; nonresident $4464 full-time, $134 per credit hour part-time. *Required fees:* $384 full-time, $12 per credit hour part-time. *Room and board:* $3500. *Payment plan:* installment.

Financial Aid Of all full-time matriculated undergraduates who enrolled in 2003, 95 Federal Work-Study jobs (averaging $1800). 50 state and other part-time jobs (averaging $1000).

Applying *Options:* common application, electronic application, early admission. *Required:* high school transcript. *Application deadlines:* 9/5 (freshmen), 9/5 (transfers). *Notification:* continuous (freshmen).

Admissions Contact Ms. Lisa Carstens, Admissions Coordinator, Southwestern Community College, 1501 West Townline Street, Creston, IA 50801. *Phone:* 641-782-7081. *Toll-free phone:* 800-247-4023. *Fax:* 641-782-3312. *E-mail:* admissions@swcc.cc.ia.us.

VATTEROTT COLLEGE
Des Moines, Iowa

- **Proprietary** 2-year
- **Calendar** semesters
- **Degree** certificates and first professional certificates
- **Urban** 25-acre campus
- **Coed**

Faculty *Student/faculty ratio:* 15:1.

Costs (2004–05) *Tuition:* $8650 full-time. *Required fees:* $525 full-time.

Admissions Contact Mr. Henry Franken, Co-Director, Vatterott College, 6100 Thornton Avenue, Suite 290, Des Moines, IA 50321. *Phone:* 515-309-9000. *Toll-free phone:* 800-353-7264.

WESTERN IOWA TECH COMMUNITY COLLEGE
Sioux City, Iowa

- **State-supported** 2-year, founded 1966, part of Iowa Department of Education Division of Community Colleges
- **Calendar** semesters
- **Degree** certificates, diplomas, and associate
- **Urban** 143-acre campus
- **Endowment** $337,763
- **Coed,** 5,370 undergraduate students, 42% full-time, 57% women, 43% men

Undergraduates 2,269 full-time, 3,101 part-time. 10% are from out of state, 2% live on campus.

Freshmen *Admission:* 2,233 applied, 2,233 admitted. *Test scores:* ACT scores over 18: 59%; ACT scores over 24: 11%.

Faculty *Total:* 321, 28% full-time, 5% with terminal degrees. *Student/faculty ratio:* 19:1.

Majors Agricultural/farm supplies retailing and wholesaling; architectural engineering technology; autobody/collision and repair technology; automobile/automotive mechanics technology; biomedical technology; business administration and management; child care and support services management; clinical/medical laboratory technology; computer programming (specific applications); computer typography and composition equipment operation; criminal justice/law enforcement administration; diesel mechanics technology; electrical, electronic and communications engineering technology; emergency medical technology (EMT paramedic); executive assistant/executive secretary; heating, air conditioning, ventilation and refrigeration maintenance technology; legal administrative assistant/secretary; liberal arts and sciences/liberal studies; machine tool

Western Iowa Tech Community College (continued)

technology; medical administrative assistant and medical secretary; nursing assistant/aide and patient care assistant; nursing (registered nurse training); occupational therapist assistant; physical therapist assistant; tool and die technology; turf and turfgrass management.

Academic Programs *Special study options:* academic remediation for entering students, accelerated degree program, adult/continuing education programs, distance learning, double majors, English as a second language, honors programs, independent study, internships, part-time degree program, services for LD students, summer session for credit.

Library Western Iowa Tech Community College Library Services with 25,696 titles, 1,886 serial subscriptions, 3,456 audiovisual materials, an OPAC.

Computers on Campus 640 computers available on campus for general student use. A campuswide network can be accessed from student residence rooms and from off campus. Internet access, at least one staffed computer lab available.

Student Life *Activities and Organizations:* Student Senate. *Campus security:* 24-hour emergency response devices and patrols. *Student services:* health clinic, personal/psychological counseling.

Athletics *Intramural sports:* basketball M/W, bowling M/W, football M/W, golf M/W, skiing (downhill) M/W, softball W, volleyball M/W, weight lifting M/W.

Costs (2005–06) *Tuition:* state resident $105 per credit hour part-time; nonresident $148 per credit hour part-time. *Payment plan:* installment.

Applying *Options:* early admission, deferred entrance. *Application fee:* $10. *Required:* high school transcript. *Application deadline:* rolling (freshmen), rolling (transfers). *Notification:* continuous (freshmen).

Admissions Contact Lora Vanderzwaag, Director of Admissions, Western Iowa Tech Community College, 4647 Stone Avenue, Sioux City, IA 51102-5199. *Phone:* 712-274-6400. *Toll-free phone:* 800-352-4649 Ext. 6403. *Fax:* 712-274-6441.

KANSAS

ALLEN COUNTY COMMUNITY COLLEGE
Iola, Kansas

- **State and locally supported** 2-year, founded 1923, part of Kansas State Board of Regents
- **Calendar** semesters
- **Degree** certificates and associate
- **Small-town** 88-acre campus
- **Endowment** $2.7 million
- **Coed**, 2,256 undergraduate students, 37% full-time, 63% women, 37% men

Undergraduates 824 full-time, 1,432 part-time. Students come from 17 states and territories, 16 other countries, 4% are from out of state, 4% African American, 0.6% Asian American or Pacific Islander, 3% Hispanic American, 1% Native American, 1% international, 76% transferred in, 10% live on campus. *Retention:* 56% of 2002 full-time freshmen returned.

Freshmen *Admission:* 893 applied, 893 admitted, 628 enrolled. *Average high school GPA:* 2.97. *Test scores:* ACT scores over 18: 64%; ACT scores over 24: 14%; ACT scores over 30: 2%.

Faculty *Total:* 32, 91% with terminal degrees. *Student/faculty ratio:* 17:1.

Majors Accounting; administrative assistant and secretarial science; agricultural production; architecture; art; athletic training; banking and financial support services; biology/biological sciences; business administration and management; business/commerce; business teacher education; chemistry; child development; computer science; computer systems networking and telecommunications; criminal justice/law enforcement administration; data processing and data processing technology; drafting and design technology; dramatic/theatre arts; economics; electrical, electronic and communications engineering technology; electrical, electronics and communications engineering; elementary education; emergency medical technology (EMT paramedic); engineering; engineering technology; English composition; equestrian studies; family and consumer sciences/human sciences; farm and ranch management; forestry; funeral service and mortuary science; general studies; geography; health aide; health and physical education; history; home health aide/home attendant; hospital and health care facilities administration; humanities; industrial arts; industrial technology; information science/studies; journalism; language interpretation and translation; library science; mathematics; music; nuclear/nuclear power technology; nursing assistant/aide and patient care assistant; parks, recreation and leisure facilities management; philosophy; physical therapy; physics; political science and government; postal management; pre-dentistry studies; pre-law studies; pre-medical studies; pre-pharmacy studies; pre-veterinary studies; psychology; religious studies; secondary education; social work; sociology; speech and rhetoric; technology/industrial arts teacher education; wood science and wood products/pulp and paper technology.

Academic Programs *Special study options:* academic remediation for entering students, adult/continuing education programs, cooperative education, part-time degree program, services for LD students, student-designed majors, summer session for credit.

Library Learning Resource Center with 49,416 titles, 159 serial subscriptions, an OPAC.

Computers on Campus 65 computers available on campus for general student use. A campuswide network can be accessed. Internet access, at least one staffed computer lab available.

Student Life *Housing:* on-campus residence required through sophomore year. *Options:* coed. Campus housing is university owned. *Activities and Organizations:* drama/theater group, student-run newspaper, choral group, intramurals, Student Senate, Biology Club, student newspaper, Phi Theta Kappa. *Campus security:* controlled dormitory access. *Student services:* personal/psychological counseling.

Athletics Member NJCAA. *Intercollegiate sports:* baseball M(s), basketball M(s)/W(s), cross-country running M(s)/W(s), golf M(s), soccer M(s)/W(s), softball W(s), track and field M(s)/W(s), volleyball W(s). *Intramural sports:* basketball M/W, football M/W, soccer M/W, softball M/W, table tennis M/W, tennis M/W, volleyball M/W.

Standardized Tests *Recommended:* ACT (for placement).

Costs (2004–05) *Tuition:* area resident $1120 full-time, $35 per credit hour part-time; state resident $1216 full-time, $38 per credit hour part-time; nonresident $1216 full-time, $38 per credit hour part-time. Full-time tuition and fees vary according to course load. Part-time tuition and fees vary according to course load. *Required fees:* $768 full-time, $24 per credit hour part-time. *Room and board:* $3500; room only: $2500. *Waivers:* senior citizens and employees or children of employees.

Financial Aid Of all full-time matriculated undergraduates who enrolled in 2003, 25 Federal Work-Study jobs (averaging $1650). 80 state and other part-time jobs (averaging $1650).

Applying *Options:* common application, early admission, deferred entrance. *Required:* high school transcript. *Application deadlines:* 8/24 (freshmen), 8/24 (transfers). *Notification:* continuous (freshmen).

Admissions Contact Mr. Randall Weber, Director of Admissions, Allen County Community College, 1801 North Cottonwood, Iola, KS 66749. *Phone:* 620-365-5116 Ext. 267.

BARTON COUNTY COMMUNITY COLLEGE
Great Bend, Kansas

- **State and locally supported** 2-year, founded 1969, part of Kansas Board of Regents
- **Calendar** semesters
- **Degree** certificates and associate
- **Rural** 140-acre campus
- **Endowment** $4.0 million
- **Coed**, 3,976 undergraduate students, 28% full-time, 54% women, 46% men

Undergraduates 1,116 full-time, 2,860 part-time. Students come from 40 states and territories, 15 other countries, 11% are from out of state, 15% African American, 2% Asian American or Pacific Islander, 7% Hispanic American, 0.8% Native American, 2% international, 3% transferred in, 4% live on campus.

Freshmen *Admission:* 1,445 enrolled.

Faculty *Total:* 193, 36% full-time, 4% with terminal degrees. *Student/faculty ratio:* 18:1.

Majors Accounting; administrative assistant and secretarial science; agricultural business and management; agriculture; anthropology; architecture; art; athletic training; automobile/automotive mechanics technology; banking and financial support services; biology/biological sciences; business administration and management; business computer programming; chemistry; child care and support services management; chiropractic assistant; clinical/medical laboratory technology; communication/speech communication and rhetoric; computer/information technology services administration related; computer science; computer systems networking and telecommunications; criminal justice/police science; crop production; cytotechnology; dance; dental hygiene; dietitian assistant; dramatic/theatre arts; early childhood education; economics; elementary education; emergency medical technology (EMT paramedic); engineering technology; English; fire science; forestry; funeral service and mortuary science; general studies; geology/earth science; graphic design; hazardous materials management and waste technology; health information/medical records administration; history; home health aide; human resources management and services related; information science/studies; journalism; kinesiology and exercise science; liberal arts and sciences/liberal studies; livestock management; marketing/marketing management; mathematics; medical administrative assistant and medical secretary; military studies; modern languages; music; nursing (registered nurse training); occupational therapy; optometric technician; pharmacy; philosophy; physical education teaching and coaching; physical sciences; physical therapist assistant; physical therapy; physician assistant; physics; political science and government; pre-dentistry studies; pre-engineering; pre-law studies; pre-medical studies; pre-veterinary studies; psychology; public administration; radiologic technology/science; religious studies; respiratory care therapy; secondary education; social work; sociology; sport and fitness administration; wildlife and wildlands science and management.

Academic Programs *Special study options:* academic remediation for entering students, accelerated degree program, adult/continuing education programs, advanced placement credit, cooperative education, distance learning, English as a second language, external degree program, honors programs, independent study, internships, part-time degree program, services for LD students, student-designed majors, summer session for credit.

Library Barton County Community College Library with 26,322 titles, 179 serial subscriptions, 1,529 audiovisual materials, an OPAC, a Web page.

Computers on Campus 350 computers available on campus for general student use. A campuswide network can be accessed from student residence rooms and from off campus. Internet access, online (class) registration, at least one staffed computer lab available.

Student Life *Housing:* on-campus residence required for freshman year. *Options:* coed, disabled students. Campus housing is university owned. Freshman campus housing is guaranteed. *Activities and Organizations:* drama/theater group, student-run newspaper, choral group, Danceline, Business Professionals, Psychology Club, Agriculture Club, Cougarettes. *Campus security:* 24-hour emergency response devices and patrols. *Student services:* health clinic, personal/psychological counseling.

Athletics Member NJCAA. *Intercollegiate sports:* baseball M(s), basketball M(s)/W(s), cheerleading M(s)/W, cross-country running M(s)/W(s), golf M(s), soccer M(s)/W(s), softball W(s), tennis M(s)/W(s), track and field M(s)/W(s), volleyball W(s). *Intramural sports:* basketball M/W, bowling M/W, football M/W, golf M/W, swimming and diving M/W, table tennis M/W, tennis M/W, track and field M/W, volleyball M/W.

Standardized Tests *Required:* ACT ASSET, ACT ACCUPLACER (for placement). *Recommended:* ACT (for placement).

Costs (2005–06) *Tuition:* state resident $1504 full-time, $47 per credit hour part-time; nonresident $2176 full-time, $68 per credit hour part-time. *Required fees:* $576 full-time, $18 per credit hour part-time. *Room and board:* $3619. Room and board charges vary according to board plan. *Payment plans:* installment, deferred payment. *Waivers:* senior citizens and employees or children of employees.

Financial Aid Of all full-time matriculated undergraduates who enrolled in 2003, 102 Federal Work-Study jobs (averaging $2400).

Applying *Options:* common application, electronic application, early admission. *Recommended:* high school transcript. *Application deadline:* rolling (freshmen), rolling (transfers).

Admissions Contact Mr. Todd Moore, Director of Admissions and Marketing, Barton County Community College, 245 Northeast 30th Road, Great Bend, KS 67530. *Phone:* 620-792-9241. *Toll-free phone:* 800-722-6842. *Fax:* 620-786-1160. *E-mail:* admissions@barton.ccc.edu.

BROWN MACKIE COLLEGE, LENEXA CAMPUS
Lenexa, Kansas

- **Proprietary** 2-year, founded 1892, part of The Brown Mackie College
- **Calendar** quarters
- **Degree** certificates, diplomas, and associate
- **Suburban** 3-acre campus with easy access to Kansas City
- **Coed**

Faculty *Student/faculty ratio:* 14:1.

Student Life *Campus security:* 24-hour emergency response devices.

Standardized Tests *Required:* ACT ASSET (for placement). *Recommended:* SAT or ACT (for placement).

Costs (2004–05) *Tuition:* $6444 full-time. *Required fees:* $432 full-time.

Applying *Options:* deferred entrance. *Application fee:* $20. *Required:* high school transcript, interview. *Recommended:* essay or personal statement, minimum 2.0 GPA.

Admissions Contact Ms. Julia M. Denniston, Director of Admissions, Brown Mackie College, Lenexa Campus, 9705 Lenexa Drive, Lenexa, KS 66215. *Phone:* 913-768-1900 Ext. 14. *Toll-free phone:* 800-635-9101. *Fax:* 913-495-9555. *E-mail:* jjohnson@amedcts.com.

BROWN MACKIE COLLEGE, SALINA CAMPUS
Salina, Kansas

Admissions Contact Ms. Diann Heath, Director of Admissions, Brown Mackie College, Salina Campus, 2106 South 9th Street, Salina, KS 67401. *Phone:* 785-825-5422 Ext. 17. *Toll-free phone:* 800-365-0433. *Fax:* 785-827-7623.

BUTLER COUNTY COMMUNITY COLLEGE
El Dorado, Kansas

- **State and locally supported** 2-year, founded 1927, part of Kansas Board of Regents
- **Calendar** semesters
- **Degree** certificates and associate
- **Small-town** 80-acre campus
- **Coed**, 8,793 undergraduate students, 40% full-time, 60% women, 40% men

Undergraduates 3,493 full-time, 5,300 part-time. Students come from 28 states and territories, 21 other countries, 5% are from out of state, 11% African American, 3% Asian American or Pacific Islander, 5% Hispanic American, 2% Native American, 3% international, 5% transferred in, 4% live on campus. *Retention:* 57% of 2002 full-time freshmen returned.

Freshmen *Admission:* 209 enrolled. *Test scores:* ACT scores over 18: 75%; ACT scores over 24: 23%; ACT scores over 30: 1%.

Faculty *Total:* 613, 23% full-time, 2% with terminal degrees. *Student/faculty ratio:* 18:1.

Majors Accounting; administrative assistant and secretarial science; agricultural business and management; art; automobile/automotive mechanics technology; biology/biological sciences; business administration and management; chemistry; child development; computer and information sciences; computer science; criminal justice/police science; data processing and data processing technology; drafting and design technology; dramatic/theatre arts; electrical, electronic and communications engineering technology; English; farm and ranch management; fire science; health information/medical records administration; history; hotel/motel administration; journalism; kindergarten/preschool education; liberal arts and sciences/liberal studies; marketing/marketing management; mass communication/media; mathematics; medical administrative assistant and medical secretary; music; music performance; nursing (registered nurse training); physical education teaching and coaching; physical therapy; physics; political science and government; pre-engineering; psychology; sociology; substance abuse/addiction counseling; welding technology.

Academic Programs *Special study options:* academic remediation for entering students, accelerated degree program, adult/continuing education programs, advanced placement credit, cooperative education, distance learning, double majors, English as a second language, honors programs, independent study, part-time degree program, services for LD students, student-designed majors, summer session for credit.

Library L.W. Nixon Library with 38,000 titles, 220 serial subscriptions, 914 audiovisual materials, an OPAC, a Web page.

Computers on Campus 90 computers available on campus for general student use. Internet access, at least one staffed computer lab available.

Student Life *Housing Options:* coed, men-only, women-only. Campus housing is university owned. *Activities and Organizations:* drama/theater group, student-run newspaper, radio and television station, choral group, Agriculture Club, Art Club, Campus Crusade for Christ, Grizzly Ambassadors, intramurals. *Campus security:* 24-hour emergency response devices and patrols, controlled dormitory access, video cameras at dormitory entrances and parking lot. *Student services:* personal/psychological counseling.

Athletics Member NJCAA. *Intercollegiate sports:* baseball M(s), basketball M(s)/W(s), cross-country running M(s)/W(s), football M(s), soccer W(s), softball W(s), tennis M(s)/W(s), track and field M(s)/W(s), volleyball W(s). *Intramural sports:* basketball M/W, bowling M/W, cheerleading M/W, football M, soccer M/W, softball W, table tennis M/W, tennis M/W, track and field M/W, volleyball W.

Standardized Tests *Required for some:* ACT ASSET. *Recommended:* ACT (for placement).

Costs (2005–06) *Tuition:* state resident $1756 full-time, $55 per credit hour part-time; nonresident $3164 full-time, $99 per credit hour part-time. *Required fees:* $448 full-time, $14 per credit hour part-time. *Room and board:* $4335. Room and board charges vary according to housing facility. *Payment plan:* installment. *Waivers:* employees or children of employees.

Financial Aid Of all full-time matriculated undergraduates who enrolled in 2003, 210 Federal Work-Study jobs (averaging $1800).

Applying *Options:* early admission, deferred entrance. *Required:* high school transcript. *Application deadlines:* 8/19 (freshmen), 8/20 (transfers). *Notification:* continuous (freshmen).

Admissions Contact Mr. Paul Kyle, Director of Enrollment Management, Butler County Community College, 901 South Haverhill Road, El Dorado, KS 67042. *Phone:* 316-321-2222 Ext. 163. *E-mail:* admissions@butlercc.edu.

CLOUD COUNTY COMMUNITY COLLEGE
Concordia, Kansas

- **State and locally supported** 2-year, founded 1965, part of Kansas Community College System
- **Calendar** semesters
- **Degree** certificates, diplomas, and associate

Cloud County Community College (continued)
- ■ **Rural** 35-acre campus
- ■ **Coed**, 3,521 undergraduate students

Undergraduates Students come from 12 states and territories, 5 other countries, 6% African American, 0.9% Asian American or Pacific Islander, 2% Hispanic American, 0.9% Native American, 0.4% international.

Faculty *Total:* 218, 17% full-time.

Majors Administrative assistant and secretarial science; agricultural business and management; art; avionics maintenance technology; behavioral sciences; biological and physical sciences; biology/biological sciences; broadcast journalism; business administration and management; child development; criminal justice/law enforcement administration; drafting and design technology; education; elementary education; family and consumer sciences/home economics teacher education; family and consumer sciences/human sciences; farm and ranch management; fashion/apparel design; history; humanities; journalism; liberal arts and sciences/liberal studies; music; nursing (registered nurse training); physical education teaching and coaching; physical sciences; pre-engineering; social sciences; tourism and travel services management.

Academic Programs *Special study options:* academic remediation for entering students, adult/continuing education programs, advanced placement credit, cooperative education, internships, part-time degree program, services for LD students, summer session for credit.

Library 18,010 titles, 142 serial subscriptions.

Computers on Campus 57 computers available on campus for general student use. Internet access, at least one staffed computer lab available.

Student Life *Activities and Organizations:* drama/theater group, student-run newspaper, radio station, choral group, Fellowship of Christian Athletes, Block and Bridle Club, Student Senate. *Campus security:* 24-hour emergency response devices. *Student services:* health clinic.

Athletics Member NJCAA. *Intercollegiate sports:* baseball M(s), basketball M(s)/W(s), cross-country running M(s)/W(s), soccer M(s)/W(s), softball W(s), tennis M(s)/W(s), track and field M(s)/W(s), volleyball W(s). *Intramural sports:* baseball M, basketball M/W, softball M/W, volleyball M/W.

Standardized Tests *Required:* ACT ASSET (for placement). *Recommended:* ACT (for placement).

Costs (2005–06) *Tuition:* state resident $1560 full-time, $52 per credit hour part-time; nonresident $2220 full-time, $74 per credit hour part-time. *Required fees:* $540 full-time, $18 per credit hour part-time. *Room and board:* $3780.

Financial Aid Of all full-time matriculated undergraduates who enrolled in 2003, 122 Federal Work-Study jobs (averaging $800).

Applying *Options:* common application, early admission, deferred entrance. *Required:* high school transcript. *Application deadlines:* 9/11 (freshmen), 9/11 (transfers). *Notification:* continuous (freshmen).

Admissions Contact Chris Burlew, Director of Admissions, Cloud County Community College, 2221 Campus Drive, PO Box 1002, Concordia, KS 66901-1002. *Phone:* 785-243-1435 Ext. 214. *Toll-free phone:* 800-729-5101. *E-mail:* thayer@mg.cloudccc.cc.ks.us.

COFFEYVILLE COMMUNITY COLLEGE

Coffeyville, Kansas

- ■ **State and locally supported** 2-year, founded 1923, part of Kansas Board of Regents
- ■ **Calendar** semesters
- ■ **Degree** certificates and associate
- ■ **Small-town** 39-acre campus with easy access to Tulsa
- ■ **Endowment** $2.8 million
- ■ **Coed**, 1,766 undergraduate students, 38% full-time, 54% women, 46% men

Undergraduates 665 full-time, 1,101 part-time. Students come from 19 states and territories, 4 other countries, 8% are from out of state, 12% African American, 0.3% Asian American or Pacific Islander, 2% Hispanic American, 2% Native American, 1% international, 38% transferred in, 27% live on campus.

Freshmen *Admission:* 1,499 applied, 1,499 admitted, 371 enrolled. *Test scores:* ACT scores over 18: 54%; ACT scores over 24: 13%; ACT scores over 30: 1%.

Faculty *Total:* 85, 60% full-time, 5% with terminal degrees. *Student/faculty ratio:* 20:1.

Majors Accounting; administrative assistant and secretarial science; agricultural business and management; agricultural economics; agricultural mechanization; agricultural teacher education; agriculture; animal sciences; applied art; art; athletic training; automobile/automotive mechanics technology; behavioral sciences; biological and physical sciences; biology/biological sciences; botany/plant biology; broadcast journalism; business administration and management; business machine repair; business teacher education; carpentry; chemistry; communications technology; computer and information sciences; computer programming; computer science; construction engineering technology; consumer merchandising/retailing management; drafting and design technology; dramatic/theatre arts; drawing; economics; education; elementary education;

emergency medical technology (EMT paramedic); engineering; English; family and consumer sciences/human sciences; history; horticultural science; humanities; industrial technology; information science/studies; journalism; legal administrative assistant/secretary; liberal arts and sciences/liberal studies; machine tool technology; marketing/marketing management; mass communication/media; mathematics; mechanical engineering/mechanical technology; medical administrative assistant and medical secretary; music; music teacher education; nursing (licensed practical/vocational nurse training); nursing (registered nurse training); occupational therapy; physical education teaching and coaching; political science and government; pre-engineering; psychology; radio and television; social sciences; social work; sociology; telecommunications; voice and opera; welding technology; wind/percussion instruments.

Academic Programs *Special study options:* academic remediation for entering students, adult/continuing education programs, advanced placement credit, cooperative education, distance learning, double majors, English as a second language, honors programs, internships, part-time degree program, services for LD students, student-designed majors, summer session for credit.

Library Russell H. Graham Learning Resource Center plus 1 other with 27,482 titles, 238 serial subscriptions, 1,415 audiovisual materials, an OPAC, a Web page.

Computers on Campus 90 computers available on campus for general student use. A campuswide network can be accessed from off campus. Internet access, at least one staffed computer lab available.

Student Life *Housing Options:* coed. Campus housing is university owned. *Activities and Organizations:* drama/theater group, student-run television station, choral group, marching band, Student Government Association, Phi Theta Kappa, Delta Psi Omega, Agriculture Club. *Campus security:* 24-hour patrols, late-night transport/escort service. *Student services:* health clinic, personal/psychological counseling, women's center.

Athletics Member NJCAA. *Intercollegiate sports:* baseball M(s), basketball M(s)/W(s), cross-country running M(s)/W(s), football M(s), golf M(s), softball W(s), track and field M(s)/W(s), volleyball W(s). *Intramural sports:* basketball M/W, bowling M/W, soccer M/W, table tennis M/W, tennis M/W, volleyball M/W, weight lifting M.

Standardized Tests *Required:* ACT (for placement), ACT COMPASS (for placement).

Costs (2005–06) *Tuition:* state resident $896 full-time, $28 per credit hour part-time; nonresident $2176 full-time, $68 per credit hour part-time. *Required fees:* $704 full-time, $22 per credit hour part-time. *Room and board:* $3380.

Financial Aid Of all full-time matriculated undergraduates who enrolled in 2003, 120 Federal Work-Study jobs (averaging $1000).

Applying *Options:* common application, early admission, deferred entrance. *Required:* high school transcript. *Application deadline:* rolling (freshmen), rolling (transfers). *Notification:* continuous (freshmen).

Admissions Contact Ms. Kim Lay, Coordinator/Advisor of Enrollment Services, Coffeyville Community College, 400 West 11th, Coffeyville, KS 67337. *Phone:* 620-252-7155. *Fax:* 620-252-7098.

COLBY COMMUNITY COLLEGE

Colby, Kansas

- ■ **State and locally supported** 2-year, founded 1964, part of Kansas Board of Regents
- ■ **Calendar** semesters
- ■ **Degree** certificates, diplomas, and associate
- ■ **Small-town** 80-acre campus
- ■ **Endowment** $3.2 million
- ■ **Coed**, 1,761 undergraduate students, 59% full-time, 54% women, 46% men

Colby Community College offers 2-year career programs in veterinary technology, beef and equine production, criminal justice, physical therapist assistant studies, nursing, office technology, midmanagement, dental hygiene, and radio/television; transfer curricula in health, education, arts and letters, behavioral science, business, mass communications, and math/science; preprofessional options in law, engineering, and medicine; and a College-owned farm operated by agriculture students.

Undergraduates 1,038 full-time, 723 part-time. Students come from 14 states and territories, 5 other countries, 13% are from out of state, 1% African American, 0.6% Asian American or Pacific Islander, 2% Hispanic American, 0.2% Native American, 2% international, 8% transferred in, 30% live on campus.

Freshmen *Admission:* 638 applied, 638 admitted, 638 enrolled. *Average high school GPA:* 3.28.

Faculty *Total:* 62, 87% full-time, 23% with terminal degrees. *Student/faculty ratio:* 20:1.

Majors Accounting; agricultural business and management; agricultural economics; agricultural teacher education; agriculture; agronomy and crop science; animal sciences; behavioral sciences; biological and physical sciences; biology/biological sciences; broadcast journalism; business administration and management; business/managerial economics; business teacher education; chemistry; child development; commercial and advertising art; computer and information sciences related; computer science; criminal justice/law enforcement administration; dental hygiene; dramatic/theatre arts; education; English; family and consumer sciences/human sciences; farm and ranch management; foods, nutrition, and wellness; forestry; geology/earth science; history; humanities; journalism; kindergarten/preschool education; liberal arts and sciences/liberal studies; library science; marketing/marketing management; mass communication/media; mathematics; music; music teacher education; nursing (licensed practical/vocational nurse training); nursing (registered nurse training); pharmacy; physical education teaching and coaching; physical therapist assistant; physical therapy; political science and government; pre-engineering; psychology; radio and television; range science and management; science teacher education; social work; sociology; veterinary sciences; veterinary technology; wildlife biology; zoology/animal biology.

Academic Programs *Special study options:* academic remediation for entering students, adult/continuing education programs, advanced placement credit, cooperative education, distance learning, double majors, honors programs, internships, part-time degree program, services for LD students, student-designed majors, summer session for credit.

Library Davis Library with 32,000 titles, 350 serial subscriptions, an OPAC.

Computers on Campus 178 computers available on campus for general student use. A campuswide network can be accessed from student residence rooms and from off campus. Internet access, at least one staffed computer lab available.

Student Life *Housing:* on-campus residence required for freshman year. *Options:* men-only, women-only. Campus housing is university owned. *Activities and Organizations:* drama/theater group, student-run newspaper, radio and television station, choral group, KSNEA, Physical Therapist Assistants Club, Block and Bridle, SVTA, COPNS. *Campus security:* 24-hour emergency response devices and patrols. *Student services:* health clinic, personal/psychological counseling.

Athletics Member NJCAA. *Intercollegiate sports:* baseball M(s), basketball M(s)/W(s), cheerleading W(s), cross-country running M(s)/W(s), equestrian sports M/W, golf M(s)/W(s), softball W(s), track and field M(s)/W(s), volleyball W(s), wrestling M(s). *Intramural sports:* basketball M/W, softball M/W, volleyball M/W.

Standardized Tests *Required:* ACT ASSET or ACT COMPASS (for placement).

Costs (2005–06) *Tuition:* state resident $1376 full-time, $43 per credit hour part-time; nonresident $2560 full-time, $80 per credit hour part-time. *Required fees:* $640 full-time, $20 per credit hour part-time. *Room and board:* $3542. Room and board charges vary according to board plan. *Payment plan:* installment. *Waivers:* senior citizens and employees or children of employees.

Financial Aid Of all full-time matriculated undergraduates who enrolled in 2003, 95 Federal Work-Study jobs (averaging $1500). 30 state and other part-time jobs (averaging $2000).

Applying *Options:* early admission, deferred entrance. *Required:* high school transcript. *Application deadline:* rolling (freshmen), rolling (transfers). *Notification:* continuous (freshmen).

Admissions Contact Mr. Skip Sharp, Dean of Students, Colby Community College, 1255 South Range, Colby, KS 67701-4099. *Phone:* 785-462-3984 Ext. 200. *Toll-free phone:* 888-634-9350 Ext. 690. *Fax:* 785-460-4691. *E-mail:* leasa@colbycc.edu.

COWLEY COUNTY COMMUNITY COLLEGE AND AREA VOCATIONAL-TECHNICAL SCHOOL
Arkansas City, Kansas

- **State and locally supported** 2-year, founded 1922, part of Kansas State Board of Education
- **Calendar** semesters
- **Degree** certificates, diplomas, and associate
- **Small-town** 19-acre campus
- **Endowment** $1.2 million
- **Coed,** 4,523 undergraduate students, 51% full-time, 59% women, 41% men

Undergraduates 2,300 full-time, 2,223 part-time. Students come from 16 states and territories, 12 other countries, 4% are from out of state, 7% African American, 5% Asian American or Pacific Islander, 3% Hispanic American, 0.9% Native American, 1% international, 7% live on campus.

Freshmen *Admission:* 1,197 applied, 1,197 admitted, 1,197 enrolled. *Average high school GPA:* 2.89. *Test scores:* ACT scores over 18: 67%; ACT scores over 24: 14%; ACT scores over 30: 1%.

Faculty *Total:* 238, 20% full-time. *Student/faculty ratio:* 28:1.

Majors Accounting; administrative assistant and secretarial science; agricultural mechanization; agriculture; agronomy and crop science; airframe mechanics and aircraft maintenance technology; art; automobile/automotive mechanics technology; business administration and management; chemistry; child development; computer graphics; consumer merchandising/retailing management; corrections; cosmetology; criminal justice/law enforcement administration; criminal justice/police science; drafting and design technology; dramatic/theatre arts;

education; elementary education; emergency medical technology (EMT paramedic); engineering technology; family and consumer economics related; farm and ranch management; hotel/motel administration; industrial arts; industrial radiologic technology; journalism; liberal arts and sciences/liberal studies; machine tool technology; marketing/marketing management; music; parks, recreation and leisure; physical education teaching and coaching; physical therapy; pre-engineering; religious studies; sign language interpretation and translation; social work; welding technology.

Academic Programs *Special study options:* academic remediation for entering students, accelerated degree program, adult/continuing education programs, advanced placement credit, cooperative education, distance learning, external degree program, independent study, part-time degree program, student-designed majors, summer session for credit.

Library Renn Memorial Library with 26,000 titles, 100 serial subscriptions.

Computers on Campus 53 computers available on campus for general student use. A campuswide network can be accessed. Internet access, at least one staffed computer lab available.

Student Life *Housing Options:* coed, men-only, women-only. *Activities and Organizations:* drama/theater group, student-run newspaper, choral group, Volunteer Club, Peers Advocating for Wellness, Phi Theta Kappa, Student Government Association, Phi Beta Lambda. *Campus security:* student patrols, late-night transport/escort service, residence hall entrances are locked at night. *Student services:* health clinic.

Athletics Member NJCAA. *Intercollegiate sports:* baseball M(s), basketball M(s)/W(s), golf M(s), softball W(s), tennis M(s)/W(s), volleyball W(s). *Intramural sports:* basketball M/W, bowling M/W, softball M/W, table tennis M/W, tennis M/W, volleyball M/W.

Standardized Tests *Required for some:* ACT ASSET, ACCUPLACER. *Recommended:* ACT (for placement).

Costs (2005–06) *Tuition:* area resident $1260 full-time, $42 per credit hour part-time; state resident $1410 full-time, $47 per credit hour part-time; nonresident $2790 full-time, $99 per credit hour part-time. Full-time tuition and fees vary according to course load. Part-time tuition and fees vary according to course load. *Required fees:* $540 full-time, $18 per credit hour part-time. *Room and board:* $3450. Room and board charges vary according to board plan.

Financial Aid Of all full-time matriculated undergraduates who enrolled in 2003, 50 Federal Work-Study jobs (averaging $1500). 75 state and other part-time jobs (averaging $2000).

Applying *Options:* early admission, deferred entrance. *Required:* high school transcript. *Application deadline:* rolling (freshmen), rolling (transfers).

Admissions Contact Ms. Sue Saia, Associate Dean of Admissions, Cowley County Community College and Area Vocational-Technical School, 125 South Second, PO Box 1147, Arkansas City, KS 67005-1147. *Phone:* 620-441-5245. *Toll-free phone:* 800-593-CCCC. *Fax:* 620-441-5264. *E-mail:* admissions@cowley.cc.ks.us.

DODGE CITY COMMUNITY COLLEGE
Dodge City, Kansas

- **State and locally supported** 2-year, founded 1935, part of Kansas State Board of Education
- **Calendar** semesters
- **Degree** certificates and associate
- **Small-town** 143-acre campus
- **Coed,** 1,956 undergraduate students

Undergraduates Students come from 20 states and territories, 5 other countries, 20% live on campus.

Faculty *Total:* 163, 34% full-time.

Majors Accounting; administrative assistant and secretarial science; agricultural business and management; agricultural economics; agricultural mechanization; agronomy and crop science; animal sciences; art; athletic training; automobile/automotive mechanics technology; behavioral sciences; biological and physical sciences; biology/biological sciences; broadcast journalism; business administration and management; chemistry; child development; clinical laboratory science/medical technology; communications technology; computer programming; computer science; construction engineering technology; cosmetology; criminal justice/law enforcement administration; data processing and data processing technology; dramatic/theatre arts; education; electrical, electronic and communications engineering technology; elementary education; engineering; engineering technology; English; equestrian studies; farm and ranch management; finance; fire science; forestry; health information/medical records administration; history; humanities; hydrology and water resources science; industrial arts; industrial technology; information science/studies; journalism; legal administrative assistant/secretary; liberal arts and sciences/liberal studies; marketing/marketing management; mass communication/media; mathematics; medical administrative assistant and medical secretary; music; music teacher education; nursing (licensed practical/vocational nurse training); nursing (registered nurse training); physical education teaching and coaching; physical sciences; physical therapy; physics; political science and government; pre-engineering; pre-pharmacy studies; psychology; radio and television; real estate;

Dodge City Community College (continued)

respiratory care therapy; social sciences; social work; speech and rhetoric; welding technology; wildlife biology.

Academic Programs *Special study options:* academic remediation for entering students, adult/continuing education programs, advanced placement credit, cooperative education, English as a second language, external degree program, internships, part-time degree program, student-designed majors, summer session for credit.

Library Learning Resource Center with 30,000 titles, 225 serial subscriptions.

Computers on Campus 125 computers available on campus for general student use. Internet access, at least one staffed computer lab available.

Student Life *Housing Options:* coed. *Activities and Organizations:* drama/theater group, student-run newspaper, radio station, choral group. *Student services:* health clinic, personal/psychological counseling.

Athletics Member NJCAA. *Intercollegiate sports:* baseball M(s), basketball M(s)/W(s), cross-country running M(s)/W(s), equestrian sports M/W, football M(s), golf M(s), softball W(s), volleyball W(s). *Intramural sports:* basketball M/W, bowling M/W, football M, golf M, racquetball M/W, volleyball M/W, weight lifting M/W.

Standardized Tests *Required:* ACT ASSET (for placement).

Costs (2005–06) *Tuition:* state resident $1120 full-time, $35 per credit hour part-time; nonresident $1344 full-time, $42 per credit hour part-time. Full-time tuition and fees vary according to course load. Part-time tuition and fees vary according to course load. *Required fees:* $806 full-time, $23 per credit hour part-time, $35 per term part-time. *Room and board:* $4060.

Applying *Options:* common application, early admission, deferred entrance. *Required:* high school transcript. *Application deadline:* rolling (freshmen), rolling (transfers). *Notification:* continuous (freshmen).

Admissions Contact Mr. Corbin Strobel, Director of Admissions, Placement, Testing and Student Services Marketing, Dodge City Community College, 2501 North 14th Avenue, Dodge City, KS 67801-2399. *Phone:* 316-225-1321. *Toll-free phone:* 800-742-9519. *Fax:* 316-225-0918. *E-mail:* admin@dccc.dodge-city.cc.ks.us.

DONNELLY COLLEGE
Kansas City, Kansas

- **Independent Roman Catholic** 2-year, founded 1949
- **Calendar** semesters
- **Degree** certificates and associate
- **Urban** 4-acre campus
- **Endowment** $4.0 million
- **Coed**

Faculty *Student/faculty ratio:* 10:1.

Student Life *Campus security:* 24-hour emergency response devices.

Costs (2004–05) *Tuition:* $4480 full-time. Full-time tuition and fees vary according to course load. Part-time tuition and fees vary according to course load.

Applying *Options:* early admission, deferred entrance. *Recommended:* high school transcript.

Admissions Contact Mr. Kevin Kelley, Vice President of Enrollment Management, Donnelly College, 608 North 18th Street, Kansas City, KS 66102. *Phone:* 913-621-8769. *Fax:* 913-621-0354. *E-mail:* bernetta@donnelly.edu.

FLINT HILLS TECHNICAL COLLEGE
Emporia, Kansas

Admissions Contact 3301 West 18th Avenue, Emporia, KS 66801. *Toll-free phone:* 800-711-6947.

FORT SCOTT COMMUNITY COLLEGE
Fort Scott, Kansas

- **State and locally supported** 2-year, founded 1919
- **Calendar** semesters
- **Degree** certificates and associate
- **Small-town** 147-acre campus
- **Coed**, 1,923 undergraduate students

Undergraduates Students come from 24 states and territories, 6% African American, 0.5% Asian American or Pacific Islander, 1% Hispanic American, 1% Native American, 0.3% international, 9% live on campus.

Freshmen *Admission:* 662 applied.

Faculty *Total:* 105, 33% full-time. *Student/faculty ratio:* 26:1.

Majors Accounting; administrative assistant and secretarial science; agricultural business and management; agricultural economics; agricultural mechanization; agricultural teacher education; agriculture; agronomy and crop science;

animal sciences; architectural engineering technology; athletic training; business administration and management; clinical laboratory science/medical technology; commercial and advertising art; computer science; consumer merchandising/retailing management; cosmetology; criminal justice/law enforcement administration; drafting and design technology; education; electrical, electronic and communications engineering technology; emergency medical technology (EMT paramedic); hydrology and water resources science; industrial arts; legal administrative assistant/secretary; liberal arts and sciences/liberal studies; medical administrative assistant and medical secretary; music; nursing (registered nurse training); photography; physical sciences; public policy analysis; quality control technology; teacher assistant/aide; transportation technology; welding technology.

Academic Programs *Special study options:* academic remediation for entering students, adult/continuing education programs, advanced placement credit, cooperative education, distance learning, English as a second language, external degree program, independent study, internships, part-time degree program, services for LD students, student-designed majors, study abroad, summer session for credit. *ROTC:* Army (c).

Library Learning Resource Center with 25,308 titles, 124 serial subscriptions, an OPAC.

Computers on Campus 95 computers available on campus for general student use. Internet access, at least one staffed computer lab available.

Student Life *Housing Options:* coed. *Activities and Organizations:* drama/theater group, choral group, marching band, Aggie Club, Student Nurses Association, student government, Soccer Club, Phi Theta Kappa. *Campus security:* controlled dormitory access, evening security from 9 pm to 6am. *Student services:* personal/psychological counseling.

Athletics Member NJCAA. *Intercollegiate sports:* baseball M(s), basketball M(s)/W(s), football M(s), softball W(s), volleyball W(s). *Intramural sports:* basketball M/W, racquetball M/W, soccer M/W, softball M/W, table tennis M/W, tennis M/W, volleyball M/W, weight lifting M/W.

Standardized Tests *Required:* ACT ASSET (for placement). *Required for some:* ACT (for placement).

Costs (2004–05) *Tuition:* state resident $990 full-time, $33 per credit hour part-time; nonresident $2670 full-time, $89 per credit hour part-time. Full-time tuition and fees vary according to course load. Part-time tuition and fees vary according to course load. *Required fees:* $694 full-time, $23 per credit hour part-time, $2 per term part-time. *Payment plan:* installment.

Applying *Options:* early admission, deferred entrance. *Application deadlines:* 8/15 (freshmen), 8/15 (transfers).

Admissions Contact Mrs. Mert Barrows, Director of Admissions, Fort Scott Community College, 2108 South Horton, Fort Scott, KS 66701. *Phone:* 316-223-2700 Ext. 353. *Toll-free phone:* 800-874-3722.

GARDEN CITY COMMUNITY COLLEGE
Garden City, Kansas

- **County-supported** 2-year, founded 1919, part of Kansas Board of Regents
- **Calendar** semesters
- **Degree** certificates and associate
- **Rural** 63-acre campus
- **Endowment** $4.9 million
- **Coed**, 2,174 undergraduate students, 43% full-time, 55% women, 45% men

Undergraduates 925 full-time, 1,249 part-time. Students come from 31 states and territories, 7% are from out of state, 9% African American, 2% Asian American or Pacific Islander, 20% Hispanic American, 0.6% Native American, 0.6% international, 12% live on campus. *Retention:* 78% of 2002 full-time freshmen returned.

Freshmen *Admission:* 845 applied, 845 admitted, 319 enrolled. *Average high school GPA:* 3.07. *Test scores:* ACT scores over 18: 64%; ACT scores over 24: 12%.

Faculty *Total:* 184, 39% full-time, 2% with terminal degrees. *Student/faculty ratio:* 17:1.

Majors Accounting; administrative assistant and secretarial science; agricultural business and management; agricultural economics; agricultural mechanization; agricultural mechanization related; agriculture; athletic training; automobile/automotive mechanics technology; biological and physical sciences; business administration and management; ceramic arts and ceramics; child development; commercial and advertising art; computer engineering technology; computer graphics; computer programming; computer science; computer systems networking and telecommunications; consumer merchandising/retailing management; cosmetology; criminal justice/law enforcement administration; criminal justice/police science; developmental and child psychology; drafting and design technology; dramatic/theatre arts; education; electrical, electronic and communications engineering technology; elementary education; emergency medical technology (EMT paramedic); engineering; engineering technology; English; family and community services; family and consumer sciences/human sciences; farm and ranch management; fashion/apparel design; fashion merchandising; fine/studio arts; health and physical education related; humanities; industrial arts; industrial technology; information science/studies; interior design; journalism; legal administrative assistant/secretary; liberal arts and sciences/liberal studies; marketing/ marketing management; mathematics; mechanical design technology; mechanical engineering/mechanical technology; metal and jewelry arts; music; nursing (registered nurse training); physical education teaching and coaching; pre-engineering; retailing; social sciences; sociology; speech and rhetoric; teacher assistant/aide; trade and industrial teacher education; welding technology.

Academic Programs *Special study options:* academic remediation for entering students, adult/continuing education programs, advanced placement credit, distance learning, English as a second language, external degree program, part-time degree program, services for LD students, student-designed majors, summer session for credit.

Library Saffell Library with 42,080 titles, 116 serial subscriptions, 303 audiovisual materials, an OPAC, a Web page.

Computers on Campus 150 computers available on campus for general student use. A campuswide network can be accessed from student residence rooms. Internet access, at least one staffed computer lab available.

Student Life *Housing Options:* coed. Campus housing is university owned. *Activities and Organizations:* drama/theater group, student-run newspaper, choral group, student government, Hispanic American Leadership Organization, Business Professionals of America, Criminal Justice Organization, Phi Theta Kappa. *Campus security:* 24-hour emergency response devices and patrols, student patrols, late-night transport/escort service, controlled dormitory access. *Student services:* health clinic, personal/psychological counseling.

Athletics Member NJCAA. *Intercollegiate sports:* baseball M(s), basketball M(s)/W(s), cheerleading M(s)/W(s), cross-country running M(s)/W(s), football M(s), soccer M/W, softball W(s), track and field M(s)/W(s), volleyball W(s). *Intramural sports:* archery M/W, basketball M/W, bowling M/W, football M/W, golf M/W, racquetball M/W, table tennis M/W, tennis M/W, track and field M/W, volleyball M/W.

Standardized Tests *Required:* ACT COMPASS (for placement).

Costs (2005–06) *Tuition:* state resident $1248 full-time, $39 per credit hour part-time; nonresident $2080 full-time, $65 per credit hour part-time. Full-time tuition and fees vary according to course load and location. Part-time tuition and fees vary according to course load and location. *Required fees:* $672 full-time, $21 per credit hour part-time. *Room and board:* $4500. Room and board charges vary according to housing facility. *Payment plan:* installment. *Waivers:* children of alumni and senior citizens.

Financial Aid Of all full-time matriculated undergraduates who enrolled in 2003, 90 Federal Work-Study jobs (averaging $1000). 100 state and other part-time jobs (averaging $900).

Applying *Required:* high school transcript. *Application deadline:* rolling (freshmen), rolling (transfers).

Admissions Contact Ms. Nikki Geier, Director of Admissions, Garden City Community College, 801 Campus Drive, Garden City, KS 67846. *Phone:* 620-276-7611 Ext. 531. *E-mail:* nikki.geier@gcccks.edu.

HESSTON COLLEGE
Hesston, Kansas

- **Independent Mennonite** 2-year, founded 1909
- **Calendar** semesters
- **Degree** associate
- **Small-town** 50-acre campus with easy access to Wichita
- **Coed,** 465 undergraduate students, 88% full-time, 52% women, 48% men

Undergraduates 411 full-time, 54 part-time. Students come from 30 states and territories, 13 other countries, 50% are from out of state, 2% African American, 0.6% Asian American or Pacific Islander, 1% Hispanic American, 11% international, 9% transferred in, 74% live on campus. *Retention:* 76% of 2002 full-time freshmen returned.

Freshmen *Admission:* 521 applied, 521 admitted, 167 enrolled. *Average high school GPA:* 3.35. *Test scores:* SAT verbal scores over 500: 62%; SAT math scores over 500: 67%; ACT scores over 18: 86%; SAT verbal scores over 600: 19%; SAT math scores over 600: 20%; ACT scores over 24: 37%; SAT verbal scores over 700: 2%; SAT math scores over 700: 3%; ACT scores over 30: 7%.

Faculty *Total:* 44, 43% full-time, 18% with terminal degrees. *Student/faculty ratio:* 12:1.

Majors Biblical studies; business administration and management; computer/ information technology services administration related; kindergarten/preschool education; liberal arts and sciences/liberal studies; nursing (registered nurse training); pastoral studies/counseling.

Academic Programs *Special study options:* academic remediation for entering students, advanced placement credit, cooperative education, double majors, English as a second language, independent study, internships, part-time degree program, services for LD students, summer session for credit.

Library Mary Miller Library with 35,000 titles, 234 serial subscriptions, 2,409 audiovisual materials, an OPAC, a Web page.

Computers on Campus 67 computers available on campus for general student use. A campuswide network can be accessed from student residence rooms and from off campus. Internet access, at least one staffed computer lab available.

Student Life *Housing:* on-campus residence required through sophomore year. *Options:* men-only, women-only. Campus housing is university owned. Freshman campus housing is guaranteed. *Activities and Organizations:* drama/theater group, student-run newspaper, choral group. *Campus security:* 24-hour emergency response devices. *Student services:* personal/psychological counseling.

Athletics Member NJCAA. *Intercollegiate sports:* baseball M(s), basketball M(s)/W(s), soccer M(s), softball W(s), tennis M/W, volleyball W(s). *Intramural sports:* basketball M/W, golf M(c)/W(c), soccer M/W, softball W, tennis M/W, volleyball M/W.

Standardized Tests *Recommended:* SAT or ACT (for placement).

Costs (2005–06) *Comprehensive fee:* $20,990 includes full-time tuition ($15,150), mandatory fees ($220), and room and board ($5620). Part-time tuition: $630 per hour. Part-time tuition and fees vary according to course load. *Required fees:* $55 per term part-time. *Payment plan:* installment. *Waivers:* senior citizens and employees or children of employees.

Financial Aid Of all full-time matriculated undergraduates who enrolled in 2003, 120 Federal Work-Study jobs (averaging $800).

Applying *Options:* electronic application, early admission, deferred entrance. *Application fee:* $15. *Required:* high school transcript, 2 letters of recommendation. *Required for some:* interview. *Application deadline:* rolling (freshmen), rolling (transfers).

Admissions Contact Mr. Clark Roth, Vice President for Admissions, Hesston College, Box 3000, Hesston, KS 67062. *Phone:* 620-327-8222. *Toll-free phone:* 800-995-2757. *Fax:* 620-327-8300. *E-mail:* admissions@hesston.edu.

HIGHLAND COMMUNITY COLLEGE
Highland, Kansas

- **State and locally supported** 2-year, founded 1858, part of Kansas Community College System
- **Calendar** semesters
- **Degree** certificates and associate
- **Rural** 20-acre campus
- **Coed,** 3,040 undergraduate students

Undergraduates Students come from 9 states and territories.

Faculty *Total:* 226, 15% full-time.

Majors Accounting; administrative assistant and secretarial science; advertising; agricultural business and management; agricultural economics; agricultural teacher education; agriculture; agronomy and crop science; animal sciences; art; athletic training; automobile/automotive mechanics technology; biology/biological sciences; business administration and management; business teacher education; carpentry; chemistry; clinical laboratory science/medical technology; commercial and advertising art; computer science; construction engineering technology; criminal justice/law enforcement administration; criminal justice/police science; cytotechnology; dairy science; data processing and data processing technology; dental hygiene; drafting and design technology; dramatic/theatre arts; education; emergency medical technology (EMT paramedic); English; family and consumer sciences/human sciences; farm and ranch management; fashion/apparel design; fiber, textile and weaving arts; food science; forestry; funeral service and mortuary science; geology/earth science; health information/medical records administration; health teacher education; history; industrial arts; industrial radiologic technology; information science/studies; journalism; legal administrative assistant/secretary; liberal arts and sciences/liberal studies; library science; mathematics; medical administrative assistant and medical secretary; music; natural resources/conservation; nursing (registered nurse training); occupational therapy; pharmacy; physical education teaching and coaching; physical sciences; physical therapy; political science and government; pre-engineering; psychology; respiratory care therapy; social work; sociology; telecommunications; theology; veterinary sciences.

Academic Programs *Special study options:* academic remediation for entering students, adult/continuing education programs, advanced placement credit, cooperative education, internships, off-campus study, part-time degree program, services for LD students, student-designed majors, summer session for credit. *ROTC:* Army (c).

Library 30,000 titles, 268 serial subscriptions.

Computers on Campus 94 computers available on campus for general student use. At least one staffed computer lab available.

Student Life *Housing Options:* coed. *Activities and Organizations:* drama/ theater group, student-run newspaper.

Athletics Member NJCAA. *Intercollegiate sports:* baseball M/W, basketball M(s)/W(s), cross-country running M(s)/W(s), football M(s), golf M(s), track and field M(s)/W(s), volleyball W(s). *Intramural sports:* basketball M/W, cross-country running M/W, football M, golf M, tennis M/W, track and field M/W, volleyball M/W.

Highland Community College (continued)

Standardized Tests *Required:* ACT ASSET (for placement). *Recommended:* ACT (for placement).

Costs (2005–06) *Tuition:* area resident $888 full-time, $37 per credit hour part-time; state resident $1080 full-time, $45 per credit hour part-time; nonresident $2280 full-time, $95 per credit hour part-time. *Required fees:* $1056 full-time, $44 per credit hour part-time. *Room and board:* $3872; room only: $2242.

Financial Aid Of all full-time matriculated undergraduates who enrolled in 2003, 75 Federal Work-Study jobs (averaging $1200). 25 state and other part-time jobs (averaging $1000).

Applying *Options:* early admission. *Required:* high school transcript. *Application deadlines:* 8/20 (freshmen), 8/20 (transfers). *Notification:* continuous (freshmen).

Admissions Contact Ms. Cheryl Rasmussen, Vice President of Student Services, Highland Community College, 606 West Main Street, Highland, KS 66035-4165. *Phone:* 785-442-6020. *Fax:* 785-442-6100.

HUTCHINSON COMMUNITY COLLEGE AND AREA VOCATIONAL SCHOOL
Hutchinson, Kansas

- **State and locally supported** 2-year, founded 1928, part of Kansas Board of Regents
- **Calendar** semesters
- **Degree** certificates and associate
- **Small-town** 47-acre campus
- **Endowment** $3.5 million
- **Coed**, 4,526 undergraduate students, 46% full-time, 58% women, 42% men

Undergraduates 2,076 full-time, 2,450 part-time. Students come from 34 states and territories, 18 other countries, 5% are from out of state, 5% African American, 0.7% Asian American or Pacific Islander, 5% Hispanic American, 1% Native American, 0.6% international, 10% transferred in, 11% live on campus. *Retention:* 60% of 2002 full-time freshmen returned.

Freshmen *Admission:* 2,908 applied, 2,908 admitted, 1,007 enrolled. *Average high school GPA:* 2.84. *Test scores:* ACT scores over 18: 69%; ACT scores over 24: 16%; ACT scores over 30: 1%.

Faculty *Total:* 328, 34% full-time, 5% with terminal degrees. *Student/faculty ratio:* 16:1.

Majors Administrative assistant and secretarial science; agricultural mechanization; agriculture; autobody/collision and repair technology; automobile/automotive mechanics technology; biology/biological sciences; business and personal/financial services marketing; business/commerce; carpentry; child care and support services management; communication/speech communication and rhetoric; communications technology; computer and information sciences; criminal justice/police science; drafting and design technology; education; educational/instructional media design; electrical/electronics equipment installation and repair; emergency medical technology (EMT paramedic); engineering; English; family and consumer sciences/human sciences; farm and ranch management; fire science; foreign languages and literatures; health information/medical records technology; legal assistant/paralegal; liberal arts and sciences/liberal studies; machine tool technology; management information systems; manufacturing technology; mathematics; medical radiologic technology; nursing (registered nurse training); physical sciences; psychology; retailing; social sciences; visual and performing arts; welding technology.

Academic Programs *Special study options:* academic remediation for entering students, adult/continuing education programs, advanced placement credit, cooperative education, distance learning, double majors, English as a second language, honors programs, independent study, internships, part-time degree program, services for LD students, student-designed majors, summer session for credit. *ROTC:* Army (c).

Library John F. Kennedy Library plus 1 other with 41,812 titles, 245 serial subscriptions, 3,039 audiovisual materials, an OPAC, a Web page.

Computers on Campus 475 computers available on campus for general student use. A campuswide network can be accessed from off campus. Internet access, at least one staffed computer lab available.

Student Life *Housing Options:* men-only, women-only. Campus housing is university owned. *Activities and Organizations:* drama/theater group, student-run newspaper, choral group, Student Government Association, Black Cultural Society, Hispanic-American Leadership Organization, Hutchinson Christian Fellowship, Campus Crusade for Christ. *Campus security:* 24-hour emergency response devices and patrols, student patrols, late-night transport/escort service, controlled dormitory access. *Student services:* health clinic, personal/psychological counseling.

Athletics Member NJCAA. *Intercollegiate sports:* baseball M(s), basketball M(s)/W(s), cheerleading W(s), cross-country running M(s)/W(s), football M(s), golf M(s), softball W(s), tennis M(s)/W(s), track and field M(s)/W(s), volleyball

W(s). *Intramural sports:* badminton M/W, basketball M/W, bowling M/W, football M/W, racquetball M/W, soccer M/W, tennis M/W, track and field M/W, volleyball M/W.

Standardized Tests *Required for some:* ACT (for placement), ACT ASSET, ACT COMPASS, ACCUPLACER. *Recommended:* ACT (for placement).

Costs (2005–06) *Tuition:* state resident $1600 full-time, $50 per hour part-time; nonresident $2816 full-time, $88 per hour part-time. *Required fees:* $480 full-time, $15 per hour part-time. *Room and board:* $4060.

Applying *Options:* electronic application, early admission, deferred entrance. *Required for some:* interview. *Recommended:* high school transcript. *Application deadline:* rolling (freshmen), rolling (transfers).

Admissions Contact Ms. Lori Bair, Director of Admissions, Hutchinson Community College and Area Vocational School, 1300 North Plum, Hutchinson, KS 67501. *Phone:* 620-665-3536. *Toll-free phone:* 800-289-3501 Ext. 3536. *Fax:* 620-665-3301. *E-mail:* bairl@hutchcc.edu.

INDEPENDENCE COMMUNITY COLLEGE
Independence, Kansas

- **State-supported** 2-year, founded 1925, part of Kansas State Board of Education
- **Calendar** semesters
- **Degree** certificates and associate
- **Small-town** 68-acre campus
- **Coed**, 1,100 undergraduate students

Undergraduates Students come from 18 states and territories, 17 other countries, 9% are from out of state, 10% live on campus.

Faculty *Total:* 47, 64% full-time, 11% with terminal degrees. *Student/faculty ratio:* 17:1.

Majors Accounting; administrative assistant and secretarial science; art teacher education; athletic training; biological and physical sciences; biology/biological sciences; business administration and management; business teacher education; chemistry; child development; civil engineering technology; cosmetology; data processing and data processing technology; drafting and design technology; electrical, electronic and communications engineering technology; elementary education; emergency medical technology (EMT paramedic); engineering; engineering technology; English; finance; French; history; humanities; kindergarten/preschool education; liberal arts and sciences/liberal studies; mathematics; modern languages; music; music management and merchandising; music teacher education; natural sciences; physical education teaching and coaching; physical sciences; political science and government; pre-engineering; psychology; science teacher education; sociology; Spanish.

Academic Programs *Special study options:* academic remediation for entering students, adult/continuing education programs, advanced placement credit, cooperative education, English as a second language, honors programs, internships, part-time degree program, summer session for credit.

Library Independence Community College Library plus 1 other with 32,408 titles, 166 serial subscriptions.

Computers on Campus 75 computers available on campus for general student use. A campuswide network can be accessed from student residence rooms and from off campus. Internet access, online (class) registration, at least one staffed computer lab available.

Student Life *Housing:* on-campus residence required through sophomore year. *Options:* Campus housing is university owned. Freshman campus housing is guaranteed. *Activities and Organizations:* drama/theater group, student-run newspaper, choral group, Student Senate, Phi Theta Kappa, Student Ambassadors, Campus Christians, multicultural student organization. *Campus security:* night patrol. *Student services:* personal/psychological counseling.

Athletics Member NJCAA. *Intercollegiate sports:* baseball M(s), basketball M(s)/W(s), cheerleading M(s)/W(s), football M(s), softball W(s), tennis M(s)/W(s), track and field M(s)/W(s), volleyball W(s). *Intramural sports:* basketball M/W.

Standardized Tests *Recommended:* SAT or ACT (for placement).

Costs (2005–06) *Tuition:* area resident $6492 full-time, $56 per credit hour part-time; state resident $6652 full-time, $61 per credit hour part-time; nonresident $6652 full-time, $61 per credit hour part-time. *Required fees:* $768 full-time, $23 per credit hour part-time. *Room and board:* $4100. *Payment plan:* installment. *Waivers:* senior citizens.

Financial Aid Of all full-time matriculated undergraduates who enrolled in 2003, 85 Federal Work-Study jobs (averaging $900).

Applying *Options:* common application, electronic application, early admission. *Required:* high school transcript. *Application deadline:* rolling (freshmen), rolling (transfers).

Admissions Contact Mr. Richard Carvajal, Dean of Student Services, Independence Community College, PO Box 708, Independence, KS 67301. *Phone:* 620-331-4100. *Toll-free phone:* 800-842-6063. *Fax:* 620-331-5344. *E-mail:* admissions@indycc.edu.

JOHNSON COUNTY COMMUNITY COLLEGE

Overland Park, Kansas

- **State and locally supported** 2-year, founded 1967, part of Kansas State Board of Education
- **Calendar** semesters
- **Degree** certificates and associate
- **Suburban** 220-acre campus with easy access to Kansas City
- **Endowment** $4.4 million
- **Coed,** 18,612 undergraduate students, 34% full-time, 55% women, 45% men

Undergraduates 6,378 full-time, 12,234 part-time. Students come from 26 states and territories, 36 other countries, 5% are from out of state, 4% African American, 4% Asian American or Pacific Islander, 3% Hispanic American, 0.7% Native American, 1% international, 1% transferred in.

Freshmen *Admission:* 2,170 enrolled.

Faculty *Total:* 837, 36% full-time. *Student/faculty ratio:* 21:1.

Majors Accounting technology and bookkeeping; administrative assistant and secretarial science; airframe mechanics and aircraft maintenance technology; automobile/automotive mechanics technology; business administration and management; chemical technology; civil engineering technology; commercial and advertising art; computer programming (specific applications); computer systems networking and telecommunications; cosmetology; criminal justice/police science; dental hygiene; drafting and design technology; education; electrical and power transmission installation; emergency medical technology (EMT paramedic); fire services administration; health information/medical records technology; heating, air conditioning and refrigeration technology; hospitality administration; hotel/motel administration; legal assistant/paralegal; liberal arts and sciences/liberal studies; machine tool technology; nursing assistant/aide and patient care assistant; nursing (licensed practical/vocational nurse training); nursing (registered nurse training); occupational therapist assistant; physical therapist assistant; respiratory care therapy; retailing; sales, distribution and marketing; sign language interpretation and translation; tourism and travel services management; veterinary technology.

Academic Programs *Special study options:* academic remediation for entering students, adult/continuing education programs, advanced placement credit, cooperative education, distance learning, double majors, English as a second language, honors programs, independent study, internships, off-campus study, part-time degree program, services for LD students, student-designed majors, summer session for credit.

Library Johnson County Community College Library with 89,400 titles, 708 serial subscriptions, 4,770 audiovisual materials, an OPAC, a Web page.

Computers on Campus 800 computers available on campus for general student use. A campuswide network can be accessed from off campus. Internet access, online (class) registration, at least one staffed computer lab available.

Student Life *Housing:* college housing not available. *Activities and Organizations:* drama/theater group, student-run newspaper. *Campus security:* 24-hour emergency response devices and patrols, late-night transport/escort service.

Athletics Member NJCAA. *Intercollegiate sports:* baseball M(s), basketball M(s)/W(s), cross-country running M(s)/W(s), soccer M(s), softball W(s), tennis M(s)/W(s), track and field M(s)/W(s), volleyball W(s). *Intramural sports:* basketball M/W, soccer M, tennis M/W, volleyball M/W.

Standardized Tests *Required for some:* ACT (for placement), ACT ASSET.

Costs (2005–06) *Tuition:* area resident $1920 full-time, $64 per credit hour part-time; state resident $2370 full-time, $79 per credit hour part-time; nonresident $4350 full-time, $145 per credit hour part-time. Full-time tuition and fees vary according to course load. Part-time tuition and fees vary according to course load.

Financial Aid Of all full-time matriculated undergraduates who enrolled in 2003, 85 Federal Work-Study jobs (averaging $4000).

Applying *Options:* early admission. *Application fee:* $10. *Required for some:* high school transcript. *Application deadline:* rolling (freshmen), rolling (transfers). *Notification:* continuous (freshmen).

Admissions Contact Dr. Charles J. Carlsen, President, Johnson County Community College, 12345 College Park Boulevard, Overland Park, KS 66210. *Phone:* 913-469-8500 Ext. 3806.

KANSAS CITY KANSAS COMMUNITY COLLEGE

Kansas City, Kansas

- **State and locally supported** 2-year, founded 1923
- **Calendar** semesters
- **Degree** certificates, diplomas, and associate
- **Urban** 148-acre campus
- **Coed,** 5,573 undergraduate students, 33% full-time, 64% women, 36% men

Undergraduates 1,845 full-time, 3,728 part-time. Students come from 29 states and territories, 23 other countries, 5% are from out of state, 26% African American, 2% Asian American or Pacific Islander, 6% Hispanic American, 1% Native American, 2% international, 7% transferred in. *Retention:* 58% of 2002 full-time freshmen returned.

Freshmen *Admission:* 732 admitted, 732 enrolled.

Faculty *Total:* 355, 30% full-time. *Student/faculty ratio:* 15:1.

Majors Administrative assistant and secretarial science; business administration and management; child care and support services management; computer engineering technology; criminal justice/police science; data processing and data processing technology; drafting and design technology; emergency medical technology (EMT paramedic); fire science; funeral service and mortuary science; hazardous materials management and waste technology; international business/trade/commerce; legal assistant/paralegal; liberal arts and sciences and humanities related; liberal arts and sciences/liberal studies; nursing (registered nurse training); physical therapist assistant; recording arts technology; respiratory care therapy; respiratory therapy technician; substance abuse/addiction counseling; web page, digital/multimedia and information resources design.

Academic Programs *Special study options:* academic remediation for entering students, adult/continuing education programs, advanced placement credit, cooperative education, distance learning, English as a second language, external degree program, freshman honors college, honors programs, independent study, internships, part-time degree program, services for LD students, summer session for credit.

Library Kansas City Kansas Community College Library with 65,000 titles, 200 serial subscriptions, 12,000 audiovisual materials, an OPAC, a Web page.

Computers on Campus 775 computers available on campus for general student use. A campuswide network can be accessed from off campus. Internet access, online (class) registration, at least one staffed computer lab available.

Student Life *Housing:* college housing not available. *Activities and Organizations:* drama/theater group, student-run newspaper, television station, choral group, Student Senate, Phi Theta Kappa, Drama Club, The African American Student Union, Christian Student Union. *Campus security:* 24-hour emergency response devices and patrols, student patrols, late-night transport/escort service. *Student services:* health clinic, personal/psychological counseling, women's center.

Athletics Member NJCAA. *Intercollegiate sports:* baseball M(s), basketball M(s)/W(s), cross-country running M(s)/W(s), golf M(s), soccer M(s), softball W(s), track and field M(s)/W(s), volleyball W(s).

Standardized Tests *Required:* ACCUPLACER (for placement).

Costs (2005–06) *Tuition:* state resident $1372 full-time, $49 per credit hour part-time; nonresident $4116 full-time, $147 per credit hour part-time. Full-time tuition and fees vary according to course load. Part-time tuition and fees vary according to course load. *Required fees:* $280 full-time, $10 per credit hour part-time. *Payment plan:* installment. *Waivers:* employees or children of employees.

Financial Aid Of all full-time matriculated undergraduates who enrolled in 2003, 125 Federal Work-Study jobs (averaging $3000).

Applying *Options:* common application, electronic application. *Required:* high school transcript. *Application deadline:* rolling (freshmen), rolling (transfers). *Notification:* continuous (freshmen).

Admissions Contact Ms. Sherri Neff, Assistant Director of Admissions, Kansas City Kansas Community College, 7250 State Avenue, Kansas City, KS 66112. *Phone:* 913-288-7201. *Fax:* 913-288-7648. *E-mail:* admiss@toto.net.

LABETTE COMMUNITY COLLEGE

Parsons, Kansas

Admissions Contact Mr. Jeff Almond, Director of Admission, Labette Community College, 200 South 14th Street, Parsons, KS 67357. *Phone:* 620-421-6700 Ext. 1228. *Toll-free phone:* 888-LABETTE. *E-mail:* jeffa@labette.edu.

MANHATTAN AREA TECHNICAL COLLEGE

Manhattan, Kansas

- **State and locally supported** 2-year, founded 1965
- **Calendar** semesters
- **Degree** certificates, diplomas, and associate
- **Suburban** 19-acre campus
- **Coed,** 350 undergraduate students, 95% full-time, 41% women, 59% men

Undergraduates 331 full-time, 19 part-time. 6% African American, 0.3% Asian American or Pacific Islander, 3% Hispanic American, 1% Native American, 43% transferred in.

Freshmen *Admission:* 372 admitted, 109 enrolled.

Faculty *Total:* 31, 94% full-time. *Student/faculty ratio:* 20:1.

Manhattan Area Technical College (continued)

Majors Autobody/collision and repair technology; automobile/automotive mechanics technology; building/construction finishing, management, and inspection related; computer systems networking and telecommunications; computer technology/computer systems technology; drafting and design technology; electrical and power transmission installation related; heating, air conditioning and refrigeration technology; management information systems; nursing (licensed practical/vocational nurse training); nursing (registered nurse training); welding technology.

Library Matc Library with an OPAC.

Computers on Campus A campuswide network can be accessed. Internet access, at least one staffed computer lab available.

Student Life *Housing:* college housing not available.

Costs (2005–06) *Tuition:* $55 per credit hour part-time; state resident $1870 full-time, $55 per credit hour part-time. *Required fees:* $85 full-time, $5 per credit hour part-time. *Payment plan:* deferred payment.

Admissions Contact Mr. Rick Smith, Coordinator of Admissions and Recruitment, Manhattan Area Technical College, 3136 Dickens Avenue, Manhattan, KS 66503-2499. *Phone:* 785-587-2800 Ext. 104. *Toll-free phone:* 800-352-7575.

NATIONAL AMERICAN UNIVERSITY
Overland Park, Kansas

Admissions Contact 10310 Mastin, Overland Park, KS 66212.

NEOSHO COUNTY COMMUNITY COLLEGE
Chanute, Kansas

Admissions Contact Ms. Lisa Last, Director of Admission/Registrar, Neosho County Community College, 800 West 14th Street, Chanute, KS 66720-2699. *Phone:* 620-431-2820 Ext. 213. *Toll-free phone:* 800-729-6222. *Fax:* 620-431-6222.

NORTH CENTRAL KANSAS TECHNICAL COLLEGE
Beloit, Kansas

Admissions Contact Ms. Judy Heidrick, Director of Admissions, North Central Kansas Technical College, PO Box 507, Beloit, KS 67420. *Phone:* 800-658-4655. *Toll-free phone:* 800-658-4655.

NORTHEAST KANSAS TECHNICAL COLLEGE
Atchison, Kansas

- **State-supported** 2-year, founded 1965
- **Calendar** semesters
- **Coed**

Costs (2004–05) *Tuition:* state resident $1996 full-time; nonresident $9820 full-time.

Admissions Contact 1501 West Riley Street, Atchison, KS 66002. *Toll-free phone:* 800-567-4890.

NORTHWEST KANSASTECHNICAL COLLEGE
Goodland, Kansas

Admissions Contact PO Box 668, 1209 Harrison Street, Goodland, KS 67735. *Toll-free phone:* 800-316-4127.

PRATT COMMUNITY COLLEGE
Pratt, Kansas

- **State and locally supported** 2-year, founded 1938, part of Kansas Board of Regents
- **Calendar** semesters
- **Degree** certificates and associate
- **Rural** 80-acre campus with easy access to Wichita
- **Coed,** 1,451 undergraduate students, 43% full-time, 51% women, 49% men

Undergraduates 629 full-time, 822 part-time. Students come from 21 states and territories, 6% African American, 1% Asian American or Pacific Islander, 3%

Hispanic American, 0.7% Native American, 1% international, 22% live on campus. *Retention:* 51% of 2002 full-time freshmen returned.

Freshmen *Admission:* 904 applied, 904 admitted, 264 enrolled.

Faculty *Total:* 91, 45% full-time, 9% with terminal degrees. *Student/faculty ratio:* 14:1.

Majors Accounting; administrative assistant and secretarial science; agricultural business and management; agricultural economics; agricultural mechanization; agricultural teacher education; agriculture; animal/livestock husbandry and production; animal sciences; applied art; art; art teacher education; athletic training; automobile/automotive mechanics technology; biological and physical sciences; biology/biological sciences; broadcast journalism; business administration and management; business teacher education; chemistry; child development; commercial and advertising art; computer systems networking and telecommunications; computer/technical support; computer typography and composition equipment operation; counselor education/school counseling and guidance; data entry/microcomputer applications; data entry/microcomputer applications related; education; education (K-12); elementary education; energy management and systems technology; English; family and consumer sciences/human sciences; farm and ranch management; fine/studio arts; fish/game management; health teacher education; history; humanities; human services; industrial arts; kindergarten/preschool education; liberal arts and sciences/liberal studies; literature; marketing/marketing management; mass communication/media; mathematics; music; nursing (registered nurse training); physical education teaching and coaching; physical sciences; pre-engineering; professional studies; psychology; social sciences; social work; sociology; speech and rhetoric; speech/theater education; trade and industrial teacher education; welding technology; wildlife and wildlands science and management; wildlife biology; word processing.

Academic Programs *Special study options:* academic remediation for entering students, adult/continuing education programs, advanced placement credit, cooperative education, distance learning, internships, part-time degree program, summer session for credit.

Library 33,000 titles, 250 serial subscriptions, 1,200 audiovisual materials, an OPAC, a Web page.

Computers on Campus 100 computers available on campus for general student use. A campuswide network can be accessed from off campus. Internet access, at least one staffed computer lab available.

Student Life *Housing:* on-campus residence required through sophomore year. *Options:* coed, men-only, women-only. Campus housing is university owned. *Activities and Organizations:* drama/theater group, student-run newspaper, choral group, Phi Theta Kappa, Student Senate, Baptist Student Union, Block and Bridle, Business Professionals Club. *Campus security:* 24-hour patrols, late-night transport/escort service, controlled dormitory access. *Student services:* health clinic, personal/psychological counseling.

Athletics Member NJCAA. *Intercollegiate sports:* baseball M(s), basketball M(s)/W(s), cheerleading W(s), cross-country running M(s)/W(s), golf M(s)/W(s), softball W(s), track and field M(s)/W(s), volleyball W(s). *Intramural sports:* basketball M/W, softball M/W, table tennis M/W, volleyball M/W, weight lifting M/W.

Standardized Tests *Required for some:* ASSET.

Costs (2005–06) *Tuition:* state resident $1280 full-time, $40 per credit hour part-time; nonresident $1280 full-time, $40 per credit hour part-time. Full-time tuition and fees vary according to course load. Part-time tuition and fees vary according to course load. *Required fees:* $928 full-time, $29 per credit hour part-time. *Room and board:* $3659. Room and board charges vary according to board plan and housing facility. *Waivers:* employees or children of employees.

Financial Aid Of all full-time matriculated undergraduates who enrolled in 2003, 77 Federal Work-Study jobs (averaging $800). 13 state and other part-time jobs (averaging $800). *Financial aid deadline:* 8/1.

Applying *Options:* common application, early admission. *Required:* high school transcript. *Application deadline:* rolling (freshmen), rolling (transfers).

Admissions Contact Ms. Mary Bolyard, Administrative Assistant, Pratt Community College, 348 Northeast State Road 61, Pratt, KS 67124. *Phone:* 620-672-5641 Ext. 217. *Toll-free phone:* 800-794-3091. *Fax:* 620-672-5288. *E-mail:* lynnp@prattcc.edu.

SEWARD COUNTY COMMUNITY COLLEGE
Liberal, Kansas

- **State and locally supported** 2-year, founded 1969, part of Kansas State Board of Regents
- **Calendar** semesters
- **Degree** certificates, diplomas, and associate
- **Rural** 120-acre campus
- **Endowment** $8.5 million
- **Coed,** 2,325 undergraduate students, 23% full-time, 58% women, 42% men

Undergraduates 538 full-time, 1,787 part-time. Students come from 8 states and territories, 7 other countries, 11% are from out of state, 21% live on campus.

Faculty *Total:* 208, 4% with terminal degrees. *Student/faculty ratio:* 18:1.

Majors Accounting; administrative assistant and secretarial science; agriculture; art; athletic training; biological and physical sciences; biology/biological sciences; business administration and management; chemistry; child development; clinical/medical laboratory technology; computer programming; computer science; criminal justice/police science; data processing and data processing technology; dramatic/theatre arts; drawing; economics; education; elementary education; English; farm and ranch management; finance; fish/game management; history; journalism; liberal arts and sciences/liberal studies; literature; marketing/marketing management; mass communication/media; mathematics; music; natural sciences; nursing (licensed practical/vocational nurse training); nursing (registered nurse training); physical education teaching and coaching; physical sciences; pre-engineering; psychology; respiratory care therapy; social work; sociology; speech and rhetoric; surgical technology; wildlife and wildlands science and management.

Academic Programs *Special study options:* academic remediation for entering students, adult/continuing education programs, cooperative education, distance learning, English as a second language, external degree program, internships, part-time degree program, student-designed majors, summer session for credit.

Library Learning Resource Center plus 1 other with 32,926 titles, 318 serial subscriptions.

Computers on Campus 102 computers available on campus for general student use. Internet access, at least one staffed computer lab available.

Student Life *Housing Options:* coed. *Activities and Organizations:* drama/theater group, student-run newspaper, choral group, HALO, ATLAS, Block and Bridle, DECA, Sigma Chi Chi. *Campus security:* 24-hour patrols, late-night transport/escort service.

Athletics Member NJCAA. *Intercollegiate sports:* baseball M(s), basketball M(s)/W(s), tennis M(s)/W(s), volleyball W(s).

Standardized Tests *Recommended:* SAT or ACT (for placement).

Costs (2004–05) *Tuition:* state resident $1710 full-time, $57 per credit hour part-time; nonresident $2400 full-time, $80 per credit hour part-time.

Financial Aid Of all full-time matriculated undergraduates who enrolled in 2003, 60 Federal Work-Study jobs (averaging $1854). 168 state and other part-time jobs (averaging $1854).

Applying *Options:* early admission, deferred entrance. *Required:* high school transcript. *Required for some:* minimum 2.0 GPA, 1 letter of recommendation, interview. *Application deadlines:* 8/15 (freshmen), 8/15 (transfers). *Notification:* continuous (freshmen).

Admissions Contact Dr. Gerald Harris, Dean of Student Services, Seward County Community College, PO Box 1137, Liberal, KS 67905-1137. *Phone:* 620-624-1951 Ext. 617. *Toll-free phone:* 800-373-9951 Ext. 710. *Fax:* 316-629-2725. *E-mail:* admit@sccc.cc.ks.us.

WICHITA AREA TECHNICAL COLLEGE
Wichita, Kansas

- **District-supported** 2-year, founded 1963
- **Calendar** semesters
- **Degree** certificates, diplomas, and associate
- **Urban** campus
- **Coed**

Faculty *Student/faculty ratio:* 17:1.

Costs (2004–05) *Tuition:* state resident $2250 full-time, $75 per credit hour part-time; nonresident $11,820 full-time, $394 per credit hour part-time. *Required fees:* $85 full-time, $3 per credit hour part-time.

Applying *Application fee:* $3.

Admissions Contact Mrs. Shirley Antes, Facilitator for Accreditation and Institutional Advancement, Wichita Area Technical College, 301 South Grove Street, Wichita, KS 67211. *Phone:* 316-677-9559.

KENTUCKY

ASHLAND COMMUNITY AND TECHNICAL COLLEGE
Ashland, Kentucky

- **State-supported** 2-year, founded 1937, part of Kentucky Community and Technical College System
- **Calendar** semesters
- **Degree** certificates, diplomas, and associate
- **Small-town** 47-acre campus
- **Endowment** $870,926
- **Coed**, 2,565 undergraduate students

Undergraduates Students come from 6 states and territories, 10% are from out of state. *Retention:* 44% of 2002 full-time freshmen returned.

Freshmen *Admission:* 404 applied, 404 admitted. *Test scores:* ACT scores over 18: 53%; ACT scores over 24: 7%.

Faculty *Total:* 132, 48% full-time. *Student/faculty ratio:* 19:1.

Majors Accounting; administrative assistant and secretarial science; business administration and management; criminal justice/police science; engineering technology; information science/studies; liberal arts and sciences/liberal studies; management information systems; nursing (registered nurse training); physical therapist assistant; real estate; respiratory care therapy.

Academic Programs *Special study options:* academic remediation for entering students, adult/continuing education programs, advanced placement credit, cooperative education, distance learning, honors programs, internships, off-campus study, part-time degree program, services for LD students, summer session for credit.

Library Joseph and Sylvia Mansbach Memorial Library with 41,379 titles, 391 serial subscriptions, an OPAC.

Computers on Campus 150 computers available on campus for general student use. A campuswide network can be accessed from off campus. Internet access, at least one staffed computer lab available.

Student Life *Housing:* college housing not available. *Activities and Organizations:* drama/theater group, student-run newspaper, choral group, Phi Theta Kappa, Phi Beta Lambda, Kentucky Association of Nursing Students, Baptist Student Union/Students for Christ, Circle K. *Campus security:* 24-hour emergency response devices and patrols, late-night transport/escort service, electronic surveillance of bookstore and business office. *Student services:* personal/psychological counseling.

Athletics *Intramural sports:* fencing M/W, tennis M/W.

Standardized Tests *Required:* ACT COMPASS (for placement). *Recommended:* ACT (for placement).

Costs (2005–06) *Tuition:* state resident $2940 full-time, $98 per credit hour part-time; nonresident $8820 full-time, $294 per credit hour part-time.

Financial Aid Of all full-time matriculated undergraduates who enrolled in 2003, 12 Federal Work-Study jobs (averaging $2500). 1 state and other part-time job (averaging $1000).

Applying *Options:* common application, early admission, deferred entrance. *Required:* high school transcript. *Application deadlines:* 8/20 (freshmen), 8/20 (transfers).

Admissions Contact Mr. Steven D. Flouhouse, Dean of Students, Ashland Community and Technical College, 1400 College Drive, Ashland, KY 41101. *Phone:* 606-326-2114. *Toll-free phone:* 800-370-7191. *Fax:* 606-326-2192. *E-mail:* willie.mccullough@kctcs.net.

BECKFIELD COLLEGE
Florence, Kentucky

- **Proprietary** 2-year
- **Calendar** quarters
- **Degree** certificates, diplomas, and associate
- **Suburban** campus
- **Coed**

Faculty *Student/faculty ratio:* 17:1.

Admissions Contact Mr. Ken Leeds, Director of Admissions, Beckfield College, 16 Spiral Drive, Florence, KY 41042. *Phone:* 859-371-9393.

BIG SANDY COMMUNITY AND TECHNICAL COLLEGE
Prestonsburg, Kentucky

- **State-supported** 2-year, founded 1964, part of Kentucky Community and Technical College System
- **Calendar** semesters
- **Degree** associate
- **Rural** 50-acre campus
- **Endowment** $700,000
- **Coed**, 4,406 undergraduate students

Undergraduates Students come from 1 other state, 0.8% African American, 0.2% Asian American or Pacific Islander, 0.2% Hispanic American, 0.1% Native American.

Faculty *Total:* 114, 61% full-time.

Majors Accounting; business administration and management; criminal justice/law enforcement administration; dental hygiene; human services; information technology; liberal arts and sciences/liberal studies; management information systems; nursing (registered nurse training); nursing related; office occupations and clerical services; real estate.

Academic Programs *Special study options:* academic remediation for entering students, adult/continuing education programs, advanced placement credit,

Big Sandy Community and Technical College (continued)
cooperative education, distance learning, independent study, off-campus study, part-time degree program, services for LD students, summer session for credit.
Library Magoffin Learning Resource Center with 34,668 titles, 259 serial subscriptions, an OPAC.
Computers on Campus 200 computers available on campus for general student use. Internet access, at least one staffed computer lab available.
Student Life *Housing:* college housing not available. *Activities and Organizations:* choral group, Phi Theta Kappa, Baptist Student Union, Student Government Association, Phi Beta Lambda, Kentucky Association of Nursing Students. *Campus security:* 24-hour emergency response devices. *Student services:* health clinic, personal/psychological counseling.
Athletics *Intramural sports:* archery M/W, bowling M/W, golf M/W, table tennis M/W, volleyball M/W.
Standardized Tests *Required:* ACT (for placement). *Recommended:* ACT ASSET.
Costs (2005–06) *Tuition:* area resident $2940 full-time, $98 per credit hour part-time; state resident $3540 full-time, $118 per credit hour part-time; nonresident $8820 full-time, $294 per credit hour part-time.
Financial Aid Of all full-time matriculated undergraduates who enrolled in 2003, 112 Federal Work-Study jobs (averaging $1749).
Applying *Options:* common application, early admission, deferred entrance. *Required:* high school transcript. *Application deadline:* rolling (freshmen), rolling (transfers).
Admissions Contact Mr. Jim Glover, Director of Admissions, Big Sandy Community and Technical College, One Bert T. Combs Drive, Prestonsburg, KY 41653-1815. *Phone:* 606-886-3863 Ext. 220. *Toll-free phone:* 888-641-4132. *Fax:* 606-886-6943. *E-mail:* jim.glover@kctcs.edu.

BOWLING GREEN TECHNICAL COLLEGE
Bowling Green, Kentucky

- **State-supported** 2-year, founded 1938
- **Calendar** semesters
- **Coed**

Costs (2004–05) *Tuition:* state resident $92 per credit hour part-time; nonresident $276 per credit hour part-time.
Admissions Contact 1845 Loop Drive, Bowling Green, KY 42101.

BROWN MACKIE COLLEGE, HOPKINSVILLE CAMPUS
Hopkinsville, Kentucky

- **Proprietary** 2-year
- **Calendar** quarters
- **Degree** diplomas and associate
- **Small-town** campus
- **Coed, primarily women**
- 100% of applicants were admitted

Faculty *Student/faculty ratio:* 16:1.
Costs (2004–05) *Tuition:* $149 per credit hour part-time. *Required fees:* $10 per credit hour part-time.
Financial Aid Of all full-time matriculated undergraduates who enrolled in 2003, 12 Federal Work-Study jobs.
Admissions Contact Jody Gray, Admissions Coordinator, Brown Mackie College, Hopkinsville Campus, 4001 Fort Campbell Boulevard, Hopkinsville, KY 42240-4962. *Phone:* 270-886-1302. *Toll-free phone:* 800-359-4753.

BROWN MACKIE COLLEGE, LOUISVILLE CAMPUS
Louisville, Kentucky

Admissions Contact Mr. Dan Squires, Director of Admissions, Brown Mackie College, Louisville Campus, 300 Highrise Drive, Louisville, KY 40213. *Phone:* 502-968-7191. *Toll-free phone:* 800-999-7387. *Fax:* 502-968-1727.

BROWN MACKIE COLLEGE, NORTHERN KENTUCKY CAMPUS
Fort Mitchell, Kentucky

- **Proprietary** 2-year, founded 1927, part of American Education Centers, Inc
- **Calendar** quarters
- **Degree** certificates, diplomas, and associate
- **Suburban** 5-acre campus with easy access to Cincinnati

- **Coed**, 400 undergraduate students

Undergraduates Students come from 3 states and territories, 8% African American, 0.5% Asian American or Pacific Islander, 2% Hispanic American.
Freshmen *Admission:* 500 applied.
Majors Accounting technology and bookkeeping; business administration and management; computer science; information science/studies; medical/clinical assistant.
Academic Programs *Special study options:* academic remediation for entering students, adult/continuing education programs, internships, part-time degree program, summer session for credit.
Library 1,500 titles, 50 serial subscriptions.
Computers on Campus 50 computers available on campus for general student use. Internet access, at least one staffed computer lab available.
Student Life *Housing:* college housing not available. *Campus security:* 24-hour emergency response devices, late-night transport/escort service. *Student services:* personal/psychological counseling.
Applying *Options:* common application. *Application deadline:* rolling (freshmen), rolling (transfers).
Admissions Contact Ms. Helen Tucker, Director of Admissions, Brown Mackie College, Northern Kentucky Campus, 309 Buttermilk Pike, Fort Mitchell, KY 41017. *Phone:* 859-341-5627. *Toll-free phone:* 800-888-1445. *E-mail:* bmcnkadm@amedcts.com.

CENTRAL KENTUCKY TECHNICAL COLLEGE
Lexington, Kentucky

Admissions Contact 308 Vo Tech Road, Lexington, KY 40511.

DAYMAR COLLEGE
Louisville, Kentucky

- **Proprietary** 2-year, founded 2001
- **Calendar** quarters
- **Degree** diplomas and associate
- **Coed**

Applying *Required:* high school transcript, interview.
Admissions Contact Mr. Patrick Carney, Director of Admissions, Daymar College, 4400 Breckenridge Lane, Suite 415, Louisville, KY 40218.

DAYMAR COLLEGE
Owensboro, Kentucky

Admissions Contact Ms. Vickie McDougal, Director of Admissions, Daymar College, 3361 Buckland Square, PO Box 22150, Owensboro, KY 42303. *Phone:* 270-926-4040. *Toll-free phone:* 800-960-4090. *Fax:* 270-685-4090. *E-mail:* info@daymarcollege.edu.

DRAUGHONS JUNIOR COLLEGE
Bowling Green, Kentucky

- **Proprietary** 2-year, founded 1989, administratively affiliated with Draughons Junior College, Inc
- **Calendar** semesters
- **Degree** diplomas and associate
- **Suburban** campus with easy access to Nashville
- **Coed, primarily women**

Faculty *Student/faculty ratio:* 13:1.
Student Life *Campus security:* 24-hour emergency response devices.
Standardized Tests *Recommended:* SAT or ACT (for placement).
Costs (2004–05) *Tuition:* $11,600 full-time, $300 per credit part-time. Full-time tuition and fees vary according to program. Part-time tuition and fees vary according to program. *Required fees:* $1000 full-time, $75 per course part-time.
Financial Aid Of all full-time matriculated undergraduates who enrolled in 2003, 2 Federal Work-Study jobs (averaging $4950).
Applying *Options:* common application. *Application fee:* $20. *Required:* high school transcript.
Admissions Contact Amye Melton, Admissions Director, Draughons Junior College, 2421 Fitzgerald Industrial Drive, Bowling Green, KY 42101. *Phone:* 270-843-6750. *Fax:* 270-843-6976.

ELIZABETHTOWN COMMUNITY AND TECHNICAL COLLEGE
Elizabethtown, Kentucky

- **State-supported** 2-year, founded 1964, part of Kentucky Community and Technical College System
- **Calendar** semesters
- **Degree** certificates, diplomas, and associate
- **Small-town** 40-acre campus with easy access to Louisville
- **Coed**, 3,615 undergraduate students, 46% full-time, 68% women, 32% men

Undergraduates 1,645 full-time, 1,970 part-time. Students come from 10 states and territories, 11% African American, 2% Asian American or Pacific Islander, 3% Hispanic American, 0.6% Native American.
Freshmen *Admission:* 737 enrolled.
Majors Administrative assistant and secretarial science; biological and physical sciences; business administration and management; child guidance; criminal justice/police science; dental hygiene; finance; information science/studies; liberal arts and sciences/liberal studies; nursing (registered nurse training); quality control technology; real estate.
Academic Programs *Special study options:* academic remediation for entering students, adult/continuing education programs, advanced placement credit, cooperative education, external degree program, internships, off-campus study, part-time degree program, services for LD students, summer session for credit.
Library Elizabethtown Community College Media Center with 35,175 titles, 240 serial subscriptions, an OPAC.
Computers on Campus 70 computers available on campus for general student use. Internet access, at least one staffed computer lab available.
Student Life *Housing:* college housing not available. *Activities and Organizations:* drama/theater group, student-run newspaper, choral group, Baptist Student Union, Kentucky Association of Nursing Students. *Campus security:* late night security.
Athletics *Intramural sports:* basketball M/W, football M, golf M, soccer M, table tennis M/W, tennis M/W, volleyball M/W.
Standardized Tests *Required for some:* ACT (for admission).
Costs (2005–06) *Tuition:* state resident $2352 full-time, $98 per credit hour part-time; nonresident $7056 full-time, $294 per credit hour part-time. Full-time tuition and fees vary according to course load. Part-time tuition and fees vary according to course load. *Payment plan:* deferred payment. *Waivers:* senior citizens and employees or children of employees.
Financial Aid Of all full-time matriculated undergraduates who enrolled in 2003, 20 Federal Work-Study jobs (averaging $2000).
Applying *Options:* common application, early admission. *Required:* essay or personal statement, high school transcript. *Application deadline:* rolling (freshmen), rolling (transfers). *Notification:* continuous (freshmen).
Admissions Contact Dr. Dale Buckles, Dean of Student Affairs, Elizabethtown Community and Technical College, 600 College Street Road, Elizabethtown, KY 42701. *Phone:* 270-769-2371 Ext. 68431. *Toll-free phone:* 877-246-2322. *Fax:* 270-769-0736.

ELIZABETHTOWN TECHNICAL COLLEGE
Elizabethtown, Kentucky

Admissions Contact 620 College Street Road, Elizabethtown, KY 42701.

GATEWAY COMMUNITY AND TECHNICAL COLLEGE
Covington, Kentucky

- **State-supported** 2-year, founded 1961
- **Calendar** semesters
- **Degree** certificates, diplomas, and associate
- **Coed**, 2,597 undergraduate students

Student Life *Housing:* college housing not available.
Standardized Tests *Required:* ACT or ACT COMPASS (for placement).
Costs (2005–06) *Tuition:* state resident $2940 full-time, $98 per credit hour part-time; nonresident $8820 full-time, $294 per credit hour part-time.
Admissions Contact Mr. Paul Brinkman, Dean of Student Affairs, Gateway Community and Technical College, 1025 Amsterdam Road, Covington, KY 41011.

HAZARD COMMUNITY AND TECHNICAL COLLEGE
Hazard, Kentucky

- **State-supported** 2-year, founded 1968, part of Kentucky Community and Technical College System

- **Calendar** semesters
- **Degree** certificates, diplomas, and associate
- **Rural** 34-acre campus
- **Coed**, 3,500 undergraduate students

Undergraduates Students come from 3 states and territories, 5% are from out of state.
Faculty *Total:* 160, 63% full-time.
Majors Administrative assistant and secretarial science; business administration and management; clinical/medical laboratory technology; computer typography and composition equipment operation; data processing and data processing technology; forestry technology; information science/studies; kindergarten/preschool education; liberal arts and sciences/liberal studies; management science; medical radiologic technology; nursing (registered nurse training); physical therapist assistant.
Academic Programs *Special study options:* academic remediation for entering students, adult/continuing education programs, honors programs, part-time degree program, summer session for credit.
Library 36,550 titles, 160 serial subscriptions.
Computers on Campus 28 computers available on campus for general student use.
Student Life *Housing Options:* coed. Campus housing is university owned and is provided by a third party. *Activities and Organizations:* drama/theater group, choral group. *Campus security:* late-night transport/escort service. *Student services:* personal/psychological counseling.
Standardized Tests *Required:* ACT (for placement).
Costs (2004–05) *Tuition:* state resident $2208 full-time, $92 per credit hour part-time; nonresident $1824 full-time, $276 per credit hour part-time. *Room and board:* $3900.
Applying *Options:* common application, early admission. *Required:* high school transcript. *Application deadline:* rolling (freshmen), rolling (transfers). *Notification:* continuous (freshmen).
Admissions Contact Mr. Steve Jones, Director of Admissions, Hazard Community and Technical College, 1 Community College Drive, Hazard, KY 41701-2403. *Phone:* 606-436-5721 Ext. 8076. *Toll-free phone:* 800-246-7521.

HENDERSON COMMUNITY COLLEGE
Henderson, Kentucky

- **State-supported** 2-year, founded 1963, part of Kentucky Community and Technical College System
- **Calendar** semesters
- **Degree** associate
- **Small-town** 120-acre campus
- **Coed**, 2,241 undergraduate students, 31% full-time, 63% women, 37% men

Undergraduates 690 full-time, 1,551 part-time. Students come from 12 states and territories, 1% are from out of state, 5% African American, 0.3% Asian American or Pacific Islander, 0.6% Hispanic American, 0.8% Native American.
Freshmen *Admission:* 1,923 applied, 1,923 admitted.
Faculty *Total:* 101, 48% full-time. *Student/faculty ratio:* 13:1.
Majors Administrative assistant and secretarial science; business administration and management; clinical laboratory science/medical technology; computer and information sciences related; computer/information technology services administration related; computer programming related; computer programming (specific applications); computer programming (vendor/product certification); computer systems networking and telecommunications; data entry/microcomputer applications; data entry/microcomputer applications related; data processing and data processing technology; electrical, electronic and communications engineering technology; engineering technology; human services; information technology; mass communication/media; nursing (registered nurse training); word processing.
Academic Programs *Special study options:* academic remediation for entering students, accelerated degree program, adult/continuing education programs, advanced placement credit, cooperative education, distance learning, double majors, English as a second language, external degree program, independent study, internships, off-campus study, part-time degree program, summer session for credit.
Library Hartfield Learning Resource Center plus 1 other with 30,206 titles, 231 serial subscriptions, 1,053 audiovisual materials, an OPAC, a Web page.
Computers on Campus 200 computers available on campus for general student use. Internet access available.
Student Life *Housing:* college housing not available. *Activities and Organizations:* drama/theater group, student-run radio station. *Campus security:* 24-hour emergency response devices. *Student services:* personal/psychological counseling.
Athletics *Intramural sports:* basketball M, football M, golf M, softball M/W, table tennis M/W.
Standardized Tests *Required:* ACT (for admission), ACT COMPASS (for admission).

Henderson Community College (continued)

Costs (2005–06) *Tuition:* state resident $2490 full-time, $98 per credit hour part-time; nonresident $8820 full-time, $294 per credit hour part-time. Full-time tuition and fees vary according to course load. Part-time tuition and fees vary according to course load. *Payment plan:* deferred payment.

Financial Aid Of all full-time matriculated undergraduates who enrolled in 2003, 31 Federal Work-Study jobs.

Applying *Options:* common application. *Required:* high school transcript. *Required for some:* essay or personal statement, letters of recommendation, interview. *Application deadlines:* 9/1 (freshmen), 9/1 (transfers).

Admissions Contact Ms. Teresa Hamiton, Admissions Counselor, Henderson Community College, 2660 South Green Street, Henderson, KY 42420-4623. *Phone:* 270-827-1867 Ext. 354.

HOPKINSVILLE COMMUNITY COLLEGE
Hopkinsville, Kentucky

- **State-supported** 2-year, founded 1965, part of Kentucky Community and Technical College System
- **Calendar** semesters
- **Degree** certificates, diplomas, and associate
- **Small-town** 70-acre campus with easy access to Nashville
- **Endowment** $2.4 million
- **Coed,** 3,104 undergraduate students, 46% full-time, 69% women, 31% men

Undergraduates 1,413 full-time, 1,691 part-time. Students come from 3 states and territories, 1 other country, 25% are from out of state, 22% African American, 1% Asian American or Pacific Islander, 4% Hispanic American, 0.4% Native American, 61% transferred in. *Retention:* 55% of 2002 full-time freshmen returned.

Freshmen *Admission:* 813 enrolled. *Test scores:* ACT scores over 18: 64%; ACT scores over 24: 15%.

Faculty *Total:* 169, 40% full-time, 7% with terminal degrees. *Student/faculty ratio:* 23:1.

Majors Administrative assistant and secretarial science; animal/livestock husbandry and production; business administration and management; child care and support services management; criminal justice/police science; early childhood education; electrical, electronic and communications engineering technology; finance; human services; industrial technology; kindergarten/preschool education; liberal arts and sciences/liberal studies; management information systems; manufacturing technology; mental health/rehabilitation; nursing (licensed practical/vocational nurse training); nursing (registered nurse training).

Academic Programs *Special study options:* academic remediation for entering students, adult/continuing education programs, advanced placement credit, distance learning, honors programs, independent study, part-time degree program, services for LD students, summer session for credit.

Library HCC Library plus 1 other with 45,674 titles, 147 serial subscriptions, 4,377 audiovisual materials, an OPAC, a Web page.

Computers on Campus 400 computers available on campus for general student use. A campuswide network can be accessed from off campus. Internet access, online (class) registration, at least one staffed computer lab available.

Student Life *Housing:* college housing not available. *Activities and Organizations:* student-run newspaper, television station, Baptist Student Union, Circle K, Minority Student Union, Donovan Scholars, Nursing Club. *Campus security:* 24-hour emergency response devices, late-night transport/escort service.

Athletics *Intramural sports:* basketball M, football M, golf M, table tennis M/W, volleyball M/W.

Standardized Tests *Required:* ACT (for placement), ACT COMPASS (for placement).

Costs (2005–06) *Tuition:* state resident $2940 full-time, $98 per credit hour part-time; nonresident $8820 full-time, $294 per credit hour part-time. Full-time tuition and fees vary according to location and reciprocity agreements. Part-time tuition and fees vary according to location and reciprocity agreements.

Financial Aid Of all full-time matriculated undergraduates who enrolled in 2003, 30 Federal Work-Study jobs (averaging $1500). *Financial aid deadline:* 6/30.

Applying *Options:* common application, early admission, deferred entrance. *Required for some:* high school transcript, interview. *Application deadline:* rolling (freshmen), rolling (transfers). *Notification:* continuous (freshmen).

Admissions Contact Ms. Ruth Ann Rettie, Registrar, Hopkinsville Community College, North Drive, PO Box 2100, Hopkinsville, KY 42241-2100. *Phone:* 270-886-3921 Ext. 6197. *Fax:* 270-886-0237. *E-mail:* admit.record@kctcs.net.

ITT TECHNICAL INSTITUTE
Louisville, Kentucky

- **Proprietary** primarily 2-year, founded 1993, part of ITT Educational Services, Inc
- **Calendar** quarters

- **Degrees** associate and bachelor's
- **Suburban** campus
- **Coed**

Standardized Tests *Required:* Wonderlic aptitude test (for admission).

Costs (2004–05) *Tuition:* Please see school catalog for specific information.

Applying *Options:* deferred entrance. *Application fee:* $100. *Required:* high school transcript, interview. *Recommended:* letters of recommendation.

Admissions Contact Mr. Chuck Taylor, Director of Recruitment, ITT Technical Institute, 10509 Timberwood Circle, Louisville, KY 40223. *Phone:* 502-327-7424. *Fax:* 502-327-7624.

JEFFERSON COMMUNITY COLLEGE
Louisville, Kentucky

- **State-supported** 2-year, founded 1968, part of Kentucky Community and Technical College System
- **Calendar** semesters
- **Degree** certificates, diplomas, and associate
- **Urban** 10-acre campus
- **Endowment** $1.1 million
- **Coed,** 10,024 undergraduate students, 39% full-time, 60% women, 40% men

Undergraduates 3,880 full-time, 6,144 part-time. Students come from 11 states and territories, 3% are from out of state, 17% African American, 1% Asian American or Pacific Islander, 2% Hispanic American, 0.1% Native American, 15% transferred in.

Freshmen *Admission:* 1,472 admitted, 1,390 enrolled.

Faculty *Total:* 453, 48% full-time. *Student/faculty ratio:* 20:1.

Majors Accounting; business administration and management; child development; commercial and advertising art; culinary arts; data processing and data processing technology; electrical, electronic and communications engineering technology; health information/medical records technology; liberal arts and sciences/liberal studies; mechanical engineering/mechanical technology; medical radiologic technology; nuclear medical technology; nursing (registered nurse training); physical therapy; real estate; respiratory care therapy; social work.

Academic Programs *Special study options:* academic remediation for entering students, adult/continuing education programs, advanced placement credit, cooperative education, distance learning, English as a second language, external degree program, honors programs, independent study, internships, off-campus study, part-time degree program, services for LD students, summer session for credit. *ROTC:* Army (c).

Library John T. Smith Learning Resource Center plus 2 others with 76,578 titles, 391 serial subscriptions, 15,103 audiovisual materials, an OPAC, a Web page.

Computers on Campus 895 computers available on campus for general student use. A campuswide network can be accessed from off campus. Internet access, at least one staffed computer lab available.

Student Life *Housing:* college housing not available. *Activities and Organizations:* drama/theater group, student-run newspaper. *Campus security:* 24-hour emergency response devices and patrols, late-night transport/escort service. *Student services:* personal/psychological counseling.

Standardized Tests *Required:* ACT COMPASS (for placement).

Costs (2005–06) *Tuition:* state resident $2940 full-time, $98 per credit hour part-time; nonresident $8820 full-time, $294 per credit hour part-time. *Required fees:* $50 full-time, $25 per term part-time.

Financial Aid Of all full-time matriculated undergraduates who enrolled in 2003, 50 Federal Work-Study jobs (averaging $4000).

Applying *Options:* early admission. *Application deadline:* rolling (freshmen), rolling (transfers). *Notification:* continuous (freshmen).

Admissions Contact Sandra Chambers, Assistant Registrar, Jefferson Community College, 109 East Broadway, Louisville, KY 40202. *Phone:* 502-213-2148. *Fax:* 502-213-2540.

JEFFERSON TECHNICAL COLLEGE
Louisville, Kentucky

- **State-supported** 2-year, founded 1967, administratively affiliated with Kentucky Community and Technical College System
- **Calendar** semesters
- **Degree** certificates, diplomas, and associate
- **Urban** campus
- **Coed,** 3,778 undergraduate students, 16% full-time, 34% women, 66% men

Undergraduates 601 full-time, 3,177 part-time. Students come from 4 states and territories, 4 other countries, 3% are from out of state, 17% African American, 0.8% Asian American or Pacific Islander, 0.7% Hispanic American, 0.6% Native American.

Freshmen *Admission:* 364 enrolled.

Faculty *Total:* 156, 53% full-time. *Student/faculty ratio:* 15:1.

Academic Programs *Special study options:* academic remediation for entering students, adult/continuing education programs, advanced placement credit, cooperative education, distance learning, English as a second language, off-campus study, part-time degree program, services for LD students, summer session for credit.

Library Main Library plus 1 other.

Computers on Campus A campuswide network can be accessed from off campus. Internet access, at least one staffed computer lab available.

Student Life *Housing:* college housing not available.

Costs (2005–06) *Tuition:* state resident $2940 full-time, $98 per credit hour part-time; nonresident $8820 full-time, $294 per credit hour part-time. *Required fees:* $25 full-time, $25 per term part-time. *Waivers:* senior citizens and employees or children of employees.

Admissions Contact Sandra Chambers, Assistant Registrar, Jefferson Technical College, 109 E. Broadway, Louisville, KY 40202. *Phone:* 502-213-2148.

LEXINGTON COMMUNITY COLLEGE
Lexington, Kentucky

- **State-supported** 2-year, founded 1965, part of Kentucky Community and Technical College System
- **Calendar** semesters
- **Degree** associate
- **Urban** 10-acre campus
- **Endowment** $750,000
- **Coed**

Faculty *Student/faculty ratio:* 19:1.

Student Life *Campus security:* 24-hour emergency response devices and patrols, late-night transport/escort service.

Standardized Tests *Required for some:* SAT or ACT (for placement).

Costs (2004–05) *Tuition:* state resident $2208 full-time, $92 per credit part-time; nonresident $6624 full-time, $276 per credit part-time. Part-time tuition and fees vary according to course load. *Required fees:* $563 full-time, $16 per term part-time. *Room and board:* $4785; room only: $3085. Room and board charges vary according to board plan.

Applying *Options:* early admission. *Application fee:* $20. *Required:* high school transcript.

Admissions Contact Mrs. Shelbie Hugle, Director of Admission Services, Lexington Community College, 200 Oswald Building, Cooper Drive, Lexington, KY 40506-0235. *Phone:* 859-257-4872 Ext. 4197. *Toll-free phone:* 866-744-4872 Ext. 5111. *E-mail:* shugl@uky.edu.

LOUISVILLE TECHNICAL INSTITUTE
Louisville, Kentucky

- **Proprietary** 2-year, founded 1961, part of Sullivan University System
- **Calendar** quarters
- **Degree** certificates, diplomas, and associate
- **Suburban** 10-acre campus
- **Coed**

Faculty *Student/faculty ratio:* 9:1.

Student Life *Campus security:* late-night transport/escort service.

Standardized Tests *Required:* ACT, SAT or CPAt (for admission).

Costs (2004–05) *Tuition:* $12,480 full-time, $260 per credit hour part-time. Full-time tuition and fees vary according to class time and program. Part-time tuition and fees vary according to program. No tuition increase for student's term of enrollment. *Required fees:* $415 full-time, $25 per course part-time. *Room only:* $3690. *Payment plans:* tuition prepayment, installment.

Applying *Options:* deferred entrance. *Application fee:* $90. *Required:* high school transcript, minimum 2.0 GPA, interview.

Admissions Contact Mr. David Ritz, Director of Admissions, Louisville Technical Institute, 3901 Atkinson Square Drive, Louisville, KY 40218. *Phone:* 502-456-6509. *Toll-free phone:* 800-884-6528. *E-mail:* dritz@louisvilletech.com.

MADISONVILLE COMMUNITY COLLEGE
Madisonville, Kentucky

Admissions Contact Mr. Jay Parent, Registrar, Madisonville Community College, 2000 College Drive, Madisonville, KY 42431. *Phone:* 270-821-2250. *Fax:* 502-821-1555. *E-mail:* dmcox@pop.uky.edu.

MAYSVILLE COMMUNITY AND TECHNICAL COLLEGE
Maysville, Kentucky

- **State-supported** 2-year, founded 1967, part of Kentucky Community and Technical College System
- **Calendar** semesters
- **Degree** certificates, diplomas, and associate
- **Rural** 12-acre campus
- **Coed**

Student Life *Campus security:* student patrols, evening parking lot security.

Standardized Tests *Required for some:* ACT (for placement).

Costs (2004–05) *Tuition:* state resident $92 per credit part-time; nonresident $276 per credit part-time. *Payment plans:* installment, deferred payment.

Financial Aid Of all full-time matriculated undergraduates who enrolled in 2003, 30 Federal Work-Study jobs (averaging $1960).

Applying *Options:* early admission. *Required:* high school transcript.

Admissions Contact Ms. Patee Massie, Registrar, Maysville Community and Technical College, 1755 US 68, Maysville, KY 41056. *Phone:* 606-759-7141 Ext. 6184. *Fax:* 606-759-5818. *E-mail:* patee.massie@kctcs.net.

NATIONAL COLLEGE OF BUSINESS & TECHNOLOGY
Danville, Kentucky

- **Proprietary** 2-year, founded 1962, part of National College of Business and Technology
- **Calendar** quarters
- **Degree** diplomas and associate
- **Coed**, 326 undergraduate students

Faculty *Total:* 30, 3% full-time. *Student/faculty ratio:* 10:1.

Majors Accounting; administrative assistant and secretarial science; business administration and management; computer and information sciences related; medical/clinical assistant.

Academic Programs *Special study options:* advanced placement credit, double majors, honors programs, internships, part-time degree program, services for LD students, summer session for credit.

Computers on Campus 30 computers available on campus for general student use. A campuswide network can be accessed. Internet access, at least one staffed computer lab available.

Student Life *Housing:* college housing not available.

Costs (2005–06) *Tuition:* $6408 full-time, $178 per credit hour part-time. *Required fees:* $75 full-time, $15 per term part-time. *Payment plans:* installment, deferred payment. *Waivers:* employees or children of employees.

Financial Aid Of all full-time matriculated undergraduates who enrolled in 2003, 1 Federal Work-Study job.

Applying *Options:* common application, electronic application. *Application fee:* $30. *Required:* high school transcript. *Application deadline:* rolling (freshmen), rolling (transfers). *Notification:* continuous (freshmen).

Admissions Contact Ms. Stacie Catlett, Campus Director, National College of Business & Technology, 115 East Lexington Avenue, Danville, KY 40422. *Phone:* 859-236-6991. *Toll-free phone:* 800-664-1886. *Fax:* 859-236-1063. *E-mail:* adm@educorp.edu.

NATIONAL COLLEGE OF BUSINESS & TECHNOLOGY
Florence, Kentucky

- **Proprietary** 2-year, founded 1941, part of National College of Business and Technology
- **Calendar** quarters
- **Degree** diplomas and associate
- **Suburban** campus
- **Coed**, 189 undergraduate students

Faculty *Total:* 23, 9% full-time. *Student/faculty ratio:* 12:1.

Majors Accounting; administrative assistant and secretarial science; business administration and management; computer and information sciences related; medical/clinical assistant.

Academic Programs *Special study options:* advanced placement credit, double majors, honors programs, internships, part-time degree program, services for LD students, summer session for credit.

Computers on Campus 30 computers available on campus for general student use. Internet access, at least one staffed computer lab available.

National College of Business & Technology (continued)

Student Life *Housing:* college housing not available. *Campus security:* 24-hour emergency response devices.

Costs (2005–06) *Tuition:* $6408 full-time, $178 per credit hour part-time. *Required fees:* $75 full-time, $15 per term part-time.

Financial Aid Of all full-time matriculated undergraduates who enrolled in 2003, 3 Federal Work-Study jobs.

Applying *Options:* electronic application. *Application fee:* $30. *Required for some:* high school transcript. *Recommended:* interview. *Application deadline:* rolling (freshmen), rolling (transfers). *Notification:* continuous (freshmen).

Admissions Contact Ron Thomas, Campus Director, National College of Business & Technology, 7627 Ewing Boulevard, Florence, KY 41042. *Phone:* 859-525-6510. *Toll-free phone:* 800-664-1886. *Fax:* 859-525-8961. *E-mail:* adm@educorp.edu.

NATIONAL COLLEGE OF BUSINESS & TECHNOLOGY
Lexington, Kentucky

- **Proprietary** 2-year, founded 1947, part of National College of Business and Technology
- **Calendar** quarters
- **Degree** diplomas and associate
- **Urban** campus
- **Coed,** 378 undergraduate students

Faculty *Total:* 45, 9% full-time. *Student/faculty ratio:* 12:1.

Majors Accounting; administrative assistant and secretarial science; business administration and management; computer and information sciences related; radio and television.

Academic Programs *Special study options:* advanced placement credit, double majors, honors programs, internships, part-time degree program, summer session for credit.

Computers on Campus 30 computers available on campus for general student use. Internet access, at least one staffed computer lab available.

Student Life *Housing:* college housing not available. *Student services:* personal/psychological counseling.

Costs (2005–06) *Tuition:* $6408 full-time, $178 per credit hour part-time. *Required fees:* $75 full-time, $15 per term part-time.

Financial Aid Of all full-time matriculated undergraduates who enrolled in 2003, 6 Federal Work-Study jobs.

Applying *Options:* electronic application. *Application fee:* $30. *Required:* high school transcript. *Application deadline:* rolling (freshmen), rolling (transfers). *Notification:* continuous (freshmen).

Admissions Contact Kim Thomasson, Campus Director, National College of Business & Technology, 628 East Main Street, Lexington, KY 40508-2312. *Phone:* 859-266-0401. *Toll-free phone:* 800-664-1886. *Fax:* 859-233-3054. *E-mail:* market@educorp.edu.

NATIONAL COLLEGE OF BUSINESS & TECHNOLOGY
Louisville, Kentucky

- **Proprietary** 2-year, founded 1990, part of National College of Business and Technology
- **Calendar** quarters
- **Degree** diplomas and associate
- **Coed,** 678 undergraduate students

Faculty *Total:* 36, 6% full-time. *Student/faculty ratio:* 10:1.

Majors Accounting; administrative assistant and secretarial science; business administration and management; computer and information sciences related; health/health care administration; medical/clinical assistant.

Academic Programs *Special study options:* advanced placement credit, double majors, honors programs, internships, part-time degree program, services for LD students, summer session for credit.

Computers on Campus 55 computers available on campus for general student use. Internet access, at least one staffed computer lab available.

Student Life *Housing:* college housing not available.

Costs (2005–06) *Tuition:* $6408 full-time, $178 per credit hour part-time. Full-time tuition and fees vary according to course load. Part-time tuition and fees vary according to course load. *Required fees:* $75 full-time, $15 per term part-time. *Payment plans:* installment, deferred payment. *Waivers:* employees or children of employees.

Financial Aid Of all full-time matriculated undergraduates who enrolled in 2003, 2 Federal Work-Study jobs.

Applying *Options:* electronic application. *Application fee:* $30. *Required for some:* high school transcript. *Application deadline:* rolling (freshmen), rolling (transfers). *Notification:* continuous (freshmen).

Admissions Contact Mike Fiore, Campus Director, National College of Business & Technology, 3950 Dixie Highway, Louisville, KY 40216. *Phone:* 502-447-7634. *Toll-free phone:* 800-664-1886. *Fax:* 502-447-7665. *E-mail:* adm@educorp.edu.

NATIONAL COLLEGE OF BUSINESS & TECHNOLOGY
Pikeville, Kentucky

- **Proprietary** 2-year, founded 1976, part of National College of Business and Technology
- **Calendar** quarters
- **Degree** diplomas and associate
- **Rural** campus
- **Coed,** 219 undergraduate students

Faculty *Total:* 15, 13% full-time. *Student/faculty ratio:* 10:1.

Majors Accounting; administrative assistant and secretarial science; business administration and management; computer and information sciences related; medical/clinical assistant.

Academic Programs *Special study options:* advanced placement credit, double majors, honors programs, internships, part-time degree program, services for LD students, summer session for credit.

Computers on Campus 24 computers available on campus for general student use. Internet access, at least one staffed computer lab available.

Student Life *Housing:* college housing not available.

Costs (2005–06) *Tuition:* $6408 full-time, $178 per credit hour part-time. *Required fees:* $75 full-time, $15 per term part-time.

Financial Aid Of all full-time matriculated undergraduates who enrolled in 2003, 4 Federal Work-Study jobs.

Applying *Application fee:* $30. *Required for some:* high school transcript. *Recommended:* interview. *Application deadline:* rolling (freshmen), rolling (transfers). *Notification:* continuous (freshmen).

Admissions Contact Mr. Jerry Lafferty, Campus Director, National College of Business & Technology, 288 South Mayo Trail, Suite 2, Pikeville, KY 41501. *Phone:* 606-432-5477. *Toll-free phone:* 800-664-1886. *Fax:* 606-437-4952. *E-mail:* adm@educorp.edu.

NATIONAL COLLEGE OF BUSINESS & TECHNOLOGY
Richmond, Kentucky

- **Proprietary** 2-year, founded 1951, part of National College of Business and Technology
- **Calendar** quarters
- **Degree** diplomas and associate
- **Suburban** campus
- **Coed,** 363 undergraduate students

Faculty *Total:* 28, 4% full-time. *Student/faculty ratio:* 12:1.

Majors Accounting; administrative assistant and secretarial science; business administration and management; computer and information sciences related; medical/clinical assistant.

Academic Programs *Special study options:* advanced placement credit, double majors, honors programs, internships, part-time degree program, summer session for credit.

Computers on Campus 20 computers available on campus for general student use. Internet access, at least one staffed computer lab available.

Student Life *Housing:* college housing not available.

Costs (2005–06) *Tuition:* $6408 full-time, $178 per credit hour part-time. *Required fees:* $75 full-time, $15 per term part-time.

Financial Aid Of all full-time matriculated undergraduates who enrolled in 2003, 1 Federal Work-Study job.

Applying *Options:* electronic application. *Application fee:* $30. *Required for some:* high school transcript. *Recommended:* interview. *Application deadline:* rolling (freshmen), rolling (transfers). *Notification:* continuous (freshmen).

Admissions Contact Ms. Keeley Gadd, Campus Director, National College of Business & Technology, 139 Killarney Lane, Richmond, KY 40475. *Phone:* 859-623-8956. *Toll-free phone:* 800-664-1886. *Fax:* 606-624-5544. *E-mail:* adm@educorp.edu.

OWENSBORO COMMUNITY AND TECHNICAL COLLEGE
Owensboro, Kentucky

- **State-supported** 2-year, founded 1986, part of Kentucky Community and Technical College System
- **Calendar** semesters
- **Degree** certificates and associate
- **Suburban** 102-acre campus
- **Endowment** $109,305
- **Coed,** 3,664 undergraduate students, 50% full-time, 60% women, 40% men

Undergraduates 1,848 full-time, 1,816 part-time. Students come from 6 states and territories, 2 other countries, 5% are from out of state, 3% African American, 0.5% Asian American or Pacific Islander, 0.3% Hispanic American, 0.2% Native American, 2% transferred in.

Freshmen *Admission:* 789 applied, 789 admitted, 700 enrolled. *Test scores:* ACT scores over 18: 72%; ACT scores over 24: 17%; ACT scores over 30: 1%.

Faculty *Total:* 203, 47% full-time. *Student/faculty ratio:* 21:1.

Majors Agriculture; business administration and management; computer and information sciences; computer/information technology services administration related; criminal justice/police science; data entry/microcomputer applications; electrical, electronic and communications engineering technology; executive assistant/executive secretary; human services; information technology; kindergarten/preschool education; liberal arts and sciences/liberal studies; medical radiologic technology; nursing (registered nurse training); social work; system administration; word processing.

Academic Programs *Special study options:* academic remediation for entering students, adult/continuing education programs, advanced placement credit, cooperative education, distance learning, double majors, external degree program, honors programs, internships, off-campus study, part-time degree program, study abroad, summer session for credit.

Library Learning Resource Center with 18,200 titles, 80 serial subscriptions, an OPAC, a Web page.

Computers on Campus 90 computers available on campus for general student use. A campuswide network can be accessed. Internet access, at least one staffed computer lab available.

Student Life *Housing:* college housing not available. *Activities and Organizations:* drama/theater group, student-run newspaper, radio and television station, choral group, student government, Psychology Club, Nursing Club. *Campus security:* 24-hour emergency response devices, late-night transport/escort service.

Athletics *Intramural sports:* basketball M, softball M/W.

Standardized Tests *Required:* ACT (for placement). *Required for some:* ACT COMPASS.

Costs (2004–05) *Tuition:* state resident $2760 full-time, $92 per credit hour part-time; nonresident $8280 full-time, $276 per credit hour part-time. Full-time tuition and fees vary according to course load. Part-time tuition and fees vary according to course load. *Room and board:* Room and board charges vary according to location. *Payment plan:* installment. *Waivers:* senior citizens and employees or children of employees.

Financial Aid Of all full-time matriculated undergraduates who enrolled in 2003, 52 Federal Work-Study jobs (averaging $2500). *Financial aid deadline:* 4/1.

Applying *Required:* high school transcript. *Application deadline:* rolling (freshmen), rolling (transfers). *Notification:* continuous (freshmen).

Admissions Contact Ms. Barbara Tipmore, Admissions Counselor, Owensboro Community and Technical College, 4800 New Hartford Road, Owensboro, KY 42303. *Phone:* 270-686-4527. *Toll-free phone:* 866-755-6282.

PADUCAH TECHNICAL COLLEGE
Paducah, Kentucky

Admissions Contact Mr. Arnold Harris, Director of Admissions, Paducah Technical College, 509 South 30th Street, PO Box 8252, Paducah, KY 42001. *Phone:* 502-444-9676. *Toll-free phone:* 800-995-4438.

ROWAN TECHNICAL COLLEGE
Morehead, Kentucky

- **State-supported** 2-year, founded 1984
- **Calendar** semesters
- **Degree** certificates, diplomas, and associate
- **Coed**

Costs (2004–05) *Tuition:* state resident $92 per credit part-time; nonresident $276 per credit part-time.

Admissions Contact Patee Massie, Registrar, Rowan Technical College, 609 Viking Drive, Morehead, KY 40351. *Phone:* 606-759-7141 Ext. 66184.

ST. CATHARINE COLLEGE
St. Catharine, Kentucky

Admissions Contact Ms. Amy C. Carrico, Director of Admissions, St. Catharine College, 2735 Bardstown Road, St. Catharine, KY 40061. *Phone:* 859-336-5082. *Toll-free phone:* 800-599-2000 Ext. 1227. *Fax:* 859-336-5031. *E-mail:* admissions@secky.edu.

SOMERSET COMMUNITY COLLEGE
Somerset, Kentucky

- **State-supported** 2-year, founded 1965, part of Kentucky Community and Technical College System
- **Calendar** semesters
- **Degree** certificates, diplomas, and associate
- **Small-town** 70-acre campus
- **Endowment** $419,000
- **Coed,** 5,850 undergraduate students

Undergraduates Students come from 3 states and territories, 0.7% African American, 0.2% Asian American or Pacific Islander, 0.3% Hispanic American, 0.2% Native American. *Retention:* 60% of 2002 full-time freshmen returned.

Freshmen *Admission:* 825 applied, 825 admitted. *Test scores:* ACT scores over 18: 60%; ACT scores over 24: 8%.

Faculty *Total:* 309, 48% full-time, 3% with terminal degrees. *Student/faculty ratio:* 19:1.

Majors Autobody/collision and repair technology; automobile/automotive mechanics technology; avionics maintenance technology; business/commerce; CAD/CADD drafting/design technology; carpentry; clinical/medical laboratory assistant; communication and media related; cosmetology; criminal justice/police science; diesel mechanics technology; early childhood education; electrical, electronic and communications engineering technology; heating, air conditioning, ventilation and refrigeration maintenance technology; industrial technology; information technology; machine tool technology; masonry; medical/clinical assistant; nail technician and manicurist; nursing (registered nurse training); nursing related; physical therapy; radiologic technology/science; respiratory care therapy; surgical technology; welding technology.

Academic Programs *Special study options:* academic remediation for entering students, adult/continuing education programs, advanced placement credit, cooperative education, distance learning, double majors, English as a second language, independent study, internships, part-time degree program, services for LD students, summer session for credit.

Library Somerset Community College Library with 58,918 titles, 154 serial subscriptions, 1,233 audiovisual materials, an OPAC, a Web page.

Computers on Campus 1000 computers available on campus for general student use. A campuswide network can be accessed. Internet access, online (class) registration, at least one staffed computer lab available.

Student Life *Housing:* college housing not available. *Activities and Organizations:* drama/theater group, student-run newspaper, choral group, Student Government Association, Students in Free Enterprise, Phi Beta Lambda, Phi Theta Kappa.

Athletics *Intramural sports:* basketball M/W, football M/W, table tennis M/W, tennis M/W.

Standardized Tests *Required:* ACT (for placement).

Costs (2004–05) *Tuition:* state resident $2760 full-time, $92 per credit hour part-time; nonresident $8280 full-time, $276 per credit hour part-time. *Waivers:* employees or children of employees.

Financial Aid Of all full-time matriculated undergraduates who enrolled in 2003, 40 Federal Work-Study jobs (averaging $2500). 25 state and other part-time jobs (averaging $2500).

Applying *Options:* common application, early admission. *Required:* high school transcript. *Application deadlines:* 8/22 (freshmen), 8/22 (transfers). *Notification:* continuous (freshmen).

Admissions Contact Mr. Sean Ayers, Recruiter, Somerset Community College, 808 Monticello Street, Somerset, KY 42501. *Phone:* 606-679-8501 Ext. 3778. *Toll-free phone:* 877-629-9722. *E-mail:* sean.ayers@kctcs.edu.

SOUTHEAST KENTUCKY COMMUNITY AND TECHNICAL COLLEGE
Cumberland, Kentucky

- **State-supported** 2-year, founded 1960, part of Kentucky Community and Technical College System
- **Calendar** semesters
- **Degree** certificates, diplomas, and associate
- **Small-town** 150-acre campus
- **Endowment** $1.8 million
- **Coed,** 4,519 undergraduate students, 43% full-time, 51% women, 49% men

Southeast Kentucky Community and Technical College (continued)

Undergraduates 1,939 full-time, 2,580 part-time. 1% African American, 0.2% Asian American or Pacific Islander, 0.3% Hispanic American, 0.2% Native American.

Faculty *Total:* 178, 64% full-time, 11% with terminal degrees. *Student/faculty ratio:* 20:1.

Majors Administrative assistant and secretarial science; business administration and management; clinical/medical laboratory technology; computer engineering technology; computer/information technology services administration related; criminal justice/police science; data processing and data processing technology; information technology; liberal arts and sciences/liberal studies; management information systems; medical radiologic technology; nursing (registered nurse training); physical therapist assistant; respiratory care therapy.

Academic Programs *Special study options:* academic remediation for entering students, accelerated degree program, adult/continuing education programs, advanced placement credit, distance learning, internships, part-time degree program, summer session for credit.

Library Gertrude Dale Library with 25,921 titles, 200 serial subscriptions, an OPAC, a Web page.

Computers on Campus 46 computers available on campus for general student use. A campuswide network can be accessed from off campus that provide access to online admissions. Internet access, at least one staffed computer lab available.

Student Life *Housing:* college housing not available. *Activities and Organizations:* drama/theater group, student-run newspaper, choral group, Professional Business Leaders, Student Government Association, Phi Theta Kappa, Black Student Union, Nursing Club.

Athletics *Intramural sports:* basketball M/W, football M/W, golf M/W, table tennis M/W, volleyball M/W.

Costs (2005–06) *Tuition:* state resident $2352 full-time, $98 per credit hour part-time; nonresident $7056 full-time, $294 per credit hour part-time. *Required fees:* $164 full-time.

Financial Aid Of all full-time matriculated undergraduates who enrolled in 2003, 90 Federal Work-Study jobs (averaging $635).

Applying *Required:* high school transcript. *Application deadline:* 8/20 (freshmen). *Notification:* continuous until 9/3 (freshmen).

Admissions Contact Ms. Cookie Baker, Director of Admissions, Southeast Kentucky Community and Technical College, 700 College Road, Cumberland, KY 40823. *Phone:* 606-589-2145 Ext. 13018. *Toll-free phone:* 888-274-SECC Ext. 2108. *Fax:* 606-589-3175. *E-mail:* cookie.baker@kctcs.net.

SOUTHWESTERN COLLEGE OF BUSINESS
Florence, Kentucky

Admissions Contact Mr. Bruce Budesheim, Director, Southwestern College of Business, 8095 Connector Drive, Florence, KY 41042. *Phone:* 859-341-6633. *Fax:* 859-341-6749.

SPENCERIAN COLLEGE
Louisville, Kentucky

- **Proprietary** 2-year, founded 1892, part of The Sullivan University System
- **Calendar** quarters
- **Degree** certificates, diplomas, and associate
- **Urban** 10-acre campus
- **Coed**, 1,326 undergraduate students, 100% full-time, 91% women, 9% men

Undergraduates 1,326 full-time. Students come from 11 states and territories, 16% are from out of state, 25% African American, 0.7% Asian American or Pacific Islander, 0.3% Hispanic American, 0.6% Native American.

Freshmen *Admission:* 1,254 admitted.

Faculty *Total:* 87, 55% full-time, 7% with terminal degrees. *Student/faculty ratio:* 14:1.

Majors Accounting; business administration and management; medical office management.

Academic Programs *Special study options:* academic remediation for entering students, accelerated degree program, advanced placement credit, cooperative education, distance learning, double majors, external degree program, honors programs, independent study, internships, part-time degree program, services for LD students.

Library Laura Diener with an OPAC, a Web page.

Computers on Campus 81 computers available on campus for general student use. A campuswide network can be accessed from off campus. Internet access, online (class) registration, at least one staffed computer lab available.

Student Life *Housing Options:* coed. Campus housing is leased by the school and is provided by a third party. *Activities and Organizations:* student-run

newspaper, Spencerian Business Leaders. *Campus security:* 24-hour emergency response devices. *Student services:* personal/psychological counseling.

Standardized Tests *Recommended:* SAT or ACT (for admission).

Costs (2005–06) *Tuition:* $12,120 full-time, $202 per credit hour part-time. *Required fees:* $575 full-time, $30 per course part-time. *Room only:* $3960.

Applying *Options:* common application, electronic application. *Application fee:* $90. *Required:* high school transcript, interview. *Required for some:* essay or personal statement, letters of recommendation. *Notification:* continuous until 9/1 (freshmen).

Admissions Contact Terri D. Thomas, Director of Admissions, Spencerian College, 4627 Dixie Highway, Louisville, KY 40299. *Phone:* 502-447-1000 Ext. 7808. *Toll-free phone:* 800-264-1799.

SPENCERIAN COLLEGE-LEXINGTON
Lexington, Kentucky

- **Proprietary** 2-year, part of Sullivan Colleges System
- **Calendar** quarters
- **Degree** certificates, diplomas, and associate
- **Urban** campus with easy access to Louisville
- **Coed**, 376 undergraduate students, 81% full-time, 21% women, 79% men

Undergraduates 306 full-time, 70 part-time. Students come from 1 other state, 1 other country, 6% African American, 2% Hispanic American, 0.3% Native American, 0.3% international, 13% live on campus.

Freshmen *Admission:* 158 applied, 125 admitted. *Average high school GPA:* 2.35.

Faculty *Total:* 40, 43% full-time. *Student/faculty ratio:* 9:1.

Majors Architectural drafting and CAD/CADD; computer graphics; electrical, electronic and communications engineering technology; mechanical drafting and CAD/CADD.

Academic Programs *Special study options:* academic remediation for entering students, cooperative education, independent study, part-time degree program, services for LD students, summer session for credit.

Library Spencerian College Library with 450 titles, 30 serial subscriptions, 25 audiovisual materials.

Computers on Campus 14 computers available on campus for general student use. A campuswide network can be accessed from off campus. Internet access, at least one staffed computer lab available.

Student Life *Housing Options:* men-only, women-only. Campus housing is leased by the school. *Activities and Organizations:* student-run newspaper. *Campus security:* 24-hour emergency response devices.

Standardized Tests *Required for some:* CPAt.

Costs (2004–05) *Comprehensive fee:* $18,223 includes full-time tuition ($12,480), mandatory fees ($403), and room and board ($5340). Part-time tuition: $280 per credit hour. No tuition increase for student's term of enrollment. *Required fees:* $25 per course part-time. *Room and board:* college room only: $3690. *Payment plan:* installment. *Waivers:* employees or children of employees.

Applying *Options:* common application. *Application fee:* $90. *Required:* high school transcript, interview. *Application deadline:* rolling (freshmen).

Admissions Contact Ms. Georgia Mullins, Admissions Representative, Spencerian College-Lexington, 2355 Harrodsburg Road, Lexington, KY 40504. *Phone:* 800-456-3253 Ext. 8010. *Toll-free phone:* 800-456-3253. *Fax:* 859-224-7744. *E-mail:* admissions@spencerian.edu.

WEST KENTUCKY COMMUNITY AND TECHNICAL COLLEGE
Paducah, Kentucky

- **State-supported** 2-year, founded 1932, part of University of Kentucky Community College System
- **Calendar** semesters
- **Degree** certificates, diplomas, and associate
- **Small-town** 117-acre campus
- **Coed**, 3,545 undergraduate students, 41% full-time, 59% women, 41% men

Undergraduates 1,455 full-time, 2,090 part-time. Students come from 12 states and territories, 6% African American, 0.4% Asian American or Pacific Islander, 0.6% Hispanic American, 0.4% Native American.

Freshmen *Average high school GPA:* 2.35.

Faculty *Total:* 153, 50% full-time. *Student/faculty ratio:* 15:1.

Majors Accounting; administrative assistant and secretarial science; business administration and management; consumer merchandising/retailing management; electrical, electronic and communications engineering technology; industrial radiologic technology; information science/studies; mass communication/media; nursing (registered nurse training); physical therapy.

Academic Programs *Special study options:* academic remediation for entering students, adult/continuing education programs, cooperative education, honors programs, internships, part-time degree program, services for LD students, summer session for credit.

Library Paducah Community College Library with 31,339 titles, 152 serial subscriptions, an OPAC, a Web page.

Computers on Campus 160 computers available on campus for general student use. At least one staffed computer lab available.

Student Life *Housing:* college housing not available. *Activities and Organizations:* drama/theater group, student-run newspaper, choral group. *Campus security:* 14-hour patrols by trained security personnel. *Student services:* women's center.

Athletics *Intramural sports:* basketball M/W, golf M/W, soccer M/W, volleyball M/W.

Standardized Tests *Required for some:* ACT (for placement).

Costs (2005–06) *Tuition:* $98 per credit hour part-time; state resident $118 per credit hour part-time; nonresident $294 per credit hour part-time.

Financial Aid Of all full-time matriculated undergraduates who enrolled in 2003, 50 Federal Work-Study jobs (averaging $1650).

Applying *Options:* early admission. *Required for some:* high school transcript. *Application deadline:* rolling (freshmen), rolling (transfers).

Admissions Contact Mr. Jerry Anderson, Admissions Counselor, West Kentucky Community and Technical College, 4810 Alben Barkley Drive, PO Box 7380, Paducah, KY 42002-7380. *Phone:* 270-554-9200.

LOUISIANA

BATON ROUGE COMMUNITY COLLEGE
Baton Rouge, Louisiana

- **State-supported** 2-year, founded 1995
- **Calendar** semesters
- **Degree** associate
- **Coed,** 5,761 undergraduate students

Costs (2005–06) *Tuition:* state resident $1656 full-time; nonresident $4464 full-time. Full-time tuition and fees vary according to course load. Part-time tuition and fees vary according to course load. *Required fees:* $432 full-time. *Payment plans:* installment, deferred payment.

Admissions Contact Ms. Michelle L. Hill, Associate Dean, Enrollment Services, Baton Rouge Community College, 5310 Florida Boulevard, Baton Rouge, LA 70806. *Phone:* 225-216-8700. *Toll-free phone:* 800-601-4558.

BATON ROUGE SCHOOL OF COMPUTERS
Baton Rouge, Louisiana

Admissions Contact 10425 Plaza Americana, Baton Rouge, LA 70816.

BOSSIER PARISH COMMUNITY COLLEGE
Bossier City, Louisiana

- **State-supported** 2-year, founded 1967, part of University of Louisiana System
- **Calendar** semesters
- **Degree** certificates, diplomas, and associate
- **Urban** 64-acre campus
- **Coed,** 4,121 undergraduate students

Undergraduates 24% African American, 0.9% Asian American or Pacific Islander, 2% Hispanic American, 0.1% Native American.

Faculty *Total:* 220, 55% full-time.

Majors Business administration and management; corrections; criminal justice/police science; drafting and design technology; electrical, electronic and communications engineering technology; emergency medical technology (EMT paramedic); information science/studies; liberal arts and sciences/liberal studies; medical/clinical assistant; physical therapy; respiratory care therapy; telecommunications.

Academic Programs *Special study options:* academic remediation for entering students, adult/continuing education programs, advanced placement credit, distance learning, double majors, part-time degree program, services for LD students, summer session for credit.

Library Bossier Parish Community College Library with 29,600 titles, 384 serial subscriptions, an OPAC.

Computers on Campus 83 computers available on campus for general student use. At least one staffed computer lab available.

Student Life *Housing:* college housing not available. *Activities and Organizations:* drama/theater group, student-run newspaper, choral group, Student Government Association, Cavalier Players Drama Club, Data Processing Management Association. *Campus security:* student patrols. *Student services:* personal/psychological counseling.

Athletics Member NJCAA. *Intercollegiate sports:* baseball M(s), basketball M(s), soccer M, softball W(s). *Intramural sports:* badminton M/W, bowling M/W, football M, racquetball M, softball M, table tennis M/W, volleyball M/W.

Standardized Tests *Required:* ACT (for placement).

Costs (2005–06) *Tuition:* state resident $1720 full-time, $254 per credit part-time; nonresident $3860 full-time, $414 per credit part-time. *Required fees:* $448 full-time, $19 per credit part-time, $55 per term part-time.

Financial Aid Of all full-time matriculated undergraduates who enrolled in 2003, 53 Federal Work-Study jobs.

Applying *Options:* early admission. *Application fee:* $15. *Required:* high school transcript. *Application deadlines:* 8/10 (freshmen), 8/10 (transfers).

Admissions Contact Ms. Ann Jempole, Director of Admissions, Bossier Parish Community College, 2719 Airline Drive North, Bossier City, LA 71111-5801. *Phone:* 318-678-6166. *Fax:* 318-742-8664.

BRYMAN COLLEGE
New Orleans, Louisiana

Admissions Contact 1201 Elmwood Park Boulevard, Suite 600, New Orleans, LA 70123.

CAMELOT COLLEGE
Baton Rouge, Louisiana

Admissions Contact Rev. Ronny L. Williams, President, Camelot College, 2618 Wooddale Boulevard, Suite A, Baton Rouge, LA 70805. *Phone:* 225-928-3005. *Toll-free phone:* 800-470-3320.

CAMERON COLLEGE
New Orleans, Louisiana

Admissions Contact 2740 Canal Street, New Orleans, LA 70119.

CAREER TECHNICAL COLLEGE
Monroe, Louisiana

Admissions Contact 2319 Louisville Avenue, Monroe, LA 71201. *Toll-free phone:* 800-234-6766.

DELGADO COMMUNITY COLLEGE
New Orleans, Louisiana

- **State-supported** 2-year, founded 1921, part of Louisiana Community and Technical College System
- **Calendar** semesters
- **Degree** certificates and associate
- **Urban** 57-acre campus
- **Endowment** $1.0 million
- **Coed**

Faculty *Student/faculty ratio:* 20:1.

Student Life *Campus security:* 24-hour patrols, student patrols.

Athletics Member NJCAA.

Standardized Tests *Required for some:* ACT (for placement). *Recommended:* ACT (for placement).

Costs (2004–05) *One-time required fee:* $15. *Tuition:* state resident $1482 full-time, $420 per term part-time; nonresident $4462 full-time, $1275 per term part-time. Part-time tuition and fees vary according to course load. *Required fees:* $174 full-time, $5 per credit part-time, $10 per term part-time.

Financial Aid Of all full-time matriculated undergraduates who enrolled in 2003, 308 Federal Work-Study jobs (averaging $1375).

Applying *Application fee:* $15. *Required for some:* high school transcript. *Recommended:* high school transcript, proof of immunization.

Admissions Contact Ms. Gwen Boute, Director of Admissions, Delgado Community College, 615 City Park Avenue, New Orleans, LA 70119. *Phone:* 504-483-4004. *Fax:* 504-483-1895. *E-mail:* enroll@dcc.edu.

DELTA COLLEGE OF ARTS AND TECHNOLOGY
Baton Rouge, Louisiana

- **Proprietary** 2-year
- **Calendar** continuous (for most programs)
- **Degree** certificates, diplomas, and associate
- **Urban** 3-acre campus
- **Coed, primarily women**

Applying *Application fee:* $100.
Admissions Contact Ms. Beulah Laverghe-Brown, Admissions Director, Delta College of Arts and Technology, 7380 Exchange Place, Baton Rouge, LA 70806. *Phone:* 225-928-7770. *Fax:* 225-927-9096. *E-mail:* dcat@deltacollege.com.

DELTA SCHOOL OF BUSINESS & TECHNOLOGY
Lake Charles, Louisiana

Admissions Contact Mr. Gary J. Holt, President, Delta School of Business & Technology, 517 Broad Street, Lake Charles, LA 70601. *Phone:* 337-439-5765.

ELAINE P. NUNEZ COMMUNITY COLLEGE
Chalmette, Louisiana

- **State-supported** 2-year, founded 1992, part of Louisiana Community and Technical Colleges System
- **Calendar** semesters
- **Degree** certificates and associate
- **Suburban** 20-acre campus with easy access to New Orleans
- **Endowment** $770,000
- **Coed**

Faculty *Student/faculty ratio:* 18:1.
Student Life *Campus security:* 24-hour emergency response devices, late-night transport/escort service.
Standardized Tests *Required for some:* ACT ASSET or ACT COMPASS. *Recommended:* ACT (for placement).
Costs (2004–05) *Tuition:* state resident $1740 full-time, $145 per credit hour part-time; nonresident $3822 full-time, $319 per credit hour part-time. *Required fees:* $325 full-time, $20 per credit hour part-time.
Financial Aid Of all full-time matriculated undergraduates who enrolled in 2003, 70 Federal Work-Study jobs (averaging $1452).
Applying *Options:* deferred entrance. *Application fee:* $10. *Required for some:* high school transcript. *Recommended:* minimum 2.0 GPA.
Admissions Contact Ms. Donna Clark, Dean of Student Affairs, Elaine P. Nunez Community College, 3710 Paris Road, Chalmette, LA 70043. *Phone:* 504-680-2457. *Fax:* 504-278-7353.

GRETNA CAREER COLLEGE
Gretna, Louisiana

Admissions Contact 1415 Whitney Avenue, Gretna, LA 70053-5835.

HERZING COLLEGE
Kenner, Louisiana

Admissions Contact Genny Bordelon, Director of Admissions, Herzing College, 2400 Veterans Boulevard, Kenner, LA 70062. *Phone:* 504-733-0074.

ITI TECHNICAL COLLEGE
Baton Rouge, Louisiana

- **Proprietary** 2-year, founded 1973
- **Calendar** continuous
- **Degree** certificates and associate
- **Suburban** 10-acre campus
- **Coed**
- 83% of applicants were admitted

Faculty *Student/faculty ratio:* 20:1.
Costs (2004–05) *Tuition:* $10,000 full-time.

Admissions Contact Mr. Joe Martin III, President, ITI Technical College, 13944 Airline Highway, Baton Rouge, LA 70817. *Phone:* 225-752-4230 Ext. 213. *Toll-free phone:* 800-467-4484.

ITT TECHNICAL INSTITUTE
St. Rose, Louisiana

- **Proprietary** primarily 2-year, part of ITT Educational Services, Inc
- **Calendar** quarters
- **Degrees** associate and bachelor's
- **Coed**

Standardized Tests *Required:* Wonderlic aptitude test (for admission).
Costs (2004–05) *Tuition:* Please see school catalog for specific information.
Applying *Options:* deferred entrance. *Application fee:* $100. *Required:* high school transcript, interview. *Recommended:* letters of recommendation.
Admissions Contact Heidi Munoz, Director of Recruitment, ITT Technical Institute, 140 James Drive East, Saint Rose, LA 70087. *Phone:* 504-463-0338. *Toll-free phone:* 866-463-0338. *Fax:* 504-463-0979.

LOUISIANA STATE UNIVERSITY AT ALEXANDRIA
Alexandria, Louisiana

Admissions Contact Ms. Shelly Kieffer, Recruiter/Admissions Counselor, Louisiana State University at Alexandria, 8100 Highway 71 South, Alexandria, LA 71302-9121. *Phone:* 318-473-6508. *Toll-free phone:* 888-473-6417. *Fax:* 318-473-6418. *E-mail:* skieffer@lsua.edu.

LOUISIANA STATE UNIVERSITY AT EUNICE
Eunice, Louisiana

Admissions Contact Ms. Gracie Guillory, Director of Financial Aid, Louisiana State University at Eunice, PO Box 1129, Eunice, LA 70535-1129. *Phone:* 337-550-1282. *Toll-free phone:* 888-367-5783. *Fax:* 337-550-1306.

LOUISIANA TECHNICAL COLLEGE
Baton Rouge, Louisiana

- **State-supported** 2-year, founded 1930
- **Degree** certificates, diplomas, and associate
- **Coed**, 15,481 undergraduate students, 54% full-time, 47% women, 53% men

Undergraduates 8,416 full-time, 7,065 part-time. 40% African American, 0.9% Asian American or Pacific Islander, 1% Hispanic American, 0.7% Native American.
Freshmen *Admission:* 3,767 applied, 3,767 admitted, 3,767 enrolled.
Faculty *Total:* 1,086, 65% full-time. *Student/faculty ratio:* 14:1.
Student Life *Housing:* college housing not available.
Costs (2005–06) *Tuition:* state resident $552 full-time, $23 per credit hour part-time; nonresident $1104 full-time, $46 per credit hour part-time. *Required fees:* $214 full-time, $9 per credit hour part-time, $5 per term part-time.
Admissions Contact Janice M. Bolden, Vice Chancellor of Student Affairs, Enrollment Management, and College Registrar, Louisiana Technical College, 150 3rd Street, Baton Rouge, LA 70801. *Phone:* 800-351-7611. *Toll-free phone:* 800-351-7611.

MEDVANCE INSTITUTE
Baton Rouge, Louisiana

Admissions Contact Ms. Sheri Kirley, Associate Director of Admissions, MedVance Institute, 4173 Government Street, Baton Rouge, LA 70806. *Phone:* 225-248-1015. *Fax:* 225-343-5426.

METROPOLITAN COMMUNITY COLLEGE
Gretna, Louisiana

Admissions Contact 2550 Belle Chasse Highway, Gretna, LA 70053. *Toll-free phone:* 866-838-3159.

REMINGTON COLLEGE-BATON ROUGE CAMPUS
Baton Rouge, Louisiana

Admissions Contact Mr. Gregg Falcon, Campus President, Remington College-Baton Rouge Campus, 1900 North Lobdell, Baton Rouge, LA 70806. *Phone:* 225-922-3990.

REMINGTON COLLEGE-LAFAYETTE CAMPUS

Lafayette, Louisiana

- **Proprietary** 2-year, founded 1940, part of Education America Inc
- **Calendar** continuous
- **Degree** diplomas and associate
- **Urban** 4-acre campus
- **Coed**

Faculty *Student/faculty ratio:* 15:1.
Student Life *Campus security:* 24-hour emergency response devices.
Costs (2004–05) *Tuition:* $11,355 full-time, $308 per credit part-time. *Payment plans:* tuition prepayment, installment, deferred payment.
Applying *Options:* early admission, deferred entrance. *Application fee:* $50. *Required:* high school transcript, interview.
Admissions Contact Mr. William Duncan, Director of Recruiting, Remington College-Lafayette Campus, 303 Rue Louis XIV, Lafayette, LA 70508. *Phone:* 337-981-9010. *Toll-free phone:* 800-736-2687. *Fax:* 337-983-7130.

REMINGTON COLLEGE-NEW ORLEANS CAMPUS

Metairie, Louisiana

Admissions Contact Mr. Roy Kimble, Director of Recruitment, Remington College-New Orleans Campus, 321 Veterans Memorial Boulevard, Metairie, LA 70005. *Phone:* 504-831-8889. *Fax:* 504-831-6803.

RIVER PARISHES COMMUNITY COLLEGE

Sorrento, Louisiana

- **State-supported** 2-year, founded 1997
- **Calendar** semesters
- **Degree** certificates, diplomas, and associate
- **Coed,** 724 undergraduate students

Faculty *Total:* 33, 48% full-time, 15% with terminal degrees.
Majors Chemical technology; liberal arts and sciences/liberal studies; physical sciences.
Costs (2005–06) *Tuition:* state resident $1458 full-time, $66 per credit hour part-time; nonresident $4174 full-time, $66 per credit hour part-time. *Required fees:* $310 full-time, $40 per term part-time.
Applying *Application fee:* $10.
Admissions Contact Ms. Allison Dauzat, Dean of Students and Enrollment Management, River Parishes Community College, P.O. Box 310, 7384 John LeBlanc Boulevard, Sorrento, LA 70778. *Phone:* 225-675-8270. *Fax:* 225-675-5478.

SCHOOL OF URBAN MISSIONS-NEW ORLEANS

New Orleans, Louisiana

Admissions Contact PO Box 53344, New Orleans, LA 70153. *Toll-free phone:* 800-385-6364.

SOUTHERN UNIVERSITY AT SHREVEPORT

Shreveport, Louisiana

Admissions Contact Ms. Juanita Johnson, Acting Admissions Records Technician, Southern University at Shreveport, 3050 Martin Luther King, Jr. Drive, Shreveport, LA 71107. *Phone:* 318-674-3342. *Toll-free phone:* 800-458-1472 Ext. 342.

MAINE

ANDOVER COLLEGE

Portland, Maine

- **Proprietary** 2-year, founded 1966
- **Calendar** modular
- **Degree** certificates and associate
- **Urban** 2-acre campus
- **Coed,** 502 undergraduate students, 98% full-time, 79% women, 21% men

Associate degrees offered at Portland and Lewiston campuses in 24 months or less in accounting, business administration, computer technology, criminal justice, early childhood education, paralegal studies, medical assisting, office administration, and travel and hospitality management. Certificates include early childhood education, paralegal studies, medical transcription, office administration, and travel and hospitality management. Facilities and services include 5 computer labs, all-digital high-speed Internet access, an Academic Assistance Center, internships, and lifetime placement services.

Undergraduates 490 full-time, 12 part-time. Students come from 4 states and territories, 3 other countries.
Freshmen *Admission:* 103 applied, 103 admitted.
Faculty *Total:* 36, 33% full-time. *Student/faculty ratio:* 19:1.
Majors Accounting; administrative assistant and secretarial science; business administration and management; computer/information technology services administration related; computer management; computer programming; computer science; criminal justice/law enforcement administration; health information/medical records administration; kindergarten/preschool education; legal administrative assistant/secretary; legal assistant/paralegal; medical administrative assistant and medical secretary; medical/clinical assistant; system administration; web/multimedia management and webmaster.
Academic Programs *Special study options:* academic remediation for entering students, adult/continuing education programs, cooperative education, independent study, internships, part-time degree program, summer session for credit.
Library Andover Library with 6,500 titles, 110 serial subscriptions, 59 audiovisual materials.
Computers on Campus 100 computers available on campus for general student use. Internet access, at least one staffed computer lab available.
Student Life *Housing:* college housing not available. *Activities and Organizations:* Student Advisors, Andover Computer, Student Advisors Group, Andover Student Medical Assistants, C.O.P.S. *Campus security:* 24-hour emergency response devices. *Student services:* personal/psychological counseling.
Costs (2004–05) *Tuition:* $5940 full-time, $495 per course part-time. *Required fees:* $1500 full-time, $80 per term part-time.
Financial Aid Of all full-time matriculated undergraduates who enrolled in 2003, 25 Federal Work-Study jobs (averaging $3000).
Applying *Options:* common application, early admission, deferred entrance. *Application fee:* $25. *Required:* high school transcript. *Recommended:* interview. *Application deadline:* rolling (freshmen), rolling (transfers).
Admissions Contact Mr. David Blessing, Director of Enrollment Management, Andover College, 901 Washington Avenue, Portland, ME 04103-2791. *Phone:* 207-774-6126 Ext. 261. *Toll-free phone:* 800-639-3110 Ext. 240 (in-state); 800-639-3110 Ext. 242 (out-of-state). *Fax:* 207-774-1715 Ext. 243. *E-mail:* enroll@andovercollege.com.

BEAL COLLEGE

Bangor, Maine

Admissions Contact Ms. Susan Palmer, Admissions Assistant, Beal College, 629 Main Street, Bangor, ME 04401. *Phone:* 207-947-4591. *Toll-free phone:* 800-660-7351. *Fax:* 207-947-0208.

CENTRAL MAINE COMMUNITY COLLEGE

Auburn, Maine

Admissions Contact Ms. Elizabeth Oken, Director of Admissions, Central Maine Community College, 1250 Turner Street, Auburn, ME 04210-6498. *Phone:* 207-755-5334 Ext. 334. *Toll-free phone:* 800-891-2002. *Fax:* 207-755-5493. *E-mail:* enroll@cmtc.net.

CENTRAL MAINE MEDICAL CENTER SCHOOL OF NURSING

Lewiston, Maine

- **Independent** 2-year, founded 1891
- **Calendar** semesters
- **Degree** certificates and associate
- **Urban** campus
- **Coed, primarily women,** 114 undergraduate students, 19% full-time, 86% women, 14% men

Undergraduates 22 full-time, 92 part-time. Students come from 2 states and territories, 1% are from out of state, 0.9% Native American, 2% live on campus.
Freshmen *Admission:* 252 applied, 61 admitted, 3 enrolled. *Average high school GPA:* 3.52. *Test scores:* SAT verbal scores over 500: 100%; SAT math scores over 500: 100%; SAT verbal scores over 600: 50%; SAT math scores over 600: 50%.

Central Maine Medical Center School of Nursing (continued)

Faculty *Total:* 12, 75% full-time, 8% with terminal degrees. *Student/faculty ratio:* 5:1.

Majors Nursing (registered nurse training).

Academic Programs *Special study options:* advanced placement credit, off-campus study.

Library Gerrish True Health Sciences Library plus 1 other with 1,975 titles, 339 serial subscriptions, an OPAC, a Web page.

Computers on Campus 10 computers available on campus for general student use. Internet access, at least one staffed computer lab available.

Student Life *Housing Options:* coed. Campus housing is university owned. *Activities and Organizations:* Student Communication Council, student government, Student Nurses Association. *Campus security:* 24-hour emergency response devices and patrols, late-night transport/escort service, controlled dormitory access. *Student services:* health clinic, personal/psychological counseling.

Standardized Tests *Required:* SAT (for admission).

Costs (2005–06) *Tuition:* $2898 full-time, $138 per credit part-time. *Required fees:* $1205 full-time, $20 per term part-time. *Room only:* $1500.

Applying *Application fee:* $40. *Required:* essay or personal statement, high school transcript, 2 letters of recommendation. *Application deadline:* 3/1 (freshmen). *Notification:* 3/15 (freshmen).

Admissions Contact Mrs. Kathleen C. Jacques, Registrar, Central Maine Medical Center School of Nursing, 70 Middle Street, Lewiston, ME 04240-0305. *Phone:* 207-795-2858. *Fax:* 207-795-2849. *E-mail:* jacqueka@cmhc.org.

EASTERN MAINE COMMUNITY COLLEGE

Bangor, Maine

- **State-supported** 2-year, founded 1966, part of Maine Community College System
- **Calendar** semesters
- **Degree** certificates, diplomas, and associate
- **Small-town** 72-acre campus
- **Endowment** $1.5 million
- **Coed,** 1,790 undergraduate students, 42% full-time, 52% women, 48% men

Undergraduates 744 full-time, 1,046 part-time. Students come from 2 states and territories, 1% are from out of state, 0.1% African American, 0.3% Asian American or Pacific Islander, 0.1% Hispanic American, 1% Native American, 20% live on campus.

Freshmen *Admission:* 1,407 applied, 705 admitted, 410 enrolled.

Faculty *Total:* 142, 38% full-time, 8% with terminal degrees. *Student/faculty ratio:* 11:1.

Majors Administrative assistant and secretarial science; automobile/automotive mechanics technology; banking and financial support services; business administration and management; carpentry; computer technology/computer systems technology; construction engineering technology; culinary arts; drafting and design technology; electrical, electronic and communications engineering technology; heating, air conditioning, ventilation and refrigeration maintenance technology; heavy equipment maintenance technology; kindergarten/preschool education; liberal arts and sciences/liberal studies; machine tool technology; nursing (licensed practical/vocational nurse training); nursing (registered nurse training); radiologic technology/science; welding technology.

Academic Programs *Special study options:* academic remediation for entering students, adult/continuing education programs, advanced placement credit, part-time degree program, summer session for credit.

Library Eastern Maine Technical College Library plus 1 other with 17,554 titles, 159 serial subscriptions, an OPAC, a Web page.

Computers on Campus 85 computers available on campus for general student use. A campuswide network can be accessed from off campus. Internet access, at least one staffed computer lab available.

Student Life *Housing Options:* coed. Campus housing is university owned. *Activities and Organizations:* student-run newspaper, Student Senate, Phi Theta Kappa, Senior Council, Resident's Council, Associated General Contractors Student Chapter. *Campus security:* late-night transport/escort service, controlled dormitory access. *Student services:* health clinic, personal/psychological counseling.

Athletics Member NSCAA. *Intercollegiate sports:* basketball M, soccer M/W. *Intramural sports:* badminton M/W, basketball M/W, bowling M/W, ice hockey M(c)/W(c), skiing (cross-country) M/W, skiing (downhill) M/W, soccer M/W, table tennis M/W, volleyball M/W, weight lifting M/W.

Standardized Tests *Required:* ACCUPLACER (for admission). *Required for some:* SAT (for admission).

Costs (2004–05) *Tuition:* state resident $2448 full-time, $68 per credit part-time; nonresident $5364 full-time, $149 per credit part-time. *Required fees:* $612 full-time, $17 per credit part-time. *Room and board:* $5519.

Financial Aid Of all full-time matriculated undergraduates who enrolled in 2003, 100 Federal Work-Study jobs (averaging $1000).

Applying *Options:* deferred entrance. *Application fee:* $20. *Required:* essay or personal statement, high school transcript, letters of recommendation. *Required for some:* interview. *Recommended:* minimum 2.0 GPA. *Application deadline:* rolling (freshmen). *Notification:* continuous (freshmen).

Admissions Contact Ms. Veronica Delcort, Director of Admissions, Eastern Maine Community College, 354 Hogan Road, Bangor, ME 04401. *Phone:* 207-974-4680. *Toll-free phone:* 800-286-9357. *Fax:* 207-974-4683. *E-mail:* admissions@emcc.edu.

KENNEBEC VALLEY COMMUNITY COLLEGE

Fairfield, Maine

- **State-supported** 2-year, founded 1970, part of Maine Community College System
- **Calendar** semesters
- **Degree** certificates, diplomas, and associate
- **Small-town** 58-acre campus
- **Endowment** $222,809
- **Coed,** 1,772 undergraduate students, 32% full-time, 71% women, 29% men

Undergraduates 568 full-time, 1,204 part-time. Students come from 4 states and territories, 0.2% African American, 0.2% Asian American or Pacific Islander, 1% Hispanic American, 0.8% Native American.

Freshmen *Admission:* 476 applied, 340 admitted, 321 enrolled.

Faculty *Total:* 159, 25% full-time. *Student/faculty ratio:* 22:1.

Majors Accounting; administrative assistant and secretarial science; biology/biological sciences; business administration and management; child care and support services management; child care provision; communications systems installation and repair technology; computer/information technology services administration related; computer installation and repair technology; computer management; computer programming related; computer software and media applications related; computer systems networking and telecommunications; data modeling/warehousing and database administration; drafting and design technology; education; electrical/electronics equipment installation and repair; emergency medical technology (EMT paramedic); executive assistant/executive secretary; general studies; health information/medical records administration; industrial electronics technology; industrial mechanics and maintenance technology; legal administrative assistant/secretary; liberal arts and sciences/liberal studies; machine tool technology; marketing/marketing management; medical/clinical assistant; nursing (registered nurse training); occupational therapist assistant; physical therapist assistant; respiratory care therapy; sales, distribution and marketing; web/multimedia management and webmaster; web page, digital/multimedia and information resources design; wood science and wood products/pulp and paper technology.

Academic Programs *Special study options:* academic remediation for entering students, accelerated degree program, adult/continuing education programs, advanced placement credit, distance learning, external degree program, independent study, internships, part-time degree program, services for LD students, summer session for credit.

Library Lunder Library with 19,629 titles, 25,734 serial subscriptions, 1,373 audiovisual materials, an OPAC, a Web page.

Computers on Campus 250 computers available on campus for general student use. A campuswide network can be accessed from off campus. Internet access, at least one staffed computer lab available.

Student Life *Housing:* college housing not available. *Activities and Organizations:* Vocational Industrial Clubs of America (VICA) Skills USA, Student Senate, Phi Theta Kappa, Glee Club. *Campus security:* Evening security patrol. *Student services:* personal/psychological counseling.

Athletics *Intramural sports:* basketball M/W, bowling M/W, ultimate Frisbee M/W, volleyball M/W.

Standardized Tests *Required for some:* nursing exam, HOBET, ACCUPLACER.

Costs (2005–06) *Tuition:* state resident $2040 full-time, $68 per credit hour part-time; nonresident $4470 full-time, $149 per credit hour part-time. *Required fees:* $450 full-time.

Financial Aid Of all full-time matriculated undergraduates who enrolled in 2003, 34 Federal Work-Study jobs (averaging $1207).

Applying *Options:* electronic application, deferred entrance. *Application fee:* $20. *Required:* essay or personal statement, high school transcript. *Required for some:* letters of recommendation, interview. *Application deadline:* rolling (freshmen), rolling (transfers). *Notification:* continuous (freshmen).

Admissions Contact Mr. Jim Bourgoin, Director of Recruitment, Kennebec Valley Community College, 92 Western Avenue, Fairfield, ME 04937-1367. *Phone:* 207-453-5035. *Toll-free phone:* 800-528-5882 Ext. 5035. *Fax:* 207-453-5011. *E-mail:* admissions@kvcc.me.edu.

NORTHERN MAINE COMMUNITY COLLEGE
Presque Isle, Maine

- **State-related** 2-year, founded 1963, part of Maine Technical College System
- **Calendar** semesters
- **Degree** certificates, diplomas, and associate
- **Small-town** 86-acre campus
- **Coed**

Student Life *Campus security:* 24-hour patrols.
Athletics Member NSCAA.
Standardized Tests *Required:* Assessment and Placement Services for Community Colleges (for placement).
Costs (2004–05) *Tuition:* state resident $1632 full-time, $68 per credit part-time; nonresident $3576 full-time, $149 per credit part-time. *Required fees:* $229 full-time. *Room and board:* $4460; room only: $1680.
Financial Aid Of all full-time matriculated undergraduates who enrolled in 2003, 55 Federal Work-Study jobs (averaging $3000).
Applying *Options:* common application, electronic application, early admission. *Application fee:* $20. *Required:* high school transcript. *Required for some:* letters of recommendation. *Recommended:* essay or personal statement, minimum 2.0 GPA.
Admissions Contact Ms. Nancy Gagnon, Admissions Secretary, Northern Maine Community College, 33 Edgemont Drive, Presque Isle, ME 04769-2016. *Phone:* 207-768-2785. *Toll-free phone:* 800-535-6682. *Fax:* 207-768-2831. *E-mail:* wcasavant@nmtc.net.

SOUTHERN MAINE COMMUNITY COLLEGE
South Portland, Maine

- **State-supported** 2-year, founded 1946, part of Maine Community College System
- **Calendar** semesters
- **Degree** certificates, diplomas, and associate
- **Small-town** 65-acre campus
- **Endowment** $513,726
- **Coed,** 4,103 undergraduate students, 52% full-time, 51% women, 49% men

Undergraduates 2,135 full-time, 1,968 part-time. Students come from 9 states and territories, 6% are from out of state, 3% African American, 1% Asian American or Pacific Islander, 1% Hispanic American, 1% Native American, 0.5% international, 10% live on campus.
Freshmen *Admission:* 1,060 enrolled.
Faculty *Total:* 259, 34% full-time. *Student/faculty ratio:* 18:1.
Majors Agronomy and crop science; architectural engineering technology; automobile/automotive mechanics technology; botany/plant biology; business administration and management; business machine repair; cardiovascular technology; carpentry; child development; cinematography and film/video production; communications technology; computer engineering technology; computer management; construction engineering technology; criminal justice/law enforcement administration; criminal justice/police science; culinary arts; dietetics; drafting and design technology; electrical, electronic and communications engineering technology; engineering related; environmental engineering technology; fire science; food services technology; general studies; heating, air conditioning, ventilation and refrigeration maintenance technology; horticultural science; hospitality administration; hotel/motel administration; industrial radiologic technology; information science/studies; kindergarten/preschool education; landscaping and groundskeeping; liberal arts and sciences/liberal studies; machine tool technology; management information systems; marine biology and biological oceanography; medical/clinical assistant; nursing (licensed practical/vocational nurse training); nursing (registered nurse training); oceanography (chemical and physical); pipefitting and sprinkler fitting; radiologic technology/science; respiratory care therapy; special products marketing; surgical technology.
Academic Programs *Special study options:* academic remediation for entering students, advanced placement credit, cooperative education, distance learning, double majors, English as a second language, internships, off-campus study, part-time degree program, services for LD students, study abroad, summer session for credit.
Library Southern Maine Community College Library with 15,000 titles, 350 serial subscriptions, an OPAC, a Web page.
Computers on Campus 200 computers available on campus for general student use. A campuswide network can be accessed from student residence rooms and from off campus. Internet access, at least one staffed computer lab available.
Student Life *Housing Options:* coed. Campus housing is university owned and is provided by a third party. *Activities and Organizations:* drama/theater group, student-run newspaper, choral group, SEA Club, student government, Phi Theta

Kappa, VICA. *Campus security:* 24-hour emergency response devices, student patrols, late-night transport/escort service. *Student services:* health clinic, personal/psychological counseling, women's center.
Athletics Member NSCAA. *Intercollegiate sports:* baseball M, basketball M, golf M/W, soccer M/W, softball W, volleyball M/W. *Intramural sports:* basketball M/W, football M/W, golf M/W, soccer M/W, volleyball M/W.
Standardized Tests *Required for some:* ACCUPLACER. *Recommended:* SAT (for placement).
Costs (2005–06) *Tuition:* state resident $2220 full-time; nonresident $4650 full-time. *Room and board:* $5824; room only: $2678.
Financial Aid Of all full-time matriculated undergraduates who enrolled in 2003, 130 Federal Work-Study jobs (averaging $1500).
Applying *Options:* electronic application. *Application fee:* $20. *Required:* high school transcript. *Application deadline:* rolling (freshmen), rolling (transfers). *Notification:* continuous (freshmen).
Admissions Contact David Tracy, Assistant Dean for Enrollment Services, Southern Maine Community College, Admissions, 2 Fort Road, South Portland, ME 04106. *Phone:* 207-741-5664. *Toll-free phone:* 877-282-2182. *Fax:* 207-741-5671. *E-mail:* admissions@smccme.edu.

WASHINGTON COUNTY COMMUNITY COLLEGE
Calais, Maine

Admissions Contact Mr. Kent Lyons, Admissions Counselor, Washington County Community College, RR#1, Box 22C River Road, Calais, ME 04619. *Phone:* 207-454-1000. *Toll-free phone:* 800-210-6932 Ext. 41049. *Fax:* 207-454-1026.

YORK COUNTY COMMUNITY COLLEGE
Wells, Maine

- **State-supported** 2-year, founded 1994, part of Maine Technical College System
- **Calendar** semesters
- **Degree** certificates and associate
- **Small-town** 84-acre campus with easy access to Boston
- **Coed**

Faculty *Student/faculty ratio:* 13:1.
Student Life *Campus security:* 24-hour emergency response devices.
Standardized Tests *Recommended:* SAT (for placement).
Costs (2004–05) *Tuition:* state resident $2040 full-time, $68 per credit part-time; nonresident $4470 full-time, $149 per credit part-time. Full-time tuition and fees vary according to course load and program. Part-time tuition and fees vary according to course load and program. *Required fees:* $710 full-time, $24 per credit part-time.
Financial Aid Of all full-time matriculated undergraduates who enrolled in 2003, 20 Federal Work-Study jobs (averaging $1200).
Applying *Application fee:* $20. *Required:* essay or personal statement, high school transcript.
Admissions Contact Ms. Leisa Collins, Director of Admissions, York County Community College, 112 College Drive, Wells, ME 04090. *Phone:* 207-646-9282 Ext. 305. *Toll-free phone:* 800-580-3820. *Fax:* 207-641-0837. *E-mail:* admissions@yctc.net.

MARYLAND

ALLEGANY COLLEGE OF MARYLAND
Cumberland, Maryland

- **State and locally supported** 2-year, founded 1961, part of Maryland State Community Colleges System
- **Calendar** semesters
- **Degree** certificates and associate
- **Small-town** 311-acre campus
- **Endowment** $5.9 million
- **Coed,** 3,705 undergraduate students, 57% full-time, 68% women, 32% men

Undergraduates 2,102 full-time, 1,603 part-time. Students come from 21 states and territories, 49% are from out of state, 7% African American, 0.5% Asian American or Pacific Islander, 0.8% Hispanic American, 0.4% Native American.
Freshmen *Admission:* 2,529 applied, 2,477 admitted, 843 enrolled.
Faculty *Total:* 245, 42% full-time. *Student/faculty ratio:* 17:1.

Allegany College of Maryland (continued)

Majors Accounting technology and bookkeeping; administrative assistant and secretarial science; automobile/automotive mechanics technology; business administration and management; clinical/medical laboratory assistant; clinical/medical laboratory technology; communications technology; computer engineering technology; cosmetology and personal grooming arts related; criminal justice/police science; culinary arts; dental hygiene; forest/forest resources management; health professions related; hospitality administration; legal assistant/paralegal; liberal arts and sciences/liberal studies; management information systems; marketing/marketing management; medical radiologic technology; nursing (registered nurse training); occupational therapist assistant; occupational therapy; physical therapist assistant; psychiatric/mental health services technology; respiratory care therapy.

Academic Programs *Special study options:* academic remediation for entering students, adult/continuing education programs, advanced placement credit, distance learning, double majors, honors programs, independent study, internships, part-time degree program, summer session for credit. *ROTC:* Army (c).

Library Allegany College of Maryland Library with 86,636 titles, 313 serial subscriptions, 3,395 audiovisual materials, an OPAC, a Web page.

Computers on Campus 700 computers available on campus for general student use. A campuswide network can be accessed from off campus. Internet access, online (class) registration, at least one staffed computer lab available.

Student Life *Housing:* college housing not available. *Activities and Organizations:* choral group, SAHDA, Honors Club, EMT Club, Forestry Club. *Campus security:* 24-hour emergency response devices and patrols, late-night transport/escort service. *Student services:* personal/psychological counseling, women's center.

Athletics Member NJCAA. *Intercollegiate sports:* baseball M, basketball M/W, soccer M/W, softball W, tennis M/W, volleyball W.

Standardized Tests *Required for some:* ACT (for admission).

Costs (2004–05) *Tuition:* area resident $2550 full-time, $85 per credit part-time; state resident $5010 full-time, $167 per credit part-time; nonresident $5910 full-time, $197 per credit part-time. Full-time tuition and fees vary according to course load and location. Part-time tuition and fees vary according to course load and location. *Required fees:* $184 full-time, $7 per credit part-time, $39 per term part-time. *Waivers:* employees or children of employees.

Applying *Options:* electronic application, early admission. *Required:* high school transcript. *Application deadline:* rolling (freshmen), rolling (transfers).

Admissions Contact Ms. Cathy Nolan, Director of Admissions and Registration, Allegany College of Maryland, 12401 Willowbrook Road, SE, Cumberland, MD 21502. *Phone:* 301-784-5000 Ext. 5202. *Fax:* 301-784-5220. *E-mail:* cnolan@allegany.edu.

ANNE ARUNDEL COMMUNITY COLLEGE
Arnold, Maryland

- **State and locally supported** 2-year, founded 1961
- **Calendar** semesters
- **Degree** certificates and associate
- **Suburban** 230-acre campus with easy access to Baltimore and Washington, DC
- **Endowment** $2.4 million
- **Coed,** 14,290 undergraduate students, 33% full-time, 62% women, 38% men

Undergraduates 4,780 full-time, 9,510 part-time. Students come from 12 states and territories, 19 other countries, 0.8% are from out of state, 12% African American, 3% Asian American or Pacific Islander, 2% Hispanic American, 0.6% Native American, 0.7% international, 19% transferred in. *Retention:* 58% of 2002 full-time freshmen returned.

Freshmen *Admission:* 3,228 admitted, 2,737 enrolled.

Faculty *Total:* 827, 29% full-time, 9% with terminal degrees. *Student/faculty ratio:* 18:1.

Majors Accounting; administrative assistant and secretarial science; American studies; applied art; architectural engineering technology; art; astronomy; behavioral sciences; biological and physical sciences; biology/biological sciences; botany/plant biology; broadcast journalism; business administration and management; business/managerial economics; chemistry; cinematography and film/video production; clinical laboratory science/medical technology; communications technology; computer and information sciences related; computer engineering technology; computer management; computer programming; computer science; computer/technical support; consumer merchandising/retailing management; corrections; criminal justice/law enforcement administration; criminal justice/police science; data entry/microcomputer applications; data processing and data processing technology; economics; education; electrical, electronic and communications engineering technology; elementary education; emergency medical technology (EMT paramedic); engineering technology; English; environmental studies; European studies; food services technology; health teacher education; horticultural science; hotel/motel administration; humanities; human services; industrial radiologic technology; industrial technology; information science/studies; kindergarten/preschool education; landscape architecture; legal assistant/

paralegal; liberal arts and sciences/liberal studies; marine science/merchant marine officer; marketing/marketing management; mass communication/media; mathematics; mechanical engineering/mechanical technology; medical/clinical assistant; mental health/rehabilitation; music; nursing (registered nurse training); photography; physical education teaching and coaching; public administration; public policy analysis; real estate; social sciences; system administration; telecommunications.

Academic Programs *Special study options:* academic remediation for entering students, accelerated degree program, adult/continuing education programs, advanced placement credit, cooperative education, distance learning, English as a second language, freshman honors college, honors programs, independent study, internships, part-time degree program, services for LD students, summer session for credit. *ROTC:* Army (c), Air Force (c).

Library Andrew G. Truxal Library with 144,694 titles, 403 serial subscriptions, 8,060 audiovisual materials, an OPAC, a Web page.

Computers on Campus 250 computers available on campus for general student use. A campuswide network can be accessed from off campus. Internet access, online (class) registration, at least one staffed computer lab available.

Student Life *Housing:* college housing not available. *Activities and Organizations:* drama/theater group, student-run newspaper, choral group, Drama Club, student association, Black Student Union, International Student Association, Chemistry Club. *Campus security:* 24-hour emergency response devices and patrols, student patrols, late-night transport/escort service. *Student services:* health clinic, personal/psychological counseling.

Athletics Member NJCAA. *Intercollegiate sports:* baseball M(s), basketball M/W, cross-country running M(s)/W(s), golf M, lacrosse M(s), soccer M(s)/W(s), softball W(s), volleyball W. *Intramural sports:* lacrosse W.

Standardized Tests *Recommended:* SAT or ACT (for placement).

Costs (2005–06) *Tuition:* area resident $1992 full-time, $83 per credit hour part-time; state resident $3816 full-time, $159 per credit hour part-time; nonresident $6768 full-time, $282 per credit hour part-time. Full-time tuition and fees vary according to course load. Part-time tuition and fees vary according to course load. *Required fees:* $232 full-time, $8 per credit hour part-time, $20 per term part-time. *Waivers:* employees or children of employees.

Financial Aid Of all full-time matriculated undergraduates who enrolled in 2003, 104 Federal Work-Study jobs (averaging $1900). 55 state and other part-time jobs (averaging $1740).

Applying *Options:* early admission, deferred entrance. *Application deadline:* rolling (freshmen), rolling (transfers).

Admissions Contact Mr. Thomas McGinn, Director of Enrollment Development and Admissions, Anne Arundel Community College, 101 College Parkway, Arnold, MD 21012-1895. *Phone:* 410-777-2240. *Fax:* 410-777-2246. *E-mail:* 4info@aacc.edu.

BALTIMORE CITY COMMUNITY COLLEGE
Baltimore, Maryland

- **State-supported** 2-year, founded 1947
- **Calendar** semesters
- **Degree** certificates and associate
- **Urban** 19-acre campus
- **Endowment** $139,215
- **Coed,** 7,095 undergraduate students

Undergraduates Students come from 4 states and territories, 1% are from out of state.

Freshmen *Admission:* 1,380 applied.

Faculty *Total:* 436, 28% full-time. *Student/faculty ratio:* 17:1.

Majors Accounting; administrative assistant and secretarial science; biological and physical sciences; business administration and management; commercial and advertising art; computer graphics; computer science; computer/technical support; corrections; criminal justice/police science; data processing and data processing technology; dental hygiene; dietetics; drafting and design technology; electrical, electronic and communications engineering technology; emergency medical technology (EMT paramedic); engineering; fashion/apparel design; fashion merchandising; gerontology; health information/medical records administration; hospitality administration; human services; information science/studies; kindergarten/preschool education; legal administrative assistant/secretary; legal assistant/paralegal; liberal arts and sciences/liberal studies; marketing/marketing management; medical administrative assistant and medical secretary; nursing (registered nurse training); physical therapy; respiratory care therapy; surgical technology; word processing.

Academic Programs *Special study options:* academic remediation for entering students, adult/continuing education programs, advanced placement credit, cooperative education, distance learning, double majors, English as a second language, honors programs, internships, part-time degree program, services for LD students, study abroad, summer session for credit.

Library Bard Library with 72,413 titles, 150 serial subscriptions, 1,074 audiovisual materials, an OPAC, a Web page.

Computers on Campus A campuswide network can be accessed. Internet access, at least one staffed computer lab available.

Student Life *Housing:* college housing not available. *Activities and Organizations:* student-run newspaper, radio station, choral group. *Student services:* health clinic, personal/psychological counseling.

Athletics *Intercollegiate sports:* basketball M/W, cross-country running M/W, track and field M/W.

Standardized Tests *Recommended:* SAT Subject Tests (for placement).

Costs (2004–05) *Tuition:* $69 per credit hour part-time; state resident $2070 full-time, $159 per credit hour part-time; nonresident $4770 full-time. *Required fees:* $240 full-time, $7 per credit hour part-time, $25 per term part-time.

Financial Aid Of all full-time matriculated undergraduates who enrolled in 2003, 331 Federal Work-Study jobs (averaging $1879).

Applying *Options:* common application, early admission, deferred entrance. *Application fee:* $10. *Required:* high school transcript. *Recommended:* interview. *Application deadlines:* 8/9 (freshmen), 8/9 (transfers). *Notification:* continuous (freshmen).

Admissions Contact Mrs. Scheherazade Forman, Admissions Coordinator, Baltimore City Community College, 2901 Liberty Heights Avenue, Baltimore, MD 21215. *Phone:* 410-462-8300. *Toll-free phone:* 888-203-1261 Ext. 8300. *Fax:* 410-462-7677. *E-mail:* sforman@bccc.state.md.us.

BALTIMORE INTERNATIONAL COLLEGE
Baltimore, Maryland

- **Independent** primarily 2-year, founded 1972
- **Calendar** semesters
- **Degrees** certificates, associate, and bachelor's
- **Urban** 6-acre campus with easy access to Washington, DC
- **Endowment** $25,960
- **Coed,** 556 undergraduate students, 95% full-time, 55% women, 45% men

Undergraduates 529 full-time, 27 part-time. Students come from 19 states and territories, 5 other countries, 4% are from out of state, 50% African American, 4% Asian American or Pacific Islander, 2% Hispanic American, 0.4% Native American, 1% international, 19% transferred in, 24% live on campus. *Retention:* 50% of 2002 full-time freshmen returned.

Freshmen *Admission:* 252 applied, 131 admitted, 130 enrolled. *Average high school GPA:* 2.50.

Faculty *Total:* 32, 41% full-time, 75% with terminal degrees. *Student/faculty ratio:* 9:1.

Majors Business administration and management; culinary arts; hospitality administration; hotel/motel administration.

Academic Programs *Special study options:* academic remediation for entering students, accelerated degree program, adult/continuing education programs, advanced placement credit, cooperative education, double majors, honors programs, internships, off-campus study, study abroad.

Library George A. Piendak Library plus 1 other with 13,000 titles, 200 serial subscriptions, 1,000 audiovisual materials.

Computers on Campus 35 computers available on campus for general student use. A campuswide network can be accessed from off campus. Internet access, at least one staffed computer lab available.

Student Life *Housing:* on-campus residence required for freshman year. *Options:* coed. Campus housing is university owned. Freshman campus housing is guaranteed. *Activities and Organizations:* student-run newspaper, American Culinary Federation, Beta Iota Kappa. *Campus security:* late-night transport/escort service, controlled dormitory access. *Student services:* health clinic, personal/psychological counseling.

Standardized Tests *Required for some:* SAT or ACT (for admission).

Costs (2005–06) *Comprehensive fee:* $20,313 includes full-time tuition ($14,751), mandatory fees ($107), and room and board ($5455). *Room and board:* college room only: $3255. Room and board charges vary according to housing facility. *Payment plans:* tuition prepayment, installment. *Waivers:* employees or children of employees.

Applying *Options:* common application, electronic application, early action, deferred entrance. *Application fee:* $35. *Required:* high school transcript. *Required for some:* essay or personal statement. *Recommended:* interview. *Application deadline:* rolling (freshmen), rolling (transfers). *Notification:* continuous until 8/15 (freshmen), 8/15 (early action).

Admissions Contact Kristin Ciarlo, Director of Admissions, Baltimore International College, Commerce Exchange, 17 Commerce Street, Baltimore, MD 21202-3230. *Phone:* 410-752-4710 Ext. 124. *Toll-free phone:* 800-624-9926 Ext. 120. *Fax:* 410-752-3730. *E-mail:* admissions@bic.edu.

▶ **See page 462 for a narrative description.**

CARROLL COMMUNITY COLLEGE
Westminster, Maryland

- **State and locally supported** 2-year, founded 1993, part of Maryland Higher Education Commission
- **Calendar** semesters plus winter session
- **Degree** certificates and associate
- **Small-town** 80-acre campus with easy access to Baltimore
- **Endowment** $913,301
- **Coed,** 3,073 undergraduate students, 44% full-time, 65% women, 35% men

Undergraduates 1,359 full-time, 1,714 part-time. Students come from 3 states and territories, 4 other countries, 1% are from out of state, 3% African American, 1% Asian American or Pacific Islander, 2% Hispanic American, 0.4% Native American, 0.2% international.

Freshmen *Admission:* 756 enrolled.

Faculty *Total:* 227, 22% full-time, 3% with terminal degrees. *Student/faculty ratio:* 17:1.

Majors Accounting; business administration and management; computer and information sciences; computer graphics; data processing and data processing technology; education (multiple levels); general studies; health science; human services; kindergarten/preschool education; liberal arts and sciences/liberal studies; mechanical design technology; music; nursing (registered nurse training); physical therapist assistant.

Academic Programs *Special study options:* academic remediation for entering students, advanced placement credit, distance learning, English as a second language, honors programs, independent study, internships, part-time degree program, services for LD students, summer session for credit.

Library Random House Learning Resources Center with 39,187 titles, 318 serial subscriptions, 3,151 audiovisual materials, an OPAC, a Web page.

Computers on Campus 674 computers available on campus for general student use. A campuswide network can be accessed. Internet access, at least one staffed computer lab available.

Student Life *Housing:* college housing not available. *Activities and Organizations:* drama/theater group, student-run newspaper, choral group, Student Government Organization, Carroll Community Chorus, Programming Board. *Campus security:* late-night transport/escort service. *Student services:* personal/psychological counseling.

Standardized Tests *Recommended:* SAT or ACT (for placement).

Costs (2005–06) *Tuition:* area resident $3234 full-time, $92 per credit part-time; state resident $4476 full-time, $128 per credit part-time; nonresident $6788 full-time, $195 per credit part-time. *Payment plan:* installment. *Waivers:* senior citizens and employees or children of employees.

Financial Aid Of all full-time matriculated undergraduates who enrolled in 2003, 22 Federal Work-Study jobs (averaging $1772).

Applying *Options:* early admission. *Required:* high school transcript. *Application deadline:* rolling (freshmen), rolling (transfers). *Notification:* continuous (freshmen).

Admissions Contact Ms. Janenne Corcoran, Director of Advising, Counseling & Admissions, Carroll Community College, 1601 Washington Road, Westminster, MD 21157. *Phone:* 410-386-8430. *Toll-free phone:* 888-221-9748. *Fax:* 410-386-8446. *E-mail:* jcorcoran@carrollcc.edu.

CECIL COMMUNITY COLLEGE
North East, Maryland

- **County-supported** 2-year, founded 1968
- **Calendar** semesters
- **Degree** certificates and associate
- **Small-town** 100-acre campus with easy access to Baltimore
- **Coed,** 1,781 undergraduate students, 35% full-time, 67% women, 33% men

Undergraduates 622 full-time, 1,159 part-time. Students come from 5 states and territories, 4 other countries, 11% are from out of state, 9% African American, 2% Asian American or Pacific Islander, 1% Hispanic American, 0.5% Native American, 0.5% international, 0.6% transferred in.

Freshmen *Admission:* 422 applied, 422 admitted, 420 enrolled.

Faculty *Total:* 206, 19% full-time, 8% with terminal degrees. *Student/faculty ratio:* 11:1.

Majors Accounting; administrative assistant and secretarial science; air traffic control; art; artificial intelligence and robotics; biology/biological sciences; business administration and management; carpentry; computer engineering technology; computer graphics; computer programming; construction engineering technology; criminal justice/law enforcement administration; data processing and data processing technology; education; education (K-12); electrical, electronic and communications engineering technology; elementary education; general studies; hydrology and water resources science; information science/studies; information technology; kindergarten/preschool education; liberal arts and sciences/liberal studies; marketing/marketing management; mathematics; medical laboratory technology; nursing (registered nurse training); photography;

Cecil Community College (continued)

physical sciences; physics; pipefitting and sprinkler fitting; transportation and materials moving related; welding technology.

Academic Programs *Special study options:* academic remediation for entering students, adult/continuing education programs, advanced placement credit, cooperative education, distance learning, double majors, English as a second language, independent study, internships, part-time degree program, services for LD students, summer session for credit.

Library Cecil County Veteran's Memorial Library with 35,575 titles, 192 serial subscriptions, 1,148 audiovisual materials, an OPAC, a Web page.

Computers on Campus 69 computers available on campus for general student use. A campuswide network can be accessed from off campus. Internet access, online (class) registration, at least one staffed computer lab available.

Student Life *Housing:* college housing not available. *Activities and Organizations:* drama/theater group, student-run newspaper, student government, Non-traditional Student Organization, Student Nurses Association, student newspaper, national fraternities. *Campus security:* 24-hour emergency response devices, late-night transport/escort service. *Student services:* personal/psychological counseling, women's center.

Athletics Member NJCAA. *Intercollegiate sports:* baseball M(s), basketball M(s)/W(s), cheerleading W, softball W, volleyball W(s). *Intramural sports:* basketball M/W, tennis M/W.

Costs (2004–05) *Tuition:* area resident $2400 full-time, $80 per credit part-time; state resident $5100 full-time, $170 per credit part-time; nonresident $6450 full-time, $215 per credit part-time. Full-time tuition and fees vary according to reciprocity agreements. *Required fees:* $350 full-time, $15 per credit part-time, $35 per term part-time. *Payment plan:* installment. *Waivers:* children of alumni, senior citizens, and employees or children of employees.

Financial Aid Of all full-time matriculated undergraduates who enrolled in 2003, 59 Federal Work-Study jobs (averaging $1421).

Applying *Options:* common application, electronic application, early admission, deferred entrance. *Recommended:* high school transcript. *Application deadline:* rolling (freshmen), rolling (transfers). *Notification:* continuous (freshmen).

Admissions Contact Ms. Sandra S. Rajaski, Registrar, Cecil Community College, One Seahawk Drive, North East, MD 21901. *Phone:* 410-287-1004 Ext. 567. *Fax:* 410-287-1026. *E-mail:* srajaski@cecilcc.edu.

CHESAPEAKE COLLEGE
Wye Mills, Maryland

- **State and locally supported** 2-year, founded 1965
- **Calendar** semesters
- **Degree** certificates and associate
- **Rural** 170-acre campus with easy access to Baltimore and Washington, DC
- **Coed**

Faculty *Student/faculty ratio:* 16:1.

Student Life *Campus security:* 24-hour patrols.

Athletics Member NJCAA.

Financial Aid Of all full-time matriculated undergraduates who enrolled in 2003, 32 Federal Work-Study jobs (averaging $1482).

Applying *Options:* early admission, deferred entrance. *Required:* high school transcript.

Admissions Contact Ms. Kathy Petrichenko, Director of Admissions, Chesapeake College, PO Box 8, Wye Mills, MD 21679. *Phone:* 410-822-5400 Ext. 257. *Fax:* 410-827-9466.

COLLEGE OF SOUTHERN MARYLAND
La Plata, Maryland

- **State and locally supported** 2-year, founded 1958
- **Calendar** semesters
- **Degree** certificates and associate
- **Rural** 175-acre campus with easy access to Washington, DC
- **Coed**, 7,423 undergraduate students, 34% full-time, 66% women, 34% men

Undergraduates 2,558 full-time, 4,865 part-time. Students come from 10 states and territories, 1% are from out of state, 18% African American, 3% Asian American or Pacific Islander, 3% Hispanic American, 1% Native American, 46% transferred in.

Freshmen *Admission:* 1,663 applied, 1,663 admitted, 1,093 enrolled. *Average high school GPA:* 2.86.

Faculty *Total:* 426, 27% full-time, 12% with terminal degrees. *Student/faculty ratio:* 20:1.

Majors Accounting; business administration and management; computer programming; education; electrical, electronic and communications engineering technology; elementary education; engineering; human services; information science/studies; kindergarten/preschool education; legal assistant/paralegal; lib-

eral arts and sciences/liberal studies; nursing (licensed practical/vocational nurse training); nursing (registered nurse training).

Academic Programs *Special study options:* academic remediation for entering students, accelerated degree program, adult/continuing education programs, advanced placement credit, cooperative education, distance learning, honors programs, internships, part-time degree program, services for LD students, study abroad, summer session for credit.

Library College of Southern Maryland Library with 44,896 titles, 166 serial subscriptions, 14,013 audiovisual materials, an OPAC, a Web page.

Computers on Campus 130 computers available on campus for general student use. A campuswide network can be accessed from off campus. Internet access, online (class) registration, at least one staffed computer lab available.

Student Life *Housing:* college housing not available. *Activities and Organizations:* drama/theater group, student-run newspaper, choral group, Spanish Club, Nursing Student Association, Science Club, Black Student Union, BACCHUS. *Campus security:* 24-hour emergency response devices and patrols. *Student services:* personal/psychological counseling, women's center.

Athletics Member NJCAA. *Intercollegiate sports:* baseball M, basketball M, golf M/W, soccer M/W, softball W, tennis M/W, volleyball W.

Costs (2005–06) *Tuition:* area resident $2136 full-time, $89 per credit part-time; state resident $3672 full-time, $153 per credit part-time; nonresident $4656 full-time, $194 per credit part-time. Full-time tuition and fees vary according to course load. Part-time tuition and fees vary according to course load. *Required fees:* $427 full-time, $18 per credit part-time. *Payment plan:* deferred payment. *Waivers:* senior citizens and employees or children of employees.

Financial Aid Of all full-time matriculated undergraduates who enrolled in 2003, 25 Federal Work-Study jobs (averaging $1200).

Applying *Options:* electronic application, early admission, deferred entrance. *Recommended:* high school transcript. *Application deadline:* rolling (freshmen), rolling (transfers). *Notification:* continuous (freshmen).

Admissions Contact Ms. Charlotte Hill, Admissions Coordinator, College of Southern Maryland, PO Box 910, La Plata, MD 20646-0910. *Phone:* 301-934-2251 Ext. 7044. *Toll-free phone:* 800-933-9177. *Fax:* 301-934-7698. *E-mail:* info@csmd.edu.

THE COMMUNITY COLLEGE OF BALTIMORE COUNTY
Baltimore, Maryland

- **County-supported** 2-year, founded 1957
- **Calendar** semesters
- **Degree** certificates and associate
- **Suburban** 350-acre campus
- **Coed**, 20,025 undergraduate students

Undergraduates 28% African American, 4% Asian American or Pacific Islander, 2% Hispanic American, 0.4% Native American, 2% international.

Faculty *Total:* 1,006, 35% full-time, 10% with terminal degrees. *Student/faculty ratio:* 20:1.

Costs (2004–05) *Tuition:* area resident $2610 full-time, $87 per hour part-time; state resident $4500 full-time, $150 per hour part-time; nonresident $6150 full-time, $205 per hour part-time. *Required fees:* $340 full-time.

Admissions Contact Diane Drake, Director of Admissions, The Community College of Baltimore County, 800 South Rolling Road, Baltimore, MD 21228-5381. *Phone:* 410-455-4392.

FREDERICK COMMUNITY COLLEGE
Frederick, Maryland

- **State and locally supported** 2-year, founded 1957
- **Calendar** semesters
- **Degree** certificates and associate
- **Small-town** 125-acre campus with easy access to Baltimore and Washington, DC
- **Endowment** $4.0 million
- **Coed**, 4,736 undergraduate students, 38% full-time, 63% women, 37% men

Undergraduates 1,791 full-time, 2,945 part-time. Students come from 9 states and territories, 1% are from out of state, 7% African American, 2% Asian American or Pacific Islander, 2% Hispanic American, 0.5% Native American.

Freshmen *Admission:* 917 applied, 917 admitted.

Faculty *Total:* 326, 24% full-time.

Majors Accounting; administrative assistant and secretarial science; agricultural business and management; agriculture; art; avionics maintenance technology; biology/biological sciences; business administration and management; chemistry; child development; computer engineering technology; construction management; criminal justice/law enforcement administration; data processing and data processing technology; drafting and design technology; education;

electrical, electronic and communications engineering technology; elementary education; engineering; English; finance; human services; international business/trade/commerce; kindergarten/preschool education; legal administrative assistant/secretary; legal assistant/paralegal; liberal arts and sciences/liberal studies; marketing/marketing management; mass communication/media; mathematics; medical administrative assistant and medical secretary; medical laboratory technology; music teacher education; nursing (registered nurse training); parks, recreation and leisure; parks, recreation and leisure facilities management; physical education teaching and coaching; physical sciences; psychology; respiratory care therapy; wildlife and wildlands science and management.

Academic Programs *Special study options:* academic remediation for entering students, adult/continuing education programs, advanced placement credit, cooperative education, distance learning, external degree program, honors programs, independent study, off-campus study, part-time degree program, services for LD students, study abroad, summer session for credit. *ROTC:* Army (c).

Library FCC Library with 40,000 titles, 5,150 serial subscriptions, 1,400 audiovisual materials, an OPAC, a Web page.

Computers on Campus A campuswide network can be accessed from off campus. Internet access, online (class) registration, at least one staffed computer lab available.

Student Life *Housing:* college housing not available. *Activities and Organizations:* drama/theater group, student-run newspaper. *Campus security:* 24-hour emergency response devices and patrols. *Student services:* personal/psychological counseling.

Athletics Member NJCAA. *Intercollegiate sports:* baseball M, basketball M/W, golf M/W, soccer M/W, softball W, volleyball W.

Standardized Tests *Recommended:* SAT or ACT (for placement).

Costs (2005–06) *Tuition:* area resident $2040 full-time, $85 per credit hour part-time; state resident $4368 full-time, $187 per credit hour part-time; nonresident $6096 full-time, $254 per credit hour part-time. *Required fees:* $292 full-time, $11 per credit hour part-time, $18 per term part-time.

Financial Aid Of all full-time matriculated undergraduates who enrolled in 2003, 25 Federal Work-Study jobs (averaging $1368). 14 state and other part-time jobs (averaging $2715).

Applying *Options:* early admission, deferred entrance. *Application deadlines:* 9/1 (freshmen), 9/1 (transfers). *Notification:* continuous (freshmen).

Admissions Contact Ms. Kathy Frawley, Associate Vice President, Registrar, Frederick Community College, Welcome and Registration Center, 7932 Opossumtown Pike, Frederick, MD 21702. *Phone:* 301-846-2432. *Fax:* 301-624-2799.

GARRETT COLLEGE
McHenry, Maryland

- **State and locally supported** 2-year, founded 1966
- **Calendar** semesters
- **Degree** certificates and associate
- **Rural** 62-acre campus
- **Coed,** 613 undergraduate students, 59% full-time, 55% women, 45% men

Undergraduates 360 full-time, 253 part-time. Students come from 12 states and territories, 1 other country, 20% are from out of state, 9% African American, 2% Hispanic American, 0.8% Native American, 2% international, 48% transferred in, 8% live on campus.

Freshmen *Admission:* 182 enrolled.

Faculty *Total:* 49, 37% full-time, 18% with terminal degrees. *Student/faculty ratio:* 13:1.

Majors Administrative assistant and secretarial science; agricultural mechanization; art; behavioral sciences; biology/biological sciences; business administration and management; criminal justice/safety; education; elementary education; fish/game management; general studies; hotel/motel administration; liberal arts and sciences/liberal studies; mathematics; music; natural resources management and policy; parks, recreation and leisure; parks, recreation and leisure facilities management; physical education teaching and coaching; psychology; social sciences; sociology; wildlife and wildlands science and management; wildlife biology.

Academic Programs *Special study options:* academic remediation for entering students, adult/continuing education programs, advanced placement credit, distance learning, double majors, external degree program, honors programs, independent study, internships, part-time degree program, services for LD students, summer session for credit.

Library Learning Resource Center with 24,230 titles, 87 serial subscriptions, 2,151 audiovisual materials, an OPAC, a Web page.

Computers on Campus 60 computers available on campus for general student use. A campuswide network can be accessed. Internet access, at least one staffed computer lab available. Computer purchase or lease plan available.

Student Life *Housing Options:* coed. Campus housing is provided by a third party. *Activities and Organizations:* drama/theater group, student-run newspaper, Wildlife Club, Raiders of the Lost Arts, student government, national fraternities. *Student services:* personal/psychological counseling.

Athletics Member NJCAA. *Intercollegiate sports:* baseball M(s), basketball M(s)/W(s), golf M, skiing (downhill) M(c)/W(c), volleyball W(s). *Intramural sports:* softball W.

Standardized Tests *Recommended:* SAT or ACT (for placement).

Costs (2005–06) *Tuition:* area resident $2340 full-time, $78 per credit hour part-time; state resident $5460 full-time, $182 per credit hour part-time; nonresident $6540 full-time, $218 per credit hour part-time. *Required fees:* $570 full-time, $18 per credit hour part-time, $15 per semester part-time. *Room and board:* $4970; room only: $2550.

Financial Aid Of all full-time matriculated undergraduates who enrolled in 2003, 55 Federal Work-Study jobs (averaging $1018). 75 state and other part-time jobs (averaging $954).

Applying *Options:* common application, early admission, deferred entrance. *Required:* high school transcript, interview. *Application deadline:* rolling (freshmen), rolling (transfers). *Notification:* continuous (freshmen).

Admissions Contact Robin Swearengen, Coordinator of Student Assistance Center, Garrett College, 687 Mosser Road, McHenry, MD 21541. *Phone:* 301-387-3044. *Fax:* 301-387-3038. *E-mail:* admissions@garrettcollege.edu.

HAGERSTOWN BUSINESS COLLEGE
Hagerstown, Maryland

- **Proprietary** 2-year, founded 1938, part of Kaplan Higher Education Corporation
- **Calendar** quarters
- **Degree** certificates and associate
- **Small-town** 8-acre campus with easy access to Baltimore and Washington, DC
- **Coed,** 932 undergraduate students, 83% full-time, 74% women, 26% men

Undergraduates 770 full-time, 162 part-time. 64% are from out of state, 10% African American, 1% Asian American or Pacific Islander, 2% Hispanic American, 0.1% Native American, 3% live on campus.

Faculty *Total:* 65, 31% full-time, 5% with terminal degrees. *Student/faculty ratio:* 18:1.

Majors Accounting; administrative assistant and secretarial science; business administration and management; computer and information systems security; criminal justice/law enforcement administration; data processing and data processing technology; health information/medical records administration; information science/studies; legal administrative assistant/secretary; legal assistant/paralegal; marketing/marketing management; medical administrative assistant and medical secretary; medical/clinical assistant.

Academic Programs *Special study options:* academic remediation for entering students, accelerated degree program, adult/continuing education programs, advanced placement credit, internships, summer session for credit.

Library HBC library plus 1 other with 8,000 titles, 70 serial subscriptions, 400 audiovisual materials.

Computers on Campus 207 computers available on campus for general student use. A campuswide network can be accessed. Internet access, at least one staffed computer lab available.

Student Life *Housing Options:* coed. Campus housing is university owned. *Activities and Organizations:* Phi Beta Lambda, Association of Legal Students, Health Information Technology Students Organization, Student Government Association, Caduceus Club. *Campus security:* 24-hour emergency response devices. *Student services:* personal/psychological counseling.

Costs (2004–05) *Tuition:* Contact college for current tuition, fees, and room and board expenses.

Financial Aid Of all full-time matriculated undergraduates who enrolled in 2003, 21 Federal Work-Study jobs (averaging $1343).

Applying *Options:* early admission, deferred entrance. *Required:* high school transcript, interview. *Application deadline:* rolling (freshmen), rolling (transfers).

Admissions Contact Mr. Jim Klein, Director of Admissions, Hagerstown Business College, 18618 Crestwood Drive, Hagerstown, MD 21742-2797. *Phone:* 301-739-2670. *Toll-free phone:* 800-422-2670. *Fax:* 301-791-7661. *E-mail:* info@hagerstownbusinesscol.org.

HAGERSTOWN COMMUNITY COLLEGE
Hagerstown, Maryland

- **State and locally supported** 2-year, founded 1946
- **Calendar** semesters
- **Degree** certificates and associate
- **Suburban** 187-acre campus with easy access to Baltimore and Washington, DC
- **Endowment** $5.4 million
- **Coed,** 3,528 undergraduate students, 33% full-time, 63% women, 37% men

Undergraduates 1,172 full-time, 2,356 part-time. Students come from 6 states and territories, 1 other country, 23% are from out of state, 8% African American,

Hagerstown Community College (continued)

1% Asian American or Pacific Islander, 2% Hispanic American, 0.5% Native American, 5% transferred in. *Retention:* 63% of 2002 full-time freshmen returned.

Freshmen *Admission:* 1,445 applied, 1,445 admitted, 781 enrolled.

Faculty *Total:* 238, 26% full-time. *Student/faculty ratio:* 14:1.

Majors Accounting technology and bookkeeping; business administration and management; business/commerce; child care and support services management; commercial and advertising art; computer and information sciences; criminal justice/police science; education; electromechanical technology; elementary education; emergency medical technology (EMT paramedic); engineering; liberal arts and sciences and humanities related; liberal arts and sciences/liberal studies; management information systems; mechanical engineering/mechanical technology; medical radiologic technology; nursing (registered nurse training); psychiatric/mental health services technology.

Academic Programs *Special study options:* academic remediation for entering students, accelerated degree program, adult/continuing education programs, advanced placement credit, cooperative education, distance learning, English as a second language, honors programs, independent study, internships, off-campus study, part-time degree program, services for LD students, student-designed majors, summer session for credit.

Library William Brish Library with 45,705 titles, 228 serial subscriptions, 1,585 audiovisual materials, an OPAC, a Web page.

Computers on Campus 500 computers available on campus for general student use. A campuswide network can be accessed from off campus. Internet access, online (class) registration, at least one staffed computer lab available. Computer purchase or lease plan available.

Student Life *Housing:* college housing not available. *Activities and Organizations:* drama/theater group, student-run newspaper, choral group, Phi Theta Kappa, Robinwood Players, Association of Nursing Students, Theta Lambda Upsilon, Art Club. *Campus security:* 24-hour patrols. *Student services:* health clinic, personal/psychological counseling.

Athletics Member NJCAA. *Intercollegiate sports:* baseball M(s), basketball M(s)/W(s), cross-country running M(s)/W(s), golf M/W, soccer M(s), softball W(s), track and field M(s)/W(s), volleyball W(s). *Intramural sports:* cheerleading M/W, golf M/W, lacrosse M/W, table tennis M/W, tennis M/W.

Standardized Tests *Required for some:* ACT (for placement).

Costs (2005–06) *Tuition:* area resident $2670 full-time, $89 per credit hour part-time; state resident $4260 full-time, $142 per credit hour part-time; nonresident $5580 full-time, $186 per credit hour part-time. Full-time tuition and fees vary according to course load. Part-time tuition and fees vary according to course load. *Required fees:* $330 full-time, $8 per credit hour part-time, $20 per semester part-time. *Payment plan:* installment. *Waivers:* senior citizens and employees or children of employees.

Financial Aid Of all full-time matriculated undergraduates who enrolled in 2003, 27 Federal Work-Study jobs (averaging $2955).

Applying *Options:* common application, electronic application, early admission, deferred entrance. *Required for some:* high school transcript, minimum 2.0 GPA, ACT composite score of 21, 1 lab chemistry and algebra for admission into nursing and radiography programs. *Application deadline:* rolling (freshmen), rolling (transfers). *Notification:* continuous (freshmen).

Admissions Contact Dr. Daniel Bock, Assistant Director, Admissions, Records and Registration, Hagerstown Community College, 11400 Robinwood Drive, Hagerstown, MD 21742-6590. *Phone:* 301-790-2800 Ext. 335. *Fax:* 301-791-4165. *E-mail:* mattosk@hagerstowncc.edu.

HARFORD COMMUNITY COLLEGE
Bel Air, Maryland

- **State and locally supported** 2-year, founded 1957
- **Calendar** semesters
- **Degree** certificates, diplomas, and associate
- **Small-town** 331-acre campus with easy access to Baltimore
- **Endowment** $4.1 million
- **Coed,** 5,492 undergraduate students, 39% full-time, 62% women, 38% men

Undergraduates 2,157 full-time, 3,335 part-time. Students come from 10 states and territories, 17 other countries, 1% are from out of state, 11% African American, 2% Asian American or Pacific Islander, 3% Hispanic American, 0.4% Native American, 0.4% international, 60% transferred in. *Retention:* 66% of 2002 full-time freshmen returned.

Freshmen *Admission:* 1,197 applied, 1,197 admitted, 1,197 enrolled.

Faculty *Total:* 293, 34% full-time. *Student/faculty ratio:* 20:1.

Majors Accounting technology and bookkeeping; administrative assistant and secretarial science; audio engineering; business administration and management; business/commerce; child care and support services management; commercial and advertising art; communications technologies and support services related; computer and information sciences; education; electroneurodiagnostic/electroencephalographic technology; elementary education; engineering; engineering technologies related; environmental engineering technology; interior design; legal assistant/paralegal; liberal arts and sciences and humanities related;

liberal arts and sciences/liberal studies; management information systems; mechanical engineering/mechanical technology; medical laboratory technology; multi-/interdisciplinary studies related; nursing (registered nurse training); philosophy; political science and government; psychology; science technologies related; security and loss prevention.

Academic Programs *Special study options:* academic remediation for entering students, adult/continuing education programs, advanced placement credit, cooperative education, distance learning, double majors, English as a second language, independent study, internships, part-time degree program, services for LD students, student-designed majors, summer session for credit.

Library Learning Resources Center with 74,731 titles, 422 serial subscriptions, 6,700 audiovisual materials, an OPAC, a Web page.

Computers on Campus 267 computers available on campus for general student use. A campuswide network can be accessed from off campus. Internet access, online (class) registration, at least one staffed computer lab available.

Student Life *Housing:* college housing not available. *Activities and Organizations:* drama/theater group, student-run newspaper, radio station, choral group, Student Association, Paralegal Club, Multi-National Students Association, Student Nurses Association, Video Club. *Campus security:* 24-hour patrols, late-night transport/escort service. *Student services:* personal/psychological counseling.

Athletics Member NJCAA. *Intercollegiate sports:* baseball M(s), basketball M(s)/W(s), field hockey W(s)(c), golf M(s), lacrosse M(s)/W(s), soccer M(s)/W(s), softball W(s), tennis M/W.

Standardized Tests *Required for some:* ACCUPLACER.

Costs (2005–06) *Tuition:* area resident $2250 full-time, $75 per credit part-time; state resident $4500 full-time, $150 per credit part-time; nonresident $6750 full-time, $225 per credit part-time. Full-time tuition and fees vary according to course load. *Required fees:* $225 full-time, $8 per credit part-time. *Payment plan:* installment. *Waivers:* senior citizens and employees or children of employees.

Financial Aid Of all full-time matriculated undergraduates who enrolled in 2003, 55 Federal Work-Study jobs (averaging $1800).

Applying *Options:* electronic application. *Application deadline:* rolling (freshmen), rolling (transfers).

Admissions Contact Ms. Donna Strasavich, Enrollment Specialist, Harford Community College, 401 Thomas Run Road, Bel Air, MD 21015-1698. *Phone:* 410-836-4311. *Fax:* 410-836-4169. *E-mail:* sendinfo@harford.edu.

HOWARD COMMUNITY COLLEGE
Columbia, Maryland

- **State and locally supported** 2-year, founded 1966
- **Calendar** semesters
- **Degree** certificates and associate
- **Suburban** 122-acre campus with easy access to Baltimore and Washington, DC
- **Endowment** $2.0 million
- **Coed,** 6,711 undergraduate students, 36% full-time, 60% women, 40% men

Undergraduates 2,433 full-time, 4,278 part-time. Students come from 4 states and territories, 1% are from out of state, 21% African American, 10% Asian American or Pacific Islander, 4% Hispanic American, 0.3% Native American.

Faculty *Total:* 481, 23% full-time, 9% with terminal degrees. *Student/faculty ratio:* 18:1.

Majors Accounting; administrative assistant and secretarial science; applied art; architecture; art; biological and physical sciences; biomedical technology; biotechnology; business administration and management; cardiovascular technology; child development; clinical laboratory science/medical technology; computer and information sciences related; computer graphics; computer/information technology services administration related; computer science; computer systems networking and telecommunications; consumer merchandising/retailing management; criminal justice/law enforcement administration; data entry/microcomputer applications; dramatic/theatre arts; electrical, electronic and communications engineering technology; elementary education; emergency medical technology (EMT paramedic); engineering; environmental studies; fashion merchandising; financial planning and services; general studies; health teacher education; information science/studies; information technology; kindergarten/preschool education; legal administrative assistant/secretary; liberal arts and sciences/liberal studies; medical administrative assistant and medical secretary; music; nuclear medical technology; nursing (licensed practical/vocational nurse training); nursing (registered nurse training); office management; ophthalmic/optometric services; photography; physical sciences; pre-dentistry studies; pre-medical studies; pre-pharmacy studies; pre-veterinary studies; psychology; secondary education; social sciences; sport and fitness administration; substance abuse/addiction counseling; telecommunications; theatre design and technology.

Academic Programs *Special study options:* academic remediation for entering students, adult/continuing education programs, advanced placement credit, cooperative education, distance learning, double majors, English as a second language, honors programs, off-campus study, part-time degree program, services for LD students, study abroad, summer session for credit.

Library Howard Community College Library with 40,380 titles, 1,201 serial subscriptions, 6,253 audiovisual materials, an OPAC, a Web page.

Computers on Campus 750 computers available on campus for general student use. Internet access, online (class) registration, at least one staffed computer lab available.

Student Life *Housing:* college housing not available. *Activities and Organizations:* drama/theater group, student-run newspaper, choral group, Secretarial Club, Nursing Club, Black Leadership Organization, student newspaper, Student Government Association. *Campus security:* 24-hour emergency response devices and patrols, late-night transport/escort service. *Student services:* personal/psychological counseling.

Athletics Member NJCAA. *Intercollegiate sports:* basketball M/W, cross-country running M/W, lacrosse M, soccer M/W, tennis M/W, track and field M/W, volleyball W. *Intramural sports:* baseball M, basketball M/W, lacrosse M, softball W.

Standardized Tests *Required for some:* SAT or ACT (for admission).

Costs (2004–05) *Tuition:* area resident $3000 full-time, $100 per credit part-time; state resident $5490 full-time, $183 per credit part-time; nonresident $6840 full-time, $228 per credit part-time. *Required fees:* $408 full-time, $14 per credit part-time. *Payment plan:* installment. *Waivers:* senior citizens and employees or children of employees.

Applying *Options:* electronic application, early admission, deferred entrance. *Application fee:* $15. *Required for some:* essay or personal statement, high school transcript, minimum 3.0 GPA, 2 letters of recommendation, interview. *Application deadline:* rolling (freshmen), rolling (transfers). *Notification:* continuous (freshmen).

Admissions Contact Ms. Christy Thomson, Assistant Director of Admissions, Howard Community College, 10901 Little Patuxent Parkway, Columbia, MD 21044-3197. *Phone:* 410-772-4856. *Fax:* 410-772-4589. *E-mail:* hsinfo@howardcc.edu.

MONTGOMERY COLLEGE
Rockville, Maryland

- **State and locally supported** 2-year
- **Calendar** semesters
- **Degree** certificates and associate
- **Suburban** campus with easy access to Washington D.C.
- **Coed**

Faculty *Student/faculty ratio:* 20:1.

Student Life *Campus security:* 24-hour emergency response devices and patrols, late-night transport/escort service.

Athletics Member NJCAA.

Costs (2004–05) *Tuition:* area resident $2670 full-time, $89 per credit part-time; state resident $5490 full-time, $183 per credit part-time; nonresident $7350 full-time, $245 per credit part-time. *Required fees:* $894 full-time, $12 per credit part-time.

Financial Aid Of all full-time matriculated undergraduates who enrolled in 2003, 216 Federal Work-Study jobs (averaging $3050). 250 state and other part-time jobs (averaging $2000).

Applying *Options:* common application. *Application fee:* $25.

Admissions Contact Mr. Sherman Helberg, Acting Director of Admissions and Enrollment, Montgomery College, 51 Mannakee Street, Rockville, MD 20850. *Phone:* 301-279-5034.

PRINCE GEORGE'S COMMUNITY COLLEGE
Largo, Maryland

- **County-supported** 2-year, founded 1958
- **Calendar** semesters plus 2 summer sessions
- **Degree** certificates and associate
- **Suburban** 150-acre campus with easy access to Washington, DC
- **Coed**

Faculty *Student/faculty ratio:* 18:1.

Student Life *Campus security:* 24-hour emergency response devices and patrols, late-night transport/escort service.

Athletics Member NJCAA.

Standardized Tests *Required for some:* ACCUPLACER.

Costs (2004–05) *Tuition:* area resident $2808 full-time, $90 per credit part-time; state resident $4464 full-time, $159 per credit part-time; nonresident $6528 full-time, $245 per credit part-time. Full-time tuition and fees vary according to program and reciprocity agreements. Part-time tuition and fees vary according to program and reciprocity agreements. *Required fees:* $74 full-time, $1 per credit part-time, $25 per semester part-time.

Financial Aid Of all full-time matriculated undergraduates who enrolled in 2003, 99 Federal Work-Study jobs (averaging $2000).

Applying *Options:* early admission. *Application fee:* $25. *Required for some:* high school transcript. *Recommended:* minimum 2.0 GPA.

Admissions Contact Ms. Vera Bagley, Director of Admissions and Records, Prince George's Community College, 301 Largo Road, Largo, MD 20774-2199. *Phone:* 301-322-0801. *Fax:* 301-322-0119.

TESST COLLEGE OF TECHNOLOGY
Baltimore, Maryland

Admissions Contact Ms. Susan Sherwood, Director, TESST College of Technology, 1520 South Caton Avenue, Baltimore, MD 21227-1063. *Phone:* 410-644-6400.

TESST COLLEGE OF TECHNOLOGY
Beltsville, Maryland

Admissions Contact Mr. Reginald M. Morton, Executive Director, TESST College of Technology, 4600 Powder Mill Road, Beltsville, MD 20705. *Phone:* 301-937-8448.

TESST COLLEGE OF TECHNOLOGY
Towson, Maryland

- **Proprietary** 2-year, founded 1992
- **Calendar** quarters
- **Degree** associate
- **Coed**

Admissions Contact Ms. Diane McRae, President, TESST College of Technology, 803 Glen Eagles Court, Towson, MD 21286. *Phone:* 410-296-5350. *Toll-free phone:* 410-296-5350.

WOR-WIC COMMUNITY COLLEGE
Salisbury, Maryland

- **State and locally supported** 2-year, founded 1976, part of Maryland State Community Colleges System
- **Calendar** semesters
- **Degree** certificates and associate
- **Small-town** 202-acre campus
- **Endowment** $2.7 million
- **Coed**, 3,110 undergraduate students, 29% full-time, 68% women, 32% men

Undergraduates 893 full-time, 2,217 part-time. Students come from 15 states and territories, 2% are from out of state, 27% African American, 1% Asian American or Pacific Islander, 1% Hispanic American, 0.6% Native American, 8% transferred in.

Freshmen *Admission:* 1,006 applied, 1,006 admitted, 661 enrolled.

Faculty *Total:* 170, 32% full-time, 12% with terminal degrees. *Student/faculty ratio:* 19:1.

Majors Accounting technology and bookkeeping; administrative assistant and secretarial science; business administration and management; business/commerce; child care and support services management; computer and information sciences; computer systems analysis; criminal justice/police science; education; electrical, electronic and communications engineering technology; elementary education; emergency medical technology (EMT paramedic); engineering technologies related; hospitality administration; liberal arts and sciences and humanities related; medical radiologic technology; nursing (registered nurse training); substance abuse/addiction counseling.

Academic Programs *Special study options:* academic remediation for entering students, accelerated degree program, adult/continuing education programs, advanced placement credit, distance learning, double majors, English as a second language, honors programs, independent study, internships, part-time degree program, services for LD students, summer session for credit.

Library Patricia M. Hazel Media Center plus 2 others with 25 titles, 37 serial subscriptions, 272 audiovisual materials, a Web page.

Computers on Campus 478 computers available on campus for general student use. A campuswide network can be accessed from off campus. Internet access, at least one staffed computer lab available.

Student Life *Housing:* college housing not available. *Activities and Organizations:* drama/theater group, student-run newspaper, choral group, Student Government Association, Arts Club, Bioneer Club, Future Educators of America Club, student newspaper. *Campus security:* 24-hour emergency response devices, late-night transport/escort service, patrols by trained security personnel 9 a.m. to midnight. *Student services:* personal/psychological counseling.

Standardized Tests *Required for some:* ACT (for admission).

Wor-Wic Community College (continued)

Costs (2005–06) *Tuition:* area resident $2190 full-time, $73 per credit hour part-time; state resident $5520 full-time, $184 per credit hour part-time; nonresident $6450 full-time, $215 per credit hour part-time. *Required fees:* $56 full-time, $1 per credit hour part-time, $13 per credit hour part-time. *Payment plan:* deferred payment. *Waivers:* senior citizens and employees or children of employees.

Applying *Options:* early admission. *Recommended:* high school transcript. *Application deadline:* rolling (freshmen), rolling (transfers).

Admissions Contact Mr. Richard Webster, Director of Admissions, Wor-Wic Community College, 32000 Campus Drive, Salisbury, MD 21804. *Phone:* 410-334-2895. *Fax:* 410-334-2954. *E-mail:* admissions@worwic.edu.

MASSACHUSETTS

BAY STATE COLLEGE
Boston, Massachusetts

- **Independent** primarily 2-year, founded 1946
- **Calendar** semesters
- **Degrees** associate and bachelor's
- **Urban** campus
- **Coed,** 757 undergraduate students, 69% full-time, 78% women, 22% men

Undergraduates 522 full-time, 235 part-time. Students come from 11 states and territories, 11 other countries, 11% are from out of state, 18% African American, 8% Asian American or Pacific Islander, 10% Hispanic American, 0.9% international, 21% live on campus. *Retention:* 50% of 2002 full-time freshmen returned.

Freshmen *Admission:* 1,405 applied, 1,119 admitted. *Average high school GPA:* 2.00.

Faculty *Total:* 66, 29% full-time. *Student/faculty ratio:* 13:1.

Majors Accounting; administrative assistant and secretarial science; business administration and management; consumer merchandising/retailing management; fashion/apparel design; fashion merchandising; hospitality administration; hotel/motel administration; kindergarten/preschool education; legal administrative assistant/secretary; legal studies; liberal arts and sciences/liberal studies; marketing/marketing management; medical administrative assistant and medical secretary; medical/clinical assistant; occupational therapy; physical therapy; tourism and travel services management.

Academic Programs *Special study options:* academic remediation for entering students, adult/continuing education programs, advanced placement credit, cooperative education, English as a second language, independent study, internships, part-time degree program.

Library Bay State College Library with 4,490 titles, 262 serial subscriptions, 471 audiovisual materials, an OPAC.

Computers on Campus 55 computers available on campus for general student use. A campuswide network can be accessed. At least one staffed computer lab available.

Student Life *Housing Options:* coed, women-only. Campus housing is provided by a third party. *Activities and Organizations:* Activities Club, Hospitality Travel Association, Fashion Club, Early Childhood Education Club, Student Medical Assisting Society. *Campus security:* late-night transport/escort service, controlled dormitory access, 14-hour patrols by trained security personnel. *Student services:* personal/psychological counseling.

Costs (2005–06) *Comprehensive fee:* $25,475 includes full-time tuition ($15,300), mandatory fees ($350), and room and board ($9825). Part-time tuition: $220 per credit.

Financial Aid Of all full-time matriculated undergraduates who enrolled in 2003, 20 Federal Work-Study jobs (averaging $2600).

Applying *Options:* common application, early admission. *Application fee:* $25. *Required:* essay or personal statement, high school transcript. *Recommended:* minimum 2.0 GPA, interview. *Application deadline:* rolling (freshmen), rolling (transfers).

Admissions Contact Ms. Pam Notemyer-Rogers, Director of Admissions, Bay State College, 122 Commonwealth Avenue, Boston, MA 02116. *Phone:* 617-236-8006. *Toll-free phone:* 800-81-LEARN. *Fax:* 617-536-1735. *E-mail:* admissions@baystate.edu.

▶ **See page 464 for a narrative description.**

BENJAMIN FRANKLIN INSTITUTE OF TECHNOLOGY
Boston, Massachusetts

Admissions Contact Norman R. Kraft, Dean of Enrollment Management, Benjamin Franklin Institute of Technology, 41 Berkeley Street, Boston, MA 02116-6296. *Phone:* 617-423-4630 Ext. 122. *Fax:* 617-482-3706. *E-mail:* admissions@bfit.edu.

▶ **See page 466 for a narrative description.**

BERKSHIRE COMMUNITY COLLEGE
Pittsfield, Massachusetts

- **State-supported** 2-year, founded 1960, part of Massachusetts Public Higher Education System
- **Calendar** semesters
- **Degree** certificates and associate
- **Suburban** 100-acre campus
- **Endowment** $2.6 million
- **Coed,** 2,364 undergraduate students, 41% full-time, 64% women, 36% men

Undergraduates 963 full-time, 1,401 part-time. Students come from 4 states and territories, 14 other countries, 4% are from out of state, 4% African American, 1% Asian American or Pacific Islander, 3% Hispanic American, 0.7% Native American, 2% international, 13% transferred in.

Freshmen *Admission:* 425 applied, 425 admitted, 425 enrolled.

Faculty *Total:* 160, 33% full-time, 53% with terminal degrees. *Student/faculty ratio:* 14:1.

Majors Administrative assistant and secretarial science; business administration and management; business automation/technology/data entry; business/commerce; community organization and advocacy; computer and information sciences; criminal justice/safety; electrical, electronic and communications engineering technology; engineering; environmental science; fire science; health professions related; hospitality administration; liberal arts and sciences/liberal studies; nursing (registered nurse training); physical therapist assistant; respiratory care therapy; visual and performing arts.

Academic Programs *Special study options:* academic remediation for entering students, adult/continuing education programs, advanced placement credit, distance learning, double majors, English as a second language, honors programs, independent study, internships, off-campus study, part-time degree program, services for LD students, student-designed majors, summer session for credit.

Library Jonathan Edwards Library plus 1 other with 74,271 titles, 319 serial subscriptions, 3,247 audiovisual materials, an OPAC, a Web page.

Computers on Campus 354 computers available on campus for general student use. A campuswide network can be accessed from off campus. Internet access, at least one staffed computer lab available. Computer purchase or lease plan available.

Student Life *Housing:* college housing not available. *Activities and Organizations:* drama/theater group, choral group, Mass PIRG, Student Nurse Organization, Student Senate, Diversity Club, LPN Organization. *Campus security:* 24-hour emergency response devices and patrols. *Student services:* personal/psychological counseling.

Athletics Member NJCAA.

Standardized Tests *Required:* ACCUPLACER (for placement).

Costs (2005–06) *Tuition:* state resident $780 full-time, $26 per credit part-time; nonresident $7800 full-time, $260 per credit part-time. Full-time tuition and fees vary according to course load. Part-time tuition and fees vary according to course load. *Required fees:* $2610 full-time, $87 per credit part-time. *Payment plans:* installment, deferred payment. *Waivers:* employees or children of employees.

Financial Aid Of all full-time matriculated undergraduates who enrolled in 2003, 72 Federal Work-Study jobs (averaging $1600).

Applying *Options:* common application, deferred entrance. *Application fee:* $10. *Required:* high school transcript. *Recommended:* interview. *Application deadline:* rolling (freshmen), rolling (transfers). *Notification:* continuous (freshmen).

Admissions Contact Ms. Margo J. Handschu, Admissions Counselor, Berkshire Community College, 1350 West Street, Pittsfield, MA 01201-5786. *Phone:* 413-499-4660 Ext. 425. *Toll-free phone:* 800-816-1233 Ext. 242. *Fax:* 413-496-9511. *E-mail:* admissions@berkshirecc.edu.

BRISTOL COMMUNITY COLLEGE
Fall River, Massachusetts

- **State-supported** 2-year, founded 1965
- **Calendar** semesters
- **Degree** certificates and associate

■ **Urban** 105-acre campus with easy access to Boston
■ **Coed,** 6,639 undergraduate students, 44% full-time, 63% women, 37% men

Undergraduates 2,901 full-time, 3,738 part-time. Students come from 7 states and territories, 25 other countries, 9% are from out of state, 5% African American, 2% Asian American or Pacific Islander, 3% Hispanic American, 0.5% Native American, 0.8% international, 5% transferred in. *Retention:* 67% of 2002 full-time freshmen returned.
Freshmen *Admission:* 4,172 applied, 3,280 admitted, 1,451 enrolled.
Faculty *Total:* 432, 24% full-time. *Student/faculty ratio:* 19:1.
Majors Accounting; applied art; banking and financial support services; business administration and management; business automation/technology/data entry; business, management, and marketing related; business operations support and secretarial services related; business teacher education; child care/guidance; civil engineering related; civil engineering technology; clinical/medical laboratory technology; communication disorders sciences and services related; communication/speech communication and rhetoric; communications systems installation and repair technology; computer and information sciences; computer and information sciences related; computer programming; computer programming (specific applications); computer science; computer typography and composition equipment operation; cosmetology and personal grooming arts related; criminal justice/safety; data processing and data processing technology; dental hygiene; design and visual communications; dramatic/theatre arts and stagecraft related; early childhood education; electrical, electronic and communications engineering technology; electrical/electronics equipment installation and repair; elementary education; engineering; engineering related; engineering science; engineering technologies related; entrepreneurship; environmental engineering technology; environmental/environmental health engineering; environmental science; environmental studies; finance and financial management services related; fine/studio arts; fire science; fishing and fisheries sciences and management; general studies; graphic design; health information/medical records technology; humanities; human services; information science/studies; information technology; intermedia/multimedia; legal administrative assistant/secretary; liberal arts and sciences/liberal studies; management information systems; manufacturing engineering; marketing/marketing management; mathematics and statistics related; mechanical engineering; medical administrative assistant and medical secretary; nursing (registered nurse training); occupational therapist assistant; occupational therapy; real estate; receptionist; social sciences; social work; structural engineering; visual and performing arts; water quality and wastewater treatment management and recycling technology; water resources engineering.
Academic Programs *Special study options:* academic remediation for entering students, adult/continuing education programs, cooperative education, distance learning, English as a second language, honors programs, independent study, internships, off-campus study, part-time degree program, services for LD students, student-designed majors, summer session for credit.
Library Learning Resources Center with 65,000 titles, 380 serial subscriptions, an OPAC, a Web page.
Computers on Campus 150 computers available on campus for general student use. A campuswide network can be accessed from off campus. Internet access, at least one staffed computer lab available.
Student Life *Housing:* college housing not available. *Activities and Organizations:* drama/theater group, student-run newspaper, International Club, MASS/PIRG WaterWatch, Criminal Justice Society, Society for Students in Free Enterprise, Portuguese Club. *Campus security:* 24-hour emergency response devices and patrols, student patrols, late-night transport/escort service. *Student services:* health clinic, personal/psychological counseling, women's center.
Standardized Tests *Required for some:* SAT (for admission).
Costs (2005–06) *Tuition:* state resident $576 full-time, $24 per credit part-time; nonresident $5520 full-time, $230 per credit part-time. *Required fees:* $2436 full-time, $99 per credit part-time, $30 per term part-time.
Financial Aid Of all full-time matriculated undergraduates who enrolled in 2003, 205 Federal Work-Study jobs (averaging $1627). 65 state and other part-time jobs (averaging $1478).
Applying *Options:* common application. *Application fee:* $10. *Required:* high school transcript. *Notification:* continuous (freshmen).
Admissions Contact Mr. Rodney S. Clark, Director of Admissions, Bristol Community College, 777 Elsbree Street, Hudnall Administration Building, Fall River, MA 02720. *Phone:* 508-678-2811 Ext. 2947. *Fax:* 508-730-3265. *E-mail:* rclark@bristol.mass.edu.

BUNKER HILL COMMUNITY COLLEGE
Boston, Massachusetts

■ **State-supported** 2-year, founded 1973
■ **Calendar** semesters
■ **Degree** certificates and associate
■ **Urban** 21-acre campus
■ **Endowment** $2.0 million
■ **Coed,** 7,821 undergraduate students, 33% full-time, 60% women, 40% men

Undergraduates 2,581 full-time, 5,240 part-time. Students come from 18 states and territories, 93 other countries, 1% are from out of state, 29% African American, 16% Asian American or Pacific Islander, 14% Hispanic American, 0.5% Native American, 4% international, 3% transferred in.
Freshmen *Admission:* 4,369 applied, 3,136 admitted, 1,443 enrolled.
Faculty *Total:* 424, 28% full-time. *Student/faculty ratio:* 19:1.
Majors Accounting; art; business administration and management; cardiovascular technology; chemistry; communication/speech communication and rhetoric; computer and information sciences and support services related; computer programming; computer programming (specific applications); computer science; computer systems networking and telecommunications; criminal justice/law enforcement administration; culinary arts; data entry/microcomputer applications; design and visual communications; dramatic/theatre arts; early childhood education; education; electrical/electronics maintenance and repair technology related; English; finance; fire protection and safety technology; general studies; health information/medical records administration; history; hospitality administration; hotel/motel administration; human services; international business/trade/commerce; mass communication/media; mathematics; medical radiologic technology; nursing (registered nurse training); operations management; physics; psychology; sociology; tourism and travel services management; web page, digital/multimedia and information resources design.
Academic Programs *Special study options:* academic remediation for entering students, advanced placement credit, cooperative education, distance learning, English as a second language, external degree program, honors programs, independent study, internships, part-time degree program, services for LD students, study abroad, summer session for credit.
Library Bunker Hill Community College Library with 65,953 titles, 330 serial subscriptions, 934 audiovisual materials, an OPAC, a Web page.
Computers on Campus 585 computers available on campus for general student use. A campuswide network can be accessed from off campus that provide access to online advising; academic support services. Internet access, online (class) registration, at least one staffed computer lab available.
Student Life *Housing:* college housing not available. *Activities and Organizations:* drama/theater group, student-run newspaper, radio station, African-American Cultural Society, Asian-Pacific Students Association, Arab Students Association, Hospitality Club, Radio station. *Campus security:* 24-hour emergency response devices and patrols, late-night transport/escort service. *Student services:* health clinic, personal/psychological counseling.
Athletics Member NSCAA, NJCAA. *Intercollegiate sports:* baseball M, basketball M/W, golf M/W, soccer M/W, softball W. *Intramural sports:* basketball M/W, table tennis M/W, tennis M/W.
Standardized Tests *Required for some:* TEAS.
Costs (2005–06) *Tuition:* state resident $576 full-time, $24 per credit part-time; nonresident $5520 full-time, $230 per credit part-time. Full-time tuition and fees vary according to course load. Part-time tuition and fees vary according to course load. *Required fees:* $1824 full-time, $76 per credit part-time. *Payment plan:* installment. *Waivers:* minority students, senior citizens, and employees or children of employees.
Financial Aid Of all full-time matriculated undergraduates who enrolled in 2003, 116 Federal Work-Study jobs (averaging $1500).
Applying *Options:* deferred entrance. *Application fee:* $10. *Required:* high school transcript. *Application deadline:* rolling (freshmen), rolling (transfers). *Notification:* continuous (freshmen).
Admissions Contact Ms. Debra Boyer, Registrar/Director of Enrollment Services, Bunker Hill Community College, BHCC Enrollment Services Center, 250 New Rutherford Avenue, Boston, MA 02129. *Phone:* 617-228-2420. *Fax:* 617-228-2082.

▶ **See page 476 for a narrative description.**

CAPE COD COMMUNITY COLLEGE
West Barnstable, Massachusetts

■ **State-supported** 2-year, founded 1961, part of Massachusetts Public Higher Education System
■ **Calendar** semesters
■ **Degree** certificates and associate
■ **Rural** 120-acre campus with easy access to Boston
■ **Endowment** $3.8 million
■ **Coed,** 4,243 undergraduate students, 35% full-time, 65% women, 35% men

Undergraduates 1,470 full-time, 2,773 part-time. Students come from 24 states and territories, 5 other countries, 1% are from out of state, 4% African American, 0.9% Asian American or Pacific Islander, 2% Hispanic American, 1% Native American, 0.9% international, 10% transferred in.
Freshmen *Admission:* 1,179 applied, 1,151 admitted, 730 enrolled.
Faculty *Total:* 331, 24% full-time, 24% with terminal degrees. *Student/faculty ratio:* 18:1.
Majors Accounting; administrative assistant and secretarial science; art; biological and physical sciences; business administration and management; com-

Cape Cod Community College (continued)

puter and information sciences related; computer graphics; computer science; computer systems networking and telecommunications; criminal justice/law enforcement administration; dental hygiene; dramatic/theatre arts; education; environmental engineering technology; environmental studies; executive assistant/executive secretary; fire science; history; hotel/motel administration; information science/studies; information technology; kindergarten/preschool education; legal administrative assistant/secretary; legal assistant/paralegal; liberal arts and sciences/liberal studies; management science; mass communication/media; mathematics; medical administrative assistant and medical secretary; modern languages; music; nursing (registered nurse training); parks, recreation and leisure; philosophy; physical education teaching and coaching; physical therapist assistant; pre-engineering; psychology; system administration; web/multimedia management and webmaster; web page, digital/multimedia and information resources design.

Academic Programs *Special study options:* academic remediation for entering students, adult/continuing education programs, advanced placement credit, cooperative education, distance learning, English as a second language, freshman honors college, honors programs, independent study, internships, off-campus study, part-time degree program, services for LD students, study abroad, summer session for credit.

Library Cape Cod Community College Learning Resource Center with 54,342 titles, 705 serial subscriptions, 6,107 audiovisual materials, an OPAC.

Computers on Campus 240 computers available on campus for general student use. A campuswide network can be accessed from off campus. Internet access, at least one staffed computer lab available.

Student Life *Housing:* college housing not available. *Activities and Organizations:* drama/theater group, student-run newspaper, radio station, choral group, Innkeepers Club, Phi Theta Kappa, Student Senate, Learning Disabilities Support Group, Ethnic Diversity. *Campus security:* 24-hour patrols. *Student services:* health clinic, personal/psychological counseling, women's center.

Athletics *Intramural sports:* badminton M/W, baseball M, basketball M/W, crew M/W, racquetball M/W, sailing M/W, skiing (downhill) M/W, soccer M, softball M/W, tennis M/W, volleyball M/W, weight lifting M/W.

Costs (2005–06) *Tuition:* state resident $720 full-time, $24 per credit hour part-time; nonresident $6900 full-time, $230 per credit hour part-time. *Required fees:* $2940 full-time, $98 per credit hour part-time.

Financial Aid Of all full-time matriculated undergraduates who enrolled in 2003, 50 Federal Work-Study jobs (averaging $1500).

Applying *Options:* deferred entrance. *Application fee:* $10. *Required:* high school transcript. *Required for some:* essay or personal statement, letters of recommendation. *Application deadlines:* 8/10 (freshmen), 8/10 (transfers). *Notification:* continuous (freshmen).

Admissions Contact Ms. Susan Kline-Symington, Director of Admissions, Cape Cod Community College, 2240 Lyanough Road, West Barnstable, MA 02668-1599. *Phone:* 508-362-2131 Ext. 4311. *Toll-free phone:* 877-846-3672. *Fax:* 508-375-4089. *E-mail:* info@capecod.mass.edu.

DEAN COLLEGE
Franklin, Massachusetts

- **Independent** primarily 2-year, founded 1865
- **Calendar** semesters
- **Degrees** certificates, associate, and bachelor's
- **Small-town** 100-acre campus with easy access to Boston and Providence
- **Endowment** $15.5 million
- **Coed**

Faculty *Student/faculty ratio:* 22:1.

Student Life *Campus security:* 24-hour emergency response devices and patrols, late-night transport/escort service, controlled dormitory access.

Athletics Member NJCAA.

Standardized Tests *Required:* SAT or ACT (for admission).

Costs (2004–05) *Comprehensive fee:* $30,680 includes full-time tuition ($19,420), mandatory fees ($1960), and room and board ($9300). Full-time tuition and fees vary according to program. Part-time tuition and fees vary according to program. *Room and board:* college room only: $5880.

Applying *Options:* common application, electronic application, deferred entrance. *Application fee:* $35. *Required:* essay or personal statement, high school transcript, letters of recommendation. *Recommended:* minimum 2.0 GPA, interview.

Admissions Contact Mr. Jay Leiendecker, Vice President for Enrollment Services, Dean College, 99 Main Street, Franklin, MA 02038. *Phone:* 508-541-1508. *Toll-free phone:* 877-TRY-DEAN. *Fax:* 508-541-8726. *E-mail:* admissions@dean.edu.

FINE MORTUARY COLLEGE
Westwood, Massachusetts

Admissions Contact 77 University Avenue, Westwood, MA 02090.

FISHER COLLEGE
Boston, Massachusetts

- **Independent** primarily 2-year, founded 1903
- **Calendar** semesters
- **Degrees** associate and bachelor's
- **Urban** campus
- **Endowment** $12.9 million
- **Coed**

Student Life *Campus security:* 24-hour emergency response devices and patrols, controlled dormitory access.

Athletics Member NAIA.

Costs (2004–05) *Comprehensive fee:* $27,550 includes full-time tuition ($15,975), mandatory fees ($1600), and room and board ($9975). Part-time tuition: $200 per credit. Part-time tuition and fees vary according to class time, course load, and program.

Applying *Options:* deferred entrance. *Application fee:* $25. *Required:* high school transcript. *Required for some:* essay or personal statement, letters of recommendation, interview. *Recommended:* minimum 2.0 GPA.

Admissions Contact Mr. William Graceffa, Director Admissions, Fisher College, 118 Beacon Street, Boston, MA 02116. *Phone:* 617-236-8800 Ext. 8822. *Toll-free phone:* 800-821-3050 (in-state); 800-446-1226 (out-of-state). *Fax:* 617-236-5473. *E-mail:* admissions@fisher.edu.

▶ **See page 496 for a narrative description.**

GIBBS COLLEGE
Boston, Massachusetts

Admissions Contact Mr. Robert A. Andriola, Director of Admissions, Gibbs College, 126 Newbury Street, Boston, MA 02116-2904. *Phone:* 617-578-7150. *Toll-free phone:* 800-6SKILLS. *Fax:* 617-262-2610.

GREENFIELD COMMUNITY COLLEGE
Greenfield, Massachusetts

- **State-supported** 2-year, founded 1962
- **Calendar** semesters
- **Degree** certificates and associate
- **Small-town** 120-acre campus
- **Coed**, 2,353 undergraduate students, 44% full-time, 64% women, 36% men

Undergraduates 1,040 full-time, 1,313 part-time. Students come from 5 states and territories, 7 other countries, 5% are from out of state, 3% African American, 4% Asian American or Pacific Islander, 3% Hispanic American, 0.5% Native American, 0.1% international, 11% transferred in. *Retention:* 55% of 2002 full-time freshmen returned.

Freshmen *Admission:* 697 applied, 697 admitted, 458 enrolled.

Faculty *Total:* 190, 29% full-time. *Student/faculty ratio:* 23:1.

Majors Accounting; administrative assistant and secretarial science; American studies; art; behavioral sciences; biological and physical sciences; business administration and management; commercial and advertising art; computer programming; criminal justice/law enforcement administration; education; engineering science; fire science; food science; human ecology; humanities; human services; industrial technology; information science/studies; kindergarten/preschool education; liberal arts and sciences/liberal studies; marketing/marketing management; mass communication/media; mathematics; natural resources management and policy; nursing (registered nurse training); parks, recreation and leisure; photography; pre-engineering.

Academic Programs *Special study options:* academic remediation for entering students, adult/continuing education programs, advanced placement credit, cooperative education, distance learning, double majors, English as a second language, honors programs, independent study, internships, part-time degree program, services for LD students, summer session for credit.

Library Greenfield Community College Library with 52,690 titles, 356 serial subscriptions.

Computers on Campus 115 computers available on campus for general student use. A campuswide network can be accessed from off campus. Internet access, at least one staffed computer lab available.

Student Life *Housing:* college housing not available. *Activities and Organizations:* drama/theater group, choral group. *Campus security:* 24-hour emergency response devices and patrols, late-night transport/escort service. *Student services:* health clinic, personal/psychological counseling, women's center.

Standardized Tests *Required for some:* Psychological Corporation Practical Nursing Entrance Examination.

Costs (2004–05) *Tuition:* state resident $780 full-time, $26 per credit part-time; nonresident $8340 full-time, $281 per credit part-time. Full-time tuition and fees vary according to class time. Part-time tuition and fees vary according to class time. *Required fees:* $2866 full-time, $153 per credit part-time, $61 per semester part-time. *Payment plan:* installment. *Waivers:* senior citizens and employees or children of employees.

Applying *Application fee:* $10. *Required for some:* high school transcript, interview. *Application deadline:* rolling (freshmen), rolling (transfers).

Admissions Contact Mr. Herbert Hentz, Assistant Director of Admission, Greenfield Community College, 1 College Drive, Greenfield, MA 01301-9739. *Phone:* 413-775-1000. *E-mail:* admission@gcc.mass.edu.

HOLYOKE COMMUNITY COLLEGE
Holyoke, Massachusetts

- **State-supported** 2-year, founded 1946, part of Massachusetts Public Higher Education System
- **Calendar** semesters
- **Degree** certificates and associate
- **Suburban** 135-acre campus
- **Endowment** $4.6 million
- **Coed,** 6,298 undergraduate students, 51% full-time, 65% women, 35% men

Undergraduates 3,215 full-time, 3,083 part-time. Students come from 18 states and territories, 11 other countries, 1% are from out of state, 6% African American, 2% Asian American or Pacific Islander, 13% Hispanic American, 0.5% Native American, 0.2% international, 5% transferred in.

Freshmen *Admission:* 1,565 enrolled.

Faculty *Total:* 498, 22% full-time. *Student/faculty ratio:* 18:1.

Majors Accounting; administrative assistant and secretarial science; American studies; biology/biological sciences; business administration and management; business teacher education; chemistry; cinematography and film/video production; clinical laboratory science/medical technology; commercial and advertising art; computer typography and composition equipment operation; consumer merchandising/retailing management; criminal justice/police science; dramatic/theatre arts; elementary education; engineering science; environmental studies; family and consumer sciences/human sciences; fine/studio arts; foods, nutrition, and wellness; health information/medical records administration; hospitality administration; hotel/motel administration; human services; information science/studies; kindergarten/preschool education; legal administrative assistant/secretary; liberal arts and sciences/liberal studies; mass communication/media; music; nursing (registered nurse training); photography; physics; pre-engineering; radiologic technology/science; sport and fitness administration; tourism and travel services management; veterinary sciences; veterinary technology; visual and performing arts.

Academic Programs *Special study options:* academic remediation for entering students, adult/continuing education programs, advanced placement credit, cooperative education, English as a second language, honors programs, independent study, internships, off-campus study, part-time degree program, services for LD students, student-designed majors, study abroad, summer session for credit. *ROTC:* Army (c), Air Force (c).

Library Elaine Marieb Library with 75,222 titles, 365 serial subscriptions, 7,489 audiovisual materials, an OPAC, a Web page.

Computers on Campus 450 computers available on campus for general student use. A campuswide network can be accessed from off campus. Internet access, online (class) registration, at least one staffed computer lab available.

Student Life *Housing:* college housing not available. *Activities and Organizations:* drama/theater group, student-run newspaper, radio station, choral group, Drama Club, Music Club, Student Advisory Board. *Campus security:* 24-hour emergency response devices and patrols, student patrols, late-night transport/escort service. *Student services:* health clinic, personal/psychological counseling, women's center.

Athletics Member NJCAA. *Intercollegiate sports:* baseball M, basketball M/W, golf M/W, skiing (downhill) M(c)/W(c), soccer M/W, softball W, tennis M/W, volleyball W.

Standardized Tests *Required for some:* Assessment and Placement Services for Community Colleges, Health Occupations Exam.

Costs (2005–06) *Tuition:* area resident $2498 full-time, $100 per credit part-time; nonresident $7442 full-time, $230 per credit part-time. *Waivers:* senior citizens and employees or children of employees.

Applying *Options:* common application, electronic application, early admission, deferred entrance. *Application fee:* $10. *Required:* high school transcript. *Recommended:* interview. *Application deadline:* rolling (freshmen), rolling (transfers). *Notification:* continuous (freshmen).

Admissions Contact Edwin Sanchez, Director of Admissions and Transfer Affairs, Holyoke Community College, Holyoke Community College, Attn: Admission Office, Holyoke, MA 01040. *Phone:* 413-552-2850. *Toll-free phone:* 888-530-8855 (in-state); 413-552-2850 (out-of-state). *Fax:* 413-552-2045. *E-mail:* admissions@hcc.mass.edu.

ITT TECHNICAL INSTITUTE
Norwood, Massachusetts

- **Proprietary** 2-year, founded 1990, part of ITT Educational Services, Inc
- **Calendar** quarters
- **Degree** associate
- **Suburban** campus with easy access to Boston
- **Coed**

Standardized Tests *Required:* Wonderlic aptitude test (for admission).

Costs (2004–05) *Tuition:* Please see school catalog for specific information.

Applying *Options:* deferred entrance. *Application fee:* $100. *Required:* high school transcript, interview. *Recommended:* letters of recommendation.

Admissions Contact Mr. Thomas F. Ryan III, Director of Recruitment, ITT Technical Institute, 333 Providence Highway, Norwood, MA 02062. *Phone:* 781-278-7200. *Toll-free phone:* 800-879-8324. *Fax:* 781-278-0766.

ITT TECHNICAL INSTITUTE
Woburn, Massachusetts

- **Proprietary** 2-year, part of ITT Educational Services, Inc
- **Calendar** quarters
- **Degree** associate
- **Coed**

Standardized Tests *Required:* Wonderlic aptitude test (for admission).

Costs (2004–05) *Tuition:* Please see school catalog for specific information.

Applying *Options:* deferred entrance. *Application fee:* $100. *Required:* high school transcript, interview. *Recommended:* letters of recommendation.

Admissions Contact Mr. David Lundgren, ITT Technical Institute, 10 Forbes Road, Woburn, MA 01801. *Phone:* 781-937-8324. *Toll-free phone:* 800-430-5097. *Fax:* 781-937-3402.

LABOURE COLLEGE
Boston, Massachusetts

- **Independent Roman Catholic** 2-year, founded 1971
- **Calendar** semesters
- **Degree** certificates and associate
- **Urban** campus
- **Endowment** $951,296
- **Coed**

Faculty *Student/faculty ratio:* 8:1.

Student Life *Campus security:* 24-hour emergency response devices.

Costs (2004–05) *Tuition:* $375 per credit part-time.

Financial Aid Of all full-time matriculated undergraduates who enrolled in 2003, 18 Federal Work-Study jobs (averaging $1000).

Applying *Options:* deferred entrance. *Application fee:* $25. *Required:* high school transcript, letters of recommendation.

Admissions Contact Ms. Gina M. Morrissette, Director of Admissions, Laboure College, 2120 Dorchester Avenue, Boston, MA 02124. *Phone:* 617-296-8300. *Fax:* 617-296-7947. *E-mail:* admit@laboure.edu.

MARIAN COURT COLLEGE
Swampscott, Massachusetts

Admissions Contact Mrs. Lisa Emerson Parker, Director of Admissions, Marian Court College, 35 Little's Point Road, Swampscott, MA 01907-2840. *Phone:* 781-595-6768 Ext. 139. *Fax:* 781-595-3560. *E-mail:* marianct@shore.net.

MASSACHUSETTS BAY COMMUNITY COLLEGE
Wellesley Hills, Massachusetts

- **State-supported** 2-year, founded 1961
- **Calendar** semesters
- **Degree** certificates and associate
- **Suburban** 84-acre campus with easy access to Boston
- **Coed,** 5,132 undergraduate students, 44% full-time, 58% women, 42% men

Undergraduates 2,283 full-time, 2,849 part-time. Students come from 7 states and territories, 50 other countries, 2% are from out of state, 11% African American, 4% Asian American or Pacific Islander, 7% Hispanic American, 0.4% Native American, 2% international, 37% transferred in.

Freshmen *Admission:* 2,528 applied, 2,457 admitted, 1,349 enrolled.

Massachusetts Bay Community College (continued)

Faculty *Total:* 395, 18% full-time. *Student/faculty ratio:* 18:1.

Majors Accounting; automotive engineering technology; biological and physical sciences; biology/biotechnology laboratory technician; business administration and management; business/commerce; chemical technology; child care and support services management; communication/speech communication and rhetoric; computer and information sciences; computer engineering technology; computer science; court reporting; criminal justice/law enforcement administration; drafting and design technology; dramatic/theatre arts; engineering technology; environmental engineering technology; forensic science and technology; general studies; hospitality administration; human services; information science/studies; international relations and affairs; laser and optical technology; legal assistant/paralegal; liberal arts and sciences/liberal studies; marine biology and biological oceanography; mechanical engineering/mechanical technology; medical radiologic technology; nursing (registered nurse training); occupational therapist assistant; physical therapist assistant; respiratory care therapy; social sciences; telecommunications.

Academic Programs *Special study options:* academic remediation for entering students, adult/continuing education programs, advanced placement credit, cooperative education, distance learning, honors programs, internships, part-time degree program, services for LD students, summer session for credit.

Library Perkins Library with 50,333 titles, 291 serial subscriptions, 4,650 audiovisual materials, an OPAC, a Web page.

Computers on Campus 400 computers available on campus for general student use. A campuswide network can be accessed from off campus. Internet access, at least one staffed computer lab available.

Student Life *Housing:* college housing not available. *Activities and Organizations:* drama/theater group, student-run newspaper, Student Government Association, Latino Student Organization, New World Society Club, Mass Bay Players, Student Occupational Therapy Association. *Campus security:* 24-hour emergency response devices and patrols. *Student services:* health clinic, personal/psychological counseling.

Athletics Member NJCAA. *Intercollegiate sports:* baseball M, basketball M/W, cross-country running M/W, golf M/W, soccer M, tennis M/W. *Intramural sports:* ice hockey M, soccer M/W.

Costs (2005–06) *Tuition:* state resident $720 full-time, $119 per credit part-time; nonresident $6900 full-time, $325 per credit part-time. *Required fees:* $2890 full-time.

Financial Aid Of all full-time matriculated undergraduates who enrolled in 2003, 25 Federal Work-Study jobs (averaging $2000).

Applying *Options:* electronic application, deferred entrance. *Application fee:* $20. *Application deadline:* rolling (freshmen), rolling (transfers). *Notification:* continuous (freshmen).

Admissions Contact Ms. Donna Raposa, Director for Admissions, Massachusetts Bay Community College, 50 Oakland Street, Wellesley Hills, MA 02481. *Phone:* 781-239-2501. *Fax:* 781-239-1047. *E-mail:* info@massbay.edu.

► **See page 522 for a narrative description.**

MASSASOIT COMMUNITY COLLEGE
Brockton, Massachusetts

- **State-supported** 2-year, founded 1966
- **Calendar** semesters
- **Degree** certificates and associate
- **Suburban** campus with easy access to Boston
- **Coed**

Student Life *Campus security:* 24-hour patrols.

Athletics Member NJCAA.

Costs (2004–05) *Tuition:* state resident $576 full-time, $24 per credit part-time; nonresident $5520 full-time, $230 per credit part-time. *Required fees:* $2088 full-time, $87 per credit part-time.

Financial Aid Of all full-time matriculated undergraduates who enrolled in 2003, 45 Federal Work-Study jobs (averaging $3200).

Admissions Contact Ms. Michelle Hughes, Director of Admissions, Massasoit Community College, 1 Massasoit Boulevard, Brockton, MA 02302-3996. *Phone:* 508-588-9100 Ext. 1412. *Toll-free phone:* 800-CAREERS.

MIDDLESEX COMMUNITY COLLEGE
Bedford, Massachusetts

- **State-supported** 2-year, founded 1970, part of Massachusetts Public Higher Education System
- **Calendar** semesters
- **Degree** certificates and associate
- **Suburban** 200-acre campus with easy access to Boston
- **Endowment** $1.1 million
- **Coed**

Student Life *Campus security:* 24-hour emergency response devices and patrols.

Standardized Tests *Required for some:* CPT.

Financial Aid Of all full-time matriculated undergraduates who enrolled in 2003, 63 Federal Work-Study jobs (averaging $2392).

Applying *Options:* common application, electronic application, early admission. *Required for some:* essay or personal statement, high school transcript, 3 letters of recommendation, interview.

Admissions Contact Ms. Laurie Dimitrov, Director, Admissions and Recruitment, Middlesex Community College, 33 Kearney Square, Lowell, MA 01852. *Phone:* 978-656-3207. *Toll-free phone:* 800-818-3434. *Fax:* 978-656-3322. *E-mail:* middlesex@middlesex.mass.edu.

MOUNT WACHUSETT COMMUNITY COLLEGE
Gardner, Massachusetts

- **State-supported** 2-year, founded 1963, part of Massachusetts Public Higher Education System
- **Calendar** semesters
- **Degree** certificates and associate
- **Small-town** 270-acre campus with easy access to Boston
- **Endowment** $1.0 million
- **Coed**, 4,165 undergraduate students, 44% full-time, 65% women, 35% men

MWCC is a 2-year public community college that offers more than 40 associate degree and certificate programs and noncredit and professional development courses. At MWCC, students gain education and training to build new skills, start a career, or transfer to a 4-year public or private college or university. Students may visit the College's Web site at http://www.mwcc.edu.

Undergraduates 1,821 full-time, 2,344 part-time. Students come from 6 states and territories, 8 other countries, 5% are from out of state, 4% African American, 2% Asian American or Pacific Islander, 8% Hispanic American, 0.3% Native American, 0.9% international, 8% transferred in.

Freshmen *Admission:* 2,043 applied, 1,942 admitted, 962 enrolled.

Faculty *Total:* 205, 34% full-time. *Student/faculty ratio:* 15:1.

Majors Accounting; art; automobile/automotive mechanics technology; broadcast journalism; business administration and management; computer graphics; computer technology/computer systems technology; criminal justice/law enforcement administration; electrical, electronic and communications engineering technology; environmental studies; fine/studio arts; fire science; general studies; human services; industrial engineering; industrial technology; information science/studies; kinesiology and exercise science; legal assistant/paralegal; liberal arts and sciences/liberal studies; management information systems; medical/clinical assistant; nursing (registered nurse training); physical therapy; plastics engineering technology; sign language interpretation and translation; speech therapy; telecommunications.

Academic Programs *Special study options:* academic remediation for entering students, adult/continuing education programs, advanced placement credit, cooperative education, distance learning, double majors, English as a second language, honors programs, independent study, internships, part-time degree program, services for LD students, study abroad, summer session for credit.

Library Mount Wachusett Community College Library with 56,344 titles, 532 serial subscriptions, 2,185 audiovisual materials, an OPAC, a Web page.

Computers on Campus 415 computers available on campus for general student use. A campuswide network can be accessed. Internet access, online (class) registration, at least one staffed computer lab available.

Student Life *Housing:* college housing not available. *Activities and Organizations:* drama/theater group, choral group, Sophomore Nursing Club, Freshman Nursing Club, Alpha Beta Gamma, Physical Therapist Assistant Club, Multicultural Club. *Campus security:* 24-hour emergency response devices and patrols. *Student services:* health clinic, personal/psychological counseling, women's center.

Costs (2004–05) *Tuition:* state resident $750 full-time, $25 per credit part-time; nonresident $6900 full-time, $230 per credit part-time. Full-time tuition and fees vary according to program and reciprocity agreements. Part-time tuition and fees vary according to program and reciprocity agreements. *Required fees:* $3330 full-time, $106 per credit part-time, $55 per term part-time. *Payment plans:* tuition prepayment, installment, deferred payment. *Waivers:* senior citizens and employees or children of employees.

Financial Aid Of all full-time matriculated undergraduates who enrolled in 2003, 60 Federal Work-Study jobs (averaging $1870).

Applying *Options:* common application, early admission. *Application fee:* $10. *Required:* high school transcript. *Required for some:* essay or personal statement, 2 letters of recommendation. *Application deadline:* rolling (freshmen), rolling (transfers). *Notification:* continuous (freshmen).

Admissions Contact John D. Walsh, Director of Admissions, Mount Wachusett Community College, 444 Green Street, Gardner, MA 01440-1000. *Phone:* 978-632-6600 Ext. 110. *Fax:* 978-630-9554. *E-mail:* admissions@ mwcc.mass.edu.

NEW ENGLAND COLLEGE OF FINANCE
Boston, Massachusetts

- **Independent** 2-year, founded 1909
- **Calendar** semesters
- **Degrees** certificates and associate (offers primarily part-time evening degree programs; bachelor's degree offered jointly with Bentley College, Assumption College, Providence College, University of Hartford, and University System College for Lifelong Learning)
- **Urban** campus
- **Coed, primarily women,** 812 undergraduate students, 80% women, 20% men

Undergraduates 812 part-time. Students come from 4 states and territories, 5% are from out of state, 3% African American, 2% Asian American or Pacific Islander, 4% Hispanic American, 0.1% Native American.

Faculty *Total:* 216. *Student/faculty ratio:* 11:1.

Majors Accounting; business administration and management; computer science; finance; management information systems; marketing/marketing management.

Academic Programs *Special study options:* academic remediation for entering students, adult/continuing education programs, distance learning, independent study, internships, part-time degree program, summer session for credit.

Computers on Campus 10 computers available on campus for general student use.

Student Life *Housing:* college housing not available. *Campus security:* reception desk in lobby of building.

Costs (2004–05) *Tuition:* $230 per quarter hour part-time.

Applying *Options:* common application. *Required:* essay or personal statement, high school transcript, 1 letter of recommendation, interview. *Application deadline:* rolling (freshmen), rolling (transfers). *Notification:* continuous (freshmen).

Admissions Contact Mr. Robert Wagstaff, Registrar, New England College of Finance, 1 Lincoln Plaza, Boston, MA 02111-2645. *Phone:* 617-951-2350 Ext. 230. *Toll-free phone:* 888-696-NECF. *Fax:* 617-951-2533.

NORTHERN ESSEX COMMUNITY COLLEGE
Haverhill, Massachusetts

- **State-supported** 2-year, founded 1960
- **Calendar** semesters
- **Degree** certificates and associate
- **Suburban** 106-acre campus with easy access to Boston
- **Endowment** $1.6 million
- **Coed,** 7,194 undergraduate students, 46% full-time, 57% women, 43% men

Northern Essex Community College is a two-year public community college with an open and rolling admission process, offering more than 70 degree and certificate programs in arts and sciences, business, computer information sciences, electronic technology and engineering science, health, human services, and paralegal studies. Students can prepare for a career or begin a bachelor's degree through the Joint Admissions Program or transfer agreements with 4-year colleges and universities.

Undergraduates 3,280 full-time, 3,914 part-time. Students come from 4 states and territories, 16% are from out of state, 3% African American, 2% Asian American or Pacific Islander, 22% Hispanic American, 0.2% Native American, 1% international. *Retention:* 54% of 2002 full-time freshmen returned.

Freshmen *Admission:* 3,314 applied, 3,164 admitted.

Faculty *Total:* 527, 19% full-time. *Student/faculty ratio:* 20:1.

Majors Accounting; administrative assistant and secretarial science; biological and physical sciences; business administration and management; business teacher education; civil engineering technology; commercial and advertising art; computer and information sciences; computer engineering technology; computer graphics; computer programming; computer programming related; computer programming (specific applications); computer science; computer systems networking and telecommunications; computer typography and composition equipment operation; criminal justice/law enforcement administration; dance; data processing and data processing technology; dental assisting; dramatic/theatre arts; education; electrical, electronic and communications engineering technology; elementary education; engineering science; finance; general studies; health information/medical records administration; history; hotel/motel administration; human services; industrial radiologic technology; international relations and affairs; journalism; kindergarten/preschool education; legal assistant/paralegal;

liberal arts and sciences/liberal studies; machine tool technology; marketing/ marketing management; materials science; medical administrative assistant and medical secretary; medical transcription; mental health/rehabilitation; music; nursing (registered nurse training); parks, recreation and leisure; physical education teaching and coaching; political science and government; radiologic technology/science; real estate; respiratory care therapy; respiratory therapy technician; sign language interpretation and translation; telecommunications technology; tourism and travel services management; web/multimedia management and webmaster; web page, digital/multimedia and information resources design; women's studies; word processing.

Academic Programs *Special study options:* academic remediation for entering students, adult/continuing education programs, advanced placement credit, cooperative education, distance learning, double majors, English as a second language, freshman honors college, honors programs, independent study, internships, off-campus study, part-time degree program, services for LD students, study abroad, summer session for credit. *ROTC:* Air Force (c).

Library Bentley Library with 61,120 titles, 598 serial subscriptions, an OPAC.

Computers on Campus 250 computers available on campus for general student use. A campuswide network can be accessed from off campus. At least one staffed computer lab available.

Student Life *Housing:* college housing not available. *Activities and Organizations:* drama/theater group, student-run newspaper. *Campus security:* 24-hour emergency response devices and patrols. *Student services:* health clinic, personal/ psychological counseling, women's center.

Athletics Member NJCAA. *Intercollegiate sports:* baseball M, basketball M/W, golf M/W, soccer M/W, softball W. *Intramural sports:* basketball M/W, cross-country running M/W, football M/W, golf M/W, racquetball M/W, skiing (cross-country) M/W, skiing (downhill) M/W, weight lifting M/W.

Standardized Tests *Required:* Psychological Corporation Aptitude Test for Practical Nursing (for admission).

Costs (2004–05) *Tuition:* $105 per credit part-time; state resident $3150 full-time, $105 per credit part-time; nonresident $3660 full-time, $346 per credit part-time. Full-time tuition and fees vary according to course load and degree level. Part-time tuition and fees vary according to course load and degree level. *Waivers:* employees or children of employees.

Financial Aid Of all full-time matriculated undergraduates who enrolled in 2003, 113 Federal Work-Study jobs (averaging $1668).

Applying *Options:* early admission. *Required:* high school transcript. *Application deadline:* rolling (freshmen), rolling (transfers). *Notification:* continuous (freshmen).

Admissions Contact Nora Sheridan, Director of Admissions, Northern Essex Community College, 100 Elliott Street, Haverhill,, MA 01830. *Phone:* 978-556-3616. *Toll-free phone:* 800-NECC-123. *Fax:* 978-556-3155.

NORTH SHORE COMMUNITY COLLEGE
Danvers, Massachusetts

- **State-supported** 2-year, founded 1965
- **Calendar** semesters
- **Degree** certificates and associate
- **Suburban** campus with easy access to Boston
- **Endowment** $3.9 million
- **Coed,** 6,690 undergraduate students, 41% full-time, 63% women, 37% men

Undergraduates 2,773 full-time, 3,917 part-time. Students come from 5 states and territories, 8 other countries, 1% are from out of state, 8% African American, 3% Asian American or Pacific Islander, 11% Hispanic American, 0.4% Native American, 0.3% international, 9% transferred in.

Freshmen *Admission:* 2,804 applied, 2,280 admitted, 1,487 enrolled.

Faculty *Total:* 398, 33% full-time. *Student/faculty ratio:* 18:1.

Majors Accounting; administrative assistant and secretarial science; airline pilot and flight crew; applied horticulture; biology/biotechnology laboratory technician; business administration and management; child development; computer and information sciences related; computer engineering technology; computer graphics; computer programming; computer programming (specific applications); computer science; criminal justice/law enforcement administration; culinary arts; data entry/microcomputer applications; engineering science; fire science; foods, nutrition, and wellness; forestry; gerontology; health science; hospitality administration; information science/studies; interdisciplinary studies; kindergarten/preschool education; landscaping and groundskeeping; legal administrative assistant/secretary; legal assistant/paralegal; liberal arts and sciences/ liberal studies; marketing/marketing management; medical administrative assistant and medical secretary; medical radiologic technology; mental health/rehabilitation; nursing (registered nurse training); occupational therapy; physical therapist assistant; pre-engineering; respiratory care therapy; substance abuse/addiction counseling; tourism and travel services management; veterinary technology.

Academic Programs *Special study options:* academic remediation for entering students, adult/continuing education programs, advanced placement credit, cooperative education, distance learning, English as a second language, honors programs, independent study, internships, part-time degree program, services for LD students, summer session for credit.

North Shore Community College (continued)

Library Learning Resource Center plus 2 others with 97,818 titles, 408 serial subscriptions, 7,795 audiovisual materials, an OPAC.

Computers on Campus 380 computers available on campus for general student use. A campuswide network can be accessed. Internet access, online (class) registration, at least one staffed computer lab available.

Student Life *Housing:* college housing not available. *Activities and Organizations:* drama/theater group, student-run newspaper, Program Council, student government, performing arts, student newspaper, Phi Theta Kappa. *Campus security:* 24-hour emergency response devices and patrols, late-night transport/escort service. *Student services:* health clinic, personal/psychological counseling, women's center.

Standardized Tests *Required for some:* nursing exam.

Costs (2005–06) *Tuition:* state resident $600 full-time, $25 per credit part-time; nonresident $6168 full-time, $257 per credit part-time. *Required fees:* $2112 full-time, $88 per credit part-time. *Payment plans:* installment, deferred payment. *Waivers:* senior citizens and employees or children of employees.

Financial Aid Of all full-time matriculated undergraduates who enrolled in 2003, 62 Federal Work-Study jobs (averaging $2385).

Applying *Options:* electronic application, early admission. *Required for some:* high school transcript, minimum 2.0 GPA, interview. *Application deadline:* rolling (freshmen), rolling (transfers). *Notification:* continuous (freshmen).

Admissions Contact Dr. Joanne Light, Dean of Enrollment Services, North Shore Community College, PO Box 3340, Danvers, MA 01923. *Phone:* 978-762-4000 Ext. 4337. *Fax:* 978-762-4015. *E-mail:* info@northshore.edu.

QUINCY COLLEGE
Quincy, Massachusetts

Admissions Contact Ms. Kristen Caputo, Assistant Director of Admissions, Quincy College, 34 Coddington Street, Quincy, MA 02169. *Phone:* 617-984-1704. *Toll-free phone:* 800-698-1700. *Fax:* 617-984-1669. *E-mail:* kcaputo@quincycollege.com.

QUINSIGAMOND COMMUNITY COLLEGE
Worcester, Massachusetts

- **State-supported** 2-year, founded 1963
- **Calendar** semesters
- **Degree** certificates and associate
- **Urban** 57-acre campus with easy access to Boston
- **Coed**

Student Life *Campus security:* 24-hour emergency response devices and patrols, late-night transport/escort service.

Athletics Member NJCAA.

Costs (2004–05) *Tuition:* state resident $576 full-time, $24 per credit part-time; nonresident $5520 full-time, $230 per credit part-time. *Required fees:* $2359 full-time, $91 per credit part-time, $75 per term part-time.

Financial Aid Of all full-time matriculated undergraduates who enrolled in 2003, 70 Federal Work-Study jobs (averaging $2200).

Applying *Options:* common application. *Application fee:* $10. *Required:* high school transcript. *Required for some:* interview.

Admissions Contact Mr. Ronald C. Smith, Director of Admissions, Quinsigamond Community College, 670 West Boylston Street, Worcester, MA 01606-2092. *Phone:* 508-854-4262. *Fax:* 508-854-4357. *E-mail:* qccadm@qcc.mass.edu.

ROXBURY COMMUNITY COLLEGE
Roxbury Crossing, Massachusetts

Admissions Contact Milton Samuels, Director/Admissions, Roxbury Community College, 1234 Columbus Avenue, Roxbury Crossing, MA 02120-3400. *Phone:* 617-541-5310. *Fax:* 617-427-5316.

SPRINGFIELD TECHNICAL COMMUNITY COLLEGE
Springfield, Massachusetts

- **State-supported** 2-year, founded 1967
- **Calendar** semesters
- **Degree** certificates and associate
- **Urban** 34-acre campus
- **Endowment** $2.5 million
- **Coed**, 6,114 undergraduate students, 45% full-time, 56% women, 44% men

Undergraduates 2,760 full-time, 3,354 part-time. Students come from 10 states and territories, 4% are from out of state, 15% African American, 2% Asian American or Pacific Islander, 14% Hispanic American, 0.5% Native American, 0.8% international.

Freshmen *Admission:* 2,695 applied, 2,060 admitted, 1,022 enrolled.

Faculty *Total:* 524, 29% full-time. *Student/faculty ratio:* 22:1.

Majors Accounting; administrative assistant and secretarial science; architectural engineering technology; automotive engineering technology; biology/biological sciences; biotechnology; business administration and management; business/commerce; CAD/CADD drafting/design technology; chemistry; civil engineering technology; clinical/medical laboratory technology; commercial and advertising art; communications technologies and support services related; computer and information sciences and support services related; computer engineering technology; computer science; cosmetology; criminal justice/police science; dental hygiene; desktop publishing and digital imaging design; diagnostic medical sonography and ultrasound technology; electrical and electronic engineering technologies related; electrical, electronic and communications engineering technology; electromechanical technology; elementary education; engineering; entrepreneurship; finance; fine/studio arts; fire science; general studies; graphic design; health aide; heating, air conditioning and refrigeration technology; kindergarten/preschool education; landscaping and groundskeeping; laser and optical technology; liberal arts and sciences/liberal studies; logistics and materials management; marketing/marketing management; massage therapy; mathematics; mechanical engineering/mechanical technology; medical administrative assistant and medical secretary; medical/clinical assistant; medical insurance coding; medical radiologic technology; nuclear medical technology; nursing (registered nurse training); occupational therapist assistant; physical therapist assistant; quality control technology; rehabilitation and therapeutic professions related; respiratory care therapy; surgical technology; web/multimedia management and webmaster.

Academic Programs *Special study options:* academic remediation for entering students, adult/continuing education programs, advanced placement credit, cooperative education, distance learning, English as a second language, honors programs, independent study, internships, off-campus study, part-time degree program, services for LD students, summer session for credit.

Library Springfield Technical Community College Library with 63,945 titles, 259 serial subscriptions, 17,586 audiovisual materials, an OPAC, a Web page.

Computers on Campus 1175 computers available on campus for general student use. A campuswide network can be accessed from off campus. Internet access, at least one staffed computer lab available.

Student Life *Housing:* college housing not available. *Activities and Organizations:* drama/theater group, student-run television station, Phi Theta Kappa Honor Society, Landscape Club, Dental Hygiene Club, Clinical Lab Club, Physical Therapist Assistant Club. *Campus security:* 24-hour emergency response devices and patrols, late-night transport/escort service. *Student services:* health clinic, personal/psychological counseling.

Athletics Member NJCAA. *Intercollegiate sports:* basketball M/W, golf M/W, soccer M/W, tennis M/W, wrestling M/W. *Intramural sports:* basketball M/W, cross-country running M/W, golf M/W, skiing (cross-country) M/W, volleyball M/W, weight lifting M/W.

Standardized Tests *Required for some:* SAT (for admission).

Costs (2005–06) *Tuition:* state resident $750 full-time, $25 per credit hour part-time; nonresident $7260 full-time, $242 per credit hour part-time. Full-time tuition and fees vary according to course load. Part-time tuition and fees vary according to course load. No tuition increase for student's term of enrollment. *Required fees:* $2454 full-time, $75 per credit hour part-time, $116 per term part-time. *Payment plan:* deferred payment. *Waivers:* senior citizens and employees or children of employees.

Financial Aid Of all full-time matriculated undergraduates who enrolled in 2003, 124 Federal Work-Study jobs (averaging $2400).

Applying *Application fee:* $10. *Required:* high school transcript. *Required for some:* interview. *Application deadline:* rolling (freshmen), rolling (transfers).

Admissions Contact Ms. Andrea Lucy-Allen, Director of Admissions, Springfield Technical Community College, One Armory Square, Springfield, MA 01105. *Phone:* 413-781-7822 Ext. 4380. *E-mail:* admissions@stcc.edu.

URBAN COLLEGE OF BOSTON
Boston, Massachusetts

- **Independent** 2-year, founded 1993
- **Calendar** semesters
- **Degree** certificates and associate
- **Urban** campus
- **Coed, primarily women**
- 100% of applicants were admitted

Faculty *Student/faculty ratio:* 20:1.

Costs (2004–05) *Tuition:* $3000 full-time, $125 per credit part-time. *Required fees:* $30 full-time, $10 per term part-time.

Applying *Application fee:* $10.

Admissions Contact Dr. Henry J. Johnson, Director of Enrollment Services/Registrar, Urban College of Boston, 178 Tremont Street, Boston, MA 02111-1093. *Phone:* 617-292-4723 Ext. 6357. *Fax:* 617-423-4758.

MICHIGAN

ALPENA COMMUNITY COLLEGE
Alpena, Michigan

- **State and locally supported** 2-year, founded 1952
- **Calendar** semesters
- **Degree** certificates and associate
- **Small-town** 700-acre campus
- **Endowment** $3.3 million
- **Coed,** 1,937 undergraduate students, 51% full-time, 58% women, 42% men

Undergraduates 984 full-time, 953 part-time. Students come from 4 states and territories, 0.8% African American, 0.5% Asian American or Pacific Islander, 0.2% Hispanic American, 0.4% Native American, 2% transferred in, 2% live on campus. *Retention:* 55% of 2002 full-time freshmen returned.
Freshmen *Admission:* 1,163 applied, 1,163 admitted, 423 enrolled. *Average high school GPA:* 2.67.
Faculty *Total:* 121, 42% full-time, 2% with terminal degrees. *Student/faculty ratio:* 17:1.
Majors Accounting; administrative assistant and secretarial science; automobile/automotive mechanics technology; biology/biological sciences; business administration and management; business automation/technology/data entry; chemical engineering; chemistry; computer and information sciences; computer/information technology services administration related; computer systems networking and telecommunications; corrections; criminal justice/police science; data processing and data processing technology; drafting and design technology; elementary education; English; general studies; information science/studies; liberal arts and sciences/liberal studies; manufacturing technology; mathematics; medical office assistant; nursing (licensed practical/vocational nurse training); nursing (registered nurse training); office management; operations management; pre-engineering; secondary education.
Academic Programs *Special study options:* academic remediation for entering students, advanced placement credit, distance learning, double majors, internships, part-time degree program, services for LD students, summer session for credit.
Library Stephen Fletcher Library with 29,000 titles, 183 serial subscriptions, an OPAC, a Web page.
Computers on Campus 75 computers available on campus for general student use. A campuswide network can be accessed from off campus. Internet access, at least one staffed computer lab available.
Student Life *Housing Options:* coed, men-only, women-only. Campus housing is provided by a third party. *Activities and Organizations:* drama/theater group, student-run newspaper, choral group, Nursing Association, Student Senate, Phi Theta Kappa, Lumberjack Newspaper, Law Enforcement Club. *Campus security:* 24-hour emergency response devices. *Student services:* personal/psychological counseling, women's center.
Athletics Member NJCAA. *Intercollegiate sports:* basketball M(s)/W(s), golf M, softball W(s), volleyball W(s). *Intramural sports:* basketball M/W, bowling M/W, football M, soccer M, softball M/W, volleyball M/W.
Standardized Tests *Required:* ACT COMPASS (for placement). *Recommended:* ACT (for placement).
Costs (2005–06) *Tuition:* area resident $2532 full-time, $68 per contact hour part-time; state resident $3545 full-time, $102 per contact hour part-time; nonresident $4550 full-time, $135 per contact hour part-time. *Required fees:* $500 full-time, $16 per contact hour part-time, $10 per term part-time. *Room and board:* room only: $3000.
Financial Aid Of all full-time matriculated undergraduates who enrolled in 2003, 80 Federal Work-Study jobs (averaging $1200). 20 state and other part-time jobs (averaging $800).
Applying *Options:* electronic application, early admission, deferred entrance. *Required:* high school transcript. *Application deadline:* rolling (freshmen), rolling (transfers). *Notification:* continuous (freshmen).
Admissions Contact Mr. Mike Kollien, Admissions Technician, Alpena Community College, 666 Johnson Street, Alpena, MI 49707-1495. *Phone:* 989-358-7339. *Toll-free phone:* 888-468-6222. *Fax:* 989-358-7561.

BAY DE NOC COMMUNITY COLLEGE
Escanaba, Michigan

- **County-supported** 2-year, founded 1963, part of Michigan Department of Education
- **Calendar** semesters
- **Degree** certificates and associate
- **Rural** 150-acre campus
- **Endowment** $2.1 million
- **Coed,** 2,549 undergraduate students

Undergraduates Students come from 2 states and territories, 2 other countries, 1% are from out of state, 0.4% African American, 0.1% Asian American or Pacific Islander, 0.2% Hispanic American, 4% Native American, 0.1% international.
Freshmen *Average high school GPA:* 2.89.
Faculty *Total:* 127, 33% full-time.
Majors Accounting; accounting technology and bookkeeping; administrative assistant and secretarial science; automobile/automotive mechanics technology; business administration and management; business/commerce; child care and support services management; community health services counseling; criminal justice/law enforcement administration; criminal justice/police science; drafting and design technology; electrical, electronic and communications engineering technology; environmental engineering technology; human services; hydrology and water resources science; information science/studies; liberal arts and sciences/liberal studies; machine tool technology; marketing/marketing management; medical administrative assistant and medical secretary; nursing (licensed practical/vocational nurse training); nursing (registered nurse training); pre-engineering; sanitation technology; social work; water quality and wastewater treatment management and recycling technology; wood science and wood products/pulp and paper technology.
Academic Programs *Special study options:* academic remediation for entering students, adult/continuing education programs, advanced placement credit, cooperative education, distance learning, internships, part-time degree program, summer session for credit.
Library Learning Resources Center plus 1 other with 30,000 titles, 200 serial subscriptions.
Computers on Campus 200 computers available on campus for general student use. A campuswide network can be accessed from off campus. Internet access, online (class) registration, at least one staffed computer lab available.
Student Life *Housing Options:* Campus housing is university owned. *Activities and Organizations:* student-run newspaper. *Campus security:* evening housing security personnel.
Athletics *Intramural sports:* basketball M/W, skiing (cross-country) M/W, skiing (downhill) M/W, tennis M/W, volleyball M/W.
Standardized Tests *Required:* ACT COMPASS (for placement).
Costs (2004–05) *Tuition:* area resident $1466 full-time, $61 per contact hour part-time; state resident $2106 full-time, $88 per contact hour part-time; nonresident $3312 full-time, $138 per contact hour part-time. *Required fees:* $164 full-time, $5 per contact hour part-time, $25 per term part-time.
Financial Aid Of all full-time matriculated undergraduates who enrolled in 2003, 80 Federal Work-Study jobs (averaging $2500). 40 state and other part-time jobs (averaging $2500).
Applying *Options:* early admission. *Required:* high school transcript. *Application deadlines:* 8/15 (freshmen), 8/15 (transfers). *Notification:* continuous (freshmen).
Admissions Contact Ms. Cynthia Aird, Director of Admissions, Bay de Noc Community College, Student Center, 2001 North Lincoln Road, Escanaba, MI 49829-2511. *Phone:* 906-786-5802 Ext. 1276. *Toll-free phone:* 800-221-2001 Ext. 1276. *Fax:* 906-786-8515. *E-mail:* wallbern@baydenoc.cc.mi.us.

BAY MILLS COMMUNITY COLLEGE
Brimley, Michigan

- **District-supported** 2-year, founded 1984
- **Calendar** semesters
- **Degree** certificates, diplomas, and associate
- **Rural** campus
- **Coed,** 489 undergraduate students

Faculty *Total:* 19, 47% full-time. *Student/faculty ratio:* 10:1.
Majors Administrative assistant and secretarial science; business administration and management; cultural studies; health science; hotel/motel administration; human services; information science/studies; liberal arts and sciences/liberal studies; modern languages; public administration; reading teacher education; social sciences.
Academic Programs *Special study options:* academic remediation for entering students, internships, part-time degree program.
Computers on Campus 60 computers available on campus for general student use. A campuswide network can be accessed. Internet access, at least one staffed computer lab available.
Student Life *Housing Options:* Campus housing is university owned. *Campus security:* 24-hour emergency response devices. *Student services:* personal/psychological counseling.
Standardized Tests *Required:* ACT ASSET (for placement).

Bay Mills Community College (continued)

Costs (2005–06) *Tuition:* state resident $2040 full-time, $85 per credit hour part-time. *Required fees:* $300 full-time, $10 per credit hour part-time, $30 per term part-time.

Financial Aid Of all full-time matriculated undergraduates who enrolled in 2003, 7 Federal Work-Study jobs (averaging $2466). 6 state and other part-time jobs (averaging $2634).

Applying *Options:* common application, early admission. *Required:* high school transcript. *Application deadline:* rolling (freshmen), rolling (transfers).

Admissions Contact Ms. Elaine Lehre, Admissions Officer, Bay Mills Community College, 12214 West Lakeshore Drive, Brimley, MI 49715. *Phone:* 906-248-3354. *Toll-free phone:* 800-844-BMCC. *Fax:* 906-248-3351.

DAVENPORT UNIVERSITY
Alma, Michigan

- **Independent** primarily 2-year, founded 1977, part of Davenport Educational System
- **Calendar** semesters
- **Degrees** diplomas, associate, and bachelor's
- **Coed**

Faculty *Student/faculty ratio:* 16:1.

Academic Programs *Special study options:* accelerated degree program, distance learning, English as a second language, independent study, internships, student-designed majors.

Costs (2004–05) *Tuition:* $5736 full-time, $239 per credit hour part-time. *Required fees:* $100 full-time, $50 per term part-time.

Applying *Options:* deferred entrance. *Application fee:* $25. *Application deadline:* rolling (freshmen), rolling (transfers). *Notification:* continuous (freshmen).

Admissions Contact Admissions, Davenport University, 415 East Fulton Street, Grand Rapids, MI 49503. *Toll-free phone:* 800-632-9569. *Fax:* 616-732-1142. *E-mail:* gradmiss@davenport.edu.

DAVENPORT UNIVERSITY
Bad Axe, Michigan

- **Independent** primarily 2-year, founded 1996, part of Davenport Educational System
- **Calendar** semesters
- **Degrees** diplomas, associate, and bachelor's
- **Coed**

Faculty *Student/faculty ratio:* 16:1.

Academic Programs *Special study options:* accelerated degree program, distance learning, English as a second language, independent study, internships, student-designed majors.

Costs (2004–05) *Tuition:* $6216 full-time, $259 per credit hour part-time. *Required fees:* $100 full-time, $50 per term part-time.

Applying *Options:* deferred entrance. *Application fee:* $25. *Application deadline:* rolling (freshmen), rolling (transfers). *Notification:* continuous (freshmen).

Admissions Contact Admissions, Davenport University, 415 East Fulton Street, Grand Rapids, MI 49503. *Toll-free phone:* 800-632-9569. *Fax:* 616-732-1142. *E-mail:* gradmiss@davenport.edu.

DAVENPORT UNIVERSITY
Bay City, Michigan

- **Independent** primarily 2-year, founded 1996, part of Davenport Educational System
- **Calendar** semesters
- **Degrees** diplomas, associate, and bachelor's
- **Coed**

Faculty *Student/faculty ratio:* 16:1.

Academic Programs *Special study options:* accelerated degree program, distance learning, English as a second language, independent study, internships, student-designed majors.

Costs (2004–05) *Tuition:* $6216 full-time, $259 per credit hour part-time. *Required fees:* $100 full-time, $50 per term part-time.

Applying *Options:* deferred entrance. *Application fee:* $25. *Application deadline:* rolling (freshmen), rolling (transfers). *Notification:* continuous (freshmen).

Admissions Contact Admissions, Davenport University, 415 East Fulton Street, Grand Rapids, MI 49503. *Toll-free phone:* 800-632-9569. *Fax:* 616-732-1142. *E-mail:* gradmiss@davenport.edu.

DAVENPORT UNIVERSITY
Caro, Michigan

- **Independent** primarily 2-year, founded 1996, part of Davenport Educational System
- **Calendar** semesters
- **Degrees** diplomas, associate, and bachelor's
- **Coed**

Faculty *Student/faculty ratio:* 16:1.

Academic Programs *Special study options:* accelerated degree program, distance learning, English as a second language, independent study, internships, student-designed majors.

Costs (2004–05) *Tuition:* $6216 full-time, $259 per credit hour part-time. *Required fees:* $100 full-time.

Applying *Options:* deferred entrance. *Application fee:* $25. *Application deadline:* rolling (freshmen), rolling (transfers). *Notification:* continuous (freshmen).

Admissions Contact Admissions, Davenport University, 415 East Fulton Street, Grand Rapids, MI 49503. *Toll-free phone:* 800-632-9569. *Fax:* 616-732-1142. *E-mail:* gradmiss@davenport.edu.

DAVENPORT UNIVERSITY
Midland, Michigan

- **Independent** primarily 2-year, founded 1996, part of Davenport Educational System
- **Calendar** semesters
- **Degrees** certificates, associate, and bachelor's
- **Urban** campus
- **Coed**

Faculty *Student/faculty ratio:* 16:1.

Majors Accounting; accounting technology and bookkeeping; administrative assistant and secretarial science; business administration and management; business automation/technology/data entry; carpentry; computer engineering technology; computer programming; computer typography and composition equipment operation; data processing and data processing technology; electrical, electronic and communications engineering technology; emergency medical technology (EMT paramedic); finance; hospitality administration; legal assistant/paralegal; medical administrative assistant and medical secretary; medical/clinical assistant; nursing (registered nurse training).

Academic Programs *Special study options:* academic remediation for entering students, accelerated degree program, cooperative education, distance learning, double majors, English as a second language, independent study, internships, part-time degree program, student-designed majors, summer session for credit.

Computers on Campus 197 computers available on campus for general student use. A campuswide network can be accessed. Internet access, at least one staffed computer lab available.

Student Life *Housing:* college housing not available. *Campus security:* 24-hour emergency response devices.

Costs (2004–05) *Tuition:* $6216 full-time, $259 per credit hour part-time. *Required fees:* $100 full-time, $50 per term part-time.

Applying *Options:* deferred entrance. *Application fee:* $25. *Required:* high school transcript. *Application deadline:* rolling (freshmen), rolling (transfers). *Notification:* continuous (freshmen).

Admissions Contact Admissions, Davenport University, 415 East Fulton Street, Grand Rapids, MI 49503. *Toll-free phone:* 800-632-9569. *Fax:* 616-732-1142. *E-mail:* gradmiss@davenport.edu.

DAVENPORT UNIVERSITY
Romeo, Michigan

- **Independent** primarily 2-year, founded 1985, part of Davenport Educational System
- **Calendar** semesters
- **Degrees** diplomas, associate, and bachelor's
- **Coed**

Faculty *Student/faculty ratio:* 16:1.

Academic Programs *Special study options:* accelerated degree program, distance learning, English as a second language, independent study, internships, student-designed majors.

Costs (2004–05) *Tuition:* $5736 full-time, $239 per credit hour part-time. *Required fees:* $100 full-time, $50 per term part-time.

Applying *Options:* deferred entrance. *Application fee:* $25. *Application deadline:* rolling (freshmen), rolling (transfers). *Notification:* continuous (freshmen).

Admissions Contact Admissions, Davenport University, 415 East Fulton Street, Grand Rapids, MI 49503. *Toll-free phone:* 800-632-9569. *Fax:* 616-732-1142. *E-mail:* gradmiss@davenport.edu.

DAVENPORT UNIVERSITY
Saginaw, Michigan

- **Independent** primarily 2-year, founded 1996, part of Davenport Educational System
- **Calendar** semesters
- **Degrees** diplomas, associate, and bachelor's
- **Coed**

Faculty *Student/faculty ratio:* 16:1.
Academic Programs *Special study options:* accelerated degree program, distance learning, English as a second language, independent study, internships, student-designed majors.
Costs (2004–05) *Tuition:* $6216 full-time, $259 per credit hour part-time. *Required fees:* $100 full-time, $50 per term part-time.
Applying *Options:* deferred entrance. *Application fee:* $25. *Application deadline:* rolling (freshmen), rolling (transfers). *Notification:* continuous (freshmen).
Admissions Contact Admissions, Davenport University, 415 East Fulton Street, Grand Rapids, MI 49503. *Toll-free phone:* 800-632-9569. *Fax:* 616-732-1142. *E-mail:* gradmiss@davenport.edu.

DELTA COLLEGE
University Center, Michigan

- **District-supported** 2-year, founded 1961
- **Calendar** semesters
- **Degree** certificates and associate
- **Rural** 640-acre campus
- **Endowment** $8.0 million
- **Coed,** 10,343 undergraduate students, 38% full-time, 58% women, 42% men

Undergraduates 3,915 full-time, 6,428 part-time. Students come from 22 other countries, 7% African American, 1% Asian American or Pacific Islander, 4% Hispanic American, 0.8% Native American, 0.9% international, 4% transferred in.
Freshmen *Admission:* 3,655 applied, 3,655 admitted, 2,285 enrolled.
Faculty *Total:* 502, 44% full-time. *Student/faculty ratio:* 21:1.
Majors Accounting; administrative assistant and secretarial science; agricultural business and management; agricultural mechanization; agriculture; apparel and textile marketing management; applied art; architectural engineering technology; art teacher education; automobile/automotive mechanics technology; avionics maintenance technology; biology/biological sciences; broadcast journalism; business administration and management; business automation/technology/data entry; business teacher education; carpentry; chemical engineering; chemistry; child development; computer and information sciences; computer and information sciences related; computer graphics; computer management; computer programming; computer programming related; computer programming (specific applications); computer science; computer software and media applications related; construction engineering technology; construction management; construction trades; consumer merchandising/retailing management; corrections; corrections and criminal justice related; cosmetology; criminal justice/law enforcement administration; criminal justice/police science; data entry/microcomputer applications; data entry/microcomputer applications related; data processing and data processing technology; dental assisting; dental hygiene; dietetics; drafting and design technology; dramatic/theatre arts; education; electrician; elementary education; emergency medical technology (EMT paramedic); engineering; engineering technology; English; environmental science; environmental studies; executive assistant/executive secretary; family and consumer sciences/human sciences; fashion merchandising; finance; fire science; forestry; funeral service and mortuary science; funeral service and mortuary science related; geology/earth science; graphic and printing equipment operation/production; heating, air conditioning and refrigeration technology; heating, air conditioning, ventilation and refrigeration maintenance technology; hydrology and water resources science; industrial arts; industrial radiologic technology; information science/studies; information technology; interior design; journalism; legal administrative assistant/secretary; legal assistant/paralegal; legal studies; liberal arts and sciences/liberal studies; machine tool technology; marketing/marketing management; mathematics; mechanical design technology; mechanical engineering; mechanical engineering/mechanical technology; medical administrative assistant and medical secretary; medical/clinical assistant; mortuary science and embalming; music; music teacher education; natural resources/conservation; natural resources management and policy; nursing (licensed practical/vocational nurse training); nursing (registered nurse training); office management; office occupations and clerical services; physical therapist assistant; physical therapy; physician assistant; pipefitting and sprinkler fitting; pre-engineering; pre-pharmacy studies; psychology; quality control technology; radio and television; radiologic technology/science; real estate; respiratory care therapy; social work; surgical technology; teacher assistant/aide; water quality and wastewater treatment management and recycling technology; web/multimedia management and webmaster; web page, digital/multimedia and information resources design; welding technology; word processing.

Academic Programs *Special study options:* academic remediation for entering students, adult/continuing education programs, advanced placement credit, cooperative education, distance learning, double majors, external degree program, freshman honors college, honors programs, independent study, internships, off-campus study, part-time degree program, services for LD students, student-designed majors, summer session for credit.
Library Library Learning Information Center with 93,167 titles, 400 serial subscriptions, 4,200 audiovisual materials, an OPAC, a Web page.
Computers on Campus 550 computers available on campus for general student use. A campuswide network can be accessed from off campus. Internet access, online (class) registration, at least one staffed computer lab available.
Student Life *Housing:* college housing not available. *Activities and Organizations:* student-run newspaper, radio and television station, intramural activities, Student Senate, Phi Theta Kappa, Inter-Varsity Christian Fellowship, DECA. *Campus security:* 24-hour emergency response devices and patrols, student patrols, late-night transport/escort service. *Student services:* personal/psychological counseling.
Athletics Member NJCAA. *Intercollegiate sports:* basketball M(s)/W(s), golf M(s), soccer M(s), softball W(s), volleyball W(s). *Intramural sports:* baseball M, basketball M/W, football M, golf M/W, racquetball M/W, soccer M/W, softball M/W, volleyball M/W.
Standardized Tests *Required:* ACT ASSET or ACT COMPASS (for placement). *Recommended:* ACT (for placement).
Costs (2004–05) *Tuition:* area resident $2484 full-time, $69 per credit part-time; state resident $3564 full-time, $99 per credit part-time; nonresident $5087 full-time, $141 per credit part-time. *Required fees:* $60 full-time, $30 per term part-time. *Waivers:* senior citizens and employees or children of employees.
Financial Aid Of all full-time matriculated undergraduates who enrolled in 2003, 156 Federal Work-Study jobs (averaging $1640). 386 state and other part-time jobs (averaging $1722).
Applying *Options:* common application, electronic application, early admission, deferred entrance. *Application fee:* $20. *Required for some:* essay or personal statement. *Recommended:* high school transcript. *Application deadline:* rolling (freshmen), rolling (transfers).
Admissions Contact Mr. Duff Zube, Director of Admissions, Delta College, 1961 Delta Road, University Center, MI 48710. *Phone:* 989-686-9449. *Toll-free phone:* 800-285-1705. *Fax:* 989-667-2202. *E-mail:* admit@delta.edu.

GLEN OAKS COMMUNITY COLLEGE
Centreville, Michigan

- **State and locally supported** 2-year, founded 1965, part of Michigan Department of Career Development
- **Calendar** semesters
- **Degree** certificates and associate
- **Rural** 300-acre campus
- **Endowment** $1.4 million
- **Coed,** 1,710 undergraduate students, 39% full-time, 61% women, 39% men

Undergraduates 659 full-time, 1,051 part-time. Students come from 3 states and territories, 6% are from out of state, 2% African American, 0.8% Asian American or Pacific Islander, 2% Hispanic American, 0.9% Native American, 0.1% international.
Freshmen *Admission:* 227 admitted, 214 enrolled.
Faculty *Total:* 109, 27% full-time. *Student/faculty ratio:* 16:1.
Majors Automobile/automotive mechanics technology; biological and physical sciences; business administration and management; liberal arts and sciences/liberal studies; nursing (registered nurse training).
Academic Programs *Special study options:* academic remediation for entering students, adult/continuing education programs, advanced placement credit, distance learning, internships, part-time degree program, services for LD students, summer session for credit.
Library E. J. Shaheen Library with 37,087 titles, 347 serial subscriptions, an OPAC.
Computers on Campus 50 computers available on campus for general student use. A campuswide network can be accessed. Internet access, at least one staffed computer lab available.
Student Life *Housing:* college housing not available. *Activities and Organizations:* student government, choir, band, Phi Theta Kappa. *Campus security:* 24-hour emergency response devices. *Student services:* personal/psychological counseling.
Athletics Member NJCAA. *Intercollegiate sports:* baseball M(s), basketball M(s)/W(s), golf M(s), softball W(s), tennis W(s), volleyball W(s). *Intramural sports:* baseball M, basketball M/W, table tennis M/W, tennis W.
Standardized Tests *Required:* ACT ASSET (for placement).
Costs (2005–06) *Tuition:* area resident $1800 full-time, $60 per credit hour part-time; state resident $2670 full-time, $89 per credit hour part-time; nonresident $3450 full-time, $114 per credit hour part-time. *Required fees:* $255 full-time, $8 per credit hour part-time, $31 per term part-time.

Glen Oaks Community College (continued)

Financial Aid Of all full-time matriculated undergraduates who enrolled in 2003, 70 Federal Work-Study jobs (averaging $1100). 38 state and other part-time jobs (averaging $1200).

Applying *Required:* high school transcript. *Application deadline:* rolling (freshmen), rolling (transfers).

Admissions Contact Ms. Beverly M. Andrews, Director of Admissions/Registrar, Glen Oaks Community College, 62249 Shimmel Road, Centreville, MI 49032-9719. *Phone:* 269-467-9945 Ext. 248. *Toll-free phone:* 888-994-7818. *Fax:* 269-467-9068. *E-mail:* webmaster@glenoaks.cc.mi.us.

GOGEBIC COMMUNITY COLLEGE
Ironwood, Michigan

- **State and locally supported** 2-year, founded 1932, part of Michigan Department of Education
- **Calendar** semesters
- **Degree** certificates and associate
- **Small-town** 195-acre campus
- **Endowment** $675,000
- **Coed,** 981 undergraduate students, 53% full-time, 62% women, 38% men

Undergraduates 517 full-time, 464 part-time. Students come from 7 states and territories, 4 other countries, 22% are from out of state, 0.6% African American, 0.4% Asian American or Pacific Islander, 0.8% Hispanic American, 3% Native American, 1% international, 3% transferred in.

Freshmen *Admission:* 261 enrolled.

Faculty *Total:* 90, 33% full-time. *Student/faculty ratio:* 13:1.

Majors Accounting; administrative assistant and secretarial science; automobile/automotive mechanics technology; biology/biological sciences; business administration and management; business automation/technology/data entry; carpentry; child care and support services management; child development; commercial and advertising art; computer engineering technology; computer graphics; computer/information technology services administration related; computer programming (specific applications); computer science; computer typography and composition equipment operation; construction engineering technology; construction management; corrections; criminal justice/law enforcement administration; data processing and data processing technology; drafting and design technology; education; engineering; forest sciences and biology; graphic and printing equipment operation/production; health information/medical records administration; humanities; information technology; kindergarten/preschool education; legal administrative assistant/secretary; liberal arts and sciences/liberal studies; mathematics; medical administrative assistant and medical secretary; nursing (licensed practical/vocational nurse training); nursing (registered nurse training); office management; psychology; social sciences; social work; sociology; system administration; word processing.

Academic Programs *Special study options:* academic remediation for entering students, adult/continuing education programs, advanced placement credit, cooperative education, distance learning, honors programs, internships, part-time degree program, services for LD students, summer session for credit.

Library Alex D. Chisholm Learning Resources Center with 22,000 titles, 220 serial subscriptions, an OPAC, a Web page.

Computers on Campus 210 computers available on campus for general student use. A campuswide network can be accessed from off campus. Internet access, online (class) registration, at least one staffed computer lab available.

Student Life *Housing:* college housing not available. *Activities and Organizations:* drama/theater group, choral group, Drama Club, Student Senate, Phi Theta Kappa, intramural sports. *Student services:* personal/psychological counseling.

Athletics Member NJCAA. *Intercollegiate sports:* basketball M(s)/W(s), cheerleading M/W. *Intramural sports:* basketball M/W, bowling M/W, football M/W, golf M/W, skiing (cross-country) M/W, skiing (downhill) M/W, softball M/W, tennis M/W, track and field M/W, volleyball M/W.

Costs (2004–05) *Tuition:* area resident $2046 full-time, $66 per credit part-time; state resident $2666 full-time, $86 per credit part-time; nonresident $3472 full-time, $112 per credit part-time. Full-time tuition and fees vary according to course load and reciprocity agreements. Part-time tuition and fees vary according to course load and reciprocity agreements. *Required fees:* $350 full-time, $5 per credit part-time. *Waivers:* senior citizens and employees or children of employees.

Financial Aid Of all full-time matriculated undergraduates who enrolled in 2003, 75 Federal Work-Study jobs (averaging $1800). 50 state and other part-time jobs (averaging $1800).

Applying *Options:* electronic application, early admission, deferred entrance. *Application fee:* $10. *Required:* high school transcript. *Application deadlines:* rolling (freshmen), 8/15 (out-of-state freshmen), 8/15 (transfers). *Notification:* continuous (freshmen).

Admissions Contact Ms. Jeanne Graham, Director of Admissions, Gogebic Community College, E-4946 Jackson Road, Ironwood, MI 49938. *Phone:*

906-932-4231 Ext. 306. *Toll-free phone:* 800-682-5910 Ext. 207. *Fax:* 906-932-0229. *E-mail:* nancyg@gogebic.edu.

GRAND RAPIDS COMMUNITY COLLEGE
Grand Rapids, Michigan

- **District-supported** 2-year, founded 1914, part of Michigan Department of Education
- **Calendar** semesters
- **Degree** certificates and associate
- **Urban** 35-acre campus
- **Endowment** $11.7 million
- **Coed,** 14,144 undergraduate students, 45% full-time, 52% women, 48% men

Undergraduates 6,338 full-time, 7,806 part-time. Students come from 13 states and territories, 35 other countries, 1% are from out of state, 10% African American, 2% Asian American or Pacific Islander, 5% Hispanic American, 0.9% Native American, 1% international, 43% transferred in. *Retention:* 55% of 2002 full-time freshmen returned.

Freshmen *Admission:* 5,989 applied, 4,997 admitted, 3,161 enrolled. *Average high school GPA:* 2.76.

Faculty *Total:* 649, 39% full-time, 7% with terminal degrees. *Student/faculty ratio:* 22:1.

Majors Administrative assistant and secretarial science; architectural engineering technology; art; automobile/automotive mechanics technology; business administration and management; computer engineering technology; computer programming; computer science; corrections; criminal justice/law enforcement administration; criminal justice/police science; culinary arts; dental hygiene; drafting and design technology; electrical, electronic and communications engineering technology; fashion merchandising; forestry; geology/earth science; heating, air conditioning, ventilation and refrigeration maintenance technology; industrial technology; legal administrative assistant/secretary; liberal arts and sciences/liberal studies; mass communication/media; medical administrative assistant and medical secretary; music; nursing (licensed practical/vocational nurse training); nursing (registered nurse training); plastics engineering technology; quality control technology; welding technology.

Academic Programs *Special study options:* academic remediation for entering students, adult/continuing education programs, advanced placement credit, cooperative education, distance learning, English as a second language, off-campus study, part-time degree program, services for LD students, study abroad, summer session for credit.

Library Arthur Andrews Memorial Library plus 1 other with 101,077 titles, 10,552 serial subscriptions, an OPAC, a Web page.

Computers on Campus 1048 computers available on campus for general student use. A campuswide network can be accessed from off campus. Internet access, at least one staffed computer lab available.

Student Life *Housing:* college housing not available. *Activities and Organizations:* drama/theater group, student-run newspaper, choral group, Student Congress, Phi Theta Kappa, Hispanic Student Organization, Asian Student Organization, Service Learning Advisory Board, national fraternities, national sororities. *Campus security:* 24-hour emergency response devices, late-night transport/escort service. *Student services:* personal/psychological counseling.

Athletics Member NJCAA. *Intercollegiate sports:* baseball M/W(s), basketball M(s)/W(s), football M(s), golf M(s), softball W(s), swimming and diving M(s)/W(s), tennis M(s)/W(s), track and field M(s), volleyball W(s), wrestling M(s). *Intramural sports:* badminton M/W, basketball M/W, skiing (cross-country) M/W, skiing (downhill) M/W, soccer M/W, swimming and diving M/W, tennis M/W, volleyball M/W.

Standardized Tests *Required for some:* ACT ASSET. *Recommended:* SAT or ACT (for admission).

Costs (2004–05) *Tuition:* area resident $1980 full-time, $66 per credit hour part-time; state resident $3300 full-time, $110 per credit hour part-time; nonresident $4500 full-time, $150 per credit hour part-time. Full-time tuition and fees vary according to course load. Part-time tuition and fees vary according to course load. *Required fees:* $100 full-time, $45 per term part-time. *Payment plan:* installment. *Waivers:* employees or children of employees.

Financial Aid Of all full-time matriculated undergraduates who enrolled in 2003, 196 Federal Work-Study jobs (averaging $1799). 66 state and other part-time jobs (averaging $1348).

Applying *Options:* early admission, deferred entrance. *Application fee:* $20. *Required:* high school transcript. *Application deadline:* 8/30 (freshmen). *Notification:* continuous (freshmen).

Admissions Contact Ms. Diane Patrick, Director of Admissions, Grand Rapids Community College, 143 Bostwick Avenue, NE, Grand Rapids, MI 49503-3201. *Phone:* 616-234-4100. *Fax:* 616-234-4005. *E-mail:* dpatrick@grcc.edu.

HENRY FORD COMMUNITY COLLEGE
Dearborn, Michigan

- **District-supported** 2-year, founded 1938
- **Calendar** semesters
- **Degree** certificates and associate
- **Suburban** 75-acre campus with easy access to Detroit
- **Coed**, 12,123 undergraduate students

Undergraduates Students come from 3 states and territories, 17% African American, 2% Asian American or Pacific Islander, 3% Hispanic American, 0.8% Native American, 0.2% international.

Faculty *Total:* 770, 29% full-time.

Majors Accounting; administrative assistant and secretarial science; applied art; art; artificial intelligence and robotics; automobile/automotive mechanics technology; business administration and management; business machine repair; ceramic arts and ceramics; commercial and advertising art; computer and information sciences; computer science; construction engineering technology; corrections; criminal justice/law enforcement administration; criminal justice/police science; culinary arts; dance; data processing and data processing technology; drafting and design technology; dramatic/theatre arts; drawing; electrical, electronic and communications engineering technology; emergency medical technology (EMT paramedic); energy management and systems technology; fire science; food services technology; health information/medical records administration; heating, air conditioning, ventilation and refrigeration maintenance technology; hospitality administration; hotel/motel administration; industrial radiologic technology; industrial technology; information science/studies; instrumentation technology; interior design; kinesiology and exercise science; legal administrative assistant/secretary; legal assistant/paralegal; liberal arts and sciences/liberal studies; marketing/marketing management; mass communication/media; materials science; medical administrative assistant and medical secretary; medical/clinical assistant; nursing (registered nurse training); pre-engineering; quality control technology; radiologic technology/science; real estate; respiratory care therapy; special products marketing; transportation technology.

Academic Programs *Special study options:* academic remediation for entering students, adult/continuing education programs, advanced placement credit, cooperative education, freshman honors college, honors programs, internships, part-time degree program, services for LD students, summer session for credit.

Library Eshleman Library with 80,000 titles, 650 serial subscriptions, an OPAC, a Web page.

Computers on Campus 250 computers available on campus for general student use. A campuswide network can be accessed from off campus. Internet access, at least one staffed computer lab available.

Student Life *Housing:* college housing not available. *Activities and Organizations:* drama/theater group, student-run newspaper, radio station, choral group, Phi Theta Kappa, Student Nurses, Future Teachers, ASAD (American Students of African Descent), Inter-Varsity Christian Fellowship. *Campus security:* 24-hour emergency response devices and patrols, late-night transport/escort service. *Student services:* personal/psychological counseling, women's center.

Athletics Member NJCAA. *Intercollegiate sports:* baseball M(s), basketball M(s)/W(s), golf M(s), softball W(s), tennis W(s), track and field M(s), volleyball W(s). *Intramural sports:* badminton M/W, basketball M/W, bowling M/W, racquetball M/W, sailing M/W, softball W, tennis M/W, volleyball M/W, weight lifting M/W.

Standardized Tests *Recommended:* ACT (for placement).

Costs (2004–05) *Tuition:* area resident $1710 full-time, $57 per credit hour part-time; state resident $3360 full-time, $112 per credit hour part-time; nonresident $3600 full-time, $120 per credit hour part-time. Full-time tuition and fees vary according to course load. Part-time tuition and fees vary according to course load. No tuition increase for student's term of enrollment. *Required fees:* $402 full-time, $11 per credit hour part-time, $36 per term part-time. *Payment plan:* installment.

Applying *Options:* early admission, deferred entrance. *Application fee:* $30. *Recommended:* high school transcript. *Application deadline:* rolling (freshmen), rolling (transfers). *Notification:* continuous (freshmen).

Admissions Contact Ms. Dorothy A. Murphy, Coordinator of Recruitment, Henry Ford Community College, 5101 Evergreen Road, Dearborn, MI 48128-1495. *Phone:* 313-845-9766. *E-mail:* dorothy@mail.henryford.cc.mi.us.

ITT TECHNICAL INSTITUTE
Canton, Michigan

- **Proprietary** 2-year, founded 2002, part of ITT Educational Services, Inc
- **Calendar** quarters
- **Degree** associate
- **Coed**

Standardized Tests *Required:* (for admission).

Costs (2004–05) *Tuition:* Please see school catalog for specific information.

Applying *Options:* deferred entrance. *Application fee:* $100. *Required:* high school transcript, interview. *Recommended:* letters of recommendation.

Admissions Contact Mr. Dudley Layfield III, Director of Recruitment, ITT Technical Institute, 1905 South Haggerty Road, Canton, MI 48188. *Phone:* 784-397-7800. *Toll-free phone:* 800-247-4477. *Fax:* 734-397-1945.

ITT TECHNICAL INSTITUTE
Grand Rapids, Michigan

- **Proprietary** 2-year, part of ITT Educational Services, Inc
- **Calendar** quarters
- **Degree** associate
- **Coed**

Standardized Tests *Required:* Wonderlic aptitude test (for admission).

Costs (2004–05) *Tuition:* Please see school catalog for specific information.

Applying *Options:* deferred entrance. *Application fee:* $100. *Required:* high school transcript, interview. *Recommended:* letters of recommendation.

Admissions Contact Director of Recruitment, ITT Technical Institute, 4020 Sparks Drive SE, Grand Rapids, MI 49546. *Phone:* 616-956-1060. *Toll-free phone:* 800-632-4676. *Fax:* 616-956-5606.

ITT TECHNICAL INSTITUTE
Troy, Michigan

- **Proprietary** 2-year, founded 1987, part of ITT Educational Services, Inc
- **Calendar** quarters
- **Degree** associate
- **Coed**

Standardized Tests *Required:* Wonderlic aptitude test (for admission).

Costs (2004–05) *Tuition:* Please see school catalog for specific information.

Applying *Options:* deferred entrance. *Application fee:* $100. *Required:* high school transcript, interview. *Recommended:* letters of recommendation.

Admissions Contact Ms. Patricia Hyman, ITT Technical Institute, 1522 East Big Beaver Road, Troy, MI 48083. *Phone:* 248-524-1800. *Toll-free phone:* 800-832-6817. *Fax:* 248-524-1965.

JACKSON COMMUNITY COLLEGE
Jackson, Michigan

- **County-supported** 2-year, founded 1928
- **Calendar** semesters
- **Degree** certificates and associate
- **Suburban** 580-acre campus with easy access to Detroit
- **Endowment** $9.0 million
- **Coed**, 5,837 undergraduate students, 37% full-time, 65% women, 35% men

Undergraduates 2,185 full-time, 3,652 part-time. 1% are from out of state, 4% African American, 0.8% Asian American or Pacific Islander, 3% Hispanic American, 0.9% Native American, 0.1% international.

Freshmen *Admission:* 524 enrolled.

Faculty *Total:* 335, 28% full-time, 5% with terminal degrees. *Student/faculty ratio:* 19:1.

Majors Accounting and finance; administrative assistant and secretarial science; airline pilot and flight crew; automobile/automotive mechanics technology; business administration and management; computer and information sciences and support services related; construction trades related; corrections; criminal justice/law enforcement administration; data processing and data processing technology; diagnostic medical sonography and ultrasound technology; early childhood education; electrical, electronic and communications engineering technology; emergency medical technology (EMT paramedic); executive assistant/executive secretary; general studies; graphic design; heating, air conditioning and refrigeration technology; liberal arts and sciences/liberal studies; marketing/marketing management; medical/clinical assistant; medical insurance/medical billing; medical radiologic technology; medical transcription; nursing (licensed practical/vocational nurse training); nursing (registered nurse training).

Academic Programs *Special study options:* academic remediation for entering students, adult/continuing education programs, advanced placement credit, cooperative education, distance learning, English as a second language, independent study, internships, part-time degree program, services for LD students, summer session for credit.

Library Atkinson Learning Resources Center plus 1 other with 67,000 titles, 300 serial subscriptions, 2,000 audiovisual materials, an OPAC, a Web page.

Computers on Campus 356 computers available on campus for general student use. A campuswide network can be accessed from off campus. Internet access, online (class) registration, at least one staffed computer lab available.

Student Life *Housing:* college housing not available. *Activities and Organizations:* drama/theater group, student-run newspaper, choral group. *Campus security:* 24-hour patrols.

Jackson Community College (continued)

Standardized Tests *Recommended:* ACT (for placement).

Costs (2004–05) *Tuition:* area resident $1836 full-time, $71 per credit hour part-time; state resident $2961 full-time, $95 per credit hour part-time; nonresident $2928 full-time, $116 per credit hour part-time. Full-time tuition and fees vary according to location. Part-time tuition and fees vary according to location. *Required fees:* $5 per credit hour part-time, $18 per term part-time. *Payment plan:* deferred payment. *Waivers:* senior citizens and employees or children of employees.

Financial Aid Of all full-time matriculated undergraduates who enrolled in 2003, 60 Federal Work-Study jobs (averaging $1304). 19 state and other part-time jobs (averaging $1192).

Applying *Options:* electronic application, early admission. *Application deadline:* rolling (freshmen), rolling (transfers). *Notification:* continuous (freshmen).

Admissions Contact Ms. Julie Hand, Director of Enrollment Services Team Leader, Jackson Community College, 2111 Emmons Road, Jackson, MI 49201. *Phone:* 517-796-8425. *Toll-free phone:* 888-522-7344. *Fax:* 517-796-8631. *E-mail:* admissions@jccmi.edu.

KALAMAZOO VALLEY COMMUNITY COLLEGE
Kalamazoo, Michigan

- **State and locally supported** 2-year, founded 1966
- **Calendar** semesters
- **Degree** certificates and associate
- **Suburban** 187-acre campus
- **Coed**, 10,634 undergraduate students, 37% full-time, 53% women, 47% men

Undergraduates 3,959 full-time, 6,675 part-time. Students come from 3 states and territories, 46 other countries, 1% are from out of state, 9% African American, 1% Asian American or Pacific Islander, 3% Hispanic American, 0.9% Native American, 1% international.

Freshmen *Admission:* 2,230 enrolled.

Faculty *Total:* 464, 27% full-time. *Student/faculty ratio:* 26:1.

Majors Accounting technology and bookkeeping; automobile/automotive mechanics technology; business administration and management; chemical technology; commercial and advertising art; computer programming; criminal justice/police science; dental hygiene; drafting and design technology; electrical, electronic and communications engineering technology; elementary education; emergency medical technology (EMT paramedic); executive assistant/executive secretary; fire science; health science; heating, air conditioning and refrigeration technology; legal administrative assistant/secretary; liberal arts and sciences/liberal studies; machine tool technology; management information systems; marketing/marketing management; mechanical engineering/mechanical technology; medical administrative assistant and medical secretary; medical/clinical assistant; nursing (registered nurse training); plastics engineering technology; pre-engineering; respiratory care therapy; welding technology.

Academic Programs *Special study options:* academic remediation for entering students, advanced placement credit, cooperative education, distance learning, English as a second language, honors programs, independent study, internships, off-campus study, part-time degree program, services for LD students, student-designed majors, summer session for credit. *ROTC:* Army (c).

Library Kalamazoo Valley Community College Library with 88,791 titles, 420 serial subscriptions, an OPAC, a Web page.

Computers on Campus 1000 computers available on campus for general student use. A campuswide network can be accessed from off campus. Internet access, at least one staffed computer lab available.

Student Life *Housing:* college housing not available. *Activities and Organizations:* student-run newspaper, choral group. *Campus security:* 24-hour emergency response devices and patrols, late-night transport/escort service. *Student services:* personal/psychological counseling, women's center.

Athletics Member NJCAA. *Intercollegiate sports:* baseball M(s), basketball M(s)/W(s), golf M, softball W(s), tennis M(s)/W(s), volleyball W(s). *Intramural sports:* basketball M/W.

Standardized Tests *Recommended:* ACT (for placement).

Costs (2004–05) *Tuition:* area resident $1252 full-time, $55 per credit part-time; state resident $2136 full-time, $94 per credit part-time; nonresident $2973 full-time, $128 per credit part-time. *Payment plan:* installment. *Waivers:* senior citizens and employees or children of employees.

Financial Aid Of all full-time matriculated undergraduates who enrolled in 2003, 54 Federal Work-Study jobs (averaging $1100). 10 state and other part-time jobs (averaging $1050).

Applying *Options:* early admission, deferred entrance. *Application deadline:* rolling (freshmen), rolling (transfers). *Notification:* continuous (freshmen).

Admissions Contact Mr. Michael McCall, Director of Admissions, Registration and Records, Kalamazoo Valley Community College, PO Box 4070, Kalamazoo, MI 49003-4070. *Phone:* 269-488-4207. *Fax:* 616-372-5161. *E-mail:* admissions@kvcc.edu.

KELLOGG COMMUNITY COLLEGE
Battle Creek, Michigan

- **State and locally supported** 2-year, founded 1956, part of Michigan Department of Education
- **Calendar** semesters
- **Degree** certificates and associate
- **Urban** 120-acre campus
- **Endowment** $91,005
- **Coed**

Faculty *Student/faculty ratio:* 15:1.

Student Life *Campus security:* 24-hour emergency response devices and patrols, late-night transport/escort service.

Athletics Member NJCAA.

Standardized Tests *Required for some:* SAT or ACT (for admission).

Costs (2004–05) *Tuition:* area resident $1770 full-time, $64 per credit hour part-time; state resident $2873 full-time, $101 per credit hour part-time; nonresident $4327 full-time, $149 per credit hour part-time. Full-time tuition and fees vary according to reciprocity agreements. Part-time tuition and fees vary according to reciprocity agreements. *Required fees:* $150 full-time.

Financial Aid Of all full-time matriculated undergraduates who enrolled in 2003, 41 Federal Work-Study jobs (averaging $2251). 43 state and other part-time jobs (averaging $2058).

Applying *Options:* common application, early admission, deferred entrance. *Required for some:* high school transcript, minimum 2.0 GPA.

Admissions Contact Mr. Sedgwick Harris, Director of Admissions, Kellogg Community College, 450 North Avenue, Battle Creek, MI 49017. *Phone:* 269-965-3931 Ext. 2641. *Fax:* 269-965-4133.

KIRTLAND COMMUNITY COLLEGE
Roscommon, Michigan

- **District-supported** 2-year, founded 1966, part of Michigan Department of Education
- **Calendar** semesters
- **Degree** certificates and associate
- **Rural** 180-acre campus
- **Coed**

Student Life *Campus security:* student patrols, late-night transport/escort service.

Standardized Tests *Required:* ACT ASSET (for placement). *Recommended:* SAT or ACT (for placement).

Costs (2004–05) *Tuition:* area resident $2008 full-time, $63 per credit part-time; state resident $3685 full-time, $115 per credit part-time; nonresident $4552 full-time, $142 per credit part-time. *Required fees:* $631 full-time. *Room and board:* $4350.

Financial Aid Of all full-time matriculated undergraduates who enrolled in 2003, 46 Federal Work-Study jobs (averaging $1282). 82 state and other part-time jobs (averaging $1578).

Applying *Options:* early admission, deferred entrance.

Admissions Contact Ms. Stacey Thompson, Registrar, Kirtland Community College, 10775 North St Helen Road, Roscommon, MI 48653-9699. *Phone:* 517-275-5121 Ext. 248.

LAKE MICHIGAN COLLEGE
Benton Harbor, Michigan

Admissions Contact Mrs. Linda Steinberger, Manager of Admissions, Lake Michigan College, 2755 East Napier, Benton Harbor, MI 49022-1899. *Phone:* 616-927-8100 Ext. 5205. *Toll-free phone:* 800-252-1LMC. *Fax:* 269-927-6874.

LANSING COMMUNITY COLLEGE
Lansing, Michigan

- **State and locally supported** 2-year, founded 1957, part of Michigan Department of Education
- **Calendar** semesters
- **Degree** certificates and associate
- **Urban** 28-acre campus
- **Endowment** $3.5 million
- **Coed**, 19,471 undergraduate students, 32% full-time, 56% women, 44% men

Undergraduates 6,203 full-time, 13,268 part-time. Students come from 29 states and territories, 69 other countries, 1% are from out of state, 9% African American, 3% Asian American or Pacific Islander, 4% Hispanic American, 1% Native American, 2% international.

Freshmen *Admission:* 10,810 applied, 10,810 admitted, 1,569 enrolled.

Faculty *Total:* 1,391, 17% full-time. *Student/faculty ratio:* 14:1.

Majors Accounting; administrative assistant and secretarial science; airline pilot and flight crew; architectural engineering technology; art; automobile/automotive mechanics technology; avionics maintenance technology; biological and physical sciences; biology/biological sciences; biology/biotechnology laboratory technician; broadcast journalism; business administration and management; carpentry; chemical engineering; chemistry; child development; cinematography and film/video production; civil engineering technology; clinical laboratory science/medical technology; commercial and advertising art; computer engineering technology; computer graphics; computer management; computer programming; computer typography and composition equipment operation; construction engineering technology; consumer merchandising/retailing management; corrections; court reporting; criminal justice/law enforcement administration; criminal justice/police science; dance; dental hygiene; developmental and child psychology; diagnostic medical sonography and ultrasound technology; drafting and design technology; dramatic/theatre arts; education; electrical, electronic and communications engineering technology; electromechanical technology; elementary education; emergency medical technology (EMT paramedic); engineering; engineering technology; English; film/cinema studies; finance; fine/studio arts; fire science; geography; geology/earth science; gerontology; heating, air conditioning, ventilation and refrigeration maintenance technology; heavy equipment maintenance technology; horticultural science; hospitality administration; hotel/motel administration; human resources management; human services; industrial technology; information science/studies; international business/trade/commerce; journalism; kindergarten/preschool education; labor and industrial relations; landscape architecture; legal administrative assistant/secretary; legal assistant/paralegal; liberal arts and sciences/liberal studies; machine tool technology; management information systems; marketing/marketing management; mass communication/media; mathematics; mechanical design technology; mechanical engineering/mechanical technology; medical/clinical assistant; medical radiologic technology; music; nursing (licensed practical/vocational nurse training); nursing (registered nurse training); philosophy; photography; physical education teaching and coaching; pre-engineering; public administration; public relations/image management; quality control technology; radio and television; real estate; religious studies; respiratory care therapy; sign language interpretation and translation; social work; special products marketing; speech and rhetoric; surgical technology; survey technology; teacher assistant/aide; telecommunications; tourism and travel services management; veterinary technology; voice and opera; welding technology.

Academic Programs *Special study options:* academic remediation for entering students, adult/continuing education programs, advanced placement credit, cooperative education, distance learning, double majors, English as a second language, external degree program, honors programs, independent study, internships, part-time degree program, services for LD students, study abroad, summer session for credit. *ROTC:* Army (c), Air Force (c).

Library Abel Sykes Technology and Learning Center plus 1 other with 98,125 titles, 600 serial subscriptions, 11,653 audiovisual materials, an OPAC, a Web page.

Computers on Campus 1146 computers available on campus for general student use. A campuswide network can be accessed from off campus. At least one staffed computer lab available.

Student Life *Housing:* college housing not available. *Activities and Organizations:* drama/theater group, student-run newspaper, radio station, choral group, Student Marketing, Legal Assistants Club, Student Nursing Club, Phi Theta Kappa, Student Advising Club, national fraternities, national sororities. *Campus security:* 24-hour emergency response devices and patrols, student patrols, late-night transport/escort service. *Student services:* personal/psychological counseling, women's center.

Athletics Member NJCAA. *Intercollegiate sports:* basketball M(s)/W(s), cross-country running M(s)/W(s), golf M(s), track and field M(s)/W(s), volleyball W(s). *Intramural sports:* baseball M, basketball M/W, cross-country running M/W, ice hockey M, soccer M/W, softball W, track and field M/W, volleyball W.

Standardized Tests *Required for some:* SAT or ACT (for placement).

Costs (2004–05) *Tuition:* area resident $1705 full-time, $55 per contact hour part-time; state resident $2728 full-time, $88 per contact hour part-time; nonresident $3720 full-time, $120 per contact hour part-time. Part-time tuition and fees vary according to course load. *Required fees:* $40 full-time, $20 per term part-time. *Payment plan:* installment. *Waivers:* senior citizens and employees or children of employees.

Financial Aid Of all full-time matriculated undergraduates who enrolled in 2003, 125 Federal Work-Study jobs (averaging $2636). 122 state and other part-time jobs (averaging $2563).

Applying *Options:* common application, electronic application, early admission, deferred entrance. *Required for some:* essay or personal statement, high school transcript, 2 letters of recommendation, interview. *Application deadline:* rolling (freshmen), rolling (transfers).

Admissions Contact Mr. Lucian Leone, Director of Enrollment Services, Lansing Community College, PO Box 40010, Lansing, MI 48901-7210. *Phone:* 517-483-1058. *Toll-free phone:* 800-644-4LCC. *Fax:* 517-483-9668. *E-mail:* jhearns@lcc.edu.

LEWIS COLLEGE OF BUSINESS
Detroit, Michigan

Admissions Contact Ms. Frances Ambrose, Admissions Secretary, Lewis College of Business, 17370 Meyers Road, Detroit, MI 48235-1423. *Phone:* 313-862-6300.

MACOMB COMMUNITY COLLEGE
Warren, Michigan

- **District-supported** 2-year, founded 1954
- **Calendar** semesters
- **Degree** certificates and associate
- **Suburban** 384-acre campus with easy access to Detroit
- **Endowment** $8.0 million
- **Coed**, 20,471 undergraduate students, 34% full-time, 53% women, 47% men

Undergraduates 6,868 full-time, 13,603 part-time. Students come from 5 states and territories, 5% African American, 3% Asian American or Pacific Islander, 1% Hispanic American, 0.6% Native American, 1% international.

Freshmen *Admission:* 1,831 enrolled.

Faculty *Total:* 942, 25% full-time, 11% with terminal degrees. *Student/faculty ratio:* 28:1.

Majors Accounting; administrative assistant and secretarial science; agriculture; architectural drafting and CAD/CADD; automobile/automotive mechanics technology; automotive engineering technology; biology/biological sciences; business administration and management; business automation/technology/data entry; business/commerce; cabinetmaking and millwork; chemistry; child care and support services management; civil engineering technology; commercial and advertising art; communication/speech communication and rhetoric; computer programming; computer programming (specific applications); construction engineering technology; criminal justice/law enforcement administration; criminal justice/police science; culinary arts; drafting and design technology; electrical, electronic and communications engineering technology; electrical/electronics equipment installation and repair; electromechanical technology; emergency medical technology (EMT paramedic); energy management and systems technology; engineering related; finance; fire protection and safety technology; forensic science and technology; general studies; graphic and printing equipment operation/production; heating, air conditioning and refrigeration technology; heating, air conditioning, ventilation and refrigeration maintenance technology; industrial mechanics and maintenance technology; industrial technology; international/global studies; legal assistant/paralegal; legal studies; liberal arts and sciences/liberal studies; machine tool technology; manufacturing technology; marketing/marketing management; mathematics; mechanical design technology; mechanical drafting and CAD/CADD; mechanical engineering/mechanical technology; mechanic and repair technologies related; medical/clinical assistant; mental health/rehabilitation; metallurgical technology; music performance; nursing (registered nurse training); occupational therapist assistant; operations management; physical therapist assistant; plastics engineering technology; plumbing technology; pre-engineering; quality control technology; respiratory care therapy; robotics technology; safety/security technology; sheet metal technology; social psychology; surgical technology; survey technology; tool and die technology; veterinary/animal health technology; veterinary sciences; welding technology.

Academic Programs *Special study options:* academic remediation for entering students, adult/continuing education programs, advanced placement credit, cooperative education, English as a second language, honors programs, internships, off-campus study, part-time degree program, services for LD students, student-designed majors, summer session for credit.

Library 159,226 titles, 4,240 serial subscriptions, an OPAC.

Computers on Campus 2000 computers available on campus for general student use. A campuswide network can be accessed from off campus. At least one staffed computer lab available.

Student Life *Housing:* college housing not available. *Activities and Organizations:* drama/theater group, Phi Beta Kappa, Adventure Unlimited, Alpha Rho Rho, SADD. *Campus security:* 24-hour emergency response devices and patrols, late-night transport/escort service, security phones in parking lots, surveillance cameras. *Student services:* health clinic, personal/psychological counseling.

Athletics Member NJCAA. *Intercollegiate sports:* baseball M(s), basketball M(s), cross-country running M(s)/W(s), soccer M(s), softball W(s), track and field M(s)/W(s), volleyball W(s). *Intramural sports:* baseball M, basketball M, bowling M/W, cross-country running M/W, football M/W, skiing (cross-country) M/W, skiing (downhill) M/W, volleyball M/W.

Standardized Tests *Required for some:* ACT ASSET, ACT COMPASS.

Costs (2004–05) *Tuition:* area resident $1891 full-time, $61 per credit hour part-time; state resident $2759 full-time, $89 per credit hour part-time; nonresident $3224 full-time, $104 per credit hour part-time. *Required fees:* $40 full-time, $20 per term part-time.

Financial Aid Of all full-time matriculated undergraduates who enrolled in 2003, 800 Federal Work-Study jobs (averaging $2800).

Macomb Community College (continued)

Applying *Options:* common application, early admission, deferred entrance. *Application deadline:* rolling (freshmen), rolling (transfers).

Admissions Contact Mr. Richard P. Stevens, Coordinator of Admissions and Assessment, Macomb Community College, G312, 14500 East 12 Mile Road, Warren, MI 48088-3896. *Phone:* 586-445-7246. *Toll-free phone:* 866-622-6624. *Fax:* 586-445-7140.

MID MICHIGAN COMMUNITY COLLEGE
Harrison, Michigan

- **State and locally supported** 2-year, founded 1965, part of Michigan Department of Education
- **Calendar** semesters
- **Degree** certificates and associate
- **Rural** 560-acre campus
- **Coed,** 3,232 undergraduate students, 45% full-time, 63% women, 37% men

Undergraduates 1,465 full-time, 1,767 part-time. Students come from 6 states and territories, 0.5% are from out of state, 2% African American, 0.7% Asian American or Pacific Islander, 2% Hispanic American, 2% Native American, 0.3% international, 6% transferred in. *Retention:* 8% of 2002 full-time freshmen returned.

Freshmen *Admission:* 1,383 applied, 1,383 admitted, 1,139 enrolled. *Test scores:* ACT scores over 18: 69%; ACT scores over 24: 9%; ACT scores over 30: 2%.

Faculty *Total:* 256, 23% full-time, 2% with terminal degrees. *Student/faculty ratio:* 15:1.

Majors Accounting; administrative assistant and secretarial science; art; automobile/automotive mechanics technology; biochemical technology; biological and physical sciences; biology/biological sciences; biology/biotechnology laboratory technician; business administration and management; chemistry; child care provision; child development; commercial and advertising art; computer graphics; computer science; corrections; criminal justice/law enforcement administration; drafting and design technology; dramatic/theatre arts; education (K-12); elementary education; emergency medical technology (EMT paramedic); engineering technologies related; engineering technology; environmental studies; fire science; fish/game management; general studies; heating, air conditioning, ventilation and refrigeration maintenance technology; hospitality administration; hospitality and recreation marketing; industrial radiologic technology; information science/studies; legal administrative assistant/secretary; liberal arts and sciences/liberal studies; machine tool technology; marketing/marketing management; mathematics; medical administrative assistant and medical secretary; medical/clinical assistant; medical transcription; nursing (licensed practical/vocational nurse training); nursing (registered nurse training); ophthalmic and optometric support services and allied professions related; pharmacy; physical therapy; pre-engineering; psychology; secondary education; sociology; speech and rhetoric; speech/theater education.

Academic Programs *Special study options:* academic remediation for entering students, adult/continuing education programs, advanced placement credit, cooperative education, distance learning, honors programs, independent study, internships, part-time degree program, services for LD students, summer session for credit.

Library Charles A. Amble Library with 29,450 titles, 200 serial subscriptions.

Computers on Campus 175 computers available on campus for general student use. A campuswide network can be accessed. At least one staffed computer lab available.

Student Life *Housing:* college housing not available. *Activities and Organizations:* drama/theater group, student-run newspaper, choral group, Commission of Student Activities Services, Phi Theta Kappa. *Campus security:* 24-hour emergency response devices.

Standardized Tests *Recommended:* ACT (for placement).

Costs (2005–06) *Tuition:* area resident $2000 full-time; state resident $3500 full-time; nonresident $6400 full-time. *Required fees:* $150 full-time.

Financial Aid Of all full-time matriculated undergraduates who enrolled in 2003, 50 Federal Work-Study jobs (averaging $3600). 50 state and other part-time jobs (averaging $3600).

Applying *Options:* early admission. *Required for some:* interview. *Recommended:* high school transcript. *Application deadline:* rolling (freshmen), rolling (transfers). *Notification:* continuous (freshmen).

Admissions Contact Ms. Brenda Mather, Admissions Specialist, Mid Michigan Community College, 1375 South Clare Avenue, Harrison, MI 48625. *Phone:* 989-386-6661. *Fax:* 989-386-6613. *E-mail:* apply@midmich.edu.

MONROE COUNTY COMMUNITY COLLEGE
Monroe, Michigan

- **County-supported** 2-year, founded 1964, part of Michigan Department of Education
- **Calendar** semesters
- **Degree** certificates and associate
- **Small-town** 150-acre campus with easy access to Detroit and Toledo
- **Coed**

Student Life *Campus security:* police patrols during open hours.

Standardized Tests *Required:* ACT ASSET, ACT COMPASS (for admission). *Required for some:* ACT (for admission). *Recommended:* ACT (for admission).

Costs (2004–05) *Tuition:* area resident $1440 full-time, $60 per credit part-time; state resident $2256 full-time, $96 per credit part-time; nonresident $2448 full-time, $104 per credit part-time. *Required fees:* $146 full-time.

Applying *Options:* early admission, deferred entrance. *Application fee:* $25. *Required:* high school transcript.

Admissions Contact Mr. Randell W. Daniels, Director of Admissions and Guidance Services, Monroe County Community College, 155 South Raisinville Road, Monroe, MI 48161-9047. *Phone:* 734-384-4261. *Toll-free phone:* 877-YES MCCC. *Fax:* 734-242-9711. *E-mail:* rdaniels@monroeccc.edu.

MONTCALM COMMUNITY COLLEGE
Sidney, Michigan

- **State and locally supported** 2-year, founded 1965, part of Michigan Department of Education
- **Calendar** semesters
- **Degree** certificates and associate
- **Rural** 240-acre campus with easy access to Grand Rapids
- **Endowment** $3.4 million
- **Coed,** 2,080 undergraduate students, 32% full-time, 69% women, 31% men

Undergraduates 674 full-time, 1,406 part-time. Students come from 1 other state, 0.2% African American, 0.3% Asian American or Pacific Islander, 2% Hispanic American, 1% Native American, 6% transferred in.

Freshmen *Admission:* 589 applied, 589 admitted, 389 enrolled. *Average high school GPA:* 2.19. *Test scores:* ACT scores over 18: 74%; ACT scores over 24: 15%.

Faculty *Total:* 133, 19% full-time, 9% with terminal degrees. *Student/faculty ratio:* 13:1.

Majors Accounting; administrative assistant and secretarial science; business administration and management; child care and support services management; child care provision; computer installation and repair technology; corrections; cosmetology; criminal justice/law enforcement administration; data processing and data processing technology; drafting and design technology; electrical, electronic and communications engineering technology; emergency medical technology (EMT paramedic); entrepreneurship; executive assistant/executive secretary; industrial radiologic technology; industrial technology; liberal arts and sciences/liberal studies; management information systems; medical administrative assistant and medical secretary; medical radiologic technology; nursing (registered nurse training).

Academic Programs *Special study options:* academic remediation for entering students, adult/continuing education programs, advanced placement credit, cooperative education, distance learning, double majors, independent study, internships, off-campus study, part-time degree program, services for LD students, summer session for credit.

Library Montcalm Community College Library with 29,848 titles, 3,670 serial subscriptions, 580 audiovisual materials, an OPAC, a Web page.

Computers on Campus 450 computers available on campus for general student use. A campuswide network can be accessed from off campus. Internet access, online (class) registration, at least one staffed computer lab available.

Student Life *Housing:* college housing not available. *Activities and Organizations:* drama/theater group, choral group, Nursing Club, Native American Club, Phi Theta Kappa, Business Club, Judo Club. *Student services:* personal/psychological counseling.

Athletics *Intramural sports:* volleyball M/W.

Standardized Tests *Required:* ACT ASSET, ACT COMPASS (for placement). *Recommended:* ACT (for placement).

Costs (2004–05) *Tuition:* area resident $1830 full-time, $61 per credit hour part-time; state resident $2790 full-time, $93 per credit hour part-time; nonresident $3600 full-time, $120 per credit hour part-time. Full-time tuition and fees vary according to course load. Part-time tuition and fees vary according to course load. *Required fees:* $165 full-time, $6 per credit hour part-time. *Payment plan:* installment. *Waivers:* senior citizens and employees or children of employees.

Financial Aid Of all full-time matriculated undergraduates who enrolled in 2003, 57 Federal Work-Study jobs (averaging $2000).

Applying *Options:* early admission, deferred entrance. *Recommended:* high school transcript. *Application deadline:* rolling (freshmen), rolling (transfers). *Notification:* continuous (freshmen).

Admissions Contact Ms. Debra Alexander, Director of Admissions, Montcalm Community College, 2800 College Drive, Sidney, MI 48885. *Phone:* 989-328-1276. *Toll-free phone:* 877-328-2111. *Fax:* 989-328-2950. *E-mail:* admissions@montcalm.edu.

MOTT COMMUNITY COLLEGE
Flint, Michigan

- **District-supported** 2-year, founded 1923, part of Michigan Labor and Economic Growth Department
- **Calendar** semesters
- **Degree** certificates and associate
- **Urban** 20-acre campus with easy access to Detroit
- **Endowment** $33.7 million
- **Coed,** 10,328 undergraduate students, 34% full-time, 61% women, 39% men

Undergraduates 3,538 full-time, 6,790 part-time. Students come from 10 states and territories, 33 other countries, 0.1% are from out of state, 18% African American, 0.9% Asian American or Pacific Islander, 3% Hispanic American, 1% Native American, 0.3% international, 3% transferred in.

Freshmen *Admission:* 2,640 applied, 979 admitted, 979 enrolled.

Faculty *Total:* 474, 31% full-time, 10% with terminal degrees. *Student/faculty ratio:* 23:1.

Majors Accounting technology and bookkeeping; administrative assistant and secretarial science; architectural engineering technology; autobody/collision and repair technology; automobile/automotive mechanics technology; business administration and management; business/commerce; child care provision; communications technology; community health services counseling; computer and information sciences and support services related; computer systems networking and telecommunications; criminal justice/police science; culinary arts; dental assisting; dental hygiene; drafting and design technology; early childhood education; electrical, electronic and communications engineering technology; elementary education; emergency medical technology (EMT paramedic); engineering technologies related; entrepreneurship; fire protection and safety technology; foodservice systems administration; general studies; graphic design; heating, air conditioning and refrigeration technology; histologic technician; information resources management; international business/trade/commerce; legal administrative assistant/secretary; legal assistant/paralegal; liberal arts and sciences/liberal studies; management information systems; manufacturing technology; marketing/marketing management; mechanical engineering/mechanical technology; medical administrative assistant and medical secretary; medical radiologic technology; nursing (licensed practical/vocational nurse training); nursing (registered nurse training); occupational therapist assistant; office management; photography; physical therapist assistant; precision production related; quality control technology; respiratory care therapy; sign language interpretation and translation; survey technology.

Academic Programs *Special study options:* academic remediation for entering students, accelerated degree program, adult/continuing education programs, advanced placement credit, cooperative education, distance learning, double majors, English as a second language, honors programs, independent study, internships, part-time degree program, services for LD students, summer session for credit.

Library Charles Stewart Mott Library with 112,251 titles, 325 serial subscriptions, an OPAC, a Web page.

Computers on Campus 1290 computers available on campus for general student use. A campuswide network can be accessed from off campus. Internet access, online (class) registration, at least one staffed computer lab available.

Student Life *Housing:* college housing not available. *Activities and Organizations:* choral group, Criminal Justice Association, Phi Theta Kappa, Dental Assisting Club, Connoisseur's Club, Social Work Club. *Campus security:* 24-hour emergency response devices and patrols, student patrols, late-night transport/escort service. *Student services:* health clinic, personal/psychological counseling.

Athletics Member NJCAA. *Intercollegiate sports:* baseball M(s), basketball M(s)/W(s), cross-country running M(s)/W(s), golf M(s), softball W(s), volleyball W(s).

Standardized Tests *Required:* Michigan Test of English Language Proficiency, CPT (for placement). *Recommended:* SAT or ACT (for placement).

Costs (2005–06) *Tuition:* area resident $2117 full-time, $71 per contact hour part-time; state resident $3167 full-time, $106 per contact hour part-time; nonresident $4226 full-time, $141 per contact hour part-time. *Required fees:* $95 full-time, $48 per term part-time. *Payment plan:* installment. *Waivers:* senior citizens and employees or children of employees.

Financial Aid Of all full-time matriculated undergraduates who enrolled in 2003, 300 Federal Work-Study jobs (averaging $1000). 300 state and other part-time jobs (averaging $1000).

Applying *Options:* electronic application, early admission, deferred entrance. *Required:* high school transcript. *Application deadline:* 8/31 (freshmen).

Admissions Contact Mr. Marc Payne, Executive Director of Admissions, Mott Community College, 1401 East Court Street, Flint, MI 48503. *Phone:* 810-762-0316. *Toll-free phone:* 800-852-8614. *Fax:* 810-232-9442. *E-mail:* admissions@mcc.edu.

MUSKEGON COMMUNITY COLLEGE
Muskegon, Michigan

- **State and locally supported** 2-year, founded 1926, part of Michigan Department of Education
- **Calendar** semesters
- **Degree** associate
- **Urban** 112-acre campus with easy access to Grand Rapids
- **Coed,** 5,000 undergraduate students

Undergraduates Students come from 3 states and territories, 5 other countries.

Faculty *Total:* 150, 67% full-time.

Majors Accounting; administrative assistant and secretarial science; advertising; anthropology; applied art; applied mathematics; art; art history, criticism and conservation; art teacher education; automobile/automotive mechanics technology; biology/biotechnology laboratory technician; biomedical technology; business administration and management; business machine repair; chemical engineering; child development; commercial and advertising art; criminal justice/law enforcement administration; data processing and data processing technology; developmental and child psychology; drafting and design technology; economics; education; electrical, electronic and communications engineering technology; electromechanical technology; elementary education; emergency medical technology (EMT paramedic); engineering technology; finance; hospitality administration; hospitality and recreation marketing; hotel/motel administration; industrial arts; industrial technology; information science/studies; legal administrative assistant/secretary; liberal arts and sciences/liberal studies; machine tool technology; marketing/marketing management; medical administrative assistant and medical secretary; nursing (registered nurse training); parks, recreation and leisure; special products marketing; transportation technology; welding technology.

Academic Programs *Special study options:* academic remediation for entering students, adult/continuing education programs, cooperative education, honors programs, part-time degree program, student-designed majors, summer session for credit.

Library 48,597 titles, 450 serial subscriptions.

Computers on Campus 30 computers available on campus for general student use.

Student Life *Housing:* college housing not available. *Activities and Organizations:* drama/theater group, choral group. *Student services:* personal/psychological counseling.

Athletics Member NJCAA. *Intercollegiate sports:* baseball M, basketball M(s)/W(s), golf M/W, softball W, tennis M/W, volleyball W(s), wrestling M. *Intramural sports:* basketball M/W, skiing (downhill) M(c)/W(c).

Standardized Tests *Recommended:* SAT or ACT (for placement).

Costs (2004–05) *Tuition:* $57 per credit hour part-time; state resident $84 per credit hour part-time; nonresident $102 per credit hour part-time. *Required fees:* $25 per term part-time.

Financial Aid Of all full-time matriculated undergraduates who enrolled in 2003, 250 Federal Work-Study jobs (averaging $2500). 50 state and other part-time jobs (averaging $2500).

Applying *Options:* early admission, deferred entrance. *Application deadline:* rolling (freshmen), rolling (transfers). *Notification:* continuous (freshmen).

Admissions Contact Ms. Lynda Schwartz, Admissions Coordinator, Muskegon Community College, 221 South Quarterline Road, Muskegon, MI 49442-1493. *Phone:* 231-773-9131 Ext. 366.

NORTH CENTRAL MICHIGAN COLLEGE
Petoskey, Michigan

Admissions Contact Ms. Julieanne Tobin, Director of Enrollment Management, North Central Michigan College, 1515 Howard Street, Petoskey, MI 49770-8717. *Phone:* 231-439-6511. *Toll-free phone:* 888-298-6605. *E-mail:* advisor@ncmc.cc.mi.us.

NORTHWESTERN MICHIGAN COLLEGE
Traverse City, Michigan

- **State and locally supported** 2-year, founded 1951
- **Calendar** semesters
- **Degree** certificates and associate
- **Small-town** 180-acre campus
- **Coed,** 4,609 undergraduate students, 44% full-time, 59% women, 41% men

Northwestern Michigan College (continued)

Undergraduates 2,011 full-time, 2,598 part-time. Students come from 19 states and territories, 2% are from out of state, 0.5% African American, 0.8% Asian American or Pacific Islander, 1% Hispanic American, 2% Native American, 11% transferred in, 5% live on campus. *Retention:* 49% of 2002 full-time freshmen returned.

Freshmen *Admission:* 2,521 applied, 2,397 admitted, 1,036 enrolled.

Faculty *Total:* 307, 30% full-time. *Student/faculty ratio:* 23:1.

Majors Accounting technology and bookkeeping; agricultural production related; airline pilot and flight crew; art; automobile/automotive mechanics technology; biology/biological sciences; business administration and management; business and personal/financial services marketing; business automation/technology/data entry; business, management, and marketing related; child care and support services management; commercial and advertising art; communication/speech communication and rhetoric; corrections and criminal justice related; crop production; culinary arts; dental assisting; drafting and design technology; dramatic/theatre arts; education; electrical, electronic and communications engineering technology; electromechanical and instrumentation and maintenance technologies related; engineering; English; executive assistant/executive secretary; forest/forest resources management; health professions related; industrial technology; landscaping and groundskeeping; legal administrative assistant/secretary; liberal arts and sciences/liberal studies; machine shop technology; management information systems; marine science/merchant marine officer; marine transportation related; maritime science; marketing/marketing management; mathematics; medical/clinical assistant; music; nursing (registered nurse training); physical sciences; social sciences; turf and turfgrass management.

Academic Programs *Special study options:* academic remediation for entering students, adult/continuing education programs, advanced placement credit, cooperative education, distance learning, honors programs, independent study, internships, part-time degree program, services for LD students, summer session for credit.

Library Mark and Helen Osterlin Library plus 1 other with 97,458 titles, 9,820 serial subscriptions, 3,000 audiovisual materials, an OPAC, a Web page.

Computers on Campus 625 computers available on campus for general student use. A campuswide network can be accessed from student residence rooms and from off campus. Internet access, online (class) registration, at least one staffed computer lab available.

Student Life *Housing Options:* coed, men-only, women-only. Campus housing is university owned. *Activities and Organizations:* drama/theater group, student-run newspaper, radio station, choral group, Residence Hall Council, honors fraternity, student newspaper, student magazine, student radio station. *Campus security:* 24-hour emergency response devices and patrols, student patrols, late-night transport/escort service, controlled dormitory access, well-lit campus. *Student services:* health clinic, personal/psychological counseling.

Athletics *Intramural sports:* basketball M/W, football M/W, golf M/W, sailing M(c)/W(c), skiing (downhill) M(c)/W(c), softball M/W, volleyball M/W.

Standardized Tests *Required:* ACT COMPASS (for placement).

Costs (2005–06) *Tuition:* area resident $2339 full-time, $69 per contact hour part-time; state resident $4077 full-time, $120 per contact hour part-time; nonresident $5087 full-time, $149 per contact hour part-time. Full-time tuition and fees vary according to location. Part-time tuition and fees vary according to course load and location. *Required fees:* $383 full-time, $10 per contact hour part-time, $16 per term part-time. *Room and board:* $6285. Room and board charges vary according to board plan and housing facility. *Payment plans:* installment, deferred payment. *Waivers:* employees or children of employees.

Financial Aid Of all full-time matriculated undergraduates who enrolled in 2003, 66 Federal Work-Study jobs (averaging $1606). 5 state and other part-time jobs (averaging $1000).

Applying *Options:* common application, early admission, deferred entrance. *Application fee:* $15. *Required for some:* high school transcript. *Recommended:* minimum 2.0 GPA. *Application deadline:* rolling (freshmen), rolling (transfers). *Notification:* continuous until 8/28 (freshmen).

Admissions Contact Mr. James Bensley, Coordinator of Admissions, Northwestern Michigan College, 1701 East Front Street, Traverse City, MI 49686. *Phone:* 231-995-1034. *Toll-free phone:* 800-748-0566. *Fax:* 616-955-1339. *E-mail:* welcome@nmc.edu.

OAKLAND COMMUNITY COLLEGE
Bloomfield Hills, Michigan

- **State and locally supported** 2-year, founded 1964, part of Michigan Department of Career Development
- **Calendar** semesters
- **Degrees** certificates, associate, and postbachelor's certificates
- **Suburban** 540-acre campus with easy access to Detroit
- **Endowment** $1.2 million
- **Coed,** 24,296 undergraduate students, 29% full-time, 58% women, 42% men

Undergraduates 7,159 full-time, 17,137 part-time. Students come from 12 states and territories, 73 other countries, 15% African American, 2% Asian American or Pacific Islander, 2% Hispanic American, 0.6% Native American, 8% international, 2% transferred in.

Freshmen *Admission:* 2,510 applied, 2,510 admitted, 1,614 enrolled.

Faculty *Total:* 926, 30% full-time. *Student/faculty ratio:* 26:1.

Majors Accounting; allied health diagnostic, intervention, and treatment professions related; applied horticulture; architectural engineering technology; architecture; automobile/automotive mechanics technology; aviation/airway management; business administration and management; business automation/technology/data entry; cabinetmaking and millwork; carpentry; ceramic arts and ceramics; child care and support services management; clinical/medical laboratory science and allied professions related; computer and information sciences; computer programming; computer technology/computer systems technology; construction management; consumer merchandising/retailing management; corrections and criminal justice related; cosmetology; court reporting; criminal justice/law enforcement administration; criminal justice/police science; culinary arts; dental hygiene; diagnostic medical sonography and ultrasound technology; electrical, electronic and communications engineering technology; electromechanical technology; electroneurodiagnostic/electroencephalographic technology; emergency medical technology (EMT paramedic); engineering; entrepreneurship; environmental control technologies related; fashion merchandising; fine arts related; fire science; foodservice systems administration; forensic science and technology; general studies; gerontology; graphic design; health and physical education related; health/health care administration; health professions related; heating, air conditioning and refrigeration technology; histologic technician; hotel/motel administration; industrial electronics technology; industrial technology; interior design; international business/trade/commerce; kinesiology and exercise science; landscape architecture; landscaping and groundskeeping; legal assistant/paralegal; liberal arts and sciences and humanities related; liberal arts and sciences/liberal studies; library assistant; machine tool technology; management information systems and services related; management science; manufacturing technology; marketing related; massage therapy; mechanical drafting and CAD/CADD; medical/clinical assistant; medical radiologic technology; medical transcription; mental and social health services and allied professions related; nuclear medical technology; nursing (licensed practical/vocational nurse training); nursing (registered nurse training); office management; operations management; ornamental horticulture; pharmacy technician; photography; precision metal working related; pre-engineering; radio and television broadcasting technology; respiratory care therapy; restaurant/food services management; robotics technology; salon/beauty salon management; sport and fitness administration; surgical technology; tool and die technology; welding technology; woodworking related.

Academic Programs *Special study options:* academic remediation for entering students, adult/continuing education programs, advanced placement credit, cooperative education, distance learning, English as a second language, internships, off-campus study, part-time degree program, services for LD students, study abroad, summer session for credit.

Library Main Library plus 5 others with 243,137 titles, 2,139 serial subscriptions, 8,315 audiovisual materials, an OPAC, a Web page.

Computers on Campus 2065 computers available on campus for general student use. A campuswide network can be accessed from off campus. Internet access, online (class) registration, at least one staffed computer lab available.

Student Life *Housing:* college housing not available. *Activities and Organizations:* drama/theater group, choral group, Phi Theta Kappa, International Student Organization, organizations related to student majors. *Campus security:* 24-hour emergency response devices, late-night transport/escort service. *Student services:* personal/psychological counseling, women's center.

Athletics Member NJCAA. *Intercollegiate sports:* basketball M(s)/W(s), cross-country running M(s)/W(s), golf M(s), soccer M, softball W(s), tennis W(s), volleyball W(s). *Intramural sports:* basketball M/W, racquetball M/W, tennis W, volleyball M/W.

Standardized Tests *Required:* ACT COMPASS (for placement).

Costs (2004–05) *Tuition:* area resident $1611 full-time, $54 per credit hour part-time; state resident $2727 full-time, $91 per credit hour part-time; nonresident $3825 full-time, $128 per credit hour part-time. *Required fees:* $70 full-time, $35 per term part-time. *Waivers:* senior citizens and employees or children of employees.

Financial Aid Of all full-time matriculated undergraduates who enrolled in 2003, 135 Federal Work-Study jobs (averaging $2800). 70 state and other part-time jobs (averaging $2800).

Applying *Options:* deferred entrance. *Recommended:* high school transcript, interview. *Application deadline:* rolling (freshmen), rolling (transfers). *Notification:* continuous (freshmen).

Admissions Contact Dr. Maurice H. McCall, Registrar and Director of Enrollment Services, Oakland Community College, 2480 Opdyke Road, Bloomfield Hills, MI 48304-2266. *Phone:* 248-341-2186.

SAGINAW CHIPPEWA TRIBAL COLLEGE
Mount Pleasant, Michigan

Admissions Contact Tracy Reed, Director of Admissions/Registrar, Saginaw Chippewa Tribal College, 2274 Enterprise Drive, Mount Pleasant, MI 48858. *Phone:* 989-775-4123.

ST. CLAIR COUNTY COMMUNITY COLLEGE
Port Huron, Michigan

- **State and locally supported** 2-year, founded 1923, part of Michigan Department of Education
- **Calendar** semesters
- **Degree** certificates and associate
- **Small-town** 25-acre campus with easy access to Detroit
- **Endowment** $2.5 million
- **Coed**

Student Life *Campus security:* patrols by security until 10 p.m.

Athletics Member NJCAA.

Standardized Tests *Recommended:* ACT (for placement).

Costs (2004–05) *Tuition:* area resident $2106 full-time; state resident $3216 full-time; nonresident $4295 full-time. *Required fees:* $58 full-time.

Financial Aid Of all full-time matriculated undergraduates who enrolled in 2003, 61 Federal Work-Study jobs (averaging $2543). 14 state and other part-time jobs (averaging $2113).

Applying *Options:* early admission. *Required:* high school transcript.

Admissions Contact Mr. Pete Lacey, Registrar, St. Clair County Community College, 323 Erie Street, PO Box 5015, PO Box 5015, Port Huron, MI 48061-5015. *Phone:* 810-989-5500. *Toll-free phone:* 800-553-2427. *Fax:* 810-984-4730. *E-mail:* enrollment@stclair.cc.mi.us.

SCHOOLCRAFT COLLEGE
Livonia, Michigan

- **District-supported** 2-year, founded 1961, part of Michigan Department of Education
- **Calendar** semesters
- **Degree** certificates and associate
- **Suburban** 183-acre campus with easy access to Detroit
- **Endowment** $8.9 million
- **Coed,** 10,213 undergraduate students, 33% full-time, 57% women, 43% men

Undergraduates 3,377 full-time, 6,836 part-time. Students come from 4 states and territories, 1% are from out of state, 8% African American, 2% Asian American or Pacific Islander, 2% Hispanic American, 0.7% Native American, 0.2% international, 13% transferred in.

Freshmen *Admission:* 3,570 applied, 3,570 admitted, 1,657 enrolled. *Average high school GPA:* 2.44.

Faculty *Total:* 435, 23% full-time, 4% with terminal degrees. *Student/faculty ratio:* 27:1.

Majors Accounting; administrative assistant and secretarial science; biomedical technology; business administration and management; child care and support services management; commercial and advertising art; computer programming; computer technology/computer systems technology; corrections; criminal justice/police science; culinary arts; data processing and data processing technology; drafting and design technology; education; electrical, electronic and communications engineering technology; electromechanical technology; emergency medical technology (EMT paramedic); engineering; entrepreneurship; environmental engineering technology; fire science; health information/medical records technology; industrial technology; laser and optical technology; liberal arts and sciences/liberal studies; marketing/marketing management; mechanical engineering/mechanical technology; medical laboratory technology; metallurgical technology; music teacher education; nursing (registered nurse training); occupational therapist assistant; physical sciences related; radio and television broadcasting technology; robotics technology; welding technology.

Academic Programs *Special study options:* academic remediation for entering students, accelerated degree program, adult/continuing education programs, advanced placement credit, cooperative education, distance learning, part-time degree program, services for LD students, summer session for credit.

Library Bradner Library plus 1 other with 96,216 titles, 634 serial subscriptions, an OPAC.

Computers on Campus 775 computers available on campus for general student use. A campuswide network can be accessed from off campus. Internet access, online (class) registration, at least one staffed computer lab available.

Student Life *Housing:* college housing not available. *Activities and Organizations:* drama/theater group, student-run newspaper, choral group, Student Activities Board, Ski Club, student newspaper, Music Club, Phi Theta Kappa, national fraternities. *Campus security:* 24-hour emergency response devices and patrols, late-night transport/escort service. *Student services:* health clinic, women's center, legal services.

Athletics Member NJCAA. *Intercollegiate sports:* basketball M(s)/W(s), cross-country running W(s), golf M(s)/W(s), soccer M(s)/W(s), volleyball W(s).

Standardized Tests *Required:* ACT or CPT (for placement). *Recommended:* ACT (for placement).

Costs (2004–05) *Tuition:* area resident $1875 full-time, $63 per credit hour part-time; state resident $2790 full-time, $93 per credit hour part-time; nonresident $4110 full-time, $137 per credit hour part-time. *Required fees:* $110 full-time. *Waivers:* senior citizens and employees or children of employees.

Financial Aid Of all full-time matriculated undergraduates who enrolled in 2003, 42 Federal Work-Study jobs (averaging $1722).

Applying *Options:* early admission, deferred entrance. *Required for some:* high school transcript. *Recommended:* high school transcript. *Application deadline:* rolling (freshmen), rolling (transfers).

Admissions Contact Ms. Cheryl Wright, Dean of Student Services, Schoolcraft College, 18600 Hagerty Road, Livonia, MI 48152-2696. *Phone:* 734-462-4426. *Fax:* 734-462-4553. *E-mail:* admissions@schoolcraft.edu.

SOUTHWESTERN MICHIGAN COLLEGE
Dowagiac, Michigan

- **State and locally supported** 2-year, founded 1964, part of Michigan Department of Education
- **Calendar** semesters
- **Degree** certificates and associate
- **Rural** 240-acre campus
- **Coed,** 2,777 undergraduate students, 37% full-time, 65% women, 35% men

Undergraduates 1,032 full-time, 1,745 part-time. Students come from 4 states and territories, 29 other countries, 9% are from out of state, 8% African American, 0.9% Asian American or Pacific Islander, 3% Hispanic American, 0.9% Native American, 3% international.

Freshmen *Admission:* 491 applied, 491 admitted, 491 enrolled.

Faculty *Total:* 161, 29% full-time, 16% with terminal degrees. *Student/faculty ratio:* 19:1.

Majors Accounting technology and bookkeeping; administrative assistant and secretarial science; airframe mechanics and aircraft maintenance technology; automobile/automotive mechanics technology; business administration and management; business, management, and marketing related; child care and support services management; computer and information sciences related; computer programming; data entry/microcomputer applications related; drafting and design technology; electrical and electronic engineering technologies related; engineering technology; general studies; graphic and printing equipment operation/production; health professions related; heavy/industrial equipment maintenance technologies related; industrial mechanics and maintenance technology; legal assistant/paralegal; liberal arts and sciences and humanities related; liberal arts and sciences/liberal studies; machine shop technology; merchandising, sales, and marketing operations related (general); nursing (registered nurse training); precision production related; precision systems maintenance and repair technologies related; welding technology.

Academic Programs *Special study options:* academic remediation for entering students, accelerated degree program, adult/continuing education programs, advanced placement credit, cooperative education, distance learning, double majors, English as a second language, honors programs, independent study, internships, part-time degree program, services for LD students, student-designed majors, summer session for credit.

Library Fred L. Mathews Library with 38,000 titles, 1,100 serial subscriptions, 1,750 audiovisual materials, an OPAC, a Web page.

Computers on Campus 200 computers available on campus for general student use. A campuswide network can be accessed. Internet access, at least one staffed computer lab available.

Student Life *Housing:* college housing not available. *Activities and Organizations:* drama/theater group, student-run newspaper, television station, choral group, Phi Theta Kappa. *Campus security:* 24-hour emergency response devices, evening police patrols.

Athletics *Intramural sports:* archery M/W, badminton M/W, basketball M/W, cross-country running M/W, football M/W, golf M/W, racquetball M/W, skiing (cross-country) M/W, skiing (downhill) M/W, soccer M/W, softball M/W, track and field M/W, volleyball M/W, weight lifting M/W.

Standardized Tests *Recommended:* SAT or ACT (for placement).

Costs (2005–06) *Tuition:* area resident $2101 full-time; state resident $2659 full-time; nonresident $2868 full-time. Full-time tuition and fees vary according to course load. Part-time tuition and fees vary according to course load. *Required fees:* $465 full-time. *Payment plan:* installment. *Waivers:* senior citizens and employees or children of employees.

Southwestern Michigan College (continued)

Financial Aid Of all full-time matriculated undergraduates who enrolled in 2003, 125 Federal Work-Study jobs (averaging $1000). 75 state and other part-time jobs (averaging $1000).

Applying *Options:* electronic application, deferred entrance. *Required:* high school transcript. *Required for some:* letters of recommendation, interview. *Application deadline:* rolling (freshmen), rolling (transfers). *Notification:* continuous until 9/10 (freshmen).

Admissions Contact Dr. Margaret Hay, Dean of Academic Support, Southwestern Michigan College, 58900 Cherry Grove Road, Dowagiac, MI 49047. *Phone:* 269-782-1000 Ext. 1306. *Toll-free phone:* 800-456-8675. *Fax:* 269-782-1331. *E-mail:* cchurch@swmich.edu.

WASHTENAW COMMUNITY COLLEGE
Ann Arbor, Michigan

- **State and locally supported** 2-year, founded 1965
- **Calendar** semesters
- **Degree** certificates and associate
- **Suburban** 235-acre campus with easy access to Detroit
- **Endowment** $3.5 million
- **Coed**

Faculty *Student/faculty ratio:* 17:1.

Student Life *Campus security:* 24-hour emergency response devices and patrols, late-night transport/escort service.

Standardized Tests *Recommended:* SAT or ACT (for admission), SAT or ACT (for placement).

Costs (2004–05) *Tuition:* area resident $1800 full-time, $60 per credit hour part-time; state resident $3030 full-time, $101 per credit hour part-time; nonresident $4020 full-time, $134 per credit hour part-time. *Required fees:* $210 full-time, $7 per credit hour part-time.

Financial Aid Of all full-time matriculated undergraduates who enrolled in 2003, 120 Federal Work-Study jobs (averaging $4100).

Applying *Options:* common application, electronic application, early admission, deferred entrance. *Required for some:* high school transcript.

Admissions Contact Mr. Bradley D. Hoth, Admissions Representative, Washtenaw Community College, 4800 East Huron River Drive, PO Box D-1, Ann Arbor, MI 48106. *Phone:* 734-973-3676. *Fax:* 734-677-5408.

WAYNE COUNTY COMMUNITY COLLEGE DISTRICT
Detroit, Michigan

- **State and locally supported** 2-year, founded 1967
- **Calendar** semesters
- **Degree** certificates and associate
- **Urban** campus
- **Coed,** 11,673 undergraduate students, 25% full-time, 73% women, 27% men

Undergraduates 2,912 full-time, 8,761 part-time.

Freshmen *Admission:* 8,265 admitted.

Faculty *Total:* 400, 38% full-time.

Majors Accounting; administrative assistant and secretarial science; automobile/automotive mechanics technology; avionics maintenance technology; business administration and management; child development; clinical/medical laboratory technology; computer science; court reporting; criminal justice/law enforcement administration; criminal justice/police science; culinary arts; data processing and data processing technology; dental hygiene; dietetics; drafting and design technology; education; electrical, electronic and communications engineering technology; emergency medical technology (EMT paramedic); engineering technology; environmental engineering technology; finance; industrial technology; labor and industrial relations; legal administrative assistant/secretary; liberal arts and sciences/liberal studies; marketing/marketing management; medical administrative assistant and medical secretary; natural resources management and policy; Near and Middle Eastern studies; nursing (registered nurse training); occupational therapy; veterinary technology; welding technology.

Academic Programs *Special study options:* academic remediation for entering students, adult/continuing education programs, cooperative education, English as a second language, honors programs, part-time degree program, summer session for credit.

Library Learning Resource Center with 70,000 titles, an OPAC.

Computers on Campus 118 computers available on campus for general student use.

Student Life *Housing:* college housing not available. *Activities and Organizations:* student-run newspaper, national sororities. *Campus security:* 24-hour emergency response devices.

Athletics Member NJCAA. *Intercollegiate sports:* basketball M(s)/W(s), golf M(s)/W(s), volleyball W(s).

Standardized Tests *Required:* ACT ASSET (for placement).

Costs (2004–05) *Tuition:* $54 per credit hour part-time.

Financial Aid Of all full-time matriculated undergraduates who enrolled in 2003, 239 Federal Work-Study jobs (averaging $2360). 147 state and other part-time jobs (averaging $1200).

Applying *Options:* common application, early admission, deferred entrance. *Application fee:* $10. *Application deadline:* rolling (freshmen), rolling (transfers).

Admissions Contact Office of Enrollment Management and Student Services, Wayne County Community College District, 801 West Fort Street, Detroit, MI 48226-2539. *Phone:* 313-496-2600. *Fax:* 313-961-2791. *E-mail:* caafjh@wccc.edu.

▶ See page 560 for a narrative description.

WEST SHORE COMMUNITY COLLEGE
Scottville, Michigan

Admissions Contact Mr. Tom Bell, Director of Admissions, West Shore Community College, PO Box 277, 3000 North Stiles Road, Scottville, MI 49454-0277. *Phone:* 231-845-6211 Ext. 3117. *Fax:* 231-845-3944. *E-mail:* admissions@westshore.cc.mi.us.

MICRONESIA

COLLEGE OF MICRONESIA-FSM
Kolonia Pohnpei, Federated States of Micronesia, Micronesia

Admissions Contact Mr. Wilson J. Kalio, Coordinator of Admissions and Records, College of Micronesia-FSM, PO Box 159, Kolonia Pohnpei, FM 96941-0159, Micronesia. *Phone:* 691-320-2480 Ext. 6200. *Fax:* 691-320-2479.

MINNESOTA

ACADEMY COLLEGE
Minneapolis, Minnesota

- **Proprietary** primarily 2-year
- **Calendar** quarters
- **Degrees** certificates, associate, and bachelor's
- **Urban** campus
- **Coed,** 320 undergraduate students

Undergraduates Students come from 5 states and territories.

Faculty *Total:* 54, 7% full-time. *Student/faculty ratio:* 8:1.

Majors Accounting; airline pilot and flight crew; aviation/airway management; business administration and management; business/commerce; commercial and advertising art; computer and information sciences; computer and information sciences and support services related; computer and information systems security; computer graphics; computer programming; computer science; computer systems networking and telecommunications; data processing and data processing technology; design and visual communications; finance; graphic design; intermedia/multimedia; management information systems; office management; sales, distribution and marketing; system administration; system, networking, and LAN/WAN management; web/multimedia management and webmaster; web page, digital/multimedia and information resources design.

Academic Programs *Special study options:* academic remediation for entering students, accelerated degree program, adult/continuing education programs, advanced placement credit, cooperative education, distance learning, double majors, English as a second language, honors programs, internships, part-time degree program, services for LD students, summer session for credit.

Library Learning Resource Center plus 1 other with 1,309 titles, 22 serial subscriptions, 88 audiovisual materials, an OPAC, a Web page.

Computers on Campus 75 computers available on campus for general student use. A campuswide network can be accessed. Internet access, online (class) registration, at least one staffed computer lab available.

Student Life *Housing:* college housing not available.

Costs (2004–05) *Tuition:* $16,415 full-time, $299 per credit part-time. Full-time tuition and fees vary according to course level. Part-time tuition and fees vary according to course level. *Required fees:* $280 full-time. *Payment plan:* installment.

Applying *Options:* common application, electronic application, early admission, deferred entrance. *Application fee:* $30. *Required:* high school transcript, interview. *Notification:* continuous (freshmen).

Admissions Contact Mr. Paul Burhhartzmeyer, Director of Admissions, Academy College, 1101 East 78th Street, Suite 100, Minneapolis, MN 55420. *Phone:* 952-851-0066. *Toll-free phone:* 800-292-9149. *Fax:* 952-851-0094. *E-mail:* admissions@academycollege.edu.

ALEXANDRIA TECHNICAL COLLEGE
Alexandria, Minnesota

- **State-supported** 2-year, founded 1961, part of Minnesota State Colleges and Universities System
- **Calendar** semesters
- **Degree** certificates, diplomas, and associate
- **Small-town** 40-acre campus
- **Coed,** 2,028 undergraduate students, 80% full-time, 44% women, 56% men

Undergraduates 1,621 full-time, 407 part-time. Students come from 14 states and territories, 4% are from out of state, 0.3% African American, 0.8% Asian American or Pacific Islander, 0.4% Hispanic American, 0.5% Native American.

Freshmen *Admission:* 1,934 applied, 1,338 admitted.

Faculty *Total:* 115, 72% full-time, 32% with terminal degrees. *Student/faculty ratio:* 20:1.

Majors Accounting; administrative assistant and secretarial science; banking and financial support services; business administration and management; CAD/CADD drafting/design technology; carpentry; cartography; child care and support services management; child care provision; clinical/medical laboratory technology; commercial and advertising art; computer and information sciences; computer programming (specific applications); computer systems networking and telecommunications; computer technology/computer systems technology; criminal justice/police science; diesel mechanics technology; dietitian assistant; farm and ranch management; fashion merchandising; health and physical education; hospitality administration; hotel/motel administration; human services; hydraulics and fluid power technology; industrial technology; interior design; legal administrative assistant/secretary; legal assistant/paralegal; machine tool technology; marine maintenance and ship repair technology; marketing/marketing management; masonry; mechanical drafting and CAD/CADD; medical administrative assistant and medical secretary; medical insurance coding; medical reception; medical transcription; nursing assistant/aide and patient care assistant; nursing (licensed practical/vocational nurse training); office management; office occupations and clerical services; operations management; phlebotomy; receptionist; selling skills and sales; small business administration; small engine mechanics and repair technology; telecommunications technology; truck and bus driver/commercial vehicle operation; web page, digital/multimedia and information resources design; welding technology.

Academic Programs *Special study options:* academic remediation for entering students, advanced placement credit, distance learning, double majors, internships, part-time degree program, services for LD students.

Library Learning Resource Center with 16,636 titles, 346 serial subscriptions, 1,219 audiovisual materials, an OPAC, a Web page.

Computers on Campus 467 computers available on campus for general student use. A campuswide network can be accessed from off campus. Internet access, online (class) registration, at least one staffed computer lab available. Computer purchase or lease plan available.

Student Life *Housing:* college housing not available. *Activities and Organizations:* VICA (Vocational Industrial Clubs of America) Skills USA, BPA (Business Professionals of America), DECA (Delta Epsilon Club), Student Senate, Phi Theta Kappa. *Campus security:* late-night transport/escort service, security cameras inside and outside. *Student services:* personal/psychological counseling.

Athletics *Intercollegiate sports:* basketball M, volleyball M/W. *Intramural sports:* basketball M/W, football M/W, golf M/W, softball M/W, volleyball M/W.

Standardized Tests *Required:* ACT COMPASS (for placement).

Costs (2005–06) *Tuition:* state resident $3863 full-time, $121 per credit part-time; nonresident $7726 full-time, $240 per credit part-time. Full-time tuition and fees vary according to class time and reciprocity agreements. Part-time tuition and fees vary according to class time and reciprocity agreements. *Required fees:* $296 full-time, $9 per credit part-time. *Payment plan:* deferred payment. *Waivers:* senior citizens and employees or children of employees.

Financial Aid Of all full-time matriculated undergraduates who enrolled in 2003, 94 Federal Work-Study jobs (averaging $1871).

Applying *Options:* common application, electronic application, early admission. *Application fee:* $20. *Required:* high school transcript, interview. *Application deadline:* rolling (freshmen).

Admissions Contact Mr. Bruce Smith, Associate Dean of Marketing and Enrollment, Alexandria Technical College, 1601 Jefferson Street, Alexandria, MN 56308. *Phone:* 320-762-0221 Ext. 4483. *Toll-free phone:* 888-234-1222. *Fax:* 320-762-4603. *E-mail:* michelleg@alextech.edu.

ANOKA-RAMSEY COMMUNITY COLLEGE
Coon Rapids, Minnesota

- **State-supported** 2-year, founded 1965, part of Minnesota State Colleges and Universities System
- **Calendar** semesters
- **Degree** certificates and associate
- **Suburban** 100-acre campus with easy access to Minneapolis-St. Paul
- **Coed,** 5,606 undergraduate students, 43% full-time, 65% women, 35% men

Undergraduates 2,436 full-time, 3,170 part-time. 1% are from out of state, 4% African American, 3% Asian American or Pacific Islander, 0.7% Hispanic American, 0.7% Native American, 0.4% international.

Freshmen *Admission:* 3,190 applied, 3,190 admitted.

Faculty *Total:* 210, 41% full-time. *Student/faculty ratio:* 27:1.

Majors Accounting; administrative assistant and secretarial science; business administration and management; cartography; clinical laboratory science/medical technology; computer science; computer systems networking and telecommunications; computer/technical support; liberal arts and sciences/liberal studies; marketing/marketing management; nursing (registered nurse training); physical therapist assistant; pre-engineering; system administration.

Academic Programs *Special study options:* academic remediation for entering students, accelerated degree program, advanced placement credit, cooperative education, distance learning, honors programs, independent study, internships, off-campus study, part-time degree program, services for LD students, study abroad, summer session for credit. *ROTC:* Air Force (c).

Library Coon Rapids Campus Library with 40,651 titles, 232 serial subscriptions, 1,517 audiovisual materials, an OPAC, a Web page.

Computers on Campus 600 computers available on campus for general student use. A campuswide network can be accessed from off campus. Internet access, online (class) registration, at least one staffed computer lab available.

Student Life *Housing:* college housing not available. *Activities and Organizations:* drama/theater group, student-run newspaper, choral group, Phi Theta Kappa, Student Senate, student newspaper, International Student Club, Inter-Varsity Christian Fellowship. *Campus security:* 24-hour emergency response devices and patrols, late-night transport/escort service. *Student services:* personal/psychological counseling.

Athletics Member NJCAA. *Intercollegiate sports:* baseball M, basketball M/W, volleyball W. *Intramural sports:* basketball M/W, bowling M/W, football M/W, golf M/W, ice hockey M/W, soccer M/W, softball M/W, tennis M/W, volleyball M/W.

Costs (2004–05) *Tuition:* state resident $3073 full-time, $102 per credit part-time; nonresident $6145 full-time, $205 per credit part-time. Full-time tuition and fees vary according to course load and reciprocity agreements. Part-time tuition and fees vary according to course load and reciprocity agreements. *Required fees:* $383 full-time, $13 per credit part-time. *Waivers:* senior citizens and employees or children of employees.

Financial Aid Of all full-time matriculated undergraduates who enrolled in 2003, 88 Federal Work-Study jobs (averaging $4000). 106 state and other part-time jobs (averaging $4000).

Applying *Options:* early admission, deferred entrance. *Application fee:* $20. *Required for some:* high school transcript. *Application deadline:* rolling (freshmen), rolling (transfers). *Notification:* continuous (freshmen).

Admissions Contact Mr. Tom Duval, Admissions Counselor, Anoka-Ramsey Community College, 11200 Mississippi Boulevard NW, Coon Rapids, MN 55433. *Phone:* 763-422-3458. *Fax:* 763-422-3341. *E-mail:* matthew.crawford@anolcaramsey.edu.

ANOKA-RAMSEY COMMUNITY COLLEGE, CAMBRIDGE CAMPUS
Cambridge, Minnesota

- **State-supported** 2-year, part of Minnesota State Colleges and Universities System
- **Calendar** semesters
- **Degree** certificates and associate
- **Small-town** campus
- **Coed,** 1,777 undergraduate students, 31% full-time, 69% women, 31% men

Undergraduates 550 full-time, 1,227 part-time. 1% are from out of state, 1% African American, 0.8% Asian American or Pacific Islander, 2% Hispanic American, 0.9% Native American.

Freshmen *Admission:* 965 applied, 965 admitted.

Faculty *Total:* 67, 34% full-time. *Student/faculty ratio:* 25:1.

Majors Accounting; administrative assistant and secretarial science; business administration and management; cartography; clinical laboratory science/medical technology; computer science; computer systems networking and tele-

Anoka-Ramsey Community College, Cambridge Campus (continued)
communications; computer/technical support; liberal arts and sciences/liberal studies; marketing/marketing management; nursing (registered nurse training); pre-engineering.

Academic Programs *Special study options:* academic remediation for entering students, accelerated degree program, advanced placement credit, cooperative education, distance learning, honors programs, independent study, internships, off-campus study, part-time degree program, services for LD students, study abroad, summer session for credit. *ROTC:* Air Force (c).

Library Cambridge Campus Library with 18,927 titles, 122 serial subscriptions, 1,536 audiovisual materials, an OPAC, a Web page.

Computers on Campus 200 computers available on campus for general student use. A campuswide network can be accessed from off campus. Internet access, online (class) registration, at least one staffed computer lab available.

Student Life *Housing:* college housing not available.

Athletics Member NJCAA. *Intercollegiate sports:* baseball M, basketball M/W, volleyball W. *Intramural sports:* bowling M/W, golf M/W, volleyball M/W.

Costs (2004–05) *Tuition:* state resident $3073 full-time, $102 per credit part-time; nonresident $6145 full-time, $205 per credit part-time. Full-time tuition and fees vary according to course load and reciprocity agreements. Part-time tuition and fees vary according to course load and reciprocity agreements. *Required fees:* $383 full-time, $13 per credit part-time. *Waivers:* senior citizens and employees or children of employees.

Applying *Options:* early admission, deferred entrance. *Application fee:* $20. *Required for some:* high school transcript. *Application deadline:* rolling (freshmen), rolling (transfers). *Notification:* continuous (freshmen).

Admissions Contact Admissions/Records, Anoka-Ramsey Community College, Cambridge Campus, 300 Polk Street South, Cambridge, MN 55008. *Phone:* 763-689-7027. *Fax:* 763-689-7050. *E-mail:* matthew.crawford@anokaramsey.edu.

ANOKA TECHNICAL COLLEGE
Anoka, Minnesota

- **State-supported** 2-year, founded 1967, part of Minnesota State Colleges and Universities System
- **Calendar** semesters
- **Degree** certificates, diplomas, and associate
- **Small-town** campus with easy access to Minneapolis-St. Paul
- **Coed**

Faculty *Student/faculty ratio:* 16:1.

Student Life *Campus security:* late-night transport/escort service.

Costs (2004–05) *Tuition:* state resident $3632 full-time, $121 per credit part-time; nonresident $7264 full-time, $242 per credit part-time. Full-time tuition and fees vary according to program and reciprocity agreements. Part-time tuition and fees vary according to program and reciprocity agreements. *Required fees:* $420 full-time, $14 per credit part-time.

Applying *Options:* common application, electronic application, deferred entrance. *Application fee:* $20. *Required:* high school transcript. *Required for some:* interview.

Admissions Contact Mr. Robert Hoenie, Director of Admissions, Anoka Technical College, 1355 West Highway 10, Anoka, MN 55303. *Phone:* 763-576-4746. *Fax:* 763-576-4756. *E-mail:* info@ank.tec.mn.us.

ARGOSY UNIVERSITY/TWIN CITIES
Eagan, Minnesota

- **Proprietary** upper-level, founded 1987, part of Education Management Corporation
- **Calendar** semesters
- **Degrees** bachelor's, master's, doctoral, and post-master's certificates
- **Suburban** campus with easy access to Minneapolis and St. Paul
- **Coed, primarily women**
- 86% of applicants were admitted

Faculty *Student/faculty ratio:* 12:1.

Student Life *Campus security:* 24-hour emergency response devices.

Costs (2004–05) *Tuition:* $11,400 full-time, $380 per credit hour part-time. *Required fees:* $200 full-time, $4 per term part-time.

Financial Aid Of all full-time matriculated undergraduates who enrolled in 2003, 8 Federal Work-Study jobs (averaging $2219).

Applying *Application fee:* $50.

Admissions Contact Jeanne Stoneking, Vice President of Enrollment Services, Argosy University/Twin Cities, 1515 Central Parkway, Eagan, MN 55121. *Phone:* 651-846-3331. *Toll-free phone:* 888-844-2004. *Fax:* 651-994-7956. *E-mail:* tcadmissions@argosyu.edu.

▶ **See page 450 for a narrative description.**

BROWN COLLEGE
Mendota Heights, Minnesota

Admissions Contact Mr. Mike Price, Director of Admissions, Brown College, 1440 Northland Drive, Mendota Heights, MN 55120. *Phone:* 651-905-3400. *Toll-free phone:* 800-6BROWN6. *Fax:* 651-905-3510.

CENTRAL LAKES COLLEGE
Brainerd, Minnesota

- **State-supported** 2-year, founded 1938, part of Minnesota State Colleges and Universities System
- **Calendar** semesters
- **Degree** certificates, diplomas, and associate
- **Small-town** 1-acre campus
- **Coed**

Faculty *Student/faculty ratio:* 17:1.

Student Life *Campus security:* late-night transport/escort service.

Athletics Member NJCAA.

Standardized Tests *Recommended:* ACT (for placement).

Applying *Options:* deferred entrance. *Application fee:* $20.

Admissions Contact Charlotte Daniels, Director of Admissions, Central Lakes College, 501 West College Drive, Brainerd, MN 56401-3904. *Phone:* 218-828-2525. *Toll-free phone:* 800-933-0346 Ext. 2586. *E-mail:* rtretter@clcmn.edu.

CENTURY COLLEGE
White Bear Lake, Minnesota

- **State-supported** 2-year, founded 1970, part of Minnesota State Colleges and Universities System
- **Calendar** semesters
- **Degree** certificates, diplomas, and associate
- **Suburban** 150-acre campus with easy access to Minneapolis-St. Paul
- **Endowment** $1.0 million
- **Coed,** 8,650 undergraduate students, 48% full-time, 59% women, 41% men

Undergraduates 4,138 full-time, 4,512 part-time. Students come from 28 states and territories, 60 other countries, 8% African American, 9% Asian American or Pacific Islander, 2% Hispanic American, 0.8% Native American, 2% international, 21% transferred in. *Retention:* 48% of 2002 full-time freshmen returned.

Freshmen *Admission:* 3,003 applied, 3,003 admitted, 1,832 enrolled.

Faculty *Total:* 388, 46% full-time. *Student/faculty ratio:* 24:1.

Majors Accounting; administrative assistant and secretarial science; autobody/collision and repair technology; automobile/automotive mechanics technology; business administration and management; computer engineering technology; cosmetology; criminal justice/police science; dental assisting; dental hygiene; dental laboratory technology; diesel mechanics technology; educational/instructional media design; emergency medical technology (EMT paramedic); environmental studies; fashion merchandising; general retailing/wholesaling; heating, air conditioning, ventilation and refrigeration maintenance technology; industrial technology; interior design; legal administrative assistant/secretary; liberal arts and sciences/liberal studies; machine tool technology; management information systems; medical administrative assistant and medical secretary; medical/clinical assistant; medical radiologic technology; music management and merchandising; nursing (registered nurse training); orthotics/prosthetics; pharmacy technician; quality control technology; selling skills and sales; small engine mechanics and repair technology; social work; substance abuse/addiction counseling.

Academic Programs *Special study options:* academic remediation for entering students, adult/continuing education programs, advanced placement credit, distance learning, double majors, English as a second language, external degree program, honors programs, internships, part-time degree program, services for LD students, summer session for credit. *ROTC:* Air Force (c).

Library Century College Main Library plus 1 other with 56,867 titles, 486 serial subscriptions, 3,569 audiovisual materials, an OPAC, a Web page.

Computers on Campus 985 computers available on campus for general student use. A campuswide network can be accessed from off campus. Internet access, online (class) registration, at least one staffed computer lab available.

Student Life *Housing:* college housing not available. *Activities and Organizations:* drama/theater group, student-run newspaper, choral group, Student Senate, Phi Theta Kappa, Dental Assistants Club, Creative Arts Alliance, Christian Club. *Campus security:* late-night transport/escort service, day patrols. *Student services:* personal/psychological counseling, women's center.

Athletics *Intramural sports:* badminton M/W, basketball M/W, golf M/W, soccer M/W, softball M/W.

Costs (2004–05) *Tuition:* state resident $3267 full-time, $109 per credit part-time; nonresident $6504 full-time, $217 per credit part-time. *Required fees:* $366 full-time, $12 per credit part-time. *Payment plan:* installment. *Waivers:* senior citizens and employees or children of employees.

Financial Aid Of all full-time matriculated undergraduates who enrolled in 2003, 70 Federal Work-Study jobs (averaging $2379). 123 state and other part-time jobs (averaging $1908).

Applying *Application fee:* $20. *Required:* high school transcript. *Application deadline:* rolling (freshmen), rolling (transfers).

Admissions Contact Ms. Christine Paulos, Admissions Director, Century College, 3300 Century Avenue North, White Bear Lake, MN 55110. *Phone:* 651-779-2619. *Toll-free phone:* 800-228-1978. *Fax:* 651-779-5810.

DAKOTA COUNTY TECHNICAL COLLEGE
Rosemount, Minnesota

- **State-supported** 2-year, founded 1970, part of Minnesota State Colleges and Universities System
- **Calendar** semesters
- **Degree** certificates, diplomas, and associate
- **Suburban** 100-acre campus with easy access to Minneapolis and St. Paul
- **Endowment** $1.3 million
- **Coed**

Faculty *Student/faculty ratio:* 20:1.

Student Life *Campus security:* 24-hour emergency response devices, late-night transport/escort service.

Athletics Member NJCAA.

Standardized Tests *Required for some:* ACCUPLACER/CPT.

Costs (2004–05) *Tuition:* state resident $3702 full-time, $116 per semester hour part-time; nonresident $7405 full-time, $231 per semester hour part-time. Full-time tuition and fees vary according to reciprocity agreements. Part-time tuition and fees vary according to reciprocity agreements. *Required fees:* $538 full-time, $17 per semester hour part-time. *Payment plans:* installment, deferred payment.

Financial Aid Of all full-time matriculated undergraduates who enrolled in 2003, 33 Federal Work-Study jobs (averaging $2372). 85 state and other part-time jobs (averaging $1279).

Applying *Options:* common application, electronic application. *Application fee:* $20. *Required for some:* high school transcript, letters of recommendation. *Recommended:* interview.

Admissions Contact Mr. Patrick Lair, Admissions Director, Dakota County Technical College, 1300 145th Street East, Rosemount, MN 55068. *Phone:* 651-423-8399. *Toll-free phone:* 877-YES-DCTC Ext. 302 (in-state); 877-YES-DCTC (out-of-state). *Fax:* 651-423-8775. *E-mail:* admissions@dctc.mnscu.edu.

DULUTH BUSINESS UNIVERSITY
Duluth, Minnesota

- **Proprietary** 2-year, founded 1891
- **Calendar** quarters
- **Degree** diplomas and associate
- **Urban** campus
- **Coed, primarily women**

Admissions Contact Mr. Mark Traux, Director of Admissions, Duluth Business University, 4724 Mike Colalillo Drive, Duluth, MN 55807. *Phone:* 800-777-8406. *Toll-free phone:* 800-777-8406.

DUNWOODY COLLEGE OF TECHNOLOGY
Minneapolis, Minnesota

- **Independent** 2-year, founded 1914
- **Calendar** quarters
- **Degree** diplomas and associate
- **Urban** 12-acre campus
- **Endowment** $31.2 million
- **Coed, primarily men**

Faculty *Student/faculty ratio:* 15:1.

Student Life *Campus security:* 24-hour emergency response devices, late-night transport/escort service.

Costs (2004–05) *Tuition:* $20,742 full-time, $227 per credit part-time. *Required fees:* $1155 full-time, $1155 per year part-time.

Financial Aid Of all full-time matriculated undergraduates who enrolled in 2003, 20 Federal Work-Study jobs (averaging $3000). 20 state and other part-time jobs (averaging $3000).

Applying *Options:* electronic application, early admission, deferred entrance. *Application fee:* $50. *Required:* high school transcript, interview, institutional entrance test.

Admissions Contact Ms. Yun-bok Christenson, Records Coordinator, Dunwoody College of Technology, 818 Dunwoody Boulevard, Minneapolis, MN 55403. *Phone:* 612-374-5800 Ext. 2019. *Toll-free phone:* 800-292-4625. *Fax:* 612-374-4128. *E-mail:* aylreb@dunwoody.tec.mn.us.

FOND DU LAC TRIBAL AND COMMUNITY COLLEGE
Cloquet, Minnesota

Admissions Contact Ms. Nancy Gordon, Admissions Representative, Fond du Lac Tribal and Community College, 2101 14th Street, Cloquet, MN 55720. *Phone:* 218-879-0808. *Toll-free phone:* 800-657-3712. *Fax:* 218-879-0814. *E-mail:* admissions@fdltcc.edu.

GLOBE COLLEGE
Oakdale, Minnesota

- **Private** primarily 2-year, founded 1885
- **Calendar** quarters
- **Degrees** certificates, diplomas, associate, and bachelor's
- **Suburban** campus
- **Coed,** 997 undergraduate students

Undergraduates Students come from 1 other country, 8% are from out of state.

Faculty *Student/faculty ratio:* 15:1.

Majors Accounting; administrative assistant and secretarial science; business administration and management; business systems networking/ telecommunications; computer graphics; computer software engineering; computer systems networking and telecommunications; cosmetology; information technology; intermedia/multimedia; kinesiology and exercise science; legal administrative assistant/secretary; massage therapy; medical administrative assistant; music related; paralegal/legal assistant; physician assistant; taxation; veterinary technology; web page, digital/multimedia and information resources design.

Academic Programs *Special study options:* academic remediation for entering students, accelerated degree program, adult/continuing education programs, cooperative education, distance learning, internships, part-time degree program, summer session for credit.

Library Globe College Library with 1,432 titles, 106 serial subscriptions, 13 audiovisual materials, an OPAC, a Web page.

Computers on Campus 180 computers available on campus for general student use. Internet access, online (class) registration, at least one staffed computer lab available.

Standardized Tests *Required:* CPAt (for admission).

Costs (2004–05) *Tuition:* $11,340 full-time, $315 per credit part-time. Full-time tuition and fees vary according to course load. Part-time tuition and fees vary according to course load. *Payment plan:* installment. *Waivers:* employees or children of employees.

Applying *Options:* common application, electronic application. *Application fee:* $50. *Required:* high school transcript, interview. *Required for some:* essay or personal statement. *Application deadline:* 10/6 (freshmen).

Admissions Contact Mr. Rob Harker, Director of Admissions, Globe College, 7166 10th Street North, Oakdale, MN 55128. *Phone:* 651-714-7313. *Fax:* 651-730-5151. *E-mail:* admissions@globecollege.edu.

HENNEPIN TECHNICAL COLLEGE
Brooklyn Park, Minnesota

Admissions Contact Mrs. Joy Bodin, Director of Admissions, Hennepin Technical College, 9000 Brooklyn Boulevard, Brooklyn Park, MN 55445. *Phone:* 763-488-2415. *Fax:* 763-550-2119.

HERZING COLLEGE
Minneapolis, Minnesota

- **Proprietary** primarily 2-year, part of Herzing College
- **Calendar** semesters
- **Degrees** certificates, diplomas, associate, and bachelor's
- **Suburban** 1-acre campus
- **Coed, primarily women,** 346 undergraduate students, 59% full-time, 79% women, 21% men

Undergraduates 205 full-time, 141 part-time. Students come from 3 states and territories, 1% are from out of state, 14% African American, 5% Asian American or Pacific Islander, 1% Hispanic American, 1% Native American.

Freshmen *Admission:* 128 applied, 96 admitted, 96 enrolled.

Faculty *Total:* 32, 66% full-time, 25% with terminal degrees. *Student/faculty ratio:* 14:1.

Herzing College (continued)

Majors Computer and information sciences; computer systems networking and telecommunications; dental assisting; dental hygiene; management information systems; massage therapy; medical/clinical assistant; medical insurance coding.

Academic Programs *Special study options:* adult/continuing education programs, distance learning, internships, part-time degree program.

Library Main Library plus 1 other.

Computers on Campus 50 computers available on campus for general student use. Internet access, at least one staffed computer lab available.

Student Life *Housing:* college housing not available. *Campus security:* 24-hour emergency response devices, late-night transport/escort service. *Student services:* personal/psychological counseling.

Standardized Tests *Required:* ACCUPLACER (for admission). *Recommended:* SAT and SAT Subject Tests or ACT (for admission), SAT II: Writing Test (for admission).

Costs (2004–05) *Tuition:* $9680 full-time, $303 per credit part-time. Full-time tuition and fees vary according to course load and program. Part-time tuition and fees vary according to course load and program. *Required fees:* $25 full-time. *Payment plan:* installment. *Waivers:* employees or children of employees.

Applying *Required:* high school transcript, interview.

Admissions Contact Mr. James Decker, Director of Admissions, Herzing College, 5700 West Broadway, Minneapolis, MN 55428. *Phone:* 763-231-3152. *Toll-free phone:* 800-878-DRAW. *Fax:* 763-535-9205. *E-mail:* info@mpls.herzing.edu.

HIBBING COMMUNITY COLLEGE
Hibbing, Minnesota

- **State-supported** 2-year, founded 1916, part of Minnesota State Colleges and Universities System
- **Calendar** semesters
- **Degree** certificates, diplomas, and associate
- **Small-town** 100-acre campus
- **Coed,** 1,832 undergraduate students

Undergraduates Students come from 20 states and territories, 11% are from out of state, 2% African American, 0.3% Asian American or Pacific Islander, 0.4% Hispanic American, 1% Native American, 10% live on campus.

Freshmen *Admission:* 1,029 applied, 1,029 admitted.

Faculty *Total:* 86, 73% full-time, 2% with terminal degrees. *Student/faculty ratio:* 17:1.

Majors Administrative assistant and secretarial science; business administration and management; clinical/medical laboratory technology; computer and information sciences; computer installation and repair technology; computer systems networking and telecommunications; criminal justice/police science; culinary arts; dental assisting; drafting and design technology; educational/instructional media design; foodservice systems administration; legal administrative assistant/secretary; liberal arts and sciences/liberal studies; medical administrative assistant and medical secretary; nursing (registered nurse training); pre-engineering; selling skills and sales; web page, digital/multimedia and information resources design.

Academic Programs *Special study options:* academic remediation for entering students, adult/continuing education programs, advanced placement credit, cooperative education, distance learning, internships, off-campus study, part-time degree program, services for LD students, study abroad, summer session for credit.

Library Hibbing Community College Library with 19,536 titles, 190 serial subscriptions, a Web page.

Computers on Campus 150 computers available on campus for general student use. A campuswide network can be accessed from off campus. At least one staffed computer lab available.

Student Life *Activities and Organizations:* drama/theater group, student-run newspaper, choral group, Phi Theta Kappa, Performing Music Ensembles Club, Student Senate, Engineering Club, VICA. *Campus security:* late-night transport/escort service. *Student services:* personal/psychological counseling.

Athletics Member NJCAA. *Intercollegiate sports:* baseball M, basketball M/W, football M, golf M/W, softball W, volleyball W. *Intramural sports:* basketball M/W, bowling M/W, field hockey M/W, skiing (cross-country) M/W, skiing (downhill) M/W, tennis M/W, volleyball M/W.

Standardized Tests *Recommended:* SAT or ACT (for placement).

Costs (2004–05) *Tuition:* state resident $3300 full-time, $110 per credit part-time; nonresident $3300 full-time, $110 per credit part-time. Full-time tuition and fees vary according to course load and reciprocity agreements. Part-time tuition and fees vary according to course load and reciprocity agreements. *Required fees:* $458 full-time, $15 per credit part-time. *Room and board:* $4275. *Payment plan:* installment. *Waivers:* senior citizens and employees or children of employees.

Applying *Options:* common application, early admission, deferred entrance. *Application fee:* $20. *Required:* high school transcript. *Application deadline:* rolling (freshmen), rolling (transfers). *Notification:* continuous (freshmen).

Admissions Contact Ms. Shelly Corradi, Admissions, Hibbing Community College, 1515 East 25th Street, Hibbing, MN 55746. *Phone:* 218-262-7207. *Toll-free phone:* 800-224-4HCC. *Fax:* 218-262-6717. *E-mail:* admissions@hcc.mnscu.edu.

HIGH-TECH INSTITUTE
St. Louis Park, Minnesota

Admissions Contact 5100 Gamble Drive, St. Louis Park, MN 55416. *Toll-free phone:* 800-987-0110.

INVER HILLS COMMUNITY COLLEGE
Inver Grove Heights, Minnesota

Admissions Contact Ms. Susan Merkling, Admissions, Inver Hills Community College, 2500 East 80th Street, Inver Grove Heights, MN 55076-3224. *Phone:* 651-450-8501. *Fax:* 651-450-8677. *E-mail:* shandwe@inverhills.mnscu.edu.

ITASCA COMMUNITY COLLEGE
Grand Rapids, Minnesota

- **State-supported** 2-year, founded 1922, part of Minnesota State Colleges and Universities System
- **Calendar** semesters
- **Degree** certificates, diplomas, and associate
- **Rural** 24-acre campus
- **Endowment** $3.5 million
- **Coed,** 1,117 undergraduate students, 77% full-time, 50% women, 50% men

Undergraduates 865 full-time, 252 part-time. Students come from 10 states and territories, 2 other countries, 3% are from out of state, 0.8% African American, 0.7% Asian American or Pacific Islander, 0.8% Hispanic American, 3% Native American, 2% international. *Retention:* 54% of 2002 full-time freshmen returned.

Freshmen *Admission:* 617 applied, 617 admitted, 506 enrolled. *Average high school GPA:* 2.78.

Faculty *Total:* 71, 61% full-time, 3% with terminal degrees. *Student/faculty ratio:* 16:1.

Majors Accounting; American Indian/Native American studies; business administration and management; chemical engineering; civil engineering; computer engineering; computer engineering related; education; education (K-12); engineering related; engineering science; engineering technology; environmental studies; fish/game management; forestry; forestry technology; general studies; geography; human services; liberal arts and sciences/liberal studies; mechanical engineering; natural resources/conservation; natural resources management and policy; nuclear engineering; nursing (licensed practical/vocational nurse training); pre-engineering; psychology; wildlife and wildlands science and management.

Academic Programs *Special study options:* academic remediation for entering students, adult/continuing education programs, advanced placement credit, cooperative education, double majors, independent study, internships, off-campus study, part-time degree program, services for LD students, study abroad, summer session for credit.

Library Itasca Community College Library with 28,790 titles, 280 serial subscriptions, 2,443 audiovisual materials, an OPAC, a Web page.

Computers on Campus 250 computers available on campus for general student use. A campuswide network can be accessed from student residence rooms and from off campus. Internet access, online (class) registration, at least one staffed computer lab available.

Student Life *Housing Options:* Campus housing is university owned. *Activities and Organizations:* student association, Circle K, Student Ambassadors, Minority Student Club, Psychology Club. *Campus security:* late-night transport/escort service, evening patrols by trained security personnel.

Athletics Member NJCAA. *Intercollegiate sports:* baseball M, basketball M/W, football M, softball W, volleyball W, wrestling M. *Intramural sports:* basketball M, bowling M/W, golf W, softball M/W, table tennis M/W, volleyball M/W.

Costs (2004–05) *Tuition:* state resident $3790 full-time, $118 per credit part-time; nonresident $7581 full-time, $237 per credit part-time. Full-time tuition and fees vary according to reciprocity agreements. Part-time tuition and fees vary according to reciprocity agreements. *Required fees:* $481 full-time, $15 per credit part-time. *Room and board:* room only: $2680. *Payment plans:* installment, deferred payment. *Waivers:* employees or children of employees.

Financial Aid Of all full-time matriculated undergraduates who enrolled in 2003, 63 Federal Work-Study jobs (averaging $1350). 155 state and other part-time jobs (averaging $910).

Applying *Options:* common application, electronic application. *Application fee:* $20. *Required:* high school transcript. *Required for some:* 3 letters of recommendation. *Application deadline:* rolling (freshmen). *Notification:* continuous (freshmen).
Admissions Contact Ms. Candace Perry, Director of Enrollment Services, Itasca Community College, 1851 East Highway 169, Grand Rapids, MN 55744. *Phone:* 218-327-4464 Ext. 4464. *Toll-free phone:* 800-996-6422 Ext. 4464. *Fax:* 218-327-4350. *E-mail:* iccinfo@it.cc.mn.us.

ITT TECHNICAL INSTITUTE
Eden Prairie, Minnesota

- **Proprietary** 2-year, founded 2003
- **Calendar** quarters
- **Coed**

Admissions Contact 8911 Columbine Road, Eden Prairie, MN 55347.

LAKE SUPERIOR COLLEGE
Duluth, Minnesota

- **State-supported** 2-year, founded 1995, part of Minnesota State Colleges and Universities System
- **Calendar** semesters
- **Degree** certificates, diplomas, and associate
- **Urban** 105-acre campus
- **Endowment** $148,576
- **Coed,** 4,281 undergraduate students, 56% full-time, 59% women, 41% men

Undergraduates 2,411 full-time, 1,870 part-time. 12% are from out of state, 1% African American, 1% Asian American or Pacific Islander, 0.9% Hispanic American, 2% Native American.
Freshmen *Admission:* 1,171 admitted.
Faculty *Total:* 256, 38% full-time, 4% with terminal degrees. *Student/faculty ratio:* 20:1.
Majors Accounting; airline pilot and flight crew; architectural drafting and CAD/CADD; automobile/automotive mechanics technology; business administration and management; carpentry; civil engineering technology; clinical/medical laboratory technology; computer programming (specific applications); computer technology/computer systems technology; dental hygiene; electrical, electronic and communications engineering technology; electrician; emergency medical technology (EMT paramedic); executive assistant/executive secretary; fire science; fire services administration; human resources management and services related; legal administrative assistant/secretary; legal assistant/paralegal; liberal arts and sciences and humanities related; liberal arts and sciences/liberal studies; machine tool technology; management information systems; mechanical drafting and CAD/CADD; medical administrative assistant and medical secretary; medical radiologic technology; nursing (registered nurse training); occupational therapist assistant; physical therapist assistant; quality control and safety technologies related; respiratory care therapy; selling skills and sales; surgical technology.
Academic Programs *Special study options:* academic remediation for entering students, advanced placement credit, distance learning, double majors, English as a second language, independent study, internships, part-time degree program, services for LD students, summer session for credit.
Library Harold P. Erickson Library with 2,869 titles, 100 serial subscriptions, 280 audiovisual materials, an OPAC, a Web page.
Computers on Campus 230 computers available on campus for general student use. A campuswide network can be accessed from off campus. Internet access, at least one staffed computer lab available.
Student Life *Housing:* college housing not available. *Activities and Organizations:* Business Professionals of America, Gus Gus Players, Art Club, All Nations, PTK Phi Theta Kappa. *Campus security:* late-night transport/escort service, 15-hour patrols by trained security personnel. *Student services:* health clinic, personal/psychological counseling, women's center.
Athletics *Intramural sports:* basketball M/W, softball M/W, volleyball M/W.
Standardized Tests *Required:* ASAP, ACCUPLACER (for placement).
Costs (2004–05) *Tuition:* state resident $3015 full-time, $101 per credit part-time; nonresident $6030 full-time, $201 per credit part-time. *Required fees:* $463 full-time, $15 per credit part-time. *Payment plans:* installment, deferred payment. *Waivers:* senior citizens and employees or children of employees.
Financial Aid Of all full-time matriculated undergraduates who enrolled in 2003, 100 Federal Work-Study jobs (averaging $2380). 100 state and other part-time jobs (averaging $2380).
Applying *Options:* early admission, deferred entrance. *Application fee:* $20. *Required for some:* high school transcript. *Application deadline:* rolling (freshmen), rolling (transfers). *Notification:* continuous (freshmen).

Admissions Contact Ms. Melissa Leno, Director of Admissions, Lake Superior College, 2101 Trinity Road, Duluth, MN 55811. *Phone:* 218-723-4895. *Toll-free phone:* 800-432-2884. *Fax:* 218-733-5945. *E-mail:* enroll@lsc.mnscu.edu.

LEECH LAKE TRIBAL COLLEGE
Cass Lake, Minnesota

Admissions Contact Admissions Director, Leech Lake Tribal College, PO Box 180, Cass Lake, MN 56633-0180. *Phone:* 218-335-4200. *Toll-free phone:* 888-829-4240.

McNALLY SMITH COLLEGE OF MUSIC
Saint Paul, Minnesota

- **Proprietary** 2-year, founded 1985
- **Calendar** semesters
- **Degree** certificates, diplomas, and associate
- **Urban** campus
- **Coed,** 454 undergraduate students, 87% full-time, 15% women, 85% men

Undergraduates 396 full-time, 58 part-time. Students come from 23 states and territories, 46% are from out of state, 5% African American, 0.2% Asian American or Pacific Islander, 0.9% Hispanic American, 0.7% Native American, 1% international, 8% transferred in.
Freshmen *Admission:* 136 enrolled.
Faculty *Total:* 86, 60% full-time. *Student/faculty ratio:* 6:1.
Majors Engineering technologies related; music management and merchandising.
Academic Programs *Special study options:* adult/continuing education programs, advanced placement credit, independent study, internships, summer session for credit.
Library McNally Smith College Learning Center plus 1 other.
Computers on Campus 20 computers available on campus for general student use. Internet access, at least one staffed computer lab available.
Student Life *Housing:* college housing not available. *Activities and Organizations:* student-run newspaper, Student Advisory Board, Audio Engineering Society, Minnesota Songwriters Association. *Campus security:* 24-hour emergency response devices. *Student services:* personal/psychological counseling.
Standardized Tests *Recommended:* ACT (for admission).
Costs (2004–05) *Tuition:* $15,725 full-time, $590 per credit part-time. Full-time tuition and fees vary according to course load and program. Part-time tuition and fees vary according to course load and program. No tuition increase for student's term of enrollment. *Required fees:* $75 full-time. *Payment plan:* installment. *Waivers:* employees or children of employees.
Applying *Application fee:* $25. *Required:* essay or personal statement, high school transcript, 2 letters of recommendation, interview. *Required for some:* audition. *Application deadline:* 8/1 (freshmen). *Notification:* 8/1 (freshmen).
Admissions Contact Ms. Debbie Sandridge, Director of Admissions, McNally Smith College of Music, 19 Exchange Street East, St. Paul, MN 55101. *Phone:* 651-291-0177 Ext. 2382. *Toll-free phone:* 800-594-9500. *Fax:* 651-291-0366. *E-mail:* dsandridge@mcnallysmith.edu.

MESABI RANGE COMMUNITY AND TECHNICAL COLLEGE
Virginia, Minnesota

- **State-supported** 2-year, founded 1918, part of Minnesota State Colleges and Universities System
- **Calendar** semesters
- **Degree** certificates, diplomas, and associate
- **Small-town** 30-acre campus
- **Coed,** 1,509 undergraduate students, 65% full-time, 48% women, 52% men

Undergraduates 988 full-time, 521 part-time. Students come from 6 states and territories, 10% live on campus.
Faculty *Total:* 77, 64% full-time. *Student/faculty ratio:* 18:1.
Majors Administrative assistant and secretarial science; business/commerce; computer graphics; computer/information technology services administration related; computer programming related; computer programming (specific applications); computer software and media applications related; computer systems networking and telecommunications; electrical/electronics equipment installation and repair; human services; information technology; instrumentation technology; liberal arts and sciences/liberal studies; pre-engineering; substance abuse/addiction counseling; web page, digital/multimedia and information resources design.
Academic Programs *Special study options:* academic remediation for entering students, adult/continuing education programs, advanced placement credit,

Mesabi Range Community and Technical College (continued)
cooperative education, internships, off-campus study, part-time degree program, services for LD students, student-designed majors, summer session for credit.

Library Mesabi Library with 23,000 titles, 167 serial subscriptions.

Computers on Campus 120 computers available on campus for general student use. At least one staffed computer lab available.

Student Life *Housing Options:* coed. Campus housing is provided by a third party. *Activities and Organizations:* drama/theater group, choral group, Student Senate, Human Services Club, Native American Club, Student Life Club, Black Awareness Club. *Campus security:* late-night transport/escort service. *Student services:* personal/psychological counseling.

Athletics Member NJCAA. *Intercollegiate sports:* baseball M, basketball M/W, football M, softball W, volleyball W. *Intramural sports:* badminton M/W, basketball M/W, bowling M/W, field hockey M/W, football M/W, golf M/W, ice hockey M/W, skiing (cross-country) M/W, skiing (downhill) M/W, tennis M/W, volleyball M/W.

Standardized Tests *Recommended:* ACT (for placement).

Costs (2004–05) *Tuition:* state resident $3889 full-time, $130 per credit hour part-time; nonresident $3889 full-time, $130 per credit hour part-time. *Room and board:* room only: $2752. *Waivers:* employees or children of employees.

Financial Aid Of all full-time matriculated undergraduates who enrolled in 2003, 209 Federal Work-Study jobs (averaging $1725). 100 state and other part-time jobs (averaging $2100).

Applying *Options:* common application, early admission, deferred entrance. *Application fee:* $20. *Application deadline:* rolling (freshmen), rolling (transfers). *Notification:* continuous (freshmen).

Admissions Contact Ms. Brenda K. Kochevar, Enrollment Services Director, Mesabi Range Community and Technical College, 1001 Chestnut Street West, Virginia, MN 55792. *Phone:* 218-749-0314. *Toll-free phone:* 800-657-3860. *Fax:* 218-749-0318.

MINNEAPOLIS BUSINESS COLLEGE
Roseville, Minnesota

- **Proprietary** 2-year, founded 1874, part of The Bradford School
- **Degree** diplomas and associate
- **Coed, primarily women**

Faculty *Student/faculty ratio:* 30:1.

Student Life *Campus security:* 24-hour emergency response devices.

Applying *Application fee:* $50.

Admissions Contact Mr. David Whitman, President, Minneapolis Business College, 1711 West County Road B, Roseville, MN 55113. *Phone:* 651-604-4118. *Toll-free phone:* 800-279-5200. *Fax:* 651-636-8185. *E-mail:* info@mplsbusinesscollege.com.

MINNEAPOLIS COMMUNITY AND TECHNICAL COLLEGE
Minneapolis, Minnesota

- **State-supported** 2-year, founded 1965, part of Minnesota State Colleges and Universities System
- **Calendar** semesters
- **Degree** certificates, diplomas, and associate
- **Urban** 4-acre campus
- **Coed**, 7,091 undergraduate students

Undergraduates Students come from 45 states and territories, 81 other countries, 3% are from out of state, 25% African American, 5% Asian American or Pacific Islander, 3% Hispanic American, 2% Native American, 3% international. *Retention:* 51% of 2002 full-time freshmen returned.

Freshmen *Admission:* 4,022 applied, 3,931 admitted.

Faculty *Total:* 367, 28% full-time. *Student/faculty ratio:* 23:1.

Majors Accounting technology and bookkeeping; administrative assistant and secretarial science; aircraft powerplant technology; airframe mechanics and aircraft maintenance technology; automobile/automotive mechanics technology; avionics maintenance technology; business administration and management; business/commerce; child guidance; cinematography and film/video production; commercial and advertising art; computer and information sciences related; computer programming; criminal justice/police science; criminal justice/safety; culinary arts; human services; information science/studies; legal administrative assistant/secretary; liberal arts and sciences/liberal studies; nursing (registered nurse training); parks, recreation and leisure; substance abuse/addiction counseling; web/multimedia management and webmaster; web page, digital/multimedia and information resources design.

Academic Programs *Special study options:* academic remediation for entering students, adult/continuing education programs, advanced placement credit, distance learning, English as a second language, honors programs, independent

study, internships, off-campus study, part-time degree program, services for LD students, student-designed majors, summer session for credit.

Library Minneapolis Community and Technical College Library with 60,352 titles, 600 serial subscriptions, 1,374 audiovisual materials, an OPAC.

Computers on Campus 150 computers available on campus for general student use. A campuswide network can be accessed. Internet access, online (class) registration, at least one staffed computer lab available.

Student Life *Housing:* college housing not available. *Activities and Organizations:* drama/theater group, student-run newspaper, choral group, Student Senate, National Vocational-Technical Honor Society, Phi Theta Kappa, Association of Black Collegiates, Soccer Club. *Campus security:* 24-hour emergency response devices, late-night transport/escort service. *Student services:* personal/psychological counseling, women's center.

Athletics Member NJCAA. *Intercollegiate sports:* basketball M/W, golf M/W. *Intramural sports:* soccer M(c)/W(c).

Costs (2004–05) *Tuition:* state resident $3886 full-time, $118 per credit part-time; nonresident $7411 full-time, $235 per credit part-time. Full-time tuition and fees vary according to program and reciprocity agreements. Part-time tuition and fees vary according to program and reciprocity agreements. *Required fees:* $361 full-time, $12 per credit part-time. *Payment plan:* installment. *Waivers:* senior citizens and employees or children of employees.

Financial Aid Of all full-time matriculated undergraduates who enrolled in 2003, 188 Federal Work-Study jobs (averaging $5000). 190 state and other part-time jobs (averaging $5000).

Applying *Options:* early admission, deferred entrance. *Application fee:* $20. *Required:* high school transcript. *Application deadline:* 8/31 (freshmen), rolling (transfers). *Notification:* continuous (freshmen).

Admissions Contact Dena Russell, Interim Director of Admissions, Minneapolis Community and Technical College, 1501 Hennepin Avenue, Minneapolis, MN 55403. *Phone:* 612-659-6206. *Toll-free phone:* 800-247-0911. *Fax:* 612-659-1357.

MINNESOTA SCHOOL OF BUSINESS-BROOKLYN CENTER
Brooklyn Center, Minnesota

- **Proprietary** primarily 2-year, founded 1989
- **Calendar** quarters
- **Degrees** certificates, diplomas, associate, and bachelor's
- **Suburban** campus
- **Coed**, 809 undergraduate students

Faculty *Student/faculty ratio:* 13:1.

Majors Accounting; administrative assistant and secretarial science; business administration and management; business systems networking/ telecommunications; computer graphics; computer software engineering; computer systems networking and telecommunications; cosmetology; information technology; intermedia/multimedia; legal administrative assistant/secretary; massage therapy; medical administrative assistant; music related; paralegal/legal assistant; physician assistant; taxation; veterinary technology; web page, digital/multimedia and information resources design.

Academic Programs *Special study options:* academic remediation for entering students, accelerated degree program, adult/continuing education programs, cooperative education, distance learning, internships, part-time degree program.

Library Minnesota School of Business—Brooklyn Center with 1,534 titles, 99 serial subscriptions, 53 audiovisual materials, an OPAC, a Web page.

Computers on Campus 179 computers available on campus for general student use. A campuswide network can be accessed. Internet access, at least one staffed computer lab available.

Student Life *Housing:* college housing not available.

Standardized Tests *Required:* CPAt (for admission).

Costs (2004–05) *Tuition:* $11,340 full-time, $315 per credit part-time. Full-time tuition and fees vary according to course load. Part-time tuition and fees vary according to course load. *Payment plan:* installment. *Waivers:* employees or children of employees.

Applying *Options:* common application, electronic application. *Application fee:* $50. *Required:* high school transcript, interview. *Required for some:* essay or personal statement. *Application deadline:* 10/6 (freshmen).

Admissions Contact Mr. Jeffrey Georgeson, Director of Admissions, Minnesota School of Business-Brooklyn Center, 5910 Shingle Creek Parkway, Brooklyn Center, MN 55430. *Phone:* 763-585-7777.

MINNESOTA SCHOOL OF BUSINESS-PLYMOUTH
Minneapolis, Minnesota

- **Proprietary** primarily 2-year, founded 2002
- **Calendar** quarters

- **Degrees** certificates, diplomas, associate, and bachelor's
- **Suburban** 3-acre campus
- **Coed,** 500 undergraduate students

Faculty *Student/faculty ratio:* 10:1.
Majors Accounting; administrative assistant and secretarial science; business administration and management; business systems networking/ telecommunications; computer graphics; computer software engineering; computer systems networking and telecommunications; cosmetology; information technology; intermedia/multimedia; kinesiology and exercise science; legal administrative assistant/secretary; massage therapy; medical administrative assistant; music related; paralegal/legal assistant; physician assistant; taxation; veterinary technology; web page, digital/multimedia and information resources design.
Academic Programs *Special study options:* academic remediation for entering students, accelerated degree program, adult/continuing education programs, cooperative education, distance learning, internships, part-time degree program, summer session for credit.
Library Minnesota School of Business-Plymouth with 1,189 titles, 106 serial subscriptions, 12 audiovisual materials, an OPAC, a Web page.
Computers on Campus 62 computers available on campus for general student use. A campuswide network can be accessed. Internet access, at least one staffed computer lab available.
Student Life *Housing:* college housing not available.
Standardized Tests *Required:* CPAt (for admission).
Costs (2004–05) *Tuition:* $11,340 full-time, $315 per credit part-time. Full-time tuition and fees vary according to course load. Part-time tuition and fees vary according to course load. *Payment plan:* installment.
Applying *Options:* common application, electronic application. *Application fee:* $50. *Required:* high school transcript, interview. *Required for some:* essay or personal statement. *Application deadline:* 10/6 (freshmen).
Admissions Contact Mr. Don Baker, Director of Admissions, Minnesota School of Business-Plymouth, 1455 County Road 101 N, Plymouth, MN 55447. *Phone:* 763-476-2000. *Fax:* 763-476-1000.

MINNESOTA SCHOOL OF BUSINESS-RICHFIELD
Richfield, Minnesota

- **Proprietary** primarily 2-year, founded 1877
- **Calendar** quarters
- **Degrees** certificates, diplomas, associate, and bachelor's
- **Urban** 3-acre campus with easy access to Minneapolis-St. Paul
- **Coed,** 944 undergraduate students

Undergraduates Students come from 5 states and territories.
Faculty *Student/faculty ratio:* 14:1.
Majors Accounting; administrative assistant and secretarial science; business administration and management; business systems networking/ telecommunications; computer graphics; computer software engineering; computer systems networking and telecommunications; cosmetology; information science/studies; intermedia/multimedia; kinesiology and exercise science; legal administrative assistant/secretary; legal assistant/paralegal; massage therapy; medical/clinical assistant; medical office management; music related; taxation; veterinary/animal health technology; web page, digital/multimedia and information resources design.
Academic Programs *Special study options:* academic remediation for entering students, accelerated degree program, adult/continuing education programs, cooperative education, distance learning, internships, part-time degree program, summer session for credit.
Library Minnesota School of Business-Richfield with 2,420 titles, 93 serial subscriptions, 93 audiovisual materials, an OPAC, a Web page.
Computers on Campus 168 computers available on campus for general student use. A campuswide network can be accessed from off campus. Internet access, online (class) registration, at least one staffed computer lab available.
Student Life *Housing:* college housing not available.
Standardized Tests *Required:* CPAt (for admission).
Costs (2004–05) *Tuition:* $11,340 full-time, $315 per credit part-time. Full-time tuition and fees vary according to course load. Part-time tuition and fees vary according to course load. *Payment plan:* installment. *Waivers:* employees or children of employees.
Applying *Options:* common application, electronic application. *Application fee:* $50. *Required:* high school transcript, interview. *Required for some:* essay or personal statement. *Application deadline:* 10/6 (freshmen).
Admissions Contact Ms. Patricia Murray, Director of Admissions, Minnesota School of Business-Richfield, 1401 West 76th Street, Richfield, MN 55430. *Phone:* 612-861-2000 Ext. 720. *Toll-free phone:* 800-752-4223. *Fax:* 612-861-5548. *E-mail:* pmurray@msbcollege.com.

MINNESOTA SCHOOL OF BUSINESS-ST. CLOUD
Waite Park, Minnesota

- **Proprietary** primarily 2-year
- **Degrees** certificates, diplomas, associate, and bachelor's
- **Coed,** 226 undergraduate students

Faculty *Student/faculty ratio:* 13:1.
Academic Programs *Special study options:* academic remediation for entering students, accelerated degree program, adult/continuing education programs, cooperative education, distance learning, internships, part-time degree program, summer session for credit.
Library Minnesota School of Business-St. Cloud with 724 titles, 88 serial subscriptions, an OPAC, a Web page.
Computers on Campus 52 computers available on campus for general student use. A campuswide network can be accessed. Internet access available.
Student Life *Housing:* college housing not available.
Standardized Tests *Required:* CPAt (for admission).
Costs (2004–05) *Tuition:* $11,340 full-time, $315 per credit part-time. Full-time tuition and fees vary according to course load. Part-time tuition and fees vary according to course load. *Payment plan:* installment. *Waivers:* employees or children of employees.
Applying *Options:* common application, electronic application. *Application fee:* $50. *Required:* high school transcript, interview. *Required for some:* essay or personal statement. *Application deadline:* 10/6 (freshmen).
Admissions Contact Mr. Jim Beck, Director of Admissions, Minnesota School of Business-St. Cloud, 1201 2nd Street S, Waite Park, MN 56387. *Phone:* 320-257-2000. *Toll-free phone:* 866-403-3333. *E-mail:* rkuhl@msbcollege.edu.

MINNESOTA SCHOOL OF BUSINESS-SHAKOPEE
Shakopee, Minnesota

- **Proprietary** primarily 2-year
- **Degrees** certificates, diplomas, associate, and bachelor's
- **Coed**

Faculty *Student/faculty ratio:* 12:1.
Academic Programs *Special study options:* academic remediation for entering students, accelerated degree program, adult/continuing education programs, cooperative education, distance learning, internships, part-time degree program, summer session for credit.
Library Minnesota School of Business-Shakopee with 919 titles, 95 serial subscriptions, an OPAC, a Web page.
Computers on Campus 48 computers available on campus for general student use. A campuswide network can be accessed. At least one staffed computer lab available.
Student Life *Housing:* college housing not available.
Standardized Tests *Required:* CPAt (for admission).
Costs (2004–05) *Tuition:* $11,340 full-time, $315 per credit part-time. Full-time tuition and fees vary according to course load. Part-time tuition and fees vary according to course load. *Payment plan:* installment. *Waivers:* employees or children of employees.
Applying *Options:* common application, electronic application. *Application fee:* $50. *Required:* high school transcript, interview. *Required for some:* essay or personal statement. *Application deadline:* 10/6 (freshmen).
Admissions Contact Ms. Jennifer Foss-Wille, Director of Admissions, Minnesota School of Business-Shakopee, 1200 Shakopee Town Square, Shakopee, MN 55379. *Phone:* 952-516-7015. *Toll-free phone:* 866-766-1200.

MINNESOTA STATE COLLEGE-SOUTHEAST TECHNICAL
Winona, Minnesota

- **State-supported** 2-year, founded 1992, part of Minnesota State Colleges and Universities System
- **Calendar** semesters
- **Degree** certificates, diplomas, and associate
- **Small-town** campus with easy access to Minneapolis-St. Paul
- **Endowment** $110,000
- **Coed,** 1,817 undergraduate students, 58% full-time, 56% women, 44% men

Undergraduates 1,060 full-time, 757 part-time. Students come from 20 states and territories, 2% African American, 1% Asian American or Pacific Islander, 0.6% Hispanic American, 1% Native American, 0.1% international.

Minnesota State College-Southeast Technical (continued)

Freshmen *Admission:* 1,263 applied, 1,104 admitted, 604 enrolled. *Average high school GPA:* 2.56.

Faculty *Total:* 118, 47% full-time.

Majors Accounting; administrative assistant and secretarial science; automobile/automotive mechanics technology; avionics maintenance technology; business machine repair; carpentry; child development; computer engineering technology; computer programming; computer typography and composition equipment operation; consumer merchandising/retailing management; cosmetology; drafting and design technology; electrical, electronic and communications engineering technology; emergency medical technology (EMT paramedic); heating, air conditioning, ventilation and refrigeration maintenance technology; industrial technology; kindergarten/preschool education; legal administrative assistant/secretary; machine tool technology; marketing/marketing management; mechanical design technology; medical administrative assistant and medical secretary; musical instrument fabrication and repair; nursing (licensed practical/vocational nurse training); nursing (registered nurse training); violin, viola, guitar and other stringed instruments; welding technology.

Academic Programs *Special study options:* academic remediation for entering students, English as a second language, internships, part-time degree program, services for LD students.

Library Learning Resource Center plus 1 other with 8,000 titles, 150 serial subscriptions, an OPAC, a Web page.

Computers on Campus 50 computers available on campus for general student use. A campuswide network can be accessed from off campus. Internet access, at least one staffed computer lab available.

Student Life *Housing:* college housing not available. *Activities and Organizations:* Student Senate. *Campus security:* 24-hour emergency response devices, late-night transport/escort service.

Costs (2004–05) *Tuition:* state resident $115 per credit part-time; nonresident $230 per credit part-time. Full-time tuition and fees vary according to reciprocity agreements. Part-time tuition and fees vary according to reciprocity agreements. *Required fees:* $12 per credit part-time.

Financial Aid Of all full-time matriculated undergraduates who enrolled in 2003, 65 Federal Work-Study jobs (averaging $2500). 65 state and other part-time jobs (averaging $2500).

Applying *Options:* common application, electronic application. *Application fee:* $20. *Required:* high school transcript. *Application deadline:* rolling (freshmen), rolling (transfers).

Admissions Contact Ms. Christine Humble, Director of Enrollment Services, Minnesota State College-Southeast Technical, PO Box 409, Winona, MN 55987. *Phone:* 507-453-2732. *Toll-free phone:* 800-372-8164. *Fax:* 507-453-2715. *E-mail:* enrollmentservices@southeasttech.mnscu.edu.

MINNESOTA STATE COMMUNITY AND TECHNICAL COLLEGE-DETROIT LAKES

Detroit Lakes, Minnesota

- **State-supported** 2-year, founded 1966
- **Calendar** semesters
- **Degree** certificates and associate
- **Coed,** 650 undergraduate students

Student Life *Housing:* college housing not available.

Costs (2004–05) *Tuition:* state resident $3864 full-time, $121 per credit part-time; nonresident $7728 full-time, $242 per credit part-time. *Required fees:* $265 full-time, $8 per credit part-time.

Applying *Application fee:* $20. *Required:* high school transcript, immunization record.

Admissions Contact Mr. Dale Westley, Enrollment Manager, Minnesota State Community and Technical College-Detroit Lakes, 900 Highway 34, E, Detroit Lakes, MN 56501. *Phone:* 218-846-3777. *Toll-free phone:* 800-492-4836.

MINNESOTA STATE COMMUNITY AND TECHNICAL COLLEGE-FERGUS FALLS

Fergus Falls, Minnesota

- **State-supported** 2-year, founded 1960, part of Minnesota State Colleges and Universities System
- **Calendar** semesters
- **Degree** certificates, diplomas, and associate
- **Rural** 146-acre campus
- **Endowment** $1.4 million
- **Coed**

Faculty *Student/faculty ratio:* 18:1.

Student Life *Campus security:* late-night transport/escort service, security for special events.

Athletics Member NJCAA.

Standardized Tests *Recommended:* ACT (for placement).

Costs (2004–05) *Tuition:* state resident $3840 full-time, $120 per credit part-time; nonresident $7680 full-time, $240 per credit part-time. Full-time tuition and fees vary according to course load, location, and reciprocity agreements. Part-time tuition and fees vary according to course load, location, and reciprocity agreements. *Required fees:* $560 full-time, $18 per credit part-time. *Room and board:* Room and board charges vary according to housing facility.

Financial Aid Of all full-time matriculated undergraduates who enrolled in 2003, 80 Federal Work-Study jobs (averaging $1900). 80 state and other part-time jobs (averaging $1900).

Applying *Options:* common application, electronic application, early admission, deferred entrance. *Application fee:* $20. *Required:* high school transcript.

Admissions Contact Ms. Carrie Brimhall, Director of Enrollment Management, Minnesota State Community and Technical College-Fergus Falls, 1414 College Way, Fergus Falls, MN 56537-1009. *Phone:* 218-739-7425. *Toll-free phone:* 888-MY-MSCTC. *Fax:* 218-739-7475.

MINNESOTA STATE COMMUNITY AND TECHNICAL COLLEGE-MOORHEAD

Moorhead, Minnesota

- **State-supported** 2-year
- **Calendar** semesters
- **Degree** certificates and associate
- **Coed,** 2,300 undergraduate students

Student Life *Housing:* college housing not available.

Costs (2004–05) *Tuition:* state resident $3864 full-time, $121 per credit part-time; nonresident $7728 full-time, $142 per credit hour part-time. *Required fees:* $329 full-time, $10 per credit hour part-time.

Applying *Application fee:* $20. *Required:* high school transcript, immunization record.

Admissions Contact Laurie McKeever, Enrollment Manager, Minnesota State Community and Technical College-Moorhead, 1900 28th Avenue, South, Moorhead, MN 56560. *Phone:* 218-299-6583. *Toll-free phone:* 800-426-5603.

MINNESOTA STATE COMMUNITY AND TECHNICAL COLLEGE-WADENA

Wadena, Minnesota

- **State-supported** 2-year
- **Calendar** semesters
- **Degree** certificates and associate
- **Coed,** 635 undergraduate students

Student Life *Housing:* college housing not available.

Costs (2004–05) *Tuition:* state resident $3874 full-time, $121 per credit part-time; nonresident $7728 full-time, $242 per credit part-time. *Required fees:* $233 full-time, $8 per credit part-time.

Applying *Application fee:* $20. *Required:* high school transcript, immunization record.

Admissions Contact Mr. Paul Drange, Enrollment Manager, Minnesota State Community and Technical College-Wadena, 405 Colfax Avenue, SW, PO Box 566, Wadena, MN 56482. *Phone:* 218-631-7818. *Toll-free phone:* 800-247-2007.

MINNESOTA WEST COMMUNITY AND TECHNICAL COLLEGE

Pipestone, Minnesota

- **State-supported** 2-year, founded 1967, part of Minnesota State Colleges and Universities System
- **Calendar** semesters
- **Degrees** certificates, diplomas, and associate (profile contains information from Canby, Granite Falls, Jackson, and Worthington campuses)
- **Rural** 103-acre campus
- **Coed,** 2,917 undergraduate students, 76% full-time, 50% women, 50% men

Undergraduates 2,207 full-time, 710 part-time. Students come from 25 states and territories, 3 other countries, 11% are from out of state, 2% African American, 2% Asian American or Pacific Islander, 2% Hispanic American, 0.8% Native American, 5% transferred in. *Retention:* 63% of 2002 full-time freshmen returned.

Freshmen *Admission:* 1,911 applied, 1,580 admitted, 651 enrolled. *Average high school GPA:* 2.50.

Faculty *Total:* 232, 41% full-time. *Student/faculty ratio:* 17:1.

Majors Accounting; administrative assistant and secretarial science; clinical/medical laboratory technology; medical administrative assistant and medical secretary; medical/clinical assistant.

Academic Programs *Special study options:* academic remediation for entering students, advanced placement credit, cooperative education, distance learning, double majors, external degree program, honors programs, independent study, internships, part-time degree program, services for LD students, summer session for credit.

Library Minnesota West Library plus 4 others with 46,057 titles, 313 serial subscriptions, 4,632 audiovisual materials, an OPAC.

Computers on Campus A campuswide network can be accessed. Internet access, online (class) registration, at least one staffed computer lab available. Computer purchase or lease plan available.

Student Life *Housing:* college housing not available. *Student services:* personal/psychological counseling.

Athletics Member NJCAA. *Intercollegiate sports:* baseball M, basketball M/W, football M, golf M/W, softball W, volleyball W, wrestling M. *Intramural sports:* softball M/W, volleyball M/W.

Costs (2005–06) *Tuition:* state resident $3968 full-time. Full-time tuition and fees vary according to reciprocity agreements. *Required fees:* $351 full-time. *Payment plans:* installment, deferred payment. *Waivers:* senior citizens and employees or children of employees.

Applying *Options:* common application, electronic application. *Application fee:* $20. *Required:* high school transcript. *Application deadline:* rolling (freshmen), rolling (transfers).

Admissions Contact Mr. Gary Gillin, Dean of Communication and Enrollment, Minnesota West Community and Technical College, 1314 North Hiawatha Avenue, Pipestone, MN 56164. *Phone:* 507-825-6804. *Toll-free phone:* 800-658-2330. *Fax:* 507-825-4656. *E-mail:* garyg@ps.mnwest.mnscu.edu.

NATIONAL AMERICAN UNIVERSITY
Bloomington, Minnesota

Admissions Contact 112 West Market, Bloomington, MN 55425.

NATIONAL AMERICAN UNIVERSITY
Brooklyn Center, Minnesota

Admissions Contact 6120 Earle Brown Drive, Suite 100, Brooklyn Center, MN 55430.

NORMANDALE COMMUNITY COLLEGE
Bloomington, Minnesota

- **State-supported** 2-year, founded 1968, part of Minnesota State Colleges and Universities System
- **Calendar** semesters
- **Degree** certificates and associate
- **Suburban** 90-acre campus with easy access to Minneapolis-St. Paul
- **Endowment** $1.4 million
- **Coed**

Faculty *Student/faculty ratio:* 28:1.

Student Life *Campus security:* 24-hour emergency response devices, student patrols, late-night transport/escort service.

Standardized Tests *Recommended:* ACT (for placement).

Costs (2004–05) *Tuition:* state resident $3675 full-time, $123 per credit part-time; nonresident $7079 full-time, $236 per credit part-time.

Financial Aid Of all full-time matriculated undergraduates who enrolled in 2003, 480 Federal Work-Study jobs (averaging $4000). 1,200 state and other part-time jobs (averaging $4000).

Applying *Options:* common application, early admission, deferred entrance. *Application fee:* $20. *Required for some:* high school transcript.

Admissions Contact Information Center, Normandale Community College, 9700 France Avenue South, Bloomington, MN 55431. *Phone:* 952-487-8201. *Toll-free phone:* 866-880-8740. *Fax:* 952-487-8230. *E-mail:* information@normandale.edu.

NORTH HENNEPIN COMMUNITY COLLEGE
Brooklyn Park, Minnesota

- **State-supported** 2-year, founded 1966, part of Minnesota State Colleges and Universities System
- **Calendar** semesters
- **Degree** certificates and associate

- **Suburban** 80-acre campus
- **Endowment** $648,485
- **Coed**, 6,602 undergraduate students, 37% full-time, 62% women, 38% men

Undergraduates 2,461 full-time, 4,141 part-time. Students come from 4 states and territories, 96 other countries, 0.3% are from out of state, 14% African American, 7% Asian American or Pacific Islander, 2% Hispanic American, 0.5% Native American, 1% international, 29% transferred in.

Freshmen *Admission:* 1,618 applied, 1,618 admitted, 1,541 enrolled.

Faculty *Total:* 194, 45% full-time, 100% with terminal degrees. *Student/faculty ratio:* 28:1.

Majors Accounting; administrative assistant and secretarial science; architectural drafting and CAD/CADD; automobile/automotive mechanics technology; business administration and management; cardiovascular technology; clinical/medical laboratory technology; commercial and advertising art; construction management; consumer merchandising/retailing management; criminal justice/police science; electrical, electronic and communications engineering technology; fire science; health information/medical records technology; hydraulics and fluid power technology; industrial technology; legal assistant/paralegal; liberal arts and sciences/liberal studies; management information systems; marketing/marketing management; materials science; mechanical drafting and CAD/CADD; medical radiologic technology; nursing (registered nurse training); pre-engineering; transportation technology.

Academic Programs *Special study options:* academic remediation for entering students, accelerated degree program, adult/continuing education programs, advanced placement credit, distance learning, English as a second language, honors programs, independent study, internships, off-campus study, part-time degree program, services for LD students, study abroad, summer session for credit.

Library Learning Resource Center with 69,375 titles, 2,500 serial subscriptions, 3,406 audiovisual materials, an OPAC, a Web page.

Computers on Campus 250 computers available on campus for general student use. A campuswide network can be accessed. Internet access, online (class) registration, at least one staffed computer lab available.

Student Life *Housing:* college housing not available. *Activities and Organizations:* drama/theater group, student-run newspaper, choral group. *Campus security:* 24-hour patrols, late-night transport/escort service. *Student services:* personal/psychological counseling.

Athletics Member NJCAA. *Intramural sports:* basketball M/W, bowling M/W, football M, golf M/W, soccer M, tennis M/W, volleyball M/W.

Costs (2004–05) *Tuition:* state resident $2892 full-time, $121 per credit part-time; nonresident $5355 full-time, $223 per credit part-time. *Required fees:* $247 full-time, $10 per credit part-time. *Payment plan:* deferred payment.

Applying *Options:* early admission, deferred entrance. *Application fee:* $20. *Recommended:* high school transcript. *Application deadline:* rolling (freshmen), rolling (transfers). *Notification:* continuous (freshmen).

Admissions Contact Ms. Lori Kirkeby, Director of Admissions and Registration, North Hennepin Community College, 7411 85th Avenue North, Brooklyn Park, MN 55445-2231. *Phone:* 763-424-0713.

NORTHLAND COMMUNITY AND TECHNICAL COLLEGE-EAST GRAND FORKS
East Grand Forks, Minnesota

- **State-supported** 2-year, founded 1973
- **Calendar** semesters
- **Degree** certificates, diplomas, and associate
- **Coed**, 1,442 undergraduate students

Faculty *Total:* 60. *Student/faculty ratio:* 24:1.

Costs (2004–05) *Tuition:* state resident $3623 full-time, $121 per credit part-time. Full-time tuition and fees vary according to course load and reciprocity agreements. Part-time tuition and fees vary according to course load and reciprocity agreements. *Required fees:* $293 full-time, $13 per credit part-time. *Waivers:* senior citizens.

Applying *Application fee:* $20.

Admissions Contact Ms. Rita Lealos, Enrollment Specialist, Northland Community and Technical College-East Grand Forks, 2022 Central Avenue, NW, East Grand Forks, MN 56721-2702. *Phone:* 218-773-4546. *Toll-free phone:* 800-451-3441.

NORTHLAND COMMUNITY AND TECHNICAL COLLEGE-THIEF RIVER FALLS
Thief River Falls, Minnesota

- **State-supported** 2-year, founded 1965, part of Minnesota State Colleges and Universities System
- **Calendar** semesters
- **Degree** diplomas and associate
- **Rural** campus
- **Coed,** 3,109 undergraduate students, 65% full-time, 57% women, 43% men

Undergraduates 2,029 full-time, 1,080 part-time. Students come from 27 states and territories, 3 other countries, 9% are from out of state, 3% African American, 0.8% Asian American or Pacific Islander, 2% Hispanic American, 3% Native American, 0.2% international. *Retention:* 56% of 2002 full-time freshmen returned.

Freshmen *Admission:* 1,511 applied, 1,511 admitted.

Faculty *Total:* 91, 67% full-time, 10% with terminal degrees. *Student/faculty ratio:* 23:1.

Majors Accounting; administrative assistant and secretarial science; aeronautics/aviation/aerospace science and technology; architectural engineering technology; athletic training; automobile/automotive mechanics technology; aviation/airway management; avionics maintenance technology; broadcast journalism; business administration and management; child care provision; child development; computer and information sciences related; computer graphics; computer science; computer software and media applications related; computer systems networking and telecommunications; computer/technical support; consumer merchandising/retailing management; cosmetology; criminal justice/law enforcement administration; criminal justice/police science; criminology; data entry/microcomputer applications; data entry/microcomputer applications related; data modeling/warehousing and database administration; drafting and design technology; electrical, electronic and communications engineering technology; farm and ranch management; industrial electronics technology; information technology; international business/trade/commerce; legal administrative assistant/secretary; legal assistant/paralegal; legal studies; liberal arts and sciences/liberal studies; marketing/marketing management; mass communication/media; nursing (licensed practical/vocational nurse training); nursing (registered nurse training); radio and television; system administration; web/multimedia management and webmaster; web page, digital/multimedia and information resources design; welding technology; word processing.

Academic Programs *Special study options:* academic remediation for entering students, adult/continuing education programs, advanced placement credit, distance learning, internships, off-campus study, part-time degree program, services for LD students, summer session for credit.

Library Northland College Library.

Computers on Campus 567 computers available on campus for general student use. A campuswide network can be accessed from off campus. Internet access, online (class) registration, at least one staffed computer lab available. Computer purchase or lease plan available.

Student Life *Housing:* college housing not available. *Activities and Organizations:* drama/theater group, student-run newspaper, radio station, choral group, Law Enforcement Club, All-Nations Club, Environmental Club, PAMA, VICA. *Campus security:* student patrols, late-night transport/escort service. *Student services:* personal/psychological counseling, women's center.

Athletics Member NJCAA. *Intercollegiate sports:* baseball M, basketball M/W, football M, golf M(s)/W(s), softball W, volleyball W. *Intramural sports:* basketball M/W, bowling M/W, golf M/W, softball M/W, tennis M/W, volleyball M/W.

Standardized Tests *Recommended:* SAT or ACT (for placement).

Costs (2005–06) *Tuition:* area resident $4018 full-time, $126 per credit part-time. Full-time tuition and fees vary according to course load and location. Part-time tuition and fees vary according to course load and location. *Required fees:* $480 full-time, $15 per credit part-time. *Payment plan:* installment. *Waivers:* senior citizens and employees or children of employees.

Financial Aid Of all full-time matriculated undergraduates who enrolled in 2003, 75 Federal Work-Study jobs (averaging $2500). 40 state and other part-time jobs (averaging $2500).

Applying *Options:* common application, electronic application, early admission, deferred entrance. *Application fee:* $20. *Required:* high school transcript. *Application deadlines:* 9/2 (freshmen), 9/2 (transfers). *Notification:* continuous (freshmen).

Admissions Contact Mr. Eugene Klinke, Director of Enrollment Management, Northland Community and Technical College-Thief River Falls, 1101 Highway #1 East, Thief River Falls, MN 56701. *Phone:* 218-681-0862. *Toll-free phone:* 800-959-6282. *Fax:* 218-681-0774. *E-mail:* eugene.klinke@northlandcollege.edu.

NORTHWEST TECHNICAL COLLEGE
Bemidji, Minnesota

- **State-supported** 2-year, founded 1993, part of Minnesota State Colleges and Universities System
- **Calendar** semesters
- **Degree** certificates, diplomas, and associate
- **Small-town** campus
- **Coed,** 4,500 undergraduate students

Faculty *Total:* 400, 75% full-time.

Majors Accounting; administrative assistant and secretarial science; architectural engineering technology; autobody/collision and repair technology; automobile/automotive mechanics technology; banking and financial support services; biomedical technology; cardiovascular technology; carpentry; child care and support services management; civil engineering technology; clinical/medical laboratory technology; commercial and advertising art; communications technology; computer programming; computer systems networking and telecommunications; construction management; dental hygiene; diesel mechanics technology; electrical, electronic and communications engineering technology; emergency medical technology (EMT paramedic); fashion merchandising; health information/medical records technology; heating, air conditioning and refrigeration technology; human resources management; industrial technology; legal administrative assistant/secretary; library science; marine technology; marketing/marketing management; mechanical design technology; medical administrative assistant and medical secretary; medical/clinical assistant; nursing (licensed practical/vocational nurse training); occupational therapist assistant; pharmacy technician; physical therapist assistant; radiologic technology/science; respiratory care therapy; surgical technology; telecommunications.

Academic Programs *Special study options:* cooperative education, distance learning, external degree program, independent study, internships, part-time degree program, services for LD students, summer session for credit.

Computers on Campus A campuswide network can be accessed from off campus. Internet access, at least one staffed computer lab available.

Student Life *Housing:* college housing not available. *Activities and Organizations:* student-run newspaper. *Campus security:* late-night transport/escort service. *Student services:* personal/psychological counseling.

Standardized Tests *Required:* ACCUPLACER (for placement).

Costs (2004–05) *Tuition:* state resident $2898 full-time, $121 per credit part-time; nonresident $5796 full-time, $242 per credit part-time. *Required fees:* $187 full-time, $8 per credit part-time.

Financial Aid Of all full-time matriculated undergraduates who enrolled in 2003, 20 Federal Work-Study jobs (averaging $1500). 10 state and other part-time jobs (averaging $1500).

Applying *Application fee:* $20.

Admissions Contact Mr. Tom Whelihan, Director, Admissions, Northwest Technical College, 905 Grant Avenue, SE, Bemidji, MN 56601. *Phone:* 218-846-7444. *Toll-free phone:* 800-942-8324.

NORTHWEST TECHNICAL INSTITUTE
Eden Prairie, Minnesota

- **Proprietary** 2-year, founded 1957
- **Calendar** semesters
- **Degree** associate
- **Suburban** 2-acre campus with easy access to Minneapolis-St. Paul
- **Coed**

Faculty *Student/faculty ratio:* 12:1.

Student Life *Campus security:* 24-hour emergency response devices and patrols, late-night transport/escort service.

Costs (2004–05) *Tuition:* $13,200 full-time. *Required fees:* $25 full-time.

Applying *Application fee:* $25. *Required:* high school transcript, interview.

Admissions Contact Mr. John Hartman, Director of Admissions, Northwest Technical Institute, 11995 Singletree Lane, Eden Prairie, MN 55344-5351. *Phone:* 952-944-0080 Ext. 103. *Toll-free phone:* 800-443-4223. *Fax:* 952-944-9274. *E-mail:* info@nti.edu.

PINE TECHNICAL COLLEGE
Pine City, Minnesota

Admissions Contact Mr. Phil Schroeder, Dean, Student Affairs, Pine Technical College, 900 Fourth Street, SE, Pine City, MN 55063. *Phone:* 320-629-5100. *Toll-free phone:* 800-521-7463.

RAINY RIVER COMMUNITY COLLEGE
International Falls, Minnesota

- **State-supported** 2-year, founded 1967, part of Minnesota State Colleges and Universities System

- **Calendar** semesters
- **Degree** certificates, diplomas, and associate
- **Small-town** 80-acre campus
- **Coed,** 384 undergraduate students, 69% full-time, 56% women, 44% men

Undergraduates 265 full-time, 119 part-time. Students come from 8 states and territories, 18% African American, 0.5% Asian American or Pacific Islander, 1% Hispanic American, 3% Native American, 10% live on campus.

Freshmen *Admission:* 230 applied, 230 admitted.

Faculty *Total:* 32, 53% full-time.

Majors Administrative assistant and secretarial science; biological and physical sciences; business administration and management; liberal arts and sciences/liberal studies; pre-engineering; real estate.

Academic Programs *Special study options:* academic remediation for entering students, adult/continuing education programs, advanced placement credit, cooperative education, English as a second language, honors programs, independent study, internships, part-time degree program, services for LD students, summer session for credit.

Library Rainy River Community College Library with 20,000 titles, an OPAC.

Computers on Campus 70 computers available on campus for general student use. A campuswide network can be accessed from off campus. Internet access, at least one staffed computer lab available.

Student Life *Housing Options:* coed, disabled students. *Activities and Organizations:* drama/theater group, Anishinaabe Student Coalition, Student Senate, Black Student Association. *Campus security:* 24-hour emergency response devices, late-night transport/escort service, controlled dormitory access. *Student services:* personal/psychological counseling.

Athletics Member NJCAA. *Intercollegiate sports:* basketball M/W, softball W, volleyball W. *Intramural sports:* archery M/W, badminton M/W, bowling M/W, skiing (cross-country) M/W, skiing (downhill) M/W, swimming and diving M/W, tennis M/W, volleyball M/W, weight lifting M/W.

Standardized Tests *Required:* CPT (for placement). *Recommended:* ACT (for placement).

Costs (2004–05) *Tuition:* state resident $2795 full-time, $116 per credit part-time. *Required fees:* $408 full-time, $17 per credit part-time.

Financial Aid Of all full-time matriculated undergraduates who enrolled in 2003, 110 Federal Work-Study jobs (averaging $2000). 55 state and other part-time jobs (averaging $2000).

Applying *Options:* common application, early admission, deferred entrance. *Application fee:* $20. *Required:* high school transcript. *Application deadline:* rolling (freshmen), rolling (transfers). *Notification:* continuous (freshmen).

Admissions Contact Ms. Berta Hagen, Registrar, Rainy River Community College, 1501 Highway 71, International Falls, MN 56649. *Phone:* 218-285-2207. *Toll-free phone:* 800-456-3996. *Fax:* 218-285-2239. *E-mail:* djohnson@rrcc.mnscu.edu.

RASMUSSEN COLLEGE EAGAN
Eagan, Minnesota

Admissions Contact Ms. Jacinda Miller, Admissions Coordinator, Rasmussen College Eagan, 3500 Federal Drive, Eagan, MN 55122-1346. *Phone:* 651-687-9000. *Toll-free phone:* 651-687-0507 (in-state); 800-852-6367 (out-of-state). *E-mail:* admission@rasmussen.edu.

RASMUSSEN COLLEGE MANKATO
Mankato, Minnesota

- **Proprietary** 2-year, founded 1904, part of Rasmussen College System
- **Calendar** quarters
- **Degree** certificates, diplomas, and associate
- **Suburban** campus with easy access to Minneapolis-St. Paul
- **Coed, primarily women**

Faculty *Student/faculty ratio:* 18:1.

Student Life *Campus security:* limited access to buildings after hours.

Standardized Tests *Required:* ACT COMPASS (for admission).

Costs (2004–05) *Tuition:* $13,200 full-time, $275 per credit part-time. *Required fees:* $60 full-time.

Financial Aid Of all full-time matriculated undergraduates who enrolled in 2003, 5 Federal Work-Study jobs (averaging $4000). 3 state and other part-time jobs (averaging $4000).

Applying *Options:* common application, deferred entrance. *Application fee:* $60. *Required:* high school transcript, minimum 2.0 GPA, interview.

Admissions Contact Ms. Kathy Clifford, Director of Admissions, Rasmussen College Mankato, 501 Holly Lane, Mankato, MN 56001-6803. *Phone:* 507-625-6556. *Toll-free phone:* 800-657-6767. *E-mail:* rascoll@ic.mankato.mn.us.

RASMUSSEN COLLEGE MINNETONKA
Minnetonka, Minnesota

- **Proprietary** 2-year, founded 1904, part of Rasmussen College System
- **Calendar** quarters
- **Degree** certificates, diplomas, and associate
- **Suburban** 2-acre campus with easy access to Minneapolis-St. Paul
- **Coed**

Faculty *Student/faculty ratio:* 11:1.

Student Life *Campus security:* late-night transport/escort service.

Costs (2004–05) *Tuition:* $19,800 full-time.

Financial Aid Of all full-time matriculated undergraduates who enrolled in 2003, 3 state and other part-time jobs (averaging $4338).

Applying *Options:* early admission, deferred entrance. *Application fee:* $60. *Required:* high school transcript, interview.

Admissions Contact Mr. Ethan Campbell, Director of Admissions, Rasmussen College Minnetonka, 12450 Wayzata Boulevard, Suite 315, Minnetonka, MN 55305-1928. *Phone:* 952-545-2000. *Toll-free phone:* 800-852-0929.

RASMUSSEN COLLEGE ST. CLOUD
St. Cloud, Minnesota

- **Proprietary** 2-year, founded 1904, part of Rasmussen College System
- **Calendar** quarters
- **Degree** certificates, diplomas, and associate
- **Urban** campus with easy access to Minneapolis-St. Paul
- **Coed, primarily women,** 533 undergraduate students, 47% full-time, 82% women, 18% men

Undergraduates 252 full-time, 281 part-time. Students come from 3 states and territories, 1% are from out of state, 2% African American, 0.9% Asian American or Pacific Islander, 2% Hispanic American, 2% Native American.

Freshmen *Admission:* 197 enrolled.

Faculty *Total:* 28, 46% full-time, 68% with terminal degrees. *Student/faculty ratio:* 19:1.

Majors Accounting; administrative assistant and secretarial science; business administration and management; court reporting; health information/medical records administration; legal administrative assistant/secretary; marketing/marketing management; medical administrative assistant and medical secretary; tourism and travel services management.

Academic Programs *Special study options:* academic remediation for entering students, adult/continuing education programs, distance learning, double majors, internships, part-time degree program, summer session for credit.

Library St. Cloud Rasmussen College Library with 689 titles, 31 serial subscriptions, 173 audiovisual materials, an OPAC, a Web page.

Computers on Campus 123 computers available on campus for general student use. A campuswide network can be accessed from off campus that provide access to Web-based e-mail, remote file access. Internet access, at least one staffed computer lab available.

Student Life *Housing:* college housing not available. *Activities and Organizations:* student-run newspaper, Student Senate.

Standardized Tests *Required:* ACT COMPASS (for admission).

Costs (2004–05) *Tuition:* $12,375 full-time, $275 per credit part-time. Full-time tuition and fees vary according to course load and program. Part-time tuition and fees vary according to course load and program. *Required fees:* $60 full-time. *Payment plan:* installment. *Waivers:* employees or children of employees.

Financial Aid Of all full-time matriculated undergraduates who enrolled in 2003, 34 Federal Work-Study jobs (averaging $866). 51 state and other part-time jobs (averaging $700).

Applying *Options:* common application, electronic application, early admission, deferred entrance. *Application fee:* $60. *Required:* high school transcript, minimum 2.0 GPA, interview. *Application deadline:* rolling (freshmen), rolling (transfers).

Admissions Contact Ms. Andrea Peters, Director of Admissions, Rasmussen College St. Cloud, 226 Park Avenue South, St. Cloud, MN 56301. *Phone:* 320-251-5600. *Toll-free phone:* 800-852-0460. *Fax:* 320-251-3702. *E-mail:* admstc@rasmussen.edu.

RIDGEWATER COLLEGE
Willmar, Minnesota

Admissions Contact Ms. Linda Barron, Admissions Assistant, Ridgewater College, PO Box 1097, Willmar, MN 56201-1097. *Phone:* 320-231-2906 Ext. 2906. *Toll-free phone:* 800-722-1151 Ext. 2906. *Fax:* 320-231-7677. *E-mail:* skerfield@ridgewater.mnscu.edu.

RIVERLAND COMMUNITY COLLEGE
Austin, Minnesota

- **State-supported** 2-year, founded 1940, part of Minnesota State Colleges and Universities System
- **Calendar** semesters
- **Degree** certificates, diplomas, and associate
- **Small-town** 187-acre campus with easy access to Minneapolis-St. Paul
- **Coed**, 4,000 undergraduate students, 58% full-time, 52% women, 48% men

Undergraduates 2,320 full-time, 1,680 part-time. Students come from 5 states and territories, 3% African American, 0.3% Asian American or Pacific Islander, 3% Hispanic American, 0.3% Native American, 2% live on campus.

Freshmen *Admission:* 2,400 admitted. *Average high school GPA:* 3.08.

Faculty *Total:* 158, 64% full-time. *Student/faculty ratio:* 18:1.

Majors Administrative assistant and secretarial science; autobody/collision and repair technology; business administration and management; computer and information systems security; computer installation and repair technology; computer programming (specific applications); computer programming (vendor/product certification); computer software and media applications related; computer systems networking and telecommunications; computer/technical support; corrections; criminal justice/police science; data entry/microcomputer applications; data entry/microcomputer applications related; diesel mechanics technology; electrical/electronics equipment installation and repair; health unit coordinator/ward clerk; human services; industrial mechanics and maintenance technology; legal administrative assistant/secretary; liberal arts and sciences/liberal studies; machine shop technology; medical administrative assistant and medical secretary; medical radiologic technology; nursing (registered nurse training); web/multimedia management and webmaster; web page, digital/multimedia and information resources design; word processing.

Academic Programs *Special study options:* academic remediation for entering students, adult/continuing education programs, advanced placement credit, distance learning, double majors, English as a second language, independent study, internships, off-campus study, part-time degree program, services for LD students, study abroad, summer session for credit.

Library Riverland Community College Library plus 2 others with 33,500 titles, 278 serial subscriptions, an OPAC.

Computers on Campus 175 computers available on campus for general student use. A campuswide network can be accessed from student residence rooms. At least one staffed computer lab available.

Student Life *Housing Options:* Campus housing is provided by a third party. *Activities and Organizations:* drama/theater group, student-run newspaper, choral group, College Choir, student newspaper, Student Activities Board, Phi Theta Kappa, Theater Club. *Campus security:* late-night transport/escort service. *Student services:* personal/psychological counseling, women's center.

Athletics Member NJCAA. *Intercollegiate sports:* baseball M, basketball M/W, golf M/W, softball W, volleyball W. *Intramural sports:* basketball M.

Standardized Tests *Required:* ASAP (for placement). *Recommended:* ACT (for placement).

Costs (2004–05) *Tuition:* state resident $3390 full-time, $113 per credit part-time; nonresident $6780 full-time, $226 per credit part-time. Full-time tuition and fees vary according to program and reciprocity agreements. Part-time tuition and fees vary according to program and reciprocity agreements. *Required fees:* $480 full-time, $16 per credit part-time. *Room and board:* room only: $2590. *Payment plans:* installment, deferred payment. *Waivers:* senior citizens and employees or children of employees.

Applying *Options:* early admission. *Application fee:* $20. *Required:* high school transcript. *Application deadline:* rolling (freshmen), rolling (transfers).

Admissions Contact Renee Wjos, Admission Secretary, Riverland Community College, 1900 8th Avenue NW, Austin, MN 55912. *Phone:* 507-433-0820. *Toll-free phone:* 800-247-5039. *Fax:* 507-433-0515. *E-mail:* admissions@river.cc.mn.us.

ROCHESTER COMMUNITY AND TECHNICAL COLLEGE
Rochester, Minnesota

- **State-supported** primarily 2-year, founded 1915, part of Minnesota State Colleges and Universities System
- **Calendar** semesters
- **Degrees** certificates, diplomas, associate, and bachelor's (also offers 13 programs that lead to a bachelor's degree with Winona State University or University of Minnesota)
- **Small-town** 460-acre campus
- **Endowment** $437,000
- **Coed**, 5,862 undergraduate students

Undergraduates Students come from 39 states and territories, 36 other countries, 10% are from out of state.

Freshmen *Admission:* 2,428 applied, 2,400 admitted.

Faculty *Total:* 225, 41% full-time.

Majors Administrative assistant and secretarial science; business administration and management; child guidance; civil engineering technology; clinical/medical laboratory technology; computer science; criminal justice/police science; dental hygiene; developmental and child psychology; electrical, electronic and communications engineering technology; fashion merchandising; general studies; greenhouse management; human services; landscaping and groundskeeping; legal administrative assistant/secretary; liberal arts and sciences/liberal studies; mechanical engineering/mechanical technology; medical administrative assistant and medical secretary; natural resources/conservation; nursing (registered nurse training); pre-engineering; respiratory care therapy; surgical technology; turf and turfgrass management.

Academic Programs *Special study options:* academic remediation for entering students, advanced placement credit, distance learning, English as a second language, honors programs, independent study, internships, off-campus study, part-time degree program, services for LD students, summer session for credit.

Library Goddard Library plus 1 other with 62,000 titles, 600 serial subscriptions.

Computers on Campus 170 computers available on campus for general student use. A campuswide network can be accessed. At least one staffed computer lab available.

Student Life *Housing:* college housing not available. *Activities and Organizations:* drama/theater group, student-run newspaper, choral group, choir, band, football, theater, Program Council. *Campus security:* student patrols, late-night transport/escort service. *Student services:* health clinic, personal/psychological counseling.

Athletics Member NJCAA. *Intercollegiate sports:* baseball M, basketball M/W, football M, golf M/W, soccer W, softball W, volleyball W, wrestling M. *Intramural sports:* basketball M/W, football M, soccer M(c)/W(c), softball M/W, table tennis M/W, tennis M/W, volleyball M/W.

Costs (2004–05) *Tuition:* state resident $2798 full-time, $117 per credit part-time; nonresident $5596 full-time, $233 per credit part-time.

Financial Aid Of all full-time matriculated undergraduates who enrolled in 2003, 500 Federal Work-Study jobs (averaging $3000). 300 state and other part-time jobs (averaging $3000).

Applying *Options:* early admission. *Application fee:* $20. *Required:* high school transcript. *Application deadlines:* 8/24 (freshmen), 8/24 (transfers). *Notification:* continuous (freshmen).

Admissions Contact Mr. Troy Tynsky, Director of Admissions, Rochester Community and Technical College, 851 30th Avenue, SE, Rochester, MN 55904-4999. *Phone:* 507-280-3509. *Fax:* 507-285-7496.

ST. CLOUD TECHNICAL COLLEGE
St. Cloud, Minnesota

- **State-supported** 2-year, founded 1948, part of Minnesota State Colleges and Universities System
- **Calendar** semesters
- **Degree** certificates, diplomas, and associate
- **Urban** 35-acre campus with easy access to Minneapolis-St. Paul
- **Coed**, 3,329 undergraduate students, 67% full-time, 51% women, 49% men

Undergraduates 2,235 full-time, 1,094 part-time. Students come from 19 states and territories, 5 other countries, 2% are from out of state, 2% African American, 1% Asian American or Pacific Islander, 0.3% Hispanic American, 0.8% Native American, 0.2% international, 9% transferred in.

Freshmen *Admission:* 3,572 applied, 1,675 admitted, 987 enrolled. *Average high school GPA:* 2.70.

Faculty *Total:* 189, 57% full-time, 3% with terminal degrees. *Student/faculty ratio:* 21:1.

Majors Accounting; accounting technology and bookkeeping; administrative assistant and secretarial science; advertising; architectural drafting and CAD/CADD; architectural engineering technology; autobody/collision and repair technology; automobile/automotive mechanics technology; banking and financial support services; business administration and management; carpentry; child care and support services management; child development; civil engineering technology; commercial and advertising art; computer/information technology services administration related; computer programming; computer programming related; computer programming (specific applications); computer systems networking and telecommunications; computer/technical support; computer typography and composition equipment operation; construction engineering technology; consumer merchandising/retailing management; culinary arts; dental assisting; dental hygiene; diagnostic medical sonography and ultrasound technology; diesel mechanics technology; electrical and power transmission installation; electrical, electronic and communications engineering technology; emergency medical technology (EMT paramedic); finance; general retailing/wholesaling; graphic and printing equipment operation/production; heating, air conditioning and refrigeration technology; heating, air conditioning, ventilation and refrigeration maintenance technology; information technology; instrumentation technology; kindergarten/preschool education; legal administrative assistant/secretary; machine tool technology; marketing/marketing management; mechanical design technology; mechanical drafting and CAD/CADD; medical administrative assistant and medical secretary; medical office management; nursing (licensed practical/vocational nurse training); office management; ophthalmic laboratory technology; pipefitting and sprinkler fitting; surgical technology; teacher assistant/aide; water quality and wastewater treatment management and recycling technology; welding technology; word processing.

Academic Programs *Special study options:* academic remediation for entering students, adult/continuing education programs, advanced placement credit, cooperative education, distance learning, English as a second language, internships, part-time degree program, services for LD students, summer session for credit.

Library Learning Resource Center plus 1 other with 10,000 titles, 600 serial subscriptions, an OPAC, a Web page.

Computers on Campus 500 computers available on campus for general student use. A campuswide network can be accessed. Internet access, online (class) registration, at least one staffed computer lab available. Computer purchase or lease plan available.

Student Life *Housing:* college housing not available. *Activities and Organizations:* student-run newspaper, Student Senate, Distributive Education Club of America, Business Professionals of America, Child and Adult Care Education, Central Minnesota Builders Association. *Campus security:* late-night transport/escort service. *Student services:* personal/psychological counseling, women's center.

Athletics Member NJCAA. *Intercollegiate sports:* basketball M/W, softball M/W. *Intramural sports:* golf M/W, volleyball M/W.

Standardized Tests *Required:* ACT ASSET or ACCUPLACER (for placement).

Costs (2004–05) *Tuition:* state resident $3520 full-time, $117 per credit part-time; nonresident $7039 full-time, $235 per credit part-time. Full-time tuition and fees vary according to program. Part-time tuition and fees vary according to program. *Required fees:* $290 full-time, $10 per credit part-time. *Waivers:* senior citizens and employees or children of employees.

Financial Aid Of all full-time matriculated undergraduates who enrolled in 2003, 38 Federal Work-Study jobs (averaging $4000). 38 state and other part-time jobs (averaging $4000).

Applying *Options:* electronic application, early admission, deferred entrance. *Application fee:* $20. *Required:* high school transcript. *Required for some:* interview. *Application deadline:* rolling (freshmen), rolling (transfers). *Notification:* continuous until 8/1 (freshmen).

Admissions Contact Ms. Jodi Elness, Admissions Office, St. Cloud Technical College, 1540 Northway Drive, St. Cloud, MN 56303. *Phone:* 320-308-5089. *Toll-free phone:* 800-222-1009. *Fax:* 320-308-5981. *E-mail:* enroll@sctc.edu.

SAINT PAUL COLLEGE-A COMMUNITY & TECHNICAL COLLEGE
St. Paul, Minnesota

- **State-related** 2-year, founded 1919, part of Minnesota State Colleges and Universities System
- **Calendar** semesters
- **Degree** certificates, diplomas, and associate
- **Urban** campus
- **Coed,** 5,442 undergraduate students, 29% full-time, 48% women, 52% men

Undergraduates 1,584 full-time, 3,858 part-time. 20% African American, 8% Asian American or Pacific Islander, 3% Hispanic American, 1% Native American, 1% international, 6% transferred in.

Freshmen *Admission:* 3,194 applied, 2,826 admitted, 1,655 enrolled.

Faculty *Total:* 265, 43% full-time, 64% with terminal degrees. *Student/faculty ratio:* 20:1.

Majors Accounting; administrative assistant and secretarial science; child development; civil engineering technology; clinical/medical laboratory technology; computer programming; electrical, electronic and communications engineering technology; human resources management; industrial technology; international business/trade/commerce; medical administrative assistant and medical secretary; respiratory care therapy; sign language interpretation and translation.

Academic Programs *Special study options:* academic remediation for entering students, adult/continuing education programs, distance learning, English as a second language, honors programs, internships, off-campus study.

Library Saint Paul College Library with 12,000 titles, 110 serial subscriptions, 260 audiovisual materials, an OPAC.

Computers on Campus A campuswide network can be accessed from off campus. Internet access, online (class) registration, at least one staffed computer lab available.

Student Life *Housing:* college housing not available. *Activities and Organizations:* Student Senate. *Campus security:* late-night transport/escort service. *Student services:* personal/psychological counseling, women's center.

Standardized Tests *Required:* CPT, ACCUPLACER (for placement).

Costs (2004–05) *Tuition:* state resident $3500 full-time; nonresident $7000 full-time. Full-time tuition and fees vary according to reciprocity agreements. Part-time tuition and fees vary according to reciprocity agreements. *Required fees:* $235 full-time. *Payment plan:* installment. *Waivers:* senior citizens.

Financial Aid Of all full-time matriculated undergraduates who enrolled in 2003, 48 Federal Work-Study jobs (averaging $2500). 94 state and other part-time jobs (averaging $2500).

Applying *Options:* electronic application, early admission. *Application fee:* $20. *Required for some:* high school transcript, interview. *Application deadline:* rolling (freshmen).

Admissions Contact Thomas Matos, Admissions Director, Saint Paul College-A Community & Technical College, 235 Marshall Avenue, Saint Paul, MN 55102. *Phone:* 651-846-1424. *Toll-free phone:* 800-227-6029. *Fax:* 651-221-1416. *E-mail:* admissions@saintpaul.edu.

SOUTH CENTRAL TECHNICAL COLLEGE
North Mankato, Minnesota

- **State-supported** 2-year, founded 1946, part of Minnesota State Colleges and Universities System
- **Calendar** semesters
- **Degree** certificates, diplomas, and associate
- **Urban** campus
- **Coed,** 2,350 undergraduate students, 100% full-time, 57% women, 43% men
- 100% of applicants were admitted

Undergraduates 2,350 full-time. Students come from 7 states and territories, 3 other countries, 1% African American, 1% Asian American or Pacific Islander, 1% Hispanic American, 0.2% Native American, 11% transferred in.

Freshmen *Admission:* 1,100 applied, 1,100 admitted, 900 enrolled.

Faculty *Total:* 210, 43% full-time. *Student/faculty ratio:* 18:1.

Majors Accounting; administrative assistant and secretarial science; agribusiness; agricultural mechanization; agricultural production; architectural drafting and CAD/CADD; autobody/collision and repair technology; automobile/automotive mechanics technology; business administration and management; computer programming; culinary arts; dental assisting; emergency medical technology (EMT paramedic); heating, air conditioning, ventilation and refrigeration maintenance technology; machine tool technology; mechanical drafting and CAD/CADD; nursing (registered nurse training).

Academic Programs *Special study options:* academic remediation for entering students, advanced placement credit, cooperative education, distance learning, independent study, part-time degree program, services for LD students.

Library Main Library plus 1 other.

Computers on Campus 700 computers available on campus for general student use. A campuswide network can be accessed from student residence rooms and from off campus. Internet access, online (class) registration, at least one staffed computer lab available.

Student Life *Housing:* college housing not available.

Costs (2005–06) *Tuition:* $115 per credit part-time; state resident $3800 full-time. *Required fees:* $16 per credit part-time. *Payment plans:* installment, deferred payment. *Waivers:* senior citizens.

Applying *Application fee:* $20. *Required:* high school transcript. *Application deadlines:* 8/1 (freshmen), 8/1 (transfers). *Notification:* continuous (freshmen).

Admissions Contact Ms. Beverly Herda, Director of Admissions, South Central Technical College, 1920 Lee Boulevard, North Mankato, MN 56003. *Phone:* 507-389-7334.

VERMILION COMMUNITY COLLEGE
Ely, Minnesota

- **State-supported** 2-year, founded 1922, part of Minnesota State Colleges and Universities System
- **Calendar** semesters
- **Degree** certificates, diplomas, and associate
- **Rural** 5-acre campus
- **Coed**

Student Life *Campus security:* student patrols, late-night transport/escort service, controlled dormitory access.

Athletics Member NJCAA.

Costs (2004–05) *Tuition:* state resident $4050 full-time, $135 per credit part-time; nonresident $7622 full-time, $254 per credit part-time. *Room and board:* $4570; room only: $2800.

Financial Aid Of all full-time matriculated undergraduates who enrolled in 2003, 150 Federal Work-Study jobs (averaging $1000). 30 state and other part-time jobs (averaging $1000).

Vermilion Community College (continued)

Applying *Options:* common application, electronic application, early admission, deferred entrance. *Application fee:* $20. *Required:* high school transcript.
Admissions Contact Mr. Todd Heiman, Director of Enrollment Services, Vermilion Community College, 1900 East Camp Street, Ely, MN 55731-1996. *Phone:* 218-365-7224. *Toll-free phone:* 800-657-3608.

MISSISSIPPI

ANTONELLI COLLEGE
Hattiesburg, Mississippi

Admissions Contact Ms. Connie Sharp, Director of Admissions, Antonelli College, 1500 North 31st Avenue, Hattiesburg, MS 39401. *Phone:* 601-583-4100.

ANTONELLI COLLEGE
Jackson, Mississippi

Admissions Contact Ms. Page McDaniel, Senior Admissions Officer, Antonelli College, 480 East Woodrow Wilson Drive, Jackson, MS 39216. *Phone:* 601-362-9991.

COAHOMA COMMUNITY COLLEGE
Clarksdale, Mississippi

- **State and locally supported** 2-year, founded 1949, part of Mississippi State Board for Community and Junior Colleges
- **Calendar** semesters
- **Degree** certificates and associate
- **Small-town** 29-acre campus with easy access to Memphis
- **Coed,** 1,400 undergraduate students

Undergraduates Students come from 8 states and territories.
Faculty *Total:* 55, 55% full-time.
Majors Accounting; administrative assistant and secretarial science; art; biology/biological sciences; business administration and management; chemistry; clinical laboratory science/medical technology; computer science; criminal justice/law enforcement administration; elementary education; English; health teacher education; kindergarten/preschool education; liberal arts and sciences/liberal studies; radio and television; social work; sport and fitness administration.
Academic Programs *Special study options:* adult/continuing education programs, part-time degree program.
Library Dickerson-Johnson Library.
Computers on Campus 25 computers available on campus for general student use. A campuswide network can be accessed. Internet access available.
Student Life *Housing Options:* Campus housing is university owned. *Activities and Organizations:* drama/theater group, student-run newspaper, choral group, marching band, Student Government Association, VICA, Phi Theta Kappa Honor Society. *Campus security:* 24-hour patrols. *Student services:* health clinic, personal/psychological counseling.
Athletics Member NJCAA. *Intercollegiate sports:* baseball M, basketball M(s)/W(s), football M.
Standardized Tests *Required:* SAT or ACT (for placement).
Costs (2005–06) *Tuition:* area resident $1400 full-time; state resident $2900 full-time, $80 per semester hour part-time; nonresident $3100 full-time. *Required fees:* $140 full-time, $25 per term part-time. *Room and board:* $2844.
Financial Aid Of all full-time matriculated undergraduates who enrolled in 2003, 350 Federal Work-Study jobs (averaging $600). 45 state and other part-time jobs (averaging $1000).
Applying *Options:* common application. *Required:* high school transcript. *Application deadline:* rolling (freshmen), rolling (transfers). *Notification:* continuous (freshmen).
Admissions Contact Mrs. Wanda Holmes, Director of Admissions and Records, Coahoma Community College, Route 1, PO Box 616, Clarksdale, MS 38614-9799. *Phone:* 662-621-4205. *Toll-free phone:* 800-844-1222.

COPIAH-LINCOLN COMMUNITY COLLEGE
Wesson, Mississippi

- **State and locally supported** 2-year, founded 1928, part of Mississippi State Board for Community and Junior Colleges

- **Calendar** semesters
- **Degree** certificates and associate
- **Rural** 525-acre campus with easy access to Jackson
- **Coed,** 2,161 undergraduate students, 66% full-time, 60% women, 40% men

Undergraduates 1,430 full-time, 731 part-time. Students come from 7 states and territories, 2 other countries, 2% are from out of state, 35% African American, 0.4% Asian American or Pacific Islander, 0.4% Hispanic American, 0.2% Native American, 0.1% international, 30% live on campus.
Freshmen *Admission:* 1,108 enrolled.
Faculty *Total:* 127, 65% full-time.
Majors Accounting; agribusiness; agricultural business and management; agricultural business and management related; agricultural business technology; agricultural economics; agricultural/farm supplies retailing and wholesaling; agriculture; architecture; art teacher education; biological and physical sciences; biology/biological sciences; business administration and management; chemistry; child development; civil engineering technology; clinical/medical laboratory technology; computer programming; cosmetology; criminal justice/police science; data processing and data processing technology; drafting and design technology; economics; education; electrical, electronic and communications engineering technology; elementary education; engineering; English; family and consumer sciences/home economics teacher education; farm and ranch management; food technology and processing; forestry; French; health teacher education; history; industrial radiologic technology; journalism; liberal arts and sciences/liberal studies; library science; music teacher education; nursing (registered nurse training); physical education teaching and coaching; special products marketing; trade and industrial teacher education; wood science and wood products/pulp and paper technology.
Academic Programs *Special study options:* academic remediation for entering students, adult/continuing education programs, advanced placement credit, honors programs, part-time degree program, student-designed majors, summer session for credit.
Library Oswalt Memorial Library with 38,900 titles, 255 serial subscriptions.
Computers on Campus 300 computers available on campus for general student use. At least one staffed computer lab available.
Student Life *Housing Options:* Campus housing is university owned. *Activities and Organizations:* drama/theater group, student-run newspaper, radio station, choral group, marching band. *Campus security:* 24-hour patrols. *Student services:* health clinic, personal/psychological counseling.
Athletics Member NJCAA. *Intercollegiate sports:* baseball M(s), basketball M(s)/W(s), football M(s), golf M/W, softball W, tennis M/W, track and field M. *Intramural sports:* basketball M/W, football M, golf M/W, tennis M/W, volleyball M/W.
Standardized Tests *Required for some:* ACT (for placement).
Costs (2005–06) *Tuition:* state resident $1600 full-time, $100 per semester hour part-time; nonresident $3400 full-time, $175 per semester hour part-time. *Required fees:* $100 full-time, $5 per semester hour part-time. *Room and board:* $2750; room only: $1000.
Financial Aid Of all full-time matriculated undergraduates who enrolled in 2003, 125 Federal Work-Study jobs (averaging $1000).
Applying *Options:* early admission. *Required:* high school transcript. *Application deadline:* rolling (freshmen), rolling (transfers).
Admissions Contact Dr. Phillilp H. Broome, Director of Admissions and Records, Copiah-Lincoln Community College, PO Box 371, Wesson, MS 39191-0457. *Phone:* 601-643-8307.

COPIAH-LINCOLN COMMUNITY COLLEGE-NATCHEZ CAMPUS
Natchez, Mississippi

- **State and locally supported** 2-year, founded 1972, part of Mississippi State Board for Community and Junior Colleges
- **Calendar** semesters
- **Degree** certificates and associate
- **Small-town** 24-acre campus
- **Coed,** 900 undergraduate students, 62% full-time, 73% women, 27% men

Undergraduates 554 full-time, 346 part-time. Students come from 4 states and territories, 53% African American, 0.3% Asian American or Pacific Islander, 0.3% Hispanic American.
Freshmen *Admission:* 363 enrolled.
Faculty *Total:* 53, 45% full-time, 100% with terminal degrees. *Student/faculty ratio:* 20:1.
Majors Administrative assistant and secretarial science; elementary education; family and consumer sciences/human sciences; forestry; general studies; hotel/motel administration; instrumentation technology; liberal arts and sciences/liberal studies; marketing/marketing management; political science and government; respiratory care therapy.

Academic Programs *Special study options:* academic remediation for entering students, adult/continuing education programs, advanced placement credit, distance learning, internships, part-time degree program, student-designed majors, summer session for credit.

Library Willie Mae Dunn Library with 19,000 titles, 112 serial subscriptions, 700 audiovisual materials, an OPAC, a Web page.

Computers on Campus 175 computers available on campus for general student use. A campuswide network can be accessed from off campus. Internet access, at least one staffed computer lab available.

Student Life *Housing Options:* Campus housing is provided by a third party. *Activities and Organizations:* student-run newspaper, student newspaper. *Campus security:* 24-hour patrols.

Athletics Member NJCAA.

Standardized Tests *Required for some:* ACT (for admission), TABE.

Costs (2005–06) *Tuition:* state resident $1600 full-time, $100 per semester hour part-time; nonresident $3400 full-time, $175 per semester hour part-time. *Required fees:* $100 full-time, $5 per semester hour part-time, $10 per year part-time. *Room and board:* $2600.

Financial Aid Of all full-time matriculated undergraduates who enrolled in 2003, 96 Federal Work-Study jobs, 14 state and other part-time jobs.

Applying *Options:* early admission. *Required:* high school transcript. *Application deadline:* rolling (freshmen), rolling (transfers). *Notification:* continuous (freshmen).

Admissions Contact Mrs. Gwen S. McCalip, Director of Admissions and Records, Copiah-Lincoln Community College-Natchez Campus, 11 Co-Lin Circle, Natchez, MS 39120. *Phone:* 601-442-9111 Ext. 224. *Fax:* 601-446-1222. *E-mail:* gwen.mccalip@colin.edu.

EAST CENTRAL COMMUNITY COLLEGE
Decatur, Mississippi

- **State and locally supported** 2-year, founded 1928, part of Mississippi State Board for Community and Junior Colleges
- **Calendar** semesters
- **Degree** certificates and associate
- **Rural** 200-acre campus
- **Coed,** 2,382 undergraduate students

Undergraduates Students come from 9 states and territories, 2% are from out of state, 27% live on campus.

Faculty *Total:* 144, 55% full-time.

Majors Accounting; art; art teacher education; behavioral sciences; biological and physical sciences; biology/biological sciences; business administration and management; carpentry; chemistry; computer science; cosmetology; data processing and data processing technology; drafting and design technology; drawing; economics; education; electrical, electronic and communications engineering technology; elementary education; engineering; English; health information/medical records administration; health teacher education; history; journalism; kindergarten/preschool education; liberal arts and sciences/liberal studies; library science; literature; mathematics; music; music teacher education; nursing (registered nurse training); occupational therapy; pharmacy; physical sciences; physical therapy; political science and government; pre-engineering; psychology; science teacher education; social sciences.

Academic Programs *Special study options:* academic remediation for entering students, adult/continuing education programs, advanced placement credit, honors programs, part-time degree program, services for LD students, summer session for credit.

Library Burton Library.

Computers on Campus 80 computers available on campus for general student use. A campuswide network can be accessed from off campus. At least one staffed computer lab available.

Student Life *Housing Options:* men-only, women-only. *Activities and Organizations:* drama/theater group, student-run newspaper, choral group, marching band. *Campus security:* 24-hour patrols. *Student services:* health clinic, personal/psychological counseling.

Athletics Member NJCAA. *Intercollegiate sports:* baseball M, basketball M(s)/W(s), football M(s), golf M(s)/W, softball W(s), tennis M/W. *Intramural sports:* basketball M/W, football M/W, table tennis M/W, volleyball M/W.

Standardized Tests *Required:* ACT (for placement).

Costs (2004–05) *Tuition:* state resident $1400 full-time; nonresident $3500 full-time. *Room and board:* $2530.

Financial Aid Of all full-time matriculated undergraduates who enrolled in 2003, 90 Federal Work-Study jobs (averaging $850). 38 state and other part-time jobs (averaging $1020).

Applying *Options:* common application, early admission. *Required:* high school transcript. *Application deadline:* rolling (freshmen). *Notification:* continuous (freshmen).

Admissions Contact Ms. Donna Luke, Director of Admissions, Records, and Research, East Central Community College, PO Box 129, Decatur, MS 39327-0129. *Phone:* 601-635-2111 Ext. 206. *Toll-free phone:* 877-462-3222. *Fax:* 601-635-2150.

EAST MISSISSIPPI COMMUNITY COLLEGE
Scooba, Mississippi

- **State and locally supported** 2-year, founded 1927, part of Mississippi State Board for Community and Junior Colleges
- **Calendar** semesters
- **Degree** certificates and associate
- **Rural** 25-acre campus
- **Endowment** $134,022
- **Coed,** 3,417 undergraduate students, 61% full-time, 60% women, 40% men

Undergraduates 2,068 full-time, 1,349 part-time. Students come from 4 states and territories, 1% are from out of state, 51% African American, 0.4% Asian American or Pacific Islander, 0.5% Hispanic American, 0.1% Native American, 25% live on campus.

Freshmen *Admission:* 2,245 applied, 1,402 admitted. *Test scores:* ACT scores over 18: 39%; ACT scores over 24: 5%.

Faculty *Total:* 191, 48% full-time. *Student/faculty ratio:* 22:1.

Majors Accounting; administrative assistant and secretarial science; art; automobile/automotive mechanics technology; banking and financial support services; biological and physical sciences; business administration and management; business teacher education; computer programming; computer science; cosmetology; criminal justice/law enforcement administration; drafting and design technology; economics; education; electrical, electronic and communications engineering technology; elementary education; English; fire science; forestry technology; funeral service and mortuary science; health teacher education; history; hotel/motel administration; instrumentation technology; liberal arts and sciences/liberal studies; mathematics; music; office occupations and clerical services; ophthalmic laboratory technology; pre-engineering; psychology; reading teacher education; real estate; social sciences; sociology.

Academic Programs *Special study options:* academic remediation for entering students, adult/continuing education programs, advanced placement credit, cooperative education, distance learning, double majors, honors programs, part-time degree program, services for LD students, summer session for credit.

Library Tubb-May Library with 27,840 titles, 116 serial subscriptions, 3,478 audiovisual materials, an OPAC, a Web page.

Computers on Campus 100 computers available on campus for general student use. A campuswide network can be accessed from student residence rooms and from off campus. Internet access available.

Student Life *Housing Options:* men-only, women-only. Campus housing is university owned. *Activities and Organizations:* drama/theater group, student-run newspaper, choral group, marching band. *Campus security:* 24-hour emergency response devices and patrols. *Student services:* personal/psychological counseling.

Athletics Member NJCAA. *Intercollegiate sports:* baseball M(s), basketball M(s)/W(s), cheerleading W(s), football M(s), golf M(s), soccer M(s)/W(s), softball W(s). *Intramural sports:* basketball M/W, football M, golf M, gymnastics M/W, tennis M/W.

Standardized Tests *Required for some:* ACT (for placement).

Costs (2004–05) *Tuition:* state resident $1400 full-time, $90 per semester hour part-time; nonresident $2850 full-time, $100 per semester hour part-time. *Required fees:* $200 full-time, $40 per term part-time. *Room and board:* $2520.

Financial Aid Of all full-time matriculated undergraduates who enrolled in 2003, 200 Federal Work-Study jobs (averaging $1200).

Applying *Options:* common application, electronic application, deferred entrance. *Required:* high school transcript. *Application deadline:* rolling (freshmen), rolling (transfers).

Admissions Contact Ms. Melinda Sciple, Admissions Officer, East Mississippi Community College, PO Box 158, Scooba, MS 39358-0158. *Phone:* 662-476-5041.

HINDS COMMUNITY COLLEGE
Raymond, Mississippi

- **State and locally supported** 2-year, founded 1917, part of Mississippi State Board for Community and Junior Colleges
- **Calendar** semesters
- **Degree** certificates, diplomas, and associate
- **Small-town** 671-acre campus
- **Endowment** $948,556
- **Coed,** 9,961 undergraduate students, 72% full-time, 65% women, 35% men

Undergraduates 7,145 full-time, 2,816 part-time. Students come from 16 states and territories, 1 other country, 3% are from out of state, 52% African

Hinds Community College (continued)

American, 0.5% Asian American or Pacific Islander, 0.6% Hispanic American, 0.2% Native American, 15% live on campus.

Freshmen *Admission:* 4,298 enrolled. *Average high school GPA:* 2.7. *Test scores:* ACT scores over 18: 16%; ACT scores over 24: 3%.

Faculty *Total:* 656, 54% full-time, 13% with terminal degrees. *Student/faculty ratio:* 17:1.

Majors Accounting; administrative assistant and secretarial science; agricultural business and management; agricultural economics; agricultural mechanization; agricultural teacher education; agronomy and crop science; art; avionics maintenance technology; biology/biological sciences; business administration and management; carpentry; child development; civil engineering technology; clinical/medical laboratory technology; clothing/textiles; commercial and advertising art; computer and information sciences related; computer graphics; computer programming; computer programming related; computer science; computer/technical support; criminal justice/law enforcement administration; criminal justice/police science; data entry/microcomputer applications; data entry/microcomputer applications related; data processing and data processing technology; dental hygiene; developmental and child psychology; dietetics; drafting and design technology; dramatic/theatre arts; economics; electrical, electronic and communications engineering technology; emergency medical technology (EMT paramedic); English; family and consumer sciences/human sciences; fashion/apparel design; finance; food services technology; graphic and printing equipment operation/production; health information/medical records administration; hotel/motel administration; humanities; industrial arts; industrial radiologic technology; information technology; journalism; landscaping and groundskeeping; legal assistant/paralegal; liberal arts and sciences/liberal studies; machine tool technology; marketing/marketing management; mass communication/media; mathematics; music; nursing (licensed practical/vocational nurse training); nursing (registered nurse training); political science and government; postal management; pre-engineering; psychology; public administration; real estate; respiratory care therapy; social sciences; sociology; special products marketing; surgical technology; system administration; telecommunications; veterinary sciences; veterinary technology; welding technology.

Academic Programs *Special study options:* academic remediation for entering students, accelerated degree program, adult/continuing education programs, advanced placement credit, cooperative education, distance learning, double majors, freshman honors college, honors programs, independent study, part-time degree program, services for LD students, summer session for credit. *ROTC:* Army (c).

Library McLendon Library with 165,260 titles, 1,178 serial subscriptions, an OPAC.

Computers on Campus 55 computers available on campus for general student use. A campuswide network can be accessed. Internet access, online (class) registration, at least one staffed computer lab available.

Student Life *Housing Options:* men-only, women-only. *Activities and Organizations:* drama/theater group, student-run newspaper, choral group, marching band, Phi Theta Kappa, Baptist Student Union, Residence Hall Association, Hi-Steppers Dance Team, band. *Campus security:* 24-hour emergency response devices and patrols, controlled dormitory access. *Student services:* personal/psychological counseling, women's center.

Athletics Member NJCAA. *Intercollegiate sports:* baseball M(s), basketball M(s)/W(s), cross-country running M(s), football M(s), golf M(s), soccer M(s), softball W(s), tennis M(s)/W(s), track and field M(s). *Intramural sports:* basketball M/W, football M/W, softball M/W, volleyball M/W.

Standardized Tests *Required for some:* SAT and SAT Subject Tests or ACT (for admission).

Costs (2004–05) *Tuition:* state resident $1660 full-time, $85 per semester hour part-time; nonresident $3866 full-time, $170 per semester hour part-time. *Room and board:* $2310; room only: $1010.

Financial Aid Of all full-time matriculated undergraduates who enrolled in 2003, 300 Federal Work-Study jobs (averaging $1250). 200 state and other part-time jobs (averaging $1000).

Applying *Options:* common application, early admission. *Required:* high school transcript. *Application deadline:* rolling (freshmen), rolling (transfers). *Notification:* continuous (freshmen).

Admissions Contact Mr. Jay Allen, Director of Admissions and Records, Hinds Community College, PO Box 1100, Raymond, MS 39154-1100. *Phone:* 601-857-3280. *Toll-free phone:* 800-HINDSCC. *Fax:* 601-857-3539.

HOLMES COMMUNITY COLLEGE

Goodman, Mississippi

- **State and locally supported** 2-year, founded 1928, part of Mississippi State Board for Community and Junior Colleges
- **Calendar** semesters
- **Degree** certificates and associate
- **Small-town** 196-acre campus
- **Endowment** $2.4 million
- **Coed,** 4,494 undergraduate students, 72% full-time, 66% women, 34% men

Undergraduates 3,251 full-time, 1,243 part-time. Students come from 11 states and territories, 1% are from out of state, 45% African American, 0.3% Hispanic American, 0.1% Native American, 12% live on campus. *Retention:* 55% of 2002 full-time freshmen returned.

Freshmen *Admission:* 1,789 enrolled.

Faculty *Total:* 351, 36% full-time, 3% with terminal degrees. *Student/faculty ratio:* 19:1.

Majors Administrative assistant and secretarial science; agriculture; biology/biological sciences; business administration and management; business teacher education; child development; clinical laboratory science/medical technology; computer and information sciences related; computer science; computer/technical support; data processing and data processing technology; drafting and design technology; elementary education; engineering; finance; forestry; health information/medical records administration; liberal arts and sciences/liberal studies; music teacher education; nursing (registered nurse training); pharmacy; physical therapy; radio and television; respiratory care therapy; science teacher education; social work; system administration; veterinary sciences; wildlife biology.

Academic Programs *Special study options:* academic remediation for entering students, adult/continuing education programs, advanced placement credit, cooperative education, distance learning, services for LD students, summer session for credit.

Library McMorrough Library plus 2 others with 53,000 titles, 550 serial subscriptions, an OPAC.

Computers on Campus 150 computers available on campus for general student use. A campuswide network can be accessed from off campus. Internet access, online (class) registration, at least one staffed computer lab available.

Student Life *Housing Options:* men-only, women-only, disabled students. Campus housing is university owned. *Activities and Organizations:* drama/theater group, student-run newspaper, choral group, marching band, Student Government Association, Drama/Theater Club, Baptist Student Union, FCA, Vocational Industrial Clubs of America. *Campus security:* 24-hour emergency response devices and patrols. *Student services:* personal/psychological counseling.

Athletics Member NJCAA. *Intercollegiate sports:* baseball M(s), basketball M(s)/W, football M(s), golf M(s)/W(s), soccer M(s)/W(s), softball W(s), tennis M(s)/W(s). *Intramural sports:* basketball M/W, football M/W, softball M/W, volleyball M/W.

Standardized Tests *Required:* ACT (for placement).

Costs (2004–05) *Tuition:* state resident $1430 full-time, $65 per semester hour part-time. Part-time tuition and fees vary according to course load. *Required fees:* $330 full-time, $10 per term part-time. *Room and board:* $3800. Room and board charges vary according to housing facility. *Waivers:* senior citizens and employees or children of employees.

Financial Aid Of all full-time matriculated undergraduates who enrolled in 2003, 160 Federal Work-Study jobs (averaging $700).

Applying *Options:* early admission. *Required:* high school transcript. *Application deadline:* rolling (freshmen), rolling (transfers). *Notification:* continuous (freshmen).

Admissions Contact Dr. Lynn Wright, Dean of Admissions and Records, Holmes Community College, PO Box 369, Goodman, MS 39079-0369. *Phone:* 601-472-2312 Ext. 1023.

ITAWAMBA COMMUNITY COLLEGE

Fulton, Mississippi

- **State and locally supported** 2-year, founded 1947, part of Mississippi State Board for Community and Junior Colleges
- **Calendar** semesters
- **Degree** associate
- **Small-town** 300-acre campus
- **Coed,** 4,000 undergraduate students

Undergraduates Students come from 9 states and territories, 3 other countries.

Faculty *Total:* 70.

Majors Accounting; administrative assistant and secretarial science; agricultural business and management; art; art teacher education; biological and physical sciences; biology/biological sciences; business administration and management; chemistry; civil engineering technology; computer and information sciences; computer science; construction engineering technology; criminal justice/police science; data processing and data processing technology; developmental and child psychology; drafting and design technology; economics; education; electrical, electronic and communications engineering technology; elementary education; English; family and consumer sciences/home economics teacher education; family and consumer sciences/human sciences; fashion/apparel design; forestry technology; health information/medical records administration; history; human services; industrial arts; journalism; kindergarten/preschool education; liberal arts and sciences/liberal studies; library science; marketing/marketing management; mathematics; medical radiologic technology; modern languages; music; music teacher education; nursing (registered nurse training); physical education teaching and coaching; piano and organ; political science and government; pre-engineering; psychology; public administration; respiratory care therapy; science teacher education; social sciences; social work; sociology; speech and rhetoric; trade and industrial teacher education; veterinary sciences; wind/percussion instruments.

Academic Programs *Special study options:* academic remediation for entering students, adult/continuing education programs, honors programs, part-time degree program, services for LD students, summer session for credit. *ROTC:* Army (b).

Library 36,816 titles, 231 serial subscriptions.

Computers on Campus 40 computers available on campus for general student use. At least one staffed computer lab available.

Student Life *Housing Options:* Campus housing is university owned.

Athletics Member NJCAA. *Intercollegiate sports:* basketball M(s)/W(s), football M(s), golf M(s), tennis M/W, track and field M. *Intramural sports:* badminton M/W, basketball M/W, football M/W, golf M/W, tennis M/W, volleyball M/W.

Standardized Tests *Required:* ACT (for placement).

Costs (2004–05) *Tuition:* state resident $1400 full-time, $75 per semester hour part-time; nonresident $3150 full-time, $75 per semester hour part-time. *Required fees:* $60 full-time, $30 per term part-time. *Room and board:* $2440; room only: $1000.

Financial Aid Of all full-time matriculated undergraduates who enrolled in 2003, 250 Federal Work-Study jobs (averaging $2300). 30 state and other part-time jobs (averaging $2300).

Applying *Options:* early admission. *Required:* high school transcript. *Application deadline:* rolling (freshmen), rolling (transfers). *Notification:* continuous (freshmen).

Admissions Contact Mr. Max Munn, Director of Recruiting, Itawamba Community College, 602 West Hill Street, Fulton, MS 38843. *Phone:* 601-862-8252.

JONES COUNTY JUNIOR COLLEGE
Ellisville, Mississippi

Admissions Contact Mrs. Dianne Speed, Director of Admissions and Records, Jones County Junior College, 900 South Court Street, Ellisville, MS 39437. *Phone:* 601-477-4025. *Fax:* 601-477-4258.

MERIDIAN COMMUNITY COLLEGE
Meridian, Mississippi

- **State and locally supported** 2-year, founded 1937, part of Mississippi State Board for Community and Junior Colleges
- **Calendar** semesters
- **Degree** certificates and associate
- **Small-town** 62-acre campus
- **Endowment** $4.8 million
- **Coed**, 3,572 undergraduate students, 74% full-time, 70% women, 30% men

Undergraduates 2,649 full-time, 923 part-time. Students come from 16 states and territories, 3% are from out of state, 39% African American, 0.4% Asian American or Pacific Islander, 0.8% Hispanic American, 2% Native American, 0.1% international, 12% live on campus.

Freshmen *Admission:* 882 admitted.

Faculty *Total:* 256, 56% full-time, 3% with terminal degrees.

Majors Administrative assistant and secretarial science; athletic training; broadcast journalism; clinical/medical laboratory technology; computer engineering technology; computer graphics; dental hygiene; drafting and design technology; electrical, electronic and communications engineering technology; emergency medical technology (EMT paramedic); fire science; health information/medical records administration; horticultural science; hotel/motel administration; machine tool technology; marketing/marketing management; medical radiologic technology; nursing (registered nurse training); physical therapy; respiratory care therapy; telecommunications.

Academic Programs *Special study options:* academic remediation for entering students, adult/continuing education programs, advanced placement credit, cooperative education, distance learning, English as a second language, independent study, part-time degree program, services for LD students, summer session for credit.

Library L.O. Todd Library with 50,000 titles, 600 serial subscriptions.

Computers on Campus 123 computers available on campus for general student use. A campuswide network can be accessed from student residence rooms and from off campus. Internet access, online (class) registration, at least one staffed computer lab available.

Student Life *Housing Options:* coed, men-only, women-only. Campus housing is university owned and leased by the school. *Activities and Organizations:* drama/theater group, student-run newspaper, radio station, choral group, Phi Theta Kappa, Vocational Industrial Clubs of America, Health Occupations

Students of America, Organization of Student Nurses, Distributive Education Clubs of America. *Campus security:* 24-hour patrols, student patrols. *Student services:* health clinic, personal/psychological counseling.

Athletics Member NJCAA. *Intercollegiate sports:* baseball M(s), basketball M(s)/W(s), cross-country running M(s)/W(s), golf M(s), soccer M(s), softball W(s), tennis M(s)/W(s), track and field M(s)/W(s). *Intramural sports:* basketball M/W, bowling M/W, cross-country running M/W, swimming and diving M/W, tennis M/W, volleyball M/W.

Standardized Tests *Required:* SAT or ACT (for placement). *Recommended:* ACCUPLACER.

Costs (2004–05) *Tuition:* state resident $1300 full-time, $70 per credit hour part-time; nonresident $2740 full-time, $137 per credit hour part-time. *Required fees:* $156 full-time, $4 per credit hour part-time, $20 per term part-time. *Room and board:* $2550. Room and board charges vary according to board plan. *Payment plan:* installment. *Waivers:* employees or children of employees.

Financial Aid Of all full-time matriculated undergraduates who enrolled in 2003, 100 Federal Work-Study jobs (averaging $2100).

Applying *Options:* early admission. *Required:* high school transcript, minimum 2.0 GPA. *Required for some:* essay or personal statement. *Application deadline:* rolling (freshmen), rolling (transfers).

Admissions Contact Ms. Dianne Walton, Director of Enrollment Services, Meridian Community College, 910 Highway 19 North, Meridian, MS 39307. *Phone:* 601-484-8895. *Toll-free phone:* 800-622-8731. *E-mail:* dwalton@mcc.cc.ms.us.

MISSISSIPPI DELTA COMMUNITY COLLEGE
Moorhead, Mississippi

Admissions Contact Mr. Joseph F. Ray Jr., Vice President of Admissions, Mississippi Delta Community College, PO Box 668, Moorhead, MS 38761-0668. *Phone:* 662-246-6308.

MISSISSIPPI GULF COAST COMMUNITY COLLEGE
Perkinston, Mississippi

- **District-supported** 2-year, founded 1911, part of Mississippi State Board for Community and Junior Colleges
- **Calendar** semesters
- **Degree** certificates, diplomas, and associate
- **Small-town** 600-acre campus with easy access to New Orleans
- **Endowment** $3.0 million
- **Coed**

Faculty *Student/faculty ratio:* 26:1.

Student Life *Campus security:* 24-hour emergency response devices and patrols.

Athletics Member NJCAA.

Standardized Tests *Required for some:* ACT (for placement).

Costs (2004–05) *One-time required fee:* $30. *Tuition:* state resident $1490 full-time, $75 per semester hour part-time; nonresident $3336 full-time, $142 per semester hour part-time. *Required fees:* $112 full-time, $3 per hour part-time, $20 per term part-time. *Room and board:* $2120; room only: $750. Room and board charges vary according to board plan.

Applying *Options:* common application, electronic application, early admission. *Required:* high school transcript.

Admissions Contact Ms. Michelle Sekul, Director of Admissions, Mississippi Gulf Coast Community College, PO Box 548, Perkinston, MS 39573. *Phone:* 601-928-6264. *E-mail:* michelle.sekul@mgccc.edu.

NORTHEAST MISSISSIPPI COMMUNITY COLLEGE
Booneville, Mississippi

- **State-supported** 2-year, founded 1948, part of Mississippi State Board for Community and Junior Colleges
- **Calendar** semesters
- **Degree** certificates and associate
- **Small-town** 100-acre campus
- **Coed**

Student Life *Campus security:* 24-hour patrols, student patrols, controlled dormitory access.

Athletics Member NJCAA.

Standardized Tests *Required for some:* SAT or ACT (for admission).

Northeast Mississippi Community College (continued)

Costs (2004–05) *Tuition:* state resident $1500 full-time, $83 per hour part-time; nonresident $3220 full-time, $179 per hour part-time. *Required fees:* $104 full-time. *Room and board:* $2862.

Applying *Options:* early admission.

Admissions Contact Office of Enrollment Services, Northeast Mississippi Community College, 101 Cunningham Boulevard, Booneville, MS 38829. *Phone:* 662-720-7239. *Toll-free phone:* 800-555-2154.

NORTHWEST MISSISSIPPI COMMUNITY COLLEGE

Senatobia, Mississippi

Admissions Contact Ms. Deanna Ferguson, Director of Admissions and Recruiting, Northwest Mississippi Community College, 4975 Highway 51 North, Senatobia, MS 38668-1701. *Phone:* 662-562-3222.

PEARL RIVER COMMUNITY COLLEGE

Poplarville, Mississippi

Admissions Contact Mr. J. Dow Ford, Director of Admissions, Pearl River Community College, 101 Highway 11 North, Poplarville, MS 39470. *Phone:* 601-795-6801 Ext. 216. *E-mail:* jdowford@teclink.net.

SOUTHWEST MISSISSIPPI COMMUNITY COLLEGE

Summit, Mississippi

- **State and locally supported** 2-year, founded 1918, part of Mississippi State Board for Community and Junior Colleges
- **Calendar** semesters
- **Degree** certificates and associate
- **Rural** 701-acre campus
- **Coed**

Faculty *Student/faculty ratio:* 25:1.

Student Life *Campus security:* 24-hour patrols.

Athletics Member NJCAA.

Standardized Tests *Required for some:* ACT (for placement).

Costs (2004–05) *Tuition:* state resident $750 full-time, $70 per hour part-time; nonresident $1850 full-time, $165 per hour part-time. *Required fees:* $50 full-time, $25 per term part-time. *Room and board:* $1050.

Financial Aid Of all full-time matriculated undergraduates who enrolled in 2003, 85 Federal Work-Study jobs (averaging $698). 6 state and other part-time jobs (averaging $550).

Applying *Required:* high school transcript.

Admissions Contact Alicia C. Shows, Director of Admissions, Southwest Mississippi Community College, College Drive, Summit, MS 39666. *Phone:* 601-276-2000. *Fax:* 601-276-3888.

VIRGINIA COLLEGE AT JACKSON

Jackson, Mississippi

- **Proprietary** 2-year, founded 2000
- **Calendar** quarters
- **Degree** diplomas and associate
- **Urban** 3-acre campus
- **Coed**

Faculty *Student/faculty ratio:* 11:1.

Student Life *Campus security:* 24-hour emergency response devices and patrols.

Standardized Tests *Required:* CPAt (for admission).

Applying *Application fee:* $100. *Required:* high school transcript, interview, GED.

Admissions Contact Mr. Bill Milstead, Vice President of Admissions, Virginia College at Jackson, Interstate 55 North, Jackson, MS 39211. *Phone:* 601-977-0960 Ext. 2704. *E-mail:* bmilstead@vc.edu.

MISSOURI

ALLIED COLLEGE

Saint Ann, Missouri

Admissions Contact Mr. Larkin Hicks, President, Allied College, 500 Northwest Plaza Tower, Suite 400, Saint Ann, MO 63074. *Phone:* 314-739-4450.

BLUE RIVER COMMUNITY COLLEGE

Independence, Missouri

- **State and locally supported** 2-year, part of Metropolitan Community Colleges System
- **Calendar** semesters
- **Degree** certificates and associate
- **Suburban** campus with easy access to Kansas City
- **Endowment** $1.9 million
- **Coed,** 2,290 undergraduate students, 43% full-time, 63% women, 37% men

Undergraduates 978 full-time, 1,312 part-time. Students come from 2 states and territories, 0.2% are from out of state, 2% African American, 0.9% Asian American or Pacific Islander, 2% Hispanic American, 0.2% Native American, 0.1% international, 6% transferred in. *Retention:* 48% of 2002 full-time freshmen returned.

Freshmen *Admission:* 347 applied, 347 admitted, 347 enrolled.

Faculty *Total:* 249, 12% full-time. *Student/faculty ratio:* 26:1.

Majors Accounting technology and bookkeeping; administrative assistant and secretarial science; business administration and management; computer and information sciences related; computer science; criminal justice/police science; fire science; information science/studies; liberal arts and sciences/liberal studies.

Academic Programs *Special study options:* academic remediation for entering students, accelerated degree program, adult/continuing education programs, advanced placement credit, cooperative education, distance learning, English as a second language, honors programs, internships, off-campus study, part-time degree program, services for LD students, summer session for credit.

Library Blue River Community College Library with 10,312 titles, 66 serial subscriptions, 567 audiovisual materials, an OPAC, a Web page.

Computers on Campus 375 computers available on campus for general student use. A campuswide network can be accessed from off campus. Internet access, at least one staffed computer lab available.

Student Life *Housing:* college housing not available. *Activities and Organizations:* choral group. *Campus security:* 24-hour emergency response devices and patrols.

Standardized Tests *Required:* ACT ASSET (for placement). *Recommended:* ACT (for placement).

Costs (2005–06) *Tuition:* area resident $2130 full-time, $71 per hour part-time; state resident $3870 full-time, $129 per hour part-time; nonresident $5250 full-time, $175 per hour part-time. Full-time tuition and fees vary according to course level and program. Part-time tuition and fees vary according to course level and program. *Required fees:* $150 full-time, $5 per hour part-time. *Payment plan:* installment. *Waivers:* employees or children of employees.

Applying *Options:* early admission, deferred entrance. *Application deadline:* rolling (freshmen), rolling (transfers).

Admissions Contact Mr. Jon Burke, Dean of Student Services, Blue River Community College, 20301 East 78 Highway, Independence, MO 64057. *Phone:* 816-655-6118. *Fax:* 816-655-6014.

CONCORDE CAREER INSTITUTE

Kansas City, Missouri

Admissions Contact 3239 Broadway, Kansas City, MO 64111-2407.

COTTEY COLLEGE

Nevada, Missouri

Admissions Contact Ms. Marjorie J. Cooke, Dean of Enrollment Management, Cottey College, 1000 West Austin, Nevada, MO 64772. *Phone:* 417-667-8181. *Toll-free phone:* 888-526-8839. *Fax:* 417-667-8103. *E-mail:* enrollmgt@cottey.edu.

▶ **See page 490 for a narrative description.**

CROWDER COLLEGE

Neosho, Missouri

- **State and locally supported** 2-year, founded 1963, part of Missouri Coordinating Board for Higher Education
- **Calendar** semesters
- **Degree** certificates and associate
- **Rural** 608-acre campus
- **Coed,** 2,611 undergraduate students, 54% full-time, 65% women, 35% men

Undergraduates 1,403 full-time, 1,208 part-time. Students come from 15 states and territories, 15 other countries, 1% are from out of state, 1% African American, 1% Asian American or Pacific Islander, 5% Hispanic American, 2% Native American, 0.6% international, 5% transferred in, 10% live on campus.

Freshmen *Admission:* 1,024 applied, 1,024 admitted, 588 enrolled.

Faculty *Total:* 214, 30% full-time. *Student/faculty ratio:* 19:1.

Majors Administrative assistant and secretarial science; agribusiness; agriculture; art; biology/biological sciences; business administration and management; business automation/technology/data entry; computer systems networking and telecommunications; construction engineering technology; drafting and design technology; dramatic/theatre arts; education; electrical, electronic and communications engineering technology; elementary education; environmental engineering technology; environmental health; executive assistant/executive secretary; farm and ranch management; fire science; general studies; industrial technology; legal administrative assistant/secretary; liberal arts and sciences/liberal studies; mass communication/media; mathematics; mathematics and computer science; medical administrative assistant and medical secretary; music; nursing (registered nurse training); physical education teaching and coaching; physical sciences; poultry science; pre-engineering; psychology; public relations/image management.

Academic Programs *Special study options:* academic remediation for entering students, adult/continuing education programs, advanced placement credit, cooperative education, English as a second language, freshman honors college, honors programs, internships, part-time degree program, study abroad, summer session for credit.

Library Crowder College Learning Resources Center with 37,452 titles, 163 serial subscriptions, 3,632 audiovisual materials, an OPAC, a Web page.

Computers on Campus 515 computers available on campus for general student use. A campuswide network can be accessed. Internet access, at least one staffed computer lab available.

Student Life *Housing Options:* men-only, women-only. Campus housing is university owned. *Activities and Organizations:* drama/theater group, student-run newspaper, choral group, Phi Beta Lambda, Students in Free Enterprise, Baptist Student Union, Student Senate, Student Ambassadors. *Campus security:* 24-hour patrols. *Student services:* personal/psychological counseling.

Athletics Member NJCAA. *Intercollegiate sports:* baseball M(s), basketball W(s). *Intramural sports:* soccer M.

Standardized Tests *Required:* ACT COMPASS (for placement). *Recommended:* ACT (for placement).

Costs (2004–05) *Tuition:* area resident $1740 full-time, $58 per semester hour part-time; state resident $2460 full-time, $82 per semester hour part-time; nonresident $3210 full-time, $107 per semester hour part-time. *Required fees:* $210 full-time, $7 per semester hour part-time. *Room and board:* $3870. *Waivers:* employees or children of employees.

Financial Aid Of all full-time matriculated undergraduates who enrolled in 2003, 150 Federal Work-Study jobs (averaging $1000).

Applying *Application fee:* $25. *Required:* high school transcript. *Application deadline:* rolling (freshmen), rolling (transfers). *Notification:* continuous (freshmen).

Admissions Contact Mr. Jim Riggs, Admissions Coordinator, Crowder College, 601 Laclede Avenue, Neosho, MO 64850. *Phone:* 417-451-3223 Ext. 5466. *Toll-free phone:* 866-238-7788. *Fax:* 417-455-5731.

EAST CENTRAL COLLEGE
Union, Missouri

- **District-supported** 2-year, founded 1959, part of Missouri Coordinating Board for Higher Education
- **Calendar** semesters
- **Degree** certificates and associate
- **Rural** 207-acre campus with easy access to St. Louis
- **Endowment** $1.8 million
- **Coed,** 3,337 undergraduate students, 45% full-time, 61% women, 39% men

Undergraduates 1,512 full-time, 1,825 part-time. Students come from 4 states and territories, 0.2% are from out of state, 0.6% African American, 0.7% Asian American or Pacific Islander, 0.8% Hispanic American, 0.3% Native American, 6% transferred in.

Freshmen *Admission:* 1,297 applied, 1,297 admitted, 1,128 enrolled. *Average high school GPA:* 2.50.

Faculty *Total:* 186, 30% full-time, 7% with terminal degrees. *Student/faculty ratio:* 21:1.

Majors Accounting; administrative assistant and secretarial science; anthropology; archeology; art; automobile/automotive mechanics technology; biology/biological sciences; botany/plant biology; business administration and management; chemistry; commercial and advertising art; computer programming; computer science; construction engineering technology; criminal justice/law enforcement administration; criminal justice/police science; data processing and data processing technology; design and visual communications; drafting and design technology; dramatic/theatre arts; ecology; economics; education; electrical, electronic and communications engineering technology; elementary education; emergency medical technology (EMT paramedic); English; family and consumer sciences/human sciences; fire science; fish/game management; forestry; French; geography; geology/earth science; German; heating, air conditioning, ventilation and refrigeration maintenance technology; history; horticultural

science; hospitality administration; hotel/motel administration; humanities; industrial technology; information science/studies; interior design; journalism; legal administrative assistant/secretary; liberal arts and sciences/liberal studies; library science; machine tool technology; management information systems; marketing/marketing management; mass communication/media; mathematics; medical administrative assistant and medical secretary; modern languages; music; nursing (registered nurse training); parks, recreation and leisure; pharmacy; philosophy; physical education teaching and coaching; physics; political science and government; pre-engineering; psychology; public administration; religious studies; social work; sociology; Spanish; special products marketing; speech and rhetoric; tourism and travel services management; welding technology; wildlife and wildlands science and management; zoology/animal biology.

Academic Programs *Special study options:* academic remediation for entering students, adult/continuing education programs, advanced placement credit, distance learning, English as a second language, honors programs, independent study, internships, part-time degree program, services for LD students, study abroad, summer session for credit.

Library East Central College Library with 38,863 titles, 278 serial subscriptions, 1,420 audiovisual materials, an OPAC, a Web page.

Computers on Campus 372 computers available on campus for general student use. A campuswide network can be accessed from off campus. Internet access, online (class) registration, at least one staffed computer lab available.

Student Life *Housing:* college housing not available. *Activities and Organizations:* drama/theater group, student-run newspaper, choral group, student government, Phi Theta Kappa, Amnesty International, Multicultural Club. *Campus security:* 24-hour emergency response devices, late-night transport/escort service.

Athletics Member NJCAA. *Intercollegiate sports:* soccer M(s), softball W(s).

Standardized Tests *Required:* ACT ASSET, ACT COMPASS (for placement). *Recommended:* ACT (for placement).

Costs (2005–06) *Tuition:* area resident $1464 full-time, $61 per credit hour part-time; state resident $2088 full-time, $87 per credit hour part-time; nonresident $3144 full-time, $113 per credit hour part-time. Full-time tuition and fees vary according to course load and program. Part-time tuition and fees vary according to course load and program. *Required fees:* $240 full-time, $10 per credit hour part-time. *Payment plans:* installment, deferred payment. *Waivers:* employees or children of employees.

Financial Aid Of all full-time matriculated undergraduates who enrolled in 2003, 35 Federal Work-Study jobs (averaging $1500). 35 state and other part-time jobs (averaging $1500).

Applying *Options:* common application, early admission, deferred entrance. *Required:* high school transcript. *Application deadline:* rolling (freshmen), rolling (transfers).

Admissions Contact Mrs. Karen Wieda, Registrar, East Central College, 1964 Prairie Dell Road, Union, MO 63084. *Phone:* 636-583-5195 Ext. 2220. *Fax:* 636-583-1897. *E-mail:* wiedaks@eastcentral.edu.

HERITAGE COLLEGE
Kansas City, Missouri

Admissions Contact 534 East 99th Street, Kansas City, MO 64131-4203.

HICKEY COLLEGE
St. Louis, Missouri

- **Proprietary** primarily 2-year, founded 1933
- **Calendar** semesters
- **Degrees** diplomas, associate, and bachelor's
- **Suburban** campus
- **Coed**

Founded in 1933, Hickey College offers diploma, associate, and bachelor's degree programs. Eight- to 16-month programs include accounting, administrative assistant studies, computer applications and programming, computer specialist, graphic design, legal administrative assistant studies, and paralegal studies. Tuition and fees vary by program. Financial assistance is available for those who qualify. Housing is offered. The College is an accredited member of ACICS. For more information, students should call 314-434-2212 or 800-777-1544 (toll-free) or visit the Web at http://www.hickeycollege.edu.

Faculty *Student/faculty ratio:* 30:1.

Costs (2004–05) *Tuition:* $10,480 full-time, $300 per credit hour part-time. *Room only:* $4800.

Applying *Application fee:* $50. *Required:* high school transcript, interview.

Admissions Contact Ms. Michelle Hayes, Director of Admissions, Hickey College, 940 West Port Plaza Drive, St. Louis, MO 63146. *Phone:* 314-434-2212 Ext. 136. *Toll-free phone:* 800-777-1544. *Fax:* 314-434-1974. *E-mail:* admin@hickeycollege.edu.

HIGH-TECH INSTITUTE
Kansas City, Missouri

Admissions Contact 9001 State Line Road, Kansas City, MO 64114.

IHM HEALTH STUDIES CENTER
St. Louis, Missouri

- **Independent** 2-year, founded 1977
- **Calendar** trimesters
- **Degree** certificates and associate
- **Suburban** campus
- **Coed**

Costs (2004–05) *Comprehensive fee:* $12,820 includes full-time tuition ($3988), mandatory fees ($210), and room and board ($8622). Part-time tuition: $145 per credit hour.
Admissions Contact Mr. Taz A. Meyer, Director of Education, IHM Health Studies Center, 2500 Abbott Place, St. Louis, MO 63143-2636. *Phone:* 314-768-1234 Ext. 1128.

ITT TECHNICAL INSTITUTE
Arnold, Missouri

- **Proprietary** primarily 2-year, part of ITT Educational Services, Inc
- **Calendar** quarters
- **Degrees** associate and bachelor's
- **Coed**

Standardized Tests *Required:* Wonderlic aptitude test (for admission).
Costs (2004–05) *Tuition:* Please see school catalog for specific information.
Applying *Options:* deferred entrance. *Application fee:* $100. *Required:* high school transcript, interview. *Recommended:* letters of recommendation.
Admissions Contact Mr. James R. Rowe, Director of Recruitment, ITT Technical Institute, 1930 Meyer Drury Drive, Arnold, MO 63010. *Phone:* 636-464-6600. *Toll-free phone:* 888-488-1082. *Fax:* 636-464-6611.

ITT TECHNICAL INSTITUTE
Earth City, Missouri

- **Proprietary** primarily 2-year, founded 1936, part of ITT Educational Services, Inc
- **Calendar** quarters
- **Degrees** associate and bachelor's
- **Suburban** 2-acre campus with easy access to St. Louis
- **Coed**

Standardized Tests *Required:* Wonderlic aptitude test (for admission).
Costs (2004–05) *Tuition:* Please see school catalog for specific information.
Applying *Options:* deferred entrance. *Application fee:* $100. *Required:* high school transcript, interview. *Recommended:* letters of recommendation.
Admissions Contact Mr. Randal Hayes, ITT Technical Institute, 13505 Lakefront Drive, Earth City, MO 63045. *Phone:* 314-298-7800. *Toll-free phone:* 800-235-5488. *Fax:* 314-298-0559.

JEFFERSON COLLEGE
Hillsboro, Missouri

- **State-supported** 2-year, founded 1963, part of Missouri Coordinating Board for Higher Education
- **Calendar** semesters
- **Degree** certificates and associate
- **Rural** 480-acre campus with easy access to St. Louis
- **Endowment** $769,631
- **Coed**

Faculty *Student/faculty ratio:* 18:1.
Student Life *Campus security:* 24-hour patrols.
Athletics Member NJCAA.
Standardized Tests *Required:* ACT COMPASS (for placement). *Recommended:* ACT (for placement).
Costs (2004–05) *Tuition:* area resident $1530 full-time, $51 per credit part-time; state resident $2230 full-time, $76 per credit part-time; nonresident $3060 full-time, $102 per credit part-time. Full-time tuition and fees vary according to program. Part-time tuition and fees vary according to program. *Required fees:* $300 full-time, $10 per credit part-time. *Room and board:* $6111. Room and board charges vary according to housing facility.
Financial Aid Of all full-time matriculated undergraduates who enrolled in 2003, 82 Federal Work-Study jobs (averaging $1525).

Applying *Options:* electronic application, early admission. *Application fee:* $20. *Required:* high school transcript.
Admissions Contact Ms. Amy Martin-Small, Director of Admissions and Financial Aid, Jefferson College, 1000 Viking Drive, Hillsboro, MO 63050. *Phone:* 636-797-3000 Ext. 218. *Toll-free phone:* 636-797-3000 Ext. 217. *Fax:* 636-789-5103. *E-mail:* admissions@jeffco.edu.

LINN STATE TECHNICAL COLLEGE
Linn, Missouri

- **State-supported** 2-year, founded 1961
- **Calendar** semesters
- **Degree** certificates and associate
- **Rural** 249-acre campus
- **Endowment** $41,867
- **Coed, primarily men,** 868 undergraduate students, 90% full-time, 10% women, 90% men

Undergraduates 779 full-time, 89 part-time. Students come from 11 states and territories, 2 other countries, 1% are from out of state, 0.8% African American, 0.8% Asian American or Pacific Islander, 0.9% Hispanic American, 0.9% Native American, 0.2% international, 9% transferred in, 15% live on campus. *Retention:* 58% of 2002 full-time freshmen returned.
Freshmen *Admission:* 1,725 applied, 568 admitted, 355 enrolled. *Average high school GPA:* 2.78. *Test scores:* ACT scores over 18: 61%; ACT scores over 24: 7%.
Faculty *Total:* 83, 93% full-time. *Student/faculty ratio:* 10:1.
Majors Aircraft powerplant technology; autobody/collision and repair technology; automobile/automotive mechanics technology; civil engineering technology; computer programming; computer systems analysis; drafting and design technology; electrical, electronic and communications engineering technology; electrical/electronics equipment installation and repair; electrician; heating, air conditioning, ventilation and refrigeration maintenance technology; heavy equipment maintenance technology; industrial production technologies related; information science/studies; laser and optical technology; lineworker; machine tool technology; nuclear and industrial radiologic technologies related; physical therapist assistant; turf and turfgrass management.
Academic Programs *Special study options:* academic remediation for entering students, accelerated degree program, adult/continuing education programs, advanced placement credit, cooperative education, distance learning, double majors, English as a second language, independent study, internships, off-campus study, part-time degree program, services for LD students, summer session for credit. *ROTC:* Army (b).
Library Linn State Technical College Library plus 2 others with 13,774 titles, 132 serial subscriptions, 729 audiovisual materials, an OPAC, a Web page.
Computers on Campus 51 computers available on campus for general student use. A campuswide network can be accessed from student residence rooms. Internet access, at least one staffed computer lab available.
Student Life *Housing Options:* coed, men-only, women-only, disabled students. Campus housing is university owned. *Activities and Organizations:* Skills USA-VICA, Phi Theta Kappa, Student Government Association, Aviation Club, Electricity Club. *Campus security:* 24-hour emergency response devices, student patrols, controlled dormitory access, indoor and outdoor surveillance cameras. *Student services:* personal/psychological counseling.
Athletics *Intercollegiate sports:* archery M/W, basketball M/W, bowling M/W, softball M/W, table tennis M/W, volleyball M/W. *Intramural sports:* archery M/W, basketball M/W, bowling M/W, golf M/W, riflery M/W, softball M/W, table tennis M/W, volleyball M/W.
Standardized Tests *Required:* ACT ASSET, ACT COMPASS (for admission). *Required for some:* ACT (for admission), ACT (for placement), ACT ASSET, ACT COMPASS.
Costs (2005–06) *Tuition:* state resident $3900 full-time, $130 per credit part-time; nonresident $7800 full-time, $260 per credit part-time. *Required fees:* $630 full-time, $21 per credit part-time. *Room and board:* $2006; room only: $1406. Room and board charges vary according to board plan. *Payment plan:* installment. *Waivers:* employees or children of employees.
Financial Aid Of all full-time matriculated undergraduates who enrolled in 2003, 70 Federal Work-Study jobs (averaging $769).
Applying *Options:* common application, electronic application. *Required:* high school transcript. *Required for some:* essay or personal statement, 3 letters of recommendation, interview, driving record, physical examination. *Notification:* continuous (freshmen).
Admissions Contact Ms. Becky Dunn, Assistant Director of Admissions, Linn State Technical College, One Technology Drive, Linn, MO 65051. *Phone:* 573-897-5196. *Toll-free phone:* 800-743-TECH. *Fax:* 573-897-5026. *E-mail:* admissions@linnstate.edu.

LONGVIEW COMMUNITY COLLEGE
Lee's Summit, Missouri

- **State and locally supported** 2-year, founded 1969, part of Metropolitan Community Colleges System
- **Calendar** semesters
- **Degree** certificates and associate
- **Suburban** 147-acre campus with easy access to Kansas City
- **Endowment** $1.9 million
- **Coed,** 5,603 undergraduate students, 44% full-time, 58% women, 42% men

Undergraduates 2,483 full-time, 3,120 part-time. Students come from 6 states and territories, 1% are from out of state, 12% African American, 0.9% Asian American or Pacific Islander, 2% Hispanic American, 0.2% Native American, 5% transferred in. *Retention:* 42% of 2002 full-time freshmen returned.

Freshmen *Admission:* 707 applied, 707 admitted, 632 enrolled.

Faculty *Total:* 330, 25% full-time. *Student/faculty ratio:* 27:1.

Majors Accounting; administrative assistant and secretarial science; agricultural mechanization; automobile/automotive mechanics technology; biological and physical sciences; biology/biological sciences; business administration and management; chemistry; computer and information sciences related; computer programming; computer science; computer typography and composition equipment operation; corrections; criminal justice/law enforcement administration; criminal justice/police science; data processing and data processing technology; drafting and design technology; electrical, electronic and communications engineering technology; engineering; heavy equipment maintenance technology; human services; legal administrative assistant/secretary; liberal arts and sciences/liberal studies; marketing/marketing management; medical administrative assistant and medical secretary; postal management; pre-engineering; quality control technology.

Academic Programs *Special study options:* academic remediation for entering students, accelerated degree program, adult/continuing education programs, advanced placement credit, cooperative education, distance learning, English as a second language, honors programs, internships, off-campus study, part-time degree program, services for LD students, summer session for credit.

Library Longview Community College Library with 56,266 titles, 288 serial subscriptions, 806 audiovisual materials, an OPAC, a Web page.

Computers on Campus 650 computers available on campus for general student use. A campuswide network can be accessed from off campus. Internet access, at least one staffed computer lab available.

Student Life *Housing:* college housing not available. *Activities and Organizations:* drama/theater group, student-run newspaper, choral group, student newspaper, student government, Phi Theta Kappa, Longview Mighty Voices Choir, Longview Broadcasting Network, national fraternities. *Campus security:* 24-hour patrols. *Student services:* personal/psychological counseling.

Athletics Member NJCAA. *Intercollegiate sports:* baseball M(s), volleyball W(s). *Intramural sports:* basketball M/W, swimming and diving M/W, volleyball M/W.

Standardized Tests *Required:* ACT ASSET (for placement). *Recommended:* ACT (for placement).

Costs (2005–06) *Tuition:* area resident $2130 full-time, $79 per hour part-time; state resident $3870 full-time, $129 per hour part-time; nonresident $5250 full-time, $175 per hour part-time. Full-time tuition and fees vary according to degree level and program. Part-time tuition and fees vary according to degree level and program. *Required fees:* $150 full-time, $5 per hour part-time.

Applying *Options:* early admission, deferred entrance. *Application deadline:* rolling (freshmen), rolling (transfers).

Admissions Contact Ms. Kathy Hale, Registrar, Longview Community College, 500 Southwest Longview Road, Lee's Summit, MO 64081-2105. *Phone:* 816-672-2249. *Fax:* 816-672-2040.

MAPLE WOODS COMMUNITY COLLEGE
Kansas City, Missouri

- **State and locally supported** 2-year, founded 1969, part of Metropolitan Community Colleges System
- **Calendar** semesters
- **Degree** certificates and associate
- **Suburban** 205-acre campus
- **Endowment** $1.9 million
- **Coed,** 4,461 undergraduate students, 43% full-time, 60% women, 40% men

Undergraduates 1,917 full-time, 2,544 part-time. Students come from 4 states and territories, 1% are from out of state, 3% African American, 2% Asian American or Pacific Islander, 2% Hispanic American, 0.5% Native American, 5% transferred in. *Retention:* 40% of 2002 full-time freshmen returned.

Freshmen *Admission:* 893 applied, 893 admitted, 554 enrolled.

Faculty *Total:* 314, 17% full-time. *Student/faculty ratio:* 25:1.

Majors Accounting; administrative assistant and secretarial science; avionics maintenance technology; biological and physical sciences; biology/biological

sciences; business administration and management; chemistry; computer and information sciences related; computer programming; computer science; criminal justice/law enforcement administration; criminal justice/police science; data processing and data processing technology; electrical, electronic and communications engineering technology; heating, air conditioning, ventilation and refrigeration maintenance technology; legal administrative assistant/secretary; liberal arts and sciences/liberal studies; machine shop technology; machine tool technology; marketing/marketing management; medical administrative assistant and medical secretary; pre-engineering; tourism and travel services management; veterinary technology.

Academic Programs *Special study options:* academic remediation for entering students, accelerated degree program, adult/continuing education programs, advanced placement credit, cooperative education, distance learning, English as a second language, honors programs, internships, off-campus study, part-time degree program, services for LD students, summer session for credit.

Library Maple Woods Community College Library with 32,906 titles, 250 serial subscriptions, 783 audiovisual materials, an OPAC.

Computers on Campus 400 computers available on campus for general student use. A campuswide network can be accessed from off campus. Internet access, at least one staffed computer lab available.

Student Life *Housing:* college housing not available. *Activities and Organizations:* drama/theater group, student-run newspaper, choral group, Student Activities Council, Art Club, Friends of All Cultures, Phi Theta Kappa, Engineering Club, national fraternities. *Campus security:* 24-hour patrols, late-night transport/escort service. *Student services:* personal/psychological counseling.

Athletics Member NJCAA. *Intercollegiate sports:* baseball M(s). *Intramural sports:* softball M/W, volleyball M/W.

Standardized Tests *Required:* ACT ASSET (for placement).

Costs (2005–06) *Tuition:* area resident $2130 full-time, $71 per hour part-time; state resident $3870 full-time, $129 per hour part-time; nonresident $5250 full-time, $175 per hour part-time. Full-time tuition and fees vary according to course level and program. Part-time tuition and fees vary according to course level and program. *Required fees:* $150 full-time, $5 per hour part-time. *Payment plan:* installment. *Waivers:* employees or children of employees.

Applying *Options:* early admission, deferred entrance. *Application deadline:* rolling (freshmen), rolling (transfers). *Notification:* continuous (freshmen).

Admissions Contact Ms. Dawn Hatterman, Registrar, Maple Woods Community College, 2601 Northeast Barry Road, Kansas City, MO 64156-1299. *Phone:* 816-437-3108. *Fax:* 816-437-3351.

METRO BUSINESS COLLEGE
Cape Girardeau, Missouri

Admissions Contact Ms. Kyla Evans, Admissions Director, Metro Business College, 1732 North Kingshighway, Cape Girardeau, MO 63701. *Phone:* 573-334-9181.

METRO BUSINESS COLLEGE
Jefferson City, Missouri

Admissions Contact Ms. Cherie Chockley, Campus Director, Metro Business College, 1407 Southwest Boulevard, Jefferson City, MO 65109. *Phone:* 573-635-6600. *Toll-free phone:* 800-467-0786.

METRO BUSINESS COLLEGE
Rolla, Missouri

Admissions Contact Ms. Cristie Barker, Director, Metro Business College, 1202 East State Route 72, Rolla, MO 65401. *Phone:* 314-364-8464. *Toll-free phone:* 800-467-0785.

METROPOLITAN COMMUNITY COLLEGE-BUSINESS & TECHNOLOGY COLLEGE
Kansas City, Missouri

- **State and locally supported** 2-year, founded 1995, part of Metropolitan Community Colleges
- **Calendar** semesters
- **Degree** certificates and associate
- **Urban** 23-acre campus
- **Endowment** $1.9 million
- **Coed, primarily men,** 357 undergraduate students, 25% full-time, 10% women, 90% men
- 100% of applicants were admitted

Undergraduates 90 full-time, 267 part-time. Students come from 2 states and territories, 2 other countries, 2% are from out of state, 6% African American,

Metropolitan Community College-Business & Technology College (continued)
0.8% Asian American or Pacific Islander, 3% Hispanic American, 0.3% Native American, 0.6% international, 3% transferred in.

Freshmen *Admission:* 95 applied, 95 admitted, 32 enrolled.

Faculty *Total:* 34, 26% full-time. *Student/faculty ratio:* 14:1.

Majors Accounting; accounting technology and bookkeeping; artificial intelligence and robotics; building/construction site management; business administration and management; business/commerce; carpentry; computer and information sciences; computer and information sciences and support services related; computer and information sciences related; computer and information systems security; computer graphics; computer/information technology services administration related; computer programming; computer programming related; computer programming (specific applications); computer programming (vendor/product certification); computer science; computer software and media applications related; computer systems analysis; computer systems networking and telecommunications; data entry/microcomputer applications; data entry/microcomputer applications related; data modeling/warehousing and database administration; data processing and data processing technology; drafting and design technology; electrical, electronic and communications engineering technology; engineering; engineering-related technologies; environmental engineering technology; glazier; information science/studies; information technology; liberal arts and sciences/liberal studies; machine shop technology; management information systems and services related; masonry; quality control technology; system administration; system, networking, and LAN/WAN management; web/multimedia management and webmaster; web page, digital/multimedia and information resources design; word processing.

Library Learning Resource Center/Library with an OPAC.

Computers on Campus 355 computers available on campus for general student use.

Student Life *Housing:* college housing not available. *Campus security:* 24-hour patrols, late-night transport/escort service.

Standardized Tests *Required:* ACT ASSET and ACT COMPASS (for placement). *Recommended:* ACT (for placement).

Costs (2005–06) *Tuition:* area resident $2130 full-time, $71 per hour part-time; state resident $3870 full-time, $129 per hour part-time; nonresident $5250 full-time, $175 per hour part-time. Full-time tuition and fees vary according to course level. Part-time tuition and fees vary according to course level. *Required fees:* $150 full-time, $5 per hour part-time. *Payment plan:* installment. *Waivers:* employees or children of employees.

Admissions Contact Mr. Jim Everett, Technical Education and Enrollment Management, Metropolitan Community College-Business & Technology College, 1775 Universal Avenue, Kansas City, MO 64120. *Toll-free phone:* 800-841-7158.

MIDWEST INSTITUTE
Earth City, Missouri

Admissions Contact 4260 Shoreline Drive, Earth City, MO 63045.

MIDWEST INSTITUTE
Kirkwood, Missouri

Admissions Contact 10910 Manchester Road, Kirkwood, MO 63122.

MINERAL AREA COLLEGE
Park Hills, Missouri

- **District-supported** 2-year, founded 1922, part of Missouri Coordinating Board for Higher Education
- **Calendar** semesters
- **Degree** certificates and associate
- **Rural** 240-acre campus with easy access to St. Louis
- **Endowment** $2.1 million
- **Coed,** 2,820 undergraduate students, 57% full-time, 68% women, 32% men

Undergraduates 1,605 full-time, 1,215 part-time. Students come from 6 states and territories, 1% are from out of state, 2% African American, 0.3% Asian American or Pacific Islander, 0.5% Hispanic American, 0.6% Native American, 0.4% international, 3% transferred in.

Freshmen *Admission:* 697 applied, 697 admitted, 697 enrolled. *Average high school GPA:* 2.84. *Test scores:* ACT scores over 18: 69%; ACT scores over 24: 12%.

Faculty *Total:* 238, 22% full-time, 8% with terminal degrees. *Student/faculty ratio:* 18:1.

Majors Accounting; administrative assistant and secretarial science; agribusiness; applied horticulture; banking and financial support services; business administration and management; child care provision; clinical laboratory science/medical technology; clinical/medical laboratory technology; commercial and

advertising art; computer management; computer programming; construction engineering technology; corrections; criminal justice/police science; drafting and design technology; electrical, electronic and communications engineering technology; fire science; health/health care administration; hospitality administration related; industrial technology; liberal arts and sciences/liberal studies; marketing/marketing management; mass communication/media; medical radiologic technology; nursing assistant/aide and patient care assistant; nursing (licensed practical/vocational nurse training); nursing (registered nurse training); occupational safety and health technology; operations management; parks, recreation and leisure; radio and television broadcasting technology; system administration; tourism and travel services management.

Academic Programs *Special study options:* academic remediation for entering students, advanced placement credit, distance learning, honors programs, internships, off-campus study, part-time degree program, services for LD students, summer session for credit.

Library C. H. Cozen Learning Resource Center with 32,228 titles, 214 serial subscriptions, 4,859 audiovisual materials, an OPAC, a Web page.

Computers on Campus 226 computers available on campus for general student use. A campuswide network can be accessed from student residence rooms and from off campus. Internet access, at least one staffed computer lab available.

Student Life *Housing Options:* coed. Campus housing is university owned. *Activities and Organizations:* drama/theater group, choral group, Student Senate, Phi Theta Kappa, Psi Beta, MAC Ambassadors, Phi Beta Lambda. *Campus security:* 24-hour patrols. *Student services:* personal/psychological counseling.

Athletics Member NJCAA. *Intercollegiate sports:* baseball M(s), basketball M(s)/W(s), volleyball W(s).

Standardized Tests *Required for some:* ACT (for placement), ACT COMPASS.

Costs (2005–06) *Tuition:* area resident $2160 full-time, $72 per credit hour part-time; state resident $2880 full-time, $96 per credit hour part-time; nonresident $3540 full-time, $118 per credit hour part-time. *Room and board:* room only: $2475.

Financial Aid Of all full-time matriculated undergraduates who enrolled in 2003, 65 Federal Work-Study jobs (averaging $3708).

Applying *Options:* electronic application, early admission. *Application fee:* $15. *Required:* high school transcript. *Application deadline:* rolling (freshmen), rolling (transfers). *Notification:* continuous (freshmen).

Admissions Contact Mrs. Linda Huffman, Registrar, Mineral Area College, PO Box 1000, Park Hills, MO 63601-1000. *Phone:* 573-518-2130. *Fax:* 573-518-2166. *E-mail:* jsheets@mineralarea.edu.

MISSOURI COLLEGE
St. Louis, Missouri

Admissions Contact Mr. Doug Brinker, Admissions Director, Missouri College, 10121 Manchester Road, St. Louis, MO 63122-1583. *Phone:* 314-821-7700.

MOBERLY AREA COMMUNITY COLLEGE
Moberly, Missouri

- **State and locally supported** 2-year, founded 1927
- **Calendar** semesters
- **Degree** certificates and associate
- **Small-town** 32-acre campus
- **Endowment** $1.2 million
- **Coed,** 3,696 undergraduate students, 49% full-time, 63% women, 37% men

Undergraduates 1,821 full-time, 1,875 part-time. Students come from 17 states and territories, 12 other countries, 1% are from out of state, 7% African American, 1% Asian American or Pacific Islander, 1% Hispanic American, 0.3% Native American, 0.2% international, 4% transferred in, 1% live on campus. *Retention:* 57% of 2002 full-time freshmen returned.

Freshmen *Admission:* 940 admitted, 940 enrolled. *Average high school GPA:* 2.85. *Test scores:* ACT scores over 18: 67%; ACT scores over 24: 14%; ACT scores over 30: 1%.

Faculty *Total:* 239, 24% full-time, 8% with terminal degrees. *Student/faculty ratio:* 20:1.

Majors Accounting technology and bookkeeping; administrative assistant and secretarial science; child guidance; computer and information sciences; criminal justice/police science; drafting and design technology; electrical, electronic and communications engineering technology; graphic and printing equipment operation/production; industrial technology; liberal arts and sciences/liberal studies; marketing/marketing management; nursing (registered nurse training); pre-engineering; welding technology.

Academic Programs *Special study options:* academic remediation for entering students, adult/continuing education programs, advanced placement credit, cooperative education, distance learning, internships, part-time degree program, services for LD students, study abroad, summer session for credit.

Library Kate Stamper Wilhite Library with 23,027 titles, 88 serial subscriptions, 1,393 audiovisual materials, an OPAC, a Web page.

Computers on Campus 750 computers available on campus for general student use. A campuswide network can be accessed from off campus. Internet access, at least one staffed computer lab available.

Student Life *Housing Options:* men-only, women-only. Campus housing is university owned. *Activities and Organizations:* drama/theater group, student-run newspaper, choral group, Phi Theta Kappa, Student Nurses Association, Child Care Club, Delta Epsilon Chi, Brother Ox. *Campus security:* student patrols, extensive surveillance.

Athletics Member NJCAA. *Intercollegiate sports:* basketball M(s)/W(s), cheerleading M(s)/W(s). *Intramural sports:* basketball M/W, volleyball M/W.

Standardized Tests *Required for some:* ACT (for admission), ACT ASSET. *Recommended:* ACT (for admission), ACT ASSET.

Costs (2005–06) *Tuition:* area resident $1650 full-time, $55 per credit hour part-time; state resident $2430 full-time, $81 per credit hour part-time; nonresident $3840 full-time, $128 per credit hour part-time. *Required fees:* $240 full-time, $8 per credit hour part-time. *Room and board:* room only: $1800. *Payment plan:* installment. *Waivers:* senior citizens and employees or children of employees.

Financial Aid Of all full-time matriculated undergraduates who enrolled in 2003, 89 Federal Work-Study jobs (averaging $4193).

Applying *Options:* electronic application. *Required:* high school transcript. *Application deadline:* rolling (freshmen), rolling (transfers). *Notification:* continuous until 9/1 (freshmen).

Admissions Contact Dr. James Grant, Dean of Student Services, Moberly Area Community College, 101 College Avenue, Moberly, MO 65270-1304. *Phone:* 660-263-4110 Ext. 235. *Toll-free phone:* 800-622-2070 Ext. 270. *Fax:* 660-263-2406. *E-mail:* info@macc.edu.

NORTH CENTRAL MISSOURI COLLEGE
Trenton, Missouri

- **District-supported** 2-year, founded 1925
- **Calendar** semesters
- **Degree** certificates and associate
- **Small-town** 2-acre campus
- **Endowment** $437,671
- **Coed,** 1,406 undergraduate students, 51% full-time, 71% women, 29% men

Undergraduates 724 full-time, 682 part-time. Students come from 7 states and territories, 1 other country, 19% are from out of state, 4% transferred in, 9% live on campus.

Freshmen *Admission:* 549 applied, 422 admitted, 401 enrolled.

Faculty *Total:* 108, 27% full-time, 6% with terminal degrees. *Student/faculty ratio:* 16:1.

Majors Accounting; administrative assistant and secretarial science; agricultural business and management; automobile/automotive mechanics technology; business administration and management; carpentry; computer engineering technology; construction engineering technology; criminal justice/law enforcement administration; data processing and data processing technology; drafting and design technology; electrical, electronic and communications engineering technology; emergency medical technology (EMT paramedic); farm and ranch management; liberal arts and sciences/liberal studies; marketing/marketing management; nursing (registered nurse training).

Academic Programs *Special study options:* academic remediation for entering students, accelerated degree program, adult/continuing education programs, advanced placement credit, cooperative education, distance learning, internships, part-time degree program, services for LD students, summer session for credit.

Library North Central Missouri College Library with 20,627 titles, 104 serial subscriptions.

Computers on Campus 159 computers available on campus for general student use. A campuswide network can be accessed. Internet access, at least one staffed computer lab available.

Student Life *Housing Options:* men-only, women-only. Campus housing is university owned. *Activities and Organizations:* drama/theater group, student-run newspaper. *Campus security:* controlled dormitory access. *Student services:* personal/psychological counseling.

Athletics Member NJCAA. *Intercollegiate sports:* baseball M(s), basketball M(s)/W(s), softball W(s).

Standardized Tests *Required for some:* SAT or ACT (for placement), nursing exam, ACT ASSET. *Recommended:* SAT or ACT (for placement).

Costs (2004–05) *Tuition:* area resident $1560 full-time, $52 per credit part-time; state resident $2430 full-time, $81 per credit part-time; nonresident $3450 full-time, $115 per credit part-time. Full-time tuition and fees vary according to course load and location. Part-time tuition and fees vary according to location. *Required fees:* $450 full-time, $15 per credit part-time. *Room and*

board: $3990; room only: $2160. Room and board charges vary according to board plan. *Payment plan:* installment. *Waivers:* employees or children of employees.

Financial Aid Of all full-time matriculated undergraduates who enrolled in 2003, 40 Federal Work-Study jobs (averaging $1500). 25 state and other part-time jobs (averaging $1200).

Applying *Required:* high school transcript. *Application deadline:* rolling (freshmen), rolling (transfers).

Admissions Contact Blaire Birdsong, Director of Admissions, North Central Missouri College, 1301 Main Street, Trenton, MO 64683. *Phone:* 660-359-3948 Ext. 401. *Toll-free phone:* 800-880-6180 Ext. 401. *E-mail:* bbirdsong@mail.ncmissouri.edu.

OZARKS TECHNICAL COMMUNITY COLLEGE
Springfield, Missouri

Admissions Contact Mr. Jeff Jochems, Dean of Student Development, Ozarks Technical Community College, PO Box 5958, Springfield, MO 65801. *Phone:* 417-895-7136. *Fax:* 417-895-7161.

PATRICIA STEVENS COLLEGE
St. Louis, Missouri

- **Proprietary** 2-year, founded 1947
- **Calendar** quarters
- **Degree** diplomas and associate
- **Urban** campus
- **Coed, primarily women**

Faculty *Student/faculty ratio:* 9:1.

Student Life *Campus security:* 24-hour emergency response devices and patrols.

Costs (2004–05) *Tuition:* $8993 full-time, $180 per credit hour part-time.

Applying *Options:* deferred entrance. *Application fee:* $15. *Required:* high school transcript, interview. *Recommended:* essay or personal statement, letters of recommendation.

Admissions Contact Mr. John Willmon, Director of Admissions, Patricia Stevens College, 330 North Fourth Street, Suite 306, St. Louis, MO 63102. *Phone:* 314-421-0949 Ext. 12. *Toll-free phone:* 800-871-0949. *Fax:* 314-421-0304. *E-mail:* info@patriciastevenscollege.com.

PENN VALLEY COMMUNITY COLLEGE
Kansas City, Missouri

- **State and locally supported** 2-year, founded 1969, part of Metropolitan Community Colleges System
- **Calendar** semesters
- **Degree** certificates and associate
- **Urban** 25-acre campus
- **Endowment** $1.9 million
- **Coed,** 4,839 undergraduate students, 34% full-time, 73% women, 27% men

Undergraduates 1,623 full-time, 3,216 part-time. Students come from 6 states and territories, 73 other countries, 5% are from out of state, 31% African American, 3% Asian American or Pacific Islander, 4% Hispanic American, 0.4% Native American, 2% international, 5% transferred in. *Retention:* 39% of 2002 full-time freshmen returned.

Freshmen *Admission:* 621 applied, 621 admitted, 506 enrolled.

Faculty *Total:* 403, 24% full-time. *Student/faculty ratio:* 23:1.

Majors Accounting; administrative assistant and secretarial science; biological and physical sciences; biology/biological sciences; business administration and management; chemistry; child care provision; commercial and advertising art; computer and information sciences related; computer science; corrections; criminal justice/law enforcement administration; criminal justice/police science; culinary arts; data processing and data processing technology; electrical, electronic and communications engineering technology; emergency medical technology (EMT paramedic); engineering; family and consumer sciences/human sciences; fashion/apparel design; fashion merchandising; fire science; health information/medical records administration; heating, air conditioning, ventilation and refrigeration maintenance technology; hotel/motel administration; industrial radiologic technology; kindergarten/preschool education; legal administrative assistant/secretary; legal assistant/paralegal; liberal arts and sciences/liberal studies; marketing/marketing management; medical administrative assistant and medical secretary; nursing (registered nurse training); occupational therapy; ophthalmic technology; physical therapy; respiratory care therapy; special products marketing.

Academic Programs *Special study options:* academic remediation for entering students, accelerated degree program, adult/continuing education programs,

Penn Valley Community College (continued)
advanced placement credit, cooperative education, distance learning, English as a second language, honors programs, internships, off-campus study, part-time degree program, services for LD students, summer session for credit.

Library Penn Valley Community College Library with 91,428 titles, 89,242 serial subscriptions, 355 audiovisual materials, an OPAC.

Computers on Campus 1058 computers available on campus for general student use. A campuswide network can be accessed from off campus. Internet access, at least one staffed computer lab available.

Student Life *Housing:* college housing not available. *Activities and Organizations:* drama/theater group, student-run newspaper, choral group, Black Student Association, Los Americanos, Phi Theta Kappa, Fashion Club, national fraternities. *Campus security:* 24-hour patrols. *Student services:* personal/psychological counseling.

Athletics Member NJCAA. *Intercollegiate sports:* basketball M(s).

Standardized Tests *Required:* ACT ASSET (for placement).

Costs (2005–06) *Tuition:* area resident $2130 full-time, $71 per hour part-time; state resident $3870 full-time, $129 per hour part-time; nonresident $5250 full-time, $175 per hour part-time. *Required fees:* $150 full-time, $5 per hour part-time.

Applying *Options:* common application, early admission. *Required:* high school transcript. *Application deadline:* rolling (freshmen), rolling (transfers).

Admissions Contact Mrs. Carroll O'Neal, Registrar, Penn Valley Community College, 3201 Southwest Trafficway, Kansas City, MO 64111. *Phone:* 816-759-4101. *Fax:* 816-759-4478.

PINNACLE CAREER INSTITUTE
Kansas City, Missouri

Admissions Contact Ms. Ruth Matous, Director of Admissions, Pinnacle Career Institute, 15329 Kensington Avenue, Kansas City, MO 64147-1212. *Phone:* 816-331-5700 Ext. 212.

RANKEN TECHNICAL COLLEGE
St. Louis, Missouri

- **Independent** primarily 2-year, founded 1907
- **Calendar** semesters
- **Degrees** certificates, associate, and bachelor's
- **Urban** 10-acre campus
- **Endowment** $39.0 million
- **Coed, primarily men,** 1,423 undergraduate students, 52% full-time, 4% women, 96% men

Undergraduates 743 full-time, 680 part-time. Students come from 3 states and territories, 40% are from out of state, 1% live on campus.

Freshmen *Admission:* 920 applied, 850 admitted, 321 enrolled.

Faculty *Total:* 67, 88% full-time. *Student/faculty ratio:* 15:1.

Majors Architectural engineering technology; autobody/collision and repair technology; automobile/automotive mechanics technology; carpentry; computer and information sciences; computer and information sciences and support services related; computer engineering technology; electrical, electronic and communications engineering technology; heating, air conditioning, ventilation and refrigeration maintenance technology; machine tool technology; pipefitting and sprinkler fitting.

Academic Programs *Special study options:* academic remediation for entering students, adult/continuing education programs, advanced placement credit, cooperative education, distance learning, independent study, internships, part-time degree program, services for LD students, summer session for credit.

Library Ashley Gray Jr. Learning Center with 11,000 titles, 182 serial subscriptions, an OPAC, a Web page.

Computers on Campus 85 computers available on campus for general student use. A campuswide network can be accessed. Internet access, at least one staffed computer lab available.

Student Life *Housing Options:* men-only, women-only. Campus housing is provided by a third party. *Activities and Organizations:* student-run newspaper, Phi Theta Kappa, student government, Women's Support Group, Instrumentation Society of America, Vocational Industrial Clubs of America. *Campus security:* 24-hour emergency response devices and patrols. *Student services:* personal/psychological counseling, women's center.

Standardized Tests *Required:* SAT or ACT (for placement).

Costs (2005–06) *Tuition:* $10,000 full-time, $725 per term part-time. *Required fees:* $140 full-time, $95 per term part-time. *Payment plan:* installment.

Financial Aid Of all full-time matriculated undergraduates who enrolled in 2003, 30 Federal Work-Study jobs (averaging $2000).

Applying *Options:* common application, electronic application. *Application fee:* $95. *Required:* essay or personal statement, high school transcript, interview. *Application deadline:* rolling (freshmen).

Admissions Contact Ms. Elizabeth Keserauskis, Director of Admissions, Ranken Technical College, 4431 Finney Avenue, St. Louis, MO 63113. *Phone:* 314-371-0233 Ext. 4811. *Toll-free phone:* 866-4RANKEN. *Fax:* 314-371-0241. *E-mail:* admissions@ranken.edu.

SAINT CHARLES COMMUNITY COLLEGE
St. Peters, Missouri

- **State-supported** 2-year, founded 1986, part of Missouri Coordinating Board for Higher Education
- **Calendar** semesters
- **Degree** certificates and associate
- **Small-town** 234-acre campus with easy access to St. Louis
- **Endowment** $6.6 million
- **Coed,** 6,772 undergraduate students, 49% full-time, 61% women, 39% men

Undergraduates 3,339 full-time, 3,433 part-time. Students come from 4 states and territories, 6 other countries, 4% African American, 1% Asian American or Pacific Islander, 2% Hispanic American, 0.5% Native American, 0.3% international, 6% transferred in.

Freshmen *Admission:* 1,710 applied, 1,710 admitted, 1,493 enrolled.

Faculty *Total:* 414, 20% full-time. *Student/faculty ratio:* 22:1.

Majors Accounting; administrative assistant and secretarial science; business administration and management; child development; commercial and advertising art; computer programming related; computer programming (specific applications); computer science; computer systems networking and telecommunications; criminal justice/law enforcement administration; criminal justice/police science; drafting and design technology; health information/medical records administration; human services; liberal arts and sciences/liberal studies; marketing/marketing management; medical transcription; nursing (registered nurse training); occupational therapy; office management; pre-engineering; web/multimedia management and webmaster.

Academic Programs *Special study options:* academic remediation for entering students, adult/continuing education programs, advanced placement credit, distance learning, double majors, English as a second language, independent study, internships, part-time degree program, services for LD students, summer session for credit.

Library Learning Resource Center with 54,110 titles, 8,282 serial subscriptions, 7,624 audiovisual materials, an OPAC, a Web page.

Computers on Campus 117 computers available on campus for general student use. A campuswide network can be accessed from off campus. Internet access, online (class) registration, at least one staffed computer lab available.

Student Life *Housing:* college housing not available. *Activities and Organizations:* drama/theater group, student-run newspaper, choral group, Phi Theta Kappa, SCCCC Roller Hockey Club, Student Senate, Criminal Justice Student Organization, Human Services Student Organization. *Campus security:* 24-hour emergency response devices and patrols, late-night transport/escort service. *Student services:* personal/psychological counseling.

Athletics Member NJCAA. *Intercollegiate sports:* baseball M(s), softball W(s). *Intramural sports:* basketball M/W, football M, soccer M/W, softball M/W, volleyball M/W.

Standardized Tests *Required:* ACT COMPASS (for placement). *Recommended:* ACT (for placement).

Costs (2005–06) *Tuition:* area resident $2130 full-time, $71 per credit hour part-time; state resident $3120 full-time, $104 per credit hour part-time; nonresident $4590 full-time, $153 per credit hour part-time. *Waivers:* employees or children of employees.

Financial Aid Of all full-time matriculated undergraduates who enrolled in 2003, 21 Federal Work-Study jobs (averaging $1848).

Applying *Options:* common application, early admission, deferred entrance. *Required for some:* high school transcript. *Recommended:* high school transcript. *Application deadline:* rolling (freshmen), rolling (transfers). *Notification:* continuous (freshmen).

Admissions Contact Ms. Kathy Brockgreitens, Director of Admissions/Registrar/Financial Assistance, Saint Charles Community College, 4601 Mid Rivers Mall Drive, St. Peters, MO 63376-0975. *Phone:* 636-922-8229. *Fax:* 636-922-8236. *E-mail:* regist@stchas.edu.

ST. LOUIS COMMUNITY COLLEGE AT FLORISSANT VALLEY
St. Louis, Missouri

- **District-supported** 2-year, founded 1963, part of St. Louis Community College System
- **Calendar** semesters
- **Degree** certificates and associate
- **Suburban** 108-acre campus
- **Coed**

Student Life *Campus security:* 24-hour emergency response devices and patrols, late-night transport/escort service.
Athletics Member NAIA, NJCAA.
Standardized Tests *Recommended:* SAT or ACT (for placement).
Costs (2004–05) *Tuition:* $72 per credit hour part-time; state resident $93 per credit hour part-time; nonresident $128 per credit hour part-time.
Applying *Options:* electronic application, early admission. *Required:* high school transcript.
Admissions Contact Mr. Mitchell Egeston, Manager of Admissions and Registration, St. Louis Community College at Florissant Valley, 3400 Pershall Road, St. Louis, MO 63135-1499. *Phone:* 314-595-4245. *Fax:* 314-595-2224.

ST. LOUIS COMMUNITY COLLEGE AT FOREST PARK
St. Louis, Missouri

■ **District-supported** 2-year, founded 1962, part of St. Louis Community College System
■ **Calendar** semesters
■ **Degree** associate
■ **Suburban** 34-acre campus
■ **Coed,** 7,610 undergraduate students

Undergraduates Students come from 11 states and territories, 4% are from out of state, 43% African American, 4% Asian American or Pacific Islander, 1% Hispanic American, 0.4% Native American, 0.2% international.
Freshmen *Admission:* 1,282 applied, 1,282 admitted.
Faculty *Total:* 314, 36% full-time. *Student/faculty ratio:* 19:1.
Majors Accounting; administrative assistant and secretarial science; African-American/Black studies; art; artificial intelligence and robotics; automobile/automotive mechanics technology; biology/biological sciences; biomedical technology; business administration and management; child development; clinical/medical laboratory technology; commercial and advertising art; computer and information sciences related; computer programming related; computer programming (specific applications); computer programming (vendor/product certification); computer science; computer systems networking and telecommunications; criminal justice/law enforcement administration; culinary arts; data entry/microcomputer applications; data entry/microcomputer applications related; data processing and data processing technology; dental hygiene; developmental and child psychology; electrical, electronic and communications engineering technology; engineering; engineering science; engineering technology; finance; fire science; funeral service and mortuary science; hotel/motel administration; human services; industrial radiologic technology; industrial technology; information technology; international business/trade/commerce; liberal arts and sciences/liberal studies; mass communication/media; mathematics; mechanical engineering/mechanical technology; music; nursing (registered nurse training); photography; pipefitting and sprinkler fitting; pre-engineering; respiratory care therapy; surgical technology; tourism and travel services management; word processing.
Academic Programs *Special study options:* academic remediation for entering students, adult/continuing education programs, distance learning, English as a second language, honors programs, part-time degree program, services for LD students, study abroad, summer session for credit.
Library St. Louis Community College Library with 72,713 titles, 511 serial subscriptions, an OPAC, a Web page.
Computers on Campus 369 computers available on campus for general student use. A campuswide network can be accessed from off campus. Internet access, at least one staffed computer lab available.
Student Life *Housing:* college housing not available. *Activities and Organizations:* drama/theater group, student-run newspaper. *Campus security:* 24-hour patrols. *Student services:* personal/psychological counseling.
Athletics Member NJCAA. *Intercollegiate sports:* baseball W, basketball M(s)/W(s), soccer M(s), volleyball W(s).
Costs (2004–05) *Tuition:* $72 per credit hour part-time; state resident $93 per credit hour part-time; nonresident $128 per credit hour part-time.
Financial Aid Of all full-time matriculated undergraduates who enrolled in 2003, 165 Federal Work-Study jobs (averaging $3000).
Applying *Options:* electronic application, early admission. *Required:* high school transcript. *Application deadlines:* 8/22 (freshmen), 2/28 (transfers). *Notification:* continuous (freshmen).
Admissions Contact Mr. Glenn Marshall, Coordinator of Enrollment Services, St. Louis Community College at Forest Park, 5600 Oakland Avenue, St. Louis, MO 63110. *Phone:* 314-644-9125. *Fax:* 314-644-9375.

ST. LOUIS COMMUNITY COLLEGE AT MERAMEC
Kirkwood, Missouri

■ **District-supported** 2-year, founded 1963, part of St. Louis Community College System
■ **Calendar** semesters
■ **Degree** certificates and associate
■ **Suburban** 80-acre campus with easy access to St. Louis
■ **Coed,** 12,607 undergraduate students

Undergraduates Students come from 10 states and territories, 4% African American, 3% Asian American or Pacific Islander, 2% Hispanic American, 0.5% Native American.
Faculty *Total:* 570, 32% full-time.
Majors Accounting; administrative assistant and secretarial science; advertising; architectural engineering technology; art; biological and physical sciences; broadcast journalism; business administration and management; child development; cinematography and film/video production; commercial and advertising art; computer programming; computer science; corrections; court reporting; creative writing; criminal justice/law enforcement administration; criminal justice/police science; dramatic/theatre arts; education; electrical, electronic and communications engineering technology; elementary education; emergency medical technology (EMT paramedic); engineering science; finance; horticultural science; human services; information science/studies; interior design; journalism; legal administrative assistant/secretary; legal assistant/paralegal; liberal arts and sciences/liberal studies; literature; materials science; mathematics; modern languages; music; nursing (registered nurse training); occupational therapy; photography; physical therapy; public relations/image management; real estate; speech and rhetoric.
Academic Programs *Special study options:* academic remediation for entering students, adult/continuing education programs, advanced placement credit, English as a second language, freshman honors college, honors programs, internships, off-campus study, part-time degree program, services for LD students, study abroad, summer session for credit. *ROTC:* Army (c), Air Force (c).
Library Meramec Library with 58,911 titles, 500 serial subscriptions.
Computers on Campus 420 computers available on campus for general student use. Internet access, at least one staffed computer lab available.
Student Life *Housing:* college housing not available. *Activities and Organizations:* drama/theater group, student-run newspaper, choral group, Phi Theta Kappa, Scuba Club, International Club, Inter-Varsity Christian Fellowship, Horticulture Club. *Campus security:* 24-hour emergency response devices and patrols. *Student services:* health clinic, personal/psychological counseling.
Athletics Member NJCAA. *Intercollegiate sports:* baseball M(s), basketball M(s), soccer M(s)/W(s), softball W(s), volleyball W(s), wrestling M(s). *Intramural sports:* basketball M, ice hockey M(c), soccer M/W, volleyball W.
Standardized Tests *Required for some:* Michigan Test of English Language Proficiency.
Costs (2004–05) *Tuition:* $72 per credit hour part-time; state resident $93 per credit hour part-time; nonresident $128 per credit hour part-time.
Applying *Options:* early admission, deferred entrance. *Required for some:* high school transcript, interview. *Application deadline:* rolling (freshmen), rolling (transfers). *Notification:* continuous (freshmen).
Admissions Contact Mr. Mike Cundiff, Coordinator of Admissions, St. Louis Community College at Meramec, 11333 Big Bend Boulevard, Kirkwood, MO 63122-5720. *Phone:* 314-984-7608. *Fax:* 314-984-7051.

SANFORD-BROWN COLLEGE
Fenton, Missouri

Admissions Contact Ms. Judy Wilga, Director of Admissions, Sanford-Brown College, 1203 Smizer Mill Road, Fenton, MO 63026. *Phone:* 636-349-4900 Ext. 102. *Toll-free phone:* 800-456-7222. *Fax:* 636-349-9170.

SANFORD-BROWN COLLEGE
Hazelwood, Missouri

■ **Proprietary** 2-year, founded 1868
■ **Calendar** quarters
■ **Degree** diplomas and associate
■ 1-acre campus with easy access to St. Louis
■ **Coed**

Student Life *Campus security:* 24-hour emergency response devices and patrols.
Applying *Options:* common application, deferred entrance. *Required:* high school transcript, interview.

Sanford-Brown College (continued)

Admissions Contact Sherri Bremer, Director of Admissions, Sanford-Brown College, 75 Village Square, Hazelwood, MO 63042. *Phone:* 314-731-5200 Ext. 201.

SANFORD-BROWN COLLEGE
North Kansas City, Missouri

Admissions Contact Mr. Edward A. Beauchamp, Director of Admissions, Sanford-Brown College, 520 East 19th Avenue, North Kansas City, MO 64116. *Phone:* 816-472-0275. *Toll-free phone:* 800-456-7222.

SANFORD-BROWN COLLEGE
St. Charles, Missouri

Admissions Contact Karl J. Petersen, Executive Director, Sanford-Brown College, 3555 Franks Drive, St. Charles, MO 63301. *Phone:* 636-949-2620. *Toll-free phone:* 800-456-7222.

SOUTHEAST MISSOURI HOSPITAL COLLEGE OF NURSING AND HEALTH SCIENCES
Cape Girardeau, Missouri

Admissions Contact Tonya L. Buttry, President, Southeast Missouri Hospital College of Nursing and Health Sciences, 1819 Broadway, Cape Girardeau, MO 63701. *Phone:* 534-334-6825.

SOUTHWEST MISSOURI STATE UNIVERSITY-WEST PLAINS
West Plains, Missouri

- **State-supported** 2-year, founded 1963, part of Southwest Missouri State University
- **Calendar** semesters
- **Degree** certificates and associate
- **Small-town** 11-acre campus
- **Endowment** $448,596
- **Coed**

Faculty *Student/faculty ratio:* 17:1.
Student Life *Campus security:* late-night transport/escort service, controlled dormitory access.
Athletics Member NJCAA.
Standardized Tests *Required for some:* ACT (for placement).
Costs (2004–05) *Tuition:* state resident $2910 full-time, $97 per credit hour part-time; nonresident $5820 full-time, $194 per credit hour part-time. Full-time tuition and fees vary according to course load and location. Part-time tuition and fees vary according to course load and location. *Required fees:* $210 full-time, $100 per term part-time. *Room and board:* $4512.
Financial Aid Of all full-time matriculated undergraduates who enrolled in 2003, 63 Federal Work-Study jobs (averaging $2000).
Applying *Application fee:* $15. *Required for some:* high school transcript.
Admissions Contact Ms. Melissa Jett, Admissions Assistant, Southwest Missouri State University-West Plains, 128 Garfield, West Plains, MO 65775. *Phone:* 417-255-7955. *Fax:* 417-255-7959. *E-mail:* admissions@wp.smsu.edu.

SPRINGFIELD COLLEGE
Springfield, Missouri

Admissions Contact Gerald F. Terrebrood, President, Springfield College, 1010 West Sunshine Street, Springfield, MO 65807. *Phone:* 417-864-7220. *Toll-free phone:* 800-864-5697 (in-state); 800-475-2669 (out-of-state). *Fax:* 417-864-5697.

STATE FAIR COMMUNITY COLLEGE
Sedalia, Missouri

Admissions Contact Mrs. Sharon Peacock, Registrar, State Fair Community College, 3201 West 16th, Sedalia, MO 65301. *Phone:* 660-530-5800 Ext. 293. *Toll-free phone:* 877-311-SFCC Ext. 217 (in-state); 877-311-SFCC (out-of-state). *Fax:* 660-530-5546.

THREE RIVERS COMMUNITY COLLEGE
Poplar Bluff, Missouri

- **State and locally supported** 2-year, founded 1966, part of Missouri Coordinating Board for Higher Education
- **Calendar** semesters
- **Degree** certificates and associate
- **Rural** 70-acre campus
- **Endowment** $641,067
- **Coed,** 3,273 undergraduate students, 53% full-time, 68% women, 32% men

Undergraduates 1,749 full-time, 1,524 part-time. Students come from 11 states and territories, 2% are from out of state, 9% African American, 0.4% Asian American or Pacific Islander, 1% Hispanic American, 0.5% Native American, 1% transferred in, 10% live on campus.
Freshmen *Admission:* 753 applied, 753 admitted, 753 enrolled. *Test scores:* ACT scores over 18: 71%; ACT scores over 24: 16%; ACT scores over 30: 1%.
Faculty *Total:* 168, 34% full-time, 7% with terminal degrees. *Student/faculty ratio:* 24:1.
Majors Accounting; administrative assistant and secretarial science; agricultural business and management; agricultural mechanization; business administration and management; clinical/medical laboratory technology; computer and information sciences related; computer engineering technology; computer/technical support; construction engineering technology; criminal justice/law enforcement administration; criminal justice/police science; data entry/microcomputer applications; data entry/microcomputer applications related; education; elementary education; engineering technology; industrial technology; information technology; liberal arts and sciences/liberal studies; marketing/marketing management; music; nursing (registered nurse training); word processing.
Academic Programs *Special study options:* academic remediation for entering students, accelerated degree program, adult/continuing education programs, advanced placement credit, distance learning, double majors, English as a second language, external degree program, honors programs, independent study, internships, part-time degree program, services for LD students, summer session for credit.
Library Rutland Library with 36,960 titles, 238 serial subscriptions, 1,027 audiovisual materials, an OPAC, a Web page.
Computers on Campus 200 computers available on campus for general student use. A campuswide network can be accessed from student residence rooms. Internet access, online (class) registration, at least one staffed computer lab available.
Student Life *Housing Options:* coed. Campus housing is university owned. *Activities and Organizations:* student government, PTK, PBL, Alpha Beta Gamma, Lambda Alpha Epsilon. *Campus security:* 24-hour patrols.
Athletics Member NJCAA. *Intercollegiate sports:* baseball M(s), basketball M(s)/W(s), cheerleading M(s)/W(s), softball W(s), volleyball W(s).
Standardized Tests *Recommended:* ACT (for placement), ACT ASSET.
Costs (2005–06) *Tuition:* area resident $1770 full-time, $59 per credit hour part-time; state resident $2790 full-time, $89 per credit hour part-time; nonresident $3480 full-time, $116 per credit hour part-time. Full-time tuition and fees vary according to course load and program. Part-time tuition and fees vary according to course load and program. *Required fees:* $356 full-time, $9 per credit hour part-time. *Room and board:* room only: $3948. Room and board charges vary according to board plan. *Payment plan:* installment. *Waivers:* senior citizens and employees or children of employees.
Applying *Options:* early admission. *Application fee:* $20. *Required:* high school transcript.
Admissions Contact Ms. Marcia Fields, Director of Admissions and Recruiting, Three Rivers Community College, 2080 Three Rivers Boulevard, Poplar Bluff, MO 63901. *Phone:* 573-840-9675. *Toll-free phone:* 877-TRY-TRCC Ext. 605 (in-state); 877-TRY-TRCC (out-of-state). *E-mail:* trytrcc@trcc.edu.

VATTEROTT COLLEGE
Kansas City, Missouri

Admissions Contact 8955 East 38th Terrace, Kansas City, MO 64129. *Toll-free phone:* 800-466-3997.

VATTEROTT COLLEGE
St. Ann, Missouri

- **Proprietary** primarily 2-year, founded 1969
- **Calendar** continuous
- **Degrees** diplomas, associate, and bachelor's
- **Suburban** 5-acre campus with easy access to St. Louis
- **Coed**

Faculty *Student/faculty ratio:* 25:1.

Applying *Options:* common application.
Admissions Contact Mrs. Shari H. Cobb, Director of Admissions, Vatterott College, 3925 Industrial Drive, St. Ann, MO 63074-1807. *Phone:* 314-428-5900 Ext. 215. *Toll-free phone:* 800-345-6018. *Fax:* 314-428-5956.

VATTEROTT COLLEGE
St. Joseph, Missouri

- **Proprietary** 2-year
- **Calendar** semesters
- **Degree** diplomas and associate
- **Urban** campus
- **Coed**

Faculty *Total:* 19, 95% full-time.
Majors Administrative assistant and secretarial science; computer systems networking and telecommunications; computer technology/computer systems technology; medical/clinical assistant.
Admissions Contact Ms. Sandra Wisdom, Director of Admissions, Vatterott College, 3131 Frederick Avenue, St. Joseph, MO 64506. *Phone:* 816-364-5399 Ext. 110. *Toll-free phone:* 800-282-5327.

VATTEROTT COLLEGE
Sunset Hills, Missouri

Admissions Contact Ms. Michelle Tinsley, Director of Admission, Vatterott College, 12970 Maurer Industrial Drive, St. Louis, MO 63127. *Phone:* 314-843-4200. *Fax:* 314-843-1709. *E-mail:* sunsethills@vatterott-college.edu.

VATTEROTT COLLEGE
Springfield, Missouri

- **Proprietary** 2-year, part of Vatterott College
- **Calendar** quarters
- **Degree** diplomas and associate
- **Urban** 2-acre campus
- **Coed**

Faculty *Total:* 19, 79% full-time.
Majors CAD/CADD drafting/design technology; computer programming; medical/clinical assistant; pharmacy technician; system, networking, and LAN/WAN management.
Academic Programs *Special study options:* internships.
Library Vattercott College.
Computers on Campus 200 computers available on campus for general student use. A campuswide network can be accessed. Internet access, at least one staffed computer lab available.
Student Life *Housing:* college housing not available. *Activities and Organizations:* Computer Club. *Campus security:* alarm devices and personnel during open hours; security alarms during closed hours.
Costs (2004–05) *Tuition:* $8800 full-time. Full-time tuition and fees vary according to degree level and program. *Required fees:* $900 full-time. *Payment plan:* installment. *Waivers:* employees or children of employees.
Applying *Required:* high school transcript, interview.
Admissions Contact Ms. Jennifer Danzer, Co-Director, Vatterott College, 3850 South Campbell, Springfield, MO 65807. *Phone:* 417-831-8116 Ext. 223. *Toll-free phone:* 800-766-5829. *E-mail:* springfield@vatterott-college.edu.

WENTWORTH MILITARY ACADEMY AND JUNIOR COLLEGE
Lexington, Missouri

Admissions Contact Maj. Todd Kitchen, Dean of Admissions, Wentworth Military Academy and Junior College, 1880 Washington Avenue, Lexington, MO 64067. *Phone:* 660-259-2221. *Fax:* 660-259-2677. *E-mail:* admissions@wma1880.org.

MONTANA

BLACKFEET COMMUNITY COLLEGE
Browning, Montana

- **Independent** 2-year, founded 1974
- **Calendar** semesters
- **Degree** certificates, diplomas, and associate
- **Small-town** 5-acre campus
- **Endowment** $300,688
- **Coed,** 503 undergraduate students, 84% full-time, 64% women, 36% men

Undergraduates 424 full-time, 79 part-time. Students come from 2 states and territories, 0.4% Hispanic American, 92% Native American, 6% transferred in.
Freshmen *Admission:* 137 enrolled.
Faculty *Total:* 63, 43% full-time, 2% with terminal degrees. *Student/faculty ratio:* 12:1.
Majors Administrative assistant and secretarial science; American Indian/Native American studies; bilingual and multilingual education; business administration and management; computer and information sciences and support services related; construction engineering technology; elementary education; entrepreneurship; general studies; health/medical preparatory programs related; hospitality administration; human services; kindergarten/preschool education; liberal arts and sciences/liberal studies; natural resources management and policy; teacher assistant/aide.
Academic Programs *Special study options:* academic remediation for entering students, adult/continuing education programs, off-campus study, part-time degree program.
Library 10,000 titles, 175 serial subscriptions.
Computers on Campus 55 computers available on campus for general student use. A campuswide network can be accessed. At least one staffed computer lab available.
Student Life *Housing:* college housing not available. *Campus security:* 16 hour patrols by security personnel.
Athletics *Intramural sports:* basketball M/W.
Costs (2004–05) *Tuition:* state resident $1650 full-time, $69 per credit part-time; nonresident $1650 full-time, $69 per credit part-time. Full-time tuition and fees vary according to course load. Part-time tuition and fees vary according to course load. *Required fees:* $350 full-time, $175 per term part-time. *Payment plan:* installment. *Waivers:* senior citizens and employees or children of employees.
Financial Aid Of all full-time matriculated undergraduates who enrolled in 2003, 10 Federal Work-Study jobs (averaging $2316). *Financial aid deadline:* 6/30.
Applying *Options:* early admission. *Application fee:* $20. *Required:* high school transcript, immunization with 2nd MMR, certificate of Indian blood. *Application deadline:* 8/29 (freshmen), rolling (transfers). *Notification:* continuous (freshmen).
Admissions Contact Ms. Deana M. McNabb, Registrar and Admissions Officer, Blackfeet Community College, PO Box 819, Browning, MT 59417. *Phone:* 406-338-5421 Ext. 243. *Toll-free phone:* 800-549-7457. *Fax:* 406-338-3272. *E-mail:* helen_morris@bfcc.org.

CHIEF DULL KNIFE COLLEGE
Lame Deer, Montana

Admissions Contact Mr. William L. Wertman, Registrar and Director of Admissions, Chief Dull Knife College, PO Box 98, Lame Deer, MT 59043-0098. *Phone:* 406-477-6215.

DAWSON COMMUNITY COLLEGE
Glendive, Montana

- **State and locally supported** 2-year, founded 1940, part of Montana University System
- **Calendar** semesters
- **Degree** certificates and associate
- **Rural** 300-acre campus
- **Endowment** $344,944
- **Coed,** 539 undergraduate students, 73% full-time, 55% women, 45% men

Undergraduates 395 full-time, 144 part-time. Students come from 10 states and territories, 2 other countries, 2% African American, 1% Hispanic American, 3% Native American, 6% transferred in, 19% live on campus.
Freshmen *Admission:* 208 applied, 208 admitted, 115 enrolled. *Test scores:* ACT scores over 18: 67%; ACT scores over 24: 17%.
Faculty *Total:* 49, 43% full-time. *Student/faculty ratio:* 16:1.
Majors Administrative assistant and secretarial science; agricultural business and management; automobile/automotive mechanics technology; business/commerce; child care and support services management; clinical/medical social work; computer and information sciences; criminal justice/police science; liberal arts and sciences/liberal studies; substance abuse/addiction counseling.
Academic Programs *Special study options:* academic remediation for entering students, adult/continuing education programs, independent study, internships, part-time degree program, services for LD students, summer session for credit.

Dawson Community College (continued)

Library Jane Carey Memorial Library with 18,870 titles, 1,112 audiovisual materials, an OPAC, a Web page.

Computers on Campus 70 computers available on campus for general student use. A campuswide network can be accessed from student residence rooms and from off campus. Internet access, at least one staffed computer lab available.

Student Life *Housing Options:* coed. Campus housing is university owned. *Activities and Organizations:* drama/theater group, choral group, Human Services Club, Law Enforcement Club, Associated Student Body, VICA, United Badlands Indian Club. *Campus security:* 24-hour emergency response devices.

Athletics Member NJCAA. *Intercollegiate sports:* baseball M, basketball M(s)/W(s), equestrian sports M(s)/W(s), softball W. *Intramural sports:* basketball M/W, bowling M/W, golf M/W, racquetball M/W, softball M/W, table tennis M/W, tennis M/W, volleyball M/W.

Standardized Tests *Required for some:* ACT (for placement). *Recommended:* ACT (for placement).

Costs (2004–05) *Tuition:* area resident $1943 full-time, $40 per credit part-time; state resident $2741 full-time, $69 per credit part-time; nonresident $6098 full-time, $189 per credit part-time. Full-time tuition and fees vary according to reciprocity agreements. Part-time tuition and fees vary according to reciprocity agreements. *Required fees:* $812 full-time, $29 per credit part-time. *Room and board:* room only: $1650. *Payment plan:* installment. *Waivers:* employees or children of employees.

Financial Aid Of all full-time matriculated undergraduates who enrolled in 2003, 45 Federal Work-Study jobs (averaging $1200). 17 state and other part-time jobs (averaging $1200).

Applying *Options:* deferred entrance. *Application fee:* $30. *Required:* high school transcript. *Application deadline:* rolling (freshmen), rolling (transfers). *Notification:* continuous (freshmen).

Admissions Contact Ms. Jolene Myers, Director of Admissions and Financial Aid, Dawson Community College, Box 421, Glendive, MT 59330-0421. *Phone:* 406-377-3396 Ext. 410. *Toll-free phone:* 800-821-8320. *Fax:* 406-377-8132.

FLATHEAD VALLEY COMMUNITY COLLEGE
Kalispell, Montana

- **State and locally supported** 2-year, founded 1967
- **Calendar** semesters
- **Degree** certificates and associate
- **Small-town** 40-acre campus
- **Endowment** $865,025
- **Coed,** 2,100 undergraduate students, 46% full-time, 65% women, 35% men

Undergraduates 972 full-time, 1,128 part-time. Students come from 25 states and territories, 2 other countries, 2% are from out of state, 0.5% African American, 0.7% Asian American or Pacific Islander, 1% Hispanic American, 2% Native American, 0.5% international, 2% transferred in. *Retention:* 55% of 2002 full-time freshmen returned.

Freshmen *Admission:* 381 applied, 338 admitted, 270 enrolled.

Faculty *Total:* 186, 22% full-time. *Student/faculty ratio:* 15:1.

Majors Accounting; administrative assistant and secretarial science; business administration and management; computer engineering technology; computer/information technology services administration related; computer typography and composition equipment operation; construction engineering technology; criminal justice/law enforcement administration; data entry/microcomputer applications; developmental and child psychology; forestry technology; hospitality and recreation marketing; hotel/motel administration; human services; liberal arts and sciences/liberal studies; medical administrative assistant and medical secretary; medical/clinical assistant; metal and jewelry arts; survey technology; web/multimedia management and webmaster; wildlife and wildlands science and management; word processing.

Academic Programs *Special study options:* academic remediation for entering students, adult/continuing education programs, advanced placement credit, distance learning, double majors, independent study, internships, part-time degree program, services for LD students, summer session for credit.

Library Flathead Valley Community College Library with 19,038 titles, 125 serial subscriptions, 514 audiovisual materials, an OPAC, a Web page.

Computers on Campus 132 computers available on campus for general student use. A campuswide network can be accessed. Internet access, at least one staffed computer lab available.

Student Life *Housing:* college housing not available. *Activities and Organizations:* drama/theater group, student-run newspaper, Forestry Club, Pi-Ta Club. *Student services:* personal/psychological counseling.

Athletics Member NJCAA. *Intercollegiate sports:* cross-country running M/W, soccer M/W. *Intramural sports:* basketball M/W, football M/W, racquetball M/W, soccer M/W, tennis M/W, volleyball M/W, weight lifting M/W.

Standardized Tests *Required:* ACT ASSET, ACT COMPASS (for placement).

Costs (2005–06) *Tuition:* area resident $1739 full-time, $62 per credit part-time; state resident $2856 full-time, $102 per credit part-time; nonresident $7146 full-time, $255 per credit part-time. Part-time tuition and fees vary according to course load. *Required fees:* $26 per credit part-time, $610 per year part-time. *Payment plan:* deferred payment. *Waivers:* senior citizens and employees or children of employees.

Financial Aid Of all full-time matriculated undergraduates who enrolled in 2003, 52 Federal Work-Study jobs (averaging $1000). 46 state and other part-time jobs (averaging $1020).

Applying *Options:* early admission, deferred entrance. *Application fee:* $15. *Required:* high school transcript. *Application deadline:* rolling (freshmen), rolling (transfers).

Admissions Contact Ms. Marlene C. Stoltz, Admissions/Graduation Coordinator, Flathead Valley Community College, 777 Grandview Avenue, Kalispell, MT 59901-2622. *Phone:* 406-756-3846. *Toll-free phone:* 800-313-3822. *Fax:* 406-756-3965.

FORT BELKNAP COLLEGE
Harlem, Montana

Admissions Contact Ms. Dixie Brockie, Registrar and Admissions Officer, Fort Belknap College, PO Box 159, Harlem, MT 59526-0159. *Phone:* 406-353-2607 Ext. 219.

FORT PECK COMMUNITY COLLEGE
Poplar, Montana

- **District-supported** 2-year, founded 1978
- **Calendar** semesters
- **Degree** certificates and associate
- **Small-town** campus
- **Coed,** 428 undergraduate students

Faculty *Total:* 31, 55% full-time.

Majors Administrative assistant and secretarial science; agricultural mechanization; American Indian/Native American studies; automobile/automotive mechanics technology; business administration and management; computer science; construction engineering technology; criminal justice/law enforcement administration; electrical, electronic and communications engineering technology; human services; kindergarten/preschool education; liberal arts and sciences/liberal studies; mental health/rehabilitation; natural resources management and policy.

Academic Programs *Special study options:* off-campus study, part-time degree program, summer session for credit.

Computers on Campus 50 computers available on campus for general student use. At least one staffed computer lab available.

Student Life *Housing:* college housing not available.

Standardized Tests *Required:* ACT ASSET (for placement).

Costs (2004–05) *Tuition:* state resident $1440 full-time, $60 per credit part-time. *Required fees:* $400 full-time, $15 per credit part-time, $30 per term part-time.

Applying *Options:* electronic application, early admission. *Application fee:* $15. *Application deadline:* rolling (freshmen).

Admissions Contact Mr. Robert McAnally, Vice President for Student Services, Fort Peck Community College, PO Box 398, Poplar, MT 59255-0398. *Phone:* 406-768-6329.

LITTLE BIG HORN COLLEGE
Crow Agency, Montana

Admissions Contact Ms. Ann Bullis, Dean of Student Services, Little Big Horn College, Box 370, Crow Agency, MT 59022-0370. *Phone:* 406-638-2228 Ext. 50.

MILES COMMUNITY COLLEGE
Miles City, Montana

- **State and locally supported** 2-year, founded 1939, part of Montana University System
- **Calendar** semesters
- **Degree** certificates and associate
- **Small-town** 8-acre campus
- **Endowment** $2.7 million
- **Coed**

Faculty *Student/faculty ratio:* 14:1.

Student Life *Campus security:* 24-hour emergency response devices.
Athletics Member NJCAA.
Standardized Tests *Required for some:* SAT or ACT (for placement). *Recommended:* SAT or ACT (for placement).
Costs (2004–05) *Tuition:* area resident $2550 full-time, $85 per credit part-time; state resident $3300 full-time, $110 per credit part-time; nonresident $5250 full-time, $175 per credit part-time. *Room and board:* Room and board charges vary according to board plan, housing facility, and location. *Payment plans:* installment, deferred payment.
Financial Aid Of all full-time matriculated undergraduates who enrolled in 2003, 25 Federal Work-Study jobs (averaging $1400). 22 state and other part-time jobs (averaging $1300).
Applying *Options:* common application, early admission, deferred entrance. *Application fee:* $40. *Required:* high school transcript.
Admissions Contact Ms. Laura J. Pierce, Chief Student Services Officer, Miles Community College, 2715 Dickinson, Miles City, MT 59301-4799. *Phone:* 406-874-6159. *Toll-free phone:* 800-541-9281. *Fax:* 406-234-3599.

MONTANA STATE UNIVERSITY-GREAT FALLS COLLEGE OF TECHNOLOGY
Great Falls, Montana

- **State-supported** 2-year, founded 1969, part of Montana University System
- **Calendar** semesters
- **Degree** certificates and associate
- **Urban** 35-acre campus
- **Coed**

Faculty *Student/faculty ratio:* 15:1.
Student Life *Campus security:* 24-hour emergency response devices.
Standardized Tests *Required:* SAT I, ACT, or ACT ASSET (for placement).
Costs (2004–05) *Tuition:* state resident $2370 full-time, $99 per credit part-time; nonresident $7556 full-time, $315 per credit part-time. Full-time tuition and fees vary according to program. Part-time tuition and fees vary according to program. *Required fees:* $438 full-time, $20 per credit part-time, $38 per term part-time.
Financial Aid Of all full-time matriculated undergraduates who enrolled in 2003, 48 Federal Work-Study jobs (averaging $2000). 13 state and other part-time jobs (averaging $2000).
Applying *Options:* deferred entrance. *Application fee:* $30. *Required:* high school transcript, proof of immunization. *Required for some:* essay or personal statement, 3 letters of recommendation.
Admissions Contact Ms. Carol Schopfer, Registrar, Montana State University-Great Falls College of Technology, 2100 16th Avenue South, Great Falls, MT 59405. *Phone:* 406-771-4300. *Toll-free phone:* 800-446-2698. *Fax:* 406-771-4317. *E-mail:* information@msugf.edu.

SALISH KOOTENAI COLLEGE
Pablo, Montana

Admissions Contact Ms. Jackie Moran, Admissions Officer, Salish Kootenai College, PO 117, Highway 93, Pablo, MT 59855. *Phone:* 406-275-4866. *Fax:* 406-275-4810. *E-mail:* jackie_moran@skc.edu.

STONE CHILD COLLEGE
Box Elder, Montana

Admissions Contact Mr. Ted Whitford, Director of Admissions/Registrar, Stone Child College, RR1, Box 1082, Box Elder, MT 59521. *Phone:* 406-395-4313 Ext. 110. *Fax:* 406-395-4836. *E-mail:* uanet337@quest.ocsc.montana.edu.

THE UNIVERSITY OF MONTANA-HELENA COLLEGE OF TECHNOLOGY
Helena, Montana

Admissions Contact Ms. Vicki Cavanaugh, Director of Admissions, The University of Montana-Helena College of Technology, 1115 North Roberts Street, Helena, MT 59601. *Phone:* 406-444-6800. *Toll-free phone:* 800-241-4882. *Fax:* 406-444-6892.

NEBRASKA

CENTRAL COMMUNITY COLLEGE-COLUMBUS CAMPUS
Columbus, Nebraska

- **State and locally supported** 2-year, founded 1968, part of Central Community College
- **Calendar** semesters plus six-week summer session
- **Degree** certificates, diplomas, and associate
- **Small-town** 90-acre campus
- **Coed,** 1,995 undergraduate students, 26% full-time, 63% women, 37% men

Undergraduates 523 full-time, 1,472 part-time. Students come from 21 states and territories, 4% are from out of state, 0.5% African American, 0.9% Asian American or Pacific Islander, 5% Hispanic American, 0.3% Native American, 2% transferred in, 17% live on campus.
Freshmen *Admission:* 125 enrolled.
Faculty *Total:* 89, 43% full-time, 6% with terminal degrees. *Student/faculty ratio:* 15:1.
Majors Accounting; administrative assistant and secretarial science; agricultural business and management; automobile/automotive mechanics technology; business administration and management; commercial and advertising art; computer and information sciences; computer programming (specific applications); drafting and design technology; electrical, electronic and communications engineering technology; electromechanical technology; family and consumer sciences/human sciences; industrial technology; information technology; liberal arts and sciences/liberal studies; machine tool technology; marketing/marketing management; nursing (licensed practical/vocational nurse training); quality control technology; system administration; web/multimedia management and webmaster; welding technology.
Academic Programs *Special study options:* academic remediation for entering students, accelerated degree program, adult/continuing education programs, advanced placement credit, cooperative education, distance learning, English as a second language, external degree program, independent study, internships, off-campus study, part-time degree program, services for LD students, student-designed majors, summer session for credit.
Library Learning Resources Center with 22,000 titles, 118 serial subscriptions, 1,390 audiovisual materials, an OPAC.
Computers on Campus 100 computers available on campus for general student use. A campuswide network can be accessed from student residence rooms and from off campus. Internet access, online (class) registration, at least one staffed computer lab available.
Student Life *Housing Options:* coed. Campus housing is university owned. *Activities and Organizations:* choral group, Phi Theta Kappa, Drama Club, Art Club, Cantari, Chorale. *Campus security:* late-night transport/escort service, controlled dormitory access, night security. *Student services:* personal/psychological counseling, women's center.
Athletics Member NJCAA. *Intercollegiate sports:* basketball M(s), volleyball W(s). *Intramural sports:* basketball M/W, football M, softball M/W, table tennis M/W, volleyball M/W.
Standardized Tests *Required for some:* ACT (for placement). *Recommended:* ACT ASSET or ACT COMPASS.
Costs (2005–06) *Tuition:* state resident $1392 full-time, $58 per credit part-time; nonresident $2088 full-time, $87 per credit part-time. *Required fees:* $96 full-time, $4 per credit part-time. *Room and board:* $3744. Room and board charges vary according to board plan. *Payment plan:* deferred payment. *Waivers:* employees or children of employees.
Applying *Options:* common application, electronic application, early admission. *Required:* high school transcript. *Required for some:* 3 letters of recommendation, interview. *Application deadline:* rolling (freshmen), rolling (transfers). *Notification:* continuous (freshmen).
Admissions Contact Ms. Mary Young, Records Coordinator, Central Community College-Columbus Campus, PO Box 1027, Columbus, NE 68602-1027. *Phone:* 402-562-1296. *Toll-free phone:* 800-642-1083. *E-mail:* myoung@cccneb.edu.

CENTRAL COMMUNITY COLLEGE-GRAND ISLAND CAMPUS
Grand Island, Nebraska

- **State and locally supported** 2-year, founded 1976, part of Central Community College
- **Calendar** semesters plus six-week summer session
- **Degree** certificates, diplomas, and associate
- **Small-town** 64-acre campus
- **Coed,** 2,756 undergraduate students, 18% full-time, 70% women, 30% men

Central Community College-Grand Island Campus (continued)

Undergraduates 495 full-time, 2,261 part-time. Students come from 22 states and territories, 1 other country, 4% are from out of state, 1% African American, 0.8% Asian American or Pacific Islander, 8% Hispanic American, 0.2% Native American, 2% transferred in, 10% live on campus.

Freshmen *Admission:* 149 enrolled.

Faculty *Total:* 112, 38% full-time, 4% with terminal degrees. *Student/faculty ratio:* 15:1.

Majors Accounting; administrative assistant and secretarial science; automobile/automotive mechanics technology; business administration and management; child development; clinical/medical social work; computer and information sciences; computer programming (specific applications); criminal justice/safety; data processing and data processing technology; drafting and design technology; electrical, electronic and communications engineering technology; heating, air conditioning, ventilation and refrigeration maintenance technology; industrial technology; information technology; legal assistant/paralegal; liberal arts and sciences/liberal studies; nursing (licensed practical/vocational nurse training); nursing (registered nurse training); system administration; web/multimedia management and webmaster; welding technology.

Academic Programs *Special study options:* academic remediation for entering students, accelerated degree program, adult/continuing education programs, advanced placement credit, cooperative education, distance learning, English as a second language, external degree program, independent study, internships, off-campus study, part-time degree program, services for LD students, student-designed majors, summer session for credit.

Library Central Community College-Grand Island Campus Library with 5,700 titles, 94 serial subscriptions, 150 audiovisual materials, an OPAC, a Web page.

Computers on Campus 156 computers available on campus for general student use. A campuswide network can be accessed from off campus. Internet access, online (class) registration, at least one staffed computer lab available.

Student Life *Housing Options:* coed. Campus housing is provided by a third party. Freshman applicants given priority for college housing. *Activities and Organizations:* Mid-Nebraska Users of Computers, Student Activities Organization, intramurals. *Student services:* personal/psychological counseling.

Athletics *Intramural sports:* bowling M/W, table tennis M/W, volleyball M/W.

Standardized Tests *Required for some:* ACT (for placement). *Recommended:* ACT ASSET or ACT COMPASS.

Costs (2005–06) *Tuition:* state resident $1392 full-time, $58 per credit part-time; nonresident $2088 full-time, $87 per credit part-time. *Required fees:* $96 full-time, $4 per credit part-time. *Payment plan:* deferred payment. *Waivers:* employees or children of employees.

Financial Aid Of all full-time matriculated undergraduates who enrolled in 2003, 155 Federal Work-Study jobs (averaging $1200). 40 state and other part-time jobs (averaging $1000).

Applying *Options:* common application, electronic application, early admission. *Required:* high school transcript. *Required for some:* 3 letters of recommendation, interview. *Application deadline:* rolling (freshmen), rolling (transfers). *Notification:* continuous (freshmen).

Admissions Contact Ms. Angie Pacheco, Admissions Director, Central Community College-Grand Island Campus, PO Box 4903, Grand Island, NE 68802-4903. *Phone:* 308-398-7406 Ext. 406. *Toll-free phone:* 800-652-9177. *Fax:* 308-398-7398. *E-mail:* apacheco@cccneb.edu.

CENTRAL COMMUNITY COLLEGE-HASTINGS CAMPUS
Hastings, Nebraska

- **State and locally supported** 2-year, founded 1966, part of Central Community College
- **Calendar** semesters plus six-week summer session
- **Degree** certificates, diplomas, and associate
- **Small-town** 600-acre campus
- **Coed,** 2,545 undergraduate students, 40% full-time, 57% women, 43% men

Undergraduates 1,027 full-time, 1,518 part-time. Students come from 36 states and territories, 4% are from out of state, 0.4% African American, 1% Asian American or Pacific Islander, 4% Hispanic American, 0.3% Native American, 3% transferred in, 26% live on campus.

Freshmen *Admission:* 267 enrolled.

Faculty *Total:* 90, 68% full-time, 4% with terminal degrees. *Student/faculty ratio:* 15:1.

Majors Accounting; administrative assistant and secretarial science; agricultural business and management; applied horticulture; autobody/collision and repair technology; automobile/automotive mechanics technology; business administration and management; child development; clinical/medical social work; commercial and advertising art; computer and information sciences; computer programming (specific applications); construction engineering technology; dental assisting; dental hygiene; diesel mechanics technology; drafting and design technology; electrical, electronic and communications engineering technology;

graphic and printing equipment operation/production; health information/medical records technology; heating, air conditioning, ventilation and refrigeration maintenance technology; hospital and health care facilities administration; hospitality administration; hotel/motel administration; industrial technology; information technology; liberal arts and sciences/liberal studies; machine tool technology; mass communication/media; medical administrative assistant and medical secretary; medical/clinical assistant; radio and television broadcasting technology; system administration; vehicle/petroleum products marketing; web/multimedia management and webmaster; welding technology.

Academic Programs *Special study options:* academic remediation for entering students, accelerated degree program, adult/continuing education programs, advanced placement credit, cooperative education, distance learning, English as a second language, external degree program, independent study, internships, off-campus study, part-time degree program, services for LD students, student-designed majors, summer session for credit.

Library Nuckolls Library with 4,025 titles, 52 serial subscriptions, 150 audiovisual materials, an OPAC.

Computers on Campus 190 computers available on campus for general student use. A campuswide network can be accessed from student residence rooms and from off campus. Internet access, online (class) registration, at least one staffed computer lab available.

Student Life *Housing Options:* coed. Campus housing is university owned. *Activities and Organizations:* student-run radio station, Student Senate, Central Dormitory Council, Judicial Board, Seeds and Soils, Young Farmers and Ranchers. *Campus security:* 24-hour patrols, controlled dormitory access. *Student services:* personal/psychological counseling, women's center.

Athletics *Intramural sports:* basketball M/W, bowling M/W, golf M/W, softball M/W, volleyball M/W, weight lifting M/W.

Standardized Tests *Required for some:* ACT (for placement). *Recommended:* ACT ASSET or ACT COMPASS.

Costs (2005–06) *Tuition:* state resident $1392 full-time, $58 per credit part-time; nonresident $2088 full-time, $87 per credit part-time. *Required fees:* $96 full-time, $4 per credit part-time. *Room and board:* $3744. Room and board charges vary according to board plan. *Payment plan:* deferred payment. *Waivers:* employees or children of employees.

Financial Aid Of all full-time matriculated undergraduates who enrolled in 2003, 70 Federal Work-Study jobs (averaging $1200). 12 state and other part-time jobs (averaging $1250).

Applying *Options:* common application, electronic application, early admission. *Required:* high school transcript. *Required for some:* 3 letters of recommendation, interview. *Application deadline:* rolling (freshmen), rolling (transfers). *Notification:* continuous (freshmen).

Admissions Contact Mr. Robert Glenn, Admissions and Recruiting Director, Central Community College-Hastings Campus, PO Box 1024, East Highway 6, Hastings, NE 68902-1024. *Phone:* 402-461-2428. *Toll-free phone:* 800-742-7872. *E-mail:* rglenn@cccneb.edu.

THE CREATIVE CENTER
Omaha, Nebraska

- **Proprietary** 2-year
- **Calendar** semesters
- **Degree** associate
- **Urban** campus
- **Coed**

Majors Computer graphics; design and visual communications; illustration.

Costs (2004–05) *Tuition:* $1480 per course part-time. *Required fees:* $100 per course part-time.

Admissions Contact Ms. Sandy LaRocca, Admissions and Placement Coordinator, The Creative Center, 10850 Emmet Street, Omaha, NE 68164. *Phone:* 402-898-1000 Ext. 224. *Toll-free phone:* 888-898-1789. *E-mail:* admission@thecreativecenter.com.

HAMILTON COLLEGE-LINCOLN
Lincoln, Nebraska

Admissions Contact Mr. Andy Bossler, Director of Admissions, Hamilton College-Lincoln, 1821 K Street, Lincoln, NE 68508. *Phone:* 402-474-5315. *Toll-free phone:* 800-742-7738. *Fax:* 402-474-5302. *E-mail:* lsc@ix.netcom.com.

HAMILTON COLLEGE-OMAHA
Omaha, Nebraska

- **Proprietary** primarily 2-year, founded 1891, part of Educational Medical, Inc
- **Calendar** quarters
- **Degrees** diplomas, associate, and bachelor's
- **Urban** 3-acre campus
- **Coed**

Faculty *Student/faculty ratio:* 20:1.
Student Life *Campus security:* 24-hour emergency response devices.
Standardized Tests *Required:* CPAt (for admission).
Applying *Options:* early admission, deferred entrance. *Application fee:* $50. *Required:* high school transcript, interview.
Admissions Contact Mr. Mark Stoltenberger, Director of Admissions, Hamilton College-Omaha, 3350 North 90 Street, Omaha, NE 68134. *Phone:* 402-572-8500. *Toll-free phone:* 800-642-1456. *Fax:* 402-573-1341.

ITT TECHNICAL INSTITUTE
Omaha, Nebraska

- **Proprietary** primarily 2-year, founded 1991, part of ITT Educational Services, Inc
- **Calendar** quarters
- **Degrees** associate and bachelor's
- **Urban** 1-acre campus
- **Coed**

Standardized Tests *Required:* Wonderlic aptitude test (for admission).
Costs (2004–05) *Tuition:* Please see school catalog for specific information.
Applying *Options:* deferred entrance. *Application fee:* $100. *Required:* high school transcript, interview. *Recommended:* letters of recommendation.
Admissions Contact Ms. Jacqueline M. Hawthorne, Director of Recruitment, ITT Technical Institute, 9814 M Street, Omaha, NE 68127. *Phone:* 402-331-2900. *Toll-free phone:* 800-677-9260. *Fax:* 402-331-9495.

LITTLE PRIEST TRIBAL COLLEGE
Winnebago, Nebraska

- **Independent** 2-year
- **Degree** certificates, diplomas, and associate
- **Rural** campus
- 130 undergraduate students, 52% full-time
- 100% of applicants were admitted

Faculty *Student/faculty ratio:* 11:1.
Financial Aid Of all full-time matriculated undergraduates who enrolled in 2003, 8 Federal Work-Study jobs (averaging $750).
Admissions Contact Ms. Karen Kemling, Director of Admissions and Records, Little Priest Tribal College, PO Box 270, Winnebago, NE 68071. *Phone:* 402-878-2380.

METROPOLITAN COMMUNITY COLLEGE
Omaha, Nebraska

- **State and locally supported** 2-year, founded 1974, part of Nebraska Coordinating Commission for Postsecondary Education
- **Calendar** quarters
- **Degree** certificates, diplomas, and associate
- **Urban** 172-acre campus
- **Endowment** $1.4 million
- **Coed**, 12,461 undergraduate students, 39% full-time, 56% women, 44% men

Metropolitan Community College offers the advantages of a comprehensive, multicampus institution with small-college friendliness. Located in Omaha, Nebraska, Metro provides personalized services and high-quality programs in business administration, computer and office technologies, food arts, industrial and construction technologies, nursing and allied health, social sciences and services, and visual and electronic technologies as well as academic transfer programs. Many courses are offered through distance learning. Students can visit the College's Web site at http://www.mccneb.edu.

Undergraduates 4,798 full-time, 7,663 part-time. 3% are from out of state, 9% transferred in. *Retention:* 46% of 2002 full-time freshmen returned.
Freshmen *Admission:* 3,674 applied, 3,674 admitted, 1,413 enrolled.
Faculty *Total:* 718, 25% full-time. *Student/faculty ratio:* 13:1.
Majors Accounting; administrative assistant and secretarial science; architectural engineering technology; automobile/automotive mechanics technology; business administration and management; child development; civil engineering technology; commercial and advertising art; computer programming; construction engineering technology; criminal justice/police science; culinary arts; drafting and design technology; electrical, electronic and communications engineering technology; graphic and printing equipment operation/production; heating, air conditioning, ventilation and refrigeration maintenance technology; heavy equipment maintenance technology; human services; interior design; kindergarten/preschool education; legal administrative assistant/secretary; legal assistant/paralegal; legal studies; liberal arts and sciences/liberal studies; mental health/rehabilitation; nursing (licensed practical/vocational nurse training); nursing (registered nurse training); ornamental horticulture; photography; pre-engineering; respiratory care therapy; surgical technology; welding technology.

Academic Programs *Special study options:* academic remediation for entering students, adult/continuing education programs, advanced placement credit, cooperative education, distance learning, English as a second language, independent study, internships, part-time degree program, services for LD students, summer session for credit. *ROTC:* Army (c).
Library Metropolitan Community College plus 2 others with 41,161 titles, 544 serial subscriptions, 10,702 audiovisual materials, an OPAC, a Web page.
Computers on Campus 1700 computers available on campus for general student use. A campuswide network can be accessed from off campus that provide access to on-line classes, e-mail. Internet access, online (class) registration, at least one staffed computer lab available.
Student Life *Housing:* college housing not available. *Campus security:* 24-hour emergency response devices and patrols, late-night transport/escort service, security on duty 9 pm to 6 am. *Student services:* personal/psychological counseling.
Standardized Tests *Recommended:* ACT (for placement), ACT ASSET or ACT COMPASS.
Costs (2005–06) *Tuition:* state resident $1733 full-time, $39 per credit hour part-time; nonresident $2610 full-time, $61 per credit hour part-time. *Required fees:* $135 full-time, $3 per credit hour part-time.
Financial Aid Of all full-time matriculated undergraduates who enrolled in 2003, 180 Federal Work-Study jobs (averaging $1339).
Applying *Options:* early admission. *Recommended:* high school transcript. *Application deadline:* rolling (freshmen), rolling (transfers). *Notification:* continuous (freshmen).
Admissions Contact Ms. Arlene Jordan, Director of Enrollment Management, Metropolitan Community College, PO Box 3777, Omaha, NE 69103-0777. *Phone:* 402-457-2563. *Toll-free phone:* 800-228-9553. *Fax:* 402-457-2564.

MID-PLAINS COMMUNITY COLLEGE
North Platte, Nebraska

- **District-supported** 2-year
- **Calendar** semesters
- **Degree** certificates, diplomas, and associate
- **Small-town** campus
- **Coed**

Faculty *Student/faculty ratio:* 14:1.
Student Life *Campus security:* controlled dormitory access, patrols by trained security personnel.
Athletics Member NJCAA.
Standardized Tests *Required:* ACT COMPASS (for placement). *Recommended:* ACT (for placement).
Costs (2004–05) *Tuition:* state resident $1620 full-time, $54 per semester hour part-time; nonresident $2025 full-time, $68 per semester hour part-time. *Required fees:* $6 per semester hour part-time. *Room and board:* $3200. Room and board charges vary according to housing facility and location.
Applying *Required:* high school transcript.
Admissions Contact Ms. Mary Schriefer, Advisor, Mid-Plains Community College, 1101 Halligan Drive, North Platte, NE 69101. *Phone:* 308-535-3710. *Toll-free phone:* 800-658-4308 (in-state); 800-658-4348 (out-of-state). *Fax:* 308-634-2522.

MYOTHERAPY INSTITUTE
Lincoln, Nebraska

Admissions Contact Ms. Gerri Allen, Director of Admissions, Myotherapy Institute, 6020 South 58th Street, Lincoln, NE 68516. *Phone:* 801-485-6600. *Toll-free phone:* 800-896-3363.

NEBRASKA COLLEGE OF TECHNICAL AGRICULTURE
Curtis, Nebraska

Admissions Contact Mr. Gerald Sundquist, Director of Instruction, Nebraska College of Technical Agriculture, RR3, Box 23A, Curtis, NE 69025-9205. *Phone:* 308-367-4124 Ext. 205. *Toll-free phone:* 800-3CURTIS. *Fax:* 308-367-5203. *E-mail:* ncta@unlvm.unl.edu.

NEBRASKA INDIAN COMMUNITY COLLEGE
Macy, Nebraska

- **Federally supported** 2-year, founded 1979
- **Calendar** semesters

Nebraska Indian Community College (continued)
- **Degree** certificates and associate
- **Rural** 2-acre campus with easy access to Omaha, NE
- **Endowment** $68,020
- **Coed,** 190 undergraduate students, 51% full-time, 68% women, 32% men

Undergraduates 97 full-time, 93 part-time. Students come from 2 states and territories, 13% are from out of state, 4% African American, 0.5% Hispanic American, 82% Native American.

Freshmen *Admission:* 68 enrolled.

Faculty *Total:* 38, 16% full-time, 3% with terminal degrees. *Student/faculty ratio:* 8:1.

Majors American Indian/Native American studies; business administration and management; carpentry; corrections and criminal justice related; data entry/microcomputer applications; early childhood education; human services; information technology; liberal arts and sciences/liberal studies; natural resources/conservation; social work.

Academic Programs *Special study options:* academic remediation for entering students, adult/continuing education programs, double majors, part-time degree program, summer session for credit.

Computers on Campus 10 computers available on campus for general student use. Internet access, at least one staffed computer lab available.

Student Life *Housing:* college housing not available.

Costs (2004–05) *Tuition:* $1920 full-time, $80 per credit hour part-time. Full-time tuition and fees vary according to course load. Part-time tuition and fees vary according to course load. *Required fees:* $314 full-time, $11 per credit hour part-time, $25 per term part-time. *Payment plan:* installment. *Waivers:* senior citizens and employees or children of employees.

Applying *Options:* early admission, deferred entrance. *Application fee:* $10. *Required:* high school transcript, certificate of tribal enrollment if applicable. *Application deadline:* rolling (freshmen), rolling (transfers). *Notification:* continuous (freshmen).

Admissions Contact Mr. Ed Stevens, Admission Counselor, Nebraska Indian Community College, 2451 Saint Mary's Avenue, Omaha, NE 68105. *Phone:* 402-344-8428. *Toll-free phone:* 888-843-6432 Ext. 14. *Fax:* 402-344-8358.

NORTHEAST COMMUNITY COLLEGE

Norfolk, Nebraska

- **State and locally supported** 2-year, founded 1973, part of Nebraska Coordinating Commission for Postsecondary Education
- **Calendar** semesters
- **Degree** certificates, diplomas, and associate
- **Small-town** 205-acre campus
- **Endowment** $1.5 million
- **Coed**

Faculty *Student/faculty ratio:* 20:1.

Student Life *Campus security:* 24-hour patrols, controlled dormitory access.

Athletics Member NJCAA.

Standardized Tests *Required:* ACT ASSET (for placement). *Recommended:* ACT (for placement).

Costs (2004–05) *Tuition:* state resident $1620 full-time, $54 per hour part-time; nonresident $2025 full-time, $68 per hour part-time. *Required fees:* $225 full-time, $8 per hour part-time. *Room and board:* $3870. Room and board charges vary according to board plan and housing facility.

Financial Aid Of all full-time matriculated undergraduates who enrolled in 2003, 90 Federal Work-Study jobs (averaging $1700).

Applying *Options:* electronic application, early admission. *Recommended:* high school transcript.

Admissions Contact Ms. Maureen Baker, Dean of Enrollment Management, Northeast Community College, PO Box 469, Norfolk, NE 68702-0469. *Phone:* 402-844-7258. *Toll-free phone:* 800-348-9033 Ext. 7260. *Fax:* 402-844-7400. *E-mail:* admission@northeastcollege.com.

SOUTHEAST COMMUNITY COLLEGE, BEATRICE CAMPUS

Beatrice, Nebraska

- **District-supported** 2-year, founded 1976, part of Southeast Community College System
- **Calendar** semesters
- **Degree** certificates, diplomas, and associate
- **Small-town** 640-acre campus
- **Coed**

Faculty *Student/faculty ratio:* 12:1.

Student Life *Campus security:* controlled dormitory access, evening security.

Athletics Member NJCAA.

Standardized Tests *Required for some:* ACT ASSET, ACT COMPASS. *Recommended:* SAT or ACT (for admission), ACT ASSET, ACT COMPASS.

Applying *Options:* common application, electronic application, early admission, deferred entrance. *Required:* high school transcript. *Recommended:* minimum 2.0 GPA.

Admissions Contact Ms. Mary Ann Harms, Admissions Technician, Southeast Community College, Beatrice Campus, 4771 W. Scott Road, Beatrice, NE 68310-7042. *Phone:* 800-233-5027 Ext. 214. *Toll-free phone:* 800-233-5027 Ext. 214.

SOUTHEAST COMMUNITY COLLEGE, LINCOLN CAMPUS

Lincoln, Nebraska

- **District-supported** 2-year, founded 1973, part of Southeast Community College System
- **Calendar** quarters
- **Degree** certificates, diplomas, and associate
- **Suburban** 115-acre campus with easy access to Omaha
- **Coed,** 7,917 undergraduate students, 52% full-time, 57% women, 43% men

Undergraduates 4,095 full-time, 3,822 part-time. Students come from 23 states and territories, 4% are from out of state, 3% African American, 2% Asian American or Pacific Islander, 3% Hispanic American, 0.5% Native American, 0.1% international.

Freshmen *Admission:* 2,612 enrolled.

Faculty *Total:* 548, 25% full-time, 2% with terminal degrees. *Student/faculty ratio:* 15:1.

Majors Administrative assistant and secretarial science; automobile/automotive mechanics technology; business administration and management; child development; clinical/medical laboratory technology; computer and information sciences; culinary arts; dietetics; drafting and design technology; electrical, electronic and communications engineering technology; environmental studies; fire science; food services technology; human services; liberal arts and sciences/liberal studies; machine tool technology; medical radiologic technology; nursing (registered nurse training); respiratory care therapy; welding technology.

Academic Programs *Special study options:* academic remediation for entering students, adult/continuing education programs, advanced placement credit, cooperative education, distance learning, English as a second language, independent study, internships, off-campus study, part-time degree program, services for LD students, summer session for credit.

Library Lincoln Campus Learning Resource Center with 14,081 titles, 375 serial subscriptions, an OPAC.

Computers on Campus 380 computers available on campus for general student use. A campuswide network can be accessed. Internet access, online (class) registration, at least one staffed computer lab available.

Student Life *Housing:* college housing not available. *Activities and Organizations:* Student Senate, Phi Theta Kappa, Multicultural Student Organization, Single Parents Club, Vocational Industrial Clubs of America. *Campus security:* late-night transport/escort service. *Student services:* personal/psychological counseling.

Athletics *Intramural sports:* basketball M/W, softball M/W, table tennis M/W, tennis M/W, volleyball M/W.

Standardized Tests *Recommended:* SAT or ACT (for placement).

Costs (2005–06) *Tuition:* state resident $1755 full-time, $39 per quarter hour part-time; nonresident $2138 full-time, $4705 per quarter hour part-time. *Required fees:* $45 full-time, $1 per quarter hour part-time.

Applying *Options:* electronic application, early admission, deferred entrance. *Required:* high school transcript. *Application deadline:* rolling (freshmen), rolling (transfers).

Admissions Contact Ms. Pat Frakes, Admissions Representative, Southeast Community College, Lincoln Campus, 8800 "O" Street, Lincoln, NE 68520. *Phone:* 402-437-2600 Ext. 2600. *Toll-free phone:* 800-642-4075 Ext. 2600.

SOUTHEAST COMMUNITY COLLEGE, MILFORD CAMPUS

Milford, Nebraska

- **District-supported** 2-year, founded 1941, part of Southeast Community College System
- **Calendar** quarters
- **Degree** diplomas and associate
- **Small-town** 50-acre campus with easy access to Omaha
- **Coed, primarily men,** 922 undergraduate students, 97% full-time, 6% women, 94% men

Undergraduates 890 full-time, 32 part-time. 0.4% Asian American or Pacific Islander, 0.6% Hispanic American, 0.6% Native American, 33% live on campus.
Freshmen *Admission:* 350 enrolled.
Faculty *Total:* 89, 97% full-time. *Student/faculty ratio:* 20:1.
Majors Architectural engineering technology; automobile/automotive mechanics technology; carpentry; civil engineering technology; commercial and advertising art; computer and information sciences; computer engineering technology; computer programming; construction engineering technology; data processing and data processing technology; drafting and design technology; electrical, electronic and communications engineering technology; electromechanical technology; heating, air conditioning, ventilation and refrigeration maintenance technology; industrial arts; industrial design; industrial technology; machine tool technology; mechanical design technology; mechanical engineering/mechanical technology; metallurgical technology; physical sciences related; pipefitting and sprinkler fitting; plastics engineering technology; quality control technology; solar energy technology; survey technology; transportation technology; welding technology.
Academic Programs *Special study options:* academic remediation for entering students, cooperative education, distance learning, internships, services for LD students.
Library Milford Campus Learning Resource Center with 10,000 titles, 300 serial subscriptions.
Computers on Campus 72 computers available on campus for general student use. At least one staffed computer lab available.
Student Life *Housing Options:* men-only, women-only, disabled students. *Campus security:* 24-hour patrols, late-night transport/escort service.
Athletics *Intramural sports:* archery M/W, basketball M/W, bowling M/W, football M, golf M/W, racquetball M/W, softball M/W, swimming and diving M/W, table tennis M/W, tennis M/W, volleyball M/W, weight lifting M/W, wrestling M.
Standardized Tests *Recommended:* SAT (for admission), ACT (for admission).
Costs (2004–05) *Tuition:* state resident $2160 full-time, $36 per quarter hour part-time; nonresident $2610 full-time, $44 per quarter hour part-time. Full-time tuition and fees vary according to course load. Part-time tuition and fees vary according to course load. *Required fees:* $60 full-time, $1 per quarter hour part-time. *Room and board:* $2880. Room and board charges vary according to housing facility. *Waivers:* minority students, adult students, and employees or children of employees.
Applying *Options:* common application. *Required:* high school transcript. *Application deadline:* rolling (freshmen), rolling (transfers). *Notification:* continuous (freshmen).
Admissions Contact Mr. Larry E. Meyer, Dean of Students, Southeast Community College, Milford Campus, 600 State Street, Milford, NE 68405. *Phone:* 402-761-2131 Ext. 8270. *Toll-free phone:* 800-933-7223 Ext. 8243. *Fax:* 402-761-2324. *E-mail:* lmeyer@southeast.edu.

VATTEROTT COLLEGE
Omaha, Nebraska

- **Proprietary** 2-year, founded 1967
- **Calendar** semesters
- **Degree** diplomas and associate
- **Urban** 1-acre campus
- **Coed**

Faculty *Student/faculty ratio:* 14:1.
Student Life *Campus security:* 24-hour emergency response devices.
Standardized Tests *Required:* Wonderlic aptitude test (for admission). *Recommended:* SAT or ACT (for admission).
Costs (2004–05) *Tuition:* $17,918 full-time. *Required fees:* $900 full-time.
Applying *Options:* early admission, deferred entrance. *Required:* high school transcript.
Admissions Contact Dr. James G. Hadley, Campus Director, Vatterott College, 225 North 80th Street, Omaha, NE 68114. *Phone:* 402-392-1300 Ext. 207. *Toll-free phone:* 800-865-8628.

VATTEROTT COLLEGE
Omaha, Nebraska

- **Proprietary** 2-year
- **Calendar** semesters
- **Coed**

Admissions Contact 5318 South 136th Street, Omaha, NE 68137.

WESTERN NEBRASKA COMMUNITY COLLEGE
Sidney, Nebraska

Admissions Contact Mr. Troy Archuleta, Admissions and Recruitment Director, Western Nebraska Community College, 371 College Drive, Sidney, NE 69162. *Phone:* 308-635-6015. *Toll-free phone:* 800-222-9682 (in-state); 800-348-4435 (out-of-state). *Fax:* 308-635-6100. *E-mail:* rhovey@wncc.net.

NEVADA

CAREER COLLEGE OF NORTHERN NEVADA
Reno, Nevada

- **Proprietary** 2-year, founded 1984
- **Calendar** quarters six-week terms
- **Degree** diplomas and associate
- **Urban** 1-acre campus
- **Coed**

Faculty *Student/faculty ratio:* 20:1.
Student Life *Campus security:* 24-hour emergency response devices.
Costs (2004–05) *Tuition:* $5580 full-time, $155 per credit hour part-time. *Required fees:* $150 full-time.
Financial Aid Of all full-time matriculated undergraduates who enrolled in 2003, 6 Federal Work-Study jobs (averaging $3000).
Applying *Application fee:* $25. *Required:* essay or personal statement, high school transcript, interview.
Admissions Contact Ms. Laura Goldhammer, Director of Admissions, Career College of Northern Nevada, 1195-A Corporate Boulevard, Reno, NV 89502. *Phone:* 775-856-2266 Ext. 11. *Fax:* 775-856-0935. *E-mail:* lgoldhammer@ccnn4u.com.

COMMUNITY COLLEGE OF SOUTHERN NEVADA
North Las Vegas, Nevada

- **State-supported** 2-year, founded 1971, part of University and Community College System of Nevada
- **Calendar** semesters
- **Degree** certificates and associate
- **Suburban** 89-acre campus with easy access to Las Vegas
- **Endowment** $2.6 million
- **Coed,** 34,204 undergraduate students, 23% full-time, 57% women, 43% men

Undergraduates 7,850 full-time, 26,354 part-time. Students come from 55 states and territories, 13 other countries, 2% are from out of state, 0.8% transferred in.
Freshmen *Admission:* 1,592 enrolled.
Faculty *Total:* 2,280, 17% full-time.
Majors Accounting; administrative assistant and secretarial science; anthropology; art; automobile/automotive mechanics technology; behavioral sciences; biological and physical sciences; biology/biological sciences; business administration and management; chemistry; child development; clinical laboratory science/medical technology; clinical/medical laboratory technology; commercial and advertising art; computer engineering technology; computer programming; computer science; computer typography and composition equipment operation; construction engineering technology; construction management; consumer merchandising/retailing management; corrections; criminal justice/law enforcement administration; criminal justice/police science; culinary arts; data processing and data processing technology; dental hygiene; drafting and design technology; dramatic/theatre arts; economics; electrical, electronic and communications engineering technology; emergency medical technology (EMT paramedic); English; environmental studies; finance; fire science; food services technology; graphic and printing equipment operation/production; health information/medical records administration; heating, air conditioning, ventilation and refrigeration maintenance technology; heavy equipment maintenance technology; history; horticultural science; hospitality administration; hotel/motel administration; industrial radiologic technology; information science/studies; kindergarten/preschool education; landscaping and groundskeeping; legal administrative assistant/secretary; legal assistant/paralegal; liberal arts and sciences/liberal studies; literature; marketing/marketing management; mass communication/media; mathematics; mechanical design technology; mechanical engineering/

Community College of Southern Nevada (continued)
mechanical technology; medical administrative assistant and medical secretary; medical/clinical assistant; music; nursing (licensed practical/vocational nurse training); nursing (registered nurse training); occupational therapy; ornamental horticulture; parks, recreation and leisure; pharmacy; photography; radio and television; radiologic technology/science; real estate; respiratory care therapy; science teacher education; sign language interpretation and translation; social sciences; sociology; special products marketing; survey technology; teacher assistant/aide; veterinary technology; welding technology; wildlife and wildlands science and management.

Academic Programs *Special study options:* academic remediation for entering students, accelerated degree program, adult/continuing education programs, advanced placement credit, cooperative education, distance learning, double majors, English as a second language, honors programs, independent study, internships, part-time degree program, services for LD students, summer session for credit. *ROTC:* Army (b).

Library Learning Assistance Center with 100,000 titles, 500 serial subscriptions, 5,400 audiovisual materials, an OPAC, a Web page.

Computers on Campus 500 computers available on campus for general student use. A campuswide network can be accessed from off campus. Internet access, online (class) registration, at least one staffed computer lab available.

Student Life *Housing:* college housing not available. *Activities and Organizations:* drama/theater group, student-run newspaper, choral group, Culinary Club, Art Club, Black Student Association, Student Organization of Latinos, Student Nurses Club. *Campus security:* 24-hour emergency response devices and patrols. *Student services:* health clinic, personal/psychological counseling, women's center, legal services.

Athletics Member NJCAA. *Intercollegiate sports:* baseball M. *Intramural sports:* basketball M/W, bowling M/W, racquetball M/W, tennis M/W, weight lifting M/W.

Costs (2005–06) *Tuition:* state resident $1523 full-time, $51 per credit part-time; nonresident $6557 full-time, $107 per credit part-time. *Required fees:* $120 full-time, $4 per credit part-time.

Financial Aid Of all full-time matriculated undergraduates who enrolled in 2003, 355 Federal Work-Study jobs (averaging $2000).

Applying *Options:* early admission. *Application fee:* $5. *Required:* student data form. *Application deadline:* rolling (freshmen).

Admissions Contact Mr. Arlie J. Stops, Associate Vice President for Admissions and Records, Community College of Southern Nevada, 3200 East Cheyenne Avenue, North Las Vegas, NV 89030-4296. *Phone:* 702-651-4060. *Toll-free phone:* 800-492-5728. *Fax:* 702-643-1474. *E-mail:* stops@ccsn.nevada.edu.

GREAT BASIN COLLEGE
Elko, Nevada

- **State-supported** primarily 2-year, founded 1967, part of University and Community College System of Nevada
- **Calendar** semesters
- **Degrees** certificates, associate, and bachelor's
- **Small-town** 45-acre campus
- **Endowment** $150,000
- **Coed,** 2,731 undergraduate students, 100% full-time, 69% women, 31% men

Undergraduates 2,731 full-time. 0.7% African American, 1% Asian American or Pacific Islander, 9% Hispanic American, 4% Native American.

Faculty *Total:* 225, 24% full-time. *Student/faculty ratio:* 12:1.

Majors Anthropology; art; business administration and management; business/commerce; chemistry; criminal justice/safety; data processing and data processing technology; diesel mechanics technology; electrical, electronic and communications engineering technology; elementary education; English; environmental studies; geology/earth science; history; industrial technology; interdisciplinary studies; kindergarten/preschool education; mathematics; nursing (registered nurse training); office management; operations management; physics; psychology; sociology; welding technology.

Academic Programs *Special study options:* academic remediation for entering students, adult/continuing education programs, cooperative education, distance learning, English as a second language, external degree program, independent study, part-time degree program, services for LD students, summer session for credit.

Library Learning Resources Center with 27,521 titles, 250 serial subscriptions, an OPAC.

Computers on Campus 95 computers available on campus for general student use. A campuswide network can be accessed from off campus. Internet access, online (class) registration, at least one staffed computer lab available.

Student Life *Housing Options:* Campus housing is university owned. *Activities and Organizations:* drama/theater group, choral group. *Campus security:* evening patrols by trained security personnel. *Student services:* personal/psychological counseling.

Athletics *Intramural sports:* badminton M/W, basketball M/W, volleyball M/W, weight lifting M/W.

Standardized Tests *Recommended:* SAT or ACT (for placement).

Costs (2005–06) *Tuition:* state resident $1643 full-time, $55 per credit part-time; nonresident $4100 full-time, $111 per credit part-time. *Room and board:* $4420; room only: $1800.

Financial Aid Of all full-time matriculated undergraduates who enrolled in 2003, 35 Federal Work-Study jobs (averaging $1000). 50 state and other part-time jobs (averaging $1800).

Applying *Options:* common application, electronic application, early admission, deferred entrance. *Application fee:* $5. *Required:* high school transcript. *Application deadline:* rolling (freshmen), rolling (transfers). *Notification:* continuous (freshmen).

Admissions Contact Ms. Julie Byrnes, Director of Enrollment Management, Great Basin College, 1500 College Parkway, Elko, NV 89801-3348. *Phone:* 775-753-2271. *Fax:* 775-753-2311. *E-mail:* stdsvc@gbcnv.edu.

HERITAGE COLLEGE
Las Vegas, Nevada

Admissions Contact 3305 Spring Mountain Road, Suite 7, Las Vegas, NV 89102.

HIGH-TECH INSTITUTE
Las Vegas, Nevada

Admissions Contact Mr. Alvin J. Hollander, Director, High-Tech Institute, 2320 South Rancho Drive, Las Vegas, NV 89102. *Phone:* 702-385-6700. *Toll-free phone:* 800-987-0110.

ITT TECHNICAL INSTITUTE
Henderson, Nevada

- **Proprietary** primarily 2-year, part of ITT Educational Services, Inc
- **Degrees** associate and bachelor's
- **Coed**

Standardized Tests *Required:* Wonderlic aptitude test (for admission).

Costs (2004–05) *Tuition:* Please see school catalog for specific information.

Financial Aid Of all full-time matriculated undergraduates who enrolled in 2003, 6 Federal Work-Study jobs (averaging $5000).

Applying *Options:* deferred entrance. *Application fee:* $100. *Required:* high school transcript, interview. *Recommended:* letters of recommendation.

Admissions Contact Ms. Sandra Turkington, Director of Recruitment, ITT Technical Institute, 168 North Gibson Road, Henderson, NV 89014. *Phone:* 702-558-5404. *Toll-free phone:* 800-488-8459. *Fax:* 702-558-5412.

LAS VEGAS COLLEGE
Las Vegas, Nevada

Admissions Contact Mr. Bill Hall, Director of Admissions, Las Vegas College, 4100 West Flamingo Road, Suite 2100, Las Vegas, NV 89103-3926. *Phone:* 702-368-6200. *Toll-free phone:* 800-903-3101. *Fax:* 702-368-6464. *E-mail:* mmiloro@cci.edu.

LE CORDON BLEU COLLEGE OF CULINARY ARTS, LAS VEGAS
Las Vegas, Nevada

Admissions Contact 1451 Center Crossing Road, Las Vegas, NV 89144.

PIMA MEDICAL INSTITUTE
Las Vegas, Nevada

- **Proprietary** 2-year, founded 2003, part of Vocational Training Institutes, Inc
- **Calendar** modular
- **Degree** certificates and associate
- **Urban** campus
- **Coed,** 329 undergraduate students, 100% full-time, 87% women, 13% men

Undergraduates 329 full-time. 10% are from out of state.

Freshmen *Admission:* 34 applied, 28 admitted.

Faculty *Total:* 12, 58% full-time. *Student/faculty ratio:* 20:1.

Majors Radiologic technology/science; respiratory therapy technician.

Academic Programs *Special study options:* advanced placement credit, internships.

Computers on Campus 25 computers available on campus for general student use. Internet access available.

Student Life *Housing:* college housing not available.

Standardized Tests *Required:* Wonderlic Scholastic Level Exam (for admission).

Applying *Required:* interview. *Required for some:* essay or personal statement, high school transcript.

Admissions Contact Admissions Office, Pima Medical Institute, Pima Medical Institute, 3333 East Flamingo Road, Las Vegas, NV 89121. *Phone:* 702-458-9650 Ext. 202. *Toll-free phone:* 800-477-PIMA.

TRUCKEE MEADOWS COMMUNITY COLLEGE
Reno, Nevada

- **State-supported** 2-year, founded 1971, part of University and Community College System of Nevada
- **Calendar** semesters
- **Degree** certificates and associate
- **Suburban** 63-acre campus
- **Endowment** $5.6 million
- **Coed,** 9,697 undergraduate students, 20% full-time, 55% women, 45% men

Undergraduates 1,963 full-time, 7,734 part-time. Students come from 12 states and territories, 3 other countries, 2% African American, 6% Asian American or Pacific Islander, 9% Hispanic American, 2% Native American, 2% international.

Freshmen *Admission:* 865 enrolled.

Faculty *Total:* 480, 30% full-time. *Student/faculty ratio:* 31:1.

Majors Accounting; administrative assistant and secretarial science; architectural engineering technology; automobile/automotive mechanics technology; business administration and management; carpentry; child development; commercial and advertising art; computer engineering technology; computer programming; computer programming related; construction engineering technology; corrections; criminal justice/law enforcement administration; criminal justice/police science; culinary arts; data processing and data processing technology; dental assisting; dental hygiene; dietitian assistant; drafting and design technology; education (K-12); electrical, electronic and communications engineering technology; elementary education; engineering technology; environmental biology; environmental studies; fire science; heating, air conditioning, ventilation and refrigeration maintenance technology; hospitality administration; industrial radiologic technology; information science/studies; kindergarten/preschool education; landscape architecture; legal administrative assistant/secretary; liberal arts and sciences/liberal studies; marketing/marketing management; medical administrative assistant and medical secretary; mental health/rehabilitation; military science; nursing (registered nurse training); pipefitting and sprinkler fitting; radiologic technology/science; real estate; safety/security technology; secondary education; solar energy technology; substance abuse/addiction counseling; welding technology.

Academic Programs *Special study options:* academic remediation for entering students, adult/continuing education programs, advanced placement credit, cooperative education, distance learning, English as a second language, internships, part-time degree program, services for LD students, summer session for credit. *ROTC:* Army (c).

Library Elizabeth Storm Library plus 1 other with 42,110 titles, 816 serial subscriptions, an OPAC, a Web page.

Computers on Campus A campuswide network can be accessed from off campus. Internet access, online (class) registration, at least one staffed computer lab available.

Student Life *Housing:* college housing not available. *Activities and Organizations:* drama/theater group, student-run newspaper, choral group, Associated Students of Truckee Meadows, Phi Theta Kappa, International Students Organization, Latino Student Organization, Asian and Pacific Islander Student Association. *Campus security:* 24-hour emergency response devices and patrols, late-night transport/escort service. *Student services:* health clinic, personal/psychological counseling.

Standardized Tests *Recommended:* SAT or ACT (for placement).

Costs (2005–06) *Tuition:* state resident $0 full-time; nonresident $4915 full-time, $56 per credit part-time. *Required fees:* $1314 full-time, $55 per credit part-time.

Financial Aid Of all full-time matriculated undergraduates who enrolled in 2003, 126 Federal Work-Study jobs (averaging $5000). 368 state and other part-time jobs (averaging $5000).

Applying *Options:* early admission, deferred entrance. *Application fee:* $10. *Application deadline:* rolling (freshmen), rolling (transfers).

Admissions Contact Mr. Dave Harbeck, Director of Admissions and Records, Truckee Meadows Community College, Mail Station #15, 7000 Dandini Boulevard, MS RDMT 319, Reno, NV 89512-3901. *Phone:* 775-674-7623.

WESTERN NEVADA COMMUNITY COLLEGE
Carson City, Nevada

- **State-supported** 2-year, founded 1971, part of University and Community College System of Nevada
- **Calendar** semesters
- **Degree** certificates, diplomas, and associate
- **Small-town** 200-acre campus
- **Endowment** $116,247
- **Coed,** 4,897 undergraduate students, 19% full-time, 60% women, 40% men

Undergraduates 936 full-time, 3,961 part-time. 3% are from out of state.

Freshmen *Admission:* 640 applied, 640 admitted.

Faculty *Total:* 365, 21% full-time.

Majors Accounting; accounting technology and bookkeeping; administrative assistant and secretarial science; automobile/automotive mechanics technology; biology/biological sciences; business administration and management; business automation/technology/data entry; business/commerce; carpentry; child care and support services management; clinical/medical laboratory technology; computer and information sciences; computer programming; construction management; corrections; criminal justice/law enforcement administration; criminal justice/police science; drafting and design technology; electrical and power transmission installation; electrical, electronic and communications engineering technology; engineering; environmental studies; fire protection and safety technology; general studies; heating, air conditioning, ventilation and refrigeration maintenance technology; industrial technology; legal assistant/paralegal; liberal arts and sciences/liberal studies; machine tool technology; management information systems; management science; marketing/marketing management; masonry; mathematics; nursing (registered nurse training); parks, recreation and leisure facilities management; physical sciences; pipefitting and sprinkler fitting; real estate; sheet metal technology; vehicle/equipment operation; welding technology.

Academic Programs *Special study options:* academic remediation for entering students, adult/continuing education programs, advanced placement credit, cooperative education, distance learning, English as a second language, honors programs, independent study, internships, part-time degree program, services for LD students, summer session for credit.

Library Western Nevada Community College Library and Media Services plus 2 others with 42,500 titles, 228 serial subscriptions, 26,695 audiovisual materials, an OPAC, a Web page.

Computers on Campus 678 computers available on campus for general student use. A campuswide network can be accessed from off campus. Internet access, online (class) registration, at least one staffed computer lab available.

Student Life *Housing:* college housing not available. *Activities and Organizations:* drama/theater group, choral group, Phi Theta Kappa, writers group, Infinity Society, Golf Club, Physics and Engineering Club. *Campus security:* late-night transport/escort service. *Student services:* personal/psychological counseling.

Athletics *Intercollegiate sports:* baseball M, equestrian sports M/W, soccer W.

Standardized Tests *Recommended:* SAT or ACT (for placement).

Costs (2005–06) *Tuition:* $51 per credit part-time; state resident $1523 full-time, $80 per credit part-time; nonresident $6588 full-time, $110 per credit part-time. Full-time tuition and fees vary according to course load and reciprocity agreements. Part-time tuition and fees vary according to course load and reciprocity agreements. *Required fees:* $120 full-time, $4 per credit part-time. *Payment plans:* installment, deferred payment. *Waivers:* senior citizens and employees or children of employees.

Financial Aid Of all full-time matriculated undergraduates who enrolled in 2003, 24 Federal Work-Study jobs (averaging $4500). 48 state and other part-time jobs (averaging $4500).

Applying *Options:* early admission. *Application fee:* $15. *Required for some:* high school transcript. *Application deadline:* rolling (freshmen), rolling (transfers).

Admissions Contact Ms. Dianne Hilliard, Director Admissions and Records, Western Nevada Community College, 2201 West College Parkway, Carson City, NV 89703-7399. *Phone:* 775-445-3271. *Fax:* 775-445-3147. *E-mail:* wncc_aro@wncc.edu.

NEW HAMPSHIRE

HESSER COLLEGE
Manchester, New Hampshire

- **Proprietary** primarily 2-year, founded 1900, part of Quest Education Corporation

Hesser College (continued)

- **Calendar** semesters
- **Degrees** certificates, diplomas, associate, and bachelor's (also offers a graduate law program with Massachusetts School of Law at Andover)
- **Urban** 1-acre campus with easy access to Boston
- **Coed,** 3,398 undergraduate students, 62% full-time, 71% women, 29% men

Undergraduates 2,104 full-time, 1,294 part-time. Students come from 12 states and territories, 50% live on campus.

Freshmen *Admission:* 1,725 applied, 1,562 admitted, 1,018 enrolled. *Average high school GPA:* 2.3.

Faculty *Total:* 215, 18% full-time.

Majors Accounting; business administration and management; business and personal/financial services marketing; child care and support services management; commercial and advertising art; computer and information sciences; computer engineering technology; computer management; computer programming; computer science; computer systems analysis; corrections; criminal justice/law enforcement administration; criminal justice/police science; criminal justice/safety; human services; information science/studies; interior design; kindergarten/preschool education; legal assistant/paralegal; liberal arts and sciences/liberal studies; management information systems; marketing/marketing management; mass communication/media; medical administrative assistant and medical secretary; medical/clinical assistant; physical therapist assistant; psychology; radio and television; sales, distribution and marketing; security and loss prevention; social work; sport and fitness administration.

Academic Programs *Special study options:* accelerated degree program, adult/continuing education programs, advanced placement credit, cooperative education, double majors, internships, part-time degree program, student-designed majors, summer session for credit.

Library Kenneth W. Galeucia Memorial Library with 38,000 titles, 200 serial subscriptions, 60 audiovisual materials, an OPAC, a Web page.

Computers on Campus 60 computers available on campus for general student use. A campuswide network can be accessed from student residence rooms. Internet access, at least one staffed computer lab available.

Student Life *Housing Options:* coed. Campus housing is university owned. Freshman campus housing is guaranteed. *Activities and Organizations:* student-run radio and television station, student government, Ski Club, Amnesty International, yearbook, student ambassadors. *Campus security:* 24-hour emergency response devices and patrols, student patrols, late-night transport/escort service, controlled dormitory access. *Student services:* health clinic, personal/psychological counseling.

Athletics *Intercollegiate sports:* basketball M(s)/W(s), soccer M(s)/W(s), volleyball M(s)/W(s). *Intramural sports:* baseball M, basketball M/W, bowling M/W, skiing (downhill) M/W, softball M/W, table tennis M/W, volleyball M/W.

Standardized Tests *Recommended:* SAT (for admission).

Costs (2005–06) *Comprehensive fee:* $18,940 includes full-time tuition ($11,340), mandatory fees ($1000), and room and board ($6600). Part-time tuition: $410 per credit. *Room and board:* college room only: $3600.

Financial Aid Of all full-time matriculated undergraduates who enrolled in 2003, 700 Federal Work-Study jobs (averaging $1000).

Applying *Options:* common application, electronic application, deferred entrance. *Application fee:* $10. *Required:* high school transcript, interview. *Required for some:* essay or personal statement, letters of recommendation. *Recommended:* minimum 2.0 GPA. *Application deadline:* rolling (freshmen), rolling (transfers). *Notification:* continuous (freshmen).

Admissions Contact Ms. Julie English, Director of Admissions, Hesser College, 3 Sundial Avenue, Manchester, NH 03103. *Phone:* 603-668-6660 Ext. 2101. *Toll-free phone:* 800-526-9231 Ext. 2110. *E-mail:* admissions@hesser.edu.

▶ See page 500 for a narrative description.

McIntosh College
Dover, New Hampshire

- **Proprietary** 2-year, founded 1896
- **Calendar** trimesters
- **Degree** certificates and associate
- **Small-town** 11-acre campus with easy access to Boston
- **Coed,** 750 undergraduate students

Undergraduates Students come from 20 states and territories, 10% are from out of state, 5% African American, 0.9% Asian American or Pacific Islander, 3% Hispanic American, 0.9% Native American, 0.6% international, 25% live on campus. *Retention:* 96% of 2002 full-time freshmen returned.

Freshmen *Admission:* 2,250 applied, 750 admitted. *Average high school GPA:* 2.78.

Faculty *Total:* 100, 42% full-time, 3% with terminal degrees. *Student/faculty ratio:* 25:1.

Majors Accounting; administrative assistant and secretarial science; business administration and management; computer and information sciences; computer management; computer science; computer systems analysis; criminal justice/law

enforcement administration; culinary arts; information science/studies; kindergarten/preschool education; legal administrative assistant/secretary; legal assistant/paralegal; medical administrative assistant and medical secretary; medical/clinical assistant; office management; sales, distribution and marketing; telecommunications; tourism and travel services management.

Academic Programs *Special study options:* accelerated degree program, adult/continuing education programs, advanced placement credit, cooperative education, double majors, internships, part-time degree program, services for LD students, summer session for credit.

Library McIntosh College Library with 11,000 titles, 130 serial subscriptions.

Computers on Campus 150 computers available on campus for general student use. Internet access, online (class) registration, at least one staffed computer lab available.

Student Life *Housing Options:* coed. Campus housing is university owned and leased by the school. *Activities and Organizations:* drama/theater group, Student Activities Committee, Drama Club, Business Club, Culture Club, Collegiate Secretaries International. *Campus security:* 24-hour emergency response devices and patrols, student patrols, controlled dormitory access. *Student services:* personal/psychological counseling.

Standardized Tests *Recommended:* SAT II: Writing Test (for placement).

Costs (2005–06) *Comprehensive fee:* $36,230 includes full-time tuition ($26,500), mandatory fees ($100), and room and board ($9630). Part-time tuition: $442 per credit.

Applying *Options:* common application, electronic application, early admission, deferred entrance. *Application fee:* $15. *Required:* high school transcript. *Recommended:* interview. *Application deadline:* rolling (freshmen). *Notification:* continuous (freshmen).

Admissions Contact Mrs. Jody LaBrie, Vice President of Admissions and Marketing, McIntosh College, 23 Cataract Avenue, Dover, NH 03820-3990. *Phone:* 603-742-1234. *Toll-free phone:* 800-McINTOSH. *Fax:* 603-743-0060. *E-mail:* admissions@mcintosh.dover.nh.us.

▶ See page 524 for a narrative description.

New Hampshire Community Technical College, Berlin/Laconia
Berlin, New Hampshire

- **State-supported** 2-year, founded 1966, part of New Hampshire Community Technical College System
- **Calendar** semesters
- **Degree** certificates, diplomas, and associate
- **Rural** 325-acre campus
- **Coed**

Athletics Member NSCAA.

Standardized Tests *Required:* ACT ASSET (for admission).

Costs (2004–05) *Tuition:* state resident $148 per credit part-time; nonresident $340 per credit part-time. *Required fees:* $3 per credit part-time. *Payment plans:* installment, deferred payment.

Applying *Application fee:* $10. *Required:* high school transcript, placement test. *Required for some:* essay or personal statement.

Admissions Contact Ms. Martha P. Laflamme, Vice President of Student Affairs, New Hampshire Community Technical College, Berlin/Laconia, 2020 Riverside Drive, Berlin, NH 03570-3717. *Phone:* 603-752-1113 Ext. 1004. *Toll-free phone:* 800-445-4525. *Fax:* 603-752-6335. *E-mail:* berlin4u@nhctc.edu.

New Hampshire Community Technical College, Manchester/Stratham
Manchester, New Hampshire

- **State-supported** 2-year, founded 1945, part of New Hampshire Community Technical College System
- **Calendar** semesters
- **Degree** certificates, diplomas, and associate
- **Urban** 60-acre campus with easy access to Boston
- **Coed,** 4,644 undergraduate students, 21% full-time, 55% women, 45% men

Undergraduates 967 full-time, 3,677 part-time. Students come from 5 states and territories.

Freshmen *Admission:* 1,199 applied, 862 admitted, 679 enrolled.

Faculty *Total:* 190, 25% full-time, 3% with terminal degrees. *Student/faculty ratio:* 14:1.

Majors Accounting; administrative assistant and secretarial science; athletic training; automobile/automotive mechanics technology; business administration and management; child development; commercial and advertising art; community organization and advocacy; construction engineering technology; drafting and design technology; heating, air conditioning, ventilation and refrigeration maintenance technology; human services; information science/studies; kindergarten/preschool education; kinesiology and exercise science; liberal arts and sciences/liberal studies; management information systems; marketing/marketing management; mechanical design technology; medical administrative assistant and medical secretary; nursing (registered nurse training); physical therapy; welding technology.

Academic Programs *Special study options:* academic remediation for entering students, adult/continuing education programs, advanced placement credit, cooperative education, distance learning, English as a second language, external degree program, independent study, internships, part-time degree program, services for LD students, summer session for credit.

Library New Hampshire Community Technical College Library plus 1 other with 18,000 titles, 160 serial subscriptions, an OPAC.

Computers on Campus 210 computers available on campus for general student use. A campuswide network can be accessed. Internet access, online (class) registration, at least one staffed computer lab available.

Student Life *Housing:* college housing not available. *Activities and Organizations:* Student Senate, Phi Theta Kappa, American Society of Welders, Student Nurses Association. *Campus security:* trained security personnel. *Student services:* personal/psychological counseling.

Athletics *Intercollegiate sports:* baseball W, basketball M, skiing (downhill) M/W, soccer M/W, volleyball M/W. *Intramural sports:* basketball M/W, bowling M/W, ice hockey M, skiing (cross-country) M/W, skiing (downhill) M/W, volleyball M/W.

Costs (2004–05) *Tuition:* area resident $3552 full-time, $148 per credit part-time; state resident $5328 full-time, $222 per credit part-time; nonresident $8160 full-time, $390 per credit part-time. *Required fees:* $3 per credit part-time.

Applying *Options:* early admission, deferred entrance. *Application fee:* $10. *Required:* high school transcript, interview. *Recommended:* letters of recommendation. *Application deadline:* rolling (freshmen), rolling (transfers). *Notification:* continuous (freshmen).

Admissions Contact Dr. Nancy L. Travers, Vice President of Student and Community Services, New Hampshire Community Technical College, Manchester/Stratham, 1066 Front Street, Manchester, NH 03102-8518. *Phone:* 603-668-6706 Ext. 224.

NEW HAMPSHIRE COMMUNITY TECHNICAL COLLEGE, NASHUA/CLAREMONT
Nashua, New Hampshire

Admissions Contact Ms. Patricia Goodman, Director of Student Services, New Hampshire Community Technical College, Nashua/Claremont, 505 Amherst Street, Nashua, NH 03063. *Phone:* 603-882-6923 Ext. 1529. *Fax:* 603-882-8690. *E-mail:* nashua@nhctc.edu.

NEW HAMPSHIRE TECHNICAL INSTITUTE
Concord, New Hampshire

- **State-supported** 2-year, founded 1964, part of New Hampshire Community Technical College System
- **Calendar** semesters
- **Degree** certificates, diplomas, and associate
- **Small-town** 225-acre campus with easy access to Boston
- **Coed**

Faculty *Student/faculty ratio:* 12:1.

Student Life *Campus security:* 24-hour patrols, late-night transport/escort service, controlled dormitory access.

Athletics Member NSCAA.

Standardized Tests *Required for some:* National League of Nursing Exam. *Recommended:* SAT or ACT (for admission).

Costs (2004–05) *Tuition:* state resident $4440 full-time, $148 per credit part-time; nonresident $10,200 full-time, $340 per credit part-time. Full-time tuition and fees vary according to class time and program. Part-time tuition and fees vary according to class time and program. *Required fees:* $510 full-time, $15 per credit part-time. *Room and board:* $5910; room only: $3850.

Financial Aid Of all full-time matriculated undergraduates who enrolled in 2003, 182 Federal Work-Study jobs (averaging $1000).

Applying *Options:* electronic application. *Application fee:* $10. *Required:* high school transcript. *Required for some:* essay or personal statement, letters of recommendation, interview. *Recommended:* minimum 2.0 GPA.

Admissions Contact Mr. Francis P. Meyer, Director of Admissions, New Hampshire Technical Institute, 11 Institute Drive, Concord, NH 03301-7412.

Phone: 603-271-7131. *Toll-free phone:* 800-247-0179. *Fax:* 603-271-7139. *E-mail:* nhtiadm@tec.nh.us.

NEW JERSEY

ASSUMPTION COLLEGE FOR SISTERS
Mendham, New Jersey

- **Independent Roman Catholic** 2-year, founded 1953
- **Calendar** semesters
- **Degree** certificates, diplomas, and associate
- **Rural** 112-acre campus with easy access to New York City
- **Endowment** $81,287
- **Women only,** 33 undergraduate students, 64% full-time

Undergraduates 21 full-time, 12 part-time. Students come from 3 states and territories, 5 other countries, 67% are from out of state, 5% Asian American or Pacific Islander, 86% international.

Freshmen *Admission:* 7 enrolled. *Test scores:* SAT verbal scores over 500: 100%; SAT math scores over 500: 100%.

Faculty *Total:* 10, 10% full-time, 10% with terminal degrees. *Student/faculty ratio:* 6:1.

Majors Liberal arts and sciences/liberal studies; theology.

Academic Programs *Special study options:* academic remediation for entering students, advanced placement credit, English as a second language, part-time degree program, services for LD students, summer session for credit.

Library Assumption College for Sisters Library with 25,000 titles, 50 serial subscriptions, 3,000 audiovisual materials, an OPAC.

Computers on Campus 16 computers available on campus for general student use. A campuswide network can be accessed. Internet access, at least one staffed computer lab available.

Student Life *Housing:* college housing not available. *Options:* Campus housing is provided by a third party. *Activities and Organizations:* choral group. *Campus security:* 24-hour emergency response devices.

Costs (2005–06) *Tuition:* $3300 full-time, $100 per credit part-time. *Required fees:* $50 full-time.

Applying *Required:* high school transcript, 1 letter of recommendation, women religious or women in religious formation. *Required for some:* interview.

Admissions Contact Sr. Gerardine Tantsits, Academic Dean/Registrar, Assumption College for Sisters, 350 Bernardsville Road, Mendham, NJ 07945-2923. *Phone:* 973-543-6528 Ext. 228. *Fax:* 973-543-1738.

ATLANTIC CAPE COMMUNITY COLLEGE
Mays Landing, New Jersey

- **County-supported** 2-year, founded 1964
- **Calendar** semesters
- **Degree** certificates, diplomas, and associate
- **Small-town** 537-acre campus with easy access to Philadelphia
- **Endowment** $576,000
- **Coed,** 6,515 undergraduate students, 46% full-time, 64% women, 36% men

Undergraduates 2,974 full-time, 3,541 part-time. Students come from 3 states and territories, 17 other countries, 1% are from out of state, 14% African American, 7% Asian American or Pacific Islander, 10% Hispanic American, 0.2% Native American, 4% transferred in.

Freshmen *Admission:* 3,393 applied, 2,261 admitted, 2,175 enrolled.

Faculty *Total:* 382, 20% full-time. *Student/faculty ratio:* 26:1.

Majors Accounting; biology/biological sciences; business administration and management; chemistry; child development; computer and information sciences and support services related; computer and information systems security; computer programming; corrections; criminal justice/police science; culinary arts; data entry/microcomputer applications; demography and population; education; fine/studio arts; foodservice systems administration; general studies; health services/allied health/health sciences; history; hospitality administration; humanities; legal assistant/paralegal; liberal arts and sciences/liberal studies; literature; mathematics; nursing (registered nurse training); physical therapist assistant; psychology; respiratory care therapy; social sciences; social work; sociology; visual and performing arts; web/multimedia management and webmaster.

Academic Programs *Special study options:* academic remediation for entering students, adult/continuing education programs, advanced placement credit, cooperative education, distance learning, double majors, English as a second language, independent study, internships, part-time degree program, services for LD students, summer session for credit.

Library William Spangler Library with 78,000 titles, 300 serial subscriptions, 1,000 audiovisual materials, an OPAC, a Web page.

Atlantic Cape Community College (continued)

Computers on Campus 350 computers available on campus for general student use. A campuswide network can be accessed from off campus. At least one staffed computer lab available.

Student Life *Housing:* college housing not available. *Activities and Organizations:* drama/theater group, student-run newspaper, radio station, Culinary Student Association, Phi Theta Kappa, History/Government Club, Student Nurses Club, Occupational Therapy Club. *Campus security:* 24-hour emergency response devices and patrols. *Student services:* personal/psychological counseling.

Athletics Member NJCAA. *Intercollegiate sports:* archery M/W, basketball M. *Intramural sports:* baseball M/W, cheerleading M/W, cross-country running M/W, football M/W, soccer M/W, softball M/W, table tennis M/W, volleyball M/W.

Standardized Tests *Recommended:* SAT (for placement), ACCUPLACER.

Costs (2004–05) *Tuition:* area resident $2195 full-time, $73 per credit part-time; state resident $4390 full-time, $146 per credit part-time; nonresident $7680 full-time, $256 per credit part-time. Full-time tuition and fees vary according to program. Part-time tuition and fees vary according to program. *Required fees:* $420 full-time, $14 per credit part-time. *Payment plans:* installment, deferred payment. *Waivers:* senior citizens and employees or children of employees.

Financial Aid Of all full-time matriculated undergraduates who enrolled in 2003, 90 Federal Work-Study jobs (averaging $2000). 1,800 state and other part-time jobs (averaging $1500).

Applying *Options:* common application, electronic application, early admission, deferred entrance. *Application fee:* $35. *Recommended:* high school transcript. *Application deadlines:* 7/1 (freshmen), 7/1 (transfers).

Admissions Contact Mrs. Linda McLeod, Assistant Director, Admissions and College Recruitment, Atlantic Cape Community College, 5100 Black Horse Pike, Mays Landing, NJ 08330-2699. *Phone:* 609-343-5000 Ext. 5009. *Toll-free phone:* 800-645-CHIEF. *Fax:* 609-343-4921. *E-mail:* accadmit@atlantic.edu.

▶ **See page 460 for a narrative description.**

BERGEN COMMUNITY COLLEGE
Paramus, New Jersey

- **County-supported** 2-year, founded 1965
- **Calendar** semesters
- **Degree** certificates and associate
- **Suburban** 167-acre campus with easy access to New York City
- **Coed,** 14,325 undergraduate students, 51% full-time, 56% women, 44% men

Undergraduates 7,258 full-time, 7,067 part-time. Students come from 120 other countries, 6% African American, 10% Asian American or Pacific Islander, 24% Hispanic American, 0.2% Native American, 7% international.

Freshmen *Admission:* 2,634 enrolled.

Faculty *Total:* 749, 40% full-time, 20% with terminal degrees. *Student/faculty ratio:* 20:1.

Majors Accounting; administrative assistant and secretarial science; art; automobile/automotive mechanics technology; biology/biological sciences; broadcast journalism; business administration and management; chemistry; clinical/medical laboratory technology; commercial and advertising art; computer engineering technology; computer programming; computer science; computer typography and composition equipment operation; consumer merchandising/retailing management; criminal justice/law enforcement administration; dance; dental hygiene; drafting and design technology; dramatic/theatre arts; economics; education; electrical, electronic and communications engineering technology; engineering science; finance; health science; history; hotel/motel administration; industrial radiologic technology; industrial technology; kindergarten/preschool education; kinesiology and exercise science; legal administrative assistant/secretary; legal assistant/paralegal; liberal arts and sciences/liberal studies; literature; mass communication/media; mathematics; medical administrative assistant and medical secretary; medical/clinical assistant; music; nursing (registered nurse training); ornamental horticulture; parks, recreation and leisure; philosophy; photography; physics; political science and government; psychology; real estate; respiratory care therapy; sociology; special products marketing; tourism and travel services management; veterinary technology; women's studies.

Academic Programs *Special study options:* academic remediation for entering students, adult/continuing education programs, cooperative education, distance learning, English as a second language, honors programs, internships, part-time degree program, services for LD students, study abroad, summer session for credit.

Library Sidney Silverman Library and Learning Resources Center plus 1 other with an OPAC.

Computers on Campus At least one staffed computer lab available.

Student Life *Housing:* college housing not available. *Activities and Organizations:* drama/theater group, student-run newspaper, choral group. *Campus security:* 24-hour patrols. *Student services:* health clinic, personal/psychological counseling.

Athletics Member NJCAA. *Intercollegiate sports:* baseball M, basketball M/W, cross-country running M/W, golf M, soccer M/W, softball W, tennis M/W, track and field M/W, volleyball W, wrestling M. *Intramural sports:* basketball M, soccer M, tennis M/W, volleyball M/W.

Costs (2004–05) *Tuition:* area resident $1982 full-time, $83 per credit part-time; state resident $4104 full-time, $171 per credit part-time; nonresident $4344 full-time, $181 per credit part-time. *Required fees:* $403 full-time, $17 per credit part-time.

Financial Aid Of all full-time matriculated undergraduates who enrolled in 2003, 159 Federal Work-Study jobs (averaging $1575).

Applying *Application fee:* $25. *Notification:* continuous (freshmen).

Admissions Contact Director of Admissions and Recruitment, Bergen Community College, 400 Paramus Road, Paramus, NJ 07652-1595. *Phone:* 201-447-7193. *Fax:* 201-670-7973. *E-mail:* admsoffice@bergen.edu.

BERKELEY COLLEGE
West Paterson, New Jersey

- **Proprietary** primarily 2-year, founded 1931
- **Calendar** quarters
- **Degrees** certificates, associate, and bachelor's
- **Suburban** 25-acre campus with easy access to New York City
- **Coed,** 2,313 undergraduate students, 85% full-time, 74% women, 26% men

Undergraduates 1,966 full-time, 347 part-time. Students come from 8 states and territories, 25 other countries, 15% African American, 5% Asian American or Pacific Islander, 34% Hispanic American, 0.3% Native American, 2% international, 5% transferred in, 1% live on campus.

Freshmen *Admission:* 745 enrolled.

Faculty *Total:* 158, 39% full-time. *Student/faculty ratio:* 22:1.

Majors Accounting; business administration and management; business/commerce; computer management; fashion merchandising; interior design; international business/trade/commerce; legal assistant/paralegal; marketing/marketing management; system administration; web page, digital/multimedia and information resources design.

Academic Programs *Special study options:* academic remediation for entering students, adult/continuing education programs, advanced placement credit, cooperative education, distance learning, English as a second language, internships, off-campus study, part-time degree program, study abroad, summer session for credit.

Library Walter A. Brower Library with 49,584 titles, 224 serial subscriptions, 2,659 audiovisual materials, an OPAC, a Web page.

Computers on Campus 300 computers available on campus for general student use. A campuswide network can be accessed from student residence rooms and from off campus. At least one staffed computer lab available.

Student Life *Housing Options:* coed. Campus housing is university owned. *Activities and Organizations:* student-run newspaper, Student Government Association, Athletics Club, Paralegal Student Association, International Club, Fashion and Marketing Club. *Campus security:* 24-hour emergency response devices, controlled dormitory access, security patrols. *Student services:* personal/psychological counseling.

Athletics *Intramural sports:* basketball M/W, football M/W, soccer M/W, softball M/W, volleyball M/W.

Standardized Tests *Required:* SAT or ACT (for admission).

Costs (2005–06) *Comprehensive fee:* $25,950 includes full-time tuition ($16,200), mandatory fees ($750), and room and board ($9000). Part-time tuition: $395 per credit. *Required fees:* $75 per term part-time. *Room and board:* college room only: $5400.

Financial Aid Of all full-time matriculated undergraduates who enrolled in 2003, 150 Federal Work-Study jobs (averaging $1200).

Applying *Options:* electronic application, deferred entrance. *Application fee:* $40. *Required:* high school transcript. *Recommended:* interview. *Application deadline:* rolling (freshmen), rolling (transfers).

Admissions Contact Mrs. Carol Covino, Director of High School Admissions, Berkeley College, 44 Rifle Camp Road, West Paterson, NJ 07424. *Phone:* 973-278-5400 Ext. 1210. *Toll-free phone:* 800-446-5400. *E-mail:* info@berkeleycollege.edu.

▶ **See page 468 for a narrative description.**

BROOKDALE COMMUNITY COLLEGE
Lincroft, New Jersey

- **County-supported** 2-year, founded 1967, part of New Jersey Commission on Higher Education

- **Calendar** semesters plus 1 ten-week and 2 six-week summer terms
- **Degree** certificates and associate
- **Small-town** 221-acre campus with easy access to New York City
- **Coed,** 12,724 undergraduate students, 52% full-time, 57% women, 43% men

Undergraduates 6,588 full-time, 6,136 part-time. Students come from 6 states and territories, 50 other countries, 0.1% are from out of state, 12% African American, 4% Asian American or Pacific Islander, 7% Hispanic American, 0.2% Native American, 1% international, 5% transferred in. *Retention:* 66% of 2002 full-time freshmen returned.

Freshmen *Admission:* 4,081 applied, 4,081 admitted, 2,806 enrolled.

Faculty *Total:* 713, 31% full-time. *Student/faculty ratio:* 22:1.

Majors Accounting; administrative assistant and secretarial science; architecture; art; audio engineering; automobile/automotive mechanics technology; biological and physical sciences; business administration and management; chemistry; clinical/medical laboratory technology; commercial and advertising art; computer engineering technology; computer programming; criminal justice/law enforcement administration; culinary arts; design and visual communications; desktop publishing and digital imaging design; drafting and design technology; dramatic/theatre arts; education; educational/instructional media design; electrical, electronic and communications engineering technology; engineering; English; fashion merchandising; humanities; human services; interior design; international relations and affairs; journalism; kindergarten/preschool education; legal assistant/paralegal; liberal arts and sciences/liberal studies; library science; marketing/marketing management; mass communication/media; mathematics; mechanical drafting and CAD/CADD; modern languages; multi-/interdisciplinary studies related; music; nursing (registered nurse training); photography; physics; political science and government; psychology; public relations/image management; radio and television broadcasting technology; radiologic technology/science; respiratory care therapy; social sciences; social work; sociology; special products marketing; speech and rhetoric; telecommunications; visual and performing arts.

Academic Programs *Special study options:* academic remediation for entering students, adult/continuing education programs, advanced placement credit, cooperative education, distance learning, English as a second language, honors programs, independent study, internships, part-time degree program, services for LD students, study abroad, summer session for credit. *ROTC:* Army (c), Air Force (c).

Library Brookdale Community College Library with 150,000 titles, 709 serial subscriptions, 33,000 audiovisual materials, an OPAC.

Computers on Campus 1100 computers available on campus for general student use. A campuswide network can be accessed from off campus. Internet access, online (class) registration, at least one staffed computer lab available.

Student Life *Housing:* college housing not available. *Activities and Organizations:* drama/theater group, student-run newspaper, radio station, Circle K, SAGE, Outdoor Club. *Campus security:* 24-hour emergency response devices and patrols. *Student services:* personal/psychological counseling, women's center.

Athletics Member NJCAA. *Intercollegiate sports:* baseball M, basketball M/W, cross-country running M/W, golf M, soccer M/W, softball W, tennis M/W. *Intramural sports:* basketball M/W, volleyball M/W.

Standardized Tests *Required for some:* ACCUPLACER.

Costs (2005–06) *Tuition:* area resident $2202 full-time, $92 per credit part-time; state resident $4404 full-time, $184 per credit part-time; nonresident $5400 full-time, $225 per credit part-time. *Required fees:* $462 full-time, $19 per credit part-time.

Applying *Options:* early admission, deferred entrance. *Application fee:* $25. *Required:* high school transcript. *Application deadline:* rolling (freshmen), rolling (transfers). *Notification:* continuous (freshmen).

Admissions Contact Ms. Kim Toomey, Registrar, Brookdale Community College, 765 Newman Springs Road, Lincroft, NJ 07738. *Phone:* 732-224-2268. *Fax:* 732-576-1643.

BURLINGTON COUNTY COLLEGE
Pemberton, New Jersey

- **County-supported** 2-year, founded 1966, part of New Jersey Commission on Higher Education
- **Calendar** semesters plus 2 summer terms
- **Degree** certificates and associate
- **Suburban** 225-acre campus with easy access to Philadelphia
- **Coed**

Faculty *Student/faculty ratio:* 27:1.

Student Life *Campus security:* 24-hour emergency response devices and patrols, late-night transport/escort service, electronic entrances to buildings and rooms, surveillance cameras.

Athletics Member NJCAA.

Standardized Tests *Required:* New Jersey Basic Skills Exam (for placement).

Costs (2004–05) *Tuition:* area resident $1716 full-time, $66 per credit part-time; state resident $2550 full-time, $85 per credit part-time; nonresident $4500 full-time, $150 per credit part-time. Part-time tuition and fees vary according to course load. *Required fees:* $375 full-time, $13 per credit part-time. *Payment plans:* installment, deferred payment.

Financial Aid Of all full-time matriculated undergraduates who enrolled in 2003, 100 Federal Work-Study jobs (averaging $1200). 100 state and other part-time jobs (averaging $2000).

Applying *Options:* common application, electronic application, early admission, deferred entrance. *Application fee:* $20. *Required:* high school transcript.

Admissions Contact Ms. Elva DeJesus-Lopez, Admissions Coordinator, Burlington County College, 601 Pemberton-Browns Mills Road, Pemberton, NJ 08068-1599. *Phone:* 609-894-9311 Ext. 7282.

CAMDEN COUNTY COLLEGE
Blackwood, New Jersey

- **State and locally supported** 2-year, founded 1967, part of New Jersey Commission on Higher Education
- **Calendar** semesters
- **Degree** certificates and associate
- **Suburban** 320-acre campus with easy access to Philadelphia
- **Coed**

New Jersey's largest community college enrolls nearly 15,000 students in more than 130 degree and certificate programs at locations in Blackwood, Camden, and Cherry Hill. In addition to credit programs in allied health, business, education, liberal arts and sciences, and technology, the College offers cultural programming, customized training, and professional and personal development courses.

Student Life *Campus security:* 24-hour emergency response devices.

Athletics Member NJCAA.

Financial Aid Of all full-time matriculated undergraduates who enrolled in 2003, 117 Federal Work-Study jobs (averaging $1126).

Applying *Options:* common application, early admission. *Required for some:* high school transcript.

Admissions Contact Jacqueline Baldwin, Enrollment Services, Camden County College, PO Box 200, College Drive, Blackwood, NJ 08012-0200. *Phone:* 856-227-7200 Ext. 4200. *Toll-free phone:* 888-228-2466. *Fax:* 856-374-4917.

COUNTY COLLEGE OF MORRIS
Randolph, New Jersey

- **County-supported** 2-year, founded 1966, part of New Jersey Commission on Higher Education
- **Calendar** semesters
- **Degree** certificates and associate
- **Suburban** 218-acre campus with easy access to New York City
- **Endowment** $1.3 million
- **Coed**

Faculty *Student/faculty ratio:* 17:1.

Student Life *Campus security:* 24-hour emergency response devices and patrols, late-night transport/escort service.

Athletics Member NJCAA.

Standardized Tests *Required:* New Jersey Basic Skills Exam (for placement). *Required for some:* SAT or ACT (for placement).

Costs (2004–05) *Tuition:* $82 per credit hour part-time; state resident $164 per credit hour part-time; nonresident $229 per credit hour part-time. *Required fees:* $13 per credit hour part-time.

Financial Aid Of all full-time matriculated undergraduates who enrolled in 2003, 848 Federal Work-Study jobs (averaging $1947).

Applying *Options:* common application, early admission. *Application fee:* $25. *Required:* high school transcript. *Required for some:* letters of recommendation.

Admissions Contact Ms. Jessica Chambers, Director of Admissions, County College of Morris, 214 Center Grove Road, Randolph, NJ 07869-2086. *Phone:* 973-328-5100. *Toll-free phone:* 888-226-8001. *Fax:* 973-328-1282. *E-mail:* admiss@ccm.edu.

CUMBERLAND COUNTY COLLEGE
Vineland, New Jersey

- **State and locally supported** 2-year, founded 1963, part of New Jersey Commission on Higher Education
- **Calendar** semesters
- **Degree** certificates and associate
- **Small-town** 100-acre campus with easy access to Philadelphia
- **Coed,** 3,176 undergraduate students, 52% full-time, 67% women, 33% men

Cumberland County College (continued)

Undergraduates 1,639 full-time, 1,537 part-time. Students come from 1 other state, 19% African American, 2% Asian American or Pacific Islander, 16% Hispanic American, 2% Native American. *Retention:* 64% of 2002 full-time freshmen returned.

Faculty *Total:* 227, 19% full-time, 4% with terminal degrees. *Student/faculty ratio:* 19:1.

Majors Accounting; administrative assistant and secretarial science; agricultural business and management; agriculture; artificial intelligence and robotics; avionics maintenance technology; biological and physical sciences; broadcast journalism; business administration and management; cinematography and film/video production; community organization and advocacy; computer science; computer systems networking and telecommunications; computer typography and composition equipment operation; corrections; criminal justice/police science; drafting and design technology; dramatic/theatre arts; education; elementary and middle school administration/principalship; engineering; fine/studio arts; horticultural science; hospitality and recreation marketing; human resources management; industrial radiologic technology; industrial technology; information science/studies; kindergarten/preschool education; legal administrative assistant/secretary; liberal arts and sciences/liberal studies; marketing/marketing management; mathematics; nursing (registered nurse training); ornamental horticulture; plastics engineering technology; pre-engineering; social work; system administration.

Academic Programs *Special study options:* academic remediation for entering students, adult/continuing education programs, advanced placement credit, cooperative education, distance learning, double majors, English as a second language, honors programs, part-time degree program, services for LD students, summer session for credit.

Library Cumberland County College Library with 51,000 titles, 213 serial subscriptions, 480 audiovisual materials, an OPAC, a Web page.

Computers on Campus 275 computers available on campus for general student use. A campuswide network can be accessed from off campus. Internet access, at least one staffed computer lab available.

Student Life *Housing:* college housing not available. *Activities and Organizations:* drama/theater group, student-run newspaper, choral group, Student Activities Board, Student Senate. *Campus security:* 24-hour emergency response devices, late-night transport/escort service. *Student services:* personal/psychological counseling.

Athletics Member NJCAA. *Intercollegiate sports:* baseball M, basketball M/W, softball W, track and field M. *Intramural sports:* fencing M/W, soccer M.

Costs (2005–06) *Tuition:* area resident $1848 full-time, $77 per credit part-time; state resident $3696 full-time, $154 per credit part-time; nonresident $7392 full-time, $308 per credit part-time. *Required fees:* $600 full-time, $25 per credit part-time.

Financial Aid Of all full-time matriculated undergraduates who enrolled in 2003, 100 Federal Work-Study jobs (averaging $500). 100 state and other part-time jobs (averaging $600).

Applying *Options:* electronic application, early admission, deferred entrance. *Application fee:* $25. *Required:* high school transcript. *Application deadline:* rolling (freshmen), rolling (transfers). *Notification:* continuous (freshmen).

Admissions Contact Ms. Maud Fried-Goodnight, Executive Director of Enrollment Services, Cumberland County College, College Drive, Vineland, NJ 08362-1500. *Phone:* 856-691-8600 Ext. 228.

ESSEX COUNTY COLLEGE
Newark, New Jersey

- **County-supported** 2-year, founded 1966, part of New Jersey Commission on Higher Education
- **Calendar** semesters
- **Degree** certificates and associate
- **Urban** 22-acre campus with easy access to New York City
- **Coed**, 11,268 undergraduate students, 54% full-time, 64% women, 36% men

Undergraduates 6,037 full-time, 5,231 part-time. Students come from 10 states and territories, 69 other countries, 51% African American, 3% Asian American or Pacific Islander, 17% Hispanic American, 0.2% Native American, 8% international, 2% transferred in. *Retention:* 57% of 2002 full-time freshmen returned.

Freshmen *Admission:* 4,446 applied, 4,446 admitted, 2,721 enrolled.

Faculty *Total:* 567, 28% full-time. *Student/faculty ratio:* 28:1.

Majors Accounting; accounting technology and bookkeeping; administrative assistant and secretarial science; architectural engineering technology; art; biology/biological sciences; business administration and management; business teacher education; chemical technology; chemistry; civil engineering technology; communications technology; computer programming; computer programming (specific applications); computer science; criminal justice/law enforcement administration; criminal justice/police science; data processing and data processing technology; dental assisting; dental hygiene; education; electrical, electronic and communications engineering technology; elementary education; emergency

medical technology (EMT paramedic); engineering; engineering technology; fire science; health/health care administration; health professions related; hotel/motel administration; human services; industrial production technologies related; information science/studies; kindergarten/preschool education; legal assistant/paralegal; legal professions and studies related; liberal arts and sciences/liberal studies; mathematics; medical administrative assistant and medical secretary; medical radiologic technology; music; nursing (registered nurse training); opticianry; physical education teaching and coaching; physical therapist assistant; physical therapy; pre-engineering; respiratory care therapy; secondary education; social sciences; social work.

Academic Programs *Special study options:* academic remediation for entering students, accelerated degree program, adult/continuing education programs, advanced placement credit, cooperative education, distance learning, double majors, English as a second language, independent study, internships, off-campus study, part-time degree program, services for LD students, summer session for credit. *ROTC:* Army (c).

Library Martin Luther King, Jr. Library with 91,000 titles, 639 serial subscriptions, 3,618 audiovisual materials, an OPAC, a Web page.

Computers on Campus 700 computers available on campus for general student use. A campuswide network can be accessed from off campus. Internet access, at least one staffed computer lab available.

Student Life *Housing:* college housing not available. *Activities and Organizations:* drama/theater group, student-run newspaper, choral group, Fashion Entertainment Board, Phi Theta Kappa, Latin Student Union, DECA, Black Student Association. *Campus security:* 24-hour emergency response devices and patrols. *Student services:* health clinic, personal/psychological counseling, women's center.

Athletics Member NJCAA. *Intercollegiate sports:* basketball M(s)/W(s), cross-country running M(s)/W(s), soccer M, track and field M/W. *Intramural sports:* table tennis M, weight lifting M.

Standardized Tests *Required:* ACCUPLACER (for placement).

Costs (2005–06) *Tuition:* area resident $2318 full-time, $77 per credit hour part-time; state resident $4635 full-time, $155 per credit hour part-time. *Required fees:* $650 full-time, $26 per credit hour part-time.

Financial Aid Of all full-time matriculated undergraduates who enrolled in 2003, 250 Federal Work-Study jobs (averaging $2880).

Applying *Options:* deferred entrance. *Application fee:* $25. *Required:* high school transcript. *Application deadline:* 8/15 (freshmen), rolling (transfers). *Notification:* continuous (freshmen).

Admissions Contact Ms. Marva Mack, Director of Admissions, Essex County College, 303 University Avenue, Newark, NJ 07102. *Phone:* 973-877-3119. *Fax:* 973-623-6449.

GIBBS COLLEGE
Montclair, New Jersey

Admissions Contact Mrs. Mary-Jo Greco, President, Gibbs College, 33 Plymouth Street, Montclair, NJ 07042-2699. *Phone:* 201-744-2010.

GLOUCESTER COUNTY COLLEGE
Sewell, New Jersey

- **County-supported** 2-year, founded 1967, part of New Jersey Commission on Higher Education
- **Calendar** semesters
- **Degree** certificates and associate
- **Rural** 270-acre campus with easy access to Philadelphia
- **Coed**

Faculty *Student/faculty ratio:* 33:1.

Student Life *Campus security:* 24-hour emergency response devices and patrols, late-night transport/escort service.

Athletics Member NJCAA.

Standardized Tests *Required for some:* SAT or ACT (for admission).

Financial Aid Of all full-time matriculated undergraduates who enrolled in 2003, 25 Federal Work-Study jobs (averaging $1000). *Financial aid deadline:* 6/1.

Applying *Options:* electronic application, deferred entrance. *Application fee:* $10. *Required:* high school transcript.

Admissions Contact Ms. Carol L. Lange, Admissions and Recruitment Coordinator, Gloucester County College, 1400 Tanyard Road, Sewell, NJ 08080. *Phone:* 856-468-5000. *Fax:* 856-468-8498. *E-mail:* hsimmons@gccnj.edu.

HUDSON COUNTY COMMUNITY COLLEGE

Jersey City, New Jersey

- **State and locally supported** 2-year, founded 1974, part of New Jersey Commission on Higher Education
- **Calendar** semesters
- **Degree** certificates, diplomas, and associate
- **Urban** campus with easy access to New York City
- **Endowment** $56,000
- **Coed,** 6,489 undergraduate students, 66% full-time, 68% women, 32% men

Undergraduates 4,277 full-time, 2,212 part-time. 19% African American, 18% Asian American or Pacific Islander, 42% Hispanic American, 0.2% Native American, 3% international.
Freshmen *Admission:* 6,350 applied, 6,350 admitted, 1,965 enrolled.
Faculty *Total:* 374, 23% full-time.
Majors Accounting; business administration and management; child development; computer engineering technology; computer science; criminal justice/safety; culinary arts; data processing and data processing technology; electrical, electronic and communications engineering technology; engineering science; health information/medical records technology; human services; legal assistant/paralegal; liberal arts and sciences/liberal studies; medical/clinical assistant; nursing (registered nurse training).
Academic Programs *Special study options:* academic remediation for entering students, adult/continuing education programs, advanced placement credit, distance learning, double majors, English as a second language, honors programs, independent study, internships, part-time degree program, services for LD students, summer session for credit.
Library Hudson County Community College Library/Learning Resources Center with 32,000 titles, 251 serial subscriptions, 940 audiovisual materials.
Computers on Campus 351 computers available on campus for general student use. A campuswide network can be accessed from off campus that provide access to class materials. Internet access, at least one staffed computer lab available.
Student Life *Housing:* college housing not available. *Activities and Organizations:* drama/theater group, student-run newspaper, choral group, Psychology Club, Hispanos Unidos Pura El Progreso, International Student Organization, Drama Society. *Campus security:* 24-hour emergency response devices. *Student services:* personal/psychological counseling.
Standardized Tests *Required:* ACCUPLACER (for placement).
Costs (2004–05) *Tuition:* area resident $2070 full-time; state resident $4140 full-time; nonresident $6210 full-time. *Required fees:* $888 full-time. *Payment plans:* installment, deferred payment.
Financial Aid Of all full-time matriculated undergraduates who enrolled in 2003, 102 Federal Work-Study jobs (averaging $3000).
Applying *Application fee:* $15. *Required:* high school transcript. *Application deadlines:* 9/1 (freshmen), 9/1 (transfers). *Notification:* continuous until 9/1 (freshmen).
Admissions Contact Mr. Robert Martin, Assistant Dean of Admissions, Hudson County Community College, 162 Sip Avenue, Jersey City, NJ 07306. *Phone:* 201-714-2115. *Fax:* 201-714-2136. *E-mail:* rmartin@mail.hccc.edu.

MERCER COUNTY COMMUNITY COLLEGE

Trenton, New Jersey

Admissions Contact Dr. Carol Tosh, Dean of Enrollment Services, Mercer County Community College, 1200 Old Trenton Road, PO Box B, Trenton, NJ 08690-1004. *Phone:* 609-586-4800 Ext. 3209. *Toll-free phone:* 800-392-MCCC. *Fax:* 609-586-6944. *E-mail:* admiss@mccc.edu.

MIDDLESEX COUNTY COLLEGE

Edison, New Jersey

- **County-supported** 2-year, founded 1964
- **Calendar** semesters
- **Degree** certificates and associate
- **Suburban** 200-acre campus with easy access to New York City
- **Coed**

Faculty *Student/faculty ratio:* 21:1.
Student Life *Campus security:* 24-hour emergency response devices and patrols.
Athletics Member NJCAA.
Standardized Tests *Required for some:* National League of Nursing Exam for most health-related programs.

Costs (2004–05) *Tuition:* area resident $1764 full-time, $74 per credit part-time; state resident $3528 full-time, $147 per credit part-time. Full-time tuition and fees vary according to course load. Part-time tuition and fees vary according to course load. *Required fees:* $420 full-time, $18 per credit part-time.
Financial Aid Of all full-time matriculated undergraduates who enrolled in 2003, 69 Federal Work-Study jobs (averaging $3350).
Applying *Options:* early admission, deferred entrance. *Application fee:* $25. *Required:* high school transcript.
Admissions Contact Mr. Peter W. Rice, Director of Admissions and Recruitment, Middlesex County College, 2600 Woodbridge Avenue, PO Box 3050, Edison, NJ 08818-3050. *Phone:* 732-906-4243. *Fax:* 732-906-7728. *E-mail:* admissions@middlesexcc.edu.

▶ **See page 528 for a narrative description.**

OCEAN COUNTY COLLEGE

Toms River, New Jersey

- **County-supported** 2-year, founded 1964, part of New Jersey Commission on Higher Education
- **Calendar** semesters
- **Degree** certificates, diplomas, and associate
- **Small-town** 275-acre campus with easy access to Philadelphia
- **Coed**

Student Life *Campus security:* 24-hour emergency response devices and patrols, late-night transport/escort service.
Athletics Member NJCAA.
Costs (2004–05) *Tuition:* area resident $2310 full-time, $77 per credit part-time; state resident $3159 full-time, $105 per credit part-time; nonresident $5190 full-time, $173 per credit part-time. *Required fees:* $40 full-time, $20 per term part-time.
Financial Aid Of all full-time matriculated undergraduates who enrolled in 2003, 76 Federal Work-Study jobs (averaging $1300). 45 state and other part-time jobs (averaging $850).
Applying *Options:* early admission, deferred entrance. *Application fee:* $15. *Required for some:* high school transcript, minimum 3.0 GPA.
Admissions Contact Mr. Carey Trevisan, Director of Admissions and Records, Ocean County College, College Drive, PO Box 2001, Toms River, NJ 08754-2001. *Phone:* 732-255-0304 Ext. 2016.

PASSAIC COUNTY COMMUNITY COLLEGE

Paterson, New Jersey

Admissions Contact Mr. Patrick Noonan, Director of Admissions, Passaic County Community College, One College Boulevard, Patterson, NJ 07505. *Phone:* 973-684-6304.

RARITAN VALLEY COMMUNITY COLLEGE

Somerville, New Jersey

- **County-supported** 2-year, founded 1965
- **Calendar** semesters
- **Degree** certificates and associate
- **Small-town** 225-acre campus with easy access to New York City and Philadelphia
- **Coed,** 6,451 undergraduate students, 39% full-time, 59% women, 41% men

Undergraduates 2,497 full-time, 3,954 part-time. 7% are from out of state, 8% African American, 8% Asian American or Pacific Islander, 10% Hispanic American, 0.1% Native American, 3% international, 7% transferred in. *Retention:* 66% of 2002 full-time freshmen returned.
Freshmen *Admission:* 2,443 applied, 1,657 admitted, 1,055 enrolled.
Faculty *Total:* 371, 26% full-time, 22% with terminal degrees. *Student/faculty ratio:* 20:1.
Majors Accounting; administrative assistant and secretarial science; aeronautics/aviation/aerospace science and technology; artificial intelligence and robotics; automobile/automotive mechanics technology; biology/biological sciences; business administration and management; chemistry; commercial and advertising art; computer programming; computer science; construction engineering technology; consumer merchandising/retailing management; criminal justice/law enforcement administration; data processing and data processing technology; diesel mechanics technology; dramatic/theatre arts; education; electrical, electronic and communications engineering technology; electromechanical technology; elementary education; engineering; environmental studies; heating, air conditioning, ventilation and refrigeration maintenance technology; hospitality

Raritan Valley Community College (continued)
and recreation marketing; hotel/motel administration; human services; industrial technology; information science/studies; intermedia/multimedia; international business/trade/commerce; kindergarten/preschool education; legal assistant/paralegal; liberal arts and sciences/liberal studies; management information systems; marketing/marketing management; mathematics; mechanical design technology; music; nursing (registered nurse training); ophthalmic laboratory technology; real estate; respiratory care therapy; social sciences; tourism and travel services management; visual and performing arts.

Academic Programs *Special study options:* academic remediation for entering students, adult/continuing education programs, advanced placement credit, cooperative education, distance learning, English as a second language, honors programs, independent study, internships, off-campus study, part-time degree program, services for LD students, summer session for credit. *ROTC:* Army (c), Air Force (c).

Library Evelyn S. Field Learning Resources Center with 82,942 titles, 354 serial subscriptions, 1,140 audiovisual materials, an OPAC, a Web page.

Computers on Campus 844 computers available on campus for general student use. A campuswide network can be accessed from off campus that provide access to library services, degree audits, grades, class schedules. Internet access, online (class) registration, at least one staffed computer lab available.

Student Life *Housing:* college housing not available. *Activities and Organizations:* drama/theater group, student-run newspaper, radio station, choral group, International Club, The Latin Pride Club, Student Nurses Association, The Record (student newspaper), Christian Fellowship Club. *Campus security:* 24-hour emergency response devices and patrols, 24-hour outdoor surveillance cameras. *Student services:* health clinic, personal/psychological counseling.

Athletics Member NJCAA. *Intercollegiate sports:* baseball M, basketball M, softball W. *Intramural sports:* golf M/W.

Costs (2005–06) *Tuition:* state resident $2340 full-time, $78 per credit part-time; nonresident $2340 full-time, $78 per credit part-time. Full-time tuition and fees vary according to course load. Part-time tuition and fees vary according to course load. *Required fees:* $740 full-time, $22 per credit part-time, $80 per term part-time. *Payment plan:* installment. *Waivers:* senior citizens and employees or children of employees.

Financial Aid Of all full-time matriculated undergraduates who enrolled in 2003, 12 Federal Work-Study jobs (averaging $2500).

Applying *Options:* electronic application, early admission. *Application fee:* $25. *Required:* high school transcript. *Application deadline:* rolling (freshmen), rolling (transfers).

Admissions Contact Mr. Richard Cole, Registrar, Enrollment Services, Raritan Valley Community College, PO Box 3300, Somerville, NJ 08876-1265. *Phone:* 908-526-1200 Ext. 8206. *Fax:* 908-704-3442.

SALEM COMMUNITY COLLEGE

Carneys Point, New Jersey

- **County-supported** 2-year, founded 1972, part of New Jersey Commission on Higher Education
- **Calendar** semesters
- **Degree** certificates and associate
- **Small-town** campus with easy access to Philadelphia
- **Coed**

Student Life *Campus security:* 24-hour emergency response devices and patrols, late-night transport/escort service.

Athletics Member NJCAA.

Standardized Tests *Required:* New Jersey Basic Skills Exam (for placement).

Costs (2004–05) *Tuition:* area resident $2265 full-time, $76 per credit part-time; state resident $2550 full-time, $85 per credit part-time; nonresident $2550 full-time, $85 per credit part-time. Full-time tuition and fees vary according to course load. Part-time tuition and fees vary according to course load. *Required fees:* $800 full-time, $25 per credit part-time, $25 per term part-time. *Payment plans:* installment, deferred payment.

Financial Aid Of all full-time matriculated undergraduates who enrolled in 2003, 63 Federal Work-Study jobs (averaging $1000).

Applying *Options:* early admission, deferred entrance. *Application fee:* $25. *Required:* essay or personal statement, high school transcript.

Admissions Contact Mr. Patrick Moore, Coordinator of Admissions/Enrollment Management, Salem Community College, 460 Hollywood Avenue, Carney's Point, NJ 08069. *Phone:* 856-351-2698. *Fax:* 856-299-9193. *E-mail:* info@salemcc.edu.

SOMERSET CHRISTIAN COLLEGE

Zarephath, New Jersey

Admissions Contact Ms. Cheryl L. Burdick, Dean of Enrollment Management, Somerset Christian College, 10 Liberty Square, Zarephath, NJ 08890.

Phone: 732-356-1595 Ext. 106. *Toll-free phone:* 800-234-9305. *Fax:* 732-356-4846. *E-mail:* info@somerset.edu.

SUSSEX COUNTY COMMUNITY COLLEGE

Newton, New Jersey

- **State and locally supported** 2-year, founded 1981, part of New Jersey Commission on Higher Education
- **Calendar** semesters
- **Degree** certificates and associate
- **Small-town** 160-acre campus with easy access to New York City
- **Endowment** $349,969
- **Coed,** 3,153 undergraduate students, 46% full-time, 60% women, 40% men

Undergraduates 1,444 full-time, 1,709 part-time. Students come from 3 states and territories, 11% are from out of state, 2% African American, 1% Asian American or Pacific Islander, 6% Hispanic American, 0.2% Native American, 0.8% international, 6% transferred in. *Retention:* 67% of 2002 full-time freshmen returned.

Freshmen *Admission:* 566 applied, 566 admitted, 566 enrolled.

Faculty *Total:* 242, 16% full-time, 15% with terminal degrees. *Student/faculty ratio:* 19:1.

Majors Accounting; administrative assistant and secretarial science; automotive engineering technology; biological and physical sciences; broadcast journalism; business administration and management; commercial and advertising art; computer and information sciences; consumer merchandising/retailing management; corrections and criminal justice related; English; environmental studies; fine/studio arts; fire protection related; health science; human services; journalism; legal assistant/paralegal; liberal arts and sciences/liberal studies; respiratory care therapy; veterinary/animal health technology.

Academic Programs *Special study options:* academic remediation for entering students, advanced placement credit, distance learning, double majors, English as a second language, internships, part-time degree program, services for LD students, summer session for credit.

Library Sussex County Community College Library with 34,346 titles, 266 serial subscriptions, 602 audiovisual materials, an OPAC, a Web page.

Computers on Campus 302 computers available on campus for general student use. A campuswide network can be accessed. Internet access, online (class) registration, at least one staffed computer lab available.

Student Life *Housing:* college housing not available. *Activities and Organizations:* drama/theater group, student-run newspaper, choral group, Student Government Association, "The College Hill" (newspaper), Human Services Club, Arts Club, Returning Adult Support Group. *Campus security:* late-night transport/escort service, trained security personnel. *Student services:* personal/psychological counseling, women's center.

Athletics Member NJCAA. *Intercollegiate sports:* baseball M, basketball M, soccer M/W, softball W. *Intramural sports:* football M/W, volleyball M/W.

Costs (2005–06) *Tuition:* area resident $2190 full-time, $73 per credit part-time; state resident $4380 full-time, $146 per credit part-time; nonresident $4380 full-time, $146 per credit part-time. *Required fees:* $480 full-time, $12 per credit part-time, $15 per term part-time.

Financial Aid Of all full-time matriculated undergraduates who enrolled in 2003, 29 Federal Work-Study jobs (averaging $1500).

Applying *Application fee:* $15. *Required:* high school transcript. *Application deadline:* rolling (freshmen), rolling (transfers). *Notification:* continuous (freshmen).

Admissions Contact Mr. James J. Donohue, Director of Admissions and Registrar, Sussex County Community College, 1 College Hill, Newton, NJ 07860. *Phone:* 973-300-2219. *E-mail:* hdamato@sussex.cc.nj.us.

UNION COUNTY COLLEGE

Cranford, New Jersey

- **State and locally supported** 2-year, founded 1933, part of New Jersey Commission on Higher Education
- **Calendar** semesters
- **Degree** certificates, diplomas, and associate
- **Suburban** 48-acre campus with easy access to New York City
- **Coed,** 11,058 undergraduate students, 48% full-time, 66% women, 34% men

Undergraduates 5,346 full-time, 5,712 part-time. Students come from 8 states and territories, 82 other countries, 2% are from out of state, 25% African American, 6% Asian American or Pacific Islander, 24% Hispanic American, 0.3% Native American, 3% international, 9% transferred in. *Retention:* 77% of 2002 full-time freshmen returned.

Freshmen *Admission:* 6,257 applied, 6,154 admitted, 2,011 enrolled.

Faculty *Total:* 450, 43% full-time. *Student/faculty ratio:* 25:1.

Majors Accounting technology and bookkeeping; administrative assistant and secretarial science; allied health diagnostic, intervention, and treatment professions related; biology/biological sciences; business administration and management; business and personal/financial services marketing; business/commerce; chemistry; civil engineering technology; clinical/medical laboratory technology; communication/speech communication and rhetoric; criminal justice/police science; dental hygiene; electromechanical technology; engineering; fire protection and safety technology; gerontology; hotel/motel administration; industrial technology; information science/studies; language interpretation and translation; liberal arts and sciences/liberal studies; management information systems; mechanical engineering/mechanical technology; medical/clinical assistant; medical radiologic technology; nuclear medical technology; nursing (licensed practical/vocational nurse training); nursing (registered nurse training); occupational therapist assistant; physical sciences; physical therapist assistant; rehabilitation and therapeutic professions related; respiratory care therapy; sign language interpretation and translation.

Academic Programs *Special study options:* academic remediation for entering students, accelerated degree program, adult/continuing education programs, advanced placement credit, distance learning, English as a second language, honors programs, independent study, internships, off-campus study, part-time degree program, services for LD students, student-designed majors, summer session for credit. *ROTC:* Air Force (c).

Library MacKay Library plus 2 others with 135,783 titles, 2,609 serial subscriptions, 3,455 audiovisual materials, an OPAC, a Web page.

Computers on Campus 881 computers available on campus for general student use. A campuswide network can be accessed from off campus. Internet access, at least one staffed computer lab available.

Student Life *Housing:* college housing not available. *Activities and Organizations:* drama/theater group, student-run newspaper, radio and television station, SIGN, Spanish Club, Black Students Heritage Organization, Student Government Organization, International Cultural Exchange Students. *Campus security:* 24-hour emergency response devices and patrols, late-night transport/escort service. *Student services:* personal/psychological counseling.

Athletics Member NJCAA. *Intercollegiate sports:* baseball M, basketball M/W(s), golf M/W, soccer M, volleyball W. *Intramural sports:* cheerleading W.

Standardized Tests *Required for some:* SAT (for placement). *Recommended:* SAT (for placement).

Costs (2005–06) *Tuition:* area resident $2340 full-time, $78 per credit part-time; state resident $4680 full-time, $156 per credit part-time. Full-time tuition and fees vary according to course load and program. Part-time tuition and fees vary according to course load and program. *Required fees:* $669 full-time, $22 per credit part-time. *Payment plan:* deferred payment. *Waivers:* senior citizens and employees or children of employees.

Financial Aid Of all full-time matriculated undergraduates who enrolled in 2003, 150 Federal Work-Study jobs (averaging $1700).

Applying *Options:* electronic application, early admission, deferred entrance. *Application fee:* $25. *Required:* high school transcript. *Required for some:* interview. *Application deadline:* rolling (freshmen), rolling (transfers). *Notification:* continuous (freshmen).

Admissions Contact Ms. Jo Ann Davis-Wayne, Director of Admissions, Records, and Registration, Union County College, 1033 Springfield Avenue, Cranford, NJ 07016. *Phone:* 908-709-7127. *Fax:* 908-709-7125.

WARREN COUNTY COMMUNITY COLLEGE
Washington, New Jersey

Admissions Contact Admissions Advisor, Warren County Community College, 475 Route 57 West, Washington, NJ 07882-9605. *Phone:* 908-835-2300. *Fax:* 908-689-5824.

NEW MEXICO

ALBUQUERQUE TECHNICAL VOCATIONAL INSTITUTE
Albuquerque, New Mexico

- **State-supported** 2-year, founded 1965
- **Calendar** trimesters
- **Degree** certificates and associate
- **Urban** 60-acre campus
- **Coed,** 22,927 undergraduate students, 30% full-time, 60% women, 40% men

Undergraduates 6,893 full-time, 16,034 part-time. 1% are from out of state, 3% African American, 2% Asian American or Pacific Islander, 42% Hispanic American, 8% Native American, 0.2% international, 8% transferred in. *Retention:* 51% of 2002 full-time freshmen returned.

Freshmen *Admission:* 5,140 applied, 5,140 admitted, 2,681 enrolled.
Faculty *Total:* 1,038, 33% full-time. *Student/faculty ratio:* 21:1.
Majors Accounting; administrative assistant and secretarial science; architectural drafting and CAD/CADD; banking and financial support services; biotechnology; building/construction finishing, management, and inspection related; business administration and management; child care and support services management; clinical/medical laboratory technology; computer systems analysis; construction trades related; cosmetology; court reporting; criminal justice/safety; culinary arts; data processing and data processing technology; diagnostic medical sonography and ultrasound technology; electrical, electronic and communications engineering technology; electrical/electronics drafting and CAD/CADD; elementary education; engineering; engineering technologies related; environmental/environmental health engineering; fire protection and safety technology; health information/medical records administration; hospitality administration; industrial technology; information science/studies; laser and optical technology; legal assistant/paralegal; liberal arts and sciences/liberal studies; nursing (registered nurse training); parks, recreation, and leisure related; respiratory care therapy; vehicle maintenance and repair technologies related.

Academic Programs *Special study options:* academic remediation for entering students, adult/continuing education programs, advanced placement credit, cooperative education, distance learning, double majors, English as a second language, internships, part-time degree program, services for LD students, summer session for credit. *ROTC:* Air Force (c).

Library Main Campus Library with an OPAC, a Web page.

Computers on Campus A campuswide network can be accessed. Internet access, at least one staffed computer lab available.

Student Life *Housing:* college housing not available. *Activities and Organizations:* student-run newspaper, Phi Theta Kappa, student government, Hispanic Club, TVI Times (student newspaper). *Campus security:* 24-hour emergency response devices and patrols, late-night transport/escort service. *Student services:* health clinic, personal/psychological counseling.

Standardized Tests *Recommended:* SAT or ACT (for placement).

Costs (2004–05) *Tuition:* state resident $1386 full-time, $39 per credit hour part-time; nonresident $7384 full-time, $205 per credit hour part-time. Full-time tuition and fees vary according to course load. Part-time tuition and fees vary according to course load. *Required fees:* $90 full-time. *Payment plan:* deferred payment. *Waivers:* senior citizens and employees or children of employees.

Financial Aid Of all full-time matriculated undergraduates who enrolled in 2003, 175 Federal Work-Study jobs (averaging $6000). 225 state and other part-time jobs (averaging $6000).

Applying *Options:* electronic application, early admission. *Recommended:* high school transcript. *Application deadline:* rolling (freshmen), rolling (transfers). *Notification:* continuous (freshmen).

Admissions Contact Ms. Jane Campbell, Director of Enrollment Services, Albuquerque Technical Vocational Institute, 900 University, SE, Albuquerque, NM 87106-4096. *Phone:* 505-224-3160. *Fax:* 505-224-4740.

THE ART CENTER DESIGN COLLEGE
Albuquerque, New Mexico

Admissions Contact Ms. Colleen Gimbel-Froebe, Associate Director of Admissions and Placement, The Art Center Design College, 5000 Marble NE, Albuquerque, NM 87110. *Phone:* 520-325-0123. *Toll-free phone:* 800-825-8753. *Fax:* 520-325-5535.

CLOVIS COMMUNITY COLLEGE
Clovis, New Mexico

- **State-supported** 2-year, founded 1990
- **Calendar** semesters
- **Degree** certificates and associate
- **Small-town** 25-acre campus
- **Endowment** $507,909
- **Coed,** 3,093 undergraduate students, 36% full-time, 67% women, 33% men

Undergraduates 1,128 full-time, 1,965 part-time. Students come from 47 states and territories, 32% are from out of state, 6% African American, 2% Asian American or Pacific Islander, 34% Hispanic American, 0.5% Native American, 6% transferred in. *Retention:* 45% of 2002 full-time freshmen returned.
Freshmen *Admission:* 252 applied, 252 admitted, 252 enrolled.
Faculty *Total:* 259, 21% full-time, 8% with terminal degrees. *Student/faculty ratio:* 15:1.
Majors Accounting; administrative assistant and secretarial science; automobile/automotive mechanics technology; bilingual and multilingual education; business administration and management; business automation/technology/data entry; carpentry; commercial and advertising art; computer and information sciences; computer typography and composition equipment operation; construction trades; corrections; cosmetology; criminal justice/police science; electrical, electronic and communications engineering technology; electromechanical technology;

Clovis Community College (continued)

executive assistant/executive secretary; finance; fine/studio arts; health and physical education; heating, air conditioning, ventilation and refrigeration maintenance technology; legal administrative assistant/secretary; legal assistant/paralegal; liberal arts and sciences/liberal studies; library assistant; management information systems; mathematics; medical administrative assistant and medical secretary; medical office assistant; medical radiologic technology; nail technician and manicurist; nursing (registered nurse training); physical sciences; psychology; sign language interpretation and translation; teacher assistant/aide; technical and business writing; web/multimedia management and webmaster; web page, digital/multimedia and information resources design.

Academic Programs *Special study options:* academic remediation for entering students, advanced placement credit, cooperative education, distance learning, double majors, English as a second language, independent study, internships, part-time degree program, services for LD students, summer session for credit.

Library Clovis Community College Library and Learning Resources Center with 52,000 titles, 370 serial subscriptions, 2,900 audiovisual materials, an OPAC.

Computers on Campus 280 computers available on campus for general student use. A campuswide network can be accessed. Internet access, at least one staffed computer lab available.

Student Life *Housing:* college housing not available. *Activities and Organizations:* Student Senate, Student Nursing Association, Black Advisory Council, Hispanic Advisory Council, student ambassadors. *Campus security:* student patrols, late-night transport/escort service. *Student services:* personal/psychological counseling.

Athletics *Intramural sports:* basketball M/W, cross-country running M/W, racquetball M/W, tennis M/W, volleyball M/W.

Standardized Tests *Required for some:* TABE, ACCUPLACER. *Recommended:* TABE, ACCUPLACER.

Costs (2005–06) *Tuition:* area resident $712 full-time, $48 per credit hour part-time; state resident $760 full-time, $50 per credit hour part-time; nonresident $1432 full-time, $50 per credit hour part-time. *Required fees:* $36 full-time, $3 per credit hour part-time.

Applying *Options:* common application. *Required:* high school transcript.

Admissions Contact Ms. Rosie Corrie, Director of Admissions and Records/Registrar, Clovis Community College, 417 Schepps Boulevard, Clovis, NM 88101-8381. *Phone:* 505-769-4021. *Fax:* 505-769-4190. *E-mail:* admissions@clovis.edu.

CROWNPOINT INSTITUTE OF TECHNOLOGY
Crownpoint, New Mexico

Admissions Contact PO Box 849, Crownpoint, NM 87313.

DONA ANA BRANCH COMMUNITY COLLEGE
Las Cruces, New Mexico

- **State and locally supported** 2-year, founded 1973, part of New Mexico State University System
- **Calendar** semesters
- **Degree** certificates and associate
- **Urban** 15-acre campus with easy access to Ciudad Juarez and El Paso
- **Coed,** 6,347 undergraduate students, 57% full-time, 56% women, 44% men

Undergraduates 3,596 full-time, 2,751 part-time. 2% African American, 0.8% Asian American or Pacific Islander, 63% Hispanic American, 2% Native American, 0.8% international, 3% transferred in. *Retention:* 80% of 2002 full-time freshmen returned.

Freshmen *Admission:* 1,629 applied, 1,624 admitted, 1,515 enrolled. *Average high school GPA:* 2.62. *Test scores:* ACT scores over 18: 36%; ACT scores over 24: 2%.

Faculty *Total:* 396, 23% full-time. *Student/faculty ratio:* 30:1.

Majors Administrative assistant and secretarial science; architectural engineering technology; automobile/automotive mechanics technology; business administration and management; computer engineering technology; computer typography and composition equipment operation; consumer merchandising/retailing management; drafting and design technology; electrical, electronic and communications engineering technology; emergency medical technology (EMT paramedic); fashion merchandising; finance; fire science; heating, air conditioning, ventilation and refrigeration maintenance technology; hospitality administration; hydrology and water resources science; industrial radiologic technology; legal assistant/paralegal; library science; nursing (registered nurse training); respiratory care therapy; welding technology.

Academic Programs *Special study options:* academic remediation for entering students, adult/continuing education programs, advanced placement credit, cooperative education, English as a second language, freshman honors college,

honors programs, internships, part-time degree program, services for LD students, summer session for credit. *ROTC:* Army (c), Air Force (c).

Library Library/Media Center with 17,140 titles, 213 serial subscriptions, an OPAC.

Computers on Campus 433 computers available on campus for general student use. A campuswide network can be accessed from off campus. Internet access, online (class) registration, at least one staffed computer lab available.

Student Life *Housing Options:* coed. Campus housing is university owned. *Activities and Organizations:* drama/theater group, student-run newspaper, radio station, choral group, marching band. *Campus security:* 24-hour emergency response devices and patrols, late-night transport/escort service. *Student services:* health clinic, personal/psychological counseling, women's center, legal services.

Standardized Tests *Recommended:* ACT, ACT ASSET, or ACT COMPASS.

Costs (2005–06) *Tuition:* area resident $1080 full-time, $45 per credit part-time; state resident $1320 full-time, $55 per credit part-time; nonresident $3240 full-time, $135 per credit part-time. *Required fees:* $45 per credit part-time.

Financial Aid Of all full-time matriculated undergraduates who enrolled in 2003, 15 Federal Work-Study jobs (averaging $2800). 106 state and other part-time jobs (averaging $2800). *Financial aid deadline:* 6/30.

Applying *Options:* deferred entrance. *Application fee:* $15. *Required:* high school transcript. *Required for some:* letters of recommendation. *Application deadline:* rolling (freshmen).

Admissions Contact Admissions Counselor, Dona Ana Branch Community College, MSC-3DA, Box 30001, Las Cruces, NM 88003-8001. *Phone:* 505-527-7532. *Toll-free phone:* 800-903-7503. *Fax:* 505-527-7515.

EASTERN NEW MEXICO UNIVERSITY-ROSWELL
Roswell, New Mexico

Admissions Contact Mr. James Mares, Assistant Director, Eastern New Mexico University-Roswell, PO Box 6000, Roswell, NM 88202-6000. *Phone:* 505-624-7149. *Toll-free phone:* 800-243-6687. *Fax:* 505-624-7144.

INSTITUTE OF AMERICAN INDIAN ARTS
Santa Fe, New Mexico

- **Federally supported** primarily 2-year, founded 1962
- **Calendar** semesters
- **Degrees** associate and bachelor's
- **Urban** 120-acre campus
- **Endowment** $4.0 million
- **Coed,** 183 undergraduate students, 85% full-time, 46% women, 54% men

Undergraduates 156 full-time, 27 part-time. Students come from 29 states and territories, 1% Asian American or Pacific Islander, 88% Native American. *Retention:* 46% of 2002 full-time freshmen returned.

Freshmen *Admission:* 109 applied, 75 admitted, 22 enrolled.

Faculty *Total:* 33, 39% full-time. *Student/faculty ratio:* 13:1.

Majors Art; ceramic arts and ceramics; creative writing; drawing; fiber, textile and weaving arts; fine/studio arts; metal and jewelry arts; museum studies; photography; printmaking; sculpture.

Academic Programs *Special study options:* academic remediation for entering students, internships, off-campus study.

Library Fogelson Library with 15,200 titles, 60 serial subscriptions.

Computers on Campus 20 computers available on campus for general student use. Internet access, at least one staffed computer lab available.

Student Life *Housing Options:* coed. Campus housing is university owned. *Activities and Organizations:* drama/theater group, student-run newspaper, Pow-wow Club, Museum Club, Ski Club, Spring Break Club. *Campus security:* 24-hour patrols, late-night transport/escort service. *Student services:* personal/psychological counseling.

Athletics *Intramural sports:* archery M/W, basketball M/W, bowling M/W, cross-country running M/W, skiing (cross-country) M/W, skiing (downhill) M/W, swimming and diving M/W, table tennis M/W, tennis M/W, track and field M/W, volleyball M/W.

Standardized Tests *Recommended:* ACT (for placement).

Costs (2005–06) *Tuition:* state resident $2400 full-time, $100 per credit hour part-time; nonresident $2400 full-time. *Required fees:* $230 full-time, $20 per term part-time. *Room and board:* $4536; room only: $2212.

Applying *Options:* deferred entrance. *Required:* high school transcript, minimum 2.0 GPA, 3 letters of recommendation. *Recommended:* interview. *Application deadlines:* 4/15 (freshmen), 4/15 (transfers). *Notification:* continuous until 7/1 (freshmen).

Admissions Contact Myra Garro, Manager of Enrollment and Admissions, Institute of American Indian Arts, 83 Avan Nu Po Road, Santa Fe, NM 87508. *Phone:* 505-424-2328. *Fax:* 505-424-3535.

INTERNATIONAL INSTITUTE OF THE AMERICAS
Albuquerque, New Mexico

- **Independent** primarily 2-year
- **Calendar** continuous
- **Degrees** certificates, diplomas, associate, and bachelor's
- **Urban** 1-acre campus
- **Coed**
- 60% of applicants were admitted

Faculty *Student/faculty ratio:* 10:1.
Costs (2004–05) *Tuition:* $9000 full-time. *Required fees:* $350 full-time.
Admissions Contact Mr. Scott Yelton, Campus Director, International Institute of the Americas, 4201 Central Avenue NW, Suite J, Albuquerque, NM 87105-1649. *Phone:* 505-880-2877. *Toll-free phone:* 888-660-2428.

ITT TECHNICAL INSTITUTE
Albuquerque, New Mexico

- **Proprietary** primarily 2-year, founded 1989, part of ITT Educational Services, Inc
- **Calendar** quarters
- **Degrees** associate and bachelor's
- **Coed**

Standardized Tests *Required:* Wonderlic aptitude test (for admission).
Costs (2004–05) *Tuition:* Please see school catalog for specific information.
Applying *Options:* deferred entrance. *Application fee:* $100. *Required:* high school transcript, interview. *Recommended:* letters of recommendation.
Admissions Contact Mr. John Crooks, Director of Recruitment, ITT Technical Institute, 5100 Masthead Street NE, Albuquerque, NM 87109. *Phone:* 505-828-1114. *Toll-free phone:* 800-636-1114. *Fax:* 505-828-1849.

LUNA COMMUNITY COLLEGE
Las Vegas, New Mexico

- **State-supported** 2-year
- **Calendar** semesters
- **Degree** certificates, diplomas, and associate
- **Rural** 25-acre campus
- **Endowment** $12,911
- **Coed,** 2,041 undergraduate students, 25% full-time, 60% women, 40% men

Undergraduates 502 full-time, 1,539 part-time. 0.5% African American, 0.5% Asian American or Pacific Islander, 88% Hispanic American, 0.5% Native American.
Freshmen *Admission:* 154 applied, 154 admitted, 109 enrolled.
Faculty *Total:* 121, 27% full-time. *Student/faculty ratio:* 13:1.
Majors Accounting; administrative assistant and secretarial science; architectural drafting; business administration and management; civil/structural drafting; computer and information sciences; criminal justice/police science; early childhood education; electrical, electronic and communications engineering technology; industrial arts; manufacturing technology; nursing (licensed practical/vocational nurse training); physical therapy.
Academic Programs *Special study options:* academic remediation for entering students, cooperative education, distance learning, honors programs, independent study, part-time degree program.
Library Samuel F. Vigil Learning Resource Center plus 1 other with 37,343 titles, 178 serial subscriptions, 5,000 audiovisual materials, an OPAC.
Computers on Campus A campuswide network can be accessed. At least one staffed computer lab available. Computer purchase or lease plan available.
Student Life *Housing:* college housing not available.
Costs (2005–06) *Tuition:* area resident $600 full-time, $25 per credit hour part-time; state resident $888 full-time, $37 per credit hour part-time; nonresident $1824 full-time, $76 per credit hour part-time. Full-time tuition and fees vary according to course load, program, and reciprocity agreements. Part-time tuition and fees vary according to course load, program, and reciprocity agreements. *Required fees:* $44 full-time, $22 per term part-time. *Room and board:* Room and board charges vary according to housing facility. *Payment plan:* installment. *Waivers:* senior citizens and employees or children of employees.
Applying *Options:* common application, electronic application. *Required:* high school transcript.
Admissions Contact Ms. Henrietta Griego, Director of Admissions, Recruitment, and Retention, Luna Community College, 366 Luna Drive, Las Vegas, NM

87701. *Phone:* 505-454-2020 Ext. 1200. *Toll-free phone:* 800-588-7232 Ext. 1202. *Fax:* 505-454-2588. *E-mail:* hgriego@luna.cc.nm.us.

MESALANDS COMMUNITY COLLEGE
Tucumcari, New Mexico

- **State-supported** 2-year, founded 1979
- **Calendar** semesters
- **Degree** certificates and associate
- **Small-town** campus
- **Endowment** $16,000
- **Coed**

Faculty *Student/faculty ratio:* 10:1.
Student Life *Campus security:* 24-hour emergency response devices.
Standardized Tests *Required:* ACT COMPASS (for placement).
Costs (2004–05) *Tuition:* state resident $1050 full-time, $35 per credit hour part-time; nonresident $1890 full-time, $63 per credit hour part-time. *Required fees:* $274 full-time, $7 per credit hour part-time, $27 per term part-time.
Applying *Required:* high school transcript.
Admissions Contact Mr. Ken Brashear, Director of Enrollment Management, Mesalands Community College, 911 South Tenth Street, Tucumcari, NM 88401. *Phone:* 505-461-4413.

NATIONAL AMERICAN UNIVERSITY
Rio Rancho, New Mexico

Admissions Contact 1601 Rio Rancho, Suite 200, Rio Rancho, NM 87124.

NEW MEXICO JUNIOR COLLEGE
Hobbs, New Mexico

Admissions Contact Mr. Robert Bensing, Dean of Enrollment Management, New Mexico Junior College, 5317 Lovington Highway, Hobbs, NM 88240-9123. *Phone:* 505-392-5092. *Fax:* 505-392-0322. *E-mail:* rbensing@nmjc.cc.nm.us.

NEW MEXICO MILITARY INSTITUTE
Roswell, New Mexico

- **State-supported** 2-year, founded 1891, part of New Mexico Commission on Higher Education
- **Calendar** semesters
- **Degree** associate
- **Small-town** 42-acre campus
- **Endowment** $243.6 million
- **Coed, primarily men,** 423 undergraduate students

Excellence is a process achieved in stages, sustained through effort, accentuated by detail, and celebrated by all. At NMMI, excellence is a universal goal. For more than 100 years, NMMI has built a community and a world-class institute of higher learning based on shared values and disciplined behavior, which foster the highest standards of achievement in its cadets.

Undergraduates Students come from 42 states and territories, 13 other countries, 58% are from out of state, 100% live on campus.
Freshmen *Admission:* 590 applied, 370 admitted. *Test scores:* ACT scores over 18: 87%; ACT scores over 24: 23%; ACT scores over 30: 1%.
Faculty *Total:* 61. *Student/faculty ratio:* 18:1.
Majors Accounting; Army R.O.T.C./military science; art; biological and physical sciences; biology/biological sciences; business administration and management; chemistry; civil engineering technology; computer programming; computer science; criminal justice/law enforcement administration; criminal justice/police science; economics; engineering; English; finance; French; German; history; humanities; liberal arts and sciences/liberal studies; mathematics; physical education teaching and coaching; physics; pre-engineering; social sciences; Spanish; sport and fitness administration.
Academic Programs *Special study options:* academic remediation for entering students, advanced placement credit, English as a second language, summer session for credit. *ROTC:* Army (b).
Library Paul Horgan Library plus 2 others with 65,000 titles, 200 serial subscriptions, an OPAC.
Computers on Campus 700 computers available on campus for general student use. A campuswide network can be accessed from student residence rooms and from off campus. Internet access, at least one staffed computer lab available. Computer purchase or lease plan available.
Student Life *Housing:* on-campus residence required through sophomore year. *Options:* coed. *Activities and Organizations:* drama/theater group, student-run

New Mexico Military Institute (continued)
newspaper, television station, choral group, marching band, band, chorus, drill teams, Officer's Club. *Campus security:* 24-hour emergency response devices and patrols, controlled dormitory access. *Student services:* health clinic, personal/psychological counseling.

Athletics Member NJCAA. *Intercollegiate sports:* baseball M(s), basketball M(s), fencing M/W, football M(s), golf M(s), riflery M/W, tennis M(s)/W(s), track and field M(s), volleyball W(s). *Intramural sports:* basketball M/W, bowling M/W, cross-country running M/W, fencing M/W, football M, golf M/W, racquetball M/W, riflery M/W, skiing (cross-country) M/W, skiing (downhill) M/W, soccer M/W, swimming and diving M/W, tennis M/W, track and field M/W, volleyball M/W, weight lifting M/W.

Standardized Tests *Required:* SAT or ACT (for admission).

Costs (2004–05) *Tuition:* state resident $1156 full-time; nonresident $3652 full-time. *Required fees:* $1220 full-time. *Room and board:* $3452.

Financial Aid Of all full-time matriculated undergraduates who enrolled in 2003, 18 Federal Work-Study jobs (averaging $794). 1 state and other part-time job (averaging $696).

Applying *Options:* early admission, deferred entrance. *Application fee:* $60. *Required:* high school transcript, minimum 2.0 GPA. *Application deadlines:* 8/1 (freshmen), 8/1 (transfers). *Notification:* continuous (freshmen).

Admissions Contact Capt. Ky Atwood, Admissions Counselor, New Mexico Military Institute, 101 West College Boulevard, Roswell, NM 88201-5173. *Phone:* 505-624-8050. *Toll-free phone:* 800-421-5376. *Fax:* 505-624-8058. *E-mail:* admissions@nmmi.edu.

▶ **See page 534 for a narrative description.**

NEW MEXICO STATE UNIVERSITY-ALAMOGORDO
Alamogordo, New Mexico

Admissions Contact Ms. Maureen Scott, Coordinator of Admissions and Records, New Mexico State University-Alamogordo, 2400 North Scenic Drive, Alamogordo, NM 88311-0477. *Phone:* 505-439-3700. *E-mail:* advisor@nmsua.nmsu.edu.

NEW MEXICO STATE UNIVERSITY-CARLSBAD
Carlsbad, New Mexico

- **State-supported** 2-year, founded 1950, part of New Mexico State University System
- **Calendar** semesters
- **Degree** certificates and associate
- **Small-town** 40-acre campus
- **Coed**

Faculty *Student/faculty ratio:* 23:1.

Student Life *Campus security:* 24-hour emergency response devices.

Standardized Tests *Required for some:* ACT (for placement). *Recommended:* ACT (for placement).

Financial Aid Of all full-time matriculated undergraduates who enrolled in 2003, 4 Federal Work-Study jobs (averaging $2800). 36 state and other part-time jobs (averaging $2300).

Applying *Options:* electronic application, early admission, deferred entrance. *Application fee:* $15. *Required:* high school transcript.

Admissions Contact Ms. Everal Shannon, Records Specialist, New Mexico State University-Carlsbad, 1500 University Drive, Carlsbad, NM 88220-3509. *Phone:* 505-234-9222. *Fax:* 505-885-4951. *E-mail:* mcleary@nmsu.edu.

NEW MEXICO STATE UNIVERSITY-GRANTS
Grants, New Mexico

- **State-supported** 2-year, founded 1968, part of New Mexico State University System
- **Calendar** semesters
- **Degree** certificates and associate
- **Small-town** campus
- **Coed**

Standardized Tests *Required:* CPT (for admission).

Financial Aid Of all full-time matriculated undergraduates who enrolled in 2003, 3 Federal Work-Study jobs (averaging $1800). 6 state and other part-time jobs (averaging $1500).

Applying *Options:* common application, early admission. *Application fee:* $15. *Required:* high school transcript.

Admissions Contact Ms. Irene Lutz, Campus Student Services Officer, New Mexico State University-Grants, 1500 3rd Street, Grants, NM 87020-2025. *Phone:* 505-287-7981. *E-mail:* bmontoya@grants.nmsu.edu.

NORTHERN NEW MEXICO COMMUNITY COLLEGE
Espanola, New Mexico

Admissions Contact Mr. Mike L. Costello, Registrar, Northern New Mexico Community College, 921 Paseo de Onate, Espanola, NM 87532. *Phone:* 505-747-2193. *Fax:* 505-747-2180. *E-mail:* tina@nnm.cc.nm.us.

PIMA MEDICAL INSTITUTE
Albuquerque, New Mexico

- **Proprietary** 2-year, founded 1985, part of Vocational Training Institutes, Inc
- **Calendar** modular
- **Degree** certificates and associate
- **Urban** campus
- **Coed,** 576 undergraduate students, 100% full-time, 91% women, 9% men

Undergraduates 576 full-time.

Freshmen *Admission:* 72 applied, 47 admitted, 47 enrolled.

Faculty *Student/faculty ratio:* 20:1.

Majors Radiologic technology/science.

Academic Programs *Special study options:* academic remediation for entering students, cooperative education, internships, services for LD students.

Computers on Campus 56 computers available on campus for general student use. A campuswide network can be accessed from off campus. Internet access, at least one staffed computer lab available.

Student Life *Housing:* college housing not available.

Standardized Tests *Required:* Wonderlic Scholastic Level Exam (for admission).

Financial Aid Of all full-time matriculated undergraduates who enrolled in 2003, 6 Federal Work-Study jobs.

Applying *Options:* early admission. *Required:* interview. *Required for some:* high school transcript.

Admissions Contact Admissions Office, Pima Medical Institute, 2201 San Pedro N.E., Building 3, Suite 100, Albuquerque, NM 87110. *Phone:* 505-881-1234. *Toll-free phone:* 888-898-9048. *Fax:* 505-881-5329.

SAN JUAN COLLEGE
Farmington, New Mexico

- **State-supported** 2-year, founded 1958, part of New Mexico Commission on Higher Education
- **Calendar** semesters
- **Degree** certificates and associate
- **Small-town** 698-acre campus
- **Endowment** $9.4 million
- **Coed,** 5,224 undergraduate students, 51% full-time, 59% women, 41% men

Undergraduates 2,667 full-time, 2,557 part-time. Students come from 18 states and territories, 7% are from out of state, 0.4% African American, 0.7% Asian American or Pacific Islander, 11% Hispanic American, 32% Native American, 0.4% international.

Freshmen *Admission:* 1,390 applied, 1,390 admitted, 989 enrolled.

Faculty *Total:* 328, 29% full-time. *Student/faculty ratio:* 21:1.

Majors Accounting technology and bookkeeping; administrative assistant and secretarial science; airline pilot and flight crew; anthropology; art; autobody/collision and repair technology; automobile/automotive mechanics technology; banking and financial support services; biology/biological sciences; business administration and management; carpentry; chemistry; commercial and advertising art; communication/speech communication and rhetoric; computer science; criminal justice/police science; criminal justice/safety; diesel mechanics technology; drafting and design technology; dramatic/theatre arts; economics; education; engineering; English; fire protection and safety technology; foreign languages and literatures; general studies; geology/earth science; health information/medical records technology; history; human services; information science/studies; instrumentation technology; kindergarten/preschool education; legal assistant/paralegal; mathematics; music; nursing (registered nurse training); parks, recreation and leisure; philosophy; physical sciences; physical therapist assistant; physics; political science and government; pre-medical studies; psychology; public administration; real estate; social work; sociology; water quality and wastewater treatment management and recycling technology; welding technology.

Academic Programs *Special study options:* academic remediation for entering students, adult/continuing education programs, advanced placement credit,

cooperative education, distance learning, English as a second language, honors programs, independent study, internships, part-time degree program, services for LD students, summer session for credit.

Library San Juan College Library with 81,116 titles, 6,677 serial subscriptions, 1,779 audiovisual materials, an OPAC, a Web page.

Computers on Campus 900 computers available on campus for general student use. A campuswide network can be accessed from off campus. Internet access, online (class) registration, at least one staffed computer lab available.

Student Life *Housing:* college housing not available. *Activities and Organizations:* drama/theater group, student-run newspaper, radio station, choral group, national fraternities, national sororities. *Campus security:* 24-hour patrols, late-night transport/escort service. *Student services:* personal/psychological counseling.

Athletics *Intramural sports:* archery M/W, badminton M/W, basketball M/W, bowling M/W, cross-country running M/W, football M/W, golf M/W, racquetball M/W, rock climbing M/W, skiing (cross-country) M/W, skiing (downhill) M/W, soccer M/W, softball M/W, table tennis M/W, tennis M/W, volleyball M/W.

Standardized Tests *Required:* CPT (for placement).

Costs (2005–06) *Tuition:* state resident $600 full-time, $25 per credit hour part-time; nonresident $840 full-time, $35 per credit hour part-time.

Financial Aid Of all full-time matriculated undergraduates who enrolled in 2003, 150 Federal Work-Study jobs (averaging $2000). 100 state and other part-time jobs (averaging $2000).

Applying *Options:* electronic application, early admission, deferred entrance. *Required:* high school transcript. *Application deadline:* rolling (freshmen), rolling (transfers). *Notification:* continuous (freshmen).

Admissions Contact San Juan College, San Juan College, 4601 College Boulevard, Farmington, NM 87402. *Phone:* 505-566-3300. *Fax:* 505-566-3500. *E-mail:* drangc@sanjuancollege.edu.

SANTA FE COMMUNITY COLLEGE
Santa Fe, New Mexico

- **State and locally supported** 2-year, founded 1983
- **Calendar** semesters
- **Degree** certificates and associate
- **Suburban** 366-acre campus
- **Coed**

Faculty *Student/faculty ratio:* 18:1.

Student Life *Campus security:* 24-hour emergency response devices and patrols, late-night transport/escort service.

Costs (2004–05) *Tuition:* area resident $720 full-time, $27 per credit hour part-time; state resident $960 full-time, $40 per credit hour part-time; nonresident $1728 full-time, $65 per credit hour part-time. *Required fees:* $84 full-time, $4 per credit hour part-time, $5 per term part-time.

Financial Aid Of all full-time matriculated undergraduates who enrolled in 2003, 20 Federal Work-Study jobs (averaging $3900). 50 state and other part-time jobs (averaging $3900).

Applying *Options:* early admission, deferred entrance. *Required:* high school transcript.

Admissions Contact Ms. Jennifer Nollette, Admissions Counselor, Santa Fe Community College, 6401 Richards Avenue, Santa Fe, NM 87505. *Phone:* 505-428-1410. *Fax:* 505-428-1237.

SOUTHWESTERN INDIAN POLYTECHNIC INSTITUTE
Albuquerque, New Mexico

Admissions Contact Ms. Myra Garro, Recruitment, Southwestern Indian Polytechnic Institute, PO Box 10146, Albuquerque, NM 87120-3103. *Phone:* 505-346-2362. *Toll-free phone:* 800-586-7474. *Fax:* 505-346-2320.

UNIVERSITY OF NEW MEXICO-GALLUP
Gallup, New Mexico

Admissions Contact Ms. Pearl A. Morris, Admissions Representative, University of New Mexico-Gallup, 200 College Road, Gallup, NM 87301-5603. *Phone:* 505-863-7576. *Fax:* 505-863-7610. *E-mail:* pmorris@gallup.unm.edu.

UNIVERSITY OF NEW MEXICO-LOS ALAMOS BRANCH
Los Alamos, New Mexico

Admissions Contact Ms. Anna Mae Apodaca, Associate Campus Director for Student Services, University of New Mexico-Los Alamos Branch, 4000 University Drive, Los Alamos, NM 87544-2233. *Phone:* 505-661-4692.

UNIVERSITY OF NEW MEXICO-TAOS
Taos, New Mexico

Admissions Contact 115 Civic Plaza Drive, Taos, NM 87571.

UNIVERSITY OF NEW MEXICO-VALENCIA CAMPUS
Los Lunas, New Mexico

Admissions Contact Ms. Lucy Sanchez, Registrar, University of New Mexico-Valencia Campus, 280 La Entrada, Los Lunas, NM 87031-7633. *Phone:* 505-925-8580. *Fax:* 505-925-8563.

NEW YORK

ADIRONDACK COMMUNITY COLLEGE
Queensbury, New York

- **State and locally supported** 2-year, founded 1960, part of State University of New York System
- **Calendar** semesters
- **Degree** certificates and associate
- **Small-town** 141-acre campus
- **Endowment** $1.0 million
- **Coed,** 3,200 undergraduate students

Undergraduates Students come from 5 states and territories, 5 other countries, 2% are from out of state.

Freshmen *Admission:* 1,328 applied, 1,211 admitted. *Average high school GPA:* 2.40.

Faculty *Total:* 244, 41% full-time. *Student/faculty ratio:* 20:1.

Majors Accounting; administrative assistant and secretarial science; banking and financial support services; behavioral sciences; biological and physical sciences; biology/biological sciences; broadcast journalism; business administration and management; business automation/technology/data entry; computer and information sciences related; computer graphics; computer science; computer systems networking and telecommunications; corrections; criminal justice/law enforcement administration; criminal justice/police science; culinary arts; data processing and data processing technology; drafting and design technology; electrical, electronic and communications engineering technology; engineering; engineering science; executive assistant/executive secretary; finance; food services technology; general studies; health information/medical records administration; history; hospitality administration; humanities; information science/studies; information technology; liberal arts and sciences/liberal studies; marketing/marketing management; mass communication/media; mathematics; mathematics and computer science; mechanical design technology; mechanical drafting and CAD/CADD; mechanical engineering/mechanical technology; medical administrative assistant and medical secretary; music; nursing (registered nurse training); occupational therapist assistant; photography; physical therapist assistant; pre-engineering; radio and television; receptionist; social sciences; system administration; tourism and travel services management; web page, digital/multimedia and information resources design; word processing.

Academic Programs *Special study options:* academic remediation for entering students, accelerated degree program, adult/continuing education programs, advanced placement credit, cooperative education, double majors, external degree program, independent study, internships, part-time degree program, services for LD students, study abroad, summer session for credit.

Library Adirondack Community College Library with 65,000 titles, 391 serial subscriptions, an OPAC, a Web page.

Computers on Campus 250 computers available on campus for general student use. A campuswide network can be accessed. At least one staffed computer lab available.

Student Life *Housing:* college housing not available. *Activities and Organizations:* drama/theater group, student-run radio station, choral group, New Horizons, Broadcasting Club, Humanities Club, College Activity Board, Ski and Adventure Club. *Campus security:* late-night transport/escort service, patrols by trained security personnel 8 a.m. to 10 p.m. *Student services:* personal/psychological counseling.

Athletics Member NJCAA. *Intercollegiate sports:* baseball M, basketball M/W, bowling M/W, golf M, skiing (cross-country) M(c)/W(c), skiing (downhill) M(c)/W(c), soccer M/W, softball W, tennis M/W, volleyball W. *Intramural sports:* badminton M/W, basketball M/W, football M/W, skiing (downhill) M/W, softball M/W, tennis M/W, volleyball M/W, weight lifting M/W.

Costs (2004–05) *One-time required fee:* $40. *Tuition:* state resident $2730 full-time, $114 per credit hour part-time; nonresident $5460 full-time, $228 per

Adirondack Community College (continued)
credit hour part-time. Full-time tuition and fees vary according to course load. Part-time tuition and fees vary according to course load. *Required fees:* $89 full-time, $8 per credit hour part-time.
Financial Aid Of all full-time matriculated undergraduates who enrolled in 2003, 98 Federal Work-Study jobs (averaging $462).
Applying *Options:* early admission, deferred entrance. *Application fee:* $30. *Required:* high school transcript. *Required for some:* minimum 2.0 GPA. *Application deadlines:* 8/15 (freshmen), 8/15 (transfers). *Notification:* continuous until 9/1 (freshmen).
Admissions Contact Office of Admissions, Adirondack Community College, 640 Bay Road, Queensbury, NY 12804. *Phone:* 518-743-2264. *Fax:* 518-745-1433. *E-mail:* info@acc.sunyacc.edu.

AMERICAN ACADEMY MCALLISTER INSTITUTE OF FUNERAL SERVICE
New York, New York

Admissions Contact Mr. Norman Provost, Registrar, American Academy McAllister Institute of Funeral Service, 450 West 56th Street, New York, NY 10019-3602. *Phone:* 212-757-1190. *Fax:* 212-765-5923.

AMERICAN ACADEMY OF DRAMATIC ARTS
New York, New York

- **Independent** 2-year, founded 1884
- **Calendar** continuous
- **Degree** certificates and associate
- **Urban** campus
- **Endowment** $4.3 million
- **Coed**

Faculty *Student/faculty ratio:* 16:1.
Student Life *Campus security:* 24-hour emergency response devices, trained security guard during hours of operation.
Costs (2004–05) *Tuition:* $15,350 full-time.
Financial Aid Of all full-time matriculated undergraduates who enrolled in 2003, 40 Federal Work-Study jobs (averaging $2000). 10 state and other part-time jobs (averaging $2000). *Financial aid deadline:* 5/15.
Applying *Options:* deferred entrance. *Application fee:* $50. *Required:* essay or personal statement, 2 letters of recommendation, interview, audition. *Required for some:* high school transcript. *Recommended:* high school transcript, minimum 2.0 GPA.
Admissions Contact Ms. Karen Higginbotham, Director of Admissions, American Academy of Dramatic Arts, 120 Madison Avenue, New York, NY 10016. *Phone:* 800-463-8990. *Toll-free phone:* 800-463-8990. *Fax:* 212-696-1284. *E-mail:* admissions-ny@aada.org.

▶ See page 446 for a narrative description.

THE ART INSTITUTE OF NEW YORK CITY
New York, New York

- **Proprietary** 2-year, founded 1980, part of Education Management Corporation
- **Calendar** quarters
- **Degree** certificates, diplomas, and associate
- **Urban** campus
- **Coed,** 1,716 undergraduate students, 59% full-time, 53% women, 47% men

Undergraduates 1,016 full-time, 700 part-time. Students come from 3 states and territories, 25% are from out of state.
Freshmen *Admission:* 523 enrolled. *Average high school GPA:* 2.5.
Faculty *Total:* 98, 81% full-time, 5% with terminal degrees. *Student/faculty ratio:* 22:1.
Majors Animation, interactive technology, video graphics and special effects; cinematography and film/video production; fashion/apparel design; graphic design; restaurant, culinary, and catering management.
Academic Programs *Special study options:* academic remediation for entering students, advanced placement credit, cooperative education, internships, summer session for credit.
Library Metropolitan College of NYC.
Computers on Campus 20 computers available on campus for general student use. Internet access, at least one staffed computer lab available.
Student Life *Housing:* college housing not available.

Costs (2004–05) *Tuition:* $420 per credit part-time. Full-time tuition and fees vary according to course load and degree level. Part-time tuition and fees vary according to course load and degree level. No tuition increase for student's term of enrollment. Contact school directly as tuition and fees vary according to program. *Payment plans:* tuition prepayment, installment. *Waivers:* children of alumni and employees or children of employees.
Applying *Options:* common application. *Required:* high school transcript, interview. *Required for some:* essay or personal statement.
Admissions Contact Mr. Rich Clark, Director of Admissions, The Art Institute of New York City, 75 Varick Street, 16th Floor, New York, NY 10013. *Phone:* 212-226-5500 Ext. 6005. *Toll-free phone:* 800-654-2433. *Fax:* 212-966-0706.

▶ See page 454 for a narrative description.

ASA INSTITUTE, THE COLLEGE OF ADVANCED TECHNOLOGY
Brooklyn, New York

Admissions Contact Ms. Alice Perez, Director of Admissions, ASA Institute, The College of Advanced Technology, 151 Lawrence Street, 2nd Floor, Brooklyn, NY 11201. *Phone:* 718-534-0773.

BERKELEY COLLEGE-NEW YORK CITY CAMPUS
New York, New York

- **Proprietary** primarily 2-year, founded 1936
- **Calendar** quarters
- **Degrees** certificates, associate, and bachelor's
- **Urban** campus
- **Coed,** 2,012 undergraduate students, 92% full-time, 70% women, 30% men

Undergraduates 1,861 full-time, 151 part-time. Students come from 14 states and territories, 66 other countries, 9% are from out of state, 27% African American, 6% Asian American or Pacific Islander, 32% Hispanic American, 0.3% Native American, 13% international, 6% transferred in.
Freshmen *Admission:* 1,295 applied, 1,123 admitted, 503 enrolled.
Faculty *Total:* 140, 29% full-time. *Student/faculty ratio:* 26:1.
Majors Accounting; business administration and management; business/commerce; fashion merchandising; international business/trade/commerce; legal assistant/paralegal; marketing/marketing management; office management.
Academic Programs *Special study options:* academic remediation for entering students, adult/continuing education programs, advanced placement credit, cooperative education, distance learning, English as a second language, internships, off-campus study, part-time degree program, study abroad, summer session for credit.
Library 13,164 titles, 138 serial subscriptions, 949 audiovisual materials, an OPAC, a Web page.
Computers on Campus 200 computers available on campus for general student use. A campuswide network can be accessed from off campus. Internet access, at least one staffed computer lab available.
Student Life *Housing:* college housing not available. *Activities and Organizations:* student-run newspaper, student government, International Club, Paralegal Club, Accounting Club. *Campus security:* 24-hour emergency response devices. *Student services:* personal/psychological counseling.
Standardized Tests *Required:* SAT or ACT (for admission).
Costs (2005–06) *Tuition:* $16,200 full-time, $395 per credit part-time. *Required fees:* $750 full-time, $75 per term part-time.
Financial Aid Of all full-time matriculated undergraduates who enrolled in 2003, 120 Federal Work-Study jobs (averaging $1500).
Applying *Options:* electronic application, deferred entrance. *Application fee:* $40. *Required:* high school transcript. *Recommended:* interview. *Application deadline:* rolling (freshmen), rolling (transfers).
Admissions Contact Mr. Stuart Siegman, Director, High School Admissions, Berkeley College-New York City Campus, 3 East 43rd Street, New York, NY 10017. *Phone:* 212-986-4343 Ext. 123. *Toll-free phone:* 800-446-5400. *Fax:* 212-818-1079. *E-mail:* info@berkeleycollege.edu.

▶ See page 470 for a narrative description.

BERKELEY COLLEGE-WESTCHESTER CAMPUS
White Plains, New York

- **Proprietary** primarily 2-year, founded 1945
- **Calendar** quarters

- **Degrees** certificates, associate, and bachelor's
- **Suburban** 10-acre campus with easy access to New York City
- **Coed,** 658 undergraduate students, 92% full-time, 71% women, 29% men

Undergraduates 608 full-time, 50 part-time. Students come from 9 states and territories, 28 other countries, 14% are from out of state, 30% African American, 3% Asian American or Pacific Islander, 23% Hispanic American, 0.2% Native American, 4% international, 13% transferred in, 10% live on campus.

Freshmen *Admission:* 517 applied, 455 admitted, 225 enrolled.

Faculty *Total:* 53, 32% full-time. *Student/faculty ratio:* 22:1.

Majors Accounting; business administration and management; business/commerce; fashion merchandising; international business/trade/commerce; legal assistant/paralegal; marketing/marketing management; office management.

Academic Programs *Special study options:* academic remediation for entering students, adult/continuing education programs, advanced placement credit, cooperative education, distance learning, English as a second language, internships, off-campus study, part-time degree program, services for LD students, study abroad, summer session for credit.

Library 9,526 titles, 66 serial subscriptions, 777 audiovisual materials, an OPAC, a Web page.

Computers on Campus 175 computers available on campus for general student use. A campuswide network can be accessed from off campus. Internet access, at least one staffed computer lab available.

Student Life *Housing Options:* coed. Campus housing is university owned. *Activities and Organizations:* student-run newspaper, student government, Paralegal Club, Fashion Club, Phi Theta Kappa. *Campus security:* monitored entrance with front desk security guard. *Student services:* personal/psychological counseling.

Standardized Tests *Required:* SAT or ACT (for admission).

Costs (2005–06) *Tuition:* $16,200 full-time, $395 per credit part-time. *Required fees:* $750 full-time, $75 per term part-time. *Room only:* $5850. Room and board charges vary according to board plan. *Payment plan:* installment. *Waivers:* employees or children of employees.

Financial Aid Of all full-time matriculated undergraduates who enrolled in 2003, 40 Federal Work-Study jobs (averaging $1100).

Applying *Options:* electronic application, deferred entrance. *Application fee:* $40. *Required:* high school transcript. *Recommended:* interview. *Application deadline:* rolling (freshmen), rolling (transfers).

Admissions Contact Mr. David Bertrone, Director of High School Admissions, Berkeley College-Westchester Campus, 99 Church Street, White Plains, NY 10601. *Phone:* 914-694-1122 Ext. 3110. *Toll-free phone:* 800-446-5400. *Fax:* 914-328-9469. *E-mail:* info@berkeleycollege.edu.

▶ See page 470 for a narrative description.

BOROUGH OF MANHATTAN COMMUNITY COLLEGE OF THE CITY UNIVERSITY OF NEW YORK

New York, New York

- **State and locally supported** 2-year, founded 1963, part of City University of New York System
- **Calendar** semesters
- **Degree** certificates and associate
- **Urban** 5-acre campus
- **Endowment** $2.2 million
- **Coed,** 17,629 undergraduate students, 63% full-time, 64% women, 36% men

Undergraduates 11,140 full-time, 6,489 part-time. Students come from 3 states and territories, 100 other countries, 12% are from out of state, 37% African American, 10% Asian American or Pacific Islander, 29% Hispanic American, 0.1% Native American, 12% international, 11% transferred in.

Freshmen *Admission:* 6,446 applied, 5,718 admitted, 3,325 enrolled. *Average high school GPA:* 2.01. *Test scores:* SAT verbal scores over 500: 12%; SAT math scores over 500: 10%; SAT verbal scores over 600: 2%; SAT math scores over 600: 2%; SAT verbal scores over 700: 1%; SAT math scores over 700: 1%.

Faculty *Total:* 1,006, 33% full-time. *Student/faculty ratio:* 24:1.

Majors Accounting; administrative assistant and secretarial science; biological and physical sciences; business administration and management; child development; computer programming; data processing and data processing technology; emergency medical technology (EMT paramedic); engineering science; health science; human services; kindergarten/preschool education; liberal arts and sciences/liberal studies; marketing/marketing management; mathematics; nursing (registered nurse training); respiratory care therapy.

Academic Programs *Special study options:* academic remediation for entering students, adult/continuing education programs, advanced placement credit, cooperative education, distance learning, English as a second language, honors programs, independent study, internships, off-campus study, part-time degree program, services for LD students, study abroad, summer session for credit.

Library A. Philip Randolph Library with 101,869 titles, 8,594 serial subscriptions, 1,343 audiovisual materials, an OPAC, a Web page.

Computers on Campus Internet access, online (class) registration, at least one staffed computer lab available. Computer purchase or lease plan available.

Student Life *Housing:* college housing not available. *Activities and Organizations:* drama/theater group, student-run newspaper, choral group, Caribbean Students Association, Dominican Students Association, When One Voice is Not Enough (WOVINE), Students of Indian Descent Association, Asian Society. *Campus security:* 24-hour patrols. *Student services:* health clinic, personal/psychological counseling, women's center.

Athletics Member NJCAA. *Intercollegiate sports:* baseball M, basketball M/W, soccer M. *Intramural sports:* basketball M/W, soccer M, volleyball M/W.

Costs (2004–05) *Tuition:* state resident $2800 full-time, $120 per credit part-time; nonresident $4560 full-time, $190 per credit part-time. *Required fees:* $248 full-time, $64 per term part-time.

Applying *Options:* electronic application, deferred entrance. *Application fee:* $60. *Required:* high school transcript. *Application deadline:* rolling (freshmen), rolling (transfers). *Notification:* continuous (freshmen).

Admissions Contact Mr. Eugenio Barrios, Director of Admissions, Borough of Manhattan Community College of the City University of New York, 199 Chambers Street, Room S-300, New York, NY 10007. *Phone:* 212-220-1265. *Fax:* 212-220-2366. *E-mail:* bmadmrpre@cunyum.cuny.edu.

BRAMSON ORT COLLEGE

Forest Hills, New York

Admissions Contact Admissions Office, Bramson ORT College, 69-30 Austin Street, Forest Hills, NY 11375-4239. *Phone:* 718-261-5800.

BRONX COMMUNITY COLLEGE OF THE CITY UNIVERSITY OF NEW YORK

Bronx, New York

- **State and locally supported** 2-year, founded 1959, part of City University of New York System
- **Calendar** semesters
- **Degree** certificates and associate
- **Urban** 50-acre campus
- **Coed,** 7,952 undergraduate students, 59% full-time, 65% women, 35% men

Undergraduates 4,725 full-time, 3,227 part-time. Students come from 16 states and territories, 100 other countries, 5% are from out of state, 38% African American, 3% Asian American or Pacific Islander, 49% Hispanic American, 0.1% Native American, 6% international, 6% transferred in. *Retention:* 65% of 2002 full-time freshmen returned.

Freshmen *Admission:* 1,409 enrolled.

Faculty *Total:* 548, 41% full-time.

Majors Accounting; administrative assistant and secretarial science; African-American/Black studies; art; biology/biological sciences; business administration and management; business teacher education; chemistry; child development; clinical/medical laboratory technology; computer science; data processing and data processing technology; electrical, electronic and communications engineering technology; history; human services; international relations and affairs; legal assistant/paralegal; liberal arts and sciences/liberal studies; marketing/marketing management; mathematics; medical administrative assistant and medical secretary; music; nuclear medical technology; nursing (registered nurse training); ornamental horticulture; pre-engineering; psychology.

Academic Programs *Special study options:* academic remediation for entering students, adult/continuing education programs, advanced placement credit, cooperative education, distance learning, English as a second language, honors programs, independent study, internships, part-time degree program, services for LD students, study abroad, summer session for credit.

Library 75,000 titles, 800 serial subscriptions.

Computers on Campus 300 computers available on campus for general student use.

Student Life *Housing:* college housing not available. *Activities and Organizations:* drama/theater group, student-run newspaper, radio station, choral group. *Campus security:* 24-hour patrols. *Student services:* personal/psychological counseling.

Athletics Member NJCAA. *Intercollegiate sports:* basketball M/W, soccer M, tennis M/W, track and field M/W, volleyball W, wrestling M. *Intramural sports:* basketball M/W, soccer M, tennis M/W, track and field M/W, volleyball W, wrestling M.

Costs (2004–05) *Tuition:* state resident $2800 full-time, $120 per credit part-time; nonresident $4560 full-time, $190 per credit part-time. *Required fees:* $284 full-time, $80 per term part-time.

Applying *Application fee:* $65. *Required:* high school transcript. *Application deadline:* rolling (freshmen), rolling (transfers). *Notification:* continuous (freshmen).

Bronx Community College of the City University of New York (continued)
Admissions Contact Ms. Alba N. Cancetty, Admissions Officer, Bronx Community College of the City University of New York, University Avenue and West 181st Street, Bronx, NY 10453. *Phone:* 718-289-5888. *E-mail:* admission@bcc.cuny.edu.

BROOME COMMUNITY COLLEGE
Binghamton, New York

- **State and locally supported** 2-year, founded 1946, part of State University of New York System
- **Calendar** semesters
- **Degree** certificates and associate
- **Suburban** 223-acre campus
- **Coed**, 6,590 undergraduate students, 63% full-time, 58% women, 42% men

Undergraduates 4,132 full-time, 2,458 part-time. Students come from 36 states and territories, 30 other countries, 5% are from out of state. *Retention:* 62% of 2002 full-time freshmen returned.
Freshmen *Admission:* 2,703 applied, 1,419 admitted, 1,419 enrolled.
Faculty *Total:* 399, 36% full-time. *Student/faculty ratio:* 21:1.
Majors Accounting technology and bookkeeping; business administration and management; child care and support services management; civil engineering technology; clinical/medical laboratory technology; communication/speech communication and rhetoric; communications systems installation and repair technology; computer and information sciences; computer engineering technology; corrections; criminal justice/police science; data processing and data processing technology; dental hygiene; electrical, electronic and communications engineering technology; emergency medical technology (EMT paramedic); engineering science; executive assistant/executive secretary; financial planning and services; fire science; health information/medical records technology; hotel/motel administration; industrial production technologies related; information science/studies; international finance; legal assistant/paralegal; liberal arts and sciences/liberal studies; mechanical engineering/mechanical technology; medical/clinical assistant; medical radiologic technology; mental and social health services and allied professions related; merchandising, sales, and marketing operations related (general); nursing (registered nurse training); physical therapist assistant; quality control technology; substance abuse/addiction counseling.
Academic Programs *Special study options:* academic remediation for entering students, adult/continuing education programs, advanced placement credit, distance learning, English as a second language, external degree program, honors programs, independent study, internships, off-campus study, part-time degree program, services for LD students, student-designed majors, study abroad, summer session for credit.
Library Cecil C. Tyrrell Learning Resources Center plus 1 other with 60,518 titles, 301 serial subscriptions, 2,145 audiovisual materials, an OPAC, a Web page.
Computers on Campus 550 computers available on campus for general student use. A campuswide network can be accessed from off campus. Internet access, at least one staffed computer lab available.
Student Life *Housing:* college housing not available. *Activities and Organizations:* student-run newspaper, choral group, Broome Early Childhood Organization, Differentially Disabled Student Association, Ecology Club, Phi Theta Kappa, Criminal Justice Club. *Campus security:* 24-hour emergency response devices and patrols. *Student services:* health clinic, personal/psychological counseling.
Athletics Member NJCAA. *Intercollegiate sports:* baseball M, basketball M/W, cross-country running M/W, golf M, ice hockey M, lacrosse M, soccer M/W, softball W, tennis M/W, volleyball W. *Intramural sports:* basketball M/W, volleyball M/W.
Standardized Tests *Required for some:* ACCUPLACER.
Costs (2004–05) *One-time required fee:* $45. *Tuition:* state resident $2690 full-time, $113 per credit hour part-time; nonresident $5380 full-time, $226 per credit hour part-time. Full-time tuition and fees vary according to course load and location. Part-time tuition and fees vary according to course load and location. *Required fees:* $242 full-time, $5 per credit hour part-time, $29 per term part-time. *Waivers:* senior citizens and employees or children of employees.
Applying *Options:* electronic application, early admission. *Required:* high school transcript. *Required for some:* interview. *Application deadline:* rolling (freshmen), rolling (transfers). *Notification:* continuous (freshmen).
Admissions Contact Mr. Anthony Fiorelli, Director of Admissions, Broome Community College, PO Box 1017, Upper Front Street, Binghamton, NY 13902. *Phone:* 607-778-5001. *E-mail:* admissions@sunybroome.edu.

BRYANT AND STRATTON COLLEGE
Albany, New York

- **Proprietary** 2-year, founded 1857, part of Bryant and Stratton College, Inc
- **Calendar** semesters
- **Degree** diplomas and associate
- **Suburban** campus
- **Coed**, 391 undergraduate students, 82% full-time, 78% women, 22% men

Undergraduates 319 full-time, 72 part-time. Students come from 1 other state, 47% African American, 2% Asian American or Pacific Islander, 8% Hispanic American. *Retention:* 52% of 2002 full-time freshmen returned.
Freshmen *Admission:* 103 applied, 93 admitted, 81 enrolled.
Faculty *Total:* 47, 17% full-time, 28% with terminal degrees. *Student/faculty ratio:* 8:1.
Majors Accounting; administrative assistant and secretarial science; business administration and management; information science/studies; information technology; legal assistant/paralegal; medical/clinical assistant.
Academic Programs *Special study options:* academic remediation for entering students, distance learning, double majors, independent study, internships, part-time degree program, services for LD students, summer session for credit.
Library Library with 3,500 titles, 5 serial subscriptions, 136 audiovisual materials, an OPAC, a Web page.
Computers on Campus 110 computers available on campus for general student use. A campuswide network can be accessed. Internet access, at least one staffed computer lab available.
Student Life *Housing:* college housing not available. *Activities and Organizations:* student-run newspaper. *Campus security:* 24-hour emergency response devices. *Student services:* personal/psychological counseling.
Standardized Tests *Required:* CPAt, Accuplacer (for admission).
Costs (2005–06) *Tuition:* $11,820 full-time, $394 per credit hour part-time. Full-time tuition and fees vary according to course load. Part-time tuition and fees vary according to course load. *Payment plan:* installment. *Waivers:* employees or children of employees.
Financial Aid Of all full-time matriculated undergraduates who enrolled in 2003, 10 Federal Work-Study jobs (averaging $800).
Applying *Options:* deferred entrance. *Application fee:* $25. *Required:* high school transcript, interview. *Required for some:* letters of recommendation. *Application deadline:* rolling (freshmen), rolling (transfers).
Admissions Contact Mr. Robert Ferrell, Director of Admissions, Bryant and Stratton College, 1259 Central Avenue, Albany, NY 12205. *Phone:* 518-437-1802 Ext. 205. *Fax:* 518-437-1048.

BRYANT AND STRATTON COLLEGE
Rochester, New York

Admissions Contact Ms. Maria Scalise, Director of Admissions, Bryant and Stratton College, 150 Bellwood Drive, Greece Campus, Rochester, NY 14606. *Phone:* 585-720-0660 Ext. 220. *Fax:* 716-292-6015.

BRYANT AND STRATTON COLLEGE
Rochester, New York

Admissions Contact Ms. Maria Scalise, Director of Admissions, Bryant and Stratton College, 1225 Jefferson Road, Henrietta Campus, Rochester, NY 14623. *Phone:* 585-292-5627 Ext. 103.

BRYANT AND STRATTON COLLEGE
Syracuse, New York

- **Proprietary** 2-year, founded 1854, part of Bryant and Stratton Business Institute, Inc
- **Calendar** semesters
- **Degree** diplomas and associate
- **Urban** campus
- **Coed**

Faculty *Student/faculty ratio:* 15:1.
Student Life *Campus security:* 24-hour emergency response devices, controlled dormitory access.
Athletics Member NJCAA.
Standardized Tests *Required:* CPAt (for admission). *Recommended:* SAT or ACT (for admission).
Costs (2004–05) *Comprehensive fee:* $17,870 includes full-time tuition ($12,120) and room and board ($5750). Full-time tuition and fees vary according to class time, degree level, program, and student level. Part-time tuition: $364 per credit. *Room and board:* college room only: $3000.
Applying *Application fee:* $25. *Required:* essay or personal statement, high school transcript, interview, entrance, placement evaluations. *Required for some:* letters of recommendation. *Recommended:* minimum 2.0 GPA.
Admissions Contact Mrs. Amy Graham, Associate Director of Admissions, Bryant and Stratton College, 953 James Street, Syracuse, NY 13203-2502. *Phone:* 315-472-6603 Ext. 247.

BRYANT AND STRATTON COLLEGE, AMHERST CAMPUS

Clarence, New York

- **Proprietary** primarily 2-year, founded 1977, part of Bryant and Stratton College
- **Calendar** semesters
- **Degrees** diplomas, associate, and bachelor's
- **Suburban** 12-acre campus with easy access to Buffalo
- **Coed,** 341 undergraduate students, 59% full-time, 71% women, 29% men

Undergraduates 202 full-time, 139 part-time. 13% African American, 0.9% Asian American or Pacific Islander, 1% Hispanic American, 0.9% Native American, 21% transferred in.
Freshmen *Admission:* 82 applied, 66 admitted, 66 enrolled.
Faculty *Total:* 38, 21% full-time, 34% with terminal degrees.
Majors Accounting; administrative assistant and secretarial science; business administration, management and operations related; commercial and advertising art; computer and information sciences; electrical, electronic and communications engineering technology; legal assistant/paralegal.
Academic Programs *Special study options:* academic remediation for entering students, advanced placement credit, cooperative education, distance learning, double majors, independent study, internships, part-time degree program, summer session for credit.
Library Library Resource Center with 4,500 titles, 25 serial subscriptions, 150 audiovisual materials, an OPAC, a Web page.
Computers on Campus 70 computers available on campus for general student use. Internet access, at least one staffed computer lab available.
Student Life *Housing:* college housing not available. *Activities and Organizations:* Phi Beta Lambda, Student Government Association, Information Technology Club, Ambassadors.
Standardized Tests *Required:* TABE, CPAt or ACCUPLACER (for admission). *Recommended:* SAT or ACT (for admission).
Costs (2005–06) *One-time required fee:* $25. *Tuition:* $10,920 full-time, $394 per credit part-time. Full-time tuition and fees vary according to class time, course load, and location. Part-time tuition and fees vary according to class time and course load. *Required fees:* $300 full-time, $100 per term part-time. *Payment plan:* installment. *Waivers:* employees or children of employees.
Applying *Options:* common application, deferred entrance. *Application fee:* $25. *Required:* high school transcript, interview. *Required for some:* essay or personal statement, interview. *Application deadline:* rolling (freshmen), rolling (transfers).
Admissions Contact Ms. Cathy Oddo, Dean of Students, Bryant and Stratton College, Amherst Campus, 40 Hazelwood Drive, Amherst, NY 14228. *Phone:* 716-691-0012. *Fax:* 716-691-6716.

BRYANT AND STRATTON COLLEGE, BUFFALO CAMPUS

Buffalo, New York

- **Proprietary** 2-year, founded 1854, part of Bryant and Stratton College
- **Calendar** semesters
- **Degree** certificates, diplomas, and associate
- **Urban** 2-acre campus
- **Coed,** 625 undergraduate students, 86% full-time, 76% women, 24% men

Undergraduates 540 full-time, 85 part-time. 68% African American, 0.2% Asian American or Pacific Islander, 6% Hispanic American, 1% Native American, 4% transferred in.
Freshmen *Admission:* 260 applied, 220 admitted, 220 enrolled.
Faculty *Total:* 48, 21% full-time, 31% with terminal degrees. *Student/faculty ratio:* 10:1.
Majors Accounting; administrative assistant and secretarial science; business administration, management and operations related; computer and information sciences; medical/clinical assistant.
Academic Programs *Special study options:* academic remediation for entering students, advanced placement credit, cooperative education, distance learning, double majors, independent study, internships, part-time degree program, summer session for credit.
Library Learning Center/Library with 30,000 titles, 28,217 serial subscriptions, 252 audiovisual materials, an OPAC.
Computers on Campus 125 computers available on campus for general student use. Internet access, at least one staffed computer lab available.
Student Life *Housing:* college housing not available. *Activities and Organizations:* Med-Assisting Club, Secretarial Club, Accounting/Business Club.
Standardized Tests *Required:* TABE, CPAt or ACCUPLACER (for admission). *Recommended:* SAT or ACT (for admission).

Costs (2005–06) *Tuition:* $10,920 full-time, $394 per credit part-time. Full-time tuition and fees vary according to class time and course load. Part-time tuition and fees vary according to course load. *Required fees:* $300 full-time. *Payment plan:* installment. *Waivers:* employees or children of employees.
Applying *Options:* common application, deferred entrance. *Application fee:* $25. *Required:* high school transcript, interview. *Required for some:* letters of recommendation. *Recommended:* minimum 2.0 GPA. *Application deadline:* rolling (freshmen), rolling (transfers).
Admissions Contact Mr. Phil Strubel, Director of Admissions, Bryant and Stratton College, Buffalo Campus, 465 Main Street, Suite 400, Buffalo, NY 14203-1713. *Phone:* 716-884-9120. *Fax:* 716-884-0091.

BRYANT AND STRATTON COLLEGE, LACKAWANNA CAMPUS

Lackawanna, New York

- **Proprietary** 2-year, founded 1989, part of Bryant and Stratton College
- **Calendar** semesters
- **Degree** diplomas and associate
- **Suburban** campus with easy access to Buffalo
- **Coed,** 256 undergraduate students, 80% full-time, 74% women, 26% men

Undergraduates 204 full-time, 52 part-time. 5% African American, 6% Hispanic American, 1% Native American.
Freshmen *Admission:* 79 enrolled.
Faculty *Total:* 40, 18% full-time, 10% with terminal degrees.
Majors Accounting; administrative assistant and secretarial science; business administration, management and operations related; computer and information sciences; hotel/motel administration.
Academic Programs *Special study options:* academic remediation for entering students, advanced placement credit, cooperative education, distance learning, double majors, independent study, internships, part-time degree program, summer session for credit.
Library Southtowns Library with 1,402 titles, 42 serial subscriptions, 128 audiovisual materials, an OPAC, a Web page.
Computers on Campus 112 computers available on campus for general student use. Internet access, at least one staffed computer lab available.
Student Life *Housing:* college housing not available. *Activities and Organizations:* Accounting/Business Club, Administrative Professionals Club, Micro Club, Honor Society, student newsletter. *Campus security:* 24-hour emergency response devices, late-night transport/escort service.
Standardized Tests *Required:* TABE, CPAt or ACCUPLACER (for admission). *Recommended:* SAT or ACT (for admission).
Costs (2005–06) *Tuition:* $10,920 full-time, $394 per credit part-time. Full-time tuition and fees vary according to class time and course load. Part-time tuition and fees vary according to course load. *Required fees:* $300 full-time, $100 per term part-time. *Payment plan:* installment. *Waivers:* employees or children of employees.
Applying *Options:* common application, deferred entrance. *Application fee:* $25. *Required:* essay or personal statement, high school transcript, interview. *Required for some:* letters of recommendation. *Recommended:* minimum 2.0 GPA. *Application deadline:* rolling (freshmen), rolling (transfers).
Admissions Contact Ms. Dee Edwards, Associate Director of Admissions, Bryant and Stratton College, Lackawanna Campus, Sterling Park, 200 Redtail, Orchard Park, NY 14127. *Phone:* 716-677-9500. *Fax:* 716-821-9343.

BRYANT AND STRATTON COLLEGE, NORTH CAMPUS

Liverpool, New York

Admissions Contact Ms. Heather Macnik, Director of Admissions, Bryant and Stratton College, North Campus, 8687 Carling Road, Liverpool, NY 13090-1315. *Phone:* 315-652-6500. *Fax:* 315-652-5500.

BUSINESS INFORMATICS CENTER, INC.

Valley Stream, New York

Admissions Contact 134 South Central Avenue, Valley Stream, NY 11580-5431.

CAYUGA COUNTY COMMUNITY COLLEGE

Auburn, New York

- **State and locally supported** 2-year, founded 1953, part of State University of New York System

Cayuga County Community College (continued)
- **Calendar** semesters
- **Degree** certificates and associate
- **Small-town** 50-acre campus with easy access to Rochester and Syracuse
- **Endowment** $6.5 million
- **Coed**, 3,896 undergraduate students, 57% full-time, 60% women, 40% men

Undergraduates 2,220 full-time, 1,676 part-time. Students come from 9 states and territories, 3 other countries, 1% are from out of state, 3% African American, 0.7% Asian American or Pacific Islander, 1% Hispanic American, 1% Native American, 0.5% international, 4% transferred in.

Freshmen *Admission:* 1,429 applied, 1,201 admitted, 676 enrolled. *Average high school GPA:* 2.45. *Test scores:* SAT verbal scores over 500: 33%; SAT math scores over 500: 47%; SAT verbal scores over 600: 5%; SAT math scores over 600: 9%; SAT verbal scores over 700: 1%; SAT math scores over 700: 1%.

Faculty *Total:* 155, 28% full-time, 15% with terminal degrees.

Majors Accounting; business administration and management; computer and information sciences; computer and information sciences related; computer/information technology services administration related; computer management; computer programming; computer science; consumer merchandising/retailing management; corrections; criminal justice/law enforcement administration; criminal justice/police science; data processing and data processing technology; drafting and design technology; electrical, electronic and communications engineering technology; humanities; information science/studies; kindergarten/preschool education; liberal arts and sciences/liberal studies; marketing/marketing management; mathematics; mechanical design technology; nursing (registered nurse training); radio and television; radio and television broadcasting technology; telecommunications.

Academic Programs *Special study options:* academic remediation for entering students, accelerated degree program, adult/continuing education programs, advanced placement credit, distance learning, double majors, honors programs, independent study, internships, part-time degree program, services for LD students, study abroad, summer session for credit.

Library Norman F. Bourke Memorial Library with 82,205 titles, 527 serial subscriptions, 8,930 audiovisual materials, an OPAC, a Web page.

Computers on Campus 240 computers available on campus for general student use. A campuswide network can be accessed from off campus. Internet access, at least one staffed computer lab available.

Student Life *Housing Options:* Campus housing is provided by a third party. *Activities and Organizations:* drama/theater group, student-run newspaper, radio and television station, choral group, Student Government Association, Student Activities Board, Radio and Television Guild, honors and business fraternities, Phi Beta Lambda. *Campus security:* security from 8 a.m. to 9 p.m. *Student services:* health clinic, personal/psychological counseling.

Athletics Member NJCAA. *Intercollegiate sports:* basketball M/W, cross-country running M/W, lacrosse M/W, soccer M/W. *Intramural sports:* archery M/W, basketball M/W, racquetball M/W, skiing (cross-country) M/W, soccer M/W, softball M/W, tennis M/W, volleyball M/W.

Standardized Tests *Required for some:* ACT ASSET, ACCUPLACER. *Recommended:* SAT or ACT (for placement).

Costs (2005–06) *Tuition:* state resident $2900 full-time, $105 per credit part-time; nonresident $5800 full-time, $210 per credit part-time. Full-time tuition and fees vary according to class time, course load, and program. Part-time tuition and fees vary according to class time, course load, and program. *Required fees:* $311 full-time, $12 per credit part-time, $2 per term part-time. *Payment plan:* installment. *Waivers:* senior citizens and employees or children of employees.

Financial Aid Of all full-time matriculated undergraduates who enrolled in 2003, 150 Federal Work-Study jobs (averaging $1800). 200 state and other part-time jobs (averaging $1000).

Applying *Options:* electronic application, deferred entrance. *Required:* high school transcript. *Required for some:* interview. *Application deadline:* rolling (freshmen), rolling (transfers). *Notification:* continuous (freshmen).

Admissions Contact Mr. Bruce M. Blodgett, Director of Admissions, Cayuga County Community College, 197 Franklin Street, Auburn, NY 13021-3099. *Phone:* 315-255-1743 Ext. 2244. *E-mail:* admissions@cayuga-cc.edu.

CLINTON COMMUNITY COLLEGE
Plattsburgh, New York

- **State and locally supported** 2-year, founded 1969, part of State University of New York System
- **Calendar** semesters
- **Degree** certificates and associate
- **Small-town** 100-acre campus
- **Endowment** $1.0 million
- **Coed**, 2,192 undergraduate students, 57% full-time, 57% women, 43% men

Undergraduates 1,259 full-time, 933 part-time. Students come from 5 states and territories, 9 other countries, 1% are from out of state, 3% African American,

0.6% Asian American or Pacific Islander, 2% Hispanic American, 0.9% Native American, 2% international, 6% transferred in, 6% live on campus.

Freshmen *Admission:* 1,714 applied, 1,406 admitted, 383 enrolled. *Average high school GPA:* 2.50.

Faculty *Total:* 142, 35% full-time, 8% with terminal degrees. *Student/faculty ratio:* 18:1.

Majors Accounting; administrative assistant and secretarial science; biological and physical sciences; business administration and management; clinical/medical laboratory technology; community organization and advocacy; computer/information technology services administration related; consumer merchandising/retailing management; criminal justice/law enforcement administration; criminal justice/police science; electrical, electronic and communications engineering technology; humanities; industrial technology; liberal arts and sciences/liberal studies; nursing (registered nurse training); physical education teaching and coaching; social sciences.

Academic Programs *Special study options:* academic remediation for entering students, adult/continuing education programs, advanced placement credit, cooperative education, distance learning, English as a second language, external degree program, independent study, internships, off-campus study, part-time degree program, services for LD students, student-designed majors, summer session for credit.

Library Clinton Community College Learning Resource Center plus 1 other with 33,862 titles, 288 serial subscriptions, 257 audiovisual materials, an OPAC, a Web page.

Computers on Campus 250 computers available on campus for general student use. A campuswide network can be accessed from off campus. Internet access, at least one staffed computer lab available.

Student Life *Housing Options:* coed, disabled students. Campus housing is provided by a third party. Freshman campus housing is guaranteed. *Activities and Organizations:* drama/theater group, student-run newspaper, choral group, Criminal Justice Club, Business Club, Tomorrow's New Teachers, Ski Club, Nursing Club. *Campus security:* 24-hour emergency response devices, late-night transport/escort service, controlled dormitory access, security during class hours. *Student services:* health clinic, personal/psychological counseling.

Athletics Member NJCAA. *Intercollegiate sports:* baseball M, basketball M/W, soccer M/W, softball W. *Intramural sports:* fencing M/W, volleyball M/W.

Standardized Tests *Recommended:* SAT or ACT (for placement).

Costs (2005–06) *Tuition:* state resident $3020 full-time, $125 per credit hour part-time; nonresident $7550 full-time, $312 per credit hour part-time. *Required fees:* $166 full-time, $5 per credit hour part-time. *Room and board:* $6340; room only: $3800.

Financial Aid Of all full-time matriculated undergraduates who enrolled in 2003, 45 Federal Work-Study jobs (averaging $1260).

Applying *Options:* common application, electronic application, deferred entrance. *Required:* high school transcript. *Required for some:* essay or personal statement, minimum 2.5 GPA, 3 letters of recommendation, interview. *Application deadlines:* 8/26 (freshmen), 9/3 (transfers). *Notification:* continuous (freshmen).

Admissions Contact Mrs. Karen L. Burnam, Director of Admissions and Financial Aid, Clinton Community College, 136 Clinton Point Drive, Plattsburgh, NY 12901. *Phone:* 518-562-4170. *Toll-free phone:* 800-552-1160. *Fax:* 518-562-4158. *E-mail:* cccadm@clintoncc.suny.edu.

COCHRAN SCHOOL OF NURSING
Yonkers, New York

- **Independent** 2-year, founded 1894
- **Calendar** semesters
- **Degree** associate
- **Urban** campus with easy access to New York City
- **Coed, primarily women**

Faculty *Student/faculty ratio:* 5:1.

Student Life *Campus security:* 24-hour emergency response devices and patrols, late-night transport/escort service.

Standardized Tests *Required:* nursing exam (for admission). *Required for some:* SAT (for admission).

Applying *Options:* deferred entrance. *Application fee:* $25. *Required:* essay or personal statement, high school transcript, interview.

Admissions Contact Ms. Sandra Sclafani, Registrar, Cochran School of Nursing, 967 North Broadway, Yonkers, NY 10701. *Phone:* 914-964-4296. *Fax:* 914-964-4796. *E-mail:* ssclafani@riversidehealth.org.

THE COLLEGE OF WESTCHESTER
White Plains, New York

- **Proprietary** 2-year, founded 1915
- **Calendar** quarters for day division, semesters for evening and weekend divisions

■ **Degree** certificates and associate
■ **Suburban** campus with easy access to New York City
■ **Coed**

Faculty *Student/faculty ratio:* 15:1.

Standardized Tests *Recommended:* SAT (for admission).

Costs (2004–05) *Tuition:* $16,203 full-time, $491 per credit part-time. Full-time tuition and fees vary according to course load and program. Part-time tuition and fees vary according to course load and program. *Required fees:* $780 full-time, $160 per term part-time.

Applying *Options:* common application, electronic application, deferred entrance. *Application fee:* $30. *Required:* high school transcript, interview. *Required for some:* essay or personal statement.

Admissions Contact Mr. Dale T. Smith, Vice President, The College of Westchester, 325 Central Avenue, PO Box 710, White Plains, NY 10602. *Phone:* 914-948-4442 Ext. 311. *Toll-free phone:* 800-333-4924 Ext. 318. *Fax:* 914-948-5441. *E-mail:* admissions@wbi.org.

▶ **See page 482 for a narrative description.**

COLUMBIA-GREENE COMMUNITY COLLEGE
Hudson, New York

■ **State and locally supported** 2-year, founded 1969, part of State University of New York System
■ **Calendar** semesters
■ **Degree** certificates and associate
■ **Rural** 143-acre campus
■ **Endowment** $450,000
■ **Coed,** 1,715 undergraduate students, 55% full-time, 64% women, 36% men

Undergraduates 938 full-time, 777 part-time. Students come from 5 states and territories, 5 other countries, 1% are from out of state, 5% transferred in.

Freshmen *Admission:* 631 applied, 499 admitted, 366 enrolled.

Faculty *Total:* 107, 45% full-time. *Student/faculty ratio:* 18:1.

Majors Accounting; administrative assistant and secretarial science; art; automobile/automotive mechanics technology; biological and physical sciences; business administration and management; computer and information sciences related; computer graphics; computer science; computer systems networking and telecommunications; criminal justice/law enforcement administration; data processing and data processing technology; humanities; human services; information science/studies; interdisciplinary studies; kinesiology and exercise science; liberal arts and sciences/liberal studies; mathematics; nursing (registered nurse training); real estate; social sciences; web/multimedia management and webmaster.

Academic Programs *Special study options:* academic remediation for entering students, adult/continuing education programs, advanced placement credit, distance learning, honors programs, internships, part-time degree program, services for LD students, student-designed majors, summer session for credit.

Library 52,484 titles, 627 serial subscriptions, an OPAC, a Web page.

Computers on Campus 150 computers available on campus for general student use. A campuswide network can be accessed from off campus. Internet access, at least one staffed computer lab available.

Student Life *Housing:* college housing not available. *Activities and Organizations:* drama/theater group, student-run radio station, choral group, student council/government, Student Ambassadors, Nursing Club. *Campus security:* 24-hour patrols, late-night transport/escort service.

Athletics Member NJCAA. *Intercollegiate sports:* baseball M, basketball M, soccer M/W, softball W. *Intramural sports:* archery M/W, badminton M/W, baseball M, basketball M/W, fencing M/W, soccer M/W, table tennis M/W, tennis M/W, volleyball M/W, weight lifting M/W.

Standardized Tests *Required:* College Qualifying Test (for placement). *Recommended:* SAT or ACT (for placement).

Costs (2004–05) *Tuition:* state resident $2688 full-time, $112 per credit hour part-time; nonresident $5376 full-time, $224 per credit hour part-time. *Required fees:* $162 full-time, $10 per credit hour part-time. *Payment plans:* installment, deferred payment. *Waivers:* senior citizens and employees or children of employees.

Applying *Options:* early admission, deferred entrance. *Application fee:* $30. *Required:* high school transcript. *Required for some:* interview. *Application deadline:* rolling (freshmen), rolling (transfers). *Notification:* continuous (freshmen).

Admissions Contact Mrs. Patricia Hallenbeck, Assistant Dean of Student Affairs, Columbia-Greene Community College, 4400 Route 23, Hudson, NY 12534-0327. *Phone:* 518-828-4181 Ext. 5513. *Fax:* 518-828-8543. *E-mail:* hallenbeck@vaxa.cis.sunycgcc.edu.

CORNING COMMUNITY COLLEGE
Corning, New York

■ **State and locally supported** 2-year, founded 1956, part of State University of New York System
■ **Calendar** semesters
■ **Degree** certificates and associate
■ **Rural** 275-acre campus
■ **Endowment** $1.2 million
■ **Coed,** 4,443 undergraduate students, 53% full-time, 59% women, 41% men

Undergraduates 2,356 full-time, 2,087 part-time. Students come from 13 states and territories, 4% are from out of state, 3% African American, 0.7% Asian American or Pacific Islander, 0.7% Hispanic American, 0.2% Native American, 0.1% international, 4% transferred in. *Retention:* 67% of 2002 full-time freshmen returned.

Freshmen *Admission:* 1,622 applied, 1,464 admitted, 988 enrolled.

Faculty *Total:* 243, 39% full-time, 8% with terminal degrees. *Student/faculty ratio:* 19:1.

Majors Accounting; administrative assistant and secretarial science; automobile/automotive mechanics technology; automotive engineering technology; biological and physical sciences; business administration and management; chemical technology; child care provision; computer and information sciences; computer and information sciences related; computer graphics; computer/information technology services administration related; computer programming; computer programming related; computer science; computer systems networking and telecommunications; computer technology/computer systems technology; corrections and criminal justice related; criminal justice/law enforcement administration; drafting and design technology; education related; electrical, electronic and communications engineering technology; elementary education; emergency medical technology (EMT paramedic); fire science; general studies; health and physical education; humanities; human services; industrial technology; information technology; legal assistant/paralegal; liberal arts and sciences/liberal studies; machine shop technology; machine tool technology; mathematics; mechanical engineering/mechanical technology; nursing (registered nurse training); optical sciences; pre-engineering; social sciences; substance abuse/addiction counseling; tourism and travel services management; word processing.

Academic Programs *Special study options:* academic remediation for entering students, accelerated degree program, advanced placement credit, distance learning, double majors, honors programs, independent study, internships, part-time degree program, services for LD students, student-designed majors, summer session for credit. *ROTC:* Army (c), Navy (c), Air Force (c).

Library Arthur A. Houghton, Jr. Library with 71,233 titles, 2,500 serial subscriptions, 4,290 audiovisual materials, an OPAC, a Web page.

Computers on Campus 350 computers available on campus for general student use. A campuswide network can be accessed from off campus that provide access to e-mail, Internet courses. Internet access, at least one staffed computer lab available.

Student Life *Housing:* college housing not available. *Activities and Organizations:* drama/theater group, student-run newspaper, radio station, choral group, student association, WCEB, Two-Bit Players, Activities Programming Committee, Nursing Society. *Campus security:* 24-hour emergency response devices and patrols, late-night transport/escort service. *Student services:* health clinic, personal/psychological counseling.

Athletics Member NJCAA. *Intercollegiate sports:* basketball M/W, cheerleading W, soccer M/W, softball W, volleyball W. *Intramural sports:* archery M/W, badminton M/W, basketball M/W, bowling M/W, golf M/W, soccer M/W, softball M/W, table tennis M/W, volleyball M/W, weight lifting M/W.

Costs (2004–05) *Tuition:* state resident $3064 full-time, $128 per credit hour part-time; nonresident $6128 full-time, $256 per credit hour part-time. Part-time tuition and fees vary according to course load. *Required fees:* $400 full-time. *Payment plan:* installment. *Waivers:* senior citizens and employees or children of employees.

Financial Aid Of all full-time matriculated undergraduates who enrolled in 2003, 264 Federal Work-Study jobs (averaging $1128).

Applying *Options:* electronic application, early admission. *Application fee:* $25. *Required:* high school transcript. *Required for some:* interview. *Application deadline:* rolling (freshmen), rolling (transfers). *Notification:* continuous (freshmen).

Admissions Contact Ms. Donna A. Hastings, Interim Director of Admissions, Corning Community College, 1 Academic Drive, Corning, NY 14830. *Phone:* 607-962-9220. *Toll-free phone:* 800-358-7171 Ext. 220. *Fax:* 607-962-9520. *E-mail:* admissions@corning-cc.edu.

CROUSE HOSPITAL SCHOOL OF NURSING
Syracuse, New York

■ **Independent** 2-year, founded 1913
■ **Calendar** semesters

Crouse Hospital School of Nursing (continued)
- **Degree** associate
- **Urban** campus
- **Coed,** 252 undergraduate students, 56% full-time, 88% women, 12% men

Undergraduates 140 full-time, 112 part-time. Students come from 4 states and territories, 2% are from out of state, 7% African American, 2% Asian American or Pacific Islander, 1% Hispanic American, 14% live on campus.

Freshmen *Admission:* 19 admitted, 19 enrolled.

Faculty *Total:* 25, 64% full-time. *Student/faculty ratio:* 9:1.

Majors Nursing (registered nurse training).

Academic Programs *Special study options:* part-time degree program.

Student Life *Campus security:* 24-hour emergency response devices and patrols, late-night transport/escort service, controlled dormitory access. *Student services:* health clinic, personal/psychological counseling.

Standardized Tests *Required for some:* SAT or ACT (for admission). *Recommended:* SAT or ACT (for admission).

Costs (2005–06) *Tuition:* $7352 full-time, $225 per credit hour part-time. *Required fees:* $360 full-time, $130 per term part-time. *Room only:* $1750.

Financial Aid Of all full-time matriculated undergraduates who enrolled in 2003, 18 Federal Work-Study jobs (averaging $880).

Applying *Options:* deferred entrance. *Application fee:* $30. *Required:* essay or personal statement, high school transcript, minimum 2.5 GPA, 3 letters of recommendation, interview. *Application deadlines:* 2/1 (freshmen), 2/1 (transfers).

Admissions Contact Ms. Karen Van Sise, Enrollment Management Supervisor, Crouse Hospital School of Nursing, 736 Irving Avenue, Syracuse, NY 13210. *Phone:* 315-470-7481. *Fax:* 315-470-7925.

DOROTHEA HOPFER SCHOOL OF NURSING AT THE MOUNT VERNON HOSPITAL
Mount Vernon, New York

Admissions Contact Office of Admissions, Dorothea Hopfer School of Nursing at The Mount Vernon Hospital, 53 Valentine Street, Mount Vernon, NY 10550. *Phone:* 914-664-8000 Ext. 3221. *Fax:* 914-665-7047.

DUTCHESS COMMUNITY COLLEGE
Poughkeepsie, New York

- **State and locally supported** 2-year, founded 1957, part of State University of New York System
- **Calendar** semesters
- **Degree** certificates and associate
- **Suburban** 130-acre campus with easy access to New York City
- **Coed,** 7,810 undergraduate students

Freshmen *Admission:* 1,030 applied, 1,012 admitted. *Average high school GPA:* 2.5.

Faculty *Total:* 396.

Majors Accounting; administrative assistant and secretarial science; architectural engineering technology; artificial intelligence and robotics; biological and physical sciences; business administration and management; business machine repair; child development; child guidance; clinical/medical laboratory technology; commercial and advertising art; communication/speech communication and rhetoric; computer and information sciences; computer science; construction engineering technology; consumer merchandising/retailing management; criminal justice/law enforcement administration; criminal justice/safety; dietetics; electrical, electronic and communications engineering technology; electrical, electronics and communications engineering; electromechanical technology; elementary education; emergency medical technology (EMT paramedic); engineering science; foods, nutrition, and wellness; humanities; information science/studies; kindergarten/preschool education; legal assistant/paralegal; liberal arts and sciences/liberal studies; mass communication/media; mathematics; medical/clinical assistant; mental health/rehabilitation; nursing (registered nurse training); parks, recreation and leisure; physical therapist assistant; psychiatric/mental health services technology; science teacher education; social sciences; special products marketing; telecommunications; tourism and travel services management.

Academic Programs *Special study options:* academic remediation for entering students, adult/continuing education programs, advanced placement credit, English as a second language, freshman honors college, honors programs, internships, off-campus study, part-time degree program, summer session for credit.

Library Dutchess Library with 103,272 titles, 540 serial subscriptions, an OPAC, a Web page.

Computers on Campus 50 computers available on campus for general student use. A campuswide network can be accessed from off campus. Internet access, at least one staffed computer lab available.

Student Life *Housing:* college housing not available. *Activities and Organizations:* drama/theater group, student-run newspaper, radio station, choral group. *Campus security:* 24-hour emergency response devices and patrols, late-night transport/escort service. *Student services:* health clinic, personal/psychological counseling.

Athletics Member NJCAA. *Intercollegiate sports:* baseball M, basketball M/W, bowling M/W, golf M, soccer M/W, softball W, tennis M/W, volleyball W. *Intramural sports:* badminton M/W, basketball M/W, football M, soccer M/W, tennis M/W, volleyball M/W.

Costs (2005–06) *Tuition:* state resident $2600 full-time, $105 per credit part-time; nonresident $5200 full-time, $210 per credit part-time. *Required fees:* $387 full-time, $8 per credit part-time, $25 per term part-time.

Financial Aid Of all full-time matriculated undergraduates who enrolled in 2003, 500 Federal Work-Study jobs (averaging $1500).

Applying *Options:* early admission, deferred entrance. *Required:* high school transcript. *Application deadline:* rolling (freshmen), rolling (transfers). *Notification:* continuous (freshmen).

Admissions Contact Ms. Rita Banner, Director of Admissions, Dutchess Community College, 53 Pendell Road, Poughkeepsie, NY 12601. *Phone:* 845-431-8010. *Toll-free phone:* 800-763-3933. *E-mail:* banner@sunydutchess.edu.

ELLIS HOSPITAL SCHOOL OF NURSING
Schenectady, New York

Admissions Contact Mary Lee Pollard, Director of School, Ellis Hospital School of Nursing, 1101 Nott Street, Schenectady, NY 12308. *Phone:* 518-243-4471.

ELMIRA BUSINESS INSTITUTE
Elmira, New York

- **Private** 2-year, founded 1858
- **Degree** certificates and associate
- **Coed, primarily women**
- 71% of applicants were admitted

Faculty *Student/faculty ratio:* 12:1.

Applying *Options:* common application, electronic application. *Required:* high school transcript, interview.

Admissions Contact Ms. Lisa Roan, Admissions Director, Elmira Business Institute, 303 North Main Street, Langdon Plaza, Elmira, NY 14901. *Phone:* 800-843-1812 Ext. 210. *Toll-free phone:* 800-843-1812. *Fax:* 607-733-7178. *E-mail:* lroan@ebi-college.com.

ERIE COMMUNITY COLLEGE
Buffalo, New York

- **State and locally supported** 2-year, founded 1971, part of State University of New York System
- **Calendar** semesters
- **Degrees** certificates, diplomas, and associate (profile also includes information from North and South campuses)
- **Urban** 1-acre campus
- **Coed,** 2,870 undergraduate students, 74% full-time, 63% women, 37% men

Undergraduates 2,110 full-time, 760 part-time. Students come from 12 states and territories, 3 other countries, 1% are from out of state, 41% African American, 1% Asian American or Pacific Islander, 8% Hispanic American, 1% Native American, 0.1% international, 6% transferred in.

Freshmen *Admission:* 4,778 applied, 4,033 admitted, 653 enrolled. *Test scores:* SAT verbal scores over 500: 23%; SAT math scores over 500: 24%; SAT verbal scores over 600: 3%; SAT math scores over 600: 3%; SAT math scores over 700: 1%.

Faculty *Total:* 1,191, 31% full-time. *Student/faculty ratio:* 17:1.

Majors Administrative assistant and secretarial science; building/property maintenance and management; business administration and management; child care and support services management; community health services counseling; criminal justice/law enforcement administration; culinary arts; hotel/motel administration; humanities; industrial production technologies related; information science/studies; legal assistant/paralegal; liberal arts and sciences/liberal studies; medical radiologic technology; nursing (registered nurse training); office management; substance abuse/addiction counseling.

Academic Programs *Special study options:* academic remediation for entering students, adult/continuing education programs, advanced placement credit, cooperative education, distance learning, double majors, English as a second language, honors programs, independent study, internships, part-time degree program, services for LD students, student-designed majors, study abroad, summer session for credit. *ROTC:* Army (c).

Library Leon E. Butler Library with 24,927 titles, 208 serial subscriptions, 2,492 audiovisual materials, an OPAC, a Web page.

Computers on Campus 341 computers available on campus for general student use. A campuswide network can be accessed from off campus. Internet access, online (class) registration, at least one staffed computer lab available.

Student Life *Housing:* college housing not available. *Activities and Organizations:* student-run newspaper, Alpha Beta Gamma, Anthropology Club, Black Student Union, Business Club, Campus Ministry Club. *Campus security:* 24-hour emergency response devices and patrols, late-night transport/escort service. *Student services:* health clinic, personal/psychological counseling, women's center.

Athletics Member NJCAA. *Intercollegiate sports:* baseball M, basketball M/W, bowling M/W, cheerleading W, cross-country running M/W, football M, golf M/W, ice hockey M, soccer M/W, softball W, swimming and diving M/W, track and field M/W, volleyball W.

Standardized Tests *Required:* ACT ASSET (for placement). *Recommended:* SAT (for placement), SAT Subject Tests (for placement).

Costs (2004–05) *Tuition:* area resident $2900 full-time, $121 per credit hour part-time; state resident $5800 full-time, $242 per credit hour part-time; nonresident $5800 full-time, $242 per credit hour part-time. *Required fees:* $300 full-time, $5 per credit hour part-time, $30 per term part-time. *Payment plans:* installment, deferred payment. *Waivers:* senior citizens and employees or children of employees.

Financial Aid Of all full-time matriculated undergraduates who enrolled in 2003, 300 Federal Work-Study jobs (averaging $2000).

Applying *Options:* common application, electronic application. *Application fee:* $25. *Required:* high school transcript. *Required for some:* interview. *Application deadline:* rolling (freshmen), rolling (transfers). *Notification:* continuous (freshmen).

Admissions Contact Ms. Petrina Hill-Cheatom, Director of Admissions, Erie Community College, 121 Ellicott Street, Buffalo, NY 14203-2698. *Phone:* 716-851-1588. *Fax:* 716-851-1129.

ERIE COMMUNITY COLLEGE, NORTH CAMPUS
Williamsville, New York

- **State and locally supported** 2-year, founded 1946, part of State University of New York System
- **Calendar** 4-1-4 plus summer sessions
- **Degree** certificates, diplomas, and associate
- **Suburban** 20-acre campus with easy access to Buffalo
- **Coed,** 6,170 undergraduate students, 62% full-time, 47% women, 53% men

Undergraduates 3,828 full-time, 2,342 part-time. Students come from 17 states and territories, 24 other countries, 1% are from out of state, 11% African American, 2% Asian American or Pacific Islander, 2% Hispanic American, 0.5% Native American, 1% international, 5% transferred in.

Freshmen *Admission:* 4,778 applied, 4,033 admitted, 1,203 enrolled. *Test scores:* SAT verbal scores over 500: 29%; SAT math scores over 500: 37%; SAT verbal scores over 600: 3%; SAT math scores over 600: 5%.

Faculty *Total:* 1,191, 31% full-time. *Student/faculty ratio:* 16:1.

Majors Administrative assistant and secretarial science; business administration and management; chemical technology; civil engineering technology; clinical/medical laboratory technology; computer and information sciences; construction trades related; criminal justice/law enforcement administration; criminal justice/police science; dental hygiene; dietitian assistant; electrical, electronic and communications engineering technology; engineering; health information/medical records technology; humanities; information science/studies; liberal arts and sciences/liberal studies; machine shop technology; mechanical engineering/mechanical technology; medical office management; nursing (registered nurse training); occupational therapist assistant; office management; opticianry; respiratory care therapy; restaurant, culinary, and catering management.

Academic Programs *Special study options:* academic remediation for entering students, adult/continuing education programs, advanced placement credit, cooperative education, distance learning, double majors, English as a second language, honors programs, independent study, internships, part-time degree program, services for LD students, student-designed majors, study abroad, summer session for credit. *ROTC:* Army (c).

Library Richard R. Dry Memorial Library with 71,220 titles, 359 serial subscriptions, 8,084 audiovisual materials, an OPAC, a Web page.

Computers on Campus 457 computers available on campus for general student use. A campuswide network can be accessed from off campus. Internet access, online (class) registration, at least one staffed computer lab available.

Student Life *Housing:* college housing not available. *Activities and Organizations:* student-run newspaper, APWA (American Public Works Association),

Dental Hygiene Club, Environmental Awareness Club, Flame and Ice, Future Teachers. *Campus security:* 24-hour emergency response devices and patrols, late-night transport/escort service. *Student services:* health clinic, personal/psychological counseling, women's center.

Athletics Member NJCAA. *Intercollegiate sports:* baseball M, basketball M/W, bowling M/W, cheerleading W, cross-country running M/W, football M, golf M/W, ice hockey M, soccer M/W, softball W, swimming and diving M/W, track and field M/W, volleyball W.

Standardized Tests *Required:* ACT ASSET (for placement). *Recommended:* SAT (for placement), SAT Subject Tests (for placement).

Costs (2004–05) *Tuition:* area resident $2900 full-time, $121 per credit hour part-time; state resident $5800 full-time, $242 per credit hour part-time; nonresident $5800 full-time, $242 per credit hour part-time. *Required fees:* $300 full-time, $5 per credit hour part-time, $30 per term part-time. *Payment plans:* installment, deferred payment. *Waivers:* senior citizens and employees or children of employees.

Financial Aid Of all full-time matriculated undergraduates who enrolled in 2003, 300 Federal Work-Study jobs (averaging $2000).

Applying *Options:* common application, electronic application. *Application fee:* $25. *Required:* high school transcript. *Required for some:* interview. *Application deadline:* rolling (freshmen), rolling (transfers). *Notification:* continuous (freshmen).

Admissions Contact Ms. Petrina Hill-Cheatom, Director of Admissions, Erie Community College, North Campus, 6205 Main Street, Williamsville, NY 14221-7095. *Phone:* 716-851-1588. *Fax:* 716-851-1429.

ERIE COMMUNITY COLLEGE, SOUTH CAMPUS
Orchard Park, New York

- **State and locally supported** 2-year, founded 1974, part of State University of New York System
- **Calendar** 4-1-4 plus summer sessions
- **Degree** certificates, diplomas, and associate
- **Suburban** 20-acre campus with easy access to Buffalo
- **Coed,** 3,793 undergraduate students, 65% full-time, 44% women, 56% men

Undergraduates 2,456 full-time, 1,337 part-time. Students come from 19 states and territories, 4 other countries, 1% are from out of state, 4% African American, 1% Asian American or Pacific Islander, 2% Hispanic American, 1% Native American, 0.2% international, 5% transferred in.

Freshmen *Admission:* 4,778 applied, 4,033 admitted, 921 enrolled. *Test scores:* SAT verbal scores over 500: 33%; SAT math scores over 500: 42%; SAT verbal scores over 600: 3%; SAT math scores over 600: 6%.

Faculty *Total:* 1,191, 31% full-time. *Student/faculty ratio:* 16:1.

Majors Administrative assistant and secretarial science; architectural engineering technology; autobody/collision and repair technology; automobile/automotive mechanics technology; biomedical technology; business administration and management; communication/speech communication and rhetoric; communications systems installation and repair technology; computer technology/computer systems technology; dental laboratory technology; fire services administration; graphic and printing equipment operation/production; humanities; information science/studies; liberal arts and sciences/liberal studies; mechanical drafting and CAD/CADD; office management; parks, recreation and leisure facilities management.

Academic Programs *Special study options:* academic remediation for entering students, adult/continuing education programs, advanced placement credit, cooperative education, distance learning, double majors, English as a second language, honors programs, independent study, internships, part-time degree program, services for LD students, student-designed majors, study abroad, summer session for credit. *ROTC:* Army (c).

Library 57,029 titles, 286 serial subscriptions, 5,401 audiovisual materials, an OPAC, a Web page.

Computers on Campus 434 computers available on campus for general student use. A campuswide network can be accessed from off campus. Internet access, online (class) registration, at least one staffed computer lab available.

Student Life *Housing:* college housing not available. *Activities and Organizations:* student-run newspaper, radio station, Habitat for Humanity, Honors Society, Phi Theta Kappa, Photo Club, Recreation Leadership Club. *Campus security:* 24-hour emergency response devices and patrols, late-night transport/escort service. *Student services:* health clinic, personal/psychological counseling, women's center.

Athletics Member NJCAA. *Intercollegiate sports:* baseball M, basketball M/W, bowling M/W, cheerleading W, cross-country running M/W, football M, golf M/W, ice hockey M, soccer M/W, softball W, swimming and diving M/W, track and field M/W, volleyball W.

Standardized Tests *Required:* ACT ASSET (for placement). *Recommended:* SAT (for placement), SAT Subject Tests (for placement).

Costs (2004–05) *Tuition:* area resident $2900 full-time, $121 per credit hour part-time; state resident $5800 full-time, $242 per credit hour part-time; nonresi-

Erie Community College, South Campus (continued)

dent $5800 full-time, $242 per credit hour part-time. *Required fees:* $300 full-time, $5 per credit hour part-time, $30 per term part-time. *Payment plans:* installment, deferred payment. *Waivers:* senior citizens and employees or children of employees.

Financial Aid Of all full-time matriculated undergraduates who enrolled in 2003, 300 Federal Work-Study jobs (averaging $2000).

Applying *Options:* common application, electronic application. *Application fee:* $25. *Required:* high school transcript. *Required for some:* interview. *Application deadline:* rolling (freshmen), rolling (transfers). *Notification:* continuous (freshmen).

Admissions Contact Ms. Petrina Hill-Cheatom, Director of Admissions, Erie Community College, South Campus, 4041 Southwestern Boulevard, Orchard Park, NY 14127-2199. *Phone:* 716-851-1588. *Fax:* 716-851-1629.

EUGENIO MARIA DE HOSTOS COMMUNITY COLLEGE OF THE CITY UNIVERSITY OF NEW YORK

Bronx, New York

- **State and locally supported** 2-year, founded 1968, part of City University of New York System
- **Calendar** semesters
- **Degree** certificates and associate
- **Urban** 8-acre campus
- **Endowment** $211,655
- **Coed,** 4,340 undergraduate students, 67% full-time, 74% women, 26% men

Undergraduates 2,917 full-time, 1,423 part-time. Students come from 4 states and territories, 91 other countries, 1% are from out of state, 29% African American, 2% Asian American or Pacific Islander, 58% Hispanic American, 0.1% Native American, 8% international, 12% transferred in.

Freshmen *Admission:* 1,316 applied, 1,316 admitted, 772 enrolled.

Faculty *Total:* 329, 50% full-time, 43% with terminal degrees. *Student/faculty ratio:* 14:1.

Majors Accounting; administrative assistant and secretarial science; business administration and management; clinical/medical laboratory technology; data entry/microcomputer applications related; data processing and data processing technology; dental hygiene; electrical and electronic engineering technologies related; gerontology; kindergarten/preschool education; legal assistant/paralegal; liberal arts and sciences/liberal studies; medical administrative assistant and medical secretary; medical radiologic technology; nursing (licensed practical/vocational nurse training); nursing (registered nurse training); public administration.

Academic Programs *Special study options:* academic remediation for entering students, adult/continuing education programs, distance learning, double majors, English as a second language, internships, part-time degree program, services for LD students, study abroad, summer session for credit.

Library Hostos Community College Library with 56,100 titles, 846 serial subscriptions, 710 audiovisual materials, an OPAC, a Web page.

Computers on Campus 800 computers available on campus for general student use. A campuswide network can be accessed from off campus. Internet access, online (class) registration, at least one staffed computer lab available.

Student Life *Housing:* college housing not available. *Activities and Organizations:* student-run newspaper, Dominican Association, Puerto Rican Student Organization, Student Government Association, Black Student Union, Veterans Club. *Campus security:* 24-hour emergency response devices and patrols, late-night transport/escort service. *Student services:* health clinic, personal/psychological counseling, women's center, legal services.

Athletics Member NJCAA. *Intercollegiate sports:* baseball M, basketball M/W, volleyball W. *Intramural sports:* basketball M/W, soccer M/W, volleyball W.

Standardized Tests *Required:* CUNY Skills Assessment Tests (for placement). *Required for some:* SAT (for placement), ACT (for placement), SAT Subject Tests (for placement).

Costs (2005–06) *Tuition:* state resident $2500 full-time, $105 per credit part-time; nonresident $3076 full-time, $130 per credit part-time. *Payment plans:* installment, deferred payment. *Waivers:* senior citizens and employees or children of employees.

Financial Aid Of all full-time matriculated undergraduates who enrolled in 2003, 1,482 Federal Work-Study jobs (averaging $1600).

Applying *Options:* common application. *Application fee:* $65. *Required:* high school transcript. *Application deadline:* rolling (freshmen), rolling (transfers). *Notification:* continuous until 8/15 (freshmen).

Admissions Contact Mr. Roland Velez, Director of Admissions, Eugenio Maria de Hostos Community College of the City University of New York, 120 149th Street, Room D-210, Bronx, NY 10451. *Phone:* 718-518-4406. *Fax:* 718-518-4256. *E-mail:* admissions2@hostos.cuny.edu.

FINGER LAKES COMMUNITY COLLEGE

Canandaigua, New York

- **State and locally supported** 2-year, founded 1965, part of State University of New York System
- **Calendar** semesters
- **Degree** certificates and associate
- **Small-town** 300-acre campus with easy access to Rochester
- **Coed,** 4,884 undergraduate students, 54% full-time, 58% women, 42% men

Undergraduates 2,637 full-time, 2,247 part-time. Students come from 6 states and territories, 3 other countries, 1% are from out of state.

Freshmen *Admission:* 3,805 applied, 2,709 admitted.

Faculty *Total:* 258, 41% full-time. *Student/faculty ratio:* 18:1.

Majors Accounting; administrative assistant and secretarial science; architectural engineering technology; banking and financial support services; biological and physical sciences; biology/biological sciences; biology/biotechnology laboratory technician; broadcast journalism; business administration and management; chemistry; commercial and advertising art; computer and information sciences; computer science; consumer merchandising/retailing management; criminal justice/law enforcement administration; criminal justice/police science; data processing and data processing technology; drafting and design technology; dramatic/theatre arts; engineering science; environmental studies; fine/studio arts; fish/game management; hotel/motel administration; humanities; human services; kindergarten/preschool education; legal assistant/paralegal; liberal arts and sciences/liberal studies; marketing/marketing management; mass communication/media; mathematics; mechanical engineering/mechanical technology; music; natural resources/conservation; natural resources management; natural resources management and policy; nursing (registered nurse training); ornamental horticulture; parks, recreation and leisure facilities management; physical education teaching and coaching; physics; political science and government; pre-engineering; psychology; social sciences; sociology; substance abuse/addiction counseling; tourism and travel services management.

Academic Programs *Special study options:* academic remediation for entering students, advanced placement credit, distance learning, English as a second language, honors programs, internships, off-campus study, part-time degree program, services for LD students, summer session for credit. *ROTC:* Army (c).

Library Charles Meder Library with 73,305 titles, 464 serial subscriptions, an OPAC.

Computers on Campus 425 computers available on campus for general student use. A campuswide network can be accessed from off campus. Internet access, at least one staffed computer lab available.

Student Life *Housing:* college housing not available. *Options:* Campus housing is provided by a third party. *Activities and Organizations:* drama/theater group, student-run newspaper, radio station, choral group, national fraternities, national sororities. *Campus security:* 24-hour emergency response devices and patrols, late-night transport/escort service. *Student services:* health clinic, personal/psychological counseling, legal services.

Athletics Member NJCAA. *Intercollegiate sports:* baseball M, basketball M/W, cross-country running M/W, lacrosse M/W, soccer M/W, softball W. *Intramural sports:* basketball M/W, tennis M/W, volleyball M/W.

Standardized Tests *Recommended:* SAT or ACT (for placement).

Costs (2004–05) *Tuition:* state resident $2750 full-time, $108 per credit hour part-time; nonresident $5500 full-time, $216 per credit hour part-time. *Required fees:* $230 full-time, $15 per credit hour part-time.

Financial Aid Of all full-time matriculated undergraduates who enrolled in 2003, 150 Federal Work-Study jobs (averaging $1800). 150 state and other part-time jobs (averaging $1800).

Applying *Options:* electronic application, early admission, deferred entrance. *Required:* high school transcript. *Recommended:* interview. *Application deadline:* rolling (freshmen), rolling (transfers). *Notification:* continuous until 8/31 (freshmen).

Admissions Contact Ms. Bonnie B. Ritts, Director of Admissions, Finger Lakes Community College, 4355 Lake Shore Drive, Canandaigua, NY 14424-8395. *Phone:* 585-394-3500 Ext. 7278. *Fax:* 585-394-5005. *E-mail:* admissions@flcc.edu.

FIORELLO H. LAGUARDIA COMMUNITY COLLEGE OF THE CITY UNIVERSITY OF NEW YORK

Long Island City, New York

- **State and locally supported** 2-year, founded 1970, part of City University of New York System
- **Calendar** modified semester
- **Degree** certificates and associate
- **Urban** 6-acre campus

■ **Coed**

LaGuardia offers 30 degree programs; day, evening, and weekend classes; a world-renowned internship program; an honors program; a Career and Transfer Center; and strong support services to ensure student success. Recently recognized as one of 13 national Institutions of Excellence by the Policy Center for the First Year of College, LaGuardia, as part of CUNY, also has the lowest college tuition in New York City. Based in Queens, the College is less than 10 minutes from Manhattan and Brooklyn by subway or bus.

Faculty *Student/faculty ratio:* 24:1.

Student Life *Campus security:* 24-hour patrols.

Standardized Tests *Recommended:* SAT or ACT (for placement).

Costs (2004–05) *Tuition:* state resident $2800 full-time, $120 per unit part-time; nonresident $4560 full-time, $190 per unit part-time. *Required fees:* $272 full-time, $64 per term part-time.

Financial Aid Of all full-time matriculated undergraduates who enrolled in 2003, 1,425 Federal Work-Study jobs (averaging $1194).

Applying *Options:* electronic application, early admission, deferred entrance. *Application fee:* $65. *Required:* high school transcript.

Admissions Contact Ms. LaVora Desvigne, Director of Admissions, Fiorello H. LaGuardia Community College of the City University of New York, RM-147, 31-10 Thomson Avenue, Long Island City, NY 11101. *Phone:* 718-482-5114. *Fax:* 718-482-5112. *E-mail:* admissions@lagcc.cuny.edu.

FULTON-MONTGOMERY COMMUNITY COLLEGE

Johnstown, New York

- ■ **State and locally supported** 2-year, founded 1964, part of State University of New York System
- ■ **Calendar** semesters plus winter session
- ■ **Degree** certificates and associate
- ■ **Rural** 195-acre campus
- ■ **Endowment** $1.5 million
- ■ **Coed**, 2,071 undergraduate students, 68% full-time, 58% women, 42% men

Undergraduates 1,404 full-time, 667 part-time. Students come from 2 states and territories, 20 other countries, 4% African American, 0.6% Asian American or Pacific Islander, 5% Hispanic American, 0.3% Native American, 7% international, 2% transferred in.

Freshmen *Admission:* 1,375 applied, 1,375 admitted, 457 enrolled.

Faculty *Total:* 128, 41% full-time, 14% with terminal degrees. *Student/faculty ratio:* 21:1.

Majors Accounting; administrative assistant and secretarial science; art; automobile/automotive mechanics technology; behavioral sciences; biological and physical sciences; biology/biological sciences; business administration and management; carpentry; commercial and advertising art; computer engineering technology; computer science; computer typography and composition equipment operation; construction engineering technology; criminal justice/law enforcement administration; data processing and data processing technology; developmental and child psychology; dramatic/theatre arts; electrical, electronic and communications engineering technology; elementary education; engineering science; English; environmental studies; finance; fine/studio arts; graphic and printing equipment operation/production; health teacher education; history; humanities; human services; information science/studies; kindergarten/preschool education; legal administrative assistant/secretary; liberal arts and sciences/liberal studies; mass communication/media; mathematics; medical administrative assistant and medical secretary; natural resources/conservation; nursing (registered nurse training); physical education teaching and coaching; physical sciences; psychology; social sciences; teacher assistant/aide.

Academic Programs *Special study options:* academic remediation for entering students, accelerated degree program, adult/continuing education programs, advanced placement credit, cooperative education, distance learning, double majors, English as a second language, external degree program, honors programs, independent study, internships, off-campus study, part-time degree program, services for LD students, student-designed majors, study abroad, summer session for credit.

Library Evans Library with 51,517 titles, 143 serial subscriptions, 1,041 audiovisual materials, an OPAC, a Web page.

Computers on Campus 400 computers available on campus for general student use. A campuswide network can be accessed from off campus. Internet access, at least one staffed computer lab available.

Student Life *Housing:* college housing not available. *Activities and Organizations:* drama/theater group, student-run newspaper, choral group, Business Students' Association, Criminal Justice Club, WAU (We Are United), Ski Club. *Campus security:* weekend and night security. *Student services:* personal/psychological counseling.

Athletics Member NJCAA. *Intercollegiate sports:* baseball M, basketball M/W, soccer M/W, softball W, volleyball W. *Intramural sports:* baseball M, basketball M/W, skiing (cross-country) M(c)/W(c), skiing (downhill) M(c)/W(c), volleyball M/W.

Costs (2004–05) *Tuition:* state resident $2800 full-time, $116 per credit hour part-time; nonresident $5600 full-time, $232 per credit hour part-time. Part-time tuition and fees vary according to course load. *Required fees:* $280 full-time, $2 per credit hour part-time, $38 per credit hour part-time. *Payment plans:* installment, deferred payment. *Waivers:* senior citizens and employees or children of employees.

Financial Aid Of all full-time matriculated undergraduates who enrolled in 2003, 87 Federal Work-Study jobs (averaging $1000).

Applying *Options:* common application, electronic application, early admission, deferred entrance. *Required:* high school transcript. *Application deadlines:* 9/10 (freshmen), 9/10 (transfers). *Notification:* continuous (freshmen).

Admissions Contact Ms. Jane Kelley, Associate Dean for Enrollment Management, Fulton-Montgomery Community College, 2805 State Highway 67, Johnstown, NY 12095-3790. *Phone:* 518-762-4651 Ext. 8301. *Fax:* 518-762-4334. *E-mail:* geninfo@fmcc.suny.edu.

GAMLA COLLEGE

Brooklyn, New York

Admissions Contact 1213 Elm Avenue, Brooklyn, NY 11230.

GENESEE COMMUNITY COLLEGE

Batavia, New York

- ■ **State and locally supported** 2-year, founded 1966, part of State University of New York System
- ■ **Calendar** semesters
- ■ **Degree** certificates and associate
- ■ **Small-town** 256-acre campus with easy access to Buffalo
- ■ **Endowment** $890,901
- ■ **Coed**, 5,204 undergraduate students, 48% full-time, 65% women, 35% men

Undergraduates 2,478 full-time, 2,726 part-time. Students come from 13 states and territories, 26 other countries, 1% are from out of state, 4% African American, 2% Asian American or Pacific Islander, 1% Hispanic American, 0.8% Native American, 2% international, 7% transferred in.

Freshmen *Admission:* 3,090 applied, 3,090 admitted, 915 enrolled.

Faculty *Total:* 229, 28% full-time. *Student/faculty ratio:* 20:1.

Majors Accounting; administrative assistant and secretarial science; business administration and management; clinical/medical laboratory technology; commercial and advertising art; computer and information sciences related; computer engineering technology; computer graphics; computer software and media applications related; consumer merchandising/retailing management; criminal justice/law enforcement administration; drafting and design technology; dramatic/theatre arts; education; electrical, electronic and communications engineering technology; elementary education; engineering science; fashion merchandising; gerontology; hotel/motel administration; human services; information science/studies; kindergarten/preschool education; legal assistant/paralegal; liberal arts and sciences/liberal studies; marketing/marketing management; mass communication/media; mathematics; nursing (registered nurse training); occupational therapy; physical education teaching and coaching; physical therapy; psychology; respiratory care therapy; substance abuse/addiction counseling; system administration; tourism and travel services management.

Academic Programs *Special study options:* academic remediation for entering students, adult/continuing education programs, advanced placement credit, cooperative education, distance learning, honors programs, independent study, internships, part-time degree program, services for LD students, summer session for credit. *ROTC:* Army (c).

Library Alfred C. O'Connell Library with 78,273 titles, 332 serial subscriptions, 4,729 audiovisual materials, an OPAC, a Web page.

Computers on Campus 408 computers available on campus for general student use. A campuswide network can be accessed from off campus that provide access to applications software. Internet access, at least one staffed computer lab available.

Student Life *Activities and Organizations:* drama/theater group, student-run newspaper, radio station, choral group, Student Government Association, Phi Theta Kappa, DECA, Student Activities Council, Forum Players. *Campus security:* 24-hour emergency response devices and patrols, late-night transport/escort service. *Student services:* health clinic, personal/psychological counseling.

Athletics Member NJCAA. *Intercollegiate sports:* baseball M, basketball M(s)/W(s), cross-country running M/W, soccer M/W(s), softball W, swimming and diving M/W, volleyball M/W(s). *Intramural sports:* badminton M/W, basketball M/W, football M/W, golf M/W, soccer M/W, softball M/W, swimming and diving M/W, table tennis M/W, tennis M/W, track and field M/W, volleyball M/W, water polo M/W, weight lifting M/W.

Genesee Community College (continued)

Standardized Tests *Required:* ACT ASSET, ACT COMPASS (for placement).

Costs (2005–06) *Tuition:* state resident $3000 full-time; nonresident $3340 full-time. *Required fees:* $290 full-time.

Financial Aid Of all full-time matriculated undergraduates who enrolled in 2003, 135 Federal Work-Study jobs (averaging $1450).

Applying *Options:* common application, electronic application. *Required:* high school transcript. *Required for some:* 1 letter of recommendation. *Application deadline:* rolling (freshmen), rolling (transfers). *Notification:* continuous (freshmen).

Admissions Contact Mrs. Tanya Lane-Martin, Director of Admissions, Genesee Community College, 1 College Road, Batavia, NY 14020. *Phone:* 585-343-0055 Ext. 6413. *Toll-free phone:* 800-CALL GCC. *Fax:* 585-345-6892.

HELENE FULD COLLEGE OF NURSING OF NORTH GENERAL HOSPITAL
New York, New York

Admissions Contact Mrs. Gladys Pineda, Student Services, Helene Fuld College of Nursing of North General Hospital, 1879 Madison Avenue, New York, NY 10035. *Phone:* 212-423-2768.

HERKIMER COUNTY COMMUNITY COLLEGE
Herkimer, New York

- **State and locally supported** 2-year, founded 1966, part of State University of New York System
- **Calendar** semesters
- **Degree** certificates and associate
- **Small-town** 500-acre campus with easy access to Syracuse
- **Endowment** $1.7 million
- **Coed,** 3,477 undergraduate students

Undergraduates Students come from 23 states and territories, 17 other countries, 2% are from out of state, 25% live on campus.

Freshmen *Test scores:* SAT verbal scores over 500: 30%; SAT math scores over 500: 31%; SAT verbal scores over 600: 5%; SAT math scores over 600: 3%; SAT verbal scores over 700: 1%.

Faculty *Total:* 128, 62% full-time, 9% with terminal degrees. *Student/faculty ratio:* 22:1.

Majors Accounting; art; broadcast journalism; business administration and management; computer and information sciences and support services related; computer and information sciences related; computer systems networking and telecommunications; corrections; criminal justice/law enforcement administration; criminal justice/police science; data entry/microcomputer applications; emergency medical technology (EMT paramedic); English; entrepreneurial and small business related; fashion merchandising; fine/studio arts; general studies; health/health care administration; humanities; human resources management; human resources management and services related; human services; international business/trade/commerce; legal assistant/paralegal; liberal arts and sciences/liberal studies; marketing/marketing management; mathematics; photography; physical education teaching and coaching; physical therapy; radio and television; social sciences; telecommunications; tourism and travel services management; tourism and travel services marketing; tourism promotion.

Academic Programs *Special study options:* academic remediation for entering students, adult/continuing education programs, advanced placement credit, English as a second language, honors programs, internships, part-time degree program, services for LD students, summer session for credit.

Library Herkimer County Community College Library with 70,000 titles, 220 serial subscriptions, an OPAC.

Computers on Campus 222 computers available on campus for general student use. A campuswide network can be accessed from off campus. At least one staffed computer lab available.

Student Life *Housing Options:* coed. *Activities and Organizations:* drama/theater group, student-run newspaper, radio and television station, Criminal Justice Club, Travel Club, Student Senate, Physical Therapy Club. *Campus security:* 24-hour emergency response devices and patrols. *Student services:* personal/psychological counseling.

Athletics Member NJCAA. *Intercollegiate sports:* baseball M, basketball M/W, cross-country running M/W, lacrosse M/W, soccer M/W, softball W, swimming and diving M/W, tennis M/W, track and field M/W, volleyball W. *Intramural sports:* baseball M, basketball M/W, lacrosse M, soccer M/W, softball W, swimming and diving M/W, tennis M/W, volleyball M/W.

Standardized Tests *Recommended:* SAT or ACT (for placement).

Financial Aid Of all full-time matriculated undergraduates who enrolled in 2003, 150 Federal Work-Study jobs (averaging $700).

Applying *Options:* early admission. *Required:* high school transcript. *Application deadlines:* 8/20 (freshmen), 8/20 (transfers). *Notification:* continuous (freshmen).

Admissions Contact Mr. Scott J. Hughes, Associate Dean for Enrollment Management, Herkimer County Community College, Herkimer, NY 13350. *Phone:* 315-866-0300 Ext. 278. *Toll-free phone:* 888-464-4222 Ext. 8278. *Fax:* 315-866-0062. *E-mail:* admission@herkimer.edu.

HUDSON VALLEY COMMUNITY COLLEGE
Troy, New York

- **State and locally supported** 2-year, founded 1953, part of State University of New York System
- **Calendar** semesters
- **Degree** certificates and associate
- **Suburban** 135-acre campus
- **Coed,** 11,405 undergraduate students

Undergraduates Students come from 21 states and territories, 18 other countries.

Freshmen *Average high school GPA:* 2.5.

Faculty *Total:* 511, 52% full-time.

Majors Accounting; administrative assistant and secretarial science; automobile/automotive mechanics technology; business administration and management; chemical engineering; chemistry; civil engineering technology; clinical/medical laboratory technology; construction engineering technology; criminal justice/law enforcement administration; data processing and data processing technology; dental hygiene; electrical, electronic and communications engineering technology; emergency medical technology (EMT paramedic); environmental studies; finance; funeral service and mortuary science; heating, air conditioning, ventilation and refrigeration maintenance technology; human services; industrial technology; insurance; interdisciplinary studies; international business/trade/commerce; kindergarten/preschool education; liberal arts and sciences/liberal studies; machine tool technology; marketing/marketing management; mathematics; mechanical engineering/mechanical technology; medical administrative assistant and medical secretary; nursing (registered nurse training); parks, recreation and leisure; physical education teaching and coaching; physician assistant; pre-engineering; radiologic technology/science; real estate; respiratory care therapy; safety/security technology; telecommunications.

Academic Programs *Special study options:* academic remediation for entering students, adult/continuing education programs, advanced placement credit, cooperative education, external degree program, internships, off-campus study, part-time degree program, services for LD students, student-designed majors, summer session for credit. *ROTC:* Army (b), Air Force (c).

Library Marvin Library with 148,189 titles, 691 serial subscriptions.

Computers on Campus 500 computers available on campus for general student use. A campuswide network can be accessed from off campus. Internet access, at least one staffed computer lab available.

Student Life *Housing:* college housing not available. *Activities and Organizations:* drama/theater group, student-run newspaper, radio station. *Campus security:* 24-hour emergency response devices and patrols, late-night transport/escort service. *Student services:* health clinic, personal/psychological counseling, women's center, legal services.

Athletics Member NJCAA. *Intercollegiate sports:* basketball M/W, bowling M/W, cross-country running M/W, football M, golf M/W, lacrosse M, soccer M, tennis M/W, track and field M/W, volleyball W. *Intramural sports:* archery M/W, badminton M/W, baseball M, basketball M/W, bowling M/W, football M, lacrosse M, racquetball M/W, softball W, table tennis M/W, tennis M/W, track and field M/W, volleyball M/W.

Standardized Tests *Required for some:* SAT or ACT (for placement). *Recommended:* SAT or ACT (for placement).

Costs (2005–06) *Tuition:* state resident $2700 full-time, $112 per credit hour part-time; nonresident $8100 full-time, $336 per credit hour part-time. *Required fees:* $480 full-time, $14 per credit hour part-time.

Financial Aid Of all full-time matriculated undergraduates who enrolled in 2003, 100 Federal Work-Study jobs (averaging $2000).

Applying *Options:* early admission, deferred entrance. *Application fee:* $30. *Required:* high school transcript. *Application deadline:* rolling (freshmen), rolling (transfers). *Notification:* continuous (freshmen).

Admissions Contact Ms. MaryClaire Bauer, Director of Admissions, Hudson Valley Community College, 80 Vandenburgh Avenue, Troy, NY 12180-6096. *Phone:* 518-629-4603. *E-mail:* panzajul@hvcc.edu.

INSTITUTE OF DESIGN AND CONSTRUCTION
Brooklyn, New York

Admissions Contact Mr. Kevin Giannetti, Director of Admissions, Institute of Design and Construction, 141 Willoughby Street, Brooklyn, NY 11201-5317. *Phone:* 718-855-3661. *Fax:* 718-852-5889.

INTERBORO INSTITUTE
New York, New York

Admissions Contact Ms. Cheryl Ryan, Director of Admissions, Interboro Institute, 450 West 56th Street, New York, NY 10019. *Phone:* 212-399-0091 Ext. 6406. *Fax:* 212-399-9746. *E-mail:* ryan@interboro.com.

ISLAND DRAFTING AND TECHNICAL INSTITUTE
Amityville, New York

- **Proprietary** 2-year, founded 1957
- **Calendar** semesters
- **Degree** certificates, diplomas, and associate
- **Suburban** campus
- **Coed, primarily men**

Faculty *Student/faculty ratio:* 15:1.
Costs (2004–05) *Tuition:* $10,800 full-time, $360 per credit part-time. No tuition increase for student's term of enrollment. *Required fees:* $350 full-time, $18 per credit part-time.
Applying *Options:* early admission. *Required:* interview. *Recommended:* high school transcript.
Admissions Contact Mr. Gary Weiller, Island Drafting and Technical Institute, 128 Broadway, Amityville, NY 11701. *Phone:* 631-691-8733. *Fax:* 631-691-8738. *E-mail:* info@islanddrafting.com.

ITT TECHNICAL INSTITUTE
Albany, New York

- **Proprietary** 2-year, part of ITT Educational Services, Inc
- **Calendar** quarters
- **Degree** associate
- **Coed**

Standardized Tests *Required:* Wonderlic aptitude test (for admission).
Costs (2004–05) *Tuition:* Please see school catalog for specific information.
Applying *Options:* deferred entrance. *Application fee:* $100. *Required:* high school transcript, interview. *Recommended:* letters of recommendation.
Admissions Contact Mr. John Henebry, Director of Recruitment, ITT Technical Institute, 13 Airline Drive, Albany, NY 12205. *Phone:* 518-452-9300. *Toll-free phone:* 800-489-1191. *Fax:* 518-452-9300.

ITT TECHNICAL INSTITUTE
Getzville, New York

- **Proprietary** 2-year, part of ITT Educational Services, Inc
- **Degree** associate
- **Coed**

Standardized Tests *Required:* Wonderlic aptitude test (for admission).
Costs (2004–05) *Tuition:* Please see school catalog for specific information.
Applying *Options:* deferred entrance. *Application fee:* $100. *Required:* high school transcript, interview. *Recommended:* letters of recommendation.
Admissions Contact Ms. Suzanne Noel, Director of Recruitment, ITT Technical Institute, 2295 Millersport Highway, PO Box 327, Getzville, NY 14068. *Phone:* 716-689-2200. *Toll-free phone:* 800-469-7593. *Fax:* 716-689-2828.

ITT TECHNICAL INSTITUTE
Liverpool, New York

- **Proprietary** 2-year, part of ITT Educational Services, Inc
- **Calendar** semesters
- **Degree** associate
- **Coed**

Standardized Tests *Required:* Wonderlic aptitude test (for admission).
Costs (2004–05) *Tuition:* Please see school catalog for specific information.

Applying *Options:* deferred entrance. *Application fee:* $100. *Required:* high school transcript, interview. *Recommended:* letters of recommendation.
Admissions Contact Terry Riesel, Director of Recruitment, ITT Technical Institute, 235 Greenfield Parkway, Liverpool, NY 13088. *Phone:* 315-461-8000. *Toll-free phone:* 877-488-0011. *Fax:* 315-461-8008.

JAMESTOWN BUSINESS COLLEGE
Jamestown, New York

- **Proprietary** 2-year, founded 1886
- **Calendar** quarters
- **Degree** certificates and associate
- **Small-town** 1-acre campus
- **Coed**

Faculty *Student/faculty ratio:* 24:1.
Student Life *Campus security:* 24-hour emergency response devices.
Costs (2004–05) *Tuition:* $8100 full-time, $225 per credit hour part-time. *Required fees:* $450 full-time, $75 per term part-time.
Applying *Application fee:* $25. *Required:* essay or personal statement, high school transcript, interview.
Admissions Contact Ms. Brenda Salemme, Director of Admissions and Placement, Jamestown Business College, 7 Fairmount Avenue, Jamestown, NY 14701. *Phone:* 716-664-5100. *Fax:* 716-664-3144. *E-mail:* admissions@ jbcny.org.

JAMESTOWN COMMUNITY COLLEGE
Jamestown, New York

- **State and locally supported** 2-year, founded 1950, part of State University of New York System
- **Calendar** semesters
- **Degree** certificates and associate
- **Small-town** 107-acre campus
- **Coed,** 3,274 undergraduate students, 75% full-time, 59% women, 41% men

Undergraduates 2,452 full-time, 822 part-time. Students come from 11 states and territories, 9% are from out of state, 2% African American, 0.7% Asian American or Pacific Islander, 2% Hispanic American, 0.8% Native American.
Freshmen *Admission:* 1,004 enrolled.
Faculty *Total:* 348, 25% full-time, 7% with terminal degrees. *Student/faculty ratio:* 16:1.
Majors Accounting; airline pilot and flight crew; business administration and management; clinical/medical laboratory technology; communication/speech communication and rhetoric; computer and information sciences; computer and information sciences related; computer and information systems security; computer engineering technology; computer science; criminal justice/police science; criminal justice/safety; electrical, electronic and communications engineering technology; electrical, electronics and communications engineering; engineering; fine/studio arts; forestry; heating, air conditioning, ventilation and refrigeration maintenance technology; liberal arts and sciences/liberal studies; mechanical engineering/mechanical technology; music performance; nursing (registered nurse training); occupational therapist assistant; social sciences.
Academic Programs *Special study options:* academic remediation for entering students, adult/continuing education programs, advanced placement credit, cooperative education, distance learning, double majors, honors programs, independent study, internships, off-campus study, part-time degree program, services for LD students, study abroad, summer session for credit.
Library Hultquist Library with 66,808 titles, 370 serial subscriptions, 4,605 audiovisual materials, an OPAC, a Web page.
Computers on Campus 400 computers available on campus for general student use. A campuswide network can be accessed from off campus that provide access to Angel course, management system. Internet access, online (class) registration, at least one staffed computer lab available.
Student Life *Housing:* college housing not available. *Activities and Organizations:* drama/theater group, student-run newspaper, radio station, choral group, Nursing Club, Inter-Varsity Christian Fellowship, Earth Awareness, Adult Student Network, Student Senate. *Student services:* health clinic, personal/psychological counseling.
Athletics Member NJCAA. *Intercollegiate sports:* baseball M, basketball M/W, golf M, soccer M(s)/W, softball W, swimming and diving M/W, volleyball W, wrestling M. *Intramural sports:* basketball M/W, bowling M/W, table tennis M/W, volleyball M/W.
Standardized Tests *Required:* ACT ASSET (for placement).
Costs (2004–05) *One-time required fee:* $60. *Tuition:* state resident $2950 full-time, $123 per credit hour part-time; nonresident $5900 full-time, $224 per credit hour part-time. Full-time tuition and fees vary according to program. *Required fees:* $526 full-time. *Payment plans:* installment, deferred payment. *Waivers:* senior citizens and employees or children of employees.

Jamestown Community College (continued)

Financial Aid Of all full-time matriculated undergraduates who enrolled in 2003, 120 Federal Work-Study jobs (averaging $1000). 110 state and other part-time jobs (averaging $1000).

Applying *Options:* deferred entrance. *Application fee:* $40. *Required:* high school transcript. *Required for some:* standardized test scores. *Application deadline:* rolling (freshmen), rolling (transfers). *Notification:* continuous (freshmen).

Admissions Contact Ms. Wendy Present, Director of Admissions and Recruitment, Jamestown Community College, 525 Falconer Street, PO Box 20, Jamestown, NY 14702-0020. *Phone:* 716-665-5220 Ext. 2240. *Toll-free phone:* 800-388-8557. *E-mail:* admissions@mail.sunyjcc.edu.

JEFFERSON COMMUNITY COLLEGE
Watertown, New York

- **State and locally supported** 2-year, founded 1961, part of State University of New York System
- **Calendar** semesters
- **Degree** certificates and associate
- **Small-town** 90-acre campus with easy access to Syracuse
- **Endowment** $2.3 million
- **Coed,** 3,481 undergraduate students, 54% full-time, 62% women, 38% men

Undergraduates 1,868 full-time, 1,613 part-time. Students come from 26 states and territories, 3 other countries, 1% are from out of state, 5% African American, 1% Asian American or Pacific Islander, 4% Hispanic American, 0.5% Native American, 0.2% international, 4% transferred in.

Freshmen *Admission:* 692 enrolled.

Faculty *Total:* 180, 42% full-time, 9% with terminal degrees. *Student/faculty ratio:* 18:1.

Majors Accounting; administrative assistant and secretarial science; biology/biotechnology laboratory technician; business administration and management; chemical technology; computer science; computer systems networking and telecommunications; computer typography and composition equipment operation; consumer merchandising/retailing management; criminal justice/law enforcement administration; engineering science; forestry technology; hospitality administration; hotel/motel administration; humanities; human services; information science/studies; interdisciplinary studies; kindergarten/preschool education; legal assistant/paralegal; liberal arts and sciences/liberal studies; marketing/marketing management; mathematics; medical administrative assistant and medical secretary; medical laboratory technology; natural sciences; nursing (registered nurse training); pre-engineering; tourism and travel services management.

Academic Programs *Special study options:* academic remediation for entering students, advanced placement credit, cooperative education, distance learning, double majors, honors programs, independent study, internships, part-time degree program, services for LD students, student-designed majors, summer session for credit.

Library Melvil Dewey Library with 62,503 titles, 247 serial subscriptions, 4,097 audiovisual materials, an OPAC, a Web page.

Computers on Campus 354 computers available on campus for general student use. A campuswide network can be accessed. Internet access, at least one staffed computer lab available.

Student Life *Housing:* college housing not available. *Activities and Organizations:* drama/theater group, student-run newspaper, choral group, Student Nursing Association, newspaper, The Melting Pot, Paralegal Club, Criminal Justice Club. *Campus security:* 24-hour emergency response devices and patrols. *Student services:* health clinic, personal/psychological counseling.

Athletics Member NJCAA. *Intercollegiate sports:* baseball M, basketball M/W, golf M/W, lacrosse M/W, soccer M/W, softball W, tennis W, volleyball W. *Intramural sports:* badminton M/W, basketball M/W, soccer M/W, softball M/W, volleyball M/W.

Standardized Tests *Recommended:* SAT or ACT (for admission).

Costs (2004–05) *Tuition:* state resident $2722 full-time, $113 per credit hour part-time; nonresident $4192 full-time, $174 per credit hour part-time. *Required fees:* $282 full-time, $10 per credit hour part-time.

Financial Aid Of all full-time matriculated undergraduates who enrolled in 2003, 125 Federal Work-Study jobs (averaging $1200). 50 state and other part-time jobs (averaging $1000).

Applying *Options:* early admission, deferred entrance. *Required:* high school transcript. *Required for some:* letters of recommendation, interview. *Application deadline:* 9/6 (freshmen), rolling (transfers). *Notification:* continuous (freshmen).

Admissions Contact Ms. Rosanne N. Weir, Director of Admissions, Jefferson Community College, 1220 Coffeen Street, Watertown, NY 13601. *Phone:* 315-786-2277. *Fax:* 315-786-2459. *E-mail:* admissions@sunyjefferson.edu.

KATHARINE GIBBS SCHOOL
Melville, New York

Admissions Contact Ms. Cynthia Gamache, Director of Admissions, Katharine Gibbs School, 320 South Service Road, Melville, NY 11747-3785. *Phone:* 631-370-3307. *Fax:* 516-293-2709.

KATHARINE GIBBS SCHOOL
New York, New York

Admissions Contact Ms. Pat Martin, Admissions Director, Katharine Gibbs School, 50 West 40th Street, New York, NY 10018. *Phone:* 212-867-9300.

KINGSBOROUGH COMMUNITY COLLEGE OF THE CITY UNIVERSITY OF NEW YORK
Brooklyn, New York

- **State and locally supported** 2-year, founded 1963, part of City University of New York System
- **Calendar** semesters
- **Degree** associate
- **Urban** 72-acre campus with easy access to New York City
- **Coed,** 15,357 undergraduate students, 52% full-time, 59% women, 41% men

Undergraduates 7,945 full-time, 7,412 part-time. 2% are from out of state, 34% African American, 8% Asian American or Pacific Islander, 14% Hispanic American, 0.1% Native American, 6% international, 9% transferred in.

Freshmen *Admission:* 3,403 applied, 2,905 admitted, 1,927 enrolled. *Average high school GPA:* 2.70. *Test scores:* SAT verbal scores over 500: 8%; SAT math scores over 500: 12%; SAT verbal scores over 600: 1%; SAT math scores over 600: 2%.

Faculty *Total:* 652, 42% full-time, 40% with terminal degrees. *Student/faculty ratio:* 27:1.

Majors Accounting; administrative assistant and secretarial science; applied art; art; biology/biological sciences; broadcast journalism; business administration and management; chemistry; commercial and advertising art; community health services counseling; computer and information sciences; computer science; data processing and data processing technology; dramatic/theatre arts; early childhood education; education; elementary education; engineering science; fashion merchandising; health and physical education related; human services; journalism; labor and industrial relations; liberal arts and sciences/liberal studies; marine technology; marketing/marketing management; mathematics; mental health/rehabilitation; music; nursing (registered nurse training); parks, recreation and leisure; physical therapist assistant; physical therapy; physics; psychiatric/mental health services technology; sport and fitness administration; teacher assistant/aide; tourism and travel services management.

Academic Programs *Special study options:* academic remediation for entering students, adult/continuing education programs, advanced placement credit, English as a second language, honors programs, internships, off-campus study, part-time degree program, services for LD students, student-designed majors, summer session for credit.

Library Robert J. Kibbee Library with 185,912 titles, 458 serial subscriptions, 2,388 audiovisual materials, an OPAC.

Computers on Campus 900 computers available on campus for general student use. A campuswide network can be accessed. Internet access, at least one staffed computer lab available.

Student Life *Housing:* college housing not available. *Activities and Organizations:* drama/theater group, student-run newspaper, radio station, choral group, Peer Advisors, Caribbean Club, DECA. *Campus security:* 24-hour emergency response devices and patrols. *Student services:* health clinic, personal/psychological counseling, women's center.

Athletics Member NJCAA. *Intercollegiate sports:* baseball M, basketball M/W, soccer M, softball W, tennis M/W, track and field M/W, volleyball W. *Intramural sports:* baseball M, basketball M/W, soccer M, softball W, tennis M/W, track and field M/W, volleyball W.

Costs (2005–06) *Tuition:* state resident $2800 full-time, $120 per credit part-time; nonresident $4560 full-time, $190 per credit part-time. *Required fees:* $280 full-time, $70 per term part-time. *Payment plan:* installment. *Waivers:* senior citizens.

Applying *Options:* common application. *Application fee:* $50. *Required:* high school transcript. *Application deadline:* 8/23 (freshmen), rolling (transfers).

Admissions Contact Mr. Robert Ingenito, Director of Admissions Information Center, Kingsborough Community College of the City University of New York, 2001 Oriental Boulevard, Brooklyn, NY 11235. *Phone:* 718-368-4600. *E-mail:* info@kbcc.cuny.edu.

LONG ISLAND BUSINESS INSTITUTE
Commack, New York

- **Proprietary** 2-year, founded 1968
- **Calendar** trimesters
- **Degree** certificates, diplomas, and associate
- **Suburban** campus with easy access to New York City
- **Coed, primarily women,** 261 undergraduate students, 40% full-time, 93% women, 7% men

Undergraduates 104 full-time, 157 part-time. Students come from 1 other state, 13% African American, 2% Asian American or Pacific Islander, 8% Hispanic American.
Freshmen *Admission:* 36 applied, 36 admitted, 36 enrolled.
Faculty *Total:* 21, 19% full-time. *Student/faculty ratio:* 15:1.
Majors Accounting; administrative assistant and secretarial science; business administration and management; court reporting.
Academic Programs *Special study options:* academic remediation for entering students, adult/continuing education programs, advanced placement credit, independent study, internships, part-time degree program, summer session for credit.
Library Mendon W. Smith Memorial Library with 1,484 titles, 15 serial subscriptions, 184 audiovisual materials, an OPAC.
Computers on Campus 77 computers available on campus for general student use. Internet access, at least one staffed computer lab available.
Student Life *Housing:* college housing not available. *Campus security:* 24-hour emergency response devices. *Student services:* personal/psychological counseling.
Standardized Tests *Required:* CPAt (for placement).
Costs (2005–06) *Tuition:* $8500 full-time, $275 per credit part-time. Full-time tuition and fees vary according to course load and program. Part-time tuition and fees vary according to course load and program. *Required fees:* $400 full-time, $50 per year part-time. *Payment plans:* installment, deferred payment.
Applying *Application fee:* $50. *Required:* essay or personal statement, high school transcript, interview. *Application deadline:* rolling (freshmen), rolling (transfers).
Admissions Contact Ms. Shannon Paul, Admissions Representative, Long Island Business Institute, 6500 Jericho Turnpike, Commack, NY 11725. *Phone:* 631-499-7100. *Fax:* 631-499-7114.

LONG ISLAND COLLEGE HOSPITAL SCHOOL OF NURSING
Brooklyn, New York

Admissions Contact Ms. Barbara J. Evans, Admissions Assistant, Long Island College Hospital School of Nursing, 397 Hicks Street, Brooklyn, NY 11201-5940. *Phone:* 718-780-1898. *Fax:* 718-780-1936.

MARIA COLLEGE
Albany, New York

- **Independent** 2-year, founded 1958
- **Calendar** semesters
- **Degree** certificates and associate
- **Urban** 9-acre campus
- **Coed,** 788 undergraduate students, 35% full-time, 87% women, 13% men

Clinical facilities for nursing, physical therapist studies, and occupational therapy assistant studies majors are among the institutional leaders. Laboratory school for education majors is among the finest in the Capital District. Liberal arts, early childhood education, and business majors are highly transferable. Also offered are associate degrees in computer information systems and legal assistant studies. One-year certificate programs include legal assistant studies, bereavement studies, complementary therapy, and gerontology.

Undergraduates 277 full-time, 511 part-time. Students come from 5 states and territories, 4 other countries, 2% are from out of state, 20% African American, 2% Asian American or Pacific Islander, 3% Hispanic American, 0.5% Native American, 0.5% international, 30% transferred in.
Freshmen *Admission:* 232 applied, 168 admitted, 84 enrolled. *Average high school GPA:* 2.53.
Faculty *Total:* 65, 45% full-time, 17% with terminal degrees. *Student/faculty ratio:* 10:1.
Majors Accounting; business administration and management; computer/information technology services administration related; kindergarten/preschool education; legal assistant/paralegal; legal studies; liberal arts and sciences/liberal studies; nursing (licensed practical/vocational nurse training); nursing (registered nurse training); occupational therapist assistant; physical therapist assistant; science technologies related.

Academic Programs *Special study options:* academic remediation for entering students, adult/continuing education programs, advanced placement credit, independent study, off-campus study, part-time degree program, services for LD students, summer session for credit. *ROTC:* Air Force (c).
Library Maria College Library with 56,746 titles, 160 serial subscriptions, 375 audiovisual materials, an OPAC, a Web page.
Computers on Campus 78 computers available on campus for general student use. A campuswide network can be accessed. Internet access, online (class) registration, at least one staffed computer lab available.
Student Life *Housing:* college housing not available. *Campus security:* late-night transport/escort service. *Student services:* personal/psychological counseling.
Standardized Tests *Required:* SAT or ACT (for admission).
Costs (2004–05) *Tuition:* $7100 full-time, $260 per credit part-time. Full-time tuition and fees vary according to program. Part-time tuition and fees vary according to program. *Required fees:* $160 full-time, $40 per term part-time. *Payment plan:* installment.
Financial Aid Of all full-time matriculated undergraduates who enrolled in 2003, 25 Federal Work-Study jobs (averaging $1000).
Applying *Options:* early admission. *Application fee:* $35. *Required:* essay or personal statement, high school transcript, minimum 2.0 GPA, 1 letter of recommendation, interview. *Application deadlines:* 8/26 (freshmen), 8/26 (transfers).
Admissions Contact Ms. Laurie A. Gilmore, Director of Admissions, Maria College, 700 New Scotland Avenue, Albany, NY 12208. *Phone:* 518-438-3111 Ext. 217. *Fax:* 518-453-1366. *E-mail:* admissions@mariacollege.edu.

▶ **See page 520 for a narrative description.**

MEMORIAL HOSPITAL SCHOOL OF NURSING
Albany, New York

Admissions Contact 600 Northern Boulevard, Albany, NY 12204.

MILDRED ELLEY
Latham, New York

- **Private** 2-year
- **Degree** certificates, diplomas, and associate
- **Suburban** campus with easy access to Albany
- 394 undergraduate students, 100% full-time
- 98% of applicants were admitted

Faculty *Student/faculty ratio:* 20:1.
Standardized Tests *Required:* CPAt (for admission).
Costs (2004–05) *Tuition:* $7800 full-time, $325 per credit part-time. Full-time tuition and fees vary according to program. *Required fees:* $300 full-time.
Admissions Contact Mr. Michael Cahalan, Enrollment Manager, Mildred Elley, 800 New Loudon Road, Suite 5120, Latham, NY 12110. *Phone:* 518-786-3171 Ext. 227. *Toll-free phone:* 800-622-6327. *Fax:* 518-786-0011. *E-mail:* michael.cahalan@mildred-elley.edu.

MOHAWK VALLEY COMMUNITY COLLEGE
Utica, New York

- **State and locally supported** 2-year, founded 1946, part of State University of New York System
- **Calendar** semesters
- **Degree** certificates and associate
- **Suburban** 80-acre campus
- **Endowment** $2.8 million
- **Coed,** 6,068 undergraduate students, 63% full-time, 53% women, 47% men

Undergraduates 3,851 full-time, 2,217 part-time. Students come from 18 states and territories, 11 other countries, 1% are from out of state, 6% African American, 2% Asian American or Pacific Islander, 3% Hispanic American, 0.9% Native American, 1% international, 5% transferred in, 6% live on campus. *Retention:* 58% of 2002 full-time freshmen returned.
Freshmen *Admission:* 3,337 applied, 3,030 admitted, 1,479 enrolled.
Faculty *Total:* 309, 45% full-time. *Student/faculty ratio:* 23:1.
Majors Accounting technology and bookkeeping; administrative assistant and secretarial science; advertising; airframe mechanics and aircraft maintenance technology; art; banking and financial support services; building/property maintenance and management; business administration and management; chemical technology; civil engineering technology; commercial and advertising art; com-

Mohawk Valley Community College (continued)

mercial photography; communications systems installation and repair technology; community organization and advocacy; computer and information sciences; computer and information sciences and support services related; computer programming; criminal justice/law enforcement administration; design and applied arts related; drafting and design technology; dramatic/theatre arts; electrical and electronic engineering technologies related; electrical, electronic and communications engineering technology; electrical/electronics maintenance and repair technology related; emergency medical technology (EMT paramedic); engineering; entrepreneurship; food services technology; foodservice systems administration; health information/medical records technology; heating, air conditioning and refrigeration technology; hotel/motel administration; humanities; human services; industrial production technologies related; liberal arts and sciences/liberal studies; management information systems and services related; mechanical design technology; mechanical engineering/mechanical technology; medical/clinical assistant; medical laboratory technology; medical radiologic technology; mental health/rehabilitation; nursing (registered nurse training); nutrition sciences; parks, recreation and leisure facilities management; pre-engineering; public administration; respiratory care therapy; restaurant, culinary, and catering management; substance abuse/addiction counseling; survey technology; telecommunications.

Academic Programs *Special study options:* academic remediation for entering students, adult/continuing education programs, advanced placement credit, distance learning, double majors, English as a second language, honors programs, independent study, internships, off-campus study, part-time degree program, services for LD students, student-designed majors, study abroad, summer session for credit. *ROTC:* Army (c).

Library Mohawk Valley Community College Library plus 2 others with 91,000 titles, 925 serial subscriptions, an OPAC, a Web page.

Computers on Campus 380 computers available on campus for general student use. A campuswide network can be accessed from off campus. Internet access, online (class) registration, at least one staffed computer lab available.

Student Life *Housing Options:* coed. Freshman campus housing is guaranteed. *Activities and Organizations:* drama/theater group, student-run newspaper, radio station, choral group, Drama Club, Student Congress, Returning Adult Student Association, Black Student Union, Program Board. *Campus security:* 24-hour emergency response devices and patrols, late-night transport/escort service, controlled dormitory access. *Student services:* health clinic, personal/psychological counseling.

Athletics Member NJCAA. *Intercollegiate sports:* baseball M, basketball M/W, bowling M/W, cross-country running M/W, golf M/W, ice hockey M, lacrosse M, soccer M/W, softball W, tennis M/W, track and field M/W, volleyball W. *Intramural sports:* basketball M/W, cheerleading W, football M, racquetball M/W, softball M/W, table tennis M/W, tennis M/W, volleyball M/W, weight lifting M.

Costs (2004–05) *Tuition:* state resident $2850 full-time, $115 per credit hour part-time; nonresident $5700 full-time, $230 per credit hour part-time. Part-time tuition and fees vary according to course load. *Required fees:* $344 full-time, $1 per credit hour part-time, $35 per term part-time. *Room and board:* $6470; room only: $3730. Room and board charges vary according to board plan. *Payment plans:* installment, deferred payment. *Waivers:* employees or children of employees.

Financial Aid Of all full-time matriculated undergraduates who enrolled in 2003, 229 Federal Work-Study jobs (averaging $1750).

Applying *Options:* electronic application, early admission, early decision, deferred entrance. *Required:* high school transcript. *Application deadline:* rolling (freshmen), rolling (transfers).

Admissions Contact Mrs. Sandra Fiebiger, Electronic Data Processing Clerk, Admissions, Mohawk Valley Community College, 1101 Sherman Drive, Utica, NY 13501. *Phone:* 315-792-5640. *Toll-free phone:* 800-SEE-MVCC. *Fax:* 315-792-5527. *E-mail:* admissions@mvcc.edu.

► **See page 530 for a narrative description.**

MONROE COLLEGE
Bronx, New York

■ **Proprietary** primarily 2-year, founded 1933
■ **Calendar** trimesters
■ **Degrees** associate and bachelor's
■ **Urban** campus
■ **Coed,** 4,284 undergraduate students, 89% full-time, 72% women, 28% men

Monroe is a private, coeducational institution that offers associate and bachelor's (2+2) degrees, with New York City and Westchester County campuses. Programs encompass a variety of majors that develop the student's career. Monroe's dynamic faculty members and strong support services foster professional development opportunities for students. At Monroe, the focus is on each student's future.

Undergraduates 3,818 full-time, 466 part-time. Students come from 7 states and territories, 8 other countries, 1% are from out of state, 42% African American, 1% Asian American or Pacific Islander, 52% Hispanic American,

0.1% Native American, 1% international, 7% transferred in, 1% live on campus. *Retention:* 43% of 2002 full-time freshmen returned.

Freshmen *Admission:* 1,470 applied, 1,112 admitted, 966 enrolled.

Faculty *Total:* 201, 33% full-time, 18% with terminal degrees. *Student/faculty ratio:* 21:1.

Majors Accounting; business administration and management; computer science; criminal justice/law enforcement administration; criminal justice/police science; hospitality administration; information science/studies; medical administrative assistant and medical secretary.

Academic Programs *Special study options:* academic remediation for entering students, adult/continuing education programs, cooperative education, English as a second language, internships, part-time degree program, summer session for credit.

Library Main Library plus 1 other with 28,000 titles, 301 serial subscriptions, an OPAC, a Web page.

Computers on Campus 541 computers available on campus for general student use. A campuswide network can be accessed. Internet access, at least one staffed computer lab available.

Student Life *Housing Options:* coed. Campus housing is university owned and leased by the school. Freshman applicants given priority for college housing. *Activities and Organizations:* drama/theater group, student-run newspaper. *Campus security:* late-night transport/escort service. *Student services:* personal/psychological counseling.

Athletics Member NJCAA. *Intercollegiate sports:* basketball M/W, soccer M, softball W, volleyball W. *Intramural sports:* basketball M/W, bowling M/W, cheerleading W.

Costs (2004–05) *Comprehensive fee:* $23,370 includes full-time tuition ($8760), mandatory fees ($600), and room and board ($14,010). Full-time tuition and fees vary according to course load. Part-time tuition: $365 per credit. *Required fees:* $150 per term part-time. *Room and board:* Room and board charges vary according to housing facility. *Payment plan:* installment. *Waivers:* adult students.

Financial Aid Of all full-time matriculated undergraduates who enrolled in 2003, 132 Federal Work-Study jobs (averaging $3100).

Applying *Options:* early admission, deferred entrance. *Application fee:* $35. *Required:* high school transcript, interview. *Application deadlines:* 8/26 (freshmen), 8/26 (transfers). *Notification:* continuous until 9/3 (freshmen).

Admissions Contact Mr. Brad Allison, Director of Admissions, Monroe College, Monroe College Way, 2501 Jerome Avenue, Bronx, NY 10468. *Phone:* 718-933-6700 Ext. 536. *Toll-free phone:* 800-55MONROE.

MONROE COLLEGE
New Rochelle, New York

■ **Proprietary** primarily 2-year, founded 1983
■ **Calendar** trimesters
■ **Degrees** associate and bachelor's
■ **Suburban** campus with easy access to New York City
■ **Coed,** 1,570 undergraduate students, 85% full-time, 69% women, 31% men

Undergraduates 1,334 full-time, 236 part-time. Students come from 9 states and territories, 10 other countries, 2% are from out of state, 64% African American, 0.7% Asian American or Pacific Islander, 14% Hispanic American, 0.1% Native American, 13% international, 9% transferred in, 20% live on campus. *Retention:* 46% of 2002 full-time freshmen returned.

Freshmen *Admission:* 642 applied, 469 admitted, 441 enrolled.

Faculty *Total:* 201, 33% full-time, 18% with terminal degrees. *Student/faculty ratio:* 20:1.

Majors Accounting; business administration and management; computer science; corrections and criminal justice related; hospitality administration; information science/studies; medical administrative assistant and medical secretary.

Academic Programs *Special study options:* academic remediation for entering students, adult/continuing education programs, cooperative education, English as a second language, external degree program, internships, part-time degree program, summer session for credit.

Library Main Library plus 1 other with 8,400 titles, 211 serial subscriptions.

Computers on Campus 214 computers available on campus for general student use. A campuswide network can be accessed from student residence rooms. Internet access, at least one staffed computer lab available.

Student Life *Housing Options:* coed. Campus housing is university owned and leased by the school. Freshman applicants given priority for college housing. *Activities and Organizations:* drama/theater group, student-run newspaper. *Campus security:* late-night transport/escort service. *Student services:* personal/psychological counseling.

Athletics Member NJCAA. *Intercollegiate sports:* baseball M, basketball M/W, soccer M, softball W, volleyball W. *Intramural sports:* basketball M/W, bowling M/W, cheerleading W, soccer M, volleyball M/W.

Costs (2004–05) *Comprehensive fee:* $23,370 includes full-time tuition ($8760), mandatory fees ($600), and room and board ($14,010). Part-time tuition: $1095 per course. *Required fees:* $150 per term part-time. *Room and board:* Room and board charges vary according to board plan.

Financial Aid Of all full-time matriculated undergraduates who enrolled in 2003, 50 Federal Work-Study jobs (averaging $4000).

Applying *Options:* common application, electronic application, early admission, deferred entrance. *Application fee:* $35. *Required:* high school transcript, interview. *Application deadlines:* 8/26 (freshmen), 8/26 (transfers). *Notification:* continuous until 9/3 (freshmen).

Admissions Contact Ms. Lisa Scorca, High School Admissions, Monroe College, 434 Main Street, New Rochelle, NY 10801. *Phone:* 914-632-5400 Ext. 407. *Toll-free phone:* 800-55MONROE. *E-mail:* ejerome@monroecollege.edu.

MONROE COMMUNITY COLLEGE
Rochester, New York

Admissions Contact Mr. Anthony Felicetti, Associate Vice President, Enrollment Management, Monroe Community College, 1000 East Henrietta Road, Rochester, NY 14623-5780. *Phone:* 585-292-2000 Ext. 2221. *Fax:* 585-292-3860. *E-mail:* admissions@monroecc.edu.

NASSAU COMMUNITY COLLEGE
Garden City, New York

■ **State and locally supported** 2-year, founded 1959, part of State University of New York System
■ **Calendar** semesters
■ **Degree** certificates and associate
■ **Suburban** 225-acre campus with easy access to New York City
■ **Coed,** 21,446 undergraduate students, 64% full-time, 54% women, 46% men

Undergraduates 13,788 full-time, 7,658 part-time. 18% African American, 5% Asian American or Pacific Islander, 12% Hispanic American, 0.3% Native American, 5% international, 9% transferred in.

Freshmen *Admission:* 7,838 applied, 7,203 admitted, 5,275 enrolled.

Faculty *Total:* 1,407, 75% with terminal degrees. *Student/faculty ratio:* 18:1.

Majors Accounting; accounting technology and bookkeeping; administrative assistant and secretarial science; African-American/Black studies; art; business administration and management; civil engineering technology; clinical/medical laboratory technology; commercial and advertising art; communication/speech communication and rhetoric; computer and information sciences; computer and information sciences related; computer graphics; computer science; computer systems networking and telecommunications; criminal justice/law enforcement administration; criminal justice/safety; dance; data processing and data processing technology; design and visual communications; dramatic/theatre arts; engineering; entrepreneurship; fashion/apparel design; fashion merchandising; funeral service and mortuary science; general retailing/wholesaling; general studies; health science; hotel/motel administration; instrumentation technology; insurance; interior design; kindergarten/preschool education; legal administrative assistant/secretary; legal assistant/paralegal; liberal arts and sciences/liberal studies; management information systems; marketing/marketing management; mass communication/media; mathematics; medical administrative assistant and medical secretary; medical radiologic technology; music performance; nursing (registered nurse training); photography; physical therapist assistant; real estate; rehabilitation therapy; respiratory care therapy; security and loss prevention; surgical technology; theatre design and technology; transportation technology; visual and performing arts.

Academic Programs *Special study options:* academic remediation for entering students, adult/continuing education programs, advanced placement credit, cooperative education, distance learning, English as a second language, honors programs, internships, off-campus study, part-time degree program, services for LD students, summer session for credit. *ROTC:* Army (c).

Library A. Holly Patterson Library with 171,938 titles, 753 serial subscriptions, 55,514 audiovisual materials, an OPAC, a Web page.

Computers on Campus 700 computers available on campus for general student use. A campuswide network can be accessed from off campus. At least one staffed computer lab available.

Student Life *Housing:* college housing not available. *Activities and Organizations:* drama/theater group, student-run newspaper, radio station, choral group, Student Organization of Latinos, Student Government Association, Programming Board, Caribbean Student Organization, NYPIRG. *Campus security:* 24-hour emergency response devices and patrols, late-night transport/escort service. *Student services:* health clinic, personal/psychological counseling, women's center.

Athletics Member NJCAA. *Intercollegiate sports:* baseball M, basketball M/W, bowling M/W, cheerleading W, cross-country running M/W, equestrian sports M/W, football M, golf M/W, lacrosse M, soccer M/W, softball W, tennis M/W, track and field M/W, volleyball M/W, wrestling M. *Intramural sports:* badminton M/W, basketball M/W, cross-country running M/W, football M, ice hockey M, lacrosse M/W, racquetball M/W, soccer M/W, softball M/W, table tennis M/W, tennis M/W, volleyball M/W.

Standardized Tests *Recommended:* SAT or ACT (for admission).

Costs (2004–05) *Tuition:* state resident $2900 full-time, $121 per credit part-time; nonresident $5800 full-time, $242 per credit part-time. *Required fees:* $242 full-time. *Payment plan:* installment.

Financial Aid Of all full-time matriculated undergraduates who enrolled in 2003, 400 Federal Work-Study jobs (averaging $3300).

Applying *Options:* deferred entrance. *Application fee:* $30. *Required:* high school transcript. *Required for some:* minimum 3.0 GPA, interview. *Recommended:* minimum 2.0 GPA. *Application deadlines:* 8/1 (freshmen), 8/1 (transfers). *Notification:* continuous (freshmen).

Admissions Contact Mr. Craig Wright, Vice President of Student Academic Affairs, Nassau Community College, One Education Drive, Garden City, NY 11530. *Phone:* 516-572-7345. *E-mail:* admissions@sunynassau.edu.

NEW YORK CAREER INSTITUTE
New York, New York

Admissions Contact Ms. Cindy McMahon, Enrollment Coordinator, New York Career Institute, 15 Park Row, 4th Floor, New York, NY 10038-2301. *Phone:* 212-962-0002 Ext. 101.

NEW YORK CITY COLLEGE OF TECHNOLOGY OF THE CITY UNIVERSITY OF NEW YORK
Brooklyn, New York

Admissions Contact Mr. Joseph Lento, Director of Admissions, New York City College of Technology of the City University of New York, 300 Jay Street, Brooklyn, NY 11201-2983. *Phone:* 718-260-5500. *E-mail:* jlento@nyctc.cuny.edu.

NEW YORK COLLEGE OF HEALTH PROFESSIONS
Syosset, New York

■ **Independent** founded 1981
■ **Calendar** trimesters
■ **Degrees** associate, incidental bachelor's, and master's
■ **Suburban** campus with easy access to New York City
■ **Coed**

Student Life *Campus security:* 24-hour patrols, security guard evening and weekend hours.

Costs (2004–05) *Tuition:* $9900 full-time, $275 per credit part-time. *Required fees:* $400 full-time.

Financial Aid Of all full-time matriculated undergraduates who enrolled in 2003, 15 Federal Work-Study jobs.

Applying *Options:* common application, electronic application, deferred entrance. *Application fee:* $85. *Required:* high school transcript, minimum 2.5 GPA, interview.

Admissions Contact Dr. Mary Rodas, Director of Admissions, New York College of Health Professions, 6801 Jericho Turnpike, Syosset, NY 11791. *Phone:* 800-922-7337 Ext. 354. *Toll-free phone:* 800-922-7337 Ext. 351. *E-mail:* admission@nycollege.edu.

▶ **See page 536 for a narrative description.**

NIAGARA COUNTY COMMUNITY COLLEGE
Sanborn, New York

■ **State and locally supported** 2-year, founded 1962, part of State University of New York System
■ **Calendar** semesters
■ **Degree** certificates and associate
■ **Rural** 287-acre campus with easy access to Buffalo
■ **Endowment** $1.7 million
■ **Coed,** 5,546 undergraduate students, 63% full-time, 59% women, 41% men

Undergraduates 3,505 full-time, 2,041 part-time. Students come from 15 states and territories, 1% are from out of state, 7% African American, 1% Asian American or Pacific Islander, 1% Hispanic American, 1% Native American, 0.6% international, 5% transferred in.

Freshmen *Admission:* 2,344 applied, 2,076 admitted, 1,387 enrolled. *Average high school GPA:* 2.48.

Faculty *Total:* 299, 45% full-time, 13% with terminal degrees. *Student/faculty ratio:* 18:1.

Niagara County Community College (continued)

Majors Accounting; administrative assistant and secretarial science; animal sciences; biochemical technology; biological and physical sciences; business administration and management; computer science; consumer merchandising/retailing management; criminal justice/law enforcement administration; culinary arts; design and applied arts related; drafting and design technology; dramatic/theatre arts; electrical, electronic and communications engineering technology; electroneurodiagnostic/electroencephalographic technology; fine/studio arts; general studies; humanities; human services; information science/studies; liberal arts and sciences/liberal studies; mass communication/media; mathematics; mechanical design technology; medical/clinical assistant; music; natural resources/conservation; nursing (registered nurse training); occupational health and industrial hygiene; physical education teaching and coaching; physical therapist assistant; radiologic technology/science; social sciences; surgical technology; telecommunications.

Academic Programs *Special study options:* academic remediation for entering students, adult/continuing education programs, advanced placement credit, cooperative education, double majors, honors programs, independent study, internships, off-campus study, part-time degree program, services for LD students, student-designed majors, study abroad, summer session for credit. *ROTC:* Army (c).

Library Library Learning Center with 93,055 titles, 524 serial subscriptions, 20,207 audiovisual materials, an OPAC, a Web page.

Computers on Campus 414 computers available on campus for general student use. A campuswide network can be accessed. Internet access, at least one staffed computer lab available.

Student Life *Housing:* college housing not available. *Activities and Organizations:* drama/theater group, student-run newspaper, radio station, choral group, student radio station, Student Nurses Association, Phi Theta Kappa, Alpha Beta Gamma, Physical Education Club. *Campus security:* student patrols, late-night transport/escort service, emergency telephones. *Student services:* health clinic, personal/psychological counseling.

Athletics Member NJCAA. *Intercollegiate sports:* baseball M, basketball M(s)/W, golf M/W, soccer M/W, softball W, volleyball W, wrestling M(s). *Intramural sports:* basketball M/W, bowling M/W, cheerleading W, skiing (cross-country) M(c)/W(c), volleyball M/W.

Costs (2004–05) *Tuition:* state resident $2976 full-time, $124 per credit hour part-time; nonresident $4464 full-time, $186 per credit hour part-time. Full-time tuition and fees vary according to program. Part-time tuition and fees vary according to program. *Required fees:* $294 full-time, $60 per term part-time. *Payment plan:* installment. *Waivers:* employees or children of employees.

Financial Aid Of all full-time matriculated undergraduates who enrolled in 2003, 139 Federal Work-Study jobs (averaging $1108). 102 state and other part-time jobs (averaging $490).

Applying *Options:* electronic application, early admission. *Required:* high school transcript. *Required for some:* minimum 2.0 GPA. *Notification:* continuous until 8/31 (freshmen).

Admissions Contact Ms. Kathy Saunders, Director of Enrollment Services, Niagara County Community College, 3111 Saunders Settlement Road, Sanborn, NY 14132. *Phone:* 716-614-6201. *Fax:* 716-614-6820. *E-mail:* admissions@niagaracc.suny.edu.

NORTH COUNTRY COMMUNITY COLLEGE
Saranac Lake, New York

- **State and locally supported** 2-year, founded 1967, part of State University of New York System
- **Calendar** semesters
- **Degree** certificates and associate
- **Rural** 100-acre campus
- **Coed,** 1,407 undergraduate students, 70% full-time, 64% women, 36% men

Undergraduates 983 full-time, 424 part-time. Students come from 13 states and territories, 4 other countries, 3% are from out of state, 2% African American, 0.5% Asian American or Pacific Islander, 0.9% Hispanic American, 3% Native American, 1% international, 9% transferred in, 7% live on campus.

Freshmen *Admission:* 818 applied, 662 admitted, 359 enrolled. *Test scores:* SAT verbal scores over 500: 29%; SAT math scores over 500: 31%; ACT scores over 18: 64%; SAT verbal scores over 600: 2%; SAT math scores over 600: 2%; ACT scores over 24: 8%; SAT verbal scores over 700: 1%.

Faculty *Total:* 111, 35% full-time, 13% with terminal degrees. *Student/faculty ratio:* 17:1.

Majors Biological and physical sciences; business administration and management; computer graphics; consumer merchandising/retailing management; criminal justice/safety; interdisciplinary studies; kinesiology and exercise science; liberal arts and sciences/liberal studies; mathematics; medical radiologic technology; mental health/rehabilitation; nursing (registered nurse training); office occupations and clerical services; parks, recreation and leisure facilities management.

Academic Programs *Special study options:* academic remediation for entering students, advanced placement credit, distance learning, double majors, internships, part-time degree program, services for LD students, student-designed majors, summer session for credit.

Library North Country Community College Library with 58,556 titles, 177 serial subscriptions, 1,217 audiovisual materials.

Computers on Campus 140 computers available on campus for general student use. Internet access, at least one staffed computer lab available.

Student Life *Housing Options:* coed. Campus housing is university owned. *Activities and Organizations:* drama/theater group, student-run newspaper, Student Government Association, Wilderness Recreation Club, Nursing Club, Radiology Club, Criminal Justice Club. *Student services:* personal/psychological counseling.

Athletics Member NJCAA. *Intercollegiate sports:* basketball M/W, ice hockey M, soccer M/W, softball W, volleyball W. *Intramural sports:* archery M/W, badminton M/W, basketball M/W, bowling M/W, football M/W, soccer M/W, softball M/W, swimming and diving M/W, tennis M/W, volleyball M/W, weight lifting M/W.

Standardized Tests *Recommended:* SAT or ACT (for admission).

Costs (2005–06) *One-time required fee:* $35. *Tuition:* state resident $3050 full-time, $140 per credit hour part-time; nonresident $6100 full-time, $280 per credit hour part-time. *Required fees:* $605 full-time, $24 per credit hour part-time. *Room and board:* $3850; room only: $3080. *Payment plan:* installment. *Waivers:* senior citizens and employees or children of employees.

Financial Aid Of all full-time matriculated undergraduates who enrolled in 2003, 104 Federal Work-Study jobs (averaging $1164). 27 state and other part-time jobs (averaging $1600).

Applying *Options:* electronic application, early admission, early decision, deferred entrance. *Required:* high school transcript. *Recommended:* essay or personal statement, 1 letter of recommendation, interview. *Application deadline:* rolling (freshmen), rolling (transfers). *Early decision:* 11/15. *Notification:* continuous (freshmen), 12/15 (early decision).

Admissions Contact Enrollment Management Assistant, North Country Community College, 23 Santanoni Avenue, PO Box 89, Saranac Lake, NY 12983-0089. *Phone:* 518-891-2915 Ext. 686. *Toll-free phone:* 888-TRY-NCCC Ext. 233. *Fax:* 518-891-0898. *E-mail:* info@nccc.edu.

OLEAN BUSINESS INSTITUTE
Olean, New York

Admissions Contact Ms. Lori Kincaid, Director of Admissions, Olean Business Institute, 301 North Union Street, Olean, NY 14760-2691. *Phone:* 716-372-7978. *Fax:* 716-372-2120.

ONONDAGA COMMUNITY COLLEGE
Syracuse, New York

Admissions Contact Mr. Monty R. Flynn, Director of Admissions, Onondaga Community College, 4941 Onondaga Road, Syracuse, NY 13215. *Phone:* 315-498-2201. *Fax:* 315-498-2107. *E-mail:* admissions@sunyocc.edu.

ORANGE COUNTY COMMUNITY COLLEGE
Middletown, New York

- **State and locally supported** 2-year, founded 1950, part of State University of New York System
- **Calendar** semesters
- **Degree** certificates and associate
- **Suburban** 37-acre campus with easy access to New York City
- **Coed,** 6,269 undergraduate students, 51% full-time, 61% women, 39% men

Undergraduates 3,222 full-time, 3,047 part-time. Students come from 22 states and territories, 20 other countries, 1% are from out of state, 10% African American, 2% Asian American or Pacific Islander, 12% Hispanic American, 0.4% Native American, 3% transferred in.

Freshmen *Admission:* 2,024 applied, 2,024 admitted, 1,710 enrolled. *Average high school GPA:* 2.25.

Faculty *Total:* 382, 36% full-time. *Student/faculty ratio:* 15:1.

Majors Accounting; administrative assistant and secretarial science; architectural engineering technology; biological and physical sciences; biology/biological sciences; business administration and management; child development; clinical/medical laboratory technology; computer and information sciences; computer and information sciences related; computer engineering related; computer engineering technology; computer programming; computer science; construction engineering technology; consumer merchandising/retailing management; criminal justice/law enforcement administration; criminal justice/police science; data entry/microcomputer applications; data processing and data processing technology; dental hygiene; drafting and design technology; electrical, electronic and communications engineering technology; elementary education; engineering science; finance; humanities; industrial radiologic technology; information science/studies; information technology; kinesiology and exercise science; liberal arts and sciences/liberal studies; marketing/marketing management; mental health/rehabilitation; nursing (registered nurse training); occupational therapy; parks, recreation and leisure; physical sciences; physical therapy; real estate; word processing.

Academic Programs *Special study options:* academic remediation for entering students, accelerated degree program, adult/continuing education programs, English as a second language, external degree program, honors programs, internships, part-time degree program, services for LD students, summer session for credit.

Library Learning Resource Center with 101,342 titles, 345 serial subscriptions, 1,408 audiovisual materials, an OPAC, a Web page.

Computers on Campus 200 computers available on campus for general student use. A campuswide network can be accessed. Internet access, at least one staffed computer lab available.

Student Life *Housing:* college housing not available. *Activities and Organizations:* drama/theater group, student-run newspaper, radio station, choral group, Phi Theta Kappa, Masters of the Elements, Computer Club, Agassiz Society, Apprentice Players. *Campus security:* 24-hour emergency response devices, late-night transport/escort service. *Student services:* health clinic, personal/psychological counseling.

Athletics Member NJCAA. *Intercollegiate sports:* baseball M(s), basketball M(s)/W(s), golf M/W, soccer M(s)/W(s), softball W(s), tennis M(s)/W(s), volleyball W. *Intramural sports:* basketball M/W, field hockey M, football M, racquetball M/W, soccer M/W, tennis M/W, volleyball M/W.

Costs (2005–06) *Tuition:* state resident $2900 full-time, $118 per credit part-time; nonresident $5800 full-time, $236 per credit part-time. *Required fees:* $315 full-time.

Financial Aid Of all full-time matriculated undergraduates who enrolled in 2003, 70 Federal Work-Study jobs (averaging $2000). 25 state and other part-time jobs (averaging $2000).

Applying *Options:* common application, early admission, deferred entrance. *Application fee:* $30. *Required:* high school transcript. *Application deadlines:* 8/1 (freshmen), 8/1 (transfers). *Notification:* continuous (freshmen).

Admissions Contact Ms. Margot St. Lawrence, Director of Admissions, Orange County Community College, 115 South Street, Middletown, NY 10940. *Phone:* 845-341-4030. *E-mail:* admssns@sunyorange.edu.

PHILLIPS BETH ISRAEL SCHOOL OF NURSING
New York, New York

- **Independent** 2-year, founded 1904
- **Calendar** semesters
- **Degree** associate
- **Urban** campus
- **Endowment** $1.2 million
- **Coed, primarily women,** 175 undergraduate students, 21% full-time, 75% women, 25% men

Undergraduates 36 full-time, 139 part-time. Students come from 8 states and territories, 5 other countries, 10% are from out of state, 15% African American, 22% Asian American or Pacific Islander, 14% Hispanic American, 4% international, 35% transferred in.

Freshmen *Admission:* 57 applied, 7 admitted, 7 enrolled. *Average high school GPA:* 2.90. *Test scores:* SAT verbal scores over 500: 100%; SAT math scores over 500: 100%.

Faculty *Total:* 18, 56% full-time, 44% with terminal degrees. *Student/faculty ratio:* 8:1.

Majors Nursing (registered nurse training).

Academic Programs *Special study options:* advanced placement credit, off-campus study, part-time degree program.

Library Phillips Health Science Library with 600 serial subscriptions, an OPAC.

Computers on Campus 15 computers available on campus for general student use. Internet access, at least one staffed computer lab available.

Student Life *Housing:* college housing not available. *Activities and Organizations:* student-run newspaper, choral group, Student Government Organization, National Student Nurses Association. *Campus security:* 24-hour emergency response devices. *Student services:* health clinic, personal/psychological counseling.

Standardized Tests *Required:* nursing exam (for admission). *Recommended:* SAT (for admission).

Costs (2005–06) *Tuition:* $11,890 full-time, $290 per credit part-time. Full-time tuition and fees vary according to course level. *Required fees:* $2095 full-time. *Waivers:* employees or children of employees.

Financial Aid *Financial aid deadline:* 6/1.

Applying *Options:* deferred entrance. *Application fee:* $35. *Required:* essay or personal statement, high school transcript, minimum 2.5 GPA, 2 letters of recommendation, interview. *Application deadlines:* 4/1 (freshmen), 4/1 (transfers). *Notification:* continuous (freshmen).

Admissions Contact Mrs. Bernice Pass-Stern, Assistant Dean, Phillips Beth Israel School of Nursing, 310 East 22nd Street, 9th Floor, New York, NY 10010-5702. *Phone:* 212-614-6176. *Fax:* 212-614-6109. *E-mail:* bstern@bethisraelny.org.

PLAZA INSTITUTE
Jackson Heights, New York

Admissions Contact Mr. Michael Talarico, Director of Admissions, Plaza Institute, 7409 37th Avenue, Jackson Heights, NY 11372-6300. *Phone:* 718-779-1430. *Toll-free phone:* 877-752-9233.

QUEENSBOROUGH COMMUNITY COLLEGE OF THE CITY UNIVERSITY OF NEW YORK
Bayside, New York

- **State and locally supported** 2-year, founded 1958, part of City University of New York System
- **Calendar** semesters
- **Degree** certificates and associate
- **Urban** 34-acre campus with easy access to New York City
- **Endowment** $1.0 million
- **Coed,** 12,798 undergraduate students, 48% full-time, 59% women, 41% men

Undergraduates 6,195 full-time, 6,603 part-time. Students come from 2 states and territories, 132 other countries, 1% are from out of state, 27% African American, 20% Asian American or Pacific Islander, 22% Hispanic American, 0.2% Native American, 6% international, 5% transferred in.

Freshmen *Admission:* 3,485 applied, 3,485 admitted, 2,329 enrolled. *Average high school GPA:* 1.7. *Test scores:* SAT math scores over 500: 5%.

Faculty *Total:* 808, 36% full-time. *Student/faculty ratio:* 21:1.

Majors Accounting; business administration and management; business, management, and marketing related; clinical/medical laboratory technology; communication and journalism related; computer engineering technology; electrical, electronic and communications engineering technology; engineering science; environmental design/architecture; environmental health; fine/studio arts; health science; information science/studies; information technology; laser and optical technology; liberal arts and sciences/liberal studies; mechanical engineering/mechanical technology; musical instrument fabrication and repair; nursing (registered nurse training); telecommunications; visual and performing arts.

Academic Programs *Special study options:* academic remediation for entering students, adult/continuing education programs, advanced placement credit, cooperative education, English as a second language, honors programs, internships, part-time degree program, services for LD students, student-designed majors, summer session for credit. *ROTC:* Army (c).

Library The Kurt R. Schmeller with 140,000 titles, 600 serial subscriptions.

Computers on Campus 1001 computers available on campus for general student use. Internet access, online (class) registration, at least one staffed computer lab available.

Student Life *Housing:* college housing not available. *Activities and Organizations:* drama/theater group, student-run newspaper, radio station, choral group, Student Orientation Leaders, Student Nurses Association, Newman Club, Accounting Club, Flip Culture Society. *Campus security:* 24-hour patrols, late-night transport/escort service. *Student services:* health clinic, personal/psychological counseling.

Athletics Member NJCAA. *Intercollegiate sports:* baseball M, basketball M/W, cross-country running M/W, soccer M, softball W, tennis M/W, track and field M/W, volleyball M/W. *Intramural sports:* archery M/W, badminton M/W, basketball M/W, fencing M/W, soccer M/W, softball M/W, swimming and diving M/W, table tennis M/W, tennis M/W, track and field M/W, volleyball M/W, weight lifting M/W.

Costs (2004–05) *Tuition:* state resident $3066 full-time, $120 per credit part-time; nonresident $4826 full-time, $190 per credit part-time. *Required fees:* $256 full-time. *Payment plan:* installment. *Waivers:* senior citizens and employees or children of employees.

Applying *Options:* electronic application, deferred entrance. *Application fee:* $40. *Required:* high school transcript. *Application deadline:* rolling (freshmen), rolling (transfers). *Notification:* continuous (freshmen).

Admissions Contact Ms. Ann Tullio, Director of Registration, Queensborough Community College of the City University of New York, 222-05 56th Avenue, Bayside, NY 11364. *Phone:* 718-631-6307. *Fax:* 718-281-5189.

ROCHESTER BUSINESS INSTITUTE
Rochester, New York

■ **Proprietary** 2-year, founded 1863, part of Corinthian Colleges, Inc
■ **Calendar** quarters
■ **Degree** certificates, diplomas, and associate
■ **Suburban** 2-acre campus
■ **Coed**

Faculty *Student/faculty ratio:* 18:1.
Standardized Tests *Required:* CPAt (for admission).
Applying *Options:* early admission, deferred entrance. *Required:* high school transcript, interview.
Admissions Contact Ms. Deanna Pfluke, Director of Admissions, Rochester Business Institute, 1630 Portland Avenue, Rochester, NY 14621. *Phone:* 585-266-0430. *Fax:* 585-266-8243. *E-mail:* csilvio@cci.edu.

ROCKLAND COMMUNITY COLLEGE
Suffern, New York

■ **State and locally supported** 2-year, founded 1959, part of State University of New York System
■ **Calendar** semesters
■ **Degree** certificates and associate
■ **Suburban** 150-acre campus with easy access to New York City
■ **Coed,** 6,549 undergraduate students, 56% full-time, 55% women, 45% men

Undergraduates 3,697 full-time, 2,852 part-time. Students come from 4 states and territories, 25 other countries, 4% are from out of state, 18% African American, 6% Asian American or Pacific Islander, 10% Hispanic American, 0.3% Native American, 5% international, 8% transferred in.
Freshmen *Admission:* 1,904 applied, 1,904 admitted, 1,428 enrolled.
Faculty *Total:* 577, 22% full-time. *Student/faculty ratio:* 17:1.
Majors Accounting; administrative assistant and secretarial science; advertising; applied art; art; automobile/automotive mechanics technology; biological and physical sciences; business administration and management; commercial and advertising art; computer and information sciences related; computer graphics; computer/information technology services administration related; computer programming; computer programming related; computer programming (specific applications); computer systems networking and telecommunications; criminal justice/law enforcement administration; culinary arts; data processing and data processing technology; developmental and child psychology; dietetics; drafting and design technology; dramatic/theatre arts; electrical, electronic and communications engineering technology; emergency medical technology (EMT paramedic); finance; fine/studio arts; fire science; health information/medical records administration; hospitality administration; human services; liberal arts and sciences/liberal studies; marketing/marketing management; mass communication/media; mathematics; nursing (registered nurse training); occupational therapy; photography; respiratory care therapy; system administration; tourism and travel services management.
Academic Programs *Special study options:* academic remediation for entering students, adult/continuing education programs, advanced placement credit, cooperative education, English as a second language, external degree program, honors programs, internships, part-time degree program, services for LD students, student-designed majors, study abroad, summer session for credit. *ROTC:* Navy (b), Air Force (b).
Library Rockland Community College Library with 122,194 titles, 541 serial subscriptions, an OPAC.
Computers on Campus 177 computers available on campus for general student use. A campuswide network can be accessed. Internet access, at least one staffed computer lab available.
Student Life *Housing:* college housing not available. *Activities and Organizations:* drama/theater group, student-run newspaper, radio station, Hospitality Club, Student Senate, Student Ambassadors, Student Nurses Association, Latino Club. *Campus security:* 24-hour emergency response devices and patrols, student patrols, late-night transport/escort service. *Student services:* personal/psychological counseling, legal services.
Athletics Member NJCAA. *Intercollegiate sports:* baseball M(s), basketball M/W, bowling M/W, golf M(s), soccer M/W, softball W, tennis M/W, volleyball W. *Intramural sports:* basketball M/W, bowling M/W, field hockey M/W, football M/W, golf M, racquetball M/W, soccer M/W, softball M/W, tennis M/W, volleyball M/W.
Standardized Tests *Recommended:* SAT or ACT (for placement).
Costs (2004–05) *Tuition:* area resident $2800 full-time, $116 per credit part-time; state resident $5600 full-time, $232 per credit part-time. *Required fees:* $235 full-time, $8 per credit part-time.
Applying *Options:* early admission, deferred entrance. *Application fee:* $25. *Required:* high school transcript. *Application deadline:* rolling (freshmen), rolling (transfers).

Admissions Contact Ms. Lucy Hirsch, Admissions Office Secretary, Rockland Community College, 145 College Road, Suffern, NY 10901-3699. *Phone:* 845-574-4237. *Toll-free phone:* 800-722-7666. *Fax:* 845-574-4433. *E-mail:* info@sunyrockland.edu.

ST. ELIZABETH COLLEGE OF NURSING
Utica, New York

Admissions Contact Ms. Marianne Monahan, Dean, St. Elizabeth College of Nursing, 2215 Genesee Street, Utica, NY 13501. *Phone:* 315-798-8253.

SAINT JOSEPH'S HOSPITAL HEALTH CENTER SCHOOL OF NURSING
Syracuse, New York

■ **Independent** 2-year
■ **Calendar** semesters
■ **Degree** associate
■ **Urban** campus
■ **Coed, primarily women**

Faculty *Student/faculty ratio:* 9:1.
Student Life *Campus security:* 24-hour patrols.
Standardized Tests *Required:* SAT or ACT (for admission).
Costs (2004–05) *Tuition:* $6500 full-time, $245 per credit hour part-time. *Required fees:* $1300 full-time, $680 per term part-time. *Room only:* $3100.
Applying *Options:* deferred entrance. *Application fee:* $30. *Required:* essay or personal statement, high school transcript, minimum 3.0 GPA, 4 letters of recommendation, interview.
Admissions Contact Ms. JoAnne Kiggins, Admission and Recruitment Coordinator, Saint Joseph's Hospital Health Center School of Nursing, 206 Prospect Avenue, Syracuse, NY 13203. *Phone:* 315-448-5040.

SAINT VINCENT CATHOLIC MEDICAL CENTERS SCHOOL OF NURSING
Fresh Meadows, New York

■ **Independent** 2-year, founded 1969
■ **Calendar** semesters
■ **Degree** associate
■ **Suburban** 2-acre campus
■ **Coed**

Faculty *Student/faculty ratio:* 10:1.
Student Life *Campus security:* 24-hour patrols.
Standardized Tests *Required:* nursing exam (for admission).
Costs (2004–05) *Tuition:* $205 per credit part-time.
Financial Aid Of all full-time matriculated undergraduates who enrolled in 2003, 11 Federal Work-Study jobs (averaging $900).
Applying *Options:* deferred entrance. *Application fee:* $20. *Required:* essay or personal statement, high school transcript.
Admissions Contact Nancy Wolinski, Chairperson of Admissions, Saint Vincent Catholic Medical Centers School of Nursing, 175-05 Horace Harding Expressway, Fresh Meadows, NY 11365. *Phone:* 718-357-0500 Ext. 131. *Fax:* 718-357-4683.

SAMARITAN HOSPITAL SCHOOL OF NURSING
Troy, New York

Admissions Contact Ms. Jennifer DeBlois, Student Services Coordinator, Samaritan Hospital School of Nursing, 2215 Burdett Avenue, Troy, NY 12180. *Phone:* 518-271-3734. *E-mail:* gallagherl@nehealth.com.

SCHENECTADY COUNTY COMMUNITY COLLEGE
Schenectady, New York

■ **State and locally supported** 2-year, founded 1969, part of State University of New York System
■ **Calendar** semesters
■ **Degree** certificates and associate
■ **Urban** 50-acre campus
■ **Coed**

Faculty *Student/faculty ratio:* 22:1.
Student Life *Campus security:* 24-hour emergency response devices and patrols, late-night transport/escort service.
Athletics Member NJCAA.
Standardized Tests *Recommended:* SAT or ACT (for placement).
Costs (2004–05) *Tuition:* state resident $2640 full-time, $102 per credit hour part-time; nonresident $5280 full-time, $204 per credit hour part-time. Full-time tuition and fees vary according to course load. Part-time tuition and fees vary according to course load. *Required fees:* $118 full-time, $2 per credit hour part-time.
Financial Aid Of all full-time matriculated undergraduates who enrolled in 2003, 50 Federal Work-Study jobs.
Applying *Options:* electronic application, early admission, deferred entrance. *Required:* high school transcript.
Admissions Contact Mr. David Sampson, Director of Admissions, Schenectady County Community College, 78 Washington Avenue, Schenectady, NY 12305. *Phone:* 518-381-1370. *E-mail:* sampsodg@gw.sunysccc.edu.

SIMMONS INSTITUTE OF FUNERAL SERVICE
Syracuse, New York

Admissions Contact Ms. Vera Wightman, Director of Admissions, Simmons Institute of Funeral Service, 1828 South Avenue, Syracuse, NY 13207. *Phone:* 315-475-5142. *Toll-free phone:* 800-727-3536. *Fax:* 315-477-3817. *E-mail:* vwightman6@aol.com.

STATE UNIVERSITY OF NEW YORK COLLEGE OF AGRICULTURE AND TECHNOLOGY AT MORRISVILLE
Morrisville, New York

- **State-supported** primarily 2-year, founded 1908, part of State University of New York System
- **Calendar** semesters
- **Degrees** certificates, associate, and bachelor's
- **Rural** 185-acre campus with easy access to Syracuse
- **Endowment** $681,026
- **Coed**

Faculty *Student/faculty ratio:* 19:1.
Student Life *Campus security:* 24-hour emergency response devices and patrols, late-night transport/escort service, controlled dormitory access.
Athletics Member NJCAA.
Standardized Tests *Required for some:* SAT (for admission). *Recommended:* SAT and SAT Subject Tests or ACT (for admission).
Costs (2004–05) *Tuition:* state resident $4350 full-time, $140 per credit part-time; nonresident $7000 full-time, $292 per credit part-time. Full-time tuition and fees vary according to degree level and student level. Part-time tuition and fees vary according to course load. *Required fees:* $1270 full-time, $15 per term part-time. *Room and board:* $6610; room only: $3540. Room and board charges vary according to board plan and housing facility.
Financial Aid Of all full-time matriculated undergraduates who enrolled in 2003, 300 Federal Work-Study jobs (averaging $1500).
Applying *Options:* electronic application, early admission, deferred entrance. *Application fee:* $40. *Required:* high school transcript. *Required for some:* essay or personal statement, letters of recommendation. *Recommended:* minimum 2.0 GPA, letters of recommendation, interview.
Admissions Contact Mr. Timothy Williams, Dean of Enrollment Management, State University of New York College of Agriculture and Technology at Morrisville, Box 901, Morrisville, NY 13408. *Phone:* 315-684-6046. *Toll-free phone:* 800-258-0111. *Fax:* 315-684-6427. *E-mail:* admissions@morrisville.edu.

STATE UNIVERSITY OF NEW YORK COLLEGE OF ENVIRONMENTAL SCIENCE & FORESTRY, RANGER SCHOOL
Wanakena, New York

- **State-supported** 2-year, founded 1912, part of State University of New York System
- **Calendar** semesters
- **Degree** associate
- **Rural** 2800-acre campus
- **Endowment** $524,891

■ **Coed, primarily men**

Faculty *Student/faculty ratio:* 7:1.
Standardized Tests *Required:* SAT or ACT (for admission).
Costs (2004–05) *Tuition:* state resident $4350 full-time, $181 per credit hour part-time; nonresident $10,300 full-time, $429 per credit hour part-time. *Required fees:* $869 full-time. *Room and board:* $7650.
Financial Aid Of all full-time matriculated undergraduates who enrolled in 2003, 30 Federal Work-Study jobs (averaging $1500). 15 state and other part-time jobs (averaging $1200).
Applying *Options:* electronic application, deferred entrance. *Application fee:* $30.
Admissions Contact Ms. Susan H. Sanford, Director of Admissions, State University of New York College of Environmental Science & Forestry, Ranger School, Bray 106, Syracuse, NY 13210-2779. *Phone:* 315-470-6600. *Toll-free phone:* 800-777-7373. *Fax:* 315-470-6933. *E-mail:* esfinfo@mailbox.syr.edu.

▶ **See page 554 for a narrative description.**

STATE UNIVERSITY OF NEW YORK COLLEGE OF TECHNOLOGY AT ALFRED
Alfred, New York

- **State-supported** primarily 2-year, founded 1908, part of State University of New York System
- **Calendar** semesters
- **Degrees** certificates, associate, and bachelor's
- **Rural** 175-acre campus
- **Endowment** $2.6 million
- **Coed**, 3,500 undergraduate students

Undergraduates Students come from 29 states and territories, 1% are from out of state, 3% African American, 1% Asian American or Pacific Islander, 3% Hispanic American, 0.3% Native American, 70% live on campus. *Retention:* 96% of 2002 full-time freshmen returned.
Freshmen *Admission:* 4,448 applied, 2,965 admitted.
Faculty *Total:* 191, 77% full-time, 14% with terminal degrees. *Student/faculty ratio:* 19:1.
Majors Accounting; agricultural business and management; agriculture; animal sciences; architectural engineering technology; autobody/collision and repair technology; automobile/automotive mechanics technology; biological and physical sciences; biology/biotechnology laboratory technician; business administration and management; carpentry; civil engineering technology; computer and information sciences; computer engineering technology; computer graphics; computer hardware engineering; computer/information technology services administration related; computer installation and repair technology; computer science; computer/technical support; computer typography and composition equipment operation; construction engineering; construction engineering technology; court reporting; culinary arts; dairy science; data processing and data processing technology; drafting and design technology; electrical, electronic and communications engineering technology; electrical/electronics equipment installation and repair; electromechanical technology; engineering science; environmental studies; finance; health information/medical records administration; heating, air conditioning, ventilation and refrigeration maintenance technology; heavy equipment maintenance technology; humanities; human services; industrial electronics technology; landscaping and groundskeeping; liberal arts and sciences/liberal studies; machine tool technology; marketing/marketing management; masonry; mathematics; mechanical design technology; mechanical engineering/mechanical technology; medical/clinical assistant; nursing (registered nurse training); pipefitting and sprinkler fitting; restaurant, culinary, and catering management; sales, distribution and marketing; social sciences; sport and fitness administration; survey technology; system administration; veterinary sciences; welding technology.
Academic Programs *Special study options:* academic remediation for entering students, adult/continuing education programs, advanced placement credit, cooperative education, distance learning, external degree program, honors programs, independent study, internships, off-campus study, part-time degree program, services for LD students, student-designed majors, study abroad, summer session for credit. *ROTC:* Army (c).
Library Walter C. Hinkle Memorial Library plus 1 other with 71,243 titles, 594 serial subscriptions, 8,148 audiovisual materials, an OPAC, a Web page.
Computers on Campus 1600 computers available on campus for general student use. A campuswide network can be accessed from student residence rooms and from off campus. Internet access, online (class) registration, at least one staffed computer lab available. Computer purchase or lease plan available.
Student Life *Housing Options:* coed, disabled students. Campus housing is university owned. Freshman campus housing is guaranteed. *Activities and Organizations:* drama/theater group, student-run newspaper, radio station, choral group, Outdoor Activity Club, BACCHUS, Sondai Society, Drama Club, choir. *Campus security:* 24-hour emergency response devices and patrols, late-night

State University of New York College of Technology at Alfred (continued)
transport/escort service, residence hall entrance guards. *Student services:* health clinic, personal/psychological counseling.

Athletics Member NJCAA. *Intercollegiate sports:* baseball M, basketball M(s)/W(s), cheerleading M/W, cross-country running M(s)/W(s), football M(s), lacrosse M(s), soccer M(s)/W(s), softball W(s), swimming and diving M/W, track and field M(s)/W(s), volleyball W, wrestling M. *Intramural sports:* basketball M/W, bowling M/W, cross-country running M/W, football M, golf M/W, lacrosse M/W, racquetball M/W, rock climbing M/W, rugby M/W, skiing (cross-country) M/W, soccer M/W, softball M/W, table tennis M/W, tennis M/W, ultimate Frisbee M/W, volleyball M/W, water polo M/W.

Standardized Tests *Recommended:* SAT or ACT (for admission).

Costs (2005–06) *Tuition:* state resident $4350 full-time; nonresident $7210 full-time. Full-time tuition and fees vary according to degree level. *Required fees:* $930 full-time. *Room and board:* $6700; room only: $3770. Room and board charges vary according to board plan and housing facility. *Payment plan:* installment.

Financial Aid Of all full-time matriculated undergraduates who enrolled in 2003, 350 Federal Work-Study jobs (averaging $1100).

Applying *Options:* common application, electronic application, deferred entrance. *Application fee:* $40. *Required:* high school transcript. *Required for some:* minimum 2.0 GPA. *Recommended:* essay or personal statement, letters of recommendation, interview. *Application deadline:* rolling (freshmen), rolling (transfers). *Notification:* continuous (freshmen).

Admissions Contact Ms. Deborah J. Goodrich, Director of Admissions, State University of New York College of Technology at Alfred, Huntington Administration Building, 10 Upper College Drive, Alfred, NY 14802. *Phone:* 607-587-4215. *Toll-free phone:* 800-4-ALFRED. *Fax:* 607-587-4299. *E-mail:* admissions@alfredstate.edu.

STATE UNIVERSITY OF NEW YORK COLLEGE OF TECHNOLOGY AT CANTON
Canton, New York

- **State-supported** primarily 2-year, founded 1906, part of State University of New York System
- **Calendar** semesters
- **Degrees** certificates, associate, and bachelor's
- **Small-town** 555-acre campus
- **Endowment** $5.6 million
- **Coed,** 2,518 undergraduate students, 82% full-time, 53% women, 47% men

Undergraduates 2,055 full-time, 463 part-time. Students come from 15 states and territories, 5 other countries, 3% are from out of state, 8% African American, 0.6% Asian American or Pacific Islander, 2% Hispanic American, 2% Native American, 0.5% international, 8% transferred in, 48% live on campus. *Retention:* 82% of 2002 full-time freshmen returned.

Freshmen *Admission:* 2,984 applied, 2,470 admitted, 857 enrolled.

Faculty *Total:* 131, 62% full-time, 14% with terminal degrees. *Student/faculty ratio:* 23:1.

Majors Accounting; automobile/automotive mechanics technology; banking and financial support services; biological and physical sciences; business administration and management; business/managerial economics; carpentry; civil engineering technology; clinical/medical laboratory technology; computer/information technology services administration related; construction engineering technology; corrections; criminal justice/law enforcement administration; criminal justice/police science; electrical, electronic and communications engineering technology; engineering science; engineering technology; environmental studies; forestry technology; funeral service and mortuary science; health/health care administration; heating, air conditioning, ventilation and refrigeration maintenance technology; humanities; industrial technology; information science/studies; interdisciplinary studies; kindergarten/preschool education; liberal arts and sciences/liberal studies; mechanical engineering/mechanical technology; nursing (registered nurse training); occupational therapist assistant; office management; physical therapist assistant; pipefitting and sprinkler fitting; social sciences; veterinary technology.

Academic Programs *Special study options:* academic remediation for entering students, adult/continuing education programs, advanced placement credit, distance learning, independent study, internships, off-campus study, part-time degree program, services for LD students, student-designed majors, summer session for credit. *ROTC:* Army (c), Air Force (c).

Library Southworth Library with 64,912 titles, 303 serial subscriptions, 1,569 audiovisual materials, an OPAC, a Web page.

Computers on Campus 300 computers available on campus for general student use. A campuswide network can be accessed. Internet access, at least one staffed computer lab available. Computer purchase or lease plan available.

Student Life *Housing:* on-campus residence required through sophomore year. *Options:* coed, men-only, women-only. Campus housing is university owned. *Activities and Organizations:* drama/theater group, student-run newspaper, radio station, choral group, Karate Club, Automotive Club, Outing Club, WATC Radio,

Afro-Latin Society, national fraternities, national sororities. *Campus security:* 24-hour emergency response devices and patrols, late-night transport/escort service, controlled dormitory access. *Student services:* health clinic, personal/psychological counseling.

Athletics Member NJCAA. *Intercollegiate sports:* baseball M, basketball M/W, ice hockey M, lacrosse M/W, soccer M/W, softball W, volleyball W. *Intramural sports:* badminton M/W, basketball M/W, cheerleading W, skiing (cross-country) M/W, soccer M/W, softball M/W, tennis M/W, volleyball M/W.

Costs (2005–06) *One-time required fee:* $20. *Tuition:* state resident $4350 full-time, $181 per credit hour part-time; nonresident $10,610 full-time, $442 per credit hour part-time. Full-time tuition and fees vary according to degree level, location, and program. Part-time tuition and fees vary according to degree level, location, and program. *Required fees:* $1065 full-time, $39 per credit hour part-time, $5 per semester part-time. *Room and board:* $7350; room only: $4220. Room and board charges vary according to housing facility. *Payment plans:* installment, deferred payment. *Waivers:* employees or children of employees.

Financial Aid Of all full-time matriculated undergraduates who enrolled in 2003, 250 Federal Work-Study jobs (averaging $1200). 10 state and other part-time jobs (averaging $1200).

Applying *Options:* electronic application, early admission, deferred entrance. *Application fee:* $40. *Required:* high school transcript. *Required for some:* interview. *Recommended:* minimum 2.0 GPA. *Application deadline:* rolling (freshmen), rolling (transfers). *Notification:* continuous (freshmen).

Admissions Contact Ms. Jodi L. Revill, Director of Admissions, State University of New York College of Technology at Canton, 34 Cornell Drive, Canton, NY 13617. *Phone:* 315-386-7123. *Toll-free phone:* 800-388-7123. *Fax:* 315-386-7929. *E-mail:* admissions@canton.edu.

STATE UNIVERSITY OF NEW YORK COLLEGE OF TECHNOLOGY AT DELHI
Delhi, New York

- **State-supported** primarily 2-year, founded 1913, part of State University of New York System
- **Calendar** semesters
- **Degrees** certificates, associate, and bachelor's
- **Rural** 405-acre campus
- **Endowment** $1.2 million
- **Coed,** 2,170 undergraduate students, 90% full-time, 43% women, 57% men

Undergraduates 1,961 full-time, 209 part-time. Students come from 7 states and territories, 3 other countries, 2% are from out of state, 12% African American, 2% Asian American or Pacific Islander, 7% Hispanic American, 0.2% Native American, 2% international, 8% transferred in, 61% live on campus.

Freshmen *Admission:* 3,650 applied, 2,236 admitted, 1,065 enrolled.

Faculty *Total:* 130, 75% full-time. *Student/faculty ratio:* 17:1.

Majors Accounting; architectural engineering technology; business administration and management; carpentry; computer/information technology services administration related; construction engineering technology; construction management; culinary arts; drafting and design technology; electrical and power transmission installation; engineering science; engineering technology; forestry; general studies; health and physical education; heating, air conditioning and refrigeration technology; heating, air conditioning, ventilation and refrigeration maintenance technology; horticultural science; hospitality and recreation marketing; hotel/motel administration; humanities; information science/studies; landscape architecture; landscaping and groundskeeping; marketing/marketing management; masonry; mathematics; nursing (registered nurse training); parks, recreation and leisure; parks, recreation and leisure facilities management; physical education teaching and coaching; pipefitting and sprinkler fitting; restaurant, culinary, and catering management; social sciences; tourism and travel services management; turf and turfgrass management; veterinary technology; web page, digital/multimedia and information resources design; welding technology; woodworking.

Academic Programs *Special study options:* academic remediation for entering students, adult/continuing education programs, advanced placement credit, distance learning, English as a second language, honors programs, internships, part-time degree program, services for LD students, student-designed majors, summer session for credit.

Library Louis and Mildred Resnick Library with 47,909 titles, 384 serial subscriptions, an OPAC.

Computers on Campus 350 computers available on campus for general student use. A campuswide network can be accessed from off campus. Internet access, online (class) registration, at least one staffed computer lab available.

Student Life *Housing:* on-campus residence required through sophomore year. *Options:* coed. *Activities and Organizations:* drama/theater group, student-run newspaper, radio station, Latin American Student Organization, Hotel Sales Management Association, student radio station, Phi Theta Kappa, Student Programming Board, national fraternities. *Campus security:* 24-hour emergency response devices and patrols. *Student services:* health clinic, personal/psychological counseling, legal services.

Athletics Member NAIA, NJCAA. *Intercollegiate sports:* basketball M/W, cross-country running M/W, golf M/W, lacrosse M, soccer M/W, softball W, swimming and diving M/W, tennis M/W, track and field M/W, volleyball W, wrestling M. *Intramural sports:* basketball M/W, bowling M/W, cross-country running M/W, football M/W, golf M/W, racquetball M/W, skiing (cross-country) M/W, skiing (downhill) M/W, swimming and diving M/W, tennis M/W, volleyball M/W, weight lifting M/W.

Costs (2004–05) *Tuition:* state resident $4350 full-time; nonresident $10,300 full-time. *Required fees:* $1115 full-time. *Room and board:* $6830.

Financial Aid Of all full-time matriculated undergraduates who enrolled in 2003, 150 Federal Work-Study jobs (averaging $1050).

Applying *Options:* electronic application, early admission, deferred entrance. *Application fee:* $30. *Required:* high school transcript. *Required for some:* minimum 2.0 GPA. *Application deadline:* rolling (freshmen), rolling (transfers). *Notification:* continuous (freshmen).

Admissions Contact Mr. Larry Barrett, Dean of Enrollment, State University of New York College of Technology at Delhi, 2 Main Street, Delhi, NY 13753. *Phone:* 607-746-4000 Ext. 4856. *Toll-free phone:* 800-96-DELHI. *Fax:* 607-746-4104. *E-mail:* enroll@delhi.edu.

SUFFOLK COUNTY COMMUNITY COLLEGE
Selden, New York

Admissions Contact Executive Director of Admissions and Enrollment Management, Suffolk County Community College, 533 College Road, Selden, NY 11784-2899. *Phone:* 631-451-4000. *Fax:* 631-451-4415.

SULLIVAN COUNTY COMMUNITY COLLEGE
Loch Sheldrake, New York

- **State and locally supported** 2-year, founded 1962, part of State University of New York System
- **Calendar** 4-1-4
- **Degree** certificates and associate
- **Rural** 405-acre campus
- **Endowment** $657,688
- **Coed**

Faculty *Student/faculty ratio:* 16:1.

Student Life *Campus security:* 24-hour emergency response devices and patrols.

Athletics Member NJCAA.

Standardized Tests *Recommended:* SAT or ACT (for placement).

Costs (2004–05) *Tuition:* state resident $2900 full-time, $115 per credit part-time; nonresident $5800 full-time, $149 per credit part-time. *Required fees:* $301 full-time. *Room and board:* $6050; room only: $3800. *Payment plans:* installment, deferred payment.

Financial Aid Of all full-time matriculated undergraduates who enrolled in 2003, 105 Federal Work-Study jobs (averaging $800). 57 state and other part-time jobs (averaging $841).

Applying *Options:* common application, electronic application, early admission, deferred entrance. *Required:* high school transcript.

Admissions Contact Mr. Ray Sheenan, Director of Admissions and Registration Services, Sullivan County Community College, 112 College Road, Loch Sheldrake, NY 12759. *Phone:* 914-434-5750 Ext. 4480. *Toll-free phone:* 800-577-5243. *Fax:* 914-434-4806. *E-mail:* dbrown@sullivan.suny.edu.

TAYLOR BUSINESS INSTITUTE
New York, New York

Admissions Contact Mr. Orlando Mangual, Director of Admissions, Taylor Business Institute, 269 West 40th Street, New York, NY 10018. *Phone:* 212-302-4000.

TCI-THE COLLEGE OF TECHNOLOGY
New York, New York

Admissions Contact Ms. Sandra Germer, Director of Admission, TCI-The College of Technology, 320 West 31st Street, New York, NY 10001-2705. *Phone:* 212-594-4000 Ext. 437. *Fax:* 212-629-3937. *E-mail:* admissions@tciedu.com.

TOMPKINS CORTLAND COMMUNITY COLLEGE
Dryden, New York

- **State and locally supported** 2-year, founded 1968, part of State University of New York System
- **Calendar** semesters
- **Degree** certificates and associate
- **Rural** 250-acre campus with easy access to Syracuse
- **Endowment** $2.0 million
- **Coed,** 3,201 undergraduate students, 67% full-time, 60% women, 40% men

Undergraduates 2,129 full-time, 1,072 part-time. Students come from 22 states and territories, 43 other countries, 1% are from out of state, 6% African American, 2% Asian American or Pacific Islander, 3% Hispanic American, 0.4% Native American, 3% international, 10% transferred in, 4% live on campus.

Freshmen *Admission:* 760 enrolled. *Average high school GPA:* 2.52. *Test scores:* SAT verbal scores over 500: 31%; SAT math scores over 500: 38%; ACT scores over 18: 65%; SAT verbal scores over 600: 6%; SAT math scores over 600: 6%; ACT scores over 24: 7%; SAT math scores over 700: 1%.

Faculty *Total:* 263, 25% full-time, 20% with terminal degrees. *Student/faculty ratio:* 19:1.

Majors Accounting; administrative assistant and secretarial science; aeronautics/aviation/aerospace science and technology; biological and physical sciences; business administration and management; child care provision; child development; commercial and advertising art; computer and information sciences related; computer and information systems security; computer graphics; computer hardware engineering; computer/information technology services administration related; computer programming related; computer science; computer software engineering; computer/technical support; construction engineering technology; criminal justice/law enforcement administration; data entry/microcomputer applications; electrical, electronic and communications engineering technology; engineering science; environmental studies; hotel/motel administration; humanities; human services; information science/studies; international business/trade/commerce; kindergarten/preschool education; legal assistant/paralegal; liberal arts and sciences/liberal studies; marketing/marketing management; mass communication/media; mathematics; nursing (registered nurse training); parks, recreation and leisure; radio and television; social sciences; sport and fitness administration; substance abuse/addiction counseling; system administration; tourism and travel services management; tourism and travel services marketing; web page, digital/multimedia and information resources design; women's studies.

Academic Programs *Special study options:* academic remediation for entering students, adult/continuing education programs, advanced placement credit, cooperative education, English as a second language, honors programs, internships, off-campus study, part-time degree program, services for LD students, summer session for credit. *ROTC:* Army (c).

Library Gerald A. Barry Memorial Library with 50,630 titles, 489 serial subscriptions, an OPAC, a Web page.

Computers on Campus 350 computers available on campus for general student use. A campuswide network can be accessed from student residence rooms. Internet access, online (class) registration, at least one staffed computer lab available.

Student Life *Housing Options:* coed. Campus housing is provided by a third party. *Activities and Organizations:* drama/theater group, Art Works, Accounting Club, Nurse's Association. *Campus security:* 24-hour emergency response devices and patrols. *Student services:* personal/psychological counseling.

Athletics Member NJCAA. *Intercollegiate sports:* basketball M/W, golf M/W, soccer M/W, softball W, tennis W, volleyball W, wrestling M. *Intramural sports:* badminton M/W, basketball M/W, bowling M/W, football M/W, golf M/W, lacrosse M/W, racquetball M/W, skiing (cross-country) M/W, soccer M/W, softball M/W, swimming and diving M/W, table tennis M/W, tennis M/W, volleyball M/W, water polo M/W.

Standardized Tests *Required for some:* SAT or ACT (for placement). *Recommended:* ACT (for placement).

Costs (2005–06) *Tuition:* state resident $3100 full-time, $120 per credit part-time; nonresident $6500 full-time, $250 per credit part-time. *Required fees:* $553 full-time, $15 per credit part-time. *Room and board:* room only: $5000.

Financial Aid Of all full-time matriculated undergraduates who enrolled in 2003, 150 Federal Work-Study jobs (averaging $1000). 150 state and other part-time jobs (averaging $1000).

Applying *Options:* early admission, deferred entrance. *Application fee:* $15. *Required:* high school transcript. *Application deadline:* rolling (freshmen), rolling (transfers). *Notification:* continuous (freshmen).

Admissions Contact Mr. Sandy Drumluk, Director of Admissions, Tompkins Cortland Community College, 170 North Street, PO Box 139, Dryden, NY 13053-0139. *Phone:* 607-844-8222. *Toll-free phone:* 888-567-8211. *Fax:* 607-844-6538. *E-mail:* admissions@sunytccc.edu.

TROCAIRE COLLEGE
Buffalo, New York

Admissions Contact Mrs. Theresa Horner, Director of Records, Trocaire College, 360 Choate Avenue, Buffalo, NY 14220. *Phone:* 716-826-1200 Ext. 1259. *Fax:* 716-828-6107. *E-mail:* info@trocaire.edu.

ULSTER COUNTY COMMUNITY COLLEGE
Stone Ridge, New York

Admissions Contact Admissions Office, Ulster County Community College, Cottekill Road, Stone Ridge, NY 12484. *Phone:* 914-687-5022. *Toll-free phone:* 800-724-0833. *Fax:* 914-687-5083. *E-mail:* reqinfo@sunyulster.edu.

UTICA SCHOOL OF COMMERCE
Utica, New York

Admissions Contact Chris Tacea, Dean of Enrollment Management, Utica School of Commerce, 201 Bleecker Street, Utica, NY 13501. *Phone:* 315-733-2300. *Toll-free phone:* 800-321-4USC. *Fax:* 315-733-9281. *E-mail:* swilliams@uscny.edu.

VILLA MARIA COLLEGE OF BUFFALO
Buffalo, New York

- **Independent** 2-year, founded 1960, affiliated with Roman Catholic Church
- **Calendar** semesters
- **Degree** associate
- **Suburban** 9-acre campus
- **Endowment** $339,861
- **Coed,** 504 undergraduate students, 76% full-time, 75% women, 25% men

Undergraduates 385 full-time, 119 part-time. Students come from 3 states and territories, 5 other countries, 1% are from out of state, 31% African American, 1% Asian American or Pacific Islander, 2% Hispanic American, 0.6% Native American, 11% transferred in.
Freshmen *Admission:* 343 applied, 273 admitted, 149 enrolled. *Average high school GPA:* 2.5. *Test scores:* SAT verbal scores over 500: 25%; SAT math scores over 500: 22%; ACT scores over 18: 67%; SAT verbal scores over 600: 3%.
Faculty *Total:* 67, 37% full-time, 31% with terminal degrees. *Student/faculty ratio:* 11:1.
Majors Administrative assistant and secretarial science; business administration and management; commercial and advertising art; computer management; education; health science; interior design; kindergarten/preschool education; liberal arts and sciences/liberal studies; music; music management and merchandising; photography; physical therapist assistant.
Academic Programs *Special study options:* academic remediation for entering students, advanced placement credit, cooperative education, double majors, independent study, internships, off-campus study, part-time degree program, services for LD students, study abroad, summer session for credit.
Library Villa Maria College Library with 37,000 titles, 130 serial subscriptions, 3,500 audiovisual materials, an OPAC, a Web page.
Computers on Campus 127 computers available on campus for general student use. A campuswide network can be accessed. Internet access, at least one staffed computer lab available.
Student Life *Housing:* college housing not available. *Activities and Organizations:* drama/theater group, student-run newspaper, radio station, choral group, Design and Beyond, Teachers Love Children, Multicultural Club, Phi Theta Kappa, Helping Adults New Dreams Succeed. *Campus security:* late-night transport/escort service. *Student services:* health clinic, personal/psychological counseling.
Costs (2004–05) *Tuition:* $10,150 full-time, $340 per credit hour part-time. *Required fees:* $400 full-time. *Payment plan:* installment. *Waivers:* employees or children of employees.
Financial Aid Of all full-time matriculated undergraduates who enrolled in 2003, 136 Federal Work-Study jobs (averaging $485).
Applying *Options:* electronic application, deferred entrance. *Application fee:* $35. *Required:* essay or personal statement, high school transcript, writing sample. *Application deadline:* rolling (freshmen), rolling (transfers). *Notification:* continuous (freshmen).
Admissions Contact Mr. Kevin Donovan, Director of Admissions, Villa Maria College of Buffalo, 240 Pine Ridge Road, Buffalo, NY 14225-3999. *Phone:* 716-896-0700 Ext. 1802. *Fax:* 716-896-0705. *E-mail:* admissions@villa.edu.

WESTCHESTER COMMUNITY COLLEGE
Valhalla, New York

- **State and locally supported** 2-year, founded 1946, part of State University of New York System
- **Calendar** semesters
- **Degree** certificates and associate
- **Suburban** 218-acre campus with easy access to New York City
- **Endowment** $8.5 million
- **Coed,** 11,935 undergraduate students, 46% full-time, 57% women, 43% men

Undergraduates 5,502 full-time, 6,433 part-time. Students come from 14 states and territories, 70 other countries, 0.5% are from out of state, 21% African American, 4% Asian American or Pacific Islander, 19% Hispanic American, 1% Native American, 3% international, 8% transferred in. *Retention:* 63% of 2002 full-time freshmen returned.
Freshmen *Admission:* 6,432 applied, 6,432 admitted, 2,909 enrolled.
Faculty *Total:* 752, 21% full-time. *Student/faculty ratio:* 16:1.
Majors Accounting; administrative assistant and secretarial science; applied art; automobile/automotive mechanics technology; biological and physical sciences; business administration and management; chemical engineering; child care provision; child development; civil engineering technology; clinical laboratory science/medical technology; clinical/medical laboratory technology; computer and information sciences; computer and information sciences related; computer science; computer systems networking and telecommunications; consumer merchandising/retailing management; corrections; criminal justice/law enforcement administration; criminal justice/police science; culinary arts; dance; data processing and data processing technology; dietetics; electrical, electronic and communications engineering technology; emergency medical technology (EMT paramedic); engineering science; engineering technology; environmental engineering technology; finance; fine/studio arts; food services technology; hotel/motel administration; humanities; human services; industrial radiologic technology; information science/studies; international business/trade/commerce; legal administrative assistant/secretary; legal assistant/paralegal; liberal arts and sciences/liberal studies; marketing/marketing management; mass communication/media; mechanical engineering/mechanical technology; nursing (registered nurse training); public administration; respiratory care therapy; social sciences; special products marketing; substance abuse/addiction counseling; tourism and travel services management; tourism promotion.
Academic Programs *Special study options:* academic remediation for entering students, adult/continuing education programs, cooperative education, distance learning, double majors, English as a second language, honors programs, independent study, internships, off-campus study, part-time degree program, services for LD students, student-designed majors, study abroad, summer session for credit.
Library Harold L. Drimmer Library with 96,419 titles, 531 serial subscriptions, 5,163 audiovisual materials, an OPAC, a Web page.
Computers on Campus 1200 computers available on campus for general student use. A campuswide network can be accessed. Internet access, online (class) registration, at least one staffed computer lab available.
Student Life *Housing:* college housing not available. *Activities and Organizations:* drama/theater group, student-run newspaper, radio station, choral group, Student Senate, African Culture Club, Italian Club, International Friendship Club, Alpha Beta Gamma. *Campus security:* 24-hour emergency response devices and patrols, late-night transport/escort service. *Student services:* health clinic, personal/psychological counseling, women's center.
Athletics Member NJCAA. *Intercollegiate sports:* baseball M, basketball M/W, bowling M/W, golf M, soccer M, softball W, volleyball W. *Intramural sports:* badminton M/W, basketball M/W, softball M/W, swimming and diving M/W, tennis M/W, volleyball M/W, weight lifting M/W.
Costs (2005–06) *Tuition:* state resident $2950 full-time, $123 per credit part-time; nonresident $7376 full-time, $308 per credit part-time. *Required fees:* $343 full-time, $76 per term part-time. *Waivers:* employees or children of employees.
Financial Aid Of all full-time matriculated undergraduates who enrolled in 2003, 200 Federal Work-Study jobs (averaging $1000).
Applying *Options:* electronic application, early admission. *Application fee:* $25. *Required:* high school transcript. *Recommended:* interview. *Application deadline:* rolling (freshmen), rolling (transfers). *Notification:* continuous until 2/2 (freshmen).
Admissions Contact Ms. Terre Wisell, Director of Admissions, Westchester Community College, 75 Grasslands Road, Administration Building, Valhalla, NY 10595-1698. *Phone:* 914-606-6735. *E-mail:* admissions@sunywcc.edu.

WOOD TOBE-COBURN SCHOOL
New York, New York

Admissions Contact Ms. Sandra L. Andujar, Director of Admissions, Wood Tobe-Coburn School, 8 East 40th Street, New York, NY 10016. *Phone:* 212-686-9040 Ext. 103.

NORTH CAROLINA

ALAMANCE COMMUNITY COLLEGE
Graham, North Carolina

- **State-supported** 2-year, founded 1959, part of North Carolina Community College System
- **Calendar** semesters
- **Degree** certificates, diplomas, and associate
- **Small-town** 48-acre campus
- **Endowment** $2.9 million
- **Coed,** 4,627 undergraduate students, 34% full-time, 65% women, 35% men

Undergraduates 1,570 full-time, 3,057 part-time. Students come from 23 states and territories, 3 other countries, 1% are from out of state, 23% African American, 1% Asian American or Pacific Islander, 2% Hispanic American, 0.4% Native American, 0.5% international, 9% transferred in.

Freshmen *Admission:* 1,733 applied, 1,733 admitted, 774 enrolled. *Average high school GPA:* 2.00.

Faculty *Total:* 238, 39% full-time, 6% with terminal degrees. *Student/faculty ratio:* 16:1.

Majors Accounting technology and bookkeeping; animal sciences; applied horticulture; automobile/automotive mechanics technology; banking and financial support services; biotechnology; business administration and management; carpentry; clinical/medical laboratory technology; commercial and advertising art; computer programming; criminal justice/safety; culinary arts; electrical, electronic and communications engineering technology; electromechanical technology; executive assistant/executive secretary; general retailing/wholesaling; heating, air conditioning and refrigeration technology; information science/studies; kindergarten/preschool education; legal administrative assistant/secretary; liberal arts and sciences/liberal studies; machine tool technology; mechanical engineering/mechanical technology; medical administrative assistant and medical secretary; medical/clinical assistant; nursing (registered nurse training); office occupations and clerical services; operations management; real estate; social work; teacher assistant/aide; welding technology.

Academic Programs *Special study options:* academic remediation for entering students, adult/continuing education programs, cooperative education, distance learning, double majors, English as a second language, independent study, off-campus study, part-time degree program, services for LD students, summer session for credit.

Library Learning Resources Center with 22,114 titles, 185 serial subscriptions, 3,033 audiovisual materials, an OPAC, a Web page.

Computers on Campus 56 computers available on campus for general student use. A campuswide network can be accessed. Internet access, at least one staffed computer lab available.

Student Life *Housing:* college housing not available. *Campus security:* 24-hour emergency response devices and patrols, student patrols, late-night transport/escort service. *Student services:* personal/psychological counseling.

Athletics *Intramural sports:* basketball M/W, bowling M/W, tennis M/W, volleyball M/W.

Standardized Tests *Recommended:* SAT or ACT (for placement).

Costs (2004–05) *Tuition:* state resident $1136 full-time, $38 per credit hour part-time; nonresident $6304 full-time, $211 per credit hour part-time. Part-time tuition and fees vary according to course load. *Required fees:* $30 full-time, $5 per term part-time. *Waivers:* senior citizens.

Financial Aid Of all full-time matriculated undergraduates who enrolled in 2003, 150 Federal Work-Study jobs (averaging $3000).

Applying *Options:* common application, deferred entrance. *Required:* high school transcript. *Application deadline:* rolling (freshmen), rolling (transfers). *Notification:* continuous (freshmen).

Admissions Contact Ms. Suzanne Lucier, Director for Enrollment Management, Alamance Community College, Jimmy Kerr Road, Graham, NC 27253-8000. *Phone:* 336-578-2002 Ext. 4138. *Fax:* 336-578-1987. *E-mail:* admissions@alamance.cc.nc.us.

THE ART INSTITUTE OF CHARLOTTE
Charlotte, North Carolina

- **Proprietary** primarily 2-year, founded 1973, part of Education Management Corporation
- **Calendar** quarters
- **Degrees** certificates, associate, and bachelor's
- **Suburban** campus
- **Coed,** 716 undergraduate students, 70% full-time, 66% women, 34% men

Undergraduates 501 full-time, 215 part-time. 29% African American, 3% Asian American or Pacific Islander, 3% Hispanic American, 26% live on campus.

Freshmen *Admission:* 285 applied, 275 admitted, 195 enrolled. *Test scores:* SAT verbal scores over 500: 45%; SAT math scores over 500: 50%; ACT scores over 18: 33%; SAT verbal scores over 600: 5%; SAT math scores over 600: 5%; ACT scores over 24: 33%.

Faculty *Total:* 52, 40% full-time, 12% with terminal degrees. *Student/faculty ratio:* 13:1.

Academic Programs *Special study options:* academic remediation for entering students, accelerated degree program, advanced placement credit, distance learning, independent study, internships, part-time degree program, services for LD students, summer session for credit.

Library The Art Institute of Charlotte Library with 15,000 titles, 130 serial subscriptions, 825 audiovisual materials, an OPAC.

Computers on Campus 150 computers available on campus for general student use. A campuswide network can be accessed. Internet access, online (class) registration, at least one staffed computer lab available.

Student Life *Housing Options:* Campus housing is leased by the school. Freshman campus housing is guaranteed.

Standardized Tests *Required:* ACCUPLACER (for admission). *Required for some:* SAT or ACT (for admission). *Recommended:* SAT or ACT (for admission).

Costs (2004–05) *Tuition:* $21,376 full-time, $343 per credit part-time. No tuition increase for student's term of enrollment. *Required fees:* $200 full-time, $50 per term part-time. *Room only:* $5416. *Payment plans:* installment, deferred payment. *Waivers:* employees or children of employees.

Applying *Options:* electronic application, deferred entrance. *Required:* essay or personal statement, high school transcript. *Required for some:* interview. *Application deadline:* rolling (freshmen).

Admissions Contact Mrs. Elizabeth Guinan, College President, The Art Institute of Charlotte, 2110 Water Ridge Parkway, Charlotte, NC 28217. *Phone:* 704-357-8020 Ext. 2541.

▶ **See page 452 for a narrative description.**

ASHEVILLE-BUNCOMBE TECHNICAL COMMUNITY COLLEGE
Asheville, North Carolina

- **State-supported** 2-year, founded 1959, part of North Carolina Community College System
- **Calendar** semesters
- **Degree** certificates, diplomas, and associate
- **Urban** 126-acre campus
- **Endowment** $98,442
- **Coed,** 5,627 undergraduate students, 36% full-time, 55% women, 45% men

Undergraduates 2,042 full-time, 3,585 part-time. 2% are from out of state, 6% African American, 0.5% Asian American or Pacific Islander, 1% Hispanic American, 0.5% Native American, 0.6% international.

Freshmen *Admission:* 2,792 applied, 2,792 admitted, 522 enrolled.

Faculty *Total:* 584, 21% full-time, 5% with terminal degrees. *Student/faculty ratio:* 17:1.

Majors Accounting technology and bookkeeping; automobile/automotive mechanics technology; business administration and management; child care and support services management; civil engineering technology; clinical/medical laboratory technology; computer programming; computer systems networking and telecommunications; criminal justice/police science; culinary arts; dental hygiene; emergency medical technology (EMT paramedic); executive assistant/executive secretary; general retailing/wholesaling; heating, air conditioning, ventilation and refrigeration maintenance technology; hotel/motel administration; institutional food workers; liberal arts and sciences/liberal studies; machine tool technology; mechanical design technology; mechanical engineering/mechanical technology; medical radiologic technology; nursing (registered nurse training); operations management; social work; survey technology; tool and die technology.

Academic Programs *Special study options:* academic remediation for entering students, adult/continuing education programs, advanced placement credit, cooperative education, distance learning, double majors, independent study, internships, part-time degree program, services for LD students, summer session for credit.

Library Holly Learning Resources Center with 37,439 titles, 195 serial subscriptions, an OPAC.

Computers on Campus 414 computers available on campus for general student use. A campuswide network can be accessed from off campus. Internet access, at least one staffed computer lab available.

Student Life *Housing:* college housing not available. *Activities and Organizations:* drama/theater group, student-run newspaper, Student Government Association, Phi Beta Lambda. *Campus security:* 24-hour emergency response devices and patrols. *Student services:* personal/psychological counseling.

Athletics *Intramural sports:* basketball M/W, softball M/W, volleyball M/W.

Standardized Tests *Required:* CPT, SAT I, or ACT (for placement).

Asheville-Buncombe Technical Community College (continued)

Costs (2005–06) *Tuition:* state resident $1216 full-time, $38 per credit hour part-time; nonresident $6752 full-time, $211 per credit hour part-time. *Required fees:* $28 full-time, $11 per term part-time.

Applying *Options:* deferred entrance. *Required:* high school transcript. *Required for some:* letters of recommendation, interview. *Application deadline:* rolling (freshmen), rolling (transfers). *Notification:* continuous (freshmen).

Admissions Contact Ms. Lisa Bush, Director, Admissions, Asheville-Buncombe Technical Community College, 340 Victoria Road, Asheville, NC 28801. *Phone:* 828-254-1921 Ext. 202. *Fax:* 828-251-6718. *E-mail:* admissions@abtech.edu.

BEAUFORT COUNTY COMMUNITY COLLEGE
Washington, North Carolina

- **State-supported** 2-year, founded 1967, part of North Carolina Community College System
- **Calendar** semesters
- **Degree** certificates, diplomas, and associate
- **Rural** 67-acre campus
- **Coed,** 1,669 undergraduate students

Undergraduates 1% are from out of state, 36% African American, 0.1% Asian American or Pacific Islander, 2% Hispanic American, 0.3% international.

Faculty *Total:* 136, 43% full-time, 3% with terminal degrees.

Majors Accounting; administrative assistant and secretarial science; agricultural mechanization; automobile/automotive mechanics technology; business administration and management; clinical/medical laboratory technology; computer programming; computer systems networking and telecommunications; criminal justice/police science; drafting and design technology; electrical, electronic and communications engineering technology; heavy equipment maintenance technology; human resources management; information science/studies; kindergarten/preschool education; liberal arts and sciences/liberal studies; medical administrative assistant and medical secretary; medical office management; nursing (registered nurse training); social work; welding technology.

Academic Programs *Special study options:* academic remediation for entering students, advanced placement credit, cooperative education, distance learning, part-time degree program, services for LD students, summer session for credit.

Library Beaufort Community College Library with 25,734 titles, 214 serial subscriptions, an OPAC, a Web page.

Computers on Campus 60 computers available on campus for general student use. A campuswide network can be accessed from off campus. Internet access, at least one staffed computer lab available.

Student Life *Housing:* college housing not available. *Activities and Organizations:* Student Government Association, Gama Beta Phi, Phi Beta Lambda, Hope Club. *Campus security:* 24-hour emergency response devices and patrols, late-night transport/escort service. *Student services:* personal/psychological counseling.

Standardized Tests *Required:* CPT (for admission). *Recommended:* SAT and SAT Subject Tests or ACT (for admission).

Costs (2005–06) *Tuition:* state resident $1248 full-time; nonresident $6784 full-time. Part-time tuition and fees vary according to course load. *Required fees:* $32 full-time. *Waivers:* senior citizens and employees or children of employees.

Financial Aid Of all full-time matriculated undergraduates who enrolled in 2003, 21 Federal Work-Study jobs (averaging $1600). *Financial aid deadline:* 7/15.

Applying *Options:* electronic application. *Required:* high school transcript. *Required for some:* essay or personal statement, letters of recommendation, interview. *Application deadline:* 8/18 (freshmen), rolling (transfers). *Notification:* continuous (freshmen).

Admissions Contact Mr. Gary Burbage, Director of Admissions, Beaufort County Community College, PO Box 1069, 5337 US Highway 264 East, Washington, NC 27889-1069. *Phone:* 252-940-6233. *Fax:* 252-940-6393. *E-mail:* garyb@email.beaufort.cc.nc.us.

BLADEN COMMUNITY COLLEGE
Dublin, North Carolina

- **State and locally supported** 2-year, founded 1967, part of North Carolina Community College System
- **Calendar** semesters
- **Degree** certificates, diplomas, and associate
- **Rural** 45-acre campus
- **Endowment** $72,151
- **Coed,** 1,407 undergraduate students, 60% full-time, 77% women, 23% men

Undergraduates 838 full-time, 569 part-time. Students come from 3 states and territories, 48% African American, 0.2% Asian American or Pacific Islander, 0.6% Hispanic American, 10% Native American. *Retention:* 35% of 2002 full-time freshmen returned.

Freshmen *Admission:* 267 enrolled. *Average high school GPA:* 2.6.

Faculty *Total:* 85, 38% full-time, 5% with terminal degrees. *Student/faculty ratio:* 15:1.

Majors Administrative assistant and secretarial science; biotechnology; business administration and management; child care provision; computer programming; computer programming (specific applications); cosmetology; criminal justice/police science; electrical, electronic and communications engineering technology; general studies; industrial technology; information technology; liberal arts and sciences/liberal studies; nursing (registered nurse training); welding technology.

Academic Programs *Special study options:* academic remediation for entering students, adult/continuing education programs, advanced placement credit, distance learning, double majors, independent study, part-time degree program, services for LD students, summer session for credit.

Library Learning Resource Center with 19,881 titles, 52 serial subscriptions, 2,364 audiovisual materials, an OPAC, a Web page.

Computers on Campus 150 computers available on campus for general student use. A campuswide network can be accessed from off campus. Internet access, at least one staffed computer lab available.

Student Life *Housing:* college housing not available. *Campus security:* 14-hour patrols. *Student services:* personal/psychological counseling.

Standardized Tests *Required:* ACT COMPASS (for placement).

Costs (2005–06) *Tuition:* area resident $1216 full-time; state resident $38 per semester hour part-time; nonresident $6752 full-time, $211 per semester hour part-time. *Required fees:* $66 full-time, $26 per term part-time. *Waivers:* senior citizens and employees or children of employees.

Financial Aid Of all full-time matriculated undergraduates who enrolled in 2003, 30 Federal Work-Study jobs (averaging $1200).

Applying *Options:* common application, electronic application, deferred entrance. *Required:* high school transcript. *Recommended:* minimum 2.0 GPA. *Application deadlines:* 8/1 (freshmen), 8/1 (transfers). *Notification:* continuous until 8/15 (freshmen).

Admissions Contact Ms. Yvonne Willoughby, Admissions Secretary, Bladen Community College, PO Box 266, Dublin, NC 28332. *Phone:* 910-879-5593. *Fax:* 910-879-5564. *E-mail:* ywilloughby@bladen.cc.nc.us.

BLUE RIDGE COMMUNITY COLLEGE
Flat Rock, North Carolina

- **State and locally supported** 2-year, founded 1969, part of North Carolina Community College System
- **Calendar** semesters
- **Degree** certificates, diplomas, and associate
- **Small-town** 109-acre campus
- **Endowment** $51,500
- **Coed,** 1,959 undergraduate students, 40% full-time, 63% women, 37% men

Undergraduates 787 full-time, 1,172 part-time. Students come from 18 states and territories, 14 other countries, 5% African American, 0.6% Asian American or Pacific Islander, 2% Hispanic American, 0.2% Native American, 2% international, 6% transferred in.

Freshmen *Admission:* 740 applied, 740 admitted, 412 enrolled.

Faculty *Total:* 302, 25% full-time, 7% with terminal degrees. *Student/faculty ratio:* 14:1.

Majors Administrative assistant and secretarial science; art; business administration and management; computer programming; computer programming related; cosmetology; drafting and design technology; electrical, electronic and communications engineering technology; environmental engineering technology; horticultural science; industrial technology; information science/studies; kindergarten/preschool education; liberal arts and sciences/liberal studies; machine tool technology; marketing/marketing management; mechanical engineering/mechanical technology; nursing (registered nurse training); sign language interpretation and translation; surgical technology; system administration; tourism and travel services management.

Academic Programs *Special study options:* academic remediation for entering students, adult/continuing education programs, advanced placement credit, cooperative education, distance learning, double majors, English as a second language, internships, part-time degree program, services for LD students, summer session for credit.

Library Blue Ridge Community College Library plus 1 other with 47,655 titles, 3,875 serial subscriptions, 1,692 audiovisual materials, an OPAC.

Computers on Campus 225 computers available on campus for general student use. A campuswide network can be accessed. Internet access available.

Student Life *Housing:* college housing not available. *Activities and Organizations:* drama/theater group, student-run newspaper, Student Government Association, Phi Theta Kappa, Spanish Club, Rotaract. *Campus security:* sheriff's deputy during class hours. *Student services:* personal/psychological counseling.

Athletics Member NJCAA. *Intercollegiate sports:* baseball M.

Costs (2004–05) *Tuition:* state resident $1216 full-time, $38 per credit hour part-time; nonresident $6752 full-time, $211 per credit hour part-time. *Required fees:* $71 full-time.

Financial Aid Of all full-time matriculated undergraduates who enrolled in 2003, 35 Federal Work-Study jobs (averaging $1920). 34 state and other part-time jobs (averaging $1920).

Applying *Options:* common application, early admission. *Required:* high school transcript. *Application deadline:* rolling (freshmen), rolling (transfers). *Notification:* continuous (freshmen).

Admissions Contact Ms. Sarah Jones, Registrar, Blue Ridge Community College, 180 West Campus Drive, Flat Rock, NC 28731. *Phone:* 828-694-1810. *E-mail:* sarahj@blueridge.edu.

BRUNSWICK COMMUNITY COLLEGE
Supply, North Carolina

- **State-supported** 2-year, founded 1979, part of North Carolina Community College System
- **Calendar** semesters
- **Degree** certificates, diplomas, and associate
- **Rural** 266-acre campus
- **Endowment** $1.3 million
- **Coed,** 1,003 undergraduate students, 49% full-time, 70% women, 30% men

Undergraduates 493 full-time, 510 part-time. Students come from 5 states and territories, 1% are from out of state, 21% African American, 0.4% Asian American or Pacific Islander, 0.8% Hispanic American, 0.2% Native American, 4% transferred in.

Freshmen *Admission:* 226 enrolled.

Faculty *Total:* 109, 27% full-time, 10% with terminal degrees. *Student/faculty ratio:* 12:1.

Majors Administrative assistant and secretarial science; applied horticulture; aquaculture; business administration and management; child care provision; computer/information technology services administration related; computer programming; computer programming related; electrical, electronic and communications engineering technology; engineering technology; fishing and fisheries sciences and management; health information/medical records administration; industrial technology; liberal arts and sciences/liberal studies; nursing (registered nurse training); teacher assistant/aide; turf and turfgrass management.

Academic Programs *Special study options:* academic remediation for entering students, advanced placement credit, cooperative education, distance learning, English as a second language, independent study, internships, part-time degree program, services for LD students, summer session for credit.

Library Brunswick Community College Library plus 1 other with 20,032 titles, 69 serial subscriptions, 986 audiovisual materials, an OPAC.

Computers on Campus 146 computers available on campus for general student use. A campuswide network can be accessed. Internet access, at least one staffed computer lab available.

Student Life *Housing:* college housing not available. *Activities and Organizations:* Student Government Association, Phi Theta Kappa Honor Society, National Vocational-Technical Honor Society. *Campus security:* late-night transport/escort service, campus police. *Student services:* personal/psychological counseling.

Athletics Member NJCAA. *Intercollegiate sports:* basketball M/W, golf M, softball W. *Intramural sports:* volleyball M/W.

Standardized Tests *Required:* ACT ASSET (for placement).

Costs (2004–05) *Tuition:* state resident $1140 full-time, $38 per semester hour part-time; nonresident $6360 full-time, $211 per semester hour part-time. Part-time tuition and fees vary according to course load. *Required fees:* $73 full-time, $73 per term part-time. *Waivers:* senior citizens.

Applying *Options:* electronic application. *Required:* high school transcript. *Required for some:* letters of recommendation, interview. *Application deadline:* rolling (freshmen), rolling (transfers). *Notification:* continuous (freshmen).

Admissions Contact Ms. Julie Olsen, Admissions Counselor, Brunswick Community College, PO Box 30, Supply, NC 28462. *Phone:* 910-755-7324. *Toll-free phone:* 800-754-1050 Ext. 324. *Fax:* 910-754-9609. *E-mail:* olsenj@brunswick.cc.nc.us.

CALDWELL COMMUNITY COLLEGE AND TECHNICAL INSTITUTE
Hudson, North Carolina

- **State-supported** 2-year, founded 1964, part of North Carolina Community College System
- **Calendar** semesters
- **Degree** certificates, diplomas, and associate
- **Small-town** 50-acre campus
- **Coed,** 3,613 undergraduate students, 33% full-time, 55% women, 45% men

Undergraduates 1,203 full-time, 2,410 part-time. Students come from 24 states and territories, 5% African American, 0.8% Asian American or Pacific Islander, 1% Hispanic American, 0.1% Native American, 9% transferred in.

Freshmen *Admission:* 744 applied, 744 admitted, 601 enrolled.

Faculty *Total:* 414, 28% full-time, 5% with terminal degrees.

Majors Accounting; aeronautics/aviation/aerospace science and technology; art; biological and physical sciences; biomedical technology; business administration and management; business systems networking/ telecommunications; cardiovascular technology; child care/guidance; computer programming (specific applications); cosmetology; diagnostic medical sonography and ultrasound technology; drafting and design technology; electrical, electronic and communications engineering technology; health/health care administration; information technology; landscaping and groundskeeping; legal assistant/paralegal; liberal arts and sciences/liberal studies; medical radiologic technology; music; nuclear medical technology; nursing (registered nurse training); physical therapy; preengineering.

Academic Programs *Special study options:* academic remediation for entering students, adult/continuing education programs, advanced placement credit, cooperative education, distance learning, double majors, independent study, part-time degree program, services for LD students, summer session for credit.

Library Broyhill Center for Learning Resources with 50,770 titles, 251 serial subscriptions, 5,352 audiovisual materials, an OPAC, a Web page.

Computers on Campus 750 computers available on campus for general student use. A campuswide network can be accessed from off campus. Internet access, online (class) registration, at least one staffed computer lab available.

Student Life *Housing:* college housing not available. *Activities and Organizations:* drama/theater group, choral group. *Campus security:* trained security personnel during open hours.

Athletics Member NJCAA. *Intercollegiate sports:* basketball M, volleyball W. *Intramural sports:* basketball M/W, tennis M/W.

Standardized Tests *Required:* CPT (for placement).

Costs (2004–05) *Tuition:* state resident $1368 full-time, $38 per credit hour part-time; nonresident $7596 full-time, $211 per credit hour part-time. *Required fees:* $4 per course part-time.

Financial Aid Of all full-time matriculated undergraduates who enrolled in 2003, 40 Federal Work-Study jobs (averaging $960).

Applying *Options:* early admission. *Required:* high school transcript. *Application deadline:* rolling (freshmen), rolling (transfers). *Notification:* continuous (freshmen).

Admissions Contact Mrs. Johnna Coffey, Director of Enrollment Management Services, Caldwell Community College and Technical Institute, 2855 Hickory Boulevard, Hudson, NC 28638. *Phone:* 828-726-2702. *Fax:* 828-726-2709.

CAPE FEAR COMMUNITY COLLEGE
Wilmington, North Carolina

- **State-supported** 2-year, founded 1959, part of North Carolina Community College System
- **Calendar** semesters
- **Degree** certificates, diplomas, and associate
- **Urban** 150-acre campus
- **Endowment** $1.7 million
- **Coed,** 7,073 undergraduate students, 48% full-time, 55% women, 45% men

Undergraduates 3,406 full-time, 3,667 part-time. Students come from 29 states and territories, 2 other countries, 5% are from out of state, 14% African American, 0.8% Asian American or Pacific Islander, 2% Hispanic American, 0.7% Native American.

Freshmen *Admission:* 1,541 applied, 1,080 admitted, 1,080 enrolled.

Faculty *Total:* 381, 59% full-time, 7% with terminal degrees. *Student/faculty ratio:* 13:1.

Majors Accounting technology and bookkeeping; architectural engineering technology; automobile/automotive mechanics technology; business administration and management; chemical technology; child care and support services management; computer systems analysis; computer systems networking and telecommunications; computer technology/computer systems technology; criminal justice/police science; dental hygiene; diagnostic medical sonography and ultrasound technology; electrical, electronic and communications engineering technology; electrical/electronics equipment installation and repair; engineering/industrial management; environmental studies; executive assistant/executive secretary; hotel/motel administration; industrial production technologies related; institutional food workers; instrumentation technology; interior design; landscaping and groundskeeping; liberal arts and sciences/liberal studies; machine shop technology; marine maintenance and ship repair technology; marine technology;

Cape Fear Community College (continued)

mechanical engineering/mechanical technology; medical radiologic technology; nursing (registered nurse training); occupational therapist assistant.

Academic Programs *Special study options:* academic remediation for entering students, adult/continuing education programs, cooperative education, distance learning, part-time degree program, services for LD students.

Library Cape Fear Community College Library with 47,761 titles, 936 serial subscriptions, 6,317 audiovisual materials, an OPAC, a Web page.

Computers on Campus 80 computers available on campus for general student use. A campuswide network can be accessed from off campus. At least one staffed computer lab available.

Student Life *Housing:* college housing not available. *Activities and Organizations:* student-run newspaper, choral group, Nursing Club, Dental Hygiene Club, Pineapple Guild. *Campus security:* 24-hour emergency response devices and patrols, late-night transport/escort service. *Student services:* personal/psychological counseling.

Athletics Member NJCAA. *Intercollegiate sports:* basketball M, cheerleading M/W, golf M, softball M/W, tennis M/W, volleyball M/W. *Intramural sports:* soccer M.

Standardized Tests *Required:* ACT ASSET (for placement).

Costs (2005–06) *Tuition:* state resident $1216 full-time, $38 per credit part-time; nonresident $6752 full-time, $211 per credit part-time. Full-time tuition and fees vary according to course load. Part-time tuition and fees vary according to course load. *Required fees:* $70 full-time, $7 per credit part-time. *Payment plan:* deferred payment. *Waivers:* senior citizens and employees or children of employees.

Financial Aid Of all full-time matriculated undergraduates who enrolled in 2003, 50 Federal Work-Study jobs.

Applying *Options:* electronic application, early admission, deferred entrance. *Required:* high school transcript, placement testing. *Application deadline:* 8/18 (freshmen), rolling (transfers). *Notification:* continuous (freshmen).

Admissions Contact Ms. Linda Kasyan, Director of Enrollment Management, Cape Fear Community College, 411 North Front Street, Wilmington, NC 28401-3993. *Phone:* 910-362-7054. *Toll-free phone:* 910-362-7557. *Fax:* 910-362-7080. *E-mail:* admissions@cfcc.edu.

CAROLINAS COLLEGE OF HEALTH SCIENCES
Charlotte, North Carolina

- **Independent** 2-year, founded 1990, part of Carolinas Healthcare System
- **Calendar** semesters
- **Degree** certificates, diplomas, and associate
- **Urban** 3-acre campus
- **Endowment** $2.0 million
- **Coed, primarily women,** 458 undergraduate students, 32% full-time, 86% women, 14% men

Undergraduates 146 full-time, 312 part-time. Students come from 3 states and territories, 6% are from out of state, 15% African American, 2% Asian American or Pacific Islander, 2% Hispanic American, 0.4% Native American, 5% live on campus.

Freshmen *Admission:* 28 enrolled. *Average high school GPA:* 3.18. *Test scores:* SAT verbal scores over 500: 63%; SAT math scores over 500: 53%; ACT scores over 18: 63%; SAT verbal scores over 600: 3%; SAT math scores over 600: 3%; ACT scores over 24: 13%.

Faculty *Total:* 51, 59% full-time, 6% with terminal degrees. *Student/faculty ratio:* 7:1.

Majors Medical radiologic technology; nursing (registered nurse training); radiologic technology/science.

Academic Programs *Special study options:* advanced placement credit, distance learning, independent study, internships.

Library AHEC Library with 9,810 titles, 503 serial subscriptions, an OPAC.

Computers on Campus 36 computers available on campus for general student use. A campuswide network can be accessed. Internet access, at least one staffed computer lab available.

Student Life *Housing Options:* Campus housing is provided by a third party. *Activities and Organizations:* Student Government Association. *Campus security:* 24-hour emergency response devices and patrols, student patrols, late-night transport/escort service. *Student services:* health clinic, personal/psychological counseling, legal services.

Standardized Tests *Required for some:* SAT or ACT (for admission).

Costs (2005–06) *Tuition:* $6145 full-time, $175 per credit part-time. Full-time tuition and fees vary according to course load and program. Part-time tuition and fees vary according to course load and program. *Required fees:* $250 full-time. *Waivers:* employees or children of employees.

Financial Aid Of all full-time matriculated undergraduates who enrolled in 2003, 12 Federal Work-Study jobs (averaging $1500).

Applying *Application fee:* $35. *Required:* high school transcript. *Required for some:* letters of recommendation, interview. *Recommended:* minimum 2.5 GPA. *Application deadline:* 2/6 (freshmen). *Notification:* 3/15 (freshmen).

Admissions Contact Ms. Elizabeth West, Admissions Officer, Carolinas College of Health Sciences, PO Box 32861, Charlotte, NC 28232-2861. *Phone:* 704-355-5043. *Fax:* 704-355-9336. *E-mail:* cchsinformation@carolinashealthcare.org.

CARTERET COMMUNITY COLLEGE
Morehead City, North Carolina

- **State-supported** 2-year, founded 1963, part of North Carolina Community College System
- **Calendar** semesters
- **Degree** certificates, diplomas, and associate
- **Small-town** 25-acre campus
- **Coed,** 1,732 undergraduate students, 39% full-time, 69% women, 31% men

Undergraduates 679 full-time, 1,053 part-time. Students come from 24 states and territories, 12% African American, 1% Asian American or Pacific Islander, 2% Hispanic American, 0.3% Native American.

Faculty *Total:* 94, 41% full-time.

Majors Administrative assistant and secretarial science; business administration and management; computer engineering technology; computer software and media applications related; computer systems networking and telecommunications; criminal justice/law enforcement administration; industrial radiologic technology; information technology; interior design; legal administrative assistant/secretary; legal assistant/paralegal; liberal arts and sciences/liberal studies; medical/clinical assistant; nursing (licensed practical/vocational nurse training); photography; respiratory care therapy; teacher assistant/aide; therapeutic recreation.

Academic Programs *Special study options:* academic remediation for entering students, adult/continuing education programs, cooperative education, distance learning, double majors, internships, part-time degree program, services for LD students, summer session for credit.

Library Michael J. Smith Learning Resource Center with 22,000 titles, 168 serial subscriptions.

Computers on Campus 150 computers available on campus for general student use. A campuswide network can be accessed. Internet access, at least one staffed computer lab available.

Student Life *Housing:* college housing not available. *Activities and Organizations:* student-run newspaper.

Athletics *Intercollegiate sports:* softball M/W, volleyball M/W.

Standardized Tests *Recommended:* SAT (for placement).

Costs (2004–05) *Tuition:* state resident $1136 full-time, $38 per semester hour part-time; nonresident $6304 full-time, $211 per semester hour part-time. *Required fees:* $47 full-time, $14 per term part-time.

Financial Aid Of all full-time matriculated undergraduates who enrolled in 2003, 40 Federal Work-Study jobs (averaging $750).

Applying *Options:* common application, electronic application, early admission. *Required:* high school transcript. *Application deadline:* rolling (freshmen), rolling (transfers). *Notification:* continuous (freshmen).

Admissions Contact Mr. Rick Hill, Director of Student Enrollment Resources, Carteret Community College, 3505 Arendell Street, Morehead City, NC 28557-2989. *Phone:* 252-222-6153 Ext. 6153. *Fax:* 252-222-6265. *E-mail:* mhw@carteret.edu.

CATAWBA VALLEY COMMUNITY COLLEGE
Hickory, North Carolina

- **State and locally supported** 2-year, founded 1960, part of North Carolina Community College System
- **Calendar** semesters
- **Degree** certificates, diplomas, and associate
- **Small-town** 50-acre campus with easy access to Charlotte
- **Endowment** $591,181
- **Coed,** 3,943 undergraduate students, 39% full-time, 56% women, 44% men

Undergraduates 1,524 full-time, 2,419 part-time. Students come from 3 states and territories, 2 other countries, 1% are from out of state, 24% transferred in.

Freshmen *Admission:* 575 enrolled. *Average high school GPA:* 2.76.

Faculty *Total:* 443, 23% full-time, 1% with terminal degrees. *Student/faculty ratio:* 11:1.

Majors Accounting technology and bookkeeping; administrative assistant and secretarial science; architectural engineering technology; automobile/automotive mechanics technology; banking and financial support services; business administration and management; business, management, and marketing related; commercial and advertising art; computer engineering related; computer engineering technology; computer programming; computer programming (specific applications); computer science; computer systems networking and telecommunications; criminal justice/police science; criminology; data processing and data processing technology; dental hygiene; electrical, electronic and communications engineering technology; emergency medical technology (EMT paramedic); engineering technologies related; fire protection and safety technology; funeral service and mortuary science; furniture design and manufacturing; health and medical administrative services related; health information/medical records technology; industrial technology; information technology; legal assistant/paralegal; liberal arts and sciences/liberal studies; marketing/marketing management; mechanical engineering/mechanical technology; medical radiologic technology; nursing (registered nurse training); operations management; photographic and film/video technology; photography; real estate; respiratory care therapy; retailing; speech-language pathology; teacher assistant/aide.

Academic Programs *Special study options:* academic remediation for entering students, adult/continuing education programs, advanced placement credit, cooperative education, distance learning, double majors, English as a second language, independent study, part-time degree program, services for LD students, student-designed majors, summer session for credit.

Library Learning Resource Center with 46,000 titles, 274 serial subscriptions, 3,644 audiovisual materials, an OPAC.

Computers on Campus 1144 computers available on campus for general student use. A campuswide network can be accessed from off campus. Internet access, at least one staffed computer lab available.

Student Life *Housing:* college housing not available. *Activities and Organizations:* student-run newspaper, choral group, NCANS (Nursing), Phi Theta Kappa, Catawba Valley Outing Club, Respiratory Care Club, Rotoract. *Campus security:* 24-hour patrols. *Student services:* personal/psychological counseling.

Athletics Member NJCAA. *Intercollegiate sports:* golf M(s), volleyball W.

Standardized Tests *Required:* ACT ASSET (for placement).

Costs (2004–05) *Tuition:* state resident $1216 full-time, $38 per semester hour part-time; nonresident $6752 full-time, $211 per semester hour part-time. *Required fees:* $337 full-time, $1 per semester hour part-time, $1 per term part-time.

Applying *Options:* common application, early admission, deferred entrance. *Required:* high school transcript. *Application deadline:* rolling (freshmen), rolling (transfers). *Notification:* continuous (freshmen).

Admissions Contact Mrs. Caroline Farmer, Director of Admissions and Records, Catawba Valley Community College, 2550 Highway 70 SE, Hickory, NC 28602-9699. *Phone:* 828-327-7000 Ext. 4218. *Fax:* 828-327-7000 Ext. 4224. *E-mail:* cfarmer@cvcc.cc.nc.us.

CENTRAL CAROLINA COMMUNITY COLLEGE
Sanford, North Carolina

- **State and locally supported** 2-year, founded 1962, part of North Carolina Community College System
- **Calendar** semesters
- **Degree** certificates, diplomas, and associate
- **Small-town** 41-acre campus
- **Endowment** $1.0 million
- **Coed,** 4,857 undergraduate students, 38% full-time, 62% women, 38% men

Undergraduates 1,845 full-time, 3,012 part-time. Students come from 36 states and territories, 5 other countries, 6% are from out of state, 25% African American, 1% Asian American or Pacific Islander, 4% Hispanic American, 0.8% Native American, 0.2% international, 20% transferred in.

Freshmen *Admission:* 2,844 applied, 1,227 admitted, 1,100 enrolled. *Test scores:* SAT verbal scores over 500: 25%; SAT math scores over 500: 25%; ACT scores over 18: 25%.

Faculty *Total:* 425, 37% full-time, 4% with terminal degrees. *Student/faculty ratio:* 8:1.

Majors Accounting; administrative assistant and secretarial science; automobile/automotive mechanics technology; business administration and management; computer/information technology services administration related; computer programming; computer programming (specific applications); computer systems networking and telecommunications; criminal justice/law enforcement administration; drafting and design technology; electrical, electronic and communications engineering technology; information science/studies; information technology; instrumentation technology; kindergarten/preschool education; laser and optical technology; legal administrative assistant/secretary; legal assistant/paralegal; liberal arts and sciences/liberal studies; marketing/marketing management; medical administrative assistant and medical secretary; medical/clinical assistant; nursing (registered nurse training); operations management; quality control technology; radio and television; social work; telecommunications; veterinary technology.

Academic Programs *Special study options:* academic remediation for entering students, adult/continuing education programs, advanced placement credit,

distance learning, double majors, English as a second language, independent study, internships, part-time degree program, services for LD students, summer session for credit.

Library Library/Learning Resources Center plus 2 others with 50,479 titles, 240 serial subscriptions, 5,946 audiovisual materials, an OPAC, a Web page.

Computers on Campus 100 computers available on campus for general student use. A campuswide network can be accessed from off campus. Internet access, at least one staffed computer lab available.

Student Life *Housing:* college housing not available. *Activities and Organizations:* student-run radio station. *Campus security:* patrols by trained security personnel during operating hours. *Student services:* personal/psychological counseling.

Athletics Member NJCAA. *Intercollegiate sports:* basketball M/W, golf M/W, softball W, volleyball W. *Intramural sports:* bowling M/W, golf M/W, softball W, volleyball W.

Standardized Tests *Required:* CPT, ACCUPLACER, ACT COMPASS, ACT ASSET (for placement). *Recommended:* SAT or ACT (for placement).

Costs (2004–05) *Tuition:* state resident $1216 full-time, $38 per credit hour part-time; nonresident $6752 full-time, $211 per credit hour part-time. *Required fees:* $36 full-time, $9 per term part-time. *Waivers:* senior citizens.

Financial Aid Of all full-time matriculated undergraduates who enrolled in 2003, 70 Federal Work-Study jobs (averaging $1361). *Financial aid deadline:* 5/4.

Applying *Options:* electronic application, early admission, deferred entrance. *Required:* high school transcript. *Application deadline:* rolling (freshmen), rolling (transfers). *Notification:* continuous (freshmen).

Admissions Contact Mr. Ken R. Hoyle Jr., Dean of Student Services, Central Carolina Community College, 1105 Kelly Drive, Sanford, NC 27330. *Phone:* 919-775-5401. *Toll-free phone:* 800-682-8353 Ext. 7300. *Fax:* 919-718-7380. *E-mail:* tgraves@cccc.edu.

CENTRAL PIEDMONT COMMUNITY COLLEGE
Charlotte, North Carolina

- **State and locally supported** 2-year, founded 1963, part of North Carolina Community College System
- **Calendar** semesters
- **Degree** certificates, diplomas, and associate
- **Urban** 37-acre campus
- **Endowment** $13.9 million
- **Coed,** 16,400 undergraduate students, 36% full-time, 59% women, 41% men

Undergraduates 5,945 full-time, 10,455 part-time. Students come from 13 states and territories, 117 other countries, 4% are from out of state, 34% African American, 3% Asian American or Pacific Islander, 3% Hispanic American, 0.4% Native American, 9% international, 29% transferred in.

Freshmen *Admission:* 1,257 applied, 1,257 admitted, 1,257 enrolled.

Faculty *Total:* 1,732, 17% full-time. *Student/faculty ratio:* 20:1.

Majors Accounting; administrative assistant and secretarial science; advertising; applied art; architectural engineering technology; art; automobile/automotive mechanics technology; biology/biological sciences; business administration and management; business machine repair; child development; civil engineering technology; clinical laboratory science/medical technology; clinical/medical laboratory technology; commercial and advertising art; computer engineering technology; computer programming; computer programming (specific applications); computer science; consumer merchandising/retailing management; criminal justice/law enforcement administration; criminal justice/police science; culinary arts; dance; data processing and data processing technology; dental hygiene; drafting and design technology; electrical, electronic and communications engineering technology; electromechanical technology; engineering technology; environmental engineering technology; fashion merchandising; finance; fire science; food science; food services technology; graphic and printing equipment operation/production; health/health care administration; health information/medical records administration; horticultural science; hospitality administration; hotel/motel administration; human services; industrial technology; insurance; interior design; kindergarten/preschool education; legal administrative assistant/secretary; legal assistant/paralegal; liberal arts and sciences/liberal studies; machine tool technology; marketing/marketing management; mechanical engineering/mechanical technology; medical administrative assistant and medical secretary; medical/clinical assistant; music; nursing (licensed practical/vocational nurse training); nursing (registered nurse training); physical therapy; postal management; real estate; respiratory care therapy; sign language interpretation and translation; social work; special products marketing; survey technology; tourism and travel services management; transportation technology; welding technology.

Academic Programs *Special study options:* academic remediation for entering students, accelerated degree program, advanced placement credit, cooperative education, distance learning, English as a second language, honors programs,

Central Piedmont Community College (continued)

off-campus study, part-time degree program, services for LD students, student-designed majors, summer session for credit.

Library Hagemeyer Learning Center plus 5 others with 102,649 titles, 750 serial subscriptions, 17,802 audiovisual materials, an OPAC, a Web page.

Computers on Campus A campuswide network can be accessed from off campus. Internet access, online (class) registration, at least one staffed computer lab available.

Student Life *Housing:* college housing not available. *Activities and Organizations:* drama/theater group, student-run newspaper, choral group, Phi Theta Kappa, Black Students Organization, Students for Environmental Sanity, Sierra Club, Nursing Club. *Campus security:* 24-hour emergency response devices and patrols. *Student services:* personal/psychological counseling, women's center.

Athletics Member NJCAA. *Intramural sports:* soccer M/W.

Standardized Tests *Required for some:* Nelson Denny Reading Test or CPT.

Costs (2004–05) *Tuition:* state resident $1216 full-time, $38 per semester hour part-time; nonresident $6752 full-time, $211 per semester hour part-time. *Required fees:* $170 full-time, $56 per semester part-time. *Waivers:* senior citizens and employees or children of employees.

Financial Aid Of all full-time matriculated undergraduates who enrolled in 2003, 102 Federal Work-Study jobs (averaging $2988).

Applying *Options:* common application. *Required for some:* high school transcript. *Application deadline:* rolling (freshmen), rolling (transfers). *Notification:* continuous (freshmen).

Admissions Contact Ms. Linda McComb, Associate Dean, Central Piedmont Community College, PO Box 35009, Charlotte, NC 28235-5009. *Phone:* 704-330-6784.

CLEVELAND COMMUNITY COLLEGE
Shelby, North Carolina

- **State-supported** 2-year, founded 1965, part of North Carolina Community College System
- **Calendar** semesters
- **Degree** certificates, diplomas, and associate
- **Small-town** 43-acre campus with easy access to Charlotte
- **Endowment** $450,000
- **Coed**, 2,943 undergraduate students, 43% full-time, 66% women, 34% men

Undergraduates 1,273 full-time, 1,670 part-time. Students come from 3 states and territories, 1% are from out of state, 25% African American, 0.7% Asian American or Pacific Islander, 1% Hispanic American, 0.2% Native American, 0.8% transferred in.

Freshmen *Admission:* 251 applied, 251 admitted, 251 enrolled. *Average high school GPA:* 2.71.

Faculty *Total:* 243, 28% full-time, 2% with terminal degrees.

Majors Accounting; administrative assistant and secretarial science; biological and physical sciences; business administration and management; communications technology; computer engineering technology; computer programming (specific applications); criminal justice/law enforcement administration; criminal justice/safety; data entry/microcomputer applications; electrical, electronic and communications engineering technology; electrician; engineering technologies related; executive assistant/executive secretary; fashion merchandising; fire protection and safety technology; industrial radiologic technology; information science/studies; information technology; liberal arts and sciences and humanities related; liberal arts and sciences/liberal studies; management information systems and services related; mechanical engineering/mechanical technology; medical administrative assistant and medical secretary; medical radiologic technology; nursing (registered nurse training); operations management; Spanish; special education; system administration; teacher assistant/aide.

Academic Programs *Special study options:* academic remediation for entering students, adult/continuing education programs, advanced placement credit, distance learning, double majors, English as a second language, independent study, off-campus study, part-time degree program, summer session for credit.

Library Cleveland Community College Library with 34,000 titles, 280 serial subscriptions, 3,619 audiovisual materials, an OPAC, a Web page.

Computers on Campus 325 computers available on campus for general student use. A campuswide network can be accessed. Internet access, at least one staffed computer lab available.

Student Life *Housing:* college housing not available. *Activities and Organizations:* drama/theater group, student-run television station, choral group, Gamma Beta Phi Honor Society, Student Government Association, Lamplighters, Mu Epsilon Delta, Black Awareness Club. *Campus security:* security personnel during open hours. *Student services:* personal/psychological counseling.

Costs (2005–06) *Tuition:* state resident $1136 full-time, $36 per credit hour part-time; nonresident $6304 full-time, $197 per credit hour part-time. Full-time tuition and fees vary according to course load. Part-time tuition and fees vary according to course load. *Required fees:* $38 full-time. *Waivers:* senior citizens.

Financial Aid Of all full-time matriculated undergraduates who enrolled in 2003, 18 Federal Work-Study jobs.

Applying *Options:* common application, electronic application, deferred entrance. *Required:* high school transcript. *Application deadline:* rolling (freshmen), rolling (transfers). *Notification:* continuous (freshmen).

Admissions Contact Mr. Alan Price, Dean of Enrollment Management, Cleveland Community College, 137 South Post Road, Shelby, NC 28152. *Phone:* 704-484-4073. *Fax:* 704-484-5305. *E-mail:* price@cleveland.cc.nc.us.

COASTAL CAROLINA COMMUNITY COLLEGE
Jacksonville, North Carolina

- **State and locally supported** 2-year, founded 1964, part of North Carolina Community College System
- **Calendar** semesters
- **Degree** certificates, diplomas, and associate
- **Small-town** 98-acre campus
- **Endowment** $1.7 million
- **Coed**, 4,158 undergraduate students, 52% full-time, 66% women, 34% men

Undergraduates 2,167 full-time, 1,991 part-time. Students come from 48 states and territories, 5 other countries, 28% are from out of state, 22% African American, 3% Asian American or Pacific Islander, 8% Hispanic American, 1% Native American, 0.6% international, 13% transferred in.

Freshmen *Admission:* 3,606 applied, 2,724 admitted, 871 enrolled.

Faculty *Total:* 266, 46% full-time, 12% with terminal degrees. *Student/faculty ratio:* 16:1.

Majors Accounting; architectural engineering technology; business administration and management; child care provision; clinical/medical laboratory technology; computer/information technology services administration related; computer programming (specific applications); computer systems analysis; computer systems networking and telecommunications; criminal justice/law enforcement administration; dental hygiene; emergency medical technology (EMT paramedic); executive assistant/executive secretary; fire science; legal assistant/paralegal; liberal arts and sciences/liberal studies; medical administrative assistant and medical secretary; nursing (registered nurse training); surgical technology.

Academic Programs *Special study options:* academic remediation for entering students, adult/continuing education programs, advanced placement credit, distance learning, double majors, English as a second language, independent study, internships, part-time degree program, services for LD students, summer session for credit.

Library C. Louis Shields Learning Resources Center with 44,062 titles, 266 serial subscriptions, 10,460 audiovisual materials, an OPAC.

Computers on Campus 830 computers available on campus for general student use. A campuswide network can be accessed from off campus. Internet access, at least one staffed computer lab available.

Student Life *Housing:* college housing not available. *Activities and Organizations:* drama/theater group, SHELL (environmental group), SPYS (social sciences group), student government, Star of Life, Association of Nursing Students. *Campus security:* 24-hour emergency response devices and patrols, late-night transport/escort service. *Student services:* personal/psychological counseling.

Standardized Tests *Required:* ACT ASSET (for placement).

Costs (2004–05) *Tuition:* state resident $1216 full-time, $38 per semester hour part-time; nonresident $6752 full-time, $211 per semester hour part-time. *Required fees:* $30 full-time, $5 per term part-time. *Waivers:* senior citizens.

Applying *Options:* deferred entrance. *Required:* high school transcript. *Required for some:* 2 letters of recommendation, interview. *Application deadline:* rolling (freshmen), rolling (transfers). *Notification:* continuous (freshmen).

Admissions Contact Mr. Jerry W. Snead, Director of Admissions, Coastal Carolina Community College, 444 Western Boulevard, Jacksonville, NC 28546. *Phone:* 910-938-6246. *Fax:* 910-455-2767.

COLLEGE OF THE ALBEMARLE
Elizabeth City, North Carolina

Admissions Contact Mr. Kenny Krentz, Director of Admissions and International Students, College of The Albemarle, PO Box 2327, 1208 N. Road Street, Elizabeth City, NC 27909-2327. *Phone:* 252-335-0821 Ext. 2220. *Fax:* 252-335-2011. *E-mail:* kkrentz@albemarle.edu.

CRAVEN COMMUNITY COLLEGE
New Bern, North Carolina

- **State-supported** 2-year, founded 1965, part of North Carolina Community College System
- **Calendar** semesters
- **Degree** certificates, diplomas, and associate

■ **Suburban** 100-acre campus
■ **Endowment** $576,211
■ **Coed,** 2,555 undergraduate students

Undergraduates Students come from 25 states and territories, 2 other countries, 17% are from out of state, 26% African American, 2% Asian American or Pacific Islander, 3% Hispanic American, 1% Native American, 0.2% international.

Faculty *Total:* 166, 38% full-time. *Student/faculty ratio:* 14:1.

Majors Accounting; automobile/automotive mechanics technology; business administration and management; child care and support services management; computer programming (specific applications); computer systems networking and telecommunications; criminal justice/law enforcement administration; electrical, electronic and communications engineering technology; electromechanical technology; executive assistant/executive secretary; general retailing/wholesaling; heating, air conditioning, ventilation and refrigeration maintenance technology; legal administrative assistant/secretary; liberal arts and sciences/liberal studies; management information systems; mechanical engineering/mechanical technology; medical administrative assistant and medical secretary; nursing (registered nurse training); tool and die technology.

Academic Programs *Special study options:* academic remediation for entering students, adult/continuing education programs, advanced placement credit, cooperative education, distance learning, double majors, independent study, internships, part-time degree program, services for LD students, student-designed majors, summer session for credit.

Library R. C. Godwin Memorial Library with 21,000 titles, 301 serial subscriptions, an OPAC.

Computers on Campus 350 computers available on campus for general student use. Internet access, at least one staffed computer lab available.

Student Life *Housing:* college housing not available. *Activities and Organizations:* drama/theater group, choral group, Accounting Club, Alumni Association, Association of Information Technology Professionals, Criminal Justice Society, Phi Theta Kappa. *Campus security:* 24-hour patrols. *Student services:* personal/psychological counseling.

Athletics Member NJCAA. *Intercollegiate sports:* basketball M, softball M/W.

Standardized Tests *Recommended:* SAT or ACT (for placement).

Costs (2004–05) *Tuition:* state resident $1216 full-time, $38 per semester hour part-time; nonresident $6792 full-time, $211 per semester hour part-time. *Required fees:* $970 full-time, $15 per semester hour part-time, $5 per term part-time.

Financial Aid Of all full-time matriculated undergraduates who enrolled in 2003, 64 Federal Work-Study jobs (averaging $1446).

Applying *Required:* high school transcript, interview. *Application deadline:* rolling (freshmen), rolling (transfers).

Admissions Contact Ms. Millicent Fulford, Recruiter, Craven Community College, 800 College Court, New Bern, NC 28562-4984. *Phone:* 252-638-7232. *Fax:* 252-638-4649.

DAVIDSON COUNTY COMMUNITY COLLEGE
Lexington, North Carolina

■ **State and locally supported** 2-year, founded 1958, part of North Carolina Community College System
■ **Calendar** semesters
■ **Degree** certificates, diplomas, and associate
■ **Rural** 83-acre campus
■ **Endowment** $6.5 million
■ **Coed,** 2,303 undergraduate students, 36% full-time, 61% women, 39% men

Undergraduates 829 full-time, 1,474 part-time. Students come from 7 states and territories, 1% are from out of state, 13% African American, 1% Asian American or Pacific Islander, 1% Hispanic American, 0.4% Native American.

Freshmen *Admission:* 692 applied, 692 admitted, 337 enrolled.

Faculty *Total:* 212, 34% full-time, 3% with terminal degrees. *Student/faculty ratio:* 11:1.

Majors Accounting; administrative assistant and secretarial science; business administration and management; clinical/medical laboratory technology; computer engineering technology; computer programming; criminal justice/law enforcement administration; criminal justice/police science; data processing and data processing technology; electrical, electronic and communications engineering technology; emergency medical technology (EMT paramedic); engineering technology; fire science; health information/medical records administration; legal assistant/paralegal; liberal arts and sciences/liberal studies; medical/clinical assistant; nursing (registered nurse training); plastics engineering technology; pre-engineering.

Academic Programs *Special study options:* academic remediation for entering students, adult/continuing education programs, advanced placement credit, cooperative education, double majors, internships, off-campus study, part-time degree program, services for LD students, summer session for credit.

Library Grady E. Love Learning Resource Center plus 1 other with 56,445 titles, 454 serial subscriptions, 7,564 audiovisual materials, an OPAC, a Web page.

Computers on Campus 400 computers available on campus for general student use. A campuswide network can be accessed from off campus. Internet access, at least one staffed computer lab available.

Student Life *Housing:* college housing not available. *Activities and Organizations:* drama/theater group. *Campus security:* late-night transport/escort service, security guards.

Standardized Tests *Required:* (for placement).

Costs (2005–06) *Tuition:* state resident $1140 full-time, $38 per credit hour part-time; nonresident $6330 full-time, $211 per credit hour part-time. *Required fees:* $1088 full-time, $27 per credit hour part-time.

Financial Aid Of all full-time matriculated undergraduates who enrolled in 2003, 20 Federal Work-Study jobs (averaging $1800).

Applying *Options:* early admission, deferred entrance. *Required:* high school transcript. *Required for some:* interview. *Application deadline:* rolling (freshmen), rolling (transfers). *Notification:* continuous (freshmen).

Admissions Contact Mr. Rick Travis, Director, Career Services, Davidson County Community College, PO Box 1287, Lexington, NC 27293-1287. *Phone:* 336-249-8186 Ext. 224. *Fax:* 336-249-0379. *E-mail:* admissions@davidson.cc.nc.us.

DURHAM TECHNICAL COMMUNITY COLLEGE
Durham, North Carolina

■ **State-supported** 2-year, founded 1961, part of North Carolina Community College System
■ **Calendar** semesters
■ **Degree** certificates, diplomas, and associate
■ **Urban** campus
■ **Coed,** 5,642 undergraduate students, 26% full-time, 63% women, 37% men

Undergraduates 1,464 full-time, 4,178 part-time. Students come from 50 states and territories, 1% are from out of state, 41% African American, 3% Asian American or Pacific Islander, 2% Hispanic American, 0.2% Native American, 8% international, 59% transferred in.

Freshmen *Admission:* 732 enrolled.

Faculty *Total:* 477, 25% full-time. *Student/faculty ratio:* 16:1.

Majors Accounting; administrative assistant and secretarial science; architectural engineering technology; automobile/automotive mechanics technology; business administration and management; child development; computer programming; computer programming related; computer typography and composition equipment operation; criminal justice/law enforcement administration; criminal justice/police science; data processing and data processing technology; dental hygiene; electrical, electronic and communications engineering technology; fire science; general studies; health information/medical records administration; information science/studies; information technology; kindergarten/preschool education; laser and optical technology; legal assistant/paralegal; liberal arts and sciences/liberal studies; machine tool technology; medical administrative assistant and medical secretary; nursing (licensed practical/vocational nurse training); nursing (registered nurse training); occupational safety and health technology; occupational therapy; operations management; ophthalmic laboratory technology; pharmacy; real estate; respiratory care therapy; surgical technology; system administration; teacher assistant/aide.

Academic Programs *Special study options:* academic remediation for entering students, accelerated degree program, adult/continuing education programs, advanced placement credit, cooperative education, distance learning, English as a second language, internships, off-campus study, part-time degree program, services for LD students, student-designed majors, summer session for credit.

Library Educational Resource Center with 36,388 titles, 1,348 audiovisual materials, an OPAC.

Computers on Campus 664 computers available on campus for general student use. A campuswide network can be accessed from off campus. Internet access, at least one staffed computer lab available.

Student Life *Housing:* college housing not available. *Activities and Organizations:* drama/theater group, Amigos Unidos, Gamma Beta Phi, Student Senate, Student Nurses Association, Practical Nurses Students Club. *Campus security:* 24-hour patrols, late-night transport/escort service. *Student services:* personal/psychological counseling.

Standardized Tests *Required:* ACT ASSET or ACT COMPASS (for placement).

Costs (2004–05) *Tuition:* state resident $1216 full-time, $38 per credit hour part-time; nonresident $6752 full-time, $211 per credit hour part-time. Full-time tuition and fees vary according to course load. *Required fees:* $45 full-time, $22 per term part-time. *Waivers:* senior citizens and employees or children of employees.

Financial Aid Of all full-time matriculated undergraduates who enrolled in 2003, 35 Federal Work-Study jobs (averaging $2000).

Durham Technical Community College (continued)

Applying *Options:* deferred entrance. *Required:* high school transcript. *Recommended:* interview. *Application deadline:* rolling (freshmen), rolling (transfers). *Notification:* continuous (freshmen).

Admissions Contact Ms. Penny Augustine, Director of Admissions and Testing, Durham Technical Community College, 1637 Lawson Street, Durham, NC 27703. *Phone:* 919-686-3619.

ECPI TECHNICAL COLLEGE
Raleigh, North Carolina

Admissions Contact Mr. Rich Wechner, Campus Director, ECPI Technical College, 4101 Doie Cope Road, Raleigh, NC 27613-7387. *Phone:* 919-571-0057. *Toll-free phone:* 800-986-1200.

EDGECOMBE COMMUNITY COLLEGE
Tarboro, North Carolina

- **State and locally supported** 2-year, founded 1968, part of North Carolina Community College System
- **Calendar** semesters
- **Degree** certificates, diplomas, and associate
- **Small-town** 90-acre campus
- **Endowment** $1.0 million
- **Coed,** 2,553 undergraduate students, 37% full-time, 74% women, 26% men

Undergraduates 947 full-time, 1,606 part-time. Students come from 3 states and territories, 4 other countries, 1% are from out of state, 62% African American, 0.4% Asian American or Pacific Islander, 1% Hispanic American, 0.8% Native American, 0.1% international, 2% transferred in.

Freshmen *Admission:* 374 applied, 354 admitted, 235 enrolled.

Faculty *Total:* 150, 54% full-time, 7% with terminal degrees. *Student/faculty ratio:* 16:1.

Majors Accounting; administrative assistant and secretarial science; business administration and management; criminal justice/law enforcement administration; data entry/microcomputer applications; electrical, electronic and communications engineering technology; health information/medical records administration; human services; information technology; kindergarten/preschool education; liberal arts and sciences/liberal studies; mechanical drafting and CAD/CADD; mechanical engineering/mechanical technology; mechanical engineering technologies related; medical/clinical assistant; nursing (licensed practical/vocational nurse training); nursing (registered nurse training); plastics engineering technology; radiologic technology/science; respiratory care therapy; respiratory therapy technician; social work; surgical technology; system administration; word processing.

Academic Programs *Special study options:* academic remediation for entering students, adult/continuing education programs, advanced placement credit, cooperative education, distance learning, double majors, English as a second language, independent study, off-campus study, part-time degree program, services for LD students, summer session for credit.

Library 42,460 titles, 239 serial subscriptions, 2,527 audiovisual materials, an OPAC, a Web page.

Computers on Campus 180 computers available on campus for general student use. A campuswide network can be accessed from off campus. Internet access, at least one staffed computer lab available.

Student Life *Housing:* college housing not available. *Activities and Organizations:* Student Government Association.

Athletics *Intramural sports:* basketball M.

Standardized Tests *Recommended:* SAT or ACT (for placement), MAPS.

Costs (2004–05) *Tuition:* state resident $1216 full-time, $38 per credit part-time; nonresident $6752 full-time, $211 per credit part-time. *Required fees:* $24 full-time, $1 per credit part-time. *Payment plan:* installment. *Waivers:* senior citizens and employees or children of employees.

Financial Aid Of all full-time matriculated undergraduates who enrolled in 2003, 45 Federal Work-Study jobs (averaging $800).

Applying *Options:* common application, electronic application. *Required:* high school transcript, minimum 2.0 GPA. *Required for some:* letters of recommendation. *Application deadline:* rolling (freshmen), rolling (transfers). *Notification:* continuous (freshmen).

Admissions Contact Ms. Jackie Heath, Admissions Officer, Edgecombe Community College, 2009 West Wilson Street, Tarboro, NC 27886. *Phone:* 252-823-5166 Ext. 254. *Fax:* 252-823-6817. *E-mail:* heathj@edgecombe.edu.

FAYETTEVILLE TECHNICAL COMMUNITY COLLEGE
Fayetteville, North Carolina

- **State-supported** 2-year, founded 1961, part of North Carolina Community College System

- **Calendar** semesters
- **Degree** certificates, diplomas, and associate
- **Suburban** 135-acre campus with easy access to Raleigh
- **Endowment** $39,050
- **Coed,** 10,175 undergraduate students, 44% full-time, 67% women, 33% men

Undergraduates 4,519 full-time, 5,656 part-time. Students come from 50 states and territories, 9 other countries, 21% are from out of state, 38% African American, 2% Asian American or Pacific Islander, 7% Hispanic American, 3% Native American, 2% international, 21% transferred in.

Freshmen *Admission:* 4,306 applied, 4,306 admitted, 2,219 enrolled. *Average high school GPA:* 2.43.

Faculty *Total:* 845, 36% full-time. *Student/faculty ratio:* 35:1.

Majors Accounting; advertising; anatomy; applied horticulture; architectural engineering technology; autobody/collision and repair technology; automobile/automotive mechanics technology; business administration and management; business automation/technology/data entry; cabinetmaking and millwork; carpentry; child care and support services management; child care provision; civil engineering technology; commercial and advertising art; communications systems installation and repair technology; computer and information sciences; computer and information sciences related; computer engineering related; computer graphics; computer programming; computer programming related; computer programming (specific applications); computer software and media applications related; computer systems networking and telecommunications; computer/technical support; cosmetology; criminal justice/safety; culinary arts related; data entry/microcomputer applications; dental assisting; dental hygiene; electrical, electronic and communications engineering technology; electrical, electronics and communications engineering; emergency medical technology (EMT paramedic); engineering technology; finance; food services technology; funeral service and mortuary science; general studies; health information/medical records technology; heating, air conditioning, ventilation and refrigeration maintenance technology; horticultural science; hospitality administration related; human resources management and services related; industrial mechanics and maintenance technology; industrial technology; information science/studies; information technology; kindergarten/preschool education; legal assistant/paralegal; liberal arts and sciences/liberal studies; machine tool technology; management information systems; management science; marketing/marketing management; masonry; medical laboratory technology; medical office management; nursing (licensed practical/vocational nurse training); nursing (registered nurse training); parks, recreation and leisure; pharmacy technician; physical therapist assistant; pipefitting and sprinkler fitting; postal management; public administration; radiologic technology/science; respiratory care therapy; sales, distribution and marketing; speech-language pathology; surgical technology; survey technology; system administration; tool and die technology; web/multimedia management and webmaster; web page, digital/multimedia and information resources design; welding technology; word processing.

Academic Programs *Special study options:* academic remediation for entering students, adult/continuing education programs, advanced placement credit, cooperative education, distance learning, double majors, English as a second language, independent study, internships, off-campus study, part-time degree program, services for LD students, student-designed majors, summer session for credit.

Library Paul H. Thompson Library with 61,580 titles, 398 serial subscriptions, 6,657 audiovisual materials, an OPAC, a Web page.

Computers on Campus 400 computers available on campus for general student use. A campuswide network can be accessed from off campus. Internet access, at least one staffed computer lab available.

Student Life *Housing:* college housing not available. *Activities and Organizations:* Criminal Justice Association, Early Childhood Club, Phi Beta Lambda, Student Nurses Club, Data Processing Management Association. *Campus security:* 24-hour emergency response devices and patrols, late-night transport/escort service. *Student services:* health clinic, personal/psychological counseling.

Athletics *Intramural sports:* basketball M/W, table tennis M/W, volleyball M/W.

Standardized Tests *Required:* ACCUPLACER (for placement).

Financial Aid Of all full-time matriculated undergraduates who enrolled in 2003, 75 Federal Work-Study jobs (averaging $2000). *Financial aid deadline:* 6/1.

Applying *Options:* electronic application, deferred entrance. *Required for some:* high school transcript. *Application deadline:* rolling (freshmen), rolling (transfers). *Notification:* continuous (freshmen).

Admissions Contact Mr. James Kelley, Director of Admissions, Fayetteville Technical Community College, PO Box 35236, Fayetteville, NC 28303. *Phone:* 910-678-8274. *Fax:* 910-678-8407. *E-mail:* collinsv@faytechcc.edu.

FORSYTH TECHNICAL COMMUNITY COLLEGE
Winston-Salem, North Carolina

- **State-supported** 2-year, founded 1964, part of North Carolina Community College System
- **Calendar** semesters
- **Degree** certificates, diplomas, and associate
- **Suburban** 38-acre campus
- **Coed,** 7,157 undergraduate students, 39% full-time, 64% women, 36% men

Undergraduates 2,784 full-time, 4,373 part-time. 25% African American, 1% Asian American or Pacific Islander, 3% Hispanic American, 0.6% Native American.
Freshmen *Admission:* 9,275 applied, 5,268 admitted.
Faculty *Total:* 360, 48% full-time. *Student/faculty ratio:* 19:1.
Majors Accounting; administrative assistant and secretarial science; architectural engineering technology; automobile/automotive mechanics technology; business administration and management; carpentry; child development; commercial and advertising art; computer engineering technology; computer science; construction engineering technology; criminal justice/law enforcement administration; criminal justice/police science; data processing and data processing technology; drafting and design technology; electrical, electronic and communications engineering technology; electromechanical technology; engineering technology; finance; funeral service and mortuary science; graphic and printing equipment operation/production; heating, air conditioning, ventilation and refrigeration maintenance technology; horticultural science; industrial radiologic technology; industrial technology; kindergarten/preschool education; legal assistant/paralegal; machine tool technology; marketing/marketing management; mechanical design technology; medical/clinical assistant; nuclear medical technology; nursing (registered nurse training); ornamental horticulture; pipefitting and sprinkler fitting; real estate; respiratory care therapy; welding technology.
Academic Programs *Special study options:* academic remediation for entering students, adult/continuing education programs, English as a second language, part-time degree program, services for LD students, summer session for credit.
Library Forsyth Technical Community College Library plus 1 other with 41,606 titles, 358 serial subscriptions.
Computers on Campus 450 computers available on campus for general student use. At least one staffed computer lab available.
Student Life *Housing:* college housing not available. *Activities and Organizations:* student-run newspaper. *Campus security:* 24-hour patrols. *Student services:* personal/psychological counseling.
Athletics *Intramural sports:* basketball M/W, bowling M/W, softball W, volleyball M/W.
Standardized Tests *Required:* Assessment and Placement Services for Community Colleges (for placement). *Recommended:* SAT or ACT (for placement).
Costs (2004–05) *Tuition:* state resident $912 full-time, $38 per credit hour part-time; nonresident $5064 full-time, $211 per credit hour part-time. Full-time tuition and fees vary according to course load. Part-time tuition and fees vary according to course load. *Required fees:* $50 full-time, $19 per term part-time.
Financial Aid Of all full-time matriculated undergraduates who enrolled in 2003, 42 Federal Work-Study jobs (averaging $2083).
Applying *Required:* high school transcript. *Application deadlines:* 8/25 (freshmen), 9/1 (transfers). *Notification:* continuous until 8/25 (freshmen).
Admissions Contact Ms. Patrice Mitchell, Director of Admissions, Forsyth Technical Community College, 2100 Silas Creek Parkway, Winston-Salem, NC 27103-5197. *Phone:* 336-734-7331. *Fax:* 336-761-2098. *E-mail:* admissions@forsythtech.edu.

GASTON COLLEGE
Dallas, North Carolina

- **State and locally supported** 2-year, founded 1963, part of North Carolina Community College System
- **Calendar** semesters
- **Degree** certificates, diplomas, and associate
- **Small-town** 166-acre campus with easy access to Charlotte
- **Endowment** $716,546
- **Coed**

Faculty *Student/faculty ratio:* 18:1.
Student Life *Campus security:* 24-hour patrols.
Standardized Tests *Required:* ACT COMPASS (for placement). *Required for some:* ACT (for placement).
Financial Aid Of all full-time matriculated undergraduates who enrolled in 2003, 50 Federal Work-Study jobs (averaging $1800). 30 state and other part-time jobs (averaging $1533).
Applying *Required for some:* high school transcript.

Admissions Contact Ms. Alice D. Hopper, Admissions Specialist, Gaston College, 201 Highway 321 South, Dallas, NC 28034. *Phone:* 704-922-6214.

GUILFORD TECHNICAL COMMUNITY COLLEGE
Jamestown, North Carolina

- **State and locally supported** 2-year, founded 1958, part of North Carolina Community College System
- **Calendar** semesters
- **Degree** certificates, diplomas, and associate
- **Suburban** 158-acre campus
- **Coed,** 8,491 undergraduate students, 35% full-time, 57% women, 43% men

Undergraduates 2,930 full-time, 5,561 part-time. Students come from 21 states and territories, 34% African American, 3% Asian American or Pacific Islander, 2% Hispanic American, 0.5% Native American, 2% international.
Freshmen *Admission:* 4,910 enrolled.
Faculty *Total:* 1,222, 44% full-time, 5% with terminal degrees.
Majors Accounting; airline pilot and flight crew; architectural engineering technology; automobile/automotive mechanics technology; aviation/airway management; avionics maintenance technology; biological and physical sciences; biology/biotechnology laboratory technician; building/construction finishing, management, and inspection related; business administration and management; business operations support and secretarial services related; chemistry related; cinematography and film/video production; civil engineering technology; clinical/medical laboratory technology; commercial and advertising art; computer/information technology services administration related; computer programming; computer systems networking and telecommunications; cosmetology; criminal justice/law enforcement administration; criminal justice/police science; culinary arts; dental hygiene; drafting and design technology; dramatic/theatre arts; education related; electrical, electronic and communications engineering technology; electrical/electronics equipment installation and repair; emergency medical technology (EMT paramedic); fire science; heating, air conditioning, ventilation and refrigeration maintenance technology; heavy equipment maintenance technology; human services; industrial arts; industrial mechanics and maintenance technology; industrial technology; information science/studies; kindergarten/preschool education; legal assistant/paralegal; liberal arts and sciences/liberal studies; machine tool technology; medical/clinical assistant; nursing (registered nurse training); occupational therapist assistant; physical therapist assistant; respiratory care therapy; speech-language pathology; surgical technology; survey technology; turf and turfgrass management; web page, digital/multimedia and information resources design.
Academic Programs *Special study options:* academic remediation for entering students, adult/continuing education programs, advanced placement credit, cooperative education, distance learning, English as a second language, external degree program, independent study, internships, off-campus study, part-time degree program, services for LD students, student-designed majors, summer session for credit. *ROTC:* Army (c), Air Force (c).
Library M. W. Bell Library plus 2 others with 74,958 titles, 381 serial subscriptions, 7,286 audiovisual materials, an OPAC, a Web page.
Computers on Campus 90 computers available on campus for general student use. A campuswide network can be accessed from off campus. Internet access, at least one staffed computer lab available.
Student Life *Housing:* college housing not available. *Activities and Organizations:* drama/theater group.
Standardized Tests *Required:* ACT COMPASS (for placement).
Costs (2005–06) *Tuition:* state resident $1216 full-time; nonresident $6752 full-time. *Required fees:* $75 full-time. *Payment plan:* installment. *Waivers:* senior citizens and employees or children of employees.
Financial Aid Of all full-time matriculated undergraduates who enrolled in 2003, 84 Federal Work-Study jobs (averaging $3302).
Applying *Options:* early admission, deferred entrance. *Required:* high school transcript. *Required for some:* interview. *Application deadline:* rolling (freshmen), rolling (transfers). *Notification:* continuous (freshmen).
Admissions Contact Ms. Jean Groome, Director of Admissions, Guilford Technical Community College, PO Box 309, Jamestown, NC 27282. *Phone:* 336-334-4822 Ext. 2396. *E-mail:* knighte@gtcc.cc.nc.us.

HALIFAX COMMUNITY COLLEGE
Weldon, North Carolina

- **State and locally supported** 2-year, founded 1967, part of North Carolina Community College System
- **Calendar** semesters
- **Degree** certificates, diplomas, and associate
- **Rural** 109-acre campus
- **Coed,** 1,580 undergraduate students

Halifax Community College (continued)

Undergraduates Students come from 2 states and territories.

Faculty *Total:* 147, 44% full-time.

Majors Administrative assistant and secretarial science; art teacher education; business administration and management; business teacher education; clinical/medical laboratory technology; commercial and advertising art; corrections; criminal justice/police science; education; industrial technology; interior design; liberal arts and sciences/liberal studies; marketing/marketing management; medical administrative assistant and medical secretary; nursing (registered nurse training); social work.

Academic Programs *Special study options:* academic remediation for entering students, adult/continuing education programs, cooperative education, part-time degree program, summer session for credit.

Library Halifax Community College Library with 26,527 titles, 122 serial subscriptions.

Computers on Campus 100 computers available on campus for general student use. At least one staffed computer lab available.

Student Life *Housing:* college housing not available. *Campus security:* 12-hour patrols by trained security personnel.

Costs (2005–06) *Tuition:* state resident $1216 full-time, $38 per credit part-time; nonresident $6752 full-time, $211 per credit part-time. *Required fees:* $80 full-time, $5 per credit part-time.

Applying *Options:* deferred entrance. *Required:* high school transcript. *Application deadline:* rolling (freshmen), rolling (transfers). *Notification:* continuous (freshmen).

Admissions Contact Mrs. Scottie Dickens, Director of Admissions, Halifax Community College, PO Drawer 809, Weldon, NC 27890-0809. *Phone:* 252-536-7220.

HAYWOOD COMMUNITY COLLEGE

Clyde, North Carolina

- **State and locally supported** 2-year, founded 1964, part of North Carolina Community College System
- **Calendar** semesters
- **Degree** certificates, diplomas, and associate
- **Rural** 85-acre campus
- **Coed,** 1,988 undergraduate students, 44% full-time, 56% women, 44% men

Undergraduates 876 full-time, 1,112 part-time. Students come from 7 states and territories, 1% are from out of state, 1% African American, 0.7% Asian American or Pacific Islander, 1% Hispanic American, 1% Native American, 13% transferred in.

Freshmen *Admission:* 1,018 applied, 681 admitted, 189 enrolled.

Faculty *Total:* 123, 54% full-time. *Student/faculty ratio:* 12:1.

Majors Business administration and management; ceramic arts and ceramics; cosmetology; crafts, folk art and artisanry; criminal justice/law enforcement administration; education; fiber, textile and weaving arts; fish/game management; forestry technology; horticultural science; industrial arts; industrial technology; information science/studies; liberal arts and sciences/liberal studies; machine tool technology; management information systems; medical/clinical assistant; metal and jewelry arts; nursing (registered nurse training); wildlife and wildlands science and management; wood science and wood products/pulp and paper technology.

Academic Programs *Special study options:* academic remediation for entering students, adult/continuing education programs, advanced placement credit, cooperative education, distance learning, double majors, English as a second language, independent study, internships, part-time degree program, services for LD students.

Library Freedlander Learning Resource Center with 26,788 titles, 167 serial subscriptions.

Computers on Campus 10 computers available on campus for general student use. A campuswide network can be accessed. Internet access available.

Student Life *Housing:* college housing not available. *Activities and Organizations:* Student Government Association, Phi Theta Kappa, Phi Beta Lambda, Outdoor Club, Cosmetology Club. *Campus security:* 24-hour patrols. *Student services:* personal/psychological counseling.

Athletics *Intramural sports:* basketball M/W, bowling M/W, football M/W, golf M/W, softball M/W, volleyball M/W.

Costs (2005–06) *Tuition:* state resident $1216 full-time, $38 per credit hour part-time; nonresident $6752 full-time, $211 per credit hour part-time. *Required fees:* $49 full-time, $13 per term part-time.

Financial Aid Of all full-time matriculated undergraduates who enrolled in 2003, 59 Federal Work-Study jobs (averaging $907).

Applying *Required:* high school transcript. *Required for some:* interview. *Application deadline:* rolling (freshmen), rolling (transfers).

Admissions Contact Ms. Debbie Rowland, Coordinator of Admissions, Haywood Community College, 185 Freedlander Drive, Clyde, NC 28721-9453. *Phone:* 828-627-4505. *Fax:* 828-627-4513. *E-mail:* drowland@haywood.cc.nc.us.

ISOTHERMAL COMMUNITY COLLEGE

Spindale, North Carolina

- **State-supported** 2-year, founded 1965, part of North Carolina Community College System
- **Calendar** semesters
- **Degree** certificates, diplomas, and associate
- **Rural** 120-acre campus
- **Coed,** 2,005 undergraduate students, 49% full-time, 65% women, 35% men

Undergraduates 988 full-time, 1,017 part-time. Students come from 40 states and territories, 3 other countries, 16% African American, 0.3% Asian American or Pacific Islander, 0.9% Hispanic American, 0.3% Native American, 0.3% international. *Retention:* 33% of 2002 full-time freshmen returned.

Freshmen *Admission:* 274 enrolled.

Faculty *Total:* 114, 53% full-time, 7% with terminal degrees. *Student/faculty ratio:* 17:1.

Majors Administrative assistant and secretarial science; automobile/automotive mechanics technology; biological and physical sciences; broadcast journalism; business administration and management; business teacher education; commercial and advertising art; computer programming; computer science; cosmetology; criminal justice/law enforcement administration; criminal justice/police science; drafting and design technology; education; electrical, electronic and communications engineering technology; elementary education; insurance; kindergarten/preschool education; liberal arts and sciences/liberal studies; machine tool technology; marketing/marketing management; mechanical design technology; mechanical engineering/mechanical technology; music; nursing (licensed practical/vocational nurse training); pharmacy; plastics engineering technology; pre-engineering; radio and television; real estate; teacher assistant/aide; trade and industrial teacher education; veterinary sciences; welding technology.

Academic Programs *Special study options:* academic remediation for entering students, adult/continuing education programs, advanced placement credit, cooperative education, English as a second language, external degree program, honors programs, part-time degree program, services for LD students, student-designed majors, summer session for credit.

Library 35,200 titles, 289 serial subscriptions, an OPAC, a Web page.

Computers on Campus Internet access, at least one staffed computer lab available.

Student Life *Housing:* college housing not available. *Activities and Organizations:* student-run newspaper, radio station, choral group. *Student services:* personal/psychological counseling.

Athletics *Intramural sports:* basketball M/W, football M/W, volleyball M/W.

Standardized Tests *Required:* ACT ASSET (for placement).

Costs (2004–05) *Tuition:* state resident $1216 full-time, $38 per hour part-time; nonresident $6752 full-time, $211 per hour part-time. *Required fees:* $28 full-time.

Financial Aid Of all full-time matriculated undergraduates who enrolled in 2003, 21 Federal Work-Study jobs (averaging $2365).

Applying *Options:* early admission, deferred entrance. *Required:* high school transcript. *Application deadline:* rolling (freshmen), rolling (transfers). *Notification:* continuous (freshmen).

Admissions Contact Ms. Betty Gabriel, Director of Counseling, Isothermal Community College, PO Box 804, Spindale, NC 28160-0804. *Phone:* 828-286-3636 Ext. 243. *Fax:* 828-286-8109. *E-mail:* smonday@isothermal.cc.nc.us.

JAMES SPRUNT COMMUNITY COLLEGE

Kenansville, North Carolina

- **State-supported** 2-year, founded 1964, part of North Carolina Community College System
- **Calendar** semesters
- **Degree** certificates, diplomas, and associate
- **Rural** 51-acre campus
- **Endowment** $16,912
- **Coed,** 1,324 undergraduate students, 49% full-time, 70% women, 30% men

Undergraduates 654 full-time, 670 part-time. Students come from 2 states and territories, 1% are from out of state, 41% African American, 3% Hispanic American, 0.1% Native American, 0.6% international, 6% transferred in.

Freshmen *Admission:* 249 applied, 214 admitted, 178 enrolled.

Faculty *Total:* 137, 41% full-time, 1% with terminal degrees. *Student/faculty ratio:* 21:1.

Majors Accounting; administrative assistant and secretarial science; agribusiness; animal sciences; business administration and management; commercial and advertising art; computer systems analysis; cosmetology; criminal justice/police science; kindergarten/preschool education; liberal arts and sciences/liberal studies; medical/clinical assistant; nursing (registered nurse training).

Academic Programs *Special study options:* academic remediation for entering students, accelerated degree program, adult/continuing education programs, advanced placement credit, cooperative education, distance learning, double majors, English as a second language, external degree program, independent study, internships, part-time degree program, summer session for credit.

Library James Sprunt Community College Library with 23,497 titles, 235 serial subscriptions, 1,392 audiovisual materials, an OPAC.

Computers on Campus 100 computers available on campus for general student use. A campuswide network can be accessed from off campus. Internet access, at least one staffed computer lab available.

Student Life *Housing:* college housing not available. *Activities and Organizations:* student-run newspaper, Student Nurses Association, Art Club, Alumni Association, National Technical-Vocational Honor Society, Phi Theta Kappa. *Campus security:* trained security personnel. *Student services:* personal/psychological counseling.

Athletics *Intercollegiate sports:* softball W, volleyball M/W.

Standardized Tests *Required:* ACT ASSET (for placement).

Costs (2004–05) *Tuition:* state resident $1216 full-time, $38 per semester hour part-time; nonresident $6752 full-time, $211 per semester hour part-time. *Required fees:* $70 full-time, $70 per term part-time. *Waivers:* senior citizens and employees or children of employees.

Financial Aid Of all full-time matriculated undergraduates who enrolled in 2003, 55 Federal Work-Study jobs (averaging $1387).

Applying *Options:* common application, electronic application, early admission, deferred entrance. *Required:* high school transcript. *Application deadline:* rolling (freshmen), rolling (transfers). *Notification:* continuous (freshmen).

Admissions Contact Ms. Rita B. Brown, Director of Admissions and Records, James Sprunt Community College, Highway 11 South, 133 James Sprunt Drive, Kenansville, NC 28349. *Phone:* 910-296-2500. *Fax:* 910-296-1222. *E-mail:* rbrown@jscc.cc.nc.us.

JOHNSTON COMMUNITY COLLEGE
Smithfield, North Carolina

- **State-supported** 2-year, founded 1969, part of North Carolina Community College System
- **Calendar** semesters
- **Degree** certificates, diplomas, and associate
- **Rural** 100-acre campus
- **Endowment** $1.9 million
- **Coed,** 3,758 undergraduate students, 41% full-time, 64% women, 36% men

Undergraduates 1,556 full-time, 2,202 part-time. Students come from 10 states and territories, 1 other country, 1% are from out of state, 21% African American, 0.7% Asian American or Pacific Islander, 3% Hispanic American, 0.6% Native American, 0.2% international.

Freshmen *Admission:* 1,368 enrolled.

Faculty *Total:* 333, 37% full-time, 75% with terminal degrees. *Student/faculty ratio:* 18:1.

Majors Accounting technology and bookkeeping; administrative assistant and secretarial science; business administration and management; commercial and advertising art; computer programming; criminal justice/police science; diesel mechanics technology; electrical, electronic and communications engineering technology; heating, air conditioning, ventilation and refrigeration maintenance technology; kindergarten/preschool education; landscaping and groundskeeping; legal assistant/paralegal; liberal arts and sciences/liberal studies; machine tool technology; medical administrative assistant and medical secretary; medical/clinical assistant; medical radiologic technology; nursing (registered nurse training); operations management.

Academic Programs *Special study options:* academic remediation for entering students, adult/continuing education programs, advanced placement credit, cooperative education, distance learning, double majors, honors programs, independent study, part-time degree program, services for LD students, summer session for credit.

Library Johnston Community College Library plus 1 other with 31,550 titles, 348 serial subscriptions, 4,445 audiovisual materials, an OPAC, a Web page.

Computers on Campus 186 computers available on campus for general student use. Internet access, at least one staffed computer lab available.

Student Life *Housing:* college housing not available. *Campus security:* 24-hour patrols. *Student services:* personal/psychological counseling.

Athletics *Intercollegiate sports:* golf M/W, softball M/W, volleyball M/W. *Intramural sports:* basketball M/W.

Standardized Tests *Recommended:* SAT or ACT (for placement).

Costs (2004–05) *Tuition:* state resident $1216 full-time, $38 per semester hour part-time; nonresident $6752 full-time, $211 per semester hour part-time. Full-time tuition and fees vary according to course load. Part-time tuition and fees vary according to course load. *Required fees:* $70 full-time, $1 per semester hour part-time, $19 per term part-time. *Waivers:* senior citizens and employees or children of employees.

Financial Aid Of all full-time matriculated undergraduates who enrolled in 2003, 35 Federal Work-Study jobs (averaging $1853).

Applying *Options:* electronic application. *Required:* high school transcript. *Application deadline:* rolling (freshmen), rolling (transfers). *Notification:* continuous (freshmen).

Admissions Contact Dr. Pam Harrell, Dean of Students Services, Johnston Community College, PO Box 2350, Smithfield, NC 27577-2350. *Phone:* 919-209-2048. *Fax:* 919-989-7862.

KING'S COLLEGE
Charlotte, North Carolina

Admissions Contact Ms. Barbara Rockecharlie, School Director, King's College, 322 Lamar Avenue, Charlotte, NC 28204-2436. *Phone:* 704-688-3613. *Toll-free phone:* 800-768-2255.

LENOIR COMMUNITY COLLEGE
Kinston, North Carolina

- **State-supported** 2-year, founded 1960, part of North Carolina Community College System
- **Calendar** semesters
- **Degree** certificates, diplomas, and associate
- **Small-town** 86-acre campus
- **Coed**

Student Life *Campus security:* 24-hour emergency response devices and patrols, student patrols.

Athletics Member NJCAA.

Standardized Tests *Required:* Assessment and Placement Services for Community Colleges (for placement). *Recommended:* SAT or ACT (for placement).

Costs (2004–05) *Tuition:* state resident $1216 full-time, $38 per credit hour part-time; nonresident $6752 full-time, $211 per credit hour part-time. *Required fees:* $96 full-time, $3 per credit hour part-time.

Applying *Options:* early admission. *Required:* high school transcript.

Admissions Contact Ms. Tammy Buck, Director of Enrollment Management, Lenoir Community College, PO Box 188, Kinston, NC 28502-0188. *Phone:* 252-527-6223 Ext. 309.

LOUISBURG COLLEGE
Louisburg, North Carolina

Admissions Contact Ms. Stephanie Buchanan, Director of Admissions, Louisburg College, 501 North Main Street, Louisburg, NC 27549-2399. *Phone:* 919-497-3228. *Toll-free phone:* 800-775-0208. *Fax:* 919-496-1788. *E-mail:* admissions@earthlink.net.

MARTIN COMMUNITY COLLEGE
Williamston, North Carolina

Admissions Contact Ms. Sonya C. Atkinson, Registrar and Admissions Officer, Martin Community College, 1161 Kehukee Park Road, Williamston, NC 27892. *Phone:* 252-792-1521 Ext. 243. *Fax:* 252-792-0826.

MAYLAND COMMUNITY COLLEGE
Spruce Pine, North Carolina

- **State and locally supported** 2-year, founded 1971, part of North Carolina Community College System
- **Calendar** semesters
- **Degree** certificates, diplomas, and associate
- **Rural** 38-acre campus
- **Coed,** 1,019 undergraduate students, 48% full-time, 54% women, 46% men

Undergraduates 487 full-time, 532 part-time. Students come from 3 states and territories, 5% African American, 0.5% Asian American or Pacific Islander, 1% Hispanic American, 1% Native American, 3% transferred in.

Freshmen *Admission:* 355 applied, 310 admitted, 39 enrolled.

Faculty *Total:* 132, 36% full-time. *Student/faculty ratio:* 10:1.

Majors Accounting; administrative assistant and secretarial science; business administration and management; carpentry; computer programming; criminal justice/law enforcement administration; criminal justice/police science; electrical, electronic and communications engineering technology; electrical, electronics and communications engineering; finance; horticultural science; information technology; kindergarten/preschool education; liberal arts and sciences/liberal studies; medical administrative assistant and medical secretary; medical/clinical assistant; nursing (registered nurse training); plumbing technology.

Academic Programs *Special study options:* academic remediation for entering students, adult/continuing education programs, advanced placement credit,

Mayland Community College (continued)
cooperative education, distance learning, double majors, independent study, internships, part-time degree program, services for LD students, summer session for credit.

Library Carolyn Munro Wilson Learning Resources Center plus 1 other with 19,041 titles, 225 serial subscriptions, 1,707 audiovisual materials, an OPAC, a Web page.

Computers on Campus 200 computers available on campus for general student use. A campuswide network can be accessed. Internet access, online (class) registration, at least one staffed computer lab available.

Student Life *Housing:* college housing not available. *Student services:* personal/psychological counseling.

Athletics Member NJCAA. *Intercollegiate sports:* basketball M. *Intramural sports:* basketball W.

Standardized Tests *Required for some:* CPT required for all for placement, required for admission to nursing program.

Costs (2004–05) *Tuition:* state resident $1229 full-time; nonresident $3376 full-time.

Financial Aid Of all full-time matriculated undergraduates who enrolled in 2003, 20 Federal Work-Study jobs (averaging $1350).

Applying *Options:* common application, electronic application, deferred entrance. *Required:* high school transcript. *Application deadline:* rolling (freshmen), rolling (transfers). *Notification:* continuous (freshmen).

Admissions Contact Ms. Cathy Morrison, Director of Admissions, Mayland Community College, PO Box 547, Spruce Pine, NC 28777. *Phone:* 828-765-7351 Ext. 224. *E-mail:* mayland@cc.nc.us.

McDOWELL TECHNICAL COMMUNITY COLLEGE
Marion, North Carolina

- **State-supported** 2-year, founded 1964, part of North Carolina Community College System
- **Calendar** semesters
- **Degree** certificates, diplomas, and associate
- **Rural** 31-acre campus
- **Coed,** 1,078 undergraduate students

Undergraduates Students come from 2 other countries.

Faculty *Total:* 58, 69% full-time.

Majors Accounting; administrative assistant and secretarial science; automobile/automotive mechanics technology; business administration and management; child development; commercial and advertising art; computer programming; construction engineering technology; cosmetology; criminal justice/law enforcement administration; electrical, electronic and communications engineering technology; heavy equipment maintenance technology; liberal arts and sciences/liberal studies; machine tool technology; marketing/marketing management; nursing (registered nurse training); photography; teacher assistant/aide; welding technology.

Academic Programs *Special study options:* academic remediation for entering students, accelerated degree program, adult/continuing education programs, cooperative education, distance learning, English as a second language, independent study, part-time degree program, services for LD students, summer session for credit.

Library 18,055 titles, 156 serial subscriptions.

Computers on Campus 70 computers available on campus for general student use. At least one staffed computer lab available.

Student Life *Housing:* college housing not available. *Campus security:* 24-hour emergency response devices. *Student services:* personal/psychological counseling.

Athletics *Intercollegiate sports:* tennis M. *Intramural sports:* basketball M/W, table tennis M/W, tennis M/W, volleyball M/W.

Standardized Tests *Required for some:* CPT.

Costs (2004–05) *Tuition:* state resident $1216 full-time, $38 per semester hour part-time; nonresident $6752 full-time, $211 per semester hour part-time. *Required fees:* $50 full-time, $1 per credit hour part-time, $5 per term part-time.

Financial Aid Of all full-time matriculated undergraduates who enrolled in 2003, 15 Federal Work-Study jobs (averaging $1900).

Applying *Options:* common application, early admission, deferred entrance. *Required for some:* high school transcript. *Application deadline:* rolling (freshmen), rolling (transfers). *Notification:* continuous (freshmen).

Admissions Contact Ms. Lisa D. Byrd, Admissions Officer, McDowell Technical Community College, Route 1, Box 170, Marion, NC 28752-9724. *Phone:* 828-652-6024. *Fax:* 828-652-1014.

MITCHELL COMMUNITY COLLEGE
Statesville, North Carolina

- **State-supported** 2-year, founded 1852, part of North Carolina Community College System
- **Calendar** semesters
- **Degree** certificates, diplomas, and associate
- **Small-town** 8-acre campus with easy access to Charlotte
- **Coed**

Faculty *Student/faculty ratio:* 17:1.

Student Life *Campus security:* day and evening security guards.

Costs (2004–05) *Tuition:* state resident $1216 full-time, $38 per credit hour part-time; nonresident $6752 full-time, $211 per credit hour part-time. *Required fees:* $62 full-time, $2 per credit hour part-time.

Financial Aid Of all full-time matriculated undergraduates who enrolled in 2003, 30 Federal Work-Study jobs.

Applying *Required:* high school transcript.

Admissions Contact Mr. Doug Rhoney, Counselor, Mitchell Community College, 500 West Broad, Statesville, NC 28677-5293. *Phone:* 704-878-3280. *Fax:* 704-878-0872.

MONTGOMERY COMMUNITY COLLEGE
Troy, North Carolina

- **State-supported** 2-year, founded 1967, part of North Carolina Community College System
- **Calendar** semesters
- **Degree** certificates, diplomas, and associate
- **Rural** 159-acre campus
- **Endowment** $3000
- **Coed,** 827 undergraduate students, 40% full-time, 63% women, 37% men

Undergraduates 333 full-time, 494 part-time. Students come from 4 states and territories, 1% are from out of state, 19% African American, 3% Asian American or Pacific Islander, 3% Hispanic American, 0.8% Native American, 0.5% international, 14% transferred in.

Freshmen *Admission:* 225 applied, 190 admitted, 190 enrolled.

Faculty *Total:* 73, 42% full-time, 1% with terminal degrees.

Majors Accounting; administrative assistant and secretarial science; automobile/automotive mechanics technology; business administration and management; ceramic arts and ceramics; child care and support services management; criminal justice/police science; electrical, electronic and communications engineering technology; emergency medical technology (EMT paramedic); forestry technology; liberal arts and sciences/liberal studies; management information systems; medical/clinical assistant.

Academic Programs *Special study options:* academic remediation for entering students, advanced placement credit, cooperative education, distance learning, double majors, English as a second language, part-time degree program, services for LD students, summer session for credit.

Library 14,859 titles, 99 serial subscriptions, 500 audiovisual materials, an OPAC.

Computers on Campus 80 computers available on campus for general student use. Internet access, at least one staffed computer lab available.

Student Life *Housing:* college housing not available. *Activities and Organizations:* Gunsmithing Club, Student Government Association, Literary Club, Forestry Club. *Student services:* personal/psychological counseling.

Standardized Tests *Required:* ACT ASSET or ACT COMPASS (for placement).

Costs (2004–05) *Tuition:* state resident $1216 full-time, $38 per semester hour part-time; nonresident $6752 full-time, $211 per semester hour part-time. Full-time tuition and fees vary according to course load. Part-time tuition and fees vary according to course load. *Required fees:* $57 full-time, $28 per term part-time. *Waivers:* senior citizens and employees or children of employees.

Financial Aid Of all full-time matriculated undergraduates who enrolled in 2003, 24 Federal Work-Study jobs (averaging $500).

Applying *Options:* early admission, deferred entrance. *Required:* high school transcript. *Application deadline:* rolling (freshmen), rolling (transfers). *Notification:* continuous (freshmen).

Admissions Contact Ms. Karen Frye, Admissions Officer, Montgomery Community College, 1011 Page Street, Troy, NC 27371. *Phone:* 910-576-6222 Ext. 240. *Toll-free phone:* 800-839-6222. *E-mail:* fryek@montgomery.edu.

NASH COMMUNITY COLLEGE
Rocky Mount, North Carolina

- **State-supported** 2-year, founded 1967, part of North Carolina Community College System
- **Calendar** semesters

- **Degree** certificates, diplomas, and associate
- **Rural** 69-acre campus
- **Endowment** $147,220
- **Coed**

Faculty *Student/faculty ratio:* 22:1.

Student Life *Campus security:* 24-hour emergency response devices, late-night transport/escort service.

Standardized Tests *Required for some:* SAT or ACT (for admission), SAT and SAT Subject Tests or ACT (for admission), ACT ASSET or ACT COMPASS.

Costs (2004–05) *Tuition:* state resident $1216 full-time, $38 per credit hour part-time; nonresident $6752 full-time, $211 per credit hour part-time. *Required fees:* $32 full-time, $1 per credit hour part-time.

Applying *Options:* common application, deferred entrance. *Required:* high school transcript. *Recommended:* interview.

Admissions Contact Ms. Mary Blount, Admissions Officer, Nash Community College, PO Box 7488, Rocky Mount, NC 27804-0488. *Phone:* 252-443-4011 Ext. 300. *Fax:* 252-443-0828.

PAMLICO COMMUNITY COLLEGE
Grantsboro, North Carolina

Admissions Contact Mr. Floyd H. Hardison, Admissions Counselor, Pamlico Community College, PO Box 185, Grantsboro, NC 28529-0185. *Phone:* 252-249-1851 Ext. 28. *Fax:* 252-249-2377. *E-mail:* jjones@pamlicocommunitycollege.cc.nc.us.

PIEDMONT COMMUNITY COLLEGE
Roxboro, North Carolina

- **State-supported** 2-year, founded 1970, part of North Carolina Community College System
- **Calendar** semesters
- **Degree** certificates, diplomas, and associate
- **Small-town** 178-acre campus
- **Endowment** $1.8 million
- **Coed,** 2,189 undergraduate students, 38% full-time, 56% women, 44% men

Undergraduates 826 full-time, 1,363 part-time. Students come from 10 states and territories, 2 other countries, 1% are from out of state, 42% African American, 0.4% Asian American or Pacific Islander, 0.6% Hispanic American, 0.8% Native American, 0.2% international.

Freshmen *Admission:* 947 applied, 947 admitted, 669 enrolled.

Faculty *Total:* 157, 45% full-time. *Student/faculty ratio:* 28:1.

Majors Accounting; business administration and management; cinematography and film/video production; computer engineering technology; computer graphics; criminal justice/law enforcement administration; electrical, electronic and communications engineering technology; liberal arts and sciences/liberal studies; medical administrative assistant and medical secretary; nursing (registered nurse training); social sciences.

Academic Programs *Special study options:* academic remediation for entering students, adult/continuing education programs, advanced placement credit, cooperative education, English as a second language, off-campus study, part-time degree program, summer session for credit.

Library Learning Resource Center with 24,166 titles, 278 serial subscriptions.

Computers on Campus 75 computers available on campus for general student use. Internet access, at least one staffed computer lab available.

Student Life *Housing:* college housing not available. *Campus security:* security guard during certain evening and weekend hours. *Student services:* personal/psychological counseling.

Athletics *Intramural sports:* volleyball M/W.

Standardized Tests *Required:* ACT ASSET (for placement).

Costs (2004–05) *Tuition:* state resident $38 per semester hour part-time; nonresident $211 per semester hour part-time. *Required fees:* $15 per term part-time.

Financial Aid Of all full-time matriculated undergraduates who enrolled in 2003, 30 Federal Work-Study jobs (averaging $1500).

Applying *Options:* early admission, deferred entrance. *Required for some:* high school transcript. *Application deadline:* rolling (freshmen), rolling (transfers). *Notification:* continuous until 9/29 (freshmen).

Admissions Contact Ms. Sheila Williamson, Director of Admissions, Piedmont Community College, PO Box 1197, 1715 College Drive, Roxboro, NC 27573. *Phone:* 336-599-1181 Ext. 219. *Fax:* 336-598-9283.

PITT COMMUNITY COLLEGE
Greenville, North Carolina

- **State and locally supported** 2-year, founded 1961, part of North Carolina Community College System

- **Calendar** semesters
- **Degree** certificates, diplomas, and associate
- **Small-town** 172-acre campus
- **Endowment** $199,213
- **Coed**

Faculty *Student/faculty ratio:* 18:1.

Student Life *Campus security:* 24-hour patrols, student patrols, late-night transport/escort service.

Athletics Member NJCAA.

Standardized Tests *Required:* ACT ASSET or ACT COMPASS (for placement).

Costs (2004–05) *Tuition:* state resident $1216 full-time, $38 per semester hour part-time; nonresident $6752 full-time, $211 per semester hour part-time. Full-time tuition and fees vary according to course load. Part-time tuition and fees vary according to course load. *Required fees:* $76 full-time.

Financial Aid Of all full-time matriculated undergraduates who enrolled in 2003, 79 Federal Work-Study jobs (averaging $1772).

Applying *Options:* electronic application, deferred entrance. *Required:* high school transcript.

Admissions Contact Ms. Mary Tate, Director of Counseling, Pitt Community College, PO Drawer 7007, 1986 Pitt Tech Road, Greenville, NC 27835-7007. *Phone:* 252-321-4217. *Fax:* 252-321-4612. *E-mail:* pittadm@pcc.pitt.cc.nc.us.

RANDOLPH COMMUNITY COLLEGE
Asheboro, North Carolina

- **State-supported** 2-year, founded 1962, part of North Carolina Community College System
- **Calendar** semesters
- **Degree** certificates, diplomas, and associate
- **Small-town** 27-acre campus
- **Endowment** $6.4 million
- **Coed,** 2,291 undergraduate students

Undergraduates Students come from 4 states and territories, 1 other country, 1% are from out of state, 8% African American, 0.8% Asian American or Pacific Islander, 2% Hispanic American, 0.9% Native American, 0.1% international.

Freshmen *Admission:* 520 applied, 520 admitted.

Faculty *Total:* 161, 30% full-time. *Student/faculty ratio:* 23:1.

Majors Accounting technology and bookkeeping; automobile/automotive mechanics technology; business administration and management; commercial and advertising art; commercial photography; computer systems analysis; criminal justice/police science; electromechanical technology; executive assistant/executive secretary; fine/studio arts; graphic and printing equipment operation/production; historic preservation and conservation; information technology; interior design; liberal arts and sciences/liberal studies; machine tool technology; nursing (registered nurse training); photographic and film/video technology; photography; plastics engineering technology; speech-language pathology; system administration; welding technology.

Academic Programs *Special study options:* academic remediation for entering students, adult/continuing education programs, advanced placement credit, cooperative education, distance learning, double majors, English as a second language, independent study, internships, off-campus study, part-time degree program, services for LD students, summer session for credit.

Library R. Alton Cox Learning Resources Center with 36,776 titles, 288 serial subscriptions, 5,841 audiovisual materials, an OPAC, a Web page.

Computers on Campus 100 computers available on campus for general student use. A campuswide network can be accessed. Internet access, at least one staffed computer lab available.

Student Life *Housing:* college housing not available. *Activities and Organizations:* student-run newspaper, Student Government Association. *Campus security:* security officer during open hours. *Student services:* personal/psychological counseling.

Standardized Tests *Required for some:* ACT ASSET or ACT COMPASS.

Costs (2004–05) *Tuition:* state resident $1216 full-time, $38 per credit hour part-time; nonresident $6752 full-time, $211 per credit hour part-time. *Required fees:* $32 full-time, $2 per credit hour part-time.

Applying *Options:* common application, deferred entrance. *Required:* high school transcript. *Application deadline:* rolling (freshmen), rolling (transfers). *Notification:* continuous (freshmen).

Admissions Contact Mrs. Carol M. Elmore, Director of Admissions and Registrar, Randolph Community College, PO Box 1009, Asheboro, NC 27204-1009. *Phone:* 336-633-0213. *Fax:* 336-629-4695. *E-mail:* info@randolph.edu.

RICHMOND COMMUNITY COLLEGE
Hamlet, North Carolina

- **State-supported** 2-year, founded 1964, part of North Carolina Community College System

Richmond Community College (continued)
- **Calendar** semesters
- **Degree** diplomas and associate
- **Rural** 163-acre campus
- **Coed,** 1,690 undergraduate students, 53% full-time, 72% women, 28% men

Undergraduates 891 full-time, 799 part-time. Students come from 3 states and territories, 31% African American, 1% Asian American or Pacific Islander, 0.5% Hispanic American, 9% Native American, 6% transferred in.
Freshmen *Admission:* 154 enrolled.
Faculty *Total:* 47, 85% full-time, 6% with terminal degrees. *Student/faculty ratio:* 30:1.
Majors Accounting; administrative assistant and secretarial science; business administration and management; child care and support services management; computer engineering technology; computer systems analysis; criminal justice/law enforcement administration; electrical, electronic and communications engineering technology; human services; industrial production technologies related; liberal arts and sciences/liberal studies; machine tool technology; mechanical engineering/mechanical technology; medical/clinical assistant; nursing (registered nurse training); web page, digital/multimedia and information resources design.
Academic Programs *Special study options:* academic remediation for entering students, adult/continuing education programs, advanced placement credit, cooperative education, distance learning, double majors, English as a second language, independent study, internships, part-time degree program, student-designed majors, summer session for credit.
Library Richmond Community College Library with 26,381 titles, 192 serial subscriptions, 1,676 audiovisual materials, an OPAC.
Computers on Campus 600 computers available on campus for general student use. A campuswide network can be accessed from off campus. Internet access, at least one staffed computer lab available.
Student Life *Housing:* college housing not available. *Activities and Organizations:* Criminal Justice Club, Human Services Club, Native American Club. *Campus security:* 24-hour emergency response devices, security guard during evening hours. *Student services:* personal/psychological counseling.
Costs (2004–05) *Tuition:* state resident $1140 full-time, $38 per credit hour part-time; nonresident $6330 full-time, $211 per credit hour part-time. *Required fees:* $38 full-time, $12 per term part-time.
Financial Aid Of all full-time matriculated undergraduates who enrolled in 2003, 35 Federal Work-Study jobs (averaging $2000).
Applying *Options:* deferred entrance. *Required:* high school transcript. *Application deadline:* rolling (freshmen), rolling (transfers). *Notification:* continuous until 8/1 (freshmen).
Admissions Contact Ms. Wanda B. Watts, Director of Admissions/Registrar, Richmond Community College, PO Box 1189, Hamlet, NC 28345. *Phone:* 910-582-7113. *Fax:* 910-582-7102.

ROANOKE-CHOWAN COMMUNITY COLLEGE
Ahoskie, North Carolina

- **State-supported** 2-year, founded 1967, part of North Carolina Community College System
- **Calendar** semesters
- **Degree** certificates, diplomas, and associate
- **Rural** 39-acre campus
- **Endowment** $125,000
- **Coed,** 1,014 undergraduate students, 48% full-time, 79% women, 21% men

Undergraduates 491 full-time, 523 part-time. 67% African American, 0.4% Asian American or Pacific Islander, 0.4% Hispanic American, 0.9% Native American. *Retention:* 59% of 2002 full-time freshmen returned.
Freshmen *Admission:* 327 applied, 327 admitted, 159 enrolled.
Faculty *Total:* 108, 35% full-time. *Student/faculty ratio:* 11:1.
Majors Administrative assistant and secretarial science; architectural engineering technology; automobile/automotive mechanics technology; business administration and management; computer programming; construction engineering technology; cosmetology; criminal justice/law enforcement administration; education; electrical, electronic and communications engineering technology; environmental engineering technology; heating, air conditioning, ventilation and refrigeration maintenance technology; kindergarten/preschool education; liberal arts and sciences/liberal studies; nursing (registered nurse training); welding technology.
Academic Programs *Special study options:* academic remediation for entering students, adult/continuing education programs, cooperative education, distance learning, part-time degree program, summer session for credit.
Library 29,268 titles, 207 serial subscriptions, an OPAC, a Web page.
Computers on Campus 90 computers available on campus for general student use. A campuswide network can be accessed. Internet access available.
Student Life *Housing:* college housing not available.

Athletics *Intramural sports:* basketball M/W, volleyball M/W.
Standardized Tests *Required:* ACT ASSET (for placement).
Costs (2004–05) *Tuition:* state resident $1216 full-time, $38 per credit part-time; nonresident $6752 full-time, $211 per credit part-time. Part-time tuition and fees vary according to course load. *Required fees:* $70 full-time, $12 per credit part-time.
Financial Aid Of all full-time matriculated undergraduates who enrolled in 2003, 50 Federal Work-Study jobs (averaging $1120).
Applying *Options:* early admission. *Required for some:* interview. *Application deadline:* rolling (freshmen), rolling (transfers). *Notification:* continuous (freshmen).
Admissions Contact Miss Sandra Copeland, Director, Counseling Services, Roanoke-Chowan Community College, 109 Community College Road, Ahoskie, NC 27910. *Phone:* 252-862-1225.

ROBESON COMMUNITY COLLEGE
Lumberton, North Carolina

Admissions Contact Ms. Judy Revels, Director of Admissions, Robeson Community College, PO Box 1420, 5160 Fayetteville Road, Lumberton, NC 28359. *Phone:* 910-618-5680 Ext. 251. *Fax:* 910-618-5686.

ROCKINGHAM COMMUNITY COLLEGE
Wentworth, North Carolina

- **State-supported** 2-year, founded 1964, part of North Carolina Community College System
- **Calendar** semesters
- **Degree** certificates, diplomas, and associate
- **Rural** 257-acre campus
- **Coed,** 2,141 undergraduate students, 48% full-time, 67% women, 33% men

Undergraduates 1,037 full-time, 1,104 part-time. Students come from 9 states and territories, 1 other country, 23% African American, 0.3% Asian American or Pacific Islander, 0.9% Hispanic American, 0.3% Native American, 1% international.
Freshmen *Admission:* 481 enrolled.
Faculty *Total:* 111, 59% full-time, 5% with terminal degrees. *Student/faculty ratio:* 18:1.
Majors Accounting; administrative assistant and secretarial science; art; biological and physical sciences; business administration and management; business machine repair; carpentry; child development; construction engineering technology; consumer services and advocacy; cosmetology; criminal justice/law enforcement administration; criminal justice/police science; electromechanical technology; heating, air conditioning, ventilation and refrigeration maintenance technology; horticultural science; human resources management; industrial arts; information science/studies; labor and industrial relations; legal administrative assistant/secretary; legal assistant/paralegal; liberal arts and sciences/liberal studies; medical administrative assistant and medical secretary; medical/clinical assistant; nursing (licensed practical/vocational nurse training); nursing (registered nurse training); occupational therapist assistant; physical therapist assistant; respiratory care therapy; teacher assistant/aide; tourism and travel services management.
Academic Programs *Special study options:* academic remediation for entering students, adult/continuing education programs, advanced placement credit, cooperative education, part-time degree program, student-designed majors, summer session for credit.
Library Gerald B. James Library with 43,044 titles, 374 serial subscriptions, 3,990 audiovisual materials, an OPAC, a Web page.
Computers on Campus 150 computers available on campus for general student use. A campuswide network can be accessed. Internet access, at least one staffed computer lab available.
Student Life *Housing:* college housing not available. *Activities and Organizations:* student-run newspaper, Phi Theta Kappa, Cultural Diversity Club, Paralegal Club. *Campus security:* late-night transport/escort service. *Student services:* personal/psychological counseling.
Athletics Member NJCAA. *Intercollegiate sports:* baseball M, basketball M/W, volleyball W. *Intramural sports:* archery M/W, badminton M/W, basketball M/W, cheerleading W, table tennis M/W, tennis M/W, volleyball M/W.
Standardized Tests *Required for some:* CGP.
Costs (2004–05) *Tuition:* state resident $1216 full-time; nonresident $6752 full-time. Full-time tuition and fees vary according to course load and program. *Required fees:* $37 full-time.
Financial Aid Of all full-time matriculated undergraduates who enrolled in 2003, 37 Federal Work-Study jobs (averaging $2300).
Applying *Options:* early admission, deferred entrance. *Application deadline:* rolling (freshmen), rolling (transfers). *Notification:* continuous (freshmen).

Admissions Contact Mrs. Leigh Hawkins, Director of Enrollment Services, Rockingham Community College, PO Box 38, Wentworth, NC 27375-0038. *Phone:* 336-342-4261 Ext. 2333.

ROWAN-CABARRUS COMMUNITY COLLEGE
Salisbury, North Carolina

- **State-supported** 2-year, founded 1963, part of North Carolina Community College System
- **Calendar** semesters
- **Degree** diplomas and associate
- **Small-town** 100-acre campus
- **Coed,** 5,200 undergraduate students, 43% full-time, 67% women, 33% men

Undergraduates 2,255 full-time, 2,945 part-time. Students come from 2 other countries, 20% African American, 1% Asian American or Pacific Islander, 2% Hispanic American, 0.4% Native American.
Freshmen *Admission:* 1,909 applied, 1,909 admitted, 1,561 enrolled.
Faculty *Total:* 251, 48% full-time.
Majors Accounting; automobile/automotive mechanics technology; biomedical technology; business administration and management; criminal justice/law enforcement administration; electrical, electronic and communications engineering technology; health information/medical records technology; industrial technology; information science/studies; kindergarten/preschool education; legal assistant/paralegal; liberal arts and sciences/liberal studies; mechanical drafting and CAD/CADD; medical laboratory technology; nursing (registered nurse training); radiologic technology/science.
Academic Programs *Special study options:* academic remediation for entering students, adult/continuing education programs, advanced placement credit, cooperative education, distance learning, English as a second language, internships, part-time degree program, services for LD students, summer session for credit.
Library Learning Resource Center with 23,005 titles, 313 serial subscriptions.
Computers on Campus 200 computers available on campus for general student use. Internet access, at least one staffed computer lab available.
Student Life *Housing:* college housing not available. *Campus security:* on-campus security during operating hours. *Student services:* personal/psychological counseling.
Athletics *Intramural sports:* basketball M/W.
Standardized Tests *Required:* ACT ASSET (for placement).
Costs (2004–05) *Tuition:* state resident $1216 full-time, $38 per credit hour part-time; nonresident $6752 full-time, $211 per credit hour part-time. No tuition increase for student's term of enrollment. *Required fees:* $64 full-time, $14 per term part-time. *Payment plan:* deferred payment. *Waivers:* senior citizens.
Applying *Required:* high school transcript. *Application deadline:* rolling (freshmen), rolling (transfers).
Admissions Contact Mr. Kenneth C. Hayes, Director of Admissions and Recruitment, Rowan-Cabarrus Community College, PO Box 1595, Salisbury, NC 28145. *Phone:* 704-637-0760 Ext. 212. *Fax:* 704-633-6804.

SAMPSON COMMUNITY COLLEGE
Clinton, North Carolina

Admissions Contact Mr. William R. Jordan, Director of Admissions, Sampson Community College, PO Box 318, Clinton, NC 28329. *Phone:* 910-592-8084 Ext. 2022. *Fax:* 910-592-8048. *E-mail:* bjordan@sampson.cc.nc.us.

SANDHILLS COMMUNITY COLLEGE
Pinehurst, North Carolina

- **State and locally supported** 2-year, founded 1963, part of North Carolina Community College System
- **Calendar** semesters
- **Degree** certificates, diplomas, and associate
- **Small-town** campus
- **Endowment** $4.1 million
- **Coed,** 3,502 undergraduate students

Undergraduates Students come from 42 states and territories, 23 other countries, 1% are from out of state, 28% African American, 0.6% Asian American or Pacific Islander, 1% Hispanic American, 6% Native American.
Faculty *Total:* 171, 65% full-time. *Student/faculty ratio:* 18:1.
Majors Accounting; administrative assistant and secretarial science; architectural engineering technology; art; art teacher education; automobile/automotive mechanics technology; biological and physical sciences; business administration and management; business, management, and marketing related; child development; civil engineering technology; clinical/medical laboratory technology;

computer engineering related; computer engineering technology; computer/information technology services administration related; computer programming; computer programming (specific applications); cosmetology; criminal justice/law enforcement administration; criminal justice/police science; culinary arts; fine/studio arts; gerontology; hotel/motel administration; human services; information science/studies; kindergarten/preschool education; landscaping and groundskeeping; liberal arts and sciences/liberal studies; mathematics; medical administrative assistant and medical secretary; mental health/rehabilitation; music; music teacher education; nursing assistant/aide and patient care assistant; nursing (licensed practical/vocational nurse training); nursing (registered nurse training); pre-engineering; radiologic technology/science; respiratory care therapy; science teacher education; substance abuse/addiction counseling; surgical technology; survey technology; system administration; teacher assistant/aide; turf and turfgrass management; web/multimedia management and webmaster.
Academic Programs *Special study options:* academic remediation for entering students, advanced placement credit, cooperative education, distance learning, double majors, honors programs, independent study, internships, part-time degree program, services for LD students, summer session for credit.
Library Boyd Library with 76,080 titles, 286 serial subscriptions, 2,317 audiovisual materials, an OPAC, a Web page.
Computers on Campus 300 computers available on campus for general student use. A campuswide network can be accessed from off campus. Internet access, at least one staffed computer lab available.
Student Life *Housing:* college housing not available. *Activities and Organizations:* student-run newspaper, choral group, Student Government Association, Minority Students for Academic and Cultural Enrichment, Circle K. *Campus security:* 24-hour emergency response devices, security on duty until 12 a.m. *Student services:* personal/psychological counseling.
Standardized Tests *Required:* ACT ASSET or ACT COMPASS (for placement).
Costs (2004–05) *Tuition:* state resident $38 per credit hour part-time; nonresident $211 per credit hour part-time. *Required fees:* $35 per term part-time.
Financial Aid Of all full-time matriculated undergraduates who enrolled in 2003, 59 Federal Work-Study jobs (averaging $1750).
Applying *Options:* common application, deferred entrance. *Required:* high school transcript. *Application deadline:* rolling (freshmen), rolling (transfers). *Notification:* continuous (freshmen).
Admissions Contact Ms. Rosa McAllister-McRae, Admissions Coordinator, Sandhills Community College, 3395 Airport Road, Pinehurst, NC 28374. *Phone:* 910-692-6185 Ext. 729. *Toll-free phone:* 800-338-3944. *Fax:* 910-692-5076. *E-mail:* mcallisterr@sandhills.edu.

SCHOOL OF COMMUNICATION ARTS
Raleigh, North Carolina

Admissions Contact 3000 Wakefield Crossing Drive, Raleigh, NC 27614. *Toll-free phone:* 800-288-7442.

SOUTH COLLEGE-ASHEVILLE
Asheville, North Carolina

- **Proprietary** 2-year, founded 1905
- **Calendar** quarters
- **Degree** certificates and associate
- **Urban** 8-acre campus
- **Coed**

Faculty *Student/faculty ratio:* 9:1.
Student Life *Campus security:* night security.
Standardized Tests *Required:* CPAt (for admission).
Applying *Options:* deferred entrance. *Application fee:* $40. *Required:* high school transcript.
Admissions Contact Mr. Michael Darnell, Director of Admissions, South College-Asheville, 1567 Patton Avenue, Asheville, NC 28806. *Phone:* 828-252-2486. *Fax:* 828-252-8558. *E-mail:* ccdean@ioa.com.

SOUTHEASTERN COMMUNITY COLLEGE
Whiteville, North Carolina

- **State-supported** 2-year, founded 1964, part of North Carolina Community College System
- **Calendar** semesters
- **Degree** certificates, diplomas, and associate
- **Rural** 106-acre campus
- **Coed**

Student Life *Campus security:* 24-hour emergency response devices.
Athletics Member NJCAA.

Southeastern Community College (continued)

Standardized Tests *Required:* ACT ASSET, ACT COMPASS (for placement).

Costs (2004–05) *Tuition:* state resident $1216 full-time, $38 per semester hour part-time; nonresident $6752 full-time, $211 per semester hour part-time. *Required fees:* $64 full-time, $32 per term part-time.

Financial Aid Of all full-time matriculated undergraduates who enrolled in 2003, 80 Federal Work-Study jobs (averaging $1580).

Applying *Options:* common application, electronic application, early admission, deferred entrance. *Required:* high school transcript.

Admissions Contact Ms. Linda Nelms, Coordinator of Student Records, Southeastern Community College, PO Box 151, Whiteville, NC 28472. *Phone:* 910-642-7141 Ext. 264. *Fax:* 910-642-5658. *E-mail:* jfowler@mail.southeast.cc.nc.us.

SOUTH PIEDMONT COMMUNITY COLLEGE

Polkton, North Carolina

Admissions Contact Ms. Jeania Martin, Admissions Coordinator, South Piedmont Community College, PO Box 126, Polkton, NC 28135. *Phone:* 704-272-7635. *Toll-free phone:* 800-766-0319. *Fax:* 704-272-8904. *E-mail:* j-martin@spcc.cc.nc.us.

SOUTHWESTERN COMMUNITY COLLEGE

Sylva, North Carolina

- **State-supported** 2-year, founded 1964, part of North Carolina Community College System
- **Calendar** semesters
- **Degree** certificates, diplomas, and associate
- **Small-town** 55-acre campus
- **Coed,** 2,014 undergraduate students, 45% full-time, 67% women, 33% men

Undergraduates 899 full-time, 1,115 part-time. Students come from 6 states and territories, 1 other country, 1% are from out of state, 1% African American, 0.3% Asian American or Pacific Islander, 1% Hispanic American, 10% Native American, 0.3% international, 8% transferred in.

Freshmen *Admission:* 277 enrolled. *Average high school GPA:* 2.90. *Test scores:* SAT verbal scores over 500: 5%; SAT math scores over 500: 5%; ACT scores over 18: 20%.

Faculty *Total:* 244, 28% full-time, 5% with terminal degrees. *Student/faculty ratio:* 12:1.

Majors Accounting; administrative assistant and secretarial science; automobile/automotive mechanics technology; business administration and management; child development; clinical/medical laboratory technology; commercial and advertising art; computer engineering technology; cosmetology; criminal justice/police science; culinary arts; electrical, electronic and communications engineering technology; emergency medical technology (EMT paramedic); environmental studies; health information/medical records administration; health information/medical records technology; information science/studies; legal assistant/paralegal; liberal arts and sciences/liberal studies; marketing/marketing management; massage therapy; medical radiologic technology; mental health/rehabilitation; nursing (licensed practical/vocational nurse training); nursing (registered nurse training); parks, recreation, and leisure related; physical therapist assistant; physical therapy; respiratory care therapy; substance abuse/addiction counseling; system, networking, and LAN/WAN management; trade and industrial teacher education.

Academic Programs *Special study options:* academic remediation for entering students, adult/continuing education programs, cooperative education, distance learning, double majors, English as a second language, independent study, off-campus study, part-time degree program, services for LD students, summer session for credit.

Library Learning Resources Center with 27,428 titles, 257 serial subscriptions, 18,410 audiovisual materials, an OPAC.

Computers on Campus 400 computers available on campus for general student use. A campuswide network can be accessed from off campus. Internet access, at least one staffed computer lab available.

Student Life *Housing:* college housing not available. *Activities and Organizations:* Electronics Club, EMT Club, HIT Club, Cyber Crime Club, National Vocational-Technical Honor Society. *Campus security:* security during hours college is open. *Student services:* personal/psychological counseling.

Standardized Tests *Recommended:* SAT or ACT (for admission).

Costs (2004–05) *Tuition:* state resident $1216 full-time, $38 per credit hour part-time; nonresident $6752 full-time, $211 per credit hour part-time. *Required fees:* $65 full-time, $2 per credit hour part-time.

Financial Aid Of all full-time matriculated undergraduates who enrolled in 2003, 55 Federal Work-Study jobs (averaging $900).

Applying *Options:* common application, early admission, deferred entrance. *Required:* high school transcript. *Required for some:* minimum 2.0 GPA, letters of recommendation, interview. *Application deadline:* rolling (freshmen), rolling (transfers). *Notification:* continuous (freshmen).

Admissions Contact Dr. Phil Weast, Director of Enrollment Management, Southwestern Community College, 447 College Drive, Sylva, NC 28779. *Phone:* 828-586-4091 Ext. 431. *Toll-free phone:* 800-447-4091. *Fax:* 828-586-3129. *E-mail:* pweast@southwest.cc.nc.us.

STANLY COMMUNITY COLLEGE

Albemarle, North Carolina

- **State-supported** 2-year, founded 1971, part of North Carolina Community College System
- **Calendar** semesters
- **Degree** certificates, diplomas, and associate
- **Small-town** 150-acre campus with easy access to Charlotte
- **Coed,** 2,000 undergraduate students

Undergraduates Students come from 13 states and territories, 3 other countries, 3% are from out of state.

Freshmen *Admission:* 642 applied, 642 admitted.

Faculty *Total:* 106, 50% full-time. *Student/faculty ratio:* 9:1.

Majors Accounting technology and bookkeeping; autobody/collision and repair technology; biomedical technology; business administration and management; child care and support services management; computer hardware engineering; computer/information technology services administration related; computer programming related; computer programming (specific applications); computer systems networking and telecommunications; computer/technical support; computer technology/computer systems technology; cosmetology; criminal justice/police science; electrical, electronic and communications engineering technology; executive assistant/executive secretary; human services; industrial technology; information science/studies; legal administrative assistant/secretary; mechanical drafting and CAD/CADD; medical administrative assistant and medical secretary; medical/clinical assistant; nursing (registered nurse training); occupational therapist assistant; physical therapist assistant; respiratory care therapy; system administration; web/multimedia management and webmaster; web page, digital/multimedia and information resources design; word processing.

Academic Programs *Special study options:* academic remediation for entering students, adult/continuing education programs, advanced placement credit, cooperative education, distance learning, double majors, English as a second language, independent study, internships, part-time degree program, services for LD students, summer session for credit.

Library 23,966 titles, 200 serial subscriptions, 2,500 audiovisual materials, an OPAC, a Web page.

Computers on Campus 100 computers available on campus for general student use. A campuswide network can be accessed. Internet access, at least one staffed computer lab available.

Student Life *Housing:* college housing not available. *Activities and Organizations:* student-run newspaper, television station. *Student services:* personal/psychological counseling.

Standardized Tests *Required:* ACT ASSET (for placement). *Recommended:* SAT (for placement).

Costs (2004–05) *Tuition:* state resident $1174 full-time, $37 per semester hour part-time; nonresident $6342 full-time, $198 per semester hour part-time.

Financial Aid Of all full-time matriculated undergraduates who enrolled in 2003, 20 Federal Work-Study jobs (averaging $1800).

Applying *Options:* early admission, deferred entrance. *Required:* high school transcript. *Application deadline:* rolling (freshmen), rolling (transfers). *Notification:* continuous (freshmen).

Admissions Contact Mr. Ronnie Hinson, Director of Admissions, Stanly Community College, 141 College Drive, Albemarle, NC 28001. *Phone:* 704-982-0121 Ext. 233. *Fax:* 704-982-0819. *E-mail:* parksdf@stanly.cc.nc.us.

SURRY COMMUNITY COLLEGE

Dobson, North Carolina

- **State-supported** 2-year, founded 1965, part of North Carolina Community College System
- **Calendar** semesters
- **Degree** certificates, diplomas, and associate
- **Rural** 100-acre campus
- **Coed,** 3,600 undergraduate students

Undergraduates Students come from 3 states and territories, 4% are from out of state, 5% African American, 0.3% Asian American or Pacific Islander, 2% Hispanic American, 0.3% Native American, 0.2% international.

Faculty *Total:* 450, 33% full-time. *Student/faculty ratio:* 27:1.

Majors Accounting; administrative assistant and secretarial science; advertising; agricultural business and management; automobile/automotive mechanics technology; business administration and management; child care provision;

commercial and advertising art; computer engineering related; computer engineering technology; computer programming; computer programming related; computer systems networking and telecommunications; construction engineering technology; cosmetology; criminal justice/law enforcement administration; drafting and design technology; electrical, electronic and communications engineering technology; heating, air conditioning, ventilation and refrigeration maintenance technology; horticultural science; information science/studies; information technology; legal assistant/paralegal; liberal arts and sciences/liberal studies; machine tool technology; medical administrative assistant and medical secretary; nursing (licensed practical/vocational nurse training); nursing (registered nurse training); poultry science.

Academic Programs *Special study options:* academic remediation for entering students, adult/continuing education programs, advanced placement credit, cooperative education, distance learning, English as a second language, independent study, internships, off-campus study, part-time degree program, summer session for credit.

Library Resource Center with 47,526 titles, 362 serial subscriptions, 3,233 audiovisual materials, an OPAC, a Web page.

Computers on Campus 200 computers available on campus for general student use. A campuswide network can be accessed. Internet access, at least one staffed computer lab available.

Student Life *Housing:* college housing not available. *Activities and Organizations:* drama/theater group, student-run radio station, choral group, Student Government Association, Phi Beta Lambda, Phi Theta Kappa, BSU. *Campus security:* security guard during day and evening hours.

Athletics Member NJCAA. *Intercollegiate sports:* baseball M, basketball M, volleyball W. *Intramural sports:* basketball M/W, softball M/W, volleyball M/W.

Standardized Tests *Required:* CPT (for placement).

Costs (2004–05) *Tuition:* state resident $38 per credit hour part-time; nonresident $211 per credit hour part-time. *Required fees:* $4 per credit hour part-time.

Financial Aid Of all full-time matriculated undergraduates who enrolled in 2003, 35 Federal Work-Study jobs (averaging $2800).

Applying *Options:* electronic application, early admission, deferred entrance. *Required:* high school transcript.

Admissions Contact Mr. Michael McHone, Vice President of Student Services, Surry Community College, PO Box 304, Dobson, NC 27017-0304. *Phone:* 336-386-3238. *Fax:* 336-386-8951. *E-mail:* mchonem@surry.cc.nc.us.

TRI-COUNTY COMMUNITY COLLEGE
Murphy, North Carolina

- **State-supported** 2-year, founded 1964
- **Calendar** semesters
- **Degree** certificates, diplomas, and associate
- **Rural** 40-acre campus
- **Coed,** 1,155 undergraduate students, 44% full-time, 67% women, 33% men

Undergraduates 503 full-time, 652 part-time. Students come from 8 states and territories, 3% are from out of state, 0.9% African American, 1% Hispanic American, 2% Native American.

Freshmen *Admission:* 518 applied, 518 admitted. *Average high school GPA:* 2.9.

Faculty *Total:* 80, 58% full-time, 5% with terminal degrees. *Student/faculty ratio:* 21:1.

Majors Accounting; automobile/automotive mechanics technology; business administration and management; computer management; early childhood education; electrical, electronic and communications engineering technology; information technology; liberal arts and sciences/liberal studies; medical/clinical assistant; nursing (registered nurse training); welding technology.

Academic Programs *Special study options:* academic remediation for entering students, adult/continuing education programs, distance learning, double majors, part-time degree program, services for LD students, summer session for credit.

Library 16,224 titles, 306 serial subscriptions.

Computers on Campus 33 computers available on campus for general student use. A campuswide network can be accessed. Internet access available.

Student Life *Housing:* college housing not available. *Activities and Organizations:* student-run newspaper. *Student services:* personal/psychological counseling.

Standardized Tests *Required for some:* Assessment and Placement Services for Community Colleges. *Recommended:* SAT (for placement).

Costs (2005–06) *Tuition:* state resident $970 full-time, $38 per credit hour part-time; nonresident $5122 full-time, $211 per credit hour part-time. *Required fees:* $60 full-time, $29 per term part-time.

Financial Aid Of all full-time matriculated undergraduates who enrolled in 2003, 11 Federal Work-Study jobs.

Applying *Required:* high school transcript. *Application deadline:* rolling (freshmen), rolling (transfers). *Notification:* continuous (freshmen).

Admissions Contact Mr. Jason Chambers, Director of Admissions, Tri-County Community College, 4600 East US 64, Murphy, NC 28906-7919. *Phone:* 828-837-6810 Ext. 4225.

VANCE-GRANVILLE COMMUNITY COLLEGE
Henderson, North Carolina

- **State-supported** 2-year, founded 1969, part of North Carolina Community College System
- **Calendar** semesters
- **Degree** certificates, diplomas, and associate
- **Rural** 83-acre campus with easy access to Raleigh
- **Endowment** $3.0 million
- **Coed**

Faculty *Student/faculty ratio:* 9:1.

Student Life *Campus security:* 24-hour emergency response devices and patrols.

Standardized Tests *Required for some:* ACT (for placement), nursing exam, Health Occupations Exam.

Costs (2004–05) *Tuition:* state resident $912 full-time, $38 per credit hour part-time; nonresident $5064 full-time, $211 per credit hour part-time. *Required fees:* $38 full-time, $14 per term part-time.

Financial Aid Of all full-time matriculated undergraduates who enrolled in 2003, 38 Federal Work-Study jobs (averaging $1750).

Applying *Options:* common application, early admission, deferred entrance. *Required:* high school transcript.

Admissions Contact Ms. Brenda W. Beck, Admissions Officer, Vance-Granville Community College, PO Box 917, State Road 1126, Henderson, NC 27536. *Phone:* 252-492-2061 Ext. 267. *Fax:* 252-430-0460.

WAKE TECHNICAL COMMUNITY COLLEGE
Raleigh, North Carolina

- **State and locally supported** 2-year, founded 1958, part of North Carolina Community College System
- **Calendar** semesters
- **Degree** certificates, diplomas, and associate
- **Suburban** 79-acre campus
- **Coed,** 11,372 undergraduate students, 34% full-time, 55% women, 45% men

Undergraduates 3,891 full-time, 7,481 part-time. Students come from 15 states and territories, 41 other countries, 15% transferred in.

Freshmen *Admission:* 5,104 admitted. *Test scores:* SAT verbal scores over 500: 33%; SAT math scores over 500: 41%; ACT scores over 18: 60%; SAT verbal scores over 600: 7%; SAT math scores over 600: 13%; ACT scores over 24: 14%; ACT scores over 30: 3%.

Faculty *Total:* 895, 30% full-time, 5% with terminal degrees. *Student/faculty ratio:* 11:1.

Majors Accounting; architectural engineering technology; artificial intelligence and robotics; business administration and management; civil engineering technology; clinical/medical laboratory technology; computer and information sciences; computer engineering technology; computer graphics; computer programming; computer programming (specific applications); computer systems networking and telecommunications; computer/technical support; criminal justice/law enforcement administration; criminal justice/police science; culinary arts; electrical and power transmission installation; electrical, electronic and communications engineering technology; electromechanical technology; emergency medical technology (EMT paramedic); environmental engineering technology; general studies; heavy equipment maintenance technology; hotel/motel administration; human resources management; industrial technology; instrumentation technology; kindergarten/preschool education; landscape architecture; legal administrative assistant/secretary; liberal arts and sciences/liberal studies; machine tool technology; mechanical drafting and CAD/CADD; mechanical engineering/mechanical technology; medical administrative assistant and medical secretary; medical radiologic technology; nursing (registered nurse training); pharmacy technician; plastics engineering technology; pre-engineering; survey technology; system administration; telecommunications; tool and die technology; web/multimedia management and webmaster; web page, digital/multimedia and information resources design; word processing.

Academic Programs *Special study options:* academic remediation for entering students, adult/continuing education programs, advanced placement credit, cooperative education, double majors, English as a second language, part-time degree program, services for LD students, summer session for credit.

Library Bruce M. Howell Library plus 1 other with 70,617 titles, 474 serial subscriptions, 6,141 audiovisual materials, an OPAC, a Web page.

Wake Technical Community College (continued)

Computers on Campus 23 computers available on campus for general student use. A campuswide network can be accessed. Internet access, at least one staffed computer lab available.

Student Life *Housing:* college housing not available. *Activities and Organizations:* drama/theater group, student-run newspaper, choral group, Science Club, History Club, Drama Club, Amateur Radio Club, Design and Garden Club. *Campus security:* 24-hour patrols. *Student services:* personal/psychological counseling.

Standardized Tests *Required:* ACT ASSET or ACT COMPASS (for placement). *Recommended:* SAT or ACT (for placement).

Costs (2004–05) *Tuition:* state resident $1216 full-time, $38 per credit hour part-time; nonresident $6736 full-time, $211 per credit hour part-time. *Required fees:* $72 full-time, $1 per credit hour part-time, $10 per term part-time.

Financial Aid Of all full-time matriculated undergraduates who enrolled in 2003, 35 Federal Work-Study jobs (averaging $2000). 15 state and other part-time jobs (averaging $2000).

Applying *Options:* common application, electronic application, early admission. *Required:* high school transcript. *Application deadline:* rolling (freshmen), rolling (transfers).

Admissions Contact Ms. Susan Bloomfield, Director of Admissions, Wake Technical Community College, 9101 Fayetteville Road, Raleigh, NC 27603-5696. *Phone:* 919-662-3357. *Fax:* 919-662-3529. *E-mail:* srbloomf@waketech.edu.

WAYNE COMMUNITY COLLEGE
Goldsboro, North Carolina

Admissions Contact Ms. Susan Mooring Sasser, Director of Admissions and Records, Wayne Community College, PO Box 8002, Goldsboro, NC 27533-8002. *Phone:* 919-735-5151 Ext. 216. *Fax:* 919-736-3204. *E-mail:* msm@wcc.wayne.cc.nc.us.

WESTERN PIEDMONT COMMUNITY COLLEGE
Morganton, North Carolina

Admissions Contact Mrs. Susan Williams, Director of Admissions, Western Piedmont Community College, 1001 Burkemont Avenue, Morganton, NC 28655-4511. *Phone:* 828-438-6051.

WILKES COMMUNITY COLLEGE
Wilkesboro, North Carolina

- **State-supported** 2-year, founded 1965, part of North Carolina Community College System
- **Calendar** semesters
- **Degree** certificates, diplomas, and associate
- **Small-town** 140-acre campus
- **Endowment** $2.6 million
- **Coed**, 2,532 undergraduate students, 52% full-time, 64% women, 36% men

Undergraduates 1,304 full-time, 1,228 part-time. Students come from 13 states and territories, 15 other countries, 1% are from out of state, 5% African American, 0.6% Asian American or Pacific Islander, 1% Hispanic American, 0.2% Native American, 3% transferred in. *Retention:* 53% of 2002 full-time freshmen returned.

Freshmen *Admission:* 1,162 applied, 1,162 admitted, 665 enrolled.

Faculty *Total:* 362, 20% full-time, 6% with terminal degrees. *Student/faculty ratio:* 10:1.

Majors Accounting technology and bookkeeping; applied horticulture; architectural engineering technology; automobile/automotive mechanics technology; building/construction finishing, management, and inspection related; business administration and management; child care and support services management; computer programming (specific applications); computer systems analysis; computer systems networking and telecommunications; criminal justice/police science; diesel mechanics technology; electrical, electronic and communications engineering technology; electromechanical technology; executive assistant/executive secretary; hotel/motel administration; institutional food workers; liberal arts and sciences/liberal studies; medical/clinical assistant; nursing (registered nurse training); psychiatric/mental health services technology; radio and television broadcasting technology; speech-language pathology.

Academic Programs *Special study options:* academic remediation for entering students, accelerated degree program, adult/continuing education programs, advanced placement credit, cooperative education, distance learning, double majors, English as a second language, independent study, internships, part-time degree program, services for LD students, summer session for credit.

Library Learning Resources Center with 56,142 titles, 127 serial subscriptions, 6,867 audiovisual materials, an OPAC, a Web page.

Computers on Campus 255 computers available on campus for general student use. A campuswide network can be accessed. Internet access, at least one staffed computer lab available.

Student Life *Housing:* college housing not available. *Activities and Organizations:* drama/theater group, student-run newspaper, radio station, choral group, Student Government Association, Phi Theta Kappa, Phi Beta Lambda, Rotaract, Baptist Student Union. *Campus security:* 24-hour emergency response devices, student patrols, late-night transport/escort service. *Student services:* personal/psychological counseling.

Athletics Member NJCAA. *Intercollegiate sports:* baseball M, basketball M/W, volleyball W. *Intramural sports:* basketball M/W, table tennis M/W.

Standardized Tests *Required:* ACT COMPASS (for placement). *Recommended:* SAT or ACT (for placement).

Costs (2005–06) *Tuition:* state resident $1216 full-time, $38 per credit hour part-time; nonresident $6752 full-time, $211 per credit hour part-time. *Required fees:* $58 full-time, $2 per credit hour part-time, $11 per term part-time.

Financial Aid Of all full-time matriculated undergraduates who enrolled in 2003, 50 Federal Work-Study jobs (averaging $1800).

Applying *Options:* electronic application, deferred entrance. *Required:* high school transcript. *Application deadline:* rolling (freshmen), rolling (transfers). *Notification:* continuous (freshmen).

Admissions Contact Mr. Mac Warren, Director of Admissions, Wilkes Community College, PO Box 120, Wilkesboro, NC 28697. *Phone:* 336-838-6141. *Fax:* 336-838-6547. *E-mail:* mac.warren@wilkescc.edu.

WILSON TECHNICAL COMMUNITY COLLEGE
Wilson, North Carolina

- **State-supported** 2-year, founded 1958, part of North Carolina Community College System
- **Calendar** semesters
- **Degree** certificates, diplomas, and associate
- **Small-town** 35-acre campus
- **Endowment** $837,822
- **Coed**, 2,077 undergraduate students, 51% full-time, 72% women, 28% men

Undergraduates 1,054 full-time, 1,023 part-time. Students come from 4 states and territories, 4 other countries, 21% are from out of state, 49% African American, 0.3% Asian American or Pacific Islander, 2% Hispanic American, 0.1% Native American, 0.2% international, 15% transferred in.

Freshmen *Admission:* 507 applied, 491 admitted, 360 enrolled.

Faculty *Total:* 106, 54% full-time, 7% with terminal degrees. *Student/faculty ratio:* 20:1.

Majors Accounting; administrative assistant and secretarial science; business administration and management; computer programming; criminal justice/law enforcement administration; electrical, electronic and communications engineering technology; emergency medical technology (EMT paramedic); fire science; general studies; industrial technology; information science/studies; kindergarten/preschool education; language interpretation and translation; legal assistant/paralegal; liberal arts and sciences/liberal studies; mechanical engineering/mechanical technology; nursing (registered nurse training); sign language interpretation and translation; tool and die technology.

Academic Programs *Special study options:* academic remediation for entering students, advanced placement credit, cooperative education, distance learning, double majors, English as a second language, independent study, internships, part-time degree program, services for LD students, summer session for credit.

Library 38,466 titles, 7,658 audiovisual materials, an OPAC.

Computers on Campus 33 computers available on campus for general student use. A campuswide network can be accessed. Internet access, at least one staffed computer lab available.

Student Life *Housing:* college housing not available. *Campus security:* 11-hour patrols by trained security personnel. *Student services:* personal/psychological counseling.

Standardized Tests *Required:* ACT COMPASS or ACT Asset (for placement).

Costs (2004–05) *Tuition:* state resident $1216 full-time, $38 per credit hour part-time; nonresident $6752 full-time, $211 per credit hour part-time. *Required fees:* $38 full-time, $1 per credit hour part-time.

Financial Aid Of all full-time matriculated undergraduates who enrolled in 2003, 65 Federal Work-Study jobs (averaging $1500).

Applying *Options:* common application, electronic application, deferred entrance. *Required:* high school transcript. *Application deadline:* rolling (freshmen), rolling (transfers). *Notification:* continuous (freshmen).

Admissions Contact Barbara Page, Admissions Technician, Wilson Technical Community College, PO Box 4305, Wilson, NC 27893-0305. *Phone:* 252-246-1285. *Fax:* 252-246-1285. *E-mail:* bpage@wilsontech.edu.

NORTH DAKOTA

AAKERS BUSINESS COLLEGE
Fargo, North Dakota

Admissions Contact Ms. Elizabeth Largent, Director, Aakers Business College, 4012 19th Avenue, SW, Fargo, ND 58103. *Phone:* 701-277-3889. *Toll-free phone:* 800-817-0009.

BISMARCK STATE COLLEGE
Bismarck, North Dakota

- **State-supported** 2-year, founded 1939, part of North Dakota University System
- **Calendar** semesters
- **Degree** certificates, diplomas, and associate
- **Suburban** 100-acre campus
- **Coed,** 3,541 undergraduate students, 66% full-time, 47% women, 53% men

Undergraduates 2,329 full-time, 1,212 part-time. Students come from 18 states and territories, 11 other countries, 8% are from out of state, 0.9% African American, 0.4% Asian American or Pacific Islander, 0.8% Hispanic American, 3% Native American, 0.3% international, 11% transferred in, 8% live on campus.
Freshmen *Admission:* 1,050 applied, 1,050 admitted, 985 enrolled.
Faculty *Total:* 251, 43% full-time. *Student/faculty ratio:* 18:1.
Majors Administrative assistant and secretarial science; agricultural business and management; autobody/collision and repair technology; automobile/automotive mechanics technology; business automation/technology/data entry; business/commerce; carpentry; clinical/medical laboratory technology; commercial and advertising art; computer systems networking and telecommunications; construction engineering technology; emergency medical technology (EMT paramedic); energy management and systems technology; heating, air conditioning, ventilation and refrigeration maintenance technology; hotel/motel administration; industrial technology; legal administrative assistant/secretary; liberal arts and sciences/liberal studies; lineworker; medical administrative assistant and medical secretary; nursing (licensed practical/vocational nurse training); surgical technology; welding technology.
Academic Programs *Special study options:* academic remediation for entering students, adult/continuing education programs, advanced placement credit, cooperative education, distance learning, part-time degree program, services for LD students, summer session for credit. *ROTC:* Army (c), Air Force (c).
Library Bismarck State College Library with 69,142 titles, 374 serial subscriptions, 6,518 audiovisual materials, an OPAC, a Web page.
Computers on Campus 420 computers available on campus for general student use. A campuswide network can be accessed from student residence rooms and from off campus. Internet access, online (class) registration, at least one staffed computer lab available.
Student Life *Housing Options:* men-only, women-only. Campus housing is university owned. *Activities and Organizations:* drama/theater group, student-run newspaper, choral group, Phi Theta Kappa, Drama Club, Art Club, Anime Club. *Campus security:* 24-hour emergency response devices and patrols, controlled dormitory access.
Athletics Member NJCAA. *Intercollegiate sports:* baseball M, basketball M(s)/W(s), golf M/W, tennis M/W, volleyball W(s). *Intramural sports:* basketball M, softball M, volleyball M/W.
Standardized Tests *Required:* SAT or ACT (for admission).
Costs (2005–06) *Tuition:* state resident $3459 full-time, $93 per credit hour part-time; nonresident $8113 full-time, $248 per credit hour part-time. *Required fees:* $500 full-time, $22 per credit hour part-time. *Room and board:* $4288.
Financial Aid Of all full-time matriculated undergraduates who enrolled in 2003, 84 Federal Work-Study jobs (averaging $1096).
Applying *Options:* common application, electronic application. *Application fee:* $35. *Required:* high school transcript. *Application deadlines:* rolling (freshmen), 8/1 (transfers). *Notification:* continuous (freshmen).
Admissions Contact Ms. Karla Gabriel, Dean of Admissions and Enrollment Services, Bismarck State College, PO Box 5587, Bismarck, ND 58506-5587. *Phone:* 701-224-5426. *Toll-free phone:* 800-445-5073 Ext. 45429 (in-state); 800-445-5073 (out-of-state). *Fax:* 701-224-5643. *E-mail:* karla.gabriel@bsc.nodak.edu.

CANKDESKA CIKANA COMMUNITY COLLEGE
Fort Totten, North Dakota

Admissions Contact Mr. Ermen Brown Jr., Registrar, Cankdeska Cikana Community College, PO Box 269, Fort Totten, ND 58335. *Phone:* 701-766-1342. *E-mail:* info@littlehoop.cc.

FORT BERTHOLD COMMUNITY COLLEGE
New Town, North Dakota

Admissions Contact Mr. Russell Mason Jr., President, Fort Berthold Community College, PO Box 490, New Town, ND 58763-0490. *Phone:* 701-627-3665. *Fax:* 701-627-3609. *E-mail:* rmason@nt1.fort.berthold.cc.nd.us.

LAKE REGION STATE COLLEGE
Devils Lake, North Dakota

- **State-supported** 2-year, founded 1941, part of North Dakota University System
- **Calendar** semesters
- **Degree** certificates, diplomas, and associate
- **Small-town** 120-acre campus
- **Endowment** $2.2 million
- **Coed,** 1,464 undergraduate students, 29% full-time, 55% women, 45% men

Undergraduates 421 full-time, 1,043 part-time. Students come from 28 states and territories, 12 other countries, 10% are from out of state, 4% African American, 2% Asian American or Pacific Islander, 2% Hispanic American, 4% Native American, 4% international, 4% transferred in, 30% live on campus. *Retention:* 47% of 2002 full-time freshmen returned.
Freshmen *Admission:* 183 applied, 183 admitted, 183 enrolled.
Faculty *Total:* 103, 29% full-time, 8% with terminal degrees. *Student/faculty ratio:* 15:1.
Majors Accounting; accounting technology and bookkeeping; administrative assistant and secretarial science; agricultural business and management; automobile/automotive mechanics technology; avionics maintenance technology; business administration and management; child care and support services management; child care provision; computer and information sciences; computer programming (specific applications); computer programming (vendor/product certification); computer science; computer systems networking and telecommunications; criminal justice/police science; diesel mechanics technology; electrical, electronics and communications engineering; electrical/electronics equipment installation and repair; executive assistant/executive secretary; fashion merchandising; information technology; legal administrative assistant/secretary; legal assistant/paralegal; liberal arts and sciences/liberal studies; management information systems; marketing research; medical administrative assistant and medical secretary; nursing assistant/aide and patient care assistant; nursing (licensed practical/vocational nurse training); office management; office occupations and clerical services; sales, distribution and marketing; sign language interpretation and translation; small business administration; technical teacher education.
Academic Programs *Special study options:* academic remediation for entering students, adult/continuing education programs, cooperative education, distance learning, double majors, English as a second language, freshman honors college, honors programs, internships, part-time degree program, summer session for credit.
Library Paul Hoghaug Library plus 1 other with 42,000 titles, 200 serial subscriptions, 2,000 audiovisual materials, an OPAC.
Computers on Campus 275 computers available on campus for general student use. A campuswide network can be accessed from student residence rooms and from off campus. Internet access, online (class) registration, at least one staffed computer lab available. Computer purchase or lease plan available.
Student Life *Housing Options:* men-only, women-only. Campus housing is university owned. *Activities and Organizations:* drama/theater group, DECA, drama, SOTA (Students Other than Average), Student Senate, Computer Club. *Campus security:* 24-hour emergency response devices, controlled dormitory access. *Student services:* personal/psychological counseling.
Athletics Member NJCAA. *Intercollegiate sports:* basketball M(s)/W(s). *Intramural sports:* basketball M/W, bowling M, football M/W, golf M/W, ice hockey M/W, softball M/W, table tennis M/W, volleyball M/W.
Standardized Tests *Required:* ACT (for placement), ACT COMPASS (for placement).
Costs (2004–05) *Tuition:* state resident $2328 full-time, $97 per credit hour part-time; nonresident $2328 full-time, $97 per credit hour part-time. Full-time tuition and fees vary according to location and reciprocity agreements. Part-time tuition and fees vary according to location and reciprocity agreements. *Required fees:* $737 full-time, $24 per credit hour part-time, $368 per term part-time. *Room and board:* $3640. Room and board charges vary according to board plan and housing facility. *Waivers:* minority students, senior citizens, and employees or children of employees.
Financial Aid Of all full-time matriculated undergraduates who enrolled in 2003, 40 Federal Work-Study jobs (averaging $1600).
Applying *Options:* electronic application. *Application fee:* $35. *Required:* high school transcript, immunizations. *Application deadline:* rolling (freshmen), rolling (transfers). *Notification:* continuous (freshmen).
Admissions Contact Ms. Denise Anderson, Administrative Assistant, Lake Region State College, 1801 College Drive North, Devils Lake, ND 58301.

Lake Region State College (continued)
Phone: 701-662-1514. *Toll-free phone:* 800-443-1313 Ext. 514. *Fax:* 701-662-1581. *E-mail:* denise.d.anderson@lrsc.nodak.edu.

MINOT STATE UNIVERSITY-BOTTINEAU CAMPUS
Bottineau, North Dakota

- **State-supported** 2-year, founded 1906, part of North Dakota University System
- **Calendar** semesters
- **Degree** certificates, diplomas, and associate
- **Rural** 35-acre campus
- **Endowment** $1.0 million
- **Coed**

Faculty *Student/faculty ratio:* 11:1.
Student Life *Campus security:* controlled dormitory access.
Athletics Member NJCAA.
Standardized Tests *Recommended:* SAT or ACT (for placement).
Costs (2004–05) *Tuition:* state resident $2362 full-time, $98 per credit part-time; nonresident $6307 full-time, $263 per credit part-time. *Required fees:* $576 full-time, $24 per credit part-time. *Room and board:* $3282.
Financial Aid Of all full-time matriculated undergraduates who enrolled in 2003, 50 Federal Work-Study jobs (averaging $1100).
Applying *Options:* common application, electronic application, early admission, deferred entrance. *Application fee:* $35. *Required:* high school transcript.
Admissions Contact Ms. Jody Klier, Admissions Counselor, Minot State University-Bottineau Campus, 105 Simrall Boulevard, Bottineau, ND 58318. *Phone:* 701-228-5426. *Toll-free phone:* 800-542-6866. *Fax:* 701-228-5499. *E-mail:* bergpla@misu.nodak.edu.

NORTH DAKOTA STATE COLLEGE OF SCIENCE
Wahpeton, North Dakota

- **State-supported** 2-year, founded 1903, part of North Dakota University System
- **Calendar** semesters
- **Degree** certificates, diplomas, and associate
- **Rural** 125-acre campus
- **Endowment** $4000
- **Coed,** 2,468 undergraduate students, 79% full-time, 37% women, 63% men

Undergraduates 1,954 full-time, 514 part-time. Students come from 54 states and territories, 11 other countries, 27% are from out of state, 1% African American, 0.3% Asian American or Pacific Islander, 0.6% Hispanic American, 2% Native American, 1% international, 9% transferred in, 56% live on campus.
Freshmen *Admission:* 2,468 admitted, 886 enrolled. *Average high school GPA:* 2.73. *Test scores:* ACT scores over 18: 58%; ACT scores over 24: 10%.
Faculty *Total:* 140, 91% full-time, 1% with terminal degrees. *Student/faculty ratio:* 15:1.
Majors Administrative assistant and secretarial science; agricultural business and management related; agricultural/farm supplies retailing and wholesaling; agricultural mechanization; agricultural production; architectural engineering technology; autobody/collision and repair technology; automobile/automotive mechanics technology; business/commerce; civil engineering technology; computer programming (specific applications); construction engineering technology; dental hygiene; diesel mechanics technology; electrical, electronic and communications engineering technology; foodservice systems administration; health information/medical records technology; heating, air conditioning and refrigeration technology; heating, air conditioning, ventilation and refrigeration maintenance technology; industrial electronics technology; industrial technology; liberal arts and sciences/liberal studies; machine shop technology; nursing (licensed practical/vocational nurse training); occupational therapist assistant; pharmacy technician; psychiatric/mental health services technology; small engine mechanics and repair technology; technical teacher education; vehicle maintenance and repair technologies related; welding technology.
Academic Programs *Special study options:* academic remediation for entering students, adult/continuing education programs, cooperative education, distance learning, double majors, English as a second language, independent study, internships, part-time degree program, services for LD students, student-designed majors, summer session for credit.
Library Mildred Johnson Library with 124,508 titles, 852 serial subscriptions, 4,178 audiovisual materials, an OPAC, a Web page.
Computers on Campus 450 computers available on campus for general student use. A campuswide network can be accessed from student residence rooms and from off campus. Internet access, at least one staffed computer lab available. Computer purchase or lease plan available.

Student Life *Housing:* on-campus residence required for freshman year. *Options:* coed, men-only, women-only. Campus housing is university owned. *Activities and Organizations:* drama/theater group, choral group, marching band, Student Health Advisory Club, Drama Club, Inter-Varsity Christian Fellowship, Cultural Diversity, Habitat for Humanity. *Campus security:* 24-hour emergency response devices and patrols, student patrols, late-night transport/escort service, controlled dormitory access. *Student services:* health clinic, personal/psychological counseling, legal services.
Athletics Member NJCAA. *Intercollegiate sports:* basketball M(s)/W(s), football M(s), volleyball W(s). *Intramural sports:* baseball M, basketball M/W, cheerleading W, field hockey M/W, football M, racquetball M/W, softball M/W, volleyball M/W.
Standardized Tests *Required:* ACT (for placement).
Costs (2004–05) *Tuition:* state resident $3298 full-time; nonresident $8054 full-time. Full-time tuition and fees vary according to reciprocity agreements. Part-time tuition and fees vary according to reciprocity agreements. *Required fees:* $450 full-time. *Room and board:* $4170; room only: $1745. Room and board charges vary according to board plan. *Payment plans:* installment, deferred payment. *Waivers:* employees or children of employees.
Financial Aid Of all full-time matriculated undergraduates who enrolled in 2003, 90 Federal Work-Study jobs (averaging $1500).
Applying *Options:* common application, electronic application, early admission. *Application fee:* $35. *Required:* high school transcript. *Application deadline:* rolling (freshmen), rolling (transfers). *Notification:* continuous (freshmen).
Admissions Contact Ms. Karen Reilly, Director of Admissions and Records, North Dakota State College of Science, 800 North 6th Street, Wahpeton, ND 58076. *Phone:* 701-671-2202. *Toll-free phone:* 800-342-4325 Ext. 2202. *Fax:* 701-671-2332.

SITTING BULL COLLEGE
Fort Yates, North Dakota

Admissions Contact Ms. Melody Silk, Director of Registration and Admissions, Sitting Bull College, 1341 92nd Street, Fort Yates, ND 58538-9701. *Phone:* 701-854-3864.

TURTLE MOUNTAIN COMMUNITY COLLEGE
Belcourt, North Dakota

Admissions Contact Ms. Joni LaFontaine, Admissions/Records Officer, Turtle Mountain Community College, Box 340, Belcourt, ND 58316-0340. *Phone:* 701-477-5605 Ext. 217. *Fax:* 701-477-8967.

UNITED TRIBES TECHNICAL COLLEGE
Bismarck, North Dakota

- **Federally supported** 2-year, founded 1969
- **Calendar** semesters
- **Degree** certificates and associate
- **Small-town** 105-acre campus
- **Coed**

Faculty *Student/faculty ratio:* 8:1.
Student Life *Campus security:* 24-hour emergency response devices and patrols.
Athletics Member NJCAA.
Standardized Tests *Recommended:* TABE.
Costs (2004–05) *One-time required fee:* $100. *Tuition:* state resident $2800 full-time; nonresident $2800 full-time. *Required fees:* $530 full-time. *Room and board:* $3000. Room and board charges vary according to housing facility.
Applying *Required:* high school transcript.
Admissions Contact Ms. Vivian Gillett, Director of Admissions, United Tribes Technical College, 3315 University Drive, Bismarck, ND 58504. *Phone:* 701-255-3285 Ext. 1334. *Fax:* 701-530-0640. *E-mail:* ndvivian@hotmail.com.

WILLISTON STATE COLLEGE
Williston, North Dakota

- **State-supported** 2-year, founded 1957, part of North Dakota University System
- **Calendar** semesters
- **Degree** certificates, diplomas, and associate
- **Small-town** 80-acre campus
- **Endowment** $52,200
- **Coed,** 937 undergraduate students, 60% full-time, 71% women, 29% men

Undergraduates 565 full-time, 372 part-time. Students come from 9 states and territories, 3 other countries, 14% are from out of state, 1% African American, 0.2% Asian American or Pacific Islander, 1% Hispanic American, 4% Native American, 2% international, 85% transferred in, 13% live on campus.

Freshmen *Admission:* 540 applied, 529 admitted, 174 enrolled.

Faculty *Total:* 93, 32% full-time, 2% with terminal degrees. *Student/faculty ratio:* 14:1.

Majors Accounting technology and bookkeeping; administrative assistant and secretarial science; agriculture; automobile/automotive mechanics technology; computer and information sciences and support services related; data processing and data processing technology; diesel mechanics technology; entrepreneurial and small business related; health information/medical records technology; liberal arts and sciences/liberal studies; marketing/marketing management; medical transcription; multi-/interdisciplinary studies related; nursing (licensed practical/vocational nurse training); physical therapist assistant.

Academic Programs *Special study options:* academic remediation for entering students, advanced placement credit, cooperative education, distance learning, honors programs, independent study, off-campus study, part-time degree program, services for LD students, student-designed majors, summer session for credit.

Library Williston State College Library with 16,218 titles, 214 serial subscriptions, 475 audiovisual materials, an OPAC, a Web page.

Computers on Campus 70 computers available on campus for general student use. A campuswide network can be accessed from student residence rooms and from off campus. Internet access, at least one staffed computer lab available. Computer purchase or lease plan available.

Student Life *Housing Options:* coed, men-only, women-only, cooperative. Campus housing is university owned. *Activities and Organizations:* drama/theater group, student-run newspaper, choral group, PTK, PBL, Student Senate, VICA, Student Nurses Association, national sororities. *Campus security:* controlled dormitory access. *Student services:* personal/psychological counseling.

Athletics Member NJCAA. *Intercollegiate sports:* baseball M(s), basketball M(s)/W(s), volleyball W(s). *Intramural sports:* basketball M/W, volleyball M/W.

Standardized Tests *Required for some:* ACT (for placement).

Costs (2005–06) *Tuition:* state resident $2073 full-time, $80 per credit part-time; nonresident $3111 full-time, $120 per credit part-time. *Required fees:* $575 full-time, $22 per credit part-time. *Room and board:* $3500; room only: $1000. *Payment plan:* installment. *Waivers:* employees or children of employees.

Financial Aid Of all full-time matriculated undergraduates who enrolled in 2003, 30 Federal Work-Study jobs (averaging $1500). 15 state and other part-time jobs (averaging $1000).

Applying *Options:* common application, electronic application. *Application fee:* $35. *Required:* high school transcript. *Application deadline:* rolling (freshmen), rolling (transfers). *Notification:* continuous (freshmen).

Admissions Contact Ms. Jan Solem, Director for Admission and Records, Williston State College, PO Box 1326, Williston, ND 58802-1326. *Phone:* 701-774-4554. *Toll-free phone:* 888-863-9455. *Fax:* 701-774-4211. *E-mail:* wsc.admission@wsc.nodak.edu.

NORTHERN MARIANA ISLANDS

NORTHERN MARIANAS COLLEGE
Saipan, Northern Mariana Islands

Admissions Contact Ms. Joyce Taro, Admission Specialist, Northern Marianas College, PO Box 501250, Saipan, MP 96950-1250. *Phone:* 670-234-3690 Ext. 1528. *Fax:* 670-235-4967. *E-mail:* joycet@nmcnet.edu.

OHIO

ACADEMY OF COURT REPORTING
Cleveland, Ohio

Admissions Contact Ms. Sheila Woods, Director of Admissions, Academy of Court Reporting, 2044 Euclid Avenue, Cleveland, OH 44115. *Phone:* 216-861-3222.

ANTONELLI COLLEGE
Cincinnati, Ohio

- **Proprietary** 2-year, founded 1947
- **Calendar** quarters
- **Degree** diplomas and associate
- **Urban** campus
- **Coed**

Faculty *Student/faculty ratio:* 10:1.

Student Life *Campus security:* 24-hour emergency response devices, security personnel while classes are in session.

Costs (2004–05) *Tuition:* $15,400 full-time, $325 per credit hour part-time. Full-time tuition and fees vary according to course load and program. Part-time tuition and fees vary according to course load and program. *Required fees:* $1440 full-time, $350 per term part-time.

Applying *Options:* early admission, deferred entrance. *Application fee:* $100. *Required:* high school transcript, interview. *Required for some:* art portfolio.

Admissions Contact Ms. Connie D. Sharp, Director, Antonelli College, 124 East Seventh Street, Cincinnati, OH 45202. *Phone:* 513-241-4338. *Toll-free phone:* 800-505-4338. *Fax:* 513-241-9396. *E-mail:* tess@antonellic.com.

THE ART INSTITUTE OF CINCINNATI
Cincinnati, Ohio

- **Proprietary** 2-year, part of Education Management Corporation
- **Degree** associate
- **Coed**, 74 undergraduate students, 100% full-time, 53% women, 47% men

Undergraduates 74 full-time. 1% are from out of state, 1% African American, 7% transferred in.

Freshmen *Admission:* 40 enrolled. *Average high school GPA:* 3.40.

Faculty *Total:* 13, 62% full-time. *Student/faculty ratio:* 9:1.

Library The Art Institute of Cincinnati Library with 1,500 titles.

Computers on Campus 48 computers available on campus for general student use. Internet access, at least one staffed computer lab available.

Student Life *Housing:* college housing not available. *Campus security:* 24-hour emergency response devices.

Costs (2004–05) *Tuition:* $13,996 full-time. No tuition increase for student's term of enrollment. *Required fees:* $2616 full-time.

Applying *Options:* common application. *Required:* high school transcript, letters of recommendation, interview, portfolio. *Application deadline:* 9/8 (freshmen).

Admissions Contact Ms. Cyndi Mendell, Admissions, The Art Institute of Cincinnati, 1171 East Kemper Road, Cincinnati, OH 45246. *Phone:* 513-751-1206. *E-mail:* aic @theartinstituteofcincinnati.com.

▶ **See page 456 for a narrative description.**

THE ART INSTITUTE OF OHIO-CINCINNATI
Cincinnati, Ohio

- **Proprietary** 2-year, part of The Art Institutes
- **Degree** associate
- **Coed**, 108 undergraduate students, 100% full-time, 56% women, 44% men

Undergraduates 108 full-time. Students come from 3 states and territories, 9% are from out of state, 36% African American, 0.9% Asian American or Pacific Islander, 0.9% Hispanic American, 2% transferred in.

Freshmen *Admission:* 108 enrolled.

Faculty *Total:* 5, 20% full-time. *Student/faculty ratio:* 25:1.

Academic Programs *Special study options:* accelerated degree program, cooperative education, distance learning, internships, part-time degree program, services for LD students.

Library Library with 7,018 titles, 75 serial subscriptions, 493 audiovisual materials, an OPAC.

Computers on Campus 229 computers available on campus for general student use. A campuswide network can be accessed. Internet access, at least one staffed computer lab available.

Costs (2004–05) *Tuition:* $16,128 full-time.

Applying *Options:* early admission, early decision, early action, deferred entrance. *Required:* high school transcript, interview.

Admissions Contact Mr. Jerry Foust, President, The Art Institute of Ohio-Cincinnati, 1011 Glendale-Milford Road, Cincinnati, OH 45215-1107. *Phone:* 513-771-2821.

ATS INSTITUTE OF TECHNOLOGY
Highland Heights, Ohio

Admissions Contact 230 Alpha Park, Highland Heights, OH 44143.

BELMONT TECHNICAL COLLEGE
St. Clairsville, Ohio

- **State-supported** 2-year, founded 1971, part of Ohio Board of Regents
- **Calendar** quarters
- **Degree** diplomas and associate
- **Rural** 55-acre campus
- **Coed,** 1,740 undergraduate students, 68% full-time, 58% women, 42% men

Undergraduates 1,180 full-time, 560 part-time. Students come from 10 states and territories, 3% are from out of state, 3% African American, 0.2% Asian American or Pacific Islander, 0.1% Hispanic American, 0.5% Native American. *Retention:* 56% of 2002 full-time freshmen returned.
Freshmen *Admission:* 199 enrolled.
Faculty *Total:* 101, 41% full-time.
Majors Accounting; administrative assistant and secretarial science; business administration and management; civil engineering technology; computer engineering technology; computer programming; corrections; electrical, electronic and communications engineering technology; electromechanical technology; emergency medical technology (EMT paramedic); heating, air conditioning, ventilation and refrigeration maintenance technology; historic preservation and conservation; medical/clinical assistant; mental health/rehabilitation; nursing (licensed practical/vocational nurse training); nursing (registered nurse training); welding technology.
Academic Programs *Special study options:* academic remediation for entering students, distance learning, independent study, part-time degree program, summer session for credit.
Library 5,612 titles, 217 serial subscriptions.
Computers on Campus 85 computers available on campus for general student use. Internet access, at least one staffed computer lab available.
Student Life *Housing:* college housing not available. *Student services:* personal/psychological counseling.
Standardized Tests *Required:* ACT COMPASS (for placement).
Costs (2005–06) *Tuition:* state resident $2520 full-time, $56 per credit hour part-time; nonresident $5220 full-time, $116 per credit hour part-time. *Required fees:* $1050 full-time, $23 per credit hour part-time, $5 per term part-time.
Financial Aid Of all full-time matriculated undergraduates who enrolled in 2003, 15 Federal Work-Study jobs (averaging $4500).
Applying *Options:* early admission. *Application deadline:* rolling (freshmen).
Admissions Contact Mr. Gregory A. Fehr, Executive Director of Marketing and Advancement, Belmont Technical College, 120 Fox Shannon Place, St. Clairsville, OH 43950-9735. *Phone:* 740-695-9500 Ext. 1018. *Toll-free phone:* 800-423-1188.

BOHECKER'S BUSINESS COLLEGE
Ravenna, Ohio

Admissions Contact 326 East Main Street, Ravenna, OH 44266.

BOWLING GREEN STATE UNIVERSITY-FIRELANDS COLLEGE
Huron, Ohio

- **State-supported** 2-year, founded 1968, part of Bowling Green State University System
- **Calendar** semesters
- **Degrees** certificates and associate (also offers some upper-level and graduate courses)
- **Rural** 216-acre campus with easy access to Cleveland and Toledo
- **Endowment** $1.6 million
- **Coed,** 1,918 undergraduate students, 54% full-time, 66% women, 34% men

Undergraduates 1,042 full-time, 876 part-time. Students come from 2 states and territories, 6% African American, 0.2% Asian American or Pacific Islander, 3% Hispanic American, 0.5% Native American, 22% transferred in. *Retention:* 42% of 2002 full-time freshmen returned.
Freshmen *Admission:* 528 applied, 496 admitted, 393 enrolled. *Average high school GPA:* 2.71. *Test scores:* SAT verbal scores over 500: 8%; SAT math scores over 500: 16%; ACT scores over 18: 71%; SAT verbal scores over 600: 8%; SAT math scores over 600: 8%; ACT scores over 24: 10%; SAT math scores over 700: 8%; ACT scores over 30: 1%.
Faculty *Total:* 108, 40% full-time, 31% with terminal degrees. *Student/faculty ratio:* 19:1.

Majors Accounting technology and bookkeeping; biological and physical sciences; business operations support and secretarial services related; communications technologies and support services related; computer engineering technology; computer programming; computer systems networking and telecommunications; computer/technical support; criminal justice/safety; design and visual communications; education; electrical, electronic and communications engineering technology; engineering technologies related; family and community services; health information/medical records administration; health professions related; humanities; human services; industrial technology; interdisciplinary studies; kindergarten/preschool education; liberal arts and sciences/liberal studies; mechanical design technology; nursing (registered nurse training); operations management; pre-engineering; respiratory care therapy; social sciences.
Academic Programs *Special study options:* academic remediation for entering students, adult/continuing education programs, advanced placement credit, distance learning, double majors, independent study, internships, part-time degree program, services for LD students, student-designed majors, summer session for credit. *ROTC:* Army (c), Air Force (c).
Library Firelands College Library with 41,281 titles, 241 serial subscriptions, 2,331 audiovisual materials, an OPAC, a Web page.
Computers on Campus 300 computers available on campus for general student use. A campuswide network can be accessed from off campus. Internet access, at least one staffed computer lab available.
Student Life *Housing:* college housing not available. *Activities and Organizations:* drama/theater group, Speech Activities Organization, Allied Health Club, student government, Intramural Club, Campus Fellowship. *Campus security:* 24-hour emergency response devices, late-night transport/escort service, patrols by trained security personnel.
Athletics *Intramural sports:* basketball M/W, football M/W, skiing (downhill) M(c)/W(c), softball M/W, volleyball M/W, weight lifting M(c)/W(c).
Standardized Tests *Required for some:* SAT or ACT (for placement).
Costs (2004–05) *Tuition:* state resident $3782 full-time, $185 per credit hour part-time; nonresident $11,090 full-time, $534 per credit hour part-time. Full-time tuition and fees vary according to course load. Part-time tuition and fees vary according to course load. *Required fees:* $178 full-time, $10 per credit hour part-time, $89 per term part-time. *Payment plans:* installment, deferred payment. *Waivers:* children of alumni and employees or children of employees.
Applying *Options:* electronic application, early admission, deferred entrance. *Application fee:* $35. *Required:* high school transcript. *Application deadlines:* 8/15 (freshmen), 8/15 (transfers). *Notification:* continuous until 8/15 (freshmen).
Admissions Contact Ms. Debralee Divers, Director of Admissions and Financial Aid, Bowling Green State University-Firelands College, One University Drive, Huron, OH 44839. *Phone:* 419-433-5560. *Toll-free phone:* 800-322-4787. *Fax:* 419-372-0604. *E-mail:* divers@bgnet.bgsu.edu.

BRADFORD SCHOOL
Columbus, Ohio

- **Proprietary** 2-year, founded 1911
- **Calendar** semesters
- **Degree** diplomas and associate
- **Suburban** campus
- **Coed**

Faculty *Student/faculty ratio:* 25:1.
Student Life *Campus security:* 24-hour patrols.
Costs (2004–05) *Tuition:* $11,000 full-time. No tuition increase for student's term of enrollment. *Room only:* $5000.
Applying *Options:* common application, electronic application. *Application fee:* $50. *Required:* high school transcript, interview.
Admissions Contact Ms. Raeann Lee, Director of Admissions, Bradford School, 2469 Stelzer Road, Columbus, OH 43219. *Phone:* 614-416-6200. *Toll-free phone:* 800-678-7981. *Fax:* 614-416-6210. *E-mail:* info@bradfordschoolcolumbus.edu.

BROWN MACKIE COLLEGE, AKRON CAMPUS
Akron, Ohio

Admissions Contact Ms. Sheila Freeman, Director of Admissions, Brown Mackie College, Akron Campus, 2791 Mogadore Road, Akron, OH 44312-1596. *Phone:* 330-733-8766.

BROWN MACKIE COLLEGE, CINCINNATI CAMPUS
Cincinnati, Ohio

Admissions Contact Ms. Cherie McNeel, Director of Admissions, Brown Mackie College, Cincinnati Campus, 1011 Glendale-Milford Road, Cincinnati, OH 45215. *Phone:* 513-771-2424. *Fax:* 513-771-3413.

BROWN MACKIE COLLEGE, FINDLAY CAMPUS
Findlay, Ohio

- **Proprietary** 2-year, founded 1929, administratively affiliated with Education Management Corporation
- **Calendar** continuous
- **Degree** diplomas and associate
- **Rural** 1-acre campus
- **Coed,** 526 undergraduate students, 85% full-time, 86% women, 14% men

Undergraduates 449 full-time, 77 part-time. Students come from 2 states and territories, 6% African American, 6% Hispanic American, 4% transferred in.
Freshmen *Admission:* 150 applied, 125 admitted, 21 enrolled. *Average high school GPA:* 2.86.
Faculty *Total:* 54, 26% full-time, 6% with terminal degrees. *Student/faculty ratio:* 15:1.
Majors Accounting; business administration and management; computer/information technology services administration related; computer programming (specific applications); executive assistant/executive secretary; health/health care administration; medical/clinical assistant; medical office management.
Academic Programs *Special study options:* advanced placement credit, cooperative education, double majors, external degree program, independent study, internships.
Library 3,134 titles, 41 serial subscriptions, 26 audiovisual materials, an OPAC, a Web page.
Computers on Campus 74 computers available on campus for general student use. A campuswide network can be accessed. Internet access, at least one staffed computer lab available. Computer purchase or lease plan available.
Student Life *Housing:* college housing not available. *Campus security:* 24-hour emergency response devices.
Standardized Tests *Required:* ACT ASSET (for placement).
Costs (2005–06) *Tuition:* $7267 full-time, $169 per credit part-time. Full-time tuition and fees vary according to course load. Part-time tuition and fees vary according to course load. No tuition increase for student's term of enrollment. *Required fees:* $430 full-time, $10 per credit hour part-time. *Payment plan:* installment.
Financial Aid Of all full-time matriculated undergraduates who enrolled in 2003, 14 Federal Work-Study jobs (averaging $1928).
Applying *Options:* common application. *Required:* high school transcript, interview. *Application deadline:* rolling (freshmen).
Admissions Contact Ms. Angelique Walker, Director of Admissions, Brown Mackie College, Findlay Campus, 1700 Fostoria Avenue, Suite 100, Findlay, OH 45840. *Phone:* 419-423-2211. *Toll-free phone:* 800-842-3687. *Fax:* 419-423-0725.

BROWN MACKIE COLLEGE, NORTH CANTON CAMPUS
North Canton, Ohio

- **Proprietary** 2-year, founded 1929, part of Educational Management Corporation
- **Calendar** quarters
- **Degree** diplomas and associate
- **Suburban** campus
- **Coed**

Standardized Tests *Required:* ACT ASSET (for admission).
Costs (2004–05) *Tuition:* $14,976 full-time, $156 per credit hour part-time.
Applying *Options:* common application.
Admissions Contact Mr. Greg Laudermilt, Admissions Director, Brown Mackie College, North Canton Campus, 1320 West Maple Street, NW, North Canton, OH 44720-2854. *Phone:* 330-494-1214.

BRYANT AND STRATTON COLLEGE
Parma, Ohio

- **Proprietary** 2-year, founded 1981, part of Bryant and Stratton Business Institute, Inc
- **Calendar** semesters
- **Degree** associate
- **Suburban** 4-acre campus with easy access to Cleveland
- **Coed,** 252 undergraduate students, 56% full-time, 76% women, 24% men

Undergraduates 142 full-time, 110 part-time. Students come from 1 other state, 24% African American, 0.4% Asian American or Pacific Islander, 10% Hispanic American, 3% transferred in. *Retention:* 47% of 2002 full-time freshmen returned.
Freshmen *Admission:* 83 applied, 77 admitted, 77 enrolled. *Average high school GPA:* 2.39.
Faculty *Total:* 28, 29% full-time, 4% with terminal degrees. *Student/faculty ratio:* 12:1.
Majors Accounting; administrative assistant and secretarial science; business administration and management; computer and information sciences; medical administrative assistant and medical secretary; medical/clinical assistant.
Academic Programs *Special study options:* academic remediation for entering students, cooperative education, distance learning, double majors, independent study, internships, part-time degree program, summer session for credit.
Library Main Library plus 1 other with 1,500 titles, 20 serial subscriptions, an OPAC.
Computers on Campus 96 computers available on campus for general student use. Internet access available.
Student Life *Housing:* college housing not available. *Activities and Organizations:* student-run newspaper, Business Professionals of America, Association for Computing Machinery, Baccus Gamma. *Campus security:* 24-hour emergency response devices. *Student services:* personal/psychological counseling.
Standardized Tests *Required:* CPAt (for admission). *Recommended:* SAT or ACT (for admission).
Costs (2005–06) *Tuition:* $10,920 full-time, $364 per credit part-time. *Required fees:* $225 full-time.
Applying *Options:* deferred entrance. *Application fee:* $25. *Required:* essay or personal statement, high school transcript, interview. *Required for some:* 2 letters of recommendation. *Recommended:* minimum 2.0 GPA. *Application deadline:* 6/30 (freshmen), rolling (transfers).
Admissions Contact Ms. Shari Grasso, Director of Admissions, Bryant and Stratton College, 12955 Snow Road, Parma, OH 44130. *Phone:* 216-265-3151 Ext. 229. *Toll-free phone:* 800-327-3151. *Fax:* 216-265-0325. *E-mail:* slgrasso@bryantstratton.edu.

BRYANT AND STRATTON COLLEGE
Willoughby Hills, Ohio

Admissions Contact Mr. James Pettit, Director of Admissions, Bryant and Stratton College, 27557 Chardon Road, Willoughby Hills, OH 44092. *Phone:* 440-944-6800. *Fax:* 440-944-9260. *E-mail:* jwpettit@bryantstratton.edu.

CENTRAL OHIO TECHNICAL COLLEGE
Newark, Ohio

Admissions Contact Admissions Representative, Central Ohio Technical College, 1179 University Drive, Newark, OH 43055-1767. *Phone:* 740-366-9222. *Toll-free phone:* 800-9NEWARK. *Fax:* 740-366-5047. *E-mail:* lnelson@bigvax.newark.ohio-state.edu.

CHATFIELD COLLEGE
St. Martin, Ohio

- **Independent** 2-year, founded 1970, affiliated with Roman Catholic Church
- **Calendar** semesters
- **Degree** associate
- **Rural** 200-acre campus with easy access to Cincinnati and Dayton
- **Endowment** $700,000
- **Coed, primarily women**

Faculty *Student/faculty ratio:* 12:1.
Student Life *Campus security:* 12-hour night patrols by security.
Costs (2004–05) *Tuition:* $235 per credit hour part-time. *Required fees:* $130 per term part-time.
Financial Aid Of all full-time matriculated undergraduates who enrolled in 2003, 10 Federal Work-Study jobs (averaging $800). 4 state and other part-time jobs (averaging $600). *Financial aid deadline:* 8/1.
Applying *Options:* common application, early admission, deferred entrance. *Application fee:* $10. *Required:* high school transcript.
Admissions Contact Mr. Bill F. Balzano PhD, Director of Admissions, Chatfield College, St. Martin, OH 45118. *Phone:* 513-875-3344. *Fax:* 513-875-3912. *E-mail:* chatfield@chatfield.edu.

CINCINNATI COLLEGE OF MORTUARY SCIENCE
Cincinnati, Ohio

- **Independent** primarily 2-year, founded 1882
- **Calendar** quarters
- **Degrees** associate and bachelor's

Cincinnati College of Mortuary Science (continued)
- **Urban** 10-acre campus
- **Coed**

Faculty *Student/faculty ratio:* 5:1.
Costs (2004–05) *Tuition:* $12,900 full-time, $172 per credit hour part-time. *Required fees:* $120 full-time, $60 per term part-time.
Applying *Options:* deferred entrance. *Application fee:* $25. *Required:* high school transcript. *Recommended:* letters of recommendation.
Admissions Contact Ms. Pat Leon, Director of Financial Aid, Cincinnati College of Mortuary Science, 645 West North Bend Road, Cincinnati, OH 45224-1462. *Phone:* 513-761-2020. *Fax:* 513-761-3333.

CINCINNATI STATE TECHNICAL AND COMMUNITY COLLEGE
Cincinnati, Ohio

- **State-supported** 2-year, founded 1966, part of Ohio Board of Regents
- **Calendar** 5 ten-week terms
- **Degree** certificates and associate
- **Urban** 46-acre campus
- **Endowment** $1.3 million
- **Coed,** 8,472 undergraduate students, 39% full-time, 57% women, 43% men

Undergraduates 3,296 full-time, 5,176 part-time. Students come from 9 states and territories, 62 other countries, 11% are from out of state, 27% African American, 0.8% Asian American or Pacific Islander, 0.7% Hispanic American, 0.1% Native American, 2% international. *Retention:* 48% of 2002 full-time freshmen returned.
Faculty *Total:* 577, 31% full-time. *Student/faculty ratio:* 16:1.
Majors Accounting; administrative assistant and secretarial science; aeronautical/aerospace engineering technology; allied health and medical assisting services related; applied horticulture/horticultural business services related; architectural engineering technology; automotive engineering technology; biomedical technology; business administration and management; business, management, and marketing related; chemical technology; child care provision; cinematography and film/video production; civil engineering technology; clinical/medical laboratory technology; commercial and advertising art; computer and information sciences; computer engineering technology; computer programming; computer programming (specific applications); criminal justice/police science; culinary arts; diagnostic medical sonography and ultrasound technology; dietetics; electrical and electronic engineering technologies related; electrical, electronic and communications engineering technology; electromechanical technology; emergency medical technology (EMT paramedic); entrepreneurship; environmental engineering technology; executive assistant/executive secretary; fire science; general studies; health information/medical records technology; health professions related; heating, air conditioning and refrigeration technology; hotel/motel administration; information science/studies; international business/trade/commerce; landscaping and groundskeeping; laser and optical technology; liberal arts and sciences/liberal studies; management information systems; marketing/marketing management; mechanical engineering/mechanical technology; mechanic and repair technologies related; medical/clinical assistant; nursing (registered nurse training); nursing related; occupational therapist assistant; office management; parks, recreation, and leisure related; plastics engineering technology; purchasing, procurement/acquisitions and contracts management; real estate; respiratory care therapy; restaurant, culinary, and catering management; science technologies related; security and loss prevention; sign language interpretation and translation; surgical technology; survey technology; technical and business writing; telecommunications; turf and turfgrass management.
Academic Programs *Special study options:* academic remediation for entering students, advanced placement credit, cooperative education, distance learning, double majors, English as a second language, honors programs, internships, off-campus study, part-time degree program, services for LD students, student-designed majors, summer session for credit.
Library Johnnie Mae Berry Library with 30,762 titles, 268 serial subscriptions, 3,428 audiovisual materials, an OPAC, a Web page.
Computers on Campus 150 computers available on campus for general student use. A campuswide network can be accessed from off campus. Internet access, online (class) registration, at least one staffed computer lab available.
Student Life *Housing:* college housing not available. *Activities and Organizations:* drama/theater group, student government, Nursing Student Association, Phi Theta Kappa, American Society of Civil Engineers, Students in Free Enterprise. *Campus security:* 24-hour emergency response devices and patrols, late-night transport/escort service. *Student services:* personal/psychological counseling.
Athletics Member NJCAA. *Intercollegiate sports:* basketball M/W, golf M/W, soccer M. *Intramural sports:* cheerleading W.
Standardized Tests *Required:* ACT COMPASS (for placement).
Costs (2005–06) *Tuition:* state resident $4152 full-time, $71 per credit hour part-time; nonresident $8019 full-time, $143 per credit hour part-time. Full-time

tuition and fees vary according to reciprocity agreements. Part-time tuition and fees vary according to reciprocity agreements. *Required fees:* $155 full-time, $31 per term part-time. *Waivers:* senior citizens and employees or children of employees.
Financial Aid Of all full-time matriculated undergraduates who enrolled in 2003, 100 Federal Work-Study jobs (averaging $3500).
Applying *Options:* electronic application. *Required:* high school transcript. *Application deadline:* rolling (freshmen), rolling (transfers). *Notification:* continuous (freshmen).
Admissions Contact Ms. Gabriele Boeckermann, Director of Admission, Cincinnati State Technical and Community College, 3520 Central Parkway, Cincinnati, OH 45223-2690. *Phone:* 513-569-1550. *Fax:* 513-569-1562. *E-mail:* adm@cincinnatistate.edu.

CLARK STATE COMMUNITY COLLEGE
Springfield, Ohio

- **State-supported** 2-year, founded 1962, part of Ohio Board of Regents
- **Calendar** quarters
- **Degree** certificates and associate
- **Suburban** 60-acre campus with easy access to Columbus and Dayton
- **Coed,** 3,510 undergraduate students, 43% full-time, 69% women, 31% men

Undergraduates 1,502 full-time, 2,008 part-time. 14% African American, 0.8% Asian American or Pacific Islander, 0.8% Hispanic American, 0.5% Native American, 0.2% international, 4% transferred in.
Freshmen *Admission:* 1,461 applied, 1,461 admitted, 738 enrolled.
Faculty *Total:* 329, 18% full-time. *Student/faculty ratio:* 15:1.
Majors Accounting; administrative assistant and secretarial science; agricultural business and management; agricultural mechanization; agriculture; business administration and management; civil engineering technology; clinical/medical laboratory technology; commercial and advertising art; computer programming; computer programming related; computer systems networking and telecommunications; computer/technical support; corrections; court reporting; criminal justice/law enforcement administration; criminal justice/police science; drafting and design technology; dramatic/theatre arts; electrical, electronic and communications engineering technology; emergency medical technology (EMT paramedic); horticultural science; human services; industrial technology; information science/studies; information technology; kindergarten/preschool education; kinesiology and exercise science; landscaping and groundskeeping; legal assistant/paralegal; liberal arts and sciences/liberal studies; mechanical engineering/mechanical technology; medical administrative assistant and medical secretary; nursing (licensed practical/vocational nurse training); nursing (registered nurse training); physical therapy; social work.
Academic Programs *Special study options:* academic remediation for entering students, adult/continuing education programs, advanced placement credit, cooperative education, distance learning, off-campus study, part-time degree program, services for LD students, summer session for credit. *ROTC:* Army (c).
Library Clark State Community College Library with 31,988 titles, 378 serial subscriptions, an OPAC, a Web page.
Computers on Campus 350 computers available on campus for general student use. A campuswide network can be accessed from off campus. Internet access, at least one staffed computer lab available.
Student Life *Housing:* college housing not available. *Activities and Organizations:* drama/theater group, student-run newspaper, choral group, Student Government Association, Minority Student Forum. *Campus security:* late-night transport/escort service. *Student services:* health clinic, personal/psychological counseling.
Athletics Member NJCAA. *Intercollegiate sports:* basketball M/W, softball W, volleyball W. *Intramural sports:* basketball M/W, tennis M/W, volleyball M/W.
Standardized Tests *Required for some:* SAT or ACT (for placement). *Recommended:* SAT or ACT (for placement).
Costs (2005–06) *Tuition:* state resident $3492 full-time, $74 per credit hour part-time; nonresident $6492 full-time, $136 per credit hour part-time. *Required fees:* $1100 full-time.
Applying *Options:* common application, electronic application, early admission, deferred entrance. *Application fee:* $15. *Required:* high school transcript. *Application deadline:* rolling (freshmen), rolling (transfers). *Notification:* continuous (freshmen).
Admissions Contact Mr. Todd Jones, Director of Admissions, Clark State Community College, PO Box 570, Springfield, OH 45501-0570. *Phone:* 937-328-6027. *Fax:* 937-328-3853. *E-mail:* admissions@clarkstate.edu.

CLEVELAND INSTITUTE OF ELECTRONICS
Cleveland, Ohio

- **Proprietary** 2-year, founded 1934
- **Calendar** continuous

- **Degrees** associate (offers only external degree programs conducted through home study)
- **Coed, primarily men**

Costs (2004–05) *Tuition:* $1645 per term part-time. No tuition increase for student's term of enrollment. *Payment plans:* tuition prepayment, installment.

Applying *Options:* common application, electronic application, early admission. *Required:* high school transcript.

Admissions Contact Mr. Scott Katzenmeyer, Registrar, Cleveland Institute of Electronics, 1776 East 17th Street, Cleveland, OH 44114. *Phone:* 216-781-9400. *Toll-free phone:* 800-243-6446. *Fax:* 216-781-0331. *E-mail:* instruct@cie-wc.edu.

COLLEGE OF ART ADVERTISING
Cincinnati, Ohio

Admissions Contact Ms. Janet Bussberg, Director of Admissions, College of Art Advertising, 4343 Bridgetown Road, Cincinnati, OH 45211-4427. *Phone:* 937-294-0592.

COLUMBUS STATE COMMUNITY COLLEGE
Columbus, Ohio

- **State-supported** 2-year, founded 1963, part of Ohio Board of Regents
- **Calendar** quarters
- **Degree** certificates and associate
- **Urban** 75-acre campus
- **Coed,** 21,872 undergraduate students, 39% full-time, 59% women, 41% men

Undergraduates 8,530 full-time, 13,342 part-time. Students come from 41 states and territories, 127 other countries, 1% are from out of state, 23% African American, 3% Asian American or Pacific Islander, 2% Hispanic American, 0.5% Native American, 0.8% international, 3% transferred in. *Retention:* 48% of 2002 full-time freshmen returned.

Freshmen *Admission:* 3,058 applied, 3,058 admitted, 2,498 enrolled.

Faculty *Total:* 1,667, 16% full-time. *Student/faculty ratio:* 19:1.

Majors Accounting; accounting and computer science; accounting technology and bookkeeping; administrative assistant and secretarial science; aircraft powerplant technology; airframe mechanics and aircraft maintenance technology; architectural engineering technology; architectural technology; automobile/automotive mechanics technology; avionics maintenance technology; business administration and management; child development; civil engineering technology; clinical laboratory science/medical technology; clinical/medical laboratory assistant; clinical/medical laboratory technology; commercial and advertising art; computer engineering technology; computer programming; construction management; consumer merchandising/retailing management; corrections; criminal justice/police science; culinary arts; dental hygiene; dental laboratory technology; dietetics; dietetic technician; electrical and electronic engineering technologies related; electrical, electronic and communications engineering technology; electromechanical technology; emergency care attendant (EMT ambulance); emergency medical technology (EMT paramedic); environmental engineering technology; finance; food services technology; gerontology; health information/medical records administration; health information/medical records technology; heating, air conditioning, ventilation and refrigeration maintenance technology; histologic technician; hotel/motel administration; human resources management; industrial radiologic technology; kindergarten/preschool education; landscape architecture; legal administrative assistant/secretary; legal assistant/paralegal; liberal arts and sciences/liberal studies; logistics and materials management; marketing/marketing management; massage therapy; mechanical engineering/mechanical technology; medical administrative assistant and medical secretary; medical insurance coding; mental health/rehabilitation; nursing (licensed practical/vocational nurse training); nursing (registered nurse training); phlebotomy; purchasing, procurement/acquisitions and contracts management; quality control technology; radiologic technology/science; real estate; respiratory care therapy; respiratory therapy technician; restaurant/food services management; sign language interpretation and translation; sport and fitness administration; substance abuse/addiction counseling; surgical technology; technical and business writing; tourism and travel services management; veterinary/animal health technology; veterinary technology.

Academic Programs *Special study options:* academic remediation for entering students, adult/continuing education programs, advanced placement credit, cooperative education, distance learning, English as a second language, honors programs, internships, off-campus study, part-time degree program, services for LD students, student-designed majors, summer session for credit. *ROTC:* Army (b), Air Force (c).

Library Educational Resources Center plus 1 other with 38,192 titles, 489 serial subscriptions, 7,903 audiovisual materials, an OPAC, a Web page.

Computers on Campus 960 computers available on campus for general student use. A campuswide network can be accessed from off campus. Internet access, online (class) registration, at least one staffed computer lab available.

Student Life *Housing:* college housing not available. *Activities and Organizations:* choral group, Phi Theta Kappa, Alpha Xi Tau, African-American Women's Support Group, Society of Manufacturing Engineers, Student Organization for Legal Assistants. *Campus security:* 24-hour emergency response devices and patrols, late-night transport/escort service. *Student services:* health clinic, personal/psychological counseling.

Athletics Member NJCAA. *Intercollegiate sports:* baseball M, basketball M(s)/W(s), cross-country running M/W, equestrian sports M/W, golf M, soccer M, softball W, volleyball W. *Intramural sports:* basketball M/W, volleyball M/W, weight lifting M/W.

Standardized Tests *Required:* ACT COMPASS (for placement).

Costs (2005–06) *One-time required fee:* $35. *Tuition:* state resident $2736 full-time, $76 per credit part-time; nonresident $6048 full-time, $168 per credit part-time. *Waivers:* employees or children of employees.

Financial Aid Of all full-time matriculated undergraduates who enrolled in 2003, 133 Federal Work-Study jobs (averaging $1500).

Applying *Options:* common application, early admission, deferred entrance. *Application fee:* $10. *Recommended:* high school transcript. *Application deadline:* rolling (freshmen), rolling (transfers). *Notification:* continuous (freshmen).

Admissions Contact Mr. Kenneth Conner, Dean of Enrollment Services, Columbus State Community College, 550 East Spring Street, Madison Hall, Columbus, OH 43215. *Phone:* 614-287-2669 Ext. 3669. *Toll-free phone:* 800-621-6407 Ext. 2669. *Fax:* 614-287-6019.

CUYAHOGA COMMUNITY COLLEGE
Cleveland, Ohio

- **State and locally supported** 2-year, founded 1963
- **Calendar** semesters
- **Degree** certificates and associate
- **Urban** campus
- **Coed,** 25,214 undergraduate students, 40% full-time, 64% women, 36% men

Undergraduates 10,169 full-time, 15,045 part-time. Students come from 21 states and territories, 63 other countries, 30% African American, 2% Asian American or Pacific Islander, 4% Hispanic American, 0.7% Native American, 2% international, 3% transferred in.

Freshmen *Admission:* 4,257 applied, 4,257 admitted, 2,419 enrolled.

Faculty *Total:* 1,667, 20% full-time, 6% with terminal degrees. *Student/faculty ratio:* 19:1.

Majors Accounting; administrative assistant and secretarial science; automobile/automotive mechanics technology; avionics maintenance technology; business administration and management; clinical laboratory science/medical technology; commercial and advertising art; computer engineering technology; computer typography and composition equipment operation; court reporting; criminal justice/police science; engineering technology; finance; fire science; industrial radiologic technology; kindergarten/preschool education; legal assistant/paralegal; liberal arts and sciences/liberal studies; marketing/marketing management; merchandising; nursing (registered nurse training); opticianry; photography; physician assistant; real estate; respiratory care therapy; restaurant, culinary, and catering management; safety/security technology; sales, distribution and marketing; selling skills and sales; surgical technology; veterinary technology.

Academic Programs *Special study options:* adult/continuing education programs, advanced placement credit, cooperative education, distance learning, English as a second language, external degree program, independent study, part-time degree program, services for LD students, summer session for credit.

Library 177,767 titles, 1,135 serial subscriptions, an OPAC, a Web page.

Computers on Campus 1275 computers available on campus for general student use. A campuswide network can be accessed from off campus. Internet access, at least one staffed computer lab available.

Student Life *Housing:* college housing not available. *Activities and Organizations:* drama/theater group, student-run newspaper, choral group, Student Senate, Student Nursing Organization, Business Focus, Phi Theta Kappa. *Campus security:* 24-hour emergency response devices and patrols, late-night transport/escort service. *Student services:* health clinic, personal/psychological counseling.

Athletics Member NJCAA. *Intercollegiate sports:* baseball M(s), basketball M(s), cross-country running M(s)/W(s), soccer M(s), softball W(s). *Intramural sports:* basketball M, tennis M/W, track and field M/W, volleyball M/W.

Costs (2005–06) *Tuition:* area resident $2301 full-time, $77 per credit hour part-time; state resident $3042 full-time, $101 per credit hour part-time; nonresident $6228 full-time, $208 per credit hour part-time.

Financial Aid Of all full-time matriculated undergraduates who enrolled in 2003, 802 Federal Work-Study jobs (averaging $3300).

Applying *Options:* early admission, deferred entrance. *Required for some:* high school transcript. *Application deadline:* rolling (freshmen), rolling (transfers). *Notification:* continuous (freshmen).

Admissions Contact Mr. Kevin McDaniel, Director of Admissions and Records, Cuyahoga Community College, 2900 Community College Avenue, Cleveland, OH 44115. *Phone:* 216-987-4030. *Toll-free phone:* 800-954-8742. *Fax:* 216-696-2567.

DAVIS COLLEGE
Toledo, Ohio

- **Proprietary** 2-year, founded 1858
- **Calendar** quarters
- **Degree** diplomas and associate
- **Urban** 1-acre campus with easy access to Detroit
- **Coed**

Faculty *Student/faculty ratio:* 14:1.
Student Life *Campus security:* 24-hour emergency response devices, security cameras for parking lot.
Standardized Tests *Required:* CPAt (for admission).
Costs (2004–05) *Tuition:* $7740 full-time, $215 per credit hour part-time. *Required fees:* $480 full-time.
Financial Aid Of all full-time matriculated undergraduates who enrolled in 2003, 10 Federal Work-Study jobs (averaging $3500).
Applying *Options:* common application, electronic application, early admission, deferred entrance. *Application fee:* $30. *Required:* high school transcript, interview.
Admissions Contact Ms. Dana Stern, Senior Career Coordinator, Davis College, 4747 Monroe Street, Toledo, OH 43623-4307. *Phone:* 419-473-2700. *Toll-free phone:* 800-477-7021. *Fax:* 419-473-2472. *E-mail:* dstern@daviscollege.edu.

EDISON STATE COMMUNITY COLLEGE
Piqua, Ohio

- **State-supported** 2-year, founded 1973, part of Ohio Board of Regents
- **Calendar** semesters
- **Degree** certificates and associate
- **Small-town** 130-acre campus with easy access to Cincinnati and Dayton
- **Coed,** 3,000 undergraduate students, 34% full-time, 64% women, 36% men

Undergraduates 1,028 full-time, 1,972 part-time. Students come from 5 states and territories, 2% African American, 0.7% Asian American or Pacific Islander, 0.5% Hispanic American, 0.3% Native American, 4% transferred in.
Freshmen *Admission:* 611 enrolled.
Faculty *Total:* 298, 14% full-time. *Student/faculty ratio:* 19:1.
Majors Accounting; administrative assistant and secretarial science; advertising; art; business administration and management; commercial and advertising art; computer engineering technology; computer graphics; computer programming; computer science; consumer merchandising/retailing management; criminal justice/law enforcement administration; criminal justice/police science; data processing and data processing technology; drafting and design technology; electrical, electronic and communications engineering technology; elementary education; engineering; engineering related; engineering technology; English; finance; health information/medical records administration; human resources management; human services; industrial technology; kindergarten/preschool education; legal assistant/paralegal; legal studies; liberal arts and sciences/liberal studies; marketing/marketing management; mathematics; mechanical design technology; medical administrative assistant and medical secretary; nursing (registered nurse training); pre-engineering; quality control technology; real estate.
Academic Programs *Special study options:* academic remediation for entering students, accelerated degree program, adult/continuing education programs, advanced placement credit, distance learning, double majors, independent study, internships, off-campus study, part-time degree program, services for LD students, student-designed majors, summer session for credit. *ROTC:* Army (c), Air Force (c).
Library Edison Community College Library with 29,851 titles, 542 serial subscriptions, 2,424 audiovisual materials, an OPAC, a Web page.
Computers on Campus 251 computers available on campus for general student use. A campuswide network can be accessed from off campus. Internet access, online (class) registration, at least one staffed computer lab available. Computer purchase or lease plan available.
Student Life *Housing:* college housing not available. *Activities and Organizations:* drama/theater group. *Campus security:* late-night transport/escort service, 18-hour patrols by trained security personnel. *Student services:* personal/psychological counseling.
Athletics Member NJCAA. *Intercollegiate sports:* basketball M/W, volleyball W.
Standardized Tests *Required for some:* SAT or ACT (for placement), ACT ASSET, ACT COMPASS. *Recommended:* ACT ASSET, ACT COMPASS.
Costs (2004–05) *Tuition:* state resident $2088 full-time, $87 per credit hour part-time; nonresident $4176 full-time, $174 per credit hour part-time. Full-time tuition and fees vary according to course load. Part-time tuition and fees vary according to course load. *Required fees:* $384 full-time, $16 per credit hour part-time. *Payment plan:* installment. *Waivers:* employees or children of employees.

Financial Aid Of all full-time matriculated undergraduates who enrolled in 2003, 42 Federal Work-Study jobs (averaging $3000).
Applying *Options:* electronic application, early admission, deferred entrance. *Application fee:* $15. *Required:* high school transcript. *Application deadline:* rolling (freshmen), rolling (transfers).
Admissions Contact Ms. Beth Iams Culbertson, Director of Admissions, Edison State Community College, 1973 Edison Drive, Piqua, OH 45356. *Phone:* 937-778-8600 Ext. 317. *Toll-free phone:* 800-922-3722. *Fax:* 937-778-4692. *E-mail:* info@edisonohio.edu.

ETI TECHNICAL COLLEGE OF NILES
Niles, Ohio

Admissions Contact Ms. Diane Marstellar, Director of Admissions, ETI Technical College of Niles, 2076 Youngstown-Warren Road, Niles, OH 44446-4398. *Phone:* 330-652-9919. *Fax:* 330-652-4399.

GALLIPOLIS CAREER COLLEGE
Gallipolis, Ohio

- **Independent** 2-year, founded 1962
- **Calendar** quarters
- **Degree** certificates, diplomas, and associate
- **Small-town** campus
- **Coed, primarily women**

Faculty *Student/faculty ratio:* 8:1.
Standardized Tests *Required:* Wonderlic aptitude test (for admission).
Costs (2004–05) *Tuition:* $8160 full-time, $170 per quarter hour part-time. *Required fees:* $100 full-time.
Applying *Application fee:* $50. *Required:* high school transcript, interview.
Admissions Contact Mr. Jack Henson, Director of Admissions, Gallipolis Career College, 1176 Jackson Pike, Suite 312, Gallipolis, OH 45631. *Phone:* 740-446-4124 Ext. 12. *Toll-free phone:* 800-214-0452. *E-mail:* admissions@gallipoliscareercollege.com.

HOCKING COLLEGE
Nelsonville, Ohio

Admissions Contact Ms. Lyn Hull, Director of Admissions, Hocking College, 3301 Hocking Parkway, Nelsonville, OH 45764-9588. *Phone:* 740-753-3591 Ext. 2803. *Toll-free phone:* 800-282-4163. *Fax:* 740-753-1452. *E-mail:* admissions@hocking.edu.

HONDROS COLLEGE
Westerville, Ohio

Admissions Contact Ms. Carol Thomas, Operations Manager, Hondros College, 4140 Executive Parkway, Westerville, OH 43081. *Phone:* 614-508-7244. *Toll-free phone:* 800-783-0095. *Fax:* 614-508-7279. *E-mail:* hondras@hondras.com.

INTERNATIONAL COLLEGE OF BROADCASTING
Dayton, Ohio

- **Private** 2-year
- **Calendar** semesters
- **Degree** diplomas and associate
- **Urban** 1-acre campus
- **Coed,** 87 undergraduate students, 100% full-time, 26% women, 74% men
- **67% of applicants were admitted**

Undergraduates 87 full-time. 31% African American, 1% Hispanic American.
Freshmen *Admission:* 21 applied, 14 admitted, 11 enrolled. *Average high school GPA:* 2.30.
Faculty *Total:* 12, 50% full-time. *Student/faculty ratio:* 10:1.
Majors Audio engineering; radio and television.
Admissions Contact Mr. Aan McIntosh, Director of Admissions, International College of Broadcasting, 6 South Smithville Road, Dayton, OH 45431. *Phone:* 937-258-8251. *Fax:* 937-258-8714. *E-mail:* micicb@aol.com.

ITT TECHNICAL INSTITUTE
Dayton, Ohio

- **Proprietary** 2-year, founded 1935, part of ITT Educational Services, Inc
- **Calendar** quarters

- **Degree** associate
- **Suburban** 7-acre campus
- **Coed**

Standardized Tests *Required:* Wonderlic aptitude test (for admission).
Costs (2004–05) *Tuition:* Please see school catalog for specific information.
Applying *Options:* deferred entrance. *Application fee:* $100. *Required:* high school transcript, interview. *Recommended:* letters of recommendation.
Admissions Contact Mr. Sean G. Kuhn, Director of Recruitment, ITT Technical Institute, 3325 Stop 8 Road, Dayton, OH 45414. *Phone:* 937-454-2267. *Toll-free phone:* 800-568-3241. *Fax:* 937-454-2278.

ITT TECHNICAL INSTITUTE
Hilliard, Ohio

- **Proprietary** 2-year, founded 2003
- **Calendar** quarters
- **Degree** associate
- **Coed**

Admissions Contact Jim Tussing, Director of Recruitment, ITT Technical Institute, 3781 Park Mill Run Drive, Hilliard, OH 43026. *Phone:* 614-771-4888. *Toll-free phone:* 888-483-4888.

ITT TECHNICAL INSTITUTE
Norwood, Ohio

- **Proprietary** 2-year, part of ITT Educational Services, Inc
- **Calendar** quarters
- **Degree** associate
- **Coed**

Standardized Tests *Required:* Wonderlic aptitude test (for admission).
Costs (2004–05) *Tuition:* Please see school catalog for specific information.
Applying *Options:* deferred entrance. *Application fee:* $100. *Required:* high school transcript, interview. *Recommended:* letters of recommendation.
Admissions Contact Mr. Bill Bradford, Director of Recruitment, ITT Technical Institute, 4750 Wesley Avenue, Norwood, OH 45212. *Phone:* 513-531-8300. *Toll-free phone:* 800-314-8324. *Fax:* 513-531-8368.

ITT TECHNICAL INSTITUTE
Strongsville, Ohio

- **Proprietary** 2-year, part of ITT Educational Services, Inc
- **Calendar** quarters
- **Degree** associate
- **Coed**

Standardized Tests *Required:* Wonderlic aptitude test (for admission).
Costs (2004–05) *Tuition:* Please see school catalog for specific information.
Applying *Options:* deferred entrance. *Application fee:* $100. *Required:* high school transcript, interview. *Recommended:* letters of recommendation.
Admissions Contact Mr. James Tussing, Director of Recruitment, ITT Technical Institute, 14955 Sprague Road, Strongsville, OH 44136. *Phone:* 440-234-9091. *Toll-free phone:* 800-331-1488. *Fax:* 440-234-7568.

ITT TECHNICAL INSTITUTE
Youngstown, Ohio

- **Proprietary** 2-year, founded 1967, part of ITT Educational Services, Inc
- **Calendar** quarters
- **Degree** associate
- **Suburban** campus with easy access to Cleveland and Pittsburgh
- **Coed**

Standardized Tests *Required:* Wonderlic aptitude test (for admission).
Costs (2004–05) *Tuition:* Please see school catalog for specific information.
Financial Aid Of all full-time matriculated undergraduates who enrolled in 2003, 5 Federal Work-Study jobs (averaging $3979).
Applying *Options:* deferred entrance. *Application fee:* $100. *Required:* high school transcript, interview. *Recommended:* letters of recommendation.
Admissions Contact Mr. Tom Flynn, Director of Recruitment, ITT Technical Institute, 1030 North Meridian Road, Youngstown, OH 44509. *Phone:* 330-270-1600. *Toll-free phone:* 800-832-5001. *Fax:* 330-270-8333.

JAMES A. RHODES STATE COLLEGE
Lima, Ohio

- **State-supported** 2-year, founded 1971
- **Calendar** quarters

- **Degree** certificates and associate
- **Rural** 565-acre campus
- **Endowment** $849,362
- **Coed**

Faculty *Student/faculty ratio:* 25:1.
Student Life *Campus security:* student patrols, late-night transport/escort service.
Standardized Tests *Required for some:* ACT (for placement), ACT ASSET and ACT COMPASS.
Costs (2004–05) *Tuition:* state resident $3756 full-time, $84 per quarter hour part-time; nonresident $7512 full-time, $167 per quarter hour part-time. Full-time tuition and fees vary according to course load and program. Part-time tuition and fees vary according to program. *Required fees:* $20 full-time, $20 per term part-time. *Payment plans:* installment, deferred payment.
Financial Aid Of all full-time matriculated undergraduates who enrolled in 2003, 110 Federal Work-Study jobs (averaging $1000).
Applying *Options:* common application, early admission, deferred entrance. *Application fee:* $25. *Required:* high school transcript.
Admissions Contact Mr. Scot Lingrell, Director, Student Advising and Development, James A. Rhodes State College, 4240 Campus Drive, Lima, OH 45804-3597. *Phone:* 419-995-8050. *Fax:* 419-995-8098. *E-mail:* lingrel.s@rhodesstate.edu.

JEFFERSON COMMUNITY COLLEGE
Steubenville, Ohio

- **State and locally supported** 2-year, founded 1966, part of Ohio Board of Regents
- **Calendar** semesters
- **Degree** certificates and associate
- **Small-town** 83-acre campus with easy access to Pittsburgh
- **Endowment** $197,077
- **Coed,** 1,260 undergraduate students, 53% full-time, 64% women, 36% men

Undergraduates 668 full-time, 592 part-time. Students come from 23 states and territories, 16% are from out of state, 4% African American, 1% Asian American or Pacific Islander, 0.7% Hispanic American, 0.1% Native American, 38% transferred in.
Freshmen *Admission:* 890 applied, 890 admitted, 398 enrolled. *Average high school GPA:* 2.53.
Faculty *Total:* 124, 28% full-time, 6% with terminal degrees. *Student/faculty ratio:* 16:1.
Majors Accounting; administrative assistant and secretarial science; business administration and management; child care and support services management; computer engineering related; consumer merchandising/retailing management; corrections; criminal justice/police science; data processing and data processing technology; dental assisting; developmental and child psychology; drafting and design technology; electrical, electronic and communications engineering technology; emergency medical technology (EMT paramedic); finance; industrial radiologic technology; industrial technology; legal administrative assistant/secretary; mechanical engineering/mechanical technology; medical administrative assistant and medical secretary; medical/clinical assistant; nursing (licensed practical/vocational nurse training); real estate; respiratory care therapy; special products marketing.
Academic Programs *Special study options:* academic remediation for entering students, adult/continuing education programs, internships, off-campus study, part-time degree program, services for LD students, summer session for credit.
Library Jefferson Community College Library with 12,500 titles, 180 serial subscriptions, 246 audiovisual materials, an OPAC.
Computers on Campus 325 computers available on campus for general student use. At least one staffed computer lab available.
Student Life *Housing:* college housing not available. *Activities and Organizations:* Student Senate, SADD, AITP (Association for Information Technology Professionals), American Drafting and Design Association, Writers Club. *Campus security:* student patrols.
Athletics *Intercollegiate sports:* basketball M/W. *Intramural sports:* basketball M/W, bowling M/W, football M/W, softball M/W, tennis M/W, volleyball M/W.
Standardized Tests *Required for some:* SAT or ACT (for admission).
Costs (2004–05) *Tuition:* area resident $2430 full-time, $81 per credit part-time; state resident $2580 full-time, $86 per credit part-time; nonresident $3240 full-time, $108 per credit part-time. Full-time tuition and fees vary according to reciprocity agreements. Part-time tuition and fees vary according to reciprocity agreements. *Required fees:* $600 full-time. *Payment plan:* deferred payment. *Waivers:* senior citizens and employees or children of employees.
Financial Aid Of all full-time matriculated undergraduates who enrolled in 2003, 30 Federal Work-Study jobs (averaging $1500).

Jefferson Community College (continued)

Applying *Options:* early admission, deferred entrance. *Application fee:* $20. *Required for some:* high school transcript. *Application deadlines:* 8/20 (freshmen), 8/20 (transfers). *Notification:* continuous until 8/20 (freshmen).

Admissions Contact Mr. Chuck Mascellino, Director of Admissions, Jefferson Community College, 4000 Sunset Boulevard, Steubenville, OH 43952. *Phone:* 740-264-5591 Ext. 142. *Toll-free phone:* 800-68-COLLEGE Ext. 142. *Fax:* 740-266-2944.

KENT STATE UNIVERSITY, ASHTABULA CAMPUS
Ashtabula, Ohio

Admissions Contact Ms. Kelly Sanford, Director, Enrollment Management and Student Services, Kent State University, Ashtabula Campus, 3325 West 13th Street, Ashtabula, OH 44004-2299. *Phone:* 440-964-4217. *E-mail:* robinson@ashtabula.kent.edu.

KENT STATE UNIVERSITY, EAST LIVERPOOL CAMPUS
East Liverpool, Ohio

Admissions Contact Mrs. Jamie Kenneally, Director of Enrollment Management and Student Services, Kent State University, East Liverpool Campus, 400 East Fourth Street, East Liverpool, OH 43920. *Phone:* 330-382-7414. *Fax:* 330-385-6348. *E-mail:* admissions@eliv.kent.edu.

KENT STATE UNIVERSITY, GEAUGA CAMPUS
Burton, Ohio

Admissions Contact Ms. Betty Landrus, Admissions and Records Secretary, Kent State University, Geauga Campus, 14111 Claridon-Troy Road, Burton, OH 44021. *Phone:* 440-834-4187. *Fax:* 440-834-8846. *E-mail:* cbaker@geauga.kent.edu.

KENT STATE UNIVERSITY, SALEM CAMPUS
Salem, Ohio

- **State-supported** primarily 2-year, founded 1966, part of Kent State University System
- **Calendar** semesters
- **Degrees** associate and bachelor's (also offers some upper-level and graduate courses)
- **Rural** 98-acre campus
- **Coed**

Faculty *Student/faculty ratio:* 13:1.
Student Life *Campus security:* 24-hour emergency response devices, late-night transport/escort service.
Standardized Tests *Required for some:* ACT (for admission), SAT or ACT (for placement). *Recommended:* SAT or ACT (for placement).
Costs (2004–05) *Tuition:* state resident $4326 full-time, $198 per credit part-time; nonresident $11,338 full-time, $518 per credit part-time. Full-time tuition and fees vary according to course level. Part-time tuition and fees vary according to course level. *Payment plans:* installment, deferred payment.
Financial Aid Of all full-time matriculated undergraduates who enrolled in 2003, 16 Federal Work-Study jobs (averaging $3021).
Applying *Options:* early admission, deferred entrance. *Application fee:* $30. *Required:* high school transcript. *Required for some:* essay or personal statement, minimum X GPA, letters of recommendation.
Admissions Contact Mrs. Judy Heisler, Admissions Secretary, Kent State University, Salem Campus, 2491 State Route 45 South, Salem, OH 44460-9412. *Phone:* 330-332-0361 Ext. 74201.

KENT STATE UNIVERSITY, STARK CAMPUS
Canton, Ohio

- **State-supported** primarily 2-year, founded 1967, part of Kent State University System
- **Calendar** semesters
- **Degrees** associate and bachelor's (also offers some graduate courses)
- **Suburban** 200-acre campus with easy access to Cleveland
- **Coed**

Faculty *Student/faculty ratio:* 19:1.
Student Life *Campus security:* 24-hour emergency response devices, late-night transport/escort service.
Standardized Tests *Required for some:* SAT or ACT (for admission).
Costs (2004–05) *Tuition:* state resident $4326 full-time, $198 per credit hour part-time; nonresident $11,338 full-time, $518 per credit hour part-time. No tuition increase for student's term of enrollment.
Financial Aid Of all full-time matriculated undergraduates who enrolled in 2003, 54 Federal Work-Study jobs (averaging $2389).
Applying *Options:* early admission, deferred entrance. *Application fee:* $30. *Required:* high school transcript. *Required for some:* interview.
Admissions Contact Ms. Deborah Ann Speck, Director of Admissions, Kent State University, Stark Campus, 6000 Frank Avenue NW, Canton, OH 44720-7599. *Phone:* 330-499-9600 Ext. 53259. *Fax:* 330-499-0301. *E-mail:* aspeck@stark.kent.edu.

KENT STATE UNIVERSITY, TRUMBULL CAMPUS
Warren, Ohio

- **State-supported** 2-year, founded 1954, part of Kent State University System
- **Calendar** semesters
- **Degrees** certificates and associate (also offers some upper-level and graduate courses)
- **Suburban** 200-acre campus with easy access to Cleveland
- **Endowment** $1.1 million
- **Coed**

Student Life *Campus security:* 24-hour emergency response devices, late-night transport/escort service, patrols by trained security personnel during open hours.
Standardized Tests *Required:* ACT COMPASS (for placement). *Required for some:* SAT or ACT (for placement).
Costs (2004–05) *Tuition:* state resident $4326 full-time, $198 per credit hour part-time; nonresident $11,338 full-time, $518 per credit hour part-time. Full-time tuition and fees vary according to course level. Part-time tuition and fees vary according to course level. *Payment plans:* installment, deferred payment.
Financial Aid Of all full-time matriculated undergraduates who enrolled in 2003, 31 Federal Work-Study jobs (averaging $2708).
Applying *Options:* early admission, deferred entrance. *Application fee:* $30. *Required:* high school transcript.
Admissions Contact Ms. Kerrianne Aulet, Admissions Specialist, Kent State University, Trumbull Campus, 4314 Mahoning Avenue, NW, Warren, OH 44483-1998. *Phone:* 330-847-0571 Ext. 2367. *E-mail:* info@lyceum.trumbull.kent.edu.

KENT STATE UNIVERSITY, TUSCARAWAS CAMPUS
New Philadelphia, Ohio

- **State-supported** primarily 2-year, founded 1962, part of Kent State University System
- **Calendar** semesters
- **Degrees** certificates, diplomas, associate, bachelor's, and master's (also offers some upper-level and graduate courses)
- **Small-town** 172-acre campus with easy access to Cleveland
- **Coed**, 1,802 undergraduate students

Undergraduates 1% African American, 0.2% Asian American or Pacific Islander, 0.4% Hispanic American, 0.2% Native American, 0.4% international.
Faculty *Total:* 163, 28% full-time, 18% with terminal degrees. *Student/faculty ratio:* 17:1.
Majors Accounting; administrative assistant and secretarial science; animation, interactive technology, video graphics and special effects; business administration and management; communications technology; computer engineering technology; criminal justice/police science; early childhood education; electrical, electronic and communications engineering technology; engineering technology; environmental studies; industrial technology; liberal arts and sciences/liberal studies; mechanical engineering/mechanical technology; nursing (registered nurse training); plastics engineering technology.
Academic Programs *Special study options:* academic remediation for entering students, accelerated degree program, adult/continuing education programs, advanced placement credit, distance learning, double majors, freshman honors college, honors programs, internships, part-time degree program, services for LD students, student-designed majors, summer session for credit. *ROTC:* Army (c), Air Force (c).

Library Tuscarawas Campus Library with 62,783 titles, 250 serial subscriptions, 800 audiovisual materials, an OPAC, a Web page.

Computers on Campus 194 computers available on campus for general student use. A campuswide network can be accessed from off campus. Internet access, online (class) registration, at least one staffed computer lab available.

Student Life *Housing:* college housing not available. *Activities and Organizations:* choral group, Society of Mechanical Engineers, IEEE, Imagineers, Criminal Justice Club, Salt and Light.

Athletics *Intercollegiate sports:* basketball M/W, golf M/W. *Intramural sports:* basketball M/W, volleyball M/W.

Standardized Tests *Required for some:* SAT or ACT (for placement).

Costs (2004–05) *Tuition:* state resident $4326 full-time, $198 per credit hour part-time; nonresident $11,138 full-time. Full-time tuition and fees vary according to course level, course load, and location. Part-time tuition and fees vary according to course level, course load, and location. *Payment plan:* installment. *Waivers:* senior citizens and employees or children of employees.

Financial Aid Of all full-time matriculated undergraduates who enrolled in 2003, 26 Federal Work-Study jobs (averaging $2699).

Applying *Options:* common application, early admission, deferred entrance. *Application fee:* $30. *Required:* high school transcript. *Application deadlines:* 9/1 (freshmen), 9/1 (transfers). *Notification:* continuous (freshmen).

Admissions Contact Ms. Denise L. Testa, Director of Admissions, Kent State University, Tuscarawas Campus, 330 University Drive NE, New Philadelphia, OH 44663-9403. *Phone:* 330-339-3391 Ext. 47425. *Fax:* 330-339-3321.

KETTERING COLLEGE OF MEDICAL ARTS
Kettering, Ohio

- **Independent Seventh-day Adventist** primarily 2-year, founded 1967
- **Calendar** semesters
- **Degrees** certificates, associate, bachelor's, and postbachelor's certificates
- **Suburban** 35-acre campus
- **Coed, primarily women**

Student Life *Campus security:* 24-hour emergency response devices and patrols, late-night transport/escort service.

Standardized Tests *Required:* ACT (for admission). *Recommended:* SAT (for admission).

Costs (2004–05) *Comprehensive fee:* $18,138 includes full-time tuition ($10,824), mandatory fees ($960), and room and board ($6354). Full-time tuition and fees vary according to program. Part-time tuition: $260 per credit hour. Part-time tuition and fees vary according to program. *Required fees:* $110 per semester part-time. *Room and board:* college room only: $2994.

Applying *Options:* early admission. *Application fee:* $25. *Required:* high school transcript, minimum 2.0 GPA, 3 letters of recommendation. *Recommended:* minimum 3.0 GPA, interview.

Admissions Contact Mr. David Lofthouse, Director of Enrollment Services, Kettering College of Medical Arts, 3737 Southern Boulevard, Kettering, OH 45429-1299. *Phone:* 937-296-7228. *Toll-free phone:* 800-433-5262. *Fax:* 937-296-4238.

LAKELAND COMMUNITY COLLEGE
Kirtland, Ohio

- **State and locally supported** 2-year, founded 1967, part of Ohio Board of Regents
- **Calendar** semesters
- **Degree** certificates and associate
- **Suburban** 380-acre campus with easy access to Cleveland
- **Endowment** $1.4 million
- **Coed**

Faculty *Student/faculty ratio:* 17:1.

Student Life *Campus security:* 24-hour emergency response devices and patrols, student patrols, late-night transport/escort service.

Athletics Member NJCAA.

Standardized Tests *Required for some:* SAT or ACT (for placement), ACT ASSET or ACT COMPASS. *Recommended:* SAT or ACT (for placement).

Costs (2004–05) *Tuition:* area resident $2243 full-time, $70 per semester hour part-time; state resident $2748 full-time, $87 per semester hour part-time; nonresident $5873 full-time, $200 per semester hour part-time. Full-time tuition and fees vary according to course load. Part-time tuition and fees vary according to course load. *Required fees:* $10 per semester hour part-time, $14 per term part-time.

Financial Aid Of all full-time matriculated undergraduates who enrolled in 2003, 71 Federal Work-Study jobs (averaging $2500). 166 state and other part-time jobs (averaging $1700).

Applying *Options:* common application, electronic application, early admission, deferred entrance. *Application fee:* $15. *Required:* high school transcript.

Admissions Contact Ms. Tracey Cooper, Director for Admissions/Registrar, Lakeland Community College, 7700 Clocktower Drive, Kirtland, OH 44094. *Phone:* 440-525-7230. *Toll-free phone:* 800-589-8520. *Fax:* 440-975-4330. *E-mail:* tcooper@lakelandcc.edu.

LORAIN COUNTY COMMUNITY COLLEGE
Elyria, Ohio

- **State and locally supported** 2-year, founded 1963, part of Ohio Board of Regents
- **Calendar** semesters
- **Degree** certificates and associate
- **Suburban** 480-acre campus with easy access to Cleveland
- **Coed**

Faculty *Student/faculty ratio:* 19:1.

Student Life *Campus security:* 24-hour emergency response devices and patrols, late-night transport/escort service.

Standardized Tests *Required for some:* ACT ASSET, ACT COMPASS. *Recommended:* SAT or ACT (for placement).

Costs (2004–05) *Tuition:* area resident $2106 full-time, $81 per credit hour part-time; state resident $2560 full-time, $99 per credit hour part-time; nonresident $5288 full-time, $203 per credit hour part-time. *Required fees:* $111 full-time, $4 per credit hour part-time. *Payment plans:* installment, deferred payment.

Financial Aid Of all full-time matriculated undergraduates who enrolled in 2003, 100 Federal Work-Study jobs.

Applying *Options:* early admission, deferred entrance. *Required for some:* high school transcript.

Admissions Contact Ms. Dione Somervile, Director of Enrollment Services, Lorain County Community College, 1005 Abbe Road, North, Elyria, OH 44035. *Phone:* 440-366-7566. *Toll-free phone:* 800-995-5222 Ext. 4032. *Fax:* 440-365-6519.

MARION TECHNICAL COLLEGE
Marion, Ohio

- **State-supported** 2-year, founded 1971, part of Ohio Board of Regents
- **Calendar** quarters
- **Degree** certificates and associate
- **Small-town** 180-acre campus with easy access to Columbus
- **Coed**

Faculty *Student/faculty ratio:* 18:1.

Student Life *Campus security:* 24-hour emergency response devices.

Standardized Tests *Required for some:* ACT (for placement).

Costs (2004–05) *Tuition:* state resident $3276 full-time, $91 per credit hour part-time; nonresident $5076 full-time, $141 per credit hour part-time. Full-time tuition and fees vary according to course load and program. Part-time tuition and fees vary according to course load and program. *Required fees:* $375 full-time.

Financial Aid Of all full-time matriculated undergraduates who enrolled in 2003, 28 Federal Work-Study jobs (averaging $1200). 45 state and other part-time jobs (averaging $1000).

Applying *Options:* early admission, deferred entrance. *Application fee:* $20. *Required:* high school transcript.

Admissions Contact Mr. Joel O. Liles, Director of Admissions and Career Services, Marion Technical College, 1467 Mt. Vernon Avenue, Marion, OH 43302. *Phone:* 740-389-4636 Ext. 249. *E-mail:* enroll@mtc.tec.oh.us.

MERCY COLLEGE OF NORTHWEST OHIO
Toledo, Ohio

- **Independent** primarily 2-year, founded 1993, affiliated with Roman Catholic Church
- **Calendar** semesters
- **Degrees** associate and bachelor's
- **Urban** campus with easy access to Detroit
- **Endowment** $3.5 million
- **Coed, primarily women,** 688 undergraduate students, 53% full-time, 86% women, 14% men

Undergraduates 365 full-time, 323 part-time. Students come from 5 states and territories, 14% are from out of state, 8% African American, 1% Asian American or Pacific Islander, 3% Hispanic American, 0.4% Native American, 19% transferred in, 8% live on campus. *Retention:* 100% of 2002 full-time freshmen returned.

Mercy College of Northwest Ohio (continued)

Freshmen *Admission:* 101 applied, 85 admitted, 74 enrolled. *Average high school GPA:* 3.24. *Test scores:* ACT scores over 18: 87%; ACT scores over 24: 18%; ACT scores over 30: 1%.

Faculty *Total:* 78, 63% full-time, 14% with terminal degrees. *Student/faculty ratio:* 17:1.

Majors General studies; health/health care administration; health information/medical records technology; massage therapy; medical radiologic technology; nursing (registered nurse training).

Academic Programs *Special study options:* academic remediation for entering students, advanced placement credit, independent study, internships, part-time degree program, services for LD students, summer session for credit.

Library Mercy College of Northwest Ohio Library with 6,400 titles, 172 serial subscriptions, 351 audiovisual materials, an OPAC.

Computers on Campus 40 computers available on campus for general student use. A campuswide network can be accessed from student residence rooms and from off campus. Internet access, at least one staffed computer lab available.

Student Life *Housing Options:* coed. Campus housing is provided by a third party. *Activities and Organizations:* student-run newspaper, Campus Ministry, Student Senate, Mercy College Musical Ensemble, Student Nurses Association, Stress Busters. *Campus security:* 24-hour patrols, late-night transport/escort service, controlled dormitory access. *Student services:* personal/psychological counseling.

Standardized Tests *Required for some:* SAT or ACT (for admission). *Recommended:* SAT or ACT (for admission).

Costs (2005–06) *One-time required fee:* $15. *Tuition:* $8160 full-time, $282 per credit hour part-time. Full-time tuition and fees vary according to course load. Part-time tuition and fees vary according to course load. *Required fees:* $434 full-time, $5 per credit hour part-time, $434 per year part-time. *Room only:* Room and board charges vary according to housing facility. *Payment plans:* installment, deferred payment. *Waivers:* employees or children of employees.

Financial Aid Of all full-time matriculated undergraduates who enrolled in 2003, 18 Federal Work-Study jobs.

Applying *Application fee:* $25. *Required:* high school transcript. *Required for some:* minimum 2.3 GPA. *Application deadline:* rolling (freshmen), rolling (transfers). *Notification:* continuous (freshmen).

Admissions Contact Ms. Erin Jones, Secretary, Mercy College of Northwest Ohio, 2221 Madison Avenue, Toledo, OH 43624-1197. *Phone:* 419-251-1313 Ext. 11723. *Toll-free phone:* 888-80-Mercy. *Fax:* 419-251-1462. *E-mail:* admissions@mercycollege.edu.

MIAMI-JACOBS COLLEGE
Dayton, Ohio

Admissions Contact Mary Percell, Vice President of Information Services, Miami-Jacobs College, 110 North Patterson Street, PO Box 1433, Dayton, OH 45402. *Phone:* 937-461-5174 Ext. 118.

MIAMI UNIVERSITY HAMILTON
Hamilton, Ohio

- **State-supported** founded 1968, part of Miami University System
- **Calendar** semesters plus summer sessions
- **Degrees** certificates, associate, bachelor's, and master's (degrees awarded by Miami University main campus)
- **Suburban** 78-acre campus with easy access to Cincinnati
- **Coed,** 3,330 undergraduate students, 73% full-time, 57% women, 43% men

Undergraduates 2,432 full-time, 898 part-time. 6% African American, 2% Asian American or Pacific Islander, 1% Hispanic American, 0.2% Native American, 4% transferred in.

Freshmen *Admission:* 947 applied, 839 admitted, 639 enrolled.

Faculty *Total:* 218, 40% full-time. *Student/faculty ratio:* 21:1.

Majors Accounting; American studies; anthropology; architectural history and criticism; architecture; art; art teacher education; athletic training; audiology and speech-language pathology; biochemistry; botany/plant biology related; business administration and management; business administration, management and operations related; business/commerce; business/managerial economics; chemistry; chemistry teacher education; city/urban, community and regional planning; classics and languages, literatures and linguistics; clinical laboratory science/medical technology; communication/speech communication and rhetoric; computer and information sciences related; computer engineering; computer science; computer systems analysis; computer technology/computer systems technology; creative writing; dietetics; early childhood education; econometrics and quantitative economics; economics; education (multiple levels); electrical and electronic engineering technologies related; electromechanical technology; engineering/industrial management; engineering physics; engineering technology; English; English composition; English/language arts teacher education; environmental

science; environmental studies; ethnic, cultural minority, and gender studies related; exercise physiology; finance; French; French language teacher education; general studies; geography; geology/earth science; German; German language teacher education; gerontology; graphic design; health teacher education; history; human resources management and services related; interior design; international/global studies; journalism; Latin; Latin teacher education; linguistics; management information systems; marketing/marketing management; marketing related; mass communication/media; mathematics; mathematics and statistics related; mathematics teacher education; mechanical engineering/mechanical technology; microbiology; multi-/interdisciplinary studies related; music; music teacher education; office management; philosophy; physical education teaching and coaching; physics; physics teacher education; political science and government; psychology; public administration; purchasing, procurement/acquisitions and contracts management; real estate; Russian; science teacher education; social studies teacher education; social work related; sociology; Spanish; Spanish language teacher education; special education; speech-language pathology; statistics; technical and business writing; theatre/theatre arts management; work and family studies; zoology/animal biology.

Academic Programs *Special study options:* academic remediation for entering students, adult/continuing education programs, advanced placement credit, cooperative education, double majors, English as a second language, honors programs, internships, part-time degree program, services for LD students, student-designed majors, study abroad, summer session for credit. *ROTC:* Navy (c), Air Force (c).

Library Rentschler Library with 68,000 titles, 400 serial subscriptions, an OPAC, a Web page.

Computers on Campus 300 computers available on campus for general student use. A campuswide network can be accessed from off campus. Internet access, online (class) registration, at least one staffed computer lab available.

Student Life *Housing:* college housing not available. *Activities and Organizations:* drama/theater group, choral group, student government, Campus Activities Committee, Ski Club, Student Nursing Association, Minority Action Committee. *Campus security:* 24-hour emergency response devices and patrols, late-night transport/escort service. *Student services:* personal/psychological counseling.

Athletics *Intercollegiate sports:* baseball M(c), basketball M(c)/W(c), cheerleading W, golf M(c), softball W(c), tennis M(c)/W(c), volleyball W(c). *Intramural sports:* basketball M/W, bowling M/W, skiing (cross-country) M/W, soccer M/W, softball M/W, tennis M/W, volleyball M/W, weight lifting M/W.

Costs (2004–05) *Tuition:* state resident $3492 full-time, $146 per credit part-time; nonresident $14,071 full-time, $586 per credit part-time. *Required fees:* $384 full-time, $15 per credit part-time, $18 per term part-time. *Payment plan:* installment. *Waivers:* employees or children of employees.

Applying *Options:* electronic application. *Application fee:* $25. *Required:* high school transcript. *Application deadline:* rolling (freshmen). *Notification:* continuous (freshmen).

Admissions Contact Mr. Archie Nelson, Director of Admission and Financial Aid, Miami University Hamilton, 1601 University Boulevard, Hamilton, OH 45011-3399. *Phone:* 513-785-3111. *Fax:* 513-785-3148.

MIAMI UNIVERSITY-MIDDLETOWN CAMPUS
Middletown, Ohio

Admissions Contact Mrs. Mary Lou Flynn, Director of Enrollment Services, Miami University-Middletown Campus, 4200 East University Boulevard, Middletown, OH 45042. *Phone:* 513-727-3346. *Toll-free phone:* 800-622-2262. *Fax:* 513-727-3223. *E-mail:* flynnml@muohio.edu.

NATIONAL INSTITUTE OF TECHNOLOGY
Cuyahoga Falls, Ohio

Admissions Contact 2545 Bailey Road, Cuyahoga Falls, OH 44221.

NORTH CENTRAL STATE COLLEGE
Mansfield, Ohio

- **State-supported** 2-year, founded 1961, part of Ohio Board of Regents
- **Calendar** quarters
- **Degree** certificates and associate
- **Suburban** 600-acre campus with easy access to Cleveland and Columbus
- **Endowment** $624,998
- **Coed,** 3,333 undergraduate students, 29% full-time, 65% women, 35% men

Undergraduates 969 full-time, 2,364 part-time. Students come from 1 other state, 5% African American, 0.7% Asian American or Pacific Islander, 1% Hispanic American, 0.4% Native American.

Freshmen *Admission:* 1,056 applied, 1,056 admitted.

Faculty *Total:* 199, 35% full-time.

Majors Accounting; administrative assistant and secretarial science; business administration and management; computer systems networking and telecommunications; criminal justice/law enforcement administration; criminal justice/safety; drafting and design technology; electrical, electronic and communications engineering technology; finance; heating, air conditioning, ventilation and refrigeration maintenance technology; human services; industrial technology; information science/studies; kindergarten/preschool education; legal assistant/paralegal; machine tool technology; mechanical engineering/mechanical technology; nursing (registered nurse training); operations management; pharmacy technician; physical therapist assistant; quality control technology; radiologic technology/science; respiratory care therapy; therapeutic recreation; welding technology.

Academic Programs *Special study options:* academic remediation for entering students, adult/continuing education programs, advanced placement credit, distance learning, independent study, internships, part-time degree program, services for LD students, student-designed majors, summer session for credit.

Library Bromfield Library plus 1 other with 52,700 titles, 410 serial subscriptions, an OPAC.

Computers on Campus 144 computers available on campus for general student use. A campuswide network can be accessed. Internet access, at least one staffed computer lab available.

Student Life *Housing:* college housing not available. *Activities and Organizations:* student-run radio station, choral group, Student Programming Board, choral group. *Campus security:* 24-hour emergency response devices and patrols, late-night transport/escort service. *Student services:* personal/psychological counseling.

Athletics *Intramural sports:* basketball M/W, football M/W, golf M/W, softball M/W, table tennis M/W, tennis M/W, volleyball M/W.

Standardized Tests *Required:* ACT COMPASS (for placement). *Required for some:* ACT (for placement).

Costs (2005–06) *Tuition:* state resident $3431 full-time, $76 per credit hour part-time; nonresident $6863 full-time, $153 per credit hour part-time. Full-time tuition and fees vary according to course load. Part-time tuition and fees vary according to course load. *Required fees:* $245 full-time, $12 per credit hour part-time. *Payment plan:* deferred payment. *Waivers:* employees or children of employees.

Applying *Options:* early admission, deferred entrance. *Required for some:* high school transcript. *Application deadline:* rolling (freshmen), rolling (transfers). *Notification:* continuous (freshmen).

Admissions Contact Ms. Nikia L. Fletcher, Director of Admissions, North Central State College, PO Box 698, Mansfield, OH 44901-0698. *Phone:* 419-755-4813. *Toll-free phone:* 888-755-4899.

NORTHWEST STATE COMMUNITY COLLEGE
Archbold, Ohio

- **State-supported** 2-year, founded 1968, part of Ohio Board of Regents
- **Calendar** semesters
- **Degree** certificates and associate
- **Rural** 80-acre campus with easy access to Toledo
- **Endowment** $529,395
- **Coed,** 3,145 undergraduate students, 35% full-time, 58% women, 42% men

Undergraduates 1,088 full-time, 2,057 part-time. Students come from 6 states and territories, 2% are from out of state, 1% African American, 0.5% Asian American or Pacific Islander, 6% Hispanic American, 0.3% Native American, 0.1% international, 3% transferred in. *Retention:* 55% of 2002 full-time freshmen returned.

Freshmen *Admission:* 649 applied, 649 admitted, 471 enrolled. *Average high school GPA:* 2.83. *Test scores:* ACT scores over 18: 69%; ACT scores over 24: 16%; ACT scores over 30: 2%.

Faculty *Total:* 172, 26% full-time, 14% with terminal degrees. *Student/faculty ratio:* 18:1.

Majors Accounting; business administration and management; business/commerce; business, management, and marketing related; child development; computer programming; corrections; criminal justice/law enforcement administration; criminal justice/police science; criminal justice/safety; design and visual communications; education; electrical, electronic and communications engineering technology; engineering related; executive assistant/executive secretary; health professions related; human development and family studies related; legal administrative assistant/secretary; legal assistant/paralegal; machine tool technology; marketing/marketing management; mechanical engineering; mechanical engineering/mechanical technology; medical administrative assistant and medical secretary; nursing (registered nurse training); plastics engineering technology; precision metal working related; quality control technology; sheet metal technology; social work; tool and die technology; transportation management.

Academic Programs *Special study options:* academic remediation for entering students, adult/continuing education programs, advanced placement credit,

cooperative education, distance learning, double majors, external degree program, independent study, internships, off-campus study, part-time degree program, services for LD students, student-designed majors, summer session for credit.

Library Northwest State Community College Library with 15,321 titles, 1,680 serial subscriptions, 1,913 audiovisual materials, an OPAC, a Web page.

Computers on Campus 425 computers available on campus for general student use. A campuswide network can be accessed. Internet access, online (class) registration, at least one staffed computer lab available.

Student Life *Housing:* college housing not available. *Activities and Organizations:* Student Body Organization, Phi Theta Kappa, Campus Crusade for Christ. *Campus security:* security patrols. *Student services:* personal/psychological counseling.

Athletics *Intramural sports:* basketball M/W, bowling M/W, soccer M/W, table tennis M/W, volleyball M/W.

Costs (2005–06) *Tuition:* state resident $3540 full-time, $112 per credit part-time; nonresident $6900 full-time, $224 per credit part-time. Full-time tuition and fees vary according to course load. Part-time tuition and fees vary according to course load. *Required fees:* $180 full-time, $6 per credit part-time, $30 per term part-time. *Payment plan:* deferred payment. *Waivers:* senior citizens.

Financial Aid Of all full-time matriculated undergraduates who enrolled in 2003, 42 Federal Work-Study jobs (averaging $1222).

Applying *Options:* electronic application, early admission, deferred entrance. *Application fee:* $20. *Required:* high school transcript. *Application deadline:* rolling (freshmen), rolling (transfers). *Notification:* continuous (freshmen).

Admissions Contact Mr. Jeffrey Ferezan, Dean of Student Success and Advocacy Center, Northwest State Community College, 22600 State Route 34, Archbold, OH 43502-9542. *Phone:* 419-267-1213. *Fax:* 419-267-5604. *E-mail:* admissions@northweststate.edu.

OHIO BUSINESS COLLEGE
Lorain, Ohio

Admissions Contact Mr. Jim Unger, Admissions Director, Ohio Business College, 1907 North Ridge Road, Lorain, OH 44055. *Toll-free phone:* 888-514-3126.

OHIO BUSINESS COLLEGE
Sandusky, Ohio

- **Proprietary** 2-year, founded 1982
- **Calendar** quarters
- **Degree** diplomas and associate
- **Suburban** 1-acre campus
- **Coed**

Applying *Application fee:* $25.

Admissions Contact Ms. Cecilia Blevins, Director of Admissions, Ohio Business College, 4020 Milan Road, Sandusky, OH 44870-5894. *Toll-free phone:* 888-627-8345.

OHIO COLLEGE OF MASSOTHERAPY
Akron, Ohio

Admissions Contact Ms. Sherri Becker, Vice President, Ohio College of Massotherapy, 225 Heritage Woods Drive, Akron, OH 44321. *Phone:* 330-665-1084.

OHIO INSTITUTE OF PHOTOGRAPHY AND TECHNOLOGY
Dayton, Ohio

- **Proprietary** 2-year, founded 1971, part of Kaplan Higher Education
- **Calendar** quarters
- **Degree** diplomas and associate
- **Urban** 2-acre campus with easy access to Cincinnati and Columbus
- **Coed,** 581 undergraduate students, 100% full-time, 74% women, 26% men

Undergraduates 581 full-time. Students come from 20 states and territories, 19% are from out of state, 14% African American, 1% Hispanic American, 0.7% Native American.

Freshmen *Admission:* 270 applied, 153 admitted, 111 enrolled.

Faculty *Total:* 53, 38% full-time.

Majors Criminal justice/law enforcement administration; graphic design; medical/clinical assistant; photography.

Ohio Institute of Photography and Technology (continued)

Academic Programs *Special study options:* cooperative education, internships, part-time degree program, student-designed majors, summer session for credit.

Library Main Library with 640 titles, 35 serial subscriptions.

Computers on Campus 90 computers available on campus for general student use. Internet access, at least one staffed computer lab available.

Student Life *Housing:* college housing not available. *Campus security:* 24-hour emergency response devices.

Costs (2004–05) *Tuition:* $17,035 full-time. Full-time tuition and fees vary according to program.

Applying *Options:* common application, early admission, deferred entrance. *Required:* high school transcript, interview, entrance exam. *Application deadline:* rolling (freshmen), rolling (transfers). *Notification:* continuous (freshmen).

Admissions Contact Mr. Norman Dorn, Director of Admissions, Ohio Institute of Photography and Technology, 2029 Edgefield Road, Dayton, OH 45439-1917. *Phone:* 937-294-6155. *Toll-free phone:* 800-932-9698. *Fax:* 937-294-2259. *E-mail:* info@oipt.com.

THE OHIO STATE UNIVERSITY AGRICULTURAL TECHNICAL INSTITUTE
Wooster, Ohio

- **State-supported** 2-year, founded 1971, part of Ohio State University
- **Calendar** quarters
- **Degree** certificates, diplomas, and associate
- **Small-town** campus with easy access to Cleveland and Columbus
- **Endowment** $2.1 million
- **Coed,** 791 undergraduate students, 86% full-time, 38% women, 62% men

Undergraduates 682 full-time, 109 part-time. Students come from 13 states and territories, 2 other countries, 2% are from out of state, 0.6% African American, 0.8% Hispanic American, 0.5% Native American, 0.3% international, 7% transferred in, 22% live on campus. *Retention:* 65% of 2002 full-time freshmen returned.

Freshmen *Admission:* 507 applied, 492 admitted, 288 enrolled. *Test scores:* SAT verbal scores over 500: 22%; SAT math scores over 500: 22%; SAT verbal scores over 600: 11%.

Faculty *Total:* 70, 47% full-time, 33% with terminal degrees. *Student/faculty ratio:* 16:1.

Majors Agribusiness; agricultural business and management; agricultural business technology; agricultural communication/journalism; agricultural economics; agricultural mechanization; agricultural power machinery operation; agricultural teacher education; agronomy and crop science; animal/livestock husbandry and production; animal sciences; biology/biotechnology laboratory technician; building/construction site management; clinical/medical laboratory technology; construction engineering technology; construction management; crop production; dairy husbandry and production; dairy science; environmental science; equestrian studies; floriculture/floristry management; greenhouse management; heavy equipment maintenance technology; horse husbandry/equine science and management; horticultural science; hydraulics and fluid power technology; industrial technology; landscaping and groundskeeping; livestock management; medical laboratory technology; natural resources management; natural resources management and policy; plant nursery management; pre-veterinary studies; soil conservation; turf and turfgrass management.

Academic Programs *Special study options:* academic remediation for entering students, accelerated degree program, adult/continuing education programs, advanced placement credit, cooperative education, honors programs, internships, part-time degree program, services for LD students, student-designed majors, summer session for credit. *ROTC:* Army (c), Navy (c), Air Force (c).

Library Agricultural Technical Institute Library with 19,009 titles, 595 serial subscriptions, an OPAC.

Computers on Campus 85 computers available on campus for general student use.

Student Life *Housing:* on-campus residence required for freshman year. *Options:* coed. Campus housing is university owned. *Activities and Organizations:* Hoof-n-Hide Club, Horticulture Club, Campus Crusade for Christ, Phi Theta Kappa, Artist de Fleur Club. *Campus security:* 24-hour emergency response devices and patrols, controlled dormitory access. *Student services:* health clinic, personal/psychological counseling.

Athletics *Intramural sports:* basketball M/W, football M/W, racquetball M/W, softball M/W, volleyball M/W.

Standardized Tests *Required for some:* SAT or ACT (for admission).

Costs (2004–05) *Tuition:* state resident $5115 full-time; nonresident $15,702 full-time. Full-time tuition and fees vary according to course load. Part-time tuition and fees vary according to course load. *Required fees:* $27 full-time. *Room and board:* room only: $4419. Room and board charges vary according to board plan. *Payment plan:* installment. *Waivers:* employees or children of employees.

Applying *Options:* early admission. *Application fee:* $40. *Required:* high school transcript. *Application deadlines:* 7/1 (freshmen), 7/1 (transfers). *Notification:* continuous until 9/15 (freshmen).

Admissions Contact Ms. Jill Byers, Coordinator of Admissions, The Ohio State University Agricultural Technical Institute, 1328 Dover Road, Wooster, OH 44691. *Phone:* 330-287-1236. *Toll-free phone:* 800-647-8283 Ext. 1327. *Fax:* 330-262-7634. *E-mail:* ati@ohio-state.edu.

OHIO TECHNICAL COLLEGE
Cleveland, Ohio

Admissions Contact Mr. Marc Brenner, President, Ohio Technical College, 1374 East 51st Street, Cleveland, OH 44103. *Phone:* 216-881-1700. *Toll-free phone:* 800-322-7000.

OHIO VALLEY COLLEGE OF TECHNOLOGY
East Liverpool, Ohio

- **Proprietary** 2-year, founded 1886
- **Calendar** semesters
- **Degree** diplomas and associate
- **Small-town** campus with easy access to Pittsburgh
- **Coed, primarily women**

Faculty *Student/faculty ratio:* 18:1.

Standardized Tests *Required:* CPAt (for admission).

Applying *Required:* high school transcript, interview.

Admissions Contact Ms. Jessica M. Ewing, Program Information Coordinator, Ohio Valley College of Technology, PO Box 7000, East Liverpool, OH 43920. *Phone:* 330-385-1070. *Toll-free phone:* 877-777-8451. *E-mail:* info@ohiovalleytech.com.

OWENS COMMUNITY COLLEGE
Findlay, Ohio

- **State-supported** 2-year, founded 1983, administratively affiliated with Owens Community College-Toledo Campus
- **Calendar** semesters
- **Degree** certificates and associate
- **Small-town** 9-acre campus
- **Coed,** 2,163 undergraduate students, 44% full-time, 61% women, 39% men

Undergraduates 945 full-time, 1,218 part-time. Students come from 5 states and territories, 8 other countries, 4% African American, 1% Asian American or Pacific Islander, 5% Hispanic American, 0.5% Native American, 0.2% international.

Freshmen *Admission:* 286 enrolled. *Average high school GPA:* 2.6.

Faculty *Total:* 170, 17% full-time. *Student/faculty ratio:* 18:1.

Majors Accounting; accounting technology and bookkeeping; administrative assistant and secretarial science; business administration and management; business/commerce; commercial and advertising art; corrections; criminal justice/law enforcement administration; criminal justice/police science; early childhood education; electrical, electronic and communications engineering technology; electromechanical technology; fashion merchandising; general studies; marketing/marketing management; mechanical engineering/mechanical technology; medical administrative assistant and medical secretary; nursing (registered nurse training); operations management.

Academic Programs *Special study options:* academic remediation for entering students, adult/continuing education programs, advanced placement credit, cooperative education, distance learning, double majors, external degree program, honors programs, independent study, internships, part-time degree program, services for LD students, summer session for credit. *ROTC:* Army (c), Air Force (b).

Library an OPAC, a Web page.

Computers on Campus 105 computers available on campus for general student use. A campuswide network can be accessed from off campus. Internet access, online (class) registration, at least one staffed computer lab available.

Student Life *Housing:* college housing not available. *Campus security:* 24-hour emergency response devices and patrols, student patrols. *Student services:* health clinic, personal/psychological counseling.

Athletics Member NJCAA. *Intercollegiate sports:* baseball M, basketball M(s)/W(s), soccer M, softball W, volleyball W. *Intramural sports:* basketball M/W, bowling M/W, football M/W, golf M/W, softball M/W, table tennis M/W, tennis M/W, volleyball M/W, weight lifting M/W.

Standardized Tests *Required for some:* ACT (for placement). *Recommended:* ACT (for placement), ACT ASSET.

Costs (2005–06) *Tuition:* state resident $2280 full-time, $95 per credit part-time; nonresident $4560 full-time, $190 per credit part-time. Full-time tuition and fees vary according to course load. *Required fees:* $400 full-time, $15 per credit part-time, $10 per term part-time. *Payment plans:* installment, deferred payment. *Waivers:* senior citizens and employees or children of employees.

Financial Aid Of all full-time matriculated undergraduates who enrolled in 2003, 75 Federal Work-Study jobs (averaging $4500).

Applying *Options:* common application, early admission, deferred entrance. *Required:* high school transcript. *Required for some:* minimum 2.0 GPA. *Recommended:* essay or personal statement, letters of recommendation, interview. *Application deadline:* rolling (freshmen), rolling (transfers). *Notification:* continuous (freshmen).

Admissions Contact Mr. Verne Walker, Admissions Director, Owens Community College, 300 Davis Street, Findlay, OH 45840. *Phone:* 567-429-3509. *Toll-free phone:* 800-FINDLAY. *Fax:* 567-423-0246.

OWENS COMMUNITY COLLEGE
Toledo, Ohio

- **State-supported** 2-year, founded 1966
- **Calendar** semesters
- **Degree** certificates and associate
- **Small-town** 100-acre campus
- **Coed,** 17,917 undergraduate students, 36% full-time, 47% women, 53% men

Undergraduates 6,528 full-time, 11,389 part-time. Students come from 15 states and territories, 49 other countries, 14% African American, 1% Asian American or Pacific Islander, 4% Hispanic American, 0.6% Native American, 0.1% international.

Freshmen *Admission:* 1,803 enrolled. *Average high school GPA:* 2.62.

Faculty *Total:* 1,164, 16% full-time. *Student/faculty ratio:* 23:1.

Majors Accounting technology and bookkeeping; agricultural business and management; automotive engineering technology; business/commerce; CAD/CADD drafting/design technology; commercial and advertising art; criminal justice/law enforcement administration; early childhood education; electrical, electronic and communications engineering technology; fashion merchandising; fire protection and safety technology; food services technology; general studies; health information/medical records technology; management information systems; manufacturing technology; marketing/marketing management; mechanical design technology; mechanical engineering/mechanical technology; nursing (registered nurse training); occupational therapist assistant; physical therapist assistant; survey technology; telecommunications.

Academic Programs *Special study options:* academic remediation for entering students, adult/continuing education programs, advanced placement credit, cooperative education, distance learning, double majors, English as a second language, external degree program, freshman honors college, honors programs, independent study, internships, part-time degree program, services for LD students, summer session for credit. *ROTC:* Army (c), Air Force (b).

Library Owens Community College Library with 78,344 titles, 6,230 serial subscriptions, 9,021 audiovisual materials, an OPAC, a Web page.

Computers on Campus 1000 computers available on campus for general student use. A campuswide network can be accessed from off campus. Internet access, online (class) registration, at least one staffed computer lab available.

Student Life *Housing:* college housing not available. *Activities and Organizations:* drama/theater group, student-run newspaper, choral group, intramurals, Alpha Beta Gamma, Drama Club, Student Association for Young Children, Phi Theta Kappa. *Campus security:* 24-hour emergency response devices and patrols, student patrols. *Student services:* health clinic, personal/psychological counseling.

Athletics Member NJCAA. *Intercollegiate sports:* baseball M, basketball M(s)/W(s), soccer M, softball W, volleyball W. *Intramural sports:* basketball M/W, bowling M/W, football M/W, golf M/W, softball M/W, table tennis M/W, tennis M/W, volleyball M/W, weight lifting M/W.

Standardized Tests *Required for some:* SAT or ACT (for placement). *Recommended:* SAT or ACT (for placement), ACT ASSET.

Costs (2005–06) *Tuition:* state resident $2280 full-time, $95 per credit part-time; nonresident $4560 full-time, $190 per credit part-time. Full-time tuition and fees vary according to course load. *Required fees:* $400 full-time, $15 per credit part-time, $10 per term part-time. *Payment plans:* installment, deferred payment. *Waivers:* senior citizens and employees or children of employees.

Financial Aid Of all full-time matriculated undergraduates who enrolled in 2003, 200 Federal Work-Study jobs (averaging $4500).

Applying *Options:* common application, early admission. *Required:* high school transcript. *Required for some:* minimum 2.0 GPA. *Recommended:* essay or personal statement, letters of recommendation, interview. *Application deadline:* rolling (freshmen), rolling (transfers). *Notification:* continuous (freshmen).

Admissions Contact Mr. Jim Welling, Admissions Coordinator, Owens Community College, PO Box 1000, Toledo, OH 43699. *Phone:* 567-429-3509. *Toll-free phone:* 800-GO-OWENS. *Fax:* 567-661-7607.

PROFESSIONAL SKILLS INSTITUTE
Toledo, Ohio

Admissions Contact Ms. Hope Finch, Director of Marketing, Professional Skills Institute, 20 Arco Drive, Toledo, OH 43607. *Phone:* 419-531-9610. *Fax:* 419-531-4732.

REMINGTON COLLEGE-CLEVELAND CAMPUS
Cleveland, Ohio

- **Proprietary** 2-year
- **Calendar** continuous
- **Degree** diplomas and associate
- **Urban** 2-acre campus
- **Coed,** 676 undergraduate students, 100% full-time, 85% women, 15% men

Undergraduates 676 full-time.

Freshmen *Admission:* 369 applied, 281 admitted, 155 enrolled.

Faculty *Total:* 65, 62% full-time, 2% with terminal degrees. *Student/faculty ratio:* 15:1.

Academic Programs *Special study options:* cooperative education.

Library Main Library plus 2 others.

Computers on Campus A campuswide network can be accessed. At least one staffed computer lab available.

Student Life *Housing:* college housing not available.

Costs (2005–06) *Tuition:* $15,745 full-time. Full-time tuition and fees vary according to program.

Applying *Application fee:* $50. *Required:* essay or personal statement, high school transcript, interview.

Admissions Contact Mr. William Cassidy, Director of Recruitment, Remington College-Cleveland Campus, 14445 Broadway Avenue, Cleveland 44125-1957. *Phone:* 216-475-7520. *Fax:* 216-475-6055.

REMINGTON COLLEGE-CLEVELAND WEST CAMPUS
North Olmstead, Ohio

- **Proprietary** 2-year, founded 2003
- **Calendar** quarters
- **Degree** diplomas and associate
- **Coed,** 407 undergraduate students, 100% full-time, 83% women, 17% men

Undergraduates 407 full-time. 16% African American, 0.5% Asian American or Pacific Islander, 8% Hispanic American, 0.7% Native American.

Costs (2004–05) *Tuition:* $11,280 full-time.

Admissions Contact Mr. Gary Azotea, Vice President, Remington College-Cleveland West Campus, 26350 Brookpark Road, North Olmstead, OH 44070. *Phone:* 440-777-2560.

RETS TECH CENTER
Centerville, Ohio

- **Proprietary** 2-year, founded 1953
- **Calendar** semesters
- **Degree** diplomas and associate
- **Suburban** 4-acre campus with easy access to Dayton
- **Coed,** 556 undergraduate students, 100% full-time, 58% women, 42% men

Undergraduates 556 full-time. Students come from 2 states and territories, 1% are from out of state, 22% African American, 1% Hispanic American, 0.9% transferred in.

Freshmen *Admission:* 206 enrolled.

Faculty *Total:* 83, 33% full-time, 7% with terminal degrees.

Majors Computer engineering technology; computer programming; computer science; electrical, electronic and communications engineering technology; legal assistant/paralegal; medical/clinical assistant.

Academic Programs *Special study options:* advanced placement credit, internships, summer session for credit.

Library RETS Library with 2,200 titles, 27 serial subscriptions, 66 audiovisual materials.

Computers on Campus 220 computers available on campus for general student use. A campuswide network can be accessed. Internet access, at least one staffed computer lab available.

Student Life *Housing:* college housing not available. *Campus security:* 24-hour emergency response devices. *Student services:* personal/psychological counseling.

RETS Tech Center (continued)

Standardized Tests *Required:* (for placement).

Costs (2004–05) *Tuition:* $7535 full-time. *Required fees:* $340 full-time. *Payment plan:* installment.

Applying *Options:* early admission, deferred entrance. *Required:* high school transcript, interview. *Application deadline:* rolling (freshmen), rolling (transfers).

Admissions Contact Mr. Rich Elkin, Director of Admissions, RETS Tech Center, 555 East Alex Bell Road, Centerville, OH 45459-2712. *Phone:* 937-433-3410. *Toll-free phone:* 800-837-7387. *Fax:* 937-435-6516. *E-mail:* rets@erinet.com.

ROSEDALE BIBLE COLLEGE

Irwin, Ohio

Admissions Contact Mr. John Showalter, Director of Enrollment Services, Rosedale Bible College, 2270 Rosedale Road, Irwin, OH 43029-9501. *Phone:* 740-857-1311.

SCHOOL OF ADVERTISING ART

Kettering, Ohio

- **Proprietary** 2-year, founded 1983
- **Calendar** trimesters
- **Degree** diplomas and associate
- **Suburban** 5-acre campus with easy access to Dayton, Ohio; Cincinnati, Ohio
- **Coed**, 121 undergraduate students, 100% full-time, 45% women, 55% men
- 80% of applicants were admitted

Undergraduates 121 full-time. Students come from 4 states and territories, 2% are from out of state, 4% African American, 0.8% Asian American or Pacific Islander, 2% Hispanic American, 0.8% Native American. *Retention:* 75% of 2002 full-time freshmen returned.

Freshmen *Admission:* 190 applied, 152 admitted, 66 enrolled. *Average high school GPA:* 2.75.

Faculty *Total:* 16, 50% full-time. *Student/faculty ratio:* 12:1.

Majors Commercial and advertising art.

Student Life *Housing:* college housing not available. *Student services:* personal/psychological counseling.

Costs (2005–06) *Tuition:* $17,775 full-time. *Required fees:* $450 full-time.

Applying *Application fee:* $90. *Required:* interview, portfolio. *Required for some:* essay or personal statement, high school transcript, minimum 2.0 GPA, 1 letter of recommendation. *Application deadlines:* 8/15 (freshmen), 8/15 (transfers). *Notification:* continuous until 8/15 (freshmen).

Admissions Contact Mrs. Jayne Fahncke, Admissions, School of Advertising Art, 1725 East David Road, Kettering, OH 45440. *Phone:* 937-294-0592 Ext. 102. *Toll-free phone:* 877-300-9866. *Fax:* 937-294-5869. *E-mail:* info@saacollege.com.

SINCLAIR COMMUNITY COLLEGE

Dayton, Ohio

- **State and locally supported** 2-year, founded 1887, part of Ohio Board of Regents
- **Calendar** quarters
- **Degree** certificates and associate
- **Urban** 50-acre campus with easy access to Cincinnati
- **Endowment** $25.0 million
- **Coed**, 19,563 undergraduate students, 39% full-time, 57% women, 43% men

Undergraduates 7,550 full-time, 12,013 part-time. Students come from 31 states and territories, 4% are from out of state, 16% African American, 1% Asian American or Pacific Islander, 1% Hispanic American, 0.4% Native American, 0.7% international, 6% transferred in. *Retention:* 56% of 2002 full-time freshmen returned.

Freshmen *Admission:* 6,271 applied, 6,271 admitted, 2,235 enrolled.

Faculty *Total:* 1,117, 42% full-time, 61% with terminal degrees. *Student/faculty ratio:* 23:1.

Majors Accounting; administrative assistant and secretarial science; African studies; applied art; architectural engineering technology; art; artificial intelligence and robotics; automobile/automotive mechanics technology; aviation/airway management; biotechnology; business administration and management; child development; civil engineering technology; commercial and advertising art; computer and information sciences; computer and information sciences related; computer engineering related; computer graphics; computer hardware engineering; computer/information technology services administration related; computer programming related; computer programming (specific applications); computer programming (vendor/product certification); computer software engineering; computer systems networking and telecommunications; consumer merchandising/retailing management; corrections; criminal justice/law enforcement administration; criminal justice/police science; culinary arts; dance; data entry/microcomputer applications; data entry/microcomputer applications related; dental hygiene; dietetics; drafting and design technology; dramatic/theatre arts; education; electrical, electronic and communications engineering technology; electromechanical technology; emergency medical technology (EMT paramedic); engineering; finance; fine/studio arts; fire science; foods, nutrition, and wellness; gerontology; graphic and printing equipment operation/production; health information/medical records administration; hotel/motel administration; human services; industrial radiologic technology; industrial technology; information science/studies; information technology; interior design; kindergarten/preschool education; labor and industrial relations; legal administrative assistant/secretary; legal assistant/paralegal; liberal arts and sciences/liberal studies; logistics and materials management; machine tool technology; marketing/marketing management; mass communication/media; mechanical engineering/mechanical technology; medical administrative assistant and medical secretary; medical/clinical assistant; mental health/rehabilitation; music; nursing (registered nurse training); occupational therapy; physical education teaching and coaching; physical therapy; plastics engineering technology; public administration; quality control technology; radiologic technology/science; real estate; respiratory care therapy; sign language interpretation and translation; special products marketing; surgical technology; survey technology; system administration; tourism and travel services management; transportation technology; web/multimedia management and webmaster; word processing.

Academic Programs *Special study options:* academic remediation for entering students, adult/continuing education programs, cooperative education, distance learning, English as a second language, external degree program, honors programs, independent study, internships, off-campus study, part-time degree program, services for LD students, student-designed majors, summer session for credit. *ROTC:* Army (c), Air Force (c).

Library Learning Resources Center with 147,613 titles, 576 serial subscriptions, 9,293 audiovisual materials, an OPAC, a Web page.

Computers on Campus 1800 computers available on campus for general student use. A campuswide network can be accessed from off campus that provide access to Portal. Internet access, at least one staffed computer lab available.

Student Life *Housing:* college housing not available. *Activities and Organizations:* drama/theater group, student-run newspaper, choral group, African-American Men of the Future, Ohio Fellows, Phi Theta Kappa, student government, student newspaper. *Campus security:* 24-hour emergency response devices and patrols, student patrols, late-night transport/escort service. *Student services:* personal/psychological counseling.

Athletics Member NJCAA. *Intercollegiate sports:* baseball M(s), basketball M(s)/W(s), golf M(s), tennis M(s)/W(s), volleyball W(s).

Standardized Tests *Required for some:* ACCUPLACER COMPASS.

Costs (2004–05) *Tuition:* area resident $1803 full-time, $40 per credit part-time; state resident $2943 full-time, $65 per credit part-time; nonresident $5310 full-time, $118 per credit part-time. Full-time tuition and fees vary according to course load. Part-time tuition and fees vary according to course load.

Financial Aid Of all full-time matriculated undergraduates who enrolled in 2003, 50 Federal Work-Study jobs (averaging $800). *Financial aid deadline:* 8/15.

Applying *Options:* electronic application, early admission, deferred entrance. *Application fee:* $10. *Required for some:* high school transcript, interview. *Application deadline:* rolling (freshmen), rolling (transfers). *Notification:* continuous (freshmen).

Admissions Contact Ms. Sara P. Smith, Director and Systems Manager, Outreach Services, Sinclair Community College, 444 West Third Street, Dayton, OH 45402-1460. *Phone:* 937-512-3060. *Toll-free phone:* 800-315-3000. *Fax:* 937-512-2393.

SOUTHEASTERN BUSINESS COLLEGE

Chillicothe, Ohio

Admissions Contact Ms. Elizabeth Scott, Admissions Representative, Southeastern Business College, 1855 Western Avenue, Chillicothe, OH 45601-1038. *Phone:* 740-774-6300.

SOUTHEASTERN BUSINESS COLLEGE

Jackson, Ohio

Admissions Contact Mr. Todd A. Riegel, Director of Education, Southeastern Business College, 504 McCarty Lane, Jackson, OH 45640. *Phone:* 740-286-1554.

SOUTHEASTERN BUSINESS COLLEGE
Lancaster, Ohio

Admissions Contact Mr. Ray Predmore, Director, Southeastern Business College, 1522 Sheridan Drive, Lancaster, OH 43130-1303. *Phone:* 740-687-6126.

SOUTHERN STATE COMMUNITY COLLEGE
Hillsboro, Ohio

- **State-supported** 2-year, founded 1975
- **Calendar** quarters
- **Degree** certificates and associate
- **Rural** 60-acre campus
- **Endowment** $443,111
- **Coed**, 2,356 undergraduate students, 53% full-time, 72% women, 28% men

Undergraduates 1,260 full-time, 1,096 part-time. 1% African American, 0.3% Asian American or Pacific Islander, 0.4% Hispanic American, 0.4% Native American.
Freshmen *Admission:* 1,005 applied, 1,005 admitted.
Faculty *Total:* 132, 36% full-time, 5% with terminal degrees. *Student/faculty ratio:* 20:1.
Majors Accounting technology and bookkeeping; agricultural production; business/commerce; computer programming (specific applications); corrections; drafting and design technology; emergency medical technology (EMT paramedic); executive assistant/executive secretary; human services; kindergarten/preschool education; liberal arts and sciences/liberal studies; medical/clinical assistant; nursing (registered nurse training); real estate.
Academic Programs *Special study options:* academic remediation for entering students, advanced placement credit, cooperative education, distance learning, double majors, independent study, internships, off-campus study, part-time degree program, services for LD students, student-designed majors, summer session for credit.
Library Learning Resources Center plus 3 others with 79,000 titles, 1,107 serial subscriptions, 7,428 audiovisual materials, an OPAC, a Web page.
Computers on Campus 300 computers available on campus for general student use. A campuswide network can be accessed from off campus. Internet access, online (class) registration, at least one staffed computer lab available.
Student Life *Housing:* college housing not available. *Activities and Organizations:* drama/theater group, choral group, Student Leadership, Student Nurses Association, Drama Club, Association of Medical Assistants, Phi Theta Kappa, national fraternities. *Student services:* personal/psychological counseling.
Athletics Member NJCAA. *Intercollegiate sports:* baseball M(c), basketball M(s)/W(s), soccer M(s), softball W(s), volleyball W(s).
Standardized Tests *Required for some:* ACT (for placement). *Recommended:* ACT (for placement).
Costs (2004–05) *Tuition:* state resident $3120 full-time, $80 per credit hour part-time; nonresident $6009 full-time, $154 per credit hour part-time. Full-time tuition and fees vary according to course load. Part-time tuition and fees vary according to course load. *Payment plan:* deferred payment. *Waivers:* senior citizens and employees or children of employees.
Applying *Options:* common application, early admission, deferred entrance. *Recommended:* high school transcript. *Application deadline:* rolling (freshmen), rolling (transfers). *Notification:* continuous (freshmen).
Admissions Contact Ms. Wendy Johnson, Director of Admissions, Southern State Community College, 100 Hobart Drive, Hillsboro, OH 45133. *Phone:* 937-393-3431 Ext. 2720. *Toll-free phone:* 800-628-7722. *Fax:* 937-393-6682. *E-mail:* info@sscc.edu.

SOUTHWESTERN COLLEGE OF BUSINESS
Cincinnati, Ohio

Admissions Contact Mr. Greg Petree, Director of Admissions, Southwestern College of Business, 149 Northland Boulevard, Cincinnati, OH 45246-1122. *Phone:* 513-874-0432.

SOUTHWESTERN COLLEGE OF BUSINESS
Cincinnati, Ohio

Admissions Contact Ms. Betty Streber, Director of Admissions, Southwestern College of Business, 632 Vine Street, Suite 200, Cincinnati, OH 45202-4304. *Phone:* 513-421-3212.

SOUTHWESTERN COLLEGE OF BUSINESS
Dayton, Ohio

Admissions Contact Ms. Kathie Day, Director of Admissions, Southwestern College of Business, 111 West First Street, Dayton, OH 45402-3003. *Phone:* 937-224-0061 Ext. 17.

SOUTHWESTERN COLLEGE OF BUSINESS
Franklin, Ohio

Admissions Contact Ms. Susan Knodel, Director of Admissions, Southwestern College of Business, 201 East Second Street, Franklin, OH 45005. *Phone:* 937-746-6633. *Fax:* 937-746-6757.

STARK STATE COLLEGE OF TECHNOLOGY
Canton, Ohio

- **State and locally supported** 2-year, founded 1970, part of Ohio Board of Regents
- **Calendar** semesters
- **Degree** certificates and associate
- **Suburban** 34-acre campus with easy access to Cleveland
- **Coed**

Faculty *Student/faculty ratio:* 19:1.
Student Life *Campus security:* 24-hour emergency response devices, late-night transport/escort service.
Standardized Tests *Recommended:* SAT or ACT (for placement).
Costs (2004–05) *Tuition:* state resident $3528 full-time, $114 per credit hour part-time; nonresident $4608 full-time, $144 per credit hour part-time. *Required fees:* $288 full-time, $16 per credit hour part-time.
Financial Aid Of all full-time matriculated undergraduates who enrolled in 2003, 194 Federal Work-Study jobs (averaging $2383).
Applying *Options:* electronic application, early admission, deferred entrance. *Application fee:* $35. *Required:* high school transcript.
Admissions Contact Mr. Wallace Hoffer, Dean of Student Services, Stark State College of Technology, 6200 Frank Road, N.W., Canton, OH 44720. *Phone:* 330-966-5450. *Toll-free phone:* 800-797-8275. *Fax:* 330-497-6313.

STAUTZENBERGER COLLEGE
Toledo, Ohio

- **Proprietary** 2-year
- **Calendar** quarters
- **Degree** certificates, diplomas, and associate
- **Urban** campus
- **Coed**
- 95% of applicants were admitted

Faculty *Student/faculty ratio:* 28:1.
Costs (2004–05) *Tuition:* $7200 full-time. *Required fees:* $100 full-time.
Financial Aid Of all full-time matriculated undergraduates who enrolled in 2003, 2 Federal Work-Study jobs (averaging $5000).
Admissions Contact Ms. Karen Fitzgerald, Director of Admissions and Marketing, Stautzenberger College, 5355 Southwyck Boulevard, Toledo, OH 43614. *Phone:* 419-866-0261. *Toll-free phone:* 800-552-5099.

TECHNOLOGY EDUCATION COLLEGE
Columbus, Ohio

Admissions Contact Michael Mongomery, Executive Director, Technology Education College, 288 South Hamilton Road, Columbus, OH 43213-2087. *Phone:* 614-456-4600. *Toll-free phone:* 800-838-3233.

TERRA STATE COMMUNITY COLLEGE
Fremont, Ohio

- **State-supported** 2-year, founded 1968, part of Ohio Board of Regents
- **Calendar** quarters
- **Degree** certificates, diplomas, and associate
- **Small-town** 100-acre campus with easy access to Toledo

Terra State Community College (continued)
- **Endowment** $907,000
- **Coed**

Faculty *Student/faculty ratio:* 21:1.

Student Life *Campus security:* 24-hour emergency response devices, late-night transport/escort service.

Athletics Member NJCAA.

Standardized Tests *Required:* ACT COMPASS (for placement). *Recommended:* SAT or ACT (for placement).

Costs (2004–05) *Tuition:* state resident $3025 full-time, $63 per credit hour part-time; nonresident $7095 full-time, $148 per credit hour part-time. Full-time tuition and fees vary according to course load. Part-time tuition and fees vary according to course load. *Required fees:* $305 full-time, $6 per credit hour part-time. *Payment plans:* installment, deferred payment.

Financial Aid Of all full-time matriculated undergraduates who enrolled in 2003, 45 Federal Work-Study jobs (averaging $2000).

Applying *Options:* electronic application, early admission, deferred entrance. *Application fee:* $15. *Required:* high school transcript.

Admissions Contact Mr. Dale Stearns, Associate Dean of Student Services, Terra State Community College, 2830 Napoleon Road, Fremont, OH 43420. *Phone:* 419-334-8400 Ext. 347. *Toll-free phone:* 800-334-3886. *Fax:* 419-334-9035. *E-mail:* thensley@terra.edu.

TRUMBULL BUSINESS COLLEGE
Warren, Ohio

- **Proprietary** 2-year, founded 1972
- **Calendar** quarters
- **Degree** diplomas and associate
- **Small-town** 6-acre campus
- **Coed, primarily women**

Faculty *Student/faculty ratio:* 28:1.

Costs (2004–05) *Tuition:* $6480 full-time, $180 per credit hour part-time. Full-time tuition and fees vary according to program. Part-time tuition and fees vary according to program. No tuition increase for student's term of enrollment. *Required fees:* $350 full-time.

Financial Aid Of all full-time matriculated undergraduates who enrolled in 2003, 2 Federal Work-Study jobs. *Financial aid deadline:* 9/30.

Applying *Application fee:* $70. *Required:* high school transcript, interview.

Admissions Contact Admissions Office, Trumbull Business College, 3200 Ridge Road, Warren, OH 44484. *Phone:* 330-369-3200 Ext. 0. *E-mail:* admissions@tbc-trumbullbusiness.com.

THE UNIVERSITY OF AKRON-WAYNE COLLEGE
Orrville, Ohio

- **State-supported** 2-year, founded 1972, part of The University of Akron
- **Calendar** semesters
- **Degree** certificates and associate
- **Rural** 157-acre campus
- **Coed,** 1,798 undergraduate students, 57% full-time, 62% women, 38% men

Undergraduates 1,025 full-time, 773 part-time. Students come from 1 other state, 3% African American, 0.6% Asian American or Pacific Islander, 0.3% Hispanic American, 0.4% Native American, 5% transferred in.

Freshmen *Admission:* 398 applied, 350 admitted, 294 enrolled. *Average high school GPA:* 2.93. *Test scores:* ACT scores over 18: 77%; ACT scores over 24: 16%; ACT scores over 30: 1%.

Faculty *Total:* 142, 22% full-time, 19% with terminal degrees. *Student/faculty ratio:* 18:1.

Majors Accounting; accounting technology and bookkeeping; administrative assistant and secretarial science; business administration and management; business automation/technology/data entry; computer science; computer systems networking and telecommunications; data processing and data processing technology; engineering; environmental health; executive assistant/executive secretary; general studies; interdisciplinary studies; legal administrative assistant/secretary; liberal arts and sciences/liberal studies; management information systems; medical administrative assistant and medical secretary; medical office management; occupational safety and health technology; office management; social work.

Academic Programs *Special study options:* academic remediation for entering students, adult/continuing education programs, advanced placement credit, cooperative education, distance learning, double majors, English as a second language, honors programs, independent study, internships, off-campus study, part-time degree program, services for LD students, summer session for credit. *ROTC:* Army (c), Air Force (c).

Library Wayne College Library with 23,450 titles, 219 serial subscriptions, 822 audiovisual materials, an OPAC.

Computers on Campus 240 computers available on campus for general student use. A campuswide network can be accessed from off campus. Internet access, online (class) registration, at least one staffed computer lab available. Computer purchase or lease plan available.

Student Life *Housing:* college housing not available. *Campus security:* late-night transport/escort service. *Student services:* personal/psychological counseling.

Athletics *Intercollegiate sports:* basketball M/W, cheerleading W, golf M, volleyball W. *Intramural sports:* basketball M/W, golf M, volleyball M/W.

Standardized Tests *Required for some:* SAT or ACT (for admission), ACT COMPASS. *Recommended:* SAT or ACT (for admission), ACT COMPASS.

Costs (2004–05) *Tuition:* state resident $5759 full-time, $192 per credit hour part-time; nonresident $12,455 full-time, $415 per credit hour part-time. Full-time tuition and fees vary according to course load and program. Part-time tuition and fees vary according to course load and program. *Required fees:* $557 full-time, $13 per credit hour part-time, $12 per term part-time. *Payment plan:* installment. *Waivers:* minority students, adult students, senior citizens, and employees or children of employees.

Financial Aid Of all full-time matriculated undergraduates who enrolled in 2003, 8 Federal Work-Study jobs (averaging $2200).

Applying *Options:* common application, electronic application, early admission, deferred entrance. *Application fee:* $30. *Required for some:* high school transcript. *Application deadlines:* 8/30 (freshmen), 8/30 (transfers). *Notification:* continuous until 8/30 (freshmen).

Admissions Contact Ms. Alicia Broadus, Admissions Student Services Office, The University of Akron-Wayne College, 1901 Smucker Road, Orrville, OH 44667. *Phone:* 800-221-8308 Ext. 8901. *Toll-free phone:* 800-221-8308 Ext. 8900. *E-mail:* wayneadmissions@uakron.edu.

UNIVERSITY OF CINCINNATI CLERMONT COLLEGE
Batavia, Ohio

Admissions Contact Ms. Tanya Bohart, Admissions Assistant, University of Cincinnati Clermont College, 4200 Clermont College Drive, Batavia, OH 45103-1785. *Phone:* 513-732-5202. *E-mail:* tanya.bohart@uc.edu.

UNIVERSITY OF CINCINNATI RAYMOND WALTERS COLLEGE
Cincinnati, Ohio

- **State-supported** 2-year, founded 1967, part of University of Cincinnati System
- **Calendar** quarters
- **Degrees** certificates, associate, and postbachelor's certificates
- **Suburban** 120-acre campus
- **Endowment** $43,625
- **Coed,** 4,421 undergraduate students, 49% full-time, 68% women, 32% men

Undergraduates 2,177 full-time, 2,244 part-time. Students come from 19 states and territories, 3% are from out of state, 15% African American, 2% Asian American or Pacific Islander, 2% Hispanic American, 0.3% Native American, 6% transferred in.

Freshmen *Admission:* 1,488 applied, 1,240 admitted, 746 enrolled. *Average high school GPA:* 2.62. *Test scores:* SAT verbal scores over 500: 36%; SAT math scores over 500: 37%; ACT scores over 18: 66%; SAT verbal scores over 600: 10%; SAT math scores over 600: 8%; ACT scores over 24: 12%; SAT verbal scores over 700: 2%; SAT math scores over 700: 1%.

Faculty *Total:* 121, 97% full-time, 44% with terminal degrees. *Student/faculty ratio:* 25:1.

Majors Accounting; administrative assistant and secretarial science; automobile/automotive mechanics technology; biochemical technology; biology/biological sciences; business administration and management; chemistry; clinical laboratory science/medical technology; commercial and advertising art; computer engineering technology; computer programming; computer science; dental hygiene; dietetics; economics; education; emergency medical technology (EMT paramedic); environmental studies; industrial radiologic technology; industrial technology; information science/studies; legal administrative assistant/secretary; liberal arts and sciences/liberal studies; library science; management information systems; marketing/marketing management; medical administrative assistant and medical secretary; medical laboratory technology; nuclear medical technology; nursing (registered nurse training); pharmacy; physical therapy; pre-engineering; real estate; social work; urban studies/affairs; veterinary technology.

Academic Programs *Special study options:* academic remediation for entering students, accelerated degree program, adult/continuing education programs, advanced placement credit, cooperative education, distance learning, double majors, English as a second language, honors programs, internships, off-campus study, part-time degree program, services for LD students, student-designed majors, study abroad, summer session for credit. *ROTC:* Army (c), Air Force (c).

Library Raymond Walters College Library with 48,226 titles, 636 serial subscriptions, 2,220 audiovisual materials, an OPAC, a Web page.

Computers on Campus 250 computers available on campus for general student use. A campuswide network can be accessed from off campus. Internet access, online (class) registration, at least one staffed computer lab available.

Student Life *Housing:* college housing not available. *Activities and Organizations:* drama/theater group, student-run newspaper, choral group, marching band, student government, African-American Cultural Association, Phi Theta Kappa, College Secretaries International, American Dental Hygiene Students Association, national fraternities, national sororities. *Campus security:* 24-hour emergency response devices and patrols, student patrols, late-night transport/escort service. *Student services:* health clinic, personal/psychological counseling, women's center.

Athletics *Intercollegiate sports:* baseball M(s), basketball M(s)/W(s), crew W(s), cross-country running M(s)/W(s), football M(s), golf M(s), soccer M(s)/W(s), swimming and diving M(s)/W(s), tennis M(s)/W(s), track and field M(s)/W(s), volleyball M(c)/W(s). *Intramural sports:* basketball M/W, cheerleading M/W, cross-country running M/W, equestrian sports M/W, fencing M/W, football M/W, golf M, ice hockey M, sailing M/W, soccer M/W, softball W, swimming and diving M/W, tennis M/W, track and field M/W, volleyball M/W, wrestling M.

Costs (2004–05) *Tuition:* state resident $4659 full-time, $130 per quarter hour part-time; nonresident $12,075 full-time, $336 per quarter hour part-time. *Required fees:* $214 full-time. *Payment plan:* installment. *Waivers:* senior citizens and employees or children of employees.

Financial Aid Of all full-time matriculated undergraduates who enrolled in 2003, 285 Federal Work-Study jobs (averaging $2903).

Applying *Options:* electronic application, deferred entrance. *Application fee:* $35. *Required:* high school transcript. *Application deadline:* rolling (freshmen), rolling (transfers). *Notification:* continuous (freshmen).

Admissions Contact Ms. Angelica Kennedy, Admission Counselor, University of Cincinnati Raymond Walters College, 9555 Plainfield Road, Cincinnati, OH 45236-1007. *Phone:* 513-745-5700. *Fax:* 513-745-5768. *E-mail:* colrel@ucrwcu.rwc.uc.edu.

UNIVERSITY OF NORTHWESTERN OHIO
Lima, Ohio

- **Independent** primarily 2-year, founded 1920
- **Calendar** quarters
- **Degrees** diplomas, associate, and bachelor's
- **Small-town** 35-acre campus with easy access to Dayton and Toledo
- **Coed,** 2,971 undergraduate students, 90% full-time, 21% women, 79% men

The University of Northwestern Ohio (UNOH) is a private, nonprofit university established in 1920. Located in Lima, Ohio, UNOH has a population of 3,200 students and offers associate degrees and diplomas in automotive, high performance, diesel, agriculture, alternative fuels, and HVAC/R. Associate degrees and diplomas are awarded in the College of Business for accounting, business, computers, and medical, as well as various other majors.

Undergraduates 2,688 full-time, 283 part-time. Students come from 34 states and territories, 15% are from out of state, 0.6% African American, 0.1% Hispanic American, 2% transferred in, 45% live on campus.

Freshmen *Admission:* 3,758 applied, 3,699 admitted, 2,152 enrolled. *Average high school GPA:* 2.5.

Faculty *Total:* 130, 61% full-time, 4% with terminal degrees. *Student/faculty ratio:* 23:1.

Majors Accounting; administrative assistant and secretarial science; agricultural business and management; automobile/automotive mechanics technology; business administration and management; computer programming; diesel mechanics technology; health/health care administration; heating, air conditioning, ventilation and refrigeration maintenance technology; legal administrative assistant/secretary; legal assistant/paralegal; marketing/marketing management; medical administrative assistant and medical secretary; medical/clinical assistant; pharmacy technician; tourism and travel services management.

Academic Programs *Special study options:* academic remediation for entering students, accelerated degree program, adult/continuing education programs, advanced placement credit, cooperative education, distance learning, double majors, part-time degree program, summer session for credit.

Library University of Northwestern Ohio Library with 4,553 titles, 95 serial subscriptions, an OPAC, a Web page.

Computers on Campus 149 computers available on campus for general student use. A campuswide network can be accessed from off campus. Internet access, at least one staffed computer lab available.

Student Life *Housing Options:* men-only, women-only, disabled students. Campus housing is university owned and leased by the school. Freshman campus housing is guaranteed. *Activities and Organizations:* student-run newspaper, Students in Free Enterprise. *Campus security:* 24-hour emergency response devices and patrols, late-night transport/escort service. *Student services:* personal/psychological counseling.

Athletics *Intramural sports:* basketball M, bowling M/W, volleyball M/W.

Costs (2004–05) *Comprehensive fee:* $15,695 includes full-time tuition ($10,935), mandatory fees ($150), and room and board ($4610). Part-time tuition: $180 per credit hour. No tuition increase for student's term of enrollment. *Room and board:* college room only: $2550. *Payment plan:* installment. *Waivers:* employees or children of employees.

Financial Aid Of all full-time matriculated undergraduates who enrolled in 2003, 40 Federal Work-Study jobs (averaging $2000).

Applying *Options:* electronic application, early admission, deferred entrance. *Application fee:* $50. *Required:* high school transcript. *Application deadline:* rolling (freshmen), rolling (transfers).

Admissions Contact Mr. Dan Klopp, Vice President for Enrollment Management, University of Northwestern Ohio, 1441 North Cable Road, Lima, OH 45805-1498. *Phone:* 419-227-3141. *Fax:* 419-229-6926. *E-mail:* info@nc.edu.

VATTEROTT COLLEGE
Broadview Heights, Ohio

Admissions Contact Mr. Jack Chalk, Director of Admissions, Vatterott College, 5025 East Royalton Road, Broadview Heights, OH 44147. *Phone:* 440-526-1660. *Toll-free phone:* 800-864-5644.

VIRGINIA MARTI COLLEGE OF ART AND DESIGN
Lakewood, Ohio

Admissions Contact Quinn Marti, Head of Admissions, Virginia Marti College of Art and Design, 11724 Detroit Avenue, PO Box 580, Lakewood, OH 44107-3002. *Phone:* 216-221-8584. *E-mail:* dmarti@vmcad.edu.

WASHINGTON STATE COMMUNITY COLLEGE
Marietta, Ohio

Admissions Contact Ms. Rebecca Peroni, Director of Admissions, Washington State Community College, 710 Colegate Drive, Marietta, OH 45750-9225. *Phone:* 740-374-8716. *Fax:* 740-376-0257.

WRIGHT STATE UNIVERSITY, LAKE CAMPUS
Celina, Ohio

Admissions Contact Mrs. B.J. Hobler, Student Services Officer, Wright State University, Lake Campus, 7600 State Route 703, Celina, OH 45822-2921. *Phone:* 419-586-0324. *Toll-free phone:* 800-237-1477.

ZANE STATE COLLEGE
Zanesville, Ohio

Admissions Contact Mr. Paul Young, Director of Admissions, Zane State College, 1555 Newark Road, Zanesville, OH 43701-2626. *Phone:* 740-454-2501 Ext. 1225. *Toll-free phone:* 800-686-TECH Ext. 1225.

OKLAHOMA

CARL ALBERT STATE COLLEGE
Poteau, Oklahoma

Admissions Contact Ms. Dee Ann Dickerson, Director of Admissions, Carl Albert State College, 1507 South McKenna, Poteau, OK 74953-5208. *Phone:* 918-647-1301. *Fax:* 918-647-1306. *E-mail:* ddickerson@carlalbert.edu.

COMMUNITY CARE COLLEGE
Tulsa, Oklahoma

- **Proprietary** 2-year, founded 1995, part of Dental Directions, Inc.
- **Calendar** semesters

Community Care College (continued)
■ **Degree** certificates and associate
■ **Coed**

Applying *Required:* high school transcript.
Admissions Contact C. J. Dewil, Admissions Director, Community Care College, 4242 South Sheridan, Tulsa, OK 74145. *Fax:* 918-610-0029. *E-mail:* tknox@communitycarecollege.com.

CONNORS STATE COLLEGE
Warner, Oklahoma

■ **State-supported** 2-year, founded 1908, part of Oklahoma State Regents for Higher Education
■ **Calendar** semesters
■ **Degree** certificates, diplomas, and associate
■ **Rural** 1658-acre campus
■ **Endowment** $19,200
■ **Coed**

Faculty *Student/faculty ratio:* 21:1.
Student Life *Campus security:* late-night transport/escort service, trained security personnel.
Athletics Member NJCAA.
Standardized Tests *Required for some:* SAT or ACT (for placement), ACT COMPASS.
Costs (2004–05) *Tuition:* state resident $1651 full-time, $44 per credit hour part-time; nonresident $3979 full-time, $134 per credit hour part-time. Full-time tuition and fees vary according to course level. Part-time tuition and fees vary according to course level. *Required fees:* $600 full-time, $20 per credit hour part-time. *Room and board:* $5636; room only: $3436. Room and board charges vary according to board plan.
Financial Aid Of all full-time matriculated undergraduates who enrolled in 2003, 100 Federal Work-Study jobs (averaging $800).
Applying *Options:* early admission, deferred entrance. *Required for some:* high school transcript.
Admissions Contact Mr. John A. Turnbull, Director of Admissions/Registrar, Connors State College, Route 1 Box 1000 College Road, Warner, OK 74469. *Phone:* 918-463-6233 Ext. 6233. *Toll-free phone:* 918-463-2931 Ext. 6241.

EASTERN OKLAHOMA STATE COLLEGE
Wilburton, Oklahoma

■ **State-supported** 2-year, founded 1908, part of Oklahoma State Regents for Higher Education
■ **Calendar** semesters
■ **Degree** certificates and associate
■ **Rural** 4000-acre campus
■ **Coed**

Athletics Member NJCAA.
Standardized Tests *Required:* ACT (for placement).
Applying *Options:* common application, early admission, deferred entrance. *Application fee:* $25. *Required:* high school transcript.
Admissions Contact Ms. Leah Miller, Director of Admissions, Eastern Oklahoma State College, 1301 West Main, Wilburton, OK 74578-4999. *Phone:* 918-465-2361 Ext. 240. *Fax:* 918-465-2431. *E-mail:* edavis@eosc.cc.ok.us.

HERITAGE COLLEGE OF HAIR DESIGN
Oklahoma City, Oklahoma

Admissions Contact 7100 I-35 Services Road, Suite 7118, Oklahoma City, OK 73149.

MURRAY STATE COLLEGE
Tishomingo, Oklahoma

Admissions Contact Mrs. Ann Beck, Registrar and Director of Admissions, Murray State College, 1Murray Campus, Tishomingo, OK 73460. *Phone:* 580-371-2371 Ext. 171. *Fax:* 580-371-9844.

NORTHEASTERN OKLAHOMA AGRICULTURAL AND MECHANICAL COLLEGE
Miami, Oklahoma

■ **State-supported** 2-year, founded 1919, part of Oklahoma State Regents for Higher Education
■ **Calendar** semesters
■ **Degree** certificates and associate
■ **Small-town** 340-acre campus
■ **Coed**

Faculty *Student/faculty ratio:* 23:1.
Student Life *Campus security:* 24-hour patrols.
Athletics Member NJCAA.
Standardized Tests *Required:* SAT or ACT (for placement).
Costs (2004–05) *Tuition:* state resident $1838 full-time, $61 per credit part-time; nonresident $4478 full-time, $149 per credit part-time. Full-time tuition and fees vary according to location. Part-time tuition and fees vary according to location. *Room and board:* Room and board charges vary according to board plan.
Financial Aid Of all full-time matriculated undergraduates who enrolled in 2003, 100 Federal Work-Study jobs (averaging $2500). 100 state and other part-time jobs (averaging $1000).
Applying *Options:* electronic application. *Required:* high school transcript.
Admissions Contact Amy Ishmael, Dean of Enrollment Management, Northeastern Oklahoma Agricultural and Mechanical College, PO Box 3842, 200 I Street NE, Miami, OK 74354. *Phone:* 918-540-6212. *Toll-free phone:* 800-464-6636. *Fax:* 918-540-6946. *E-mail:* neoadmission@neoam.edu.

NORTHERN OKLAHOMA COLLEGE
Tonkawa, Oklahoma

Admissions Contact Ms. Sheri Snyder, Director of College Relations, Northern Oklahoma College, PO Box 310, Tonkawa, OK 74653. *Phone:* 580-628-6290. *Toll-free phone:* 800-429-5715. *Fax:* 580-628-6371.

OKLAHOMA CITY COMMUNITY COLLEGE
Oklahoma City, Oklahoma

■ **State-supported** 2-year, founded 1969, part of Oklahoma State Regents for Higher Education
■ **Calendar** semesters
■ **Degree** certificates and associate
■ **Urban** 143-acre campus
■ **Endowment** $91,544
■ **Coed**

Faculty *Student/faculty ratio:* 23:1.
Student Life *Campus security:* 24-hour emergency response devices and patrols, late-night transport/escort service.
Standardized Tests *Required for some:* ACT (for placement), ACT COMPASS.
Financial Aid Of all full-time matriculated undergraduates who enrolled in 2003, 305 Federal Work-Study jobs (averaging $2667).
Applying *Options:* early admission, deferred entrance. *Application fee:* $25. *Required:* high school transcript.
Admissions Contact Ms. Gloria Cardenas-Barton, Dean of Admissions/Registrar, Oklahoma City Community College, 7777 South May Avenue, Oklahoma City, OK 73159. *Phone:* 405-682-7515. *E-mail:* sedwards@okccc.edu.

OKLAHOMA STATE UNIVERSITY, OKLAHOMA CITY
Oklahoma City, Oklahoma

■ **State-supported** 2-year, founded 1961, part of Oklahoma State University
■ **Calendar** semesters
■ **Degree** certificates and associate
■ **Urban** 80-acre campus
■ **Coed**

Faculty *Student/faculty ratio:* 20:1.
Student Life *Campus security:* 24-hour patrols, late-night transport/escort service.
Standardized Tests *Required for some:* SAT or ACT (for placement), ACT COMPASS.
Costs (2004–05) *Tuition:* state resident $2304 full-time, $77 per credit hour part-time; nonresident $5754 full-time, $192 per credit hour part-time. *Required fees:* $35 full-time.
Financial Aid Of all full-time matriculated undergraduates who enrolled in 2003, 75 Federal Work-Study jobs (averaging $2500).
Applying *Options:* early admission.
Admissions Contact Ms. Jeanne Kubier, Director of Admissions and Registrar, Oklahoma State University, Oklahoma City, 900 North Portland Avenue, Oklahoma City, OK 73107. *Phone:* 405-945-3287. *Fax:* 405-945-3277.

OKLAHOMA STATE UNIVERSITY, OKMULGEE
Okmulgee, Oklahoma

Admissions Contact Kelly Hildebrant, Director of Admissions, Oklahoma State University, Okmulgee, 1801 East Fourth Street, Okmulgee, OK 74447-3901. *Phone:* 918-293-5298. *Toll-free phone:* 800-722-4471. *Fax:* 918-293-4650. *E-mail:* francie@okway.okstate.edu.

PLATT COLLEGE
Oklahoma City, Oklahoma

Admissions Contact Ms. Jane Nowlin, Director, Platt College, 309 South Ann Arbor Avenue, Oklahoma City, OK 73128. *Phone:* 405-946-7799.

PLATT COLLEGE
Tulsa, Oklahoma

Admissions Contact Mrs. Susan Rone, Director, Platt College, 3801 South Sheridan Road, Tulsa, OK 74145-111. *Phone:* 918-663-9000.

REDLANDS COMMUNITY COLLEGE
El Reno, Oklahoma

Admissions Contact Vice President for Student Services, Redlands Community College, El Reno, OK 73036. *Phone:* 405-262-2552 Ext. 1282. *E-mail:* frenchr@redlands.cc.net.

ROSE STATE COLLEGE
Midwest City, Oklahoma

Admissions Contact Ms. Evelyn K. Hutchings, Registrar and Director of Admissions, Rose State College, 6420 Southeast 15th Street, Midwest City, OK 73110-2799. *Phone:* 405-733-7673. *Fax:* 405-736-0309. *E-mail:* ekhutchings@ms.rose.cc.ok.us.

SEMINOLE STATE COLLEGE
Seminole, Oklahoma

- **State-supported** 2-year, founded 1931, part of Oklahoma State Regents for Higher Education
- **Calendar** semesters
- **Degree** diplomas and associate
- **Small-town** 40-acre campus with easy access to Oklahoma City
- **Coed,** 2,482 undergraduate students, 88% full-time, 69% women, 31% men

Undergraduates 2,178 full-time, 304 part-time. Students come from 13 states and territories, 5 other countries, 2% are from out of state, 6% African American, 0.3% Asian American or Pacific Islander, 2% Hispanic American, 21% Native American, 0.8% international, 44% transferred in, 8% live on campus.
Freshmen *Admission:* 2,178 applied, 2,178 admitted, 1,246 enrolled. *Test scores:* ACT scores over 18: 51%; ACT scores over 24: 19%.
Faculty *Total:* 95, 51% full-time, 6% with terminal degrees. *Student/faculty ratio:* 19:1.
Majors Accounting; administrative assistant and secretarial science; art; behavioral sciences; biology/biological sciences; business administration and management; clinical/medical laboratory technology; computer science; criminal justice/police science; elementary education; English; liberal arts and sciences/liberal studies; mathematics; nursing (registered nurse training); physical education teaching and coaching; physical sciences; pre-engineering; social sciences.
Academic Programs *Special study options:* academic remediation for entering students, accelerated degree program, adult/continuing education programs, advanced placement credit, cooperative education, distance learning, honors programs, independent study, off-campus study, part-time degree program, services for LD students, summer session for credit.
Library Boren Library with 27,507 titles, 200 serial subscriptions, an OPAC.
Computers on Campus 100 computers available on campus for general student use. A campuswide network can be accessed from off campus. Internet access, at least one staffed computer lab available.
Student Life *Housing Options:* coed. Campus housing is university owned. *Activities and Organizations:* student-run newspaper, choral group, Student Government Association, Native American Student Association, Psi Beta Honor Society, Student Nurses Association, Phi Theta Kappa. *Campus security:* 24-hour patrols. *Student services:* personal/psychological counseling.
Athletics Member NJCAA. *Intercollegiate sports:* baseball M(s), basketball M(s)/W(s), cheerleading M(s)/W(s), golf M(s)/W(s), softball W(s), tennis M(s)/W(s), volleyball W(s).

Standardized Tests *Required:* SAT I, ACT, or ACT COMPASS (for placement).
Costs (2004–05) *One-time required fee:* $15. *Tuition:* state resident $1726 full-time, $44 per credit hour part-time; nonresident $4066 full-time, $142 per credit hour part-time. *Required fees:* $839 full-time, $28 per credit hour part-time. *Room and board:* $4316. Room and board charges vary according to location. *Payment plans:* installment, deferred payment. *Waivers:* employees or children of employees.
Applying *Options:* common application, early admission, deferred entrance. *Application fee:* $15. *Required:* high school transcript. *Application deadline:* rolling (freshmen), rolling (transfers). *Notification:* continuous (freshmen).
Admissions Contact Mr. Chris Lindley, Director of Enrollment Management, Seminole State College, PO Box 351, 2701 Boren Boulevard, Seminole, OK 74818-0351. *Phone:* 405-382-9272. *Fax:* 405-382-9524. *E-mail:* lindley_c@ssc.cc.ok.us.

SOUTHWESTERN OKLAHOMA STATE UNIVERSITY AT SAYRE
Sayre, Oklahoma

- **State and locally supported** 2-year, founded 1938, part of Southwestern Oklahoma State University
- **Calendar** semesters
- **Degree** diplomas and associate
- **Rural** 6-acre campus
- **Coed,** 585 undergraduate students, 58% full-time, 75% women, 25% men

Undergraduates 337 full-time, 248 part-time. Students come from 2 states and territories, 4% are from out of state, 1% African American, 0.3% Asian American or Pacific Islander, 5% Hispanic American, 11% Native American.
Freshmen *Admission:* 124 applied, 124 admitted, 124 enrolled. *Test scores:* ACT scores over 18: 75%; ACT scores over 24: 9%.
Faculty *Total:* 19, 63% full-time. *Student/faculty ratio:* 18:1.
Majors Business administration and management; clinical/medical laboratory technology; computer science; corrections; criminal justice/safety; general studies; medical radiologic technology; nursing (registered nurse training); occupational therapist assistant; physical therapist assistant.
Academic Programs *Special study options:* academic remediation for entering students, adult/continuing education programs, advanced placement credit, cooperative education, distance learning, independent study, part-time degree program, services for LD students, summer session for credit.
Library Oscar McMahan Library with 9,975 titles, 45 serial subscriptions, an OPAC, a Web page.
Computers on Campus 100 computers available on campus for general student use. A campuswide network can be accessed. Internet access, online (class) registration, at least one staffed computer lab available.
Student Life *Housing:* college housing not available.
Standardized Tests *Required for some:* ACT (for admission).
Costs (2004–05) *Tuition:* state resident $2240 full-time, $70 per credit hour part-time; nonresident $6720 full-time, $210 per credit hour part-time. Full-time tuition and fees vary according to course level, course load, and program. Part-time tuition and fees vary according to course level, course load, and program. *Required fees:* $960 full-time, $30 per credit hour part-time. *Payment plan:* installment. *Waivers:* employees or children of employees.
Applying *Options:* common application, early admission, deferred entrance. *Application fee:* $15. *Required:* high school transcript. *Application deadline:* rolling (freshmen), rolling (transfers).
Admissions Contact Ms. Kim Seymour, Registrar, Southwestern Oklahoma State University at Sayre, 409 East Mississippi Street, Sayre, OK 73662-1236. *Phone:* 580-928-5533 Ext. 101. *Fax:* 580-928-1140.

SPARTAN COLLEGE OF AERONAUTICS AND TECHNOLOGY
Tulsa, Oklahoma

Admissions Contact Mr. Mark Fowler, Vice President of Student Records and Finance, Spartan College of Aeronautics and Technology, 8820 East Pine Street, PO Box 582833, Tulsa, OK 74158-2833. *Phone:* 918-836-6886.

TULSA COMMUNITY COLLEGE
Tulsa, Oklahoma

Admissions Contact Ms. Leanne Brewer, Director of Admissions and Records, Tulsa Community College, 6111 East Skelly Drive, Tulsa, OK 74135. *Phone:* 918-595-7811. *E-mail:* lbrewer@tulsacc.edu.

TULSA WELDING SCHOOL
Tulsa, Oklahoma

- **Proprietary** 2-year, founded 1949, administratively affiliated with Tulsa Welding School, Jacksonville Branch
- **Calendar** continuous (phased start every 3 weeks)
- **Degree** diplomas and associate
- **Urban** 5-acre campus
- **Coed, primarily men,** 362 undergraduate students, 100% full-time, 4% women, 96% men

Undergraduates 362 full-time. Students come from 21 states and territories, 41% are from out of state, 13% African American, 0.6% Asian American or Pacific Islander, 3% Hispanic American, 9% Native American.
Faculty *Total:* 17, 94% full-time. *Student/faculty ratio:* 16:1.
Majors Welding technology.
Library Technical Resource Center with 389 titles, 2 serial subscriptions, a Web page.
Computers on Campus 3 computers available on campus for general student use. A campuswide network can be accessed. Internet access available.
Student Life *Housing:* college housing not available. *Campus security:* 24-hour emergency response devices.
Costs (2005–06) *Tuition:* $23,620 per degree program part-time.
Admissions Contact Mr. Mike Thurber, Director of Admissions, Tulsa Welding School, 2545 East 11th Street, Tulsa, OK 74104. *Phone:* 800-331-2934 Ext. 240. *Toll-free phone:* 800-WELD-PRO. *E-mail:* tws@ionet.net.

VATTEROTT COLLEGE
Oklahoma City, Oklahoma

- **Proprietary** 2-year
- **Calendar** semesters
- **Degrees** diplomas, associate, and first professional
- **Urban** campus
- **Coed,** 249 undergraduate students, 100% full-time, 49% women, 51% men

Undergraduates 249 full-time. 36% African American, 2% Asian American or Pacific Islander, 5% Hispanic American, 7% Native American.
Freshmen *Admission:* 145 applied, 90 admitted.
Faculty *Total:* 21, 71% full-time, 14% with terminal degrees. *Student/faculty ratio:* 12:1.
Majors Computer programming; electrical and electronic engineering technologies related; heating, air conditioning and refrigeration technology; information technology; medical office assistant.
Costs (2004–05) *Tuition:* $20,000 full-time. *Required fees:* $900 full-time.
Applying *Required:* essay or personal statement, high school transcript, interview.
Admissions Contact Mark Hybers, Director of Admissions, Vatterott College, 4629 Northwest 23rd Street, Oklahoma City, OK 73127. *Phone:* 405-945-0088. *Toll-free phone:* 888-948-0088.

VATTEROTT COLLEGE
Tulsa, Oklahoma

- **Proprietary** 2-year
- **Calendar** semesters
- **Degree** diplomas and associate
- **Urban** 3-acre campus
- **Coed, primarily women**
- 68% of applicants were admitted

Faculty *Student/faculty ratio:* 15:1.
Costs (2004–05) *Tuition:* $7729 full-time. *Required fees:* $450 full-time.
Admissions Contact Mr. Tim Maloukis, Director of Admissions, Vatterott College, 555 South Memorial Drive, Tulsa, OK 74112. *Phone:* 918-836-6656. *Toll-free phone:* 888-857-4016.

WESTERN OKLAHOMA STATE COLLEGE
Altus, Oklahoma

- **State-supported** 2-year, founded 1926, part of Oklahoma State Regents for Higher Education
- **Calendar** semesters
- **Degree** certificates and associate
- **Rural** 142-acre campus
- **Endowment** $2.5 million
- **Coed,** 1,919 undergraduate students

Undergraduates Students come from 30 states and territories, 1 other country, 10% African American, 3% Asian American or Pacific Islander, 11% Hispanic American, 3% Native American. *Retention:* 50% of 2002 full-time freshmen returned.
Freshmen *Admission:* 494 applied, 494 admitted.
Faculty *Total:* 90, 40% full-time, 3% with terminal degrees. *Student/faculty ratio:* 20:1.
Majors Agricultural business and management; airline pilot and flight crew; art teacher education; aviation/airway management; avionics maintenance technology; behavioral sciences; biology/biological sciences; business administration and management; child development; computer and information sciences; computer and information sciences related; computer programming related; computer programming (specific applications); computer programming (vendor/product certification); computer science; computer software and media applications related; computer systems networking and telecommunications; construction engineering technology; corrections; criminal justice/police science; data entry/microcomputer applications; data entry/microcomputer applications related; data processing and data processing technology; drafting and design technology; education; elementary education; emergency medical technology (EMT paramedic); English; forestry; history; humanities; information science/studies; information technology; liberal arts and sciences/liberal studies; management information systems; mathematics; medical radiologic technology; music teacher education; nursing (registered nurse training); physical education teaching and coaching; physical sciences; political science and government; pre-engineering; psychology; sociology; Spanish; speech and rhetoric; veterinary sciences; welding technology; wildlife and wildlands science and management; word processing.
Academic Programs *Special study options:* academic remediation for entering students, adult/continuing education programs, advanced placement credit, honors programs, off-campus study, part-time degree program, services for LD students, student-designed majors, summer session for credit.
Library Learning Resources Center with 33,000 titles, 1,000 serial subscriptions, an OPAC, a Web page.
Computers on Campus 50 computers available on campus for general student use. A campuswide network can be accessed from student residence rooms and from off campus. At least one staffed computer lab available.
Student Life *Housing Options:* coed. Campus housing is university owned. *Activities and Organizations:* drama/theater group, choral group, Baptist Student Union, Phi Theta Kappa, Student Senate, Behavioral Science Club, Aggie Club, national fraternities. *Campus security:* 24-hour emergency response devices. *Student services:* personal/psychological counseling.
Athletics Member NJCAA. *Intercollegiate sports:* baseball M(s), basketball M(s)/W(s), softball W(s). *Intramural sports:* basketball M/W, football M, golf M/W, tennis M/W, volleyball M/W.
Standardized Tests *Required for some:* ACT (for admission).
Costs (2005–06) *Tuition:* state resident $2043 full-time, $68 per semester hour part-time; nonresident $4952 full-time, $165 per semester hour part-time. *Room and board:* $4400.
Financial Aid Of all full-time matriculated undergraduates who enrolled in 2003, 85 Federal Work-Study jobs (averaging $1978).
Applying *Options:* electronic application, early admission. *Application fee:* $15. *Required:* high school transcript. *Application deadline:* rolling (freshmen), rolling (transfers). *Notification:* continuous (freshmen).
Admissions Contact Mr. Larry W. Paxton, Director of Academic Services, Western Oklahoma State College, 2801 North Main Street, Altus, OK 73521-1397. *Phone:* 580-477-7720. *Fax:* 580-477-7723. *E-mail:* larry.paston@wosc.edu.

OREGON

BLUE MOUNTAIN COMMUNITY COLLEGE
Pendleton, Oregon

- **State and locally supported** 2-year, founded 1962
- **Calendar** quarters
- **Degree** certificates and associate
- **Rural** 170-acre campus
- **Endowment** $1.7 million
- **Coed,** 1,878 undergraduate students, 46% full-time, 61% women, 39% men

Undergraduates 872 full-time, 1,006 part-time. Students come from 9 states and territories, 6 other countries, 2% are from out of state, 0.5% African American, 0.5% Asian American or Pacific Islander, 6% Hispanic American, 4% Native American, 0.6% international.
Freshmen *Admission:* 468 enrolled.
Faculty *Total:* 224, 34% full-time, 5% with terminal degrees. *Student/faculty ratio:* 25:1.

Majors Accounting; administrative assistant and secretarial science; agricultural business and management; animal sciences; automobile/automotive mechanics technology; business administration and management; civil drafting and CAD/CADD; civil engineering technology; dental assisting; diesel mechanics technology; electrical, electronic and communications engineering technology; health and physical education; health information/medical records technology; industrial technology; information science/studies; liberal arts and sciences/liberal studies; marketing/marketing management; mathematics; medical administrative assistant and medical secretary; nursing (licensed practical/vocational nurse training); nursing (registered nurse training); social work.

Academic Programs *Special study options:* academic remediation for entering students, adult/continuing education programs, advanced placement credit, cooperative education, distance learning, English as a second language, part-time degree program, services for LD students, summer session for credit.

Library Blue Mountain Community College Library with 39,026 titles, 271 serial subscriptions, 1,879 audiovisual materials, an OPAC, a Web page.

Computers on Campus 180 computers available on campus for general student use. A campuswide network can be accessed from off campus. Internet access, online (class) registration, at least one staffed computer lab available.

Student Life *Housing:* college housing not available. *Activities and Organizations:* drama/theater group, choral group, Multicultural Club, Campus Crusade for Christ. *Student services:* personal/psychological counseling.

Athletics Member NJCAA. *Intercollegiate sports:* baseball M(s), basketball M(s)/W(s), softball W(s), volleyball W(s). *Intramural sports:* basketball M.

Standardized Tests *Required:* ACT ASSET and ACT COMPASS (for placement).

Costs (2004–05) *Tuition:* state resident $2624 full-time, $58 per credit hour part-time; nonresident $5247 full-time, $117 per credit hour part-time. Full-time tuition and fees vary according to course load. Part-time tuition and fees vary according to course load. *Required fees:* $107 full-time, $2 per credit hour part-time, $13 per term part-time. *Payment plans:* installment, deferred payment. *Waivers:* employees or children of employees.

Financial Aid Of all full-time matriculated undergraduates who enrolled in 2003, 60 Federal Work-Study jobs (averaging $1800). 100 state and other part-time jobs (averaging $1200).

Applying *Options:* electronic application. *Required:* high school transcript. *Application deadline:* rolling (freshmen), rolling (transfers). *Notification:* continuous (freshmen).

Admissions Contact Ms. Valerie Fouquette, Director, Admissions, Blue Mountain Community College, PO Box 100, Pendleton, OR 97801. *Phone:* 541-278-5774. *Fax:* 541-278-5871. *E-mail:* onlineinquiry@bluecc.edu.

CENTRAL OREGON COMMUNITY COLLEGE
Bend, Oregon

- **District-supported** 2-year, founded 1949, part of Oregon Community College Association
- **Calendar** quarters
- **Degree** certificates and associate
- **Small-town** 193-acre campus
- **Endowment** $5.5 million
- **Coed,** 4,048 undergraduate students, 38% full-time, 58% women, 42% men

Located in Bend, Oregon, Central Oregon Community College (COCC) offers more than 50 certificate and degree options, affordable tuition, outstanding faculty members, small classes, and access to more than 20 bachelor's degree programs through Oregon State University's Cascades campus. COCC also features on-campus housing, intramural sports, and exceptional outdoor recreation opportunities.

Undergraduates 1,536 full-time, 2,512 part-time. Students come from 7 states and territories, 4% are from out of state, 0.2% African American, 1% Asian American or Pacific Islander, 4% Hispanic American, 3% Native American, 3% live on campus.

Freshmen *Admission:* 1,410 applied, 740 enrolled.

Faculty *Total:* 312, 28% full-time, 15% with terminal degrees. *Student/faculty ratio:* 24:1.

Majors Accounting; administrative assistant and secretarial science; art; automobile/automotive mechanics technology; biological and physical sciences; business administration and management; cartography; computer and information sciences related; computer science; criminal justice/law enforcement administration; culinary arts; dental assisting; early childhood education; education; emergency medical technology (EMT paramedic); fire science; fish/game management; forestry; forestry technology; health information/medical records technology; hospitality administration; hospitality and recreation marketing; hotel/motel administration; humanities; industrial technology; kinesiology and exercise science; liberal arts and sciences/liberal studies; marketing/marketing management; mathematics; medical/clinical assistant; nursing (licensed practical/vocational nurse training); nursing (registered nurse training); physical sciences;

pre-engineering; social sciences; sport and fitness administration; tourism promotion; welding technology.

Academic Programs *Special study options:* academic remediation for entering students, cooperative education, distance learning, double majors, English as a second language, independent study, internships, part-time degree program, student-designed majors, study abroad.

Library COCC Library plus 1 other with 76,421 titles, 329 serial subscriptions, 3,570 audiovisual materials, an OPAC, a Web page.

Computers on Campus 335 computers available on campus for general student use. A campuswide network can be accessed from student residence rooms and from off campus that provide access to e-mail. Internet access, online (class) registration, at least one staffed computer lab available.

Student Life *Housing Options:* coed. Campus housing is provided by a third party. *Activities and Organizations:* student-run newspaper, choral group, student government, club sports, Phi Theta Kappa, DEC, Science Learning Center. *Campus security:* 24-hour emergency response devices and patrols, late-night transport/escort service. *Student services:* health clinic, personal/psychological counseling.

Athletics *Intramural sports:* badminton M/W, baseball M/W, basketball M/W, cross-country running M/W, football M, soccer M/W, softball M/W, table tennis M/W, tennis M/W, track and field M/W, volleyball M/W, water polo M/W, weight lifting M/W.

Standardized Tests *Required:* (for placement).

Costs (2005–06) *Tuition:* area resident $2745 full-time; state resident $3735 full-time; nonresident $7740 full-time. Part-time tuition and fees vary according to course load. *Required fees:* $114 full-time. *Room and board:* $6060. *Waivers:* employees or children of employees.

Financial Aid Of all full-time matriculated undergraduates who enrolled in 2003, 400 Federal Work-Study jobs (averaging $1900).

Applying *Options:* electronic application. *Application fee:* $25. *Application deadline:* rolling (freshmen), rolling (transfers). *Notification:* continuous (freshmen).

Admissions Contact Ms. Alicia Moore, Director, Admissions, Central Oregon Community College, 2600 Northwest College Way, Bend, OR 97701-5998. *Phone:* 541-383-7211. *Fax:* 541-383-7506. *E-mail:* welcome@cocc.edu.

CHEMEKETA COMMUNITY COLLEGE
Salem, Oregon

- **State and locally supported** 2-year, founded 1955
- **Calendar** quarters
- **Degree** certificates, diplomas, and associate
- **Urban** 72-acre campus with easy access to Portland
- **Coed,** 14,454 undergraduate students, 25% full-time, 54% women, 46% men

Undergraduates 3,647 full-time, 10,807 part-time. Students come from 5 states and territories, 1% are from out of state, 1% African American, 3% Asian American or Pacific Islander, 8% Hispanic American, 2% Native American, 0.1% international.

Freshmen *Admission:* 781 enrolled.

Faculty *Total:* 632, 36% full-time. *Student/faculty ratio:* 25:1.

Majors Accounting; administrative assistant and secretarial science; agricultural teacher education; art teacher education; automobile/automotive mechanics technology; business administration and management; civil engineering technology; computer engineering technology; computer programming; computer science; construction engineering technology; criminal justice/law enforcement administration; dental hygiene; drafting and design technology; economics; education; electrical, electronic and communications engineering technology; emergency medical technology (EMT paramedic); engineering; English; finance; fire science; forestry; forestry technology; graphic and printing equipment operation/production; health/health care administration; health information/medical records administration; health teacher education; hospitality administration; hotel/motel administration; humanities; human services; industrial technology; kindergarten/preschool education; liberal arts and sciences/liberal studies; mathematics; mechanical design technology; medical administrative assistant and medical secretary; medical/clinical assistant; nursing (licensed practical/vocational nurse training); nursing (registered nurse training); physical education teaching and coaching; political science and government; real estate; science teacher education; social sciences; teacher assistant/aide; welding technology.

Academic Programs *Special study options:* academic remediation for entering students, adult/continuing education programs, advanced placement credit, cooperative education, distance learning, double majors, English as a second language, independent study, internships, part-time degree program, services for LD students, summer session for credit.

Library Chemeketa Community College Library plus 1 other with 801 audiovisual materials, an OPAC, a Web page.

Computers on Campus A campuswide network can be accessed from off campus. Internet access, at least one staffed computer lab available.

Student Life *Housing:* college housing not available. *Activities and Organizations:* drama/theater group, student-run newspaper, choral group, Health

Chemeketa Community College *(continued)*

Occupations Students of America, International Conference of Building Officials, Ski Club, Christian Fellowship. *Campus security:* 24-hour emergency response devices and patrols, late-night transport/escort service. *Student services:* personal/psychological counseling, women's center.

Athletics *Intercollegiate sports:* baseball M(s), basketball M(s)/W(s), cross-country running M(s)/W(s), track and field M(s)/W(s), volleyball W(s).

Standardized Tests *Required for some:* ACT ASSET.

Costs (2005–06) *Tuition:* state resident $2610 full-time, $58 per quarter hour part-time; nonresident $8955 full-time, $199 per quarter hour part-time. *Required fees:* $180 full-time, $4 per quarter hour part-time.

Financial Aid Of all full-time matriculated undergraduates who enrolled in 2003, 316 Federal Work-Study jobs (averaging $1290).

Applying *Options:* deferred entrance. *Required for some:* high school transcript. *Application deadline:* rolling (freshmen), rolling (transfers). *Notification:* continuous (freshmen).

Admissions Contact Ms. Carolyn Brownell, Admissions Specialist, Chemeketa Community College, 4000 Lancaster Drive, NE, Salem, OR 97305-7070. *Phone:* 503-399-5006. *Fax:* 503-399-3918. *E-mail:* broc@chemeketa.edu.

CLACKAMAS COMMUNITY COLLEGE
Oregon City, Oregon

- **District-supported** 2-year, founded 1966
- **Calendar** quarters
- **Degree** certificates, diplomas, and associate
- **Suburban** 175-acre campus with easy access to Portland
- **Endowment** $5.6 million
- **Coed,** 6,866 undergraduate students, 42% full-time, 51% women, 49% men

Undergraduates 2,852 full-time, 4,014 part-time. Students come from 38 states and territories, 16 other countries, 7% are from out of state, 1% African American, 4% Asian American or Pacific Islander, 4% Hispanic American, 1% Native American, 0.1% international, 31% transferred in.

Freshmen *Admission:* 1,190 enrolled.

Faculty *Total:* 525, 27% full-time. *Student/faculty ratio:* 19:1.

Majors Accounting; autobody/collision and repair technology; automobile/automotive mechanics technology; community organization and advocacy; computer technology/computer systems technology; corrections; criminal justice/police science; drafting and design technology; general studies; liberal arts and sciences/liberal studies; machine tool technology; nursing (registered nurse training); office management; ornamental horticulture; water quality and wastewater treatment management and recycling technology.

Academic Programs *Special study options:* academic remediation for entering students, accelerated degree program, adult/continuing education programs, advanced placement credit, cooperative education, distance learning, double majors, English as a second language, honors programs, independent study, internships, part-time degree program, services for LD students, study abroad, summer session for credit. *ROTC:* Air Force (c).

Library Dye Learning Resource Center plus 1 other with 41,263 titles, 274 serial subscriptions, 1,141 audiovisual materials, an OPAC, a Web page.

Computers on Campus 500 computers available on campus for general student use. A campuswide network can be accessed. Internet access, online (class) registration, at least one staffed computer lab available.

Student Life *Housing:* college housing not available. *Activities and Organizations:* drama/theater group, student-run newspaper, choral group, Ski Club, Spanish Club, Phi Theta Kappa, Horticulture Club, Speech Club, national fraternities. *Campus security:* 24-hour emergency response devices and patrols, student patrols, late-night transport/escort service. *Student services:* personal/psychological counseling, women's center.

Athletics Member NJCAA. *Intercollegiate sports:* baseball M(s), basketball M(s)/W(s), cross-country running M(s)/W(s), soccer W, softball W(s), track and field M(s)/W(s), volleyball W(s), wrestling M(s). *Intramural sports:* basketball M/W, football M, soccer M/W, tennis M/W.

Standardized Tests *Required:* Assessment and Placement Services for Community Colleges (for placement). *Recommended:* SAT or ACT (for placement).

Costs (2004–05) *Tuition:* state resident $2520 full-time, $56 per credit hour part-time; nonresident $8730 full-time, $194 per credit hour part-time. *Required fees:* $180 full-time, $4 per credit hour part-time.

Financial Aid Of all full-time matriculated undergraduates who enrolled in 2003, 115 Federal Work-Study jobs (averaging $1330).

Applying *Options:* early admission. *Recommended:* high school transcript. *Application deadline:* rolling (freshmen), rolling (transfers).

Admissions Contact Ms. Diane Drebin, Registrar, Clackamas Community College, 19600 South Molalla Avenue, Oregon City, OR 97045. *Phone:* 503-657-6958 Ext. 2742. *Fax:* 503-650-6654. *E-mail:* pattyw@clackamas.edu.

CLATSOP COMMUNITY COLLEGE
Astoria, Oregon

- **County-supported** 2-year, founded 1958
- **Calendar** quarters
- **Degree** certificates and associate
- **Small-town** 20-acre campus
- **Endowment** $2.0 million
- **Coed,** 1,824 undergraduate students, 24% full-time, 48% women, 52% men

Undergraduates 445 full-time, 1,379 part-time. Students come from 28 states and territories, 1 other country, 15% are from out of state, 0.7% African American, 2% Asian American or Pacific Islander, 4% Hispanic American, 3% Native American, 0.9% international, 0.4% transferred in.

Freshmen *Admission:* 340 applied, 277 admitted, 205 enrolled.

Faculty *Total:* 198, 20% full-time, 3% with terminal degrees.

Majors Accounting; administrative assistant and secretarial science; business administration and management; business automation/technology/data entry; computer engineering technology; computer systems networking and telecommunications; criminal justice/law enforcement administration; fire science; legal administrative assistant/secretary; liberal arts and sciences/liberal studies; medical administrative assistant and medical secretary; nursing (registered nurse training).

Academic Programs *Special study options:* academic remediation for entering students, adult/continuing education programs, advanced placement credit, cooperative education, distance learning, English as a second language, external degree program, internships, part-time degree program, services for LD students, summer session for credit.

Library Dora Badollet Library plus 1 other with 48,517 titles, 180 serial subscriptions, 5,000 audiovisual materials, an OPAC, a Web page.

Computers on Campus 76 computers available on campus for general student use. A campuswide network can be accessed from off campus. Internet access, at least one staffed computer lab available.

Student Life *Housing:* college housing not available. *Activities and Organizations:* drama/theater group, student-run television station, Lives in Transition, Phi Theta Kappa, Nursing Club, Spanish Club, Fine Arts Club. *Campus security:* 24-hour emergency response devices, late-night transport/escort service. *Student services:* personal/psychological counseling.

Standardized Tests *Required:* ACT ASSET (for placement).

Costs (2004–05) *Tuition:* state resident $2430 full-time, $54 per credit part-time; nonresident $4860 full-time, $108 per credit part-time. *Required fees:* $270 full-time, $6 per credit part-time.

Financial Aid Of all full-time matriculated undergraduates who enrolled in 2003, 220 Federal Work-Study jobs (averaging $2175).

Applying *Options:* early admission. *Application fee:* $15. *Recommended:* high school transcript. *Application deadlines:* rolling (freshmen), 9/29 (transfers). *Notification:* continuous (freshmen).

Admissions Contact Ms. Joanne Swenson, Admissions Coordinator/Registrar, Clatsop Community College, 1653 Jerome, Astoria, OR 97103-3698. *Phone:* 503-338-2325. *Toll-free phone:* 866-252-8767. *Fax:* 503-325-5738. *E-mail:* admissions@clatsop.cc.or.us.

COLUMBIA GORGE COMMUNITY COLLEGE
The Dalles, Oregon

- **State-supported** 2-year, founded 1977
- **Calendar** quarters
- **Degree** certificates, diplomas, and associate
- **Coed**

Faculty *Total:* 90, 17% full-time.

Costs (2004–05) *Tuition:* state resident $59 per credit part-time. Full-time tuition and fees vary according to course load. Part-time tuition and fees vary according to course load. *Required fees:* $8 per credit part-time. *Payment plan:* installment. *Waivers:* adult students.

Admissions Contact Ms. Karen Carter, Dean of Student Services, Columbia Gorge Community College, 400 East Scenic Drive, The Dalles, OR 97058. *Phone:* 541-298-3110. *E-mail:* mmartin@cgcc.cc.or.us.

HEALD COLLEGE-PORTLAND
Portland, Oregon

Admissions Contact Director of Admissions, Heald College-Portland, 625 Southwest Broadway, Suite 200, Portland, OR 97205. *Phone:* 503-229-0492. *Toll-free phone:* 800-755-3550. *E-mail:* info@heald.edu.

ITT TECHNICAL INSTITUTE
Portland, Oregon

- **Proprietary** primarily 2-year, founded 1971, part of ITT Educational Services, Inc
- **Calendar** quarters
- **Degrees** associate and bachelor's
- **Urban** 4-acre campus
- **Coed**

Standardized Tests *Required:* Wonderlic aptitude test (for admission).

Costs (2004–05) *Tuition:* Please see school catalog for specific information.

Financial Aid Of all full-time matriculated undergraduates who enrolled in 2003, 15 Federal Work-Study jobs (averaging $4000).

Applying *Options:* deferred entrance. *Application fee:* $100. *Required:* high school transcript, interview. *Recommended:* letters of recommendation.

Admissions Contact Mr. Ed Yakimchick, Director of Recruitment, ITT Technical Institute, 6035 Northeast 78th Court, Portland, OR 97218. *Phone:* 503-255-6500. *Toll-free phone:* 800-234-5488. *Fax:* 503-255-8381.

KLAMATH COMMUNITY COLLEGE
Klamath Falls, Oregon

Admissions Contact Mr. Greg Brown, Dean for Student Services, Klamath Community College, 7390 South 6th Street, Klamath Falls, OR 97603. *Phone:* 541-882-3521.

LANE COMMUNITY COLLEGE
Eugene, Oregon

- **State and locally supported** 2-year, founded 1964
- **Calendar** quarters
- **Degree** certificates and associate
- **Suburban** 240-acre campus
- **Endowment** $6.0 million
- **Coed,** 11,834 undergraduate students, 39% full-time, 64% women, 36% men

Undergraduates 4,565 full-time, 7,269 part-time. Students come from 28 states and territories, 27 other countries, 1% African American, 2% Asian American or Pacific Islander, 4% Hispanic American, 2% Native American, 2% international. *Retention:* 62% of 2002 full-time freshmen returned.

Faculty *Total:* 585, 44% full-time. *Student/faculty ratio:* 22:1.

Majors Accounting; administrative assistant and secretarial science; agricultural mechanization; airline pilot and flight crew; automobile/automotive mechanics technology; avionics maintenance technology; broadcast journalism; business administration and management; child development; cinematography and film/video production; commercial and advertising art; community organization and advocacy; computer engineering technology; computer programming; construction engineering technology; criminal justice/law enforcement administration; culinary arts; dental hygiene; drafting and design technology; electrical, electronic and communications engineering technology; energy management and systems technology; food services technology; heating, air conditioning, ventilation and refrigeration maintenance technology; heavy equipment maintenance technology; hospitality administration; hotel/motel administration; industrial technology; kindergarten/preschool education; liberal arts and sciences/liberal studies; nursing (registered nurse training); radio and television; real estate; respiratory care therapy; special products marketing; substance abuse/addiction counseling; welding technology.

Academic Programs *Special study options:* academic remediation for entering students, adult/continuing education programs, advanced placement credit, English as a second language, internships, part-time degree program, services for LD students, summer session for credit.

Library Lane Community College Library plus 1 other with 67,051 titles, 513 serial subscriptions, an OPAC, a Web page.

Computers on Campus 1600 computers available on campus for general student use. A campuswide network can be accessed. At least one staffed computer lab available.

Student Life *Housing:* college housing not available. *Activities and Organizations:* drama/theater group, student-run newspaper, radio and television station, choral group, Associated Students of Lane, Multicultural Club, Native American Club, Lane Writing Club, Forensics Club. *Campus security:* 24-hour emergency response devices and patrols, student patrols, late-night transport/escort service. *Student services:* health clinic, personal/psychological counseling, women's center, legal services.

Athletics *Intercollegiate sports:* baseball M(s), basketball M(s)/W(s), cross-country running M(s)/W(s), track and field M(s)/W(s), volleyball W(s). *Intramural sports:* badminton M/W, basketball M/W, bowling M/W, football M/W, golf M/W, skiing (cross-country) M/W, skiing (downhill) M/W, soccer M/W, softball M/W, tennis M/W, volleyball M, weight lifting M/W.

Costs (2004–05) *Tuition:* state resident $2322 full-time, $65 per credit hour part-time; nonresident $7956 full-time, $221 per credit hour part-time. *Required fees:* $250 full-time. *Payment plan:* installment. *Waivers:* senior citizens and employees or children of employees.

Financial Aid Of all full-time matriculated undergraduates who enrolled in 2003, 400 Federal Work-Study jobs (averaging $3600).

Applying *Options:* common application, early admission. *Application deadline:* rolling (freshmen), rolling (transfers). *Notification:* continuous (freshmen).

Admissions Contact Ms. Helen Garrett, Director of Admissions/Registrar, Lane Community College, 4000 East 30th Avenue, Eugene, OR 97405-0640. *Phone:* 541-747-4501 Ext. 2686. *E-mail:* williamss@lanecc.edu.

LINN-BENTON COMMUNITY COLLEGE
Albany, Oregon

- **State and locally supported** 2-year, founded 1966
- **Calendar** quarters
- **Degree** certificates and associate
- **Small-town** 104-acre campus
- **Endowment** $2.1 million
- **Coed,** 5,398 undergraduate students, 54% full-time, 55% women, 45% men

Undergraduates 2,891 full-time, 2,507 part-time. Students come from 5 states and territories, 10 other countries, 3% are from out of state, 0.8% African American, 3% Asian American or Pacific Islander, 4% Hispanic American, 2% Native American, 0.6% international.

Freshmen *Admission:* 3,014 applied, 2,740 admitted, 1,200 enrolled.

Faculty *Total:* 489, 33% full-time.

Majors Accounting; administrative assistant and secretarial science; agricultural business and management; agricultural teacher education; agriculture; animal sciences; art; automobile/automotive mechanics technology; biological and physical sciences; biology/biological sciences; business administration and management; chemistry; child care and support services management; civil engineering technology; commercial and advertising art; computer and information sciences; computer programming (specific applications); computer/technical support; criminal justice/police science; criminal justice/safety; culinary arts; culinary arts related; dairy husbandry and production; desktop publishing and digital imaging design; diesel mechanics technology; drafting and design technology; dramatic/theatre arts; economics; education; elementary education; engineering; English; family and consumer sciences/human sciences; foreign languages and literatures; graphic communications related; horse husbandry/equine science and management; horticultural science; industrial technology; journalism; juvenile corrections; legal administrative assistant/secretary; liberal arts and sciences/liberal studies; machine tool technology; mathematics; medical administrative assistant and medical secretary; medical/clinical assistant; metallurgical technology; multi-/interdisciplinary studies related; nursing (registered nurse training); photography; physical education teaching and coaching; physical sciences; physics; pre-engineering; restaurant, culinary, and catering management; speech and rhetoric; system administration; teacher assistant/aide; technical and business writing; water quality and wastewater treatment management and recycling technology; welding technology.

Academic Programs *Special study options:* academic remediation for entering students, adult/continuing education programs, advanced placement credit, cooperative education, distance learning, English as a second language, independent study, internships, part-time degree program, services for LD students, student-designed majors, summer session for credit. *ROTC:* Army (c), Air Force (c).

Library Linn-Benton Community College Library with 42,561 titles, 91 serial subscriptions, 8,758 audiovisual materials, an OPAC, a Web page.

Computers on Campus 500 computers available on campus for general student use. A campuswide network can be accessed from off campus. Internet access, online (class) registration, at least one staffed computer lab available.

Student Life *Housing:* college housing not available. *Activities and Organizations:* drama/theater group, student-run newspaper, choral group, EBOP Club, Multicultural Club, Campus Family Co-op, Horticulture Club, Collegiate Secretary Club. *Campus security:* 24-hour emergency response devices and patrols, student patrols, late-night transport/escort service. *Student services:* personal/psychological counseling.

Athletics *Intercollegiate sports:* baseball M(s), basketball M(s)/W(s), volleyball W(s). *Intramural sports:* basketball M/W, tennis M/W, ultimate Frisbee M/W, volleyball M/W.

Standardized Tests *Required:* CPT (for placement).

Costs (2005–06) *Tuition:* state resident $2790 full-time, $58 per credit hour part-time; nonresident $7335 full-time, $163 per credit hour part-time. *Required fees:* $4 per credit hour part-time.

Financial Aid Of all full-time matriculated undergraduates who enrolled in 2003, 290 Federal Work-Study jobs (averaging $1800).

Applying *Options:* deferred entrance. *Application fee:* $25. *Required for some:* high school transcript. *Application deadline:* rolling (freshmen), rolling (transfers).

Linn-Benton Community College (continued)

Admissions Contact Ms. Christine Baker, Outreach Coordinator, Linn-Benton Community College, 6500 Pacific Boulevard, SW, Albany, OR 97321. *Phone:* 541-917-4813. *E-mail:* admissions@linnbenton.edu.

MT. HOOD COMMUNITY COLLEGE
Gresham, Oregon

Admissions Contact Dr. Craig Kolins, Associate Vice President of Enrollment Services, Mt. Hood Community College, 26000 Southeast Stark Street, Gresham, OR 97030-3300. *Phone:* 503-491-7265.

OREGON COAST COMMUNITY COLLEGE
Newport, Oregon

- **Public** 2-year
- **Degree** certificates and associate
- **Coed,** 504 undergraduate students, 20% full-time, 66% women, 34% men

Undergraduates 99 full-time, 405 part-time. Students come from 5 states and territories, 1% are from out of state, 0.3% African American, 1% Asian American or Pacific Islander, 6% Hispanic American, 3% Native American, 51% transferred in.

Freshmen *Admission:* 76 admitted, 76 enrolled.

Faculty *Total:* 45, 7% full-time, 20% with terminal degrees. *Student/faculty ratio:* 14:1.

Academic Programs *Special study options:* academic remediation for entering students, cooperative education, distance learning, English as a second language, honors programs, internships, part-time degree program, services for LD students, summer session for credit.

Library Oregon Coast Community College Library with 8,652 titles, 51 serial subscriptions, 1,210 audiovisual materials, an OPAC, a Web page.

Computers on Campus 40 computers available on campus for general student use. A campuswide network can be accessed. Internet access, at least one staffed computer lab available.

Student Life *Housing:* college housing not available.

Costs (2004–05) *Tuition:* area resident $2700 full-time, $60 per credit part-time; nonresident $7740 full-time, $172 per credit part-time. Full-time tuition and fees vary according to course load. Part-time tuition and fees vary according to course load. *Required fees:* $90 full-time, $5 per credit part-time, $30 per term part-time. *Payment plan:* deferred payment. *Waivers:* employees or children of employees.

Applying *Options:* common application.

Admissions Contact Student Services, Oregon Coast Community College, 332 SW Coast Highway, Newport, OR 97365. *Phone:* 541-574-7101. *Toll-free phone:* 541-574-7125. *Fax:* 541-574-7159. *E-mail:* webinfo@occc.cc.or.us.

PIONEER PACIFIC COLLEGE
Wilsonville, Oregon

- **Proprietary** primarily 2-year, founded 1981
- **Calendar** continuous
- **Degrees** diplomas, associate, and bachelor's
- **Suburban** campus with easy access to Portland
- **Coed,** 1,015 undergraduate students, 100% full-time, 74% women, 26% men

Undergraduates 1,014 full-time, 1 part-time. Students come from 2 states and territories, 1 other country, 6% are from out of state, 3% African American, 2% Asian American or Pacific Islander, 5% Hispanic American, 1% Native American, 0.1% international, 19% transferred in.

Freshmen *Admission:* 752 applied, 631 admitted, 151 enrolled.

Faculty *Total:* 121, 34% full-time, 6% with terminal degrees. *Student/faculty ratio:* 15:1.

Majors Accounting; business administration and management; criminal justice/police science; health/health care administration; information science/studies; information technology; legal assistant/paralegal; medical/clinical assistant; sales, distribution and marketing; web/multimedia management and webmaster.

Academic Programs *Special study options:* accelerated degree program, honors programs, internships.

Library 2,500 titles.

Computers on Campus 300 computers available on campus for general student use. A campuswide network can be accessed. Internet access available. Computer purchase or lease plan available.

Student Life *Housing:* college housing not available. *Activities and Organizations:* Phi Beta Lambda.

Standardized Tests *Required:* CPAt (for admission).

Costs (2005–06) *One-time required fee:* $150. *Tuition:* $8100 full-time, $180 per credit hour part-time. Full-time tuition and fees vary according to program.

Required fees: $150 full-time. *Payment plans:* installment, deferred payment. *Waivers:* employees or children of employees.

Applying *Application fee:* $50. *Required:* high school transcript, interview. *Application deadline:* rolling (freshmen).

Admissions Contact Ms. Mary Harris, Vice President of Marketing, Pioneer Pacific College, 27501 Southwest Parkway Avenue, Wilsonville, OR 97070. *Phone:* 503-654-8000. *Toll-free phone:* 866-772-4636. *Fax:* 503-682-1514. *E-mail:* inquiries@pioneerpacific.edu.

PORTLAND COMMUNITY COLLEGE
Portland, Oregon

- **State and locally supported** 2-year, founded 1961
- **Calendar** quarters
- **Degree** certificates, diplomas, and associate
- **Urban** 400-acre campus
- **Coed**

Faculty *Student/faculty ratio:* 25:1.

Student Life *Campus security:* 24-hour emergency response devices and patrols, late-night transport/escort service.

Athletics Member NJCAA.

Costs (2004–05) *Tuition:* state resident $2975 full-time, $62 per credit part-time; nonresident $8735 full-time, $190 per credit part-time. *Required fees:* $240 full-time, $4 per credit part-time.

Applying *Options:* electronic application.

Admissions Contact Mr. Dennis Bailey-Fougnier, Director of Admissions, Portland Community College, PO Box 19000, Portland, OR 97280. *Phone:* 503-977-4519. *Fax:* 503-977-4740. *E-mail:* admissions@pcc.edu.

ROGUE COMMUNITY COLLEGE
Grants Pass, Oregon

- **State and locally supported** 2-year, founded 1970
- **Calendar** quarters
- **Degree** certificates, diplomas, and associate
- **Rural** 90-acre campus
- **Endowment** $5.7 million
- **Coed,** 4,211 undergraduate students, 41% full-time, 59% women, 41% men

Undergraduates 1,734 full-time, 2,477 part-time. Students come from 5 states and territories, 5 other countries, 0.4% are from out of state, 0.9% African American, 1% Asian American or Pacific Islander, 5% Hispanic American, 3% Native American, 0.3% international, 25% transferred in.

Freshmen *Admission:* 483 applied, 483 admitted, 483 enrolled.

Faculty *Total:* 492, 20% full-time. *Student/faculty ratio:* 11:1.

Majors Accounting; administrative assistant and secretarial science; art history, criticism and conservation; automobile/automotive mechanics technology; biological and physical sciences; business administration and management; child development; computer science; criminal justice/law enforcement administration; education related; electrical, electronic and communications engineering technology; fire science; heavy equipment maintenance technology; humanities; human services; industrial technology; journalism related; liberal arts and sciences/liberal studies; massage therapy; mathematics; nursing (registered nurse training); respiratory care therapy; social sciences; substance abuse/addiction counseling; welding technology.

Academic Programs *Special study options:* academic remediation for entering students, adult/continuing education programs, advanced placement credit, cooperative education, distance learning, double majors, English as a second language, internships, part-time degree program, services for LD students, summer session for credit.

Library Rogue Community College Library with 33,000 titles, 275 serial subscriptions, an OPAC.

Computers on Campus 96 computers available on campus for general student use. A campuswide network can be accessed. Internet access, online (class) registration, at least one staffed computer lab available.

Student Life *Housing:* college housing not available. *Activities and Organizations:* drama/theater group, student-run newspaper, choral group. *Campus security:* 24-hour patrols, late-night transport/escort service. *Student services:* personal/psychological counseling, women's center.

Athletics *Intramural sports:* basketball M/W, soccer M/W, tennis M/W, volleyball M/W.

Standardized Tests *Required:* ACT ASSET/COMPASS (for placement).

Costs (2004–05) *Tuition:* state resident $2124 full-time, $59 per credit hour part-time; nonresident $2556 full-time, $71 per credit hour part-time. *Required fees:* $294 full-time, $4 per credit hour part-time. *Payment plan:* deferred payment. *Waivers:* employees or children of employees.

Financial Aid Of all full-time matriculated undergraduates who enrolled in 2003, 210 Federal Work-Study jobs (averaging $3200). 300 state and other part-time jobs (averaging $3000).

Applying *Options:* early admission. *Application deadline:* rolling (freshmen), rolling (transfers).
Admissions Contact Claudia Sullivan, Director of Admissions, Rogue Community College, 3345 Redwood Highway, Grants Pass, OR 97527-9298. *Phone:* 541-956-7176. *E-mail:* csullivan@roguecc.edu.

SOUTHWESTERN OREGON COMMUNITY COLLEGE
Coos Bay, Oregon

- **State and locally supported** 2-year, founded 1961
- **Calendar** quarters
- **Degree** certificates, diplomas, and associate
- **Small-town** 125-acre campus
- **Endowment** $637,301
- **Coed,** 2,114 undergraduate students, 43% full-time, 60% women, 40% men

Undergraduates 914 full-time, 1,200 part-time. Students come from 4 other countries, 1% African American, 1% Asian American or Pacific Islander, 3% Hispanic American, 5% Native American, 0.7% international.
Freshmen *Admission:* 636 applied, 636 admitted, 474 enrolled. *Average high school GPA:* 2.40.
Faculty *Total:* 205, 34% full-time. *Student/faculty ratio:* 23:1.
Majors Accounting; adult development and aging; athletic training; banking and financial support services; biological and physical sciences; business administration and management; criminal justice/police science; engineering; environmental studies; fire science; forestry; industrial technology; kindergarten/preschool education; liberal arts and sciences/liberal studies; machine tool technology; management information systems; marketing/marketing management; mathematics; medical/clinical assistant; music; nursing (registered nurse training); office management; social work; substance abuse/addiction counseling; turf and turfgrass management; welding technology.
Academic Programs *Special study options:* academic remediation for entering students, adult/continuing education programs, advanced placement credit, cooperative education, distance learning, English as a second language, internships, part-time degree program, services for LD students, summer session for credit.
Library Southwestern Oregon Community College Library with 40,505 titles, 218 serial subscriptions, 3,673 audiovisual materials, an OPAC, a Web page.
Computers on Campus 65 computers available on campus for general student use. A campuswide network can be accessed. Internet access, online (class) registration, at least one staffed computer lab available.
Student Life *Housing:* on-campus residence required for freshman year. *Options:* coed. Campus housing is university owned. *Activities and Organizations:* drama/theater group, student-run newspaper, choral group. *Campus security:* controlled dormitory access. *Student services:* personal/psychological counseling.
Athletics Member NJCAA. *Intercollegiate sports:* baseball M(s), basketball M(s)/W(s), cheerleading M(s)/W(s), cross-country running M(s)/W(s), golf M(s)/W(s), soccer M(s)/W(s), softball W(s), track and field M(s)/W(s), volleyball W(s), wrestling M(s). *Intramural sports:* basketball M, volleyball M/W.
Standardized Tests *Recommended:* SAT or ACT (for placement).
Costs (2004–05) *Tuition:* area resident $2520 full-time, $56 per credit part-time. Full-time tuition and fees vary according to class time, course level, course load, degree level, location, program, reciprocity agreements, and student level. Part-time tuition and fees vary according to class time, course level, course load, degree level, location, program, reciprocity agreements, and student level. *Required fees:* $315 full-time, $7 per credit part-time. *Room and board:* $5750. Room and board charges vary according to board plan and housing facility. *Payment plans:* installment, deferred payment. *Waivers:* employees or children of employees.
Financial Aid Of all full-time matriculated undergraduates who enrolled in 2003, 140 Federal Work-Study jobs (averaging $874). 42 state and other part-time jobs (averaging $545).
Applying *Options:* early admission. *Application fee:* $30. *Required for some:* high school transcript. *Application deadline:* rolling (freshmen), rolling (transfers). *Notification:* continuous (freshmen).
Admissions Contact Mr. Tom Nicholls, Recruitment, Southwestern Oregon Community College, Student First Stop, 1988 Newmark Avenue, Coos Bay, OR 97420. *Phone:* 541-888-7611. *Toll-free phone:* 800-962-2838. *E-mail:* lwells@socc.edu.

TILLAMOOK BAY COMMUNITY COLLEGE
Tillamook, Oregon

- **District-supported** 2-year, founded 1984, administratively affiliated with Portland Community College
- **Calendar** quarters
- **Degree** certificates, diplomas, and associate
- **Coed,** 250 undergraduate students, 12% full-time, 67% women, 33% men
- **100% of applicants were admitted**

Undergraduates 31 full-time, 219 part-time. Students come from 2 states and territories, 1 other country, 2% are from out of state, 2% African American, 0.8% Asian American or Pacific Islander, 3% Hispanic American, 0.8% Native American, 4% transferred in.
Freshmen *Admission:* 52 applied, 52 admitted, 52 enrolled.
Faculty *Total:* 27, 19% full-time, 19% with terminal degrees. *Student/faculty ratio:* 8:1.
Majors Accounting; accounting technology and bookkeeping; administrative assistant and secretarial science; business automation/technology/data entry; criminal justice/law enforcement administration; early childhood education; emergency medical technology (EMT paramedic); general studies; liberal arts and sciences/liberal studies; management science; marketing related; nursing related; office management; substance abuse/addiction counseling.
Student Life *Housing:* college housing not available. *Activities and Organizations:* student-run newspaper. *Campus security:* Evening security guard.
Costs (2004–05) *Tuition:* state resident $55 per credit hour part-time; nonresident $75 per credit hour part-time. *Required fees:* $7 per credit part-time.
Admissions Contact Ms. Shiela Fitch, Enrollment Services Supervisor, Tillamook Bay Community College, 2510 First Street, Tillamook, OR 97141. *Phone:* 503-842-8222. *Fax:* 503-842-2214. *E-mail:* sfitch@tbcc.cc.or.us.

TREASURE VALLEY COMMUNITY COLLEGE
Ontario, Oregon

Admissions Contact Ms. Suzanne Bergam, Office of Admissions and Student Services, Treasure Valley Community College, 650 College Boulevard, Ontario, OR 97914. *Phone:* 541-881-8822 Ext. 239. *Fax:* 541-881-2721.

UMPQUA COMMUNITY COLLEGE
Roseburg, Oregon

- **State and locally supported** 2-year, founded 1964
- **Calendar** quarters
- **Degree** certificates and associate
- **Rural** 100-acre campus
- **Endowment** $2.9 million
- **Coed,** 2,141 undergraduate students, 46% full-time, 58% women, 42% men

Undergraduates 987 full-time, 1,154 part-time. Students come from 5 states and territories, 1% are from out of state, 1% African American, 1% Asian American or Pacific Islander, 2% Hispanic American, 2% Native American.
Faculty *Student/faculty ratio:* 18:1.
Majors Accounting; administrative assistant and secretarial science; agriculture; anthropology; art; art history, criticism and conservation; art teacher education; automobile/automotive mechanics technology; behavioral sciences; biological and physical sciences; biology/biological sciences; business administration and management; chemistry; child development; civil engineering technology; computer engineering technology; computer science; cosmetology; criminal justice/law enforcement administration; desktop publishing and digital imaging design; dramatic/theatre arts; economics; education; electrical, electronic and communications engineering technology; elementary education; emergency medical technology (EMT paramedic); engineering; English; fire science; forestry; health teacher education; history; humanities; human resources management; journalism; kindergarten/preschool education; legal administrative assistant/secretary; liberal arts and sciences/liberal studies; marketing/marketing management; mathematics; medical administrative assistant and medical secretary; music; music teacher education; natural sciences; nursing (registered nurse training); physical education teaching and coaching; physical sciences; political science and government; pre-engineering; psychology; social sciences; social work; sociology.
Academic Programs *Special study options:* academic remediation for entering students, accelerated degree program, adult/continuing education programs, advanced placement credit, cooperative education, distance learning, English as a second language, honors programs, part-time degree program, services for LD students, student-designed majors, summer session for credit.
Library Umpqua Community College Library with 41,000 titles, 350 serial subscriptions, an OPAC, a Web page.
Computers on Campus 300 computers available on campus for general student use. A campuswide network can be accessed from off campus. Internet access, at least one staffed computer lab available. Computer purchase or lease plan available.
Student Life *Housing:* college housing not available. *Activities and Organizations:* drama/theater group, student-run newspaper, choral group, Phi Theta Kappa, Computer Club, Phi Beta Lambda, Nursing Club, Umpqua Accounting Associates. *Student services:* personal/psychological counseling.

Oregon

Umpqua Community College (continued)

Athletics *Intercollegiate sports:* basketball M(s)/W(s). *Intramural sports:* basketball M/W.

Costs (2004–05) *Tuition:* state resident $2655 full-time, $59 per credit part-time; nonresident $159 per credit part-time. *Required fees:* $45 full-time, $15 per term part-time. *Payment plan:* deferred payment. *Waivers:* senior citizens and employees or children of employees.

Financial Aid Of all full-time matriculated undergraduates who enrolled in 2003, 120 Federal Work-Study jobs (averaging $3000).

Applying *Options:* early admission, deferred entrance. *Application fee:* $25. *Recommended:* high school transcript. *Application deadline:* rolling (freshmen), rolling (transfers).

Admissions Contact Lindsay Cameron, Recruiter/Admissions Officer, Umpqua Community College, PO Box 967, 1140 College Road, Roseburg, OR 97470. *Phone:* 541-440-4616. *Fax:* 541-440-4612. *E-mail:* lindsay.cameron@umpqua.edu.

WESTERN BUSINESS COLLEGE
Portland, Oregon

Admissions Contact 425 Southwest Washington, Portland, OR 97204.

WESTERN CULINARY INSTITUTE
Portland, Oregon

Admissions Contact 1235 Southwest 12th Avenue, Suite 100, Portland, OR 97201. *Toll-free phone:* 800-666-0312.

PENNSYLVANIA

ACADEMY OF MEDICAL ARTS AND BUSINESS
Harrisburg, Pennsylvania

- **Proprietary** 2-year, founded 1980
- **Calendar** continuous
- **Degree** diplomas and associate
- **Suburban** 8-acre campus
- **Coed, primarily women**

Faculty *Student/faculty ratio:* 20:1.

Costs (2004–05) *Tuition:* $8650 full-time. *Required fees:* $1790 full-time.

Financial Aid Of all full-time matriculated undergraduates who enrolled in 2003, 25 Federal Work-Study jobs (averaging $6000).

Applying *Options:* common application. *Application fee:* $150. *Required:* high school transcript, interview.

Admissions Contact Mr. Gary Kay, Director of Admissions, Academy of Medical Arts and Business, 2301 Academy Drive, Harrisburg, PA 17112. *Phone:* 717-545-4747. *Toll-free phone:* 800-400-3322. *Fax:* 717-901-9090. *E-mail:* info@acadcampus.com.

ALLIED MEDICAL AND TECHNICAL CAREERS
Forty Fort, Pennsylvania

Admissions Contact 166 Slocum Street, Forty Fort, PA 18704-2936.

ANTONELLI INSTITUTE
Erdenheim, Pennsylvania

- **Proprietary** 2-year, founded 1938
- **Calendar** semesters
- **Degree** associate
- **Suburban** 15-acre campus with easy access to Philadelphia
- **Coed,** 147 undergraduate students, 100% full-time, 71% women, 29% men

Undergraduates 147 full-time. Students come from 9 states and territories, 23% are from out of state, 4% African American, 0.7% Asian American or Pacific Islander, 0.7% Hispanic American, 40% live on campus. *Retention:* 100% of 2002 full-time freshmen returned.

Freshmen *Admission:* 136 applied, 100 admitted, 80 enrolled. *Average high school GPA:* 2.65.

Faculty *Total:* 17, 65% full-time. *Student/faculty ratio:* 11:1.

Majors Commercial and advertising art; photography.

Academic Programs *Special study options:* adult/continuing education programs, part-time degree program.

Library Antonelli Institute Library with 4,000 titles, 70 serial subscriptions, 50 audiovisual materials.

Computers on Campus 21 computers available on campus for general student use. A campuswide network can be accessed. Internet access, at least one staffed computer lab available. Computer purchase or lease plan available.

Student Life *Housing Options:* coed. Campus housing is leased by the school. Freshman applicants given priority for college housing. *Campus security:* 24-hour emergency response devices. *Student services:* personal/psychological counseling.

Costs (2005–06) *Tuition:* $15,600 full-time, $525 per credit part-time. *Required fees:* $25 full-time. *Room only:* $5900. *Payment plan:* installment.

Financial Aid Of all full-time matriculated undergraduates who enrolled in 2003, 5 Federal Work-Study jobs (averaging $2000).

Applying *Options:* common application, deferred entrance. *Application fee:* $25. *Required:* high school transcript, interview. *Recommended:* 1 letter of recommendation. *Application deadlines:* 9/1 (freshmen), 9/1 (transfers).

Admissions Contact Mr. Anthony Detore, Director of Admissions, Antonelli Institute, 300 Montgomery Avenue, Erdenheim, PA 19038. *Phone:* 215-836-2222. *Toll-free phone:* 800-722-7871. *Fax:* 215-836-2794.

THE ART INSTITUTE OF PHILADELPHIA
Philadelphia, Pennsylvania

- **Proprietary** primarily 2-year, founded 1966, part of Education Management Corporation
- **Calendar** quarters
- **Degrees** associate and bachelor's
- **Urban** campus
- **Coed,** 3,271 undergraduate students, 67% full-time, 43% women, 57% men

Undergraduates 2,186 full-time, 1,085 part-time. Students come from 30 states and territories, 17% African American, 5% Asian American or Pacific Islander, 5% Hispanic American, 0.8% Native American, 0.4% international, 27% live on campus.

Freshmen *Admission:* 2,100 applied, 1,760 admitted. *Average high school GPA:* 2.7. *Test scores:* SAT verbal scores over 500: 54%; SAT math scores over 500: 54%; SAT verbal scores over 600: 24%; SAT math scores over 600: 24%; SAT verbal scores over 700: 1%; SAT math scores over 700: 1%.

Faculty *Total:* 171, 50% full-time. *Student/faculty ratio:* 22:1.

Majors Applied art; art; cinematography and film/video production; commercial and advertising art; commercial photography; culinary arts; fashion/apparel design; fashion merchandising; film/video and photographic arts related; graphic design; industrial design; interior design; intermedia/multimedia; photography; visual and performing arts related.

Academic Programs *Special study options:* academic remediation for entering students, adult/continuing education programs, advanced placement credit, cooperative education, external degree program, independent study, internships, off-campus study, part-time degree program, services for LD students, summer session for credit.

Library The Art Institute of Philadelphia Library with 25,000 titles, 150 serial subscriptions, 2,000 audiovisual materials, an OPAC, a Web page.

Computers on Campus 368 computers available on campus for general student use. A campuswide network can be accessed. Internet access, online (class) registration, at least one staffed computer lab available. Computer purchase or lease plan available.

Student Life *Housing Options:* coed, disabled students. Campus housing is university owned. Freshman campus housing is guaranteed. *Activities and Organizations:* drama/theater group, student-run newspaper. *Campus security:* 24-hour patrols, controlled dormitory access. *Student services:* personal/psychological counseling.

Athletics *Intramural sports:* basketball M/W, softball M/W.

Standardized Tests *Recommended:* SAT or ACT (for placement).

Costs (2004–05) *One-time required fee:* $100. *Tuition:* $22,800 full-time, $380 per credit part-time. Full-time tuition and fees vary according to course load and program. No tuition increase for student's term of enrollment. *Required fees:* $17,100 full-time. *Room only:* $8400. Room and board charges vary according to housing facility. *Payment plans:* tuition prepayment, installment.

Financial Aid Of all full-time matriculated undergraduates who enrolled in 2003, 230 Federal Work-Study jobs (averaging $3500).

Applying *Options:* electronic application, early admission, early decision, deferred entrance. *Application fee:* $50. *Required:* essay or personal statement, high school transcript, interview. *Recommended:* minimum 2.5 GPA, letters of recommendation. *Application deadline:* rolling (freshmen), rolling (transfers). *Notification:* continuous (freshmen).

Admissions Contact Mr. Tim Howard, Director of Admissions, The Art Institute of Philadelphia, 1622 Chestnut Street, Philadelphia, PA 19103. *Phone:* 215-567-7080 Ext. 6337. *Toll-free phone:* 800-275-2474. *Fax:* 215-405-6399.

BEREAN INSTITUTE
Philadelphia, Pennsylvania

- **Independent** 2-year, founded 1899
- **Calendar** quarters
- **Degree** certificates, diplomas, and associate
- **Urban** 3-acre campus
- **Endowment** $135,000
- **Coed**

Faculty *Student/faculty ratio:* 15:1.
Student Life *Campus security:* 24-hour emergency response devices and patrols.
Applying *Options:* common application, deferred entrance. *Application fee:* $20. *Required:* high school transcript, interview.
Admissions Contact Director of Recruitment, Berean Institute, 1901 West Girard Avenue, Philadelphia, PA 19130. *Phone:* 215-763-4833 Ext. 135. *Fax:* 215-236-6011 Ext. 104.

BERKS TECHNICAL INSTITUTE
Wyomissing, Pennsylvania

Admissions Contact Mr. Freddy Gonzales, Director of Admissions, Berks Technical Institute, 2205 Ridgewood Road, Wyomissing, PA 19610-1168. *Phone:* 610-372-1722. *Toll-free phone:* 800-284-4672 (in-state); 800-821-4662 (out-of-state).

BIDWELL TRAINING CENTER
Pittsburgh, Pennsylvania

Admissions Contact 1815 Metropolitan Street, Pittsburgh, PA 15233-2234.

BRADFORD SCHOOL
Pittsburgh, Pennsylvania

Admissions Contact Mr. Vincent S. Graziano, President, Bradford School, 707 Grant Street, Gulf Tower, Pittsburgh, PA 15219. *Phone:* 412-391-6710. *E-mail:* info@bradfordschoolpgh.com.

BRADLEY ACADEMY FOR THE VISUAL ARTS
York, Pennsylvania

Admissions Contact Ms. Alicia Laughman, Senior Admissions Representative, Bradley Academy for the Visual Arts, 1409 Williams Road, York, PA 17402. *Phone:* 717-755-2711. *Toll-free phone:* 800-864-7725. *Fax:* 717-840-1951. *E-mail:* info@bradleyacademy.net.

▶ See page 472 for a narrative description.

BUCKS COUNTY COMMUNITY COLLEGE
Newtown, Pennsylvania

- **County-supported** 2-year, founded 1964
- **Calendar** semesters
- **Degree** certificates and associate
- **Suburban** 200-acre campus with easy access to Philadelphia
- **Endowment** $2.4 million
- **Coed,** 9,947 undergraduate students, 41% full-time, 59% women, 41% men

Undergraduates 4,074 full-time, 5,873 part-time. Students come from 5 states and territories, 15 other countries, 1% are from out of state, 3% African American, 2% Asian American or Pacific Islander, 2% Hispanic American, 0.3% Native American, 6% international, 4% transferred in.
Freshmen *Admission:* 5,176 applied, 5,128 admitted, 2,657 enrolled.
Faculty *Total:* 594, 25% full-time. *Student/faculty ratio:* 20:1.
Majors Accounting; administrative assistant and secretarial science; American studies; art; banking and financial support services; biology/biological sciences; business administration and management; chemistry; cinematography and film/video production; commercial and advertising art; computer and information sciences; computer and information sciences related; computer engineering technology; computer/information technology services administration related; computer programming; computer programming related; computer program-

ming (specific applications); computer science; consumer merchandising/retailing management; corrections; criminal justice/law enforcement administration; criminal justice/police science; culinary arts; data processing and data processing technology; dramatic/theatre arts; education; electrical, electronic and communications engineering technology; engineering; entrepreneurship; environmental studies; health science; health teacher education; historic preservation and conservation; hospitality administration; hotel/motel administration; humanities; information science/studies; information technology; journalism; kindergarten/preschool education; legal assistant/paralegal; liberal arts and sciences/liberal studies; marketing/marketing management; mass communication/media; mathematics; medical/clinical assistant; music; nursing (registered nurse training); physical education teaching and coaching; psychology; radio and television; social sciences; social work; sport and fitness administration; teacher assistant/aide; visual and performing arts; woodworking.
Academic Programs *Special study options:* academic remediation for entering students, adult/continuing education programs, advanced placement credit, cooperative education, distance learning, English as a second language, external degree program, independent study, internships, part-time degree program, services for LD students, student-designed majors, summer session for credit.
Library Bucks County Community College Library with 155,779 titles, 515 serial subscriptions, an OPAC, a Web page.
Computers on Campus 1600 computers available on campus for general student use. A campuswide network can be accessed from off campus that provide access to e-mail, online course work, WEBCT. Internet access, online (class) registration, at least one staffed computer lab available.
Student Life *Housing:* college housing not available. *Activities and Organizations:* drama/theater group, student-run newspaper, radio station, choral group, Phi Theta Kappa, Students in Free Enterprise, student council, The Centurion (student newspaper). *Campus security:* 24-hour emergency response devices and patrols, late-night transport/escort service. *Student services:* personal/psychological counseling.
Athletics Member NJCAA. *Intercollegiate sports:* baseball M, basketball M, equestrian sports M/W, golf M/W, soccer M/W, tennis M/W, volleyball W. *Intramural sports:* basketball M/W, soccer M/W, softball M/W, tennis M/W, volleyball W.
Costs (2005–06) *Tuition:* area resident $2670 full-time, $89 per credit part-time; state resident $5340 full-time, $178 per credit part-time; nonresident $8010 full-time, $267 per credit part-time. *Required fees:* $434 full-time. *Payment plans:* installment, deferred payment. *Waivers:* senior citizens and employees or children of employees.
Financial Aid Of all full-time matriculated undergraduates who enrolled in 2003, 200 Federal Work-Study jobs.
Applying *Options:* electronic application, early admission. *Application fee:* $30. *Required:* high school transcript. *Required for some:* essay or personal statement, interview. *Application deadlines:* 5/1 (freshmen), 5/1 (transfers).
Admissions Contact Ms. Amy Wilson, Assistant Director of Admissions, Bucks County Community College, 275 Swamp Road, Newtown, PA 18940. *Phone:* 215-968-8119. *Fax:* 215-968-8110. *E-mail:* gleasonj@bucks.edu.

BUSINESS INSTITUTE OF PENNSYLVANIA
Meadville, Pennsylvania

- **Proprietary** 2-year, founded 1987
- **Calendar** quarters
- **Degree** certificates, diplomas, and associate
- **Coed,** 76 undergraduate students, 100% full-time, 93% women, 7% men
- **91% of applicants were admitted**

Undergraduates 76 full-time. 8% African American, 1% Native American.
Freshmen *Admission:* 32 applied, 29 admitted, 18 enrolled. *Average high school GPA:* 3.6.
Faculty *Total:* 5, 60% full-time, 100% with terminal degrees. *Student/faculty ratio:* 20:1.
Student Life *Housing:* college housing not available.
Costs (2005–06) *Tuition:* $7500 full-time, $250 per credit part-time. *Required fees:* $600 full-time.
Admissions Contact Anne Burger, Admissions Officer, Business Institute of Pennsylvania, 628 Arch Street, Suite B105, Meadville, PA 16335. *Phone:* 814-724-0700.

BUSINESS INSTITUTE OF PENNSYLVANIA
Sharon, Pennsylvania

- **Proprietary** 2-year, founded 1926
- **Calendar** quarters
- **Degree** certificates, diplomas, and associate

Business Institute of Pennsylvania (continued)
- **Small-town** 2-acre campus
- **Coed,** 106 undergraduate students, 92% full-time, 93% women, 7% men
- 80% of applicants were admitted

Undergraduates 98 full-time, 8 part-time. 5% African American.
Freshmen *Admission:* 49 applied, 39 admitted, 39 enrolled. *Average high school GPA:* 3.1.
Faculty *Total:* 9, 56% full-time, 100% with terminal degrees. *Student/faculty ratio:* 16:1.
Majors Administrative assistant and secretarial science; business administration and management; business automation/technology/data entry; computer programming; executive assistant/executive secretary; health information/medical records administration; legal administrative assistant/secretary; medical administrative assistant and medical secretary; medical/clinical assistant.
Student Life *Housing:* college housing not available.
Standardized Tests *Required:* ACT (for admission).
Costs (2005–06) *Tuition:* $7500 full-time, $250 per credit part-time. *Required fees:* $600 full-time.
Applying *Required:* high school transcript, interview.
Admissions Contact Ms. Shannon P. McNamara, President, Business Institute of Pennsylvania, 335 Boyd Drive, Sharon, PA 16146. *Phone:* 724-983-0700. *Toll-free phone:* 800-289-2069. *Fax:* 724-983-8355.

BUTLER COUNTY COMMUNITY COLLEGE
Butler, Pennsylvania

- **County-supported** 2-year, founded 1965
- **Calendar** semesters
- **Degree** certificates, diplomas, and associate
- **Rural** 300-acre campus with easy access to Pittsburgh
- **Coed,** 3,731 undergraduate students, 51% full-time, 60% women, 40% men

Undergraduates 1,904 full-time, 1,827 part-time. Students come from 8 states and territories, 1 other country, 1% are from out of state.
Freshmen *Admission:* 1,285 applied, 1,285 admitted.
Faculty *Total:* 72, 100% full-time. *Student/faculty ratio:* 19:1.
Majors Accounting; administrative assistant and secretarial science; architectural drafting and CAD/CADD; architectural engineering technology; biology/biological sciences; business administration and management; civil engineering technology; commercial and advertising art; computer and information sciences; computer programming; criminal justice/police science; criminology; dietetics; drafting and design technology; education; electrical, electronic and communications engineering technology; elementary education; emergency medical technology (EMT paramedic); English; executive assistant/executive secretary; food services technology; general studies; hospitality administration; humanities; instrumentation technology; kindergarten/preschool education; kinesiology and exercise science; legal administrative assistant/secretary; liberal arts and sciences/liberal studies; machine tool technology; marketing/marketing management; mass communication/media; mathematics; mechanical design technology; mechanical drafting and CAD/CADD; medical administrative assistant and medical secretary; medical/clinical assistant; nursing (registered nurse training); office occupations and clerical services; parks, recreation and leisure facilities management; physical education teaching and coaching; physical sciences; physical therapist assistant; pre-engineering; psychology; quality control technology; sport and fitness administration; therapeutic recreation; tourism and travel services management.
Academic Programs *Special study options:* academic remediation for entering students, adult/continuing education programs, advanced placement credit, cooperative education, English as a second language, internships, part-time degree program, services for LD students, summer session for credit.
Library John A. Beck, Jr. Library with 70,000 titles, 305 serial subscriptions.
Computers on Campus 350 computers available on campus for general student use. Internet access, at least one staffed computer lab available.
Student Life *Housing:* college housing not available. *Activities and Organizations:* drama/theater group, student-run newspaper, choral group, student government, Ski Club, Drama Club, Outdoor Recreation Club. *Campus security:* 24-hour emergency response devices, late-night transport/escort service. *Student services:* personal/psychological counseling.
Athletics Member NJCAA. *Intercollegiate sports:* baseball M, basketball M, golf M/W, softball W, volleyball W. *Intramural sports:* badminton M/W, basketball M/W, racquetball M/W, soccer M/W, softball M, table tennis M/W, tennis M/W, volleyball M/W, weight lifting M/W.
Standardized Tests *Required:* ACT ASSET (for placement).
Costs (2004–05) *Tuition:* area resident $2400 full-time, $80 per credit part-time; state resident $4400 full-time, $147 per credit part-time; nonresident $6400 full-time, $214 per credit part-time. *Required fees:* $400 full-time. *Waivers:* senior citizens and employees or children of employees.
Financial Aid Of all full-time matriculated undergraduates who enrolled in 2003, 65 Federal Work-Study jobs (averaging $1545).

Applying *Options:* common application, early admission, deferred entrance. *Application fee:* $15. *Application deadlines:* 8/15 (freshmen), 8/15 (transfers). *Notification:* continuous until 8/15 (freshmen).
Admissions Contact Mr. William L. Miller, Director of Admissions, Butler County Community College, College Drive, PO Box 1203, Butler, PA 16003-1203. *Phone:* 724-287-8711 Ext. 344. *Toll-free phone:* 888-826-2829. *Fax:* 724-287-4961.

CAMBRIA-ROWE BUSINESS COLLEGE
Indiana, Pennsylvania

- **Proprietary** 2-year, founded 1959
- **Calendar** quarters
- **Degree** diplomas and associate
- **Small-town** 1-acre campus
- **Coed, primarily women**
- 72% of applicants were admitted

Faculty *Student/faculty ratio:* 14:1.
Costs (2004–05) *Tuition:* $6900 full-time, $195 per credit part-time. *Required fees:* $990 full-time, $840 per term part-time.
Admissions Contact Laurie Price, Representative at Indiana Campus, Cambria-Rowe Business College, 422 South 13th Street, Indiana, PA 15701. *Phone:* 724-483-0222.

CAMBRIA-ROWE BUSINESS COLLEGE
Johnstown, Pennsylvania

- **Proprietary** 2-year, founded 1891
- **Calendar** quarters
- **Degree** diplomas and associate
- **Small-town** campus with easy access to Pittsburgh
- **Coed, primarily women**

Faculty *Student/faculty ratio:* 20:1.
Costs (2004–05) *One-time required fee:* $25. *Tuition:* $9200 full-time, $195 per credit part-time. *Required fees:* $1200 full-time.
Financial Aid *Financial aid deadline:* 8/1.
Applying *Options:* common application, electronic application, early admission. *Application fee:* $15. *Required:* high school transcript, entrance exam. *Recommended:* minimum 2.0 GPA, interview.
Admissions Contact Mrs. Amanda C. Artim, Director of Admissions, Cambria-Rowe Business College, 221 Central Avenue, Johnstown, PA 15902-2494. *Phone:* 814-536-5168. *Fax:* 814-536-5160. *E-mail:* admissions@crbc.net.

CAREER TRAINING ACADEMY
Monroeville, Pennsylvania

Admissions Contact 105 Mall Boulevard, Suite 300 West, Expo Mart, Monroeville, PA 15146.

CAREER TRAINING ACADEMY
New Kensington, Pennsylvania

Admissions Contact 950 Fifth Avenue, New Kensington, PA 15068-6301.

CAREER TRAINING ACADEMY
Pittsburgh, Pennsylvania

Admissions Contact 1500 Northway Mall, Suite 200, Pittsburgh, PA 15237.

CENTER FOR ADVANCED MANUFACTURING & TECHNOLOGY
Erie, Pennsylvania

Admissions Contact Ms. Lisa Peszel, Director of Admissions, Center for Advanced Manufacturing & Technology, 5451 Merwin Lane, Erie, PA 16510. *Phone:* 814-897-0391 Ext. 226. *Toll-free phone:* 888-834-4226.

CHI INSTITUTE
Southampton, Pennsylvania

- **Proprietary** 2-year, founded 1981, part of Quest Education
- **Calendar** quarters
- **Degree** certificates, diplomas, and associate

■ **Suburban** 6-acre campus with easy access to Philadelphia
■ **Coed**

Faculty *Student/faculty ratio:* 20:1.
Financial Aid Of all full-time matriculated undergraduates who enrolled in 2003, 30 Federal Work-Study jobs (averaging $2050).
Applying *Options:* common application, deferred entrance. *Required:* high school transcript, interview.
Admissions Contact Mr. Michael Herbert, Director of Admissions, CHI Institute, 520 Street Road, Southampton, PA 18966. *Phone:* 215-357-5100 Ext. 114. *Toll-free phone:* 800-336-7696.

CHI INSTITUTE, RETS CAMPUS
Broomall, Pennsylvania

Admissions Contact Mr. Stuart Kahn, Director of Admissions, CHI Institute, RETS Campus, Lawrence Park Shopping Center, Rt. 320 & Lawrence Road, Broomall, PA 19008. *Phone:* 610-353-7630.

COMMONWEALTH TECHNICAL INSTITUTE
Johnstown, Pennsylvania

■ **State-supported** 2-year
■ **Calendar** trimesters
■ **Degree** certificates, diplomas, and associate
■ **Coed,** 231 undergraduate students, 100% full-time, 39% women, 61% men

Undergraduates 231 full-time. 14% African American, 1% Asian American or Pacific Islander. *Retention:* 64% of 2002 full-time freshmen returned.
Freshmen *Admission:* 102 enrolled.
Faculty *Total:* 30, 100% full-time.
Majors Accounting; architectural drafting and CAD/CADD; computer science; culinary arts; dental laboratory technology; mechanical drafting and CAD/CADD; medical/clinical assistant.
Library Commonwealth Technical Institute at the Hiram G. Andrews Center Library.
Student Life *Campus security:* 24-hour patrols.
Costs (2004–05) *Tuition:* state resident $16,836 full-time.
Financial Aid Of all full-time matriculated undergraduates who enrolled in 2003, 20 Federal Work-Study jobs.
Admissions Contact Ms. Barbara Peterson, Director of Admissions, Commonwealth Technical Institute, 727 Goucher Street, Johnstown, PA 15905-3092. *Phone:* 814-255-8200 Ext. 8372. *Toll-free phone:* 800-762-4211 Ext. 8237.

COMMUNITY COLLEGE OF ALLEGHENY COUNTY
Pittsburgh, Pennsylvania

■ **County-supported** 2-year, founded 1966
■ **Calendar** semesters
■ **Degree** certificates, diplomas, and associate
■ **Urban** 242-acre campus
■ **Coed,** 18,964 undergraduate students, 41% full-time, 56% women, 44% men

Undergraduates 7,818 full-time, 11,146 part-time. Students come from 17 states and territories, 79 other countries, 2% are from out of state, 15% African American, 1% Asian American or Pacific Islander, 0.6% Hispanic American, 0.7% Native American, 0.9% international, 11% transferred in.
Freshmen *Admission:* 6,273 applied, 5,392 admitted, 2,383 enrolled.
Faculty *Total:* 2,180, 13% full-time. *Student/faculty ratio:* 4:1.
Majors Accounting technology and bookkeeping; administrative assistant and secretarial science; airline pilot and flight crew; applied horticulture; architectural drafting and CAD/CADD; art; athletic training; automotive engineering technology; aviation/airway management; banking and financial support services; biology/biological sciences; building/property maintenance and management; business administration and management; business automation/technology/data entry; business machine repair; carpentry; chemical technology; chemistry; child care provision; child development; civil drafting and CAD/CADD; civil engineering technology; clinical/medical laboratory technology; commercial and advertising art; communications technologies and support services related; community health services counseling; computer engineering technology; computer systems networking and telecommunications; computer technology/computer systems technology; construction engineering technology; construction trades related; corrections; cosmetology and personal grooming arts related; court reporting; criminal justice/police science; culinary arts; diagnostic medical sonography and ultrasound technology; dietitian assistant; drafting and design

technology; drafting/design engineering technologies related; dramatic/theatre arts; education (specific levels and methods) related; education (specific subject areas) related; electrical, electronic and communications engineering technology; electroneurodiagnostic/electroencephalographic technology; energy management and systems technology; engineering technologies related; English; entrepreneurship; environmental engineering technology; fire protection and safety technology; foodservice systems administration; foreign languages and literatures; general studies; greenhouse management; health and physical education; health information/medical records technology; health professions related; health unit coordinator/ward clerk; heating, air conditioning, ventilation and refrigeration maintenance technology; hotel/motel administration; housing and human environments related; human development and family studies related; humanities; human resources management; industrial technology; insurance; journalism; landscaping and groundskeeping; legal administrative assistant/secretary; legal assistant/paralegal; liberal arts and sciences/liberal studies; machine shop technology; management information systems; marketing/marketing management; mathematics; mechanical design technology; mechanical drafting and CAD/CADD; medical administrative assistant and medical secretary; medical/clinical assistant; medical radiologic technology; music; nuclear medical technology; nursing assistant/aide and patient care assistant; nursing (licensed practical/vocational nurse training); nursing (registered nurse training); occupational therapist assistant; office management; ornamental horticulture; perioperative/operating room and surgical nursing; pharmacy technician; physical therapist assistant; physics; plant nursery management; psychiatric/mental health services technology; psychology; quality control technology; real estate; respiratory care therapy; restaurant, culinary, and catering management; retailing; robotics technology; science technologies related; sheet metal technology; sign language interpretation and translation; social sciences; social work; sociology; solar energy technology; substance abuse/addiction counseling; surgical technology; therapeutic recreation; tourism promotion; turf and turfgrass management; visual and performing arts related; welding technology.
Academic Programs *Special study options:* academic remediation for entering students, advanced placement credit, distance learning, English as a second language, external degree program, honors programs, independent study, off-campus study, part-time degree program, services for LD students, study abroad, summer session for credit.
Library Community College of Allegheny County Library plus 4 others with 272,697 titles, 933 serial subscriptions, 13,165 audiovisual materials, an OPAC, a Web page.
Computers on Campus 3100 computers available on campus for general student use. A campuswide network can be accessed from off campus. Internet access, online (class) registration, at least one staffed computer lab available.
Student Life *Housing:* college housing not available. *Activities and Organizations:* drama/theater group, student-run newspaper, choral group, Phi Theta Kappa. *Campus security:* 24-hour emergency response devices and patrols, late-night transport/escort service. *Student services:* health clinic, personal/psychological counseling, women's center.
Athletics Member NJCAA. *Intercollegiate sports:* baseball M, basketball M/W, bowling M/W, golf M/W, ice hockey M, softball W, table tennis M/W, tennis M/W, volleyball W. *Intramural sports:* badminton M/W, basketball M/W, bowling M/W, cross-country running M/W, football M, golf M/W, lacrosse M, racquetball M/W, softball M/W, table tennis M/W, tennis M/W, volleyball M/W, weight lifting M/W.
Costs (2005–06) *Tuition:* area resident $2400 full-time, $80 per credit part-time; state resident $4800 full-time, $160 per credit part-time; nonresident $7200 full-time, $240 per credit part-time. *Required fees:* $305 full-time, $11 per credit part-time.
Applying *Options:* deferred entrance. *Recommended:* high school transcript. *Application deadline:* rolling (freshmen), rolling (transfers). *Notification:* continuous (freshmen).
Admissions Contact Admissions, Community College of Allegheny County, 800 Allegheny Avenue, Pittsburgh, PA 15233.

▶ **See page 486 for a narrative description.**

COMMUNITY COLLEGE OF BEAVER COUNTY
Monaca, Pennsylvania

■ **State-supported** 2-year, founded 1966
■ **Calendar** semesters
■ **Degree** certificates, diplomas, and associate
■ **Small-town** 75-acre campus with easy access to Pittsburgh
■ **Coed,** 2,500 undergraduate students

Undergraduates Students come from 7 states and territories, 2 other countries, 3% are from out of state.
Freshmen *Admission:* 920 applied, 920 admitted.
Faculty *Total:* 106, 45% full-time.
Majors Accounting; administrative assistant and secretarial science; aeronautics/aviation/aerospace science and technology; airline pilot and flight crew; air

Community College of Beaver County (continued)

traffic control; architectural engineering technology; avionics maintenance technology; biology/biological sciences; business administration and management; clinical/medical laboratory technology; communications technology; computer and information sciences; computer programming; computer typography and composition equipment operation; criminal justice/law enforcement administration; criminal justice/police science; culinary arts; data processing and data processing technology; drafting and design technology; education; electrical, electronic and communications engineering technology; industrial arts; information science/studies; liberal arts and sciences/liberal studies; marketing/marketing management; medical administrative assistant and medical secretary; nursing (licensed practical/vocational nurse training); nursing (registered nurse training); public relations/image management; telecommunications.

Academic Programs *Special study options:* academic remediation for entering students, adult/continuing education programs, advanced placement credit, cooperative education, distance learning, double majors, independent study, internships, off-campus study, part-time degree program, services for LD students, summer session for credit.

Library Community College of Beaver County Library with 52,857 titles, 300 serial subscriptions.

Computers on Campus A campuswide network can be accessed. Internet access, at least one staffed computer lab available.

Student Life *Housing:* college housing not available. *Campus security:* 24-hour emergency response devices and patrols, late-night transport/escort service.

Athletics Member NJCAA. *Intercollegiate sports:* baseball M, basketball M, softball W, tennis M/W, volleyball W. *Intramural sports:* basketball M, table tennis M/W, volleyball M/W.

Standardized Tests *Required:* ACT ASSET, ACT, or nursing exam depending on program (for placement).

Costs (2005–06) *Tuition:* area resident $2400 full-time, $80 per credit part-time; state resident $4800 full-time, $160 per credit part-time; nonresident $7200 full-time, $240 per credit part-time. *Required fees:* $525 full-time, $18 per credit part-time.

Financial Aid Of all full-time matriculated undergraduates who enrolled in 2003, 50 Federal Work-Study jobs (averaging $1400).

Applying *Options:* early admission. *Application fee:* $25. *Recommended:* high school transcript, interview. *Application deadline:* rolling (freshmen), rolling (transfers). *Notification:* continuous (freshmen).

Admissions Contact Mr. Michael Macon, Vice President for Enrollment Management, Community College of Beaver County, One Campus Drive, Monaca, PA 15061-2588. *Phone:* 724-775-8561 Ext. 151. *Toll-free phone:* 800-335-0222. *Fax:* 724-775-4055.

COMMUNITY COLLEGE OF PHILADELPHIA
Philadelphia, Pennsylvania

- **State and locally supported** 2-year, founded 1964
- **Calendar** semesters
- **Degree** certificates, diplomas, and associate
- **Urban** 14-acre campus
- **Coed,** 22,671 undergraduate students

Faculty *Total:* 1,207, 33% full-time.

Majors Accounting; administrative assistant and secretarial science; architectural engineering technology; art; automobile/automotive mechanics technology; biological and physical sciences; biomedical technology; business administration and management; business teacher education; chemical engineering; clinical/medical laboratory technology; communications technology; community organization and advocacy; computer engineering technology; computer science; construction engineering technology; consumer merchandising/retailing management; criminal justice/law enforcement administration; culinary arts; data processing and data processing technology; dental hygiene; dietetics; drafting and design technology; education; electrical, electronic and communications engineering technology; engineering; engineering technology; environmental engineering technology; fashion merchandising; finance; fire science; foods, nutrition, and wellness; gerontology; health information/medical records administration; hotel/motel administration; industrial radiologic technology; international business/trade/commerce; kindergarten/preschool education; legal administrative assistant/secretary; legal assistant/paralegal; liberal arts and sciences/liberal studies; library science; marketing/marketing management; medical administrative assistant and medical secretary; medical/clinical assistant; mental health/rehabilitation; music; nursing (registered nurse training); photography; pre-engineering; real estate; respiratory care therapy; sign language interpretation and translation; special products marketing.

Academic Programs *Special study options:* academic remediation for entering students, accelerated degree program, adult/continuing education programs,

English as a second language, honors programs, internships, part-time degree program, services for LD students, student-designed majors, summer session for credit.

Library 92,698 titles, 376 serial subscriptions, a Web page.

Computers on Campus 350 computers available on campus for general student use. At least one staffed computer lab available.

Student Life *Housing:* college housing not available. *Activities and Organizations:* drama/theater group, student-run newspaper, radio station, choral group. *Campus security:* 24-hour emergency response devices and patrols. *Student services:* health clinic, personal/psychological counseling, women's center.

Athletics *Intercollegiate sports:* baseball M, basketball M/W, cross-country running M/W, soccer M, softball W, tennis M/W, volleyball W. *Intramural sports:* basketball M/W, soccer M/W, tennis M/W, track and field M/W, volleyball M/W.

Costs (2005–06) *Tuition:* $104 per credit hour part-time; state resident $208 per credit hour part-time; nonresident $312 per credit hour part-time.

Applying *Options:* early admission, deferred entrance. *Application fee:* $20. *Required for some:* high school transcript. *Application deadline:* rolling (freshmen), rolling (transfers). *Notification:* continuous (freshmen).

Admissions Contact Daivd Norris, Director of Admissions, Community College of Philadelphia, 1700 Spring Garden Street, Philadelphia, PA 19130-3991. *Phone:* 215-751-8199. *E-mail:* admissions@ccp.edu.

CONSOLIDATED SCHOOL OF BUSINESS
Lancaster, Pennsylvania

Admissions Contact Ms. Millie Liberatore, Director of Admission, Consolidated School of Business, 2124 Ambassador Circle, Lancaster, PA 17603. *Phone:* 717-764-9550. *Toll-free phone:* 800-541-8298. *Fax:* 717-394-6213. *E-mail:* admissions@csb.edu.

CONSOLIDATED SCHOOL OF BUSINESS
York, Pennsylvania

- **Proprietary** 2-year, founded 1981
- **Calendar** continuous
- **Degree** diplomas and associate
- **Suburban** 6-acre campus with easy access to Baltimore
- **Coed, primarily women**

Faculty *Student/faculty ratio:* 15:1.

Standardized Tests *Required:* TABE (for placement).

Costs (2004–05) *Tuition:* $15,500 full-time. No tuition increase for student's term of enrollment.

Applying *Options:* common application. *Application fee:* $25. *Required:* high school transcript, interview.

Admissions Contact Ms. Millie Liberatore, Director of Admissions, Consolidated School of Business, 1605 Clugston Road, York, PA 17404. *Phone:* 717-764-9550. *Toll-free phone:* 800-520-0691. *Fax:* 717-764-9469. *E-mail:* admissions@csb.edu.

DEAN INSTITUTE OF TECHNOLOGY
Pittsburgh, Pennsylvania

- **Proprietary** 2-year, founded 1947
- **Calendar** quarters
- **Degree** diplomas and associate
- **Urban** 2-acre campus
- **Coed**

Faculty *Student/faculty ratio:* 10:1.

Student Life *Campus security:* 24-hour emergency response devices.

Applying *Options:* early admission, deferred entrance. *Application fee:* $50.

Admissions Contact Mr. Richard D. Ali, Admissions Director, Dean Institute of Technology, 1501 West Liberty Avenue, Pittsburgh, PA 15226-1103. *Phone:* 412-531-4433. *Fax:* 412-531-4435.

DELAWARE COUNTY COMMUNITY COLLEGE
Media, Pennsylvania

- **State and locally supported** 2-year, founded 1967
- **Calendar** semesters
- **Degree** certificates and associate
- **Suburban** 123-acre campus with easy access to Philadelphia
- **Endowment** $676,410
- **Coed,** 10,608 undergraduate students, 40% full-time, 56% women, 44% men

Undergraduates 4,263 full-time, 6,345 part-time. Students come from 13 states and territories, 46 other countries, 1% are from out of state, 15% African American, 4% Asian American or Pacific Islander, 2% Hispanic American, 0.2% Native American, 1% international.

Freshmen *Admission:* 3,840 applied, 3,840 admitted, 2,616 enrolled.

Faculty *Total:* 665, 22% full-time. *Student/faculty ratio:* 20:1.

Majors Accounting technology and bookkeeping; anthropology; architectural engineering technology; automobile/automotive mechanics technology; biological and physical sciences; biomedical technology; building/property maintenance and management; business administration and management; business administration, management and operations related; commercial and advertising art; communication and journalism related; communication/speech communication and rhetoric; computer and information sciences; computer programming (specific applications); computer systems networking and telecommunications; computer technology/computer systems technology; construction engineering technology; criminal justice/police science; drafting and design technology; education (multiple levels); electrical, electronic and communications engineering technology; energy management and systems technology; engineering; entrepreneurship; fire protection and safety technology; general studies; health unit management/ward supervision; heating, air conditioning and refrigeration technology; heating, air conditioning, ventilation and refrigeration maintenance technology; hotel/motel administration; information science/studies; journalism; legal assistant/paralegal; liberal arts and sciences/liberal studies; machine tool technology; management information systems; mechanical engineering/mechanical technology; mechanical engineering technologies related; medical/clinical assistant; nursing (registered nurse training); office management; psychology; respiratory care therapy; robotics technology; science technologies related; sociology; surgical technology; teacher assistant/aide; web page, digital/multimedia and information resources design.

Academic Programs *Special study options:* academic remediation for entering students, adult/continuing education programs, advanced placement credit, cooperative education, distance learning, double majors, English as a second language, independent study, internships, part-time degree program, services for LD students, student-designed majors, summer session for credit.

Library Delaware County Community College Library with 58,692 titles, 421 serial subscriptions, 3,251 audiovisual materials, an OPAC, a Web page.

Computers on Campus 1200 computers available on campus for general student use. A campuswide network can be accessed from off campus. Internet access, online (class) registration, at least one staffed computer lab available.

Student Life *Housing:* college housing not available. *Activities and Organizations:* drama/theater group, student-run newspaper, radio station, choral group, student government, student radio station, Phi Theta Kappa, Business Society, Student Pennsylvania State Education Association. *Campus security:* 24-hour emergency response devices and patrols, late-night transport/escort service. *Student services:* health clinic, personal/psychological counseling.

Athletics Member NJCAA. *Intercollegiate sports:* baseball M, basketball M/W, golf M/W, soccer M, softball W, tennis M/W, volleyball W. *Intramural sports:* basketball M/W, lacrosse M(c), volleyball W.

Costs (2005–06) *Tuition:* area resident $1968 full-time, $82 per credit part-time; state resident $3936 full-time, $164 per credit part-time; nonresident $5904 full-time, $246 per credit part-time. *Required fees:* $544 full-time, $21 per credit part-time, $20 per term part-time.

Financial Aid Of all full-time matriculated undergraduates who enrolled in 2003, 95 Federal Work-Study jobs (averaging $900).

Applying *Options:* early admission, deferred entrance. *Application fee:* $20. *Required:* high school transcript. *Application deadline:* rolling (freshmen), rolling (transfers). *Notification:* continuous (freshmen).

Admissions Contact Ms. Hope Lentine, Director of Admissions, Delaware County Community College, Admissions Office, 901 South Media Line Road, Media, PA 19063-1094. *Phone:* 610-359-5333. *Toll-free phone:* 800-872-1102 (in-state); 800-543-0146 (out-of-state). *Fax:* 610-359-5343. *E-mail:* admiss@dccc.edu.

DOUGLAS EDUCATION CENTER
Monessen, Pennsylvania

Admissions Contact Ms. Linda Gambattista, Director of Admissions, Douglas Education Center, 130 Seventh Street, Monessen, PA 15062. *Phone:* 724-684-3684. *Fax:* 724-684-7463. *E-mail:* dec@douglas-school.com.

DUBOIS BUSINESS COLLEGE
DuBois, Pennsylvania

Admissions Contact Ms. Lisa Stanford, Director of Admissions, DuBois Business College, 1 Beaver Drive, DuBois, PA 15801-2401. *Phone:* 814-371-6920. *Toll-free phone:* 800-692-6213.

DUFF'S BUSINESS INSTITUTE
Pittsburgh, Pennsylvania

Admissions Contact Ms. Lynn Fischer, Director of Admissions, Duff's Business Institute, 100 Forbes Avenue, Suite 1200, Pittsburgh, PA 15222. *Phone:* 412-261-4520 Ext. 212. *Toll-free phone:* 888-279-3314.

EDUCATION DIRECT CENTER FOR DEGREE STUDIES
Scranton, Pennsylvania

- **Proprietary** 2-year, founded 1975
- **Calendar** semesters
- **Degrees** associate (offers only external degree programs conducted through home study)
- **Coed**

Costs (2004–05) *Tuition:* $3765 per degree program part-time. Part-time tuition and fees vary according to program.

Applying *Required:* high school transcript.

Admissions Contact Ms. Connie Dempsey, Director of Compliance and Academic Affairs, Education Direct Center for Degree Studies, 925 Oak Street, Scranton, PA 18515. *Phone:* 570-342-7701 Ext. 4692. *Toll-free phone:* 800-233-4191.

ERIE BUSINESS CENTER, MAIN
Erie, Pennsylvania

- **Proprietary** 2-year, founded 1884
- **Calendar** trimesters
- **Degree** diplomas and associate
- **Urban** 1-acre campus with easy access to Cleveland and Buffalo
- **Coed**, 480 undergraduate students, 60% full-time, 65% women, 35% men

Undergraduates 289 full-time, 191 part-time. Students come from 3 states and territories, 5% are from out of state, 36% African American, 5% Hispanic American, 0.6% transferred in, 1% live on campus.

Freshmen *Admission:* 253 enrolled. *Average high school GPA:* 3.20.

Faculty *Total:* 56, 25% full-time. *Student/faculty ratio:* 10:1.

Majors Administrative assistant and secretarial science; business administration and management; computer programming related; computer science; computer systems networking and telecommunications; information science/studies; legal administrative assistant/secretary; legal assistant/paralegal; marketing/marketing management; medical administrative assistant and medical secretary; medical/clinical assistant; medical transcription; tourism and travel services management; web page, digital/multimedia and information resources design.

Academic Programs *Special study options:* adult/continuing education programs, advanced placement credit, independent study, part-time degree program, summer session for credit.

Library EBC Blackmer Library with 3,035 titles, 84 serial subscriptions, an OPAC.

Computers on Campus 114 computers available on campus for general student use. A campuswide network can be accessed from off campus. Internet access, at least one staffed computer lab available.

Student Life *Housing Options:* coed. Campus housing is leased by the school. *Activities and Organizations:* drama/theater group, Student Ambassadors, Spring trip, Fall Festival, Holiday Dinner Dance, Flag football. *Campus security:* 24-hour emergency response devices, security guard.

Standardized Tests *Required:* Wonderlic aptitude test (for admission).

Costs (2005–06) *Tuition:* $9000 full-time. *Required fees:* $800 full-time. *Payment plan:* installment. *Waivers:* employees or children of employees.

Financial Aid Of all full-time matriculated undergraduates who enrolled in 2003, 15 Federal Work-Study jobs (averaging $600).

Applying *Options:* common application, deferred entrance. *Application fee:* $25. *Required:* essay or personal statement, high school transcript, interview. *Application deadline:* rolling (freshmen), rolling (transfers). *Notification:* continuous (freshmen).

Admissions Contact Mrs. Donna B. Perino, Director, Erie Business Center, Main, 220 West Ninth Street, Erie, PA 16501-1392. *Phone:* 814-456-7504 Ext. 17. *Toll-free phone:* 800-352-3743. *Fax:* 814-456-4370. *E-mail:* admissions@eriebc.com.

ERIE BUSINESS CENTER SOUTH
New Castle, Pennsylvania

- **Proprietary** 2-year, founded 1894
- **Calendar** quarters

Erie Business Center South (continued)
- **Degree** diplomas and associate
- **Small-town** 1-acre campus with easy access to Pittsburgh
- **Coed, primarily women,** 100 undergraduate students, 100% full-time, 74% women, 26% men

Undergraduates 100 full-time. 8% African American. *Retention:* 80% of 2002 full-time freshmen returned.

Freshmen *Admission:* 45 applied, 39 admitted.

Faculty *Total:* 5, 80% full-time. *Student/faculty ratio:* 14:1.

Majors Accounting; administrative assistant and secretarial science; advertising; business administration and management; computer science; health information/medical records administration; legal administrative assistant/secretary; marketing/marketing management; medical administrative assistant and medical secretary; tourism and travel services management.

Academic Programs *Special study options:* academic remediation for entering students, adult/continuing education programs, internships, part-time degree program.

Library 1,725 titles, 20 serial subscriptions, 8 audiovisual materials.

Computers on Campus 60 computers available on campus for general student use. A campuswide network can be accessed. Internet access, at least one staffed computer lab available.

Student Life *Housing:* college housing not available. *Activities and Organizations:* student government, Business Club, Medical Club, Travel Club, Ambassadors Club. *Campus security:* 24-hour patrols. *Student services:* personal/psychological counseling.

Athletics *Intramural sports:* basketball M/W, bowling M/W, softball M/W, volleyball M/W.

Standardized Tests *Recommended:* SAT and SAT Subject Tests or ACT (for admission).

Costs (2004–05) *Tuition:* $4560 full-time, $456 per course part-time. Full-time tuition and fees vary according to course load. Part-time tuition and fees vary according to course load. *Required fees:* $300 full-time, $152 per credit part-time. *Payment plan:* installment. *Waivers:* employees or children of employees.

Applying *Options:* common application, electronic application, deferred entrance. *Application fee:* $25. *Required:* high school transcript. *Recommended:* interview. *Application deadline:* rolling (freshmen), rolling (transfers).

Admissions Contact Mr. Nick DeSalvo, Administrative Representative, Erie Business Center South, 170 Cascade Galleria, New Castle, PA 16101-3950. *Phone:* 724-658-9066. *Toll-free phone:* 800-722-6227. *E-mail:* hallr@eriebcs.com.

ERIE INSTITUTE OF TECHNOLOGY

Erie, Pennsylvania

- **Proprietary** 2-year
- **Calendar** 4 3-month terms
- **Degree** diplomas and associate
- **Suburban** campus
- **Coed**

Faculty *Student/faculty ratio:* 15:1.

Applying *Application fee:* $25.

Admissions Contact Mr. Ken Haas, Admissions Representative, Erie Institute of Technology, 5539 Peach Street, Erie, PA 16509. *Phone:* 814-868-9900. *Toll-free phone:* 866-868-3743.

HARCUM COLLEGE

Bryn Mawr, Pennsylvania

- **Independent** 2-year, founded 1915
- **Calendar** semesters
- **Degree** certificates and associate
- **Suburban** 12-acre campus with easy access to Philadelphia
- **Endowment** $9.0 million
- **Coed, primarily women,** 573 undergraduate students, 67% full-time, 88% women, 12% men

Undergraduates 385 full-time, 188 part-time. Students come from 8 states and territories, 6 other countries, 10% are from out of state, 20% African American, 3% Asian American or Pacific Islander, 3% Hispanic American, 0.3% Native American, 0.9% international, 21% transferred in, 23% live on campus. *Retention:* 90% of 2002 full-time freshmen returned.

Freshmen *Admission:* 302 applied, 256 admitted, 97 enrolled. *Average high school GPA:* 2.38.

Faculty *Total:* 108, 28% full-time, 11% with terminal degrees. *Student/faculty ratio:* 9:1.

Majors Allied health diagnostic, intervention, and treatment professions related; animal sciences; business administration and management; child development;

clinical/medical laboratory technology; consumer merchandising/retailing management; dental assisting; dental hygiene; fashion/apparel design; fashion merchandising; health science; information science/studies; interdisciplinary studies; interior design; kindergarten/preschool education; liberal arts and sciences/liberal studies; nursing (registered nurse training); occupational therapist assistant; physical therapist assistant; psychology; veterinary technology.

Academic Programs *Special study options:* academic remediation for entering students, adult/continuing education programs, advanced placement credit, distance learning, double majors, English as a second language, honors programs, independent study, internships, off-campus study, part-time degree program, services for LD students, summer session for credit.

Library Main Library plus 1 other with 39,000 titles, 300 serial subscriptions, 1,000 audiovisual materials.

Computers on Campus 65 computers available on campus for general student use. Internet access, at least one staffed computer lab available.

Student Life *Housing Options:* coed, women-only. Campus housing is university owned. Freshman campus housing is guaranteed. *Activities and Organizations:* student-run newspaper, choral group, OATS (Organization for Animal Tech Students), Student Association of Dental Hygienist of America, Ebony Club, Dental Assisting Club, FLA International Club. *Campus security:* 24-hour emergency response devices and patrols, controlled dormitory access. *Student services:* health clinic, personal/psychological counseling, women's center.

Athletics *Intramural sports:* badminton W, basketball W, soccer W, softball W, tennis W, volleyball W.

Standardized Tests *Required:* SAT or ACT (for admission).

Costs (2005–06) *Comprehensive fee:* $21,422 includes full-time tuition ($14,322), mandatory fees ($200), and room and board ($6900). Part-time tuition: $478 per credit.

Financial Aid Of all full-time matriculated undergraduates who enrolled in 2003, 161 Federal Work-Study jobs (averaging $1100).

Applying *Options:* common application, electronic application, early admission, deferred entrance. *Application fee:* $25. *Required:* essay or personal statement, high school transcript, letters of recommendation. *Recommended:* interview. *Application deadline:* rolling (freshmen), rolling (transfers). *Notification:* continuous (freshmen).

Admissions Contact Office of Enrollment Management, Harcum College, 750 Montgomery Avenue, Melville Hall, Bryn Mawr, PA 19010-3476. *Phone:* 610-526-6050. *Toll-free phone:* 800-345-2600. *Fax:* 610-526-6147. *E-mail:* enroll@harcum.edu.

▶ **See page 498 for a narrative description.**

HARRISBURG AREA COMMUNITY COLLEGE

Harrisburg, Pennsylvania

- **State and locally supported** 2-year, founded 1964
- **Calendar** semesters
- **Degree** certificates, diplomas, and associate
- **Urban** 212-acre campus
- **Endowment** $30.1 million
- **Coed,** 16,109 undergraduate students, 40% full-time, 65% women, 35% men

Undergraduates 6,413 full-time, 9,696 part-time. Students come from 14 states and territories, 8 other countries, 1% are from out of state, 10% African American, 3% Asian American or Pacific Islander, 6% Hispanic American, 0.3% Native American, 0.9% international, 30% transferred in.

Freshmen *Admission:* 5,068 applied, 5,024 admitted, 1,663 enrolled.

Faculty *Total:* 955, 27% full-time, 5% with terminal degrees. *Student/faculty ratio:* 23:1.

Majors Accounting; actuarial science; administrative assistant and secretarial science; agricultural business and management; architectural engineering technology; architecture; art; automobile/automotive mechanics technology; automotive engineering technology; banking and financial support services; biology/biological sciences; business administration and management; business/commerce; business, management, and marketing related; business teacher education; cardiovascular technology; chemistry; civil engineering technology; clinical/medical laboratory assistant; clinical/medical laboratory technology; commercial and advertising art; computer and information sciences; computer and information sciences and support services related; computer installation and repair technology; computer systems networking and telecommunications; construction engineering technology; consumer merchandising/retailing management; criminal justice/law enforcement administration; criminal justice/police science; culinary arts; dental hygiene; design and visual communications; dietetics; dramatic/theatre arts; education; electrical, electronic and communications engineering technology; elementary education; emergency medical technology (EMT paramedic); engineering; engineering technologies related; engineering technology; environmental studies; fire science; foods, nutrition, and wellness; general retailing/wholesaling; health information/medical records administration; heating, air conditioning and refrigeration technology; hospital and health care facilities administration; hotel/motel administration; human services; industrial mechanics and maintenance technology; information technology; institutional food workers; international relations and affairs; journalism; kindergarten/preschool education; legal administrative assistant/secretary; legal assistant/paralegal; liberal arts and sciences/liberal studies; management information systems; management science; marketing/marketing management; mass communication/media; mathematics; mechanical engineering/mechanical technology; medical office assistant; medical radiologic technology; music; nuclear medical technology; nursing (registered nurse training); opticianry; pharmacy technician; photography; physical education teaching and coaching; physical sciences; psychology; real estate; respiratory care therapy; respiratory therapy technician; science teacher education; social sciences; social work; tourism and travel services management; tourism and travel services marketing; web/multimedia management and webmaster.

Academic Programs *Special study options:* academic remediation for entering students, adult/continuing education programs, advanced placement credit, distance learning, double majors, English as a second language, honors programs, independent study, internships, part-time degree program, services for LD students, student-designed majors, study abroad, summer session for credit. *ROTC:* Army (b).

Library McCormick Library with 119,000 titles, 873 serial subscriptions, 12,733 audiovisual materials, an OPAC, a Web page.

Computers on Campus 974 computers available on campus for general student use. A campuswide network can be accessed from off campus. Internet access, online (class) registration, at least one staffed computer lab available.

Student Life *Housing:* college housing not available. *Activities and Organizations:* drama/theater group, student-run newspaper, radio station, Student Government Association, Phi Theta Kappa, African American Student Association, Mosiaco Club, Fourth Estate. *Campus security:* 24-hour emergency response devices and patrols, late-night transport/escort service. *Student services:* personal/psychological counseling.

Athletics *Intercollegiate sports:* basketball M/W, soccer M/W, swimming and diving M/W, tennis M/W, volleyball M/W. *Intramural sports:* basketball M/W, football M/W, golf M/W, racquetball M/W, skiing (downhill) M/W, soccer M, softball M/W, squash M/W, tennis M/W, volleyball W.

Standardized Tests *Required for some:* ACT (for placement).

Costs (2004–05) *Tuition:* area resident $2625 full-time, $76 per credit hour part-time; state resident $4950 full-time, $151 per credit hour part-time; nonresident $7275 full-time, $226 per credit hour part-time. *Required fees:* $360 full-time, $12 per credit hour part-time. *Waivers:* employees or children of employees.

Applying *Options:* electronic application, early admission. *Application fee:* $30. *Required:* high school transcript. *Application deadline:* rolling (freshmen), rolling (transfers).

Admissions Contact Mrs. Vanita Cowan, Administrative Clerk, Admissions, Harrisburg Area Community College, 1 HACC Drive, Harrisburg, PA 17110. *Phone:* 717-780-2406. *Toll-free phone:* 800-ABC-HACC. *E-mail:* admit@hacc.edu.

ICM SCHOOL OF BUSINESS & MEDICAL CAREERS
Pittsburgh, Pennsylvania

- **Proprietary** 2-year, founded 1963
- **Calendar** continuous
- **Degree** diplomas and associate
- **Urban** campus
- **Coed,** 1,095 undergraduate students, 97% full-time, 70% women, 30% men

Undergraduates 1,065 full-time, 30 part-time. Students come from 3 states and territories, 2% are from out of state, 48% African American, 0.3% Asian American or Pacific Islander, 0.7% Hispanic American, 0.5% Native American, 0.1% international.

Freshmen *Admission:* 496 applied, 310 admitted, 310 enrolled. *Average high school GPA:* 2.0.

Faculty *Total:* 65, 49% full-time, 8% with terminal degrees. *Student/faculty ratio:* 18:1.

Majors Accounting; administrative assistant and secretarial science; business administration and management; computer engineering technology; computer management; computer programming; computer science; criminal justice/law enforcement administration; fashion merchandising; legal administrative assistant/secretary; medical administrative assistant and medical secretary; medical/clinical assistant; occupational therapy; tourism and travel services management.

Academic Programs *Special study options:* academic remediation for entering students, advanced placement credit, cooperative education, independent study, internships, part-time degree program, summer session for credit.

Library ICM Learning Resource Center with 3,100 titles, 48 serial subscriptions.

Computers on Campus 120 computers available on campus for general student use. Internet access, at least one staffed computer lab available.

Student Life *Housing:* college housing not available. *Activities and Organizations:* Association of Information Technology Professionals, American Association of Information Professionals, Student Activities Association, American Association of Medical Assistants, Travel and Tourism Club. *Campus security:* 24-hour emergency response devices, evening security personnel.

Standardized Tests *Required:* Wonderlic aptitude test, CPAt (for admission). *Required for some:* SAT and SAT Subject Tests or ACT (for admission).

Costs (2005–06) *Tuition:* $24,400 full-time. *Required fees:* $130 full-time.

Applying *Options:* common application. *Application fee:* $30. *Required:* essay or personal statement, high school transcript, interview. *Application deadline:* rolling (freshmen), rolling (transfers). *Notification:* continuous (freshmen).

Admissions Contact Mrs. Marcia Rosenberg, Director of Admissions, ICM School of Business & Medical Careers, 10 Wood Street, Pittsburgh, PA 15222. *Phone:* 412-261-2647 Ext. 229. *Toll-free phone:* 800-441-5222. *E-mail:* icm@citynet.com.

INFORMATION COMPUTER SYSTEMS INSTITUTE
Allentown, Pennsylvania

Admissions Contact Bill Barber, Director, Information Computer Systems Institute, 2201 Hangar Place, Allentown, PA 18103-9504. *Phone:* 610-264-8029.

INTERNATIONAL ACADEMY OF DESIGN & TECHNOLOGY
Pittsburgh, Pennsylvania

Admissions Contact Ms. Debbie Love, Chief Admissions Officer, International Academy of Design & Technology, 555 Grant Street, Pittsburgh, PA 15219. *Phone:* 412-391-4197. *Toll-free phone:* 800-447-8324.

JNA INSTITUTE OF CULINARY ARTS
Philadelphia, Pennsylvania

Admissions Contact 1212 South Broad Street, Philadelphia, PA 19146.

JOHNSON COLLEGE
Scranton, Pennsylvania

Admissions Contact Ms. Melissa Turlip, Acting Director of Enrollment Management, Johnson College, 3427 North Main Avenue, Scranton, PA 18508. *Phone:* 570-342-6404 Ext. 122. *Toll-free phone:* 800-2-WE-WORK Ext. 125. *Fax:* 570-348-2181. *E-mail:* admit@johnson.edu.

▶ See page 506 for a narrative description.

KATHARINE GIBBS SCHOOL
Norristown, Pennsylvania

Admissions Contact Mr. Joseph Carretta, President, Katharine Gibbs School, 2501 Monroe Boulevard, Norristown, PA 19403. *Phone:* 610-676-0500. *Toll-free phone:* 866-PAGIBBS.

KEYSTONE COLLEGE
La Plume, Pennsylvania

- **Independent** primarily 2-year, founded 1868
- **Calendar** semesters
- **Degrees** certificates, associate, bachelor's, and postbachelor's certificates
- **Rural** 270-acre campus
- **Endowment** $8.9 million
- **Coed,** 1,658 undergraduate students, 74% full-time, 62% women, 38% men

Undergraduates 1,231 full-time, 427 part-time. Students come from 12 states and territories, 7 other countries, 6% are from out of state, 4% African American, 0.6% Asian American or Pacific Islander, 2% Hispanic American, 0.5% Native American, 0.7% international, 10% transferred in, 24% live on campus. *Retention:* 58% of 2002 full-time freshmen returned.

Freshmen *Admission:* 870 applied, 806 admitted, 448 enrolled. *Test scores:* SAT verbal scores over 500: 21%; SAT math scores over 500: 16%; ACT scores over 18: 45%; SAT verbal scores over 600: 3%; SAT math scores over 600: 2%.

Faculty *Total:* 206, 30% full-time, 13% with terminal degrees. *Student/faculty ratio:* 12:1.

Majors Accounting; accounting and business/management; accounting related; art; art teacher education; biological and physical sciences; biology/biological sciences; business administration and management; business administration,

Keystone College (continued)

management and operations related; business/commerce; communication and journalism related; communication and media related; communication/speech communication and rhetoric; computer/information technology services administration related; computer programming; computer programming (specific applications); computer systems networking and telecommunications; criminal justice/law enforcement administration; criminal justice/safety; culinary arts; culinary arts related; data processing and data processing technology; diagnostic medical sonography and ultrasound technology; drawing; early childhood education; education; education (K-12); elementary education; environmental studies; family and community services; fine/studio arts; food preparation; forensic science and technology; forestry; forestry technology; graphic design; hotel/motel administration; human resources management; illustration; information technology; journalism; kindergarten/preschool education; landscape architecture; liberal arts and sciences and humanities related; liberal arts and sciences/liberal studies; medical radiologic technology; natural resources management; occupational therapy; painting; parks, recreation and leisure facilities management; photography; physical therapy; physician assistant; pre-medical studies; pre-nursing studies; pre-pharmacy studies; pre-veterinary studies; printmaking; public relations, advertising, and applied communication related; radio and television; radiologic technology/science; radio, television, and digital communication related; restaurant, culinary, and catering management; restaurant/food services management; sculpture; sport and fitness administration; system administration; therapeutic recreation; water, wetlands, and marine resources management; wildlife and wildlands science and management; wildlife biology.

Academic Programs *Special study options:* academic remediation for entering students, adult/continuing education programs, advanced placement credit, cooperative education, distance learning, external degree program, freshman honors college, honors programs, independent study, internships, part-time degree program, services for LD students, student-designed majors, summer session for credit. *ROTC:* Army (c), Air Force (c).

Library Miller Library with 65,000 titles, 309 serial subscriptions, 10,000 audiovisual materials, an OPAC, a Web page.

Computers on Campus 120 computers available on campus for general student use. A campuswide network can be accessed from student residence rooms and from off campus that provides access to wireless campus. Internet access, online (class) registration, at least one staffed computer lab available. Computer purchase or lease plan available.

Student Life *Housing Options:* coed, women-only, disabled students. Campus housing is university owned. Freshman campus housing is guaranteed. *Activities and Organizations:* drama/theater group, student-run newspaper, radio station, choral group, Campus Activity Board, Student Senate, Art Society, Inter-Hall Council, Commuter Council. *Campus security:* 24-hour emergency response devices and patrols, student patrols, late-night transport/escort service, controlled dormitory access. *Student services:* health clinic, personal/psychological counseling, women's center.

Athletics Member NCAA. *Intercollegiate sports:* baseball M, basketball M/W, cross-country running M/W, golf M, soccer M/W, softball W, tennis M/W, track and field M/W, volleyball W. *Intramural sports:* basketball M/W, cheerleading M(c)/W(c), equestrian sports M(c)/W(c), football M/W, lacrosse M/W, skiing (downhill) M(c)/W(c), soccer M/W, softball M/W, table tennis M/W, tennis M/W, volleyball M/W, weight lifting M/W.

Standardized Tests *Required for some:* SAT or ACT (for admission). *Recommended:* SAT or ACT (for admission).

Costs (2005–06) *Comprehensive fee:* $22,810 includes full-time tuition ($14,100), mandatory fees ($920), and room and board ($7790). Part-time tuition: $325 per credit. *Required fees:* $110 per term part-time. *Room and board:* Room and board charges vary according to board plan and housing facility. *Payment plan:* installment. *Waivers:* senior citizens and employees or children of employees.

Financial Aid Of all full-time matriculated undergraduates who enrolled in 2003, 125 Federal Work-Study jobs (averaging $1000). 100 state and other part-time jobs (averaging $1000).

Applying *Options:* common application, electronic application, early admission, deferred entrance. *Application fee:* $25. *Required:* high school transcript, 1 letter of recommendation. *Required for some:* interview, art portfolio. *Recommended:* essay or personal statement, minimum 2.0 GPA, interview. *Application deadlines:* 7/1 (freshmen), 8/1 (transfers).

Admissions Contact Ms. Sarah Keating, Director of Admissions, Keystone College, One College Green, La Plume, PA 18440-1099. *Phone:* 570-945-8112. *Toll-free phone:* 877-4COLLEGE Ext. 1. *Fax:* 570-945-7916. *E-mail:* admissions@keystone.edu.

▶ **See page 508 for a narrative description.**

LACKAWANNA COLLEGE
Scranton, Pennsylvania

- **Independent** 2-year, founded 1894
- **Calendar** semesters
- **Degree** certificates, diplomas, and associate

- **Urban** 4-acre campus
- **Endowment** $1.2 million
- **Coed,** 1,197 undergraduate students, 63% full-time, 53% women, 47% men

Undergraduates 758 full-time, 439 part-time. Students come from 20 states and territories, 3% are from out of state, 11% African American, 0.5% Asian American or Pacific Islander, 2% Hispanic American, 0.3% Native American, 11% transferred in, 12% live on campus.

Freshmen *Admission:* 626 admitted, 362 enrolled.

Faculty *Total:* 56, 36% full-time, 11% with terminal degrees. *Student/faculty ratio:* 13:1.

Majors Accounting technology and bookkeeping; administrative assistant and secretarial science; banking and financial support services; biotechnology; business administration and management; business/commerce; communication/speech communication and rhetoric; communications technology; computer and information sciences; criminal justice/safety; diagnostic medical sonography and ultrasound technology; early childhood education; education; emergency medical technology (EMT paramedic); general studies; humanities; industrial technology; legal assistant/paralegal; liberal arts and sciences/liberal studies; management information systems; mass communication/media; medical administrative assistant and medical secretary; mental health/rehabilitation.

Academic Programs *Special study options:* academic remediation for entering students, adult/continuing education programs, cooperative education, double majors, English as a second language, internships, part-time degree program, services for LD students, summer session for credit. *ROTC:* Army (c), Air Force (c).

Library Seeley Memorial Library with 15,276 titles, 58 serial subscriptions, 491 audiovisual materials, an OPAC, a Web page.

Computers on Campus 200 computers available on campus for general student use. A campuswide network can be accessed from student residence rooms and from off campus. Internet access, at least one staffed computer lab available.

Student Life *Housing:* on-campus residence required through sophomore year. *Options:* men-only. Campus housing is university owned. *Activities and Organizations:* drama/theater group, student-run newspaper, student government, Student/Alumni Association, Diversity Club, student newspaper, Phi Beta Lambda. *Campus security:* 24-hour emergency response devices, late-night transport/escort service, patrols by college liaison staff. *Student services:* personal/psychological counseling.

Athletics Member NJCAA. *Intercollegiate sports:* baseball M(s), basketball M(s)/W(s), football M(s), golf M(s)/W(s), softball W(s), volleyball W(s). *Intramural sports:* weight lifting M/W.

Standardized Tests *Recommended:* SAT (for admission), ACT (for admission), SAT or ACT (for admission).

Costs (2005–06) *Comprehensive fee:* $15,500 includes full-time tuition ($9200), mandatory fees ($100), and room and board ($6200). Part-time tuition: $310 per credit. *Required fees:* $80 per term part-time. *Payment plan:* installment. *Waivers:* employees or children of employees.

Financial Aid Of all full-time matriculated undergraduates who enrolled in 2003, 78 Federal Work-Study jobs (averaging $1450).

Applying *Options:* electronic application, early admission, deferred entrance. *Application fee:* $30. *Required:* high school transcript, interview. *Application deadline:* rolling (freshmen), rolling (transfers).

Admissions Contact Mr. Mark Duda, Director of Admissions, Lackawanna College, 501 Vine Street, Scranton, PA 18509. *Phone:* 570-961-7852. *Toll-free phone:* 877-346-3552. *Fax:* 570-961-7853. *E-mail:* dudam@lackawanna.edu.

LANSDALE SCHOOL OF BUSINESS
North Wales, Pennsylvania

Admissions Contact Ms. Marianne H. Johnson, Director of Admissions, Lansdale School of Business, 201 Church Road, North Wales, PA 19454-4148. *Phone:* 215-699-5700 Ext. 112. *Fax:* 215-699-8770.

LAUREL BUSINESS INSTITUTE
Uniontown, Pennsylvania

- **Proprietary** 2-year, founded 1985
- **Calendar** trimesters
- **Degree** certificates, diplomas, and associate
- **Small-town** 10-acre campus with easy access to Pittsburgh
- **Coed,** 378 undergraduate students, 97% full-time, 71% women, 29% men

Undergraduates 365 full-time, 13 part-time. Students come from 2 states and territories, 9% African American, 0.3% Hispanic American, 0.3% international. *Retention:* 77% of 2002 full-time freshmen returned.

Freshmen *Admission:* 328 applied, 217 admitted, 131 enrolled. *Average high school GPA:* 2.75.

Faculty *Total:* 30, 70% full-time, 100% with terminal degrees. *Student/faculty ratio:* 12:1.

Majors Accounting; administrative assistant and secretarial science; banking and financial support services; business administration and management; business automation/technology/data entry; child guidance; computer and information sciences related; computer and information systems security; computer/information technology services administration related; computer management; computer software and media applications related; computer systems networking and telecommunications; computer/technical support; consumer merchandising/retailing management; data entry/microcomputer applications; data entry/microcomputer applications related; executive assistant/executive secretary; home health aide/home attendant; information technology; insurance; legal administrative assistant/secretary; medical administrative assistant and medical secretary; medical/clinical assistant; medical transcription; office occupations and clerical services; system administration; web page, digital/multimedia and information resources design; word processing.

Academic Programs *Special study options:* academic remediation for entering students, adult/continuing education programs, advanced placement credit, cooperative education, double majors, freshman honors college, honors programs, internships, part-time degree program, services for LD students.

Computers on Campus 75 computers available on campus for general student use. A campuswide network can be accessed from off campus. Internet access, at least one staffed computer lab available.

Student Life *Housing:* college housing not available. *Activities and Organizations:* student-run newspaper. *Student services:* personal/psychological counseling.

Standardized Tests *Required:* Wonderlic aptitude test (for placement).

Costs (2005–06) *Tuition:* $9225 full-time, $205 per credit part-time. *Required fees:* $1996 full-time, $359 per term part-time.

Financial Aid Of all full-time matriculated undergraduates who enrolled in 2003, 60 Federal Work-Study jobs (averaging $710).

Applying *Options:* common application, electronic application, deferred entrance. *Application fee:* $25. *Required:* high school transcript, interview. *Application deadline:* rolling (freshmen).

Admissions Contact Ms. Lisa Dolan, Enrollment Supervisor, Laurel Business Institute, 11-15 Penn Street, PO Box 877, Uniontown, PA 15401. *Phone:* 724-439-4900 Ext. 158. *Fax:* 724-439-3607. *E-mail:* lbi@laurelbusiness.net.

LEHIGH CARBON COMMUNITY COLLEGE
Schnecksville, Pennsylvania

- **State and locally supported** 2-year, founded 1967
- **Calendar** semesters
- **Degree** certificates, diplomas, and associate
- **Suburban** 153-acre campus with easy access to Philadelphia
- **Endowment** $841,000
- **Coed,** 6,674 undergraduate students, 39% full-time, 61% women, 39% men

Undergraduates 2,607 full-time, 4,067 part-time. Students come from 19 states and territories, 9 other countries, 1% are from out of state, 5% African American, 2% Asian American or Pacific Islander, 8% Hispanic American, 0.1% Native American, 0.1% international, 33% transferred in.

Freshmen *Admission:* 2,791 applied, 2,780 admitted, 2,708 enrolled.

Faculty *Total:* 488, 22% full-time, 3% with terminal degrees. *Student/faculty ratio:* 14:1.

Majors Accounting; accounting technology and bookkeeping; administrative assistant and secretarial science; adult development and aging; airline pilot and flight crew; art; aviation/airway management; avionics maintenance technology; biology/biological sciences; biomedical technology; biotechnology; business administration and management; chemical technology; child care provision; clinical/medical laboratory technology; commercial and advertising art; communication/speech communication and rhetoric; computer engineering technology; computer technology/computer systems technology; construction engineering technology; corrections; criminal justice/law enforcement administration; criminal justice/police science; culinary arts; digital communication and media/multimedia; drafting and design technology; education; electrical, electronic and communications engineering technology; electrical, electronics and communications engineering; engineering; executive assistant/executive secretary; forensic science and technology; general studies; health information/medical records technology; heating, air conditioning, ventilation and refrigeration maintenance technology; horticultural science; hotel/motel administration; humanities; human resources management; industrial technology; information science/studies; interior architecture; kindergarten/preschool education; legal administrative assistant/secretary; legal assistant/paralegal; liberal arts and sciences/liberal studies; lineworker; logistics and materials management; manufacturing technology; mathematics; mechanical engineering; mechanical engineering/mechanical technology; medical/clinical assistant; medical transcription; nursing (licensed practical/vocational nurse training); nursing (registered nurse training); occupational therapist assistant; office occupations and clerical services; operations management; physical sciences; physical therapist assistant; real estate; respiratory care therapy; restaurant/food services management; social sciences; social work; special education; sport and fitness administration; tourism and travel services marketing; tourism promotion; veterinary/animal health technology.

Academic Programs *Special study options:* academic remediation for entering students, adult/continuing education programs, advanced placement credit, cooperative education, distance learning, English as a second language, independent study, internships, part-time degree program, services for LD students, summer session for credit. *ROTC:* Army (c).

Library Learning Resource Center with 99,734 titles, 510 serial subscriptions, 6,016 audiovisual materials, an OPAC, a Web page.

Computers on Campus 830 computers available on campus for general student use. At least one staffed computer lab available.

Student Life *Housing:* college housing not available. *Activities and Organizations:* student-run newspaper, radio station, Phi Theta Kappa, STEP Student Association, student radio station, student government, College Activity Board. *Campus security:* 24-hour emergency response devices and patrols, student patrols, late-night transport/escort service. *Student services:* personal/psychological counseling.

Athletics Member NJCAA. *Intercollegiate sports:* baseball M/W, basketball M/W, golf M/W, soccer M, softball W, volleyball W. *Intramural sports:* archery M/W, badminton M/W, baseball M, basketball M/W, bowling M/W, field hockey W, football M/W, golf M/W, racquetball M/W, skiing (downhill) M/W, soccer M/W, softball M/W, swimming and diving M/W, table tennis M/W, tennis M/W, track and field M, volleyball M/W, weight lifting M/W.

Standardized Tests *Required for some:* ACT or ACT COMPASS.

Costs (2005–06) *Tuition:* area resident $2700 full-time, $76 per credit part-time; state resident $5250 full-time, $152 per credit part-time; nonresident $7800 full-time, $228 per credit part-time. *Required fees:* $420 full-time, $14 per credit hour part-time.

Applying *Application fee:* $25. *Required for some:* essay or personal statement, high school transcript, interview. *Application deadline:* rolling (freshmen), rolling (transfers). *Notification:* continuous (freshmen).

Admissions Contact Mr. Jack Mosser, Associate Dean of Enrollment, Lehigh Carbon Community College, 4525 Education Park Drive, Schnecksville, PA 18078-2598. *Phone:* 610-799-1575. *Fax:* 610-799-1527. *E-mail:* tellme@lccc.edu.

LEHIGH VALLEY COLLEGE
Center Valley, Pennsylvania

- **Proprietary** 2-year, founded 1869, part of Career Education Corporation
- **Calendar** quarters
- **Degree** diplomas and associate
- **Urban** 30-acre campus with easy access to Philadelphia
- **Coed**

Faculty *Student/faculty ratio:* 26:1.

Student Life *Campus security:* evening security guard.

Standardized Tests *Required:* ACCUPLACER (for admission).

Costs (2004–05) *Tuition:* $25,200 full-time. Full-time tuition and fees vary according to class time, course load, and program. Part-time tuition and fees vary according to class time and course load. No tuition increase for student's term of enrollment. *Required fees:* $600 full-time. *Room only:* Room and board charges vary according to housing facility.

Financial Aid Of all full-time matriculated undergraduates who enrolled in 2003, 30 Federal Work-Study jobs (averaging $2500).

Applying *Options:* common application, electronic application, deferred entrance. *Required:* high school transcript. *Recommended:* interview.

Admissions Contact Mr. Michael Venier, Vice President Admissions, Lehigh Valley College, 2809 East Saucon Valley Road, Center Valley, PA 18034. *Phone:* 610-791-5100. *Toll-free phone:* 800-227-9109. *Fax:* 610-791-7810.

▶ See page 512 for a narrative description.

LINCOLN TECHNICAL INSTITUTE
Allentown, Pennsylvania

Admissions Contact Admissions Office, Lincoln Technical Institute, 5151 Tilghman Street, Allentown, PA 18104-3298. *Phone:* 610-398-5301.

LINCOLN TECHNICAL INSTITUTE
Philadelphia, Pennsylvania

Admissions Contact Mr. James Kuntz, Executive Director, Lincoln Technical Institute, 9191 Torresdale Avenue, Philadelphia, PA 19136-1595. *Phone:* 215-335-0800. *Toll-free phone:* 800-238-8381.

LUZERNE COUNTY COMMUNITY COLLEGE
Nanticoke, Pennsylvania

- **County-supported** 2-year, founded 1966
- **Calendar** semesters

Luzerne County Community College (continued)
- **Degree** certificates, diplomas, and associate
- **Suburban** 122-acre campus with easy access to Philadelphia
- **Coed**

Faculty *Student/faculty ratio:* 19:1.

Student Life *Campus security:* 24-hour patrols.

Athletics Member NJCAA.

Standardized Tests *Recommended:* ACCUPLACER.

Costs (2004–05) *Tuition:* area resident $2190 full-time, $73 per credit part-time; state resident $4380 full-time, $146 per credit part-time; nonresident $6570 full-time, $219 per credit part-time. *Required fees:* $480 full-time, $16 per credit part-time.

Applying *Options:* early admission, deferred entrance. *Application fee:* $40. *Recommended:* high school transcript.

Admissions Contact Mr. Francis Curry, Director of Admissions, Luzerne County Community College, 1333 South Prospect Street, Nanticoke, PA 18634. *Phone:* 570-740-0200 Ext. 343. *Toll-free phone:* 800-377-5222 Ext. 337. *Fax:* 570-740-0238. *E-mail:* admissions@luzerne.edu.

MANOR COLLEGE
Jenkintown, Pennsylvania

Manor College, located in Jenkintown, a suburb of Philadelphia, offers associate degree and transfer programs in the allied health, business, and liberal arts fields. Areas of study include accounting, allied health, business administration, computer science, dental hygiene, early child care/human services, expanded functions dental assisting, human resource management, marketing management, paralegal studies, psychology, and veterinary technology.

Admissions Contact Ms. I. Jerry Czenstuch, Vice President of Enrollment Management, Manor College, 700 Fox Chase Road, Jenkintown, PA 19046. *Phone:* 215-884-2216. *Fax:* 215-576-6564. *E-mail:* ftadmiss@manor.edu.

▶ See page 518 for a narrative description.

McCANN SCHOOL OF BUSINESS & TECHNOLOGY
Pottsville, Pennsylvania

Admissions Contact Ms. Rachel M. Schoffstall, Director, Pottsville Campus, McCann School of Business & Technology, 2650 Woodglen Road, Pottsville, PA 17901. *Phone:* 570-622-7622. *Toll-free phone:* 888-622-2664. *Fax:* 570-622-7770.

MEDIAN SCHOOL OF ALLIED HEALTH CAREERS
Pittsburgh, Pennsylvania

Admissions Contact Ms. Kris Jackson, Admission Coordinator, Median School of Allied Health Careers, 125 7th Street, Pittsburgh, PA 15222-3400. *Phone:* 800-570-0693. *Toll-free phone:* 800-570-0693. *Fax:* 412-232-4348. *E-mail:* median@sgi.net.

METROPOLITAN CAREER CENTER
Philadelphia, Pennsylvania

Admissions Contact Mr. Ken Huselton, Director of Student Services, Metropolitan Career Center, 100 South Broad Street, Philadelphia, PA 19110. *Phone:* 215-843-6615.

MONTGOMERY COUNTY COMMUNITY COLLEGE
Blue Bell, Pennsylvania

- **County-supported** 2-year, founded 1964
- **Calendar** semesters
- **Degree** certificates and associate
- **Suburban** 186-acre campus with easy access to Philadelphia
- **Coed,** 10,842 undergraduate students, 43% full-time, 59% women, 41% men

Undergraduates 4,679 full-time, 6,163 part-time. Students come from 10 states and territories, 41 other countries, 0.2% are from out of state, 9% African American, 5% Asian American or Pacific Islander, 2% Hispanic American, 0.3% Native American, 1% international.

Freshmen *Admission:* 4,425 applied, 4,425 admitted, 3,752 enrolled.

Faculty *Total:* 644, 25% full-time. *Student/faculty ratio:* 23:1.

Majors Accounting; accounting technology and bookkeeping; administrative assistant and secretarial science; architectural drafting and CAD/CADD; art; automotive engineering technology; baking and pastry arts; biology/biological sciences; biotechnology; business administration and management; business/commerce; business/corporate communications; child care and support services management; clinical/medical laboratory technology; commercial and advertising art; communication/speech communication and rhetoric; communications technologies and support services related; computer and information sciences; computer engineering technology; computer programming; computer systems networking and telecommunications; criminal justice/police science; culinary arts; dental hygiene; electrical, electronic and communications engineering technology; electromechanical technology; elementary education; engineering science; engineering technologies related; fire protection and safety technology; food sales operations; hospitality and recreation marketing; hotel/motel services marketing operations; humanities; information science/studies; liberal arts and sciences/liberal studies; management information systems and services related; mathematics; mechanical drafting and CAD/CADD; mechanical engineering/mechanical technology; medical radiologic technology; nursing (registered nurse training); physical education teaching and coaching; physical sciences; psychiatric/mental health services technology; radiologic technology/science; real estate; respiratory care therapy; sales, distribution and marketing; secondary education; social sciences; surgical technology; teacher assistant/aide.

Academic Programs *Special study options:* academic remediation for entering students, adult/continuing education programs, advanced placement credit, distance learning, English as a second language, honors programs, independent study, internships, part-time degree program, services for LD students, student-designed majors, study abroad, summer session for credit.

Library The Brendlinger Library plus 1 other with 201,174 titles, 550 serial subscriptions, 19,450 audiovisual materials, an OPAC, a Web page.

Computers on Campus 800 computers available on campus for general student use. A campuswide network can be accessed from off campus. Internet access, online (class) registration, at least one staffed computer lab available.

Student Life *Housing:* college housing not available. *Activities and Organizations:* drama/theater group, student-run newspaper, radio and television station, choral group, student government, Meridians Non-traditional Age Club, student radio station. *Campus security:* 24-hour emergency response devices and patrols, late-night transport/escort service. *Student services:* health clinic, personal/psychological counseling.

Athletics *Intramural sports:* badminton M/W, basketball M/W, bowling M/W, cross-country running M/W, football M, racquetball M/W, soccer M/W, softball M/W, table tennis M/W, tennis M/W, volleyball M/W, weight lifting M/W.

Standardized Tests *Recommended:* SAT or ACT (for placement).

Costs (2005–06) *Tuition:* area resident $2716 full-time, $83 per credit part-time; state resident $5348 full-time, $191 per credit part-time; nonresident $7980 full-time, $285 per credit part-time. Full-time tuition and fees vary according to course load. Part-time tuition and fees vary according to course load. *Required fees:* $390 full-time, $14 per credit part-time. *Payment plan:* deferred payment. *Waivers:* senior citizens and employees or children of employees.

Financial Aid Of all full-time matriculated undergraduates who enrolled in 2003, 60 Federal Work-Study jobs (averaging $2500).

Applying *Options:* electronic application, early admission, deferred entrance. *Application fee:* $25. *Required for some:* high school transcript, interview. *Application deadline:* 5/1 (freshmen), rolling (transfers). *Notification:* continuous (freshmen).

Admissions Contact Mr. Joe Rodriguez, Director of Admissions and Records, Montgomery County Community College, Office of Admissions and Records, Blue Bell, PA 19422. *Phone:* 215-641-6551. *Fax:* 215-619-7188. *E-mail:* admrec@admin.mc3.edu.

NEW CASTLE SCHOOL OF TRADES
Pulaski, Pennsylvania

- **Independent** 2-year, founded 1945, part of Educational Enterprises Incorporated
- **Calendar** quarters
- **Degree** diplomas and associate
- **Rural** 20-acre campus with easy access to Youngstown
- **Coed, primarily men**
- 97% of applicants were admitted

Faculty *Student/faculty ratio:* 18:1.

Student Life *Campus security:* 24-hour emergency response devices.

Standardized Tests *Required:* Wonderlic aptitude test (for admission).

Costs (2004–05) *Tuition:* $12,999 full-time, $2200 per term part-time. No tuition increase for student's term of enrollment. *Required fees:* $9 per hour part-time. *Payment plans:* tuition prepayment, installment, deferred payment.

Applying *Application fee:* $25. *Required:* high school transcript, interview. *Required for some:* essay or personal statement, letters of recommendation.

Admissions Contact Mr. James Catheline, Admissions Director, New Castle School of Trades, RD 1, Route 422, Pulaski, PA 16143. *Phone:* 800-837-8299 Ext. 12. *Toll-free phone:* 800-837-8299 Ext. 12. *Fax:* 724-964-8777.

NEWPORT BUSINESS INSTITUTE
Lower Burrell, Pennsylvania

- **Proprietary** 2-year, founded 1895
- **Calendar** quarters
- **Degree** certificates, diplomas, and associate
- **Small-town** 4-acre campus with easy access to Pittsburgh
- **Coed**

Faculty *Student/faculty ratio:* 14:1.

Student Life *Campus security:* security system.

Costs (2004–05) *Tuition:* $6900 full-time, $580 per course part-time. Full-time tuition and fees vary according to program. *Required fees:* $1400 full-time.

Applying *Options:* common application, early admission. *Application fee:* $25. *Required:* high school transcript. *Recommended:* interview.

Admissions Contact Mr. William Bates, Admissions Coordinator, Newport Business Institute, Lower Burrell, PA 15068. *Phone:* 724-339-7542. *Toll-free phone:* 800-752-7695. *Fax:* 724-339-2950.

NEWPORT BUSINESS INSTITUTE
Williamsport, Pennsylvania

- **Proprietary** 2-year, founded 1955
- **Calendar** quarters
- **Degree** associate
- **Small-town** campus
- **Coed, primarily women,** 107 undergraduate students, 99% full-time, 92% women, 8% men

Undergraduates 106 full-time, 1 part-time. Students come from 1 other state, 7% African American, 0.9% Asian American or Pacific Islander, 15% transferred in. *Retention:* 88% of 2002 full-time freshmen returned.

Freshmen *Admission:* 30 applied, 30 admitted, 30 enrolled.

Faculty *Total:* 7, 86% full-time. *Student/faculty ratio:* 20:1.

Majors Administrative assistant and secretarial science; business administration and management; legal administrative assistant/secretary; medical administrative assistant and medical secretary.

Academic Programs *Special study options:* internships, part-time degree program, summer session for credit.

Computers on Campus 64 computers available on campus for general student use. Internet access, at least one staffed computer lab available.

Student Life *Housing:* college housing not available. *Activities and Organizations:* Student Council.

Costs (2005–06) *Tuition:* $8400 full-time, $700 per course part-time. *Required fees:* $400 full-time. *Waivers:* employees or children of employees.

Financial Aid *Financial aid deadline:* 8/1.

Applying *Options:* deferred entrance. *Application fee:* $25. *Required:* high school transcript. *Application deadline:* rolling (freshmen), rolling (transfers).

Admissions Contact Mr. David Andrus, Admissions Representative, Newport Business Institute, 941 West Third Street, Williamsport, PA 17701. *Phone:* 570-326-2869. *Toll-free phone:* 800-962-6971. *Fax:* 570-326-2136. *E-mail:* admissions_NBI@suscom.net.

NORTHAMPTON COUNTY AREA COMMUNITY COLLEGE
Bethlehem, Pennsylvania

- **State and locally supported** 2-year, founded 1967
- **Calendar** semesters
- **Degree** certificates, diplomas, and associate
- **Suburban** 165-acre campus with easy access to Philadelphia
- **Endowment** $12.8 million
- **Coed,** 8,246 undergraduate students, 43% full-time, 63% women, 37% men

Undergraduates 3,565 full-time, 4,681 part-time. Students come from 22 states and territories, 39 other countries, 3% are from out of state, 6% African American, 2% Asian American or Pacific Islander, 9% Hispanic American, 0.3% Native American, 1% international, 35% transferred in, 3% live on campus.

Freshmen *Admission:* 2,917 applied, 2,889 admitted, 2,570 enrolled.

Faculty *Total:* 512, 20% full-time, 21% with terminal degrees. *Student/faculty ratio:* 21:1.

Majors Accounting technology and bookkeeping; acting; architectural engineering technology; automotive engineering technology; banking and financial support services; biological and biomedical sciences related; biology/biological sciences; business administration and management; business/commerce; chemical technology; chemistry; child care and support services management; commercial and advertising art; communication disorders; computer and information sciences; computer installation and repair technology; criminal justice/law enforcement administration; culinary arts; data processing and data processing technology; dental hygiene; drafting and design technology; education (specific levels and methods) related; electrical and electronic engineering technologies related; electrical, electronic and communications engineering technology; electromechanical technology; engineering; executive assistant/executive secretary; fine/studio arts; fire services administration; funeral service and mortuary science; general studies; hotel/motel administration; interior architecture; journalism; legal administrative assistant/secretary; legal assistant/paralegal; liberal arts and sciences and humanities related; liberal arts and sciences/liberal studies; mathematics; medical administrative assistant and medical secretary; medical radiologic technology; nursing (registered nurse training); occupational health and industrial hygiene; physics; quality control technology; radio and television broadcasting technology; social work; special education; sport and fitness administration; veterinary/animal health technology.

Academic Programs *Special study options:* academic remediation for entering students, accelerated degree program, adult/continuing education programs, advanced placement credit, cooperative education, distance learning, double majors, English as a second language, internships, part-time degree program, services for LD students, student-designed majors, study abroad, summer session for credit.

Library Paul & Harriett Mack Library with 64,758 titles, 355 serial subscriptions, 9,169 audiovisual materials, an OPAC, a Web page.

Computers on Campus 1400 computers available on campus for general student use. A campuswide network can be accessed from student residence rooms and from off campus. Internet access, online (class) registration, at least one staffed computer lab available. Computer purchase or lease plan available.

Student Life *Housing Options:* coed. Campus housing is university owned. *Activities and Organizations:* drama/theater group, student-run newspaper, radio station, choral group, Phi Theta Kappa, Nursing Student Organization, NAVTA (Veterinary Technology Club), Student American Dental Hygiene Association, Video Waves. *Campus security:* 24-hour emergency response devices and patrols, controlled dormitory access. *Student services:* health clinic, personal/psychological counseling.

Athletics *Intercollegiate sports:* baseball M, basketball M/W, bowling M/W, golf M/W, ice hockey M/W, soccer M/W, softball W, tennis M/W, volleyball M/W, wrestling M(c). *Intramural sports:* basketball M/W, bowling M/W, football M/W, golf M/W, racquetball M/W, soccer M/W, volleyball M/W.

Standardized Tests *Required for some:* ACT (for placement).

Costs (2004–05) *Tuition:* area resident $2070 full-time, $69 per credit hour part-time; state resident $4140 full-time, $138 per credit hour part-time; nonresident $6210 full-time, $207 per credit hour part-time. *Required fees:* $660 full-time, $22 per credit hour part-time. *Room and board:* $5604; room only: $3262. Room and board charges vary according to board plan and housing facility. *Payment plans:* installment, deferred payment. *Waivers:* senior citizens and employees or children of employees.

Financial Aid Of all full-time matriculated undergraduates who enrolled in 2003, 300 Federal Work-Study jobs (averaging $2800). 130 state and other part-time jobs (averaging $1500).

Applying *Options:* common application, electronic application, deferred entrance. *Application fee:* $25. *Required:* high school transcript. *Required for some:* interview, Interview required for radiography, veterinary technician, and diagnostic medical sonography programs; portfolio required for communication design, fine art programs; audition required for theatre program. *Application deadline:* rolling (freshmen), rolling (transfers). *Notification:* continuous (freshmen).

Admissions Contact Mr. James McCarthy, Director of Admissions, Northampton County Area Community College, 3835 Green Pond Road, Bethlehem, PA 18020-7599. *Phone:* 610-861-5506. *Fax:* 610-861-5551. *E-mail:* adminfo@northampton.edu.

NORTH CENTRAL INDUSTRIAL TECHNICAL EDUCATION CENTER
Ridgway, Pennsylvania

Admissions Contact Lugene Inzana, Director, North Central Industrial Technical Education Center, 651 Montmorenci Avenue, Ridgway, PA 15853. *Phone:* 814-772-1012. *Toll-free phone:* 800-242-5872.

OAKBRIDGE ACADEMY OF ARTS
Lower Burrell, Pennsylvania

- **Proprietary** 2-year, founded 1972
- **Calendar** quarters
- **Degree** associate

Oakbridge Academy of Arts (continued)
■ **Small-town** 2-acre campus with easy access to Pittsburgh
■ **Coed**

Faculty *Student/faculty ratio:* 9:1.
Student Life *Campus security:* 24-hour emergency response devices.
Costs (2004–05) *Tuition:* $10,400 full-time, $600 per course part-time. Full-time tuition and fees vary according to course load and program. Part-time tuition and fees vary according to course load and program. *Required fees:* $800 full-time.
Financial Aid *Financial aid deadline:* 8/1.
Applying *Options:* common application, electronic application. *Required:* high school transcript, portfolio.
Admissions Contact Jan Schoeneberger, Admissions Representative, Oakbridge Academy of Arts, 1250 Greensburg Road, Lower Burrell, PA 15068. *Phone:* 724-335-5336. *Toll-free phone:* 800-734-5601. *Fax:* 724-335-3367.

ORLEANS TECHNICAL INSTITUTE-CENTER CITY CAMPUS
Philadelphia, Pennsylvania

■ **Proprietary** 2-year
■ **Calendar** trimesters
■ **Degree** associate
■ **Urban** campus
■ **Coed, primarily women,** 135 undergraduate students, 64% full-time, 94% women, 6% men
■ 76% of applicants were admitted

Undergraduates 87 full-time, 48 part-time. Students come from 3 states and territories, 1 other country, 60% are from out of state, 24% African American, 1% Asian American or Pacific Islander, 6% Hispanic American, 0.7% Native American, 6% transferred in.
Freshmen *Admission:* 45 applied, 34 admitted, 30 enrolled.
Faculty *Total:* 17, 18% full-time. *Student/faculty ratio:* 7:1.
Academic Programs *Special study options:* academic remediation for entering students, internships, part-time degree program, summer session for credit.
Library Library plus 1 other with 625 titles, 14 serial subscriptions.
Computers on Campus 46 computers available on campus for general student use. Internet access, at least one staffed computer lab available.
Student Life *Housing:* college housing not available.
Standardized Tests *Required:* CPAt (for admission).
Costs (2005–06) *Tuition:* $10,500 full-time, $7350 per year part-time. Full-time tuition and fees vary according to program. Part-time tuition and fees vary according to program. *Required fees:* $150 full-time. *Payment plan:* installment. *Waivers:* employees or children of employees.
Financial Aid Of all full-time matriculated undergraduates who enrolled in 2003, 5 Federal Work-Study jobs (averaging $4800). *Financial aid deadline:* 8/1.
Applying *Application fee:* $150. *Required:* high school transcript, interview. *Application deadline:* rolling (freshmen), rolling (transfers).
Admissions Contact Mr. Gary Bello, Admissions Representative, Orleans Technical Institute-Center City Campus, 1845 Walnut Street, 7th Floor, Philadphia, PA 19103. *Phone:* 215-854-1853. *Fax:* 215-854-1880. *E-mail:* gary.bello@jevs.org.

PACE INSTITUTE
Reading, Pennsylvania

Admissions Contact Mr. Ed Levandowski, Director of Enrollment Management, Pace Institute, 606 Court Street, Reading, PA 19601. *Phone:* 610-375-1212.

PENN COMMERCIAL BUSINESS AND TECHNICAL SCHOOL
Washington, Pennsylvania

Admissions Contact Mr. Michael John Joyce, Director of Admissions, Penn Commercial Business and Technical School, 242 Oak Spring Road, Washington, PA 15301. *Phone:* 724-222-5330 Ext. 1. *Fax:* 724-225-3561. *E-mail:* pcadmissions@penncommercial.net.

PENNCO TECH
Bristol, Pennsylvania

Admissions Contact Mr. Nate R. Aldsworth, Corporate Director of Admissions and Marketing, Pennco Tech, 3815 Otter Street, Bristol, PA 19007-3696. *Phone:* 215-824-3200. *E-mail:* admissions@penncotech.com.

PENNSYLVANIA COLLEGE OF TECHNOLOGY
Williamsport, Pennsylvania

■ **State-related** 4-year, founded 1965, administratively affiliated with Pennsylvania State University
■ **Calendar** semesters
■ **Degrees** certificates, associate, and bachelor's
■ **Small-town** 958-acre campus
■ **Endowment** $602,752
■ **Coed,** 6,358 undergraduate students, 84% full-time, 35% women, 65% men
■ **Noncompetitive** entrance level, 93% of applicants were admitted

Undergraduates 5,365 full-time, 993 part-time. Students come from 32 states and territories, 19 other countries, 8% are from out of state, 3% African American, 1% Asian American or Pacific Islander, 1% Hispanic American, 0.4% Native American, 0.5% international, 4% transferred in, 23% live on campus. Freshmen *Admission:* 5,014 applied, 4,649 admitted, 1,705 enrolled.
Faculty *Total:* 469, 61% full-time. *Student/faculty ratio:* 18:1.
Majors Accounting; accounting technology and bookkeeping; administrative assistant and secretarial science; adult health nursing; aeronautical/aerospace engineering technology; aircraft powerplant technology; allied health diagnostic, intervention, and treatment professions related; applied horticulture/horticultural business services related; architectural engineering technology; autobody/collision and repair technology; automotive engineering technology; avionics maintenance technology; baking and pastry arts; banking and financial support services; biology/biological sciences; biomedical technology; broadcast journalism; business administration and management; business administration, management and operations related; business automation/technology/data entry; cabinetmaking and millwork; cardiovascular technology; carpentry; child care and support services management; child care provision; civil engineering technology; commercial and advertising art; computer and information sciences; computer and information sciences and support services related; computer/information technology services administration related; computer programming (specific applications); computer systems analysis; computer systems networking and telecommunications; computer technology/computer systems technology; construction engineering technology; culinary arts; dental hygiene; diesel mechanics technology; dietitian assistant; drafting and design technology; drafting/design engineering technologies related; education (specific subject areas) related; electrical and electronic engineering technologies related; electrical, electronic and communications engineering technology; electrician; emergency medical technology (EMT paramedic); engineering science; engineering technologies related; environmental control technologies related; environmental engineering technology; forestry technology; general studies; graphic and printing equipment operation/production; health and medical administrative services related; health and physical education related; health information/medical records administration; health professions related; heating, air conditioning and refrigeration technology; heavy equipment maintenance technology; heavy/industrial equipment maintenance technologies related; industrial electronics technology; industrial mechanics and maintenance technology; industrial production technologies related; industrial technology; information technology; institutional food workers; instrumentation technology; laser and optical technology; legal assistant/paralegal; legal professions and studies related; legal studies; liberal arts and sciences and humanities related; liberal arts and sciences/liberal studies; machine shop technology; management information systems; manufacturing technology; masonry; mass communication/media; mechanical drafting and CAD/CADD; mechanical engineering/mechanical technology; mechanic and repair technologies related; medical administrative assistant and medical secretary; medical radiologic technology; mental and social health services and allied professions related; multi-/interdisciplinary studies related; nursing (licensed practical/vocational nurse training); nursing (registered nurse training); occupational therapist assistant; office occupations and clerical services; ornamental horticulture; physical sciences; plant nursery management; plastics engineering technology; platemaking/imaging; plumbing technology; psychiatric/mental health services technology; quality control technology; solar energy technology; survey technology; technical and business writing; tool and die technology; tourism and travel services management; turf and turfgrass management; vehicle and vehicle parts and accessories marketing; vehicle maintenance and repair technologies related; web page, digital/multimedia and information resources design; welding technology; woodworking related.
Academic Programs *Special study options:* academic remediation for entering students, advanced placement credit, cooperative education, distance learning, double majors, English as a second language, independent study, internships, off-campus study, part-time degree program, services for LD students, student-designed majors, summer session for credit. *ROTC:* Army (c).
Library Penn College Library plus 1 other with 96,281 titles, 9,118 serial subscriptions, 13,625 audiovisual materials, an OPAC, a Web page.
Student Life *Housing options:* coed, disabled students. Campus housing is university owned. *Activities and organizations:* student-run newspaper, radio station, Student Government Association, Resident Hall Association (RHA), Wildcats Event Board (WEB), Phi Beta Lambda, Early Educators. *Campus*

security: 24-hour emergency response devices and patrols, late-night transport/escort service. *Student services:* personal/psychological counseling, women's center.

Athletics *Intercollegiate sports:* archery M/W, baseball M, basketball M/W, bowling M/W, cross-country running M/W, golf M/W, soccer M/W, softball W, tennis M/W, volleyball M/W. *Intramural sports:* archery M/W, badminton M/W, basketball M/W, bowling M/W, football M/W, golf M/W, lacrosse M/W, racquetball M/W, soccer M/W, softball M/W, table tennis M/W, tennis M/W, ultimate Frisbee M/W, volleyball M/W, weight lifting M/W, wrestling M.

Standardized Tests *Required for some:* SAT (for admission).

Costs (2004–05) *Tuition:* state resident $8100 full-time, $270 per credit part-time; nonresident $10,560 full-time, $352 per credit part-time. Full-time tuition and fees vary according to course load and program. Part-time tuition and fees vary according to course load and program. *Required fees:* $1380 full-time, $46 per credit part-time. *Room and board:* $5132; room only: $3832. Room and board charges vary according to board plan, housing facility, and location. *Payment plan:* deferred payment. *Waivers:* employees or children of employees.

Financial Aid Of all full-time matriculated undergraduates who enrolled in 2003, 324 Federal Work-Study jobs (averaging $1281). 260 state and other part-time jobs (averaging $1117).

Applying *Options:* electronic application, early admission, deferred entrance. *Application fee:* $50. *Required:* high school transcript. *Application deadlines:* 7/1 (freshmen), 7/1 (out-of-state freshmen), rolling (transfers). *Early decision:* 7/1.

Admissions Contact Mr. Chester D. Schuman, Director of Admissions, Pennsylvania College of Technology, One College Avenue, DIF #119, Williamsport, PA 17701. *Phone:* 570-327-4761. *Toll-free phone:* 800-367-9222. *Fax:* 570-321-5551. *E-mail:* cschuman@pct.edu.

▶ **See page 540 for a narrative description.**

PENNSYLVANIA CULINARY INSTITUTE
Pittsburgh, Pennsylvania

- **Proprietary** 2-year, founded 1986
- **Calendar** semesters
- **Degree** associate
- **Urban** campus
- **Coed,** 1,040 undergraduate students, 100% full-time, 33% women, 67% men

Undergraduates 1,040 full-time. Students come from 31 states and territories, 10 other countries, 46% are from out of state, 11% African American, 1% Asian American or Pacific Islander, 2% Hispanic American, 0.2% Native American.

Freshmen *Admission:* 1,040 admitted.

Faculty *Total:* 39, 100% full-time. *Student/faculty ratio:* 18:1.

Majors Culinary arts; hotel/motel administration.

Academic Programs *Special study options:* academic remediation for entering students, double majors, internships, services for LD students.

Library L. Edwin Brown Library and Resource Center with 5,000 titles, 100 serial subscriptions, 350 audiovisual materials, an OPAC, a Web page.

Computers on Campus 102 computers available on campus for general student use. A campuswide network can be accessed from student residence rooms and from off campus. Internet access, at least one staffed computer lab available.

Student Life *Housing Options:* coed. Campus housing is university owned. Freshman applicants given priority for college housing.

Costs (2004–05) *Comprehensive fee:* $25,341 includes full-time tuition ($18,550) and room and board ($6791). No tuition increase for student's term of enrollment. *Room and board:* college room only: $4343. Room and board charges vary according to board plan and housing facility. *Payment plans:* tuition prepayment, installment. *Waivers:* employees or children of employees.

Applying *Options:* common application, electronic application. *Application fee:* $100. *Required:* high school transcript, interview. *Required for some:* entrance examination (qualifying score on either SAT or ACT will exempt applicant from examination). *Recommended:* essay or personal statement.

Admissions Contact Mr. Bob Cappel, Vice President of Admissions, Pennsylvania Culinary Institute, 717 Liberty Avenue, Pittsburgh, PA 15222-3500. *Phone:* 412-566-2433. *Toll-free phone:* 800-432-2433. *Fax:* 412-566-2434. *E-mail:* info@paculinary.com.

PENNSYLVANIA HIGHLAND COMMUNITY COLLEGE
Johnstown, Pennsylvania

- **State and locally supported** 2-year
- **Calendar** semesters
- **Degree** certificates, diplomas, and associate
- **Small-town** campus
- **Coed,** 1,327 undergraduate students, 45% full-time, 62% women, 38% men

Undergraduates 594 full-time, 733 part-time.

Freshmen *Admission:* 459 applied, 459 admitted, 386 enrolled.

Faculty *Total:* 145, 17% full-time. *Student/faculty ratio:* 14:1.

Majors Accounting; banking and financial support services; computer and information sciences; computer/information technology services administration related; computer programming; computer programming related; computer programming (specific applications); computer/technical support; construction engineering technology; consumer merchandising/retailing management; court reporting; electrical, electronic and communications engineering technology; environmental engineering technology; geography; health/health care administration; heating, air conditioning and refrigeration technology; hospitality administration; human services; industrial technology; liberal arts and sciences/liberal studies; system administration; web/multimedia management and webmaster.

Academic Programs *Special study options:* academic remediation for entering students, adult/continuing education programs, advanced placement credit, cooperative education, distance learning, honors programs, independent study, internships, part-time degree program, services for LD students.

Library Cambria County Area Community College Main Library plus 3 others with an OPAC.

Computers on Campus 100 computers available on campus for general student use. A campuswide network can be accessed. Internet access, at least one staffed computer lab available.

Costs (2005–06) *Tuition:* area resident $1680 full-time, $70 per credit hour part-time; state resident $3360 full-time, $140 per credit hour part-time; nonresident $5040 full-time, $210 per credit hour part-time. *Required fees:* $390 full-time, $15 per credit hour part-time, $15 per term part-time.

Financial Aid Of all full-time matriculated undergraduates who enrolled in 2003, 25 Federal Work-Study jobs (averaging $2500).

Applying *Options:* common application. *Application fee:* $20. *Recommended:* high school transcript, interview. *Application deadline:* 8/20 (freshmen).

Admissions Contact Mr. Jeff Maul, Admissions Officer, Pennsylvania Highland Community College, PO Box 68, Johnstown, PA 15907. *Phone:* 814-532-5327. *Fax:* 814-262-3220. *E-mail:* jmaul@mail.ccacc.cc.pa.us.

PENNSYLVANIA INSTITUTE OF TECHNOLOGY
Media, Pennsylvania

- **Independent** 2-year, founded 1953
- **Calendar** semesters
- **Degree** certificates and associate
- **Small-town** 12-acre campus with easy access to Philadelphia
- **Coed,** 215 undergraduate students, 58% full-time, 35% women, 65% men

Undergraduates 125 full-time, 90 part-time. Students come from 3 states and territories, 29% African American, 1% Asian American or Pacific Islander, 1% Hispanic American. *Retention:* 58% of 2002 full-time freshmen returned.

Freshmen *Admission:* 82 enrolled.

Faculty *Total:* 30, 37% full-time, 3% with terminal degrees. *Student/faculty ratio:* 14:1.

Majors Architectural engineering technology; business administration and management; electrical, electronic and communications engineering technology; engineering technology; mechanical engineering/mechanical technology; mechanical engineering technologies related; medical office management; office occupations and clerical services; web page, digital/multimedia and information resources design.

Academic Programs *Special study options:* academic remediation for entering students, adult/continuing education programs, advanced placement credit, cooperative education, part-time degree program, summer session for credit.

Library Pennsylvania Institute of Technology Library/Learning Resource Center with 16,500 titles, 217 serial subscriptions, an OPAC, a Web page.

Computers on Campus 85 computers available on campus for general student use. At least one staffed computer lab available.

Student Life *Housing:* college housing not available. *Campus security:* 24-hour emergency response devices. *Student services:* personal/psychological counseling.

Athletics *Intramural sports:* basketball M/W, volleyball M/W.

Standardized Tests *Recommended:* SAT or ACT (for placement).

Pennsylvania Institute of Technology (continued)

Costs (2005–06) *Tuition:* $9000 full-time, $300 per credit part-time. *Required fees:* $330 full-time, $11 per credit part-time.

Financial Aid Of all full-time matriculated undergraduates who enrolled in 2003, 15 Federal Work-Study jobs (averaging $1025). *Financial aid deadline:* 8/1.

Applying *Options:* common application, electronic application, deferred entrance. *Application fee:* $25. *Required:* high school transcript, interview. *Required for some:* 2 letters of recommendation. *Recommended:* essay or personal statement. *Application deadline:* 8/1 (freshmen), rolling (transfers). *Notification:* continuous until 9/1 (freshmen).

Admissions Contact Ms. Angela Cassetta, Dean of Enrollment Management, Pennsylvania Institute of Technology, 800 Manchester Avenue, Media, PA 19063-4036. *Phone:* 610-892-1550 Ext. 1553. *Toll-free phone:* 800-422-0025. *Fax:* 610-892-1510. *E-mail:* info@pit.edu.

THE PENNSYLVANIA STATE UNIVERSITY BEAVER CAMPUS OF THE COMMONWEALTH COLLEGE
Monaca, Pennsylvania

- **State-related** primarily 2-year, founded 1964, part of Pennsylvania State University
- **Calendar** semesters
- **Degrees** associate and bachelor's (also offers up to 2 years of most bachelor's degree programs offered at University Park campus)
- **Small-town** 91-acre campus with easy access to Pittsburgh
- **Coed,** 655 undergraduate students, 86% full-time, 40% women, 60% men

Undergraduates 563 full-time, 92 part-time. 4% are from out of state, 4% African American, 1% Asian American or Pacific Islander, 1% Hispanic American, 0.2% Native American, 0.5% international, 4% transferred in, 25% live on campus. *Retention:* 71% of 2002 full-time freshmen returned.

Freshmen *Admission:* 506 applied, 464 admitted, 196 enrolled. *Average high school GPA:* 2.97. *Test scores:* SAT verbal scores over 500: 44%; SAT math scores over 500: 51%; SAT verbal scores over 600: 8%; SAT math scores over 600: 14%; SAT verbal scores over 700: 1%; SAT math scores over 700: 2%.

Faculty *Total:* 58, 57% full-time, 40% with terminal degrees. *Student/faculty ratio:* 15:1.

Majors Accounting; acting; actuarial science; adult and continuing education administration; advertising; aerospace, aeronautical and astronautical engineering; African-American/Black studies; agribusiness; agricultural and extension education; agricultural/biological engineering and bioengineering; agricultural business and management related; agricultural mechanization; agriculture; American studies; animal sciences; animal sciences related; anthropology; applied economics; archeology; architectural engineering; art; art history, criticism and conservation; art teacher education; Asian studies (East); astronomy; atmospheric sciences and meteorology; biochemistry; biological and biomedical sciences related; biological and physical sciences; biology/biological sciences; biology/biotechnology laboratory technician; biomedical/medical engineering; biomedical technology; business administration and management; business/commerce; business/managerial economics; chemical engineering; chemistry; civil engineering; classics and languages, literatures and linguistics; communication and journalism related; communication/speech communication and rhetoric; comparative literature; computer and information sciences; computer engineering; criminal justice/law enforcement administration; economics; electrical, electronic and communications engineering technology; electrical, electronics and communications engineering; elementary education; engineering science; English; environmental/environmental health engineering; film/cinema studies; finance; food science; forestry technology; forest sciences and biology; French; geography; geological and earth sciences/geosciences related; geology/earth science; German; graphic design; health/health care administration; history; horticultural science; hospitality administration related; human development and family studies; human nutrition; industrial engineering; information science/studies; international business/trade/commerce; international relations and affairs; Italian; Japanese; Jewish/Judaic studies; journalism; kinesiology and exercise science; labor and industrial relations; landscape architecture; landscaping and groundskeeping; Latin American studies; liberal arts and sciences/liberal studies; logistics and materials management; management information systems; management sciences and quantitative methods related; marketing/marketing management; materials science; mathematics; mechanical engineering; medical microbiology and bacteriology; medieval and Renaissance studies; mining and mineral engineering; natural resources and conservation related; natural resources/conservation; nuclear engineering; nursing (registered nurse training); organizational behavior; parks, recreation and leisure facilities management; petroleum engineering; philosophy; physics; political science and government; pre-medical studies; psychology; rehabilitation and therapeutic professions related; religious studies; Russian; secondary education; sociology; soil science and agronomy;

Spanish; special education; statistics; telecommunications technology; theatre design and technology; turf and turfgrass management; visual and performing arts; women's studies.

Academic Programs *Special study options:* academic remediation for entering students, accelerated degree program, adult/continuing education programs, advanced placement credit, distance learning, double majors, English as a second language, honors programs, independent study, internships, services for LD students, study abroad, summer session for credit.

Library 39,861 titles, 222 serial subscriptions, 6,683 audiovisual materials.

Computers on Campus 106 computers available on campus for general student use. A campuswide network can be accessed from student residence rooms and from off campus. Internet access, online (class) registration, at least one staffed computer lab available. Computer purchase or lease plan available.

Student Life *Housing Options:* coed. Campus housing is university owned. Freshman campus housing is guaranteed. *Activities and Organizations:* drama/theater group, student-run newspaper, radio station. *Campus security:* 24-hour patrols, controlled dormitory access.

Athletics Member NJCAA. *Intercollegiate sports:* baseball M, basketball M, golf M, softball W, volleyball W. *Intramural sports:* basketball M/W, cheerleading M(c)/W(c), cross-country running M/W, football M, golf M/W, soccer M/W, softball M/W, table tennis M/W.

Standardized Tests *Required:* SAT or ACT (for admission).

Costs (2004–05) *Tuition:* state resident $9180 full-time, $371 per credit part-time; nonresident $14,040 full-time, $585 per credit part-time. *Required fees:* $444 full-time, $75 per term part-time. *Room and board:* $6230; room only: $3250. *Waivers:* senior citizens.

Financial Aid Of all full-time matriculated undergraduates who enrolled in 2003, 46 Federal Work-Study jobs (averaging $1146). 6 state and other part-time jobs (averaging $4570).

Applying *Options:* electronic application, early admission, deferred entrance. *Application fee:* $50. *Required:* high school transcript. *Application deadline:* rolling (freshmen), rolling (transfers). *Notification:* continuous (freshmen).

Admissions Contact Mr. Randall C. Deike, Assistant Vice President for Enrollment Management, The Pennsylvania State University Beaver Campus of the Commonwealth College, 100 University Drive, Suite 113, Monaca, PA 15061-2799. *Phone:* 814-865-5471. *Toll-free phone:* 877-564-6778. *Fax:* 724-773-3658. *E-mail:* br-admissions@psu.edu.

THE PENNSYLVANIA STATE UNIVERSITY DELAWARE COUNTY CAMPUS OF THE COMMONWEALTH COLLEGE
Media, Pennsylvania

- **State-related** primarily 2-year, founded 1966, part of Pennsylvania State University
- **Calendar** semesters
- **Degrees** associate and bachelor's (also offers up to 2 years of most bachelor's degree programs offered at University Park campus)
- **Small-town** 87-acre campus with easy access to Philadelphia
- **Coed,** 1,636 undergraduate students, 84% full-time, 44% women, 56% men

Undergraduates 1,371 full-time, 265 part-time. 3% are from out of state, 14% African American, 8% Asian American or Pacific Islander, 2% Hispanic American, 0.1% Native American, 0.4% international, 3% transferred in. *Retention:* 72% of 2002 full-time freshmen returned.

Freshmen *Admission:* 1,526 applied, 1,189 admitted, 439 enrolled. *Average high school GPA:* 2.82. *Test scores:* SAT verbal scores over 500: 36%; SAT math scores over 500: 43%; SAT verbal scores over 600: 10%; SAT math scores over 600: 13%; SAT verbal scores over 700: 1%; SAT math scores over 700: 2%.

Faculty *Total:* 128, 55% full-time, 42% with terminal degrees. *Student/faculty ratio:* 16:1.

Majors Accounting; acting; actuarial science; adult and continuing education administration; advertising; aerospace, aeronautical and astronautical engineering; African-American/Black studies; agribusiness; agricultural and extension education; agricultural/biological engineering and bioengineering; agricultural business and management related; agricultural mechanization; agriculture; American studies; animal sciences; animal sciences related; anthropology; applied economics; archeology; architectural engineering; art; art history, criticism and conservation; art teacher education; Asian studies (East); astronomy; atmospheric sciences and meteorology; biochemistry; biological and biomedical sciences related; biological and physical sciences; biology/biological sciences; biology/biotechnology laboratory technician; biomedical/medical engineering; business administration and management; business/commerce; business/managerial economics; chemical engineering; chemistry; civil engineering; classics and languages, literatures and linguistics; communication and journalism related; communication disorders; communication/speech communication and rhetoric; comparative literature; computer and information sciences; computer engineering; criminal justice/law enforcement administration; economics; electrical, electronics and communications engineering; elementary education; engineering science; English; environmental/environmental health engineering; film/cinema studies; finance; food science; forestry technology; forest sciences and biology; French; geography; geological and earth sciences/geosciences related; geology/earth science; German; graphic design; health/health care administration; history; horticultural science; hospitality administration related; human development and family studies; human nutrition; industrial engineering; information science/studies; international business/trade/commerce; international relations and affairs; Italian; Japanese; Jewish/Judaic studies; journalism; kinesiology and exercise science; labor and industrial relations; landscape architecture; landscaping and groundskeeping; Latin American studies; liberal arts and sciences/liberal studies; logistics and materials management; management information systems; management sciences and quantitative methods related; marketing/marketing management; materials science; mathematics; mechanical engineering; medical microbiology and bacteriology; medieval and Renaissance studies; mining and mineral engineering; natural resources and conservation related; natural resources/conservation; nuclear engineering; nursing (registered nurse training); organizational behavior; parks, recreation and leisure facilities management; petroleum engineering; philosophy; physics; political science and government; pre-medical studies; psychology; rehabilitation and therapeutic professions related; religious studies; Russian; secondary education; sociology; soil science and agronomy; Spanish; special education; statistics; theatre design and technology; turf and turfgrass management; visual and performing arts; women's studies.

Academic Programs *Special study options:* academic remediation for entering students, adult/continuing education programs, advanced placement credit, distance learning, double majors, English as a second language, honors programs, independent study, internships, services for LD students, study abroad, summer session for credit. *ROTC:* Air Force (c).

Library 59,930 titles, 457 serial subscriptions, 3,987 audiovisual materials.

Computers on Campus 180 computers available on campus for general student use. A campuswide network can be accessed from off campus. Internet access, online (class) registration, at least one staffed computer lab available. Computer purchase or lease plan available.

Student Life *Housing:* college housing not available. *Activities and Organizations:* drama/theater group, student-run newspaper. *Campus security:* late-night transport/escort service, part-time trained security personnel.

Athletics Member NJCAA. *Intercollegiate sports:* baseball M, basketball M/W, lacrosse M(c)/W(c), soccer M/W, tennis M/W, volleyball W. *Intramural sports:* basketball M/W, cheerleading M(c)/W(c), golf M/W, ice hockey M(c)/W(c), lacrosse M/W, soccer M/W, softball W(c), tennis M/W, volleyball M(c)/W.

Standardized Tests *Required:* SAT or ACT (for admission).

Costs (2004–05) *Tuition:* state resident $9180 full-time, $371 per credit part-time; nonresident $14,040 full-time, $585 per credit part-time. *Required fees:* $444 full-time, $75 per term part-time.

Financial Aid Of all full-time matriculated undergraduates who enrolled in 2003, 70 Federal Work-Study jobs (averaging $1030).

Applying *Options:* electronic application, early admission, deferred entrance. *Application fee:* $50. *Application deadline:* rolling (freshmen), rolling (transfers). *Notification:* continuous (freshmen).

Admissions Contact Mr. Randall C. Deike, Assistant Vice President for Enrollment Management, The Pennsylvania State University Delaware County Campus of the Commonwealth College, 25 Yearsley Mill Road, Media, PA 19063-5596. *Phone:* 814-865-5471. *Fax:* 610-892-1357. *E-mail:* admissions-delco@psu.edu.

THE PENNSYLVANIA STATE UNIVERSITY DUBOIS CAMPUS OF THE COMMONWEALTH COLLEGE

DuBois, Pennsylvania

- **State-related** primarily 2-year, founded 1935, part of Pennsylvania State University
- **Calendar** semesters
- **Degrees** associate and bachelor's (also offers up to 2 years of most bachelor's degree programs offered at University Park campus)
- **Small-town** 20-acre campus
- **Coed,** 842 undergraduate students, 73% full-time, 50% women, 50% men

Undergraduates 614 full-time, 228 part-time. 1% are from out of state, 1% African American, 0.6% Asian American or Pacific Islander, 0.3% Hispanic American, 0.3% Native American, 0.1% international, 2% transferred in. *Retention:* 75% of 2002 full-time freshmen returned.

Freshmen *Admission:* 400 applied, 362 admitted, 226 enrolled. *Average high school GPA:* 2.89. *Test scores:* SAT verbal scores over 500: 31%; SAT math scores over 500: 46%; SAT verbal scores over 600: 6%; SAT math scores over 600: 14%; SAT math scores over 700: 1%.

Faculty *Total:* 85, 53% full-time, 42% with terminal degrees. *Student/faculty ratio:* 12:1.

Majors Accounting; acting; actuarial science; adult and continuing education administration; advertising; aerospace, aeronautical and astronautical engineering; African-American/Black studies; agribusiness; agricultural and extension education; agricultural/biological engineering and bioengineering; agricultural business and management related; agricultural mechanization; agriculture; American studies; animal sciences; animal sciences related; anthropology; applied economics; archeology; architectural engineering; art; art history, criticism and conservation; art teacher education; Asian studies (East); astronomy; atmospheric sciences and meteorology; biochemistry; biological and biomedical sciences related; biological and physical sciences; biology/biological sciences; biology/biotechnology laboratory technician; biomedical/medical engineering; biomedical technology; business administration and management; business/commerce; business/managerial economics; chemical engineering; chemistry; civil engineering; classics and languages, literatures and linguistics; clinical/medical laboratory technology; communication and journalism related; communication disorders; communication/speech communication and rhetoric; comparative literature; computer and information sciences; computer engineering; criminal justice/law enforcement administration; economics; electrical, electronic and communications engineering technology; electrical, electronics and communications engineering; elementary education; engineering science; English; environmental/environmental health engineering; film/cinema studies; finance; food science; forestry technology; forest sciences and biology; French; geography; geological and earth sciences/geosciences related; geology/earth science; German; graphic design; health/health care administration; history; horticultural science; hospitality administration related; human development and family studies; human nutrition; industrial engineering; information science/studies; international business/trade/commerce; international relations and affairs; Italian; Japanese; Jewish/Judaic studies; journalism; kinesiology and exercise science; labor and industrial relations; landscape architecture; landscaping and groundskeeping; Latin American studies; liberal arts and sciences/liberal studies; logistics and materials management; management information systems; management sciences and quantitative methods related; marketing/marketing management; materials science; mathematics; mechanical engineering; mechanical engineering/mechanical technology; medical microbiology and bacteriology; medieval and Renaissance studies; metallurgical technology; mining and mineral engineering; natural resources and conservation related; natural resources/conservation; nuclear engineering; nursing (registered nurse training); occupational therapist assistant; organizational behavior; parks, recreation and leisure facilities management; petroleum engineering; philosophy; physical therapist assistant; physics; political science and government; pre-medical studies; psychology; rehabilitation and therapeutic professions related; religious studies; Russian; secondary education; sociology; soil science and agronomy; Spanish; special education; statistics; telecommunications technology; theatre design and technology; turf and turfgrass management; visual and performing arts; wildlife and wildlands science and management; women's studies.

Academic Programs *Special study options:* academic remediation for entering students, accelerated degree program, adult/continuing education programs, advanced placement credit, distance learning, double majors, honors programs, independent study, internships, services for LD students, student-designed majors, study abroad, summer session for credit.

Library 43,710 titles, 224 serial subscriptions, 1,091 audiovisual materials.

Computers on Campus 126 computers available on campus for general student use. A campuswide network can be accessed from off campus. Internet access, online (class) registration, at least one staffed computer lab available. Computer purchase or lease plan available.

Student Life *Housing:* college housing not available. *Activities and Organizations:* student-run newspaper, choral group.

Athletics Member NJCAA. *Intercollegiate sports:* basketball M, cross-country running M/W, golf M/W, volleyball W. *Intramural sports:* basketball M/W, football M, soccer M/W, table tennis M/W, volleyball M/W.

Standardized Tests *Required:* SAT or ACT (for admission).

Costs (2004–05) *Tuition:* state resident $9180 full-time, $371 per credit part-time; nonresident $14,040 full-time, $585 per credit part-time. *Required fees:* $434 full-time, $73 per term part-time.

Financial Aid Of all full-time matriculated undergraduates who enrolled in 2003, 122 Federal Work-Study jobs (averaging $1450). 1 state and other part-time job (averaging $1395).

Applying *Options:* electronic application, early admission, deferred entrance. *Application fee:* $50. *Required:* high school transcript. *Application deadline:* rolling (freshmen), rolling (transfers). *Notification:* continuous (freshmen).

Admissions Contact Mr. Randall C. Deike, Assistant Vice President for Enrollment Management, The Pennsylvania State University DuBois Campus of the Commonwealth College, 101 Hiller Building, College Place, DuBois, PA 15801-3199. *Phone:* 814-865-5471. *Toll-free phone:* 800-346-7627. *Fax:* 814-375-4784. *E-mail:* ds-admissions@psu.edu.

THE PENNSYLVANIA STATE UNIVERSITY FAYETTE CAMPUS OF THE COMMONWEALTH COLLEGE

Uniontown, Pennsylvania

- **State-related** primarily 2-year, founded 1934, part of Pennsylvania State University
- **Calendar** semesters
- **Degrees** associate and bachelor's (also offers up to 2 years of most bachelor's degree programs offered at University Park campus)
- **Small-town** 92-acre campus
- **Coed,** 1,066 undergraduate students, 74% full-time, 60% women, 40% men

Undergraduates 788 full-time, 278 part-time. 1% are from out of state, 6% African American, 0.6% Asian American or Pacific Islander, 0.5% Hispanic American, 3% transferred in. *Retention:* 67% of 2002 full-time freshmen returned.

Freshmen *Admission:* 329 applied, 290 admitted, 160 enrolled. *Average high school GPA:* 2.86. *Test scores:* SAT verbal scores over 500: 30%; SAT math scores over 500: 33%; SAT verbal scores over 600: 2%; SAT math scores over 600: 9%.

Faculty *Total:* 91, 57% full-time, 40% with terminal degrees. *Student/faculty ratio:* 14:1.

Majors Accounting; acting; actuarial science; adult and continuing education administration; advertising; aerospace, aeronautical and astronautical engineering; African-American/Black studies; agribusiness; agricultural and extension education; agricultural/biological engineering and bioengineering; agricultural business and management related; agricultural mechanization; agriculture; American studies; animal sciences; animal sciences related; anthropology; applied economics; archeology; architectural engineering; architectural engineering technology; art; art history, criticism and conservation; art teacher education; Asian studies (East); astronomy; atmospheric sciences and meteorology; biochemistry; biological and biomedical sciences related; biological and physical sciences; biology/biological sciences; biology/biotechnology laboratory technician; biomedical/medical engineering; biomedical technology; business administration and management; business/commerce; business/managerial economics; chemical engineering; chemistry; civil engineering; classics and languages, literatures and linguistics; communication and journalism related; communication disorders; communication/speech communication and rhetoric; comparative literature; computer and information sciences; computer engineering; criminal justice/law enforcement administration; criminal justice/safety; economics; electrical, electronic and communications engineering technology; electrical, electronics and communications engineering; elementary education; engineering science; English; environmental/environmental health engineering; film/cinema studies; finance; food science; forestry technology; forest sciences and biology; French; geography; geological and earth sciences/geosciences related; geology/earth science; German; graphic design; health/health care administration; history; horticultural science; hospitality administration related; human development and family studies; human nutrition; industrial engineering; information science/studies; international business/trade/commerce; international relations and affairs; Italian; Japanese; Jewish/Judaic studies; journalism; kinesiology and exercise science; labor and industrial relations; landscape architecture; landscaping and groundskeeping; Latin American studies; liberal arts and sciences/liberal studies; logistics and materials management; management information systems; management sciences and quantitative methods related; manufacturing engineering; marketing/marketing management; materials science; mathematics; mechanical engineering; medical microbiology and bacteriology; medieval and Renaissance studies; metallurgical technology; mining and mineral engineering; natural resources and conservation related; natural resources/conservation; nuclear engineering; nursing (registered nurse training); organizational behavior; parks, recreation and leisure facilities management; petroleum engineering; philosophy; physics; political science and government; pre-medical studies; psychology; rehabilitation and therapeutic professions related; religious studies; Russian; secondary education; sociology; soil science and agronomy; Spanish; special education; statistics; telecommunications technology; theatre design and technology; turf and turfgrass management; visual and performing arts; women's studies.

Academic Programs *Special study options:* academic remediation for entering students, accelerated degree program, adult/continuing education programs, advanced placement credit, distance learning, double majors, honors programs, independent study, internships, services for LD students, student-designed majors, study abroad, summer session for credit.

Library 54,610 titles, 187 serial subscriptions, 6,721 audiovisual materials.

Computers on Campus 103 computers available on campus for general student use. A campuswide network can be accessed from off campus. Internet access, online (class) registration, at least one staffed computer lab available. Computer purchase or lease plan available.

Student Life *Housing:* college housing not available. *Activities and Organizations:* drama/theater group, student-run newspaper. *Campus security:* student patrols, 8-hour patrols by trained security personnel.

Athletics Member NJCAA. *Intercollegiate sports:* baseball M, basketball M, softball W, volleyball W. *Intramural sports:* badminton M/W, basketball M/W, cheerleading M(c)/W(c), equestrian sports M(c)/W(c), football M/W, golf M(c)/W(c), softball M/W, tennis M/W, volleyball M/W, weight lifting M/W.

Standardized Tests *Required:* SAT or ACT (for admission).

Costs (2004–05) *Tuition:* state resident $9180 full-time, $371 per credit part-time; nonresident $14,040 full-time, $585 per credit part-time. *Required fees:* $434 full-time, $73 per term part-time.

Financial Aid Of all full-time matriculated undergraduates who enrolled in 2003, 65 Federal Work-Study jobs (averaging $1770).

Applying *Options:* electronic application, early admission, deferred entrance. *Application fee:* $50. *Required:* high school transcript. *Application deadline:* rolling (freshmen), rolling (transfers). *Notification:* continuous (freshmen).

Admissions Contact Mr. Randall C. Deike, Assistant Vice President for Enrollment Management, The Pennsylvania State University Fayette Campus of the Commonwealth College, PO Box 519, Route 119 North, 108 Williams Building, Uniontown, PA 15401-0519. *Phone:* 814-865-5471. *Toll-free phone:* 877-568-4130. *Fax:* 724-430-4175. *E-mail:* feadm@psu.edu.

THE PENNSYLVANIA STATE UNIVERSITY HAZLETON CAMPUS OF THE COMMONWEALTH COLLEGE

Hazleton, Pennsylvania

- **State-related** primarily 2-year, founded 1934, part of Pennsylvania State University
- **Calendar** semesters
- **Degrees** associate and bachelor's (also offers up to 2 years of most bachelor's degree programs offered at University Park campus)
- **Small-town** 98-acre campus
- **Coed,** 1,108 undergraduate students, 94% full-time, 39% women, 61% men

Undergraduates 1,043 full-time, 65 part-time. 22% are from out of state, 6% African American, 4% Asian American or Pacific Islander, 5% Hispanic American, 0.2% Native American, 0.3% international, 3% transferred in, 43% live on campus. *Retention:* 80% of 2002 full-time freshmen returned.

Freshmen *Admission:* 1,199 applied, 1,087 admitted, 477 enrolled. *Average high school GPA:* 2.90. *Test scores:* SAT verbal scores over 500: 44%; SAT math scores over 500: 54%; SAT verbal scores over 600: 10%; SAT math scores over 600: 14%; SAT verbal scores over 700: 1%; SAT math scores over 700: 2%.

Faculty *Total:* 85, 66% full-time, 40% with terminal degrees. *Student/faculty ratio:* 16:1.

Majors Accounting; acting; actuarial science; adult and continuing education administration; advertising; aerospace, aeronautical and astronautical engineering; African-American/Black studies; agribusiness; agricultural and extension education; agricultural/biological engineering and bioengineering; agricultural business and management related; agricultural mechanization; agriculture; American studies; animal sciences; animal sciences related; anthropology; applied economics; archeology; architectural engineering; art; art history, criticism and conservation; art teacher education; Asian studies (East); astronomy; atmospheric sciences and meteorology; biochemistry; biological and biomedical sciences related; biological and physical sciences; biology/biological sciences; biology/biotechnology laboratory technician; biomedical/medical engineering; biomedical technology; business administration and management; business/commerce; business/managerial economics; chemical engineering; chemistry; civil engineering; classics and languages, literatures and linguistics; clinical/medical laboratory technology; communication and journalism related; communication disorders; communication/speech communication and rhetoric; comparative literature; computer and information sciences; computer engineering; criminal justice/law enforcement administration; economics; electrical, electronic and communications engineering technology; electrical, electronics and communications engineering; elementary education; engineering science; English; environmental/environmental health engineering; film/cinema studies; finance; food science; forestry technology; forest sciences and biology; French; geography; geological and earth sciences/geosciences related; geology/earth science; German; graphic design; health/health care administration; history; horticultural science; hospitality administration related; human development and family studies; human nutrition; industrial engineering; information science/studies; international business/trade/commerce; international relations and affairs; Italian; Japanese; Jewish/Judaic studies; journalism; kinesiology and exercise science; labor and industrial relations; landscape architecture; landscaping and groundskeeping; Latin American studies; liberal arts and sciences/liberal studies; logistics and materials management; management information systems; management sciences and quantitative methods related; manufacturing engineering; marketing/marketing management; materials science; mathematics; mechanical engineering; mechanical engineering/mechanical technology; medical microbiology and bacteriology; medieval and Renaissance studies; metallurgical technology; mining and mineral engineering; natural resources and conservation related; natural resources/conservation; nuclear engineering; nursing (registered nurse training); organizational behavior; parks, recreation and leisure facilities management; petroleum engineering; philosophy; physical therapist assistant; physics; political science and government; pre-medical studies; psychology; rehabilitation and therapeutic professions related; religious studies; Russian; secondary education; sociology; soil science and agronomy; Spanish; special education; statistics; telecommunications technology; theatre design and technology; turf and turfgrass management; visual and performing arts; women's studies.

Academic Programs *Special study options:* academic remediation for entering students, accelerated degree program, adult/continuing education programs, advanced placement credit, distance learning, double majors, English as a second language, honors programs, independent study, internships, services for LD students, student-designed majors, study abroad, summer session for credit. *ROTC:* Army (b), Air Force (c).

Library 83,266 titles, 996 serial subscriptions, 6,771 audiovisual materials.

Computers on Campus 131 computers available on campus for general student use. A campuswide network can be accessed from student residence rooms and from off campus. Internet access, online (class) registration, at least one staffed computer lab available. Computer purchase or lease plan available.

Student Life *Housing Options:* coed. Campus housing is university owned. Freshman campus housing is guaranteed. *Activities and Organizations:* drama/theater group, student-run newspaper, radio station, choral group. *Campus security:* 24-hour patrols, late-night transport/escort service, controlled dormitory access.

Athletics Member NJCAA. *Intercollegiate sports:* baseball M, basketball M/W, cheerleading M/W, soccer M, softball W(s), tennis M/W, volleyball M(c)/W. *Intramural sports:* basketball M/W, skiing (downhill) M(c)/W(c), soccer M/W, volleyball M/W.

Standardized Tests *Required:* SAT or ACT (for admission).

Costs (2004–05) *Tuition:* state resident $9180 full-time, $371 per credit part-time; nonresident $14,040 full-time, $585 per credit part-time. *Required fees:* $434 full-time, $73 per term part-time. *Room and board:* $6230; room only: $3250.

Financial Aid Of all full-time matriculated undergraduates who enrolled in 2003, 135 Federal Work-Study jobs (averaging $1297). 13 state and other part-time jobs (averaging $4973).

Applying *Options:* electronic application, early admission, deferred entrance. *Application fee:* $50. *Required:* high school transcript. *Application deadline:* rolling (freshmen), rolling (transfers). *Notification:* continuous (freshmen).

Admissions Contact Mr. Randall C. Deike, Assistant Vice President for Enrollment Management, The Pennsylvania State University Hazleton Campus of the Commonwealth College, 110 Administration Building, 76 University Drive, Hazleton, PA 18202-1291. *Phone:* 814-865-5471. *Toll-free phone:* 800-279-8495. *Fax:* 570-450-3182. *E-mail:* admissions-hn@psu.edu.

THE PENNSYLVANIA STATE UNIVERSITY MCKEESPORT CAMPUS OF THE COMMONWEALTH COLLEGE

McKeesport, Pennsylvania

- **State-related** primarily 2-year, founded 1947, part of Pennsylvania State University
- **Calendar** semesters
- **Degrees** associate and bachelor's (also offers up to 2 years of most bachelor's degree programs offered at University Park campus)
- **Small-town** 40-acre campus with easy access to Pittsburgh
- **Coed,** 798 undergraduate students, 89% full-time, 40% women, 60% men

Undergraduates 707 full-time, 91 part-time. 8% are from out of state, 14% African American, 3% Asian American or Pacific Islander, 1% Hispanic American, 0.3% international, 4% transferred in, 14% live on campus. *Retention:* 79% of 2002 full-time freshmen returned.

Freshmen *Admission:* 522 applied, 470 admitted, 225 enrolled. *Average high school GPA:* 2.90. *Test scores:* SAT verbal scores over 500: 43%; SAT math scores over 500: 45%; SAT verbal scores over 600: 10%; SAT math scores over 600: 12%; SAT math scores over 700: 3%.

Faculty *Total:* 67, 58% full-time, 1% with terminal degrees. *Student/faculty ratio:* 15:1.

Majors Accounting; acting; actuarial science; adult and continuing education administration; advertising; aerospace, aeronautical and astronautical engineering; African-American/Black studies; agribusiness; agricultural and extension education; agricultural/biological engineering and bioengineering; agricultural business and management related; agricultural mechanization; agriculture; American studies; animal sciences; animal sciences related; anthropology; applied economics; archeology; architectural engineering; art; art history, criticism and conservation; art teacher education; Asian studies (East); astronomy; atmospheric sciences and meteorology; biochemistry; biological and biomedical sciences related; biological and physical sciences; biology/biological sciences; biology/biotechnology laboratory technician; biomedical/medical engineering; business administration and management; business/commerce; business/

managerial economics; chemical engineering; chemistry; civil engineering; classics and languages, literatures and linguistics; communication and journalism related; communication disorders; communication/speech communication and rhetoric; comparative literature; computer and information sciences; computer engineering; criminal justice/law enforcement administration; economics; electrical, electronics and communications engineering; elementary education; engineering science; English; environmental/environmental health engineering; film/cinema studies; finance; food science; forestry technology; forest sciences and biology; French; geography; geological and earth sciences/geosciences related; geology/earth science; German; graphic design; health/health care administration; history; horticultural science; hospitality administration related; human development and family studies; human nutrition; industrial engineering; information science/studies; international business/trade/commerce; international relations and affairs; Italian; Japanese; Jewish/Judaic studies; journalism; kinesiology and exercise science; labor and industrial relations; landscape architecture; landscaping and groundskeeping; Latin American studies; liberal arts and sciences/liberal studies; logistics and materials management; management information systems; management sciences and quantitative methods related; marketing/marketing management; materials science; mathematics; mechanical engineering; medical microbiology and bacteriology; medieval and Renaissance studies; mining and mineral engineering; natural resources and conservation related; natural resources/conservation; nuclear engineering; nursing (registered nurse training); organizational behavior; parks, recreation and leisure facilities management; petroleum engineering; philosophy; physics; political science and government; pre-medical studies; psychology; rehabilitation and therapeutic professions related; religious studies; Russian; secondary education; sociology; soil science and agronomy; Spanish; special education; statistics; theatre design and technology; turf and turfgrass management; visual and performing arts; women's studies.

Academic Programs *Special study options:* academic remediation for entering students, accelerated degree program, adult/continuing education programs, advanced placement credit, distance learning, double majors, honors programs, independent study, internships, services for LD students, study abroad, summer session for credit. *ROTC:* Air Force (c).

Library 40,851 titles, 300 serial subscriptions, 2,783 audiovisual materials.

Computers on Campus 167 computers available on campus for general student use. A campuswide network can be accessed from student residence rooms and from off campus. Internet access, online (class) registration, at least one staffed computer lab available. Computer purchase or lease plan available.

Student Life *Housing Options:* coed. Campus housing is university owned. Freshman campus housing is guaranteed. *Activities and Organizations:* drama/theater group, student-run newspaper, radio station. *Campus security:* 24-hour patrols, controlled dormitory access.

Athletics Member NJCAA. *Intercollegiate sports:* baseball M, basketball M, softball W, volleyball W. *Intramural sports:* basketball M/W, cheerleading M(c)/W(c), football M/W, ice hockey M(c), racquetball M/W, skiing (cross-country) M(c)/W(c), skiing (downhill) M(c)/W(c), soccer M(c)/W(c), softball M/W, tennis M/W, volleyball M/W.

Standardized Tests *Required:* SAT or ACT (for admission).

Costs (2004–05) *Tuition:* state resident $9180 full-time, $371 per credit part-time; nonresident $14,040 full-time, $585 per credit part-time. *Required fees:* $424 full-time, $71 per term part-time. *Room and board:* $6230; room only: $3250.

Financial Aid Of all full-time matriculated undergraduates who enrolled in 2003, 103 Federal Work-Study jobs (averaging $1315). 4 state and other part-time jobs (averaging $5630).

Applying *Options:* electronic application, early admission, deferred entrance. *Application fee:* $50. *Required:* high school transcript. *Application deadline:* rolling (freshmen), rolling (transfers). *Notification:* continuous (freshmen).

Admissions Contact Mr. Randall C. Deike, Assistant Vice President for Enrollment Management, The Pennsylvania State University McKeesport Campus of the Commonwealth College, 101 Frable Building, 4000 University Drive, McKeesport, PA 15132-7698. *Phone:* 814-865-5471. *Fax:* 412-675-9056. *E-mail:* psumk@psu.edu.

THE PENNSYLVANIA STATE UNIVERSITY MONT ALTO CAMPUS OF THE COMMONWEALTH COLLEGE

Mont Alto, Pennsylvania

- **State-related** primarily 2-year, founded 1929, part of Pennsylvania State University
- **Calendar** semesters
- **Degrees** associate and bachelor's (also offers up to 2 years of most bachelor's degree programs offered at University Park campus)
- **Small-town** 64-acre campus
- **Coed,** 1,018 undergraduate students, 69% full-time, 58% women, 42% men

Undergraduates 707 full-time, 311 part-time. 14% are from out of state, 7% African American, 2% Asian American or Pacific Islander, 3% Hispanic Ameri-

The Pennsylvania State University Mont Alto Campus of the Commonwealth College (continued)

can, 0.2% Native American, 0.1% international, 6% transferred in, 33% live on campus. *Retention:* 78% of 2002 full-time freshmen returned.

Freshmen *Admission:* 649 applied, 559 admitted, 285 enrolled. *Average high school GPA:* 2.82. *Test scores:* SAT verbal scores over 500: 40%; SAT math scores over 500: 42%; SAT verbal scores over 600: 10%; SAT math scores over 600: 13%; SAT verbal scores over 700: 1%; SAT math scores over 700: 1%.

Faculty *Total:* 95, 55% full-time, 31% with terminal degrees. *Student/faculty ratio:* 12:1.

Majors Accounting; acting; actuarial science; adult and continuing education administration; advertising; aerospace, aeronautical and astronautical engineering; African-American/Black studies; agribusiness; agricultural and extension education; agricultural/biological engineering and bioengineering; agricultural business and management related; agricultural mechanization; agriculture; American studies; animal sciences; animal sciences related; anthropology; applied economics; archeology; architectural engineering; art; art history, criticism and conservation; art teacher education; Asian studies (East); astronomy; atmospheric sciences and meteorology; biochemistry; biological and biomedical sciences related; biological and physical sciences; biology/biological sciences; biology/biotechnology laboratory technician; biomedical/medical engineering; business administration and management; business/commerce; business/managerial economics; chemical engineering; chemistry; civil engineering; classics and languages, literatures and linguistics; communication and journalism related; communication disorders; communication/speech communication and rhetoric; comparative literature; computer and information sciences; computer engineering; criminal justice/law enforcement administration; economics; electrical, electronics and communications engineering; elementary education; engineering science; English; environmental/environmental health engineering; film/cinema studies; finance; food science; forestry technology; forest sciences and biology; French; geography; geological and earth sciences/geosciences related; geology/earth science; German; graphic design; health/health care administration; history; horticultural science; hospitality administration related; human development and family studies; human nutrition; industrial engineering; information science/studies; international business/trade/commerce; international relations and affairs; Italian; Japanese; Jewish/Judaic studies; journalism; kinesiology and exercise science; labor and industrial relations; landscape architecture; landscaping and groundskeeping; Latin American studies; liberal arts and sciences/liberal studies; logistics and materials management; management information systems; management sciences and quantitative methods related; marketing/marketing management; materials science; mathematics; mechanical engineering; medical microbiology and bacteriology; medieval and Renaissance studies; mining and mineral engineering; natural resources and conservation related; natural resources/conservation; nuclear engineering; nursing (registered nurse training); occupational therapist assistant; occupational therapy; organizational behavior; parks, recreation and leisure facilities management; petroleum engineering; philosophy; physical therapist assistant; physics; political science and government; pre-medical studies; psychology; rehabilitation and therapeutic professions related; religious studies; Russian; secondary education; sociology; soil science and agronomy; Spanish; special education; statistics; theatre design and technology; turf and turfgrass management; visual and performing arts; women's studies.

Academic Programs *Special study options:* academic remediation for entering students, accelerated degree program, adult/continuing education programs, advanced placement credit, distance learning, double majors, honors programs, independent study, internships, services for LD students, study abroad, summer session for credit. *ROTC:* Army (c).

Library 38,962 titles, 273 serial subscriptions, 1,418 audiovisual materials.

Computers on Campus 182 computers available on campus for general student use. A campuswide network can be accessed from student residence rooms and from off campus. Internet access, online (class) registration, at least one staffed computer lab available. Computer purchase or lease plan available.

Student Life *Housing Options:* coed, disabled students. Campus housing is university owned. Freshman campus housing is guaranteed. *Activities and Organizations:* student-run radio station. *Campus security:* 24-hour patrols, controlled dormitory access.

Athletics Member NJCAA. *Intercollegiate sports:* basketball M/W, cheerleading M/W, cross-country running M/W, golf M/W, soccer M/W, softball W, tennis M/W, volleyball W. *Intramural sports:* badminton M/W, basketball M/W, cheerleading M(c)/W(c), racquetball M/W, soccer M/W, softball W, volleyball M/W.

Standardized Tests *Required:* SAT or ACT (for admission).

Costs (2004–05) *Tuition:* state resident $9180 full-time, $371 per credit part-time; nonresident $14,040 full-time, $585 per credit part-time. *Required fees:* $444 full-time, $75 per term part-time. *Room and board:* $6230; room only: $3250.

Financial Aid Of all full-time matriculated undergraduates who enrolled in 2003, 93 Federal Work-Study jobs (averaging $1015). 12 state and other part-time jobs (averaging $4893).

Applying *Options:* electronic application, early admission, deferred entrance. *Application fee:* $50. *Required:* high school transcript. *Application deadline:* rolling (freshmen), rolling (transfers). *Notification:* continuous (freshmen).

Admissions Contact Mr. Randall C. Deike, Assistant Vice President for Enrollment Management, The Pennsylvania State University Mont Alto Campus of the Commonwealth College, 1 Campus Drive, Mont Alto, PA 17237-9703. *Phone:* 814-865-5471. *Toll-free phone:* 800-392-6173. *Fax:* 717-749-6132. *E-mail:* psuma@psu.edu.

THE PENNSYLVANIA STATE UNIVERSITY NEW KENSINGTON CAMPUS OF THE COMMONWEALTH COLLEGE
New Kensington, Pennsylvania

- **State-related** primarily 2-year, founded 1958, part of Pennsylvania State University
- **Calendar** semesters
- **Degrees** associate and bachelor's (also offers up to 2 years of most bachelor's degree programs offered at University Park campus)
- **Small-town** 71-acre campus with easy access to Pittsburgh
- **Coed,** 977 undergraduate students, 70% full-time, 41% women, 59% men

Undergraduates 683 full-time, 294 part-time. 2% are from out of state, 2% African American, 0.3% Asian American or Pacific Islander, 0.6% Hispanic American, 0.1% Native American, 5% transferred in. *Retention:* 77% of 2002 full-time freshmen returned.

Freshmen *Admission:* 425 applied, 370 admitted, 192 enrolled. *Average high school GPA:* 2.92. *Test scores:* SAT verbal scores over 500: 44%; SAT math scores over 500: 47%; SAT verbal scores over 600: 10%; SAT math scores over 600: 13%; SAT verbal scores over 700: 1%.

Faculty *Total:* 96, 44% full-time, 38% with terminal degrees. *Student/faculty ratio:* 13:1.

Majors Accounting; acting; actuarial science; adult and continuing education administration; advertising; aerospace, aeronautical and astronautical engineering; African-American/Black studies; agribusiness; agricultural and extension education; agricultural/biological engineering and bioengineering; agricultural business and management related; agricultural mechanization; agriculture; American studies; animal sciences; animal sciences related; anthropology; applied economics; archeology; architectural engineering; art; art history, criticism and conservation; art teacher education; Asian studies (East); astronomy; atmospheric sciences and meteorology; biochemistry; biological and biomedical sciences related; biological and physical sciences; biology/biological sciences; biology/biotechnology laboratory technician; biomedical/medical engineering; biomedical technology; business administration and management; business/commerce; business/managerial economics; chemical engineering; chemistry; civil engineering; classics and languages, literatures and linguistics; communication and journalism related; communication disorders; communication/speech communication and rhetoric; comparative literature; computer and information sciences; computer engineering; computer engineering technology; criminal justice/law enforcement administration; economics; electrical, electronic and communications engineering technology; electrical, electronics and communications engineering; elementary education; engineering science; English; environmental/environmental health engineering; film/cinema studies; finance; food science; forestry technology; forest sciences and biology; French; geography; geological and earth sciences/geosciences related; geology/earth science; German; graphic design; health/health care administration; history; horticultural science; hospitality administration related; human development and family studies; human nutrition; industrial engineering; information science/studies; international business/trade/commerce; international relations and affairs; Italian; Japanese; Jewish/Judaic studies; journalism; kinesiology and exercise science; labor and industrial relations; landscape architecture; landscaping and groundskeeping; Latin American studies; liberal arts and sciences/liberal studies; logistics and materials management; management information systems; management sciences and quantitative methods related; marketing/marketing management; materials science; mathematics; mechanical engineering; mechanical engineering/mechanical technology; medical microbiology and bacteriology; medical radiologic technology; medieval and Renaissance studies; metallurgical technology; mining and mineral engineering; natural resources and conservation related; natural resources/conservation; nuclear engineering; nursing (registered nurse training); organizational behavior; parks, recreation and leisure facilities management; petroleum engineering; philosophy; physics; political science and government; pre-medical studies; psychology; rehabilitation and therapeutic professions related; religious studies; Russian; secondary education; sociology; soil science and agronomy; Spanish; special education; statistics; telecommunications technology; theatre design and technology; turf and turfgrass management; visual and performing arts; women's studies.

Academic Programs *Special study options:* academic remediation for entering students, accelerated degree program, adult/continuing education programs, advanced placement credit, distance learning, double majors, external degree program, honors programs, independent study, internships, services for LD students, summer session for credit.

Library 28,897 titles, 404 serial subscriptions, 4,294 audiovisual materials.

Computers on Campus 264 computers available on campus for general student use. A campuswide network can be accessed from off campus. Internet access, online (class) registration, at least one staffed computer lab available. Computer purchase or lease plan available.

Student Life *Housing:* college housing not available. *Activities and Organizations:* drama/theater group, student-run newspaper, choral group. *Campus security:* part-time trained security personnel.

Athletics Member NJCAA. *Intercollegiate sports:* baseball M, basketball M/W, cheerleading M/W, golf M/W, softball W, volleyball W. *Intramural sports:* badminton M/W, basketball M/W, bowling M/W, cheerleading M(c)/W(c), football M/W, ice hockey M(c)/W(c), racquetball M/W, skiing (downhill) M(c)/W(c), soccer M/W, softball W, volleyball M/W.

Standardized Tests *Required:* SAT or ACT (for admission).

Costs (2004–05) *Tuition:* state resident $9180 full-time, $371 per credit part-time; nonresident $14,040 full-time, $585 per credit part-time. *Required fees:* $444 full-time, $75 per term part-time.

Financial Aid Of all full-time matriculated undergraduates who enrolled in 2003, 65 Federal Work-Study jobs (averaging $1644).

Applying *Options:* electronic application, early admission, deferred entrance. *Application fee:* $50. *Required:* high school transcript. *Application deadline:* rolling (freshmen), rolling (transfers). *Notification:* continuous (freshmen).

Admissions Contact Mr. Randall C. Deike, Assistant Vice President for Enrollment Management, The Pennsylvania State University New Kensington Campus of the Commonwealth College, 3550 7th Street Road, Route 780, Upper Burrell, PA 15068-1798. *Phone:* 814-865-5471. *Toll-free phone:* 888-968-7297. *Fax:* 724-334-6111. *E-mail:* nkadmissions@psu.edu.

THE PENNSYLVANIA STATE UNIVERSITY SHENANGO CAMPUS OF THE COMMONWEALTH COLLEGE
Sharon, Pennsylvania

- **State-related** primarily 2-year, founded 1965, part of Pennsylvania State University
- **Calendar** semesters
- **Degrees** associate and bachelor's (also offers up to 2 years of most bachelor's degree programs offered at University Park campus)
- **Small-town** 14-acre campus
- **Coed,** 958 undergraduate students, 59% full-time, 64% women, 36% men

Undergraduates 565 full-time, 393 part-time. 11% are from out of state, 6% African American, 0.7% Asian American or Pacific Islander, 1% Hispanic American, 0.1% Native American, 4% transferred in. *Retention:* 74% of 2002 full-time freshmen returned.

Freshmen *Admission:* 297 applied, 260 admitted, 157 enrolled. *Average high school GPA:* 2.82. *Test scores:* SAT verbal scores over 500: 32%; SAT math scores over 500: 31%; SAT verbal scores over 600: 3%; SAT math scores over 600: 5%.

Faculty *Total:* 75, 40% full-time, 31% with terminal degrees. *Student/faculty ratio:* 16:1.

Majors Accounting; acting; actuarial science; adult and continuing education administration; advertising; aerospace, aeronautical and astronautical engineering; African-American/Black studies; agribusiness; agricultural and extension education; agricultural/biological engineering and bioengineering; agricultural business and management related; agricultural mechanization; agriculture; American studies; animal sciences; animal sciences related; anthropology; applied economics; archeology; architectural engineering; art; art history, criticism and conservation; art teacher education; Asian studies (East); astronomy; atmospheric sciences and meteorology; biochemistry; biological and biomedical sciences related; biological and physical sciences; biology/biological sciences; biology/biotechnology laboratory technician; biomedical/medical engineering; biomedical technology; business administration and management; business/commerce; business/managerial economics; chemical engineering; chemistry; civil engineering; classics and languages, literatures and linguistics; communication and journalism related; communication disorders; communication/speech communication and rhetoric; comparative literature; computer and information sciences; computer engineering; criminal justice/law enforcement administration; economics; electrical, electronics and communications engineering; elementary education; engineering science; English; environmental/environmental health engineering; film/cinema studies; finance; food science; forestry technology; forest sciences and biology; French; geography; geological and earth sciences/geosciences related; geology/earth science; German; graphic design; health/health care administration; history; horticultural science; hospitality administration related; human development and family studies; human nutrition; industrial engineering; information science/studies; international business/trade/commerce; international relations and affairs; Italian; Japanese; Jewish/Judaic studies;

journalism; kinesiology and exercise science; labor and industrial relations; landscape architecture; landscaping and groundskeeping; Latin American studies; liberal arts and sciences/liberal studies; logistics and materials management; management information systems; management sciences and quantitative methods related; marketing/marketing management; materials science; mathematics; mechanical engineering; mechanical engineering/mechanical technology; medical microbiology and bacteriology; medieval and Renaissance studies; metallurgical technology; mining and mineral engineering; natural resources and conservation related; natural resources/conservation; nuclear engineering; nursing (registered nurse training); organizational behavior; parks, recreation and leisure facilities management; petroleum engineering; philosophy; physical therapist assistant; physics; political science and government; pre-medical studies; psychology; rehabilitation and therapeutic professions related; religious studies; Russian; secondary education; sociology; soil science and agronomy; Spanish; special education; statistics; telecommunications technology; theatre design and technology; turf and turfgrass management; visual and performing arts; women's studies.

Academic Programs *Special study options:* academic remediation for entering students, accelerated degree program, adult/continuing education programs, advanced placement credit, distance learning, double majors, honors programs, independent study, internships, services for LD students, student-designed majors, study abroad, summer session for credit.

Library 25,273 titles, 346 serial subscriptions, 2,064 audiovisual materials.

Computers on Campus 102 computers available on campus for general student use. A campuswide network can be accessed from off campus. Internet access, online (class) registration, at least one staffed computer lab available. Computer purchase or lease plan available.

Student Life *Housing:* college housing not available. *Campus security:* part-time trained security personnel.

Athletics *Intramural sports:* basketball M(c)/W, bowling M/W, football M(c), golf M/W, softball M/W, tennis M/W, volleyball M/W.

Standardized Tests *Required:* SAT or ACT (for admission).

Costs (2004–05) *Tuition:* state resident $9180 full-time, $371 per credit part-time; nonresident $14,040 full-time, $585 per credit part-time. *Required fees:* $444 full-time, $75 per term part-time.

Financial Aid Of all full-time matriculated undergraduates who enrolled in 2003, 46 Federal Work-Study jobs (averaging $1790).

Applying *Options:* electronic application, early admission, deferred entrance. *Application fee:* $50. *Required:* high school transcript. *Application deadline:* rolling (freshmen), rolling (transfers). *Notification:* continuous (freshmen).

Admissions Contact Mr. Randall C. Deike, Assistant Vice President for Enrollment Management, The Pennsylvania State University Shenango Campus of the Commonwealth College, 147 Shenango Avenue, Sharon, PA 16146-1597. *Phone:* 814-865-5471. *Fax:* 724-983-2820. *E-mail:* psushenango@psu.edu.

THE PENNSYLVANIA STATE UNIVERSITY WILKES-BARRE CAMPUS OF THE COMMONWEALTH COLLEGE
Lehman, Pennsylvania

- **State-related** primarily 2-year, founded 1916, part of Pennsylvania State University
- **Calendar** semesters
- **Degrees** associate and bachelor's (also offers up to 2 years of most bachelor's degree programs offered at University Park campus)
- **Rural** 156-acre campus
- **Coed,** 735 undergraduate students, 79% full-time, 33% women, 67% men

Undergraduates 580 full-time, 155 part-time. 3% are from out of state, 1% African American, 1% Asian American or Pacific Islander, 1% Hispanic American, 5% transferred in. *Retention:* 79% of 2002 full-time freshmen returned.

Freshmen *Admission:* 453 applied, 281 admitted, 170 enrolled. *Average high school GPA:* 2.92. *Test scores:* SAT verbal scores over 500: 45%; SAT math scores over 500: 48%; SAT verbal scores over 600: 10%; SAT math scores over 600: 13%; SAT math scores over 700: 1%.

Faculty *Total:* 68, 54% full-time, 35% with terminal degrees. *Student/faculty ratio:* 14:1.

Majors Accounting; acting; actuarial science; adult and continuing education administration; advertising; aerospace, aeronautical and astronautical engineering; African-American/Black studies; agribusiness; agricultural and extension education; agricultural/biological engineering and bioengineering; agricultural business and management related; agricultural mechanization; agriculture; American studies; animal sciences; animal sciences related; anthropology; applied economics; archeology; architectural engineering; art; art history, criticism and conservation; art teacher education; Asian studies (East); astronomy; atmospheric sciences and meteorology; biochemistry; biological and biomedical sciences related; biological and physical sciences; biology/biological sciences; biology/biotechnology laboratory technician; biomedical/medical engineering; business administration and management; business/commerce; business/

The Pennsylvania State University Wilkes-Barre Campus of the Commonwealth College (continued)

managerial economics; chemical engineering; chemistry; civil engineering; classics and languages, literatures and linguistics; communication and journalism related; communication disorders; communication/speech communication and rhetoric; comparative literature; computer and information sciences; computer engineering; criminal justice/law enforcement administration; economics; electrical, electronic and communications engineering technology; electrical, electronics and communications engineering; elementary education; engineering science; English; environmental/environmental health engineering; film/cinema studies; finance; food science; forestry technology; forest sciences and biology; French; geography; geological and earth sciences/geosciences related; geology/earth science; German; graphic design; health/health care administration; history; horticultural science; hospitality administration related; human development and family studies; human nutrition; industrial engineering; information science/studies; international business/trade/commerce; international relations and affairs; Italian; Japanese; Jewish/Judaic studies; journalism; kinesiology and exercise science; labor and industrial relations; landscape architecture; landscaping and groundskeeping; Latin American studies; liberal arts and sciences/liberal studies; logistics and materials management; management information systems; management sciences and quantitative methods related; manufacturing engineering; marketing/marketing management; materials science; mathematics; mechanical engineering; medical microbiology and bacteriology; medieval and Renaissance studies; metallurgical technology; mining and mineral engineering; natural resources and conservation related; natural resources/conservation; nuclear engineering; nursing (registered nurse training); organizational behavior; parks, recreation and leisure facilities management; petroleum engineering; philosophy; physics; political science and government; pre-medical studies; psychology; rehabilitation and therapeutic professions related; religious studies; Russian; secondary education; sociology; soil science and agronomy; Spanish; special education; statistics; survey technology; telecommunications technology; theatre design and technology; turf and turfgrass management; visual and performing arts; women's studies.

Academic Programs *Special study options:* academic remediation for entering students, accelerated degree program, adult/continuing education programs, advanced placement credit, distance learning, double majors, honors programs, independent study, internships, services for LD students, student-designed majors, study abroad, summer session for credit. *ROTC:* Air Force (c).

Library 35,697 titles, 199 serial subscriptions, 394 audiovisual materials.

Computers on Campus 137 computers available on campus for general student use. A campuswide network can be accessed from off campus. Internet access, online (class) registration, at least one staffed computer lab available. Computer purchase or lease plan available.

Student Life *Housing:* college housing not available. *Activities and Organizations:* student-run newspaper, radio station. *Campus security:* part-time trained security personnel.

Athletics Member NJCAA. *Intercollegiate sports:* baseball M, basketball M, cross-country running M/W, golf M/W, soccer M/W, volleyball W. *Intramural sports:* basketball M/W, bowling M(c)/W(c), cheerleading M(c)/W(c), football M, racquetball M/W, softball W, volleyball M(c)/W.

Standardized Tests *Required:* SAT or ACT (for admission).

Costs (2004–05) *Tuition:* state resident $9180 full-time, $371 per credit part-time; nonresident $14,040 full-time, $585 per credit part-time. *Required fees:* $444 full-time, $75 per term part-time.

Financial Aid Of all full-time matriculated undergraduates who enrolled in 2003, 34 Federal Work-Study jobs (averaging $1074).

Applying *Options:* electronic application, early admission, deferred entrance. *Application fee:* $50. *Required:* high school transcript. *Application deadline:* rolling (freshmen), rolling (transfers). *Notification:* continuous (freshmen).

Admissions Contact Mr. Randall C. Deike, Assistant Vice President for Enrollment Management, The Pennsylvania State University Wilkes-Barre Campus of the Commonwealth College, PO Box PSU, Old Route 115, Lehman, PA 18627-9999. *Phone:* 814-865-5471. *Toll-free phone:* 800-966-6613. *Fax:* 570-675-9113. *E-mail:* wbadmissions@psu.edu.

THE PENNSYLVANIA STATE UNIVERSITY WORTHINGTON SCRANTON CAMPUS OF THE COMMONWEALTH COLLEGE

Dunmore, Pennsylvania

- **State-related** primarily 2-year, founded 1923, part of Pennsylvania State University
- **Calendar** semesters
- **Degrees** associate and bachelor's (also offers up to 2 years of most bachelor's degree programs offered at University Park campus)
- **Small-town** 43-acre campus
- **Coed,** 1,303 undergraduate students, 77% full-time, 50% women, 50% men

Undergraduates 997 full-time, 306 part-time. 1% are from out of state, 1% African American, 0.9% Asian American or Pacific Islander, 2% Hispanic American, 0.3% international, 6% transferred in. *Retention:* 77% of 2002 full-time freshmen returned.

Freshmen *Admission:* 653 applied, 517 admitted, 256 enrolled. *Average high school GPA:* 2.83. *Test scores:* SAT verbal scores over 500: 40%; SAT math scores over 500: 46%; SAT verbal scores over 600: 7%; SAT math scores over 600: 10%; SAT math scores over 700: 1%.

Faculty *Total:* 105, 59% full-time, 35% with terminal degrees. *Student/faculty ratio:* 15:1.

Majors Accounting; acting; actuarial science; adult and continuing education administration; advertising; aerospace, aeronautical and astronautical engineering; African-American/Black studies; agribusiness; agricultural and extension education; agricultural/biological engineering and bioengineering; agricultural business and management related; agricultural mechanization; agriculture; American studies; animal sciences; animal sciences related; anthropology; applied economics; archeology; architectural engineering; architectural engineering technology; art; art history, criticism and conservation; art teacher education; Asian studies (East); astronomy; atmospheric sciences and meteorology; biochemistry; biological and biomedical sciences related; biological and physical sciences; biology/biological sciences; biology/biotechnology laboratory technician; biomedical/medical engineering; business administration and management; business/commerce; business/managerial economics; chemical engineering; chemistry; civil engineering; classics and languages, literatures and linguistics; communication and journalism related; communication disorders; communication/speech communication and rhetoric; comparative literature; computer and information sciences; computer engineering; criminal justice/law enforcement administration; economics; electrical, electronics and communications engineering; elementary education; engineering science; English; environmental/environmental health engineering; film/cinema studies; finance; food science; forestry technology; forest sciences and biology; French; geography; geological and earth sciences/geosciences related; geology/earth science; German; graphic design; health/health care administration; history; horticultural science; hospitality administration related; human development and family studies; human nutrition; industrial engineering; information science/studies; international business/trade/commerce; international relations and affairs; Italian; Japanese; Jewish/Judaic studies; journalism; kinesiology and exercise science; labor and industrial relations; landscape architecture; landscaping and groundskeeping; Latin American studies; liberal arts and sciences/liberal studies; logistics and materials management; management information systems; management sciences and quantitative methods related; marketing/marketing management; materials science; mathematics; mechanical engineering; medical microbiology and bacteriology; medieval and Renaissance studies; mining and mineral engineering; natural resources and conservation related; natural resources/conservation; nuclear engineering; nursing (registered nurse training); occupational therapist assistant; organizational behavior; parks, recreation and leisure facilities management; petroleum engineering; philosophy; physics; political science and government; pre-medical studies; psychology; rehabilitation and therapeutic professions related; religious studies; Russian; secondary education; sociology; soil science and agronomy; Spanish; special education; statistics; theatre design and technology; turf and turfgrass management; visual and performing arts; women's studies.

Academic Programs *Special study options:* academic remediation for entering students, accelerated degree program, adult/continuing education programs, advanced placement credit, cooperative education, distance learning, double majors, honors programs, independent study, internships, services for LD students, study abroad, summer session for credit. *ROTC:* Air Force (c).

Library 53,572 titles, 102 serial subscriptions, 3,048 audiovisual materials.

Computers on Campus 104 computers available on campus for general student use. A campuswide network can be accessed from off campus. Internet access, online (class) registration, at least one staffed computer lab available. Computer purchase or lease plan available.

Student Life *Housing:* college housing not available. *Activities and Organizations:* drama/theater group, student-run newspaper. *Campus security:* part-time trained security personnel.

Athletics Member NJCAA. *Intercollegiate sports:* baseball M, basketball M/W, cheerleading M/W, cross-country running M/W, soccer M, softball W, volleyball W. *Intramural sports:* basketball M/W, bowling M(c)/W(c), skiing (downhill) M(c)/W(c), soccer M/W, softball M/W, volleyball M/W(c), weight lifting M(c)/W(c).

Standardized Tests *Required:* SAT or ACT (for admission).

Costs (2004–05) *Tuition:* state resident $9180 full-time, $371 per credit part-time; nonresident $14,040 full-time, $585 per credit part-time. *Required fees:* $424 full-time, $71 per term part-time.

Financial Aid Of all full-time matriculated undergraduates who enrolled in 2003, 38 Federal Work-Study jobs (averaging $1116).

Applying *Options:* electronic application, early admission, deferred entrance. *Application fee:* $50. *Required:* high school transcript. *Application deadline:* rolling (freshmen), rolling (transfers). *Notification:* continuous (freshmen).

Admissions Contact Mr. Randall C. Deike, Assistant Vice President for Enrollment Management, The Pennsylvania State University Worthington

Scranton Campus of the Commonwealth College, 120 Ridge View Drive, Dunmore, PA 18512-1699. *Phone:* 814-865-5471. *Fax:* 570-963-2524. *E-mail:* wsadmissions@psu.edu.

THE PENNSYLVANIA STATE UNIVERSITY YORK CAMPUS OF THE COMMONWEALTH COLLEGE
York, Pennsylvania

- **State-related** primarily 2-year, founded 1926, part of Pennsylvania State University
- **Calendar** semesters
- **Degrees** associate and bachelor's (also offers up to 2 years of most bachelor's degree programs offered at University Park campus)
- **Suburban** 53-acre campus
- **Coed**, 1,571 undergraduate students, 59% full-time, 43% women, 57% men

Undergraduates 934 full-time, 637 part-time. 2% are from out of state, 4% African American, 6% Asian American or Pacific Islander, 3% Hispanic American, 0.3% Native American, 0.3% international, 2% transferred in. *Retention:* 74% of 2002 full-time freshmen returned.

Freshmen *Admission:* 792 applied, 671 admitted, 300 enrolled. *Average high school GPA:* 2.77. *Test scores:* SAT verbal scores over 500: 43%; SAT math scores over 500: 47%; SAT verbal scores over 600: 13%; SAT math scores over 600: 17%; SAT verbal scores over 700: 2%; SAT math scores over 700: 2%.

Faculty *Total:* 120, 48% full-time, 40% with terminal degrees. *Student/faculty ratio:* 16:1.

Majors Accounting; acting; actuarial science; adult and continuing education administration; advertising; aerospace, aeronautical and astronautical engineering; African-American/Black studies; agribusiness; agricultural and extension education; agricultural/biological engineering and bioengineering; agricultural business and management related; agricultural mechanization; agriculture; American studies; animal sciences; animal sciences related; anthropology; applied economics; archeology; architectural engineering; art; art history, criticism and conservation; art teacher education; Asian studies (East); astronomy; atmospheric sciences and meteorology; biochemistry; biological and biomedical sciences related; biological and physical sciences; biology/biological sciences; biology/biotechnology laboratory technician; biomedical/medical engineering; biomedical technology; business/commerce; business/managerial economics; chemical engineering; chemistry; civil engineering; classics and languages, literatures and linguistics; communication and journalism related; communication disorders; communication/speech communication and rhetoric; comparative literature; computer and information sciences; computer engineering; criminal justice/law enforcement administration; economics; electrical, electronic and communications engineering technology; electrical, electronics and communications engineering; elementary education; engineering science; English; environmental/environmental health engineering; film/cinema studies; finance; food science; forestry technology; forest sciences and biology; French; geography; geological and earth sciences/geosciences related; geology/earth science; German; graphic design; health/health care administration; history; horticultural science; hospitality administration related; human development and family studies; human nutrition; industrial engineering; industrial technology; information science/studies; international business/trade/commerce; international relations and affairs; Italian; Japanese; Jewish/Judaic studies; journalism; kinesiology and exercise science; labor and industrial relations; landscape architecture; landscaping and groundskeeping; Latin American studies; liberal arts and sciences/liberal studies; logistics and materials management; management information systems; management sciences and quantitative methods related; manufacturing engineering; marketing/marketing management; materials science; mathematics; mechanical engineering; mechanical engineering/mechanical technology; medical microbiology and bacteriology; medieval and Renaissance studies; metallurgical technology; mining and mineral engineering; natural resources and conservation related; natural resources/conservation; nuclear engineering; nursing (registered nurse training); organizational behavior; parks, recreation and leisure facilities management; petroleum engineering; philosophy; physics; political science and government; pre-medical studies; psychology; rehabilitation and therapeutic professions related; religious studies; Russian; secondary education; sociology; soil science and agronomy; Spanish; special education; statistics; telecommunications technology; theatre design and technology; turf and turfgrass management; visual and performing arts; women's studies.

Academic Programs *Special study options:* academic remediation for entering students, accelerated degree program, adult/continuing education programs, advanced placement credit, distance learning, double majors, English as a second language, honors programs, independent study, internships, services for LD students, student-designed majors, study abroad, summer session for credit.

Library 49,996 titles, 243 serial subscriptions, 3,567 audiovisual materials.

Computers on Campus 155 computers available on campus for general student use. A campuswide network can be accessed from off campus. Internet access, online (class) registration, at least one staffed computer lab available. Computer purchase or lease plan available.

Student Life *Housing:* college housing not available. *Activities and Organizations:* student-run newspaper. *Campus security:* part-time trained security personnel.

Athletics Member NJCAA. *Intercollegiate sports:* basketball M/W, cross-country running M/W, soccer M, tennis M/W, volleyball W. *Intramural sports:* badminton M/W, basketball M/W, cheerleading M(c)/W(c), football M, soccer M/W, softball M/W, tennis M/W, ultimate Frisbee M/W, volleyball M/W.

Standardized Tests *Required:* SAT or ACT (for admission).

Costs (2004–05) *Tuition:* state resident $9180 full-time, $371 per credit part-time; nonresident $14,040 full-time, $585 per credit part-time. *Required fees:* $424 full-time, $71 per term part-time.

Financial Aid Of all full-time matriculated undergraduates who enrolled in 2003, 54 Federal Work-Study jobs (averaging $963).

Applying *Options:* electronic application, early admission, deferred entrance. *Application fee:* $50. *Required:* high school transcript. *Application deadline:* rolling (freshmen), rolling (transfers). *Notification:* continuous (freshmen).

Admissions Contact Mr. Randall C. Deike, Assistant Vice President for Enrollment Management, The Pennsylvania State University York Campus of the Commonwealth College, 1031 Edgecomb Avenue, York, PA 17403-3398. *Phone:* 814-865-5471. *Toll-free phone:* 800-778-6227. *Fax:* 717-771-4005. *E-mail:* ykadmission@psu.edu.

PITTSBURGH INSTITUTE OF AERONAUTICS
Pittsburgh, Pennsylvania

Admissions Contact Ms. Michaelene F. Kalinowski, Director of Admissions, Pittsburgh Institute of Aeronautics, PO Box 10897, Pittsburgh, PA 15236. *Phone:* 412-346-2100 Ext. 2123. *Toll-free phone:* 800-444-1440. *Fax:* 412-466-0513. *E-mail:* admissions@piainfo.org.

PITTSBURGH INSTITUTE OF MORTUARY SCIENCE, INCORPORATED
Pittsburgh, Pennsylvania

Admissions Contact Ms. Karen S. Rocco, Registrar, Pittsburgh Institute of Mortuary Science, Incorporated, 5808 Baum Boulevard, Pittsburgh, PA 15206-3706. *Phone:* 412-362-8500 Ext. 101. *Toll-free phone:* 800-933-5808. *Fax:* 412-362-1684. *E-mail:* pims5808@aol.com.

PITTSBURGH TECHNICAL INSTITUTE
Oakdale, Pennsylvania

- **Proprietary** 2-year, founded 1946
- **Calendar** quarters
- **Coed**

Admissions Contact Mary Lou Zook, Vice President of Admissions, Pittsburgh Technical Institute, 1111 McKee Road, Oakdale, PA 15071. *Phone:* 412-809-5100. *Toll-free phone:* 800-784-9675.

THE PJA SCHOOL
Upper Darby, Pennsylvania

Admissions Contact Mr. David Hudiak, Director, The PJA School, 7900 West Chester Pike, Upper Darby, PA 19082-1926. *Phone:* 610-789-6700. *Toll-free phone:* 800-RING-PJA.

READING AREA COMMUNITY COLLEGE
Reading, Pennsylvania

- **County-supported** 2-year, founded 1971
- **Calendar** quarters
- **Degree** certificates, diplomas, and associate
- **Urban** 14-acre campus with easy access to Philadelphia
- **Endowment** $745,770
- **Coed**

Student Life *Campus security:* 24-hour patrols.

Costs (2004–05) *Tuition:* area resident $1704 full-time, $72 per credit part-time; state resident $3192 full-time, $133 per credit part-time; nonresident $4680 full-time, $195 per credit part-time. *Required fees:* $504 full-time, $21 per credit part-time.

Financial Aid Of all full-time matriculated undergraduates who enrolled in 2003, 100 Federal Work-Study jobs (averaging $3300). 5 state and other part-time jobs (averaging $3300).

Reading Area Community College (continued)

Applying *Options:* electronic application, early admission, deferred entrance. *Application fee:* $20.

Admissions Contact Mr. David J. Adams, Director of Admissions, Reading Area Community College, PO Box 1706, Reading, PA 19603-1706. *Phone:* 610-607-6224. *Toll-free phone:* 800-626-1665. *Fax:* 610-375-8255.

THE RESTAURANT SCHOOL AT WALNUT HILL COLLEGE
Philadelphia, Pennsylvania

- **Proprietary** primarily 2-year, founded 1974
- **Calendar** semesters
- **Degrees** associate and bachelor's
- **Urban** 2-acre campus
- **Coed**

Faculty *Student/faculty ratio:* 25:1.

Standardized Tests *Recommended:* SAT or ACT (for admission).

Costs (2004–05) *Tuition:* $12,100 full-time.

Applying *Options:* common application, early admission, early decision, deferred entrance. *Application fee:* $50. *Required:* essay or personal statement, high school transcript, 2 letters of recommendation, interview. *Required for some:* entrance exam. *Recommended:* minimum 2.0 GPA.

Admissions Contact Mr. Karl D. Becker, Director of Admissions, The Restaurant School at Walnut Hill College, 4207 Walnut Street, Philadelphia, PA 19104. *Phone:* 215-222-4200 Ext. 3011. *Toll-free phone:* 877-925-6884 Ext. 3011. *Fax:* 215-222-4219. *E-mail:* info@walnuthillcollege.edu.

▶ **See page 548 for a narrative description.**

RETS INSTITUTE OF TECHNOLOGY
Pittsburgh, Pennsylvania

Admissions Contact 777 Penn Center Boulevard, Pittsburgh, PA 15235. *Toll-free phone:* 888-300-4255.

ROSEDALE TECHNICAL INSTITUTE
Pittsburgh, Pennsylvania

- **Independent** 2-year
- **Calendar** semesters
- **Degree** associate
- **Suburban** 6-acre campus
- **Coed, primarily women**
- **66% of applicants were admitted**

Faculty *Student/faculty ratio:* 20:1.

Costs (2004–05) *Tuition:* $20,140 per degree program part-time.

Admissions Contact Mr. Kevin Auld, Director, Rosedale Technical Institute, 4634 Browns Hill Road, Pittsburgh, PA 15217-2919. *Phone:* 412-521-6200. *Toll-free phone:* 800-521-6262.

SCHUYLKILL INSTITUTE OF BUSINESS AND TECHNOLOGY
Pottsville, Pennsylvania

- **Proprietary** 2-year, part of Fore Front Education, Inc
- **Calendar** quarters
- **Degree** diplomas and associate
- **Rural** campus
- **Coed,** 153 undergraduate students, 100% full-time, 68% women, 32% men

Undergraduates 153 full-time. Students come from 1 other state, 0.7% African American, 3% transferred in.

Freshmen *Admission:* 60 applied, 60 admitted, 60 enrolled. *Average high school GPA:* 3.0.

Faculty *Total:* 15, 87% full-time. *Student/faculty ratio:* 8:1.

Majors Administrative assistant and secretarial science; business administration and management; commercial and advertising art; computer and information sciences and support services related; drafting and design technology; electrical, electronic and communications engineering technology; legal assistant/paralegal; medical office management.

Academic Programs *Special study options:* academic remediation for entering students, advanced placement credit, cooperative education, independent study, internships, services for LD students.

Library Schuylkill Institute of Business and Technology Learning Resource Cent with 920 titles, 20 serial subscriptions, 300 audiovisual materials, an OPAC.

Computers on Campus 41 computers available on campus for general student use. A campuswide network can be accessed from off campus. Internet access, at least one staffed computer lab available.

Student Life *Housing:* college housing not available.

Costs (2005–06) *Tuition:* $10,000 full-time. Full-time tuition and fees vary according to degree level and program. No tuition increase for student's term of enrollment. *Required fees:* $450 full-time. *Payment plans:* installment, deferred payment. *Waivers:* employees or children of employees.

Applying *Options:* common application. *Application fee:* $50. *Required:* high school transcript, interview. *Application deadlines:* 10/25 (freshmen), 10/25 (transfers).

Admissions Contact Regina Gargano, Director of Admissions, Schuylkill Institute of Business and Technology, 171 Red Horse Road, Pottsville, PA 17901. *Phone:* 570-622-4835. *Fax:* 570-622-6563.

SOUTH HILLS SCHOOL OF BUSINESS & TECHNOLOGY
Atloona, Pennsylvania

Admissions Contact Ms. Marianne M. Beyer, Director, South Hills School of Business & Technology, 508 58th Street, Altoona, PA 16602. *Phone:* 814-944-6134. *Fax:* 814-944-4684. *E-mail:* admissions@southhills.edu.

SOUTH HILLS SCHOOL OF BUSINESS & TECHNOLOGY
State College, Pennsylvania

- **Proprietary** 2-year, founded 1970
- **Calendar** quarters
- **Degrees** certificates, diplomas, and associate (also includes Altoona campus)
- **Small-town** 6-acre campus
- **Coed,** 686 undergraduate students, 92% full-time, 69% women, 31% men

Undergraduates 628 full-time, 58 part-time. Students come from 1 other state, 1% African American, 0.3% Asian American or Pacific Islander, 0.6% Hispanic American, 0.4% Native American, 0.3% international, 16% transferred in. *Retention:* 83% of 2002 full-time freshmen returned.

Freshmen *Admission:* 632 applied, 510 admitted, 391 enrolled. *Average high school GPA:* 2.75.

Faculty *Total:* 60, 62% full-time. *Student/faculty ratio:* 15:1.

Majors Accounting; administrative assistant and secretarial science; business administration and management; computer and information sciences; computer programming (specific applications); diagnostic medical sonography and ultrasound technology; engineering technology; health information/medical records technology; legal administrative assistant/secretary; marketing/marketing management; medical administrative assistant and medical secretary; office management.

Academic Programs *Special study options:* advanced placement credit, distance learning, double majors, independent study, internships, part-time degree program.

Library Main Library plus 1 other.

Computers on Campus 360 computers available on campus for general student use. Internet access available.

Student Life *Housing:* college housing not available. *Activities and Organizations:* student-run newspaper, Phi Beta Lambda, South Hills Executives, Student Forum, newspaper. *Campus security:* 24-hour emergency response devices.

Standardized Tests *Required for some:* CPAt, CPAt.

Costs (2004–05) *Tuition:* $11,082 full-time, $308 per credit part-time. Full-time tuition and fees vary according to course load and program. Part-time tuition and fees vary according to course load and program. *Required fees:* $75 full-time, $25 per term part-time. *Waivers:* employees or children of employees.

Applying *Options:* electronic application. *Application fee:* $25. *Required:* high school transcript, minimum 1.5 GPA, interview. *Required for some:* essay or personal statement, 2 letters of recommendation. *Recommended:* minimum 3.0 GPA. *Application deadline:* 9/2 (freshmen).

Admissions Contact Ms. Diane M. Brown, Director of Admissions, South Hills School of Business & Technology, 480 Waupelani Drive, State College, PA 16801-4516. *Phone:* 814-234-7755 Ext. 2020. *Toll-free phone:* 888-282-7427 Ext. 2020. *Fax:* 814-234-0926. *E-mail:* admissions@southhills.edu.

THADDEUS STEVENS COLLEGE OF TECHNOLOGY
Lancaster, Pennsylvania

- **State-supported** 2-year, founded 1905
- **Calendar** semesters

- **Degree** associate
- **Urban** 33-acre campus with easy access to Philadelphia
- **Coed,** 660 undergraduate students, 100% full-time, 7% women, 93% men

Undergraduates 660 full-time. Students come from 1 other state, 16% African American, 1% Asian American or Pacific Islander, 6% Hispanic American, 0.6% Native American, 48% live on campus. *Retention:* 60% of 2002 full-time freshmen returned.

Freshmen *Admission:* 1,063 applied, 421 admitted. *Average high school GPA:* 2.52.

Faculty *Total:* 48, 94% full-time. *Student/faculty ratio:* 12:1.

Majors Architectural engineering technology; automobile/automotive mechanics technology; carpentry; computer programming (vendor/product certification); construction engineering technology; data entry/microcomputer applications; drafting and design technology; electrical, electronic and communications engineering technology; graphic and printing equipment operation/production; heating, air conditioning, ventilation and refrigeration maintenance technology; industrial arts; information science/studies; legal administrative assistant/ secretary; machine tool technology; mechanical design technology; pipefitting and sprinkler fitting; system administration; web page, digital/multimedia and information resources design; word processing.

Academic Programs *Special study options:* academic remediation for entering students, internships, services for LD students.

Library K.W. Schuler Learning Resources Center plus 1 other with 26,000 titles, 450 serial subscriptions, an OPAC, a Web page.

Computers on Campus 100 computers available on campus for general student use. A campuswide network can be accessed. Internet access, at least one staffed computer lab available.

Student Life *Housing Options:* coed, men-only. Campus housing is university owned. Freshman applicants given priority for college housing. *Activities and Organizations:* student-run newspaper, Tech Phi Tech. *Campus security:* 24-hour emergency response devices. *Student services:* health clinic, personal/ psychological counseling, women's center.

Athletics Member NJCAA. *Intercollegiate sports:* basketball M, cross-country running M, football M, golf M, track and field M, wrestling M. *Intramural sports:* archery M/W, baseball M, basketball M, bowling M/W, cross-country running M/W, football M, golf M, soccer M/W, softball M, table tennis M, tennis M/W, track and field M, volleyball M/W, weight lifting M/W, wrestling M/W.

Standardized Tests *Required:* ACT ASSET (for admission).

Costs (2004–05) *Tuition:* area resident $5140 full-time. *Required fees:* $30 full-time. *Room and board:* $4136; room only: $1816.

Applying *Options:* common application, electronic application, deferred entrance. *Application fee:* $25. *Required:* essay or personal statement, high school transcript, minimum 2.0 GPA, letters of recommendation, ASSET Test. *Required for some:* interview. *Application deadlines:* 6/30 (freshmen), 6/30 (transfers). *Notification:* continuous until 7/15 (freshmen).

Admissions Contact Ms. Erin Kate Nelsen, Director of Enrollment, Thaddeus Stevens College of Technology, Enrollment Services, 750 East King Street, Lancaster, PA 17602-3198. *Phone:* 717-299-7772. *Toll-free phone:* 800-842-3832. *Fax:* 717-391-6929. *E-mail:* nelsen@stevenscollege.edu.

THOMPSON INSTITUTE
Harrisburg, Pennsylvania

- **Proprietary** primarily 2-year, founded 1918, part of Kaplan Higher Education Corporation
- **Calendar** quarters
- **Degrees** certificates, diplomas, associate, and bachelor's
- **Suburban** 5-acre campus
- **Coed,** 485 undergraduate students, 100% full-time, 53% women, 47% men

Undergraduates 485 full-time. Students come from 2 states and territories, 2% are from out of state, 14% African American, 1% Asian American or Pacific Islander, 5% Hispanic American.

Freshmen *Admission:* 165 applied, 145 admitted, 103 enrolled.

Faculty *Total:* 27, 89% full-time. *Student/faculty ratio:* 25:1.

Majors Accounting; business administration and management; computer management; computer programming; computer systems networking and telecommunications; drafting and design technology; electrical, electronic and communications engineering technology; health information/medical records administration; medical/clinical assistant.

Academic Programs *Special study options:* academic remediation for entering students, adult/continuing education programs, advanced placement credit, internships, services for LD students, summer session for credit.

Library 950 titles, 20 serial subscriptions, an OPAC.

Computers on Campus 113 computers available on campus for general student use. A campuswide network can be accessed from off campus. Internet access, at least one staffed computer lab available. Computer purchase or lease plan available.

Student Life *Housing Options:* coed. Campus housing is leased by the school. *Activities and Organizations:* Electronics Club, CAD Club, DPMA, Math Club, national sororities. *Campus security:* campus facilities manager. *Student services:* personal/psychological counseling.

Costs (2005–06) *Tuition:* $8600 full-time. *Room only:* $1600. *Payment plans:* installment, deferred payment.

Applying *Options:* common application, electronic application, deferred entrance. *Application fee:* $50. *Required:* high school transcript. *Recommended:* minimum 2.0 GPA. *Application deadline:* rolling (freshmen), rolling (transfers).

Admissions Contact Mr. Charles Zimmerman, Admissions Director, Thompson Institute, 5650 Derry Street, Harrisburg, PA 17111. *Phone:* 717-564-4112. *Toll-free phone:* 800-272-4632. *Fax:* 717-564-3779. *E-mail:* czimmerman@ thompson.edu.

TRIANGLE TECH, INC.-DUBOIS SCHOOL
DuBois, Pennsylvania

- **Proprietary** 2-year, founded 1944, part of Triangle Tech, Inc
- **Calendar** semesters
- **Degree** associate
- **Small-town** 5-acre campus
- **Coed, primarily men**

Faculty *Student/faculty ratio:* 15:1.

Applying *Options:* deferred entrance. *Required:* high school transcript, minimum 2.0 GPA, interview.

Admissions Contact Mr. John Conway, Director of Admissions, Triangle Tech, Inc.-DuBois School, PO Box 551, DuBois, PA 15801. *Phone:* 412-359-1000. *Toll-free phone:* 800-874-8324. *Fax:* 814-371-9227. *E-mail:* info@triangle-tech.com.

TRIANGLE TECH, INC.-ERIE SCHOOL
Erie, Pennsylvania

Admissions Contact Jennifer Provost, Admissions Representative, Triangle Tech, Inc.-Erie School, 2000 Liberty St., Erie, PA 16502. *Phone:* 814-453-6016. *Toll-free phone:* 800-874-8324 (in-state); 800-TRI-TECH (out-of-state). *Fax:* 814-454-2818. *E-mail:* pfitzgerald@triangle-tech.com.

TRIANGLE TECH, INC.-GREENSBURG SCHOOL
Greensburg, Pennsylvania

- **Proprietary** 2-year, founded 1944, part of Triangle Tech, Inc
- **Calendar** semesters
- **Degree** diplomas and associate
- **Small-town** 1-acre campus with easy access to Pittsburgh
- **Coed, primarily men,** 255 undergraduate students, 100% full-time, 2% women, 98% men

Undergraduates 255 full-time. Students come from 2 states and territories, 1% are from out of state, 0.8% African American.

Freshmen *Admission:* 145 applied, 144 admitted, 97 enrolled.

Faculty *Total:* 26, 77% full-time. *Student/faculty ratio:* 12:1.

Majors Carpentry; construction trades; drafting and design technology; electrical/electronics equipment installation and repair; electrical/electronics maintenance and repair technology related; heating, air conditioning and refrigeration technology; heating, air conditioning, ventilation and refrigeration maintenance technology; mechanical drafting and CAD/CADD.

Academic Programs *Special study options:* academic remediation for entering students, adult/continuing education programs, advanced placement credit, summer session for credit.

Library Triangle Tech Library plus 2 others with 550 titles, 15 serial subscriptions.

Computers on Campus 100 computers available on campus for general student use. A campuswide network can be accessed from off campus. Internet access, at least one staffed computer lab available.

Student Life *Housing:* college housing not available. *Student services:* personal/ psychological counseling.

Costs (2004–05) *Tuition:* $10,864 full-time. *Required fees:* $200 full-time. *Payment plan:* installment.

Financial Aid Of all full-time matriculated undergraduates who enrolled in 2003, 5 Federal Work-Study jobs (averaging $2000).

Applying *Options:* common application, deferred entrance. *Application fee:* $75. *Required:* high school transcript. *Application deadline:* rolling (freshmen), rolling (transfers).

Triangle Tech, Inc.-Greensburg School (continued)

Admissions Contact Mr. John A. Mazzarese, Vice President of Admissions, Triangle Tech, Inc.-Greensburg School, 222 East Pittsburgh Street, Greensburg, PA 15601. *Phone:* 412-359-1000. *Toll-free phone:* 800-874-8324.

TRIANGLE TECH, INC.-PITTSBURGH SCHOOL
Pittsburgh, Pennsylvania

- **Proprietary** 2-year, founded 1944, part of Triangle Tech Group
- **Calendar** semesters
- **Degree** diplomas and associate
- **Urban** 5-acre campus
- **Coed, primarily men,** 377 undergraduate students, 100% full-time, 4% women, 96% men

Undergraduates 377 full-time. Students come from 3 states and territories, 6% are from out of state, 11% African American.
Freshmen *Admission:* 121 applied, 120 admitted, 120 enrolled. *Average high school GPA:* 2.00.
Faculty *Total:* 33, 85% full-time, 3% with terminal degrees. *Student/faculty ratio:* 10:1.
Majors Architectural engineering technology; carpentry; drafting and design technology; electrical, electronic and communications engineering technology; heating, air conditioning, ventilation and refrigeration maintenance technology; mechanical design technology.
Academic Programs *Special study options:* academic remediation for entering students, advanced placement credit.
Library 2,000 titles, 30 serial subscriptions.
Computers on Campus 50 computers available on campus for general student use. A campuswide network can be accessed from off campus. Internet access, at least one staffed computer lab available.
Student Life *Housing:* college housing not available. *Activities and Organizations:* student council. *Campus security:* 16-hour patrols by trained security personnel.
Costs (2005–06) *Tuition:* $302 per credit part-time.
Financial Aid Of all full-time matriculated undergraduates who enrolled in 2003, 16 Federal Work-Study jobs (averaging $1500). *Financial aid deadline:* 7/1.
Applying *Options:* early admission, deferred entrance. *Required:* high school transcript, minimum 2.0 GPA, interview. *Application deadline:* rolling (freshmen), rolling (transfers).
Admissions Contact Mr. John A. Mazzarese, Vice President of Admissions, Triangle Tech, Inc.-Pittsburgh School, 1940 Perrysville Avenue, Pittsburgh, PA 15214. *Phone:* 412-359-1000 Ext. 7174. *Toll-free phone:* 800-874-8324. *Fax:* 412-359-1012. *E-mail:* info@triangle-tech.edu.

TRIANGLE TECH, INC.-SUNBURY SCHOOL
Sunbury, Pennsylvania

Admissions Contact RR #1, Box 51, Sunbury, PA 17801.

TRI-STATE BUSINESS INSTITUTE
Erie, Pennsylvania

Admissions Contact Guy M. Euliano, President, Tri-State Business Institute, 5757 West 26th Street, Erie, PA 16506. *Phone:* 814-838-7673.

UNIVERSITY OF PITTSBURGH AT TITUSVILLE
Titusville, Pennsylvania

- **State-related** 2-year, founded 1963, part of University of Pittsburgh System
- **Calendar** semesters
- **Degree** certificates and associate
- **Small-town** 10-acre campus
- **Endowment** $795,000
- **Coed,** 565 undergraduate students, 75% full-time, 60% women, 40% men

Undergraduates 422 full-time, 143 part-time. Students come from 15 states and territories, 8% are from out of state, 14% African American, 2% Asian American or Pacific Islander, 2% Hispanic American, 0.4% Native American, 5% transferred in, 48% live on campus.
Freshmen *Admission:* 3,431 applied, 3,391 admitted, 232 enrolled. *Average high school GPA:* 2.85. *Test scores:* SAT verbal scores over 500: 28%; SAT math

scores over 500: 34%; ACT scores over 18: 66%; SAT verbal scores over 600: 8%; SAT math scores over 600: 5%; ACT scores over 24: 20%.
Faculty *Total:* 61, 34% full-time, 31% with terminal degrees. *Student/faculty ratio:* 12:1.
Majors Accounting; business administration and management; liberal arts and sciences/liberal studies; natural sciences; physical therapist assistant.
Academic Programs *Special study options:* academic remediation for entering students, advanced placement credit, distance learning, independent study, internships, part-time degree program, study abroad, summer session for credit.
Library Haskell Memorial Library with 49,256 titles, 126 serial subscriptions, 505 audiovisual materials, an OPAC.
Computers on Campus 62 computers available on campus for general student use. A campuswide network can be accessed from student residence rooms and from off campus. Internet access, at least one staffed computer lab available.
Student Life *Housing:* on-campus residence required through sophomore year. *Options:* coed, disabled students. Campus housing is university owned. Freshman campus housing is guaranteed. *Activities and Organizations:* drama/theater group, choral group, Phi Theta Kappa, Weight Club, SAB, SIFE, Diversity Club. *Campus security:* 24-hour emergency response devices and patrols, controlled dormitory access. *Student services:* health clinic, personal/psychological counseling.
Athletics Member NJCAA. *Intercollegiate sports:* basketball M(s)/W(s), golf M(s), volleyball W(s). *Intramural sports:* badminton M/W, basketball M/W, bowling M/W, football M/W, golf M/W, racquetball M/W, softball M/W, table tennis M/W, tennis M/W, volleyball M/W, weight lifting M/W.
Standardized Tests *Required:* SAT or ACT (for admission). *Recommended:* SAT (for admission).
Costs (2004–05) *Tuition:* state resident $8218 full-time, $293 per credit part-time; nonresident $17,098 full-time, $610 per credit part-time. Part-time tuition and fees vary according to student level. *Required fees:* $670 full-time, $88 per term part-time. *Room and board:* $6888. Room and board charges vary according to board plan. *Payment plan:* installment.
Applying *Options:* deferred entrance. *Application fee:* $35. *Required:* high school transcript, minimum 2.0 GPA. *Required for some:* essay or personal statement, 1 letter of recommendation. *Recommended:* interview. *Application deadline:* rolling (freshmen), rolling (transfers). *Notification:* continuous (freshmen).
Admissions Contact Mr. John R. Mumford, Executive Director of Enrollment Management, University of Pittsburgh at Titusville, PO Box 287, Titusville, PA 16354. *Phone:* 814-827-4409. *Toll-free phone:* 888-878-0462. *Fax:* 814-827-4519. *E-mail:* uptadm@pitt.edu.

VALLEY FORGE MILITARY COLLEGE
Wayne, Pennsylvania

- **Independent** 2-year, founded 1928
- **Calendar** 4-1-4
- **Degree** associate
- **Suburban** 119-acre campus with easy access to Philadelphia
- **Endowment** $7.2 million
- **Men only**

The College's primary goal is to prepare young men to transfer to and succeed at the 4-year college or university of their choice. For more than 95% of the graduates, that goal is achieved through challenging academic programs, a structured environment that builds confidence and character and fosters academic success, and personal transfer counseling and transfer agreements with major universities. VFMC offers the only 2-year Army ROTC commissioning program in the Northeast US, with full tuition scholarships for qualified applicants.

Faculty *Student/faculty ratio:* 10:1.
Student Life *Campus security:* 24-hour patrols, student patrols.
Standardized Tests *Required:* SAT or ACT (for admission).
Financial Aid Of all full-time matriculated undergraduates who enrolled in 2003, 20 Federal Work-Study jobs (averaging $1500).
Applying *Options:* common application, early admission, deferred entrance. *Application fee:* $25. *Required:* high school transcript, guidance counselor/teacher evaluation form. *Recommended:* minimum 2.0 GPA, interview.
Admissions Contact Maj. Kelly M. DeShane, Associate Director for College Enrollment, Valley Forge Military College, 1001 Eagle Road, Wayne, PA 19087-3695. *Phone:* 610-989-1300. *Toll-free phone:* 800-234-8362. *Fax:* 610-688-1545. *E-mail:* admissions@vfmac.edu.

▶ **See page 556 for a narrative description.**

WESTERN SCHOOL OF HEALTH AND BUSINESS CAREERS
Monroeville, Pennsylvania

Admissions Contact 1 Monroeville Center, Suite 250, Route 22, 3824 Northern Pike, Monroeville, PA 15146-2142.

WESTERN SCHOOL OF HEALTH AND BUSINESS CAREERS
Pittsburgh, Pennsylvania

Admissions Contact Mr. Bruce E. Jones, Director of Admission, Western School of Health and Business Careers, 421 Seventh Avenue, Pittsburgh, PA 15219. *Phone:* 412-281-7083 Ext. 114. *Toll-free phone:* 800-333-6607. *Fax:* 412-281-0319. *E-mail:* adm@westernschool.com.

WESTMORELAND COUNTY COMMUNITY COLLEGE
Youngwood, Pennsylvania

- **County-supported** 2-year, founded 1970
- **Calendar** semesters
- **Degree** certificates, diplomas, and associate
- **Rural** 85-acre campus with easy access to Pittsburgh
- **Coed,** 6,194 undergraduate students, 43% full-time, 63% women, 37% men

Undergraduates 2,657 full-time, 3,537 part-time. Students come from 5 states and territories, 2% African American, 0.3% Asian American or Pacific Islander, 0.5% Hispanic American, 0.2% Native American. *Retention:* 58% of 2002 full-time freshmen returned.

Freshmen *Admission:* 2,548 applied, 2,548 admitted, 1,531 enrolled.

Faculty *Total:* 398, 20% full-time. *Student/faculty ratio:* 17:1.

Majors Accounting; administrative assistant and secretarial science; architectural engineering technology; artificial intelligence and robotics; business administration and management; child development; commercial and advertising art; computer and information sciences; computer engineering technology; computer graphics; computer science; consumer merchandising/retailing management; criminal justice/law enforcement administration; criminal justice/police science; culinary arts; data processing and data processing technology; dental hygiene; dietetics; drafting and design technology; electrical, electronic and communications engineering technology; engineering; environmental engineering technology; fashion/apparel design; fashion merchandising; finance; fire science; graphic and printing equipment operation/production; health information/medical records administration; health teacher education; heating, air conditioning, ventilation and refrigeration maintenance technology; horticultural science; hospitality administration; hotel/motel administration; human services; information science/studies; legal administrative assistant/secretary; legal assistant/paralegal; liberal arts and sciences/liberal studies; marketing/marketing management; mechanical design technology; mechanical engineering/mechanical technology; medical administrative assistant and medical secretary; nuclear/nuclear power technology; nursing (licensed practical/vocational nurse training); nursing (registered nurse training); ophthalmic laboratory technology; photography; public administration; publishing; real estate; special products marketing; tourism and travel services management; welding technology.

Academic Programs *Special study options:* academic remediation for entering students, adult/continuing education programs, advanced placement credit, cooperative education, distance learning, double majors, English as a second language, honors programs, independent study, internships, off-campus study, part-time degree program, services for LD students, summer session for credit.

Library 34,522 titles, 643 serial subscriptions.

Computers on Campus 600 computers available on campus for general student use. A campuswide network can be accessed. Internet access, at least one staffed computer lab available.

Student Life *Housing:* college housing not available. *Activities and Organizations:* student-run newspaper, radio station, choral group. *Campus security:* 24-hour emergency response devices and patrols. *Student services:* personal/psychological counseling.

Athletics Member NJCAA. *Intercollegiate sports:* baseball M, golf M/W, softball W, tennis M/W, volleyball W. *Intramural sports:* basketball M/W, bowling M/W, football M/W, racquetball M/W, skiing (downhill) M/W, softball M/W, table tennis M/W, volleyball M/W, weight lifting M/W.

Standardized Tests *Required:* ACT ASSET (for placement).

Costs (2004–05) *Tuition:* area resident $1830 full-time, $61 per credit part-time; state resident $3810 full-time, $129 per credit part-time; nonresident $5640 full-time, $191 per credit part-time. Full-time tuition and fees vary according to course load. Part-time tuition and fees vary according to course load. *Required fees:* $120 full-time, $4 per credit part-time. *Waivers:* employees or children of employees.

Applying *Options:* electronic application, early admission. *Application deadline:* rolling (freshmen), rolling (transfers). *Notification:* continuous (freshmen). **Admissions Contact** Mr. Justin Tatar, Admissions Coordinator, Westmoreland County Community College, 400 Armbrust Road, Youngwood, PA 15697. *Phone:* 724-925-4064. *Toll-free phone:* 800-262-2103. *Fax:* 724-925-1150. *E-mail:* admission@wccc-pa.edu.

THE WILLIAMSON FREE SCHOOL OF MECHANICAL TRADES
Media, Pennsylvania

- **Independent** 2-year, founded 1888
- **Calendar** semesters
- **Degree** diplomas and associate
- **Small-town** 240-acre campus with easy access to Philadelphia
- **Men only**

Faculty *Student/faculty ratio:* 14:1.

Student Life *Campus security:* evening patrols, gate security.

Athletics Member NJCAA.

Standardized Tests *Required:* Armed Services Vocational Aptitude Battery (for admission).

Costs (2004–05) *Tuition:* All students attend on full scholarship which covers tuition, room and board, and textbooks.

Applying *Required:* essay or personal statement, high school transcript, minimum 2.0 GPA, 3 letters of recommendation, interview.

Admissions Contact Mr. Edward D. Bailey, Director of Enrollments, The Williamson Free School of Mechanical Trades, 106 South New Middletown Road, Media, PA 19063. *Phone:* 610-566-1776 Ext. 235. *E-mail:* wiltech@libertynet.org.

WINNER INSTITUTE OF ARTS & SCIENCES
Transfer, Pennsylvania

Admissions Contact One Winner Place, Transfer, PA 16154. *Toll-free phone:* 888-414-2433.

WYOTECH
Blairsville, Pennsylvania

Admissions Contact 500 Innovation Drive, Blairsville, PA 15717. *Toll-free phone:* 800-822-8253.

YORK TECHNICAL INSTITUTE
York, Pennsylvania

- **Private** 2-year
- **Calendar** continuous
- **Degree** diplomas and associate
- **Suburban** campus
- **Coed**

Faculty *Student/faculty ratio:* 25:1.

Costs (2004–05) *Tuition:* $22,000 full-time. *Required fees:* $1200 full-time.

Applying *Required:* high school transcript, minimum 2.0 GPA, interview. *Required for some:* essay or personal statement.

Admissions Contact Ms. Sharon Mulligan, Associate Director of Admissions, York Technical Institute, 1405 Williams Road, York, PA 17402. *Phone:* 717-757-1100 Ext. 318. *Toll-free phone:* 800-229-9675 (in-state); 800-227-9675 (out-of-state). *E-mail:* crb@yhi.edu.

YORKTOWNE BUSINESS INSTITUTE
York, Pennsylvania

Admissions Contact Ms. Bonnie Gillespie, Director of Admissions, Yorktowne Business Institute, West Seventh Avenue, York, PA 17404. *Phone:* 717-846-5000 Ext. 124. *Toll-free phone:* 800-840-1004. *Fax:* 717-848-4584. *E-mail:* info@ybi.edu.

PUERTO RICO

CENTRO DE ESTUDIOS MULTIDISCIPLINARIOS
San Juan, Puerto Rico

Admissions Contact URB San Agustin, 1206 13th Street, San Juan, PR 00926.

COLUMBIA COLLEGE
Yauco, Puerto Rico

Admissions Contact Box 3062, Yauco, PR 00698.

ELECTRONIC DATA PROCESSING COLLEGE OF PUERTO RICO-SAN SEBASTIAN
San Sebastian, Puerto Rico

Admissions Contact 48 Betances Street, PO Box 1674, San Sebastian, PR 00685.

HUERTAS JUNIOR COLLEGE
Caguas, Puerto Rico

Admissions Contact Mrs. Barbara Hassim, Director of Admissions, Huertas Junior College, PO Box 8429, Caguas, PR 00726. *Phone:* 787-743-1242.

HUMACAO COMMUNITY COLLEGE
Humacao, Puerto Rico

Admissions Contact Ms. Paula Serrano, Director of Admissions, Humacao Community College, PO Box 9139, Humacao, PR 00792. *Phone:* 787-852-2525.

INSTITUTO COMERCIAL DE PUERTO RICO JUNIOR COLLEGE
San Juan, Puerto Rico

- **Proprietary** 2-year, founded 1946
- **Calendar** trimesters
- **Degree** certificates, diplomas, and associate
- **Urban** 1-acre campus
- **Coed**, 1,270 undergraduate students, 86% full-time, 63% women, 37% men

Undergraduates 1,086 full-time, 184 part-time. 1% are from out of state, 100% Hispanic American.
Freshmen *Admission:* 1,429 applied, 697 admitted, 516 enrolled.
Faculty *Total:* 89, 38% full-time. *Student/faculty ratio:* 17:1.
Majors Accounting; administrative assistant and secretarial science; business administration and management; hotel/motel administration; information science/studies.
Academic Programs *Special study options:* adult/continuing education programs, double majors, English as a second language, independent study, part-time degree program. *ROTC:* Army (c).
Library Pedro Negron Library plus 1 other with 40,858 titles, 173 serial subscriptions, 320 audiovisual materials.
Computers on Campus 76 computers available on campus for general student use. At least one staffed computer lab available.
Student Life *Campus security:* 24-hour emergency response devices. *Student services:* personal/psychological counseling.
Costs (2005–06) *Comprehensive fee:* $7716 includes full-time tuition ($4680), mandatory fees ($180), and room and board ($2856). Part-time tuition: $130 per credit. *Room and board:* college room only: $1142.
Applying *Options:* common application, early admission. *Application fee:* $25. *Required:* high school transcript, interview, proficiency in Spanish. *Recommended:* letters of recommendation. *Application deadline:* 8/15 (freshmen). *Notification:* continuous (freshmen).
Admissions Contact Admissions Office, Instituto Comercial de Puerto Rico Junior College, PO Box 190304, San Juan, PR 00919-0304. *Phone:* 787-753-6335. *Fax:* 787-763-7249. *E-mail:* 1a_f_mena@icprjc.edu.

INTERNATIONAL JUNIOR COLLEGE
San Juan, Puerto Rico

Admissions Contact PO Box 8245, San Juan, PR 00910.

NATIONAL COLLEGE OF BUSINESS & TECHNOLOGY
Bayamon, Puerto Rico

Admissions Contact Mr. Desi Lopez, Vice President of Financial Aid and Compliance, National College of Business & Technology, PO Box 2036, Bayamon, PR 00960. *Phone:* 787-780-5134. *Toll-free phone:* 800-780-5188.

PUERTO RICO TECHNICAL JUNIOR COLLEGE
Mayaguez, Puerto Rico

Admissions Contact Calle Santiago R. Palmer #15 Est, Mayaguez, PR 00680.

PUERTO RICO TECHNICAL JUNIOR COLLEGE
San Juan, Puerto Rico

Admissions Contact 703 Ponce De Leon Avenue, Hato Rey, San Juan, PR 00917.

RAMIREZ COLLEGE OF BUSINESS AND TECHNOLOGY
San Juan, Puerto Rico

Admissions Contact Mrs. Evelyn Mercado, Director of Admissions, Ramirez College of Business and Technology, PO Box 8340, San Juan, PR 00910-0340. *Phone:* 787-763-3120.

TECHNOLOGICAL COLLEGE OF SAN JUAN
San Juan, Puerto Rico

Admissions Contact Mrs. Nilsa E. Rivera-Almenas, Director of Enrollment Management, Technological College of San Juan, 180 Jose R. Oliver Street, Tres Monjitas Industrial Park, San Juan, PR 00918. *Phone:* 787-250-7111 Ext. 2271. *Fax:* 787-250-7395.

UNIVERSITY COLLEGE OF CRIMINAL JUSTICE OF PUERTO RICO
Gurabo, Puerto Rico

Admissions Contact HC 02 Box 12000, Gurabo, PR 00778-9601.

UNIVERSITY OF PUERTO RICO AT CAROLINA
Carolina, Puerto Rico

Admissions Contact Mrs. Ivonne Calderon, Admissions Officer, University of Puerto Rico at Carolina, PO Box 4800, Carolina, PR 00984-4800. *Phone:* 787-257-0000 Ext. 3347.

RHODE ISLAND

COMMUNITY COLLEGE OF RHODE ISLAND
Warwick, Rhode Island

- **State-supported** 2-year, founded 1964
- **Calendar** semesters
- **Degree** certificates and associate
- **Suburban** 205-acre campus with easy access to Boston

■ **Endowment** $1.2 million
■ **Coed**, 16,293 undergraduate students, 35% full-time, 64% women, 36% men

Undergraduates 5,731 full-time, 10,562 part-time. Students come from 17 states and territories, 14 other countries, 7% African American, 3% Asian American or Pacific Islander, 10% Hispanic American, 0.6% Native American, 0.1% international, 3% transferred in.

Freshmen *Admission:* 6,510 applied, 4,657 admitted, 3,165 enrolled.

Faculty *Total:* 736, 45% full-time.

Majors Accounting; administrative assistant and secretarial science; adult development and aging; art; banking and financial support services; biological and physical sciences; business administration and management; business/commerce; chemical technology; clinical/medical laboratory technology; computer engineering technology; computer programming; criminal justice/police science; dental hygiene; dramatic/theatre arts; electrical, electronic and communications engineering technology; engineering; fashion merchandising; fire science; general retailing/wholesaling; general studies; instrumentation technology; kindergarten/preschool education; labor and industrial relations; legal administrative assistant/secretary; legal assistant/paralegal; liberal arts and sciences/liberal studies; marketing/marketing management; medical administrative assistant and medical secretary; medical radiologic technology; music; nursing (registered nurse training); occupational therapist assistant; physical therapist assistant; psychiatric/mental health services technology; rehabilitation and therapeutic professions related; respiratory care therapy; retailing; social work; special education; substance abuse/addiction counseling; theatre design and technology; urban studies/affairs.

Academic Programs *Special study options:* academic remediation for entering students, adult/continuing education programs, advanced placement credit, cooperative education, distance learning, double majors, English as a second language, external degree program, honors programs, independent study, internships, off-campus study, part-time degree program, services for LD students, study abroad, summer session for credit. *ROTC:* Army (c).

Library Community College of Rhode Island Learning Resources Center plus 3 others with 98,140 titles, 872 serial subscriptions, 20,231 audiovisual materials, an OPAC, a Web page.

Computers on Campus 1200 computers available on campus for general student use. A campuswide network can be accessed from off campus that provide access to e-mail. Internet access, online (class) registration, at least one staffed computer lab available.

Student Life *Housing:* college housing not available. *Activities and Organizations:* drama/theater group, choral group, Distributive Education Clubs of America, theater group, ABLE, Phi Theta Kappa. *Campus security:* 24-hour emergency response devices and patrols. *Student services:* health clinic, personal/psychological counseling.

Athletics Member NJCAA. *Intercollegiate sports:* baseball M(s), basketball M(s)/W(s), cross-country running M/W, golf M/W, soccer M(s)/W(s), softball W(s), tennis M/W, track and field M/W, volleyball W(s). *Intramural sports:* basketball M/W, cross-country running M/W, volleyball M/W, water polo M/W.

Costs (2004–05) *Tuition:* state resident $2040 full-time, $96 per credit hour part-time; nonresident $5992 full-time, $287 per credit hour part-time. Part-time tuition and fees vary according to course load. *Required fees:* $270 full-time, $7 per credit hour part-time, $32 per term part-time. *Payment plan:* deferred payment. *Waivers:* senior citizens and employees or children of employees.

Financial Aid Of all full-time matriculated undergraduates who enrolled in 2003, 500 Federal Work-Study jobs (averaging $2500). 70 state and other part-time jobs (averaging $2000).

Applying *Options:* deferred entrance. *Application fee:* $20. *Application deadline:* rolling (freshmen), rolling (transfers). *Notification:* continuous (freshmen).

Admissions Contact Dr. Heather C. Smith, Dean, Community College of Rhode Island, 400 East Avenue, Warwick, RI 02886. *Phone:* 401-333-7302. *Fax:* 401-825-2394. *E-mail:* webadmission@ccri.cc.ri.us.

NEW ENGLAND INSTITUTE OF TECHNOLOGY
Warwick, Rhode Island

Admissions Contact Mr. Michael Kwiatkowski, Director of Admissions, New England Institute of Technology, 2500 Post Road, Warwick, RI 02886-2266. *Phone:* 401-739-5000. *E-mail:* neit@ids.net.

SOUTH CAROLINA

AIKEN TECHNICAL COLLEGE
Aiken, South Carolina

Admissions Contact Mr. Dennis Harville, Director of Admissions and Records, Aiken Technical College, PO Drawer 696, Aiken, SC 29802-0696. *Phone:* 803-593-9231. *E-mail:* harden@aik.tec.sc.us.

CENTRAL CAROLINA TECHNICAL COLLEGE
Sumter, South Carolina

■ **State-supported** 2-year, founded 1963, part of South Carolina State Board for Technical and Comprehensive Education
■ **Calendar** semesters
■ **Degree** certificates, diplomas, and associate
■ **Small-town** 70-acre campus
■ **Coed**, 3,259 undergraduate students, 31% full-time, 71% women, 29% men

Undergraduates 1,016 full-time, 2,243 part-time. Students come from 2 states and territories, 1% are from out of state, 48% African American, 1% Asian American or Pacific Islander, 1% Hispanic American, 0.3% Native American, 0.2% international, 13% transferred in.

Freshmen *Admission:* 657 enrolled. *Test scores:* SAT verbal scores over 500: 24%; SAT math scores over 500: 22%; ACT scores over 18: 40%; SAT verbal scores over 600: 10%; SAT math scores over 600: 3%; ACT scores over 24: 3%.

Faculty *Total:* 160, 48% full-time, 16% with terminal degrees. *Student/faculty ratio:* 19:1.

Majors Accounting; administrative assistant and secretarial science; business administration and management; child care and support services management; civil engineering technology; criminal justice/safety; data processing and data processing technology; environmental control technologies related; industrial electronics technology; legal assistant/paralegal; liberal arts and sciences/liberal studies; mechanical drafting and CAD/CADD; multi-/interdisciplinary studies related; natural resources management and policy; nursing (registered nurse training); sales, distribution and marketing; surgical technology.

Academic Programs *Special study options:* academic remediation for entering students, adult/continuing education programs, advanced placement credit, cooperative education, distance learning, external degree program, independent study, internships, part-time degree program, summer session for credit.

Library Central Carolina Technical College Library with 20,356 titles, 245 serial subscriptions, 1,317 audiovisual materials, an OPAC, a Web page.

Computers on Campus 556 computers available on campus for general student use. A campuswide network can be accessed from off campus that provide access to student account and grade information. Internet access, online (class) registration, at least one staffed computer lab available.

Student Life *Housing:* college housing not available. *Activities and Organizations:* Creative Arts Society, Phi Theta Kappa, Computer Club, National Student Nurses Association (local chapter), Natural Resources Management Club. *Campus security:* 24-hour emergency response devices. *Student services:* personal/psychological counseling.

Standardized Tests *Required:* ACT COMPASS (for placement). *Required for some:* SAT or ACT (for placement).

Costs (2005–06) *Tuition:* area resident $2700 full-time, $113 per credit hour part-time; state resident $3180 full-time, $133 per credit hour part-time; nonresident $5388 full-time, $225 per credit hour part-time. *Payment plan:* installment. *Waivers:* senior citizens.

Applying *Options:* electronic application. *Application fee:* $25. *Required:* high school transcript. *Application deadline:* rolling (freshmen), rolling (transfers).

Admissions Contact Ms. Nita Colman, Director of Admissions and Counseling, Central Carolina Technical College, 506 North Guignard Drive, Sumter, SC 29150. *Phone:* 803-778-1961 Ext. 467. *Toll-free phone:* 800-221-8711 Ext. 455 (in-state); 803-778-1961 Ext. 455 (out-of-state). *Fax:* 803-778-6696. *E-mail:* colmanjh@cctech.edu.

CLINTON JUNIOR COLLEGE
Rock Hill, South Carolina

Admissions Contact Dr. Janis Pen, President, Clinton Junior College, PO Box 968, 1029 Crawford Road, Rock Hill, SC 29730. *Phone:* 803-327-7402.

DENMARK TECHNICAL COLLEGE
Denmark, South Carolina

Admissions Contact Mrs. Michelle McDowell, Director of Admission and Records, Denmark Technical College, Solomon Blatt Boulevard, Box 327, Denmark, SC 29042-0327. *Phone:* 803-793-5176. *Fax:* 803-793-5942.

FLORENCE-DARLINGTON TECHNICAL COLLEGE
Florence, South Carolina

Admissions Contact Mr. Kevin Qualls, Director of Enrollment Services, Florence-Darlington Technical College, 2715 West Lucas Street, PO Box 100548,

Florence-Darlington Technical College (continued)
Florence, SC 29501-0548. *Phone:* 843-661-8153. *Toll-free phone:* 800-228-5745. *Fax:* 843-661-8041. *E-mail:* kirvenp@flo.tec.sc.us.

FORREST JUNIOR COLLEGE
Anderson, South Carolina

- **Proprietary** 2-year, founded 1946
- **Calendar** quarters
- **Degree** certificates, diplomas, and associate
- **Small-town** 3-acre campus
- **Coed, primarily women,** 165 undergraduate students, 69% full-time, 92% women, 8% men

Undergraduates 114 full-time, 51 part-time. Students come from 2 states and territories, 26% are from out of state, 47% African American.
Freshmen *Admission:* 26 applied, 24 admitted.
Faculty *Total:* 18, 22% full-time. *Student/faculty ratio:* 16:1.
Majors Business administration and management.
Academic Programs *Special study options:* accelerated degree program, advanced placement credit, cooperative education, distance learning, double majors, English as a second language, freshman honors college, internships, part-time degree program, summer session for credit.
Library Forrest Junior College Library plus 1 other with an OPAC.
Computers on Campus 37 computers available on campus for general student use. A campuswide network can be accessed from off campus. Internet access, online (class) registration, at least one staffed computer lab available.
Student Life *Housing:* college housing not available. *Campus security:* late-night transport/escort service. *Student services:* health clinic, legal services.
Costs (2004–05) *Tuition:* $4950 full-time, $110 per quarter hour part-time. Full-time tuition and fees vary according to course load and program. Part-time tuition and fees vary according to course load and program. *Required fees:* $450 full-time, $150 per term part-time. *Payment plan:* installment.
Financial Aid Of all full-time matriculated undergraduates who enrolled in 2003, 18 Federal Work-Study jobs (averaging $700).
Applying *Options:* deferred entrance. *Application fee:* $25. *Required:* essay or personal statement, high school transcript, letters of recommendation, interview. *Application deadline:* 9/30 (freshmen).
Admissions Contact Ms. Janie Turmon, Admissions Representative, Forrest Junior College, 601 East River Street, Anderson, SC 29624. *Phone:* 864-225-7653 Ext. 206. *Fax:* 864-261-7471. *E-mail:* janieturmon@forrestcollege.com.

GREENVILLE TECHNICAL COLLEGE
Greenville, South Carolina

Admissions Contact Ms. Martha S. White, Director of Admissions, Greenville Technical College, PO Box 5616, Greenville, SC 29606-5616. *Phone:* 864-250-8109. *Toll-free phone:* 800-922-1183 (in-state); 800-723-0673 (out-of-state). *Fax:* 864-250-8534.

HORRY-GEORGETOWN TECHNICAL COLLEGE
Conway, South Carolina

Admissions Contact Ms. Teresa Hilburn, Associate Vice President for Enrollment Development, Horry-Georgetown Technical College, 2050 Highway 501 East, PO Box 261966, Conway, SC 29528-6066. *Phone:* 843-349-5277. *Fax:* 843-234-2213. *E-mail:* jackson@hor.tec.sc.us.

ITT TECHNICAL INSTITUTE
Greenville, South Carolina

- **Proprietary** primarily 2-year, founded 1992, part of ITT Educational Services, Inc
- **Calendar** quarters
- **Degrees** associate and bachelor's
- **Coed**

Standardized Tests *Required:* Wonderlic aptitude test (for admission).
Costs (2004–05) *Tuition:* Please see school catalog for specific information.
Financial Aid Of all full-time matriculated undergraduates who enrolled in 2003, 3 Federal Work-Study jobs.
Applying *Options:* deferred entrance. *Application fee:* $100. *Required:* high school transcript, interview. *Recommended:* letters of recommendation.
Admissions Contact Ms. Pamela Carpenter, Director of Recruitment, ITT Technical Institute, One Marcus Drive, Building 4, Suite 402, Greenville, SC 29615. *Phone:* 864-288-0777. *Toll-free phone:* 800-932-4488. *Fax:* 864-297-0930.

MIDLANDS TECHNICAL COLLEGE
Columbia, South Carolina

- **State and locally supported** 2-year, founded 1974, part of South Carolina State Board for Technical and Comprehensive Education
- **Calendar** semesters
- **Degree** certificates, diplomas, and associate
- **Suburban** 113-acre campus
- **Endowment** $2.4 million
- **Coed,** 10,710 undergraduate students, 45% full-time, 63% women, 37% men

Undergraduates 4,834 full-time, 5,876 part-time. Students come from 33 states and territories, 3% are from out of state, 37% African American, 2% Asian American or Pacific Islander, 2% Hispanic American, 0.9% Native American, 0.4% international.
Freshmen *Admission:* 2,229 admitted, 2,229 enrolled.
Faculty *Total:* 656, 34% full-time. *Student/faculty ratio:* 21:1.
Majors Accounting; architectural engineering technology; automobile/automotive mechanics technology; business administration and management; business/commerce; child care provision; civil engineering technology; clinical/medical laboratory technology; commercial and advertising art; computer and information sciences and support services related; computer systems networking and telecommunications; construction engineering technology; data processing and data processing technology; dental assisting; dental hygiene; electrical, electronic and communications engineering technology; electrician; engineering technology; graphic and printing equipment operation/production; health information/medical records technology; heating, air conditioning, ventilation and refrigeration maintenance technology; industrial electronics technology; legal assistant/paralegal; liberal arts and sciences/liberal studies; mechanical drafting and CAD/CADD; mechanical engineering/mechanical technology; medical radiologic technology; multi-/interdisciplinary studies related; nuclear medical technology; nursing assistant/aide and patient care assistant; nursing (licensed practical/vocational nurse training); nursing (registered nurse training); occupational therapist assistant; pharmacy technician; physical therapist assistant; precision production related; respiratory care therapy; surgical technology.
Academic Programs *Special study options:* academic remediation for entering students, adult/continuing education programs, advanced placement credit, cooperative education, distance learning, double majors, English as a second language, internships, part-time degree program, services for LD students, student-designed majors, summer session for credit.
Library 89,618 titles, 551 serial subscriptions, 1,036 audiovisual materials, an OPAC, a Web page.
Computers on Campus 125 computers available on campus for general student use. A campuswide network can be accessed from off campus. Internet access, online (class) registration, at least one staffed computer lab available.
Student Life *Housing:* college housing not available. *Activities and Organizations:* student-run newspaper. *Campus security:* 24-hour emergency response devices and patrols. *Student services:* personal/psychological counseling, women's center.
Athletics *Intramural sports:* basketball M, football M, softball M/W, volleyball M/W.
Standardized Tests *Required:* ACT ASSET (for admission). *Recommended:* SAT or ACT (for admission).
Costs (2004–05) *Tuition:* area resident $2808 full-time, $117 per credit part-time; state resident $3504 full-time, $146 per credit part-time; nonresident $8424 full-time, $351 per credit part-time. *Required fees:* $100 full-time. *Waivers:* senior citizens and employees or children of employees.
Financial Aid Of all full-time matriculated undergraduates who enrolled in 2003, 138 Federal Work-Study jobs (averaging $2496).
Applying *Options:* common application, electronic application, early admission, deferred entrance. *Recommended:* high school transcript. *Application deadline:* rolling (freshmen), rolling (transfers). *Notification:* continuous (freshmen).
Admissions Contact Ms. Sylvia Littlejohn, Director of Admissions, Midlands Technical College, PO Box 2408, Columbia, SC 29202. *Phone:* 803-738-8324. *Fax:* 803-738-7840.

MILLER-MOTTE TECHNICAL COLLEGE
Charleston, South Carolina

- **Proprietary** 2-year, founded 2000
- **Calendar** quarters
- **Degree** diplomas
- **Urban** campus
- **Coed**

Admissions Contact Ms. Julie Corner, Campus President, Miller-Motte Technical College, 8085 Rivers Avenue, Suite E, Charleston, SC 29418. *Phone:* 843-574-0101. *Toll-free phone:* 877-617-4740.

NORTHEASTERN TECHNICAL COLLEGE
Cheraw, South Carolina

- **State and locally supported** 2-year, founded 1967, part of South Carolina State Board for Technical and Comprehensive Education
- **Calendar** semesters
- **Degree** certificates, diplomas, and associate
- **Rural** 59-acre campus
- **Endowment** $27,621
- **Coed,** 1,115 undergraduate students

Undergraduates Students come from 2 states and territories, 1% are from out of state, 46% African American, 0.4% Asian American or Pacific Islander, 0.4% Hispanic American, 2% Native American.

Freshmen *Admission:* 468 applied, 468 admitted.

Faculty *Total:* 103, 27% full-time, 3% with terminal degrees. *Student/faculty ratio:* 25:1.

Majors Accounting; administrative assistant and secretarial science; business administration and management; computer programming; computer science; data processing and data processing technology; electrical, electronic and communications engineering technology; liberal arts and sciences/liberal studies; machine tool technology; marketing/marketing management; mechanical design technology.

Academic Programs *Special study options:* academic remediation for entering students, adult/continuing education programs, advanced placement credit, part-time degree program, summer session for credit.

Library Northeastern Technical College Library with 20,502 titles, 261 serial subscriptions, 690 audiovisual materials, an OPAC, a Web page.

Computers on Campus 125 computers available on campus for general student use. A campuswide network can be accessed from off campus. Internet access, at least one staffed computer lab available.

Student Life *Housing:* college housing not available. *Campus security:* 24-hour emergency response devices. *Student services:* personal/psychological counseling.

Standardized Tests *Required for some:* SAT (for admission).

Costs (2004–05) *Tuition:* area resident $2346 full-time, $98 per hour part-time; state resident $2448 full-time, $102 per hour part-time; nonresident $3936 full-time, $164 per hour part-time. *Required fees:* $100 full-time, $4 per hour part-time. *Waivers:* senior citizens.

Financial Aid Of all full-time matriculated undergraduates who enrolled in 2003, 25 Federal Work-Study jobs (averaging $2700).

Applying *Options:* early admission. *Application fee:* $13. *Required:* high school transcript, interview. *Application deadline:* rolling (transfers).

Admissions Contact Mrs. Mary K. Newton, Dean of Students, Northeastern Technical College, PO Drawer 1007, Cheraw, SC 29520-1007. *Phone:* 843-921-6935. *Fax:* 843-537-6148. *E-mail:* mpace@netc.edu.

ORANGEBURG-CALHOUN TECHNICAL COLLEGE
Orangeburg, South Carolina

- **State and locally supported** 2-year, founded 1968, part of State Board for Technical and Comprehensive Education, South Carolina
- **Calendar** semesters
- **Degree** certificates, diplomas, and associate
- **Small-town** 100-acre campus with easy access to Columbia
- **Endowment** $2.5 million
- **Coed**

Student Life *Campus security:* 24-hour emergency response devices and patrols.

Standardized Tests *Required for some:* ACT ASSET.

Costs (2004–05) *Tuition:* area resident $2640 full-time, $110 per semester hour part-time; state resident $3000 full-time, $125 per semester hour part-time; nonresident $4368 full-time, $182 per semester hour part-time. *Required fees:* $96 full-time, $4 per semester hour part-time.

Applying *Options:* common application, early admission. *Application fee:* $15. *Required:* high school transcript. *Required for some:* interview.

Admissions Contact Dana Rickards, Director of Recruitment, Orangeburg-Calhoun Technical College, 3250 St. Matthews Road, Highway 601, Orangeburg, SC 29118. *Phone:* 803-535-1219. *Toll-free phone:* 800-813-6519. *Fax:* 803-535-1388. *E-mail:* rickardsd@octech.edu.

PIEDMONT TECHNICAL COLLEGE
Greenwood, South Carolina

Admissions Contact Mr. Steve Coleman, Director of Admissions, Piedmont Technical College, PO Box 1467, Emerald Road, Greenwood, SC 29648. *Phone:* 864-941-8603. *Toll-free phone:* 800-868-5528. *E-mail:* coleman_s@piedmont.tec.sc.us.

SOUTH UNIVERSITY
Columbia, South Carolina

- **Proprietary** primarily 2-year, founded 1935, part of South University-Savannah
- **Calendar** quarters
- **Degrees** certificates, associate, bachelor's, and postbachelor's certificates
- **Urban** 2-acre campus
- **Coed,** 361 undergraduate students, 59% full-time, 84% women, 16% men

Undergraduates 212 full-time, 149 part-time. Students come from 1 other state, 89% African American, 0.3% Asian American or Pacific Islander, 0.6% Hispanic American, 0.3% Native American, 22% transferred in.

Freshmen *Admission:* 157 applied, 102 admitted, 14 enrolled. *Average high school GPA:* 2.6.

Faculty *Total:* 32, 44% full-time, 56% with terminal degrees. *Student/faculty ratio:* 14:1.

Majors Accounting; business administration and management; information technology; legal assistant/paralegal; legal studies; medical/clinical assistant.

Academic Programs *Special study options:* academic remediation for entering students, accelerated degree program, adult/continuing education programs, advanced placement credit, cooperative education, distance learning, double majors, internships, part-time degree program, services for LD students, summer session for credit.

Library South University Library with 10,765 titles, 100 serial subscriptions, 250 audiovisual materials, an OPAC.

Computers on Campus 40 computers available on campus for general student use. A campuswide network can be accessed from off campus. Internet access available.

Student Life *Housing:* college housing not available. *Campus security:* 24-hour emergency response devices. *Student services:* personal/psychological counseling.

Standardized Tests *Required:* SAT or ACT (for admission). *Recommended:* SAT (for admission), ACT (for admission), SAT or ACT (for admission), SAT and SAT Subject Tests or ACT (for admission), SAT Subject Tests (for admission).

Costs (2004–05) *One-time required fee:* $70. *Tuition:* $8685 per year part-time. Part-time tuition and fees vary according to course load. *Required fees:* $2895 per year part-time. *Room only:* Room and board charges vary according to board plan. *Payment plan:* installment. *Waivers:* employees or children of employees.

Applying *Options:* electronic application, deferred entrance. *Application fee:* $25. *Required:* high school transcript, interview, admissions test. *Application deadline:* rolling (freshmen), rolling (transfers).

Admissions Contact Trisha Sherwood, Director of Admissions, South University, 3810 Main Street, Columbia, SC 29203-6443. *Phone:* 803-799-9082. *Toll-free phone:* 866-629-3031. *Fax:* 803-799-9038.

SPARTANBURG METHODIST COLLEGE
Spartanburg, South Carolina

- **Independent Methodist** 2-year, founded 1911
- **Calendar** semesters
- **Degree** certificates, diplomas, and associate
- **Urban** 111-acre campus with easy access to Charlotte, NC
- **Endowment** $14.0 million
- **Coed,** 784 undergraduate students, 92% full-time, 48% women, 52% men

Spartanburg Methodist College (SMC) is the only private, 2-year, residential, liberal arts, coeducational college in South Carolina. Located in the college town of Spartanburg, South Carolina, and affiliated with the United Methodist Church, the College offers the Associate in Arts, the Associate in Science, and the Associate in Criminal Justice degrees. SMC offers a caring, nurturing environment that promotes success, with more than 90 percent of its graduates continuing their education at some of the finest colleges and universities in the nation.

Undergraduates 721 full-time, 63 part-time. Students come from 9 states and territories, 6 other countries, 7% are from out of state, 32% African American, 0.8% Asian American or Pacific Islander, 3% Hispanic American, 0.1% Native American, 2% international, 4% transferred in, 75% live on campus. *Retention:* 74% of 2002 full-time freshmen returned.

Spartanburg Methodist College (continued)

Freshmen *Admission:* 999 applied, 836 admitted, 441 enrolled. *Average high school GPA:* 3.02. *Test scores:* SAT verbal scores over 500: 17%; SAT math scores over 500: 21%; ACT scores over 18: 37%; SAT verbal scores over 600: 2%; SAT math scores over 600: 2%; ACT scores over 24: 3%.

Faculty *Total:* 43, 51% full-time, 33% with terminal degrees. *Student/faculty ratio:* 18:1.

Majors Administrative assistant and secretarial science; criminal justice/law enforcement administration; information technology; liberal arts and sciences/liberal studies.

Academic Programs *Special study options:* academic remediation for entering students, advanced placement credit, English as a second language, honors programs, independent study, part-time degree program, services for LD students, summer session for credit. *ROTC:* Army (c).

Library Marie Blair Burgess Learning Resource Center with 75,000 titles, 5,000 serial subscriptions, 3,150 audiovisual materials, an OPAC, a Web page.

Computers on Campus 48 computers available on campus for general student use. A campuswide network can be accessed from student residence rooms and from off campus. Internet access, at least one staffed computer lab available.

Student Life *Housing:* on-campus residence required through sophomore year. *Options:* coed, men-only, women-only. Campus housing is university owned. *Activities and Organizations:* drama/theater group, student-run newspaper, choral group, College Christian Movement, Alpha Phi Omega, Campus Union, Fellowship of Christian Athletes, Kappa Sigma Alpha. *Campus security:* 24-hour emergency response devices and patrols, student patrols, late-night transport/escort service, controlled dormitory access. *Student services:* health clinic, personal/psychological counseling.

Athletics Member NJCAA. *Intercollegiate sports:* baseball M(s), basketball M(s)/W(s), cheerleading M(s)/W(s), cross-country running M(s)/W(s), golf M(s)/W(s), soccer M(s)/W(s), softball W(s), tennis M(s)/W(s), volleyball W(s), wrestling M(s). *Intramural sports:* basketball M/W, football M/W, golf M/W, racquetball M/W, soccer M/W, softball M/W, table tennis M/W, tennis M/W, volleyball M/W.

Standardized Tests *Required:* SAT or ACT (for admission).

Costs (2005–06) *Comprehensive fee:* $15,476 includes full-time tuition ($9816), mandatory fees ($150), and room and board ($5510). Part-time tuition: $260 per credit. Part-time tuition and fees vary according to course load. *Room and board:* college room only: $2784. Room and board charges vary according to housing facility. *Payment plan:* installment. *Waivers:* employees or children of employees.

Financial Aid Of all full-time matriculated undergraduates who enrolled in 2003, 80 Federal Work-Study jobs (averaging $1600). 90 state and other part-time jobs (averaging $1600). *Financial aid deadline:* 8/30.

Applying *Options:* common application, electronic application, deferred entrance. *Application fee:* $20. *Required:* essay or personal statement, high school transcript, minimum 2.0 GPA, rank in top 75% of high school class. *Required for some:* letters of recommendation, interview. *Recommended:* interview. *Application deadline:* rolling (freshmen), rolling (transfers). *Notification:* continuous (freshmen).

Admissions Contact Mr. Daniel L. Philbeck, Vice President for Enrollment Management, Spartanburg Methodist College, 1000 Powell Mill Road, Spartanburg, SC 29301-5899. *Phone:* 864-587-4223. *Toll-free phone:* 800-772-7286. *Fax:* 864-587-4355. *E-mail:* admiss@smcsc.edu.

▶ **See page 552 for a narrative description.**

SPARTANBURG TECHNICAL COLLEGE
Spartanburg, South Carolina

- **State-supported** 2-year, founded 1961, part of South Carolina State Board for Technical and Comprehensive Education
- **Calendar** semesters plus summer sessions
- **Degree** certificates, diplomas, and associate
- **Suburban** 104-acre campus
- **Coed,** 4,095 undergraduate students, 53% full-time, 64% women, 36% men

Undergraduates 2,163 full-time, 1,932 part-time. 3% are from out of state, 29% African American, 1% Asian American or Pacific Islander, 1% Hispanic American, 0.2% Native American.

Faculty *Total:* 100.

Majors Accounting; administrative assistant and secretarial science; architectural engineering technology; automobile/automotive mechanics technology; biological and physical sciences; business administration and management; civil engineering technology; clinical/medical laboratory technology; computer and information sciences; drafting and design technology; electrical, electronic and communications engineering technology; engineering technology; heating, air conditioning, ventilation and refrigeration maintenance technology; horticultural science; liberal arts and sciences/liberal studies; machine tool technology; marketing/marketing management; mechanical engineering/mechanical technology; medical administrative assistant and medical secretary; medical radiologic

technology; respiratory care therapy; robotics technology; sign language interpretation and translation; trade and industrial teacher education.

Academic Programs *Special study options:* academic remediation for entering students, adult/continuing education programs, advanced placement credit, cooperative education, distance learning, part-time degree program, services for LD students, summer session for credit.

Library Spartanburg Technical College Library with 36,173 titles, 295 serial subscriptions, 3,534 audiovisual materials, an OPAC, a Web page.

Computers on Campus 360 computers available on campus for general student use. A campuswide network can be accessed from off campus. At least one staffed computer lab available.

Student Life *Housing:* college housing not available. *Activities and Organizations:* drama/theater group, student-run newspaper. *Campus security:* 24-hour patrols. *Student services:* personal/psychological counseling, women's center.

Standardized Tests *Required:* SAT or ACT (for placement), ACT ASSET, ACT COMPASS (for placement).

Costs (2005–06) *Tuition:* area resident $2666 full-time, $112 per hour part-time; state resident $3334 full-time, $139 per hour part-time; nonresident $5230 full-time, $218 per hour part-time. *Required fees:* $140 full-time, $5 per hour part-time, $20 per term part-time.

Financial Aid Of all full-time matriculated undergraduates who enrolled in 2003, 80 Federal Work-Study jobs (averaging $2600).

Applying *Options:* early admission. *Required:* high school transcript. *Application deadline:* rolling (freshmen), rolling (transfers). *Notification:* continuous (freshmen).

Admissions Contact Mr. Michael Harvey, Dean of Enrollment Management, Spartanburg Technical College, PO Box 4386, Spartanburg, SC 29305. *Phone:* 864-591-3800. *Toll-free phone:* 800-922-3679. *Fax:* 864-591-3916.

TECHNICAL COLLEGE OF THE LOWCOUNTRY
Beaufort, South Carolina

- **State-supported** 2-year, founded 1972, part of South Carolina Technical and Comprehensive Education System
- **Calendar** semesters
- **Degree** certificates, diplomas, and associate
- **Small-town** 12-acre campus
- **Coed,** 1,765 undergraduate students

Faculty *Total:* 69, 59% full-time.

Majors Accounting; administrative assistant and secretarial science; automobile/automotive mechanics technology; biological and physical sciences; business administration and management; carpentry; computer engineering technology; computer typography and composition equipment operation; construction engineering technology; criminal justice/law enforcement administration; data processing and data processing technology; electrical, electronic and communications engineering technology; environmental studies; fashion merchandising; heating, air conditioning, ventilation and refrigeration maintenance technology; horticultural science; human services; kindergarten/preschool education; legal administrative assistant/secretary; legal assistant/paralegal; liberal arts and sciences/liberal studies; marketing/marketing management; nursing (licensed practical/vocational nurse training); nursing (registered nurse training).

Academic Programs *Special study options:* academic remediation for entering students, adult/continuing education programs, advanced placement credit, internships, part-time degree program, student-designed majors, summer session for credit.

Library 25,226 titles, 244 serial subscriptions.

Computers on Campus 106 computers available on campus for general student use.

Student Life *Housing:* college housing not available. *Campus security:* security during class hours.

Athletics *Intramural sports:* tennis M/W.

Standardized Tests *Required:* ACT ASSET (for admission). *Recommended:* SAT and SAT Subject Tests or ACT (for admission).

Costs (2004–05) *Tuition:* state resident $2750 full-time, $115 per credit hour part-time; nonresident $3710 full-time, $155 per credit hour part-time. *Required fees:* $150 full-time, $5 per credit hour part-time, $25 per term part-time.

Financial Aid Of all full-time matriculated undergraduates who enrolled in 2003, 56 Federal Work-Study jobs (averaging $1700).

Applying *Options:* early admission, deferred entrance. *Application fee:* $10. *Application deadline:* rolling (freshmen), rolling (transfers).

Admissions Contact Mr. Les Brediger, Director of Admissions, Technical College of the Lowcountry, 921 Ribaut Road, PO Box 1288, Beaufort, SC 29901-1288. *Phone:* 843-525-8307.

TRI-COUNTY TECHNICAL COLLEGE
Pendleton, South Carolina

- **State-supported** 2-year, founded 1962, part of South Carolina State Board for Technical and Comprehensive Education
- **Calendar** semesters
- **Degree** certificates, diplomas, and associate
- **Rural** 100-acre campus
- **Coed,** 4,100 undergraduate students

Undergraduates Students come from 3 states and territories, 7 other countries, 11% African American, 0.8% Asian American or Pacific Islander, 0.8% Hispanic American, 0.3% Native American, 2% international.
Faculty *Total:* 400, 55% full-time. *Student/faculty ratio:* 25:1.
Majors Accounting; administrative assistant and secretarial science; business administration and management; clinical/medical laboratory technology; clothing/textiles; computer programming; criminal justice/law enforcement administration; data processing and data processing technology; drafting and design technology; electrical, electronic and communications engineering technology; electromechanical technology; health science; heating, air conditioning, ventilation and refrigeration maintenance technology; liberal arts and sciences/liberal studies; machine tool technology; medical/clinical assistant; nursing (registered nurse training); quality control technology; radio and television; veterinary technology.
Academic Programs *Special study options:* academic remediation for entering students, adult/continuing education programs, advanced placement credit, cooperative education, English as a second language, internships, part-time degree program, summer session for credit. *ROTC:* Army (c), Air Force (c).
Library Tri-County Technical College Library with 34,513 titles, 356 serial subscriptions, an OPAC, a Web page.
Computers on Campus 600 computers available on campus for general student use. Internet access, at least one staffed computer lab available.
Student Life *Housing:* college housing not available. *Activities and Organizations:* student-run newspaper. *Campus security:* 24-hour emergency response devices and patrols.
Standardized Tests *Required for some:* SAT (for placement), National League of Nursing Exam.
Costs (2004–05) *Tuition:* area resident $2450 full-time, $102 per credit hour part-time; state resident $2736 full-time, $114 per credit hour part-time; nonresident $5820 full-time, $242 per credit hour part-time. *Required fees:* $96 full-time, $4 per credit hour part-time.
Applying *Options:* early admission. *Application fee:* $20. *Application deadline:* rolling (freshmen), rolling (transfers). *Notification:* continuous (freshmen).
Admissions Contact Ms. Rachel Campbell, Director, Admission and Counseling, Tri-County Technical College, PO Box 587, Highway 76, Pendleton, SC 29670-0587. *Phone:* 864-646-1500. *Fax:* 864-646-8256. *E-mail:* admstaff@tricty.tricounty.tec.sc.us.

TRIDENT TECHNICAL COLLEGE
Charleston, South Carolina

- **State and locally supported** 2-year, founded 1964, part of South Carolina State Board for Technical and Comprehensive Education
- **Calendar** semesters
- **Degree** certificates, diplomas, and associate
- **Urban** campus
- **Coed,** 11,795 undergraduate students, 45% full-time, 63% women, 37% men

Undergraduates 5,270 full-time, 6,525 part-time. 1% are from out of state, 28% African American, 2% Asian American or Pacific Islander, 2% Hispanic American, 0.5% Native American.
Freshmen *Admission:* 2,094 enrolled.
Faculty *Total:* 637, 41% full-time.
Majors Accounting; administrative assistant and secretarial science; airframe mechanics and aircraft maintenance technology; automobile/automotive mechanics technology; biological and physical sciences; broadcast journalism; business administration and management; child care provision; civil engineering technology; clinical/medical laboratory technology; commercial and advertising art; computer engineering technology; computer graphics; computer/information technology services administration related; computer programming (specific applications); computer systems networking and telecommunications; criminal justice/law enforcement administration; culinary arts; dental hygiene; electrical, electronic and communications engineering technology; engineering technology; horticultural science; hotel/motel administration; human services; industrial technology; legal assistant/paralegal; legal studies; liberal arts and sciences/liberal studies; machine tool technology; marketing/marketing management; mechanical engineering/mechanical technology; medical administrative assistant and medical secretary; nursing (registered nurse training); occupational therapy; physical therapy; respiratory care therapy; telecommunications; veteri-

nary technology; web/multimedia management and webmaster; web page, digital/multimedia and information resources design.
Academic Programs *Special study options:* academic remediation for entering students, advanced placement credit, cooperative education, English as a second language, part-time degree program, services for LD students, summer session for credit.
Library Learning Resources Center plus 3 others with 68,462 titles, 868 serial subscriptions.
Computers on Campus 500 computers available on campus for general student use. A campuswide network can be accessed. At least one staffed computer lab available. Computer purchase or lease plan available.
Student Life *Housing:* college housing not available. *Activities and Organizations:* student-run newspaper. *Campus security:* 24-hour emergency response devices and patrols, late-night transport/escort service. *Student services:* personal/psychological counseling.
Standardized Tests *Required:* SAT I, ACT, or in-house test (for placement).
Costs (2005–06) *Tuition:* area resident $2950 full-time, $120 per credit hour part-time; state resident $3276 full-time, $134 per credit hour part-time; nonresident $5586 full-time, $230 per credit hour part-time. *Required fees:* $50 full-time, $5 per credit hour part-time.
Financial Aid Of all full-time matriculated undergraduates who enrolled in 2003, 117 Federal Work-Study jobs (averaging $3000).
Applying *Options:* common application, early admission. *Application fee:* $25. *Required for some:* high school transcript. *Application deadlines:* 8/4 (freshmen), 8/4 (transfers). *Notification:* continuous (freshmen).
Admissions Contact Ms. Clara Martin, Admissions Director (Interim), Trident Technical College, 7000 Rivers Avenue, Charleston, SC 29423-8067. *Phone:* 843-574-6483.

UNIVERSITY OF SOUTH CAROLINA LANCASTER
Lancaster, South Carolina

Admissions Contact Ms. Rebecca D. Parker, Director of Admissions, University of South Carolina Lancaster, PO Box 889, Lancaster, SC 29721-0889. *Phone:* 803-313-7000. *E-mail:* bparker@gwm.sc.edu.

UNIVERSITY OF SOUTH CAROLINA SALKEHATCHIE
Allendale, South Carolina

- **State-supported** 2-year, founded 1965, part of University of South Carolina System
- **Calendar** semesters
- **Degree** associate
- **Rural** 95-acre campus
- **Coed**

Student Life *Campus security:* 24-hour emergency response devices.
Athletics Member NJCAA.
Standardized Tests *Required:* SAT or ACT (for admission).
Costs (2004–05) *One-time required fee:* $50. *Tuition:* state resident $3798 full-time, $158 per semester hour part-time. *Required fees:* $130 full-time, $10 per semester hour part-time.
Financial Aid Of all full-time matriculated undergraduates who enrolled in 2003, 53 Federal Work-Study jobs (averaging $2500). 68 state and other part-time jobs.
Applying *Required:* high school transcript, minimum 2.0 GPA.
Admissions Contact Ms. Jane T. Brewer, Associate Dean for Student Services, University of South Carolina Salkehatchie, PO Box 617, Allendale, SC 29810-0617. *Phone:* 803-584-3446. *Toll-free phone:* 800-922-5500.

UNIVERSITY OF SOUTH CAROLINA SUMTER
Sumter, South Carolina

- **State-supported** 2-year, founded 1966, part of University of South Carolina System
- **Calendar** semesters
- **Degree** associate
- **Urban** 50-acre campus
- **Endowment** $1.5 million
- **Coed,** 1,042 undergraduate students, 53% full-time, 60% women, 40% men

Undergraduates 552 full-time, 490 part-time. Students come from 2 states and territories, 4 other countries, 1% are from out of state, 27% African

University of South Carolina Sumter (continued)

American, 2% Asian American or Pacific Islander, 3% Hispanic American, 1% Native American, 0.4% international, 11% transferred in. *Retention:* 58% of 2002 full-time freshmen returned.

Freshmen *Admission:* 449 applied, 289 admitted, 238 enrolled. *Average high school GPA:* 3.11. *Test scores:* SAT verbal scores over 500: 50%; SAT math scores over 500: 50%; ACT scores over 18: 65%; SAT verbal scores over 600: 5%; SAT math scores over 600: 5%; ACT scores over 24: 6%.

Faculty *Total:* 66, 59% full-time, 62% with terminal degrees. *Student/faculty ratio:* 19:1.

Majors Interdisciplinary studies; liberal arts and sciences/liberal studies.

Academic Programs *Special study options:* adult/continuing education programs, advanced placement credit, distance learning, honors programs, independent study, part-time degree program, services for LD students, summer session for credit. *ROTC:* Army (c), Air Force (c).

Library University of South Carolina at Sumter Library with 81,114 titles, 1,114 serial subscriptions, 913 audiovisual materials, an OPAC, a Web page.

Computers on Campus 355 computers available on campus for general student use. A campuswide network can be accessed from off campus that provide access to online course evaluation, online student surveys. Internet access, online (class) registration, at least one staffed computer lab available.

Student Life *Housing:* college housing not available. *Activities and Organizations:* drama/theater group, choral group, Association of African-American Students, Baptist Student Union, Student Education Association, Gamecock Ambassadors, Environmental Club. *Campus security:* late-night transport/escort service. *Student services:* personal/psychological counseling.

Athletics Member NSCAA. *Intramural sports:* badminton M/W, basketball M/W, bowling M/W, gymnastics M/W, racquetball M/W, rock climbing M/W, soccer M, softball M/W, table tennis M/W, volleyball M/W.

Standardized Tests *Required:* SAT or ACT (for admission).

Costs (2004–05) *Tuition:* state resident $3798 full-time, $158 per semester hour part-time; nonresident $9460 full-time, $394 per semester hour part-time. *Required fees:* $260 full-time, $10 per semester hour part-time. *Waivers:* senior citizens.

Financial Aid Of all full-time matriculated undergraduates who enrolled in 2003, 47 Federal Work-Study jobs (averaging $1337).

Applying *Options:* common application, electronic application. *Application fee:* $40. *Required:* high school transcript, minimum 2.0 GPA. *Application deadline:* 8/8 (freshmen), rolling (transfers).

Admissions Contact Dr. Robert Ferrell, Director of Admissions, University of South Carolina Sumter, 200 Miller Road, Sumter, SC 29150-2498. *Phone:* 803-938-3762. *Fax:* 803-938-3901. *E-mail:* bobf@usc.sumter.edu.

UNIVERSITY OF SOUTH CAROLINA UNION
Union, South Carolina

- **State-supported** 2-year, founded 1965, part of University of South Carolina System
- **Calendar** semesters
- **Degree** associate
- **Small-town** campus with easy access to Charlotte
- **Coed,** 406 undergraduate students, 41% full-time, 63% women, 37% men

Undergraduates 165 full-time, 241 part-time. Students come from 2 states and territories, 20% African American, 0.2% Asian American or Pacific Islander, 0.2% Hispanic American, 0.2% Native American.

Freshmen *Admission:* 126 applied, 116 admitted. *Test scores:* SAT verbal scores over 500: 15%; SAT math scores over 500: 18%.

Faculty *Total:* 25, 52% full-time. *Student/faculty ratio:* 14:1.

Majors Biological and physical sciences; liberal arts and sciences/liberal studies.

Academic Programs *Special study options:* part-time degree program.

Computers on Campus 30 computers available on campus for general student use. A campuswide network can be accessed from off campus.

Student Life *Housing:* college housing not available. *Activities and Organizations:* drama/theater group, student-run newspaper, choral group.

Standardized Tests *Required:* SAT or ACT (for admission).

Costs (2004–05) *Tuition:* state resident $3798 full-time, $158 per hour part-time; nonresident $9460 full-time, $394 per hour part-time. *Required fees:* $200 full-time, $8 per hour part-time. *Payment plan:* deferred payment. *Waivers:* senior citizens and employees or children of employees.

Financial Aid Of all full-time matriculated undergraduates who enrolled in 2003, 16 Federal Work-Study jobs (averaging $3400).

Applying *Application fee:* $40. *Required:* high school transcript. *Application deadline:* rolling (freshmen).

Admissions Contact Mr. Terry E. Young, Director of Enrollment Services, University of South Carolina Union, PO Drawer 729, Union, SC 29379-0729. *Phone:* 864-429-8728.

WILLIAMSBURG TECHNICAL COLLEGE
Kingstree, South Carolina

- **State-supported** 2-year, founded 1969, part of South Carolina State Board for Technical and Comprehensive Education
- **Calendar** semesters
- **Degree** certificates, diplomas, and associate
- **Rural** 41-acre campus
- **Endowment** $52,987
- **Coed, primarily women**

Faculty *Student/faculty ratio:* 13:1.

Student Life *Campus security:* late-night transport/escort service.

Standardized Tests *Required:* ACT ASSET, ACT COMPASS (for placement). *Recommended:* SAT or ACT (for placement).

Costs (2004–05) *Tuition:* state resident $2550 full-time, $106 per credit hour part-time; nonresident $4848 full-time, $202 per credit hour part-time. *Required fees:* $4 per credit hour part-time, $10 per term part-time.

Financial Aid Of all full-time matriculated undergraduates who enrolled in 2003, 22 Federal Work-Study jobs (averaging $2800).

Applying *Options:* common application, early admission, deferred entrance. *Application fee:* $10. *Required:* high school transcript.

Admissions Contact Ms. Elaine M. Hanna, Director of Admissions, Williamsburg Technical College, 601 Martin Luther King, Jr. Avenue, Kingstree, SC 29556-4197. *Phone:* 843-355-4110 Ext. 4162. *Toll-free phone:* 800-768-2021 Ext. 4162. *Fax:* 843-355-4269. *E-mail:* admissions@wil.tec.sc.us.

YORK TECHNICAL COLLEGE
Rock Hill, South Carolina

- **State-supported** 2-year, founded 1961, part of South Carolina State Board for Technical and Comprehensive Education
- **Calendar** semesters
- **Degree** certificates, diplomas, and associate
- **Small-town** 110-acre campus with easy access to Charlotte
- **Coed**

Student Life *Campus security:* 24-hour patrols.

Standardized Tests *Required:* SAT I, ACT, or ACT ASSET, ACT COMPASS (for admission).

Costs (2004–05) *Tuition:* area resident $2750 full-time, $115 per semester hour part-time; state resident $3100 full-time, $130 per semester hour part-time; nonresident $6200 full-time, $259 per semester hour part-time. Full-time tuition and fees vary according to location. Part-time tuition and fees vary according to location. *Required fees:* $136 full-time, $4 per semester hour part-time, $20 per term part-time.

Financial Aid Of all full-time matriculated undergraduates who enrolled in 2003, 56 Federal Work-Study jobs (averaging $3500).

Applying *Options:* electronic application. *Required for some:* high school transcript.

Admissions Contact Mr. Kenny Aldridge, Admissions Department Manager, York Technical College, 452 South Anderson Road, Rock Hill, SC 29730. *Phone:* 803-327-8008. *Toll-free phone:* 800-922-8324. *Fax:* 803-981-7237. *E-mail:* kaldridge@yorktech.com.

SOUTH DAKOTA

KILIAN COMMUNITY COLLEGE
Sioux Falls, South Dakota

- **Independent** 2-year, founded 1977
- **Calendar** trimesters
- **Degree** certificates and associate
- **Urban** 2-acre campus
- **Endowment** $1587
- **Coed**

Faculty *Student/faculty ratio:* 8:1.

Student Life *Campus security:* late-night transport/escort service.

Standardized Tests *Required for some:* ACT ASSET.

Costs (2004–05) *Tuition:* $6660 full-time, $185 per credit part-time. *Required fees:* $150 full-time.
Financial Aid Of all full-time matriculated undergraduates who enrolled in 2003, 31 Federal Work-Study jobs (averaging $1200).
Applying *Options:* early admission, deferred entrance. *Application fee:* $25. *Required:* high school transcript.
Admissions Contact Ms. Jacque Danielson, Director of Admissions, Kilian Community College, 224 North Phillips Avenue, Sioux Falls, SD 57104-6014. *Phone:* 605-221-3100. *Toll-free phone:* 800-888-1147. *Fax:* 605-336-2606. *E-mail:* info@kilian.edu.

LAKE AREA TECHNICAL INSTITUTE
Watertown, South Dakota

- **State-supported** 2-year, founded 1964
- **Calendar** semesters
- **Degree** diplomas and associate
- **Small-town** 16-acre campus
- **Coed**

Faculty *Student/faculty ratio:* 15:1.
Standardized Tests *Required:* ACT (for admission).
Costs (2004–05) *Tuition:* Full-time tuition and fees vary according to program. Tuition varies by program.
Financial Aid Of all full-time matriculated undergraduates who enrolled in 2003, 100 Federal Work-Study jobs (averaging $1200).
Applying *Options:* electronic application. *Application fee:* $15. *Required:* high school transcript. *Required for some:* essay or personal statement, 3 letters of recommendation, interview.
Admissions Contact Ms. Debra Shephard, Assistant Director, Lake Area Technical Institute, 230 11th Street Northeast, Watertown, SD 57201. *Phone:* 605-882-5284. *Toll-free phone:* 800-657-4344. *E-mail:* latiinfo@lati.tec.sd.us.

MITCHELL TECHNICAL INSTITUTE
Mitchell, South Dakota

- **District-supported** 2-year, founded 1968
- **Calendar** semesters
- **Degree** diplomas and associate
- **Rural** 90-acre campus
- **Coed**

Faculty *Student/faculty ratio:* 16:1.
Standardized Tests *Required for some:* TABE. *Recommended:* ACT (for admission).
Costs (2004–05) *Tuition:* $60 per credit hour part-time; state resident $2500 full-time; nonresident $2500 full-time. Full-time tuition and fees vary according to course level and program. Part-time tuition and fees vary according to course level and program. *Required fees:* $600 full-time, $20 per credit hour part-time. *Room and board:* Room and board charges vary according to housing facility.
Financial Aid Of all full-time matriculated undergraduates who enrolled in 2003, 67 Federal Work-Study jobs (averaging $1100).
Applying *Options:* electronic application. *Application fee:* $25. *Required:* high school transcript. *Required for some:* essay or personal statement, interview. *Recommended:* minimum 2.0 GPA.
Admissions Contact Mr. Clayton Deuter, Admissions Representative, Mitchell Technical Institute, 821 North Capital, Mitchell, SD 57301. *Phone:* 605-995-3025. *Toll-free phone:* 800-952-0042. *Fax:* 605-996-3299. *E-mail:* questions@mti.tec.sd.us.

NATIONAL AMERICAN UNIVERSITY
Ellsworth AFB, South Dakota

Admissions Contact 2700 Doolittle Drive, Ellsworth AFB, SD 57706.

SISSETON-WAHPETON COMMUNITY COLLEGE
Sisseton, South Dakota

- **Federally supported** 2-year, founded 1979
- **Calendar** semesters
- **Degree** certificates and associate
- **Rural** 2-acre campus
- **Endowment** $253,820
- **Coed,** 274 undergraduate students, 54% full-time, 70% women, 30% men

Undergraduates 147 full-time, 127 part-time. Students come from 3 states and territories, 82% Native American, 5% transferred in.

Freshmen *Admission:* 53 applied, 53 admitted, 53 enrolled.
Faculty *Total:* 25, 40% full-time, 40% with terminal degrees. *Student/faculty ratio:* 10:1.
Majors Accounting; American Indian/Native American studies; business administration and management; electrical, electronic and communications engineering technology; hospitality administration; information science/studies; kindergarten/preschool education; liberal arts and sciences/liberal studies; natural sciences; nursing (registered nurse training); nutrition sciences; substance abuse/addiction counseling.
Academic Programs *Special study options:* academic remediation for entering students, adult/continuing education programs, cooperative education, double majors, internships, off-campus study, part-time degree program, summer session for credit.
Library Sisseton-Wahpeton Community College Library with 15,481 titles, 162 serial subscriptions, 885 audiovisual materials, an OPAC, a Web page.
Computers on Campus 28 computers available on campus for general student use. A campuswide network can be accessed from off campus. Internet access, at least one staffed computer lab available.
Student Life *Housing:* college housing not available. *Activities and Organizations:* Student Senate. *Campus security:* 24-hour emergency response devices. *Student services:* personal/psychological counseling.
Standardized Tests *Required:* Assessment and Placement Services for Community Colleges (for placement).
Costs (2005–06) *Tuition:* state resident $2880 full-time. No tuition increase for student's term of enrollment. *Required fees:* $490 full-time. *Waivers:* senior citizens.
Financial Aid Of all full-time matriculated undergraduates who enrolled in 2003, 5 Federal Work-Study jobs (averaging $1200).
Applying *Options:* common application, deferred entrance. *Required:* high school transcript. *Recommended:* minimum 2.0 GPA, letters of recommendation, interview. *Application deadline:* rolling (freshmen), rolling (transfers).
Admissions Contact Ms. Darlene Redday, Director of Admissions, Sisseton-Wahpeton Community College, Old Agency Box 689, Sisseton, SD 57262. *Phone:* 605-698-3966 Ext. 1110.

SOUTHEAST TECHNICAL INSTITUTE
Sioux Falls, South Dakota

- **State-supported** 2-year, founded 1968
- **Calendar** semesters
- **Degree** certificates, diplomas, and associate
- **Urban** 169-acre campus
- **Endowment** $238,427
- **Coed,** 2,363 undergraduate students, 81% full-time, 47% women, 53% men

Undergraduates 1,915 full-time, 448 part-time. Students come from 7 states and territories, 1 other country, 21% are from out of state, 0.5% African American, 0.4% Asian American or Pacific Islander, 0.3% Hispanic American, 0.4% Native American, 1% live on campus.
Freshmen *Admission:* 1,876 applied, 1,256 admitted, 621 enrolled. *Average high school GPA:* 2.70.
Faculty *Total:* 143, 55% full-time, 4% with terminal degrees. *Student/faculty ratio:* 16:1.
Majors Accounting; architectural engineering technology; artificial intelligence and robotics; autobody/collision and repair technology; automobile/automotive mechanics technology; biomedical technology; business administration and management; cardiovascular technology; civil engineering technology; clinical/medical laboratory technology; commercial and advertising art; computer and information sciences related; computer graphics; computer/information technology services administration related; computer programming; computer programming related; computer programming (specific applications); computer programming (vendor/product certification); computer software and media applications related; computer software engineering; computer systems networking and telecommunications; computer/technical support; computer technology/computer systems technology; diesel mechanics technology; drafting and design technology; electrical, electronic and communications engineering technology; electromechanical technology; engineering technology; finance; graphic and printing equipment operation/production; health unit coordinator/ward clerk; heating, air conditioning, ventilation and refrigeration maintenance technology; horticultural science; industrial technology; information science/studies; information technology; laser and optical technology; machine tool technology; marketing/marketing management; mechanical engineering/mechanical technology; medical transcription; nuclear medical technology; nursing related; sign language interpretation and translation; surgical technology; survey technology; system administration; turf and turfgrass management; web/multimedia management and webmaster; web page, digital/multimedia and information resources design.
Academic Programs *Special study options:* academic remediation for entering students, accelerated degree program, advanced placement credit, double majors, independent study, internships, part-time degree program, services for LD students, summer session for credit.

Southeast Technical Institute (continued)

Library Southeast Library with 10,643 titles, 158 serial subscriptions, 182 audiovisual materials, an OPAC.

Computers on Campus 400 computers available on campus for general student use. A campuswide network can be accessed from off campus. Internet access, at least one staffed computer lab available. Computer purchase or lease plan available.

Student Life *Housing Options:* coed. Campus housing is provided by a third party. *Activities and Organizations:* VICA, ICON, PBL, American Landscape Contractors Association, Silent Tones. *Campus security:* 24-hour emergency response devices and patrols. *Student services:* personal/psychological counseling.

Athletics *Intramural sports:* basketball M/W, volleyball M/W.

Standardized Tests *Recommended:* ACT (for admission).

Costs (2004–05) *Tuition:* state resident $1920 full-time, $60 per credit part-time; nonresident $60 per credit part-time. Full-time tuition and fees vary according to course load and program. Part-time tuition and fees vary according to course load and program. *Required fees:* $1195 full-time, $37 per credit part-time. *Room and board:* room only: $4200. *Payment plan:* installment.

Financial Aid Of all full-time matriculated undergraduates who enrolled in 2003, 35 Federal Work-Study jobs (averaging $2550).

Applying *Required:* high school transcript, minimum 2.0 GPA. *Required for some:* interview. *Application deadline:* rolling (freshmen), rolling (transfers). *Notification:* continuous (freshmen).

Admissions Contact Mr. Scott Dorman, Recruiter, Southeast Technical Institute, 2320 North Career Avenue, Sioux Falls, SD 57107. *Phone:* 605-367-7624. *Toll-free phone:* 800-247-0789. *Fax:* 605-367-8305. *E-mail:* scott.dorman@southeasttech.com.

WESTERN DAKOTA TECHNICAL INSTITUTE
Rapid City, South Dakota

- **State-supported** 2-year, founded 1968
- **Calendar** semesters
- **Degree** certificates, diplomas, and associate
- **Small-town** 5-acre campus
- **Coed**

Faculty *Student/faculty ratio:* 15:1.

Standardized Tests *Required:* TABE/NET for nursing applicants, HOBET for other medical programs (for placement). *Recommended:* ACT (for placement).

Costs (2004–05) *Tuition:* state resident $2160 full-time, $60 per credit hour part-time; nonresident $2160 full-time, $60 per credit hour part-time. Full-time tuition and fees vary according to program. Part-time tuition and fees vary according to program. *Required fees:* $1562 full-time, $48 per credit hour part-time.

Financial Aid Of all full-time matriculated undergraduates who enrolled in 2003, 85 Federal Work-Study jobs (averaging $1400).

Applying *Options:* common application, electronic application. *Application fee:* $10. *Required:* essay or personal statement, high school transcript. *Required for some:* letters of recommendation, interview. *Recommended:* minimum 2.0 GPA.

Admissions Contact Janell Oberlander, Director of Admissions, Western Dakota Technical Institute, 800 Mickelson Drive, Rapid City, SD 57703. *Phone:* 605-394-4034 Ext. 111. *Toll-free phone:* 800-544-8765. *E-mail:* joberlander@wdti.tec.sd.us.

TENNESSEE

AMERICAN ACADEMY OF NUTRITION, COLLEGE OF NUTRITION
Knoxville, Tennessee

- **Proprietary** 2-year, founded 1984
- **Calendar** continuous
- **Degrees** certificates, diplomas, and associate (offers only external degree programs conducted through home study)
- **Suburban** campus
- **Coed**

Faculty *Student/faculty ratio:* 29:1.

Costs (2004–05) *Tuition:* $3950 full-time, $132 per credit hour part-time. *Required fees:* $200 full-time. *Payment plans:* tuition prepayment, installment.

Applying *Options:* common application, electronic application, deferred entrance. *Required for some:* high school transcript, interview. *Recommended:* minimum 2.0 GPA.

Admissions Contact Ms. Jennifer Green, Faculty, American Academy of Nutrition, College of Nutrition, 1204-D Kenesaw Avenue, Knoxville, TN 37919. *Phone:* 865-524-8079. *Toll-free phone:* 800-290-4226. *Fax:* 865-524-8339. *E-mail:* info@nutritioneducation.com.

CHATTANOOGA STATE TECHNICAL COMMUNITY COLLEGE
Chattanooga, Tennessee

- **State-supported** 2-year, founded 1965, part of Tennessee Board of Regents
- **Calendar** semesters
- **Degree** certificates, diplomas, and associate
- **Urban** 100-acre campus
- **Coed,** 8,121 undergraduate students, 47% full-time, 62% women, 38% men

Undergraduates 3,782 full-time, 4,339 part-time. Students come from 5 states and territories, 19% African American, 1% Asian American or Pacific Islander, 1% Hispanic American, 0.4% Native American, 22% transferred in.

Freshmen *Admission:* 1,343 applied, 1,343 admitted, 1,343 enrolled.

Faculty *Total:* 626, 32% full-time. *Student/faculty ratio:* 22:1.

Majors Accounting; administrative assistant and secretarial science; advertising; airline pilot and flight crew; applied art; artificial intelligence and robotics; automobile/automotive mechanics technology; aviation/airway management; avionics maintenance technology; biology/biological sciences; broadcast journalism; business administration and management; chemical engineering; chemistry; child development; civil engineering technology; commercial and advertising art; computer engineering technology; computer programming; computer science; consumer merchandising/retailing management; criminal justice/law enforcement administration; data processing and data processing technology; dental hygiene; drafting and design technology; electrical, electronic and communications engineering technology; emergency medical technology (EMT paramedic); energy management and systems technology; engineering related; environmental engineering technology; finance; fire science; fish/game management; food services technology; forestry; forestry technology; graphic and printing equipment operation/production; health information/medical records administration; heating, air conditioning, ventilation and refrigeration maintenance technology; hotel/motel administration; industrial radiologic technology; information science/studies; instrumentation technology; kindergarten/preschool education; legal administrative assistant/secretary; liberal arts and sciences/liberal studies; machine tool technology; mass communication/media; mechanical design technology; mechanical engineering/mechanical technology; medical administrative assistant and medical secretary; nuclear medical technology; nuclear/nuclear power technology; nursing (registered nurse training); occupational therapy; physical therapy; radio and television; respiratory care therapy; sign language interpretation and translation; survey technology; transportation technology; welding technology; wildlife and wildlands science and management.

Academic Programs *Special study options:* academic remediation for entering students, accelerated degree program, adult/continuing education programs, advanced placement credit, cooperative education, distance learning, English as a second language, honors programs, independent study, internships, part-time degree program, services for LD students, summer session for credit.

Library Augusta R. Kolwyck Library with 73,334 titles, 803 serial subscriptions, an OPAC, a Web page.

Computers on Campus 500 computers available on campus for general student use. A campuswide network can be accessed from off campus. Internet access, at least one staffed computer lab available.

Student Life *Housing:* college housing not available. *Activities and Organizations:* student-run newspaper, radio station, choral group, Black Student Association, Adult Connections, Human Services Specialists, Student Government Association, Student Nurses Association. *Campus security:* 24-hour emergency response devices and patrols, late-night transport/escort service. *Student services:* personal/psychological counseling, women's center.

Athletics Member NJCAA. *Intercollegiate sports:* baseball M(s), basketball M(s)/W(s), softball W(s). *Intramural sports:* softball W.

Standardized Tests *Required for some:* SAT or ACT (for placement).

Costs (2004–05) *Tuition:* state resident $1952 full-time; nonresident $6072 full-time. *Required fees:* $339 full-time.

Financial Aid Of all full-time matriculated undergraduates who enrolled in 2003, 377 Federal Work-Study jobs (averaging $652).

Applying *Options:* early admission, deferred entrance. *Application fee:* $10. *Required:* high school transcript. *Application deadline:* rolling (freshmen), rolling (transfers). *Notification:* continuous (freshmen).

Admissions Contact Ms. Diane Norris, Director of Admissions, Chattanooga State Technical Community College, 4501 Amnicola Highway, Chattanooga, TN 37406-1097. *Phone:* 423-697-4401 Ext. 3107. *Fax:* 423-697-4709. *E-mail:* admsis@cstcc.cc.tn.us.

CLEVELAND STATE COMMUNITY COLLEGE
Cleveland, Tennessee

- **State-supported** 2-year, founded 1967, part of Tennessee Board of Regents
- **Calendar** semesters
- **Degree** certificates and associate
- **Small-town** 105-acre campus
- **Endowment** $4.4 million
- **Coed,** 2,962 undergraduate students, 55% full-time, 60% women, 40% men

Undergraduates 1,635 full-time, 1,327 part-time. Students come from 9 states and territories, 1% are from out of state, 4% African American, 1% Asian American or Pacific Islander, 1% Hispanic American, 0.7% Native American, 5% transferred in.

Freshmen *Admission:* 1,034 applied, 570 admitted, 570 enrolled. *Average high school GPA:* 2.8.

Faculty *Total:* 169, 40% full-time, 18% with terminal degrees. *Student/faculty ratio:* 21:1.

Majors Administrative assistant and secretarial science; business administration and management; child development; community organization and advocacy; general studies; industrial arts; industrial technology; kindergarten/preschool education; liberal arts and sciences/liberal studies; nursing (registered nurse training); public administration and social service professions related.

Academic Programs *Special study options:* academic remediation for entering students, adult/continuing education programs, advanced placement credit, cooperative education, distance learning, double majors, English as a second language, external degree program, honors programs, independent study, internships, off-campus study, part-time degree program, services for LD students, summer session for credit.

Library Cleveland State Community College Library with 65,347 titles, 368 serial subscriptions, 10,116 audiovisual materials, an OPAC, a Web page.

Computers on Campus 450 computers available on campus for general student use. A campuswide network can be accessed from off campus. Internet access, online (class) registration, at least one staffed computer lab available.

Student Life *Housing:* college housing not available. *Activities and Organizations:* student-run newspaper, television station, choral group, Student Senate, International Association of Administration Professionals, Phi Theta Kappa, Student Nursing Association. *Campus security:* 24-hour emergency response devices and patrols, late-night transport/escort service. *Student services:* personal/psychological counseling.

Athletics Member NJCAA. *Intercollegiate sports:* baseball M(s), basketball M(s)/W(s), softball W(s). *Intramural sports:* archery M/W, badminton M/W, basketball M/W, bowling M/W, golf M/W, softball M/W, table tennis M/W, tennis M/W, volleyball M/W.

Standardized Tests *Required for some:* ACT (for placement).

Costs (2004–05) *Tuition:* state resident $1952 full-time, $83 per semester hour part-time; nonresident $7798 full-time, $336 per semester hour part-time. Full-time tuition and fees vary according to course load. *Required fees:* $263 full-time, $28 per semester hour part-time. *Payment plan:* deferred payment. *Waivers:* senior citizens and employees or children of employees.

Financial Aid Of all full-time matriculated undergraduates who enrolled in 2003, 52 Federal Work-Study jobs (averaging $1025).

Applying *Options:* early admission, deferred entrance. *Application fee:* $10. *Required:* high school transcript. *Application deadline:* rolling (freshmen), rolling (transfers). *Notification:* continuous (freshmen).

Admissions Contact Ms. Midge Burnette, Director of Admissions and Recruitment, Cleveland State Community College, 3535 Adkisson Drive, Cleveland, TN 37320-3570. *Phone:* 423-478-6212. *Toll-free phone:* 800-604-2722. *Fax:* 423-478-6255. *E-mail:* mburnette@clevelandstatecc.edu.

COLUMBIA STATE COMMUNITY COLLEGE
Columbia, Tennessee

- **State-supported** 2-year, founded 1966
- **Calendar** semesters
- **Degree** certificates and associate
- **Small-town** 179-acre campus with easy access to Nashville
- **Endowment** $707,627
- **Coed,** 4,613 undergraduate students, 53% full-time, 66% women, 34% men

Undergraduates 2,423 full-time, 2,190 part-time. Students come from 6 states and territories, 2 other countries, 8% African American, 0.7% Asian American or Pacific Islander, 2% Hispanic American, 0.4% Native American, 0.1% international, 10% transferred in. *Retention:* 61% of 2002 full-time freshmen returned.

Freshmen *Admission:* 837 enrolled. *Average high school GPA:* 2.84. *Test scores:* SAT verbal scores over 500: 33%; SAT math scores over 500: 33%; ACT

scores over 18: 67%; SAT verbal scores over 600: 17%; ACT scores over 24: 12%; SAT verbal scores over 700: 17%; ACT scores over 30: 1%.

Faculty *Total:* 257, 38% full-time.

Majors Accounting; administrative assistant and secretarial science; agricultural business and management; art; biology/biological sciences; business/commerce; chemistry; clinical/medical laboratory technology; dental hygiene; economics; electrical, electronic and communications engineering technology; elementary education; geography; history; industrial radiologic technology; information science/studies; kindergarten/preschool education; liberal arts and sciences/liberal studies; mass communication/media; mathematics; music; nursing (registered nurse training); pharmacy; physical education teaching and coaching; physical therapy; physics; political science and government; pre-engineering; psychology; respiratory care therapy; sociology; speech and rhetoric; veterinary technology.

Academic Programs *Special study options:* academic remediation for entering students, adult/continuing education programs, advanced placement credit, double majors, honors programs, part-time degree program, services for LD students, summer session for credit.

Library John W. Finney Memorial Learning Resources Center with 61,200 titles, 460 serial subscriptions, an OPAC.

Computers on Campus 260 computers available on campus for general student use. A campuswide network can be accessed from off campus. Internet access, at least one staffed computer lab available.

Student Life *Housing:* college housing not available. *Activities and Organizations:* drama/theater group, Student Government Association, Student Tennessee Education Association, Circle K, Gamma Beta Phi, Students in Free Enterprise. *Campus security:* 24-hour patrols. *Student services:* health clinic, personal/psychological counseling.

Athletics Member NJCAA. *Intercollegiate sports:* baseball M(s), basketball M(s)/W(s), softball W(s). *Intramural sports:* basketball M/W, softball M/W, table tennis M/W, volleyball M/W.

Standardized Tests *Required for some:* SAT or ACT (for placement).

Costs (2004–05) *Tuition:* state resident $1952 full-time, $83 per semester hour part-time; nonresident $7798 full-time, $336 per semester hour part-time. Full-time tuition and fees vary according to course load. Part-time tuition and fees vary according to course load. *Required fees:* $231 full-time, $10 per semester hour part-time, $3 per term part-time.

Financial Aid Of all full-time matriculated undergraduates who enrolled in 2003, 50 Federal Work-Study jobs (averaging $1250).

Applying *Options:* early admission. *Application fee:* $10. *Required:* high school transcript. *Application deadline:* rolling (freshmen), rolling (transfers).

Admissions Contact Mr. Joey Scruggs, Coordinator of Recruitment, Columbia State Community College, PO Box 1315, Columbia, TN 38402-1315. *Phone:* 931-540-2540. *Fax:* 931-540-2830. *E-mail:* scruggs@columbiastate.edu.

CONCORDE CAREER COLLEGE
Memphis, Tennessee

Admissions Contact 5100 Poplar Avenue, Suite 132, Memphis, TN 38137.

DRAUGHONS JUNIOR COLLEGE
Clarksville, Tennessee

Admissions Contact Admissions Office, Draughons Junior College, 1860 Wilma Rudolph Boulevard, Clarksville, TN 37040. *Fax:* 931-552-3624.

DRAUGHONS JUNIOR COLLEGE
Nashville, Tennessee

Admissions Contact Admissions Office, Draughons Junior College, 340 Plus Park, Nashville, TN 37217. *Phone:* 615-361-7555. *Fax:* 615-367-2736.

DYERSBURG STATE COMMUNITY COLLEGE
Dyersburg, Tennessee

- **State-supported** 2-year, founded 1969, part of Tennessee Board of Regents
- **Calendar** semesters
- **Degree** certificates and associate
- **Small-town** 100-acre campus with easy access to Memphis
- **Endowment** $3.2 million
- **Coed,** 2,477 undergraduate students, 58% full-time, 72% women, 28% men

Undergraduates 1,447 full-time, 1,030 part-time. Students come from 5 states and territories, 2% are from out of state, 19% African American, 0.5% Asian American or Pacific Islander, 2% Hispanic American, 0.5% Native American, 7% transferred in.

Dyersburg State Community College (continued)

Freshmen *Admission:* 861 applied, 856 admitted, 594 enrolled. *Average high school GPA:* 2.56. *Test scores:* ACT scores over 18: 56%; ACT scores over 24: 5%.

Faculty *Total:* 204, 29% full-time, 13% with terminal degrees. *Student/faculty ratio:* 24:1.

Majors Business administration and management; child development; computer/information technology services administration related; criminal justice/police science; electrical, electronic and communications engineering technology; health information/medical records technology; liberal arts and sciences/liberal studies; nursing (registered nurse training).

Academic Programs *Special study options:* academic remediation for entering students, adult/continuing education programs, advanced placement credit, distance learning, double majors, honors programs, independent study, part-time degree program, services for LD students, summer session for credit.

Library Learning Resource Center with 44,033 titles, 85 serial subscriptions, 2,231 audiovisual materials, an OPAC, a Web page.

Computers on Campus 501 computers available on campus for general student use. A campuswide network can be accessed from off campus. At least one staffed computer lab available.

Student Life *Housing:* college housing not available. *Activities and Organizations:* drama/theater group, student-run newspaper, choral group, student government, Phi Theta Kappa, Minority Association for Successful Students, Video Club, Psychology Club. *Campus security:* 24-hour patrols. *Student services:* personal/psychological counseling.

Athletics Member NJCAA. *Intercollegiate sports:* baseball M(s), basketball M(s)/W(s), cheerleading W(s), softball W(s).

Standardized Tests *Required for some:* ACT (for placement).

Costs (2004–05) *Tuition:* state resident $1952 full-time, $83 per hour part-time; nonresident $8049 full-time, $336 per hour part-time. Part-time tuition and fees vary according to course load. *Required fees:* $251 full-time. *Payment plan:* deferred payment. *Waivers:* senior citizens.

Financial Aid Of all full-time matriculated undergraduates who enrolled in 2003, 84 Federal Work-Study jobs (averaging $997). 115 state and other part-time jobs (averaging $837).

Applying *Options:* common application, early admission. *Application fee:* $10. *Required:* high school transcript. *Application deadline:* rolling (freshmen), rolling (transfers). *Notification:* continuous (freshmen).

Admissions Contact Mr. Dan J. Gullett, Assistant Vice President for Academic Affairs, Dyersburg State Community College, 1510 Lake Road, Dyersburg, TN 38024. *Phone:* 731-286-3327. *Fax:* 731-286-3325. *E-mail:* gulett@dscc.edu.

ELECTRONIC COMPUTER PROGRAMMING COLLEGE
Chattanooga, Tennessee

Admissions Contact Toney McFadden, Admission Director, Electronic Computer Programming College, 3805 Brainerd Road, Chattanooga, TN 37411-3798. *Phone:* 423-624-0077.

FOUNTAINHEAD COLLEGE OF TECHNOLOGY
Knoxville, Tennessee

- **Proprietary** primarily 2-year, founded 1947
- **Calendar** semesters
- **Degrees** associate and bachelor's
- **Suburban** 1-acre campus
- **Coed**

Student Life *Campus security:* 24-hour emergency response devices.

Applying *Application fee:* $100. *Recommended:* high school transcript.

Admissions Contact Ms. Casey Rackley, Director of Administration, Fountainhead College of Technology, 3203 Tazewell Pike, Knoxville, TN 37918-2530. *Phone:* 865-688-9422. *Toll-free phone:* 888-218-7335.

HIGH-TECH INSTITUTE
Memphis, Tennessee

Admissions Contact 5865 Shelby Oaks Circle, Memphis, TN 38134.

HIGH-TECH INSTITUTE
Nashville, Tennessee

Admissions Contact Mr. David Martinez, College Director, High-Tech Institute, 2710 Old Lebanon Road, Suite 12, Nashville, TN 37214. *Phone:* 615-902-9705. *Toll-free phone:* 800-987-0110.

ITT TECHNICAL INSTITUTE
Knoxville, Tennessee

- **Proprietary** primarily 2-year, founded 1988, part of ITT Educational Services, Inc
- **Calendar** quarters
- **Degrees** associate and bachelor's
- **Suburban** 5-acre campus
- **Coed**

Standardized Tests *Required:* Wonderlic aptitude test (for admission).

Costs (2004–05) *Tuition:* Please see school catalog for specific information.

Applying *Options:* deferred entrance. *Application fee:* $100. *Required:* high school transcript, interview. *Recommended:* letters of recommendation.

Admissions Contact Mr. Mike Burke, Director of Recruitment, ITT Technical Institute, 10208 Technology Drive, Knoxville, TN 37932. *Phone:* 865-671-2800. *Toll-free phone:* 800-671-2801. *Fax:* 865-671-2811.

ITT TECHNICAL INSTITUTE
Memphis, Tennessee

- **Proprietary** primarily 2-year, founded 1994, part of ITT Educational Services, Inc
- **Calendar** quarters
- **Degrees** associate and bachelor's
- **Suburban** 1-acre campus
- **Coed**

Standardized Tests *Required:* Wonderlic aptitude test (for admission).

Costs (2004–05) *Tuition:* Please see school catalog for specific information.

Applying *Options:* deferred entrance. *Application fee:* $100. *Required:* high school transcript, interview. *Recommended:* letters of recommendation.

Admissions Contact Mr. James R. Mills, Director of Recruitment, ITT Technical Institute, 1255 Lynnfield Road, Suite 192, Memphis, TN 38119. *Phone:* 901-762-0556. *Fax:* 901-762-0566.

ITT TECHNICAL INSTITUTE
Nashville, Tennessee

- **Proprietary** primarily 2-year, founded 1984, part of ITT Educational Services, Inc
- **Calendar** quarters
- **Degrees** associate and bachelor's
- **Urban** 21-acre campus
- **Coed**

Standardized Tests *Required:* Wonderlic aptitude test (for admission).

Costs (2004–05) *Tuition:* Please see school catalog for specific information.

Applying *Options:* deferred entrance. *Application fee:* $100. *Required:* high school transcript, interview. *Recommended:* letters of recommendation.

Admissions Contact Mr. Ronald Binkley, Director of Recruitment, ITT Technical Institute, 441 Donelson Pike, Nashville, TN 37214. *Phone:* 615-889-8700. *Toll-free phone:* 800-331-8386. *Fax:* 615-872-7209.

JACKSON STATE COMMUNITY COLLEGE
Jackson, Tennessee

- **State-supported** 2-year, founded 1967, part of Tennessee Board of Regents
- **Calendar** semesters
- **Degree** certificates and associate
- **Small-town** 104-acre campus
- **Endowment** $557,781
- **Coed,** 3,970 undergraduate students, 56% full-time, 66% women, 34% men

Undergraduates 2,224 full-time, 1,746 part-time. Students come from 9 states and territories, 0.2% are from out of state, 18% African American, 0.5% Asian American or Pacific Islander, 1% Hispanic American, 0.4% Native American, 17% transferred in. *Retention:* 57% of 2002 full-time freshmen returned.

Freshmen *Admission:* 791 applied, 791 admitted, 791 enrolled. *Average high school GPA:* 2.75. *Test scores:* ACT scores over 18: 57%; ACT scores over 24: 8%.

Faculty *Total:* 209, 54% full-time, 16% with terminal degrees. *Student/faculty ratio:* 19:1.

Majors Agricultural business and management; business administration and management; child development; clinical/medical laboratory technology; commercial and advertising art; computer science; electromechanical technology; industrial technology; liberal arts and sciences/liberal studies; management information systems; medical radiologic technology; nursing (registered nurse training); physical therapist assistant; respiratory care therapy; tool and die technology.

Academic Programs *Special study options:* academic remediation for entering students, adult/continuing education programs, advanced placement credit, cooperative education, distance learning, honors programs, internships, part-time degree program, summer session for credit.

Library Jackson State Community College Library with 63,620 titles, 225 serial subscriptions, 2,000 audiovisual materials, an OPAC, a Web page.

Computers on Campus 725 computers available on campus for general student use. A campuswide network can be accessed from off campus. Internet access, online (class) registration, at least one staffed computer lab available. Computer purchase or lease plan available.

Student Life *Housing:* college housing not available. *Activities and Organizations:* drama/theater group, student-run newspaper, choral group, Student Government Organization, Spanish Club, Biology Club, Art Club, Black Student Association. *Campus security:* 24-hour patrols. *Student services:* health clinic, personal/psychological counseling.

Athletics Member NJCAA. *Intercollegiate sports:* baseball M(s), basketball M(s)/W(s), cheerleading W(s), softball W(s). *Intramural sports:* basketball M/W, football M, golf M, tennis M/W, volleyball W.

Standardized Tests *Required for some:* SAT or ACT (for placement).

Costs (2004–05) *Tuition:* state resident $1952 full-time, $83 per semester hour part-time; nonresident $5846 full-time, $336 per semester hour part-time. *Required fees:* $253 full-time, $23 per semester hour part-time. *Payment plan:* deferred payment. *Waivers:* senior citizens and employees or children of employees.

Financial Aid Of all full-time matriculated undergraduates who enrolled in 2003, 60 Federal Work-Study jobs (averaging $3000). 10 state and other part-time jobs (averaging $3000).

Applying *Options:* electronic application, early admission, deferred entrance. *Application fee:* $10. *Required for some:* high school transcript. *Application deadline:* 8/22 (freshmen), rolling (transfers). *Notification:* continuous (freshmen).

Admissions Contact Ms. Monica Ray, Director of Admissions and Records, Jackson State Community College, 2046 North Parkway, Jackson, TN 38301. *Phone:* 731-425-2644. *Toll-free phone:* 800-355-5722. *Fax:* 731-425-9559. *E-mail:* mray@jscc.edu.

JOHN A. GUPTON COLLEGE
Nashville, Tennessee

Admissions Contact Ms. Lisa Bolin, Registrar, John A. Gupton College, 1616 Church Street, Nashville, TN 37203. *Phone:* 615-327-3927. *Toll-free phone:* 615-327-3927. *E-mail:* spann@guptoncollege.com.

MEDVANCE INSTITUTE
Cookeville, Tennessee

Admissions Contact Ms. Sharon Mellott, Director of Admissions, MedVance Institute, 1065 East 10th Street, Cookeville, TN 38501-1907. *Phone:* 931-526-3660. *Toll-free phone:* 800-259-3659 (in-state); 800-256-9085 (out-of-state). *Fax:* 931-372-2603. *E-mail:* briddell@medvance.org.

MID-AMERICA BAPTIST THEOLOGICAL SEMINARY
Germantown, Tennessee

- **Independent Southern Baptist** founded 1972
- **Calendar** semesters
- **Degrees** associate, master's, doctoral, and first professional
- **Suburban** campus with easy access to Memphis
- **Endowment** $3.6 million
- **Coed, primarily men,** 49 undergraduate students, 63% full-time, 100% men

Undergraduates 31 full-time, 18 part-time. Students come from 26 states and territories, 4% African American.

Faculty *Total:* 27, 100% full-time. *Student/faculty ratio:* 14:1.

Majors Theology.

Academic Programs *Special study options:* summer session for credit.

Library Ora Byram Allison Memorial Library with 119,000 titles, 931 serial subscriptions, an OPAC, a Web page.

Computers on Campus 10 computers available on campus for general student use. Internet access, at least one staffed computer lab available.

Student Life *Housing Options:* Campus housing is university owned. *Campus security:* 24-hour emergency response devices.

Costs (2005–06) *Tuition:* $3280 full-time. Full-time tuition and fees vary according to course load. Part-time tuition and fees vary according to course load.

Applying *Options:* common application. *Application fee:* $25. *Required:* high school transcript, 2 letters of recommendation. *Application deadline:* 8/7 (freshmen).

Admissions Contact Miss Kim Powers, Admissions Counselor, Mid-America Baptist Theological Seminary, 2216 Germantown Road South, Germantown, TN 38138. *Phone:* 901-751-8453 Ext. 3066. *Fax:* 901-751-8454. *E-mail:* info@mabts.edu.

MILLER-MOTTE TECHNICAL COLLEGE
Clarksville, Tennessee

Admissions Contact Ms. Lisa Teague, Director of Admissions, Miller-Motte Technical College, 1820 Business Park Drive, Clarksville, TN 37040. *Phone:* 800-558-0071.

MOTLOW STATE COMMUNITY COLLEGE
Tullahoma, Tennessee

- **State-supported** 2-year, founded 1969, part of Tennessee Board of Regents
- **Calendar** semesters
- **Degree** certificates and associate
- **Small-town** 187-acre campus with easy access to Nashville
- **Endowment** $3.0 million
- **Coed,** 3,540 undergraduate students, 58% full-time, 63% women, 37% men

Undergraduates 2,041 full-time, 1,499 part-time. Students come from 11 states and territories, 8 other countries, 0.9% are from out of state, 7% African American, 1% Asian American or Pacific Islander, 1% Hispanic American, 0.4% Native American, 0.3% international, 7% transferred in. *Retention:* 62% of 2002 full-time freshmen returned.

Freshmen *Admission:* 1,189 applied, 1,095 admitted, 1,079 enrolled. *Average high school GPA:* 2.8. *Test scores:* ACT scores over 18: 62%; ACT scores over 24: 7%.

Faculty *Total:* 187, 40% full-time. *Student/faculty ratio:* 32:1.

Majors Business administration and management; engineering technology; liberal arts and sciences/liberal studies; nursing (registered nurse training); special education (early childhood).

Academic Programs *Special study options:* academic remediation for entering students, adult/continuing education programs, advanced placement credit, cooperative education, distance learning, double majors, honors programs, independent study, part-time degree program, services for LD students, summer session for credit.

Library Crouch Library with 54,968 titles, 211 serial subscriptions, 4,464 audiovisual materials, an OPAC, a Web page.

Computers on Campus 600 computers available on campus for general student use. A campuswide network can be accessed from off campus that provide access to e-mail. Internet access, online (class) registration, at least one staffed computer lab available.

Student Life *Housing:* college housing not available. *Activities and Organizations:* drama/theater group, student-run newspaper, choral group, Photography Club, Psychology Club, Student Government Association, Outing Club, Baptist Student Union. *Campus security:* 24-hour patrols, late-night transport/escort service. *Student services:* health clinic, personal/psychological counseling.

Athletics Member NJCAA. *Intercollegiate sports:* baseball M(s), basketball M(s)/W(s), softball W(s). *Intramural sports:* archery M/W, badminton M/W, basketball M/W, bowling M/W, golf M/W, tennis M/W, volleyball M/W.

Standardized Tests *Required for some:* SAT or ACT (for placement).

Costs (2004–05) *Tuition:* state resident $1952 full-time, $83 per credit part-time; nonresident $7798 full-time, $336 per credit part-time. Full-time tuition and fees vary according to program. Part-time tuition and fees vary according to course load and program. *Required fees:* $247 full-time, $144 per credit part-time. *Payment plans:* installment, deferred payment. *Waivers:* senior citizens and employees or children of employees.

Financial Aid Of all full-time matriculated undergraduates who enrolled in 2003, 66 Federal Work-Study jobs (averaging $12,185).

Applying *Options:* electronic application, early admission, deferred entrance. *Application fee:* $10. *Required:* high school transcript. *Application deadline:* 8/13 (freshmen), rolling (transfers). *Notification:* continuous (freshmen).

Admissions Contact Wendi Patton, Director of New Student Admissions, Motlow State Community College, PO Box 8500, Lynchburg, TN 37352. *Phone:* 931-393-1764. *Toll-free phone:* 800-654-4877. *Fax:* 931-393-1681. *E-mail:* galsup@mscc.edu.

NASHVILLE AUTO DIESEL COLLEGE
Nashville, Tennessee

- **Proprietary** 2-year, founded 1919
- **Calendar** continuous

Nashville Auto Diesel College (continued)
- **Degree** diplomas and associate
- **Urban** 13-acre campus
- **Coed, primarily men**

Faculty *Student/faculty ratio:* 30:1.

Student Life *Campus security:* 24-hour emergency response devices and patrols.

Costs (2004–05) *Tuition:* $17,750 full-time. Full-time tuition and fees vary according to degree level and program. No tuition increase for student's term of enrollment. *Required fees:* $100 full-time. *Room only:* $4372. Room and board charges vary according to housing facility.

Applying *Options:* deferred entrance. *Application fee:* $100. *Required:* high school transcript, interview. *Required for some:* minimum 2.3 GPA.

Admissions Contact Ms. Peggie Werrbach, Director of Admissions, Nashville Auto Diesel College, 1524 Gallatin Road, Nashville, TN 37206. *Phone:* 615-226-3990 Ext. 8465. *Toll-free phone:* 800-228-NADC. *Fax:* 615-262-8466. *E-mail:* wpruitt@nadcedu.com.

NASHVILLE STATE TECHNICAL COMMUNITY COLLEGE

Nashville, Tennessee

- **State-supported** 2-year, founded 1970, part of Tennessee Board of Regents
- **Calendar** semesters
- **Degree** certificates and associate
- **Urban** 85-acre campus
- **Coed,** 7,021 undergraduate students, 34% full-time, 58% women, 42% men

Undergraduates 2,421 full-time, 4,600 part-time. Students come from 36 states and territories, 55 other countries, 2% are from out of state, 26% African American, 4% Asian American or Pacific Islander, 2% Hispanic American, 0.4% Native American, 3% international, 3% transferred in.

Freshmen *Admission:* 908 enrolled.

Faculty *Total:* 412, 33% full-time.

Majors Accounting; administrative assistant and secretarial science; architectural engineering technology; automobile/automotive mechanics technology; business administration and management; civil engineering technology; commercial and advertising art; computer engineering technology; computer systems networking and telecommunications; criminal justice/police science; culinary arts; electrical, electronic and communications engineering technology; industrial engineering; industrial technology; information science/studies; kindergarten/preschool education; occupational therapy; photography; sign language interpretation and translation.

Academic Programs *Special study options:* academic remediation for entering students, adult/continuing education programs, advanced placement credit, cooperative education, distance learning, English as a second language, off-campus study, part-time degree program, services for LD students, summer session for credit.

Library Jane G. Kisber Memorial Library with 38,502 titles, 275 serial subscriptions, an OPAC, a Web page.

Computers on Campus 518 computers available on campus for general student use. A campuswide network can be accessed from off campus.

Student Life *Housing:* college housing not available. *Activities and Organizations:* student-run newspaper, Data Processing Management Association, Occupational Therapy Club, Phi Theta Kappa, Student Government Association, Black Student Association. *Campus security:* 24-hour emergency response devices and patrols, late-night transport/escort service. *Student services:* personal/psychological counseling.

Standardized Tests *Required for some:* SAT or ACT (for placement).

Costs (2004–05) *One-time required fee:* $25. *Tuition:* state resident $2177 full-time, $83 per credit hour part-time; nonresident $8023 full-time, $336 per credit hour part-time. Part-time tuition and fees vary according to course load. *Required fees:* $235 full-time, $10 per credit hour part-time, $5 per term part-time. *Payment plan:* deferred payment. *Waivers:* senior citizens and employees or children of employees.

Financial Aid Of all full-time matriculated undergraduates who enrolled in 2003, 66 Federal Work-Study jobs (averaging $806). 97 state and other part-time jobs (averaging $917).

Applying *Options:* electronic application, deferred entrance. *Application fee:* $5. *Required:* high school transcript. *Application deadline:* rolling (freshmen), rolling (transfers). *Notification:* continuous (freshmen).

Admissions Contact Ms. Laura Potter, Coordinator of Recruitment, Nashville State Technical Community College, 120 White Bridge Road, Nashville, TN 37209. *Phone:* 615-353-3265. *Toll-free phone:* 800-272-7363. *Fax:* 615-353-3243. *E-mail:* laura.potter@nscc.edu.

NATIONAL COLLEGE OF BUSINESS & TECHNOLOGY

Bristol, Tennessee

- **Proprietary** 2-year, founded 1992, part of National College of Business and Technology
- **Calendar** quarters
- **Degree** diplomas and associate
- **Small-town** campus
- **Coed,** 319 undergraduate students

Faculty *Total:* 30, 23% full-time. *Student/faculty ratio:* 12:1.

Majors Accounting; administrative assistant and secretarial science; business administration and management; computer and information sciences related; medical/clinical assistant.

Academic Programs *Special study options:* advanced placement credit, double majors, honors programs, internships, part-time degree program, services for LD students, summer session for credit.

Library National Business College-Bristol Campus Library.

Computers on Campus 35 computers available on campus for general student use. A campuswide network can be accessed. Internet access, at least one staffed computer lab available.

Student Life *Housing:* college housing not available.

Costs (2005–06) *Tuition:* $6408 full-time, $178 per credit hour part-time. *Required fees:* $75 full-time, $15 per term part-time.

Financial Aid Of all full-time matriculated undergraduates who enrolled in 2003, 3 Federal Work-Study jobs.

Applying *Options:* electronic application. *Application fee:* $30. *Required:* high school transcript. *Recommended:* interview. *Application deadline:* rolling (freshmen), rolling (transfers).

Admissions Contact Ms. Angela Carrier, Campus Director, National College of Business & Technology, 300 A Piedmont Avenue, Bristol, VA 24201. *Phone:* 423-878-4440. *Fax:* 540-669-4793. *E-mail:* adm@educorp.edu.

NATIONAL COLLEGE OF BUSINESS & TECHNOLOGY

Knoxville, Tennessee

- **Proprietary** 2-year, founded 2003, part of National College of Business and Technology
- **Calendar** quarters
- **Degree** diplomas and associate
- **Suburban** 2-acre campus
- **Coed**

Faculty *Student/faculty ratio:* 12:1.

Costs (2004–05) *Tuition:* $6120 full-time, $170 per credit hour part-time. Full-time tuition and fees vary according to course load. Part-time tuition and fees vary according to course load. *Required fees:* $75 full-time. *Payment plans:* installment, deferred payment.

Admissions Contact Mr. Andy W. Wills, Director, National College of Business & Technology, 8415 Kingston Pike, Knoxville, TN 37919. *Phone:* 865-539-2011. *Toll-free phone:* 800-664-1886.

NATIONAL COLLEGE OF BUSINESS & TECHNOLOGY

Nashville, Tennessee

- **Proprietary** 2-year, founded 1915, part of National College of Business and Technology
- **Calendar** quarters
- **Degree** diplomas and associate
- **Urban** 1-acre campus
- **Coed,** 466 undergraduate students

Faculty *Total:* 41, 5% full-time. *Student/faculty ratio:* 10:1.

Majors Administrative assistant and secretarial science; business administration and management; computer and information sciences related; medical/clinical assistant.

Academic Programs *Special study options:* double majors, honors programs, part-time degree program, services for LD students, summer session for credit.

Computers on Campus 35 computers available on campus for general student use. Internet access, at least one staffed computer lab available.

Student Life *Housing:* college housing not available.

Costs (2005–06) *Tuition:* $6408 full-time, $178 per credit hour part-time. *Required fees:* $75 full-time, $15 per term part-time.

Financial Aid Of all full-time matriculated undergraduates who enrolled in 2003, 3 Federal Work-Study jobs.

Applying *Options:* electronic application. *Application fee:* $30. *Recommended:* interview. *Application deadline:* rolling (freshmen), rolling (transfers). *Notification:* continuous (freshmen).

Admissions Contact Mr. Robert Leonard, Campus Director, National College of Business & Technology, 3748 Nolensville Pike, Nashville, TN 37211. *Phone:* 615-333-3344. *Toll-free phone:* 800-664-1886. *Fax:* 615-333-3429. *E-mail:* adm@educorp.edu.

NORTH CENTRAL INSTITUTE
Clarksville, Tennessee

- **Proprietary** 2-year, founded 1988
- **Calendar** continuous
- **Degree** associate
- **Suburban** 14-acre campus
- **Coed, primarily men,** 107 undergraduate students, 49% full-time, 13% women, 87% men

Undergraduates 52 full-time, 55 part-time. Students come from 50 states and territories, 95% are from out of state, 17% African American, 0.9% Asian American or Pacific Islander, 12% Hispanic American, 8% Native American.

Freshmen *Admission:* 14 enrolled.

Faculty *Total:* 18, 39% full-time. *Student/faculty ratio:* 10:1.

Majors Aircraft powerplant technology; airframe mechanics and aircraft maintenance technology.

Academic Programs *Special study options:* advanced placement credit, external degree program, independent study, part-time degree program, summer session for credit.

Library Media Resource Center plus 1 other with 200 titles, 12 serial subscriptions, 20 audiovisual materials.

Student Life *Housing:* college housing not available. *Activities and Organizations:* Alpha Eta Rho (aviation fraternity). *Campus security:* 24-hour emergency response devices. *Student services:* personal/psychological counseling.

Costs (2005–06) *Tuition:* $11,760 full-time.

Applying *Options:* common application, electronic application, early admission. *Application fee:* $35.

Admissions Contact Mrs. Sheri Nash-Kutch, Dean of Student Services, North Central Institute, 168 Jack Miller Boulevard, Clarksville, TN 37042. *Phone:* 931-431-9700 Ext. 247. *Fax:* 931-431-9771. *E-mail:* admissions@nci.edu.

NORTHEAST STATE TECHNICAL COMMUNITY COLLEGE
Blountville, Tennessee

- **State-supported** 2-year, founded 1966, part of Tennessee Board of Regents
- **Calendar** semesters
- **Degree** certificates and associate
- **Small-town** 100-acre campus
- **Endowment** $2.4 million
- **Coed,** 5,084 undergraduate students, 55% full-time, 55% women, 45% men

Undergraduates 2,798 full-time, 2,286 part-time. Students come from 3 states and territories, 3% are from out of state, 3% African American, 0.7% Asian American or Pacific Islander, 0.7% Hispanic American, 0.3% Native American, 5% transferred in. *Retention:* 58% of 2002 full-time freshmen returned.

Freshmen *Admission:* 2,824 applied, 2,824 admitted, 924 enrolled. *Average high school GPA:* 2.51. *Test scores:* ACT scores over 18: 57%; ACT scores over 24: 8%; ACT scores over 30: 1%.

Faculty *Total:* 241, 40% full-time, 12% with terminal degrees. *Student/faculty ratio:* 22:1.

Majors Accounting; administrative assistant and secretarial science; automobile/automotive mechanics technology; business administration and management; cardiovascular technology; chemistry; computer programming; computer programming related; computer systems networking and telecommunications; data processing and data processing technology; drafting and design technology; electrical, electronic and communications engineering technology; emergency medical technology (EMT paramedic); engineering technology; industrial technology; instrumentation technology; kindergarten/preschool education; liberal arts and sciences/liberal studies; machine tool technology; medical/clinical assistant; surgical technology; welding technology.

Academic Programs *Special study options:* academic remediation for entering students, advanced placement credit, cooperative education, distance learning, double majors, honors programs, part-time degree program, services for LD students, summer session for credit.

Library Wayne G. Basler Library plus 1 other with 44,997 titles, 438 serial subscriptions, 8,591 audiovisual materials, an OPAC, a Web page.

Computers on Campus 910 computers available on campus for general student use. A campuswide network can be accessed from off campus that provide access to WebCT, online transcripts. Internet access, online (class) registration, at least one staffed computer lab available.

Student Life *Housing:* college housing not available. *Activities and Organizations:* drama/theater group, Phi Theta Kappa, Student Government Association, Student Tennessee Education Association, Students in Free Enterprise, Student Ambassadors. *Campus security:* 24-hour patrols, late-night transport/escort service. *Student services:* health clinic, personal/psychological counseling.

Athletics *Intramural sports:* basketball M/W, golf M/W, volleyball M/W.

Standardized Tests *Required:* SAT or ACT (for placement).

Costs (2004–05) *Tuition:* state resident $1952 full-time, $83 per credit hour part-time; nonresident $7798 full-time, $336 per credit hour part-time. Full-time tuition and fees vary according to course load. Part-time tuition and fees vary according to course load. *Required fees:* $260 full-time, $12 per credit hour part-time, $18 per credit hour part-time. *Waivers:* senior citizens and employees or children of employees.

Financial Aid Of all full-time matriculated undergraduates who enrolled in 2003, 109 Federal Work-Study jobs (averaging $1318). 35 state and other part-time jobs.

Applying *Options:* electronic application. *Application fee:* $10. *Required:* high school transcript, minimum 2.0 GPA. *Application deadline:* rolling (freshmen), rolling (transfers). *Notification:* continuous (freshmen).

Admissions Contact Dr. Jon P. Harr, Dean of Admissions and Records, Northeast State Technical Community College, PO Box 246, Blountville, TN 37617. *Phone:* 423-323-0231. *Toll-free phone:* 800-836-7822. *Fax:* 423-323-0215. *E-mail:* jpharr@nstcc.edu.

NOSSI COLLEGE OF ART
Goodlettsville, Tennessee

Admissions Contact Ms. Mary Alexander, Admissions Director, Nossi College of Art, 907 Rivergate Parkway, Goodlettsville, TN 37072. *Phone:* 615-851-1088. *E-mail:* admissions@nossi.com.

PELLISSIPPI STATE TECHNICAL COMMUNITY COLLEGE
Knoxville, Tennessee

- **State-supported** 2-year, founded 1974, part of Tennessee Board of Regents
- **Calendar** semesters
- **Degree** certificates and associate
- **Suburban** 144-acre campus
- **Endowment** $2.8 million
- **Coed**

Faculty *Student/faculty ratio:* 21:1.

Student Life *Campus security:* 24-hour patrols.

Standardized Tests *Required for some:* ACT (for placement).

Costs (2004–05) *Tuition:* state resident $2224 full-time; nonresident $8070 full-time.

Applying *Options:* common application, electronic application, early admission, deferred entrance. *Application fee:* $5. *Required:* high school transcript.

Admissions Contact Admissions Coordinator, Pellissippi State Technical Community College, PO Box 22990, Knoxville, TN 37933. *Phone:* 865-694-6681. *E-mail:* latouzeau@pstcc.cc.tn.us.

REMINGTON COLLEGE-MEMPHIS CAMPUS
Memphis, Tennessee

Admissions Contact Dr. Lori May, Campus President, Remington College-Memphis Campus, 2731 Nonconnah Boulevard, Memphis, TN 38132-2131. *Phone:* 901-291-4225.

REMINGTON COLLEGE-NASHVILLE CAMPUS
Nashville, Tennessee

Admissions Contact Mr. Frank Vivelo, Campus President, Remington College-Nashville Campus, 441 Donnelson Pike, Suite 150, Nashville, TN 37214. *Phone:* 615-889-5520.

ROANE STATE COMMUNITY COLLEGE
Harriman, Tennessee

- **State-supported** 2-year, founded 1971, part of Tennessee Board of Regents
- **Calendar** semesters
- **Degree** certificates and associate
- **Rural** 104-acre campus with easy access to Knoxville
- **Endowment** $18,123
- **Coed**

Faculty *Student/faculty ratio:* 19:1.

Student Life *Campus security:* 24-hour patrols.

Athletics Member NJCAA.

Standardized Tests *Required for some:* SAT or ACT (for placement).

Costs (2004–05) *Tuition:* state resident $1824 full-time, $78 per semester hour part-time; nonresident $7288 full-time, $314 per semester hour part-time. Full-time tuition and fees vary according to course load and program. Part-time tuition and fees vary according to program. *Required fees:* $265 full-time, $15 per semester hour part-time, $15 per term part-time.

Financial Aid Of all full-time matriculated undergraduates who enrolled in 2003, 150 Federal Work-Study jobs (averaging $3000).

Applying *Options:* common application, electronic application, early admission, deferred entrance. *Application fee:* $10. *Required:* high school transcript.

Admissions Contact Ms. Brenda Rector, Director of Records and Registration, Roane State Community College, 276 Patton Lane, Harriman, TN 37748. *Phone:* 865-882-4526. *Toll-free phone:* 800-343-9104. *Fax:* 865-882-4562. *E-mail:* marine_gl@a1.rscc.cc.tn.us.

SOUTH COLLEGE
Knoxville, Tennessee

- **Proprietary** primarily 2-year, founded 1882
- **Calendar** quarters
- **Degrees** certificates, associate, and bachelor's
- **Urban** 2-acre campus
- **Coed, primarily women**

Faculty *Student/faculty ratio:* 11:1.

Student Life *Campus security:* evening and morning security patrols.

Standardized Tests *Recommended:* SAT I, ACT, or CPT.

Applying *Options:* common application, early admission, deferred entrance. *Application fee:* $40. *Required:* high school transcript, interview.

Admissions Contact Mr. Walter Hosea, Director of Admissions, South College, 720 North Fifth Avenue, Knoxville, TN 37917. *Phone:* 865-524-3043 Ext. 1825. *Fax:* 865-637-0127.

SOUTHEASTERN CAREER COLLEGE
Nashville, Tennessee

Admissions Contact 2416 South 21st Avenue, Suite 300, Nashville, TN 37212. *Toll-free phone:* 800-336-4457.

SOUTHWEST TENNESSEE COMMUNITY COLLEGE
Memphis, Tennessee

Admissions Contact Ms. Cindy Meziere, Assistant Director of Recruiting, Southwest Tennessee Community College, PO Box 780, Memphis, TN 38103-0780. *Phone:* 901-333-4195. *Toll-free phone:* 877-717-STCC. *Fax:* 901-333-4473.

VATTEROTT COLLEGE
Memphis, Tennessee

Admissions Contact 6152 Macon Road, Memphis, TN 38134.

VOLUNTEER STATE COMMUNITY COLLEGE
Gallatin, Tennessee

- **State-supported** 2-year, founded 1970, part of Tennessee Board of Regents
- **Calendar** semesters
- **Degree** certificates and associate
- **Small-town** 100-acre campus with easy access to Nashville
- **Endowment** $103,626

- **Coed,** 7,044 undergraduate students, 49% full-time, 63% women, 37% men

Undergraduates 3,468 full-time, 3,576 part-time. Students come from 8 states and territories, 24 other countries, 1% are from out of state, 9% African American, 1% Asian American or Pacific Islander, 2% Hispanic American, 0.4% Native American, 9% transferred in. *Retention:* 54% of 2002 full-time freshmen returned.

Freshmen *Admission:* 1,995 applied, 1,995 admitted, 1,219 enrolled. *Average high school GPA:* 2.76. *Test scores:* ACT scores over 18: 63%; ACT scores over 24: 9%; ACT scores over 30: 1%.

Faculty *Total:* 402, 37% full-time. *Student/faculty ratio:* 20:1.

Majors Business administration and management; fire science; health information/medical records technology; health professions related; industrial arts; legal assistant/paralegal; liberal arts and sciences/liberal studies; medical radiologic technology; ophthalmic technology; physical therapist assistant; respiratory care therapy.

Academic Programs *Special study options:* academic remediation for entering students, accelerated degree program, adult/continuing education programs, advanced placement credit, distance learning, double majors, English as a second language, honors programs, independent study, part-time degree program, services for LD students, summer session for credit.

Library Thigpen Learning Resource Center with 52,571 titles, 274 serial subscriptions, 3,212 audiovisual materials, an OPAC, a Web page.

Computers on Campus 600 computers available on campus for general student use. A campuswide network can be accessed from off campus. Internet access, online (class) registration, at least one staffed computer lab available.

Student Life *Housing:* college housing not available. *Activities and Organizations:* drama/theater group, student-run newspaper, radio station, choral group, Gamma Beta Phi, Returning Women's Organization, Phi Theta Kappa, Student Government Association, The Settler. *Campus security:* 24-hour emergency response devices and patrols, late-night transport/escort service. *Student services:* health clinic, personal/psychological counseling.

Athletics Member NJCAA. *Intercollegiate sports:* baseball M(s), basketball M(s)/W(s), softball W(s). *Intramural sports:* basketball M/W.

Standardized Tests *Required for some:* ACT (for placement).

Costs (2005–06) *Tuition:* state resident $2108 full-time, $97 per credit hour part-time; nonresident $8421 full-time, $370 per credit hour part-time. Full-time tuition and fees vary according to course load. Part-time tuition and fees vary according to course load. *Required fees:* $241 full-time, $9 per credit hour part-time, $8 per term part-time. *Payment plan:* deferred payment. *Waivers:* senior citizens and employees or children of employees.

Financial Aid Of all full-time matriculated undergraduates who enrolled in 2003, 45 Federal Work-Study jobs (averaging $1900). 15 state and other part-time jobs (averaging $2000).

Applying *Options:* electronic application, early admission, deferred entrance. *Application fee:* $10. *Required:* high school transcript. *Required for some:* essay or personal statement, minimum 2.0 GPA. *Application deadlines:* 9/1 (freshmen), 9/1 (transfers). *Notification:* continuous (freshmen).

Admissions Contact Mr. Tim Amyx, Director of Admission and Records, Volunteer State Community College, 1480 Nashville Pike, Gallatin, TN 37066-3188. *Phone:* 615-452-8600 Ext. 3614. *Toll-free phone:* 888-335-8722. *Fax:* 615-230-3577.

WALTERS STATE COMMUNITY COLLEGE
Morristown, Tennessee

- **State-supported** 2-year, founded 1970, part of Tennessee Board of Regents
- **Calendar** semesters
- **Degree** certificates and associate
- **Small-town** 100-acre campus
- **Endowment** $6.9 million
- **Coed,** 5,964 undergraduate students, 52% full-time, 65% women, 35% men

Undergraduates 3,101 full-time, 2,863 part-time. Students come from 8 states and territories, 6 other countries, 1% are from out of state, 4% African American, 0.7% Asian American or Pacific Islander, 1% Hispanic American, 0.2% Native American, 0.1% international, 4% transferred in.

Freshmen *Admission:* 1,698 applied, 1,698 admitted, 1,066 enrolled. *Average high school GPA:* 2.80. *Test scores:* SAT verbal scores over 500: 50%; SAT math scores over 500: 50%; ACT scores over 18: 55%; SAT verbal scores over 600: 20%; SAT math scores over 600: 20%; ACT scores over 24: 21%; SAT verbal scores over 700: 10%; SAT math scores over 700: 10%; ACT scores over 30: 1%.

Faculty *Total:* 288, 44% full-time, 15% with terminal degrees. *Student/faculty ratio:* 22:1.

Majors Administrative assistant and secretarial science; agricultural mechanization; art; art teacher education; business administration and management; child development; clinical/medical laboratory technology; computer and information sciences related; computer science; criminal justice/law enforcement administration; education; industrial radiologic technology; information technology; interdisciplinary studies; liberal arts and sciences/liberal studies; medical administrative assistant and medical secretary; music teacher education; nursing (registered nurse training); physical education teaching and coaching; pre-engineering.

Academic Programs *Special study options:* academic remediation for entering students, accelerated degree program, adult/continuing education programs, advanced placement credit, distance learning, freshman honors college, honors programs, part-time degree program, summer session for credit. *ROTC:* Army (c).

Library Walters State Library with 47,559 titles, 189 serial subscriptions, 22,677 audiovisual materials, an OPAC, a Web page.

Computers on Campus 686 computers available on campus for general student use. A campuswide network can be accessed from off campus. Internet access, online (class) registration, at least one staffed computer lab available.

Student Life *Housing:* college housing not available. *Activities and Organizations:* student-run newspaper, choral group. *Campus security:* 24-hour emergency response devices. *Student services:* health clinic.

Athletics Member NJCAA. *Intercollegiate sports:* baseball M(s), basketball M(s)/W(s), golf M(s), softball W(s). *Intramural sports:* baseball M, basketball M/W.

Standardized Tests *Required:* SAT or ACT (for admission).

Costs (2004–05) *Tuition:* state resident $1952 full-time, $83 per hour part-time; nonresident $7798 full-time, $358 per hour part-time. *Required fees:* $238 full-time, $15 per hour part-time, $7 per term part-time. *Waivers:* senior citizens and employees or children of employees.

Financial Aid Of all full-time matriculated undergraduates who enrolled in 2003, 60 Federal Work-Study jobs (averaging $2400).

Applying *Options:* early admission. *Application fee:* $10. *Required:* high school transcript. *Application deadline:* rolling (freshmen), rolling (transfers). *Notification:* continuous (freshmen).

Admissions Contact Mr. Michael Campbell, Director of Admissions and Registration Services, Walters State Community College, 500 South Davy Crockett Parkway, Morristown, TN 37813-6899. *Phone:* 423-585-2682. *Toll-free phone:* 800-225-4770. *Fax:* 423-585-6876. *E-mail:* mary.hopper@ws.edu.

TEXAS

THE ACADEMY OF HEALTH CARE PROFESSIONS
Houston, Texas

Admissions Contact Ms. Wanda Federick, Director of Admissions, The Academy of Health Care Professions, 1900 North Loop West, Suite 100, Houston, TX 77018. *Phone:* 713-425-3111.

ALVIN COMMUNITY COLLEGE
Alvin, Texas

- **State and locally supported** 2-year, founded 1949
- **Calendar** semesters
- **Degree** certificates, diplomas, and associate
- **Small-town** 114-acre campus with easy access to Houston
- **Coed,** 3,932 undergraduate students, 41% full-time, 56% women, 44% men

Undergraduates 1,611 full-time, 2,321 part-time. Students come from 17 states and territories, 5 other countries, 0.8% are from out of state, 8% African American, 2% Asian American or Pacific Islander, 20% Hispanic American, 0.7% Native American, 0.3% international, 6% transferred in.

Freshmen *Admission:* 590 applied, 590 admitted, 590 enrolled.

Faculty *Total:* 275, 35% full-time. *Student/faculty ratio:* 15:1.

Majors Accounting; administrative assistant and secretarial science; aeronautics/aviation/aerospace science and technology; art; biology/biological sciences; business administration and management; chemical technology; child development; computer engineering technology; computer programming; corrections; court reporting; criminal justice/police science; drafting and design technology; dramatic/theatre arts; electrical, electronic and communications engineering technology; emergency medical technology (EMT paramedic); legal administrative assistant/secretary; legal assistant/paralegal; legal studies; liberal arts and sciences/liberal studies; marketing/marketing management; mathematics; medical administrative assistant and medical secretary; mental health/rehabilitation; music; nursing (registered nurse training); physical education teaching and coaching; physical sciences; radio and television; respiratory care therapy; substance abuse/addiction counseling; voice and opera.

Academic Programs *Special study options:* academic remediation for entering students, accelerated degree program, adult/continuing education programs, advanced placement credit, distance learning, double majors, English as a second language, honors programs, independent study, internships, part-time degree program, services for LD students, student-designed majors, study abroad, summer session for credit.

Library Alvin Community College Library with 28,361 titles, 146 serial subscriptions, 5 audiovisual materials, an OPAC, a Web page.

Computers on Campus 622 computers available on campus for general student use. A campuswide network can be accessed from off campus. Internet access, online (class) registration, at least one staffed computer lab available.

Student Life *Housing:* college housing not available. *Activities and Organizations:* drama/theater group, student-run radio and television station, choral group, Student Government Association, Baptist Student Union, Pan American College Forum, Catholic Newman Association, Phi Theta Kappa. *Campus security:* 24-hour patrols, late-night transport/escort service. *Student services:* personal/psychological counseling.

Athletics Member NJCAA. *Intercollegiate sports:* baseball M(s), softball W(s), volleyball W(s). *Intramural sports:* soccer M(c)/W(c).

Standardized Tests *Required:* THEA, ACCUPLACER (for placement).

Costs (2004–05) *Tuition:* area resident $624 full-time, $26 per credit part-time; state resident $1248 full-time, $52 per credit part-time; nonresident $2304 full-time, $96 per credit part-time. Full-time tuition and fees vary according to course load. Part-time tuition and fees vary according to course load. *Required fees:* $276 full-time, $5 per course part-time, $78 per term part-time. *Payment plan:* installment.

Financial Aid Of all full-time matriculated undergraduates who enrolled in 2003, 50 Federal Work-Study jobs (averaging $2200). 1 state and other part-time job (averaging $2500).

Applying *Required for some:* high school transcript. *Application deadline:* rolling (freshmen), rolling (transfers).

Admissions Contact Ms. Stephanie Stockstill, Director of Admissions and Advising, Alvin Community College, 3110 Mustang Road, Alvin, TX 77511. *Phone:* 281-756-3531. *Fax:* 281-756-3531. *E-mail:* admiss@alvincollege.edu.

AMARILLO COLLEGE
Amarillo, Texas

- **State and locally supported** 2-year, founded 1929
- **Calendar** semesters
- **Degree** certificates and associate
- **Suburban** 58-acre campus
- **Endowment** $13.6 million
- **Coed,** 10,196 undergraduate students, 34% full-time, 60% women, 40% men

Undergraduates 3,436 full-time, 6,760 part-time. Students come from 9 states and territories, 1% are from out of state, 3% African American, 3% Asian American or Pacific Islander, 22% Hispanic American, 0.9% Native American.

Faculty *Total:* 237. *Student/faculty ratio:* 17:1.

Majors Accounting; administrative assistant and secretarial science; airframe mechanics and aircraft maintenance technology; architectural engineering technology; art; automobile/automotive mechanics technology; behavioral sciences; biblical studies; biology/biological sciences; broadcast journalism; business administration and management; business teacher education; chemical technology; chemistry; child development; clinical laboratory science/medical technology; commercial and advertising art; computer engineering technology; computer programming; computer science; computer systems analysis; corrections; criminal justice/law enforcement administration; criminal justice/police science; dental hygiene; drafting and design technology; dramatic/theatre arts; electrical, electronic and communications engineering technology; elementary education; emergency medical technology (EMT paramedic); engineering; English; environmental health; fine/studio arts; fire science; funeral service and mortuary science; general studies; geology/earth science; health information/medical records administration; heating, air conditioning, ventilation and refrigeration maintenance technology; heavy equipment maintenance technology; history; industrial radiologic technology; information science/studies; instrumentation technology; interior design; journalism; laser and optical technology; legal administrative assistant/secretary; liberal arts and sciences/liberal studies; machine tool technology; mass communication/media; mathematics; medical administrative assistant and medical secretary; modern languages; music; music teacher education; natural sciences; nuclear medical technology; nursing (licensed practical/vocational nurse training); nursing (registered nurse training); occupational therapy; photography; physical education teaching and coaching; physical sciences; physical therapy; physics; pre-engineering; pre-pharmacy studies; psychology; public relations/image management; radio and television; radiologic technology/science; real estate; religious studies; respiratory care therapy; social sciences; social work; speech and rhetoric; substance abuse/addiction counseling; telecommunications; tourism and travel services management; visual and performing arts.

Academic Programs *Special study options:* academic remediation for entering students, adult/continuing education programs, advanced placement credit, distance learning, English as a second language, honors programs, part-time degree program, services for LD students, summer session for credit.

Amarillo College (continued)

Library Lynn Library Learning Center plus 1 other with 75,200 titles, 325 serial subscriptions, an OPAC.

Computers on Campus 450 computers available on campus for general student use. A campuswide network can be accessed. Internet access, at least one staffed computer lab available.

Student Life *Housing:* college housing not available. *Options:* coed. *Activities and Organizations:* drama/theater group, student-run newspaper, radio station, choral group, Student Government Association, College Republicans. *Campus security:* 24-hour patrols, late-night transport/escort service. *Student services:* personal/psychological counseling.

Athletics *Intramural sports:* basketball M/W, tennis M/W, volleyball M/W.

Standardized Tests *Required:* THEA, MAPS (for placement).

Costs (2005–06) *Tuition:* area resident $1278 full-time, $53 per credit part-time; state resident $1638 full-time, $68 per credit part-time; nonresident $5478 full-time, $228 per credit part-time. *Payment plan:* installment. *Waivers:* senior citizens and employees or children of employees.

Financial Aid Of all full-time matriculated undergraduates who enrolled in 2003, 100 Federal Work-Study jobs (averaging $3000).

Applying *Options:* early admission, deferred entrance. *Required:* high school transcript. *Notification:* continuous (freshmen).

Admissions Contact Mr. Robert Austin, Associate Dean of Student Services, Amarillo College, PO Box 447, Amarillo, TX 79178-0001. *Phone:* 806-371-5024. *Fax:* 806-371-5066. *E-mail:* austin-rc@actx.edu.

ANGELINA COLLEGE
Lufkin, Texas

Admissions Contact Ms. Judith Cutting, Registrar/Enrollment Director, Angelina College, PO Box 1768, Lufkin, TX 75902-1768. *Phone:* 936-639-1301 Ext. 213. *Fax:* 936-639-4299.

ATI TECHNICAL TRAINING CENTER
Dallas, Texas

Admissions Contact Mr. Brian DeLozier, Director, ATI Technical Training Center, 6627 Maple Avenue, Dallas, TX 75235. *Phone:* 214-352-2222.

AUSTIN BUSINESS COLLEGE
Austin, Texas

Admissions Contact Ms. Pam Binns, Director of Admissions, Austin Business College, 2101 Interstate Highway 35, Suite 300, Austin, TX 78741. *Phone:* 512-447-9415. *Toll-free phone:* 512-447-9415. *Fax:* 512-447-0194. *E-mail:* abc@austinbusinesscollege.org.

AUSTIN COMMUNITY COLLEGE
Austin, Texas

- **District-supported** 2-year, founded 1972
- **Calendar** semesters
- **Degree** certificates and associate
- **Urban** campus
- **Coed,** 35,576 undergraduate students

Undergraduates Students come from 93 other countries, 0.2% are from out of state, 7% African American, 6% Asian American or Pacific Islander, 22% Hispanic American, 0.9% Native American, 2% international.

Freshmen *Admission:* 4,701 applied, 4,701 admitted.

Faculty *Total:* 1,479, 28% full-time. *Student/faculty ratio:* 20:1.

Majors Accounting; administrative assistant and secretarial science; art; astronomy; automobile/automotive mechanics technology; biology/biological sciences; business administration and management; chemistry; clinical/medical laboratory technology; commercial and advertising art; computer and information sciences related; computer programming; computer programming related; computer science; computer systems networking and telecommunications; construction engineering technology; consumer merchandising/retailing management; criminal justice/law enforcement administration; criminal justice/police science; data entry/microcomputer applications; developmental and child psychology; drafting and design technology; economics; electrical, electronic and communications engineering technology; emergency medical technology (EMT paramedic); English; fashion merchandising; finance; fire science; French; geology/earth science; German; graphic and printing equipment operation/production; heating, air conditioning, ventilation and refrigeration maintenance technology; history; hospitality and recreation marketing; hotel/motel administration; human services; industrial radiologic technology; industrial technology; information science/studies; information technology; insurance; Japanese; journalism; legal administrative assistant/secretary; legal assistant/paralegal; liberal arts and sciences/liberal studies; marketing/marketing management; mass communication/media; mathematics; medical/clinical assistant; music; nursing (registered nurse training); occupational therapy; photography; physical sciences; physics; political science and government; pre-engineering; psychology; quality control technology; radio and television; real estate; Russian; sign language interpretation and translation; social work; sociology; Spanish; speech and rhetoric; surgical technology; survey technology; system administration; technical and business writing; welding technology.

Academic Programs *Special study options:* academic remediation for entering students, accelerated degree program, adult/continuing education programs, advanced placement credit, cooperative education, distance learning, English as a second language, external degree program, honors programs, independent study, internships, part-time degree program, services for LD students, summer session for credit. *ROTC:* Army (c), Air Force (c).

Library Main Library plus 6 others with 115,567 titles, 1,974 serial subscriptions, 14,044 audiovisual materials, an OPAC, a Web page.

Computers on Campus 225 computers available on campus for general student use. A campuswide network can be accessed from off campus. Internet access, at least one staffed computer lab available.

Student Life *Housing:* college housing not available. *Activities and Organizations:* drama/theater group, student-run newspaper. *Student services:* personal/psychological counseling.

Athletics *Intramural sports:* basketball M/W, football M, golf M, racquetball M/W, volleyball M/W, weight lifting M/W.

Costs (2005–06) *Tuition:* area resident $936 full-time; state resident $2328 full-time; nonresident $4416 full-time. *Required fees:* $336 full-time.

Financial Aid Of all full-time matriculated undergraduates who enrolled in 2003, 296 Federal Work-Study jobs (averaging $2000). 12 state and other part-time jobs (averaging $2000).

Applying *Options:* electronic application. *Application deadline:* rolling (freshmen), rolling (transfers).

Admissions Contact Ms. Linda Kluck, Director, Admissions and Records, Austin Community College, 5930 Middle Fiskville Road, Austin, TX 78752-4390. *Phone:* 512-223-7766. *Fax:* 512-223-7665. *E-mail:* outreach@austincc.edu.

BLINN COLLEGE
Brenham, Texas

Admissions Contact Ms. Brandi Bothe, Coordinator, Recruitment and Admissions, Blinn College, 902 College Avenue, Brenham, TX 77833-4049. *Phone:* 979-830-4152. *Fax:* 979-830-4110. *E-mail:* recruit@blinn.edu.

BORDER INSTITUTE OF TECHNOLOGY
El Paso, Texas

- **Proprietary** 2-year
- **Calendar** quarters
- **Degree** certificates, diplomas, and associate
- **Suburban** campus
- **Coed, primarily men**

Faculty *Student/faculty ratio:* 7:1.

Financial Aid Of all full-time matriculated undergraduates who enrolled in 2003, 83 Federal Work-Study jobs (averaging $410).

Admissions Contact Mr. Miguel Gamino, Admissions Director, Border Institute of Technology, 9611 Acer Avenue, El Paso, TX 79925-6744. *Phone:* 915-593-7328 Ext. 24.

BRAZOSPORT COLLEGE
Lake Jackson, Texas

- **State and locally supported** 2-year, founded 1968
- **Calendar** semesters
- **Degree** certificates and associate
- **Small-town** 160-acre campus with easy access to Houston
- **Endowment** $3.3 million
- **Coed,** 3,389 undergraduate students, 28% full-time, 54% women, 46% men

Undergraduates 960 full-time, 2,429 part-time. Students come from 12 states and territories, 11 other countries, 1% are from out of state, 6% African American, 1% Asian American or Pacific Islander, 24% Hispanic American, 0.4% Native American, 0.5% international, 4% transferred in.

Freshmen *Admission:* 941 applied, 941 admitted, 354 enrolled.

Faculty *Total:* 166, 43% full-time, 10% with terminal degrees. *Student/faculty ratio:* 18:1.

Majors Accounting; administrative assistant and secretarial science; agricultural business and management; architecture; art; automobile/automotive mechanics technology; biology/biological sciences; business administration and management; business/commerce; chemical technology; chemistry; child care and support services management; child development; computer and information sciences; computer hardware technology; computer programming; computer programming related; computer programming (specific applications); computer technology/computer systems technology; construction engineering technology; construction/heavy equipment/earthmoving equipment operation; corrections and criminal justice related; criminal justice/police science; data processing and data processing technology; drafting and design technology; dramatic/theatre arts; economics; education; electrical, electronic and communications engineering technology; electrician; elementary education; emergency medical technology (EMT paramedic); engineering; English; environmental health; ethnic, cultural minority, and gender studies related; family and consumer sciences/human sciences; finance; fine/studio arts; foreign languages and literatures; general studies; geology/earth science; health and physical education; health professions related; heating, air conditioning, ventilation and refrigeration maintenance technology; history; information technology; instrumentation technology; journalism; legal assistant/paralegal; liberal arts and sciences/liberal studies; library science; machine tool technology; marketing/marketing management; mathematics; music; nursing (registered nurse training); occupational safety and health technology; physical education teaching and coaching; physics; pipefitting and sprinkler fitting; political science and government; pre-law studies; pre-medical studies; psychology; public administration; purchasing, procurement/acquisitions and contracts management; quality control technology; secondary education; sheet metal technology; social sciences; sociology; speech and rhetoric; theology; vehicle/equipment operation; welding technology.

Academic Programs *Special study options:* academic remediation for entering students, adult/continuing education programs, advanced placement credit, cooperative education, distance learning, honors programs, internships, part-time degree program, summer session for credit.

Library Brazosport College Library with 85,425 titles, 339 serial subscriptions, 397 audiovisual materials, an OPAC, a Web page.

Computers on Campus 420 computers available on campus for general student use. A campuswide network can be accessed from off campus. Internet access, online (class) registration, at least one staffed computer lab available.

Student Life *Housing:* college housing not available. *Activities and Organizations:* drama/theater group, student-run newspaper, choral group, Phi Theta Kappa, Baptist Student Ministry, Student Senate, Fencing Club. *Campus security:* 24-hour patrols.

Athletics *Intramural sports:* archery M/W, basketball M/W, bowling M/W, fencing M/W, football M/W, golf M/W, soccer M/W, softball M/W, table tennis M/W, tennis M/W, volleyball M/W.

Standardized Tests *Required for some:* THEA, ACT COMPASS.

Costs (2005–06) *Tuition:* area resident $840 full-time, $28 per hour part-time; state resident $1470 full-time, $49 per hour part-time; nonresident $2880 full-time, $96 per hour part-time. Full-time tuition and fees vary according to course load. Part-time tuition and fees vary according to course load. *Required fees:* $300 full-time, $9 per hour part-time, $15 per term part-time. *Payment plan:* installment. *Waivers:* employees or children of employees.

Applying *Options:* early admission, deferred entrance. *Required for some:* high school transcript. *Application deadlines:* 8/15 (freshmen), 8/15 (transfers).

Admissions Contact Ms. Patricia S. Leyendecker, Director of Admissions/Registrar, Brazosport College, 500 College Drive, Lake Jackson, TX 77566. *Phone:* 979-230-3217. *Fax:* 979-230-3376. *E-mail:* regist@brazosport.edu.

BROOKHAVEN COLLEGE
Farmers Branch, Texas

Admissions Contact Thoa Vo, Registrar, Brookhaven College, 3939 Valley View Lane, Farmers Branch, TX 75244-4997. *Phone:* 972-860-4604. *Fax:* 972-860-4897. *E-mail:* bhc2310@dcccd.edu.

CEDAR VALLEY COLLEGE
Lancaster, Texas

■ **State-supported** 2-year, founded 1977, part of Dallas County Community College District System
■ **Calendar** semesters
■ **Degree** certificates and associate
■ **Suburban** 353-acre campus with easy access to Dallas-Fort Worth
■ **Endowment** $17.2 million
■ **Coed,** 4,290 undergraduate students, 34% full-time, 62% women, 38% men

Undergraduates 1,447 full-time, 2,843 part-time. Students come from 5 other countries, 2% are from out of state, 55% African American, 1% Asian American or Pacific Islander, 12% Hispanic American, 0.4% Native American, 0.5% international, 74% transferred in.

Freshmen *Admission:* 1,956 applied, 1,956 admitted, 547 enrolled.

Faculty *Total:* 174, 37% full-time. *Student/faculty ratio:* 26:1.

Majors Accounting; administrative assistant and secretarial science; automobile/automotive mechanics technology; business administration and management; computer programming; computer programming (specific applications); criminal justice/law enforcement administration; data processing and data processing technology; heating, air conditioning, ventilation and refrigeration maintenance technology; liberal arts and sciences/liberal studies; management information systems and services related; marketing/marketing management; music; radio and television broadcasting technology; real estate; veterinary/animal health technology.

Academic Programs *Special study options:* academic remediation for entering students, advanced placement credit, cooperative education, distance learning, English as a second language, part-time degree program, services for LD students, summer session for credit. *ROTC:* Army (c).

Library Cedar Valley College Library with 43,788 titles, 217 serial subscriptions, 16,460 audiovisual materials, an OPAC, a Web page.

Computers on Campus 675 computers available on campus for general student use. A campuswide network can be accessed from off campus that provide access to video conferencing. Internet access, online (class) registration, at least one staffed computer lab available.

Student Life *Housing:* college housing not available. *Activities and Organizations:* drama/theater group, choral group, African-American Student Organization, Latin-American Student Organization, Veterinary Technology Club, Phi Theta Kappa, Police Academy Club. *Campus security:* 24-hour emergency response devices and patrols. *Student services:* health clinic, personal/psychological counseling.

Athletics Member NJCAA. *Intercollegiate sports:* baseball M, basketball M, soccer W, volleyball W. *Intramural sports:* cheerleading W.

Standardized Tests *Required:* THEA (for admission). *Recommended:* SAT or ACT (for admission).

Costs (2005–06) *Tuition:* area resident $990 full-time, $33 per credit part-time; state resident $1800 full-time, $60 per credit part-time; nonresident $2880 full-time, $200 per credit part-time. *Payment plan:* installment.

Applying *Options:* electronic application, early admission. *Required for some:* letters of recommendation, interview. *Recommended:* high school transcript. *Application deadline:* rolling (freshmen), rolling (transfers). *Notification:* continuous (freshmen).

Admissions Contact Ms. Carolyn Ward, Director of Admissions/Registrar, Cedar Valley College, 3030 North Dallas Avenue, Lancaster, TX 75134-3799. *Phone:* 972-860-8201. *E-mail:* jww3310@dcccd.edu.

CENTER FOR ADVANCED LEGAL STUDIES
Houston, Texas

Admissions Contact 3910 Kirby Drive, Suite 200, Houston, TX 77098-4151.

CENTRAL TEXAS COLLEGE
Killeen, Texas

■ **State and locally supported** 2-year, founded 1967
■ **Calendar** semesters
■ **Degree** certificates and associate
■ **Suburban** 500-acre campus with easy access to Austin
■ **Endowment** $1.5 million
■ **Coed,** 18,351 undergraduate students, 16% full-time, 44% women, 56% men

Undergraduates 2,986 full-time, 15,365 part-time. Students come from 48 states and territories, 19 other countries, 28% African American, 4% Asian American or Pacific Islander, 15% Hispanic American, 1% Native American, 0.2% international, 1% live on campus.

Freshmen *Admission:* 3,791 enrolled.

Faculty *Total:* 1,970, 11% full-time, 12% with terminal degrees. *Student/faculty ratio:* 40:1.

Majors Administrative assistant and secretarial science; agriculture; aircraft powerplant technology; airline pilot and flight crew; automobile/automotive mechanics technology; biology/biological sciences; business administration and management; chemistry; child care and support services management; clinical/medical laboratory technology; commercial and advertising art; computer and information sciences; computer programming; computer programming related; computer programming (specific applications); computer programming (vendor/product certification); cosmetology; criminal justice/police science; criminal justice/safety; data processing and data processing technology; drafting and design technology; electrical, electronic and communications engineering technology; emergency medical technology (EMT paramedic); engineering; environmental studies; equestrian studies; farm and ranch management; geology/earth science; graphic and printing equipment operation/production; heating, air conditioning, ventilation and refrigeration maintenance technology; hotel/motel administration; interdisciplinary studies; journalism; legal assistant/paralegal; liberal arts and sciences/liberal studies; marketing/marketing management; math-

Central Texas College (continued)

ematics; medical administrative assistant and medical secretary; medical radiologic technology; music; nursing (licensed practical/vocational nurse training); nursing (registered nurse training); office management; physical education teaching and coaching; radio and television; social sciences; substance abuse/addiction counseling; welding technology.

Academic Programs *Special study options:* academic remediation for entering students, accelerated degree program, adult/continuing education programs, advanced placement credit, distance learning, English as a second language, external degree program, internships, part-time degree program, services for LD students, student-designed majors, summer session for credit. *ROTC:* Army (b).

Library Oveta Culp Hobby Memorial Library with 80,381 titles, 467 serial subscriptions, 2,590 audiovisual materials, an OPAC, a Web page.

Computers on Campus 130 computers available on campus for general student use. A campuswide network can be accessed from student residence rooms and from off campus. Internet access, online (class) registration, at least one staffed computer lab available.

Student Life *Housing Options:* coed. *Activities and Organizations:* drama/theater group, student-run newspaper, International Student Association, We Can Do It Club, Students in Free Enterprise, Student Nurses Association, NAACP. *Campus security:* 24-hour emergency response devices and patrols.

Athletics *Intramural sports:* badminton M/W, basketball M/W, bowling M/W, football M/W, golf M/W, soccer M/W, softball M/W, table tennis M/W, tennis M/W, volleyball M/W.

Standardized Tests *Required:* THEA (for placement). *Recommended:* SAT or ACT (for placement), SAT Subject Tests (for placement), SAT II: Writing Test (for placement).

Costs (2005–06) *Tuition:* area resident $912 full-time, $38 per hour part-time; state resident $1104 full-time, $46 per hour part-time; nonresident $2880 full-time, $60 per hour part-time. Full-time tuition and fees vary according to course load and location. Part-time tuition and fees vary according to course load and location. *Required fees:* $390 full-time, $8 per hour part-time. *Room and board:* $2990. *Payment plan:* installment. *Waivers:* employees or children of employees.

Financial Aid Of all full-time matriculated undergraduates who enrolled in 2003, 68 Federal Work-Study jobs.

Applying *Options:* electronic application, early admission, deferred entrance. *Required:* high school transcript, minimum 2.0 GPA. *Application deadline:* rolling (freshmen), rolling (transfers).

Admissions Contact Admissions Office, Central Texas College, PO Box 1800, Killeen, TX 76540-1800. *Phone:* 254-526-1696. *Toll-free phone:* 800-792-3348 Ext. 1696. *Fax:* 254-526-1545. *E-mail:* admrec@ctcd.edu.

▶ **See page 478 for a narrative description.**

CISCO JUNIOR COLLEGE
Cisco, Texas

Admissions Contact Mr. Olin O. Odom III, Dean of Admission/Registrar, Cisco Junior College, 101 College Heights, Cisco, TX 76437-9321. *Phone:* 254-442-2567 Ext. 130.

CLARENDON COLLEGE
Clarendon, Texas

- **State and locally supported** 2-year, founded 1898
- **Calendar** semesters
- **Degree** certificates and associate
- **Rural** 88-acre campus
- **Coed,** 1,021 undergraduate students, 39% full-time, 44% women, 56% men

Undergraduates 402 full-time, 619 part-time. Students come from 14 states and territories, 3 other countries, 10% African American, 0.8% Asian American or Pacific Islander, 15% Hispanic American, 0.7% Native American, 0.5% international.

Freshmen *Admission:* 634 applied, 620 admitted, 461 enrolled.

Faculty *Total:* 69, 42% full-time, 4% with terminal degrees. *Student/faculty ratio:* 15:1.

Majors Accounting; agribusiness; agricultural economics; agriculture; behavioral sciences; biology/biological sciences; business administration and management; chemistry; computer and information sciences; dramatic/theatre arts; education; electrical, electronic and communications engineering technology; elementary education; English; farm and ranch management; finance; health services/allied health/health sciences; history; horse husbandry/equine science and management; kinesiology and exercise science; liberal arts and sciences/liberal studies; marketing/marketing management; mathematics; music; nursing (registered nurse training); physical education teaching and coaching; physical therapy; political science and government related; pre-dentistry studies; premedical studies; psychology; secondary education; social sciences; social work related; sociology; speech and rhetoric.

Academic Programs *Special study options:* academic remediation for entering students, adult/continuing education programs, advanced placement credit, distance learning, double majors, independent study, part-time degree program, services for LD students, summer session for credit.

Library Vera Dial Dickey Library plus 1 other with 22,000 titles, 89 serial subscriptions, 350 audiovisual materials, an OPAC, a Web page.

Computers on Campus 57 computers available on campus for general student use. A campuswide network can be accessed from student residence rooms and from off campus. Internet access, online (class) registration, at least one staffed computer lab available. Computer purchase or lease plan available.

Student Life *Housing:* on-campus residence required through sophomore year. *Options:* Campus housing is university owned. *Activities and Organizations:* drama/theater group, choral group. *Campus security:* 8-hour patrols by trained security personnel.

Athletics Member NJCAA. *Intercollegiate sports:* baseball M(s), basketball M(s)/W(s), cheerleading M(s)/W(s), softball W(s), volleyball W(s). *Intramural sports:* basketball M/W, football M/W, volleyball M/W.

Standardized Tests *Required:* THEA (for placement).

Costs (2005–06) *Tuition:* area resident $1140 full-time, $38 per credit hour part-time; state resident $1650 full-time, $55 per credit hour part-time; nonresident $2100 full-time, $20 per credit hour part-time. Full-time tuition and fees vary according to program. Part-time tuition and fees vary according to course load and program. *Required fees:* $720 full-time, $24 per credit hour part-time, $72 per term part-time. *Room and board:* $3250; room only: $1190. *Payment plan:* installment. *Waivers:* senior citizens.

Financial Aid Of all full-time matriculated undergraduates who enrolled in 2003, 41 Federal Work-Study jobs (averaging $985). 9 state and other part-time jobs (averaging $860).

Applying *Options:* early admission, deferred entrance. *Required:* high school transcript. *Required for some:* letters of recommendation, interview. *Application deadline:* rolling (freshmen), rolling (transfers). *Notification:* continuous (freshmen).

Admissions Contact Ms. Sharon Hannon, Admissions Director/Registrar, Clarendon College, PO Box 968, Clarendon, TX 79226-0968. *Phone:* 806-874-3571 Ext. 107. *Toll-free phone:* 800-687-9737. *Fax:* 806-874-3201.

COASTAL BEND COLLEGE
Beeville, Texas

- **County-supported** 2-year, founded 1965
- **Calendar** semesters
- **Degree** certificates and associate
- **Rural** 100-acre campus
- **Endowment** $825,011
- **Coed,** 4,013 undergraduate students, 45% full-time, 59% women, 41% men

Undergraduates 1,789 full-time, 2,224 part-time. Students come from 15 states and territories, 3 other countries, 1% are from out of state, 5% African American, 0.6% Asian American or Pacific Islander, 62% Hispanic American, 0.5% Native American, 0.3% international, 55% transferred in, 5% live on campus. *Retention:* 62% of 2002 full-time freshmen returned.

Freshmen *Admission:* 1,250 applied, 1,250 admitted, 1,250 enrolled.

Faculty *Total:* 171, 54% full-time, 6% with terminal degrees. *Student/faculty ratio:* 21:1.

Majors Accounting; administrative assistant and secretarial science; agriculture; applied art; art; art teacher education; automobile/automotive mechanics technology; biological and physical sciences; biology/biological sciences; business administration and management; chemistry; child development; commercial and advertising art; computer and information sciences related; computer engineering technology; computer programming related; computer programming (specific applications); computer programming (vendor/product certification); computer science; computer systems networking and telecommunications; cosmetology; criminal justice/law enforcement administration; criminal justice/police science; data entry/microcomputer applications; data entry/microcomputer applications related; data processing and data processing technology; dental hygiene; developmental and child psychology; drafting and design technology; dramatic/theatre arts; economics; education; elementary education; engineering; English; environmental engineering technology; finance; fine/studio arts; French; geology/earth science; German; health teacher education; history; information technology; journalism; legal administrative assistant/secretary; liberal arts and sciences/liberal studies; mathematics; music; music teacher education; nursing (licensed practical/vocational nurse training); nursing (registered nurse training); parks, recreation and leisure; petroleum technology; pharmacy; physical education teaching and coaching; physical sciences; physics; political science and government; psychology; public relations/image management; sociology; speech and rhetoric; system administration; voice and opera; welding technology; word processing.

Academic Programs *Special study options:* academic remediation for entering students, adult/continuing education programs, advanced placement credit,

cooperative education, distance learning, internships, part-time degree program, services for LD students, summer session for credit. *ROTC:* Army (c), Air Force (c).

Library Grady C. Hogue Learning Resource Center with 37,971 titles, 268 serial subscriptions, 2,974 audiovisual materials, an OPAC.

Computers on Campus 970 computers available on campus for general student use. A campuswide network can be accessed from off campus. Internet access, online (class) registration, at least one staffed computer lab available.

Student Life *Housing Options:* coed, men-only, women-only, disabled students. Campus housing is university owned. *Activities and Organizations:* drama/theater group, choral group, student government, Computer Science Club, Creative Writing Club, Drama Club, Art Club. *Campus security:* 24-hour emergency response devices. *Student services:* personal/psychological counseling.

Athletics *Intramural sports:* archery M/W, badminton M/W, basketball M/W, bowling M/W, cross-country running M/W, golf M/W, soccer M/W, softball M/W, table tennis M/W, tennis M/W, track and field M/W, volleyball M/W, weight lifting M/W.

Standardized Tests *Required:* THEA or ACT COMPASS (for placement).

Costs (2004–05) *Tuition:* area resident $1232 full-time, $48 per hour part-time; state resident $1928 full-time, $84 per hour part-time; nonresident $2192 full-time, $114 per hour part-time. *Required fees:* $80 full-time, $40 per term part-time. *Room and board:* room only: $1300. *Payment plan:* installment.

Financial Aid Of all full-time matriculated undergraduates who enrolled in 2003, 80 Federal Work-Study jobs (averaging $1484). 11 state and other part-time jobs (averaging $1159).

Applying *Options:* deferred entrance. *Required:* high school transcript. *Application deadline:* rolling (freshmen), rolling (transfers). *Notification:* continuous (freshmen).

Admissions Contact Ms. Alicia Ulloa, Director of Admissions/Registrar, Coastal Bend College, 3800 Charco Road, Beeville, TX 78102-2197. *Phone:* 361-354-2251. *Fax:* 361-354-2254. *E-mail:* register@coastalbend.edu.

COLLEGE OF THE MAINLAND
Texas City, Texas

- **State and locally supported** 2-year, founded 1967
- **Calendar** semesters
- **Degree** certificates, diplomas, and associate
- **Suburban** 120-acre campus with easy access to Houston
- **Coed,** 3,948 undergraduate students, 37% full-time, 60% women, 40% men

Undergraduates 1,464 full-time, 2,484 part-time. Students come from 8 states and territories, 1% are from out of state, 17% African American, 2% Asian American or Pacific Islander, 18% Hispanic American, 0.8% Native American, 0.1% international, 8% transferred in.

Freshmen *Admission:* 548 admitted, 548 enrolled.

Faculty *Total:* 234, 38% full-time, 7% with terminal degrees. *Student/faculty ratio:* 17:1.

Majors Accounting technology and bookkeeping; administrative assistant and secretarial science; business administration and management; chemical technology; child development; computer programming; computer systems networking and telecommunications; criminal justice/law enforcement administration; criminal justice/safety; drafting and design technology; emergency medical technology (EMT paramedic); fire protection and safety technology; general studies; liberal arts and sciences/liberal studies; nursing (registered nurse training); web page, digital/multimedia and information resources design.

Academic Programs *Special study options:* academic remediation for entering students, adult/continuing education programs, cooperative education, distance learning, English as a second language, honors programs, part-time degree program, services for LD students, summer session for credit.

Library Com Library plus 1 other with 84,128 titles, 19,000 serial subscriptions, 492 audiovisual materials, an OPAC, a Web page.

Computers on Campus 307 computers available on campus for general student use. A campuswide network can be accessed from off campus that provide access to wireless access throughout campus to Com network and Internet. Internet access, online (class) registration, at least one staffed computer lab available.

Student Life *Housing:* college housing not available. *Activities and Organizations:* drama/theater group, student-run newspaper, choral group, Student Activities Board, Student Government Association, COM Amigos, COM Soccer Club, Phi Theta Kappa. *Campus security:* 24-hour emergency response devices and patrols, student patrols. *Student services:* personal/psychological counseling, women's center.

Athletics *Intramural sports:* basketball M/W, football M/W, golf M/W, racquetball M/W, soccer M, softball M/W, swimming and diving M/W, table tennis M/W, tennis M/W, track and field M/W, volleyball M/W.

Standardized Tests *Required for some:* THEA (for placement).

Costs (2005–06) *Tuition:* area resident $624 full-time, $26 per credit part-time; state resident $1416 full-time, $59 per credit part-time; nonresident $2136

full-time, $89 per credit part-time. Full-time tuition and fees vary according to course load. Part-time tuition and fees vary according to course load. *Required fees:* $167 full-time, $7 per credit part-time, $84 per term part-time. *Payment plan:* installment. *Waivers:* employees or children of employees.

Financial Aid Of all full-time matriculated undergraduates who enrolled in 2003, 137 Federal Work-Study jobs (averaging $1127). 145 state and other part-time jobs (averaging $936).

Applying *Options:* electronic application, early admission, deferred entrance. *Required for some:* high school transcript. *Application deadline:* rolling (freshmen), rolling (transfers). *Notification:* continuous (freshmen).

Admissions Contact Ms. Kelly Musick, Registrar/Director of Admissions, College of the Mainland, 1200 Amburn Road, Texas City, TX 77591. *Phone:* 409-938-1211 Ext. 469. *Toll-free phone:* 888-258-8859 Ext. 264. *Fax:* 409-938-3126. *E-mail:* sem@com.edu.

COLLIN COUNTY COMMUNITY COLLEGE DISTRICT
Plano, Texas

- **State and locally supported** 2-year, founded 1985
- **Calendar** semesters
- **Degree** certificates and associate
- **Suburban** 333-acre campus with easy access to Dallas-Fort Worth
- **Endowment** $925,270
- **Coed,** 17,702 undergraduate students, 40% full-time, 57% women, 43% men

Undergraduates 7,061 full-time, 10,641 part-time. Students come from 44 states and territories, 86 other countries, 3% are from out of state, 8% African American, 7% Asian American or Pacific Islander, 9% Hispanic American, 0.6% Native American, 6% international, 11% transferred in.

Freshmen *Admission:* 3,417 admitted, 3,417 enrolled.

Faculty *Total:* 1,049, 21% full-time. *Student/faculty ratio:* 21:1.

Majors Biology/biotechnology laboratory technician; business administration and management; business automation/technology/data entry; commercial and advertising art; computer and information sciences; computer engineering technology; computer programming; computer systems networking and telecommunications; dental hygiene; drafting and design technology; educational/instructional media design; electrical, electronic and communications engineering technology; electrical/electronics drafting and CAD/CADD; electrical/electronics equipment installation and repair; emergency medical technology (EMT paramedic); environmental engineering technology; family and community services; fire protection and safety technology; hospitality administration; interior design; legal assistant/paralegal; liberal arts and sciences/liberal studies; music management and merchandising; nursing (registered nurse training); real estate; respiratory care therapy; sales, distribution and marketing; sign language interpretation and translation; telecommunications technology; water quality and wastewater treatment management and recycling technology; web page, digital/multimedia and information resources design.

Academic Programs *Special study options:* academic remediation for entering students, adult/continuing education programs, advanced placement credit, cooperative education, distance learning, English as a second language, honors programs, internships, part-time degree program, services for LD students, study abroad, summer session for credit.

Library Main Library plus 3 others with 129,032 titles, 940 serial subscriptions, 17,342 audiovisual materials, an OPAC, a Web page.

Computers on Campus 1858 computers available on campus for general student use. A campuswide network can be accessed from student residence rooms. Internet access, online (class) registration, at least one staffed computer lab available. Computer purchase or lease plan available.

Student Life *Housing:* college housing not available. *Activities and Organizations:* drama/theater group, choral group, Phi Theta Kappa, LULAC/BSN, Baptist Student Ministry, Psi Beta, Collin Nursing Student Association. *Campus security:* 24-hour emergency response devices and patrols, late-night transport/escort service, controlled dormitory access. *Student services:* personal/psychological counseling.

Athletics Member NJCAA. *Intercollegiate sports:* basketball M(s)/W(s), tennis M(s)/W(s), volleyball W(s).

Standardized Tests *Required:* THEA (for admission).

Costs (2005–06) *Tuition:* area resident $810 full-time, $27 per credit hour part-time; state resident $990 full-time, $33 per credit hour part-time; nonresident $2400 full-time, $80 per credit hour part-time. *Required fees:* $308 full-time, $10 per credit hour part-time, $4 per term part-time.

Financial Aid Of all full-time matriculated undergraduates who enrolled in 2003, 80 Federal Work-Study jobs (averaging $3490).

Applying *Options:* electronic application. *Application deadline:* rolling (freshmen). *Notification:* continuous (freshmen).

Admissions Contact Ms. Stephanie Meinhardt, Registrar, Collin County Community College District, 2200 West University Drive, McKinney, TX 75070-8001. *Phone:* 972-881-5174. *Fax:* 972-881-5175. *E-mail:* smeinhardt@ccccd.edu.

COMMONWEALTH INSTITUTE OF FUNERAL SERVICE
Houston, Texas

- **Independent** 2-year, founded 1988
- **Calendar** quarters
- **Degree** certificates and associate
- **Urban** campus
- **Coed,** 164 undergraduate students, 96% full-time, 53% women, 47% men

Undergraduates 157 full-time, 7 part-time. Students come from 11 states and territories, 20% are from out of state, 30% African American, 0.6% Asian American or Pacific Islander, 17% Hispanic American, 7% transferred in.
Freshmen *Admission:* 51 enrolled.
Faculty *Total:* 13, 31% full-time, 8% with terminal degrees. *Student/faculty ratio:* 23:1.
Majors Funeral service and mortuary science.
Academic Programs *Special study options:* adult/continuing education programs, external degree program.
Library Commonwealth Institute Library and York Learning Resource Center with 1,500 titles, 12 serial subscriptions.
Computers on Campus 15 computers available on campus for general student use. At least one staffed computer lab available.
Student Life *Housing:* college housing not available. *Activities and Organizations:* student council. *Campus security:* 24-hour emergency response devices.
Standardized Tests *Required for some:* Wonderlic aptitude test or THEA. *Recommended:* SAT or ACT (for admission).
Costs (2005–06) *Tuition:* $9400 full-time, $13 per contact hour part-time. *Required fees:* $100 full-time.
Applying *Options:* common application. *Application fee:* $50. *Required:* high school transcript. *Application deadline:* rolling (freshmen). *Notification:* continuous (freshmen).
Admissions Contact Mrs. Patricia Moreno, Registrar, Commonwealth Institute of Funeral Service, 415 Barren Springs Drive, Houston, TX 77090. *Phone:* 281-873-0262. *Toll-free phone:* 800-628-1580. *Fax:* 281-873-5232.

COMPUTER CAREER CENTER
El Paso, Texas

Admissions Contact Ms. Sarah Hernandez, Registrar, Computer Career Center, 6101 Montana Avenue, El Paso, TX 79925. *Phone:* 915-779-8031.

COURT REPORTING INSTITUTE OF DALLAS
Dallas, Texas

- **Proprietary** 2-year, founded 1978
- **Calendar** quarters
- **Degree** associate
- **Urban** campus
- **Coed, primarily women**

Faculty *Student/faculty ratio:* 35:1.
Student Life *Campus security:* 24-hour patrols, late-night transport/escort service.
Costs (2004–05) *Tuition:* $2222 full-time, $1500 per term part-time. Part-time tuition and fees vary according to program. *Required fees:* $100 full-time, $25 per term part-time.
Applying *Options:* early decision. *Application fee:* $100. *Required:* high school transcript, interview.
Admissions Contact Ms. Debra Smith-Armstrong, Director of Admissions, Court Reporting Institute of Dallas, 8585 North Stemmons, #200 North, Dallas, TX 75247. *Phone:* 214-350-9722 Ext. 227. *Toll-free phone:* 800-880-9722.

COURT REPORTING INSTITUTE OF HOUSTON
Houston, Texas

Admissions Contact 13101 Northwest Freeway, Suite 100, Houston, TX 77040. *Toll-free phone:* 866-996-8300.

CY-FAIR COLLEGE
Houston, Texas

- **State and locally supported** 2-year, founded 2002, part of North Harris Montgomery Community Course District
- **Calendar** semesters
- **Degree** certificates, diplomas, and associate
- **Suburban** 200-acre campus
- **Coed,** 8,540 undergraduate students, 22% full-time, 59% women, 41% men

Undergraduates 1,895 full-time, 6,645 part-time. Students come from 36 other countries, 9% African American, 8% Asian American or Pacific Islander, 21% Hispanic American, 0.4% Native American, 3% international.
Freshmen *Admission:* 1,447 enrolled.
Faculty *Total:* 449, 29% full-time. *Student/faculty ratio:* 17:1.
Academic Programs *Special study options:* academic remediation for entering students, adult/continuing education programs, advanced placement credit, cooperative education, distance learning, English as a second language, external degree program, honors programs, independent study, internships, part-time degree program, services for LD students.
Student Life *Housing:* college housing not available.
Standardized Tests *Required for some:* SAT or ACT (for placement).
Costs (2005–06) *Tuition:* area resident $768 full-time, $32 per credit hour part-time; state resident $1728 full-time, $72 per credit hour part-time; nonresident $2088 full-time, $87 per credit hour part-time. *Required fees:* $216 full-time, $8 per credit hour part-time, $12 per term part-time.
Applying *Options:* electronic application.
Admissions Contact Dr. Earl Campa, Vice President of Student Success, Cy-Fair College, 9191 Barker Cypress Road, Cypress, TX 77433-1383. *Phone:* 281-290-3950.

DALLAS INSTITUTE OF FUNERAL SERVICE
Dallas, Texas

- **Independent** 2-year, founded 1945
- **Calendar** quarters
- **Degree** associate
- **Urban** 8-acre campus with easy access to Dallas/Ft. Worth
- **Coed,** 234 undergraduate students, 100% full-time, 46% women, 54% men

Undergraduates 234 full-time. Students come from 12 states and territories, 10% are from out of state, 29% African American, 0.4% Asian American or Pacific Islander, 11% Hispanic American, 0.4% Native American, 10% transferred in.
Freshmen *Admission:* 95 applied, 88 admitted, 83 enrolled.
Faculty *Total:* 10, 50% full-time, 20% with terminal degrees. *Student/faculty ratio:* 23:1.
Majors Funeral service and mortuary science.
Student Life *Housing:* college housing not available. *Campus security:* 24-hour emergency response devices.
Costs (2005–06) *Tuition:* $10,000 full-time, $200 per hour part-time. Part-time tuition and fees vary according to course load. No tuition increase for student's term of enrollment. *Required fees:* $50 full-time. *Payment plan:* installment.
Applying *Application fee:* $50. *Required:* high school transcript.
Admissions Contact Terry Parrish, Director of Admissions, Dallas Institute of Funeral Service, 3909 S. Buckner Boulevard, Dallas, TX 75227. *Phone:* 214-388-5466. *Toll-free phone:* 800-235-5444. *E-mail:* difs@dallasinstitute.edu.

DEL MAR COLLEGE
Corpus Christi, Texas

- **State and locally supported** 2-year, founded 1935
- **Calendar** semesters
- **Degree** certificates and associate
- **Urban** 159-acre campus
- **Endowment** $29.1 million
- **Coed**

Faculty *Student/faculty ratio:* 18:1.
Student Life *Campus security:* 24-hour emergency response devices and patrols.
Standardized Tests *Required:* THEA or ACT ASSET (for placement).
Financial Aid Of all full-time matriculated undergraduates who enrolled in 2003, 259 Federal Work-Study jobs (averaging $960). 449 state and other part-time jobs (averaging $1082).
Applying *Options:* early admission, deferred entrance. *Required:* high school transcript.
Admissions Contact Ms. Frances P. Jordan, Assistant Dean of Enrollment Services and Registrar, Del Mar College, 101 Baldwin Boulevard, Corpus Christi, TX 78404-3897. *Phone:* 361-698-1248. *Toll-free phone:* 800-652-3357.

EASTFIELD COLLEGE
Mesquite, Texas

- **State and locally supported** 2-year, founded 1970, part of Dallas County Community College District System
- **Calendar** semesters
- **Degree** certificates and associate
- **Suburban** 244-acre campus with easy access to Dallas-Fort Worth
- **Coed,** 11,666 undergraduate students, 19% full-time, 59% women, 41% men

Undergraduates 2,239 full-time, 9,427 part-time. Students come from 18 states and territories, 1% are from out of state, 22% African American, 6% Asian American or Pacific Islander, 21% Hispanic American, 0.7% Native American, 2% international, 3% transferred in. *Retention:* 39% of 2002 full-time freshmen returned.

Freshmen *Admission:* 516 applied, 516 admitted, 516 enrolled.

Faculty *Total:* 484, 22% full-time. *Student/faculty ratio:* 23:1.

Majors Accounting; autobody/collision and repair technology; automobile/automotive mechanics technology; business administration and management; child care and support services management; computer and information sciences related; computer engineering technology; computer hardware engineering; computer/information technology services administration related; computer programming; computer programming related; computer systems networking and telecommunications; criminal justice/safety; data entry/microcomputer applications; data processing and data processing technology; drafting and design technology; electrical, electronic and communications engineering technology; electrical/electronics drafting and CAD/CADD; executive assistant/executive secretary; graphic and printing equipment operation/production; heating, air conditioning, ventilation and refrigeration maintenance technology; legal administrative assistant/secretary; liberal arts and sciences/liberal studies; psychiatric/mental health services technology; sign language interpretation and translation; social work; substance abuse/addiction counseling; system administration; word processing.

Academic Programs *Special study options:* academic remediation for entering students, adult/continuing education programs, advanced placement credit, cooperative education, distance learning, English as a second language, honors programs, part-time degree program, services for LD students, summer session for credit.

Library Eastfield College Learning Resource Center with 66,988 titles, 415 serial subscriptions, 2,620 audiovisual materials, an OPAC, a Web page.

Computers on Campus 50 computers available on campus for general student use. A campuswide network can be accessed from off campus. Internet access, at least one staffed computer lab available.

Student Life *Housing:* college housing not available. *Activities and Organizations:* drama/theater group, student-run newspaper, choral group, LULAC, Rodeo Club, PTK, Rising Star, Communications Club. *Campus security:* 24-hour emergency response devices and patrols. *Student services:* health clinic, personal/psychological counseling, women's center.

Athletics Member NJCAA. *Intercollegiate sports:* baseball M, basketball M, golf M, soccer W, tennis M/W, volleyball M/W. *Intramural sports:* basketball M, football M, softball M/W, volleyball M/W.

Costs (2005–06) *Tuition:* area resident $900 full-time, $30 per credit part-time; state resident $1500 full-time, $50 per credit part-time; nonresident $2400 full-time, $80 per credit part-time.

Applying *Options:* early admission, deferred entrance. *Recommended:* high school transcript. *Application deadline:* rolling (freshmen), rolling (transfers). *Notification:* continuous (freshmen).

Admissions Contact Ms. Linda Richardson, Director of Admissions/Registrar, Eastfield College, 3737 Motley Drive, Mesquite, TX 75150-2099. *Phone:* 972-860-7105. *Fax:* 912-860-8306. *E-mail:* efc@dcccd.edu.

EL CENTRO COLLEGE
Dallas, Texas

- **County-supported** 2-year, founded 1966, part of Dallas County Community College District System
- **Calendar** semesters
- **Degree** certificates and associate
- **Urban** 2-acre campus
- **Coed**

Faculty *Student/faculty ratio:* 16:1.

Student Life *Campus security:* 24-hour emergency response devices and patrols, late-night transport/escort service.

Standardized Tests *Required:* THEA, ACCUPLACER (for placement). *Recommended:* SAT or ACT (for placement).

Costs (2004–05) *Tuition:* area resident $720 full-time, $30 per credit part-time; state resident $1200 full-time, $50 per credit part-time; nonresident $1920 full-time, $80 per credit part-time.

Applying *Options:* electronic application, early admission. *Required for some:* high school transcript, 1 letter of recommendation.

Admissions Contact Ms. Stevie Stewart, Director of Admissions and Registrar, El Centro College, 801 Main Street, Dallas, TX 75202. *Phone:* 214-860-2618. *Fax:* 214-860-2233. *E-mail:* sgs5310@dcccd.edu.

EL PASO COMMUNITY COLLEGE
El Paso, Texas

- **County-supported** 2-year, founded 1969
- **Calendar** semesters
- **Degree** certificates and associate
- **Urban** campus
- **Endowment** $24,000
- **Coed,** 19,953 undergraduate students

Undergraduates Students come from 47 states and territories, 40 other countries, 5% are from out of state.

Freshmen *Admission:* 3,672 applied, 3,672 admitted.

Faculty *Total:* 1,183, 30% full-time.

Majors Accounting; administrative assistant and secretarial science; architectural engineering technology; art; automobile/automotive mechanics technology; biology/biological sciences; broadcast journalism; business administration and management; chemistry; child development; clinical/medical laboratory technology; commercial and advertising art; computer and information sciences; computer and information sciences related; computer graphics; computer programming; computer programming related; computer programming (specific applications); computer software and media applications related; computer systems networking and telecommunications; computer/technical support; construction management; corrections; court reporting; criminal justice/police science; data entry/microcomputer applications; data entry/microcomputer applications related; data modeling/warehousing and database administration; dental hygiene; dietetics; drafting and design technology; dramatic/theatre arts; education; electrical, electronic and communications engineering technology; elementary education; English; fashion/apparel design; fashion merchandising; finance; fire science; geology/earth science; health information/medical records administration; health science; health teacher education; heating, air conditioning, ventilation and refrigeration maintenance technology; history; human services; industrial arts; industrial radiologic technology; information technology; interior design; international business/trade/commerce; liberal arts and sciences/liberal studies; mass communication/media; mathematics; medical/clinical assistant; mental health/rehabilitation; music; nursing (registered nurse training); ophthalmic laboratory technology; photography; physical therapist assistant; physics; political science and government; pre-engineering; psychology; real estate; respiratory care therapy; sign language interpretation and translation; social sciences; sociology; speech and rhetoric; system administration; tourism and travel services management; web/multimedia management and webmaster; web page, digital/multimedia and information resources design; word processing.

Academic Programs *Special study options:* academic remediation for entering students, adult/continuing education programs, advanced placement credit, cooperative education, distance learning, English as a second language, external degree program, honors programs, internships, off-campus study, part-time degree program, services for LD students, summer session for credit. *ROTC:* Army (c).

Library El Paso Community College Learning Resource Center plus 4 others with 442,879 titles, 938 serial subscriptions, 12,035 audiovisual materials, an OPAC, a Web page.

Computers on Campus 1200 computers available on campus for general student use. A campuswide network can be accessed from off campus. Internet access, at least one staffed computer lab available.

Student Life *Housing:* college housing not available. *Activities and Organizations:* drama/theater group, student-run newspaper, radio and television station, choral group, African-American Coalition, Art Student Society, Phi Theta Kappa, Architecture Club, Social Science Club. *Campus security:* 24-hour patrols, late-night transport/escort service. *Student services:* personal/psychological counseling.

Athletics Member NJCAA. *Intercollegiate sports:* baseball M(s), softball W(s). *Intramural sports:* basketball M/W, bowling M/W, cross-country running M/W, softball M/W, table tennis M/W, tennis M/W, volleyball M/W, weight lifting M/W.

Standardized Tests *Required:* THEA (for placement).

Costs (2004–05) *Tuition:* state resident $1096 full-time, $34 per credit part-time; nonresident $1566 full-time. Part-time tuition and fees vary according to course load. *Required fees:* $240 full-time, $10 per credit part-time. *Payment plan:* installment. *Waivers:* senior citizens and employees or children of employees.

Financial Aid Of all full-time matriculated undergraduates who enrolled in 2003, 750 Federal Work-Study jobs (averaging $1800). 50 state and other part-time jobs (averaging $1800).

Applying *Options:* early admission, deferred entrance. *Application fee:* $10. *Application deadlines:* 8/3 (freshmen), 8/3 (transfers).

El Paso Community College (continued)
Admissions Contact Daryle Hendry, Director of Admissions, El Paso Community College, PO Box 20500, El Paso, TX 79998-0500. *Phone:* 915-831-2580.

EVEREST COLLEGE
Arlington, Texas

Admissions Contact 2801 East Division Street, Suite 250, Arlington, TX 76011.

EVEREST COLLEGE
Dallas, Texas

Admissions Contact 6060 North Central Expressway, Suite 101, Dallas, TX 75206-5209.

FRANK PHILLIPS COLLEGE
Borger, Texas

- **State and locally supported** 2-year, founded 1948
- **Calendar** semesters
- **Degree** certificates and associate
- **Small-town** 60-acre campus
- **Endowment** $402,582
- **Coed,** 1,100 undergraduate students

Undergraduates Students come from 11 states and territories, 12 other countries.
Faculty *Total:* 97, 29% full-time.
Majors Accounting; administrative assistant and secretarial science; agricultural business and management; agricultural economics; agricultural mechanization; agricultural teacher education; agriculture; agronomy and crop science; airline pilot and flight crew; anatomy; art; art teacher education; athletic training; biological and physical sciences; biology/biological sciences; botany/plant biology; business administration and management; business machine repair; business/managerial economics; business teacher education; chemistry; computer and information sciences; computer engineering technology; computer science; cosmetology; criminal justice/law enforcement administration; criminal justice/police science; data processing and data processing technology; developmental and child psychology; economics; education; electrical, electronic and communications engineering technology; elementary education; engineering; engineering technology; English; farm and ranch management; finance; fire science; heating, air conditioning, ventilation and refrigeration maintenance technology; history; horticultural science; information science/studies; legal administrative assistant/secretary; liberal arts and sciences/liberal studies; mathematics; music; music teacher education; natural resources management and policy; nursing (registered nurse training); petroleum technology; physical education teaching and coaching; physical sciences; piano and organ; political science and government; postal management; pre-engineering; pre-pharmacy studies; psychology; sociology; survey technology; welding technology; zoology/animal biology.
Academic Programs *Special study options:* academic remediation for entering students, accelerated degree program, adult/continuing education programs, advanced placement credit, cooperative education, distance learning, honors programs, internships, part-time degree program, services for LD students, summer session for credit.
Library Frank Phillips College Learning Resource Center with 35,700 titles, 138 serial subscriptions, an OPAC.
Computers on Campus 29 computers available on campus for general student use. A campuswide network can be accessed. Internet access, at least one staffed computer lab available.
Student Life *Housing Options:* men-only, women-only. Campus housing is university owned. *Activities and Organizations:* choral group, Rodeo Club, Music Club, Computer Club, Phi Theta Kappa, student government. *Campus security:* 24-hour emergency response devices and patrols, controlled dormitory access. *Student services:* personal/psychological counseling.
Athletics Member NJCAA. *Intercollegiate sports:* baseball M(s), basketball M(s)/W(s), volleyball W(s). *Intramural sports:* basketball M/W, racquetball M/W, volleyball M/W.
Standardized Tests *Required:* THEA (for placement).
Costs (2005–06) *Tuition:* area resident $720 full-time, $30 per semester hour part-time; state resident $1128 full-time, $47 per semester hour part-time; nonresident $1296 full-time, $54 per semester hour part-time. *Required fees:* $914 full-time, $36 per semester hour part-time, $50 per term part-time.
Financial Aid Of all full-time matriculated undergraduates who enrolled in 2003, 9 Federal Work-Study jobs (averaging $3000). 1 state and other part-time job (averaging $3000).

Applying *Options:* common application, early admission, deferred entrance. *Required:* high school transcript. *Application deadline:* 8/25 (freshmen). *Notification:* continuous until 8/25 (freshmen).
Admissions Contact Ms. Beth Raper, Director of Admissions, Frank Phillips College, Borger, TX 79008-5118. *Phone:* 806-457-4200 Ext. 741. *Toll-free phone:* 800-687-2056. *Fax:* 806-274-6835. *E-mail:* dtrimble@fpc.cc.tx.us.

GALVESTON COLLEGE
Galveston, Texas

- **State and locally supported** 2-year, founded 1967
- **Calendar** semesters
- **Degree** certificates and associate
- **Urban** 11-acre campus with easy access to Houston
- **Coed**

Student Life *Campus security:* 24-hour emergency response devices, late-night transport/escort service.
Athletics Member NJCAA.
Costs (2004–05) *Tuition:* state resident $900 full-time, $180 per term part-time; nonresident $1800 full-time, $360 per term part-time. *Required fees:* $478 full-time, $102 per term part-time.
Financial Aid Of all full-time matriculated undergraduates who enrolled in 2003, 36 Federal Work-Study jobs (averaging $2000).
Applying *Options:* common application. *Required for some:* high school transcript.
Admissions Contact MaEsther Francis, Dean of Enrollment Management and Student Success, Galveston College, 4015 Avenue Q, Galveston, TX 77550. *Phone:* 409-944-1238. *Fax:* 409-944-1501. *E-mail:* lhumphries@gc.edu.

GRAYSON COUNTY COLLEGE
Denison, Texas

Admissions Contact Dr. David Petrash, Associate Vice President for Admissions, Records and Institutional Research, Grayson County College, 6101 Grayson Drive, Denison, TX 75020. *Phone:* 903-465-6030. *Fax:* 903-463-5284.

HALLMARK INSTITUTE OF AERONAUTICS
San Antonio, Texas

Admissions Contact Mr. David McSorley, Director, Hallmark Institute of Aeronautics, 8901 Wetmore Road, San Antonio, TX 78216. *Phone:* 210-690-9000. *Toll-free phone:* 800-683-3600.

HALLMARK INSTITUTE OF TECHNOLOGY
San Antonio, Texas

Admissions Contact Ms. Sonia Ross, Director of Admissions, Hallmark Institute of Technology, 10401 IH 10 West, San Antonio, TX 78230-1737. *Phone:* 210-690-9000 Ext. 212. *Toll-free phone:* 800-880-6600. *Fax:* 210-697-8225.

HIGH-TECH INSTITUTE
Irving, Texas

Admissions Contact Ms. Cindy M. Lewellen, Director, High-Tech Institute, 4250 North Belt Line Road, Irving, TX 75038. *Phone:* 972-871-2824. *Toll-free phone:* 800-987-0110.

HILL COLLEGE OF THE HILL JUNIOR COLLEGE DISTRICT
Hillsboro, Texas

- **District-supported** 2-year, founded 1923
- **Calendar** semesters
- **Degree** certificates and associate
- **Small-town** 80-acre campus with easy access to Dallas-Fort Worth
- **Endowment** $416,886
- **Coed**

Faculty *Student/faculty ratio:* 25:1.
Student Life *Campus security:* late-night transport/escort service, controlled dormitory access, security officers.
Athletics Member NJCAA.

Standardized Tests *Required:* THEA (for placement). *Recommended:* SAT or ACT (for placement).

Financial Aid Of all full-time matriculated undergraduates who enrolled in 2003, 51 Federal Work-Study jobs (averaging $858). 20 state and other part-time jobs (averaging $230).

Applying *Options:* early admission, deferred entrance. *Required:* high school transcript.

Admissions Contact Ms. Diane Harvey, Director of Admissions/Registrar, Hill College of the Hill Junior College District, PO Box 619, Hillsboro, TX 76645-0619. *Phone:* 254-582-2555 Ext. 315. *Fax:* 254-582-7591. *E-mail:* diharvey@hill-college.cc.tx.us.

HOUSTON COMMUNITY COLLEGE SYSTEM
Houston, Texas

- **State and locally supported** 2-year, founded 1971
- **Calendar** semesters
- **Degree** certificates and associate
- **Urban** campus
- **Coed,** 39,838 undergraduate students, 42% full-time, 69% women, 31% men

Undergraduates 16,609 full-time, 23,229 part-time.

Faculty *Total:* 3,128, 26% full-time. *Student/faculty ratio:* 21:1.

Majors Accounting; administrative assistant and secretarial science; agriculture; automobile/automotive mechanics technology; business administration and management; business/corporate communications; cartography; child care and support services management; child development; civil engineering technology; clinical/medical laboratory technology; commercial and advertising art; commercial photography; computer and information sciences; computer engineering technology; computer science; construction engineering technology; court reporting; criminal justice/police science; drafting and design technology; dramatic/theatre arts; electrical, electronic and communications engineering technology; emergency medical technology (EMT paramedic); engineering technology; family and consumer sciences/human sciences; fashion/apparel design; fashion merchandising; finance; fire science; graphic and printing equipment operation/production; health/health care administration; health information/medical records administration; health information/medical records technology; horticultural science; hotel/motel administration; human resources management; industrial radiologic technology; industrial technology; insurance; interior design; kinesiology and exercise science; legal assistant/paralegal; liberal arts and sciences/liberal studies; logistics and materials management; marketing/marketing management; mass communication/media; medical administrative assistant and medical secretary; medical radiologic technology; mental health/rehabilitation; music management and merchandising; music theory and composition; nuclear medical technology; nursing (registered nurse training); occupational safety and health technology; occupational therapist assistant; physical therapist assistant; psychiatric/mental health services technology; radio and television broadcasting technology; real estate; respiratory care therapy; sign language interpretation and translation; social sciences; technical and business writing; tourism and travel services management; transportation technology.

Academic Programs *Special study options:* academic remediation for entering students, adult/continuing education programs, advanced placement credit, cooperative education, distance learning, English as a second language, honors programs, independent study, internships, part-time degree program, services for LD students, study abroad, summer session for credit. *ROTC:* Army (c).

Library Main Library plus 19 others with 140,674 titles, 2,012 serial subscriptions, 16,334 audiovisual materials, an OPAC, a Web page.

Computers on Campus 3200 computers available on campus for general student use. A campuswide network can be accessed from off campus. At least one staffed computer lab available.

Student Life *Housing:* college housing not available. *Activities and Organizations:* drama/theater group, student-run newspaper, television station, Phi Theta Kappa, Eastwood Student Association, Eagle's Club, Society of Hispanic Professional Engineers, International Student Association. *Campus security:* 24-hour emergency response devices and patrols, late-night transport/escort service. *Student services:* personal/psychological counseling.

Costs (2004–05) *Tuition:* area resident $1470 full-time, $49 per semester hour part-time; state resident $3090 full-time, $103 per semester hour part-time; nonresident $3690 full-time, $129 per semester hour part-time. *Payment plan:* installment.

Applying *Required for some:* high school transcript, interview. *Application deadline:* rolling (freshmen).

Admissions Contact Ms. Mary Lemburg, Registrar, Houston Community College System, 3100 Main Street, PO Box 667517, Houston, TX 77266-7517. *Phone:* 713-718-8500. *Fax:* 713-718-2111.

HOWARD COLLEGE
Big Spring, Texas

- **State and locally supported** 2-year, founded 1945, part of Howard County Junior College District System
- **Calendar** semesters
- **Degree** certificates and associate
- **Small-town** 120-acre campus
- **Endowment** $1.2 million
- **Coed,** 2,728 undergraduate students, 36% full-time, 63% women, 37% men

Undergraduates 986 full-time, 1,742 part-time. Students come from 10 states and territories, 2 other countries, 0.5% are from out of state, 5% African American, 0.5% Asian American or Pacific Islander, 34% Hispanic American, 0.4% Native American, 0.1% international, 0.4% transferred in, 18% live on campus.

Freshmen *Admission:* 597 applied, 597 admitted, 597 enrolled.

Faculty *Total:* 216, 59% full-time, 3% with terminal degrees. *Student/faculty ratio:* 14:1.

Majors Accounting; agriculture; art; automobile/automotive mechanics technology; behavioral sciences; biology/biological sciences; business administration and management; chemistry; child development; computer and information sciences related; computer programming; computer science; cosmetology; criminal justice/police science; dental hygiene; drafting and design technology; dramatic/theatre arts; English; finance; health information/medical records administration; industrial arts; mathematics; music teacher education; nursing (licensed practical/vocational nurse training); nursing (registered nurse training); ornamental horticulture; physical education teaching and coaching; respiratory care therapy; social sciences; speech and rhetoric; substance abuse/addiction counseling.

Academic Programs *Special study options:* academic remediation for entering students, adult/continuing education programs, advanced placement credit, cooperative education, distance learning, English as a second language, independent study, internships, part-time degree program, services for LD students, summer session for credit.

Library Howard College Library with 30,921 titles, 16,006 serial subscriptions, 1,710 audiovisual materials, an OPAC, a Web page.

Computers on Campus 300 computers available on campus for general student use. A campuswide network can be accessed from student residence rooms. Internet access, at least one staffed computer lab available.

Student Life *Housing:* on-campus residence required for freshman year. *Options:* men-only, women-only. Campus housing is university owned. Freshman applicants given priority for college housing. *Activities and Organizations:* drama/theater group, choral group, Phi Theta Kappa, Student Government Association, Mexican-American Student Association, Baptist Student Ministries. *Campus security:* 24-hour patrols. *Student services:* personal/psychological counseling.

Athletics Member NJCAA. *Intercollegiate sports:* baseball M(s), basketball M(s)/W(s), cheerleading M(s)/W(s), softball W(s). *Intramural sports:* basketball M/W, bowling M/W, football M/W, racquetball M/W, softball W, volleyball M/W.

Standardized Tests *Required:* THEA (for placement). *Required for some:* SAT or ACT (for placement).

Costs (2005–06) *Tuition:* area resident $900 full-time, $30 per credit hour part-time; state resident $1200 full-time, $40 per credit hour part-time; nonresident $1800 full-time, $60 per credit hour part-time. Full-time tuition and fees vary according to course load, location, and program. Part-time tuition and fees vary according to course load, location, and program. *Required fees:* $200 full-time, $50 per term part-time. *Room and board:* $3140. *Payment plan:* installment. *Waivers:* senior citizens.

Applying *Options:* early admission. *Required:* high school transcript. *Application deadline:* rolling (freshmen), rolling (transfers). *Notification:* continuous until 8/31 (freshmen).

Admissions Contact Ms. Rebecca Villanueva, Outreach Coordinator, Howard College, 1001 Birdwell Lane, Big Spring, TX 79720-3702. *Phone:* 866-HC-HAWKS Ext. 5114. *Toll-free phone:* 866-HC-HAWKS. *E-mail:* rvillanueva@howardcollege.edu.

ITT TECHNICAL INSTITUTE
Arlington, Texas

- **Proprietary** 2-year, founded 1982, part of ITT Educational Services, Inc
- **Calendar** quarters
- **Degree** associate
- **Suburban** campus with easy access to Dallas-Fort Worth
- **Coed**

Standardized Tests *Required:* Wonderlic aptitude test (for admission).

Costs (2004–05) *Tuition:* Please see school catalog for specific information.

ITT Technical Institute (continued)

Applying *Options:* deferred entrance. *Application fee:* $100. *Required:* high school transcript, interview. *Recommended:* letters of recommendation.
Admissions Contact Mr. Ed Leal, Director of Recruitment, ITT Technical Institute, 551 Ryan Plaza Drive, Arlington, TX 76011. *Phone:* 817-794-5100. *Toll-free phone:* 888-288-4950. *Fax:* 817-275-8446.

ITT TECHNICAL INSTITUTE
Austin, Texas

- **Proprietary** 2-year, founded 1985, part of ITT Educational Services, Inc
- **Calendar** quarters
- **Degree** associate
- **Urban** campus
- **Coed**

Standardized Tests *Required:* Wonderlic aptitude test (for admission).
Costs (2004–05) *Tuition:* Please see school catalog for specific information.
Financial Aid Of all full-time matriculated undergraduates who enrolled in 2003, 1 Federal Work-Study job.
Applying *Options:* deferred entrance. *Application fee:* $100. *Required:* high school transcript, interview. *Recommended:* letters of recommendation.
Admissions Contact Mr. Steve Shanabarger, Director of Recruitment, ITT Technical Institute, 6330 Highway 290 East, Suite 150, Austin, TX 78723. *Phone:* 512-467-6800. *Toll-free phone:* 800-431-0677. *Fax:* 512-467-6677.

ITT TECHNICAL INSTITUTE
Houston, Texas

- **Proprietary** 2-year, founded 1985, part of ITT Educational Services, Inc
- **Calendar** quarters
- **Degree** associate
- **Suburban** 1-acre campus
- **Coed**

Standardized Tests *Required:* Wonderlic aptitude test (for admission).
Costs (2004–05) *Tuition:* Please see school catalog for specific information.
Applying *Options:* deferred entrance. *Application fee:* $100. *Required:* high school transcript, interview. *Recommended:* letters of recommendation.
Admissions Contact Mr. Robert Roloff, Director of Recruitment, ITT Technical Institute, 15621 Blue Ash Drive, Suite 160, Houston, TX 77090. *Phone:* 281-873-0512. *Toll-free phone:* 800-879-6486. *Fax:* 281-873-0518.

ITT TECHNICAL INSTITUTE
Houston, Texas

- **Proprietary** 2-year, founded 1995, part of ITT Educational Services, Inc
- **Calendar** quarters
- **Degree** associate
- **Coed**

Standardized Tests *Required:* Wonderlic aptitude test (for admission).
Costs (2004–05) *Tuition:* Please see school catalog for specific information.
Applying *Options:* deferred entrance. *Application fee:* $100. *Required:* high school transcript, interview. *Recommended:* letters of recommendation.
Admissions Contact Mr. Ricky J. Kana, Director of Recruitment, ITT Technical Institute, 2222 Bay Area Boulevard, Houston, TX 77058. *Phone:* 281-486-2630. *Toll-free phone:* 888-488-9347. *Fax:* 281-486-6099.

ITT TECHNICAL INSTITUTE
Houston, Texas

- **Proprietary** 2-year, founded 1983, part of ITT Educational Services, Inc
- **Calendar** quarters
- **Degree** associate
- **Urban** 4-acre campus
- **Coed**

Standardized Tests *Required:* Wonderlic aptitude test (for admission).
Costs (2004–05) *Tuition:* Please see school catalog for specific information.
Applying *Options:* deferred entrance. *Application fee:* $100. *Required:* high school transcript, interview. *Recommended:* letters of recommendation.
Admissions Contact Gaynelle Sanders, Director of Recruitment, ITT Technical Institute, 2950 South Gessner, Houston, TX 77063. *Phone:* 713-952-2294. *Toll-free phone:* 800-235-4787. *Fax:* 713-952-2393.

ITT TECHNICAL INSTITUTE
Richardson, Texas

- **Proprietary** 2-year, founded 1989, part of ITT Educational Services, Inc
- **Calendar** quarters
- **Degree** associate
- **Suburban** campus with easy access to Dallas-Fort Worth
- **Coed**

Standardized Tests *Required:* Wonderlic aptitude test (for admission).
Costs (2004–05) *Tuition:* Please see school catalog for specific information.
Financial Aid Of all full-time matriculated undergraduates who enrolled in 2003, 5 Federal Work-Study jobs (averaging $5000).
Applying *Options:* deferred entrance. *Application fee:* $100. *Required:* high school transcript, interview. *Recommended:* letters of recommendation.
Admissions Contact Mr. Fred Garcia, Director of Recruitment, ITT Technical Institute, 2101 Waterview Parkway, Richardson, TX 75080. *Phone:* 972-690-9100. *Toll-free phone:* 888-488-5761. *Fax:* 972-690-0853.

ITT TECHNICAL INSTITUTE
San Antonio, Texas

- **Proprietary** 2-year, founded 1988, part of ITT Educational Services, Inc
- **Calendar** quarters
- **Degree** associate
- **Urban** campus
- **Coed**

Standardized Tests *Required:* Wonderlic aptitude test (for admission).
Costs (2004–05) *Tuition:* Please see school catalog for specific information.
Applying *Options:* deferred entrance. *Application fee:* $100. *Required:* high school transcript, interview. *Recommended:* letters of recommendation.
Admissions Contact Mr. Doug Howard, Director of Recruitment, ITT Technical Institute, 5700 Northwest Parkway, San Antonio, TX 78249. *Phone:* 210-694-4612. *Toll-free phone:* 800-880-0570. *Fax:* 210-694-4651.

JACKSONVILLE COLLEGE
Jacksonville, Texas

- **Independent Baptist** 2-year, founded 1899
- **Calendar** semesters
- **Degree** diplomas and associate
- **Small-town** 20-acre campus
- **Coed**

Faculty *Student/faculty ratio:* 14:1.
Student Life *Campus security:* 24-hour emergency response devices, evening security personnel.
Athletics Member NJCAA.
Standardized Tests *Required:* THEA (for placement).
Costs (2004–05) *Comprehensive fee:* $6778 includes full-time tuition ($3750), mandatory fees ($400), and room and board ($2628). Part-time tuition: $165 per hour. Part-time tuition and fees vary according to course load.
Applying *Options:* electronic application, early admission. *Application fee:* $15.
Admissions Contact Mrs. Johnnie Ross, Director of Admissions, Jacksonville College, 105 B.J. Albritton Drive, Jacksonville, TX 75766. *Phone:* 903-586-2518 Ext. 7134. *Toll-free phone:* 800-256-8522. *Fax:* 903-586-0743. *E-mail:* admissions@jacksonville-college.org.

KD STUDIO
Dallas, Texas

- **Proprietary** 2-year, founded 1979
- **Calendar** semesters
- **Degree** associate
- **Urban** campus
- **Coed**

Faculty *Student/faculty ratio:* 15:1.
Student Life *Campus security:* 24-hour emergency response devices and patrols.
Costs (2004–05) *Tuition:* $19,400 full-time. No tuition increase for student's term of enrollment. *Required fees:* $250 full-time.
Applying *Options:* common application, deferred entrance. *Application fee:* $100. *Required:* essay or personal statement, high school transcript, interview, audition. *Required for some:* letters of recommendation.

Admissions Contact Mr. T. A. Taylor, Director of Education, KD Studio, 2600 Stemmons Freeway, #117, Dallas, TX 75207. *Phone:* 214-638-0484. *Fax:* 214-630-5140. *E-mail:* information@kdstudio.com.

KILGORE COLLEGE
Kilgore, Texas

- **State and locally supported** 2-year, founded 1935
- **Calendar** semesters
- **Degree** certificates and associate
- **Small-town** 35-acre campus with easy access to Dallas-Fort Worth
- **Endowment** $5.2 million
- **Coed,** 4,957 undergraduate students, 55% full-time, 62% women, 38% men

Undergraduates 2,749 full-time, 2,208 part-time. Students come from 21 states and territories, 36 other countries, 1% are from out of state, 15% African American, 0.5% Asian American or Pacific Islander, 4% Hispanic American, 0.1% Native American, 2% international, 6% transferred in, 12% live on campus. *Retention:* 45% of 2002 full-time freshmen returned.

Freshmen *Admission:* 1,706 applied, 1,079 admitted, 1,079 enrolled. *Test scores:* SAT verbal scores over 500: 43%; SAT math scores over 500: 45%; ACT scores over 18: 70%; SAT verbal scores over 600: 8%; SAT math scores over 600: 9%; ACT scores over 24: 17%; SAT math scores over 700: 1%.

Faculty *Total:* 247, 52% full-time, 9% with terminal degrees. *Student/faculty ratio:* 19:1.

Majors Accounting; accounting technology and bookkeeping; administrative assistant and secretarial science; aerospace, aeronautical and astronautical engineering; agriculture; art; automobile/automotive mechanics technology; biological and physical sciences; business administration and management; business/commerce; chemistry; child care and support services management; clinical laboratory science/medical technology; clinical/medical laboratory technology; commercial and advertising art; commercial photography; computer and information sciences; computer programming; computer systems networking and telecommunications; corrections; criminal justice/law enforcement administration; criminal justice/police science; criminal justice/safety; dance; data processing and data processing technology; design and visual communications; diesel mechanics technology; drafting and design technology; dramatic/theatre arts; electrical, electronic and communications engineering technology; elementary education; emergency medical technology (EMT paramedic); English; executive assistant/executive secretary; fashion merchandising; finance; fire science; forestry; general studies; geology/earth science; graphic and printing equipment operation/production; health teacher education; heating, air conditioning, ventilation and refrigeration maintenance technology; industrial technology; journalism; legal assistant/paralegal; machine tool technology; management information systems; mathematics; medical/clinical assistant; medical radiologic technology; metallurgical technology; music; nursing (registered nurse training); occupational safety and health technology; operations management; physical education teaching and coaching; physical therapist assistant; physics; pre-pharmacy studies; psychology; religious studies; social sciences; speech and rhetoric; trade and industrial teacher education.

Academic Programs *Special study options:* academic remediation for entering students, adult/continuing education programs, advanced placement credit, cooperative education, English as a second language, internships, part-time degree program, services for LD students, student-designed majors, summer session for credit. *ROTC:* Army (c).

Library Randolph C. Watson Library plus 1 other with 65,000 titles, 6,679 serial subscriptions, 13,351 audiovisual materials, an OPAC, a Web page.

Computers on Campus 302 computers available on campus for general student use. Internet access, online (class) registration, at least one staffed computer lab available.

Student Life *Housing:* on-campus residence required for freshman year. *Options:* coed, men-only, women-only. Campus housing is university owned. *Activities and Organizations:* drama/theater group, choral group, marching band, Phi Theta Kappa, Student Government Association, Ambucs. *Campus security:* 24-hour emergency response devices and patrols.

Athletics Member NJCAA. *Intercollegiate sports:* basketball M(s)/W(s), cheerleading M(s)/W(s), football M(s). *Intramural sports:* basketball M/W, football M/W, golf M/W, racquetball M/W, swimming and diving M/W, tennis M/W, volleyball M/W.

Standardized Tests *Required:* THEA (for placement). *Recommended:* SAT or ACT (for placement).

Costs (2005–06) *Tuition:* area resident $540 full-time, $18 per hour part-time; state resident $1680 full-time, $56 per hour part-time; nonresident $2520 full-time, $84 per hour part-time. *Required fees:* $510 full-time. *Room and board:* $3580; room only: $1580.

Financial Aid Of all full-time matriculated undergraduates who enrolled in 2003, 80 Federal Work-Study jobs (averaging $2500). *Financial aid deadline:* 6/1.

Applying *Options:* early admission. *Required:* high school transcript. *Required for some:* interview. *Application deadline:* rolling (freshmen), rolling (transfers).

Admissions Contact Ms. Jeanna Centers, Admissions Specialist, Kilgore College, 1100 Broadway, Kilgore, TX 75662. *Phone:* 903-983-8202. *Fax:* 903-983-8607. *E-mail:* register@kilgore.cc.tx.us.

KINGWOOD COLLEGE
Kingwood, Texas

- **State and locally supported** 2-year, founded 1984, part of North Harris Montgomery Community College District
- **Calendar** semesters
- **Degree** certificates and associate
- **Suburban** 264-acre campus with easy access to Houston
- **Coed,** 6,403 undergraduate students, 21% full-time, 65% women, 35% men

Undergraduates 1,343 full-time, 5,060 part-time. Students come from 44 other countries, 0.7% are from out of state, 8% African American, 3% Asian American or Pacific Islander, 14% Hispanic American, 0.6% Native American, 2% international, 4% transferred in.

Freshmen *Admission:* 3,898 applied, 3,898 admitted, 905 enrolled.

Faculty *Total:* 331, 29% full-time. *Student/faculty ratio:* 16:1.

Majors Accounting; biology/biological sciences; business administration and management; computer and information sciences; computer engineering technology; computer graphics; computer typography and composition equipment operation; education; English; foreign languages and literatures; information science/studies; mathematics; nursing (licensed practical/vocational nurse training); occupational therapy; psychology; social sciences; visual and performing arts.

Academic Programs *Special study options:* academic remediation for entering students, accelerated degree program, advanced placement credit, cooperative education, distance learning, double majors, English as a second language, external degree program, honors programs, independent study, internships, part-time degree program, services for LD students, summer session for credit.

Library Kingwood College Library with 38,000 titles, 262 serial subscriptions, 3,177 audiovisual materials, an OPAC, a Web page.

Computers on Campus 540 computers available on campus for general student use. A campuswide network can be accessed from off campus. Internet access, online (class) registration, at least one staffed computer lab available.

Student Life *Housing:* college housing not available. *Activities and Organizations:* drama/theater group, student-run television station, choral group, Phi Theta Kappa, Office Administration Club, African American Student Association, Student Government Association, Delta Epsilon Chi. *Campus security:* 24-hour emergency response devices and patrols, late-night transport/escort service. *Student services:* personal/psychological counseling.

Athletics *Intramural sports:* baseball M.

Standardized Tests *Required for some:* SAT or ACT (for placement), ACT ASSET.

Costs (2005–06) *Tuition:* area resident $984 full-time, $52 per credit part-time; state resident $1944 full-time, $92 per credit part-time; nonresident $2304 full-time, $220 per credit part-time. Full-time tuition and fees vary according to course load and program. Part-time tuition and fees vary according to course load. *Payment plans:* installment, deferred payment. *Waivers:* employees or children of employees.

Financial Aid Of all full-time matriculated undergraduates who enrolled in 2003, 13 Federal Work-Study jobs, 4 state and other part-time jobs. *Financial aid deadline:* 5/15.

Applying *Options:* common application, early admission. *Required:* high school transcript. *Required for some:* essay or personal statement. *Application deadline:* rolling (freshmen), rolling (transfers).

Admissions Contact Mr. Ike Williams, Director of Enrollment Management, Kingwood College, 20000 Kingwood Drive, Kingwood, TX 77339. *Phone:* 281-312-1562. *Fax:* 281-312-1477. *E-mail:* ronald.shade@nhmccd.edu.

LAMAR INSTITUTE OF TECHNOLOGY
Beaumont, Texas

Admissions Contact Mr. James Rush, Director of Admissions, Lamar Institute of Technology, PO Box 10043, Beaumont, TX 77710. *Phone:* 409-880-8354. *Toll-free phone:* 800-950-8321.

LAMAR STATE COLLEGE-ORANGE
Orange, Texas

- **State-supported** 2-year, founded 1969, part of The Texas State University System
- **Calendar** semesters
- **Degree** certificates and associate
- **Small-town** 21-acre campus
- **Endowment** $5524
- **Coed**

Lamar State College-Orange (continued)

Faculty *Student/faculty ratio:* 18:1.
Student Life *Campus security:* 24-hour emergency response devices, late-night transport/escort service.
Standardized Tests *Required for some:* THEA.
Costs (2004–05) *Tuition:* state resident $1728 full-time, $168 per credit part-time; nonresident $8976 full-time, $374 per credit part-time. Full-time tuition and fees vary according to course load. Part-time tuition and fees vary according to course load. *Required fees:* $716 full-time, $61 per credit part-time.
Financial Aid Of all full-time matriculated undergraduates who enrolled in 2003, 20 Federal Work-Study jobs (averaging $3000). 2 state and other part-time jobs (averaging $2000).
Applying *Options:* common application, early admission, deferred entrance. *Required:* high school transcript. *Recommended:* minimum 2.0 GPA.
Admissions Contact Kerry Olson, Director of Admissions and Financial Aid, Lamar State College-Orange, 410 Front Street, Orange, TX 77632. *Phone:* 409-882-3362.

LAMAR STATE COLLEGE-PORT ARTHUR
Port Arthur, Texas

■ **State-supported** 2-year, founded 1909, part of The Texas State University System
■ **Calendar** semesters
■ **Degree** certificates and associate
■ **Suburban** 34-acre campus with easy access to Houston
■ **Coed**

Faculty *Student/faculty ratio:* 30:1.
Student Life *Campus security:* 24-hour emergency response devices, student patrols, late-night transport/escort service.
Standardized Tests *Required for some:* SAT (for placement), THEA.
Costs (2004–05) *Tuition:* state resident $2160 full-time, $72 per credit part-time; nonresident $9900 full-time, $330 per credit part-time. *Required fees:* $820 full-time, $48 per term part-time.
Applying *Options:* common application, early admission, deferred entrance. *Required:* high school transcript. *Required for some:* interview.
Admissions Contact Ms. Connie Nicholas, Registrar, Lamar State College-Port Arthur, PO Box 310, Port Arthur, TX 77641-0310. *Phone:* 409-984-6165. *Toll-free phone:* 800-477-5872. *Fax:* 409-984-6025. *E-mail:* connie.nicholas@lamarpa.edu.

LAREDO COMMUNITY COLLEGE
Laredo, Texas

■ **State and locally supported** 2-year, founded 1946
■ **Calendar** semesters
■ **Degree** certificates and associate
■ **Urban** 186-acre campus
■ **Endowment** $389,879
■ **Coed,** 9,032 undergraduate students, 33% full-time, 59% women, 41% men

Undergraduates 3,018 full-time, 6,014 part-time. Students come from 4 states and territories, 5 other countries, 0.2% African American, 0.2% Asian American or Pacific Islander, 94% Hispanic American, 3% international. *Retention:* 83% of 2002 full-time freshmen returned.
Freshmen *Admission:* 1,482 applied, 1,482 admitted, 1,482 enrolled.
Faculty *Total:* 376, 55% full-time, 10% with terminal degrees. *Student/faculty ratio:* 19:1.
Majors Administrative assistant and secretarial science; child development; clinical/medical laboratory technology; computer programming; computer programming related; computer software and media applications related; computer systems networking and telecommunications; construction engineering technology; criminal justice/police science; data entry/microcomputer applications; data entry/microcomputer applications related; data processing and data processing technology; electrical, electronic and communications engineering technology; emergency medical technology (EMT paramedic); fashion merchandising; fire science; hotel/motel administration; industrial radiologic technology; information science/studies; information technology; international business/trade/commerce; liberal arts and sciences/liberal studies; marketing/marketing management; medical/clinical assistant; nursing (registered nurse training); physical therapy; radiologic technology/science; real estate; social sciences.
Academic Programs *Special study options:* academic remediation for entering students, adult/continuing education programs, advanced placement credit, distance learning, double majors, English as a second language, freshman honors college, honors programs, independent study, internships, part-time degree program, services for LD students, summer session for credit.
Library Yeary Library with 88,006 titles, 555 serial subscriptions, an OPAC.

Student Life *Housing Options:* coed. Campus housing is university owned. *Activities and Organizations:* drama/theater group, student-run newspaper, choral group. *Campus security:* 24-hour emergency response devices and patrols, student patrols. *Student services:* personal/psychological counseling, women's center.
Athletics Member NJCAA. *Intercollegiate sports:* baseball M(s), tennis M(s)/W(s), volleyball W(s). *Intramural sports:* cross-country running M/W, gymnastics M/W, swimming and diving M/W, tennis M/W, track and field M/W, volleyball M/W.
Standardized Tests *Recommended:* ACT (for placement).
Costs (2005–06) *Tuition:* area resident $1188 full-time, $32 per credit hour part-time; state resident $1904 full-time, $64 per credit hour part-time; nonresident $2628 full-time, $96 per credit hour part-time. *Required fees:* $24 per credit hour part-time, $28 per term part-time. *Room and board:* $4000. *Payment plans:* installment, deferred payment. *Waivers:* senior citizens and employees or children of employees.
Financial Aid Of all full-time matriculated undergraduates who enrolled in 2003, 282 Federal Work-Study jobs (averaging $1854). 127 state and other part-time jobs (averaging $1884).
Applying *Options:* common application, early admission, deferred entrance. *Required:* high school transcript. *Application deadline:* rolling (freshmen), rolling (transfers).
Admissions Contact Ms. Josie Soliz, Admissions Records Supervisor, Laredo Community College, West End Washington Street, Laredo, TX 78040-4395. *Phone:* 956-721-5177. *Fax:* 956-721-5493.

LEE COLLEGE
Baytown, Texas

Admissions Contact Ms. Becki Griffith, Registrar, Lee College, PO Box 818, Baytown, TX 77522-0818. *Phone:* 281-425-6399. *Toll-free phone:* 800-621-8724. *Fax:* 281-425-6831.

LON MORRIS COLLEGE
Jacksonville, Texas

■ **Independent United Methodist** 2-year, founded 1854
■ **Calendar** semesters
■ **Degree** associate
■ **Small-town** 76-acre campus
■ **Endowment** $20.1 million
■ **Coed**

Faculty *Student/faculty ratio:* 10:1.
Student Life *Campus security:* late-night transport/escort service, controlled dormitory access.
Athletics Member NJCAA.
Standardized Tests *Required:* SAT or ACT (for admission).
Costs (2004–05) *Comprehensive fee:* $13,400 includes full-time tuition ($6800), mandatory fees ($1800), and room and board ($4800). Full-time tuition and fees vary according to course load. Part-time tuition and fees vary according to course load. *Room and board:* college room only: $2300. Room and board charges vary according to board plan. *Payment plans:* installment, deferred payment.
Financial Aid Of all full-time matriculated undergraduates who enrolled in 2003, 63 Federal Work-Study jobs (averaging $1300). 9 state and other part-time jobs (averaging $700).
Applying *Options:* common application, electronic application, deferred entrance. *Application fee:* $35. *Required:* high school transcript.
Admissions Contact Mr. Craig Lee, Director of Admissions, Lon Morris College, 800 College Avenue, Jacksonville, TX 75766-2923. *Phone:* 903-589-4000 Ext. 4063. *Toll-free phone:* 800-259-5753. *Fax:* 903-589-4006.

McLENNAN COMMUNITY COLLEGE
Waco, Texas

■ **County-supported** 2-year, founded 1965
■ **Calendar** semesters
■ **Degree** certificates and associate
■ **Urban** 200-acre campus
■ **Coed,** 7,562 undergraduate students, 44% full-time, 68% women, 32% men

Undergraduates 3,354 full-time, 4,208 part-time. Students come from 10 other countries, 17% African American, 1% Asian American or Pacific Islander, 15% Hispanic American, 0.3% Native American, 0.4% international.
Freshmen *Admission:* 2,646 applied, 2,646 admitted, 1,186 enrolled.
Faculty *Total:* 351, 14% with terminal degrees.

Majors Accounting; administrative assistant and secretarial science; art teacher education; business administration and management; clinical/medical laboratory technology; computer engineering technology; criminal justice/law enforcement administration; criminal justice/police science; developmental and child psychology; finance; health information/medical records administration; industrial radiologic technology; information science/studies; kindergarten/preschool education; legal administrative assistant/secretary; legal assistant/paralegal; liberal arts and sciences/liberal studies; medical administrative assistant and medical secretary; mental health/rehabilitation; music; nursing (registered nurse training); physical education teaching and coaching; physical therapy; real estate; respiratory care therapy; sign language interpretation and translation.

Academic Programs *Special study options:* academic remediation for entering students, adult/continuing education programs, advanced placement credit, cooperative education, distance learning, honors programs, internships, off-campus study, part-time degree program, services for LD students, student-designed majors, study abroad, summer session for credit. *ROTC:* Air Force (c).

Library McLennan Community College Library with 93,000 titles, 400 serial subscriptions, an OPAC, a Web page.

Computers on Campus 425 computers available on campus for general student use. A campuswide network can be accessed from off campus. Internet access, at least one staffed computer lab available.

Student Life *Housing:* college housing not available. *Activities and Organizations:* drama/theater group, student-run newspaper, choral group. *Campus security:* 24-hour emergency response devices and patrols. *Student services:* personal/psychological counseling.

Athletics Member NJCAA. *Intercollegiate sports:* baseball M(s), basketball M(s)/W(s), golf M(s)/W(s), softball W(s). *Intramural sports:* basketball M/W, football M, gymnastics M, volleyball M/W.

Standardized Tests *Required:* THEA (for placement).

Costs (2005–06) *Tuition:* area resident $1272 full-time; state resident $1560 full-time; nonresident $2712 full-time. *Required fees:* $216 full-time.

Financial Aid Of all full-time matriculated undergraduates who enrolled in 2003, 265 Federal Work-Study jobs (averaging $850). 35 state and other part-time jobs (averaging $1000).

Applying *Options:* early admission. *Required:* high school transcript. *Application deadline:* rolling (freshmen), rolling (transfers). *Notification:* continuous until 9/2 (freshmen).

Admissions Contact Ms. Vivian G. Jefferson, Director, Admissions and Recruitment, McLennan Community College, 1400 College Drive, Waco, TX 76708-1499. *Phone:* 254-299-8689. *Fax:* 254-299-8694. *E-mail:* ad1@mclennan.edu.

MIDLAND COLLEGE
Midland, Texas

- **State and locally supported** primarily 2-year, founded 1969
- **Calendar** semesters
- **Degrees** certificates, associate, and bachelor's
- **Suburban** 163-acre campus
- **Endowment** $3.3 million
- **Coed,** 5,531 undergraduate students, 37% full-time, 57% women, 43% men

Undergraduates 2,027 full-time, 3,504 part-time. Students come from 22 states and territories, 31 other countries, 2% are from out of state, 5% African American, 1% Asian American or Pacific Islander, 29% Hispanic American, 0.5% Native American, 1% international, 5% transferred in, 5% live on campus.

Freshmen *Admission:* 2,457 applied, 2,457 admitted, 739 enrolled.

Faculty *Total:* 269, 48% full-time, 14% with terminal degrees. *Student/faculty ratio:* 18:1.

Majors Airline pilot and flight crew; anthropology; art; automobile/automotive mechanics technology; behavioral sciences; biology/biological sciences; business automation/technology/data entry; business/commerce; chemistry; child care provision; commercial and advertising art; computer programming (specific applications); criminal justice/police science; data modeling/warehousing and database administration; developmental and child psychology; drafting and design technology; drawing; economics; electrical, electronic and communications engineering technology; emergency medical technology (EMT paramedic); English; fine/studio arts; fire science; fire services administration; foreign languages and literatures; French; geology/earth science; German; health information/medical records technology; heating, air conditioning, ventilation and refrigeration maintenance technology; history; journalism; legal assistant/paralegal; liberal arts and sciences/liberal studies; literature; mass communication/media; mathematics; medical radiologic technology; modern languages; music; music teacher education; nursing (registered nurse training); physical education teaching and coaching; physics; political science and government; pre-engineering; psychology; radiologic technology/science; respiratory care therapy; sociology; Spanish; speech and rhetoric; substance abuse/addiction counseling; system administration; system, networking, and LAN/WAN management; veterinary/animal health technology; veterinary technology; welding technology.

Academic Programs *Special study options:* academic remediation for entering students, adult/continuing education programs, advanced placement credit, distance learning, honors programs, services for LD students.

Library Murray Fasken Learning Resource Center plus 1 other with 65,760 titles, 285 serial subscriptions, 359 audiovisual materials, an OPAC, a Web page.

Computers on Campus 1200 computers available on campus for general student use. A campuswide network can be accessed from student residence rooms and from off campus. Internet access, online (class) registration, at least one staffed computer lab available.

Student Life *Housing Options:* coed, men-only, women-only. Campus housing is university owned. *Activities and Organizations:* drama/theater group, student-run newspaper, choral group, OIKOS, Midland College Latin American Student Society, Student Government Association, Student Nurses Association, Baptist Student Ministries. *Campus security:* 24-hour patrols. *Student services:* personal/psychological counseling.

Athletics Member NJCAA. *Intercollegiate sports:* baseball M(s), basketball M(s)/W(s), cheerleading M(s)/W(s), golf M(s), softball W(s), volleyball W(s). *Intramural sports:* football M/W, soccer M/W, table tennis M/W, tennis M/W, ultimate Frisbee M, volleyball M/W.

Standardized Tests *Required:* THEA or ACT COMPASS (for placement). *Recommended:* ACT (for placement).

Costs (2005–06) *Tuition:* area resident $1100 full-time, $46 per credit hour part-time; state resident $1270 full-time, $51 per credit hour part-time; nonresident $2280 full-time, $170 per credit hour part-time. Full-time tuition and fees vary according to course load, degree level, and program. Part-time tuition and fees vary according to course load, degree level, and program. *Required fees:* $288 full-time. *Room and board:* $3600. *Payment plan:* installment. *Waivers:* senior citizens and employees or children of employees.

Financial Aid Of all full-time matriculated undergraduates who enrolled in 2003, 75 Federal Work-Study jobs (averaging $2000). 5 state and other part-time jobs (averaging $2000).

Applying *Options:* common application. *Required:* high school transcript. *Application deadline:* rolling (freshmen), rolling (transfers). *Notification:* continuous (freshmen).

Admissions Contact Mr. Trey Wetendorf, Admissions Coordinator, Midland College, 3600 North Garfield, Midland, TX 79705-6399. *Phone:* 432-685-5502. *Toll-free phone:* 432-685-5502. *Fax:* 432-685-6401. *E-mail:* twetendorf@midland.edu.

MONTGOMERY COLLEGE
Conroe, Texas

Admissions Contact Ms. Suzy Englert, Admissions/Advising Coordinator, Montgomery College, 3200 College Park Drive, Conroe, TX 77384. *Phone:* 936-273-7236. *E-mail:* suzye@nhmccd.edu.

MOUNTAIN VIEW COLLEGE
Dallas, Texas

- **State and locally supported** 2-year, founded 1970, part of Dallas County Community College District System
- **Calendar** semesters
- **Degree** certificates and associate
- **Urban** 200-acre campus
- **Coed**

Student Life *Campus security:* 24-hour patrols, late-night transport/escort service.

Athletics Member NJCAA.

Standardized Tests *Required:* SAT I, ACT, THEA, or MAPS (for placement).

Costs (2004–05) *Tuition:* area resident $360 full-time, $30 per credit hour part-time; state resident $600 full-time, $50 per credit hour part-time; nonresident $960 full-time, $200 per credit hour part-time.

Financial Aid Of all full-time matriculated undergraduates who enrolled in 2003, 145 Federal Work-Study jobs (averaging $2700).

Applying *Options:* common application, electronic application, early admission, deferred entrance. *Required:* high school transcript.

Admissions Contact Ms. Glenda Hall, Associate Dean Student Services, Mountain View College, 4849 West Illinois Avenue, Dallas, TX 75211-6599. *Phone:* 214-860-8666. *Fax:* 214-860-8570. *E-mail:* jctorres@dcccd.edu.

MTI COLLEGE OF BUSINESS AND TECHNOLOGY
Houston, Texas

- **Proprietary** 2-year, founded 1984
- **Calendar** semesters

MTI College of Business and Technology (continued)
- **Degree** certificates, diplomas, and associate
- **Suburban** 3-acre campus
- **Coed,** 217 undergraduate students, 100% full-time, 59% women, 41% men

Undergraduates 217 full-time. 12% African American, 0.9% Asian American or Pacific Islander, 48% Hispanic American.
Faculty *Total:* 15, 60% full-time. *Student/faculty ratio:* 20:1.
Majors Administrative assistant and secretarial science; business operations support and secretarial services related; computer technology/computer systems technology; medical office assistant.
Academic Programs *Special study options:* advanced placement credit, cooperative education, English as a second language.
Computers on Campus 120 computers available on campus for general student use. Internet access, at least one staffed computer lab available.
Student Life *Housing:* college housing not available.
Costs (2004–05) *Tuition:* Degree programs range from $19,400 to $23,600. Contact institution for further information.
Applying *Options:* electronic application. *Required:* high school transcript, interview. *Application deadline:* rolling (freshmen).
Admissions Contact Mr. Derrell Beck, Admissions Manager, MTI College of Business and Technology, 1275 Space Park Drive, Houston, TX 77058. *Phone:* 281-333-3363. *Toll-free phone:* 888-532-7675. *Fax:* 281-333-4118. *E-mail:* info@mti.edu.

MTI COLLEGE OF BUSINESS AND TECHNOLOGY

Houston, Texas

- **Proprietary** 2-year
- **Calendar** semesters
- **Degree** certificates, diplomas, and associate
- **Urban** 6-acre campus with easy access to Houston
- 718 undergraduate students, 100% full-time

Undergraduates 718 full-time. Students come from 1 other state.
Freshmen *Admission:* 521 enrolled.
Faculty *Total:* 31. *Student/faculty ratio:* 25:1.
Majors Administrative assistant and secretarial science; business automation/technology/data entry; computer and information systems security; medical office assistant; system administration; system, networking, and LAN/WAN management.
Student Life *Housing:* college housing not available. *Campus security:* late-night transport/escort service.
Costs (2004–05) *Tuition:* $22,500 full-time. *Payment plan:* installment. *Waivers:* employees or children of employees.
Admissions Contact Mr. David Wood, Director of Admissions, MTI College of Business and Technology, 7277 Regency Square Boulevard, Houston, TX 77036-3163. *Phone:* 713-974-7181. *Toll-free phone:* 800-344-1990.

NAVARRO COLLEGE

Corsicana, Texas

Admissions Contact Mr. Dewayne Gragg, Registrar, Navarro College, 3200 West 7th Avenue, Corsicana, TX 75110-4899. *Phone:* 903-874-6501 Ext. 221. *Toll-free phone:* 800-NAVARRO (in-state); 800-628-2776 (out-of-state).

NORTH CENTRAL TEXAS COLLEGE

Gainesville, Texas

Admissions Contact Condoa Parrent, Director of Admissions/Registrar, North Central Texas College, 1525 West California Street, Gainesville, TX 76240-4699. *Phone:* 940-668-4222. *Fax:* 940-668-6049. *E-mail:* cparrent@nctc.cc.tx.us.

NORTHEAST TEXAS COMMUNITY COLLEGE

Mount Pleasant, Texas

- **State and locally supported** 2-year, founded 1985
- **Calendar** semesters
- **Degree** certificates and associate
- **Rural** 175-acre campus
- **Coed**

Student Life *Campus security:* 24-hour patrols.

Athletics Member NJCAA.
Standardized Tests *Required for some:* SAT or ACT (for placement).
Costs (2004–05) *Tuition:* area resident $555 full-time, $45 per hour part-time; state resident $783 full-time, $64 per hour part-time; nonresident $903 full-time, $74 per hour part-time. *Room and board:* $1630.
Financial Aid Of all full-time matriculated undergraduates who enrolled in 2003, 79 Federal Work-Study jobs (averaging $1600). 8 state and other part-time jobs (averaging $1600).
Applying *Options:* early admission. *Required:* high school transcript.
Admissions Contact Ms. Sherry Keys, Director of Admissions, Northeast Texas Community College, PO Box 1307, 1735 Farm to Market Road, Mount Pleasant, TX 75456-1307. *Phone:* 903-572-1911 Ext. 263. *Fax:* 903-572-6712. *E-mail:* skeys@ntcc.edu.

NORTH HARRIS COLLEGE

Houston, Texas

- **State and locally supported** 2-year, founded 1972, part of North Harris Montgomery Community College District
- **Calendar** semesters
- **Degree** certificates and associate
- **Suburban** 185-acre campus
- **Coed**

Student Life *Campus security:* 24-hour emergency response devices and patrols, late-night transport/escort service.
Standardized Tests *Required for some:* SAT or ACT (for placement), ACT ASSET/THEA/ACCUPLACER/MAPS/ACT COMPASS.
Costs (2004–05) *Tuition:* area resident $1236 full-time; state resident $2436 full-time; nonresident $2886 full-time. *Required fees:* $276 full-time.
Financial Aid Of all full-time matriculated undergraduates who enrolled in 2003, 61 Federal Work-Study jobs (averaging $1390). 9 state and other part-time jobs (averaging $1153).
Applying *Options:* electronic application, early admission. *Required for some:* high school transcript, interview.
Admissions Contact Mr. Michael Code, Assistant Dean, North Harris College, 2700 W.W. Thorne Drive, Houston, TX 77073. *Phone:* 281-618-5794. *Fax:* 281-618-7141. *E-mail:* nhc.startcollege@nhmccd.edu.

NORTH LAKE COLLEGE

Irving, Texas

- **County-supported** 2-year, founded 1977, part of Dallas County Community College District System
- **Calendar** semesters
- **Degree** certificates, diplomas, and associate
- **Suburban** 250-acre campus with easy access to Dallas-Fort Worth
- **Coed,** 8,779 undergraduate students, 33% full-time, 52% women, 48% men

Undergraduates 2,925 full-time, 5,854 part-time. Students come from 14 other countries, 16% African American, 13% Asian American or Pacific Islander, 20% Hispanic American, 0.6% Native American, 6% international.
Freshmen *Admission:* 1,027 enrolled.
Faculty *Total:* 537, 18% full-time, 7% with terminal degrees. *Student/faculty ratio:* 19:1.
Majors Accounting; administrative assistant and secretarial science; business administration and management; carpentry; communications technology; computer programming; construction engineering technology; data processing and data processing technology; electrical, electronic and communications engineering technology; heating, air conditioning, ventilation and refrigeration maintenance technology; information science/studies; kinesiology and exercise science; legal administrative assistant/secretary; liberal arts and sciences/liberal studies; real estate.
Academic Programs *Special study options:* academic remediation for entering students, advanced placement credit, cooperative education, distance learning, English as a second language, part-time degree program, services for LD students, summer session for credit.
Library North Lake College Library with 34,000 titles, 400 serial subscriptions, a Web page.
Computers on Campus 65 computers available on campus for general student use. A campuswide network can be accessed. Internet access, at least one staffed computer lab available.
Student Life *Housing:* college housing not available. *Activities and Organizations:* drama/theater group, student-run newspaper, choral group. *Campus security:* late-night transport/escort service. *Student services:* health clinic, personal/psychological counseling, women's center.
Athletics Member NJCAA. *Intercollegiate sports:* baseball M, basketball M, softball W, volleyball W.

Costs (2004–05) *Tuition:* area resident $972 full-time, $33 per credit hour part-time; state resident $1440 full-time, $60 per credit hour part-time; nonresident $1920 full-time, $80 per credit hour part-time.

Applying *Options:* early admission. *Recommended:* high school transcript. *Application deadlines:* 8/24 (freshmen), 8/24 (transfers). *Notification:* continuous (freshmen).

Admissions Contact Mr. Steve Twenge, Director of Admissions and Registration, North Lake College, 5001 North MacArthur Boulevard, Irving, TX 75038-3899. *Phone:* 972-273-3109.

NORTHWEST VISTA COLLEGE
San Antonio, Texas

Admissions Contact Ms. Jill Weston, Director of Enrollment Management, Northwest Vista College, 3535 North Ellison Drive, San Antonio, TX 78251. *Phone:* 210-348-2016.

ODESSA COLLEGE
Odessa, Texas

- **State and locally supported** 2-year, founded 1946
- **Calendar** semesters
- **Degree** certificates and associate
- **Urban** 87-acre campus
- **Endowment** $2.5 million
- **Coed,** 4,569 undergraduate students, 39% full-time, 60% women, 40% men

Undergraduates 1,799 full-time, 2,770 part-time. Students come from 32 states and territories, 1% are from out of state, 4% African American, 1% Asian American or Pacific Islander, 44% Hispanic American, 0.7% Native American, 0.2% international, 0.1% transferred in, 3% live on campus.

Freshmen *Admission:* 1,101 applied, 1,101 admitted, 842 enrolled.

Faculty *Total:* 265, 45% full-time, 9% with terminal degrees. *Student/faculty ratio:* 15:1.

Majors Accounting; administrative assistant and secretarial science; agriculture; applied art; art; athletic training; automobile/automotive mechanics technology; biology/biological sciences; business administration and management; chemistry; child development; clinical/medical laboratory technology; computer and information sciences; computer science; computer systems networking and telecommunications; construction engineering technology; cosmetology; criminal justice/law enforcement administration; criminal justice/police science; culinary arts; data processing and data processing technology; drafting and design technology; education; electrical, electronic and communications engineering technology; emergency medical technology (EMT paramedic); English; fashion merchandising; fire science; geology/earth science; hazardous materials management and waste technology; heating, air conditioning, ventilation and refrigeration maintenance technology; history; human services; industrial radiologic technology; information science/studies; kindergarten/preschool education; legal administrative assistant/secretary; liberal arts and sciences/liberal studies; machine tool technology; mathematics; modern languages; music; nursing (registered nurse training); petroleum technology; photography; physical education teaching and coaching; physical therapy; physics; political science and government; pre-engineering; psychology; radio and television; respiratory care therapy; social sciences; sociology; speech and rhetoric; substance abuse/addiction counseling; surgical technology; teacher assistant/aide; welding technology.

Academic Programs *Special study options:* academic remediation for entering students, adult/continuing education programs, advanced placement credit, cooperative education, internships, part-time degree program, services for LD students, student-designed majors, summer session for credit.

Library Murray H. Fly Learning Resource Center with 79,882 titles, 496 serial subscriptions.

Computers on Campus 300 computers available on campus for general student use. A campuswide network can be accessed from off campus. Internet access, at least one staffed computer lab available.

Student Life *Housing Options:* coed. Campus housing is university owned and is provided by a third party. *Activities and Organizations:* choral group, Baptist Student Union, Student Government Association, Rodeo Club, Physical Therapy Assistant Club, American Chemical Society. *Campus security:* 24-hour emergency response devices and patrols, late-night transport/escort service. *Student services:* personal/psychological counseling.

Athletics Member NJCAA. *Intercollegiate sports:* baseball M(s), basketball M(s)/W(s), golf M(s), softball W(s). *Intramural sports:* basketball M/W, bowling M/W, football M, racquetball M/W, softball M/W, table tennis M/W, volleyball M/W, weight lifting M/W.

Costs (2005–06) *Tuition:* area resident $1110 full-time; state resident $1410 full-time; nonresident $1860 full-time. Full-time tuition and fees vary according to course load. Part-time tuition and fees vary according to course load. *Required fees:* $330 full-time. *Room and board:* $4948; room only: $3500. Room and

board charges vary according to board plan and housing facility. *Payment plans:* installment, deferred payment. *Waivers:* senior citizens.

Financial Aid Of all full-time matriculated undergraduates who enrolled in 2003, 105 Federal Work-Study jobs (averaging $1667). 11 state and other part-time jobs (averaging $2046).

Applying *Options:* common application, electronic application, early admission, deferred entrance. *Application deadline:* rolling (freshmen), rolling (transfers). *Notification:* continuous (freshmen).

Admissions Contact Ms. Norma Garcia, Director of Admissions, Odessa College, 201 West University Avenue, Odessa, TX 79764-7127. *Phone:* 432-335-6815. *Fax:* 432-335-6824. *E-mail:* thughes@odessa.edu.

PALO ALTO COLLEGE
San Antonio, Texas

- **State and locally supported** 2-year, founded 1987, part of Alamo Community College District System
- **Calendar** semesters
- **Degree** associate
- **Urban** campus
- **Coed**

Faculty *Student/faculty ratio:* 18:1.

Student Life *Campus security:* 24-hour emergency response devices and patrols.

Athletics Member NJCAA.

Standardized Tests *Required:* ACT ASSET (for placement). *Required for some:* SAT or ACT (for placement).

Costs (2004–05) *Tuition:* area resident $1140 full-time; state resident $2280 full-time; nonresident $4560 full-time. *Required fees:* $210 full-time.

Financial Aid Of all full-time matriculated undergraduates who enrolled in 2003, 272 Federal Work-Study jobs (averaging $2000).

Applying *Options:* early admission. *Required:* high school transcript.

Admissions Contact Ms. Rachel Montejano, Associate Director of Admissions and Records, Palo Alto College, 1400 West Villaret Boulevard, San Antonio, TX 78224. *Phone:* 210-921-5279. *Fax:* 210-921-5310. *E-mail:* pacar@accd.edu.

PANOLA COLLEGE
Carthage, Texas

- **State and locally supported** 2-year, founded 1947
- **Calendar** semesters
- **Degree** certificates and associate
- **Small-town** 35-acre campus
- **Endowment** $1.4 million
- **Coed,** 1,780 undergraduate students, 53% full-time, 67% women, 33% men

Undergraduates 950 full-time, 830 part-time. Students come from 15 states and territories, 5 other countries, 9% are from out of state, 18% African American, 0.2% Asian American or Pacific Islander, 4% Hispanic American, 0.6% Native American, 0.5% international, 12% live on campus.

Freshmen *Admission:* 440 applied, 440 admitted, 440 enrolled.

Faculty *Total:* 60, 100% full-time, 5% with terminal degrees. *Student/faculty ratio:* 22:1.

Majors Administrative assistant and secretarial science; cosmetology; forestry technology; information science/studies; nursing (registered nurse training).

Academic Programs *Special study options:* academic remediation for entering students, adult/continuing education programs, advanced placement credit, cooperative education, distance learning, English as a second language, part-time degree program, services for LD students, summer session for credit.

Library M. P. Baker Library with 88,897 titles, 347 serial subscriptions, 4,133 audiovisual materials, an OPAC, a Web page.

Computers on Campus 500 computers available on campus for general student use. A campuswide network can be accessed from off campus. Internet access, online (class) registration, at least one staffed computer lab available.

Student Life *Housing:* on-campus residence required through sophomore year. *Options:* coed, men-only, women-only. Campus housing is university owned. *Activities and Organizations:* drama/theater group, student-run newspaper, choral group, Student Senate, Excel Club, Baptist Student Union, Panola Pipers, Phi Theta Kappa. *Campus security:* controlled dormitory access.

Athletics Member NJCAA. *Intercollegiate sports:* baseball M(s), basketball M(s)/W(s), volleyball W(s). *Intramural sports:* basketball M/W, football M/W, racquetball M/W, table tennis M/W, volleyball M/W, weight lifting M/W.

Standardized Tests *Required:* THEA, ACT ASSET, or ACT COMPASS (for placement). *Required for some:* SAT or ACT (for placement). *Recommended:* SAT or ACT (for placement).

Costs (2004–05) *Tuition:* area resident $1008 full-time, $42 per semester hour part-time; state resident $1460 full-time, $65 per semester hour part-time;

Panola College (continued)

nonresident $1872 full-time, $78 per semester hour part-time. Full-time tuition and fees vary according to course load. Part-time tuition and fees vary according to course load. *Room and board:* $3150. *Waivers:* employees or children of employees.

Financial Aid Of all full-time matriculated undergraduates who enrolled in 2003, 50 Federal Work-Study jobs (averaging $1236).

Applying *Options:* common application, electronic application, early admission. *Required for some:* high school transcript. *Recommended:* high school transcript. *Application deadline:* rolling (freshmen), rolling (transfers). *Notification:* continuous (freshmen).

Admissions Contact Ms. Barbara Simpson, Registrar/Director of Admissions, Panola College, 1109 West Panola Street, Carthage, TX 75633-2397. *Phone:* 903-693-2009. *Fax:* 903-693-2031.

PARIS JUNIOR COLLEGE
Paris, Texas

- **State and locally supported** 2-year, founded 1924
- **Calendar** semesters
- **Degree** certificates, diplomas, and associate
- **Rural** 54-acre campus
- **Coed**

Faculty *Student/faculty ratio:* 24:1.

Student Life *Campus security:* 24-hour emergency response devices and patrols, late-night transport/escort service.

Athletics Member NJCAA.

Standardized Tests *Required:* THEA (for placement).

Costs (2004–05) *Tuition:* area resident $1068 full-time; state resident $1596 full-time; nonresident $2436 full-time. *Required fees:* $260 full-time. *Room and board:* $2000; room only: $500.

Applying *Options:* early admission. *Required:* high school transcript.

Admissions Contact Ms. Sheila Reece, Director of Admissions, Paris Junior College, 2400 Clarksville Street, Paris, TX 75460-6298. *Phone:* 903-782-0425. *Toll-free phone:* 800-232-5804.

RANGER COLLEGE
Ranger, Texas

Admissions Contact Dr. Jim Davis, Dean of Students, Ranger College, College Circle, Ranger, TX 76470. *Phone:* 254-647-3234 Ext. 110.

REMINGTON COLLEGE-DALLAS CAMPUS
Garland, Texas

Admissions Contact Mr. Skip Walls, Campus President, Remington College-Dallas Campus, 1800 East Gate Drive, Garland, TX 75041-5513. *Phone:* 972-686-7878.

REMINGTON COLLEGE-FORT WORTH CAMPUS
Fort Worth, Texas

Admissions Contact Ms. Lynn Wey, Campus President, Remington College-Fort Worth Campus, 300 East Loop 820, Fort Worth, TX 76112. *Phone:* 817-451-0017.

REMINGTON COLLEGE-HOUSTON CAMPUS
Houston, Texas

Admissions Contact Mr. Lance Stribling, Director of Recruitment, Remington College-Houston Campus, 3110 Hayes Road, Suite 380, Houston, TX 77082. *Phone:* 281-89-1240.

RICHLAND COLLEGE
Dallas, Texas

Admissions Contact Ms. Carol McKinney, Department Assistant, Richland College, 12800 Abrams Road, Dallas, TX 75243-2199. *Phone:* 972-238-6100.

ST. PHILIP'S COLLEGE
San Antonio, Texas

- **District-supported** 2-year, founded 1898, part of Alamo Community College District System
- **Calendar** semesters
- **Degree** certificates, diplomas, and associate
- **Urban** 16-acre campus
- **Coed,** 10,164 undergraduate students, 45% full-time, 57% women, 43% men

Undergraduates 4,575 full-time, 5,589 part-time. Students come from 35 states and territories, 8 other countries, 17% African American, 2% Asian American or Pacific Islander, 48% Hispanic American, 0.5% Native American, 0.1% international, 10% transferred in.

Freshmen *Admission:* 1,964 enrolled.

Faculty *Total:* 597, 34% full-time, 7% with terminal degrees. *Student/faculty ratio:* 19:1.

Majors Accounting; administrative assistant and secretarial science; aircraft powerplant technology; airframe mechanics and aircraft maintenance technology; art; autobody/collision and repair technology; automobile/automotive mechanics technology; biology/biological sciences; biomedical technology; business administration and management; CAD/CADD drafting/design technology; chemistry; clinical/medical laboratory technology; communications technology; computer and information systems security; computer maintenance technology; computer systems networking and telecommunications; construction engineering technology; construction management; criminal justice/law enforcement administration; culinary arts; data entry/microcomputer applications; diesel mechanics technology; dramatic/theatre arts; dramatic/theatre arts and stagecraft related; early childhood education; e-commerce; economics; education; electrical/electronics equipment installation and repair; electromechanical technology; English; environmental science; health information/medical records technology; heating, air conditioning, ventilation and refrigeration maintenance technology; history; home furnishings and equipment installation; hotel/motel administration; interior architecture; interior design; kinesiology and exercise science; leatherworking/upholstery; legal administrative assistant/secretary; liberal arts and sciences/liberal studies; mathematics; medical administrative assistant and medical secretary; medical radiologic technology; music; nursing (licensed practical/vocational nurse training); occupational therapist assistant; philosophy; physical therapist assistant; political science and government; pre-dentistry studies; pre-engineering; pre-law studies; pre-medical studies; pre-nursing studies; pre-pharmacy studies; psychology; respiratory care therapy; restaurant/food services management; social work; sociology; Spanish; speech and rhetoric; system, networking, and LAN/WAN management; teacher assistant/aide; tourism and travel services management; urban studies/affairs; web/multimedia management and webmaster; welding technology.

Academic Programs *Special study options:* academic remediation for entering students, adult/continuing education programs, advanced placement credit, cooperative education, distance learning, double majors, English as a second language, honors programs, independent study, internships, off-campus study, part-time degree program, services for LD students, summer session for credit. *ROTC:* Army (c).

Library St. Philip's College Learning Resource Center plus 1 other with 112,197 titles, 577 serial subscriptions, 11,300 audiovisual materials, an OPAC, a Web page.

Computers on Campus 885 computers available on campus for general student use. A campuswide network can be accessed from off campus that provide access to e-mail. Internet access, online (class) registration, at least one staffed computer lab available.

Student Life *Housing:* college housing not available. *Activities and Organizations:* drama/theater group, student-run newspaper, choral group, student government, Delta Epsilon Chi, Radiography Club, Respiratory Therapy Club, Diagnostic Imaging Club. *Campus security:* 24-hour emergency response devices and patrols, late-night transport/escort service. *Student services:* health clinic, women's center.

Athletics *Intramural sports:* basketball M/W, cheerleading M/W, table tennis M/W, tennis M/W, volleyball M/W, weight lifting M/W.

Costs (2004–05) *Tuition:* area resident $1140 full-time, $38 per hour part-time; state resident $2280 full-time, $76 per hour part-time; nonresident $4560 full-time, $152 per hour part-time. *Required fees:* $258 full-time. *Payment plan:* installment. *Waivers:* senior citizens and employees or children of employees.

Applying *Options:* common application, electronic application, early admission. *Required:* high school transcript. *Application deadline:* rolling (freshmen), rolling (transfers). *Notification:* continuous (freshmen).

Admissions Contact Ms. Ana Lisa Garza, Recruiter, St. Philip's College, 1801 Martin Luther King Drive, San Antonio, TX 78203-2098. *Phone:* 210-531-4861. *Fax:* 210-531-4836. *E-mail:* xallen@accd.edu.

SAN ANTONIO COLLEGE
San Antonio, Texas

- **State and locally supported** 2-year, founded 1925, part of Alamo Community College District System
- **Calendar** semesters
- **Degree** certificates and associate
- **Urban** 45-acre campus
- **Coed,** 22,226 undergraduate students, 39% full-time, 60% women, 40% men

Undergraduates 8,587 full-time, 13,639 part-time. Students come from 54 states and territories, 112 other countries, 2% are from out of state, 5% African American, 2% Asian American or Pacific Islander, 49% Hispanic American, 0.5% Native American, 2% international, 8% transferred in.

Freshmen *Admission:* 4,265 enrolled.

Faculty *Total:* 1,036, 43% full-time. *Student/faculty ratio:* 20:1.

Majors Biological and physical sciences; business administration and management; business machine repair; child care and support services management; child care provision; child development; civil engineering technology; commercial and advertising art; computer engineering technology; computer graphics; computer/information technology services administration related; computer programming; computer programming related; computer programming (specific applications); computer programming (vendor/product certification); corrections; court reporting; criminal justice/law enforcement administration; criminal justice/police science; data entry/microcomputer applications; data processing and data processing technology; dental hygiene; developmental and child psychology; drafting and design technology; electrical, electronic and communications engineering technology; engineering technology; fire science; funeral service and mortuary science; industrial technology; legal administrative assistant/secretary; liberal arts and sciences/liberal studies; mechanical engineering/mechanical technology; medical/clinical assistant; metal and jewelry arts; nursing (registered nurse training); postal management; psychology; public administration; radio and television; real estate; speech/theater education; system administration; web page, digital/multimedia and information resources design; word processing.

Academic Programs *Special study options:* academic remediation for entering students, adult/continuing education programs, advanced placement credit, cooperative education, distance learning, double majors, English as a second language, honors programs, independent study, internships, part-time degree program, services for LD students, summer session for credit. *ROTC:* Army (b), Air Force (c).

Library San Antonio College Library and Media Services with 233,714 titles, 1,498 serial subscriptions, 6,082 audiovisual materials, an OPAC, a Web page.

Computers on Campus 1700 computers available on campus for general student use. A campuswide network can be accessed from off campus. Internet access, online (class) registration, at least one staffed computer lab available.

Student Life *Housing:* college housing not available. *Activities and Organizations:* drama/theater group, student-run newspaper, radio station, choral group. *Campus security:* 24-hour patrols, late-night transport/escort service. *Student services:* health clinic, personal/psychological counseling, women's center.

Athletics *Intramural sports:* basketball M(c)/W(c), football M/W, golf W(c), soccer W(c), volleyball W(c).

Standardized Tests *Required for some:* ACT ASSET, THEA, ACCUPLACER. *Recommended:* SAT or ACT (for placement), ACT ASSET, THEA, ACCUPLACER.

Costs (2005–06) *Tuition:* area resident $1398 full-time, $40 per semester hour part-time; state resident $2538 full-time, $80 per semester hour part-time; nonresident $4818 full-time, $160 per semester hour part-time. *Required fees:* $270 full-time, $129 per term part-time. *Payment plan:* installment. *Waivers:* senior citizens and employees or children of employees.

Financial Aid Of all full-time matriculated undergraduates who enrolled in 2003, 500 Federal Work-Study jobs (averaging $3000).

Applying *Options:* early admission. *Required:* minimum 2.0 GPA. *Required for some:* high school transcript. *Recommended:* high school transcript. *Application deadline:* rolling (freshmen), rolling (transfers).

Admissions Contact Ms. Rosemarie Hoopes, Director of Admissions and Records, San Antonio College, 1300 San Pedro Avenue, San Antonio, TX 78212-4299. *Phone:* 210-733-2582. *Toll-free phone:* 800-944-7575.

SAN JACINTO COLLEGE DISTRICT
Pasadena, Texas

Admissions Contact 4624 Fairmont Parkway, Pasadena, TX 77504-3323.

SOUTHEASTERN CAREER INSTITUTE
Dallas, Texas

Admissions Contact 5440 Harvest Hill, Suite 200, Dallas, TX 75230-1600. *Toll-free phone:* 800-525-1446.

SOUTH PLAINS COLLEGE
Levelland, Texas

- **State and locally supported** 2-year, founded 1958
- **Calendar** semesters
- **Degree** certificates and associate
- **Small-town** 177-acre campus
- **Endowment** $3.0 million
- **Coed**

Faculty *Student/faculty ratio:* 23:1.

Student Life *Campus security:* 24-hour emergency response devices and patrols.

Athletics Member NJCAA.

Standardized Tests *Required:* THEA (for placement).

Costs (2004–05) *Tuition:* area resident $4600 full-time; state resident $5000 full-time; nonresident $5400 full-time. *Room and board:* $2900.

Financial Aid Of all full-time matriculated undergraduates who enrolled in 2003, 80 Federal Work-Study jobs (averaging $2000). 22 state and other part-time jobs (averaging $2000).

Applying *Options:* early admission. *Required:* high school transcript.

Admissions Contact Mrs. Andrea Rangel, Dean of Admissions and Records, South Plains College, 1401 College Avenue, Levelland, TX 78336. *Phone:* 806-894-9611 Ext. 2370. *Fax:* 806-897-3167. *E-mail:* arangel@southplainscollege.edu.

SOUTH TEXAS COLLEGE
McAllen, Texas

- **District-supported** primarily 2-year, founded 1993
- **Calendar** semesters
- **Degrees** certificates, associate, and bachelor's
- **Suburban** 20-acre campus
- **Endowment** $17,971
- **Coed,** 15,334 undergraduate students, 46% full-time, 62% women, 38% men

Undergraduates 6,991 full-time, 8,343 part-time. 0.1% African American, 0.8% Asian American or Pacific Islander, 94% Hispanic American, 0.4% international. *Retention:* 56% of 2002 full-time freshmen returned.

Freshmen *Admission:* 1,844 enrolled. *Test scores:* SAT verbal scores over 500: 8%; SAT math scores over 500: 9%; SAT verbal scores over 600: 1%; SAT math scores over 600: 1%.

Faculty *Total:* 542, 61% full-time. *Student/faculty ratio:* 11:1.

Majors Accounting; automobile/automotive mechanics technology; behavioral sciences; business administration and management; clinical laboratory science/medical technology; computer science; computer typography and composition equipment operation; developmental and child psychology; education; emergency medical technology (EMT paramedic); heating, air conditioning, ventilation and refrigeration maintenance technology; heavy equipment maintenance technology; hospitality administration; hotel/motel administration; human services; industrial radiologic technology; industrial technology; information science/studies; interdisciplinary studies; legal administrative assistant/secretary; legal assistant/paralegal; liberal arts and sciences/liberal studies; machine tool technology; nursing (registered nurse training); occupational therapy; plastics engineering technology.

Academic Programs *Special study options:* academic remediation for entering students, accelerated degree program, adult/continuing education programs, cooperative education, off-campus study, part-time degree program, services for LD students, summer session for credit. *ROTC:* Army (c).

Library Learning Resources Center with 12,611 titles, 177 serial subscriptions, an OPAC, a Web page.

Computers on Campus 240 computers available on campus for general student use. A campuswide network can be accessed from off campus. At least one staffed computer lab available.

Student Life *Housing:* college housing not available. *Activities and Organizations:* Beta Epsilon Mu Honor Society, Automotive Technology Club, Child Care and Development Association Club, Heating, Air Conditioning, and Ventilation Club, Writing in Literary Discussion Club. *Campus security:* 24-hour emergency response devices and patrols, late-night transport/escort service. *Student services:* personal/psychological counseling.

Athletics *Intramural sports:* badminton M/W, basketball M/W, bowling M/W, football M/W, golf M/W, racquetball M/W, soccer M/W, softball M/W, table tennis M/W, volleyball M/W.

Standardized Tests *Required for some:* THEA.

Costs (2004–05) *One-time required fee:* $75. *Tuition:* area resident $1069 full-time; state resident $1241 full-time; nonresident $2436 full-time. Part-time tuition and fees vary according to course load.

Applying *Options:* common application, early admission, deferred entrance. *Required:* high school transcript. *Application deadline:* rolling (freshmen), rolling (transfers).

South Texas College (continued)

Admissions Contact Ms. Sarah Gomez, Director of Enrollment Services and Registrar, South Texas College, 3201 West Pecan, McAllen, TX 78501. *Phone:* 956-688-2011. *Toll-free phone:* 800-742-7822.

SOUTHWEST INSTITUTE OF TECHNOLOGY
Austin, Texas

- **Proprietary** 2-year
- **Calendar** continuous
- **Degree** diplomas and associate
- **Urban** 1-acre campus
- **Coed, primarily men**
- 82% of applicants were admitted

Faculty *Student/faculty ratio:* 6:1.
Costs (2004–05) *Tuition:* $25,600 full-time.
Applying *Application fee:* $100.
Admissions Contact Fredrico Garcia, Director of Admissions, Southwest Institute of Technology, 5424 Highway 290 West, Suite 200, Austin, TX 78735-8800. *Phone:* 512-892-2640.

SOUTHWEST TEXAS JUNIOR COLLEGE
Uvalde, Texas

Admissions Contact Mr. Joe C. Barker, Dean of Admissions and Student Services, Southwest Texas Junior College, 2401 Garner Field Road, Uvalde, TX 78801. *Phone:* 830-278-4401 Ext. 7284.

TARRANT COUNTY COLLEGE DISTRICT
Fort Worth, Texas

Admissions Contact Dr. Cathie Jackson, Director of Admissions and Records, Tarrant County College District, 1500 Houston Street, Fort Worth, TX 76102-6599. *Phone:* 817-515-5291.

TEMPLE COLLEGE
Temple, Texas

- **District-supported** 2-year, founded 1926
- **Calendar** semesters
- **Degree** certificates and associate
- **Suburban** 114-acre campus
- **Coed,** 4,068 undergraduate students, 38% full-time, 64% women, 36% men

Undergraduates 1,533 full-time, 2,535 part-time. Students come from 20 states and territories, 8 other countries, 1% are from out of state, 14% African American, 2% Asian American or Pacific Islander, 15% Hispanic American, 0.6% Native American, 0.2% international, 7% transferred in, 1% live on campus. *Retention:* 51% of 2002 full-time freshmen returned.
Freshmen *Admission:* 753 applied, 753 admitted, 723 enrolled.
Faculty *Total:* 224, 38% full-time, 16% with terminal degrees. *Student/faculty ratio:* 18:1.
Majors Administrative assistant and secretarial science; art; automobile/automotive mechanics technology; business administration and management; clinical laboratory science/medical technology; clinical/medical laboratory technology; computer programming; computer science; criminal justice/law enforcement administration; criminal justice/police science; data processing and data processing technology; dental hygiene; drafting and design technology; electrical, electronic and communications engineering technology; industrial technology; liberal arts and sciences/liberal studies; medical administrative assistant and medical secretary; nursing (licensed practical/vocational nurse training); nursing (registered nurse training); respiratory care therapy.
Academic Programs *Special study options:* academic remediation for entering students, adult/continuing education programs, distance learning, English as a second language, internships, off-campus study, part-time degree program, summer session for credit.
Library Hubert Dawson Library with 55,536 titles, 391 serial subscriptions, 2,170 audiovisual materials, an OPAC, a Web page.
Computers on Campus 100 computers available on campus for general student use. A campuswide network can be accessed from student residence rooms and from off campus. Internet access, at least one staffed computer lab available.
Student Life *Housing Options:* disabled students. Campus housing is provided by a third party. *Activities and Organizations:* drama/theater group. *Campus security:* 24-hour emergency response devices and patrols. *Student services:* personal/psychological counseling.

Athletics Member NJCAA. *Intercollegiate sports:* baseball M(s), basketball M(s)/W(s), softball W(s), tennis M(s)/W(s). *Intramural sports:* basketball M/W, golf M/W, racquetball M/W, soccer M/W, tennis M/W, volleyball M/W.
Standardized Tests *Required:* THEA (for placement). *Recommended:* ACT (for placement).
Costs (2005–06) *Tuition:* area resident $1740 full-time, $58 per hour part-time; state resident $2640 full-time, $88 per hour part-time; nonresident $4500 full-time, $150 per hour part-time. *Required fees:* $65 full-time.
Financial Aid Of all full-time matriculated undergraduates who enrolled in 2003, 86 Federal Work-Study jobs (averaging $826). 7 state and other part-time jobs (averaging $951).
Applying *Options:* early admission. *Required for some:* high school transcript. *Application deadlines:* 8/19 (freshmen), 8/23 (transfers).
Admissions Contact Ms. Angela Balch, Director of Admissions and Records, Temple College, 2600 South First Street, Temple, TX 76504-7435. *Phone:* 254-298-8308. *Toll-free phone:* 800-460-4636. *Fax:* 254-298-8288. *E-mail:* angela.balch@templejc.edu.

TEXARKANA COLLEGE
Texarkana, Texas

Admissions Contact Mr. Van Miller, Director of Admissions, Texarkana College, 2500 North Robison Road, Texarkana, TX 75599. *Phone:* 903-838-4541 Ext. 3358. *Fax:* 903-832-5030. *E-mail:* vmiller@texarkanacollege.edu.

TEXAS CULINARY ACADEMY
Austin, Texas

- **Independent** 2-year
- **Calendar** continuous
- **Degree** certificates, diplomas, and associate
- **Urban** campus
- **Coed**

Faculty *Student/faculty ratio:* 16:1.
Student Life *Campus security:* 24-hour emergency response devices.
Costs (2004–05) *Tuition:* $37,500 full-time, $9375 per term part-time. Full-time tuition and fees vary according to program. No tuition increase for student's term of enrollment. *Required fees:* $2500 full-time.
Applying *Application fee:* $100. *Required:* essay or personal statement, high school transcript.
Admissions Contact Paula Paulette, Vice President of Marketing and Admissions, Texas Culinary Academy, 11400 Burnet Road, Austin, TX 78758. *Phone:* 512-837-2665. *Toll-free phone:* 888-553-2433.

TEXAS SOUTHMOST COLLEGE
Brownsville, Texas

Admissions Contact Mr. Rene Villarreal, Director of Admissions, Texas Southmost College, 80 Fort Brown, Brownsville, TX 78520-4991. *Phone:* 956-544-8992. *E-mail:* admissions@utb.edu.

TEXAS STATE TECHNICAL COLLEGE HARLINGEN
Harlingen, Texas

- **State-supported** 2-year, founded 1967, part of Texas State Technical College System
- **Calendar** semesters
- **Degree** certificates and associate
- **Small-town** 125-acre campus
- **Coed**

Faculty *Student/faculty ratio:* 17:1.
Student Life *Campus security:* 24-hour emergency response devices and patrols, late-night transport/escort service, night watchman for housing area.
Standardized Tests *Required:* THEA (for placement). *Recommended:* SAT or ACT (for placement).
Costs (2004–05) *Tuition:* state resident $2088 full-time, $58 per credit hour part-time; nonresident $5832 full-time, $162 per credit hour part-time. *Required fees:* $686 full-time, $8 per credit hour part-time, $1 per credit hour part-time. *Room and board:* $4017; room only: $2085.
Financial Aid Of all full-time matriculated undergraduates who enrolled in 2003, 150 Federal Work-Study jobs (averaging $2800). 5 state and other part-time jobs (averaging $2800).
Applying *Options:* common application, early admission, deferred entrance. *Required:* high school transcript.

Admissions Contact Mrs. Elva Short, Director of Admissions, Texas State Technical College Harlingen, 1902 North Loop 499, Harlingen, TX 78550-3697. *Phone:* 956-364-4100. *Toll-free phone:* 800-852-8784. *Fax:* 956-364-5117. *E-mail:* arangel@harlingen.tstc.edu.

TEXAS STATE TECHNICAL COLLEGE WACO

Waco, Texas

- **State-supported** 2-year, founded 1965, part of Texas State Technical College System
- **Calendar** trimesters
- **Degree** certificates and associate
- **Suburban** 200-acre campus
- **Coed,** 4,417 undergraduate students, 68% full-time, 21% women, 79% men

Undergraduates 3,000 full-time, 1,417 part-time. Students come from 30 states and territories, 5 other countries, 16% African American, 1% Asian American or Pacific Islander, 16% Hispanic American, 0.7% Native American.
Freshmen *Admission:* 3,325 applied, 3,325 admitted, 1,450 enrolled.
Faculty *Total:* 278, 87% full-time. *Student/faculty ratio:* 30:1.
Majors Aeronautics/aviation/aerospace science and technology; agricultural and food products processing; aircraft powerplant technology; airframe mechanics and aircraft maintenance technology; airline pilot and flight crew; audio engineering; autobody/collision and repair technology; automobile/automotive mechanics technology; avionics maintenance technology; biomedical technology; chemical engineering; chemical technology; commercial and advertising art; computer and information sciences; computer engineering technology; computer programming; computer science; computer technology/computer systems technology; culinary arts; dental assisting; diesel mechanics technology; drafting and design technology; educational/instructional media design; electrical, electronic and communications engineering technology; electrical/electronics drafting and CAD/CADD; food services technology; graphic and printing equipment operation/production; heating, air conditioning and refrigeration technology; heating, air conditioning, ventilation and refrigeration maintenance technology; heavy equipment maintenance technology; industrial technology; information science/studies; institutional food workers; instrumentation technology; laser and optical technology; machine tool technology; mechanical engineering/mechanical technology; nuclear/nuclear power technology; occupational safety and health technology; ornamental horticulture; photographic and film/video technology; quality control technology; turf and turfgrass management; welding technology.
Academic Programs *Special study options:* academic remediation for entering students, adult/continuing education programs, cooperative education, distance learning, internships, part-time degree program, services for LD students, summer session for credit.
Library Texas State Technical College-Waco Campus Library with 60,000 titles, 400 serial subscriptions, 2,324 audiovisual materials, an OPAC, a Web page.
Computers on Campus 900 computers available on campus for general student use. A campuswide network can be accessed from student residence rooms that provide access to various software packages. At least one staffed computer lab available.
Student Life *Housing:* on-campus residence required for freshman year. *Options:* coed, men-only, women-only, disabled students. *Activities and Organizations:* student-run newspaper, Automotive VICA, Society of Mexican-American Engineers and Scientists, Texas Association of Black Persons In Higher Education, Phi Theta Kappa. *Campus security:* 24-hour emergency response devices and patrols, late-night transport/escort service, controlled dormitory access. *Student services:* health clinic, personal/psychological counseling, women's center.
Athletics *Intramural sports:* basketball M/W, football M, golf M/W, racquetball M/W, softball M/W, volleyball M/W, weight lifting M.
Standardized Tests *Required:* CPT, THEA, ACCUPLACER (for placement).
Costs (2005–06) *Tuition:* state resident $1740 full-time, $58 per credit hour part-time; nonresident $4860 full-time, $162 per credit hour part-time. *Required fees:* $1908 full-time, $21 per credit hour part-time. *Room and board:* $4030; room only $1860.
Financial Aid Of all full-time matriculated undergraduates who enrolled in 2003, 125 Federal Work-Study jobs (averaging $2500). 150 state and other part-time jobs.
Applying *Options:* common application, electronic application, early admission. *Required:* high school transcript. *Required for some:* interview. *Application deadline:* rolling (freshmen), rolling (transfers). *Notification:* continuous (freshmen).
Admissions Contact Mr. Marcus Balch, Director, Recruiting Services, Texas State Technical College Waco, 3801 Campus Drive, Waco, TX 76705. *Phone:* 254-867-2026. *Toll-free phone:* 800-792-8784 Ext. 2362.

TEXAS STATE TECHNICAL COLLEGE WEST TEXAS

Sweetwater, Texas

Admissions Contact Ms. Maria Aguirre-Acuna, Coordinator of New Students, Texas State Technical College West Texas, 300 College Drive, Sweetwater, TX 79556-4108. *Phone:* 915-235-7349. *Toll-free phone:* 800-592-8784. *Fax:* 915-235-7416. *E-mail:* juanita.garcia@sweetwater.tstc.edu.

TOMBALL COLLEGE

Tomball, Texas

Admissions Contact Mr. Larry Rideaux, Dean of Enrollment Services, Tomball College, 30555 Tomball Parkway, Tomball, TX 77375-4036. *Phone:* 281-351-3334. *Fax:* 281-357-3773. *E-mail:* tc.advisors@nhmccd.edu.

TRINITY VALLEY COMMUNITY COLLEGE

Athens, Texas

- **State and locally supported** 2-year, founded 1946
- **Calendar** semesters
- **Degree** certificates, diplomas, and associate
- **Small-town** 65-acre campus with easy access to Dallas-Fort Worth
- **Endowment** $1.5 million
- **Coed,** 5,821 undergraduate students, 42% full-time, 56% women, 44% men

Undergraduates 2,442 full-time, 3,379 part-time. Students come from 48 states and territories, 13% African American, 0.3% Asian American or Pacific Islander, 6% Hispanic American, 0.3% Native American, 0.5% international.
Freshmen *Admission:* 1,160 enrolled.
Faculty *Total:* 257, 48% full-time, 5% with terminal degrees.
Majors Accounting; agricultural teacher education; animal sciences; art; automobile/automotive mechanics technology; biology/biological sciences; business administration and management; business teacher education; chemistry; child development; computer science; corrections; cosmetology; criminal justice/law enforcement administration; criminal justice/police science; dance; data processing and data processing technology; developmental and child psychology; drafting and design technology; dramatic/theatre arts; education; elementary education; emergency medical technology (EMT paramedic); English; farm and ranch management; fashion merchandising; finance; geology/earth science; heating, air conditioning, ventilation and refrigeration maintenance technology; history; horticultural science; insurance; journalism; kindergarten/preschool education; legal administrative assistant/secretary; liberal arts and sciences/liberal studies; marketing/marketing management; mathematics; music; nursing (licensed practical/vocational nurse training); nursing (registered nurse training); physical education teaching and coaching; physical sciences; political science and government; pre-engineering; psychology; range science and management; real estate; religious studies; sociology; Spanish; speech and rhetoric; surgical technology; welding technology.
Academic Programs *Special study options:* academic remediation for entering students, adult/continuing education programs, advanced placement credit, cooperative education, distance learning, honors programs, internships, part-time degree program, services for LD students, summer session for credit.
Library Ginger Murchison Learning Resource Center plus 3 others with 54,940 titles, 257 serial subscriptions, 1,954 audiovisual materials, an OPAC, a Web page.
Computers on Campus 66 computers available on campus for general student use. A campuswide network can be accessed. Internet access, at least one staffed computer lab available.
Student Life *Housing Options:* coed, men-only, women-only. Campus housing is university owned. *Activities and Organizations:* drama/theater group, student-run newspaper, choral group, marching band, Student Senate, Phi Theta Kappa, Delta Epsilon Chi. *Campus security:* 24-hour emergency response devices and patrols, controlled dormitory access. *Student services:* personal/psychological counseling.
Athletics Member NJCAA. *Intercollegiate sports:* basketball M(s)/W(s), cheerleading M(s)/W(s), football M(s). *Intramural sports:* baseball M/W, basketball M/W, football M, table tennis M/W, volleyball M/W.
Standardized Tests *Required:* THEA (for placement).
Costs (2005–06) *Tuition:* area resident $1200 full-time; state resident $1650 full-time; nonresident $2400 full-time. *Room and board:* $3430. Room and board charges vary according to board plan. *Payment plan:* installment. *Waivers:* employees or children of employees.
Financial Aid Of all full-time matriculated undergraduates who enrolled in 2003, 80 Federal Work-Study jobs (averaging $1544). 40 state and other part-time jobs (averaging $1544).
Applying *Options:* early admission. *Application fee:* $80. *Application deadline:* rolling (freshmen), rolling (transfers). *Notification:* continuous (freshmen).

Trinity Valley Community College (continued)
Admissions Contact Dr. Collette Hilliard, Dean of Enrollment Management and Registrar, Trinity Valley Community College, 100 Cardinal Drive, Athens, TX 75751. *Phone:* 903-675-6209 Ext. 209.

TYLER JUNIOR COLLEGE
Tyler, Texas

Admissions Contact Ms. Janna Chancey, Director of Enrollment Management, Tyler Junior College, PO Box 9020, Tyler, TX 75711. *Phone:* 903-510-2396. *Toll-free phone:* 800-687-5680. *Fax:* 903-510-2634. *E-mail:* klew@tjc.edu.

UNIVERSAL TECHNICAL INSTITUTE
Houston, Texas

Admissions Contact Randy Whitman, Director of Admissions, Universal Technical Institute, 721 Lockhaven Drive, Houston, TX 77073-5598. *Phone:* 281-443-6262 Ext. 261.

VERNON COLLEGE
Vernon, Texas

Admissions Contact Mr. Joe Hite, Dean of Admissions/Registrar, Vernon College, 4400 College Drive, Vernon, TX 76384-4092. *Phone:* 940-552-6291 Ext. 2204. *Fax:* 940-553-1753. *E-mail:* sdavenport@vrjc.cc.tx.us.

VICTORIA COLLEGE
Victoria, Texas

Admissions Contact Laverne Dentler, Registrar, Victoria College, 2200 East Red River, Victoria, TX 77901-4494. *Phone:* 361-573-3291 Ext. 6407. *Fax:* 361-582-2525.

VIRGINIA COLLEGE AT AUSTIN
Austin, Texas

Admissions Contact 6301 East Highway 290, Austin, TX 78723.

WADE COLLEGE
Dallas, Texas

Admissions Contact Ms. Suzan Wade, Admissions Director, Wade College, International Apparel Mart at Dallas Market Center, 2350 Stemmons Expressway, Suite M5120, PO Box 586343, Dallas, TX 75258. *Phone:* 214-637-3530. *Toll-free phone:* 800-624-4850. *Fax:* 214-637-0827. *E-mail:* lfreeman@wadecollege.edu.

▶ **See page 558 for a narrative description.**

WEATHERFORD COLLEGE
Weatherford, Texas

- **State and locally supported** 2-year, founded 1869
- **Calendar** semesters
- **Degree** certificates, diplomas, and associate
- **Small-town** 94-acre campus with easy access to Dallas-Fort Worth
- **Endowment** $42.5 million
- **Coed**

Faculty *Student/faculty ratio:* 42:1.
Student Life *Campus security:* 24-hour emergency response devices and patrols, late-night transport/escort service.
Athletics Member NJCAA.
Standardized Tests *Required:* THEA (for placement). *Recommended:* SAT or ACT (for placement).
Costs (2004–05) *Tuition:* area resident $1232 full-time, $44 per hour part-time; state resident $1624 full-time, $58 per hour part-time; nonresident $2660 full-time, $95 per hour part-time. *Required fees:* $50 full-time. *Room and board:* $5700.
Applying *Options:* early admission.
Admissions Contact Mr. Ralph Willingham, Dean of Admissions, Weatherford College, 225 College Park Drive, Weatherford, TX 76086-5699. *Phone:* 817-598-6248. *Toll-free phone:* 800-287-5471 Ext. 248. *Fax:* 817-598-6205.

WESTERN TECHNICAL COLLEGE
El Paso, Texas

- **Private** 2-year
- **Degree** certificates and associate
- 825 undergraduate students, 73% full-time

Undergraduates 600 full-time, 225 part-time. 3% African American, 85% Hispanic American.
Faculty *Total:* 134, 75% full-time. *Student/faculty ratio:* 18:1.
Majors Automobile/automotive mechanics technology; computer engineering technology; heating, air conditioning, ventilation and refrigeration maintenance technology.
Computers on Campus 25 computers available on campus for general student use. A campuswide network can be accessed from off campus. Internet access, at least one staffed computer lab available. Computer purchase or lease plan available.
Student Life *Housing:* college housing not available.
Applying *Options:* early admission, deferred entrance.
Admissions Contact Mr. Bill Terrell, Chief Admissions Officer, Western Technical College, 1000 Texas Avenue, El Paso, TX 79901-1536. *Phone:* 915-532-3737 Ext. 117.

WESTERN TECHNICAL INSTITUTE
El Paso, Texas

Admissions Contact Mr. Bill Terrell, Chief Admissions Officer, Western Technical Institute, 9451 Diana, El Paso, TX 79930-2610. *Phone:* 800-225-5984.

WESTERN TEXAS COLLEGE
Snyder, Texas

Admissions Contact Dr. Jim Clifton, Dean of Student Services, Western Texas College, 6200 College Avenue, Snyder, TX 79549-6105. *Phone:* 325-573-8511 Ext. 204. *Toll-free phone:* 888-GO-TO-WTC.

WESTWOOD COLLEGE-DALLAS
Dallas, Texas

- **Proprietary** 2-year, founded 2002
- **Calendar** continuous
- **Degree** associate
- **Urban** campus with easy access to Dallas
- **Coed**

Applying *Required:* interview, HS diploma or GED, AND passing score on ACT/SAT or Accuplacer test.
Admissions Contact Eric Southwell, Director of Admissions, Westwood College-Dallas, Executive Plaza I, Suite 100, Dallas, TX 75243. *Phone:* 800-803-3140.

▶ **See page 576 for a narrative description.**

WESTWOOD COLLEGE-FORT WORTH
Euless, Texas

- **Proprietary** 2-year
- **Calendar** continuous
- **Degree** associate
- **Urban** campus with easy access to Dallas, TX
- **Coed**

Applying *Required:* interview, H.S. diploma/GED and passing scores on ACT/SAT or Accuplacer exam.
Admissions Contact Ms. Lisa Hecht, Director of Admissions, Westwood College-Fort Worth, 1331 Airport Freeway, Suite 402, Euless, TX 76040. *Phone:* 817-685-9994. *Toll-free phone:* 866-533-9997. *Fax:* 817-685-8929. *E-mail:* info@westwood.edu.

▶ **See page 582 for a narrative description.**

WESTWOOD COLLEGE-HOUSTON SOUTH CAMPUS
Houston, Texas

- **Proprietary** 2-year, founded 2003
- **Calendar** continuous

- **Degree** associate
- **Urban** campus with easy access to Houston, TX
- **Coed**
- 66% of applicants were admitted

Applying *Required:* interview, HS diploma/GED and passing ACT/SAT or Accuplacer scores.
Admissions Contact Admissions, Westwood College-Houston South Campus, 7322 Southwest Freeway #1900, Houston, TX 77074. *Phone:* 713-777-4433. *E-mail:* info@westwood.edu.

▶ **See page 584 for a narrative description.**

WHARTON COUNTY JUNIOR COLLEGE
Wharton, Texas

Admissions Contact Mr. Albert Barnes, Dean of Admissions and Registration, Wharton County Junior College, 911 Boling Highway, Wharton, TX 77488-3298. *Phone:* 979-532-6381.

UTAH

COLLEGE OF EASTERN UTAH
Price, Utah

- **State-supported** 2-year, founded 1937, part of Utah System of Higher Education
- **Calendar** semesters
- **Degree** certificates and associate
- **Small-town** 15-acre campus
- **Coed**

Faculty *Student/faculty ratio:* 17:1.
Student Life *Campus security:* 24-hour emergency response devices and patrols, late-night transport/escort service.
Athletics Member NJCAA.
Standardized Tests *Required:* ACT ASSET or ABLE (for placement). *Recommended:* SAT or ACT (for placement).
Costs (2004–05) *Tuition:* state resident $1505 full-time, $76 per credit hour part-time; nonresident $6309 full-time, $298 per credit hour part-time. Part-time tuition and fees vary according to course load. *Required fees:* $356 full-time, $18 per credit hour part-time. *Room and board:* $3690; room only: $1990. Room and board charges vary according to board plan, housing facility, and location.
Financial Aid Of all full-time matriculated undergraduates who enrolled in 2003, 66 Federal Work-Study jobs (averaging $1369). 27 state and other part-time jobs (averaging $773).
Applying *Options:* electronic application, early admission. *Application fee:* $25. *Recommended:* high school transcript.
Admissions Contact Mr. Todd Olsen, Director of Admissions, High School Relations, College of Eastern Utah, 451 East 400 North, Price, UT 84501. *Phone:* 435-613-5217. *Fax:* 435-613-5814. *E-mail:* janyoung@ceu.edu.

DIXIE STATE COLLEGE OF UTAH
St. George, Utah

- **State-supported** primarily 2-year, founded 1911, part of Utah System of Higher Education
- **Calendar** semesters
- **Degrees** certificates, diplomas, associate, and bachelor's
- **Small-town** 60-acre campus
- **Endowment** $9.9 million
- **Coed,** 8,373 undergraduate students, 42% full-time, 52% women, 48% men

Undergraduates 3,531 full-time, 4,842 part-time. Students come from 44 states and territories, 19 other countries, 13% are from out of state, 0.7% African American, 2% Asian American or Pacific Islander, 3% Hispanic American, 1% Native American, 0.7% international, 5% transferred in, 2% live on campus. *Retention:* 48% of 2002 full-time freshmen returned.
Freshmen *Admission:* 2,745 applied, 2,341 admitted, 1,495 enrolled. *Average high school GPA:* 3.3. *Test scores:* SAT verbal scores over 500: 41%; SAT math scores over 500: 34%; ACT scores over 18: 75%; SAT verbal scores over 600: 19%; SAT math scores over 600: 10%; ACT scores over 24: 20%; ACT scores over 30: 1%.
Faculty *Total:* 353, 27% full-time. *Student/faculty ratio:* 24:1.
Majors Accounting; administrative assistant and secretarial science; agriculture; airline pilot and flight crew; architectural drafting and CAD/CADD; art; art history, criticism and conservation; autobody/collision and repair technology;

automobile/automotive mechanics technology; aviation/airway management; biology/biological sciences; biotechnology; botany/plant biology; broadcast journalism; business administration and management; cartography; ceramic arts and ceramics; chemistry; child care and support services management; commercial and advertising art; communication/speech communication and rhetoric; computer science; criminal justice/safety; dance; data processing and data processing technology; dental hygiene; diesel mechanics technology; dramatic/theatre arts; drawing; ecology; economics; elementary education; emergency medical technology (EMT paramedic); engineering; English; environmental studies; foreign languages and literatures; forestry; general retailing/wholesaling; geology/earth science; health professions related; history; humanities; interior design; journalism; kindergarten/preschool education; liberal arts and sciences/liberal studies; marine biology and biological oceanography; mathematics; mechanical drafting and CAD/CADD; music; natural resources/conservation; natural resources management and policy; nursing (registered nurse training); painting; philosophy; photographic and film/video technology; photography; physical education teaching and coaching; physics; plant pathology/phytopathology; plant protection and integrated pest management; political science and government; pre-law studies; printmaking; psychology; radio and television; range science and management; sculpture; secondary education; social work; sociology; soil science and agronomy; tourism and travel services marketing; water resources engineering; web page, digital/multimedia and information resources design; wildlife and wildlands science and management; zoology/animal biology.
Academic Programs *Special study options:* academic remediation for entering students, adult/continuing education programs, advanced placement credit, cooperative education, distance learning, English as a second language, honors programs, off-campus study, part-time degree program, services for LD students, summer session for credit.
Library Val A. Browning Library with 94,747 titles, 263 serial subscriptions, 13,411 audiovisual materials, an OPAC, a Web page.
Computers on Campus A campuswide network can be accessed from student residence rooms. Internet access, online (class) registration, at least one staffed computer lab available.
Student Life *Housing Options:* coed, men-only, disabled students. Campus housing is university owned. *Activities and Organizations:* drama/theater group, student-run newspaper, radio and television station, choral group, Dixie Spirit, Outdoor Club, Association of Women Students. *Campus security:* 24-hour emergency response devices and patrols. *Student services:* health clinic, personal/psychological counseling.
Athletics Member NJCAA. *Intercollegiate sports:* baseball M(s), basketball M(s)/W(s), football M(s), golf M(s), soccer W(s), softball W(s), volleyball W(s). *Intramural sports:* basketball M/W, football M, golf M/W, soccer M/W, softball M/W, tennis M/W, ultimate Frisbee M/W, volleyball M/W.
Standardized Tests *Required:* SAT I, ACT, CPT or ACT COMPASS (for placement). *Recommended:* SAT or ACT (for placement).
Costs (2005–06) *Tuition:* state resident $1984 full-time, $67 per credit part-time; nonresident $7390 full-time, $292 per credit part-time. Full-time tuition and fees vary according to course level. Part-time tuition and fees vary according to course level and course load. *Required fees:* $382 full-time. *Room and board:* $2380. *Payment plan:* installment. *Waivers:* employees or children of employees.
Financial Aid Of all full-time matriculated undergraduates who enrolled in 2003, 100 Federal Work-Study jobs (averaging $2700). 20 state and other part-time jobs (averaging $2700).
Applying *Options:* electronic application, early admission, deferred entrance. *Application fee:* $25. *Required:* high school transcript. *Application deadline:* rolling (freshmen).
Admissions Contact Ms. Darla Rollins, Admissions Coordinator, Dixie State College of Utah, 225 South 700 East Street, St. George, UT 84770-3876. *Phone:* 435-652-7702. *Toll-free phone:* 888-GO2DIXIE. *Fax:* 435-656-4005. *E-mail:* admissions@dixie.edu.

ITT TECHNICAL INSTITUTE
Murray, Utah

- **Proprietary** primarily 2-year, founded 1984, part of ITT Educational Services, Inc
- **Calendar** quarters
- **Degrees** associate and bachelor's
- **Suburban** 3-acre campus with easy access to Salt Lake City
- **Coed**

Standardized Tests *Required:* Wonderlic aptitude test (for admission).
Costs (2004–05) *Tuition:* Please see school catalog for specific information.
Applying *Options:* deferred entrance. *Application fee:* $100. *Required:* high school transcript, interview. *Recommended:* letters of recommendation.
Admissions Contact Ms. JoAnn Meron, Director of Recruitment, ITT Technical Institute, 920 West LeVoy Drive, Murray, UT 84123. *Phone:* 801-263-3313. *Toll-free phone:* 800-365-2136. *Fax:* 801-263-3497.

LDS BUSINESS COLLEGE
Salt Lake City, Utah

- **Independent** 2-year, founded 1886, affiliated with The Church of Jesus Christ of Latter-day Saints, part of Latter-day Saints Church Educational System
- **Calendar** semesters
- **Degree** certificates and associate
- **Urban** campus
- **Coed**

Faculty *Student/faculty ratio:* 20:1.
Student Life *Campus security:* 24-hour emergency response devices, controlled dormitory access.
Standardized Tests *Recommended:* ACT (for placement).
Costs (2004–05) *Tuition:* $2400 full-time, $100 per credit hour part-time. Full-time tuition and fees vary according to course load. Part-time tuition and fees vary according to course load. *Room only:* $2236.
Applying *Options:* electronic application, early admission, deferred entrance. *Application fee:* $25. *Required:* high school transcript, interview.
Admissions Contact Mr. Matt D. Tittle, Assistant Dean of Students, LDS Business College, 411 East South Temple, Salt Lake City, UT 84111-1392. *Phone:* 801-524-8146. *Toll-free phone:* 800-999-5767. *Fax:* 801-524-1900. *E-mail:* admissions@ldsbc.edu.

MOUNTAIN WEST COLLEGE
West Valley City, Utah

- **Proprietary** 2-year, founded 1982, part of Corinthian Colleges, Inc
- **Calendar** quarters
- **Degree** diplomas and associate
- **Suburban** campus
- **Coed**

Faculty *Student/faculty ratio:* 15:1.
Standardized Tests *Required:* CPAt (for admission). *Recommended:* SAT or ACT (for admission).
Costs (2004–05) *Tuition:* $9144 full-time, $254 per quarter hour part-time. *Required fees:* $100 full-time, $25 per term part-time.
Applying *Options:* deferred entrance. *Required:* high school transcript, interview.
Admissions Contact Mr. Jason Peterson, Director of Admissions, Mountain West College, 3280 West 3500 South, West Valley City, UT 84119. *Phone:* 801-840-4800. *Toll-free phone:* 888-741-4271. *Fax:* 801-840-4800. *E-mail:* jrios@cci.edu.

PROVO COLLEGE
Provo, Utah

Admissions Contact Mr. Gordon Peters, College Director, Provo College, 1450 West 820 North, Provo, UT 84601. *Phone:* 801-375-1861. *Toll-free phone:* 800-748-4834.

SALT LAKE COMMUNITY COLLEGE
Salt Lake City, Utah

- **State-supported** 2-year, founded 1948, part of Utah System of Higher Education
- **Calendar** semesters
- **Degree** certificates, diplomas, and associate
- **Urban** 114-acre campus
- **Endowment** $2.0 million
- **Coed,** 24,725 undergraduate students, 34% full-time, 49% women, 51% men

Undergraduates 8,471 full-time, 16,254 part-time. 5% are from out of state, 1% African American, 4% Asian American or Pacific Islander, 7% Hispanic American, 1% Native American, 0.9% international, 6% transferred in.
Freshmen *Admission:* 3,805 applied, 3,805 admitted, 3,805 enrolled.
Faculty *Total:* 1,418, 23% full-time. *Student/faculty ratio:* 21:1.
Majors Accounting; administrative assistant and secretarial science; airframe mechanics and aircraft maintenance technology; airline pilot and flight crew; architectural engineering technology; art; automobile/automotive mechanics technology; avionics maintenance technology; biology/biological sciences; business administration and management; carpentry; child development; civil engineering technology; clinical/medical laboratory technology; commercial and advertising art; computer and information sciences; computer and information sciences related; computer and information systems security; computer engineering related; computer engineering technology; computer graphics; computer programming related; computer science; computer software and media applica-

tions related; computer software engineering; computer systems networking and telecommunications; construction engineering technology; construction management; cosmetology; criminal justice/law enforcement administration; culinary arts; dental hygiene; drafting and design technology; education; electrical, electronic and communications engineering technology; elementary education; engineering; engineering related; engineering technology; environmental studies; finance; geography; health science; heating, air conditioning, ventilation and refrigeration maintenance technology; heavy equipment maintenance technology; humanities; human resources management; human services; industrial radiologic technology; industrial technology; information science/studies; information technology; international relations and affairs; legal assistant/paralegal; liberal arts and sciences/liberal studies; machine tool technology; marketing/marketing management; mass communication/media; mechanical engineering/mechanical technology; medical administrative assistant and medical secretary; medical/clinical assistant; nursing (licensed practical/vocational nurse training); nursing (registered nurse training); occupational therapist assistant; physical sciences; physical therapist assistant; pipefitting and sprinkler fitting; pre-engineering; sign language interpretation and translation; social sciences; social work; surgical technology; survey technology; system administration; transportation technology; web page, digital/multimedia and information resources design; welding technology; word processing.
Academic Programs *Special study options:* academic remediation for entering students, advanced placement credit, cooperative education, distance learning, double majors, English as a second language, internships, part-time degree program, services for LD students, student-designed majors, study abroad, summer session for credit. *ROTC:* Army (c), Air Force (c).
Library Markosian Library plus 2 others with 96,470 titles, 781 serial subscriptions, 29,810 audiovisual materials, an OPAC, a Web page.
Computers on Campus 2905 computers available on campus for general student use. A campuswide network can be accessed from off campus. Internet access, online (class) registration, at least one staffed computer lab available.
Student Life *Housing:* college housing not available. *Activities and Organizations:* drama/theater group, student-run newspaper, television station, choral group, LDSSA, VICA, Phi Theta Kappa, PBL, Student Nurse Alliance. *Campus security:* 24-hour emergency response devices and patrols, late-night transport/escort service. *Student services:* health clinic, personal/psychological counseling.
Athletics Member NJCAA. *Intercollegiate sports:* baseball M(s), basketball M(s)/W(s), cheerleading M(s)/W(s), soccer M(c)/W(c), softball W(s), volleyball W(s).
Standardized Tests *Recommended:* ACT (for placement), CPT.
Costs (2004–05) *Tuition:* state resident $1832 full-time; nonresident $6412 full-time. *Required fees:* $342 full-time.
Applying *Options:* electronic application, early admission, deferred entrance. *Application fee:* $35. *Application deadline:* rolling (freshmen), rolling (transfers).
Admissions Contact Ms. Terri Blau, Assistant Director of Admissions for School Relations, Salt Lake Community College, Salt Lake City, UT 84130. *Phone:* 801-957-4299. *Fax:* 801-957-4958.

SNOW COLLEGE
Ephraim, Utah

- **State-supported** 2-year, founded 1888, part of Utah System of Higher Education
- **Calendar** semesters
- **Degree** certificates, diplomas, and associate
- **Rural** 50-acre campus
- **Endowment** $3.8 million
- **Coed,** 2,975 undergraduate students, 83% full-time, 56% women, 44% men

Undergraduates 2,473 full-time, 502 part-time. Students come from 34 states and territories, 15 other countries, 8% are from out of state, 1% African American, 2% Asian American or Pacific Islander, 2% Hispanic American, 0.9% Native American, 2% international, 1% transferred in, 10% live on campus.
Freshmen *Admission:* 1,973 applied, 1,973 admitted, 1,229 enrolled. *Average high school GPA:* 3.72. *Test scores:* ACT scores over 18: 71%; ACT scores over 24: 22%; ACT scores over 30: 1%.
Faculty *Total:* 148, 74% full-time, 13% with terminal degrees. *Student/faculty ratio:* 21:1.
Majors Accounting; administrative assistant and secretarial science; agricultural business and management; agricultural economics; agriculture; agronomy and crop science; animal physiology; animal sciences; art; automobile/automotive mechanics technology; biology/biological sciences; botany/plant biology; business administration and management; business teacher education; carpentry; chemistry; child development; computer science; construction engineering technology; construction management; criminal justice/law enforcement administration; dance; dramatic/theatre arts; economics; education; electrical, electronic and communications engineering technology; elementary education; engineering; entomology; family and community services; family and consumer sciences/human sciences; farm and ranch management; foods, nutrition, and wellness;

forestry; French; geography; geology/earth science; history; humanities; information science/studies; Japanese; kindergarten/preschool education; liberal arts and sciences/liberal studies; mass communication/media; mathematics; music; music history, literature, and theory; music teacher education; natural resources management and policy; natural sciences; philosophy; physical education teaching and coaching; physical sciences; physics; political science and government; pre-engineering; range science and management; science teacher education; sociology; soil conservation; Spanish; trade and industrial teacher education; veterinary sciences; voice and opera; wildlife and wildlands science and management; zoology/animal biology.

Academic Programs *Special study options:* academic remediation for entering students, adult/continuing education programs, advanced placement credit, cooperative education, English as a second language, external degree program, honors programs, independent study, part-time degree program, services for LD students, summer session for credit.

Library Lucy Phillips Library with 31,911 titles, 1,870 audiovisual materials, an OPAC, a Web page.

Computers on Campus 220 computers available on campus for general student use. A campuswide network can be accessed from off campus. At least one staffed computer lab available.

Student Life *Housing Options:* coed. Campus housing is university owned. *Activities and Organizations:* drama/theater group, student-run newspaper, radio station, choral group, marching band, Drama Club, Latter-Day Saints Singers, Dead Cats Society, Associated Women Students, Associated Men Students. *Campus security:* student patrols. *Student services:* health clinic, personal/psychological counseling.

Athletics Member NJCAA. *Intercollegiate sports:* baseball M, basketball M(s)/W(s), football M(s), golf M(s), softball W, volleyball W(s). *Intramural sports:* badminton M/W, basketball M/W, bowling M/W, football M/W, golf M/W, racquetball M/W, soccer M, softball M/W, tennis M/W, volleyball M/W, wrestling M.

Costs (2004–05) *Tuition:* state resident $1370 full-time; nonresident $6072 full-time. Part-time tuition and fees vary according to class time, location, and program. *Required fees:* $300 full-time. *Room and board:* $3800. Room and board charges vary according to board plan. *Payment plan:* installment. *Waivers:* employees or children of employees.

Financial Aid Of all full-time matriculated undergraduates who enrolled in 2003, 92 Federal Work-Study jobs (averaging $1200).

Applying *Options:* early admission. *Application fee:* $30. *Required:* high school transcript. *Application deadlines:* 6/15 (freshmen), 6/1 (transfers). *Notification:* continuous (freshmen).

Admissions Contact Mr. Brach Schleuter, Coordinator of High School Relations, Snow College, 150 East College Avenue, Ephraim, UT 84627. *Phone:* 435-283-7151. *Fax:* 435-283-6879.

STEVENS-HENAGER COLLEGE
Ogden, Utah

Admissions Contact Admissions Office, Stevens-Henager College, PO Box 9428, Ogden, UT 84409. *Phone:* 801-394-7791. *Toll-free phone:* 800-371-7791.

UTAH CAREER COLLEGE
West Jordan, Utah

- **Proprietary** 2-year
- **Calendar** quarters
- **Degree** certificates, diplomas, and associate
- **Suburban** 1-acre campus with easy access to Salt Lake City
- **Coed**
- 100% of applicants were admitted

Faculty *Student/faculty ratio:* 9:1.

Costs (2004–05) *Tuition:* $10,260 full-time, $285 per credit part-time. Full-time tuition and fees vary according to course load. Part-time tuition and fees vary according to course load. *Payment plans:* tuition prepayment, installment.

Applying *Required:* high school transcript, interview.

Admissions Contact Mr. Richard Flanders, Director of Admissions, Utah Career College, 1902 West 7800 South, West Jordan, UT 84088. *Phone:* 801-304-4224 Ext. 103. *Toll-free phone:* 866-304-4224. *E-mail:* rflanders@utahcollege.com.

VERMONT

COMMUNITY COLLEGE OF VERMONT
Waterbury, Vermont

- **State-supported** 2-year, founded 1970, part of Vermont State Colleges System
- **Calendar** semesters
- **Degree** certificates, diplomas, and associate
- **Rural** campus
- **Coed,** 5,801 undergraduate students

Undergraduates Students come from 16 states and territories, 3% are from out of state, 2% African American, 1% Asian American or Pacific Islander, 1% Hispanic American, 0.8% Native American, 0.2% international.

Freshmen *Admission:* 602 applied, 602 admitted.

Faculty *Total:* 635.

Majors Accounting; administrative assistant and secretarial science; business administration and management; child development; community organization and advocacy; computer science; data entry/microcomputer applications; developmental and child psychology; education; human services; industrial technology; information technology; liberal arts and sciences/liberal studies; social sciences; teacher assistant/aide.

Academic Programs *Special study options:* academic remediation for entering students, accelerated degree program, adult/continuing education programs, cooperative education, distance learning, double majors, English as a second language, external degree program, independent study, internships, part-time degree program, services for LD students, student-designed majors, summer session for credit.

Library Vermont Community and Technical College Library with an OPAC.

Computers on Campus 200 computers available on campus for general student use. A campuswide network can be accessed from off campus. Internet access, online (class) registration, at least one staffed computer lab available.

Student Life *Housing:* college housing not available.

Standardized Tests *Required:* ACCUPLACER (for placement).

Costs (2005–06) *Tuition:* state resident $3912 full-time, $163 per credit part-time; nonresident $7824 full-time, $326 per credit part-time. *Required fees:* $100 full-time, $50 per term part-time.

Financial Aid Of all full-time matriculated undergraduates who enrolled in 2003, 35 Federal Work-Study jobs (averaging $2000).

Applying *Application deadline:* rolling (freshmen), rolling (transfers).

Admissions Contact Ms. Susan Henry, Dean of Administration, Community College of Vermont, PO Box 120, Waterbury, VT 05676-0120. *Phone:* 802-865-4422.

LANDMARK COLLEGE
Putney, Vermont

- **Independent** 2-year, founded 1983
- **Calendar** semesters
- **Degrees** associate (offers degree program for high-potential students with dyslexia, ADHD, or specific learning disabilities)
- **Rural** 125-acre campus
- **Endowment** $1.2 million
- **Coed,** 334 undergraduate students, 67% full-time, 30% women, 70% men

Undergraduates 223 full-time, 111 part-time. Students come from 37 states and territories, 11 other countries, 94% are from out of state, 3% African American, 3% Asian American or Pacific Islander, 2% Hispanic American, 0.3% Native American, 4% international, 10% transferred in, 94% live on campus. *Retention:* 40% of 2002 full-time freshmen returned.

Freshmen *Admission:* 291 applied, 178 admitted, 54 enrolled.

Faculty *Total:* 106, 97% full-time, 12% with terminal degrees. *Student/faculty ratio:* 4:1.

Majors Liberal arts and sciences/liberal studies.

Academic Programs *Special study options:* academic remediation for entering students, adult/continuing education programs, advanced placement credit, services for LD students, study abroad, summer session for credit.

Library Landmark College Library with 30,066 titles, 135 serial subscriptions, 1,555 audiovisual materials.

Computers on Campus 50 computers available on campus for general student use. A campuswide network can be accessed from student residence rooms and from off campus. Internet access, at least one staffed computer lab available. Computer purchase or lease plan available.

Student Life *Housing:* on-campus residence required for freshman year. *Options:* coed. Campus housing is university owned. Freshman campus housing is guaranteed. *Activities and Organizations:* drama/theater group, Student Government Association, Campus Activities Board, Phi Theta Kappa Honor Society, Jazz Band Club, Cultural Diversity Club. *Campus security:* 24-hour emergency response devices and patrols, controlled dormitory access. *Student services:* health clinic, personal/psychological counseling, women's center.

Athletics *Intercollegiate sports:* baseball M(c), basketball M(c)/W(c), cross-country running M(c)/W(c), rock climbing M(c)/W(c), soccer M(c)/W(c), softball W(c). *Intramural sports:* badminton M/W, fencing M/W, golf M/W, ice hockey M/W, skiing (cross-country) M/W, soccer M/W, softball W, tennis M/W, volleyball M/W.

Landmark College (continued)

Standardized Tests *Required:* Wechsler Adult Intelligence Scale III and Nelson Denny Reading Test (for admission).

Costs (2005–06) *Comprehensive fee:* $44,538 includes full-time tuition ($37,000), mandatory fees ($738), and room and board ($6800). *Room and board:* college room only: $3400. *Waivers:* employees or children of employees.

Financial Aid Of all full-time matriculated undergraduates who enrolled in 2003, 60 Federal Work-Study jobs (averaging $1600).

Applying *Options:* deferred entrance. *Application fee:* $75. *Required:* essay or personal statement, high school transcript, 2 letters of recommendation, interview, diagnosis of LD and/or AD/HD. *Application deadline:* rolling (freshmen), rolling (transfers). *Notification:* continuous (freshmen).

Admissions Contact Mrs. Dale Herold, Vice President for Enrollment Management, Landmark College, 1 River Road South, Putney, VT 05346. *Phone:* 802-387-6716. *Fax:* 802-387-6868. *E-mail:* admissions@landmark.edu.

▶ **See page 510 for a narrative description.**

NEW ENGLAND CULINARY INSTITUTE
Montpelier, Vermont

- **Proprietary** primarily 2-year, founded 1980
- **Calendar** quarters
- **Degrees** certificates, associate, and bachelor's
- **Small-town** campus
- **Endowment** $291,550
- **Coed**

Faculty *Student/faculty ratio:* 6:1.

Student Life *Campus security:* 24-hour emergency response devices, student patrols, Mod patrols in the evening.

Standardized Tests *Recommended:* SAT (for placement).

Costs (2004–05) *Comprehensive fee:* $27,500 includes full-time tuition ($20,995), mandatory fees ($450), and room and board ($6055). Full-time tuition and fees vary according to program and student level. *Room and board:* college room only: $3810.

Financial Aid Of all full-time matriculated undergraduates who enrolled in 2003, 320 Federal Work-Study jobs (averaging $1000).

Applying *Options:* common application, electronic application, early admission, deferred entrance. *Required:* essay or personal statement, high school transcript, 1 letter of recommendation, interview. *Required for some:* minimum TOEFL scores for foreign students.

Admissions Contact Ms. Dawn Hayward, Director of Admissions, New England Culinary Institute, 250 Main Street, Montpelier, VT 05602. *Phone:* 877-223-6324 Ext. 3211. *Toll-free phone:* 877-223-6324. *Fax:* 802-225-3280. *E-mail:* info@neci.edu.

NEW ENGLAND CULINARY INSTITUTE AT ESSEX
Essex Junction, Vermont

Admissions Contact 48½ Park Street, Essex Junction, VT 05452.

VIRGINIA

BLUE RIDGE COMMUNITY COLLEGE
Weyers Cave, Virginia

- **State-supported** 2-year, founded 1967, part of Virginia Community College System
- **Calendar** semesters
- **Degree** certificates, diplomas, and associate
- **Rural** 65-acre campus
- **Endowment** $1.5 million
- **Coed**, 3,942 undergraduate students, 37% full-time, 58% women, 42% men

Undergraduates 1,445 full-time, 2,497 part-time. Students come from 29 states and territories, 2 other countries, 2% are from out of state, 4% African American, 1% Asian American or Pacific Islander, 1% Hispanic American, 0.3% Native American, 41% transferred in. *Retention:* 42% of 2002 full-time freshmen returned.

Freshmen *Admission:* 625 applied, 625 admitted, 625 enrolled.

Faculty *Total:* 172, 30% full-time. *Student/faculty ratio:* 23:1.

Majors Accounting; administrative assistant and secretarial science; business administration and management; computer systems networking and telecommu-

nications; electrical, electronic and communications engineering technology; information science/studies; information technology; liberal arts and sciences/liberal studies; mechanical design technology; mental health/rehabilitation; nursing (registered nurse training); veterinary technology.

Academic Programs *Special study options:* academic remediation for entering students, adult/continuing education programs, advanced placement credit, cooperative education, distance learning, double majors, English as a second language, honors programs, internships, off-campus study, part-time degree program, services for LD students, study abroad, summer session for credit.

Library Houff Library with 59,735 titles, 206 serial subscriptions, 1,646 audiovisual materials, an OPAC, a Web page.

Computers on Campus 285 computers available on campus for general student use. A campuswide network can be accessed. Internet access, at least one staffed computer lab available.

Student Life *Housing:* college housing not available. *Activities and Organizations:* Student Government Association, Phi Theta Kappa, Christian Fellowship, intramural athletics, special interest groups. *Campus security:* 24-hour emergency response devices and patrols, late-night transport/escort service. *Student services:* personal/psychological counseling, women's center.

Athletics *Intramural sports:* basketball M.

Standardized Tests *Recommended:* SAT (for placement).

Costs (2005–06) *Tuition:* state resident $1911 full-time, $64 per credit hour part-time; nonresident $6290 full-time, $210 per credit hour part-time. *Required fees:* $146 full-time, $5 per credit hour part-time. *Waivers:* senior citizens.

Financial Aid Of all full-time matriculated undergraduates who enrolled in 2003, 25 Federal Work-Study jobs (averaging $1582).

Applying *Options:* electronic application, early admission. *Required for some:* high school transcript, interview. *Application deadline:* rolling (freshmen), rolling (transfers). *Notification:* continuous (freshmen).

Admissions Contact Mr. Robert Clemmer, Coordinator of Admissions and Records, Blue Ridge Community College, PO Box 80, Weyers Cave, VA 24486-0080. *Phone:* 540-453-2251.

BRYANT AND STRATTON COLLEGE, RICHMOND
Richmond, Virginia

Admissions Contact Mr. Mark Sarver, Director of Admissions, Bryant and Stratton College, Richmond, 8141 Hull Street Road, Richmond, VA 23235-6411. *Phone:* 804-745-2444. *Fax:* 804-745-6884.

BRYANT AND STRATTON COLLEGE, VIRGINIA BEACH
Virginia Beach, Virginia

Admissions Contact Mr. Greg Smith, Director of Admissions, Bryant and Stratton College, Virginia Beach, 301 Centre Pointe Drive, Virginia Beach, VA 23462-4417. *Phone:* 757-499-7900.

CENTRAL VIRGINIA COMMUNITY COLLEGE
Lynchburg, Virginia

Admissions Contact Ms. Judy Wilhelm, Enrollment Services Coordinator, Central Virginia Community College, 3506 Wards Road, Lynchburg, VA 24502-2498. *Phone:* 434-832-7630. *Toll-free phone:* 800-562-3060. *Fax:* 804-386-4681.

DABNEY S. LANCASTER COMMUNITY COLLEGE
Clifton Forge, Virginia

- **State-supported** 2-year, founded 1964, part of Virginia Community College System
- **Calendar** semesters
- **Degree** certificates, diplomas, and associate
- **Rural** 117-acre campus
- **Coed**, 1,443 undergraduate students

Undergraduates Students come from 5 states and territories, 5% African American, 0.5% Asian American or Pacific Islander, 0.7% Hispanic American, 0.3% Native American.

Faculty *Total:* 95, 22% full-time.

Majors Administrative assistant and secretarial science; biological and physical sciences; business administration and management; computer programming;

criminal justice/law enforcement administration; data processing and data processing technology; drafting and design technology; education; electrical, electronic and communications engineering technology; forestry technology; information science/studies; legal administrative assistant/secretary; liberal arts and sciences/liberal studies; mechanical design technology; medical administrative assistant and medical secretary; nursing (registered nurse training); wood science and wood products/pulp and paper technology.

Academic Programs *Special study options:* academic remediation for entering students, adult/continuing education programs, advanced placement credit, cooperative education, honors programs, internships, part-time degree program, services for LD students, summer session for credit.

Library 37,716 titles, 376 serial subscriptions.

Student Life *Housing:* college housing not available. *Activities and Organizations:* drama/theater group. *Student services:* personal/psychological counseling.

Athletics *Intercollegiate sports:* basketball M. *Intramural sports:* basketball M/W, bowling M/W, equestrian sports M/W, football M/W, golf M/W, skiing (downhill) M/W, soccer M/W, tennis M/W, volleyball M/W.

Standardized Tests *Required:* CGP (for placement).

Costs (2005–06) *Tuition:* state resident $1633 full-time, $68 per credit part-time; nonresident $5172 full-time, $216 per credit part-time.

Applying *Options:* early admission, deferred entrance. *Application deadline:* rolling (freshmen), rolling (transfers). *Notification:* continuous (freshmen).

Admissions Contact Dr. Benjamin T. King, Vice President for Instruction and Student Services, Dabney S. Lancaster Community College, 100 Dabney Drive, PO Box 1000, Clifton Forge, VA 24422. *Phone:* 540-863-2812.

DANVILLE COMMUNITY COLLEGE
Danville, Virginia

- **State-supported** 2-year, founded 1967, part of Virginia Community College System
- **Calendar** semesters
- **Degree** certificates, diplomas, and associate
- **Urban** 76-acre campus
- **Coed,** 4,089 undergraduate students, 33% full-time, 61% women, 39% men

Undergraduates 1,366 full-time, 2,723 part-time. Students come from 9 states and territories, 3 other countries, 2% are from out of state, 34% African American, 0.3% Asian American or Pacific Islander, 0.5% Hispanic American, 0.1% Native American. *Retention:* 100% of 2002 full-time freshmen returned.

Freshmen *Admission:* 404 enrolled.

Faculty *Total:* 201, 26% full-time. *Student/faculty ratio:* 19:1.

Majors Accounting; administrative assistant and secretarial science; biological and physical sciences; business administration and management; computer programming; education; engineering technology; liberal arts and sciences/liberal studies; marketing/marketing management.

Academic Programs *Special study options:* academic remediation for entering students, adult/continuing education programs, advanced placement credit, cooperative education, distance learning, honors programs, part-time degree program, summer session for credit.

Library Learning Resource Center with 41,600 titles, 345 serial subscriptions, an OPAC, a Web page.

Computers on Campus 265 computers available on campus for general student use. Internet access, at least one staffed computer lab available.

Student Life *Housing:* college housing not available. *Campus security:* 24-hour patrols.

Athletics *Intramural sports:* basketball M/W, bowling M/W, football M, golf M, softball M/W, volleyball M/W.

Standardized Tests *Required for some:* ACT ASSET.

Costs (2005–06) *Tuition:* state resident $2040 full-time, $68 per credit hour part-time; nonresident $6486 full-time, $216 per credit hour part-time. *Required fees:* $110 full-time, $4 per credit hour part-time.

Financial Aid Of all full-time matriculated undergraduates who enrolled in 2003, 40 Federal Work-Study jobs (averaging $1700).

Applying *Options:* early admission, deferred entrance. *Required:* high school transcript. *Application deadline:* rolling (freshmen), rolling (transfers). *Notification:* continuous (freshmen).

Admissions Contact Mr. Peter Castiglione, Director of Student Development and Enrollment Management, Danville Community College, 1008 South Main Street, Danville, VA 24541-4088. *Phone:* 434-797-8490. *Toll-free phone:* 800-560-4291.

EASTERN SHORE COMMUNITY COLLEGE
Melfa, Virginia

- **State-supported** 2-year, founded 1971, part of Virginia Community College System

- **Calendar** semesters
- **Degree** certificates and associate
- **Rural** 117-acre campus
- **Coed,** 807 undergraduate students, 32% full-time, 72% women, 28% men

Undergraduates 260 full-time, 547 part-time. 44% African American, 0.7% Asian American or Pacific Islander, 1% Hispanic American. *Retention:* 36% of 2002 full-time freshmen returned.

Freshmen *Admission:* 390 applied, 322 admitted. *Average high school GPA:* 2.60.

Faculty *Total:* 57, 32% full-time, 7% with terminal degrees. *Student/faculty ratio:* 13:1.

Majors Administrative assistant and secretarial science; biological and physical sciences; business administration and management; computer/information technology services administration related; computer/technical support; education; electrical, electronic and communications engineering technology; liberal arts and sciences/liberal studies; nursing (registered nurse training).

Academic Programs *Special study options:* academic remediation for entering students, adult/continuing education programs, advanced placement credit, cooperative education, distance learning, English as a second language, off-campus study, part-time degree program, services for LD students, summer session for credit.

Library Learning Resources Center with 20,479 titles, 95 serial subscriptions, an OPAC, a Web page.

Computers on Campus 53 computers available on campus for general student use. A campuswide network can be accessed. At least one staffed computer lab available.

Student Life *Housing:* college housing not available. *Campus security:* night security guard. *Student services:* personal/psychological counseling.

Costs (2005–06) *Tuition:* state resident $2040 full-time, $68 per credit part-time; nonresident $6420 full-time, $214 per credit part-time. *Required fees:* $110 full-time, $4 per credit part-time.

Financial Aid Of all full-time matriculated undergraduates who enrolled in 2003, 11 Federal Work-Study jobs.

Applying *Required:* high school transcript. *Application deadline:* rolling (freshmen), rolling (transfers). *Notification:* continuous (freshmen).

Admissions Contact Ms. Faye Wilson, Enrollment Services Assistant for Admissions, Eastern Shore Community College, 29300 Lankford Highway, Melfa, VA 23410. *Phone:* 757-789-1731. *Toll-free phone:* 877-871-8455. *Fax:* 757-787-5984. *E-mail:* eswilsf@es.cc.va.us.

ECPI COLLEGE OF TECHNOLOGY
Newport News, Virginia

- **Proprietary** 2-year, founded 1966
- **Calendar** trimesters
- **Degree** certificates, diplomas, and associate
- **Suburban** campus
- **Coed,** 576 undergraduate students, 100% full-time, 36% women, 64% men

Undergraduates 576 full-time. Students come from 34 states and territories, 2% are from out of state, 47% African American, 3% Asian American or Pacific Islander, 6% Hispanic American, 0.3% Native American, 74% transferred in.

Freshmen *Admission:* 256 applied, 182 admitted, 121 enrolled.

Faculty *Total:* 130, 51% full-time, 2% with terminal degrees. *Student/faculty ratio:* 16:1.

Majors Accounting; communications technology; computer and information sciences; computer engineering technology; computer management; computer science; computer typography and composition equipment operation; electrical, electronic and communications engineering technology; electromechanical technology; engineering technology; health/health care administration; health information/medical records administration; information science/studies; mechanical engineering/mechanical technology; medical administrative assistant and medical secretary; telecommunications; trade and industrial teacher education.

Academic Programs *Special study options:* adult/continuing education programs, advanced placement credit, freshman honors college, honors programs, internships, part-time degree program, summer session for credit.

Library ECPI-Virginia Beach Library with 13,014 titles, 168 serial subscriptions, an OPAC, a Web page.

Computers on Campus 100 computers available on campus for general student use. A campuswide network can be accessed from off campus. Internet access, at least one staffed computer lab available.

Student Life *Housing:* college housing not available. *Activities and Organizations:* SETA, IEEE, NVTHS, Accounting Society, CSI. *Campus security:* building and parking lot security. *Student services:* personal/psychological counseling.

Costs (2004–05) *Tuition:* Contact school directly for currents costs.

Financial Aid Of all full-time matriculated undergraduates who enrolled in 2003, 30 Federal Work-Study jobs (averaging $2000).

ECPI College of Technology (continued)

Applying *Options:* common application, deferred entrance. *Application fee:* $100. *Required:* high school transcript, minimum 2.0 GPA, interview. *Notification:* continuous (freshmen).

Admissions Contact Mr. John Olsen, Provost, ECPI College of Technology, 1001 Omni Boulevard, #100, Newport News, VA 23606. *Phone:* 757-838-9191.

ECPI COLLEGE OF TECHNOLOGY
Virginia Beach, Virginia

- **Proprietary** primarily 2-year, founded 1966
- **Calendar** trimesters
- **Degrees** certificates, diplomas, associate, and bachelor's
- **Suburban** 8-acre campus
- **Coed,** 4,391 undergraduate students, 98% full-time, 47% women, 53% men

Undergraduates 4,312 full-time, 79 part-time. Students come from 6 states and territories, 10% are from out of state, 43% African American, 3% Asian American or Pacific Islander, 4% Hispanic American, 0.4% Native American.

Freshmen *Admission:* 1,433 applied, 982 admitted, 737 enrolled.

Faculty *Total:* 130, 51% full-time, 2% with terminal degrees. *Student/faculty ratio:* 16:1.

Majors Accounting; biomedical technology; business machine repair; communications technology; computer and information sciences; computer engineering technology; computer management; computer programming; computer science; computer typography and composition equipment operation; data processing and data processing technology; electrical, electronic and communications engineering technology; electromechanical technology; engineering technology; health/health care administration; health information/medical records administration; information science/studies; mechanical engineering/mechanical technology; medical administrative assistant and medical secretary; telecommunications.

Academic Programs *Special study options:* adult/continuing education programs, advanced placement credit, distance learning, freshman honors college, internships, part-time degree program, summer session for credit.

Library ECPI-Virginia Beach Library with an OPAC, a Web page.

Computers on Campus 600 computers available on campus for general student use. A campuswide network can be accessed from off campus. Internet access, at least one staffed computer lab available.

Student Life *Housing Options:* Campus housing is provided by a third party. *Activities and Organizations:* SETA, IEEE, NVTHS, ITE, Accounting Society. *Campus security:* building and parking lot security. *Student services:* personal/psychological counseling.

Standardized Tests *Recommended:* SAT or ACT (for admission).

Costs (2004–05) *Tuition:* Contact school directly for currents costs.

Financial Aid Of all full-time matriculated undergraduates who enrolled in 2003, 80 Federal Work-Study jobs (averaging $2000).

Applying *Options:* common application, electronic application, deferred entrance. *Application fee:* $100. *Required:* high school transcript, interview. *Notification:* continuous (freshmen).

Admissions Contact Mr. Ronald Ballance, Vice President, ECPI College of Technology, 5555 Greenwich Road, Suite 100, Virginia Beach, VA 23462. *Phone:* 804-330-5533. *Toll-free phone:* 800-986-1200.

ECPI TECHNICAL COLLEGE
Glen Allen, Virginia

- **Proprietary** primarily 2-year
- **Calendar** semesters
- **Degrees** certificates, diplomas, associate, and bachelor's
- **Urban** campus with easy access to Richmond
- **Coed,** 427 undergraduate students, 100% full-time, 29% women, 71% men
- **82%** of applicants were admitted

Undergraduates 427 full-time. Students come from 2 states and territories, 1% are from out of state, 38% African American, 4% Asian American or Pacific Islander, 4% Hispanic American, 0.5% Native American.

Freshmen *Admission:* 148 applied, 121 admitted, 82 enrolled.

Faculty *Student/faculty ratio:* 15:1.

Majors Computer and information systems security; computer programming; computer technology/computer systems technology; data entry/microcomputer applications; telecommunications technology; web page, digital/multimedia and information resources design.

Student Life *Housing:* college housing not available. *Activities and Organizations:* CSI, OPMA, SETA, NVTHS, ITE. *Campus security:* building and parking lot security.

Standardized Tests *Recommended:* SAT and SAT Subject Tests or ACT (for admission).

Costs (2004–05) *Tuition:* Contact college directly as tuition and fees vary by program.

Applying *Required:* high school transcript, interview. *Application deadline:* rolling (freshmen), rolling (transfers). *Notification:* continuous (freshmen).

Admissions Contact Mr. Keith Hennett, Director, ECPI Technical College, 4305 Cox Road, Glen Allen, VA 23060. *Phone:* 804-934-0100. *Toll-free phone:* 800-986-1200.

ECPI TECHNICAL COLLEGE
Richmond, Virginia

- **Proprietary** primarily 2-year, founded 1966
- **Calendar** semesters
- **Degrees** certificates, diplomas, associate, and bachelor's
- **Urban** campus
- **Coed,** 512 undergraduate students, 100% full-time, 36% women, 64% men

Undergraduates 512 full-time. Students come from 2 states and territories, 1% are from out of state, 43% African American, 1% Asian American or Pacific Islander, 0.6% Hispanic American, 0.6% Native American.

Freshmen *Admission:* 176 applied, 132 admitted, 106 enrolled.

Faculty *Student/faculty ratio:* 15:1.

Majors Accounting; business machine repair; communications technology; computer and information sciences; computer and information sciences related; computer and information systems security; computer management; computer programming; computer science; computer technology/computer systems technology; computer typography and composition equipment operation; data entry/microcomputer applications; data processing and data processing technology; electrical, electronic and communications engineering technology; electromechanical technology; engineering technology; health/health care administration; health information/medical records administration; information science/studies; mechanical engineering/mechanical technology; medical administrative assistant and medical secretary; telecommunications; telecommunications technology; trade and industrial teacher education; web page, digital/multimedia and information resources design.

Academic Programs *Special study options:* adult/continuing education programs, advanced placement credit, freshman honors college, honors programs, internships, part-time degree program, summer session for credit.

Library ECPI-Richmond Library with 3,165 titles, 81 serial subscriptions, an OPAC, a Web page.

Computers on Campus 190 computers available on campus for general student use. A campuswide network can be accessed from off campus. Internet access, at least one staffed computer lab available.

Student Life *Housing:* college housing not available. *Activities and Organizations:* Collegiate Secretaries International, Data Processing Management Association, Student Electronics Technicians Association, Future Office Assistants, National Vocational-Technical Honor Society. *Campus security:* building and parking lot security.

Standardized Tests *Recommended:* SAT and SAT Subject Tests or ACT (for admission).

Costs (2004–05) *Tuition:* Contact college directly as tuition and fees vary by program. *Payment plan:* installment. *Waivers:* employees or children of employees.

Financial Aid Of all full-time matriculated undergraduates who enrolled in 2003, 40 Federal Work-Study jobs (averaging $2000).

Applying *Options:* common application, deferred entrance. *Application fee:* $100. *Required:* high school transcript, interview. *Application deadline:* rolling (freshmen), rolling (transfers). *Notification:* continuous (freshmen).

Admissions Contact Ms. Ada Gerard, Director, ECPI Technical College, 800 Moorefield Park Drive, Richmond, VA 23236. *Phone:* 804-330-5533. *Toll-free phone:* 800-986-1200.

ECPI TECHNICAL COLLEGE
Roanoke, Virginia

- **Proprietary** primarily 2-year, founded 1966
- **Calendar** semesters
- **Degrees** certificates, diplomas, associate, and bachelor's
- **Suburban** 3-acre campus
- **Coed,** 340 undergraduate students, 100% full-time, 39% women, 61% men

Undergraduates 340 full-time. Students come from 4 states and territories, 1% are from out of state, 22% African American, 0.3% Asian American or Pacific Islander, 1% Hispanic American, 0.6% Native American.

Freshmen *Admission:* 159 applied, 103 admitted, 66 enrolled.

Faculty *Student/faculty ratio:* 15:1.

Majors Accounting; communications technology; computer and information sciences; computer and information sciences related; computer and information systems security; computer engineering technology; computer science; computer technology/computer systems technology; computer typography and composition equipment operation; data entry/microcomputer applications; electrical, electronic and communications engineering technology; electromechanical technology; engineering technology; health/health care administration; health information/medical records administration; information science/studies; mechanical engineering/mechanical technology; medical administrative assistant and medical secretary; medical/clinical assistant; telecommunications; telecommunications technology.

Academic Programs *Special study options:* accelerated degree program, adult/continuing education programs, advanced placement credit, distance learning, internships, part-time degree program, summer session for credit.

Library ECPI-Roanoke Library plus 1 other with 1,703 titles, 43 serial subscriptions, a Web page.

Computers on Campus 80 computers available on campus for general student use. A campuswide network can be accessed from off campus. Internet access, at least one staffed computer lab available.

Student Life *Housing:* college housing not available. *Activities and Organizations:* SETA, NVTHS, SAFA, FOAMA, ITE. *Campus security:* building and parking lot security.

Standardized Tests *Recommended:* SAT and SAT Subject Tests or ACT (for admission).

Costs (2004–05) *Tuition:* Contact college directly as tuition and fees vary by program. *Payment plan:* installment. *Waivers:* employees or children of employees.

Financial Aid Of all full-time matriculated undergraduates who enrolled in 2003, 20 Federal Work-Study jobs (averaging $2000).

Applying *Options:* common application, electronic application, deferred entrance. *Application fee:* $100. *Required:* high school transcript, interview. *Application deadline:* rolling (freshmen), rolling (transfers). *Notification:* continuous (freshmen).

Admissions Contact Mr. Elmer Haas, Director, ECPI Technical College, 5234 Airport Road, Roanoke, VA 24012. *Phone:* 540-362-5400. *Toll-free phone:* 800-986-1200.

GERMANNA COMMUNITY COLLEGE
Locust Grove, Virginia

- **State-supported** 2-year, founded 1970, part of Virginia Community College System
- **Calendar** semesters
- **Degree** certificates and associate
- **Rural** 100-acre campus with easy access to Washington, DC
- **Coed,** 4,799 undergraduate students, 28% full-time, 66% women, 34% men

Undergraduates 1,359 full-time, 3,440 part-time. Students come from 5 states and territories, 1 other country, 13% African American, 3% Asian American or Pacific Islander, 3% Hispanic American, 0.5% Native American.

Freshmen *Admission:* 838 applied, 838 admitted, 838 enrolled.

Faculty *Total:* 272, 18% full-time. *Student/faculty ratio:* 20:1.

Majors Accounting; administrative assistant and secretarial science; biological and physical sciences; business administration and management; criminal justice/police science; data processing and data processing technology; education; electrical, electronic and communications engineering technology; general studies; liberal arts and sciences/liberal studies; nursing (registered nurse training).

Academic Programs *Special study options:* academic remediation for entering students, adult/continuing education programs, off-campus study, part-time degree program, summer session for credit.

Library 22,412 titles, 160 serial subscriptions.

Computers on Campus 55 computers available on campus for general student use. At least one staffed computer lab available.

Student Life *Housing:* college housing not available. *Activities and Organizations:* student-run newspaper, Student Nurses Association, Student Government Association, Phi Theta Kappa, Students Against Substance Abuse. *Campus security:* 24-hour patrols. *Student services:* personal/psychological counseling.

Athletics *Intramural sports:* archery M/W, basketball M/W, bowling M/W, football M/W, golf M/W, tennis M/W, volleyball M/W.

Costs (2005–06) *Tuition:* state resident $1632 full-time, $68 per credit part-time; nonresident $5136 full-time, $214 per credit part-time. Full-time tuition and fees vary according to course load. Part-time tuition and fees vary according to course load. *Required fees:* $118 full-time, $5 per credit part-time. *Payment plans:* installment, deferred payment. *Waivers:* senior citizens.

Financial Aid Of all full-time matriculated undergraduates who enrolled in 2003, 35 Federal Work-Study jobs (averaging $1212). 15 state and other part-time jobs (averaging $1667).

Applying *Options:* early admission. *Required for some:* high school transcript. *Application deadline:* rolling (freshmen), rolling (transfers). *Notification:* continuous (freshmen).

Admissions Contact Ms. Rita Dunston, Registrar, Germanna Community College, 10000 Germanna Point Drive, Fredericksburg, VA 22408. *Phone:* 540-727-3034. *Fax:* 540-710-2101.

ITT TECHNICAL INSTITUTE
Chantilly, Virginia

- **Proprietary** 2-year, founded 2002, part of ITT Educational Services, Inc
- **Calendar** quarters
- **Degree** associate
- **Coed**

Standardized Tests *Required:* (for admission).

Costs (2004–05) *Tuition:* Please see school catalog for specific information.

Applying *Options:* deferred entrance. *Application fee:* $100. *Required:* high school transcript, interview. *Recommended:* letters of recommendation.

Admissions Contact Foy Ann Roach, Director of Recruitment, ITT Technical Institute, 14420 Albemarle Point Place, Chantilly, VA 20151. *Phone:* 703-263-2541. *Toll-free phone:* 888-895-8324. *Fax:* 703-263-0846.

ITT TECHNICAL INSTITUTE
Norfolk, Virginia

- **Proprietary** primarily 2-year, founded 1988, part of ITT Educational Services, Inc
- **Calendar** quarters
- **Degrees** associate and bachelor's
- **Suburban** 2-acre campus
- **Coed**

Standardized Tests *Required:* Wonderlic aptitude test (for admission).

Costs (2004–05) *Tuition:* Please see school catalog for specific information.

Financial Aid Of all full-time matriculated undergraduates who enrolled in 2003, 3 Federal Work-Study jobs (averaging $5000).

Applying *Options:* deferred entrance. *Application fee:* $100. *Required:* high school transcript, interview. *Recommended:* letters of recommendation.

Admissions Contact Mr. Jack Keesee, Director of Recruitment, ITT Technical Institute, 863 Glenrock Road, Norfolk, VA 23502. *Phone:* 757-466-1260. *Toll-free phone:* 888-253-8324. *Fax:* 757-466-7630.

ITT TECHNICAL INSTITUTE
Richmond, Virginia

- **Proprietary** primarily 2-year, part of ITT Educational Services, Inc
- **Calendar** quarters
- **Degrees** associate and bachelor's
- **Coed**

Standardized Tests *Required:* Wonderlic aptitude test (for admission).

Costs (2004–05) *Tuition:* Please see school catalog for specific information.

Applying *Options:* deferred entrance. *Application fee:* $100. *Required:* high school transcript, interview. *Recommended:* letters of recommendation.

Admissions Contact Mr. Marc Wright, Director of Recruitment, ITT Technical Institute, 300 Gateway Centre Parkway, Richmond, VA 23235. *Phone:* 804-330-4992. *Toll-free phone:* 888-330-4888. *Fax:* 804-330-4993.

ITT TECHNICAL INSTITUTE
Springfield, Virginia

- **Proprietary** primarily 2-year, founded 2002, part of ITT Educational Services, Inc
- **Calendar** quarters
- **Degrees** associate and bachelor's
- **Coed**

Standardized Tests *Required:* Wonderlic aptitude test (for admission).

Costs (2004–05) *Tuition:* Please see school catalog for specific information.

Applying *Options:* deferred entrance. *Application fee:* $100. *Required:* high school transcript, interview. *Recommended:* letters of recommendation.

Admissions Contact Mr. Paul M. Ochoa, Director of Recruitment, ITT Technical Institute, 7300 Boston Boulevard, Springfield, VA 22153. *Phone:* 703-440-9535. *Toll-free phone:* 866-817-8324. *Fax:* 703-440-9561.

JOHN TYLER COMMUNITY COLLEGE
Chester, Virginia

- **State-supported** 2-year, founded 1967, part of Virginia Community College System
- **Calendar** semesters
- **Degree** certificates and associate
- **Suburban** 160-acre campus with easy access to Richmond

John Tyler Community College (continued)
■ **Endowment** $2.0 million
■ **Coed,** 6,054 undergraduate students, 24% full-time, 63% women, 37% men

Undergraduates 1,428 full-time, 4,626 part-time. Students come from 38 states and territories, 2% are from out of state, 25% African American, 3% Asian American or Pacific Islander, 2% Hispanic American, 0.5% Native American, 0.3% international, 15% transferred in.
Freshmen *Admission:* 378 enrolled.
Faculty *Total:* 402, 14% full-time. *Student/faculty ratio:* 27:1.
Majors Administrative assistant and secretarial science; architectural engineering technology; biology/biotechnology laboratory technician; business/commerce; electrical, electronics and communications engineering; environmental engineering technology; funeral service and mortuary science; human services; liberal arts and sciences/liberal studies; management information systems; mechanical engineering/mechanical technology; nursing (registered nurse training); physical therapy; safety/security technology.
Academic Programs *Special study options:* academic remediation for entering students, adult/continuing education programs, advanced placement credit, distance learning, external degree program, honors programs, off-campus study, part-time degree program, services for LD students, study abroad, summer session for credit. *ROTC:* Army (c).
Library John Tyler Community College Learning Resource and Technology Center with 49,393 titles, 179 serial subscriptions, 1,544 audiovisual materials, an OPAC, a Web page.
Computers on Campus 465 computers available on campus for general student use. A campuswide network can be accessed from off campus. Internet access, at least one staffed computer lab available.
Student Life *Housing:* college housing not available. *Campus security:* 24-hour patrols. *Student services:* personal/psychological counseling.
Athletics *Intramural sports:* golf M/W, softball M/W, tennis M/W, volleyball M/W.
Costs (2005–06) *Tuition:* state resident $1708 full-time, $71 per credit part-time; nonresident $5264 full-time, $219 per credit part-time. *Required fees:* $50 full-time, $25 per term part-time.
Applying *Options:* common application, early admission, deferred entrance. *Recommended:* high school transcript. *Application deadline:* rolling (freshmen). *Notification:* continuous (freshmen).
Admissions Contact Ms. Joy James, Registrar and Enrollment Services Coordinator, John Tyler Community College, 13101 Jefferson Davis Highway, Chester, VA 23831. *Phone:* 804-796-4150. *Toll-free phone:* 800-552-3490. *Fax:* 804-796-4163.

J. SARGEANT REYNOLDS COMMUNITY COLLEGE
Richmond, Virginia

■ **State-supported** 2-year, founded 1972, part of Virginia Community College System
■ **Calendar** semesters
■ **Degree** certificates and associate
■ **Suburban** 207-acre campus
■ **Endowment** $2.3 million
■ **Coed,** 11,678 undergraduate students, 25% full-time, 61% women, 39% men

Undergraduates 2,871 full-time, 8,807 part-time. 36% African American, 3% Asian American or Pacific Islander, 2% Hispanic American, 0.6% Native American, 0.4% international.
Freshmen *Admission:* 1,252 enrolled.
Faculty *Total:* 567, 21% full-time. *Student/faculty ratio:* 22:1.
Majors Accounting technology and bookkeeping; administrative assistant and secretarial science; architectural engineering technology; biological and physical sciences; business administration and management; child care and support services management; civil engineering technology; clinical/medical laboratory technology; community organization and advocacy; computer and information sciences; computer and information sciences related; computer engineering technology; computer programming; computer programming related; construction engineering technology; criminal justice/safety; culinary arts; data processing and data processing technology; dental laboratory technology; dietetics; electrical, electronic and communications engineering technology; engineering; executive assistant/executive secretary; fashion merchandising; fire science; hospitality administration; hotel/motel administration; information technology; landscaping and groundskeeping; legal assistant/paralegal; liberal arts and sciences/liberal studies; marketing/marketing management; music; nursing (registered nurse training); occupational therapist assistant; opticianry; ornamental horticulture; respiratory care therapy; social sciences.
Academic Programs *Special study options:* academic remediation for entering students, adult/continuing education programs, advanced placement credit,

distance learning, English as a second language, independent study, internships, off-campus study, part-time degree program, services for LD students, summer session for credit.
Library Learning Resource Center plus 2 others with 80,736 titles, 465 serial subscriptions, 1,575 audiovisual materials, an OPAC, a Web page.
Computers on Campus 1069 computers available on campus for general student use. A campuswide network can be accessed from off campus that provide access to telephone registration for returning students. Internet access, online (class) registration, at least one staffed computer lab available.
Student Life *Housing:* college housing not available. *Activities and Organizations:* drama/theater group, choral group, Phi Theta Kappa, Student Nurses Association, SGA, Phi Beta Lambda. *Campus security:* security during open hours. *Student services:* personal/psychological counseling.
Costs (2004–05) *Tuition:* state resident $2123 full-time, $71 per credit hour part-time; nonresident $6546 full-time, $218 per credit hour part-time. *Required fees:* $9 per credit hour part-time. *Payment plan:* installment. *Waivers:* senior citizens.
Financial Aid Of all full-time matriculated undergraduates who enrolled in 2003, 527 Federal Work-Study jobs (averaging $1711).
Applying *Options:* electronic application. *Required:* high school transcript. *Required for some:* interview. *Application deadline:* rolling (freshmen), rolling (transfers). *Notification:* continuous (freshmen).
Admissions Contact Ms. Karen Pettis-Walden, Acting Director of Admissions and Records, J. Sargeant Reynolds Community College, PO Box 85622, Richmond, VA 23285-5622. *Phone:* 804-371-3029. *Fax:* 804-371-3650. *E-mail:* kpettis-walden@jsr.vccs.edu.

LORD FAIRFAX COMMUNITY COLLEGE
Middletown, Virginia

■ **State-supported** 2-year, founded 1969, part of Virginia Community College System
■ **Calendar** semesters
■ **Degree** certificates and associate
■ **Rural** 100-acre campus with easy access to Washington, DC
■ **Coed**

Student Life *Campus security:* late-night transport/escort service.
Financial Aid Of all full-time matriculated undergraduates who enrolled in 2003, 28 Federal Work-Study jobs (averaging $1600).
Applying *Options:* early admission. *Recommended:* high school transcript.
Admissions Contact Ms. Cynthia Bambara, Vice President of Student Success, Lord Fairfax Community College, 173 Skirmisher Lane, Middletown, VA 22645. *Phone:* 540-868-7105. *Toll-free phone:* 800-906-5322 Ext. 7107. *Fax:* 540-868-7005. *E-mail:* lfsmitt@lfcc.edu.

MEDICAL CAREERS INSTITUTE
Newport News, Virginia

Admissions Contact 1001 Omni Boulevard, Suite 200, Newport News, VA 23606.

MEDICAL CAREERS INSTITUTE
Richmond, Virginia

Admissions Contact David K. Mayle, Director of Admissions, Medical Careers Institute, 800 Moorefield Park Drive, Suite 302, Richmond, VA 23236-3659. *Phone:* 804-521-0400.

MEDICAL CAREERS INSTITUTE
Virginia Beach, Virginia

Admissions Contact 5501 Greenwich Road, Virginia Beach, VA 23462.

MOUNTAIN EMPIRE COMMUNITY COLLEGE
Big Stone Gap, Virginia

■ **State-supported** 2-year, founded 1972, part of Virginia Community College System
■ **Calendar** semesters
■ **Degree** certificates, diplomas, and associate
■ **Small-town** campus with easy access to Kingsport
■ **Coed**

Faculty *Student/faculty ratio:* 18:1.
Student Life *Campus security:* 24-hour emergency response devices and patrols.
Standardized Tests *Required:* ACT ASSET, ACT COMPASS (for placement).

Costs (2004–05) *Tuition:* state resident $2516 full-time, $70 per credit hour part-time; nonresident $7823 full-time, $217 per credit hour part-time.
Financial Aid Of all full-time matriculated undergraduates who enrolled in 2003, 150 Federal Work-Study jobs (averaging $1200). 30 state and other part-time jobs (averaging $650).
Applying *Options:* early admission, deferred entrance. *Required:* high school transcript. *Required for some:* minimum 2.0 GPA.
Admissions Contact Mr. Perry Carroll, Director of Enrollment Services, Mountain Empire Community College, 3441 Mountain Empire Road, Big Stone Gap, VA 24219. *Phone:* 276-523-2400 Ext. 219. *E-mail:* pcarroll@me.vccs.edu.

NATIONAL COLLEGE OF BUSINESS & TECHNOLOGY
Bluefield, Virginia

- **Proprietary** 2-year, founded 1886, part of National College of Business and Technology
- **Calendar** quarters
- **Degree** diplomas and associate
- **Small-town** campus
- **Coed,** 203 undergraduate students

Faculty *Total:* 21, 10% full-time. *Student/faculty ratio:* 10:1.
Majors Accounting; administrative assistant and secretarial science; business administration and management; computer and information sciences related; medical/clinical assistant.
Academic Programs *Special study options:* advanced placement credit, double majors, honors programs, internships, part-time degree program, services for LD students, summer session for credit.
Computers on Campus 35 computers available on campus for general student use. A campuswide network can be accessed. Internet access, at least one staffed computer lab available.
Student Life *Housing:* college housing not available.
Costs (2005–06) *Tuition:* $6408 full-time, $178 per credit hour part-time. Full-time tuition and fees vary according to course load. Part-time tuition and fees vary according to course load. *Required fees:* $75 full-time, $15 per term part-time. *Payment plans:* installment, deferred payment. *Waivers:* employees or children of employees.
Financial Aid Of all full-time matriculated undergraduates who enrolled in 2003, 5 Federal Work-Study jobs.
Applying *Options:* electronic application. *Application fee:* $30. *Recommended:* interview. *Application deadline:* rolling (freshmen), rolling (transfers).
Admissions Contact Ms. Jennifer Hooper, Admissions Representative, National College of Business & Technology, 100 Logan Street, Bluefield, VA 24605. *Phone:* 540-326-6321. *Toll-free phone:* 800-664-1886. *Fax:* 540-322-5731. *E-mail:* adm@educorp.edu.

NATIONAL COLLEGE OF BUSINESS & TECHNOLOGY
Charlottesville, Virginia

- **Proprietary** 2-year, founded 1975, part of National College of Business and Technology
- **Calendar** quarters
- **Degree** certificates, diplomas, and associate
- **Small-town** campus with easy access to Richmond
- **Coed,** 163 undergraduate students

Faculty *Total:* 14, 14% full-time. *Student/faculty ratio:* 12:1.
Majors Accounting; administrative assistant and secretarial science; business/commerce; computer and information sciences related; medical/clinical assistant.
Academic Programs *Special study options:* advanced placement credit, double majors, honors programs, internships, part-time degree program, services for LD students, summer session for credit.
Computers on Campus 35 computers available on campus for general student use. A campuswide network can be accessed. Internet access, at least one staffed computer lab available.
Student Life *Housing:* college housing not available.
Costs (2005–06) *Tuition:* $6408 full-time, $178 per credit hour part-time. Full-time tuition and fees vary according to course load. Part-time tuition and fees vary according to course load. *Required fees:* $75 full-time, $15 per term part-time. *Payment plans:* installment, deferred payment. *Waivers:* employees or children of employees.
Financial Aid Of all full-time matriculated undergraduates who enrolled in 2003, 4 Federal Work-Study jobs.

Applying *Options:* electronic application. *Application fee:* $30. *Required for some:* high school transcript. *Recommended:* interview. *Application deadline:* rolling (freshmen), rolling (transfers).
Admissions Contact Ms. Adrienne D. Granitz, Campus Director, National College of Business & Technology, 1819 Emmet Street, Charlottesville, VA 22903. *Phone:* 434-295-0136. *Toll-free phone:* 800-664-1886. *Fax:* 434-979-8061. *E-mail:* mthomas@educorp.edu.

NATIONAL COLLEGE OF BUSINESS & TECHNOLOGY
Danville, Virginia

Admissions Contact Ms. Amy Bracey, Campus Director, National College of Business & Technology, 734 Main Street, Danville, VA 24541. *Phone:* 434-793-6822. *Toll-free phone:* 800-664-1886. *Fax:* 434-793-3634. *E-mail:* adm@educorp.edu.

NATIONAL COLLEGE OF BUSINESS & TECHNOLOGY
Harrisonburg, Virginia

- **Proprietary** 2-year, founded 1988, part of National College of Business and Technology
- **Calendar** quarters
- **Degree** diplomas and associate
- **Small-town** campus
- **Coed,** 233 undergraduate students

Faculty *Total:* 20, 10% full-time. *Student/faculty ratio:* 12:1.
Majors Accounting; administrative assistant and secretarial science; business administration and management; computer and information sciences related; medical/clinical assistant.
Academic Programs *Special study options:* advanced placement credit, double majors, honors programs, internships, part-time degree program, services for LD students, summer session for credit.
Computers on Campus 35 computers available on campus for general student use. A campuswide network can be accessed. Internet access, at least one staffed computer lab available.
Student Life *Housing:* college housing not available.
Costs (2005–06) *Tuition:* $6408 full-time, $178 per credit hour part-time. Full-time tuition and fees vary according to course load. Part-time tuition and fees vary according to course load. *Required fees:* $75 full-time, $15 per term part-time. *Payment plans:* installment, deferred payment. *Waivers:* employees or children of employees.
Financial Aid Of all full-time matriculated undergraduates who enrolled in 2003, 2 Federal Work-Study jobs.
Applying *Options:* electronic application. *Application fee:* $30. *Required for some:* high school transcript. *Recommended:* interview. *Application deadline:* rolling (freshmen), rolling (transfers). *Notification:* continuous (freshmen).
Admissions Contact Jack Evey, Campus Director, National College of Business & Technology, 51 B Burgess Road, Harrisonburg, VA 22801. *Phone:* 540-432-0943. *Toll-free phone:* 800-664-1886. *Fax:* 540-432-1133. *E-mail:* adm@educorp.edu.

NATIONAL COLLEGE OF BUSINESS & TECHNOLOGY
Lynchburg, Virginia

- **Proprietary** 2-year, founded 1979, part of National College of Business and Technology
- **Calendar** quarters
- **Degree** diplomas and associate
- **Small-town** 2-acre campus
- **Coed,** 383 undergraduate students

Undergraduates Students come from 15 other countries.
Faculty *Total:* 33, 3% full-time. *Student/faculty ratio:* 12:1.
Majors Accounting; administrative assistant and secretarial science; business administration and management; computer and information sciences related; medical/clinical assistant.
Academic Programs *Special study options:* advanced placement credit, double majors, honors programs, internships, part-time degree program, services for LD students, summer session for credit.
Library 10 serial subscriptions.
Computers on Campus 35 computers available on campus for general student use. A campuswide network can be accessed. Internet access, at least one staffed computer lab available.

National College of Business & Technology (continued)

Student Life *Housing:* college housing not available.

Costs (2005–06) *Tuition:* $6408 full-time, $178 per credit hour part-time. Full-time tuition and fees vary according to course load. Part-time tuition and fees vary according to course load. *Required fees:* $75 full-time, $15 per term part-time. *Payment plans:* installment, deferred payment. *Waivers:* employees or children of employees.

Financial Aid Of all full-time matriculated undergraduates who enrolled in 2003, 3 Federal Work-Study jobs.

Applying *Options:* electronic application. *Application fee:* $30. *Required for some:* high school transcript. *Recommended:* interview. *Application deadline:* rolling (freshmen), rolling (transfers).

Admissions Contact Mr. George Wheelous, Admissions Representative, National College of Business & Technology, 104 Candlewood Court, Lynchburg, VA 24502. *Phone:* 804-239-3500. *Toll-free phone:* 800-664-1886. *Fax:* 434-239-3948. *E-mail:* adm@educorp.edu.

NATIONAL COLLEGE OF BUSINESS & TECHNOLOGY
Martinsville, Virginia

- **Proprietary** 2-year, founded 1975, part of National College of Business and Technology
- **Calendar** quarters
- **Degree** diplomas and associate
- **Small-town** campus
- **Coed**, 383 undergraduate students

Faculty *Total:* 15, 13% full-time. *Student/faculty ratio:* 12:1.

Majors Accounting; administrative assistant and secretarial science; business administration and management; computer and information sciences related.

Academic Programs *Special study options:* advanced placement credit, double majors, honors programs, internships, part-time degree program, services for LD students, summer session for credit.

Computers on Campus 35 computers available on campus for general student use. A campuswide network can be accessed. Internet access, at least one staffed computer lab available.

Student Life *Housing:* college housing not available.

Costs (2005–06) *Tuition:* $6408 full-time, $178 per credit hour part-time. *Required fees:* $75 full-time, $15 per term part-time.

Financial Aid Of all full-time matriculated undergraduates who enrolled in 2003, 2 Federal Work-Study jobs.

Applying *Options:* electronic application. *Application fee:* $30. *Required for some:* high school transcript. *Recommended:* interview. *Application deadline:* rolling (freshmen), rolling (transfers).

Admissions Contact Mr. John Scott, Campus Director, National College of Business & Technology, 10 Church Street, Martinsville, VA 24114. *Phone:* 276-632-5621. *Toll-free phone:* 800-664-1886 (in-state); 800-664-1866 (out-of-state). *Fax:* 276-632-7915. *E-mail:* adm@educorp.edu.

NATIONAL COLLEGE OF BUSINESS & TECHNOLOGY
Salem, Virginia

- **Proprietary** primarily 2-year, founded 1886, part of National College of Business and Technology
- **Calendar** quarters
- **Degrees** certificates, diplomas, associate, bachelor's, and master's
- **Urban** 3-acre campus
- **Coed**, 756 undergraduate students

Undergraduates Students come from 15 other countries, 24% are from out of state. *Retention:* 70% of 2002 full-time freshmen returned.

Freshmen *Admission:* 346 applied, 346 admitted.

Faculty *Total:* 75, 17% full-time. *Student/faculty ratio:* 12:1.

Majors Accounting; accounting technology and bookkeeping; administrative assistant and secretarial science; business/commerce; computer and information sciences; executive assistant/executive secretary; hospitality administration; hotel/motel administration; marketing/marketing management; medical/clinical assistant; office management; tourism and travel services marketing.

Academic Programs *Special study options:* academic remediation for entering students, advanced placement credit, double majors, internships, part-time degree program, summer session for credit.

Library Main Library plus 1 other with 25,867 titles, 40 serial subscriptions.

Computers on Campus 35 computers available on campus for general student use. A campuswide network can be accessed. Internet access, at least one staffed computer lab available.

Student Life *Housing:* college housing not available. *Options:* coed.

Costs (2005–06) *Tuition:* $6408 full-time, $178 per credit hour part-time. *Required fees:* $75 full-time, $15 per term part-time.

Financial Aid Of all full-time matriculated undergraduates who enrolled in 2003, 6 Federal Work-Study jobs.

Applying *Application fee:* $30. *Required:* high school transcript. *Recommended:* interview. *Application deadline:* rolling (freshmen), rolling (transfers). *Notification:* continuous (freshmen).

Admissions Contact Ms. Bunnie Hancock, Admissions Representative, National College of Business & Technology, PO Box 6400, Roanoke, VA 24017. *Phone:* 540-986-1800. *Toll-free phone:* 800-664-1886. *Fax:* 540-986-1344. *E-mail:* market@educorp.edu.

NEW RIVER COMMUNITY COLLEGE
Dublin, Virginia

- **State-supported** 2-year, founded 1969, part of Virginia Community College System
- **Calendar** semesters
- **Degree** certificates, diplomas, and associate
- **Rural** 100-acre campus
- **Endowment** $1.9 million
- **Coed**

Faculty *Student/faculty ratio:* 22:1.

Student Life *Campus security:* 24-hour patrols.

Costs (2004–05) *Tuition:* state resident $1911 full-time, $64 per semester hour part-time; nonresident $6290 full-time, $210 per semester hour part-time. Full-time tuition and fees vary according to course load. Part-time tuition and fees vary according to course load. *Required fees:* $153 full-time, $5 per semester hour part-time.

Financial Aid Of all full-time matriculated undergraduates who enrolled in 2003, 150 Federal Work-Study jobs (averaging $2000).

Applying *Options:* early admission, deferred entrance. *Required for some:* high school transcript.

Admissions Contact Ms. Margaret G. Taylor, Coordinator of Admissions and Records and Student Services, New River Community College, PO Box 1127, 5251 College Drive, Dublin, VA 24084. *Phone:* 540-674-3600 Ext. 4205. *Fax:* 540-674-3644. *E-mail:* nrtaylm@nr.cc.va.us.

NORTHERN VIRGINIA COMMUNITY COLLEGE
Annandale, Virginia

- **State-supported** 2-year, founded 1965, part of Virginia Community College System
- **Calendar** semesters
- **Degree** certificates and associate
- **Suburban** 435-acre campus with easy access to Washington, DC
- **Endowment** $1.1 million
- **Coed**, 39,353 undergraduate students

Undergraduates 2% are from out of state, 15% African American, 12% Asian American or Pacific Islander, 10% Hispanic American, 2% Native American, 4% international.

Faculty *Total:* 1,606, 36% full-time.

Majors Accounting; administrative assistant and secretarial science; airline pilot and flight crew; applied art; architectural engineering technology; art; art history, criticism and conservation; automobile/automotive mechanics technology; avionics maintenance technology; biological and physical sciences; business administration and management; civil engineering technology; clinical/medical laboratory technology; commercial and advertising art; computer graphics; computer science; criminal justice/law enforcement administration; criminal justice/police science; dental hygiene; dietetics; electrical, electronic and communications engineering technology; emergency medical technology (EMT paramedic); engineering; fire science; gerontology; health information/medical records administration; heating, air conditioning, ventilation and refrigeration maintenance technology; horticultural science; hotel/motel administration; human services; industrial radiologic technology; information science/studies; interior design; international business/trade/commerce; kindergarten/preschool education; legal assistant/paralegal; liberal arts and sciences/liberal studies; marketing/marketing management; mathematics; mechanical engineering/mechanical technology; music; nursing (registered nurse training); parks, recreation and leisure; photography; physical therapy; pre-engineering; psychology; purchasing, procurement/acquisitions and contracts management; religious studies; respiratory care therapy; special products marketing; speech and rhetoric; substance abuse/addiction counseling; tourism and travel services management; veterinary technology.

Academic Programs *Special study options:* academic remediation for entering students, adult/continuing education programs, advanced placement credit, cooperative education, distance learning, double majors, English as a second language, external degree program, honors programs, part-time degree program, services for LD students, study abroad, summer session for credit.
Library 228,009 titles, 1,949 serial subscriptions, 12,227 audiovisual materials, an OPAC, a Web page.
Computers on Campus 2000 computers available on campus for general student use. A campuswide network can be accessed. Internet access, at least one staffed computer lab available.
Student Life *Housing:* college housing not available. *Activities and Organizations:* student-run newspaper, television station. *Campus security:* 24-hour emergency response devices, campus police.
Athletics *Intramural sports:* basketball M/W, football M/W, soccer M/W, volleyball M/W.
Costs (2004–05) *Tuition:* state resident $1528 full-time, $64 per credit hour part-time; nonresident $5031 full-time, $210 per credit hour part-time. *Required fees:* $96 full-time, $4 per credit hour part-time.
Applying *Options:* common application, early admission, deferred entrance. *Required for some:* high school transcript. *Application deadline:* rolling (freshmen), rolling (transfers). *Notification:* continuous (freshmen).
Admissions Contact Dr. Max L. Bassett, Dean of Academic and Student Services, Northern Virginia Community College, 4001 Wakefield Chapel Road, Annandale, VA 22003-3796. *Phone:* 703-323-3195.

PARKS COLLEGE
Arlington, Virginia

- **Proprietary** 2-year, founded 2001
- **Calendar** quarters
- **Degree** certificates and associate
- **Urban** campus
- **Coed**

Admissions Contact Lachelle Green, Director of Admissions, Parks College, 801 North Quincy Street, Arlington, VA 22203. *Phone:* 703-248-8887.

PATRICK HENRY COMMUNITY COLLEGE
Martinsville, Virginia

- **State-supported** 2-year, founded 1962, part of Virginia Community College System
- **Calendar** semesters
- **Degree** associate
- **Rural** 137-acre campus
- **Coed,** 3,456 undergraduate students

Undergraduates Students come from 3 states and territories. *Retention:* 48% of 2002 full-time freshmen returned.
Faculty *Total:* 139, 28% full-time.
Majors Accounting; administrative assistant and secretarial science; biological and physical sciences; business administration and management; computer programming; computer programming related; computer systems networking and telecommunications; data entry/microcomputer applications related; data processing and data processing technology; electrical, electronic and communications engineering technology; engineering technology; industrial technology; information technology; liberal arts and sciences/liberal studies; nursing (registered nurse training).
Academic Programs *Special study options:* academic remediation for entering students, adult/continuing education programs, advanced placement credit, cooperative education, English as a second language, internships, part-time degree program, services for LD students, summer session for credit.
Library Lester Library with 26,160 titles, 259 serial subscriptions, an OPAC, a Web page.
Computers on Campus 505 computers available on campus for general student use. A campuswide network can be accessed from off campus. At least one staffed computer lab available.
Student Life *Housing:* college housing not available. *Activities and Organizations:* drama/theater group, Student Government Association, Student Support Services, Phi Theta Kappa, Gospel Choir, Black Student Association. *Campus security:* 24-hour emergency response devices and patrols, late-night transport/escort service.
Athletics *Intramural sports:* baseball M, basketball M/W, soccer M, table tennis M/W, tennis M/W, volleyball M/W, weight lifting M/W.
Standardized Tests *Required:* ACT ASSET (for placement).
Costs (2005–06) *Tuition:* state resident $1632 full-time, $68 per credit hour part-time; nonresident $5136 full-time, $214 per credit hour part-time. *Required fees:* $81 full-time, $3 per credit hour part-time, $5 per term part-time.

Financial Aid Of all full-time matriculated undergraduates who enrolled in 2003, 41 Federal Work-Study jobs (averaging $2000).
Applying *Options:* early admission, deferred entrance. *Required:* high school transcript. *Application deadline:* rolling (freshmen), rolling (transfers). *Notification:* continuous (freshmen).
Admissions Contact Dr. Joanne B. Whitley, Vice President of Academic and Student Development, Patrick Henry Community College, PO Box 5311, 645 Patriot Avenue, Martinsville, VA 24115. *Phone:* 276-656-0315. *Toll-free phone:* 800-232-7997. *Fax:* 276-656-0247. *E-mail:* qvalentine@ph.vccs.edu.

PAUL D. CAMP COMMUNITY COLLEGE
Franklin, Virginia

- **State-supported** 2-year, founded 1971, part of Virginia Community College System
- **Calendar** semesters
- **Degree** certificates and associate
- **Small-town** 99-acre campus
- **Endowment** $16,121
- **Coed**

Faculty *Student/faculty ratio:* 17:1.
Student Life *Campus security:* security staff until 7 p.m.
Standardized Tests *Required:* ACT COMPASS (for placement).
Costs (2004–05) *Tuition:* state resident $1883 full-time, $63 per credit hour part-time; nonresident $6306 full-time, $210 per credit hour part-time. Full-time tuition and fees vary according to course load. Part-time tuition and fees vary according to course load. *Required fees:* $95 full-time, $3 per credit hour part-time.
Financial Aid Of all full-time matriculated undergraduates who enrolled in 2003, 30 Federal Work-Study jobs (averaging $2000).
Applying *Options:* deferred entrance. *Required:* high school transcript.
Admissions Contact Ms. Monette Williams, Acting Director of Admissions and Records, Paul D. Camp Community College, PO Box 737, 100 North College Drive, Franklin, VA 23851-0737. *Phone:* 757-569-6725. *Fax:* 757-569-6795. *E-mail:* jstandahl@pc.cc.va.us.

PIEDMONT VIRGINIA COMMUNITY COLLEGE
Charlottesville, Virginia

- **State-supported** 2-year, founded 1972, part of Virginia Community College System
- **Calendar** semesters
- **Degree** certificates and associate
- **Suburban** 114-acre campus with easy access to Richmond
- **Coed,** 4,358 undergraduate students, 25% full-time, 61% women, 39% men

Undergraduates 1,077 full-time, 3,281 part-time. Students come from 12 states and territories, 1% are from out of state, 14% African American, 3% Asian American or Pacific Islander, 2% Hispanic American, 0.5% Native American, 0.8% international, 46% transferred in.
Freshmen *Admission:* 464 admitted, 464 enrolled.
Faculty *Total:* 205, 26% full-time, 11% with terminal degrees. *Student/faculty ratio:* 20:1.
Majors Accounting; administrative assistant and secretarial science; art; automobile/automotive mechanics technology; biological and physical sciences; business administration and management; computer programming; construction management; criminal justice/law enforcement administration; criminal justice/police science; data processing and data processing technology; dramatic/theatre arts; education; electrical, electronic and communications engineering technology; liberal arts and sciences/liberal studies; marketing/marketing management; nursing (registered nurse training); pre-engineering.
Academic Programs *Special study options:* academic remediation for entering students, adult/continuing education programs, advanced placement credit, cooperative education, distance learning, English as a second language, honors programs, independent study, internships, part-time degree program, services for LD students, summer session for credit. *ROTC:* Army (c).
Library Jessup Library with 72,574 titles, 209 serial subscriptions, 10,254 audiovisual materials, an OPAC, a Web page.
Computers on Campus 60 computers available on campus for general student use. A campuswide network can be accessed from off campus that provide access to e-mail. Internet access, online (class) registration, at least one staffed computer lab available.
Student Life *Housing:* college housing not available. *Activities and Organizations:* drama/theater group, student-run newspaper, choral group, Phi Theta Kappa, Black Student Alliance, Science Club, Masquers, Christian Fellowship Club. *Campus security:* 24-hour patrols.

Piedmont Virginia Community College (continued)

Athletics *Intramural sports:* basketball M/W, bowling M/W, football M/W, golf M/W, lacrosse M/W, skiing (cross-country) M/W, soccer M/W, softball M/W, tennis M/W, volleyball M/W, weight lifting M/W.

Standardized Tests *Recommended:* ACT (for placement), SAT Subject Tests (for placement).

Costs (2005–06) *Tuition:* state resident $2040 full-time, $68 per credit part-time; nonresident $6420 full-time, $214 per credit part-time. Full-time tuition and fees vary according to course load. Part-time tuition and fees vary according to course load. *Required fees:* $134 full-time, $4 per credit part-time, $49 per term part-time. *Waivers:* senior citizens.

Financial Aid Of all full-time matriculated undergraduates who enrolled in 2003, 50 Federal Work-Study jobs.

Applying *Options:* common application, electronic application, early admission. *Required for some:* high school transcript. *Application deadline:* 8/26 (transfers). *Notification:* continuous (freshmen).

Admissions Contact Ms. Mary Lee Walsh, Director of Student Services, Piedmont Virginia Community College, 501 College Drive, Charlottesville, VA 22902-7589. *Phone:* 434-961-5400. *Fax:* 434-961-5425.

RAPPAHANNOCK COMMUNITY COLLEGE
Glenns, Virginia

Admissions Contact Ms. Wilnet Willis, Admissions and Records Officer, Rappahannock Community College, Glenns Campus, 12745 College Drive, Glenns, VA 23149-2616. *Phone:* 804-758-6742. *Fax:* 804-758-3852.

RICHARD BLAND COLLEGE OF THE COLLEGE OF WILLIAM AND MARY
Petersburg, Virginia

- **State-supported** 2-year, founded 1961, part of College of William and Mary
- **Calendar** semesters
- **Degree** associate
- **Rural** 712-acre campus with easy access to Richmond
- **Endowment** $377,780
- **Coed,** 1,409 undergraduate students, 55% full-time, 67% women, 33% men

Undergraduates 778 full-time, 631 part-time. Students come from 8 states and territories, 1% are from out of state, 19% African American, 2% Asian American or Pacific Islander, 2% Hispanic American, 0.6% Native American, 7% transferred in. *Retention:* 64% of 2002 full-time freshmen returned.

Freshmen *Admission:* 651 applied, 552 admitted, 462 enrolled. *Average high school GPA:* 2.7. *Test scores:* SAT verbal scores over 500: 34%; SAT math scores over 500: 29%; SAT verbal scores over 600: 2%; SAT math scores over 600: 2%.

Faculty *Total:* 61, 54% full-time, 31% with terminal degrees. *Student/faculty ratio:* 22:1.

Majors Liberal arts and sciences/liberal studies.

Academic Programs *Special study options:* academic remediation for entering students, accelerated degree program, advanced placement credit, part-time degree program, services for LD students, summer session for credit. *ROTC:* Army (c).

Library Richard Bland College Library with 91,000 titles, 9,000 serial subscriptions, 2,400 audiovisual materials, an OPAC, a Web page.

Computers on Campus 128 computers available on campus for general student use. A campuswide network can be accessed from off campus that provide access to e-mail, Blackboard. Internet access, at least one staffed computer lab available.

Student Life *Housing:* college housing not available. *Activities and Organizations:* drama/theater group, student-run newspaper, choral group, RBC Newspaper, Multicultural Alliance, student government, Spanish Club, Biology Club. *Campus security:* 24-hour patrols.

Athletics *Intramural sports:* basketball M/W, cheerleading M/W, golf M/W, tennis M/W, volleyball M/W.

Standardized Tests *Required:* ACT COMPASS (for admission). *Recommended:* SAT or ACT (for admission).

Costs (2005–06) *Tuition:* state resident $2350 full-time, $91 per credit hour part-time; nonresident $9608 full-time, $398 per credit hour part-time. *Required fees:* $170 full-time, $4 per credit hour part-time.

Financial Aid Of all full-time matriculated undergraduates who enrolled in 2003, 10 Federal Work-Study jobs (averaging $2000).

Applying *Application fee:* $20. *Required:* essay or personal statement, high school transcript, minimum 2.0 GPA. *Required for some:* letters of recommendation, interview. *Application deadline:* 8/15 (freshmen), rolling (transfers). *Notification:* continuous (freshmen).

Admissions Contact Mr. Randy Dean, Director of Admissions and Student Services, Richard Bland College of The College of William and Mary, 11301

Johnson Road, Petersburg, VA 23805-7100. *Phone:* 804-862-6225. *Fax:* 804-862-6490. *E-mail:* admit@rbc.edu.

SOUTHSIDE VIRGINIA COMMUNITY COLLEGE
Alberta, Virginia

- **State-supported** 2-year, founded 1970, part of Virginia Community College System
- **Calendar** semesters
- **Degree** certificates, diplomas, and associate
- **Rural** 207-acre campus
- **Endowment** $428,604
- **Coed,** 4,686 undergraduate students, 29% full-time, 65% women, 35% men

Undergraduates 1,359 full-time, 3,327 part-time. Students come from 3 states and territories, 2 other countries, 1% are from out of state, 46% African American, 0.7% Asian American or Pacific Islander, 0.5% Hispanic American, 0.2% Native American.

Freshmen *Admission:* 380 enrolled.

Faculty *Total:* 295, 24% full-time, 6% with terminal degrees. *Student/faculty ratio:* 17:1.

Majors Administrative assistant and secretarial science; biological and physical sciences; business administration and management; criminal justice/law enforcement administration; drafting and design technology; education; electrical, electronic and communications engineering technology; general studies; human services; information science/studies; information technology; liberal arts and sciences/liberal studies; nursing (registered nurse training); respiratory care therapy.

Academic Programs *Special study options:* academic remediation for entering students, advanced placement credit, distance learning, honors programs, off-campus study, part-time degree program, services for LD students, study abroad, summer session for credit. *ROTC:* Army (c).

Library Julian M. Howell Library plus 1 other with 27,691 titles, 164 serial subscriptions, 1,307 audiovisual materials, an OPAC, a Web page.

Computers on Campus 200 computers available on campus for general student use. A campuswide network can be accessed. Internet access, online (class) registration, at least one staffed computer lab available.

Student Life *Housing:* college housing not available. *Activities and Organizations:* choral group, Student Forum, Phi Theta Kappa, Phi Beta Lambda, Alpha Delta Omega.

Athletics *Intramural sports:* basketball M, softball M/W, table tennis M/W, tennis M/W, volleyball M/W.

Standardized Tests *Required:* ACT ASSET, ACT COMPASS (for placement).

Costs (2005–06) *Tuition:* state resident $2040 full-time, $68 per credit part-time; nonresident $6420 full-time, $214 per credit part-time. Full-time tuition and fees vary according to course load. Part-time tuition and fees vary according to course load. *Required fees:* $155 full-time, $5 per credit part-time. *Payment plan:* installment. *Waivers:* senior citizens.

Applying *Options:* common application, electronic application, deferred entrance. *Required:* high school transcript, interview. *Application deadline:* rolling (freshmen), rolling (transfers). *Notification:* continuous (freshmen).

Admissions Contact Dr. Ronald E. Mattox, Dean of Admissions, Records, and Institutional Research, Southside Virginia Community College, 109 Campus Drive, Alberta, VA 23821. *Phone:* 434-949-1012. *Fax:* 434-949-7863. *E-mail:* rhina.jones@sv.vccs.edu.

SOUTHWEST VIRGINIA COMMUNITY COLLEGE
Richlands, Virginia

Admissions Contact Mr. Roderick B. Moore, Director of Admissions, Records, and Financial Aid, Southwest Virginia Community College, Box SVCC, Richlands, VA 24641. *Phone:* 276-964-7294. *Toll-free phone:* 800-822-7822. *Fax:* 540-964-7716.

TESST COLLEGE OF TECHNOLOGY
Alexandria, Virginia

Admissions Contact Mr. Bob Somers, Director, TESST College of Technology, 6315 Bren Mar Drive, Alexandria, VA 22312-6342. *Phone:* 703-548-4800. *Toll-free phone:* 800-48-TESST.

THOMAS NELSON COMMUNITY COLLEGE
Hampton, Virginia

- **State-supported** 2-year, founded 1968, part of Virginia Community College System
- **Calendar** semesters
- **Degree** certificates, diplomas, and associate
- **Suburban** 85-acre campus with easy access to Virginia Beach
- **Coed**

Student Life *Campus security:* 24-hour patrols.
Standardized Tests *Recommended:* SAT (for placement).
Costs (2004–05) *Tuition:* state resident $1911 full-time, $60 per credit hour part-time; nonresident $6335 full-time, $207 per credit hour part-time. *Required fees:* $116 full-time, $3 per credit hour part-time, $11 per term part-time.
Financial Aid Of all full-time matriculated undergraduates who enrolled in 2003, 110 Federal Work-Study jobs (averaging $3000).
Applying *Options:* early admission, deferred entrance. *Required:* high school transcript.
Admissions Contact Ms. Aileen Girard, Admissions Office Manager, Thomas Nelson Community College, PO Box 9407, 99 Thomas Nelson Drive, Hampton, VA 23670. *Phone:* 757-825-2800.

TIDEWATER COMMUNITY COLLEGE
Norfolk, Virginia

- **State-supported** 2-year, founded 1968, part of Virginia Community College System
- **Calendar** semesters
- **Degree** certificates, diplomas, and associate
- **Suburban** 520-acre campus
- **Coed**

Student Life *Campus security:* 24-hour patrols.
Standardized Tests *Required for some:* ACT COMPASS. *Recommended:* ACT COMPASS.
Costs (2004–05) *Tuition:* state resident $1528 full-time, $64 per credit part-time; nonresident $5032 full-time, $210 per credit part-time. *Required fees:* $204 full-time, $9 per credit part-time.
Financial Aid Of all full-time matriculated undergraduates who enrolled in 2003, 64 Federal Work-Study jobs (averaging $2000).
Applying *Options:* early admission, deferred entrance.
Admissions Contact Mr. Randy Shannon, Associate Dean, Student Services, Tidewater Community College, 7000 College Drive, Portsmouth, VA 23703. *Phone:* 757-822-1068.

TIDEWATER TECH
Virginia Beach, Virginia

Admissions Contact 2697 Dean Drive, Suite 100, Virginia Beach, VA 23452.

VIRGINIA HIGHLANDS COMMUNITY COLLEGE
Abingdon, Virginia

Admissions Contact Mr. David N. Matlock, Director of Admissions, Records, and Financial Aid, Virginia Highlands Community College, PO Box 828, Abingdon, VA 24212-0828. *Phone:* 276-739-2414 Ext. 290. *Toll-free phone:* 877-207-6115. *Fax:* 540-676-5591.

VIRGINIA WESTERN COMMUNITY COLLEGE
Roanoke, Virginia

- **State-supported** 2-year, founded 1966, part of Virginia Community College System
- **Calendar** semesters
- **Degree** certificates and associate
- **Suburban** 70-acre campus
- **Coed**

Faculty *Student/faculty ratio:* 25:1.
Standardized Tests *Recommended:* SAT or ACT (for placement).
Applying *Options:* common application, early admission, deferred entrance. *Required:* high school transcript.

Admissions Contact Admissions Office, Virginia Western Community College, 3095 Colonial Avenue, Roanoke, VA 24038. *Phone:* 540-857-7231. *Fax:* 540-857-6102. *E-mail:* infocenter@vw.vccs.edu.

WYTHEVILLE COMMUNITY COLLEGE
Wytheville, Virginia

Admissions Contact Ms. Sherry K. Dix, Registrar, Wytheville Community College, 1000 East Main Street, Wytheville, VA 24382-3308. *Phone:* 276-223-4755. *Toll-free phone:* 800-468-1195. *Fax:* 276-223-4860. *E-mail:* wcdixxs@wcc.vccs.edu.

WASHINGTON

APOLLO COLLEGE
Spokane, Washington

Admissions Contact Deanna Baker, Campus Director, Apollo College, 1101 North Francher Road, Spokane, WA 99212. *Phone:* 509-532-8888.

THE ART INSTITUTE OF SEATTLE
Seattle, Washington

- **Proprietary** 4-year, founded 1982, part of Education Management Corporation
- **Calendar** quarters
- **Degrees** diplomas, associate, and bachelor's
- **Urban** campus
- **Endowment** $1950
- **Coed**, 2,492 undergraduate students, 52% full-time, 49% women, 51% men
- **Moderately difficult** entrance level, 67% of applicants were admitted

Undergraduates 1,298 full-time, 1,194 part-time. Students come from 49 states and territories, 21 other countries, 17% are from out of state, 3% African American, 8% Asian American or Pacific Islander, 3% Hispanic American, 1% Native American, 6% international, 2% transferred in. *Retention:* 66% of 2002 full-time freshmen returned.
Freshmen *Admission:* 693 applied, 466 admitted, 466 enrolled. *Average high school GPA:* 2.40.
Faculty *Total:* 162, 47% full-time, 13% with terminal degrees. *Student/faculty ratio:* 19:1.
Majors Audio engineering; culinary arts; design and applied arts related; fashion/apparel design; fashion merchandising; film/video and photographic arts related; graphic design; industrial design; interior design; intermedia/multimedia; photography.
Academic Programs *Special study options:* academic remediation for entering students, adult/continuing education programs, honors programs, internships, off-campus study, part-time degree program, services for LD students, summer session for credit.
Library AIS Library plus 1 other with 17,164 titles, 303 serial subscriptions, 5,416 audiovisual materials, an OPAC, a Web page.
Student Life *Housing options:* coed. Campus housing is leased by the school. Freshman campus housing is guaranteed. *Activities and organizations:* Multicultural Affairs Organization, American Society of Interior Designers, DECA, Student Advisory Board. *Campus security:* 24-hour emergency response devices and patrols, controlled dormitory access, patrols by trained security personnel for 17 hours. *Student services:* personal/psychological counseling.
Athletics *Intramural sports:* soccer M/W.
Standardized Tests *Recommended:* SAT or ACT (for admission).
Costs (2005–06) *Tuition:* $16,020 full-time, $369 per credit part-time. *Room only:* $8355. *Payment plans:* installment, deferred payment. *Waivers:* employees or children of employees.
Financial Aid Of all full-time matriculated undergraduates who enrolled in 2003, 18 Federal Work-Study jobs (averaging $1795).
Applying *Options:* electronic application, deferred entrance. *Application fee:* $50. *Required:* essay or personal statement, high school transcript, interview. *Recommended:* 3 letters of recommendation. *Application deadline:* rolling (freshmen). *Notification:* continuous (freshmen).
Admissions Contact Ms. Karen Shea, Director of Admissions, The Art Institute of Seattle, 2323 Elliott Avenue, Seattle, WA 98121-1622. *Phone:* 800-275-2471. *Toll-free phone:* 800-275-2471. *Fax:* 206-269-0275. *E-mail:* adm@ais.edu.

▶ **See page 458 for a narrative description.**

BATES TECHNICAL COLLEGE
Tacoma, Washington

- **State-supported** 2-year, part of Washington State Board for Community and Technical Colleges
- **Calendar** quarters
- **Degree** certificates, diplomas, and associate
- **Urban** campus with easy access to Seattle
- **Coed**

Faculty *Student/faculty ratio:* 18:1.
Student Life *Campus security:* 24-hour emergency response devices, on-campus weekday security to 10 p.m.
Standardized Tests *Required:* ACT ASSET (for placement).
Costs (2004–05) *Tuition:* state resident $3500 full-time. Full-time tuition and fees vary according to program.
Financial Aid Of all full-time matriculated undergraduates who enrolled in 2003, 15 Federal Work-Study jobs (averaging $3500). 35 state and other part-time jobs (averaging $3500).
Applying *Application fee:* $49.
Admissions Contact Ms. Gwen Sailer, Vice President for Student Services, Bates Technical College, 1101 South Yakima Avenue, Tacoma, WA 98405. *Phone:* 253-680-7000. *Toll-free phone:* 800-562-7099. *Fax:* 253-680-7101. *E-mail:* sashpole@bates.ctc.edu.

BELLEVUE COMMUNITY COLLEGE
Bellevue, Washington

- **State-supported** 2-year, founded 1966, part of Washington State Board for Community and Technical Colleges
- **Calendar** quarters
- **Degree** certificates and associate
- **Suburban** 96-acre campus with easy access to Seattle
- **Coed**

Faculty *Student/faculty ratio:* 36:1.
Athletics Member NJCAA.
Costs (2004–05) *Tuition:* state resident $2523 full-time, $76 per credit part-time; nonresident $7731 full-time, $248 per credit part-time.
Financial Aid Of all full-time matriculated undergraduates who enrolled in 2003, 75 Federal Work-Study jobs (averaging $3400). 23 state and other part-time jobs (averaging $3000).
Applying *Options:* electronic application.
Admissions Contact Ms. Tika Esler, Associate Dean of Enrollment Services, Bellevue Community College, 3000 Landerholm Circle SE, Bellerne, WA 98007. *Phone:* 425-564-2222. *Fax:* 425-564-4065.

BELLINGHAM TECHNICAL COLLEGE
Bellingham, Washington

Admissions Contact Mr. David Klaffke, Vice President, Student Services, Bellingham Technical College, 3028 Lindbergh Avenue, Bellingham, WA 98225-1599. *Phone:* 360-738-3105 Ext. 440. *E-mail:* beltcadm@belltc.ctc.edu.

BIG BEND COMMUNITY COLLEGE
Moses Lake, Washington

- **State-supported** 2-year, founded 1962
- **Calendar** quarters
- **Degree** certificates and associate
- **Small-town** 159-acre campus
- **Endowment** $951,594
- **Coed**, 2,102 undergraduate students, 61% full-time, 57% women, 43% men

Undergraduates 1,274 full-time, 828 part-time. Students come from 4 states and territories, 2 other countries, 5% are from out of state, 0.8% African American, 0.8% Asian American or Pacific Islander, 19% Hispanic American, 1% Native American, 0.3% international, 6% transferred in, 5% live on campus.
Freshmen *Admission:* 519 applied, 519 admitted, 338 enrolled.
Faculty *Total:* 132, 41% full-time, 3% with terminal degrees. *Student/faculty ratio:* 20:1.
Majors Accounting technology and bookkeeping; airline pilot and flight crew; automobile/automotive mechanics technology; avionics maintenance technology; civil engineering technology; heavy/industrial equipment maintenance technologies related; industrial electronics technology; information science/studies; liberal arts and sciences/liberal studies; nursing (licensed practical/vocational nurse training); nursing (registered nurse training); office management; teacher assistant/aide; welding technology.

Academic Programs *Special study options:* academic remediation for entering students, advanced placement credit, cooperative education, distance learning, part-time degree program, services for LD students, summer session for credit.
Library Big Bend Community College Library with 41,900 titles, 3,700 serial subscriptions, 3,150 audiovisual materials, an OPAC, a Web page.
Computers on Campus 430 computers available on campus for general student use. A campuswide network can be accessed from off campus. Internet access, online (class) registration, at least one staffed computer lab available.
Student Life *Housing Options:* coed. Campus housing is university owned. *Activities and Organizations:* student-run newspaper, choral group. *Campus security:* 24-hour emergency response devices, student patrols. *Student services:* personal/psychological counseling.
Athletics *Intercollegiate sports:* baseball M(s), basketball M(s)/W(s), softball W(s), volleyball W(s).
Costs (2005–06) *Tuition:* state resident $2570 full-time, $77 per credit part-time; nonresident $3015 full-time, $92 per credit part-time. *Room and board:* $5200. Room and board charges vary according to board plan. *Waivers:* senior citizens.
Financial Aid Of all full-time matriculated undergraduates who enrolled in 2003, 50 Federal Work-Study jobs (averaging $2700). 100 state and other part-time jobs (averaging $3240).
Applying *Options:* early admission, deferred entrance. *Application fee:* $30. *Required for some:* high school transcript. *Application deadline:* rolling (freshmen), rolling (transfers). *Notification:* continuous (freshmen).
Admissions Contact Ms. Candis Lacher, Dean of Enrollment Services, Big Bend Community College, 7662 Chanute Street, Moses Lake, WA 98837. *Phone:* 509-793-2061. *Fax:* 509-762-6243. *E-mail:* admissions@bigbend.edu.

CASCADIA COMMUNITY COLLEGE
Bothell, Washington

- **State-supported** 2-year, founded 1999
- **Calendar** quarters
- **Degree** certificates and associate
- **Suburban** 128-acre campus
- **Coed**, 1,889 undergraduate students, 50% full-time, 49% women, 51% men

Undergraduates 952 full-time, 937 part-time. 2% African American, 6% Asian American or Pacific Islander, 4% Hispanic American, 0.2% Native American. *Retention:* 60% of 2002 full-time freshmen returned.
Freshmen *Admission:* 316 enrolled.
Faculty *Total:* 101, 21% full-time, 27% with terminal degrees. *Student/faculty ratio:* 26:1.
Majors Liberal arts and sciences and humanities related; liberal arts and sciences/liberal studies; science technologies related.
Academic Programs *Special study options:* academic remediation for entering students, accelerated degree program, adult/continuing education programs, advanced placement credit, cooperative education, distance learning, English as a second language, external degree program, independent study, internships, off-campus study, part-time degree program, services for LD students, study abroad.
Library UWB/CCC Campus Library with 67,943 titles, 979 serial subscriptions, 6,100 audiovisual materials, an OPAC, a Web page.
Computers on Campus 75 computers available on campus for general student use. A campuswide network can be accessed from off campus. Internet access, online (class) registration, at least one staffed computer lab available. Computer purchase or lease plan available.
Student Life *Housing:* college housing not available. *Campus security:* 24-hour emergency response devices, late-night transport/escort service.
Costs (2005–06) *Tuition:* state resident $2230 full-time, $74 per credit part-time; nonresident $7738 full-time, $258 per credit part-time. *Required fees:* $75 full-time, $4 per credit part-time. *Waivers:* adult students, senior citizens, and employees or children of employees.
Admissions Contact Ms. Marla Coan, Dean for Student Success, Cascadia Community College, 18345 Campus Way, NE, Bothell, WA 98011. *Phone:* 425-352-8000. *Fax:* 425-352-8137. *E-mail:* admissions@cascadia.ctc.edu.

CENTRALIA COLLEGE
Centralia, Washington

- **State-supported** 2-year, founded 1925, part of Washington State Board for Community and Technical Colleges
- **Calendar** quarters
- **Degree** certificates and associate
- **Small-town** 31-acre campus
- **Endowment** $3.0 million
- **Coed**, 3,685 undergraduate students, 51% full-time, 63% women, 37% men

Undergraduates 1,863 full-time, 1,822 part-time. Students come from 4 states and territories, 1% are from out of state, 0.6% African American, 1% Asian American or Pacific Islander, 8% Hispanic American, 2% Native American. *Retention:* 72% of 2002 full-time freshmen returned.

Freshmen *Admission:* 2,346 applied, 2,346 admitted.

Faculty *Total:* 240, 24% full-time, 8% with terminal degrees. *Student/faculty ratio:* 24:1.

Majors Administrative assistant and secretarial science; applied art; art; biological and physical sciences; biology/biological sciences; botany/plant biology; broadcast journalism; business administration and management; business and personal/financial services marketing; business/commerce; chemistry; child care and support services management; child development; civil engineering technology; commercial and advertising art; computer and information sciences related; computer programming related; computer systems networking and telecommunications; consumer merchandising/retailing management; corrections; criminal justice/law enforcement administration; diesel mechanics technology; dramatic/theatre arts; electrical, electronic and communications engineering technology; engineering; English; family living/parenthood; French; geology/earth science; German; heavy equipment maintenance technology; history; humanities; kindergarten/preschool education; legal administrative assistant/secretary; liberal arts and sciences/liberal studies; marketing/marketing management; mass communication/media; mathematics; medical administrative assistant and medical secretary; music; natural sciences; nursing (licensed practical/vocational nurse training); nursing (registered nurse training); parks, recreation and leisure; physical sciences; political science and government; pre-dentistry studies; pre-engineering; pre-law studies; pre-medical studies; pre-pharmacy studies; pre-veterinary studies; psychology; radio and television; receptionist; retailing; sales, distribution and marketing; social sciences; sociology; Spanish; survey technology; system administration; teacher assistant/aide; welding technology; zoology/animal biology.

Academic Programs *Special study options:* academic remediation for entering students, adult/continuing education programs, advanced placement credit, cooperative education, distance learning, English as a second language, external degree program, freshman honors college, honors programs, independent study, part-time degree program, services for LD students, study abroad, summer session for credit.

Library Kirk Library with 38,000 titles, 225 serial subscriptions, an OPAC, a Web page.

Computers on Campus 125 computers available on campus for general student use. A campuswide network can be accessed from off campus that provide access to online degree audits, transcripts. Internet access, online (class) registration, at least one staffed computer lab available. Computer purchase or lease plan available.

Student Life *Housing:* college housing not available. *Activities and Organizations:* drama/theater group, student-run newspaper, radio and television station, choral group, marching band, Phi Theta Kappa, Diesel Tech Club, Business Management Association, Student Activities/Admissions Team, International Club. *Campus security:* 24-hour patrols, late-night transport/escort service. *Student services:* personal/psychological counseling, women's center.

Athletics Member NJCAA. *Intercollegiate sports:* baseball M(s), basketball M(s)/W(s), golf W(s), softball W(s), volleyball W(s).

Standardized Tests *Required:* ACT ASSET or ACT COMPASS (for placement).

Costs (2005–06) *Tuition:* state resident $2445 full-time, $72 per credit part-time; nonresident $2835 full-time, $85 per credit part-time. *Required fees:* $258 full-time, $5 per term part-time.

Applying *Options:* electronic application. *Required:* high school transcript. *Application deadline:* rolling (freshmen), rolling (transfers). *Notification:* continuous until 9/15 (freshmen).

Admissions Contact Mr. Scott A. Copeland, Director of Enrollment Services and College Registrar, Centralia College, 600 West Locust, Centralia, WA 98531. *Phone:* 360-736-9391 Ext. 682. *Fax:* 360-330-7503. *E-mail:* admissions@centralia.ctc.edu.

CLARK COLLEGE
Vancouver, Washington

- **State-supported** 2-year, founded 1933, part of Washington State Board for Community and Technical Colleges
- **Calendar** quarters
- **Degree** certificates, diplomas, and associate
- **Urban** 80-acre campus with easy access to Portland
- **Endowment** $42.0 million
- **Coed,** 9,946 undergraduate students, 43% full-time, 60% women, 40% men

Undergraduates 4,314 full-time, 5,632 part-time. Students come from 6 states and territories, 16 other countries, 4% are from out of state, 2% African American, 5% Asian American or Pacific Islander, 5% Hispanic American, 0.9% Native American, 0.4% international, 9% transferred in. *Retention:* 64% of 2002 full-time freshmen returned.

Freshmen *Admission:* 2,246 applied, 2,246 admitted, 1,078 enrolled.

Faculty *Total:* 576, 34% full-time, 10% with terminal degrees. *Student/faculty ratio:* 23:1.

Majors Accounting technology and bookkeeping; applied horticulture; automobile/automotive mechanics technology; baking and pastry arts; business administration and management; business automation/technology/data entry; computer systems networking and telecommunications; construction engineering technology; culinary arts; data entry/microcomputer applications; dental hygiene; diesel mechanics technology; early childhood education; electrical, electronic and communications engineering technology; emergency medical technology (EMT paramedic); executive assistant/executive secretary; human resources management; landscaping and groundskeeping; legal assistant/paralegal; liberal arts and sciences/liberal studies; machine tool technology; manufacturing technology; medical administrative assistant and medical secretary; medical/clinical assistant; nursing (registered nurse training); substance abuse/addiction counseling; telecommunications technology; welding technology.

Academic Programs *Special study options:* academic remediation for entering students, accelerated degree program, adult/continuing education programs, advanced placement credit, cooperative education, distance learning, English as a second language, independent study, internships, part-time degree program, services for LD students, study abroad, summer session for credit. *ROTC:* Army (c), Air Force (c).

Library Lewis D. Cannell Library with 63,525 titles, 417 serial subscriptions, 2,147 audiovisual materials, an OPAC, a Web page.

Computers on Campus 750 computers available on campus for general student use. A campuswide network can be accessed from off campus. Internet access, online (class) registration, at least one staffed computer lab available.

Student Life *Housing:* college housing not available. *Activities and Organizations:* drama/theater group, student-run newspaper, choral group, Phi Theta Kappa, Baptist Student Ministries, Multicultural Students United, Peace Project, Students for Political Activism Now (SPAN). *Campus security:* 24-hour patrols, late-night transport/escort service, security staff during hours of operation. *Student services:* health clinic, personal/psychological counseling, legal services.

Athletics *Intercollegiate sports:* basketball M(s)/W(s), cross-country running M(s)/W(s), fencing M(c)/W(c), soccer M(s)/W(s), track and field M(s)/W(s), volleyball W(s). *Intramural sports:* basketball M/W, fencing M/W, football M/W, soccer M/W, softball M/W, table tennis M/W, volleyball M/W.

Standardized Tests *Required:* ACT ASSET (for placement).

Costs (2004–05) *Tuition:* state resident $2572 full-time, $75 per quarter hour part-time; nonresident $2572 full-time, $75 per quarter hour part-time. Full-time tuition and fees vary according to course load and reciprocity agreements. Part-time tuition and fees vary according to course load and reciprocity agreements. *Waivers:* senior citizens and employees or children of employees.

Financial Aid Of all full-time matriculated undergraduates who enrolled in 2003, 170 Federal Work-Study jobs (averaging $1900). 164 state and other part-time jobs (averaging $2150).

Applying *Options:* early admission, deferred entrance. *Required for some:* high school transcript, interview. *Application deadlines:* 8/8 (freshmen), 8/8 (transfers). *Notification:* continuous (freshmen).

Admissions Contact Ms. Sheryl Anderson, Director of Admissions, Clark College, 1800 East McLoughlin Boulevard, Vancouver, WA 98663. *Phone:* 360-992-2308. *Toll-free phone:* 360-992-2107. *Fax:* 360-992-2867. *E-mail:* sanderson@clark.edu.

CLOVER PARK TECHNICAL COLLEGE
Lakewood, Washington

- **State-supported** 2-year, founded 1942, part of Washington State Community and Technical College System
- **Degree** certificates and associate
- **Coed,** 8,488 undergraduate students, 22% full-time, 61% women, 39% men

Undergraduates 1,848 full-time, 6,640 part-time. Students come from 3 states and territories, 12% African American, 7% Asian American or Pacific Islander, 3% Hispanic American, 1% Native American, 1% international.

Freshmen *Admission:* 208 enrolled.

Faculty *Total:* 299, 37% full-time. *Student/faculty ratio:* 22:1.

Majors Accounting technology and bookkeeping; agriculture; airline pilot and flight crew; architectural engineering technology; automobile/automotive mechanics technology; avionics maintenance technology; business machine repair; clinical/medical laboratory assistant; computer and information sciences and support services related; computer and information systems security; computer programming; computer systems networking and telecommunications; early childhood education; environmental engineering technology; graphic and printing equipment operation/production; heating, air conditioning, ventilation and refrigeration maintenance technology; heavy equipment maintenance technology; interior design; landscaping and groundskeeping; legal administrative assistant/secretary; machine tool technology; marketing/marketing management;

Clover Park Technical College (continued)

massage therapy; mechanical engineering/mechanical technology; office management; radio and television broadcasting technology; rehabilitation and therapeutic professions related; security and protective services related; teacher assistant/aide; web page, digital/multimedia and information resources design.

Academic Programs *Special study options:* academic remediation for entering students, accelerated degree program, cooperative education, distance learning, English as a second language, internships, part-time degree program, services for LD students.

Library CPTC Library with 11,219 titles, 97 serial subscriptions, 2,322 audiovisual materials, an OPAC, a Web page.

Computers on Campus 1510 computers available on campus for general student use. A campuswide network can be accessed from off campus. Internet access, at least one staffed computer lab available.

Student Life *Housing:* college housing not available. *Activities and Organizations:* student-run newspaper, Accounting Numbers Club, Auto Tech Club, Computer Users Club, Social Services Club. *Campus security:* 24-hour patrols, late-night transport/escort service. *Student services:* personal/psychological counseling.

Standardized Tests *Required:* ACT COMPASS (for placement).

Costs (2004–05) *Tuition:* state resident $2369 full-time, $48 per credit hour part-time. *Required fees:* $513 full-time.

Applying *Options:* common application, electronic application. *Application fee:* $36. *Required for some:* high school transcript, interview. *Application deadline:* 9/27 (freshmen). *Notification:* continuous until 9/27 (freshmen).

Admissions Contact Ms. Judy Richardson, Registrar, Clover Park Technical College, 4500 Steilacoom Boulevard Southwest, Lakewood, WA 98499. *Phone:* 253-589-5570. *Fax:* 253-589-5852. *E-mail:* admissions@cptc.edu.

COLUMBIA BASIN COLLEGE
Pasco, Washington

Admissions Contact Ms. Donna Korstad, Program Support Supervisor, Enrollment Management, Columbia Basin College, 2600 North 20th Avenue, Pasco, WA 99301. *Phone:* 509-547-0511 Ext. 2250. *Toll-free phone:* 509-547-0511 Ext. 2250. *Fax:* 509-546-0401.

CROWN COLLEGE
Tacoma, Washington

- **Proprietary** primarily 2-year, founded 1969, administratively affiliated with Killebrew Dalton, Inc
- **Calendar** continuous
- **Degrees** associate and bachelor's (bachelor's degree in public administration only)
- **Urban** campus with easy access to Seattle
- **Coed**
- 95% of applicants were admitted

Faculty *Student/faculty ratio:* 20:1.

Student Life *Campus security:* 24-hour emergency response devices.

Applying *Options:* common application, electronic application. *Application fee:* $135. *Required:* high school transcript, interview. *Required for some:* essay or personal statement.

Admissions Contact Ms. Sheila Millineaux, Admissions Director, Crown College, 8739 South Hosmer, Tacoma, WA 98444. *Phone:* 253-531-3123. *Toll-free phone:* 800-755-9525 (in-state); 888-689-3688 (out-of-state). *Fax:* 253-531-3521. *E-mail:* admissions@crowncollege.edu.

DIGIPEN INSTITUTE OF TECHNOLOGY
Redmond, Washington

Admissions Contact Ms. Gina Corpening, Admissions and Outreach Coordinator, DigiPen Institute of Technology, 5001 150th Avenue, NE, Redmond, WA 98052. *Phone:* 425-558-0299.

EDMONDS COMMUNITY COLLEGE
Lynnwood, Washington

- **State and locally supported** 2-year, founded 1967, part of Washington State Board for Community and Technical Colleges
- **Calendar** quarters
- **Degree** certificates and associate
- **Suburban** 115-acre campus with easy access to Seattle
- **Coed,** 8,385 undergraduate students, 45% full-time, 56% women, 44% men

Undergraduates 3,787 full-time, 4,598 part-time. Students come from 55 other countries, 4% African American, 11% Asian American or Pacific Islander, 5% Hispanic American, 1% Native American, 5% international.

Faculty *Total:* 419, 34% full-time. *Student/faculty ratio:* 24:1.

Majors Accounting technology and bookkeeping; business administration and management; chemical technology; child care and support services management; community health services counseling; computer and information sciences and support services related; computer technology/computer systems technology; construction engineering technology; culinary arts; data processing and data processing technology; electrical, electronic and communications engineering technology; entrepreneurship; fire services administration; gerontology; health aide; hospitality and recreation marketing; human resources management; international business/trade/commerce; landscaping and groundskeeping; legal administrative assistant/secretary; legal assistant/paralegal; liberal arts and sciences/liberal studies; marketing/marketing management; office management; plant nursery management; retailing; social work; substance abuse/addiction counseling; therapeutic recreation; tourism and travel services marketing; vocational rehabilitation counseling.

Academic Programs *Special study options:* academic remediation for entering students, adult/continuing education programs, advanced placement credit, cooperative education, distance learning, English as a second language, honors programs, internships, off-campus study, part-time degree program, services for LD students, student-designed majors, study abroad, summer session for credit.

Library Edmonds Community College Library with 47,947 titles, 312 serial subscriptions, 7,735 audiovisual materials, an OPAC, a Web page.

Computers on Campus 1129 computers available on campus for general student use. A campuswide network can be accessed from off campus. Internet access, online (class) registration, at least one staffed computer lab available.

Student Life *Housing:* college housing not available. *Activities and Organizations:* student-run newspaper, choral group, Phi Theta Kappa, AITP, AAWCC, International Club, Pottery/Art Club. *Campus security:* 24-hour emergency response devices and patrols, student patrols, late-night transport/escort service. *Student services:* personal/psychological counseling, women's center.

Athletics *Intercollegiate sports:* baseball M(s), basketball M(s)/W(s), golf M(s)/W(s), soccer M(s)/W(s), softball W(s), volleyball W(s). *Intramural sports:* badminton M/W, baseball M, basketball M/W, bowling M/W, football M/W, golf M/W, soccer M, softball W, table tennis M/W, volleyball M/W.

Costs (2005–06) *Tuition:* state resident $2445 full-time, $72 per credit hour part-time; nonresident $7653 full-time, $2551 per credit hour part-time. Full-time tuition and fees vary according to course load. Part-time tuition and fees vary according to course load. *Required fees:* $128 full-time, $4 per credit hour part-time.

Financial Aid Of all full-time matriculated undergraduates who enrolled in 2003, 125 Federal Work-Study jobs (averaging $7200). 100 state and other part-time jobs (averaging $7200).

Applying *Options:* common application, electronic application, early admission, deferred entrance. *Application fee:* $15. *Application deadline:* rolling (freshmen), rolling (transfers). *Notification:* continuous (freshmen).

Admissions Contact Ms. Sharon Bench, Admissions Director, Edmonds Community College, 20000 68th Avenue West, Lynnwood, WA 98036-5999. *Phone:* 425-640-1416. *Fax:* 425-640-1159. *E-mail:* info@edcc.edu.

EVERETT COMMUNITY COLLEGE
Everett, Washington

- **State-supported** 2-year, founded 1941, part of Washington State Board for Community and Technical Colleges
- **Calendar** quarters
- **Degree** certificates, diplomas, and associate
- **Suburban** 25-acre campus with easy access to Seattle
- **Endowment** $1.5 million
- **Coed,** 7,188 undergraduate students, 45% full-time, 62% women, 38% men

Undergraduates 3,262 full-time, 3,926 part-time. Students come from 17 states and territories, 13 other countries, 3% are from out of state, 2% African American, 5% Asian American or Pacific Islander, 4% Hispanic American, 2% Native American, 0.4% international, 3% transferred in. *Retention:* 59% of 2002 full-time freshmen returned.

Freshmen *Admission:* 612 admitted, 612 enrolled.

Faculty *Total:* 363, 36% full-time. *Student/faculty ratio:* 20:1.

Majors Accounting; animal sciences; anthropology; art; atmospheric sciences and meteorology; avionics maintenance technology; biology/biological sciences; botany/plant biology; business administration and management; chemistry; cinematography and film/video production; civil engineering technology; commercial and advertising art; computer science; consumer merchandising/retailing management; cosmetology; criminal justice/law enforcement administration; criminal justice/police science; data processing and data processing technology; dental hygiene; drafting and design technology; dramatic/theatre arts; drawing; ecology; economics; education; elementary education; engineering; engineering science; engineering technology; English; environmental studies; fire science; funeral service and mortuary science; geology/earth science; German; history; human services; industrial arts; industrial technology; Japanese; journalism; kindergarten/preschool education; liberal arts and sciences/

liberal studies; marketing/marketing management; mathematics; medical administrative assistant and medical secretary; medical/clinical assistant; modern languages; music; nursing (licensed practical/vocational nurse training); nursing (registered nurse training); occupational therapy; oceanography (chemical and physical); ophthalmic laboratory technology; pharmacy technician; philosophy; photography; physical education teaching and coaching; physical therapist assistant; physics; political science and government; pre-engineering; psychology; Russian; sociology; Spanish; speech and rhetoric; welding technology; wildlife biology; zoology/animal biology.

Academic Programs *Special study options:* academic remediation for entering students, adult/continuing education programs, advanced placement credit, cooperative education, distance learning, English as a second language, independent study, internships, part-time degree program, services for LD students, study abroad, summer session for credit.

Library John Terrey Library/Media Center with 49,600 titles, 279 serial subscriptions, 5,997 audiovisual materials, an OPAC, a Web page.

Computers on Campus 600 computers available on campus for general student use. A campuswide network can be accessed from off campus. Internet access, online (class) registration, at least one staffed computer lab available.

Student Life *Housing:* college housing not available. *Activities and Organizations:* drama/theater group, student-run newspaper, choral group, United Native American Council, Nippon Friendship Club, Student Nurses Association, International Students Club, Math, Engineering and Science Student Organization. *Campus security:* 24-hour emergency response devices and patrols, late-night transport/escort service. *Student services:* personal/psychological counseling, women's center.

Athletics Member NJCAA. *Intercollegiate sports:* baseball M(s), basketball M(s)/W(s), cross-country running M(s)/W(s), soccer M(s)/W(s), softball W(s), volleyball W(s). *Intramural sports:* basketball M/W, bowling M/W, crew M(c)/W(c), football M/W, golf M/W, soccer M/W, softball M/W, tennis M/W, volleyball M/W, weight lifting M/W.

Standardized Tests *Recommended:* ACT ASSET, ACT COMPASS.

Costs (2005–06) *Tuition:* state resident $2313 full-time, $69 per credit part-time; nonresident $3807 full-time, $122 per credit part-time.

Financial Aid Of all full-time matriculated undergraduates who enrolled in 2003, 152 Federal Work-Study jobs (averaging $3000). 48 state and other part-time jobs (averaging $3000).

Applying *Options:* common application, electronic application, early admission, deferred entrance. *Recommended:* high school transcript. *Application deadline:* rolling (freshmen), rolling (transfers). *Notification:* continuous (freshmen).

Admissions Contact Ms. Linda Baca, Admissions Manager, Everett Community College, 2000 Tower Street, Everett, WA 98201-1352. *Phone:* 425-388-9219. *Fax:* 425-388-9173. *E-mail:* admissions@everettcc.edu.

GRAYS HARBOR COLLEGE
Aberdeen, Washington

Admissions Contact Ms. Brenda Dell, Admissions Officer, Grays Harbor College, 1620 Edward P. Smith Drive, Aberdeen, WA 98520-7599. *Phone:* 360-532-9020 Ext. 4026. *Toll-free phone:* 800-562-4830. *Fax:* 360-538-4293. *E-mail:* bdell@ghc.edu.

GREEN RIVER COMMUNITY COLLEGE
Auburn, Washington

- **State-supported** 2-year, founded 1965, part of Washington State Board for Community and Technical Colleges
- **Calendar** quarters
- **Degree** certificates, diplomas, and associate
- **Rural** 168-acre campus with easy access to Seattle
- **Coed,** 6,621 undergraduate students, 59% full-time, 56% women, 44% men

Undergraduates 3,883 full-time, 2,738 part-time. Students come from 30 other countries, 1% are from out of state, 3% African American, 7% Asian American or Pacific Islander, 5% Hispanic American, 1% Native American, 4% international.

Freshmen *Admission:* 1,098 enrolled.

Faculty *Total:* 368, 35% full-time. *Student/faculty ratio:* 22:1.

Majors Accounting technology and bookkeeping; airline pilot and flight crew; air traffic control; autobody/collision and repair technology; automobile/automotive mechanics technology; carpentry; child care and support services management; court reporting; criminal justice/police science; drafting and design technology; forestry technology; information science/studies; legal administrative assistant/secretary; liberal arts and sciences/liberal studies; machine tool technology; marketing/marketing management; mechanical engineering/mechanical technology; medical administrative assistant and medical secretary; nursing (licensed practical/vocational nurse training); occupational therapist assistant; office management; physical therapist assistant; water quality and wastewater treatment management and recycling technology; welding technology.

Academic Programs *Special study options:* academic remediation for entering students, adult/continuing education programs, advanced placement credit, cooperative education, distance learning, English as a second language, internships, off-campus study, part-time degree program, services for LD students, summer session for credit.

Library Holman Library with 32,500 titles, 2,100 serial subscriptions, 4,471 audiovisual materials, an OPAC, a Web page.

Computers on Campus 104 computers available on campus for general student use. A campuswide network can be accessed. Internet access, at least one staffed computer lab available.

Student Life *Housing:* college housing not available. *Activities and Organizations:* drama/theater group, student-run newspaper, radio station, choral group, Phi Theta Kappa, Green River Active Christian Encounter, Vocational and Industrial Clubs of America (VICA), Multicultural Student Alliance. *Campus security:* 24-hour emergency response devices and patrols, student patrols, late-night transport/escort service. *Student services:* health clinic, personal/psychological counseling, women's center.

Athletics Member NJCAA. *Intercollegiate sports:* baseball M(s), basketball M(s)/W(s), golf M(s)/W(s), soccer M(s)/W(s), softball W(s), tennis M(s)/W(s), volleyball W(s). *Intramural sports:* badminton M/W, basketball M/W, football M/W, tennis M/W, volleyball M/W, weight lifting M/W.

Standardized Tests *Required:* ACT ASSET or ACT COMPASS (for placement).

Costs (2004–05) *Tuition:* state resident $2313 full-time, $69 per credit part-time; nonresident $2776 full-time, $83 per credit part-time. Part-time tuition and fees vary according to course load. *Required fees:* $308 full-time. *Payment plan:* installment.

Financial Aid Of all full-time matriculated undergraduates who enrolled in 2003, 113 Federal Work-Study jobs (averaging $2356). 174 state and other part-time jobs.

Applying *Options:* electronic application, early admission, deferred entrance. *Required for some:* high school transcript. *Application deadline:* rolling (freshmen), rolling (transfers). *Notification:* continuous (freshmen).

Admissions Contact Ms. Peggy Morgan, Program Support Supervisor, Green River Community College, 12401 Southeast 320th Street, Auburn, WA 98092-3699. *Phone:* 253-833-9111 Ext. 2513. *Fax:* 253-288-3454.

HIGHLINE COMMUNITY COLLEGE
Des Moines, Washington

- **State-supported** 2-year, founded 1961, part of Washington State Board for Community and Technical Colleges
- **Calendar** quarters
- **Degree** certificates, diplomas, and associate
- **Suburban** 81-acre campus with easy access to Seattle
- **Coed,** 6,372 undergraduate students, 51% full-time, 64% women, 36% men

Highline Community College is one of the premier 2-year schools in Washington State. The main 80-acre campus overlooks the Puget Sound and the Olympic Mountains. Conveniently located between Seattle and Tacoma, Highline serves one of the most diverse student bodies in the region. Exceptional student services staff and faculty members, high-quality transfer and professional/technical programs, and affordable cost combine to make Highline a great choice for a promising future.

Undergraduates 3,229 full-time, 3,143 part-time. 11% African American, 17% Asian American or Pacific Islander, 5% Hispanic American, 1% Native American, 0.2% international. *Retention:* 60% of 2002 full-time freshmen returned.

Freshmen *Admission:* 3,933 applied, 3,933 admitted, 667 enrolled.

Faculty *Total:* 356, 39% full-time.

Majors Accounting; administrative assistant and secretarial science; art; behavioral sciences; biological and physical sciences; business administration and management; clinical/medical laboratory science and allied professions related; computer engineering technology; computer programming; computer systems networking and telecommunications; computer typography and composition equipment operation; criminal justice/law enforcement administration; criminal justice/police science; cultural studies; data entry/microcomputer applications related; dental hygiene; drafting and design technology; education; engineering; engineering technology; English; graphic and printing equipment operation/production; hotel/motel administration; humanities; human services; industrial technology; interior design; international business/trade/commerce; journalism; kindergarten/preschool education; legal administrative assistant/secretary; legal assistant/paralegal; library science; marine technology; mathematics; medical/clinical assistant; music; natural sciences; nursing (registered nurse training); plastics engineering technology; pre-engineering; psychology; respiratory care therapy; Romance languages; social sciences; tourism and travel services management; transportation technology; web page, digital/multimedia and information resources design.

Academic Programs *Special study options:* academic remediation for entering students, advanced placement credit, cooperative education, English as a second language, freshman honors college, honors programs, internships, part-

Highline Community College (continued)
time degree program, services for LD students, student-designed majors, study abroad, summer session for credit. *ROTC:* Army (c), Air Force (c).
Library Highline Community College Library with 57,678 titles, 585 serial subscriptions, an OPAC.
Computers on Campus 300 computers available on campus for general student use. A campuswide network can be accessed. At least one staffed computer lab available.
Student Life *Housing:* college housing not available. *Activities and Organizations:* drama/theater group, student-run newspaper, choral group, Campus Crusade for Christ, Phi Theta Kappa, International Club, Respiratory Care. *Campus security:* 24-hour patrols. *Student services:* health clinic, personal/psychological counseling, women's center.
Athletics Member NJCAA. *Intercollegiate sports:* basketball M(s)/W(s), cross-country running M(s)/W(s), soccer M(s)/W(s), softball W(s), track and field M(s)/W(s), volleyball W(s), wrestling M(s).
Standardized Tests *Recommended:* ACT COMPASS.
Costs (2004–05) *Tuition:* state resident $2313 full-time, $69 per credit part-time; nonresident $7521 full-time, $241 per credit part-time. *Required fees:* $75 full-time, $3 per credit part-time.
Applying *Application fee:* $20. *Application deadline:* rolling (freshmen), rolling (transfers).
Admissions Contact Ms. Debbie Faison, Assistant Registrar, Highline Community College, PO Box 98000, 2400 South 240th Street, Des Moines, WA 98198-9800. *Phone:* 206-878-3710 Ext. 3363. *Fax:* 206-870-4855. *E-mail:* dfaison@hcc.ctc.edu.

ITT TECHNICAL INSTITUTE
Bothell, Washington

- **Proprietary** primarily 2-year, founded 1993, part of ITT Educational Services, Inc
- **Calendar** quarters
- **Degrees** associate and bachelor's
- **Coed**

Standardized Tests *Required:* Wonderlic aptitude test (for admission).
Costs (2004–05) *Tuition:* Please see school catalog for specific information.
Applying *Options:* deferred entrance. *Application fee:* $100. *Required:* high school transcript, interview. *Recommended:* letters of recommendation.
Admissions Contact Mr. Jon L. Scherrer, Director of Recruitment, ITT Technical Institute, 2525 223rd Street SE, Bothell, WA 98021. *Phone:* 425-485-0303. *Toll-free phone:* 800-272-3791. *Fax:* 425-485-3438.

ITT TECHNICAL INSTITUTE
Seattle, Washington

- **Proprietary** primarily 2-year, founded 1932, part of ITT Educational Services, Inc
- **Calendar** quarters
- **Degrees** associate and bachelor's
- **Urban** campus
- **Coed**

Standardized Tests *Required:* Wonderlic aptitude test (for admission).
Costs (2004–05) *Tuition:* Please see school catalog for specific information.
Applying *Options:* deferred entrance. *Application fee:* $100. *Required:* high school transcript, interview. *Recommended:* letters of recommendation.
Admissions Contact Mr. Rocco Liace, Director of Recruitment, ITT Technical Institute, 12720 Gateway Drive, Suite 100, Seattle, WA 98168. *Phone:* 206-244-3300. *Toll-free phone:* 800-422-2029. *Fax:* 206-246-7635.

ITT TECHNICAL INSTITUTE
Spokane, Washington

- **Proprietary** primarily 2-year, founded 1985, part of ITT Educational Services, Inc
- **Calendar** quarters
- **Degrees** associate and bachelor's
- **Suburban** 3-acre campus
- **Coed**

Standardized Tests *Required:* Wonderlic aptitude test (for admission).
Costs (2004–05) *Tuition:* Please see school catalog for specific information.
Financial Aid Of all full-time matriculated undergraduates who enrolled in 2003, 9 Federal Work-Study jobs (averaging $4000).
Applying *Options:* deferred entrance. *Application fee:* $100. *Required:* high school transcript, interview. *Recommended:* letters of recommendation.

Admissions Contact Mr. Gregory L. Alexander, Director of Recruitment, ITT Technical Institute, North 1050 Argonne Road, Spokane, WA 99212. *Phone:* 509-926-2900. *Toll-free phone:* 800-777-8324. *Fax:* 509-926-2908.

LAKE WASHINGTON TECHNICAL COLLEGE
Kirkland, Washington

- **District-supported** 2-year, founded 1949, part of Washington State Board for Community and Technical Colleges
- **Calendar** quarters
- **Degree** certificates and associate
- **Suburban** 57-acre campus with easy access to Seattle
- **Endowment** $198,295
- **Coed**

Faculty *Student/faculty ratio:* 8:1.
Student Life *Campus security:* 24-hour emergency response devices, late-night transport/escort service, parking lot security, security cameras.
Standardized Tests *Required:* ACT ASSET (for placement).
Costs (2004–05) *Tuition:* state resident $3193 full-time, $64 per credit part-time. Full-time tuition and fees vary according to course load and program. Part-time tuition and fees vary according to course load and program.
Financial Aid Of all full-time matriculated undergraduates who enrolled in 2003, 38 Federal Work-Study jobs (averaging $1800). 69 state and other part-time jobs (averaging $2259).
Applying *Options:* common application, early admission. *Required for some:* high school transcript.
Admissions Contact Mr. Jim West, Director of Admissions and Registration, Lake Washington Technical College, 11605 132nd Avenue NE, Kirkland, WA 98034-8506. *Phone:* 425-739-8233.

LOWER COLUMBIA COLLEGE
Longview, Washington

- **State-supported** 2-year, founded 1934, part of Washington State Board for Community and Technical Colleges
- **Calendar** quarters
- **Degree** certificates, diplomas, and associate
- **Small-town** 30-acre campus with easy access to Portland
- **Endowment** $2.4 million
- **Coed**, 3,223 undergraduate students, 55% full-time, 62% women, 38% men

Undergraduates 1,758 full-time, 1,465 part-time. Students come from 5 states and territories, 15% are from out of state, 1% African American, 2% Asian American or Pacific Islander, 3% Hispanic American, 1% Native American, 0.1% international, 11% transferred in. *Retention:* 48% of 2002 full-time freshmen returned.
Freshmen *Admission:* 332 applied, 332 admitted, 332 enrolled.
Faculty *Total:* 165, 51% full-time. *Student/faculty ratio:* 20:1.
Majors Accounting; accounting technology and bookkeeping; administrative assistant and secretarial science; anthropology; art; automobile/automotive mechanics technology; biology/biological sciences; business administration and management; business/commerce; CAD/CADD drafting/design technology; computer and information sciences; computer engineering technology; computer programming; computer science; computer systems analysis; computer systems networking and telecommunications; computer technology/computer systems technology; corrections; criminal justice/law enforcement administration; criminal justice/police science; criminal justice/safety; data entry/microcomputer applications; data processing and data processing technology; diesel mechanics technology; dramatic/theatre arts; early childhood education; economics; electrical, electronic and communications engineering technology; electrician; engineering; engineering technology; English; environmental studies; fire science; fire services administration; foreign languages and literatures; geography; geology/earth science; heavy equipment maintenance technology; history; industrial mechanics and maintenance technology; industrial technology; information science/studies; information technology; instrumentation technology; kindergarten/preschool education; legal administrative assistant/secretary; liberal arts and sciences/liberal studies; lineworker; machine tool technology; management information systems; mathematics; mechanical engineering/mechanical technology; medical administrative assistant and medical secretary; medical/clinical assistant; medical reception; medical transcription; music; nursing assistant/aide and patient care assistant; nursing (licensed practical/vocational nurse training); nursing (registered nurse training); office management; philosophy; photography; physical education teaching and coaching; physics; political science and government; pre-engineering; pre-law studies; psychology; receptionist; social sciences; sociology; speech and rhetoric; substance abuse/addiction counseling; teacher assistant/aide; welding technology; wood science and wood products/pulp and paper technology; word processing.

Academic Programs *Special study options:* academic remediation for entering students, adult/continuing education programs, cooperative education, English as a second language, honors programs, part-time degree program, services for LD students, study abroad, summer session for credit.

Library Allan Thompson Library plus 1 other with 41,991 titles, 217 serial subscriptions, 3,376 audiovisual materials, an OPAC.

Computers on Campus 250 computers available on campus for general student use. A campuswide network can be accessed. At least one staffed computer lab available.

Student Life *Housing:* college housing not available. *Activities and Organizations:* drama/theater group, student-run newspaper, choral group, Campus Entertainment, Phi Theta Kappa, Services and Relations Club, Multicultural Students Club, Theater Club. *Campus security:* 24-hour emergency response devices and patrols. *Student services:* health clinic, personal/psychological counseling.

Athletics *Intercollegiate sports:* baseball M(s), basketball M(s)/W(s), soccer M(s)/W(s), softball W(s), volleyball W(s).

Standardized Tests *Required:* ACT COMPASS (for placement).

Costs (2004–05) *Tuition:* state resident $2445 full-time, $73 per credit part-time; nonresident $3120 full-time, $95 per credit part-time. Full-time tuition and fees vary according to course load. Part-time tuition and fees vary according to course load. *Required fees:* $44 full-time. *Payment plan:* deferred payment. *Waivers:* senior citizens and employees or children of employees.

Financial Aid Of all full-time matriculated undergraduates who enrolled in 2003, 440 Federal Work-Study jobs (averaging $708). 447 state and other part-time jobs (averaging $2415).

Applying *Options:* early admission, deferred entrance. *Recommended:* high school transcript. *Application deadline:* rolling (freshmen), rolling (transfers). *Notification:* continuous (freshmen).

Admissions Contact Ms. Mary Harding, Vice President for Student Success, Lower Columbia College, 1600 Maple Street, Longview, WA 98632. *Phone:* 360-442-2301. *Fax:* 360-442-2379. *E-mail:* registration@lcc.ctc.edu.

NORTH SEATTLE COMMUNITY COLLEGE
Seattle, Washington

- **State-supported** 2-year, founded 1970, part of Seattle Community College District System
- **Calendar** quarters
- **Degree** certificates, diplomas, and associate
- **Urban** 65-acre campus
- **Coed,** 6,125 undergraduate students, 48% full-time, 61% women, 39% men

Undergraduates 2,918 full-time, 3,207 part-time. Students come from 50 states and territories, 1% are from out of state, 7% African American, 17% Asian American or Pacific Islander, 5% Hispanic American, 2% Native American, 0.3% international, 38% transferred in.

Freshmen *Admission:* 5,726 applied, 5,726 admitted, 1,110 enrolled.

Faculty *Total:* 283, 36% full-time, 4% with terminal degrees. *Student/faculty ratio:* 19:1.

Majors Accounting technology and bookkeeping; art; biomedical technology; business administration and management; civil drafting and CAD/CADD; communications systems installation and repair technology; computer systems networking and telecommunications; culinary arts; data processing and data processing technology; early childhood education; electrical, electronic and communications engineering technology; electrical/electronics drafting and CAD/CADD; heating, air conditioning, ventilation and refrigeration maintenance technology; industrial electronics technology; information science/studies; liberal arts and sciences/liberal studies; mechanical drafting and CAD/CADD; medical/clinical assistant; music; nursing (licensed practical/vocational nurse training); nursing (registered nurse training); office management; pharmacy technician; watchmaking and jewelrymaking; web/multimedia management and webmaster; web page, digital/multimedia and information resources design.

Academic Programs *Special study options:* academic remediation for entering students, adult/continuing education programs, advanced placement credit, cooperative education, distance learning, English as a second language, external degree program, independent study, internships, part-time degree program, services for LD students, summer session for credit. *ROTC:* Army (c).

Library North Seattle Community College Library with 52,496 titles, 594 serial subscriptions, 2,957 audiovisual materials, an OPAC, a Web page.

Computers on Campus 1600 computers available on campus for general student use. A campuswide network can be accessed from off campus. Internet access, online (class) registration, at least one staffed computer lab available.

Student Life *Housing:* college housing not available. *Activities and Organizations:* drama/theater group, student-run newspaper, television station, choral group, Muslim Students Association, Indonesian Community Club, Literary Guild, Phi Theta Kappa, Vietnamese Student Association, national sororities. *Campus security:* 24-hour emergency response devices and patrols, student patrols, late-night transport/escort service, patrols by security. *Student services:* personal/psychological counseling, women's center, legal services.

Athletics *Intercollegiate sports:* basketball M/W. *Intramural sports:* basketball M/W.

Costs (2005–06) *Tuition:* state resident $2709 full-time, $74 per credit part-time; nonresident $8281 full-time, $240 per credit part-time. Full-time tuition and fees vary according to course load. Part-time tuition and fees vary according to course load. *Required fees:* $341 full-time, $35 per term part-time. *Waivers:* senior citizens and employees or children of employees.

Applying *Options:* common application, electronic application, early admission, deferred entrance. *Required:* high school transcript. *Required for some:* essay or personal statement. *Application deadline:* rolling (freshmen), rolling (transfers). *Notification:* continuous until 9/24 (freshmen).

Admissions Contact Ms. Betsy Abts, Registrar, North Seattle Community College, 9600 College Way North, Seattle, WA 98103-3599. *Phone:* 206-527-3796. *Fax:* 206-527-3671. *E-mail:* babts@sccd.ctc.edu.

NORTHWEST AVIATION COLLEGE
Auburn, Washington

Admissions Contact Mr. Shawn Pratt, Assistant Director of Education, Northwest Aviation College, 506 23rd, NE, Auburn, WA 98002. *Phone:* 253-854-4960. *Toll-free phone:* 800-246-4960. *Fax:* 253-931-0768. *E-mail:* afsnac@nventure.com.

NORTHWEST INDIAN COLLEGE
Bellingham, Washington

Admissions Contact Ms. Lisa Santana, Director of Admissions, Northwest Indian College, 2522 Kwina Road, Bellingham, WA 98226. *Phone:* 360-676-2772 Ext. 4270. *Toll-free phone:* 866-676-2772 Ext. 4264. *E-mail:* admissions@orca.nwic.edu.

NORTHWEST SCHOOL OF WOODEN BOATBUILDING
Port Townsend, Washington

Admissions Contact Ms. Gretchen Siegfried, Student Services Coordinator, Northwest School of Wooden Boatbuilding, 251 Otto Street, Port Townsend, WA 98368. *Phone:* 360-385-4948.

OLYMPIC COLLEGE
Bremerton, Washington

- **State-supported** 2-year, founded 1946, part of Washington State Board for Community and Technical Colleges
- **Calendar** quarters
- **Degree** certificates, diplomas, and associate
- **Suburban** 32-acre campus with easy access to Seattle
- **Endowment** $3.3 million
- **Coed,** 6,390 undergraduate students, 51% full-time, 55% women, 45% men

Undergraduates 3,253 full-time, 3,137 part-time. Students come from 50 states and territories, 4 other countries, 3% African American, 9% Asian American or Pacific Islander, 5% Hispanic American, 2% Native American, 0.1% international, 0.5% transferred in.

Freshmen *Admission:* 4,022 applied, 4,022 admitted, 738 enrolled.

Faculty *Total:* 307, 32% full-time, 12% with terminal degrees. *Student/faculty ratio:* 25:1.

Majors Accounting technology and bookkeeping; administrative assistant and secretarial science; aesthetician/esthetician and skin care; animation, interactive technology, video graphics and special effects; audiovisual communications technologies related; automobile/automotive mechanics technology; barbering; business administration and management; child care and support services management; computer and information sciences related; computer graphics; computer programming; computer programming related; computer software and media applications related; computer systems networking and telecommunications; cosmetology; cosmetology, barber/styling, and nail instruction; criminal justice/law enforcement administration; criminal justice/police science; culinary arts; culinary arts related; digital communication and media/multimedia; drafting and design technology; early childhood education; electrical, electronic and communications engineering technology; engineering; fire science; fire services administration; industrial technology; information science/studies; information technology; legal administrative assistant/secretary; liberal arts and sciences/liberal studies; marine maintenance and ship repair technology; medical/clinical assistant; nail technician and manicurist; nursing (licensed practical/vocational nurse training); nursing (registered nurse training); office management; photographic and film/video technology; recording arts technology; special education (early childhood); system administration; system, networking, and LAN/WAN management; web/multimedia management and webmaster; welding technology.

Olympic College (continued)

Academic Programs *Special study options:* academic remediation for entering students, adult/continuing education programs, advanced placement credit, cooperative education, distance learning, English as a second language, honors programs, independent study, off-campus study, part-time degree program, services for LD students, summer session for credit.

Library Haselwood Library with 51,443 titles, 541 serial subscriptions, 3,007 audiovisual materials, an OPAC, a Web page.

Computers on Campus 634 computers available on campus for general student use. A campuswide network can be accessed from off campus. Internet access, online (class) registration, at least one staffed computer lab available.

Student Life *Housing:* college housing not available. *Activities and Organizations:* drama/theater group, student-run newspaper, choral group, Phi Theta Kappa, Aware, Oceans (Nursing), ASOC, ASAD. *Campus security:* 24-hour emergency response devices and patrols, student patrols, late-night transport/escort service. *Student services:* personal/psychological counseling, women's center.

Athletics *Intercollegiate sports:* baseball M(s), basketball M(s)/W(s), golf M/W, softball W(s), volleyball W(s). *Intramural sports:* basketball M/W, volleyball M/W.

Standardized Tests *Required for some:* ACT ASSET.

Costs (2004–05) *Tuition:* state resident $2313 full-time, $69 per credit part-time; nonresident $3792 full-time, $115 per credit part-time. Full-time tuition and fees vary according to course load. Part-time tuition and fees vary according to course load. *Required fees:* $232 full-time, $60 per term part-time. *Payment plan:* deferred payment. *Waivers:* senior citizens and employees or children of employees.

Financial Aid Of all full-time matriculated undergraduates who enrolled in 2003, 105 Federal Work-Study jobs (averaging $2380). 31 state and other part-time jobs (averaging $2880).

Applying *Options:* early admission. *Required for some:* high school transcript. *Application deadline:* rolling (freshmen), rolling (transfers). *Notification:* continuous (freshmen).

Admissions Contact Ms. Gerry Stamm, Director of Admissions and Outreach, Olympic College, 1600 Chester Avenue, Bremerton, WA 98337-1699. *Phone:* 360-475-7126. *Toll-free phone:* 800-259-6718. *Fax:* 360-475-7020. *E-mail:* gstamm@oc.ctc.edu.

PENINSULA COLLEGE
Port Angeles, Washington

- **State-supported** 2-year, founded 1961
- **Calendar** quarters
- **Degree** certificates and associate
- **Small-town** 75-acre campus
- **Coed,** 4,132 undergraduate students, 36% full-time, 57% women, 43% men

Undergraduates 1,492 full-time, 2,640 part-time. Students come from 5 other countries, 2% African American, 2% Asian American or Pacific Islander, 2% Hispanic American, 3% Native American, 0.9% international.

Freshmen *Admission:* 164 applied, 164 admitted, 164 enrolled.

Faculty *Total:* 230, 27% full-time, 13% with terminal degrees. *Student/faculty ratio:* 19:1.

Majors Accounting; automobile/automotive mechanics technology; biological and physical sciences; business administration and management; child care and support services management; child development; civil engineering technology; commercial fishing; computer programming (vendor/product certification); criminal justice/law enforcement administration; data entry/microcomputer applications related; diesel mechanics technology; electrical, electronic and communications engineering technology; engineering technology; fishing and fisheries sciences and management; nursing (registered nurse training); office management; substance abuse/addiction counseling; web page, digital/multimedia and information resources design.

Academic Programs *Special study options:* academic remediation for entering students, adult/continuing education programs, advanced placement credit, distance learning, English as a second language, honors programs, internships, part-time degree program, services for LD students, summer session for credit.

Library 33,736 titles, 383 serial subscriptions.

Computers on Campus 38 computers available on campus for general student use. A campuswide network can be accessed from student residence rooms and from off campus. At least one staffed computer lab available.

Student Life *Housing Options:* coed. Campus housing is university owned. *Activities and Organizations:* drama/theater group, student-run newspaper, choral group, Phi Theta Kappa, SAGE (Students Advocating Global Environmentalism). *Campus security:* 8-hour patrols by trained security personnel. *Student services:* women's center.

Athletics *Intercollegiate sports:* basketball M/W, soccer M, softball W. *Intramural sports:* badminton M/W, basketball M/W, bowling M/W, football M, golf M, skiing (cross-country) M/W, soccer M/W, softball M/W, table tennis M/W, tennis M/W, volleyball M/W.

Standardized Tests *Required:* ACT ASSET or ACT COMPASS (for placement). *Recommended:* SAT (for placement).

Costs (2005–06) *Tuition:* state resident $2400 full-time, $72 per credit part-time; nonresident $2789 full-time, $85 per credit part-time. *Required fees:* $130 full-time, $3 per credit part-time, $13 per term part-time.

Financial Aid Of all full-time matriculated undergraduates who enrolled in 2003, 30 Federal Work-Study jobs (averaging $3600). 25 state and other part-time jobs (averaging $3600).

Applying *Options:* common application, electronic application, deferred entrance. *Required for some:* high school transcript. *Application deadline:* rolling (freshmen), rolling (transfers). *Notification:* continuous (freshmen).

Admissions Contact Mr. Jack Huls, Vice President of Student Services, Peninsula College, 1502 East Lauridsen Boulevard, Port Angeles, WA 98362-2779. *Phone:* 360-417-6225. *Fax:* 360-457-8100. *E-mail:* admissions@pcadmin.ctc.edu.

PIERCE COLLEGE
Puyallup, Washington

Admissions Contact Ms. Cindy Burbank, Director of Admissions, Pierce College, 1601 39th Avenue SE, Puyallup, WA 98374-2222. *Phone:* 253-964-6686. *Fax:* 253-964-6427.

PIMA MEDICAL INSTITUTE
Seattle, Washington

- **Proprietary** 2-year, founded 1989, part of Vocational Training Institutes, Inc
- **Calendar** modular
- **Degree** certificates and associate
- **Urban** campus
- **Coed,** 289 undergraduate students, 100% full-time, 74% women, 26% men

Undergraduates 289 full-time.

Freshmen *Admission:* 109 applied, 67 admitted, 67 enrolled.

Faculty *Student/faculty ratio:* 10:1.

Majors Radiologic technology/science.

Student Life *Housing:* college housing not available.

Standardized Tests *Required:* Wonderlic aptitude test (for admission).

Costs (2005–06) *Tuition:* Costs vary by program. *Required fees:* $275 full-time.

Applying *Required:* interview. *Required for some:* high school transcript.

Admissions Contact Admissions Office, Pima Medical Institute, 1627 Eastlake Avenue East, Seattle, WA 98102. *Phone:* 206-322-6100. *Toll-free phone:* 888-898-9048.

RENTON TECHNICAL COLLEGE
Renton, Washington

Admissions Contact Mr. Jon Pozega, Vice President for Student Services, Renton Technical College, 3000 Fourth Street, NE, Renton, WA 98056. *Phone:* 425-235-2463. *Fax:* 425-235-7832. *E-mail:* cdaniels@rtc.ctc.edu.

SEATTLE CENTRAL COMMUNITY COLLEGE
Seattle, Washington

- **State-supported** 2-year, founded 1966, part of Seattle Community College District System
- **Calendar** quarters
- **Degree** certificates and associate
- **Urban** 15-acre campus
- **Coed,** 10,721 undergraduate students

Undergraduates 11% African American, 14% Asian American or Pacific Islander, 8% Hispanic American, 1% Native American, 7% international.

Faculty *Total:* 607, 27% full-time.

Majors Accounting; administrative assistant and secretarial science; biological and physical sciences; biology/biotechnology laboratory technician; carpentry; cinematography and film/video production; commercial and advertising art; computer typography and composition equipment operation; cosmetology; culinary arts; drafting and design technology; fashion/apparel design; graphic and printing equipment operation/production; hospitality administration; hotel/motel administration; human services; kindergarten/preschool education; liberal arts and sciences/liberal studies; marine technology; nursing (registered nurse training); ophthalmic laboratory technology; photography; respiratory care therapy; sign language interpretation and translation; substance abuse/addiction counseling.

Academic Programs *Special study options:* academic remediation for entering students, adult/continuing education programs, cooperative education, English as a second language, external degree program, internships, part-time degree program, services for LD students, summer session for credit. *ROTC:* Army (c), Navy (c), Air Force (c).

Library Main Library with 56,338 titles, 425 serial subscriptions.

Computers on Campus 366 computers available on campus for general student use. At least one staffed computer lab available.

Student Life *Housing:* college housing not available. *Activities and Organizations:* drama/theater group, student-run newspaper, choral group, Triangle Club, African Brothers of Unity, MECHA, Asian/Pacific Islander Student Union, Sea-King Club for the Deaf. *Campus security:* 24-hour emergency response devices. *Student services:* personal/psychological counseling, women's center.

Athletics *Intramural sports:* basketball M/W, softball M/W, tennis M/W, volleyball M/W, weight lifting M/W, wrestling M/W.

Standardized Tests *Required:* ACT ASSET (for placement).

Costs (2004–05) *Tuition:* state resident $69 per credit part-time; nonresident $241 per credit part-time. *Required fees:* $3 per credit part-time, $30 per term part-time.

Applying *Application deadline:* rolling (freshmen), rolling (transfers).

Admissions Contact Admissions Office, Seattle Central Community College, 1701 Broadway, Seattle, WA 98122-2400. *Phone:* 206-587-5450.

SHORELINE COMMUNITY COLLEGE
Shoreline, Washington

- **State-supported** 2-year, founded 1964, part of Washington State Board for Community and Technical Colleges
- **Calendar** quarters
- **Degree** certificates, diplomas, and associate
- **Suburban** 80-acre campus
- **Coed,** 8,591 undergraduate students

Freshmen *Admission:* 1,877 admitted.

Faculty *Total:* 415, 37% full-time. *Student/faculty ratio:* 21:1.

Majors Accounting; audio engineering; automobile/automotive mechanics technology; biology/biotechnology laboratory technician; business administration and management; chemical engineering; child development; cinematography and film/video production; civil engineering technology; clinical/medical laboratory technology; commercial and advertising art; computer and information sciences; computer graphics; consumer merchandising/retailing management; cosmetology; dental hygiene; dietetics; drafting and design technology; education; engineering technology; environmental engineering technology; graphic and printing equipment operation/production; health information/medical records administration; human development and family studies; industrial technology; international business/trade/commerce; kindergarten/preschool education; liberal arts and sciences/liberal studies; machine tool technology; marine biology and biological oceanography; marine technology; marketing/marketing management; mechanical engineering/mechanical technology; medical administrative assistant and medical secretary; medical laboratory technology; music; nursing (registered nurse training); oceanography (chemical and physical); photography; pre-engineering; purchasing, procurement/acquisitions and contracts management; teacher assistant/aide.

Academic Programs *Special study options:* academic remediation for entering students, adult/continuing education programs, advanced placement credit, cooperative education, English as a second language, internships, part-time degree program, services for LD students, study abroad, summer session for credit.

Library Ray W. Howard Library/Media Center with 79,554 titles, 1,735 serial subscriptions, an OPAC, a Web page.

Computers on Campus 385 computers available on campus for general student use. Internet access, at least one staffed computer lab available.

Student Life *Housing:* college housing not available. *Activities and Organizations:* drama/theater group, student-run newspaper, choral group, Arts and Entertainment Board, International Club, music groups. *Campus security:* 24-hour emergency response devices and patrols. *Student services:* personal/psychological counseling, women's center.

Athletics *Intercollegiate sports:* archery M/W, baseball M(s), basketball M(s)/W(s), cross-country running M/W, soccer M(s)/W, softball W(s), tennis M/W(s), volleyball W(s). *Intramural sports:* archery M/W, badminton M/W, basketball M/W, fencing M/W, gymnastics W, racquetball M/W, skiing (cross-country) M/W, skiing (downhill) M/W, softball M/W, swimming and diving M/W, volleyball M/W.

Standardized Tests *Required for some:* SAT or ACT (for placement), ACT ASSET or ACT COMPASS.

Costs (2004–05) *Tuition:* state resident $2293 full-time, $69 per credit part-time; nonresident $5091 full-time, $161 per credit part-time. *Required fees:* $165 full-time, $6 per credit part-time.

Applying *Options:* early admission. *Required:* high school transcript. *Application deadline:* rolling (freshmen), rolling (transfers).

Admissions Contact Ms. Robin Young, Registrar, Shoreline Community College, 16101 Greenwood Avenue North, Seattle, WA 98133. *Phone:* 206-546-4581. *Fax:* 206-546-5835. *E-mail:* sccadmis@ctc.edu.

SKAGIT VALLEY COLLEGE
Mount Vernon, Washington

Admissions Contact Ms. Karen Ackelson, Admissions and Recruitment Coordinator, Skagit Valley College, 2405 College Way, Mount Vernon, WA 98273-5899. *Phone:* 360-416-7620. *Fax:* 360-416-7890. *E-mail:* ackelson@skagit.ctc.edu.

SOUTH PUGET SOUND COMMUNITY COLLEGE
Olympia, Washington

- **State-supported** 2-year, founded 1970, part of Washington State Board for Community and Technical Colleges
- **Calendar** quarters
- **Degree** certificates, diplomas, and associate
- **Suburban** 86-acre campus with easy access to Seattle
- **Coed**

Faculty *Student/faculty ratio:* 20:1.

Student Life *Campus security:* 24-hour emergency response devices and patrols, late-night transport/escort service.

Standardized Tests *Required:* CPT, ACCUPLACER (for placement). *Recommended:* SAT or ACT (for placement).

Costs (2004–05) *Tuition:* state resident $2307 full-time, $69 per credit part-time; nonresident $2695 full-time, $82 per credit part-time. *Required fees:* $35 full-time, $3 per credit part-time.

Financial Aid Of all full-time matriculated undergraduates who enrolled in 2003, 42 Federal Work-Study jobs (averaging $3150). 14 state and other part-time jobs (averaging $4400). *Financial aid deadline:* 6/29.

Applying *Options:* electronic application, early admission, deferred entrance. *Application fee:* $15.

Admissions Contact Mr. Jerry Haynes, Dean of Enrollment Services, South Puget Sound Community College, 2011 Mottman Road, SW, Olympia, WA 98512. *Phone:* 360-754-7711 Ext. 5240. *Fax:* 360-664-0780. *E-mail:* enrollmentservices@spscc.ctc.edu.

SOUTH SEATTLE COMMUNITY COLLEGE
Seattle, Washington

Admissions Contact Ms. Kim Manderbach, Dean of Student Services/Registration, South Seattle Community College, 6000 16th Avenue, SW, Seattle, WA 98106-1499. *Phone:* 206-764-5378.

SPOKANE COMMUNITY COLLEGE
Spokane, Washington

- **State-supported** 2-year, founded 1963, part of Washington State Board for Community and Technical Colleges
- **Calendar** quarters
- **Degree** certificates, diplomas, and associate
- **Urban** 108-acre campus
- **Endowment** $33,508
- **Coed**

Faculty *Student/faculty ratio:* 21:1.

Student Life *Campus security:* 24-hour emergency response devices and patrols, student patrols, late-night transport/escort service.

Athletics Member NJCAA.

Financial Aid Of all full-time matriculated undergraduates who enrolled in 2003, 291 Federal Work-Study jobs (averaging $3600). 250 state and other part-time jobs (averaging $3600).

Applying *Options:* early admission, deferred entrance. *Application fee:* $15. *Recommended:* high school transcript.

Admissions Contact Ms. Colleen Straight, Manager, District Institutional Research, Spokane Community College, North 1810 Greene Street, Spokane, WA 99217-5399. *Phone:* 509-434-5240. *Toll-free phone:* 800-248-5644.

SPOKANE FALLS COMMUNITY COLLEGE
Spokane, Washington

- **State-supported** 2-year, founded 1967, part of State Board for Washington Community and Technical Colleges

Spokane Falls Community College (continued)
- **Calendar** quarters
- **Degree** certificates, diplomas, and associate
- **Urban** 125-acre campus
- **Endowment** $33,407
- **Coed**

Faculty *Student/faculty ratio:* 22:1.

Student Life *Campus security:* late-night transport/escort service, 24-hour emergency dispatch.

Athletics Member NJCAA.

Standardized Tests *Required:* ACT ASSET (for placement).

Financial Aid Of all full-time matriculated undergraduates who enrolled in 2003, 250 Federal Work-Study jobs (averaging $3600). 260 state and other part-time jobs (averaging $4500).

Applying *Options:* early admission, deferred entrance. *Application fee:* $15. *Recommended:* high school transcript.

Admissions Contact Ms. Carol Green, Vice President of Student Services, Spokane Falls Community College, 3410 West Fort George Wright Drive, Spokane, WA 99224-5288. *Phone:* 509-533-3682. *Toll-free phone:* 888-509-7944.

TACOMA COMMUNITY COLLEGE

Tacoma, Washington

- **State-supported** 2-year, founded 1965, part of Washington State Board for Community and Technical Colleges
- **Calendar** quarters
- **Degree** certificates, diplomas, and associate
- **Urban** 150-acre campus with easy access to Seattle
- **Coed,** 6,056 undergraduate students

Undergraduates Students come from 20 other countries, 4% are from out of state, 12% African American, 10% Asian American or Pacific Islander, 7% Hispanic American, 2% Native American, 3% international.

Freshmen *Admission:* 5,295 applied, 5,295 admitted.

Faculty *Total:* 334, 31% full-time. *Student/faculty ratio:* 27:1.

Majors Accounting; administrative assistant and secretarial science; American studies; anthropology; art; behavioral sciences; biological and physical sciences; biology/biological sciences; botany/plant biology; business administration and management; business/managerial economics; chemistry; computer and information sciences related; computer programming (specific applications); computer science; computer systems networking and telecommunications; computer/technical support; criminal justice/law enforcement administration; criminal justice/police science; data processing and data processing technology; economics; education; emergency medical technology (EMT paramedic); engineering; English; environmental studies; fine/studio arts; forestry; general studies; geology/earth science; health information/medical records administration; history; humanities; human services; information science/studies; information technology; international business/trade/commerce; international relations and affairs; Japanese; journalism; liberal arts and sciences/liberal studies; literature; mathematics; medical administrative assistant and medical secretary; museum studies; music; nursing (registered nurse training); occupational therapy; oceanography (chemical and physical); pharmacy technician; philosophy; physical education teaching and coaching; physical sciences; physical therapy; physics; political science and government; pre-engineering; pre-pharmacy studies; psychology; radiologic technology/science; respiratory care therapy; Romance languages; Russian; social sciences; sociology; Spanish; speech and rhetoric; substance abuse/addiction counseling; system administration; web page, digital/multimedia and information resources design; wildlife and wildlands science and management; wildlife biology; wood science and wood products/pulp and paper technology; word processing; zoology/animal biology.

Academic Programs *Special study options:* academic remediation for entering students, accelerated degree program, adult/continuing education programs, advanced placement credit, distance learning, English as a second language, honors programs, independent study, internships, off-campus study, part-time degree program, services for LD students, student-designed majors, summer session for credit. *ROTC:* Army (c).

Library Pearl Wanamaker Library with 90,192 titles, 269 serial subscriptions, 5,281 audiovisual materials, an OPAC, a Web page.

Computers on Campus 310 computers available on campus for general student use. A campuswide network can be accessed. Internet access, online (class) registration, at least one staffed computer lab available.

Student Life *Housing:* college housing not available. *Activities and Organizations:* drama/theater group, student-run newspaper, choral group. *Campus security:* Sonitrol electronic system. *Student services:* personal/psychological counseling, women's center.

Athletics *Intercollegiate sports:* baseball M(s), basketball M(s)/W(s), golf M(s)/W(s), soccer M(s)/W(s), volleyball W(s). *Intramural sports:* basketball M/W, bowling M/W, fencing M/W, football M/W, golf M/W, skiing (downhill) M/W, soccer M/W, softball M/W, tennis M/W, volleyball W.

Standardized Tests *Required:* ACCUPLACER (for placement).

Costs (2005–06) *Tuition:* state resident $2543 full-time; nonresident $2932 full-time. *Required fees:* $68 full-time.

Financial Aid Of all full-time matriculated undergraduates who enrolled in 2003, 81 Federal Work-Study jobs (averaging $2916). 146 state and other part-time jobs (averaging $2830). *Financial aid deadline:* 5/14.

Applying *Options:* early admission. *Application deadline:* rolling (freshmen), rolling (transfers).

Admissions Contact Ms. Annette Hayward, Admissions Officer, Tacoma Community College, 6501 South 19th Street, Tacoma, WA 98466. *Phone:* 253-566-5108. *Fax:* 253-566-6011. *E-mail:* admissions@tcc.ctc.edu.

WALLA WALLA COMMUNITY COLLEGE

Walla Walla, Washington

- **State-supported** 2-year, founded 1967, part of Washington State Board for Community and Technical Colleges
- **Calendar** quarters
- **Degree** certificates, diplomas, and associate
- **Small-town** 125-acre campus
- **Endowment** $4.0 million
- **Coed,** 4,440 undergraduate students, 49% full-time, 51% women, 49% men

Undergraduates 2,164 full-time, 2,276 part-time. Students come from 5 other countries, 12% are from out of state, 4% African American, 1% Asian American or Pacific Islander, 6% Hispanic American, 1% Native American, 0.2% international.

Freshmen *Admission:* 1,256 applied, 1,144 admitted, 407 enrolled.

Faculty *Total:* 359, 32% full-time. *Student/faculty ratio:* 21:1.

Majors Accounting technology and bookkeeping; administrative assistant and secretarial science; agricultural business and management; agricultural mechanization; agricultural production; autobody/collision and repair technology; automobile/automotive mechanics technology; business administration and management; carpentry; child care and support services management; civil engineering technology; computer technology/computer systems technology; corrections; cosmetology; criminal justice/safety; data entry/microcomputer applications; fire services administration; general retailing/wholesaling; heating, air conditioning, ventilation and refrigeration maintenance technology; information science/studies; legal administrative assistant/secretary; liberal arts and sciences/liberal studies; machine tool technology; medical administrative assistant and medical secretary; nursing (licensed practical/vocational nurse training); nursing (registered nurse training); office management; office occupations and clerical services; teacher assistant/aide; turf and turfgrass management; welding technology.

Academic Programs *Special study options:* academic remediation for entering students, adult/continuing education programs, advanced placement credit, cooperative education, distance learning, double majors, English as a second language, external degree program, honors programs, independent study, internships, off-campus study, part-time degree program, services for LD students, summer session for credit.

Library Walla Walla Community College Library with 45,814 titles, 428 serial subscriptions, 3,715 audiovisual materials, an OPAC.

Computers on Campus 180 computers available on campus for general student use. A campuswide network can be accessed from off campus. Internet access, online (class) registration, at least one staffed computer lab available.

Student Life *Housing:* college housing not available. *Activities and Organizations:* drama/theater group, choral group, Drama Club, Computer Club, intramurals, Nursing Club, Business Leadership Club. *Campus security:* student patrols, late-night transport/escort service. *Student services:* personal/psychological counseling.

Athletics Member NJCAA. *Intercollegiate sports:* baseball M(s), basketball M(s)/W(s), cross-country running W(s), equestrian sports M(s)/W(s), golf M(s)/W(s), soccer M(s)/W(s), softball W(s), tennis M(s)/W(s), volleyball W(s). *Intramural sports:* basketball M/W, racquetball M/W, soccer M/W, softball M/W, table tennis M/W, tennis M/W, volleyball M/W, weight lifting M/W.

Standardized Tests *Required:* ACT ASSET and ACT COMPASS (for placement).

Costs (2004–05) *Tuition:* state resident $2463 full-time; nonresident $3532 full-time.

Financial Aid Of all full-time matriculated undergraduates who enrolled in 2003, 95 Federal Work-Study jobs (averaging $1600). 20 state and other part-time jobs (averaging $2000).

Applying *Options:* common application, electronic application. *Application fee:* $40. *Required for some:* interview. *Recommended:* high school transcript. *Application deadline:* rolling (freshmen), rolling (transfers).

Admissions Contact Ms. Sally Wagoner, Director of Admissions and Records, Walla Walla Community College, 500 Tausick Way, Walla Walla, WA 99362-9267. *Phone:* 509-527-4283. *Toll-free phone:* 877-992-9282 (in-state); 877-992-9292 (out-of-state). *Fax:* 509-527-3361. *E-mail:* admissions@wccc.ctc.edu.

WENATCHEE VALLEY COLLEGE
Wenatchee, Washington

Admissions Contact Ms. Marlene Sinko, Registrar/Admissions Coordinator, Wenatchee Valley College, 1300 Fifth Street, Wenatchee, WA 98801-1799. *Phone:* 509-664-2564. *Fax:* 509-664-2511. *E-mail:* atyrrell@wvcmail.ctc.edu.

WESTERN BUSINESS COLLEGE
Vancouver, Washington

Admissions Contact Ms. Maryann Green, Director of Admission, Western Business College, 120 Northeast 136th Avenue, Suite300, Vancouver, WA 98684. *Phone:* 360-254-3282. *Fax:* 360-254-3035.

WHATCOM COMMUNITY COLLEGE
Bellingham, Washington

- **State-supported** 2-year, founded 1970, part of Washington State Board for Community and Technical Colleges
- **Calendar** quarters
- **Degree** certificates, diplomas, and associate
- **Small-town** 52-acre campus with easy access to Vancouver
- **Endowment** $2.0 million
- **Coed**, 4,173 undergraduate students

Undergraduates 5% are from out of state.
Faculty *Total:* 223, 24% full-time.
Majors Accounting; administrative assistant and secretarial science; business administration and management; commercial and advertising art; computer engineering technology; computer science; criminal justice/police science; kindergarten/preschool education; legal assistant/paralegal; liberal arts and sciences/liberal studies; medical administrative assistant and medical secretary; medical/clinical assistant; nursing (registered nurse training); physical therapist assistant.
Academic Programs *Special study options:* academic remediation for entering students, accelerated degree program, adult/continuing education programs, advanced placement credit, cooperative education, distance learning, English as a second language, external degree program, honors programs, independent study, internships, part-time degree program, services for LD students, student-designed majors, study abroad, summer session for credit.
Library Whatcom Community College Library with 14,680 titles, 193 serial subscriptions, 3,653 audiovisual materials, an OPAC, a Web page.
Computers on Campus 79 computers available on campus for general student use. A campuswide network can be accessed from off campus. Internet access, online (class) registration, at least one staffed computer lab available.
Student Life *Housing:* college housing not available. *Activities and Organizations:* drama/theater group, student-run newspaper, choral group, Anime Anonymous, Deaf Student Fellowship Club, Health and Wellness Club, Phi Theta Kappa, International Friendship Club. *Campus security:* 24-hour emergency response devices. *Student services:* personal/psychological counseling.
Athletics *Intercollegiate sports:* basketball M(s)/W(s), cheerleading M/W, soccer M(s), volleyball W(s). *Intramural sports:* basketball M/W, soccer M/W, tennis M/W, ultimate Frisbee M/W, volleyball M/W, weight lifting M/W.
Costs (2004–05) *Tuition:* state resident $2352 full-time, $71 per credit part-time; nonresident $7560 full-time, $242 per credit part-time. *Waivers:* senior citizens and employees or children of employees.
Financial Aid Of all full-time matriculated undergraduates who enrolled in 2003, 50 Federal Work-Study jobs (averaging $3500). 80 state and other part-time jobs (averaging $3690).
Applying *Options:* electronic application. *Application deadline:* rolling (freshmen). *Notification:* continuous (freshmen).
Admissions Contact Entry and Advising Center, Whatcom Community College, 237 West Kellogg Road, Bellingham, WA 98226. *Phone:* 360-650-5358. *Fax:* 360-676-2171. *E-mail:* admit@whatcom.ctc.edu.

YAKIMA VALLEY COMMUNITY COLLEGE
Yakima, Washington

- **State-supported** 2-year, founded 1928, part of Washington State Board for Community and Technical Colleges
- **Calendar** quarters
- **Small-town** 20-acre campus
- **Endowment** $5.4 million
- **Coed**, 6,770 undergraduate students, 55% full-time, 65% women, 35% men

Undergraduates 3,690 full-time, 3,080 part-time. Students come from 10 other countries, 2% are from out of state, 1% live on campus.

Freshmen *Admission:* 2,204 applied, 2,204 admitted.
Faculty *Total:* 120. *Student/faculty ratio:* 20:1.
Majors Accounting; administrative assistant and secretarial science; agricultural business and management; agricultural mechanization; agriculture; agronomy and crop science; animal sciences; automobile/automotive mechanics technology; broadcast journalism; business administration and management; child development; civil engineering technology; computer engineering technology; computer graphics; computer science; criminal justice/law enforcement administration; criminal justice/police science; dental hygiene; electrical, electronic and communications engineering technology; family and consumer economics related; fire science; hotel/motel administration; industrial radiologic technology; industrial technology; instrumentation technology; kindergarten/preschool education; legal administrative assistant/secretary; liberal arts and sciences/liberal studies; management information systems; marketing/marketing management; medical administrative assistant and medical secretary; nursing (registered nurse training); occupational therapy; pre-engineering; special products marketing; substance abuse/addiction counseling; tourism and travel services management; veterinary technology.
Academic Programs *Special study options:* academic remediation for entering students, adult/continuing education programs, advanced placement credit, cooperative education, distance learning, English as a second language, internships, part-time degree program, services for LD students, summer session for credit.
Library Raymond Library with 31,716 titles, 860 serial subscriptions, an OPAC.
Computers on Campus 369 computers available on campus for general student use. A campuswide network can be accessed. Internet access, online (class) registration, at least one staffed computer lab available.
Student Life *Housing Options:* coed. Campus housing is university owned. *Activities and Organizations:* drama/theater group, student-run newspaper, choral group, Veterans with Supporters, Business Management/Marketing Club, Image Makers, Agri-Business Club. *Campus security:* 24-hour emergency response devices, student patrols, late-night transport/escort service, controlled dormitory access. *Student services:* health clinic, personal/psychological counseling, women's center.
Athletics Member NJCAA. *Intercollegiate sports:* baseball M(s), basketball M(s)/W(s), softball W(s), volleyball W(s), wrestling M(s). *Intramural sports:* basketball M/W, volleyball W, wrestling M.
Standardized Tests *Required:* ACT ASSET (for placement).
Costs (2004–05) *Tuition:* state resident $2418 full-time, $73 per credit part-time; nonresident $2807 full-time, $245 per credit part-time. Full-time tuition and fees vary according to course load. Part-time tuition and fees vary according to course load. *Room and board:* $4425. *Payment plan:* installment. *Waivers:* senior citizens.
Financial Aid Of all full-time matriculated undergraduates who enrolled in 2003, 133 Federal Work-Study jobs (averaging $1164). 156 state and other part-time jobs (averaging $2083).
Applying *Options:* common application, electronic application, deferred entrance. *Application fee:* $20. *Required for some:* high school transcript, minimum 2.0 GPA, letters of recommendation, interview. *Recommended:* high school transcript. *Application deadlines:* 9/15 (freshmen), 9/15 (transfers). *Notification:* continuous until 9/15 (freshmen).
Admissions Contact Tessa Southards, Admissions Assistant, Yakima Valley Community College, PO Box 22520, Yakima, WA 98907-2520. *Phone:* 509-574-4713. *Fax:* 509-574-6860. *E-mail:* admis@yvcc.edu.

WEST VIRGINIA

COMMUNITY & TECHNICAL COLLEGE AT WEST VIRGINIA UNIVERSITY INSTITUTE OF TECHNOLOGY
Montgomery, West Virginia

- **County-supported** 2-year
- **Degree** certificates and associate
- **Coed**

Faculty *Total:* 30.
Majors Accounting; administrative assistant and secretarial science; automobile/automotive mechanics technology; automotive engineering technology; business administration and management; civil engineering technology; corrections; culinary arts; data processing and data processing technology; dental hygiene; drafting and design technology; electrical, electronic and communications engineering technology; graphic and printing equipment operation/production; health/health care administration; legal administrative assistant/secretary; liberal arts

Community & Technical College at West Virginia University Institute of Technology (continued)

and sciences/liberal studies; mechanical engineering/mechanical technology; medical administrative assistant and medical secretary; respiratory care therapy; surgical technology.

Costs (2004–05) *Tuition:* state resident $3786 full-time, $132 per credit hour part-time; nonresident $9486 full-time, $397 per credit hour part-time. *Room and board:* $4960; room only: $2420.

Admissions Contact Ms. Lisa Graham, Director of Admissions, Community & Technical College at West Virginia University Institute of Technology, Box 10, Old Main, Montgomery, WV 25136. *Phone:* 304-442-3167. *Toll-free phone:* 888-554-8324. *Fax:* 304-442-3097. *E-mail:* admissions@wvutech.edu.

COMMUNITY AND TECHNICAL COLLEGE OF SHEPHERD
Martinsburg, West Virginia

- **County-supported** 2-year
- **Degree** certificates and associate
- **Coed**, 1,520 undergraduate students

Majors Automobile/automotive mechanics technology; business, management, and marketing related; criminal justice/safety; culinary arts; design and visual communications; electromechanical technology; emergency medical technology (EMT paramedic); fashion merchandising; fire science; general studies; heating, air conditioning, ventilation and refrigeration maintenance technology; information technology; office occupations and clerical services; paralegal/legal assistant; safety/security technology.

Costs (2004–05) *Tuition:* state resident $2968 full-time, $123 per credit hour part-time; nonresident $8542 full-time, $355 per credit hour part-time. *Room and board:* room only: $788.

Applying *Application fee:* $35.

Admissions Contact Director of Enrollment Management, Community and Technical College of Shepherd, 400 West Stephen Street, Martinsburg, WV 25401. *Phone:* 304-260-4380. *Fax:* 304-260-4376.

EASTERN WEST VIRGINIA COMMUNITY AND TECHNICAL COLLEGE
Moorefield, West Virginia

- **State-supported** 2-year, founded 1999
- **Calendar** semesters
- **Degree** certificates and associate
- **Rural** campus
- **Coed**, 694 undergraduate students, 11% full-time, 73% women, 27% men
- **100% of applicants were admitted**

Undergraduates 73 full-time, 621 part-time. 2% African American, 0.4% Native American.

Freshmen *Admission:* 96 applied, 96 admitted, 64 enrolled.

Faculty *Total:* 40, 8% with terminal degrees. *Student/faculty ratio:* 22:1.

Student Life *Housing:* college housing not available.

Costs (2005–06) *Tuition:* state resident $1708 full-time, $71 per credit part-time; nonresident $6824 full-time, $284 per credit part-time.

Admissions Contact Ms. Sharon Bungard, Dean for Learner Support Services, Eastern West Virginia Community and Technical College, 1929 State Road 55, Moorefield, WV 26836. *Phone:* 304-434-8000. *Toll-free phone:* 877-982-2322. *Fax:* 304-434-8000.

FAIRMONT STATE COMMUNITY & TECHNICAL COLLEGE
Fairmont, West Virginia

- **State-supported** 2-year, administratively affiliated with Fairmont State College
- **Calendar** semesters
- **Degree** certificates and associate
- **Small-town** 90-acre campus
- **Endowment** $91,000
- **Coed**, 3,355 undergraduate students, 56% full-time, 57% women, 43% men

Undergraduates 1,878 full-time, 1,477 part-time. Students come from 11 states and territories, 5% African American, 1% Asian American or Pacific Islander, 0.6% Hispanic American, 0.5% Native American.

Freshmen *Admission:* 1,267 applied, 1,120 admitted, 513 enrolled.

Faculty *Total:* 242, 17% full-time.

Majors Aeronautical/aerospace engineering technology; American Sign Language (ASL); architectural engineering technology; business/commerce; child

development; civil engineering technology; communications technology; drafting/design engineering technologies related; electrical and electronic engineering technologies related; electrical, electronic and communications engineering technology; emergency medical technology (EMT paramedic); finance; food service and dining room management; general studies; graphic communications; mechanical engineering/mechanical technology; nursing (registered nurse training); physician assistant.

Academic Programs *Special study options:* adult/continuing education programs, external degree program, part-time degree program, summer session for credit.

Student Life *Housing Options:* Campus housing is university owned. *Activities and Organizations:* drama/theater group, student-run newspaper, choral group, marching band, national fraternities, national sororities. *Student services:* health clinic, personal/psychological counseling.

Athletics Member NCAA.

Standardized Tests *Required:* SAT or ACT (for admission). *Required for some:* ACT COMPASS.

Costs (2004–05) *Tuition:* state resident $3008 full-time, $67 per credit hour part-time; nonresident $7020 full-time, $183 per credit hour part-time. Full-time tuition and fees vary according to location. Part-time tuition and fees vary according to location. *Room and board:* $5228; room only: $2680. Room and board charges vary according to board plan and housing facility. *Payment plan:* installment.

Applying *Options:* common application, electronic application, deferred entrance. *Recommended:* high school transcript, minimum 2.25 GPA. *Application deadline:* rolling (freshmen), rolling (transfers). *Notification:* continuous (freshmen).

Admissions Contact Mr. Douglas Dobbins, Executive Director of Enrollment Services, Fairmont State Community & Technical College, 1201 Locust Avenue, Fairmont, WV 26554. *Phone:* 304-367-4062. *Toll-free phone:* 800-641-5678. *Fax:* 304-367-4584. *E-mail:* fscinfo@mail.fscwv.edu.

▶ **See page 492 for a narrative description.**

HUNTINGTON JUNIOR COLLEGE
Huntington, West Virginia

Admissions Contact Mr. James Garrett, Educational Services Director, Huntington Junior College, 900 Fifth Avenue, Huntington, WV 25701-2004. *Phone:* 304-697-7550.

INTERNATIONAL ACADEMY OF DESIGN & TECHNOLOGY
Fairmont, West Virginia

Admissions Contact Mr. Dennis A. Hirsh, President, International Academy of Design & Technology, 2000 Green River Drive, Fairmont, WV 26554-9790. *Phone:* 888-406-8324. *Toll-free phone:* 888-406-8324.

MARSHALL COMMUNITY AND TECHNICAL COLLEGE
Huntington, West Virginia

- **County-supported** 2-year, part of Community and Technical College System of West Virginia, administratively affiliated with Marshall University
- **Degree** certificates and associate
- **Coed**, 2,400 undergraduate students, 57% full-time, 41% women, 59% men
- **69% of applicants were admitted**

Undergraduates 1,371 full-time, 1,029 part-time. Students come from 24 states and territories, 3 other countries, 15% are from out of state, 6% African American, 0.4% Asian American or Pacific Islander, 1% Hispanic American, 0.1% Native American, 0.1% international, 8% transferred in.

Freshmen *Admission:* 658 applied, 455 admitted, 455 enrolled. *Average high school GPA:* 2.64.

Faculty *Total:* 202, 18% full-time, 4% with terminal degrees. *Student/faculty ratio:* 25:1.

Majors Accounting technology and bookkeeping; administrative assistant and secretarial science; business/commerce; computer engineering technology; criminal justice/police science; data processing and data processing technology; dental laboratory technology; electrical, electronic and communications engineering technology; emergency medical technology (EMT paramedic); finance; health information/medical records technology; hospitality administration; interior design; legal assistant/paralegal; liberal arts and sciences/liberal studies; manufacturing technology; medical/clinical assistant; medical radiologic technology; medical transcription; multi-/interdisciplinary studies related; physical therapist assistant; respiratory care therapy; science technologies related.

Academic Programs *Special study options:* academic remediation for entering students, accelerated degree program, cooperative education, distance learning, double majors, English as a second language, independent study, internships, off-campus study, part-time degree program, services for LD students, summer session for credit. *ROTC:* Army (b).

Library John Deaver Drinko Library plus 2 others with 478,274 titles, 5,314 serial subscriptions, 24,759 audiovisual materials, an OPAC, a Web page.

Computers on Campus 1854 computers available on campus for general student use. A campuswide network can be accessed from student residence rooms and from off campus. Internet access, online (class) registration, at least one staffed computer lab available.

Student Life *Housing:* on-campus residence required for freshman year. *Options:* coed, men-only, women-only, disabled students. Campus housing is university owned. Freshman campus housing is guaranteed.

Standardized Tests *Recommended:* SAT or ACT (for placement).

Costs (2004–05) *Tuition:* state resident $3818 full-time, $151 per credit hour part-time; nonresident $10,128 full-time, $414 per credit hour part-time. Full-time tuition and fees vary according to program and reciprocity agreements. Part-time tuition and fees vary according to program and reciprocity agreements. *Required fees:* $478 full-time, $12 per credit hour part-time. *Room and board:* $6060. Room and board charges vary according to board plan and housing facility. *Payment plans:* installment, deferred payment. *Waivers:* employees or children of employees.

Applying *Options:* common application, electronic application, early admission. *Application fee:* $25. *Required:* high school transcript, minimum 2.0 GPA. *Application deadline:* rolling (freshmen), rolling (transfers). *Notification:* continuous (freshmen).

Admissions Contact Mr. Craig Grooms, Admissions Director, Marshall Community and Technical College, 1 John Marshall Drive, Huntington, WV 25755. *Phone:* 304-696-3160. *Toll-free phone:* 800-642-3499. *Fax:* 304-696-3135. *E-mail:* admissions@marshall.edu.

MOUNTAIN STATE COLLEGE
Parkersburg, West Virginia

- **Proprietary** 2-year, founded 1888
- **Calendar** quarters
- **Degree** diplomas and associate
- **Small-town** campus
- **Coed, primarily women**

Faculty *Student/faculty ratio:* 17:1.

Standardized Tests *Required:* CPAt (for admission).

Costs (2004–05) *Tuition:* $7050 full-time. *Required fees:* $115 full-time.

Applying *Required:* interview.

Admissions Contact Ms. Linda Craig, Director, Student Services, Mountain State College, 1508 Spring Street, Parkersburg, WV 26101-3993. *Phone:* 304-485-5487. *Toll-free phone:* 800-841-0201. *Fax:* 304-485-3524. *E-mail:* adm@mountainstate.org.

NATIONAL INSTITUTE OF TECHNOLOGY
Cross Lanes, West Virginia

- **Proprietary** 2-year, founded 1938, part of Corinthian Schools, Inc
- **Calendar** quarters
- **Degree** certificates, diplomas, and associate
- **Small-town** campus
- **Coed**

Financial Aid Of all full-time matriculated undergraduates who enrolled in 2003, 4 Federal Work-Study jobs (averaging $4000).

Applying *Options:* deferred entrance. *Required:* high school transcript, interview.

Admissions Contact Mrs. Karen Wilkinson, Director of Admissions, National Institute of Technology, 5514 Big Tyler Road, Cross Lanes, WV 25313. *Phone:* 304-776-6290. *Toll-free phone:* 888-741-4271. *Fax:* 304-776-6262.

NEW RIVER COMMUNITY AND TECHNICAL COLLEGE
Beckley, West Virginia

- **County-supported** 2-year
- **Degree** certificates and associate
- **Coed**

Faculty *Total:* 23.

Majors Accounting; administrative assistant and secretarial science; biological and physical sciences; business/commerce; communications technology; computer and information sciences; corrections; criminal justice/police science; hotel/motel administration; interdisciplinary studies; legal assistant/paralegal;

liberal arts and sciences/liberal studies; marketing/marketing management; medical/clinical assistant; psychology.

Costs (2004–05) *Tuition:* state resident $2624 full-time, $109 per credit part-time; nonresident $6894 full-time, $289 per credit part-time.

Admissions Contact Mr. Michael Palm, Director of Student Services, New River Community and Technical College, 101 Church Street, Lewisburg, WV 24901. *Phone:* 304-647-6564. *E-mail:* bscadmit@bluefieldstate.edu.

POTOMAC STATE COLLEGE OF WEST VIRGINIA UNIVERSITY
Keyser, West Virginia

Admissions Contact Ms. Beth Little, Director of Enrollment Services, Potomac State College of West Virginia University, One Grand Central Business Center, Suite 2090, Keyser, WV 26726. *Phone:* 304-788-6820. *Toll-free phone:* 800-262-7332 Ext. 6820. *Fax:* 304-788-6939. *E-mail:* go2psc@mail.wvu.edu.

SOUTHERN WEST VIRGINIA COMMUNITY AND TECHNICAL COLLEGE
Mount Gay, West Virginia

- **State-supported** 2-year, founded 1971, part of State College System of West Virginia
- **Calendar** semesters
- **Degree** certificates and associate
- **Rural** 23-acre campus
- **Coed**

Faculty *Student/faculty ratio:* 25:1.

Standardized Tests *Required for some:* ACT (for placement).

Costs (2004–05) *Tuition:* $68 per credit hour part-time; state resident $1634 full-time; nonresident $6486 full-time, $270 per credit hour part-time.

Financial Aid Of all full-time matriculated undergraduates who enrolled in 2003, 45 Federal Work-Study jobs (averaging $1500). *Financial aid deadline:* 3/1.

Applying *Options:* early admission, deferred entrance. *Required:* high school transcript.

Admissions Contact Mr. Roy Simmons, Registrar, Southern West Virginia Community and Technical College, PO Box 2900, Mt. Gay, WV 25637. *Phone:* 304-792-7160 Ext. 120. *E-mail:* admissions@southern.wvnet.edu.

VALLEY COLLEGE OF TECHNOLOGY
Martinsburg, West Virginia

- **Proprietary** 2-year, founded 1983
- **Calendar** continuous
- **Degree** certificates and associate
- **Suburban** campus
- **Coed, primarily women**

Faculty *Student/faculty ratio:* 14:1.

Admissions Contact Ms. Leslie C. See, Admissions Director, Valley College of Technology, 2600 Aikens Center, Edwin Miller Boulevard, Martinsburg, WV 25401. *Phone:* 304-263-0979.

WEST VIRGINIA BUSINESS COLLEGE
Nutter Fort, West Virginia

Admissions Contact 116 Pennsylvania Avenue, Nutter Fort, WV 26301.

WEST VIRGINIA BUSINESS COLLEGE
Wheeling, West Virginia

- **Proprietary** 2-year, founded 1881
- **Calendar** quarters
- **Degree** diplomas and associate
- **Urban** 5-acre campus
- **Coed, primarily women**
- **100% of applicants were admitted**

Faculty *Student/faculty ratio:* 6:1.

Costs (2004–05) *Tuition:* $15,000 full-time. No tuition increase for student's term of enrollment. *Required fees:* $175 full-time.

Admissions Contact Ms. Karen D. Shaw, Director, West Virginia Business College, 1052 Main Street, Wheeling, WV 26003. *Phone:* 304-232-0361. *E-mail:* wbbcwheeling@juno.com.

WEST VIRGINIA JUNIOR COLLEGE
Bridgeport, West Virginia

Admissions Contact Ms. Cheryl Stickley, Executive Assistant, West Virginia Junior College, 176 Thompson Drive, Bridgeport, WV 26330. *Phone:* 304-363-8824.

WEST VIRGINIA JUNIOR COLLEGE
Charleston, West Virginia

Admissions Contact Admission Department, West Virginia Junior College, 1000 Virginia Street East, Charleston, WV 25301-2817. *Phone:* 304-345-2820.

WEST VIRGINIA JUNIOR COLLEGE
Morgantown, West Virginia

Admissions Contact Admissions Office, West Virginia Junior College, 148 Willey Street, Morgantown, WV 26505-5521. *Phone:* 304-296-8282.

WEST VIRGINIA NORTHERN COMMUNITY COLLEGE
Wheeling, West Virginia

- **State-supported** 2-year, founded 1972
- **Calendar** semesters
- **Degree** certificates and associate
- **Small-town** campus with easy access to Pittsburgh
- **Endowment** $700,706
- **Coed**

Faculty *Student/faculty ratio:* 21:1.

Student Life *Campus security:* security personnel during evening and night classes.

Standardized Tests *Required:* ACT ASSET (for placement). *Required for some:* SAT or ACT (for placement).

Costs (2004–05) *Tuition:* state resident $1752 full-time, $73 per credit part-time; nonresident $5592 full-time, $233 per credit part-time. Full-time tuition and fees vary according to course load and reciprocity agreements. Part-time tuition and fees vary according to course load and reciprocity agreements. *Required fees:* $6 full-time, $3 per term part-time.

Financial Aid Of all full-time matriculated undergraduates who enrolled in 2003, 35 Federal Work-Study jobs (averaging $1650).

Applying *Options:* common application, electronic application, early admission, deferred entrance. *Required for some:* high school transcript.

Admissions Contact Ms. Janet M. Fike, Associate Dean of Enrollment Management, West Virginia Northern Community College, 1704 Market Street, Wheeling, WV 26003-3699. *Phone:* 304-233-5900 Ext. 4363. *Fax:* 304-233-5900.

WEST VIRGINIA STATE COMMUNITY AND TECHNICAL COLLEGE
Institute, West Virginia

- **County-supported** 2-year
- **Degree** certificates and associate
- **Coed**

Undergraduates 7% are from out of state.

Faculty *Total:* 93, 28% full-time.

Majors Accounting; architectural drafting; banking and financial support services; behavioral sciences; business administration, management and operations related; CAD/CADD drafting/design technology; chemical technology; computer science; criminal justice/safety; electrical and electronic engineering technologies related; electrical/electronics maintenance and repair technology related; general studies; gerontology; health services/allied health/health sciences; heating, air conditioning, ventilation and refrigeration maintenance technology; legal assistant/paralegal; marketing related; meteorology; nuclear medical technology; office occupations and clerical services.

Costs (2004–05) *Tuition:* state resident $3222 full-time, $134 per credit hour part-time; nonresident $7400 full-time, $308 per credit hour part-time. *Room and board:* $4720; room only: $2200.

Admissions Contact Mr. Tyreno N. Sowell Sr., Interim Director, Admissions and Recruitment Services, West Virginia State Community and Technical College, PO Box 1000, Institute, WV 25112-1000. *Phone:* 304-766-3033. *Toll-free phone:* 800-987-2112. *Fax:* 304-766-4105.

WEST VIRGINIA UNIVERSITY AT PARKERSBURG
Parkersburg, West Virginia

- **State-supported** primarily 2-year, founded 1961, administratively affiliated with West Virginia University
- **Calendar** semesters
- **Degrees** certificates, associate, and bachelor's
- **Small-town** 140-acre campus
- **Coed,** 3,722 undergraduate students, 58% full-time, 63% women, 37% men

Undergraduates 2,148 full-time, 1,574 part-time. Students come from 5 states and territories, 2% are from out of state, 0.5% African American, 0.6% Asian American or Pacific Islander, 0.3% Hispanic American, 0.3% Native American, 5% transferred in. *Retention:* 56% of 2002 full-time freshmen returned.

Freshmen *Admission:* 663 applied, 663 admitted, 584 enrolled. *Average high school GPA:* 2.92. *Test scores:* SAT verbal scores over 500: 40%; SAT math scores over 500: 30%; ACT scores over 18: 55%; SAT verbal scores over 600: 15%; SAT math scores over 600: 20%; ACT scores over 24: 10%; ACT scores over 30: 1%.

Faculty *Total:* 209, 41% full-time, 11% with terminal degrees. *Student/faculty ratio:* 20:1.

Majors Accounting; administrative assistant and secretarial science; automobile/automotive mechanics technology; business administration and management; chemical engineering; criminal justice/law enforcement administration; data processing and data processing technology; drafting and design technology; education; electrical, electronic and communications engineering technology; electromechanical technology; elementary education; environmental engineering technology; finance; liberal arts and sciences/liberal studies; machine tool technology; marketing/marketing management; mechanical engineering/mechanical technology; nursing (registered nurse training); pre-engineering; social work; welding technology.

Academic Programs *Special study options:* academic remediation for entering students, adult/continuing education programs, advanced placement credit, cooperative education, distance learning, English as a second language, independent study, internships, part-time degree program, services for LD students, study abroad, summer session for credit. *ROTC:* Army (c).

Library WVUP Library plus 1 other with 41,300 titles, 248 serial subscriptions, an OPAC, a Web page.

Computers on Campus 200 computers available on campus for general student use. A campuswide network can be accessed from off campus. Internet access, at least one staffed computer lab available.

Student Life *Housing:* college housing not available. *Activities and Organizations:* drama/theater group, student-run newspaper. *Student services:* health clinic, personal/psychological counseling.

Athletics *Intramural sports:* badminton M/W, basketball M/W, bowling M/W, cross-country running M/W, football M/W, golf M/W, table tennis M/W, tennis M/W, volleyball M/W, weight lifting M/W.

Standardized Tests *Required:* ACT (for placement).

Costs (2004–05) *Tuition:* state resident $2232 full-time, $70 per credit hour part-time; nonresident $5904 full-time, $241 per credit hour part-time. Full-time tuition and fees vary according to degree level and reciprocity agreements. Part-time tuition and fees vary according to degree level and reciprocity agreements. *Payment plan:* installment.

Applying *Options:* common application, electronic application, early admission, deferred entrance. *Required for some:* high school transcript. *Application deadline:* rolling (freshmen). *Notification:* continuous (freshmen).

Admissions Contact Ms. Violet Mosser, Senior Admissions Counselor, West Virginia University at Parkersburg, 300 Campus Drive, Parkersburg, WV 26101. *Phone:* 304-424-8223 Ext. 223. *Toll-free phone:* 800-WVA-WVUP. *Fax:* 304-424-8332.

WISCONSIN

BLACKHAWK TECHNICAL COLLEGE
Janesville, Wisconsin

- **District-supported** 2-year, founded 1968, part of Wisconsin Technical College System
- **Calendar** semesters
- **Degree** associate
- **Rural** 84-acre campus
- **Coed**

Costs (2004–05) *Tuition:* state resident $76 per credit part-time; nonresident $488 per credit part-time.

Financial Aid Of all full-time matriculated undergraduates who enrolled in 2003, 40 Federal Work-Study jobs (averaging $1900).
Applying *Options:* common application, electronic application. *Application fee:* $30. *Required:* high school transcript.
Admissions Contact Ms. Barbara Erlandson, Student Services Manager, Blackhawk Technical College, PO Box 5009, Janesville, WI 53547-5009. *Phone:* 608-757-7713. *Toll-free phone:* 800-472-0024. *Fax:* 608-743-4407.

BRYANT AND STRATTON COLLEGE
Milwaukee, Wisconsin

- **Proprietary** primarily 2-year, founded 1863, part of Bryant and Stratton Business Institute, Inc
- **Calendar** semesters
- **Degrees** associate and bachelor's
- **Urban** 2-acre campus
- **Coed**

Faculty *Student/faculty ratio:* 14:1.
Student Life *Campus security:* 24-hour emergency response devices and patrols.
Standardized Tests *Required:* TABE (for admission). *Recommended:* SAT or ACT (for admission).
Applying *Application fee:* $25. *Required:* high school transcript. *Required for some:* letters of recommendation, interview. *Recommended:* minimum 2.0 GPA.
Admissions Contact Ms. Kathryn Cotey, Director of Admissions, Bryant and Stratton College, 310 West Wisconsin Avenue, Milwaukee, WI 53203-2214. *Phone:* 414-276-5200.

CHIPPEWA VALLEY TECHNICAL COLLEGE
Eau Claire, Wisconsin

Admissions Contact Mr. Timothy Shepardson, Director of Admissions, Chippewa Valley Technical College, 620 West Clairemont Avenue, Eau Claire, WI 54701-6162. *Phone:* 715-833-6245. *Toll-free phone:* 800-547-2882. *Fax:* 715-833-6470.

COLLEGE OF MENOMINEE NATION
Keshena, Wisconsin

Admissions Contact Ms. Cynthia Norton, Admissions Representative, College of Menominee Nation, PO Box 1179, Keshena, WI 54135. *Phone:* 715-799-5600 Ext. 3053. *Fax:* 715-799-1326.

FOX VALLEY TECHNICAL COLLEGE
Appleton, Wisconsin

- **State and locally supported** 2-year, founded 1967, part of Wisconsin Technical College System
- **Calendar** semesters
- **Degree** certificates, diplomas, and associate
- **Suburban** 100-acre campus
- **Coed,** 7,523 undergraduate students, 30% full-time, 50% women, 50% men

Undergraduates 2,265 full-time, 5,258 part-time. Students come from 11 states and territories, 1% are from out of state, 0.9% African American, 2% Asian American or Pacific Islander, 2% Hispanic American, 0.9% Native American.
Freshmen *Admission:* 3,531 applied, 2,516 admitted, 968 enrolled.
Faculty *Total:* 848, 33% full-time. *Student/faculty ratio:* 18:1.
Majors Accounting; administrative assistant and secretarial science; agricultural business and management; airline pilot and flight crew; automobile/automotive mechanics technology; business administration and management; child development; commercial and advertising art; computer programming; computer typography and composition equipment operation; consumer merchandising/retailing management; criminal justice/law enforcement administration; criminal justice/police science; culinary arts; drafting and design technology; electrical, electronic and communications engineering technology; finance; fire science; fish/game management; forestry technology; graphic and printing equipment operation/production; hospitality administration; industrial technology; insurance; interior design; legal administrative assistant/secretary; marketing/marketing management; mechanical design technology; mechanical engineering/mechanical technology; natural resources/conservation; nursing (registered nurse training); occupational therapy; special products marketing; welding technology; wood science and wood products/pulp and paper technology.
Academic Programs *Special study options:* academic remediation for entering students, accelerated degree program, adult/continuing education programs,

advanced placement credit, cooperative education, distance learning, double majors, English as a second language, honors programs, independent study, internships, off-campus study, part-time degree program, services for LD students, student-designed majors, study abroad, summer session for credit.
Library William Sirek Educational Resource Center with 45,139 titles, 297 serial subscriptions, 7,953 audiovisual materials, an OPAC, a Web page.
Computers on Campus 300 computers available on campus for general student use. A campuswide network can be accessed from off campus that provide access to e-mail, personal web pages. Internet access, online (class) registration, at least one staffed computer lab available.
Student Life *Housing:* college housing not available. *Activities and Organizations:* student-run newspaper, Business Professionals of America, Delta Epsilon Chi, Vocational Industrial Clubs of America. *Campus security:* late-night transport/escort service, 16-hour patrols by trained security personnel. *Student services:* health clinic, personal/psychological counseling, women's center.
Athletics *Intramural sports:* archery M/W, basketball M/W, bowling M/W, skiing (downhill) M/W, tennis M/W, volleyball M/W, weight lifting M/W.
Standardized Tests *Required:* prefer ACCUPLACER; will accept ACT/SAT or ACT COMPASS (for placement).
Costs (2005–06) *Tuition:* state resident $2550 full-time; nonresident $15,926 full-time. *Required fees:* $575 full-time.
Financial Aid Of all full-time matriculated undergraduates who enrolled in 2003, 165 Federal Work-Study jobs (averaging $2300).
Applying *Options:* common application, electronic application, early admission, deferred entrance. *Application fee:* $30. *Required:* high school transcript. *Application deadline:* rolling (freshmen), rolling (transfers).
Admissions Contact Mr. Robert Burdick, Dean of Student Services, Fox Valley Technical College, 1825 North Bluemound Drive, PO Box 2277, Appleton, WI 54912-2277. *Phone:* 920-735-5643. *Fax:* 920-735-2582.

GATEWAY TECHNICAL COLLEGE
Kenosha, Wisconsin

Admissions Contact Ms. Susan Roberts, Manager Admissions and Testing, Gateway Technical College, 3520 30th Avenue, Kenosha, WI 53144-1690. *Phone:* 262-564-3224. *Fax:* 262-564-2301. *E-mail:* admissions@gateway.tec.wi.us.

HERZING COLLEGE
Madison, Wisconsin

- **Proprietary** primarily 2-year, founded 1948, part of Herzing Institutes, Inc
- **Calendar** semesters
- **Degrees** diplomas, associate, and bachelor's
- **Suburban** campus with easy access to Milwaukee
- **Coed, primarily men,** 650 undergraduate students

Undergraduates Students come from 5 states and territories, 2 other countries, 33% are from out of state.
Freshmen *Average high school GPA:* 2.5.
Faculty *Total:* 46, 33% full-time, 15% with terminal degrees. *Student/faculty ratio:* 13:1.
Majors Computer and information sciences; computer programming related; computer systems networking and telecommunications; drafting and design technology; electrical, electronic and communications engineering technology.
Academic Programs *Special study options:* academic remediation for entering students, accelerated degree program, adult/continuing education programs, advanced placement credit, cooperative education, distance learning, double majors, honors programs, independent study, internships, part-time degree program, services for LD students.
Library Herzing College Library with 1,500 titles, 15 serial subscriptions, an OPAC, a Web page.
Computers on Campus 210 computers available on campus for general student use. A campuswide network can be accessed from off campus. Internet access, at least one staffed computer lab available. Computer purchase or lease plan available.
Student Life *Housing:* college housing not available. *Options:* Campus housing is provided by a third party. *Campus security:* 24-hour emergency response devices.
Costs (2005–06) *Tuition:* $10,000 full-time, $290 per credit part-time. Full-time tuition and fees vary according to location and program. Part-time tuition and fees vary according to location and program. *Required fees:* $25 full-time. *Payment plan:* installment. *Waivers:* employees or children of employees.
Financial Aid *Financial aid deadline:* 6/30.
Applying *Options:* common application, electronic application, early admission. *Required:* high school transcript, interview, college entrance examination. *Application deadlines:* rolling (freshmen), 10/10 (transfers).

Herzing College (continued)

Admissions Contact Ms. Rebecca Abrams, Admissions Director, Herzing College, 5218 East Terrace Drive, Madison, WI 53718. *Phone:* 608-249-6611 Ext. 804. *Toll-free phone:* 800-582-1227. *Fax:* 608-249-8593. *E-mail:* info@ msn.herzing.edu.

ITT TECHNICAL INSTITUTE
Green Bay, Wisconsin

- **Proprietary** primarily 2-year, founded 2000, part of ITT Educational Services, Inc
- **Calendar** quarters
- **Degrees** associate and bachelor's
- **Coed**

Standardized Tests *Required:* (for admission).
Costs (2004–05) *Tuition:* Please see school catalog for specific information.
Applying *Options:* deferred entrance. *Application fee:* $100. *Required:* high school transcript, interview. *Recommended:* letters of recommendation.
Admissions Contact Mr. Raymond Sweetman, ITT Technical Institute, 470 Security Boulevard, Green Bay, WI 54313. *Phone:* 920-662-9000. *Toll-free phone:* 888-884-3626. *Fax:* 920-662-9384.

ITT TECHNICAL INSTITUTE
Greenfield, Wisconsin

- **Proprietary** primarily 2-year, founded 1968, part of ITT Educational Services, Inc
- **Calendar** quarters
- **Degrees** associate and bachelor's
- **Suburban** campus with easy access to Milwaukee
- **Coed**

Standardized Tests *Required:* Wonderlic aptitude test (for admission).
Costs (2004–05) *Tuition:* Please see school catalog for specific information.
Applying *Options:* deferred entrance. *Application fee:* $100. *Required:* high school transcript, interview. *Recommended:* letters of recommendation.
Admissions Contact Mr. Al Hedin, Director of Recruitment, ITT Technical Institute, 6300 West Layton Avenue, Greenfield, WI 53220. *Phone:* 414-282-9494. *Fax:* 414-282-9698.

LAC COURTE OREILLES OJIBWA COMMUNITY COLLEGE
Hayward, Wisconsin

- **Federally supported** 2-year, founded 1982
- **Calendar** semesters
- **Degree** certificates and associate
- **Rural** 2-acre campus
- **Endowment** $950,616
- **Coed,** 460 undergraduate students, 60% full-time, 77% women, 23% men

Undergraduates 275 full-time, 185 part-time. Students come from 1 other state, 0.9% African American, 0.2% Hispanic American, 69% Native American.
Freshmen *Admission:* 118 admitted, 118 enrolled.
Faculty *Total:* 61, 28% full-time. *Student/faculty ratio:* 20:1.
Majors Administrative assistant and secretarial science; American Indian/Native American studies; business administration and management; liberal arts and sciences/liberal studies; medical/clinical assistant; natural resources management and policy; nursing (registered nurse training); social work; substance abuse/addiction counseling.
Academic Programs *Special study options:* academic remediation for entering students, adult/continuing education programs, distance learning, double majors, external degree program, honors programs, independent study, part-time degree program.
Library Lac Courte Oreilles Ojibwa Community College Library with 13,800 titles, 100 serial subscriptions, an OPAC.
Computers on Campus 25 computers available on campus for general student use. A campuswide network can be accessed. Internet access, at least one staffed computer lab available.
Student Life *Housing:* college housing not available. *Activities and Organizations:* student association. *Campus security:* 24-hour emergency response devices.
Athletics *Intramural sports:* basketball M, softball W, volleyball M/W, weight lifting M/W.
Standardized Tests *Required:* TABE (for placement).
Costs (2005–06) *Tuition:* area resident $3300 full-time, $110 per credit part-time. *Required fees:* $40 full-time.

Financial Aid Of all full-time matriculated undergraduates who enrolled in 2003, 15 Federal Work-Study jobs (averaging $1400).
Applying *Options:* common application, early admission. *Application fee:* $10. *Required:* high school transcript. *Application deadline:* rolling (freshmen), rolling (transfers).
Admissions Contact Ms. Annette Wiggins, Registrar, Lac Courte Oreilles Ojibwa Community College, 13466 West Trepania Road, Hayward, WI 54843-2181. *Phone:* 715-634-4790 Ext. 104. *Toll-free phone:* 888-526-6221.

LAKESHORE TECHNICAL COLLEGE
Cleveland, Wisconsin

- **State and locally supported** 2-year, founded 1967, part of Wisconsin Technical College System
- **Calendar** semesters
- **Degree** certificates, diplomas, and associate
- **Rural** 160-acre campus with easy access to Milwaukee
- **Coed**

Faculty *Student/faculty ratio:* 14:1.
Student Life *Campus security:* 24-hour patrols.
Standardized Tests *Required:* SAT or ACT (for admission), ACCUPLACER/ACT ASSET (for admission).
Costs (2004–05) *Tuition:* state resident $76 per credit part-time. Full-time tuition and fees vary according to course load and program. Part-time tuition and fees vary according to course load and program. *Required fees:* $7 per credit part-time.
Financial Aid Of all full-time matriculated undergraduates who enrolled in 2003, 37 Federal Work-Study jobs.
Applying *Options:* common application, electronic application, early admission, deferred entrance. *Application fee:* $30. *Required for some:* high school transcript, interview.
Admissions Contact Ms. Donna Gorzelitz, Enrollment Specialist, Lakeshore Technical College, 1290 North Avenue, Cleveland, WI 53015. *Phone:* 920-693-1339. *Toll-free phone:* 888-GO TO LTC. *Fax:* 920-693-3561. *E-mail:* enroll@ltc.tec.wi.us.

MADISON AREA TECHNICAL COLLEGE
Madison, Wisconsin

Admissions Contact Ms. Maureen Menendez, Interim Admissions Administrator, Madison Area Technical College, 3550 Anderson Street, Madison, WI 53704-2599. *Phone:* 608-246-6212.

MADISON MEDIA INSTITUTE
Madison, Wisconsin

Admissions Contact Mr. Chris K. Hutchings, President / Director, Madison Media Institute, 2702 Agriculture Drive, Suite 1, Madison, WI 53718. *Phone:* 608-663-2000. *Toll-free phone:* 800-236-4997.

MID-STATE TECHNICAL COLLEGE
Wisconsin Rapids, Wisconsin

Admissions Contact Ms. Carole Prochnow, Admissions Assistant, Mid-State Technical College, 500 32nd Street North, Wisconsin Rapids, WI 54494-5599. *Phone:* 715-422-5444. *Toll-free phone:* 888-575-6782. *Fax:* 715-422-5440.

MILWAUKEE AREA TECHNICAL COLLEGE
Milwaukee, Wisconsin

- **District-supported** 2-year, founded 1912, part of Wisconsin Technical College System
- **Calendar** semesters
- **Degree** certificates, diplomas, and associate
- **Urban** campus
- **Coed,** 55,992 undergraduate students

Freshmen *Admission:* 10,500 applied, 10,500 admitted.
Faculty *Total:* 1,843, 32% full-time. *Student/faculty ratio:* 16:1.
Majors Accounting technology and bookkeeping; administrative assistant and secretarial science; agricultural business and management; automobile/automotive mechanics technology; baking and pastry arts; barbering; biomedical technology; business administration and management; business, management, and marketing related; cardiovascular technology; chemical engineering; child development; civil engineering technology; clinical/medical laboratory technology;

commercial and advertising art; communications technology; computer and information sciences related; computer graphics; computer/information technology services administration related; computer programming related; computer programming (specific applications); computer programming (vendor/product certification); computer science; computer systems analysis; construction engineering technology; consumer merchandising/retailing management; cooking and related culinary arts; cosmetology; cosmetology and personal grooming arts related; criminal justice/law enforcement administration; criminal justice/police science; culinary arts; data entry/microcomputer applications; data processing and data processing technology; dental assisting; dental hygiene; dietetics; dietetic technician; drafting and design technology; e-commerce; educational/instructional media design; electrical, electronic and communications engineering technology; electrical/electronics equipment installation and repair; electrocardiograph technology; electromechanical technology; environmental engineering technology; environmental health; fashion merchandising; film/cinema studies; finance; fire science; food services technology; funeral service and mortuary science; funeral service and mortuary science related; furniture design and manufacturing; graphic and printing equipment operation/production; hair styling and hair design; health unit coordinator/ward clerk; heating, air conditioning and refrigeration technology; heating, air conditioning, ventilation and refrigeration maintenance technology; hospitality and recreation marketing; hotel/motel administration; human services; hydrology and water resources science; industrial design; industrial radiologic technology; industrial technology; information technology; landscaping and groundskeeping; legal administrative assistant/secretary; legal assistant/paralegal; liberal arts and sciences/liberal studies; machine tool technology; marketing/marketing management; mechanical engineering/mechanical technology; medical administrative assistant and medical secretary; music; nursing (licensed practical/vocational nurse training); nursing (registered nurse training); occupational therapy; opticianry; photography; physical therapy; pre-engineering; publishing; radio and television broadcasting technology; real estate; respiratory care therapy; substance abuse/addiction counseling; survey technology; system administration; tool and die technology; tourism and travel services marketing; transportation management; transportation technology; web/multimedia management and webmaster; welding technology; word processing.

Academic Programs *Special study options:* academic remediation for entering students, accelerated degree program, adult/continuing education programs, advanced placement credit, cooperative education, distance learning, double majors, English as a second language, external degree program, freshman honors college, honors programs, independent study, internships, off-campus study, part-time degree program, services for LD students, student-designed majors, summer session for credit.

Library William F. Rasche Library plus 4 others with 60,847 titles, 856 serial subscriptions, an OPAC, a Web page.

Computers on Campus 1000 computers available on campus for general student use. A campuswide network can be accessed. Internet access, online (class) registration, at least one staffed computer lab available.

Student Life *Housing:* college housing not available. *Activities and Organizations:* student-run newspaper, television station, choral group. *Campus security:* 24-hour emergency response devices and patrols, student patrols, late-night transport/escort service. *Student services:* personal/psychological counseling, women's center, legal services.

Athletics Member NJCAA. *Intercollegiate sports:* baseball M/W, basketball M/W, bowling M/W, cross-country running M/W, golf M/W, soccer M, softball M/W, tennis M/W, track and field M/W, volleyball W. *Intramural sports:* badminton M/W, baseball M/W, basketball M, bowling M/W, soccer M/W, table tennis M/W, tennis M/W, volleyball M/W.

Standardized Tests *Required:* ACCUPLACER (for admission).

Costs (2005–06) *Tuition:* state resident $2624 full-time, $78 per credit part-time; nonresident $15,812 full-time, $494 per credit part-time. Full-time tuition and fees vary according to course level and program. Part-time tuition and fees vary according to course level and program. *Required fees:* $215 full-time, $7 per credit part-time. *Payment plan:* installment.

Financial Aid Of all full-time matriculated undergraduates who enrolled in 2003, 300 Federal Work-Study jobs (averaging $3900).

Applying *Options:* common application, electronic application. *Application fee:* $30. *Required:* high school transcript. *Application deadline:* rolling (freshmen), rolling (transfers). *Notification:* continuous until 8/20 (freshmen).

Admissions Contact Mr. Robert Bullock, Director, Admissions and Testing, Milwaukee Area Technical College, 700 West State Street, Milwaukee, WI 53233. *Phone:* 414-297-6274. *Fax:* 414-297-7999. *E-mail:* apply@matc.edu.

MORAINE PARK TECHNICAL COLLEGE
Fond du Lac, Wisconsin

- **State and locally supported** 2-year, founded 1967, part of Wisconsin Technical College System
- **Calendar** semesters
- **Degree** certificates, diplomas, and associate
- **Small-town** 40-acre campus with easy access to Milwaukee
- **Endowment** $21,500
- **Coed**

Student Life *Campus security:* 24-hour emergency response devices.

Standardized Tests *Required:* ACT ASSET, ACCUPLACER (for admission). *Required for some:* ACT (for admission).

Costs (2004–05) *Tuition:* state resident $2280 full-time, $76 per credit part-time; nonresident $16,923 full-time, $564 per credit part-time. *Required fees:* $114 full-time, $4 per credit part-time.

Financial Aid Of all full-time matriculated undergraduates who enrolled in 2003, 47 Federal Work-Study jobs (averaging $989).

Applying *Options:* electronic application, deferred entrance. *Application fee:* $30. *Required:* interview. *Recommended:* high school transcript.

Admissions Contact Ms. Karen Jarvis, Student Services, Moraine Park Technical College, 235 North National Ave, PO Box 1940, Fond du Lac, WI 54936-1940. *Phone:* 920-924-3200. *Toll-free phone:* 800-472-4554. *Fax:* 920-924-3421.

NICOLET AREA TECHNICAL COLLEGE
Rhinelander, Wisconsin

Admissions Contact Ms. Susan Kordula, Director of Admissions and Marketing, Nicolet Area Technical College, Box 518, Rhinelander, WI 54501-0518. *Phone:* 715-365-4451. *Toll-free phone:* 800-544-3039 Ext. 4451. *Fax:* 715-365-4411. *E-mail:* inquire@nicolet.tec.wi.us.

NORTHCENTRAL TECHNICAL COLLEGE
Wausau, Wisconsin

- **District-supported** 2-year, founded 1912, part of Wisconsin Technical College System
- **Calendar** semesters
- **Degree** certificates, diplomas, and associate
- **Rural** 96-acre campus
- **Endowment** $1.4 million
- **Coed**

Faculty *Student/faculty ratio:* 13:1.

Student Life *Campus security:* 24-hour emergency response devices, late-night transport/escort service.

Standardized Tests *Required for some:* ACCUPLACER.

Costs (2004–05) *Tuition:* state resident $2280 full-time, $76 per credit part-time; nonresident $14,643 full-time, $488 per credit part-time. Full-time tuition and fees vary according to course load and program. Part-time tuition and fees vary according to course load and program. *Required fees:* $138 full-time, $5 per credit part-time. *Room and board:* Room and board charges vary according to board plan.

Financial Aid Of all full-time matriculated undergraduates who enrolled in 2003, 366 Federal Work-Study jobs (averaging $2000).

Applying *Options:* common application, electronic application, early admission, deferred entrance. *Application fee:* $25. *Required:* high school transcript. *Required for some:* interview.

Admissions Contact Ms. Carolyn Michalski, Team Leader, Student Services, Northcentral Technical College, 1000 West Campus Drive, Wausau, WI 54401-1899. *Phone:* 715-675-3331 Ext. 4285. *Fax:* 715-675-9776.

NORTHEAST WISCONSIN TECHNICAL COLLEGE
Green Bay, Wisconsin

- **State and locally supported** 2-year, founded 1913, part of Wisconsin Technical College System
- **Calendar** semesters
- **Degree** certificates, diplomas, and associate
- **Suburban** 192-acre campus
- **Coed**

Faculty *Student/faculty ratio:* 39:1.

Student Life *Campus security:* 24-hour emergency response devices, late-night transport/escort service.

Standardized Tests *Required for some:* SAT or ACT (for placement).

Costs (2004–05) *Tuition:* state resident $2205 full-time, $74 per credit part-time; nonresident $13,222 full-time, $441 per credit part-time. *Required fees:* $375 full-time, $8 per credit part-time.

Financial Aid Of all full-time matriculated undergraduates who enrolled in 2003, 80 Federal Work-Study jobs (averaging $1991).

Applying *Options:* early admission. *Application fee:* $30. *Required for some:* high school transcript.

Admissions Contact Ms. Heather Hill, Program Enrollment Team Supervisor, Northeast Wisconsin Technical College, 2740 West Mason Street, PO Box

Northeast Wisconsin Technical College (continued)
19042, Green Bay, WI 54307-9042. *Phone:* 920-498-5612. *Toll-free phone:* 800-498-5444 (in-state); 800-422-6982 (out-of-state). *Fax:* 920-498-6882. *E-mail:* heather.hill@nwtc.edu.

SOUTHWEST WISCONSIN TECHNICAL COLLEGE
Fennimore, Wisconsin

- **State and locally supported** 2-year, founded 1967, part of Wisconsin Technical College System
- **Calendar** semesters
- **Degree** certificates, diplomas, and associate
- **Rural** 53-acre campus
- **Endowment** $935,000
- **Coed,** 1,861 undergraduate students, 42% full-time, 52% women, 48% men

Undergraduates 778 full-time, 1,083 part-time. Students come from 4 states and territories, 1% are from out of state, 1% African American, 0.5% Asian American or Pacific Islander, 1% Hispanic American, 0.3% Native American, 3% live on campus.
Freshmen *Admission:* 352 enrolled.
Faculty *Total:* 89, 97% full-time, 1% with terminal degrees. *Student/faculty ratio:* 13:1.
Majors Accounting; administrative assistant and secretarial science; agribusiness; agricultural mechanization; autobody/collision and repair technology; automobile/automotive mechanics technology; child development; computer management; computer programming; cosmetology; culinary arts; dairy science; data processing and data processing technology; dental assisting; drafting and design technology; electrical, electronic and communications engineering technology; electromechanical technology; finance; food services technology; human services; legal administrative assistant/secretary; machine tool technology; marketing/marketing management; masonry; mechanical design technology; medical/clinical assistant; medical transcription; nursing assistant/aide and patient care assistant; nursing (licensed practical/vocational nurse training); nursing (registered nurse training); welding technology.
Academic Programs *Special study options:* academic remediation for entering students, adult/continuing education programs, advanced placement credit, distance learning, double majors, English as a second language, internships, part-time degree program, services for LD students, student-designed majors, summer session for credit.
Library Southwest Technical College Library plus 1 other with 25,000 titles, 307 serial subscriptions, 5,000 audiovisual materials, an OPAC.
Computers on Campus 250 computers available on campus for general student use. A campuswide network can be accessed from off campus. Internet access, at least one staffed computer lab available.
Student Life *Housing Options:* coed. Campus housing is provided by a third party. *Activities and Organizations:* student-run newspaper, Business Professionals of America, Vocational Industrial Clubs of America, Health Occupations Students of America, Marketing and Management Association. *Student services:* health clinic, personal/psychological counseling, women's center.
Athletics *Intramural sports:* basketball M/W, bowling M/W, softball M/W, volleyball M/W.
Standardized Tests *Required:* TABE (for placement).
Applying *Options:* electronic application, early admission. *Application fee:* $30. *Required:* high school transcript, interview. *Application deadline:* rolling (freshmen).
Admissions Contact Ms. Kathy Kreul, Admissions, Southwest Wisconsin Technical College, 1800 Bronson Boulevard, Fennimore, WI 53813. *Phone:* 608-822-3262 Ext. 2355. *Toll-free phone:* 800-362-3322 Ext. 2355. *Fax:* 608-822-6019. *E-mail:* kkreul@southwest.tec.wi.us.

UNIVERSITY OF WISCONSIN-BARABOO/SAUK COUNTY
Baraboo, Wisconsin

- **State-supported** 2-year, founded 1968, part of University of Wisconsin System
- **Calendar** semesters
- **Degree** associate
- **Small-town** 68-acre campus
- **Coed,** 561 undergraduate students, 66% full-time, 56% women, 44% men

Undergraduates 371 full-time, 190 part-time. Students come from 3 states and territories, 3 other countries, 1% are from out of state, 1% African American, 1% Asian American or Pacific Islander, 2% Hispanic American, 2% Native American, 0.2% international.
Freshmen *Admission:* 343 applied, 292 admitted.

Faculty *Total:* 41, 49% full-time, 54% with terminal degrees. *Student/faculty ratio:* 21:1.
Majors Liberal arts and sciences/liberal studies.
Academic Programs *Special study options:* academic remediation for entering students, advanced placement credit, distance learning, external degree program, honors programs, independent study, internships, off-campus study, part-time degree program, services for LD students, student-designed majors, study abroad, summer session for credit.
Library T. N. Savides Library with 45,000 titles, 300 serial subscriptions, 940 audiovisual materials, an OPAC.
Computers on Campus 50 computers available on campus for general student use. A campuswide network can be accessed from off campus that provide access to financial aid application. Internet access, online (class) registration, at least one staffed computer lab available.
Student Life *Housing:* college housing not available. *Activities and Organizations:* drama/theater group, student-run newspaper, choral group, Student Government Association, chorus and band, dance team, Gaming Club, Business Club.
Athletics Member NJCAA. *Intercollegiate sports:* basketball M(s), golf M(s)/W(s), soccer M(s)/W(s), tennis M/W, volleyball W(s). *Intramural sports:* racquetball M/W, softball M/W, table tennis M/W, volleyball M/W, weight lifting M/W.
Standardized Tests *Required:* SAT or ACT (for admission). *Recommended:* ACT (for admission).
Costs (2004–05) *Tuition:* state resident $3985 full-time, $165 per credit part-time; nonresident $12,685 full-time, $529 per credit part-time. Part-time tuition and fees vary according to course load. *Payment plans:* installment, deferred payment. *Waivers:* senior citizens.
Applying *Options:* electronic application, early admission, deferred entrance. *Application fee:* $35. *Required:* high school transcript. *Required for some:* interview. *Application deadline:* rolling (freshmen), rolling (transfers). *Notification:* continuous until 8/31 (freshmen).
Admissions Contact Ms. Jan Gerlach, Assistant Director of Student Services, University of Wisconsin-Baraboo/Sauk County, 1006 Connie Road, Baraboo, WI 53913-1015. *Phone:* 608-356-8724 Ext. 270. *Fax:* 608-356-4074. *E-mail:* boouinfo@uwc.edu.

UNIVERSITY OF WISCONSIN-BARRON COUNTY
Rice Lake, Wisconsin

- **State-supported** 2-year, founded 1966, part of University of Wisconsin System
- **Calendar** semesters
- **Degree** associate
- **Small-town** 142-acre campus
- **Coed,** 616 undergraduate students, 50% full-time, 58% women, 42% men

Undergraduates 308 full-time, 308 part-time. Students come from 2 states and territories.
Freshmen *Admission:* 300 applied, 298 admitted.
Faculty *Total:* 33, 64% full-time, 42% with terminal degrees.
Majors Liberal arts and sciences/liberal studies.
Academic Programs *Special study options:* academic remediation for entering students, adult/continuing education programs, advanced placement credit, distance learning, independent study, internships, off-campus study, part-time degree program, services for LD students, study abroad, summer session for credit.
Library Main Library plus 1 other with 39,479 titles, 233 serial subscriptions, an OPAC.
Computers on Campus 50 computers available on campus for general student use. A campuswide network can be accessed from off campus. Internet access, online (class) registration, at least one staffed computer lab available. Computer purchase or lease plan available.
Student Life *Housing:* college housing not available. *Activities and Organizations:* drama/theater group, student-run newspaper, choral group, Phi Theta Kappa, student government, Encore, Delta Psi Omega, Sociology Club. *Student services:* health clinic.
Athletics Member NJCAA. *Intercollegiate sports:* baseball M, basketball M/W, golf M/W, volleyball W. *Intramural sports:* softball M/W, volleyball M/W.
Standardized Tests *Required:* ACT (for admission), SAT or ACT (for placement).
Costs (2004–05) *Tuition:* state resident $3700 full-time, $154 per credit part-time; nonresident $12,400 full-time, $516 per credit part-time. Full-time tuition and fees vary according to reciprocity agreements. Part-time tuition and fees vary according to reciprocity agreements. *Required fees:* $356 full-time, $15 per credit part-time. *Payment plan:* installment.

Applying *Options:* electronic application, deferred entrance. *Application fee:* $35. *Required:* high school transcript. *Required for some:* essay or personal statement, 1 letter of recommendation. *Application deadlines:* 9/15 (freshmen), 9/15 (transfers). *Notification:* continuous (freshmen).

Admissions Contact Mr. Dale Fenton, Assistant Dean for Student Services, University of Wisconsin-Barron County, 1800 College Drive, Rice Lake, WI 54868. *Phone:* 715-234-8024. *E-mail:* uwbcinfo@wwc.edu.

UNIVERSITY OF WISCONSIN-FOND DU LAC

Fond du Lac, Wisconsin

Admissions Contact Ms. Linda A. Reiss, Director of Student Services, University of Wisconsin-Fond du Lac, 400 University Drive, Fond du Lac, WI 54935-2950. *Phone:* 920-929-3606. *E-mail:* lreiss@uwc.edu.

UNIVERSITY OF WISCONSIN-FOX VALLEY

Menasha, Wisconsin

Admissions Contact Ms. Rhonda Uschan, Director of Student Services, University of Wisconsin-Fox Valley, 1478 Midway Road, Menasha, WI 54952. *Phone:* 920-832-2620. *Toll-free phone:* 888-INFOUWC. *E-mail:* foxinfo@uwc.edu.

UNIVERSITY OF WISCONSIN-MANITOWOC

Manitowoc, Wisconsin

- **State-supported** 2-year, founded 1935, part of University of Wisconsin System
- **Calendar** semesters
- **Degree** associate
- **Small-town** 50-acre campus with easy access to Milwaukee
- **Coed**

Faculty *Student/faculty ratio:* 21:1.

Standardized Tests *Required:* SAT or ACT (for admission).

Costs (2004–05) *Tuition:* state resident $3880 full-time, $161 per credit part-time; nonresident $12,300 full-time, $516 per credit part-time.

Applying *Options:* electronic application, early admission. *Application fee:* $35. *Required:* high school transcript.

Admissions Contact Dr. Michael A. Herrity, Director of Student Services, University of Wisconsin-Manitowoc, 705 Viebahn Street, Manitowoc, WI 54220-6699. *Phone:* 920-683-4708. *E-mail:* mherrity@uwc.edu.

UNIVERSITY OF WISCONSIN-MARATHON COUNTY

Wausau, Wisconsin

- **State-supported** 2-year, founded 1933, part of University of Wisconsin System
- **Calendar** semesters
- **Degree** associate
- **Small-town** 7-acre campus
- **Coed**, 1,303 undergraduate students, 68% full-time, 54% women, 46% men

Undergraduates 883 full-time, 420 part-time. Students come from 130 states and territories, 0.7% African American, 7% Asian American or Pacific Islander, 0.8% Hispanic American, 0.5% Native American, 16% live on campus. *Retention:* 100% of 2002 full-time freshmen returned.

Freshmen *Admission:* 892 enrolled. *Average high school GPA:* 2.80.

Faculty *Total:* 84, 70% full-time. *Student/faculty ratio:* 24:1.

Majors Liberal arts and sciences/liberal studies.

Academic Programs *Special study options:* academic remediation for entering students, adult/continuing education programs, advanced placement credit, honors programs, off-campus study, part-time degree program, student-designed majors, study abroad, summer session for credit. *ROTC:* Army (c).

Library University of Wisconsin-Marathon Library with 37,000 titles, 150 serial subscriptions, an OPAC, a Web page.

Computers on Campus 50 computers available on campus for general student use. A campuswide network can be accessed. Internet access, at least one staffed computer lab available.

Student Life *Housing Options:* coed. Campus housing is university owned. *Activities and Organizations:* drama/theater group, student-run newspaper, cho-

ral group, Fiercely Independent Theatre, Ski Club, Ten Percent Society, Unity, Tempo. *Campus security:* 24-hour emergency response devices, controlled dormitory access. *Student services:* personal/psychological counseling.

Athletics Member NJCAA. *Intercollegiate sports:* basketball M/W, golf M/W, soccer M/W, tennis M/W, volleyball W. *Intramural sports:* archery M/W, badminton M/W, basketball M/W, bowling M/W, cross-country running M/W, fencing M/W, football M/W, golf M/W, racquetball M/W, skiing (cross-country) M/W, skiing (downhill) M/W, soccer M/W, squash M/W, swimming and diving M/W, table tennis M/W, tennis M/W, volleyball M/W, water polo M/W, weight lifting M/W.

Standardized Tests *Required:* ACT (for admission).

Costs (2004–05) *Tuition:* state resident $3914 full-time, $165 per credit part-time; nonresident $12,614 full-time, $528 per credit part-time. *Room and board:* $3728. Room and board charges vary according to board plan. *Payment plan:* deferred payment.

Applying *Options:* common application, electronic application, early admission, deferred entrance. *Application fee:* $35. *Required for some:* interview. *Recommended:* minimum 2.0 GPA. *Application deadline:* rolling (transfers).

Admissions Contact Dr. Nolan Beck, Director of Student Services, University of Wisconsin-Marathon County, 518 South Seventh Avenue, Wausau, WI 54401-5396. *Phone:* 715-261-6238. *Toll-free phone:* 888-367-8962. *Fax:* 715-848-3568.

UNIVERSITY OF WISCONSIN-MARINETTE

Marinette, Wisconsin

- **State-supported** 2-year, founded 1965, part of University of Wisconsin System
- **Calendar** semesters
- **Degree** associate
- **Small-town** 36-acre campus
- **Endowment** $200,000
- **Coed**, 486 undergraduate students, 100% full-time, 59% women, 41% men

Undergraduates 486 full-time. Students come from 2 states and territories, 16 other countries, 1% Asian American or Pacific Islander, 2% Hispanic American, 0.6% Native American, 6% international.

Faculty *Total:* 30, 53% full-time. *Student/faculty ratio:* 21:1.

Majors Liberal arts and sciences/liberal studies.

Academic Programs *Special study options:* academic remediation for entering students, adult/continuing education programs, advanced placement credit, cooperative education, distance learning, English as a second language, independent study, internships, off-campus study, part-time degree program, services for LD students, summer session for credit.

Library Main Library plus 1 other with 23,000 titles, 135 serial subscriptions.

Computers on Campus 48 computers available on campus for general student use. A campuswide network can be accessed. Internet access, at least one staffed computer lab available.

Student Life *Housing:* college housing not available. *Activities and Organizations:* drama/theater group, student-run newspaper, choral group, Student Senate, Writers Club/Literature Club, Phi Theta Kappa, Student Ambassadors. *Student services:* personal/psychological counseling.

Athletics *Intercollegiate sports:* basketball M/W, volleyball W. *Intramural sports:* basketball M/W, football M/W, volleyball M/W.

Standardized Tests *Recommended:* SAT or ACT (for admission).

Costs (2004–05) *Tuition:* state resident $3868 full-time, $154 per credit part-time; nonresident $12,400 full-time, $516 per credit part-time. *Required fees:* $150 full-time, $7 per credit part-time. *Payment plans:* installment, deferred payment.

Applying *Options:* electronic application. *Application fee:* $35. *Required:* high school transcript. *Application deadline:* rolling (freshmen), rolling (transfers). *Notification:* continuous (freshmen).

Admissions Contact Ms. Cynthia M. Bailey, Director of Student Services, University of Wisconsin-Marinette, 750 West Bay Shore, Marinette, WI 54143-4299. *Phone:* 715-735-4301. *E-mail:* ssinfo@mai.uwc.edu.

UNIVERSITY OF WISCONSIN-MARSHFIELD/WOOD COUNTY

Marshfield, Wisconsin

Admissions Contact Mr. Jeff Meece, Director of Student Services, University of Wisconsin-Marshfield/Wood County, 2000 West Fifth Street, Marshfield, WI 54449. *Phone:* 715-389-6500. *Fax:* 715-384-1718.

UNIVERSITY OF WISCONSIN-RICHLAND
Richland Center, Wisconsin

- **State-supported** 2-year, founded 1967, part of University of Wisconsin System
- **Calendar** semesters
- **Degree** associate
- **Rural** 135-acre campus
- **Coed,** 516 undergraduate students, 79% full-time, 55% women, 45% men

Undergraduates 407 full-time, 109 part-time. Students come from 4 states and territories, 15 other countries, 1% are from out of state, 0.2% African American, 0.4% Asian American or Pacific Islander, 0.2% Hispanic American, 0.2% Native American, 4% international, 6% transferred in, 35% live on campus. *Retention:* 55% of 2002 full-time freshmen returned.

Freshmen *Admission:* 353 enrolled. *Test scores:* ACT scores over 18: 91%; ACT scores over 24: 19%.

Faculty *Total:* 26, 50% full-time, 35% with terminal degrees. *Student/faculty ratio:* 18:1.

Majors Biological and physical sciences; liberal arts and sciences/liberal studies.

Academic Programs *Special study options:* academic remediation for entering students, adult/continuing education programs, advanced placement credit, distance learning, external degree program, independent study, off-campus study, part-time degree program, services for LD students, study abroad, summer session for credit.

Library Miller Memorial Library with 45,000 titles, 200 serial subscriptions, an OPAC, a Web page.

Computers on Campus 45 computers available on campus for general student use. A campuswide network can be accessed from off campus. Internet access, at least one staffed computer lab available.

Student Life *Housing Options:* coed. Campus housing is provided by a third party. *Activities and Organizations:* drama/theater group, student-run newspaper, choral group. *Student services:* personal/psychological counseling.

Athletics *Intercollegiate sports:* basketball M/W, soccer M/W, volleyball W. *Intramural sports:* badminton M/W, basketball M/W, football M/W, golf M/W, racquetball M/W, swimming and diving M/W, table tennis M/W, tennis M/W, volleyball M/W.

Standardized Tests *Required:* SAT or ACT (for admission). *Recommended:* ACT (for admission).

Costs (2004–05) *Tuition:* state resident $4078 full-time, $170 per credit part-time; nonresident $12,777 full-time, $533 per credit part-time. *Required fees:* $377 full-time. *Room and board:* $4630; room only: $2890. *Payment plan:* installment. *Waivers:* senior citizens.

Applying *Options:* electronic application, early admission. *Application fee:* $35. *Required:* high school transcript. *Required for some:* letters of recommendation, interview. *Application deadlines:* rolling (freshmen), 9/1 (transfers). *Notification:* continuous until 9/1 (freshmen).

Admissions Contact Mr. John D. Poole, Director of Student Services, University of Wisconsin-Richland, 1200 Highway 14 West, Richland Center, WI 53581. *Phone:* 608-647-8422 Ext. 223. *Fax:* 608-647-6225. *E-mail:* jpoole@uwc.edu.

UNIVERSITY OF WISCONSIN-ROCK COUNTY
Janesville, Wisconsin

- **State-supported** 2-year, founded 1966, part of University of Wisconsin System
- **Calendar** semesters
- **Degree** certificates and associate
- **Suburban** 50-acre campus with easy access to Milwaukee
- **Coed,** 880 undergraduate students, 85% full-time, 55% women, 45% men

Undergraduates 751 full-time, 129 part-time. Students come from 10 states and territories, 4 other countries, 1% are from out of state, 11% transferred in.

Freshmen *Admission:* 371 applied, 360 admitted, 281 enrolled.

Faculty *Total:* 44, 45% full-time, 57% with terminal degrees. *Student/faculty ratio:* 16:1.

Majors Liberal arts and sciences/liberal studies.

Academic Programs *Special study options:* academic remediation for entering students, adult/continuing education programs, advanced placement credit, distance learning, off-campus study, part-time degree program, services for LD students, summer session for credit.

Library University of Wisconsin-Rock County Library with 79,972 titles, 4,466 audiovisual materials, an OPAC, a Web page.

Computers on Campus 50 computers available on campus for general student use. A campuswide network can be accessed. At least one staffed computer lab available.

Student Life *Housing:* college housing not available. *Activities and Organizations:* drama/theater group, choral group, Student Government Association, Multicultural Student Union, U-Rock Players, Education Club, Adult Student Club.

Athletics *Intercollegiate sports:* soccer M/W, tennis M/W, volleyball W. *Intramural sports:* basketball M/W, weight lifting M/W.

Standardized Tests *Required:* ACT (for admission).

Costs (2004–05) *Tuition:* state resident $3952 full-time, $163 per credit part-time; nonresident $12,614 full-time, $526 per credit part-time. *Required fees:* $2 per term part-time.

Applying *Options:* electronic application, deferred entrance. *Application fee:* $35. *Required:* high school transcript. *Application deadlines:* rolling (freshmen), 8/15 (transfers). *Notification:* continuous (freshmen).

Admissions Contact Ms. Donna Johnson, Program Manager, University of Wisconsin-Rock County, 2909 Kellogg Avenue, Janesville, WI 53456. *Phone:* 608-758-6523. *Toll-free phone:* 888-INFO-UWC. *Fax:* 608-755-2732. *E-mail:* tpickart@uwc.edu.

UNIVERSITY OF WISCONSIN-SHEBOYGAN
Sheboygan, Wisconsin

- **State-supported** 2-year, founded 1933, part of University of Wisconsin System
- **Calendar** semesters
- **Degree** associate
- **Small-town** 75-acre campus with easy access to Milwaukee
- **Coed,** 731 undergraduate students

Undergraduates Students come from 5 other countries, 1% African American, 6% Asian American or Pacific Islander, 3% Hispanic American, 0.5% Native American, 0.1% international.

Freshmen *Average high school GPA:* 2.54.

Faculty *Total:* 44, 52% full-time, 43% with terminal degrees. *Student/faculty ratio:* 15:1.

Majors Liberal arts and sciences/liberal studies.

Academic Programs *Special study options:* academic remediation for entering students, adult/continuing education programs, advanced placement credit, distance learning, English as a second language, independent study, off-campus study, part-time degree program, services for LD students, summer session for credit.

Library Battig Memorial Library with 40,100 titles, 160 serial subscriptions, an OPAC, a Web page.

Computers on Campus 60 computers available on campus for general student use. A campuswide network can be accessed. Internet access, at least one staffed computer lab available.

Student Life *Housing:* college housing not available. *Activities and Organizations:* drama/theater group, student-run newspaper, choral group, Student Ambassadors, Phi Theta Kappa, student government, Circle K, Zoomers (nontraditional students). *Campus security:* 24-hour patrols by city police.

Athletics Member NJCAA. *Intercollegiate sports:* basketball M/W, golf M/W, tennis M/W, volleyball W. *Intramural sports:* archery M, basketball M/W, soccer M/W, softball M/W, volleyball M/W.

Standardized Tests *Required:* ACT (for placement).

Costs (2004–05) *One-time required fee:* $75. *Tuition:* state resident $3952 full-time, $167 per credit hour part-time; nonresident $12,652 full-time, $529 per credit hour part-time. *Payment plans:* installment, deferred payment. *Waivers:* senior citizens.

Applying *Options:* common application, electronic application. *Application fee:* $35. *Required:* high school transcript. *Required for some:* interview. *Application deadline:* rolling (freshmen), rolling (transfers).

Admissions Contact Beth Raffaelli, Assistant Campus Dean for Student Services, University of Wisconsin-Sheboygan, One University Drive, Sheboygan, WI 53081-4789. *Phone:* 920-459-6633. *Fax:* 920-459-6662. *E-mail:* braffael@uwc.edu.

UNIVERSITY OF WISCONSIN-WASHINGTON COUNTY
West Bend, Wisconsin

- **State-supported** 2-year, founded 1968, part of University of Wisconsin System
- **Calendar** semesters
- **Degree** associate
- **Small-town** 87-acre campus with easy access to Milwaukee
- **Coed,** 942 undergraduate students, 72% full-time, 53% women, 47% men

Undergraduates 680 full-time, 262 part-time. Students come from 2 states and territories, 2 other countries, 1% are from out of state, 0.6% African American, 1% Asian American or Pacific Islander, 2% Hispanic American, 0.7% Native American, 0.2% international, 7% transferred in.

Freshmen *Admission:* 487 enrolled. *Test scores:* ACT scores over 18: 58%; ACT scores over 24: 21%.

Faculty *Total:* 49, 55% full-time, 63% with terminal degrees. *Student/faculty ratio:* 25:1.

Majors Liberal arts and sciences/liberal studies.

Academic Programs *Special study options:* academic remediation for entering students, advanced placement credit, distance learning, double majors, honors programs, independent study, off-campus study, part-time degree program, services for LD students, summer session for credit.

Library University of Wisconsin-Washington County Library with 46,429 titles, 247 serial subscriptions, 4,998 audiovisual materials, an OPAC, a Web page.

Computers on Campus 78 computers available on campus for general student use. A campuswide network can be accessed from off campus. Internet access, at least one staffed computer lab available.

Student Life *Housing:* college housing not available. *Activities and Organizations:* drama/theater group, student-run newspaper, choral group, Student Government Association, Business Club, Phi Theta Kappa, Writers' Guild, Student Impact. *Student services:* personal/psychological counseling.

Athletics Member NAIA. *Intercollegiate sports:* basketball M/W, golf M/W, soccer M/W, tennis M/W, volleyball W. *Intramural sports:* basketball M/W, football M/W, softball M/W, volleyball M/W.

Standardized Tests *Required:* ACT (for admission).

Costs (2004–05) *Tuition:* state resident $3947 full-time, $154 per credit part-time; nonresident $12,647 full-time, $516 per credit part-time. Part-time tuition and fees vary according to course load. *Required fees:* $336 full-time, $10 per credit part-time, $122 per term part-time. *Payment plans:* installment, deferred payment.

Applying *Options:* electronic application, deferred entrance. *Application fee:* $35. *Required:* high school transcript. *Required for some:* essay or personal statement, interview. *Application deadline:* rolling (freshmen), rolling (transfers).

Admissions Contact Mr. Dan Cebrario, Associate Director of Student Services, University of Wisconsin-Washington County, Student Services Office, 400 University Drive, West Bend, WI 53095. *Phone:* 262-335-5201. *Fax:* 262-335-5220.

UNIVERSITY OF WISCONSIN-WAUKESHA
Waukesha, Wisconsin

- **State-supported** 2-year, founded 1966, part of University of Wisconsin System
- **Calendar** semesters
- **Degree** associate
- **Suburban** 86-acre campus with easy access to Milwaukee
- **Coed**

Faculty *Student/faculty ratio:* 14:1.

Student Life *Campus security:* late-night transport/escort service, part-time patrols by trained security personnel.

Athletics Member NJCAA.

Standardized Tests *Required:* ACT (for admission). *Required for some:* SAT (for admission).

Costs (2004–05) *Tuition:* state resident $3921 full-time, $163 per credit part-time; nonresident $12,621 full-time, $526 per credit part-time. *Required fees:* $109 full-time, $9 per credit part-time.

Applying *Options:* early admission, deferred entrance. *Application fee:* $35. *Required:* high school transcript. *Required for some:* letters of recommendation, interview.

Admissions Contact Ms. Susan Adams, Coordinator of Admissions, University of Wisconsin-Waukesha, 1500 North University Drive, Waukesha, WI 53188. *Phone:* 262-521-5200. *Fax:* 262-521-5491. *E-mail:* sadams@uwc.edu.

WAUKESHA COUNTY TECHNICAL COLLEGE
Pewaukee, Wisconsin

Admissions Contact Ms. Dianna Skornicka, Interim Director of Admissions, Waukesha County Technical College, 800 Main Street, Pewaukee, WI 53072-4601. *Phone:* 262-691-5464. *Toll-free phone:* 888-892-WCTC.

WESTERN WISCONSIN TECHNICAL COLLEGE
La Crosse, Wisconsin

- **District-supported** 2-year, founded 1911, part of Wisconsin Technical College System
- **Calendar** semesters
- **Degree** certificates, diplomas, and associate
- **Urban** 10-acre campus
- **Coed**

Faculty *Student/faculty ratio:* 16:1.

Student Life *Campus security:* 24-hour emergency response devices and patrols, student patrols, late-night transport/escort service, controlled dormitory access.

Athletics Member NJCAA.

Standardized Tests *Required for some:* ACT ASSET. *Recommended:* ACT (for admission).

Costs (2004–05) *Tuition:* state resident $2280 full-time, $76 per credit part-time; nonresident $14,894 full-time, $488 per credit part-time. *Required fees:* $251 full-time. *Room and board:* room only: $2200. Room and board charges vary according to housing facility.

Financial Aid Of all full-time matriculated undergraduates who enrolled in 2003, 102 Federal Work-Study jobs (averaging $1444).

Applying *Options:* common application, electronic application, early admission. *Application fee:* $30. *Required:* high school transcript. *Recommended:* interview.

Admissions Contact Ms. Jane Wells, Manager of Admissions, Registration and Records, Western Wisconsin Technical College, PO Box 908, La Crosse, WI 54602-0908. *Phone:* 608-785-9158. *Toll-free phone:* 800-322-9982 (in-state); 800-248-9982 (out-of-state). *Fax:* 608-785-9094. *E-mail:* mildes@wwtc.edu.

WISCONSIN INDIANHEAD TECHNICAL COLLEGE
Shell Lake, Wisconsin

- **District-supported** 2-year, founded 1912, part of Wisconsin Technical College System
- **Calendar** semesters
- **Degree** certificates, diplomas, and associate
- **Urban** 113-acre campus
- **Endowment** $1.7 million
- **Coed**

Faculty *Student/faculty ratio:* 6:1.

Costs (2004–05) *Tuition:* state resident $2432 full-time, $76 per credit part-time; nonresident $15,619 full-time, $488 per credit part-time. Full-time tuition and fees vary according to course load, program, and reciprocity agreements. Part-time tuition and fees vary according to course load, program, and reciprocity agreements. *Required fees:* $200 full-time.

Applying *Application fee:* $35.

Admissions Contact Ms. Mimi Crandall, Dean, Student Services, Wisconsin Indianhead Technical College, 505 Pine Ridge Drive, Shell Lake, WI 54871. *Phone:* 715-468-2815 Ext. 2280. *Toll-free phone:* 800-243-9482. *Fax:* 715-468-2819.

WYOMING

CASPER COLLEGE
Casper, Wyoming

- **District-supported** 2-year, founded 1945, part of Wyoming Community College Commission
- **Calendar** semesters
- **Degree** certificates and associate
- **Small-town** 125-acre campus
- **Coed**, 4,023 undergraduate students, 47% full-time, 61% women, 39% men

Undergraduates 1,875 full-time, 2,148 part-time. Students come from 40 states and territories, 15 other countries, 7% are from out of state, 0.8% African American, 0.4% Asian American or Pacific Islander, 4% Hispanic American, 1% Native American, 0.8% international, 7% transferred in, 15% live on campus. *Retention:* 59% of 2002 full-time freshmen returned.

Freshmen *Admission:* 996 applied, 996 admitted, 646 enrolled. *Average high school GPA:* 3.00. *Test scores:* SAT verbal scores over 500: 50%; SAT math

Casper College (continued)

scores over 500: 40%; ACT scores over 18: 74%; SAT verbal scores over 600: 20%; ACT scores over 24: 20%; ACT scores over 30: 1%.

Faculty *Total:* 251, 59% full-time, 14% with terminal degrees. *Student/faculty ratio:* 14:1.

Majors Accounting; administrative assistant and secretarial science; agricultural business and management; agricultural mechanization; agriculture; airline pilot and flight crew; animal sciences; anthropology; applied art; art; automobile/automotive mechanics technology; behavioral sciences; biological and physical sciences; biology/biological sciences; botany/plant biology; business administration and management; business teacher education; carpentry; ceramic arts and ceramics; chemistry; clinical laboratory science/medical technology; commercial and advertising art; computer engineering technology; computer programming; computer science; construction engineering technology; consumer merchandising/retailing management; corrections; criminal justice/law enforcement administration; criminal justice/police science; data processing and data processing technology; drafting and design technology; dramatic/theatre arts; ecology; economics; education; electrical, electronic and communications engineering technology; elementary education; emergency medical technology (EMT paramedic); engineering; English; fire science; French; geology/earth science; German; history; humanities; industrial arts; industrial radiologic technology; Italian; journalism; kindergarten/preschool education; legal administrative assistant/secretary; legal assistant/paralegal; liberal arts and sciences/liberal studies; machine tool technology; marketing/marketing management; mass communication/media; mathematics; mining technology; music; music teacher education; natural sciences; nursing (licensed practical/vocational nurse training); nursing (registered nurse training); occupational therapy; pharmacy; pharmacy technician; photography; physical education teaching and coaching; physical sciences; physical therapy; physics; political science and government; pre-engineering; psychology; social sciences; social work; sociology; Spanish; speech and rhetoric; veterinary sciences; welding technology; wildlife and wildlands science and management; zoology/animal biology.

Academic Programs *Special study options:* academic remediation for entering students, accelerated degree program, adult/continuing education programs, advanced placement credit, cooperative education, distance learning, English as a second language, independent study, internships, part-time degree program, services for LD students, summer session for credit. *ROTC:* Army (c).

Library Goodstein Library with 118,000 titles, 500 serial subscriptions, an OPAC, a Web page.

Computers on Campus 130 computers available on campus for general student use. A campuswide network can be accessed from student residence rooms. Internet access, online (class) registration, at least one staffed computer lab available.

Student Life *Housing Options:* coed. Campus housing is university owned. *Activities and Organizations:* drama/theater group, student-run newspaper, choral group, Student Senate, Student Activities Board, Agriculture Club, Theater Club, Phi Theta Kappa. *Campus security:* 24-hour patrols, late-night transport/escort service. *Student services:* health clinic, personal/psychological counseling, women's center.

Athletics Member NJCAA. *Intercollegiate sports:* basketball M(s)/W(s), cheerleading M/W, volleyball W(s). *Intramural sports:* badminton M/W, basketball M/W, bowling M/W, football M/W, golf M/W, racquetball M/W, soccer M/W, softball M/W, tennis M/W.

Standardized Tests *Recommended:* ACT (for placement).

Costs (2005–06) *Tuition:* state resident $1368 full-time, $57 per credit part-time; nonresident $4128 full-time, $172 per credit part-time. *Required fees:* $168 full-time, $7 per credit part-time. *Room and board:* $3460. Room and board charges vary according to board plan. *Payment plan:* installment. *Waivers:* children of alumni, senior citizens, and employees or children of employees.

Financial Aid Of all full-time matriculated undergraduates who enrolled in 2003, 104 Federal Work-Study jobs (averaging $1410).

Applying *Options:* electronic application, early admission. *Required:* high school transcript. *Required for some:* minimum 2.0 GPA. *Application deadlines:* 8/15 (freshmen), 8/15 (transfers). *Notification:* continuous until 8/15 (freshmen).

Admissions Contact Ms. Donna Hoffman, Admission Specialist, Casper College, 125 College Drive, Casper, WY 82601. *Phone:* 307-268-2458. *Toll-free phone:* 800-442-2963. *E-mail:* mfrank@caspercollege.edu.

CENTRAL WYOMING COLLEGE
Riverton, Wyoming

- **State and locally supported** 2-year, founded 1966, part of Wyoming Community College Commission
- **Calendar** semesters
- **Degree** certificates and associate
- **Small-town** 200-acre campus
- **Endowment** $3.8 million
- **Coed,** 1,732 undergraduate students, 42% full-time, 66% women, 34% men

Undergraduates 733 full-time, 999 part-time. Students come from 39 states and territories, 6 other countries, 6% are from out of state, 0.4% African

American, 0.4% Asian American or Pacific Islander, 3% Hispanic American, 19% Native American, 0.8% international, 11% transferred in, 9% live on campus. *Retention:* 57% of 2002 full-time freshmen returned.

Freshmen *Admission:* 344 applied, 344 admitted, 211 enrolled. *Average high school GPA:* 3.07. *Test scores:* ACT scores over 18: 78%; ACT scores over 24: 20%.

Faculty *Total:* 173, 25% full-time, 49% with terminal degrees. *Student/faculty ratio:* 12:1.

Majors Accounting; accounting technology and bookkeeping; agricultural business and management; agriculture; American Indian/Native American studies; art; automobile/automotive mechanics technology; biology/biological sciences; business administration and management; business automation/technology/data entry; child care and support services management; computer science; computer systems networking and telecommunications; computer technology/computer systems technology; criminal justice/law enforcement administration; dramatic/theatre arts; elementary education; English; environmental science; equestrian studies; general studies; horse husbandry/equine science and management; human services; management information systems; music; nursing (registered nurse training); parts, warehousing, and inventory management; physical sciences; pre-law studies; psychology; radio and television broadcasting technology; range science and management; secondary education; social sciences; surgical technology; web page, digital/multimedia and information resources design; welding technology.

Academic Programs *Special study options:* academic remediation for entering students, adult/continuing education programs, advanced placement credit, cooperative education, distance learning, English as a second language, honors programs, independent study, off-campus study, part-time degree program, services for LD students, student-designed majors, summer session for credit.

Library Central Wyoming College Library with 78,167 titles, 183 serial subscriptions, 1,256 audiovisual materials, an OPAC, a Web page.

Computers on Campus 323 computers available on campus for general student use. A campuswide network can be accessed from student residence rooms and from off campus. Internet access, online (class) registration, at least one staffed computer lab available.

Student Life *Housing Options:* coed. Campus housing is university owned. *Activities and Organizations:* drama/theater group, student-run radio and television station, choral group, Multi-Cultural Club, La Vida Nueva Club, Fellowship of College Christians, Quality Leaders, Science Club. *Campus security:* 24-hour patrols. *Student services:* personal/psychological counseling.

Athletics *Intercollegiate sports:* equestrian sports M(s)/W(s). *Intramural sports:* badminton M/W, basketball M/W, football M/W, skiing (downhill) M/W, soccer M/W, softball M/W, swimming and diving M/W, table tennis M/W, tennis M/W, volleyball M/W, weight lifting M/W.

Standardized Tests *Required for some:* ACT COMPASS. *Recommended:* SAT or ACT (for placement).

Costs (2005–06) *Tuition:* state resident $1368 full-time, $57 per credit part-time; nonresident $4104 full-time, $171 per credit part-time. *Required fees:* $504 full-time. *Room and board:* $2690; room only: $1300.

Financial Aid Of all full-time matriculated undergraduates who enrolled in 2003, 36 Federal Work-Study jobs (averaging $2045).

Applying *Options:* early admission, deferred entrance. *Recommended:* high school transcript. *Application deadline:* rolling (freshmen), rolling (transfers).

Admissions Contact Admissions Officer, Central Wyoming College, 2660 Peck Avenue, Riverton, WY 82501-2273. *Phone:* 307-855-2119. *Toll-free phone:* 800-735-8418 Ext. 2119. *Fax:* 307-855-2065. *E-mail:* admit@cwc.edu.

EASTERN WYOMING COLLEGE
Torrington, Wyoming

- **State and locally supported** 2-year, founded 1948, part of Wyoming Community College Commission
- **Calendar** semesters
- **Degree** certificates, diplomas, and associate
- **Rural** 40-acre campus
- **Coed**

Faculty *Student/faculty ratio:* 13:1.

Student Life *Campus security:* 24-hour emergency response devices, controlled dormitory access.

Athletics Member NJCAA.

Standardized Tests *Recommended:* ACT (for placement).

Costs (2004–05) *Tuition:* state resident $1320 full-time, $55 per credit hour part-time; nonresident $3960 full-time, $165 per credit hour part-time. Full-time tuition and fees vary according to reciprocity agreements. Part-time tuition and fees vary according to reciprocity agreements. *Required fees:* $384 full-time, $16 per credit hour part-time. *Room and board:* $3124; room only: $1364.

Financial Aid Of all full-time matriculated undergraduates who enrolled in 2003, 100 Federal Work-Study jobs (averaging $700). 60 state and other part-time jobs (averaging $700).

Applying *Options:* electronic application, early admission. *Recommended:* high school transcript, minimum 2.0 GPA.

Admissions Contact Mrs. Marilyn Cotant, Dean of Students, Eastern Wyoming College, 3200 West C Street, Torrington, WY 82240. *Phone:* 307-532-8257. *Toll-free phone:* 800-658-3195. *Fax:* 307-532-8222. *E-mail:* bbates@ewc.cc.wy.us.

LARAMIE COUNTY COMMUNITY COLLEGE
Cheyenne, Wyoming

- **State-supported** 2-year, founded 1968, part of Wyoming Community College Commission
- **Calendar** semesters
- **Degree** certificates and associate
- **Small-town** 270-acre campus
- **Endowment** $5.8 million
- **Coed,** 4,522 undergraduate students, 38% full-time, 60% women, 40% men

Undergraduates 1,708 full-time, 2,814 part-time. Students come from 40 states and territories, 14 other countries, 7% are from out of state, 3% African American, 1% Asian American or Pacific Islander, 7% Hispanic American, 1% Native American, 0.3% international, 4% transferred in, 2% live on campus.

Freshmen *Admission:* 2,493 applied, 2,493 admitted, 371 enrolled.

Faculty *Total:* 264, 33% full-time. *Student/faculty ratio:* 18:1.

Majors Accounting; agribusiness; agricultural business technology; agricultural production; agriculture; anthropology; art; autobody/collision and repair technology; automobile/automotive mechanics technology; biological and physical sciences; biology/biological sciences; business administration and management; business/commerce; business operations support and secretarial services related; carpentry; chemistry; civil engineering technology; communication/speech communication and rhetoric; computer and information sciences; computer and information sciences and support services related; computer hardware technology; computer programming; computer science; computer systems analysis; construction engineering technology; construction trades; construction trades related; corrections; criminal justice/law enforcement administration; customer service support/call center/teleservice operation; data modeling/warehousing and database administration; dental assisting; dental hygiene; diagnostic medical sonography and ultrasound technology; diesel mechanics technology; digital communication and media/multimedia; dramatic/theatre arts; early childhood education; economics; education; education (specific levels and methods) related; electrician; engineering; engineering technology; English; entrepreneurship; equestrian studies; health/medical preparatory programs related; history; humanities; industrial radiologic technology; information technology; journalism; mass communication/media; mathematics; multi-/interdisciplinary studies related; music; nursing assistant/aide and patient care assistant; nursing (registered nurse training); philosophy; physical education teaching and coaching; political science and government; pre-dentistry studies; pre-engineering; pre-law studies; pre-medical studies; pre-pharmacy studies; pre-veterinary studies; psychology; public administration; radiologic technology/science; religious studies; social sciences; sociology; Spanish; visual and performing arts; web/multimedia management and webmaster; web page, digital/multimedia and information resources design; wildlife and wildlands science and management.

Academic Programs *Special study options:* academic remediation for entering students, adult/continuing education programs, advanced placement credit, cooperative education, distance learning, double majors, English as a second language, honors programs, independent study, internships, off-campus study, part-time degree program, services for LD students, summer session for credit. *ROTC:* Air Force (c).

Library Laramie County Community College Library with 51,872 titles, 323 serial subscriptions, 31,514 audiovisual materials, an OPAC, a Web page.

Computers on Campus 720 computers available on campus for general student use. A campuswide network can be accessed from off campus. Internet access, online (class) registration, at least one staffed computer lab available.

Student Life *Housing Options:* coed. Campus housing is university owned. *Activities and Organizations:* drama/theater group, student-run newspaper, choral group, Block and Bridle Club, Phi Theta Kappa, music, Student Nurses Association, STAR Club. *Campus security:* 24-hour patrols, controlled dormitory access. *Student services:* personal/psychological counseling.

Athletics Member NJCAA. *Intercollegiate sports:* basketball M(s), cheerleading M(s)/W(s), soccer M(s)/W(s), volleyball W(s). *Intramural sports:* basketball M/W, golf M/W, racquetball M/W, rock climbing M/W, skiing (cross-country) M/W, soccer M/W, table tennis M/W, ultimate Frisbee M/W, volleyball M/W.

Standardized Tests *Recommended:* ACT (for placement).

Costs (2005–06) *Tuition:* state resident $1368 full-time, $57 per credit hour part-time; nonresident $4128 full-time, $172 per credit hour part-time. Part-time tuition and fees vary according to course load. *Required fees:* $588 full-time, $25 per credit hour part-time. *Room and board:* $4640. *Payment plan:* installment. *Waivers:* senior citizens and employees or children of employees.

Applying *Options:* electronic application, early admission. *Application fee:* $20. *Required:* high school transcript. *Required for some:* interview. *Application deadline:* rolling (freshmen), rolling (transfers). *Notification:* continuous until 8/31 (freshmen).

Admissions Contact Ms. Jenny Hargett, Assistant Director of Enrollment Management, Laramie County Community College, 1400 East College Drive, Cheyenne, WY 82007. *Phone:* 307-778-5222 Ext. 1117. *Toll-free phone:* 800-522-2993 Ext. 1357. *Fax:* 307-778-1360. *E-mail:* learnmore@lccc.wy.edu.

NORTHWEST COLLEGE
Powell, Wyoming

- **State and locally supported** 2-year, founded 1946, part of Wyoming Community College Commission
- **Calendar** semesters
- **Degree** certificates and associate
- **Rural** 75-acre campus
- **Endowment** $6.1 million
- **Coed**

Faculty *Student/faculty ratio:* 16:1.

Student Life *Campus security:* 24-hour emergency response devices and patrols, late-night transport/escort service, controlled dormitory access.

Athletics Member NJCAA.

Standardized Tests *Required for some:* SAT or ACT (for admission), ACT COMPASS.

Costs (2004–05) *Tuition:* state resident $1320 full-time, $55 per credit part-time; nonresident $3960 full-time, $165 per credit part-time. Full-time tuition and fees vary according to program. Part-time tuition and fees vary according to program. *Required fees:* $488 full-time, $18 per credit part-time. *Room and board:* $3306. Room and board charges vary according to board plan and housing facility.

Financial Aid Of all full-time matriculated undergraduates who enrolled in 2003, 107 Federal Work-Study jobs (averaging $1200). 245 state and other part-time jobs (averaging $1200).

Applying *Options:* common application, electronic application, early admission, deferred entrance. *Required:* high school transcript. *Recommended:* minimum 2.0 GPA.

Admissions Contact Assistant Director of Admissions, Northwest College, 231 West Sixth Street, Powell, WY 82435. *Phone:* 307-754-6043. *Toll-free phone:* 800-560-4692. *Fax:* 307-754-6249. *E-mail:* admissions@northwestcollege.edu.

SHERIDAN COLLEGE
Sheridan, Wyoming

- **State and locally supported** 2-year, founded 1948, part of Wyoming Community College Commission
- **Calendar** semesters
- **Degree** certificates and associate
- **Small-town** 124-acre campus
- **Coed,** 2,761 undergraduate students, 37% full-time, 60% women, 40% men

Undergraduates 1,012 full-time, 1,749 part-time. Students come from 31 states and territories, 3 other countries, 9% are from out of state, 0.6% African American, 0.5% Asian American or Pacific Islander, 3% Hispanic American, 2% Native American, 0.5% international, 3% transferred in, 20% live on campus.

Freshmen *Admission:* 406 admitted, 406 enrolled.

Faculty *Total:* 171, 44% full-time, 9% with terminal degrees. *Student/faculty ratio:* 17:1.

Majors Administrative assistant and secretarial science; agricultural business and management; agriculture; art; biological and physical sciences; biology/biological sciences; business administration and management; business/commerce; computer programming (specific applications); computer software and media applications related; computer systems networking and telecommunications; criminal justice/law enforcement administration; criminal justice/police science; data entry/microcomputer applications; dental hygiene; diesel mechanics technology; drafting and design technology; education; elementary education; engineering; engineering technology; English; foreign languages and literatures; general studies; health and physical education; heavy equipment maintenance technology; history; hospitality administration; humanities; information science/studies; liberal arts and sciences/liberal studies; machine tool technology; mathematics; music; nursing (registered nurse training); respiratory care therapy; sign language interpretation and translation; social sciences; system administration; web/multimedia management and webmaster; web page, digital/multimedia and information resources design; welding technology.

Academic Programs *Special study options:* academic remediation for entering students, adult/continuing education programs, advanced placement credit, cooperative education, distance learning, double majors, English as a second language, independent study, internships, off-campus study, part-time degree program, services for LD students, student-designed majors, summer session for credit.

Sheridan College (continued)

Library Griffith Memorial Library plus 1 other with 46,589 titles, 545 serial subscriptions, 17,122 audiovisual materials, an OPAC, a Web page.

Computers on Campus 200 computers available on campus for general student use. A campuswide network can be accessed from student residence rooms and from off campus. Internet access, at least one staffed computer lab available.

Student Life *Housing Options:* coed, women-only, disabled students. Campus housing is university owned. *Activities and Organizations:* drama/theater group, student-run newspaper, choral group, student government, Phi Theta Kappa, Art Club, Nursing Club, Police Science Club. *Campus security:* 24-hour emergency response devices, student patrols, controlled dormitory access, night patrols by certified officers. *Student services:* personal/psychological counseling.

Athletics Member NJCAA. *Intercollegiate sports:* basketball M(s)/W(s), volleyball W(s). *Intramural sports:* basketball M/W, bowling M/W, soccer M/W, softball M/W, table tennis M/W, tennis M/W, ultimate Frisbee M/W, volleyball M/W.

Costs (2005–06) *Tuition:* state resident $1368 full-time, $57 per credit hour part-time; nonresident $4104 full-time, $171 per credit hour part-time. Full-time tuition and fees vary according to course load and reciprocity agreements. Part-time tuition and fees vary according to reciprocity agreements. *Required fees:* $480 full-time, $20 per credit hour part-time. *Room and board:* $3840. Room and board charges vary according to board plan and housing facility. *Payment plans:* installment, deferred payment. *Waivers:* senior citizens and employees or children of employees.

Financial Aid Of all full-time matriculated undergraduates who enrolled in 2003, 86 Federal Work-Study jobs (averaging $1044).

Applying *Options:* electronic application, early admission, deferred entrance. *Required for some:* high school transcript. *Recommended:* high school transcript. *Application deadline:* rolling (freshmen), rolling (transfers). *Notification:* continuous (freshmen).

Admissions Contact Mr. Zane Garstad, Director of Admissions, Sheridan College, PO Box 1500, Sheridan, WY 82801-1500. *Phone:* 307-674-6446 Ext. 2002. *Toll-free phone:* 800-913-9139 Ext. 2002. *Fax:* 307-674-7205. *E-mail:* admissions@sheridan.edu.

WESTERN WYOMING COMMUNITY COLLEGE
Rock Springs, Wyoming

- **State and locally supported** 2-year, founded 1959
- **Calendar** semesters
- **Degree** certificates, diplomas, and associate
- **Small-town** 10-acre campus
- **Endowment** $6.0 million
- **Coed,** 2,654 undergraduate students, 41% full-time, 63% women, 37% men

Western Wyoming Community College is a public, 2-year, comprehensive community college located in Rock Springs, Wyoming. This small-town campus provides easy access to a variety of outdoor recreational opportunities, and its location makes travel to metropolitan areas such as Denver and Salt Lake City very easy. The modern, fully enclosed campus is designed to provide comfort and safety for college students as well as up-to-date equipment and facilities. The low student-teacher ratio of 15:1 ensures that students get individualized attention in their classes. Students major in transfer programs as well as occupational programs designed to lead directly to the workforce. Western is committed to both quality and success.

Undergraduates 1,099 full-time, 1,555 part-time. Students come from 12 states and territories, 17 other countries, 7% are from out of state, 0.6% African American, 0.5% Asian American or Pacific Islander, 7% Hispanic American, 0.8% Native American, 3% international, 3% transferred in, 13% live on campus. *Retention:* 47% of 2002 full-time freshmen returned.

Freshmen *Admission:* 1,137 applied, 894 admitted, 477 enrolled. *Average high school GPA:* 3.00. *Test scores:* ACT scores over 18: 90%; ACT scores over 24: 10%.

Faculty *Total:* 195, 33% full-time. *Student/faculty ratio:* 17:1.

Majors Accounting; administrative assistant and secretarial science; anthropology; archeology; art; automobile/automotive mechanics technology; biological and physical sciences; biology/biological sciences; business administration and management; chemistry; communication/speech communication and rhetoric; computer and information sciences; computer programming (specific applications); computer science; criminal justice/law enforcement administration; criminology; dance; data entry/microcomputer applications; data processing and data processing technology; diesel mechanics technology; dramatic/theatre arts; early childhood education; economics; education; education (multiple levels); electrical, electronic and communications engineering technology; electrical/electronics equipment installation and repair; electrician; elementary education; engineering technology; English; environmental science; forestry; general studies; geography; geology/earth science; health/medical preparatory programs related; health services/allied health/health sciences; heavy equipment maintenance technology; history; humanities; human services; industrial electronics technology; industrial mechanics and maintenance technology; information science/studies; information technology; instrumentation technology; international relations and affairs; journalism; kinesiology and exercise science; legal administrative assistant/secretary; liberal arts and sciences/liberal studies; marketing/marketing management; mathematics; mechanics and repair; medical administrative assistant and medical secretary; medical/clinical assistant; medical office assistant; medical office computer specialist; mining technology; music; nursing assistant/aide and patient care assistant; nursing (licensed practical/vocational nurse training); photography; political science and government; pre-dentistry studies; pre-engineering; pre-law studies; pre-medical studies; pre-nursing studies; pre-pharmacy studies; pre-veterinary studies; psychology; secondary education; social sciences; social work; sociology; Spanish; special education; theatre design and technology; visual and performing arts; web/multimedia management and webmaster; web page, digital/multimedia and information resources design; welding technology; wildlife and wildlands science and management; word processing.

Academic Programs *Special study options:* academic remediation for entering students, adult/continuing education programs, advanced placement credit, cooperative education, distance learning, English as a second language, freshman honors college, honors programs, independent study, internships, part-time degree program, services for LD students, summer session for credit.

Library Hay Library with 115,000 titles, 175 serial subscriptions, 3,500 audiovisual materials, an OPAC, a Web page.

Computers on Campus 350 computers available on campus for general student use. A campuswide network can be accessed from student residence rooms and from off campus. Internet access, online (class) registration, at least one staffed computer lab available.

Student Life *Housing Options:* coed, disabled students. Campus housing is university owned. *Activities and Organizations:* drama/theater group, student-run newspaper, choral group, Phi Theta Kappa, Students Without Borders (international club), Residence Hall Association, Associated Student Government, LDSSA. *Campus security:* 24-hour emergency response devices, late-night transport/escort service, controlled dormitory access, patrols by trained security personnel from 4 p.m. to 8 a.m., 24-hour patrols on weekends and holidays. *Student services:* personal/psychological counseling.

Athletics Member NJCAA. *Intercollegiate sports:* basketball M(s)/W(s), cheerleading M(s)/W(s), soccer M(s)(c)/W(s)(c), volleyball W(s), wrestling M(s). *Intramural sports:* badminton M/W, basketball M/W, bowling M/W, football M/W, rock climbing M/W, skiing (downhill) M/W, soccer M/W, softball M/W, table tennis M/W, tennis M/W, ultimate Frisbee M/W, volleyball M/W, water polo M/W.

Standardized Tests *Required:* ACT COMPASS (for placement). *Recommended:* SAT or ACT (for placement).

Costs (2005–06) *Tuition:* state resident $1658 full-time, $70 per credit hour part-time; nonresident $4418 full-time, $185 per credit hour part-time. Full-time tuition and fees vary according to reciprocity agreements. Part-time tuition and fees vary according to course load and reciprocity agreements. *Room and board:* $3033; room only: $1474. Room and board charges vary according to board plan and housing facility. *Payment plan:* installment. *Waivers:* children of alumni, senior citizens, and employees or children of employees.

Financial Aid Of all full-time matriculated undergraduates who enrolled in 2003, 20 Federal Work-Study jobs (averaging $1500).

Applying *Options:* common application, electronic application, early admission, deferred entrance. *Required:* high school transcript. *Application deadline:* rolling (freshmen), rolling (transfers).

Admissions Contact Ms. Laurie Watkins, Director of Admissions, Western Wyoming Community College, PO Box 428, 2500 College Drive, Rock Springs, WY 82902-0428. *Phone:* 307-382-1647. *Toll-free phone:* 800-226-1181. *Fax:* 307-382-1636. *E-mail:* admissions@wwcc.wy.edu.

WYOTECH
Laramie, Wyoming

Admissions Contact Mr. Troy Chaney, Director of Admissions, WyoTech, 4373 North Third Street, Laramie, WY 82072-9519. *Phone:* 307-742-3776. *Toll-free phone:* 800-521-7158.

INTERNATIONAL

MARSHALL ISLANDS

COLLEGE OF THE MARSHALL ISLANDS
Majuro, Marshall Islands

Admissions Contact PO Box 1258, Majuro 96960, Marshall Islands.

MEXICO

WESTHILL UNIVERSITY
Sante Fe, Mexico

Admissions Contact 56 Domingo Garcia Ramos, Zona Escolar, Prados de la Montana I, Sante Fe, Cuajimalpa CP 05610, Mexico.

PALAU

PALAU COMMUNITY COLLEGE
Koror, Palau

Admissions Contact Ms. Elsie Skang, Admissions Counselor, Palau Community College, PO Box 9, Koror, PW 96940-0009, Palau. *Phone:* 680-488-2470 Ext. 265. *Fax:* 680-488-4468.

SWITZERLAND

SCHILLER INTERNATIONAL UNIVERSITY
Engelberg, Switzerland

- **Independent** 2-year, founded 1988, part of Schiller International University
- **Calendar** semesters
- **Degree** certificates, diplomas, and associate
- **Urban** campus with easy access to Zurich
- **Coed**

Faculty *Student/faculty ratio:* 7:1.

Student Life *Campus security:* 24-hour emergency response devices.

Financial Aid *Financial aid deadline:* 6/1.

Applying *Options:* common application, deferred entrance. *Application fee:* $55. *Required:* high school transcript, interview.

Admissions Contact Ms. Annelies Muff, Administrative Assistant, Schiller International University, Hotel Europe, Dorfstrasse 40, Engelberg 6390, Switzerland. *Phone:* 41-41-639 74 74. *Fax:* 41-41-639 7475. *E-mail:* info@schiller-university.ch.

In-Depth Descriptions of Two-Year
COLLEGES

AMERICAN ACADEMY OF DRAMATIC ARTS
NEW YORK, NEW YORK, AND LOS ANGELES, CALIFORNIA

The College and Its Mission

Founded in New York in 1884, the American Academy of Dramatic Arts (AADA) was the first school in the United States to provide a professional education for actors. Since 1974, the Academy has operated an additional campus in the Los Angeles area, making AADA the only degree granting conservatory for actors offering programs in both of the major centers of theatrical activity in the country. Now in its second century, the Academy remains dedicated to a single purpose: training actors. The love of acting, as an art and as an occupation, is the spirit that impels the school. For the serious, well-motivated student ready to make a commitment to acting and to concentrated professional training, the Academy offers more than a century of success; a well-balanced, carefully structured curriculum; and a vital, dedicated, and caring faculty. Academy training involves the student intellectually, physically, and emotionally. Designed for the individual, it stresses self-discovery and self-discipline. Underlying the training are the beliefs that an actor prepared to work on the stage has the best foundation for acting in any medium and that classroom learning must be put to the test in the practical arena of a theater. The soundness of this approach is reflected in the achievements of the alumni, a diverse body of professionals unmatched by the alumni of any other institution. (Performances by Academy alumni have received nominations for 72 Oscars, 57 Tonys, and 202 Emmys.) The time spent at the Academy can be an important period of development for those who become professional actors as well as for those who eventually choose other paths. All students are expected to make a commitment to professionalism, excellence, and discipline while enrolled at the Academy. The American Academy of Dramatic Arts is a nonprofit educational institution, chartered in New York by the Board of Regents of the University of the State of New York. In New York the Academy is accredited by the Middle States Association of Colleges and Schools and in California by the Western Association of Schools and Colleges. Both schools are accredited by the National Association of Schools of Theatre.

Academic Programs

The Professional Training Program requires two years to complete. Students who meet the requirements of the program receive an associate degree. A third-year performance program is offered to selected graduates. Students who successfully complete this program earn the Certificate of Advanced Studies in Actor training.

The first year consists of two 12-week terms and one 6-week term, providing a total of 30 transferable college credits. Classes include acting, movement, voice and speech, vocal production, acting styles, and theater history. The primary goals of the first-year program are to achieve relaxed, free, and truthful use of oneself in imaginary circumstances; to gain awareness of the body in terms of alignment, flexibility, and strength; to develop an open, well-placed, and well-supported vocal tone; to acquire clearly articulated standard American speech; and to increase understanding of the historical and stylistic backgrounds of drama. Students may enter the first year in mid-September or late January for the course in Los Angeles; late October or early February for New York. Admission to the second year is by invitation. Selection is made on the basis of progress, potential, and readiness to benefit from advanced training, as evidenced by the quality of first-year classwork and examination play performances. The second year begins with advanced classwork designed to reinforce and build upon the learning experiences of the first year. Emphasis is gradually shifted to performance opportunities. Additional courses are given in fencing and stage makeup. The second-year course provides 30 transferable undergraduate credits. Workshops to deal with specific acting problems are set up as needed, and, toward the end of the second year, seminars are scheduled to familiarize students with basic procedures for attaining professional employment. Upon completion of the second year, students graduate from the Professional Training Program with associate degrees. Admission to the third-year program, which emphasizes performance, is also by invitation. Students who undertake a third year of study become members of the Academy Company, the school's performance ensemble. Selection is based on the individual's potential and the overall concept of a balanced acting company. The practical development of the actor is continued through study, rehearsal, and performance of fully-produced plays in Academy theaters over a thirty-week period from late summer to late winter. Agents, casting directors, and other professional personnel are invited to see Academy Company productions, and counseling is offered to assist third-year students in launching professional careers. Students completing the third-year program earn an additional 30 college credits and are awarded a certificate. Guest speakers from the professional world are regularly invited to the Academy to share insights with the students at special assemblies.

The Academy also offers a six-week summer conservatory for those who would like to begin to study, to refresh basic skills, or to test interest and ability in an environment of professional training. Classes begin shortly after the Fourth of July and are open to anyone of high school age or older. Teaching standards are identical to those of the Academy's degree and certificate programs.

Costs

In 2004–05, the cost of the full-time program was $14,900 for tuition and $450 for the general fee. (The general fee covers the cost of accident insurance, costume and production costs, use of the library, and student identification.) Students need to budget an additional $600 for purchasing books and scripts, dance attire for movement class, a makeup kit, and other expenses related to the training. The cost of housing varies. On the average, housing, food, transportation, and personal expenses can amount to approximately $11,000 to $13,000.

Financial Aid

The Academy makes every effort to assist students in need of financial aid. The Academy participates in various financial aid programs, including government administered grants, loans, and college work-study. Grant awards are determined by financial need. (Only United States citizens and permanent residents are eligible for government-sponsored aid programs.) Payment plans (for those eligible) assist students by extending the payment of tuition over a period of time. Scholarships, awarded on the basis of both need and merit, are available to qualified students, including a limited number of Trustee Awards to first-year students. New York City and Los Angeles offer numerous job opportunities for students desiring part-time employment, including on-campus employment (work-study).

Faculty

To achieve its objectives, the Academy requires that its faculty members be well trained in the various performing arts disciplines; seasoned by professional experience; mature, objective, and sympathetic in their relations with students; and exemplars of the commitment to excellence that the Academy hopes to instill in its students. In their own training, the Academy's faculty members represent all of the master teachers and significant systems and philosophies of the performing arts of the past half-century. Their professional experience is diversified, encompassing a variety of positions in film, television, and theater. In selecting faculty members to support its specialized programs, the Academy places more importance on an instructor's professional training and experience and teaching ability than on traditional academic credentials. The student-faculty ratio ranges from 16:1 in classroom instruction, to 4:1 or 3:1 in some performance situations.

Student Body Profile

Academy students reflect a wide diversity of backgrounds and geographical origin; they come from every region of the United States, from Canada, and from many other countries. Enrollment in 2004 was 275 in California and 265 in New York, with a combined average of 20 percent members of minority groups and 20 percent international students. Forty percent of the students are men. The average age of an entering Academy student is 22. Less than half of all first-year students come directly after high school; others enroll after a range of experiences, including college, military service, or other careers.

Student Activities

Students at the American Academy of Dramatic Arts are bonded by their love of acting. A common interest and the collaborative nature of the training contribute to genial social relations among the student body, and, accordingly, school-arranged activities are usually related to the performing arts. Academy students are frequently invited to attend all types of theatrical events for free or given the opportunity to purchase reduced-priced tickets. Every effort is made by the school to facilitate the cultural enrichment of the students.

Facilities and Resources

The Academy in New York is housed in a six-story building that is a registered New York City landmark. It includes classrooms, rehearsal studios, dance studios, a video studio, a student lounge, locker areas, and dressing rooms. A library, made possible by a grant from CBS, is a handsome facility, organized to serve the special research and study needs of the actor. Three theaters—a 160-seat proscenium theater, an intimate 160-seat thrust-stage theater, and a semiarena theater that seats 103—are used for classes, rehearsals, and productions. Production facilities include a prop department, a costume department, a scene shop, and a sound room.

After housing its West Coast operation in leased space in Pasadena for more than twenty-five years, the Academy purchased a campus in the heart of Hollywood and took residence in 2000. Situated on 2.25 acres adjacent to the historic Charlie Chaplin Studios, the new campus includes a theater, ample parking, a library, and spacious classrooms and studios.

In place of on-campus housing, AADA offers a variety of attractive off-campus options through special arrangements with local housing resources.

Location

Located in midtown Manhattan, the New York home of the Academy is within walking distance of the Grand Central and Pennsylvania train stations, the Port Authority bus terminal, and Broadway and off-Broadway theaters.

AADA Los Angeles is located in the center of the motion picture and television production capital of the world. The new campus is a short walk from Hollywood Boulevard and is surrounded by film and television production companies. The California Freeway system affords access to beaches, deserts, and mountains.

At each location, the training at the Academy is enhanced by the exciting variety of nearby cultural and recreational opportunities afforded by New York and Los Angeles.

Admission Requirements

AADA seeks talented and highly motivated applicants. An audition/interview is the cornerstone of the admission process. The overall policy is to admit individuals who seem both artistically and academically qualified to undertake a rigorous conservatory program of professional training. Readiness to benefit fully from such training is assessed in the audition/interview. Auditions, whether for entrance into the program in New York City or Los Angeles, may be held at either school. In addition, regional auditions are held annually in major cities in the United States, Canada, and London. The audition requires the performance of two contrasting, memorized speeches (one comedic and one dramatic) from published plays (one period and one contemporary), the total performance time to be no more than 4 minutes. The audition appointment includes an interview. In the audition/interview, special attention is given to the quality of the applicant's instinctive emotional connection to the audition material. Since good listening is so fundamental to good acting, the auditioner notes how well the applicant listens in the "real world" context of the interview. Other criteria include sensitivity, sense of language, sense of humor, vitality, presence, vocal quality, cultural interests, a realistic sense of self, and the challenge involved in pursuing an acting career.

All entering students must hold a diploma from an accredited secondary school or its equivalent. Transcripts of all previous academic work must be submitted; previous college credits may not be transferred. High school seniors should submit SAT or ACT scores. Two letters of recommendation are required before an audition is scheduled. International students who are fluent in English are welcome to apply. AADA is approved for the training of veterans.

Application and Information

The Academy operates on a rolling admission basis, but early application is encouraged. There is a nonrefundable application fee of $50. Admission decisions are made within four weeks of the audition. Further information may be obtained from:

For AADA New York:
Karen Higginbotham
Director of Admissions
American Academy of Dramatic Arts
120 Madison Avenue
New York, New York 10016
Telephone: 212-686-0620
        800-463-8990 (toll-free)
E-mail: admissions-ny@aada.org

For AADA Los Angeles:
Dan Justin
Director of Admissions
American Academy of Dramatic Arts
1336 North La Brea Avenue
Hollywood, California 90028
Telephone: 800-222-2867 (toll-free)
E-mail: admissions-ca@aada.org
World Wide Web: http://www.aada.org (both campuses)

Robert Redford presents fellow AADA alumnus Jason Robards with the Alumni Achievement Award at the Centennial Gala.

ANDREW COLLEGE
CUTHBERT, GEORGIA

The College and Its Mission

Founded in 1854, Andrew College is a small, two-year, residential college related to the United Methodist Church. Its mission is to provide an academically challenging liberal arts curriculum within a nurturing community. As a two-year, senior college–parallel, church-related college, Andrew exists to provide students with a better beginning to their college careers. Andrew specializes in the education of freshmen and sophomores. Historically, 100 percent of Andrew College's graduates are accepted into four-year colleges and universities.

For a quarter of a century, the Andrew College chapter of Phi Theta Kappa, the international honor society for two-year colleges, has won national recognition and was the number one chapter during five of those years. There are more than 1,000 chapters of Phi Theta Kappa, and no other chapter, in public or private institutions, has established a more impressive record. Andrew College seeks to achieve its goals by providing several advantages, many of which are unique to a small campus with a church-related environment: the opportunity for intellectual, social, and spiritual development; a professionally competent faculty that is dedicated to teaching; individual attention to students at all levels of operation within the College; a two-year curriculum that parallels that of four-year colleges and universities; a cultural enrichment program that encourages students to appreciate the arts; the opportunity to learn leisure-time skills that lead to the development of a healthy body; remediation in the basic skills; orientation experiences for successful adjustment to college life; academic advising; a student community committed to the earning of a college education; and cultural and academic resources for the community and churches in the area.

Andrew College is accredited by the Commission on Colleges of the Southern Association of Colleges and Schools (1866 Southern Lane, Decatur, Georgia 30033-4097; telephone: 404-679-4501) to award associate degrees. Andrew College is listed by the University Senate of the United Methodist Church.

Academic Programs

The academic program at Andrew College is specifically designed for freshman and sophomore students. The faculty members serve at Andrew because they enjoy teaching freshmen and sophomores. This attitude and expertise contribute significantly to the quality of education that students receive.

Andrew College offers programs that lead to advanced degrees in the arts and sciences. The College offers the Associate of Arts degree, the Associate of Science degree, and the Associate of Music degree. To be eligible for graduation, a student must have earned at least a 2.0 cumulative grade point average on the work attempted at Andrew College. All associate degrees have a core curriculum of liberal studies, including a required curriculum of essential skills, humanities/fine arts, science/mathematics/technology, social science, and physical education. Each student must satisfactorily complete a course in religion or philosophy and satisfy Cultural Enrichment Program requirements. All students who graduate from Andrew College must demonstrate proficiency in computer and oral communication skills.

All students entering Andrew College are assigned a faculty adviser who assists students in all matters relating to their academic progress. Andrew College schedules free tutoring during each term for students who need extra help with their studies. Some students, including students on academic probation and those admitted on a conditional basis, are assigned to mandatory study and tutoring sessions. Enrichment seminars are offered in areas beyond those covered in regular class study. These courses provide students with a challenge to do in-depth study and carry institutional credit only. Andrew College offers a number of programs that assist students in reaching their educational potential. For a variety of reasons, some applicants to Andrew College may need to improve their academic skills in order to be successful in a full-time schedule of college-level courses. The Strategic Studies Program serves students who need to improve their academic skills before embarking on a full-time

schedule of college-level courses. The program contains a selected schedule of college-level course work as well as other specially designed courses that provide intensive study and individual guidance at a pace that is compatible with the students' abilities. Tutorial assistance is provided.

Andrew College has established an intensive level of academic support services designed for and limited to specifically identified and accepted students with documented learning disabilities and/or attention deficit disorders. While the Focus Program supplements and complements the tutorial and advising services available to all students, it provides an additional level of professional assistance and monitoring to enhance the students' probability for success.

Andrew College offers an English as a Second Language (ESL) Program for students whose native language is not English and gives them a choice in the selection of the instructional program.

Through the Cultural Enrichment Program (CEP), Andrew College recognizes the fact that exposure to the cultural arts is an essential part of a liberal arts education. As a graduation requirement, all degree-seeking students must attend designated programs relating to the cultural arts during their enrollment.

Costs

Although Andrew College is a private college, an Andrew education is affordable. Tuition and fees for the 2005–06 academic year are $8550. Room and board are $5385 for the academic year. Books and supplies average $600 to $700 per academic year. Approximately $2300 per year should be allowed for other costs, including transportation and personal expenses.

Financial Aid

Approximately 90 percent of Andrew College students receive some type of federal or institutional aid. Students from Georgia are eligible for the Georgia Tuition Equalization Grant and may be eligible for the HOPE Scholarship. Scholarships are given for academic excellence, community service, intercollegiate sports, spiritual life, and programs such as chorus, art, drama, piano, photography, yearbook, and journalism.

Every year, the Office of Admission holds a Scholarship Day program, where students who have a 3.0 GPA or above and at least a 1000 on the SAT I are invited to compete for academic scholarships. Four Andrew Scholar awards (full tuition, room, and board scholarships) are presented at the competition, along with other academic awards. Scholarships or loans may be awarded to students who are members of the United Methodist Church. Other churches, religious and community organizations, and fraternal or business groups may also sponsor financial awards. Government programs at the federal and state levels provide a variety of grants, low-interest educational loans, and work-study employment opportunities for students. Eligibility for many of these programs is based on need.

Faculty

The faculty at Andrew College is committed to the education of freshmen and sophomores. The success of the students at the next level and beyond is the focus of the faculty and the academic program at Andrew.

The College employs 29 full-time and 5 part-time faculty members. The student-faculty ratio varies each year but is maintained at or below 16:1, resulting in lively discussions, teacher-student interaction, and individual attention. The student-faculty ratio for 2003–04 was 13:1. Eight members of the full-time faculty hold doctoral degrees, two have terminal degrees in their field, and the remainder hold master's degrees in their area of specialty.

Student Body Profile

Andrew College has a diverse population of students from all over the world. Approximately 3 percent of the College population is international students from countries such as Japan, Nigeria, Trinidad, Mexico, Guatemala, and Korea. Based on figures from fall 2003, 80 percent of students were from Georgia, 10 percent were from Florida,

5 percent were from Alabama, and 2 percent were from other states. The total student population in fall 2003 was 320 students. The College plans to grow to 500 students by 2005. Ninety percent of Andrew College students live in a College residence hall.

While most students transfer to schools in Georgia, graduates have chosen to transfer to schools as far away as New England or California.

Student Activities

The student life program at Andrew College is designed to promote activities and programs that are supportive of the College's aims and purposes. The first two years of college are critical for academic success; therefore, programs that support and enhance students' lives are very important.

Andrew College is committed to the idea that total education involves more than academic pursuit. Activities, including intramural recreation, student activities, religious activities, career and transfer services, student government, and residential and commuter student programs, are among the many programs offered. All freshman students are required to complete a student orientation program.

Informal recreation opportunities available to students include basketball, indoor and outdoor volleyball, racquetball, walleyball, weight training, and tennis. Formalized recreational opportunities exist under the umbrella of intramurals and include team and individual sports and exercise programs. Off-campus recreational opportunities are promoted throughout the year. A wide variety of student activities take place at Andrew. Many organizations and various offices of the College provide a diversity of programs. The Student Events and Activities (SEA) Board is the chief programming committee in the student life area and sponsors events such as Homecoming, major dances, movies, coffeehouse performers, speakers, and comedy acts. Student organizations at Andrew College offer many leadership opportunities and operate under the jurisdiction of the Student Development Committee. Such organizations include the Student Government Association, International Student Association, Outdoor Adventure Club, Phi Theta Kappa Honor Society, AndrewServes, and the Residence Hall Association.

Sports Andrew College maintains membership in the National Junior College Athletic Association and the Georgia Junior College Athletic Association. Andrew offers scholarships in all intercollegiate sports in which the College participates. Andrew participates competitively in baseball, golf, and soccer for men and soccer and fast-pitch softball for women.

Facilities and Resources

Pitts Library subscribes to more than 100 periodicals, five daily newspapers, and three weekly newspapers. These publications supplement the library's holdings and provide reading and sources for the students and faculty members. Library computers provide students with access to holdings at other libraries and access to the World Wide Web through the Internet. A substantial collection of audiovisual and microfilm materials is maintained. An attractive main reading room provides areas for individual study, and a special reference section supplies ample space for research work.

The Andrew College Interactive Distance Learning Center is located adjacent to the main reading room and contains videoconferencing and Web-based instructional program development facilities.

In 1999, the College completed construction of an athletic complex, which contains baseball, soccer, and softball fields. The Fort Residence

Building was completed and ready for occupancy by 142 students in fall 2000. The Phyllis and Jack Jones Chapel was completed in September 2001.

Location

Andrew College is located in southwest Georgia in the town of Cuthbert. Cuthbert is the county seat of Randolph County, which has a total population of 8,000 people. The Cuthbert area is a safe, friendly community located 40 miles east of Albany, Georgia; 161 miles southwest of Atlanta; 60 miles south of Columbus, Georgia; and 30 miles east of Eufaula, Alabama. The weather year-round is ideally suited to the many recreational opportunities in the region. A championship state park golf course is located 20 minutes from the campus of Andrew College. Lake George is also 20 minutes away and provides an ideal place for fishing, boating, and waterskiing. Large cities and shopping malls are within 1 hour's drive. Providence Canyon, for hiking, picnicking, and nature watching, is only a 20-minute drive from the campus.

Admission Requirements

Andrew College admits applicants who demonstrate abilities that are necessary for successful completion of the program. Admission decisions are based on the applicant's previous academic record, test scores, recommendations, and, in some cases, a personal interview. Equal educational opportunities are offered to students regardless of race, color, religion, disability, gender, age, creed, or national origin.

Applicants may be admitted for any term. In order to ensure proper processing, all credentials should be on file in the Office of Admission approximately thirty days prior to semester registration. All applicants must submit the following materials: a completed application for admission, a $20 application fee, transcripts of high school (or GED) and/or college course work attempted, and scores from either the SAT I or ACT. Transfer students who have successfully completed college-level courses in English and math need not submit SAT I/ACT scores. In addition, applicants whose native language is not English must submit scores from the Test of English as a Foreign Language (TOEFL) or an acceptable score on an equivalent English language examination.

Admission to Andrew College is gained through an individual selection process. Minimum academic requirements for nonconditional acceptance include a high school diploma, graduation from an accredited high school, an evaluated high school GPA of 2.0 or better on a 4.0 scale, and SAT I scores of at least 460 on verbal and 430 on math or the ACT equivalent. Students not meeting the minimum academic requirements for nonconditional acceptance may be conditionally accepted but are required to take placement examinations prior to registering for their first semester.

Application and Information

A new student may enter Andrew College at the beginning of the fall, spring, and summer semesters. There is an application deadline set at two weeks prior to the registration date for each term.

For an application and further information about Andrew College, students should contact:

Office of Admission and Financial Aid
Andrew College
413 College Street
Cuthbert, Georgia 39840

Telephone: 800-664-9250 (toll-free)
Fax: 229-732-2176
E-mail: admissions@andrewcollege.edu
World Wide Web: http://www.andrewcollege.edu

ARGOSY UNIVERSITY/TWIN CITIES
College of Health Sciences
EAGAN, MINNESOTA

The University and Its Mission

Argosy University is a private institution of higher education dedicated to providing high-quality professional educational programs at doctoral, master's, baccalaureate, and associate degree levels, as well as continuing education to individuals who seek to advance their professional and personal lives. The University emphasizes programs in the behavioral sciences, business, education, and the health-care professions. A limited number of preprofessional programs and general education offerings are provided to permit students to prepare for entry into these professional fields. The programs of Argosy University are designed to instill the knowledge, skills, and ethical values of professional practice and to foster values of social responsibility in a supportive, learning-centered environment of mutual respect and professional excellence.

Argosy University/Twin Cities is part of Argosy University, a national university made up of thirteen campuses. Argosy's staff and practitioner-oriented faculty members believe that a high-quality education is a key component of a successful career. The Argosy University/Twin Cities campus offers an educational environment that meets the needs of busy individuals with convenient, flexible class schedules that enable them to earn their degrees while fulfilling other responsibilities.

Argosy University is accredited by the Higher Learning Commission of the North Central Association of Colleges and Schools (30 North LaSalle Street, Suite 2400, Chicago, Illinois 60602; telephone: 312-263-0456; Web site: http://www.ncahlc.org).

The Associate of Science in Dental Hygiene Degree Program is accredited by the Commission on Dental Accreditation (211 East Chicago Avenue, Chicago, Illinois 60611; telephone: 312-440-4653.) The commission is a specialized accrediting body recognized by the United States Department of Education.

The Associate of Applied Science in Veterinary Technology Degree Program is accredited through the Council on Education of the American Veterinary Medical Association (1931 North Meachum Road, Suite 100, Schaumburg, Illinois 60173; telephone: 847-925-8070).

The Associate of Applied Science in Medical Assisting Degree Program is accredited by the Commission on Accreditation of Allied Health Education Programs on recommendation of the Committee on Accreditation for Medical Assistant Education (35 East Wacker Drive, Suite 1970, Chicago, Illinois 60601-2208; telephone: 312-553-9355).

The Associate of Applied Science in Diagnostic Medical Sonography Degree Program is accredited by the Commission on Accreditation of Allied Health Education Programs on recommendation of the Joint Review Committee on Education in Diagnostic Medical Sonography (35 East Wacker Drive, Suite 1970, Chicago, Illinois 60601-2208; telephone: 312-553-9355).

The Associate of Applied Science in Radiologic Technology and the Associate of Science in Radiation Therapy Degree Programs are accredited by the Joint Review Committee on Education in Radiologic Technology (20 North Wacker Drive, Suite 900, Chicago, Illinois 60606; telephone: 312-704-5300).

The Associate of Applied Science in Histotechnology and the Associate of Science in Medical Laboratory Technology Degree

Programs are accredited by the National Accrediting Agency for Clinical Laboratory Sciences (8410 West Bryn Mawr, Suite 670, Chicago, Illinois 60631; telephone: 773-714-8880).

Academic Programs

The programs at Argosy University/Twin Cities are designed to develop skills in high-demand fields and to provide students with industry-relevant instruction from experienced professors. Since 1961, nearly 6,000 students have successfully completed the health science programs and joined the health-care community as practicing health-care and veterinary professionals.

Associate Degree Programs The Argosy University/Twin Cities College of Health Sciences offers associate degree programs in dental hygiene, diagnostic medical sonography, histotechnology, medical assisting, medical laboratory technology, radiation therapy, radiologic technology, and veterinary technology. Typically, associate degree programs are completed in one to two years. These programs follow a semester calendar.

Costs

Tuition information can be obtained from Argosy University/Twin Cities.

Financial Aid

A wide range of financial aid options is available to students who qualify. Argosy University/Twin Cities offers access to federal aid programs, work-study, and merit-based awards. As a first step, students should complete the Free Application for Federal Student Aid (FAFSA), which may be done electronically at http://fafsa.ed.gov or at the campus. To receive consideration for the maximum amount of aid and ensure timely receipt of funds, it is best to submit the application promptly. Depending on the individual's circumstances, financial aid payments may be deferred until after graduation.

Faculty

The most outstanding aspect of the institution is the dedication of the faculty members and their ability to cultivate a supportive learning environment. From them, students learn to integrate formal knowledge with professional practice. Argosy University/Twin Cities faculty members believe that their primary roles are those of mentor, teacher, and co-learner. They are dedicated to training students to assume leadership roles within various health science fields. Students have access to faculty members and counseling with regard to course and program matters. In addition, the Student Services Office personnel advise students in a number of areas.

Student Activities

Argosy University/Twin Cities offers a number of activities designed to involve students in experiences not normally available through academic courses. A student organization group meets with faculty and administration members regularly to discuss issues pertinent to the campus. In addition, most faculty committees include a student representative.

Facilities and Resources

Argosy University libraries provide such curriculum support and educational resources as current text materials, diagnostic training documents, reference materials and databases, journals and dissertations, and major and current titles in program areas. The University provides an online public-access catalog encompassing library resources throughout the Argosy University system. Students have full remote access to their campus library's database, enabling them to study and conduct research at home. The available academic databases offer dissertation abstracts, academic journals, and professional periodicals. All library computers are Internet accessible. Software applications include Word, Excel, PowerPoint, SPSS, and various test-scoring programs. All electronic resources are Web based and therefore accessible from the library or home.

Location

The new Argosy University/Twin Cities campus is in a convenient location, with easy freeway access and within 10 miles of the airport and the Mall of America. Located in a very pleasant suburban area that has many shops, restaurants, and housing nearby, the new campus is in a parklike setting next to the new Eagan Community Center, which offers numerous amenities, including walking paths, a fitness center, meeting rooms, and an outdoor amphitheater.

The Twin Cities of Minneapolis and St. Paul have been rated as one of the most livable metropolitan areas in the country. With a population of 2.5 million, the area offers an abundance of recreational opportunities. Year-round outdoor activities, nationally acclaimed theater and arts, music venues, and professional sports teams attract and inspire residents and visitors alike.

Admission Requirements

Students who have successfully completed a program of secondary education or the equivalent (GED) are eligible for admission to the health sciences programs. Entrance requirements include either an ACT composite score of 18 or above, a combined math and verbal SAT score of 850 or above, or a passing score on the Argosy University entrance exam. In addition, a minimum TOEFL score of 173 (computer version) or 500 (paper version) is required for applicants whose native language is not English or who have not graduated from an institution in which English is the language of instruction. All applicants must include a completed application form, proof of high school graduation or successful completion of the GED test, official postsecondary transcripts, and SAT, ACT, or Argosy University exam scores. Additional materials are required prior to matriculation. Some programs have additional application requirements. An admissions representative can provide further detailed information.

Application and Information

Argosy University/Twin Cities accepts students on a rolling admissions basis year-round, depending on availability of required courses. Applications for admission are available online or by contacting the campus, using the information listed in this In-Depth Description.

Admissions Office
Argosy University/Twin Cities
1515 Central Parkway
Eagan, Minnesota 55121
Telephone: 651-846-2882
           888-844-2004 (toll-free)
E-mail: tcadmissions@argosyu.edu
World Wide Web: http://www.argosyu.edu/pg

THE ART INSTITUTE OF CHARLOTTE
CHARLOTTE, NORTH CAROLINA

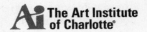

The Institute and Its Mission

The Art Institute of Charlotte prepares students for entry-level employment in the creative arts. Students learn through programs of study that reflect the needs of a changing job market. Courses are taught by faculty members who have professional experience in their fields of expertise. The school offers twelve bachelor's, associate, and certificate programs.

Of all 2003 Art Institute of Charlotte graduates available for employment, 88.7 percent were working in a field related to their program of study within six months of graduation and earning an average salary of $26,722.

Student housing options include apartments that comfortably accommodate four students in two-bedroom, two-bath units complete with living room, dining area, and full kitchen. Students submit a roommate preference form and are assigned to apartments by the housing staff. The apartments are located close to the Art Institute of Charlotte and shopping, dining, and entertainment venues.

Services are available to assist students with resume writing, networking, and keeping abreast of what employers are looking for in job applicants.

The school is accredited by the Accrediting Council for Independent Colleges and Schools (ACICS) and is licensed by the North Carolina Department of Community Colleges and the University of North Carolina Board of Governors.

Academic Programs

Bachelor of Arts degrees are available in fashion marketing and management and in interior design. Associate in Applied Science degrees are offered in culinary arts, fashion marketing, graphic design, interactive media design, and Interior design. Certificate programs are available in art of cooking, digital design, fashion merchandising, residential design, and Web design.

Costs

Program tuition varies by the student's chosen course of study. Interested students should check the school's Web site or contact the Admissions Office for the current program costs.

Financial Aid

Financial aid is available to those who qualify. Financial aid programs are designed to supplement, rather than replace, a student's resources. Most financial aid is based on individual economic circumstances and is determined by analyzing the financial information provided by the student on the Free Application for Federal Student Aid (FAFSA) form.

Faculty

The Art Institute of Charlotte's faculty members are experienced instructors, many of whom have professional experience outside of the classroom.

Student Body Profile

Students come to the Art Institute of Charlotte from throughout the southeastern United States and abroad. There are more than 700 students enrolled at the Art Institute of Charlotte. The average age of the students is 23, and 66 percent are women. The student population includes recent high school graduates, transfer students, and those who have left a previous employment situation to study and train for a new career. Students are creative, competitive, and open to new ideas. They place great value on an education that prepares them for an exciting entry-level position in the arts.

Student Activities

Students enrolled in the Art Institute of Charlotte can get involved in student-led activities through the Student Affairs Department. Activities stimulate cultural awareness, creativity, and social and professional development. Students enrolled in the interior design program may join the Interior Design Student Association. In addition, academic departments regularly organize trips to the International Home Furnishing Market in High Point, North Carolina, as well as to local museums and galleries.

Facilities and Resources

The Art Institute of Charlotte facility has six computer labs for student use. Additional computers are available in the library. Studios, classrooms, and meetings rooms are available for students and faculty members.

Location

Charlotte mixes the characteristics of a large urban center with the charm of suburban life. With a mild climate and central location, Charlotte residents are only 2 hours from the Blue Ridge Mountains and 3 hours from the Atlantic coast. Charlotte is known for its arts community, sports, shopping, and restaurants. More than 300 Fortune 500 companies have offices in Charlotte, the nation's second largest banking center. The city is the nation's fifth-largest urban region, with 6.3 million people living within a 100-mile radius.

Admission Requirements

Applicants must be high school graduates or have a GED certificate. A 150-word written essay is required, as are high school transcripts and any records from other academic institutions attended. All interested students are interviewed in person or over the phone. Following this interview, prospective students complete an application for admission and an Enrollment Agreement. These documents must be submitted to the Art Institute of Charlotte with a $50 application fee. Applicants who have taken the SAT or ACT are encouraged to submit their scores to the Admissions Office for evaluation.

Application and Information

The Art Institute of Charlotte
Three LakePointe Plaza
2110 Water Ridge Parkway
Charlotte, North Carolina 28217
Telephone: 704-357-8020
Fax: 704) 357-1133
E-mail: aichadm@aii.edu
World Wide Web: http://www.aich.artinstitutes.edu

THE ART INSTITUTE OF NEW YORK CITY

NEW YORK, NEW YORK

The Institute and Its Mission

The Art Institute of New York City prepares students for entry-level employment in the creative arts. Students learn through programs of study that reflect the needs of a changing job market. Courses are taught by faculty members who have professional experience in their fields of expertise.

The maximum number of students in a class is 36 per lecture, 21 per kitchen lab, and 25 per computer lab. Of all 2003 Art Institute of New York City graduates available for employment, 91.7 percent were working in a field related to their program of study within six months and earning an average salary of $26,137. In addition, assistance is available to help students with resume writing, networking, and keeping abreast of what employers are looking for in job candidates.

The Art Institute of New York City is accredited by the Accrediting Council for Independent Colleges and Schools (ACICS).

Academic Programs

The Art Institute of New York City offers associate degree programs in advertising, culinary arts and restaurant management, fashion design, graphic design, interactive media design, interior design, and video production. A diploma program is available in graphic design, and certificate programs are offered in culinary arts, pastry arts, and restaurant management. Each academic program is offered on a year-round basis, allowing students to continue to work uninterrupted toward their degrees.

Costs

Tuition and fees vary from program to program. Students should visit the school's Web site for a current listing of tuition costs per program.

Financial Aid

Financial aid is available to those who qualify. The Art Institute of New York City participates in federal, state, and other financial aid programs. Financial aid is divided into grants, loans, and work-study. Students may be eligible for

several loans, including the Federal Stafford Student Loan, the Federal PLUS loan (parents), and the Creative Education Loan. Application deadlines and eligibility requirements vary.

Faculty

Faculty members at the Art Institute of New York City are professionals, many of whom have experience in their respective fields. There are 79 full-time and 19 part-time faculty members at the school.

Student Body Profile

There are nearly 1,720 students enrolled in the Art Institute of New York City. Students come to the school from throughout the United States and abroad. The student population includes recent high school graduates, transfer students, and those who have left a previous employment situation to study and train for a new career. Students are creative, competitive, and open to new ideas. They place great value on an education that prepares them for an exciting entry-level position in the arts.

Student Activities

There are several events for students throughout the year that celebrate culture, health, and holidays. The Student Activities Office also provides shape-up and wellness programs for students, along with the Art Institute of New York City Celebrates Women program. Students are offered many opportunities to volunteer throughout the year. Culinary students work at various events throughout the city as well as open-house programs at the school.

Academic Facilities

The Art Institute of New York City occupies approximately 42,000 square feet of space at 75 Varick Street and 33,000 square feet at 11 Beach Street in the SoHo/Tribeca district of New York City.

Students study culinary techniques at the Varick Street location in nine kitchens that include ovens, broilers, food slicers, mixers, charcoal grills, stove tops, convection ovens, dishwashers, and refrigerators. One Hudson Place, the Art Institute of New York City's restaurant, provides students with the opportunity to cook and serve in a professional setting. The Education Department is situated at the Varick Street location, as are library resources, facilities, and services that are shared with Metropolitan College.

The school's Beach Street location houses the Graphic Design, Interactive Media Design, Video Production, Interior Design, Advertising, and Fashion Design Departments. There are thirteen classrooms, four computer labs (two Macintosh and two PC), two drawing studios (one for life drawing), and a dining room for wine seminars and service management classes. A large bookstore and an art gallery are located on the first floor. All lecture classes are housed at the Beach Street site, many in classrooms equipped with TV monitors, VCRs, and overhead projectors.

Location

The Art Institute of New York City is located in downtown Manhattan's SoHo/Tribeca area, a hub of contemporary style. SoHo is a focal point for individuals who appreciate and possess creative talents. West Broadway is the district's main thoroughfare, lined with avant-garde boutiques and trendsetting galleries, including a branch of the Guggenheim Museum, which exhibits both contemporary collec-tions and selections from the museum's permanent collection. The New Museum of Contemporary Art is a major venue for innovative shows.

Admission Requirements

Applicants must complete an application form, pay a $50 application fee, and complete a 150-word essay to apply for admission to the Art Institute of New York City. A personal interview with an admissions representative is required. Applicants must provide official high school transcripts, proof of successful completion of the General Educational Development (GED) test, or transcripts from any college previously attended.

Application and Information

To obtain an application or make arrangements for an interview or tour of the school, students should contact:

The Art Institute of New York City
75 Varick Street, 16th Floor
New York, New York 10013-1917
Telephone: 212-226-5500
        800-654-2433 (toll-free)
World Wide Web: http://www.ainyc.artinstitutes.edu

THE ART INSTITUTE OF OHIO–CINCINNATI

CINCINNATI, OHIO

The Institute and Its Mission

The Art Institute of Ohio–Cincinnati prepares students for entry-level employment in the creative arts. The Institute offers three associate degree programs.

Founded in 2004, the Art Institute of Ohio–Cincinnati includes more than 57,000 square feet of classroom, laboratory, and office space designed according to the school's specifications for its design programs. The Art Institute of Ohio–Cincinnati shares facility space with Brown Mackie College–Cincinnati Campus.

The Art Institute of Ohio–Cincinnati is accredited by the Accrediting Council for Independent Colleges and Schools (ACICS) to award the associate degree. ACICS is listed as a nationally recognized accrediting agency by the United States Department of Education (USDE). Its accreditation of degree-granting institutions also is recognized by the Council for Higher Education Accreditation (CHEA). The school is a branch of Brown Mackie College in Findlay, and the campus is approved under Chapter 3332 of the Ohio Revised Code for the offering of all programs by the State Board of Career Colleges and Schools. The Art Institute of Ohio–Cincinnati is a member of the Ohio Council of Private Colleges and Schools.

The Art Institute of Ohio–Cincinnati is nonresidential; students who are unable to commute daily from their homes may request assistance from the Office of Admissions in locating off-campus housing. The school is accessible by public transportation and provides ample student parking at no additional cost.

The Art Institute of Ohio–Cincinnati affords its students the opportunity to work for major corporations, hear speakers of international acclaim, volunteer for civic organizations, and enjoy all the culture and excitement that a large city has to offer.

Assistance is available to help students with resume writing, networking, and keeping abreast of what employers are looking for in job candidates.

Academic Programs

Students attending the Art Institute of Ohio–Cincinnati can pursue an Associate of Applied Science (A.A.S.) degree in graphic design, interactive media design, or interior design. Each program requires the successful completion of 96 credits.

Costs

Total tuition and fees are $32,256 for the 2005–06 academic year. Costs are the same for each degree program.

Financial Aid

Financial aid is available for those who qualify. The Art Institute of Ohio–Cincinnati offers student financial planning. The goal of Student Financial Services is to structure affordable monthly payment plans so that students may concentrate on fulfilling their educational and career aspirations.

Available resources include federal and state aid, student loans from private lenders, and Federal Work-Study (FWS) Program opportunities, both on and off campus. Students seeking financial aid must complete the Free Application for Federal Student Aid (FAFSA). Application deadlines and eligibility requirements vary.

Faculty

The Art Institute of Ohio–Cincinnati has 12 full-time faculty members, who are qualified and experienced teachers committed to the academic and technical preparation of their students.

Student Body Profile

Students come to the Art Institute of Ohio–Cincinnati from throughout the United States. The student population includes recent high school graduates, transfer students, and those who have left a previous employment situation to study and train for a new career. Students are creative, competitive, and open to new ideas. They place great value on an education that prepares them for an exciting entry-level position in the arts.

Student Activities

Student life is an integral part of the Art Institute of Ohio–Cincinnati experience. The Office of Student Affairs sponsors a variety of events, including intramural sports, dances, parties, lunch-and-learn sessions, and off-campus trips.

Academic Facilities

The Art Institute of Ohio–Cincinnati provides easy access to the technology, tools, and facilities needed to complete projects in all disciplines. Students may produce work in an environment that is appropriate for their chosen creative endeavors. The facilities include media presentation rooms for special instructional needs, libraries that provide instructional resources, and academic support for both faculty members and students.

Location

Cincinnati is home to major-league sporting events, concerts, a professional symphony, theater, Paramount's Kings Island, award-winning restaurants, and downtown entertainment districts that offer exciting nightlife.

The city is known for its great beauty—with steep hills, wooded suburbs, a picturesque downtown riverfront, and four distinct seasons. Cincinnati is an affordable city in which to live and is designated by *Fortune* magazine as one of the top ten places to live and work in the United States.

Admission Requirements

Applicants to the Art Institute of Ohio–Cincinnati must demonstrate proof of high school graduation or its equivalent.

An official copy of the high school transcript or General Educational Development (GED) certificate is required. Candidates are interviewed and must write an essay on how an education at the Art Institute of Ohio–Cincinnati can help them reach their career goals.

Each applicant's academic transcript and completed essay is evaluated by the Admissions Acceptance Committee. A separate application and enrollment form must be completed and signed by the applicant and then submitted to the Art Institute of Ohio–Cincinnati.

Application and Information

To obtain an application or make arrangements for an interview or tour of the school, students should contact:

The Art Institute of Ohio–Cincinnati
1011 Glendale-Milford Road
Cincinnati, Ohio 45215-1107
Telephone: 513-771-2821
     866-613-5184 (toll-free)
Fax: 877-477-8486 (toll-free)
World Wide Web: http://www.aioc.artinstitutes.edu

THE ART INSTITUTE OF SEATTLE

SEATTLE, WASHINGTON

The Institute and Its Mission

The Art Institute of Seattle provides programs that prepare graduates for entry-level employment in the creative arts. Programs are developed with and taught by experienced educators. The Art Institute of Seattle has a proud history both as a part of the Seattle community and as a contributor to the Northwest's creative industries.

The average class size is 19 students. The school offers three bachelor's degree programs and eleven associate degree programs.

The Career Services Department works with students to refine their presentations to potential employers. The department also helps provide student advisers with insight into each student's specialized skills and interests. Specific career advising occurs during the last two quarters of a student's education. Interviewing techniques and resume-writing skills are developed, and students receive portfolio advising from faculty members. Of all 2003 Art Institute of Seattle graduates available for employment, 79.7 percent were working in a field related to their program of study within six months of graduation and earning an average salary of $26,115.

The Student Affairs Department offers a variety of services to students to help them make the most of their educational experience. These services include both school-sponsored and independent housing options.

The Art Institute of Seattle is accredited by the Northwest Commission on Colleges and Universities (NWCCU) and is licensed by the Washington Workforce Training and Education Coordinating Board. The Art Institute of Seattle is approved for the training of veterans and eligible veterans' dependents and is authorized to enroll nonimmigrant international students.

Academic Programs

The Art Institute of Seattle operates on a year-round, quarterly basis. Each quarter totals eleven weeks. Bachelor's degree programs are available in graphic design, interior design, and media arts and animation. Associate degrees are offered in animation art and design, audio production, culinary arts, fashion design, fashion marketing, graphic design, industrial design technology, interactive media design, interior design, photography, and video production. Diploma programs are available in the art of cooking, baking and pastry, digital graphic production, and residential design.

Bachelor's degree programs are twelve quarters in length. Associate degree programs vary between six and nine quarters in length, and diploma programs require four quarters for completion.

Costs

The Art Institute of Seattle follows a tuition lock-in policy that allows students to keep their tuition at a constant level for the duration of their studies. As long as students stay in school, they are unaffected by any future tuition increases.

Tuition is charged on a per-credit-hour basis. The costs for tuition and fees vary, depending upon the program of study. For current costs, students should contact the Art Institute of Seattle's Admissions Office or visit the school's Web site.

Financial Aid

Financial aid is available for those who qualify. The school's student financial aid officers take a holistic approach to developing a plan to assist the student in meeting projected education costs.

Eligible students may apply for financial assistance under various federal and state programs, including the Federal Pell Grant, Federal Supplemental Educational Opportunity Grant (FSEOG), Federal Perkins Loan, Federal Stafford Student Loan (subsidized and unsubsidized), Federal Work-Study Program (FWS), Alaska State Student Loan, Federal PLUS loan (for parents), Washington State Need Grant, Vocational Rehabilitation Assistance, Veterans' Administration benefits, and Bureau of Indian Affairs awards. Awards are based on individual need and the availability of funds.

The Art Institute of Seattle offers scholarships based on merit, motivation, and financial need. Scholarships include the Advantage Grant Program, the Art Institute of Seattle Excellence Award, the Art Institute of Seattle Scholarship Competition, the Art Institute of Seattle Culinary Scholarship Competition, the National Art Honor Society Scholarship, the Evelyn Keedy Memorial Scholarship, VICA Skills USA Championship, Scholastic Arts Competition, HERO, IACP Foundation, C-Cap, ProStart, Technology Student Association Competition, and New York City Public Schools Scholarship Competition. Application deadlines and eligibility requirements vary.

Faculty

Faculty members at the Art Institute of Seattle include 140 instructors who are experienced in what they teach and bring real-world knowledge into the classroom.

Student Body Profile

Students come to the Art Institute of Seattle from throughout the United States and abroad. The student population includes recent high school graduates, transfer students, and those who have left a previous employment situation to study and train for a new career. Students are creative, competitive, and open to new ideas. They place great value on an education that prepares them for an exciting entry-level position in the arts.

Student Activities

The Art Institute of Seattle places high importance on student life, both inside and outside the classroom. The school provides an environment that encourages involvement in a wide variety of activities, including clubs and organizations, community service opportunities, and various committees designed to enhance the quality of student life. Numerous all-school programs and events are planned throughout the year to meet students' needs.

Academic Facilities

The Art Institute of Seattle is an urban campus that comprises three facilities. The school houses classrooms, audio and video studios, a student store, student lounges, copy centers, a gallery, a woodshop, a sculpture room, fashion display windows, a resource center, a technology center, and culinary facilities. The Art Institute of Seattle is also home to a public restaurant.

Location

The Art Institute of Seattle is located in the city's Belltown district. Founded by Native Americans and traders, the city has retained respect for its different cultures and customs. People from all over the world come to study, work, and live in this city, known for its friendly people and beautiful natural surroundings.

World-class companies, such as Microsoft, Boeing, Starbucks, Amazon.com, and Nordstrom, make their global headquarters in Seattle. As a gateway to the Pacific Rim, Seattle is a crossroads where creativity, technology, and business meet.

Admission Requirements

A student seeking admission to the Art Institute of Seattle is required to interview with an admissions representative (in person or over the phone). Applicants are required to have a high school diploma or a General Educational Development (GED) certificate and to submit an admissions application, the $50 application fee, and an essay describing how an education at the Art Institute of Seattle may help the student to achieve creative goals. Prospective students must complete an Enrollment Agreement and pay a $100 tuition deposit within ten days after the application is submitted. For advanced placement, additional information, including college transcripts, letters of recommendation, or portfolio work, may be required. Students may apply for admission online.

The Art Institute of Seattle follows a rolling admissions schedule. Students are encouraged to apply for their chosen quarter early so that they may take advantage of orientation activities. Students may also apply until the actual start date for any given quarter, depending on space availability.

Application and Information

To obtain an application or make arrangements for an interview or tour of the school, students should contact:

The Art Institute of Seattle
2323 Elliott Avenue
Seattle, Washington 98121-1622
Telephone: 206-448-6600
          800-275-2471 (toll-free)
Fax: 206-269-0275
World Wide Web: http://www.ais.edu

The Art Institute of Seattle's faculty members bring their professional experience into the classroom to create a collaborative, real-world learning environment.

ATLANTIC CAPE COMMUNITY COLLEGE

MAYS LANDING, ATLANTIC CITY, AND CAPE MAY COUNTY,
NEW JERSEY

The College and Its Mission

Founded in 1964, Atlantic Cape Community College (ACCC) held its first classes in fall 1966 in rented facilities in Atlantic City, New Jersey. In February 1968, the College moved to its present main campus location in Mays Landing, the Atlantic County seat. ACCC was the second community college organized in the state.

ACCC is a comprehensive, two-year public institution serving the residents of Atlantic and Cape May counties, enrolling more than 6,500 credit students. The College operates nationally recognized casino career and culinary arts programs and is a leader in online education. In addition to the College's main campus in Mays Landing, ACCC operates an extension center in Atlantic City and opened a full-service branch campus in Cape May County in fall 2005.

The Casino Career Institute (CCI), located at the Charles D. Worthington Atlantic City Center, was the first casino gaming school in the nation affiliated with a community college and the only licensed slot training school in New Jersey. Opened in 1978, CCI has trained more than 46,000 people for careers in the casino industry. It has provided training for members of several federal governments and many state police forces as other jurisdictions prepare themselves for legalized gaming.

In 1981, as another extension of its role to train workers for the southern New Jersey hospitality industry, ACCC opened the Academy of Culinary Arts, a chefs' training program that has graduated more than 2,400 students. The Academy of Culinary Arts has a full-time enrollment of nearly 300 students.

Academic Programs

ACCC offers twenty-one transfer and career degree programs with twenty-one options and thirty-three professional series programs as well as noncredit professional development and customized training services. ACCC requires a minimum of 64 credits for its associate degrees.

Associate Degree Programs Associate in Arts degree programs are designed for students who wish to continue their education at a four-year college or university and pursue studies in the liberal arts, humanities, or social sciences. The A.A. degree requires a minimum of 45 credits in general education. One basic program of study in liberal arts is available, with options in business administration, child development/child care, education, history, humanities, literature, performing arts, philosophy, psychology, social science, sociology, or studio art.

Associate in Science degrees are awarded to students who successfully complete programs that emphasize mathematics, the biological or physical sciences, and business programs intended as prebaccalaureate work. The A.S. degree requires a minimum of 30 credits in general education. Degree programs are available in business administration (with an option in economics), computer information systems, criminal justice (with an option in corrections), general studies, health sciences, paralegal studies, science and mathematics (with options in biology, chemistry, and mathematics), and social work.

Associate in Applied Science degree programs emphasize preparation for careers, typically at the technical or semiprofessional level. The A.A.S. degree requires a minimum of 20 credits in general education. Degree programs are available in accounting (with an option in accounting information systems), baking and pastry, business administration, computer programming, computer systems support (with options in microcomputer technologies and Web technologies), culinary arts, food service management, hospitality management, nursing, office systems technology, paralegal studies, respiratory therapy, and travel and tourism.

In addition, ACCC offers a number of certificate programs to meet the short-term training needs of the local workforce.

The largest cooking school in New Jersey, the Academy of Culinary Arts, was founded in 1981 to meet the growing need for highly skilled chefs and food service professionals for the Atlantic City hospitality industry. Facilities include eight teaching kitchens with overhead mirrors, a bake shop, classrooms, a computer lab, a banquet room, a pastry/baking retail store, and a gourmet public restaurant.

The culinary arts program, including the option in baking and pastry, features hands-on and academic training and an externship program. Classes meet five hours a day, Monday through Friday, in a morning or afternoon session from January through May and August/September through December. Part-time evening courses are also available. As part of their training, students operate a gourmet restaurant on the college's campus. Specialized certificate programs are available in catering, food service management, hot food, and baking and pastry.

The food service management program combines liberal arts classes, hands-on culinary training, and management-related courses in the specifics of the hospitality industry. The combination of front-of-the-house and back-of-the-house courses provides students with the broad-based knowledge of the industry that is key to succeeding in the field.

Off-Campus Programs

Cooperative education is an academic program that allows students to receive college credits for working in jobs related to their major while pursuing their studies at ACCC. A cooperative education component is required for the culinary arts program and is optional for office systems technology and paralegal studies students.

ACCC, a leader in educational technology, now offers eleven associate degrees and several professional series programs online through distance education. The degree programs available through distance education are business administration (A.A.S. and A.S.), computer information systems (A.S.), general studies (A.S.), liberal arts (A.A., with options in business administration, history, humanities, literature, psychology, and social science), and office systems technology (A.A.S.). ACCC offers more than 100 online courses and has trained faculty members from colleges across New Jersey to use the technology for instruction. It hosts the New Jersey Virtual Community College Consortium (NJVCCC).

Costs

In 2005–06, full-time tuition for Atlantic and Cape May County residents or out-of-county New Jersey residents with a chargeback is $2200 per year. Part-time tuition is $73.15 per credit. Out-of-county New Jersey residents without chargebacks pay $146.30 per credit. Out-of-state and out-of-country residents pay $256 per credit.

The 2005–06 tuition and fees for the Academy of Culinary Arts are $219.45 per credit for Atlantic and Cape May County residents, $292.60 per credit for out-of-county residents without chargeback, and $402.35 per credit for out-of-state and out-of-country residents. Students also pay required fees of $14 per credit and a program fee of $137 per credit for culinary arts courses only. Full-time tuition and fees for in-county and out-of-county residents with chargeback is approximately $4500 per semester.

There are also parking and mandatory accident and health insurance fees. Some classes require special lab or material costs or other fees.

Tuition for online courses is $93 per credit.

Financial Aid

About 65 percent of ACCC students who apply receive some form of financial aid, including scholarships, grants, loans, and work-study assistance. Funds are available from federal, state, and private sources for those with a demonstrated need or who meet eligibility requirements. All applicants for aid must complete the Free Application for Federal Student Aid (FAFSA), available online or from ACCC's financial aid office or most high school guidance offices.

Faculty

ACCC has 78 full-time and approximately 300 part-time faculty members. Full-time faculty members hold master's degrees, and many also have doctoral degrees in their field of study. Most faculty members also serve as academic advisers. ACCC's student-faculty ratio is 26:1.

Student Body Profile

In fall 2004, there were 6,515 students at Atlantic Cape Community College. Atlantic County residents accounted for 73 percent of the student body; Cape May County residents accounted for 20 percent. Members of minority groups were as follows: Hispanic, 9.84 percent; Asian, 7.43 percent; Native American, 0.21 percent; and African American, 13.88 percent. International students made up 3 percent of the total. The average age of students was 27.

Student Activities

Every ACCC student is a member of the Student Government Association (SGA). The main policy making body of the SGA is the Student Senate, which charters student clubs and organizations, approves budgets, determines student policy, and works with the faculty and administration to improve the College. There are numerous special interest clubs and organizations open to all students, including *Atlantic Cape Review* (student newspaper), Art Club, Black Student Alliance, Computer Club, Criminal Justice Club, Cross-Cultural Student Association, Culinary Student Association, Future Teachers of America Club, International Club, Jewish Student Association, Latino Experience Club, Performing Arts Club, Phi Theta Kappa International Honor Society, *Rewrites* literary magazine, Shakespeare Club, Student Nurses Club, and WACC, the campus radio station.

ACCC intercollegiate sports include men's basketball, coed archery, and coed cheerleading. Intramural sports include men's soccer, volleyball, basketball, Ping-Pong, and bowling.

Facilities and Resources

ACCC's main campus is built around a quadrangle of lawn. The buildings, designed of split-face brick, natural cedar shakes, and tinted glass, are joined by a system of walkways. A central loop connects buildings and parking areas with the Black Horse Pike (Route 322). ACCC's indoor athletic facilities include a gymnasium with a seating capacity of 800 and a weight room with lockers and showers. Outdoor facilities include baseball, softball, and soccer fields; two basketball courts; a nature trail; and an archery range. ACCC's housing program assists culinary students who are not Atlantic or Cape May County residents in obtaining quality living arrangements in an off-campus setting. There is no on-campus housing available.

The College's cultural events are staged in a 460-seat theater located in Walter E. Edge Hall. The resources and facilities of the William Spangler Library are available to the College community and to the residents of Atlantic and Cape May counties. The library owns more than 81,000 books, audiocassettes, videocassettes, music CD's and art reproductions, as well as subscriptions to more than 300 periodicals. More than 200 videos are accessible from the College's new video server. Twelve computer workstations and sixteen wireless laptops are available for student and faculty use in the library. Students have access to Science Direct, Dialog, EBSCO Host, Literature Resource Center, and LexisNexis (1,000 full-text journals); a variety of CD-ROM databases; and the World Wide Web.

Location

Located on 537 acres in the picturesque New Jersey Pinelands, Atlantic Cape Community College is in Atlantic County, New Jersey, 17 miles west of Atlantic City's boardwalk, 45 miles from Philadelphia, and 115 miles from New York City. It operates an extension center in Atlantic City and opened a full-service campus in Middle Township, Cape May County, in fall 2005.

Admission Requirements

Admission is available to all applicants who are 18 years of age and older whose high school class has graduated. Applicants who have graduated from an accredited secondary or preparatory school, or those with a state equivalency certificate, are accepted to ACCC. Applicants under 18 years of age, not currently enrolled in a high school or not having a high school diploma or GED certificate do not qualify for admission to a community college. Applicants who are 18 years of age and older and do not have a high school diploma or GED certificate may apply to the College for admission under special conditions.

Admission to specific programs, such as culinary arts or nursing, is dependent upon students meeting the necessary program requirements and completing course prerequisites.

Application and Information

Applications are reviewed on a continuous basis. The preferred deadline for fall admission is July 1; for spring admission, November 1. There is a $35 application fee, which includes the cost of administering the placement test. Culinary applicants must pay an additional, nonrefundable $300 deposit. The deposit reserves a seat for a maximum of two semesters and is applied toward the semester tuition bill when the student registers. Seats are assigned on a first-come, first-served basis according to the completion of the steps toward admission.

For an application or additional information, students should contact:

Admissions Office
Atlantic Cape Community College
5100 Black Horse Pike
Mays Landing, New Jersey 08330-2699
Telephone: 609-343-5000
       800-645-CHEF (toll-free)
E-mail: accadmit@atlantic.edu
World Wide Web: http://www.atlantic.edu

The Academy of Culinary Arts, housed at Atlantic Cape Community College, is New Jersey's largest cooking school, with nearly 300 students.

BALTIMORE INTERNATIONAL COLLEGE
BALTIMORE, MARYLAND; VIRGINIA, COUNTY CAVAN, IRELAND

The College and Its Mission

The Baltimore International College, a regionally accredited, independent college, was founded in 1972 to provide theoretical and technical skills education for individuals seeking careers as hospitality professionals. The College is committed to providing students with the knowledge and ability necessary for employment and success in the hospitality industry.

In 1985, the College was authorized by the state of Maryland to grant associate degrees. As part of the College's continued growth, restaurant and food service management and innkeeping management were added to its curriculum. In 1987, the Virginia Park Campus in Ireland was founded, enabling students to study under European chefs and hoteliers in a European environment. In 1996, the College was granted accreditation by the Commission on Higher Education of the Middle States Association of College and Schools. In 1998, the College was authorized by the state of Maryland to grant four-year baccalaureate degrees. In addition to classrooms, offices, and dorms, the College's campus in Baltimore includes a campus bookstore, a student union, a hotel, an inn, two restaurants, parking, student dining facilities, a Career Development Center, and a Learning Resource Center comprising a library, two academic computer labs, and an art gallery.

Freshman students who are single, under 21, and live farther than 50 miles from campus are required to live in student housing.

Academic Programs

The College provides a comprehensive curriculum, which includes an honors study abroad program at the Baltimore International College Virginia Park Campus near Dublin, Ireland.

The College's professional cooking program and the combined programs in professional cooking and baking and baking and pastry operate throughout the calendar year; new classes begin in the spring, summer, and fall. The College's business and management programs accept freshmen in the fall and spring semesters. The culinary arts certificate, which combines cooking and baking, and the certificate in professional marketing are available through evening classes and begin in the fall and spring semesters.

Associate Degree Programs Baltimore International College awards the associate degree in the following programs: food and beverage management, hotel/motel/innkeeping management, professional baking and pastry, professional cooking, and professional cooking and baking. The associate degree is offered separately and as part of the 2+2 program at Baltimore International College. In the 2+2 program, students receive their two-year associate degree and then continue two additional years to complete the four-year bachelor's degree. Bachelor's degree programs require 125 to 133 credits.

To earn an associate degree in professional cooking, professional baking and pastry, or professional cooking and baking, the student must complete 62–66 credits. To earn an associate degree in food and beverage management or hotel/motel/ innkeeping management, the student must complete approximately 65 credits. Certificate candidates must complete 54 credits. The certificate program concentrates on technical courses and is intended for students who already have a strong academic background. The associate degree program combines technical hands-on courses with general education courses

such as nutrition, sanitation, psychology, English, and mathematics, as well as an internship or externship.

Off-Campus Programs

The Honors Program has been developed for qualified culinary arts and business and management majors. The Honors Program is taught at the College's historic, 100-acre Virginia Park campus in County Cavan, Ireland. Culinary students who are selected for the Honors Program further enhance their skills in and knowledge of European cuisine, baking and pastry, and a la carte service. Business and management students selected for the honors program have the opportunity to learn the day-to-day operation of a hotel and restaurant, from reception to housekeeping and from restaurant management to accounting. Students fully enjoy the cross-cultural experience of living in an English-speaking foreign country.

Costs

Tuition for 2004–05 was $7024. Student housing costs ranged from $3100 to $5196 per semester for dormitory-style housing (includes meal plan).

Financial Aid

Students receive financial aid from federal, state, institutional, and private sources and may be employed during their attendance as full-time students. The forms of financial aid available at the College through federal sources include the Federal Pell Grant, the Federal Supplemental Educational Opportunity Grant, the Federal Work-Study Program, the Federal Subsidized and Unsubsidized Stafford Student Loans, FPLUS loans, and veterans' educational benefits. Students are encouraged to investigate the scholarship programs in their home state and apply for state scholarships if the grants can be used in Maryland. The College also offers its own series of scholarships and payment options. In 2003–04, College-funded scholarships averaged $3300 per academic year. Students can request a financial aid application from the Student Financial Planning Office. The College employs the Federal Methodology of Need Analysis, approved by the U.S. Department of Education, as a fair and equitable means of determining the family's ability to contribute to the student's educational expenses, as well as eligibility for other financial aid programs.

Faculty

Baltimore International College faculty members include 29 chefs and academic instructors of high academic distinction. The student-faculty ratio averages 16:1 in culinary labs and 25:1 in academic classes. Each student is assigned a faculty adviser who oversees the student's progress and answers questions about academic and career concerns. Students are encouraged to discuss program-related issues with the Director of Student Counseling.

Student Body Profile

Current enrollment is 750 annually, with 52 percent men and 48 percent women. Approximately 17 percent of students are from out-of-state, representing twenty-four states and several other countries. Students can join the Greater Baltimore Chapter of the American Culinary Federation and can participate in a variety of other activities through Student Affairs.

Student Activities

The College offers general academic counseling for all students, peer tutoring on request, and a variety of referrals for support services. In addition, student services provide many recreation and leisure activities, including the student union, a series of activities sponsored by the College, and information about cultural programs around the city. Student services also provides ongoing support to the College's alumni through surveys, mailings about the College's growth, and involvement in College-sponsored events such as open houses, resume referrals, and career fairs.

Facilities and Resources

The Baltimore campus includes kitchens, storerooms, cooking demonstration theaters, academic classrooms, multipurpose rooms, a library, computer labs, a student union, and auxiliary services. Public operations that function as in-house training for students include the Mount Vernon Hotel, the Bay Atlantic Club Restaurant, and the Hopkins Inn.

The Virginia Park Campus is located on 100 acres, 50 miles from Dublin student housing, with laboratory kitchens and lecture facilities. The complex also includes the Park Hotel, with public operations that function as in-house training for students, including the Marquis Dining Room and the Marchioness Ballroom. The Park Hotel has thirty-six guest rooms. All students enjoy unlimited golf and fishing as well as hiking trails.

Career Planning/Placement Offices The College's Career Development Center offers students access to information about careers in food service and hospitality management. The College's career development services are located in the Career Information Center where coordinators organize on-campus recruiting and offer workshops and assistance in resume writing and interviewing skills.

Library and Audiovisual Services The College's Learning Resource Center is a member of an interlibrary loan network that enables users to borrow from public, academic, and private libraries throughout Maryland. The library's current core collection has approximately 13,000 volumes, 200 periodicals, and almost 800 audiovisual selections. The library offers students access to the Internet, a worldwide network of electronic information. In-house services include two academic computer labs, electronic databases for research, and a photocopier.

The College's art gallery is part of the Learning Resource Center and features a permanent display of edible art. Student participation in all exhibits is encouraged.

Location

The College's main campus, located in downtown Baltimore, is just two blocks from the city's famous Inner Harbor, a location that puts the College in the midst of numerous hotels and restaurants. The city offers year-round cultural and entertainment opportunities, such as theater, opera, the Baltimore Symphony Orchestra, museums, sporting events, and festivals. Other attractions in Baltimore, within walking distance of the College, are the National Aquarium, Harborplace, Oriole Park at Camden Yards, Ravens Stadium, Maryland Science Center, and many historic sites, including Fort McHenry, Mount Vernon, and the Walters Art Museum. Baltimore also has parks and miles of waterfront for those who enjoy outdoor recreation. Washington, D.C., the nation's capital, is just 30 miles from downtown Baltimore. The city of Baltimore is easily accessed by major highways and bus, rail, and air service. Baltimore/Washington International Airport is a short drive from the campus.

Admission Requirements

Creativity and skill of students must be matched by dedication. The College seeks candidates who desire a professional career in the hospitality industry.

Individuals seeking admission to the College must have earned a high school diploma or have passed the GED. Applicants must either pass the College's Admissions Test, take developmental courses during their first semester, or have one of the following: minimum SAT I scores of 430 verbal and 420 math, a minimum composite ACT score of 16, minimum CLEP scores in the 50th percentile in math and English composition with essay, a secondary degree, or 16 credit hours at the postsecondary level with a minimum average of C in math and English. Transfer students must submit an official college transcript as well as catalog course descriptions for credits they wish to transfer.

The College affords equally to all students the rights, privileges, programs, activities, scholarships and loan programs, and other programs administered by the College without regard to race, color, creed, sex, age, handicap, or national or ethnic origin.

Application and Information

Applicants are required to submit an application form along with a $35 nonrefundable fee. Requests by the College for additional information must be handled in a timely manner. An admission decision is made as soon as a file is complete. Upon acceptance, applicants are asked to submit a $100 tuition deposit.

For additional information, students should contact:

Office of Admissions
Commerce Exchange
Baltimore International College
17 Commerce Street
Baltimore, Maryland 21202-3230
Telephone: 410-752-4710 Ext. 120
         800-624-9926 Ext. 120 (toll-free)
E-mail: admissions@bic.edu
World Wide Web: http://www.bic.edu

Small classes at Baltimore International College enable students to receive individual instruction that helps them perfect their skills.

BAY STATE COLLEGE

BOSTON, MASSACHUSETTS

The College and Its Mission

Bay State College, a private, two-year, independent, coeducational institution, is located in Boston's historic Back Bay. Since 1946, Bay State College has been preparing young men and women with the skills necessary to attain outstanding careers in the business and allied health disciplines.

The College's goal is to prepare and educate students for successful and rewarding professional opportunities. Bay State College accomplishes this by providing the best possible education, which enables students to go out into the working world equipped with all the skills needed to succeed professionally or to transfer to a four-year college of choice. Bay State College assists, encourages, supports, and educates students in all their academic, professional, and personal goals and aspirations.

Bay State College is accredited by the New England Association of Schools and Colleges, is authorized to award the Associate in Science and Associate in Applied Science degrees by the Commonwealth of Massachusetts, and is a member of several professional educational associations.

Bay State College's allied health programs are accredited by the Accrediting Bureau of Health Education Schools (ABHES). The Physical Therapist Assistant Program is accredited by the Commission on Accreditation in Physical Therapy Education (CAPTE) of the American Physical Therapy Association (APTA).

Academic Programs

Bay State College offers unique courses preparing students for careers in accounting, business, criminal justice, early childhood education, fashion design, fashion merchandising, general studies, medical assisting studies, and physical therapist assistant studies. In addition, students are exceptionally prepared to transfer to four-year colleges and universities.

The College's current programs include accounting (A.A.S.), business administration (A.A.S.), early childhood education (A.S.), entertainment management (A.A.S.), fashion design (A.S.), fashion merchandising (A.A.S.), general studies (A.S.), medical assisting studies (A.S.), physical therapist assistant studies (A.S.), retail business management (A.A.S.), and travel and hospitality management (A.A.S.).

In addition, Bay State is now offering three baccalaureate degrees in entertainment management, fashion merchandising, and management.

Bay State College's Day and Continuing Education Divisions offer day and evening classes. Two satellite campuses for continuing education are located in Gloucester and Middleborough, Massachusetts.

Off-Campus Programs

The internship program, available in all major areas of study, provides practical field experience so that the students gain the skills and experience with the technologies used in the business and medical settings.

Students from Bay State College are among the 250 students participating in the Walt Disney World College Program. During their stay at Walt Disney World, students receive on-the-job training and classroom experience. This is just one of the many internship possibilities for students each year at Bay State College.

Costs

For the 2004–05 academic year, the College's Day Division charged a comprehensive fee of $24,400, which included full-time tuition ($14,900) and room and board ($9500). There is an allied health lab fee of $475 per year (medical assisting studies and physical therapist assistant studies only). Textbooks are estimated at $600 per year. Bay State College's Continuing Education Division, the Boston, Middleborough, and Gloucester campuses, charged $220 per credit. Tuition, dormitory charges, and fees are subject to change.

Financial Aid

Personal financial planning and counseling is completed with all students and families. Approximately 85 percent of students receive some form of financial assistance. Bay State College requires a completed Free Application for Federal Student Aid (FAFSA) form and signed federal tax forms. The College's institutional financial aid priority deadline is March 1. Financial aid is granted on a rolling basis.

Faculty

There are 50 faculty members, with 53 percent holding advanced degrees and 6 percent holding doctoral degrees. The student-faculty ratio is 15:1.

Student Body Profile

There are 567 students in terminal programs. The average age is 18. The student body is ethnically and culturally diverse; 85 percent are state residents, 9 percent are transfer students, 4 percent are international students, 60 percent are women, 19 percent are African American, 11 percent are Hispanic, and 10 percent are Asian American. In the past year, 33 percent of Bay State College's graduating class continued on to a four-year college.

Bay State College's residence halls are located on Commonwealth Avenue. There are 174 college housing spaces available. Each residence hall is designed to accommodate from 1 to 5 students per room. Housing is guaranteed to freshmen who complete and submit a dorm contract by May 1.

Each hall is staffed by professional live-in directors and a paraprofessional staff of resident assistants. The staff members strive to foster a living and learning environment that complements the academic mission. All residents have the opportunity to experience a wide variety of programs such as in-house educational, cultural, and awareness seminars; study breaks; discounts to area movies and theater productions; and holiday celebrations. Twenty-four-hour quiet hours are in effect during midterm and final periods. A campus dining facility is available, as are microwaves, laundry facilities, cable-ready outlets, and computer labs.

Student Activities

Students participate in a multitude of activities offered by the College through student groups. These include the Travel Club, Fashion Club, Early Childhood Education Club, Accounting Club, Student Leader Organization, Medical Assisting Society, Physical Therapist Assistant Club, a talent show, a student-produced fashion show, a literary magazine, literary readings, and access to a gym.

Facilities and Resources

Advisement/Counseling Trained staff members assist students in selecting courses and programs of study to satisfy their educational objectives. A counseling center is available to provide mental and physical health referrals to all Bay State students in need of such services. Referral networks are extensive, within a wide range of geographic areas, and provide access to a variety of public and private health agencies.

Specialized Services The Learning Center has been renamed the Center for Learning and Academic Support (CLAS). A learning center serves as a supplementary learning tool for those individuals wishing to improve their skills through self-paced individualized instruction. The center offers assistance through the use of peer and faculty tutors, individualized learning packets, and audio, visual, and other self-study resources. Introductory studies courses are designed for a diverse population of students, including workers returning to school, recent high school graduates seeking academic reinforcement, and ESL students. Their individual needs are met so they can be successful in the traditional course of study leading to an associate degree.

Career Planning/Placement Of the number of students seeking assistance from the Career Services Office, there was a 95 percent job placement rate. The primary purpose of the Career Services Office at Bay State College is to see that every graduating senior secures the best possible position in his or her chosen career. The Career Services Office, offering lifelong service to all alumni, continually posts job openings for current students and graduates. An average of 10,000 job openings are posted every year. The Career Services Office,

under the guidance of Mr. Timothy Mosehauer, Assistant Director of Student Career Services (telephone: 617-236-8030), assists each student through one-on-one career counseling. Services include career fairs on campus, with more than seventy attending companies; resume preparation; career counseling; the career library; and a professional dynamics course.

Library and Audiovisual Services The library has a combined book collection of approximately 5,300 books. In addition, Bay State College has 100 periodicals and 200 audiovisual titles. The College's sixty computers have access to the Internet and several databases for magazine and journal articles, including ProQuest, LexisNexis Academic, and Westlaw legal database.

Location

The location of Bay State College makes it the perfect place to attend to get a complete education. While the academics are great, students are also within a mile of major-league sports, free concerts, museums, the Freedom Trail, Boston Symphony Hall, the Boston Public Library, the Boston Public Garden, and much more. The city is known for its college atmosphere. Tree-lined streets are mirrored in the skyscrapers of the Back Bay. Major shopping, cultural, and sporting events make College life an experience that students will always remember. The College's location is accessible by public transportation and in proximity to Boston Logan International Airport.

Admission Requirements

Students must be in pursuit of a high school diploma or GED certificate in order to apply and must receive it before the start of classes at Bay State College. A personal interview is strongly recommended for all students. Transcripts are requested once a student has applied. A decision is made by the Admissions Office upon completion and receipt of all documents. International students must complete an International Student Application and provide a transcript, a TOEFL score, and final documents in order to be considered for admission.

Application and Information

Bay State College accepts applications on a rolling basis, so students may apply at any time. A $25 fee is required at the time of application, but application fee waivers are available upon request.

Applications should be submitted to:

Admissions Office
Bay State College
122 Commonwealth Avenue
Boston, Massachusetts 02116
Telephone: 800-81-LEARN (toll-free)
Fax: 617-536-1735
World Wide Web: http://www.baystate.edu

BENJAMIN FRANKLIN INSTITUTE OF TECHNOLOGY

BOSTON, MASSACHUSETTS

The Institute and Its Mission

Benjamin Franklin Institute of Technology (BFIT) is a small technical college offering a variety of instructional programs based on science, engineering, and technology. Programs of one, two, three, and four years' duration are provided for various levels of interest, abilities, and objectives. The aim of the Franklin Institute is to prepare the students in each program for immediate employment upon graduation in a chosen career field and at the same time to give students a technical education upon which they can continue to build. Because of the Institute's student-teacher ratio of 11:1, students receive a great deal of individual attention with a hands-on approach to learning.

The objectives of the Franklin Institute are threefold: to provide educational opportunities in science and technology for men and women in order that they may better themselves both economically and socially, to provide a sound educational foundation upon which the graduates of the Institute's programs may continue to grow both in personal terms as well as professional and educational terms, and to assess the present and future needs of industry and technology in order to anticipate and respond to those needs through curriculum revisions and the addition of new programs.

Academic Programs

Bachelor's Degree Programs Franklin Institute is one of the few colleges in the nation to offer a **Bachelor of Science** degree in automotive technology. The program follows completion of all requirements at the Franklin associate level. Its primary objective is to prepare students for middle management positions in the automotive industry and raise the standards for education industry-wide in an increasingly complex and technical profession. The curriculum is a combination of technical and business management courses. A total of eight semesters and 134 credit hours must be successfully completed for graduation.

Associate Degree Programs Franklin Institute grants the **Associate in Science** degree in automotive technology. The **Associate in Engineering** degree is awarded in architectural technology, computer engineering technology, computer technology, electrical engineering technology, electronic engineering technology, mechanical engineering technology, and medical electronics engineering technology.

The engineering technology associate degree programs require four semesters for completion, with a total of 74 semester hours of credit. Half of the total curriculum in each engineering technology program is devoted to the technical specialty. One fourth of the total curriculum is devoted to physical science and mathematics, courses in college algebra and trigonometry, analytic geometry, calculus, and college physics. The remaining fourth of the curriculum includes English, humanities, and social studies. Most of the graduates of the engineering technology associate degree programs are employed by industry in various capacities in engineering and scientific fields. A high percentage of graduates continue their education at other colleges and universities.

The computer engineering technology program includes both fundamental and advanced courses in digital computer circuits, systems and languages, and electronic devices and circuit theory.

The electrical engineering technology program includes basic and advanced courses in the design and construction of electrical distribution systems for modern commercial and industrial buildings, commercial lighting design, and electrical estimating.

The electronic engineering technology program includes basic and advanced courses in electric and electronic circuit theory, semiconductor devices, principles and design of electrical and electronic equipment, and measurement techniques up to and including microwave frequencies.

The mechanical engineering technology program includes fundamental and advanced courses in applied mechanics, mechanics of materials, thermodynamics, heat transfer, machine design, fluid power, and instrumentation.

The medical electronics engineering technology curriculum incorporates basic and advanced courses in minicomputers and microcomputers, electronic devices, electric and electronic circuit theory, medical instrumentation, human physiology, medical instrument safety and grounding techniques, semiconductor circuitry, and principles and design of medical electronic instruments.

The industrial technology associate degree programs require four semesters for completion, with a total of 70 semester hours of credit. More than half of the total curriculum in each industrial technology program is devoted to the technical specialty. About one fourth of the total curriculum is devoted to basic science and mathematics, including algebra, trigonometry, and precalculus mathematics. The remainder of the curriculum includes English, humanities, and social studies.

More than half of the automotive technology two-year program is devoted to automotive technical specialties, including actual work on vehicles in the student instructional garage. About one third of the program is devoted to basic mathematics, physics, humanities, and social sciences, and the remaining time is devoted to basic mechanical technology studies.

The computer technology program prepares students to meet the rapidly growing demand for technicians who can install, maintain, and repair computer equipment and digital electronic systems.

The architectural technology program is designed to enable its graduates to become skilled and knowledgeable architectural draftspersons, capable of making important contributions to the architectural and/or engineering team that produces the complete working drawings from which buildings, residences, and other structures are erected.

Transfer Arrangements Transfer credit received for courses completed at Franklin Institute is dependent on the policies of the transferring institution. Many graduates receive a full two years' credit toward a baccalaureate degree.

Certificate Programs The BFIT certificate programs require two to three semesters for completion, with a total of 18 to 36 semester hours of credit. Instruction is concentrated in the student's main area of interest. The Institute currently offers certificate programs in digital photography and imaging technology (DPIT), marine technology, pharmacy technology, and practical electricity.

Costs

For the 2004–05 academic year, tuition was $12,500 per year. Books and supplies average $600. While the Institute does not maintain its own residence halls, various housing options exist.

Financial Aid

Franklin Institute offers financial assistance to students on the basis of demonstrated financial need and satisfactory academic progress. All students are encouraged to file the Free Application for Federal Student Aid (FAFSA). The Institute participates in the Federal Pell Grant, Federal Supplemental Educational Opportunity Grant, Federal Direct Loan, and Federal Work-Study programs and offers Franklin Institute grants and academic scholarships. State scholarships, VA assistance, rehabilitation funding, and payment plans are available for eligible students.

Faculty

The faculty at Franklin Institute consists of instructors with practical experience in their field of expertise and many years of instruction. Instructors meet annually with the Industrial Advisory Board for each program to review and update the curricula. There are 32 full-time and 9 part-time faculty members.

Student Body Profile

Ninety-two percent of students are state residents, 8 percent are transfer students, and 3 percent are international students. Fourteen percent of the student body are 25 years of age or older, and 14 percent are women. The student body is ethnically and culturally diverse: 30 percent are African American, 15 percent are Hispanic, and 14 percent are Asian American. Thirty-five percent of students work full-time.

Student Activities

All students are encouraged to participate in the campus environment. Activities include student government, Women's Support Group, engineering week competitions, yearbook, professional honor societies, and athletics.

Sports Franklin Institute offers outdoor recreation programs, including basketball and soccer. Indoor activities include table tennis.

Facilities and Resources

The Union building houses the library, which holds 10,000 bound volumes, 160 periodical subscriptions, eighty-five computer terminals, and a word processing lab for student use. Other labs associated with individual programs include digital and analog electronics, electrical wiring, computer systems, materials testing, machine tool, CAD, automotive engines, transmissions, drivability, and electrical as well as a full-service garage.

Location

The land on which the Institute stands, at the corner of Berkeley and Appleton Streets in the South End of Boston, was provided by the city in 1906. The Institute complex consists of three buildings, a plaza, a landscaped mall connecting the buildings on Berkeley and Appleton Streets, and a modern underground automotive technology shop. The facilities of the Kendall Administration Building and the Dunham Building are handicapped accessible. The Institute is readily accessible by public transportation and is within close walking distance of many cultural, social, and recreational activities offered in the city of Boston. Franklin Institute students have the opportunity to meet other college students from around the world, as there are more than seventy postsecondary institutions in the greater Boston area.

Admission Requirements

All applicants must possess a high school diploma or its equivalent and must have completed four full-year courses in high school English. For associate degrees in engineering technology, satisfactory completion of the following courses in mathematics and science is also required: algebra I, algebra II, and a laboratory science, preferably physics, although courses in chemistry or biology are acceptable. Additional courses in mathematics, such as trigonometry, math analysis, or precalculus, are helpful but not required.

Admission requirements for associate degree in industrial technology programs include a minimum of two high school courses in mathematics, including the study of elementary algebra, and one course in science.

Admission requirements for the Certificate of Proficiency include a minimum of two high school courses in mathematics and one course in science. The study of elementary algebra is recommended and in some cases required.

Application and Information

All applicants should complete a Franklin Institute Application for Admission and submit it with the required $25 processing fee to the Office of Admission. Official transcripts of high school records, including first-term senior-year grades, should be requested by the student and sent directly from the high school to the Office of Admission. Because applications are processed on a rolling basis, applicants are notified of their admission status shortly after all required documents have been received. International applicants are also required to demonstrate English language proficiency and provide a financial statement showing proof of ability to pay the first year's costs.

State and institutional financial aid resources can be exhausted early in the application process. For financial aid priority consideration, applicants should apply for admission and financial aid no later than April 15.

Requests for additional information and application forms should be addressed to:

Office of Admission
Benjamin Franklin Institute of Technology
41 Berkeley Street
Boston, Massachusetts 02116
Telephone: 617-423-4630
Fax: 617-482-3706
E-mail: admissions@bfit.edu
World Wide Web: http://www.bfit.edu

BERKELEY COLLEGE
WEST PATERSON, PARAMUS, AND WOODBRIDGE, NEW JERSEY

The College and Its Mission

Since its inception in 1931, Berkeley College has been committed to providing an exceptional, student-centered undergraduate business education. Today, Berkeley College is recognized across the nation as a premier school, preparing students for successful careers in business in the modern world. Berkeley College's strong academic program succeeds through a blend of traditional education, professional training, and real-world experience.

At Berkeley, students benefit from small class sizes, personalized academic and career counseling, and the chance to develop their analytical and creative skills. Berkeley believes that teaching should provide a practical perspective to traditional material, and Berkeley's distinguished faculty brings academic preparation and professional experience to the classroom. Faculty members are chosen not just for their academic achievements, but also for their applicable backgrounds in the business world.

All campuses are accredited by the Middle States Commission on Higher Education of the Middle States Association of Colleges and Schools. The New Jersey campuses are licensed as a college and are authorized by the New Jersey Commission on Higher Education to confer the degrees of Associate in Science (A.S.), Associate in Applied Science (A.A.S.), and Bachelor of Science (B.S.) in business administration. The American Bar Association (ABA) approves the paralegal studies program at all campuses.

Berkeley programs provide the comprehensive foundation necessary to begin a successful business career or to advance in a current career. The Academic Support Centers provide students with a wide range of support services to help improve their study skills as well as their reading, writing, and mathematical abilities. Academic, career, individual advisement, and free tutorial services are also available. At Berkeley, the traditional undergraduate curriculum is enhanced with professional training and experience. Berkeley's internship requirement provides valuable work experience and often leads to a full-time position. Students work in their fields of study, earn academic credits toward their degrees, establish a network of business connections for the future, and offset college costs.

Academic Programs

Berkeley offers a wide range of career-focused associate and bachelor's degree programs that prepare students for immediate marketability and professional growth. The academic curriculum combines leading-edge theory, real-world practicality, and extensive training in the latest computer technologies. Berkeley's commitment to excellence constitutes the primary objective of the College. Small classes, individualized advisement and counseling, and the development of the students' creative and analytical skills support this commitment.

Berkeley College provides exceptional flexibility and convenience, as students have the option of combining day, evening, weekend, and online classes. With Berkeley College's online program, Berkeley brings the classroom to students online with the same high standards of its on-site classes. The carefully developed program provides everything students need to pursue a wide range of associate or bachelor's degrees, backed by Berkeley's commitment to excellence in education and value. The Bachelor of Science degree in business administration is offered entirely online. The Associate in Applied Science degree is offered entirely online in international business, business administration marketing, and business administration management.

The College operates year-round on the quarter system, with classes starting in September, January, April, and July. The flexible quarter system provides students enrolled in the day division with the opportunity to complete their associate degree in only eighteen months or in the traditional two years or earn their bachelor's degree in as little as three years or in the traditional four years. Associate degree credits are easily transferred to bachelor's degree programs.

Associate Degree Programs Associate degrees are offered in business administration, with specializations in accounting, information systems management, management, and marketing. Additional associate degree programs include fashion marketing and management, interior design, international business, network management, paralegal studies, and Web design. Not all programs are offered at all locations.

Bachelor's Degree Programs Bachelor of Science degrees are offered in accounting, business administration, fashion marketing and management, international business, management, and marketing. Not all programs are offered at all locations. Highly student-supportive and flexible online programs leading to a Bachelor of Science degree in business administration and an Associate in Applied Science degree in international business, business administration marketing, and business administration management are also available for those whose busy lives and daily responsibilities do not allow them to attend classes on campus.

Certificate Programs Berkeley College offers a certificate program in computer applications. This program, which can be completed in a year or less, provides students with the opportunity to get a head start in a gratifying career. Credits earned in a certificate program are transferable to Berkeley's degree programs. Students enrolled in a certificate program receive all the benefits of a Berkeley education, including lifetime placement assistance and software refresher courses.

Costs

In 2005-06, full-time students pay $16,950 in tuition and fees for the academic year. Berkeley offers protection from any tuition increase to students who maintain continuous, full-time enrollment. A variety of housing options are available, depending on the campus attended. Students who choose to live in residence housing pay an additional $5400 to $7500 per academic year for a double- or single-room preference and an additional $3600 per academic year for fifteen meals weekly. Students are securely housed in Garret Hall and Knuppel Hall, which are three-story, brick, coed residence halls. Rooms are designed to house 1 or 2 students and are comfortably furnished. The buildings also include lounges, kitchens, and a laundry room in addition to overnight security.

Financial Aid

Berkeley is committed to helping students find the financing options that will make their education possible. Financial assistance programs are available from federal and state sources and through Berkeley in the form of scholarships, grants, loans, and other awards. Berkeley College itself awards more than $12 million each year in scholarships and institutional aid based on academic achievement or financial need. Financial aid aministrators are available to meet one on one with students and their families to develop a plan best suited to individual goals and circumstances.

Faculty

Because Berkeley believes that teaching should encompass both a conceptual and practical perspective, faculty members are chosen for both their professional experience and their academic credentials. Their business experience brings an added intellectual reality to the classroom, resulting in a challenging and stimulating learning environment. Several of Berkeley's faculty members are nationally recognized authors, lecturers, consultants, and leaders in business education.

Student Body Profile

Berkeley's total enrollment of nearly 5,000 students at six locations in New Jersey and New York includes day and evening and full- and part-time students who represent eighty countries.

Student Activities

All students are members of the Student Government Association (SGA). Elected SGA officers meet regularly and act as liaisons between students and the administration concerning social and academic matters. Berkeley offers a number of organizations, clubs, and activities designed to meet the educational, cultural, and social needs and interests of students. Activities include, but are not limited to, picnics, intramural sports, ski weekends, theater events, and charity drives.

Facilities and Resources

Libraries and Computer Labs Berkeley College maintains comprehensive libraries on each campus. Each library houses a collection of print and nonprint resources, periodicals, study areas, computers, and audiovisual equipment. The libraries provide a variety of services, including orientations, reference assistance, and course-related, course-integrated, and point-of-use instruction. A systemwide catalog, encompassing the holdings of all Berkeley libraries, consists of approximately 93,400 items. Library Web pages provide 24-hours-a-day, seven-days-a-week access to the online catalogs, electronic databases, reference tools, Internet search engines, library service and staff members, and links to the institution-wide portals. Each academic facility is staffed with librarians committed to teaching independent research and literacy skills. Throughout Berkeley's campuses are state-of-the-art computer labs with more than 700 classroom computer stations.

Advisement/Counseling From academic, career, and individual counseling to free tutorial services, Berkeley is committed to providing a supportive, highly personalized environment.

Placement Berkeley's full-service Career Services division has 20 career professionals who specialize in each major field of study. Berkeley's Career Services counselors work with students to identify career options, develop and refine resume and interviewing skills, set up and place students in internship positions, and schedule interviews in the areas surrounding the six New Jersey/New York locations. Lifetime career assistance is available to all Berkeley graduates. Consistently, year after year, more than 90 percent of all graduates available for placement are employed in positions related to their studies at Berkeley College.

Location

The Garret Mountain campus offers all the amenities of college life and is located on 25 acres of wooded countryside and situated atop Garret Mountain in the suburban West Paterson–Little Falls region. Students enjoy the complete college experience with diverse student activities, residence halls, student center, full-service cafeteria, and the friendliness and warmth of the Berkeley community. The Middlesex campus, located in Woodbridge, and the Bergen campus, located in Paramus, are ideal for students who prefer a smaller setting and the intimacy and the extrapersonalized attention that comes with it. Berkeley's Middlesex campus in central New Jersey is located in downtown Woodbridge. It is within easy reach of Woodbridge Center, which is the focus for fashion, the arts, shopping, recreation, and government in the region. The Bergen campus, located in Paramus, is in the heart of Bergen County's business district. The corporate atmosphere of the campus reflects the area. Internship and employment opportunities can be found nearby.

Admission Requirements

The basic requirements for admission to Berkeley College include graduation from an accredited high school or the equivalent and an entrance exam or SAT/ACT scores. A personal interview is strongly recommended. The following credentials must be submitted as part of the application process: a completed application form, a nonrefundable $40 application fee, and an unofficial transcript for currently enrolled high school students or an official high school transcript or its equivalent (GED) for high school graduates.

Students who graduated from an accredited high school or who have earned a GED and then attended another college or university are considered transfer students. A transfer student must submit an application for admission and the nonrefundable $40 application fee, a final transcript from each college or university attended, and a final high school transcript or GED certificate.

Berkeley accepts transfer credits from regionally accredited postsecondary institutions for courses in which the student earned a minimum grade of C and that are applicable to a student's program at Berkeley. Academic advisers can also explore with transfer students the possibility of receiving credit for acceptable scores on national standardized exams and professional certification exams. Knowledge gained outside the classroom, either through work or life experience, can often translate into college credit at Berkeley. A prior-learning academic adviser counsels students, reviews the possibilities for credit recognition, and determines the best method for assessment.

Application and Information

Applications are accepted on an ongoing basis. Prospective students should contact the Director of Admissions at the campus that is most convenient to them or visit the College's Web site.

Garret Mountain Campus
Berkeley College
44 Rifle Camp Road
West Paterson, New Jersey

Middlesex Campus
Berkeley College
430 Rahway Avenue
Woodbridge, New Jersey

Bergen Campus
Berkeley College
64 East Midland Avenue
Paramus, New Jersey

To reach all campuses:
Telephone: 800-446-5400 Ext. G28 (toll-free)
E-mail: info@berkeleycollege.edu
World Wide Web: http://www.berkeleycollege.edu

Berkeley College's career-oriented curriculum includes training in the latest computer technologies.

BERKELEY COLLEGE

NEW YORK CITY AND WHITE PLAINS, NEW YORK

Berkeley College

The College and Its Mission

Since its inception in 1931, Berkeley College has been committed to providing an exceptional, student-centered undergraduate business education. Today, Berkeley College is recognized across the nation as a premier school that prepares students for successful careers in business in the modern world. Berkeley College's strong academic program succeeds through a blend of traditional education, professional training, and real-world experience.

At Berkeley, students benefit from small class sizes, personal academic and career counseling, and the chance to develop their analytical and creative skills. Berkeley believes that teaching should provide a practical perspective to traditional material, and Berkeley's distinguished faculty members bring academic preparation and professional experience to the classroom. Faculty members are chosen not just for their academic achievements but also for their applicable background in the business world.

The Middle States Commission on Higher Education of the Middle States Association of Colleges and Schools accredits Berkeley College, and the New York State Board of Regents authorizes the New York City and Westchester campuses to confer the degrees of Associate in Science (A.S.), Associate in Applied Science (A.A.S.), and Bachelor of Business Administration (B.B.A.). Their programs are registered by the New York State Education Department. The paralegal studies program at all campuses is approved by the American Bar Association (ABA).

Berkeley programs provide the comprehensive foundation necessary to begin a successful business career or to advance in a current career. At Berkeley, the traditional undergraduate curriculum is enhanced with professional training and experience. Berkeley's internship requirement provides valuable work experience and often leads to a full-time position. Students work in their fields of study, earn academic credits toward their degrees, establish a network of business connections for the future, and offset college costs.

Academic Programs

Berkeley offers a wide range of career-focused associate and bachelor's degrees that prepare students for immediate marketability and professional growth. The academic curriculum combines leading-edge theory, real-world practicality, and extensive training in the latest computer technologies. Berkeley's commitment to excellence constitutes the primary objective of the College. Small classes, individualized advisement and counseling, and the development of the students' creative and analytical skills support this commitment.

Berkeley College provides exceptional flexibility and convenience, as students have the option of combining day, evening, weekend, and online classes. With Berkeley College's online program, Berkeley brings the classroom to students online with the same high standards of its on-site classes. The carefully developed program provides everything students need to pursue a wide range of associate or bachelor's degrees backed by Berkeley's commitment to excellence in education and value. The Bachelor of Business Administration degree in general business is offered entirely online. The Associate in Applied Science degree is offered entirely online in international business, business administration marketing, and business administration management.

The College operates year-round on the quarter system, with classes starting in September, January, April, and July. The flexible quarter system provides students enrolled in the day division with the opportunity to complete their associate degree in only eighteen months or in the traditional two years or earn their bachelor's degree in as little as three years or in the traditional four years. Associate degree credits are easily transferred to bachelor's degree programs.

Majors and Degrees Associate degree programs are offered in business administration, with specializations in accounting, information systems management, management, and marketing. Additional associate degree programs include fashion marketing and management, health information management, international business, and paralegal studies. Bachelor of Business Administration degree programs are offered in accounting, fashion marketing and management, general business, information systems management, international business, management, and marketing. Not all programs are offered at all locations.

Certificate Programs Berkeley College offers certificate programs in computer applications and software management. These programs, which can be completed in a year or less, provide students with the opportunity to get a head start in a gratifying career. Credits earned in certificate programs are transferable to Berkeley's degree programs, and students enrolled in certificate programs receive all the benefits of a Berkeley education, including lifetime placement assistance and software refresher courses.

Credit for Nontraditional Learning Experiences

Knowledge gained outside the classroom, through either work or life experience, can often translate into college credit at Berkeley. Academic advisers counsel students, review the possibilities for credit recognition, and determine the best method for assessment.

Costs

In 2005–06, full-time students pay $16,900 in tuition and fees for the academic year. Berkeley offers protection from any tuition increase to students who maintain continuous full-time enrollment. A variety of housing options are available, depending on the campus attended. A variety of residence facilities are available in Manhattan and nearby boroughs. Rates vary according to location and accommodations. Westchester students are housed in Cottage Place Apartments, a new six-story residence adjacent to the White Plains campus. Cottage Place comprises studio apartments with kitchenettes and two- or three-bedroom apartments with full kitchens and living rooms. All studios and bedrooms are designed for double occupancy, and the three-bedroom apartments have two bathrooms. Bright, cheerful, and attractively furnished, each apartment is air conditioned and wired for voice, data, and cable TV. Amenities include overnight security, laundry facilities, and electronic key-card access. Cottage Place is within easy walking distance of commuter train and bus lines. Housing costs are $6600 per academic year. Living expenses can vary considerably.

Financial Aid

Berkeley is committed to helping students find the financing options that make their education possible. Financial assistance programs are available from federal and state sources and through Berkeley in the forms of scholarships, grants, loans, and other awards. Berkeley College itself awards more than $12 million annually for student aid, based on academic achievement or financial need. Financial aid administrators are available to meet one-on-one with students and their families to develop a plan that is best suited to individual goals and circumstances.

Faculty

Because Berkeley believes that teaching should encompass a conceptual and practical perspective, faculty members are chosen for both their professional experience and their academic credentials. Their business experience brings an added intellectual reality to the classroom, creating a challenging and stimulating learning environment. Several of Berkeley's faculty members are nationally recognized authors, lecturers, consultants, and leaders in business education.

Student Body Profile

Berkeley's total enrollment of nearly 5,000 students at six locations in New York and New Jersey includes day and evening and full- and part-time students, who represent eighty countries.

Student Activities

Berkeley offers a number of organizations, clubs, and activities designed to meet the educational, cultural, and social needs and interests of students. Activities include, but are not limited to, picnics, intramural sports, ski weekends, theater events, and charity drives. All students are members of the Student Government Association (SGA). Elected SGA officers meet regularly and act as liaisons between students and the administration concerning social and academic matters.

Facilities and Resources

Berkeley College maintains comprehensive libraries on each campus. Each library houses a collection of print and nonprint resources, periodicals, study areas, computers, and audiovisual equipment. The libraries provide a variety of services, including orientations, reference assistance, and course-related, course-integrated, and point-of-use instruction. A systemwide catalog encompassing the holdings of all Berkeley libraries consists of approximately 93,400 items. Library Web pages provide access 24 hours a day, seven days a week to online catalogs, electronic databases, reference tools, Internet search engines, library service and staff members, and links to institution-wide portals. Each academic facility is staffed with librarians committed to teaching independent research and literacy skills.

The Academic Support Centers provide students with a wide range of support services to help improve their study skills as well as their reading, writing, and mathematical abilities. Academic, career, individual advisement, and free tutorial services are also available. Throughout Berkeley's campuses are state-of-the-art computer labs with more than 700 classroom computer stations.

Berkeley's full-service Career Services division has 20 career professionals who specialize in each major field of study. Berkeley's Career Services counselors work with students to identify career options, develop and refine resume and interviewing skills, set up and place students in internship positions, and schedule interviews in the areas surrounding the six New York/New Jersey locations. Lifetime career assistance is available to all Berkeley graduates. Consistently, year after year, more than 90 percent of all graduates available for placement are employed in positions related to their studies at Berkeley College.

Location

Berkeley College provides students with the choices and opportunities of both urban and suburban locations. The New York City campus, found in the heart of Manhattan's east side next to Grand Central Station, is for students who want to take advantage of the total metropolitan experience. The Lower Manhattan Extension Center is approximately 4 miles from Berkeley's midtown campus. Easily accessible by public transportation from the five boroughs, the center is within walking distance of New York's dynamic financial district, allowing students to take advantage of invaluable internship opportunities. Berkeley's Westchester campus, which was recently relocated to the heart of the business district in downtown White Plains, is easily accessible and centrally located near commuter train and bus lines.

Admission Requirements

The basic requirements for admission to Berkeley College include graduation from an accredited high school or the equivalent and entrance exam or SAT/ACT scores. A personal interview is strongly recommended. The following must be submitted as part of the application process: a completed application form, a nonrefundable $40 application fee, and an unofficial transcript for currently enrolled high school students or an official high school transcript or its equivalent for high school graduates.

Students who graduated from an accredited high school or the equivalent and then attended another college or university are considered transfer students. A transfer student must submit an application for admission and the nonrefundable $40 application fee, a final transcript from each college or university attended, and a final high school transcript or GED certificate.

Berkeley accepts transfer credits from regionally accredited postsecondary institutions for courses in which the student earned a minimum grade of C and that are applicable to a student's program at Berkeley. Academic advisers can also explore with transfer students the possibility of receiving credit for acceptable scores on national standardized exams and professional certification exams.

Application and Information

Applications are accepted on an ongoing basis. Prospective students should contact the Director of Admissions at the Berkeley College campus that is most convenient to them.

Midtown Campus
Berkeley College
3 East 43rd Street
New York, New York 10017

Lower Manhattan Extension Center
Berkeley College
130 William Street
New York, New York 10038

Westchester Campus
Berkeley College
99 Church Street
White Plains, New York 10601

To reach all campuses:
Telephone: 800-446-5400 Ext. G28 (toll-free)
E-mail: info@berkeleycollege.edu
World Wide Web: http://www.berkeleycollege.edu

Berkeley College's career-oriented curriculum includes training in the latest computer technologies.

BRADLEY ACADEMY FOR THE VISUAL ARTS

YORK, PENNSYLVANIA

The Academy and Its Mission

Bradley Academy for the Visual Arts provides students with an educational environment and dedicated faculty members who are committed to preparing students for entry-level positions in the creative arts. Professional academic courses encourage the achievement of self-knowledge and the development of critical thinking. Under the guidance of industry professionals, students learn by doing the types of tasks they are likely to encounter in the workplace. In addition, assistance is available to help students with resume writing, networking, and keeping abreast of what employers are looking for in job candidates.

Whenever possible and appropriate, courses are taught in a studio or lab setting. While at the school, students can access the wireless network to check mail, hand in assignments, and work on a project—anywhere on campus.

Bradley Academy for the Visual Arts is accredited by the Accrediting Commission of Career Schools and Colleges of Technology (ACCSCT), which is listed by the U.S. Department of Education as a nationally recognized accrediting agency. Bradley Academy for the Visual Arts is also licensed by the State Board of Private Licensed Schools (Pennsylvania Department of Education).

Academic Programs

Bradley Academy for the Visual Arts operates on a year-round, four-quarter system. Associate degrees are offered in animation, digital arts, fashion marketing, graphic design, interior design, and Web design.

Costs

Tuition for the 2004–05 academic year was $390 per credit or $4680 per term. In addition to the $50 application fee and $150 tuition deposit, students are responsible for the costs of textbooks and supplies. An initial supply kit ranges in cost from $500 to $900, depending upon the program of study. A $20 graduation processing fee is charged to all students to cover the costs of maintaining academic records, ID cards, parking stickers, printing, and graduation.

Financial Aid

Financial aid is available to those who qualify. Eligible students may apply for federal and state financial aid, including student loans, grants, and scholarships. Work-study programs are also available for qualifying students. Bradley Academy for the Visual Arts participates in the Imagine America Scholarship Program, which is sponsored by the Career Training Foundation. These scholarships are matched by the school and are awarded to qualifying high school seniors through the guidance offices at their high schools. Bradley Academy for the Visual Arts has committed to matching most Dollars for Scholars awards up to a maximum of $1000 per student, provided the student has demonstrated financial need. Application deadlines and eligibility requirements vary.

Faculty

Faculty members at Bradley Academy for the Visual Arts are professional artists and designers who work in their fields of expertise. The school's 40 faculty members have a broad range of experience with technology, fashion, art, and design trends, which allows them to provide their students with a unique, relevant educational experience.

Student Body Profile

There are currently 477 students enrolled in the school. The average age of students is 22, and many students come from the York, Harrisburg, and Philadelphia, Pennsylvania, areas. An additional 50 to 75 students are enrolled in short-term enrichment and self-improvement courses, which usually meet in the evenings or on Saturdays.

The student population includes recent high school graduates, transfer students, and those who have left a previous employment situation to study and train for a new career. Students are creative, competitive, and open to new ideas. They place great value on an education that prepares them for an exciting entry-level position in the arts.

Student Activities

In addition to a traditional student government association, many professional organizations exist on campus, including the American Society of Interior Designers (ASID), the National Kitchen and Bath Association (NKBA), the Baltimore chapter of the American Institute of Graphic Arts (AIGA), and DECA/Delta Epsilon Chi. Students maintaining a GPA of 3.5 or higher at the end of the fifth term are considered for induction into Alpha Beta Kappa, a national honor society.

Academic Facilities

Bradley Academy for the Visual Arts is housed within a 38,000-square-foot building in suburban York, Pennsylvania. The new facility contains twenty classrooms and studios, a student computer commons, a gallery, an art store, and a library.

Two computer labs contain more than forty Macintosh G4 computers, and two additional PC labs run Windows 2000. All labs are equipped with color scanners and have access to more than 200 gigabytes of network storage. Each lab is supported by desktop and high-resolution printers. The school also has a graphics lab, display windows, and vignette space to allow students to apply skills learned in the classroom.

In association with the York Martin Memorial Library, Bradley Academy houses a 1,000-square-foot library on the first floor of the school. In addition to general reference books, the library houses titles specifically related to programs offered at the school. Eight Windows NT workstations with direct access to the Internet and to Martin Library's catalog are available for students. Open every weekday, the library features full-time staffing, interlibrary loan, CD-ROM–based reference materials, and PC business software for use by students and the public.

Location

Bradley Academy for the Visual Arts is located in York, a suburban area in south central Pennsylvania. Surrounded by sprawling hills and Amish farmlands, York offers visitors an abundance of shopping areas and museums and three centuries of American history, including the battle sites of the Revolutionary and Civil Wars. York is a 30-minute drive from Hershey and Harrisburg, Pennsylvania; approximately a 90-minute drive from Philadelphia; and a 1-hour drive from Baltimore, Maryland.

Admission Requirements

Bradley Academy for the Visual Arts encourages interested students to apply early. To apply, students must possess a high school diploma or GED and a minimum SAT score of 800 (at least 400 math, 400 verbal) or a minimum ACT score of 16. A portfolio review is required for students majoring in graphic design and animation and is welcomed from students pursuing a degree in digital arts, interior design, or Web design.

Upon acceptance, students must sign and return the Enrollment Agreement along with a tuition deposit of $150 within fifteen days to confirm enrollment.

Application and Information

To obtain an application or make arrangements for an interview or tour of the school, prospective students should contact:

Bradley Academy for the Visual Arts
1409 Williams Road
York, Pennsylvania 17402-9012
Telephone: 717-755-2300
          800-864-7725 (toll-free)
Fax: 717-840-1951
World Wide Web: http://www.bradleyacademy.edu

BRIARWOOD COLLEGE
SOUTHINGTON, CONNECTICUT

The College and Its Mission

Briarwood College is a coed, two-year private college whose mission is to develop students' critical-thinking, self-discipline, and communication skills within the context of career and technical programs. An emphasis on small classes, comprehensive academic support services, and programs closely connected to opportunities in the employment market account for more than 85 percent of Briarwood's graduates being placed in jobs in their field within six months of graduation.

The College offers full- and part-time opportunities, evening classes, an accelerated option on Saturdays that is designed for working adults, and a variety of continuing education offerings through the Division of Lifelong Learning. In addition, alumni of the College receive a unique benefit, *Education for Life®*, which allows them to return for further course work tuition-free for the rest of their lives.

Academic Programs

Briarwood College offers a variety of career-oriented programs, both full- and part-time, leading to a certificate, diploma, or associate degree. In general, an associate degree program requires two years of study and a certificate program, one year. Diploma programs may take up to one year.

Associate Degree Programs Briarwood College offers associate degrees in twenty-seven majors. The **Associate in Arts** (A.A.) degree is offered in general studies, with concentrations in ballet, biotechnology, computer information systems, English, environmental technology, fine arts, history, mathematics, psychology, and science. The **Associate in Applied Science** (A.A.S.) degree is offered in accounting, administrative technology (with concentrations in executive, legal, and management), child development, communication, computer information systems, criminal justice, dental administrative assistant studies, dietetic technician studies, executive medical assistant studies, fashion merchandising, fitness technician studies, health information technology, hospitality (with concentrations in hotel and restaurant management and travel and tourism management), marketing, medical office management, mortuary science, occupational therapy assistant studies, and paralegal studies.

Certificate Programs The following programs lead to a certificate after one year: administrative legal professional studies, administrative medical professional studies, child development assistant studies, dental chairside assistant studies, health information coding, health information processing, medical assistant studies, medical transcription, pharmacy technician studies, and word processing. Most of these programs may be applied toward an associate degree program. The College also offers noncredit certificate programs in acupuncture and court reporting.

Diploma Programs Briarwood also offers diploma courses in computer information systems, leading to certification in Microsoft certified systems engineer, Microsoft certified system administrator, certified Novell administrator, and Computer Technology Industry Association: A+ certification for hardware repair.

Saturday College Saturday College is an accelerated degree program for mature adults who want to complete their studies while continuing to work full-time. Students complete two courses every eight weeks, enabling them to complete an associate degree in twenty months.

Education for Life® is a unique benefit offered to graduates of Briarwood College who complete associate degrees after at least three full-time semesters of study. Graduates are able to return to Briarwood for additional credit or noncredit courses tuition-free for the rest of their lives.

Costs

For the 2005–06 academic year, costs are as follows: tuition is $15,200 for resident and commuter students; part-time students pay $485 per credit. Resident students are also charged a $3320 residency fee. The nonrefundable registration fee for resident and commuter students is $95; part-time students pay $95 per semester.

Financial Aid

The following types of financial aid are available individually or in combination with other resources: presidential scholarships, state scholarships, and the Capitol Scholarship Program. Briarwood College, in conjunction with outside professional associations, also awards several scholarships in the business, health, and office administration fields. As other scholarships become available in specific program fields, they are announced in Briarwood College publications and posted outside the Financial Aid Office. A number of scholarships are awarded annually to students by local civic groups, churches, and fraternal and union organizations. Students are encouraged to explore all outside possibilities, utilizing the assistance of high school guidance officers or the Briarwood College Financial Aid Office. Recipients are selected on the basis of their academic achievement, extracurricular activities, recommendation letters, and personal essays. Eligible students are encouraged to seek, and are assisted in obtaining, educational benefits from the Veterans Administration, G.I. Bill, and state agencies. There are also grants and loans available, including Connecticut Independent College Student Grants (CICS), Federal Pell Grants, Federal Stafford Student Loans, Federal PLUS loans, Federal Supplemental Educational Opportunity Grants, and Federal Perkins Loans. For more information, students should contact the Financial Aid Office at 860-628-4751 or 800-952-2444 (toll-free).

Faculty

The teaching experience among the faculty members at Briarwood College is distinct in its variety of professional, business, and years of teaching experience. There are several faculty members who remain active in their line of work. For example, the Allied Health Division has on its staff several faculty members who are currently active in their vocation who bring expertise to their students. The faculty members in this category include the Program Director of the Pharmacy Technician Program, who is a practicing pharmacist; the Program Director of Travel and Tourism, who has more than twenty years of experience in the travel industry and is still active in the field; and adjunct faculty members in the Mortuary Science Program, who are presently working in the funeral service business.

Student Body Profile

There were 637 full- and part-time students enrolled in fall 2004. Students come from eight states and two other countries. Approximately 33 percent (218 students) live on campus.

Student Activities

The Dean of Student Life and her staff coordinate a variety of recreational opportunities, including clubs, fitness activities, student organizations, volunteer opportunities, and special events. Popular events include an annual fashion show, international night, a formal dinner/dance, award ceremonies, trips, picnics, and noon-hour programs on a variety of topics.

Briarwood students participate in a number of community volunteer activities, including America Reads, food and toy drives, a soup kitchen, and a blood drive.

The College Culture Committee coordinates cultural and educational events with various academic departments. Recent events have included presentations by visiting authors, films, and panel discussions.

Sports Briarwood College is a member of the National Junior College Athletic Association and competes with other colleges in Region 21. The College currently offers men's basketball and women's soccer at the varsity level. Students may also become involved in a wide variety of outdoor/indoor recreational activities, such as softball, volleyball, and golf. Skiing is available locally at Mount Southington, only 1 mile from the College. Annual trips to area ski resorts are also planned.

Briarwood has an affiliation with a local gym that enables students to use the facilities for a nominal fee. The gym is a 24,000-square-foot facility with large cardiovascular and free-weight areas, as well as areas for yoga, group cycling, pilates, and group exercise. Briarwood also has an affiliation with the Southington YMCA that allows students to use this facility during the academic year for a greatly reduced rate. This facility includes a gym and a pool as well as a complete line of cardiovascular and strength-training equipment.

Facilities and Resources

There are two residential facilities on campus: Eder Hall, with its town house–style apartments, and Palmisano Hall. All units have furnished bedrooms, kitchens, and living rooms as well as laundry facilities. The residence halls also have Internet and cable access. A student center provides recreation space, pool tables, lounge chairs, and a large-screen television. A softball/soccer field is located adjacent to the residence halls.

Career Services The Career Service Office at Briarwood College provides a comprehensive career development program designed to assist students in making appropriate career choices and in developing plans to achieve their goals. Both individual and group sessions are offered to assist students with resume writing, interviewing, and job search skills.

Counseling Services Students who experience academic, personal, learning, or study problems are urged to seek help as soon as the problem is recognized. Counselors provide academic intervention activities designed to assist students who are experiencing academic difficulties. These activities include Early Alert notices, midterm intervention sessions, and individual assistance. A counselor is available to assist students who are having academic difficulties by working with them individually or by referring them to the services of the College Learning Center.

College counselors are available to aid students in resolving many types of problems, including social, emotional, vocational, and personal concerns. All information is handled in a confidential setting. Services of the Counseling Center include short-term personal counseling, crisis intervention, career development, and administering and interpreting self-assessment inventories.

In some cases, a counselor determines that the needs of a student would be best met through a community agency off campus. Referrals are made when the student is in crisis; has a long-term, ongoing problem; or can otherwise benefit from the resources of an outside agency. Counselors assist students in obtaining such services when appropriate.

Disability Services The Disability Services Office is responsible for all disability-related concerns of Briarwood College students. Briarwood College encourages qualified students with disabilities to take advantage of its educational programs. The College is responsible for ensuring that courses, programs, services, activities, and facilities are available and usable in the most integrated and appropriate settings. Students with disabilities seeking accommodations must identify themselves as individuals with disabilities, request needed accommodations, and provide documentation from the appropriate professional as to how the disabilities limit their participation in courses, programs, activities, and use of facilities. Upon receipt of documentation of a disability, it is the responsibility of the Disability Services Office to explore and facilitate reasonable accommodations, academic adjustments, and/or auxiliary aids and services for individuals with disabilities in courses, programs, services, activities, and facilities. Students

anticipating the need for accommodations, both before and after enrollment, are encouraged to contact the Dean of Student Services, whose office is located in the lower level of Eder Hall Center.

Health and Wellness Services The Health Office provides basic first aid and health education information to Briarwood College students. In some cases, a nurse determines that the needs of a student would be best met through an off-campus community facility. All students are required by federal law to provide their medical history and documentation of illnesses and immunizations prior to matriculation at Briarwood College. This information is used by the nurse in providing routine and emergency care.

Library and Audiovisual Services The Dr. Anthony A. Pupillo Library, staffed by a professional librarian and knowledgeable library assistants, plays an integral part in the education process of the students. The library is committed to providing support for the various courses and programs of study offered by Briarwood College. Although the library's resources are richest in the curricula taught at the College, a wide variety of works for individual interest and personal growth are also offered. The library offers a wide variety of electronic resources to facilitate student research. Novice users quickly learn to utilize the capabilities of the library's computer technology. The library offers research-only computers for student use and one-on-one sessions with students to familiarize them with its resources. Interlibrary loan is available to the students.

Location

Briarwood College is located in Southington, Connecticut, only 2 hours from Boston and New York. Students find skiing and Connecticut beaches readily accessible, and the school is minutes from the Hartford and New Haven metropolitan areas. The picturesque 35-acre campus is nestled at the base of Mount Southington, next to an 18-hole golf course and close to Lake Compounce Amusement Park, the Mount Southington ski area, and ESPN. Hartford, Connecticut's capital city, is just 15 minutes from the campus and offers numerous restaurants, indoor and outdoor concert venues, theaters, museums, parks, and shopping centers. The greater Hartford area is also home to seven colleges and universities.

Admission Requirements

The College requires applicants for full-time study to submit a completed application form, a $25 application fee, official high school transcripts or GED scores, a personal statement, and one letter of recommendation. SAT scores are not required but are recommended for students interested in scholarship opportunities. International students for whom English is not the first language are required to show proof of English competency. Part-time and transfer applicants are ordinarily not required to submit a personal statement and recommendation letter. Transfer applicants are also required to submit transcripts from all colleges or universities previously attended. Interviews with the program directors are also required for applicants to the dental assisting and occupational therapy assisting programs. Applications are reviewed on a rolling basis and acceptances are mailed, usually within one week of receipt of all required documents. Applicants for fall semester are encouraged to apply by March 30 for priority scholarship consideration.

Application and Information

For more information, students should contact:

Admissions Department
Briarwood College
2279 Mt. Vernon Road
Southington, Connecticut 06489
Telephone: 860-628-4751
            800-952-2444 (toll-free)
E-mail: admis@briarwood.edu
World Wide Web: http://www.briarwood.edu

BUNKER HILL COMMUNITY COLLEGE

BOSTON, MASSACHUSETTS

The College and Its Mission

A public institution of higher education, Bunker Hill Community College (BHCC) offers wide-ranging workforce education curricula interwoven throughout comprehensive programs and courses of study, including nursing and allied health, an extensive information technology program, criminal justice, hospitality and culinary arts, business, and early childhood development. Accredited by the Commission on Institutions of Higher Education of the New England Association of Schools and Colleges, BHCC supports open access to postsecondary education by providing a strong liberal arts foundation and a range of educational opportunities that include distance learning, self-directed learning, an honors program, and, for nonnative English-speaking students, a variety of levels of English as a second language (ESL) instruction. BHCC graduates have gone on to continue their education at many four-year institutions, including the University of Massachusetts, Brandeis University, Northeastern University, Tufts University, Smith College, Suffolk University, and Wellesley College. BHCC seeks to enhance its position as a primary educational and economic asset for the commonwealth through cooperative planning and program implementation involving neighboring institutions of higher education, the public schools, community organizations, and area businesses and industries.

Academic Programs

BHCC offers numerous programs of study. They include Associate in Arts (A.A.) degrees, Associate in Science (A.S.) degrees, and certificate programs. Associate in Arts concentrations are designed to permit the student to transfer smoothly to four-year colleges and universities. Although extreme care has been taken in fashioning these transfer-focused degrees, students are advised to consult the institution to which they wish to transfer to ensure the wisest choice of courses at BHCC. These students should also work with the BHCC transfer counselor and academic advisers in planning both the curriculum at BHCC and the transfer process.

Associate in Science programs are designed to develop the knowledge and skills required for employment at the conclusion of the associate degree. In addition to employment preparation, many Associate in Science programs have transfer options. To ensure smooth transfer to four-year programs, students are advised to consult the institution to which they wish to transfer.

A wide variety of certificate programs provide skills training and job-upgrade opportunities for students who successfully complete these programs.

The honors program offers students the opportunity to study and learn in an academically challenging and enriching learning environment.

Associate Degree Programs Associate in Arts degrees are available in biological science, business, chemical science, communication, computer information systems, computer science, education, English, fine arts, foreign language, general concentration, history and government, mathematics, music, physics/engineering, psychology, sociology, and theater. Students enrolling in any A.A. degree program can earn world-studies emphasis certification simultaneously.

Associate in Science degrees are offered in business administration (accounting, finance, international business, management), computer information technology (computer

support specialist studies, database programming and administration, network technology and administration), criminal justice, culinary arts, early childhood development, fire protection and safety, graphic arts and visual communication, hotel/restaurant/travel (hotel/restaurant management, travel and tourism management), human services, media technology, medical imaging (cardiac sonography, general sonography, medical radiography, medical radiography–part-time evening), nursing (day, evening, or weekend), office and information management (administrative information management, medical information management), and pharmacy technology.

Certificate Programs Certificates are available in allied health (medical assistant studies, medical lab assistant studies, patient-care assistant studies, phlebotomy technician studies), business administration (accounting, e-commerce marketing management, international business, paralegal studies), computer information technology (computer support specialist studies, database programming and administration, network technology and administration, object-oriented computer programming and design), culinary arts, early childhood development, human services, office and information management (information management specialist studies, medical coding, medical information management assistant studies), surgical technology (central processing (sterile processing and distribution management), surgical technology), and travel and tourism management.

Off-Campus Programs

Bunker Hill Community College offers home study and online distance learning courses as a convenient alternative to the traditional classroom. These courses are designed for self-directed, motivated learners. The courses are equivalent in content and academic rigor to traditional classroom courses but offer students the flexibility and convenience of learning virtually anytime and anywhere. The College also offers hybrid courses. These courses incorporate both traditional classroom and online components. Hybrid courses generally meet on-site for 50 percent of the instructional time, with the remaining instruction conducted online.

BHCC offers a range of educational opportunities at its five satellite campuses, each intended to serve the distinct needs and interests of the host communities—Cambridge, Chinatown, Revere, Somerville, and Boston's South End. The curricula available at the satellites allow students to prepare for workforce advancement while earning credits toward an associate degree or certificate in several of the wide variety of fields offered by the College. Programs include foundation courses that fulfill general education requirements as well as courses in response to community interest, such as offerings in computer technology, business management, and hospitality.

Bunker Hill Community College has a comprehensive study-abroad program that allows students to experience different cultures. Each year, approximately twenty scholarships are awarded to further assist BHCC students in realizing their dream of studying abroad. Faculty, staff, and interested community members are also invited to take part in the programs, although scholarships are available only to qualified BHCC students.

Credit for Nontraditional Learning Experiences

The Prior Learning Assessment Program provides an opportunity to students to condense their time of study by granting credits for college-level knowledge and skills. This program assists students in examining their outside learning experiences and identifying those that might be considered for college credits. Common sources for this kind of learning are jobs, volunteer work, skills training, workshops or study groups, and community involvement.

Students can earn college credits in four ways: portfolio evaluation, the College-Level Examination Program (CLEP), military evaluation, and departmental challenge exams.

Costs

Tuition for Massachusetts residents is $100 per credit; for non-Massachusetts residents, it is $306 per credit. The New England Regional Student Program costs $112 per credit. The health course fee is $35 per credit (for health program courses only).

Financial Aid

The Financial Aid Office at Bunker Hill Community College assists students and their families in meeting the costs of a college education. Bunker Hill Community College participates in a wide variety of federal, state, and private financial aid programs. Students should be aware that all institutions, including Bunker Hill Community College, are subject to adjustments in funding allocations from both the commonwealth of Massachusetts and the United States Department of Education.

In order to be eligible for financial aid, an applicant must be a United States citizen or an eligible noncitizen enrolled or accepted for enrollment in an eligible program. In addition, the applicant must maintain satisfactory academic progress, comply with Federal Selective Service Law, and not be in default on any educational loans or owe a refund on any federal grants or loans to any institution. Students who have obtained a previous bachelor's degree at any U.S. or international institution are not eligible for financial aid.

Financial aid awards are subject to change if any of the factors used to calculate eligibility from the Free Application for Federal Student Aid (FAFSA) change after the date of original application. Other examples of factors that impact eligibility include increases in income and changes in family size and/or in the number of family members enrolled in college. Students are strongly advised to consult with the Financial Aid Office if they are contemplating a change in enrollment status.

Faculty

There are 117 full-time faculty members and 350 adjunct faculty members at BHCC. The average class size is 19.

Student Body Profile

The student body reflects the diversity of the urban community, and an essential part of the College's mission is to encourage this diversity. The average student age is 28. Nearly 60 percent of the students are women, more than half are people of color, and most are employed while attending school.

Student Activities

Bunker Hill Community College has an active student life program. The activities coordinated through the Student Activities and Athletics Office provide students with the opportunity to have fun, meet people, and make a difference in campus life at the College. BHCC celebrates cultural diversity and encourages cultural interaction.

There are twenty-five student organizations and athletic teams at Bunker Hill Community College, which provide the campus with social, cultural, and educational programs as well as competitive sports, intramural/recreational programs, and leisure-time activities. New members are always welcome.

Athletic programs provide opportunities for students to participate in competitive or recreational activities on the intercollegiate and intramural levels. The Intercollegiate Athletic Program consists of men's baseball, basketball, and soccer; women's basketball, soccer, and softball; and co-ed golf. The Intramural Athletic Program includes basketball, flag football, table tennis, and tennis.

Student clubs and organizations include ACT (Activism, Commitment, and Teamwork); African-American Cultural Society; Alpha Kappa Mu Honor Society; Arab Students Association; Asian Students Association; Brazilian Cultural Club; Business Club; Campus Activities Board; Cape Verdean Club; Criminal Justice Society; Debating Society; Drama Club; Evening Student Association; Gay, Lesbian, and Bisexual Student Union; Gospel Choir; Haitian Club; Hillel Club; Hospitality Club; Islamic Students Association; Latinos Unidos Club; Multicultural Club; Nurse Mentor Club; Real Life Club; Student Government Association; Upsidedown Club; and WBCC radio station.

Facilities and Resources

Facilities available at BHCC include the library and information center, advising and counseling center, tutoring and academic support center, career center, international center, and technology support services center.

Location

All Bunker Hill Community College sites are located in urban communities within 5 miles of downtown Boston. The main campus is located in the historic Charlestown neighborhood of Boston. An annex campus is located in Bellingham Square in Chelsea. The satellites are in Cambridge, Chinatown, Revere, Somerville, and the South End. All locations are easily accessible via public transportation. A subway stop is located steps from the Charlestown Campus.

Admission Requirements

Bunker Hill Community College is committed to an open admission policy. This policy offers the opportunity to enroll to those who have earned a high school diploma, a GED certificate, or an associate degree or higher and who express a desire to pursue a college education. All students admitted to degree or certificate programs are required to take computerized placement tests (CPTs) in English, reading, and mathematics. Students whose first language is not English, and who have not earned a high school diploma or GED in the United States, must take the English Placement Test (EPT). International students must take the Levels of English Proficiency (LOEP) assessment if they have not scored at least 500 on the TOEFL paper test or 173 on the computerized version. The purpose of these tests is to determine the levels at which students will begin their study. Based upon test results, the College may prescribe developmental courses or limit a student's enrollment, in an effort to enhance that student's ability to succeed. Applicants to health careers and technical programs must comply with program entrance requirements and application deadlines.

Application and Information

Although the College has a rolling admissions process, students should contact the Admissions and Transfer Counseling Office for program-specific application deadlines.

Admissions and Transfer Counseling
Bunker Hill Community College
Charlestown Campus, Room B130
250 New Rutherford Avenue
Boston, Massachusetts 02129
Telephone: 617-228-2019
Fax: 617-228-3336
E-mail: admissions@bhcc.mass.edu
World Wide Web: http://www.bhcc.mass.edu

CENTRAL TEXAS COLLEGE

KILLEEN, TEXAS

The College and Its Mission

Founded in 1965, Central Texas College (CTC) is a public, open-admission community college, offering associate degrees and certificate programs in academic, professional, and vocational/technical fields. Central Texas College consists of six campuses: Central Campus in Killeen, Texas; the Continental Campus; the Europe Campus; the Fort Hood and Service Area Campus; the Navy Campus; and the Pacific Far East Campus. With more than 100 locations around the world, CTC serves more than 50,000 students on military installations, in correctional facilities, in embassies, and on ships at sea. Central Texas College is evolving and expanding to meet its role in the changing needs of the local, national, and military communities. Its mission is to provide students with high-quality education.

Academic Programs

Central Texas College confers the Associate in Arts degree, the Associate in Science degree, the Associate in Applied Science degree, and the Associate of General Studies degree upon students who have successfully completed the minimum requirements and all the specific requirements for graduation. In addition, a Certificate of Completion is awarded to students who fulfill the curricular requirements of special courses and programs.

Degree programs are offered in the major subjects of agriculture science, art, auto collision studies, automotive mechanic studies, aviation science, biology, business administration, business management, chemistry, computer science, criminal justice, diesel studies, drafting and design, drama, early childhood studies, electronics, emergency medical technician studies, engineering, environmental science, geology, graphics and printing, heating and air conditioning, hospitality management, interdisciplinary studies, journalism/communication, legal assistant studies, kinesiology, maintenance technology, mathematics, medical laboratory technician studies, mental health services, modern language, music, nursing, office technology, radio and television broadcasting, social science, and welding.

The English as a second language (ESL) program provides training for non-English speaking students. New students who have not taken the TOEFL, or those with TOEFL scores below 520 on the paper-based test, are required to take the Comprehensive English Language Test (CELT) upon arrival to determine the appropriate level of English instruction required. The ESL program is comprised of three levels of English, which include listening and speaking, reading and vocabulary, and grammar/writing. Classes operate under the traditional semester system. Fall and spring semesters are sixteen weeks, and summer semester is ten weeks. Students with a TOEFL score of 520 or higher are required to take a placement test. ESL classes are only offered on Central Campus in Killeen, Texas.

Costs

Tuition ranges from $30 per credit hour (minimum of $90) for a Texas resident to $1325 (full-time) for a non-Texas resident or international student per semester. Fees are not included in these amounts. The complete tuition and fee schedule may be found on the College Web site. Books are not included in the cost of tuition and fees.

Financial Aid

Central Texas College participates in numerous financial aid programs designed to assist students who demonstrate financial need. To be considered for financial aid, students must complete the Free Application for Federal Student Aid (FAFSA). International students (visa or nonimmigrant) are not eligible to receive federal financial aid.

The CTC Foundation offers scholarships to students currently enrolled in CTC and who are in good academic standing. Application guidelines and a current list of scholarships offered are listed in the Alumni/CTC Foundation section on the CTC Web site.

Faculty

Central Texas College's faculty members strive to provide high-quality instruction with individual attention while serving a culturally diverse and mobile population. The College faculty and staff members share a common commitment to the personal development of each student. Most of CTC's instructors hold advanced degrees in their areas of specialization and continually seek further education and professional development

Student Body Profile

At the CTC Central Campus, there are 9,500 students, of whom 62.9 percent are women and 37.1 percent are men. The ethnicity of the student body is made up of 5.5 percent Asian, 31.7 percent black, 17 percent Hispanic, 0.8 percent Native American, 43.6 percent white, and 1.4 percent international.

Student Activities

The Office of Student Life supports student development by providing opportunities through student organizations, tournaments, multicultural celebrations, and other social activities. The Roy J. Smith Student Center is the social center of the campus. The first floor contains the Student Life Office, the campus bookstore, the cafeteria, the snack bar, and offices for Student Support Services. The second floor contains the Student Government Association Office, a game room, a recreational center, and a television lounge and is the main site for student organization meetings and activities.

A host of intramural sports activities, which take place in and around the new Natatorium and Physical Education Complex, are available and include volleyball, three-on-three basketball, and softball.

Facilities and Resources

Central Texas College seeks constant improvement by building new facilities and upgrading existing structures. The attractively landscaped campus provides a modern classroom, a laboratory, a library, on-campus housing, and athletic and recreational facilities. The most recent addition to Central Campus was the $8.5-million Technology Complex and Planetarium. Other examples of CTC's commitment to growth include the recently opened Natatorium and Physical Education Center, and the expanded Oveta Culp Hobby Library. On the Central Campus, Central Texas College operates an air-conditioned, coeducational residence hall that accommodates approximately 120 students. A comprehensive campus tour is available under the Alumni and Community section of the College Web site.

Project PASS (Partners in Academic Success Services) provides a wide range of tutoring, textbook lending and library services, and noncredit refresher courses in math and English. Disability Support Services assist students with physical and/or learning disabilities through the lending of equipment, such as Braille textbooks, tape recorders, tutoring, and providing note-taker services. Other services include Single Parent/Homemaker Support Services, the Gender Equity Program, the Learning Resource Center, and transportation assistance, which offers bus service to CTC from many pick-up points in the area. All of these services are free to CTC students.

Location

The CTC Central Campus is located in Killeen, Texas, approximately 60 miles north of the capital city of Austin and adjacent to Fort Hood, the largest Army installation in the U.S.

Admission Requirements

Application forms and procedures are available under Admissions and Registration on the College Web site. International students must meet additional admission requirements and should contact the Office of International Student Services for assistance.

Application and Information

Admissions and Records
Central Texas College
P.O. Box 1800
Killeen, Texas 76540-1800
Telephone: 254-526-1696
            800-792-3348 Ext. 1696 (toll-free)
E-mail: admissions.registrar@ctcd.edu
World Wide Web: http://www.ctcd.edu

International Student Services
Central Texas College
P.O. Box 1800
Killeen, Texas 76540-1800
Telephone: 254-526-1107
            800-792-3348 Ext. 1107 (toll-free)
E-mail: ctc.international@ctcd.edu

COLLEGE OF BUSINESS AND TECHNOLOGY
MIAMI, FLORIDA

The College and Its Mission

The mission of the College of Business and Technology (CBT) is to provide education and training in accordance with the demand of the present and future job market. The College's ultimate goal is to graduate individuals of moral, technical, and professional excellence who can make a better life for themselves and their families and lead the way toward a better society for everyone.

To fulfill this mission, CBT encourages the development of the knowledge base, study skills, and personal motivation necessary for competent scholarly inquiry and the lifelong pursuit of learning. The College also provides outstanding technical and educational facilities to offer students the best hands-on training possible, and it introduces the essential skills necessary to meet day-to-day tasks demanded by the business environment to people who are looking to better their environment. Graduates of the College are well-prepared for entry-level positions in management, visual media, and information technology.

The College of Business and Technology is accredited by the Accrediting Council for Independent Colleges and Schools (ACICS) and is licensed by the Commission for Independent Education (CIE).

Academic Programs

The College offers associate degree programs in animation, accounting, business administration, computer networking, criminal justice, game design, graphic design, and medical assisting.

Diplomas programs include administrative assistant studies, desktop support technician studies, English as a second language, NCLEX test prep, office technology, and Web design.

The following certifications are offered at the College of Business and Technology: A+, Certified Bookkeeper, Cisco Certified Network Administrator (CCNA), Certified Internet Webmaster (CIW), Microsoft Certified Professional (MCP), Microsoft Certified Systems Administrator (MCSA), Network+, and TOEFL.

The College of Business and Technology also offers online classes through the Blackboard Learning System. For more information, prospective students should visit the College's Web site at http://www.cbt.edu and follow the links for online learning.

Costs

Tuition is $260 per semester credit. Other costs include a registration fee of $100, lab and equipment fees of $30 per course for some courses, a software supply fee of $24 per semester, and an Internet-access fee of $20 per semester.

Financial Aid

Pell Grants are awarded to undergraduate students who demonstrate financial need. The amount is determined based on income earned, number of dependents, working status, and other situations. Supplemental Educational Opportunity Grants of $100 to $4000 per year are awarded to undergraduates who show the greatest financial need. Through the Ford Direct Student Loan, offered by the federal government, students can receive up to $2625 per academic year, but the loan must be paid back within six months after graduation. Students can also request up to $4000 of an unsubsidized loan. The Fernando Llerena Scholarship awards $100 to $500 to students who are enrolled in the ESL Program and maintain a minimum 3.0 GPA and an attendance record of 80 percent. The College also participates in the Federal Work-Study Program, which places students from low-income families in jobs that require 5 to 20 hours of work per week.

Faculty

The faculty consists of part-time and full-time instructors. Class size is limited to 16 students. The student-faculty ratio is 12:1, which allows faculty members to become more familiar with their students' specific strengths and career goals.

Student Body Profile

There are approximately 515 students attending the College of Business and Technology. Fifty-three percent of the students are women, 19 percent are African American, and 69 percent are Hispanic. There are 74 international students from thirty-one countries.

Student Activities

At the College of Business and Technology, students are able to participate in the Student Government Association (SGA). Students also are active in the College's intramural athletic program, which includes baseball, basketball, and soccer.

Location

Known as the "magic city," Miami is located between the Florida Everglades and the Atlantic Ocean and is renowned for its diverse culture and ethnicities. Blessed with year-round mild climates and unrivaled ocean access, Miami was ranked the nation's Number One Healthiest City by *Natural Health* magazine in 2002. The city offers some of the world's top golf, tennis, and sporting facilities, and its sparkling waters are a magnet for boating enthusiasts, fishermen, windsurfers, divers, and water-sports aficionados. Other nearby attractions include the Everglades National Park, Loxahatchee River, and Tropical Park.

Admission Requirements

Requirements for admission include evidence of a high school diploma or GED, an interview with a College Academic Counselor, and a completed Enrollment Agreement. Applicants lacking a high school diploma or its equivalent may be admitted to the up-to-one-year diploma program at the discretion of the College.

Application and Information

Prospective students who are interested in the College of Business and Technology are encouraged to make an appointment for an interview and to tour the College's classrooms and facilities. An enrollment agreement is filled out when the prospective student decides to enroll and the admission requirements are met. The College representative reviews this agreement and a new appointment is made for final acceptance.

An online application is available at http://www.cbt.edu. For additional information, prospective students should contact:

Admissions Department
Kendall Campus
College of Business and Technology
8991 Southwest 107 Avenue
Suite 200
Miami, Florida 33176
Telephone: 305-CALL-CBT (225-5228)
E-mail: admissions@cbt.edu
World Wide Web: http://www.cbt.edu

THE COLLEGE OF WESTCHESTER

WHITE PLAINS, NEW YORK

The College and Its Mission

Founded in 1915, the College of Westchester (CW) has a rich history of providing the community with affordable, private education at the collegiate level. The beautiful, state-of-the-art campus in White Plains offers an environment that is conducive to learning. Programs are designed for college-bound students with an interest in a career-focused education leading to long-term security and financial success.

The College's mission is to offer high-quality, career-oriented programs that challenge both the traditional and returning student to advanced levels of intellectual and personal development. This commitment to educational excellence is reflected in a carefully constructed and distinctive curriculum that is designed to provide students with sophisticated, marketable skills and to promote in students those attributes that contribute to personal and career success and a desire for lifelong learning. In order to maximize student success, the College maintains a student-centered environment.

CW is a junior college accredited by the Commission on Higher Education (CHE) of the Middle States Association of Colleges and Schools (3624 Market Street, Philadelphia, Pennsylvania 19104; telephone: 215-662-5606). The CHE is an institutional accrediting agency recognized by the U.S. Department of Education and the Council for Higher Education Accreditation.

Academic Programs

The Associate in Applied Science (A.A.S.) degree or the Associate in Occupational Studies (A.O.S.) degree is awarded upon successful completion of a two-year program. The requirements include courses in basic college skills, courses pertaining to the student's major, and, for those students pursuing an A.A.S. degree, courses in general education.

The Business Administration–Management/Marketing program provides students with an opportunity to concentrate in either e-commerce marketing, entrepreneurial management, or information systems. Three new concentrations have been added to the day program: entertainment, music, and sports management; fashion/retail merchandising; and hotel and resort management. Graduates pursue management training, Internet marketing, and sales positions. The program also affords self-employment opportunities through an appropriate educational background.

The Computer Network Administration program provides students with a leading-edge career education for today's technical world. Students study administration, design, support, and maintenance of local area networks through lectures and by using Microsoft Windows 2000 systems and software. The program includes additional nontechnical courses to enhance the student's career opportunities.

The Multimedia Development and Management program provides students with the tools to design and develop multimedia applications for the general media, business, education, the Internet, and entertainment markets. The program utilizes the most current multimedia technologies that enable students to create portfolios of their work.

The Computer Applications Management program prepares students for various professional-level employment opportunities in the rapidly expanding information processing and office technology fields. Graduates of this program are qualified to seek office technology and information processing positions that require expert computer applications skills and knowledge of technical office procedures.

The Business Systems–Management Applications program prepares students to become competent business-applications programmers and systems specialists. Instruction in computer languages in microcomputer environments gives students the flexibility to become competent in diverse business usages. Students can choose a concentration in database management or Web development.

The Business Administration–Accounting/Computer Applications program provides students with a business administration accounting curriculum, which places a strong focus on computer applications. Upon graduation, students are prepared for a variety of career possibilities in which a thorough understanding of the principles of accounting is essential.

The Office Administration program prepares students for various professional-level employment opportunities. Graduates of the program are qualified to seek office administration, executive administrative assistant, executive assistant, or office management positions.

The Medical Office Systems Management program prepares students for entry-level employment in such administrative positions as medical billers, coders, collectors, and office managers in organizations ranging from small medical practices to large health-care institutions.

Students in nondegree programs receive a certificate from CW if all courses are successfully completed. Credits may be transferred to the associate degree programs, providing a 2.0 or better cumulative grade point average has been achieved in addition to the successful completion of all required courses.

In a short certificate program, students can obtain specialized job skills to launch or upgrade their career. These programs are popular among students who already have some advanced skills or education as well as those who want to be employable and promotable in the shortest possible time.

Certificate programs include Computer Applications Specialist, Computer Networking Specialist, Computer Programming, E-Commerce, Intensive Accounting/Computer Applications, Multimedia Technology, and Word Processing Specialist.

Costs

The cost of tuition and fees varies, depending on the student's program. Current costs are available from the CW admissions office.

Financial Aid

All students at CW are encouraged to apply for financial assistance and meet with a financial assistance counselor who conducts a confidential analysis detailing the funds available to finance their education. In addition to federal- and state-funded programs, the College offers a variety of institutional scholarships, grants, and payment plans each year.

Faculty

CW instructors are highly qualified, dedicated, and respected educators who are committed to excellence in teaching and service to students. Most faculty members have advanced degrees and all have extensive business experience. A comprehensive faculty development program ensures that all instructors remain current in their field of expertise and utilizes state-of-the-art technology and teaching methodologies.

Student Body Profile

Students come to CW from throughout the New York metropolitan area. The present student body represents 117 high schools, five states, and six countries. The breadth of racial, ethnic, and socioeconomic backgrounds represented in the student body creates a genuinely diverse institution. There are nearly equal numbers of women and men enrolled and a sizable population of mature, nontraditional students who primarily attend convenient evening and weekend classes.

Student Activities

CW offers an array of student activities and support services designed to help students achieve their fullest potential for growth. Activities include Student Government Association, Alpha Beta Kappa honor society, business- and technology-related clubs, field trips to businesses and corporations, and social events.

Academic Facilities

The College of Westchester is located in a beautiful five-story, 50,000-square-foot building. The College's academic facilities include nineteen classrooms; a library; a student life center that houses all student organizations and clubs; an academic advancement center, an open computer lab that also serves as a tutoring and study center; a student lounge; and faculty offices. The facility also includes the Admissions Office; the Academic Center, where the academic administrators, including academic advisers, are housed; the Financial Services Center; and Career Placement Services.

CW's Career Placement Services specializes in finding part-time work for currently enrolled students and full-time, career-related positions for graduates. The staff members work with students to secure internships, co-op opportunities, and work-study positions while they are attending the College and also carefully guide students through the many facets of planning and preparing for job searches. This may include guidance in areas such as properly completing resumes, writing letters of application, securing job interviews, researching companies, and conducting interviews.

At CW, leading-edge technology defines the teaching and learning environment. The computer classrooms feature Pentium-based personal computers, outfitted with an extensive selection of current software applications. The recent addition of a G5 Macintosh lab has enabled CW students to learn applications on both Macintosh and PC platforms.

Location

CW is located in White Plains, the county seat and hub of Westchester County. Many of the College's graduates work for area corporations, including IBM, Verizon, Kraft General Foods USA, the Bank of New York, PepsiCo, AT&T, the Reader's Digest Association, Philip Morris, MasterCard, Citibank, Con Ed, CIBA, Texaco, MCI, Bayer Corporation, MBIA, Lillian Vernon, Fuji Film USA, Sunburst Communications, Hitachi America, Ltd., MetLife Corporation, MTA, Nine West, Avon Products, Carolee Designs, Online Design, Pitney Bowes, American Express, Coca Cola Corporation, Dannon Corporation, Doral Arrowwood, FedEx, International Paper, *The Journal News*, KPMG Peat Marwick, Lincoln Center for the Performing Arts, MCS Cannon, Manulife Wood Logan, Marsh & McLennan, the United Way, Xerox, and Zurich Reinsurance.

The New York Metro North Railroad Station and the transportation center are both a short walk from CW.

Admission Requirements

To properly assist applicants in selecting the program that is best suited to their needs, a personal interview is conducted with an admissions associate. Prospective students should call the Admissions Office for an appointment. In addition to the interview, all applicants must be graduates of an accredited high school or its equivalent or have received a high school equivalency diploma (GED). In some cases, mature, non–high school graduates who have demonstrated an ability to benefit based upon an interview, counseling, and testing may be admitted. These individuals may qualify for a high school equivalency diploma through CW from the New York State Education Department by successfully completing 36 quarter hours of academic work with a minimum of a 2.0 GPA in one of the College programs.

Application and Information

CW has a rolling admissions policy. Students may apply at any time up to the beginning of the quarter; although, students are strongly encouraged to apply as early as possible. To be considered for admission, the following must be submitted: an application for admission, a $30 nonrefundable application fee, and an official high school transcript, its equivalent, or a GED equivalency diploma. If transferring credits from a prior college, students must submit an official college transcript. Students seeking to transfer credits from another institution of higher education should request that an official transcript be mailed to Transfer Credits, Office of Admissions. Students who have attended another accredited college or university may obtain credit toward graduation for courses taken at that institution. Credit is transferable for comparable courses in the student's selected curriculum in which the applicant has obtained a grade of C (2.0) or higher. A maximum of 50 percent of the credits required for program completion may be transferred. Official documentation of successful completion of high school or the equivalent must be received prior to the completion of the first quarter at the College.

For application materials and additional information, prospective students should contact:

Office of Admissions
The College of Westchester
325 Central Park Avenue
White Plains, New York 10606
Telephone: 800-333-4924
E-mail: admissions@cw.edu
World Wide Web: http://www.cw.edu

COLORADO MOUNTAIN COLLEGE
GLENWOOD SPRINGS, COLORADO

The College and Its Mission

There is a different view of the Rocky Mountains at each Colorado Mountain College campus. Learning is personal; classes are small; faculty members are friendly. Colorado Mountain College is a multicampus community college with three residential campuses and twelve commuter locations. This coeducational public institution began operation in 1967. Colorado Mountain College is a district-supported college with its own governing board. Colorado Mountain College operates on a semester system with a limited summer session and is accredited by the North Central Association of Colleges and Secondary Schools.

The three residential campuses include Alpine Campus in Steamboat Springs, Spring Valley Campus outside of Glenwood Springs, and Timberline Campus in Leadville. At these locations, students still find a traditional college experience, including residence halls, cafeterias, extensive libraries, laboratories, and many opportunities to participate in campus life. The commuter campuses serve primarily local residents, and classes are scheduled for the convenience of working adults. Commuter sites are located in Aspen, Basalt, Breckenridge, Buena Vista, Carbondale, Dillon, Eagle, Glenwood Springs, Rifle, Salida, and Vail.

Colorado Mountain College offers academic programs for transfer, career training in several specialty areas, and courses to enrich the lives and livelihoods of local residents. Students can begin their four-year degree because the State Guaranteed Transfer courses are guaranteed to satisfy general education requirements at all Colorado public higher-education institutions.

Students may also choose to start a career with occupational training programs. In one or two years, students can learn the skills for employment in some unique and exciting programs. The mountain environment gives students many opportunities to learn outside the classroom.

Academic Programs

Colorado Mountain College offers both occupational and transfer programs. Degrees awarded include the **Associate in Arts** degree, **Associate in Science** degree, **Associate in General Studies** degree, **Associate in Applied Science** degree, and a one-year Occupational Proficiency certificate. The Associate in Arts degree is available at all Colorado Mountain College campuses.

Degrees and programs vary by campus, with the residential campuses offering the fullest range of degrees and certificates. Alpine Campus offerings include the Associate in Arts (areas of specialization are business, fine arts, liberal arts, and wilderness studies), the Associate in Science (areas of specialization are biology, chemistry, geology, and mathematics), and the Associate in Applied Science and Certificates of Occupational Proficiency (offerings include accounting, business, microcomputer support specialist, resort management, and ski and snowboard business). Spring Valley Campus offerings include the Associate in Arts (areas of specialization are business, liberal arts, outdoor education, and theater), Associate in Science (areas of specialization are biology, chemistry, geology, mathematics, and nursing), and Associate in Applied Science and Certificates of Occupational Proficiency (offerings include accounting, business, graphic design, law enforcement, microcomputer support specialist studies, photography, practical nursing, and veterinary technology). Timberline Campus offerings include the Associate in Arts (areas of specialization are business, liberal arts, and Outdoor Semester in the Rockies), the Associate in General Studies degree in outdoor recreational leadership, the Associate in Science (areas of specialization are biology, chemistry, geology,

and mathematics), and the Associate in Applied Science and Certificates of Occupational Proficiency (offerings include accounting, business, microcomputer support specialist studies, natural resources management, natural resources recreation management, and ski area operations).

Off-Campus Programs

One of the most popular off-campus programs is the Outdoor Semester in the Rockies. This program blends outdoor adventure with the disciplines of college classes such as science and philosophy. Colorado Mountain College encourages students to take advantage of several study-abroad class tours. The College also offers exciting distance education opportunities to district and residential campus students through telecourses, an interactive video system, and some Internet courses.

Credit for Nontraditional Learning Experiences

Colorado Mountain College awards credit through national standardized exams, challenge exams, and credit for life experience. To be awarded credit, testing options are used if possible, and students must be enrolled in a degree or certificate program. Credits posted to a student's academic record through one of these nontraditional methods are noted, indicating the method by which they were awarded.

Costs

Colorado Mountain College's tuition for the academic year 2004–05 was $41 per credit hour for in-district students, $69 per credit hour for in-state students, and $220 per credit hour for out-of-state students. Residential campuses had student activity fees of $180 per academic year. Room and board costs averaged $6100 per year, and the housing reservation deposit was $300. Books average $650 per academic year.

Financial Aid

Colorado Mountain College is approved for participation in all major federal and state financial aid programs, including Federal Pell Grant, loan programs, and work-study. Financial assistance is awarded through a central district office for all Colorado Mountain College campuses and education centers. The application for financial assistance is the Free Application for Federal Student Aid (FAFSA). First priority is given to those students applying on or before March 31. Applications received after this date are processed pending availability of funds. Questions may be addressed to Student Financial Assistance, District Office, P.O. 10001, Glenwood Springs, Colorado 81602.

Faculty

Colorado Mountain College faculty members are accessible to students. They are at Colorado Mountain College because they believe in teaching. There are 72 full-time faculty members and 144 part-time faculty members at the three residential campuses. The faculty members pride themselves on the high-quality education students receive in the classroom, with classes averaging 15 students. The student-faculty ratio is 12:1. Many faculty members have taught at colleges and universities and have chosen to teach at Colorado Mountain College because of their love for teaching and the blend of invigorating environments and stimulating learning.

Student Body Profile

Colorado Mountain College students are from the local area, forty-eight states, and six other countries. Undergraduate full-time and part-time students at the residential campuses number 1,500 at the Alpine Campus, 1,000 at the Spring Valley Campus, and 1,100 at the Timberline Campus. Alpine has approximately 500 full-time students, and Timberline has about 300 full-time students. Colorado Mountain College opened new residence halls in fall 1997 at all three residential locations. The Alpine Campus can house about 220 students on campus, the Spring Valley Campus about 200 students, and the Timberline Campus about 100 students.

Student Activities

Each residential campus has active student government organizations. Each student government determines the student activity fee and how the funds are utilized on each campus. Student government helps to sponsor student activities, clubs and organizations, and guest speakers. Colorado Mountain College's ski team holds six national titles. But there is more than snow available for outdoor activities. Students actively participate in hiking, biking, and water sports. Student Activities Offices organize basketball and volleyball intramurals. Men's and women's varsity soccer teams are offered at the Spring Valley Campus. Every season brings new activities and celebrations to the mountain resort towns.

Facilities and Resources

The residential campuses offer a full college experience with residence halls, cafeterias, libraries, academic classrooms, learning labs, laboratories, and student center facilities.

The Alpine Campus offers residence halls and classroom buildings. Fall 1992 marked the opening of an academic building that includes faculty offices, a library, classrooms, instructional and computer laboratories, and recreational space. Spring 1995 saw the opening of a remodeled cafeteria, bookstore, and student center. At the Spring Valley Campus, students can enjoy the hot springs pool in Glenwood Springs, the charm of Carbondale, and the culture of Aspen. Spring Valley offers residence halls, a cafeteria, a gymnasium and climbing wall, a student center, a bookstore, classrooms, a working farm, laboratories, and an extensive library. A new academic building opened in fall 1998. This building houses a theater, photography labs and studio, a graphic design computer lab, a student computer center, and classrooms. The faculty offices surround the classrooms so students can easily access their instructors and professors. At the Timberline Campus, many students combine their environmental interests and their college education. Colorado's highest mountain peak is in the backyard, cross-country skiing begins at the edge of campus, and many of Colorado's big name slopes are no more than an hour away. The campus offers classroom facilities, a library and learning lab, a computer lab, and a bookstore. In fall 1999, a new academic building opened at the Timberline Campus. It houses classrooms, a computer center, laboratories, student services, and faculty offices. Students enjoy a relaxing student center and cafeteria and have access to Leadville's modern recreation complex.

Location

Like the Rockies that surround it, Colorado Mountain College is wide open and full of possibilities. There are miles of spruce and aspen, wildflowers, backroads, whitewater and bareback ranchland, three national forests, six wilderness areas, and most of Colorado's major ski resorts. There is a spirit among the teachers and students, an atmosphere of encouragement, and an attitude of confidence. **Alpine Campus** is situated above the downtown area on the west end of Steamboat Springs. In Leadville, **Timberline Campus** is less than an hour's drive from Vail and is surrounded by Colorado's highest peaks and the legends of a town built by silver. High above the Roaring Fork River, **Spring Valley Campus** is located 10 miles south of Glenwood Springs and within 40 miles of Aspen. All Colorado Mountain College locations are resort or mountain communities accessible by air, rail, or bus, and provide excellent outdoor opportunities.

Admission Requirements

Colorado Mountain College seeks, encourages, and assists all interested students beyond high-school age who demonstrate a desire to learn. With a few exceptions, admission follows an open-door policy. Even though Colorado Mountain College has open admission, certain occupational programs have selective admission. Programs with selection or testing requirements and admission deadlines include culinary arts, nursing, outdoor recreation leadership, paramedicine, professional photography, and veterinary technology.

To apply for admission, students must complete and return the Colorado Mountain College admissions application and official high school and/or college transcripts. There is no application fee. All entering students should submit ACT or SAT I scores for scholarship, advising, and placement purposes. Some programs require testing for admission.

Transfer students are welcome and should have attained a cumulative grade point average of at least 2.0 on any college work attempted. Nongraduates may take the General Educational Development test (GED) to meet graduation equivalence. International students may be considered for admission to the residential campuses. International admission packets are available and must be completed and returned to apply for admission, and a minimum TOEFL score of 500 on the paper exam or a minimum score of 173 on the computerized exam is required for admission.

Students are encouraged to apply as soon as possible to secure on-campus housing. After applying for admission to a residential campus, students receive housing reservation information.

Application and Information

For more information, students should contact:

Director of Pre-Enrollment Services
Colorado Mountain College
P.O. Box 10001
Glenwood Springs, Colorado 81602
Telephone: 970-945-8691
          800-621-8559 (toll-free)
Fax: 970-947-8324
E-mail: joinus@coloradomtn.edu
World Wide Web: http://www.coloradomtn.edu

The Colorado Rockies are a classroom for Colorado Mountain College students.

COMMUNITY COLLEGE OF ALLEGHENY COUNTY

PITTSBURGH, MONROEVILLE, NORTH HILLS, AND WEST MIFFLIN, PENNSYLVANIA

The College and Its Mission

The Community College of Allegheny County (CCAC) has been helping students plan their futures for nearly forty years. CCAC's educational influence extends far beyond the 350 acres that compose its four campuses. The College reaches deep into the communities. Classes are offered at **Allegheny Campus** on Pittsburgh's North Shore, **Boyce Campus** in Monroeville, **South Campus** in West Mifflin, and **North Campus** in the North Hills section of Pittsburgh. Classes are also offered at more than 400 other locations in Allegheny County. CCAC is the largest community college in Pennsylvania. Its size is a great advantage in terms of the depth and breadth of academic opportunities. However, it is the deep personal commitment that CCAC brings to each student's academic life that makes this college especially effective. High school graduates seeking to begin their college studies find themselves challenged by supporting faculty members who have made a commitment to teaching. Nontraditional students who are returning to school and have family responsibilities can find a wide range of course offerings scheduled at convenient times and locations. CCAC is fully accredited by the Middle States Association of Colleges and Schools.

Academic Programs

CCAC offers academic, career, and technical programs that prepare students for the workforce or to transfer into baccalaureate degree programs at other colleges or universities. The College offers both full- and part-time programs leading to certificates or associate degrees. Program requirements vary, but in general, an associate degree program requires two years of study, and a certificate program requires one year or less.

Associate Degree Programs The associate degrees offered by CCAC can be grouped into seven different areas. University Parallel and transfer programs offer associate degrees in accounting, Africana and ethnic studies, art, biology, business, chemistry, computer information science, cosmetology management, criminal justice and criminology, engineering science, engineering technology, foreign language, humanities, journalism, liberal arts and sciences, manufacturing engineering, mathematics, music, physics, pre–athletic training, pre–health professions, psychology, social sciences, sociology/anthropology, teacher education, and theater.

Career programs in business offer associate degrees in accounting specialist studies, aviation management, aviation technology, business management, court reporter studies, culinary arts, hotel-restaurant management, marketing management, paralegal studies, personnel management, public administration, and tourism management.

Career programs in computer information technology offer associate degrees in application software development, e-commerce development, network administration, and user support.

Career programs in health offer associate degrees in biotechnology, children with special needs, diagnostic medical sonographer studies, dietary manager studies, health information technology, massage therapy, medical assistant studies, medical laboratory technician studies, nuclear medicine technologist studies, nursing, occupational therapy assistant studies, pharmacy technician studies, physical therapy assistant studies, radiation therapy technologist studies, radiologic technologist studies, respiratory therapy technician studies, and surgical technologist studies.

Career programs in social service offer associate degrees in child and family studies, criminal justice and criminology, fire science and administration, mental health/mental retardation specialist studies, social work technician studies and teacher's assistant studies.

Career programs in applied arts technologies offer associate degrees in graphics communications, horticulture technology (floriculture), horticulture technology (landscape design), horticulture technology (landscape and turfgrass management), industrial design and art, and multimedia communications.

Career programs in applied service and trade technologies offer associate degrees in automotive service education, automotive technology, building construction estimating, building construction supervision, building construction technology, building maintenance technology, electrical distribution technology, heating and air-conditioning technology, mechanical electronics technology, mechanical maintenance technology, motor winding technology, and welding technology.

Career programs in engineering and science technologies offer associate degrees in architectural drafting and design technology, chemical technology, civil engineering technology, computer-aided drafting and design technology, electronic engineering technology, laboratory technology, mechanical drafting and design technology, microcomputer electronics technology, robotics and automated systems technology, and science and engineering technology.

Certificate Programs CCAC offers the following certificate programs: accounting, Africana and ethnic studies, American Sign Language, automotive technology, basic CAD, basic electronics, basic preparation cook studies, biotechnology, building construction, building maintenance technology, business management, carpentry, case management, CAT scanning, central services technology, child and family studies, child care, child development, CIT application software development, CIT computer programming, CIT e-commerce development, CIT network administration, CIT survivability and information assurance, CIT user support, CIT Web designer studies, commercial art and design, computer numerical control programming, construction estimating, court reporting, deaf studies, diagnostic medical sonography, dietary manager studies, digital electronics, digital graphic design, drafting and/or surveying, drug and alcohol, electronics (basic or digital), families of prisoners intervention, families with children with special needs, family intervention, floral art and design, floriculture, foreman training, geriatric studies, health unit coordinator studies, heating and air conditioning, hotel management, ironworking, landscape horticulture, landscape maintenance, machine studies (basic), massage therapy, mechanical electronic technology, mechanical maintenance technology, medical assistant studies, medical insurance specialist studies, medical transcription, mental health specialist studies, mental retardation technician studies, motor winding technology, MRI scanning, nanofabrication, network cable, nuclear medicine, office technology professional studies, operating room nursing, paralegal studies, personnel administration, pharmacy technician studies, phlebotomist studies, plumbing, practical nursing, private pilot, public administration, radiation therapy, rehabilitation aide studies, restaurant management, sheet-metal studies, social work, surgical technology, teacher's assistant studies, technical theater, training for persons needing learning support (food service, greenhouse/nursery, human services aide, janitorial/housekeeping, or nursing assistant), travel specialist studies, turfgrass maintenance, and welding.

Costs

For residents of Allegheny County, CCAC's tuition was $80 per credit. Residents of other Pennsylvania counties that do not have a community college paid $91.50 per credit. Residents of Pennsylvania counties with community colleges paid $155 per credit. Students living out of state paid $232.50 per credit. A College fee of $50.40 per semester was charged to students taking classes at each campus location. Some courses offered by CCAC require special course or lab fees in addition to the tuition and College fee. All of these costs were estimated for the 2004–05 academic year. CCAC reserves the right to change the tuition and fees at any time and without prior notice.

Financial Aid

Financial aid programs at CCAC are designed to assist students whose family circumstances limit their ability to contribute toward educational costs. Under federal guidelines, students are expected to seek assistance first from funds that are available through their own personal resources and then from the government. Most awards are need-based, which means that a determination of the expected family contribution is made through a formula established by the U.S. Department of Education. Financial aid consists of scholarships, grants, loans, and employment. Aid may be offered in some combination of these sources, depending on the student's financial need and the requirements for each program. Awards are based on the enrollment of the student, the expected family contribution of the student, and the availability of funding at the time the application for aid is received. Students who have taken out student loans in the past and who are in default on those loans are not eligible for any type of federal, state, or institutional financial aid. Students must complete the Free Application for Federal Student Aid (FAFSA) to be considered for financial aid. Other supporting documents may be required by the Financial Aid Office. Students are notified as to which forms are required once the FAFSA results are received.

Faculty

CCAC has 254 full-time professors and a staff of part-time educators who are experienced, knowledgeable, and committed to teaching. While most faculty members continue their studies and research to remain current in their respective fields, their first commitment is to the students. The average class size is 20.

Student Body Profile

There are currently 19,674 students enrolled as full- and part-time credit students. The average age of this student population is 28. In a typical fall semester, the CCAC minority group enrollment is approximately 19 percent. Eighty-three percent of the students enrolled in credit courses live within Allegheny County. Students enrolled in noncredit course work currently number 22,191.

Student Activities

CCAC student activities include acquiring leadership potential as part of student government or participation in creative endeavors, including student publications, drama productions, and art programs. Many cultural clubs and organizations exist as well. Students may also enrich their chosen field of studies as a member of an academically related club or organization. For those who prefer the competitive edge, athletic programs for both men and women are available at designated CCAC campuses. Basketball, baseball, golf, tennis, bowling, softball, volleyball, cross-country, racquetball, and weightlifting are just some of the intramural and intercollegiate athletic programs available at designated campuses.

Academic Facilities

The Community College of Allegheny County is committed to students' success. The modern facilities available provide the stimulus to enhance the educational experience. Each of the four CCAC campuses provides a developmental child-care center, staffed by professionals who not only care for each child's physical needs but also provide a stimulating learning environment. CCAC Adult Re-entry Services provide educational and emotional support for these students returning to an academic environment after a long absence. Services offered include career and educational planning, basic skills instruction, and confidence building. Facilities at CCAC are designed to accommodate students with physical disabilities. Paved walkways, accessible building entrances, and elevator systems provide easy access to classrooms and laboratories. In addition, interpreters for the deaf, Braille materials, note-taking, scanning, voice output, and use of technology are available for students with documented disabilities. The College maintains excellent computer facilities at each of its four campuses. Students receive hands-on experience on state-of-the-art computers and instructional equipment ranging from a powerful IBM mainframe computer that is used for both instructional and administrative purposes to microcomputers. Campus and center computer labs offer convenient day and evening hours.

CCAC's four campus libraries house more than 200,000 volumes and subscribe to 847 periodicals. Quiet private reading and study areas are available with knowledgeable librarians who provide the research assistance to help students succeed. Tutoring services and workshops in test taking, study techniques, and basic academic skills are provided at no cost to students through CCAC's Learning Assistance Centers. In support of classroom instruction, audiovisual instructional and technical support services are provided to faculty members.

CCAC provides valuable job search assistance for its students and graduates through its Career Services Departments. In 2003 through early 2004, local employers posted more than 2,000 jobs on the CCAC Job Bank Web site. Through the CCAC Career Services Departments, CCAC belongs as a community center to Pennsylvania CareerLink, which maintains a database containing more than 5,000 annual job listings.

Location

The College is composed of four campuses and seven college centers located strategically throughout Allegheny County. The city of Pittsburgh, located in Allegheny County, is one of the largest sites of corporate headquarters in the United States and has an abundance of cultural activities.

Admission Requirements

As an open-door institution, CCAC provides learning opportunities for all students regardless of prior educational background. CCAC can help applicants with a high school diploma or a General Educational Development (GED) certificate or those who are 18 years of age or older with reasonably equivalent experience to achieve their academic goals. The college placement tests may be given to first-time college students. These tests are intended to assist students in selecting courses that are most appropriate for their current academic skill level. These are not admissions tests. Students who have completed college-level course work at another school or have ACT or SAT scores may be exempt from testing. Students should check with the registration and advisement offices for exemption criteria.

Students should request an admission application form from the admission office on any CCAC campus and should return the completed application to the admission office. Students can also apply online at CCAC's Web site. There is no application fee.

Application and Information

Application forms and additional information are available at the following CCAC campus locations:

Allegheny Campus (North Shore)
Community College of Allegheny County
808 Ridge Avenue
Pittsburgh, Pennsylvania 15212
Telephone: 412-237-2511

North Campus (North Hills)
Community College of Allegheny County
8701 Perry Highway
Pittsburgh, Pennsylvania 15237
Telephone: 412-369-3600

Boyce Campus (Monroeville)
Community College of Allegheny County
595 Beatty Road
Monroeville, Pennsylvania 15146
Telephone: 724-325-6614

South Campus (West Mifflin)
Community College of Allegheny County
1750 Clairton Road and Route 885
West Mifflin, Pennsylvania 15122
Telephone: 412-469-4301
World Wide Web: http://www.ccac.edu

COOKING AND HOSPITALITY INSTITUTE OF CHICAGO

CHICAGO, ILLINOIS

C H I C

The Institute and Its Mission

The mission of the Le Cordon Bleu Program at the Cooking and Hospitality Institute of Chicago is to prepare students to fulfill their career ambitions and meet the needs of the food service industry. To this end, the Institute has set up a dynamic curriculum that continually adapts to the needs of employers while providing students with the flexibility to receive the education that best meets their career needs. Founded in 1983, the Institute was established to provide culinary education using the traditional European hands-on approach. In 1991, the Institute received degree-granting authority from the Illinois Board of Higher Education and began offering an Associate of Applied Science degree in culinary arts. In 2000, the Cooking and Hospitality Institute of Chicago introduced the Le Cordon Bleu Culinary Program to its Associate of Applied Science degree program. With its reputation for excellence, the demand for graduates by employers far exceeds the number of graduates available.

The Cooking and Hospitality Institute of Chicago is accredited by the Higher Learning Commission of the North Central Association of Colleges and Schools. The Institute is also accredited by the Accrediting Commission of Career Schools and Colleges of Technology (ACCSCT) and the American Culinary Federation (ACF).

Academic Programs

The Cooking and Hospitality Institute of Chicago offers accredited Associate of Applied Sciences (A.A.S.) degrees in Le Cordon Bleu culinary arts and Le Cordon Bleu patisserie and baking. The Cooking and Hospitality Institute of Chicago is devoted to fostering a lifelong love of learning and holding students to high academic standards. The Institute's premier Le Cordon Bleu A.A.S. program combines course work in three areas: culinary, baking and pastry, and management. Students at the Cooking and Hospitality Institute of Chicago can complete the program in as little as fifteen months. There are currently eight start dates available per year. Morning, afternoon, and evening courses are offered to accommodate most students' schedules. Students enrolled in the Le Cordon Bleu programs show commitment to those programs, as well as to the culinary profession, by completing their education in a timely manner.

Associate Degree Programs The Cooking and Hospitality Institute of Chicago offers an Associate of Applied Science degree in Le Cordon Bleu patisserie and baking. This program teaches the principles and techniques of professional pastry and baking production and is intended for students who have an interest in large-quantity baking or who want to work for establishments that have in-house baking and pastry operations.

The Cooking and Hospitality Institute of Chicago also offers an Associate of Applied Science degree in Le Cordon Bleu culinary arts. The program includes professional cooking skills, baking and pastry skills, restaurant management skills, nutrition sciences, and general education. This well-rounded program is designed to give students the technical skills and theoretical expertise that are necessary for a career in the food service industry. Graduates can expect employment in entry-level to midlevel positions as well as rapid advancement into management and sous chef positions and further. Students with or without prior experience find that this program offers everything that they need to begin a fast-track career in the fastest-growing industry in the United States.

Transfer Arrangements The Cooking and Hospitality Institute of Chicago accepts transfer credits from any accredited college provided that the credits are in courses comparable to the courses required under the student's program of study at the Institute. The school registrar determines if credits are transferable.

Off-Campus Programs

The Cooking and Hospitality Institute of Chicago has entered into cooperative agreements with three area colleges that allow students to transfer credits from the Institute toward a bachelor's degree. At Dominican University in River Forest, Illinois, students can continue on for a Bachelor of General Studies (B.G.S.) in culinary arts and management or a Bachelor of Science (B.S.) in nutrition and dietetics, food science management, or food science and nutrition. Students may opt to include in these programs elective courses for nursing home administrator licensure in Illinois. Students may also continue their studies at Robert Morris College, which has campuses in Chicago, Orland Park, Naperville, and Springfield, Illinois, to pursue a Bachelor of Business Administration (B.B.A.). Graduates of the Institute who transfer to Robert Morris with a GPA of at least 3.0 may also receive a tuition scholarship of up to $4800. Students also have the opportunity to continue their studies at Roosevelt University, which accepts 39 credits from the Cooking and Hospitality Institute of Chicago toward their B.S. in hospitality and tourism.

Credit for Nontraditional Learning Experiences

The Institute awards credit to students who have demonstrated proficiency through the Advanced Placement (AP) program and the College-Level Examination Program (CLEP).

Costs

As of January 2005, tuition for the entire culinary program is $38,250. The current tuition for the entire patisserie and baking program is $32,950. In addition, students can expect a one-time purchase of a supply kit. Books, uniforms, and supplies can cost up to approximately $3200 per year.

Financial Aid

Tuition planning is provided free of charge to all applicants. The Institute participates in Federal Title IV assistance programs such as Federal Stafford Student Loans, Federal PLUS loans, Federal Pell Grants, Federal Supplemental Educational Opportunity Grants, and the Federal Work-Study Program. Students may also receive funding from a variety of institutional and industry-related scholarships, which include the Nancy Abrams Academic Excellence Scholarship, the Educational Foundation's ProMgmt. Scholarship, and the Career College Association's Imagine America Scholarships for high school seniors as well as scholarships from the James Beard Foundation, the International Association of Culinary Professionals, the Illinois Restaurant Association, and the National Restaurant Association. Scholarships range from $500 to $10,000.

Nongovernmental loans are available through Sallie Mae. These loans may be used to supplement federal financial aid and in cases where students do not qualify for federal aid. The loan terms are similar to federal student loans, but the application procedure is greatly simplified.

Faculty

Faculty members are selected for their professional backgrounds, academic experience, and certification from the American

Culinary Federation as culinary educators. This allows faculty members to bring daily real-life experiences to their students.

Student Body Profile

The Cooking and Hospitality Institute of Chicago is both ethnically and culturally diverse, with international students representing more than fifteen different countries. Students range in age from 17 to 70. Twenty percent of the students are recent high school graduates, while more than half are career changers whose average age is about 30. In addition, 20 percent of the students are from out of state and have relocated to Chicago in order to participate in the Le Cordon Bleu programs.

Student Activities

The Cooking and Hospitality Institute of Chicago supports many student organizations that provide students with interesting networking and experiential opportunities. Under the advisement of the Dean of Education and faculty advisers, these organizations are the Student Recipe Development Association, the Alpha Beta Kappa Society, the Student Board, the Cellar Club, the Pastry Display Club, the Bread Guild, the Culinary Competition Team, and many more. The Culinary Competition Team has won medals and certificates around the country.

Facilities and Resources

The main campus of the Institute is housed on the ground, first, and second floors of a two-story building. The 60,000-square-foot facility features large air-conditioned classrooms, a student lounge, men's and women's locker rooms, a student communication center, the Learning Resource Center (LRC), and eight kitchens. In addition, the Institute's showcase is the 100-seat student-run restaurant, the CHIC Café, which is open for lunch seven days a week as well as for dinner on Friday and Saturday nights.

In August 2004, the Institute opened a "south campus" across the parking lot from the main building. The new "south campus" features five industry-current kitchens, two large classrooms, a computer lab, a student lounge, and changing rooms. With a total of thirteen kitchens, the Cooking and Hospitality Institute of Chicago is now one of the largest culinary schools in the Midwest.

Student Housing A student housing program is available to students through a real estate firm. Apartments (shared housing) are competitively priced and accessible to the campus via public transportation.

Learning Resource Center Students and faculty members have full access to a collection of more than 5,000 volumes, forty related periodicals and newsletters, and reference materials in hospitality-related areas as well as CD-ROMs and numerous online resources. Online services include a reference catalog, Internet access, ProQuest, and Infotrac. In addition to the current holdings, the library has cooperative arrangements with various local libraries and professional associations. Interlibrary loan service is available through Illinet (Illinois Library and Information Network). The LRC also maintains a staffed computer laboratory for student use, with access to the Internet, various hospitality and purchasing software, word processing, and scanners.

Career Planning/Placement Offices The Career Services Department serves as the liaison between employers and graduates and students seeking career positions. The Institute has developed relationships with many industry leaders who support the educational endeavors of the students. Current students are encouraged to seek part-time positions through the department. Permanent placement upon graduation is readily available, and alumni who wish to advance their careers find a number of opportunities through the department. The Institute currently receives more employer inquiries than it has students and graduates to fill them. For this reason, the Institute screens employers so that they meet the desires of its students.

Location

The Institute is located in the River North area of Chicago, within walking distance of some of the finest restaurants and art galleries in the city. It is eight blocks west of Chicago's famed shopping district, the Magnificent Mile, and only a few blocks north of Chicago's business district, the Loop. It is easily accessible by public transportation, two major expressways, and two international airports.

Admission Requirements

All applicants must be beyond compulsory school age and must furnish documentation of at least a high school diploma or a GED diploma. In addition, applicants must demonstrate their math and English abilities by providing high school or college transcripts or ACT or SAT scores, or they may take the Institute's math and/or English placement exams. International students may submit TOEFL scores for initial acceptance and issuance of an I-20 visa, but they must take the Institute's placement tests upon arrival for course determination.

Application and Information

Applications are accepted on an ongoing basis. Prospective students should contact:

Director of Admissions
Cooking and Hospitality Institute of Chicago
361 West Chestnut
Chicago, Illinois 60610
Telephone: 312-944-0882
         877-828-7772 (toll-free)
Fax: 312-944-8557
E-mail: chic@chicnet.org
World Wide Web: http://www.chic.edu

Students receive hands-on instruction in the kitchens of the Cooking and Hospitality Institute of Chicago.

COTTEY COLLEGE

NEVADA, MISSOURI

The College and Its Mission

Cottey College is a two-year independent, residential, liberal arts and sciences college for women. Virginia Alice Cottey founded the College in 1884 with the firm belief that women deserved the same quality of education as men. When the founder became a member of the P.E.O. Sisterhood—a philanthropic educational organization of more than 250,000 members dedicated to providing educational opportunities for women—she realized the organization paralleled her own goals and ideas about higher education for women. The P.E.O. Sisterhood accepted the College as a gift from the founder in 1927, which made it the only nonsectarian college owned and supported by women.

Cottey College concentrates on what it does best—providing two years of very focused and rigorous academics to move students closer to earning a four-year degree. A Cottey education emphasizes high academic standards with unique opportunities for personal growth through residential, cultural, and intellectual experiences. Cottey College educates qualified women in the arts and sciences to prepare them to transfer to programs beyond the associate degree by enhancing their intellectual ability, their store of knowledge, their personal skills, and, thereby, their capacity for contribution to society and their chosen fields.

Cottey is a member of the Missouri American Council on Education (ACE) Network for the Office of Women in Higher Education (OWHE) and hosts the state Web site on its server.

Academic Programs

The academic tradition at Cottey College is firmly established in the liberal arts. Because its mission is, in part, "to educate qualified women in arts and sciences to prepare them for transfer to programs beyond the associate degree," Cottey emphasizes general education. Fields of study are, in effect, prospective majors for Cottey students, allowing them to focus on specialized personal interests growing out of a general education in the liberal arts and sciences. A Cottey education in a chosen field of study permits students to start learning and working toward careers that interest them and prepares them to enter a major or preprofessional program when they transfer to another institution to complete their bachelor's degree.

Cottey College grants the Associate in Arts (A.A.) and the Associate in Science (A.S.) degrees. Both associate degrees require the completion of 62 credit hours with a cumulative grade point average (GPA) of 2.0 or higher. Thirty-two credit hours must be completed at Cottey College. All students must complete a 24-credit common core curriculum. The core includes 11 credits in basic skills, such as English composition (writing), mathematics, and physical activities. The other 13 credits are distribution requirements in the fine arts, humanities, natural sciences, and social sciences. Depending on their interests and prospective majors, Cottey graduates earn either the A.A. or A.S. degree by meeting additional degree requirements beyond the core curriculum. The A.A. degree requires 12 additional credits focusing on the humanities, foreign languages, and fine arts. The A.S. degree requires 11 additional credits focusing on the sciences and mathematics.

More than 95 percent of graduates transfer to four-year institutions, including such top schools as MIT, Smith, Grinnell, Pepperdine, and the University of Washington, to name a few. As a two-year college, Cottey does not pressure students to declare a major, but they are prepared to declare one at their next college or university.

Off-Campus Programs

In March 2000, for the first time in the College's history, second-year Cottey students spent the first week of the spring break in London, England. The Cottey College Board of Trustees approved a three-year pilot program that sends students to a European city during the spring break of their second year. The program continues to receive approval from the Board and in the last six years, the College has traveled to London, Paris, and Madrid. In 2006, the second-year class is scheduled to return to London for the first time since 2001. There are no additional costs in terms of tuition increases or program or transportation fees placed upon students to participate in this program. Members of the Cottey faculty and staff are involved in the planning of this program and integrate on-campus instruction and activities with the trip preparations. Professors selected for the international trip create educational modules related to their disciplines or interests that they present during two days of the trip. Students have ample time for individual sight-seeing and group-touring opportunities, and all participants attend a farewell dinner at a first-class restaurant.

Costs

In the 2005–06 academic year, the total cost was $17,510. This included tuition, room and board, and all fees.

Financial Aid

Approximately 97 percent of the students receive some form of need- or merit-based aid. Assistance programs include P.E.O. and Cottey scholarships, grants, campus employment, and loans. Amounts depend on financial need, talents, high school GPA, and ACT and/or SAT scores. More information can be obtained from the financial aid office.

Faculty

There are 35 full-time faculty members, of whom more than 94 percent hold doctoral degrees or the terminal degrees in their fields. Twenty-two hold a Ph.D. degree. The student-faculty ratio is 10:1, and the average class size is 13 students. The faculty members are first and foremost teachers. Their subject areas are obvious and inspiring, and their primary interest is in teaching and mentoring young women of promise. All classes are taught by Cottey professors, not teaching assistants. Students know their professors, and this access to faculty members allows students to ask questions and get the answers they need. Many faculty members accept calls at home, and some are known to regularly visit campus study groups on nights or weekends for last-minute tutoring sessions before a test.

Student Body Profile

Cottey students come from everywhere. Generally, no more than 10 percent of students come from any one state, and approximately 10 percent come from outside the United States.

Cottey's residential student population of 350 women typically represents forty states, Canada, and ten to fourteen countries.

Student Activities

Many outstanding cultural events, performances, lectures, workshops, and recreational activities are offered without charge to students. More than thirty-five clubs and organizations at Cottey represent varying student interests in academics, culture, recreation, social concerns, religion, and volunteerism. The clubs and organizations also offer many leadership positions for students each year, enabling women to gain valuable leadership experiences that can help shape their future, their education, and their career paths. Many students become involved in the programs at Cottey's Helen and George Washburn Center for Women's Leadership (CWL), which was established to build girls' and women's lives through enrichment, education, and leadership development. The CWL offers special guest lecturers and notable speakers, and Cottey students can obtain leadership certification through its Leadership, Education, Opportunities (LEO) program, which provides student leaders with an opportunity to document and receive recognition for their experiences inside and outside the classroom and to further develop leadership skills. The LEO program offers four levels of certification.

Cottey's regular slate of national and international guests and performers makes Nevada seem like a larger city. The CLASS series brings to campus such artists, experts, and entertainers as the National Theatre for the Deaf, a Japanese storyteller, the Preservation Hall Jazz Band, Alvin Ailey II Dance Company, Tibetan monks performing sacred music and dance, the Kansas City Symphony, State Ballet, and folk singer Karla Bonhoff. Cottey students take the lead in celebrating International Focus Week, during which they share the food, stories, artifacts, and artistry of their native or ancestral cultures.

Cottey College offers volleyball and basketball in its intercollegiate sports program. Cottey is a member of the National Junior College Athletic Association (NJCAA) Division II, Region XVI. The NJCAA is the athletic association for all two-year colleges. Division II is a mix of small and large two-year colleges. Region XVI is the state of Missouri. There are six colleges that are Division II in Missouri, and those colleges compete in the Regional Tournament.

Facilities and Resources

Completed in 1963, the Blanche Skiff Ross Memorial Library was named in honor of Mrs. Frank Ross of Oak Park, Illinois, niece of Alice Virginia Coffin, one of the 7 founders of the P.E.O. Sisterhood. Browsing the shelves of more than 50,000 volumes of books, videos, DVDs, CDs, slides, maps, and music scores can lead to exploring a broad range of subjects, viewpoints, and cultures. More than 180 current periodical subscriptions reflect the variety of today's interests; some titles extend to 150 years of history. On campus, the library Web site links to databases with full texts of more than 2,000 periodicals as well as news services, government documents, and scholarly databases. The library is a member of the Missouri Bibliographic Information User System (MOBIUS), a group of more than fifty libraries in Missouri, as well as SouthWest Academic Libraries (SWAN),

which is a regional branch of the MOBIUS system. MOBIUS and SWAN allow a Cottey student to request a book from libraries within this system. Items requested from MOBIUS and SWAN are delivered to Cottey's library usually within three to four days. This gives students access to resources and information beyond what Cottey can offer.

Location

A community of about 9,000 people, Nevada, Missouri, is approximately 100 miles south of Kansas City. The campus occupies fourteen buildings on eleven city blocks and a 33-acre wooded recreational area with a lodge. Nevada is a fairly self-sufficient town, with grocery stores, restaurants, local shops, and a Wal-Mart. In addition, there are several large cities and recreational areas within a 90-minute drive of the Cottey campus.

Admission Requirements

All applicants for admission to Cottey College should take a college preparatory sequence. The minimum required high school curriculum includes 4 years of study in English composition and literature, 3 years of math (algebra I and II and geometry), 2 years of history and government, 2 years of a laboratory science, and 2 years of the same foreign language. Acceptance to Cottey is based on prior performance, academic aptitude, and the student's likelihood for success.

Students can apply online or by mail. If applying by mail, there is a $20 nonrefundable application fee. Along with a completed application, students must submit an evaluation form completed by a high school teacher or guidance counselor, an official copy of the high school transcript (showing the completion of at least six semesters of course work), and official ACT or SAT scores. All international students must complete the international application for admission, even if they are currently living in the United States.

Application and Information

The application for admission should be on file with the Office of Enrollment Management as early as possible. The College accepts students for admission only until it reaches its capacity of 350 residential students. If a student has a high school GPA of at least 2.6 and standardized test results that meet the current eligibility requirements (ACT composite of 21 or better or an SAT total of 970 or better on the critical thinking and math sections), she is notified of an admission decision within two to four weeks after completing the application process. Cottey College does not require the Writing section of the SAT at this time.

Office of Enrollment Management
Cottey College
1000 West Austin Boulevard
Nevada, Missouri 64772
Telephone: 417-667-8181
       888-5-COTTEY (toll-free)
Fax: 417-667-8103
E-mail: enrollmgt@cottey.edu
World Wide Web: http://www.cottey.edu

FAIRMONT STATE COMMUNITY & TECHNICAL COLLEGE

FAIRMONT, WEST VIRGINIA

The College and Its Mission

Fairmont State Community & Technical College (FSC&TC) has an enrollment of approximately 3,500 students. Founded in 1974, the College is located in Fairmont, West Virginia.

FSC&TC enhances the quality of life for the people of north-central West Virginia through accessible, affordable, comprehensive, responsive, workforce-related training and high-quality higher education opportunities.

FSC&TC offers a variety of courses at more than twenty-five sites each semester in its thirteen-county service area through its Off-Campus Programs and provides job training for the region through its Center for Workforce Education in downtown Fairmont. The Weekend College program allows adults the opportunity to earn degrees by attending classes on Saturdays on the main campus in Fairmont and at the Gaston Caperton Center in Clarksburg. The Televised Classes Program offers adult students the opportunity to earn College credits from home. The Community Education Program has been developed to meet the needs of the community by offering noncredit classes as an introduction to lifetime learning.

Academic Programs

FSC&TC offers more than forty associate degrees, certificates, skill-set certificates, and occupational development classes. A complete list of majors and programs offered is available on the College's Web site.

Associate degree programs are offered in the following areas: aviation, business technology, criminal justice, culinary arts, health information technology, homeland security, interior design, physical therapist assistant studies, and veterinary technology. Certificates are available in accounting paraprofessional studies, administrative assistant studies, avionics line maintenance, laboratory assistant studies, and office technology. Skill-set certificates include ballroom dancing, classroom teacher's aide studies, computer-aided design, early childhood teaching aide studies, ProMgmt, and Serve Safe. Occupational development classes are offered for those in building and construction trades, child-care practitioners, correctional officers, EMS specialists, and firefighters.

Costs

During the 2004–05 academic year, per-semester charges for Fairmont State students from West Virginia were $1504 for tuition and fees, $2614 for room and board, and $600 for books and supplies, for a total of $4718. Out-of-state students paid $3510 for tuition and fees, $2614 for room and board, and $600 for books and supplies each semester, for a total of $6724.

Financial Aid

About 80 percent of Fairmont State students receive some form of aid. Guidelines and forms for West Virginia and out-of-state residents are available from high school guidance counselors or the Fairmont State Financial Aid Office. Fairmont State awards more than $30 million in financial assistance each year.

Faculty

FSC&TC employs 50 full-time faculty members, ensuring a low student-teacher ratio. Dedicated academic advisers and faculty members work one-on-one with students to meet their individual needs.

Student Activities

Fairmont State is a member of the NCAA Division II and the West Virginia Intercollegiate Athletic Conference. Varsity programs for men are offered in football, basketball, baseball, cross-country, golf, tennis, and swimming. Intercollegiate athletic programs for women include tennis, golf, basketball, volleyball, swimming, softball, and cross-country.

Fairmont State offers more than eighty clubs, organizations, student publications, honoraries, sororities, and fraternities as well as a wide range of intramural sports. Many fine arts performances and exhibits are planned each semester. Nationally prominent speakers are invited to the campus.

Student Government actively seeks to supplement the academic atmosphere with intellectual, cultural, and social activities. Student Government members are involved in all aspects of life on campus and work cooperatively with the administration.

The new Student Activity Center features 7,000 square feet of fitness equipment; five versatile courts for indoor sports; space for fitness classes; a four-lane pool with a whirlpool, sauna, and outdoor sunning deck; a four-lane cushioned jogging/walking track; game rooms; and more.

Academic Facilities

The Ruth Ann Musick Library has a collection of more than 200,000 books and more than 15,000 bound periodicals, microfilms, and other materials, including a large collection of audiotapes and videotapes. The library also has sites at the Caperton Center and the National Aerospace Education Center.

Fairmont State's state-of-the-art technology infrastructure includes thirty computer labs and high-speed network connections that are accessible from the library, classrooms, and every residence hall room, as well as the most up-to-date teaching software.

Location

Fairmont, a city of more than 19,000 in north-central West Virginia, is the county seat of Marion County. Located along Interstate 79 approximately 90 miles south of Pittsburgh, the city and the College are easily accessible to all travelers. Shopping malls, restaurants, cultural entertainment, and nightlife are easily found throughout the area.

West Virginia's natural treasures—mountains, rivers, waterfalls, wildlife, wildflowers, clean air, and vast tracts of national forest—are all close at hand. In and near Fairmont are popular trails for hiking and biking; rivers for white-water rafting; excellent spots for rock and mountain climbing, camping, and fishing; and some of the best skiing in the East.

FSC&TC shares a main campus with Fairmont State University. The campus features fifteen buildings on more than 90 acres. From the historic administration building, Hardway Hall, to the brand-new residence hall, Bryant Place, the facilities are a blend of tradition and technology. Facilities also include the Robert C. Byrd National Aerospace Education Center in Bridgeport, West Virginia, and the Gaston Caperton Center in Clarksburg, West Virginia.

Admission Requirements

First-time freshmen who are applying to Fairmont State must submit an application for admission; an official high school transcript from an accredited high school (partial or complete), a GED certificate (for homeschooled students or for students who don't have a high school diploma), or placement test results (this test is administered by the College to all students without ACT or SAT scores; ACT or SAT scores are required for admission into most health career programs); immunization records (for students born after January 1, 1957); and a statement of activities (for students out of high school six months or longer). Transfer students must submit an application for admission, college transcripts from accredited institutions (if there are fewer than 16 earned credit hours, ACT, SAT, or COMPASS scores are also required), a statement of activities, and immunization records. Non–degree seeking students (those with fewer than 15 hours who are not seeking a degree) and transient students (those enrolled at another school who are returning to that institution) must submit an application for admission. Current high school students must submit an application for admission, have completed their junior year of high school with a GPA of at least 3.0, and submit a recommendation letter from their high school principal.

Application and Information

On a Saturday each fall, Fairmont State schedules a Campus Visitation Day so that potential students and their family members and friends can visit the campus and attend information sessions on admissions, financial aid, and living on campus. An Academic Fair is also scheduled so that students can meet with faculty members about the academic schools and departments.

Campus tours through the Office of Admissions are available Mondays through Fridays. To set up a tour, students should call 800-641-5678 Ext. 2 (toll-free) or 304-367-4855. Tours can also be scheduled online at Fairmont State's Web site.

Office of Admissions
Fairmont State Community & Technical College
1201 Locust Avenue
Fairmont, West Virginia 26554
Telephone: 304-367-4892
  800-641-5678 (toll-free)
  304-367-4213 (financial aid)
  304-367-4216 (residence life)
  304-367-4000 (campus operator)
  304-367-4026 (Gaston Caperton Center)
  304-842-8300 (Robert C. Byrd National
    Aerospace Education Center)
  304-367-4200 (TDD)
Fax: 304-367-4789
E-mail: admit@fairmontstate.edu
World Wide Web: http://www.fairmontstate.edu

Fairmont State students have an opportunity to relax and socialize in the inviting plaza in front of the Education Building.

FIDM/FASHION INSTITUTE OF DESIGN & MERCHANDISING, LOS ANGELES CAMPUS

LOS ANGELES, CALIFORNIA

The Institute and Its Mission

FIDM/The Fashion Institute of Design and Merchandising provides a dynamic and exciting community of learning in the fashion, graphics, interior design, and entertainment industries. The purpose of the Institute is to provide an educational environment designed to combine student goals with industry needs.

FIDM has a reputation for graduating professionally competent and confident men and women capable of creative thought. It has graduated more than 30,000 students in its thirty-five-year history.

FIDM is accredited by the Accrediting Commission for Community and Junior Colleges of the Western Association of Schools and Colleges (WASC) and the National Association of Schools of Art and Design (NASAD).

Academic Programs

FIDM operates on a four-quarter academic calendar. New students may begin their studies any quarter throughout the year. The requirement for a two-year Associate of Arts degree is the completion of 90 units.

Associate Degree Programs FIDM offers Associate of Arts degrees in apparel manufacturing management, beauty industry merchandising and marketing, fashion design, film and TV production, footwear design, graphic design, interior design, international manufacturing and product development, merchandise marketing (fashion merchandising or product development), textile design, theater costume, TV and film costume design, and visual communication. All of these programs offer the highly specialized curriculum of a specific major combined with a core general education/liberal arts foundation.

Transfer Arrangements FIDM accepts course work from other accredited colleges if there is an equivalent course at FIDM and the grade is a C or better. FIDM courses at the 100, 200, and 300 levels are certified by FIDM to be baccalaureate level. FIDM maintains articulation agreements with selected colleges with the intent of enhancing a student's transfer opportunities. Academic counselors will provide assistance to students interested in transferring to other institutions to attain a four-year degree.

Internship and Co-op Programs Internships are available within each of the various majors. Paid and volunteer positions provide work experience for students to gain practical application of classroom skills.

Special Programs and Services FIDM offers Associate of Arts professional designation degrees for individuals with substantial academic and professional experience who wish to add a new field of specialization. These are nine- or twelve-month programs of intensive study in one of the Institute's specialized majors. Students from other regionally accredited programs have the opportunity to complement their previous education by enrolling in a professional designation program. Requirements for completion range from 45 to 66 units, depending on the field of study. FIDM also offers Associate of Arts Advanced Study Programs that develop specialized expertise in the student's unique area of study.

These programs are open to students who possess extensive prior academic and professional experience within the discipline area. These areas include fashion design advanced study, interior design advanced study, theater costume advanced study, and international manufacturing and product development. Completion requirements for these programs are 45 units. Some classes are offered online.

In response to student needs, FIDM has established an evening program in addition to the regular daytime courses. The program has been designed to accommodate the time requirements of working students. The entire evening program for the Associate in Arts degree can be completed in 2½ years.

FIDM offers English as a second language (ESL) for students requiring English development to complete their major field of study. The program is concurrent and within FIDM's existing college-level course work. These classes focus on the special needs of students in the areas of oral communication, reading comprehension, and English composition.

Community Programs Community service programs are offered both independently and in cooperation with various community groups. General studies course credit may be awarded to participating students. Each FIDM campus identifies community projects that allow students to support local service agencies.

Off-Campus Programs

FIDM provides the opportunity for students to participate in academic study tours in Europe, Asia, and New York. These tours are specifically designed to broaden and enhance the specialized education offered at the Institute. Study tour participants may earn academic credit under faculty-supervised directed studies. Exchange programs are also available with Esmod, Paris; Instituto Artictico dell' Abbigliamento Marangoni, Milan; Accademia Internazionale d'Alta Mode e d'Arte del Costume Koefia, Rome; St. Martins School of Art, London; College of Distributive Trades, London; and Janette Klein Design School, Mexico City.

Credit for Nontraditional Learning Experiences

The Institute may give credit for demonstrated proficiency in areas related to college-level courses. Sources used to determine proficiency are the College-Level Examination Program (CLEP) and Credit for Academically Relevant Experience (CARE), an Institute-sponsored program.

Costs

For the 2005–06 academic year, tuition started at $17,660, depending on the major selected by the student. Textbooks and supplies started at $1400 per year, depending on the major. Yearly fees were $500. First-year application fees started at $225 for California residents and ranged up to $525 for international students.

Financial Aid

There are several sources of financial funding available to the student, including federal financial aid and education loan programs, California state aid programs, institutional loan programs, and FIDM awards and scholarships.

Faculty

FIDM faculty members are selected as specialists in their fields. Many are actively employed in their respective fields of expertise. They bring daily exposure to their industry into the classroom for the benefit of the students. In pursuit of the best faculty members, consideration is given to both academic excellence as well as practical experience. FIDM has a 16:1 student-instructor ratio.

Student Body Profile

FIDM's ethnically and culturally diverse student body is one of the attractions to the Institute. Fifteen percent of the current student body are international students from more than thirty different countries. Twenty percent of the students are more than 25 years of age. Fifty percent of all students complete their associate degree. More than 90 percent find career positions within one year of graduation.

Student Activities

The Student Activities Committee plans and coordinates social activities, cultural events, and community projects, including the ASID Student Chapter, International Club, Delta Epsilon Chi (DEX), Association of Manufacturing Students, Honor Society, and the Alumni Association. The students also produce their own trend newsletter, *The Mode.*

Facilities and Resources

Advisement/Counseling Department Chairs and other trained staff members provide assistance to students in selecting the correct sequence of courses to allow each student to complete degree requirements. The counseling department provides personal guidance and referral to outside counseling services as well as matching peer tutors to specific students' needs. Individual Development and Education Assistance (IDEA) centers at each campus provide students with additional educational assistance to supplement classroom instruction. Services are available in the areas of writing, mathematics, computer competency, study skills, research skills, and reading comprehension.

Career Planning/Placement Offices Career planning and job placement are among the most important services offered by the Institute. Career assistance includes job search techniques, preparation for employment interviews, resume preparation, and job adjustment assistance. Services provided by the center include undergraduate placement, graduate placement, alumni placement, internships, and industry work/study programs.

Library and Audiovisual Services FIDM's library goes beyond the traditional sources of information. In addition to more than 12,000 books and reference materials, FIDM also features an international video library, subscriptions to major predictive services, international and domestic periodicals, interior design workrooms, textile samples, a trimmings/findings collection, and access to the Internet. FIDM's Costume Museum houses more than 4,500 garments from the seventeenth century to present day. The collection includes items from the California Historical Society (First Families), the Hollywood Collection, and the Rudi Gernreich Collection.

State-of-the-art computer labs support and enhance the educational programs of the Institute. Specialized labs offer computerized cutting and marking, graphic and textile design, word processing, and database management.

Location

Established in 1969, FIDM is a private college that is proud to enroll more than 5,000 students a year. The main campus is in the heart of downtown Los Angeles near the famed California Mart and Garment District. This campus is adjacent to the beautiful Grand Hope Park. There are additional California branch campuses located in San Francisco, San Diego, and Irvine.

Admission Requirements

The Institute provides educational opportunities to high school graduates or applicants that meet the Institute's Ability to Benefit (ATB) criteria to pursue a two-year Associate of Arts degree. Qualifications for professional designation programs include students that meet the general education core requirements or who have a U.S. accredited degree. All applicants must have an initial interview with an admissions representative. In addition, students must submit references and specific portfolio projects if applicable to the chosen major. The Institute is on the approved list of the U.S. Department of Justice for nonimmigrant students and is authorized to issue Certificates of Eligibility (Form I-20).

Application and Information

Applications are accepted on an ongoing basis. All prospective students should contact:

Director of Admissions
FIDM/The Fashion Institute of Design & Merchandising, Los
  Angeles Campus
919 South Grand Avenue
Los Angeles, California 90015
Telephone: 800-624-1200 (toll-free)
Fax: 213-624-4799
World Wide Web: http://www.fidm.edu/

Debut. Student designer: Kim Yen Cao.

FISHER COLLEGE
BOSTON, MASSACHUSETTS

The College and Its Mission

Fisher College, a small, private college for men and women, celebrated its centennial in 2003. Fisher has been a leader in preparing students for challenging careers and facilitating transfer options to four-year colleges. Transfer options also include the College's baccalaureate degree in management. Currently, more than 550 students comprise the College's student body. Students come from all parts of the United States and more than fifteen other countries.

The Academic Center for Enrichment (ACE) is staffed by 20 learning skills specialists and provides a supportive environment in which students develop writing, mathematics, and test-taking skills. The majority of the tutors also serve as instructors, so the tutors have firsthand experience with the subject matter and the students themselves.

Fisher students who graduate with their associate degree have three options once they have completed their program. An increasing number of students are transferring into Fisher College's Management Program. Currently, there are four concentrations in the B.S. Management Program: general management, hospitality management, human resources management, and retail management. Other students join the workforce upon graduation. Still others transfer to a different four-year college or university. Fisher College is fully accredited by the New England Association of Schools and Colleges. Therefore, other institutions accept qualified courses with adequate grades for transfer credit. Academic advisers assist students with the transfer process. Fisher also has several articulation agreements with colleges and universities throughout New England and beyond.

Academic Programs

The programs at Fisher College are designed to help students develop academic and professional skills.

Associate Degree Programs Fisher offers associate degrees in business administration, early childhood education, fashion design, fashion merchandising, health science, interdisciplinary studies/liberal arts, and psychology.

Bachelor's Degree Programs Fisher College now offers a B.S. in management. There are four concentrations in the Management Program: general management, hospitality management, human resource management, and retail management.

Certificate programs are also available.

Internship Program Some of the majors offered at Fisher College require internships. Through the internship program, students gain professional experience that often becomes an employment opportunity upon graduation. Students learn valuable skills that help them build their resumes and they also have the opportunity to establish professional contacts.

Fisher's location in downtown Boston creates the opportunity for countless internship possibilities. Students who take internships gain professional skills, learn business practices, and benefit from hands-on experience. Students have secured internships at businesses such as American Express Financial, Louis of Boston, Bright Horizons, Hilton Hotels, Park Plaza Hotel, and Saks Fifth Avenue.

Special Programs and Services Fisher College offers a summer English as a second language program. The majority of the students attending the Summer Language Institute matriculate into the College full-time in the fall semester. Students entering this program are required to have taken the Test of English as Foreign Language (TOEFL) and attained a minimum score of 400 (paper-based test) or 97 (computer-based test). For further details, students should visit the College's Web site, which is listed in the Application and Information section.

Costs

For the 2005–06 academic year, tuition is $16,775, room and board are $10,475, and the comprehensive fee is $1675.

Financial Aid

The vast majority of students at Fisher qualify for some form of financial aid. Fisher offers both need-based and merit-based scholarships. Need-based awards include the Fisher Trustee Scholarship, Federal Pell Grants, Federal Perkins Loans, Federal Stafford Student Loans, Massachusetts State (Gilbert) Grants, and Federal Work-Study Program positions. Merit-based funds include eight different types of scholarships for incoming freshmen and several different options for transfer students. Students who have graduated from a Massachusetts public high school after June 2003 must pass the MCAS in order to be eligible for state and federal financial aid.

Faculty

The instructors at Fisher College are aware of and are sensitive to students' needs and aspirations. Faculty members are chosen for their academic qualifications and experience. Students find that the instructors are involved in promoting the progress and success of each student. The student-faculty ratio is 20:1. Faculty members and course advisers counsel students during posted office hours and informally throughout the day. Many instructors also work as tutors in the ACE.

Student Body Profile

Ninety percent of all students enter Fisher immediately after high school. Students come from fifteen different states and twelve other countries. The mean GPA for students applying for the 2005–06 academic year is 2.51 on a 4.0 scale.

Fifty percent of all students complete a full-time two-year associate degree program. Sixty percent transfer to a four-year college or university. This includes the students who continue at Fisher and earn their bachelor's degree in the Management Program.

Student Activities

The Office of Co-Curricular Programming is the focal point of campus life and offers a full range of extracurricular activities. Clubs and activities offered vary from year to year, depending on the interest of the students. Recently, the active clubs have included intramural sports, the Multicultural Club, Outdoors Club, Management Club, Ski Club, the Honors Program, Phi Theta Kappa, and the Fashion Show.

Sports Fisher College offers intercollegiate men's and women's baseball, basketball, and softball. All teams are recognized by the NAIA and compete at the Division II level in the Sunrise Conference.

Facilities and Resources

Advisement/Counseling The Office of Co-Curricular Life consists of Residence Life, Co-Curricular Programming, Athletics, Health and Counseling Service, and Career Placement. A faculty adviser is assigned to each student to assist with the selection of courses.

Career Planning/Placement Offices Fisher College's Placement Office offers students a full range of professional services designed to help guide students along the path to a successful career. Trained staff members assist students with developing resumes and interviewing techniques and identifying specific job opportunities. With a 98 percent placement success rate and lifetime assistance, the Placement Office is an invaluable resource.

Library and Audiovisual Services The Fisher College Library contains more than 35,000 volumes and 200 printed periodicals as well as a comprehensive supply of audiovisual materials. The library also provides students with Internet access in the computer labs and residence halls. Students have access to PCs in the computer labs when classes are not held and there are banks of computers in the library and the Academic Support Center. Students also use the Boston Public Library, which is located only a few blocks from the College.

Location

Located in the Back Bay section of Boston, Fisher is a small college in a world-class city. Within a 6-mile radius of Boston, there are more than thirty-six schools and colleges that draw more than 250,000 students to the city annually. This creates an environment that is truly unique—the individual attention and structure that only a small college can offer and the social, cultural, historical, and educational opportunities that make Boston famous.

The campus facilities, dorms, and classrooms overlook either Beacon Street or the Charles River and the Esplanade. The Back Bay is one of the most exclusive and safest neighborhoods of Boston. The city itself becomes a part of the student's college experience. Many of the city's world-famous attractions are within walking distance of the campus, and there is nothing in Boston that is not accessible via subway or bus.

Boston has an outstanding public transportation system; there is a subway stop within four blocks of the College. South Station and North Station offer both bus and rail service for local and interstate travel. Both are only a few stops away on the subway. Logan International Airport is approximately 20 minutes away via taxi. Airport shuttle service is available.

Admission Requirements

The College advocates an admission policy that focuses on the positive attributes in a student's record. Applicants are evaluated based on their academic performance in secondary school. Applicants must submit an official transcript for acceptance and a final, official copy upon graduation from high school.

Students must have a minimum grade point average (GPA) of 2.0 in college preparatory classes, 4 units of English, 3 units of math, 3 units of history/social science, and 2 units of science. Fisher College recalculates a student's GPA and does not factor electives into the new GPA. Improvements over the course of the applicant's high school career, recommendations, a personal statement, an interview, and other supporting credentials are also considered in the decision-making process but are not required.

International students are required to submit original copies of transcripts, state exam results, and results from the Test of English as a Foreign Language (TOEFL). Photocopies are not acceptable forms of documentation. International students should visit the College's Web site (listed in the Application and Information section) for examples of proper documentation.

Application and Information

Applications are received on a rolling basis. The Admissions Committee reviews an application when it is complete with proper documentation. Following a preliminary assessment, the Admissions Committee may request additional documents or require a personal interview. Students interested in Fisher College should contact:

Director of Admissions
Fisher College
118 Beacon Street
Boston, Massachusetts 02116
Telephone: 617-236-8818
Fax: 617-236-5473
E-mail: admissions@fisher.edu
World Wide Web: http://www.fisher.edu

The Administration Building, located on Beacon Street in Boston's Back Bay.

HARCUM COLLEGE

BRYN MAWR, PENNSYLVANIA

The College and Its Mission

Harcum College seeks to provide men and women with outstanding career preparation that meets or exceeds the standards of their chosen professions. At Harcum, self-realization and preparation for participative citizenship are also of great importance. Intent upon remaining among the foremost independent two-year colleges in America, Harcum aims to provide every student with the opportunity not only for a rewarding career but also for a fulfilling life.

Academic Programs

Harcum's academic programs are diverse and fall under four centers: the Center for Allied Health, the Center for Business and Professional Studies, the Center for Legal Studies, and the Center for Liberal Studies and Education. In addition, there are the School of Continuing and Professional Studies, which includes an evening/weekend college, and the Center for International Studies, which includes the English Language Academy. The four centers offer associate degrees and certificates.

Transfer Arrangements The Career and Transfer Services staff assists students in preparing for transfer to a four-year institution. Harcum students have been accepted by more than 200 colleges and universities nationwide and abroad. Harcum has close relationships with many colleges. The College has a number of articulation agreements with four-year colleges, whereby credit is seamlessly transferred to the four-year institution.

Internship and Co-op Programs All of Harcum's programs require an internship as part of the curriculum. Students spend a period of time gaining valuable work experience in a workplace appropriate to their program, where they apply the knowledge they have acquired in the classroom. Many students subsequently receive job offers from their internship sponsors.

Special Programs and Services The College offers a number of special programs to assist students in succeeding at college. Summer Advance is a five-week summer program that gives students an opportunity to adjust to college life while strengthening their academic preparation in reading, writing, math, and other areas. Achieving Individual Motivation for Success (A.I.M.) develops academic and personal skills, cultural awareness, career plans, and lifelong learning tools for students who have disabilities, are economically disadvantaged, or are first-generation college attendees. The English Language Academy offers full- and part-time instruction in English as a second language. The Developmental Program provides courses to strengthen skills in English, math, and reading. Independent study is offered for students who want to study a topic that deeply interests them. A qualified, conscientious instructor guides students in their study, independent of regular classroom attendance. Periodic meetings and discussion seminars are held. The Center for Student Development and Counseling offers personal and individualized career and academic counseling.

Continuing Education Programs The College's School of Continuing and Professional Studies offers programs year-round. Courses are offered for professional development and personal enrichment. Continuing Education Units (CEUs) may be earned in the dental and veterinary fields and in many other fields related to the College's degree programs. Other popular programs include the pharmacy technician training course and the phlebotomy technician training course. For adult students looking to further their education in the evenings and on weekends, Harcum College offers flexible scheduling, a large selection of Internet courses, and an accelerated core curriculum to make the associate degree attainable. The College also offers a full schedule of evening and weekend classes for credit at reduced tuition.

Credit for Nontraditional Learning Experiences

The College awards credit for knowledge acquired outside the usual educational setting by accepting College-Level Examination Program (CLEP) scores for credit toward a degree. The College accepts general and subject examination CLEP scores based on the American Council on Education's recommended cut scores. Students working toward an associate degree may earn a total of 30 credits through CLEP, challenge exams, portfolio-assisted assessment, or traditional transfer.

Costs

The 2004–05 annual tuition for full-time students was $6945 per semester. Tuition for part-time students was $455 per credit. There are additional miscellaneous fees and deposits. Annual room and board charges were $3400 per semester in 2004–05. All fees and tuition are subject to change. In addition, tuition for classes in the evening/weekend college was $185 per credit.

Financial Aid

More than 90 percent of students at Harcum receive some form of financial aid. Available aid includes Harcum grants-in-aid, scholarships, Federal Pell Grants, Federal Supplemental Educational Opportunity Grants, state grants, Federal Perkins Loans, and Federal Work-Study Program awards. The priority deadline for financial aid applications is May 1 for fall enrollment.

Faculty

All of Harcum's programs are led by full-time directors and have full-time professors. Their expertise is augmented by part-time adjunct instructors who usually are practicing professionals in their fields. There are 26 full-time faculty members. Eighty percent of full-time faculty members have advanced degrees, including 13 percent who hold doctorates. The student-faculty ratio is 9:1.

Student Body Profile

The student body is 85 percent women. The largest age group is between 18 and 26, but nearly as many are between 26 and 39 years of age. Seventy percent of the students are white, 16 percent are African American, and 3 percent are Asian. Full-time students make up 68 percent of the total. Commuters account for 83 percent. Eighty-nine percent of the students are from Pennsylvania, primarily from the five-county Philadelphia region. The next-largest group (4 percent) is from New Jersey. International students make up 2 percent. Sixty percent of those accepted to Harcum College enroll. Of those who enroll, 60 percent graduate.

Student Activities

It is easy to get involved on campus. Harcum has clubs and organizations for students with many different interests. Students make their mark on campus by joining one of more than twenty clubs, such as the student newspaper, the yearbook, the Organization for Animal Technician Students, or the Student

American Dental Hygienists Association. The College has a chapter of Phi Theta Kappa, the national honor society for two-year colleges, and Chi Alpha Epsilon, a national honor society for A.I.M. students. The College also organizes many community service activities and events. Students participate in volunteer projects on and off campus, such as peer tutoring, clothing drives, and Earth Day.

Facilities and Resources

Harcum gives students full support throughout their time at the College and after graduation. At the Center for Student Development and Counseling, counselors give a hand with everything from advice on balancing a schedule to resolving a personal problem. The College also has academic tutors to help students with course work.

Students at Harcum have the option of living on campus in the residence halls, which is a great way to make friends and be in the middle of everything that is happening on campus. The residence hall staff plans programs and events, including seminars and discussion groups on topics ranging from study skills to current events, and stress-buster pizza parties.

Students feel at home at Harcum College. Even the students who commute say they do not feel like outsiders. Harcum is a small community, and students quickly find that they recognize friendly faces all over the campus.

Library and Audiovisual Services The library collection has 39,000 volumes, 300 periodicals, and more than 1,000 audiovisual items. It is a member of the Tri-State College Library Cooperative, a forty-two-college consortium, which provides access to more than 6 million volumes. Harcum's library also provides connections to the Internet and FirstSearch, an online database, and it is networked with 20 CD-ROM databases.

Location

Harcum is located in Bryn Mawr, Pennsylvania, 12 miles west of Philadelphia, in the heart of the Main Line, a string of attractive, safe, friendly suburban communities. The College is in the midst of one of the largest concentrations of educational institutions in the country. There are fifty-five colleges and universities in the Philadelphia area. The campus is on a parklike 12-acre site next to a commuter railroad station, which makes travel to Philadelphia and throughout the area easy. Available in Philadelphia are the world-renowned Philadelphia Orchestra, the Pennsylvania Ballet, the Opera Company of Philadelphia, and the world-famous Philadelphia Museum of Art. The city has major-league teams in baseball, football, ice hockey, and basketball. There are numerous historic sites in and around Philadelphia to visit, including Independence Hall, the Liberty Bell, and Valley Forge National Park.

Admission Requirements

All applicants are required to submit official academic transcripts, results of any standardized tests taken, a written essay, and a letter of recommendation. An interview is recommended. The dental hygiene application deadline is February 15. All other programs follow a rolling admission policy. Prospective students should consult the enrollment office for additional requirements specific to each program.

Application and Information

For more information, students should contact:

Office of Enrollment Management
Harcum College
750 Montgomery Avenue
Bryn Mawr, Pennsylvania 19010-3476
Telephone: 610-526-6050
           800-345-2600 (toll-free)
Fax: 610-526-6147
E-mail: enroll@harcum.edu
World Wide Web: http://www.harcum.edu

Library and Academic Center.

HESSER COLLEGE

MANCHESTER, NEW HAMPSHIRE

The College and Its Mission

The primary purpose of Hesser College is to provide a high-quality education that is personalized, cost effective, and employment oriented. Hesser College's innovative approach to higher education provides students increased flexibility compared to traditional colleges. After two years of college, students earn an associate degree and are prepared to enter the workplace, or, if they prefer, students can continue on in one of Hesser's bachelor's degree programs.

Hesser College was established in 1900 as Hesser Business College, a private, nonsectarian college. Since 1972, Hesser College has expanded and enriched its curriculum in keeping with its tradition of providing an affordable career education of high quality. The physical building encompasses more than fifteen different businesses that all create the Hesser Center of Commerce and Education. This is an unusual and beneficial partnership of business and education.

Hesser College is fully accredited by the New England Association of Schools and Colleges. The association is the official accrediting agency for schools and colleges in the six New England states and is widely considered to hold the strictest academic standards. Students who choose Hesser College are assured of a high-quality education.

Academic Programs

The primary goal of the curricula is to prepare students for success in specific career areas. The general education requirements are designed to provide the skills necessary for career growth and lifelong learning. Internships, practicums, and opportunities for part-time work experience are available in all majors. An education from Hesser College provides a solid career foundation. The College's goal is quite simple: to prepare people for careers and career advancement.

Many of the Hesser College programs are for the career-minded student who wants to concentrate on the skills required to be successful in the workplace. Seventy-five percent of the courses that students take are directly related to their career choices. Upon completion of the associate degree program, a student may pursue a four-year degree by enrolling in one of Hesser's bachelor's degree programs.

Associate Degree Programs Hesser offers a wide range of programs that prepare students for high-demand careers. They include accounting; business administration; business computer applications; business science/individualized studies; communications and public relations; corrections, probation, and parole; early childhood education; graphic design; human services; interior design; law enforcement; liberal studies; marketing; medical assistant studies; medical office management; paralegal studies; physical therapist assistant studies; psychology; radio and video production and broadcasting; small-business management/entrepreneurship; and sports management.

Bachelor's Degree Programs Hesser College offers bachelor's degree programs in accounting, business administration, and criminal justice.

Off-Campus Programs

The College offers opportunities for cooperative education and internships in most of its academic programs. The early childhood education program includes practicums and supervised fieldwork in the freshman and senior years, utilizing a variety of child-care facilities. In addition, the curricula of several programs incorporate short-term study tours: business program students study on a trip to Walt Disney World, and criminal justice program students study on a trip to Washington, D.C. The physical therapist assistant studies program requires students to participate in at least 265 hours of clinical experience in a health-care setting under the direct supervision of a certified instructor or therapist. The medical assistant studies program requires 120 externship hours.

Hesser College has relationships with many businesses, and internship sites have been located in the Hesser Center of Commerce and Education, in nearby downtown Manchester, and throughout the state.

Credit for Nontraditional Learning Experiences

Hesser College offers a variety of options for students to earn college credit by means other than taking traditional college courses. These programs enable those students who have reached the college level of education in nontraditional ways (e.g., correspondence study, self-study, or company or military training) to assess the level of their achievement and to use the assessment and/or test results in seeking college credit. These programs allow the student to shorten the amount of time required to obtain a degree.

Costs

Part-time students are billed at the rate of $396 per credit for most majors. Information technology credit rates vary. Full-time expenses per semester in 2004–05 were as follows: tuition (12–16 credits), $5445, and room and board, $3200.

Financial Aid

Hesser College offers financial assistance to students based on demonstrated financial need. Seventy percent of students receive some form of aid. Scholarships are awarded each year to freshman and senior students based on academic and financial standing. The College offers low-interest loans from both internal and external sources. Federal Supplemental Educational Opportunity Grants, the Federal Work-Study Program, Federal Perkins Loans, Federal Stafford Student Loans, and state scholarship programs are available to those who qualify. Awards are made on a rolling basis and are subject to availability. In order to apply for financial aid and scholarships at Hesser College, students must complete a FAFSA and a Hesser College Institutional Financial Aid Application.

Faculty

The faculty members of Hesser College consistently receive high student evaluations for their interest in each student's success and for the high quality of their teaching. The majority of the faculty members have completed programs of advanced study, many hold doctoral degrees, and all have practical experience in business or other career fields. Faculty members participate in national and regional conferences and associations and are continually involved with program review and curriculum development. The student-faculty ratio is 18:1.

Student Body Profile

Nearly 85 percent of the students work in the afternoons, evenings, or weekends while attending Hesser. The 890 men and women currently enrolled represent several states and more than fifteen countries. A large part of the student population is from the New England region.

Student Activities

Hesser College offers intercollegiate sports teams in men's and women's basketball, soccer, and volleyball; men's baseball; and women's softball. The basketball and volleyball teams have consistently been a major power in the Northern New England Small College Conference. Students also participate in a number of intramural sports programs. Extracurricular activities are varied and include social activities, clubs, trips, and programs in the residence halls. A freshman orientation program is conducted each fall before classes begin.

Facilities and Resources

The College includes dormitories for approximately 70 percent of the 890 students. A wide range of resources are located on campus. Academic advising is coordinated through department chairpersons and the Center for Teaching, Learning, and Assessment. The size of the College allows for individual attention to the financial and career counseling needs of each student.

The academic facilities located within the Hesser Commerce and Education Center include five computer labs, a Mac-based graphic design lab, a medical assistant lab, a physical therapist assistant lab, and a radio/video production lab. The College library contains more than 30,000 titles. The Center for Teaching, Learning, and Assessment provides special tutoring and programs in study skills, reading, writing, math, and computer skills.

The College has also developed a number of learning assistance programs to help students succeed in their studies. Tutoring and special classes are provided by the faculty throughout each semester. In addition, several departments offer honor programs and special opportunities for independent study. The College also sponsors an active chapter of the national honor society Phi Theta Kappa, which promotes scholarship and service to the College and the community.

Location

Hesser College is located in Manchester, New Hampshire. With a population of more than 100,000, Manchester is a medium-sized city that offers many cultural, historical, and social events. Hesser College's central location provides easy access to entertainment, shopping, and a variety of part-time jobs and academic work experiences.

Manchester was recently named by *Money* magazine as the number one small city in the northeast United States. In addition, Manchester was recently named as one of the best cities in the United States for business. According to *U.S. News & World Report*, Manchester is "at the hub of things" in the fast-growing, high-technology, financial, and information-oriented businesses of southern New Hampshire.

Manchester is within 1 hour of Boston, and the mountains and major ski resorts are within 1–2 hours of Hesser's campus. Manchester has been called the "Gateway to Northern New England," and several major carriers serve the Manchester Airport.

Admission Requirements

Hesser College's freshman class is selected by a committee made up of administrators and admissions personnel. A high school transcript must be submitted. SAT scores are not required but may be considered in the admission decision if submitted. Transfer students are required to submit a high school and college transcript, with a minimum grade point average of 2.0 for college work.

All applicants are required to come to Hesser for an interview. Hesser recommends that all applicants submit one recommendation from a counselor, teacher, or employer. The College operates on a rolling admission basis, and notification is continuous.

Application and Information

Applicants must submit an application form with a $10 nonrefundable fee. Applications are reviewed on a first-come, first-served basis and normally take seven to fourteen days to be fully reviewed upon receipt of all required information.

Requests for additional information and application forms should be addressed to:

Director of Admissions
Hesser College
3 Sundial Avenue
Manchester, New Hampshire 03103
Telephone: 603-668-6660 Ext. 2110
          800-526-9231 Ext. 2110 (toll-free)
Fax: 603-666-4722
E-mail: admissions@hesser.edu
World Wide Web: http://www.hesser.edu

Students at Hesser College's main campus.

INDIANA BUSINESS COLLEGE
INDIANAPOLIS, INDIANA

The College and Its Mission

Indiana Business College was founded in 1902 to serve the specific education and career needs and interests of students planning to enter the business community. Indiana Business College consists of eleven campuses at convenient locations across the state. Full- and part-time programs, online classes, and day and evening classes are available at all locations. The philosophy behind the curriculum at the College is one of individual attention, allowing for flexibility and higher achievement in the classroom. The career-oriented emphasis enables course work to be highly specialized. Indiana Business College has a commitment to providing career-related education; students are trained by practical application and hands-on experience. This commitment, coupled with a reputation for offering a high-quality education, contributes to the employment opportunities for graduates. The College offers lifetime career assistance to its graduates and is continually updating the curriculum to meet the demands of today's business world. Indiana Business College is accredited by the Accrediting Council for Independent Colleges and Schools and is regulated by the Indiana Commission on Proprietary Education. The medical assisting programs at the Evansville, Fort Wayne, Medical (Indianapolis), and Terre Haute campuses are accredited by the Commission on Accreditation of Allied Health Education Programs on the recommendation of the Committee on Accreditation for Medical Assistant Education.

Academic Programs

Indiana Business College offers Associate of Applied Science degrees in accounting, administrative assistant studies, business administration, business administration/network technology, business and information technology, Cisco Network Associate studies, criminal justice, fashion merchandising, health claims examiner studies, medical assisting, medical coding technology, organizational management, and therapeutic massage and bodyworks.

Indiana Business College also offers diplomas in the areas of accounting assistant studies, medical office assistant studies, medical transcription, and office assistant studies.

Certificates are available in computer network technician studies and therapeutic massage practitioner studies.

Indiana Business College operates throughout the calendar year; classes begin quarterly in January, April, June, and September. To be awarded a degree, diploma, or certificate, students must maintain a minimum cumulative GPA of 2.0 (on a 4.0 scale).

The computer programs at Indiana Business College include courses in Cisco network administration, A+ computer technology, and Network+. The College has some of the state's top information technology programs available, including MCSE and MCSA. IBC is an associate member of CompTIA, offering A+ and Network+ certifications. The College is also a Microsoft IT Academy and one of the only Transcender Training partners in Indianapolis offering on-site testing for all IT certification programs.

The organizational management degree is designed to prepare individuals for careers in project management, where sound business principles and state-of-the-art computer skills are essential for success in today's high-speed, high-technology marketplace. Topics include project integration, human and material resource allocation, risk analysis, cost engineering, procurement management, information technology topics, and e-business. Project managers are employed in every aspect of the business community.

The accounting programs offered at Indiana Business College include courses in intermediate and cost accounting, income tax, and payroll. Both diploma and Associate of Applied Science degree accounting programs incorporate the courses necessary to prepare students for excellent positions in private business, public accounting, and departments within the government.

The Associate of Applied Science degree program in business administration includes courses in the areas of computers, accounting, marketing, management, and sales. This program helps students to develop the creativity and the supervisory skills needed for managerial positions.

Indiana Business College's administrative support programs include administrative assistant studies and office assistant studies. These programs provide students with the necessary foundation in keyboarding, information processing, and computer technology.

The Associate of Applied Science degree program in criminal justice provides students with a broad spectrum of course work in corrections, law enforcement, private security, and investigation. This program is designed to prepare students for a variety of careers in the criminal justice field in both the public and private sector.

The Associate of Applied Science degree program in fashion merchandising prepares the graduate for a career in the fashion industry. Combining business classes with fashion studies prepares the student to succeed in this competitive field. Included in this curriculum are courses such as textiles, display and design, marketing, and apparel merchandising.

Indiana Business College's medical programs include health claims examiner studies, medical assistant studies, medical coding technology, medical office assistant studies, medical transcription, surgical technology, and therapeutic massage studies. The medical assistant studies degree program provides the student with skills to be competent in both front and back office procedures. The medical assistant may assist the physician in minor surgery, perform laboratory tests, assess vital signs, administer medication, operate an EKG machine, or perform other therapeutic modalities prescribed by the physician. The Associate of Applied Science degree program in surgical technology is designed to provide students with an academic and clinical background in the field of surgical technology. Students in this program develop the skills necessary to be a knowledgeable, professional, and responsible member of the surgical team. Programs in medical coding technology provide training to analyze medical records, to assign codes to index diagnoses and procedures, and to provide information for reimbursement purposes. Courses in medical science, medical terminology, medical office administration, and medical insurance processing are offered to help students meet the needs of the industry. The therapeutic massage and bodyworks studies program at Indiana Business College allows graduates to possess the necessary skills for applications and treatment goals of muscular and general relaxation, stress reduction, pain management, recovery from injury, health promotion, education, and body awareness. The successful practitioner must therefore be proficient at more than a simple massage; he or she must understand the body and its functions, master a variety of techniques, and hone such skills as client assessment, communication, and self-evaluation.

Costs

For 2004–05 the cost per credit hour ranged from $154 to $220. Tuition varies according to the program chosen and does not include books or fees.

Financial Aid

Many Indiana Business College students qualify for some form of financial aid. The College participates in the Federal Pell Grant, Federal Supplemental Educational Opportunity Grant, Federal Stafford Student Loan, Federal PLUS programs, the Federal Work-Study Program, the Twenty-first Century Scholars Program, and state grants. Students' eligibility to participate in these programs is contingent upon demonstration of financial need. In addition, the College offers scholarships to both graduating high school seniors and nontraditional students.

Financial planning and financial aid personnel are available to assist the student in the application process.

Students are also encouraged to investigate possibilities for private scholarships.

Faculty

The faculty at Indiana Business College is composed of dedicated professionals who are committed to giving personal attention to every student. The selection of instructors is based not only on their academic credentials, professional training, and business experience, but also on their capacity to develop students' abilities in preparation for the world of work.

Student Body Profile

The student body consists of approximately 3,500 students.

Student Activities

Students may join independent student groups and student councils. Coordinating activities with an executive director or department head, student groups organize a variety of on-campus and off-campus events. Professional organizations are also available for student participation. Intramural sports and group functions vary by campus.

Facilities and Resources

Indiana Business College offers resource centers and computer labs for its students. These facilities provide access to up-to-date information and programs.

Career Planning/Placement Offices The Career Services Department at Indiana Business College assists graduates in securing employment. The Career Services Department offers lifetime career assistance to all alumni and posts job openings for current students and graduates. Students are assisted in all aspects of the job search through career development classes focusing on goal setting, resumes, interviewing, and networking.

Location

Indiana Business College has three convenient Indianapolis locations (northwest, downtown, and southeast) as well as eight other statewide locations. Situated in the heart of Indianapolis, the downtown campus of Indiana Business College houses the Corporate Office for all branches of the College. The excitement of urban living, combined with the cultural and historical sites, makes Indiana Business College's locations ideal. Indianapolis' Children's Museum, Indiana Repertory Theater, and White River Park Zoo provide a variety of educational and recreational activities. The College is within walking distance of downtown shopping centers and major sports centers, such as Circle Centre Mall, Conseco Field House, and the RCA Dome. It is also readily accessible from many different transportation systems.

In addition to the three Indianapolis locations, Indiana Business College has campuses in Anderson, Columbus, Evansville, Fort Wayne, Lafayette, Marion, Muncie, and Terre Haute.

Students may earn credits toward the completion of a program at more than one location. The convenience of having eleven locations and online classes significantly lessens the cost of an education by eliminating additional housing and transportation expenses.

Admission Requirements

Applicants must be high school graduates or have obtained a General Educational Development (GED) certificate to be considered for admission to Indiana Business College. The College reviews each application for admission and bases the admission decision on a personal interview and scores from the Wonderlic Scholastic Level Exam.

The College is open to men and women of any race, faith, or national origin. All students are given equal opportunity to pursue their educational and career goals through the programs offered at Indiana Business College.

Application and Information

All applications must be accompanied by a $50 application fee. High school transcripts are requested directly from the student's school by Indiana Business College. Applicants are notified within two weeks of the completion of all application requirements.

All inquiries should be directed to:

Admissions Office
Indiana Business College
550 East Washington Street
Indianapolis, Indiana 46204
Telephone: 800-IBC-GRAD (toll-free)
Fax: 317-264-5650
World Wide Web: http://www.ibcschools.edu

INTERNATIONAL COLLEGE OF HOSPITALITY MANAGEMENT, CÉSAR RITZ

SUFFIELD, CONNECTICUT

The College and Its Mission

The International College of Hospitality Management *César Ritz* (ICHM), located in the town of Suffield in northwest Connecticut, is the only Swiss college of hospitality management in the U.S. It is one of four internationally acclaimed HOTELCONSULT *César Ritz* colleges, with affiliate campuses in Switzerland and Australia. The mission of ICHM is to prepare students for successful careers in the hospitality industry by combining the renowned Swiss art of hotel management with American business techniques.

With a maximum of 120 students on a 56-acre residential campus set among woods and rolling lawns, the College occupies a former seminary, St. Alphonsus College. Hospitality faculty members have extensive professional experience and instruct alongside liberal studies teachers of the highest caliber. Students receive intensive course training over four 11-week terms. This training is reinforced by a paid internship in prestigious hotels of the U.S.

The internship is an essential component in the program at ICHM. The resulting combination of professional, academic, and practical training provides graduates with a firm base for managing their careers. The internship also supplies ICHM students with a competitive edge in finding employment when they leave the College. The College's Director of Internships and Placements helps guide students in their career development, and HOTELCONSULT has a network of 10,000 alumni to give yet further guidance. In addition, the College organizes career fairs twice each year. The College has a 100 percent placement rate, a record of which it is very proud.

ICHM students are encouraged to actively participate in the social and recreational life of the College, in much the same way that they assume significant responsibilities in managing their academic progress and professional comportment. Because students are very involved in many aspects of College life, a great sense of community has developed at ICHM.

Academic Programs

Associate of Science Degree in Hospitality Management
The first year of the program consists of two 11-week terms, followed by a six-month (810-hour) internship. The first two terms of study are very hands-on, with courses based in practical skills and hotel industry norms. The internship that follows is carefully structured and supervised and enhances the concepts previously introduced in the classroom.

In their second academic year, students develop skills in business planning and strategy, and learn about control procedures and staff management. The second academic year is followed by an optional 810-hour internship, with an option to prolong the internship contract by six or twelve months. Studying abroad is available to those qualifying students who want to take terms three and four in ICHM's affiliate campuses in Switzerland or Australia. (More information on study abroad is in the Off-Campus Programs section.)

Certificate in Hospitality Management
Candidates holding a bachelor's degree in a different discipline or those with professional hospitality experience may choose to enroll in the certificate program in hospitality management. This one-year program consists of two 11-week terms followed by an internship of at least 810 hours. It is designed to provide graduates with the skills and experience necessary to enter the hospitality industry with confidence.

Special Program Services
Career fairs are held twice each year, wherein students and alumni are selected for 810-hour paid internships and positions of longer duration. The fairs are attended by recruiters from approximately thirty leading hotel and resort properties, typically five-star hospitality establishments. Many students receive multiple internship offers. In addition, individual hotel and resort properties often recruit directly on campus.

Transfer Arrangements
Course-credit transfers must be comparable to ICHM courses and must have been awarded by an accredited institution. The student must have earned a minimum C grade (2.0 GPA) for transfer credits to be considered. This information must be provided on official sealed transcripts mailed directly to ICHM's Office of Admissions.

Off-Campus Programs

Students with qualifying grades may wish to take their second year of studies at either the campus on Lake Geneva, Switzerland, or at the campus in Sydney, Australia. The Switzerland option enables students to gain a Swiss Diploma in Hospitality Management. Students electing to go to Sydney receive an Australian Diploma in Hospitality Management. In addition, all students who successfully complete their program, having spent their first year of studies at ICHM, receive an American Associate of Science degree. Students who wish to complete their studies in Switzerland or Australia must give written advice to the ICHM Dean of Academic Affairs before the end of the first term of their first year.

Credit for Nontraditional Learning Experiences

Credit may be awarded for prior professional experience in the hospitality industry. For details, applicants should consult the Registrar.

Costs

Expenses for the 2005–06 academic year include tuition of $15,900 and room and board of $4978. Each student is required to purchase books, uniforms, and supplies.

Financial Aid

To help eligible students meet their educational expense, the College offers financial assistance programs such as scholarships, grants, low-interest loans, and part-time employment opportunities. The College's Financial Aid Officer is happy to work with families on an individual basis to help them plan the cost of education.

Faculty

The student-faculty ratio at the College is 15:1. All full-time faculty members have student advising responsibilities and are involved in the administration of the College. The faculty members have a wide range of international hospitality experience, a diversity that supports the College's mission of offering students an intellectually challenging education in a multicultural environment.

Student Body Profile

The College attracts students from the United States and nearly thirty different countries each year, representing many different cultures. Most students are in their early twenties and, for many, English is a second language. Some are seeking a change of career, others have already obtained advanced qualifications in a different discipline, and all are drawn to the dynamics of international hospitality.

Student Activities

The Student Committee organizes sports, activities, theme nights, and excursions and serves as a representative of all students. Officers of the Student Committee are elected by a democratic vote and arrange meetings and activities with the Coordinator of Student Services. In addition, within the College is a voluntary organization called the Ritz Guild. Its members plan and coordinate events to benefit the local community, often with the help of civic organizations such as the Lions Club and the House of Bread. Each year, Ritz Guild members are given official recognition for their contributions. The College maintains several vans for student activities around the region.

Facilities and Resources

In 2003, the College moved from rural Washington, Connecticut, to a larger, more convenient campus in Suffield, Connecticut. The new location offers an array of activities and amenities to ICHM students.

The meal plan is provided by ICHM's sister school, the Connecticut Culinary Institute, with which it shares a campus. Students can enjoy an excellent regulation-size gymnasium and a modern exercise facility. There are also sports fields and hiking trails on campus. The area has many fine theaters, music venues, restaurants, clubs, and dancing. There are also many well-regarded museums and historic sites within a short distance.

ICHM's spacious library offers more than 10,000 volumes plus numerous industry periodicals and videotapes. The College's computer labs are all connected to broadband Internet services, and the entire building is a wireless broadband environment as well.

Location

The College is situated on 56 wooded acres in Suffield, Connecticut, a charming New England town. Next door to the campus is Six Flags New England Amusement Park, with a new $140-million water park. The 135,000-square-foot building is located minutes from Springfield, Massachusetts, and Hartford, Connecticut. It is a short drive to Boston and New York City and only 10 minutes from Bradley International Airport.

Admission Requirements

The College requires U.S. applicants to submit a completed application form, $100 application fee, official high school transcripts or GED scores, and two letters of recommendation. SAT scores are not required but are highly recommended. Students for whom English is not the first language are required to show proof of English competency. The College seeks applications from both U.S. and international citizens and welcomes motivated students who have a desire to succeed in international hospitality management. The cultural mix of ICHM benefits students as they move towards their chosen profession. Because of the unique nature of the College and its program, applicants are strongly encouraged to schedule an on-campus interview. Prospective students may take advantage of the Visitor Information Program (VIP), wherein they can stay on campus for up to two nights and participate in classes and campus activities. Applicants should contact the Office of Admissions for details.

Application and Information

The College accepts applications throughout the year for its August, November, February, and April starting dates. Applicants are notified of their admission status shortly after their forms are received, usually within two weeks. For application materials and additional information, students should contact:

Office of Admissions
International College of Hospitality Management *César Ritz*
1760 Mapleton Avenue
Suffield, Connecticut 06078

Telephone: 860-668-3515
Fax: 860-668-7369
E-mail: admissions@ichm.edu
World Wide Web: http://www.ichm.edu
            http://www.ritz.edu

The elegant grounds of the International College of Hospitality Management, César Ritz.

JOHNSON COLLEGE

SCRANTON, PENNSYLVANIA

The College and Its Mission

Johnson College, a two-year technical college, was founded by Orlando S. Johnson, a wealthy coal baron in the Scranton area who died in 1912. Mr. Johnson left the bulk of his estate to establish and maintain a trade school, and his purpose became the mission of the College: to be an institution "where young men and women can be taught useful arts and trades that may enable them to make an honorable living and become contributing members of society."

A board of directors was created and a 65-acre tract in Scranton known as the William H. Richmond estate was selected as the site for the new enterprise. Opening in 1918, the school admitted young men and women who had completed a minimum of eight years of school and were at least 14 years old.

In 1964, the school became a postsecondary institution, requiring applicants to be high school graduates or to have equivalency certificates. The name of the institution changed from the Johnson Trade School to the Johnson School of Technology in 1966. The school was incorporated as a nonprofit corporation in 1967, and in 1968 it became licensed by the Commonwealth of Pennsylvania Bureau of Private Trade Schools. Approval to award an Associate in Specialized Technology degree came in 1974, with accreditation by the National Association of Trade and Technical Schools (NATTS) following in 1979. In 1985, the school changed its name to Johnson Technical Institute, and the three-year Associate in Specialized Technology degree programs were changed to two-year programs in 1987.

Responding to the continuing technological changes in society, the board, administration, faculty and staff members, and students conducted an intense two-year self-study, beginning in 1994, to assess the institution's strengths and weaknesses. The study led to a formal application to the Commission on Higher Education for two-year college status. The Pennsylvania Department of Education approved the application of Johnson Technical Institute as a two-year college in 1997. The graduating class of 1998 was the first class to receive either an Associate in Applied Science (A.A.S.) degree or an Associate in Science (A.S.) degree.

Continuing the expansion of technology programs, the College began offering veterinary science technology in 1994. Clinical classes were held off campus until the completion of a 6,500-square-foot Science Center on campus. The program received full accreditation from the American Veterinary Medical Association (AVMA) for the fall semester of 2000. In 1995, electromechanical technology was added to the curriculum, and the Bureau of Private Licensed Schools approved the diesel truck technology program in November 1996. A computer information technology program, specializing in enterprise computer networking, was approved in 2000, and a curriculum in radiographic technology received approval in 2002.

Today, approximately 400 students pursue careers in twelve different technical and clinical programs. The College has eight buildings on campus, including a library, a bookstore, a gymnasium, classrooms, shops, laboratories, administrative offices, and a student apartment complex for on-campus living.

Over the years, the College has served the region by providing a technical education program, and it continually evaluates its program to meet the technological needs of society. This evaluation process is assisted by the Program Advisory Committees of each program area, consisting of regional business and community leaders who meet several times during the year to advise the College on curriculum content, length of programs, and current materials and equipment. They also review placement and retention statistics. The College has maintained the initial intent of Mr. Johnson with a professional and dedicated staff to ensure up-to-date training that prepares graduates to readily step into responsible positions in business and industry.

The current student count is approximately 400, made up of about 60 percent men and 40 percent women. The students spend 70 percent of their time in technological programs and the remainder in general education classes. The College has extensive externships with a variety of businesses and professional organizations. One of the important success stories of Johnson College is its career placement rate. For the last reported year, 97 percent of the graduating class secured positions within twelve months of graduation (based on data gathered from the 125 graduates of the class of 2001).

Academic Programs

Johnson College offers twelve technical and clinical programs, awarding Associate in Applied Science and Associate in Science degrees.

The technology programs include architectural drafting and design, automotive technology, biomedical equipment technology, carpentry and cabinetmaking, diesel truck technology, electrical construction and maintenance technology, electronic technology, machine tool technology, and tool and diemaking technology.

The science programs include computer information technology, radiologic technology, and veterinary technology.

Johnson College is accredited by the Accrediting Commission of Career Schools and Colleges of Technology (ACCSCT), and the veterinary science technology program is accredited by the American Veterinary Medical Association (AVMA). The Pennsylvania Department of Education and the State Board of Education have approved Johnson College as a two-year college.

Transfer Arrangements The College maintains articulation agreements with the State University of New York Institute of Technology at Utica/Rome for the following programs: architectural drafting and design technology, biomedical equipment technology, and electronic technology.

Costs

The tuition for full-time attendance for 2004–05 (12 to 24 credit hours) was $5450 per semester for all programs. Books and supplies were approximately $1500 per school year; however, this amount varied by program. Program fees vary by department. On-campus housing is available in double-occupancy apartments at a rate of $300 per month per student. Students should consult the current College catalog for additional and recent financial information.

Financial Aid

Johnson College provides financial support through the Financial Aid Office, with several programs and opportunities available for students from all income categories. Scholarships are available and are awarded on the basis of merit, academic performance, and extracurricular involvement. The College also participates in the following federally sponsored programs: Federal Pell Grants, Federal Supplemental Educational Opportunity Grants (FSEOG), Federal PLUS loans, and Federal Stafford Student Loans. Other opportunities include employment programs and alternative loans at the College and state and College grants. For consideration for any financial assistance program, students must complete the Free Application for Federal Student Aid (FAFSA). In addition, the College offers $25,000 in merit scholarships for those who are eligible.

Faculty

There are 26 faculty members at the College, and the student-faculty ratio is 17:1. Counseling is available for academic, personal, and vocational issues. The College maintains strong interpersonal relationships among its students and faculty and staff members.

Student Activities

There are a variety of activities available for students on campus, including a Student Government Association, which consists of a student from each technical, trade, and clinical program. The Social Force Club, funded by Act 101, is a community service organization that involves students in on- and off-campus activities, including field trips. Students participate in an active intramural sports program, social functions, holiday parties, talent shows, clubs, and other events and functions.

Facilities and Resources

The Library Resource Center at the College is a technology-based library and is a participating member of the Northeastern Pennsylvania Library Network Consortium. Located in the Moffat Building, the collection consists of more than 4,000 volumes of books and more than 100 current periodical subscriptions. The library complements the curriculum of the academic and technical, trade, and clinical programs. This unique collection offers students the resources necessary to research issues that pertain to their fields of study and for which students should keep abreast of new technological developments. The library also offers online computer services and CD-ROM searching. A professionally staffed cafeteria is available for breakfast, lunch, and snacks. The Moffat Building contains two fitness centers that offer a variety of exercise equipment. A campus bookstore is available for student supplies, clothing items, and a variety of other items. Limited on-campus housing is available in fully furnished two-story apartment-style units.

Location

Johnson College is conveniently located in Scranton, Pennsylvania, at Exit 190 on Interstate 81. Highway exit ramps clearly indicate the location of the campus. The College is just under 2 hours from New York City and Philadelphia. The campus is minutes from great skiing and other recreational activities, along with a variety of sports, arts, music, cultural, and historical events at places like Lackawanna County Stadium (home of the Triple-A Red Barons baseball team), Montage Amphitheater, and the Steamtown National Park and Mall.

Admission Requirements

Johnson College accepts qualified students regardless of race, religion, handicap, or national origin, and admissions are on a rolling basis. The technical core of each program begins in the fall semester; however, students may enroll in general education courses at any time. Applicants should be secondary school seniors, secondary school graduates, or recipients of a secondary school equivalency certificate. Successful completion of one year of algebra is required for all programs. Veterinary and radiologic technology applicants must have successfully completed one unit of biology and chemistry (a grade of C or better is considered successful completion). To complete the radiologic technology program in two years, including summers, entering students are required to have successfully completed one unit of chemistry or biology with a grade of C or better and a minimum of one year of algebra. Each applicant is encouraged to arrange for a campus visit and a personal interview with an admissions representative, and appointments may be made for meeting with appropriate faculty members and current students.

Application and Information

Applications may be submitted in person, by mail, or online at the Web site listed below. Accompanying information must include an official secondary school or equivalency transcript, satisfactory SAT or ACT test scores, one letter of recommendation, and a $30 nonrefundable processing fee. Applicants for veterinary technology and radiologic technology are required to submit a questionnaire and observation hours as part of the application process. The College notifies prospective candidates of a decision within thirty days following the completion of the application procedures.

Additional information may be obtained by contacting:

Office of Admissions
Johnson College
3427 North Main Avenue
Scranton, Pennsylvania 18508
Telephone: 800-293-9675 (toll-free)
World Wide Web: http://www.johnson.edu

KEYSTONE COLLEGE

LA PLUME, PENNSYLVANIA

The College and Its Mission

Keystone College was founded in 1868 as Keystone Academy in Factoryville, Pennsylvania. Initially opened as the only high school between Binghamton, New York, and Scranton, Pennsylvania, Keystone flourished as a secondary school for more than sixty-five years. Rechartered as Scranton-Keystone Junior College in 1934 and then Keystone Junior College in 1944, the College served as one of the premier two-year institutions in the Northeast until 1995. In this year the school was again renamed, as Keystone College, and began its tenure as an "ideal" four-year degree-granting college. Keystone College has a current enrollment of 1,600, including students from fourteen states and seven other countries. Students can choose from twelve different four-year majors and more than twenty-five different two-year degree and certificate programs.

Academic Programs

Associate Degree Programs Associate of Applied Science degrees are offered in accounting, culinary arts, hotel and restaurant management, and information technology. The Associate in Fine Arts is offered in art. The Associate in Arts is offered in communications, forest/resource management, landscape architecture, liberal studies, liberal studies–education emphasis, and wildlife biology. The Associate in Science is offered in biology; business; criminal justice; early childhood education; health sciences with emphasis in medical technology, nursing/cytotechnology, occupational therapy/respiratory care, and radiotherapy/medical imaging/cardiac perfusion; human resource management; and sport and recreation management. In addition, there are one-year programs in Cisco, forestry technology, Microsoft Certified Systems Administrator, Microsoft Certified Systems Engineer, and pre–major studies (undeclared major).

Bachelor's Degree Programs The Bachelor of Arts degree is offered in communications and visual arts. The Bachelor of Science degree is offered in accounting, biology with tracks in the medical professions, business, criminal justice with a track in prelaw, early childhood education, elementary education, environmental biology, forensic biology, human resource management, information technology, sport and recreation management, teaching–art education, teaching–child and society, teaching–special education, and water resource management.

Postbaccalaureate certification is available in elementary education, early childhood education, and teaching–art education (K–12).

The College runs on a two-semester schedule (fall and spring) and has night and weekend classes available. The number of credit hours required to earn a degree is dependent on the field of study chosen, and students must have attained a minimum cumulative GPA of 2.0. Every student must complete a set of general core curriculum requirements as well as the courses specific to his or her major course of study. All students are required to complete one internship or co-op before graduation, depending on the course of study.

Students have the opportunity to participate in both the Army and Navy ROTC programs in conjunction with other local participating institutions. There are opportunities for double majors as well as minors in various fields of study.

Off-Campus Programs

The College maintains articulation agreements with Thomas Jefferson University, College Misericordia, and SUNY Upstate Medical for students enrolling in the health science curriculums. Students enrolled in the environmental programs may opt to pursue Keystone's articulation with State University of New York College of Environmental Science and Forestry (SUNY-ESF) in Syracuse. Other transfer opportunities exist with Marywood University, University of Scranton, Bloomsburg University, Wilkes University, Temple University, University of the Arts, Parson's School of Design, Penn State University, and many others.

Costs

Tuition and fees for Keystone College for the 2003–04 year were $6975 per semester, while room and board costs averaged $3700 per semester. Books and general supplies averaged $500 per semester and vary according to major.

Financial Aid

The Financial Aid Office provides adequate funds and resources to meet the financial needs of students from all income categories. Scholarships are awarded based on merit, academic performance, and extracurricular involvement. Keystone College also participates in the following federally sponsored programs: Federal Perkins Loan, Federal Pell Grant, Federal Supplemental Educational Opportunity Grant (FSEOG), Federal PLUS Loan, and Federal Stafford Student Loan. The College also offers college employment programs to students and alternative loans as well as state grants and Keystone grants. In order to be considered for financial aid, students must complete the Free Application for Federal Student Aid (FAFSA).

Faculty

There are 59 full-time professors and 151 part-time adjunct faculty members. The student-faculty ratio is 10:1, and the average class size is 15 students. Counseling is available for academic, personal, and vocational issues. Keystone College is supported by strong interpersonal relationships among its students and faculty and staff members. All faculty members post regular office hours and are generally available outside of these hours.

Student Activities

Student Senate is the central governing body of all student government organizations on the campus. It serves as the liaison between the student body and the College administration. Members of Student Senate are chosen by their peers and are responsible for improving and maintaining student life both on and off campus. Students may choose from more than twenty-five different clubs and organizations, including those with academic, service-oriented, and social interests.

Facilities and Resources

The Harry K. Miller Library is available on campus to all students. This facility offers standard print and online research opportunities. The Hibbard Campus Center is the setting for the student cafeteria, a full-service restaurant, and The Chef's Table (a student-run restaurant), as well as a U.S. post office, a print shop, a student-run radio station, and reception halls. The campus also includes an art gallery, a celestial observatory, and the Poinsard Greenhouse. Keystone College also serves as the home for the Urban Forestry Center, Willary Water Discovery Center, the Northeast Theatre (TNT), and the Countryside Conservancy.

There are more than 120 computers available on campus for general student use, and both the Internet and campus network can be accessed from all residence halls and most buildings on campus.

Location

Located at the foot of the Endless Mountains in northeastern Pennsylvania, the 270-acre campus is both scenic and historic, with buildings dating back to 1870. Located 13 miles from Scranton, Pennsylvania, the campus offers easy access to major East Coast cities, including New York, Philadelphia, and Baltimore.

Admission Requirements

Keystone accepts qualified students regardless of race, religion, handicap, or national origin, and admissions are on a rolling basis. Admission is based on prior academic performance and the ability of the applicant to profit from and contribute to the academic, interpersonal, and extracurricular life of the College. Keystone considers applicants who meet the following criteria: graduation from an approved secondary school or the equivalent (with official transcripts), satisfactory scores on the SAT or ACT (the SAT is preferred but is not required in all circumstances), one letter of recommendation, and evidence of potential for successful college achievement. All students are strongly encouraged to visit the campus for a personal interview with the admissions staff and a member of the faculty from the

student's area of interest. Students applying to the art and teaching–art education programs are required to participate in a portfolio interview.

Transfer students in good academic and financial standing at their current institution are also encouraged to apply to Keystone. Transfer students should contact the Office of Admissions and may be required to submit either high school transcripts or transcripts from each college attended, or both.

Admissions decisions are made within two weeks from the day all required materials are received in the Office of Admissions.

Application and Information

Students wishing to be considered for admission must submit an application and a $25 processing fee, along with official high school transcripts, college transcripts (if applicable), a letter of recommendation from someone other than a friend or relative, and scores from either the SAT or ACT (submitted directly to the Office of Admissions; Keystone's CEEB code numbers are 2351 for the SAT, 2602 for the ACT).

Applications and any additional information about Keystone College may be obtained by contacting:

Office of Admissions
Keystone College
One College Green
La Plume, Pennsylvania 18440
Telephone: 570-945-8111
        800-824-2764 Option 1 (toll-free)
E-mail: admissions@keystone.edu
World Wide Web: http://www.keystone.edu

Students on the campus of Keystone College.

LANDMARK COLLEGE
PUTNEY, VERMONT

LANDMARK COLLEGE

The College and Its Mission

Landmark College is one of only two accredited colleges in the country designed exclusively for students of average to superior intellectual potential with LD or AD/HD or other specific learning disabilities. Life-changing experiences are commonplace at Landmark College. Simply put, Landmark College, better than any other place on earth, knows how to serve students who learn differently.

Landmark's beautiful campus offers all the resources students expect at a high-quality higher education institution, including a new athletics center, a student center, a dining facility, a café, residence halls, and academic resource centers. The College has also invested substantially in technology and offers a wireless network in all of its classrooms, along with LAN, telephone, and cable connections in all the residence rooms. Notebook computers are required and are used in nearly every class session. The College's programs extensively integrate assistive technologies, such as Dragon Naturally Speaking and Kurzweil text-to-speech software.

Landmark's faculty and staff members make it unique. The College's more than 100 full-time faculty members are all highly experienced in serving students with learning disabilities and attention deficit disorders. More than 100 staff members provide an array of support services that are unusually comprehensive for a student population of slightly more than 400 students.

Academic Programs

Students can earn an associate degree in either general studies or business studies. Landmark College builds strong literacy, organizational, study, and other skills—positioning students to successfully pursue a baccalaureate or advanced degree and to be successful in their professional careers. More than 90 percent of Landmark College graduates go on to a four-year college or university.

With more than 100 faculty members and slightly more than 400 students, Landmark College's small classes and personalized instruction provide a uniquely challenging, yet supportive, academic program. At Landmark College, students learn how to learn.

The College's diverse curriculum includes English, communications, the humanities, math, science, foreign language, theater, video, music, art, physical education, and other classes taught in a multimodal, multimedia environment that is highly interactive. There is no "back of the room" in a Landmark College classroom, and all students participate in class discussions, while building strong academic skills.

Landmark College has articulation agreements with a number of other colleges. These colleges have agreed to admit Landmark College graduates as juniors and transfer all of their credits if they attain a specific grade point average on graduation from Landmark.

Through a carefully sequenced, integrated curriculum, students develop the confidence and independence needed to meet the demands of college work. When students graduate with an associate degree from Landmark College, they are ready to succeed in a four-year college, a technical or professional program, or the workforce.

Off-Campus Programs

The Landmark Study Abroad Program has developed programs with students' diverse learning styles in mind. Landmark College's faculty members design and teach experiential courses in their specific disciplines that fulfill Landmark core requirements, while helping students gain confidence and independence in new academic structures. College faculty members accompany students abroad, providing them with the Landmark College academic experience in an international setting. The College offers summer credit programs in England, Greece, Ireland, Italy, and Spain; in January, a two-week program in Costa Rica is offered.

Costs

Landmark College's tuition for the 2005–06 academic year is $37,000. Room and board costs are $6800. Single rooms or suites are available at an added cost of between $1000 and $1500. A damage deposit of $300 is required.

Since admission to Landmark College requires a medical diagnosis of a learning disability or attention deficit disorder, in most cases, the entire cost of a Landmark College education may be tax deductible as a medical expense. For more information, parents are advised to consult a tax attorney.

Financial Aid

Landmark College participates in all major federal and state financial aid programs, including the Federal Pell Grant, Federal Family Education Loans, and work-study. Institutional scholarships are available. To apply for financial assistance, students should submit the Free Application for Federal Student Aid (FAFSA), the Landmark College Financial Aid Application, and federal tax returns.

Faculty

With the College's low student-faculty ratio, Landmark College faculty members are unusually accessible to students. There are more than 100 full-time faculty members who provide classroom teaching, professional advising, and office hours to students. In addition, faculty members provide individualized instruction throughout the day and into the evening at one of three Centers for Academic Support. Landmark College does not typically employ adjunct faculty members or student teaching assistants. Regular faculty members deliver all instruction. Their depth of experience in serving students with learning differences ensures that students receive the individualized education that is most appropriate to their learning style.

Student Body Profile

Landmark College students come from around the country and from an average of six other countries annually. Approximately two thirds of the student body is men. Ninety percent of all students are residential students living on campus in one of ten residence facilities. Representatives of multicultural groups make up approximately 10 percent of Landmark College students.

Student Activities

Landmark College closely integrates academics and student life. Academic deans, advisers, and faculty members work closely with student life deans and directors to provide a comprehensive program that serves the whole student. The goal is not simply to support academic success, but also to guide and challenge students in their personal and social development. Each student has access to a comprehensive support team, including an academic adviser, classroom instructors, a resident dean, an extensive program of athletics, adventure education, and activities; and a highly trained and experienced counseling department.

For a college its size, Landmark College has an extraordinary range of student-development resources, providing general educational, social, and recreational opportunities. Clubs at Landmark are active. In the past, they have included the Running Club, Monday Night Art, the Multicultural Awareness Club, the Gay/Lesbian/Bisexual/Transgender Alliance, the Mountain Biking Club, the Jazz Ensemble, *Impressions Literary Magazine,* the Coffee House Writers Group, the International Club, the Small Business Management Club, Choral Singing, the Weight Lifting Group, and the Spirituality Group.

Landmark College outdoor programs provide students with a diverse range of outdoor and experiential learning opportunities, including wilderness first-aid training, a ropes course, rock-climbing instruction, an indoor climbing wall, and a full inventory of camping equipment, cross-country skis, snowshoes, and mountain bikes. The College has an active intercollegiate and intramural athletics program that is supported by a well-equipped athletics center that opened in 2001.

Facilities and Resources

Landmark College's residence halls, academic buildings, athletics center, and student center provide a rich array of resources and educational, recreational, and social opportunities. The traditional brick campus, designed by noted architect Edward Durell Stone in the 1960s and entirely renovated beginning in the mid-1980s, includes such amenities as a 400-seat theater, an NCAA regulation basketball court, an exercise pool, three fitness centers, a tennis court, science laboratories, an infirmary, an academic resource center, a bookstore, learning centers, a café, a game room, an indoor climbing wall, and a ropes course.

Location

Located in scenic southeastern Vermont, Landmark College overlooks the Connecticut River Valley, with sweeping views of the mountains and valleys of southern Vermont and northern Massachusetts. Wilderness areas, national forests, ski areas, lakes and streams, and other natural attractions abound. Nearby Brattleboro, Vermont, and the five-college region in the Amherst, Massachusetts, area offer opportunities for culture, the arts, fine dining, and more. Putney is a picturesque Vermont village with several shops, stores, restaurants, a bakery/coffeehouse, a bookstore, and other resources.

The College is located just off Exit 4 on Interstate 91. The most convenient airport is Bradley International Airport in Hartford, Connecticut, about 1½ hours away by car. Metropolitan areas within a 4-hour driving radius include Boston, New York, and Providence.

Admission Requirements

Applicants to Landmark College must have a diagnosis of dyslexia, attention deficit disorder, or other specific learning disability. Diagnostic testing within the last three years is required, along with a diagnosis of a learning disability or AD/HD. One of the Wechsler Scales (WAIS-III or WISC-III) administered within three years of application is required. Scores and subtest scores and their analysis are required to be submitted as well. Alternately, the Woodcock Johnson Cognitive Assessment may be substituted if administered within three years of application. Other criteria for admission include average to superior intellectual potential and high motivation to undertake the program.

The College offers rolling admission and enrolls academic semester students for fall and spring semesters. Students may begin in August (for the fall semester) or January (for the spring semester). The College offers credit-bearing courses each summer in addition to programs for students from other colleges, high school students, and students entering other colleges in the fall.

Application and Information

For more information, students should contact:

Office of Admissions
Landmark College
River Road South
Putney, Vermont 05346-0820

Telephone: 802-387-6718
Fax: 802-387-6868
E-mail: admissions@landmark.edu
World Wide Web: http://www.landmark.edu

Twenty years serving students with learning disabilities and AD/HD.

LEHIGH VALLEY COLLEGE
CENTER VALLEY, PENNSYLVANIA

The College and Its Mission

Located in the Lehigh Valley for more than 134 years, Lehigh Valley College (LVC) is steeped in a tradition of educational excellence. LVC is dedicated to developing people for career positions using hands-on teaching methods, industry-current technology, and externships. The vast majority of graduates are either employed or continuing their education within one year of graduation. Because LVC is a private college, it can put students first and promote an atmosphere in which students can learn, grow, and meet or even exceed their expectations of achievement. Lehigh Valley College is accredited by the Accrediting Council for Independent Colleges and Schools.

Academic Programs

LVC provides career training leading to a diploma or an Associate in Specialized Business or Technology degree. All programs follow the quarterly schedule. These programs are eighteen to twenty-four months long. Associate degree programs consist of prescribed subjects that are divided into periods of instruction approximately twelve weeks in length and offered every twelve weeks.

Associate Degree Programs Accounting: eighteen months (day), 1,568 clock hours, 95 credits. Graduates are qualified for such positions as junior accountant, accounts receivable/payable clerk, bookkeeper, and payroll clerk upon completion of the course.

Computer Programming: eighteen months (day), 1,568 clock hours, 91 credits. The program prepares students for careers in the field of application development and system design. The program enhances the basic philosophies with a detailed study of modern programming languages. Programming skills are applicable to the PC market, the mainframe market, or the emerging Internet programming market. Graduates are awarded the Associate in Specialized Technology degree.

Criminal Justice: eighteen months (day), twenty-four months (evening), 1,638 clock hours, 92 credits. This program prepares students for positions as corrections officers; local, county, and state police officers; campus police; investigators; detectives; child case workers; juvenile service officers; drug task officers; customs inspectors; loss prevention managers; and U.S. marshals.

Hospitality and Tourism Management: eighteen months (day), 1,638 clock hours, 93 credits. After completing their internship, students are prepared for positions in the hospitality industry and tourism field.

Medical Assisting and Office Administration: eighteen months (day), twenty-four months (evening), 1,638 clock hours, 90.5 credits. After an internship is completed in the health-care field, graduates take positions in hospitals, doctors' offices, clinics, and insurance agencies.

Management/Marketing: eighteen months (day), twenty-four months (evening), 1,568 clock hours, 98 credits. Graduates of this program are qualified for entry-level positions in business, banking, insurance, finance, and government.

Personal Computers and Network Technology: eighteen months (day), twenty-four months (evening), 1,568 clock hours, 93 credits. Students are provided with the latest technology, software, and core business subjects to perform entry-level tasks in PC and LAN setups, diagnoses, upgrades, configurations, and repairs.

Visual Communications: eighteen months (day), twenty-four months (evening), 1,568 clock hours, 90 credits. Graduates of this program find employment as entry-level production artists, layout artists, illustrators, and freelance graphic designers. Employment opportunities are in advertising agencies, design studios, art departments, printing companies, and newspaper/magazine publishers.

E-Business Management: eighteen months (day), 1,680 clock hours, 96 credits. The high level of instruction and variety of courses in this program help students gain successful employment by providing skills to design, launch, and manage Web sites for businesses.

Paralegal Studies: eighteen months (day), 1,750 clock hours, 96 credits. This program prepares students for a career in the legal field, doing work with closings, hearings, trials, and corporate meetings; in the business field, helping with contracts; and in the government field, analyzing legal material, doing research, collecting evidence, and writing memoranda.

Diploma Programs Massage Therapy: eighteen months (day), twenty-four months (evening), 1,582 clock hours, 90 credits. This program prepares students for a career in the massage field working is such places as chiropractic offices, clinics, hospitals, health and beauty spas, fitness centers and health clubs, resorts, hotels, and physical therapy centers. Graduates may work from home, an office, or onsite at public events.

Early Childhood Education: eighteen months (day), twenty-four months (evening), 1,540 clock hours, 90 credits. This program instructs students on how to effectively stimulate the emotional, physical, intellectual, and social growth of children in their care. They are also prepared to manage employees, learn about operating budgets, and establish relationships with parents and the community.

Costs

The following costs are estimates and subject to change. Costs for diploma programs include Massage Therapy: $25,200 (estimated cost of books and supplies, $2200; laptop, $2500) and Early Childhood Education: $25,200 (estimated cost of books and supplies, $2200; laptop, $2500). Business associate degree programs are estimated at $26,520 (estimated cost of books and supplies, $2200; laptop, $2500); Other associate degree program costs include E-Business Management: $29,520 (estimated cost of books/supplies, $2400; laptop, $2500); Personal Computer and Network Technology: $29,520 (estimated cost of books and supplies, $3500; laptop, $2500); and the Visual Communications program: $29,520 (estimated cost of books and supplies, $4625; laptop, $2800). All books, supplies, and laptop costs are estimates. All costs are for the entire program. Additional fees include a registration fee of $20 and a graduation fee of $150.

The Education Department evaluates any previous education and training that may be applicable to an educational program. If the education and/or training meets the standards for transfer of credit, the program may be shortened and the tuition reduced accordingly. Students who request credit for previous education or training are required to provide the Registrar's Office with an official transcript from the educational institution.

Financial Aid

The Financial Aid Department devotes personal attention to every student by individually mapping out financial options. In addition to more than $100,000 in scholarships, grants and loans available to those who qualify include Federal Pell Grant, Federal Stafford Student Loan, Federal Supplemental Educational Opportunity Grant, Federal Parent Loan for Undergraduate Students, Federal Work-Study Program, and alternative funding. Scholarships from Lehigh Valley College and Future Business Leaders of America for graduating high school seniors are also available.

Faculty

Lehigh Valley College has more than 100 full- and part-time instructors with either bachelor's, master's, or doctoral degrees in addition to occupational qualifications.

Student Body Profile

There are currently more than 1,500 students enrolled at the College. The students who attend Lehigh Valley College come from a number of areas within a 50-mile radius. All students reside off campus; however, LVC assists with housing when necessary.

Student Activities

LVC has a number of activities and organizations for the students to participate in, such as SIFE, Student Government Association, and various organizations in the program specialties. The students are also encouraged to participate in community events and help raise money for worthy causes.

Throughout the academic year, activities that encourage college spirit and develop student leadership may be offered. The College believes that participation in these activities is an important part of the educational process, and student involvement is encouraged.

Facilities and Resources

Students are provided with facilities that have the latest industry-standard equipment. LVC's new facility houses a variety of teaching and resource tools, including a library, a bookstore, and student lounges. The building also houses six PC labs, three Mac labs, two art studios, and a photography studio. The wireless environment allows students to work freely throughout the campus with access to the network at all times.

Career Planning Lehigh Valley College provides career planning services to all students and graduates. While at LVC, students may take advantage of job fairs and part-time job postings. As students prepare for graduation, career planning representatives assist them with resume writing, interviewing skills, and all other job search techniques to help maximize employment opportunities. Through relationships developed and maintained with employers, the career planning department stays informed about current hiring and industry trends to better serve students and graduates.

Lehigh Valley College assists students in finding part-time employment while they attend college. Assistance includes advice in preparing for an interview, aid with securing an interview, and offering a list of available jobs.

The College encourages students to maintain satisfactory attendance, conduct, and academic progress so they may be viewed favorably by prospective employers. While LVC cannot guarantee employment, it has been successful in placing the majority of its graduates in their field of training. All graduating students participate in the following career planning activities: preparation of resumes and letters of introduction, an important step in a well-planned job search; interviewing techniques, where students acquire effective interviewing skills through

practice exercises; job referral, as the Career Planning Services Department compiles job openings from employers in the area; and on-campus interviews, in which companies visit the College to interview graduates for employment opportunities.

All students are expected to participate in the career-planning program, and failure to do so may jeopardize these privileges.

Alumni may continue to utilize the College's career-planning program at no additional cost.

Location

Lehigh Valley College is located at 2809 East Saucon Valley Road, Center Valley, Pennsylvania. Its new 97,000-square foot building is easily accessible from I-78 and the Pennsylvania Turnpike. It is on a local bus route and within a short driving distance of the Poconos, Philadelphia, and New York. Nearby are Blue Mountain Ski Area, Doe Mountain Ski Area, Dorney Park and Wildwater Kingdom, and the Lehigh County Velodrome. Year-round activities include Musikfest, the Celtic Classic, the Great Allentown Fair, Mayfair, and the Pennsylvania Shakespeare Festival.

Admission Requirements

Students are required to have a personal interview to be accepted into the College. This can be done by meeting with an admissions representative in person. This is also a time to tour the facilities and ask any questions that the student, spouse, or parents may have. Personal interviews enable the College representative to determine whether an applicant is likely to benefit from enrollment into the program. The following items must be included at the time of application: a high school transcript or General Educational Development (GED) test scores, an enrollment agreement (if the applicant is under 18 years of age, it must be signed by the parent or guardian), financial aid forms (if the applicant wishes to apply for financial aid), and the registration fee of $20.

The College reserves the right to reject students if the requirements listed above are not successfully completed.

Prior to beginning at LVC or upon receipt of the student's records, diagnostic testing is used to assess basic learning skills and the student's ability to benefit from enrolling in the College. The diagnostic tests used are the Test of English as a Foreign Language (TOEFL) and the Accuplacer Assessment Exam.

Students who graduate from a high school outside of the United States must have successfully completed the TOEFL with a minimum score of 450.

Application and Information

Lehigh Valley College follows an open enrollment system; applications to the College are accepted at all times. Students should apply for admission as soon as possible in order to be officially accepted for a specific program and starting date. To apply, students should call to set up an interview with one of the admissions representatives. To meet with one of the representatives and tour the College or to get additional information, interested students should contact the address below.

Admissions Department
Lehigh Valley College
2809 East Saucon Valley Road
Center Valley, Pennsylvania 18034

Telephone: 610-791-5100
Fax: 610-791-7810
World Wide Web: http://www.lehighvalley.edu

LINCOLN COLLEGE
LINCOLN, ILLINOIS

The College and Its Mission

The mission of Lincoln College is to assist each student in the development and achievement of personal and educational goals and to ensure that its degree recipients are liberally educated and personally and academically prepared to succeed in four-year colleges. Lincoln College is an excellent beginning for those students with a 15–21 ACT score who desire a residential experience in a supportive atmosphere. Lincoln College has a solid reputation for a high percentage/retention of students who transfer to four-year institutions and is the only two-year residential institution in Illinois.

Academic Programs

Associate Degree Programs The majority of students graduate with an **Associate in Arts** degree. This is designed to provide the student with a liberal grounding in the fundamental areas of human knowledge and allow elective selection of courses of general interest or pre-major preparation. This degree is transfer-oriented and fulfills the general education requirements of most four-year colleges and universities nationwide.

A variety of courses and scholarships exist in the performing arts arena. Subjects include dance, music-vocal, music-instrumental, theater, technical theater, visual arts, creative writing, photography, and speech.

Costs

Costs for the 2004–05 academic year included tuition ($13,600), room and board ($5400), and fees ($570). Textbooks and supplies were estimated at $240.

Financial Aid

Financial assistance is generally determined by the need of the applicant, along with the availability of funds from federal, state, institutional, and private sources. Lincoln College considers the needs of each individual applicant in creating the financial package. Scholarships are awarded for academic, fine arts, and athletic excellence. Approximately 90 percent of Lincoln College students receive financial aid.

Faculty

The majority of Lincoln College faculty members are full-time. They are directly involved in instruction, advising, and counseling. Of full-time faculty members, 100 percent hold advanced degrees. The student-faculty ratio is 16:1, and the average class size is 16.

Student Body Profile

Fourteen different states and six other countries are represented through the Lincoln campus student body. Approximately 650 students attend Lincoln College, and 90 percent are classified as residential. The average age is 18.5. Approximately 89 percent of Lincoln College graduates enter immediately into four-year institutions.

Student Activities

Students may participate in a variety of fine arts activities, including music-vocal, music-instrumental, theater, technical theater, dance, photography, ceramics, visual art, and speech.

Sports Varsity sports for women include athletic training/management, basketball, cheerleading, cross-country, golf, soccer, softball, swimming/diving, tennis, and volleyball. Varsity sports for men include athletic training/management, baseball, basketball, cheerleading, cross-country, golf, soccer, swimming/diving, and wrestling.

Facilities and Resources

Lincoln College was established in 1865 and since that time has grown into a 60-acre campus with ten instructional buildings, a library, a swimming pool, a gymnasium, a performing arts center, a student center, two modern computer centers, an art gallery and studio, the Lincoln Museum and Museum of Presidents, administrative offices, a dance studio, a radio station, seven residential halls, a bookstore, a post office, softball and baseball diamonds, a soccer field, several intramural fields, a weight training center, tennis courts, and several supporting physical plant structures.

The original structure of Lincoln College, University Hall, has been in continuous use since 1866. For both its historic ties to Abraham Lincoln and its Italianate Victorian style of architecture, University Hall is listed on the National Registry of Historical Sites and Places.

Lincoln College is well established in its commitment to a supportive environment. Many programs are designed to assist the student both academically and socially. A very personal approach to education includes the residential component, outstanding faculty members and advising, tutorial services, enriched classes, detailed orientation, academic tracking, and a campus-wide commitment to student achievement.

Location

The city of Lincoln (population 16,000) is located in the geographic center of Illinois. The city is the hub of six major urban areas: Springfield, Decatur, Bloomington-Normal, Champaign-Urbana, Pekin, and Peoria. There are two airports within an hour's drive, and daily Amtrak service to Chicago and St. Louis is available. The College is located directly off of Interstate 55.

Admission Requirements

For freshman students, acceptance to Lincoln College is based on high school record, standardized test scores, a personal interview, and letters of recommendation. Students with an ACT composite score of 16 or better may be admitted without restriction. Those with an ACT composite score of 15 or lower may be admitted on provisional status. The admissions committee also considers high school transcript data, and high school counselor recommendations are given a high priority. Students entering Lincoln College provisionally are required to attend and successfully complete the Academic Development Seminar, which occurs one week prior to the fall semester. Students who are transferring to Lincoln College from another college or university may enter the College at the beginning of any semester. If they were on probation at the previous institution and/or maintained less than a 2.0 GPA (on a 4.0 scale), they may be admitted to Lincoln College on provisional status as well. Students for whom English is a second language must take the TOEFL examination and have their scores sent to Lincoln College. Any international student with a minimum score of 480 on the Test of English as a Foreign Language (TOEFL) will be granted admission to Lincoln College. Students whose scores are below 480 may be granted conditional acceptance if space is available.

Application and Information

Applications are accepted contingent on the availability of housing. Freshmen are encouraged to apply before July 1. Individuals interested in Lincoln College should contact:

Lincoln College Admissions
Lincoln College
300 Keokuk
Lincoln, Illinois 62656
Telephone: 217-732-3155
             800-569-0556 (toll-free)
Fax: 217-732-7715
E-mail: tschilling@lincolncollege.com
World Wide Web: http://www.lincolncollege.edu

Lincoln College is well established in its commitment to a supportive environment.

LINCOLN COLLEGE AT NORMAL

NORMAL, ILLINOIS

The College and Its Mission

Lincoln College, a private two-year residential college, has been offering students the opportunity to study and succeed in a highly supportive environment since 1865. Accredited by the North Central Association of Colleges and Schools, Lincoln offers Associate in Arts, Associate in Science, Associate in Applied Science, Bachelor of Arts, and Bachelor of Science degrees.

The mission of Lincoln College is to assist each student in the development and achievement of personal and educational goals and to ensure that degree recipients are liberally educated and personally and academically prepared to succeed in four-year colleges and/or careers. The College is an excellent beginning for those students with a 15–21 ACT score who desire a residential experience in a supportive atmosphere.

Lincoln College has a national reputation for academic achievement, and the College's associate degree graduates have continued their studies at more than 200 different four-year colleges and universities in the last decade. Small class sizes, outstanding faculty advisement, free professional tutoring, and a residential experience result in approximately 89 percent of Lincoln College graduates entering immediately into four-year institutions. In addition, the College added new bachelor's degree programs for liberal arts and business management during the 2001–02 academic year.

Lincoln College at Normal opened in 1979 as an extension of Lincoln College in Lincoln, Illinois. Today, Lincoln College at Normal has two modern academic facilities on campus, which house classrooms, laboratories, and administrative offices. In addition, five student residential units are available on campus, offering apartment/suite-style living with private bedrooms and shared kitchens and living rooms. Students also enjoy a new Student Activity Center on campus. Coexisting in the Bloomington-Normal area with a major state university as well as a private four-year college, Lincoln College at Normal offers students the excitement and diversity of a large university community while still preserving the benefits of a small-college atmosphere.

Academic Programs

The College is on a two-semester schedule, with fall and spring components. A limited number of classes are also offered in the summer.

Bachelor's Degree Programs In the fall of 2001, Lincoln College at Normal established two new bachelor's degree programs: a Bachelor of Arts in liberal arts and a Bachelor of Science in business management. These programs are organized in a "2+2" structure, where students must first complete an Associate in Arts or an Associate in Science degree (or the equivalent) before being accepted to the bachelor's degree program.

Associate Degree Programs The Associate in Arts degree is designed to provide the student with a liberal grounding in the fundamental areas of human knowledge and allow a variety of elective selection of courses of general interest or premajor preparation. This degree is transfer-oriented and fulfills the general education requirements of most four-year colleges and universities nationwide. Typical premajor interests include American studies, art, biology, business administration, chemistry/physics, criminal justice, education, English/literature, environmental science, history/political science, law enforcement, mathematics, media/journalism, music, philosophy and religion, physical education, prenursing, psychology, sociology, speech, and theater. The College also offers an Associate in Science

degree, where more emphasis is placed upon math and science, as well as Associate in Applied Science degrees in cosmetology and travel/tourism.

Certificate and Diploma Programs These programs are typically completed in one year and include cosmetology, managerial training, and travel/tourism.

Costs

Costs for the 2005–06 academic year include tuition, $14,300; room and board, $5500; and fees, $570. Textbook rentals and supplies are estimated at $300.

Financial Aid

Approximately 95 percent of students at Lincoln College at Normal benefit from some type of financial aid each year. Financial assistance is generally determined by the need of the applicant (from the Free Application for Federal Student Aid) along with the availability of funds from federal, state, institutional, and private sources. Lincoln College considers the needs of each individual applicant in creating the financial aid package. Scholarships are also awarded for academic, fine arts, and athletic excellence.

Faculty

The majority of Lincoln College faculty members are full-time. Their direct involvement with students includes instruction, advisement, and counseling. Of the full-time faculty, 100 percent hold advanced degrees. The student-faculty ratio is 14:1, and the average class size is 16.

Student Body Profile

Six different states and three other countries are represented through the approximately 550 students enrolled at Lincoln College at Normal. Approximately 70 percent of students are full-time and 64 percent of the full-time students reside on campus. The average age of the student body is 19. Typically, 72 percent of students graduate on time with a two-year degree, with 89 percent of those students transferring successfully either to the bachelor's degree program on campus or to a four-year university the following semester.

Student Activities

Student Government The members of the Student Government Association are committed to proactively effecting change in the best interests of the student body, furthering the cultural and social growth of the student body, and generally advocating the interests of the student body to the College and community.

Student Activities The Student Activities Committee works to get the student body involved both in the College and in the various extracurricular activities. Student activities include intramural sports, outdoor activities (camping, canoeing, etc.), volunteering and community service events, music concerts, shopping trips, and athletic events.

Fine Arts Students may participate in a variety of fine arts activities, including the areas of visual arts, theater, and music.

Sports Opportunities in intramural athletics are available on campus as well as through the intramural programs offered at neighboring Illinois State University. Students also have access to the Student Recreation Complex at Illinois State University for exercise and workout needs. Opportunities in varsity athletics are available through the campus in Lincoln, Illinois.

Facilities and Resources

Lincoln College at Normal consists of two modern academic facilities with classrooms, laboratories, an art center, a state-of-the-art lecture hall, and administrative offices. In addition, five student residential buildings are located on campus, offering apartment/suite-style living with private bedrooms and shared kitchens and living rooms. This represents the primary housing option for students, with private off-campus apartment housing also available in the community. In addition, the Student Activity Center opened on campus in 2002. It houses the Student Activities office and also features workout facilities, a multimedia room, a game room, a snack bar, and meeting spaces.

Advisement/Counseling Trained full-time faculty members assist students in selecting courses and programs of study to satisfy their educational objectives. The Learning Resource Center provides free professional tutoring to all students in any subject. This takes the form of one-on-one sessions as well as online tutorial programs. Students can also make up assignments and do extra credit projects under the direction of the Learning Resource Center personnel.

Recreation/Career Counseling/Placement Services Students enjoy full access and privileges to each of these facilities and offices at Illinois State University as part of their enrollment at Lincoln College at Normal.

Health Services Lincoln College students at the campus in Normal may also elect to take advantage of the student health center at Illinois State University in Normal. This offering is available on an à la carte basis and can be arranged with the assistance of the Lincoln College Housing personnel.

Library and Audiovisual Services Lincoln College students at the campus in Normal have library privileges for the Illinois State University library in Normal, with a combined book collection of 1,659,983 volumes. CD-ROM and online databases are also available for student use. The College offers two state-of-the-art computer labs for classroom, homework, and project use. These labs have more than forty computers for the students' use, all with Internet access. In addition, the student housing on campus features high-speed Internet access in every bedroom, and additional computers are also available in the Student Activity Center.

Location

Lincoln College at Normal is located in the city of Normal near the geographic center of Illinois, and with the adjoining city of Bloomington, has a population of more than 100,000. The College is situated on 10 acres of land approximately two blocks west of Route 51 (North Main Street) in north Normal, just off Interstate 55. The Bloomington/Normal area is served by three interstate highways, I-55, I-74, and I-39. It also features an airport, bus service, and Amtrak service. Driving time from Chicago and St. Louis is 2½ hours.

Admission Requirements

Associate Degree Program Acceptance to the associate degree program at Lincoln College at Normal is based on a student's high school record, standardized test scores, a personal interview, and letters of recommendation. Students with a minimum ACT composite score of 17 may be admitted without restriction. Those with an ACT composite score of 16 or less may be admitted on provisional status, based on the decision of the Admissions Committee. Students who are transferring to Lincoln College at Normal from another college or university may enter the College at the beginning of any semester. If they have been on academic probation at the previous institution and/or have maintained less than a 2.0 GPA (on a 4.0 scale), they may be admitted to the College on provisional status as well. Students for whom English is a second language must take the TOEFL examination and have their scores sent to the College. Any international student with a minimum score of 157 (computer-based) on the TOEFL may be granted admission to Lincoln College. Students whose scores are below 157 may be granted conditional acceptance if space is available.

Bachelor's Degree Program Students who are applying to the bachelor's degree program are required to have earned an Associate in Arts or Associate in Science degree or the equivalent at an accredited institution in order to be admitted without restriction. Students who have not yet met this requirement may be admitted on a conditional basis, based on the decision of the Admissions Committee.

Application and Information

Applications are accepted on a rolling basis and housing on campus is contingent on availability. All students are encouraged to apply before June 1 for the fall semester. Individuals interested in Lincoln College at Normal should contact:

Lincoln College Admissions
Lincoln College at Normal
715 West Raab Road
Normal, Illinois 61761
Telephone: 309-452-0500
           800-569-0558 (toll-free)
Fax: 309-862-3352
E-mail: admissions@lincoln.mclean.il.us
World Wide Web: http://www.lincolncollege.edu/normal

Students enjoy various activities on campus at Lincoln College at Normal.

MANOR COLLEGE
JENKINTOWN, PENNSYLVANIA

The College and Its Mission

Manor College is a private, coed Catholic college founded in 1947 by the Ukrainian Sisters of Saint Basil the Great. The College is characterized by its dedication to the education, growth, and self-actualization of the whole person through its personalized and nurturing atmosphere. Upon graduation, 40 percent of Manor's students are employed in their chosen fields; the remaining 60 percent of students transfer to four-year institutions to earn baccalaureate degrees. There are approximately 800 full- and part-time students enrolled at Manor. Extracurricular activities include honor societies and men's and women's intercollegiate soccer and basketball as well as the yearbook and special interest and cultural clubs. Manor provides free counseling and tutoring services through an on-campus learning center. Trained counselors are available to assist students on an individual and confidential basis for academic, career, and personal concerns. Upon entering Manor, students are assigned an academic adviser, who provides guidance and support throughout their Manor experience. Transfer counseling is available for students interested in pursuing a four-year degree. The College's 35-acre campus includes a modern three-story dormitory, a library/administration building, and an academic building that also houses the bookstore, dining hall, an auditorium/gymnasium, and a student lounge. The Ukrainian Heritage Studies Center and the Manor Dental Health Center are also located on the campus grounds. Manor is accredited by the Middle States Association of Colleges and Schools.

Academic Programs

Manor offers career-oriented, two-year associate degrees, as well as transfer programs for the purpose of pursuing a bachelor's degree. Internships provide theory with practice, enhancing employment opportunities. The liberal arts core ensures a common breadth of knowledge along with mobility and future advancement. Manor offers ten programs with twenty-three majors/concentrations leading to associate degrees and transfer programs through its three divisions: Liberal Arts, Allied Health/Science/Mathematics, and Business.

The Liberal Arts Division offers **Associate in Arts** degrees in early childhood education, psychology, and liberal arts. In addition, the Liberal Arts Division provides a liberal arts transfer major as well as an elementary education transfer major, an early child-care major, a three-year English as a second language (ESL) concentration, a concentration in catechetical education, and a concentration in communications. The Allied Health/Science/Mathematics Division offers **Associate in Science** degrees in dental hygiene, expanded functions dental assisting, and veterinary technology. This division also includes allied health and science transfer programs for students who seek preprofessional programs in biotechnology, cytotechnology, diagnostic imaging, funeral science, general sciences, medical technology, nursing, occupational therapy, physical therapy, prepharmacy, and pre–veterinary animal science. The Business Division offers **Associate in Science** degrees in accounting, business administration, business administration/computer science, business administration/human resource management, business administration/international business, business administration/management, business administration/marketing management, and paralegal studies. There are four certificate programs. There are a PC technician/computer support specialist studies certificate and a certificate program in paralegal studies for students who have a bachelor's degree, as well as a legal nurse consultant certificate. A certificate program in catechist/educator development is offered for both Roman and Byzantine rites. Manor also offers selected courses through two modes of distance learning: online Web-based learning and teleconferencing.

The Office of Continuing Education serves adult learners by providing educational options for those who want to attend college on a part-time basis. The office also supports the needs of the community and business and industry by offering noncredit classes and workshops, as well as on- and off-site corporate training programs, throughout the year. Approved as an authorized provider by the International Association for Continuing Education and Training, the office also grants continuing education units (CEUs) for selected professional development courses each semester.

Off-Campus Programs

Externships are incorporated into the academic studies programs. Students earn credits as they gain practical experience under the supervision of professionals in a specific field of study. Externships are offered in the career-oriented programs of study and in some transfer programs. Manor's affiliation with several area hospitals, as well as Manor College's on-campus Dental Health Center, enables the allied health program student to fulfill clinical requirements at these sites. Students in other programs serve externships in law offices, courtrooms, day-care centers, businesses, health-care organizations, and veterinary facilities. Manor has dual admissions, 2+2, and 2+3 articulation agreements with major allied health universities, hospitals, and local universities.

Credit for Nontraditional Learning Experiences

Manor College awards credit by examination for college-level learning through the College-Level Examination Program (CLEP). Manor administers exemption tests for courses not available through CLEP. Adults may also receive college credit for military experience and education through the Army/American Council on Education Registry Transcript System (AARTS), by submitting a transcript to Manor for evaluation of credits, and by requesting assessment of previous life and job experiences through nontraditional means.

Costs

Tuition for the 2004–05 academic year was $10,046 for full-time studies. Part-time study was $220 per credit hour. Students in certain allied health programs paid an additional $470 per year for full-time study or an additional $95 per credit hour for part-time study. On-campus room and board are available for men and women and cost $4900 a year. There is an additional $800 fee for a private room. Other fees included a $350 general fee per year and a $100 graduation fee.

Financial Aid

Manor College offers need-based financial aid to eligible applicants in the form of grants, loans, and campus employment. Scholarships are awarded on the basis of academic promise. Approximately 85 percent of Manor's students receive some form of financial aid. Federally funded sources include the Federal Pell Grant, Federal Supplemental Educational Opportunity Grant, Federal Perkins Loan, Federal Stafford Student Loan, Federal PLUS loan, and Federal Work-Study Program. State-funded programs offered are the PHEAA State Grant and State Work-Study programs. The institutionally funded sources are the Manor Grant and the Resident Grant. Scholarships available for attendance at Manor include the following: Manor Presidential Scholarship; Joseph and Rose Wawriw Scholarships; Henry Lewandowski Memorial Scholarship; Elizabeth A. Stahlecker Memorial Scholarship; Mary Wolchonsky Scholarship; John Woloschuk Memorial Scholarship; Lorraine Osinski Keating Memorial Scholarship; Yuri and Jaroslava Rybak Scholarship; Dr. and Mrs. Volodymyr and Lydia Bazarko Scholarship; Heritage Foundation Scholarship of First Securities Federal Savings Bank; Father Chlystun Scholarship; Sesok Family Memorial Scholarship; Eileen Freedman Memorial Scholarship; Manor Allied Health,

Science, and Math Division Scholarship; Business Division Scholarship; Liberal Arts Division Scholarship; Basilian Scholarships; Scholar Athlete Award; St. Basil Academy Scholarship; Wasyl and Jozefa Soroka Scholarships; and International Scholarships. Scholarship eligibility requirements vary; details are available from the Admissions Office.

Faculty

There are 23 full-time and 119 part-time faculty members at Manor. Forty-five percent of the faculty members have master's degrees and 32 percent possess doctorates in their field. Faculty members spend three fourths of their time teaching and the remainder counseling and advising students. The overall faculty-student ratio is 1:14. Small class size allows for personal attention in an environment conducive to learning.

Student Body Profile

Of the approximately 800 full- and part-time students enrolled at Manor, 207 entered the College as full-time freshman students in fall 2002. Twenty percent of that freshman class lived in the on-campus residence hall. Seventeen percent of the recent freshman class were members of minority groups, and 9 percent were international students from Albania, Brazil, India, Jamaica, Japan, Korea, Liberia, Nigeria, Poland, Sierra Leone, Ukraine, and Uzbekistan.

Student Activities

Manor encourages students to develop leadership skills through active participation in all aspects of College life. A variety of options for extracurricular participation fall under the umbrella of Manor's student services department, including the Student Senate, athletic teams, and clubs. The Student Senate forms an important part of the College community. The Senate, representing the student population, responds to student interests and concerns and acts as a liaison between the administration and the student body. Other extracurricular activities include intercollegiate men's and women's basketball and soccer. Manor's sports teams compete in the Eastern Pennsylvania Collegiate Conference. Additional extracurricular activities include the honor societies, intramural sports, the yearbook, and various special interest and cultural clubs. Student services is also responsible for the campus ministry, the counseling center, the residence hall, and the on-campus security force.

Facilities and Resources

The Academic Building (also called Mother of Perpetual Help Hall) includes classrooms, lecture rooms, laboratories, the chapel, and the Offices of Student Services, Campus Ministry, and Counseling. The Academic Building is equipped with up-to-date facilities, including biology, chemistry, and clinical laboratories, as well as modern IBM-compatible microsystems network labs. The Learning Center provides professional and student tutors in all College subjects and conducts workshops in study and research skills. Courses in English as a second language are also offered at the center.

The Basileiad Library has the capacity for 60,000 books, periodicals, and journals. The library includes a reserve room, reading areas, a micromedia room, and stack areas. The current library collection contains 50,000 volumes, including a special law collection, and subscriptions to 206 periodicals and newspapers. The library also houses the Small Business Resource Center, which helps local businesses with the solutions to everyday problems. An on-campus community Manor Dental Health Center was established in 1979 as an adjunct to the Expanded Functions Dental Assisting (EFDA) Program. Located on the lower level of St. Josaphat Hall, the center provides students enrolled in the EFDA Program or the Dental Hygiene Program at Manor with training under the direct supervision of faculty dentists. Currently, more than 2,000 patients receive care, including the following services: general dentistry, oral hygiene, orthodontics, prosthodontics, endodontics, and cosmetic dentistry. Because Manor Dental Health Center is a teaching facility, the fees charged for services are lower than those charged by private practitioners. Community residents are welcome as patients. The

Ukrainian Heritage Studies Center, located on the campus, preserves and promotes Ukrainian heritage, arts, and culture through four areas: academic programs, a museum collection, a library, and archives. Special events, exhibits, workshops, and seminars are offered throughout the year. The center is open to the public for tours and educational presentations by appointment.

Location

Manor is located in Jenkintown, Pennsylvania, 15 miles north of Center City Philadelphia. Manor is accessible via public transportation and is located near the Pennsylvania Turnpike, Route 611, U.S. 1, and Route 232. Centers of cultural and historic interest are found in nearby Philadelphia, Valley Forge, and beautiful Bucks County. Manor's suburban campus is within walking distance of a large shopping mall, medical offices, and a township park.

Admission Requirements

Manor is open to qualified applicants of all races, creeds, and national origins. Candidates are required to have a high school diploma or its equivalent. Admission is based on the applicant's scholastic record, test scores, and interviews. The application procedure involves submission of a completed application form, a high school transcript, SAT or ACT scores (required for students less than 21 years old), an interview, and Manor's entrance/placement test (waived for candidates who hold the baccalaureate degree). Transfer students must submit transcripts of all college work completed. International students must also submit results of the Test of English as a Foreign Language (TOEFL) or, for the Liberal Arts/ESL program, must have completed two years of English language study at the high school or college level in their native country.

Application and Information

Manor has a rolling admission policy. Students may apply for admission in either the fall or the spring semester. Interested students are invited to visit the campus and meet with admissions staff, faculty members, program directors, and students. Open houses, career days and nights, and classroom visits are scheduled throughout the year. The Admissions Office is open Monday through Friday, 8:30 a.m. to 6 p.m. (Saturday hours are by appointment). Admissions staff members can schedule visits and answer questions concerning admission, careers, programs, special features, and student life. For application forms, program-of-study bulletins, and catalogs, students should write to:

I. Jerry Czenstuch
Vice President of Enrollment Management
Manor College
700 Fox Chase Road
Jenkintown, Pennsylvania 19046
Telephone: 215-884-2216
E-mail: ftadmiss@manor.edu
World Wide Web: http://www.manor.edu

Manor College students relax between classes on the steps outside Mother of Perpetual Help Hall.

MARIA COLLEGE
ALBANY, NEW YORK

The College and Its Mission

Maria College was established in 1958 by the Religious Sisters of Mercy as an independent two-year, degree-granting institution. The College is career oriented and admits both men and women. The current enrollment is 688; about 90 percent are women. It is accredited by the Middle States Association of Colleges and Schools.

Located in a quiet corner of New York State's capital, Albany, Maria College concentrates on preparing its students for productive careers in health, education, and business. Nursing graduates are prepared for the state examination for licensure as registered nurses. The occupational therapy assistant studies and physical therapist assistant studies programs lead to certification by the state of New York upon graduation. In addition, following an examination, occupational therapy assistants are certified by the American Occupational Therapy Association.

The College's Career Planning and Placement Office is responsible for counseling students and alumni on career development, helping students obtain employment upon graduation, and assisting students in the process of transferring to other institutions. With the cooperation of program chairpersons, this office conducts seminars on resume preparation, interviewing techniques, and the job search. Individual counseling is available. Placement Office records show nearly 100 percent employment and/or transfer to four-year schools for Maria College graduates over the past fifteen years.

Academic Programs

Associate Degree Programs Maria College offers the **Associate in Applied Science (A.A.S.)** degree in allied health (nursing, occupational therapy assistant studies, and physical therapist assistant studies), business sciences (accounting, legal assistant studies, and management), computer information systems, and early childhood education. The **Associate in Arts (A.A.)** degree is offered in liberal arts. The **Associate in Science (A.S.)** degree is offered in general studies. Degrees are conferred on students who have completed at least 64 college credits through courses taken at Maria, transfer credit, credit earned through approved proficiency examinations, or life experience credit. Graduates also must complete the College's requirements of 6 credit hours in religious studies/philosophy and 6 credit hours in English. The required liberal arts core consists of 48 credit hours for an A.A., 32 credit hours for an A.S., and 22 credit hours for an A.A.S. An overall quality point average of at least 2.0 (on a 4.0 scale) is also required.

In addition to traditional day classes, Maria College's Evening Division offers degree programs in accounting, computer information systems, general studies, liberal arts, management, nursing, and physical therapist assistant studies. For those who are unable to attend during the day and seek programs for enrichment or a career change, credit-free evening courses, seminars, and workshops are also provided.

The first Weekend College to be established in northeastern New York is conducted at Maria. This innovative, degree-granting option allows students to complete degree programs in business, computer information systems, general studies, legal assistant studies, and liberal arts by attending classes every other weekend for two years. The occupational therapy assistant studies program takes three years to complete.

Students who wish to continue studies toward a baccalaureate degree may complete the first two years of study at Maria and then transfer to a senior institution for the next two years. To facilitate such a transfer, Maria College has articulation agreements with a wide range of senior colleges. For nursing students, for example, articulation agreements exist with the baccalaureate nursing program at Russell Sage College in Troy, New York, and with the College of Health Related Professions of the State University of New York Health Science Center at Syracuse.

Certificate Programs Certificate programs are available in bereavement studies, complementary therapy, gerontology, and legal assistant studies. The legal assistant studies certificate is available only for those with associate or bachelor's degrees.

Off-Campus Programs

Clinical laboratory experiences for nursing students are provided at Albany Medical Center, Our Lady of Mercy Life Center, and St. Peter's Hospital. Students in the occupational therapy assistant and physical therapist assistant programs receive clinical training in hospitals, developmental centers, nursing homes, and rehabilitation centers in New York State and at selected sites in other states. Senior students in the early childhood education program are trained in a variety of outside field agencies, which may include day-care centers, home-based centers, Head Start, and centers providing programs for infants and toddlers or for children with special needs.

Credit for Nontraditional Learning Experiences

Maria College recognizes college-level courses taken by students while they are still attending high school. Advanced Placement scores of 5, 4, and 3 normally earn college credit. Maria College grants credit for the Regents College Examinations and the College-Level Examination Program (CLEP) when these examinations cover comparable material. Proficiency credits are treated as transfer credits.

Maria College recognizes that certain adult students may have gained valuable knowledge in their lives from diverse experiences. Some of this learning may qualify as college-level course work. Students requesting credit are required to substantiate this learning experience. Total credit obtained through life experience is limited to a maximum of 16 nonduplicative transfer credits applied toward a degree, 25 percent of the required 64 credits.

The Nursing Program offers advanced placement for licensed practical nurses, who may challenge 7 credits in nursing. A series of classes is held twice a year to assist licensed practical nurses in meeting the requirements for challenge. Each candidate for advanced placement must be successful in both a written and a skill examination.

Costs

Tuition for the 2002–03 academic year was $6300 for full-time study and $230 per credit hour for part-time study. Fees were $100 per academic year (higher for those in the allied health programs). The College does not provide housing, but arrangements for off-campus housing may be made through the Admissions Office.

Financial Aid

Tuition Assistance Program (TAP) awards are available to New York State residents only. Financial aid is available to students through Federal Stafford Student Loans, Federal PLUS loans, Federal Perkins Loans, Federal Nursing Loans, Federal Pell Grants, Federal Supplemental Educational Opportunity Grants, and Federal Work-Study Program awards. Also available to those qualifying are the Regents Awards for Children of Deceased or Disabled Veterans and Disabled Policemen and Firefighters, State Aid to Native Americans, and Veterans Administration educational benefits. Approximately 50 percent of the College's students receive aid. To apply for aid, students must submit both the Free Application for Federal Student Aid (FAFSA) and the NYS TAP form.

Faculty

Maria College has full- and part-time faculty members. Every freshman is assigned to a faculty adviser, who encourages communication and a strong working relationship. The student-faculty ratio is 8:1.

Student Body Profile

For the entering fall 2001 class, 23 percent were first-time freshmen. Approximately 85 percent of all students were from a radius of 50 miles from the College. Nonresident aliens made up less than 1 percent of the student body, and approximately 22 percent of full-time enrollees belonged to a minority group. Seventy percent of students were older than 25. Maria College is a commuter-based institution; less than 10 percent of students seek housing through the Admissions Office.

Student Activities

Student government is handled on a departmental basis; each department operates independently of all other departments.

Facilities and Resources

Maria's facilities are located in three buildings. The Administration Building's modern facilities include offices, classrooms, computerized science laboratories, a computer center, a working library of 55,000 volumes, a multimedia center, and a multimedia large lecture hall. Marian Hall, Maria's allied health facility, has been renovated through grants from the Helene Fuld Foundation and gifts from the College's alumni and friends. It includes the Helene Fuld Audio-Visual Laboratory for nursing students, the Bearldean B. Burke Occupational Therapy Teaching Center, the Activities of Daily Living Suite, a multimedia auditorium, classrooms, offices, and nursing labs. Marian Hall also houses facilities for the physical therapist assistant program. The Campus School is a fully equipped teaching facility that provides preschool and full-day kindergarten classes and serves as a laboratory school for students majoring in early childhood education.

Location

Maria's urban location makes the many attractions of the capital district readily accessible. City buses provide convenient transportation to the area's sister cities of Schenectady and Troy, to many fine shopping centers, and to the impressive Nelson A. Rockefeller Empire State Plaza, which has the State Museum, indoor and outdoor entertainment areas, and performing arts facilities. Access to the Adirondack Northway—leading to the Saratoga Performing Arts Center and Canada—is minutes away. Amtrak trains are available from Schenectady and Rensselaer. Opportunities for outdoor activities in the area are numerous. The Catskills, the Helderbergs, the Adirondacks, and their many lakes provide four seasons of outdoor enjoyment.

Admission Requirements

Admission to full-time study at Maria College is based on a review of the applicant's high school and (when applicable) college performance, SAT or ACT scores and other objective test data, letters of recommendation, and the applicant's interests, maturity, and objectives. Interviews are required. An early admission program is offered for qualified high school students. Part-time study is also available.

Application and Information

It is recommended that application be made early in the first semester of the last year of high school. Applicants must submit an application form and a nonrefundable $25 fee, offer evidence of completion or anticipated completion of a high school program or its equivalent, present at least 16 units of high school work (as specified by the program selected at the College), and arrange for transcripts and SAT or ACT scores to be sent to Maria College. Students whose SAT or ACT scores fall below a particular level are required to take placement tests in the basic skills of reading, writing, and mathematics. Inquiries regarding academic programs or admission to Maria College may be directed to:

Director of Admissions
Maria College
700 New Scotland Avenue
Albany, New York 12208
Telephone: 518-438-3111
Fax: 518-453-1366
E-mail: admissions@mariacollege.edu
World Wide Web: http://www.mariacollege.edu

Students wait in the College courtyard for exam doors to open.

MASSACHUSETTS BAY COMMUNITY COLLEGE

WELLESLEY HILLS, FRAMINGHAM, AND ASHLAND, MASSACHUSETTS

The College and Its Mission

Massachusetts Bay Community College (MassBay) provides a student-centered learning environment in which a diverse student body explores, develops, and achieves educational goals. MassBay is committed to academic excellence and student success. The College is a comprehensive, two-year public institution offering career programs for immediate employability and programs paralleling the first two years of a bachelor's degree. MassBay emphasizes technology and health-care programs and has strong transfer programs in the liberal arts and business. While the majority of the students hail from the Metro West and Boston areas, its reputation has attracted students from throughout the United States and worldwide. It has been serving the academic needs of the community since it was founded in 1961.

The student body at MassBay comprises a diverse group of individuals, all with various goals and educational needs. Some may be working towards an associate degree or certificate program by taking day or evening classes. Others may have plans to transfer to a four-year college or university to continue their education. Still others may have some college experience but want to broaden their professional skills. MassBay's programs are geared to meet the needs of this diverse population, ensuring access to education and flexibility to students by offering a variety of instructional delivery systems, including day and night schedules and online courses.

Each of MassBay's programs of study belongs to one of its specialized Centers of Excellence—the Science, Technology, and Business Institute (STBI), the Health, Human Services, and Education Institute (HHSEI), and the Liberal Arts Institute (LAI). Whether a student's level of study is undergraduate, professional training, or continuing education, the goal of the Centers of Excellence is to provide students with a seamless learning and training experience. In addition, the Centers of Excellence enable students to easily plan their education to meet their career goals and at a pace that fits their lifestyle. For example, they can decide to complete a degree or certificate program to obtain an entry-level position, then return to the Center for more advanced training as they prepare for the next step of their career ladder. Because MassBay is committed to the success of its students, the Centers of Excellence are designed to provide open and enriching dialogue among faculty members and fellow students in similar programs of study. This allows for students to share experiences, compare similarities in career fields, or mentor each other in a particular project. Through the Centers of Excellence, students experience an innovative way of learning that provides a rewarding college experience and prepares them to excel in meeting the ever-changing demands of today's workforce.

MassBay students perform better than the state average on the registered nurse licensing exam (NCLEX-RN) and the practical nurse licensing exam (NCLEX-PN). All of MassBay's automotive technician training programs have received Automotive Service Excellence (ASE) MASTER certification, the highest level of achievement recognized by the National Institute for Automotive Service Excellence. MassBay students have received the prestigious and world-recognized Barry M. Goldwater Scholarship Award for mathematics, natural science, or engineering excellence. MassBay students regularly receive several Elizabeth Davis Scholarships from Wellesley College. MassBay's athletic teams routinely contend for state, regional, and national honors and championships.

MassBay is accredited by the New England Association of Schools and Colleges (NEASC), the Council for Accreditation of Allied Health Education Programs (NEASC), the Council for Accreditation for Allied Health Education Programs (CAAHEP), the Joint Review Committee on Education in Radiologic Technology (JRCERT), the National League for Nursing (NLN), Commission on Accreditation in Physical Therapy Education (CAPTE), and the National Automotive Technician Educational Foundation (NATEF).

Academic Programs

MassBay Community College offers two-year professional and liberal arts programs and certificate programs. From automotive technology, business, education, engineering, health, information systems and computer technology, liberal arts, and physical sciences, MassBay students have a wide range of choices. Many of the College's professional programs give students the opportunity to learn not only in the classroom but also in the field, with hands-on experience and state-of-the-art labs simulating the real experiences faced on the job. MassBay's liberal arts program provides the foundation for further learning and career advancement. Certificates can help students enter a new field or advance their current one. MassBay recommends that students work with an adviser in designing their specific course of study and planning for further college study or employment.

Students who complete a MassBay degree program may receive an Associate of Arts or an Associate of Science degree and are fully prepared for further study at four-year institutions for a baccalaureate degree. Students may be eligible for transfer status as a junior to many colleges and universities. Many of these programs also qualify students for immediate employment in their chosen field.

MassBay also participates in the Joint Admissions Program for students to transfer from MassBay to one of the four University of Massachusetts campuses or seven state colleges. The program is open to students who receive an associate degree in an approved major, with a 2.5 or higher grade point average. In addition, the Tuition Advantage Plan may help transferring graduates lower their tuition costs.

The associate degree programs offered are accounting, automotive technology, biotechnology, business administration, communication, computer information systems, computer science, criminal justice, early childhood education, electrical and computer engineering, electronics technology, electronics technology: semiconductor, engineering, engineering design, environmental science and occupational safety, forensic science, general business, general studies, hospitality management, human services, information systems technology and management, liberal arts, liberal arts: early childhood education, liberal arts: elementary education, liberal arts: global studies, life sciences, mechanical engineering, nursing, paralegal studies, physical therapist assistant, psychology/sociology/anthropology, and radiologic technology.

The certificate programs offered are accounting, automotive technology, central processing technology, central services and material management, communication, computer-aided design (CAD), CAD with Web option, early childhood education, early childhood education: infant-toddler teacher, emergency medical technician, hospitality management, human services, information technology, interior design, liberal arts, management, medical coding, medical interpreter, medical office administrative assistant, paralegal studies, paramedicine, personal fitness trainer, phlebotomy, practical nursing, surgical technology, and therapeutic massage.

Internships, clinicals, and co-ops play a critical role in the MassBay learning experience. Counselors in the Office of Career

Development can assist students in finding internship opportunities that fit into their career paths. Internships are valuable experiences that allow students to gain experience in the field of their interest and develop professional contacts.

Costs

For January 2005, the tuition per credit hour for Massachusetts residents was $119. For out-of-state/nonresidents, the tuition was $325 per credit hour. Fees for health insurance, student parking, lab, or material costs may be added. Continuing education tuition is $136 per credit hour for Massachusetts residents. For out-of-state/nonresidents, the cost of tuition per credit hour is $325. All evening tuition for AD nursing courses is $283 per credit hour plus additional fees. All evening tuition for practical nursing courses (CE, PN) is $245 per credit hour plus additional fees. Under the New England Regional Student Program, some New England students may attend MassBay for 150 percent of the in-state tuition rate, which is less than the out-of-state tuition rate.

Financial Aid

Financial assistance is available to all qualified students. Such aid is designed to help students meet basic college expenses. Financial assistance may be in the form of a grant, a scholarship, a loan, work-study employment, or any combination of these. MassBay's resources are obtained from federal, state, local, or private sources. Applicant eligibility and program guidelines are defined by the funding source. Grants and scholarships generally do not need to be paid back to MassBay or the sponsor. Loans can be made to the student or a student's parent and must be paid back. Loans can be need-based or non-need-based depending upon the individual circumstances of the student. A monthly payment plan through Academic Management Services (AMS) is also available.

Faculty

The faculty members at MassBay totaled 286, with 73 full-time and 211 part-time as of January 2005. Many members of the faculty are affiliated with other colleges and universities in the state, providing MassBay students with a valuable resource.

Student Body Profile

The student body at MassBay comprises a diverse group of individuals, all with various goals and educational needs. There are more than 5,000 students enrolled at MassBay. While the majority of students hail from the Metro West and the Boston vicinity, there are many international students as well, representing countries such as Brazil, Haiti, Russia, Uganda, and India. Fifty percent of MassBay students are between 17 and 22 years of age.

Student Activities

The College supports intercollegtiate athletic programs, including men's baseball; women's softball; and men's and women's soccer, basketball, volleyball, golf, tennis, and cross-country.

Some other student clubs and organizations offered by MassBay are the Student Senate and Student Government; honor societies, such as Alpha Beta Gamma, the National Business Honor Society, Alpha Kappa Lamda, Psi Beta, Sigma Delta Mus, and Silver Key; the student-run theater group, the MassBay Players; concert/lecture series; the International and Multicultural Student Development program; and the student newspaper, *The Beacon*.

For students interested in a healthy lifestyle, the Recreation Center, built in 2003, offers a variety of activities, such as exercising, weight training, and pickup basketball.

Facilities and Resources

MassBay provides the College community with resources and facilities that support the academic programs and courses offered, including a Student Development Office; Advising Center, where students can speak with an academic adviser; an Academic Achievement Center that supplements classroom instruction with one-on-one support while accommodating MassBay students' diverse learning styles; the Reading and Writing Centers, which offer one-on-one help in completing a reading or writing assignment for any college course; smart classrooms, used by faculty members and students to enhance the classroom learning experience; a library with more than 49,000 volumes; wireless technologies; and computer labs with more than 400 computers for student use.

Location

MassBay serves students from three convenient locations. The Wellesley Hills Campus is located on Route 9 approximately 10 miles west of Boston. The Framingham Campus is near Routes 9 and 126. The Technology Center in Ashland is approximately 4 miles south of the Framingham Campus off Route 126.

Admission Requirements

MassBay maintains an open-door admissions policy, and there is no application deadline. If students have proof of a GED, high school graduation, or an associate degree or higher, they will be admitted to MassBay on a first-come, first-served basis, provided there is a vacancy in the program to which they have applied.

Application and Information

MassBay enrollment is open to Massachusetts residents at the in-state tuition rate. A Massachusetts resident is currently defined as a U.S. citizen or permanent resident having a minimum of six consecutive months of verifiable domicile in the Commonwealth. Others may attend MassBay at the out-of-state tuition rate.

All applicants must include a non-refundable application fee of $20 fee with their application. Credit card payment is accepted for online application. For an application and information, students should contact the Office of Admissions at the address listed.

Office of Admissions
Massachusetts Bay Community College
50 Oakland Street
Wellesley Hills, Massachusetts 02481
Telephone: 781-239-2500
World Wide Web: http://www.massbay.edu

The MassBay Wellesley campus.

McINTOSH COLLEGE

DOVER, NEW HAMPSHIRE

The College and Its Mission

For the residential or commuting student seeking the intimate personal experience of a small college and the technical training in practical skills needed to compete in today's computer-oriented job market, McIntosh College is the answer. For more than 100 years, McIntosh has provided an exciting variety of business and professional opportunities to recent high school graduates and adults seeking career changes or re-entry into the job market. McIntosh is a two-year degree-granting institution accredited by the New England Association of Schools and Colleges. The College currently enrolls more than 1,000 students at its campus in Dover, New Hampshire.

The mission of the College combines a clearly defined educational philosophy with a profound understanding of the College's role in providing effective business-oriented associate degree and certificate programs in a fully equipped learning facility. This integration allows the College to enhance the quality of personal and professional life of the business and academic communities that it serves.

McIntosh is a career-oriented institution dedicated to the personal, intellectual, and professional growth of its students. The College has a century-long tradition of providing academic programs that integrate the acquisition of job-related skills with the development of clear, critical thinking and effective reasoning. While McIntosh recognizes its obligation to provide the specific skills necessary for the student to function in a contemporary work environment, it operates under the philosophy that a college is more than a training facility. Students must leave the college experience with a sense of competence in their chosen fields, a belief in themselves as individuals, and an enhanced critical awareness of the world around them.

Academic Programs

McIntosh College offers a unique blend of courses and programs of study designed to prepare students for careers in business, hospitality and tourism management, the computer industry, public service, allied health, paralegal studies, and criminal justice. All programs of study provide students with academic credit, which allows them to continue their studies at four-year institutions.

Associate Degree Programs McIntosh College is authorized by the Postsecondary Education Commission of the State of New Hampshire to offer associate degree programs with major areas of concentration in accounting, business studies, criminal justice, culinary arts, graphic design and professional photography, medical assisting, and paralegal studies.

Honors Programs The McIntosh College Beta Gamma Gamma Chapter of the Phi Theta Kappa Honor Society supports a number of scholarship opportunities and activities for honor students.

Transfer Arrangements McIntosh students can earn an associate degree and an articulated bachelor's degree in one continuous program of study at the Dover campus through the uniquely structured McIntosh/Southern New Hampshire University (formerly New Hampshire College) 2+2 Program.

Academic counseling is available and full support is provided for students wishing to continue their education at other institutions of higher learning.

Internship and Co-op Programs All academic departments supporting degree programs support for-credit internship opportunities for qualified students. The Office of Career Development assists students in finding appropriate internships in accounting, business, computer studies, criminal justice, culinary arts, hospitality and tourism management, information systems, medical assisting, office technology, or paralegal studies.

Credit for Nontraditional Learning Experiences

The College grants credit to students who have passed authorized advanced placement courses in high school with grades of B or better or who present evidence of having received scores of 460 or better on CLEP examinations in subject areas that directly correspond to the content of individual McIntosh courses.

Costs

The 2003–04 annual tuition for a full-time degree candidate was $20,000–$25,000. Tuition and costs are subject to change.

Financial Aid

The Office of Financial Aid provides information and personal counseling with respect to the various federal grant and loan programs and institutional scholarships available to students attending McIntosh College. McIntosh College believes that every student should have access to the financial resources needed to pursue academic or career interests. Pell Grants, Supplemental Educational Opportunity Grants, Federal Work-Study, Stafford Student Loans, Plus Loans, State Incentive Programs, direct loans, scholarships, and family discounts are all available to students attending McIntosh College.

Faculty

There are 44 full-time faculty members at McIntosh College. Of these, 67 percent hold advanced degrees and specialized certifications.

Student Body Profile

McIntosh College attracts students from a wide age spectrum. Because the College offers parallel day and evening programs, there is a substantial mix of recent high school graduates and adult students returning to school. The average age of a McIntosh student is 26, slightly higher at night and slightly lower during the day program. Students are generally career oriented. More than 50 percent of graduates continue their studies at the bachelor's degree level.

Student Activities

The College supports a variety of social clubs, organizations, and other extracurricular activities designed to enhance and enrich the student's educational experience at McIntosh. The Student Activities Committee provides a forum for students interested in planning and implementing social and cultural events at the College. There is a chapter of Delta Epsilon Chi on campus. Departmental associations include the McIntosh Paralegal Association and the Criminal Justice Association.

Facilities and Resources

In recent years, McIntosh has anticipated changes in the business environment and the need for a newly oriented work force by establishing a superior computer facility consisting of seven computer labs housing more than 209 individual and networked stations. An integrated curriculum provides specific computer instruction related to each major field of study. In addition, McIntosh students can roam the Internet, explore online services such as WestLaw, or browse through an extensive CD-ROM collection in the McIntosh academic and paralegal library facilities. A fully equipped medical lab and a real-world operative teaching kitchen provide hands-on working environments for medical assisting and culinary arts majors. At McIntosh, emphasis is placed on the practical aspects of career development. Internships are available in all departments.

On-campus student housing facilities at McIntosh College have been carefully designed to provide a warm, supportive living and learning environment that serves to nurture students' personal development and to enhance their opportunities for academic and professional success. The residential facility includes spacious furnished living units that are cable-ready and have air-conditioning, a full bath, and access to a computer lab. Residential students may choose from a variety of meal plans. Initial inquiries about eligibility requirements and the availability of on-campus housing should be directed to the Office of Admissions. Room assignments are made on a first-come, first-served basis, depending on eligibility.

Advisement/Counseling The faculty and administration of the College are committed to the principle that students should be given every possible opportunity to achieve academic and professional success. For this reason, the College offers extensive academic and career counseling to its students. Free study skills workshops are regularly available. In addition, the College provides free tutorial assistance in accounting, computer applications, English, and math.

Career Planning/Placement Offices The College provides free career counseling and placement referral services to its students and graduates through the Office of Career Development. Workshops on resume writing are frequently offered to currently enrolled students.

Location

McIntosh College consists of two separate facilities situated next to the Spaulding Turnpike in Dover, New Hampshire. Dover is a city of about 26,000, located in the Seacoast area of New Hampshire about one hour north of Boston. The College is conveniently located just a short drive from coastal beaches and world-class skiing. The academic center is located on a 13-acre tract of land on Cataract Avenue.

Admission Requirements

A high school diploma or its equivalent (GED) is required of all students accepted for admission at McIntosh College with matriculated student status. Students can apply and can be admitted at any time during the year. A student attending a full-time degree program can expect to graduate in eighteen or twenty-four months.

Application and Information

Applications for admission are accepted on an ongoing basis. Most students may begin classes at the start of any term scheduled throughout the year. For application materials, students should contact:

Office of Admissions
McIntosh College
23 Cataract Avenue
Dover, New Hampshire 03820
Telephone: 800-262-1111 (toll-free)
Fax: 603-742-3755
E-mail: admissions@mcintoshcollege.com
World Wide Web: http://www.mcintoshcollege.edu

McIntosh welcomes students from around the world.

MIAMI DADE COLLEGE

MIAMI, FLORIDA

The College and Its Mission

Miami Dade College is recognized as one of the outstanding community colleges in the nation. With 163,000 students, it is also the largest institution of higher learning in America. At Miami Dade, student success is the priority. The mission of the College is to provide accessible, affordable, high-quality education that keeps the learner's needs at the center of the decision-making process. The College is accredited by the Southern Association of Colleges and Schools and offers undergraduate study in more than 200 areas and professions.

Academic Programs

The College's instructional program is three-fold: to prepare students to enter the professional field of teaching science and math in secondary schools and K–12 exceptional students by awarding a B.A. degree; to prepare students to transfer to the upper division of senior colleges and universities by awarding an Associate in Arts (A.A.) or Associate in Science (A.S.) degree; and to prepare students for certification leading to rapid entry into career fields.

The A.A. degree, offered for students planning to transfer to a university, can be earned in 60 credits, including 36 credits of required general education and 24 credits of electives. The state of Florida has developed a set of common program prerequisites for each program to facilitate student transfer. A variety of A.S. and Associate in Applied Science (A.A.S.) degrees, college credit certificate programs, vocational credit certificate programs, and supplemental courses are offered to prepare students to enter the job market or upgrade skills. These programs vary in length. The A.S. degree includes 15 credits of general education requirements. Several A.S. and A.A.S. degree programs include courses that have articulation agreements for transfer to one or more universities; others offer advanced certificate training. The Medical Center Campus offers a wide range of allied health and nursing programs, with clinicals in major local hospitals and health-care centers. Courses are offered year-round in two major terms of sixteen weeks each and summer terms consisting of two 6-week terms or one 12-week term.

The following A.S. degree programs, which prepare students for employment and may transfer to a four-year institution, are available: accounting technology; air-conditioning, refrigeration, and heating; architectural design and construction technology; automotive service management technology; aviation administration; aviation maintenance management; biomedical engineering technology; building construction technology; business administration; civil engineering technology; computer engineering technology; computer information technology; computer programming and analysis; court reporting technology; criminal justice technology; dietetic technician studies; drafting and design technology; electronics engineering technology; environmental science technology; film production technology; financial services; fire science technology; funeral services; graphic arts technology; graphic design technology; graphic Internet technology; hospitality and tourism management; human services; industrial management technology; interior design technology; Internet services technology; landscape technology; legal assisting; marketing management; music business; networking services technology; office systems technology; photographic technology; professional pilot technology; radio and television broadcast programming; sign language interpretation; telecommunications engineering; theater and entertainment technology; translation/interpretation: English/Spanish track; and travel industry management.

Allied health A.S. degree programs offered at the Medical Center Campus include dental hygiene, diagnostic medical sonography technology, emergency medical services, health information management, histologic technology, medical laboratory technology, midwifery, nuclear medicine technology, nursing-RN, opticianry, physical therapist assistant and physician assistant studies, radiation therapy technology, respiratory care, and veterinary technology. In addition, an A.A.S. degree program is offered in radiography.

College credit certificates are offered in accounting applications, air cargo agent, airline reservation and ticketing agent studies, airline/ aviation management, business management, Cisco network associate studies, computer specialist studies, computer programming, computer-aided design assistant or operator studies, embalming, emergency medical technician studies, information technology support, interpretation studies: English/Spanish, marketing operations, microcomputer repairer/installer studies, Microsoft database administrator studies, Microsoft solutions developer studies, mortgage finance, network systems developer studies, nuclear medicine technology specialist studies, office systems specialist studies, Oracle database administrator or database developer studies, passenger service agent studies, paramedic studies, translation studies: English/ Spanish, and Web development specialist studies. An Applied Technology Diploma is offered in emergency medical technician studies.

Distance Education Through virtual college, high-quality online academic and vocational programs are offered to meet the needs of nontraditional and out-of-area students as well as students who find it difficult to attend classes during scheduled hours and at specific locations. The array of instructional activities in the Web courses is designed to engage students in interactive and collaborative learning and cover the established competencies.

Honors Programs Miami Dade's Honors College provides a rigorous and comprehensive curriculum, seminars, and enrichment activities in a scholarly and supportive environment where goal-oriented, academically gifted students explore new ideas and engage in inspired creativity and intellectual collaborations with experienced faculty members. Honors College graduates continue their studies at some of the nation's finest schools, including Columbia, Georgetown, Harvard, Smith, Yale, and the Universities of Indiana, Michigan, Texas, and Wisconsin.

Transfer Arrangements A statewide articulation agreement among all Florida institutions of higher education facilitates transfers and ensures that a student who is awarded the Associate in Arts degree at Miami Dade has met general education requirements for admission to the upper division in public and private colleges and universities. In all, Miami Dade has established articulation agreements with fifty-eight prestigious colleges and universities.

Certificate Programs Vocational credit certificates are offered in academy of international marketing, accounting operations, administrative assistant studies, architectural drafting, bail bonding, business computer programming, business supervision and management, commercial art technology, community service officer/ police service aide studies, correctional officer and correctional probation officer studies, customer assistance, early childhood education, electronic technology, fire fighting, insurance marketing, law enforcement officer studies, legal secretary studies, massage therapy, mechanical drafting, medical assisting, medical coder/biller studies, medical record transcribing, medical secretary studies, network support services, PC support services, pharmacy technician studies, phlebotomy, practical nursing, private security officer studies, public safety telecommunications, real estate marketing, television production, teller operations, and travel and tourism. Applied Technology Diplomas are offered in medical coder/biller and medical record transcribing.

Internship and Co-op Programs These programs provide an opportunity for students to obtain career-related work experience (paid or voluntary) while earning academic credit.

Special Programs and Services New World School of the Arts (NWSA) is a unique educational partnership of Miami-Dade County Public Schools, Miami Dade College, and the University of Florida. Through its sponsoring institutions, NWSA awards high school diplomas, A.A. degrees, and Bachelor of Music and Bachelor of Fine Arts degrees. Students are admitted through audition or portfolio presentation. Other special programs include academic remediation for entering students, English as a second language, services for disabled students (including learning disabled), study abroad, and advanced placement.

The College is a leader in working proactively to assist students with disabilities. Each campus has a ground floor ACCESS office to provide the guidance and technological accommodations required. Computers equipped with voice synthesizer programs are available as well as note-takers to help the physically challenged students.

Continuing Education Unit Certificate Programs Miami Dade provides students the opportunity to obtain Continuing Education Units (CEUs) for certain courses. Transcripts designating CEUs are provided.

Personal Enrichment/Noncredit Courses A wide array of noncredit courses and programs are offered both on and off campus.

Off-Campus Programs

Study-abroad programs, both short-term and full semester, are available in many countries. Internships and clinicals may be scheduled off campus.

Credit for Nontraditional Learning Experiences

The College may award credit for demonstrated proficiency in areas related to college-level courses. Sources used to determine such proficiency are the College-Level Examination Program, the Advanced Placement Program, the Proficiency Examination Program, the International Baccalaureate Program, Dual Enrollment, Tech Prep Articulation, the Defense Activity for Nontraditional Education Support, the United States Armed Forces Institute, the Institutional Credit by Exam, and the internal Miami Dade procedures for awarding credit related to specific programs for approval licensures.

Costs

For the 2004–05 academic year, tuition was $59.15 per college credit and $49.70 per vocational credit for Florida residents; it was $206.95 per college credit and $198.05 per vocational credit for nonresidents. Textbooks and supplies for full-time students were estimated at $1500. Although housing is not available on campus, there are numerous housing options near the College at varying costs.

Financial Aid

Financial aid that a student receives is determined through federal, state, and institutional guidelines and is offered to students in packages that may consist of grants, loans, employment, and scholarships. It is based upon financial need. The College also offers merit-based aid to qualified students as funds are available. Assistance includes Federal Pell Grants, Federal Supplemental Educational Opportunity Grants, the Florida Student Assistance Grant, the Florida Bright Futures Scholarship, the Federal Work-Study Program, the Florida Work Experience Program (FWEP), Federal Perkins Loans, Federal Family Education Loan Programs, and Federal PLUS Loans. The College also offers Foundation and Institutional Grants, scholarships, short-term tuition loans, and employment to students as well as funding for the purchase of special equipment for disabled students. About 45 percent of the student body receive some form of financial aid. In 2005, 36,000 students received Pell Grants.

Faculty

There are 723 full-time faculty members and 1,370 part-time faculty members. Of the full-time faculty members, 94 percent hold advanced degrees.

Student Body Profile

Of the 163,000 credit and noncredit students enrolled at Miami Dade, 1,800 are international students. Seventy-three percent of students with an A.A. degree continue their education at a four-year college. Of the upper-division students in the Florida State University System, 15 percent started college at Miami Dade. The average age of students is 27, although about 30 percent are between 21 and 25. Almost 65 percent attend on a part-time basis, and 62 percent are women. The student body is ethnically and culturally diverse. Miami Dade enrolls and graduates more Hispanic students than any other college or university and is second in African-American enrollment in the United States.

Student Activities

More than 100 organizations offer opportunities to participate in student government, student publications, music ensembles, drama productions (in English and Spanish), religious activities, service and political clubs, national and local fraternities and sororities, professional organizations, and honor societies.

Intercollegiate and intramural athletics play an important role at Miami Dade College, which is a member of NJCAA and competes at the Division I level. Intercollegiate teams include women's basketball, softball, and volleyball and men's baseball and basketball. Sports facilities include racquetball, tennis, and handball courts; wellness centers; swimming pools; and a track.

Facilities and Resources

Career Planning/Placement Offices Trained staff members assist students in selecting courses and programs of study to satisfy their educational objectives. Each campus has a career center where students may obtain career counseling and vocational interest testing. The campus Job Placement Centers provide part-time or full-time job referral services to actively enrolled students or graduates. The centers also prepare students for resume writing and successful job search. Career Fairs bring employers to the campuses.

Library and Audiovisual Services The campus libraries have a combined book collection of more than 312,000 titles and more than 17,000 periodicals. There are nearly 7,000 CD-ROMs or other audiovisual materials, and online databases are available. Computers for student use are available in computer labs, learning resource centers, labs, classrooms, and the library.

Location

Blessed with a sunny, subtropical climate, beautiful beaches, and an international flavor, Miami offers a rich variety of exciting cultural, sporting, and intellectual activities. Opportunities abound to explore unique settings, such as the historic Art Deco District of Miami Beach and Miami's colorful Little Havana or the nearby Everglades National Park. Six campuses and numerous outreach centers are located throughout the Greater Miami area. **North Campus** is located on a 245-acre, fully landscaped site, and its buildings are clustered around a beautiful lake. **Kendall Campus** is situated 23 miles southwest of the North Campus on a 185-acre site. Focal points of the campus' award-winning landscape designs are the lakes and lush tropical growth. **Wolfson Campus,** is located in the heart of downtown Miami's business community and has two award-winning buildings. **Medical Center Campus** is located in Miami's medical/civic center complex. **Homestead Campus** is located on an 8-acre site in the historic business district of Homestead. **InterAmerican Campus** is located in the heart of Little Havana. Off-campus commuter sites are located in the major suburbs.

Admission Requirements

Miami Dade has an open-door admission policy. The College provides educational opportunities to all high school graduates, including those who have a state high school equivalency diploma, and to transfer students from other colleges and universities. In addition to the College's application and the $20 application fee, students must have official transcripts from high school, college, university, or other postsecondary educational institutions sent directly to the Office of Admissions from the institutions. High school equivalency diploma or certificate holders must provide the original document and score report (which are returned) or an exact copy of the documents. Florida residents must complete a Florida residency statement. SAT, ACT, or TOEFL test scores should be sent directly to the Office of Admissions by the testing board. Students not presenting test scores are tested for placement purposes upon acceptance.

Application and Information

Applications are accepted on an ongoing basis. All prospective students should contact:

District Office of Admissions and Registration Services
Miami Dade College
11011 S.W. 104th Street
Miami, Florida 33176-3393

Telephone: 305-237-8888
Fax: 305-237-2964
World Wide Web: http://www.mdc.edu

MIDDLESEX COUNTY COLLEGE

EDISON, NEW JERSEY

The College and Its Mission

More students are choosing community colleges for their educational needs than ever before. Middlesex County College, with its diverse programs and specialized services, is the college of choice for more than 13,000 students in 2004–05. More students than ever are enrolled in full-time degree programs and are preparing to transfer as juniors to four-year colleges and universities.

Middlesex County College is one of the largest and among the oldest county colleges in New Jersey. The College, a two-year publicly supported coeducational institution, is committed to serving all those who can benefit from postsecondary learning, and the student body reflects this belief. More than 550 courses are offered during the day, evening, and on weekends. Students have the opportunity to prepare academically and through cooperative work placements, clinical experience, and laboratory work for careers in business, health, social science, and science technologies.

Middlesex County College offers modern, well-equipped facilities located on a beautiful 200-acre campus, together with excellent learning resources and dedicated faculty members. Most students commute to the College from Middlesex County. Each year, more and more students from outside the United States enroll as international students. All students have the opportunity to add to their collegiate experience through participation in a variety of student activities and clubs. The College has a recreational facility with a 25-meter pool, dance studio, wrestling and weight rooms, and racquetball courts. The College philosophy is directed toward assisting each individual in reaching his or her maximum potential, and counselors work with students to ensure this goal.

Academic Programs

More than seventy different degree and certificate programs, either transfer or career oriented, may be taken full-time or part-time during the day, evening, and on weekends. Courses are offered during the fall and spring semesters, a January winter session, and summer sessions. The College offers **Associate in Arts (A.A.)** and **Associate in Science (A.S.)** degree programs designed specifically to transfer to four-year colleges and universities in the fields of arts, business education, engineering, and sciences. Students interested in preparing for careers in medicine and law begin study at Middlesex County College with courses in science and liberal arts.

Middlesex offers formal credit articulation transfer agreements and/or dual-degree admissions programs with more than 50 four-year institutions, including Rutgers, Montclair State, Kean, and NYU. It has always been the largest "feeder" school to the New Jersey Institute of Technology (NJIT), where its graduates are continually recognized for their outstanding academic achievements.

Students who complete the requirements of a transfer curriculum earn an associate degree and are accepted into the receiving college or university as members of the junior class. Working closely with their faculty and advisers assures this seamless transition, and students find that the cost of their undergraduate education is substantially lower because of their work at Middlesex.

Many challenging programs and options designed to prepare students for entry into the job market are available in business education, engineering technologies, health technologies, and science. Graduates of career programs receive an **Associate in Applied Science (A.A.S.)** degree. Many graduates holding the A.A.S. degree transfer to four-year colleges, which may accept all or part of the credits earned at Middlesex. Certificate programs are also available.

In addition to associate degree and certificate curricula, the College offers students the opportunity to enroll in a plan of study through the Open College Program. Open College serves students who want to try out an individualized academic program prior to formally enrolling in a specific degree or certificate program. The College offers Project Connections, a nationally recognized program for students with learning disabilities. Students interested in military education may participate in the Army or Air Force ROTC program through cross-registration at Rutgers University.

Degree and certificate programs are offered in accounting, biology transfer program, biotechnology, business administration, business software applications, chemical technology, chemistry transfer program, civil construction engineering technology, computer-aided drafting, computer and information systems, computer programming, computer science transfer program, criminal justice, culinary arts certificate, dental hygiene, dietetic technology, education practitioner, electronic and computer engineering technology, engineering science, English as a second language, environmental technology, fashion merchandising, fine arts (options in art, music, and theater), fire science technology, graphics for digital media, health science, hotel restaurant and institution management, land surveying technology, liberal arts (options in business, communications, dance, English, general, health and physical education, history, journalism, media arts and design, modern languages, music, political science, psychology, sociology, social rehabilitation services, social science, theater, and visual arts), management, marketing, mathematics transfer program, mechanical manufacturing technology, mecomtronics engineering technology, medical laboratory technology, nursing, office administration, paralegal studies, pharmacy assistant, physics transfer program, psychosocial rehabilitation and treatment, radiography education, respiratory care, small business management, teacher aide, and telecommunications networking technology.

Off-Campus Programs

In addition to the main campus in Edison, Middlesex offers outreach centers in New Brunswick and Perth Amboy. Both centers offer credit-level classes as well as classes in English as a second language. Credit and noncredit courses are also offered at selected locations throughout the county.

Credit for Nontraditional Learning Experiences

There are several programs at the College through which applicants may earn credit for knowledge learned in nontraditional ways. Both Credit by Examination and the College-Level Examination Program (CLEP) are available.

Costs

Tuition for the fall 2005 semester is $79.25 per credit for a Middlesex County resident and $158.50 per credit for an out-of-county resident. There is a $12-per-credit general service fee, a $3.50-per-credit student service fee and a $7-per-credit technology fee for Middlesex residents. The fees for out-of-county residents are $24 per credit for general service, $7 per credit for student service and $14 per credit for technology. There are also mandatory accident and health insurance fees. Some classes require special laboratory, material, or other fees.

Financial Aid

Through its financial aid programs, Middlesex County College makes every effort to overcome economic barriers. Funds from federal, state, and private sources are available to those who have need and meet the eligibility requirements. To be considered for financial aid, a student must complete the Free Application for Federal Student Aid (FAFSA) and the Middlesex County College Financial Aid Form. The priority deadline for the fall semester is April 1 and November 1 for the spring semester. Before a financial aid application can be reviewed, the student must be accepted to a degree program and be matriculated for a minimum of 6 credits.

Students who graduate from a New Jersey high school and finish in the top 20 percent of their graduating class may qualify for the NJSTARS free tuition program. Students must also apply for federal financial aid, be a U.S. citizen or permanent resident, be admitted to a degree program, and register for at least 12 college level credits to be eligible for the program.

Faculty

There are 200 full-time and 500 part-time members of the faculty. The student-faculty ratio is 21:1. Of the full-time faculty members, nearly 90 percent are teaching faculty members and serve as academic advisers. Middlesex faculty members have impressive resumes, outstanding accomplishments, and degrees from some of the country's finest colleges and universities. Many bring to the classroom years of workplace experience in their field. However, most important is the faculty's commitment to help students reach their potential and gain the confidence to achieve their life goals.

Student Body Profile

There are about 13,000 students on campus, about half are full-time. The campus population is diverse, with students from more than sixty countries in attendance. Approximately half of the students come directly from high school, with an average age of 24 for the entire student body.

Student Activities

There are more than sixty chartered clubs and organizations, a College Center Program Board, College Assembly, national honor societies, special minority student activities, and a College newspaper, radio station, and literary magazine. The College offers intercollegiate competition through membership in Region XIX of the National Junior College Athletic Association and the Garden State Athletic Conference.

Facilities and Resources

The campus is comprises twenty-five buildings, including a state-of-the-art Technical Services Center, a fully equipped Recreation Center, and a 440-seat Performing Arts Center. The Counseling and Career Services Center provides students with assistance in making decisions about career choices, education programs, college transfer, job placement, and other personal concerns. Bilingual counseling is available to Spanish-speaking students.

Location

The College is located just 15 minutes from New Brunswick, New Jersey. The College is conveniently located near numerous restaurants and shopping centers. The New Jersey shore is less than 30 minutes away. Mass transit to the College is available from many surrounding areas.

Admission Requirements

The admission policy is based on the premise that the College should provide an opportunity for further education to all citizens of the community. Enrollment is open to anyone who holds a high school diploma or any non–high school graduates 18 years of age or older who can demonstrate an ability to benefit from a college education. SAT scores are optional. Applicants to most programs are not required to submit any standardized test scores.

Admission to programs that specify additional selective criteria may require a review of prior educational performance, standardized test scores, the completion of an appropriate developmental program, or, when suitable, an assessment of an applicant's aptitude and interest, as determined during an admission counseling interview.

Application and Information

Completed applications are reviewed on a continuous basis, with the exception of the limited-seat programs in dental hygiene, medical laboratory technology, nursing, psychosocial rehabilitation, radiography education, and respiratory care. Automotive technology is offered every other year. A completed application form, a required $25 nonrefundable application fee, and all supporting materials should be sent to the Office of Admissions.

For further information or to schedule a campus visit, students should contact:

Office of Admissions
Middlesex County College
2600 Woodbridge Avenue, P.O. Box 3050
Edison, New Jersey 08818-3050
Telephone: 732-906-4243
         888-YOU-4MIDDLESEX (toll-free)
Fax: 732-906-7728
E-mail: admissions@middlesexcc.edu
World Wide Web: http://www.middlesexcc.edu

MOHAWK VALLEY COMMUNITY COLLEGE

UTICA AND ROME, NEW YORK

The College and Its Mission

Mohawk Valley Community College (MVCC) offers choice, opportunity, and hope by providing accessible and affordable higher education, training, and services that emphasize academic excellence, diversity, and a global view.

Mohawk Valley Community College strives to be a college of choice through innovative educational leadership, programs, and services that address the current and future needs of rapidly changing local, regional, and global communities.

The College was founded in 1946 as the New York State Institute of Applied Arts and Sciences at Utica. One of five postsecondary institutions established on an experimental basis after World War II, the public institute offered programs leading to technical and semiprofessional employment in business and industry. After name changes in the 1950s, redefining its mission, the College moved to its current 80-acre campus location in Utica in 1960. In 1961, the College was renamed Mohawk Valley Community College. Today, the College offers a full range of academic programs.

The College is accredited by the Middle States Association of Colleges and Schools. Individual program accreditations are as follows: civil, electrical, and mechanical engineering technology and surveying technology by the Commission for Technology Accreditation of the Accreditation Board for Engineering and Technology, Inc. (ABET); nursing by the National League for Nursing Accrediting Commission (NLNAC); and respiratory care and health information technology–medical records by the Commission on Accreditation of Allied Health Education Programs, in cooperation with the Committee on Accreditation for Respiratory Care and the American Health Information Management Association's Council on Accreditation, respectively.

Academic Programs

The College has been authorized to offer the following degrees and certificates: Associate in Arts (A.A.) degree, Associate in Science (A.S.) degree, Associate in Applied Science (A.A.S.) degree, Associate in Occupational Studies (A.O.S.) degree, and the MVCC Certificate.

The structure and goals of academic programming at MVCC have two main purposes. Certificate, A.O.S., and A.A.S. programs emphasize the development of employable skills through a combination of classroom and laboratory instruction. Some programs also include internship experiences. A.A. and A.S. programs provide students with the liberal arts, science, mathematics, business, engineering, or computer course work necessary for transfer into the junior year of a preprofessional program at a four-year public or private college or university upon the completion of their associate degree.

The minimum number of credits needed to earn an associate degree is 62. The maximum credits required for a degree differ by program and degree type.

Opportunities for specialization include the honors program, independent study, internships, study abroad, and ROTC (Army).

The College operates on a semester calendar. Fall classes begin before Labor Day and end before Christmas. Spring classes begin in mid-January and end in mid-May.

Career and transfer programs are available. Majors offered include accounting (A.A.S.); air conditioning technology (A.O.S.); banking and insurance (A.A.S.); building management and maintenance (A.A.S.); business administration (A.S.); business management (A.A.S.); chemical dependency practitioner studies (A.A.S.); civil engineering technology (A.A.S.); computer-aided drafting (A.O.S.); computer information systems (A.A.S.); computer science (A.S.); criminal justice (A.A.S.); culinary arts management (A.O.S.), also with baking and pastry emphasis; digital animation (A.A.S.); electrical engineering technology (A.A.S.); electrical service technician studies (A.O.S.), with options in electrical maintenance, fiber optics, and robotics; emergency medical services/paramedic studies (A.A.S.); engineering science (A.S.); environmental analysis–chemical technology (A.A.S.); fine arts (A.S.); general studies (A.S.); general studies–childhood education (A.S., joint admission with the State University of New York (SUNY) College at Oneonta); graphic arts technology (A.A.S.); graphic design (A.A.S.); health information technology–medical records (A.A.S.); hotel technology–meeting services (A.A.S.); human services (A.A.S.); illustration (A.A.S.); individual studies (A.A., A.A.S., A.S., and A.O.S.); international studies (A.A.); liberal arts–humanities and social science (A.A.); liberal arts–psychology (A.S.); liberal arts–public policy (A.S.); liberal arts–theater (A.A.); manufacturing technology (A.O.S.); mathematics (A.S.); mechanical engineering technology (A.A.S.); mechanical technology–aircraft maintenance (A.A.S.); media marketing and management (A.A.S.); medical assisting (A.A.S.); nursing (A.A.S.); nutrition and dietetics (A.S.); office technologies (A.A.S.); photography (A.A.S.); pre–environmental science (A.S.); programming and systems (A.A.S.); radiologic technology (A.S.); recreation and leisure services (A.A.S.); respiratory care (A.A.S.); restaurant management (A.A.S.); science (A.S.), with emphasis areas in biology, chemistry, physical education, physics, and sports medicine; semiconductor manufacturing technology (A.A.S.); surveying technology (A.A.S.); telecommunications technology (A.A.S.); Web site design and management (A.A.S.); and welding technology (A.O.S.).

Certificate programs include appliance repair, refrigeration, and air conditioning; architectural drafting; carpentry and masonry; chef training; clinical lab assistant studies; CNC machinist technology; coaching; computer electronic technician studies; electronic technician studies; engineering drawing; English as a second language; finance; forensic photography; graphic communication; heating and air conditioning; individual studies: business and industry; industrial and commercial electricity; industrial engineering technician studies; insurance; machinist technology; managerial accounting; mechanical drafting; media marketing and management; medical assistant studies; metallurgy lab technician studies; office practices; phlebotomy; photography; production planning; refrigeration; small-business management; supervisory management; surveying; tool design; transportation management; Web site design and management; and welding.

A jointly registered degree program with SUNY College at Oneonta offers applicants the opportunity to complete a bachelor's degree in childhood education (grades 1–6) at MVCC.

Credit for Nontraditional Learning Experiences

MVCC offers adult students the opportunity to earn credits through the CLEP examination, MVCC-administered examinations, life experience, and course work completed in a noncollegiate setting. The accumulated credit earned cannot exceed 75 percent of the student's degree program.

Costs

Tuition for New York State residents is $1425 per semester for full-time students and $115 per credit hour for part-time students; for out-of-state and international students, it is $2850 per semester for full-time students and $230 per credit hour for part-time students. Student fees are $65 per semester for full-time students and $1 per credit hour for part-time students. Books and supplies range from $300 to $500 per semester, depending on the student's major. Residence hall occupants must purchase one of the available room and board packages each semester. Costs are approximately $3300 per semester, depending on type of accommodations and number of meals chosen. The residence hall technology fee is $100 per semester for Internet and phone access. The residence hall social fee is $10 per semester. The residence hall orientation fee is $40 and covers new-resident orientation programming and meals.

Financial Aid

One of MVCC's major objectives is to make college affordable for all. Approximately 90 percent of MVCC students receive some form of state or federal financial aid. The College offers a comprehensive financial assistance program of scholarships, loans, and grants. Most of the financial assistance received by MVCC students is need based. Non-need-based scholarships include the Presidential Scholarship Program for the top 10 percent of Oneida County (the College's sponsoring county) graduates, two similar Exceptional Student Scholarships for those not from Oneida County, and the Sodexho/MVCC Meal Plan Scholarships, which consider exceptional citizenship. Students eligible for non-need-based scholarships are expected to apply for state and federal financial assistance as applicable.

Faculty

The full-time faculty numbers 149, and the part-time faculty numbers 130. Approximately 8 percent of all faculty members have doctoral degrees. The student-faculty ratio is approximately 20:1.

Student Body Profile

MVCC enrolls approximately 5,500 students each year. Enrollment is divided between the main campus in Utica, New York, and the branch campus in Rome, New York, with approximately 80 percent of the student population enrolled on the main campus.

The College is designed to be predominantly commuter based; 85 percent of the students live within 60 miles of the campus in central New York State. For fall 2005, the College plans to add a fifth residence hall on the main campus in Utica, increasing housing capacity to 500 students. The residence life staff provides listings of off-campus apartment-style housing options.

The international student population has grown from 40 students to 100 since 1996. Twenty-one different countries are represented on campus.

The average age of students is about 22, with approximately 35 percent of the population being over the age of 25. Approximately 52 percent of the enrolled students are women. The racial/ethnic makeup of the campus is currently 80 percent white, non-Hispanic; 7 percent black, non-Hispanic; 1 percent American Indian/Alaskan native; 1 percent Asian/Pacific Islander; and 3 percent Hispanic. Of the total student body, 8 percent chose not to identify with any of the listed groups.

Enrolling students typically exhibit an 80 percent grade average in high school and a rank in the top 50 percent of their high school class.

Student Activities

The Student Activities program offers a wide variety of experiences for students through clubs, Student Congress, and other activities. On each campus, the staff assists students with the planning of events and programs. There are seventeen professional, curriculum-related clubs. In addition, there are thirty service/interest clubs that provide students with the opportunity to participate in a wide range of social, cultural, theatrical, athletic, and international activities to broaden their experiences.

MVCC participates in Division III of the National Junior College Athletic Association. Men's teams include baseball, basketball, bowling, cross-country, golf, ice hockey, indoor track, lacrosse, tennis, track and field, and soccer. Women's teams include basketball, bowling, cross-country, golf, indoor track, softball, soccer, tennis, track and field, and volleyball. The combined team win/loss record in 2004 (fall and winter sports) was 264-72-4, for a .786 winning percentage.

Facilities and Resources

MVCC has recently undergone major renovations as part of a $21-million campus master plan. As part of the plan, campus renovations have included practice lab facilities for nursing and respiratory-care students, cadaver labs for anatomy and physiology, and a student service center in Payne Hall that includes admissions, financial aid, the registrar, counseling, the business office, an advisement center, and a help desk. Other renovations to the Alumni College Center provided an expanded bookstore and a student health center.

A 65,000-square-foot information technology and performing arts conference center, the main feature of the project, houses computer labs, conferencing facilities, a state-of-the-art theater, and additional instructional computer support laboratories. It is a focal point of campus activities.

The campus collection includes 94,500 books and more than 727 periodical titles. CDs, audiotapes, DVDs, and videotapes are available for loan. Each campus library has a bestseller collection for recreational reading. The main campus library in Utica maintains a Career Center for job-search assistance. Each library provides a number of electronic resources, including Internet access.

Academic tutoring is available at no cost to students in the Learning Centers on both campuses. The centers offer instructional support in mathematics, writing, reading, study skills, life sciences, and computer and social sciences.

Location

The main campus is in Utica, New York, a small city of 50,000 people. The branch campus in Rome, New York, is located in a community of 30,000 people. The small-city atmosphere, coupled with a wide range of cultural activities, museums, access to the Adirondack Mountains, good public transportation, and sports venues, provides an excellent location for student growth and development.

Admission Requirements

The College is an open-admission, full-opportunity college. The College does not require applicants to complete standardized admissions tests such as the ACT or SAT.

Application and Information

Students can apply in a variety of ways. MVCC provides its own admission application; no processing fee is required. It is available from the Admissions Office or high schools in New York State, or it can be printed out from the College's Web site. MVCC also participates in the SUNY application process. Students can use the SUNY application, which costs $40 per college choice, as well.

For further information, interested students should contact:

Admissions Office
Mohawk Valley Community College
1101 Sherman Drive
Utica, New York 13501
Telephone: 315-792-5354
Fax: 315-792-5527
E-mail: admissions@mvcc.edu (U.S.)
　　　　international_admissions@mvcc.edu (international)
World Wide Web: http://www.mvcc.edu

MORRISON INSTITUTE OF TECHNOLOGY

MORRISON, ILLINOIS

The Institute and Its Mission

Morrison Institute of Technology is an independent, coeducational, not-for-profit, two-year college specializing in engineering technology. Founded in 1973, the college provides a cost-effective educational program that leads to a professional career in engineering technology. While many graduates go directly into industry, some transfer to four-year colleges offering a continuation of studies in the engineering technology fields.

All classes are day classes offered at the campus in Morrison, Illinois. Courses are offered on a semester basis, with semesters starting in January and August.

Morrison has an open admissions policy. Anyone with a valid high school diploma or equivalent may enroll. It has been found from experience that some students who have had an otherwise undistinguished high school career often thrive and blossom when challenged by a college program that specializes in the area in which they are interested. Many students who have found their niche at Morrison have gone on to earn advanced technical degrees and some have even founded thriving technical businesses.

The college is authorized to operate and grant degrees in the state of Illinois under the applicable state statutes administered by the Illinois Board of Higher Education. The Engineering Technology program is accredited by the Technology Accreditation Commission (TAC) of the Accreditation Board for Engineering and Technology (ABET), 111 Market Place, Suite 1050, Baltimore, Maryland 21201; telephone: 410-347-7700. In addition, the drafting design program at Morrison Institute of Technology is certified by the American Drafting Design Association, P.O. Box 11937, Columbia, South Carolina 29211 (telephone: 803-771-0008), at the design/drafter level. The college is also fully accredited by the Council on Occupational Education, 41 Perimeter Center, NE Suite 640, Atlanta, Georgia 30346; telephone: 800-917-2081 (toll-free). The state of Illinois, Department of Veterans Affairs, State Approving Agency, has approved Morrison Institute of Technology for veteran's training under Chapter 36 of Title #38, U.S. Code. The Division of Rehabilitation Services (DORS) and the Job Training Partnership Act (JTPA) both refer clients to the college for training. The college is listed in the Educational Directory, U.S. Department of Education, as a legally authorized institution of higher learning, allowing qualified students to participate in a number of federally funded student financial aid and grant programs. The college is also a member of the Service Members Opportunity Colleges (SOC), thus extending educational opportunities to service personnel while on active duty. The college is also a member of the Better Business Bureau.

Student housing facilities are available on campus in Odey Residence Hall. This facility has been designed to provide housing for students in an efficiency apartment arrangement. The residence hall is coeducational, but individual rooms are not coeducational and accommodations for married couples are not available.

Academic Programs

The engineering technology program has been developed and is kept current in accordance with suggested guidelines provided by nationally recognized technical education groups, accrediting organizations, and the college Industrial Advisory Board.

The curriculum for the engineering technology program has been designed with an appropriate balance of study in the areas of engineering and construction technology and manual drafting. In addition, to ensure that a student is prepared to assume a productive and contributing role as a citizen locally, nationally, and worldwide, a core of general education courses, including basic sciences, humanities, written and oral communications, mathematics, and computer literacy, are required to provide that academic foundation which the student must acquire to continue a lifelong learning process on a formal or informal basis. Extensive exposure to computer usage in computer-aided drafting (CAD) is also provided to all students.

The program has a very open architecture to permit students to concentrate their technical electives in the construction area or the design drafting area. A student may also elect to choose technical electives from both concentrations, if he or she desires a more general background. The minimum total number of technical elective credit hours required is 21 in order to meet the minimum total number of credit hours required to receive the Associate in Applied Science (A.A.S.) degree in engineering technology.

Costs

The tuition for 2004–05 was $5500 per semester, based upon taking a typical academic load of 12 to 19 semester credit hours. The computer usage fee was $100 per semester. Campus housing costs were $1100 per semester (not required if the student lives off campus). An additional $100 housing deposit is required for first-time residents. The housing cost figure does not include food, laundry, or general living expenses. Parking fees were $25 per semester (not required if the student does not park a car on campus). The recreation center/activity fee was $30 per semester, and the technology fee was $150.

Financial Aid

The curricula offered at Morrison Institute of Technology have been accredited by a nationally recognized accrediting agency. Qualified students, therefore, may take advantage of a number of federally funded student financial aid programs.

Grant programs at Morrison include the Federal Pell Grant, the Illinois Student Assistance Commission Monetary Award Program Grant, the Federal Supplemental Educational Opportunity Grant (FSEOG), the Federal Work-Study Program (FWS), tutorial and lab supervisors, the Department of Rehabilitation Services, the Job Training Partnership Act and the Veterans Educational Program.

Morrison Institute of Technology has available a limited number of scholarships for students now attending high school or the associated area vocational technical school, who wish to pursue engineering technology studies at Morrison Institute of Technology. These scholarships are independent of, and in addition to, any other financial aid a student may obtain. There are three areas in which a student can qualify for a Morrison Institute of Technology sponsored scholarship: the Morrison Institute of Technology Academic Scholarships, the Morrison

Institute of Technology Performance Scholarships, or the Morrison Institute of Technology Parent Scholarships.

Loan programs at Morrison include the Subsidized Federal Family Education Loan Program (student loan), the Unsubsidized Federal Family Education Loan Program (student loan), and the Federal PLUS loan.

All prospective students are encouraged to complete the Free Application for Federal Student Aid (FAFSA). Applications may be obtained from student's high school or the college Federal Aid Office or by downloading the FAFSA Express Software from the Web at http://www.ed.gov/offices/OPE/express.html.

Faculty

Morrison's faculty members are full-time employees. The student-faculty ratio is about 15:1, which means that students at Morrison receive a lot of personal attention. The faculty members are experienced in the areas they teach, and many are sought out by businesses to provide private consultative services; therefore, students learn what the profession is all about from persons who actually do the work. Approximately 30 percent of the faculty members are licensed professional engineers or surveyors. Approximately 23 percent have earned graduate-level degrees.

Student Body Profile

Morrison is a small college. The total full-time enrollment is about 200 students. The majority of the students attending are from the Midwest, mostly Illinois, Iowa, Wisconsin, and Indiana, with a few from the Eastern and Western states. Approximately 8–12 percent of the student enrollment is female, Hispanics make up 2–6 percent, African Americans number 6–10 percent, and Asians compose 1–2 percent. Approximately 75 percent of the students receive financial aid of some kind. About 60 percent are enrolled in the construction option while the remaining 40 percent are enrolled in the design drafting CAD option.

Student Activities

A student recreation center is provided for all students. The recreation center provides a place for students to relax; play pool, video games, Ping-Pong, card games, or chess; or watch TV. The facility also has a fitness room and laundromat. Vending machines are also available in the recreation center. Morrison Institute of Technology sponsors a student chapter of the Society of Manufacturing Engineers (SME). Activities associated with SME include attending regional meetings, field trips, and SME-sponsored exhibitions and seminars.

Facilities and Resources

The college has two main educational facilities, the A. E. Rambo Center, which also houses the administrative offices and student learning center, and the Technical Center, which houses mainly the computer laboratories, survey, soils laboratory, and multimedia lecture halls. The college also has the student recreation center complex and Odey Residence Hall.

Location

The campus is located on 17 acres on the south side of Morrison, Illinois. Morrison is about 45 minutes by car from the Quad-Cities area and about 2¼ hours by car from Chicago. Morrison is a picturesque small town with a population of 4,300. It is a neat, clean, and friendly town with tree-lined streets, neighborhood churches, and a small but busy business district. The college took its mascot emblem, "The Thoroughbreds," because there are many horse ranches in the area. The town is considered very safe: children play on the streets after dark here, and many people don't bother to lock their doors. Nearby is Rockwood State Park, several wildlife sanctuaries along the Mississippi River, and several park areas featuring Native American pre-Columbian settlements.

Admission Requirements

Admission to Morrison Institute of Technology is considered if the applicant has graduated from high school or has completed GED testing with scores that can be accepted as meeting high school requirements. It is recommended, but not required, that an applicant's educational background include at least one semester each of high school algebra and geometry. ACT or SAT test scores are required for academic counseling. Those students not having either test score are administered an institutional placement test.

All applicants are encouraged to schedule a tour of the campus. Tours are conducted during any of the formal open houses held by the college. If an applicant is unable to attend an open house, tours can be arranged on an individual basis by appointment. To complete the application process the following items are to be mailed to the college: a completed application for enrollment; the appropriate fees; an official high school transcript; if transfer analysis is requested, an official transcript from the institution granting the credit, mailed directly from the institution to Morrison Institute of Technology; a copy of the applicant's immunization record; and ACT, SAT, or placement test scores.

Application and Information

Students who wish to attend Morrison Institute of Technology may obtain the required admission application material and additional information by contacting:

Admissions Office
Morrison Institute of Technology
701 Portland Avenue
Morrison, Illinois 61270

Telephone: 815-772-7218
Fax: 815-772-7584
E-mail: admissions@morrison.tec.il.us
World Wide Web: http://www.morrison.tec.il.us

NEW MEXICO MILITARY INSTITUTE
ROSWELL, NEW MEXICO

The Institute and Its Mission

New Mexico Military Institute (NMMI) was established in 1891 and became a State (Territorial) School in 1893. Its purpose then and now was "for the education and training of the youth of this country with a mandate by law to be of as high a standard as like institutions in other states and territories of the United States." New Mexico Military Institute is primarily an academic institution operating within the framework of a military environment. NMMI is accredited by the North Central Association of Colleges and Schools, by the State of New Mexico Department of Education, and by the Department of the Army as a Military Junior college offering Junior and Senior ROTC. The Department of the Army has annually rated NMMI as an Honor School with Distinction or its equivalent since 1909.

Academic Programs

New Mexico Military Institute provides a comprehensive liberal arts curriculum including such disciplines as criminal justice, English, foreign language (Spanish, German, French), history, sociology, philosophy, political science, psychology, business administration, economics, computer science, chemistry, physics, biology, math through college calculus, geology, art, music, and physical education.

Associate Degree Programs The school awards an **Associate in Arts** degree, which requires 68 hours (6 in English, 6 to 8 in the humanities, 9 in social science/history, 8 in laboratory science, 6 to 12 in military science, 3 in mathematics, 2 in physical education, with the balance in electives). A normal load is 17 hours per semester. A cadet may choose to concentrate in a particular area while pursuing the Associate in Arts degree.

Many cadets are interested in pursuing a military career through the ROTC Basic Camp (Camp Challenge) approach. In order to qualify for the two-year commissioning program, a student must successfully complete a five-week training program conducted by the U.S. Army. This course occurs the summer before cadets enter their freshman (second class) year at New Mexico Military Institute. In special cases, students who have three or more years of high school ROTC or prior military service may apply for advanced placement credit. If accepted, they need not attend the Basic Camp. All eligible camp cadets can compete for a two-year scholarship that is awarded upon completion of the Basic Camp. The PMS has numerous Army ROTC two-year scholarships to award each year. Two years of advanced military science (MS III and MS IV), are required during the freshman and sophomore years, respectively. An advanced ROTC camp is required during the summer between MS III and MS IV. This camp is five weeks long. Upon successful completion of all phases, two years of college, Basic Camp, MS III, Advanced Camp, and MS IV, the cadet is commissioned as a second lieutenant in the United States Army Reserve.

Costs

For the academic year 2005–06, in-state tuition is $1156, out-of-state tuition is $3652, room is $1253, board is $2199, and the matriculation fee is $5. Accident insurance costs $200. Other fixed fees are $1157. Uniforms, books, and supplies cost $1700. This includes all uniform purchases. Additional funds are necessary for personal expenses. The amount needed varies depending on a cadet's spending habits. New Mexico Military Institute offers a deferred payment plan requiring an initial deposit of $2200. All costs are subject to change.

Financial Aid

Federal financial aid is available to all eligible college students. New Mexico Military Institute participates in the Federal Pell Grant, Federal Supplemental Educational Opportunity Grant, Federal Perkins Loan, Federal Work Study program, Stafford Loan, Parent Loan for Undergraduate Students program and specialized programs for New Mexico residents. New Mexico Military Institute offers a varied scholarship program for merit-based and need-based considerations. The New Mexico Legislator Scholarship Program is available only to New Mexico residents. Scholarships are renewable based on the continued eligibility of the recipient. In 2003–04, more than 76 percent of the college student body received either federal or scholarship assistance amounting to more than $1.3 million. Currently, 410 college students receive $1,368,295 in assistance, ranging from $500 scholarships to $7000 in federal financial aid. A full-time financial aid staff is available.

Faculty

NMMI has 63 full-time faculty members, many with terminal degrees, and all are required to have at least a master's degree. The student-faculty ratio is 18:1.

Student Body Profile

The junior college population of 450 to 500 at New Mexico Military Institute generally includes cadets from more than forty-four different states and twelve other countries. Typically, the ethnic breakdown includes 17 percent Hispanic, 8 percent African American, 6 percent Asian, and 2 percent Native American students. In 2003–04, there were 111 cadets representing thirteen different nations. Twenty-one percent of the Corps of Cadets were female. More than one third of college students are pursuing an Army commission. College cadets entering the Corps of Cadets for the first time are new cadets for one semester. New cadets receive yearling status at the completion of one semester and old cadet status with the completion of one year. The new cadet environment is stressful, formal, strict, and just. All cadets are held strictly accountable for their actions. NMMI operates with a Cadet Honor Code that states, "A cadet will not lie, cheat, or steal, or tolerate those who do. Every cadet is obligated to support and enforce the honor system." NMMI maintains a strict policy regarding the possession, use, or sale of alcoholic beverages and illegal drugs. All cadets live on campus.

Student Activities

Students enjoy video games, pool, bowling, and the snack bar during their free time. Movies on Saturday nights also contribute to weekend activities. Informal dances are held about twice a month. Recorded music is provided by students and professional disc jockeys. Two formal balls are held each year, the Homecoming Ball in the fall and the Final Ball in the spring. Escorts from all over the country attend. NMMI students can participate in outdoor activities at the nearby ski resort area of Ruidoso and the Mescalero Apache Indian Reservation. Other attractions include Carlsbad Caverns, Lincoln National Forest, Bottomless Lakes, Living Desert State Park, and the historical town of Lincoln, famous for the exploits of Billy the Kid, Pat Garrett, and John Chisum. Rounding out the Institute's extracurricular activities, students enjoy marching and concert bands, soccer, judo and karate clubs, color guards, and rifle and drill teams. Students may also participate in swimming, drama, and academic honorary societies. Student publications include *The Maverick* and the Bronco yearbook.

Facilities and Resources

NMMI's campus encompasses more than 40 acres and has some of the finest academic facilities in the country. The yellow brick buildings reflect a military style traditional to the campus since 1909. The Toles Learning Center houses the library and its 68,000-volume collection, TV/communication studio, academic computer center, 200-seat lecture hall, classrooms, and the Student Assistance Center. Available to cadets is an online catalog. Also located in the Toles Learning Center are the Computer Services Center and the Career Lab, housed in the Student Assistance Center. College faculty academic advisers are available to provide students with assistance in college exploration and selection. A computerized college scholarship search program is available in the center for cadet use. NMMI is a regional test center for the ACT, SAT, and GRE. College-Level Examination Program (CLEP) exams are available to those cadets wishing to challenge a course. A liaison officer is available whose duties include working with and assisting students interested in attending the national service academies. The Student Assistance Center provides professional advisers who offer academic and career counseling. Transfer guidance on colleges and service academy admission is also available. Approximately $15 million in cadet room renovations have allowed each cadet access to a state-of-the-art computer network, cable TV, and telephones. New Mexico Military Institute has excellent athletic facilities and athletic playing fields. They include a physical education building with four regulation basketball courts, four handball/racquetball courts, an Olympic-size swimming pool with sunning decks, Nautilus exercise equipment and Universal exercise machines. A separate building houses the varsity team locker and weight rooms and a gymnasium for varsity basketball games. The playing fields include twelve tennis courts, a baseball diamond, running tracks (quarter-mile and half-mile), football and soccer fields, and an eighteen-hole golf course.

Location

New Mexico Military Institute is located in the city of Roswell in the southeastern part of New Mexico. It is within 70 miles of skiing in the mountains of Ruidoso and within 200 miles of El Paso to the south and Albuquerque and Santa Fe to the north. The nearest regional airports are Albuquerque International Airport and Lubbock International Airport.

Admission Requirements

The minimum standards for normal admission to the college are graduation from high school with at least a 2.0 GPA (on a 4.0 scale) or equivalent and a composite score of 18 on the ACT, or a combined verbal/mathematics score of 870 on the recentered SAT I and a 2.0 GPA, or a minimum 2.5 GPA for all high school core courses and graduating in the top 50 percent of the high school class. Prospective students for the Army Commissioning program will need a composite score of 19 on the ACT, or a combined verbal/mathematics score of 920 on the recentered SAT I. Applicants and members of the Corps of Cadets must have never been married, have no dependent children, be in good physical condition, and be able to participate in athletic and leadership development activities. In addition, they cannot be more than the age of 22 at the time of admission. The admissions policy of New Mexico Military Institute is nondiscriminatory with respect to race, color, creed, or national or ethnic origin and is in compliance with federal laws with respect to sex and the handicapped. Priority of admission is given to New Mexico residents.

Application and Information

An initial inquiry is welcome at any time. Campus tours are conducted weekdays. Interested students should call to schedule an appointment at any time except for school holidays. Applications are accepted through July into all classes. Notification of acceptance is made on a rolling admissions basis.

For more information, students should contact:

Director of Admissions
New Mexico Military Institute
101 West College Boulevard
Roswell, New Mexico 88201-5173
Telephone: 505-624-8050
           800-421-5376 (toll-free)
Fax: 505-624-8058
E-mail: admissions@nmmi.edu
World Wide Web: http://www.nmmi.edu

Cadets find time to study in the New Mexico sunshine.

NEW YORK COLLEGE OF HEALTH PROFESSIONS
School of Massage Therapy
SYOSSET AND BROOKLYN, NEW YORK

The College and Its Mission

New York College of Health Professions, a private nonprofit institution, is one of the nation's premier centers of holistic medicine. The College educates students, treats patients, and conducts innovative research. Founded in 1981, New York College has been a leader in holistic education and care for more than twenty years. It is firmly rooted in the principles of blending Western and Eastern practices, or Integrative medicine.

New York College offers accredited degree programs in the field of complementary medicine. Undergraduate programs include an associate degree in massage therapy and a bachelor's degree in advanced Asian bodywork. Graduate programs include combined bachelor's and master's degrees in acupuncture or oriental medicine (the combined study of acupuncture and herbs). All programs lead to New York State licensing and/or national certification.

The College also offers a 495-clock-hour continuing education program in holistic nursing for RNs and a selection of other continuing education courses and workshops for both health-care professionals and the general public. New York College was awarded a grant from New York State to train all the RNs at Bellevue Hospital in New York City in an Introduction to Holistic Nursing course and receives grants from SEIU 1199, the health-care workers' union, for RNs from Flushing Hospital and Beth Israel Hospital Center to also participate in the College's holistic nursing programs.

New York College is chartered by the Board of Regents of the University of the State of New York, and all programs are registered by the New York State Education Department. The Acupuncture and Oriental Medicine programs are accredited by the Accrediting Commission for Acupuncture and Oriental Medicine (ACAOM). The Oriental Medicine program is also approved by the California Acupuncture Board. The College is approved as a provider of Continuing Education by the New York State Nurses Association Council on Continuing Education and the National Certification Board for Therapeutic Massage and Bodywork. The College is a member of numerous professional organizations related to the fields of oriental medicine and massage therapy.

Academic Programs

The Massage Therapy program at New York College began in 1981 and was the School's first educational program. It has since become nationally recognized and was cited for academic excellence in 1997 by the National Certification Board for Therapeutic Massage and Bodywork. In 1996, New York College became the first college in the United States to award an associate degree in massage therapy. The program exceeds national certification and state licensing requirements. First-time candidates from New York College rank among the highest pass rates on the New York State Massage Therapy Licensing Examination.

The benefits of massage therapy have become widely recognized. Documentation on the effects of massage shows that it improves circulation and lymph drainage and can help treat sports injuries and alleviate stress, headaches, and other aches and pains. When practiced in conjunction with Western medical treatment, massage can also be used to treat arthritis, hypertension, diabetes, asthma, bronchitis, and neuromuscular diseases, among others. Massage therapy most commonly falls into two categories: Western (Swedish), which focuses on the musculoskeletal system and is based on standard Western anatomy and physiology, and Eastern, or Oriental, which is based on the movement of energy through various channels in the body. At New York College, students learn both of these modalities as well as the specific techniques for sports massage, chair massage, shiatsu, reflexology, and more. Career opportunities in the field of massage therapy continue to grow and

range from owning one's own business to working in spas, health clubs, resorts, Wellness Centers, hospitals, or doctors' offices or with sports teams.

New York College's Massage Therapy program is a 72-credit program. Upon completion, graduates receive an Associate of Occupational Studies (A.O.S.) degree in massage therapy. They are eligible to sit for the New York State Licensing Exam in Massage Therapy, the National Certification Exam for Therapeutic Massage and Bodywork, and the NCCAOM National Certification Exam for Oriental Bodywork Therapy. Course work for the Massage Therapy program includes in-depth study of both Western and Eastern health sciences, Western and Oriental bodywork techniques, and tai chi chuan, qi gong, or yoga. Courses are also offered in ethics, professional development, and business practice. The culmination of the program is the intensive clinical internship that students undergo in the College's on-site teaching clinic.

New York College operates on a fifteen-week trimester system. New students are admitted to the College for the September, January, and May trimesters. Ten-week, second-cycle trimester admissions may be added when there is sufficient demand. The program can be completed in twenty months, twenty-four months, or thirty-six months on a part-time basis.

Off-Campus Programs

New York College offers travel/life-experience trips abroad to its Luo Yang Medical Center facility in the People's Republic of China. Programs are three-week immersion trips to China that include visits to hospitals as well as attendance at lectures and demonstrations at the medical center and visits to historic sites throughout the country.

Costs

Tuition is based on a per-credit charge of $275 and is paid each trimester. The application fee is $85. Students should expect to incur an additional $2000 in expenses for texts and supplies throughout their course of study.

Financial Aid

New York College is an eligible institution approved by the United States Department of Education and the New York State Education Department to participate in the following programs: Federal Pell Grant, Federal Supplemental Educational Opportunity Grant (FSEOG), Tuition Assistance Program (TAP), Aid for Part-Time Study, Federal Work-Study Program, Veterans Administration, Vocational Rehabilitation, Federal Stafford Student Loan, Federal PLUS loan, and alternative financing. For additional information, students should contact the College's Office of Financial Aid (800-922-7337 Ext. 244).

Faculty

New York College has a total of 90 faculty members, 16 of whom are full-time. The faculty-student ratio is 1:16 for technique classes, 1:40 for didactic classes, and up to 1:6 for clinical internships.

Student Body Profile

Total current enrollment at New York College is about 1,000 students, most of whom are enrolled in the Massage Therapy program. New York College does not have student housing; therefore, the majority of students are from the local area, with the largest group coming from Long Island, Brooklyn, and Queens. However, the College attracts a percentage of both international and out-of-state students.

Facilities and Resources

The main Syosset, Long Island, campus occupies 70,000 square feet in a modern facility on three levels. Within the facility are the administrative offices, classrooms for all College educational programs, a physical arts deck, the Integrative Health Center, Academic Health Care Teaching Clinics, the Herbal Dispensary, the James and Lenore Jacobson Library, the café, the bookstore, and student and faculty lounges. Classrooms are designed and used specifically for lecture or technique work and contain the most recent instructional materials. The physical arts deck for the practice of tai chi, hatha yoga, and qi gong is specifically designed with space, light, and quiet.

The James and Lenore Jacobson Library contains the most extensive collection of materials about holistic medicine available on Long Island. The library houses a collection of books and journals specializing in Oriental medicine, complementary and alternative therapies, acupuncture, herbs, massage therapy, and holistic nursing. The library belongs to a consortium of special and medical libraries that provide interloans of additional books and journal articles. Several networked workstations provide access to the computerized book collection catalog and magazine subject index, various software and CD-ROM programs, the Internet, and various online professional databases.

The Academic Health Care Teaching Clinics are an integral part of a student's educational experience through this internship. The clinics provide affordable holistic health care to members of the community, treating more than 30,000 patients annually. Supervised student treatments include Swedish massage, Amma massage, acupuncture, herbal consultations, and holistic nursing.

The Integrative Health Center is the professional clinic of the College and offers the skills and services of licensed holistic practitioners to patients of all ages. For more than twenty-five years, this fully integrated clinic has provided patients with minimally invasive therapies, including acupuncture; herbal medicine; many modalities of massage therapy, such as Swedish, sports, Amma, shiatsu, reflexology, and pregnancy massage; and chiropractic and holistic nursing. Special patient programs exist for smoking cessation, weight loss, and cancer support.

In 2004, New York College opened a center in Brooklyn, New York, and began conducting classes in all degree programs. Located in a private wing of the Brooklyn Hospital Center, Caledonian Campus, this additional location is convenient and easily reached by subway or bus for students from the outer boroughs of New York City as well as Manhattan. This center has both didactic and technique classrooms, a solarium for physical arts, a lab, administration and faculty offices, a student lounge for studying, and a student locker room. It is located close to the Brooklyn Public Library and to stores and restaurants. The College offers day, evening, and weekend classes in Brooklyn, and a massage clinic for the community where the students participate in their internship.

The Dean of Students is responsible for special-needs students, academic progress advisement, the organization of study groups, and tutoring services. New York College's Career Services Office offers graduates assistance with job placement. Currently, the College lists more than 300 employment and rental opportunities for its licensed graduates. Sponsorship opportunities for graduates waiting to sit for licensure are also available.

Location

Long Island The main campus of New York College is located in Syosset, on the North Shore of Long Island, approximately 30 miles from Manhattan. Its proximity to all major parkways and railroad service provides easy access to one of the world's most exciting cities, while capturing the serenity, beauty, and open space of the suburbs. Long Island stretches for 110 miles and is a wealth of natural, cultural, and historic treasures. Some of the world's most beautiful sandy beaches surround the island—from the popular Jones Beach to the chic Hamptons to the barrier isle of Fire Island with its pristine beaches and absence of automobiles. The island's fifteen state parks also offer an abundance of recreational opportunities and even include a polo field. There are nearly 100 museums on the island.

Brooklyn New York College operates a center in Brooklyn, located at the Brooklyn Hospital Center, Caledonian Campus, at 100 Parkside Avenue. This facility is located directly across the street from Prospect Park and is reached easily by bus or subway from all of the boroughs of New York City, including Manhattan.

China New York College owns the Luo Yang Medical Center in the People's Republic of China. Situated in the ancient capital of China, the 35-acre site is surrounded by historic and important attractions. Modern buildings are fully equipped with Western fixtures.

Admission Requirements

New York College is deeply committed to recruiting the most highly qualified and motivated candidates for admission. The College is particularly proud of its diverse population that is made up of students from a variety of cultural backgrounds, who possess many unique gifts and strengths. New York College students contribute to the friendly and supportive atmosphere at the College.

Applicants who have graduated from high school must have achieved a minimum GPA of 2.0 or have equivalent qualifications. Students may earn their GED certificate while enrolled in a massage therapy degree program by successfully completing 24 credits of specified credit courses in six subject areas. Candidates must be at least 17 years of age and, in accordance with New York State guidelines, must hold U.S. citizenship, be an alien lawfully admitted for permanent residence in the U.S., or hold a valid visa. The College is authorized under federal law to enroll nonimmigrant alien students.

Candidates must complete and submit an application along with an $85 application fee and arrange for the submission of an official high school transcript (or proof of equivalency) and official transcripts from all previously attended higher educational institutions. Candidates are notified promptly of the receipt of their application and advised which, if any, of the required documents have not been received by the Admissions Office. An admissions interview is required. The College offers on-the-spot enrollment: a student can be interviewed and conditionally admitted and enrolled in one visit.

Application and Information

New students are admitted to New York College for the September, January, and May trimesters. Additional second-cycle trimesters may be added if there is sufficient demand. It is recommended that applications be submitted three to four months prior to the desired entrance date.

Admissions Office
New York College of Health Professions
6801 Jericho Turnpike
Syosset, New York 11791

Telephone: 800-9-CAREER Ext. 351 (toll-free)
Fax: 516-364-0989
E-mail: admissions@nycollege.edu
World Wide Web: http://www.nycollege.edu

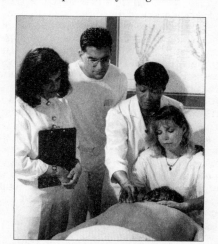

The Academic Health Care Teaching Clinics are an integral part of a student's education.

NORTHWESTERN BUSINESS COLLEGE

CHICAGO, ILLINOIS

The College and Its Mission

Northwestern Business College (NBC) was established in 1902 as Chicago's first private business college, and for nearly a century it has been helping ambitious students get started on the path to success. As business needs have changed over the years, so have the College's programs of study. Students find that today's NBC is much different from the traditional "business college" of years past. Just like its students, NBC is diversified, career-oriented, and right in step with the times. More than 2,400 students attend classes at the College's three easily accessible campuses: the first is in Jefferson Park, just northwest of the Chicago Loop; the second, in suburban Bridgeview; and the third, in Naperville on Mill Street and Diehl Road.

The College believes in its mission: "The professionals of Northwestern Business College, an institution of higher education, empower students to realize their career potential and individual goals. Our quality educational programs combined with our commitment, integrity, and personal attention provide a vital human resource to the community." These educational programs provide hands-on knowledge and training in many of today's most-sought-after professions. A highly focused curriculum and career-relevant courses make it possible for students to earn an Associate in Applied Science degree in only eighteen months or complete a certificate in less than a year.

Northwestern Business College is accredited by the Higher Learning Commission of the North Central Association of Colleges and Schools (30 North LaSalle Street, Suite 2400, Chicago, Illinois 60602-2504; telephone: 312-263-0456). The medical assisting program is accredited by the Commission on Accreditation of Allied Health Education Programs (CAAHEP) on the recommendation of the Committee on Accreditation for Medical Assistant Education, also known as the Curriculum Review Board of the American Association of Medical Assistants' Endowment (AAMAE; 35 East Wacker Drive, Suite 1970, Chicago, Illinois 60601; telephone: 312-553-9355). Graduates of the medical assisting program are eligible to sit for the national Certified Medical Assistant (CMA) exam. The health information technology program is accredited by the Commission on Accreditation of Allied Health Education Programs, in cooperation with the Council on Accreditation of the American Health Information Management Association (AHIMA). Graduates of accredited programs are eligible to take the national qualifying examination for certification as an accredited record technician (ART). The business administration, executive accounting, computer, and administrative assisting programs are accredited by the Association of Collegiate Business Schools and Programs (ACBSP; 7007 College Boulevard, Suite 420, Overland Park, Kansas 66211; telephone: 913-339-9356). The paralegal and legal nurse consultant programs are approved by the American Bar Association (ABA). The College is also approved for veterans' training under the G.I. bill for veterans' educational assistance, as well as by the United States Department of Justice Immigration and Naturalization Service as an institution of higher education for training international students. It is approved by the Board of Higher Education of the State of Illinois and authorized by the board to award the Associate in Applied Science degree.

Academic Programs

The academic calendar year is divided into four quarters: fall, winter, spring, and summer. Each term is approximately twelve weeks in length. The fall, winter, and spring terms constitute a traditional academic year. The summer quarter is ten weeks, and students who wish to graduate early attend all four quarters.

Northwestern Business College is committed to providing students with both a foundation and the essential tools necessary for continued personal and intellectual growth. To that end, the College requires that a minimum of 34 percent of a student's course work be in general education. This general education core requirement includes courses in communications, humanities, social and behavioral sciences, mathematics, and life skills and is intended to help students build a foundation for learning through study and exploration.

Associate Degree Programs The College offers Associate in Applied Science degrees in administrative assisting, business administration, business computer programming, business information systems, computer technical support, criminal justice, cyber security, executive accounting, health information technology, hospitality tourism management, massage therapy, medical assisting, and paralegal studies. In order to graduate with an Associate in Applied Science degree, each student must successfully complete a minimum of 100 quarter hours of credit, with a cumulative GPA of at least 2.0.

Certificate Programs Certificates are offered in accounting, business, coding specialist studies, gaming management, health-care billing specialist studies, IT support specialist studies, legal nurse consultant studies, massage therapy, medical machine transcriptionist studies, and meeting planning and convention management.

Externship and Co-op Programs Many programs require students to complete an externship, which puts students on-site with one of the area's major employers. Students work in their fields of study, earn college credit, and gain valuable business skills at the same time, while also opening doors to potential full-time employment. Externship participants are not paid and assume the costs of transportation, lunch, appropriate wardrobe, and other related expenses.

Credit for Nontraditional Learning Experiences

The College evaluates life experience credits through written examination. Northwestern Business College offers two types of proficiency examinations to determine a student's prior knowledge of a subject. Advanced Status Examinations are given to determine advanced class placement but do not provide college credit. Credit by Examination (CBE) is a comprehensive exam that relates specifically to the subject matter for which credit is sought, and students who pass the CBE receive credit for that course. Students should contact the Student Services Department for the list of classes for which proficiency examinations may be taken.

Costs

For the 2005–06 academic year, tuition is $290 per credit hour for lecture classes and $390 per credit hour for laboratory and computer classes.

Financial Aid

Northwestern Business College recognizes that many students need financial assistance. The College's Financial Aid Office is available to assist those students and families requiring financial assistance in addition to their own contributions to cover the cost of their NBC education. Financial assistance is available to eligible students who are enrolled for 7 or more credit hours. Available assistance includes Federal Work-Study, Pell Grants, Supplemental Educational Opportunity Grants, Federal PLUS Program, TERI Loans, and Federal Stafford Student Loans, as well as veterans' benefits and state of Illinois MAP and IIA grants. In addition, the College offers institutional scholarships and a payment plan. All students applying for financial aid must complete and submit the FAFSA as well as any other required forms, depending upon the type of aid sought.

Faculty

Because NBC's faculty comprises working professionals who have built successful careers in the same fields in which they teach, they are able to share insights and perspectives that give meaning to the "real world" outside of the classroom. The more than 130 faculty members at Northwestern include practicing lawyers, certified public accountants, travel agents, computer programmers, and medical personnel. Small class size (the College has an average student-faculty ratio of 18:1) and a comfortable atmosphere allow faculty members and students to work together on a more personal level.

Student Body Profile

The caliber of NBC's faculty members is matched by the high quality of the students who enroll. The commitment, creativity, and seriousness of the student body is one of the school's greatest strengths. NBC's enrollment includes approximately 2,400 students. Seventy percent reside within Chicago city limits. Others travel from neighboring suburbs, and some come from as far away as Indiana. Several hundred of these students attend part-time.

Nearly twenty countries are represented in the student body. NBC's international students come from diverse ethnic heritages and pride themselves on their bilingual expertise. The College encourages and welcomes economic, racial, ethnic, and religious diversity in its student body.

Student Activities

NBC believes that college is about more than simply attending classes. It is also about participating in activities, sharing interests, helping others succeed, and building lasting friendships. The College's numerous organizations encourage students to explore their career interests outside of the classroom. NBC also sponsors a chapter of Alpha Beta Gamma, a national business society established in 1970 to recognize and encourage scholarship among college students in business curricula. In addition, the College sponsors Student Ambassadors, a service organization of students responsible for representing NBC at special community and college events, and Students Helping Students, a peer tutoring program.

Facilities and Resources

Advisement/Counseling All new students are assigned a faculty adviser, who is available throughout the school year to provide advice and assistance with scheduling classes and other academic matters. The College provides personal counseling to help students with school-related problems and/or to provide referral assistance to appropriate outside agencies.

Career Development and Alumni Relations Offices Because the majority of NBC students are interested in gaining work experience while attending college, job placement is available after their first quarter. The NBC Office of Career Development and Alumni Relations also serves as an active liaison between employers and graduates. More than 95 percent of NBC's graduates have been successfully placed in the field of their choice. The College offers a lifetime placement assistance program that graduates may use at any time in the future. In addition to on-campus recruitment and career fairs, NBC offers guidance in resume writing, interviewing, and job-search techniques, which build the confidence of students and enhance their professional images.

Library Services Each campus has a library equipped with current books, periodicals, and reference material for student use

in classroom research. Students also have access to the Internet as well as Westlaw, LexisNexis, and ProQuest. In addition, videotapes and audiotapes are available for student use.

Location

Chicago The Chicago campus, located on Milwaukee Avenue and Lawrence Avenue, is 7 miles northwest of Chicago's Loop, in a residential/commercial area. It is easily accessible by bus, rapid transit, commuter train, and car and is convenient to both the Kennedy and Edens Expressways.

Bridgeview Located at 79th and Harlem, the Bridgeview campus serves the southern suburbs. This totally renovated facility offers 88,000 square feet of space, more than three times that of the former campus in Hickory Hills, which was replaced by the Bridgeview campus in 2003.

Naperville NBC's Naperville location was opened in 2002 on the corner of Mill Street and Diehl Road in an office complex near Interstate 88 and Naverville Road. This location serves DuPage, Kane, Will, and Cook Counties.

Admission Requirements

Northwestern Business College seeks students who have the desire for practical career preparation in their chosen fields and have the ability to achieve academic success. To be admitted to the College, a prospective student must be a high school graduate or hold a General Educational Development (GED) certificate and have the minimum required SAT or ACT scores (minimum conditional scores are 550–700 on the SAT and 15 on the ACT). The placement exam administered on campus may be used for admission if SAT or ACT scores are not available.

Northwestern Business College may accept credit for a course taken at another accredited college or university if the grade earned is a C or better and the course is college level, credit bearing, and equivalent to one taught at NBC in the student's major. Fifty percent of the entire program and 67 percent of the major program must be completed at NBC. If a student changes majors, his or her transferred credits are reevaluated.

International applicants are expected to meet the same admissions requirements as all other students. In addition, applicants whose native language is not English are requested to take the Test of English as a Foreign Language (TOEFL) and must achieve a minimum score of 500; or they may use the placement exam administered on campus in lieu of the TOEFL.

Application and Information

Applications are accepted on an ongoing basis. Interested students are invited to visit Northwestern Business College's Web site at http://www.northwesternbc.edu. All prospective students should contact the Admissions Department at:

Chicago Campus
Northwestern Business College
4839 North Milwaukee Avenue
Chicago, Illinois 60630
Telephone: 800-396-5613 (toll-free)

Bridgeview Campus
Northwestern Business College
7725 South Harlem Avenue
Bridgeview, Illinois 60455
Telephone: 800-682-9113 (toll-free)

Naperville Campus
Northwestern Business College
1805 F Mill Street
Naperville, Illinois 60563
Telephone: 866-622-6785 (toll-free)

PENNSYLVANIA COLLEGE OF TECHNOLOGY
An Affiliate of The Pennsylvania State University
WILLIAMSPORT, PENNSYLVANIA

Pennsylvania
College of
Technology

PENNSTATE

The College and Its Mission

Pennsylvania College of Technology (Penn College) is an affiliate of the Pennsylvania State University (Penn State) and is Pennsylvania's premier technical college. Penn College is a special mission affiliate of Penn State, committed to applied technology education. Partnerships with industry leaders, including Honda, Toyota, Ford, Mack Trucks, and Caterpillar, provide students unique opportunities to advance their careers. Graduate surveys indicate a placement rate that exceeds 90 percent annually (100 percent in some majors). Among the keys to graduate success are Penn College's emphasis on small classes (18 students is the average size of freshman classes), personal attention, and hands-on experience using the latest technology. Student projects reflect real working situations. A number of campus buildings, including a conference center, a Victorian guest house, an athletic field house, and a rustic retreat used for professional gatherings, have been designed, constructed, and maintained by students. The facilities stand as testimony to the quality of a Penn College education. State-of-the-art classrooms and laboratories on the ultramodern campus located in Williamsport, Pennsylvania, reflect the expectations of the modern workforce.

Academic Programs

Associate Degree Majors Associate degrees (A.A.S., A.A.A., or A.A.) are offered in accounting; advertising art; architectural technology; automated manufacturing technology; automotive service sales and marketing; automotive technology (including Ford and Toyota industry-sponsored majors); aviation technology; baking and pastry arts; building construction technology; building construction technology (masonry emphasis); business management; civil engineering technology; collision repair technology; computer-aided drafting; culinary arts technology; dental hygiene; diesel technology (including a Mack Trucks industry-sponsored major); early childhood education; electric power generation technology; electrical technology; electromechanical maintenance technology; electronics technology (emphases in Cisco systems, communications/fiber optics, computer-automation maintenance, electronics engineering technology, industrial process control, and semiconductor processing technology); environmental technology; floral design/interior plantscape; forest technology; general studies; graphic communications technology; health arts; health information technology; heating, ventilation, and air conditioning (HVAC) technology; heavy construction equipment technology (emphases in a Caterpillar industry-sponsored major, operator studies, and technician studies); hospitality management; human services; individual studies; information systems (emphases in Cisco technology, information technology technician studies, network technology, technical support technology, and Web and applications technology); landscape/nursery technology; landscape/nursery technology (turfgrass management emphasis); legal assistant (paralegal) studies; mass media communication; nursing; occupational therapy assistant studies; office information technology (emphases in medical office information, specialized office information, and Web design); paramedic technology; physical fitness specialist studies; plastics and polymer technology; radiography; surgical technology; surveying technology; toolmaking technology; and welding technology.

Bachelor's Degree Majors Many associate degree graduates choose to continue their education with unique **Bachelor of Science (B.S.) degrees** that focus on applied technology in traditional and emerging career fields. Majors include accounting; applied health studies; applied human services; automotive technology management; aviation maintenance technology; building automation technology; business administration (concentrations in banking and finance, management, management information systems, marketing, and small business and entrepreneurship); civil engineering technology; computer-aided product design; computer information technology (concentrations in IT security specialist studies, network specialist studies, technical support specialist studies, and Web and applications development); construction management; culinary arts technology; dental hygiene (concentrations in health policy and administration and special-population care); electronics engineering technology; environmental technology management; graphic communications management; graphic design; heating, ventilation, and air

conditioning (HVAC) technology; legal assistant/paralegal studies; manufacturing engineering technology; nursing; physician assistant studies; plastics and polymer engineering technology; residential construction technology and management; technology management; and welding and fabrication engineering technology.

Certificate Majors Certificates are offered in automotive service technician studies, aviation maintenance technician studies, cabinetmaking and millwork, computer applications technology, collision repair technician studies, construction carpentry, diesel technician studies, electrical occupations, machinist general, nurse/health-care paralegal studies, plumbing, practical nursing, and welding.

Off-Campus Programs

Cooperative education and internships give students the opportunity to gain workforce experience. Penn College students have worked throughout Pennsylvania and in eighteen other states, the District of Columbia, Canada, and Puerto Rico.

Costs

Tuition and related fees are based on a per-credit-hour charge. Yearly tuition and fees, based upon 15 credits per semester for 2004–05 (not including housing, food, living expenses, lab fees, books, tools, uniforms, supplies, and major personal expenses), were $8940 for in-state students and $11,250 for out-of-state students. The exact costs depend upon the specific courses and number of credits taken. In 2004–05, costs ranged from $1563 to $2000 per semester for on-campus housing. All on-campus housing is apartment style (kitchen, living room, bedrooms, and bathroom). On-campus housing is alcohol-free, drug-free, noise controlled, and secure. Resident and nonresident students may purchase meal plans that are accepted in the College's dining facilities, which include the main dining hall, a bistro-style restaurant, a gourmet restaurant, two convenience stores, a coffeehouse, and on-campus pizza delivery. The College Store offers an Express Pay plan for student purchases. Students can add to their meal plan and Express Pay accounts during the semester and can place College Store orders via the Internet.

Financial Aid

Approximately 4 out of 5 Penn College students receive financial assistance. Types of aid available include Federal Pell Grants, Pennsylvania Higher Education Assistance Agency grants, Federal Supplemental Educational Opportunity Grants, Federal Work-Study Program awards, Federal Stafford Student Loans, Federal PLUS loans, veterans' benefits, and Bureau of Vocational Rehabilitation benefits. A deferred-payment plan allows students to spread their tuition cost over two payments each semester. Penn College offers academic, need-based, and technical scholarships to qualified students. For detailed information on scholarships, students should contact the Financial Aid Office or visit the Web at http://www.pct.edu/scholarships.

Faculty

Penn College's 473 faculty members (288 full-time and 185 part-time) provide individual attention that students need to be successful in the classroom and the workplace. Faculty members are experienced in their fields. Each year, Penn College recognizes excellence among the faculty members through distinguished faculty award programs. Small class sizes (with a current student-faculty ratio of 18:1) promote student success. Advisory committees of faculty members and business and industry leaders work together to ensure that programs meet current workplace needs.

Student Body Profile

More than 6,300 students attend Penn College. More than 7,000 additional men and women take part in the extensive noncredit and continuing education program, which includes customized business and industry courses offered through Workforce Development and Continuing Education.

Student Activities

Penn College is a place where future technicians and designers mingle easily with chefs, health-care personnel, and business students. It is a place where students actually construct campus buildings, cater important campus functions, compute strategies for engineering technology problems, and care for children in an on-campus day-care center and kindergarten program. A magnificent Campus Center provides an opportunity to eat, shop, work out, and spend time with friends. A modern fitness center, College Store, convenience store, art gallery, TV lounge, Internet lounge, video rental and game room, coffeehouse, and bistro-style restaurant are among the features of the Campus Center. Impressive cultural activities are available both on the main campus and at Penn College's Community Arts Center, a restored 1920s-era theater in downtown Williamsport. Student ticket rates are available for performances that include Broadway shows, opera, ballet, symphony orchestras, and popular entertainers.

Student Government Association (SGA) and Wildcat Events Board (WEB) represent the student body in matters related to College policy and activities. Participation offers students the opportunity to develop leadership skills while contributing to the well-being of the College and the student body. In addition, more than forty student organizations offer opportunities for organized campus activity and leadership experiences.

The Penn College Wildcats compete in Penn State's Commonwealth Campus Athletics Conferences. Varsity sports include archery, baseball, basketball, bowling, cross-country, golf, soccer, softball, team tennis, and volleyball. Penn College's men's compound-bow archery team is a former two-time national champion in the National Archery Association (NAA).

Facilities and Resources

The hands-on experience offered at Penn College creates a need for a variety of special academic facilities. Students enjoy access to an advanced computer network through both on-campus and dial-in services. On-campus computer labs offer an average of one computer for every 4 students. Besides extensive, accessible computer labs, the main campus has an automated manufacturing center, plastics manufacturing center, printing and publishing facility, dental hygiene clinic, automotive repair center, machine shop, welding shop, building trades center, architectural studio, computer-aided drafting labs, broadcast studio, modern science laboratories, fine-dining restaurant, campus guest house, aviation and avionics instructional facility located at the regional airport, greenhouses, working sawmill, diesel center, and heavy-equipment training site.

Library Services The library houses a collection of more than 110,000 items, including books, periodicals, and audiovisual and electronic materials. The collection grows at the rate of nearly 6,000 titles per year to keep pace with student needs. The fully automated catalog of library resources, including more than 7,000 online periodical subscriptions and other databases, is available through the library's Web site and is available on and off campus. Basic library instruction is offered to each first-year student. Library hours include late evenings and weekends.

Location

The main campus is in Williamsport, a city known internationally as the home of Little League Baseball. Williamsport (population 32,500) is the seat of Lycoming County (population 121,000); it offers the advantages of a city situated in a rural environment. The surrounding area is an outdoor-lovers' paradise, offering hunting, fishing, hiking, camping, backpacking, and more, just minutes from downtown. Besides the main campus in Williamsport, Penn College also offers classes at three other locations: the Advanced Automotive Technology Center at Wahoo Drive Industrial Park in Williamsport, the Aviation Center at the Williamsport Regional Airport in Montoursville, and the Earth Science Center, 10 miles south of Williamsport near Allenwood.

Admission Requirements

Penn College offers educational opportunities to anyone who has the interest, desire, and ability to pursue advanced study. Due to the wide variety of majors, admission criteria vary according to the major. At a minimum, applicants must have a high school diploma or its equivalent. Some majors are restricted to persons who meet certain academic skill levels and prerequisites, have attained certain levels of academic achievement, and have earned an acceptable score on the SAT or ACT. Questions regarding the admission standards for specific majors should be directed to the Office of Admissions. To ensure that applicants have the entry-level skills needed for success in college majors, all students are required to take placement examinations, which are used to assess skills in math, English, and reading. The College provides opportunities for students to develop the basic skills necessary for enrollment in associate degree and certificate majors when the placement tests indicate that such help is needed. International students whose native language is not English are required to take the TOEFL, submit an affidavit of support, and comply with test regulations of the Immigration and Naturalization Service, along with meeting all other admission requirements. The College offers equal opportunity for admission without regard to age, race, color, creed, sex, national origin, disability, veteran status, or political affiliation.

Penn College offers opportunities for students to transfer the following course credits: credit earned at other institutions, college credit earned before high school graduation, service credit, DANTES credit, and credit earned through the College-Level Examination Program (CLEP).

Application and Information

College catalogs, viewbooks, financial aid information, and other informative brochures, along with applications for admission, are available from the Office of Admissions. Prospective students and their families should contact the Office of Admissions to arrange a personal interview or campus tour. Fall and spring visitation events are held annually.

All inquiries should be addressed to:

Office of Admissions
Pennsylvania College of Technology
One College Avenue
Williamsport, Pennsylvania 17701-5799
Telephone: 570-327-4761
          800-367-9222 (toll-free)
E-mail: admissions@pct.edu
World Wide Web: http://www.pct.edu/peter2

Banners representing each of the eight academic schools at Penn College adorn lampposts leading from the new main entrance to the heart of the campus.

PLATT COLLEGE

LOS ANGELES, CALIFORNIA

The College and its Mission

Platt College is a private school that was founded in Missouri in 1879. Today, Platt has three Southern California campuses, which are located in Los Angeles, Newport Beach, and Ontario (a branch of Platt College Los Angeles).

Platt College students participate in a career-focused and hands-on environment that prepares them to enter the workforce as quickly as possible.

Platt College is always looking to the future and revising its programs to meet the constant changes taking place in the related industries. Platt College is dedicated to the principle that education is the foundation for personal and professional growth and that students should have the opportunity to develop to their full potential. Platt College is accredited by the Accrediting Commission of Career Schools and Colleges of Technology and is state approved by the Bureau for Private Postsecondary and Vocational Education.

Academic Programs

Platt College offers the following programs: Bachelor of Arts (B.A.) in visual communication, Associate of Arts (A.A.) and a diploma in graphic design, Associate of Arts in paralegal studies, Associate of Science (A.S.) in information technology networking, a certificate in information technology networking, and a certificate in multimedia.

The programs vary in length from approximately five to thirty-one months, and total classroom hours vary from 350 to 2,400 hours. Classes start every five weeks, thus providing many opportunities for students to get started in fulfilling their educational and career goals.

Classes meet either two or four days each week, depending on the nature of the specific course. There are no classes on Friday, which is reserved as an open lab day so that students may work on class or individual projects.

Credit for Nontraditional Learning Experiences

Transfer and Experiential Learning Credit Many students enter Platt College having attended another college. In addition, many students with industry experience attend Platt College for the purpose of gaining a degree or enhancing their skills. Applicants with the appropriate amount of industry experience may be qualified for waiver of Platt College courses through experiential learning. Up to 50 percent of a student's program at Platt College may be waived through transfer credits from a previously attended school and/or through experiential learning.

Costs

Program costs (including tuition, books, supplies, and registration fee), as of the date of this publication, are B.A. in visual communication, $57,455; A.A. in graphic design, $26,350; A.A. in paralegal studies, $26,780; A.S. in information technology networking, $27,420; diploma in graphic design, $19,635; certificate in information technology networking, $8240; and certificate in multimedia, $10,885.

Financial Aid

Eligible applicants may benefit from the following federally sponsored programs, which provide grants, loans, and Federal Work-Study Program positions to cover portions of tuition and fees: Federal Pell Grant, Federal Supplemental Educational Opportunity Grant (FSEOG), Federal Stafford Student Loans (subsidized and unsubsidized), Federal PLUS loans for parents, and Consolidation Loans. Platt College can also provide private education loans through KeyBank and Sallie Mae. Applicants are required to complete a credit application to determine approval status.

Platt College also participates in the Cal Grant program which is offered by the State of California and administered through the California Student Aid Commission. Awards are based on need and academic achievement. Platt College also services students receiving Veterans Administration benefits.

Faculty

The faculty of the Los Angeles campus is composed of full- and part-time instructors who bring teaching and industry experience to the classrooms and computer labs. The faculty members are active in all campus activities, from new student orientation through to graduation. Platt College believes that the learning process is a partnership between the students and their instructors.

Student Body Profile

The Los Angeles campus has a student population that varies from 160 to 200 students. The average age of the student population is 23; 60 percent of the students are men and 40 percent are women; approximately 45 percent of the students have prior industry and/or college experience; and the ethnic breakdown is representative of Los Angeles County. All students are commuters.

Facilities and Resources

Facilities include general education rooms and computer labs, with each student having a dedicated workstation. The Library provides research materials, both in holdings and online as well as computers for Internet access and a service bureau.

Academic and financial aid advising is provided for the students. Campus activities focus on contacts with industries related to students' majors and opportunities for students to develop and present their portfolios.

Career Services strives to see that each graduate understands the job search process. Placement begins on orientation day, at which time the importance of attendance and productivity in class are stressed. During the course of training, the Career

Services staff meets with each student, becoming familiar with his or her special skills, background, and goals. Students participate in resume preparation, letters of application, researching and contacting potential employers, interviewing skills, and portfolio preparation.

Location

Platt College Los Angeles is located in a gated campus setting that includes other learning institutions, businesses, restaurants, and other amenities. The area surrounding the campus is Greater Los Angeles, with easy access to the beautiful California beaches, parks, entertainment industry, and other attractions associated with a large metropolitian area.

Admission Requirements

All applicants to Platt College are required to visit the campus for a personal interview with the Admissions Department, complete an application form, and tour the facility to view the classrooms, equipment, and samples of student work.

Applicants are required to take a standardized entrance examination that measures language, reading comprehension, and numerical skills. In addition to the examination, all applicants are required to complete a written essay addressing their rationale for entering one of the offered programs of study. All applicants must provide proof of either a high school diploma or successful completion of the GED program.

An Acceptance Committee reviews the examination scores and essay and then informs the applicant regarding her or his acceptance or nonacceptance to Platt College.

Application and Information

Platt College programs are based on five-week modules with rolling start dates throughout the year. Interested students should contact:

Manfred Rodriguez, Campus Director
Platt College
1000 South Fremont Ave, A9 West
Alhambra, California 91803
Telephone: 626-300-5444
        888-866-6697 (toll-free)
Fax: 626-300-3978
E-mail: mrodriguez@plattcollege.edu
World Wide Web: http://www.plattcollege.edu

PLATT COLLEGE
NEWPORT BEACH, CALIFORNIA

The College and its Mission

Platt College is a private school that was founded in Missouri in 1879. Today, Platt has three southern California campuses, which are located in Los Angeles, Newport Beach, and Ontario, a branch of Platt College Los Angeles.

Platt College students participate in a career-focused and hands-on environment that prepares them to enter the workforce as quickly as possible.

Platt College is always looking to the future and revising its programs to meet the constant changes taking place in the related industries. Platt College is dedicated to the principle that education is the foundation for personal and professional growth and that students should have the opportunity to develop to their full potential. Platt College is accredited by the Accrediting Commission of Career Schools and Colleges of Technology and is state approved by the Bureau for Private Postsecondary and Vocational Education.

Academic Programs

Platt College offers the following programs: the Bachelor of Arts (B.A.) degree in visual communication, the Associate of Arts (A.A.) degree and diploma in graphic design, the Associate of Arts (A.A.) degree in paralegal studies, the Associate of Science (A.S.) degree in information technology networking, a certificate in information technology networking, and a certificate in multimedia.

The programs vary in length from approximately five months to thirty-one months and total classroom hours vary from 350 to 2,400 hours. Classes start every five weeks, thus providing many opportunities for students to get started in fulfilling their educational and career goals.

Classes meet either two or four days each week, depending on the nature of the specific course. There are no classes on Friday, which is reserved as an open-lab day for students to work on class or individual projects.

While internships are not a requirement for graduation, students are encouraged to contact the Career Services Office to participate in an internship if their schedule allows.

Credit for Nontraditional Learning Experiences

Transfer and Experiential Learning Credit Many students enter Platt College having attended another college. In addition, many students with industry experience attend Platt College for the purpose of gaining a degree or enhancing their skills. Applicants with the appropriate amount of industry experience may be qualified for waiver of Platt College courses through experiential learning. Up to 50 percent of a student's program at Platt College may be waived through transfer credits from a previously attended school and/or through experiential learning.

Costs

Program costs (including tuition, books, supplies, and registration fee), as of the date of this publication, are B.A. in visual communication, $57,455; A.A. in graphic design, $26,350; A.A. in paralegal studies, $26,780; A.S. in information technology networking, $27,420; diploma in graphic design, $19,635; certificate in information technology networking, $8240; and certificate in multimedia, $10,885.

Financial Aid

Eligible applicants may benefit from the following federally sponsored programs which provide grants, loans, and federal work-study opportunities to cover portions of a student's tuition and fees: Federal Pell Grant, Supplemental Educational Opportunity Grant (SEOG), subsidized and unsubsidized Stafford Student Loans, Parent Loan for Undergraduate Students (PLUS), and consolidation loans. Platt College can also provide private education loans through Key Bank and SallieMae. Applicants are required to complete a credit application to determine approval status.

Platt College also participates in the Cal Grant program, which is offered by the State of California and administered through the California Student Aid Commission. Awards are based on need and academic achievement. Platt College also services students who are receiving Veterans Administration benefits.

Faculty

The faculty of the Newport Beach campus is composed of full-time and part-time instructors who bring teaching and industry experience to the classrooms and computer labs. The faculty members are active in all campus activities, from the new student orientation program through graduation day. Platt College believes that the learning process is a partnership between the students and their instructors.

Student Body Profile

The Newport Beach campus has a student population that ranges from 180 to 200 students. The average age of the student population is 23; 60 percent of the students are men and 40 percent are women; approximately 45 percent of the students have prior industry and/or college experience; and the ethnic breakdown is representative of Orange County. All students are commuters.

Student Activities

Students participate in field trips related to art and science. Graphic design students display work in local art shows and often do work for charity groups that need design services. Students may also take advantage of on-campus guest speakers and Career Nights, which are arranged by the College.

Facilities and Resources

Facilities include general education classrooms and computer labs, with each student having a dedicated workstation. The library provides research materials, both in its holdings and online; it also provides computers for Internet access.

Academic and financial aid advising is made available to all students. Campus activities focus on contacts with the related industries and opportunities for students to develop and present their portfolios.

Career Services strives to see that each graduate understands the job search process. Placement begins on orientation day, at which time the importance of the student's attendance and productivity in class is stressed. During the course of training, members of the Career Services staff meet with each student and become familiar with his or her special skills, background, and goals. Students participate in writing resumes and letters of application, portfolio preparation, and researching and contacting potential employers. Students also gain valuable interviewing skills.

Location

The area surrounding the campus is the growing and vibrant area of Orange County. The campus is conveniently located within easy access to the beautiful California beaches, amusement parks, and other attractions. The campus is serviced by Los Angeles International Airport and nearby John Wayne Airport.

Admission Requirements

All applicants for admission to Platt College are required to visit the campus for a personal interview with the Admissions Department, complete an application form, and tour the facility to view the classrooms, equipment, and samples of student work.

Applicants are required to take a standardized entrance examination that measures language, reading comprehension, and numerical skills. In addition to the examination, all applicants are required to complete a written essay addressing their rationale for entering one of the offered programs of study. An Acceptance Committee reviews the examination scores and essay and then informs the applicants regarding their acceptance to Platt College.

All applicants must provide proof of either a high school diploma or GED.

Application and Information

Platt College programs are based on five-week modules with rolling start dates throughout the year.

Interested students should contact:

Alan Purvis, Executive Director, Platt Colleges
Platt College
3901 MacArthur Boulevard
Newport Beach, California 92660
Telephone: 949-851-4991
          888-866-6697 (toll-free)
Fax: 949-833-0269
E-mail: apurvis@plattcollege.edu
World Wide Web: http://www.plattcollege.edu

PLATT COLLEGE

ONTARIO, CALIFORNIA

The College and its Mission

Platt College is a private school that was founded in Missouri in 1879. Today, Platt has three southern California campuses, which are located in Los Angeles, Newport Beach, and Ontario, a branch of Platt College Los Angeles.

Platt College students participate in a career-focused and hands-on environment that prepares them to enter the workforce as quickly as possible.

Platt College is always looking to the future and revising its programs to meet the constant changes taking place in the related industries. Platt College is dedicated to the principle that education is the foundation for personal and professional growth and that students should have the opportunity to develop to their full potential. Platt College is accredited by the Accrediting Commission of Career Schools and Colleges of Technology and is state approved by the Bureau for Private Postsecondary and Vocational Education.

Academic Programs

Platt College offers the following programs: the Bachelor of Arts (B.A.) degree in visual communication, the Associate of Arts (A.A.) degree and diploma in graphic design, the Associate of Arts (A.A.) degree and diploma in paralegal studies, the Associate of Science (A.S.) degree in information technology networking, a certificate in information technology networking, and a certificate in multimedia.

The programs vary in length from approximately five months to thirty-one months and total classroom hours vary from 350 to 2,400 hours. Classes start every five weeks, thus providing many opportunities for students to get started in fulfilling their educational and career goals.

Classes meet either two or four days each week, depending on the nature of the specific course. There are no classes on Friday, which is reserved as an open-lab day for students to work on class or individual projects.

While internships are not a requirement for graduation, students are encouraged to contact the Career Services Office to participate in an internship if their schedule allows.

Credit for Nontraditional Learning Experiences

Transfer and Experiential Learning Credit Many students enter Platt College having attended another college. In addition, many students with industry experience attend Platt College for the purpose of gaining a degree or enhancing their skills. Applicants with the appropriate amount of industry experience may be qualified for waiver of Platt College courses through experiential learning. Up to 50 percent of a student's program at Platt College may be waived through transfer credits from a previously attended school and/or through experiential learning.

Costs

Program costs (including tuition, books, supplies, and registration fee), as of the date of this publication, are B.A. in visual communication, $57,455; A.A. in graphic design, $26,350; A.A. in paralegal studies, $26,780; A.S. in information technology networking, $27,420; diploma in graphic design, $19,635; certificate in information technology networking, $8240; and certificate in multimedia, $10,885.

Financial Aid

Eligible applicants may benefit from the following federally sponsored programs which provide grants, loans, and federal work-study opportunities to cover portions of a student's tuition and fees: Federal Pell Grant, Supplemental Educational Opportunity Grant (SEOG), subsidized and unsubsidized Stafford Student Loans, Parent Loan for Undergraduate Students (PLUS), and consolidation loans. Platt College can also provide private education loans through Key Bank and SallieMae. Applicants are required to complete a credit application to determine approval status.

Platt College also participates in the Cal Grant program, which is offered by the State of California and administered through the California Student Aid Commission. Awards are based on need and academic achievement. Platt College also services students who are receiving Veterans Administration benefits.

Faculty

The faculty of the Ontario campus is composed of full-time and part-time instructors who bring teaching and industry experience to the classrooms and computer labs. The faculty members are active in all campus activities, from the new student orientation program through graduation day. Platt College believes that the learning process is a partnership between the students and their instructors.

Student Body Profile

The Ontario campus has a student population that ranges from 380 to 425 students. The average age of the student population is 23; 55 percent of the students are men and 45 percent are women; approximately 45 percent of the students have prior industry and/or college experience; and the ethnic make-up is representative of the counties comprising southern California's Inland Empire. All students are commuters.

Student Activities

Students participate in field trips related to art and science. Graphic design students display work in local art shows and often do work for charity groups that need design services. Students may also take advantage of on-campus guest speakers and Career Nights, which are arranged by the College.

Facilities and Resources

Facilities include general education classrooms and computer labs, with each student having a dedicated workstation. The library provides research materials, both in its holdings and online; it also provides computers for Internet access.

Academic and financial aid advising is made available to all students. Campus activities focus on contacts with the related industries and opportunities for students to develop and present their portfolios.

Career Services strives to see that each graduate understands the job search process. Placement begins on orientation day, at which time the importance of the student's attendance and productivity in class is stressed. During the course of training, members of the Career Services staff meet with each student and become familiar with his or her special skills, background, and goals. Students participate in writing resumes and letters of application, portfolio preparation, and researching and contacting potential employers. Students also gain valuable interviewing skills.

Location

The area surrounding the campus is the growing city of Ontario and the greater Inland Empire. The campus is close, via the freeway, to Orange and Los Angeles counties and is serviced by Ontario International Airport and local bus lines.

Admission Requirements

All applicants for admission to Platt College are required to visit the campus for a personal interview with the Admissions Department, complete an application form, and tour the facility to view the classrooms, equipment, and samples of student work.

Applicants are required to take a standardized entrance examination that measures language, reading comprehension, and numerical skills. In addition to the examination, all applicants are required to complete a written essay addressing their rationale for entering one of the offered programs of study. An Acceptance Committee reviews the examination scores and essay and then informs the applicant regarding his or her acceptance to Platt College.

All applicants must provide proof of either a high school diploma or GED.

Application and Information

Platt College programs are based on five-week modules with rolling start dates throughout the year.

Interested students should contact:

Joe Blackman, Campus Director
Platt College
3700 Inland Empire Boulevard
Ontario, California 91764
Telephone: 909-941-9410
                888-866-6697 (toll-free)
Fax: 909-941-9660
E-mail: jblackman@plattcollege.edu
World Wide Web: http://www.plattcollege.edu

THE RESTAURANT SCHOOL
AT WALNUT HILL COLLEGE
PHILADELPHIA, PENNSYLVANIA

The College and Its Mission

The Restaurant School at Walnut Hill College, *Philadelphia's Home of Hospitality Excellence*, was established in 1974 and is dedicated to inspiring the future of the restaurant and hotel industry through training that is dynamic, timely, and insightful, with a commitment of service to its students. The Restaurant School at Walnut Hill College combines both intensive classroom training and practical experience; students use their knowledge while they learn. Within eighteen months, graduates are working in the field, earning an income, building a resume, and gaining practical and professional experience.

A student's education is cultivated by the College's philosophy that hands-on training is an essential part of education. This approach has multiple benefits—it enhances learning abilities, creates marketable skills and experience for a resume, brings education to life, and, most importantly, puts the student at the center of it all.

The Restaurant School at Walnut Hill College is licensed by the Pennsylvania Department of Education State Board of Private License Schools, is a member of the Pennsylvania Association of Private School Administrators, is accredited by the Accrediting Commission of Career Schools and Colleges of Technology, is certified for veteran's training by the Veterans Administration, is approved by the United States Department of Justice to grant student visas, and is recognized as a Professional Management Development Partner of the Educational Foundation of the National Restaurant Association.

Academic Programs

Associate and Bachelor's Degree Programs There are four majors at the Restaurant School at Walnut Hill College: hotel management, restaurant management, culinary arts, and pastry arts. Each major provides the student with a broad-based knowledge of the overall workings of a fine restaurant or hotel. Beyond that, the programs prepare the student with the day-to-day skills and specific knowledge that are required as he or she develops a career as a restaurant manager, chef, pastry chef, hotel manager, or restaurateur. In partnership with the Educational Foundation of the National Restaurant Association, the College's curriculum includes up to twelve nationally recognized food service and hospitality management courses. Upon successful completion of the courses and the certification exam, students receive national certification.

All students must successfully complete four 15-week semesters to be awarded an Associate of Science degree or eight 15-week semesters to be awarded a Bachelor of Science degree.

Off-Campus Programs

The Restaurant School at Walnut Hill College was one of the first schools in the country to offer a travel experience as part of a curriculum. Culinary and pastry students participate in an eight-day tour of France, while hotel and restaurant management students participate in an eight-day Orlando resort and cruise tour. This travel experience enhances both training and resumes.

A study-abroad program to France and England is currently being formulated. Students may contact the College for detailed information.

Costs

Tuition for the two-year program for students who start September 6, 2005, is $25,200 ($12,600 per academic year). Equipment, books, activity fees, culinary whites, and management dining room attire cost approximately $960. Students may contact the College for information on on-campus housing.

Financial Aid

Financial aid programs are available to those who qualify. It is recommended that students apply early. The College participates in the Federal Pell Grant, the Pennsylvania PHEAA State Grant, the Subsidized Federal Stafford Student Loan, the Unsubsidized Federal Stafford Student Loan, and the parents' Federal PLUS loan programs. The financial aid officers assist students and their families with the creation of a personal plan that outlines expenses and identifies financial resources that are available to students. Scholarships and grants are available to incoming students; for more specific information, students may contact the College.

Faculty

Learning comes to life under the guiding hands and encouragement of the highly trained, technically skilled faculty; the Restaurant School at Walnut Hill College has on staff 1 of only 20 Certified Master Pastry Chefs in the country. The faculty members are seasoned professionals, having logged many years of experience in restaurants and food service. Through their instruction, students gain professional insight, which gives them a competitive edge upon entering the hospitality field. The chefs and instructors are committed to helping students achieve success. As professionals, they continuously keep pace with current trends in the hospitality industry and convey their professional dedication and work ethic to their students.

Student Body Profile

There is a diverse population at the Restaurant School at Walnut Hill College, with students coming from throughout the United States and abroad and ranging in age from the high school graduate to the adult who wants to change careers.

Student Activities

Whether it is a celebrity chef's cooking demonstration, dinner and a tour at a notable restaurant or hotel, or a winery tour and tasting, students at the Restaurant School at Walnut Hill College are exposed to the very best Philadelphia has to offer. There are activities and weekly special events that are sponsored by student clubs. The Culinary Salon Team holds the title of 2001–02 Pennsylvania State Champions, and the Wine Club is undefeated in their scholastic debates. Activities are both educational and fun, combining opportunities to learn and to establish camaraderie and professional development. Events are listed in the student newsletter and monthly calendar.

Facilities and Resources

Recently completing a yearlong renovation, the Restaurant School at Walnut Hill College is poised to offer one of the most dynamic hands-on learning opportunities in the country. The dining experience, situated in the breathtakingly restored 1853 Allison Mansion, turns into a dining event with the addition of three theme restaurants, including Terraza di Italia, a casual Italian trattoria that features classic pasta presentations set amidst an Italian terrace. Guests are invited to sit inside the restaurant, where they can enjoy homemade pasta or dine amongst the twinkling lights in the European Courtyard.

American cuisine is presented in an innovative new style in the American Heartland. Depicting a country farm with a painted blue sky and cornfields, this restaurant allows students to explore some of America's best cooking while guests enjoy the comfort of a country dining or veranda setting.

Most notable is the elegant Great Chefs of Philadelphia restaurant. Amidst glittering crystal chandeliers and a rich tapestry motif, guests enjoy wonderful cuisine and service designed by some of Philadelphia's and America's top chefs.

Also in the mansion is the student resource center, featuring state-of-the-art computer lab stations as well as the Alumni Library, which encompasses thousands of books, magazines, and videotapes on cooking, management, and wines. The building also houses a student conference room and a wines and bartending training salon.

The Pastry Shop and Café is filled each morning with buttery croissants, crisp French baguettes, and glistening pastries that are prepared by the pastry arts students. Also available is a selection of pastas, salads, soups, and entrées for an informal café lunch, prepared by the culinary arts students.

The education building is the focal point of a student's training. It houses four modern classroom kitchens, two lecture halls, and the College's purchasing center.

Hunter Hall is a turn-of-the-century masterpiece that features magnificent carved mahogany, marble, and fireplaces. The College's Office of Admissions, Financial Aid, and Independent Student Housing is located in this building.

Career Development and Job Placement Assistance at the Restaurant School at Walnut Hill College begins on the first day of school with training that is thorough and realistic. In the classroom, students learn how to develop effective resumes and portfolios as well as various interviewing techniques. Career development never ends—graduates can always contact the College for assistance with employment possibilities and resume updates. The College regularly invites personnel directors and proprietors of successful restaurants, hotels, and other food businesses to visit the College. Placement of Restaurant School at Walnut Hill College graduates averages 97 percent.

Location

Philadelphia is a great place to live and learn. As the fourth-largest city in the United States, Philadelphia has much to offer and is a city of firsts—the first public library, the first college, the first zoo—all in a first-class city.

The Restaurant School at Walnut Hill College is located in the University City section of Philadelphia, neighboring both the University of Pennsylvania and Drexel University. Located just across the Schuylkill River from Center City, University City has a wonderful college-town ambiance. Restaurants, museums, shops, and theaters abound, with local merchants offering discounts to students. The Amtrak train station is within walking distance of the campus, and the airport is 20 minutes away by car.

Center City is located just minutes from campus. Here, students find a bustling shopping and business district, complete with award-winning restaurant row, luxury hotels, and exclusive boutiques.

Ethnic diversity abounds in this city of neighborhoods, including Chinatown, complete with exotic restaurants and shops; South Philadelphia, with its famed Italian Market; and the ever-eclectic South Street, with blocks of restaurants, galleries, shops, and entertainment. There are also the historic district, which was the birthplace of the nation, and a waterfront that features exciting nightlife.

Philadelphia is rich in culture and heritage. Students find world-class art and science museums, theaters that feature major Broadway shows and renowned regional productions, and music, which includes everything from jazz to pop to the internationally acclaimed Philadelphia Orchestra.

Admission Requirements

Typically, the admissions procedure begins with a visit to the College. At that time, prospective students and their families tour the College, watch hands-on classes in action, and get a feel for campus life. Application for admission to the College is available to any individual with a high school diploma or its equivalent and an interest in developing a career or ownership options in fine restaurants, food service, or hospitality. Applicants are evaluated on their educational background and demonstrated or stated interest in their chosen field. Two references are required, as are high school transcripts.

Students may contact the College for information on the early decision program for high school juniors and seniors.

Application and Information

The Restaurant School at Walnut Hill College practices rolling admission; qualified applicants are accepted at any time. Applications for admission are submitted with a $50 application fee and a $150 registration fee. Prospective students should contact:

Office of Admissions
The Restaurant School at Walnut Hill College
4207 Walnut Street
Philadelphia, Pennsylvania 19104
Telephone: 215-222-4200 Ext. 3011
        877-925-6884 Ext. 3011 (toll-free)
Fax: 215-222-4219
E-mail: info@walnuthillcollege.com
World Wide Web: http://www.walnuthillcollege.com

The Restaurant School at Walnut Hill College.

SANTA MONICA COLLEGE

SANTA MONICA, CALIFORNIA

The College and Its Mission

Santa Monica College is a two-year community college, founded in 1929. The College is supported by the state of California and is accredited by the Western Association of Schools and Colleges. It has an enrollment of 27,700 students, including 2,557 students from 105 other countries.

Santa Monica College welcomes students from all countries in the world and provides special assistance to them through the International Student Center. New incoming students are given an orientation that includes an introduction to the College and its services. In addition, information on immigration issues, housing, and registration are also covered in these sessions.

Santa Monica College ranks first among the 109 community colleges in California in transferring students to the University of California. The College also has articulation agreements with the California State Universities as well as with outstanding private universities, including the University of Southern California and Pepperdine and Loyola Marymount Universities.

To a great extent, the reputation of Santa Monica as one of the leading community colleges in America is based on the quality of its teaching faculty. Unlike some universities that place more emphasis on research, Santa Monica College chooses its professors for their ability to teach as well as their expertise in their fields.

A high priority is placed on individual interaction between instructors and students. Smaller classes give students the opportunity to receive more personal attention than they would in introductory courses at large universities.

The College radio station, KCRW, is the leading public radio station in southern California, providing both local and national news and entertainment programs. The Santa Monica Associates, a community-based foundation, enables the College to bring some of the world's outstanding scientists, writers, and artists to the campus for lectures and interaction with students. Santa Monica College students also present symphony concerts, plays, and operas.

Academic Programs

Graduation from Santa Monica College with the **Associate in Arts** degree is granted upon successful completion of a program of studies that includes the mastery of minimum skill requirements in English and mathematics; a selection of courses from the natural sciences, social sciences, and humanities; and prescribed courses in the major field. Graduating students are required to complete a minimum of 60 units with at least a C (2.0) average. A unit is based on the number of hours of classroom instruction. Most courses offer 3 units of credit for classes that meet 3 hours a week for a semester. Full-time students take a minimum of 12 units per semester.

Santa Monica College offers programs of courses that parallel the lower division, or the first two years, of four-year universities and colleges. Students wishing to transfer must complete a minimum of 56 transfer-level units in fields including English, mathematics, humanities, the physical sciences, and the social sciences. Requirements vary among universities, and it is to the student's advantage to choose the university to which he or she plans to transfer as soon as possible.

All nine campuses of the University of California, including UCLA and Berkeley, give preference to California's community college students over all other applicants for third-year transfer;

however, students must complete the required courses with at least a 2.8 grade point average. In some majors, such as engineering and economics, a higher grade point average may be necessary for acceptance at high-demand campuses such as UCLA.

The twenty-three campuses of the California State University also give preference to community college students who have completed a prescribed program of lower-division courses with 56 transfer-level units and a minimum grade point average of 2.5. Campuses and majors in high demand by students may require higher grade point averages.

Associate Degree Programs Santa Monica College offers courses in sixty academic major fields of study, including accounting, anatomy, anthropology, art, astronomy, bilingual education, biological sciences, botany, broadcasting, business administration, chemistry, child development, Chinese, cinema, communication, computer information systems, economics, electronics, engineering, English, fashion merchandising, French, geography, geology, German, graphic design, history, interior design, Italian, Japanese, journalism, management, mathematics, merchandising, philosophy, photography, physical education, physics, physiology, political science, respiratory therapy, Russian, sociology, Spanish, speech, theater arts, and zoology. Courses for preprofessional study in such fields as chiropractic studies, medicine, optometry, pharmacy, physical therapy, and veterinary science are also offered.

Students who complete their first two years of undergraduate requirements may receive an Associate in Arts degree before transferring to a four-year university to complete their bachelor's degree. Occupational certificates are also granted in certain two-year programs including accounting, automotive technology, child development, computer information systems, cosmetology, electronics, fashion design, management, office information systems, photography, printing, real estate, recreational leadership, and supervision.

Credit for Nontraditional Learning Experiences

The cooperative work experience program at Santa Monica College makes it possible for students to earn College credit for work experience in technical, business, or professional settings. The program is a joint effort of the College and the community to combine on-the-job training with classroom instruction, enabling the student to acquire knowledge, skills, and attitudes necessary to enter into or progress in a chosen occupation.

Costs

For the 2005–06 academic year, California residents pay an enrollment fee of $26 per unit. Nonresidents paid an enrollment fee of $26 per unit plus $180 per unit in tuition. It is estimated that room and board in a homestay or apartment for this period cost $9832. Other costs include mandatory health insurance for F-1 international students ($684 per year) and textbooks and supplies ($1500). International students should have a minimum of $17,000 available to them to cover all of their costs for the year.

Financial Aid

U.S. students receive government support in the form of grants and loans based on their financial need. International students do not qualify for government support, but they are eligible to compete for 200 non-need scholarships (averaging $500) given by private donors.

Faculty

Santa Monica has 321 full-time faculty members and 581 part-time faculty members. All hold the equivalent of a master's degree or higher and are certified by the state of California. Although faculty members are chosen on the basis of their teaching ability, many of the professors hold doctoral degrees, particularly in the sciences. The student-faculty ratio is 40:1, although some classes are larger or smaller than 40, depending on the subject. Many faculty members maintain office hours to advise students on an individual basis. In addition, counselors on the faculty help students plan their schedules and provide special assistance for personal learning problems.

Student Body Profile

Santa Monica College has a total enrollment of 27,700 students, of whom 44 percent are men and 56 percent are women. The average age is 29. The racial breakdown of the student group includes Asian, 23 percent; African American, 9 percent; Hispanic, 24 percent; Native American, 1 percent; Pacific Islander, 1 percent; other (nonwhites), 2 percent; and white (non-Hispanic), 40 percent. Of the full-time students enrolled, 65 percent plan to transfer to a four-year college or university, 13 percent are undecided, 6 percent are taking classes for personal interest, 4 percent enroll for professional development, 3 percent enroll for a vocational certificate or an associate degree, and 9 percent enroll for other reasons. The international student population numbers 2,557.

Student Activities

All students are encouraged to join a variety of clubs supported by the Associated Students. The clubs are organized by students with special interests such as ecology, geology, biology, skiing, karate, dance, music, and drama. There is also an international club and clubs organized by students from Hong Kong, Indonesia, and India. The clubs normally meet once a week and conduct activities on and off campus throughout the year.

Sports Sports facilities at the College include off-site tennis courts, a gymnasium, an Olympic-size swimming pool, and the track built for the 1984 Olympics in Los Angeles. The College competes on the varsity level in men's football and men's and women's basketball, tennis, track, and volleyball. All students have access to the sports facilities for classes and individual training.

Facilities and Resources

Santa Monica College has excellent teaching facilities, including laboratories for science, electronics, computers, and nursing. It also has a new state-of the-art library with 103,392 bound volumes, and a learning resources center provides media-assisted individual instruction and free tutoring. There are 160 terminals/PCs available for student use at various locations throughout the campus. Other facilities include an amphitheater, a music room and auditorium, a little theater, an art gallery, a planetarium, a media center, and a student activities building.

The Associated Student Center provides study areas and a computer laboratory with free use of Macintosh computers to all students. The Student Center also includes a cafeteria, conference center, and bookstore.

The Santa Monica College Transfer Center assists students who are seeking to continue their studies at a four-year college or university. Its services include workshops on the application process, opportunities to meet with representatives from the four-year institutions, and tours of the campuses throughout California.

A Mentor Program in the arts gives exceptionally talented students in the performing and applied arts an opportunity to further develop their abilities through individual instruction. Mentor programs exist in architecture, art, dance, fashion design, music, photography, and theater arts. Students wishing to be part of the Mentor Program must demonstrate exceptional abilities and commitment. The program of study is tailored to the goals of the individual and often results in a 1-person show of the student's work or a public performance.

Location

Santa Monica College is located on the beautiful coast of Southern California in the city of Santa Monica. Because of the nearness to the ocean, Santa Monica has clean air and a mild climate throughout the year. It is just to the west of Los Angeles, one of the most cosmopolitan cities in the world. The campus provides easy access to outstanding theater, music, and museum facilities in Los Angeles as well as to Universal Studios and other centers of the entertainment industry. Santa Monica College is less than 10 miles from UCLA, USC, Pepperdine University, Loyola Marymount University, and other fine institutions of higher education in the Los Angeles area.

Admission Requirements

Santa Monica College has an open admission policy. Math and English tests are given upon entry in order to counsel students and place them at the proper course levels. International students who are below the university level in English are able to take preuniversity courses in ESL while they are taking university transfer-level courses, such as mathematics, that are not as dependent on English skills. International students are required to have an English level equivalent to a TOEFL score of 450 (133 CPT) in order to enroll in university transfer-level courses. Students who do not have the required English proficiency (TOEFL score) can enroll in the Intensive ESL Program at Santa Monica College.

Application and Information

Applications are accepted on an ongoing basis prior to the beginning of each semester. For the 2005–06 academic year, the fall semester begins August 29, the winter session begins January 3, the spring semester begins February 13, and the summer session begins June 19. All students should apply two months prior to the beginning of each semester or session in order to have the best selection of classes. International students must submit the documents required by the U.S. government for issuing I-20 student visas two months in advance. These documents include transcripts from high school and other colleges or universities attended, verification of financial support, and a certification of the minimum English level. International student applications are processed within one week, and notification of acceptance can be made by fax or express mail when necessary.

For more information, students should contact:

Teresita Rodriguez
Dean of Admissions
Santa Monica College
1900 Pico Boulevard
Santa Monica, California 90405-1628
Telephone: 310-434-4380

International students should contact:

Dr. Elena M. Garate
Dean, International Education
International Student Center
Santa Monica College
1900 Pico Boulevard
Santa Monica, California 90405-1628
Telephone: 310-434-4217
Fax: 310-434-3651

SPARTANBURG METHODIST COLLEGE

SPARTANBURG, SOUTH CAROLINA

The College and Its Mission

Spartanburg Methodist College (SMC) is the only private, residential, two-year liberal arts college in South Carolina. SMC serves the educational needs of 750 students. Most students have as their primary goal to earn a baccalaureate degree. Students are generally traditional college-age students, 80 percent of whom live on campus.

Spartanburg Methodist College was founded in 1911 by Dr. David English Camak, a visionary Methodist minister, as a work-study cooperative to serve young adults. As the first cooperative education program in the country, students worked a week and then took classes for a week. In 1927, the curriculum provided graduates with an associate degree in liberal arts for transfer to senior-level colleges.

Today, SMC serves a highly diverse student body from many states and ten different nations. Spartanburg Methodist College seeks to enable students to meet the challenges of the future and to develop the worth and abilities of students through programs that are relevant to their academic and personal needs. The College provides a values-oriented atmosphere in the Christian tradition in which students develop sensitivity to the needs of others and from which they assume responsible positions in society. The academic program offers a university-parallel curriculum that is designed to transfer to a four-year college or university for continued study in the junior and senior year.

Since 1911, Spartanburg Methodist College has believed that the first two years of college are the most critical in determining college success. Therefore, the College places all of its effort into making this the best two years of a four-year degree for its students. More than 90 percent of graduates continue their education by enrolling in the junior class of some of the finest universities and colleges in the nation. The Spartanburg curriculum insures a smooth transfer of credits.

Academic Programs

SMC has a variety of academic and special education opportunities available to traditional age and adult students. The College helps students to discover and develop their personal skills and interests, to reflect on their personal values and goals, to make decisions about their educational and vocational goals, and to prepare for their futures. SMC has transfer articulation agreements and direct-transfer agreements with colleges across the state and region to facilitate the transfer process. SMC students are well prepared for the challenges of academic work at the senior college or university of their choice.

Spartanburg Methodist offers the Associate in Arts, Associate in Science, Associate in Criminal Justice, and Associate in Information Management degrees. The Associate in Arts degree prepares students for many majors, such as business administration, English, foreign language, history, political science or government, psychology, religious studies, and sociology. The Associate in Science degree leads to majors in allied health, business, computer science, mathematics, natural and physical sciences, and preprofessional degrees. The Associate in Criminal Justice degree prepares students to enter one of the many career fields in criminal justice or law

enforcement or transfer to four-year degree programs in criminal justice. The Associate in Information Management degree meets the educational needs of students who are planning to work in the high-technology offices of the twenty-first century.

Candidates for the associate degrees must complete 64 hours of course work and maintain a 2.0 grade point average on work completed at Spartanburg Methodist College. Candidates must earn a minimum of 34 credit hours on the campus of SMC and demonstrate competency in reading, writing, basic mathematics, the basic use of computers, and oral communication.

Credit for Nontraditional Learning Experiences

Students may be granted academic credit by achieving successful scores on the CLEP and Advanced Placement tests of the College Board.

Costs

Tuition and fees for the 2004–05 year were $9322. For those students who reside on campus, there was an additional charge of $2566 for room and $2426 for board, making the total cost for a student living on campus $14,314.

Financial Aid

Financial aid assistance is determined by the financial need of the student. Determinations are made based on the filing of the Free Application for Federal Student Aid (FAFSA). Financial aid packages include funds from federal, state, institutional, and private sources. Sources include Federal Pell Grants, Federal Supplemental Educational Opportunity Grants, South Carolina State Tuition Grants, South Carolina LIFE Scholarships, Federal Subsidized and Unsubsidized Stafford Student Loans, Federal PLUS Loans, Perkins Loans, and the Federal Work-Study Program. In addition, the College offers academic, athletic, need-based, merit, and performance-related scholarship programs, the United Methodist Scholar Program, and College-funded work-study opportunities. Off-campus work positions also can be attained through the College Work/Campus Service Coordinator. South Carolina students who graduate with a rank in the top 75 percent of their high school class or with an SAT score of at least 900 or ACT score of at least 19 may qualify for a need-based state tuition grant. South Carolina LIFE Scholarships are awarded based on a student's graduation from high school with a GPA of at least 3.0 (on a 4.0 scale). South Carolina Education Lottery Scholarships are also available.

Faculty

Spartanburg Methodist College has 48 full-time faculty members and dedicated adjunct faculty members. All of the faculty members have earned graduate degrees and one fourth hold the doctorate in their subject area. The student-faculty ratio is 18:1.

Student Body Profile

Spartanburg Methodist has an enrollment of 750 students. The average age of the student body is 20. SMC has an ethnically and culturally diverse student body, with members of minority groups representing 20 percent of the student body, international students from ten countries represent 5 percent, and out-of-state students represent 30 percent. Full-time students make up

91 percent of the student body, and 48 percent are women. Seventy-six percent of the freshman class graduates with an associate degree, and 93 percent of these graduates transfer to senior colleges or universities.

Student Activities

Spartanburg Methodist College offers a variety of extracurricular activities that challenge students mentally, physically, socially, and spiritually. SMC offers students membership to academic honor societies, service fraternities, and numerous clubs associated with academic classes and activities on campus. As a member of the NJCAA, SMC fields five men's and six women's intercollegiate teams. Men's sports include baseball, basketball, cross-country, golf, and soccer. Women's sports include basketball, cross-country, soccer, softball, tennis, and volleyball. An active intramural program provides many opportunities for students who are not members of an intercollegiate team to participate in team events.

SMC enjoys a rich heritage that is closely connected to the United Methodist Church. Religious life activities include the Fellowship of Christian Athletes, the Gospel Choir, and the College Christian Movement. The Office of the Chaplain also sponsors a mission trip during spring break.

Because SMC believes that one learns how to be a leader through service, it has developed a leadership program that focuses heavily on community service. In addition to the Leadership Retreat, the Leadership Transcript, the Leadership Training Lab, and the Student Organization Fair, SMC's student leaders regularly volunteer their time to services such as the Downtown Rescue Mission, the Salvation Army, and the Red Cross.

SMC offers a fully staffed career/counseling center to assist students with selecting career paths and dealing with personal problems.

The Marie Blair Burgess Learning Resources Center includes books, periodicals, and study areas as well as a complete multimedia center, computer terminals, and the control center of the campus television cable system. The College also has state-of-the-art computer labs that are available to students throughout the day and evening with appropriate staff assistance. All dormitory rooms provide high-speed Internet access for each resident student.

Location

Spartanburg Methodist is located on a 110-acre campus in Spartanburg, South Carolina. Interstates I-26 and I-85 intersect near the campus and provide easy access to SMC. The Blue Ridge Mountains of North Carolina are within a 1-hour drive of the campus, while the beaches of South Carolina, such as Myrtle Beach and Hilton Head, are just 4 hours away. Two major airports serve the area, Charlotte International Airport in Charlotte, North Carolina, and Greenville-Spartanburg International Airport.

Admission Requirements

Spartanburg Methodist College is committed to providing opportunities to motivated, academically qualified students. The student's high school academic record, class rank, SAT or ACT scores, and extracurricular activities are all taken into consideration in admission decisions.

Application and Information

Consideration for admission to SMC requires a completed application, a $20 application fee, an official copy of the high school transcript, and scores from either the SAT or ACT. Transfer students with less than 16 transferable credit hours must submit official copies of both the college and high school transcripts. Transfer students with 16 or more transferable credit hours must submit official copies of all college transcripts. Qualified students are notified of their acceptance as soon as their files are completed and evaluated.

For more information, students should contact:

Dean of Admissions and Financial Aid
Spartanburg Methodist College
1200 Textile Road
Spartanburg, South Carolina 29301
Telephone: 864-587-4213
         800-772-7286 (toll-free)
Fax: 864-587-4355
E-mail: admiss@smcsc.edu
World Wide Web: http://www.smcsc.edu

A view of the campus at Spartanburg Methodist College.

STATE UNIVERSITY OF NEW YORK COLLEGE OF ENVIRONMENTAL SCIENCE AND FORESTRY, RANGER SCHOOL

WANAKENA, NEW YORK

The College and Its Mission

The Forest Technology Program is offered through the State University of New York College of Environmental Science and Forestry (ESF) at the Ranger School campus. Throughout its history, the College has focused on the environmental issues of the time in each of its three mission areas: instruction, research, and public service. The College is dedicated to educating future scientists and managers who, through specialized skills, will be able to use a holistic approach to solving the environmental and resource problems facing society.

More than 3,200 students have graduated from the program over the past eighty-five years, including 180 women since 1974. Established in 1912 with the gift of 1,800 acres of land in the Adirondack Mountains, the ESF Forest Technology Program is the oldest in the nation. The Ranger School's managed forest includes both hardwood and coniferous trees and is bounded on two sides by the New York State Forest Preserve. It is also adjacent to several acres of virgin timber in the Adirondack Forest preserve.

The main campus building houses the central academic, dining, and recreational facilities. Dormitory wings are located on either side of the main campus building. Dorm rooms are designed to accommodate 1 or 2 people. All second-year students live on campus, with the exception of married students accompanied by their families. These students should arrange for rental accommodations well before the start of the academic year.

A $5-million renovation and expansion of the Ranger school was just completed. This project included renovations and an addition to the main campus building, a new dining hall, distance learning classrooms, additional residence hall facilities, and a new student recreational area.

Academic Programs

Associate Degree Programs Students who complete the program earn an **Associate in Applied Science (A.A.S.)** degree in forest technology.

The two-year curriculum offers concentrations in forest technology and surveying. Students may fulfill the program's freshman liberal arts and sciences requirements at any accredited college. The second year of study takes place on the Wanakena campus. Time is equally divided between classroom and laboratory work and experience in the field. Students must also devote several hours to evening and weekend study. Forestry agencies and the wood products industry employ graduates as forest technicians, and graduates of the surveying option join surveying firms and governmental agencies.

The ESF Ranger School's 1+1 plan requires 30 credit hours of course work in general studies at the College's Syracuse campus or any accredited college during the freshman year and an additional 48 credit hours at the Wanakena campus in the

second year of the program. Field study is a large component of the curriculum. Several short field trips, made at no additional expense to the student, take place as part of the second year of study. The trips enhance courses in dendrology, silviculture, forest management and recreation, wildlife ecology, and surveying. Students who are considering later transfer to a baccalaureate program should follow the suggestions for freshman course selection outlined in the ESF catalog.

Transfer Arrangements Counseling is available for students interested in pursuing a four-year degree on the main campus in Syracuse. Students should contact the ESF admissions office.

Costs

The cost of the first year varies according to the institution attended. Estimated tuition and fees for the 2005–06 academic year at the Wanakena campus total $5219 for residents of New York State and $11,169 for out-of-state residents. Room and board at the Wanakena campus are $7650 and the estimated cost of books, personal expenses, and travel is $2550. (Books and supplies are sold on campus.)

Financial Aid

More than 80 percent of Ranger School students receive some form of financial aid, including grants and scholarships, low-interest loans, and student employment. All students are encouraged to apply for financial aid by completing the Free Application for Federal Student Aid.

Faculty

Five full-time faculty members and 1 part-time instructor teach at the Wanakena campus. The student-faculty ratio is approximately 10:1. Students have ready access to faculty members for consultations. Faculty members are housed on campus, and faculty offices are located near student living quarters. There is close contact between students and faculty members in the classroom and at fieldwork sites.

Student Body Profile

Ninety percent of all students complete the forest technology program. About 50 percent go on to careers as forest technicians or aides with private companies or government agencies; some 30 percent become surveyors. Many graduates of the Forest Technology Program go on to receive Bachelor of Science and even graduate-level degrees at ESF's main campus in Syracuse or at other colleges and universities.

Student Activities

Students have a variety of activities available to them at the Wanakena campus. Many recreational activities are readily available, including hiking, camping, canoeing, cross-country skiing, and ice-skating. Students are assigned a canoe for their use during the year. Each class forms a student government, which plans a number of class activities. A small recreational facility is available for student use. Students in the second year of the Forest Technology Program follow the ESF code of student conduct and follow the house rules of the Wanakena campus.

Location

The 2,800-acre campus is situated on the banks of the Oswegatchie River near the Adirondack Mountain hamlet of Wanakena, approximately 65 miles east of Watertown, New York, and 35 miles west of Tupper Lake on New York State's Route 3. At the Wanakena campus, social and recreational activities utilize the area's year-round opportunities for outdoor enjoyment. An excellent hospital, located in Star Lake, New York, serves the community.

Admission Requirements

Students may apply to ESF for admission to the Ranger School's Forest Technology Program during their senior year in high school for guaranteed transfer admission or during their freshman year of college for transfer admission. Prospective students should consult the current catalog for specific information concerning the application process. ESF cooperates with more than fifty colleges in cooperative transfer programs. Acceptance to the Ranger School is contingent upon satisfactory completion of first-year courses. While in high school, applicants should successfully complete a college-preparatory program with an emphasis in mathematics and science. Electives in such areas as computer applications and mechanical drawing are recommended. Transfer students are considered on the basis of college course work and interest in the program. In addition to academic requirements, applicants must be able to meet the physical requirements of the Ranger School program and must submit a full medical report. Parents of applicants under 18 years old should be aware of the field nature of the program and its rigorous study-work regimen.

Application and Information

The Forest Technology Program accepts students for fall admission only. Fall admission decisions are made beginning around the middle of January and continue on a rolling basis until the class is filled. Application forms for New York State residents are available at all high schools in the state and at all colleges in the state university system. Out-of-state students should request application forms from the Office of Undergraduate Admissions at the address below. Prospective students who wish to visit the 2,800-acre campus can do so by contacting the Director, New York State Ranger School, Wanakena, New York 13695-0106 (telephone: 315-848-2566 or fax: 315-848-3249).

Office of Undergraduate Admissions
106 Bray Hall
State University of New York College of Environmental
　　Science and Forestry
1 Forestry Drive
Syracuse, New York 13210-2779
Telephone: 315-470-6600
　　　　　　800-777-7373 (toll-free)
Fax: 315-470-6933
E-mail: esfinfo@esf.edu
World Wide Web: http://rangerschool.esf.edu

VALLEY FORGE MILITARY COLLEGE

WAYNE, PENNSYLVANIA

The College and Its Mission

Valley Forge Military College (VFMC) is a private men's residential college that offers the freshman and sophomore years of college. The primary mission of the College is to prepare students for transfer to competitive senior colleges and universities. The College, established in 1935, has a long tradition of fostering personal growth through a comprehensive system built on the five cornerstones that make Valley Forge unique: academics, character development, self-discipline, physical development, and leadership to all students regardless of race, creed, or national origin. The diverse student body represents more than twenty-seven states and twenty-three countries. The College has an excellent transfer record, with 95 percent of cadets accepted to their first or second choice. More than 65 percent were admitted to the top- and second-tier schools in the country.

Valley Forge Military College is the only college in the northeastern United States that offers qualified freshmen the opportunity to participate in an Early Commissioning Program, leading to a commission as a second lieutenant in the U.S. Army Reserves at the end of their sophomore year. The U.S. Air Force Academy, the U.S. Military Academy, the U.S. Coast Guard Academy, and the U.S. Naval Academy have all sponsored young men through their Foundation Scholars Program to attend Valley Forge Military College.

The College is accredited by the Middle States Association of Colleges and Schools and is approved by the Pennsylvania State Council of Education and the Commission on Higher Education of the Pennsylvania State Department of Education. The College is a member of the National Association of Independent Colleges and Universities, the Commission on Independent Colleges and Universities, and the Association of Military Colleges and Schools in the United States.

Academic Programs

All students are required to complete a core program of approximately 45 credits that is designed to establish the essential competencies necessary for continued intellectual development and to facilitate the transfer process. Included in the core program are two semesters of English, one semester of literature, one semester of Western civilization, two semesters of mathematics, one semester of science, and one semester of computer science. Qualified cadets must also complete a minimum of two semesters of military science. All sophomores participate in the sophomore writing seminar, a guided research experience. To satisfy the requirement for an associate degree, cadets must complete at least 15 additional credits in courses related to their selected area of concentration. Associate degrees are awarded upon completion of the degree requirements with a quality point average of 2.0 or better.

Associate Degree Programs Valley Forge Military College offers concentrations in the liberal arts, business, criminal justice, leadership and entrepreneurial studies, and general studies, leading to an Associate of Arts degree, as well as concentrations in pre-engineering, physical sciences, life sciences, and general studies, leading to an Associate of Science degree.

Transfer Arrangements Transfer of academic credits and completion of the baccalaureate degree is facilitated by established relationships with a number of outstanding colleges and universities.

Credit for Nontraditional Learning Experiences

Valley Forge Military College may give credit for demonstrated proficiency in areas related to college-level courses. Sources used to determine such proficiency are the College-Level Examination Program (CLEP), Advanced Placement Examination (AP), Defense Activity for Nontraditional Education Support (DANTES), and the Office of Education Credit and Credentials of the American Council on Education (ACE).

Costs

The annual charge for 2004–05 was $26,450. This charge included tuition, room and board, uniforms, maintenance, haircuts, and other fees. Optional expenses may include fee-based courses, such as scuba, aviation, and driver's education, or membership in the cavalry troop or artillery battery. A fee is charged for Health Center confinement over 24 hours' duration. For information on the payment plan, students should contact the Finance Office.

Financial Aid

The College offers merit-based scholarships, merit- and need-based endowed scholarships, and need-based grants to help VFMC cadets finance their education. The academic scholarship rewards incoming and returning cadets who have demonstrated academic excellence. Performance scholarships are awarded to eligible cadets who participate in the athletic teams, band, or choir. Many Friends of Valley Forge have established various special and endowed scholarships, with a range of merit- and/or need-based criteria, to help cadets finance their education. Need-based grants are offered to eligible cadets with demonstrated financial need based on the filing of the Free Application for Federal Student Aid (FAFSA). In addition, qualified cadets in the advanced ROTC commissioning program are eligible for two-year, full tuition scholarships. These scholarships are supplemented by assistance for room and board provided by the College.

Valley Forge Military College offers federal student aid to eligible cadets in the form of Federal Pell Grants, Federal Supplemental Educational Opportunity Grants (FSEOG), Federal Work-Study (FWS) Program positions, and federally guaranteed student and parent loans through the Federal Family Education Loan Program. Applicants must file the FAFSA and the VFMC financial aid application for consideration.

Faculty

There are 13 full-time and 17 part-time faculty members holding the academic rank of professor, associate professor, assistant professor, or instructor. These faculty members are selected for their professional ability and strong personal leadership qualities. Faculty members perform additional duties as athletic coaches and advisers of extracurricular activities. The Military Science Department has 5 active-duty Army officers and 4 noncommissioned officers assigned as full-time faculty members for the ROTC program. The faculty-student ratio is approximately 1:10. Classes are small, and the classroom atmosphere contributes to a harmonious relationship between faculty members and the students.

Student Body Profile

The military structure of Valley Forge provides extraordinary opportunities for the student to develop and exercise his leadership abilities. The Corps of Cadets is a self-administering body organized in nine company units along military lines, with a cadet officer and noncommissioned officer organization for cadet control and administration. The College's cadets are appointed to major command positions in the Corps. The first captain is generally a sophomore in the College. Cadet leadership and positive peer pressure within this structured setting results in a brotherhood and camaraderie among cadets. Cadets, through their student representatives, cooperate with the administration in enforcing regulations regarding student conduct. A Student Advisory Council represents the cadets in the school administration. The Dean's Council meets regularly to discuss aspects of academic life.

Student Activities

The proximity to many colleges and universities ensures a full schedule of local college-oriented events in addition to Valley Forge's own activities. Cadets are encouraged to become involved in community-service activities. The scholarship-supported Regimental Band has performed for U.S. presidents, royalty, and countless military and social events. The Regimental Chorus has performed at the Capitol Building in Washington, D.C.; the Philadelphia Academy of Music; and New York's Carnegie Hall. In addition, eligible students can participate in VFMC honor societies: Phi Theta Kappa, Lambda Alpha Epsilon, or Alpha Beta Gamma. Other available activities include business and political clubs, Rotoract, flight training, and the Mask and Spur Theater Society.

Sports Athletics and physical well-being are important elements in a Valley Forge education. The aim of the program is to develop all-around fitness, alertness, character, esprit de corps, leadership, courage, competitive spirit, and genuine desire for physical and mental achievement. For students aspiring to compete at the Division I-A or Division I-AA level, Valley Forge's residential college football and basketball programs offer a distinctive opportunity that combines such a strong academic transfer program with a highly successful athletic program that has habitually placed players at the national level. Continuing a legacy that began with its high school program, in only eight years, the College has placed 40 players on national-level teams in basketball and football. In the last three years, the Valley Forge wrestling program has also produced two National Collegiate Wrestling Association Champions and one All American National Collegiate Wrestling Association Champion. Students may also compete at the collegiate level in cross country, lacrosse, soccer, tennis, and wrestling. Club and interscholastic teams are available in golf, polo, and riflery. The Valley Forge polo team is consistently among the top-ranked polo teams in the nation.

Facilities and Resources

Campus buildings are modern and well equipped to meet student needs. A fiber-optic, Internet-capable computer network connects all classrooms, laboratories, library, and dormitory rooms on the campus. All rooms are computer accessible and provide access to CadetNET, the institutional local area network. This network provides access to the library and the Internet. College classrooms are located in two buildings and contain chemistry, biology, and physics laboratories. A recently renovated computer laboratory supports the computer science curriculum and student requirements through a local area network.

Library and Audiovisual Services The Mary H. Baker Memorial Library is a learning resource center for independent study and research. The library has more than 100,000 volumes and audiovisual materials, microfilm, and periodicals and houses the newly created Cadet Achievement Center. It provides online database access, membership in the Tri-State Library Consortium, and computer links to ACCESS Pennsylvania and other databases to support the College requirements.

Location

Valley Forge Military College is on a beautifully landscaped 120-acre campus in the Main Line community of Wayne, 15 miles west of Philadelphia and close to the Valley Forge National Historic Park. Ample opportunities exist for cadets to enjoy cultural and entertainment resources and activities in the Philadelphia area.

Admission Requirements

Admission to the College is based upon review of an applicant's SAT or ACT scores, high school transcript, recommendations from a guidance counselor, and personal interview. Students may be accepted for midyear admission. Minimum requirements for admission on a nonprobational status are a high school diploma or equivalency diploma with a minimum 2.0 average, rank in the upper half of the class, and a minimum combined SAT score of 850 or ACT score of 17. An international student for whom English is a second language must have a minimum score of 500 on the Test of English as a Foreign Language (TOEFL). Up to 20 percent of an entering class may be admitted on a conditional or probationary status, and individual entrance requirements may be waived by the dean of the College for students who display a sincere commitment to pursuing a college degree.

Application and Information

Valley Forge Military College follows a program of rolling admissions. Applicants are notified of the admission decision as soon as their files are complete. A nonrefundable registration fee of $25 is required of all applicants.

For application forms and further information, students should contact:

College Admissions Officer
Valley Forge Military College
1001 Eagle Road
Wayne, Pennsylvania 19087
Telephone: 800-234-VFMC (toll-free)
E-mail: admissions@vfmac.edu
World Wide Web: http://www.vfmac.edu

A Valley Forge College cadet rappels down the Rappel Tower.

WADE COLLEGE

DALLAS, TEXAS

The College and Its Mission

Wade College is a small private college offering an associate degree program in merchandising and design. The College is a teaching institution that emphasizes professional study and the liberal arts.

Wade College exists and operates to provide its students with the skills and knowledge that are needed to be productive members of society. It further seeks to provide them with an enriching cultural, moral, economic, and social experience. The College is committed to serving the changing requirements of the merchandising, fashion design, computer graphic design, and interior design fields.

The purpose of Wade College is to offer programs of instruction that are designed to allow students to develop the competencies necessary for immediate employment and career advancement in their chosen fields; continue and complete a formal education in upper-level and graduate colleges and universities, if so desired; develop intellectual, humanitarian, and leadership skills that will advance their potential for success; and engage in continual self-improvement.

Wade College emphasizes individual student attention. To facilitate this, class sizes are usually small.

Academic Programs

The educational program emphasizes the importance of both general education and specialized study. The values of the former are deemed important to the development of responsible citizens in a free society; the experience of the latter is regarded as indispensable to students preparing for active careers. General education is versatile and helps students to better adapt to change so that they may advance in their careers. Specialized study helps them develop the professional skills that are required in their career fields.

Through the integration of diverse disciplines in art, design, business, computers, and the liberal arts, the Associate of Arts degree program reaches beyond specialized professional skills to a broader spectrum of knowledge. The curriculum promotes a well-rounded perspective of the world in general and the field of merchandising and design in particular.

For more than forty years, Wade College has specialized in academic programs leading to careers in the fields of merchandising and design. The Associate of Arts degree is a balanced program with dual majors in merchandising and design. Concentrations are offered in fashion design, interior design, computer graphic design, merchandise marketing, fashion merchandising, and interior merchandising. A minimum of 63 semester credit hours is required for degree completion. The associate degree is normally completed in four consecutive trimesters of full-time study. Each trimester is fifteen weeks in length and is equivalent to a traditional semester. Full-time students are expected to graduate sixteen months after entering the program. Individual degree plans can be developed for students with special needs.

Costs

In 2005–06, tuition for the academic year is $8850. Optional student housing is $3360 per academic year. There are additional fees and deposits. Textbooks, supplies, and course fees are estimated at $1480 per academic year. All tuition and fee costs are subject to change. Wade College has a guaranteed tuition rate for the four trimesters of the student's program.

Financial Aid

Wade College offers financial aid counseling and assistance in applying for a variety of federal financial aid programs. The U.S. Department of Education offers several financial aid programs to help students meet educational expenses. Students at Wade College are eligible to apply for financial assistance under the following federal student aid programs: the Federal Pell Grant Program, Federal Supplemental Educational Opportunity Grants, Federal Work-Study Program, Federal Perkins Loan, William D. Ford Federal Direct Loan Program, and the Federal Parent Loan for Undergraduate Students (PLUS) program.

The College is committed to helping every student plan for educational expenses. An individual Student Financial Plan is prepared for each registered student prior to the start of classes. Various payment options are also available.

Faculty

Each educational area is headed by a full-time faculty member with an advanced degree in his or her field. There are five full-time instructors. Numerous part-time adjunct instructors are also available. Usually, these are individuals who have advanced degrees and are also practicing professionals in their fields. Approximately 85 percent of the faculty members have advanced degrees.

Student Body Profile

The student body is 90 percent female and 10 percent male. The majority of students are from Texas, but students also come from Oklahoma, Louisiana, Arkansas, Colorado, New Mexico, and from almost every other part of the U.S. and several other countries. The average age is 20.5 years old. Most students are between the ages of 18 and 24, but there are many students over 30. The ethnic composition of the student body is similar to that of the North Texas area. Approximately 45 percent are white, 35 percent are African American, 15 percent are Hispanic, and 5 percent are Asian.

Student Activities

Numerous campus organizations and activities are available for student participation. The College has a chapter of Phi Theta Kappa, the national honor society for two-year colleges. Many students participate in the seasonal fashion apparel and furniture wholesale markets held on campus at the Dallas Market Center. They are assisted through the College's Career Planning and Placement Office.

Comprehensive student services are offered in the areas of housing, financial aid, part-time employment, counseling, and graduate placement. Student needs are given a high priority. Career planning and placement for students of Wade College is offered through the offices of the Executive Director and the Director of Student Services. Career development and professional job search assistance is provided to students and alumni though individual career counseling and exploration of various career opportunities. The office also provides instruction in writing resumes and cover letters, portfolio presentations and self-promotion, interviewing skills, and networking techniques to prepare students for the job market.

Facilities and Resources

Wade College is located at the Dallas Market Center, the world's largest merchandising and design wholesale complex. The Market Center features almost 5,000 showrooms for the wholesale display of merchandise. Students have the opportunity to learn right in the heart of the industry, where the education and business worlds come together. The Dallas area is one of the largest business markets for furnishings, apparel, merchandising, and computer technology in the United States.

The student residence apartments are located in the dynamic environment of North Dallas, 12 miles from downtown.

Wade College Library is located on the campus of Wade College. The library provides access to a specialty collection of materials reflecting the College's curriculum. The library's collection contains more than 7,000 bound volumes, 150 periodical subscriptions, and 400 audiovisual and computer items. The library is a member of AMIGOS, a regional network for resource sharing and technology. The library is also a member of OCLC, providing online search capabilities.

Location

Dallas, Texas is an international business, technology, and retail center. Dallas is known for its shopping, restaurants, and entertainment. Dallas is also home to the Cowboys, the Mavericks, the Rangers, and the Stars—major professional sports teams in the NFL, NBA, MLB, and NHL, respectively. The city and surrounding areas have a population of well over 2 million. The area is served by public transportation, including bus and light rail. Situated on a major interstate highway, the campus is easily accessible by car. Fort Worth, another major urban center, is within easy driving distance. The climate of Dallas is relatively mild in winter, warm in spring and fall, and hot in the summer.

Admission Requirements

Wade College adheres to a policy of open admissions for high school graduates or those students who have passed the GED test. This policy precludes admitting students on the basis of qualitative selection procedures. The philosophy of admission is that an educationally motivated individual is entitled to an opportunity for improved professional and personal success. The College provides a supportive educational environment so that individuals with a sincere interest have the opportunity to meet the educational rigors placed on them and successfully progress through course requirements.

Prospective students may apply for admission as early as one year in advance of the desired class starting date. Since annual enrollment is limited by facility space available in the Dallas Market Center, interested students are encouraged to submit their applications as early as possible. Wade College does not have an application fee. All applicants are required to interview with a representative from the Admissions Office prior to the start of classes. It is highly recommended that this interview take place at the College; however, in circumstances where the applicant's home is a great distance from the College, the interview may be conducted on the telephone or via the Internet.

Applicants are expected to register within 30 days of their acceptance by paying a nonrefundable $125 enrollment fee. Accepted applicants must submit verification of high school graduation or successful completion of the GED program prior to entry.

Application and Information

For more information, prospective students should contact:

Admissions Office
Wade College
Dallas Market Center
2350 Stemmons Expressway, Suite M5120
P.O. Box 421149
Dallas, Texas 75342
Telephone: 214-637-3530
        800-624-4850 (toll-free)
Fax: 214-637-0827
E-mail: admissions@wadecollege.edu
World Wide Web: http://www.wadecollege.edu

WAYNE COUNTY COMMUNITY COLLEGE DISTRICT

DETROIT, MICHIGAN

The College and Its Mission

Wayne County Community College District (WCCCD) has served as a leader in providing education services and training to residents of southeast Michigan. Distinctive in its purpose and history, WCCCD was established by a public mandate and chartered in 1967. In 1969, the first classes were offered by the institution known as the "college without walls" in that WCCCD had no buildings or facilities of its own. By 1982, the College had constructed five campuses within its 550-square-mile service district. As a two-year "open door" institution, WCCCD is committed to providing an affordable high-quality education in an atmosphere of friendly support and encouragement.

Academic Programs

The College operates on a two-semester system and also offers a summer term.

WCCCD offers **Associate of General Studies, Associate of Arts, Associate of Applied Science,** and **Associate of Science** degrees plus one-year and two-year certificates.

The certificate and degree programs offered at Wayne County Community College District include the following: accounting; agriscience; architectural construction technology; automotive body repair; automotive service technology; aviation mechanics (options in airframe and power plant); business administration; business information systems (options in administrative assistant studies, general office clerical, legal secretarial, medical secretarial, and word/information processing); child-care training; computer information systems; criminal justice (options in law enforcement administration and corrections); dental assisting; dental hygiene; dental lab technology; electrical/electronics technology (options in computer technology, electronics engineering technology, industrial electronics and control technology, and telecommunications technology); emergency medical technology; environmental and natural resources; environmental, health, and safety technology; facility maintenance; fire protection; food service system management; general studies; gerontology; heating, ventilating, and air-conditioning; heavy-equipment maintenance technology; honors program; industrial computer graphic technology; lawn and ornamental plant maintenance; machine tool technology/numerical control; manufacturing technology; mental health; Muslim world studies; nursing; nursing assistant studies; occupational therapy assistant studies; optical technology; paralegal technology; pre-engineering (transfer); pharmacy assistant technology; pre–social work; real estate entrepreneurship; substance-abuse counseling; surgical technology; telecommunications technology; urban teacher studies (options in elementary education, secondary education, and special education); veterinary technology; and welding technology.

WCCCD offers a combination of programs oriented toward general education, transfer to baccalaureate institutions, and career preparation. All degree programs require the completion of at least 60 credit hours, including the last 15 at WCCCD, and specific program or academic group requirements; a varying number of credit hours in U.S. government; and a final grade point average of at least 2.0. Requirements for the Associate of Arts and Associate of Science degrees include a specified number of credit hours in English, humanities, mathematics/

sciences, and natural and social sciences. Associate of Applied Science degree requirements include a specified number of credit hours in general education, specific courses, and occupational support courses.

Many students begin their education at Wayne County Community College District and later transfer to four-year colleges or universities. Transfer is made possible in several ways. WCCCD participates in a number of articulation agreements with local colleges and universities (e.g., Wayne State, Michigan, Michigan State, etc.) These agreements provide ease of transfer to those students wishing to earn a baccalaureate degree. WCCCD is a member of the Michigan Association of Collegiate Registrars and Admissions Officers (MACRAO). Students wishing to transfer are advised of the requirements as stipulated in the MACRAO Agreement. Academic advising is made accessible to any student in any major who wishes to transfer so that the number of hours transferred into a four-year degree program is maximized.

Certificate programs are designed for students seeking job-entry skills and those aiming to improve job performance or to qualify for advancement. Specific program requirements vary by program.

Costs

Tuition for 2005–06 is $55.50 per credit hour for Wayne County residents who live in WCCCD's service district. Average fees for the academic year are approximately $90.

Financial Aid

A student must apply for admission to be considered for financial aid, which is granted based on eligibility and need. Available assistance includes Federal Pell Grants, Federal Supplemental Educational Opportunity Grants, Federal Work-Study Program awards, Federal Stafford Student Loans, Michigan Part-time Student Grants, Michigan College Work-Study awards, and Michigan Educational Opportunity Grants. Michigan's Tuition Incentive Program (TIP) provides free community-college tuition for two years to eligible high school graduates. Though applications are accepted on an ongoing basis, students are encouraged to apply early and electronically. The priority date for fall semester enrollment is June 1.

Faculty

The WCCCD faculty includes approximately 100 full-time and more than 300 part-time instructors.

Student Body Profile

WCCCD has a rich and diverse student population; approximately 70 percent are women and more than 50 percent are members of minority groups. While some 85 percent are Michigan residents, citizens from more than thirty countries are also enrolled in programs of study at the College. Seventy percent of all WCCCD students attend part-time. There are no on-campus housing facilities. Excellent child-care facilities in a safe and caring educational environment are available for a limited number of students at four of the campuses.

Student Activities

In addition to a variety of student clubs and organizations, there is a Student Government Association on each campus. Films, lectures, performing arts events, and other activities offer opportunities for students beyond the classroom.

Academic Facilities

WCCCD offers a wide range of support services to help students have a meaningful and productive educational experience.

The Career Planning and Placement Office offers aid that includes computerized career information and exploration resources, such as the Michigan Occupational Information System, Sigi-Plus, and the Perfect Resume Service. A computer job-sharing network lists a variety of opportunities.

Multi-Learning Laboratories have filmstrips, slides, programmed texts, tapes, reading machines, and textbooks at varying levels of difficulty to help students improve academically. Tutoring is also available.

The Access College Careers and Educational Supportive Services (ACCESS) helps students who are displaced homemakers, people who speak English as a second language, and those who are physically handicapped. This department can provide tutors, note takers, braille and taped materials, and interpreters for the deaf.

The Learning Resource Center at each campus is a library and more. Features include the Detroit Area Library Network (DALNET), a computer link between all WCCCD libraries and the libraries of several local colleges, universities, and hospitals.

Location

Wayne County Community College District's five facilities are located in suburban, urban, and rural areas of Wayne County.

Metropolitan Detroit offers a broad choice of cultural institutions and recreational activities, including major sports teams. In addition to being the world's automotive capital, Detroit is host to leading medical institutions, high-technology manufacturers, and international-class financial institutions.

Wayne County Community College has five campuses located in the metropolitan Detroit area. The **Downtown Campus** is at the edge of Detroit's convention center. The **Eastern Campus** is part of a medical/retail/residential corridor on the east side of the city. The **Northwest Campus** is located in a business hub and near a diverse residential community in northwest Detroit. The **Downriver Campus** is located in suburban Taylor (an industrial and residential community), and the **Western Campus** sits on more than 100 acres in the growing industrial community of Belleville.

All College facilities are easily accessible via freeways.

Admission Requirements

WCCCD has an open admission policy—acceptance is automatic for those who are age 18 or older with a high school diploma or GED certificate. Admission is granted on a nonselective basis. However, all students are assessed upon entry in English and math for placement into appropriate courses.

Students at other colleges or universities who wish to transfer credits to WCCCD should request that official copies of their transcripts be forwarded to WCCCD's Office of Admissions. Generally, credit earned from regionally accredited institutions and from all publicly supported junior and community colleges is readily accepted if it has been earned with a grade of C or better. Students should note that grades are not transferable; only credit hours can be transferred.

WCCCD welcomes applications from international students who have completed secondary education and are eligible for admission to college-level studies. International applicants should begin the admission process at the earliest possible date: from three to six months before a semester begins is recommended. In addition to meeting other admission criteria, international students must score 500 or above on the Test of English as a Foreign Language (TOEFL) or score at least 70 on the Michigan Test. The TOEFL is given in countries throughout the world. Testing information is available from TOEFL, Box 6151, Princeton, New Jersey 08541 and from the U.S. embassies or consulates. Michigan Test information is available from the English Language Institute, University of Michigan, Ann Arbor, Michigan 48109 (telephone: 313-764-2416).

Application and Information

Applications are accepted on an ongoing basis. For international students, correspondence concerning admission and all credentials in support of the application must be on file in the Office of Admissions prior to its issuance of an I-20 A-B.

For an application form and additional information, students should contact:

Division of Student Services
Wayne County Community College District
801 West Fort Street
Detroit, Michigan 48226-2539

Telephone: 313-496-2600
E-mail: info@wcccd.edu
World Wide Web: http://www.wcccd.edu

WESTWOOD AVIATION INSTITUTE–HOUSTON

HOUSTON, TEXAS

The Institute and Its Mission

Today, the variables that define career success are ever changing. In order to get ahead and stay ahead, students need the right kind of preparation. To prepare for the working world, they need a program of career-focused education that teaches the skills that employers demand and offers hands-on, practical experience with real-world applications and the right kind of job-placement assistance to help students get started in their new career.

Students also need a fast-track learning program that shortens the time from education to career, with an academic schedule that fits their lifestyle. They need a high level of student services to help reach their goals and the right financial package to make it all possible.

All of these are the focus at Westwood College and Westwood Aviation Institute, which operate eighteen campuses, with locations in California, Colorado, Illinois, Georgia, and Texas. The fifteen campuses of Westwood College offer degree programs in high-technology fields, while the three aviation campuses (Westwood College of Aviation Technology–Denver, Westwood College of Aviation Technology–Los Angeles, and Westwood Aviation Institute–Houston) offer aviation maintenance training.

Westwood Aviation Institute offers aviation maintenance curriculum in Houston.

Westwood Aviation Institute–Houston is a branch of Westwood College of Aviation Technology–Los Angeles and is accredited by the Council on Occupational Education (COE).

Academic Programs

Students are drawn to this campus to train for an aviation-maintenance career. Graduates have gone on to careers with large commercial airlines, aerospace manufacturing companies, regional airlines, fixed-base carriers, and a variety of other industry employers. A certificate program in airframe and power plant maintenance is offered.

Costs

Standard program costs can be found in the Westwood College academic catalog.

Financial Aid

Tuition assistance is available for those who qualify. Scholarships include the Westwood High School Scholarship Program, in which two scholarships are offered to every high school in the United States. In addition, several loan programs are available.

Student Body Profile

The campus has an enrollment of 450, of whom 90 percent are men and 10 percent women.

Student Activities

With the campus located in the nation's fourth-largest city, cultural and recreational opportunities abound for the student. A Southwestern flavor naturally highlights the area, with such events as the Houston Livestock Show and Rodeo and Fiesta Patrias, in addition to shopping at the Galleria.

Facilities and Resources

The campus covers 7 acres and includes more than 40,000 square feet of modern, air-conditioned classrooms and workshops. Students are given hands-on experience with a variety of essential training aids, including reciprocating power plants from manufacturers such as General Electric, Pratt & Whitney, and others. The campus also features operable subassemblies needed to learn airframe and power plant maintenance.

Location

The campus is located at 8880 Telephone Road, near Houston's Hobby Airport. It is easily reached via Interstate 45 and Airport Boulevard.

Admission Requirements

To enroll, students must be at least 17 years of age, have a high school diploma or GED certificate, and be able to speak, write, and read English.

Application and Information

Director of Admissions
Westwood Aviation Institute–Houston
8880 Telephone Road
Houston, Texas 77061-5114

Telephone: 713-645-4444
Fax: 713-644-9744
E-mail: info@westwood.edu
World Wide Web: http://www.westwood.edu/aviation

Westwood Aviation Institute–Houston campus.

WESTWOOD COLLEGE–ANAHEIM

ANAHEIM, CALIFORNIA

The College and Its Mission

Today, the variables that define career success are ever changing. In order to get ahead and stay ahead, students need the right kind of preparation. To prepare them for the working world, students need a career-focused education program that teaches the skills employers demand and offers hands-on practical experience with real-world applications and the right kind of job-placement assistance to help them get started in their new careers.

Students also need a fast-track learning program that shortens the time from education to career, with an academic schedule that fits their lifestyle. They need a high level of student services to help them reach their goals and the right financial package to make it all possible.

All of these are the focus at Westwood College, which operates eighteen campuses, with locations in California, Colorado, Illinois, Georgia, and Texas. The fifteen campuses of Westwood College offer degree programs in high-technology fields, while the three aviation campuses (Westwood College of Aviation Technology–Denver, Westwood College of Aviation Technology–Los Angeles, and Westwood Aviation Institute–Houston) offer aviation maintenance training.

Such fields as computer networking, graphic design, computer-aided design, and e-business are featured at the Westwood College campuses located in Anaheim, Inland Empire (Upland), Long Beach, and Los Angeles, California; Atlanta, Georgia; DuPage, O'Hare Airport, River Oaks, and Chicago–Loop, Illinois; Denver–North and Denver–South, Colorado; and Dallas, Fort Worth, and Houston, Texas. The Westwood College of Aviation Technology offers the aviation curriculum at the Denver, Colorado and Los Angeles, California, campuses, while Westwood Aviation Institute offers the aviation curriculum in Houston.

The Anaheim campus is accredited by the Accrediting Commission of Career Schools and Colleges of Technology (ACCSCT).

Westwood College–Anaheim is a branch of Westwood College–Denver North.

Academic Programs

The Anaheim campus focuses on computer-based technology programs that prepare graduates to take advantage of southern California's unique, high-tech career opportunities. Bachelor's degree programs are offered in computer network management, criminal justice, e-business management, game art and design, game software development, information systems security, interior design, visual communications, and Web design and multimedia. Associate degree programs are offered in computer-aided design/architectural drafting, computer network engineering, graphic design and multimedia, and software engineering.

The programs, which feature hands-on learning experience, are designed to prepare students for entry-level positions in their chosen careers.

Costs

Standard program costs can be found in the Westwood College academic catalog.

Financial Aid

Tuition assistance is available for those who qualify. Scholarships include the Westwood High School Scholarship Program, which offers two scholarships to every high school in the United States; the Colorado Undergraduate Merit State Scholarships for Colorado residents; and several loan programs.

Student Body Profile

Student enrollment at the Anaheim campus totals 780, of whom approximately 25 percent are women.

Student Activities

In addition to on-campus activities, the Anaheim area offers many cultural and recreational opportunities for students.

Facilities and Resources

The campus includes a primary building with approximately 25,000 square feet dedicated to classrooms, labs, and administrative offices. A nearby campus annex houses additional classroom space.

Location

The Anaheim campus is in Orange County, minutes from attractions such as Disneyland, Knott's Berry Farm, and Edison International Park. The area offers students an active lifestyle and is rich in career opportunities. Located directly across the street from Anaheim's arena, the Arrowhead Pond, the campus is easily accessible from I-5 at Katella.

Admission Requirements

Applicants must have either a diploma from an accredited high school or a GED certificate and passing scores on the College entrance exam (or qualifying ACT/SAT scores).

Application and Information

Emily Yost, Director of Admissions
Westwood College–Anaheim
1551 South Douglas Road
Anaheim, California 92801

Telephone: 714-704-2721
          877-650-6050 (toll-free)
Fax: 714-456-9971
E-mail: info@westwood.edu
World Wide Web: http://www.westwood.edu

Westwood College–Anaheim campus.

WESTWOOD COLLEGE–ATLANTA MIDTOWN

ATLANTA, GEORGIA

WESTWOOD COLLEGE

The College and Its Mission

Today, the variables that define career success are ever changing. In order to get ahead and stay ahead, students need the right kind of preparation. To prepare for the working world, they need a career-focused education program that teaches the skills employers demand and offers hands-on, practical experience with real-world applications and the right kind of job-placement assistance to help students get started in their new careers.

Students also need a fast-track learning program that shortens the time from education to career, with an academic schedule that fits their lifestyle. They need a high level of student services to help them reach their goals and the right financial package to make it all possible.

All of these are the focus at Westwood, which operates eighteen campuses, with locations in California, Colorado, Illinois, Georgia, and Texas. The fifteen campuses of Westwood College offer degree programs in high-technology fields, while the three aviation campuses (Westwood College of Aviation Technology–Denver, Westwood College of Aviation Technology–Los Angeles, and Westwood Aviation Institute–Houston) offer aviation maintenance training.

Such fields as computer networking, graphic design, computer-aided design, and e-business are featured at the Westwood College campuses located in Anaheim, Inland Empire (Upland), Long Beach, and Los Angeles, California; Atlanta, Georgia; DuPage, O'Hare Airport, River Oaks, and Chicago Loop, Illinois; Denver North and Denver South, Colorado; and Dallas, Fort Worth, and Houston, Texas. The Westwood College of Aviation Technology offers the aviation curriculum at the Denver, Colorado, and Los Angeles, California, campuses, while Westwood Aviation Institute offers the aviation curriculum in Houston.

The Atlanta Midtown campus is a branch of Westwood College–DuPage and is accredited by the Accrediting Council for Independent Colleges and Schools (ACICS).

Academic Programs

The Atlanta Midtown campus offers bachelor's degree programs in animation, computer network management, e-business management, interior design, visual communications, and Web design and multimedia. Associate degree programs include computer-aided design/architectural drafting, computer network engineering, and graphic design and multimedia.

Costs

Standard program costs can be found in the Westwood College academic catalog.

Financial Aid

Tuition assistance is available for those who qualify. Scholarships include the Westwood High School Scholarship Program, in which two scholarships are offered to every high school in the United States. In addition, several loan programs are available.

Student Body Profile

Student enrollment at the Atlanta Midtown campus totals 130, of whom approximately 40 percent are women.

Student Activities

In addition to on-campus activities, many cultural and recreational activities are available in the greater Atlanta area.

Facilities and Resources

Westwood offers a variety of information and research resources, including on-campus Resource Centers, links to Internet-based information services, and a bookstore at each campus. The Campus Resource Centers offer a library of program-specific materials that have been carefully selected to aid that school's career-focused educational mission. The Education Department at each campus collaborates closely with the campus' Resource Center staff to ensure that materials support the school's hands-on curriculum. Typical learning aids include books, periodicals, and Internet access. A virtual library, providing remote access to several selected databases, is also offered. Staff members are available to assist students during regular library hours and can provide instruction on how to conduct research in the library and online.

Location

Westwood College–Atlanta Midtown's convenient campus location just off I-85 and north of I-20 in midtown Atlanta is in the cultural heart of the city. Metropolitan Atlanta's population is more than 4 million, and the community offers all the entertainment advantages of a large city, including scores of galleries and alternative spaces that exhibit a broad variety of artwork; a ballet and opera; numerous movie houses showing new releases and foreign and classic films; a growing number of theater companies; and many opportunities for rock, jazz, avant-garde music, and outdoor performances. In addition, Atlanta has myriad natural areas and parks, restaurants and coffee houses of every description, and four professional sports teams. The Arts Center Station of MARTA, Atlanta's clean, safe, and efficient rapid transit system, is located just around the corner and offers easy access to many points of interest. The Georgia Institute of Technology and the Atlanta College of Design are only blocks away. Atlanta is a city full of life with a job market that values career-ready individuals such as Westwood College graduates.

Admission Requirements

A diploma from an accredited high school or a GED certificate and passing scores on the college entrance exam (or qualifying ACT/SAT scores) are required.

Application and Information

Director of Admissions
Westwood College–Atlanta Midtown
1100 Spring Street NW
Atlanta, Georgia 30309

Telephone: 404-745-9862
Fax: 404-892-7253
E-mail: info@westwood.edu
World Wide Web: http://www.westwood.edu

WESTWOOD COLLEGE–ATLANTA NORTHLAKE
ATLANTA, GEORGIA

The College and Its Mission

Today, the variables that define career success are ever changing. In order to get ahead and stay ahead, students need the right kind of preparation. To prepare for the working world, they need a career-focused education program that teaches the skills employers demand and offers hands-on, practical experience with real-world applications and the right kind of job-placement assistance to help students get started in their new careers.

Students also need a fast-track learning program that shortens the time from education to career, with an academic schedule that fits their lifestyle. They need a high level of student services to help them reach their goals and the right financial package to make it all possible.

All of these are the focus at Westwood, which operates eighteen campuses, with locations in California, Colorado, Illinois, Georgia, and Texas. The fifteen campuses of Westwood College offer degree programs in high-technology fields, while the three aviation campuses (Westwood College of Aviation Technology–Denver, Westwood College of Aviation Technology–Los Angeles, and Westwood Aviation Institute–Houston) offer aviation maintenance training.

Such fields as computer networking, graphic design, computer-aided design, and e-business are featured at the Westwood College campuses located in Anaheim, Inland Empire (Upland), Long Beach, and Los Angeles, California; Atlanta, Georgia; DuPage, O'Hare Airport, River Oaks, and Chicago Loop, Illinois; Denver North and Denver South, Colorado; and Dallas, Fort Worth, and Houston, Texas. The Westwood College of Aviation Technology offers the aviation curriculum at the Denver, Colorado, and Los Angeles, California, campuses, while Westwood Aviation Institute offers the aviation curriculum in Houston.

The Atlanta Northlake campus is a branch of Westwood College–O'Hare Airport and is accredited by the Accrediting Council for Independent Colleges and Schools (ACICS).

Academic Programs

The Atlanta Northlake campus offers bachelor's degree programs in animation, computer network management, e-business management, interior design, and visual communications. Associate degree programs include computer-aided design/architectural drafting, computer network engineering, and graphic design and multimedia.

Costs

Standard program costs can be found in the Westwood College academic catalog.

Financial Aid

Tuition assistance is available for those who qualify. Scholarships include the Westwood High School Scholarship Program, in which two scholarships are offered to every high school in the United States. In addition, several loan programs are available.

Student Body Profile

Student enrollment at the newly opened Atlanta Northlake campus totals almost 75, of whom approximately 40 percent are women.

Student Activities

In addition to on-campus activities, many cultural and recreational activities are available in the greater Atlanta area.

Facilities and Resources

Westwood offers a variety of information and research resources, including on-campus Resource Centers, links to Internet-based information services, and a bookstore at each campus. The Campus Resource Centers offer a library of program-specific materials that have been carefully selected to aid that school's career-focused educational mission. The Education Department at each campus collaborates closely with the campus' Resource Center staff to ensure that materials support the school's hands-on curriculum. Typical learning aids include books, periodicals, and Internet access. A virtual library, providing remote access to several selected databases, is also offered. Staff members are available to assist students during regular library hours and can provide instruction on how to conduct research in the library and online.

Location

Westwood College–Atlanta Northlake's convenient campus location is just off I-285 northeast of downtown Atlanta. Metropolitan Atlanta's population is more than 4 million, and the community offers all the entertainment advantages of a large city, including scores of galleries and alternative spaces that exhibit a broad variety of artwork; a ballet and opera; numerous movie houses showing new releases and foreign and classic films; a growing number of theater companies; and many opportunities for rock, jazz, avant-garde music, and outdoor performances. In addition, Atlanta has myriad natural areas and parks, restaurants and coffee houses of every description, and four professional sports teams. The Arts Center Station of MARTA, Atlanta's clean, safe, and efficient rapid transit system, is located just around the corner and offers easy access to many points of interest. The Georgia Institute of Technology and the Atlanta College of Design are only blocks away. Atlanta is a city full of life with a job market that values career-ready individuals such as Westwood College graduates.

Admission Requirements

A diploma from an accredited high school or a GED certificate and passing scores on the college entrance exam (or qualifying ACT/SAT scores) are required.

Application and Information

Director of Admissions
Westwood College–Atlanta Northlake
2220 Parklake Drive NE
Atlanta, Georgia 30345

Telephone: 404-962-2998
Fax: 770-934-9539
E-mail: info@westwood.edu
World Wide Web: http://www.westwood.edu

WESTWOOD COLLEGE–CHICAGO LOOP

CHICAGO, ILLINOIS

The College and Its Mission

Today, the variables that define career success are ever changing. In order to get ahead and stay ahead, students need the right kind of preparation. To prepare for the working world, they need a career-focused education program that teaches the skills employers demand. The curriculum should include hands-on, practical experience and real-world applications to help graduates get started in their new careers.

Students also need a fast-track learning program that shortens the time from education to career, with an academic schedule that fits their lifestyle. They need a high level of student services to help them reach their goals and the right financial package to make it all possible.

All of these are the focus at Westwood College, which operates eighteen campuses, with locations in California, Colorado, Illinois, Georgia, and Texas. The fifteen campuses of Westwood College offer degree programs in high-technology fields, while the three aviation campuses (Westwood College of Aviation Technology–Denver, Westwood College of Aviation Technology–Los Angeles, and Westwood Aviation Institute–Houston) offer aviation maintenance training.

Such fields as computer networking, graphic design, computer-aided design, and e-business are featured at the Westwood College campuses located in Anaheim, Inland Empire (Upland), Long Beach, and Los Angeles, California; Atlanta, Georgia; DuPage, O'Hare Airport, River Oaks, and Chicago–Loop, Illinois; Denver–North and Denver–South, Colorado; and Dallas, Fort Worth, and Houston, Texas. The Westwood College of Aviation Technology offers the aviation curriculum at the Denver, Colorado, and Los Angeles, California, campuses, while Westwood Aviation Institute offers the aviation curriculum in Houston.

Westwood College–Chicago Loop is a branch of Westwood College–Los Angeles and is accredited by the Accrediting Council for Independent Colleges and Schools (ACICS).

Academic Programs

At the Westwood College–Chicago Loop campus, students may obtain a bachelor's degree in thirty-six months or an associate degree in twenty months through day and evening classes. The programs are designed to help adults

move quickly into the high-technology world of work. Classes provide hands-on skills and career-focused training. Skilled technology workers with fine-tuned critical-thinking skills graduate from Westwood ready to succeed. Westwood College's career development services match students with employers to get graduates started on the right career path.

The Chicago Loop campus offers such programs as bachelor's degree programs in animation, computer network management, criminal justice, information systems security, interior design, visual communications, and Web design and multimedia. The College offers associate degree programs in computer-aided design/architectural drafting, computer network engineering, and graphic design and multimedia.

Costs

Standard program costs can be found in the Westwood College academic catalog.

Financial Aid

Tuition assistance is available for those who qualify. Scholarships include the Westwood High School Scholarship Program, in which two scholarships are offered to every high school in the United States. In addition, several loan programs are available.

Student Body Profile

Westwood College recruits recent high school graduates, young adults, and working adults who want to acquire new skills to take advantage of growing opportunities in the professional workplace. Students come to Westwood from all across the U.S. and many other countries. Currently, the Loop campus has more than 300 students, of whom 30 percent are women.

Student Activities

In addition to the many on-campus activities available at Westwood College, the greater Chicago area abounds in cultural and recreational opportunities.

Facilities and Resources

Campus Resource Centers located on each Westwood campus contain a library of program-specific materials, books, and periodicals and Internet access. A virtual library provides remote access to several selected databases and links to Internet-based information that is specific to technology study. The Resource Center also contains the campus bookstore. Resource Center staff members can assist students in navigating all the research materials that are available.

Location

Westwood College's Chicago Loop campus is located on North State Street, in the heart of downtown Chicago, one of the nation's major urban hubs. Students find plenty of diversity and activity in Chicago's Loop area, the hub of central Chicago's shopping, dining, and commerce district. Arts and theater, nightlife, and city activities abound—all within easy access by foot, trolley, or public transit. Chicago is situated on Lake Michigan, providing plenty of outdoor recreational choices as well.

Admission Requirements

Admission requirements include a diploma from an accredited four-year high school or a GED certificate and passing scores on the College placement exam or qualifying SAT/ACT scores.

Application and Information

Director of Admissions
Westwood College–Chicago Loop
17 North State Street, 15th floor
Chicago, Illinois 60602
Telephone: 312-739-0850
         800-693-5415 (toll-free)
Fax: 312-739-1004
E-mail: info@westwood.edu
World Wide Web: http://www.westwood.edu

WESTWOOD COLLEGE–CHICAGO O'HARE AIRPORT

SCHILLER PARK, ILLINOIS

WESTWOOD COLLEGE

The College and Its Mission

Today, the variables that define career success are ever changing. In order to get ahead and stay ahead, students need the right kind of preparation. To prepare for the working world, students need a programmed, career-focused education that teaches the skills employers demand—that is, hands-on, practical experience with real-world applications and the right kind of job-placement assistance to help them get started in their new career.

Students also need a fast-track learning program that shortens the time from education to career, with an academic schedule that fits their lifestyle. Students need a high level of student services to help them reach their goals and the right financial package to make it all possible.

All of these are the focus at Westwood College, which operates eighteen campuses, with locations in California, Colorado, Illinois, Georgia, and Texas. The fifteen campuses of Westwood College offer degree programs in high-technology fields, while the three aviation campuses (Westwood College of Aviation Technology–Denver, Westwood College of Aviation Technology–Los Angeles, and Westwood Aviation Institute–Houston) offer aviation maintenance training.

Such fields as computer networking, graphic design, computer-aided design, and e-business are featured at the Westwood College campuses located in Anaheim, Inland Empire (Upland), Long Beach, and Los Angeles, California; Atlanta, Georgia; DuPage, O'Hare Airport, River Oaks, and Chicago–Loop, Illinois; Denver–North and Denver–South, Colorado; and Dallas, Fort Worth, and Houston, Texas. The Westwood College of Aviation Technology offers the aviation curriculum at the Denver, Colorado, and Los Angeles, California, campuses, while Westwood Aviation Institute offers the aviation curriculum in Houston.

The Westwood–O'Hare Airport campus is accredited by the Accrediting Council for Independent Colleges and Schools (ACICS).

Academic Programs

The Westwood College–O'Hare Airport campus focuses on computer-based technology programs that prepare graduates to take advantage of their high-technology career opportunities. Associate degree programs are offered in computer-aided design/architectural drafting (CAD), computer network engineering, and graphic design and multimedia. Bachelor's degree programs are offered in animation, computer network management, e-business management, visual communications, and Web design and multimedia.

Costs

Standard program costs can be found in the Westwood College academic catalog.

Financial Aid

Tuition assistance is available for those who qualify. Scholarships include the Westwood High School Scholarship Program, in which two scholarships are offered to every high school in the United States. In addition, several loan programs are available.

Student Body Profile

A total of 400 students are enrolled at the O'Hare Airport campus, of whom approximately 75 percent are men and 25 percent are women.

Student Activities

In addition to on-campus activities, the greater Chicago area offers many cultural and recreational opportunities.

Facilities and Resources

The campus includes 27,000 square feet of classrooms, labs, and administrative offices. In addition to an on-campus Resource Center, students benefit through cooperation with the suburban Inter-Library Loan Consortium and Illinet.

Location

The campus is located in Schiller Park, close to major highways and O'Hare International Airport.

Admission Requirements

A diploma from an accredited high school or GED certificate is required, as are passing scores on the college entrance exam (or qualifying ACT/SAT scores).

Application and Information

David Traub, Director of Admissions
Westwood College–Chicago O'Hare Airport
4825 North Scott Street, Suite 100
Schiller Park, Illinois 60176-1209
Telephone: 847-928-0200
　　　　　877-877-8857 (toll-free)
Fax: 847-928-2120
E-mail: info@westwood.edu
World Wide Web: http://www.westwood.edu

Westwood College–Chicago O'Hare Airport campus.

WESTWOOD COLLEGE– CHICAGO RIVER OAKS

CALUMET CITY, ILLINOIS

The College and Its Mission

Today, the variables that define career success are ever changing. In order to get ahead and stay ahead, students need the right kind of preparation. To prepare for the working world, students need a career-focused education program that teaches the skills employers demand and offers hands-on, practical experience with real-world applications and the right kind of job-placement assistance to help them get started in their new careers.

Students also need a fast-track learning program that shortens the time from education to career, with an academic schedule that fits their lifestyle. They need a high level of student services to help them reach their goals and the right financial package to make it all possible.

All of these are the focus at Westwood College, which operates eighteen campuses, with locations in California, Colorado, Illinois, Georgia, and Texas. The fifteen campuses of Westwood College offer degree programs in high-technology fields, while the three aviation campuses (Westwood College of Aviation Technology–Denver, Westwood College of Aviation Technology–Los Angeles, and Westwood Aviation Institute–Houston) offer aviation maintenance training.

Such fields as computer networking, graphic design, computer-aided design, and e-business are featured at the Westwood College campuses located in Anaheim, Inland Empire (Upland), Long Beach, and Los Angeles, California; Atlanta, Georgia; DuPage, O'Hare Airport, River Oaks, and Chicago–Loop, Illinois; Denver–North and Denver–South, Colorado; and Dallas, Fort Worth, and Houston, Texas. The Westwood College of Aviation Technology offers the aviation curriculum at the Denver, Colorado and Los Angeles, California, campuses, while Westwood Aviation Institute offers the aviation curriculum in Houston.

The River Oaks campus is accredited by the Accrediting Council for Independent Colleges and Schools (ACICS).

Westwood College–River Oaks is a branch of Westwood College–Los Angeles.

Academic Programs

The River Oaks Campus focuses on computer-based technology programs that prepare students to take advantage of high-tech careers. Associate degree programs in computer-aided design/architectural drafting (CAD), computer network engineering, graphic design and multimedia, and software engineering are offered. Bachelor's degree programs are offered in animation, computer network management, e-business management, visual communications, and Web design and multimedia.

Costs

Standard program costs can be found in the Westwood College academic catalog.

Financial Aid

Tuition assistance is available for those who qualify. Scholarships include the Westwood High School Scholarship Program, through which two scholarships are offered to every high school in the United States; the Colorado Undergraduate Merit State Scholarships for Colorado residents; and several loan programs.

Student Body Profile

There are 640 students enrolled at this campus, of whom 25 percent are women.

Student Activities

In addition to on-campus activities, many cultural and recreational opportunities are available in the Greater Chicago area.

Facilities and Resources

The campus includes 25,000 square feet of classrooms, labs, and administrative offices. In addition to an on-campus resource center, students benefit from cooperation with the suburban Inter-Library Loan Consortium and Illinet.

Location

The campus is located an hour south of Chicago at 80 River Oaks Center in Calumet City. It is easily reached by several major freeways.

Admission Requirements

A diploma from an accredited high school or a GED certificate and passing scores on the college entrance exam (or qualifying ACT/SAT scores) are required.

Application and Information

Director of Admissions
Westwood College–Chicago River Oaks
80 River Oaks Drive, Suite D-49
Calumet City, Illinois 60409-5802

Telephone: 708-832-1988
          888-549-6873 (toll-free)
Fax: 708-832-9617
E-mail: info@westwood.edu
World Wide Web: http://www.westwood.edu

Westwood College–Chicago River Oaks campus.

WESTWOOD COLLEGE–DALLAS

DALLAS, TEXAS

The College and Its Mission

Today, the variables that define career success are ever changing. In order to get ahead and stay ahead, students need the right kind of preparation. To prepare for the working world, they need a career-focused education program that teaches the skills employers demand. The curriculum should include hands-on, practical experience and real-world applications to help graduates get started in their new career.

Students also need a fast-track learning program that shortens the time from education to career, with an academic schedule that fits their lifestyle. They need a high level of student services to help them reach their goals and the right financial package to make it all possible.

All of these are the focus at Westwood College, which operates eighteen campuses, with locations in California, Colorado, Illinois, Georgia, and Texas. The fifteen campuses of Westwood College offer degree programs in high-technology fields, while the three aviation campuses (Westwood College of Aviation Technology–Denver, Westwood College of Aviation Technology–Los Angeles, and Westwood Aviation Institute–Houston) offer aviation maintenance training.

Such fields as computer-aided design, computer networking, e-business, and graphic design are featured at the Westwood College campuses located in Anaheim, Inland Empire (Upland), Long Beach, and Los Angeles, California; Atlanta, Georgia; DuPage, O'Hare Airport, River Oaks, and Chicago–Loop, Illinois; Denver–North and Denver–South, Colorado; and Dallas, Fort Worth, and Houston, Texas. The Westwood College of Aviation Technology offers the aviation curriculum at the Denver, Colorado, and Los Angeles, California, campuses, while Westwood Aviation Institute offers the aviation curriculum in Houston.

Westwood College–Dallas is a branch of Westwood College–O'Hare Airport and is accredited by the Accrediting Council for Independent Colleges and Schools (ACICS).

Academic Programs

At the Westwood College–Dallas campus, students may obtain an associate degree in twenty months through day and evening classes. The programs are designed to help adults move into the high-tech world of work quickly.

Classes provide hands-on skills and career-focused training. Skilled technology workers with fine-tuned critical-thinking skills graduate from Westwood ready to succeed. Westwood College's career development services work to match students with employers to get graduates started on the right career path.

The Dallas campus offers associate degree programs in computer-aided design with a concentration in architectural drafting, computer-aided design with a concentration in interior finishes, computer network engineering, graphic design and multimedia, and software engineering.

The Dallas campus also offers a diploma in medical assisting and medical insurance coding and billing.

Costs

Standard program costs can be found in the Westwood College academic catalog.

Financial Aid

Tuition assistance is available for those who qualify. Scholarships include the Westwood High School Scholarship Program, in which two scholarships are offered to every high school in the United States. In addition, several loan programs are available.

Student Body Profile

Westwood College recruits recent high school graduates, young adults, and working adults who want to acquire new skills to take advantage of growing opportunities in the professional workplace. Students come to Westwood from all across the U.S. and many other countries. Students enrolled at the Dallas campus total more than 500, of whom 30 percent are women.

Student Activities

In addition to the on-campus activities available at the College, the greater Dallas area offers unlimited recreational opportunities for students.

Facilities and Resources

Campus Resource Centers located on each Westwood campus contain a library of program-specific materials, books, and periodicals and Internet access. A virtual library provides remote access to several selected databases and links to Internet-based information that is specific to technology study. The Resource Center also contains the campus bookstore. Resource Center staff members can assist students in navigating all the research materials that are available.

Location

Westwood's Dallas campus is located on LBJ Freeway in the heart of Dallas, Texas. One of the largest cities in the southern United States, Dallas offers a wide range of cultural and recreational activities in an urban setting. A 60-acre arts district is home to theater, dance, music, sculpture, and museums. The city maintains more than 20,000 acres of lake and park space within its borders.

Admission Requirements

Admission requirements include a diploma from an accredited four-year high school or a GED certificate and passing scores on the College placement exam or qualifying SAT or ACT scores.

Application and Information

Admissions Office
Westwood College–Dallas
Executive Center I, Suite 100
8390 LBJ Freeway
Dallas, Texas 75243
Telephone: 214-570-9100
          800-803-3140 (toll-free)
Fax: 214-570-8502
E-mail: info@westwood.edu
World Wide Web: http://www.westwood.edu

Westwood College–Dallas campus.

WESTWOOD COLLEGE–DENVER NORTH

DENVER, COLORADO

The College and Its Mission

Today, the variables that define career success are ever changing. In order to get ahead and stay ahead, students need the right kind of preparation. To prepare for the working world, they need a career-focused education program that teaches the skills employers demand and offers hands-on, practical experience with real-world applications and the right kind of job-placement assistance to help students get started in their new careers.

Students also need a fast-track learning program that shortens the time from education to career, with an academic schedule that fits their lifestyle. They need a high level of student services to help them reach their goals and the right financial package to make it all possible.

All of these are the focus at Westwood College, which operates eighteen campuses, with locations in California, Colorado, Illinois, Georgia, and Texas. The fifteen campuses of Westwood College offer degree programs in high-technology fields, while the three aviation campuses (Westwood College of Aviation Technology–Denver, Westwood College of Aviation Technology–Los Angeles, and Westwood Aviation Institute–Houston) offer aviation maintenance training.

Such fields as computer networking, graphic design, computer-aided design, and e-business are featured at the Westwood College campuses located in Anaheim, Inland Empire (Upland), Long Beach, and Los Angeles, California; Atlanta, Georgia; DuPage, O'Hare Airport, River Oaks, and Chicago–Loop, Illinois; Denver–North and Denver–South, Colorado; and Dallas, Fort Worth, and Houston, Texas. The Westwood College of Aviation Technology offers the aviation curriculum at the Denver, Colorado and Los Angeles, California, campuses, while Westwood Aviation Institute offers the aviation curriculum in Houston.

The Denver North campus is accredited by the Accrediting Commission of Career Schools and Colleges of Technology (ACCSCT).

Academic Programs

Denver North offers the largest variety of Westwood's bachelor's and associate degree programs. The campus, in addition to featuring high-technology opportunities, offers programs in high-demand industrial and medical fields. Bachelor's degree programs in animation, computer network management, criminal justice, e-business management, electronic engineering technology, game art and design, game software development, information systems security, interior design, visual communications, and Web design and multimedia are offered. Associate degree programs in technology are offered in computer-aided design/architectural drafting, computer-aided design/mechanical drafting, computer network engineering, electronic engineering technology, graphic design and multimedia, and software engineering. Associate degree programs in service and industrial fields are offered in automotive technology; heating, ventilation, air conditioning, and refrigeration; hotel and restaurant management; medical assisting; medical transcription; and surveying.

Westwood College welcomes students to the exciting world of fashion with the introduction of a new bachelor's degree program in fashion merchandising. The Westwood College fashion merchandising degree program gives students exposure to all of the important areas in fashion, with courses that include Apparel Analysis, Trend Forecasting, Consumer Behavior, Retail Management, Retail Buying, Visual Merchandising, and Fashion Product Development. This new program explores all aspects of the clothing industry, such as product buying, retailing, visual merchandising, and promotion. The program is available only at the Denver campuses.

Off-Campus Programs

Many of the College's degree programs are also available online. This offers students the chance to obtain a degree at any time and location through a virtual campus. Students should call 800-992-5050 Ext. 244 for information.

Costs

Standard program costs can be found in the Westwood College academic catalog.

Financial Aid

Tuition assistance is available for those who qualify. Scholarships include the Westwood High School Scholarship Program, through which two scholarships are offered to every high school in the United States; the Colorado Undergraduate Merit State Scholarships for Colorado residents; and several loan programs.

Student Body Profile

There are 1,100 students enrolled at the Denver North campus, of whom 25 percent are women.

Student Activities

With a diverse population of nearly 2 million and proximity to the Rocky Mountains, Denver offers students a unique opportunity to combine advanced learning with a healthy, active lifestyle. Skiing, snowboarding, mountain climbing, and other outdoor, recreational, and cultural activities abound.

Facilities and Resources

The Denver North campus is the largest of Westwood's campuses and recently underwent a $4-million renovation. The campus provides industry-standard classrooms and labs, which provides a completely functional learning environment that complements Westwood's mission.

Location

The campus is located at 7350 North Broadway in Denver, near the intersection of Interstate 25 and the Boulder Turnpike. Students have easy access to the downtown business districts, LoDo cultural activities, and the I-36 High-Tech Corridor.

Admission Requirements

A diploma from an accredited high school or a GED certificate and passing scores on the college placement exam (or qualifying SAT/ACT scores) are required.

Application and Information

Ben Simms, Director of Admissions
Westwood College–Denver North
7350 North Broadway
Denver, Colorado 80221-3653
Telephone: 303-650-5050
           800-992-5050 (toll-free)
Fax: 303-487-0214
E-mail: info@westwood.edu
World Wide Web: http://www.westwood.edu

Westwood College–Denver North campus.

WESTWOOD COLLEGE–DENVER SOUTH

DENVER, COLORADO

The College and Its Mission

Today, the variables that define career success are ever changing. In order to get ahead and stay ahead, students need the right kind of preparation. To prepare for the working world, they need a program of career-focused education that teaches the skills employers demand and offers hands-on, practical experience with real-world applications and the right kind of job-placement assistance to help students get started in their new careers.

Students also need a fast-track learning program that shortens the time from education to career, with an academic schedule that fits their lifestyle. They need a high level of student services to help reach their goals and the right financial package to make it all possible.

All of these are the focus at Westwood College, which operates eighteen campuses, with locations in California, Colorado, Illinois, Georgia, and Texas. The fifteen campuses of Westwood College offer degree programs in high-technology fields, while the three aviation campuses (Westwood College of Aviation Technology–Denver, Westwood College of Aviation Technology–Los Angeles, and Westwood Aviation Institute–Houston) offer aviation maintenance training.

Such fields as computer networking, graphic design, computer-aided design, and e-business are featured at the Westwood College campuses located in Anaheim, Inland Empire (Upland), Long Beach, and Los Angeles, California; Atlanta, Georgia; DuPage, O'Hare Airport, River Oaks, and Chicago-Loop, Illinois; Denver–North and Denver–South, Colorado; and Dallas, Fort Worth, and Houston, Texas. The Westwood College of Aviation Technology offers the aviation curriculum at the Denver, Colorado, and Los Angeles, California, campuses, while Westwood Aviation Institute offers the aviation curriculum in Houston.

The Denver South Campus is accredited by the Accrediting Commission of Career Schools and Colleges of Technology (ACCSCT).

Academic Programs

Denver South concentrates on computer-based high-technology bachelor's and associate degree programs. It offers daytime, evening, and weekend class schedules in order to serve as many students as possible. Bachelor's programs in animation, computer network management, criminal justice, e-business management, game art and design, game software development, interior design, technical management, visual communications, and Web design and multimedia are offered. Associate degree programs in computer-aided design/architectural drafting (CAD), computer network engineering, graphic design and multimedia, and software engineering are available.

Westwood College welcomes students to the exciting world of fashion with the introduction of a new bachelor's degree program in fashion merchandising. The Westwood College fashion merchandising degree program gives students exposure to all of the important areas in fashion, with courses that include Apparel Analysis, Trend Forecasting, Consumer Behavior, Retail Management, Retail Buying, Visual Merchandising, and Fashion Product Development. This new program explores all aspects of the clothing industry, such as product buying, retailing, visual merchandising, and promotion. The program is available only at the Denver campuses.

Costs

Standard program costs can be found in the Westwood College academic catalog.

Financial Aid

Tuition assistance is available for those who qualify. Scholarships include the Westwood High School Scholarship Program, through which two scholarships are offered to every high school in the United States; the Colorado Undergraduate Merit State Scholarships for Colorado residents; and several loan programs.

Student Body Profile

There are 350 students enrolled at Denver South, of whom 75 percent are men and 25 percent women.

Student Activities

With a diverse population of nearly 2 million and proximity to the Rocky Mountains, students have a unique opportunity to combine advanced learning with a healthy, active lifestyle. Skiing, snowboarding, mountain climbing, and other outdoor, recreational, and cultural activities abound.

Facilities and Resources

The campus includes two dedicated buildings totaling more than 30,000 square feet of classrooms, labs, and administrative offices. There is also an annex containing classroom space.

Location

The campus is located at 3150 South Sheridan Boulevard in Denver, at the intersection of South Sheridan Boulevard and Hampden Avenue (Highway 285). It is easily accessible from Lakewood, Englewood, Littleton, and Denver's entire southwest metro area.

Admission Requirements

A diploma from an accredited high school or a GED certificate and passing scores on the college entrance exam (or qualifying ACT/SAT scores) are required.

Application and Information

Ron DeJong, Director of Admissions
Westwood College–Denver South
3150 South Sheridan Boulevard
Denver, Colorado 80227-5548

Telephone: 303-934-2790
Fax: 303-934-2583
E-mail: info@westwood.edu
World Wide Web: http://www.westwood.edu

Westwood College–Denver South campus.

WESTWOOD COLLEGE–FORT WORTH

EULESS, TEXAS

The College and Its Mission

Today, the variables that define career success are ever changing. In order to get ahead and stay ahead, students need the right kind of preparation. To prepare for the working world, students need a programmed, career-focused education that teaches the skills employers demand, that is, hands-on practical experience with real-world applications and the right kind of job-placement assistance to help them get started in their new career.

Students also need a fast-track leaning program that shortens the time from education to career, with an academic schedule that fits their lifestyle. Students need a high level of student services to help them reach their goals, and the right financial package to make it all possible.

All of these are the focus at Westwood College, which operates eighteen campuses, with locations in California, Colorado, Illinois, Georgia, and Texas. The fifteen campuses of Westwood College offer degree programs in high-technology fields, while the three aviation campuses (Westwood College of Aviation Technology–Denver, Westwood College of Aviation Technology–Los Angeles, and Westwood Aviation Institute–Houston) offer aviation maintenance training.

Such fields as computer networking, graphic design, computer-aided design, and e-business are featured at the Westwood College campuses located in Anaheim, Inland Empire (Upland), Long Beach, and Los Angeles, California; Atlanta, Georgia; DuPage, O'Hare Airport, River Oaks, and Chicago–Loop, Illinois; Denver–North and Denver–South, Colorado; and Dallas, Fort Worth, and Houston, Texas. The Westwood College of Aviation Technology offers the aviation curriculum at the Denver, Colorado and Los Angeles, California, campuses, while Westwood Aviation Institute offers the aviation curriculum in Houston.

The Fort Worth campus is accredited by the Accrediting Council for Independent Colleges and Schools (ACICS).

Westwood College–Fort Worth (Euless, Texas) is a branch of Westwood College–DuPage (Woodridge, Illinois).

Academic Programs

The Fort Worth campus focuses on computer-based technology programs that prepare graduates to take advantage of the high-technology career opportunities that exist in the Dallas–Fort Worth metroplex. Associate degree programs are offered in computer-assisted design/architectural drafting, computer-aided design/interior finishes, computer network engineering, graphic design and multimedia, and software engineering. The Fort Worth campus also offers diploma programs in medical assisting and medical insurance coding and billing.

Costs

Standard program costs can be found in the Westwood College academic catalog.

Financial Aid

Tuition assistance is available for those who qualify. Scholarships include the Westwood High School Scholarship Program, in which two scholarships are offered to every high school in the United States. In addition, several loan programs are available.

Student Body Profile

Students enrolled at the Forth Worth campus total 415, of whom 30 percent are women.

Student Activities

In addition to on-campus activities, students can take advantage of a vast array of recreational and cultural activities in this dynamic area with a Southwestern flavor.

Facilities and Resources

Westwood College–Fort Worth currently occupies 12,000 square feet of administrative and instructional space. Also available is a Resource Center, with occupation-related reference materials and a number of resources that link students to library assets nationwide.

Location

The Fort Worth campus is located in Euless, Texas, between Dallas and Fort Worth.

Admission Requirements

A diploma from an accredited high school or GED certificate and passing scores on the college entrance exam (or qualifying ACT/SAT scores) are required.

Application and Information

Director of Admissions
Westwood College–Fort Worth
1331 Airport Freeway, Suite 402
Euless, Texas 76040

Telephone: 817-685-9994
              866-533-9997 (toll-free)
Fax: 817-685-8929
E-mail: info@westwood.edu
World Wide Web: http://www.westwood.edu

Westwood college–Fort Worth campus.

WESTWOOD COLLEGE–HOUSTON SOUTH

HOUSTON, TEXAS

The College and Its Mission

Today, the variables that define career success are ever changing. In order to get ahead and stay ahead, students need the right kind of preparation. To prepare for the working world, they need a career-focused education program that teaches the skills employers demand. The curriculum should include hands-on, practical experience and real-world applications to help graduates get started in their new careers.

Students also need a fast-track learning program that shortens the time from education to career, with an academic schedule that fits their lifestyle. They need a high level of student services to help them reach their goals and the right financial package to make it all possible.

All of these are the focus at Westwood College, which operates eighteen campuses, with locations in California, Colorado, Illinois, Georgia, and Texas. The fifteen campuses of Westwood College offer degree programs in high-technology fields, while the three aviation campuses (Westwood College of Aviation Technology–Denver, Westwood College of Aviation Technology–Los Angeles, and Westwood Aviation Institute–Houston) offer aviation maintenance training.

Such fields as computer networking, graphic design, computer-aided design, and e-business are featured at the Westwood College campuses located in Anaheim, Inland Empire (Upland), Long Beach, and Los Angeles, California; Atlanta, Georgia; DuPage, O'Hare Airport, River Oaks, and Chicago Loop, Illinois; Denver North and Denver South, Colorado; and Dallas, Fort Worth, and Houston South, Texas. The Westwood College of Aviation Technology offers the aviation curriculum at the Denver, Colorado, and Los Angeles, California, campuses, while Westwood Aviation Institute offers the aviation curriculum in Houston.

Westwood College–Houston South is accredited by the Accrediting Commission of Career Schools and Colleges of Technology (ACCSCT) and is a branch of Westwood College–Denver North.

Academic Programs

At the Westwood College–Houston South campus, students may obtain an associate degree in twenty months through day and evening classes. The programs are designed to help adults move into the high-technology world of work quickly. Classes provide hands-on skills and career-focused training. Skilled technology workers with fine-tuned critical-thinking skills graduate from Westwood ready to succeed. Westwood College's career development services work to match students with employers to get graduates started on the right career path.

The Houston South campus focuses on computer-based programs that prepare graduates to take advantage of the high-technology career opportunities available in Houston. Associate degree programs are offered in computer-aided design/architectural drafting (CAD), computer-aided design/interior finishes, engineering, computer network engineering, graphic design and multimedia, and software engineering. Houston South also offers diploma programs in medical assisting and medical insurance coding and billing.

Costs

Standard program costs can be found in the Westwood College academic catalog.

Financial Aid

Tuition assistance is available for those who qualify. Scholarships include the Westwood High School Scholarship Program, in which two scholarships are offered to every high school in the United States. In addition, several loan programs are available.

Student Body Profile

Student enrollment at the Houston South campus totals 160 students, 30 percent of whom are women.

Student Activities

In addition to on-campus activities, students can take advantage of the many cultural and recreational activities of the city and surrounding communities.

Facilities and Resources

The Campus Resource Center offers a library of program-specific materials that have been carefully selected to aid that school's career-focused educational mission. Typical learning aids include books, periodicals, and Internet access. A virtual library provides remote access to several selected databases, and staff members are available to assist with research and provide instruction on how to conduct research. Westwood offers tutoring at no charge, and specialized Student Success Workshops help students improve skills in areas such as test taking, time management, resume preparation, and general study skills.

Location

With the campus located in the nation's fourth-largest city, cultural and recreational opportunities abound for students. A cosmopolitan city of many cultures and world-class theater, music, museums, architecture, dance, art, sports, and shopping, Houston also offers nearby beaches, rivers, and outdoor activities.

Admission Requirements

Admission requirements include a diploma from an accredited high school or a GED certificate and passing scores on the College placement exam or qualifying SAT/ACT scores.

Application and Information

Westwood College–Houston South
One Arena Place
7322 Southwest Freeway #1900
Houston, Texas 77074

Telephone: 713-777-4433
E-mail: info@westwood.edu
World Wide Web: http://www.westwood.edu

WESTWOOD COLLEGE–INLAND EMPIRE

UPLAND, CALIFORNIA

The College and Its Mission

Today, the variables that define career success are ever changing. In order to get ahead and stay ahead, students needs the right kind of preparation. To prepare for the working world, students need a career-focused education program that teaches the skills employers demand and offers hands-on, practical experience with real-world applications and the right kind of job-placement assistance to help them get started in their new careers.

Students also need a fast-track learning program that shortens the time from education to career, with an academic schedule that fits their lifestyle. They need a high level of student services to help them reach their goals and the right financial package to make it all possible.

All of these are the focus at Westwood College, which operates eighteen campuses, with locations in California, Colorado, Illinois, Georgia, and Texas. The fifteen campuses of Westwood College offer degree programs in high-technology fields, while the three aviation campuses (Westwood College of Aviation Technology–Denver, Westwood College of Aviation Technology–Los Angeles, and Westwood Aviation Institute–Houston) offer aviation maintenance training.

Such fields as computer networking, graphic design, computer-aided design, and e-business are featured at the Westwood College campuses located in Anaheim, Inland Empire (Upland), Long Beach, and Los Angeles, California; Atlanta, Georgia; DuPage, O'Hare Airport, River Oaks, and Chicago–Loop, Illinois; Denver–North and Denver–South, Colorado; and Dallas, Fort Worth, and Houston, Texas. The Westwood College of Aviation Technology offers the aviation curriculum at the Denver, Colorado, and Los Angeles, California, campuses, while Westwood Aviation Institute offers the aviation curriculum in Houston.

The Inland Empire campus is accredited by the Accrediting Commission of Career Schools and Colleges of Technology (ACCSCT).

Westwood College–Inland Empire is a branch of Westwood College–Denver North.

Academic Programs

The Inland Empire campus focuses on computer-based programs that prepare graduates to take advantage of Southern California's high-tech career opportunities. Bachelor's degree programs are offered in computer network management, criminal justice, e-business management, game art and design, game software development, information systems security, interior design, and visual communications. Associate degree programs are offered in computer-aided design/architectural drafting (CAD), computer network engineering, graphic design and multimedia, and software engineering.

Costs

Standard program costs can be found in the Westwood College academic catalog.

Financial Aid

Tuition assistance is available to those students who qualify. Scholarships include the Westwood High School Scholarship Program, which offers two scholarships to every high school in the United States; the Colorado Undergraduate Merit State Scholarships for Colorado residents; and several loan programs.

Student Body Profile

Student enrollment at the Inland Empire campus totals more than 1,000 students, 30 percent of whom are women.

Student Activities

In addition to on-campus activities, students can take advantage of many outdoor recreational activities. Several minor-league baseball teams play in the area. Many cultural opportunities are available as well.

Facilities and Resources

The campus features an all-new facility that was designed and built specifically for Westwood College. The design, layout, and features of the facility are the product of an extensive research project that evaluated the unique requirements of Westwood's students, faculty, and staff.

Location

The campus is located on the western edge of Southern California's Inland Empire, just minutes from the Ontario International Airport. It is easily reached by Interstate 10 and Interstate 15 from surrounding communities such as Ontario, Pomona, Rancho Cucamonga, Covina, Redlands, and San Bernardino.

Admission Requirements

A diploma from an accredited high school or a GED certificate and passing scores on the college entrance exam (or qualifying ACT/SAT scores) are required.

Application and Information

Director of Admissions
Westwood College–Inland Empire
20 West 7th Street
Upland, California 91786-7148
Telephone: 909-931-7550
           866-288-9488 (toll-free)
Fax: 909-931-9195
E-mail: info@westwood.edu
World Wide Web: http://www.westwood.edu

Westwood College–Inland Empire campus.

WESTWOOD COLLEGE–LONG BEACH

LONG BEACH, CALIFORNIA

The College and Its Mission

Today, the variables that define career success are ever changing. In order to get ahead and stay ahead, students need the right kind of preparation. To prepare for the working world, they need a career-focused education program that teaches the skills employers demand. The curriculum should include hands-on, practical experience and real-world applications to help graduates get started in their new careers.

Students also need a fast-track learning program that shortens the time from education to career, with an academic schedule that fits their lifestyle. They need a high level of student services to help them reach their goals and the right financial package to make it all possible.

All of these are the focus at Westwood College, which operates eighteen campuses, with locations in California, Colorado, Illinois, Georgia, and Texas. The fifteen campuses of Westwood College offer degree programs in high-technology fields, while the three aviation campuses (Westwood College of Aviation Technology–Denver, Westwood College of Aviation Technology–Los Angeles, and Westwood Aviation Institute–Houston) offer aviation maintenance training.

Such fields as computer networking, graphic design, computer-aided design, and e-business are featured at the Westwood College campuses located in Anaheim, Inland Empire (Upland), Long Beach, and Los Angeles, California; Atlanta, Georgia; DuPage, O'Hare Airport, River Oaks, and Chicago–Loop, Illinois; Denver–North and Denver–South, Colorado; and Dallas, Fort Worth, and Houston, Texas. The Westwood College of Aviation Technology offers the aviation curriculum at the Denver, Colorado, and Los Angeles, California, campuses, while Westwood Aviation Institute offers the aviation curriculum in Houston.

Westwood College–Long Beach is accredited by the Accrediting Commission of Career Schools and Colleges of Technology (ACCSCT) and has received temporary approval from the Bureau for Private Postsecondary and Vocational Education.

Academic Programs

At the Westwood College–Long Beach campus, students may obtain a bachelor's degree in thirty-six months or an associate degree in twenty months through day and evening classes. The programs are designed to help adults move into the high-tech world of work quickly. Classes provide hands-on skills and career-focused training. Skilled technology workers with fine-tuned critical-thinking skills graduate from Westwood ready to succeed. Westwood College's career development services match students with employers to get graduates started on the right career path.

The Long Beach campus offers such bachelor's degree programs as animation, computer network management, criminal justice, information systems security, and visual communications. The College offers associate degree programs in computer-aided design/architectural drafting, computer network engineering, and graphic design and multimedia.

Costs

Standard program costs can be found in the Westwood College academic catalog.

Financial Aid

Tuition assistance is available for those who qualify. Scholarships include the Westwood High School Scholarship Program, in which two scholarships are offered to every high school in the United States. In addition, several loan programs are available.

Student Body Profile

Westwood College recruits recent high school graduates, young adults, and working adults who want to acquire new skills to take advantage of growing opportunities in the professional workplace. Students come to Westwood from all across the U.S. and many other countries. Currently, there are more than 250 students enrolled on the Westwood College–Long Beach campus, of whom 30 percent are women.

Student Activities

In addition to the many on-campus activities available at Westwood College, the greater Long Beach area abounds in cultural and recreational opportunities.

Facilities and Resources

Campus Resource Centers located on each Westwood campus contain a library of program-specific materials, books, and periodicals and Internet access. A virtual library provides remote access to several selected databases and links to Internet-based information that is specific to technology study. The Resource Center also contains the campus bookstore. Resource Center staff members can assist students in navigating all the research materials that are available.

Location

Long Beach is located in southern California, on the Pacific coast. Outstanding cultural arts and music festivals, plus a short boat ride to Catalina Island and gorgeous weather year-round, make Long Beach a paradise. Shopping, dining, sporting events, endless beaches, and an array of cultural diversity and nightlife make Long Beach a terrific place to begin a visitor's California adventure. Nearby Los Angeles as well as the many diverse towns and cities along the edge of the Pacific Ocean supply visitors with limitless opportunities for recreation, culture, and arts.

Admission Requirements

Admission requirements include a diploma from an accredited four-year high school or a GED certificate and passing scores on the College placement exam or qualifying SAT or ACT scores.

Application and Information

Westwood College–Long Beach
3901 Via Oro Avenue, #103
Long Beach, California 90810
Telephone: 310-522-2088
            888-403-3339 (toll-free)
Fax: 310-522-2093
E-mail: info@westwood.edu
World Wide Web: http://www.westwood.edu

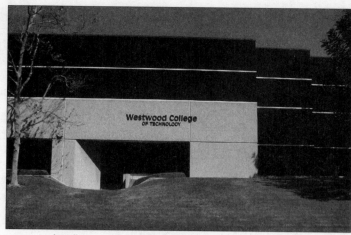

Westwood College–Long Beach campus.

WESTWOOD COLLEGE– LOS ANGELES

LOS ANGELES, CALIFORNIA

The College and Its Mission

Today, the variables that define career success are ever changing. In order to get ahead and stay ahead, students need the right kind of preparation. To prepare for the working world, they need a career-focused education program that teaches the skills employers demand and offers hands-on, practical experience with real-world applications and the right kind of job-placement assistance to help students get started in their new careers.

Students also need a fast-track learning program that shortens the time from education to career, with an academic schedule that fits their lifestyle. They need a high level of student services to help them reach their goals and the right financial package to make it all possible.

All of these are the focus at Westwood College, which operates eighteen campuses, with locations in California, Colorado, Illinois, Georgia, and Texas. The fifteen campuses of Westwood College offer degree programs in high-technology fields, while the three aviation campuses (Westwood College of Aviation Technology–Denver, Westwood College of Aviation Technology–Los Angeles, and Westwood Aviation Institute–Houston) offer aviation maintenance training.

Such fields as computer networking, graphic design, computer-aided design, and e-business are featured at the Westwood College campuses located in Anaheim, Inland Empire (Upland), Long Beach, and Los Angeles, California; Atlanta, Georgia; DuPage, O'Hare Airport, River Oaks, and Chicago–Loop, Illinois; Denver–North and Denver–South, Colorado; and Dallas, Fort Worth, and Houston, Texas. The Westwood College of Aviation Technology offers the aviation curriculum at the Denver, Colorado and Los Angeles, California, campuses, while Westwood Aviation Institute offers the aviation curriculum in Houston.

The Los Angeles campus is accredited by the Accrediting Council for Independent Colleges and Schools (ACICS).

Academic Programs

The Los Angeles campus focuses on computer-based technologies that prepare graduates to take advantage of southern California's unique career opportunities. Associate degree programs are offered in computer-aided designing/architectural drafting, computer network engineering, graphic design and multimedia, and software engineering. Bachelor's degree programs are offered in animation, computer network management, criminal justice, e-business management, game art and design, game software development, information systems security, visual communications, and Web design and multimedia.

Costs

Standard program costs can be found in the Westwood College academic catalog.

Financial Aid

Tuition assistance is available for those who qualify. Scholarships include the Westwood High School Scholarship Program, through which two scholarships are offered to every high school in the United States; the Colorado Undergraduate Merit State Scholarships for Colorado residents; and several loan programs.

Student Body Profile

The campus has an enrollment of 800, of whom 75 percent are men and 25 percent are women.

Student Activities

The Los Angeles area, given its climate and recreational and cultural diversity, offers unlimited opportunities for students.

Facilities and Resources

The campus includes computer labs, featuring both PC and Macintosh machines running the most popular software applications used throughout industry to give students the hands-on experience that employers demand. The campus offers both day and evening classes.

Location

The campus is located at 3460 Wilshire Boulevard, Suite 700, in the Central Plaza Complex, just minutes from downtown Los Angeles in an urban environment.

Admission Requirements

A diploma from an accredited high school or a GED certificate as well as passing scores on the college's entrance exam (or qualifying ACT/SAT scores) are required.

Application and Information

Ron Milman, Director of Admissions
Westwood College–Los Angeles
3460 Wilshire Boulevard, Suite 700
Los Angeles, California 90010-2210
Telephone: 213-739-9999
　　　　　　877-377-4600 (toll-free)
Fax: 213-382-2468
E-mail: info@westwood.edu
World Wide Web: http://www.westwood.edu

Westwood College–Los Angeles campus.

WESTWOOD COLLEGE OF AVIATION TECHNOLOGY–DENVER

DENVER, COLORADO

WESTWOOD COLLEGE

The College and Its Mission

Today, the variables that define career success are ever changing. In order to get ahead and stay ahead, students need the right kind of preparation. To prepare for the working world, students need a career-focused education program that teaches the skills employers demand and offers hands-on practical experience with real-world applications and the right kind of job-placement assistance to help them get started in their new careers.

Students also need a fast-track learning program that shortens the time from education to career, with an academic schedule that fits their lifestyle. They need a high level of student services to help them reach their goals and the right financial package to make it all possible.

All of these are the focus at Westwood College, which operates eighteen campuses, with locations in California, Colorado, Illinois, Georgia, and Texas. The fifteen campuses of Westwood College offer degree programs in high-technology fields, while the three aviation campuses (Westwood College of Aviation Technology–Denver, Westwood College of Aviation Technology–Los Angeles, and Westwood Aviation Institute–Houston) offer aviation maintenance training.

Such fields as computer networking, graphic design, computer-aided design, and e-business are featured at the Westwood College campuses located in Anaheim, Inland Empire (Upland), Long Beach, and Los Angeles, California; Atlanta, Georgia; DuPage, O'Hare Airport, River Oaks, and Chicago-Loop, Illinois; Denver–North and Denver–South, Colorado; and Dallas, Fort Worth, and Houston, Texas. The Westwood College of Aviation Technology offers the aviation curriculum at the Denver, Colorado, and Los Angeles, California, campuses, while Westwood Aviation Institute offers the aviation curriculum in Houston.

Westwood College of Aviation Technology–Denver is accredited by the Accrediting Commission of Career Schools and Colleges of Technology (ACCSCT).

Academic Programs

Students are drawn to this campus to train for a career in aviation maintenance or avionics. Graduates have gone on to careers with large commercial airlines, aerospace manufacturing companies, regional airlines, fixed-base carriers, and a variety of other industry employers. Programs in airframe and power plant and advanced electronics technology (avionics) are offered.

Costs

Standard program costs can be found in the Westwood College academic catalog.

Financial Aid

Tuition assistance is available for those who qualify. Scholarships include the Westwood High School Scholarship Program, which offers two scholarships to every high school in the United States; the Colorado Undergraduate Merit State Scholarships for Colorado residents; and several loan programs.

Student Body Profile

Student enrollment at the Denver Aviation campus totals 632, of whom approximately 10 percent are women.

Student Activities

Located near both the Rocky Mountain foothills and Denver, students attending this campus have a vast array of recreational and cultural opportunities at their disposal.

Facilities and Resources

The Denver Aviation campus gives students hands-on experience, with a variety of essential training aids, including reciprocating power plants and turbines from General Electric, Lycoming, Pratt & Whitney, and other manufacturers. The campus also features a complete Boeing 727 cockpit and operable subassemblies needed to learn airframe and power plant and avionics maintenance.

Location

The campus is located a few minutes northwest of Denver in the suburb of Broomfield, Colorado, at 10851 West 120th Avenue, adjacent to the Jefferson County Airport. It is easily reached from Denver, Boulder, and surrounding communities via the Boulder Turnpike (Highway 36).

Admission Requirements

To enroll, students must be at least 17 years of age, have a high school diploma or GED certificate, and be able to speak, read, and write in English.

Application and Information

Susan Cottrell, Director of Admissions
Westwood College of Aviation Technology–Denver
10851 West 120th Avenue
Broomfield, Colorado 80021-3401

Telephone: 303-466-1714
Fax: 303-469-3797
E-mail: info@westwood.edu
World Wide Web: http://www.westwood.edu/aviation

Westwood College of Aviation Technology–Denver campus.

WESTWOOD COLLEGE OF AVIATION TECHNOLOGY– LOS ANGELES

LOS ANGELES, CALIFORNIA

The College and Its Mission

Today, the variables that define career success are ever changing. In order to get ahead and stay ahead, students need the right kind of preparation. To prepare for the working world, they need a career-focused education program that teaches the skills employers demand and offers hands-on, practical experience with real-world applications and the right kind of job-placement assistance to help students get started in their new careers.

Students also need a fast-track learning program that shortens the time from education to career, with an academic schedule that fits their lifestyle. They need a high level of student services to help them reach their goals and the right financial package to make it all possible.

All of these are the focus at Westwood College, which operates eighteen campuses, with locations in California, Colorado, Illinois, Georgia, and Texas. The fifteen campuses of Westwood College offer degree programs in high-technology fields, while the three aviation campuses (Westwood College of Aviation Technology–Denver, Westwood College of Aviation Technology–Los Angeles, and Westwood Aviation Institute–Houston) offer aviation maintenance training.

Such fields as computer networking, graphic design, computer-aided design, and e-business are featured at the Westwood College campuses located in Anaheim, Inland Empire (Upland), Long Beach, and Los Angeles, California; Atlanta, Georgia; DuPage, O'Hare Airport, River Oaks, and Chicago–Loop, Illinois; Denver–North and Denver–South, Colorado; and Dallas, Fort Worth, and Houston, Texas. The Westwood College of Aviation Technology offers the aviation curriculum at the Denver, Colorado and Los Angeles, California, campuses, while Westwood Aviation Institute offers the aviation curriculum in Houston.

Westwood College of Aviation Technology–Los Angeles is accredited by the Accrediting Commission of the Council on Occupational Education (COE).

Academic Programs

Students are drawn to this campus to train for an aviation-maintenance career. Aviation maintenance careers offer the opportunity to work in a highly skilled profession. Graduates have gone on to careers with large commercial airlines, aerospace manufacturing companies, regional airlines, fixed-base carriers, and a variety of other industry employers. A certificate program in airframe and power plant maintenance is offered.

Costs

Standard program costs can be found in the Westwood College academic catalog.

Financial Aid

Tuition assistance is available for those who qualify. Scholarships include the Westwood High School Scholarship Program, in which two scholarships are offered to every high school in the United States, and the Colorado Undergraduate Merit State Scholarships for Colorado residents. In addition, several loan programs are available.

Student Body Profile

The Westwood College of Aviation Technology–Los Angeles campus has an enrollment of more than 600 students, of whom 90 percent are men and 10 percent are women.

Student Activities

The student, while preparing for a career in aviation maintenance, can take advantage of all the recreational and cultural opportunities southern California offers.

Facilities and Resources

Students are given hands-on experience with a variety of essential training aids, including reciprocating power plants from manufacturers such as General Electric, Pratt & Whitney, and others. The campus also features operable subassemblies needed to learn airframe and power plant maintenance.

Location

The campus is located minutes from Los Angeles International Airport in Inglewood, California.

Admission Requirements

To enroll, students must be at least 17 years of age, have a high school diploma or GED certificate, and be able to speak, read, and write English.

Application and Information

Lani Townsend, Director of Admissions
Westwood College of Aviation Technology–Los Angeles
8911 Aviation Boulevard
Inglewood, California 90301-2904

Telephone: 310-337-4444
      800-597-8690 (toll-free)
Fax: 310-337-1176
E-mail: info@westwood.edu
World Wide Web: http://www.westwood.edu/aviation

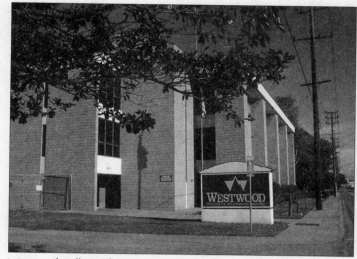

Westwood College of Aviation Technology–Los Angeles campus.

WESTWOOD COLLEGE OF TECHNOLOGY–CHICAGO DUPAGE

WOODRIDGE, ILLINOIS

The College and Its Mission

Today, the variables that define career success are ever changing. In order to get ahead and stay ahead, students need the right kind of preparation. To prepare for the working world, they need a career-focused education program that teaches the skills employers demand and offers hands-on, practical experience with real-world applications and the right kind of job-placement assistance to help students get started in their new careers.

Students also need a fast-track learning program that shortens the time from education to career, with an academic schedule that fits their lifestyle. They need a high level of student services to help them reach their goals and the right financial package to make it all possible.

All of these are the focus at Westwood College, which operates eighteen campuses, with locations in California, Colorado, Illinois, Georgia, and Texas. The fifteen campuses of Westwood College offer degree programs in high-technology fields, while the three aviation campuses (Westwood College of Aviation Technology–Denver, Westwood College of Aviation Technology–Los Angeles, and Westwood Aviation Institute–Houston) offer aviation maintenance training.

Such fields as computer networking, graphic design, computer-aided design, and e-business are featured at the Westwood College campuses located in Anaheim, Inland Empire (Upland), Long Beach, and Los Angeles, California; Atlanta, Georgia; DuPage, O'Hare Airport, River Oaks, and Chicago–Loop, Illinois; Denver–North and Denver–South, Colorado; and Dallas, Fort Worth, and Houston, Texas. The Westwood College of Aviation Technology offers the aviation curriculum at the Denver, Colorado, and Los Angeles, California, campuses, while Westwood Aviation Institute offers the aviation curriculum in Houston.

The DuPage campus is accredited by the Accrediting Council for Independent Colleges and Schools (ACICS) for Associate of Applied Science and Bachelor degrees.

Academic Programs

The DuPage campus focuses on computer-based technology programs that prepare graduates to take advantage of high-technology career opportunities. Both the faculty and campus have been designed specifically to meet the unique needs of Westwood's students. Associate degree programs in computer-assisted design (CAD), computer network engineering, graphic design and multimedia, and software engineering are offered in addition to bachelor's degree programs in computer network management, e-business, and visual communications.

Costs

Standard program costs can be found in the Westwood College academic catalog.

Financial Aid

Tuition assistance is available for those who qualify. Scholarships include the Westwood High School Scholarship Program, in which two scholarships are offered to every high school in the United States, and the Colorado Undergraduate Merit State Scholarships for Colorado residents. In addition, several loan programs are available.

Student Body Profile

Student enrollment at the DuPage campus totals 550, of whom approximately 30 percent are women.

Student Activities

The greater Chicago area offers many cultural and recreational activities.

Facilities and Resources

The campus occupies 25,000 square feet of classroom, lab, and administrative space.

Location

One of three Westwood campuses in the greater Chicago area, the DuPage campus is located an hour's drive southwest of Chicago in Woodridge, Illinois.

Admission Requirements

A diploma from an accredited four-year high school or a GED certificate is required.

Application and Information

Director of Admissions
Westwood College of Technology–Chicago DuPage
7155 Janes Avenue
Woodridge, Illinois 60517-2321

Telephone: 630-434-8244
            888-721-7646 (toll-free)
Fax: 630-434-8255
E-mail: info@westwood.edu
World Wide Web: http://www.westwood.edu

Westwood College of Technology–Chicago DuPage campus.

Appendix

2004–05 Changes in Institutions

Following is an alphabetical listing of institutions that have recently closed, merged with other institutions, or changed their name or status. In the case of a name change, the former name appears first, followed by the new name.

AEC Southern Ohio College (North Canton, OH): name changed to Brown Mackie College.

AEC Southern Ohio College, Akron Campus (Akron, OH): name changed to Brown Mackie College, Akron Campus.

AEC Southern Ohio College, Cincinnati Campus (Cincinnati, OH): name changed to The Brown Mackie College–Cincinnati Campus.

AEC Southern Ohio College, Findlay Campus (Findlay, OH): name changed to Brown Mackie College, Findlay Campus.

AEC Southern Ohio College, Northern Kentucky Campus (Fort Mitchell, KY): name changed to Brown Mackie College, Northern Kentucky Campus.

Allentown Business School (Center Valley, PA): name changed to Lehigh Valley College.

Asher School of Business (Norcross, GA): name changed to The Brown Mackie College–Atlanta Campus.

Bryant and Stratton College (Buffalo, NY): name changed to Bryant and Stratton College, Buffalo Campus.

Bryant and Stratton College (Lackawanna, NY): name changed to Bryant and Stratton College, Lackawanna Campus.

Cambria County Area Community College (Johnstown, PA): name changed to Pennsylvania Highland Community College.

College of Oceaneering (Wilmington, CA): name changed to National Polytechnic College of Engineering and Oceaneering.

Cooper Career Institute (West Palm Beach, FL): closed.

Don Bosco College of Science and Technology (Rosemead, CA): name changed to Don Bosco Technical Institute.

D-Q University (Davis, CA): no longer eligible.

East Central Technical Institute (Fitzgerald, GA): name changed to East Central Technical College.

Edison Community College (Fort Myers, FL): name changed to Edison College.

Electronic Institute (Middletow, PA): closed.

Elizabethtown Community College (Elizabethtown, KY): name changed to Elizabethtown Community and Technical College.

Fashion Institute of Design and Merchandising, Los Angeles Campus (Los Angeles, CA): name changed to FIDM/The Fashion Institute of Design & Merchandising, Los Angeles Campus.

Fashion Institute of Design and Merchandising, Orange County (Irvine, CA): name changed to FIDM/The Fashion Institute of Design & Merchandising, Orange County Campus.

Fashion Institute of Design and Merchandising, San Diego Campus (San Diego, CA): name changed to FIDM/The Fashion Institute of Design & Merchandising, San Diego Campus.

Fashion Institute of Design and Merchandising, San Francisco Campus (San Francisco, CA): name changed to FIDM/The Fashion Institute of Design & Merchandising, San Francisco Campus.

Feather River Community College District (Quincy, CA): name changed to Feather River College.

Hamilton College (Omaha, NE): name changed to Hamilton College-Omaha.

Herzing College, Lakeland Medical–Dental Division (Minneapolis, MN): closed.

Herzing College, Minneapolis Drafting School Division (Minneapolis, MN): name changed to Herzing College.

Hiwassee College Madisonville (Madisonville, TN): no longer eligible.

Keiser Career College (Port St. Lucie, FL): name changed to Keiser College.

Maysville Community College (Maysville, KY): name changed to Maysville Community and Technical College.

Michiana College (Fort Wayne, IN): name changed to The Brown Mackie College–Fort Wayne Campus.

Michiana College (South Bend, IN): name changed to The Brown Mackie College–South Bend Campus.

Musictech College (Saint Paul, MN): name changed to McNally Smith College of Music.

Okaloosa-Walton Community College (Niceville, FL): name changed to Okaloosa-Walton College.

Plaza Business Institute (Jackson Heights, NY): name changed to Plaza Institute.

Sequoia Institute (Fremont, CA): name changed to WyoTech.

Southeast Community College (Cumberland, KY): name changed to Southeast Kentucky Community and Technical College.

Spartan School of Aeronautics (Tulsa, OK): name changed to Spartan College of Aeronautics and Technology.

Trenholm State Technical College (Montgomery, AL): name changed to H. Councill Trenholm State Technical College.

Ultrasound Diagnostic School (Jacksonville, FL): name changed to Sanford-Brown Institute.

Ultrasound Diagnostic School (Lauderdale Lakes, FL): name changed to Sanford-Brown Institute.

Ultrasound Diagnostic School (Tampa, FL): name changed to Sanford-Brown Institute.

University of Kentucky, Lexington Community College (Lexington, KY): name changed to Lexington Community College.

Virginia College-Technical (Pelham, AL): name changed to VC Tech.

Webster College (Tampa, FL): name changed to Gulf Coast College.

Indexes

Associate Degree Programs at Two-Year Colleges

Accounting

Academy Coll (MN)
Adirondack Comm Coll (NY)
Alabama Southern Comm Coll (AL)
Albuquerque Tech Vocational Inst (NM)
Alexandria Tech Coll (MN)
Allen County Comm Coll (KS)
Alpena Comm Coll (MI)
Alvin Comm Coll (TX)
Amarillo Coll (TX)
American Samoa Comm Coll (AS)
Andover Coll (ME)
Anne Arundel Comm Coll (MD)
Anoka-Ramsey Comm Coll (MN)
Anoka-Ramsey Comm Coll, Cambridge Campus (MN)
Arapahoe Comm Coll (CO)
Ashland Comm and Tech Coll (KY)
Asnuntuck Comm Coll (CT)
Athens Tech Coll (GA)
Atlantic Cape Comm Coll (NJ)
Augusta Tech Coll (GA)
Austin Comm Coll (TX)
Bainbridge Coll (GA)
Baltimore City Comm Coll (MD)
Barton County Comm Coll (KS)
Bay de Noc Comm Coll (MI)
Bay State Coll (MA)
Beaufort County Comm Coll (NC)
Belmont Tech Coll (OH)
Bergen Comm Coll (NJ)
Berkeley Coll (NJ)
Berkeley Coll-New York City Campus (NY)
Berkeley Coll-Westchester Campus (NY)
Bessemer State Tech Coll (AL)
Big Sandy Comm and Tech Coll (KY)
Black Hawk Coll, Moline (IL)
Blue Mountain Comm Coll (OR)
Blue Ridge Comm Coll (VA)
Borough of Manhattan Comm Coll of City U of NY (NY)
Brazosport Coll (TX)
Brevard Comm Coll (FL)
Briarwood Coll (CT)
Bristol Comm Coll (MA)
Bronx Comm Coll of City U of NY (NY)
Brookdale Comm Coll (NJ)
Broward Comm Coll (FL)
Brown Mackie Coll, Findlay Campus (OH)
Brown Mackie Coll, Michigan City Campus (IN)
Bryant & Stratton Business Inst, Albany (NY)

Bryant and Stratton Coll, Parma (OH)
Bryant & Stratton Business Inst, Amherst Cmps (NY)
Bryant & Stratton Business Inst (NY)
Bryant & Stratton Business Inst (NY)
Bucks County Comm Coll (PA)
Bunker Hill Comm Coll (MA)
Butler County Comm Coll (KS)
Butler County Comm Coll (PA)
Caldwell Comm Coll and Tech Inst (NC)
Calhoun Comm Coll (AL)
Cape Cod Comm Coll (MA)
Capital Comm Coll (CT)
Carroll Comm Coll (MD)
Casper Coll (WY)
Cayuga County Comm Coll (NY)
Cecil Comm Coll (MD)
Cedar Valley Coll (TX)
Central Arizona Coll (AZ)
Central Carolina Comm Coll (NC)
Central Carolina Tech Coll (SC)
Central Comm Coll– Columbus Campus (NE)
Central Comm Coll–Grand Island Campus (NE)
Central Comm Coll– Hastings Campus (NE)
Central Georgia Tech Coll (GA)
Central Oregon Comm Coll (OR)
Central Piedmont Comm Coll (NC)
Central Wyoming Coll (WY)
Century Coll (MN)
Chandler-Gilbert Comm Coll (AZ)
Chattahoochee Tech Coll (GA)
Chattanooga State Tech Comm Coll (TN)
Chemeketa Comm Coll (OR)
Chipola Coll (FL)
Cincinnati State Tech and Comm Coll (OH)
City Colls of Chicago, Wilbur Wright Coll (IL)
Clackamas Comm Coll (OR)
Clarendon Coll (TX)
Clark State Comm Coll (OH)
Clatsop Comm Coll (OR)
Cleveland Comm Coll (NC)
Clinton Comm Coll (NY)
Clovis Comm Coll (NM)
Coahoma Comm Coll (MS)
Coastal Bend Coll (TX)
Coastal Carolina Comm Coll (NC)
Coconino Comm Coll (AZ)
Coffeyville Comm Coll (KS)
Colby Comm Coll (KS)
Coll of DuPage (IL)

Coll of Southern Idaho (ID)
Coll of Southern Maryland (MD)
Coll of the Canyons (CA)
Colorado Mountn Coll, Alpine Cmps (CO)
Colorado Mountn Coll (CO)
Colorado Mountn Coll, Timberline Cmps (CO)
Colorado Northwestern Comm Coll (CO)
Columbia-Greene Comm Coll (NY)
Columbia State Comm Coll (TN)
Columbus State Comm Coll (OH)
Columbus Tech Coll (GA)
Commonwealth Tech Inst (PA)
Comm & Tech Coll at West Virginia U Inst of Technology (WV)
Comm Coll of Aurora (CO)
Comm Coll of Beaver County (PA)
Comm Coll of Denver (CO)
Comm Coll of Philadelphia (PA)
Comm Coll of Rhode Island (RI)
Comm Coll of Southern Nevada (NV)
Comm Coll of Vermont (VT)
Compton Comm Coll (CA)
Copiah-Lincoln Comm Coll (MS)
Corning Comm Coll (NY)
Cowley County Comm Coll and Voc-Tech School (KS)
Craven Comm Coll (NC)
Cumberland County Coll (NJ)
Cuyahoga Comm Coll (OH)
Danville Area Comm Coll (IL)
Danville Comm Coll (VA)
Darton Coll (GA)
Davenport U, Midland (MI)
Davidson County Comm Coll (NC)
Daytona Beach Comm Coll (FL)
De Anza Coll (CA)
DeKalb Tech Coll (GA)
Delaware Tech & Comm Coll, Jack F Owens Cmps (DE)
Delaware Tech & Comm Coll, Stanton/ Wilmington Cmps (DE)
Delaware Tech & Comm Coll, Terry Cmps (DE)
Delta Coll (MI)
Des Moines Area Comm Coll (IA)
Dixie State Coll of Utah (UT)
Dodge City Comm Coll (KS)
Durham Tech Comm Coll (NC)
Dutchess Comm Coll (NY)
East Central Coll (MO)
East Central Comm Coll (MS)

Eastern Idaho Tech Coll (ID)
Eastfield Coll (TX)
East Mississippi Comm Coll (MS)
ECPI Coll of Technology, Newport News (VA)
ECPI Coll of Technology, Virginia Beach (VA)
ECPI Tech Coll, Richmond (VA)
ECPI Tech Coll, Roanoke (VA)
Edgecombe Comm Coll (NC)
Edison State Comm Coll (OH)
Elgin Comm Coll (IL)
Ellsworth Comm Coll (IA)
El Paso Comm Coll (TX)
Erie Business Center South (PA)
Essex County Coll (NJ)
Eugenio María de Hostos Comm Coll of City U of NY (NY)
Everest Coll (AZ)
Everett Comm Coll (WA)
Fayetteville Tech Comm Coll (NC)
Finger Lakes Comm Coll (NY)
Flathead Valley Comm Coll (MT)
Florida Comm Coll at Jacksonville (FL)
Florida National Coll (FL)
Foothill Coll (CA)
Forsyth Tech Comm Coll (NC)
Fort Scott Comm Coll (KS)
Fox Valley Tech Coll (WI)
Frank Phillips Coll (TX)
Frederick Comm Coll (MD)
Fulton-Montgomery Comm Coll (NY)
Gadsden State Comm Coll-Ayers Campus (AL)
Gainesville Coll (GA)
Garden City Comm Coll (KS)
GateWay Comm Coll (AZ)
Gateway Comm Coll (CT)
Genesee Comm Coll (NY)
George Corley Wallace State Comm Coll (AL)
George C. Wallace Comm Coll (AL)
Germanna Comm Coll (VA)
Glendale Comm Coll (CA)
Globe Coll (MN)
Gogebic Comm Coll (MI)
Greenfield Comm Coll (MA)
Griffin Tech Coll (GA)
Guam Comm Coll (GU)
Guilford Tech Comm Coll (NC)
Gulf Coast Comm Coll (FL)
Gwinnett Tech Coll (GA)
Hagerstown Business Coll (MD)
Harrisburg Area Comm Coll (PA)
Hawaii Business Coll (HI)
Hawkeye Comm Coll (IA)

Henry Ford Comm Coll (MI)
Herkimer County Comm Coll (NY)
Hesser Coll (NH)
Highland Comm Coll (IL)
Highland Comm Coll (KS)
Highline Comm Coll (WA)
Hillsborough Comm Coll (FL)
Hinds Comm Coll (MS)
Holyoke Comm Coll (MA)
Houston Comm Coll System (TX)
Howard Coll (TX)
Howard Comm Coll (MD)
Hudson County Comm Coll (NJ)
Hudson Valley Comm Coll (NY)
ICM School of Business & Medical Careers (PA)
Illinois Eastern Comm Colls, Olney Central Coll (IL)
Illinois Valley Comm Coll (IL)
Independence Comm Coll (KS)
Indiana Business Coll, Anderson (IN)
Indiana Business Coll, Columbus (IN)
Indiana Business Coll, Evansville (IN)
Indiana Business Coll, Fort Wayne (IN)
Indiana Business Coll, Indianapolis (IN)
Indiana Business Coll, Lafayette (IN)
Indiana Business Coll, Marion (IN)
Indiana Business Coll, Muncie (IN)
Indiana Business Coll, Terre Haute (IN)
Indian River Comm Coll (FL)
Instituto Comercial de Puerto Rico Jr Coll (PR)
Iowa Central Comm Coll (IA)
Iowa Lakes Comm Coll (IA)
Iowa Western Comm Coll (IA)
Itasca Comm Coll (MN)
Itawamba Comm Coll (MS)
Ivy Tech State Coll– Lafayette (IN)
James Sprunt Comm Coll (NC)
Jamestown Comm Coll (NY)
Jefferson Comm Coll (KY)
Jefferson Comm Coll (NY)
Jefferson Comm Coll (OH)
J. F. Drake State Tech Coll (AL)
John A. Logan Coll (IL)
John Wood Comm Coll (IL)
Kapiolani Comm Coll (HI)
Kauai Comm Coll (HI)
Keiser Coll, Fort Lauderdale (FL)

Kennebec Valley Comm Coll (ME)
Kent State U, Tuscarawas Campus (OH)
Keystone Coll (PA)
Kilgore Coll (TX)
Kingsborough Comm Coll of City U of NY (NY)
Kingwood Coll (TX)
Lake Region State Coll (ND)
Lake Superior Coll (MN)
Lane Comm Coll (OR)
Lanier Tech Coll (GA)
Lansing Comm Coll (MI)
Laramie County Comm Coll (WY)
Laurel Business Inst (PA)
Lehigh Carbon Comm Coll (PA)
Lewis and Clark Comm Coll (IL)
Linn-Benton Comm Coll (OR)
Long Beach City Coll (CA)
Long Island Business Inst (NY)
Longview Comm Coll (MO)
Lower Columbia Coll (WA)
Luna Comm Coll (NM)
Macomb Comm Coll (MI)
Manchester Comm Coll (CT)
Maple Woods Comm Coll (MO)
Maria Coll (NY)
Massachusetts Bay Comm Coll (MA)
Mayland Comm Coll (NC)
McDowell Tech Comm Coll (NC)
McIntosh Coll (NH)
McLennan Comm Coll (TX)
Metropolitan Comm Coll (NE)
Metropolitan Comm Coll-Business & Technology College (MO)
Midlands Tech Coll (SC)
Mid Michigan Comm Coll (MI)
Mineral Area Coll (MO)
Minnesota School of Business–Brooklyn Center (MN)
Minnesota School of Business–Plymouth (MN)
Minnesota School of Business–Richfield (MN)
Minnesota State Coll– Southeast Tech (MN)
Minnesota West Comm & Tech Coll-Pipestone Cmps (MN)
Modesto Jr Coll (CA)
Mohave Comm Coll (AZ)
Monroe Coll, Bronx (NY)
Monroe Coll, New Rochelle (NY)
Montcalm Comm Coll (MI)
Montgomery Comm Coll (NC)
Montgomery County Comm Coll (PA)

Mount Wachusett Comm Coll (MA)
Muscatine Comm Coll (IA)
Muskegon Comm Coll (MI)
Napa Valley Coll (CA)
Nashville State Tech Comm Coll (TN)
Nassau Comm Coll (NY)
National Coll of Business & Technology, Danville (KY)
National Coll of Business & Technology, Florence (KY)
National Coll of Business & Technology, Lexington (KY)
National Coll of Business & Technology, Louisville (KY)
National Coll of Business & Technology, Pikeville (KY)
National Coll of Business & Technology, Richmond (KY)
National Coll of Business & Technology, Bristol (TN)
National Coll of Business & Technology, Bluefield (VA)
National Coll of Business & Technology, Charlottesville (VA)
National Coll of Business & Technology, Harrisonburg (VA)
National Coll of Business & Technology, Lynchburg (VA)
National Coll of Business & Technology, Martinsville (VA)
National Coll of Business & Technology, Salem (VA)
New England Coll of Finance (MA)
New Hampshire Comm Tech Coll, Manchester/Stratham (NH)
New Mexico Military Inst (NM)
New River Comm and Tech Coll (WV)
Niagara County Comm Coll (NY)
North Central Missouri Coll (MO)
North Central State Coll (OH)
Northeastern Tech Coll (SC)
Northeast State Tech Comm Coll (TN)
Northern Essex Comm Coll (MA)
Northern Virginia Comm Coll (VA)
North Hennepin Comm Coll (MN)
North Iowa Area Comm Coll (IA)
North Lake Coll (TX)
Northland Comm and Tech Coll–Thief River Falls (MN)
North Shore Comm Coll (MA)
Northwestern Connecticut Comm–Tech Coll (CT)
Northwest-Shoals Comm Coll (AL)
Northwest State Comm Coll (OH)
Northwest Tech Coll (MN)
Oakland Comm Coll (MI)
Odessa Coll (TX)
Orange Coast Coll (CA)
Orange County Comm Coll (NY)
Ouachita Tech Coll (AR)
Owens Comm Coll, Findlay (OH)
Palm Beach Comm Coll (FL)
Paradise Valley Comm Coll (AZ)
Pasadena City Coll (CA)
Patrick Henry Comm Coll (VA)
Peninsula Coll (WA)
Pennsylvania Highland Comm Coll (PA)

Penn Valley Comm Coll (MO)
Piedmont Comm Coll (NC)
Piedmont Virginia Comm Coll (VA)
Pima Comm Coll (AZ)
Pioneer Pacific Coll (OR)
Pratt Comm Coll and Area Vocational School (KS)
Queensborough Comm Coll of City U of NY (NY)
Quinebaug Valley Comm Coll (CT)
Raritan Valley Comm Coll (NJ)
Rasmussen Coll St. Cloud (MN)
Richland Comm Coll (IL)
Richmond Comm Coll (NC)
Riverside Comm Coll District (CA)
Rockingham Comm Coll (NC)
Rockland Comm Coll (NY)
Rock Valley Coll (IL)
Rogue Comm Coll (OR)
Rowan-Cabarrus Comm Coll (NC)
Saint Charles Comm Coll (MO)
St. Cloud Tech Coll (MN)
St. Louis Comm Coll at Forest Park (MO)
St. Louis Comm Coll at Meramec (MO)
Saint Paul Coll–A Comm & Tech College (MN)
St. Philip's Coll (TX)
Salt Lake Comm Coll (UT)
Sandhills Comm Coll (NC)
San Diego City Coll (CA)
San Diego Miramar Coll (CA)
San Joaquin Delta Coll (CA)
Santa Barbara City Coll (CA)
Santa Fe Comm Coll (FL)
Sauk Valley Comm Coll (IL)
Savannah Tech Coll (GA)
Schoolcraft Coll (MI)
Scott Comm Coll (IA)
Seattle Central Comm Coll (WA)
Seminole Comm Coll (FL)
Seminole State Coll (OK)
Seward County Comm Coll (KS)
Shawnee Comm Coll (IL)
Shoreline Comm Coll (WA)
Sinclair Comm Coll (OH)
Sisseton-Wahpeton Comm Coll (SD)
Snow Coll (UT)
Solano Comm Coll (CA)
South Central Tech Coll (MN)
Southeastern Tech Coll (GA)
Southeast Tech Inst (SD)
South Hills School of Business & Technology, State College (PA)
South Texas Coll (TX)
South U (FL)
South U (SC)
Southwestern Comm Coll (IA)
Southwestern Comm Coll (NC)
Southwestern Oregon Comm Coll (OR)
Southwest Georgia Tech Coll (GA)
Southwest Wisconsin Tech Coll (WI)
Spartanburg Tech Coll (SC)
Spencerian Coll (KY)
Springfield Tech Comm Coll (MA)
State U of NY Coll of Technology at Alfred (NY)
State U of NY Coll of Technology at Canton (NY)
State U of NY Coll of Technology at Delhi (NY)
Surry Comm Coll (NC)
Sussex County Comm Coll (NJ)

Tacoma Comm Coll (WA)
Taft Coll (CA)
Tech Coll of the Lowcountry (SC)
Thompson Inst (PA)
Three Rivers Comm Coll (CT)
Three Rivers Comm Coll (MO)
Tillamook Bay Comm Coll (OR)
Tompkins Cortland Comm Coll (NY)
Tri-County Comm Coll (NC)
Tri-County Tech Coll (SC)
Trident Tech Coll (SC)
Trinidad State Jr Coll (CO)
Trinity Valley Comm Coll (TX)
Truckee Meadows Comm Coll (NV)
Tunxis Comm Coll (CT)
Umpqua Comm Coll (OR)
The U of Akron–Wayne Coll (OH)
U of Alaska Anchorage, Matanuska-Susitna Coll (AK)
U of Cincinnati Raymond Walters Coll (OH)
U of Northwestern Ohio (OH)
U of Pittsburgh at Titusville (PA)
Valencia Comm Coll (FL)
Wake Tech Comm Coll (NC)
Wayne County Comm Coll District (MI)
West Central Tech Coll (GA)
Westchester Comm Coll (NY)
Western Nevada Comm Coll (NV)
Western Wyoming Comm Coll (WY)
West Kentucky Comm and Tech Coll (KY)
Westmoreland County Comm Coll (PA)
West Virginia State Comm and Tech Coll (WV)
West Virginia U at Parkersburg (WV)
Whatcom Comm Coll (WA)
Wilson Tech Comm Coll (NC)
Yakima Valley Comm Coll (WA)
Yavapai Coll (AZ)
Yuba Coll (CA)

Accounting and Computer Science
Columbus State Comm Coll (OH)

Accounting and Finance
Jackson Comm Coll (MI)

Accounting Technology and Bookkeeping
Alamance Comm Coll (NC)
Allegany Coll of Maryland (MD)
Asheville-Buncombe Tech Comm Coll (NC)
Bay de Noc Comm Coll (MI)
Big Bend Comm Coll (WA)
Bishop State Comm Coll (AL)
Blue River Comm Coll (MO)
Bowling Green State U–Firelands Coll (OH)
Broome Comm Coll (NY)
Brown Mackie Coll, Northern Kentucky Campus (KY)
Cape Fear Comm Coll (NC)
Catawba Valley Comm Coll (NC)
Central Florida Comm Coll (FL)
Central Georgia Tech Coll (GA)
Central Wyoming Coll (WY)
Clark Coll (WA)
Clover Park Tech Coll (WA)
Coll of Lake County (IL)
Coll of the Mainland (TX)

Columbus State Comm Coll (OH)
Comm Coll of Allegheny County (PA)
Davenport U, Midland (MI)
Delaware County Comm Coll (PA)
Edmonds Comm Coll (WA)
Elgin Comm Coll (IL)
Essex County Coll (NJ)
Front Range Comm Coll (CO)
Glendale Comm Coll (AZ)
Goodwin Coll (CT)
Green River Comm Coll (WA)
Hagerstown Comm Coll (MD)
Harford Comm Coll (MD)
Iowa Lakes Comm Coll (IA)
Ivy Tech State Coll–Bloomington (IN)
Ivy Tech State Coll–Central Indiana (IN)
Ivy Tech State Coll–Columbus (IN)
Ivy Tech State Coll–Eastcentral (IN)
Ivy Tech State Coll–Kokomo (IN)
Ivy Tech State Coll–Lafayette (IN)
Ivy Tech State Coll–North Central (IN)
Ivy Tech State Coll–Northeast (IN)
Ivy Tech State Coll–Northwest (IN)
Ivy Tech State Coll–Southcentral (IN)
Ivy Tech State Coll–Southeast (IN)
Ivy Tech State Coll–Southwest (IN)
Ivy Tech State Coll–Wabash Valley (IN)
Ivy Tech State Coll–Whitewater (IN)
Jefferson State Comm Coll (AL)
Johnson County Comm Coll (KS)
Johnston Comm Coll (NC)
John Wood Comm Coll (IL)
J. Sargeant Reynolds Comm Coll (VA)
Kalamazoo Valley Comm Coll (MI)
Kilgore Coll (TX)
Lackawanna Coll (PA)
Lake Land Coll (IL)
Lake Region State Coll (ND)
Lehigh Carbon Comm Coll (PA)
Lower Columbia Coll (WA)
Marshall Comm and Tech Coll (WV)
Metropolitan Comm Coll-Business & Technology College (MO)
Miami Dade Coll (FL)
Milwaukee Area Tech Coll (WI)
Minneapolis Comm and Tech Coll (MN)
Moberly Area Comm Coll (MO)
Mohawk Valley Comm Coll (NY)
Montgomery County Comm Coll (PA)
Mott Comm Coll (MI)
Nassau Comm Coll (NY)
National Coll of Business & Technology, Salem (VA)
Northampton County Area Comm Coll (PA)
North Iowa Area Comm Coll (IA)
North Seattle Comm Coll (WA)
Northwestern Michigan Coll (MI)
Northwestern Tech Coll (GA)

Olympic Coll (WA)
Owens Comm Coll, Findlay (OH)
Owens Comm Coll, Toledo (OH)
Parkland Coll (IL)
Polk Comm Coll (FL)
Randolph Comm Coll (NC)
St. Cloud Tech Coll (MN)
St. Petersburg Coll (FL)
San Juan Coll (NM)
Southern State Comm Coll (OH)
Southwestern Michigan Coll (MI)
Stanly Comm Coll (NC)
Tillamook Bay Comm Coll (OR)
Union County Coll (NJ)
The U of Akron–Wayne Coll (OH)
Walla Walla Comm Coll (WA)
Waubonsee Comm Coll (IL)
Western Nevada Comm Coll (NV)
West Georgia Tech Coll (GA)
Wilkes Comm Coll (NC)
Williston State Coll (ND)
Wor-Wic Comm Coll (MD)

Acting
Northampton County Area Comm Coll (PA)
Santa Barbara City Coll (CA)

Actuarial Science
Harrisburg Area Comm Coll (PA)

Administrative Assistant and Secretarial Science
Adirondack Comm Coll (NY)
Alabama Southern Comm Coll (AL)
Albuquerque Tech Vocational Inst (NM)
Alexandria Tech Coll (MN)
Allegany Coll of Maryland (MD)
Allen County Comm Coll (KS)
Alpena Comm Coll (MI)
Alvin Comm Coll (TX)
Amarillo Coll (TX)
American Samoa Comm Coll (AS)
Andover Coll (ME)
Anne Arundel Comm Coll (MD)
Anoka-Ramsey Comm Coll (MN)
Anoka-Ramsey Comm Coll, Cambridge Campus (MN)
Arapahoe Comm Coll (CO)
Arizona Western Coll (AZ)
Ashland Comm and Tech Coll (KY)
Asnuntuck Comm Coll (CT)
Athens Tech Coll (GA)
Augusta Tech Coll (GA)
Austin Comm Coll (TX)
Bainbridge Coll (GA)
Baltimore City Comm Coll (MD)
Barton County Comm Coll (KS)
Bay de Noc Comm Coll (MI)
Bay Mills Comm Coll (MI)
Bay State Coll (MA)
Beaufort County Comm Coll (NC)
Belmont Tech Coll (OH)
Bergen Comm Coll (NJ)
Berkshire Comm Coll (MA)
Bessemer State Tech Coll (AL)
Bevill State Comm Coll (AL)
Bishop State Comm Coll (AL)
Bismarck State Coll (ND)
Blackfeet Comm Coll (MT)
Black Hawk Coll, Moline (IL)
Bladen Comm Coll (NC)
Blue Mountain Comm Coll (OR)
Blue Ridge Comm Coll (NC)

Blue Ridge Comm Coll (VA)
Blue River Comm Coll (MO)
Borough of Manhattan Comm Coll of City U of NY (NY)
Brazosport Coll (TX)
Briarwood Coll (CT)
Bronx Comm Coll of City U of NY (NY)
Brookdale Comm Coll (NJ)
Broward Comm Coll (FL)
Brown Mackie Coll, Michigan City Campus (IN)
Brunswick Comm Coll (NC)
Bryant & Stratton Business Inst, Albany (NY)
Bryant and Stratton Coll, Parma (OH)
Bryant & Stratton Business Inst, Amherst Cmps (NY)
Bryant & Stratton Business Inst (NY)
Bryant & Stratton Business Inst (NY)
Bucks County Comm Coll (PA)
Business Inst of Pennsylvania, Sharon (PA)
Butler County Comm Coll (KS)
Butler County Comm Coll (PA)
Cape Cod Comm Coll (MA)
Capital Comm Coll (CT)
Carteret Comm Coll (NC)
Casper Coll (WY)
Catawba Valley Comm Coll (NC)
Cecil Comm Coll (MD)
Cedar Valley Coll (TX)
Central Alabama Comm Coll (AL)
Central Arizona Coll (AZ)
Central Carolina Comm Coll (NC)
Central Carolina Tech Coll (SC)
Central Comm Coll–Columbus Campus (NE)
Central Comm Coll–Grand Island Campus (NE)
Central Comm Coll–Hastings Campus (NE)
Centralia Coll (WA)
Central Oregon Comm Coll (OR)
Central Piedmont Comm Coll (NC)
Central Texas Coll (TX)
Century Coll (MN)
Chattahoochee Valley Comm Coll (AL)
Chattanooga State Tech Comm Coll (TN)
Chemeketa Comm Coll (OR)
Cincinnati State Tech and Comm Coll (OH)
Citrus Coll (CA)
Clark State Comm Coll (OH)
Clatsop Comm Coll (OR)
Cleveland Comm Coll (NC)
Cleveland State Comm Coll (TN)
Clinton Comm Coll (IA)
Clinton Comm Coll (NY)
Cloud County Comm Coll (KS)
Clovis Comm Coll (NM)
Coahoma Comm Coll (MS)
Coastal Bend Coll (TX)
Cochise Coll, Douglas (AZ)
Coffeyville Comm Coll (KS)
Coll of DuPage (IL)
Coll of Lake County (IL)
Coll of the Canyons (CA)
Coll of the Mainland (TX)
Columbia Coll (CA)
Columbia-Greene Comm Coll (NY)
Columbia State Comm Coll (TN)
Columbus State Comm Coll (OH)
Columbus Tech Coll (GA)

Comm & Tech Coll at West Virginia U Inst of Technology (WV)
Comm Coll of Allegheny County (PA)
Comm Coll of Aurora (CO)
Comm Coll of Beaver County (PA)
Comm Coll of Denver (CO)
Comm Coll of Philadelphia (PA)
Comm Coll of Rhode Island (RI)
Comm Coll of Southern Nevada (NV)
Comm Coll of Vermont (VT)
Compton Comm Coll (CA)
Contra Costa Coll (CA)
Copiah-Lincoln Comm Coll–Natchez Campus (MS)
Corning Comm Coll (NY)
Cowley County Comm Coll and Voc-Tech School (KS)
Crowder Coll (MO)
Cumberland County Coll (NJ)
Cuyahoga Comm Coll (OH)
Dabney S. Lancaster Comm Coll (VA)
Danville Comm Coll (VA)
Darton Coll (GA)
Davenport U, Midland (MI)
Davidson County Comm Coll (NC)
Dawson Comm Coll (MT)
Daytona Beach Comm Coll (FL)
De Anza Coll (CA)
DeKalb Tech Coll (GA)
Delaware Tech & Comm Coll, Jack F Owens Cmps (DE)
Delaware Tech & Comm Coll, Stanton/ Wilmington Cmps (DE)
Delaware Tech & Comm Coll, Terry Cmps (DE)
Delta Coll (MI)
Des Moines Area Comm Coll (IA)
Dixie State Coll of Utah (UT)
Dodge City Comm Coll (KS)
Doña Ana Branch Comm Coll (NM)
Durham Tech Comm Coll (NC)
Dutchess Comm Coll (NY)
East Central Coll (MO)
Eastern Idaho Tech Coll (ID)
Eastern Maine Comm Coll (ME)
Eastern Shore Comm Coll (VA)
East Mississippi Comm Coll (MS)
Edgecombe Comm Coll (NC)
Edison State Comm Coll (OH)
Elgin Comm Coll (IL)
Elizabethtown Comm and Tech Coll (KY)
Ellsworth Comm Coll (IA)
El Paso Comm Coll (TX)
Enterprise-Ozark Comm Coll (AL)
Erie Business Center, Main (PA)
Erie Business Center South (PA)
Erie Comm Coll (NY)
Erie Comm Coll, North Campus (NY)
Erie Comm Coll, South Campus (NY)
Essex County Coll (NJ)
Eugenio María de Hostos Comm Coll of City U of NY (NY)
Everest Coll (AZ)
Feather River Coll (CA)
Finger Lakes Comm Coll (NY)

Flathead Valley Comm Coll (MT)
Florida Comm Coll at Jacksonville (FL)
Florida National Coll (FL)
Forsyth Tech Comm Coll (NC)
Fort Peck Comm Coll (MT)
Fort Scott Comm Coll (KS)
Fox Valley Tech Coll (WI)
Frank Phillips Coll (TX)
Frederick Comm Coll (MD)
Front Range Comm Coll (CO)
Fulton-Montgomery Comm Coll (NY)
Gadsden State Comm Coll (AL)
Garden City Comm Coll (KS)
Garrett Coll (MD)
Genesee Comm Coll (NY)
George C. Wallace Comm Coll (AL)
Germanna Comm Coll (VA)
Glendale Comm Coll (AZ)
Glendale Comm Coll (CA)
Globe Coll (MN)
Gogebic Comm Coll (MI)
Goodwin Coll (CT)
Gordon Coll (GA)
Grand Rapids Comm Coll (MI)
Greenfield Comm Coll (MA)
Griffin Tech Coll (GA)
Guam Comm Coll (GU)
Gulf Coast Comm Coll (FL)
Gwinnett Tech Coll (GA)
Hagerstown Business Coll (MD)
Halifax Comm Coll (NC)
Harford Comm Coll (MD)
Harrisburg Area Comm Coll (PA)
Hawkeye Comm Coll (IA)
Hazard Comm and Tech Coll (KY)
Heartland Comm Coll (IL)
Henderson Comm Coll (KY)
Henry Ford Comm Coll (MI)
Hibbing Comm Coll (MN)
Highland Comm Coll (IL)
Highland Comm Coll (KS)
Highline Comm Coll (WA)
Hillsborough Comm Coll (FL)
Hinds Comm Coll (MS)
Holmes Comm Coll (MS)
Holyoke Comm Coll (MA)
Hopkinsville Comm Coll (KY)
Houston Comm Coll System (TX)
Howard Comm Coll (MD)
Hudson Valley Comm Coll (NY)
Hutchinson Comm Coll and Area Vocational School (KS)
ICM School of Business & Medical Careers (PA)
Illinois Eastern Comm Colls, Frontier Comm Coll (IL)
Illinois Eastern Comm Colls, Olney Central Coll (IL)
Illinois Eastern Comm Colls, Wabash Valley Coll (IL)
Illinois Valley Comm Coll (IL)
Independence Comm Coll (KS)
Indiana Business Coll, Anderson (IN)
Indiana Business Coll, Columbus (IN)
Indiana Business Coll, Evansville (IN)
Indiana Business Coll, Fort Wayne (IN)
Indiana Business Coll, Indianapolis (IN)
Indiana Business Coll, Lafayette (IN)
Indiana Business Coll, Marion (IN)
Indiana Business Coll, Muncie (IN)

Indiana Business Coll, Terre Haute (IN)
Indian River Comm Coll (FL)
Instituto Comercial de Puerto Rico Jr Coll (PR)
Iowa Central Comm Coll (IA)
Iowa Lakes Comm Coll (IA)
Iowa Western Comm Coll (IA)
Isothermal Comm Coll (NC)
Itawamba Comm Coll (MS)
Jackson Comm Coll (MI)
James H. Faulkner State Comm Coll (AL)
James Sprunt Comm Coll (NC)
Jefferson Comm Coll (NY)
Jefferson Comm Coll (OH)
Jefferson State Comm Coll (AL)
J. F. Drake State Tech Coll (AL)
Johnson County Comm Coll (KS)
Johnston Comm Coll (NC)
John Tyler Comm Coll (VA)
John Wood Comm Coll (IL)
J. Sargeant Reynolds Comm Coll (VA)
Kansas City Kansas Comm Coll (KS)
Kauai Comm Coll (HI)
Kennebec Valley Comm Coll (ME)
Kent State U, Tuscarawas Campus (OH)
Kilgore Coll (TX)
Kingsborough Comm Coll of City U of NY (NY)
Lac Courte Oreilles Ojibwa Comm Coll (WI)
Lackawanna Coll (PA)
Lake Land Coll (IL)
Lake Region State Coll (ND)
Lane Comm Coll (OR)
Lansing Comm Coll (MI)
Laredo Comm Coll (TX)
Laurel Business Inst (PA)
Lehigh Carbon Comm Coll (PA)
Lewis and Clark Comm Coll (IL)
Lincoln Land Comm Coll (IL)
Linn-Benton Comm Coll (OR)
Long Beach City Coll (CA)
Long Island Business Inst (NY)
Longview Comm Coll (MO)
Lower Columbia Coll (WA)
Luna Comm Coll (NM)
Macomb Comm Coll (MI)
Manchester Comm Coll (CT)
Maple Woods Comm Coll (MO)
Marshall Comm and Tech Coll (WV)
Mayland Comm Coll (NC)
McDowell Tech Comm Coll (NC)
McIntosh Coll (NH)
McLennan Comm Coll (TX)
Meridian Comm Coll (MS)
Mesabi Range Comm and Tech Coll (MN)
Metropolitan Comm Coll (NE)
Miami Dade Coll (FL)
Mid Michigan Comm Coll (MI)
Milwaukee Area Tech Coll (WI)
Mineral Area Coll (MO)
Minneapolis Comm and Tech Coll (MN)
Minnesota School of Business–Brooklyn Center (MN)
Minnesota School of Business–Plymouth (MN)
Minnesota School of Business–Richfield (MN)
Minnesota State Coll–Southeast Tech (MN)

Minnesota West Comm & Tech Coll-Pipestone Cmps (MN)
Moberly Area Comm Coll (MO)
Modesto Jr Coll (CA)
Mohawk Valley Comm Coll (NY)
Montcalm Comm Coll (MI)
Montgomery Comm Coll (NC)
Montgomery County Comm Coll (PA)
Moraine Valley Comm Coll (IL)
Mott Comm Coll (MI)
MTI Coll of Business and Technology, Houston (TX)
MTI Coll of Business and Technology, Houston (TX)
Muscatine Comm Coll (IA)
Muskegon Comm Coll (MI)
Napa Valley Coll (CA)
Nashville State Tech Comm Coll (TN)
Nassau Comm Coll (NY)
National Coll of Business & Technology, Danville (KY)
National Coll of Business & Technology, Florence (KY)
National Coll of Business & Technology, Lexington (KY)
National Coll of Business & Technology, Louisville (KY)
National Coll of Business & Technology, Pikeville (KY)
National Coll of Business & Technology, Richmond (KY)
National Coll of Business & Technology, Bristol (TN)
National Coll of Business & Technology, Nashville (TN)
National Coll of Business & Technology, Bluefield (VA)
National Coll of Business & Technology, Charlottesville (VA)
National Coll of Business & Technology, Harrisonburg (VA)
National Coll of Business & Technology, Lynchburg (VA)
National Coll of Business & Technology, Martinsville (VA)
National Coll of Business & Technology, Salem (VA)
New Hampshire Comm Tech Coll, Manchester/Stratham (NH)
Newport Business Inst, Williamsport (PA)
New River Comm and Tech Coll (WV)
Niagara County Comm Coll (NY)
North Central Missouri Coll (MO)
North Central State Coll (OH)
North Dakota State Coll of Science (ND)
Northeast Alabama Comm Coll (AL)
Northeastern Tech Coll (SC)
Northeast State Tech Comm Coll (TN)
Northern Essex Comm Coll (MA)
Northern Virginia Comm Coll (VA)
North Hennepin Comm Coll (MN)
North Idaho Coll (ID)
North Iowa Area Comm Coll (IA)
North Lake Coll (TX)
Northland Comm and Tech Coll–Thief River Falls (MN)
North Shore Comm Coll (MA)
Northwestern Connecticut Comm-Tech Coll (CT)

Northwest-Shoals Comm Coll (AL)
Northwest Tech Coll (MN)
Odessa Coll (TX)
Olympic Coll (WA)
Orange Coast Coll (CA)
Orange County Comm Coll (NY)
Otero Jr Coll (CO)
Ouachita Tech Coll (AR)
Owens Comm Coll, Findlay (OH)
Palm Beach Comm Coll (FL)
Panola Coll (TX)
Paradise Valley Comm Coll (AZ)
Parkland Coll (IL)
Pasadena City Coll (CA)
Patrick Henry Comm Coll (VA)
Penn Valley Comm Coll (MO)
Phillips Comm Coll of the U of Arkansas (AR)
Piedmont Virginia Comm Coll (VA)
Pima Comm Coll (AZ)
Pratt Comm Coll and Area Vocational School (KS)
Pulaski Tech Coll (AR)
Quinebaug Valley Comm Coll (CT)
Rainy River Comm Coll (MN)
Raritan Valley Comm Coll (NJ)
Rasmussen Coll St. Cloud (MN)
Reid State Tech Coll (AL)
Richland Comm Coll (IL)
Richmond Comm Coll (NC)
Rich Mountain Comm Coll (AR)
Riverland Comm Coll (MN)
Roanoke-Chowan Comm Coll (NC)
Rochester Comm and Tech Coll (MN)
Rockingham Comm Coll (NC)
Rockland Comm Coll (NY)
Rogue Comm Coll (OR)
Saint Charles Comm Coll (MO)
St. Cloud Tech Coll (MN)
St. Louis Comm Coll at Forest Park (MO)
St. Louis Comm Coll at Meramec (MO)
Saint Paul Coll–A Comm & Tech College (MN)
St. Philip's Coll (TX)
Salt Lake Comm Coll (UT)
Sandhills Comm Coll (NC)
San Diego City Coll (CA)
San Diego Miramar Coll (CA)
San Juan Coll (NM)
Santa Barbara City Coll (CA)
Sauk Valley Comm Coll (IL)
Savannah Tech Coll (GA)
Schoolcraft Coll (MI)
Schuylkill Inst of Business and Technology (PA)
Scott Comm Coll (IA)
Seattle Central Comm Coll (WA)
Seminole Comm Coll (FL)
Seminole State Coll (OK)
Seward County Comm Coll (KS)
Shawnee Comm Coll (IL)
Shelton State Comm Coll (AL)
Sheridan Coll (WY)
Sinclair Comm Coll (OH)
Snow Coll (UT)
South Central Tech Coll (MN)
Southeast Comm Coll, Lincoln Campus (NE)
Southeast Kentucky Comm and Tech Coll (KY)
Southern Union State Comm Coll (AL)

South Hills School of Business & Technology, State College (PA)
South Mountain Comm Coll (AZ)
Southside Virginia Comm Coll (VA)
South U (FL)
Southwestern Comm Coll (IA)
Southwestern Comm Coll (NC)
Southwestern Michigan Coll (MI)
Southwest Georgia Tech Coll (GA)
Southwest Wisconsin Tech Coll (WI)
Spartanburg Methodist Coll (SC)
Spartanburg Tech Coll (SC)
Springfield Tech Comm Coll (MA)
Surry Comm Coll (NC)
Sussex County Comm Coll (NJ)
Tacoma Comm Coll (WA)
Taft Coll (CA)
Tech Coll of the Lowcountry (SC)
Temple Coll (TX)
Three Rivers Comm Coll (CT)
Three Rivers Comm Coll (MO)
Tillamook Bay Comm Coll (OR)
Tompkins Cortland Comm Coll (NY)
Tri-County Tech Coll (SC)
Trident Tech Coll (SC)
Trinidad State Jr Coll (CO)
Truckee Meadows Comm Coll (NV)
Tunxis Comm Coll (CT)
Umpqua Comm Coll (OR)
Union County Coll (NJ)
The U of Akron–Wayne Coll (OH)
U of Alaska Anchorage, Matanuska-Susitna Coll (AK)
U of Arkansas Comm Coll at Morrilton (AR)
U of Cincinnati Raymond Walters Coll (OH)
U of Northwestern Ohio (OH)
Valencia Comm Coll (FL)
Vatterott Coll, St. Joseph (MO)
Villa Maria Coll of Buffalo (NY)
Walla Walla Comm Coll (WA)
Walters State Comm Coll (TN)
Waubonsee Comm Coll (IL)
Wayne County Comm Coll District (MI)
West Central Tech Coll (GA)
Westchester Comm Coll (NY)
Western Nevada Comm Coll (NV)
Western Wyoming Comm Coll (WY)
West Kentucky Comm and Tech Coll (KY)
Westmoreland County Comm Coll (PA)
West Virginia U at Parkersburg (WV)
Whatcom Comm Coll (WA)
Williston State Coll (ND)
Wilson Tech Comm Coll (NC)
Wor-Wic Comm Coll (MD)
Yakima Valley Comm Coll (WA)
Yavapai Coll (AZ)
Yuba Coll (CA)

Adult Development and Aging
Comm Coll of Rhode Island (RI)

Lehigh Carbon Comm Coll (PA)
Southwestern Oregon Comm Coll (OR)

Advertising
Central Piedmont Comm Coll (NC)
Chattanooga State Tech Comm Coll (TN)
Daytona Beach Comm Coll (FL)
Edison State Comm Coll (OH)
Erie Business Center South (PA)
Fayetteville Tech Comm Coll (NC)
Highland Comm Coll (KS)
Long Beach City Coll (CA)
Mohawk Valley Comm Coll (NY)
Muskegon Comm Coll (MI)
Parkland Coll (IL)
Pasadena City Coll (CA)
Rockland Comm Coll (NY)
St. Cloud Tech Coll (MN)
St. Louis Comm Coll at Meramec (MO)
Santa Rosa Jr Coll (CA)
Surry Comm Coll (NC)
Yuba Coll (CA)

Aeronautical/Aerospace Engineering Technology
Calhoun Comm Coll (AL)
Cincinnati State Tech and Comm Coll (OH)
Fairmont State Comm & Tech Coll (WV)
GateWay Comm Coll (AZ)
Santa Rosa Jr Coll (CA)

Aeronautics/Aviation/ Aerospace Science and Technology
Alvin Comm Coll (TX)
Caldwell Comm Coll and Tech Inst (NC)
Comm Coll of Beaver County (PA)
Comm Coll of the Air Force (AL)
Delaware Tech & Comm Coll, Terry Cmps (DE)
Miami Dade Coll (FL)
Northland Comm and Tech Coll–Thief River Falls (MN)
Orange Coast Coll (CA)
Raritan Valley Comm Coll (NJ)
Texas State Tech Coll– Waco/Marshall Campus (TX)
Tompkins Cortland Comm Coll (NY)

Aerospace, Aeronautical and Astronautical Engineering
Kilgore Coll (TX)

Aesthetician/Esthetician and Skin Care
Colorado Northwestern Comm Coll (CO)
Olympic Coll (WA)

African-American/Black Studies
Atlanta Metropolitan Coll (GA)
Bronx Comm Coll of City U of NY (NY)
Compton Comm Coll (CA)
Contra Costa Coll (CA)
Nassau Comm Coll (NY)
Pasadena City Coll (CA)
St. Louis Comm Coll at Forest Park (MO)
San Diego City Coll (CA)
Santa Barbara City Coll (CA)
Solano Comm Coll (CA)
Yuba Coll (CA)

African Studies
Pasadena City Coll (CA)
Sinclair Comm Coll (OH)
Solano Comm Coll (CA)

Agribusiness
Black Hawk Coll, Moline (IL)
Clarendon Coll (TX)
Copiah-Lincoln Comm Coll (MS)
Crowder Coll (MO)
Eastern Arizona Coll (AZ)
Glendale Comm Coll (AZ)
Iowa Lakes Comm Coll (IA)
James Sprunt Comm Coll (NC)
Laramie County Comm Coll (WY)
Mineral Area Coll (MO)
Ohio State U Ag Tech Inst (OH)
South Central Tech Coll (MN)
Southwest Wisconsin Tech Coll (WI)
Yavapai Coll (AZ)

Agricultural and Food Products Processing
Texas State Tech Coll– Waco/Marshall Campus (TX)

Agricultural Business and Management
Arizona Western Coll (AZ)
Barton County Comm Coll (KS)
Bismarck State Coll (ND)
Blue Mountain Comm Coll (OR)
Brazosport Coll (TX)
Butler County Comm Coll (KS)
Casper Coll (WY)
Central Comm Coll– Columbus Campus (NE)
Central Comm Coll–Hastings Campus (NE)
Central Wyoming Coll (WY)
Clark State Comm Coll (OH)
Cloud County Comm Coll (KS)
Coastal Georgia Comm Coll (GA)
Coffeyville Comm Coll (KS)
Colby Comm Coll (KS)
Coll of Southern Idaho (ID)
Columbia State Comm Coll (TN)
Copiah-Lincoln Comm Coll (MS)
Cumberland County Coll (NJ)
Danville Area Comm Coll (IL)
Dawson Comm Coll (MT)
Delaware Tech & Comm Coll, Jack F Owens Cmps (DE)
Delta Coll (MI)
Des Moines Area Comm Coll (IA)
Dodge City Comm Coll (KS)
Ellsworth Comm Coll (IA)
Enterprise-Ozark Comm Coll (AL)
Fort Scott Comm Coll (KS)
Fox Valley Tech Coll (WI)
Frank Phillips Coll (TX)
Frederick Comm Coll (MD)
Garden City Comm Coll (KS)
Harrisburg Area Comm Coll (PA)
Hawkeye Comm Coll (IA)
Highland Comm Coll (IL)
Highland Comm Coll (KS)
Hinds Comm Coll (MS)
Illinois Eastern Comm Colls, Wabash Valley Coll (IL)
Illinois Valley Comm Coll (IL)
Indian River Comm Coll (FL)
Iowa Lakes Comm Coll (IA)
Iowa Western Comm Coll (IA)
Itawamba Comm Coll (MS)
Jackson State Comm Coll (TN)
Jefferson State Comm Coll (AL)
John Wood Comm Coll (IL)
Kaskaskia Coll (IL)

Lake Land Coll (IL)
Lake Region State Coll (ND)
Linn-Benton Comm Coll (OR)
Milwaukee Area Tech Coll (WI)
Modesto Jr Coll (CA)
North Central Missouri Coll (MO)
Ohio State U Ag Tech Inst (OH)
Otero Jr Coll (CO)
Owens Comm Coll, Toledo (OH)
Parkland Coll (IL)
Phillips Comm Coll of the U of Arkansas (AR)
Pratt Comm Coll and Area Vocational School (KS)
Richland Comm Coll (IL)
Riverside Comm Coll District (CA)
San Joaquin Delta Coll (CA)
Santa Rosa Jr Coll (CA)
Shawnee Comm Coll (IL)
Sheridan Coll (WY)
Snow Coll (UT)
Southwestern Comm Coll (IA)
State U of NY Coll of Technology at Alfred (NY)
Surry Comm Coll (NC)
Three Rivers Comm Coll (MO)
U of Northwestern Ohio (OH)
Walla Walla Comm Coll (WA)
Western Oklahoma State Coll (OK)
Yakima Valley Comm Coll (WA)
Yavapai Coll (AZ)
Yuba Coll (CA)

Agricultural Business and Management Related
Copiah-Lincoln Comm Coll (MS)
Iowa Lakes Comm Coll (IA)
North Dakota State Coll of Science (ND)
Penn State U Beaver Campus of the Commonwealth (PA)
Penn State U Delaware County Campus of the Commonwealth (PA)
Penn State U DuBois Campus of the Commonwealth (PA)
Penn State U Fayette Campus of the Commonwealth (PA)
Penn State U Hazleton Campus of the Commonwealth (PA)
Penn State U McKeesport Campus of the Commonwealth (PA)
Penn State U Mont Alto Campus of the Commonwealth (PA)
Penn State U New Kensington Campus of the Commonwealth (PA)
Penn State U Shenango Campus of the Commonwealth (PA)
Penn State U Wilkes-Barre Campus of the Commonwealth (PA)
Penn State U Worthington Scranton Cmps Commonwealth (PA)
Penn State U York Campus of the Commonwealth Coll (PA)

Agricultural Business Technology
Copiah-Lincoln Comm Coll (MS)
Iowa Lakes Comm Coll (IA)
Laramie County Comm Coll (WY)

North Iowa Area Comm Coll (IA)
Ohio State U Ag Tech Inst (OH)

Agricultural Communication/Journalism
Ohio State U Ag Tech Inst (OH)

Agricultural Economics
Clarendon Coll (TX)
Coffeyville Comm Coll (KS)
Colby Comm Coll (KS)
Copiah-Lincoln Comm Coll (MS)
Dodge City Comm Coll (KS)
Fort Scott Comm Coll (KS)
Frank Phillips Coll (TX)
Garden City Comm Coll (KS)
Highland Comm Coll (KS)
Hinds Comm Coll (MS)
Iowa Lakes Comm Coll (IA)
North Iowa Area Comm Coll (IA)
Ohio State U Ag Tech Inst (OH)
Pratt Comm Coll and Area Vocational School (KS)
Snow Coll (UT)

Agricultural/Farm Supplies Retailing and Wholesaling
Copiah-Lincoln Comm Coll (MS)
Iowa Lakes Comm Coll (IA)
Muscatine Comm Coll (IA)
North Dakota State Coll of Science (ND)
Western Iowa Tech Comm Coll (IA)

Agricultural Mechanics and Equipment Technology
Black Hawk Coll, Moline (IL)
Iowa Lakes Comm Coll (IA)

Agricultural Mechanization
American Samoa Comm Coll (AS)
Beaufort County Comm Coll (NC)
Black Hawk Coll, Moline (IL)
Casper Coll (WY)
Clark State Comm Coll (OH)
Coffeyville Comm Coll (KS)
Cowley County Comm Coll and Voc-Tech School (KS)
Delta Coll (MI)
Dodge City Comm Coll (KS)
Fort Peck Comm Coll (MT)
Fort Scott Comm Coll (KS)
Frank Phillips Coll (TX)
Garden City Comm Coll (KS)
Garrett Coll (MD)
Hawkeye Comm Coll (IA)
Highland Comm Coll (IL)
Hinds Comm Coll (MS)
Hutchinson Comm Coll and Area Vocational School (KS)
Indian Hills Comm Coll (IA)
Iowa Lakes Comm Coll (IA)
Lake Land Coll (IL)
Lane Comm Coll (OR)
Longview Comm Coll (MO)
Modesto Jr Coll (CA)
North Dakota State Coll of Science (ND)
Ohio State U Ag Tech Inst (OH)
Parkland Coll (IL)
Pratt Comm Coll and Area Vocational School (KS)
San Joaquin Delta Coll (CA)
Santa Rosa Jr Coll (CA)
South Central Tech Coll (MN)
Southwest Georgia Tech Coll (GA)
Southwest Wisconsin Tech Coll (WI)
Three Rivers Comm Coll (MO)
Walla Walla Comm Coll (WA)
Walters State Comm Coll (TN)

Yakima Valley Comm Coll (WA)
Yuba Coll (CA)

Agricultural Mechanization Related
Garden City Comm Coll (KS)

Agricultural Power Machinery Operation
Iowa Lakes Comm Coll (IA)
Ohio State U Ag Tech Inst (OH)

Agricultural Production
Allen County Comm Coll (KS)
Hillsborough Comm Coll (FL)
Illinois Eastern Comm Colls, Wabash Valley Coll (IL)
Iowa Lakes Comm Coll (IA)
John Wood Comm Coll (IL)
Lake Land Coll (IL)
Laramie County Comm Coll (WY)
Lincoln Land Comm Coll (IL)
Modesto Jr Coll (CA)
Muscatine Comm Coll (IA)
North Dakota State Coll of Science (ND)
North Iowa Area Comm Coll (IA)
South Central Tech Coll (MN)
Southern State Comm Coll (OH)
Walla Walla Comm Coll (WA)

Agricultural Production Related
Black Hawk Coll, Moline (IL)
Iowa Lakes Comm Coll (IA)
Northwestern Michigan Coll (MI)

Agricultural Teacher Education
American Samoa Comm Coll (AS)
Chemeketa Comm Coll (OR)
Coffeyville Comm Coll (KS)
Colby Comm Coll (KS)
Fort Scott Comm Coll (KS)
Frank Phillips Coll (TX)
Highland Comm Coll (KS)
Hinds Comm Coll (MS)
Iowa Lakes Comm Coll (IA)
Linn-Benton Comm Coll (OR)
Northwest-Shoals Comm Coll (AL)
Ohio State U Ag Tech Inst (OH)
Pratt Comm Coll and Area Vocational School (KS)
Trinity Valley Comm Coll (TX)

Agriculture
American Samoa Comm Coll (AS)
Andrew Coll (GA)
Arizona Western Coll (AZ)
Arkansas Northeastern Coll (AR)
Bainbridge Coll (GA)
Barton County Comm Coll (KS)
Calhoun Comm Coll (AL)
Casper Coll (WY)
Central Arizona Coll (AZ)
Central Texas Coll (TX)
Central Wyoming Coll (WY)
Chattahoochee Valley Comm Coll (AL)
Chipola Coll (FL)
Clarendon Coll (TX)
Clark State Comm Coll (OH)
Clover Park Tech Coll (WA)
Coastal Bend Coll (TX)
Cochise Coll, Douglas (AZ)
Coffeyville Comm Coll (KS)
Colby Comm Coll (KS)
Coll of Southern Idaho (ID)
Copiah-Lincoln Comm Coll (MS)
Cowley County Comm Coll and Voc-Tech School (KS)
Crowder Coll (MO)

Cumberland County Coll (NJ)
Danville Area Comm Coll (IL)
Darton Coll (GA)
Daytona Beach Comm Coll (FL)
Delta Coll (MI)
Dixie State Coll of Utah (UT)
Eastern Arizona Coll (AZ)
Fort Scott Comm Coll (KS)
Frank Phillips Coll (TX)
Frederick Comm Coll (MD)
Gainesville Coll (GA)
Garden City Comm Coll (KS)
Gordon Coll (GA)
Highland Comm Coll (KS)
Holmes Comm Coll (MS)
Houston Comm Coll System (TX)
Howard Coll (TX)
Hutchinson Comm Coll and Area Vocational School (KS)
Illinois Valley Comm Coll (IL)
Iowa Lakes Comm Coll (IA)
John A. Logan Coll (IL)
Kilgore Coll (TX)
Laramie County Comm Coll (WY)
Linn-Benton Comm Coll (OR)
Macomb Comm Coll (MI)
Miami Dade Coll (FL)
Modesto Jr Coll (CA)
Napa Valley Coll (CA)
North Idaho Coll (ID)
Odessa Coll (TX)
Owensboro Comm and Tech Coll (KY)
Pratt Comm Coll and Area Vocational School (KS)
San Joaquin Delta Coll (CA)
Santa Rosa Jr Coll (CA)
Seward County Comm Coll (KS)
Shawnee Comm Coll (IL)
Sheridan Coll (WY)
Snow Coll (UT)
State U of NY Coll of Technology at Alfred (NY)
Umpqua Comm Coll (OR)
Williston State Coll (ND)
Yakima Valley Comm Coll (WA)
Yavapai Coll (AZ)
Yuba Coll (CA)

Agronomy and Crop Science
American Samoa Comm Coll (AS)
Chipola Coll (FL)
Colby Comm Coll (KS)
Cowley County Comm Coll and Voc-Tech School (KS)
Dodge City Comm Coll (KS)
Fort Scott Comm Coll (KS)
Frank Phillips Coll (TX)
Hawkeye Comm Coll (IA)
Highland Comm Coll (KS)
Hinds Comm Coll (MS)
Iowa Lakes Comm Coll (IA)
Modesto Jr Coll (CA)
Ohio State U Ag Tech Inst (OH)
Shawnee Comm Coll (IL)
Snow Coll (UT)
Southern Maine Comm Coll (ME)
Yakima Valley Comm Coll (WA)
Yuba Coll (CA)

Aircraft Powerplant Technology
Central Texas Coll (TX)
Colorado Northwestern Comm Coll (CO)
Columbus State Comm Coll (OH)
Florida Comm Coll at Jacksonville (FL)
Linn State Tech Coll (MO)
Minneapolis Comm and Tech Coll (MN)

Aircraft Powerplant Technology

North Central Inst (TN)
Pima Comm Coll (AZ)
St. Philip's Coll (TX)
San Joaquin Valley Coll (CA)
Texas State Tech Coll–
Waco/Marshall Campus
(TX)

Airframe Mechanics and Aircraft Maintenance Technology
Amarillo Coll (TX)
Chandler-Gilbert Comm Coll
(AZ)
Cochise Coll, Douglas (AZ)
Colorado Northwestern
Comm Coll (CO)
Columbus State Comm Coll
(OH)
Comm Coll of the Air Force
(AL)
Cowley County Comm Coll
and Voc-Tech School (KS)
Enterprise-Ozark Comm Coll
(AL)
Florida Comm Coll at
Jacksonville (FL)
Glendale Comm Coll (CA)
Hawkeye Comm Coll (IA)
Ivy Tech State Coll–Wabash
Valley (IN)
Johnson County Comm Coll
(KS)
Minneapolis Comm and Tech
Coll (MN)
Mohawk Valley Comm Coll
(NY)
North Central Inst (TN)
St. Philip's Coll (TX)
Salt Lake Comm Coll (UT)
San Diego Miramar Coll (CA)
San Joaquin Valley Coll (CA)
Solano Comm Coll (CA)
Southwestern Michigan Coll
(MI)
Texas State Tech Coll–
Waco/Marshall Campus
(TX)
Trident Tech Coll (SC)

Airline Pilot and Flight Crew
Academy Coll (MN)
Big Bend Comm Coll (WA)
Broward Comm Coll (FL)
Casper Coll (WY)
Central Florida Comm Coll
(FL)
Central Texas Coll (TX)
Chattanooga State Tech
Comm Coll (TN)
Clover Park Tech Coll (WA)
Cochise Coll, Douglas (AZ)
Colorado Northwestern
Comm Coll (CO)
Comm Coll of Allegheny
County (PA)
Comm Coll of Beaver County
(PA)
Compton Comm Coll (CA)
Dixie State Coll of Utah (UT)
Florida Comm Coll at
Jacksonville (FL)
Fox Valley Tech Coll (WI)
Frank Phillips Coll (TX)
Glendale Comm Coll (CA)
Green River Comm Coll
(WA)
Guilford Tech Comm Coll
(NC)
Indian Hills Comm Coll (IA)
Indian River Comm Coll (FL)
Iowa Central Comm Coll (IA)
Iowa Lakes Comm Coll (IA)
Jackson Comm Coll (MI)
Jamestown Comm Coll (NY)
Lake Superior Coll (MN)
Lane Comm Coll (OR)
Lansing Comm Coll (MI)
Lehigh Carbon Comm Coll
(PA)
Long Beach City Coll (CA)
Miami Dade Coll (FL)
Midland Coll (TX)
Northern Virginia Comm Coll
(VA)

North Shore Comm Coll
(MA)
Northwestern Michigan Coll
(MI)
Orange Coast Coll (CA)
Palm Beach Comm Coll (FL)
Pasadena City Coll (CA)
Salt Lake Comm Coll (UT)
San Juan Coll (NM)
Scott Comm Coll (IA)
Texas State Tech Coll–
Waco/Marshall Campus
(TX)
Western Oklahoma State
Coll (OK)

Air Traffic Control
Cecil Comm Coll (MD)
Comm Coll of Beaver County
(PA)
Comm Coll of the Air Force
(AL)
Green River Comm Coll
(WA)
Miami Dade Coll (FL)

Allied Health and Medical Assisting Services Related
Cincinnati State Tech and
Comm Coll (OH)
Florida National Coll (FL)

Allied Health Diagnostic, Intervention, and Treatment Professions Related
Harcum Coll (PA)
Oakland Comm Coll (MI)
Union County Coll (NJ)

American Indian/Native American Studies
Blackfeet Comm Coll (MT)
Central Wyoming Coll (WY)
Fort Peck Comm Coll (MT)
Itasca Comm Coll (MN)
Lac Courte Oreilles Ojibwa
Comm Coll (WI)
Nebraska Indian Comm Coll
(NE)
North Idaho Coll (ID)
Pima Comm Coll (AZ)
Santa Barbara City Coll (CA)
Sisseton-Wahpeton Comm
Coll (SD)

American Sign Language (Asl)
Fairmont State Comm &
Tech Coll (WV)

American Studies
Anne Arundel Comm Coll
(MD)
Bucks County Comm Coll
(PA)
Foothill Coll (CA)
Greenfield Comm Coll (MA)
Holyoke Comm Coll (MA)
Miami Dade Coll (FL)
Tacoma Comm Coll (WA)

Anatomy
Fayetteville Tech Comm Coll
(NC)
Frank Phillips Coll (TX)
Riverside Comm Coll District
(CA)

Animal Health
Santa Rosa Jr Coll (CA)

Animal/Livestock Husbandry and Production
Black Hawk Coll, Moline (IL)
Feather River Coll (CA)
Hopkinsville Comm Coll (KY)
Iowa Lakes Comm Coll (IA)
Iowa Western Comm Coll
(IA)
John Wood Comm Coll (IL)
Ohio State U Ag Tech Inst
(OH)
Pratt Comm Coll and Area
Vocational School (KS)

Animal Physiology
Santa Rosa Jr Coll (CA)
Snow Coll (UT)

Animal Sciences
Alamance Comm Coll (NC)
Black Hawk Coll, Moline (IL)
Blue Mountain Comm Coll
(OR)
Casper Coll (WY)
Coffeyville Comm Coll (KS)
Colby Comm Coll (KS)
Dodge City Comm Coll (KS)
Everett Comm Coll (WA)
Fort Scott Comm Coll (KS)
Harcum Coll (PA)
Hawkeye Comm Coll (IA)
Highland Comm Coll (KS)
Iowa Lakes Comm Coll (IA)
James Sprunt Comm Coll
(NC)
Linn-Benton Comm Coll
(OR)
Modesto Jr Coll (CA)
Niagara County Comm Coll
(NY)
Ohio State U Ag Tech Inst
(OH)
Pratt Comm Coll and Area
Vocational School (KS)
San Joaquin Delta Coll (CA)
Shawnee Comm Coll (IL)
Snow Coll (UT)
State U of NY Coll of
Technology at Alfred (NY)
Trinity Valley Comm Coll
(TX)
Yakima Valley Comm Coll
(WA)
Yuba Coll (CA)

Animal Sciences Related
Front Range Comm Coll
(CO)

Animation, Interactive Technology, Video Graphics and Special Effects
The Art Inst of New York City
(NY)
Delaware Coll of Art and
Design (DE)
Kent State U, Tuscarawas
Campus (OH)
Olympic Coll (WA)
Platt Coll San Diego (CA)

Anthropology
Barton County Comm Coll
(KS)
Casper Coll (WY)
Cochise Coll, Douglas (AZ)
Coll of Southern Idaho (ID)
Columbia Coll (CA)
Comm Coll of Southern
Nevada (NV)
Contra Costa Coll (CA)
Darton Coll (GA)
Daytona Beach Comm Coll
(FL)
Delaware County Comm Coll
(PA)
East Central Coll (MO)
Eastern Arizona Coll (AZ)
Everett Comm Coll (WA)
Foothill Coll (CA)
Gainesville Coll (GA)
Great Basin Coll (NV)
Gulf Coast Comm Coll (FL)
Indian River Comm Coll (FL)
Laramie County Comm Coll
(WY)
Lower Columbia Coll (WA)
Miami Dade Coll (FL)
Midland Coll (TX)
Muskegon Comm Coll (MI)
North Idaho Coll (ID)
Orange Coast Coll (CA)
Pasadena City Coll (CA)
Pima Comm Coll (AZ)
Riverside Comm Coll District
(CA)
San Diego City Coll (CA)
San Diego Miramar Coll (CA)
San Joaquin Delta Coll (CA)
San Juan Coll (NM)
Santa Barbara City Coll (CA)
Santa Rosa Jr Coll (CA)
Tacoma Comm Coll (WA)

Umpqua Comm Coll (OR)
Western Wyoming Comm
Coll (WY)

Apparel and Accessories Marketing
Fashion Inst of Design &
Merchandising, LA
Campus (CA)
Fashion Inst of Design &
Merchandising, SD
Campus (CA)
Fashion Inst of Design &
Merchandising, SF
Campus (CA)

Apparel and Textile Marketing Management
Comm Coll of the Air Force
(AL)
Delta Coll (MI)

Apparel and Textiles
Fashion Inst of Design &
Merchandising, LA
Campus (CA)
Fashion Inst of Design &
Merchandising, SF
Campus (CA)
Modesto Jr Coll (CA)

Applied Art
Anne Arundel Comm Coll
(MD)
The Art Inst of Philadelphia
(PA)
Bristol Comm Coll (MA)
Casper Coll (WY)
Centralia Coll (WA)
Central Piedmont Comm Coll
(NC)
Chattanooga State Tech
Comm Coll (TN)
Coastal Bend Coll (TX)
Coffeyville Comm Coll (KS)
Delta Coll (MI)
Glendale Comm Coll (CA)
Henry Ford Comm Coll (MI)
Howard Comm Coll (MD)
Iowa Lakes Comm Coll (IA)
Kingsborough Comm Coll of
City U of NY (NY)
Muskegon Comm Coll (MI)
Northern Virginia Comm Coll
(VA)
Odessa Coll (TX)
Pratt Comm Coll and Area
Vocational School (KS)
Rockland Comm Coll (NY)
Sinclair Comm Coll (OH)
Tunxis Comm Coll (CT)
Westchester Comm Coll
(NY)

Applied Horticulture
Alamance Comm Coll (NC)
Arkansas Northeastern Coll
(AR)
Brunswick Comm Coll (NC)
Central Comm Coll–Hastings
Campus (NE)
Clark Coll (WA)
Comm Coll of Allegheny
County (PA)
Fayetteville Tech Comm Coll
(NC)
Front Range Comm Coll
(CO)
Glendale Comm Coll (AZ)
John Wood Comm Coll (IL)
Kaskaskia Coll (IL)
Mineral Area Coll (MO)
North Shore Comm Coll
(MA)
Oakland Comm Coll (MI)
Santa Barbara City Coll (CA)
Wilkes Comm Coll (NC)

Applied Horticulture/ Horticultural Business Services Related
Central Florida Comm Coll
(FL)
Cincinnati State Tech and
Comm Coll (OH)

Applied Mathematics
Muskegon Comm Coll (MI)
San Diego Miramar Coll (CA)

Aquaculture
Brunswick Comm Coll (NC)
Hillsborough Comm Coll (FL)
Yavapai Coll (AZ)

Archeology
East Central Coll (MO)
Pima Comm Coll (AZ)
Western Wyoming Comm
Coll (WY)

Architectural Drafting
Coll of Lake County (IL)
Luna Comm Coll (NM)
West Virginia State Comm
and Tech Coll (WV)

Architectural Drafting and Cad/Cadd
Albuquerque Tech Vocational
Inst (NM)
Butler County Comm Coll
(PA)
Clinton Comm Coll (IA)
Commonwealth Tech Inst
(PA)
Comm Coll of Allegheny
County (PA)
Dixie State Coll of Utah (UT)
Florida Comm Coll at
Jacksonville (FL)
Glendale Comm Coll (AZ)
Indian River Comm Coll (FL)
Kaskaskia Coll (IL)
Lake Superior Coll (MN)
Lincoln Land Comm Coll (IL)
Macomb Comm Coll (MI)
Miami Dade Coll (FL)
Montgomery County Comm
Coll (PA)
North Hennepin Comm Coll
(MN)
Pima Comm Coll (AZ)
St. Cloud Tech Coll (MN)
South Central Tech Coll (MN)
Spencerian Coll–Lexington
(KY)
Westwood Coll–Denver
North (CO)
Yavapai Coll (AZ)

Architectural Engineering Technology
Amarillo Coll (TX)
Anne Arundel Comm Coll
(MD)
Arapahoe Comm Coll (CO)
Broward Comm Coll (FL)
Butler County Comm Coll
(PA)
Cape Fear Comm Coll (NC)
Catawba Valley Comm Coll
(NC)
Central Piedmont Comm Coll
(NC)
Cincinnati State Tech and
Comm Coll (OH)
City Colls of Chicago, Wilbur
Wright Coll (IL)
Clover Park Tech Coll (WA)
Coastal Carolina Comm Coll
(NC)
Columbus State Comm Coll
(OH)
Comm Coll of Beaver County
(PA)
Comm Coll of Philadelphia
(PA)
Daytona Beach Comm Coll
(FL)
Delaware County Comm Coll
(PA)
Delaware Tech & Comm
Coll, Jack F Owens Cmps
(DE)
Delaware Tech & Comm
Coll, Stanton/ Wilmington
Cmps (DE)
Delaware Tech & Comm
Coll, Terry Cmps (DE)
Delta Coll (MI)
Doña Ana Branch Comm
Coll (NM)

Durham Tech Comm Coll
(NC)
Dutchess Comm Coll (NY)
El Paso Comm Coll (TX)
Erie Comm Coll, South
Campus (NY)
Essex County Coll (NJ)
Fairmont State Comm &
Tech Coll (WV)
Fayetteville Tech Comm Coll
(NC)
Finger Lakes Comm Coll
(NY)
Florida Comm Coll at
Jacksonville (FL)
Forsyth Tech Comm Coll
(NC)
Fort Scott Comm Coll (KS)
Front Range Comm Coll
(CO)
Grand Rapids Comm Coll
(MI)
Guam Comm Coll (GU)
Guilford Tech Comm Coll
(NC)
Harrisburg Area Comm Coll
(PA)
Hawkeye Comm Coll (IA)
Hillsborough Comm Coll (FL)
Iowa Western Comm Coll
(IA)
John Tyler Comm Coll (VA)
J. Sargeant Reynolds Comm
Coll (VA)
Lake Land Coll (IL)
Lansing Comm Coll (MI)
Long Beach City Coll (CA)
Metropolitan Comm Coll
(NE)
Miami Dade Coll (FL)
Midlands Tech Coll (SC)
Modesto Jr Coll (CA)
Mott Comm Coll (MI)
Nashville State Tech Comm
Coll (TN)
Northampton County Area
Comm Coll (PA)
North Dakota State Coll of
Science (ND)
Northern Virginia Comm Coll
(VA)
Northland Comm and Tech
Coll–Thief River Falls (MN)
Northwest Tech Coll (MN)
Oakland Comm Coll (MI)
Orange Coast Coll (CA)
Orange County Comm Coll
(NY)
Pasadena City Coll (CA)
Pennsylvania Inst of
Technology (PA)
Penn State U Fayette
Campus of the
Commonwealth Coll (PA)
Penn State U Worthington
Scranton Cmps
Commonwealth Coll (PA)
Ranken Tech Coll (MO)
Roanoke-Chowan Comm
Coll (NC)
St. Cloud Tech Coll (MN)
St. Louis Comm Coll at
Meramec (MO)
St. Petersburg Coll (FL)
Salt Lake Comm Coll (UT)
Sandhills Comm Coll (NC)
Seminole Comm Coll (FL)
Sinclair Comm Coll (OH)
Southeast Comm Coll,
Milford Campus (NE)
Southeast Tech Inst (SD)
Southern Maine Comm Coll
(ME)
Spartanburg Tech Coll (SC)
Springfield Tech Comm Coll
(MA)
State U of NY Coll of
Technology at Alfred (NY)
State U of NY Coll of
Technology at Delhi (NY)
Thaddeus Stevens Coll of
Technology (PA)
Three Rivers Comm Coll
(CT)

Triangle Tech, Inc.–Pittsburgh School (PA)
Truckee Meadows Comm Coll (NV)
Wake Tech Comm Coll (NC)
Western Iowa Tech Comm Coll (IA)
Westmoreland County Comm Coll (PA)
Wilkes Comm Coll (NC)

Architectural Technology
City Colls of Chicago, Wilbur Wright Coll (IL)
Columbus State Comm Coll (OH)

Architecture
Allen County Comm Coll (KS)
Barton County Comm Coll (KS)
Brazosport Coll (TX)
Brookdale Comm Coll (NJ)
Copiah-Lincoln Comm Coll (MS)
Harrisburg Area Comm Coll (PA)
Howard Comm Coll (MD)
Oakland Comm Coll (MI)
Riverside Comm Coll District (CA)
Sauk Valley Comm Coll (IL)

Army R.O.T.C./Military Science
New Mexico Military Inst (NM)

Art
Alabama Southern Comm Coll (AL)
Allen County Comm Coll (KS)
Alvin Comm Coll (TX)
Amarillo Coll (TX)
Andrew Coll (GA)
Anne Arundel Comm Coll (MD)
Arizona Western Coll (AZ)
The Art Inst of Philadelphia (PA)
Asnuntuck Comm Coll (CT)
Atlanta Metropolitan Coll (GA)
Austin Comm Coll (TX)
Bainbridge Coll (GA)
Barton County Comm Coll (KS)
Bergen Comm Coll (NJ)
Blue Ridge Comm Coll (NC)
Brazosport Coll (TX)
Bronx Comm Coll of City U of NY (NY)
Brookdale Comm Coll (NJ)
Bucks County Comm Coll (PA)
Bunker Hill Comm Coll (MA)
Butler County Comm Coll (KS)
Caldwell Comm Coll and Tech Inst (NC)
Cape Cod Comm Coll (MA)
Casper Coll (WY)
Cecil Comm Coll (MD)
Centralia Coll (WA)
Central Oregon Comm Coll (OR)
Central Piedmont Comm Coll (NC)
Central Wyoming Coll (WY)
Cerro Coso Comm Coll (CA)
Chipola Coll (FL)
Citrus Coll (CA)
City Colls of Chicago, Wilbur Wright Coll (IL)
Cloud County Comm Coll (KS)
Coahoma Comm Coll (MS)
Coastal Bend Coll (TX)
Coastal Georgia Comm Coll (GA)
Cochise Coll, Douglas (AZ)
Coffeyville Comm Coll (KS)
Coll of Lake County (IL)
Coll of Southern Idaho (ID)
Coll of the Canyons (CA)

Colorado Mountn Coll (CO)
Colorado Mountn Coll, Timberline Cmps (CO)
Colorado Northwestern Comm Coll (CO)
Columbia Coll (CA)
Columbia-Greene Comm Coll (NY)
Columbia State Comm Coll (TN)
Comm Coll of Allegheny County (PA)
Comm Coll of Philadelphia (PA)
Comm Coll of Rhode Island (RI)
Comm Coll of Southern Nevada (NV)
Compton Comm Coll (CA)
Contra Costa Coll (CA)
Cowley County Comm Coll and Voc-Tech School (KS)
Crowder Coll (MO)
Danville Area Comm Coll (IL)
Darton Coll (GA)
Daytona Beach Comm Coll (FL)
De Anza Coll (CA)
Dixie State Coll of Utah (UT)
Dodge City Comm Coll (KS)
East Central Coll (MO)
East Central Comm Coll (MS)
Eastern Arizona Coll (AZ)
East Mississippi Comm Coll (MS)
Edison State Comm Coll (OH)
Elgin Comm Coll (IL)
Ellsworth Comm Coll (IA)
El Paso Comm Coll (TX)
Essex County Coll (NJ)
Everett Comm Coll (WA)
Foothill Coll (CA)
Frank Phillips Coll (TX)
Frederick Comm Coll (MD)
Fulton-Montgomery Comm Coll (NY)
Gainesville Coll (GA)
Garrett Coll (MD)
Glendale Comm Coll (CA)
Gordon Coll (GA)
Grand Rapids Comm Coll (MI)
Great Basin Coll (NV)
Greenfield Comm Coll (MA)
Gulf Coast Comm Coll (FL)
Harrisburg Area Comm Coll (PA)
Henry Ford Comm Coll (MI)
Herkimer County Comm Coll (NY)
Highland Comm Coll (IL)
Highland Comm Coll (KS)
Highline Comm Coll (WA)
Hillsborough Comm Coll (FL)
Hinds Comm Coll (MS)
Howard Coll (TX)
Howard Comm Coll (MD)
Inst of American Indian Arts (NM)
Iowa Lakes Comm Coll (IA)
Itawamba Comm Coll (MS)
John A. Logan Coll (IL)
Keystone Coll (PA)
Kilgore Coll (TX)
Kingsborough Comm Coll of City U of NY (NY)
Lansing Comm Coll (MI)
Laramie County Comm Coll (WY)
Lehigh Carbon Comm Coll (PA)
Lewis and Clark Comm Coll (IL)
Lincoln Land Comm Coll (IL)
Linn-Benton Comm Coll (OR)
Long Beach City Coll (CA)
Lower Columbia Coll (WA)
Miami Dade Coll (FL)
Midland Coll (TX)
Mid Michigan Comm Coll (MI)

Modesto Jr Coll (CA)
Mohave Comm Coll (AZ)
Mohawk Valley Comm Coll (NY)
Montgomery County Comm Coll (PA)
Mount Wachusett Comm Coll (MA)
Muskegon Comm Coll (MI)
Napa Valley Coll (CA)
Nassau Comm Coll (NY)
New Mexico Military Inst (NM)
Northern Virginia Comm Coll (VA)
North Idaho Coll (ID)
North Seattle Comm Coll (WA)
Northwestern Connecticut Comm-Tech Coll (CT)
Northwestern Michigan Coll (MI)
Northwest-Shoals Comm Coll (AL)
Odessa Coll (TX)
Orange Coast Coll (CA)
Palm Beach Comm Coll (FL)
Parkland Coll (IL)
Pasadena City Coll (CA)
Phillips Comm Coll of the U of Arkansas (AR)
Piedmont Virginia Comm Coll (VA)
Pima Comm Coll (AZ)
Platt Coll San Diego (CA)
Pratt Comm Coll and Area Vocational School (KS)
Quinebaug Valley Comm Coll (CT)
Riverside Comm Coll District (CA)
Rockingham Comm Coll (NC)
Rockland Comm Coll (NY)
St. Louis Comm Coll at Forest Park (MO)
St. Louis Comm Coll at Meramec (MO)
St. Philip's Coll (TX)
Salt Lake Comm Coll (UT)
Sandhills Comm Coll (NC)
San Diego City Coll (CA)
San Diego Miramar Coll (CA)
San Joaquin Delta Coll (CA)
San Juan Coll (NM)
Santa Rosa Jr Coll (CA)
Sauk Valley Comm Coll (IL)
Seminole State Coll (OK)
Seward County Comm Coll (KS)
Sheridan Coll (WY)
Sinclair Comm Coll (OH)
Snow Coll (UT)
Solano Comm Coll (CA)
South Mountain Comm Coll (AZ)
Tacoma Comm Coll (WA)
Taft Coll (CA)
Temple Coll (TX)
Trinity Valley Comm Coll (TX)
Tunxis Comm Coll (CT)
Umpqua Comm Coll (OR)
Walters State Comm Coll (TN)
Waubonsee Comm Coll (IL)
Western Wyoming Comm Coll (WY)
Yuba Coll (CA)

Art History, Criticism and Conservation
De Anza Coll (CA)
Dixie State Coll of Utah (UT)
Foothill Coll (CA)
Glendale Comm Coll (CA)
Iowa Lakes Comm Coll (IA)
Muskegon Comm Coll (MI)
Northern Virginia Comm Coll (VA)
Palm Beach Comm Coll (FL)
Pasadena City Coll (CA)
Rogue Comm Coll (OR)
Santa Barbara City Coll (CA)
Umpqua Comm Coll (OR)

Artificial Intelligence and Robotics
Cecil Comm Coll (MD)
Chattanooga State Tech Comm Coll (TN)
Cumberland County Coll (NJ)
Des Moines Area Comm Coll (IA)
Dutchess Comm Coll (NY)
Henry Ford Comm Coll (MI)
Indian Hills Comm Coll (IA)
Metropolitan Comm Coll-Business & Technology College (MO)
Raritan Valley Comm Coll (NJ)
St. Louis Comm Coll at Forest Park (MO)
San Diego City Coll (CA)
Sinclair Comm Coll (OH)
Southeast Tech Inst (SD)
Wake Tech Comm Coll (NC)
Westmoreland County Comm Coll (PA)

Art Teacher Education
Chemeketa Comm Coll (OR)
Coastal Bend Coll (TX)
Compton Comm Coll (CA)
Copiah-Lincoln Comm Coll (MS)
Delta Coll (MI)
East Central Comm Coll (MS)
Eastern Arizona Coll (AZ)
Ellsworth Comm Coll (IA)
Frank Phillips Coll (TX)
Gainesville Coll (GA)
Halifax Comm Coll (NC)
Independence Comm Coll (KS)
Indian River Comm Coll (FL)
Iowa Lakes Comm Coll (IA)
Itawamba Comm Coll (MS)
John A. Logan Coll (IL)
McLennan Comm Coll (TX)
Miami Dade Coll (FL)
Muskegon Comm Coll (MI)
Parkland Coll (IL)
Pratt Comm Coll and Area Vocational School (KS)
Sandhills Comm Coll (NC)
Shelton State Comm Coll (AL)
Trinidad State Jr Coll (CO)
Umpqua Comm Coll (OR)
Walters State Comm Coll (TN)
Waubonsee Comm Coll (IL)
Western Oklahoma State Coll (OK)

Asian Studies
Miami Dade Coll (FL)
Pima Comm Coll (AZ)

Astronomy
Anne Arundel Comm Coll (MD)
Austin Comm Coll (TX)
Daytona Beach Comm Coll (FL)
Iowa Lakes Comm Coll (IA)
North Idaho Coll (ID)
Pasadena City Coll (CA)
Riverside Comm Coll District (CA)
Santa Rosa Jr Coll (CA)

Athletic Training
Allen County Comm Coll (KS)
Andrew Coll (GA)
Barton County Comm Coll (KS)
Coffeyville Comm Coll (KS)
Comm Coll of Allegheny County (PA)
Dodge City Comm Coll (KS)
Foothill Coll (CA)
Fort Scott Comm Coll (KS)
Frank Phillips Coll (TX)
Front Range Comm Coll (CO)
Garden City Comm Coll (KS)
Highland Comm Coll (KS)

Independence Comm Coll (KS)
Iowa Lakes Comm Coll (IA)
Meridian Comm Coll (MS)
New Hampshire Comm Tech Coll, Manchester/Stratham (NH)
North Idaho Coll (ID)
Northland Comm and Tech Coll–Thief River Falls (MN)
Odessa Coll (TX)
Orange Coast Coll (CA)
Pratt Comm Coll and Area Vocational School (KS)
Santa Barbara City Coll (CA)
Santa Rosa Jr Coll (CA)
Sauk Valley Comm Coll (IL)
Seward County Comm Coll (KS)
Southwestern Oregon Comm Coll (OR)

Atmospheric Sciences and Meteorology
Comm Coll of the Air Force (AL)
Daytona Beach Comm Coll (FL)
Everett Comm Coll (WA)
Santa Rosa Jr Coll (CA)

Audio Engineering
Brookdale Comm Coll (NJ)
Full Sail Real World Education (FL)
Harford Comm Coll (MD)
International Coll of Broadcasting (OH)
Shoreline Comm Coll (WA)
Texas State Tech Coll–Waco/Marshall Campus (TX)

Audiology and Hearing Sciences
Arkansas State U–Mountain Home (AR)

Audiovisual Communications Technologies Related
Olympic Coll (WA)

Autobody/Collision and Repair Technology
Bismarck State Coll (ND)
Black Hawk Coll, Moline (IL)
Central Comm Coll–Hastings Campus (NE)
Century Coll (MN)
Clackamas Comm Coll (OR)
Coll of Southern Idaho (ID)
Dixie State Coll of Utah (UT)
Eastfield Coll (TX)
Erie Comm Coll, South Campus (NY)
Fayetteville Tech Comm Coll (NC)
Florida Comm Coll at Jacksonville (FL)
Green River Comm Coll (WA)
Hawkeye Comm Coll (IA)
Hutchinson Comm Coll and Area Vocational School (KS)
Illinois Eastern Comm Colls, Olney Central Coll (IL)
Iowa Lakes Comm Coll (IA)
Kaskaskia Coll (IL)
Kauai Comm Coll (HI)
Laramie County Comm Coll (WY)
Linn State Tech Coll (MO)
Manhattan Area Tech Coll (KS)
Modesto Jr Coll (CA)
Mott Comm Coll (MI)
North Dakota State Coll of Science (ND)
Northwest Tech Coll (MN)
Parkland Coll (IL)
Prairie State Coll (IL)
Ranken Tech Coll (MO)
Riverland Comm Coll (MN)
St. Cloud Tech Coll (MN)
St. Philip's Coll (TX)

San Juan Coll (NM)
Scott Comm Coll (IA)
Somerset Comm Coll (KY)
South Central Tech Coll (MN)
Southeast Tech Inst (SD)
Southwestern Comm Coll (IA)
Southwest Wisconsin Tech Coll (WI)
Stanly Comm Coll (NC)
State U of NY Coll of Technology at Alfred (NY)
Texas State Tech Coll–Waco/Marshall Campus (TX)
Walla Walla Comm Coll (WA)
Waubonsee Comm Coll (IL)
Western Iowa Tech Comm Coll (IA)

Automobile/Automotive Mechanics Technology
Alamance Comm Coll (NC)
Allegany Coll of Maryland (MD)
Alpena Comm Coll (MI)
Amarillo Coll (TX)
American Samoa Comm Coll (AS)
Arapahoe Comm Coll (CO)
Arizona Western Coll (AZ)
Asheville-Buncombe Tech Comm Coll (NC)
Athens Tech Coll (GA)
Austin Comm Coll (TX)
Bainbridge Coll (GA)
Barton County Comm Coll (KS)
Bay de Noc Comm Coll (MI)
Beaufort County Comm Coll (NC)
Bergen Comm Coll (NJ)
Bessemer State Tech Coll (AL)
Big Bend Comm Coll (WA)
Bismarck State Coll (ND)
Blue Mountain Comm Coll (OR)
Brazosport Coll (TX)
Brookdale Comm Coll (NJ)
Broward Comm Coll (FL)
Butler County Comm Coll (KS)
Cape Fear Comm Coll (NC)
Casper Coll (WY)
Catawba Valley Comm Coll (NC)
Cedar Valley Coll (TX)
Central Arizona Coll (AZ)
Central Carolina Comm Coll (NC)
Central Comm Coll–Columbus Campus (NE)
Central Comm Coll–Grand Island Campus (NE)
Central Comm Coll–Hastings Campus (NE)
Central Oregon Comm Coll (OR)
Central Piedmont Comm Coll (NC)
Central Texas Coll (TX)
Central Wyoming Coll (WY)
Century Coll (MN)
Cerro Coso Comm Coll (CA)
Chattahoochee Tech Coll (GA)
Chattanooga State Tech Comm Coll (TN)
Chemeketa Comm Coll (OR)
Citrus Coll (CA)
Clackamas Comm Coll (OR)
Clark Coll (WA)
Clover Park Tech Coll (WA)
Clovis Comm Coll (NM)
Coastal Bend Coll (TX)
Coffeyville Comm Coll (KS)
Coll of DuPage (IL)
Coll of Lake County (IL)
Coll of Southern Idaho (ID)
Columbia Coll (CA)
Columbia-Greene Comm Coll (NY)
Columbus State Comm Coll (OH)

Comm & Tech Coll at West Virginia U Inst of Technology (WV)
Comm and Tech Coll of Shepherd (WV)
Comm Coll of Aurora (CO)
Comm Coll of Philadelphia (PA)
Comm Coll of Southern Nevada (NV)
Comm Coll of the Air Force (AL)
Compton Comm Coll (CA)
Contra Costa Coll (CA)
Corning Comm Coll (NY)
Cossatot Comm Coll of the U of Arkansas (AR)
Cowley County Comm Coll and Voc-Tech School (KS)
Craven Comm Coll (NC)
Cuyahoga Comm Coll (OH)
Danville Area Comm Coll (IL)
Dawson Comm Coll (MT)
Daytona Beach Comm Coll (FL)
De Anza Coll (CA)
DeKalb Tech Coll (GA)
Delaware County Comm Coll (PA)
Delaware Tech & Comm Coll, Jack F Owens Cmps (DE)
Delta Coll (MI)
Des Moines Area Comm Coll (IA)
Dixie State Coll of Utah (UT)
Dodge City Comm Coll (KS)
Doña Ana Branch Comm Coll (NM)
Durham Tech Comm Coll (NC)
East Central Coll (MO)
Eastern Arizona Coll (AZ)
Eastern Idaho Tech Coll (ID)
Eastern Maine Comm Coll (ME)
Eastfield Coll (TX)
East Mississippi Comm Coll (MS)
Elgin Comm Coll (IL)
El Paso Comm Coll (TX)
Enterprise-Ozark Comm Coll (AL)
Erie Comm Coll, South Campus (NY)
Fayetteville Tech Comm Coll (NC)
Florida Comm Coll at Jacksonville (FL)
Forsyth Tech Comm Coll (NC)
Fort Peck Comm Coll (MT)
Fox Valley Tech Coll (WI)
Front Range Comm Coll (CO)
Fulton-Montgomery Comm Coll (NY)
Gainesville Coll (GA)
Garden City Comm Coll (KS)
GateWay Comm Coll (AZ)
Gateway Comm Coll (CT)
George C. Wallace Comm Coll (AL)
Glendale Comm Coll (AZ)
Glen Oaks Comm Coll (MI)
Gogebic Comm Coll (MI)
Grand Rapids Comm Coll (MI)
Green River Comm Coll (WA)
Guam Comm Coll (GU)
Guilford Tech Comm Coll (NC)
Gwinnett Tech Coll (GA)
Harrisburg Area Comm Coll (PA)
Hawkeye Comm Coll (IA)
Henry Ford Comm Coll (MI)
Highland Comm Coll (IL)
Highland Comm Coll (KS)
Houston Comm Coll System (TX)
Howard Coll (TX)

Hudson Valley Comm Coll (NY)
Hutchinson Comm Coll and Area Vocational School (KS)
Illinois Eastern Comm Colls, Olney Central Coll (IL)
Illinois Valley Comm Coll (IL)
Indian Hills Comm Coll (IA)
Indian River Comm Coll (FL)
Iowa Central Comm Coll (IA)
Iowa Lakes Comm Coll (IA)
Iowa Western Comm Coll (IA)
Isothermal Comm Coll (NC)
Ivy Tech State Coll–Central Indiana (IN)
Ivy Tech State Coll–Columbus (IN)
Ivy Tech State Coll–Eastcentral (IN)
Ivy Tech State Coll–Kokomo (IN)
Ivy Tech State Coll–Lafayette (IN)
Ivy Tech State Coll–North Central (IN)
Ivy Tech State Coll–Northeast (IN)
Ivy Tech State Coll–Northwest (IN)
Ivy Tech State Coll–Southcentral (IN)
Ivy Tech State Coll–Southwest (IN)
Ivy Tech State Coll–Wabash Valley (IN)
Ivy Tech State Coll–Whitewater (IN)
Jackson Comm Coll (MI)
John A. Logan Coll (IL)
Johnson County Comm Coll (KS)
Kalamazoo Valley Comm Coll (MI)
Kaskaskia Coll (IL)
Kauai Comm Coll (HI)
Kilgore Coll (TX)
Lake Land Coll (IL)
Lake Region State Coll (ND)
Lake Superior Coll (MN)
Lane Comm Coll (OR)
Lansing Comm Coll (MI)
Laramie County Comm Coll (WY)
Lewis and Clark Comm Coll (IL)
Lincoln Land Comm Coll (IL)
Linn-Benton Comm Coll (OR)
Linn State Tech Coll (MO)
Long Beach City Coll (CA)
Longview Comm Coll (MO)
Lower Columbia Coll (WA)
Macomb Comm Coll (MI)
Manhattan Area Tech Coll (KS)
McDowell Tech Comm Coll (NC)
Metropolitan Comm Coll (NE)
Midland Coll (TX)
Midlands Tech Coll (SC)
Mid Michigan Comm Coll (MI)
Milwaukee Area Tech Coll (WI)
Minneapolis Comm and Tech Coll (MN)
Minnesota State Coll–Southeast Tech (MN)
Modesto Jr Coll (CA)
Mohave Comm Coll (AZ)
Montgomery Comm Coll (NC)
Moraine Valley Comm Coll (IL)
Mott Comm Coll (MI)
Mount Wachusett Comm Coll (MA)
Muskegon Comm Coll (MI)
Nashville State Tech Comm Coll (TN)

New Hampshire Comm Tech Coll, Manchester/Stratham (NH)
North Central Missouri Coll (MO)
North Dakota State Coll of Science (ND)
Northeast State Tech Comm Coll (TN)
Northern Virginia Comm Coll (VA)
North Hennepin Comm Coll (MN)
North Idaho Coll (ID)
North Iowa Area Comm Coll (IA)
Northland Comm and Tech Coll–Thief River Falls (MN)
Northwestern Michigan Coll (MI)
Northwest Tech Coll (MN)
Oakland Comm Coll (MI)
Odessa Coll (TX)
Olympic Coll (WA)
Otero Jr Coll (CO)
Ouachita Tech Coll (AR)
Parkland Coll (IL)
Pasadena City Coll (CA)
Peninsula Coll (WA)
Phillips Comm Coll of the U of Arkansas (AR)
Piedmont Virginia Comm Coll (VA)
Pima Comm Coll (AZ)
Prairie State Coll (IL)
Pratt Comm Coll and Area Vocational School (KS)
Randolph Comm Coll (NC)
Ranken Tech Coll (MO)
Raritan Valley Comm Coll (NJ)
Richland Comm Coll (IL)
Roanoke-Chowan Comm Coll (NC)
Rockland Comm Coll (NY)
Rock Valley Coll (IL)
Rogue Comm Coll (OR)
Rowan-Cabarrus Comm Coll (NC)
St. Cloud Tech Coll (MN)
St. Louis Comm Coll at Forest Park (MO)
St. Philip's Coll (TX)
Salt Lake Comm Coll (UT)
Sandhills Comm Coll (NC)
San Diego City Coll (CA)
San Diego Miramar Coll (CA)
San Joaquin Delta Coll (CA)
San Juan Coll (NM)
Santa Barbara City Coll (CA)
Santa Fe Comm Coll (FL)
Scott Comm Coll (IA)
Seminole Comm Coll (FL)
Shawnee Comm Coll (IL)
Shelton State Comm Coll (AL)
Shoreline Comm Coll (WA)
Sinclair Comm Coll (OH)
Snow Coll (UT)
Solano Comm Coll (CA)
Somerset Comm Coll (KY)
South Central Tech Coll (MN)
Southeast Comm Coll, Lincoln Campus (NE)
Southeast Comm Coll, Milford Campus (NE)
Southeast Tech Inst (SD)
Southern Maine Comm Coll (ME)
South Texas Coll (TX)
Southwestern Comm Coll (IA)
Southwestern Comm Coll (NC)
Southwestern Michigan Coll (MI)
Southwest Wisconsin Tech Coll (WI)
Spartanburg Tech Coll (SC)
State U of NY Coll of Technology at Alfred (NY)
State U of NY Coll of Technology at Canton (NY)
Surry Comm Coll (NC)

Taft Coll (CA)
Tech Coll of the Lowcountry (SC)
Temple Coll (TX)
Texas State Tech Coll–Waco/Marshall Campus (TX)
Thaddeus Stevens Coll of Technology (PA)
Tri-County Comm Coll (NC)
Trident Tech Coll (SC)
Trinidad State Jr Coll (CO)
Trinity Valley Comm Coll (TX)
Truckee Meadows Comm Coll (NV)
Umpqua Comm Coll (OR)
U of Arkansas Comm Coll at Morrilton (AR)
U of Cincinnati Raymond Walters Coll (OH)
U of Northwestern Ohio (OH)
Walla Walla Comm Coll (WA)
Waubonsee Comm Coll (IL)
Wayne County Comm Coll District (MI)
Westchester Comm Coll (NY)
Western Iowa Tech Comm Coll (IA)
Western Nevada Comm Coll (NV)
Western Tech Coll (TX)
Western Wyoming Comm Coll (WY)
West Virginia U at Parkersburg (WV)
Westwood Coll–Denver North (CO)
Wilkes Comm Coll (NC)
Williston State Coll (ND)
Yakima Valley Comm Coll (WA)
Yavapai Coll (AZ)
Yuba Coll (CA)

Automotive Engineering Technology
Central Florida Comm Coll (FL)
Cincinnati State Tech and Comm Coll (OH)
Comm & Tech Coll at West Virginia U Inst of Technology (WV)
Comm Coll of Allegheny County (PA)
Corning Comm Coll (NY)
Harrisburg Area Comm Coll (PA)
Macomb Comm Coll (MI)
Massachusetts Bay Comm Coll (MA)
Montgomery County Comm Coll (PA)
Northampton County Area Comm Coll (PA)
Owens Comm Coll, Toledo (OH)
Springfield Tech Comm Coll (MA)
Sussex County Comm Coll (NJ)

Aviation/Airway Management
Academy Coll (MN)
Broward Comm Coll (FL)
Chattanooga State Tech Comm Coll (TN)
Comm Coll of Allegheny County (PA)
Delaware Tech & Comm Coll, Terry Cmps (DE)
Dixie State Coll of Utah (UT)
Florida Comm Coll at Jacksonville (FL)
Glendale Comm Coll (CA)
Guilford Tech Comm Coll (NC)
Iowa Central Comm Coll (IA)
Iowa Lakes Comm Coll (IA)
Lehigh Carbon Comm Coll (PA)
Long Beach City Coll (CA)

Miami Dade Coll (FL)
Northland Comm and Tech Coll–Thief River Falls (MN)
Oakland Comm Coll (MI)
Pasadena City Coll (CA)
Sinclair Comm Coll (OH)
Western Oklahoma State Coll (OK)

Avionics Maintenance Technology
Big Bend Comm Coll (WA)
Black River Tech Coll (AR)
Broward Comm Coll (FL)
Chandler-Gilbert Comm Coll (AZ)
Chattanooga State Tech Comm Coll (TN)
Cloud County Comm Coll (KS)
Clover Park Tech Coll (WA)
Cochise Coll, Douglas (AZ)
Columbus State Comm Coll (OH)
Comm Coll of Beaver County (PA)
Comm Coll of the Air Force (AL)
Cumberland County Coll (NJ)
Cuyahoga Comm Coll (OH)
Delaware Tech & Comm Coll, Terry Cmps (DE)
Delta Coll (MI)
Enterprise-Ozark Comm Coll (AL)
Everett Comm Coll (WA)
Foothill Coll (CA)
Frederick Comm Coll (MD)
Gateway Comm Coll (CT)
Glendale Comm Coll (CA)
Guilford Tech Comm Coll (NC)
Hawkeye Comm Coll (IA)
Hinds Comm Coll (MS)
Indian Hills Comm Coll (IA)
Iowa Western Comm Coll (IA)
Lake Region State Coll (ND)
Lane Comm Coll (OR)
Lansing Comm Coll (MI)
Lehigh Carbon Comm Coll (PA)
Long Beach City Coll (CA)
Maple Woods Comm Coll (MO)
Minneapolis Comm and Tech Coll (MN)
Minnesota State Coll–Southeast Tech (MN)
Northern Virginia Comm Coll (VA)
Northland Comm and Tech Coll–Thief River Falls (MN)
Orange Coast Coll (CA)
Pasadena City Coll (CA)
Quinebaug Valley Comm Coll (CT)
Rock Valley Coll (IL)
Salt Lake Comm Coll (UT)
San Diego Miramar Coll (CA)
Solano Comm Coll (CA)
Somerset Comm Coll (KY)
Texas State Tech Coll–Waco/Marshall Campus (TX)
Three Rivers Comm Coll (CT)
Wayne County Comm Coll District (MI)
Western Oklahoma State Coll (OK)

Baking and Pastry Arts
Clark Coll (WA)
Coll of DuPage (IL)
Milwaukee Area Tech Coll (WI)
Montgomery County Comm Coll (PA)

Banking and Financial Support Services
Adirondack Comm Coll (NY)
Alamance Comm Coll (NC)

Albuquerque Tech Vocational Inst (NM)
Alexandria Tech Coll (MN)
Allen County Comm Coll (KS)
Barton County Comm Coll (KS)
Black Hawk Coll, Moline (IL)
Bristol Comm Coll (MA)
Bucks County Comm Coll (PA)
Catawba Valley Comm Coll (NC)
Comm Coll of Allegheny County (PA)
Comm Coll of Rhode Island (RI)
Delaware Tech & Comm Coll, Stanton/Wilmington Cmps (DE)
Eastern Maine Comm Coll (ME)
East Mississippi Comm Coll (MS)
Finger Lakes Comm Coll (NY)
Florida Comm Coll at Jacksonville (FL)
Harrisburg Area Comm Coll (PA)
Indian River Comm Coll (FL)
Jefferson State Comm Coll (AL)
Lackawanna Coll (PA)
Lanier Tech Coll (GA)
Laurel Business Inst (PA)
Mineral Area Coll (MO)
Modesto Jr Coll (CA)
Mohawk Valley Comm Coll (NY)
Northampton County Area Comm Coll (PA)
Northwest Tech Coll (MN)
Pennsylvania Highland Comm Coll (PA)
Pima Comm Coll (AZ)
St. Cloud Tech Coll (MN)
San Juan Coll (NM)
Seminole Comm Coll (FL)
Southwestern Oregon Comm Coll (OR)
Waubonsee Comm Coll (IL)
West Virginia State Comm and Tech Coll (WV)

Barbering
Milwaukee Area Tech Coll (WI)
Olympic Coll (WA)

Behavioral Sciences
Adirondack Comm Coll (NY)
Amarillo Coll (TX)
Anne Arundel Comm Coll (MD)
Casper Coll (WY)
Citrus Coll (CA)
Clarendon Coll (TX)
Cloud County Comm Coll (KS)
Cochise Coll, Douglas (AZ)
Coffeyville Comm Coll (KS)
Colby Comm Coll (KS)
Colorado Mountn Coll, Alpine Cmps (CO)
Colorado Mountn Coll (CO)
Colorado Mountn Coll, Timberline Cmps (CO)
Comm Coll of Southern Nevada (NV)
Compton Comm Coll (CA)
Daytona Beach Comm Coll (FL)
De Anza Coll (CA)
Dodge City Comm Coll (KS)
East Central Comm Coll (MS)
Fulton-Montgomery Comm Coll (NY)
Garrett Coll (MD)
Gordon Coll (GA)
Greenfield Comm Coll (MA)
Highline Comm Coll (WA)
Howard Coll (TX)
Iowa Lakes Comm Coll (IA)

Miami Dade Coll (FL)
Midland Coll (TX)
Modesto Jr Coll (CA)
Napa Valley Coll (CA)
Northwestern Connecticut Comm-Tech Coll (CT)
Orange Coast Coll (CA)
San Diego City Coll (CA)
San Joaquin Delta Coll (CA)
Santa Rosa Jr Coll (CA)
Seminole State Coll (OK)
South Texas Coll (TX)
Tacoma Comm Coll (WA)
Umpqua Comm Coll (OR)
Western Oklahoma State Coll (OK)
West Virginia State Comm and Tech Coll (WV)

Biblical Studies
Amarillo Coll (TX)
Hesston Coll (KS)

Bilingual and Multilingual Education
Blackfeet Comm Coll (MT)
Clovis Comm Coll (NM)

Biochemical Technology
Mid Michigan Comm Coll (MI)
Niagara County Comm Coll (NY)
U of Cincinnati Raymond Walters Coll (OH)

Biological and Biomedical Sciences Related
Northampton County Area Comm Coll (PA)

Biological and Physical Sciences
Adirondack Comm Coll (NY)
Andrew Coll (GA)
Anne Arundel Comm Coll (MD)
Arapahoe Comm Coll (CO)
Arizona Western Coll (AZ)
Baltimore City Comm Coll (MD)
Borough of Manhattan Comm Coll of City U of NY (NY)
Bowling Green State U-Firelands Coll (OH)
Brookdale Comm Coll (NJ)
Caldwell Comm Coll and Tech Inst (NC)
Cape Cod Comm Coll (MA)
Casper Coll (WY)
Centralia Coll (WA)
Central Oregon Comm Coll (OR)
Chipola Coll (FL)
City Colls of Chicago, Wilbur Wright Coll (IL)
Cleveland Comm Coll (NC)
Clinton Comm Coll (NY)
Cloud County Comm Coll (KS)
Coastal Bend Coll (TX)
Coconino Comm Coll (AZ)
Coffeyville Comm Coll (KS)
Colby Comm Coll (KS)
Coll of DuPage (IL)
Coll of Lake County (IL)
Coll of the Canyons (CA)
Colorado Mountn Coll, Alpine Cmps (CO)
Colorado Mountn Coll (CO)
Colorado Mountn Coll, Timberline Cmps (CO)
Columbia-Greene Comm Coll (NY)
Comm Coll of Aurora (CO)
Comm Coll of Philadelphia (PA)
Comm Coll of Rhode Island (RI)
Comm Coll of Southern Nevada (NV)
Compton Comm Coll (CA)
Copiah-Lincoln Comm Coll (MS)
Corning Comm Coll (NY)

Cumberland County Coll (NJ)
Dabney S. Lancaster Comm Coll (VA)
Danville Area Comm Coll (IL)
Danville Comm Coll (VA)
Daytona Beach Comm Coll (FL)
Delaware County Comm Coll (PA)
Dodge City Comm Coll (KS)
Dutchess Comm Coll (NY)
East Central Comm Coll (MS)
Eastern Shore Comm Coll (VA)
East Mississippi Comm Coll (MS)
Elgin Comm Coll (IL)
Elizabethtown Comm and Tech Coll (KY)
Ellsworth Comm Coll (IA)
Enterprise-Ozark Comm Coll (AL)
Finger Lakes Comm Coll (NY)
Frank Phillips Coll (TX)
Fulton-Montgomery Comm Coll (NY)
Gainesville Coll (GA)
Garden City Comm Coll (KS)
Germanna Comm Coll (VA)
Glendale Comm Coll (CA)
Glen Oaks Comm Coll (MI)
Gordon Coll (GA)
Greenfield Comm Coll (MA)
Guilford Tech Comm Coll (NC)
Heartland Comm Coll (IL)
Highland Comm Coll (IL)
Highline Comm Coll (WA)
Howard Comm Coll (MD)
Illinois Eastern Comm Colls, Frontier Comm Coll (IL)
Illinois Eastern Comm Colls, Lincoln Trail Coll (IL)
Illinois Eastern Comm Colls, Olney Central Coll (IL)
Illinois Eastern Comm Colls, Wabash Valley Coll (IL)
Independence Comm Coll (KS)
Iowa Central Comm Coll (IA)
Iowa Lakes Comm Coll (IA)
Isothermal Comm Coll (NC)
Itawamba Comm Coll (MS)
John Wood Comm Coll (IL)
J. Sargeant Reynolds Comm Coll (VA)
Kaskaskia Coll (IL)
Kilgore Coll (TX)
Lake Land Coll (IL)
Lansing Comm Coll (MI)
Laramie County Comm Coll (WY)
Lewis and Clark Comm Coll (IL)
Lincoln Land Comm Coll (IL)
Linn-Benton Comm Coll (OR)
Longview Comm Coll (MO)
Maple Woods Comm Coll (MO)
Massachusetts Bay Comm Coll (MA)
Mid Michigan Comm Coll (MI)
Moraine Valley Comm Coll (IL)
Napa Valley Coll (CA)
New Mexico Military Inst (NM)
New River Comm and Tech Coll (WV)
Niagara County Comm Coll (NY)
North Country Comm Coll (NY)
Northeast Alabama Comm Coll (AL)
Northern Essex Comm Coll (MA)
Northern Virginia Comm Coll (VA)

North Idaho Coll (ID)
Orange County Comm Coll (NY)
Otero Jr Coll (CO)
Parkland Coll (IL)
Pasadena City Coll (CA)
Patrick Henry Comm Coll (VA)
Peninsula Coll (WA)
Penn State U Beaver Campus of the Commonwealth Coll (PA)
Penn State U DuBois Campus of the Commonwealth Coll (PA)
Penn State U McKeesport Campus of the Commonwealth Coll (PA)
Penn State U New Kensington Campus of the Commonwealth Coll (PA)
Penn State U Shenango Campus of the Commonwealth Coll (PA)
Penn Valley Comm Coll (MO)
Phillips Comm Coll of the U of Arkansas (AR)
Piedmont Virginia Comm Coll (VA)
Pratt Comm Coll and Area Vocational School (KS)
Rainy River Comm Coll (MN)
Richland Comm Coll (IL)
Riverside Comm Coll District (CA)
Rockingham Comm Coll (NC)
Rockland Comm Coll (NY)
Rogue Comm Coll (OR)
St. Louis Comm Coll at Meramec (MO)
San Antonio Coll (TX)
Sandhills Comm Coll (NC)
Seattle Central Comm Coll (WA)
Seward County Comm Coll (KS)
Shawnee Comm Coll (IL)
Sheridan Coll (WY)
Solano Comm Coll (CA)
Southside Virginia Comm Coll (VA)
Southwestern Oregon Comm Coll (OR)
Spartanburg Tech Coll (SC)
State U of NY Coll of Technology at Alfred (NY)
State U of NY Coll of Technology at Canton (NY)
Sussex County Comm Coll (NJ)
Tacoma Comm Coll (WA)
Tech Coll of the Lowcountry (SC)
Tompkins Cortland Comm Coll (NY)
Trident Tech Coll (SC)
Trinidad State Jr Coll (CO)
Umpqua Comm Coll (OR)
U of South Carolina at Union (SC)
U of Wisconsin Center–Richland (WI)
Waubonsee Comm Coll (IL)
Westchester Comm Coll (NY)
Western Wyoming Comm Coll (WY)
Yuba Coll (CA)

Biology/Biological Sciences
Adirondack Comm Coll (NY)
Alabama Southern Comm Coll (AL)
Allen County Comm Coll (KS)
Alpena Comm Coll (MI)
Alvin Comm Coll (TX)
Amarillo Coll (TX)
Ancilla Coll (IN)
Andrew Coll (GA)
Anne Arundel Comm Coll (MD)
Arizona Western Coll (AZ)

Atlanta Metropolitan Coll (GA)
Atlantic Cape Comm Coll (NJ)
Austin Comm Coll (TX)
Bainbridge Coll (GA)
Barton County Comm Coll (KS)
Bergen Comm Coll (NJ)
Brazosport Coll (TX)
Bronx Comm Coll of City U of NY (NY)
Bucks County Comm Coll (PA)
Butler County Comm Coll (KS)
Butler County Comm Coll (PA)
Calhoun Comm Coll (AL)
Casper Coll (WY)
Cecil Comm Coll (MD)
Centralia Coll (WA)
Central Piedmont Comm Coll (NC)
Central Texas Coll (TX)
Central Wyoming Coll (WY)
Chattahoochee Valley Comm Coll (AL)
Chattanooga State Tech Comm Coll (TN)
Citrus Coll (CA)
Clarendon Coll (TX)
Cloud County Comm Coll (KS)
Coahoma Comm Coll (MS)
Coastal Bend Coll (TX)
Coastal Georgia Comm Coll (GA)
Cochise Coll, Douglas (AZ)
Coffeyville Comm Coll (KS)
Colby Comm Coll (KS)
Coll of Southern Idaho (ID)
Coll of the Canyons (CA)
Colorado Mountn Coll, Alpine Cmps (CO)
Colorado Mountn Coll (CO)
Colorado Mountn Coll, Timberline Cmps (CO)
Columbia Coll (CA)
Columbia State Comm Coll (TN)
Comm Coll of Allegheny County (PA)
Comm Coll of Beaver County (PA)
Comm Coll of Southern Nevada (NV)
Compton Comm Coll (CA)
Contra Costa Coll (CA)
Copiah-Lincoln Comm Coll (MS)
Crowder Coll (MO)
Danville Area Comm Coll (IL)
Darton Coll (GA)
Daytona Beach Comm Coll (FL)
De Anza Coll (CA)
Delta Coll (MI)
Dixie State Coll of Utah (UT)
Dodge City Comm Coll (KS)
East Central Coll (MO)
East Central Comm Coll (MS)
Eastern Arizona Coll (AZ)
Ellsworth Comm Coll (IA)
El Paso Comm Coll (TX)
Essex County Coll (NJ)
Everett Comm Coll (WA)
Feather River Coll (CA)
Finger Lakes Comm Coll (NY)
Foothill Coll (CA)
Frank Phillips Coll (TX)
Frederick Comm Coll (MD)
Fulton-Montgomery Comm Coll (NY)
Gainesville Coll (GA)
Garrett Coll (MD)
Gogebic Comm Coll (MI)
Gordon Coll (GA)
Gulf Coast Comm Coll (FL)
Harrisburg Area Comm Coll (PA)
Hawkeye Comm Coll (IA)

Highland Comm Coll (KS)
Hinds Comm Coll (MS)
Holmes Comm Coll (MS)
Holyoke Comm Coll (MA)
Howard Coll (TX)
Hutchinson Comm Coll and Area Vocational School (KS)
Independence Comm Coll (KS)
Indian River Comm Coll (FL)
Iowa Lakes Comm Coll (IA)
Itawamba Comm Coll (MS)
John A. Logan Coll (IL)
Kennebec Valley Comm Coll (ME)
Keystone Coll (PA)
Kingsborough Comm Coll of City U of NY (NY)
Kingwood Coll (TX)
Lansing Comm Coll (MI)
Laramie County Comm Coll (WY)
Lehigh Carbon Comm Coll (PA)
Lewis and Clark Comm Coll (IL)
Linn-Benton Comm Coll (OR)
Long Beach City Coll (CA)
Longview Comm Coll (MO)
Lower Columbia Coll (WA)
Macomb Comm Coll (MI)
Maple Woods Comm Coll (MO)
Miami Dade Coll (FL)
Midland Coll (TX)
Mid Michigan Comm Coll (MI)
Modesto Jr Coll (CA)
Montgomery County Comm Coll (PA)
New Mexico Military Inst (NM)
Northampton County Area Comm Coll (PA)
North Idaho Coll (ID)
Northwestern Connecticut Comm-Tech Coll (CT)
Northwestern Michigan Coll (MI)
Odessa Coll (TX)
Orange Coast Coll (CA)
Orange County Comm Coll (NY)
Otero Jr Coll (CO)
Palm Beach Comm Coll (FL)
Pasadena City Coll (CA)
Penn Valley Comm Coll (MO)
Phillips Comm Coll of the U of Arkansas (AR)
Pratt Comm Coll and Area Vocational School (KS)
Raritan Valley Comm Coll (NJ)
St. Louis Comm Coll at Forest Park (MO)
St. Philip's Coll (TX)
Salt Lake Comm Coll (UT)
San Diego City Coll (CA)
San Diego Miramar Coll (CA)
San Joaquin Delta Coll (CA)
San Juan Coll (NM)
Santa Barbara City Coll (CA)
Santa Rosa Jr Coll (CA)
Sauk Valley Comm Coll (IL)
Seminole State Coll (OK)
Seward County Comm Coll (KS)
Shelton State Comm Coll (AL)
Sheridan Coll (WY)
Snow Coll (UT)
Solano Comm Coll (CA)
South Mountain Comm Coll (AZ)
Springfield Tech Comm Coll (MA)
Tacoma Comm Coll (WA)
Taft Coll (CA)
Trinidad State Jr Coll (CO)
Trinity Valley Comm Coll (TX)

Umpqua Comm Coll (OR)
Union County Coll (NJ)
U of Cincinnati Raymond Walters Coll (OH)
Western Nevada Comm Coll (NV)
Western Oklahoma State Coll (OK)
Western Wyoming Comm Coll (WY)
Yuba Coll (CA)

Biology/Biotechnology Laboratory Technician
Athens Tech Coll (GA)
Collin County Comm Coll District (TX)
Contra Costa Coll (CA)
Des Moines Area Comm Coll (IA)
Ellsworth Comm Coll (IA)
Finger Lakes Comm Coll (NY)
Foothill Coll (CA)
Guilford Tech Comm Coll (NC)
Indian Hills Comm Coll (IA)
Jefferson Comm Coll (NY)
John Tyler Comm Coll (VA)
Lansing Comm Coll (MI)
Massachusetts Bay Comm Coll (MA)
Mid Michigan Comm Coll (MI)
Muskegon Comm Coll (MI)
North Shore Comm Coll (MA)
Ohio State U Ag Tech Inst (OH)
Seattle Central Comm Coll (WA)
Shoreline Comm Coll (WA)
State U of NY Coll of Technology at Alfred (NY)

Biomedical Technology
Alabama Southern Comm Coll (AL)
Caldwell Comm Coll and Tech Inst (NC)
Chattahoochee Tech Coll (GA)
Cincinnati State Tech and Comm Coll (OH)
Comm Coll of Philadelphia (PA)
Comm Coll of the Air Force (AL)
Delaware County Comm Coll (PA)
Delaware Tech & Comm Coll, Stanton/ Wilmington Cmps (DE)
ECPI Coll of Technology, Virginia Beach (VA)
Erie Comm Coll, South Campus (NY)
Florida Comm Coll at Jacksonville (FL)
Gateway Comm Coll (CT)
George Corley Wallace State Comm Coll (AL)
Hillsborough Comm Coll (FL)
Howard Comm Coll (MD)
Jefferson State Comm Coll (AL)
Lehigh Carbon Comm Coll (PA)
Miami Dade Coll (FL)
Milwaukee Area Tech Coll (WI)
Muskegon Comm Coll (MI)
Napa Valley Coll (CA)
North Seattle Comm Coll (WA)
Northwest Tech Coll (MN)
Parkland Coll (IL)
Penn State U Beaver Campus of the Commonwealth Coll (PA)
Penn State U DuBois Campus of the Commonwealth Coll (PA)

Penn State U Fayette
Campus of the
Commonwealth Coll (PA)
Penn State U Hazleton
Campus of the
Commonwealth Coll (PA)
Penn State U New
Kensington Campus of the
Commonwealth Coll (PA)
Penn State U Shenango
Campus of the
Commonwealth Coll (PA)
Penn State U York Campus
of the Commonwealth Coll
(PA)
Rowan-Cabarrus Comm Coll
(NC)
St. Louis Comm Coll at
Forest Park (MO)
St. Philip's Coll (TX)
Santa Barbara City Coll (CA)
Santa Fe Comm Coll (FL)
Savannah Tech Coll (GA)
Schoolcraft Coll (MI)
Southeast Tech Inst (SD)
Stanly Comm Coll (NC)
Texas State Tech Coll–
Waco/Marshall Campus
(TX)
Western Iowa Tech Comm
Coll (IA)

Biotechnology
Alamance Comm Coll (NC)
Albuquerque Tech Vocational
Inst (NM)
Bladen Comm Coll (NC)
Briarwood Coll (CT)
Dixie State Coll of Utah (UT)
Howard Comm Coll (MD)
Lackawanna Coll (PA)
Lehigh Carbon Comm Coll
(PA)
Montgomery County Comm
Coll (PA)
Santa Barbara City Coll (CA)
Sinclair Comm Coll (OH)
Springfield Tech Comm Coll
(MA)

Boilermaking
Ivy Tech State Coll–
Southwest (IN)

Botany/Plant Biology
Anne Arundel Comm Coll
(MD)
Casper Coll (WY)
Centralia Coll (WA)
Coffeyville Comm Coll (KS)
Coll of Southern Idaho (ID)
Dixie State Coll of Utah (UT)
East Central Coll (MO)
Everett Comm Coll (WA)
Frank Phillips Coll (TX)
Iowa Lakes Comm Coll (IA)
North Idaho Coll (ID)
Palm Beach Comm Coll (FL)
Riverside Comm Coll District
(CA)
San Joaquin Delta Coll (CA)
Santa Rosa Jr Coll (CA)
Snow Coll (UT)
Southern Maine Comm Coll
(ME)
Tacoma Comm Coll (WA)

Broadcast Journalism
Adirondack Comm Coll (NY)
Amarillo Coll (TX)
Anne Arundel Comm Coll
(MD)
Arizona Western Coll (AZ)
Bergen Comm Coll (NJ)
Centralia Coll (WA)
Chattanooga State Tech
Comm Coll (TN)
Cloud County Comm Coll
(KS)
Coffeyville Comm Coll (KS)
Colby Comm Coll (KS)
Cumberland County Coll
(NJ)
Delta Coll (MI)
Dixie State Coll of Utah (UT)
Dodge City Comm Coll (KS)
El Paso Comm Coll (TX)

Finger Lakes Comm Coll
(NY)
Herkimer County Comm Coll
(NY)
Iowa Central Comm Coll (IA)
Iowa Lakes Comm Coll (IA)
Isothermal Comm Coll (NC)
Kingsborough Comm Coll of
City U of NY (NY)
Lane Comm Coll (OR)
Lansing Comm Coll (MI)
Meridian Comm Coll (MS)
Mount Wachusett Comm Coll
(MA)
Northland Comm and Tech
Coll–Thief River Falls (MN)
Pasadena City Coll (CA)
Pratt Comm Coll and Area
Vocational School (KS)
St. Louis Comm Coll at
Meramec (MO)
San Joaquin Delta Coll (CA)
Sussex County Comm Coll
(NJ)
Trident Tech Coll (SC)
Yakima Valley Comm Coll
(WA)

**Building/Construction
Finishing, Management, and
Inspection Related**
Albuquerque Tech Vocational
Inst (NM)
Guilford Tech Comm Coll
(NC)
Manhattan Area Tech Coll
(KS)
Pima Comm Coll (AZ)
Wilkes Comm Coll (NC)

**Building/Construction Site
Management**
Metropolitan Comm
Coll-Business &
Technology College (MO)
Ohio State U Ag Tech Inst
(OH)

**Building/Home/Construction
Inspection**
Arapahoe Comm Coll (CO)
Iowa Western Comm Coll
(IA)
Modesto Jr Coll (CA)
Orange Coast Coll (CA)

**Building/Property
Maintenance and
Management**
Coll of DuPage (IL)
Comm Coll of Allegheny
County (PA)
Delaware County Comm Coll
(PA)
Erie Comm Coll (NY)
Illinois Eastern Comm Colls,
Lincoln Trail Coll (IL)
Ivy Tech State Coll–
Bloomington (IN)
Ivy Tech State Coll–Central
Indiana (IN)
Ivy Tech State Coll–
Columbus (IN)
Ivy Tech State Coll–
Eastcentral (IN)
Ivy Tech State Coll–Kokomo
(IN)
Ivy Tech State Coll–Lafayette
(IN)
Ivy Tech State Coll–North
Central (IN)
Ivy Tech State Coll–
Northeast (IN)
Ivy Tech State Coll–
Northwest (IN)
Ivy Tech State Coll–
Southcentral (IN)
Ivy Tech State Coll–
Southwest (IN)
Ivy Tech State Coll–Wabash
Valley (IN)
Ivy Tech State Coll–
Whitewater (IN)
Mohawk Valley Comm Coll
(NY)
Pima Comm Coll (AZ)

**Business Administration
and Management**
Academy Coll (MN)
Adirondack Comm Coll (NY)
Alabama Southern Comm
Coll (AL)
Alamance Comm Coll (NC)
Alexandria Tech Coll (MN)
Allegany Coll of Maryland
(MD)
Allen County Comm Coll
(KS)
Alpena Comm Coll (MI)
Alvin Comm Coll (TX)
Amarillo Coll (TX)
American Samoa Comm Coll
(AS)
Ancilla Coll (IN)
Andover Coll (ME)
Andrew Coll (GA)
Anne Arundel Comm Coll
(MD)
Anoka-Ramsey Comm Coll
(MN)
Anoka-Ramsey Comm Coll,
Cambridge Campus (MN)
Arapahoe Comm Coll (CO)
Arizona Western Coll (AZ)
Asheville-Buncombe Tech
Comm Coll (NC)
Ashland Comm and Tech
Coll (KY)
Asnuntuck Comm Coll (CT)
Atlanta Metropolitan Coll
(GA)
Atlantic Cape Comm Coll
(NJ)
Austin Comm Coll (TX)
Bainbridge Coll (GA)
Baltimore City Comm Coll
(MD)
Barton County Comm Coll
(KS)
Bay de Noc Comm Coll (MI)
Bay Mills Comm Coll (MI)
Bay State Coll (MA)
Beaufort County Comm Coll
(NC)
Belmont Tech Coll (OH)
Bergen Comm Coll (NJ)
Berkeley Coll (NJ)
Berkeley Coll-New York City
Campus (NY)
Berkeley Coll-Westchester
Campus (NY)
Berkshire Comm Coll (MA)
Bevill State Comm Coll (AL)
Big Sandy Comm and Tech
Coll (KY)
Blackfeet Comm Coll (MT)
Black Hawk Coll, Moline (IL)
Black River Tech Coll (AR)
Bladen Comm Coll (NC)
Blue Mountain Comm Coll
(OR)
Blue Ridge Comm Coll (NC)
Blue Ridge Comm Coll (VA)
Blue River Comm Coll (MO)
Borough of Manhattan
Comm Coll of City U of NY
(NY)
Bossier Parish Comm Coll
(LA)
Brazosport Coll (TX)
Brevard Comm Coll (FL)
Briarwood Coll (CT)
Bristol Comm Coll (MA)
Bronx Comm Coll of City U of
NY (NY)
Brookdale Comm Coll (NJ)
Broome Comm Coll (NY)
Broward Comm Coll (FL)
Brown Mackie Coll, Findlay
Campus (OH)
Brown Mackie Coll, Michigan
City Campus (IN)
Brown Mackie Coll, Northern
Kentucky Campus (KY)
Brunswick Comm Coll (NC)
Bryant & Stratton Business
Inst, Albany (NY)

Bryant and Stratton Coll,
Parma (OH)
Bucks County Comm Coll
(PA)
Bunker Hill Comm Coll (MA)
Business Inst of
Pennsylvania, Sharon (PA)
Butler County Comm Coll
(KS)
Butler County Comm Coll
(PA)
Caldwell Comm Coll and
Tech Inst (NC)
Calhoun Comm Coll (AL)
Cape Cod Comm Coll (MA)
Cape Fear Comm Coll (NC)
Capital Comm Coll (CT)
Carroll Comm Coll (MD)
Carteret Comm Coll (NC)
Casper Coll (WY)
Catawba Valley Comm Coll
(NC)
Cayuga County Comm Coll
(NY)
Cecil Comm Coll (MD)
Cedar Valley Coll (TX)
Central Alabama Comm Coll
(AL)
Central Arizona Coll (AZ)
Central Carolina Comm Coll
(NC)
Central Carolina Tech Coll
(SC)
Central Comm Coll–
Columbus Campus (NE)
Central Comm Coll–Grand
Island Campus (NE)
Central Comm Coll–Hastings
Campus (NE)
Central Florida Comm Coll
(FL)
Central Georgia Tech Coll
(GA)
Centralia Coll (WA)
Central Oregon Comm Coll
(OR)
Central Piedmont Comm Coll
(NC)
Central Texas Coll (TX)
Central Wyoming Coll (WY)
Century Coll (MN)
Cerro Coso Comm Coll (CA)
Chandler-Gilbert Comm Coll
(AZ)
Chattahoochee Tech Coll
(GA)
Chattahoochee Valley Comm
Coll (AL)
Chattanooga State Tech
Comm Coll (TN)
Chemeketa Comm Coll (OR)
Chipola Coll (FL)
Cincinnati State Tech and
Comm Coll (OH)
Citrus Coll (CA)
City Colls of Chicago, Wilbur
Wright Coll (IL)
Clarendon Coll (TX)
Clark Coll (WA)
Clark State Comm Coll (OH)
Clatsop Comm Coll (OR)
Cleveland Comm Coll (NC)
Cleveland State Comm Coll
(TN)
Clinton Comm Coll (IA)
Clinton Comm Coll (NY)
Cloud County Comm Coll
(KS)
Clovis Comm Coll (NM)
Coahoma Comm Coll (MS)
Coastal Bend Coll (TX)
Coastal Carolina Comm Coll
(NC)
Coastal Georgia Comm Coll
(GA)
Cochise Coll, Douglas (AZ)
Coconino Comm Coll (AZ)
Coffeyville Comm Coll (KS)
Colby Comm Coll (KS)
Coll of DuPage (IL)
Coll of Lake County (IL)
Coll of Southern Idaho (ID)
Coll of Southern Maryland
(MD)

Coll of the Canyons (CA)
Coll of the Mainland (TX)
Collin County Comm Coll
District (TX)
Colorado Mountn Coll, Alpine
Cmps (CO)
Colorado Mountn Coll (CO)
Colorado Mountn Coll,
Timberline Cmps (CO)
Colorado Northwestern
Comm Coll (CO)
Columbia Coll (CA)
Columbia-Greene Comm
Coll (NY)
Columbus State Comm Coll
(OH)
Comm & Tech Coll at West
Virginia U Inst of
Technology (WV)
Comm Coll of Allegheny
County (PA)
Comm Coll of Aurora (CO)
Comm Coll of Beaver County
(PA)
Comm Coll of Denver (CO)
Comm Coll of Philadelphia
(PA)
Comm Coll of Rhode Island
(RI)
Comm Coll of Southern
Nevada (NV)
Comm Coll of Vermont (VT)
Compton Comm Coll (CA)
Contra Costa Coll (CA)
Copiah-Lincoln Comm Coll
(MS)
Corning Comm Coll (NY)
Cossatot Comm Coll of the U
of Arkansas (AR)
Cowley County Comm Coll
and Voc-Tech School (KS)
Craven Comm Coll (NC)
Crowder Coll (MO)
Cumberland County Coll
(NJ)
Cuyahoga Comm Coll (OH)
Dabney S. Lancaster Comm
Coll (VA)
Danville Area Comm Coll (IL)
Danville Comm Coll (VA)
Darton Coll (GA)
Davenport U, Midland (MI)
Davidson County Comm Coll
(NC)
Daytona Beach Comm Coll
(FL)
De Anza Coll (CA)
Delaware County Comm Coll
(PA)
Delaware Tech & Comm
Coll, Jack F Owens Cmps
(DE)
Delaware Tech & Comm
Coll, Stanton/ Wilmington
Cmps (DE)
Delaware Tech & Comm
Coll, Terry Cmps (DE)
Delta Coll (MI)
Des Moines Area Comm Coll
(IA)
Dixie State Coll of Utah (UT)
Dodge City Comm Coll (KS)
Doña Ana Branch Comm
Coll (NM)
Durham Tech Comm Coll
(NC)
Dutchess Comm Coll (NY)
Dyersburg State Comm Coll
(TN)
East Arkansas Comm Coll
(AR)
East Central Coll (MO)
East Central Comm Coll
(MS)
Eastern Arizona Coll (AZ)
Eastern Maine Comm Coll
(ME)
Eastern Shore Comm Coll
(VA)
Eastfield Coll (TX)
East Mississippi Comm Coll
(MS)
Edgecombe Comm Coll (NC)

Edison State Comm Coll
(OH)
Edmonds Comm Coll (WA)
Elgin Comm Coll (IL)
Elizabethtown Comm and
Tech Coll (KY)
Ellsworth Comm Coll (IA)
El Paso Comm Coll (TX)
Enterprise-Ozark Comm Coll
(AL)
Erie Business Center, Main
(PA)
Erie Business Center South
(PA)
Erie Comm Coll (NY)
Erie Comm Coll, North
Campus (NY)
Erie Comm Coll, South
Campus (NY)
Essex County Coll (NJ)
Eugenio María de Hostos
Comm Coll of City U of NY
(NY)
Everett Comm Coll (WA)
Fayetteville Tech Comm Coll
(NC)
Finger Lakes Comm Coll
(NY)
Flathead Valley Comm Coll
(MT)
Florida Comm Coll at
Jacksonville (FL)
Florida Keys Comm Coll (FL)
Florida National Coll (FL)
Foothill Coll (CA)
Forrest Jr Coll (SC)
Forsyth Tech Comm Coll
(NC)
Fort Peck Comm Coll (MT)
Fort Scott Comm Coll (KS)
Fox Valley Tech Coll (WI)
Frank Phillips Coll (TX)
Frederick Comm Coll (MD)
Front Range Comm Coll
(CO)
Fulton-Montgomery Comm
Coll (NY)
Gainesville Coll (GA)
Garden City Comm Coll (KS)
Garrett Coll (MD)
Gateway Comm Coll (CT)
Genesee Comm Coll (NY)
George Corley Wallace State
Comm Coll (AL)
George C. Wallace Comm
Coll (AL)
Germanna Comm Coll (VA)
Glendale Comm Coll (AZ)
Glendale Comm Coll (CA)
Glen Oaks Comm Coll (MI)
Globe Coll (MN)
Gogebic Comm Coll (MI)
Gordon Coll (GA)
Grand Rapids Comm Coll
(MI)
Great Basin Coll (NV)
Greenfield Comm Coll (MA)
Guam Comm Coll (GU)
Guilford Tech Comm Coll
(NC)
Gulf Coast Comm Coll (FL)
Hagerstown Business Coll
(MD)
Hagerstown Comm Coll
(MD)
Halifax Comm Coll (NC)
Harcum Coll (PA)
Harford Comm Coll (MD)
Harrisburg Area Comm Coll
(PA)
Hawaii Business Coll (HI)
Hawkeye Comm Coll (IA)
Haywood Comm Coll (NC)
Hazard Comm and Tech Coll
(KY)
Heartland Comm Coll (IL)
Henderson Comm Coll (KY)
Henry Ford Comm Coll (MI)
Herkimer County Comm Coll
(NY)
Hesser Coll (NH)
Hesston Coll (KS)
Hibbing Comm Coll (MN)
Highland Comm Coll (IL)

Highland Comm Coll (KS)
Highline Comm Coll (WA)
Hillsborough Comm Coll (FL)
Hinds Comm Coll (MS)
Holmes Comm Coll (MS)
Holyoke Comm Coll (MA)
Hopkinsville Comm Coll (KY)
Houston Comm Coll System (TX)
Howard Coll (TX)
Howard Comm Coll (MD)
Hudson County Comm Coll (NJ)
Hudson Valley Comm Coll (NY)
ICM School of Business & Medical Careers (PA)
Illinois Eastern Comm Colls, Wabash Valley Coll (IL)
Illinois Valley Comm Coll (IL)
Independence Comm Coll (KS)
Indiana Business Coll, Anderson (IN)
Indiana Business Coll, Columbus (IN)
Indiana Business Coll, Evansville (IN)
Indiana Business Coll, Fort Wayne (IN)
Indiana Business Coll, Indianapolis (IN)
Indiana Business Coll, Lafayette (IN)
Indiana Business Coll, Marion (IN)
Indiana Business Coll, Muncie (IN)
Indiana Business Coll, Terre Haute (IN)
Indian Hills Comm Coll (IA)
Indian River Comm Coll (FL)
Instituto Comercial de Puerto Rico Jr Coll (PR)
Iowa Central Comm Coll (IA)
Iowa Lakes Comm Coll (IA)
Iowa Western Comm Coll (IA)
Isothermal Comm Coll (NC)
Itasca Comm Coll (MN)
Itawamba Comm Coll (MS)
Ivy Tech State Coll–Bloomington (IN)
Ivy Tech State Coll–Central Indiana (IN)
Ivy Tech State Coll–Columbus (IN)
Ivy Tech State Coll–Eastcentral (IN)
Ivy Tech State Coll–Kokomo (IN)
Ivy Tech State Coll–Lafayette (IN)
Ivy Tech State Coll–North Central (IN)
Ivy Tech State Coll–Northeast (IN)
Ivy Tech State Coll–Northwest (IN)
Ivy Tech State Coll–Southcentral (IN)
Ivy Tech State Coll–Southeast (IN)
Ivy Tech State Coll–Southwest (IN)
Ivy Tech State Coll–Wabash Valley (IN)
Ivy Tech State Coll–Whitewater (IN)
Jackson Comm Coll (MI)
Jackson State Comm Coll (TN)
James H. Faulkner State Comm Coll (AL)
James Sprunt Comm Coll (NC)
Jamestown Comm Coll (NY)
Jefferson Comm Coll (KY)
Jefferson Comm Coll (NY)
Jefferson Comm Coll (OH)
John A. Logan Coll (IL)
Johnson County Comm Coll (KS)
Johnston Comm Coll (NC)

John Wood Comm Coll (IL)
J. Sargeant Reynolds Comm Coll (VA)
Kalamazoo Valley Comm Coll (MI)
Kansas City Kansas Comm Coll (KS)
Kaskaskia Coll (IL)
Keiser Coll, Fort Lauderdale (FL)
Keiser Coll, Miami (FL)
Kennebec Valley Comm Coll (ME)
Kent State U, Tuscarawas Campus (OH)
Keystone Coll (PA)
Kilgore Coll (TX)
Kingsborough Comm Coll of City U of NY (NY)
Kingwood Coll (TX)
Lac Courte Oreilles Ojibwa Comm Coll (WI)
Lackawanna Coll (PA)
Lake Land Coll (IL)
Lake Region State Coll (ND)
Lake-Sumter Comm Coll (FL)
Lake Superior Coll (MN)
Lane Comm Coll (OR)
Lansing Comm Coll (MI)
Laramie County Comm Coll (WY)
Laurel Business Inst (PA)
Lehigh Carbon Comm Coll (PA)
Lewis and Clark Comm Coll (IL)
Lincoln Land Comm Coll (IL)
Linn-Benton Comm Coll (OR)
Long Beach City Coll (CA)
Long Island Business Inst (NY)
Longview Comm Coll (MO)
Lower Columbia Coll (WA)
Luna Comm Coll (NM)
Macomb Comm Coll (MI)
Manchester Comm Coll (CT)
Maple Woods Comm Coll (MO)
Maria Coll (NY)
Massachusetts Bay Comm Coll (MA)
Mayland Comm Coll (NC)
McDowell Tech Comm Coll (NC)
McIntosh Coll (NH)
McLennan Comm Coll (TX)
Metropolitan Comm Coll (NE)
Metropolitan Comm Coll–Business & Technology College (MO)
Miami Dade Coll (FL)
Miami U Hamilton (OH)
Middle Georgia Coll (GA)
Midlands Tech Coll (SC)
Mid Michigan Comm Coll (MI)
Milwaukee Area Tech Coll (WI)
Mineral Area Coll (MO)
Minneapolis Comm and Tech Coll (MN)
Minnesota School of Business–Brooklyn Center (MN)
Minnesota School of Business–Plymouth (MN)
Minnesota School of Business–Richfield (MN)
Modesto Jr Coll (CA)
Mohave Comm Coll (AZ)
Mohawk Valley Comm Coll (NY)
Monroe Coll, Bronx (NY)
Monroe Coll, New Rochelle (NY)
Montcalm Comm Coll (MI)
Montgomery Comm Coll (NC)
Montgomery County Comm Coll (PA)

Moraine Valley Comm Coll (IL)
Motlow State Comm Coll (TN)
Mott Comm Coll (MI)
Mount Wachusett Comm Coll (MA)
Muscatine Comm Coll (IA)
Muskegon Comm Coll (MI)
Napa Valley Coll (CA)
Nashville State Tech Comm Coll (TN)
Nassau Comm Coll (NY)
National Coll of Business & Technology, Danville (KY)
National Coll of Business & Technology, Florence (KY)
National Coll of Business & Technology, Lexington (KY)
National Coll of Business & Technology, Louisville (KY)
National Coll of Business & Technology, Pikeville (KY)
National Coll of Business & Technology, Richmond (KY)
National Coll of Business & Technology, Bristol (TN)
National Coll of Business & Technology, Nashville (TN)
National Coll of Business & Technology, Bluefield (VA)
National Coll of Business & Technology, Harrisonburg (VA)
National Coll of Business & Technology, Lynchburg (VA)
National Coll of Business & Technology, Martinsville (VA)
Nebraska Indian Comm Coll (NE)
New England Coll of Finance (MA)
New Hampshire Comm Tech Coll, Manchester/Stratham (NH)
New Mexico Military Inst (NM)
Newport Business Inst, Williamsport (PA)
Niagara County Comm Coll (NY)
Northampton County Area Comm Coll (PA)
North Central Missouri Coll (MO)
North Central State Coll (OH)
North Country Comm Coll (NY)
Northeast Alabama Comm Coll (AL)
Northeastern Tech Coll (SC)
Northeast State Tech Comm Coll (TN)
Northern Essex Comm Coll (MA)
Northern Virginia Comm Coll (VA)
North Hennepin Comm Coll (MN)
North Idaho Coll (ID)
North Iowa Area Comm Coll (IA)
North Lake Coll (TX)
Northland Comm and Tech Coll–Thief River Falls (MN)
North Seattle Comm Coll (WA)
North Shore Comm Coll (MA)
Northwestern Connecticut Comm-Tech Coll (CT)
Northwestern Michigan Coll (MI)
Northwest-Shoals Comm Coll (AL)
Northwest State Comm Coll (OH)
Oakland Comm Coll (MI)
Odessa Coll (TX)
Olympic Coll (WA)
Orange Coast Coll (CA)

Orange County Comm Coll (NY)
Otero Jr Coll (CO)
Ouachita Tech Coll (AR)
Owensboro Comm and Tech Coll (KY)
Owens Comm Coll, Findlay (OH)
Palm Beach Comm Coll (FL)
Paradise Valley Comm Coll (AZ)
Parkland Coll (IL)
Pasadena City Coll (CA)
Pasco-Hernando Comm Coll (FL)
Patrick Henry Comm Coll (VA)
Peninsula Coll (WA)
Pennsylvania Inst of Technology (PA)
Penn Valley Comm Coll (MO)
Phillips Comm Coll of the U of Arkansas (AR)
Piedmont Comm Coll (NC)
Piedmont Virginia Comm Coll (VA)
Pima Comm Coll (AZ)
Pioneer Pacific Coll (OR)
Polk Comm Coll (FL)
Pratt Comm Coll and Area Vocational School (KS)
Queensborough Comm Coll of City U of NY (NY)
Quinebaug Valley Comm Coll (CT)
Rainy River Comm Coll (MN)
Randolph Comm Coll (NC)
Raritan Valley Comm Coll (NJ)
Rasmussen Coll St. Cloud (MN)
Richland Comm Coll (IL)
Richmond Comm Coll (NC)
Riverland Comm Coll (MN)
Riverside Comm Coll District (CA)
Roanoke-Chowan Comm Coll (NC)
Rochester Comm and Tech Coll (MN)
Rockingham Comm Coll (NC)
Rockland Comm Coll (NY)
Rock Valley Coll (IL)
Rogue Comm Coll (OR)
Rowan-Cabarrus Comm Coll (NC)
Saint Charles Comm Coll (MO)
St. Cloud Tech Coll (MN)
St. Louis Comm Coll at Forest Park (MO)
St. Louis Comm Coll at Meramec (MO)
St. Petersburg Coll (FL)
St. Philip's Coll (TX)
Salt Lake Comm Coll (UT)
San Antonio Coll (TX)
Sandhills Comm Coll (NC)
San Diego City Coll (CA)
San Diego Miramar Coll (CA)
San Joaquin Delta Coll (CA)
San Juan Coll (NM)
Santa Barbara City Coll (CA)
Santa Fe Comm Coll (FL)
Santa Rosa Jr Coll (CA)
Sauk Valley Comm Coll (IL)
Schoolcraft Coll (MI)
Schuylkill Inst of Business and Technology (PA)
Scott Comm Coll (IA)
Seminole Comm Coll (FL)
Seminole State Coll (OK)
Seward County Comm Coll (KS)
Shawnee Comm Coll (IL)
Shelton State Comm Coll (AL)
Sheridan Coll (WY)
Shoreline Comm Coll (WA)
Sinclair Comm Coll (OH)
Sisseton-Wahpeton Comm Coll (SD)

Snow Coll (UT)
Solano Comm Coll (CA)
South Central Tech Coll (MN)
Southeast Comm Coll, Lincoln Campus (NE)
Southeastern Tech Coll (GA)
Southeast Kentucky Comm and Tech Coll (KY)
Southeast Tech Inst (SD)
Southern Maine Comm Coll (ME)
Southern Union State Comm Coll (AL)
South Hills School of Business & Technology, State College (PA)
South Mountain Comm Coll (AZ)
Southside Virginia Comm Coll (VA)
South Texas Coll (TX)
South U (FL)
South U (SC)
Southwestern Comm Coll (IA)
Southwestern Comm Coll (NC)
Southwestern Michigan Coll (MI)
Southwestern Oklahoma State U at Sayre (OK)
Southwestern Oregon Comm Coll (OR)
Spartanburg Tech Coll (SC)
Spencerian Coll (KY)
Springfield Tech Comm Coll (MA)
Stanly Comm Coll (NC)
State U of NY Coll of Technology at Alfred (NY)
State U of NY Coll of Technology at Canton (NY)
State U of NY Coll of Technology at Delhi (NY)
Surry Comm Coll (NC)
Sussex County Comm Coll (NJ)
Tacoma Comm Coll (WA)
Taft Coll (CA)
Tech Coll of the Lowcountry (SC)
Temple Coll (TX)
Thompson Inst (PA)
Three Rivers Comm Coll (CT)
Three Rivers Comm Coll (MO)
Tompkins Cortland Comm Coll (NY)
Tri-County Comm Coll (NC)
Tri-County Tech Coll (SC)
Trident Tech Coll (SC)
Trinidad State Jr Coll (CO)
Trinity Valley Comm Coll (TX)
Truckee Meadows Comm Coll (NV)
Tunxis Comm Coll (CT)
Umpqua Comm Coll (OR)
Union County Coll (NJ)
The U of Akron–Wayne Coll (OH)
U of Alaska Anchorage, Matanuska-Susitna Coll (AK)
U of Arkansas Comm Coll at Hope (AR)
U of Cincinnati Raymond Walters Coll (OH)
U of Northwestern Ohio (OH)
U of Pittsburgh at Titusville (PA)
Valencia Comm Coll (FL)
Villa Maria Coll of Buffalo (NY)
Volunteer State Comm Coll (TN)
Wake Tech Comm Coll (NC)
Walla Walla Comm Coll (WA)
Walters State Comm Coll (TN)
Waubonsee Comm Coll (IL)
Wayne County Comm Coll District (MI)

West Central Tech Coll (GA)
Westchester Comm Coll (NY)
Western Iowa Tech Comm Coll (IA)
Western Nevada Comm Coll (NV)
Western Oklahoma State Coll (OK)
Western Wyoming Comm Coll (WY)
West Kentucky Comm and Tech Coll (KY)
Westmoreland County Comm Coll (PA)
West Virginia U at Parkersburg (WV)
Whatcom Comm Coll (WA)
Wilkes Comm Coll (NC)
Wilson Tech Comm Coll (NC)
Wor-Wic Comm Coll (MD)
Yakima Valley Comm Coll (WA)
Yavapai Coll (AZ)
Yuba Coll (CA)

Business Administration, Management and Operations Related
Bryant & Stratton Business Inst, Amherst Cmps (NY)
Bryant & Stratton Business Inst (NY)
Bryant & Stratton Business Inst (NY)
Delaware County Comm Coll (PA)
Indiana Business Coll, Anderson (IN)
Indiana Business Coll, Columbus (IN)
Indiana Business Coll, Indianapolis (IN)
Indiana Business Coll, Lafayette (IN)
Indiana Business Coll, Muncie (IN)
Indiana Business Coll, Terre Haute (IN)
Lanier Tech Coll (GA)
West Virginia State Comm and Tech Coll (WV)

Business and Personal/Financial Services Marketing
Centralia Coll (WA)
Heartland Comm Coll (IL)
Hesser Coll (NH)
Hutchinson Comm Coll and Area Vocational School (KS)
Northwestern Michigan Coll (MI)
Union County Coll (NJ)

Business Automation/Technology/Data Entry
Adirondack Comm Coll (NY)
Alpena Comm Coll (MI)
Arkansas State U–Mountain Home (AR)
Berkshire Comm Coll (MA)
Bismarck State Coll (ND)
Bristol Comm Coll (MA)
Business Inst of Pennsylvania, Sharon (PA)
Central Wyoming Coll (WY)
Clark Coll (WA)
Clatsop Comm Coll (OR)
Clovis Comm Coll (NM)
Coll of Lake County (IL)
Collin County Comm Coll District (TX)
Comm Coll of Allegheny County (PA)
Crowder Coll (MO)
Davenport U, Midland (MI)
Delta Coll (MI)
Fayetteville Tech Comm Coll (NC)
Front Range Comm Coll (CO)
Gogebic Comm Coll (MI)
Illinois Eastern Comm Colls, Frontier Comm Coll (IL)

Illinois Eastern Comm Colls, Lincoln Trail Coll (IL)
Illinois Eastern Comm Colls, Olney Central Coll (IL)
Illinois Eastern Comm Colls, Wabash Valley Coll (IL)
Iowa Lakes Comm Coll (IA)
Kaskaskia Coll (IL)
Laurel Business Inst (PA)
Lincoln Land Comm Coll (IL)
Macomb Comm Coll (MI)
Midland Coll (TX)
MTI Coll of Business and Technology, Houston (TX)
Northwestern Michigan Coll (MI)
Oakland Comm Coll (MI)
Parkland Coll (IL)
Tillamook Bay Comm Coll (OR)
The U of Akron–Wayne Coll (OH)
Waubonsee Comm Coll (IL)
Western Nevada Comm Coll (NV)

Business/Commerce
Academy Coll (MN)
Allen County Comm Coll (KS)
Arkansas Northeastern Coll (AR)
Bay de Noc Comm Coll (MI)
Berkeley Coll (NJ)
Berkshire Comm Coll (MA)
Bismarck State Coll (ND)
Brazosport Coll (TX)
Centralia Coll (WA)
Coll of Southern Idaho (ID)
Columbia State Comm Coll (TN)
Comm Coll of Rhode Island (RI)
Dawson Comm Coll (MT)
DeKalb Tech Coll (GA)
Fairmont State Comm & Tech Coll (WV)
Feather River Coll (CA)
GateWay Comm Coll (AZ)
Glendale Comm Coll (AZ)
Goodwin Coll (CT)
Great Basin Coll (NV)
Hagerstown Comm Coll (MD)
Harford Comm Coll (MD)
Harrisburg Area Comm Coll (PA)
Hawkeye Comm Coll (IA)
Hutchinson Comm Coll and Area Vocational School (KS)
Jefferson State Comm Coll (AL)
John Tyler Comm Coll (VA)
John Wood Comm Coll (IL)
Keystone Coll (PA)
Kilgore Coll (TX)
Lackawanna Coll (PA)
Laramie County Comm Coll (WY)
Lower Columbia Coll (WA)
Macomb Comm Coll (MI)
Marshall Comm and Tech Coll (WV)
Massachusetts Bay Comm Coll (MA)
Mesabi Range Comm and Tech Coll (MN)
Metropolitan Comm Coll-Business & Technology College (MO)
Midland Coll (TX)
Midlands Tech Coll (SC)
Minneapolis Comm and Tech Coll (MN)
Montgomery County Comm Coll (PA)
Moraine Valley Comm Coll (IL)
Mott Comm Coll (MI)
National Coll of Business & Technology, Charlottesville (VA)
National Coll of Business & Technology, Salem (VA)

New River Comm and Tech Coll (WV)
Northampton County Area Comm Coll (PA)
North Dakota State Coll of Science (ND)
Northwest State Comm Coll (OH)
Owens Comm Coll, Findlay (OH)
Owens Comm Coll, Toledo (OH)
Penn State U Beaver Campus of the Commonwealth Coll (PA)
Penn State U Delaware County Campus of the Commonwealth Coll (PA)
Penn State U DuBois Campus of the Commonwealth Coll (PA)
Penn State U Fayette Campus of the Commonwealth Coll (PA)
Penn State U Hazleton Campus of the Commonwealth Coll (PA)
Penn State U McKeesport Campus of the Commonwealth Coll (PA)
Penn State U Mont Alto Campus of the Commonwealth Coll (PA)
Penn State U New Kensington Campus of the Commonwealth Coll (PA)
Penn State U Shenango Campus of the Commonwealth Coll (PA)
Penn State U Wilkes-Barre Campus of the Commonwealth Coll (PA)
Penn State U Worthington Scranton Cmps Commonwealth Coll (PA)
Penn State U York Campus of the Commonwealth Coll (PA)
San Joaquin Valley Coll (CA)
Sheridan Coll (WY)
Somerset Comm Coll (KY)
Southern State Comm Coll (OH)
Springfield Tech Comm Coll (MA)
Truett-McConnell Coll (GA)
Union County Coll (NJ)
U of Arkansas Comm Coll at Batesville (AR)
Western Nevada Comm Coll (NV)
Wor-Wic Comm Coll (MD)

Business Computer Programming
Barton County Comm Coll (KS)
Coll of Lake County (IL)

Business/Corporate Communications
Houston Comm Coll System (TX)
Montgomery County Comm Coll (PA)

Business Machine Repair
Athens Tech Coll (GA)
Central Piedmont Comm Coll (NC)
Clover Park Tech Coll (WA)
Coffeyville Comm Coll (KS)
Comm Coll of Allegheny County (PA)
De Anza Coll (CA)
Dutchess Comm Coll (NY)
ECPI Coll of Technology, Virginia Beach (VA)
ECPI Tech Coll, Richmond (VA)
Frank Phillips Coll (TX)
Henry Ford Comm Coll (MI)
Iowa Lakes Comm Coll (IA)
Minnesota State Coll–Southeast Tech (MN)
Muskegon Comm Coll (MI)

Rockingham Comm Coll (NC)
San Antonio Coll (TX)
Solano Comm Coll (CA)
Southern Maine Comm Coll (ME)

Business, Management, and Marketing Related
Bristol Comm Coll (MA)
Catawba Valley Comm Coll (NC)
Cincinnati State Tech and Comm Coll (OH)
Comm and Tech Coll of Shepherd (WV)
Eastern Arizona Coll (AZ)
Harrisburg Area Comm Coll (PA)
Heart of Georgia Tech Coll (GA)
Lanier Tech Coll (GA)
Milwaukee Area Tech Coll (WI)
Northwestern Michigan Coll (MI)
Northwest State Comm Coll (OH)
Queensborough Comm Coll of City U of NY (NY)
Sandhills Comm Coll (NC)
Southwestern Michigan Coll (MI)

Business/Managerial Economics
Anne Arundel Comm Coll (MD)
Colby Comm Coll (KS)
Frank Phillips Coll (TX)
San Joaquin Delta Coll (CA)
State U of NY Coll of Technology at Canton (NY)
Tacoma Comm Coll (WA)

Business Operations Support and Secretarial Services Related
Ancilla Coll (IN)
Bowling Green State U-Firelands Coll (OH)
Bristol Comm Coll (MA)
Eastern Arizona Coll (AZ)
Guilford Tech Comm Coll (NC)
Hillsborough Comm Coll (FL)
Laramie County Comm Coll (WY)
MTI Coll of Business and Technology, Houston (TX)

Business Systems Networking/ Telecommunications
Caldwell Comm Coll and Tech Inst (NC)
Coll of Lake County (IL)
Globe Coll (MN)
Minnesota School of Business–Brooklyn Center (MN)
Minnesota School of Business–Plymouth (MN)
Minnesota School of Business–Richfield (MN)

Business Teacher Education
Alabama Southern Comm Coll (AL)
Allen County Comm Coll (KS)
Amarillo Coll (TX)
American Samoa Comm Coll (AS)
Bainbridge Coll (GA)
Bristol Comm Coll (MA)
Bronx Comm Coll of City U of NY (NY)
Casper Coll (WY)
Coffeyville Comm Coll (KS)
Colby Comm Coll (KS)
Comm Coll of Philadelphia (PA)
Darton Coll (GA)
Delta Coll (MI)
Eastern Arizona Coll (AZ)

East Mississippi Comm Coll (MS)
Essex County Coll (NJ)
Frank Phillips Coll (TX)
Gainesville Coll (GA)
George Corley Wallace State Comm Coll (AL)
Halifax Comm Coll (NC)
Harrisburg Area Comm Coll (PA)
Highland Comm Coll (KS)
Holmes Comm Coll (MS)
Holyoke Comm Coll (MA)
Independence Comm Coll (KS)
Iowa Central Comm Coll (IA)
Iowa Lakes Comm Coll (IA)
Isothermal Comm Coll (NC)
John A. Logan Coll (IL)
Northern Essex Comm Coll (MA)
North Idaho Coll (ID)
Pasadena City Coll (CA)
Phillips Comm Coll of the U of Arkansas (AR)
Pratt Comm Coll and Area Vocational School (KS)
Shelton State Comm Coll (AL)
Snow Coll (UT)
Trinity Valley Comm Coll (TX)

Cabinetmaking and Millwork
Coll of Southern Idaho (ID)
Fayetteville Tech Comm Coll (NC)
Illinois Eastern Comm Colls, Olney Central Coll (IL)
Ivy Tech State Coll–Bloomington (IN)
Ivy Tech State Coll–Central Indiana (IN)
Ivy Tech State Coll–Columbus (IN)
Ivy Tech State Coll–Eastcentral (IN)
Ivy Tech State Coll–Kokomo (IN)
Ivy Tech State Coll–Lafayette (IN)
Ivy Tech State Coll–North Central (IN)
Ivy Tech State Coll–Northeast (IN)
Ivy Tech State Coll–Northwest (IN)
Ivy Tech State Coll–Southcentral (IN)
Ivy Tech State Coll–Southwest (IN)
Ivy Tech State Coll–Wabash Valley (IN)
Ivy Tech State Coll–Whitewater (IN)
Macomb Comm Coll (MI)
Oakland Comm Coll (MI)

Cad/Cadd Drafting/Design Technology
Alexandria Tech Coll (MN)
Black Hawk Coll, Moline (IL)
Lower Columbia Coll (WA)
Morrison Inst of Technology (IL)
Owens Comm Coll, Toledo (OH)
St. Philip's Coll (TX)
Somerset Comm Coll (KY)
Springfield Tech Comm Coll (MA)
Vatterott Coll, Springfield (MO)
West Virginia State Comm and Tech Coll (WV)
Westwood Coll–Long Beach (CA)

Cardiovascular Technology
Bunker Hill Comm Coll (MA)
Caldwell Comm Coll and Tech Inst (NC)
Comm Coll of the Air Force (AL)
Darton Coll (GA)

Harrisburg Area Comm Coll (PA)
Howard Comm Coll (MD)
Milwaukee Area Tech Coll (WI)
Northeast State Tech Comm Coll (TN)
North Hennepin Comm Coll (MN)
Northwest Tech Coll (MN)
Orange Coast Coll (CA)
Southeast Tech Inst (SD)
Southern Maine Comm Coll (ME)
Valencia Comm Coll (FL)

Carpentry
Alamance Comm Coll (NC)
Alexandria Tech Coll (MN)
Bismarck State Coll (ND)
Black Hawk Coll, Moline (IL)
Casper Coll (WY)
Cecil Comm Coll (MD)
Clovis Comm Coll (NM)
Coffeyville Comm Coll (KS)
Comm Coll of Allegheny County (PA)
Comm Coll of Aurora (CO)
Cossatot Comm Coll of the U of Arkansas (AR)
Davenport U, Midland (MI)
Delaware Tech & Comm Coll, Jack F Owens Cmps (DE)
Delta Coll (MI)
Des Moines Area Comm Coll (IA)
East Central Comm Coll (MS)
Eastern Maine Comm Coll (ME)
Fayetteville Tech Comm Coll (NC)
Forsyth Tech Comm Coll (NC)
Fulton-Montgomery Comm Coll (NY)
GateWay Comm Coll (AZ)
George C. Wallace Comm Coll (AL)
Gogebic Comm Coll (MI)
Green River Comm Coll (WA)
Highland Comm Coll (KS)
Hinds Comm Coll (MS)
Hutchinson Comm Coll and Area Vocational School (KS)
Illinois Valley Comm Coll (IL)
Indian River Comm Coll (FL)
Iowa Central Comm Coll (IA)
Iowa Lakes Comm Coll (IA)
Ivy Tech State Coll–Central Indiana (IN)
Ivy Tech State Coll–Eastcentral (IN)
Ivy Tech State Coll–Lafayette (IN)
Ivy Tech State Coll–North Central (IN)
Ivy Tech State Coll–Northwest (IN)
Ivy Tech State Coll–Southcentral (IN)
Ivy Tech State Coll–Southwest (IN)
Ivy Tech State Coll–Wabash Valley (IN)
Kaskaskia Coll (IL)
Kauai Comm Coll (HI)
Lake Superior Coll (MN)
Lansing Comm Coll (MI)
Laramie County Comm Coll (WY)
Long Beach City Coll (CA)
Mayland Comm Coll (NC)
Metropolitan Comm Coll-Business & Technology College (MO)
Minnesota State Coll–Southeast Tech (MN)
Nebraska Indian Comm Coll (NE)
North Central Missouri Coll (MO)

North Idaho Coll (ID)
North Iowa Area Comm Coll (IA)
North Lake Coll (TX)
Northwest Tech Coll (MN)
Oakland Comm Coll (MI)
Pasadena City Coll (CA)
Ranken Tech Coll (MO)
Rockingham Comm Coll (NC)
St. Cloud Tech Coll (MN)
Salt Lake Comm Coll (UT)
San Diego City Coll (CA)
San Joaquin Delta Coll (CA)
San Juan Coll (NM)
Seattle Central Comm Coll (WA)
Snow Coll (UT)
Somerset Comm Coll (KY)
Southeast Comm Coll, Milford Campus (NE)
Southern Maine Comm Coll (ME)
Southwestern Comm Coll (IA)
State U of NY Coll of Technology at Alfred (NY)
State U of NY Coll of Technology at Canton (NY)
State U of NY Coll of Technology at Delhi (NY)
Tech Coll of the Lowcountry (SC)
Thaddeus Stevens Coll of Technology (PA)
Triangle Tech, Inc.–Greensburg School (PA)
Triangle Tech, Inc.–Pittsburgh School (PA)
Trinidad State Jr Coll (CO)
Truckee Meadows Comm Coll (NV)
Walla Walla Comm Coll (WA)
Western Nevada Comm Coll (NV)

Cartography
Alexandria Tech Coll (MN)
Anoka-Ramsey Comm Coll (MN)
Anoka-Ramsey Comm Coll, Cambridge Campus (MN)
Central Oregon Comm Coll (OR)
Dixie State Coll of Utah (UT)
Houston Comm Coll System (TX)

Ceramic Arts and Ceramics
Casper Coll (WY)
De Anza Coll (CA)
Dixie State Coll of Utah (UT)
Garden City Comm Coll (KS)
Glendale Comm Coll (CA)
Haywood Comm Coll (NC)
Henry Ford Comm Coll (MI)
Inst of American Indian Arts (NM)
Iowa Lakes Comm Coll (IA)
Mohave Comm Coll (AZ)
Montgomery Comm Coll (NC)
Oakland Comm Coll (MI)
Palm Beach Comm Coll (FL)
Pasadena City Coll (CA)

Ceramic Sciences and Engineering
Pasadena City Coll (CA)

Chemical Engineering
Alpena Comm Coll (MI)
Brevard Comm Coll (FL)
Chattanooga State Tech Comm Coll (TN)
Comm Coll of Philadelphia (PA)
Delaware Tech & Comm Coll, Jack F Owens Cmps (DE)
Delaware Tech & Comm Coll, Stanton/ Wilmington Cmps (DE)
Delta Coll (MI)
Hudson Valley Comm Coll (NY)
Itasca Comm Coll (MN)

Lansing Comm Coll (MI)
Milwaukee Area Tech Coll (WI)
Muskegon Comm Coll (MI)
Shoreline Comm Coll (WA)
Texas State Tech Coll–Waco/Marshall Campus (TX)
Westchester Comm Coll (NY)
West Virginia U at Parkersburg (WV)

Chemical Technology
Alvin Comm Coll (TX)
Amarillo Coll (TX)
Brazosport Coll (TX)
Cape Fear Comm Coll (NC)
Cincinnati State Tech and Comm Coll (OH)
Coll of Lake County (IL)
Coll of the Mainland (TX)
Comm Coll of Allegheny County (PA)
Comm Coll of Rhode Island (RI)
Corning Comm Coll (NY)
Edmonds Comm Coll (WA)
Erie Comm Coll, North Campus (NY)
Essex County Coll (NJ)
Jefferson Comm Coll (NY)
Johnson County Comm Coll (KS)
Kalamazoo Valley Comm Coll (MI)
Lehigh Carbon Comm Coll (PA)
Massachusetts Bay Comm Coll (MA)
Mohawk Valley Comm Coll (NY)
Northampton County Area Comm Coll (PA)
River Parishes Comm Coll (LA)
Texas State Tech Coll–Waco/Marshall Campus (TX)
West Virginia State Comm and Tech Coll (WV)

Chemistry
Alabama Southern Comm Coll (AL)
Allen County Comm Coll (KS)
Alpena Comm Coll (MI)
Amarillo Coll (TX)
Ancilla Coll (IN)
Andrew Coll (GA)
Anne Arundel Comm Coll (MD)
Arizona Western Coll (AZ)
Atlanta Metropolitan Coll (GA)
Atlantic Cape Comm Coll (NJ)
Austin Comm Coll (TX)
Bainbridge Coll (GA)
Barton County Comm Coll (KS)
Bergen Comm Coll (NJ)
Brazosport Coll (TX)
Bronx Comm Coll of City U of NY (NY)
Brookdale Comm Coll (NJ)
Bucks County Comm Coll (PA)
Bunker Hill Comm Coll (MA)
Butler County Comm Coll (KS)
Casper Coll (WY)
Centralia Coll (WA)
Central Texas Coll (TX)
Chattahoochee Valley Comm Coll (AL)
Chattanooga State Tech Comm Coll (TN)
Clarendon Coll (TX)
Coahoma Comm Coll (MS)
Coastal Bend Coll (TX)
Coastal Georgia Comm Coll (GA)
Cochise Coll, Douglas (AZ)

Coffeyville Comm Coll (KS)
Colby Comm Coll (KS)
Coll of Southern Idaho (ID)
Coll of the Canyons (CA)
Columbia Coll (CA)
Columbia State Comm Coll (TN)
Comm Coll of Allegheny County (PA)
Comm Coll of Southern Nevada (NV)
Compton Comm Coll (CA)
Contra Costa Coll (CA)
Copiah-Lincoln Comm Coll (MS)
Cowley County Comm Coll and Voc-Tech School (KS)
Darton Coll (GA)
Daytona Beach Comm Coll (FL)
Delta Coll (MI)
Dixie State Coll of Utah (UT)
Dodge City Comm Coll (KS)
East Central Coll (MO)
East Central Comm Coll (MS)
Eastern Arizona Coll (AZ)
El Paso Comm Coll (TX)
Essex County Coll (NJ)
Everett Comm Coll (WA)
Finger Lakes Comm Coll (NY)
Foothill Coll (CA)
Frank Phillips Coll (TX)
Frederick Comm Coll (MD)
Gainesville Coll (GA)
Great Basin Coll (NV)
Harrisburg Area Comm Coll (PA)
Highland Comm Coll (IL)
Highland Comm Coll (KS)
Holyoke Comm Coll (MA)
Howard Coll (TX)
Hudson Valley Comm Coll (NY)
Independence Comm Coll (KS)
Indian River Comm Coll (FL)
Iowa Lakes Comm Coll (IA)
Itawamba Comm Coll (MS)
John A. Logan Coll (IL)
Kilgore Coll (TX)
Kingsborough Comm Coll of City U of NY (NY)
Lansing Comm Coll (MI)
Laramie County Comm Coll (WY)
Linn-Benton Comm Coll (OR)
Longview Comm Coll (MO)
Macomb Comm Coll (MI)
Maple Woods Comm Coll (MO)
Miami Dade Coll (FL)
Midland Coll (TX)
Mid Michigan Comm Coll (MI)
New Mexico Military Inst (NM)
Northampton County Area Comm Coll (PA)
Northeast State Tech Comm Coll (TN)
North Idaho Coll (ID)
Odessa Coll (TX)
Orange Coast Coll (CA)
Palm Beach Comm Coll (FL)
Pasadena City Coll (CA)
Penn Valley Comm Coll (MO)
Phillips Comm Coll of the U of Arkansas (AR)
Pratt Comm Coll and Area Vocational School (KS)
Raritan Valley Comm Coll (NJ)
Riverside Comm Coll District (CA)
St. Philip's Coll (TX)
San Diego Miramar Coll (CA)
San Joaquin Delta Coll (CA)
San Juan Coll (NM)
Santa Barbara City Coll (CA)
Santa Rosa Jr Coll (CA)

Sauk Valley Comm Coll (IL)
Seward County Comm Coll (KS)
Shelton State Comm Coll (AL)
Snow Coll (UT)
Solano Comm Coll (CA)
South Mountain Comm Coll (AZ)
Springfield Tech Comm Coll (MA)
Tacoma Comm Coll (WA)
Trinidad State Jr Coll (CO)
Trinity Valley Comm Coll (TX)
Umpqua Comm Coll (OR)
Union County Coll (NJ)
U of Cincinnati Raymond Walters Coll (OH)
Western Wyoming Comm Coll (WY)
Yuba Coll (CA)

Chemistry Related
Guilford Tech Comm Coll (NC)

Child Care and Guidance Related
Albany Tech Coll (GA)

Child Care and Support Services Management
Albuquerque Tech Vocational Inst (NM)
Alexandria Tech Coll (MN)
Arapahoe Comm Coll (CO)
Arkansas Northeastern Coll (AR)
Asheville-Buncombe Tech Comm Coll (NC)
Barton County Comm Coll (KS)
Bay de Noc Comm Coll (MI)
Brazosport Coll (TX)
Broome Comm Coll (NY)
Calhoun Comm Coll (AL)
Cape Fear Comm Coll (NC)
Central Carolina Tech Coll (SC)
Central Florida Comm Coll (FL)
Central Georgia Tech Coll (GA)
Centralia Coll (WA)
Central Texas Coll (TX)
Central Wyoming Comm Coll (WY)
Cerro Coso Comm Coll (CA)
Coll of DuPage (IL)
Colorado Northwestern Comm Coll (CO)
Craven Comm Coll (NC)
Dawson Comm Coll (MT)
Dixie State Coll of Utah (UT)
Eastfield Coll (TX)
Edmonds Comm Coll (WA)
Erie Comm Coll (NY)
Fayetteville Tech Comm Coll (NC)
Feather River Coll (CA)
Florida Comm Coll at Jacksonville (FL)
Front Range Comm Coll (CO)
Gadsden State Comm Coll (AL)
Gogebic Comm Coll (MI)
Green River Comm Coll (WA)
Hagerstown Comm Coll (MD)
Harford Comm Coll (MD)
Hesser Coll (NH)
Highland Comm Coll (IL)
Hopkinsville Comm Coll (KY)
Houston Comm Coll System (TX)
Hutchinson Comm Coll and Area Vocational School (KS)
Iowa Western Comm Coll (IA)
Ivy Tech State Coll–Bloomington (IN)
Ivy Tech State Coll–Central Indiana (IN)

Ivy Tech State Coll–Columbus (IN)
Ivy Tech State Coll–Eastcentral (IN)
Ivy Tech State Coll–Kokomo (IN)
Ivy Tech State Coll–Lafayette (IN)
Ivy Tech State Coll–North Central (IN)
Ivy Tech State Coll–Northeast (IN)
Ivy Tech State Coll–Northwest (IN)
Ivy Tech State Coll–Southcentral (IN)
Ivy Tech State Coll–Southeast (IN)
Ivy Tech State Coll–Southwest (IN)
Ivy Tech State Coll–Wabash Valley (IN)
Ivy Tech State Coll–Whitewater (IN)
Jefferson Comm Coll (OH)
Jefferson State Comm Coll (AL)
J. Sargeant Reynolds Comm Coll (VA)
Kansas City Kansas Comm Coll (KS)
Kennebec Valley Comm Coll (ME)
Kilgore Coll (TX)
Lake Land Coll (IL)
Lake Region State Coll (ND)
Linn-Benton Comm Coll (OR)
Macomb Comm Coll (MI)
Massachusetts Bay Comm Coll (MA)
Modesto Jr Coll (CA)
Montcalm Comm Coll (MI)
Montgomery Comm Coll (NC)
Montgomery County Comm Coll (PA)
Muscatine Comm Coll (IA)
Northampton County Area Comm Coll (PA)
Northwestern Michigan Coll (MI)
Northwest Tech Coll (MN)
Oakland Comm Coll (MI)
Olympic Coll (WA)
Orange Coast Coll (CA)
Ouachita Tech Coll (AR)
Peninsula Coll (WA)
Pima Comm Coll (AZ)
Richmond Comm Coll (NC)
St. Cloud Tech Coll (MN)
San Antonio Coll (TX)
Santa Barbara City Coll (CA)
Schoolcraft Coll (MI)
Scott Comm Coll (IA)
Southwestern Michigan Coll (MI)
Stanly Comm Coll (NC)
Walla Walla Comm Coll (WA)
Western Iowa Tech Comm Coll (IA)
Western Nevada Comm Coll (NV)
Wilkes Comm Coll (NC)
Wor-Wic Comm Coll (MD)

Child Care/Guidance
Bristol Comm Coll (MA)
Caldwell Comm Coll and Tech Inst (NC)
Feather River Coll (CA)

Child Care Provision
Alexandria Tech Coll (MN)
Arapahoe Comm Coll (CO)
Bladen Comm Coll (NC)
Brunswick Comm Coll (NC)
Central Florida Comm Coll (FL)
Cerro Coso Comm Coll (CA)
Cincinnati State Tech and Comm Coll (OH)
Coastal Carolina Comm Coll (NC)
Coll of DuPage (IL)

Coll of Lake County (IL)
Comm Coll of Allegheny County (PA)
Corning Comm Coll (NY)
Eastern Arizona Coll (AZ)
Fayetteville Tech Comm Coll (NC)
Florida Comm Coll at Jacksonville (FL)
Gadsden State Comm Coll-Ayers Campus (AL)
Gulf Coast Comm Coll (FL)
Heartland Comm Coll (IL)
Highland Comm Coll (IL)
Iowa Lakes Comm Coll (IA)
Iowa Western Comm Coll (IA)
Kennebec Valley Comm Coll (ME)
Lake Region State Coll (ND)
Lehigh Carbon Comm Coll (PA)
Lincoln Land Comm Coll (IL)
Midland Coll (TX)
Midlands Tech Coll (SC)
Mid Michigan Comm Coll (MI)
Mineral Area Coll (MO)
Modesto Jr Coll (CA)
Montcalm Comm Coll (MI)
Moraine Valley Comm Coll (IL)
Mott Comm Coll (MI)
Northland Comm and Tech Coll–Thief River Falls (MN)
Orange Coast Coll (CA)
Parkland Coll (IL)
Penn Valley Comm Coll (MO)
Pima Comm Coll (AZ)
San Antonio Coll (TX)
Surry Comm Coll (NC)
Tompkins Cortland Comm Coll (NY)
Trident Tech Coll (SC)
U of Arkansas Comm Coll at Hope (AR)
Waubonsee Comm Coll (IL)
Westchester Comm Coll (NY)

Child Development
Allen County Comm Coll (KS)
Alvin Comm Coll (TX)
Amarillo Coll (TX)
Athens Tech Coll (GA)
Atlanta Metropolitan Coll (GA)
Atlantic Cape Comm Coll (NJ)
Augusta Tech Coll (GA)
Black Hawk Coll, Moline (IL)
Borough of Manhattan Comm Coll of City U of NY (NY)
Brazosport Coll (TX)
Briarwood Coll (CT)
Bronx Comm Coll of City U of NY (NY)
Broward Comm Coll (FL)
Butler County Comm Coll (KS)
Central Arizona Coll (AZ)
Central Comm Coll–Grand Island Campus (NE)
Central Comm Coll–Hastings Campus (NE)
Centralia Coll (WA)
Central Piedmont Comm Coll (NC)
Chattahoochee Tech Coll (GA)
Chattanooga State Tech Comm Coll (TN)
Cleveland State Comm Coll (TN)
Cloud County Comm Coll (KS)
Coastal Bend Coll (TX)
Colby Comm Coll (KS)
Coll of DuPage (IL)
Coll of Southern Idaho (ID)
Coll of the Canyons (CA)
Coll of the Mainland (TX)

Colorado Mountn Coll, Timberline Cmps (CO)
Columbus State Comm Coll (OH)
Comm Coll of Allegheny County (PA)
Comm Coll of Southern Nevada (NV)
Comm Coll of Vermont (VT)
Compton Comm Coll (CA)
Copiah-Lincoln Comm Coll (MS)
Cowley County Comm Coll and Voc-Tech School (KS)
Danville Area Comm Coll (IL)
Daytona Beach Comm Coll (FL)
De Anza Coll (CA)
Delaware Tech & Comm Coll, Jack F Owens Cmps (DE)
Delta Coll (MI)
Des Moines Area Comm Coll (IA)
Dodge City Comm Coll (KS)
Durham Tech Comm Coll (NC)
Dutchess Comm Coll (NY)
Dyersburg State Comm Coll (TN)
Ellsworth Comm Coll (IA)
El Paso Comm Coll (TX)
Enterprise-Ozark Comm Coll (AL)
Fairmont State Comm & Tech Coll (WV)
Foothill Coll (CA)
Forsyth Tech Comm Coll (NC)
Fox Valley Tech Coll (WI)
Frederick Comm Coll (MD)
Gainesville Coll (GA)
Garden City Comm Coll (KS)
Glendale Comm Coll (CA)
Gogebic Comm Coll (MI)
Guam Comm Coll (GU)
Harcum Coll (PA)
Hawkeye Comm Coll (IA)
Heartland Comm Coll (IL)
Highland Comm Coll (IL)
Hillsborough Comm Coll (FL)
Hinds Comm Coll (MS)
Holmes Comm Coll (MS)
Houston Comm Coll System (TX)
Howard Coll (TX)
Howard Comm Coll (MD)
Hudson County Comm Coll (NJ)
Illinois Eastern Comm Colls, Wabash Valley Coll (IL)
Illinois Valley Comm Coll (IL)
Independence Comm Coll (KS)
Indian Hills Comm Coll (IA)
Indian River Comm Coll (FL)
Iowa Lakes Comm Coll (IA)
Iowa Western Comm Coll (IA)
Jackson State Comm Coll (TN)
Jefferson Comm Coll (KY)
Lane Comm Coll (OR)
Lansing Comm Coll (MI)
Laredo Comm Coll (TX)
Lewis and Clark Comm Coll (IL)
McDowell Tech Comm Coll (NC)
Metropolitan Comm Coll (NE)
Miami Dade Coll (FL)
Mid Michigan Comm Coll (MI)
Milwaukee Area Tech Coll (WI)
Minnesota State Coll–Southeast (MN)
Modesto Jr Coll (CA)
Muskegon Comm Coll (MI)
Napa Valley Coll (CA)
New Hampshire Comm Tech Coll, Manchester/Stratham (NH)

Child Development

Northland Comm and Tech Coll–Thief River Falls (MN)
North Shore Comm Coll (MA)
Northwestern Connecticut Comm-Tech Coll (CT)
Northwest-Shoals Comm Coll (AL)
Northwest State Comm Coll (OH)
Odessa Coll (TX)
Orange County Comm Coll (NY)
Otero Jr Coll (CO)
Peninsula Coll (WA)
Polk Comm Coll (FL)
Pratt Comm Coll and Area Vocational School (KS)
Richland Comm Coll (IL)
Riverside Comm Coll District (CA)
Rockingham Comm Coll (NC)
Rock Valley Coll (IL)
Rogue Comm Coll (OR)
Saint Charles Comm Coll (MO)
St. Cloud Tech Coll (MN)
St. Louis Comm Coll at Forest Park (MO)
St. Louis Comm Coll at Meramec (MO)
Saint Paul Coll–A Comm & Tech College (MN)
Salt Lake Comm Coll (UT)
San Antonio Coll (TX)
Sandhills Comm Coll (NC)
San Joaquin Delta Coll (CA)
Santa Fe Comm Coll (FL)
Seminole Comm Coll (FL)
Seward County Comm Coll (KS)
Shawnee Comm Coll (IL)
Shoreline Comm Coll (WA)
Sinclair Comm Coll (OH)
Snow Coll (UT)
Southeast Comm Coll, Lincoln Campus (NE)
Southern Maine Comm Coll (ME)
Southwestern Comm Coll (NC)
Southwest Wisconsin Tech Coll (WI)
Tompkins Cortland Comm Coll (NY)
Trinity Valley Comm Coll (TX)
Truckee Meadows Comm Coll (NV)
Umpqua Comm Coll (OR)
U of Arkansas Comm Coll at Morrilton (AR)
Walters State Comm Coll (TN)
Wayne County Comm Coll District (MI)
Westchester Comm Coll (NY)
Western Oklahoma State Coll (OK)
Westmoreland County Comm Coll (PA)
Yakima Valley Comm Coll (WA)
Yuba Coll (CA)

Child Guidance

Dutchess Comm Coll (NY)
Elizabethtown Comm and Tech Coll (KY)
Gulf Coast Comm Coll (FL)
Ivy Tech State Coll–Central Indiana (IN)
John Wood Comm Coll (IL)
Laurel Business Inst (PA)
Lincoln Land Comm Coll (IL)
Minneapolis Comm and Tech Coll (MN)
Moberly Area Comm Coll (MO)
Prairie State Coll (IL)
Rochester Comm and Tech Coll (MN)
Santa Rosa Jr Coll (CA)

Chiropractic Assistant

Barton County Comm Coll (KS)
Iowa Lakes Comm Coll (IA)
Sauk Valley Comm Coll (IL)

Cinematography and Film/Video Production

Anne Arundel Comm Coll (MD)
The Art Inst of New York City (NY)
The Art Inst of Philadelphia (PA)
Bucks County Comm Coll (PA)
Cincinnati State Tech and Comm Coll (OH)
Coll of DuPage (IL)
Coll of the Canyons (CA)
Cumberland County Coll (NJ)
Daytona Beach Comm Coll (FL)
Everett Comm Coll (WA)
Full Sail Real World Education (FL)
Glendale Comm Coll (AZ)
Guilford Tech Comm Coll (NC)
Holyoke Comm Coll (MA)
Lane Comm Coll (OR)
Lansing Comm Coll (MI)
Miami Dade Coll (FL)
Minneapolis Comm and Tech Coll (MN)
Orange Coast Coll (CA)
Piedmont Comm Coll (NC)
Platt Coll San Diego (CA)
St. Louis Comm Coll at Meramec (MO)
Seattle Central Comm Coll (WA)
Shoreline Comm Coll (WA)
Southern Maine Comm Coll (ME)
Valencia Comm Coll (FL)

Civil Drafting and Cad/Cadd

Blue Mountain Comm Coll (OR)
Comm Coll of Allegheny County (PA)
North Seattle Comm Coll (WA)

Civil Engineering

Itasca Comm Coll (MN)

Civil Engineering Related

Bristol Comm Coll (MA)

Civil Engineering Technology

Asheville-Buncombe Tech Comm Coll (NC)
Belmont Tech Coll (OH)
Big Bend Comm Coll (WA)
Bishop State Comm Coll (AL)
Black Hawk Coll, Moline (IL)
Blue Mountain Comm Coll (OR)
Bristol Comm Coll (MA)
Broome Comm Coll (NY)
Broward Comm Coll (FL)
Butler County Comm Coll (PA)
Central Arizona Coll (AZ)
Central Carolina Tech Coll (SC)
Centralia Coll (WA)
Central Piedmont Comm Coll (NC)
Chattanooga State Tech Comm Coll (TN)
Chemeketa Comm Coll (OR)
Cincinnati State Tech and Comm Coll (OH)
Clark State Comm Coll (OH)
Coll of Lake County (IL)
Columbus State Comm Coll (OH)
Comm & Tech Coll at West Virginia U Inst of Technology (WV)

Comm Coll of Allegheny County (PA)
Compton Comm Coll (CA)
Copiah-Lincoln Comm Coll (MS)
Daytona Beach Comm Coll (FL)
Delaware Tech & Comm Coll, Jack F Owens Cmps (DE)
Delaware Tech & Comm Coll, Stanton/ Wilmington Cmps (DE)
Delaware Tech & Comm Coll, Terry Cmps (DE)
Des Moines Area Comm Coll (IA)
Eastern Arizona Coll (AZ)
Erie Comm Coll, North Campus (NY)
Essex County Coll (NJ)
Everett Comm Coll (WA)
Fairmont State Comm & Tech Coll (WV)
Fayetteville Tech Comm Coll (NC)
Florida Comm Coll at Jacksonville (FL)
Gadsden State Comm Coll (AL)
Guam Comm Coll (GU)
Guilford Tech Comm Coll (NC)
Gulf Coast Comm Coll (FL)
Harrisburg Area Comm Coll (PA)
Hawkeye Comm Coll (IA)
Hinds Comm Coll (MS)
Houston Comm Coll System (TX)
Hudson Valley Comm Coll (NY)
Independence Comm Coll (KS)
Indian River Comm Coll (FL)
Iowa Western Comm Coll (IA)
Itawamba Comm Coll (MS)
Johnson County Comm Coll (KS)
J. Sargeant Reynolds Comm Coll (VA)
Lake Land Coll (IL)
Lake Superior Coll (MN)
Lansing Comm Coll (MI)
Laramie County Comm Coll (WY)
Linn-Benton Comm Coll (OR)
Linn State Tech Coll (MO)
Macomb Comm Coll (MI)
Metropolitan Comm Coll (NE)
Miami Dade Coll (FL)
Midlands Tech Coll (SC)
Milwaukee Area Tech Coll (WI)
Mohawk Valley Comm Coll (NY)
Nashville State Tech Comm Coll (TN)
Nassau Comm Coll (NY)
New Mexico Military Inst (NM)
North Dakota State Coll of Science (ND)
Northern Essex Comm Coll (MA)
Northern Virginia Comm Coll (VA)
Northwest Tech Coll (MN)
Pasadena City Coll (CA)
Peninsula Coll (WA)
Rochester Comm and Tech Coll (MN)
St. Cloud Tech Coll (MN)
Saint Paul Coll–A Comm & Tech College (MN)
Salt Lake Comm Coll (UT)
San Antonio Coll (TX)
Sandhills Comm Coll (NC)
San Joaquin Delta Coll (CA)
Savannah Tech Coll (GA)
Seminole Comm Coll (FL)

Shoreline Comm Coll (WA)
Sinclair Comm Coll (OH)
Southeast Comm Coll, Milford Campus (NE)
Southeast Tech Inst (SD)
Spartanburg Tech Coll (SC)
Springfield Tech Comm Coll (MA)
State U of NY Coll of Technology at Alfred (NY)
State U of NY Coll of Technology at Canton (NY)
Three Rivers Comm Coll (CT)
Trident Tech Coll (SC)
Trinidad State Jr Coll (CO)
Umpqua Comm Coll (OR)
Union County Coll (NJ)
Valencia Comm Coll (FL)
Wake Tech Comm Coll (NC)
Walla Walla Comm Coll (WA)
Westchester Comm Coll (NY)
Yakima Valley Comm Coll (WA)

Civil/Structural Drafting

Luna Comm Coll (NM)

Classics and Languages, Literatures And Linguistics

Foothill Coll (CA)

Clinical Laboratory Science/ Medical Technology

Amarillo Coll (TX)
Andrew Coll (GA)
Anne Arundel Comm Coll (MD)
Anoka-Ramsey Comm Coll (MN)
Anoka-Ramsey Comm Coll, Cambridge Campus (MN)
Arapahoe Comm Coll (CO)
Athens Tech Coll (GA)
Broward Comm Coll (FL)
Casper Coll (WY)
Central Piedmont Comm Coll (NC)
Chattahoochee Valley Comm Coll (AL)
Chipola Coll (FL)
Coahoma Comm Coll (MS)
Coll of Southern Idaho (ID)
Columbus State Comm Coll (OH)
Comm Coll of Southern Nevada (NV)
Cuyahoga Comm Coll (OH)
Darton Coll (GA)
Dodge City Comm Coll (KS)
Ellsworth Comm Coll (IA)
Fort Scott Comm Coll (KS)
Henderson Comm Coll (KY)
Highland Comm Coll (KS)
Holmes Comm Coll (MS)
Holyoke Comm Coll (MA)
Howard Comm Coll (MD)
Kilgore Coll (TX)
Lansing Comm Coll (MI)
Mineral Area Coll (MO)
North Idaho Coll (ID)
Northwest-Shoals Comm Coll (AL)
Orange Coast Coll (CA)
South Texas Coll (TX)
Temple Coll (TX)
U of Cincinnati Raymond Walters Coll (OH)
Westchester Comm Coll (NY)

Clinical/Medical Laboratory Assistant

Allegany Coll of Maryland (MD)
Clover Park Tech Coll (WA)
Columbus State Comm Coll (OH)
Harrisburg Area Comm Coll (PA)
Riverside Comm Coll District (CA)
Somerset Comm Coll (KY)

Clinical/Medical Laboratory Science and Allied Professions Related

Highline Comm Coll (WA)
Oakland Comm Coll (MI)

Clinical/Medical Laboratory Technology

Alabama Southern Comm Coll (AL)
Alamance Comm Coll (NC)
Albuquerque Tech Vocational Inst (NM)
Alexandria Tech Coll (MN)
Allegany Coll of Maryland (MD)
Arapahoe Comm Coll (CO)
Asheville-Buncombe Tech Comm Coll (NC)
Austin Comm Coll (TX)
Barton County Comm Coll (KS)
Beaufort County Comm Coll (NC)
Bergen Comm Coll (NJ)
Bevill State Comm Coll (AL)
Bismarck State Coll (ND)
Brevard Comm Coll (FL)
Bristol Comm Coll (MA)
Bronx Comm Coll of City U of NY (NY)
Brookdale Comm Coll (NJ)
Broome Comm Coll (NY)
Broward Comm Coll (FL)
Central Georgia Tech Coll (GA)
Central Piedmont Comm Coll (NC)
Central Texas Coll (TX)
Cincinnati State Tech and Comm Coll (OH)
Clark State Comm Coll (OH)
Clinton Comm Coll (NY)
Coastal Carolina Comm Coll (NC)
Coastal Georgia Comm Coll (GA)
Columbia State Comm Coll (TN)
Columbus State Comm Coll (OH)
Comm Coll of Allegheny County (PA)
Comm Coll of Beaver County (PA)
Comm Coll of Philadelphia (PA)
Comm Coll of Rhode Island (RI)
Comm Coll of Southern Nevada (NV)
Comm Coll of the Air Force (AL)
Copiah-Lincoln Comm Coll (MS)
Davidson County Comm Coll (NC)
DeKalb Tech Coll (GA)
Delaware Tech & Comm Coll, Jack F Owens Cmps (DE)
Des Moines Area Comm Coll (IA)
Dutchess Comm Coll (NY)
Elgin Comm Coll (IL)
El Paso Comm Coll (TX)
Erie Comm Coll, North Campus (NY)
Eugenio María de Hostos Comm Coll of City U of NY (NY)
Gadsden State Comm Coll (AL)
Gainesville Coll (GA)
Genesee Comm Coll (NY)
George Corley Wallace State Comm Coll (AL)
George C. Wallace Comm Coll (AL)
Guilford Tech Comm Coll (NC)
Halifax Comm Coll (NC)
Harcum Coll (PA)
Harrisburg Area Comm Coll (PA)

Hawkeye Comm Coll (IA)
Hazard Comm and Tech Coll (KY)
Hibbing Comm Coll (MN)
Hinds Comm Coll (MS)
Houston Comm Coll System (TX)
Hudson Valley Comm Coll (NY)
Indian River Comm Coll (FL)
Iowa Central Comm Coll (IA)
Ivy Tech State Coll–North Central (IN)
Ivy Tech State Coll–Wabash Valley (IN)
Jackson State Comm Coll (TN)
Jamestown Comm Coll (NY)
Jefferson State Comm Coll (AL)
John A. Logan Coll (IL)
John Wood Comm Coll (IL)
J. Sargeant Reynolds Comm Coll (VA)
Kapiolani Comm Coll (HI)
Keiser Coll, Fort Lauderdale (FL)
Kilgore Coll (TX)
Lake Superior Coll (MN)
Laredo Comm Coll (TX)
Lehigh Carbon Comm Coll (PA)
Manchester Comm Coll (CT)
McLennan Comm Coll (TX)
Meridian Comm Coll (MS)
Miami Dade Coll (FL)
Midlands Tech Coll (SC)
Milwaukee Area Tech Coll (WI)
Mineral Area Coll (MO)
Minnesota West Comm & Tech Coll-Pipestone Cmps (MN)
Montgomery County Comm Coll (PA)
Nassau Comm Coll (NY)
Northern Virginia Comm Coll (VA)
North Hennepin Comm Coll (MN)
North Iowa Area Comm Coll (IA)
Northwest Tech Coll (MN)
Odessa Coll (TX)
Ohio State U Ag Tech Inst (OH)
Okefenokee Tech Coll (GA)
Orange County Comm Coll (NY)
Penn State U Hazleton Campus of the Commonwealth Coll (PA)
Phillips Comm Coll of the U of Arkansas (AR)
Queensborough Comm Coll of City U of NY (NY)
Rochester Comm and Tech Coll (MN)
St. Louis Comm Coll at Forest Park (MO)
Saint Paul Coll–A Comm & Tech College (MN)
St. Petersburg Coll (FL)
St. Philip's Coll (TX)
Salt Lake Comm Coll (UT)
Sandhills Comm Coll (NC)
Scott Comm Coll (IA)
Seminole State Coll (OK)
Seward County Comm Coll (KS)
Shelton State Comm Coll (AL)
Shoreline Comm Coll (WA)
Southeast Comm Coll, Lincoln Campus (NE)
Southeast Kentucky Comm and Tech Coll (KY)
Southeast Tech Inst (SD)
Southwestern Comm Coll (NC)
Southwestern Oklahoma State U at Sayre (OK)
Southwest Georgia Tech Coll (GA)

Spartanburg Tech Coll (SC)
Springfield Tech Comm Coll (MA)
State U of NY Coll of Technology at Canton (NY)
Temple Coll (TX)
Three Rivers Comm Coll (MO)
Tri-County Tech Coll (SC)
Trident Tech Coll (SC)
Union County Coll (NJ)
Wake Tech Comm Coll (NC)
Walters State Comm Coll (TN)
Wayne County Comm Coll District (MI)
Westchester Comm Coll (NY)
Western Iowa Tech Comm Coll (IA)
Western Nevada Comm Coll (NV)
West Georgia Tech Coll (GA)

Clinical/Medical Social Work
Central Comm Coll–Grand Island Campus (NE)
Central Comm Coll–Hastings Campus (NE)
Dawson Comm Coll (MT)

Clothing/Textiles
Central Alabama Comm Coll (AL)
Hinds Comm Coll (MS)
Indian River Comm Coll (FL)
Palm Beach Comm Coll (FL)
Tri-County Tech Coll (SC)

Commercial and Advertising Art
Academy Coll (MN)
Alamance Comm Coll (NC)
Alexandria Tech Coll (MN)
Amarillo Coll (TX)
Antonelli Inst (PA)
Arapahoe Comm Coll (CO)
The Art Inst of Philadelphia (PA)
Asnuntuck Comm Coll (CT)
Austin Comm Coll (TX)
Baltimore City Comm Coll (MD)
Bergen Comm Coll (NJ)
Bismarck State Coll (ND)
Brookdale Comm Coll (NJ)
Bryant & Stratton Business Inst, Amherst Cmps (NY)
Bucks County Comm Coll (PA)
Butler County Comm Coll (PA)
Casper Coll (WY)
Catawba Valley Comm Coll (NC)
Central Comm Coll–Columbus Campus (NE)
Central Comm Coll–Hastings Campus (NE)
Centralia Coll (WA)
Central Piedmont Comm Coll (NC)
Central Texas Coll (TX)
Chattanooga State Tech Comm Coll (TN)
Cincinnati State Tech and Comm Coll (OH)
Clark State Comm Coll (OH)
Clovis Comm Coll (NM)
Coastal Bend Coll (TX)
Colby Comm Coll (KS)
Coll of DuPage (IL)
Coll of Southern Idaho (ID)
Collin County Comm Coll District (TX)
Colorado Mountn Coll (CO)
Columbus State Comm Coll (OH)
Comm Coll of Allegheny County (PA)
Comm Coll of Aurora (CO)
Comm Coll of Denver (CO)
Comm Coll of Southern Nevada (NV)
Comm Coll of the Air Force (AL)

Compton Comm Coll (CA)
Cuyahoga Comm Coll (OH)
Daytona Beach Comm Coll (FL)
De Anza Coll (CA)
Delaware County Comm Coll (PA)
Des Moines Area Comm Coll (IA)
Dixie State Coll of Utah (UT)
Dutchess Comm Coll (NY)
East Central Coll (MO)
Eastern Arizona Coll (AZ)
Edison State Comm Coll (OH)
Elgin Comm Coll (IL)
El Paso Comm Coll (TX)
Everett Comm Coll (WA)
Fayetteville Tech Comm Coll (NC)
Fashion Inst of Design & Merchandising, LA Campus (CA)
Fashion Inst of Design & Merchandising, SD Campus (CA)
Fashion Inst of Design & Merchandising, SF Campus (CA)
Finger Lakes Comm Coll (NY)
Florida Comm Coll at Jacksonville (FL)
Florida Keys Comm Coll (FL)
Foothill Coll (CA)
Forsyth Tech Comm Coll (NC)
Fort Scott Comm Coll (KS)
Fox Valley Tech Coll (WI)
Full Sail Real World Education (FL)
Fulton-Montgomery Comm Coll (NY)
Garden City Comm Coll (KS)
Genesee Comm Coll (NY)
George C. Wallace Comm Coll (AL)
Glendale Comm Coll (AZ)
Glendale Comm Coll (CA)
Gogebic Comm Coll (MI)
Greenfield Comm Coll (MA)
Guilford Tech Comm Coll (NC)
Hagerstown Comm Coll (MD)
Halifax Comm Coll (NC)
Harford Comm Coll (MD)
Harrisburg Area Comm Coll (PA)
Hawkeye Comm Coll (IA)
Henry Ford Comm Coll (MI)
Hesser Coll (NH)
Highland Comm Coll (IL)
Highland Comm Coll (KS)
Hillsborough Comm Coll (FL)
Hinds Comm Coll (MS)
Holyoke Comm Coll (MA)
Houston Comm Coll System (TX)
Iowa Lakes Comm Coll (IA)
Iowa Western Comm Coll (IA)
Isothermal Comm Coll (NC)
Jackson State Comm Coll (TN)
James H. Faulkner State Comm Coll (AL)
James Sprunt Comm Coll (NC)
Jefferson Comm Coll (KY)
J. F. Drake State Tech Coll (AL)
Johnson County Comm Coll (KS)
Johnston Comm Coll (NC)
Kalamazoo Valley Comm Coll (MI)
Kilgore Coll (TX)
Kingsborough Comm Coll of City U of NY (NY)
Lake-Sumter Comm Coll (FL)
Lane Comm Coll (OR)
Lansing Comm Coll (MI)

Lehigh Carbon Comm Coll (PA)
Linn-Benton Comm Coll (OR)
Macomb Comm Coll (MI)
Manchester Comm Coll (CT)
McDowell Tech Comm Coll (NC)
Metropolitan Comm Coll (NE)
Miami Dade Coll (FL)
Midland Coll (TX)
Midlands Tech Coll (SC)
Mid Michigan Comm Coll (MI)
Milwaukee Area Tech Coll (WI)
Mineral Area Coll (MO)
Minneapolis Comm and Tech Coll (MN)
Modesto Jr Coll (CA)
Mohawk Valley Comm Coll (NY)
Montgomery County Comm Coll (PA)
Muskegon Comm Coll (MI)
Nashville State Tech Comm Coll (TN)
Nassau Comm Coll (NY)
New Hampshire Comm Tech Coll, Manchester/Stratham (NH)
Northampton County Area Comm Coll (PA)
Northern Essex Comm Coll (MA)
Northern Virginia Comm Coll (VA)
North Hennepin Comm Coll (MN)
North Idaho Coll (ID)
Northwestern Connecticut Comm-Tech Coll (CT)
Northwestern Michigan Coll (MI)
Northwest Tech Coll (MN)
Orange Coast Coll (CA)
Owens Comm Coll, Findlay (OH)
Owens Comm Coll, Toledo (OH)
Palm Beach Comm Coll (FL)
Penn Valley Comm Coll (MO)
Pima Comm Coll (AZ)
Platt Coll San Diego (CA)
Pratt Comm Coll and Area Vocational School (KS)
Randolph Comm Coll (NC)
Raritan Valley Comm Coll (NJ)
Rockland Comm Coll (NY)
Saint Charles Comm Coll (MO)
St. Cloud Tech Coll (MN)
St. Louis Comm Coll at Forest Park (MO)
St. Louis Comm Coll at Meramec (MO)
St. Petersburg Coll (FL)
Salt Lake Comm Coll (UT)
San Antonio Coll (TX)
San Diego City Coll (CA)
San Joaquin Delta Coll (CA)
San Juan Coll (NM)
Santa Barbara City Coll (CA)
Santa Fe Comm Coll (FL)
Schoolcraft Coll (MI)
School of Advertising Art (OH)
Schuylkill Inst of Business and Technology (PA)
Seattle Central Comm Coll (WA)
Shoreline Comm Coll (WA)
Sinclair Comm Coll (OH)
Solano Comm Coll (CA)
Southeast Comm Coll, Milford Campus (NE)
Southeast Tech Inst (SD)
Southwestern Comm Coll (NC)
Springfield Tech Comm Coll (MA)

Surry Comm Coll (NC)
Sussex County Comm Coll (NJ)
Texas State Tech Coll–Waco/Marshall Campus (TX)
Tompkins Cortland Comm Coll (NY)
Trident Tech Coll (SC)
Trinidad State Jr Coll (CO)
Truckee Meadows Comm Coll (NV)
Tunxis Comm Coll (CT)
U of Arkansas Comm Coll at Morrilton (AR)
U of Cincinnati Raymond Walters Coll (OH)
Valencia Comm Coll (FL)
Villa Maria Coll of Buffalo (NY)
Westmoreland County Comm Coll (PA)
Whatcom Comm Coll (WA)
Yavapai Coll (AZ)

Commercial Fishing
Peninsula Coll (WA)

Commercial Photography
The Art Inst of Philadelphia (PA)
Houston Comm Coll System (TX)
Kilgore Coll (TX)
Mohawk Valley Comm Coll (NY)
Randolph Comm Coll (NC)

Communication and Journalism Related
Delaware County Comm Coll (PA)
Iowa Lakes Comm Coll (IA)
Keystone Coll (PA)
Queensborough Comm Coll of City U of NY (NY)

Communication and Media Related
Keystone Coll (PA)
Platt Coll San Diego (CA)
Somerset Comm Coll (KY)

Communication Disorders
Northampton County Area Comm Coll (PA)

Communication Disorders Sciences and Services Related
Bristol Comm Coll (MA)

Communication/Speech Communication and Rhetoric
Atlanta Metropolitan Coll (GA)
Barton County Comm Coll (KS)
Briarwood Coll (CT)
Bristol Comm Coll (MA)
Broome Comm Coll (NY)
Bunker Hill Comm Coll (MA)
Coll of Southern Idaho (ID)
Delaware County Comm Coll (PA)
Dixie State Coll of Utah (UT)
Dutchess Comm Coll (NY)
Erie Comm Coll, South Campus (NY)
Foothill Coll (CA)
Hutchinson Comm Coll and Area Vocational School (KS)
Jamestown Comm Coll (NY)
Keystone Coll (PA)
Lackawanna Coll (PA)
Laramie County Comm Coll (WY)
Lehigh Carbon Comm Coll (PA)
Macomb Comm Coll (MI)
Manchester Comm Coll (CT)
Massachusetts Bay Comm Coll (MA)
Montgomery County Comm Coll (PA)
Nassau Comm Coll (NY)

Northwestern Michigan Coll (MI)
San Juan Coll (NM)
Santa Barbara City Coll (CA)
Santa Rosa Jr Coll (CA)
Sauk Valley Comm Coll (IL)
Union County Coll (NJ)
Waubonsee Comm Coll (IL)
Western Wyoming Comm Coll (WY)
Yuba Coll (CA)

Communications Systems Installation and Repair Technology
Arapahoe Comm Coll (CO)
Bristol Comm Coll (MA)
Broome Comm Coll (NY)
Coll of DuPage (IL)
Erie Comm Coll, South Campus (NY)
Fayetteville Tech Comm Coll (NC)
Kennebec Valley Comm Coll (ME)
Modesto Jr Coll (CA)
Mohawk Valley Comm Coll (NY)
North Seattle Comm Coll (WA)

Communications Technologies and Support Services Related
Bowling Green State U–Firelands Coll (OH)
Comm Coll of Allegheny County (PA)
Harford Comm Coll (MD)
Montgomery County Comm Coll (PA)
Springfield Tech Comm Coll (MA)

Communications Technology
Allegany Coll of Maryland (MD)
Anne Arundel Comm Coll (MD)
Arapahoe Comm Coll (CO)
Athens Tech Coll (GA)
Black Hawk Coll, Moline (IL)
Cleveland Comm Coll (NC)
Coffeyville Comm Coll (KS)
Coll of DuPage (IL)
Comm Coll of Beaver County (PA)
Comm Coll of Philadelphia (PA)
Comm Coll of the Air Force (AL)
Dodge City Comm Coll (KS)
ECPI Coll of Technology, Newport News (VA)
ECPI Coll of Technology, Virginia Beach (VA)
ECPI Tech Coll, Richmond (VA)
ECPI Tech Coll, Roanoke (VA)
Essex County Coll (NJ)
Fairmont State Comm & Tech Coll (WV)
Hutchinson Comm Coll and Area Vocational School (KS)
Kent State U, Tuscarawas Campus (OH)
Lackawanna Coll (PA)
Milwaukee Area Tech Coll (WI)
Mott Comm Coll (MI)
Napa Valley Coll (CA)
New River Comm and Tech Coll (WV)
North Lake Coll (TX)
Northwestern Connecticut Comm-Tech Coll (CT)
Northwest Tech Coll (MN)
Orange Coast Coll (CA)
Pasadena City Coll (CA)
St. Philip's Coll (TX)
Santa Fe Comm Coll (FL)
Southern Maine Comm Coll (ME)

Community Health Services Counseling
Bay de Noc Comm Coll (MI)
Comm Coll of Allegheny County (PA)
Edmonds Comm Coll (WA)
Erie Comm Coll (NY)
Kingsborough Comm Coll of City U of NY (NY)
Mott Comm Coll (MI)

Community Organization and Advocacy
Berkshire Comm Coll (MA)
Clackamas Comm Coll (OR)
Cleveland State Comm Coll (TN)
Clinton Comm Coll (NY)
Comm Coll of Philadelphia (PA)
Comm Coll of Vermont (VT)
Cumberland County Coll (NJ)
Iowa Central Comm Coll (IA)
J. Sargeant Reynolds Comm Coll (VA)
Lane Comm Coll (OR)
Mohawk Valley Comm Coll (NY)
New Hampshire Comm Tech Coll, Manchester/Stratham (NH)

Computer and Information Sciences
Academy Coll (MN)
Albany Tech Coll (GA)
Alexandria Tech Coll (MN)
Alpena Comm Coll (MI)
Andrew Coll (GA)
Atlanta Metropolitan Coll (GA)
Berkshire Comm Coll (MA)
Bevill State Comm Coll (AL)
Bishop State Comm Coll (AL)
Brazosport Coll (TX)
Bristol Comm Coll (MA)
Broome Comm Coll (NY)
Bryant and Stratton Coll, Parma (OH)
Bryant & Stratton Business Inst, Amherst Cmps (NY)
Bryant & Stratton Business Inst (NY)
Bryant & Stratton Business Inst (NY)
Bucks County Comm Coll (PA)
Butler County Comm Coll (KS)
Butler County Comm Coll (PA)
Calhoun Comm Coll (AL)
Capital Comm Coll (CT)
Carroll Comm Coll (MD)
Cayuga County Comm Coll (NY)
Central Arizona Coll (AZ)
Central Comm Coll–Columbus Campus (NE)
Central Comm Coll–Grand Island Campus (NE)
Central Comm Coll–Hastings Campus (NE)
Central Texas Coll (TX)
Cerro Coso Comm Coll (CA)
Cincinnati State Tech and Comm Coll (OH)
City Colls of Chicago, Wilbur Wright Coll (IL)
Clarendon Coll (TX)
Clovis Comm Coll (NM)
Coffeyville Comm Coll (KS)
Collin County Comm Coll District (TX)
Comm Coll of Beaver County (PA)
Corning Comm Coll (NY)
Darton Coll (GA)
Dawson Comm Coll (MT)
Delaware County Comm Coll (PA)
Delta Coll (MI)
Dutchess Comm Coll (NY)

ECPI Coll of Technology, Newport News (VA)
ECPI Coll of Technology, Virginia Beach (VA)
ECPI Tech Coll, Richmond (VA)
ECPI Tech Coll, Roanoke (VA)
El Paso Comm Coll (TX)
Erie Comm Coll, North Campus (NY)
Fayetteville Tech Comm Coll (NC)
Finger Lakes Comm Coll (NY)
Florida Comm Coll at Jacksonville (FL)
Frank Phillips Coll (TX)
Gadsden State Comm Coll (AL)
GateWay Comm Coll (AZ)
Goodwin Coll (CT)
Hagerstown Comm Coll (MD)
Harford Comm Coll (MD)
Harrisburg Area Comm Coll (PA)
Heartland Comm Coll (IL)
Henry Ford Comm Coll (MI)
Herzing Coll (MN)
Herzing Coll (WI)
Hesser Coll (NH)
Hibbing Comm Coll (MN)
Houston Comm Coll System (TX)
Hutchinson Comm Coll and Area Vocational School (KS)
Indiana Business Coll, Indianapolis (IN)
Itawamba Comm Coll (MS)
Ivy Tech State Coll–Bloomington (IN)
Ivy Tech State Coll–Central Indiana (IN)
Ivy Tech State Coll–Columbus (IN)
Ivy Tech State Coll–Eastcentral (IN)
Ivy Tech State Coll–Kokomo (IN)
Ivy Tech State Coll–Lafayette (IN)
Ivy Tech State Coll–North Central (IN)
Ivy Tech State Coll–Northeast (IN)
Ivy Tech State Coll–Northwest (IN)
Ivy Tech State Coll–Southcentral (IN)
Ivy Tech State Coll–Southeast (IN)
Ivy Tech State Coll–Southwest (IN)
Ivy Tech State Coll–Wabash Valley (IN)
Ivy Tech State Coll–Whitewater (IN)
James H. Faulkner State Comm Coll (AL)
Jamestown Comm Coll (NY)
Jefferson State Comm Coll (AL)
J. Sargeant Reynolds Comm Coll (VA)
Kilgore Coll (TX)
Kingsborough Comm Coll of City U of NY (NY)
Kingwood Coll (TX)
Lackawanna Coll (PA)
Lake Region State Coll (ND)
Laramie County Comm Coll (WY)
Linn-Benton Comm Coll (OR)
Lower Columbia Coll (WA)
Luna Comm Coll (NM)
Massachusetts Bay Comm Coll (MA)
McIntosh Coll (NH)
Metropolitan Comm Coll-Business & Technology College (MO)

Mid-South Comm Coll (AR)
Moberly Area Comm Coll (MO)
Mohawk Valley Comm Coll (NY)
Montgomery County Comm Coll (PA)
Nassau Comm Coll (NY)
National Coll of Business & Technology, Salem (VA)
New River Comm and Tech Coll (WV)
Northampton County Area Comm Coll (PA)
Northern Essex Comm Coll (MA)
North Iowa Area Comm Coll (IA)
Northwest-Shoals Comm Coll (AL)
Oakland Comm Coll (MI)
Odessa Coll (TX)
Orange County Comm Coll (NY)
Ouachita Tech Coll (AR)
Owensboro Comm and Tech Coll (KY)
Parkland Coll (IL)
Pennsylvania Highland Comm Coll (PA)
Pima Comm Coll (AZ)
Prairie State Coll (IL)
Ranken Tech Coll (MO)
Riverside Comm Coll District (CA)
Salt Lake Comm Coll (UT)
Scott Comm Coll (IA)
Shoreline Comm Coll (WA)
Sinclair Comm Coll (OH)
Southeast Comm Coll, Lincoln Campus (NE)
Southeast Comm Coll, Milford Campus (NE)
South Hills School of Business & Technology, State College (PA)
Spartanburg Tech Coll (SC)
State U of NY Coll of Technology at Alfred (NY)
Sussex County Comm Coll (NJ)
Texas State Tech Coll–Waco/Marshall Campus (TX)
Wake Tech Comm Coll (NC)
Waubonsee Comm Coll (IL)
Westchester Comm Coll (NY)
Western Nevada Comm Coll (NV)
Western Oklahoma State Coll (OK)
Western Wyoming Comm Coll (WY)
West Georgia Tech Coll (GA)
Westmoreland County Comm Coll (PA)
Wor-Wic Comm Coll (MD)

Computer and Information Sciences And Support Services Related
Academy Coll (MN)
Atlantic Cape Comm Coll (NJ)
Blackfeet Comm Coll (MT)
Bunker Hill Comm Coll (MA)
Clover Park Tech Coll (WA)
Edmonds Comm Coll (WA)
Harrisburg Area Comm Coll (PA)
Herkimer County Comm Coll (NY)
Indiana Business Coll, Columbus (IN)
Indiana Business Coll, Indianapolis (IN)
Indiana Business Coll, Lafayette (IN)
Indiana Business Coll, Muncie (IN)
Indiana Business Coll, Terre Haute (IN)
Jackson Comm Coll (MI)

Laramie County Comm Coll (WY)
Metropolitan Comm Coll-Business & Technology College (MO)
Midlands Tech Coll (SC)
Mohawk Valley Comm Coll (NY)
Mott Comm Coll (MI)
Ranken Tech Coll (MO)
Schuylkill Inst of Business and Technology (PA)
Springfield Tech Comm Coll (MA)
Williston State Coll (ND)

Computer and Information Sciences Related
Adirondack Comm Coll (NY)
Anne Arundel Comm Coll (MD)
Austin Comm Coll (TX)
Blue River Comm Coll (MO)
Bristol Comm Coll (MA)
Bucks County Comm Coll (PA)
Cape Cod Comm Coll (MA)
Capital Comm Coll (CT)
Cayuga County Comm Coll (NY)
Centralia Coll (WA)
Central Oregon Comm Coll (OR)
Chipola Coll (FL)
Citrus Coll (CA)
Coastal Bend Coll (TX)
Colby Comm Coll (KS)
Coll of the Canyons (CA)
Columbia-Greene Comm Coll (NY)
Corning Comm Coll (NY)
Daytona Beach Comm Coll (FL)
Delta Coll (MI)
Eastfield Coll (TX)
ECPI Tech Coll, Richmond (VA)
ECPI Tech Coll, Roanoke (VA)
Ellsworth Comm Coll (IA)
El Paso Comm Coll (TX)
Fayetteville Tech Comm Coll (NC)
Florida Comm Coll at Jacksonville (FL)
GateWay Comm Coll (AZ)
Gateway Comm Coll (CT)
Genesee Comm Coll (NY)
Glendale Comm Coll (CA)
Gordon Coll (GA)
Heartland Comm Coll (IL)
Henderson Comm Coll (KY)
Herkimer County Comm Coll (NY)
Highland Comm Coll (IL)
Hinds Comm Coll (MS)
Holmes Comm Coll (MS)
Howard Coll (TX)
Howard Comm Coll (MD)
Iowa Lakes Comm Coll (IA)
Jamestown Comm Coll (NY)
J. Sargeant Reynolds Comm Coll (VA)
Lake-Sumter Comm Coll (FL)
Laurel Business Inst (PA)
Longview Comm Coll (MO)
Maple Woods Comm Coll (MO)
Metropolitan Comm Coll-Business & Technology College (MO)
Middle Georgia Coll (GA)
Milwaukee Area Tech Coll (WI)
Minneapolis Comm and Tech Coll (MN)
Mohave Comm Coll (AZ)
Nassau Comm Coll (NY)
National Coll of Business & Technology, Danville (KY)
National Coll of Business & Technology, Florence (KY)
National Coll of Business & Technology, Lexington (KY)

National Coll of Business & Technology, Louisville (KY)
National Coll of Business & Technology, Pikeville (KY)
National Coll of Business & Technology, Richmond (KY)
National Coll of Business & Technology, Bristol (TN)
National Coll of Business & Technology, Nashville (TN)
National Coll of Business & Technology, Bluefield (VA)
National Coll of Business & Technology, Charlottesville (VA)
National Coll of Business & Technology, Harrisonburg (VA)
National Coll of Business & Technology, Lynchburg (VA)
National Coll of Business & Technology, Martinsville (VA)
North Idaho Coll (ID)
Northland Comm and Tech Coll–Thief River Falls (MN)
North Shore Comm Coll (MA)
Olympic Coll (WA)
Orange County Comm Coll (NY)
Penn Valley Comm Coll (MO)
Quinebaug Valley Comm Coll (CT)
Richland Comm Coll (IL)
Rockland Comm Coll (NY)
St. Louis Comm Coll at Forest Park (MO)
Salt Lake Comm Coll (UT)
Sauk Valley Comm Coll (IL)
Seminole Comm Coll (FL)
Sinclair Comm Coll (OH)
Southeast Tech Inst (SD)
Southwestern Michigan Coll (MI)
Tacoma Comm Coll (WA)
Three Rivers Comm Coll (MO)
Tompkins Cortland Comm Coll (NY)
Trinidad State Jr Coll (CO)
Walters State Comm Coll (TN)
West Central Tech Coll (GA)
Westchester Comm Coll (NY)
Western Oklahoma State Coll (OK)
Yuba Coll (CA)

Computer and Information Systems Security
Academy Coll (MN)
Atlantic Cape Comm Coll (NJ)
City Colls of Chicago, Wilbur Wright Coll (IL)
Clover Park Tech Coll (WA)
ECPI Tech Coll, Glen Allen (VA)
ECPI Tech Coll, Richmond (VA)
ECPI Tech Coll, Roanoke (VA)
Florida Comm Coll at Jacksonville (FL)
Florida National Coll (FL)
Hagerstown Business Coll (MD)
Jamestown Comm Coll (NY)
Laurel Business Inst (PA)
Metropolitan Comm Coll-Business & Technology College (MO)
MTI Coll of Business and Technology, Houston (TX)
Riverland Comm Coll (MN)
St. Philip's Coll (TX)
Salt Lake Comm Coll (UT)
Seminole Comm Coll (FL)
Tompkins Cortland Comm Coll (NY)

Computer Engineering
Itasca Comm Coll (MN)
Santa Barbara City Coll (CA)

Computer Engineering Related
Catawba Valley Comm Coll (NC)
Coll of the Canyons (CA)
Columbus Tech Coll (GA)
Daytona Beach Comm Coll (FL)
Fayetteville Tech Comm Coll (NC)
Gateway Comm Coll (CT)
Glendale Comm Coll (CA)
Itasca Comm Coll (MN)
Jefferson Comm Coll (OH)
Middle Georgia Coll (GA)
Orange County Comm Coll (NY)
Salt Lake Comm Coll (UT)
Sandhills Comm Coll (NC)
Seminole Comm Coll (FL)
Sinclair Comm Coll (OH)
Surry Comm Coll (NC)

Computer Engineering Technology
Alabama Southern Comm Coll (AL)
Allegany Coll of Maryland (MD)
Alvin Comm Coll (TX)
Amarillo Coll (TX)
Anne Arundel Comm Coll (MD)
Belmont Tech Coll (OH)
Bergen Comm Coll (NJ)
Bowling Green State U-Firelands Coll (OH)
Brevard Comm Coll (FL)
Brookdale Comm Coll (NJ)
Broome Comm Coll (NY)
Broward Comm Coll (FL)
Bucks County Comm Coll (PA)
Capital Comm Coll (CT)
Carteret Comm Coll (NC)
Casper Coll (WY)
Catawba Valley Comm Coll (NC)
Cecil Comm Coll (MD)
Central Piedmont Comm Coll (NC)
Century Coll (MN)
Cerro Coso Comm Coll (CA)
Chandler-Gilbert Comm Coll (AZ)
Chattahoochee Tech Coll (GA)
Chattanooga State Tech Comm Coll (TN)
Chemeketa Comm Coll (OR)
Cincinnati State Tech and Comm Coll (OH)
Clatsop Comm Coll (OR)
Cleveland Comm Coll (NC)
Coastal Bend Coll (TX)
Collin County Comm Coll District (TX)
Colorado Mountn Coll, Alpine Cmps (CO)
Colorado Mountn Coll (CO)
Colorado Mountn Coll, Timberline Cmps (CO)
Columbus State Comm Coll (OH)
Comm Coll of Allegheny County (PA)
Comm Coll of Philadelphia (PA)
Comm Coll of Rhode Island (RI)
Comm Coll of Southern Nevada (NV)
Compton Comm Coll (CA)
Cuyahoga Comm Coll (OH)
Davenport U, Midland (MI)
Davidson County Comm Coll (NC)
DeKalb Tech Coll (GA)
Delaware Tech & Comm Coll, Terry Cmps (DE)

Des Moines Area Comm Coll (IA)
Doña Ana Branch Comm Coll (NM)
East Arkansas Comm Coll (AR)
Eastfield Coll (TX)
ECPI Coll of Technology, Newport News (VA)
ECPI Coll of Technology, Virginia Beach (VA)
ECPI Tech Coll, Roanoke (VA)
Edison State Comm Coll (OH)
Everest Coll (AZ)
Flathead Valley Comm Coll (MT)
Florida Comm Coll at Jacksonville (FL)
Foothill Coll (CA)
Forsyth Tech Comm Coll (NC)
Foundation Coll, San Diego (CA)
Frank Phillips Coll (TX)
Frederick Comm Coll (MD)
Fulton-Montgomery Comm Coll (NY)
Garden City Comm Coll (KS)
Gateway Comm Coll (CT)
Genesee Comm Coll (NY)
Glendale Comm Coll (CA)
Gogebic Comm Coll (MI)
Grand Rapids Comm Coll (MI)
Gulf Coast Comm Coll (FL)
Hawkeye Comm Coll (IA)
Heartland Comm Coll (IL)
Hesser Coll (NH)
Highline Comm Coll (WA)
Hillsborough Comm Coll (FL)
Houston Comm Coll System (TX)
Hudson County Comm Coll (NJ)
ICM School of Business & Medical Careers (PA)
Indian Hills Comm Coll (IA)
Indian River Comm Coll (FL)
Iowa Central Comm Coll (IA)
Jamestown Comm Coll (NY)
J. Sargeant Reynolds Comm Coll (VA)
Kansas City Kansas Comm Coll (KS)
Keiser Coll, Fort Lauderdale (FL)
Kent State U, Tuscarawas Campus (OH)
Kingwood Coll (TX)
Lane Comm Coll (OR)
Lansing Comm Coll (MI)
Lehigh Carbon Comm Coll (PA)
Lower Columbia Coll (WA)
Marshall Comm and Tech Coll (WV)
Massachusetts Bay Comm Coll (MA)
McLennan Comm Coll (TX)
Meridian Comm Coll (MS)
Miami Dade Coll (FL)
Minnesota State Coll–Southeast Tech (MN)
Montgomery County Comm Coll (PA)
Nashville State Tech Comm Coll (TN)
North Central Missouri Coll (MO)
Northern Essex Comm Coll (MA)
North Shore Comm Coll (MA)
Northwestern Connecticut Comm-Tech Coll (CT)
Northwest-Shoals Comm Coll (AL)
Orange Coast Coll (CA)
Orange County Comm Coll (NY)
Pasadena City Coll (CA)

Penn State U New Kensington Campus of the Commonwealth Coll (PA)
Piedmont Comm Coll (NC)
Pulaski Tech Coll (AR)
Queensborough Comm Coll of City U of NY (NY)
Ranken Tech Coll (MO)
RETS Tech Center (OH)
Richmond Comm Coll (NC)
Rock Valley Coll (IL)
St. Petersburg Coll (FL)
Salt Lake Comm Coll (UT)
San Antonio Coll (TX)
Sandhills Comm Coll (NC)
San Diego City Coll (CA)
San Joaquin Delta Coll (CA)
Santa Fe Comm Coll (FL)
Seminole Comm Coll (FL)
Southeast Comm Coll, Milford Campus (NE)
Southeast Kentucky Comm and Tech Coll (KY)
Southern Maine Comm Coll (ME)
Southwestern Comm Coll (NC)
Springfield Tech Comm Coll (MA)
State U of NY Coll of Technology at Alfred (NY)
Surry Comm Coll (NC)
Tech Coll of the Lowcountry (SC)
Texas State Tech Coll–Waco/Marshall Campus (TX)
Three Rivers Comm Coll (CT)
Three Rivers Comm Coll (MO)
Trident Tech Coll (SC)
Truckee Meadows Comm Coll (NV)
Umpqua Comm Coll (OR)
U of Cincinnati Raymond Walters Coll (OH)
Wake Tech Comm Coll (NC)
Western Tech Coll (TX)
Westmoreland County Comm Coll (PA)
Westwood Coll–Denver North (CO)
Whatcom Comm Coll (WA)
Yakima Valley Comm Coll (WA)

Computer Graphics
Academy Coll (MN)
Adirondack Comm Coll (NY)
Arapahoe Comm Coll (CO)
Baltimore City Comm Coll (MD)
Calhoun Comm Coll (AL)
Cape Cod Comm Coll (MA)
Carroll Comm Coll (MD)
Cecil Comm Coll (MD)
Cerro Coso Comm Coll (CA)
Columbia-Greene Comm Coll (NY)
Corning Comm Coll (NY)
Cowley County Comm Coll and Voc-Tech School (KS)
The Creative Center (NE)
Daytona Beach Comm Coll (FL)
De Anza Coll (CA)
Delta Coll (MI)
Edison State Comm Coll (OH)
Elgin Comm Coll (IL)
El Paso Comm Coll (TX)
Fayetteville Tech Comm Coll (NC)
Florida Comm Coll at Jacksonville (FL)
Florida National Coll (FL)
Full Sail Real World Education (FL)
Garden City Comm Coll (KS)
Gateway Comm Coll (CT)
Genesee Comm Coll (NY)
Globe Coll (MN)
Gogebic Comm Coll (MI)
Hinds Comm Coll (MS)

Howard Comm Coll (MD)
Iowa Lakes Comm Coll (IA)
Keiser Coll, Fort Lauderdale (FL)
Kingwood Coll (TX)
Lansing Comm Coll (MI)
Meridian Comm Coll (MS)
Mesabi Range Comm and Tech Coll (MN)
Metropolitan Comm Coll-Business & Technology College (MO)
Miami Dade Coll (FL)
Mid Michigan Comm Coll (MI)
Milwaukee Area Tech Coll (WI)
Minnesota School of Business–Brooklyn Center (MN)
Minnesota School of Business–Plymouth (MN)
Minnesota School of Business–Richfield (MN)
Modesto Jr Coll (CA)
Mount Wachusett Comm Coll (MA)
Nassau Comm Coll (NY)
North Country Comm Coll (NY)
Northeast Alabama Comm Coll (AL)
Northern Essex Comm Coll (MA)
Northern Virginia Comm Coll (VA)
Northland Comm and Tech Coll–Thief River Falls (MN)
North Shore Comm Coll (MA)
Northwestern Connecticut Comm-Tech Coll (CT)
Olympic Coll (WA)
Orange Coast Coll (CA)
Parkland Coll (IL)
Platt Coll San Diego (CA)
Prairie State Coll (IL)
Quinebaug Valley Comm Coll (CT)
Richland Comm Coll (IL)
Riverside Comm Coll District (CA)
Rockland Comm Coll (NY)
Salt Lake Comm Coll (UT)
San Antonio Coll (TX)
Seminole Comm Coll (FL)
Shoreline Comm Coll (WA)
Sinclair Comm Coll (OH)
Southeast Tech Inst (SD)
Spencerian Coll–Lexington (KY)
State U of NY Coll of Technology at Alfred (NY)
Tompkins Cortland Comm Coll (NY)
Trident Tech Coll (SC)
Wake Tech Comm Coll (NC)
Westmoreland County Comm Coll (PA)
Yakima Valley Comm Coll (WA)

Computer Hardware Engineering
Eastfield Coll (TX)
Florida Comm Coll at Jacksonville (FL)
Seminole Comm Coll (FL)
Sinclair Comm Coll (OH)
Stanly Comm Coll (NC)
Tompkins Cortland Comm Coll (NY)
Westwood Coll–Long Beach (CA)

Computer Hardware Technology
Brazosport Coll (TX)
Central Florida Comm Coll (FL)
Laramie County Comm Coll (WY)

Computer/Information Technology Services Administration Related
Alpena Comm Coll (MI)
Andover Coll (ME)
Arapahoe Comm Coll (CO)
Atlanta Metropolitan Coll (GA)
Barton County Comm Coll (KS)
Black Hawk Coll, Moline (IL)
Brevard Comm Coll (FL)
Brown Mackie Coll, Findlay Campus (OH)
Brunswick Comm Coll (NC)
Bucks County Comm Coll (PA)
Cayuga County Comm Coll (NY)
Central Carolina Comm Coll (NC)
Clinton Comm Coll (IA)
Clinton Comm Coll (NY)
Coastal Carolina Comm Coll (NC)
Corning Comm Coll (NY)
Daytona Beach Comm Coll (FL)
Dyersburg State Comm Coll (TN)
Eastern Shore Comm Coll (VA)
Eastfield Coll (TX)
Flathead Valley Comm Coll (MT)
Florida Comm Coll at Jacksonville (FL)
Gogebic Comm Coll (MI)
Guilford Tech Comm Coll (NC)
Hawkeye Comm Coll (IA)
Henderson Comm Coll (KY)
Hesston Coll (KS)
Howard Comm Coll (MD)
Iowa Lakes Comm Coll (IA)
Kennebec Valley Comm Coll (ME)
Keystone Coll (PA)
Laurel Business Inst (PA)
Maria Coll (NY)
Mesabi Range Comm and Tech Coll (MN)
Metropolitan Comm Coll-Business & Technology College (MO)
Middle Georgia Coll (GA)
Milwaukee Area Tech Coll (WI)
Modesto Jr Coll (CA)
Muscatine Comm Coll (IA)
Owensboro Comm and Tech Coll (KY)
Parkland Coll (IL)
Pennsylvania Highland Comm Coll (PA)
Rockland Comm Coll (NY)
St. Cloud Tech Coll (MN)
San Antonio Coll (TX)
Sandhills Comm Coll (NC)
Seminole Comm Coll (FL)
Sinclair Comm Coll (OH)
Southeast Kentucky Comm and Tech Coll (KY)
Southeast Tech Inst (SD)
Stanly Comm Coll (NC)
State U of NY Coll of Technology at Canton (NY)
Tompkins Cortland Comm Coll (NY)
Trident Tech Coll (SC)

Computer Installation and Repair Technology
Black Hawk Coll, Moline (IL)
Coll of DuPage (IL)
Coll of Lake County (IL)
Harrisburg Area Comm Coll (PA)
Hibbing Comm Coll (MN)
Kennebec Valley Comm Coll (ME)
Modesto Jr Coll (CA)
Montcalm Comm Coll (MI)
Northampton County Area Comm Coll (PA)

Riverland Comm Coll (MN)
State U of NY Coll of Technology at Alfred (NY)

Computer Maintenance Technology
St. Philip's Coll (TX)

Computer Management
Andover Coll (ME)
Anne Arundel Comm Coll (MD)
Berkeley Coll (NJ)
Cayuga County Comm Coll (NY)
Central Georgia Tech Coll (GA)
Cossatot Comm Coll of the U of Arkansas (AR)
Darton Coll (GA)
De Anza Coll (CA)
Delta Coll (MI)
ECPI Coll of Technology, Newport News (VA)
ECPI Coll of Technology, Virginia Beach (VA)
ECPI Tech Coll, Richmond (VA)
Hesser Coll (NH)
ICM School of Business & Medical Careers (PA)
Kennebec Valley Comm Coll (ME)
Lansing Comm Coll (MI)
Laurel Business Inst (PA)
McIntosh Coll (NH)
Mineral Area Coll (MO)
Northwestern Tech Coll (GA)
Otero Jr Coll (CO)
Southern Maine Comm Coll (ME)
Southwest Wisconsin Tech Coll (WI)
Thompson Inst (PA)
Tri-County Comm Coll (NC)
Villa Maria Coll of Buffalo (NY)

Computer Programming
Academy Coll (MN)
Alabama Southern Comm Coll (AL)
Alamance Comm Coll (NC)
Alvin Comm Coll (TX)
Amarillo Coll (TX)
Ancilla Coll (IN)
Andover Coll (ME)
Anne Arundel Comm Coll (MD)
Arapahoe Comm Coll (CO)
Asheville-Buncombe Tech Comm Coll (NC)
Athens Tech Coll (GA)
Atlantic Cape Comm Coll (NJ)
Augusta Tech Coll (GA)
Austin Comm Coll (TX)
Beaufort County Comm Coll (NC)
Belmont Tech Coll (OH)
Bergen Comm Coll (NJ)
Black Hawk Coll, Moline (IL)
Bladen Comm Coll (NC)
Blue Ridge Comm Coll (NC)
Borough of Manhattan Comm Coll of City U of NY (NY)
Bowling Green State U-Firelands Coll (OH)
Brazosport Coll (TX)
Brevard Comm Coll (FL)
Bristol Comm Coll (MA)
Brookdale Comm Coll (NJ)
Broward Comm Coll (FL)
Brunswick Comm Coll (NC)
Bucks County Comm Coll (PA)
Bunker Hill Comm Coll (MA)
Business Inst of Pennsylvania, Sharon (PA)
Butler County Comm Coll (PA)
Casper Coll (WY)
Catawba Valley Comm Coll (NC)

Cayuga County Comm Coll (NY)
Cecil Comm Coll (MD)
Cedar Valley Coll (TX)
Central Alabama Comm Coll (AL)
Central Carolina Comm Coll (NC)
Central Florida Comm Coll (FL)
Central Piedmont Comm Coll (NC)
Central Texas Coll (TX)
Chattahoochee Tech Coll (GA)
Chattanooga State Tech Comm Coll (TN)
Chemeketa Comm Coll (OR)
Cincinnati State Tech and Comm Coll (OH)
Clark State Comm Coll (OH)
Clover Park Tech Coll (WA)
Cochise Coll, Douglas (AZ)
Coffeyville Comm Coll (KS)
Coll of Southern Maryland (MD)
Collin County Comm Coll District (TX)
Columbus State Comm Coll (OH)
Comm Coll of Beaver County (PA)
Comm Coll of Denver (CO)
Comm Coll of Rhode Island (RI)
Comm Coll of Southern Nevada (NV)
Compton Comm Coll (CA)
Contra Costa Coll (CA)
Copiah-Lincoln Comm Coll (MS)
Corning Comm Coll (NY)
Dabney S. Lancaster Comm Coll (VA)
Danville Area Comm Coll (IL)
Danville Comm Coll (VA)
Darton Coll (GA)
Davenport U, Midland (MI)
Davidson County Comm Coll (NC)
Daytona Beach Comm Coll (FL)
De Anza Coll (CA)
DeKalb Tech Coll (GA)
Delaware Tech & Comm Coll, Jack F Owens Cmps (DE)
Delaware Tech & Comm Coll, Terry Cmps (DE)
Delta Coll (MI)
Des Moines Area Comm Coll (IA)
Dodge City Comm Coll (KS)
Durham Tech Comm Coll (NC)
East Central Coll (MO)
Eastfield Coll (TX)
East Mississippi Comm Coll (MS)
ECPI Coll of Technology, Virginia Beach (VA)
ECPI Tech Coll, Glen Allen (VA)
ECPI Tech Coll, Richmond (VA)
Edison State Comm Coll (OH)
El Paso Comm Coll (TX)
Essex County Coll (NJ)
Fayetteville Tech Comm Coll (NC)
Florida Comm Coll at Jacksonville (FL)
Florida Keys Comm Coll (FL)
Florida National Coll (FL)
Foundation Coll, San Diego (CA)
Fox Valley Tech Coll (WI)
Garden City Comm Coll (KS)
George Corley Wallace State Comm Coll (AL)
Grand Rapids Comm Coll (MI)

Greenfield Comm Coll (MA)
Griffin Tech Coll (GA)
Guilford Tech Comm Coll (NC)
Gulf Coast Comm Coll (FL)
Gwinnett Tech Coll (GA)
Heartland Comm Coll (IL)
Hesser Coll (NH)
Highline Comm Coll (WA)
Hillsborough Comm Coll (FL)
Hinds Comm Coll (MS)
Howard Coll (TX)
ICM School of Business & Medical Careers (PA)
Illinois Valley Comm Coll (IL)
Indiana Business Coll, Indianapolis (IN)
Indian Hills Comm Coll (IA)
Indian River Comm Coll (FL)
Iowa Lakes Comm Coll (IA)
Iowa Western Comm Coll (IA)
Isothermal Comm Coll (NC)
Johnston Comm Coll (NC)
J. Sargeant Reynolds Comm Coll (VA)
Kalamazoo Valley Comm Coll (MI)
Keiser Coll, Fort Lauderdale (FL)
Keystone Coll (PA)
Kilgore Coll (TX)
Lane Comm Coll (OR)
Lansing Comm Coll (MI)
Laramie County Comm Coll (WY)
Laredo Comm Coll (TX)
Lewis and Clark Comm Coll (IL)
Linn State Tech Coll (MO)
Long Beach City Coll (CA)
Longview Comm Coll (MO)
Lower Columbia Coll (WA)
Macomb Comm Coll (MI)
Maple Woods Comm Coll (MO)
Mayland Comm Coll (NC)
McDowell Tech Comm Coll (NC)
Metropolitan Comm Coll (NE)
Metropolitan Comm Coll-Business & Technology College (MO)
Miami Dade Coll (FL)
Mineral Area Coll (MO)
Minneapolis Comm and Tech Coll (MN)
Minnesota State Coll–Southeast Tech (MN)
Mohawk Valley Comm Coll (NY)
Montgomery County Comm Coll (PA)
New Mexico Military Inst (NM)
Northeastern Tech Coll (SC)
Northeast State Tech Comm Coll (TN)
Northern Essex Comm Coll (MA)
North Idaho Coll (ID)
North Lake Coll (TX)
North Shore Comm Coll (MA)
Northwestern Connecticut Comm-Tech Coll (CT)
Northwest-Shoals Comm Coll (AL)
Northwest State Comm Coll (OH)
Northwest Tech Coll (MN)
Oakland Comm Coll (MI)
Olympic Coll (WA)
Orange Coast Coll (CA)
Orange County Comm Coll (NY)
Palm Beach Comm Coll (FL)
Parkland Coll (IL)
Pasadena City Coll (CA)
Patrick Henry Comm Coll (VA)
Pennsylvania Highland Comm Coll (PA)

Computer Programming

Phillips Comm Coll of the U of Arkansas (AR)
Piedmont Virginia Comm Coll (VA)
Raritan Valley Comm Coll (NJ)
RETS Tech Center (OH)
Riverside Comm Coll District (CA)
Roanoke-Chowan Comm Coll (NC)
Rockland Comm Coll (NY)
St. Cloud Tech Coll (MN)
St. Louis Comm Coll at Meramec (MO)
Saint Paul Coll—A Comm & Tech College (MN)
St. Petersburg Coll (FL)
San Antonio Coll (TX)
Sandhills Comm Coll (NC)
San Joaquin Delta Coll (CA)
Santa Fe Comm Coll (FL)
Savannah Tech Coll (GA)
Schoolcraft Coll (MI)
Seminole Comm Coll (FL)
Seward County Comm Coll (KS)
Solano Comm Coll (CA)
South Central Tech Coll (MN)
Southeast Comm Coll, Milford Campus (NE)
Southeast Tech Inst (SD)
Southwestern Comm Coll (IA)
Southwestern Michigan Coll (MI)
Southwest Wisconsin Tech Coll (WI)
Surry Comm Coll (NC)
Temple Coll (TX)
Texas State Tech Coll–Waco/Marshall Campus (TX)
Thompson Inst (PA)
Three Rivers Comm Coll (CT)
Tri-County Tech Coll (SC)
Truckee Meadows Comm Coll (NV)
U of Cincinnati Raymond Walters Coll (OH)
U of Northwestern Ohio (OH)
Valencia Comm Coll (FL)
Vatterott Coll, Springfield (MO)
Vatterott Coll, Oklahoma City (OK)
Wake Tech Comm Coll (NC)
Western Nevada Comm Coll (NV)
Westwood Coll–Denver North (CO)
Wilson Tech Comm Coll (NC)

Computer Programming Related

Arapahoe Comm Coll (CO)
Austin Comm Coll (TX)
Blue Ridge Comm Coll (NC)
Brazosport Coll (TX)
Brunswick Comm Coll (NC)
Bucks County Comm Coll (PA)
Centralia Coll (WA)
Central Texas Coll (TX)
Clark State Comm Coll (OH)
Coastal Bend Coll (TX)
Corning Comm Coll (NY)
Delta Coll (MI)
Durham Tech Comm Coll (NC)
Eastfield Coll (TX)
El Paso Comm Coll (TX)
Erie Business Center, Main (PA)
Fayetteville Tech Comm Coll (NC)
Florida Comm Coll at Jacksonville (FL)
Florida National Coll (FL)
Glendale Comm Coll (CA)
Henderson Comm Coll (KY)
Herzing Coll (WI)
Hinds Comm Coll (MS)

Iowa Western Comm Coll (IA)
J. Sargeant Reynolds Comm Coll (VA)
Kennebec Valley Comm Coll (ME)
Laredo Comm Coll (TX)
Mesabi Range Comm and Tech Coll (MN)
Metropolitan Comm Coll-Business & Technology College (MO)
Milwaukee Area Tech Coll (WI)
Northeast State Tech Comm Coll (TN)
Northern Essex Comm Coll (MA)
Olympic Coll (WA)
Pasco-Hernando Comm Coll (FL)
Patrick Henry Comm Coll (VA)
Pennsylvania Highland Comm Coll (PA)
Riverside Comm Coll District (CA)
Rockland Comm Coll (NY)
Saint Charles Comm Coll (MO)
St. Cloud Tech Coll (MN)
St. Louis Comm Coll at Forest Park (MO)
Salt Lake Comm Coll (UT)
San Antonio Coll (TX)
Seminole Comm Coll (FL)
Sinclair Comm Coll (OH)
Southeast Tech Inst (SD)
Stanly Comm Coll (NC)
Surry Comm Coll (NC)
Tompkins Cortland Comm Coll (NY)
Truckee Meadows Comm Coll (NV)
Valencia Comm Coll (FL)
Western Oklahoma State Coll (OK)

Computer Programming (Specific Applications)

Alexandria Tech Coll (MN)
Arapahoe Comm Coll (CO)
Bladen Comm Coll (NC)
Brazosport Coll (TX)
Brevard Comm Coll (FL)
Bristol Comm Coll (MA)
Brown Mackie Coll, Findlay Campus (OH)
Bucks County Comm Coll (PA)
Bunker Hill Comm Coll (MA)
Caldwell Comm Coll and Tech Inst (NC)
Catawba Valley Comm Coll (NC)
Cedar Valley Coll (TX)
Central Carolina Comm Coll (NC)
Central Comm Coll–Columbus Campus (NE)
Central Comm Coll–Grand Island Campus (NE)
Central Comm Coll–Hastings Campus (NE)
Central Piedmont Comm Coll (NC)
Central Texas Coll (TX)
Cincinnati State Tech and Comm Coll (OH)
Cleveland Comm Coll (NC)
Coastal Bend Coll (TX)
Coastal Carolina Comm Coll (NC)
Coll of DuPage (IL)
Craven Comm Coll (NC)
Daytona Beach Comm Coll (FL)
Delaware County Comm Coll (PA)
Delta Coll (MI)
Des Moines Area Comm Coll (IA)
Elgin Comm Coll (IL)
El Paso Comm Coll (TX)
Essex County Coll (NJ)

Fayetteville Tech Comm Coll (NC)
Florida Comm Coll at Jacksonville (FL)
Florida National Coll (FL)
GateWay Comm Coll (AZ)
Glendale Comm Coll (CA)
Gogebic Comm Coll (MI)
Gulf Coast Comm Coll (FL)
Heartland Comm Coll (IL)
Henderson Comm Coll (KY)
Highland Comm Coll (IL)
Indiana Business Coll, Evansville (IN)
Indiana Business Coll, Indianapolis (IN)
Indiana Business Coll, Muncie (IN)
Indiana Business Coll, Terre Haute (IN)
Iowa Western Comm Coll (IA)
Johnson County Comm Coll (KS)
John Wood Comm Coll (IL)
Kaskaskia Coll (IL)
Lake Land Coll (IL)
Lake Region State Coll (ND)
Lake Superior Coll (MN)
Lincoln Land Comm Coll (IL)
Linn-Benton Comm Coll (OR)
Macomb Comm Coll (MI)
Mesabi Range Comm and Tech Coll (MN)
Metropolitan Comm Coll-Business & Technology College (MO)
Midland Coll (TX)
Milwaukee Area Tech Coll (WI)
Mohave Comm Coll (AZ)
Moraine Valley Comm Coll (IL)
North Dakota State Coll of Science (ND)
Northern Essex Comm Coll (MA)
North Shore Comm Coll (MA)
Northwestern Tech Coll (GA)
Orange Coast Coll (CA)
Palm Beach Comm Coll (FL)
Parkland Coll (IL)
Pasco-Hernando Comm Coll (FL)
Pennsylvania Highland Comm Coll (PA)
Richland Comm Coll (IL)
Riverland Comm Coll (MN)
Rockland Comm Coll (NY)
Saint Charles Comm Coll (MO)
St. Cloud Tech Coll (MN)
St. Louis Comm Coll at Forest Park (MO)
San Antonio Coll (TX)
Sandhills Comm Coll (NC)
Seminole Comm Coll (FL)
Sheridan Coll (WY)
Sinclair Comm Coll (OH)
Southeast Tech Inst (SD)
Southern State Comm Coll (OH)
South Hills School of Business & Technology, State College (PA)
Stanly Comm Coll (NC)
Tacoma Comm Coll (WA)
Trident Tech Coll (SC)
Valencia Comm Coll (FL)
Wake Tech Comm Coll (NC)
Waubonsee Comm Coll (IL)
West Central Tech Coll (GA)
Western Iowa Tech Comm Coll (IA)
Western Oklahoma State Coll (OK)
Western Wyoming Comm Coll (WY)
Wilkes Comm Coll (NC)

Computer Programming (Vendor/Product Certification)

Central Texas Coll (TX)
Coastal Bend Coll (TX)
Florida Comm Coll at Jacksonville (FL)
GateWay Comm Coll (AZ)
Guam Comm Coll (GU)
Heartland Comm Coll (IL)
Henderson Comm Coll (KY)
Lake Region State Coll (ND)
Metropolitan Comm Coll-Business & Technology College (MO)
Milwaukee Area Tech Coll (WI)
Parkland Coll (IL)
Peninsula Coll (WA)
Riverland Comm Coll (MN)
St. Louis Comm Coll at Forest Park (MO)
San Antonio Coll (TX)
Seminole Comm Coll (FL)
Sinclair Comm Coll (OH)
Southeast Tech Inst (SD)
Thaddeus Stevens Coll of Technology (PA)
Western Oklahoma State Coll (OK)

Computer Science

Adirondack Comm Coll (NY)
Alabama Southern Comm Coll (AL)
Allen County Comm Coll (KS)
Amarillo Coll (TX)
Andover Coll (ME)
Anne Arundel Comm Coll (MD)
Anoka-Ramsey Comm Coll (MN)
Anoka-Ramsey Comm Coll, Cambridge Campus (MN)
Arapahoe Comm Coll (CO)
Arizona Western Coll (AZ)
Asnuntuck Comm Coll (CT)
Atlanta Metropolitan Coll (GA)
Austin Comm Coll (TX)
Baltimore City Comm Coll (MD)
Barton County Comm Coll (KS)
Bergen Comm Coll (NJ)
Bessemer State Tech Coll (AL)
Blue River Comm Coll (MO)
Bristol Comm Coll (MA)
Bronx Comm Coll of City U of NY (NY)
Broward Comm Coll (FL)
Brown Mackie Coll, Northern Kentucky Campus (KY)
Bucks County Comm Coll (PA)
Bunker Hill Comm Coll (MA)
Butler County Comm Coll (KS)
Cape Cod Comm Coll (MA)
Career Colls of Chicago (IL)
Casper Coll (WY)
Catawba Valley Comm Coll (NC)
Cayuga County Comm Coll (NY)
Central Alabama Comm Coll (AL)
Central Arizona Coll (AZ)
Central Oregon Comm Coll (OR)
Central Piedmont Comm Coll (NC)
Central Wyoming Coll (WY)
Chattanooga State Tech Comm Coll (TN)
Chemeketa Comm Coll (OR)
Chipola Coll (FL)
Citrus Coll (CA)
Coahoma Comm Coll (MS)
Coastal Bend Coll (TX)
Coastal Georgia Comm Coll (GA)
Cochise Coll, Douglas (AZ)

Coffeyville Comm Coll (KS)
Colby Comm Coll (KS)
Coll of Southern Idaho (ID)
Coll of the Canyons (CA)
Columbia Coll (CA)
Columbia-Greene Comm Coll (NY)
Commonwealth Tech Inst (PA)
Comm Coll of Philadelphia (PA)
Comm Coll of Southern Nevada (NV)
Comm Coll of Vermont (VT)
Contra Costa Coll (CA)
Corning Comm Coll (NY)
Cumberland County Coll (NJ)
Darton Coll (GA)
Daytona Beach Comm Coll (FL)
De Anza Coll (CA)
Delta Coll (MI)
Dixie State Coll of Utah (UT)
Dodge City Comm Coll (KS)
Dutchess Comm Coll (NY)
East Central Coll (MO)
East Central Comm Coll (MS)
East Mississippi Comm Coll (MS)
ECPI Coll of Technology, Newport News (VA)
ECPI Coll of Technology, Virginia Beach (VA)
ECPI Tech Coll, Richmond (VA)
ECPI Tech Coll, Roanoke (VA)
Edison State Comm Coll (OH)
Enterprise-Ozark Comm Coll (AL)
Erie Business Center, Main (PA)
Erie Business Center South (PA)
Essex County Coll (NJ)
Everett Comm Coll (WA)
Finger Lakes Comm Coll (NY)
Florida National Coll (FL)
Foothill Coll (CA)
Forsyth Tech Comm Coll (NC)
Fort Peck Comm Coll (MT)
Fort Scott Comm Coll (KS)
Foundation Coll, San Diego (CA)
Frank Phillips Coll (TX)
Fulton-Montgomery Comm Coll (NY)
Gadsden State Comm Coll-Ayers Campus (AL)
Gainesville Coll (GA)
Garden City Comm Coll (KS)
George Corley Wallace State Comm Coll (AL)
George C. Wallace Comm Coll (AL)
Glendale Comm Coll (CA)
Gogebic Comm Coll (MI)
Gordon Coll (GA)
Grand Rapids Comm Coll (MI)
Guam Comm Coll (GU)
Gwinnett Tech Coll (GA)
Hawaii Business Coll (HI)
Heartland Comm Coll (IL)
Henry Ford Comm Coll (MI)
Hesser Coll (NH)
Highland Comm Coll (IL)
Highland Comm Coll (KS)
Hinds Comm Coll (MS)
Holmes Comm Coll (MS)
Houston Comm Coll System (TX)
Howard Coll (TX)
Howard Comm Coll (MD)
Hudson County Comm Coll (NJ)
ICM School of Business & Medical Careers (PA)
Indian River Comm Coll (FL)

Iowa Lakes Comm Coll (IA)
Isothermal Comm Coll (NC)
Itawamba Comm Coll (MS)
Jackson State Comm Coll (TN)
Jamestown Comm Coll (NY)
Jefferson Comm Coll (NY)
John A. Logan Coll (IL)
Kingsborough Comm Coll of City U of NY (NY)
Lake Region State Coll (ND)
Lake-Sumter Comm Coll (FL)
Lanier Tech Coll (GA)
Laramie County Comm Coll (WY)
Longview Comm Coll (MO)
Lower Columbia Coll (WA)
Maple Woods Comm Coll (MO)
Massachusetts Bay Comm Coll (MA)
McIntosh Coll (NH)
Metropolitan Comm Coll-Business & Technology College (MO)
Miami Dade Coll (FL)
Middle Georgia Coll (GA)
Mid Michigan Comm Coll (MI)
Milwaukee Area Tech Coll (WI)
Modesto Jr Coll (CA)
Mohave Comm Coll (AZ)
Monroe Coll, Bronx (NY)
Monroe Coll, New Rochelle (NY)
Napa Valley Coll (CA)
Nassau Comm Coll (NY)
New England Coll of Finance (MA)
New Mexico Military Inst (NM)
Niagara County Comm Coll (NY)
Northeast Alabama Comm Coll (AL)
Northeastern Tech Coll (SC)
Northern Essex Comm Coll (MA)
Northern Virginia Comm Coll (VA)
North Idaho Coll (ID)
Northland Comm and Tech Coll–Thief River Falls (MN)
North Shore Comm Coll (MA)
Northwestern Connecticut Comm-Tech Coll (CT)
Northwest-Shoals Comm Coll (AL)
Odessa Coll (TX)
Orange County Comm Coll (NY)
Palm Beach Comm Coll (FL)
Parkland Coll (IL)
Pasadena City Coll (CA)
Penn Valley Comm Coll (MO)
Raritan Valley Comm Coll (NJ)
RETS Tech Center (OH)
Rochester Comm and Tech Coll (MN)
Rock Valley Coll (IL)
Rogue Comm Coll (OR)
Saint Charles Comm Coll (MO)
St. Louis Comm Coll at Forest Park (MO)
St. Louis Comm Coll at Meramec (MO)
Salt Lake Comm Coll (UT)
San Joaquin Delta Coll (CA)
San Juan Coll (NM)
Santa Barbara City Coll (CA)
Santa Rosa Jr Coll (CA)
Seminole State Coll (OK)
Seward County Comm Coll (KS)
Shelton State Comm Coll (AL)
Snow Coll (UT)
South Texas Coll (TX)

Southwestern Oklahoma State U at Sayre (OK)
Springfield Tech Comm Coll (MA)
State U of NY Coll of Technology at Alfred (NY)
Tacoma Comm Coll (WA)
Taft Coll (CA)
Temple Coll (TX)
Texas State Tech Coll–Waco/Marshall Campus (TX)
Tompkins Cortland Comm Coll (NY)
Trinidad State Jr Coll (CO)
Trinity Valley Comm Coll (TX)
Umpqua Comm Coll (OR)
The U of Akron–Wayne Coll (OH)
U of Cincinnati Raymond Walters Coll (OH)
Walters State Comm Coll (TN)
Wayne County Comm Coll District (MI)
Westchester Comm Coll (NY)
Western Oklahoma State Coll (OK)
Western Wyoming Comm Coll (WY)
Westmoreland County Comm Coll (PA)
West Virginia State Comm and Tech Coll (WV)
Whatcom Comm Coll (WA)
Yakima Valley Comm Coll (WA)
Yuba Coll (CA)

Computer Software and Media Applications Related
Ancilla Coll (IN)
Arapahoe Comm Coll (CO)
Brevard Comm Coll (FL)
Carteret Comm Coll (NC)
Cerro Coso Comm Coll (CA)
Delta Coll (MI)
El Paso Comm Coll (TX)
Fayetteville Tech Comm Coll (NC)
Florida Comm Coll at Jacksonville (FL)
Genesee Comm Coll (NY)
Glendale Comm Coll (CA)
Kennebec Valley Comm Coll (ME)
Laredo Comm Coll (TX)
Laurel Business Inst (PA)
Mesabi Range Comm and Tech Coll (MN)
Metropolitan Comm Coll–Business & Technology College (MO)
Northland Comm and Tech Coll–Thief River Falls (MN)
Olympic Coll (WA)
Parkland Coll (IL)
Platt Coll San Diego (CA)
Riverland Comm Coll (MN)
Salt Lake Comm Coll (UT)
Seminole Comm Coll (FL)
Sheridan Coll (WY)
Southeast Tech Inst (SD)
Western Oklahoma State Coll (OK)

Computer Software Engineering
Florida Comm Coll at Jacksonville (FL)
Globe Coll (MN)
Minnesota School of Business–Brooklyn Center (MN)
Minnesota School of Business–Plymouth (MN)
Minnesota School of Business–Richfield (MN)
Salt Lake Comm Coll (UT)
Seminole Comm Coll (FL)
Sinclair Comm Coll (OH)

Southeast Tech Inst (SD)
Tompkins Cortland Comm Coll (NY)

Computer Software Technology
Iowa Lakes Comm Coll (IA)
Miami Dade Coll (FL)
Westwood Coll–Denver North (CO)

Computer Systems Analysis
Albuquerque Tech Vocational Inst (NM)
Amarillo Coll (TX)
Brevard Comm Coll (FL)
Cape Fear Comm Coll (NC)
Central Florida Comm Coll (FL)
Coastal Carolina Comm Coll (NC)
Florida Comm Coll at Jacksonville (FL)
Hesser Coll (NH)
James Sprunt Comm Coll (NC)
Laramie County Comm Coll (WY)
Linn State Tech Coll (MO)
Lower Columbia Coll (WA)
McIntosh Coll (NH)
Metropolitan Comm Coll–Business & Technology College (MO)
Milwaukee Area Tech Coll (WI)
Pima Comm Coll (AZ)
Randolph Comm Coll (NC)
Richmond Comm Coll (NC)
Wilkes Comm Coll (NC)
Wor-Wic Comm Coll (MD)

Computer Systems Networking and Telecommunications
Academy Coll (MN)
Adirondack Comm Coll (NY)
Alexandria Tech Coll (MN)
Allen County Comm Coll (KS)
Alpena Comm Coll (MI)
Ancilla Coll (IN)
Anoka-Ramsey Comm Coll (MN)
Anoka-Ramsey Comm Coll, Cambridge Campus (MN)
Arapahoe Comm Coll (CO)
Asheville-Buncombe Tech Comm Coll (NC)
Austin Comm Coll (TX)
Barton County Comm Coll (KS)
Beaufort County Comm Coll (NC)
Bismarck State Coll (ND)
Black Hawk Coll, Moline (IL)
Blue Ridge Comm Coll (VA)
Bowling Green State U–Firelands Coll (OH)
Brevard Comm Coll (FL)
Bunker Hill Comm Coll (MA)
Cape Cod Comm Coll (MA)
Cape Fear Comm Coll (NC)
Carteret Comm Coll (NC)
Catawba Valley Comm Coll (NC)
Central Carolina Comm Coll (NC)
Centralia Coll (WA)
Central Wyoming Coll (WY)
Clark Coll (WA)
Clark State Comm Coll (OH)
Clatsop Comm Coll (OR)
Clover Park Tech Coll (WA)
Coastal Bend Coll (TX)
Coastal Carolina Comm Coll (NC)
Coll of the Mainland (TX)
Collin County Comm Coll District (TX)
Colorado Mountn Coll (CO)
Columbia-Greene Comm Coll (NY)
Comm Coll of Allegheny County (PA)
Corning Comm Coll (NY)

Craven Comm Coll (NC)
Crowder Coll (MO)
Cumberland County Coll (NJ)
Daytona Beach Comm Coll (FL)
Delaware County Comm Coll (PA)
Eastern Idaho Tech Coll (ID)
Eastfield Coll (TX)
Ellsworth Comm Coll (IA)
El Paso Comm Coll (TX)
Erie Business Center, Main (PA)
Fayetteville Tech Comm Coll (NC)
Florida Comm Coll at Jacksonville (FL)
Florida National Coll (FL)
Foundation Coll, San Diego (CA)
Garden City Comm Coll (KS)
Glendale Comm Coll (AZ)
Globe Coll (MN)
Guilford Tech Comm Coll (NC)
Harrisburg Area Comm Coll (PA)
Hawkeye Comm Coll (IA)
Heartland Comm Coll (IL)
Henderson Comm Coll (KY)
Herkimer County Comm Coll (NY)
Herzing Coll (MN)
Herzing Coll (WI)
Hibbing Comm Coll (MN)
Highline Comm Coll (WA)
Hillsborough Comm Coll (FL)
Howard Comm Coll (MD)
Illinois Valley Comm Coll (IL)
Iowa Lakes Comm Coll (IA)
Jefferson Comm Coll (NY)
Johnson County Comm Coll (KS)
Keiser Coll, Miami (FL)
Kennebec Valley Comm Coll (ME)
Kilgore Coll (TX)
Lake Land Coll (IL)
Lake Region State Coll (ND)
Lanier Tech Coll (GA)
Laredo Comm Coll (TX)
Laurel Business Inst (PA)
Lincoln Land Comm Coll (IL)
Lower Columbia Coll (WA)
Manhattan Area Tech Coll (KS)
Mesabi Range Comm and Tech Coll (MN)
Metropolitan Comm Coll–Business & Technology College (MO)
Midlands Tech Coll (SC)
Minnesota School of Business–Brooklyn Center (MN)
Minnesota School of Business–Plymouth (MN)
Minnesota School of Business–Richfield (MN)
Montgomery County Comm Coll (PA)
Moraine Valley Comm Coll (IL)
Mott Comm Coll (MI)
Nashville State Tech Comm Coll (TN)
Nassau Comm Coll (NY)
North Central State Coll (OH)
Northeast State Tech Comm Coll (TN)
Northern Essex Comm Coll (MA)
Northland Comm and Tech Coll–Thief River Falls (MN)
North Seattle Comm Coll (WA)
Northwest Tech Coll (MN)
Odessa Coll (TX)
Olympic Coll (WA)
Parkland Coll (IL)
Pasco-Hernando Comm Coll (FL)

Patrick Henry Comm Coll (VA)
Pima Comm Coll (AZ)
Pratt Comm Coll and Area Vocational School (KS)
Quinebaug Valley Comm Coll (CT)
Riverland Comm Coll (MN)
Riverside Comm Coll District (CA)
Rockland Comm Coll (NY)
Saint Charles Comm Coll (MO)
St. Cloud Tech Coll (MN)
St. Louis Comm Coll at Forest Park (MO)
St. Petersburg Coll (FL)
St. Philip's Coll (TX)
Salt Lake Comm Coll (UT)
San Joaquin Valley Coll (CA)
Seminole Comm Coll (FL)
Sheridan Coll (WY)
Sinclair Comm Coll (OH)
Southeast Tech Inst (SD)
Stanly Comm Coll (NC)
Surry Comm Coll (NC)
Tacoma Comm Coll (WA)
Thompson Inst (PA)
Trident Tech Coll (SC)
Trinidad State Jr Coll (CO)
The U of Akron–Wayne Coll (OH)
U of Arkansas Comm Coll at Batesville (AR)
U of Arkansas Comm Coll at Morrilton (AR)
Vatterott Coll, St. Joseph (MO)
Wake Tech Comm Coll (NC)
Westchester Comm Coll (NY)
Western Oklahoma State Coll (OK)
Wilkes Comm Coll (NC)

Computer/Technical Support
Anne Arundel Comm Coll (MD)
Anoka-Ramsey Comm Coll (MN)
Anoka-Ramsey Comm Coll, Cambridge Campus (MN)
Arapahoe Comm Coll (CO)
Baltimore City Comm Coll (MD)
Black Hawk Coll, Moline (IL)
Bowling Green State U–Firelands Coll (OH)
Clark State Comm Coll (OH)
Colorado Mountn Coll (CO)
Eastern Shore Comm Coll (VA)
El Paso Comm Coll (TX)
Fayetteville Tech Comm Coll (NC)
Florida Comm Coll at Jacksonville (FL)
Florida National Coll (FL)
Glendale Comm Coll (CA)
Goodwin Coll (CT)
Hawkeye Comm Coll (IA)
Heartland Comm Coll (IL)
Highland Comm Coll (IL)
Hinds Comm Coll (MS)
Holmes Comm Coll (MS)
Iowa Western Comm Coll (IA)
Laurel Business Inst (PA)
Linn-Benton Comm Coll (OR)
North Idaho Coll (ID)
Northland Comm and Tech Coll–Thief River Falls (MN)
Palm Beach Comm Coll (FL)
Parkland Coll (IL)
Pennsylvania Highland Comm Coll (PA)
Pratt Comm Coll and Area Vocational School (KS)
Riverland Comm Coll (MN)
Riverside Comm Coll District (CA)
St. Cloud Tech Coll (MN)
San Joaquin Valley Coll (CA)

Seminole Comm Coll (FL)
Southeast Tech Inst (SD)
Stanly Comm Coll (NC)
Tacoma Comm Coll (WA)
Three Rivers Comm Coll (MO)
Tompkins Cortland Comm Coll (NY)
Wake Tech Comm Coll (NC)

Computer Technology/Computer Systems Technology
Alexandria Tech Coll (MN)
Brazosport Coll (TX)
Cape Fear Comm Coll (NC)
Central Wyoming Coll (WY)
Clackamas Comm Coll (OR)
Comm Coll of Allegheny County (PA)
Corning Comm Coll (NY)
Delaware County Comm Coll (PA)
Eastern Maine Comm Coll (ME)
ECPI Tech Coll, Glen Allen (VA)
ECPI Tech Coll, Richmond (VA)
ECPI Tech Coll, Roanoke (VA)
Edmonds Comm Coll (WA)
Erie Comm Coll, South Campus (NY)
Foundation Coll, San Diego (CA)
Lake Superior Coll (MN)
Lehigh Carbon Comm Coll (PA)
Lower Columbia Coll (WA)
Manhattan Area Tech Coll (KS)
Miami Dade Coll (FL)
Miami U Hamilton (OH)
Mount Wachusett Comm Coll (MA)
MTI Coll of Business and Technology, Houston (TX)
Oakland Comm Coll (MI)
Okefenokee Tech Coll (GA)
Pima Comm Coll (AZ)
Schoolcraft Coll (MI)
Southeast Tech Inst (SD)
Stanly Comm Coll (NC)
Texas State Tech Coll–Waco/Marshall Campus (TX)
Vatterott Coll, St. Joseph (MO)
Walla Walla Comm Coll (WA)

Computer Typography and Composition Equipment Operation
Bergen Comm Coll (NJ)
Bristol Comm Coll (MA)
Brown Mackie Coll, Michigan City Campus (IN)
Chattahoochee Tech Coll (GA)
Clovis Comm Coll (NM)
Coll of DuPage (IL)
Comm Coll of Beaver County (PA)
Comm Coll of Denver (CO)
Comm Coll of Southern Nevada (NV)
Cumberland County Coll (NJ)
Cuyahoga Comm Coll (OH)
Davenport U, Midland (MI)
Daytona Beach Comm Coll (FL)
Doña Ana Branch Comm Coll (NM)
Durham Tech Comm Coll (NC)
ECPI Coll of Technology, Newport News (VA)
ECPI Coll of Technology, Virginia Beach (VA)
ECPI Tech Coll, Richmond (VA)
ECPI Tech Coll, Roanoke (VA)

Elgin Comm Coll (IL)
Flathead Valley Comm Coll (MT)
Fox Valley Tech Coll (WI)
Fulton-Montgomery Comm Coll (NY)
Gateway Comm Coll (CT)
Gogebic Comm Coll (MI)
Hazard Comm and Tech Coll (KY)
Highline Comm Coll (WA)
Holyoke Comm Coll (MA)
Indian River Comm Coll (FL)
Jefferson Comm Coll (NY)
Kingwood Coll (TX)
Lansing Comm Coll (MI)
Long Beach City Coll (CA)
Longview Comm Coll (MO)
Minnesota State Coll–Southeast Tech (MN)
Northeast Alabama Comm Coll (AL)
Northern Essex Comm Coll (MA)
Northwest-Shoals Comm Coll (AL)
Orange Coast Coll (CA)
Paradise Valley Comm Coll (AZ)
Pasadena City Coll (CA)
Platt Coll San Diego (CA)
Pratt Comm Coll and Area Vocational School (KS)
St. Cloud Tech Coll (MN)
Seattle Central Comm Coll (WA)
South Mountain Comm Coll (AZ)
South Texas Coll (TX)
State U of NY Coll of Technology at Alfred (NY)
Tech Coll of the Lowcountry (SC)
Three Rivers Comm Coll (CT)
U of Arkansas Comm Coll at Morrilton (AR)
Western Iowa Tech Comm Coll (IA)

Construction Engineering
State U of NY Coll of Technology at Alfred (NY)

Construction Engineering Technology
American Samoa Comm Coll (AS)
Austin Comm Coll (TX)
Bessemer State Tech Coll (AL)
Bismarck State Coll (ND)
Blackfeet Comm Coll (MT)
Brazosport Coll (TX)
Casper Coll (WY)
Cecil Comm Coll (MD)
Central Comm Coll–Hastings Campus (NE)
Chemeketa Comm Coll (OR)
Clark Coll (WA)
Coffeyville Comm Coll (KS)
Coll of Lake County (IL)
Comm Coll of Allegheny County (PA)
Comm Coll of Philadelphia (PA)
Comm Coll of Southern Nevada (NV)
Comm Coll of the Air Force (AL)
Compton Comm Coll (CA)
Crowder Coll (MO)
Daytona Beach Comm Coll (FL)
De Anza Coll (CA)
Delaware County Comm Coll (PA)
Delaware Tech & Comm Coll, Terry Cmps (DE)
Delta Coll (MI)
Dodge City Comm Coll (KS)
Dutchess Comm Coll (NY)
East Central Coll (MO)
Eastern Maine Comm Coll (ME)

Edmonds Comm Coll (WA)
Feather River Coll (CA)
Flathead Valley Comm Coll (MT)
Florida Comm Coll at Jacksonville (FL)
Forsyth Tech Comm Coll (NC)
Fort Peck Comm Coll (MT)
Fulton-Montgomery Comm Coll (NY)
GateWay Comm Coll (AZ)
Gogebic Comm Coll (MI)
Gulf Coast Comm Coll (FL)
Harrisburg Area Comm Coll (PA)
Henry Ford Comm Coll (MI)
Highland Comm Coll (KS)
Hillsborough Comm Coll (FL)
Houston Comm Coll System (TX)
Hudson Valley Comm Coll (NY)
Iowa Lakes Comm Coll (IA)
Itawamba Comm Coll (MS)
Jefferson State Comm Coll (AL)
J. Sargeant Reynolds Comm Coll (VA)
Lane Comm Coll (OR)
Lansing Comm Coll (MI)
Laramie County Comm Coll (WY)
Laredo Comm Coll (TX)
Lehigh Carbon Comm Coll (PA)
Macomb Comm Coll (MI)
McDowell Tech Comm Coll (NC)
Metropolitan Comm Coll (NE)
Miami Dade Coll (FL)
Midlands Tech Coll (SC)
Milwaukee Area Tech Coll (WI)
Mineral Area Coll (MO)
Morrison Inst of Technology (IL)
New Hampshire Comm Tech Coll, Manchester/Stratham (NH)
North Central Missouri Coll (MO)
North Dakota State Coll of Science (ND)
North Lake Coll (TX)
Odessa Coll (TX)
Ohio State U Ag Tech Inst (OH)
Orange Coast Coll (CA)
Orange County Comm Coll (NY)
Pasadena City Coll (CA)
Pennsylvania Highland Comm Coll (PA)
Pima Comm Coll (AZ)
Raritan Valley Comm Coll (NJ)
Richland Comm Coll (IL)
Roanoke-Chowan Comm Coll (NC)
Rockingham Comm Coll (NC)
Rock Valley Coll (IL)
St. Cloud Tech Coll (MN)
St. Petersburg Coll (FL)
St. Philip's Coll (TX)
Salt Lake Comm Coll (UT)
San Joaquin Delta Coll (CA)
Santa Fe Comm Coll (FL)
Seminole Comm Coll (FL)
Snow Coll (UT)
Southeast Comm Coll, Milford Campus (NE)
Southern Maine Comm Coll (ME)
State U of NY Coll of Technology at Alfred (NY)
State U of NY Coll of Technology at Canton (NY)
State U of NY Coll of Technology at Delhi (NY)
Surry Comm Coll (NC)

Tech Coll of the Lowcountry (SC)
Thaddeus Stevens Coll of Technology (PA)
Three Rivers Comm Coll (MO)
Tompkins Cortland Comm Coll (NY)
Trinidad State Jr Coll (CO)
Truckee Meadows Comm Coll (NV)
Valencia Comm Coll (FL)
Western Oklahoma State Coll (OK)
Yavapai Coll (AZ)

Construction/Heavy Equipment/Earthmoving Equipment Operation
Brazosport Coll (TX)
Ivy Tech State Coll–Southwest (IN)
Ivy Tech State Coll–Wabash Valley (IN)

Construction Management
Arapahoe Comm Coll (CO)
Broward Comm Coll (FL)
Columbus State Comm Coll (OH)
Columbus State Comm Coll (OH)
Comm Coll of Southern Nevada (NV)
Delaware Tech & Comm Coll, Jack F Owens Cmps (DE)
Delaware Tech & Comm Coll, Terry Cmps (DE)
Delta Coll (MI)
El Paso Comm Coll (TX)
Frederick Comm Coll (MD)
Gogebic Comm Coll (MI)
Gwinnett Tech Coll (GA)
Iowa Lakes Comm Coll (IA)
Modesto Jr Coll (CA)
North Hennepin Comm Coll (MN)
Northwest Tech Coll (MN)
Oakland Comm Coll (MI)
Ohio State U Ag Tech Inst (OH)
Palm Beach Comm Coll (FL)
Parkland Coll (IL)
Piedmont Virginia Comm Coll (VA)
St. Philip's Coll (TX)
Salt Lake Comm Coll (UT)
Santa Rosa Jr Coll (CA)
Seminole Comm Coll (FL)
Snow Coll (UT)
State U of NY Coll of Technology at Delhi (NY)
Western Nevada Comm Coll (NV)

Construction Trades
Clovis Comm Coll (NM)
Delta Coll (MI)
Iowa Lakes Comm Coll (IA)
Ivy Tech State Coll–Eastcentral (IN)
Ivy Tech State Coll–Northeast (IN)
Ivy Tech State Coll–Northwest (IN)
Ivy Tech State Coll–Whitewater (IN)
Laramie County Comm Coll (WY)
Triangle Tech, Inc.–Greensburg School (PA)

Construction Trades Related
Albuquerque Tech Vocational Inst (NM)
Comm Coll of Allegheny County (PA)
Comm Coll of Denver (CO)
Erie Comm Coll, North Campus (NY)
Jackson Comm Coll (MI)
Laramie County Comm Coll (WY)

Consumer Merchandising/Retailing Management
Anne Arundel Comm Coll (MD)
Arapahoe Comm Coll (CO)
Austin Comm Coll (TX)
Bay State Coll (MA)
Bergen Comm Coll (NJ)
Bessemer State Tech Coll (AL)
Bucks County Comm Coll (PA)
Casper Coll (WY)
Cayuga County Comm Coll (NY)
Centralia Coll (WA)
Central Piedmont Comm Coll (NC)
Chattanooga State Tech Comm Coll (TN)
Clinton Comm Coll (NY)
Coffeyville Comm Coll (KS)
Colorado Mountn Coll, Alpine Cmps (CO)
Columbus State Comm Coll (OH)
Comm Coll of Philadelphia (PA)
Comm Coll of Southern Nevada (NV)
Cowley County Comm Coll and Voc-Tech School (KS)
Delaware Tech & Comm Coll, Jack F Owens Cmps (DE)
Delta Coll (MI)
Des Moines Area Comm Coll (IA)
Doña Ana Branch Comm Coll (NM)
Dutchess Comm Coll (NY)
Edison State Comm Coll (OH)
Elgin Comm Coll (IL)
Ellsworth Comm Coll (IA)
Enterprise-Ozark Comm Coll (AL)
Everett Comm Coll (WA)
Fashion Inst of Design & Merchandising, LA Campus (CA)
Fashion Inst of Design & Merchandising, SD Campus (CA)
Fashion Inst of Design & Merchandising, SF Campus (CA)
Finger Lakes Comm Coll (NY)
Fort Scott Comm Coll (KS)
Fox Valley Tech Coll (WI)
Garden City Comm Coll (KS)
Gateway Comm Coll (CT)
Genesee Comm Coll (NY)
Glendale Comm Coll (AZ)
Harcum Coll (PA)
Harrisburg Area Comm Coll (PA)
Holyoke Comm Coll (MA)
Howard Comm Coll (MD)
Indian River Comm Coll (FL)
Iowa Lakes Comm Coll (IA)
Iowa Western Comm Coll (IA)
Jefferson Comm Coll (NY)
Jefferson Comm Coll (OH)
John A. Logan Coll (IL)
Lansing Comm Coll (MI)
Laurel Business Inst (PA)
Long Beach City Coll (CA)
Milwaukee Area Tech Coll (WI)
Minnesota State Coll–Southeast Tech (MN)
Niagara County Comm Coll (NY)
North Country Comm Coll (NY)
North Hennepin Comm Coll (MN)
Northland Comm and Tech Coll–Thief River Falls (MN)
Oakland Comm Coll (MI)

Orange County Comm Coll (NY)
Parkland Coll (IL)
Pennsylvania Highland Comm Coll (PA)
Raritan Valley Comm Coll (NJ)
St. Cloud Tech Coll (MN)
Shoreline Comm Coll (WA)
Sinclair Comm Coll (OH)
Southwestern Comm Coll (IA)
Sussex County Comm Coll (NJ)
Three Rivers Comm Coll (CT)
Westchester Comm Coll (NY)
West Kentucky Comm and Tech Coll (KY)
Westmoreland County Comm Coll (PA)

Consumer Services and Advocacy
Rockingham Comm Coll (NC)
San Diego City Coll (CA)

Cooking and Related Culinary Arts
Iowa Lakes Comm Coll (IA)
Milwaukee Area Tech Coll (WI)

Corrections
Adirondack Comm Coll (NY)
Alpena Comm Coll (MI)
Alvin Comm Coll (TX)
Amarillo Coll (TX)
Anne Arundel Comm Coll (MD)
Atlantic Cape Comm Coll (NJ)
Baltimore City Comm Coll (MD)
Belmont Tech Coll (OH)
Bossier Parish Comm Coll (LA)
Brevard Comm Coll (FL)
Broome Comm Coll (NY)
Broward Comm Coll (FL)
Bucks County Comm Coll (PA)
Casper Coll (WY)
Cayuga County Comm Coll (NY)
Central Arizona Coll (AZ)
Centralia Coll (WA)
Chattahoochee Tech Coll (GA)
Clackamas Comm Coll (OR)
Clark State Comm Coll (OH)
Clovis Comm Coll (NM)
Coll of DuPage (IL)
Columbus State Comm Coll (OH)
Comm & Tech Coll at West Virginia U Inst of Technology (WV)
Comm Coll of Allegheny County (PA)
Comm Coll of Southern Nevada (NV)
Cowley County Comm Coll and Voc-Tech School (KS)
Cumberland County Coll (NJ)
Daytona Beach Comm Coll (FL)
De Anza Coll (CA)
Delaware Tech & Comm Coll, Stanton/ Wilmington Cmps (DE)
Delaware Tech & Comm Coll, Terry Cmps (DE)
Delta Coll (MI)
Des Moines Area Comm Coll (IA)
Eastern Arizona Coll (AZ)
Elgin Comm Coll (IL)
Ellsworth Comm Coll (IA)
El Paso Comm Coll (TX)
Gogebic Comm Coll (MI)
Grand Rapids Comm Coll (MI)

Guam Comm Coll (GU)
Halifax Comm Coll (NC)
Hawkeye Comm Coll (IA)
Heartland Comm Coll (IL)
Henry Ford Comm Coll (MI)
Herkimer County Comm Coll (NY)
Hesser Coll (NH)
Hillsborough Comm Coll (FL)
Illinois Eastern Comm Colls, Frontier Comm Coll (IL)
Illinois Eastern Comm Colls, Lincoln Trail Coll (IL)
Illinois Eastern Comm Colls, Olney Central Coll (IL)
Illinois Eastern Comm Colls, Wabash Valley Coll (IL)
Indian River Comm Coll (FL)
Iowa Lakes Comm Coll (IA)
Jackson Comm Coll (MI)
Jefferson Comm Coll (OH)
Kilgore Coll (TX)
Lake Land Coll (IL)
Lansing Comm Coll (MI)
Laramie County Comm Coll (WY)
Lehigh Carbon Comm Coll (PA)
Longview Comm Coll (MO)
Lower Columbia Coll (WA)
Mid Michigan Comm Coll (MI)
Mineral Area Coll (MO)
Modesto Jr Coll (CA)
Montcalm Comm Coll (MI)
Moraine Valley Comm Coll (IL)
Napa Valley Coll (CA)
New River Comm and Tech Coll (WV)
Northwest State Comm Coll (OH)
Owens Comm Coll, Findlay (OH)
Penn Valley Comm Coll (MO)
Polk Comm Coll (FL)
Riverland Comm Coll (MN)
St. Louis Comm Coll at Meramec (MO)
St. Petersburg Coll (FL)
San Antonio Coll (TX)
San Diego Miramar Coll (CA)
San Joaquin Delta Coll (CA)
San Joaquin Valley Coll (CA)
Santa Fe Comm Coll (FL)
Sauk Valley Comm Coll (IL)
Schoolcraft Coll (MI)
Sinclair Comm Coll (OH)
Southern State Comm Coll (OH)
Southwestern Oklahoma State U at Sayre (OK)
State U of NY Coll of Technology at Canton (NY)
Three Rivers Comm Coll (CT)
Trinidad State Jr Coll (CO)
Trinity Valley Comm Coll (TX)
Truckee Meadows Comm Coll (NV)
Tunxis Comm Coll (CT)
Walla Walla Comm Coll (WA)
Westchester Comm Coll (NY)
Western Nevada Comm Coll (NV)
Western Oklahoma State Coll (OK)
Yuba Coll (CA)

Corrections and Criminal Justice Related
Albany Tech Coll (GA)
Brazosport Coll (TX)
Corning Comm Coll (NY)
Delta Coll (MI)
Heart of Georgia Tech Coll (GA)
Keiser Coll, Fort Lauderdale (FL)
Lanier Tech Coll (GA)
Monroe Coll, New Rochelle (NY)

Nebraska Indian Comm Coll (NE)
Northwestern Michigan Coll (MI)
Oakland Comm Coll (MI)
Southeastern Tech Coll (GA)

Cosmetology
Albuquerque Tech Vocational Inst (NM)
Athens Tech Coll (GA)
Bladen Comm Coll (NC)
Blue Ridge Comm Coll (NC)
Caldwell Comm Coll and Tech Inst (NC)
Central Texas Coll (TX)
Century Coll (MN)
Citrus Coll (CA)
Clovis Comm Coll (NM)
Coastal Bend Coll (TX)
Copiah-Lincoln Comm Coll (MS)
Cowley County Comm Coll and Voc-Tech School (KS)
Daytona Beach Comm Coll (FL)
Delta Coll (MI)
Dodge City Comm Coll (KS)
East Central Comm Coll (MS)
East Mississippi Comm Coll (MS)
Everett Comm Coll (WA)
Fayetteville Tech Comm Coll (NC)
Fort Scott Comm Coll (KS)
Frank Phillips Coll (TX)
Garden City Comm Coll (KS)
Glendale Comm Coll (CA)
Globe Coll (MN)
Guilford Tech Comm Coll (NC)
Haywood Comm Coll (NC)
Howard Coll (TX)
Independence Comm Coll (KS)
Indian River Comm Coll (FL)
Isothermal Comm Coll (NC)
James Sprunt Comm Coll (NC)
John A. Logan Coll (IL)
Johnson County Comm Coll (KS)
McDowell Tech Comm Coll (NC)
Milwaukee Area Tech Coll (WI)
Minnesota School of Business–Brooklyn Center (MN)
Minnesota School of Business–Plymouth (MN)
Minnesota School of Business–Richfield (MN)
Minnesota State Coll–Southeast Tech (MN)
Montcalm Comm Coll (MI)
Napa Valley Coll (CA)
Northland Comm and Tech Coll–Thief River Falls (MN)
Oakland Comm Coll (MI)
Odessa Coll (TX)
Olympic Coll (WA)
Panola Coll (TX)
Pasadena City Coll (CA)
Phillips Comm Coll of the U of Arkansas (AR)
Roanoke-Chowan Comm Coll (NC)
Rockingham Comm Coll (NC)
Salt Lake Comm Coll (UT)
Sandhills Comm Coll (NC)
San Diego City Coll (CA)
Santa Barbara City Coll (CA)
Seattle Central Comm Coll (WA)
Shawnee Comm Coll (IL)
Shelton State Comm Coll (AL)
Shoreline Comm Coll (WA)
Solano Comm Coll (CA)
Somerset Comm Coll (KY)
Southwestern Comm Coll (NC)

Southwest Wisconsin Tech Coll (WI)
Springfield Tech Comm Coll (MA)
Stanly Comm Coll (NC)
Surry Comm Coll (NC)
Trinidad State Jr Coll (CO)
Trinity Valley Comm Coll (TX)
Umpqua Comm Coll (OR)
Walla Walla Comm Coll (WA)
Yuba Coll (CA)

Cosmetology and Personal Grooming Arts Related
Allegany Coll of Maryland (MD)
Bristol Comm Coll (MA)
Comm Coll of Allegheny County (PA)
Milwaukee Area Tech Coll (WI)

Cosmetology, Barber/ Styling, and Nail Instruction
Olympic Coll (WA)

Counselor Education/ School Counseling and Guidance
Pratt Comm Coll and Area Vocational School (KS)

Court Reporting
Albuquerque Tech Vocational Inst (NM)
Alvin Comm Coll (TX)
Career Colls of Chicago (IL)
Clark State Comm Coll (OH)
Comm Coll of Allegheny County (PA)
Cuyahoga Comm Coll (OH)
Daytona Beach Comm Coll (FL)
El Paso Comm Coll (TX)
Gadsden State Comm Coll (AL)
GateWay Comm Coll (AZ)
Green River Comm Coll (WA)
Houston Comm Coll System (TX)
Illinois Eastern Comm Colls, Wabash Valley Coll (IL)
James H. Faulkner State Comm Coll (AL)
Lansing Comm Coll (MI)
Long Island Business Inst (NY)
Massachusetts Bay Comm Coll (MA)
Miami Dade Coll (FL)
Oakland Comm Coll (MI)
Pennsylvania Highland Comm Coll (PA)
Rasmussen Coll St. Cloud (MN)
St. Louis Comm Coll at Meramec (MO)
San Antonio Coll (TX)
San Diego City Coll (CA)
State U of NY Coll of Technology at Alfred (NY)
Wayne County Comm Coll District (MI)

Crafts, Folk Art and Artisanry
Haywood Comm Coll (NC)

Creative Writing
Foothill Coll (CA)
Inst of American Indian Arts (NM)
St. Louis Comm Coll at Meramec (MO)

Criminal Justice/Law Enforcement Administration
Adirondack Comm Coll (NY)
Allen County Comm Coll (KS)
Amarillo Coll (TX)
Ancilla Coll (IN)
Andover Coll (ME)
Anne Arundel Comm Coll (MD)
Arapahoe Comm Coll (CO)
Arizona Western Coll (AZ)

Arkansas State U–Mountain Home (AR)
Athens Tech Coll (GA)
Atlanta Metropolitan Coll (GA)
Austin Comm Coll (TX)
Bainbridge Coll (GA)
Bay de Noc Comm Coll (MI)
Bergen Comm Coll (NJ)
Big Sandy Comm and Tech Coll (KY)
Black Hawk Coll, Moline (IL)
Brevard Comm Coll (FL)
Briarwood Coll (CT)
Brookdale Comm Coll (NJ)
Broward Comm Coll (FL)
Bucks County Comm Coll (PA)
Bunker Hill Comm Coll (MA)
Cape Cod Comm Coll (MA)
Carteret Comm Coll (NC)
Casper Coll (WY)
Cayuga County Comm Coll (NY)
Cecil Comm Coll (MD)
Cedar Valley Coll (TX)
Central Arizona Coll (AZ)
Central Carolina Comm Coll (NC)
Central Florida Comm Coll (FL)
Centralia Coll (WA)
Central Oregon Comm Coll (OR)
Central Piedmont Comm Coll (NC)
Central Wyoming Coll (WY)
Cerro Coso Comm Coll (CA)
Chattahoochee Valley Comm Coll (AL)
Chattanooga State Tech Comm Coll (TN)
Chemeketa Comm Coll (OR)
Citrus Coll (CA)
Clark State Comm Coll (OH)
Clatsop Comm Coll (OR)
Cleveland Comm Coll (NC)
Clinton Comm Coll (NY)
Cloud County Comm Coll (KS)
Coahoma Comm Coll (MS)
Coastal Bend Coll (TX)
Coastal Carolina Comm Coll (NC)
Coastal Georgia Comm Coll (GA)
Cochise Coll, Douglas (AZ)
Coconino Comm Coll (AZ)
Colby Comm Coll (KS)
Coll of DuPage (IL)
Coll of Southern Idaho (ID)
Coll of the Canyons (CA)
Coll of the Mainland (TX)
Colorado Mountn Coll (CO)
Colorado Northwestern Comm Coll (CO)
Columbia-Greene Comm Coll (NY)
Comm Coll of Aurora (CO)
Comm Coll of Beaver County (PA)
Comm Coll of Philadelphia (PA)
Comm Coll of Southern Nevada (NV)
Comm Coll of the Air Force (AL)
Compton Comm Coll (CA)
Contra Costa Coll (CA)
Corning Comm Coll (NY)
Cowley County Comm Coll and Voc-Tech School (KS)
Craven Comm Coll (NC)
Dabney S. Lancaster Comm Coll (VA)
Danville Area Comm Coll (IL)
Darton Coll (GA)
Davidson County Comm Coll (NC)
Daytona Beach Comm Coll (FL)
De Anza Coll (CA)

Delaware Tech & Comm Coll, Jack F Owens Cmps (DE)
Delaware Tech & Comm Coll, Stanton/ Wilmington Cmps (DE)
Delaware Tech & Comm Coll, Terry Cmps (DE)
Delta Coll (MI)
Des Moines Area Comm Coll (IA)
Dodge City Comm Coll (KS)
Durham Tech Comm Coll (NC)
Dutchess Comm Coll (NY)
East Arkansas Comm Coll (AR)
East Central Coll (MO)
Eastern Arizona Coll (AZ)
East Mississippi Comm Coll (MS)
Edgecombe Comm Coll (NC)
Edison State Comm Coll (OH)
Elgin Comm Coll (IL)
Ellsworth Comm Coll (IA)
Enterprise-Ozark Comm Coll (AL)
Erie Comm Coll (NY)
Erie Comm Coll, North Campus (NY)
Essex County Coll (NJ)
Everett Comm Coll (WA)
Feather River Coll (CA)
Finger Lakes Comm Coll (NY)
Flathead Valley Comm Coll (MT)
Florida Comm Coll at Jacksonville (FL)
Forsyth Tech Comm Coll (NC)
Fort Peck Comm Coll (MT)
Fort Scott Comm Coll (KS)
Fox Valley Tech Coll (WI)
Frank Phillips Coll (TX)
Frederick Comm Coll (MD)
Fulton-Montgomery Comm Coll (NY)
Gainesville Coll (GA)
Garden City Comm Coll (KS)
Genesee Comm Coll (NY)
George Corley Wallace State Comm Coll (AL)
Glendale Comm Coll (AZ)
Gogebic Comm Coll (MI)
Grand Rapids Comm Coll (MI)
Greenfield Comm Coll (MA)
Guam Comm Coll (GU)
Guilford Tech Comm Coll (NC)
Gulf Coast Comm Coll (FL)
Hagerstown Business Coll (MD)
Harrisburg Area Comm Coll (PA)
Hawkeye Comm Coll (IA)
Haywood Comm Coll (NC)
Henry Ford Comm Coll (MI)
Herkimer County Comm Coll (NY)
Hesser Coll (NH)
Highland Comm Coll (KS)
Highline Comm Coll (WA)
Hillsborough Comm Coll (FL)
Hinds Comm Coll (MS)
Howard Comm Coll (MD)
Hudson Valley Comm Coll (NY)
ICM School of Business & Medical Careers (PA)
Illinois Valley Comm Coll (IL)
Indian Hills Comm Coll (IA)
Indian River Comm Coll (FL)
Iowa Lakes Comm Coll (IA)
Iowa Western Comm Coll (IA)
Isothermal Comm Coll (NC)
Jackson Comm Coll (MI)
Jefferson Comm Coll (NY)
John A. Logan Coll (IL)
Keiser Coll, Miami (FL)
Kilgore Coll (TX)

Lake-Sumter Comm Coll (FL)
Lane Comm Coll (OR)
Lansing Comm Coll (MI)
Laramie County Comm Coll (WY)
Lehigh Carbon Comm Coll (PA)
Lewis and Clark Comm Coll (IL)
Long Beach City Coll (CA)
Longview Comm Coll (MO)
Lower Columbia Coll (WA)
Macomb Comm Coll (MI)
Manchester Comm Coll (CT)
Maple Woods Comm Coll (MO)
Massachusetts Bay Comm Coll (MA)
Mayland Comm Coll (NC)
McDowell Tech Comm Coll (NC)
McIntosh Coll (NH)
McLennan Comm Coll (TX)
Miami Dade Coll (FL)
Mid Michigan Comm Coll (MI)
Milwaukee Area Tech Coll (WI)
Modesto Jr Coll (CA)
Mohawk Valley Comm Coll (NY)
Monroe Coll, Bronx (NY)
Montcalm Comm Coll (MI)
Mount Wachusett Comm Coll (MA)
Muskegon Comm Coll (MI)
Napa Valley Coll (CA)
Nassau Comm Coll (NY)
New Mexico Military Inst (NM)
Niagara County Comm Coll (NY)
Northampton County Area Comm Coll (PA)
North Central Missouri Coll (MO)
North Central State Coll (OH)
Northern Essex Comm Coll (MA)
Northern Virginia Comm Coll (VA)
North Idaho Coll (ID)
Northland Comm and Tech Coll–Thief River Falls (MN)
North Shore Comm Coll (MA)
Northwestern Connecticut Comm-Tech Coll (CT)
Northwest-Shoals Comm Coll (AL)
Northwest State Comm Coll (OH)
Oakland Comm Coll (MI)
Odessa Coll (TX)
Ohio Inst of Photography and Technology (OH)
Olympic Coll (WA)
Orange County Comm Coll (NY)
Owens Comm Coll, Findlay (OH)
Owens Comm Coll, Toledo (OH)
Palm Beach Comm Coll (FL)
Pasadena City Coll (CA)
Pasco-Hernando Comm Coll (FL)
Peninsula Coll (WA)
Penn Valley Comm Coll (MO)
Piedmont Comm Coll (NC)
Piedmont Virginia Comm Coll (VA)
Polk Comm Coll (FL)
Prairie State Coll (IL)
Raritan Valley Comm Coll (NJ)
Richmond Comm Coll (NC)
Riverside Comm Coll District (CA)
Roanoke-Chowan Comm Coll (NC)

Rockingham Comm Coll (NC)
Rockland Comm Coll (NY)
Rock Valley Coll (IL)
Rogue Comm Coll (OR)
Rowan-Cabarrus Comm Coll (NC)
Saint Charles Comm Coll (MO)
St. Louis Comm Coll at Forest Park (MO)
St. Louis Comm Coll at Meramec (MO)
St. Philip's Coll (TX)
Salt Lake Comm Coll (UT)
San Antonio Coll (TX)
Sandhills Comm Coll (NC)
San Diego Miramar Coll (CA)
Santa Barbara City Coll (CA)
Santa Fe Comm Coll (FL)
Santa Rosa Jr Coll (CA)
Sauk Valley Comm Coll (IL)
Seminole Comm Coll (FL)
Sheridan Coll (WY)
Sinclair Comm Coll (OH)
Snow Coll (UT)
Solano Comm Coll (CA)
Southern Maine Comm Coll (ME)
Southside Virginia Comm Coll (VA)
Spartanburg Methodist Coll (SC)
State U of NY Coll of Technology at Canton (NY)
Surry Comm Coll (NC)
Tacoma Comm Coll (WA)
Taft Coll (CA)
Tech Coll of the Lowcountry (SC)
Temple Coll (TX)
Three Rivers Comm Coll (CT)
Three Rivers Comm Coll (MO)
Tillamook Bay Comm Coll (OR)
Tompkins Cortland Comm Coll (NY)
Tri-County Tech Coll (SC)
Trident Tech Coll (SC)
Trinity Valley Comm Coll (TX)
Truckee Meadows Comm Coll (NV)
Tunxis Comm Coll (CT)
Umpqua Comm Coll (OR)
U of Arkansas Comm Coll at Hope (AR)
Valencia Comm Coll (FL)
Wake Tech Comm Coll (NC)
Walters State Comm Coll (TN)
Wayne County Comm Coll District (MI)
Westchester Comm Coll (NY)
Western Iowa Tech Comm Coll (IA)
Western Nevada Comm Coll (NV)
Western Wyoming Comm Coll (WY)
Westmoreland County Comm Coll (PA)
West Virginia U at Parkersburg (WV)
Wilson Tech Comm Coll (NC)
Yakima Valley Comm Coll (WA)
Yuba Coll (CA)

Criminal Justice/Police Science
Adirondack Comm Coll (NY)
Alexandria Tech Coll (MN)
Allegany Coll of Maryland (MD)
Alpena Comm Coll (MI)
Alvin Comm Coll (TX)
Amarillo Coll (TX)
Anne Arundel Comm Coll (MD)
Arapahoe Comm Coll (CO)
Arizona Western Coll (AZ)

Arkansas Northeastern Coll (AR)
Asheville-Buncombe Tech Comm Coll (NC)
Ashland Comm and Tech Coll (KY)
Atlantic Cape Comm Coll (NJ)
Austin Comm Coll (TX)
Baltimore City Comm Coll (MD)
Barton County Comm Coll (KS)
Bay de Noc Comm Coll (MI)
Beaufort County Comm Coll (NC)
Bladen Comm Coll (NC)
Blue River Comm Coll (MO)
Bossier Parish Comm Coll (LA)
Brazosport Coll (TX)
Brevard Comm Coll (FL)
Broome Comm Coll (NY)
Broward Comm Coll (FL)
Bucks County Comm Coll (PA)
Butler County Comm Coll (KS)
Butler County Comm Coll (PA)
Calhoun Comm Coll (AL)
Cape Fear Comm Coll (NC)
Casper Coll (WY)
Catawba Valley Comm Coll (NC)
Cayuga County Comm Coll (NY)
Central Piedmont Comm Coll (NC)
Central Texas Coll (TX)
Century Coll (MN)
Chattahoochee Tech Coll (GA)
Cincinnati State Tech and Comm Coll (OH)
Citrus Coll (CA)
City Colls of Chicago, Wilbur Wright Coll (IL)
Clackamas Comm Coll (OR)
Clark State Comm Coll (OH)
Clinton Comm Coll (NY)
Clovis Comm Coll (NM)
Coastal Bend Coll (TX)
Cochise Coll, Douglas (AZ)
Coll of DuPage (IL)
Coll of Lake County (IL)
Coll of Southern Idaho (ID)
Coll of the Canyons (CA)
Columbus State Comm Coll (OH)
Comm Coll of Allegheny County (PA)
Comm Coll of Beaver County (PA)
Comm Coll of Rhode Island (RI)
Comm Coll of Southern Nevada (NV)
Compton Comm Coll (CA)
Contra Costa Coll (CA)
Copiah-Lincoln Comm Coll (MS)
Cowley County Comm Coll and Voc-Tech School (KS)
Cumberland County Coll (NJ)
Cuyahoga Comm Coll (OH)
Danville Area Comm Coll (IL)
Davidson County Comm Coll (NC)
Dawson Comm Coll (MT)
Daytona Beach Comm Coll (FL)
De Anza Coll (CA)
Delaware County Comm Coll (PA)
Delaware Tech & Comm Coll, Stanton/ Wilmington Cmps (DE)
Delta Coll (MI)
Des Moines Area Comm Coll (IA)
Durham Tech Comm Coll (NC)

Dyersburg State Comm Coll (TN)
East Arkansas Comm Coll (AR)
East Central Coll (MO)
Eastern Arizona Coll (AZ)
Edison State Comm Coll (OH)
Elgin Comm Coll (IL)
Elizabethtown Comm and Tech Coll (KY)
El Paso Comm Coll (TX)
Enterprise-Ozark Comm Coll (AL)
Erie Comm Coll, North Campus (NY)
Essex County Coll (NJ)
Everett Comm Coll (WA)
Finger Lakes Comm Coll (NY)
Florida Comm Coll at Jacksonville (FL)
Forsyth Tech Comm Coll (NC)
Fox Valley Tech Coll (WI)
Frank Phillips Coll (TX)
Gadsden State Comm Coll (AL)
Garden City Comm Coll (KS)
George Corley Wallace State Comm Coll (AL)
George C. Wallace Comm Coll (AL)
Germanna Comm Coll (VA)
Glendale Comm Coll (AZ)
Glendale Comm Coll (CA)
Grand Rapids Comm Coll (MI)
Green River Comm Coll (WA)
Griffin Tech Coll (GA)
Guam Comm Coll (GU)
Guilford Tech Comm Coll (NC)
Hagerstown Comm Coll (MD)
Halifax Comm Coll (NC)
Harrisburg Area Comm Coll (PA)
Hawkeye Comm Coll (IA)
Henry Ford Comm Coll (MI)
Herkimer County Comm Coll (NY)
Hesser Coll (NH)
Hibbing Comm Coll (MN)
Highland Comm Coll (KS)
Highline Comm Coll (WA)
Hillsborough Comm Coll (FL)
Hinds Comm Coll (MS)
Holyoke Comm Coll (MA)
Hopkinsville Comm Coll (KY)
Houston Comm Coll System (TX)
Howard Coll (TX)
Hutchinson Comm Coll and Area Vocational School (KS)
Illinois Eastern Comm Colls, Olney Central Coll (IL)
Illinois Valley Comm Coll (IL)
Indian River Comm Coll (FL)
Iowa Central Comm Coll (IA)
Iowa Lakes Comm Coll (IA)
Iowa Western Comm Coll (IA)
Isothermal Comm Coll (NC)
Itawamba Comm Coll (MS)
James Sprunt Comm Coll (NC)
Jamestown Comm Coll (NY)
Jefferson Comm Coll (OH)
Jefferson State Comm Coll (AL)
Johnson County Comm Coll (KS)
Johnston Comm Coll (NC)
John Wood Comm Coll (IL)
Kalamazoo Valley Comm Coll (MI)
Kansas City Kansas Comm Coll (KS)
Kaskaskia Coll (IL)
Kent State U, Tuscarawas Campus (OH)

Kilgore Coll (TX)
Lake Land Coll (IL)
Lake Region State Coll (ND)
Lansing Comm Coll (MI)
Laredo Comm Coll (TX)
Lehigh Carbon Comm Coll (PA)
Lincoln Land Comm Coll (IL)
Linn-Benton Comm Coll (OR)
Longview Comm Coll (MO)
Lower Columbia Coll (WA)
Luna Comm Coll (NM)
Macomb Comm Coll (MI)
Maple Woods Comm Coll (MO)
Marshall Comm and Tech Coll (WV)
Mayland Comm Coll (NC)
McLennan Comm Coll (TX)
Metropolitan Comm Coll (NE)
Miami Dade Coll (FL)
Middle Georgia Coll (GA)
Midland Coll (TX)
Milwaukee Area Tech Coll (WI)
Mineral Area Coll (MO)
Minneapolis Comm and Tech Coll (MN)
Moberly Area Comm Coll (MO)
Modesto Jr Coll (CA)
Mohave Comm Coll (AZ)
Monroe Coll, Bronx (NY)
Montgomery Comm Coll (NC)
Montgomery County Comm Coll (PA)
Moraine Valley Comm Coll (IL)
Mott Comm Coll (MI)
Napa Valley Coll (CA)
Nashville State Tech Comm Coll (TN)
New Mexico Military Inst (NM)
New River Comm and Tech Coll (WV)
Northern Virginia Comm Coll (VA)
North Hennepin Comm Coll (MN)
North Idaho Coll (ID)
North Iowa Area Comm Coll (IA)
Northland Comm and Tech Coll–Thief River Falls (MN)
Northwestern Connecticut Comm-Tech Coll (CT)
Northwest-Shoals Comm Coll (AL)
Northwest State Comm Coll (OH)
Oakland Comm Coll (MI)
Odessa Coll (TX)
Okefenokee Tech Coll (GA)
Olympic Coll (WA)
Orange County Comm Coll (NY)
Owensboro Comm and Tech Coll (KY)
Owens Comm Coll, Findlay (OH)
Palm Beach Comm Coll (FL)
Penn Valley Comm Coll (MO)
Piedmont Virginia Comm Coll (VA)
Pima Comm Coll (AZ)
Pioneer Pacific Coll (OR)
Polk Comm Coll (FL)
Randolph Comm Coll (NC)
Richland Comm Coll (IL)
Riverland Comm Coll (MN)
Rochester Comm and Tech Coll (MN)
Rockingham Comm Coll (NC)
Saint Charles Comm Coll (MO)
St. Louis Comm Coll at Meramec (MO)
St. Petersburg Coll (FL)

San Antonio Coll (TX)
Sandhills Comm Coll (NC)
San Diego Miramar Coll (CA)
San Joaquin Delta Coll (CA)
San Juan Coll (NM)
Santa Fe Comm Coll (FL)
Sauk Valley Comm Coll (IL)
Schoolcraft Coll (MI)
Scott Comm Coll (IA)
Seminole State Coll (OK)
Seward County Comm Coll (KS)
Shawnee Comm Coll (IL)
Sheridan Coll (WY)
Sinclair Comm Coll (OH)
Somerset Comm Coll (KY)
Southeast Kentucky Comm and Tech Coll (KY)
Southern Maine Comm Coll (ME)
Southwestern Comm Coll (NC)
Southwestern Oregon Comm Coll (OR)
Springfield Tech Comm Coll (MA)
Stanly Comm Coll (NC)
State U of NY Coll of Technology at Canton (NY)
Tacoma Comm Coll (WA)
Temple Coll (TX)
Three Rivers Comm Coll (MO)
Trinidad State Jr Coll (CO)
Trinity Valley Comm Coll (TX)
Truckee Meadows Comm Coll (NV)
Union County Coll (NJ)
Wake Tech Comm Coll (NC)
Waubonsee Comm Coll (IL)
Wayne Comm Coll District (MI)
Westchester Comm Coll (NY)
Western Nevada Comm Coll (NV)
Western Oklahoma State Coll (OK)
Westmoreland County Comm Coll (PA)
Whatcom Comm Coll (WA)
Wilkes Comm Coll (NC)
Wor-Wic Comm Coll (MD)
Yakima Valley Comm Coll (WA)
Yavapai Coll (AZ)
Yuba Coll (CA)

Criminal Justice/Safety

Alamance Comm Coll (NC)
Albuquerque Tech Vocational Inst (NM)
Arkansas State U–Mountain Home (AR)
Asnuntuck Comm Coll (CT)
Berkshire Comm Coll (MA)
Bowling Green State U–Firelands (OH)
Bristol Comm Coll (MA)
Central Carolina Tech Coll (SC)
Central Comm Coll–Grand Island Campus (NE)
Central Texas Coll (TX)
Cleveland Comm Coll (NC)
Coll of the Mainland (TX)
Comm and Tech Coll of Shepherd (WV)
Dixie State Coll of Utah (UT)
Dutchess Comm Coll (NY)
Eastfield Coll (TX)
Fayetteville Tech Comm Coll (NC)
Garrett Coll (MD)
Great Basin Coll (NV)
Hudson County Comm Coll (NJ)
Ivy Tech State Coll–Bloomington (IN)
Ivy Tech State Coll–Central Indiana (IN)
Ivy Tech State Coll–Eastcentral (IN)

Ivy Tech State Coll–Kokomo (IN)
Ivy Tech State Coll–North Central (IN)
Ivy Tech State Coll–Northwest (IN)
Ivy Tech State Coll–Southwest (IN)
Ivy Tech State Coll–Wabash Valley (IN)
Jamestown Comm Coll (NY)
J. Sargeant Reynolds Comm Coll (VA)
Keystone Coll (PA)
Kilgore Coll (TX)
Lackawanna Coll (PA)
Linn-Benton Comm Coll (OR)
Lower Columbia Coll (WA)
Minneapolis Comm and Tech Coll (MN)
Nassau Comm Coll (NY)
North Central State Coll (OH)
North Country Comm Coll (NY)
Northwest State Comm Coll (OH)
Parkland Coll (IL)
Pima Comm Coll (AZ)
San Juan Coll (NM)
Southwestern Oklahoma State U at Sayre (OK)
U of Arkansas Comm Coll at Batesville (AR)
Walla Walla Comm Coll (WA)
West Virginia State Comm and Tech Coll (WV)

Criminology

Butler County Comm Coll (PA)
Catawba Valley Comm Coll (NC)
Daytona Beach Comm Coll (FL)
Northland Comm and Tech Coll–Thief River Falls (MN)
Western Wyoming Comm Coll (WY)

Crop Production

Barton County Comm Coll (KS)
Iowa Lakes Comm Coll (IA)
Northwestern Michigan Coll (MI)
Ohio State U Ag Tech Inst (OH)

Culinary Arts

Adirondack Comm Coll (NY)
Alamance Comm Coll (NC)
Albany Tech Coll (GA)
Albuquerque Tech Vocational Inst (NM)
Allegany Coll of Maryland (MD)
The Art Inst of Philadelphia (PA)
Asheville-Buncombe Tech Comm Coll (NC)
Atlantic Cape Comm Coll (NJ)
Baltimore International Coll (MD)
Black Hawk Coll, Moline (IL)
Brevard Comm Coll (FL)
Brookdale Comm Coll (NJ)
Bucks County Comm Coll (PA)
Bunker Hill Comm Coll (MA)
Central Oregon Comm Coll (OR)
Central Piedmont Comm Coll (NC)
Cincinnati State Tech and Comm Coll (OH)
Clark Coll (WA)
Coll of DuPage (IL)
Coll of Southern Idaho (ID)
Columbia Coll (MO)
Columbus State Comm Coll (OH)
Commonwealth Tech Inst (PA)

Comm & Tech Coll at West Virginia U Inst of Technology (WV)
Comm and Tech Coll of Shepherd (WV)
Comm Coll of Allegheny County (PA)
Comm Coll of Beaver County (PA)
Comm Coll of Philadelphia (PA)
Comm Coll of Southern Nevada (NV)
Contra Costa Coll (CA)
Daytona Beach Comm Coll (FL)
Delaware Tech & Comm Coll, Stanton/ Wilmington Cmps (DE)
Des Moines Area Comm Coll (IA)
Eastern Maine Comm Coll (ME)
Edmonds Comm Coll (WA)
Elgin Comm Coll (IL)
Erie Comm Coll (NY)
Florida Comm Coll at Jacksonville (FL)
Fox Valley Tech Coll (WI)
Glendale Comm Coll (CA)
Grand Rapids Comm Coll (MI)
Guilford Tech Comm Coll (NC)
Gulf Coast Comm Coll (FL)
Harrisburg Area Comm Coll (PA)
Henry Ford Comm Coll (MI)
Hibbing Comm Coll (MN)
Hillsborough Comm Coll (FL)
Hudson County Comm Coll (NJ)
Illinois Eastern Comm Colls, Lincoln Trail Coll (IL)
Indian River Comm Coll (FL)
Iowa Western Comm Coll (IA)
Jefferson Comm Coll (KY)
J. Sargeant Reynolds Comm Coll (VA)
Kapiolani Comm Coll (HI)
Kaskaskia Coll (IL)
Kauai Comm Coll (HI)
Keiser Coll, Fort Lauderdale (FL)
Keystone Coll (PA)
Lane Comm Coll (OR)
Lehigh Carbon Comm Coll (PA)
Linn-Benton Comm Coll (OR)
Long Beach City Coll (CA)
Macomb Comm Coll (MI)
McIntosh Coll (NH)
Metropolitan Comm Coll (NE)
Milwaukee Area Tech Coll (WI)
Minneapolis Comm and Tech Coll (MN)
Montgomery County Comm Coll (PA)
Mott Comm Coll (MI)
Nashville State Tech Comm Coll (TN)
Niagara County Comm Coll (NY)
Northampton County Area Comm Coll (PA)
North Idaho Coll (ID)
North Seattle Comm Coll (WA)
North Shore Comm Coll (MA)
Northwestern Michigan Coll (MI)
Oakland Comm Coll (MI)
Odessa Coll (TX)
Olympic Coll (WA)
Orange Coast Coll (CA)
Pennsylvania Culinary Inst (PA)
Penn Valley Comm Coll (MO)

Riverside Comm Coll District (CA)
Rockland Comm Coll (NY)
St. Cloud Tech Coll (MN)
St. Louis Comm Coll at Forest Park (MO)
St. Philip's Coll (TX)
Salt Lake Comm Coll (UT)
Sandhills Comm Coll (NC)
San Joaquin Delta Coll (CA)
Schoolcraft Coll (MI)
Scott Comm Coll (IA)
Seattle Central Comm Coll (WA)
Sinclair Comm Coll (OH)
South Central Tech Coll (MN)
Southeast Comm Coll, Lincoln Campus (NE)
Southern Maine Comm Coll (ME)
Southwestern Comm Coll (NC)
Southwest Wisconsin Tech Coll (WI)
State U of NY Coll of Technology at Alfred (NY)
State U of NY Coll of Technology at Delhi (NY)
Texas State Tech Coll–Waco/Marshall Campus (TX)
Trident Tech Coll (SC)
Truckee Meadows Comm Coll (NV)
Valencia Comm Coll (FL)
Wake Tech Comm Coll (NC)
Wayne County Comm Coll District (MI)
Westchester Comm Coll (NY)
Westmoreland County Comm Coll (PA)

Culinary Arts Related

Fayetteville Tech Comm Coll (NC)
Hillsborough Comm Coll (FL)
Iowa Lakes Comm Coll (IA)
Keystone Coll (PA)
Linn-Benton Comm Coll (OR)
Olympic Coll (WA)
Santa Barbara City Coll (CA)

Cultural Studies

Bay Mills Comm Coll (MI)
Compton Comm Coll (CA)
De Anza Coll (CA)
Foothill Coll (CA)
Highline Comm Coll (WA)
Orange Coast Coll (CA)
Pasadena City Coll (CA)
Riverside Comm Coll District (CA)
Santa Barbara City Coll (CA)
Santa Rosa Jr Coll (CA)
Solano Comm Coll (CA)
Yuba Coll (CA)

Customer Service Support/ Call Center/Teleservice Operation

Laramie County Comm Coll (WY)

Cytotechnology

Barton County Comm Coll (KS)
Highland Comm Coll (KS)

Dairy Husbandry and Production

Linn-Benton Comm Coll (OR)
Ohio State U Ag Tech Inst (OH)

Dairy Science

Highland Comm Coll (KS)
Modesto Jr Coll (CA)
Ohio State U Ag Tech Inst (OH)
Southwest Wisconsin Tech Coll (WI)
State U of NY Coll of Technology at Alfred (NY)

Dance

Barton County Comm Coll (KS)
Bergen Comm Coll (NJ)
Central Piedmont Comm Coll (NC)
Citrus Coll (CA)
Compton Comm Coll (CA)
Daytona Beach Comm Coll (FL)
Dixie State Coll of Utah (UT)
Glendale Comm Coll (CA)
Henry Ford Comm Coll (MI)
Hillsborough Comm Coll (FL)
Kilgore Coll (TX)
Lansing Comm Coll (MI)
Long Beach City Coll (CA)
Miami Dade Coll (FL)
Nassau Comm Coll (NY)
Northern Essex Comm Coll (MA)
Orange Coast Coll (CA)
San Joaquin Delta Coll (CA)
Sinclair Comm Coll (OH)
Snow Coll (UT)
Trinity Valley Comm Coll (TX)
Westchester Comm Coll (NY)
Western Wyoming Comm Coll (WY)

Data Entry/Microcomputer Applications

Anne Arundel Comm Coll (MD)
Atlantic Cape Comm Coll (NJ)
Austin Comm Coll (TX)
Bunker Hill Comm Coll (MA)
Clark Coll (WA)
Cleveland Comm Coll (NC)
Coastal Bend Coll (TX)
Colorado Mountn Coll, Timberline Cmps (CO)
Comm Coll of Vermont (VT)
Delta Coll (MI)
Eastern Arizona Coll (AZ)
Eastfield Coll (TX)
ECPI Tech Coll, Glen Allen (VA)
ECPI Tech Coll, Richmond (VA)
ECPI Tech Coll, Roanoke (VA)
Edgecombe Comm Coll (NC)
Ellsworth Comm Coll (IA)
El Paso Comm Coll (TX)
Fayetteville Tech Comm Coll (NC)
Flathead Valley Comm Coll (MT)
Florida Comm Coll at Jacksonville (FL)
Florida National Coll (FL)
Gateway Comm Coll (CT)
Glendale Comm Coll (CA)
Heartland Comm Coll (IL)
Henderson Comm Coll (KY)
Herkimer County Comm Coll (NY)
Hinds Comm Coll (MS)
Howard Comm Coll (MD)
Iowa Lakes Comm Coll (IA)
Iowa Western Comm Coll (IA)
Laredo Comm Coll (TX)
Laurel Business Inst (PA)
Lower Columbia Coll (WA)
Metropolitan Comm Coll-Business & Technology College (MO)
Milwaukee Area Tech Coll (WI)
Modesto Jr Coll (CA)
Nebraska Indian Comm Coll (NE)
Northland Comm and Tech Coll–Thief River Falls (MN)
North Shore Comm Coll (MA)
Orange County Comm Coll (NY)
Owensboro Comm and Tech Coll (KY)

Parkland Coll (IL)
Pratt Comm Coll and Area Vocational School (KS)
Quinebaug Valley Comm Coll (CT)
Richland Comm Coll (IL)
Riverland Comm Coll (MN)
St. Louis Comm Coll at Forest Park (MO)
St. Philip's Coll (TX)
San Antonio Coll (TX)
Seminole Comm Coll (FL)
Sheridan Coll (WY)
Sinclair Comm Coll (OH)
Southeastern Tech Coll (GA)
Thaddeus Stevens Coll of Technology (PA)
Three Rivers Comm Coll (MO)
Tompkins Cortland Comm Coll (NY)
U of Arkansas Comm Coll at Batesville (AR)
Valencia Comm Coll (FL)
Walla Walla Comm Coll (WA)
West Central Tech Coll (GA)
Western Oklahoma State Coll (OK)
Western Wyoming Comm Coll (WY)

Data Entry/Microcomputer Applications Related

Capital Comm Coll (CT)
Coastal Bend Coll (TX)
Coll of DuPage (IL)
Colorado Mountn Coll, Alpine Cmps (CO)
Colorado Mountn Coll (CO)
Colorado Mountn Coll, Timberline Cmps (CO)
Delta Coll (MI)
El Paso Comm Coll (TX)
Eugenio María de Hostos Comm Coll of City U of NY (NY)
Florida Comm Coll at Jacksonville (FL)
Florida National Coll (FL)
Glendale Comm Coll (CA)
Hawkeye Comm Coll (IA)
Heartland Comm Coll (IL)
Henderson Comm Coll (KY)
Highline Comm Coll (WA)
Hinds Comm Coll (MS)
Laredo Comm Coll (TX)
Laurel Business Inst (PA)
Metropolitan Comm Coll-Business & Technology College (MO)
Northland Comm and Tech Coll–Thief River Falls (MN)
Orange Coast Coll (CA)
Patrick Henry Comm Coll (VA)
Peninsula Coll (WA)
Pratt Comm Coll and Area Vocational School (KS)
Richland Comm Coll (IL)
Riverland Comm Coll (MN)
St. Louis Comm Coll at Forest Park (MO)
Seminole Comm Coll (FL)
Sinclair Comm Coll (OH)
Southwestern Michigan Coll (MI)
Three Rivers Comm Coll (MO)
Western Oklahoma State Coll (OK)

Data Modeling/Warehousing and Database Administration

Arapahoe Comm Coll (CO)
El Paso Comm Coll (TX)
Florida Comm Coll at Jacksonville (FL)
Kennebec Valley Comm Coll (ME)
Lanier Tech Coll (GA)
Laramie County Comm Coll (WY)

Metropolitan Comm Coll-Business & Technology College (MO)
Midland Coll (TX)
Northland Comm and Tech Coll–Thief River Falls (MN)
Seminole Comm Coll (FL)

Data Processing and Data Processing Technology

Academy Coll (MN)
Adirondack Comm Coll (NY)
Albuquerque Tech Vocational Inst (NM)
Allen County Comm Coll (KS)
Alpena Comm Coll (MI)
Anne Arundel Comm Coll (MD)
Bainbridge Coll (GA)
Baltimore City Comm Coll (MD)
Black Hawk Coll, Moline (IL)
Black River Tech Coll (AR)
Borough of Manhattan Comm Coll of City U of NY (NY)
Brazosport Coll (TX)
Bristol Comm Coll (MA)
Bronx Comm Coll of City U of NY (NY)
Broome Comm Coll (NY)
Broward Comm Coll (FL)
Bucks County Comm Coll (PA)
Butler County Comm Coll (KS)
Carroll Comm Coll (MD)
Casper Coll (WY)
Catawba Valley Comm Coll (NC)
Cayuga County Comm Coll (NY)
Cecil Comm Coll (MD)
Cedar Valley Coll (TX)
Central Carolina Tech Coll (SC)
Central Comm Coll–Grand Island Campus (NE)
Central Piedmont Comm Coll (NC)
Central Texas Coll (TX)
Cerro Coso Comm Coll (CA)
Chattahoochee Tech Coll (GA)
Chattahoochee Valley Comm Coll (AL)
Chattanooga State Tech Comm Coll (TN)
Citrus Coll (CA)
City Colls of Chicago, Wilbur Wright Coll (IL)
Coastal Bend Coll (TX)
Columbia-Greene Comm Coll (NY)
Comm & Tech Coll at West Virginia U Inst of Technology (WV)
Comm Coll of Beaver County (PA)
Comm Coll of Philadelphia (PA)
Comm Coll of Southern Nevada (NV)
Compton Comm Coll (CA)
Copiah-Lincoln Comm Coll (MS)
Dabney S. Lancaster Comm Coll (VA)
Danville Area Comm Coll (IL)
Davenport U, Midland (MI)
Davidson County Comm Coll (NC)
Delaware Tech & Comm Coll, Jack F Owens Cmps (DE)
Delaware Tech & Comm Coll, Stanton/ Wilmington Cmps (DE)
Delaware Tech & Comm Coll, Terry Cmps (DE)
Delta Coll (MI)
Des Moines Area Comm Coll (IA)
Dixie State Coll of Utah (UT)

Dodge City Comm Coll (KS)
Durham Tech Comm Coll (NC)
East Central Coll (MO)
East Central Comm Coll (MS)
Eastfield Coll (TX)
ECPI Coll of Technology, Virginia Beach (VA)
ECPI Tech Coll, Richmond (VA)
Edison State Comm Coll (OH)
Edmonds Comm Coll (WA)
Ellsworth Comm Coll (IA)
Essex County Coll (NJ)
Eugenio María de Hostos Comm Coll of City U of NY (NY)
Everett Comm Coll (WA)
Finger Lakes Comm Coll (NY)
Florida National Coll (FL)
Forsyth Tech Comm Coll (NC)
Foundation Coll, San Diego (CA)
Frank Phillips Coll (TX)
Frederick Comm Coll (MD)
Fulton-Montgomery Comm Coll (NY)
Gateway Comm Coll (CT)
George C. Wallace Comm Coll (AL)
Germanna Comm Coll (VA)
Glendale Comm Coll (CA)
Gogebic Comm Coll (MI)
Great Basin Coll (NV)
Hagerstown Business Coll (MD)
Hazard Comm and Tech Coll (KY)
Henderson Comm Coll (KY)
Henry Ford Comm Coll (MI)
Highland Comm Coll (IL)
Highland Comm Coll (KS)
Hinds Comm Coll (MS)
Holmes Comm Coll (MS)
Hudson County Comm Coll (NJ)
Hudson Valley Comm Coll (NY)
Illinois Valley Comm Coll (IL)
Independence Comm Coll (KS)
Iowa Central Comm Coll (IA)
Iowa Lakes Comm Coll (IA)
Itawamba Comm Coll (MS)
Jackson Comm Coll (MI)
Jefferson Comm Coll (KY)
Jefferson Comm Coll (OH)
John A. Logan Coll (IL)
J. Sargeant Reynolds Comm Coll (VA)
Kansas City Kansas Comm Coll (KS)
Kapiolani Comm Coll (HI)
Keystone Coll (PA)
Kilgore Coll (TX)
Kingsborough Comm Coll of City U of NY (NY)
Laredo Comm Coll (TX)
Lewis and Clark Comm Coll (IL)
Long Beach City Coll (CA)
Longview Comm Coll (MO)
Lower Columbia Coll (WA)
Maple Woods Comm Coll (MO)
Marshall Comm and Tech Coll (WV)
Metropolitan Comm Coll-Business & Technology College (MO)
Miami Dade Coll (FL)
Middle Georgia Coll (GA)
Midlands Tech Coll (SC)
Milwaukee Area Tech Coll (WI)
Montcalm Comm Coll (MI)
Muskegon Comm Coll (MI)
Napa Valley Coll (CA)
Nassau Comm Coll (NY)

Northampton County Area Comm Coll (PA)
North Central Missouri Coll (MO)
Northeastern Tech Coll (SC)
Northeast State Tech Comm Coll (TN)
Northern Essex Comm Coll (MA)
North Lake Coll (TX)
North Seattle Comm Coll (WA)
Odessa Coll (TX)
Orange Coast Coll (CA)
Orange County Comm Coll (NY)
Otero Jr Coll (CO)
Palm Beach Comm Coll (FL)
Pasadena City Coll (CA)
Patrick Henry Comm Coll (VA)
Penn Valley Comm Coll (MO)
Phillips Comm Coll of the U of Arkansas (AR)
Piedmont Virginia Comm Coll (VA)
Polk Comm Coll (FL)
Raritan Valley Comm Coll (NJ)
Rockland Comm Coll (NY)
St. Louis Comm Coll at Forest Park (MO)
San Antonio Coll (TX)
San Diego City Coll (CA)
Santa Fe Comm Coll (FL)
Schoolcraft Coll (MI)
Seminole Comm Coll (FL)
Seward County Comm Coll (KS)
Shelton State Comm Coll (AL)
Southeast Comm Coll, Milford Campus (NE)
Southeast Kentucky Comm and Tech Coll (KY)
Southwest Wisconsin Tech Coll (WI)
State U of NY Coll of Technology at Alfred (NY)
Tacoma Comm Coll (WA)
Taft Coll (CA)
Tech Coll of the Lowcountry (SC)
Temple Coll (TX)
Three Rivers Comm Coll (CT)
Tri-County Tech Coll (SC)
Trinidad State Jr Coll (CO)
Trinity Valley Comm Coll (TX)
Truckee Meadows Comm Coll (NV)
Tunxis Comm Coll (CT)
The U of Akron–Wayne Coll (OH)
Wayne County Comm Coll District (MI)
Westchester Comm Coll (NY)
Western Oklahoma State Coll (OK)
Western Wyoming Comm Coll (WY)
Westmoreland County Comm Coll (PA)
West Virginia U at Parkersburg (WV)
Williston State Coll (ND)

Demography and Population

Atlantic Cape Comm Coll (NJ)

Dental Assisting

Athens Tech Coll (GA)
Black Hawk Coll, Moline (IL)
Blue Mountain Comm Coll (OR)
Briarwood Coll (CT)
Calhoun Comm Coll (AL)
Central Comm Coll–Hastings Campus (NE)
Central Oregon Comm Coll (OR)

Century Coll (MN)
Citrus Coll (CA)
Coll of Southern Idaho (ID)
Comm Coll of the Air Force (AL)
Delta Coll (MI)
Essex County Coll (NJ)
Fayetteville Tech Comm Coll (NC)
Foothill Coll (CA)
Harcum Coll (PA)
Herzing Coll (MN)
Hibbing Comm Coll (MN)
James H. Faulkner State Comm Coll (AL)
Jefferson Comm Coll (OH)
Laramie County Comm Coll (WY)
Midlands Tech Coll (SC)
Milwaukee Area Tech Coll (WI)
Modesto Jr Coll (CA)
Mott Comm Coll (MI)
Northern Essex Comm Coll (MA)
Northwestern Michigan Coll (MI)
St. Cloud Tech Coll (MN)
San Joaquin Valley Coll (CA)
South Central Tech Coll (MN)
Southwest Wisconsin Tech Coll (WI)
Texas State Tech Coll– Waco/Marshall Campus (TX)
Truckee Meadows Comm Coll (NV)

Dental Hygiene

Allegany Coll of Maryland (MD)
Amarillo Coll (TX)
Andrew Coll (GA)
Apollo Coll (ID)
Asheville-Buncombe Tech Comm Coll (NC)
Athens Tech Coll (GA)
Baltimore City Comm Coll (MD)
Barton County Comm Coll (KS)
Bergen Comm Coll (NJ)
Big Sandy Comm and Tech Coll (KY)
Brevard Comm Coll (FL)
Bristol Comm Coll (MA)
Broome Comm Coll (NY)
Broward Comm Coll (FL)
Cape Cod Comm Coll (MA)
Cape Fear Comm Coll (NC)
Catawba Valley Comm Coll (NC)
Central Comm Coll–Hastings Campus (NE)
Central Piedmont Comm Coll (NC)
Century Coll (MN)
Chattanooga State Tech Comm Coll (TN)
Chemeketa Comm Coll (OR)
Clark Coll (WA)
Coastal Bend Coll (TX)
Coastal Carolina Comm Coll (NC)
Coastal Georgia Comm Coll (GA)
Colby Comm Coll (KS)
Coll of DuPage (IL)
Coll of Lake County (IL)
Coll of Southern Idaho (ID)
Collin County Comm Coll District (TX)
Colorado Northwestern Comm Coll (CO)
Columbia State Comm Coll (TN)
Columbus State Comm Coll (OH)
Comm & Tech Coll at West Virginia U Inst of Technology (WV)
Comm Coll of Denver (CO)
Comm Coll of Philadelphia (PA)

Comm Coll of Rhode Island (RI)

Comm Coll of Southern Nevada (NV)

Contra Costa Coll (CA)

Delaware Tech & Comm Coll, Stanton/ Wilmington Cmps (DE)

Delta Coll (MI)

Des Moines Area Comm Coll (IA)

Dixie State Coll of Utah (UT)

Durham Tech Comm Coll (NC)

Elizabethtown Comm and Tech Coll (KY)

El Paso Comm Coll (TX)

Erie Comm Coll, North Campus (NY)

Essex County Coll (NJ)

Eugenio María de Hostos Comm Coll of City U of NY (NY)

Everett Comm Coll (WA)

Fayetteville Tech Comm Coll (NC)

Florida Comm Coll at Jacksonville (FL)

Florida National Coll (FL)

Foothill Coll (CA)

Gainesville Coll (GA)

Grand Rapids Comm Coll (MI)

Guilford Tech Comm Coll (NC)

Gulf Coast Comm Coll (FL)

Gwinnett Tech Coll (GA)

Harcum Coll (PA)

Harrisburg Area Comm Coll (PA)

Hawkeye Comm Coll (IA)

Herzing Coll (MN)

Highland Comm Coll (KS)

Highline Comm Coll (WA)

Hillsborough Comm Coll (FL)

Hinds Comm Coll (MS)

Howard Coll (TX)

Hudson Valley Comm Coll (NY)

Indian River Comm Coll (FL)

Iowa Western Comm Coll (IA)

John A. Logan Coll (IL)

Johnson County Comm Coll (KS)

Kalamazoo Valley Comm Coll (MI)

Lake Land Coll (IL)

Lake Superior Coll (MN)

Lane Comm Coll (OR)

Lansing Comm Coll (MI)

Laramie County Comm Coll (WY)

Lewis and Clark Comm Coll (IL)

Meridian Comm Coll (MS)

Miami Dade Coll (FL)

Midlands Tech Coll (SC)

Milwaukee Area Tech Coll (WI)

Montgomery County Comm Coll (PA)

Mott Comm Coll (MI)

Northampton County Area Comm Coll (PA)

North Dakota State Coll of Science (ND)

Northern Virginia Comm Coll (VA)

Northwest Tech Coll (MN)

Oakland Comm Coll (MI)

Orange Coast Coll (CA)

Orange County Comm Coll (NY)

Palm Beach Comm Coll (FL)

Parkland Coll (IL)

Pasadena City Coll (CA)

Pasco-Hernando Comm Coll (FL)

Pima Comm Coll (AZ)

Prairie State Coll (IL)

Riverside Comm Coll District (CA)

Rochester Comm and Tech Coll (MN)

St. Cloud Tech Coll (MN)

St. Louis Comm Coll at Forest Park (MO)

St. Petersburg Coll (FL)

Salt Lake Comm Coll (UT)

San Antonio Coll (TX)

San Joaquin Valley Coll (CA)

Santa Fe Comm Coll (FL)

Santa Rosa Jr Coll (CA)

Sheridan Coll (WY)

Shoreline Comm Coll (WA)

Sinclair Comm Coll (OH)

Springfield Tech Comm Coll (MA)

Taft Coll (CA)

Temple Coll (TX)

Trident Tech Coll (SC)

Truckee Meadows Comm Coll (NV)

Tunxis Comm Coll (CT)

Union County Coll (NJ)

U of Cincinnati Raymond Walters Coll (OH)

Valencia Comm Coll (FL)

Wayne County Comm Coll District (MI)

West Central Tech Coll (GA)

Westmoreland County Comm Coll (PA)

Yakima Valley Comm Coll (WA)

Dental Laboratory Technology

Century Coll (MN)

Columbus State Comm Coll (OH)

Commonwealth Tech Inst (PA)

Comm Coll of the Air Force (AL)

Erie Comm Coll, South Campus (NY)

J. Sargeant Reynolds Comm Coll (VA)

Marshall Comm and Tech Coll (WV)

Pima Comm Coll (AZ)

Design and Applied Arts Related

Mohawk Valley Comm Coll (NY)

Niagara County Comm Coll (NY)

Platt Coll San Diego (CA)

Design and Visual Communications

Academy Coll (MN)

Black Hawk Coll, Moline (IL)

Bristol Comm Coll (MA)

Brookdale Comm Coll (NJ)

Bunker Hill Comm Coll (MA)

Coll of DuPage (IL)

Comm and Tech Coll of Shepherd (WV)

The Creative Center (NE)

East Central Coll (MO)

Elgin Comm Coll (IL)

Fashion Inst of Design & Merchandising, LA Campus (CA)

Fashion Inst of Design & Merchandising, SD Campus (CA)

Fashion Inst of Design & Merchandising, SF Campus (CA)

Florida Comm Coll at Jacksonville (FL)

Front Range Comm Coll (CO)

Harrisburg Area Comm Coll (PA)

Ivy Tech State Coll–Central Indiana (IN)

Ivy Tech State Coll–Columbus (IN)

Ivy Tech State Coll–North Central (IN)

Ivy Tech State Coll–Southcentral (IN)

Ivy Tech State Coll–Southwest (IN)

Ivy Tech State Coll–Wabash Valley (IN)

Kilgore Coll (TX)

Moraine Valley Comm Coll (IL)

Nassau Comm Coll (NY)

Northwest State Comm Coll (OH)

Parkland Coll (IL)

Pima Comm Coll (AZ)

Platt Coll San Diego (CA)

Trinidad State Jr Coll (CO)

Waubonsee Comm Coll (IL)

Desktop Publishing and Digital Imaging Design

Brookdale Comm Coll (NJ)

Coll of DuPage (IL)

Glendale Comm Coll (CA)

Iowa Lakes Comm Coll (IA)

Lake Land Coll (IL)

Linn-Benton Comm Coll (OR)

Parkland Coll (IL)

Platt Coll San Diego (CA)

Springfield Tech Comm Coll (MA)

Umpqua Comm Coll (OR)

Developmental and Child Psychology

Arizona Western Coll (AZ)

Austin Comm Coll (TX)

Central Georgia Tech Coll (GA)

Coastal Bend Coll (TX)

Coll of the Canyons (CA)

Columbia Coll (CA)

Comm Coll of Vermont (VT)

Compton Comm Coll (CA)

De Anza Coll (CA)

Ellsworth Comm Coll (IA)

Flathead Valley Comm Coll (MT)

Frank Phillips Coll (TX)

Fulton-Montgomery Comm Coll (NY)

Garden City Comm Coll (KS)

Hinds Comm Coll (MS)

Iowa Lakes Comm Coll (IA)

Itawamba Comm Coll (MS)

Jefferson Comm Coll (OH)

Lansing Comm Coll (MI)

Long Beach City Coll (CA)

McLennan Comm Coll (TX)

Midland Coll (TX)

Muskegon Comm Coll (MI)

North Idaho Coll (ID)

Pasadena City Coll (CA)

Rochester Comm and Tech Coll (MN)

Rockland Comm Coll (NY)

St. Louis Comm Coll at Forest Park (MO)

San Antonio Coll (TX)

San Diego City Coll (CA)

San Diego Miramar Coll (CA)

San Joaquin Delta Coll (CA)

South Texas Coll (TX)

Trinity Valley Comm Coll (TX)

Diagnostic Medical Sonography and Ultrasound Technology

Albuquerque Tech Vocational Inst (NM)

Athens Tech Coll (GA)

Caldwell Comm Coll and Tech Inst (NC)

Cape Fear Comm Coll (NC)

Cincinnati State Tech and Comm Coll (OH)

Comm Coll of Allegheny County (PA)

Darton Coll (GA)

Delaware Tech & Comm Coll, Stanton/ Wilmington Cmps (DE)

Florida Comm Coll at Jacksonville (FL)

Florida Hospital Coll of Health Sciences (FL)

Florida National Coll (FL)

Foothill Coll (CA)

GateWay Comm Coll (AZ)

Hillsborough Comm Coll (FL)

Jackson Comm Coll (MI)

Keystone Coll (PA)

Lackawanna Coll (PA)

Lansing Comm Coll (MI)

Laramie County Comm Coll (WY)

Miami Dade Coll (FL)

Oakland Comm Coll (MI)

St. Cloud Tech Coll (MN)

South Hills School of Business & Technology, State College (PA)

Springfield Tech Comm Coll (MA)

Valencia Comm Coll (FL)

Diesel Mechanics Technology

Alexandria Tech Coll (MN)

Black Hawk Coll, Moline (IL)

Blue Mountain Comm Coll (OR)

Central Comm Coll–Hastings Campus (NE)

Centralia Coll (WA)

Century Coll (MN)

Clark Coll (WA)

Coll of Southern Idaho (ID)

Dixie State Coll of Utah (UT)

Eastern Idaho Tech Coll (ID)

Great Basin Coll (NV)

Illinois Eastern Comm Colls, Wabash Valley Coll (IL)

Johnston Comm Coll (NC)

Kilgore Coll (TX)

Lake Region State Coll (ND)

Laramie County Comm Coll (WY)

Linn-Benton Comm Coll (OR)

Lower Columbia Coll (WA)

North Dakota State Coll of Science (ND)

Northwest Tech Coll (MN)

Peninsula Coll (WA)

Raritan Valley Comm Coll (NJ)

Riverland Comm Coll (MN)

St. Cloud Tech Coll (MN)

St. Philip's Coll (TX)

San Juan Coll (NM)

Scott Comm Coll (IA)

Sheridan Coll (WY)

Somerset Comm Coll (KY)

Southeast Tech Inst (SD)

Texas State Tech Coll–Waco/Marshall Campus (TX)

U of Northwestern Ohio (OH)

Western Iowa Tech Comm Coll (IA)

Western Wyoming Comm Coll (WY)

Wilkes Comm Coll (NC)

Williston State Coll (ND)

Dietetics

Baltimore City Comm Coll (MD)

Black River Tech Coll (AR)

Briarwood Coll (CT)

Butler County Comm Coll (PA)

Central Arizona Coll (AZ)

Cincinnati State Tech and Comm Coll (OH)

Coll of Southern Idaho (ID)

Columbus State Comm Coll (OH)

Comm Coll of Philadelphia (PA)

Comm Coll of the Air Force (AL)

Delta Coll (MI)

Dutchess Comm Coll (NY)

El Paso Comm Coll (TX)

Florida Comm Coll at Jacksonville (FL)

Gateway Comm Coll (CT)

Harrisburg Area Comm Coll (PA)

Hinds Comm Coll (MS)

J. Sargeant Reynolds Comm Coll (VA)

Long Beach City Coll (CA)

Miami Dade Coll (FL)

Milwaukee Area Tech Coll (WI)

Northern Virginia Comm Coll (VA)

Orange Coast Coll (CA)

Riverside Comm Coll District (CA)

Rockland Comm Coll (NY)

Santa Rosa Jr Coll (CA)

Shoreline Comm Coll (WA)

Sinclair Comm Coll (OH)

Southeast Comm Coll, Lincoln Campus (NE)

Southern Maine Comm Coll (ME)

U of Cincinnati Raymond Walters Coll (OH)

Wayne County Comm Coll District (MI)

Westchester Comm Coll (NY)

Westmoreland County Comm Coll (PA)

Dietetic Technician

Columbus State Comm Coll (OH)

Miami Dade Coll (FL)

Milwaukee Area Tech Coll (WI)

Dietitian Assistant

Alexandria Tech Coll (MN)

Barton County Comm Coll (KS)

Comm Coll of Allegheny County (PA)

Erie Comm Coll, North Campus (NY)

Florida Comm Coll at Jacksonville (FL)

Front Range Comm Coll (CO)

Truckee Meadows Comm Coll (NV)

Digital Communication and Media/Multimedia

Brevard Comm Coll (FL)

Hillsborough Comm Coll (FL)

Laramie County Comm Coll (WY)

Lehigh Carbon Comm Coll (PA)

Olympic Coll (WA)

Platt Coll San Diego (CA)

Divinity/Ministry

Andrew Coll (GA)

The Salvation Army Coll for Officer Training at Crestmont (CA)

Drafting

Arkansas Northeastern Coll (AR)

Drafting and Design Technology

Adirondack Comm Coll (NY)

Albany Tech Coll (GA)

Allen County Comm Coll (KS)

Alpena Comm Coll (MI)

Alvin Comm Coll (TX)

Amarillo Coll (TX)

Arapahoe Comm Coll (CO)

Arizona Western Coll (AZ)

Athens Tech Coll (GA)

Austin Comm Coll (TX)

Bainbridge Coll (GA)

Baltimore City Comm Coll (MD)

Bay de Noc Comm Coll (MI)

Beaufort County Comm Coll (NC)

Bergen Comm Coll (NJ)

Bessemer State Tech Coll (AL)

Bevill State Comm Coll (AL)

Bishop State Comm Coll (AL)

Blue Ridge Comm Coll (NC)

Bossier Parish Comm Coll (LA)

Brazosport Coll (TX)

Brevard Comm Coll (FL)

Brookdale Comm Coll (NJ)

Butler County Comm Coll (KS)

Butler County Comm Coll (PA)

Caldwell Comm Coll and Tech Inst (NC)

Calhoun Comm Coll (AL)

Casper Coll (WY)

Cayuga County Comm Coll (NY)

Central Alabama Comm Coll (AL)

Central Carolina Comm Coll (NC)

Central Comm Coll–Columbus Campus (NE)

Central Comm Coll–Grand Island Campus (NE)

Central Comm Coll–Hastings Campus (NE)

Central Piedmont Comm Coll (NC)

Central Texas Coll (TX)

Cerro Coso Comm Coll (CA)

Chattanooga State Tech Comm Coll (TN)

Chemeketa Comm Coll (OR)

Citrus Coll (CA)

Clackamas Comm Coll (OR)

Clark State Comm Coll (OH)

Cloud County Comm Coll (KS)

Coastal Bend Coll (TX)

Cochise Coll, Douglas (AZ)

Coffeyville Comm Coll (KS)

Coll of DuPage (IL)

Coll of Southern Idaho (ID)

Coll of the Canyons (CA)

Coll of the Mainland (TX)

Collin County Comm Coll District (TX)

Comm & Tech Coll at West Virginia U Inst of Technology (WV)

Comm Coll of Allegheny County (PA)

Comm Coll of Beaver County (PA)

Comm Coll of Denver (CO)

Comm Coll of Philadelphia (PA)

Comm Coll of Southern Nevada (NV)

Compton Comm Coll (CA)

Contra Costa Coll (CA)

Copiah-Lincoln Comm Coll (MS)

Corning Comm Coll (NY)

Cowley County Comm Coll and Voc-Tech School (KS)

Crowder Coll (MO)

Cumberland County Coll (NJ)

Dabney S. Lancaster Comm Coll (VA)

Danville Area Comm Coll (IL)

Daytona Beach Comm Coll (FL)

Delaware County Comm Coll (PA)

Delaware Tech & Comm Coll, Jack F Owens Cmps (DE)

Delaware Tech & Comm Coll, Stanton/ Wilmington Cmps (DE)

Delaware Tech & Comm Coll, Terry Cmps (DE)

Delta Coll (MI)

Des Moines Area Comm Coll (IA)

Doña Ana Branch Comm Coll (NM)

East Arkansas Comm Coll (AR)

East Central Coll (MO)

East Central Comm Coll (MS)

Eastern Arizona Coll (AZ)

Eastern Maine Comm Coll (ME)
Eastfield Coll (TX)
East Mississippi Comm Coll (MS)
Edison State Comm Coll (OH)
Elgin Comm Coll (IL)
El Paso Comm Coll (TX)
Everett Comm Coll (WA)
Finger Lakes Comm Coll (NY)
Florida Comm Coll at Jacksonville (FL)
Forsyth Tech Comm Coll (NC)
Fort Scott Comm Coll (KS)
Fox Valley Tech Coll (WI)
Frederick Comm Coll (MD)
Front Range Comm Coll (CO)
Gadsden State Comm Coll-Ayers Campus (AL)
Garden City Comm Coll (KS)
Genesee Comm Coll (NY)
George Corley Wallace State Comm Coll (AL)
George C. Wallace Comm Coll (AL)
Glendale Comm Coll (CA)
Gogebic Comm Coll (MI)
Grand Rapids Comm Coll (MI)
Green River Comm Coll (WA)
Guilford Tech Comm Coll (NC)
Gulf Coast Comm Coll (FL)
Gwinnett Tech Coll (GA)
Hawkeye Comm Coll (IA)
Heartland Comm Coll (IL)
Henry Ford Comm Coll (MI)
Herzing Coll (WI)
Hibbing Comm Coll (MN)
Highland Comm Coll (IL)
Highland Comm Coll (KS)
Highline Comm Coll (WA)
Hinds Comm Coll (MS)
Holmes Comm Coll (MS)
Houston Comm Coll System (TX)
Howard Coll (TX)
Hutchinson Comm Coll and Area Vocational School (KS)
Illinois Valley Comm Coll (IL)
Independence Comm Coll (KS)
Indian Hills Comm Coll (IA)
Indian River Comm Coll (FL)
Iowa Central Comm Coll (IA)
Iowa Lakes Comm Coll (IA)
Isothermal Comm Coll (NC)
Itawamba Comm Coll (MS)
Ivy Tech State Coll–Central Indiana (IN)
Ivy Tech State Coll–Columbus (IN)
Ivy Tech State Coll–Eastcentral (IN)
Ivy Tech State Coll–Kokomo (IN)
Ivy Tech State Coll–Lafayette (IN)
Ivy Tech State Coll–North Central (IN)
Ivy Tech State Coll–Northeast (IN)
Ivy Tech State Coll–Northwest (IN)
Ivy Tech State Coll–Wabash Valley (IN)
Jefferson Comm Coll (OH)
J. F. Drake State Tech Coll (AL)
John A. Logan Coll (IL)
Johnson County Comm Coll (KS)
Kalamazoo Valley Comm Coll (MI)
Kansas City Kansas Comm Coll (KS)
Kennebec Valley Comm Coll (ME)

Kilgore Coll (TX)
Lake Land Coll (IL)
Lane Comm Coll (OR)
Lansing Comm Coll (MI)
Lehigh Carbon Comm Coll (PA)
Lewis and Clark Comm Coll (IL)
Linn-Benton Comm Coll (OR)
Linn State Tech Coll (MO)
Long Beach City Coll (CA)
Longview Comm Coll (MO)
Macomb Comm Coll (MI)
Manhattan Area Tech Coll (KS)
Massachusetts Bay Comm Coll (MA)
Meridian Comm Coll (MS)
Metropolitan Comm Coll (NE)
Metropolitan Comm Coll-Business & Technology College (MO)
Miami Dade Coll (FL)
Midland Coll (TX)
Mid Michigan Comm Coll (MI)
Milwaukee Area Tech Coll (WI)
Mineral Area Coll (MO)
Minnesota State Coll–Southeast Tech (MN)
Moberly Area Comm Coll (MO)
Modesto Jr Coll (CA)
Mohawk Valley Comm Coll (NY)
Montcalm Comm Coll (MI)
Morrison Inst of Technology (IL)
Mott Comm Coll (MI)
Muskegon Comm Coll (MI)
Napa Valley Coll (CA)
New Hampshire Comm Tech Coll, Manchester/Stratham (NH)
Niagara County Comm Coll (NY)
Northampton County Area Comm Coll (PA)
North Central Missouri Coll (MO)
North Central State Coll (OH)
Northeast State Tech Comm Coll (TN)
North Idaho Coll (ID)
Northland Comm and Tech Coll–Thief River Falls (MN)
Northwestern Michigan Coll (MI)
Northwestern Tech Coll (GA)
Northwest-Shoals Comm Coll (AL)
Odessa Coll (TX)
Olympic Coll (WA)
Orange Coast Coll (CA)
Orange County Comm Coll (NY)
Palm Beach Comm Coll (FL)
Pasadena City Coll (CA)
Pasco-Hernando Comm Coll (FL)
Phillips Comm Coll of the U of Arkansas (AR)
Pulaski Tech Coll (AR)
Richland Comm Coll (IL)
Rockland Comm Coll (NY)
Saint Charles Comm Coll (MO)
St. Petersburg Coll (FL)
Salt Lake Comm Coll (UT)
San Antonio Coll (TX)
San Diego City Coll (CA)
San Joaquin Delta Coll (CA)
San Juan Coll (NM)
Santa Barbara City Coll (CA)
Santa Fe Comm Coll (NM)
Schoolcraft Coll (MI)
Schuylkill Inst of Business and Technology (PA)
Seattle Central Comm Coll (WA)
Seminole Comm Coll (FL)

Shelton State Comm Coll (AL)
Sheridan Coll (WY)
Shoreline Comm Coll (WA)
Sinclair Comm Coll (OH)
Solano Comm Coll (CA)
Southeast Comm Coll, Lincoln Campus (NE)
Southeast Comm Coll, Milford Campus (NE)
Southeast Tech Inst (SD)
Southern Maine Comm Coll (ME)
Southern State Comm Coll (OH)
Southside Virginia Comm Coll (VA)
Southwestern Comm Coll (IA)
Southwestern Michigan Coll (MI)
Southwest Wisconsin Tech Coll (WI)
Spartanburg Tech Coll (SC)
State U of NY Coll of Technology at Alfred (NY)
State U of NY Coll of Technology at Delhi (NY)
Surry Comm Coll (NC)
Taft Coll (CA)
Temple Coll (TX)
Texas State Tech Coll–Waco/Marshall Campus (TX)
Thaddeus Stevens Coll of Technology (PA)
Thompson Inst (PA)
Three Rivers Comm Coll (CT)
Triangle Tech, Inc.–Greensburg School (PA)
Triangle Tech, Inc.–Pittsburgh School (PA)
Tri-County Tech Coll (SC)
Trinidad State Jr Coll (CO)
Trinity Valley Comm Coll (TX)
Truckee Meadows Comm Coll (NV)
U of Arkansas Comm Coll at Morrilton (AR)
Valencia Comm Coll (FL)
Wayne County Comm Coll District (MI)
Western Nevada Comm Coll (NV)
Western Oklahoma State Coll (OK)
Westmoreland County Comm Coll (PA)
West Virginia U at Parkersburg (WV)

Drafting/Design Engineering Technologies Related
Comm Coll of Allegheny County (PA)
Fairmont State Comm & Tech Coll (WV)

Dramatic/Theatre Arts
Allen County Comm Coll (KS)
Alvin Comm Coll (TX)
Amarillo Coll (TX)
Andrew Coll (GA)
Arizona Western Coll (AZ)
Bainbridge Coll (GA)
Barton County Comm Coll (KS)
Bergen Comm Coll (NJ)
Brazosport Coll (TX)
Brookdale Comm Coll (NJ)
Bucks County Comm Coll (PA)
Bunker Hill Comm Coll (MA)
Butler County Comm Coll (KS)
Calhoun Comm Coll (AL)
Cape Cod Comm Coll (MA)
Casper Coll (WY)
Centralia Coll (WA)
Central Wyoming Coll (WY)
Chattahoochee Valley Comm Coll (AL)

Citrus Coll (CA)
Clarendon Coll (TX)
Clark State Comm Coll (OH)
Coastal Bend Coll (TX)
Coffeyville Comm Coll (KS)
Colby Comm Coll (KS)
Coll of Southern Idaho (ID)
Colorado Mountn Coll (CO)
Columbia Coll (CA)
Comm Coll of Allegheny County (PA)
Comm Coll of Rhode Island (RI)
Comm Coll of Southern Nevada (NV)
Compton Comm Coll (CA)
Cowley County Comm Coll and Voc-Tech School (KS)
Crowder Coll (MO)
Cumberland County Coll (NJ)
Darton Coll (GA)
Daytona Beach Comm Coll (FL)
De Anza Coll (CA)
Delta Coll (MI)
Dixie State Coll of Utah (UT)
Dodge City Comm Coll (KS)
East Central Coll (MO)
Eastern Arizona Coll (AZ)
El Paso Comm Coll (TX)
Everett Comm Coll (WA)
Finger Lakes Comm Coll (NY)
Foothill Coll (CA)
Fulton-Montgomery Comm Coll (NY)
Gainesville Coll (GA)
Garden City Comm Coll (KS)
Genesee Comm Coll (NY)
Glendale Comm Coll (CA)
Gordon Coll (GA)
Guilford Tech Comm Coll (NC)
Harrisburg Area Comm Coll (PA)
Henry Ford Comm Coll (MI)
Highland Comm Coll (IL)
Highland Comm Coll (KS)
Hillsborough Comm Coll (FL)
Hinds Comm Coll (MS)
Holyoke Comm Coll (MA)
Houston Comm Coll System (TX)
Howard Coll (TX)
Howard Comm Coll (MD)
Indian River Comm Coll (FL)
Kilgore Coll (TX)
Kingsborough Comm Coll of City U of NY (NY)
Lansing Comm Coll (MI)
Laramie County Comm Coll (WY)
Linn-Benton Comm Coll (OR)
Long Beach City Coll (CA)
Lower Columbia Coll (WA)
Manchester Comm Coll (CT)
Massachusetts Bay Comm Coll (MA)
Miami Dade Coll (FL)
Mid Michigan Comm Coll (MI)
Modesto Jr Coll (CA)
Mohawk Valley Comm Coll (NY)
Nassau Comm Coll (NY)
Niagara County Comm Coll (NY)
Northern Essex Comm Coll (MA)
North Idaho Coll (ID)
Northwestern Michigan Coll (MI)
Orange Coast Coll (CA)
Otero Jr Coll (CO)
Palm Beach Comm Coll (FL)
Pasadena City Coll (CA)
Phillips Comm Coll of the U of Arkansas (AR)
Piedmont Virginia Comm Coll (VA)
Pima Comm Coll (AZ)

Raritan Valley Comm Coll (NJ)
Riverside Comm Coll District (CA)
Rockland Comm Coll (NY)
St. Louis Comm Coll at Meramec (MO)
St. Philip's Coll (TX)
San Diego City Coll (CA)
San Joaquin Delta Coll (CA)
San Juan Coll (NM)
Santa Barbara City Coll (CA)
Santa Rosa Jr Coll (CA)
Sauk Valley Comm Coll (IL)
Seward County Comm Coll (KS)
Sinclair Comm Coll (OH)
Snow Coll (UT)
Three Rivers Comm Coll (CT)
Trinidad State Jr Coll (CO)
Trinity Valley Comm Coll (TX)
Umpqua Comm Coll (OR)
Valencia Comm Coll (FL)
Western Wyoming Comm Coll (WY)
Yuba Coll (CA)

Dramatic/Theatre Arts and Stagecraft Related
Bristol Comm Coll (MA)
St. Philip's Coll (TX)

Drawing
Coffeyville Comm Coll (KS)
De Anza Coll (CA)
Dixie State Coll of Utah (UT)
East Central Comm Coll (MS)
Everett Comm Coll (WA)
Henry Ford Comm Coll (MI)
Inst of American Indian Arts (NM)
Iowa Lakes Comm Coll (IA)
Keystone Coll (PA)
Midland Coll (TX)
Pasadena City Coll (CA)
San Joaquin Delta Coll (CA)
Seward County Comm Coll (KS)

Early Childhood Education
Albany Tech Coll (GA)
Barton County Comm Coll (KS)
Brevard Comm Coll (FL)
Bristol Comm Coll (MA)
Bunker Hill Comm Coll (MA)
Central Oregon Comm Coll (OR)
Cerro Coso Comm Coll (CA)
Clark Coll (WA)
Clover Park Tech Coll (WA)
Colorado Northwestern Comm Coll (CO)
Heart of Georgia Tech Coll (GA)
Hopkinsville Comm Coll (KY)
Iowa Lakes Comm Coll (IA)
Jackson Comm Coll (MI)
John Wood Comm Coll (IL)
Kent State U, Tuscarawas Campus (OH)
Keystone Coll (PA)
Kingsborough Comm Coll of City U of NY (NY)
Lackawanna Coll (PA)
Lanier Tech Coll (GA)
Laramie County Comm Coll (WY)
Lower Columbia Coll (WA)
Luna Comm Coll (NM)
Mott Comm Coll (MI)
Nebraska Indian Comm Coll (NE)
North Seattle Comm Coll (WA)
Okefenokee Tech Coll (GA)
Olympic Coll (WA)
Owens Comm Coll, Findlay (OH)
Owens Comm Coll, Toledo (OH)
St. Philip's Coll (TX)
Sauk Valley Comm Coll (IL)

Somerset Comm Coll (KY)
Southeastern Tech Coll (GA)
Tillamook Bay Comm Coll (OR)
Tri-County Comm Coll (NC)
Western Wyoming Comm Coll (WY)

Ecology
Casper Coll (WY)
Colorado Mountn Coll, Timberline Cmps (CO)
Dixie State Coll of Utah (UT)
East Central Coll (MO)
Everett Comm Coll (WA)
Iowa Lakes Comm Coll (IA)

E-Commerce
Colorado Northwestern Comm Coll (CO)
Milwaukee Area Tech Coll (WI)
St. Philip's Coll (TX)

Economics
Alabama Southern Comm Coll (AL)
Allen County Comm Coll (KS)
Anne Arundel Comm Coll (MD)
Austin Comm Coll (TX)
Barton County Comm Coll (KS)
Bergen Comm Coll (NJ)
Brazosport Coll (TX)
Casper Coll (WY)
Chemeketa Comm Coll (OR)
Coastal Bend Coll (TX)
Coffeyville Comm Coll (KS)
Columbia State Comm Coll (TN)
Comm Coll of Southern Nevada (NV)
Compton Comm Coll (CA)
Copiah-Lincoln Comm Coll (MS)
Darton Coll (GA)
Daytona Beach Comm Coll (FL)
De Anza Coll (CA)
Dixie State Coll of Utah (UT)
East Central Coll (MO)
East Central Comm Coll (MS)
East Mississippi Comm Coll (MS)
Ellsworth Comm Coll (IA)
Everett Comm Coll (WA)
Foothill Coll (CA)
Frank Phillips Coll (TX)
GateWay Comm Coll (AZ)
Gulf Coast Comm Coll (FL)
Hinds Comm Coll (MS)
Indian River Comm Coll (FL)
Iowa Lakes Comm Coll (IA)
Itawamba Comm Coll (MS)
Laramie County Comm Coll (WY)
Linn-Benton Comm Coll (OR)
Lower Columbia Coll (WA)
Miami Dade Coll (FL)
Midland Coll (TX)
Muskegon Comm Coll (MI)
New Mexico Military Inst (NM)
Orange Coast Coll (CA)
Palm Beach Comm Coll (FL)
Pasadena City Coll (CA)
Riverside Comm Coll District (CA)
St. Philip's Coll (TX)
San Joaquin Delta Coll (CA)
San Juan Coll (NM)
Santa Barbara City Coll (CA)
Santa Rosa Jr Coll (CA)
Sauk Valley Comm Coll (IL)
Seward County Comm Coll (KS)
Snow Coll (UT)
Tacoma Comm Coll (WA)
Umpqua Comm Coll (OR)

Economics

U of Cincinnati Raymond Walters Coll (OH)
Western Wyoming Comm Coll (WY)

Education
Alabama Southern Comm Coll (AL)
Andrew Coll (GA)
Anne Arundel Comm Coll (MD)
Arizona Western Coll (AZ)
Atlantic Cape Comm Coll (NJ)
Bainbridge Coll (GA)
Bergen Comm Coll (NJ)
Bowling Green State U-Firelands Coll (OH)
Brazosport Coll (TX)
Brookdale Comm Coll (NJ)
Bucks County Comm Coll (PA)
Bunker Hill Comm Coll (MA)
Butler County Comm Coll (PA)
Calhoun Comm Coll (AL)
Cape Cod Comm Coll (MA)
Casper Coll (WY)
Cecil Comm Coll (MD)
Central Oregon Comm Coll (OR)
Chemeketa Comm Coll (OR)
Chipola Coll (FL)
Clarendon Coll (TX)
Cloud County Comm Coll (KS)
Coastal Bend Coll (TX)
Cochise Coll, Douglas (AZ)
Coffeyville Comm Coll (KS)
Colby Comm Coll (KS)
Coll of Southern Idaho (ID)
Coll of Southern Maryland (MD)
Colorado Northwestern Comm Coll (CO)
Comm Coll of Beaver County (PA)
Comm Coll of Philadelphia (PA)
Comm Coll of Vermont (VT)
Copiah-Lincoln Comm Coll (MS)
Cowley County Comm Coll and Voc-Tech School (KS)
Crowder Coll (MO)
Cumberland County Coll (NJ)
Dabney S. Lancaster Comm Coll (VA)
Danville Area Comm Coll (IL)
Danville Comm Coll (VA)
Darton Coll (GA)
Daytona Beach Comm Coll (FL)
Delta Coll (MI)
Des Moines Area Comm Coll (IA)
Dodge City Comm Coll (KS)
East Central Coll (MO)
East Central Comm Coll (MS)
Eastern Shore Comm Coll (VA)
East Mississippi Comm Coll (MS)
Ellsworth Comm Coll (IA)
El Paso Comm Coll (TX)
Enterprise-Ozark Comm Coll (AL)
Essex County Coll (NJ)
Everett Comm Coll (WA)
Florida National Coll (FL)
Fort Scott Comm Coll (KS)
Frank Phillips Coll (TX)
Frederick Comm Coll (MD)
Gainesville Coll (GA)
Garden City Comm Coll (KS)
Garrett Coll (MD)
GateWay Comm Coll (AZ)
Genesee Comm Coll (NY)
Germanna Comm Coll (VA)
Glendale Comm Coll (CA)
Gogebic Comm Coll (MI)
Gordon Coll (GA)
Greenfield Comm Coll (MA)

Guam Comm Coll (GU)
Hagerstown Comm Coll (MD)
Halifax Comm Coll (NC)
Harford Comm Coll (MD)
Harrisburg Area Comm Coll (PA)
Hawkeye Comm Coll (IA)
Haywood Comm Coll (NC)
Highland Comm Coll (IL)
Highland Comm Coll (KS)
Highline Comm Coll (WA)
Hillsborough Comm Coll (FL)
Hutchinson Comm Coll and Area Vocational School (KS)
Illinois Valley Comm Coll (IL)
Indian River Comm Coll (FL)
Iowa Central Comm Coll (IA)
Iowa Lakes Comm Coll (IA)
Isothermal Comm Coll (NC)
Itasca Comm Coll (MN)
Itawamba Comm Coll (MS)
John A. Logan Coll (IL)
Johnson County Comm Coll (KS)
Kennebec Valley Comm Coll (ME)
Kingsborough Comm Coll of City U of NY (NY)
Kingwood Coll (TX)
Lackawanna Coll (PA)
Lansing Comm Coll (MI)
Laramie County Comm Coll (WY)
Lehigh Carbon Comm Coll (PA)
Linn-Benton Comm Coll (OR)
Miami Dade Coll (FL)
Muskegon Comm Coll (MI)
Northern Essex Comm Coll (MA)
North Idaho Coll (ID)
Northwestern Michigan Coll (MI)
Northwest-Shoals Comm Coll (AL)
Northwest State Comm Coll (OH)
Odessa Coll (TX)
Otero Jr Coll (CO)
Palm Beach Comm Coll (FL)
Phillips Comm Coll of the U of Arkansas (AR)
Piedmont Virginia Comm Coll (VA)
Pratt Comm Coll and Area Vocational School (KS)
Raritan Valley Comm Coll (NJ)
Riverside Comm Coll District (CA)
Roanoke-Chowan Comm Coll (NC)
St. Louis Comm Coll at Meramec (MO)
St. Philip's Coll (TX)
Salt Lake Comm Coll (UT)
San Juan Coll (NM)
Santa Fe Comm Coll (FL)
Santa Rosa Jr Coll (CA)
Sauk Valley Comm Coll (IL)
Schoolcraft Coll (MI)
Seward County Comm Coll (KS)
Shelton State Comm Coll (AL)
Sheridan Coll (WY)
Shoreline Comm Coll (WA)
Sinclair Comm Coll (OH)
Snow Coll (UT)
Southside Virginia Comm Coll (VA)
South Texas Coll (TX)
Tacoma Comm Coll (WA)
Three Rivers Comm Coll (MO)
Trinidad State Jr Coll (CO)
Trinity Valley Comm Coll (TX)
Truett-McConnell Coll (GA)
Umpqua Comm Coll (OR)

U of Arkansas Comm Coll at Batesville (AR)
U of Cincinnati Raymond Walters Coll (OH)
Villa Maria Coll of Buffalo (NY)
Walters State Comm Coll (TN)
Wayne County Comm Coll District (MI)
Western Oklahoma State Coll (OK)
Western Wyoming Comm Coll (WY)
West Virginia U at Parkersburg (WV)
Wor-Wic Comm Coll (MD)
Yuba Coll (CA)

Educational/Instructional Media Design
Brookdale Comm Coll (NJ)
Century Coll (MN)
Collin County Comm Coll District (TX)
Comm Coll of the Air Force (AL)
Hibbing Comm Coll (MN)
Hutchinson Comm Coll and Area Vocational School (KS)
Ivy Tech State Coll–North Central (IN)
Milwaukee Area Tech Coll (WI)
Texas State Tech Coll–Waco/Marshall Campus (TX)

Educational Leadership and Administration
Comm Coll of the Air Force (AL)

Education (K-12)
Cecil Comm Coll (MD)
Itasca Comm Coll (MN)
Keystone Coll (PA)
Mid Michigan Comm Coll (MI)
Pratt Comm Coll and Area Vocational School (KS)
Truckee Meadows Comm Coll (NV)

Education (Multiple Levels)
Atlanta Metropolitan Coll (GA)
Carroll Comm Coll (MD)
Coastal Georgia Comm Coll (GA)
Delaware County Comm Coll (PA)
Western Wyoming Comm Coll (WY)

Education Related
Corning Comm Coll (NY)
Guilford Tech Comm Coll (NC)
Rogue Comm Coll (OR)
Yavapai Coll (AZ)

Education (Specific Levels and Methods) Related
Comm Coll of Allegheny County (PA)
Laramie County Comm Coll (WY)
Northampton County Area Comm Coll (PA)

Education (Specific Subject Areas) Related
Comm Coll of Allegheny County (PA)

Electrical and Electronic Engineering Technologies Related
Albany Tech Coll (GA)
Cincinnati State Tech and Comm Coll (OH)
Columbus State Comm Coll (OH)
Eugenio María de Hostos Comm Coll of City U of NY (NY)

Fairmont State Comm & Tech Coll (WV)
Miami Dade Coll (FL)
Miami U Hamilton (OH)
Mohawk Valley Comm Coll (NY)
Northampton County Area Comm Coll (PA)
Southwestern Michigan Coll (MI)
Springfield Tech Comm Coll (MA)
Vatterott Coll, Oklahoma City (OK)
West Virginia State Comm and Tech Coll (WV)

Electrical and Power Transmission Installation
Ivy Tech State Coll–Columbus (IN)
Johnson County Comm Coll (KS)
Orange Coast Coll (CA)
St. Cloud Tech Coll (MN)
State U of NY Coll of Technology at Delhi (NY)
Wake Tech Comm Coll (NC)
Western Nevada Comm Coll (NV)

Electrical and Power Transmission Installation Related
Calhoun Comm Coll (AL)
Manhattan Area Tech Coll (KS)

Electrical, Electronic and Communications Engineering Technology
Adirondack Comm Coll (NY)
Alamance Comm Coll (NC)
Albuquerque Tech Vocational Inst (NM)
Allen County Comm Coll (KS)
Alvin Comm Coll (TX)
Amarillo Coll (TX)
Anne Arundel Comm Coll (MD)
Arapahoe Comm Coll (CO)
Arizona Western Coll (AZ)
Athens Tech Coll (GA)
Augusta Tech Coll (GA)
Austin Comm Coll (TX)
Bainbridge Coll (GA)
Baltimore City Comm Coll (MD)
Bay de Noc Comm Coll (MI)
Beaufort County Comm Coll (NC)
Belmont Tech Coll (OH)
Bergen Comm Coll (NJ)
Berkshire Comm Coll (MA)
Bessemer State Tech Coll (AL)
Bishop State Comm Coll (AL)
Bladen Comm Coll (NC)
Blue Mountain Comm Coll (OR)
Blue Ridge Comm Coll (NC)
Blue Ridge Comm Coll (VA)
Bossier Parish Comm Coll (LA)
Bowling Green State U-Firelands Coll (OH)
Brazosport Coll (TX)
Brevard Comm Coll (FL)
Bristol Comm Coll (MA)
Bronx Comm Coll of City U of NY (NY)
Brookdale Comm Coll (NJ)
Broome Comm Coll (NY)
Broward Comm Coll (FL)
Brunswick Comm Coll (NC)
Bryant & Stratton Business Inst, Amherst Cmps (NY)
Bucks County Comm Coll (PA)
Butler County Comm Coll (KS)
Butler County Comm Coll (PA)

Caldwell Comm Coll and Tech Inst (NC)
Calhoun Comm Coll (AL)
Cape Fear Comm Coll (NC)
Capital Comm Coll (CT)
Casper Coll (WY)
Catawba Valley Comm Coll (NC)
Cayuga County Comm Coll (NY)
Cecil Comm Coll (MD)
Central Alabama Comm Coll (AL)
Central Carolina Comm Coll (NC)
Central Comm Coll–Columbus Campus (NE)
Central Comm Coll–Grand Island Campus (NE)
Central Comm Coll–Hastings Campus (NE)
Central Florida Comm Coll (FL)
Centralia Coll (WA)
Central Piedmont Comm Coll (NC)
Central Texas Coll (TX)
Chattahoochee Tech Coll (GA)
Chattanooga State Tech Comm Coll (TN)
Chemeketa Comm Coll (OR)
Cincinnati State Tech and Comm Coll (OH)
Citrus Coll (CA)
Clarendon Coll (TX)
Clark Coll (WA)
Clark State Comm Coll (OH)
Cleveland Comm Coll (NC)
Clinton Comm Coll (IA)
Clinton Comm Coll (NY)
Clovis Comm Coll (NM)
Coll of DuPage (IL)
Coll of Lake County (IL)
Coll of Southern Idaho (ID)
Coll of Southern Maryland (MD)
Coll of the Canyons (CA)
Collin County Comm Coll District (TX)
Columbia State Comm Coll (TN)
Columbus State Comm Coll (OH)
Comm & Tech Coll at West Virginia U Inst of Technology (WV)
Comm Coll of Allegheny County (PA)
Comm Coll of Beaver County (PA)
Comm Coll of Denver (CO)
Comm Coll of Philadelphia (PA)
Comm Coll of Rhode Island (RI)
Comm Coll of Southern Nevada (NV)
Comm Coll of the Air Force (AL)
Compton Comm Coll (CA)
Contra Costa Coll (CA)
Copiah-Lincoln Comm Coll (MS)
Corning Comm Coll (NY)
Craven Comm Coll (NC)
Crowder Coll (MO)
Dabney S. Lancaster Comm Coll (VA)
Danville Area Comm Coll (IL)
Davenport U, Midland (MI)
Davidson County Comm Coll (NC)
Daytona Beach Comm Coll (FL)
DeKalb Tech Coll (GA)
Delaware County Comm Coll (PA)
Delaware Tech & Comm Coll, Jack F Owens Cmps (DE)
Delaware Tech & Comm Coll, Stanton/ Wilmington Cmps (DE)

Delaware Tech & Comm Coll, Terry Cmps (DE)
Des Moines Area Comm Coll (IA)
Dodge City Comm Coll (KS)
Doña Ana Branch Comm Coll (NM)
Durham Tech Comm Coll (NC)
Dutchess Comm Coll (NY)
Dyersburg State Comm Coll (TN)
East Central Coll (MO)
East Central Comm Coll (MS)
Eastern Idaho Tech Coll (ID)
Eastern Maine Comm Coll (ME)
Eastern Shore Comm Coll (VA)
Eastfield Coll (TX)
East Mississippi Comm Coll (MS)
ECPI Coll of Technology, Newport News (VA)
ECPI Coll of Technology, Virginia Beach (VA)
ECPI Tech Coll, Richmond (VA)
ECPI Tech Coll, Roanoke (VA)
Edgecombe Comm Coll (NC)
Edison State Comm Coll (OH)
Edmonds Comm Coll (WA)
Elgin Comm Coll (IL)
El Paso Comm Coll (TX)
Erie Comm Coll, North Campus (NY)
Essex County Coll (NJ)
Fairmont State Comm & Tech Coll (WV)
Fayetteville Tech Comm Coll (NC)
Florida Comm Coll at Jacksonville (FL)
Foothill Coll (CA)
Forsyth Tech Comm Coll (NC)
Fort Peck Comm Coll (MT)
Fort Scott Comm Coll (KS)
Fox Valley Tech Coll (WI)
Frank Phillips Coll (TX)
Frederick Comm Coll (MD)
Front Range Comm Coll (CO)
Fulton-Montgomery Comm Coll (NY)
Gadsden State Comm Coll-Ayers Campus (AL)
Gainesville Coll (GA)
Garden City Comm Coll (KS)
Gateway Comm Coll (CT)
Genesee Comm Coll (NY)
George Corley Wallace State Comm Coll (AL)
George C. Wallace Comm Coll (AL)
Germanna Comm Coll (VA)
Glendale Comm Coll (AZ)
Grand Rapids Comm Coll (MI)
Great Basin Coll (NV)
Guam Comm Coll (GU)
Guilford Tech Comm Coll (NC)
Gulf Coast Comm Coll (FL)
Gwinnett Tech Coll (GA)
Harrisburg Area Comm Coll (PA)
Heartland Comm Coll (IL)
Henderson Comm Coll (KY)
Henry Ford Comm Coll (MI)
Herzing Coll (WI)
Highland Comm Coll (IL)
Hillsborough Comm Coll (FL)
Hinds Comm Coll (MS)
Hopkinsville Comm Coll (KY)
Houston Comm Coll System (TX)
Howard Comm Coll (MD)
Hudson County Comm Coll (NJ)

Hudson Valley Comm Coll (NY)
Illinois Eastern Comm Colls, Wabash Valley Coll (IL)
Illinois Valley Comm Coll (IL)
Independence Comm Coll (KS)
Indian Hills Comm Coll (IA)
Indian River Comm Coll (FL)
Iowa Central Comm Coll (IA)
Iowa Western Comm Coll (IA)
Isothermal Comm Coll (NC)
Itawamba Comm Coll (MS)
Ivy Tech State Coll–Bloomington (IN)
Ivy Tech State Coll–Central Indiana (IN)
Ivy Tech State Coll–Columbus (IN)
Ivy Tech State Coll–Eastcentral (IN)
Ivy Tech State Coll–Kokomo (IN)
Ivy Tech State Coll–Lafayette (IN)
Ivy Tech State Coll–North Central (IN)
Ivy Tech State Coll–Northeast (IN)
Ivy Tech State Coll–Northwest (IN)
Ivy Tech State Coll–Southcentral (IN)
Ivy Tech State Coll–Southeast (IN)
Ivy Tech State Coll–Southwest (IN)
Ivy Tech State Coll–Wabash Valley (IN)
Ivy Tech State Coll–Whitewater (IN)
Jackson Comm Coll (MI)
Jamestown Comm Coll (NY)
Jefferson Comm Coll (KY)
Jefferson Comm Coll (OH)
J. F. Drake State Tech Coll (AL)
John A. Logan Coll (IL)
Johnston Comm Coll (NC)
John Wood Comm Coll (IL)
J. Sargeant Reynolds Comm Coll (VA)
Kalamazoo Valley Comm Coll (MI)
Kaskaskia Coll (IL)
Kauai Comm Coll (HI)
Kent State U, Tuscarawas Campus (OH)
Kilgore Coll (TX)
Lake Land Coll (IL)
Lake Superior Coll (MN)
Lane Comm Coll (OR)
Lanier Tech Coll (GA)
Lansing Comm Coll (MI)
Laredo Comm Coll (TX)
Lehigh Carbon Comm Coll (PA)
Lincoln Land Comm Coll (IL)
Linn State Tech Coll (MO)
Long Beach City Coll (CA)
Longview Comm Coll (MO)
Lower Columbia Coll (WA)
Luna Comm Coll (NM)
Macomb Comm Coll (MI)
Maple Woods Comm Coll (MO)
Marshall Comm and Tech Coll (WV)
Mayland Comm Coll (NC)
McDowell Tech Comm Coll (NC)
Meridian Comm Coll (MS)
Metropolitan Comm Coll (NE)
Metropolitan Comm Coll–Business & Technology College (MO)
Miami Dade Coll (FL)
Midland Coll (TX)
Midlands Tech Coll (SC)
Milwaukee Area Tech Coll (WI)
Mineral Area Coll (MO)

Minnesota State Coll–Southeast Tech (MN)
Moberly Area Comm Coll (MO)
Modesto Jr Coll (CA)
Mohawk Valley Comm Coll (NY)
Montcalm Comm Coll (MI)
Montgomery Comm Coll (NC)
Montgomery County Comm Coll (PA)
Mott Comm Coll (MI)
Mount Wachusett Comm Coll (MA)
Muskegon Comm Coll (MI)
Napa Valley Coll (CA)
Nashville State Tech Comm Coll (TN)
Niagara County Comm Coll (NY)
Northampton County Area Comm Coll (PA)
North Central Missouri Coll (MO)
North Central State Coll (OH)
North Dakota State Coll of Science (ND)
Northeast Alabama Comm Coll (AL)
Northeastern Tech Coll (SC)
Northeast State Tech Comm Coll (TN)
Northern Essex Comm Coll (MA)
Northern Virginia Comm Coll (VA)
North Hennepin Comm Coll (MN)
North Idaho Coll (ID)
North Iowa Area Comm Coll (IA)
North Lake Coll (TX)
Northland Comm and Tech Coll–Thief River Falls (MN)
North Seattle Comm Coll (WA)
Northwestern Connecticut Comm-Tech Coll (CT)
Northwestern Michigan Coll (MI)
Northwest-Shoals Comm Coll (AL)
Northwest State Comm Coll (OH)
Northwest Tech Coll (MN)
Oakland Comm Coll (MI)
Odessa Coll (TX)
Olympic Coll (WA)
Orange Coast Coll (CA)
Orange County Comm Coll (NY)
Owensboro Comm and Tech Coll (KY)
Owens Comm Coll, Findlay (OH)
Owens Comm Coll, Toledo (OH)
Palm Beach Comm Coll (FL)
Pasadena City Coll (CA)
Patrick Henry Comm Coll (VA)
Peninsula Coll (WA)
Pennsylvania Highland Comm Coll (PA)
Pennsylvania Inst of Technology (PA)
Penn State U Beaver Campus of the Commonwealth Coll (PA)
Penn State U DuBois Campus of the Commonwealth Coll (PA)
Penn State U Fayette Campus of the Commonwealth Coll (PA)
Penn State U Hazleton Campus of the Commonwealth Coll (PA)
Penn State U New Kensington Campus of the Commonwealth Coll (PA)

Penn State U Wilkes-Barre Campus of the Commonwealth Coll (PA)
Penn State U York Campus of the Commonwealth Coll (PA)
Penn Valley Comm Coll (MO)
Piedmont Comm Coll (NC)
Piedmont Virginia Comm Coll (VA)
Pima Comm Coll (AZ)
Prairie State Coll (IL)
Queensborough Comm Coll of City U of NY (NY)
Ranken Tech Coll (MO)
Raritan Valley Comm Coll (NJ)
Reid State Tech Coll (AL)
RETS Tech Center (OH)
Richland Comm Coll (IL)
Richmond Comm Coll (NC)
Roanoke-Chowan Comm Coll (NC)
Rochester Comm and Tech Coll (MN)
Rockland Comm Coll (NY)
Rock Valley Coll (IL)
Rogue Comm Coll (OR)
Rowan-Cabarrus Comm Coll (NC)
St. Cloud Tech Coll (MN)
St. Louis Comm Coll at Forest Park (MO)
St. Louis Comm Coll at Meramec (MO)
Saint Paul Coll–A Comm & Tech College (MN)
St. Petersburg Coll (FL)
Salt Lake Comm Coll (UT)
San Antonio Coll (TX)
San Diego City Coll (CA)
San Joaquin Delta Coll (CA)
San Joaquin Valley Coll (CA)
Santa Barbara City Coll (CA)
Santa Fe Comm Coll (FL)
Sauk Valley Comm Coll (IL)
Savannah Tech Coll (GA)
Schoolcraft Coll (MI)
Schuylkill Inst of Business and Technology (PA)
Seminole Comm Coll (FL)
Shawnee Comm Coll (IL)
Shelton State Comm Coll (AL)
Sinclair Comm Coll (OH)
Sisseton-Wahpeton Comm Coll (SD)
Snow Coll (UT)
Solano Comm Coll (CA)
Somerset Comm Coll (KY)
Southeast Comm Coll, Lincoln Campus (NE)
Southeast Comm Coll, Milford Campus (NE)
Southeastern Tech Coll (GA)
Southeast Tech Inst (SD)
Southern Maine Comm Coll (ME)
Southside Virginia Comm Coll (VA)
Southwestern Comm Coll (NC)
Southwest Wisconsin Tech Coll (WI)
Spartanburg Tech Coll (SC)
Spencerian Coll–Lexington (KY)
Springfield Tech Comm Coll (MA)
Stanly Comm Coll (NC)
State U of NY Coll of Technology at Alfred (NY)
State U of NY Coll of Technology at Canton (NY)
Surry Comm Coll (NC)
Taft Coll (CA)
Tech Coll of the Lowcountry (SC)
Temple Coll (TX)
Texas State Tech Coll–Waco/Marshall Campus (TX)

Thaddeus Stevens Coll of Technology (PA)
Thompson Inst (PA)
Three Rivers Comm Coll (CT)
Tompkins Cortland Comm Coll (NY)
Triangle Tech, Inc.–Pittsburgh School (PA)
Tri-County Comm Coll (NC)
Tri-County Tech Coll (SC)
Trident Tech Coll (SC)
Trinidad State Jr Coll (CO)
Truckee Meadows Comm Coll (NV)
Umpqua Comm Coll (OR)
U of Alaska Anchorage, Matanuska-Susitna Coll (AK)
Valencia Comm Coll (FL)
Wake Tech Comm Coll (NC)
Waubonsee Comm Coll (IL)
Wayne County Comm Coll District (MI)
West Central Tech Coll (GA)
Westchester Comm Coll (NY)
Western Iowa Tech Comm Coll (IA)
Western Nevada Comm Coll (NV)
Western Wyoming Comm Coll (WY)
West Kentucky Comm and Tech Coll (KY)
Westmoreland County Comm Coll (PA)
West Virginia U at Parkersburg (WV)
Westwood Coll–Denver North (CO)
Wilkes Comm Coll (NC)
Wilson Tech Comm Coll (NC)
Wor-Wic Comm Coll (MD)
Yakima Valley Comm Coll (WA)
Yuba Coll (CA)

Electrical, Electronics and Communications Engineering
Allen County Comm Coll (KS)
Black Hawk Coll, Moline (IL)
Dutchess Comm Coll (NY)
Fayetteville Tech Comm Coll (NC)
Jamestown Comm Coll (NY)
John Tyler Comm Coll (VA)
Lake Region State Coll (ND)
Lehigh Carbon Comm Coll (PA)
Mayland Comm Coll (NC)

Electrical/Electronics Drafting and Cad/Cadd
Albuquerque Tech Vocational Inst (NM)
Brevard Comm Coll (FL)
Collin County Comm Coll District (TX)
Eastfield Coll (TX)
North Seattle Comm Coll (WA)
Texas State Tech Coll–Waco/Marshall Campus (TX)

Electrical/Electronics Equipment Installation and Repair
Bristol Comm Coll (MA)
Cape Fear Comm Coll (NC)
Coll of DuPage (IL)
Collin County Comm Coll District (TX)
Gadsden State Comm Coll-Ayers Campus (AL)
Guilford Tech Comm Coll (NC)
Hutchinson Comm Coll and Area Vocational School (KS)
Iowa Western Comm Coll (IA)

Kennebec Valley Comm Coll (ME)
Lake Region State Coll (ND)
Linn State Tech Coll (MO)
Macomb Comm Coll (MI)
Mesabi Range Comm and Tech Coll (MN)
Milwaukee Area Tech Coll (WI)
Modesto Jr Coll (CA)
Orange Coast Coll (CA)
Riverland Comm Coll (MN)
St. Philip's Coll (TX)
Santa Barbara City Coll (CA)
State U of NY Coll of Technology at Alfred (NY)
Triangle Tech, Inc.–Greensburg School (PA)
Western Wyoming Comm Coll (WY)

Electrical/Electronics Maintenance and Repair Technology Related
Bunker Hill Comm Coll (MA)
Mohawk Valley Comm Coll (NY)
Triangle Tech, Inc.–Greensburg School (PA)
West Virginia State Comm and Tech Coll (WV)

Electrician
Black Hawk Coll, Moline (IL)
Brazosport Coll (TX)
Cleveland Comm Coll (NC)
Coll of Lake County (IL)
Delta Coll (MI)
Ivy Tech State Coll–Bloomington (IN)
Ivy Tech State Coll–Central Indiana (IN)
Ivy Tech State Coll–Eastcentral (IN)
Ivy Tech State Coll–Kokomo (IN)
Ivy Tech State Coll–Lafayette (IN)
Ivy Tech State Coll–North Central (IN)
Ivy Tech State Coll–Northeast (IN)
Ivy Tech State Coll–Northwest (IN)
Ivy Tech State Coll–Southcentral (IN)
Ivy Tech State Coll–Southwest (IN)
Ivy Tech State Coll–Wabash Valley (IN)
Ivy Tech State Coll–Whitewater (IN)
John Wood Comm Coll (IL)
Lake Superior Coll (MN)
Laramie County Comm Coll (WY)
Linn State Tech Coll (MO)
Lower Columbia Coll (WA)
Midlands Tech Coll (SC)
Western Wyoming Comm Coll (WY)

Electrocardiograph Technology
Milwaukee Area Tech Coll (WI)

Electromechanical and Instrumentation And Maintenance Technologies Related
Calhoun Comm Coll (AL)
Gulf Coast Comm Coll (FL)
Northwestern Michigan Coll (MI)

Electromechanical Technology
Alamance Comm Coll (NC)
Belmont Tech Coll (OH)
Black Hawk Coll, Moline (IL)
Central Comm Coll–Columbus Campus (NE)
Central Piedmont Comm Coll (NC)
Chattahoochee Tech Coll (GA)

Cincinnati State Tech and Comm Coll (OH)
Clovis Comm Coll (NM)
Coll of DuPage (IL)
Columbus State Comm Coll (OH)
Comm and Tech Coll of Shepherd (WV)
Craven Comm Coll (NC)
DeKalb Tech Coll (GA)
Delaware Tech & Comm Coll, Terry Cmps (DE)
Dutchess Comm Coll (NY)
ECPI Coll of Technology, Newport News (VA)
ECPI Coll of Technology, Virginia Beach (VA)
ECPI Tech Coll, Richmond (VA)
ECPI Tech Coll, Roanoke (VA)
Forsyth Tech Comm Coll (NC)
GateWay Comm Coll (AZ)
Glendale Comm Coll (CA)
Hagerstown Comm Coll (MD)
Jackson State Comm Coll (TN)
Lake Land Coll (IL)
Lansing Comm Coll (MI)
Macomb Comm Coll (MI)
Milwaukee Area Tech Coll (WI)
Montgomery County Comm Coll (PA)
Muskegon Comm Coll (MI)
Northampton County Area Comm Coll (PA)
Northwestern Tech Coll (GA)
Oakland Comm Coll (MI)
Owens Comm Coll, Findlay (OH)
Pulaski Tech Coll (AR)
Randolph Comm Coll (NC)
Raritan Valley Comm Coll (NJ)
Rockingham Comm Coll (NC)
St. Philip's Coll (TX)
Savannah Tech Coll (GA)
Schoolcraft Coll (MI)
Sinclair Comm Coll (OH)
Southeast Comm Coll, Milford Campus (NE)
Southeast Tech Inst (SD)
Southwestern Comm Coll (IA)
Southwest Wisconsin Tech Coll (WI)
Springfield Tech Comm Coll (MA)
State U of NY Coll of Technology at Alfred (NY)
Tri-County Tech Coll (SC)
Union County Coll (NJ)
Wake Tech Comm Coll (NC)
West Virginia U at Parkersburg (WV)
Wilkes Comm Coll (NC)

Electroneurodiagnostic/ Electroencephalographic Technology
Black Hawk Coll, Moline (IL)
Comm Coll of Allegheny County (PA)
Harford Comm Coll (MD)
Niagara County Comm Coll (NY)
Oakland Comm Coll (MI)
Parkland Coll (IL)
Scott Comm Coll (IA)

Elementary and Middle School Administration/ Principalship
Cumberland County Coll (NJ)

Elementary Education
Alabama Southern Comm Coll (AL)
Albuquerque Tech Vocational Inst (NM)

Elementary Education

Allen County Comm Coll (KS)
Alpena Comm Coll (MI)
Amarillo Coll (TX)
Ancilla Coll (IN)
Anne Arundel Comm Coll (MD)
Bainbridge Coll (GA)
Barton County Comm Coll (KS)
Blackfeet Comm Coll (MT)
Brazosport Coll (TX)
Bristol Comm Coll (MA)
Broward Comm Coll (FL)
Butler County Comm Coll (PA)
Calhoun Comm Coll (AL)
Casper Coll (WY)
Cecil Comm Coll (MD)
Central Wyoming Coll (WY)
Chattahoochee Valley Comm Coll (AL)
City Colls of Chicago, Wilbur Wright Coll (IL)
Clarendon Coll (TX)
Cloud County Comm Coll (KS)
Coahoma Comm Coll (MS)
Coastal Bend Coll (TX)
Coffeyville Comm Coll (KS)
Coll of Southern Idaho (ID)
Coll of Southern Maryland (MD)
Columbia State Comm Coll (TN)
Copiah-Lincoln Comm Coll (MS)
Copiah-Lincoln Comm Coll–Natchez Campus (MS)
Corning Comm Coll (NY)
Cowley County Comm Coll and Voc-Tech School (KS)
Crowder Coll (MO)
Danville Area Comm Coll (IL)
Delta Coll (MI)
Dixie State Coll of Utah (UT)
Dodge City Comm Coll (KS)
Dutchess Comm Coll (NY)
East Central Coll (MO)
East Central Comm Coll (MS)
Eastern Arizona Coll (AZ)
East Mississippi Comm Coll (MS)
Edison State Comm Coll (OH)
El Paso Comm Coll (TX)
Essex County Coll (NJ)
Everett Comm Coll (WA)
Frank Phillips Coll (TX)
Frederick Comm Coll (MD)
Fulton-Montgomery Comm Coll (NY)
Gainesville Coll (GA)
Garden City Comm Coll (KS)
Garrett Coll (MD)
Genesee Comm Coll (NY)
Great Basin Coll (NV)
Gulf Coast Comm Coll (FL)
Hagerstown Comm Coll (MD)
Harford Comm Coll (MD)
Harrisburg Area Comm Coll (PA)
Hillsborough Comm Coll (FL)
Holmes Comm Coll (MS)
Holyoke Comm Coll (MA)
Howard Comm Coll (MD)
Illinois Valley Comm Coll (IL)
Independence Comm Coll (KS)
Iowa Lakes Comm Coll (IA)
Isothermal Comm Coll (NC)
Itawamba Comm Coll (MS)
John A. Logan Coll (IL)
Kalamazoo Valley Comm Coll (MI)
Kilgore Coll (TX)
Kingsborough Comm Coll of City U of NY (NY)
Lansing Comm Coll (MI)
Linn-Benton Comm Coll (OR)

Miami Dade Coll (FL)
Mid Michigan Comm Coll (MI)
Montgomery County Comm Coll (PA)
Mott Comm Coll (MI)
Muskegon Comm Coll (MI)
Northern Essex Comm Coll (MA)
North Idaho Coll (ID)
Northwest-Shoals Comm Coll (AL)
Orange County Comm Coll (NY)
Otero Jr Coll (CO)
Palm Beach Comm Coll (FL)
Pratt Comm Coll and Area Vocational School (KS)
Raritan Valley Comm Coll (NJ)
St. Louis Comm Coll at Meramec (MO)
Salt Lake Comm Coll (UT)
Sauk Valley Comm Coll (IL)
Seminole State Coll (OK)
Seward County Comm Coll (KS)
Shelton State Comm Coll (AL)
Sheridan Coll (WY)
Snow Coll (UT)
Springfield Tech Comm Coll (MA)
Three Rivers Comm Coll (MO)
Trinity Valley Comm Coll (TX)
Truckee Meadows Comm Coll (NV)
Umpqua Comm Coll (OR)
Western Oklahoma State Coll (OK)
Western Wyoming Comm Coll (WY)
Wor-Wic Comm Coll (MD)
Yuba Coll (CA)

Emergency Care Attendant (Emt Ambulance)

Columbus State Comm Coll (OH)
Iowa Lakes Comm Coll (IA)

Emergency Medical Technology (Emt Paramedic)

Allen County Comm Coll (KS)
Alvin Comm Coll (TX)
Amarillo Coll (TX)
Anne Arundel Comm Coll (MD)
Arapahoe Comm Coll (CO)
Arkansas State U–Mountain Home (AR)
Asheville-Buncombe Tech Comm Coll (NC)
Augusta Tech Coll (GA)
Austin Comm Coll (TX)
Baltimore City Comm Coll (MD)
Barton County Comm Coll (KS)
Belmont Tech Coll (OH)
Bevill State Comm Coll (AL)
Bismarck State Coll (ND)
Black River Tech Coll (AR)
Borough of Manhattan Comm Coll of City U of NY (NY)
Bossier Parish Comm Coll (LA)
Brazosport Coll (TX)
Brevard Comm Coll (FL)
Broome Comm Coll (NY)
Broward Comm Coll (FL)
Butler County Comm Coll (PA)
Calhoun Comm Coll (AL)
Capital Comm Coll (CT)
Casper Coll (WY)
Catawba Valley Comm Coll (NC)
Central Arizona Coll (AZ)

Central Florida Comm Coll (FL)
Central Oregon Comm Coll (OR)
Central Texas Coll (TX)
Century Coll (MN)
Cerro Coso Comm Coll (CA)
Chattanooga State Tech Comm Coll (TN)
Chemeketa Comm Coll (OR)
Cincinnati State Tech and Comm Coll (OH)
Clark Coll (WA)
Clark State Comm Coll (OH)
Clinton Comm Coll (IA)
Coastal Carolina Comm Coll (NC)
Coffeyville Comm Coll (KS)
Coll of DuPage (IL)
Coll of the Mainland (TX)
Collin County Comm Coll District (TX)
Colorado Northwestern Comm Coll (CO)
Columbus State Comm Coll (OH)
Comm and Tech Coll of Shepherd (WV)
Comm Coll of Southern Nevada (NV)
Compton Comm Coll (CA)
Contra Costa Coll (CA)
Corning Comm Coll (NY)
Cossatot Comm Coll of the U of Arkansas (AR)
Cowley County Comm Coll and Voc-Tech School (KS)
Davenport U, Midland (MI)
Davidson County Comm Coll (NC)
Daytona Beach Comm Coll (FL)
Delaware Tech & Comm Coll, Jack F Owens Cmps (DE)
Delaware Tech & Comm Coll, Stanton/ Wilmington Cmps (DE)
Delta Coll (MI)
Dixie State Coll of Utah (UT)
Doña Ana Branch Comm Coll (NM)
Dutchess Comm Coll (NY)
East Central Coll (MO)
Eastern Arizona Coll (AZ)
Elgin Comm Coll (IL)
Essex County Coll (NJ)
Fairmont State Comm & Tech Coll (WV)
Fayetteville Tech Comm Coll (NC)
Florida Comm Coll at Jacksonville (FL)
Foothill Coll (CA)
Fort Scott Comm Coll (KS)
Gadsden State Comm Coll (AL)
Garden City Comm Coll (KS)
George C. Wallace Comm Coll (AL)
Glendale Comm Coll (AZ)
Guilford Tech Comm Coll (NC)
Gulf Coast Comm Coll (FL)
Gwinnett Tech Coll (GA)
Hagerstown Comm Coll (MD)
Harrisburg Area Comm Coll (PA)
Hawkeye Comm Coll (IA)
Henry Ford Comm Coll (MI)
Herkimer County Comm Coll (NY)
Highland Comm Coll (KS)
Hillsborough Comm Coll (FL)
Hinds Comm Coll (MS)
Houston Comm Coll System (TX)
Howard Comm Coll (MD)
Hudson Valley Comm Coll (NY)
Hutchinson Comm Coll and Area Vocational School (KS)

Independence Comm Coll (KS)
Indian River Comm Coll (FL)
Iowa Lakes Comm Coll (IA)
Ivy Tech State Coll–Bloomington (IN)
Ivy Tech State Coll–Kokomo (IN)
Ivy Tech State Coll–North Central (IN)
Ivy Tech State Coll–Southwest (IN)
Ivy Tech State Coll–Wabash Valley (IN)
Jackson Comm Coll (MI)
Jefferson Comm Coll (OH)
John A. Logan Coll (IL)
Johnson County Comm Coll (KS)
John Wood Comm Coll (IL)
Kalamazoo Valley Comm Coll (MI)
Kansas City Kansas Comm Coll (KS)
Keiser Coll, Fort Lauderdale (FL)
Kennebec Valley Comm Coll (ME)
Kilgore Coll (TX)
Lackawanna Coll (PA)
Lake-Sumter Comm Coll (FL)
Lake Superior Coll (MN)
Lansing Comm Coll (MI)
Laredo Comm Coll (TX)
Macomb Comm Coll (MI)
Marshall Comm and Tech Coll (WV)
Meridian Comm Coll (MS)
Miami Dade Coll (FL)
Midland Coll (TX)
Mid Michigan Comm Coll (MI)
Minnesota State Coll–Southeast Tech (MN)
Modesto Jr Coll (CA)
Mohawk Valley Comm Coll (NY)
Montcalm Comm Coll (MI)
Montgomery Comm Coll (NC)
Mott Comm Coll (MI)
Muscatine Comm Coll (IA)
Muskegon Comm Coll (MI)
Napa Valley Coll (CA)
North Central Missouri Coll (MO)
Northeast Alabama Comm Coll (AL)
Northeast State Tech Comm Coll (TN)
Northern Virginia Comm Coll (VA)
North Iowa Area Comm Coll (IA)
Northwest Tech Coll (MN)
Oakland Comm Coll (MI)
Odessa Coll (TX)
Orange Coast Coll (CA)
Pasco-Hernando Comm Coll (FL)
Penn Valley Comm Coll (MO)
Pima Comm Coll (AZ)
Polk Comm Coll (FL)
Rockland Comm Coll (NY)
St. Cloud Tech Coll (MN)
St. Louis Comm Coll at Meramec (MO)
St. Petersburg Coll (FL)
San Diego City Coll (CA)
San Diego Miramar Coll (CA)
San Joaquin Delta Coll (CA)
Santa Fe Comm Coll (FL)
Schoolcraft Coll (MI)
Scott Comm Coll (IA)
Seminole Comm Coll (FL)
Shelton State Comm Coll (AL)
Sinclair Comm Coll (OH)
South Central Tech Coll (MN)
Southern State Comm Coll (OH)
South Texas Coll (TX)

Southwestern Comm Coll (NC)
Tacoma Comm Coll (WA)
Tillamook Bay Comm Coll (OR)
Trinity Valley Comm Coll (TX)
Umpqua Comm Coll (OR)
U of Arkansas Comm Coll at Batesville (AR)
U of Cincinnati Raymond Walters Coll (OH)
Valencia Comm Coll (FL)
Wake Tech Comm Coll (NC)
Wayne County Comm Coll District (MI)
Westchester Comm Coll (NY)
Western Iowa Tech Comm Coll (IA)
Western Oklahoma State Coll (OK)
Wilson Tech Comm Coll (NC)
Wor-Wic Comm Coll (MD)

Energy Management and Systems Technology

Bismarck State Coll (ND)
Chattanooga State Tech Comm Coll (TN)
Comm Coll of Allegheny County (PA)
Delaware County Comm Coll (PA)
Henry Ford Comm Coll (MI)
Iowa Lakes Comm Coll (IA)
Lane Comm Coll (OR)
Macomb Comm Coll (MI)
Pratt Comm Coll and Area Vocational School (KS)

Engineering

Adirondack Comm Coll (NY)
Alabama Southern Comm Coll (AL)
Albuquerque Tech Vocational Inst (NM)
Allen County Comm Coll (KS)
Amarillo Coll (TX)
Arapahoe Comm Coll (CO)
Baltimore City Comm Coll (MD)
Berkshire Comm Coll (MA)
Brazosport Coll (TX)
Bristol Comm Coll (MA)
Brookdale Comm Coll (NJ)
Bucks County Comm Coll (PA)
Casper Coll (WY)
Central Arizona Coll (AZ)
Centralia Coll (WA)
Central Texas Coll (TX)
Chemeketa Comm Coll (OR)
Citrus Coll (CA)
City Colls of Chicago, Wilbur Wright Coll (IL)
Coastal Bend Coll (TX)
Coffeyville Comm Coll (KS)
Coll of DuPage (IL)
Coll of Lake County (IL)
Coll of Southern Idaho (ID)
Coll of Southern Maryland (MD)
Comm Coll of Philadelphia (PA)
Comm Coll of Rhode Island (RI)
Compton Comm Coll (CA)
Contra Costa Coll (CA)
Copiah-Lincoln Comm Coll (MS)
Cumberland County Coll (NJ)
Danville Area Comm Coll (IL)
Daytona Beach Comm Coll (FL)
De Anza Coll (CA)
Delaware County Comm Coll (PA)
Delaware Tech & Comm Coll, Jack F Owens Cmps (DE)

Delaware Tech & Comm Coll, Stanton/ Wilmington Cmps (DE)
Delta Coll (MI)
Dixie State Coll of Utah (UT)
Dodge City Comm Coll (KS)
East Central Comm Coll (MS)
Edison State Comm Coll (OH)
Erie Comm Coll, North Campus (NY)
Essex County Coll (NJ)
Everett Comm Coll (WA)
Foothill Coll (CA)
Frank Phillips Coll (TX)
Frederick Comm Coll (MD)
Gainesville Coll (GA)
Garden City Comm Coll (KS)
Gogebic Comm Coll (MI)
Hagerstown Comm Coll (MD)
Harford Comm Coll (MD)
Harrisburg Area Comm Coll (PA)
Heartland Comm Coll (IL)
Highland Comm Coll (IL)
Highline Comm Coll (WA)
Hillsborough Comm Coll (FL)
Holmes Comm Coll (MS)
Howard Comm Coll (MD)
Hutchinson Comm Coll and Area Vocational School (KS)
Independence Comm Coll (KS)
Indian River Comm Coll (FL)
Iowa Lakes Comm Coll (IA)
Itasca Comm Coll (MN)
Jamestown Comm Coll (NY)
J. Sargeant Reynolds Comm Coll (VA)
Lansing Comm Coll (MI)
Laramie County Comm Coll (WY)
Lehigh Carbon Comm Coll (PA)
Linn-Benton Comm Coll (OR)
Long Beach City Coll (CA)
Longview Comm Coll (MO)
Lower Columbia Coll (WA)
Metropolitan Comm Coll-Business & Technology College (MO)
Miami Dade Coll (FL)
Modesto Jr Coll (CA)
Mohawk Valley Comm Coll (NY)
Napa Valley Coll (CA)
Nassau Comm Coll (NY)
New Mexico Military Inst (NM)
Northampton County Area Comm Coll (PA)
Northern Virginia Comm Coll (VA)
North Idaho Coll (ID)
Northwestern Connecticut Comm-Tech Coll (CT)
Northwestern Michigan Coll (MI)
Oakland Comm Coll (MI)
Olympic Coll (WA)
Orange Coast Coll (CA)
Pasadena City Coll (CA)
Penn Valley Comm Coll (MO)
Raritan Valley Comm Coll (NJ)
Riverside Comm Coll District (CA)
St. Louis Comm Coll at Forest Park (MO)
Salt Lake Comm Coll (UT)
San Joaquin Delta Coll (CA)
San Juan Coll (NM)
Santa Barbara City Coll (CA)
Santa Fe Comm Coll (FL)
Santa Rosa Jr Coll (CA)
Schoolcraft Coll (MI)
Sheridan Coll (WY)
Sinclair Comm Coll (OH)
Snow Coll (UT)

Southwestern Oregon Comm
Coll (OR)
Springfield Tech Comm Coll
(MA)
Tacoma Comm Coll (WA)
Three Rivers Comm Coll
(CT)
Trinidad State Jr Coll (CO)
Tunxis Comm Coll (CT)
Umpqua Comm Coll (OR)
Union County Coll (NJ)
The U of Akron–Wayne Coll
(OH)
Waubonsee Comm Coll (IL)
Western Nevada Comm Coll
(NV)
Westmoreland County
Comm Coll (PA)

**Engineering/Industrial
Management**
Cape Fear Comm Coll (NC)
St. Petersburg Coll (FL)

Engineering Related
Bristol Comm Coll (MA)
Chattanooga State Tech
Comm Coll (TN)
Edison State Comm Coll
(OH)
Itasca Comm Coll (MN)
Macomb Comm Coll (MI)
Miami Dade Coll (FL)
Northwest State Comm Coll
(OH)
Salt Lake Comm Coll (UT)
San Joaquin Delta Coll (CA)
Southern Maine Comm Coll
(ME)

**Engineering-Related
Technologies**
Metropolitan Comm
Coll-Business &
Technology College (MO)

Engineering Science
Adirondack Comm Coll (NY)
Asnuntuck Comm Coll (CT)
Bergen Comm Coll (NJ)
Borough of Manhattan
Comm Coll of City U of NY
(NY)
Bristol Comm Coll (MA)
Broome Comm Coll (NY)
Broward Comm Coll (FL)
Dutchess Comm Coll (NY)
Everett Comm Coll (WA)
Finger Lakes Comm Coll
(NY)
Fulton-Montgomery Comm
Coll (NY)
Genesee Comm Coll (NY)
Greenfield Comm Coll (MA)
Highland Comm Coll (IL)
Holyoke Comm Coll (MA)
Hudson County Comm Coll
(NJ)
Itasca Comm Coll (MN)
Jefferson Comm Coll (NY)
Kingsborough Comm Coll of
City U of NY (NY)
Manchester Comm Coll (CT)
Montgomery County Comm
Coll (PA)
Northern Essex Comm Coll
(MA)
North Shore Comm Coll
(MA)
Orange County Comm Coll
(NY)
Parkland Coll (IL)
Queensborough Comm Coll
of City U of NY (NY)
St. Louis Comm Coll at
Forest Park (MO)
St. Louis Comm Coll at
Meramec (MO)
State U of NY Coll of
Technology at Alfred (NY)
State U of NY Coll of
Technology at Canton (NY)
State U of NY Coll of
Technology at Delhi (NY)
Three Rivers Comm Coll
(CT)

Tompkins Cortland Comm
Coll (NY)
Westchester Comm Coll
(NY)

**Engineering Technologies
Related**
Albuquerque Tech Vocational
Inst (NM)
Bowling Green State
U-Firelands Coll (OH)
Bristol Comm Coll (MA)
Catawba Valley Comm Coll
(NC)
Cleveland Comm Coll (NC)
Comm Coll of Allegheny
County (PA)
Harford Comm Coll (MD)
Harrisburg Area Comm Coll
(PA)
McNally Smith Coll of Music
(MN)
Mid Michigan Comm Coll
(MI)
Montgomery County Comm
Coll (PA)
Mott Comm Coll (MI)
Wor-Wic Comm Coll (MD)

Engineering Technology
Allen County Comm Coll
(KS)
Anne Arundel Comm Coll
(MD)
Arizona Western Coll (AZ)
Ashland Comm and Tech
Coll (KY)
Athens Tech Coll (GA)
Atlanta Metropolitan Coll
(GA)
Atlanta Metropolitan Coll
(GA)
Barton County Comm Coll
(KS)
Bishop State Comm Coll
(AL)
Brunswick Comm Coll (NC)
Central Piedmont Comm Coll
(NC)
Cerro Coso Comm Coll (CA)
Cerro Coso Comm Coll (CA)
Citrus Coll (CA)
Comm Coll of Philadelphia
(PA)
Cowley County Comm Coll
and Voc-Tech School (KS)
Cuyahoga Comm Coll (OH)
Danville Comm Coll (VA)
Darton Coll (GA)
Davidson County Comm Coll
(NC)
De Anza Coll (CA)
DeKalb Tech Coll (GA)
Delaware Tech & Comm
Coll, Jack F Owens Cmps
(DE)
Delaware Tech & Comm
Coll, Terry Cmps (DE)
Delta Coll (MI)
Dodge City Comm Coll (KS)
ECPI Coll of Technology,
Newport News (VA)
ECPI Coll of Technology,
Virginia Beach (VA)
ECPI Tech Coll, Richmond
(VA)
ECPI Tech Coll, Roanoke
(VA)
Edison State Comm Coll
(OH)
Essex County Coll (NJ)
Everett Comm Coll (WA)
Fayetteville Tech Comm Coll
(NC)
Florida Comm Coll at
Jacksonville (FL)
Forsyth Tech Comm Coll
(NC)
Frank Phillips Coll (TX)
Gainesville Coll (GA)
Garden City Comm Coll (KS)
Gateway Comm Coll (CT)
Glendale Comm Coll (AZ)
Gulf Coast Comm Coll (FL)

Harrisburg Area Comm Coll
(PA)
Hawkeye Comm Coll (IA)
Henderson Comm Coll (KY)
Highland Comm Coll (IL)
Highline Comm Coll (WA)
Houston Comm Coll System
(TX)
Independence Comm Coll
(KS)
Indian River Comm Coll (FL)
Iowa Western Comm Coll
(IA)
Itasca Comm Coll (MN)
Keiser Coll, Fort Lauderdale
(FL)
Kent State U, Tuscarawas
Campus (OH)
Lansing Comm Coll (MI)
Laramie County Comm Coll
(WY)
Lower Columbia Coll (WA)
Massachusetts Bay Comm
Coll (MA)
Miami Dade Coll (FL)
Midlands Tech Coll (SC)
Mid Michigan Comm Coll
(MI)
Morrison Inst of Technology
(IL)
Motlow State Comm Coll
(TN)
Muskegon Comm Coll (MI)
Northeast State Tech Comm
Coll (TN)
Pasadena City Coll (CA)
Patrick Henry Comm Coll
(VA)
Peninsula Coll (WA)
Pennsylvania Inst of
Technology (PA)
Quinebaug Valley Comm
Coll (CT)
St. Louis Comm Coll at
Forest Park (MO)
Salt Lake Comm Coll (UT)
San Antonio Coll (TX)
San Antonio Coll (TX)
San Diego City Coll (CA)
San Joaquin Delta Coll (CA)
Santa Barbara City Coll (CA)
Santa Rosa Jr Coll (CA)
Sheridan Coll (WY)
Shoreline Comm Coll (WA)
Southeast Tech Inst (SD)
South Hills School of
Business & Technology,
State College (PA)
Southwestern Michigan Coll
(MI)
Spartanburg Tech Coll (SC)
State U of NY Coll of
Technology at Canton (NY)
State U of NY Coll of
Technology at Delhi (NY)
Three Rivers Comm Coll
(CT)
Three Rivers Comm Coll
(MO)
Trident Tech Coll (SC)
Truckee Meadows Comm
Coll (NV)
Tunxis Comm Coll (CT)
Wayne County Comm Coll
District (MI)
Westchester Comm Coll
(NY)
Western Wyoming Comm
Coll (WY)

Engine Machinist
Black Hawk Coll, Moline (IL)

English
Alabama Southern Comm
Coll (AL)
Alpena Comm Coll (MI)
Amarillo Coll (TX)
Andrew Coll (GA)
Anne Arundel Comm Coll
(MD)
Arizona Western Coll (AZ)
Atlanta Metropolitan Coll
(GA)
Austin Comm Coll (TX)

Bainbridge Coll (GA)
Barton County Comm Coll
(KS)
Brazosport Coll (TX)
Brookdale Comm Coll (NJ)
Bunker Hill Comm Coll (MA)
Butler County Comm Coll
(KS)
Butler County Comm Coll
(PA)
Calhoun Comm Coll (AL)
Casper Coll (WY)
Centralia Coll (WA)
Central Wyoming Coll (WY)
Chemeketa Comm Coll (OR)
Citrus Coll (CA)
City Colls of Chicago, Wilbur
Wright Coll (IL)
Clarendon Coll (TX)
Coahoma Comm Coll (MS)
Coastal Bend Coll (TX)
Coastal Georgia Comm Coll
(GA)
Cochise Coll, Douglas (AZ)
Coffeyville Comm Coll (KS)
Colby Comm Coll (KS)
Coll of Southern Idaho (ID)
Coll of the Canyons (CA)
Colorado Mountn Coll, Alpine
Cmps (CO)
Colorado Mountn Coll (CO)
Colorado Mountn Coll,
Timberline Cmps (CO)
Colorado Northwestern
Comm Coll (CO)
Columbia Coll (CA)
Comm Coll of Allegheny
County (PA)
Comm Coll of Southern
Nevada (NV)
Compton Comm Coll (CA)
Contra Costa Coll (CA)
Copiah-Lincoln Comm Coll
(MS)
Danville Area Comm Coll (IL)
Darton Coll (GA)
Daytona Beach Comm Coll
(FL)
De Anza Coll (CA)
Delta Coll (MI)
Dixie State Coll of Utah (UT)
Dodge City Comm Coll (KS)
East Central Coll (MO)
East Central Comm Coll
(MS)
Eastern Arizona Coll (AZ)
East Mississippi Comm Coll
(MS)
Edison State Comm Coll
(OH)
El Paso Comm Coll (TX)
Everett Comm Coll (WA)
Feather River Coll (CA)
Foothill Coll (CA)
Frank Phillips Coll (TX)
Frederick Comm Coll (MD)
Fulton-Montgomery Comm
Coll (NY)
Gainesville Coll (GA)
Garden City Comm Coll (KS)
Glendale Comm Coll (CA)
Gordon Coll (GA)
Great Basin Coll (NV)
Gulf Coast Comm Coll (FL)
Herkimer County Comm Coll
(NY)
Highland Comm Coll (KS)
Highline Comm Coll (WA)
Hinds Comm Coll (MS)
Howard Coll (TX)
Hutchinson Comm Coll and
Area Vocational School
(KS)
Illinois Valley Comm Coll (IL)
Independence Comm Coll
(KS)
Indian River Comm Coll (FL)
Iowa Lakes Comm Coll (IA)
Itawamba Comm Coll (MS)
John A. Logan Coll (IL)
Kilgore Coll (TX)
Kingwood Coll (TX)
Lansing Comm Coll (MI)

Laramie County Comm Coll
(WY)
Linn-Benton Comm Coll
(OR)
Long Beach City Coll (CA)
Lower Columbia Coll (WA)
Miami Dade Coll (FL)
Midland Coll (TX)
Modesto Jr Coll (CA)
Mohave Comm Coll (AZ)
New Mexico Military Inst
(NM)
North Idaho Coll (ID)
Northwestern Connecticut
Comm-Tech Coll (CT)
Northwestern Michigan Coll
(MI)
Odessa Coll (TX)
Orange Coast Coll (CA)
Palm Beach Comm Coll (FL)
Pasadena City Coll (CA)
Phillips Comm Coll of the U
of Arkansas (AR)
Pratt Comm Coll and Area
Vocational School (KS)
Riverside Comm Coll District
(CA)
St. Philip's Coll (TX)
San Diego City Coll (CA)
San Diego Miramar Coll (CA)
San Joaquin Delta Coll (CA)
San Juan Coll (NM)
Santa Barbara City Coll (CA)
Santa Rosa Jr Coll (CA)
Sauk Valley Comm Coll (IL)
Seminole State Coll (OK)
Seward County Comm Coll
(KS)
Sheridan Coll (WY)
Solano Comm Coll (CA)
Sussex County Comm Coll
(NJ)
Tacoma Comm Coll (WA)
Taft Coll (CA)
Trinidad State Jr Coll (CO)
Trinity Valley Comm Coll
(TX)
Umpqua Comm Coll (OR)
Western Oklahoma State
Coll (OK)
Western Wyoming Comm
Coll (WY)
Yuba Coll (CA)

English Composition
Allen County Comm Coll
(KS)

Entomology
Snow Coll (UT)

**Entrepreneurial and Small
Business Related**
Herkimer County Comm Coll
(NY)
Williston State Coll (ND)

Entrepreneurship
Blackfeet Comm Coll (MT)
Bristol Comm Coll (MA)
Bucks County Comm Coll
(PA)
Calhoun Comm Coll (AL)
Cincinnati State Tech and
Comm Coll (OH)
Colorado Northwestern
Comm Coll (CO)
Comm Coll of Allegheny
County (PA)
Delaware County Comm Coll
(PA)
Eastern Arizona Coll (AZ)
Edmonds Comm Coll (WA)
Front Range Comm Coll
(CO)
Goodwin Coll (CT)
Laramie County Comm Coll
(WY)
Mohawk Valley Comm Coll
(NY)
Montcalm Comm Coll (MI)
Moraine Valley Comm Coll
(IL)
Mott Comm Coll (MI)
Nassau Comm Coll (NY)
North Iowa Area Comm Coll
(IA)

Oakland Comm Coll (MI)
Schoolcraft Coll (MI)
Springfield Tech Comm Coll
(MA)
Waubonsee Comm Coll (IL)

Environmental Biology
Truckee Meadows Comm
Coll (NV)

**Environmental Control
Technologies Related**
Black Hawk Coll, Moline (IL)
Central Carolina Tech Coll
(SC)
Central Florida Comm Coll
(FL)
Oakland Comm Coll (MI)

**Environmental Design/
Architecture**
Iowa Lakes Comm Coll (IA)
Queensborough Comm Coll
of City U of NY (NY)

Environmental Education
Colorado Mountn Coll,
Timberline Cmps (CO)
Iowa Lakes Comm Coll (IA)

**Environmental Engineering
Technology**
Arapahoe Comm Coll (CO)
Bay de Noc Comm Coll (MI)
Blue Ridge Comm Coll (NC)
Bristol Comm Coll (MA)
Broward Comm Coll (FL)
Cape Cod Comm Coll (MA)
Central Alabama Comm Coll
(AL)
Central Piedmont Comm Coll
(NC)
Chattanooga State Tech
Comm Coll (TN)
Cincinnati State Tech and
Comm Coll (OH)
City Colls of Chicago, Wilbur
Wright Coll (IL)
Clinton Comm Coll (IA)
Clover Park Tech Coll (WA)
Coastal Bend Coll (TX)
Collin County Comm Coll
District (TX)
Columbus State Comm Coll
(OH)
Comm Coll of Allegheny
County (PA)
Comm Coll of Denver (CO)
Comm Coll of Philadelphia
(PA)
Crowder Coll (MO)
Delaware Tech & Comm
Coll, Jack F Owens Cmps
(DE)
Ellsworth Comm Coll (IA)
Front Range Comm Coll
(CO)
Harford Comm Coll (MD)
Iowa Lakes Comm Coll (IA)
James H. Faulkner State
Comm Coll (AL)
John Tyler Comm Coll (VA)
Massachusetts Bay Comm
Coll (MA)
Metropolitan Comm
Coll-Business &
Technology College (MO)
Miami Dade Coll (FL)
Milwaukee Area Tech Coll
(WI)
Muscatine Comm Coll (IA)
Napa Valley Coll (CA)
Pennsylvania Highland
Comm Coll (PA)
Pima Comm Coll (AZ)
Roanoke-Chowan Comm
Coll (NC)
San Diego City Coll (CA)
Schoolcraft Coll (MI)
Scott Comm Coll (IA)
Shoreline Comm Coll (WA)
Southern Maine Comm Coll
(ME)
Three Rivers Comm Coll
(CT)
Valencia Comm Coll (FL)
Wake Tech Comm Coll (NC)

Wayne County Comm Coll District (MI)
Westchester Comm Coll (NY)
Westmoreland County Comm Coll (PA)
West Virginia U at Parkersburg (WV)

Environmental/ Environmental Health Engineering
Albuquerque Tech Vocational Inst (NM)
Bristol Comm Coll (MA)
Santa Barbara City Coll (CA)

Environmental Health
Amarillo Coll (TX)
Black Hawk Coll, Moline (IL)
Brazosport Coll (TX)
Comm Coll of the Air Force (AL)
Crowder Coll (MO)
Milwaukee Area Tech Coll (WI)
North Idaho Coll (ID)
Queensborough Comm Coll of City U of NY (NY)
The U of Akron–Wayne Coll (OH)

Environmental Science
Berkshire Comm Coll (MA)
Bristol Comm Coll (MA)
Central Wyoming Coll (WY)
City Colls of Chicago, Wilbur Wright Coll (IL)
Colorado Northwestern Comm Coll (CO)
Darton Coll (GA)
Delta Coll (MI)
Ohio State U Ag Tech Inst (OH)
St. Philip's Coll (TX)
Western Wyoming Comm Coll (WY)

Environmental Studies
Anne Arundel Comm Coll (MD)
Arizona Western Coll (AZ)
Bristol Comm Coll (MA)
Bucks County Comm Coll (PA)
Cape Cod Comm Coll (MA)
Cape Fear Comm Coll (NC)
Central Texas Coll (TX)
Century Coll (MN)
Coll of Southern Idaho (ID)
Colorado Mountn Coll, Timberline Cmps (CO)
Columbia Coll (CA)
Comm Coll of Southern Nevada (NV)
Comm Coll of the Air Force (AL)
Cossatot Comm Coll of the U of Arkansas (AR)
De Anza Coll (CA)
Delta Coll (MI)
Dixie State Coll of Utah (UT)
Everett Comm Coll (WA)
Finger Lakes Comm Coll (NY)
Fulton-Montgomery Comm Coll (NY)
Great Basin Coll (NV)
Harrisburg Area Comm Coll (PA)
Hillsborough Comm Coll (FL)
Holyoke Comm Coll (MA)
Howard Comm Coll (MD)
Hudson Valley Comm Coll (NY)
Iowa Lakes Comm Coll (IA)
Itasca Comm Coll (MN)
Kent State U, Tuscarawas Campus (OH)
Keystone Coll (PA)
Lower Columbia Coll (WA)
Mid Michigan Comm Coll (MI)
Mount Wachusett Comm Coll (MA)
Napa Valley Coll (CA)

Raritan Valley Comm Coll (NJ)
Riverside Comm Coll District (CA)
Salt Lake Comm Coll (UT)
Santa Barbara City Coll (CA)
Santa Fe Comm Coll (FL)
Santa Rosa Jr Coll (CA)
Southeast Comm Coll, Lincoln Campus (NE)
Southwestern Comm Coll (NC)
Southwestern Oregon Comm Coll (OR)
State U of NY Coll of Technology at Alfred (NY)
State U of NY Coll of Technology at Canton (NY)
Sussex County Comm Coll (NJ)
Tacoma Comm Coll (WA)
Tech Coll of the Lowcountry (SC)
Tompkins Cortland Comm Coll (NY)
Truckee Meadows Comm Coll (NV)
U of Cincinnati Raymond Walters Coll (OH)
Western Nevada Comm Coll (NV)

Equestrian Studies
Allen County Comm Coll (KS)
Black Hawk Coll, Moline (IL)
Central Texas Coll (TX)
Central Wyoming Coll (WY)
Coll of Southern Idaho (ID)
Dodge City Comm Coll (KS)
Ellsworth Comm Coll (IA)
Laramie County Comm Coll (WY)
Ohio State U Ag Tech Inst (OH)
Parkland Coll (IL)
Scott Comm Coll (IA)
Yavapai Coll (AZ)

Ethnic, Cultural Minority, and Gender Studies Related
Brazosport Coll (TX)

European Studies
Anne Arundel Comm Coll (MD)

Executive Assistant/ Executive Secretary
Adirondack Comm Coll (NY)
Alamance Comm Coll (NC)
Asheville-Buncombe Tech Comm Coll (NC)
Broome Comm Coll (NY)
Brown Mackie Coll, Findlay Campus (OH)
Business Inst of Pennsylvania, Sharon (PA)
Butler County Comm Coll (PA)
Cape Cod Comm Coll (MA)
Cape Fear Comm Coll (NC)
Central Florida Comm Coll (FL)
Cincinnati State Tech and Comm Coll (OH)
Clark Coll (WA)
Cleveland Comm Coll (NC)
Clovis Comm Coll (NM)
Coastal Carolina Comm Coll (NC)
Craven Comm Coll (NC)
Crowder Coll (MO)
Delta Coll (MI)
Eastfield Coll (TX)
Elgin Comm Coll (IL)
Ivy Tech State Coll–Bloomington (IN)
Ivy Tech State Coll–Central Indiana (IN)
Ivy Tech State Coll–Columbus (IN)
Ivy Tech State Coll–Eastcentral (IN)
Ivy Tech State Coll–Kokomo (IN)

Ivy Tech State Coll–Lafayette (IN)
Ivy Tech State Coll–North Central (IN)
Ivy Tech State Coll–Northeast (IN)
Ivy Tech State Coll–Northwest (IN)
Ivy Tech State Coll–Southcentral (IN)
Ivy Tech State Coll–Southeast (IN)
Ivy Tech State Coll–Southwest (IN)
Ivy Tech State Coll–Wabash Valley (IN)
Ivy Tech State Coll–Whitewater (IN)
Jackson Comm Coll (MI)
John Wood Comm Coll (IL)
J. Sargeant Reynolds Comm Coll (VA)
Kalamazoo Valley Comm Coll (MI)
Kaskaskia Coll (IL)
Kennebec Valley Comm Coll (ME)
Kilgore Coll (TX)
Lake Land Coll (IL)
Lake Region State Coll (ND)
Lake Superior Coll (MN)
Laurel Business Inst (PA)
Lehigh Carbon Comm Coll (PA)
Montcalm Comm Coll (MI)
National Coll of Business & Technology, Salem (VA)
Northampton County Area Comm Coll (PA)
Northwestern Michigan Coll (MI)
Northwestern Tech Coll (GA)
Northwest State Comm Coll (OH)
Owensboro Comm and Tech Coll (KY)
Prairie State Coll (IL)
Randolph Comm Coll (NC)
Southern State Comm Coll (OH)
Stanly Comm Coll (NC)
The U of Akron–Wayne Coll (OH)
Waubonsee Comm Coll (IL)
Western Iowa Tech Comm Coll (IA)
West Georgia Tech Coll (GA)
Wilkes Comm Coll (NC)

Family and Community Services
Bowling Green State U-Firelands Coll (OH)
Collin County Comm Coll District (TX)
Garden City Comm Coll (KS)
Snow Coll (UT)

Family and Consumer Economics Related
Arizona Western Coll (AZ)
Cowley County Comm Coll and Voc-Tech School (KS)
Long Beach City Coll (CA)
Modesto Jr Coll (CA)
Orange Coast Coll (CA)
Yakima Valley Comm Coll (WA)
Yuba Coll (CA)

Family and Consumer Sciences/Home Economics Teacher Education
Cloud County Comm Coll (KS)
Copiah-Lincoln Comm Coll (MS)
Itawamba Comm Coll (MS)

Family and Consumer Sciences/Human Sciences
Allen County Comm Coll (KS)
Bainbridge Coll (GA)
Brazosport Coll (TX)
Central Comm Coll–Columbus Campus (NE)

Cloud County Comm Coll (KS)
Coffeyville Comm Coll (KS)
Colby Comm Coll (KS)
Compton Comm Coll (CA)
Contra Costa Coll (CA)
Copiah-Lincoln Comm Coll–Natchez Campus (MS)
Delta Coll (MI)
East Central Coll (MO)
Garden City Comm Coll (KS)
Highland Comm Coll (KS)
Hinds Comm Coll (MS)
Holyoke Comm Coll (MA)
Houston Comm Coll System (TX)
Hutchinson Comm Coll and Area Vocational School (KS)
Indian River Comm Coll (FL)
Iowa Lakes Comm Coll (IA)
Itawamba Comm Coll (MS)
Linn-Benton Comm Coll (OR)
Long Beach City Coll (CA)
Orange Coast Coll (CA)
Palm Beach Comm Coll (FL)
Penn Valley Comm Coll (MO)
Pratt Comm Coll and Area Vocational School (KS)
Riverside Comm Coll District (CA)
San Joaquin Delta Coll (CA)
Santa Rosa Jr Coll (CA)
Shelton State Comm Coll (AL)
Snow Coll (UT)
Solano Comm Coll (CA)
South Mountain Comm Coll (AZ)
Yuba Coll (CA)

Family Living/Parenthood
Centralia Coll (WA)

Family Resource Management
Calhoun Comm Coll (AL)

Farm and Ranch Management
Alexandria Tech Coll (MN)
Allen County Comm Coll (KS)
Butler County Comm Coll (KS)
Central Texas Coll (TX)
Clarendon Coll (TX)
Cloud County Comm Coll (KS)
Colby Comm Coll (KS)
Copiah-Lincoln Comm Coll (MS)
Cowley County Comm Coll and Voc-Tech School (KS)
Crowder Coll (MO)
Dodge City Comm Coll (KS)
Frank Phillips Coll (TX)
Garden City Comm Coll (KS)
Hawkeye Comm Coll (IA)
Highland Comm Coll (KS)
Hutchinson Comm Coll and Area Vocational School (KS)
Iowa Lakes Comm Coll (IA)
Iowa Western Comm Coll (IA)
North Central Missouri Coll (MO)
Northland Comm and Tech Coll–Thief River Falls (MN)
Pratt Comm Coll and Area Vocational School (KS)
Seward County Comm Coll (KS)
Snow Coll (UT)
Trinidad State Jr Coll (CO)
Trinity Valley Comm Coll (TX)

Fashion and Fabric Consulting
Coll of DuPage (IL)

Fashion/Apparel Design
The Art Inst of New York City (NY)
The Art Inst of Philadelphia (PA)
Baltimore City Comm Coll (MD)
Bay State Coll (MA)
Cloud County Comm Coll (KS)
Coll of DuPage (IL)
Daytona Beach Comm Coll (FL)
El Paso Comm Coll (TX)
Fashion Careers of California Coll (CA)
Fashion Inst of Design & Merchandising, LA Campus (CA)
Fashion Inst of Design & Merchandising, SD Campus (CA)
Fashion Inst of Design & Merchandising, SF Campus (CA)
Garden City Comm Coll (KS)
Glendale Comm Coll (CA)
Harcum Coll (PA)
Highland Comm Coll (KS)
Hinds Comm Coll (MS)
Houston Comm Coll System (TX)
Itawamba Comm Coll (MS)
Long Beach City Coll (CA)
Nassau Comm Coll (NY)
Palm Beach Comm Coll (FL)
Penn Valley Comm Coll (MO)
Seattle Central Comm Coll (WA)
Westmoreland County Comm Coll (PA)

Fashion Merchandising
Alexandria Tech Coll (MN)
The Art Inst of Philadelphia (PA)
Austin Comm Coll (TX)
Baltimore City Comm Coll (MD)
Bay State Coll (MA)
Berkeley Coll (NJ)
Berkeley Coll-New York City Campus (NY)
Berkeley Coll-Westchester Campus (NY)
Briarwood Coll (CT)
Brookdale Comm Coll (NJ)
Central Piedmont Comm Coll (NC)
Century Coll (MN)
Cleveland Comm Coll (NC)
Coll of DuPage (IL)
Comm and Tech Coll of Shepherd (WV)
Comm Coll of Philadelphia (PA)
Comm Coll of Rhode Island (RI)
Delta Coll (MI)
Des Moines Area Comm Coll (IA)
Doña Ana Branch Comm Coll (NM)
Ellsworth Comm Coll (IA)
El Paso Comm Coll (TX)
Fashion Careers of California Coll (CA)
Fashion Inst of Design & Merchandising, LA Campus (CA)
Fashion Inst of Design & Merchandising, SD Campus (CA)
Fashion Inst of Design & Merchandising, SF Campus (CA)
Florida Comm Coll at Jacksonville (FL)
Garden City Comm Coll (KS)
Gateway Comm Coll (CT)
Genesee Comm Coll (NY)
Grand Rapids Comm Coll (MI)
Gwinnett Tech Coll (GA)

Harcum Coll (PA)
Herkimer County Comm Coll (NY)
Houston Comm Coll System (TX)
Howard Comm Coll (MD)
ICM School of Business & Medical Careers (PA)
Indiana Business Coll, Indianapolis (IN)
Indian River Comm Coll (FL)
Iowa Lakes Comm Coll (IA)
Iowa Western Comm Coll (IA)
John A. Logan Coll (IL)
J. Sargeant Reynolds Comm Coll (VA)
Kilgore Coll (TX)
Kingsborough Comm Coll of City U of NY (NY)
Lake Region State Coll (ND)
Laredo Comm Coll (TX)
Long Beach City Coll (CA)
Middle Georgia Coll (GA)
Milwaukee Area Tech Coll (WI)
Modesto Jr Coll (CA)
Nassau Comm Coll (NY)
Northwest Tech Coll (MN)
Oakland Comm Coll (MI)
Odessa Coll (TX)
Orange Coast Coll (CA)
Owens Comm Coll, Findlay (OH)
Owens Comm Coll, Toledo (OH)
Palm Beach Comm Coll (FL)
Pasadena City Coll (CA)
Penn Valley Comm Coll (MO)
Rochester Comm and Tech Coll (MN)
San Diego City Coll (CA)
San Joaquin Delta Coll (CA)
Santa Fe Comm Coll (FL)
Solano Comm Coll (CA)
Tech Coll of the Lowcountry (SC)
Trinity Valley Comm Coll (TX)
Tunxis Comm Coll (CT)
Westmoreland County Comm Coll (PA)

Fiber, Textile and Weaving Arts
Compton Comm Coll (CA)
Haywood Comm Coll (NC)
Highland Comm Coll (KS)
Inst of American Indian Arts (NM)
Pasadena City Coll (CA)

Film/Cinema Studies
Cochise Coll, Douglas (AZ)
De Anza Coll (CA)
Lansing Comm Coll (MI)
Long Beach City Coll (CA)
Milwaukee Area Tech Coll (WI)
Orange Coast Coll (CA)
Santa Barbara City Coll (CA)
Santa Rosa Jr Coll (CA)
Yavapai Coll (AZ)

Finance
Academy Coll (MN)
Adirondack Comm Coll (NY)
Alabama Southern Comm Coll (AL)
Arapahoe Comm Coll (CO)
Arizona Western Coll (AZ)
Austin Comm Coll (TX)
Bergen Comm Coll (NJ)
Black Hawk Coll, Moline (IL)
Brazosport Coll (TX)
Broward Comm Coll (FL)
Bunker Hill Comm Coll (MA)
Central Piedmont Comm Coll (NC)
Chattanooga State Tech Comm Coll (TN)
Chemeketa Comm Coll (OR)
Chipola Coll (FL)
Clarendon Coll (TX)
Clovis Comm Coll (NM)

Coastal Bend Coll (TX)
Coll of Southern Idaho (ID)
Columbus State Comm Coll (OH)
Comm Coll of Aurora (CO)
Comm Coll of Philadelphia (PA)
Comm Coll of Southern Nevada (NV)
Comm Coll of the Air Force (AL)
Cuyahoga Comm Coll (OH)
Davenport U, Midland (MI)
Daytona Beach Comm Coll (FL)
Delta Coll (MI)
Dodge City Comm Coll (KS)
Doña Ana Branch Comm Coll (NM)
Edison State Comm Coll (OH)
Elizabethtown Comm and Tech Coll (KY)
El Paso Comm Coll (TX)
Enterprise-Ozark Comm Coll (AL)
Fairmont State Comm & Tech Coll (WV)
Fayetteville Tech Comm Coll (NC)
Forsyth Tech Comm Coll (NC)
Fox Valley Tech Coll (WI)
Frank Phillips Coll (TX)
Frederick Comm Coll (MD)
Fulton-Montgomery Comm Coll (NY)
GateWay Comm Coll (AZ)
Glendale Comm Coll (CA)
Hillsborough Comm Coll (FL)
Hinds Comm Coll (MS)
Holmes Comm Coll (MS)
Hopkinsville Comm Coll (KY)
Houston Comm Coll System (TX)
Howard Coll (TX)
Hudson Valley Comm Coll (NY)
Independence Comm Coll (KS)
Indian River Comm Coll (FL)
Iowa Lakes Comm Coll (IA)
Jefferson Comm Coll (OH)
John A. Logan Coll (IL)
Kilgore Coll (TX)
Lansing Comm Coll (MI)
Macomb Comm Coll (MI)
Marshall Comm and Tech Coll (WV)
Mayland Comm Coll (NC)
McLennan Comm Coll (TX)
Miami Dade Coll (FL)
Milwaukee Area Tech Coll (WI)
Modesto Jr Coll (CA)
Muskegon Comm Coll (MI)
New England Coll of Finance (MA)
New Mexico Military Inst (NM)
North Central State Coll (OH)
Northeast Alabama Comm Coll (AL)
Northern Essex Comm Coll (MA)
Orange County Comm Coll (NY)
Palm Beach Comm Coll (FL)
Pasadena City Coll (CA)
Polk Comm Coll (FL)
Prairie State Coll (IL)
Rockland Comm Coll (NY)
St. Cloud Tech Coll (MN)
St. Louis Comm Coll at Forest Park (MO)
St. Louis Comm Coll at Meramec (MO)
Salt Lake Comm Coll (UT)
San Diego City Coll (CA)
Santa Barbara City Coll (CA)
Santa Fe Comm Coll (FL)
Seminole Comm Coll (FL)
Seward County Comm Coll (KS)

Sinclair Comm Coll (OH)
Solano Comm Coll (CA)
Southeast Tech Inst (SD)
Southern Union State Comm Coll (AL)
Southwest Wisconsin Tech Coll (WI)
Springfield Tech Comm Coll (MA)
State U of NY Coll of Technology at Alfred (NY)
Trinity Valley Comm Coll (TX)
Wayne County Comm Coll District (MI)
Westchester Comm Coll (NY)
Westmoreland County Comm Coll (PA)
West Virginia U at Parkersburg (WV)

Finance and Financial Management Services Related
Black Hawk Coll, Moline (IL)
Bristol Comm Coll (MA)

Financial Planning and Services
Broome Comm Coll (NY)
Howard Comm Coll (MD)

Fine Arts Related
Ancilla Coll (IN)
Colorado Northwestern Comm Coll (CO)
Oakland Comm Coll (MI)
Yavapai Coll (AZ)

Fine/Studio Arts
Alabama Southern Comm Coll (AL)
Amarillo Coll (TX)
Atlantic Cape Comm Coll (NJ)
Brazosport Coll (TX)
Bristol Comm Coll (MA)
Cerro Coso Comm Coll (CA)
Clovis Comm Coll (NM)
Coastal Bend Coll (TX)
Colorado Mountn Coll, Alpine Cmps (CO)
Cumberland County Coll (NJ)
Delaware Coll of Art and Design (DE)
Finger Lakes Comm Coll (NY)
Foothill Coll (CA)
Fulton-Montgomery Comm Coll (NY)
Garden City Comm Coll (KS)
Herkimer County Comm Coll (NY)
Holyoke Comm Coll (MA)
Inst of American Indian Arts (NM)
Iowa Lakes Comm Coll (IA)
Jamestown Comm Coll (NY)
Lansing Comm Coll (MI)
Manchester Comm Coll (CT)
Midland Coll (TX)
Mount Wachusett Comm Coll (MA)
Niagara County Comm Coll (NY)
Northampton County Area Comm Coll (PA)
Pratt Comm Coll and Area Vocational School (KS)
Queensborough Comm Coll of City U of NY (NY)
Randolph Comm Coll (NC)
Rockland Comm Coll (NY)
Sandhills Comm Coll (NC)
San Diego Miramar Coll (CA)
Santa Barbara City Coll (CA)
Sinclair Comm Coll (OH)
Springfield Tech Comm Coll (MA)
Sussex County Comm Coll (NJ)
Tacoma Comm Coll (WA)
Westchester Comm Coll (NY)

Fire Protection and Safety Technology
Albuquerque Tech Vocational Inst (NM)
Bunker Hill Comm Coll (MA)
Capital Comm Coll (CT)
Catawba Valley Comm Coll (NC)
Central Florida Comm Coll (FL)
Cleveland Comm Coll (NC)
Coll of Lake County (IL)
Coll of the Mainland (TX)
Collin County Comm Coll District (TX)
Comm Coll of Allegheny County (PA)
Delaware County Comm Coll (PA)
Elgin Comm Coll (IL)
Florida Comm Coll at Jacksonville (FL)
John Wood Comm Coll (IL)
Lincoln Land Comm Coll (IL)
Macomb Comm Coll (MI)
Montgomery County Comm Coll (PA)
Moraine Valley Comm Coll (IL)
Mott Comm Coll (MI)
Owens Comm Coll, Toledo (OH)
San Juan Coll (NM)
Union County Coll (NJ)
Waubonsee Comm Coll (IL)
Western Nevada Comm Coll (NV)

Fire Protection Related
Sussex County Comm Coll (NJ)

Fire Science
Alabama Southern Comm Coll (AL)
Amarillo Coll (TX)
Arizona Western Coll (AZ)
Austin Comm Coll (TX)
Barton County Comm Coll (KS)
Berkshire Comm Coll (MA)
Black River Tech Coll (AR)
Blue River Comm Coll (MO)
Brevard Comm Coll (FL)
Bristol Comm Coll (MA)
Broome Comm Coll (NY)
Broward Comm Coll (FL)
Butler County Comm Coll (KS)
Cape Cod Comm Coll (MA)
Casper Coll (WY)
Central Oregon Comm Coll (OR)
Central Piedmont Comm Coll (NC)
Cerro Coso Comm Coll (CA)
Chattahoochee Valley Comm Coll (AL)
Chattanooga State Tech Comm Coll (TN)
Chemeketa Comm Coll (OR)
Cincinnati State Tech and Comm Coll (OH)
Clatsop Comm Coll (OR)
Coastal Carolina Comm Coll (NC)
Cochise Coll, Douglas (AZ)
Coconino Comm Coll (AZ)
Coll of DuPage (IL)
Colorado Northwestern Comm Coll (CO)
Columbia Coll (CA)
Comm and Tech Coll of Shepherd (WV)
Comm Coll of Philadelphia (PA)
Comm Coll of Rhode Island (RI)
Comm Coll of Southern Nevada (NV)
Comm Coll of the Air Force (AL)
Compton Comm Coll (CA)
Corning Comm Coll (NY)
Crowder Coll (MO)

Cuyahoga Comm Coll (OH)
Davidson County Comm Coll (NC)
Daytona Beach Comm Coll (FL)
Delaware Tech & Comm Coll, Stanton/ Wilmington Cmps (DE)
Delta Coll (MI)
Des Moines Area Comm Coll (IA)
Dodge City Comm Coll (KS)
Doña Ana Branch Comm Coll (NM)
Durham Tech Comm Coll (NC)
East Central Coll (MO)
East Mississippi Comm Coll (MS)
Elgin Comm Coll (IL)
El Paso Comm Coll (TX)
Essex County Coll (NJ)
Everett Comm Coll (WA)
Florida Comm Coll at Jacksonville (FL)
Fox Valley Tech Coll (WI)
Frank Phillips Coll (TX)
Gateway Comm Coll (CT)
George Corley Wallace State Comm Coll (AL)
Glendale Comm Coll (AZ)
Glendale Comm Coll (CA)
Greenfield Comm Coll (MA)
Guam Comm Coll (GU)
Guilford Tech Comm Coll (NC)
Gulf Coast Comm Coll (FL)
Harrisburg Area Comm Coll (PA)
Hawkeye Comm Coll (IA)
Henry Ford Comm Coll (MI)
Hillsborough Comm Coll (FL)
Houston Comm Coll System (TX)
Hutchinson Comm Coll and Area Vocational School (KS)
Indian River Comm Coll (FL)
Iowa Western Comm Coll (IA)
J. Sargeant Reynolds Comm Coll (VA)
Kalamazoo Valley Comm Coll (MI)
Kansas City Kansas Comm Coll (KS)
Keiser Coll, Fort Lauderdale (FL)
Kilgore Coll (TX)
Lake-Sumter Comm Coll (FL)
Lake Superior Coll (MN)
Lanier Tech Coll (GA)
Lansing Comm Coll (MI)
Laredo Comm Coll (TX)
Lewis and Clark Comm Coll (IL)
Long Beach City Coll (CA)
Lower Columbia Coll (WA)
Meridian Comm Coll (MS)
Miami Dade Coll (FL)
Midland Coll (TX)
Mid Michigan Comm Coll (MI)
Milwaukee Area Tech Coll (WI)
Mineral Area Coll (MO)
Modesto Jr Coll (CA)
Mohave Comm Coll (AZ)
Mount Wachusett Comm Coll (MA)
Northern Virginia Comm Coll (VA)
North Hennepin Comm Coll (MN)
North Shore Comm Coll (MA)
Northwest-Shoals Comm Coll (AL)
Oakland Comm Coll (MI)
Odessa Coll (TX)
Olympic Coll (WA)
Palm Beach Comm Coll (FL)
Pasadena City Coll (CA)

Penn Valley Comm Coll (MO)
Pima Comm Coll (AZ)
Polk Comm Coll (FL)
Prairie State Coll (IL)
Richland Comm Coll (IL)
Rockland Comm Coll (NY)
Rock Valley Coll (IL)
Rogue Comm Coll (OR)
St. Louis Comm Coll at Forest Park (MO)
St. Petersburg Coll (FL)
San Antonio Coll (TX)
San Diego Miramar Coll (CA)
San Joaquin Delta Coll (CA)
Santa Fe Comm Coll (FL)
Savannah Tech Coll (GA)
Schoolcraft Coll (MI)
Seminole Comm Coll (FL)
Sinclair Comm Coll (OH)
Solano Comm Coll (CA)
Southeast Comm Coll, Lincoln Campus (NE)
Southern Maine Comm Coll (ME)
Southwestern Oregon Comm Coll (OR)
Springfield Tech Comm Coll (MA)
Three Rivers Comm Coll (CT)
Truckee Meadows Comm Coll (NV)
Umpqua Comm Coll (OR)
U of Alaska Anchorage, Matanuska-Susitna Coll (AK)
Valencia Comm Coll (FL)
Volunteer State Comm Coll (TN)
Westmoreland County Comm Coll (PA)
Wilson Tech Comm Coll (NC)
Yakima Valley Comm Coll (WA)
Yavapai Coll (AZ)
Yuba Coll (CA)

Fire Services Administration
Black Hawk Coll, Moline (IL)
Calhoun Comm Coll (AL)
Capital Comm Coll (CT)
Edmonds Comm Coll (WA)
Erie Comm Coll, South Campus (NY)
Jefferson State Comm Coll (AL)
Johnson County Comm Coll (KS)
Lake Superior Coll (MN)
Lower Columbia Coll (WA)
Midland Coll (TX)
Northampton County Area Comm Coll (PA)
North Iowa Area Comm Coll (IA)
Olympic Coll (WA)
Walla Walla Comm Coll (WA)

Fish/Game Management
Central Oregon Comm Coll (OR)
Chattanooga State Tech Comm Coll (TN)
Coll of Southern Idaho (ID)
East Central Coll (MO)
Finger Lakes Comm Coll (NY)
Fox Valley Tech Coll (WI)
Garrett Coll (MD)
Haywood Comm Coll (NC)
Iowa Lakes Comm Coll (IA)
Itasca Comm Coll (MN)
Mid Michigan Comm Coll (MI)
North Idaho Coll (ID)
Pratt Comm Coll and Area Vocational School (KS)
Seward County Comm Coll (KS)

Fishing and Fisheries Sciences And Management
Bristol Comm Coll (MA)
Brunswick Comm Coll (NC)
Iowa Lakes Comm Coll (IA)

Peninsula Coll (WA)
Santa Rosa Jr Coll (CA)

Flight Instruction
Iowa Lakes Comm Coll (IA)

Floriculture/Floristry Management
Ohio State U Ag Tech Inst (OH)

Food/Nutrition
Indian River Comm Coll (FL)

Food Preparation
Iowa Lakes Comm Coll (IA)
Keystone Coll (PA)

Food Sales Operations
Montgomery County Comm

Foods and Nutrition Related
Front Range Comm Coll (CO)
Iowa Lakes Comm Coll (IA)

Food Science
Central Piedmont Comm Coll (NC)
Greenfield Comm Coll (MA)
Hawkeye Comm Coll (IA)
Highland Comm Coll (KS)
Miami Dade Coll (FL)
Modesto Jr Coll (CA)
Orange Coast Coll (CA)

Food Service and Dining Room Management
Fairmont State Comm & Tech Coll (WV)
Iowa Lakes Comm Coll (IA)

Food Services Technology
Adirondack Comm Coll (NY)
Anne Arundel Comm Coll (MD)
Arapahoe Comm Coll (CO)
Butler County Comm Coll (PA)
Central Piedmont Comm Coll (NC)
Chattanooga State Tech Comm Coll (TN)
Columbia Coll (CA)
Columbus State Comm Coll (OH)
Comm Coll of Southern Nevada (NV)
Delaware Tech & Comm Coll, Stanton/ Wilmington Cmps (DE)
Fayetteville Tech Comm Coll (NC)
Henry Ford Comm Coll (MI)
Hinds Comm Coll (MS)
Indian Hills Comm Coll (IA)
Iowa Western Comm Coll (IA)
Lane Comm Coll (OR)
Long Beach City Coll (CA)
Milwaukee Area Tech Coll (WI)
Modesto Jr Coll (CA)
Mohawk Valley Comm Coll (NY)
Orange Coast Coll (CA)
Owens Comm Coll, Toledo (OH)
Richland Comm Coll (IL)
San Joaquin Delta Coll (CA)
Shawnee Comm Coll (IL)
Southeast Comm Coll, Lincoln Campus (NE)
Southern Maine Comm Coll (ME)
Southwest Wisconsin Tech Coll (WI)
Texas State Tech Coll– Waco/Marshall Campus (TX)
Westchester Comm Coll (NY)

Foodservice Systems Administration
Atlantic Cape Comm Coll (NJ)
Comm Coll of Allegheny County (PA)

Florida Comm Coll at
Jacksonville (FL)
Hibbing Comm Coll (MN)
Mohawk Valley Comm Coll
(NY)
Mott Comm Coll (MI)
North Dakota State Coll of
Science (ND)
Oakland Comm Coll (MI)
Santa Barbara City Coll (CA)

**Foods, Nutrition, and
Wellness**
Colby Comm Coll (KS)
Comm Coll of Philadelphia
(PA)
Compton Comm Coll (CA)
Daytona Beach Comm Coll
(FL)
Dutchess Comm Coll (NY)
Harrisburg Area Comm Coll
(PA)
Holyoke Comm Coll (MA)
North Shore Comm Coll
(MA)
Orange Coast Coll (CA)
Palm Beach Comm Coll (FL)
Sinclair Comm Coll (OH)
Snow Coll (UT)

**Food Technology and
Processing**
Copiah-Lincoln Comm Coll
(MS)

**Foreign Languages and
Literatures**
Atlanta Metropolitan Coll
(GA)
Brazosport Coll (TX)
Coastal Georgia Comm Coll
(GA)
Coll of Southern Idaho (ID)
Comm Coll of Allegheny
County (PA)
Darton Coll (GA)
Dixie State Coll of Utah (UT)
Eastern Arizona Coll (AZ)
Glendale Comm Coll (CA)
Gulf Coast Comm Coll (FL)
Hutchinson Comm Coll and
Area Vocational School
(KS)
Iowa Lakes Comm Coll (IA)
Kingwood Coll (TX)
Linn-Benton Comm Coll
(OR)
Lower Columbia Coll (WA)
Midland Coll (TX)
Modesto Jr Coll (CA)
San Juan Coll (NM)
Sheridan Coll (WY)

**Forensic Science and
Technology**
Arkansas State U–Mountain
Home (AR)
Darton Coll (GA)
Lehigh Carbon Comm Coll
(PA)
Macomb Comm Coll (MI)
Massachusetts Bay Comm
Coll (MA)
Oakland Comm Coll (MI)
Tunxis Comm Coll (CT)

**Forest/Forest Resources
Management**
Allegany Coll of Maryland
(MD)
Northwestern Michigan Coll
(MI)

Forestry
Allen County Comm Coll
(KS)
Andrew Coll (GA)
Bainbridge Coll (GA)
Barton County Comm Coll
(KS)
Central Oregon Comm Coll
(OR)
Chattahoochee Valley Comm
Coll (AL)
Chattanooga State Tech
Comm Coll (TN)
Chemeketa Comm Coll (OR)

Coastal Georgia Comm Coll
(GA)
Colby Comm Coll (KS)
Coll of Southern Idaho (ID)
Copiah-Lincoln Comm Coll
(MS)
Copiah-Lincoln Comm
Coll–Natchez Campus
(MS)
Darton Coll (GA)
Daytona Beach Comm Coll
(FL)
Delta Coll (MI)
Dixie State Coll of Utah (UT)
Dodge City Comm Coll (KS)
East Central Coll (MO)
Eastern Arizona Coll (AZ)
Feather River Coll (CA)
Gainesville Coll (GA)
Grand Rapids Comm Coll
(MI)
Highland Comm Coll (KS)
Holmes Comm Coll (MS)
Indian River Comm Coll (FL)
Iowa Lakes Comm Coll (IA)
Itasca Comm Coll (MN)
Jamestown Comm Coll (NY)
Keystone Coll (PA)
Kilgore Coll (TX)
Miami Dade Coll (FL)
Modesto Jr Coll (CA)
North Idaho Coll (ID)
North Shore Comm Coll
(MA)
Northwest-Shoals Comm
Coll (AL)
Riverside Comm Coll District
(CA)
Santa Rosa Jr Coll (CA)
Snow Coll (UT)
Southwestern Oregon Comm
Coll (OR)
State U of NY Coll of
Technology at Delhi (NY)
Tacoma Comm Coll (WA)
Trinidad State Jr Coll (CO)
Umpqua Comm Coll (OR)
Western Oklahoma State
Coll (OK)
Western Wyoming Comm
Coll (WY)

Forestry Technology
Alabama Southern Comm
Coll (AL)
Albany Tech Coll (GA)
Central Oregon Comm Coll
(OR)
Chattanooga State Tech
Comm Coll (TN)
Chemeketa Comm Coll (OR)
Columbia Coll (CA)
Dabney S. Lancaster Comm
Coll (VA)
East Mississippi Comm Coll
(MS)
Flathead Valley Comm Coll
(MT)
Fox Valley Tech Coll (WI)
Green River Comm Coll
(WA)
Haywood Comm Coll (NC)
Hazard Comm and Tech Coll
(KY)
Itasca Comm Coll (MN)
Itawamba Comm Coll (MS)
Jefferson Comm Coll (NY)
Keystone Coll (PA)
Modesto Jr Coll (CA)
Montgomery Comm Coll
(NC)
Okefenokee Tech Coll (GA)
Panola Coll (TX)
Pasadena City Coll (CA)
Penn State U Mont Alto
Campus of the
Commonwealth Coll (PA)
State U of NY Coll of
Technology at Canton (NY)

**Forest Sciences and
Biology**
Gogebic Comm Coll (MI)

French
Austin Comm Coll (TX)
Casper Coll (WY)
Centralia Coll (WA)
Citrus Coll (CA)
Coastal Bend Coll (TX)
Coll of the Canyons (CA)
Compton Comm Coll (CA)
Contra Costa Coll (CA)
Copiah-Lincoln Comm Coll
(MS)
East Central Coll (MO)
Foothill Coll (CA)
Independence Comm Coll
(KS)
Indian River Comm Coll (FL)
Long Beach City Coll (CA)
Miami Dade Coll (FL)
Midland Coll (TX)
New Mexico Military Inst
(NM)
North Idaho Coll (ID)
Orange Coast Coll (CA)
Pasadena City Coll (CA)
Riverside Comm Coll District
(CA)
San Joaquin Delta Coll (CA)
Santa Barbara City Coll (CA)
Santa Rosa Jr Coll (CA)
Sauk Valley Comm Coll (IL)
Snow Coll (UT)
Solano Comm Coll (CA)

**Funeral Service and
Mortuary Science**
Allen County Comm Coll
(KS)
Amarillo Coll (TX)
Arapahoe Comm Coll (CO)
Arkansas State U–Mountain
Home (AR)
Barton County Comm Coll
(KS)
Bishop State Comm Coll
(AL)
Briarwood Coll (CT)
Catawba Valley Comm Coll
(NC)
Commonwealth Inst of
Funeral Service (TX)
Dallas Inst of Funeral
Service (TX)
Delta Coll (MI)
East Mississippi Comm Coll
(MS)
Everett Comm Coll (WA)
Fayetteville Tech Comm Coll
(NC)
Forsyth Tech Comm Coll
(NC)
Highland Comm Coll (KS)
Hudson Valley Comm Coll
(NY)
Jefferson State Comm Coll
(AL)
John Tyler Comm Coll (VA)
Kansas City Kansas Comm
Coll (KS)
Miami Dade Coll (FL)
Milwaukee Area Tech Coll
(WI)
Nassau Comm Coll (NY)
Northampton County Area
Comm Coll (PA)
St. Louis Comm Coll at
Forest Park (MO)
St. Petersburg Coll (FL)
San Antonio Coll (TX)
State U of NY Coll of
Technology at Canton (NY)
U of Arkansas Comm Coll at
Hope (AR)

**Funeral Service and
Mortuary Science Related**
Delta Coll (MI)
Milwaukee Area Tech Coll
(WI)

**Furniture Design and
Manufacturing**
Catawba Valley Comm Coll
(NC)
Milwaukee Area Tech Coll
(WI)

**General Retailing/
Wholesaling**
Alamance Comm Coll (NC)
Asheville-Buncombe Tech
Comm Coll (NC)
Century Coll (MN)
Comm Coll of Rhode Island
(RI)
Craven Comm Coll (NC)
Dixie State Coll of Utah (UT)
Elgin Comm Coll (IL)
Gadsden State Comm Coll
(AL)
Harrisburg Area Comm Coll
(PA)
Nassau Comm Coll (NY)
Orange Coast Coll (CA)
St. Cloud Tech Coll (MN)
Walla Walla Comm Coll (WA)

General Studies
Adirondack Comm Coll (NY)
Allen County Comm Coll
(KS)
Alpena Comm Coll (MI)
Amarillo Coll (TX)
Arkansas Northeastern Coll
(AR)
Asnuntuck Comm Coll (CT)
Atlanta Metropolitan Coll
(GA)
Atlantic Cape Comm Coll
(NJ)
Barton County Comm Coll
(KS)
Bevill State Comm Coll (AL)
Bishop State Comm Coll
(AL)
Blackfeet Comm Coll (MT)
Bladen Comm Coll (NC)
Brazosport Coll (TX)
Briarwood Coll (CT)
Bristol Comm Coll (MA)
Bunker Hill Comm Coll (MA)
Butler County Comm Coll
(PA)
Calhoun Comm Coll (AL)
Carroll Comm Coll (MD)
Cecil Comm Coll (MD)
Central Wyoming Coll (WY)
Cincinnati State Tech and
Comm Coll (OH)
City Colls of Chicago, Wilbur
Wright Coll (IL)
Clackamas Comm Coll (OR)
Cleveland State Comm Coll
(TN)
Coll of the Mainland (TX)
Colorado Northwestern
Comm Coll (CO)
Comm and Tech Coll of
Shepherd (WV)
Comm Coll of Allegheny
County (PA)
Comm Coll of Rhode Island
(RI)
Copiah-Lincoln Comm
Coll–Natchez Campus
(MS)
Corning Comm Coll (NY)
Crowder Coll (MO)
Darton Coll (GA)
Delaware County Comm Coll
(PA)
Durham Tech Comm Coll
(NC)
Estrella Mountain Comm Coll
(AZ)
Fairmont State Comm &
Tech Coll (WV)
Fayetteville Tech Comm Coll
(NC)
Florida Hospital Coll of
Health Sciences (FL)
Front Range Comm Coll
(CO)
Gadsden State Comm Coll
(AL)
Garrett Coll (MD)
GateWay Comm Coll (AZ)
Germanna Comm Coll (VA)
Gordon Coll (GA)
Herkimer County Comm Coll
(NY)
Howard Comm Coll (MD)

Illinois Eastern Comm Colls,
Frontier Comm Coll (IL)
Illinois Eastern Comm Colls,
Lincoln Trail Coll (IL)
Illinois Eastern Comm Colls,
Olney Central Coll (IL)
Illinois Eastern Comm Colls,
Wabash Valley Coll (IL)
Iowa Lakes Comm Coll (IA)
Itasca Comm Coll (MN)
Jackson Comm Coll (MI)
James H. Faulkner State
Comm Coll (AL)
Jefferson State Comm Coll
(AL)
John Wood Comm Coll (IL)
Kaskaskia Coll (IL)
Kennebec Valley Comm Coll
(ME)
Kilgore Coll (TX)
Lackawanna Coll (PA)
Lake Land Coll (IL)
Lehigh Carbon Comm Coll
(PA)
Lincoln Land Comm Coll (IL)
Macomb Comm Coll (MI)
Manchester Comm Coll (CT)
Massachusetts Bay Comm
Coll (MA)
Mercy Coll of Northwest Ohio
(OH)
Miami Dade Coll (FL)
Miami U Hamilton (OH)
Mid Michigan Comm Coll
(MI)
Modesto Jr Coll (CA)
Mott Comm Coll (MI)
Mount Wachusett Comm Coll
(MA)
Nassau Comm Coll (NY)
Niagara County Comm Coll
(NY)
Northampton County Area
Comm Coll (PA)
Northern Essex Comm Coll
(MA)
Northwest-Shoals Comm
Coll (AL)
Oakland Comm Coll (MI)
Owens Comm Coll, Findlay
(OH)
Owens Comm Coll, Toledo
(OH)
Parkland Coll (IL)
Pima Comm Coll (AZ)
Platt Coll San Diego (CA)
Rochester Comm and Tech
Coll (MN)
San Juan Coll (NM)
Sheridan Coll (WY)
Southern Maine Comm Coll
(ME)
Southside Virginia Comm
Coll (VA)
Southwestern Michigan Coll
(MI)
Southwestern Oklahoma
State U at Sayre (OK)
Springfield Tech Comm Coll
(MA)
State U of NY Coll of
Technology at Delhi (NY)
Tacoma Comm Coll (WA)
Taft Coll (CA)
Tillamook Bay Comm Coll
(OR)
Truett-McConnell Coll (GA)
The U of Akron–Wayne Coll
(OH)
Wake Tech Comm Coll (NC)
Waubonsee Comm Coll (IL)
Western Nevada Comm Coll
(NV)
Western Wyoming Comm
Coll (WY)
West Virginia State Comm
and Tech Coll (WV)
Wilson Tech Comm Coll (NC)

Geography
Allen County Comm Coll
(KS)
Coll of Southern Idaho (ID)
Coll of the Canyons (CA)

Columbia State Comm Coll
(TN)
Contra Costa Coll (CA)
Darton Coll (GA)
East Central Coll (MO)
Foothill Coll (CA)
Itasca Comm Coll (MN)
Lansing Comm Coll (MI)
Lower Columbia Coll (WA)
Orange Coast Coll (CA)
Pasadena City Coll (CA)
Pennsylvania Highland
Comm Coll (PA)
Riverside Comm Coll District
(CA)
Salt Lake Comm Coll (UT)
San Diego Miramar Coll (CA)
Santa Barbara City Coll (CA)
Santa Rosa Jr Coll (CA)
Snow Coll (UT)
Western Wyoming Comm
Coll (WY)

Geology/Earth Science
Amarillo Coll (TX)
Arizona Western Coll (AZ)
Austin Comm Coll (TX)
Barton County Comm Coll
(KS)
Brazosport Coll (TX)
Casper Coll (WY)
Centralia Coll (WA)
Central Texas Coll (TX)
Coastal Bend Coll (TX)
Coastal Georgia Comm Coll
(GA)
Colby Comm Coll (KS)
Coll of Southern Idaho (ID)
Coll of the Canyons (CA)
Colorado Mountn Coll, Alpine
Cmps (CO)
Colorado Northwestern
Comm Coll (CO)
Columbia Coll (CA)
Contra Costa Coll (CA)
Daytona Beach Comm Coll
(FL)
Delta Coll (MI)
Dixie State Coll of Utah (UT)
East Central Coll (MO)
Eastern Arizona Coll (AZ)
El Paso Comm Coll (TX)
Everett Comm Coll (WA)
Foothill Coll (CA)
Gainesville Coll (GA)
Grand Rapids Comm Coll
(MI)
Great Basin Coll (NV)
Highland Comm Coll (IL)
Highland Comm Coll (KS)
Iowa Lakes Comm Coll (IA)
Kilgore Coll (TX)
Lansing Comm Coll (MI)
Lower Columbia Coll (WA)
Miami Dade Coll (FL)
Midland Coll (TX)
North Idaho Coll (ID)
Odessa Coll (TX)
Orange Coast Coll (CA)
Pasadena City Coll (CA)
Riverside Comm Coll District
(CA)
San Joaquin Delta Coll (CA)
San Juan Coll (NM)
Santa Barbara City Coll (CA)
Santa Rosa Jr Coll (CA)
Snow Coll (UT)
Tacoma Comm Coll (WA)
Trinity Valley Comm Coll
(TX)
Western Wyoming Comm
Coll (WY)

German
Austin Comm Coll (TX)
Casper Coll (WY)
Centralia Coll (WA)
Citrus Coll (CA)
Coastal Bend Coll (TX)
Coll of the Canyons (CA)
Compton Comm Coll (CA)
Contra Costa Coll (CA)
East Central Coll (MO)
Everett Comm Coll (WA)
Foothill Coll (CA)

Long Beach City Coll (CA)
Miami Dade Coll (FL)
Midland Coll (TX)
New Mexico Military Inst (NM)
North Idaho Coll (ID)
Orange Coast Coll (CA)
Pasadena City Coll (CA)
Riverside Comm Coll District (CA)
San Joaquin Delta Coll (CA)
Santa Rosa Jr Coll (CA)
Solano Comm Coll (CA)

Gerontology
Baltimore City Comm Coll (MD)
City Colls of Chicago, Wilbur Wright Coll (IL)
Columbus State Comm Coll (OH)
Comm Coll of Philadelphia (PA)
Delaware Tech & Comm Coll, Stanton/ Wilmington Cmps (DE)
Edmonds Comm Coll (WA)
Elgin Comm Coll (IL)
Eugenio María de Hostos Comm Coll of City U of NY (NY)
Gateway Comm Coll (CT)
Genesee Comm Coll (NY)
Lansing Comm Coll (MI)
Northern Virginia Comm Coll (VA)
North Shore Comm Coll (MA)
Oakland Comm Coll (MI)
Pima Comm Coll (AZ)
Sandhills Comm Coll (NC)
Sinclair Comm Coll (OH)
Union County Coll (NJ)
West Virginia State Comm and Tech Coll (WV)

Glazier
Metropolitan Comm Coll-Business & Technology College (MO)

Graphic and Printing Equipment Operation/ Production
Austin Comm Coll (TX)
Bishop State Comm Coll (AL)
Central Comm Coll–Hastings Campus (NE)
Central Piedmont Comm Coll (NC)
Central Texas Coll (TX)
Chattanooga State Tech Comm Coll (TN)
Chemeketa Comm Coll (OR)
Clinton Comm Coll (IA)
Clover Park Tech Coll (WA)
Coll of DuPage (IL)
Comm & Tech Coll at West Virginia U Inst of Technology (WV)
Comm Coll of Denver (CO)
Comm Coll of Southern Nevada (NV)
Compton Comm Coll (CA)
Delta Coll (MI)
Des Moines Area Comm Coll (IA)
Eastfield Coll (TX)
Erie Comm Coll, South Campus (NY)
Forsyth Tech Comm Coll (NC)
Fox Valley Tech Coll (WI)
Fulton-Montgomery Comm Coll (NY)
Gogebic Comm Coll (MI)
Highline Comm Coll (WA)
Hinds Comm Coll (MS)
Houston Comm Coll System (TX)
Iowa Lakes Comm Coll (IA)
Kilgore Coll (TX)
Lake Land Coll (IL)
Macomb Comm Coll (MI)

Metropolitan Comm Coll (NE)
Midlands Tech Coll (SC)
Milwaukee Area Tech Coll (WI)
Moberly Area Comm Coll (MO)
Modesto Jr Coll (CA)
Phillips Comm Coll of the U of Arkansas (AR)
Randolph Comm Coll (NC)
St. Cloud Tech Coll (MN)
San Diego City Coll (CA)
San Joaquin Delta Coll (CA)
Seattle Central Comm Coll (WA)
Shoreline Comm Coll (WA)
Sinclair Comm Coll (OH)
Southeast Tech Inst (SD)
Southwestern Michigan Coll (MI)
Texas State Tech Coll– Waco/Marshall Campus (TX)
Thaddeus Stevens Coll of Technology (PA)
Westmoreland County Comm Coll (PA)

Graphic Communications
Fairmont State Comm & Tech Coll (WV)
Iowa Lakes Comm Coll (IA)
Platt Coll San Diego (CA)

Graphic Communications Related
Linn-Benton Comm Coll (OR)
Platt Coll San Diego (CA)

Graphic Design
Academy Coll (MN)
The Art Inst of New York City (NY)
The Art Inst of Philadelphia (PA)
Barton County Comm Coll (KS)
Bristol Comm Coll (MA)
Calhoun Comm Coll (AL)
Delaware Coll of Art and Design (DE)
Iowa Lakes Comm Coll (IA)
Ivy Tech State Coll– Southwest (IN)
Jackson Comm Coll (MI)
Keystone Coll (PA)
Mott Comm Coll (MI)
Oakland Comm Coll (MI)
Ohio Inst of Photography and Technology (OH)
Platt Coll San Diego (CA)
Springfield Tech Comm Coll (MA)
Westwood Coll–Denver North (CO)
Westwood Coll–Long Beach (CA)
Yavapai Coll (AZ)

Greenhouse Management
Comm Coll of Allegheny County (PA)
Ohio State U Ag Tech Inst (OH)
Rochester Comm and Tech Coll (MN)

Gunsmithing
Yavapai Coll (AZ)

Hair Styling and Hair Design
Colorado Northwestern Comm Coll (CO)
Milwaukee Area Tech Coll (WI)

Hazardous Materials Management and Waste Technology
Barton County Comm Coll (KS)
Kansas City Kansas Comm Coll (KS)
Odessa Coll (TX)

Health Aide
Allen County Comm Coll (KS)
Central Arizona Coll (AZ)
Edmonds Comm Coll (WA)
Springfield Tech Comm Coll (MA)

Health and Medical Administrative Services Related
Catawba Valley Comm Coll (NC)
Hawaii Business Coll (HI)
Indiana Business Coll, Marion (IN)
Keiser Coll, Miami (FL)

Health and Physical Education
Alexandria Tech Coll (MN)
Allen County Comm Coll (KS)
Atlanta Metropolitan Coll (GA)
Blue Mountain Comm Coll (OR)
Brazosport Coll (TX)
Cerro Coso Comm Coll (CA)
Citrus Coll (CA)
Clovis Comm Coll (NM)
Coastal Georgia Comm Coll (GA)
Comm Coll of Allegheny County (PA)
Corning Comm Coll (NY)
Darton Coll (GA)
Eastern Arizona Coll (AZ)
Iowa Lakes Comm Coll (IA)
John Wood Comm Coll (IL)
Riverside Comm Coll District (CA)
Sheridan Coll (WY)
State U of NY Coll of Technology at Delhi (NY)

Health and Physical Education Related
Garden City Comm Coll (KS)
Indiana Business Coll-Medical (IN)
Kingsborough Comm Coll of City U of NY (NY)
Oakland Comm Coll (MI)

Health/Health Care Administration
Brown Mackie Coll, Findlay Campus (OH)
Caldwell Comm Coll and Tech Inst (NC)
Central Piedmont Comm Coll (NC)
Chemeketa Comm Coll (OR)
Coll of DuPage (IL)
Coll of Southern Idaho (ID)
Comm & Tech Coll at West Virginia U Inst of Technology (WV)
Comm Coll of the Air Force (AL)
Des Moines Area Comm Coll (IA)
ECPI Coll of Technology, Newport News (VA)
ECPI Coll of Technology, Virginia Beach (VA)
ECPI Tech Coll, Richmond (VA)
ECPI Tech Coll, Roanoke (VA)
Essex County Coll (NJ)
GateWay Comm Coll (AZ)
Herkimer County Comm Coll (NY)
Houston Comm Coll System (TX)
Indian Hills Comm Coll (IA)
Iowa Lakes Comm Coll (IA)
Keiser Coll, Fort Lauderdale (FL)
Mineral Area Coll (MO)
National Coll of Business & Technology, Louisville (KY)
North Idaho Coll (ID)
Oakland Comm Coll (MI)

Pennsylvania Highland Comm Coll (PA)
Pioneer Pacific Coll (OR)
St. Petersburg Coll (FL)

Health Information/Medical Records Administration
Adirondack Comm Coll (NY)
Alabama Southern Comm Coll (AL)
Albuquerque Tech Vocational Inst (NM)
Amarillo Coll (TX)
Andover Coll (ME)
Arapahoe Comm Coll (CO)
Baltimore City Comm Coll (MD)
Barton County Comm Coll (KS)
Black Hawk Coll, Moline (IL)
Bowling Green State U-Firelands Coll (OH)
Briarwood Coll (CT)
Brunswick Comm Coll (NC)
Bunker Hill Comm Coll (MA)
Business Inst of Pennsylvania, Sharon (PA)
Butler County Comm Coll (KS)
Central Florida Comm Coll (FL)
Central Piedmont Comm Coll (NC)
Chattanooga State Tech Comm Coll (TN)
Chemeketa Comm Coll (OR)
Coll of DuPage (IL)
Columbus State Comm Coll (OH)
Comm Coll of Philadelphia (PA)
Comm Coll of Southern Nevada (NV)
Darton Coll (GA)
Davidson County Comm Coll (NC)
Daytona Beach Comm Coll (FL)
Dodge City Comm Coll (KS)
Durham Tech Comm Coll (NC)
East Central Comm Coll (MS)
ECPI Coll of Technology, Newport News (VA)
ECPI Coll of Technology, Virginia Beach (VA)
ECPI Tech Coll, Richmond (VA)
ECPI Tech Coll, Roanoke (VA)
Edgecombe Comm Coll (NC)
Edison State Comm Coll (OH)
Elgin Comm Coll (IL)
El Paso Comm Coll (TX)
Enterprise-Ozark Comm Coll (AL)
Erie Business Center South (PA)
Florida Comm Coll at Jacksonville (FL)
George Corley Wallace State Comm Coll (AL)
Glendale Comm Coll (CA)
Gogebic Comm Coll (MI)
Hagerstown Business Coll (MD)
Harrisburg Area Comm Coll (PA)
Henry Ford Comm Coll (MI)
Highland Comm Coll (KS)
Hinds Comm Coll (MS)
Holmes Comm Coll (MS)
Holyoke Comm Coll (MA)
Houston Comm Coll System (TX)
Howard Coll (TX)
Indiana Business Coll, Evansville (IN)
Indian Hills Comm Coll (IA)
Indian River Comm Coll (FL)
Itawamba Comm Coll (MS)
John A. Logan Coll (IL)

Kennebec Valley Comm Coll (ME)
Lake-Sumter Comm Coll (FL)
McLennan Comm Coll (TX)
Meridian Comm Coll (MS)
Miami Dade Coll (FL)
Northern Essex Comm Coll (MA)
Northern Virginia Comm Coll (VA)
Penn Valley Comm Coll (MO)
Polk Comm Coll (FL)
Rasmussen Coll St. Cloud (MN)
Rockland Comm Coll (NY)
Saint Charles Comm Coll (MO)
St. Petersburg Coll (FL)
Santa Fe Comm Coll (FL)
Shelton State Comm Coll (AL)
Shoreline Comm Coll (WA)
Sinclair Comm Coll (OH)
Southwestern Comm Coll (NC)
State U of NY Coll of Technology at Alfred (NY)
Tacoma Comm Coll (WA)
Thompson Inst (PA)
Westmoreland County Comm Coll (PA)

Health Information/Medical Records Technology
Bishop State Comm Coll (AL)
Blue Mountain Comm Coll (OR)
Bristol Comm Coll (MA)
Broome Comm Coll (NY)
Catawba Valley Comm Coll (NC)
Central Comm Coll–Hastings Campus (NE)
Central Oregon Comm Coll (OR)
Cincinnati State Tech and Comm Coll (OH)
Coll of DuPage (IL)
Columbus State Comm Coll (OH)
Comm Coll of Allegheny County (PA)
Darton Coll (GA)
Dyersburg State Comm Coll (TN)
Erie Comm Coll, North Campus (NY)
Fayetteville Tech Comm Coll (NC)
Houston Comm Coll System (TX)
Hudson County Comm Coll (NJ)
Hutchinson Comm Coll and Area Vocational School (KS)
Indiana Business Coll, Anderson (IN)
Indiana Business Coll, Muncie (IN)
Jefferson Comm Coll (KY)
Johnson County Comm Coll (KS)
Lehigh Carbon Comm Coll (PA)
Marshall Comm and Tech Coll (WV)
Mercy Coll of Northwest Ohio (OH)
Midland Coll (TX)
Midlands Tech Coll (SC)
Mohawk Valley Comm Coll (NY)
Moraine Valley Comm Coll (IL)
North Dakota State Coll of Science (ND)
North Hennepin Comm Coll (MN)
Northwest Tech Coll (MN)
Owens Comm Coll, Toledo (OH)

Rowan-Cabarrus Comm Coll (NC)
St. Philip's Coll (TX)
San Juan Coll (NM)
Santa Barbara City Coll (CA)
Schoolcraft Coll (MI)
South Hills School of Business & Technology, State College (PA)
Southwestern Comm Coll (NC)
Volunteer State Comm Coll (TN)
Williston State Coll (ND)

Health/Medical Preparatory Programs Related
Ancilla Coll (IN)
Blackfeet Comm Coll (MT)
Eastern Arizona Coll (AZ)
Laramie County Comm Coll (WY)
Western Wyoming Comm Coll (WY)

Health Professions Related
Allegany Coll of Maryland (MD)
Berkshire Comm Coll (MA)
Bowling Green State U-Firelands Coll (OH)
Brazosport Coll (TX)
Cincinnati State Tech and Comm Coll (OH)
Comm Coll of Allegheny County (PA)
Dixie State Coll of Utah (UT)
Essex County Coll (NJ)
Indiana Business Coll, Columbus (IN)
Indiana Business Coll, Fort Wayne (IN)
Indiana Business Coll, Terre Haute (IN)
Indiana Business Coll-Medical (IN)
Lanier Tech Coll (GA)
Northwestern Michigan Coll (MI)
Northwest State Comm Coll (OH)
Oakland Comm Coll (MI)
Southwestern Michigan Coll (MI)
Volunteer State Comm Coll (TN)

Health Science
American Samoa Comm Coll (AS)
Arizona Western Coll (AZ)
Bay Mills Comm Coll (MI)
Bergen Comm Coll (NJ)
Borough of Manhattan Comm Coll of City U of NY (NY)
Bucks County Comm Coll (PA)
Carroll Comm Coll (MD)
Coll of the Canyons (CA)
Compton Comm Coll (CA)
Daytona Beach Comm Coll (FL)
El Paso Comm Coll (TX)
Harcum Coll (PA)
Kalamazoo Valley Comm Coll (MI)
Mohave Comm Coll (AZ)
Nassau Comm Coll (NY)
North Shore Comm Coll (MA)
Northwestern Connecticut Comm-Tech Coll (CT)
Orange Coast Coll (CA)
Queensborough Comm Coll of City U of NY (NY)
Riverside Comm Coll District (CA)
Salt Lake Comm Coll (UT)
San Joaquin Delta Coll (CA)
Sussex County Comm Coll (NJ)
Tri-County Tech Coll (SC)
Villa Maria Coll of Buffalo (NY)

Health Services/Allied Health/Health Sciences
Atlanta Metropolitan Coll (GA)
Atlantic Cape Comm Coll (NJ)
Clarendon Coll (TX)
Colorado Northwestern Comm Coll (CO)
Florida National Coll (FL)
Keiser Coll, Miami (FL)
South U (FL)
Western Wyoming Comm Coll (WY)
West Virginia State Comm and Tech Coll (WV)

Health Teacher Education
Anne Arundel Comm Coll (MD)
Bainbridge Coll (GA)
Bucks County Comm Coll (PA)
Chemeketa Comm Coll (OR)
Coahoma Comm Coll (MS)
Coastal Bend Coll (TX)
Columbia Coll (CA)
Copiah-Lincoln Comm Coll (MS)
Daytona Beach Comm Coll (FL)
East Central Comm Coll (MS)
East Mississippi Comm Coll (MS)
El Paso Comm Coll (TX)
Fulton-Montgomery Comm Coll (NY)
Highland Comm Coll (KS)
Howard Comm Coll (MD)
Kilgore Coll (TX)
Palm Beach Comm Coll (FL)
Pratt Comm Coll and Area Vocational School (KS)
Umpqua Comm Coll (OR)
Westmoreland County Comm Coll (PA)
Yuba Coll (CA)

Health Unit Coordinator/ Ward Clerk
Comm Coll of Allegheny County (PA)
Milwaukee Area Tech Coll (WI)
Riverland Comm Coll (MN)
Southeast Tech Inst (SD)

Health Unit Management/ Ward Supervision
Delaware County Comm Coll (PA)

Heating, Air Conditioning and Refrigeration Technology
Alamance Comm Coll (NC)
Bevill State Comm Coll (AL)
Calhoun Comm Coll (AL)
Cincinnati State Tech and Comm Coll (OH)
DeKalb Tech Coll (GA)
Delaware County Comm Coll (PA)
Delta Coll (MI)
Front Range Comm Coll (CO)
Gadsden State Comm Coll (AL)
GateWay Comm Coll (AZ)
Harrisburg Area Comm Coll (PA)
Jackson Comm Coll (MI)
Johnson County Comm Coll (KS)
Kalamazoo Valley Comm Coll (MI)
Macomb Comm Coll (MI)
Manhattan Area Tech Coll (KS)
Miami Dade Coll (FL)
Milwaukee Area Tech Coll (WI)
Mohawk Valley Comm Coll (NY)
Mott Comm Coll (MI)

North Dakota State Coll of Science (ND)
Northwest Tech Coll (MN)
Oakland Comm Coll (MI)
Pennsylvania Highland Comm Coll (PA)
St. Cloud Tech Coll (MN)
Springfield Tech Comm Coll (MA)
State U of NY Coll of Technology at Delhi (NY)
Texas State Tech Coll– Waco/Marshall Campus (TX)
Triangle Tech, Inc.– Greensburg School (PA)
Vatterott Coll, Oklahoma City (OK)

Heating, Air Conditioning, Ventilation and Refrigeration Maintenance Technology
Amarillo Coll (TX)
Arizona Western Coll (AZ)
Asheville-Buncombe Tech Comm Coll (NC)
Athens Tech Coll (GA)
Austin Comm Coll (TX)
Belmont Tech Coll (OH)
Bismarck State Coll (ND)
Black Hawk Coll, Moline (IL)
Brazosport Coll (TX)
Calhoun Comm Coll (AL)
Cedar Valley Coll (TX)
Central Comm Coll–Grand Island Campus (NE)
Central Comm Coll–Hastings Campus (NE)
Central Texas Coll (TX)
Century Coll (MN)
Chattanooga State Tech Comm Coll (TN)
Clover Park Tech Coll (WA)
Clovis Comm Coll (NM)
Coll of DuPage (IL)
Coll of Lake County (IL)
Coll of Southern Idaho (ID)
Columbus State Comm Coll (OH)
Comm and Tech Coll of Shepherd (WV)
Comm Coll of Allegheny County (PA)
Comm Coll of Denver (CO)
Comm Coll of Southern Nevada (NV)
Craven Comm Coll (NC)
Daytona Beach Comm Coll (FL)
Delaware County Comm Coll (PA)
Delta Coll (MI)
Des Moines Area Comm Coll (IA)
Doña Ana Branch Comm Coll (NM)
East Central Coll (MO)
Eastern Maine Comm Coll (ME)
Eastfield Coll (TX)
Elgin Comm Coll (IL)
El Paso Comm Coll (TX)
Fayetteville Tech Comm Coll (NC)
Forsyth Tech Comm Coll (NC)
Frank Phillips Coll (TX)
Gadsden State Comm Coll–Ayers Campus (AL)
GateWay Comm Coll (AZ)
George C. Wallace Comm Coll (AL)
Grand Rapids Comm Coll (MI)
Guilford Tech Comm Coll (NC)
Hawkeye Comm Coll (IA)
Heartland Comm Coll (IL)
Henry Ford Comm Coll (MI)
Hudson Valley Comm Coll (NY)
Illinois Eastern Comm Colls, Lincoln Trail Coll (IL)
Indian River Comm Coll (FL)

Ivy Tech State Coll– Bloomington (IN)
Ivy Tech State Coll–Central Indiana (IN)
Ivy Tech State Coll– Columbus (IN)
Ivy Tech State Coll– Eastcentral (IN)
Ivy Tech State Coll–Kokomo (IN)
Ivy Tech State Coll–Lafayette (IN)
Ivy Tech State Coll–North Central (IN)
Ivy Tech State Coll– Northeast (IN)
Ivy Tech State Coll– Northwest (IN)
Ivy Tech State Coll– Southcentral (IN)
Ivy Tech State Coll– Southwest (IN)
Ivy Tech State Coll–Wabash Valley (IN)
Ivy Tech State Coll– Whitewater (IN)
Jamestown Comm Coll (NY)
John A. Logan Coll (IL)
Johnston Comm Coll (NC)
Kilgore Coll (TX)
Lane Comm Coll (OR)
Lansing Comm Coll (MI)
Lehigh Carbon Comm Coll (PA)
Linn State Tech Coll (MO)
Long Beach City Coll (CA)
Macomb Comm Coll (MI)
Maple Woods Comm Coll (MO)
Metropolitan Comm Coll (NE)
Miami Dade Coll (FL)
Midland Coll (TX)
Midlands Tech Coll (SC)
Mid Michigan Comm Coll (MI)
Milwaukee Area Tech Coll (WI)
Minnesota State Coll– Southeast Tech (MN)
Modesto Jr Coll (CA)
New Hampshire Comm Tech Coll, Manchester/Stratham (NH)
North Central State Coll (OH)
North Dakota State Coll of Science (ND)
Northern Virginia Comm Coll (VA)
North Idaho Coll (ID)
North Iowa Area Comm Coll (IA)
North Lake Coll (TX)
North Seattle Comm Coll (WA)
Odessa Coll (TX)
Orange Coast Coll (CA)
Penn Valley Comm Coll (MO)
Phillips Comm Coll of the U of Arkansas (AR)
Ranken Tech Coll (MO)
Raritan Valley Comm Coll (NJ)
Roanoke-Chowan Comm Coll (NC)
Rockingham Comm Coll (NC)
St. Cloud Tech Coll (MN)
St. Philip's Coll (TX)
Salt Lake Comm Coll (UT)
San Joaquin Delta Coll (CA)
San Joaquin Valley Coll (CA)
Sauk Valley Comm Coll (IL)
Scott Comm Coll (IA)
Shelton State Comm Coll (AL)
Somerset Comm Coll (KY)
South Central Tech Coll (MN)
Southeast Comm Coll, Milford Campus (NE)
Southeast Tech Inst (SD)
Southern Maine Comm Coll (ME)

South Texas Coll (TX)
Spartanburg Tech Coll (SC)
State U of NY Coll of Technology at Alfred (NY)
State U of NY Coll of Technology at Canton (NY)
State U of NY Coll of Technology at Delhi (NY)
Surry Comm Coll (NC)
Tech Coll of the Lowcountry (SC)
Texas State Tech Coll– Waco/Marshall Campus (TX)
Thaddeus Stevens Coll of Technology (PA)
Triangle Tech, Inc.– Greensburg School (PA)
Triangle Tech, Inc.– Pittsburgh School (PA)
Tri-County Tech Coll (SC)
Trinity Valley Comm Coll (TX)
Truckee Meadows Comm Coll (NV)
U of Alaska Anchorage, Matanuska-Susitna Coll (AK)
U of Arkansas Comm Coll at Morrilton (AR)
U of Northwestern Ohio (OH)
Walla Walla Comm Coll (WA)
Waubonsee Comm Coll (IL)
Western Iowa Tech Comm Coll (IA)
Western Nevada Comm Coll (NV)
Western Tech Coll (TX)
Westmoreland County Comm Coll (PA)
West Virginia State Comm and Tech Coll (WV)
Westwood Coll–Denver North (CO)

Heavy Equipment Maintenance Technology
Amarillo Coll (TX)
Beaufort County Comm Coll (NC)
Centralia Coll (WA)
Clover Park Tech Coll (WA)
Comm Coll of Southern Nevada (NV)
Delaware Tech & Comm Coll, Jack F Owens Cmps (DE)
Des Moines Area Comm Coll (IA)
Eastern Maine Comm Coll (ME)
Guilford Tech Comm Coll (NC)
Hawkeye Comm Coll (IA)
Illinois Eastern Comm Colls, Olney Central Coll (IL)
Indian Hills Comm Coll (IA)
Lane Comm Coll (OR)
Lansing Comm Coll (MI)
Linn State Tech Coll (MO)
Long Beach City Coll (CA)
Longview Comm Coll (MO)
Lower Columbia Coll (WA)
McDowell Tech Comm Coll (NC)
Metropolitan Comm Coll (NE)
North Idaho Coll (ID)
Ohio State U Ag Tech Inst (OH)
Rogue Comm Coll (OR)
Salt Lake Comm Coll (UT)
Sheridan Coll (WY)
South Texas Coll (TX)
Southwest Georgia Tech Coll (GA)
State U of NY Coll of Technology at Alfred (NY)
Texas State Tech Coll– Waco/Marshall Campus (TX)
Trinidad State Jr Coll (CO)
Wake Tech Comm Coll (NC)

West Central Tech Coll (GA)
Western Wyoming Comm Coll (WY)

Heavy/Industrial Equipment Maintenance Technologies Related
Big Bend Comm Coll (WA)
Southwestern Michigan Coll (MI)

Hematology Technology
Comm Coll of the Air Force (AL)

Hispanic-American, Puerto Rican, and Mexican-American/Chicano Studies
City Colls of Chicago, Wilbur Wright Coll (IL)
Compton Comm Coll (CA)
Contra Costa Coll (CA)
Pasadena City Coll (CA)
San Diego City Coll (CA)
Santa Barbara City Coll (CA)
Solano Comm Coll (CA)
Yuba Coll (CA)

Histologic Technician
Columbus State Comm Coll (OH)
Darton Coll (GA)
Miami Dade Coll (FL)
Mott Comm Coll (MI)
Oakland Comm Coll (MI)

Historic Preservation and Conservation
Belmont Tech Coll (OH)
Bucks County Comm Coll (PA)
Randolph Comm Coll (NC)

History
Adirondack Comm Coll (NY)
Alabama Southern Comm Coll (AL)
Allen County Comm Coll (KS)
Amarillo Coll (TX)
Andrew Coll (GA)
Atlanta Metropolitan Coll (GA)
Atlantic Cape Comm Coll (NJ)
Austin Comm Coll (TX)
Bainbridge Coll (GA)
Barton County Comm Coll (KS)
Bergen Comm Coll (NJ)
Brazosport Coll (TX)
Bronx Comm Coll of City U of NY (NY)
Bunker Hill Comm Coll (MA)
Butler County Comm Coll (KS)
Cape Cod Comm Coll (MA)
Casper Coll (WY)
Centralia Coll (WA)
Cerro Coso Comm Coll (CA)
Clarendon Coll (TX)
Cloud County Comm Coll (KS)
Coastal Bend Coll (TX)
Coastal Georgia Comm Coll (GA)
Cochise Coll, Douglas (AZ)
Coffeyville Comm Coll (KS)
Colby Comm Coll (KS)
Coll of Southern Idaho (ID)
Coll of the Canyons (CA)
Colorado Northwestern Comm Coll (CO)
Columbia Coll (CA)
Columbia State Comm Coll (TN)
Comm Coll of Southern Nevada (NV)
Compton Comm Coll (CA)
Contra Costa Coll (CA)
Copiah-Lincoln Comm Coll (MS)
Danville Area Comm Coll (IL)
Darton Coll (GA)
Daytona Beach Comm Coll (FL)
De Anza Coll (CA)

Dixie State Coll of Utah (UT)
Dodge City Comm Coll (KS)
East Central Coll (MO)
East Central Comm Coll (MS)
Eastern Arizona Coll (AZ)
East Mississippi Comm Coll (MS)
Ellsworth Comm Coll (IA)
El Paso Comm Coll (TX)
Everett Comm Coll (WA)
Feather River Coll (CA)
Foothill Coll (CA)
Frank Phillips Coll (TX)
Fulton-Montgomery Comm Coll (NY)
Gainesville Coll (GA)
Gordon Coll (GA)
Great Basin Coll (NV)
Gulf Coast Comm Coll (FL)
Highland Comm Coll (IL)
Highland Comm Coll (KS)
Independence Comm Coll (KS)
Indian River Comm Coll (FL)
Iowa Lakes Comm Coll (IA)
Itawamba Comm Coll (MS)
John A. Logan Coll (IL)
Laramie County Comm Coll (WY)
Lower Columbia Coll (WA)
Miami Dade Coll (FL)
Midland Coll (TX)
Mohave Comm Coll (AZ)
New Mexico Military Inst (NM)
Northern Essex Comm Coll (MA)
North Idaho Coll (ID)
Odessa Coll (TX)
Orange Coast Coll (CA)
Otero Jr Coll (CO)
Palm Beach Comm Coll (FL)
Pasadena City Coll (CA)
Pratt Comm Coll and Area Vocational School (KS)
Riverside Comm Coll District (CA)
St. Philip's Coll (TX)
San Joaquin Delta Coll (CA)
San Juan Coll (NM)
Santa Barbara City Coll (CA)
Santa Rosa Jr Coll (CA)
Sauk Valley Comm Coll (IL)
Seward County Comm Coll (KS)
Sheridan Coll (WY)
Snow Coll (UT)
Solano Comm Coll (CA)
South Mountain Comm Coll (AZ)
Tacoma Comm Coll (WA)
Trinity Valley Comm Coll (TX)
Umpqua Comm Coll (OR)
Western Oklahoma State Coll (OK)
Western Wyoming Comm Coll (WY)
Yuba Coll (CA)

Home Furnishings and Equipment Installation
Jefferson State Comm Coll (AL)
St. Philip's Coll (TX)

Home Health Aide
Barton County Comm Coll (KS)

Home Health Aide/Home Attendant
Allen County Comm Coll (KS)
Laurel Business Inst (PA)

Horse Husbandry/Equine Science and Management
Black Hawk Coll, Moline (IL)
Central Wyoming Coll (WY)
Clarendon Coll (TX)
Linn-Benton Comm Coll (OR)
Ohio State U Ag Tech Inst (OH)
Yavapai Coll (AZ)

Horticultural Science

Anne Arundel Comm Coll (MD)
Black Hawk Coll, Moline (IL)
Blue Ridge Comm Coll (NC)
Central Piedmont Comm Coll (NC)
Clark State Comm Coll (OH)
Coffeyville Comm Coll (KS)
Comm Coll of Southern Nevada (NV)
Cumberland County Coll (NJ)
Danville Area Comm Coll (IL)
Des Moines Area Comm Coll (IA)
East Central Coll (MO)
Fayetteville Tech Comm Coll (NC)
Forsyth Tech Comm Coll (NC)
Frank Phillips Coll (TX)
Gwinnett Tech Coll (GA)
Hawkeye Comm Coll (IA)
Haywood Comm Coll (NC)
Houston Comm Coll System (TX)
Indian Hills Comm Coll (IA)
Lansing Comm Coll (MI)
Lehigh Carbon Comm Coll (PA)
Linn-Benton Comm Coll (OR)
Long Beach City Coll (CA)
Mayland Comm Coll (NC)
Meridian Comm Coll (MS)
Miami Dade Coll (FL)
Northern Virginia Comm Coll (VA)
Ohio State U Ag Tech Inst (OH)
Orange Coast Coll (CA)
Rockingham Comm Coll (NC)
St. Louis Comm Coll at Meramec (MO)
Shawnee Comm Coll (IL)
Southeast Tech Inst (SD)
Southern Maine Comm Coll (ME)
Spartanburg Tech Coll (SC)
State U of NY Coll of Technology at Delhi (NY)
Surry Comm Coll (NC)
Tech Coll of the Lowcountry (SC)
Trident Tech Coll (SC)
Trinity Valley Comm Coll (TX)
U of Arkansas Comm Coll at Morrilton (AR)
Westmoreland County Comm Coll (PA)

Hospital and Health Care Facilities Administration

Allen County Comm Coll (KS)
Central Comm Coll–Hastings Campus (NE)
Coll of DuPage (IL)
Harrisburg Area Comm Coll (PA)

Hospitality Administration

Adirondack Comm Coll (NY)
Albuquerque Tech Vocational Inst (NM)
Alexandria Tech Coll (MN)
Allegany Coll of Maryland (MD)
Arizona Western Coll (AZ)
Atlantic Cape Comm Coll (NJ)
Baltimore City Comm Coll (MD)
Baltimore International Coll (MD)
Bay State Coll (MA)
Berkshire Comm Coll (MA)
Blackfeet Comm Coll (MT)
Bucks County Comm Coll (PA)
Bunker Hill Comm Coll (MA)

Butler County Comm Coll (PA)
Central Comm Coll–Hastings Campus (NE)
Central Florida Comm Coll (FL)
Central Oregon Comm Coll (OR)
Central Piedmont Comm Coll (NC)
Chemeketa Comm Coll (OR)
Coll of DuPage (IL)
Collin County Comm Coll District (TX)
Colorado Mountn Coll, Alpine Cmps (CO)
Comm Coll of Southern Nevada (NV)
Davenport U, Midland (MI)
Daytona Beach Comm Coll (FL)
Delaware Tech & Comm Coll, Jack F Owens Cmps (DE)
Des Moines Area Comm Coll (IA)
Doña Ana Branch Comm Coll (NM)
East Central Coll (MO)
Florida Comm Coll at Jacksonville (FL)
Florida National Coll (FL)
Fox Valley Tech Coll (WI)
Guam Comm Coll (GU)
Gulf Coast Comm Coll (FL)
Henry Ford Comm Coll (MI)
Hillsborough Comm Coll (FL)
Holyoke Comm Coll (MA)
International Coll of Hospitality Management, *César Ritz* (CT)
Iowa Lakes Comm Coll (IA)
Ivy Tech State Coll–Eastcentral (IN)
Ivy Tech State Coll–North Central (IN)
Ivy Tech State Coll–Northeast (IN)
James H. Faulkner State Comm Coll (AL)
Jefferson Comm Coll (NY)
Jefferson State Comm Coll (AL)
Johnson County Comm Coll (KS)
J. Sargeant Reynolds Comm Coll (VA)
Kauai Comm Coll (HI)
Keiser Coll, Fort Lauderdale (FL)
Lane Comm Coll (OR)
Lansing Comm Coll (MI)
Marshall Comm and Tech Coll (WV)
Massachusetts Bay Comm Coll (MA)
Miami Dade Coll (FL)
Mid Michigan Comm Coll (MI)
Monroe Coll, Bronx (NY)
Monroe Coll, New Rochelle (NY)
Muskegon Comm Coll (MI)
National Coll of Business & Technology, Salem (VA)
North Idaho Coll (ID)
North Shore Comm Coll (MA)
Pennsylvania Highland Comm Coll (PA)
Pima Comm Coll (AZ)
Rockland Comm Coll (NY)
St. Petersburg Coll (FL)
San Diego City Coll (CA)
Seattle Central Comm Coll (WA)
Sheridan Coll (WY)
Sisseton-Wahpeton Comm Coll (SD)
Southern Maine Comm Coll (ME)
South Texas Coll (TX)
Three Rivers Comm Coll (CT)

Truckee Meadows Comm Coll (NV)
Valencia Comm Coll (FL)
Westmoreland County Comm Coll (PA)
Wor-Wic Comm Coll (MD)

Hospitality Administration Related

Fayetteville Tech Comm Coll (NC)
Mineral Area Coll (MO)
Penn State U Beaver Campus of the Commonwealth Coll (PA)
Southwest Georgia Tech Coll (GA)

Hospitality and Recreation Marketing

Austin Comm Coll (TX)
Central Oregon Comm Coll (OR)
Cumberland County Coll (NJ)
Edmonds Comm Coll (WA)
Flathead Valley Comm Coll (MT)
Florida Comm Coll at Jacksonville (FL)
Guam Comm Coll (GU)
Iowa Central Comm Coll (IA)
Iowa Western Comm Coll (IA)
Mid Michigan Comm Coll (MI)
Milwaukee Area Tech Coll (WI)
Montgomery County Comm Coll (PA)
Muskegon Comm Coll (MI)
Raritan Valley Comm Coll (NJ)
State U of NY Coll of Technology at Delhi (NY)

Hotel and Restaurant Management

Athens Tech Coll (GA)

Hotel/Motel Administration

Alexandria Tech Coll (MN)
Anne Arundel Comm Coll (MD)
Asheville-Buncombe Tech Comm Coll (NC)
Austin Comm Coll (TX)
Baltimore International Coll (MD)
Bay Mills Comm Coll (MI)
Bay State Coll (MA)
Bergen Comm Coll (NJ)
Bismarck State Coll (ND)
Briarwood Coll (CT)
Broome Comm Coll (NY)
Broward Comm Coll (FL)
Bryant & Stratton Business Inst (NY)
Bucks County Comm Coll (PA)
Bunker Hill Comm Coll (MA)
Butler County Comm Coll (KS)
Cape Cod Comm Coll (MA)
Cape Fear Comm Coll (NC)
Central Arizona Coll (AZ)
Central Comm Coll–Hastings Campus (NE)
Central Oregon Comm Coll (OR)
Central Piedmont Comm Coll (NC)
Central Texas Coll (TX)
Chattanooga State Tech Comm Coll (TN)
Chemeketa Comm Coll (OR)
Cincinnati State Tech and Comm Coll (OH)
Coll of DuPage (IL)
Coll of Southern Idaho (ID)
Coll of the Canyons (CA)
Colorado Mountn Coll, Alpine Cmps (CO)
Columbia Coll (CA)
Columbus State Comm Coll (OH)

Comm Coll of Allegheny County (PA)
Comm Coll of Philadelphia (PA)
Comm Coll of Southern Nevada (NV)
Comm Coll of the Air Force (AL)
Copiah-Lincoln Comm Coll–Natchez Campus (MS)
Cowley County Comm Coll and Voc-Tech School (KS)
Daytona Beach Comm Coll (FL)
Delaware County Comm Coll (PA)
Delaware Tech & Comm Coll, Jack F Owens Cmps (DE)
Delaware Tech & Comm Coll, Stanton/ Wilmington Cmps (DE)
Des Moines Area Comm Coll (IA)
East Central Coll (MO)
East Mississippi Comm Coll (MS)
Elgin Comm Coll (IL)
Erie Comm Coll (NY)
Essex County Coll (NJ)
Finger Lakes Comm Coll (NY)
Flathead Valley Comm Coll (MT)
Florida Comm Coll at Jacksonville (FL)
Gainesville Coll (GA)
Garrett Coll (MD)
Gateway Comm Coll (CT)
Genesee Comm Coll (NY)
Glendale Comm Coll (CA)
Guam Comm Coll (GU)
Gwinnett Tech Coll (GA)
Harrisburg Area Comm Coll (PA)
Henry Ford Comm Coll (MI)
Highline Comm Coll (WA)
Hillsborough Comm Coll (FL)
Hinds Comm Coll (MS)
Holyoke Comm Coll (MA)
Houston Comm Coll System (TX)
Indian River Comm Coll (FL)
Instituto Comercial de Puerto Rico Jr Coll (PR)
Iowa Lakes Comm Coll (IA)
Iowa Western Comm Coll (IA)
Jefferson Comm Coll (NY)
Johnson County Comm Coll (KS)
John Wood Comm Coll (IL)
J. Sargeant Reynolds Comm Coll (VA)
Kapiolani Comm Coll (HI)
Keystone Coll (PA)
Lane Comm Coll (OR)
Lansing Comm Coll (MI)
Laredo Comm Coll (TX)
Lehigh Carbon Comm Coll (PA)
Lincoln Land Comm Coll (IL)
Long Beach City Coll (CA)
Manchester Comm Coll (CT)
Meridian Comm Coll (MS)
Milwaukee Area Tech Coll (WI)
Mohawk Valley Comm Coll (NY)
Muskegon Comm Coll (MI)
Nassau Comm Coll (NY)
National Coll of Business & Technology, Salem (VA)
New River Comm and Tech Coll (WV)
Northampton County Area Comm Coll (PA)
Northern Essex Comm Coll (MA)
Northern Virginia Comm Coll (VA)
Oakland Comm Coll (MI)
Orange Coast Coll (CA)

Palm Beach Comm Coll (FL)
Pennsylvania Culinary Inst (PA)
Penn Valley Comm Coll (MO)
Pima Comm Coll (AZ)
Raritan Valley Comm Coll (NJ)
St. Louis Comm Coll at Forest Park (MO)
St. Philip's Coll (TX)
Sandhills Comm Coll (NC)
Santa Barbara City Coll (CA)
Santa Rosa Jr Coll (CA)
Seattle Central Comm Coll (WA)
Sinclair Comm Coll (OH)
Southern Maine Comm Coll (ME)
South Texas Coll (TX)
State U of NY Coll of Technology at Delhi (NY)
Three Rivers Comm Coll (CT)
Tompkins Cortland Comm Coll (NY)
Trident Tech Coll (SC)
Union County Coll (NJ)
Wake Tech Comm Coll (NC)
Westchester Comm Coll (NY)
Westmoreland County Comm Coll (PA)
Wilkes Comm Coll (NC)
Yakima Valley Comm Coll (WA)

Hotel/Motel Services Marketing Operations

Montgomery County Comm Coll (PA)

Housing and Human Environments

Modesto Jr Coll (CA)
Orange Coast Coll (CA)

Housing and Human Environments Related

Comm Coll of Allegheny County (PA)

Human Development and Family Studies

Orange Coast Coll (CA)
Penn State U Delaware County Campus of the Commonwealth Coll (PA)
Penn State U DuBois Campus of the Commonwealth Coll (PA)
Penn State U Fayette Campus of the Commonwealth Coll (PA)
Penn State U Mont Alto Campus of the Commonwealth Coll (PA)
Penn State U New Kensington Campus of the Commonwealth Coll (PA)
Penn State U Shenango Campus of the Commonwealth Coll (PA)
Penn State U Worthington Scranton Cmps Commonwealth Coll (PA)
Penn State U York Campus of the Commonwealth Coll (PA)
Shoreline Comm Coll (WA)

Human Development and Family Studies Related

Comm Coll of Allegheny County (PA)
Northwest State Comm Coll (OH)

Human Ecology

Greenfield Comm Coll (MA)

Humanities

Adirondack Comm Coll (NY)
Allen County Comm Coll (KS)
Ancilla Coll (IN)
Andrew Coll (GA)

Anne Arundel Comm Coll (MD)
Atlantic Cape Comm Coll (NJ)
Bowling Green State U-Firelands Coll (OH)
Bristol Comm Coll (MA)
Brookdale Comm Coll (NJ)
Bucks County Comm Coll (PA)
Butler County Comm Coll (PA)
Casper Coll (WY)
Cayuga County Comm Coll (NY)
Centralia Coll (WA)
Central Oregon Comm Coll (OR)
Cerro Coso Comm Coll (CA)
Chemeketa Comm Coll (OR)
Clinton Comm Coll (NY)
Cloud County Comm Coll (KS)
Coffeyville Comm Coll (KS)
Colby Comm Coll (KS)
Coll of the Canyons (CA)
Colorado Mountn Coll, Alpine Cmps (CO)
Colorado Mountn Coll (CO)
Colorado Mountn Coll, Timberline Cmps (CO)
Columbia Coll (CA)
Columbia-Greene Comm Coll (NY)
Comm Coll of Allegheny County (PA)
Contra Costa Coll (CA)
Corning Comm Coll (NY)
Danville Area Comm Coll (IL)
Daytona Beach Comm Coll (FL)
De Anza Coll (CA)
Dixie State Coll of Utah (UT)
Dodge City Comm Coll (KS)
Dutchess Comm Coll (NY)
East Central Coll (MO)
Erie Comm Coll (NY)
Erie Comm Coll, North Campus (NY)
Erie Comm Coll, South Campus (NY)
Finger Lakes Comm Coll (NY)
Foothill Coll (CA)
Fulton-Montgomery Comm Coll (NY)
Garden City Comm Coll (KS)
Glendale Comm Coll (CA)
Gogebic Comm Coll (MI)
Greenfield Comm Coll (MA)
Herkimer County Comm Coll (NY)
Highline Comm Coll (WA)
Hinds Comm Coll (MS)
Independence Comm Coll (KS)
Indian River Comm Coll (FL)
Iowa Lakes Comm Coll (IA)
Jefferson Comm Coll (NY)
John A. Logan Coll (IL)
Lackawanna Coll (PA)
Laramie County Comm Coll (WY)
Lehigh Carbon Comm Coll (PA)
Miami Dade Coll (FL)
Modesto Jr Coll (CA)
Mohawk Valley Comm Coll (NY)
Montgomery County Comm Coll (PA)
Napa Valley Coll (CA)
New Mexico Military Inst (NM)
Niagara County Comm Coll (NY)
Orange Coast Coll (CA)
Orange County Comm Coll (NY)
Otero Jr Coll (CO)
Pratt Comm Coll and Area Vocational School (KS)
Riverside Comm Coll District (CA)

Humanities

Rogue Comm Coll (OR)
Salt Lake Comm Coll (UT)
San Diego Miramar Coll (CA)
San Joaquin Delta Coll (CA)
Sheridan Coll (WY)
Snow Coll (UT)
State U of NY Coll of Technology at Alfred (NY)
State U of NY Coll of Technology at Canton (NY)
State U of NY Coll of Technology at Delhi (NY)
Tacoma Comm Coll (WA)
Tompkins Cortland Comm Coll (NY)
Umpqua Comm Coll (OR)
Westchester Comm Coll (NY)
Western Oklahoma State Coll (OK)
Western Wyoming Comm Coll (WY)

Human Resources Management

Beaufort County Comm Coll (NC)
Central Georgia Tech Coll (GA)
Clark Coll (WA)
Columbus State Comm Coll (OH)
Comm Coll of Allegheny County (PA)
Comm Coll of the Air Force (AL)
Cumberland County Coll (NJ)
Edison State Comm Coll (OH)
Edmonds Comm Coll (WA)
Herkimer County Comm Coll (NY)
Houston Comm Coll System (TX)
Keystone Coll (PA)
Lansing Comm Coll (MI)
Lehigh Carbon Comm Coll (PA)
Moraine Valley Comm Coll (IL)
Northwestern Tech Coll (GA)
Northwest Tech Coll (MN)
Prairie State Coll (IL)
Rockingham Comm Coll (NC)
Saint Paul Coll—A Comm & Tech College (MN)
Salt Lake Comm Coll (UT)
Umpqua Comm Coll (OR)
Valencia Comm Coll (FL)
Wake Tech Comm Coll (NC)
West Georgia Tech Coll (GA)

Human Resources Management and Services Related

Barton County Comm Coll (KS)
Fayetteville Tech Comm Coll (NC)
Herkimer County Comm Coll (NY)
Iowa Lakes Comm Coll (IA)
Lake Superior Coll (MN)

Human Services

Alexandria Tech Coll (MN)
Anne Arundel Comm Coll (MD)
Arizona Western Coll (AZ)
Asnuntuck Comm Coll (CT)
Atlanta Metropolitan Coll (GA)
Austin Comm Coll (TX)
Baltimore City Comm Coll (MD)
Bay de Noc Comm Coll (MI)
Bay Mills Comm Coll (MI)
Big Sandy Comm and Tech Coll (KY)
Blackfeet Comm Coll (MT)
Borough of Manhattan Comm Coll of City U of NY (NY)

Bowling Green State U-Firelands Coll (OH)
Bristol Comm Coll (MA)
Bronx Comm Coll of City U of NY (NY)
Brookdale Comm Coll (NJ)
Bunker Hill Comm Coll (MA)
Bunker Hill Comm Coll (MA)
Carroll Comm Coll (MD)
Central Piedmont Comm Coll (NC)
Central Wyoming Coll (WY)
Chemeketa Comm Coll (OR)
Clark State Comm Coll (OH)
Coll of DuPage (IL)
Coll of DuPage (IL)
Coll of Southern Idaho (ID)
Coll of Southern Maryland (MD)
Colorado Northwestern Comm Coll (CO)
Columbia-Greene Comm Coll (NY)
Comm Coll of Denver (CO)
Comm Coll of Vermont (VT)
Compton Comm Coll (CA)
Corning Comm Coll (NY)
Danville Area Comm Coll (IL)
Daytona Beach Comm Coll (FL)
Delaware Tech & Comm Coll, Jack F Owens Cmps (DE)
Delaware Tech & Comm Coll, Stanton/ Wilmington Cmps (DE)
Delaware Tech & Comm Coll, Terry Cmps (DE)
Des Moines Area Comm Coll (IA)
Edgecombe Comm Coll (NC)
Edison State Comm Coll (OH)
Elgin Comm Coll (IL)
Ellsworth Comm Coll (IA)
El Paso Comm Coll (TX)
Essex County Coll (NJ)
Everett Comm Coll (WA)
Finger Lakes Comm Coll (NY)
Flathead Valley Comm Coll (MT)
Florida Comm Coll at Jacksonville (FL)
Fort Peck Comm Coll (MT)
Frederick Comm Coll (MD)
Fulton-Montgomery Comm Coll (NY)
Gateway Comm Coll (CT)
Genesee Comm Coll (NY)
Glendale Comm Coll (AZ)
Greenfield Comm Coll (MA)
Guilford Tech Comm Coll (NC)
Gulf Coast Comm Coll (FL)
Gulf Coast Comm Coll (FL)
Harrisburg Area Comm Coll (PA)
Harrisburg Area Comm Coll (PA)
Henderson Comm Coll (KY)
Herkimer County Comm Coll (NY)
Hesser Coll (NH)
Highland Comm Coll (IL)
Highline Comm Coll (WA)
Hillsborough Comm Coll (FL)
Holyoke Comm Coll (MA)
Hopkinsville Comm Coll (KY)
Hopkinsville Comm Coll (KY)
Hudson County Comm Coll (NJ)
Hudson Valley Comm Coll (NY)
Indian River Comm Coll (FL)
Iowa Western Comm Coll (IA)
Itasca Comm Coll (MN)
Itawamba Comm Coll (MS)
Jefferson Comm Coll (NY)
John Tyler Comm Coll (VA)
Kingsborough Comm Coll of City U of NY (NY)
Lake Land Coll (IL)

Lansing Comm Coll (MI)
Long Beach City Coll (CA)
Longview Comm Coll (MO)
Manchester Comm Coll (CT)
Massachusetts Bay Comm Coll (MA)
Mesabi Range Comm and Tech Coll (MN)
Metropolitan Comm Coll (NE)
Miami Dade Coll (FL)
Milwaukee Area Tech Coll (WI)
Minneapolis Comm and Tech Coll (MN)
Modesto Jr Coll (CA)
Mohawk Valley Comm Coll (NY)
Mount Wachusett Comm Coll (MA)
Nebraska Indian Comm Coll (NE)
Nebraska Indian Comm Coll (NE)
New Hampshire Comm Tech Coll, Manchester/Stratham (NH)
Niagara County Comm Coll (NY)
North Central State Coll (OH)
Northern Essex Comm Coll (MA)
Northern Virginia Comm Coll (VA)
North Idaho Coll (ID)
Northwestern Connecticut Comm-Tech Coll (CT)
Odessa Coll (TX)
Owensboro Comm and Tech Coll (KY)
Parkland Coll (IL)
Pasadena City Coll (CA)
Pasco-Hernando Comm Coll (FL)
Pennsylvania Highland Comm Coll (PA)
Pratt Comm Coll and Area Vocational School (KS)
Quinebaug Valley Comm Coll (CT)
Raritan Valley Comm Coll (NJ)
Richmond Comm Coll (NC)
Riverland Comm Coll (MN)
Rochester Comm and Tech Coll (MN)
Rockland Comm Coll (NY)
Rock Valley Coll (IL)
Rogue Comm Coll (OR)
Saint Charles Comm Coll (MO)
St. Louis Comm Coll at Forest Park (MO)
St. Louis Comm Coll at Meramec (MO)
St. Petersburg Coll (FL)
Salt Lake Comm Coll (UT)
Sandhills Comm Coll (NC)
San Juan Coll (NM)
Sauk Valley Comm Coll (IL)
Seattle Central Comm Coll (WA)
Shawnee Comm Coll (IL)
Sinclair Comm Coll (OH)
Southeast Comm Coll, Lincoln Campus (NE)
Southern State Comm Coll (OH)
Southside Virginia Comm Coll (VA)
Southwest Wisconsin Tech Coll (WI)
South Texas Coll (TX)
Stanly Comm Coll (NC)
State U of NY Coll of Technology at Alfred (NY)
Sussex County Comm Coll (NJ)
Tacoma Comm Coll (WA)
Tech Coll of the Lowcountry (SC)
Three Rivers Comm Coll (CT)

Tompkins Cortland Comm Coll (NY)
Trident Tech Coll (SC)
Tunxis Comm Coll (CT)
U of Alaska Anchorage, Matanuska-Susitna Coll (AK)
U of Arkansas Comm Coll at Hope (AR)
Westchester Comm Coll (NY)
Western Wyoming Comm Coll (WY)
Westmoreland County Comm Coll (PA)
Yuba Coll (CA)

Hydraulics and Fluid Power Technology

Alexandria Tech Coll (MN)
North Hennepin Comm Coll (MN)
Ohio State U Ag Tech Inst (OH)

Hydrology and Water Resources Science

Bay de Noc Comm Coll (MI)
Cecil Comm Coll (MD)
Citrus Coll (CA)
Coll of Southern Idaho (ID)
Coll of the Canyons (CA)
Colorado Mountn Coll, Timberline Cmps (CO)
Delta Coll (MI)
Dodge City Comm Coll (KS)
Doña Ana Branch Comm Coll (NM)
Fort Scott Comm Coll (KS)
Indian River Comm Coll (FL)
Iowa Lakes Comm Coll (IA)
Milwaukee Area Tech Coll (WI)
Northeast Alabama Comm Coll (AL)
St. Petersburg Coll (FL)
Three Rivers Comm Coll (CT)

Illustration

The Creative Center (NE)
Delaware Coll of Art and Design (DE)
Keystone Coll (PA)

Industrial Arts

Allen County Comm Coll (KS)
Casper Coll (WY)
Cleveland State Comm Coll (TN)
Comm Coll of Beaver County (PA)
Contra Costa Coll (CA)
Cowley County Comm Coll and Voc-Tech School (KS)
Delta Coll (MI)
Dodge City Comm Coll (KS)
El Paso Comm Coll (TX)
Everett Comm Coll (WA)
Fort Scott Comm Coll (KS)
Garden City Comm Coll (KS)
Guilford Tech Comm Coll (NC)
Haywood Comm Coll (NC)
Highland Comm Coll (KS)
Hinds Comm Coll (MS)
Howard Coll (TX)
Itawamba Comm Coll (MS)
Long Beach City Coll (CA)
Luna Comm Coll (NM)
Modesto Jr Coll (CA)
Muskegon Comm Coll (MI)
Ouachita Tech Coll (AR)
Phillips Comm Coll of the U of Arkansas (AR)
Pratt Comm Coll and Area Vocational School (KS)
Rockingham Comm Coll (NC)
San Diego City Coll (CA)
Southeast Comm Coll, Milford Campus (NE)
Taft Coll (CA)

Thaddeus Stevens Coll of Technology (PA)
Volunteer State Comm Coll (TN)

Industrial Design

Iowa Western Comm Coll (IA)
Milwaukee Area Tech Coll (WI)
Orange Coast Coll (CA)
Rock Valley Coll (IL)
Santa Rosa Jr Coll (CA)
Southeast Comm Coll, Milford Campus (NE)

Industrial Electronics Technology

Big Bend Comm Coll (WA)
Central Carolina Tech Coll (SC)
Coll of DuPage (IL)
John Wood Comm Coll (IL)
Kennebec Valley Comm Coll (ME)
Midlands Tech Coll (SC)
Modesto Jr Coll (CA)
North Dakota State Coll of Science (ND)
North Iowa Area Comm Coll (IA)
Northland Comm and Tech Coll—Thief River Falls (MN)
North Seattle Comm Coll (WA)
Northwest-Shoals Comm Coll (AL)
Oakland Comm Coll (MI)
State U of NY Coll of Technology at Alfred (NY)
Western Wyoming Comm Coll (WY)

Industrial Engineering

Manchester Comm Coll (CT)
Mount Wachusett Comm Coll (MA)
Nashville State Tech Comm Coll (TN)
Pima Comm Coll (AZ)
Santa Barbara City Coll (CA)

Industrial Mechanics and Maintenance Technology

Arkansas Northeastern Coll (AR)
Calhoun Comm Coll (AL)
Coll of Lake County (IL)
Fayetteville Tech Comm Coll (NC)
Guilford Tech Comm Coll (NC)
Harrisburg Area Comm Coll (PA)
Heartland Comm Coll (IL)
Illinois Eastern Comm Colls, Olney Central Coll (IL)
Ivy Tech State Coll—Eastcentral (IN)
John Wood Comm Coll (IL)
Kaskaskia Coll (IL)
Kennebec Valley Comm Coll (ME)
Lower Columbia Coll (WA)
Macomb Comm Coll (MI)
Northwest-Shoals Comm Coll (AL)
Riverland Comm Coll (MN)
Southwestern Michigan Coll (MI)
U of Arkansas Comm Coll at Hope (AR)
Waubonsee Comm Coll (IL)
Western Wyoming Comm Coll (WY)

Industrial Production Technologies Related

Arkansas Northeastern Coll (AR)
Broome Comm Coll (NY)
Cape Fear Comm Coll (NC)
Erie Comm Coll (NY)
Essex County Coll (NJ)
Linn State Tech Coll (MO)

Mohawk Valley Comm Coll (NY)
Richmond Comm Coll (NC)

Industrial Radiologic Technology

Amarillo Coll (TX)
Anne Arundel Comm Coll (MD)
Athens Tech Coll (GA)
Austin Comm Coll (TX)
Bergen Comm Coll (NJ)
Broward Comm Coll (FL)
Carteret Comm Coll (NC)
Casper Coll (WY)
Central Florida Comm Coll (FL)
Chattahoochee Valley Comm Coll (AL)
Chattanooga State Tech Comm Coll (TN)
Cleveland Comm Coll (NC)
Columbia State Comm Coll (TN)
Columbus State Comm Coll (OH)
Comm Coll of Denver (CO)
Comm Coll of Philadelphia (PA)
Comm Coll of Southern Nevada (NV)
Compton Comm Coll (CA)
Copiah-Lincoln Comm Coll (MS)
Cowley County Comm Coll and Voc-Tech School (KS)
Cumberland County Coll (NJ)
Cuyahoga Comm Coll (OH)
Danville Area Comm Coll (IL)
Daytona Beach Comm Coll (FL)
Delaware Tech & Comm Coll, Stanton/ Wilmington Cmps (DE)
Delta Coll (MI)
Doña Ana Branch Comm Coll (NM)
El Paso Comm Coll (TX)
Forsyth Tech Comm Coll (NC)
Gateway Comm Coll (CT)
George Corley Wallace State Comm Coll (AL)
Griffin Tech Coll (GA)
Gulf Coast Comm Coll (FL)
Gwinnett Tech Coll (GA)
Henry Ford Comm Coll (MI)
Highland Comm Coll (KS)
Hillsborough Comm Coll (FL)
Hinds Comm Coll (MS)
Houston Comm Coll System (TX)
Indian Hills Comm Coll (IA)
Indian River Comm Coll (FL)
Iowa Central Comm Coll (IA)
Jefferson Comm Coll (OH)
Kapiolani Comm Coll (HI)
Keiser Coll, Fort Lauderdale (FL)
Laramie County Comm Coll (WY)
Laredo Comm Coll (TX)
Long Beach City Coll (CA)
McLennan Comm Coll (TX)
Mid Michigan Comm Coll (MI)
Milwaukee Area Tech Coll (WI)
Montcalm Comm Coll (MI)
Northern Essex Comm Coll (MA)
Northern Virginia Comm Coll (VA)
Odessa Coll (TX)
Orange Coast Coll (CA)
Orange County Comm Coll (NY)
Palm Beach Comm Coll (FL)
Pasadena City Coll (CA)
Penn Valley Comm Coll (MO)
Phillips Comm Coll of the U of Arkansas (AR)

St. Louis Comm Coll at Forest Park (MO)
St. Petersburg Coll (FL)
Salt Lake Comm Coll (UT)
San Joaquin Delta Coll (CA)
Santa Fe Comm Coll (FL)
Sauk Valley Comm Coll (IL)
Sinclair Comm Coll (OH)
Southern Maine Comm Coll (ME)
South Texas Coll (TX)
Truckee Meadows Comm Coll (NV)
U of Cincinnati Raymond Walters Coll (OH)
Walters State Comm Coll (TN)
West Central Tech Coll (GA)
Westchester Comm Coll (NY)
West Kentucky Comm and Tech Coll (KY)
Yakima Valley Comm Coll (WA)
Yuba Coll (CA)

Industrial Technology
Albany Tech Coll (GA)
Albuquerque Tech Vocational Inst (NM)
Alexandria Tech Coll (MN)
Allen County Comm Coll (KS)
Anne Arundel Comm Coll (MD)
Arkansas Northeastern Coll (AR)
Austin Comm Coll (TX)
Bergen Comm Coll (NJ)
Bismarck State Coll (ND)
Black River Tech Coll (AR)
Bladen Comm Coll (NC)
Blue Mountain Comm Coll (OR)
Blue Ridge Comm Coll (NC)
Bowling Green State U-Firelands Coll (OH)
Brunswick Comm Coll (NC)
Catawba Valley Comm Coll (NC)
Central Arizona Coll (AZ)
Central Comm Coll–Columbus Campus (NE)
Central Comm Coll–Grand Island Campus (NE)
Central Comm Coll–Hastings Campus (NE)
Central Georgia Tech Coll (GA)
Central Oregon Comm Coll (OR)
Central Piedmont Comm Coll (NC)
Century Coll (MN)
Chemeketa Comm Coll (OR)
Clark State Comm Coll (OH)
Cleveland State Comm Coll (TN)
Clinton Comm Coll (NY)
Coffeyville Comm Coll (KS)
Coll of DuPage (IL)
Comm Coll of Allegheny County (PA)
Comm Coll of the Air Force (AL)
Comm Coll of Vermont (VT)
Corning Comm Coll (NY)
Cossatot Comm Coll of the U of Arkansas (AR)
Crowder Coll (MO)
Cumberland County Coll (NJ)
Danville Area Comm Coll (IL)
De Anza Coll (CA)
Delaware Tech & Comm Coll, Stanton/ Wilmington Cmps (DE)
Delaware Tech & Comm Coll, Terry Cmps (DE)
Dodge City Comm Coll (KS)
East Central (MO)
Edison State Comm Coll (OH)
Elgin Comm Coll (IL)
Everett Comm Coll (WA)

Fayetteville Tech Comm Coll (NC)
Forsyth Tech Comm Coll (NC)
Fox Valley Tech Coll (WI)
Front Range Comm Coll (CO)
Garden City Comm Coll (KS)
GateWay Comm Coll (AZ)
Gateway Comm Coll (CT)
Glendale Comm Coll (AZ)
Glendale Comm Coll (CA)
Grand Rapids Comm Coll (MI)
Great Basin Coll (NV)
Greenfield Comm Coll (MA)
Griffin Tech Coll (GA)
Guilford Tech Comm Coll (NC)
Halifax Comm Coll (NC)
Haywood Comm Coll (NC)
Heartland Comm Coll (IL)
Henry Ford Comm Coll (MI)
Highline Comm Coll (WA)
Hopkinsville Comm Coll (KY)
Houston Comm Coll System (TX)
Hudson Valley Comm Coll (NY)
Illinois Eastern Comm Colls, Wabash Valley Coll (IL)
Illinois Valley Comm Coll (IL)
Ivy Tech State Coll–Bloomington (IN)
Ivy Tech State Coll–Central Indiana (IN)
Ivy Tech State Coll–Columbus (IN)
Ivy Tech State Coll–Eastcentral (IN)
Ivy Tech State Coll–Kokomo (IN)
Ivy Tech State Coll–Lafayette (IN)
Ivy Tech State Coll–North Central (IN)
Ivy Tech State Coll–Northeast (IN)
Ivy Tech State Coll–Southcentral (IN)
Ivy Tech State Coll–Southeast (IN)
Ivy Tech State Coll–Southwest (IN)
Ivy Tech State Coll–Wabash Valley (IN)
Ivy Tech State Coll–Whitewater (IN)
Jackson State Comm Coll (TN)
Jefferson Comm Coll (OH)
Kent State U, Tuscarawas Campus (OH)
Kilgore Coll (TX)
Lackawanna Coll (PA)
Lake Land Coll (IL)
Lane Comm Coll (OR)
Lanier Tech Coll (GA)
Lansing Comm Coll (MI)
Lehigh Carbon Comm Coll (PA)
Linn-Benton Comm Coll (OR)
Long Beach City Coll (CA)
Lower Columbia Coll (WA)
Macomb Comm Coll (MI)
Manchester Comm Coll (CT)
Miami Dade Coll (FL)
Milwaukee Area Tech Coll (WI)
Mineral Area Coll (MO)
Minnesota State Coll–Southeast Tech (MN)
Moberly Area Comm Coll (MO)
Montcalm Comm Coll (MI)
Mount Wachusett Comm Coll (MA)
Muskegon Comm Coll (MI)
Nashville State Tech Comm Coll (TN)
North Central State Coll (OH)
North Dakota State Coll of Science (ND)

Northeast State Tech Comm Coll (TN)
North Hennepin Comm Coll (MN)
Northwestern Michigan Coll (MI)
Northwest Tech Coll (MN)
Oakland Comm Coll (MI)
Ohio State U Ag Tech Inst (OH)
Olympic Coll (WA)
Ouachita Tech Coll (AR)
Parkland Coll (IL)
Patrick Henry Comm Coll (VA)
Pennsylvania Highland Comm Coll (PA)
Penn State U York Campus of the Commonwealth Coll (PA)
Prairie State Coll (IL)
Pulaski Tech Coll (AR)
Raritan Valley Comm Coll (NJ)
Richland Comm Coll (IL)
Rock Valley Coll (IL)
Rogue Comm Coll (OR)
Rowan-Cabarrus Comm Coll (NC)
St. Louis Comm Coll at Forest Park (MO)
Saint Paul Coll–A Comm & Tech College (MN)
St. Petersburg Coll (FL)
Salt Lake Comm Coll (UT)
San Antonio Coll (TX)
San Diego City Coll (CA)
Santa Barbara City Coll (CA)
Schoolcraft Coll (MI)
Seminole Comm Coll (FL)
Shoreline Comm Coll (WA)
Sinclair Comm Coll (OH)
Somerset Comm Coll (KY)
Southeast Comm Coll, Milford Campus (NE)
Southeast Tech Inst (SD)
South Texas Coll (TX)
Southwestern Oregon Comm Coll (OR)
Stanly Comm Coll (NC)
State U of NY Coll of Technology at Canton (NY)
Temple Coll (TX)
Texas State Tech Coll–Waco/Marshall Campus (TX)
Three Rivers Comm Coll (CT)
Three Rivers Comm Coll (MO)
Trident Tech Coll (SC)
Trinidad State Jr Coll (CO)
Union County Coll (NJ)
U of Arkansas Comm Coll at Batesville (AR)
U of Cincinnati Raymond Walters Coll (OH)
Valencia Comm Coll (FL)
Wake Tech Comm Coll (NC)
Waubonsee Comm Coll (IL)
Wayne County Comm Coll District (MI)
Western Nevada Comm Coll (NV)
Wilson Tech Comm Coll (NC)
Yakima Valley Comm Coll (WA)
Yuba Coll (CA)

Information Resources Management
Mott Comm Coll (MI)

Information Science/Studies
Adirondack Comm Coll (NY)
Alamance Comm Coll (NC)
Albuquerque Tech Vocational Inst (NM)
Allen County Comm Coll (KS)
Alpena Comm Coll (MI)
Amarillo Coll (TX)
Anne Arundel Comm Coll (MD)
Arapahoe Comm Coll (CO)

Arizona Western Coll (AZ)
Arkansas State U–Mountain Home (AR)
Ashland Comm and Tech Coll (KY)
Atlanta Metropolitan Coll (GA)
Augusta Tech Coll (GA)
Austin Comm Coll (TX)
Bainbridge Coll (GA)
Baltimore City Comm Coll (MD)
Barton County Comm Coll (KS)
Bay de Noc Comm Coll (MI)
Bay Mills Comm Coll (MI)
Beaufort County Comm Coll (NC)
Big Bend Comm Coll (WA)
Black River Tech Coll (AR)
Blue Mountain Comm Coll (OR)
Blue Ridge Comm Coll (NC)
Blue Ridge Comm Coll (VA)
Blue River Comm Coll (MO)
Bossier Parish Comm Coll (LA)
Bristol Comm Coll (MA)
Broome Comm Coll (NY)
Broward Comm Coll (FL)
Brown Mackie Coll, Northern Kentucky Campus (KY)
Bryant & Stratton Business Inst, Albany (NY)
Bucks County Comm Coll (PA)
Cape Cod Comm Coll (MA)
Cayuga County Comm Coll (NY)
Cecil Comm Coll (MD)
Central Alabama Comm Coll (AL)
Central Carolina Comm Coll (NC)
Central Georgia Tech Coll (GA)
Chattahoochee Valley Comm Coll (AL)
Chattanooga State Tech Comm Coll (TN)
Cincinnati State Tech and Comm Coll (OH)
Clark State Comm Coll (OH)
Cleveland Comm Coll (NC)
Cochise Coll, Douglas (AZ)
Coconino Comm Coll (AZ)
Coffeyville Comm Coll (KS)
Coll of Southern Maryland (MD)
Coll of the Canyons (CA)
Columbia-Greene Comm Coll (NY)
Columbia State Comm Coll (TN)
Comm Coll of Aurora (CO)
Comm Coll of Beaver County (PA)
Comm Coll of Denver (CO)
Comm Coll of Southern Nevada (NV)
Compton Comm Coll (CA)
Cumberland County Coll (NJ)
Dabney S. Lancaster Comm Coll (VA)
Danville Area Comm Coll (IL)
Daytona Beach Comm Coll (FL)
De Anza Coll (CA)
Delaware County Comm Coll (PA)
Delaware Tech & Comm Coll, Stanton/ Wilmington Cmps (DE)
Delta Coll (MI)
Dodge City Comm Coll (KS)
Durham Tech Comm Coll (NC)
Dutchess Comm Coll (NY)
East Central Coll (MO)
Eastern Arizona Coll (AZ)
ECPI Coll of Technology, Newport News (VA)

ECPI Coll of Technology, Virginia Beach (VA)
ECPI Tech Coll, Richmond (VA)
ECPI Tech Coll, Roanoke (VA)
Elgin Comm Coll (IL)
Elizabethtown Comm and Tech Coll (KY)
Erie Business Center, Main (PA)
Erie Comm Coll (NY)
Erie Comm Coll, North Campus (NY)
Erie Comm Coll, South Campus (NY)
Essex County Coll (NJ)
Fayetteville Tech Comm Coll (NC)
Florida Comm Coll at Jacksonville (FL)
Frank Phillips Coll (TX)
Fulton-Montgomery Comm Coll (NY)
Garden City Comm Coll (KS)
Genesee Comm Coll (NY)
Greenfield Comm Coll (MA)
Green River Comm Coll (WA)
Guilford Tech Comm Coll (NC)
Hagerstown Business Coll (MD)
Harcum Coll (PA)
Haywood Comm Coll (NC)
Hazard Comm and Tech Coll (KY)
Heartland Comm Coll (IL)
Henry Ford Comm Coll (MI)
Hesser Coll (NH)
Highland Comm Coll (KS)
Hillsborough Comm Coll (FL)
Holyoke Comm Coll (MA)
Howard Comm Coll (MD)
Indian River Comm Coll (FL)
Instituto Comercial de Puerto Rico Jr Coll (PR)
Jefferson Comm Coll (NY)
J. F. Drake State Tech Coll (AL)
John A. Logan Coll (IL)
Kingwood Coll (TX)
Lansing Comm Coll (MI)
Laredo Comm Coll (TX)
Lehigh Carbon Comm Coll (PA)
Linn State Tech Coll (MO)
Lower Columbia Coll (WA)
Manchester Comm Coll (CT)
Massachusetts Bay Comm Coll (MA)
McIntosh Coll (NH)
McLennan Comm Coll (TX)
Metropolitan Comm Coll-Business & Technology College (MO)
Miami Dade Coll (FL)
Middle Georgia Coll (GA)
Mid Michigan Comm Coll (MI)
Minneapolis Comm and Tech Coll (MN)
Minnesota School of Business–Richfield (MN)
Monroe Coll, Bronx (NY)
Monroe Coll, New Rochelle (NY)
Montgomery County Comm Coll (PA)
Mount Wachusett Comm Coll (MA)
Muskegon Comm Coll (MI)
Nashville State Tech Comm Coll (TN)
New Hampshire Comm Tech Coll, Manchester/Stratham (NH)
Niagara County Comm Coll (NY)
North Central State Coll (OH)
Northeast Alabama Comm Coll (AL)
Northern Virginia Comm Coll (VA)

North Lake Coll (TX)
North Seattle Comm Coll (WA)
North Shore Comm Coll (MA)
Northwestern Connecticut Comm-Tech Coll (CT)
Northwest-Shoals Comm Coll (AL)
Odessa Coll (TX)
Olympic Coll (WA)
Orange Coast Coll (CA)
Orange County Comm Coll (NY)
Panola Coll (TX)
Parkland Coll (IL)
Pasadena City Coll (CA)
Penn State U Beaver Campus of the Commonwealth Coll (PA)
Penn State U DuBois Campus of the Commonwealth Coll (PA)
Penn State U Fayette Campus of the Commonwealth Coll (PA)
Penn State U Hazleton Campus of the Commonwealth Coll (PA)
Penn State U Mont Alto Campus of the Commonwealth Coll (PA)
Penn State U New Kensington Campus of the Commonwealth Coll (PA)
Penn State U Shenango Campus of the Commonwealth Coll (PA)
Penn State U Wilkes-Barre Campus of the Commonwealth Coll (PA)
Penn State U Worthington Scranton Cmps Commonwealth Coll (PA)
Penn State U York Campus of the Commonwealth Coll (PA)
Pioneer Pacific Coll (OR)
Polk Comm Coll (FL)
Pulaski Tech Coll (AR)
Queensborough Comm Coll of City U of NY (NY)
Raritan Valley Comm Coll (NJ)
Richland Comm Coll (IL)
Rockingham Comm Coll (NC)
Rowan-Cabarrus Comm Coll (NC)
St. Louis Comm Coll at Meramec (MO)
St. Petersburg Coll (FL)
Salt Lake Comm Coll (UT)
Sandhills Comm Coll (NC)
San Diego Miramar Coll (CA)
San Juan Coll (NM)
Santa Barbara City Coll (CA)
Santa Fe Comm Coll (FL)
Seminole Comm Coll (FL)
Shawnee Comm Coll (IL)
Sheridan Coll (WY)
Sinclair Comm Coll (OH)
Sisseton-Wahpeton Comm Coll (SD)
Snow Coll (UT)
Southeast Tech Inst (SD)
Southern Maine Comm Coll (ME)
Southern Union State Comm Coll (AL)
South Mountain Comm Coll (AZ)
Southside Virginia Comm Coll (VA)
South Texas Coll (TX)
South U (FL)
Southwestern Comm Coll (NC)
Southwest Georgia Tech Coll (GA)
Stanly Comm Coll (NC)
State U of NY Coll of Technology at Canton (NY)

State U of NY Coll of Technology at Delhi (NY)
Surry Comm Coll (NC)
Tacoma Comm Coll (WA)
Texas State Tech Coll–Waco/Marshall Campus (TX)
Thaddeus Stevens Coll of Technology (PA)
Tompkins Cortland Comm Coll (NY)
Trinidad State Jr Coll (CO)
Truckee Meadows Comm Coll (NV)
Tunxis Comm Coll (CT)
Union County Coll (NJ)
U of Arkansas Comm Coll at Morrilton (AR)
U of Cincinnati Raymond Walters Coll (OH)
Walla Walla Comm Coll (WA)
West Central Tech Coll (GA)
Westchester Comm Coll (NY)
Western Oklahoma State Coll (OK)
Western Wyoming Comm Coll (WY)
West Kentucky Comm and Tech Coll (KY)
Westmoreland County Comm Coll (PA)
Wilson Tech Comm Coll (NC)
Yavapai Coll (AZ)

Information Technology
Adirondack Comm Coll (NY)
Atlanta Metropolitan Coll (GA)
Austin Comm Coll (TX)
Big Sandy Comm and Tech Coll (KY)
Black Hawk Coll, Moline (IL)
Bladen Comm Coll (NC)
Blue Ridge Comm Coll (VA)
Brazosport Coll (TX)
Bristol Comm Coll (MA)
Bryant & Stratton Business Inst, Albany (NY)
Bucks County Comm Coll (PA)
Caldwell Comm Coll and Tech Inst (NC)
Cape Cod Comm Coll (MA)
Capital Comm Coll (CT)
Carteret Comm Coll (NC)
Catawba Valley Comm Coll (NC)
Cecil Comm Coll (MD)
Central Carolina Comm Coll (NC)
Central Comm Coll–Columbus Campus (NE)
Central Comm Coll–Grand Island Campus (NE)
Central Comm Coll–Hastings Campus (NE)
Clark State Comm Coll (OH)
Cleveland Comm Coll (NC)
Coastal Bend Coll (TX)
Comm and Tech Coll of Shepherd (WV)
Comm Coll of Vermont (VT)
Corning Comm Coll (NY)
Daytona Beach Comm Coll (FL)
Delta Coll (MI)
Durham Tech Comm Coll (NC)
Edgecombe Comm Coll (NC)
El Paso Comm Coll (TX)
Fayetteville Tech Comm Coll (NC)
Florida Comm Coll at Jacksonville (FL)
GateWay Comm Coll (AZ)
Globe Coll (MN)
Gogebic Comm Coll (MI)
Gordon Coll (GA)
Harrisburg Area Comm Coll (PA)
Hawkeye Comm Coll (IA)
Heartland Comm Coll (IL)
Henderson Comm Coll (KY)
Hinds Comm Coll (MS)

Howard Comm Coll (MD)
Indiana Business Coll, Columbus (IN)
Indiana Business Coll, Evansville (IN)
Indiana Business Coll, Indianapolis (IN)
Indiana Business Coll, Lafayette (IN)
Indiana Business Coll, Muncie (IN)
Indiana Business Coll, Terre Haute (IN)
Iowa Lakes Comm Coll (IA)
J. Sargeant Reynolds Comm Coll (VA)
Keystone Coll (PA)
Lake Land Coll (IL)
Lake Region State Coll (ND)
Laramie County Comm Coll (WY)
Laredo Comm Coll (TX)
Laurel Business Inst (PA)
Lower Columbia Coll (WA)
Mayland Comm Coll (NC)
Mesabi Range Comm and Tech Coll (MN)
Metropolitan Comm Coll-Business & Technology College (MO)
Milwaukee Area Tech Coll (WI)
Minnesota School of Business–Brooklyn Center (MN)
Minnesota School of Business–Plymouth (MN)
Mohave Comm Coll (AZ)
Nebraska Indian Comm Coll (NE)
Northland Comm and Tech Coll–Thief River Falls (MN)
Olympic Coll (WA)
Orange County Comm Coll (NY)
Owensboro Comm and Tech Coll (KY)
Pasco-Hernando Comm Coll (FL)
Patrick Henry Comm Coll (VA)
Queensborough Comm Coll of City U of NY (NY)
Randolph Comm Coll (NC)
St. Cloud Tech Coll (MN)
St. Louis Comm Coll at Forest Park (MO)
Salt Lake Comm Coll (UT)
Santa Barbara City Coll (CA)
Savannah Tech Coll (GA)
Seminole Comm Coll (FL)
Sinclair Comm Coll (OH)
Somerset Comm Coll (KY)
Southeast Kentucky Comm and Tech Coll (KY)
Southeast Tech Inst (SD)
Southside Virginia Comm Coll (VA)
South U (FL)
South U (SC)
Spartanburg Methodist Coll (SC)
Surry Comm Coll (NC)
Tacoma Comm Coll (WA)
Three Rivers Comm Coll (MO)
Tri-County Comm Coll (NC)
Trinidad State Jr Coll (CO)
U of Arkansas Comm Coll at Batesville (AR)
Valencia Comm Coll (FL)
Vatterott Coll, Oklahoma City (OK)
Walters State Comm Coll (TN)
Western Oklahoma State Coll (OK)
Western Wyoming Comm Coll (WY)

Institutional Food Workers
Asheville-Buncombe Tech Comm Coll (NC)
Cape Fear Comm Coll (NC)

Harrisburg Area Comm Coll (PA)
Iowa Lakes Comm Coll (IA)
Santa Barbara City Coll (CA)
Texas State Tech Coll–Waco/Marshall Campus (TX)
Wilkes Comm Coll (NC)

Instrumentation Technology
Amarillo Coll (TX)
Bishop State Comm Coll (AL)
Brazosport Coll (TX)
Butler County Comm Coll (PA)
Cape Fear Comm Coll (NC)
Central Carolina Comm Coll (NC)
Chattanooga State Tech Comm Coll (TN)
Colorado Northwestern Comm Coll (CO)
Comm Coll of Rhode Island (RI)
Copiah-Lincoln Comm Coll–Natchez Campus (MS)
DeKalb Tech Coll (GA)
Delaware Tech & Comm Coll, Stanton/ Wilmington Cmps (DE)
East Mississippi Comm Coll (MS)
Florida Comm Coll at Jacksonville (FL)
Henry Ford Comm Coll (MI)
Lower Columbia Coll (WA)
Mesabi Range Comm and Tech Coll (MN)
Moraine Valley Comm Coll (IL)
Nassau Comm Coll (NY)
Northeast State Tech Comm Coll (TN)
Phillips Comm Coll of the U of Arkansas (AR)
St. Cloud Tech Coll (MN)
San Juan Coll (NM)
Savannah Tech Coll (GA)
Texas State Tech Coll–Waco/Marshall Campus (TX)
Wake Tech Comm Coll (NC)
Western Wyoming Comm Coll (WY)
Yakima Valley Comm Coll (WA)

Insurance
Alabama Southern Comm Coll (AL)
Austin Comm Coll (TX)
Broward Comm Coll (FL)
Central Piedmont Comm Coll (NC)
Comm Coll of Allegheny County (PA)
Daytona Beach Comm Coll (FL)
Enterprise-Ozark Comm Coll (AL)
Florida Comm Coll at Jacksonville (FL)
Fox Valley Tech Coll (WI)
Houston Comm Coll System (TX)
Hudson Valley Comm Coll (NY)
Isothermal Comm Coll (NC)
Laurel Business Inst (PA)
Nassau Comm Coll (NY)
Richland Comm Coll (IL)
San Diego City Coll (CA)
Trinity Valley Comm Coll (TX)

Interdisciplinary Studies
Bowling Green State U-Firelands Coll (OH)
Central Texas Coll (TX)
Columbia-Greene Comm Coll (NY)
Great Basin Coll (NV)
Harcum Coll (PA)
Hawkeye Comm Coll (IA)

Hudson Valley Comm Coll (NY)
Jefferson Comm Coll (NY)
New River Comm and Tech Coll (WV)
North Country Comm Coll (NY)
North Shore Comm Coll (MA)
Pasadena City Coll (CA)
South Texas Coll (TX)
State U of NY Coll of Technology at Canton (NY)
The U of Akron–Wayne Coll (OH)
U of South Carolina at Sumter (SC)
Walters State Comm Coll (TN)

Interior Architecture
Lehigh Carbon Comm Coll (PA)
Northampton County Area Comm Coll (PA)
St. Philip's Coll (TX)

Interior Design
Alexandria Tech Coll (MN)
Amarillo Coll (TX)
The Art Inst of Philadelphia (PA)
Berkeley Coll (NJ)
Black Hawk Coll, Moline (IL)
Brookdale Comm Coll (NJ)
Broward Comm Coll (FL)
Cape Fear Comm Coll (NC)
Carteret Comm Coll (NC)
Central Piedmont Comm Coll (NC)
Century Coll (MN)
Clover Park Tech Coll (WA)
Coll of DuPage (IL)
Coll of the Canyons (CA)
Collin County Comm Coll District (TX)
Daytona Beach Comm Coll (FL)
Delaware Coll of Art and Design (DE)
Delta Coll (MI)
Dixie State Coll of Utah (UT)
East Central Coll (MO)
Ellsworth Comm Coll (IA)
El Paso Comm Coll (TX)
Fashion Inst of Design & Merchandising, LA Campus (CA)
Fashion Inst of Design & Merchandising, SD Campus (CA)
Fashion Inst of Design & Merchandising, SF Campus (CA)
Florida Comm Coll at Jacksonville (FL)
Fox Valley Tech Coll (WI)
Garden City Comm Coll (KS)
Gwinnett Tech Coll (GA)
Halifax Comm Coll (NC)
Harcum Coll (PA)
Harford Comm Coll (MD)
Hawkeye Comm Coll (IA)
Henry Ford Comm Coll (MI)
Hesser Coll (NH)
Highline Comm Coll (WA)
Hillsborough Comm Coll (FL)
Houston Comm Coll System (TX)
Indian River Comm Coll (FL)
Ivy Tech State Coll–North Central (IN)
Ivy Tech State Coll–Southwest (IN)
Long Beach City Coll (CA)
Marshall Comm and Tech Coll (WV)
Metropolitan Comm Coll (NE)
Miami Dade Coll (FL)
Modesto Jr Coll (CA)
Nassau Comm Coll (NY)
Northern Virginia Comm Coll (VA)
Oakland Comm Coll (MI)

Orange Coast Coll (CA)
Palm Beach Comm Coll (FL)
Pasadena City Coll (CA)
Prairie State Coll (IL)
Randolph Comm Coll (NC)
St. Louis Comm Coll at Meramec (MO)
St. Philip's Coll (TX)
San Diego City Coll (CA)
San Joaquin Delta Coll (CA)
Santa Barbara City Coll (CA)
Scott Comm Coll (IA)
Seminole Comm Coll (FL)
Sinclair Comm Coll (OH)
Villa Maria Coll of Buffalo (NY)

Intermedia/Multimedia
Academy Coll (MN)
The Art Inst of Philadelphia (PA)
Bristol Comm Coll (MA)
Comm Coll of Denver (CO)
Full Sail Real World Education (FL)
Globe Coll (MN)
Hillsborough Comm Coll (FL)
Minnesota School of Business–Brooklyn Center (MN)
Minnesota School of Business–Plymouth (MN)
Minnesota School of Business–Richfield (MN)
Platt Coll San Diego (CA)
Raritan Valley Comm Coll (NJ)

International Business/Trade/Commerce
Berkeley Coll (NJ)
Berkeley Coll-New York City Campus (NY)
Berkeley Coll-Westchester Campus (NY)
Black Hawk Coll, Moline (IL)
Brevard Comm Coll (FL)
Bunker Hill Comm Coll (MA)
Cincinnati State Tech and Comm Coll (OH)
Comm Coll of Philadelphia (PA)
Edmonds Comm Coll (WA)
El Paso Comm Coll (TX)
Foothill Coll (CA)
Frederick Comm Coll (MD)
Gainesville Coll (GA)
GateWay Comm Coll (AZ)
Herkimer County Comm Coll (NY)
Highline Comm Coll (WA)
Hudson Valley Comm Coll (NY)
Iowa Western Comm Coll (IA)
Kansas City Kansas Comm Coll (KS)
Lansing Comm Coll (MI)
Laredo Comm Coll (TX)
Long Beach City Coll (CA)
Mott Comm Coll (MI)
Northern Virginia Comm Coll (VA)
Northland Comm and Tech Coll–Thief River Falls (MN)
Oakland Comm Coll (MI)
Paradise Valley Comm Coll (AZ)
Pima Comm Coll (AZ)
Raritan Valley Comm Coll (NJ)
St. Louis Comm Coll at Forest Park (MO)
Saint Paul Coll–A Comm & Tech College (MN)
Shoreline Comm Coll (WA)
Tacoma Comm Coll (WA)
Tompkins Cortland Comm Coll (NY)
Westchester Comm Coll (NY)

International Finance
Broome Comm Coll (NY)

International/Global Studies
Macomb Comm Coll (MI)

International Relations and Affairs
Bronx Comm Coll of City U of NY (NY)
Brookdale Comm Coll (NJ)
Cochise Coll, Douglas (AZ)
De Anza Coll (CA)
Harrisburg Area Comm Coll (PA)
Massachusetts Bay Comm Coll (MA)
Miami Dade Coll (FL)
Northern Essex Comm Coll (MA)
Salt Lake Comm Coll (UT)
Santa Barbara City Coll (CA)
Tacoma Comm Coll (WA)
Western Wyoming Comm Coll (WY)

Ironworking
Ivy Tech State Coll–Lafayette (IN)
Ivy Tech State Coll–North Central (IN)
Ivy Tech State Coll–Northeast (IN)
Ivy Tech State Coll–Northwest (IN)
Ivy Tech State Coll–Southwest (IN)
Ivy Tech State Coll–Wabash Valley (IN)

Italian
Casper Coll (WY)
Contra Costa Coll (CA)
Miami Dade Coll (FL)
San Joaquin Delta Coll (CA)
Santa Rosa Jr Coll (CA)

Japanese
Austin Comm Coll (TX)
Citrus Coll (CA)
Everett Comm Coll (WA)
Foothill Coll (CA)
San Joaquin Delta Coll (CA)
Snow Coll (UT)
Tacoma Comm Coll (WA)

Jazz/Jazz Studies
Compton Comm Coll (CA)
Iowa Lakes Comm Coll (IA)

Journalism
Allen County Comm Coll (KS)
Amarillo Coll (TX)
Andrew Coll (GA)
Austin Comm Coll (TX)
Bainbridge Coll (GA)
Barton County Comm Coll (KS)
Brazosport Coll (TX)
Brookdale Comm Coll (NJ)
Bucks County Comm Coll (PA)
Butler County Comm Coll (KS)
Casper Coll (WY)
Central Texas Coll (TX)
Citrus Coll (CA)
City Colls of Chicago, Wilbur Wright Coll (IL)
Cloud County Comm Coll (KS)
Coastal Bend Coll (TX)
Cochise Coll, Douglas (AZ)
Coffeyville Comm Coll (KS)
Colby Comm Coll (KS)
Coll of the Canyons (CA)
Comm Coll of Allegheny County (PA)
Compton Comm Coll (CA)
Contra Costa Coll (CA)
Copiah-Lincoln Comm Coll (MS)
Cowley County Comm Coll and Voc-Tech School (KS)
Danville Area Comm Coll (IL)
Darton Coll (GA)
Daytona Beach Comm Coll (FL)
De Anza Coll (CA)
Delaware County Comm Coll (PA)

Delaware Tech & Comm Coll, Jack F Owens Cmps (DE)
Delta Coll (MI)
Dixie State Coll of Utah (UT)
Dodge City Comm Coll (KS)
East Central Coll (MO)
East Central Comm Coll (MS)
Enterprise-Ozark Comm Coll (AL)
Everett Comm Coll (WA)
Gainesville Coll (GA)
Garden City Comm Coll (KS)
Glendale Comm Coll (CA)
Gordon Coll (GA)
Harrisburg Area Comm Coll (PA)
Highland Comm Coll (KS)
Highline Comm Coll (WA)
Hinds Comm Coll (MS)
Illinois Valley Comm Coll (IL)
Indian River Comm Coll (FL)
Iowa Central Comm Coll (IA)
Iowa Lakes Comm Coll (IA)
Iowa Western Comm Coll (IA)
Itawamba Comm Coll (MS)
John A. Logan Coll (IL)
Keystone Coll (PA)
Kilgore Coll (TX)
Kingsborough Comm Coll of City U of NY (NY)
Lansing Comm Coll (MI)
Laramie County Comm Coll (WY)
Linn-Benton Comm Coll (OR)
Long Beach City Coll (CA)
Manchester Comm Coll (CT)
Miami Dade Coll (FL)
Midland Coll (TX)
Northampton County Area Comm Coll (PA)
Northern Essex Comm Coll (MA)
North Idaho Coll (ID)
Orange Coast Coll (CA)
Palm Beach Comm Coll (FL)
Pasadena City Coll (CA)
Pima Comm Coll (AZ)
Riverside Comm Coll District (CA)
St. Louis Comm Coll at Meramec (MO)
San Diego City Coll (CA)
San Joaquin Delta Coll (CA)
Santa Rosa Jr Coll (CA)
Seward County Comm Coll (KS)
Solano Comm Coll (CA)
Sussex County Comm Coll (NJ)
Tacoma Comm Coll (WA)
Taft Coll (CA)
Trinidad State Jr Coll (CO)
Trinity Valley Comm Coll (TX)
Umpqua Comm Coll (OR)
Western Wyoming Comm Coll (WY)

Journalism Related
Rogue Comm Coll (OR)

Juvenile Corrections
Linn-Benton Comm Coll (OR)

Kindergarten/Preschool Education
Alabama Southern Comm Coll (AL)
Alamance Comm Coll (NC)
Andover Coll (ME)
Anne Arundel Comm Coll (MD)
Asnuntuck Comm Coll (CT)
Bainbridge Coll (GA)
Baltimore City Comm Coll (MD)
Bay State Coll (MA)
Beaufort County Comm Coll (NC)
Bergen Comm Coll (NJ)
Blackfeet Comm Coll (MT)

Blue Ridge Comm Coll (NC)
Borough of Manhattan Comm Coll of City U of NY (NY)
Brookdale Comm Coll (NJ)
Broward Comm Coll (FL)
Bucks County Comm Coll (PA)
Butler County Comm Coll (KS)
Butler County Comm Coll (PA)
Cape Cod Comm Coll (MA)
Capital Comm Coll (CT)
Carroll Comm Coll (MD)
Casper Coll (WY)
Cayuga County Comm Coll (NY)
Cecil Comm Coll (MD)
Central Arizona Coll (AZ)
Central Carolina Comm Coll (NC)
Centralia Coll (WA)
Central Piedmont Comm Coll (NC)
Cerro Coso Comm Coll (CA)
Chattanooga State Tech Comm Coll (TN)
Chemeketa Comm Coll (OR)
Clark State Comm Coll (OH)
Cleveland State Comm Coll (TN)
Coahoma Comm Coll (MS)
Colby Comm Coll (KS)
Coll of Southern Maryland (MD)
Coll of the Canyons (CA)
Colorado Mountn Coll, Timberline Cmps (CO)
Columbia State Comm Coll (TN)
Columbus State Comm Coll (OH)
Comm Coll of Aurora (CO)
Comm Coll of Denver (CO)
Comm Coll of Philadelphia (PA)
Comm Coll of Rhode Island (RI)
Comm Coll of Southern Nevada (NV)
Compton Comm Coll (CA)
Contra Costa Coll (CA)
Cumberland County Coll (NJ)
Cuyahoga Comm Coll (OH)
Danville Area Comm Coll (IL)
Daytona Beach Comm Coll (FL)
Delaware Tech & Comm Coll, Stanton/ Wilmington Cmps (DE)
Delaware Tech & Comm Coll, Terry Cmps (DE)
Dixie State Coll of Utah (UT)
Durham Tech Comm Coll (NC)
Dutchess Comm Coll (NY)
East Central Comm Coll (MS)
Eastern Maine Comm Coll (ME)
Edgecombe Comm Coll (NC)
Edison State Comm Coll (OH)
Elgin Comm Coll (IL)
Ellsworth Comm Coll (IA)
Enterprise-Ozark Comm Coll (AL)
Essex County Coll (NJ)
Eugenio María de Hostos Comm Coll of City U of NY (NY)
Everett Comm Coll (WA)
Fayetteville Tech Comm Coll (NC)
Finger Lakes Comm Coll (NY)
Forsyth Tech Comm Coll (NC)
Fort Peck Comm Coll (MT)
Frederick Comm Coll (MD)
Fulton-Montgomery Comm Coll (NY)

Gainesville Coll (GA)
Gateway Comm Coll (CT)
Genesee Comm Coll (NY)
Glendale Comm Coll (AZ)
Gogebic Comm Coll (MI)
Great Basin Coll (NV)
Greenfield Comm Coll (MA)
Guam Comm Coll (GU)
Guilford Tech Comm Coll (NC)
Harcum Coll (PA)
Harrisburg Area Comm Coll (PA)
Hazard Comm and Tech Coll (KY)
Heartland Comm Coll (IL)
Hesser Coll (NH)
Hesston Coll (KS)
Highland Comm Coll (IL)
Highline Comm Coll (WA)
Holyoke Comm Coll (MA)
Hopkinsville Comm Coll (KY)
Howard Comm Coll (MD)
Hudson Valley Comm Coll (NY)
Independence Comm Coll (KS)
Indian River Comm Coll (FL)
Iowa Lakes Comm Coll (IA)
Isothermal Comm Coll (NC)
Itawamba Comm Coll (MS)
James Sprunt Comm Coll (NC)
Jefferson Comm Coll (NY)
John A. Logan Coll (IL)
Johnston Comm Coll (NC)
Kauai Comm Coll (HI)
Keystone Coll (PA)
Lane Comm Coll (OR)
Lansing Comm Coll (MI)
Lehigh Carbon Comm Coll (PA)
Lewis and Clark Comm Coll (IL)
Long Beach City Coll (CA)
Lower Columbia Coll (WA)
Manchester Comm Coll (CT)
Maria Coll (NY)
Mayland Comm Coll (NC)
McIntosh Coll (NH)
McLennan Comm Coll (TX)
Metropolitan Comm Coll (NE)
Miami Dade Coll (FL)
Minnesota State Coll– Southeast Tech (MN)
Modesto Jr Coll (CA)
Napa Valley Coll (CA)
Nashville State Tech Comm Coll (TN)
Nassau Comm Coll (NY)
New Hampshire Comm Tech Coll, Manchester/Stratham (NH)
North Central State Coll (OH)
Northeast State Tech Comm Coll (TN)
Northern Essex Comm Coll (MA)
Northern Virginia Comm Coll (VA)
North Shore Comm Coll (MA)
Northwestern Connecticut Comm-Tech Coll (CT)
Northwestern Tech Coll (GA)
Odessa Coll (TX)
Orange Coast Coll (CA)
Otero Jr Coll (CO)
Owensboro Comm and Tech Coll (KY)
Palm Beach Comm Coll (FL)
Pasadena City Coll (CA)
Penn Valley Comm Coll (MO)
Pratt Comm Coll and Area Vocational School (KS)
Raritan Valley Comm Coll (NJ)
Riverside Comm Coll District (CA)
Roanoke-Chowan Comm Coll (NC)

Rowan-Cabarrus Comm Coll (NC)
St. Cloud Tech Coll (MN)
St. Petersburg Coll (FL)
Sandhills Comm Coll (NC)
San Joaquin Delta Coll (CA)
San Juan Coll (NM)
Santa Barbara City Coll (CA)
Santa Fe Comm Coll (FL)
Seattle Central Comm Coll (WA)
Shelton State Comm Coll (AL)
Shoreline Comm Coll (WA)
Sinclair Comm Coll (OH)
Sisseton-Wahpeton Comm Coll (SD)
Snow Coll (UT)
Solano Comm Coll (CA)
Southern Maine Comm Coll (ME)
Southern State Comm Coll (OH)
Southwestern Oregon Comm Coll (OR)
Springfield Tech Comm Coll (MA)
State U of NY Coll of Technology at Canton (NY)
Taft Coll (CA)
Tech Coll of the Lowcountry (SC)
Three Rivers Comm Coll (CT)
Tompkins Cortland Comm Coll (NY)
Trinidad State Jr Coll (CO)
Trinity Valley Comm Coll (TX)
Truckee Meadows Comm Coll (NV)
Tunxis Comm Coll (CT)
Umpqua Comm Coll (OR)
U of Arkansas Comm Coll at Batesville (AR)
Villa Maria Coll of Buffalo (NY)
Wake Tech Comm Coll (NC)
Waubonsee Comm Coll (IL)
Whatcom Comm Coll (WA)
Wilson Tech Comm Coll (NC)
Yakima Valley Comm Coll (WA)
Yuba Coll (CA)

Kinesiology and Exercise Science
Barton County Comm Coll (KS)
Bergen Comm Coll (NJ)
Butler County Comm Coll (PA)
Central Oregon Comm Coll (OR)
Clarendon Coll (TX)
Clark State Comm Coll (OH)
Columbia-Greene Comm Coll (NY)
Delaware Tech & Comm Coll, Stanton/ Wilmington Cmps (DE)
Globe Coll (MN)
Henry Ford Comm Coll (MI)
Houston Comm Coll System (TX)
Minnesota School of Business–Plymouth (MN)
Minnesota School of Business–Richfield (MN)
Mount Wachusett Comm Coll (MA)
New Hampshire Comm Tech Coll, Manchester/Stratham (NH)
North Country Comm Coll (NY)
North Lake Coll (TX)
Oakland Comm Coll (MI)
Orange Coast Coll (CA)
Orange County Comm Coll (NY)
St. Philip's Coll (TX)
Santa Barbara City Coll (CA)
Western Wyoming Comm Coll (WY)

Labor and Industrial Relations
Comm Coll of Rhode Island (RI)
Kingsborough Comm Coll of City U of NY (NY)
Lansing Comm Coll (MI)
Rockingham Comm Coll (NC)
San Diego City Coll (CA)
Sinclair Comm Coll (OH)
Wayne County Comm Coll District (MI)

Landscape Architecture
Anne Arundel Comm Coll (MD)
Columbus State Comm Coll (OH)
Foothill Coll (CA)
Keystone Coll (PA)
Lansing Comm Coll (MI)
Modesto Jr Coll (CA)
Oakland Comm Coll (MI)
Pasadena City Coll (CA)
Riverside Comm Coll District (CA)
Santa Rosa Jr Coll (CA)
State U of NY Coll of Technology at Delhi (NY)
Trinidad State Jr Coll (CO)
Truckee Meadows Comm Coll (NV)
Wake Tech Comm Coll (NC)

Landscaping and Groundskeeping
Caldwell Comm Coll and Tech Inst (NC)
Cape Fear Comm Coll (NC)
Cincinnati State Tech and Comm Coll (OH)
Clark Coll (WA)
Clark State Comm Coll (OH)
Clover Park Tech Coll (WA)
Coll of DuPage (IL)
Coll of Lake County (IL)
Comm Coll of Allegheny County (PA)
Comm Coll of Southern Nevada (NV)
Danville Area Comm Coll (IL)
Edmonds Comm Coll (WA)
Glendale Comm Coll (AZ)
Hinds Comm Coll (MS)
Iowa Lakes Comm Coll (IA)
James H. Faulkner State Comm Coll (AL)
Johnston Comm Coll (NC)
J. Sargeant Reynolds Comm Coll (VA)
Lincoln Land Comm Coll (IL)
Miami Dade Coll (FL)
Milwaukee Area Tech Coll (WI)
North Shore Comm Coll (MA)
Northwestern Michigan Coll (MI)
Oakland Comm Coll (MI)
Ohio State U Ag Tech Inst (OH)
Parkland Coll (IL)
Rochester Comm and Tech Coll (MN)
St. Petersburg Coll (FL)
Sandhills Comm Coll (NC)
Santa Barbara City Coll (CA)
Southern Maine Comm Coll (ME)
Springfield Tech Comm Coll (MA)
State U of NY Coll of Technology at Alfred (NY)
State U of NY Coll of Technology at Delhi (NY)

Land Use Planning and Management
Colorado Mountn Coll, Timberline Cmps (CO)

Language Interpretation and Translation
Allen County Comm Coll (KS)
Indian River Comm Coll (FL)

Labor and Industrial Relations
Union County Coll (NJ)
Wilson Tech Comm Coll (NC)

Laser and Optical Technology
Albuquerque Tech Vocational Inst (NM)
Amarillo Coll (TX)
Central Carolina Comm Coll (NC)
Cincinnati State Tech and Comm Coll (OH)
Durham Tech Comm Coll (NC)
Front Range Comm Coll (CO)
George C. Wallace Comm Coll (AL)
Indian Hills Comm Coll (IA)
Linn State Tech Coll (MO)
Massachusetts Bay Comm Coll (MA)
Queensborough Comm Coll of City U of NY (NY)
Schoolcraft Coll (MI)
Southeast Tech Inst (SD)
Springfield Tech Comm Coll (MA)
Texas State Tech Coll– Waco/Marshall Campus (TX)
Three Rivers Comm Coll (CT)

Latin
Santa Rosa Jr Coll (CA)

Latin American Studies
Miami Dade Coll (FL)
Pasadena City Coll (CA)
San Diego City Coll (CA)

Leatherworking/Upholstery
St. Philip's Coll (TX)

Legal Administrative Assistant/Secretary
Alamance Comm Coll (NC)
Alexandria Tech Coll (MN)
Alvin Comm Coll (TX)
Amarillo Coll (TX)
Andover Coll (ME)
Arapahoe Comm Coll (CO)
Austin Comm Coll (TX)
Baltimore City Comm Coll (MD)
Bay State Coll (MA)
Bergen Comm Coll (NJ)
Bismarck State Coll (ND)
Black Hawk Coll, Moline (IL)
Briarwood Coll (CT)
Bristol Comm Coll (MA)
Broward Comm Coll (FL)
Brown Mackie Coll, Michigan City Campus (IN)
Business Inst of Pennsylvania, Sharon (PA)
Butler County Comm Coll (PA)
Cape Cod Comm Coll (MA)
Career Colls of Chicago (IL)
Carteret Comm Coll (NC)
Casper Coll (WY)
Central Arizona Coll (AZ)
Central Carolina Comm Coll (NC)
Central Florida Comm Coll (FL)
Centralia Coll (WA)
Central Piedmont Comm Coll (NC)
Century Coll (MN)
Chattahoochee Valley Comm Coll (AL)
Chattanooga State Tech Comm Coll (TN)
Clatsop Comm Coll (OR)
Clover Park Tech Coll (WA)
Clovis Comm Coll (NM)
Coastal Bend Coll (TX)
Cochise Coll, Douglas (AZ)
Coffeyville Comm Coll (KS)
Coll of DuPage (IL)
Columbus State Comm Coll (OH)

Comm & Tech Coll at West Virginia U Inst of Technology (WV)
Comm Coll of Allegheny County (PA)
Comm Coll of Denver (CO)
Comm Coll of Philadelphia (PA)
Comm Coll of Rhode Island (RI)
Comm Coll of Southern Nevada (NV)
Craven Comm Coll (NC)
Crowder Coll (MO)
Cumberland County Coll (NJ)
Dabney S. Lancaster Comm Coll (VA)
Danville Area Comm Coll (IL)
Daytona Beach Comm Coll (FL)
DeKalb Tech Coll (GA)
Delaware Tech & Comm Coll, Jack F Owens Cmps (DE)
Delta Coll (MI)
Des Moines Area Comm Coll (IA)
Dodge City Comm Coll (KS)
East Central Coll (MO)
Eastfield Coll (TX)
Edmonds Comm Coll (WA)
Elgin Comm Coll (IL)
Ellsworth Comm Coll (IA)
Enterprise-Ozark Comm Coll (AL)
Erie Business Center, Main (PA)
Erie Business Center South (PA)
Florida National Coll (FL)
Fort Scott Comm Coll (KS)
Fox Valley Tech Coll (WI)
Frank Phillips Coll (TX)
Frederick Comm Coll (MD)
Fulton-Montgomery Comm Coll (NY)
Garden City Comm Coll (KS)
Gateway Comm Coll (CT)
Glendale Comm Coll (CA)
Globe Coll (MN)
Gogebic Comm Coll (MI)
Grand Rapids Comm Coll (MI)
Green River Comm Coll (WA)
Hagerstown Business Coll (MD)
Harrisburg Area Comm Coll (PA)
Henry Ford Comm Coll (MI)
Hibbing Comm Coll (MN)
Highland Comm Coll (KS)
Highline Comm Coll (WA)
Hillsborough Comm Coll (FL)
Holyoke Comm Coll (MA)
Howard Comm Coll (MD)
ICM School of Business & Medical Careers (PA)
Indiana Business Coll, Indianapolis (IN)
Iowa Lakes Comm Coll (IA)
Iowa Western Comm Coll (IA)
Jefferson Comm Coll (OH)
John A. Logan Coll (IL)
John Wood Comm Coll (IL)
Kalamazoo Valley Comm Coll (MI)
Kapiolani Comm Coll (HI)
Kennebec Valley Comm Coll (ME)
Lake Land Coll (IL)
Lake Region State Coll (ND)
Lake Superior Coll (MN)
Lansing Comm Coll (MI)
Laurel Business Inst (PA)
Lehigh Carbon Comm Coll (PA)
Lewis and Clark Comm Coll (IL)
Lincoln Land Comm Coll (IL)
Linn-Benton Comm Coll (OR)

Long Beach City Coll (CA)
Longview Comm Coll (MO)
Lower Columbia Coll (WA)
Manchester Comm Coll (CT)
Maple Woods Comm Coll (MO)
McIntosh Coll (NH)
McLennan Comm Coll (TX)
Metropolitan Comm Coll (NE)
Miami Dade Coll (FL)
Mid Michigan Comm Coll (MI)
Milwaukee Area Tech Coll (WI)
Minneapolis Comm and Tech Coll (MN)
Minnesota School of Business–Brooklyn Center (MN)
Minnesota School of Business–Plymouth (MN)
Minnesota School of Business–Richfield (MN)
Minnesota State Coll–Southeast Tech (MN)
Mott Comm Coll (MI)
Muskegon Comm Coll (MI)
Napa Valley Coll (CA)
Nassau Comm Coll (NY)
Newport Business Inst, Williamsport (PA)
Northampton County Area Comm Coll (PA)
Northeast Alabama Comm Coll (AL)
North Idaho Coll (ID)
North Lake Coll (TX)
Northland Comm and Tech Coll–Thief River Falls (MN)
North Shore Comm Coll (MA)
Northwestern Michigan Coll (MI)
Northwest State Comm Coll (OH)
Northwest Tech Coll (MN)
Odessa Coll (TX)
Olympic Coll (WA)
Orange Coast Coll (CA)
Otero Jr Coll (CO)
Ouachita Tech Coll (AR)
Palm Beach Comm Coll (FL)
Pasadena City Coll (CA)
Penn Valley Comm Coll (MO)
Polk Comm Coll (FL)
Rasmussen Coll St. Cloud (MN)
Richland Comm Coll (IL)
Riverland Comm Coll (MN)
Rochester Comm and Tech Coll (MN)
Rockingham Comm Coll (NC)
St. Cloud Tech Coll (MN)
St. Louis Comm Coll at Meramec (MO)
St. Petersburg Coll (FL)
St. Philip's Coll (TX)
San Antonio Coll (TX)
San Diego City Coll (CA)
Santa Fe Comm Coll (FL)
Sauk Valley Comm Coll (IL)
Shawnee Comm Coll (IL)
Sinclair Comm Coll (OH)
Solano Comm Coll (CA)
South Hills School of Business & Technology, State College (PA)
South Texas Coll (TX)
Southwest Wisconsin Tech Coll (WI)
Stanly Comm Coll (NC)
Tech Coll of the Lowcountry (SC)
Thaddeus Stevens Coll of Technology (PA)
Three Rivers Comm Coll (CT)
Trinity Valley Comm Coll (TX)
Truckee Meadows Comm Coll (NV)

Tunxis Comm Coll (CT)
Umpqua Comm Coll (OR)
The U of Akron–Wayne Coll (OH)
U of Cincinnati Raymond Walters (OH)
U of Northwestern Ohio (OH)
Valencia Comm Coll (FL)
Wake Tech Comm Coll (NC)
Walla Walla Comm Coll (WA)
Wayne County Comm Coll District (MI)
Westchester Comm Coll (NY)
Western Iowa Tech Comm Coll (IA)
Western Wyoming Comm Coll (WY)
Westmoreland County Comm Coll (PA)
Yakima Valley Comm Coll (WA)
Yavapai Coll (AZ)

Legal Assistant/Paralegal
Albuquerque Tech Vocational Inst (NM)
Alexandria Tech Coll (MN)
Allegany Coll of Maryland (MD)
Alvin Comm Coll (TX)
Andover Coll (ME)
Anne Arundel Comm Coll (MD)
Arapahoe Comm Coll (CO)
Athens Tech Coll (GA)
Atlantic Cape Comm Coll (NJ)
Austin Comm Coll (TX)
Baltimore City Comm Coll (MD)
Bergen Comm Coll (NJ)
Berkeley Coll (NJ)
Berkeley Coll–New York City Campus (NY)
Berkeley Coll–Westchester Campus (NY)
Black Hawk Coll, Moline (IL)
Brazosport Coll (TX)
Brevard Comm Coll (FL)
Briarwood Coll (CT)
Bronx Comm Coll of City U of NY (NY)
Brookdale Comm Coll (NJ)
Broome Comm Coll (NY)
Broward Comm Coll (FL)
Bryant & Stratton Business Inst, Albany (NY)
Bryant & Stratton Business Inst, Amherst Cmps (NY)
Bucks County Comm Coll (PA)
Caldwell Comm Coll and Tech Inst (NC)
Calhoun Comm Coll (AL)
Cape Cod Comm Coll (MA)
Carteret Comm Coll (NC)
Casper Coll (WY)
Catawba Valley Comm Coll (NC)
Central Carolina Comm Coll (NC)
Central Carolina Tech Coll (SC)
Central Comm Coll–Grand Island Campus (NE)
Central Florida Comm Coll (FL)
Central Piedmont Comm Coll (NC)
Central Texas Coll (TX)
Clark Coll (WA)
Clark State Comm Coll (OH)
Clovis Comm Coll (NM)
Coastal Carolina Comm Coll (NC)
Coll of Southern Maryland (MD)
Collin County Comm Coll District (TX)
Colorado Northwestern Comm Coll (CO)
Columbus State Comm Coll (OH)

Comm Coll of Allegheny County (PA)
Comm Coll of Aurora (CO)
Comm Coll of Denver (CO)
Comm Coll of Philadelphia (PA)
Comm Coll of Rhode Island (RI)
Comm Coll of Southern Nevada (NV)
Comm Coll of the Air Force (AL)
Compton Comm Coll (CA)
Corning Comm Coll (NY)
Cuyahoga Comm Coll (OH)
Davenport U, Midland (MI)
Davidson County Comm Coll (NC)
Daytona Beach Comm Coll (FL)
De Anza Coll (CA)
Delaware County Comm Coll (PA)
Delta Coll (MI)
Des Moines Area Comm Coll (IA)
Doña Ana Branch Comm Coll (NM)
Durham Tech Comm Coll (NC)
Dutchess Comm Coll (NY)
Eastern Idaho Tech Coll (ID)
Edison State Comm Coll (OH)
Edmonds Comm Coll (WA)
Elgin Comm Coll (IL)
Erie Business Center, Main (PA)
Erie Comm Coll (NY)
Essex County Coll (NJ)
Eugenio María de Hostos Comm Coll of City U of NY (NY)
Everest Coll (AZ)
Fayetteville Tech Comm Coll (NC)
Finger Lakes Comm Coll (NY)
Florida Comm Coll at Jacksonville (FL)
Florida National Coll (FL)
Forsyth Tech Comm Coll (NC)
Frederick Comm Coll (MD)
Gadsden State Comm Coll (AL)
Gainesville Coll (GA)
Genesee Comm Coll (NY)
Guilford Tech Comm Coll (NC)
Gulf Coast Comm Coll (FL)
Hagerstown Business Coll (MD)
Harford Comm Coll (MD)
Harrisburg Area Comm Coll (PA)
Henry Ford Comm Coll (MI)
Herkimer County Comm Coll (NY)
Hesser Coll (NH)
Highline Comm Coll (WA)
Hinds Comm Coll (MS)
Houston Comm Coll System (TX)
Hudson County Comm Coll (NJ)
Hutchinson Comm Coll and Area Vocational School (KS)
Indian River Comm Coll (FL)
Iowa Lakes Comm Coll (IA)
Iowa Western Comm Coll (IA)
Ivy Tech State Coll–Bloomington (IN)
Ivy Tech State Coll–Central Indiana (IN)
Ivy Tech State Coll–Columbus (IN)
Ivy Tech State Coll–Eastcentral (IN)
Ivy Tech State Coll–Kokomo (IN)

Ivy Tech State Coll–Lafayette (IN)
Ivy Tech State Coll–North Central (IN)
Ivy Tech State Coll–Northeast (IN)
Ivy Tech State Coll–Northwest (IN)
Ivy Tech State Coll–Southcentral (IN)
Ivy Tech State Coll–Southeast (IN)
Ivy Tech State Coll–Southwest (IN)
Ivy Tech State Coll–Wabash Valley (IN)
Ivy Tech State Coll–Whitewater (IN)
James H. Faulkner State Comm Coll (AL)
Jefferson Comm Coll (NY)
Johnson County Comm Coll (KS)
Johnston Comm Coll (NC)
J. Sargeant Reynolds Comm Coll (VA)
Kansas City Kansas Comm Coll (KS)
Kapiolani Comm Coll (HI)
Keiser Coll, Fort Lauderdale (FL)
Keiser Coll, Miami (FL)
Kilgore Coll (TX)
Lackawanna Coll (PA)
Lake Region State Coll (ND)
Lake-Sumter Comm Coll (FL)
Lake Superior Coll (MN)
Lansing Comm Coll (MI)
Lehigh Carbon Comm Coll (PA)
Macomb Comm Coll (MI)
Manchester Comm Coll (CT)
Maria Coll (NY)
Marshall Comm and Tech Coll (WV)
Massachusetts Bay Comm Coll (MA)
McIntosh Coll (NH)
McLennan Comm Coll (TX)
Metropolitan Comm Coll (NE)
Miami Dade Coll (FL)
Midland Coll (TX)
Midlands Tech Coll (SC)
Milwaukee Area Tech Coll (WI)
Minnesota School of Business–Richfield (MN)
Mott Comm Coll (MI)
Mount Wachusett Comm Coll (MA)
Napa Valley Coll (CA)
Nassau Comm Coll (NY)
New River Comm and Tech Coll (WV)
Northampton County Area Comm Coll (PA)
North Central State Coll (OH)
Northeast Alabama Comm Coll (AL)
Northern Essex Comm Coll (MA)
Northern Virginia Comm Coll (VA)
North Hennepin Comm Coll (MN)
North Idaho Coll (ID)
Northland Comm and Tech Coll–Thief River Falls (MN)
North Shore Comm Coll (MA)
Northwestern Connecticut Comm-Tech Coll (CT)
Northwest State Comm Coll (OH)
Oakland Comm Coll (MI)
Ouachita Tech Coll (AR)
Pasco-Hernando Comm Coll (FL)
Penn Valley Comm Coll (MO)
Pima Comm Coll (AZ)
Pioneer Pacific Coll (OR)

Raritan Valley Comm Coll (NJ)
RETS Tech Center (OH)
Rockingham Comm Coll (NC)
Rowan-Cabarrus Comm Coll (NC)
St. Louis Comm Coll at Meramec (MO)
St. Petersburg Coll (FL)
Salt Lake Comm Coll (UT)
San Diego City Coll (CA)
San Diego Miramar Coll (CA)
San Juan Coll (NM)
Schuylkill Inst of Business and Technology (PA)
Seminole Comm Coll (FL)
Sinclair Comm Coll (OH)
South Texas Coll (TX)
South U (FL)
South U (SC)
Southwestern Comm Coll (NC)
Southwestern Michigan Coll (MI)
Surry Comm Coll (NC)
Sussex County Comm Coll (NJ)
Tech Coll of the Lowcountry (SC)
Tompkins Cortland Comm Coll (NY)
Trident Tech Coll (SC)
U of Northwestern Ohio (OH)
Valencia Comm Coll (FL)
Volunteer State Comm Coll (TN)
Westchester Comm Coll (NY)
Western Nevada Comm Coll (NV)
Westmoreland County Comm Coll (PA)
West Virginia State Comm and Tech Coll (WV)
Whatcom Comm Coll (WA)
Wilson Tech Comm Coll (NC)
Yavapai Coll (AZ)

Legal Professions and Studies Related
Essex County Coll (NJ)
Florida National Coll (FL)

Legal Studies
Alvin Comm Coll (TX)
Bay State Coll (MA)
Delta Coll (MI)
Edison State Comm Coll (OH)
Florida National Coll (FL)
Foothill Coll (CA)
Hillsborough Comm Coll (FL)
Iowa Lakes Comm Coll (IA)
Macomb Comm Coll (MI)
Maria Coll (NY)
Metropolitan Comm Coll (NE)
Northland Comm and Tech Coll–Thief River Falls (MN)
Pasadena City Coll (CA)
Santa Barbara City Coll (CA)
Santa Fe Comm Coll (FL)
Trident Tech Coll (SC)

Liberal Arts and Sciences And Humanities Related
Cascadia Comm Coll (WA)
Cleveland Comm Coll (NC)
Hagerstown Comm Coll (MD)
Harford Comm Coll (MD)
Iowa Lakes Comm Coll (IA)
Kansas City Kansas Comm Coll (KS)
Lake Superior Coll (MN)
Northampton County Area Comm Coll (PA)
Oakland Comm Coll (MI)
Platt Coll San Diego (CA)
Southwestern Michigan Coll (MI)
Wor-Wic Comm Coll (MD)

Liberal Arts and Sciences/ Liberal Studies
Adirondack Comm Coll (NY)

Alabama Southern Comm Coll (AL)
Alamance Comm Coll (NC)
Albuquerque Tech Vocational Inst (NM)
Allegany Coll of Maryland (MD)
Alpena Comm Coll (MI)
Alvin Comm Coll (TX)
Amarillo Coll (TX)
American Samoa Comm Coll (AS)
Ancilla Coll (IN)
Anne Arundel Comm Coll (MD)
Anoka-Ramsey Comm Coll (MN)
Anoka-Ramsey Comm Coll, Cambridge Campus (MN)
Arapahoe Comm Coll (CO)
Arizona Western Coll (AZ)
Arkansas State U–Mountain Home (AR)
Asheville-Buncombe Tech Comm Coll (NC)
Ashland Comm and Tech Coll (KY)
Asnuntuck Comm Coll (CT)
Assumption Coll for Sisters (NJ)
Atlantic Cape Comm Coll (NJ)
Austin Comm Coll (TX)
Bainbridge Coll (GA)
Baltimore City Comm Coll (MD)
Barton County Comm Coll (KS)
Bay de Noc Comm Coll (MI)
Bay Mills Comm Coll (MI)
Bay State Coll (MA)
Beaufort County Comm Coll (NC)
Bergen Comm Coll (NJ)
Berkshire Comm Coll (MA)
Bevill State Comm Coll (AL)
Big Bend Comm Coll (WA)
Big Sandy Comm and Tech Coll (KY)
Bishop State Comm Coll (AL)
Bismarck State Coll (ND)
Blackfeet Comm Coll (MT)
Black River Tech Coll (AR)
Bladen Comm Coll (NC)
Blue Mountain Comm Coll (OR)
Blue Ridge Comm Coll (NC)
Blue Ridge Comm Coll (VA)
Blue River Comm Coll (MO)
Borough of Manhattan Comm Coll of City U of NY (NY)
Bossier Parish Comm Coll (LA)
Bowling Green State U-Firelands Coll (OH)
Brazosport Coll (TX)
Brevard Comm Coll (FL)
Bristol Comm Coll (MA)
Bronx Comm Coll of City U of NY (NY)
Brookdale Comm Coll (NJ)
Broome Comm Coll (NY)
Broward Comm Coll (FL)
Brunswick Comm Coll (NC)
Bucks County Comm Coll (PA)
Butler County Comm Coll (KS)
Butler County Comm Coll (PA)
Caldwell Comm Coll and Tech Inst (NC)
Calhoun Comm Coll (AL)
Cape Cod Comm Coll (MA)
Cape Fear Comm Coll (NC)
Capital Comm Coll (CT)
Carroll Comm Coll (MD)
Carteret Comm Coll (NC)
Cascadia Comm Coll (WA)
Casper Coll (WY)
Catawba Valley Comm Coll (NC)

Cayuga County Comm Coll (NY)
Cecil Comm Coll (MD)
Cedar Valley Coll (TX)
Central Alabama Comm Coll (AL)
Central Arizona Coll (AZ)
Central Carolina Comm Coll (NC)
Central Carolina Tech Coll (SC)
Central Comm Coll–Columbus Campus (NE)
Central Comm Coll–Grand Island Campus (NE)
Central Comm Coll–Hastings Campus (NE)
Central Florida Comm Coll (FL)
Centralia Coll (WA)
Central Oregon Comm Coll (OR)
Central Piedmont Comm Coll (NC)
Central Texas Coll (TX)
Century Coll (MN)
Cerro Coso Comm Coll (CA)
Chandler-Gilbert Comm Coll (AZ)
Chattahoochee Valley Comm Coll (AL)
Chattanooga State Tech Comm Coll (TN)
Chemeketa Comm Coll (OR)
Chipola Coll (FL)
Cincinnati State Tech and Comm Coll (OH)
Citrus Coll (CA)
City Colls of Chicago, Wilbur Wright Coll (IL)
Clackamas Comm Coll (OR)
Clarendon Coll (TX)
Clark Coll (WA)
Clark State Comm Coll (OH)
Clatsop Comm Coll (OR)
Cleveland Comm Coll (NC)
Cleveland State Comm Coll (TN)
Clinton Comm Coll (IA)
Clinton Comm Coll (NY)
Cloud County Comm Coll (KS)
Clovis Comm Coll (NM)
Coahoma Comm Coll (MS)
Coastal Bend Coll (TX)
Coastal Carolina Comm Coll (NC)
Coastal Georgia Comm Coll (GA)
Cochise Coll, Douglas (AZ)
Coconino Comm Coll (AZ)
Coffeyville Comm Coll (KS)
Colby Comm Coll (KS)
Coll of DuPage (IL)
Coll of Lake County (IL)
Coll of Southern Idaho (ID)
Coll of Southern Maryland (MD)
Coll of the Canyons (CA)
Coll of the Mainland (TX)
Collin County Comm Coll District (TX)
Colorado Mountn Coll, Alpine Cmps (CO)
Colorado Mountn Coll (CO)
Colorado Mountn Coll, Timberline Cmps (CO)
Colorado Northwestern Comm Coll (CO)
Columbia Coll (CA)
Columbia-Greene Comm Coll (NY)
Columbia State Comm Coll (TN)
Columbus State Comm Coll (OH)
Comm & Tech Coll at West Virginia U Inst of Technology (WV)
Comm Coll of Allegheny County (PA)
Comm Coll of Aurora (CO)
Comm Coll of Beaver County (PA)

Comm Coll of Denver (CO)
Comm Coll of Philadelphia (PA)
Comm Coll of Rhode Island (RI)
Comm Coll of Southern Nevada (NV)
Comm Coll of Vermont (VT)
Compton Comm Coll (CA)
Contra Costa Coll (CA)
Copiah-Lincoln Comm Coll (MS)
Copiah-Lincoln Comm Coll–Natchez Campus (MS)
Corning Comm Coll (NY)
Cossatot Comm Coll of the U of Arkansas (AR)
Cowley County Comm Coll and Voc-Tech School (KS)
Craven Comm Coll (NC)
Crowder Coll (MO)
Cumberland County Coll (NJ)
Cuyahoga Comm Coll (OH)
Dabney S. Lancaster Comm Coll (VA)
Danville Area Comm Coll (IL)
Danville Comm Coll (VA)
Davidson County Comm Coll (NC)
Dawson Comm Coll (MT)
Daytona Beach Comm Coll (FL)
De Anza Coll (CA)
Delaware County Comm Coll (PA)
Delta Coll (MI)
Des Moines Area Comm Coll (IA)
Dixie State Coll of Utah (UT)
Dodge City Comm Coll (KS)
Durham Tech Comm Coll (NC)
Dutchess Comm Coll (NY)
Dyersburg State Comm Coll (TN)
East Arkansas Comm Coll (AR)
East Central Coll (MO)
East Central Comm Coll (MS)
Eastern Arizona Coll (AZ)
Eastern Maine Comm Coll (ME)
Eastern Shore Comm Coll (VA)
Eastfield Coll (TX)
East Mississippi Comm Coll (MS)
Edgecombe Comm Coll (NC)
Edison State Comm Coll (OH)
Edmonds Comm Coll (WA)
Elgin Comm Coll (IL)
Elizabethtown Comm and Tech Coll (KY)
Ellsworth Comm Coll (IA)
El Paso Comm Coll (TX)
Enterprise-Ozark Comm Coll (AL)
Erie Comm Coll (NY)
Erie Comm Coll, North Campus (NY)
Erie Comm Coll, South Campus (NY)
Essex County Coll (NJ)
Estrella Mountain Comm Coll (AZ)
Eugenio María de Hostos Comm Coll of City U of NY (NY)
Everett Comm Coll (WA)
Fayetteville Tech Comm Coll (NC)
Feather River Coll (CA)
Finger Lakes Comm Coll (NY)
Flathead Valley Comm Coll (MT)
Florida Comm Coll at Jacksonville (FL)
Florida Keys Comm Coll (FL)
Florida National Coll (FL)

Foothill Coll (CA)
Fort Peck Comm Coll (MT)
Fort Scott Comm Coll (KS)
Frank Phillips Coll (TX)
Frederick Comm Coll (MD)
Front Range Comm Coll (CO)
Fulton-Montgomery Comm Coll (NY)
Gadsden State Comm Coll (AL)
Gainesville Coll (GA)
Garden City Comm Coll (KS)
Garrett Coll (MD)
GateWay Comm Coll (AZ)
Gateway Comm Coll (CT)
Genesee Comm Coll (NY)
George C. Wallace Comm Coll (AL)
Germanna Comm Coll (VA)
Glendale Comm Coll (AZ)
Glendale Comm Coll (CA)
Glen Oaks Comm Coll (MI)
Gogebic Comm Coll (MI)
Grand Rapids Comm Coll (MI)
Greenfield Comm Coll (MA)
Green River Comm Coll (WA)
Guilford Tech Comm Coll (NC)
Gulf Coast Comm Coll (FL)
Hagerstown Comm Coll (MD)
Halifax Comm Coll (NC)
Harcum Coll (PA)
Harford Comm Coll (MD)
Harrisburg Area Comm Coll (PA)
Hawkeye Comm Coll (IA)
Haywood Comm Coll (NC)
Hazard Comm and Tech Coll (KY)
Heartland Comm Coll (IL)
Henry Ford Comm Coll (MI)
Herkimer County Comm Coll (NY)
Hesser Coll (NH)
Hesston Coll (KS)
Hibbing Comm Coll (MN)
Highland Comm Coll (IL)
Highland Comm Coll (KS)
Hillsborough Comm Coll (FL)
Hinds Comm Coll (MS)
Holmes Comm Coll (MS)
Holy Cross Coll (IN)
Holyoke Comm Coll (MA)
Hopkinsville Comm Coll (KY)
Houston Comm Coll System (TX)
Howard Comm Coll (MD)
Hudson County Comm Coll (NJ)
Hudson Valley Comm Coll (NY)
Hutchinson Comm Coll and Area Vocational School (KS)
Illinois Eastern Comm Colls, Frontier Comm Coll (IL)
Illinois Eastern Comm Colls, Lincoln Trail Coll (IL)
Illinois Eastern Comm Colls, Olney Central Coll (IL)
Illinois Eastern Comm Colls, Wabash Valley Coll (IL)
Illinois Valley Comm Coll (IL)
Independence Comm Coll (KS)
Indian Hills Comm Coll (IA)
Indian River Comm Coll (FL)
Iowa Central Comm Coll (IA)
Iowa Lakes Comm Coll (IA)
Iowa Western Comm Coll (IA)
Isothermal Comm Coll (NC)
Itasca Comm Coll (MN)
Itawamba Comm Coll (MS)
Ivy Tech State Coll–Bloomington (IN)
Ivy Tech State Coll–Central Indiana (IN)
Ivy Tech State Coll–Columbus (IN)

Ivy Tech State Coll–Eastcentral (IN)
Ivy Tech State Coll–Kokomo (IN)
Ivy Tech State Coll–Lafayette (IN)
Ivy Tech State Coll–North Central (IN)
Ivy Tech State Coll–Northeast (IN)
Ivy Tech State Coll–Southcentral (IN)
Ivy Tech State Coll–Southeast (IN)
Ivy Tech State Coll–Southwest (IN)
Ivy Tech State Coll–Wabash Valley (IN)
Ivy Tech State Coll–Whitewater (IN)
Jackson Comm Coll (MI)
Jackson State Comm Coll (TN)
James H. Faulkner State Comm Coll (AL)
James Sprunt Comm Coll (NC)
Jamestown Comm Coll (NY)
Jefferson Comm Coll (KY)
Jefferson Comm Coll (NY)
Jefferson State Comm Coll (AL)
John A. Logan Coll (IL)
Johnson County Comm Coll (KS)
Johnston Comm Coll (NC)
John Tyler Comm Coll (VA)
John Wood Comm Coll (IL)
J. Sargeant Reynolds Comm Coll (VA)
Kalamazoo Valley Comm Coll (MI)
Kansas City Kansas Comm Coll (KS)
Kapiolani Comm Coll (HI)
Kaskaskia Coll (IL)
Kauai Comm Coll (HI)
Kennebec Valley Comm Coll (ME)
Kent State U, Tuscarawas Campus (OH)
Keystone Coll (PA)
Kingsborough Comm Coll of City U of NY (NY)
Lac Courte Oreilles Ojibwa Comm Coll (WI)
Lackawanna Coll (PA)
Lake Land Coll (IL)
Lake Region State Coll (ND)
Lake-Sumter Comm Coll (FL)
Lake Superior Coll (MN)
Landmark Coll (VT)
Lane Comm Coll (OR)
Lansing Comm Coll (MI)
Laredo Comm Coll (TX)
Lehigh Carbon Comm Coll (PA)
Lewis and Clark Comm Coll (IL)
Lincoln Land Comm Coll (IL)
Linn-Benton Comm Coll (OR)
Long Beach City Coll (CA)
Longview Comm Coll (MO)
Lower Columbia Coll (WA)
Macomb Comm Coll (MI)
Manchester Comm Coll (CT)
Maple Woods Comm Coll (MO)
Maria Coll (NY)
Marshall Comm and Tech Coll (WV)
Massachusetts Bay Comm Coll (MA)
Mayland Comm Coll (NC)
McDowell Tech Comm Coll (NC)
McLennan Comm Coll (TX)
Mesabi Range Comm and Tech Coll (MN)
Metropolitan Comm Coll (NE)

Metropolitan Comm Coll-Business & Technology College (MO)
Middle Georgia Coll (GA)
Midland Coll (TX)
Midlands Tech Coll (SC)
Mid Michigan Comm Coll (MI)
Mid-South Comm Coll (AR)
Milwaukee Area Tech Coll (WI)
Mineral Area Coll (MO)
Minneapolis Comm and Tech Coll (MN)
Moberly Area Comm Coll (MO)
Mohave Comm Coll (AZ)
Mohawk Valley Comm Coll (NY)
Montcalm Comm Coll (MI)
Montgomery Comm Coll (NC)
Montgomery County Comm Coll (PA)
Moraine Valley Comm Coll (IL)
Motlow State Comm Coll (TN)
Mott Comm Coll (MI)
Mount Wachusett Comm Coll (MA)
Muscatine Comm Coll (IA)
Muskegon Comm Coll (MI)
Nassau Comm Coll (NY)
Nebraska Indian Comm Coll (NE)
New Hampshire Comm Tech Coll, Manchester/Stratham (NH)
New Mexico Military Inst (NM)
New River Comm and Tech Coll (WV)
Niagara County Comm Coll (NY)
Northampton County Area Comm Coll (PA)
North Central Missouri Coll (MO)
North Country Comm Coll (NY)
North Dakota State Coll of Science (ND)
Northeast Alabama Comm Coll (AL)
Northeastern Tech Coll (SC)
Northeast State Tech Comm Coll (TN)
Northern Essex Comm Coll (MA)
Northern Virginia Comm Coll (VA)
North Hennepin Comm Coll (MN)
North Idaho Coll (ID)
North Iowa Area Comm Coll (IA)
North Lake Coll (TX)
Northland Comm and Tech Coll–Thief River Falls (MN)
North Seattle Comm Coll (WA)
North Shore Comm Coll (MA)
Northwestern Connecticut Comm-Tech Coll (CT)
Northwestern Michigan Coll (MI)
Northwest-Shoals Comm Coll (AL)
Oakland Comm Coll (MI)
Odessa Coll (TX)
Olympic Coll (WA)
Orange Coast Coll (CA)
Orange County Comm Coll (NY)
Otero Jr Coll (CO)
Ouachita Tech Coll (AR)
Owensboro Comm and Tech Coll (KY)
Palm Beach Comm Coll (FL)
Paradise Valley Comm Coll (AZ)
Parkland Coll (IL)

Pasadena City Coll (CA)
Pasco-Hernando Comm Coll (FL)
Patrick Henry Comm Coll (VA)
Pennsylvania Highland Comm Coll (PA)
Penn State U Beaver Campus of the Commonwealth Coll (PA)
Penn State U Delaware County Campus of the Commonwealth Coll (PA)
Penn State U DuBois Campus of the Commonwealth Coll (PA)
Penn State U Fayette Campus of the Commonwealth Coll (PA)
Penn State U Hazleton Campus of the Commonwealth Coll (PA)
Penn State U McKeesport Campus of the Commonwealth Coll (PA)
Penn State U Mont Alto Campus of the Commonwealth Coll (PA)
Penn State U New Kensington Campus of the Commonwealth Coll (PA)
Penn State U Shenango Campus of the Commonwealth Coll (PA)
Penn State U Wilkes-Barre Campus of the Commonwealth Coll (PA)
Penn State U Worthington Scranton Cmps Commonwealth Coll (PA)
Penn State U York Campus of the Commonwealth Coll (PA)
Penn Valley Comm Coll (MO)
Phillips Comm Coll of the U of Arkansas (AR)
Piedmont Comm Coll (NC)
Piedmont Virginia Comm Coll (VA)
Pima Comm Coll (AZ)
Polk Comm Coll (FL)
Prairie State Coll (IL)
Pratt Comm Coll and Area Vocational School (KS)
Queensborough Comm Coll of City U of NY (NY)
Quinebaug Valley Comm Coll (CT)
Rainy River Comm Coll (MN)
Randolph Comm Coll (NC)
Raritan Valley Comm Coll (NJ)
Richard Bland Coll of the Coll of William and Mary (VA)
Richland Comm Coll (IL)
Richmond Comm Coll (NC)
Rich Mountain Comm Coll (AR)
Riverland Comm Coll (MN)
River Parishes Comm Coll (LA)
Riverside Comm Coll District (CA)
Roanoke-Chowan Comm Coll (NC)
Rochester Comm and Tech Coll (MN)
Rockingham Comm Coll (NC)
Rockland Comm Coll (NY)
Rock Valley Coll (IL)
Rogue Comm Coll (OR)
Rowan-Cabarrus Comm Coll (NC)
Saint Charles Comm Coll (MO)
St. Louis Comm Coll at Forest Park (MO)
St. Louis Comm Coll at Meramec (MO)
St. Petersburg Coll (FL)
St. Philip's Coll (TX)

Salt Lake Comm Coll (UT)
San Antonio Coll (TX)
Sandhills Comm Coll (NC)
San Diego City Coll (CA)
San Diego Miramar Coll (CA)
San Joaquin Delta Coll (CA)
Santa Barbara City Coll (CA)
Santa Fe Comm Coll (FL)
Santa Rosa Jr Coll (CA)
Sauk Valley Comm Coll (IL)
Schoolcraft Coll (MI)
Scott Comm Coll (IA)
Seattle Central Comm Coll (WA)
Seminole Comm Coll (FL)
Seminole State Coll (OK)
Seward County Comm Coll (KS)
Shawnee Comm Coll (IL)
Shelton State Comm Coll (AL)
Sheridan Coll (WY)
Shoreline Comm Coll (WA)
Sinclair Comm Coll (OH)
Sisseton-Wahpeton Comm Coll (SD)
Snow Coll (UT)
Solano Comm Coll (CA)
Southeast Comm Coll, Lincoln Campus (NE)
Southeast Kentucky Comm and Tech Coll (KY)
Southern Maine Comm Coll (ME)
Southern State Comm Coll (OH)
Southern Union State Comm Coll (AL)
South Mountain Comm Coll (AZ)
Southside Virginia Comm Coll (VA)
South Texas Coll (TX)
Southwestern Comm Coll (IA)
Southwestern Comm Coll (NC)
Southwestern Michigan Coll (MI)
Southwestern Oregon Comm Coll (OR)
Spartanburg Methodist Coll (SC)
Spartanburg Tech Coll (SC)
Springfield Tech Comm Coll (MA)
State U of NY Coll of Technology at Alfred (NY)
State U of NY Coll of Technology at Canton (NY)
Surry Comm Coll (NC)
Sussex County Comm Coll (NJ)
Tacoma Comm Coll (WA)
Taft Coll (CA)
Tech Coll of the Lowcountry (SC)
Temple Coll (TX)
Three Rivers Comm Coll (CT)
Three Rivers Comm Coll (MO)
Tillamook Bay Comm Coll (OR)
Tompkins Cortland Comm Coll (NY)
Tri-County Comm Coll (NC)
Tri-County Tech Coll (SC)
Trident Tech Coll (SC)
Trinidad State Jr Coll (CO)
Trinity Valley Comm Coll (TX)
Truckee Meadows Comm Coll (NV)
Truett-McConnell Coll (GA)
Tunxis Comm Coll (CT)
Umpqua Comm Coll (OR)
Union County Coll (NJ)
The U of Akron–Wayne Coll (OH)
U of Alaska Anchorage, Matanuska-Susitna Coll (AK)

U of Arkansas Comm Coll at Hope (AR)
U of Arkansas Comm Coll at Morrilton (AR)
U of Cincinnati Raymond Walters Coll (OH)
U of Pittsburgh at Titusville (PA)
U of South Carolina at Sumter (SC)
U of South Carolina at Union (SC)
U of Wisconsin Center–Baraboo/ Sauk County (WI)
U of Wisconsin Center–Barron County (WI)
U of Wisconsin Center–Marathon County (WI)
U of Wisconsin Center–Marinette (WI)
U of Wisconsin Center–Richland (WI)
U of Wisconsin Center–Rock County (WI)
U of Wisconsin Center–Sheboygan County (WI)
U of Wisconsin Center–Washington County (WI)
Valencia Comm Coll (FL)
Villa Maria Coll of Buffalo (NY)
Volunteer State Comm Coll (TN)
Wake Tech Comm Coll (NC)
Walla Walla Comm Coll (WA)
Walters State Comm Coll (TN)
Waubonsee Comm Coll (IL)
Wayne County Comm Coll District (MI)
Westchester Comm Coll (NY)
Western Iowa Tech Comm Coll (IA)
Western Nevada Comm Coll (NV)
Western Oklahoma State Coll (OK)
Western Wyoming Comm Coll (WY)
Westmoreland County Comm Coll (PA)
West Virginia U at Parkersburg (WV)
Whatcom Comm Coll (WA)
Wilkes Comm Coll (NC)
Williston State Coll (ND)
Wilson Tech Comm Coll (NC)
Windward Comm Coll (HI)
Yakima Valley Comm Coll (WA)
Yavapai Coll (AZ)

Library Assistant
Black Hawk Coll, Moline (IL)
Citrus Coll (CA)
Clovis Comm Coll (NM)
Coll of DuPage (IL)
Oakland Comm Coll (MI)

Library Science
Allen County Comm Coll (KS)
American Samoa Comm Coll (AS)
Brazosport Coll (TX)
Brookdale Comm Coll (NJ)
Citrus Coll (CA)
City Colls of Chicago, Wilbur Wright Coll (IL)
Colby Comm Coll (KS)
Coll of DuPage (IL)
Coll of Southern Idaho (ID)
Comm Coll of Philadelphia (PA)
Copiah-Lincoln Comm Coll (MS)
Doña Ana Branch Comm Coll (NM)
East Central Coll (MO)
East Central Comm Coll (MS)
Foothill Coll (CA)
Highland Comm Coll (KS)

Highline Comm Coll (WA)
Indian River Comm Coll (FL)
Itawamba Comm Coll (MS)
Northwest Tech Coll (MN)
Pasadena City Coll (CA)
Riverside Comm Coll District (CA)
U of Cincinnati Raymond Walters Coll (OH)

Lineworker
Bismarck State Coll (ND)
Ivy Tech State Coll–Lafayette (IN)
Lehigh Carbon Comm Coll (PA)
Linn State Tech Coll (MO)
Lower Columbia Coll (WA)

Linguistics
Foothill Coll (CA)

Literature
Andrew Coll (GA)
Atlantic Cape Comm Coll (NJ)
Bergen Comm Coll (NJ)
Comm Coll of Southern Nevada (NV)
Compton Comm Coll (CA)
East Central Comm Coll (MS)
Foothill Coll (CA)
Iowa Lakes Comm Coll (IA)
Lincoln Land Comm Coll (IL)
Miami Dade Coll (FL)
Midland Coll (TX)
Otero Jr Coll (CO)
Palm Beach Comm Coll (FL)
Pratt Comm Coll and Area Vocational School (KS)
St. Louis Comm Coll at Meramec (MO)
San Joaquin Delta Coll (CA)
Seward County Comm Coll (KS)
Tacoma Comm Coll (WA)

Livestock Management
Barton County Comm Coll (KS)
Ohio State U Ag Tech Inst (OH)

Logistics and Materials Management
Columbus State Comm Coll (OH)
Comm Coll of the Air Force (AL)
Houston Comm Coll System (TX)
Lehigh Carbon Comm Coll (PA)
Prairie State Coll (IL)
Sinclair Comm Coll (OH)
Springfield Tech Comm Coll (MA)
Waubonsee Comm Coll (IL)

Machine Shop Technology
Cape Fear Comm Coll (NC)
Coll of Lake County (IL)
Comm Coll of Allegheny County (PA)
Corning Comm Coll (NY)
Eastern Arizona Coll (AZ)
Erie Comm Coll, North Campus (NY)
Florida Comm Coll at Jacksonville (FL)
Front Range Comm Coll (CO)
Gadsden State Comm Coll-Ayers Campus (AL)
Illinois Eastern Comm Colls, Wabash Valley Coll (IL)
Ivy Tech State Coll–Central Indiana (IN)
Maple Woods Comm Coll (MO)
Metropolitan Comm Coll-Business & Technology College (MO)
Modesto Jr Coll (CA)
North Dakota State Coll of Science (ND)

North Iowa Area Comm Coll (IA)
Northwestern Michigan Coll (MI)
Orange Coast Coll (CA)
Pima Comm Coll (AZ)
Riverland Comm Coll (MN)
Southwestern Michigan Coll (MI)
U of Arkansas Comm Coll at Hope (AR)

Machine Tool Technology
Alamance Comm Coll (NC)
Alexandria Tech Coll (MN)
Amarillo Coll (TX)
Asheville-Buncombe Tech Comm Coll (NC)
Athens Tech Coll (GA)
Bay de Noc Comm Coll (MI)
Black Hawk Coll, Moline (IL)
Blue Ridge Comm Coll (NC)
Brazosport Coll (TX)
Butler County Comm Coll (PA)
Calhoun Comm Coll (AL)
Casper Coll (WY)
Central Comm Coll–Columbus Campus (NE)
Central Comm Coll–Hastings Campus (NE)
Central Piedmont Comm Coll (NC)
Century Coll (MN)
Cerro Coso Comm Coll (CA)
Chattanooga State Tech Comm Coll (TN)
City Colls of Chicago, Wilbur Wright Coll (IL)
Clackamas Comm Coll (OR)
Clark Coll (WA)
Clinton Comm Coll (IA)
Clover Park Tech Coll (WA)
Coffeyville Comm Coll (KS)
Coll of DuPage (IL)
Compton Comm Coll (CA)
Corning Comm Coll (NY)
Cowley County Comm Coll and Voc-Tech School (KS)
De Anza Coll (CA)
Delaware County Comm Coll (PA)
Delta Coll (MI)
Des Moines Area Comm Coll (IA)
Durham Tech Comm Coll (NC)
East Central Coll (MO)
Eastern Maine Comm Coll (ME)
Elgin Comm Coll (IL)
Fayetteville Tech Comm Coll (NC)
Forsyth Tech Comm Coll (NC)
Gadsden State Comm Coll-Ayers Campus (AL)
George Corley Wallace State Comm Coll (AL)
George C. Wallace Comm Coll (AL)
Glendale Comm Coll (CA)
Green River Comm Coll (WA)
Guilford Tech Comm Coll (NC)
Gwinnett Tech Coll (GA)
Hawkeye Comm Coll (IA)
Haywood Comm Coll (NC)
Heartland Comm Coll (IL)
Hinds Comm Coll (MS)
Hudson Valley Comm Coll (NY)
Hutchinson Comm Coll and Area Vocational School (KS)
Indian Hills Comm Coll (IA)
Iowa Central Comm Coll (IA)
Iowa Western Comm Coll (IA)
Isothermal Comm Coll (NC)
Ivy Tech State Coll–Bloomington (IN)
Ivy Tech State Coll–Central Indiana (IN)

Ivy Tech State Coll–Columbus (IN)
Ivy Tech State Coll–Eastcentral (IN)
Ivy Tech State Coll–Kokomo (IN)
Ivy Tech State Coll–Lafayette (IN)
Ivy Tech State Coll–North Central (IN)
Ivy Tech State Coll–Northeast (IN)
Ivy Tech State Coll–Northwest (IN)
Ivy Tech State Coll–Southcentral (IN)
Ivy Tech State Coll–Southwest (IN)
Ivy Tech State Coll–Wabash Valley (IN)
Ivy Tech State Coll–Whitewater (IN)
J. F. Drake State Tech Coll (AL)
John A. Logan Coll (IL)
Johnson County Comm Coll (KS)
Johnston Comm Coll (NC)
Kalamazoo Valley Comm Coll (MI)
Kennebec Valley Comm Coll (ME)
Kilgore Coll (TX)
Lake Superior Coll (MN)
Lansing Comm Coll (MI)
Lewis and Clark Comm Coll (IL)
Linn-Benton Comm Coll (OR)
Linn State Tech Coll (MO)
Long Beach City Coll (CA)
Lower Columbia Coll (WA)
Macomb Comm Coll (MI)
Maple Woods Comm Coll (MO)
McDowell Tech Comm Coll (NC)
Meridian Comm Coll (MS)
Mid Michigan Comm Coll (MI)
Milwaukee Area Tech Coll (WI)
Minnesota State Coll–Southeast Tech (MN)
Modesto Jr Coll (CA)
Muscatine Comm Coll (IA)
Muskegon Comm Coll (MI)
Napa Valley Coll (CA)
North Central State Coll (OH)
Northeastern Tech Coll (SC)
Northeast State Tech Comm Coll (TN)
Northern Essex Comm Coll (MA)
North Idaho Coll (ID)
North Iowa Area Comm Coll (IA)
Northwest State Comm Coll (OH)
Oakland Comm Coll (MI)
Odessa Coll (TX)
Orange Coast Coll (CA)
Ouachita Tech Coll (AR)
Pasadena City Coll (CA)
Randolph Comm Coll (NC)
Ranken Tech Coll (MO)
Richmond Comm Coll (NC)
St. Cloud Tech Coll (MN)
Salt Lake Comm Coll (UT)
San Diego City Coll (CA)
San Joaquin Delta Coll (CA)
Scott Comm Coll (IA)
Shawnee Comm Coll (IL)
Sheridan Coll (WY)
Shoreline Comm Coll (WA)
Sinclair Comm Coll (OH)
Solano Comm Coll (CA)
Somerset Comm Coll (KY)
South Central Tech Coll (MN)
Southeast Comm Coll, Lincoln Campus (NE)
Southeast Comm Coll, Milford Campus (NE)
Southeast Tech Inst (SD)

Southern Maine Comm Coll (ME)
South Texas Coll (TX)
Southwestern Oregon Comm Coll (OR)
Southwest Wisconsin Tech Coll (WI)
Spartanburg Tech Coll (SC)
State U of NY Coll of Technology at Alfred (NY)
Surry Comm Coll (NC)
Texas State Tech Coll–Waco/Marshall Campus (TX)
Thaddeus Stevens Coll of Technology (PA)
Tri-County Tech Coll (SC)
Trident Tech Coll (SC)
U of Arkansas Comm Coll at Morrilton (AR)
Wake Tech Comm Coll (NC)
Walla Walla Comm Coll (WA)
Western Iowa Tech Comm Coll (IA)
Western Nevada Comm Coll (NV)
West Virginia U at Parkersburg (WV)
Yuba Coll (CA)

Management Information Systems
Academy Coll (MN)
Allegany Coll of Maryland (MD)
Arapahoe Comm Coll (CO)
Ashland Comm and Tech Coll (KY)
Big Sandy Comm and Tech Coll (KY)
Bristol Comm Coll (MA)
Central Wyoming Coll (WY)
Century Coll (MN)
Chandler-Gilbert Comm Coll (AZ)
Cincinnati State Tech and Comm Coll (OH)
Clovis Comm Coll (NM)
Comm Coll of Allegheny County (PA)
Comm Coll of the Air Force (AL)
Craven Comm Coll (NC)
Delaware County Comm Coll (PA)
Delaware Tech & Comm Coll, Stanton/ Wilmington Cmps (DE)
East Central Coll (MO)
Fayetteville Tech Comm Coll (NC)
Front Range Comm Coll (CO)
Glendale Comm Coll (AZ)
Gwinnett Tech Coll (GA)
Hagerstown Comm Coll (MD)
Harford Comm Coll (MD)
Harrisburg Area Comm Coll (PA)
Haywood Comm Coll (NC)
Heartland Comm Coll (IL)
Hesser Coll (NH)
Hopkinsville Comm Coll (KY)
Hutchinson Comm Coll and Area Vocational School (KS)
Jackson State Comm Coll (TN)
John Tyler Comm Coll (VA)
Kalamazoo Valley Comm Coll (MI)
Kilgore Coll (TX)
Lackawanna Coll (PA)
Lake Region State Coll (ND)
Lake Superior Coll (MN)
Lansing Comm Coll (MI)
Lower Columbia Coll (WA)
Manchester Comm Coll (CT)
Manhattan Area Tech Coll (KS)
Miami Dade Coll (FL)
Miami U Hamilton (OH)
Modesto Jr Coll (CA)
Montcalm Comm Coll (MI)

Montgomery Comm Coll (NC)
Mott Comm Coll (MI)
Mount Wachusett Comm Coll (MA)
Napa Valley Coll (CA)
Nassau Comm Coll (NY)
New England Coll of Finance (MA)
New Hampshire Comm Tech Coll, Manchester/Stratham (NH)
North Hennepin Comm Coll (MN)
Northwestern Michigan Coll (MI)
Ouachita Tech Coll (AR)
Owens Comm Coll, Toledo (OH)
Raritan Valley Comm Coll (NJ)
Southeast Kentucky Comm and Tech Coll (KY)
Southern Maine Comm Coll (ME)
Southwestern Oregon Comm Coll (OR)
Trinidad State Jr Coll (CO)
Union County Coll (NJ)
The U of Akron–Wayne Coll (OH)
U of Cincinnati Raymond Walters Coll (OH)
Western Nevada Comm Coll (NV)
Western Oklahoma State Coll (OK)
Yakima Valley Comm Coll (WA)

Management Information Systems and Services Related
Cedar Valley Coll (TX)
Central Florida Comm Coll (FL)
Cleveland Comm Coll (NC)
Indiana Business Coll, Columbus (IN)
Indiana Business Coll, Indianapolis (IN)
Indiana Business Coll, Lafayette (IN)
Indiana Business Coll, Muncie (IN)
Indiana Business Coll, Terre Haute (IN)
Metropolitan Comm Coll-Business & Technology College (MO)
Mid-South Comm Coll (AR)
Mohawk Valley Comm Coll (NY)
Montgomery County Comm Coll (PA)
Oakland Comm Coll (MI)

Management Science
Black Hawk Coll, Moline (IL)
Cape Cod Comm Coll (MA)
Fayetteville Tech Comm Coll (NC)
GateWay Comm Coll (AZ)
Harrisburg Area Comm Coll (PA)
Hazard Comm and Tech Coll (KY)
Oakland Comm Coll (MI)
Prairie State Coll (IL)
Tillamook Bay Comm Coll (OR)
Western Nevada Comm Coll (NV)

Manufacturing Engineering
Bristol Comm Coll (MA)
Penn State U Fayette Campus of the Commonwealth Coll (PA)
Penn State U Hazleton Campus of the Commonwealth Coll (PA)

Penn State U Wilkes-Barre Campus of the Commonwealth Coll (PA)
Penn State U York Campus of the Commonwealth Coll (PA)

Manufacturing Technology
Albany Tech Coll (GA)
Alpena Comm Coll (MI)
Black Hawk Coll, Moline (IL)
Brevard Comm Coll (FL)
Clark Coll (WA)
Coll of DuPage (IL)
Hopkinsville Comm Coll (KY)
Hutchinson Comm Coll and Area Vocational School (KS)
Lehigh Carbon Comm Coll (PA)
Luna Comm Coll (NM)
Macomb Comm Coll (MI)
Marshall Comm and Tech Coll (WV)
Mott Comm Coll (MI)
Oakland Comm Coll (MI)
Owens Comm Coll, Toledo (OH)

Marine Biology and Biological Oceanography
Colorado Northwestern Comm Coll (CO)
Daytona Beach Comm Coll (FL)
Dixie State Coll of Utah (UT)
Florida Keys Comm Coll (FL)
Massachusetts Bay Comm Coll (MA)
Shoreline Comm Coll (WA)
Southern Maine Comm Coll (ME)

Marine Maintenance and Ship Repair Technology
Alexandria Tech Coll (MN)
Cape Fear Comm Coll (NC)
Iowa Lakes Comm Coll (IA)
Olympic Coll (WA)

Marine Science/Merchant Marine Officer
Anne Arundel Comm Coll (MD)
Indian River Comm Coll (FL)
Northwestern Michigan Coll (MI)

Marine Technology
Cape Fear Comm Coll (NC)
Florida Keys Comm Coll (FL)
Highline Comm Coll (WA)
Kingsborough Comm Coll of City U of NY (NY)
North Idaho Coll (ID)
Northwest Tech Coll (MN)
Orange Coast Coll (CA)
Santa Barbara City Coll (CA)
Seattle Central Comm Coll (WA)
Shoreline Comm Coll (WA)

Marine Transportation Related
Northwestern Michigan Coll (MI)

Maritime Science
Northwestern Michigan Coll (MI)

Marketing/Marketing Management
Adirondack Comm Coll (NY)
Alexandria Tech Coll (MN)
Allegany Coll of Maryland (MD)
Alvin Comm Coll (TX)
Anne Arundel Comm Coll (MD)
Anoka-Ramsey Comm Coll (MN)
Anoka-Ramsey Comm Coll, Cambridge Campus (MN)
Arapahoe Comm Coll (CO)
Athens Tech Coll (GA)
Augusta Tech Coll (GA)
Austin Comm Coll (TX)
Bainbridge Coll (GA)

Baltimore City Comm Coll (MD)
Barton County Comm Coll (KS)
Bay de Noc Comm Coll (MI)
Berkeley Coll (NJ)
Berkeley Coll-New York City Campus (NY)
Berkeley Coll-Westchester Campus (NY)
Blue Mountain Comm Coll (OR)
Blue Ridge Comm Coll (NC)
Borough of Manhattan Comm Coll of City U of NY (NY)
Brazosport Coll (TX)
Bristol Comm Coll (MA)
Bronx Comm Coll of City U of NY (NY)
Brookdale Comm Coll (NJ)
Broward Comm Coll (FL)
Bucks County Comm Coll (PA)
Butler County Comm Coll (KS)
Butler County Comm Coll (PA)
Casper Coll (WY)
Catawba Valley Comm Coll (NC)
Cayuga County Comm Coll (NY)
Cecil Comm Coll (MD)
Cedar Valley Coll (TX)
Central Arizona Coll (AZ)
Central Carolina Comm Coll (NC)
Central Comm Coll-Columbus Campus (NE)
Central Florida Comm Coll (FL)
Centralia Coll (WA)
Central Oregon Comm Coll (OR)
Central Piedmont Comm Coll (NC)
Central Texas Coll (TX)
Chattahoochee Tech Coll (GA)
Cincinnati State Tech and Comm Coll (OH)
City Colls of Chicago, Wilbur Wright Coll (IL)
Clarendon Coll (TX)
Clover Park Tech Coll (WA)
Coffeyville Comm Coll (KS)
Colby Comm Coll (KS)
Coll of DuPage (IL)
Coll of Southern Idaho (ID)
Colorado Mountn Coll, Alpine Cmps (CO)
Columbus State Comm Coll (OH)
Comm Coll of Allegheny County (PA)
Comm Coll of Aurora (CO)
Comm Coll of Beaver County (PA)
Comm Coll of Philadelphia (PA)
Comm Coll of Rhode Island (RI)
Comm Coll of Southern Nevada (NV)
Copiah-Lincoln Comm Coll–Natchez Campus (MS)
Cowley County Comm Coll and Voc-Tech School (KS)
Cumberland County Coll (NJ)
Cuyahoga Comm Coll (OH)
Danville Area Comm Coll (IL)
Danville Comm Coll (VA)
Daytona Beach Comm Coll (FL)
De Anza Coll (CA)
DeKalb Tech Coll (GA)
Delaware Tech & Comm Coll, Jack F Owens Cmps (DE)

Delaware Tech & Comm Coll, Stanton/ Wilmington Cmps (DE)
Delta Coll (MI)
Des Moines Area Comm Coll (IA)
Dodge City Comm Coll (KS)
East Central Coll (MO)
Eastern Idaho Tech Coll (ID)
Edison State Comm Coll (OH)
Edmonds Comm Coll (WA)
Elgin Comm Coll (IL)
Ellsworth Comm Coll (IA)
Enterprise-Ozark Comm Coll (AL)
Erie Business Center, Main (PA)
Erie Business Center South (PA)
Everett Comm Coll (WA)
Fayetteville Tech Comm Coll (NC)
Finger Lakes Comm Coll (NY)
Florida Comm Coll at Jacksonville (FL)
Forsyth Tech Comm Coll (NC)
Fox Valley Tech Coll (WI)
Frederick Comm Coll (MD)
Gainesville Coll (GA)
Garden City Comm Coll (KS)
Genesee Comm Coll (NY)
Greenfield Comm Coll (MA)
Green River Comm Coll (WA)
Guam Comm Coll (GU)
Gwinnett Tech Coll (GA)
Hagerstown Business Coll (MD)
Halifax Comm Coll (NC)
Harrisburg Area Comm Coll (PA)
Hawkeye Comm Coll (IA)
Henry Ford Comm Coll (MI)
Herkimer County Comm Coll (NY)
Hesser Coll (NH)
Highland Comm Coll (IL)
Hillsborough Comm Coll (FL)
Hinds Comm Coll (MS)
Houston Comm Coll System (TX)
Hudson Valley Comm Coll (NY)
Illinois Valley Comm Coll (IL)
Indian River Comm Coll (FL)
Iowa Lakes Comm Coll (IA)
Iowa Western Comm Coll (IA)
Isothermal Comm Coll (NC)
Itawamba Comm Coll (MS)
Jackson Comm Coll (MI)
Jefferson Comm Coll (NY)
John A. Logan Coll (IL)
J. Sargeant Reynolds Comm Coll (VA)
Kalamazoo Valley Comm Coll (MI)
Kapiolani Comm Coll (HI)
Kennebec Valley Comm Coll (ME)
Kingsborough Comm Coll of City U of NY (NY)
Lake Land Coll (IL)
Lansing Comm Coll (MI)
Laredo Comm Coll (TX)
Long Beach City Coll (CA)
Longview Comm Coll (MO)
Macomb Comm Coll (MI)
Manchester Comm Coll (CT)
Maple Woods Comm Coll (MO)
McDowell Tech Comm Coll (NC)
Meridian Comm Coll (MS)
Miami Dade Coll (FL)
Miami U Hamilton (OH)
Mid Michigan Comm Coll (MI)
Milwaukee Area Tech Coll (WI)
Mineral Area Coll (MO)

Minnesota State Coll–Southeast Tech (MN)
Moberly Area Comm Coll (MO)
Modesto Jr Coll (CA)
Mohave Comm Coll (AZ)
Mott Comm Coll (MI)
Muskegon Comm Coll (MI)
Napa Valley Coll (CA)
Nassau Comm Coll (NY)
National Coll of Business & Technology, Salem (VA)
New England Coll of Finance (MA)
New Hampshire Comm Tech Coll, Manchester/Stratham (NH)
New River Comm and Tech Coll (WV)
North Central Missouri Coll (MO)
Northeastern Tech Coll (SC)
Northern Essex Comm Coll (MA)
Northern Virginia Comm Coll (VA)
North Hennepin Comm Coll (MN)
Northland Comm and Tech Coll–Thief River Falls (MN)
North Shore Comm Coll (MA)
Northwestern Michigan Coll (MI)
Northwest State Comm Coll (OH)
Northwest Tech Coll (MN)
Orange Coast Coll (CA)
Orange County Comm Coll (NY)
Ouachita Tech Coll (AR)
Owens Comm Coll, Findlay (OH)
Owens Comm Coll, Toledo (OH)
Palm Beach Comm Coll (FL)
Pasadena City Coll (CA)
Pasco-Hernando Comm Coll (FL)
Penn Valley Comm Coll (MO)
Piedmont Virginia Comm Coll (VA)
Polk Comm Coll (FL)
Pratt Comm Coll and Area Vocational School (KS)
Raritan Valley Comm Coll (NJ)
Rasmussen Coll St. Cloud (MN)
Rockland Comm Coll (NY)
Rock Valley Coll (IL)
Saint Charles Comm Coll (MO)
St. Cloud Tech Coll (MN)
St. Petersburg Coll (FL)
Salt Lake Comm Coll (UT)
San Diego City Coll (CA)
San Joaquin Delta Coll (CA)
Santa Barbara City Coll (CA)
Santa Fe Comm Coll (FL)
Sauk Valley Comm Coll (IL)
Schoolcraft Coll (MI)
Seminole Comm Coll (FL)
Seward County Comm Coll (KS)
Shoreline Comm Coll (WA)
Sinclair Comm Coll (OH)
Solano Comm Coll (CA)
Southeastern Tech Coll (GA)
Southeast Tech Inst (SD)
South Hills School of Business & Technology, State College (PA)
Southwestern Comm Coll (IA)
Southwestern Comm Coll (NC)
Southwestern Oregon Comm Coll (OR)
Southwest Wisconsin Tech Coll (WI)
Spartanburg Tech Coll (SC)

Springfield Tech Comm Coll (MA)
State U of NY Coll of Technology at Alfred (NY)
State U of NY Coll of Technology at Delhi (NY)
Tech Coll of the Lowcountry (SC)
Three Rivers Comm Coll (CT)
Three Rivers Comm Coll (MO)
Tompkins Cortland Comm Coll (NY)
Trident Tech Coll (SC)
Trinidad State Jr Coll (CO)
Trinity Valley Comm Coll (TX)
Truckee Meadows Comm Coll (NV)
Tunxis Comm Coll (CT)
Umpqua Comm Coll (OR)
U of Arkansas Comm Coll at Morrilton (AR)
U of Cincinnati Raymond Walters Coll (OH)
U of Northwestern Ohio (OH)
Valencia Comm Coll (FL)
Wayne County Comm Coll District (MI)
West Central Tech Coll (GA)
Westchester Comm Coll (NY)
Western Nevada Comm Coll (NV)
Western Wyoming Comm Coll (WY)
West Georgia Tech Coll (GA)
Westmoreland County Comm Coll (PA)
West Virginia U at Parkersburg (WV)
Williston State Coll (ND)
Yakima Valley Comm Coll (WA)

Marketing Related
Black Hawk Coll, Moline (IL)
Oakland Comm Coll (MI)
Tillamook Bay Comm Coll (OR)
West Virginia State Comm and Tech Coll (WV)

Marketing Research
Guam Comm Coll (GU)
Lake Region State Coll (ND)
Riverside Comm Coll District (CA)

Masonry
Alexandria Tech Coll (MN)
Fayetteville Tech Comm Coll (NC)
Florida Comm Coll at Jacksonville (FL)
Ivy Tech State Coll–Central Indiana (IN)
Ivy Tech State Coll–Columbus (IN)
Ivy Tech State Coll–Eastcentral (IN)
Ivy Tech State Coll–Lafayette (IN)
Ivy Tech State Coll–North Central (IN)
Ivy Tech State Coll–Northeast (IN)
Ivy Tech State Coll–Northwest (IN)
Ivy Tech State Coll–Southcentral (IN)
Ivy Tech State Coll–Southwest (IN)
Ivy Tech State Coll–Wabash Valley (IN)
Metropolitan Comm Coll-Business & Technology College (MO)
Somerset Comm Coll (KY)
Southwest Wisconsin Tech Coll (WI)
State U of NY Coll of Technology at Alfred (NY)

State U of NY Coll of Technology at Delhi (NY)
Western Nevada Comm Coll (NV)

Massage Therapy
Clover Park Tech Coll (WA)
Coll of DuPage (IL)
Columbus State Comm Coll (OH)
Globe Coll (MN)
Herzing Coll (MN)
Indiana Business Coll-Medical (IN)
Iowa Lakes Comm Coll (IA)
Mercy Coll of Northwest Ohio (OH)
Minnesota School of Business–Brooklyn Center (MN)
Minnesota School of Business–Plymouth (MN)
Minnesota School of Business–Richfield (MN)
Oakland Comm Coll (MI)
Rogue Comm Coll (OR)
Southwestern Comm Coll (NC)
Springfield Tech Comm Coll (MA)
Waubonsee Comm Coll (IL)

Mass Communication/Media
Adirondack Comm Coll (NY)
Amarillo Coll (TX)
Andrew Coll (GA)
Anne Arundel Comm Coll (MD)
Asnuntuck Comm Coll (CT)
Austin Comm Coll (TX)
Bergen Comm Coll (NJ)
Brookdale Comm Coll (NJ)
Bucks County Comm Coll (PA)
Bunker Hill Comm Coll (MA)
Butler County Comm Coll (KS)
Butler County Comm Coll (PA)
Cape Cod Comm Coll (MA)
Casper Coll (WY)
Central Comm Coll–Hastings Campus (NE)
Centralia Coll (WA)
Chattanooga State Tech Comm Coll (TN)
Chipola Coll (FL)
Cochise Coll, Douglas (AZ)
Coffeyville Comm Coll (KS)
Colby Comm Coll (KS)
Columbia State Comm Coll (TN)
Comm Coll of Southern Nevada (NV)
Crowder Coll (MO)
Daytona Beach Comm Coll (FL)
De Anza Coll (CA)
Dodge City Comm Coll (KS)
Dutchess Comm Coll (NY)
East Central Coll (MO)
El Paso Comm Coll (TX)
Enterprise-Ozark Comm Coll (AL)
Finger Lakes Comm Coll (NY)
Frederick Comm Coll (MD)
Fulton-Montgomery Comm Coll (NY)
Genesee Comm Coll (NY)
Glendale Comm Coll (CA)
Grand Rapids Comm Coll (MI)
Greenfield Comm Coll (MA)
Harrisburg Area Comm Coll (PA)
Henderson Comm Coll (KY)
Henry Ford Comm Coll (MI)
Hesser Coll (NH)
Hillsborough Comm Coll (FL)
Hinds Comm Coll (MS)
Holyoke Comm Coll (MA)
Houston Comm Coll System (TX)
Iowa Central Comm Coll (IA)

Iowa Lakes Comm Coll (IA)
Lackawanna Coll (PA)
Lansing Comm Coll (MI)
Laramie County Comm Coll (WY)
Miami Dade Coll (FL)
Midland Coll (TX)
Mineral Area Coll (MO)
Modesto Jr Coll (CA)
Nassau Comm Coll (NY)
Niagara County Comm Coll (NY)
North Idaho Coll (ID)
Northland Comm and Tech Coll–Thief River Falls (MN)
Orange Coast Coll (CA)
Palm Beach Comm Coll (FL)
Pasadena City Coll (CA)
Pratt Comm Coll and Area Vocational School (KS)
Rockland Comm Coll (NY)
St. Louis Comm Coll at Forest Park (MO)
Salt Lake Comm Coll (UT)
Seward County Comm Coll (KS)
Sinclair Comm Coll (OH)
Snow Coll (UT)
South Mountain Comm Coll (AZ)
Tompkins Cortland Comm Coll (NY)
Waubonsee Comm Coll (IL)
Westchester Comm Coll (NY)
West Kentucky Comm and Tech Coll (KY)
Yuba Coll (CA)

Materials Science
Central Arizona Coll (AZ)
Contra Costa Coll (CA)
GateWay Comm Coll (AZ)
Henry Ford Comm Coll (MI)
Northern Essex Comm Coll (MA)
North Hennepin Comm Coll (MN)
St. Louis Comm Coll at Meramec (MO)

Mathematics
Adirondack Comm Coll (NY)
Alabama Southern Comm Coll (AL)
Allen County Comm Coll (KS)
Alpena Comm Coll (MI)
Alvin Comm Coll (TX)
Amarillo Coll (TX)
Ancilla Coll (IN)
Andrew Coll (GA)
Anne Arundel Comm Coll (MD)
Arizona Western Coll (AZ)
Atlanta Metropolitan Coll (GA)
Atlantic Cape Comm Coll (NJ)
Austin Comm Coll (TX)
Bainbridge Coll (GA)
Barton County Comm Coll (KS)
Bergen Comm Coll (NJ)
Blue Mountain Comm Coll (OR)
Borough of Manhattan Comm Coll of City U of NY (NY)
Brazosport Coll (TX)
Bronx Comm Coll of City U of NY (NY)
Brookdale Comm Coll (NJ)
Bucks County Comm Coll (PA)
Bunker Hill Comm Coll (MA)
Butler County Comm Coll (KS)
Butler County Comm Coll (PA)
Calhoun Comm Coll (AL)
Cape Cod Comm Coll (MA)
Casper Coll (WY)
Cayuga County Comm Coll (NY)

Cecil Comm Coll (MD)
Centralia Coll (WA)
Central Oregon Comm Coll (OR)
Central Texas Coll (TX)
Chattahoochee Valley Comm Coll (AL)
Chemeketa Comm Coll (OR)
Citrus Coll (CA)
Clarendon Coll (TX)
Clovis Comm Coll (NM)
Coastal Bend Coll (TX)
Coastal Georgia Comm Coll (GA)
Coffeyville Comm Coll (KS)
Colby Comm Coll (KS)
Coll of Southern Idaho (ID)
Coll of the Canyons (CA)
Colorado Mountn Coll, Alpine Cmps (CO)
Colorado Mountn Coll (CO)
Colorado Mountn Coll, Timberline Cmps (CO)
Columbia Coll (CA)
Columbia-Greene Comm Coll (NY)
Columbia State Comm Coll (TN)
Comm Coll of Allegheny County (PA)
Comm Coll of Southern Nevada (NV)
Compton Comm Coll (CA)
Contra Costa Coll (CA)
Corning Comm Coll (NY)
Crowder Coll (MO)
Cumberland County Coll (NJ)
Danville Area Comm Coll (IL)
Darton Coll (GA)
Daytona Beach Comm Coll (FL)
De Anza Coll (CA)
Delta Coll (MI)
Dixie State Coll of Utah (UT)
Dodge City Comm Coll (KS)
Dutchess Comm Coll (NY)
East Central Coll (MO)
East Central Comm Coll (MS)
Eastern Arizona Coll (AZ)
East Mississippi Comm Coll (MS)
Edison State Comm Coll (OH)
Ellsworth Comm Coll (IA)
El Paso Comm Coll (TX)
Essex County Coll (NJ)
Everett Comm Coll (WA)
Feather River Coll (CA)
Finger Lakes Comm Coll (NY)
Foothill Coll (CA)
Frank Phillips Coll (TX)
Frederick Comm Coll (MD)
Fulton-Montgomery Comm Coll (NY)
Gainesville Coll (GA)
Garden City Comm Coll (KS)
Garrett Coll (MD)
Genesee Comm Coll (NY)
Glendale Comm Coll (CA)
Gogebic Comm Coll (MI)
Gordon Coll (GA)
Great Basin Coll (NV)
Greenfield Comm Coll (MA)
Gulf Coast Comm Coll (FL)
Harrisburg Area Comm Coll (PA)
Herkimer County Comm Coll (NY)
Highland Comm Coll (IL)
Highland Comm Coll (KS)
Highline Comm Coll (WA)
Hinds Comm Coll (MS)
Howard Coll (TX)
Hudson Valley Comm Coll (NY)
Hutchinson Comm Coll and Area Vocational School (KS)
Independence Comm Coll (KS)
Indian River Comm Coll (FL)

Iowa Lakes Comm Coll (IA)
Itawamba Comm Coll (MS)
Jefferson Comm Coll (NY)
John A. Logan Coll (IL)
Kilgore Coll (TX)
Kingsborough Comm Coll of City U of NY (NY)
Kingwood Coll (TX)
Lansing Comm Coll (MI)
Laramie County Comm Coll (WY)
Lehigh Carbon Comm Coll (PA)
Linn-Benton Comm Coll (OR)
Long Beach City Coll (CA)
Lower Columbia Coll (WA)
Macomb Comm Coll (MI)
Miami Dade Coll (FL)
Midland Coll (TX)
Mid Michigan Comm Coll (MI)
Modesto Jr Coll (CA)
Mohave Comm Coll (AZ)
Montgomery County Comm Coll (PA)
Nassau Comm Coll (NY)
New Mexico Military Inst (NM)
Niagara County Comm Coll (NY)
Northampton County Area Comm Coll (PA)
North Country Comm Coll (NY)
Northern Virginia Comm Coll (VA)
North Idaho Coll (ID)
Northwestern Connecticut Comm-Tech Coll (CT)
Northwestern Michigan Coll (MI)
Odessa Coll (TX)
Orange Coast Coll (CA)
Otero Jr Coll (CO)
Palm Beach Comm Coll (FL)
Pasadena City Coll (CA)
Phillips Comm Coll of the U of Arkansas (AR)
Pratt Comm Coll and Area Vocational School (KS)
Raritan Valley Comm Coll (NJ)
Riverside Comm Coll District (CA)
Rockland Comm Coll (NY)
Rogue Comm Coll (OR)
St. Louis Comm Coll at Forest Park (MO)
St. Louis Comm Coll at Meramec (MO)
St. Philip's Coll (TX)
Sandhills Comm Coll (NC)
San Diego City Coll (CA)
San Diego Miramar Coll (CA)
San Joaquin Delta Coll (CA)
San Juan Coll (NM)
Santa Barbara City Coll (CA)
Santa Rosa Jr Coll (CA)
Sauk Valley Comm Coll (IL)
Seminole State Coll (OK)
Seward County Comm Coll (KS)
Sheridan Coll (WY)
Snow Coll (UT)
Solano Comm Coll (CA)
South Mountain Comm Coll (AZ)
Southwestern Oregon Comm Coll (OR)
Springfield Tech Comm Coll (MA)
State U of NY Coll of Technology at Alfred (NY)
State U of NY Coll of Technology at Delhi (NY)
Tacoma Comm Coll (WA)
Taft Coll (CA)
Tompkins Cortland Comm Coll (NY)
Trinity Valley Comm Coll (TX)
Umpqua Comm Coll (OR)

Western Nevada Comm Coll (NV)
Western Oklahoma State Coll (OK)
Western Wyoming Comm Coll (WY)
Yuba Coll (CA)

Mathematics and Computer Science
Adirondack Comm Coll (NY)
Crowder Coll (MO)

Mathematics and Statistics Related
Bristol Comm Coll (MA)

Mechanical Design Technology
Adirondack Comm Coll (NY)
Arapahoe Comm Coll (CO)
Asheville-Buncombe Tech Comm Coll (NC)
Blue Ridge Comm Coll (VA)
Bowling Green State U-Firelands Coll (OH)
Butler County Comm Coll (PA)
Carroll Comm Coll (MD)
Cayuga County Comm Coll (NY)
Chattanooga State Tech Comm Coll (TN)
Chemeketa Comm Coll (OR)
Coll of DuPage (IL)
Comm Coll of Allegheny County (PA)
Comm Coll of Southern Nevada (NV)
Dabney S. Lancaster Comm Coll (VA)
De Anza Coll (CA)
Delta Coll (MI)
Edison State Comm Coll (OH)
Forsyth Tech Comm Coll (NC)
Fox Valley Tech Coll (WI)
Garden City Comm Coll (KS)
Hawkeye Comm Coll (IA)
Heartland Comm Coll (IL)
Illinois Valley Comm Coll (IL)
Iowa Western Comm Coll (IA)
Isothermal Comm Coll (NC)
Lansing Comm Coll (MI)
Macomb Comm Coll (MI)
Minnesota State Coll–Southeast Tech (MN)
Mohawk Valley Comm Coll (NY)
New Hampshire Comm Tech Coll, Manchester/Stratham (NH)
Niagara County Comm Coll (NY)
Northeastern Tech Coll (SC)
Northwest Tech Coll (MN)
Owens Comm Coll, Toledo (OH)
Prairie State Coll (IL)
Raritan Valley Comm Coll (NJ)
Rock Valley Coll (IL)
St. Cloud Tech Coll (MN)
Southeast Comm Coll, Milford Campus (NE)
Southwest Wisconsin Tech Coll (WI)
State U of NY Coll of Technology at Alfred (NY)
Thaddeus Stevens Coll of Technology (PA)
Triangle Tech, Inc.– Pittsburgh School (PA)
Westmoreland County Comm Coll (PA)

Mechanical Drafting and Cad/Cadd
Adirondack Comm Coll (NY)
Alexandria Tech Coll (MN)
Brookdale Comm Coll (NJ)
Butler County Comm Coll (PA)
Central Carolina Tech Coll (SC)

Commonwealth Tech Inst (PA)
Comm Coll of Allegheny County (PA)
Dixie State Coll of Utah (UT)
Edgecombe Comm Coll (NC)
Erie Comm Coll, South Campus (NY)
John Wood Comm Coll (IL)
Lake Superior Coll (MN)
Macomb Comm Coll (MI)
Midlands Tech Coll (SC)
Montgomery County Comm Coll (PA)
Morrison Inst of Technology (IL)
North Hennepin Comm Coll (MN)
North Seattle Comm Coll (WA)
Oakland Comm Coll (MI)
Rowan-Cabarrus Comm Coll (NC)
St. Cloud Tech Coll (MN)
South Central Tech Coll (MN)
Spencerian Coll–Lexington (KY)
Stanly Comm Coll (NC)
Triangle Tech, Inc.– Greensburg School (PA)
Wake Tech Comm Coll (NC)
Westwood Coll–Denver North (CO)

Mechanical Engineering
Bristol Comm Coll (MA)
Delta Coll (MI)
Itasca Comm Coll (MN)
Lehigh Carbon Comm Coll (PA)
Northwest State Comm Coll (OH)

Mechanical Engineering/ Mechanical Technology
Adirondack Comm Coll (NY)
Alamance Comm Coll (NC)
Anne Arundel Comm Coll (MD)
Asheville-Buncombe Tech Comm Coll (NC)
Augusta Tech Coll (GA)
Blue Ridge Comm Coll (NC)
Broome Comm Coll (NY)
Broward Comm Coll (FL)
Cape Fear Comm Coll (NC)
Catawba Valley Comm Coll (NC)
Central Piedmont Comm Coll (NC)
Chattanooga State Tech Comm Coll (TN)
Cincinnati State Tech and Comm Coll (OH)
Citrus Coll (CA)
Clark State Comm Coll (OH)
Cleveland Comm Coll (NC)
Clover Park Tech Coll (WA)
Coffeyville Comm Coll (KS)
Coll of Lake County (IL)
Columbus State Comm Coll (OH)
Columbus Tech Coll (GA)
Comm & Tech Coll at West Virginia U Inst of Technology (WV)
Comm Coll of Southern Nevada (NV)
Compton Comm Coll (CA)
Corning Comm Coll (NY)
Craven Comm Coll (NC)
Danville Area Comm Coll (IL)
Delaware County Comm Coll (PA)
Delaware Tech & Comm Coll, Stanton/ Wilmington Cmps (DE)
Delta Coll (MI)
ECPI Coll of Technology, Newport News (VA)
ECPI Coll of Technology, Virginia Beach (VA)
ECPI Tech Coll, Richmond (VA)

ECPI Tech Coll, Roanoke (VA)
Edgecombe Comm Coll (NC)
Erie Comm Coll, North Campus (NY)
Fairmont State Comm & Tech Coll (WV)
Finger Lakes Comm Coll (NY)
Fox Valley Tech Coll (WI)
Gadsden State Comm Coll (AL)
Garden City Comm Coll (KS)
Gateway Comm Coll (CT)
Green River Comm Coll (WA)
Hagerstown Comm Coll (MD)
Harford Comm Coll (MD)
Harrisburg Area Comm Coll (PA)
Hawkeye Comm Coll (IA)
Highland Comm Coll (IL)
Hudson Valley Comm Coll (NY)
Illinois Eastern Comm Colls, Lincoln Trail Coll (IL)
Illinois Valley Comm Coll (IL)
Iowa Western Comm Coll (IA)
Isothermal Comm Coll (NC)
Jamestown Comm Coll (NY)
Jefferson Comm Coll (KY)
Jefferson Comm Coll (OH)
John Tyler Comm Coll (VA)
Kalamazoo Valley Comm Coll (MI)
Kent State U, Tuscarawas Campus (OH)
Lansing Comm Coll (MI)
Lehigh Carbon Comm Coll (PA)
Lower Columbia Coll (WA)
Macomb Comm Coll (MI)
Massachusetts Bay Comm Coll (MA)
Miami U Hamilton (OH)
Midlands Tech Coll (SC)
Milwaukee Area Tech Coll (WI)
Mohawk Valley Comm Coll (NY)
Montgomery County Comm Coll (PA)
Moraine Valley Comm Coll (IL)
Mott Comm Coll (MI)
North Central State Coll (OH)
Northern Virginia Comm Coll (VA)
Northwest State Comm Coll (OH)
Owens Comm Coll, Findlay (OH)
Owens Comm Coll, Toledo (OH)
Pasadena City Coll (CA)
Pennsylvania Inst of Technology (PA)
Penn State U DuBois Campus of the Commonwealth Coll (PA)
Penn State U Hazleton Campus of the Commonwealth Coll (PA)
Penn State U New Kensington Campus of the Commonwealth Coll (PA)
Penn State U Shenango Campus of the Commonwealth Coll (PA)
Penn State U York Campus of the Commonwealth Coll (PA)
Queensborough Comm Coll of City U of NY (NY)
Richmond Comm Coll (NC)
Rochester Comm and Tech Coll (MN)
St. Louis Comm Coll at Forest Park (MO)
Salt Lake Comm Coll (UT)
San Antonio Coll (TX)
San Joaquin Delta Coll (CA)

Sauk Valley Comm Coll (IL)
Schoolcraft Coll (MI)
Shoreline Comm Coll (WA)
Sinclair Comm Coll (OH)
Southeast Comm Coll, Milford Campus (NE)
Southeast Tech Inst (SD)
Spartanburg Tech Coll (SC)
Springfield Tech Comm Coll (MA)
State U of NY Coll of Technology at Alfred (NY)
State U of NY Coll of Technology at Canton (NY)
Texas State Tech Coll– Waco/Marshall Campus (TX)
Three Rivers Comm Coll (CT)
Trident Tech Coll (SC)
Union County Coll (NJ)
Wake Tech Comm Coll (NC)
Westchester Comm Coll (NY)
Westmoreland County Comm Coll (PA)
West Virginia U at Parkersburg (WV)
Wilson Tech Comm Coll (NC)

Mechanical Engineering Technologies Related
Delaware County Comm Coll (PA)
Edgecombe Comm Coll (NC)
Pennsylvania Inst of Technology (PA)

Mechanic and Repair Technologies Related
Cincinnati State Tech and Comm Coll (OH)
Macomb Comm Coll (MI)

Mechanics and Repair
Black Hawk Coll, Moline (IL)
Ivy Tech State Coll– Bloomington (IN)
Ivy Tech State Coll–Central Indiana (IN)
Ivy Tech State Coll– Columbus (IN)
Ivy Tech State Coll–Kokomo (IN)
Ivy Tech State Coll–Lafayette (IN)
Ivy Tech State Coll–North Central (IN)
Ivy Tech State Coll– Northeast (IN)
Ivy Tech State Coll– Northwest (IN)
Ivy Tech State Coll– Southcentral (IN)
Ivy Tech State Coll– Southwest (IN)
Ivy Tech State Coll–Wabash Valley (IN)
Ivy Tech State Coll– Whitewater (IN)
Western Wyoming Comm Coll (WY)

Medical Administrative Assistant
Globe Coll (MN)
Minnesota School of Business–Brooklyn Center (MN)
Minnesota School of Business–Plymouth (MN)

Medical Administrative Assistant and Medical Secretary
Adirondack Comm Coll (NY)
Alamance Comm Coll (NC)
Alexandria Tech Coll (MN)
Alvin Comm Coll (TX)
Amarillo Coll (TX)
Andover Coll (ME)
Athens Tech Coll (GA)
Baltimore City Comm Coll (MD)
Barton County Comm Coll (KS)
Bay de Noc Comm Coll (MI)

Bay State Coll (MA)
Beaufort County Comm Coll (NC)
Bergen Comm Coll (NJ)
Bismarck State Coll (ND)
Blue Mountain Comm Coll (OR)
Brevard Comm Coll (FL)
Briarwood Coll (CT)
Bristol Comm Coll (MA)
Bronx Comm Coll of City U of NY (NY)
Broward Comm Coll (FL)
Brown Mackie Coll, Michigan City Campus (IN)
Bryant and Stratton Coll, Parma (OH)
Business Inst of Pennsylvania, Sharon (PA)
Butler County Comm Coll (KS)
Butler County Comm Coll (PA)
Cape Cod Comm Coll (MA)
Career Colls of Chicago (IL)
Central Arizona Coll (AZ)
Central Carolina Comm Coll (NC)
Central Comm Coll–Hastings Campus (NE)
Centralia Coll (WA)
Central Piedmont Comm Coll (NC)
Central Texas Coll (TX)
Century Coll (MN)
Chattanooga State Tech Comm Coll (TN)
Chemeketa Comm Coll (OR)
Clark Coll (WA)
Clark State Comm Coll (OH)
Clatsop Comm Coll (OR)
Cleveland Comm Coll (NC)
Clovis Comm Coll (NM)
Coastal Carolina Comm Coll (NC)
Cochise Coll, Douglas (AZ)
Coffeyville Comm Coll (KS)
Columbus State Comm Coll (OH)
Comm & Tech Coll at West Virginia U Inst of Technology (WV)
Comm Coll of Allegheny County (PA)
Comm Coll of Aurora (CO)
Comm Coll of Beaver County (PA)
Comm Coll of Denver (CO)
Comm Coll of Philadelphia (PA)
Comm Coll of Rhode Island (RI)
Comm Coll of Southern Nevada (NV)
Craven Comm Coll (NC)
Crowder Coll (MO)
Dabney S. Lancaster Comm Coll (VA)
Danville Area Comm Coll (IL)
Davenport U, Midland (MI)
Daytona Beach Comm Coll (FL)
Delaware Tech & Comm Coll, Jack F Owens Cmps (DE)
Delaware Tech & Comm Coll, Stanton/ Wilmington Cmps (DE)
Delta Coll (MI)
Des Moines Area Comm Coll (IA)
Dodge City Comm Coll (KS)
Durham Tech Comm Coll (NC)
East Central Coll (MO)
ECPI Coll of Technology, Newport News (VA)
ECPI Coll of Technology, Virginia Beach (VA)
ECPI Tech Coll, Richmond (VA)
ECPI Tech Coll, Roanoke (VA)

Edison State Comm Coll (OH)
Elgin Comm Coll (IL)
Ellsworth Comm Coll (IA)
Enterprise-Ozark Comm Coll (AL)
Erie Business Center, Main (PA)
Erie Business Center South (PA)
Essex County Coll (NJ)
Eugenio María de Hostos Comm Coll of City U of NY (NY)
Everett Comm Coll (WA)
Flathead Valley Comm Coll (MT)
Florida National Coll (FL)
Fort Scott Comm Coll (KS)
Frederick Comm Coll (MD)
Fulton-Montgomery Comm Coll (NY)
Gateway Comm Coll (CT)
George C. Wallace Comm Coll (AL)
Glendale Comm Coll (CA)
Gogebic Comm Coll (MI)
Goodwin Coll (CT)
Grand Rapids Comm Coll (MI)
Green River Comm Coll (WA)
Hagerstown Business Coll (MD)
Halifax Comm Coll (NC)
Hawkeye Comm Coll (IA)
Henry Ford Comm Coll (MI)
Hesser Coll (NH)
Hibbing Comm Coll (MN)
Highland Comm Coll (KS)
Hillsborough Comm Coll (FL)
Houston Comm Coll System (TX)
Howard Comm Coll (MD)
Hudson Valley Comm Coll (NY)
ICM School of Business & Medical Careers (PA)
Illinois Eastern Comm Colls, Olney Central Coll (IL)
Indian River Comm Coll (FL)
Iowa Lakes Comm Coll (IA)
Iowa Western Comm Coll (IA)
Jefferson Comm Coll (NY)
Jefferson Comm Coll (OH)
Johnston Comm Coll (NC)
John Wood Comm Coll (IL)
Kalamazoo Valley Comm Coll (MI)
Lackawanna Coll (PA)
Lake Land Coll (IL)
Lake Region State Coll (ND)
Lake Superior Coll (MN)
Laurel Business Inst (PA)
Lewis and Clark Comm Coll (IL)
Linn-Benton Comm Coll (OR)
Long Beach City Coll (CA)
Longview Comm Coll (MO)
Lower Columbia Coll (WA)
Manchester Comm Coll (CT)
Maple Woods Comm Coll (MO)
Mayland Comm Coll (NC)
McIntosh Coll (NH)
McLennan Comm Coll (TX)
Mid Michigan Comm Coll (MI)
Milwaukee Area Tech Coll (WI)
Minnesota State Coll– Southeast Tech (MN)
Minnesota West Comm & Tech Coll-Pipestone Cmps (MN)
Monroe Coll, Bronx (NY)
Monroe Coll, New Rochelle (NY)
Montcalm Comm Coll (MI)
Mott Comm Coll (MI)
Muskegon Comm Coll (MI)
Nassau Comm Coll (NY)

New Hampshire Comm Tech Coll, Manchester/Stratham (NH)
Newport Business Inst, Williamsport (PA)
Northampton County Area Comm Coll (PA)
Northeast Alabama Comm Coll (AL)
Northern Essex Comm Coll (MA)
North Idaho Coll (ID)
North Shore Comm Coll (MA)
Northwest State Comm Coll (OH)
Northwest Tech Coll (MN)
Orange Coast Coll (CA)
Otero Jr Coll (CO)
Ouachita Tech Coll (AR)
Owens Comm Coll, Findlay (OH)
Penn Valley Comm Coll (MO)
Phillips Comm Coll of the U of Arkansas (AR)
Piedmont Comm Coll (NC)
Pima Comm Coll (AZ)
Polk Comm Coll (FL)
Rasmussen Coll St. Cloud (MN)
Richland Comm Coll (IL)
Riverland Comm Coll (MN)
Rochester Comm and Tech Coll (MN)
Rockingham Comm Coll (NC)
St. Cloud Tech Coll (MN)
Saint Paul Coll–A Comm & Tech College (MN)
St. Philip's Coll (TX)
Salt Lake Comm Coll (UT)
Sandhills Comm Coll (NC)
San Joaquin Valley Coll (CA)
Santa Fe Comm Coll (FL)
Shawnee Comm Coll (IL)
Shelton State Comm Coll (AL)
Shoreline Comm Coll (WA)
Sinclair Comm Coll (OH)
South Hills School of Business & Technology, State College (PA)
Spartanburg Tech Coll (SC)
Springfield Tech Comm Coll (MA)
Stanly Comm Coll (NC)
Surry Comm Coll (NC)
Tacoma Comm Coll (WA)
Temple Coll (TX)
Three Rivers Comm Coll (CT)
Trident Tech Coll (SC)
Truckee Meadows Comm Coll (NV)
Tunxis Comm Coll (CT)
Umpqua Comm Coll (OR)
The U of Akron–Wayne Coll (OH)
U of Cincinnati Raymond Walters Coll (OH)
U of Northwestern Ohio (OH)
Valencia Comm Coll (FL)
Wake Tech Comm Coll (NC)
Walla Walla Comm Coll (WA)
Walters State Comm Coll (TN)
Wayne County Comm Coll District (MI)
Western Iowa Tech Comm Coll (IA)
Western Wyoming Comm Coll (WY)
Westmoreland County Comm Coll (PA)
Whatcom Comm Coll (WA)
Yakima Valley Comm Coll (WA)

Medical/Clinical Assistant
Alamance Comm Coll (NC)
Andover Coll (ME)
Anne Arundel Comm Coll (MD)
Arapahoe Comm Coll (CO)

Athens Tech Coll (GA)
Austin Comm Coll (TX)
Bay State Coll (MA)
Belmont Tech Coll (OH)
Bergen Comm Coll (NJ)
Bossier Parish Comm Coll (LA)
Brevard Comm Coll (FL)
Briarwood Coll (CT)
Broome Comm Coll (NY)
Broward Comm Coll (FL)
Brown Mackie Coll, Findlay Campus (OH)
Brown Mackie Coll, Michigan City Campus (IN)
Brown Mackie Coll, Northern Kentucky Campus (KY)
Bryant & Stratton Business Inst, Albany (NY)
Bryant and Stratton Coll, Parma (OH)
Bryant & Stratton Business Inst (NY)
Bucks County Comm Coll (PA)
Business Inst of Pennsylvania, Sharon (PA)
Butler County Comm Coll (PA)
Capital Comm Coll (CT)
Carteret Comm Coll (NC)
Central Carolina Comm Coll (NC)
Central Comm Coll—Hastings Campus (NE)
Central Oregon Comm Coll (OR)
Central Piedmont Comm Coll (NC)
Century Coll (MN)
Chemeketa Comm Coll (OR)
Cincinnati State Tech and Comm Coll (OH)
Clark Coll (WA)
Commonwealth Tech Inst (PA)
Comm Coll of Allegheny County (PA)
Comm Coll of Aurora (CO)
Comm Coll of Philadelphia (PA)
Comm Coll of Southern Nevada (NV)
Cossatot Comm Coll of the U of Arkansas (AR)
Davenport U, Midland (MI)
Davidson County Comm Coll (NC)
De Anza Coll (CA)
DeKalb Tech Coll (GA)
Delaware County Comm Coll (PA)
Delaware Tech & Comm Coll, Jack F Owens Cmps (DE)
Delta Coll (MI)
Des Moines Area Comm Coll (IA)
Dutchess Comm Coll (NY)
Eastern Idaho Tech Coll (ID)
ECPI Tech Coll, Roanoke (VA)
Edgecombe Comm Coll (NC)
El Paso Comm Coll (TX)
Erie Business Center, Main (PA)
Everett Comm Coll (WA)
Flathead Valley Comm Coll (MT)
Florida National Coll (FL)
Forsyth Tech Comm Coll (NC)
George Corley Wallace State Comm Coll (AL)
Glendale Comm Coll (CA)
Goodwin Coll (CT)
Guam Comm Coll (GU)
Guilford Tech Comm Coll (NC)
Gwinnett Tech Coll (GA)
Hagerstown Business Coll (MD)
Haywood Comm Coll (NC)
Henry Ford Comm Coll (MI)

Herzing Coll (MN)
Hesser Coll (NH)
Highline Comm Coll (WA)
Hudson County Comm Coll (NJ)
ICM School of Business & Medical Careers (PA)
Indiana Business Coll, Anderson (IN)
Indiana Business Coll, Columbus (IN)
Indiana Business Coll, Evansville (IN)
Indiana Business Coll, Fort Wayne (IN)
Indiana Business Coll, Terre Haute (IN)
Indiana Business Coll-Medical (IN)
Iowa Central Comm Coll (IA)
Iowa Lakes Comm Coll (IA)
Iowa Western Comm Coll (IA)
Ivy Tech State Coll—Central Indiana (IN)
Ivy Tech State Coll—Columbus (IN)
Ivy Tech State Coll—Eastcentral (IN)
Ivy Tech State Coll—Kokomo (IN)
Ivy Tech State Coll—Lafayette (IN)
Ivy Tech State Coll—North Central (IN)
Ivy Tech State Coll—Northeast (IN)
Ivy Tech State Coll—Northwest (IN)
Ivy Tech State Coll—Southcentral (IN)
Ivy Tech State Coll—Southeast (IN)
Ivy Tech State Coll—Southwest (IN)
Ivy Tech State Coll—Wabash Valley (IN)
Ivy Tech State Coll—Whitewater (IN)
Jackson Comm Coll (MI)
James Sprunt Comm Coll (NC)
Jefferson Comm Coll (OH)
Johnston Comm Coll (NC)
Kalamazoo Valley Comm Coll (MI)
Kapiolani Comm Coll (HI)
Keiser Coll, Fort Lauderdale (FL)
Kennebec Valley Comm Coll (ME)
Kilgore Coll (TX)
Lac Courte Oreilles Ojibwa Comm Coll (WI)
Lansing Comm Coll (MI)
Laredo Comm Coll (TX)
Laurel Business Inst (PA)
Lehigh Carbon Comm Coll (PA)
Linn-Benton Comm Coll (OR)
Long Beach City Coll (CA)
Lower Columbia Coll (WA)
Macomb Comm Coll (MI)
Marshall Comm and Tech Coll (WV)
Mayland Comm Coll (NC)
McIntosh Coll (NH)
Miami Dade Coll (FL)
Mid Michigan Comm Coll (MI)
Minnesota School of Business—Richfield (MN)
Minnesota West Comm & Tech Coll-Pipestone Cmps (MN)
Modesto Jr Coll (CA)
Mohawk Valley Comm Coll (NY)
Montgomery Comm Coll (NC)
Mount Wachusett Comm Coll (MA)

National Coll of Business & Technology, Danville (KY)
National Coll of Business & Technology, Florence (KY)
National Coll of Business & Technology, Louisville (KY)
National Coll of Business & Technology, Pikeville (KY)
National Coll of Business & Technology, Richmond (KY)
National Coll of Business & Technology, Bristol (TN)
National Coll of Business & Technology, Nashville (TN)
National Coll of Business & Technology, Bluefield (VA)
National Coll of Business & Technology, Charlottesville (VA)
National Coll of Business & Technology, Harrisonburg (VA)
National Coll of Business & Technology, Lynchburg (VA)
National Coll of Business & Technology, Salem (VA)
New River Comm and Tech Coll (WV)
Niagara County Comm Coll (NY)
Northeast State Tech Comm Coll (TN)
North Iowa Area Comm Coll (IA)
North Seattle Comm Coll (WA)
Northwestern Connecticut Comm-Tech Coll (CT)
Northwestern Michigan Coll (MI)
Northwest Tech Coll (MN)
Oakland Comm Coll (MI)
Ohio Inst of Photography and Technology (OH)
Olympic Coll (WA)
Orange Coast Coll (CA)
Pasadena City Coll (CA)
Pioneer Pacific Coll (OR)
Quinebaug Valley Comm Coll (CT)
RETS Tech Center (OH)
Richmond Comm Coll (NC)
Rockingham Comm Coll (NC)
Salt Lake Comm Coll (UT)
San Antonio Coll (TX)
San Joaquin Valley Coll (CA)
Shelton State Comm Coll (AL)
Sinclair Comm Coll (OH)
Somerset Comm Coll (KY)
Southern Maine Comm Coll (ME)
Southern State Comm Coll (OH)
South U (FL)
South U (SC)
Southwestern Oregon Comm Coll (OR)
Southwest Wisconsin Tech Coll (WI)
Springfield Tech Comm Coll (MA)
Stanly Comm Coll (NC)
State U of NY Coll of Technology at Alfred (NY)
Thompson Inst (PA)
Tri-County Comm Coll (NC)
Tri-County Tech Coll (SC)
Union County Coll (NJ)
U of Northwestern Ohio (OH)
Vatterott Coll, St. Joseph (MO)
Vatterott Coll, Springfield (MO)
Waubonsee Comm Coll (IL)
Western Wyoming Comm Coll (WY)
Westwood Coll—Denver North (CO)
Whatcom Comm Coll (WA)
Wilkes Comm Coll (NC)

Medical Insurance Coding
Alexandria Tech Coll (MN)
Columbus State Comm Coll (OH)
Goodwin Coll (CT)
Herzing Coll (MN)
Springfield Tech Comm Coll (MA)

Medical Insurance/Medical Billing
Jackson Comm Coll (MI)

Medical Laboratory Technology
Athens Tech Coll (GA)
Cecil Comm Coll (MD)
Delaware Tech & Comm Coll, Jack F Owens Cmps (DE)
Ellsworth Comm Coll (IA)
Fayetteville Tech Comm Coll (NC)
Florida Comm Coll at Jacksonville (FL)
Frederick Comm Coll (MD)
Harford Comm Coll (MD)
Iowa Lakes Comm Coll (IA)
Jefferson Comm Coll (NY)
Mohawk Valley Comm Coll (NY)
Northwest-Shoals Comm Coll (AL)
Ohio State U Ag Tech Inst (OH)
Rowan-Cabarrus Comm Coll (NC)
Schoolcraft Coll (MI)
Shoreline Comm Coll (WA)
U of Cincinnati Raymond Walters Coll (OH)

Medical Microbiology and Bacteriology
Riverside Comm Coll District (CA)

Medical Office Assistant
Alpena Comm Coll (MI)
Clovis Comm Coll (NM)
Harrisburg Area Comm Coll (PA)
Indiana Business Coll, Muncie (IN)
Iowa Lakes Comm Coll (IA)
Keiser Coll, Miami (FL)
MTI Coll of Business and Technology, Houston (TX)
MTI Coll of Business and Technology, Houston (TX)
Sauk Valley Comm Coll (IL)
Vatterott Coll, Oklahoma City (OK)
Western Wyoming Comm Coll (WY)

Medical Office Computer Specialist
Iowa Lakes Comm Coll (IA)
Western Wyoming Comm Coll (WY)

Medical Office Management
Apollo Coll (ID)
Beaufort County Comm Coll (NC)
Briarwood Coll (CT)
Brown Mackie Coll, Findlay Campus (OH)
Coll of Lake County (IL)
Erie Comm Coll, North Campus (NY)
Fayetteville Tech Comm Coll (NC)
Florida Comm Coll at Jacksonville (FL)
Minnesota School of Business—Richfield (MN)
Pennsylvania Inst of Technology (PA)
St. Cloud Tech Coll (MN)
Schuylkill Inst of Business and Technology (PA)
Spencerian Coll (KY)
The U of Akron—Wayne Coll (OH)
U of Arkansas Comm Coll at Batesville (AR)

Medical Physiology
Comm Coll of the Air Force (AL)

Medical Radiologic Technology
Allegany Coll of Maryland (MD)
Asheville-Buncombe Tech Comm Coll (NC)
Broome Comm Coll (NY)
Bunker Hill Comm Coll (MA)
Caldwell Comm Coll and Tech Inst (NC)
Cape Fear Comm Coll (NC)
Capital Comm Coll (CT)
Carolinas Coll of Health Sciences (NC)
Catawba Valley Comm Coll (NC)
Central Texas Coll (TX)
Century Coll (MN)
City Colls of Chicago, Wilbur Wright Coll (IL)
Cleveland Comm Coll (NC)
Clovis Comm Coll (NM)
Coastal Georgia Comm Coll (GA)
Coll of DuPage (IL)
Coll of Lake County (IL)
Coll of Southern Idaho (ID)
Comm Coll of Allegheny County (PA)
Comm Coll of Rhode Island (RI)
Comm Coll of the Air Force (AL)
Erie Comm Coll (NY)
Essex County Coll (NJ)
Eugenio María de Hostos Comm Coll of City U of NY (NY)
Florida Comm Coll at Jacksonville (FL)
Foothill Coll (CA)
Gadsden State Comm Coll (AL)
GateWay Comm Coll (AZ)
Hagerstown Comm Coll (MD)
Harrisburg Area Comm Coll (PA)
Hazard Comm and Tech Coll (KY)
Houston Comm Coll System (TX)
Hutchinson Comm Coll and Area Vocational School (KS)
Illinois Eastern Comm Colls, Olney Central Coll (IL)
Itawamba Comm Coll (MS)
Ivy Tech State Coll—Central Indiana (IN)
Ivy Tech State Coll—Columbus (IN)
Ivy Tech State Coll—Eastcentral (IN)
Ivy Tech State Coll—Wabash Valley (IN)
Jackson Comm Coll (MI)
Jackson State Comm Coll (TN)
Jefferson Comm Coll (KY)
Jefferson State Comm Coll (AL)
Johnston Comm Coll (NC)
John Wood Comm Coll (IL)
Kaskaskia Coll (IL)
Keiser Coll, Fort Lauderdale (FL)
Keystone Coll (PA)
Kilgore Coll (TX)
Lake Superior Coll (MN)
Lansing Comm Coll (MI)
Lincoln Land Comm Coll (IL)
Marshall Comm and Tech Coll (WV)
Massachusetts Bay Comm Coll (MA)
Mercy Coll of Northwest Ohio (OH)
Meridian Comm Coll (MS)
Midland Coll (TX)
Midlands Tech Coll (SC)

Mineral Area Coll (MO)
Mohawk Valley Comm Coll (NY)
Montcalm Comm Coll (MI)
Montgomery County Comm Coll (PA)
Moraine Valley Comm Coll (IL)
Mott Comm Coll (MI)
Nassau Comm Coll (NY)
Northampton County Area Comm Coll (PA)
North Country Comm Coll (NY)
North Hennepin Comm Coll (MN)
North Shore Comm Coll (MA)
Oakland Comm Coll (MI)
Owensboro Comm and Tech Coll (KY)
Parkland Coll (IL)
Penn State U New Kensington Campus of the Commonwealth Coll (PA)
Pima Comm Coll (AZ)
Riverland Comm Coll (MN)
St. Philip's Coll (TX)
Santa Barbara City Coll (CA)
Scott Comm Coll (IA)
Southeast Comm Coll, Lincoln Campus (NE)
Southeast Kentucky Comm and Tech Coll (KY)
Southwestern Comm Coll (NC)
Southwestern Oklahoma State U at Sayre (OK)
Southwest Georgia Tech Coll (GA)
Spartanburg Tech Coll (SC)
Springfield Tech Comm Coll (MA)
Union County Coll (NJ)
Valencia Comm Coll (FL)
Volunteer State Comm Coll (TN)
Wake Tech Comm Coll (NC)
Western Oklahoma State Coll (OK)
Wor-Wic Comm Coll (MD)

Medical Reception
Alexandria Tech Coll (MN)
Iowa Lakes Comm Coll (IA)
Lower Columbia Coll (WA)

Medical Transcription
Alexandria Tech Coll (MN)
Black Hawk Coll, Moline (IL)
Central Arizona Coll (AZ)
Elgin Comm Coll (IL)
Erie Business Center, Main (PA)
Iowa Lakes Comm Coll (IA)
Jackson Comm Coll (MI)
Laurel Business Inst (PA)
Lehigh Carbon Comm Coll (PA)
Lower Columbia Coll (WA)
Marshall Comm and Tech Coll (WV)
Mid Michigan Comm Coll (MI)
Northern Essex Comm Coll (MA)
Oakland Comm Coll (MI)
Saint Charles Comm Coll (MO)
Southeast Tech Inst (SD)
Southwest Wisconsin Tech Coll (WI)
Westwood Coll—Denver North (CO)
Williston State Coll (ND)

Mental and Social Health Services And Allied Professions Related
Broome Comm Coll (NY)
Oakland Comm Coll (MI)

Mental Health/Rehabilitation
Alvin Comm Coll (TX)
Anne Arundel Comm Coll (MD)
Belmont Tech Coll (OH)

Blue Ridge Comm Coll (VA)
Columbus State Comm Coll (OH)
Comm Coll of Philadelphia (PA)
Comm Coll of the Air Force (AL)
Dutchess Comm Coll (NY)
Elgin Comm Coll (IL)
El Paso Comm Coll (TX)
Fort Peck Comm Coll (MT)
Gateway Comm Coll (CT)
Glendale Comm Coll (CA)
Hopkinsville Comm Coll (KY)
Houston Comm Coll System (TX)
Kingsborough Comm Coll of City U of NY (NY)
Lackawanna Coll (PA)
Macomb Comm Coll (MI)
McLennan Comm Coll (TX)
Metropolitan Comm Coll (NE)
Mohawk Valley Comm Coll (NY)
North Country Comm Coll (NY)
Northern Essex Comm Coll (MA)
North Shore Comm Coll (MA)
Orange County Comm Coll (NY)
Prairie State Coll (IL)
Sandhills Comm Coll (NC)
Sinclair Comm Coll (OH)
Southwestern Comm Coll (NC)
Truckee Meadows Comm Coll (NV)

Merchandising
Coll of DuPage (IL)
Cuyahoga Comm Coll (OH)

Merchandising, Sales, and Marketing Operations Related (General)
Broome Comm Coll (NY)
Iowa Lakes Comm Coll (IA)
Southwestern Michigan Coll (MI)

Metal and Jewelry Arts
Flathead Valley Comm Coll (MT)
Garden City Comm Coll (KS)
Haywood Comm Coll (NC)
Inst of American Indian Arts (NM)
Mohave Comm Coll (AZ)
Pasadena City Coll (CA)
San Antonio Coll (TX)

Metallurgical Technology
Arkansas Northeastern Coll (AR)
Comm Coll of the Air Force (AL)
Elgin Comm Coll (IL)
Kilgore Coll (TX)
Linn-Benton Comm Coll (OR)
Macomb Comm Coll (MI)
Penn State U DuBois Campus of the Commonwealth Coll (PA)
Penn State U Fayette Campus of the Commonwealth Coll (PA)
Penn State U Hazleton Campus of the Commonwealth Coll (PA)
Penn State U New Kensington Campus of the Commonwealth Coll (PA)
Penn State U Shenango Campus of the Commonwealth Coll (PA)
Penn State U Wilkes-Barre Campus of the Commonwealth Coll (PA)
Penn State U York Campus of the Commonwealth Coll (PA)

Schoolcraft Coll (MI)
Southeast Comm Coll, Milford Campus (NE)

Meteorology
West Virginia State Comm and Tech Coll (WV)

Middle School Education
Arkansas Northeastern Coll (AR)
Arkansas State U–Mountain Home (AR)
Gainesville Coll (GA)
Miami Dade Coll (FL)

Military Studies
Barton County Comm Coll (KS)
Truckee Meadows Comm Coll (NV)

Military Technologies
Calhoun Comm Coll (AL)
Comm Coll of the Air Force (AL)

Mining Technology
Casper Coll (WY)
Eastern Arizona Coll (AZ)
Illinois Eastern Comm Colls, Wabash Valley Coll (IL)
Trinidad State Jr Coll (CO)
Western Wyoming Comm Coll (WY)

Modern Languages
Amarillo Coll (TX)
Barton County Comm Coll (KS)
Bay Mills Comm Coll (MI)
Brookdale Comm Coll (NJ)
Cape Cod Comm Coll (MA)
Citrus Coll (CA)
City Colls of Chicago, Wilbur Wright Coll (IL)
East Central Coll (MO)
Everett Comm Coll (WA)
Independence Comm Coll (KS)
Itawamba Comm Coll (MS)
Midland Coll (TX)
Odessa Coll (TX)
Otero Jr Coll (CO)
Pasadena City Coll (CA)
St. Louis Comm Coll at Meramec (MO)
San Diego City Coll (CA)

Mortuary Science and Embalming
Delta Coll (MI)

Motorcycle Maintenance and Repair Technology
Iowa Lakes Comm Coll (IA)

Multi-/Interdisciplinary Studies Related
Brookdale Comm Coll (NJ)
Central Carolina Tech Coll (SC)
Harford Comm Coll (MD)
Laramie County Comm Coll (WY)
Linn-Benton Comm Coll (OR)
Marshall Comm and Tech Coll (WV)
Midlands Tech Coll (SC)
Mid-South Comm Coll (AR)
Northwest-Shoals Comm Coll (AL)
Williston State Coll (ND)

Museum Studies
Inst of American Indian Arts (NM)
Tacoma Comm Coll (WA)

Music
Adirondack Comm Coll (NY)
Allen County Comm Coll (KS)
Alvin Comm Coll (TX)
Amarillo Coll (TX)
Andrew Coll (GA)
Anne Arundel Comm Coll (MD)
Arizona Western Coll (AZ)

Atlanta Metropolitan Coll (GA)
Austin Comm Coll (TX)
Barton County Comm Coll (KS)
Bergen Comm Coll (NJ)
Brazosport Coll (TX)
Bronx Comm Coll of City U of NY (NY)
Brookdale Comm Coll (NJ)
Bucks County Comm Coll (PA)
Butler County Comm Coll (KS)
Caldwell Comm Coll and Tech Inst (NC)
Calhoun Comm Coll (AL)
Cape Cod Comm Coll (MA)
Carroll Comm Coll (MD)
Casper Coll (WY)
Cedar Valley Coll (TX)
Centralia Coll (WA)
Central Piedmont Comm Coll (NC)
Central Texas Coll (TX)
Central Wyoming Coll (WY)
Chattahoochee Valley Comm Coll (AL)
Citrus Coll (CA)
City Colls of Chicago, Wilbur Wright Coll (IL)
Clarendon Coll (TX)
Cloud County Comm Coll (KS)
Coastal Bend Coll (TX)
Coffeyville Comm Coll (KS)
Colby Comm Coll (KS)
Coll of Lake County (IL)
Coll of Southern Idaho (ID)
Colorado Northwestern Comm Coll (CO)
Columbia Coll (CA)
Columbia State Comm Coll (TN)
Comm Coll of Allegheny County (PA)
Comm Coll of Philadelphia (PA)
Comm Coll of Rhode Island (RI)
Comm Coll of Southern Nevada (NV)
Compton Comm Coll (CA)
Contra Costa Coll (CA)
Cowley County Comm Coll and Voc-Tech School (KS)
Crowder Coll (MO)
Darton Coll (GA)
Daytona Beach Comm Coll (FL)
De Anza Coll (CA)
Delta Coll (MI)
Dixie State Coll of Utah (UT)
Dodge City Comm Coll (KS)
East Central Coll (MO)
East Central Comm Coll (MS)
Eastern Arizona Coll (AZ)
East Mississippi Comm Coll (MS)
El Paso Comm Coll (TX)
Essex County Coll (NJ)
Everett Comm Coll (WA)
Finger Lakes Comm Coll (NY)
Foothill Coll (CA)
Fort Scott Comm Coll (KS)
Frank Phillips Coll (TX)
Gainesville Coll (GA)
Garden City Comm Coll (KS)
Garrett Coll (MD)
Glendale Comm Coll (CA)
Grand Rapids Comm Coll (MI)
Gulf Coast Comm Coll (FL)
Harrisburg Area Comm Coll (PA)
Highland Comm Coll (KS)
Highline Comm Coll (WA)
Hillsborough Comm Coll (FL)
Hinds Comm Coll (MS)
Holyoke Comm Coll (MA)
Howard Comm Coll (MD)

Illinois Eastern Comm Colls, Lincoln Trail Coll (IL)
Illinois Eastern Comm Colls, Olney Central Coll (IL)
Independence Comm Coll (KS)
Indian River Comm Coll (FL)
Iowa Lakes Comm Coll (IA)
Isothermal Comm Coll (NC)
Itawamba Comm Coll (MS)
J. Sargeant Reynolds Comm Coll (VA)
Kilgore Coll (TX)
Kingsborough Comm Coll of City U of NY (NY)
Lansing Comm Coll (MI)
Laramie County Comm Coll (WY)
Lewis and Clark Comm Coll (IL)
Lincoln Land Comm Coll (IL)
Long Beach City Coll (CA)
Lower Columbia Coll (WA)
Manchester Comm Coll (CT)
McLennan Comm Coll (TX)
Miami Dade Coll (FL)
Midland Coll (TX)
Milwaukee Area Tech Coll (WI)
Modesto Jr Coll (CA)
Mohave Comm Coll (AZ)
Napa Valley Coll (CA)
Niagara County Comm Coll (NY)
Northern Essex Comm Coll (MA)
Northern Virginia Comm Coll (VA)
North Idaho Coll (ID)
North Seattle Comm Coll (WA)
Northwestern Michigan Coll (MI)
Northwest-Shoals Comm Coll (AL)
Odessa Coll (TX)
Orange Coast Coll (CA)
Palm Beach Comm Coll (FL)
Pasadena City Coll (CA)
Phillips Comm Coll of the U of Arkansas (AR)
Pima Comm Coll (AZ)
Pratt Comm Coll and Area Vocational School (KS)
Raritan Valley Comm Coll (NJ)
Riverside Comm Coll District (CA)
St. Louis Comm Coll at Forest Park (MO)
St. Louis Comm Coll at Meramec (MO)
St. Philip's Coll (TX)
Sandhills Comm Coll (NC)
San Diego City Coll (CA)
San Joaquin Delta Coll (CA)
San Juan Coll (NM)
Santa Barbara City Coll (CA)
Santa Rosa Jr Coll (CA)
Sauk Valley Comm Coll (IL)
Seward County Comm Coll (KS)
Shelton State Comm Coll (AL)
Sheridan Coll (WY)
Shoreline Comm Coll (WA)
Sinclair Comm Coll (OH)
Snow Coll (UT)
Solano Comm Coll (CA)
South Mountain Comm Coll (AZ)
Southwestern Comm Coll (IA)
Southwestern Oregon Comm Coll (OR)
Tacoma Comm Coll (WA)
Three Rivers Comm Coll (MO)
Trinidad State Jr Coll (CO)
Trinity Valley Comm Coll (TX)
Truett-McConnell Coll (GA)
Umpqua Comm Coll (OR)

Villa Maria Coll of Buffalo (NY)
Waubonsee Comm Coll (IL)
Western Wyoming Comm Coll (WY)
Yuba Coll (CA)

Musical Instrument Fabrication and Repair
Minnesota State Coll–Southeast Tech (MN)
Orange Coast Coll (CA)
Queensborough Comm Coll of City U of NY (NY)

Music History, Literature, and Theory
Snow Coll (UT)

Music Management and Merchandising
Century Coll (MN)
Collin County Comm Coll District (TX)
Full Sail Real World Education (FL)
Houston Comm Coll System (TX)
Independence Comm Coll (KS)
McNally Smith Coll of Music (MN)
Orange Coast Coll (CA)
Villa Maria Coll of Buffalo (NY)

Music Performance
Butler County Comm Coll (KS)
Comm Coll of the Air Force (AL)
Jamestown Comm Coll (NY)
Macomb Comm Coll (MI)
Miami Dade Coll (FL)
Nassau Comm Coll (NY)
Parkland Coll (IL)

Music Related
Globe Coll (MN)
Minnesota School of Business–Brooklyn Center (MN)
Minnesota School of Business–Plymouth (MN)
Minnesota School of Business–Richfield (MN)

Music Teacher Education
Amarillo Coll (TX)
Casper Coll (WY)
Chattahoochee Valley Comm Coll (AL)
Coastal Bend Coll (TX)
Coffeyville Comm Coll (KS)
Colby Comm Coll (KS)
Coll of Lake County (IL)
Copiah-Lincoln Comm Coll (MS)
Delta Coll (MI)
Dodge City Comm Coll (KS)
East Central Comm Coll (MS)
Frank Phillips Coll (TX)
Frederick Comm Coll (MD)
Gainesville Coll (GA)
Highland Comm Coll (IL)
Holmes Comm Coll (MS)
Howard Coll (TX)
Illinois Eastern Comm Colls, Lincoln Trail Coll (IL)
Illinois Eastern Comm Colls, Olney Central Coll (IL)
Independence Comm Coll (KS)
Iowa Lakes Comm Coll (IA)
Itawamba Comm Coll (MS)
Miami Dade Coll (FL)
Midland Coll (TX)
North Idaho Coll (ID)
Parkland Coll (IL)
Sandhills Comm Coll (NC)
Schoolcraft Coll (MI)
Shelton State Comm Coll (AL)
Snow Coll (UT)
Umpqua Comm Coll (OR)
Walters State Comm Coll (TN)

Waubonsee Comm Coll (IL)
Western Oklahoma State Coll (OK)

Music Theory and Composition
Houston Comm Coll System (TX)

Music Therapy
Pasadena City Coll (CA)

Nail Technician and Manicurist
Clovis Comm Coll (NM)
Colorado Northwestern Comm Coll (CO)
Olympic Coll (WA)
Somerset Comm Coll (KY)

Natural Resources/ Conservation
Colorado Northwestern Comm Coll (CO)
Delta Coll (MI)
Dixie State Coll of Utah (UT)
Ellsworth Comm Coll (IA)
Finger Lakes Comm Coll (NY)
Fox Valley Tech Coll (WI)
Fulton-Montgomery Comm Coll (NY)
Highland Comm Coll (KS)
Iowa Lakes Comm Coll (IA)
Itasca Comm Coll (MN)
Muscatine Comm Coll (IA)
Nebraska Indian Comm Coll (NE)
Niagara County Comm Coll (NY)
Rochester Comm and Tech Coll (MN)

Natural Resources Management
Feather River Coll (CA)
Finger Lakes Comm Coll (NY)
Ohio State U Ag Tech Inst (OH)
St. Petersburg Coll (FL)

Natural Resources Management and Policy
Blackfeet Comm Coll (MT)
Central Carolina Tech Coll (SC)
Cerro Coso Comm Coll (CA)
Coll of Lake County (IL)
Columbia Coll (CA)
Delta Coll (MI)
Dixie State Coll of Utah (UT)
Finger Lakes Comm Coll (NY)
Fort Peck Comm Coll (MT)
Frank Phillips Coll (TX)
Garrett Coll (MD)
Greenfield Comm Coll (MA)
Hawkeye Comm Coll (IA)
Itasca Comm Coll (MN)
Lac Courte Oreilles Ojibwa Comm Coll (WI)
Ohio State U Ag Tech Inst (OH)
San Joaquin Delta Coll (CA)
Santa Rosa Jr Coll (CA)
Snow Coll (UT)
Trinidad State Jr Coll (CO)
Wayne County Comm Coll District (MI)

Natural Sciences
Amarillo Coll (TX)
Andrew Coll (GA)
Casper Coll (WY)
Centralia Coll (WA)
Citrus Coll (CA)
Coll of Southern Idaho (ID)
Coll of the Canyons (CA)
Colorado Mountn Coll (CO)
Highline Comm Coll (WA)
Independence Comm Coll (KS)
Iowa Lakes Comm Coll (IA)
Jefferson Comm Coll (NY)
Miami Dade Coll (FL)
Orange Coast Coll (CA)
San Joaquin Delta Coll (CA)

Seward County Comm Coll (KS)
Sisseton-Wahpeton Comm Coll (SD)
Snow Coll (UT)
Umpqua Comm Coll (OR)
U of Pittsburgh at Titusville (PA)

Near and Middle Eastern Studies
Wayne County Comm Coll District (MI)

Non-Profit Management
Goodwin Coll (CT)
Miami Dade Coll (FL)

Nuclear and Industrial Radiologic Technologies Related
Linn State Tech Coll (MO)

Nuclear Engineering
Itasca Comm Coll (MN)

Nuclear Medical Technology
Amarillo Coll (TX)
Bronx Comm Coll of City U of NY (NY)
Broward Comm Coll (FL)
Caldwell Comm Coll and Tech Inst (NC)
Chattanooga State Tech Comm Coll (TN)
Coll of DuPage (IL)
Comm Coll of Allegheny County (PA)
Comm Coll of the Air Force (AL)
Compton Comm Coll (CA)
Darton Coll (GA)
Delaware Tech & Comm Coll, Stanton/ Wilmington Cmps (DE)
Florida Hospital Coll of Health Sciences (FL)
Forsyth Tech Comm Coll (NC)
GateWay Comm Coll (AZ)
Gateway Comm Coll (CT)
Harrisburg Area Comm Coll (PA)
Hillsborough Comm Coll (FL)
Houston Comm Coll System (TX)
Howard Comm Coll (MD)
Jefferson Comm Coll (KY)
Miami Dade Coll (FL)
Midlands Tech Coll (SC)
Oakland Comm Coll (MI)
Orange Coast Coll (CA)
Santa Fe Comm Coll (FL)
Southeast Tech Inst (SD)
Springfield Tech Comm Coll (MA)
Union County Coll (NJ)
U of Cincinnati Raymond Walters Coll (OH)
West Virginia State Comm and Tech Coll (WV)

Nuclear/Nuclear Power Technology
Allen County Comm Coll (KS)
Central Florida Comm Coll (FL)
Chattanooga State Tech Comm Coll (TN)
Florida Comm Coll at Jacksonville (FL)
Texas State Tech Coll– Waco/Marshall Campus (TX)
Three Rivers Comm Coll (CT)
Westmoreland County Comm Coll (PA)

Nursing Assistant/Aide and Patient Care Assistant
Alexandria Tech Coll (MN)
Allen County Comm Coll (KS)
Colorado Northwestern Comm Coll (CO)

Comm Coll of Allegheny County (PA)
Glendale Comm Coll (AZ)
Johnson County Comm Coll (KS)
Lake Region State Coll (ND)
Laramie County Comm Coll (WY)
Lower Columbia Coll (WA)
Midlands Tech Coll (SC)
Mineral Area Coll (MO)
Modesto Jr Coll (CA)
North Iowa Area Comm Coll (IA)
Sandhills Comm Coll (NC)
Southwest Wisconsin Tech Coll (WI)
Trinidad State Jr Coll (CO)
Waubonsee Comm Coll (IL)
Western Iowa Tech Comm Coll (IA)
Western Wyoming Comm Coll (WY)

Nursing (Licensed Practical/ Vocational Nurse Training)
Alexandria Tech Coll (MN)
Alpena Comm Coll (MI)
Amarillo Coll (TX)
American Samoa Comm Coll (AS)
Arizona Western Coll (AZ)
Athens Tech Coll (GA)
Atlanta Metropolitan Coll (GA)
Bainbridge Coll (GA)
Bay de Noc Comm Coll (MI)
Belmont Tech Coll (OH)
Bessemer State Tech Coll (AL)
Big Bend Comm Coll (WA)
Bismarck State Coll (ND)
Black Hawk Coll, Moline (IL)
Blue Mountain Comm Coll (OR)
Carteret Comm Coll (NC)
Casper Coll (WY)
Central Arizona Coll (AZ)
Central Comm Coll– Columbus Campus (NE)
Central Comm Coll–Grand Island Campus (NE)
Centralia Coll (WA)
Central Oregon Comm Coll (OR)
Central Piedmont Comm Coll (NC)
Central Texas Coll (TX)
Cerro Coso Comm Coll (CA)
Chattahoochee Valley Comm Coll (AL)
Chemeketa Comm Coll (OR)
Citrus Coll (CA)
Clark State Comm Coll (OH)
Clinton Comm Coll (IA)
Coastal Bend Coll (TX)
Coffeyville Comm Coll (KS)
Colby Comm Coll (KS)
Coll of Southern Maryland (MD)
Coll of the Canyons (CA)
Colorado Mountn Coll (CO)
Columbus State Comm Coll (OH)
Comm Coll of Allegheny County (PA)
Comm Coll of Beaver County (PA)
Comm Coll of Southern Nevada (NV)
Contra Costa Coll (CA)
Danville Area Comm Coll (IL)
Darton Coll (GA)
Daytona Beach Comm Coll (FL)
De Anza Coll (CA)
Delaware Tech & Comm Coll, Jack F Owens Cmps (DE)
Delaware Tech & Comm Coll, Terry Cmps (DE)
Delta Coll (MI)
Des Moines Area Comm Coll (IA)
Dodge City Comm Coll (KS)

Durham Tech Comm Coll (NC)
East Arkansas Comm Coll (AR)
Eastern Maine Comm Coll (ME)
Edgecombe Comm Coll (NC)
Elgin Comm Coll (IL)
Eugenio María de Hostos Comm Coll of City U of NY (NY)
Everett Comm Coll (WA)
Fayetteville Tech Comm Coll (NC)
Feather River Coll (CA)
George Corley Wallace State Comm Coll (AL)
Glendale Comm Coll (CA)
Gogebic Comm Coll (MI)
Gordon Coll (GA)
Grand Rapids Comm Coll (MI)
Green River Comm Coll (WA)
Hawkeye Comm Coll (IA)
Heartland Comm Coll (IL)
Hinds Comm Coll (MS)
Hopkinsville Comm Coll (KY)
Howard Coll (TX)
Howard Comm Coll (MD)
Illinois Eastern Comm Colls, Olney Central Coll (IL)
Indian Hills Comm Coll (IA)
Indian River Comm Coll (FL)
Iowa Central Comm Coll (IA)
Iowa Western Comm Coll (IA)
Isothermal Comm Coll (NC)
Itasca Comm Coll (MN)
Jackson Comm Coll (MI)
James H. Faulkner State Comm Coll (AL)
Jefferson Comm Coll (OH)
John A. Logan Coll (IL)
Johnson County Comm Coll (KS)
Kingwood Coll (TX)
Lake Region State Coll (ND)
Lansing Comm Coll (MI)
Lehigh Carbon Comm Coll (PA)
Lower Columbia Coll (WA)
Luna Comm Coll (NM)
Manhattan Area Tech Coll (KS)
Maria Coll (NY)
Metropolitan Comm Coll (NE)
Midlands Tech Coll (SC)
Mid Michigan Comm Coll (MI)
Milwaukee Area Tech Coll (WI)
Mineral Area Coll (MO)
Minnesota State Coll– Southeast Tech (MN)
Mott Comm Coll (MI)
Muscatine Comm Coll (IA)
North Dakota State Coll of Science (ND)
North Idaho Coll (ID)
North Iowa Area Comm Coll (IA)
Northland Comm and Tech Coll–Thief River Falls (MN)
North Seattle Comm Coll (WA)
Northwest-Shoals Comm Coll (AL)
Northwest Tech Coll (MN)
Oakland Comm Coll (MI)
Olympic Coll (WA)
Ouachita Tech Coll (AR)
Pasadena City Coll (CA)
Phillips Comm Coll of the U of Arkansas (AR)
Rockingham Comm Coll (NC)
St. Cloud Tech Coll (MN)
St. Philip's Coll (TX)
Salt Lake Comm Coll (UT)
Sandhills Comm Coll (NC)
San Diego City Coll (CA)
San Joaquin Delta Coll (CA)

San Joaquin Valley Coll (CA)
Santa Barbara City Coll (CA)
Scott Comm Coll (IA)
Seward County Comm Coll (KS)
Shelton State Comm Coll (AL)
Southern Maine Comm Coll (ME)
Southwestern Comm Coll (IA)
Southwestern Comm Coll (NC)
Southwest Wisconsin Tech Coll (WI)
Surry Comm Coll (NC)
Tech Coll of the Lowcountry (SC)
Temple Coll (TX)
Trinidad State Jr Coll (CO)
Trinity Valley Comm Coll (TX)
Union County Coll (NJ)
U of Arkansas Comm Coll at Morrilton (AR)
Walla Walla Comm Coll (WA)
Western Wyoming Comm Coll (WY)
Westmoreland County Comm Coll (PA)
Williston State Coll (ND)
Yuba Coll (CA)

Nursing Midwifery
Miami Dade Coll (FL)

Nursing (Registered Nurse Training)
Adirondack Comm Coll (NY)
Alabama Southern Comm Coll (AL)
Alamance Comm Coll (NC)
Albuquerque Tech Vocational Inst (NM)
Allegany Coll of Maryland (MD)
Alpena Comm Coll (MI)
Alvin Comm Coll (TX)
Amarillo Coll (TX)
American Samoa Comm Coll (AS)
Andrew Coll (GA)
Anne Arundel Comm Coll (MD)
Anoka-Ramsey Comm Coll (MN)
Anoka-Ramsey Comm Coll, Cambridge Campus (MN)
Arapahoe Comm Coll (CO)
Arizona Western Coll (AZ)
Arkansas Northeastern Coll (AR)
Asheville-Buncombe Tech Comm Coll (NC)
Ashland Comm and Tech Coll (KY)
Athens Tech Coll (GA)
Atlantic Cape Comm Coll (NJ)
Austin Comm Coll (TX)
Bainbridge Coll (GA)
Baltimore City Comm Coll (MD)
Barton County Comm Coll (KS)
Bay de Noc Comm Coll (MI)
Beaufort County Comm Coll (NC)
Belmont Tech Coll (OH)
Bergen Comm Coll (NJ)
Berkshire Comm Coll (MA)
Bevill State Comm Coll (AL)
Big Bend Comm Coll (WA)
Big Sandy Comm and Tech Coll (KY)
Bishop State Comm Coll (AL)
Black Hawk Coll, Moline (IL)
Black River Tech Coll (AR)
Bladen Comm Coll (NC)
Blue Mountain Comm Coll (OR)
Blue Ridge Comm Coll (NC)
Blue Ridge Comm Coll (VA)

Borough of Manhattan Comm Coll of City U of NY (NY)
Bowling Green State U–Firelands Coll (OH)
Brazosport Coll (TX)
Brevard Comm Coll (FL)
Bristol Comm Coll (MA)
Bronx Comm Coll of City U of NY (NY)
Brookdale Comm Coll (NJ)
Broome Comm Coll (NY)
Broward Comm Coll (FL)
Brunswick Comm Coll (NC)
Bucks County Comm Coll (PA)
Bunker Hill Comm Coll (MA)
Butler County Comm Coll (KS)
Butler County Comm Coll (PA)
Caldwell Comm Coll and Tech Inst (NC)
Calhoun Comm Coll (AL)
Cape Cod Comm Coll (MA)
Cape Fear Comm Coll (NC)
Capital Comm Coll (CT)
Carolinas Coll of Health Sciences (NC)
Carroll Comm Coll (MD)
Casper Coll (WY)
Catawba Valley Comm Coll (NC)
Cayuga County Comm Coll (NY)
Cecil Comm Coll (MD)
Central Alabama Comm Coll (AL)
Central Arizona Coll (AZ)
Central Carolina Comm Coll (NC)
Central Carolina Tech Coll (SC)
Central Comm Coll–Grand Island Campus (NE)
Central Florida Comm Coll (FL)
Centralia Coll (WA)
Central Maine Medical Center School of Nursing (ME)
Central Oregon Comm Coll (OR)
Central Piedmont Comm Coll (NC)
Central Texas Coll (TX)
Central Wyoming Coll (WY)
Century Coll (MN)
Chattahoochee Valley Comm Coll (AL)
Chattanooga State Tech Comm Coll (TN)
Chemeketa Comm Coll (OR)
Chipola Coll (FL)
Cincinnati State Tech and Comm Coll (OH)
Clackamas Comm Coll (OR)
Clarendon Coll (TX)
Clark Coll (WA)
Clark State Comm Coll (OH)
Clatsop Comm Coll (OR)
Cleveland Comm Coll (NC)
Cleveland State Comm Coll (TN)
Clinton Comm Coll (IA)
Clinton Comm Coll (NY)
Cloud County Comm Coll (KS)
Clovis Comm Coll (NM)
Coastal Bend Coll (TX)
Coastal Carolina Comm Coll (NC)
Coastal Georgia Comm Coll (GA)
Cochise Coll, Douglas (AZ)
Coffeyville Comm Coll (KS)
Colby Comm Coll (KS)
Coll of DuPage (IL)
Coll of Lake County (IL)
Coll of Southern Idaho (ID)
Coll of Southern Maryland (MD)
Coll of the Canyons (CA)
Coll of the Mainland (TX)

Collin County Comm Coll District (TX)
Colorado Mountn Coll (CO)
Colorado Northwestern Comm Coll (CO)
Columbia-Greene Comm Coll (NY)
Columbia State Comm Coll (TN)
Columbus State Comm Coll (OH)
Comm Coll of Allegheny County (PA)
Comm Coll of Beaver County (PA)
Comm Coll of Denver (CO)
Comm Coll of Philadelphia (PA)
Comm Coll of Rhode Island (RI)
Comm Coll of Southern Nevada (NV)
Compton Comm Coll (CA)
Contra Costa Coll (CA)
Copiah-Lincoln Comm Coll (MS)
Corning Comm Coll (NY)
Craven Comm Coll (NC)
Crouse Hospital School of Nursing (NY)
Crowder Coll (MO)
Cumberland County Coll (NJ)
Cuyahoga Comm Coll (OH)
Dabney S. Lancaster Comm Coll (VA)
Danville Area Comm Coll (IL)
Darton Coll (GA)
Davenport U, Midland (MI)
Davidson County Comm Coll (NC)
Daytona Beach Comm Coll (FL)
De Anza Coll (CA)
Delaware County Comm Coll (PA)
Delaware Tech & Comm Coll, Jack F Owens Cmps (DE)
Delaware Tech & Comm Coll, Stanton/ Wilmington Cmps (DE)
Delaware Tech & Comm Coll, Terry Cmps (DE)
Delta Coll (MI)
Des Moines Area Comm Coll (IA)
Dixie State Coll of Utah (UT)
Dodge City Comm Coll (KS)
Doña Ana Branch Comm Coll (NM)
Durham Tech Comm Coll (NC)
Dutchess Comm Coll (NY)
Dyersburg State Comm Coll (TN)
East Central Coll (MO)
East Central Comm Coll (MS)
Eastern Arizona Coll (AZ)
Eastern Maine Comm Coll (ME)
Eastern Shore Comm Coll (VA)
Edgecombe Comm Coll (NC)
Edison State Comm Coll (OH)
Elgin Comm Coll (IL)
Elizabethtown Comm and Tech Coll (KY)
Ellsworth Comm Coll (IA)
El Paso Comm Coll (TX)
Erie Comm Coll (NY)
Erie Comm Coll, North Campus (NY)
Essex County Coll (NJ)
Eugenio María de Hostos Comm Coll of City U of NY (NY)
Everett Comm Coll (WA)
Fairmont State Comm & Tech Coll (WV)
Fayetteville Tech Comm Coll (NC)

Finger Lakes Comm Coll (NY)
Florida Comm Coll at Jacksonville (FL)
Florida Hospital Coll of Health Sciences (FL)
Florida Keys Comm Coll (FL)
Forsyth Tech Comm Coll (NC)
Fort Scott Comm Coll (KS)
Fox Valley Tech Coll (WI)
Frank Phillips Coll (TX)
Frederick Comm Coll (MD)
Front Range Comm Coll (CO)
Fulton-Montgomery Comm Coll (NY)
Gadsden State Comm Coll (AL)
Garden City Comm Coll (KS)
GateWay Comm Coll (AZ)
Genesee Comm Coll (NY)
George Corley Wallace State Comm Coll (AL)
George C. Wallace Comm Coll (AL)
Germanna Comm Coll (VA)
Glendale Comm Coll (AZ)
Glendale Comm Coll (CA)
Glen Oaks Comm Coll (MI)
Gogebic Comm Coll (MI)
Goodwin Coll (CT)
Gordon Coll (GA)
Grand Rapids Comm Coll (MI)
Great Basin Coll (NV)
Greenfield Comm Coll (MA)
Guilford Tech Comm Coll (NC)
Gulf Coast Comm Coll (FL)
Hagerstown Comm Coll (MD)
Halifax Comm Coll (NC)
Harcum Coll (PA)
Harford Comm Coll (MD)
Harrisburg Area Comm Coll (PA)
Hawkeye Comm Coll (IA)
Haywood Comm Coll (NC)
Hazard Comm and Tech Coll (KY)
Heartland Comm Coll (IL)
Henderson Comm Coll (KY)
Henry Ford Comm Coll (MI)
Hesston Coll (KS)
Hibbing Comm Coll (MN)
Highland Comm Coll (IL)
Highland Comm Coll (KS)
Highline Comm Coll (WA)
Hillsborough Comm Coll (FL)
Hinds Comm Coll (MS)
Holmes Comm Coll (MS)
Holyoke Comm Coll (MA)
Hopkinsville Comm Coll (KY)
Houston Comm Coll System (TX)
Howard Coll (TX)
Howard Comm Coll (MD)
Hudson County Comm Coll (NJ)
Hudson Valley Comm Coll (NY)
Hutchinson Comm Coll and Area Vocational School (KS)
Illinois Eastern Comm Colls, Frontier Comm Coll (IL)
Illinois Eastern Comm Colls, Olney Central Coll (IL)
Illinois Valley Comm Coll (IL)
Indian Hills Comm Coll (IA)
Indian River Comm Coll (FL)
Iowa Central Comm Coll (IA)
Iowa Lakes Comm Coll (IA)
Iowa Western Comm Coll (IA)
Itawamba Comm Coll (MS)
Ivy Tech State Coll–Bloomington (IN)
Ivy Tech State Coll–Central Indiana (IN)
Ivy Tech State Coll–Eastcentral (IN)

Ivy Tech State Coll–Lafayette (IN)
Ivy Tech State Coll–North Central (IN)
Ivy Tech State Coll–Northwest (IN)
Ivy Tech State Coll–Southcentral (IN)
Ivy Tech State Coll–Southeast (IN)
Ivy Tech State Coll–Southwest (IN)
Ivy Tech State Coll–Wabash Valley (IN)
Ivy Tech State Coll–Whitewater (IN)
Jackson Comm Coll (MI)
Jackson State Comm Coll (TN)
James H. Faulkner State Comm Coll (AL)
James Sprunt Comm Coll (NC)
Jamestown Comm Coll (NY)
Jefferson Comm Coll (KY)
Jefferson Comm Coll (NY)
Jefferson State Comm Coll (AL)
John A. Logan Coll (IL)
Johnson County Comm Coll (KS)
Johnston Comm Coll (NC)
John Tyler Comm Coll (VA)
John Wood Comm Coll (IL)
J. Sargeant Reynolds Comm Coll (VA)
Kalamazoo Valley Comm Coll (MI)
Kansas City Kansas Comm Coll (KS)
Kapiolani Comm Coll (HI)
Kaskaskia Coll (IL)
Kauai Comm Coll (HI)
Keiser Coll, Miami (FL)
Kennebec Valley Comm Coll (ME)
Kent State U, Tuscarawas Campus (OH)
Kilgore Coll (TX)
Kingsborough Comm Coll of City U of NY (NY)
Lac Courte Oreilles Ojibwa Comm Coll (WI)
Lake Land Coll (IL)
Lake-Sumter Comm Coll (FL)
Lake Superior Coll (MN)
Lane Comm Coll (OR)
Lansing Comm Coll (MI)
Laramie County Comm Coll (WY)
Laredo Comm Coll (TX)
Lehigh Carbon Comm Coll (PA)
Lewis and Clark Comm Coll (IL)
Lincoln Land Comm Coll (IL)
Linn-Benton Comm Coll (OR)
Long Beach City Coll (CA)
Lower Columbia Coll (WA)
Macomb Comm Coll (MI)
Manhattan Area Tech Coll (KS)
Maria Coll (NY)
Massachusetts Bay Comm Coll (MA)
Mayland Comm Coll (NC)
McDowell Tech Comm Coll (NC)
McLennan Comm Coll (TX)
Mercy Coll of Northwest Ohio (OH)
Meridian Comm Coll (MS)
Metropolitan Comm Coll (NE)
Miami Dade Coll (FL)
Middle Georgia Coll (GA)
Midland Coll (TX)
Midlands Tech Coll (SC)
Mid Michigan Comm Coll (MI)
Milwaukee Area Tech Coll (WI)

Mineral Area Coll (MO)
Minneapolis Comm and Tech Coll (MN)
Minnesota State Coll–Southeast Tech (MN)
Moberly Area Comm Coll (MO)
Modesto Jr Coll (CA)
Mohave Comm Coll (AZ)
Mohawk Valley Comm Coll (NY)
Montcalm Comm Coll (MI)
Montgomery County Comm Coll (PA)
Moraine Valley Comm Coll (IL)
Motlow State Comm Coll (TN)
Mott Comm Coll (MI)
Mount Wachusett Comm Coll (MA)
Muskegon Comm Coll (MI)
Napa Valley Coll (CA)
Nassau Comm Coll (NY)
New Hampshire Comm Tech Coll, Manchester/Stratham (NH)
Niagara County Comm Coll (NY)
Northampton County Area Comm Coll (PA)
North Central Missouri Coll (MO)
North Central State Coll (OH)
North Country Comm Coll (NY)
Northeast Alabama Comm Coll (AL)
Northern Essex Comm Coll (MA)
Northern Virginia Comm Coll (VA)
North Hennepin Comm Coll (MN)
North Idaho Coll (ID)
North Iowa Area Comm Coll (IA)
Northland Comm and Tech Coll–Thief River Falls (MN)
North Seattle Comm Coll (WA)
North Shore Comm Coll (MA)
Northwestern Michigan Coll (MI)
Northwest-Shoals Comm Coll (AL)
Northwest State Comm Coll (OH)
Oakland Comm Coll (MI)
Odessa Coll (TX)
Olympic Coll (WA)
Orange County Comm Coll (NY)
Otero Jr Coll (CO)
Owensboro Comm and Tech Coll (KY)
Owens Comm Coll, Findlay (OH)
Owens Comm Coll, Toledo (OH)
Palm Beach Comm Coll (FL)
Panola Coll (TX)
Parkland Coll (IL)
Pasadena City Coll (CA)
Pasco-Hernando Comm Coll (FL)
Patrick Henry Comm Coll (VA)
Peninsula Coll (WA)
Penn State U Fayette Campus of the Commonwealth Coll (PA)
Penn State U Mont Alto Campus of the Commonwealth Coll (PA)
Penn State U Worthington Scranton Cmps Commonwealth Coll (PA)
Penn Valley Comm Coll (MO)
Phillips Beth Israel School of Nursing (NY)

Phillips Comm Coll of the U of Arkansas (AR)
Piedmont Comm Coll (NC)
Piedmont Virginia Comm Coll (VA)
Pima Comm Coll (AZ)
Polk Comm Coll (FL)
Prairie State Coll (IL)
Pratt Comm Coll and Area Vocational School (KS)
Queensborough Comm Coll of City U of NY (NY)
Randolph Comm Coll (NC)
Raritan Valley Comm Coll (NJ)
Richland Comm Coll (IL)
Richmond Comm Coll (NC)
Riverland Comm Coll (MN)
Riverside Comm Coll District (CA)
Roanoke-Chowan Comm Coll (NC)
Rochester Comm and Tech Coll (MN)
Rockingham Comm Coll (NC)
Rockland Comm Coll (NY)
Rock Valley Coll (IL)
Rogue Comm Coll (OR)
Rowan-Cabarrus Comm Coll (NC)
Saint Charles Comm Coll (MO)
St. Louis Comm Coll at Forest Park (MO)
St. Louis Comm Coll at Meramec (MO)
St. Luke's Coll (IA)
St. Petersburg Coll (FL)
Salt Lake Comm Coll (UT)
San Antonio Coll (TX)
Sandhills Comm Coll (NC)
San Diego City Coll (CA)
San Joaquin Delta Coll (CA)
San Juan Coll (NM)
Santa Barbara City Coll (CA)
Santa Fe Comm Coll (FL)
Santa Rosa Jr Coll (CA)
Sauk Valley Comm Coll (IL)
Schoolcraft Coll (MI)
Scott Comm Coll (IA)
Seattle Central Comm Coll (WA)
Seminole Comm Coll (FL)
Seminole State Coll (OK)
Seward County Comm Coll (KS)
Shawnee Comm Coll (IL)
Shelton State Comm Coll (AL)
Sheridan Coll (WY)
Shoreline Comm Coll (WA)
Sinclair Comm Coll (OH)
Sisseton-Wahpeton Comm Coll (SD)
Solano Comm Coll (CA)
Somerset Comm Coll (KY)
South Central Tech Coll (MN)
Southeast Comm Coll, Lincoln Campus (NE)
Southeast Kentucky Comm and Tech Coll (KY)
Southern Maine Comm Coll (ME)
Southern State Comm Coll (OH)
Southern Union State Comm Coll (AL)
Southside Virginia Comm Coll (VA)
South Texas Coll (TX)
Southwestern Comm Coll (IA)
Southwestern Comm Coll (NC)
Southwestern Michigan Coll (MI)
Southwestern Oklahoma State U at Sayre (OK)
Southwestern Oregon Comm Coll (OR)
Southwest Wisconsin Tech Coll (WI)

Springfield Tech Comm Coll (MA)
Stanly Comm Coll (NC)
State U of NY Coll of Technology at Alfred (NY)
State U of NY Coll of Technology at Canton (NY)
State U of NY Coll of Technology at Delhi (NY)
Surry Comm Coll (NC)
Tacoma Comm Coll (WA)
Tech Coll of the Lowcountry (SC)
Temple Coll (TX)
Three Rivers Comm Coll (CT)
Three Rivers Comm Coll (MO)
Tompkins Cortland Comm Coll (NY)
Tri-County Comm Coll (NC)
Tri-County Tech Coll (SC)
Trident Tech Coll (SC)
Trinidad State Jr Coll (CO)
Trinity Valley Comm Coll (TX)
Truckee Meadows Comm Coll (NV)
Umpqua Comm Coll (OR)
Union County Coll (NJ)
U of Arkansas Comm Coll at Batesville (AR)
U of Cincinnati Raymond Walters Coll (OH)
Valencia Comm Coll (FL)
Wake Tech Comm Coll (NC)
Walla Walla Comm Coll (WA)
Walters State Comm Coll (TN)
Waubonsee Comm Coll (IL)
Wayne County Comm Coll District (MI)
Westchester Comm Coll (NY)
Western Iowa Tech Comm Coll (IA)
Western Nevada Comm Coll (NV)
Western Oklahoma State Coll (OK)
West Kentucky Comm and Tech Coll (KY)
Westmoreland County Comm Coll (PA)
West Virginia U at Parkersburg (WV)
Whatcom Comm Coll (WA)
Wilkes Comm Coll (NC)
Wilson Tech Comm Coll (NC)
Wor-Wic Comm Coll (MD)
Yakima Valley Comm Coll (WA)
Yavapai Coll (AZ)
Yuba Coll (CA)

Nursing Related
Big Sandy Comm and Tech Coll (KY)
Cincinnati State Tech and Comm Coll (OH)
Somerset Comm Coll (KY)
Southeast Tech Inst (SD)
Tillamook Bay Comm Coll (OR)

Nutrition Sciences
Mohawk Valley Comm Coll (NY)
Sisseton-Wahpeton Comm Coll (SD)

Occupational Health and Industrial Hygiene
Niagara County Comm Coll (NY)
Northampton County Area Comm Coll (PA)

Occupational Safety and Health Technology
Brazosport Coll (TX)
Clinton Comm Coll (IA)
Comm Coll of the Air Force (AL)
Cossatot Comm Coll of the U of Arkansas (AR)

Delaware Tech & Comm Coll, Stanton/ Wilmington Cmps (DE)
Durham Tech Comm Coll (NC)
GateWay Comm Coll (AZ)
Houston Comm Coll System (TX)
Ivy Tech State Coll–Central Indiana (IN)
Ivy Tech State Coll–Northeast (IN)
Ivy Tech State Coll–Northwest (IN)
Ivy Tech State Coll–Wabash Valley (IN)
Kilgore Coll (TX)
Lanier Tech Coll (GA)
Mineral Area Coll (MO)
Muscatine Comm Coll (IA)
Okefenokee Tech Coll (GA)
Paradise Valley Comm Coll (AZ)
San Diego City Coll (CA)
San Diego Miramar Coll (CA)
Scott Comm Coll (IA)
Texas State Tech Coll–Waco/Marshall Campus (TX)
Trinidad State Jr Coll (CO)
The U of Akron–Wayne Coll (OH)

Occupational Therapist Assistant
Adirondack Comm Coll (NY)
Allegany Coll of Maryland (MD)
Apollo Coll (ID)
Briarwood Coll (CT)
Bristol Comm Coll (MA)
Cape Fear Comm Coll (NC)
Cincinnati State Tech and Comm Coll (OH)
Coll of DuPage (IL)
Comm Coll of Allegheny County (PA)
Comm Coll of Rhode Island (RI)
Darton Coll (GA)
Delaware Tech & Comm Coll, Stanton/ Wilmington Cmps (DE)
Erie Comm Coll, North Campus (NY)
Florida Hospital Coll of Health Sciences (FL)
Green River Comm Coll (WA)
Guilford Tech Comm Coll (NC)
Harcum Coll (PA)
Houston Comm Coll System (TX)
Ivy Tech State Coll–Central Indiana (IN)
Jamestown Comm Coll (NY)
Johnson County Comm Coll (KS)
J. Sargeant Reynolds Comm Coll (VA)
Kennebec Valley Comm Coll (ME)
Lake Superior Coll (MN)
Lehigh Carbon Comm Coll (PA)
Lewis and Clark Comm Coll (IL)
Lincoln Land Comm Coll (IL)
Macomb Comm Coll (MI)
Manchester Comm Coll (CT)
Maria Coll (NY)
Massachusetts Bay Comm Coll (MA)
Middle Georgia Coll (GA)
Midlands Tech Coll (SC)
Mott Comm Coll (MI)
North Dakota State Coll of Science (ND)
Northwestern Tech Coll (GA)
Northwest Tech Coll (MN)
Owens Comm Coll, Toledo (OH)
Parkland Coll (IL)

Penn State U DuBois
Campus of the
Commonwealth Coll (PA)
Penn State U Mont Alto
Campus of the
Commonwealth Coll (PA)
Penn State U Worthington
Scranton Cmps
Commonwealth Coll (PA)
Polk Comm Coll (FL)
Rockingham Comm Coll
(NC)
St. Philip's Coll (TX)
Salt Lake Comm Coll (UT)
Schoolcraft Coll (MI)
Scott Comm Coll (IA)
Southwestern Oklahoma
State U at Sayre (OK)
Southwest Georgia Tech Coll
(GA)
Springfield Tech Comm Coll
(MA)
Stanly Comm Coll (NC)
State U of NY Coll of
Technology at Canton (NY)
Union County Coll (NJ)
Western Iowa Tech Comm
Coll (IA)

Occupational Therapy
Alabama Southern Comm
Coll (AL)
Allegany Coll of Maryland
(MD)
Amarillo Coll (TX)
Andrew Coll (GA)
Austin Comm Coll (TX)
Barton County Comm Coll
(KS)
Bay State Coll (MA)
Bristol Comm Coll (MA)
Casper Coll (WY)
Chattanooga State Tech
Comm Coll (TN)
City Colls of Chicago, Wilbur
Wright Coll (IL)
Coastal Georgia Comm Coll
(GA)
Coffeyville Comm Coll (KS)
Coll of DuPage (IL)
Coll of Southern Idaho (ID)
Comm Coll of Southern
Nevada (NV)
Danville Area Comm Coll (IL)
Daytona Beach Comm Coll
(FL)
Durham Tech Comm Coll
(NC)
East Central Comm Coll
(MS)
Everett Comm Coll (WA)
Fox Valley Tech Coll (WI)
Genesee Comm Coll (NY)
George Corley Wallace State
Comm Coll (AL)
Highland Comm Coll (KS)
Hillsborough Comm Coll (FL)
ICM School of Business &
Medical Careers (PA)
Iowa Central Comm Coll (IA)
John A. Logan Coll (IL)
Kapiolani Comm Coll (HI)
Keiser Coll, Fort Lauderdale
(FL)
Keystone Coll (PA)
Kingwood Coll (TX)
Milwaukee Area Tech Coll
(WI)
Nashville State Tech Comm
Coll (TN)
North Shore Comm Coll
(MA)
Orange County Comm Coll
(NY)
Palm Beach Comm Coll (FL)
Pasadena City Coll (CA)
Penn Valley Comm Coll
(MO)
Rockland Comm Coll (NY)
Saint Charles Comm Coll
(MO)
St. Louis Comm Coll at
Meramec (MO)
Santa Rosa Jr Coll (CA)
Sauk Valley Comm Coll (IL)

Sinclair Comm Coll (OH)
South Texas Coll (TX)
Tacoma Comm Coll (WA)
Trident Tech Coll (SC)
Wayne County Comm Coll
District (MI)
Yakima Valley Comm Coll
(WA)

**Oceanography (Chemical
and Physical)**
Arizona Western Coll (AZ)
Everett Comm Coll (WA)
Riverside Comm Coll District
(CA)
Santa Rosa Jr Coll (CA)
Shoreline Comm Coll (WA)
Southern Maine Comm Coll
(ME)
Tacoma Comm Coll (WA)

Office Management
Academy Coll (MN)
Alexandria Tech Coll (MN)
Alpena Comm Coll (MI)
Berkeley Coll–New York City
Campus (NY)
Berkeley Coll–Westchester
Campus (NY)
Big Bend Comm Coll (WA)
Calhoun Comm Coll (AL)
Central Texas Coll (TX)
Cincinnati State Tech and
Comm Coll (OH)
Clackamas Comm Coll (OR)
Clover Park Tech Coll (WA)
Coll of DuPage (IL)
Comm Coll of Allegheny
County (PA)
Comm Coll of the Air Force
(AL)
Delaware County Comm Coll
(PA)
Delta Coll (MI)
Edmonds Comm Coll (WA)
Erie Comm Coll (NY)
Erie Comm Coll, North
Campus (NY)
Erie Comm Coll, South
Campus (NY)
Florida Comm Coll at
Jacksonville (FL)
Gadsden State Comm
Coll-Ayers Campus (AL)
Gogebic Comm Coll (MI)
Great Basin Coll (NV)
Green River Comm Coll
(WA)
Howard Comm Coll (MD)
Iowa Lakes Comm Coll (IA)
Lake Land Coll (IL)
Lake Region State Coll (ND)
Lake-Sumter Comm Coll
(FL)
Lower Columbia Coll (WA)
McIntosh Coll (NH)
Modesto Jr Coll (CA)
Mott Comm Coll (MI)
National Coll of Business &
Technology, Salem (VA)
North Seattle Comm Coll
(WA)
Oakland Comm Coll (MI)
Olympic Coll (WA)
Peninsula Coll (WA)
Saint Charles Comm Coll
(MO)
St. Cloud Tech Coll (MN)
South Hills School of
Business & Technology,
State College (PA)
Southwestern Oregon Comm
Coll (OR)
State U of NY Coll of
Technology at Canton (NY)
Tillamook Bay Comm Coll
(OR)
The U of Akron–Wayne Coll
(OH)
Valencia Comm Coll (FL)
Walla Walla Comm Coll (WA)

**Office Occupations and
Clerical Services**
Alamance Comm Coll (NC)
Alexandria Tech Coll (MN)

Big Sandy Comm and Tech
Coll (KY)
Butler County Comm Coll
(PA)
Comm and Tech Coll of
Shepherd (WV)
Darton Coll (GA)
Delta Coll (MI)
East Mississippi Comm Coll
(MS)
Florida Comm Coll at
Jacksonville (FL)
GateWay Comm Coll (AZ)
Hillsborough Comm Coll (FL)
Iowa Lakes Comm Coll (IA)
Lake Region State Coll (ND)
Lanier Tech Coll (GA)
Laurel Business Inst (PA)
Lehigh Carbon Comm Coll
(PA)
Modesto Jr Coll (CA)
North Country Comm Coll
(NY)
Okefenokee Tech Coll (GA)
Pennsylvania Inst of
Technology (PA)
Walla Walla Comm Coll (WA)
West Virginia State Comm
and Tech Coll (WV)

Operations Management
Alamance Comm Coll (NC)
Alexandria Tech Coll (MN)
Alpena Comm Coll (MI)
Asheville-Buncombe Tech
Comm Coll (NC)
Atlanta Metropolitan Coll
(GA)
Bowling Green State
U-Firelands Coll (OH)
Bunker Hill Comm Coll (MA)
Catawba Valley Comm Coll
(NC)
Central Carolina Comm Coll
(NC)
Cleveland Comm Coll (NC)
DeKalb Tech Coll (GA)
Durham Tech Comm Coll
(NC)
Goodwin Coll (CT)
Great Basin Coll (NV)
Guam Comm Coll (GU)
Johnston Comm Coll (NC)
Kilgore Coll (TX)
Lehigh Carbon Comm Coll
(PA)
Macomb Comm Coll (MI)
Mineral Area Coll (MO)
North Central State Coll (OH)
Oakland Comm Coll (MI)
Owens Comm Coll, Findlay
(OH)
Waubonsee Comm Coll (IL)

**Ophthalmic and Optometric
Support Services And Allied
Professions Related**
Mid Michigan Comm Coll
(MI)

**Ophthalmic Laboratory
Technology**
Comm Coll of Aurora (CO)
Comm Coll of the Air Force
(AL)
DeKalb Tech Coll (GA)
Durham Tech Comm Coll
(NC)
East Mississippi Comm Coll
(MS)
El Paso Comm Coll (TX)
Everett Comm Coll (WA)
Hillsborough Comm Coll (FL)
Raritan Valley Comm Coll
(NJ)
St. Cloud Tech Coll (MN)
Santa Rosa Jr Coll (CA)
Seattle Central Comm Coll
(WA)
Westmoreland County
Comm Coll (PA)

**Ophthalmic/Optometric
Services**
Howard Comm Coll (MD)

Ophthalmic Technology
Miami Dade Coll (FL)
Penn Valley Comm Coll
(MO)
Pima Medical Inst, Denver
(CO)
Volunteer State Comm Coll
(TN)

Optical Sciences
Corning Comm Coll (NY)

Opticianry
Arkansas State U–Mountain
Home (AR)
Cuyahoga Comm Coll (OH)
Erie Comm Coll, North
Campus (NY)
Essex County Coll (NJ)
Harrisburg Area Comm Coll
(PA)
J. Sargeant Reynolds Comm
Coll (VA)
Milwaukee Area Tech Coll
(WI)

Optometric Technician
Barton County Comm Coll
(KS)
Darton Coll (GA)
Sauk Valley Comm Coll (IL)

Ornamental Horticulture
Bergen Comm Coll (NJ)
Bessemer State Tech Coll
(AL)
Bronx Comm Coll of City U of
NY (NY)
Central Florida Comm Coll
(FL)
Clackamas Comm Coll (OR)
Coll of DuPage (IL)
Coll of Lake County (IL)
Comm Coll of Allegheny
County (PA)
Comm Coll of Southern
Nevada (NV)
Cumberland County Coll
(NJ)
Danville Area Comm Coll (IL)
Finger Lakes Comm Coll
(NY)
Foothill Coll (CA)
Forsyth Tech Comm Coll
(NC)
Gwinnett Tech Coll (GA)
Hawkeye Comm Coll (IA)
Hillsborough Comm Coll (FL)
Howard Coll (TX)
J. Sargeant Reynolds Comm
Coll (VA)
Long Beach City Coll (CA)
Metropolitan Comm Coll
(NE)
Miami Dade Coll (FL)
Modesto Jr Coll (CA)
Oakland Comm Coll (MI)
Orange Coast Coll (CA)
San Joaquin Delta Coll (CA)
Santa Barbara City Coll (CA)
Santa Fe Comm Coll (FL)
Solano Comm Coll (CA)
Texas State Tech Coll–
Waco/Marshall Campus
(TX)
U of Arkansas Comm Coll at
Morrilton (AR)
Valencia Comm Coll (FL)

Orthotics/Prosthetics
Century Coll (MN)

Painting
Dixie State Coll of Utah (UT)
Keystone Coll (PA)

Painting and Wall Covering
Ivy Tech State Coll–Central
Indiana (IN)
Ivy Tech State Coll–
Eastcentral (IN)
Ivy Tech State Coll–Lafayette
(IN)
Ivy Tech State Coll–North
Central (IN)
Ivy Tech State Coll–
Northeast (IN)

Ivy Tech State Coll–
Northwest (IN)
Ivy Tech State Coll–
Southwest (IN)
Ivy Tech State Coll–Wabash
Valley (IN)

Paralegal/Legal Assistant
Comm and Tech Coll of
Shepherd (WV)
Globe Coll (MN)
Minnesota School of
Business–Brooklyn Center
(MN)
Minnesota School of
Business–Plymouth (MN)

**Parks, Recreation and
Leisure**
Bergen Comm Coll (NJ)
Cape Cod Comm Coll (MA)
Centralia Coll (WA)
Coastal Bend Coll (TX)
Colorado Mountn Coll,
Timberline Cmps (CO)
Colorado Northwestern
Comm Coll (CO)
Comm Coll of Denver (CO)
Comm Coll of Southern
Nevada (NV)
Comm Coll of the Air Force
(AL)
Compton Comm Coll (CA)
Cowley County Comm Coll
and Voc-Tech School (KS)
Dutchess Comm Coll (NY)
East Central Coll (MO)
Enterprise-Ozark Comm Coll
(AL)
Fayetteville Tech Comm Coll
(NC)
Florida Keys Comm Coll (FL)
Frederick Comm Coll (MD)
Garrett Coll (MD)
Glendale Comm Coll (CA)
Gordon Coll (GA)
Greenfield Comm Coll (MA)
Hudson Valley Comm Coll
(NY)
Iowa Lakes Comm Coll (IA)
Kingsborough Comm Coll of
City U of NY (NY)
Miami Dade Coll (FL)
Mineral Area Coll (MO)
Minneapolis Comm and Tech
Coll (MN)
Muskegon Comm Coll (MI)
Northern Essex Comm Coll
(MA)
Northern Virginia Comm Coll
(VA)
Northwestern Connecticut
Comm-Tech Coll (CT)
Orange County Comm Coll
(NY)
Pasadena City Coll (CA)
San Diego City Coll (CA)
San Juan Coll (NM)
Santa Barbara City Coll (CA)
State U of NY Coll of
Technology at Delhi (NY)
Taft Coll (CA)
Tompkins Cortland Comm
Coll (NY)

**Parks, Recreation and
Leisure Facilities
Management**
Allen County Comm Coll
(KS)
Andrew Coll (GA)
Butler County Comm Coll
(PA)
Cerro Coso Comm Coll (CA)
Coastal Georgia Comm Coll
(GA)
Colorado Mountn Coll, Alpine
Cmps (CO)
Colorado Mountn Coll,
Timberline Cmps (CO)
Compton Comm Coll (CA)
Erie Comm Coll, South
Campus (NY)
Feather River Coll (CA)
Finger Lakes Comm Coll
(NY)

Frederick Comm Coll (MD)
Garrett Coll (MD)
Hawkeye Comm Coll (IA)
James H. Faulkner State
Comm Coll (AL)
Keystone Coll (PA)
Modesto Jr Coll (CA)
Mohawk Valley Comm Coll
(NY)
Moraine Valley Comm Coll
(IL)
North Country Comm Coll
(NY)
Northwestern Connecticut
Comm-Tech Coll (CT)
Santa Fe Comm Coll (FL)
State U of NY Coll of
Technology at Delhi (NY)
Western Nevada Comm Coll
(NV)

**Parks, Recreation, and
Leisure Related**
Albuquerque Tech Vocational
Inst (NM)
Cincinnati State Tech and
Comm Coll (OH)
Feather River Coll (CA)
Southwestern Comm Coll
(NC)

**Parts, Warehousing, and
Inventory Management**
Central Wyoming Coll (WY)

Pastoral Studies/Counseling
Hesston Coll (KS)

**Perioperative/Operating
Room and Surgical Nursing**
Comm Coll of Allegheny
County (PA)

**Personal and Culinary
Services Related**
Arizona Western Coll (AZ)

Petroleum Technology
Coastal Bend Coll (TX)
Frank Phillips Coll (TX)
Odessa Coll (TX)

Pharmacy
Arapahoe Comm Coll (CO)
Barton County Comm Coll
(KS)
Casper Coll (WY)
Coastal Bend Coll (TX)
Colby Comm Coll (KS)
Columbia State Comm Coll
(TN)
Comm Coll of Southern
Nevada (NV)
Durham Tech Comm Coll
(NC)
East Central Coll (MO)
East Central Comm Coll
(MS)
Gateway Comm Coll (CT)
Highland Comm Coll (KS)
Holmes Comm Coll (MS)
Indian River Comm Coll (FL)
Iowa Lakes Comm Coll (IA)
Isothermal Comm Coll (NC)
Mid Michigan Comm Coll
(MI)
Northwest-Shoals Comm
Coll (AL)
Pasadena City Coll (CA)
Riverside Comm Coll District
(CA)
Shelton State Comm Coll
(AL)
U of Cincinnati Raymond
Walters Coll (OH)

Pharmacy Technician
Albany Tech Coll (GA)
Casper Coll (WY)
Century Coll (MN)
Clinton Comm Coll (IA)
Comm Coll of Allegheny
County (PA)
Comm Coll of the Air Force
(AL)
Darton Coll (GA)
Everett Comm Coll (WA)
Fayetteville Tech Comm Coll
(NC)

Harrisburg Area Comm Coll (PA)
Hillsborough Comm Coll (FL)
Midlands Tech Coll (SC)
Muscatine Comm Coll (IA)
North Central State Coll (OH)
North Dakota State Coll of Science (ND)
North Seattle Comm Coll (WA)
Northwest Tech Coll (MN)
Oakland Comm Coll (MI)
Pima Comm Coll (AZ)
San Joaquin Valley Coll (CA)
Scott Comm Coll (IA)
Tacoma Comm Coll (WA)
U of Northwestern Ohio (OH)
Vatterott Coll, Springfield (MO)
Wake Tech Comm Coll (NC)

Philosophy
Allen County Comm Coll (KS)
Andrew Coll (GA)
Barton County Comm Coll (KS)
Bergen Comm Coll (NJ)
Cape Cod Comm Coll (MA)
Coastal Georgia Comm Coll (GA)
Compton Comm Coll (CA)
Contra Costa Coll (CA)
Danville Area Comm Coll (IL)
Darton Coll (GA)
Daytona Beach Comm Coll (FL)
De Anza Coll (CA)
Dixie State Coll of Utah (UT)
East Central Coll (MO)
Everett Comm Coll (WA)
Foothill Coll (CA)
Harford Comm Coll (MD)
Indian River Comm Coll (FL)
Iowa Lakes Comm Coll (IA)
Lansing Comm Coll (MI)
Laramie County Comm Coll (WY)
Lower Columbia Coll (WA)
Miami Dade Coll (FL)
Orange Coast Coll (CA)
Palm Beach Comm Coll (FL)
Pasadena City Coll (CA)
Riverside Comm Coll District (CA)
St. Philip's Coll (TX)
San Diego Miramar Coll (CA)
San Joaquin Delta Coll (CA)
San Juan Coll (NM)
Santa Barbara City Coll (CA)
Santa Rosa Jr Coll (CA)
Snow Coll (UT)
Tacoma Comm Coll (WA)
Yuba Coll (CA)

Phlebotomy
Alexandria Tech Coll (MN)
Columbus State Comm Coll (OH)

Photographic and Film/Video Technology
Calhoun Comm Coll (AL)
Catawba Valley Comm Coll (NC)
Dixie State Coll of Utah (UT)
Miami Dade Coll (FL)
Olympic Coll (WA)
Platt Coll San Diego (CA)
Randolph Comm Coll (NC)
Texas State Tech Coll–Waco/Marshall Campus (TX)

Photography
Adirondack Comm Coll (NY)
Amarillo Coll (TX)
Anne Arundel Comm Coll (MD)
Antonelli Inst (PA)
The Art Inst of Philadelphia (PA)
Austin Comm Coll (TX)
Bergen Comm Coll (NJ)
Brookdale Comm Coll (NJ)
Carteret Comm Coll (NC)
Casper Coll (WY)

Catawba Valley Comm Coll (NC)
Cecil Comm Coll (MD)
Citrus Coll (CA)
Coll of DuPage (IL)
Coll of Southern Idaho (ID)
Colorado Mountn Coll (CO)
Columbia Coll (CA)
Comm Coll of Denver (CO)
Comm Coll of Philadelphia (PA)
Comm Coll of Southern Nevada (NV)
Compton Comm Coll (CA)
Cuyahoga Comm Coll (OH)
Daytona Beach Comm Coll (FL)
De Anza Coll (CA)
Delaware Coll of Art and Design (DE)
Dixie State Coll of Utah (UT)
El Paso Comm Coll (TX)
Everett Comm Coll (WA)
Foothill Coll (CA)
Fort Scott Comm Coll (KS)
Glendale Comm Coll (CA)
Greenfield Comm Coll (MA)
Gwinnett Tech Coll (GA)
Harrisburg Area Comm Coll (PA)
Hawkeye Comm Coll (IA)
Herkimer County Comm Coll (NY)
Holyoke Comm Coll (MA)
Howard Comm Coll (MD)
Inst of American Indian Arts (NM)
Iowa Lakes Comm Coll (IA)
Keystone Coll (PA)
Lansing Comm Coll (MI)
Linn-Benton Comm Coll (OR)
Long Beach City Coll (CA)
Lower Columbia Coll (WA)
McDowell Tech Comm Coll (NC)
Metropolitan Comm Coll (NE)
Miami Dade Coll (FL)
Milwaukee Area Tech Coll (WI)
Modesto Jr Coll (CA)
Mott Comm Coll (MI)
Napa Valley Coll (CA)
Nashville State Tech Comm Coll (TN)
Nassau Comm Coll (NY)
Northern Virginia Comm Coll (VA)
Oakland Comm Coll (MI)
Odessa Coll (TX)
Ohio Inst of Photography and Technology (OH)
Orange Coast Coll (CA)
Palm Beach Comm Coll (FL)
Pasadena City Coll (CA)
Prairie State Coll (IL)
Randolph Comm Coll (NC)
Rockland Comm Coll (NY)
St. Louis Comm Coll at Forest Park (MO)
St. Louis Comm Coll at Meramec (MO)
San Diego City Coll (CA)
San Joaquin Delta Coll (CA)
Seattle Central Comm Coll (WA)
Shoreline Comm Coll (WA)
Solano Comm Coll (CA)
Villa Maria Coll of Buffalo (NY)
Western Wyoming Comm Coll (WY)
Westmoreland County Comm Coll (PA)
Yuba Coll (CA)

Physical Education Teaching and Coaching
Alabama Southern Comm Coll (AL)
Alvin Comm Coll (TX)
Amarillo Coll (TX)
Andrew Coll (GA)

Anne Arundel Comm Coll (MD)
Arizona Western Coll (AZ)
Barton County Comm Coll (KS)
Brazosport Coll (TX)
Bucks County Comm Coll (PA)
Butler County Comm Coll (KS)
Butler County Comm Coll (PA)
Cape Cod Comm Coll (MA)
Casper Coll (WY)
Central Texas Coll (TX)
Chattahoochee Valley Comm Coll (AL)
Chemeketa Comm Coll (OR)
Citrus Coll (CA)
Clarendon Coll (TX)
Clinton Comm Coll (NY)
Cloud County Comm Coll (KS)
Coastal Bend Coll (TX)
Cochise Coll, Douglas (AZ)
Coffeyville Comm Coll (KS)
Colby Comm Coll (KS)
Coll of Southern Idaho (ID)
Coll of the Canyons (CA)
Columbia Coll (CA)
Columbia State Comm Coll (TN)
Compton Comm Coll (CA)
Copiah-Lincoln Comm Coll (MS)
Cowley County Comm Coll and Voc-Tech School (KS)
Crowder Coll (MO)
Danville Area Comm Coll (IL)
Daytona Beach Comm Coll (FL)
De Anza Coll (CA)
Dixie State Coll of Utah (UT)
Dodge City Comm Coll (KS)
East Central Coll (MO)
Ellsworth Comm Coll (IA)
Essex County Coll (NJ)
Everett Comm Coll (WA)
Finger Lakes Comm Coll (NY)
Foothill Coll (CA)
Frank Phillips Coll (TX)
Frederick Comm Coll (MD)
Fulton-Montgomery Comm Coll (NY)
Gadsden State Comm Coll (AL)
Gainesville Coll (GA)
Garden City Comm Coll (KS)
Garrett Coll (MD)
Genesee Comm Coll (NY)
Harrisburg Area Comm Coll (PA)
Herkimer County Comm Coll (NY)
Highland Comm Coll (KS)
Hillsborough Comm Coll (FL)
Howard Coll (TX)
Hudson Valley Comm Coll (NY)
Independence Comm Coll (KS)
Indian River Comm Coll (FL)
Iowa Lakes Comm Coll (IA)
Itawamba Comm Coll (MS)
John A. Logan Coll (IL)
Kilgore Coll (TX)
Lansing Comm Coll (MI)
Laramie County Comm Coll (WY)
Linn-Benton Comm Coll (OR)
Long Beach City Coll (CA)
Lower Columbia Coll (WA)
McLennan Comm Coll (TX)
Miami Dade Coll (FL)
Midland Coll (TX)
Modesto Jr Coll (CA)
Montgomery County Comm Coll (PA)
New Mexico Military Inst (NM)
Niagara County Comm Coll (NY)

Northern Essex Comm Coll (MA)
Odessa Coll (TX)
Orange Coast Coll (CA)
Palm Beach Comm Coll (FL)
Pasadena City Coll (CA)
Pratt Comm Coll and Area Vocational School (KS)
San Diego City Coll (CA)
San Diego Miramar Coll (CA)
San Joaquin Delta Coll (CA)
Santa Barbara City Coll (CA)
Santa Rosa Jr Coll (CA)
Sauk Valley Comm Coll (IL)
Seminole State Coll (OK)
Seward County Comm Coll (KS)
Shelton State Comm Coll (AL)
Sinclair Comm Coll (OH)
Snow Coll (UT)
Solano Comm Coll (CA)
South Mountain Comm Coll (AZ)
State U of NY Coll of Technology at Delhi (NY)
Tacoma Comm Coll (WA)
Taft Coll (CA)
Trinidad State Jr Coll (CO)
Trinity Valley Comm Coll (TX)
Umpqua Comm Coll (OR)
Valencia Comm Coll (FL)
Walters State Comm Coll (TN)
Western Oklahoma State Coll (OK)
Yuba Coll (CA)

Physical Sciences
Alvin Comm Coll (TX)
Amarillo Coll (TX)
Austin Comm Coll (TX)
Barton County Comm Coll (KS)
Butler County Comm Coll (PA)
Casper Coll (WY)
Cecil Comm Coll (MD)
Centralia Coll (WA)
Central Oregon Comm Coll (OR)
Central Wyoming Coll (WY)
Cerro Coso Comm Coll (CA)
Citrus Coll (CA)
City Colls of Chicago, Wilbur Wright Coll (IL)
Cloud County Comm Coll (KS)
Clovis Comm Coll (NM)
Coastal Bend Coll (TX)
Coll of the Canyons (CA)
Colorado Mountn Coll, Alpine Cmps (CO)
Colorado Northwestern Comm Coll (CO)
Columbia Coll (CA)
Compton Comm Coll (CA)
Crowder Coll (MO)
Dodge City Comm Coll (KS)
East Central Comm Coll (MS)
Ellsworth Comm Coll (IA)
Feather River Coll (CA)
Fort Scott Comm Coll (KS)
Frank Phillips Coll (TX)
Frederick Comm Coll (MD)
Fulton-Montgomery Comm Coll (NY)
Gordon Coll (GA)
Harrisburg Area Comm Coll (PA)
Highland Comm Coll (IL)
Highland Comm Coll (KS)
Howard Comm Coll (MD)
Hutchinson Comm Coll and Area Vocational School (KS)
Independence Comm Coll (KS)
Iowa Lakes Comm Coll (IA)
Lehigh Carbon Comm Coll (PA)
Linn-Benton Comm Coll (OR)

Long Beach City Coll (CA)
Miami Dade Coll (FL)
Montgomery County Comm Coll (PA)
North Idaho Coll (ID)
Northwestern Connecticut Comm-Tech Coll (CT)
Northwestern Michigan Coll (MI)
Orange County Comm Coll (NY)
Otero Jr Coll (CO)
Palm Beach Comm Coll (FL)
Pasadena City Coll (CA)
Pratt Comm Coll and Area Vocational School (KS)
River Parishes Comm Coll (LA)
Riverside Comm Coll District (CA)
Salt Lake Comm Coll (UT)
San Diego City Coll (CA)
San Diego Miramar Coll (CA)
San Joaquin Delta Coll (CA)
San Juan Coll (NM)
Santa Rosa Jr Coll (CA)
Seminole State Coll (OK)
Seward County Comm Coll (KS)
Snow Coll (UT)
Tacoma Comm Coll (WA)
Taft Coll (CA)
Trinity Valley Comm Coll (TX)
Umpqua Comm Coll (OR)
Union County Coll (NJ)
Western Nevada Comm Coll (NV)
Western Oklahoma State Coll (OK)

Physical Sciences Related
Schoolcraft Coll (MI)
Southeast Comm Coll, Milford Campus (NE)

Physical Therapist Assistant
Adirondack Comm Coll (NY)
Allegany Coll of Maryland (MD)
Anoka-Ramsey Comm Coll (MN)
Ashland Comm and Tech Coll (KY)
Atlantic Cape Comm Coll (NJ)
Barton County Comm Coll (KS)
Berkshire Comm Coll (MA)
Bishop State Comm Coll (AL)
Black Hawk Coll, Moline (IL)
Broome Comm Coll (NY)
Butler County Comm Coll (PA)
Cape Cod Comm Coll (MA)
Capital Comm Coll (CT)
Carroll Comm Coll (MD)
Central Florida Comm Coll (FL)
Colby Comm Coll (KS)
Coll of DuPage (IL)
Comm Coll of Allegheny County (PA)
Comm Coll of Rhode Island (RI)
Comm Coll of the Air Force (AL)
Darton Coll (GA)
Delaware Tech & Comm Coll, Stanton/ Wilmington Cmps (DE)
Delta Coll (MI)
Dutchess Comm Coll (NY)
El Paso Comm Coll (TX)
Essex County Coll (NJ)
Everett Comm Coll (WA)
Fayetteville Tech Comm Coll (NC)
Florida Comm Coll at Jacksonville (FL)
GateWay Comm Coll (AZ)
Green River Comm Coll (WA)

Guilford Tech Comm Coll (NC)
Gulf Coast Comm Coll (FL)
Harcum Coll (PA)
Hazard Comm and Tech Coll (KY)
Hesser Coll (NH)
Houston Comm Coll System (TX)
Indian River Comm Coll (FL)
Ivy Tech State Coll–Eastcentral (IN)
Jackson State Comm Coll (TN)
Jefferson State Comm Coll (AL)
Johnson County Comm Coll (KS)
Kansas City Kansas Comm Coll (KS)
Kaskaskia Coll (IL)
Keiser Coll, Fort Lauderdale (FL)
Kennebec Valley Comm Coll (ME)
Kilgore Coll (TX)
Kingsborough Comm Coll of City U of NY (NY)
Lake Land Coll (IL)
Lake Superior Coll (MN)
Lehigh Carbon Comm Coll (PA)
Lincoln Land Comm Coll (IL)
Linn State Tech Coll (MO)
Macomb Comm Coll (MI)
Manchester Comm Coll (CT)
Maria Coll (NY)
Marshall Comm and Tech Coll (WV)
Massachusetts Bay Comm Coll (MA)
Miami Dade Coll (FL)
Middle Georgia Coll (GA)
Midlands Tech Coll (SC)
Mott Comm Coll (MI)
Nassau Comm Coll (NY)
Niagara County Comm Coll (NY)
North Central State Coll (OH)
North Iowa Area Comm Coll (IA)
North Shore Comm Coll (MA)
Northwest Tech Coll (MN)
Owens Comm Coll, Toledo (OH)
Pasco-Hernando Comm Coll (FL)
Penn State U DuBois Campus of the Commonwealth Coll (PA)
Penn State U Hazleton Campus of the Commonwealth Coll (PA)
Penn State U Mont Alto Campus of the Commonwealth Coll (PA)
Penn State U Shenango Campus of the Commonwealth Coll (PA)
Pima Medical Inst, Tucson (AZ)
Pima Medical Inst, Denver (CO)
Polk Comm Coll (FL)
Rockingham Comm Coll (NC)
St. Petersburg Coll (FL)
St. Philip's Coll (TX)
Salt Lake Comm Coll (UT)
San Juan Coll (NM)
Southeast Kentucky Comm and Tech Coll (KY)
South U (FL)
Southwestern Comm Coll (NC)
Southwestern Oklahoma State U at Sayre (OK)
Springfield Tech Comm Coll (MA)
Stanly Comm Coll (NC)
State U of NY Coll of Technology at Canton (NY)
Union County Coll (NJ)

U of Pittsburgh at Titusville (PA)
Villa Maria Coll of Buffalo (NY)
Volunteer State Comm Coll (TN)
Western Iowa Tech Comm Coll (IA)
Whatcom Comm Coll (WA)
Williston State Coll (ND)

Physical Therapy
Alabama Southern Comm Coll (AL)
Allen County Comm Coll (KS)
Amarillo Coll (TX)
Andrew Coll (GA)
Arapahoe Comm Coll (CO)
Athens Tech Coll (GA)
Baltimore City Comm Coll (MD)
Barton County Comm Coll (KS)
Bay State Coll (MA)
Bossier Parish Comm Coll (LA)
Broward Comm Coll (FL)
Butler County Comm Coll (KS)
Caldwell Comm Coll and Tech Inst (NC)
Casper Coll (WY)
Central Piedmont Comm Coll (NC)
Chattanooga State Tech Comm Coll (TN)
Clarendon Coll (TX)
Clark State Comm Coll (OH)
Coastal Georgia Comm Coll (GA)
Colby Comm Coll (KS)
Coll of Southern Idaho (ID)
Columbia State Comm Coll (TN)
Cowley County Comm Coll and Voc-Tech School (KS)
Danville Area Comm Coll (IL)
Daytona Beach Comm Coll (FL)
De Anza Coll (CA)
Delta Coll (MI)
Dodge City Comm Coll (KS)
East Central Comm Coll (MS)
Essex County Coll (NJ)
Genesee Comm Coll (NY)
George Corley Wallace State Comm Coll (AL)
Gwinnett Tech Coll (GA)
Herkimer County Comm Coll (NY)
Highland Comm Coll (KS)
Hillsborough Comm Coll (FL)
Holmes Comm Coll (MS)
Indian Hills Comm Coll (IA)
Indian River Comm Coll (FL)
Iowa Central Comm Coll (IA)
Jefferson Comm Coll (KY)
John Tyler Comm Coll (VA)
Kapiolani Comm Coll (HI)
Keystone Coll (PA)
Kingsborough Comm Coll of City U of NY (NY)
Laredo Comm Coll (TX)
Luna Comm Coll (NM)
McLennan Comm Coll (TX)
Meridian Comm Coll (MS)
Miami Dade Coll (FL)
Mid Michigan Comm Coll (MI)
Milwaukee Area Tech Coll (WI)
Mount Wachusett Comm Coll (MA)
New Hampshire Comm Tech Coll, Manchester/Stratham (NH)
Northern Virginia Comm Coll (VA)
Odessa Coll (TX)
Orange County Comm Coll (NY)
Palm Beach Comm Coll (FL)

Penn Valley Comm Coll (MO)
Riverside Comm Coll District (CA)
St. Louis Comm Coll at Meramec (MO)
Santa Rosa Jr Coll (CA)
Sauk Valley Comm Coll (IL)
Scott Comm Coll (IA)
Seminole Comm Coll (FL)
Sinclair Comm Coll (OH)
Somerset Comm Coll (KY)
Southwestern Comm Coll (NC)
Southwest Georgia Tech Coll (GA)
Tacoma Comm Coll (WA)
Trident Tech Coll (SC)
Tunxis Comm Coll (CT)
U of Cincinnati Raymond Walters Coll (OH)
West Kentucky Comm and Tech Coll (KY)

Physician Assistant
Barton County Comm Coll (KS)
Coastal Georgia Comm Coll (GA)
Coll of Southern Idaho (ID)
Cuyahoga Comm Coll (OH)
Darton Coll (GA)
Delta Coll (MI)
Fairmont State Comm & Tech Coll (WV)
Foothill Coll (CA)
Globe Coll (MN)
Hudson Valley Comm Coll (NY)
Keystone Coll (PA)
Minnesota School of Business–Brooklyn Center (MN)
Minnesota School of Business–Plymouth (MN)
Santa Rosa Jr Coll (CA)

Physics
Allen County Comm Coll (KS)
Amarillo Coll (TX)
Andrew Coll (GA)
Arizona Western Coll (AZ)
Atlanta Metropolitan Coll (GA)
Austin Comm Coll (TX)
Barton County Comm Coll (KS)
Bergen Comm Coll (NJ)
Brazosport Coll (TX)
Brookdale Comm Coll (NJ)
Bunker Hill Comm Coll (MA)
Butler County Comm Coll (KS)
Casper Coll (WY)
Cecil Comm Coll (MD)
Chattahoochee Valley Comm Coll (AL)
Coastal Bend Coll (TX)
Coastal Georgia Comm Coll (GA)
Coll of Southern Idaho (ID)
Columbia Coll (CA)
Columbia State Comm Coll (TN)
Comm Coll of Allegheny County (PA)
Compton Comm Coll (CA)
Contra Costa Coll (CA)
Darton Coll (GA)
Daytona Beach Comm Coll (FL)
De Anza Coll (CA)
Dixie State Coll of Utah (UT)
Dodge City Comm Coll (KS)
East Central Coll (MO)
Eastern Arizona Coll (AZ)
El Paso Comm Coll (TX)
Everett Comm Coll (WA)
Finger Lakes Comm Coll (NY)
Foothill Coll (CA)
Gainesville Coll (GA)
Great Basin Coll (NV)
Highland Comm Coll (IL)

Holyoke Comm Coll (MA)
Indian River Comm Coll (FL)
John A. Logan Coll (IL)
Kilgore Coll (TX)
Kingsborough Comm Coll of City U of NY (NY)
Linn-Benton Comm Coll (OR)
Lower Columbia Coll (WA)
Miami Dade Coll (FL)
Midland Coll (TX)
New Mexico Military Inst (NM)
Northampton County Area Comm Coll (PA)
North Idaho Coll (ID)
Odessa Coll (TX)
Orange Coast Coll (CA)
Pasadena City Coll (CA)
Phillips Comm Coll of the U of Arkansas (AR)
San Diego Miramar Coll (CA)
San Juan Coll (NM)
Santa Barbara City Coll (CA)
Santa Rosa Jr Coll (CA)
Sauk Valley Comm Coll (IL)
Snow Coll (UT)
Solano Comm Coll (CA)
South Mountain Comm Coll (AZ)
Tacoma Comm Coll (WA)

Piano and Organ
Frank Phillips Coll (TX)
Iowa Lakes Comm Coll (IA)
Itawamba Comm Coll (MS)

Pipefitting and Sprinkler Fitting
Brazosport Coll (TX)
Cecil Comm Coll (MD)
Delta Coll (MI)
Fayetteville Tech Comm Coll (NC)
Forsyth Tech Comm Coll (NC)
GateWay Comm Coll (AZ)
Ivy Tech State Coll–Bloomington (IN)
Ivy Tech State Coll–Central Indiana (IN)
Ivy Tech State Coll–Columbus (IN)
Ivy Tech State Coll–Eastcentral (IN)
Ivy Tech State Coll–Kokomo (IN)
Ivy Tech State Coll–Lafayette (IN)
Ivy Tech State Coll–North Central (IN)
Ivy Tech State Coll–Northeast (IN)
Ivy Tech State Coll–Northwest (IN)
Ivy Tech State Coll–Southcentral (IN)
Ivy Tech State Coll–Southwest (IN)
Ivy Tech State Coll–Wabash Valley (IN)
Ivy Tech State Coll–Whitewater (IN)
Ranken Tech Coll (MO)
St. Cloud Tech Coll (MN)
St. Louis Comm Coll at Forest Park (MO)
Salt Lake Comm Coll (UT)
Southeast Comm Coll, Milford Campus (NE)
Southern Maine Comm Coll (ME)
State U of NY Coll of Technology at Alfred (NY)
State U of NY Coll of Technology at Canton (NY)
State U of NY Coll of Technology at Delhi (NY)
Thaddeus Stevens Coll of Technology (PA)
Truckee Meadows Comm Coll (NV)
Western Nevada Comm Coll (NV)

Plant Nursery Management
Comm Coll of Allegheny County (PA)
Edmonds Comm Coll (WA)
Foothill Coll (CA)
Miami Dade Coll (FL)
Modesto Jr Coll (CA)
Ohio State U Ag Tech Inst (OH)

Plant Pathology/ Phytopathology
Dixie State Coll of Utah (UT)

Plant Protection and Integrated Pest Management
Dixie State Coll of Utah (UT)

Plastics Engineering Technology
Cincinnati State Tech and Comm Coll (OH)
Coll of DuPage (IL)
Cumberland County Coll (NJ)
Davidson County Comm Coll (NC)
Edgecombe Comm Coll (NC)
Grand Rapids Comm Coll (MI)
Highline Comm Coll (WA)
Isothermal Comm Coll (NC)
Kalamazoo Valley Comm Coll (MI)
Kent State U, Tuscarawas Campus (OH)
Macomb Comm Coll (MI)
Mount Wachusett Comm Coll (MA)
Northwest State Comm Coll (OH)
Quinebaug Valley Comm Coll (CT)
Randolph Comm Coll (NC)
St. Petersburg Coll (FL)
Sinclair Comm Coll (OH)
Southeast Comm Coll, Milford Campus (NE)
South Texas Coll (TX)
Wake Tech Comm Coll (NC)

Plumbing Technology
Macomb Comm Coll (MI)
Mayland Comm Coll (NC)

Political Science and Government
Allen County Comm Coll (KS)
Atlanta Metropolitan Coll (GA)
Austin Comm Coll (TX)
Bainbridge Coll (GA)
Barton County Comm Coll (KS)
Bergen Comm Coll (NJ)
Brazosport Coll (TX)
Brookdale Comm Coll (NJ)
Butler County Comm Coll (KS)
Casper Coll (WY)
Centralia Coll (WA)
Chemeketa Comm Coll (OR)
Coastal Bend Coll (TX)
Coastal Georgia Comm Coll (GA)
Cochise Coll, Douglas (AZ)
Coffeyville Comm Coll (KS)
Colby Comm Coll (KS)
Coll of Southern Idaho (ID)
Coll of the Canyons (CA)
Colorado Northwestern Comm Coll (CO)
Columbia State Comm Coll (TN)
Contra Costa Coll (CA)
Copiah-Lincoln Comm Coll–Natchez Campus (MS)
Darton Coll (GA)
De Anza Coll (CA)
Dixie State Coll of Utah (UT)
Dodge City Comm Coll (KS)
East Central Coll (MO)
East Central Comm Coll (MS)
Eastern Arizona Coll (AZ)

Ellsworth Comm Coll (IA)
El Paso Comm Coll (TX)
Everett Comm Coll (WA)
Finger Lakes Comm Coll (NY)
Foothill Coll (CA)
Frank Phillips Coll (TX)
Gainesville Coll (GA)
Gordon Coll (GA)
Gulf Coast Comm Coll (FL)
Harford Comm Coll (MD)
Highland Comm Coll (IL)
Highland Comm Coll (KS)
Hinds Comm Coll (MS)
Independence Comm Coll (KS)
Indian River Comm Coll (FL)
Iowa Lakes Comm Coll (IA)
Itawamba Comm Coll (MS)
John A. Logan Coll (IL)
Laramie County Comm Coll (WY)
Lower Columbia Coll (WA)
Miami Dade Coll (FL)
Midland Coll (TX)
Northern Essex Comm Coll (MA)
North Idaho Coll (ID)
Odessa Coll (TX)
Orange Coast Coll (CA)
Otero Jr Coll (CO)
Palm Beach Comm Coll (FL)
Pasadena City Coll (CA)
Pima Comm Coll (AZ)
Riverside Comm Coll District (CA)
St. Philip's Coll (TX)
San Diego City Coll (CA)
San Joaquin Delta Coll (CA)
San Juan Coll (NM)
Santa Barbara City Coll (CA)
Santa Rosa Jr Coll (CA)
Sauk Valley Comm Coll (IL)
Snow Coll (UT)
Solano Comm Coll (CA)
South Mountain Comm Coll (AZ)
Tacoma Comm Coll (WA)
Trinity Valley Comm Coll (TX)
Umpqua Comm Coll (OR)
Western Oklahoma State Coll (OK)
Western Wyoming Comm Coll (WY)

Political Science and Government Related
Clarendon Coll (TX)

Portuguese
Miami Dade Coll (FL)

Postal Management
Allen County Comm Coll (KS)
Central Piedmont Comm Coll (NC)
Comm Coll of Denver (CO)
Daytona Beach Comm Coll (FL)
Fayetteville Tech Comm Coll (NC)
Frank Phillips Coll (TX)
Hinds Comm Coll (MS)
Longview Comm Coll (MO)
San Antonio Coll (TX)
San Diego City Coll (CA)

Poultry Science
Crowder Coll (MO)
Gainesville Coll (GA)
Modesto Jr Coll (CA)
Surry Comm Coll (NC)

Precision Metal Working Related
Northwest State Comm Coll (OH)
Oakland Comm Coll (MI)

Precision Production Related
Midlands Tech Coll (SC)
Mott Comm Coll (MI)
Southwestern Michigan Coll (MI)

Precision Production Trades
Coll of DuPage (IL)

Precision Systems Maintenance and Repair Technologies Related
Southwestern Michigan Coll (MI)

Pre-Dentistry Studies
Allen County Comm Coll (KS)
Barton County Comm Coll (KS)
Calhoun Comm Coll (AL)
Centralia Coll (WA)
Clarendon Coll (TX)
Coastal Georgia Comm Coll (GA)
Darton Coll (GA)
Howard Comm Coll (MD)
Iowa Lakes Comm Coll (IA)
Laramie County Comm Coll (WY)
Miami Dade Coll (FL)
St. Philip's Coll (TX)
Sauk Valley Comm Coll (IL)
Western Wyoming Comm Coll (WY)

Pre-Engineering
Adirondack Comm Coll (NY)
Alabama Southern Comm Coll (AL)
Alpena Comm Coll (MI)
Amarillo Coll (TX)
Andrew Coll (GA)
Anoka-Ramsey Comm Coll (MN)
Anoka-Ramsey Comm Coll, Cambridge Campus (MN)
Arizona Western Coll (AZ)
Austin Comm Coll (TX)
Barton County Comm Coll (KS)
Bay de Noc Comm Coll (MI)
Bowling Green State U-Firelands Coll (OH)
Bronx Comm Coll of City U of NY (NY)
Broward Comm Coll (FL)
Butler County Comm Coll (KS)
Butler County Comm Coll (PA)
Caldwell Comm Coll and Tech Inst (NC)
Cape Cod Comm Coll (MA)
Casper Coll (WY)
Centralia Coll (WA)
Central Oregon Comm Coll (OR)
Cerro Coso Comm Coll (CA)
Chattahoochee Valley Comm Coll (AL)
Chipola Coll (FL)
City Colls of Chicago, Wilbur Wright Coll (IL)
Cloud County Comm Coll (KS)
Coastal Georgia Comm Coll (GA)
Cochise Coll, Douglas (AZ)
Coffeyville Comm Coll (KS)
Colby Comm Coll (KS)
Coll of the Canyons (CA)
Columbia State Comm Coll (TN)
Comm Coll of Philadelphia (PA)
Compton Comm Coll (CA)
Corning Comm Coll (NY)
Cowley County Comm Coll and Voc-Tech School (KS)
Crowder Coll (MO)
Cumberland County Coll (NJ)
Danville Area Comm Coll (IL)
Darton Coll (GA)
Davidson County Comm Coll (NC)
De Anza Coll (CA)
Delta Coll (MI)
Dodge City Comm Coll (KS)
East Central Coll (MO)

East Central Comm Coll (MS)
East Mississippi Comm Coll (MS)
Edison State Comm Coll (OH)
Elgin Comm Coll (IL)
Ellsworth Comm Coll (IA)
El Paso Comm Coll (TX)
Enterprise-Ozark Comm Coll (AL)
Essex County Coll (NJ)
Everett Comm Coll (WA)
Finger Lakes Comm Coll (NY)
Frank Phillips Coll (TX)
Garden City Comm Coll (KS)
Greenfield Comm Coll (MA)
Henry Ford Comm Coll (MI)
Hibbing Comm Coll (MN)
Highland Comm Coll (IL)
Highland Comm Coll (KS)
Highline Comm Coll (WA)
Hinds Comm Coll (MS)
Holyoke Comm Coll (MA)
Hudson Valley Comm Coll (NY)
Illinois Valley Comm Coll (IL)
Independence Comm Coll (KS)
Indian River Comm Coll (FL)
Iowa Lakes Comm Coll (IA)
Isothermal Comm Coll (NC)
Itasca Comm Coll (MN)
Itawamba Comm Coll (MS)
Jefferson Comm Coll (NY)
John A. Logan Coll (IL)
Kalamazoo Valley Comm Coll (MI)
Lansing Comm Coll (MI)
Laramie County Comm Coll (WY)
Lewis and Clark Comm Coll (IL)
Lincoln Land Comm Coll (IL)
Linn-Benton Comm Coll (OR)
Long Beach City Coll (CA)
Longview Comm Coll (MO)
Lower Columbia Coll (WA)
Macomb Comm Coll (MI)
Maple Woods Comm Coll (MO)
Mesabi Range Comm and Tech Coll (MN)
Metropolitan Comm Coll (NE)
Miami Dade Coll (FL)
Midland Coll (TX)
Mid Michigan Comm Coll (MI)
Milwaukee Area Tech Coll (WI)
Moberly Area Comm Coll (MO)
Mohawk Valley Comm Coll (NY)
New Mexico Military Inst (NM)
Northeast Alabama Comm Coll (AL)
Northern Virginia Comm Coll (VA)
North Hennepin Comm Coll (MN)
North Shore Comm Coll (MA)
Northwestern Connecticut Comm-Tech Coll (CT)
Northwest-Shoals Comm Coll (AL)
Oakland Comm Coll (MI)
Odessa Coll (TX)
Otero Jr Coll (CO)
Palm Beach Comm Coll (FL)
Piedmont Virginia Comm Coll (VA)
Polk Comm Coll (FL)
Pratt Comm Coll and Area Vocational School (KS)
Quinebaug Valley Comm Coll (CT)
Rainy River Comm Coll (MN)
Richland Comm Coll (IL)

Rochester Comm and Tech Coll (MN)
Rock Valley Coll (IL)
Saint Charles Comm Coll (MO)
St. Louis Comm Coll at Forest Park (MO)
St. Philip's Coll (TX)
Salt Lake Comm Coll (UT)
Sandhills Comm Coll (NC)
San Diego City Coll (CA)
Seminole State Coll (OK)
Seward County Comm Coll (KS)
Shoreline Comm Coll (WA)
Snow Coll (UT)
South Mountain Comm Coll (AZ)
Tacoma Comm Coll (WA)
Taft Coll (CA)
Three Rivers Comm Coll (CT)
Trinidad State Jr Coll (CO)
Trinity Valley Comm Coll (TX)
Umpqua Comm Coll (OR)
U of Cincinnati Raymond Walters Coll (OH)
Valencia Comm Coll (FL)
Wake Tech Comm Coll (NC)
Walters State Comm Coll (TN)
Western Oklahoma State Coll (OK)
Western Wyoming Comm Coll (WY)
West Virginia U at Parkersburg (WV)
Yakima Valley Comm Coll (WA)
Yuba Coll (CA)

Pre-Law Studies
Allen County Comm Coll (KS)
Barton County Comm Coll (KS)
Brazosport Coll (TX)
Calhoun Comm Coll (AL)
Centralia Coll (WA)
Central Wyoming Coll (WY)
Darton Coll (GA)
Dixie State Coll of Utah (UT)
Eastern Arizona Coll (AZ)
Gulf Coast Comm Coll (FL)
Iowa Lakes Comm Coll (IA)
Laramie County Comm Coll (WY)
Lower Columbia Coll (WA)
Riverside Comm Coll District (CA)
St. Philip's Coll (TX)
Western Wyoming Comm Coll (WY)

Pre-Medical Studies
Allen County Comm Coll (KS)
Barton County Comm Coll (KS)
Brazosport Coll (TX)
Calhoun Comm Coll (AL)
Centralia Coll (WA)
Clarendon Coll (TX)
Coastal Georgia Comm Coll (GA)
Darton Coll (GA)
Eastern Arizona Coll (AZ)
Howard Comm Coll (MD)
Iowa Lakes Comm Coll (IA)
Laramie County Comm Coll (WY)
Miami Dade Coll (FL)
St. Philip's Coll (TX)
San Juan Coll (NM)
Sauk Valley Comm Coll (IL)
Western Wyoming Comm Coll (WY)

Pre-Nursing Studies
Iowa Lakes Comm Coll (IA)
Keystone Coll (PA)
Miami Dade Coll (FL)
St. Philip's Coll (TX)

South U (FL)
Western Wyoming Comm Coll (WY)

Pre-Pharmacy Studies
Allen County Comm Coll (KS)
Amarillo Coll (TX)
Andrew Coll (GA)
Calhoun Comm Coll (AL)
Centralia Coll (WA)
Coastal Georgia Comm Coll (GA)
Coll of Southern Idaho (ID)
Darton Coll (GA)
Delta Coll (MI)
Dodge City Comm Coll (KS)
Eastern Arizona Coll (AZ)
Frank Phillips Coll (TX)
Howard Comm Coll (MD)
Iowa Lakes Comm Coll (IA)
Kilgore Coll (TX)
Laramie County Comm Coll (WY)
Miami Dade Coll (FL)
St. Philip's Coll (TX)
Santa Rosa Jr Coll (CA)
Sauk Valley Comm Coll (IL)
Tacoma Comm Coll (WA)
Western Wyoming Comm Coll (WY)

Pre-Veterinary Studies
Allen County Comm Coll (KS)
Barton County Comm Coll (KS)
Calhoun Comm Coll (AL)
Centralia Coll (WA)
Coastal Georgia Comm Coll (GA)
Darton Coll (GA)
Howard Comm Coll (MD)
Iowa Lakes Comm Coll (IA)
Laramie County Comm Coll (WY)
Miami Dade Coll (FL)
Ohio State U Ag Tech Inst (OH)
Sauk Valley Comm Coll (IL)
Western Wyoming Comm Coll (WY)

Printing Press Operation
Iowa Lakes Comm Coll (IA)
Lake Land Coll (IL)

Printmaking
De Anza Coll (CA)
Dixie State Coll of Utah (UT)
Florida Comm Coll at Jacksonville (FL)
Inst of American Indian Arts (NM)
Keystone Coll (PA)

Professional Studies
Pratt Comm Coll and Area Vocational School (KS)
Windward Comm Coll (HI)

Psychiatric/Mental Health Services Technology
Allegany Coll of Maryland (MD)
Central Florida Comm Coll (FL)
Comm Coll of Allegheny County (PA)
Comm Coll of Rhode Island (RI)
Darton Coll (GA)
Dutchess Comm Coll (NY)
Eastfield Coll (TX)
Hagerstown Comm Coll (MD)
Houston Comm Coll System (TX)
Ivy Tech State Coll–Bloomington (IN)
Ivy Tech State Coll–Central Indiana (IN)
Ivy Tech State Coll–Columbus (IN)
Ivy Tech State Coll–Eastcentral (IN)
Ivy Tech State Coll–Kokomo (IN)

Ivy Tech State Coll–Lafayette (IN)
Ivy Tech State Coll–Northeast (IN)
Ivy Tech State Coll–Northwest (IN)
Ivy Tech State Coll–Southcentral (IN)
Ivy Tech State Coll–Southeast (IN)
Ivy Tech State Coll–Southwest (IN)
Ivy Tech State Coll–Wabash Valley (IN)
Ivy Tech State Coll–Whitewater (IN)
Kingsborough Comm Coll of City U of NY (NY)
Montgomery County Comm Coll (PA)
North Dakota State Coll of Science (ND)
San Joaquin Delta Coll (CA)
Wilkes Comm Coll (NC)
Yuba Coll (CA)

Psychology
Alabama Southern Comm Coll (AL)
Allen County Comm Coll (KS)
Amarillo Coll (TX)
Andrew Coll (GA)
Atlanta Metropolitan Coll (GA)
Atlantic Cape Comm Coll (NJ)
Austin Comm Coll (TX)
Bainbridge Coll (GA)
Barton County Comm Coll (KS)
Bergen Comm Coll (NJ)
Brazosport Coll (TX)
Bronx Comm Coll of City U of NY (NY)
Brookdale Comm Coll (NJ)
Bucks County Comm Coll (PA)
Bunker Hill Comm Coll (MA)
Butler County Comm Coll (KS)
Butler County Comm Coll (PA)
Cape Cod Comm Coll (MA)
Casper Coll (WY)
Centralia Coll (WA)
Central Wyoming Coll (WY)
Clarendon Coll (TX)
Clovis Comm Coll (NM)
Coastal Bend Coll (TX)
Coastal Georgia Comm Coll (GA)
Cochise Coll, Douglas (AZ)
Coffeyville Comm Coll (KS)
Colby Comm Coll (KS)
Coll of Southern Idaho (ID)
Coll of the Canyons (CA)
Colorado Mountn Coll (CO)
Colorado Mountn Coll, Timberline Cmps (CO)
Colorado Northwestern Comm Coll (CO)
Columbia Coll (CA)
Columbia State Comm Coll (TN)
Comm Coll of Allegheny County (PA)
Compton Comm Coll (CA)
Crowder Coll (MO)
Danville Area Comm Coll (IL)
Darton Coll (GA)
Daytona Beach Comm Coll (FL)
De Anza Coll (CA)
Delaware County Comm Coll (PA)
Delta Coll (MI)
Dixie State Coll of Utah (UT)
Dodge City Comm Coll (KS)
East Central Coll (MO)
East Central Comm Coll (MS)
Eastern Arizona Coll (AZ)
East Mississippi Comm Coll (MS)

Ellsworth Comm Coll (IA)
El Paso Comm Coll (TX)
Everett Comm Coll (WA)
Finger Lakes Comm Coll (NY)
Foothill Coll (CA)
Frank Phillips Coll (TX)
Frederick Comm Coll (MD)
Fulton-Montgomery Comm Coll (NY)
Gainesville Coll (GA)
Garrett Coll (MD)
GateWay Comm Coll (AZ)
Genesee Comm Coll (NY)
Gogebic Comm Coll (MI)
Gordon Coll (GA)
Great Basin Coll (NV)
Gulf Coast Comm Coll (FL)
Harcum Coll (PA)
Harford Comm Coll (MD)
Harrisburg Area Comm Coll (PA)
Hesser Coll (NH)
Highland Comm Coll (IL)
Highland Comm Coll (KS)
Highline Comm Coll (WA)
Hinds Comm Coll (MS)
Howard Comm Coll (MD)
Hutchinson Comm Coll and Area Vocational School (KS)
Independence Comm Coll (KS)
Indian River Comm Coll (FL)
Iowa Lakes Comm Coll (IA)
Itasca Comm Coll (MN)
Itawamba Comm Coll (MS)
John A. Logan Coll (IL)
John Wood Comm Coll (IL)
Kilgore Coll (TX)
Kingwood Coll (TX)
Laramie County Comm Coll (WY)
Lower Columbia Coll (WA)
Miami Dade Coll (FL)
Midland Coll (TX)
Mid Michigan Comm Coll (MI)
Mohave Comm Coll (AZ)
New River Comm and Tech Coll (WV)
Northern Virginia Comm Coll (VA)
North Idaho Coll (ID)
Odessa Coll (TX)
Otero Jr Coll (CO)
Palm Beach Comm Coll (FL)
Pasadena City Coll (CA)
Pratt Comm Coll and Area Vocational School (KS)
Riverside Comm Coll District (CA)
St. Philip's Coll (TX)
San Antonio Coll (TX)
San Diego City Coll (CA)
San Diego Miramar Coll (CA)
San Joaquin Delta Coll (CA)
San Juan Coll (NM)
Santa Barbara City Coll (CA)
Santa Rosa Jr Coll (CA)
Sauk Valley Comm Coll (IL)
Seward County Comm Coll (KS)
Solano Comm Coll (CA)
South Mountain Comm Coll (AZ)
Tacoma Comm Coll (WA)
Trinidad State Jr Coll (CO)
Trinity Valley Comm Coll (TX)
Umpqua Comm Coll (OR)
Western Oklahoma State Coll (OK)
Western Wyoming Comm Coll (WY)
Yuba Coll (CA)

Public Administration
American Samoa Comm Coll (AS)
Anne Arundel Comm Coll (MD)
Barton County Comm Coll (KS)
Bay Mills Comm Coll (MI)

Brazosport Coll (TX)
Citrus Coll (CA)
East Central Coll (MO)
Eugenio María de Hostos Comm Coll of City U of NY (NY)
Fayetteville Tech Comm Coll (NC)
Hinds Comm Coll (MS)
Itawamba Comm Coll (MS)
Keiser Coll, Fort Lauderdale (FL)
Lansing Comm Coll (MI)
Laramie County Comm Coll (WY)
Miami Dade Coll (FL)
Middle Georgia Coll (GA)
Mohawk Valley Comm Coll (NY)
San Antonio Coll (TX)
San Joaquin Delta Coll (CA)
San Juan Coll (NM)
Sinclair Comm Coll (OH)
Solano Comm Coll (CA)
Three Rivers Comm Coll (CT)
Westchester Comm Coll (NY)
Westmoreland County Comm Coll (PA)

Public Administration and Social Service Professions Related
Cleveland State Comm Coll (TN)
Sauk Valley Comm Coll (IL)

Public Health Education and Promotion
Coll of Southern Idaho (ID)

Public Policy Analysis
Anne Arundel Comm Coll (MD)
Fort Scott Comm Coll (KS)

Public Relations, Advertising, and Applied Communication Related
Keystone Coll (PA)

Public Relations/Image Management
Amarillo Coll (TX)
Brookdale Comm Coll (NJ)
Coastal Bend Coll (TX)
Comm Coll of Beaver County (PA)
Comm Coll of the Air Force (AL)
Crowder Coll (MO)
Glendale Comm Coll (AZ)
Lansing Comm Coll (MI)
St. Louis Comm Coll at Meramec (MO)

Publishing
Milwaukee Area Tech Coll (WI)
Westmoreland County Comm Coll (PA)

Purchasing, Procurement/Acquisitions and Contracts Management
Brazosport Coll (TX)
Cincinnati State Tech and Comm Coll (OH)
Columbus State Comm Coll (OH)
Comm Coll of the Air Force (AL)
De Anza Coll (CA)
Miami U Hamilton (OH)
Northern Virginia Comm Coll (VA)
Shoreline Comm Coll (WA)

Quality Control and Safety Technologies Related
Lake Superior Coll (MN)

Quality Control Technology
Austin Comm Coll (TX)
Brazosport Coll (TX)
Broome Comm Coll (NY)
Butler County Comm Coll (PA)

Central Carolina Comm Coll (NC)
Central Comm Coll–Columbus Campus (NE)
Century Coll (MN)
Coll of the Canyons (CA)
Columbus State Comm Coll (OH)
Comm Coll of Allegheny County (PA)
Contra Costa Coll (CA)
Delta Coll (MI)
Des Moines Area Comm Coll (IA)
Edison State Comm Coll (OH)
Elizabethtown Comm and Tech Coll (KY)
Fort Scott Comm Coll (KS)
Grand Rapids Comm Coll (MI)
Heartland Comm Coll (IL)
Henry Ford Comm Coll (MI)
Illinois Eastern Comm Colls, Frontier Comm Coll (IL)
Illinois Eastern Comm Colls, Lincoln Trail Coll (IL)
Ivy Tech State Coll–Lafayette (IN)
Lansing Comm Coll (MI)
Longview Comm Coll (MO)
Macomb Comm Coll (MI)
Metropolitan Comm Coll-Business & Technology College (MO)
Mott Comm Coll (MI)
Northampton County Area Comm Coll (PA)
North Central State Coll (OH)
Northwestern Tech Coll (GA)
Northwest State Comm Coll (OH)
Rock Valley Coll (IL)
St. Petersburg Coll (FL)
Sinclair Comm Coll (OH)
Southeast Comm Coll, Milford Campus (NE)
Springfield Tech Comm Coll (MA)
Texas State Tech Coll–Waco/Marshall Campus (TX)
Tri-County Tech Coll (SC)
Waubonsee Comm Coll (IL)

Radio and Television
Adirondack Comm Coll (NY)
Alvin Comm Coll (TX)
Amarillo Coll (TX)
Austin Comm Coll (TX)
Brevard Comm Coll (FL)
Bucks County Comm Coll (PA)
Cayuga County Comm Coll (NY)
Central Carolina Comm Coll (NC)
Centralia Coll (WA)
Central Texas Coll (TX)
Chattanooga State Tech Comm Coll (TN)
Coahoma Comm Coll (MS)
Coffeyville Comm Coll (KS)
Colby Comm Coll (KS)
Comm Coll of Southern Nevada (NV)
Daytona Beach Comm Coll (FL)
De Anza Coll (CA)
Delta Coll (MI)
Dixie State Coll of Utah (UT)
Dodge City Comm Coll (KS)
Foothill Coll (CA)
Gulf Coast Comm Coll (FL)
Herkimer County Comm Coll (NY)
Hesser Coll (NH)
Hillsborough Comm Coll (FL)
Holmes Comm Coll (MS)
Illinois Eastern Comm Colls, Wabash Valley Coll (IL)
International Coll of Broadcasting (OH)
Iowa Central Comm Coll (IA)
Iowa Lakes Comm Coll (IA)

Isothermal Comm Coll (NC)
Keystone Coll (PA)
Lake Land Coll (IL)
Lane Comm Coll (OR)
Lansing Comm Coll (MI)
Lewis and Clark Comm Coll (IL)
Long Beach City Coll (CA)
Miami Dade Coll (FL)
Modesto Jr Coll (CA)
Napa Valley Coll (CA)
National Coll of Business & Technology, Lexington (KY)
Northland Comm and Tech Coll–Thief River Falls (MN)
Odessa Coll (TX)
Parkland Coll (IL)
Pasadena City Coll (CA)
Pima Comm Coll (AZ)
San Antonio Coll (TX)
San Diego City Coll (CA)
Tompkins Cortland Comm Coll (NY)
Tri-County Tech Coll (SC)

Radio and Television Broadcasting Technology
Black Hawk Coll, Moline (IL)
Briarwood Coll (CT)
Brookdale Comm Coll (NJ)
Cayuga County Comm Coll (NY)
Cedar Valley Coll (TX)
Central Comm Coll–Hastings Campus (NE)
Central Wyoming Coll (WY)
Clover Park Tech Coll (WA)
Gadsden State Comm Coll (AL)
Hillsborough Comm Coll (FL)
Houston Comm Coll System (TX)
Iowa Lakes Comm Coll (IA)
Jefferson State Comm Coll (AL)
Miami Dade Coll (FL)
Milwaukee Area Tech Coll (WI)
Mineral Area Coll (MO)
Northampton County Area Comm Coll (PA)
Oakland Comm Coll (MI)
Parkland Coll (IL)
Schoolcraft Coll (MI)
Scott Comm Coll (IA)
Wilkes Comm Coll (NC)

Radiologic Technology/Science
Amarillo Coll (TX)
Barton County Comm Coll (KS)
Black Hawk Coll, Moline (IL)
Brevard Comm Coll (FL)
Brookdale Comm Coll (NJ)
Carolinas Coll of Health Sciences (NC)
Columbus State Comm Coll (OH)
Comm Coll of Denver (CO)
Comm Coll of Southern Nevada (NV)
Delta Coll (MI)
Eastern Maine Comm Coll (ME)
Edgecombe Comm Coll (NC)
Fayetteville Tech Comm Coll (NC)
Florida Hospital Coll of Health Sciences (FL)
Florida National Coll (FL)
Foothill Coll (CA)
Henry Ford Comm Coll (MI)
Hillsborough Comm Coll (FL)
Holyoke Comm Coll (MA)
Hudson Valley Comm Coll (NY)
Keiser Coll, Miami (FL)
Keystone Coll (PA)
Laramie County Comm Coll (WY)
Laredo Comm Coll (TX)
Miami Dade Coll (FL)
Midland Coll (TX)

Montgomery County Comm Coll (PA)
Niagara County Comm Coll (NY)
North Central State Coll (OH)
Northern Essex Comm Coll (MA)
Northwest Tech Coll (MN)
Pasco-Hernando Comm Coll (FL)
Pima Medical Inst, Mesa (AZ)
Pima Medical Inst, Tucson (AZ)
Pima Medical Inst (CA)
Pima Medical Inst, Denver (CO)
Pima Medical Inst (NV)
Pima Medical Inst (NM)
Pima Medical Inst (WA)
Polk Comm Coll (FL)
Rowan-Cabarrus Comm Coll (NC)
St. Luke's Coll (IA)
St. Petersburg Coll (FL)
Sandhills Comm Coll (NC)
Sinclair Comm Coll (OH)
Somerset Comm Coll (KY)
Southern Maine Comm Coll (ME)
Tacoma Comm Coll (WA)
Truckee Meadows Comm Coll (NV)

Radio, Television, and Digital Communication Related
Hillsborough Comm Coll (FL)
Keystone Coll (PA)

Range Science and Management
Central Wyoming Coll (WY)
Colby Comm Coll (KS)
Coll of Southern Idaho (ID)
Dixie State Coll of Utah (UT)
Santa Rosa Jr Coll (CA)
Snow Coll (UT)
Trinity Valley Comm Coll (TX)

Reading Teacher Education
Bay Mills Comm Coll (MI)
East Mississippi Comm Coll (MS)

Real Estate
Alamance Comm Coll (NC)
Amarillo Coll (TX)
Anne Arundel Comm Coll (MD)
Ashland Comm and Tech Coll (KY)
Austin Comm Coll (TX)
Bergen Comm Coll (NJ)
Big Sandy Comm and Tech Coll (KY)
Bristol Comm Coll (MA)
Calhoun Comm Coll (AL)
Catawba Valley Comm Coll (NC)
Cedar Valley Coll (TX)
Central Piedmont Comm Coll (NC)
Chemeketa Comm Coll (OR)
Cincinnati State Tech and Comm Coll (OH)
Citrus Coll (CA)
Coll of DuPage (IL)
Coll of Southern Idaho (ID)
Coll of the Canyons (CA)
Collin County Comm Coll District (TX)
Columbia-Greene Comm Coll (NY)
Columbus State Comm Coll (OH)
Comm Coll of Allegheny County (PA)
Comm Coll of Philadelphia (PA)
Comm Coll of Southern Nevada (NV)
Compton Comm Coll (CA)
Contra Costa Coll (CA)
Cuyahoga Comm Coll (OH)
Danville Area Comm Coll (IL)

De Anza Coll (CA)
Delta Coll (MI)
Dodge City Comm Coll (KS)
Durham Tech Comm Coll (NC)
East Mississippi Comm Coll (MS)
Edison State Comm Coll (OH)
Elizabethtown Comm and Tech Coll (KY)
El Paso Comm Coll (TX)
Enterprise-Ozark Comm Coll (AL)
Florida Comm Coll at Jacksonville (FL)
Foothill Coll (CA)
Forsyth Tech Comm Coll (NC)
GateWay Comm Coll (AZ)
Glendale Comm Coll (AZ)
Glendale Comm Coll (CA)
Harrisburg Area Comm Coll (PA)
Henry Ford Comm Coll (MI)
Hinds Comm Coll (MS)
Houston Comm Coll System (TX)
Hudson Valley Comm Coll (NY)
Iowa Lakes Comm Coll (IA)
Isothermal Comm Coll (NC)
Jefferson Comm Coll (KY)
Jefferson Comm Coll (OH)
Lane Comm Coll (OR)
Lansing Comm Coll (MI)
Laredo Comm Coll (TX)
Lehigh Carbon Comm Coll (PA)
Long Beach City Coll (CA)
McLennan Comm Coll (TX)
Miami U Hamilton (OH)
Milwaukee Area Tech Coll (WI)
Modesto Jr Coll (CA)
Montgomery County Comm Coll (PA)
Napa Valley Coll (CA)
Nassau Comm Coll (NY)
Northeast Alabama Comm Coll (AL)
Northern Essex Comm Coll (MA)
North Lake Coll (TX)
Orange County Comm Coll (NY)
Pasadena City Coll (CA)
Pima Comm Coll (AZ)
Rainy River Comm Coll (MN)
Raritan Valley Comm Coll (NJ)
St. Louis Comm Coll at Meramec (MO)
San Antonio Coll (TX)
San Diego City Coll (CA)
San Juan Coll (NM)
Santa Barbara City Coll (CA)
Sinclair Comm Coll (OH)
Southern State Comm Coll (OH)
Trinity Valley Comm Coll (TX)
Truckee Meadows Comm Coll (NV)
U of Cincinnati Raymond Walters Coll (OH)
Western Nevada Comm Coll (NV)
Westmoreland County Comm Coll (PA)

Receptionist
Adirondack Comm Coll (NY)
Alexandria Tech Coll (MN)
Bristol Comm Coll (MA)
Centralia Coll (WA)
Iowa Lakes Comm Coll (IA)
Lower Columbia Coll (WA)

Recording Arts Technology
Kansas City Kansas Comm Coll (KS)
Miami Dade Coll (FL)
Olympic Coll (WA)

Rehabilitation and Therapeutic Professions Related
Clover Park Tech Coll (WA)
Comm Coll of Rhode Island (RI)
Springfield Tech Comm Coll (MA)
Union County Coll (NJ)

Rehabilitation Therapy
Iowa Lakes Comm Coll (IA)
Nassau Comm Coll (NY)

Religious Studies
Allen County Comm Coll (KS)
Amarillo Coll (TX)
Andrew Coll (GA)
Barton County Comm Coll (KS)
Cowley County Comm Coll and Voc-Tech School (KS)
East Central Coll (MO)
Kilgore Coll (TX)
Lansing Comm Coll (MI)
Laramie County Comm Coll (WY)
Northern Virginia Comm Coll (VA)
Orange Coast Coll (CA)
Palm Beach Comm Coll (FL)
Pasadena City Coll (CA)
San Joaquin Delta Coll (CA)
Trinity Valley Comm Coll (TX)

Respiratory Care Therapy
Alabama Southern Comm Coll (AL)
Albuquerque Tech Vocational Inst (NM)
Allegany Coll of Maryland (MD)
Alvin Comm Coll (TX)
Amarillo Coll (TX)
Andrew Coll (GA)
Ashland Comm and Tech Coll (KY)
Athens Tech Coll (GA)
Atlantic Cape Comm Coll (NJ)
Augusta Tech Coll (GA)
Baltimore City Comm Coll (MD)
Barton County Comm Coll (KS)
Bergen Comm Coll (NJ)
Berkshire Comm Coll (MA)
Borough of Manhattan Comm Coll of City U of NY (NY)
Bossier Parish Comm Coll (LA)
Bowling Green State U-Firelands Coll (OH)
Brookdale Comm Coll (NJ)
Broward Comm Coll (FL)
Carteret Comm Coll (NC)
Catawba Valley Comm Coll (NC)
Central Piedmont Comm Coll (NC)
Chattanooga State Tech Comm Coll (TN)
Cincinnati State Tech and Comm Coll (OH)
Coastal Georgia Comm Coll (GA)
Coll of DuPage (IL)
Coll of Southern Idaho (ID)
Collin County Comm Coll District (TX)
Columbia State Comm Coll (TN)
Columbus State Comm Coll (OH)
Comm & Tech Coll at West Virginia U Inst of Technology (WV)
Comm Coll of Allegheny County (PA)
Comm Coll of Philadelphia (PA)
Comm Coll of Rhode Island (RI)

Comm Coll of Southern Nevada (NV)
Compton Comm Coll (CA)
Copiah-Lincoln Comm Coll–Natchez Campus (MS)
Cuyahoga Comm Coll (OH)
Danville Area Comm Coll (IL)
Darton Coll (GA)
Daytona Beach Comm Coll (FL)
Delaware County Comm Coll (PA)
Delaware Tech & Comm Coll, Stanton/ Wilmington Cmps (DE)
Delta Coll (MI)
Des Moines Area Comm Coll (IA)
Dodge City Comm Coll (KS)
Doña Ana Branch Comm Coll (NM)
Durham Tech Comm Coll (NC)
Edgecombe Comm Coll (NC)
El Paso Comm Coll (TX)
Erie Comm Coll, North Campus (NY)
Essex County Coll (NJ)
Fayetteville Tech Comm Coll (NC)
Florida Comm Coll at Jacksonville (FL)
Foothill Coll (CA)
Forsyth Tech Comm Coll (NC)
Frederick Comm Coll (MD)
Front Range Comm Coll (CO)
GateWay Comm Coll (AZ)
Genesee Comm Coll (NY)
George Corley Wallace State Comm Coll (AL)
George C. Wallace Comm Coll (AL)
Guilford Tech Comm Coll (NC)
Gulf Coast Comm Coll (FL)
Gwinnett Tech Coll (GA)
Harrisburg Area Comm Coll (PA)
Hawkeye Comm Coll (IA)
Henry Ford Comm Coll (MI)
Highland Comm Coll (KS)
Highline Comm Coll (WA)
Hillsborough Comm Coll (FL)
Hinds Comm Coll (MS)
Holmes Comm Coll (MS)
Houston Comm Coll System (TX)
Howard Coll (TX)
Hudson Valley Comm Coll (NY)
Indian River Comm Coll (FL)
Itawamba Comm Coll (MS)
Ivy Tech State Coll–Central Indiana (IN)
Ivy Tech State Coll–Lafayette (IN)
Ivy Tech State Coll–Northeast (IN)
Ivy Tech State Coll–Northwest (IN)
Ivy Tech State Coll–Southcentral (IN)
Jackson State Comm Coll (TN)
Jefferson Comm Coll (KY)
Jefferson Comm Coll (KY)
Johnson County Comm Coll (KS)
J. Sargeant Reynolds Comm Coll (VA)
Kalamazoo Valley Comm Coll (MI)
Kansas City Kansas Comm Coll (KS)
Kapiolani Comm Coll (HI)
Kaskaskia Coll (IL)
Kennebec Valley Comm Coll (ME)
Lake Superior Coll (MN)
Lane Comm Coll (OR)
Lansing Comm Coll (MI)

Lehigh Carbon Comm Coll (PA)
Lincoln Land Comm Coll (IL)
Macomb Comm Coll (MI)
Manchester Comm Coll (CT)
Marshall Comm and Tech Coll (WV)
Massachusetts Bay Comm Coll (MA)
McLennan Comm Coll (TX)
Meridian Comm Coll (MS)
Metropolitan Comm Coll (NE)
Miami Dade Coll (FL)
Midland Coll (TX)
Midlands Tech Coll (SC)
Milwaukee Area Tech Coll (WI)
Modesto Jr Coll (CA)
Mohawk Valley Comm Coll (NY)
Montgomery County Comm Coll (PA)
Moraine Valley Comm Coll (IL)
Mott Comm Coll (MI)
Napa Valley Coll (CA)
Nassau Comm Coll (NY)
North Central State Coll (OH)
Northern Essex Comm Coll (MA)
Northern Virginia Comm Coll (VA)
North Shore Comm Coll (MA)
Northwest Tech Coll (MN)
Oakland Comm Coll (MI)
Odessa Coll (TX)
Orange Coast Coll (CA)
Parkland Coll (IL)
Penn Valley Comm Coll (MO)
Pima Comm Coll (AZ)
Raritan Valley Comm Coll (NJ)
Rochester Comm and Tech Coll (MN)
Rockingham Comm Coll (NC)
Rockland Comm Coll (NY)
Rock Valley Coll (IL)
Rogue Comm Coll (OR)
St. Louis Comm Coll at Forest Park (MO)
St. Luke's Coll (IA)
Saint Paul Coll–A Comm & Tech College (MN)
St. Petersburg Coll (FL)
St. Philip's Coll (TX)
Sandhills Comm Coll (NC)
San Joaquin Valley Coll (CA)
Santa Fe Comm Coll (FL)
Scott Comm Coll (IA)
Seattle Central Comm Coll (WA)
Seminole Comm Coll (FL)
Seward County Comm Coll (KS)
Shelton State Comm Coll (AL)
Sheridan Coll (WY)
Sinclair Comm Coll (OH)
Somerset Comm Coll (KY)
Southeast Comm Coll, Lincoln Campus (NE)
Southeast Kentucky Comm and Tech Coll (KY)
Southern Maine Comm Coll (ME)
Southside Virginia Comm Coll (VA)
Southwestern Comm Coll (NC)
Southwest Georgia Tech Coll (GA)
Spartanburg Tech Coll (SC)
Springfield Tech Comm Coll (MA)
Stanly Comm Coll (NC)
Sussex County Comm Coll (NJ)
Tacoma Comm Coll (WA)
Temple Coll (TX)
Trident Tech Coll (SC)

Union County Coll (NJ)
U of Arkansas Comm Coll at Hope (AR)
Valencia Comm Coll (FL)
Volunteer State Comm Coll (TN)
Westchester Comm Coll (NY)

Respiratory Therapy Technician
Columbus State Comm Coll (OH)
Edgecombe Comm Coll (NC)
Harrisburg Area Comm Coll (PA)
Heart of Georgia Tech Coll (GA)
Kansas City Kansas Comm Coll (KS)
Miami Dade Coll (FL)
Northern Essex Comm Coll (MA)
Okefenokee Tech Coll (GA)
Pima Medical Inst, Mesa (AZ)
Pima Medical Inst, Tucson (AZ)
Pima Medical Inst (CA)
Pima Medical Inst, Denver (CO)
Pima Medical Inst (NV)

Restaurant, Culinary, and Catering Management
The Art Inst of New York City (NY)
Central Florida Comm Coll (FL)
Cincinnati State Tech and Comm Coll (OH)
Coll of DuPage (IL)
Coll of Lake County (IL)
Comm Coll of Allegheny County (PA)
Cuyahoga Comm Coll (OH)
Erie Comm Coll, North Campus (NY)
Hillsborough Comm Coll (FL)
Iowa Lakes Comm Coll (IA)
John Wood Comm Coll (IL)
Keystone Coll (PA)
Linn-Benton Comm Coll (OR)
Mohawk Valley Comm Coll (NY)
Moraine Valley Comm Coll (IL)
Orange Coast Coll (CA)
Pima Comm Coll (AZ)
State U of NY Coll of Technology at Alfred (NY)
State U of NY Coll of Technology at Delhi (NY)

Restaurant/Food Services Management
Columbus State Comm Coll (OH)
Iowa Lakes Comm Coll (IA)
Keystone Coll (PA)
Lehigh Carbon Comm Coll (PA)
Oakland Comm Coll (MI)
St. Philip's Coll (TX)

Retailing
Black Hawk Coll, Moline (IL)
Catawba Valley Comm Coll (NC)
Centralia Coll (WA)
Coll of DuPage (IL)
Comm Coll of Allegheny County (PA)
Comm Coll of Rhode Island (RI)
Edmonds Comm Coll (WA)
Ellsworth Comm Coll (IA)
Florida Comm Coll at Jacksonville (FL)
Garden City Comm Coll (KS)
Hutchinson Comm Coll and Area Vocational School (KS)
Iowa Lakes Comm Coll (IA)
Johnson County Comm Coll (KS)

Moraine Valley Comm Coll (IL)
Orange Coast Coll (CA)
Waubonsee Comm Coll (IL)

Robotics Technology
Coll of DuPage (IL)
Comm Coll of Allegheny County (PA)
Delaware County Comm Coll (PA)
Ivy Tech State Coll–Columbus (IN)
Ivy Tech State Coll–Southwest (IN)
Ivy Tech State Coll–Wabash Valley (IN)
Ivy Tech State Coll–Whitewater (IN)
Jefferson State Comm Coll (AL)
Macomb Comm Coll (MI)
Oakland Comm Coll (MI)
Schoolcraft Coll (MI)
Spartanburg Tech Coll (SC)
Waubonsee Comm Coll (IL)
Yuba Coll (CA)

Romance Languages
Highline Comm Coll (WA)
Tacoma Comm Coll (WA)

Russian
Austin Comm Coll (TX)
Everett Comm Coll (WA)
Tacoma Comm Coll (WA)

Safety/Security Technology
Comm and Tech Coll of Shepherd (WV)
Cuyahoga Comm Coll (OH)
Des Moines Area Comm Coll (IA)
Guam Comm Coll (GU)
Hudson Valley Comm Coll (NY)
John Tyler Comm Coll (VA)
Macomb Comm Coll (MI)
Truckee Meadows Comm Coll (NV)

Sales and Marketing/ Marketing And Distribution Teacher Education
Parkland Coll (IL)

Sales, Distribution and Marketing
Academy Coll (MN)
Central Carolina Tech Coll (SC)
Centralia Coll (WA)
Coll of DuPage (IL)
Collin County Comm Coll District (TX)
Cuyahoga Comm Coll (OH)
Fayetteville Tech Comm Coll (NC)
Hesser Coll (NH)
Iowa Lakes Comm Coll (IA)
Iowa Western Comm Coll (IA)
Johnson County Comm Coll (KS)
John Wood Comm Coll (IL)
Kennebec Valley Comm Coll (ME)
Lake Region State Coll (ND)
McIntosh Coll (NH)
Montgomery County Comm Coll (PA)
Pioneer Pacific Coll (OR)
Santa Barbara City Coll (CA)
State U of NY Coll of Technology at Alfred (NY)

Sales Operations
Coll of Lake County (IL)

Salon/Beauty Salon Management
Oakland Comm Coll (MI)

Sanitation Technology
Bay de Noc Comm Coll (MI)

Science Teacher Education
Chemeketa Comm Coll (OR)
Colby Comm Coll (KS)

Comm Coll of Southern Nevada (NV)
Dutchess Comm Coll (NY)
East Central Comm Coll (MS)
Harrisburg Area Comm Coll (PA)
Holmes Comm Coll (MS)
Independence Comm Coll (KS)
Iowa Central Comm Coll (IA)
Iowa Lakes Comm Coll (IA)
Itawamba Comm Coll (MS)
Miami Dade Coll (FL)
Sandhills Comm Coll (NC)
Snow Coll (UT)

Science Technologies Related
Cascadia Comm Coll (WA)
Cincinnati State Tech and Comm Coll (OH)
Comm Coll of Allegheny County (PA)
Delaware County Comm Coll (PA)
Front Range Comm Coll (CO)
Harford Comm Coll (MD)
Maria Coll (NY)
Marshall Comm and Tech Coll (WV)

Sculpture
De Anza Coll (CA)
Dixie State Coll of Utah (UT)
Inst of American Indian Arts (NM)
Keystone Coll (PA)

Secondary Education
Allen County Comm Coll (KS)
Alpena Comm Coll (MI)
Barton County Comm Coll (KS)
Brazosport Coll (TX)
Calhoun Comm Coll (AL)
Central Wyoming Coll (WY)
Clarendon Coll (TX)
Dixie State Coll of Utah (UT)
Eastern Arizona Coll (AZ)
Essex County Coll (NJ)
Gulf Coast Comm Coll (FL)
Howard Comm Coll (MD)
Mid Michigan Comm Coll (MI)
Montgomery County Comm Coll (PA)
Northwest-Shoals Comm Coll (AL)
Sauk Valley Comm Coll (IL)
Truckee Meadows Comm Coll (NV)
Western Wyoming Comm Coll (WY)

Security and Loss Prevention
Cincinnati State Tech and Comm Coll (OH)
Comm Coll of the Air Force (AL)
Harford Comm Coll (MD)
Hesser Coll (NH)
Nassau Comm Coll (NY)
San Joaquin Valley Coll (CA)

Security and Protective Services Related
Black Hawk Coll, Moline (IL)
Clover Park Tech Coll (WA)
Pima Comm Coll (AZ)

Selling Skills and Sales
Alexandria Tech Coll (MN)
Century Coll (MN)
Coll of DuPage (IL)
Cuyahoga Comm Coll (OH)
Hibbing Comm Coll (MN)
Iowa Lakes Comm Coll (IA)
Iowa Western Comm Coll (IA)
Lake Superior Coll (MN)
Lincoln Land Comm Coll (IL)
Moraine Valley Comm Coll (IL)

Orange Coast Coll (CA)
Santa Barbara City Coll (CA)

Sheet Metal Technology
Black Hawk Coll, Moline (IL)
Brazosport Coll (TX)
Comm Coll of Allegheny County (PA)
Ivy Tech State Coll–Central Indiana (IN)
Ivy Tech State Coll–Lafayette (IN)
Ivy Tech State Coll–North Central (IN)
Ivy Tech State Coll–Northeast (IN)
Ivy Tech State Coll–Northwest (IN)
Ivy Tech State Coll–Southcentral (IN)
Ivy Tech State Coll–Southwest (IN)
Ivy Tech State Coll–Wabash Valley (IN)
Macomb Comm Coll (MI)
Northwest State Comm Coll (OH)
Western Nevada Comm Coll (NV)

Sign Language Interpretation
Black Hawk Coll, Moline (IL)

Sign Language Interpretation and Translation
Austin Comm Coll (TX)
Blue Ridge Comm Coll (NC)
Central Piedmont Comm Coll (NC)
Chattanooga State Tech Comm Coll (TN)
Cincinnati State Tech and Comm Coll (OH)
Clovis Comm Coll (NM)
Collin County Comm Coll District (TX)
Columbus State Comm Coll (OH)
Comm Coll of Allegheny County (PA)
Comm Coll of Philadelphia (PA)
Comm Coll of Southern Nevada (NV)
Cowley County Comm Coll and Voc-Tech School (KS)
Delaware Tech & Comm Coll, Stanton/ Wilmington Cmps (DE)
Eastfield Coll (TX)
El Paso Comm Coll (TX)
Florida Comm Coll at Jacksonville (FL)
Front Range Comm Coll (CO)
Guam Comm Coll (GU)
Hillsborough Comm Coll (FL)
Houston Comm Coll System (TX)
Iowa Western Comm Coll (IA)
John A. Logan Coll (IL)
Johnson County Comm Coll (KS)
Lake Region State Coll (ND)
Lansing Comm Coll (MI)
McLennan Comm Coll (TX)
Miami Dade Coll (FL)
Mott Comm Coll (MI)
Mount Wachusett Comm Coll (MA)
Nashville State Tech Comm Coll (TN)
Northern Essex Comm Coll (MA)
Northwestern Connecticut Comm-Tech Coll (CT)
Pasadena City Coll (CA)
Pima Comm Coll (AZ)
Riverside Comm Coll District (CA)
Saint Paul Coll–A Comm & Tech College (MN)
St. Petersburg Coll (FL)

Orange Coast Coll (CA)
Santa Barbara City Coll (CA)

Sheet Metal Technology

Salt Lake Comm Coll (UT)
Scott Comm Coll (IA)
Seattle Central Comm Coll (WA)
Sheridan Coll (WY)
Sinclair Comm Coll (OH)
Southeast Tech Inst (SD)
Spartanburg Tech Coll (SC)
Union County Coll (NJ)
Waubonsee Comm Coll (IL)
Wilson Tech Comm Coll (NC)

Small Business Administration
Alexandria Tech Coll (MN)
Black Hawk Coll, Moline (IL)
Iowa Lakes Comm Coll (IA)
Lake Region State Coll (ND)

Small Engine Mechanics and Repair Technology
Alexandria Tech Coll (MN)
Century Coll (MN)
Iowa Lakes Comm Coll (IA)
North Dakota State Coll of Science (ND)

Social Psychology
Macomb Comm Coll (MI)

Social Sciences
Adirondack Comm Coll (NY)
Alabama Southern Comm Coll (AL)
Amarillo Coll (TX)
Ancilla Coll (IN)
Andrew Coll (GA)
Anne Arundel Comm Coll (MD)
Arizona Western Coll (AZ)
Atlantic Cape Comm Coll (NJ)
Bay Mills Comm Coll (MI)
Bowling Green State U-Firelands Coll (OH)
Brazosport Coll (TX)
Bristol Comm Coll (MA)
Brookdale Comm Coll (NJ)
Bucks County Comm Coll (PA)
Casper Coll (WY)
Centralia Coll (WA)
Central Oregon Comm Coll (OR)
Central Texas Coll (TX)
Central Wyoming Coll (WY)
Chemeketa Comm Coll (OR)
Citrus Coll (CA)
Clarendon Coll (TX)
Clinton Comm Coll (NY)
Cloud County Comm Coll (KS)
Cochise Coll, Douglas (AZ)
Coffeyville Comm Coll (KS)
Coll of the Canyons (CA)
Colorado Mountn Coll, Alpine Cmps (CO)
Colorado Mountn Coll (CO)
Colorado Mountn Coll, Timberline Cmps (CO)
Columbia-Greene Comm Coll (NY)
Comm Coll of Allegheny County (PA)
Comm Coll of Southern Nevada (NV)
Comm Coll of Vermont (VT)
Compton Comm Coll (CA)
Corning Comm Coll (NY)
Danville Area Comm Coll (IL)
Daytona Beach Comm Coll (FL)
De Anza Coll (CA)
Dodge City Comm Coll (KS)
Dutchess Comm Coll (NY)
East Central Comm Coll (MS)
East Mississippi Comm Coll (MS)
El Paso Comm Coll (TX)
Enterprise-Ozark Comm Coll (AL)
Essex County Coll (NJ)
Feather River Coll (CA)
Finger Lakes Comm Coll (NY)
Foothill Coll (CA)

Fulton-Montgomery Comm Coll (NY)
Garden City Comm Coll (KS)
Garrett Coll (MD)
Glendale Comm Coll (CA)
Gogebic Comm Coll (MI)
Harrisburg Area Comm Coll (PA)
Herkimer County Comm Coll (NY)
Highline Comm Coll (WA)
Hinds Comm Coll (MS)
Houston Comm Coll System (TX)
Howard Coll (TX)
Howard Comm Coll (MD)
Hutchinson Comm Coll and Area Vocational School (KS)
Indian River Comm Coll (FL)
Iowa Lakes Comm Coll (IA)
Itawamba Comm Coll (MS)
Jamestown Comm Coll (NY)
J. Sargeant Reynolds Comm Coll (VA)
Kilgore Coll (TX)
Kingwood Coll (TX)
Laramie County Comm Coll (WY)
Laredo Comm Coll (TX)
Lehigh Carbon Comm Coll (PA)
Long Beach City Coll (CA)
Lower Columbia Coll (WA)
Massachusetts Bay Comm Coll (MA)
Miami Dade Coll (FL)
Modesto Jr Coll (CA)
Montgomery County Comm Coll (PA)
New Mexico Military Inst (NM)
Niagara County Comm Coll (NY)
North Idaho Coll (ID)
Northwestern Connecticut Comm-Tech Coll (CT)
Northwestern Michigan Coll (MI)
Odessa Coll (TX)
Orange Coast Coll (CA)
Otero Jr Coll (CO)
Palm Beach Comm Coll (FL)
Pasadena City Coll (CA)
Phillips Comm Coll of the U of Arkansas (AR)
Piedmont Comm Coll (NC)
Pratt Comm Coll and Area Vocational School (KS)
Raritan Valley Comm Coll (NJ)
Riverside Comm Coll District (CA)
Rogue Comm Coll (OR)
Salt Lake Comm Coll (UT)
San Diego City Coll (CA)
San Diego Miramar Coll (CA)
San Joaquin Delta Coll (CA)
Santa Rosa Jr Coll (CA)
Seminole State Coll (OK)
Sheridan Coll (WY)
Solano Comm Coll (CA)
State U of NY Coll of Technology at Alfred (NY)
State U of NY Coll of Technology at Canton (NY)
State U of NY Coll of Technology at Delhi (NY)
Tacoma Comm Coll (WA)
Taft Coll (CA)
Tompkins Cortland Comm Coll (NY)
Umpqua Comm Coll (OR)
Westchester Comm Coll (NY)
Western Wyoming Comm Coll (WY)
Yuba Coll (CA)

Social Work
Alamance Comm Coll (NC)
Allen County Comm Coll (KS)
Amarillo Coll (TX)
Andrew Coll (GA)

Asheville-Buncombe Tech Comm Coll (NC)
Atlanta Metropolitan Coll (GA)
Atlantic Cape Comm Coll (NJ)
Austin Comm Coll (TX)
Barton County Comm Coll (KS)
Bay de Noc Comm Coll (MI)
Beaufort County Comm Coll (NC)
Blue Mountain Comm Coll (OR)
Bristol Comm Coll (MA)
Brookdale Comm Coll (NJ)
Bucks County Comm Coll (PA)
Capital Comm Coll (CT)
Casper Coll (WY)
Central Carolina Comm Coll (NC)
Central Piedmont Comm Coll (NC)
Century Coll (MN)
Chipola Coll (FL)
Clark State Comm Coll (OH)
Coahoma Comm Coll (MS)
Coffeyville Comm Coll (KS)
Colby Comm Coll (KS)
Coll of Lake County (IL)
Comm Coll of Allegheny County (PA)
Comm Coll of Rhode Island (RI)
Comm Coll of the Air Force (AL)
Compton Comm Coll (CA)
Cowley County Comm Coll and Voc-Tech School (KS)
Cumberland County Coll (NJ)
Danville Area Comm Coll (IL)
Darton Coll (GA)
Delta Coll (MI)
Des Moines Area Comm Coll (IA)
Dixie State Coll of Utah (UT)
Dodge City Comm Coll (KS)
East Central Coll (MO)
Eastfield Coll (TX)
Edgecombe Comm Coll (NC)
Edmonds Comm Coll (WA)
Elgin Comm Coll (IL)
Ellsworth Comm Coll (IA)
Essex County Coll (NJ)
Gainesville Coll (GA)
GateWay Comm Coll (AZ)
Gogebic Comm Coll (MI)
Halifax Comm Coll (NC)
Harrisburg Area Comm Coll (PA)
Hesser Coll (NH)
Highland Comm Coll (KS)
Holmes Comm Coll (MS)
Illinois Eastern Comm Colls, Wabash Valley Coll (IL)
Indian River Comm Coll (FL)
Iowa Central Comm Coll (IA)
Iowa Lakes Comm Coll (IA)
Itawamba Comm Coll (MS)
Jefferson Comm Coll (KY)
John A. Logan Coll (IL)
Lac Courte Oreilles Ojibwa Comm Coll (WI)
Lake Land Coll (IL)
Lansing Comm Coll (MI)
Lehigh Carbon Comm Coll (PA)
Manchester Comm Coll (CT)
Miami Dade Coll (FL)
Nebraska Indian Comm Coll (NE)
Northampton County Area Comm Coll (PA)
Northwest State Comm Coll (OH)
Owensboro Comm and Tech Coll (KY)
Palm Beach Comm Coll (FL)
Pratt Comm Coll and Area Vocational School (KS)
St. Philip's Coll (TX)

Salt Lake Comm Coll (UT)
San Diego City Coll (CA)
San Juan Coll (NM)
Sauk Valley Comm Coll (IL)
Seward County Comm Coll (KS)
Shawnee Comm Coll (IL)
Southwestern Oregon Comm Coll (OR)
Umpqua Comm Coll (OR)
The U of Akron–Wayne Coll (OH)
U of Cincinnati Raymond Walters Coll (OH)
Waubonsee Comm Coll (IL)
Western Wyoming Comm Coll (WY)
West Virginia U at Parkersburg (WV)

Social Work Related
Clarendon Coll (TX)

Sociology
Allen County Comm Coll (KS)
Andrew Coll (GA)
Atlantic Cape Comm Coll (NJ)
Austin Comm Coll (TX)
Bainbridge Coll (GA)
Barton County Comm Coll (KS)
Bergen Comm Coll (NJ)
Brazosport Coll (TX)
Brookdale Comm Coll (NJ)
Bunker Hill Comm Coll (MA)
Butler County Comm Coll (KS)
Casper Coll (WY)
Centralia Coll (WA)
Clarendon Coll (TX)
Coastal Bend Coll (TX)
Coastal Georgia Comm Coll (GA)
Coffeyville Comm Coll (KS)
Colby Comm Coll (KS)
Coll of Southern Idaho (ID)
Columbia Coll (CA)
Columbia State Comm Coll (TN)
Comm Coll of Allegheny County (PA)
Comm Coll of Southern Nevada (NV)
Compton Comm Coll (CA)
Contra Costa Coll (CA)
Darton Coll (GA)
Daytona Beach Comm Coll (FL)
De Anza Coll (CA)
Delaware County Comm Coll (PA)
Dixie State Coll of Utah (UT)
East Central Coll (MO)
Eastern Arizona Coll (AZ)
East Mississippi Comm Coll (MS)
Ellsworth Comm Coll (IA)
El Paso Comm Coll (TX)
Everett Comm Coll (WA)
Finger Lakes Comm Coll (NY)
Foothill Coll (CA)
Frank Phillips Coll (TX)
Gainesville Coll (GA)
Garden City Comm Coll (KS)
Garrett Coll (MD)
Gogebic Comm Coll (MI)
Gordon Coll (GA)
Great Basin Coll (NV)
Gulf Coast Comm Coll (FL)
Highland Comm Coll (IL)
Highland Comm Coll (KS)
Hinds Comm Coll (MS)
Independence Comm Coll (KS)
Indian River Comm Coll (FL)
Iowa Central Comm Coll (IA)
Iowa Lakes Comm Coll (IA)
Itawamba Comm Coll (MS)
John Wood Comm Coll (IL)
Laramie County Comm Coll (WY)
Lower Columbia Coll (WA)

Miami Dade Coll (FL)
Midland Coll (TX)
Mid Michigan Comm Coll (MI)
Mohave Comm Coll (AZ)
North Idaho Coll (ID)
Odessa Coll (TX)
Orange Coast Coll (CA)
Pasadena City Coll (CA)
Pima Comm Coll (AZ)
Pratt Comm Coll and Area Vocational School (KS)
St. Philip's Coll (TX)
San Diego City Coll (CA)
San Diego Miramar Coll (CA)
San Joaquin Delta Coll (CA)
San Juan Coll (NM)
Santa Barbara City Coll (CA)
Santa Rosa Jr Coll (CA)
Sauk Valley Comm Coll (IL)
Seward County Comm Coll (KS)
Snow Coll (UT)
South Mountain Comm Coll (AZ)
Tacoma Comm Coll (WA)
Trinity Valley Comm Coll (TX)
Umpqua Comm Coll (OR)
Western Oklahoma State Coll (OK)
Western Wyoming Comm Coll (WY)

Soil Conservation
Ohio State U Ag Tech Inst (OH)
Snow Coll (UT)
Trinidad State Jr Coll (CO)

Soil Science and Agronomy
Dixie State Coll of Utah (UT)
Iowa Lakes Comm Coll (IA)

Solar Energy Technology
Comm Coll of Allegheny County (PA)
Southeast Comm Coll, Milford Campus (NE)
Truckee Meadows Comm Coll (NV)

Spanish
Arizona Western Coll (AZ)
Austin Comm Coll (TX)
Casper Coll (WY)
Centralia Coll (WA)
Citrus Coll (CA)
Cleveland Comm Coll (NC)
Cochise Coll, Douglas (AZ)
Coll of the Canyons (CA)
Compton Comm Coll (CA)
Contra Costa Coll (CA)
De Anza Coll (CA)
East Central Coll (MO)
Everett Comm Coll (WA)
Foothill Coll (CA)
Gordon Coll (GA)
Independence Comm Coll (KS)
Indian River Comm Coll (FL)
Iowa Lakes Comm Coll (IA)
Laramie County Comm Coll (WY)
Long Beach City Coll (CA)
Miami Dade Coll (FL)
Midland Coll (TX)
New Mexico Military Inst (NM)
North Idaho Coll (ID)
Orange Coast Coll (CA)
Pasadena City Coll (CA)
Riverside Comm Coll District (CA)
St. Philip's Coll (TX)
San Diego Miramar Coll (CA)
San Joaquin Delta Coll (CA)
Santa Barbara City Coll (CA)
Santa Rosa Jr Coll (CA)
Sauk Valley Comm Coll (IL)
Snow Coll (UT)
Solano Comm Coll (CA)
Tacoma Comm Coll (WA)
Trinity Valley Comm Coll (TX)

Western Oklahoma State Coll (OK)
Western Wyoming Comm Coll (WY)

Special Education
Cleveland Comm Coll (NC)
Comm Coll of Rhode Island (RI)
Lehigh Carbon Comm Coll (PA)
Northampton County Area Comm Coll (PA)
Sauk Valley Comm Coll (IL)
Western Wyoming Comm Coll (WY)

Special Education (Early Childhood)
Calhoun Comm Coll (AL)
Motlow State Comm Coll (TN)
Olympic Coll (WA)

Special Education (Hearing Impaired)
Bishop State Comm Coll (AL)

Special Products Marketing
Asnuntuck Comm Coll (CT)
Bergen Comm Coll (NJ)
Brookdale Comm Coll (NJ)
Broward Comm Coll (FL)
Central Piedmont Comm Coll (NC)
Columbia Coll (CA)
Comm Coll of Philadelphia (PA)
Comm Coll of Southern Nevada (NV)
Copiah-Lincoln Comm Coll (MS)
Daytona Beach Comm Coll (FL)
Des Moines Area Comm Coll (IA)
Dutchess Comm Coll (NY)
East Central Coll (MO)
Enterprise-Ozark Comm Coll (AL)
Fox Valley Tech Coll (WI)
Gateway Comm Coll (CT)
Henry Ford Comm Coll (MI)
Hinds Comm Coll (MS)
Indian River Comm Coll (FL)
Iowa Western Comm Coll (IA)
Jefferson Comm Coll (OH)
Kapiolani Comm Coll (HI)
Lane Comm Coll (OR)
Lansing Comm Coll (MI)
Long Beach City Coll (CA)
Modesto Jr Coll (CA)
Muskegon Comm Coll (MI)
Northern Virginia Comm Coll (VA)
Orange Coast Coll (CA)
Palm Beach Comm Coll (FL)
Penn Valley Comm Coll (MO)
San Diego City Coll (CA)
San Joaquin Delta Coll (CA)
Sinclair Comm Coll (OH)
Southern Maine Comm Coll (ME)
Three Rivers Comm Coll (CT)
Westchester Comm Coll (NY)
Westmoreland County Comm Coll (PA)
Yakima Valley Comm Coll (WA)

Speech and Rhetoric
Allen County Comm Coll (KS)
Amarillo Coll (TX)
Andrew Coll (GA)
Atlanta Metropolitan Coll (GA)
Austin Comm Coll (TX)
Bainbridge Coll (GA)
Brazosport Coll (TX)
Brookdale Comm Coll (NJ)
Casper Coll (WY)

City Colls of Chicago, Wilbur Wright Coll (IL)
Clarendon Coll (TX)
Coastal Bend Coll (TX)
Columbia State Comm Coll (TN)
Compton Comm Coll (CA)
Darton Coll (GA)
De Anza Coll (CA)
Dodge City Comm Coll (KS)
East Central Coll (MO)
El Paso Comm Coll (TX)
Everett Comm Coll (WA)
Foothill Coll (CA)
Gainesville Coll (GA)
Garden City Comm Coll (KS)
Glendale Comm Coll (CA)
Howard Coll (TX)
Indian River Comm Coll (FL)
Iowa Lakes Comm Coll (IA)
Itawamba Comm Coll (MS)
Kilgore Coll (TX)
Lansing Comm Coll (MI)
Linn-Benton Comm Coll (OR)
Long Beach City Coll (CA)
Lower Columbia Coll (WA)
Midland Coll (TX)
Mid Michigan Comm Coll (MI)
Modesto Jr Coll (CA)
Northern Virginia Comm Coll (VA)
Odessa Coll (TX)
Pasadena City Coll (CA)
Pima Comm Coll (AZ)
Pratt Comm Coll and Area Vocational School (KS)
Riverside Comm Coll District (CA)
St. Louis Comm Coll at Meramec (MO)
St. Philip's Coll (TX)
San Diego City Coll (CA)
San Joaquin Delta Coll (CA)
Sauk Valley Comm Coll (IL)
Seward County Comm Coll (KS)
Tacoma Comm Coll (WA)
Trinity Valley Comm Coll (TX)
Western Oklahoma State Coll (OK)

Speech-Language Pathology
Catawba Valley Comm Coll (NC)
Coll of DuPage (IL)
Fayetteville Tech Comm Coll (NC)
Guilford Tech Comm Coll (NC)
Parkland Coll (IL)
Randolph Comm Coll (NC)
Santa Rosa Jr Coll (CA)
Wilkes Comm Coll (NC)

Speech/Theater Education
Highland Comm Coll (IL)
Iowa Western Comm Coll (IA)
Mid Michigan Comm Coll (MI)
Pratt Comm Coll and Area Vocational School (KS)
San Antonio Coll (TX)

Speech Therapy
Mount Wachusett Comm Coll (MA)

Sport and Fitness Administration
Barton County Comm Coll (KS)
Bucks County Comm Coll (PA)
Butler County Comm Coll (PA)
Central Oregon Comm Coll (OR)
Coahoma Comm Coll (MS)
Columbus State Comm Coll (OH)
Hesser Coll (NH)
Holyoke Comm Coll (MA)

Howard Comm Coll (MD)
Iowa Lakes Comm Coll (IA)
Keystone Coll (PA)
Kingsborough Comm Coll of City U of NY (NY)
Lake-Sumter Comm Coll (FL)
Lehigh Carbon Comm Coll (PA)
New Mexico Military Inst (NM)
Northampton County Area Comm Coll (PA)
North Iowa Area Comm Coll (IA)
Oakland Comm Coll (MI)
State U of NY Coll of Technology at Alfred (NY)
Tompkins Cortland Comm Coll (NY)

Statistics
Daytona Beach Comm Coll (FL)
Pasadena City Coll (CA)

Structural Engineering
Bristol Comm Coll (MA)

Substance Abuse/Addiction Counseling
Alvin Comm Coll (TX)
Amarillo Coll (TX)
Asnuntuck Comm Coll (CT)
Broome Comm Coll (NY)
Butler County Comm Coll (KS)
Central Texas Coll (TX)
Century Coll (MN)
Clark Coll (WA)
Coll of DuPage (IL)
Coll of Lake County (IL)
Columbus State Comm Coll (OH)
Comm Coll of Allegheny County (PA)
Comm Coll of Rhode Island (RI)
Corning Comm Coll (NY)
Danville Area Comm Coll (IL)
Dawson Comm Coll (MT)
Delaware Tech & Comm Coll, Stanton/ Wilmington Cmps (DE)
Eastfield Coll (TX)
Edmonds Comm Coll (WA)
Elgin Comm Coll (IL)
Erie Comm Coll (NY)
Finger Lakes Comm Coll (NY)
Florida Comm Coll at Jacksonville (FL)
Gadsden State Comm Coll (AL)
Gateway Comm Coll (CT)
Genesee Comm Coll (NY)
Howard Coll (TX)
Howard Comm Coll (MD)
Iowa Western Comm Coll (IA)
Kansas City Kansas Comm Coll (KS)
Lac Courte Oreilles Ojibwa Comm Coll (WI)
Lane Comm Coll (OR)
Lower Columbia Coll (WA)
Mesabi Range Comm and Tech Coll (MN)
Miami Dade Coll (FL)
Midland Coll (TX)
Milwaukee Area Tech Coll (WI)
Minneapolis Comm and Tech Coll (MN)
Mohawk Valley Comm Coll (NY)
Northern Virginia Comm Coll (VA)
North Shore Comm Coll (MA)
Northwestern Connecticut Comm-Tech Coll (CT)
Odessa Coll (TX)
Peninsula Coll (WA)
Prairie State Coll (IL)

Quinebaug Valley Comm Coll (CT)
Rogue Comm Coll (OR)
St. Petersburg Coll (FL)
Sandhills Comm Coll (NC)
Seattle Central Comm Coll (WA)
Sisseton-Wahpeton Comm Coll (SD)
Southwestern Comm Coll (NC)
Southwestern Oregon Comm Coll (OR)
Tacoma Comm Coll (WA)
Three Rivers Comm Coll (CT)
Tillamook Bay Comm Coll (OR)
Tompkins Cortland Comm Coll (NY)
Truckee Meadows Comm Coll (NV)
Tunxis Comm Coll (CT)
Westchester Comm Coll (NY)
Wor-Wic Comm Coll (MD)
Yakima Valley Comm Coll (WA)
Yuba Coll (CA)

Surgical Technology
Athens Tech Coll (GA)
Austin Comm Coll (TX)
Baltimore City Comm Coll (MD)
Bismarck State Coll (ND)
Blue Ridge Comm Coll (NC)
Brevard Comm Coll (FL)
Central Carolina Tech Coll (SC)
Central Wyoming Coll (WY)
Cincinnati State Tech and Comm Coll (OH)
Coastal Carolina Comm Coll (NC)
Coll of DuPage (IL)
Coll of Southern Idaho (ID)
Columbus State Comm Coll (OH)
Comm & Tech Coll at West Virginia U Inst of Technology (WV)
Comm Coll of Allegheny County (PA)
Comm Coll of the Air Force (AL)
Cuyahoga Comm Coll (OH)
DeKalb Tech Coll (GA)
Delaware County Comm Coll (PA)
Delta Coll (MI)
Durham Tech Comm Coll (NC)
Eastern Idaho Tech Coll (ID)
Edgecombe Comm Coll (NC)
Fayetteville Tech Comm Coll (NC)
GateWay Comm Coll (AZ)
Guilford Tech Comm Coll (NC)
Hinds Comm Coll (MS)
Iowa Lakes Comm Coll (IA)
Ivy Tech State Coll–Central Indiana (IN)
Ivy Tech State Coll–Columbus (IN)
Ivy Tech State Coll–Eastcentral (IN)
Ivy Tech State Coll–Kokomo (IN)
Ivy Tech State Coll–Lafayette (IN)
Ivy Tech State Coll–Northwest (IN)
Ivy Tech State Coll–Southwest (IN)
Ivy Tech State Coll–Wabash Valley (IN)
James H. Faulkner State Comm Coll (AL)
Lake Superior Coll (MN)
Lanier Tech Coll (GA)
Lansing Comm Coll (MI)
Macomb Comm Coll (MI)
Manchester Comm Coll (CT)

Metropolitan Comm Coll (NE)
Midlands Tech Coll (SC)
Montgomery County Comm Coll (PA)
Nassau Comm Coll (NY)
Niagara County Comm Coll (NY)
Northeast State Tech Comm Coll (TN)
Northwest Tech Coll (MN)
Oakland Comm Coll (MI)
Okefenokee Tech Coll (GA)
Polk Comm Coll (FL)
Rochester Comm and Tech Coll (MN)
St. Cloud Tech Coll (MN)
St. Louis Comm Coll at Forest Park (MO)
Salt Lake Comm Coll (UT)
Sandhills Comm Coll (NC)
San Joaquin Valley Coll (CA)
Savannah Tech Coll (GA)
Seward County Comm Coll (KS)
Sinclair Comm Coll (OH)
Somerset Comm Coll (KY)
Southeast Tech Inst (SD)
Southern Maine Comm Coll (ME)
Springfield Tech Comm Coll (MA)
Trinity Valley Comm Coll (TX)

Survey Technology
Asheville-Buncombe Tech Comm Coll (NC)
Austin Comm Coll (TX)
Centralia Coll (WA)
Central Piedmont Comm Coll (NC)
Chattanooga State Tech Comm Coll (TN)
Cincinnati State Tech and Comm Coll (OH)
Comm Coll of Southern Nevada (NV)
Delaware Tech & Comm Coll, Terry Cmps (DE)
Fayetteville Tech Comm Coll (NC)
Flathead Valley Comm Coll (MT)
Frank Phillips Coll (TX)
Guilford Tech Comm Coll (NC)
Hawkeye Comm Coll (IA)
Indian River Comm Coll (FL)
Lansing Comm Coll (MI)
Macomb Comm Coll (MI)
Middle Georgia Coll (GA)
Milwaukee Area Tech Coll (WI)
Mohawk Valley Comm Coll (NY)
Morrison Inst of Technology (IL)
Mott Comm Coll (MI)
Owens Comm Coll, Toledo (OH)
Palm Beach Comm Coll (FL)
Penn State U Wilkes-Barre Campus of the Commonwealth Coll (PA)
Salt Lake Comm Coll (UT)
Sandhills Comm Coll (NC)
Sinclair Comm Coll (OH)
Southeast Comm Coll, Milford Campus (NE)
Southeast Tech Inst (SD)
State U of NY Coll of Technology at Alfred (NY)
U of Arkansas Comm Coll at Morrilton (AR)
Valencia Comm Coll (FL)
Wake Tech Comm Coll (NC)
Westwood Coll–Denver North (CO)

System Administration
Academy Coll (MN)
Adirondack Comm Coll (NY)
Andover Coll (ME)

Anne Arundel Comm Coll (MD)
Anoka-Ramsey Comm Coll (MN)
Austin Comm Coll (TX)
Berkeley Coll (NJ)
Blue Ridge Comm Coll (NC)
Brevard Comm Coll (FL)
Cape Cod Comm Coll (MA)
Central Comm Coll–Columbus Campus (NE)
Central Comm Coll–Grand Island Campus (NE)
Central Comm Coll–Hastings Campus (NE)
Centralia Coll (WA)
Cleveland Comm Coll (NC)
Coastal Bend Coll (TX)
Cumberland County Coll (NJ)
Durham Tech Comm Coll (NC)
Eastfield Coll (TX)
Edgecombe Comm Coll (NC)
El Paso Comm Coll (TX)
Fayetteville Tech Comm Coll (NC)
Florida Comm Coll at Jacksonville (FL)
Florida National Coll (FL)
Gadsden State Comm Coll-Ayers Campus (AL)
GateWay Comm Coll (AZ)
Genesee Comm Coll (NY)
Gogebic Comm Coll (MI)
Hawkeye Comm Coll (IA)
Heartland Comm Coll (IL)
Hinds Comm Coll (MS)
Holmes Comm Coll (MS)
Iowa Lakes Comm Coll (IA)
Keiser Coll, Fort Lauderdale (FL)
Laurel Business Inst (PA)
Linn-Benton Comm Coll (OR)
Metropolitan Comm Coll-Business & Technology College (MO)
Midland Coll (TX)
Milwaukee Area Tech Coll (WI)
Mineral Area Coll (MO)
MTI Coll of Business and Technology, Houston (TX)
Northland Comm and Tech Coll–Thief River Falls (MN)
Olympic Coll (WA)
Owensboro Comm and Tech Coll (KY)
Palm Beach Comm Coll (FL)
Parkland Coll (IL)
Pennsylvania Highland Comm Coll (PA)
Quinebaug Valley Comm Coll (CT)
Randolph Comm Coll (NC)
Rockland Comm Coll (NY)
Salt Lake Comm Coll (UT)
San Antonio Coll (TX)
Sandhills Comm Coll (NC)
Santa Barbara City Coll (CA)
Seminole Comm Coll (FL)
Sheridan Coll (WY)
Sinclair Comm Coll (OH)
Southeast Tech Inst (SD)
Stanly Comm Coll (NC)
Tacoma Comm Coll (WA)
Thaddeus Stevens Coll of Technology (PA)
Tompkins Cortland Comm Coll (NY)
U of Arkansas Comm Coll at Batesville (AR)
Wake Tech Comm Coll (NC)

System, Networking, and Lan/Wan Management
Academy Coll (MN)
Brevard Comm Coll (FL)
Iowa Lakes Comm Coll (IA)
Metropolitan Comm Coll-Business & Technology College (MO)
Midland Coll (TX)

MTI Coll of Business and Technology, Houston (TX)
Olympic Coll (WA)
St. Philip's Coll (TX)
Southeastern Tech Coll (GA)
Southwestern Comm Coll (NC)
Vatterott Coll, Springfield (MO)

Taxation
Globe Coll (MN)
Minnesota School of Business–Brooklyn Center (MN)
Minnesota School of Business–Plymouth (MN)
Minnesota School of Business–Richfield (MN)

Teacher Assistant/Aide
Alamance Comm Coll (NC)
Athens Tech Coll (GA)
Big Bend Comm Coll (WA)
Blackfeet Comm Coll (MT)
Black Hawk Coll, Moline (IL)
Brunswick Comm Coll (NC)
Bucks County Comm Coll (PA)
Carteret Comm Coll (NC)
Catawba Valley Comm Coll (NC)
Centralia Coll (WA)
Chemeketa Comm Coll (OR)
Cleveland Comm Coll (NC)
Clover Park Tech Coll (WA)
Clovis Comm Coll (NM)
Cochise Coll, Douglas (AZ)
Colorado Northwestern Comm Coll (CO)
Comm Coll of Southern Nevada (NV)
Comm Coll of Vermont (VT)
Compton Comm Coll (CA)
Danville Area Comm Coll (IL)
Delaware County Comm Coll (PA)
Delta Coll (MI)
Des Moines Area Comm Coll (IA)
Durham Tech Comm Coll (NC)
Ellsworth Comm Coll (IA)
Fort Scott Comm Coll (KS)
Fulton-Montgomery Comm Coll (NY)
Garden City Comm Coll (KS)
Illinois Eastern Comm Colls, Lincoln Trail Coll (IL)
Indian River Comm Coll (FL)
Isothermal Comm Coll (NC)
John A. Logan Coll (IL)
Kingsborough Comm Coll of City U of NY (NY)
Lansing Comm Coll (MI)
Lewis and Clark Comm Coll (IL)
Linn-Benton Comm Coll (OR)
Lower Columbia Coll (WA)
Manchester Comm Coll (CT)
McDowell Tech Comm Coll (NC)
Miami Dade Coll (FL)
Montgomery County Comm Coll (PA)
Odessa Coll (TX)
Pasadena City Coll (CA)
Prairie State Coll (IL)
Rockingham Comm Coll (NC)
St. Cloud Tech Coll (MN)
St. Philip's Coll (TX)
Sandhills Comm Coll (NC)
San Diego City Coll (CA)
Shoreline Comm Coll (WA)
Walla Walla Comm Coll (WA)

Technical and Business Writing
Austin Comm Coll (TX)
Cincinnati State Tech and Comm Coll (OH)
Clovis Comm Coll (NM)
Coll of Lake County (IL)

Columbus State Comm Coll (OH)
De Anza Coll (CA)
Florida National Coll (FL)
Houston Comm Coll System (TX)
Linn-Benton Comm Coll (OR)
Three Rivers Comm Coll (CT)

Technical Teacher Education
Lake Region State Coll (ND)
North Dakota State Coll of Science (ND)

Technology/Industrial Arts Teacher Education
Allen County Comm Coll (KS)
Eastern Arizona Coll (AZ)
Iowa Lakes Comm Coll (IA)

Telecommunications
Amarillo Coll (TX)
Anne Arundel Comm Coll (MD)
Bossier Parish Comm Coll (LA)
Brookdale Comm Coll (NJ)
Cayuga County Comm Coll (NY)
Central Carolina Comm Coll (NC)
Cincinnati State Tech and Comm Coll (OH)
Coffeyville Comm Coll (KS)
Comm Coll of Beaver County (PA)
Compton Comm Coll (CA)
Daytona Beach Comm Coll (FL)
DeKalb Tech Coll (GA)
Des Moines Area Comm Coll (IA)
Dutchess Comm Coll (NY)
ECPI Coll of Technology, Newport News (VA)
ECPI Coll of Technology, Virginia Beach (VA)
ECPI Tech Coll, Richmond (VA)
ECPI Tech Coll, Roanoke (VA)
Gadsden State Comm Coll (AL)
Gwinnett Tech Coll (GA)
Herkimer County Comm Coll (NY)
Highland Comm Coll (KS)
Hinds Comm Coll (MS)
Howard Comm Coll (MD)
Hudson Valley Comm Coll (NY)
Illinois Eastern Comm Colls, Lincoln Trail Coll (IL)
Iowa Central Comm Coll (IA)
Lake Land Coll (IL)
Lansing Comm Coll (MI)
Massachusetts Bay Comm Coll (MA)
McIntosh Coll (NH)
Meridian Comm Coll (MS)
Mohawk Valley Comm Coll (NY)
Mount Wachusett Comm Coll (MA)
Napa Valley Coll (CA)
Niagara County Comm Coll (NY)
Northwest Tech Coll (MN)
Owens Comm Coll, Toledo (OH)
Pasadena City Coll (CA)
Queensborough Comm Coll of City U of NY (NY)
St. Petersburg Coll (FL)
San Diego City Coll (CA)
Seminole Comm Coll (FL)
Solano Comm Coll (CA)
Trident Tech Coll (SC)
Wake Tech Comm Coll (NC)

Telecommunications Technology

Alexandria Tech Coll (MN)
Clark Coll (WA)
Collin County Comm Coll District (TX)
ECPI Tech Coll, Glen Allen (VA)
ECPI Tech Coll, Richmond (VA)
ECPI Tech Coll, Roanoke (VA)
Miami Dade Coll (FL)
Northern Essex Comm Coll (MA)
Penn State U Beaver Campus of the Commonwealth Coll (PA)
Penn State U DuBois Campus of the Commonwealth Coll (PA)
Penn State U Fayette Campus of the Commonwealth Coll (PA)
Penn State U Hazleton Campus of the Commonwealth Coll (PA)
Penn State U New Kensington Campus of the Commonwealth Coll (PA)
Penn State U Shenango Campus of the Commonwealth Coll (PA)
Penn State U Wilkes-Barre Campus of the Commonwealth Coll (PA)
Penn State U York Campus of the Commonwealth Coll (PA)

Theatre Design and Technology

Comm Coll of Rhode Island (RI)
Florida Comm Coll at Jacksonville (FL)
Howard Comm Coll (MD)
Lake-Sumter Comm Coll (FL)
Nassau Comm Coll (NY)
Santa Barbara City Coll (CA)
Western Wyoming Comm Coll (WY)

Theatre/Theatre Arts Management

Gulf Coast Comm Coll (FL)

Theology

Assumption Coll for Sisters (NJ)
Brazosport Coll (TX)
Highland Comm Coll (KS)
Mid-America Baptist Theological Seminary (TN)
Riverside Comm Coll District (CA)

Therapeutic Recreation

Butler County Comm Coll (PA)
Carteret Comm Coll (NC)
Colorado Mountn Coll (CO)
Comm Coll of Allegheny County (PA)
Edmonds Comm Coll (WA)
Keystone Coll (PA)
Moraine Valley Comm Coll (IL)
North Central State Coll (OH)
Northwestern Connecticut Comm-Tech Coll (CT)
Santa Barbara City Coll (CA)

Tool and Die Technology

Asheville-Buncombe Tech Comm Coll (NC)
Bevill State Comm Coll (AL)
Black Hawk Coll, Moline (IL)
Craven Comm Coll (NC)
Fayetteville Tech Comm Coll (NC)
Gadsden State Comm Coll (AL)
Hawkeye Comm Coll (IA)
Ivy Tech State Coll–Bloomington (IN)

Ivy Tech State Coll–Central Indiana (IN)
Ivy Tech State Coll–Columbus (IN)
Ivy Tech State Coll–Eastcentral (IN)
Ivy Tech State Coll–Kokomo (IN)
Ivy Tech State Coll–Lafayette (IN)
Ivy Tech State Coll–North Central (IN)
Ivy Tech State Coll–Northeast (IN)
Ivy Tech State Coll–Northwest (IN)
Ivy Tech State Coll–Southcentral (IN)
Ivy Tech State Coll–Southwest (IN)
Ivy Tech State Coll–Wabash Valley (IN)
Ivy Tech State Coll–Whitewater (IN)
Jackson State Comm Coll (TN)
Macomb Comm Coll (MI)
Milwaukee Area Tech Coll (WI)
North Iowa Area Comm Coll (IA)
Northwest State Comm Coll (OH)
Oakland Comm Coll (MI)
Prairie State Coll (IL)
Wake Tech Comm Coll (NC)
Western Iowa Tech Comm Coll (IA)
Wilson Tech Comm Coll (NC)

Tourism and Travel Services Management

Adirondack Comm Coll (NY)
Amarillo Coll (TX)
Arapahoe Comm Coll (CO)
Bay State Coll (MA)
Bergen Comm Coll (NJ)
Blue Ridge Comm Coll (NC)
Briarwood Coll (CT)
Broward Comm Coll (FL)
Bunker Hill Comm Coll (MA)
Butler County Comm Coll (PA)
Central Piedmont Comm Coll (NC)
Cloud County Comm Coll (KS)
Columbus State Comm Coll (OH)
Comm Coll of Denver (CO)
Corning Comm Coll (NY)
Danville Area Comm Coll (IL)
Daytona Beach Comm Coll (FL)
Dutchess Comm Coll (NY)
East Central Coll (MO)
Elgin Comm Coll (IL)
El Paso Comm Coll (TX)
Erie Business Center, Main (PA)
Erie Business Center South (PA)
Finger Lakes Comm Coll (NY)
Florida National Coll (FL)
Foothill Coll (CA)
Genesee Comm Coll (NY)
Guam Comm Coll (GU)
Gwinnett Tech Coll (GA)
Harrisburg Area Comm Coll (PA)
Hawaii Business Coll (HI)
Herkimer County Comm Coll (NY)
Highline Comm Coll (WA)
Holyoke Comm Coll (MA)
Houston Comm Coll System (TX)
ICM School of Business & Medical Careers (PA)
Iowa Lakes Comm Coll (IA)
Jefferson Comm Coll (NY)
John A. Logan Coll (IL)

Johnson County Comm Coll (KS)
Kapiolani Comm Coll (HI)
Kingsborough Comm Coll of City U of NY (NY)
Lansing Comm Coll (MI)
Long Beach City Coll (CA)
Maple Woods Comm Coll (MO)
McIntosh Coll (NH)
Miami Dade Coll (FL)
Mineral Area Coll (MO)
Northern Essex Comm Coll (MA)
Northern Virginia Comm Coll (VA)
North Shore Comm Coll (MA)
Pasadena City Coll (CA)
Pima Comm Coll (AZ)
Raritan Valley Comm Coll (NJ)
Rasmussen Coll St. Cloud (MN)
Rockingham Comm Coll (NC)
Rockland Comm Coll (NY)
St. Louis Comm Coll at Forest Park (MO)
St. Petersburg Coll (FL)
St. Philip's Coll (TX)
San Diego City Coll (CA)
San Joaquin Valley Coll (CA)
Shelton State Comm Coll (AL)
Sinclair Comm Coll (OH)
State U of NY Coll of Technology at Delhi (NY)
Three Rivers Comm Coll (CT)
Tompkins Cortland Comm Coll (NY)
U of Northwestern Ohio (OH)
Valencia Comm Coll (FL)
Westchester Comm Coll (NY)
Westmoreland County Comm Coll (PA)
Yakima Valley Comm Coll (WA)

Tourism and Travel Services Marketing

Coll of DuPage (IL)
Dixie State Coll of Utah (UT)
Edmonds Comm Coll (WA)
Florida Comm Coll at Jacksonville (FL)
Guam Comm Coll (GU)
Harrisburg Area Comm Coll (PA)
Herkimer County Comm Coll (NY)
Iowa Lakes Comm Coll (IA)
Lehigh Carbon Comm Coll (PA)
Milwaukee Area Tech Coll (WI)
Moraine Valley Comm Coll (IL)
National Coll of Business & Technology, Salem (VA)
Tompkins Cortland Comm Coll (NY)
Waubonsee Comm Coll (IL)

Tourism Promotion

Central Oregon Comm Coll (OR)
Coll of DuPage (IL)
Comm Coll of Allegheny County (PA)
Florida National Coll (FL)
Guam Comm Coll (GU)
Herkimer County Comm Coll (NY)
Iowa Lakes Comm Coll (IA)
Lehigh Carbon Comm Coll (PA)
Westchester Comm Coll (NY)

Trade and Industrial Teacher Education

Compton Comm Coll (CA)

Copiah-Lincoln Comm Coll (MS)
ECPI Coll of Technology, Newport News (VA)
ECPI Tech Coll, Richmond (VA)
Ellsworth Comm Coll (IA)
Gainesville Coll (GA)
Garden City Comm Coll (KS)
Iowa Lakes Comm Coll (IA)
Isothermal Comm Coll (NC)
Itawamba Comm Coll (MS)
Kilgore Coll (TX)
Pratt Comm Coll and Area Vocational School (KS)
Snow Coll (UT)
Southwestern Comm Coll (NC)
Spartanburg Tech Coll (SC)
U of Arkansas Comm Coll at Hope (AR)

Transportation and Materials Moving Related

Cecil Comm Coll (MD)

Transportation Management

Calhoun Comm Coll (AL)
Milwaukee Area Tech Coll (WI)
Northwest State Comm Coll (OH)

Transportation Technology

Central Piedmont Comm Coll (NC)
Chattanooga State Tech Comm Coll (TN)
Coll of DuPage (IL)
Delaware Tech & Comm Coll, Stanton/ Wilmington Cmps (DE)
Fort Scott Comm Coll (KS)
Henry Ford Comm Coll (MI)
Highline Comm Coll (WA)
Houston Comm Coll System (TX)
Milwaukee Area Tech Coll (WI)
Muskegon Comm Coll (MI)
Nassau Comm Coll (NY)
North Hennepin Comm Coll (MN)
Salt Lake Comm Coll (UT)
San Diego City Coll (CA)
San Diego Miramar Coll (CA)
Sinclair Comm Coll (OH)
Southeast Comm Coll, Milford Campus (NE)

Truck and Bus Driver/Commercial Vehicle Operation

Alexandria Tech Coll (MN)
Black Hawk Coll, Moline (IL)

Turf and Turfgrass Management

Brunswick Comm Coll (NC)
Cincinnati State Tech and Comm Coll (OH)
Coll of Lake County (IL)
Comm Coll of Allegheny County (PA)
Guilford Tech Comm Coll (NC)
Iowa Lakes Comm Coll (IA)
Linn State Tech Coll (MO)
Northwestern Michigan Coll (MI)
Ohio State U Ag Tech Inst (OH)
Rochester Comm and Tech Coll (MN)
Sandhills Comm Coll (NC)
Southeast Tech Inst (SD)
Southwestern Oregon Comm Coll (OR)
State U of NY Coll of Technology at Delhi (NY)
Texas State Tech Coll–Waco/Marshall Campus (TX)
Walla Walla Comm Coll (WA)
Western Iowa Tech Comm Coll (IA)

Urban Studies/Affairs

Comm Coll of Rhode Island (RI)
Riverside Comm Coll District (CA)
St. Philip's Coll (TX)
U of Cincinnati Raymond Walters Coll (OH)

Vehicle and Vehicle Parts And Accessories Marketing

Guam Comm Coll (GU)

Vehicle/Equipment Operation

Brazosport Coll (TX)
Comm Coll of the Air Force (AL)
Western Nevada Comm Coll (NV)

Vehicle Maintenance and Repair Technologies Related

Albuquerque Tech Vocational Inst (NM)
Black Hawk Coll, Moline (IL)
North Dakota State Coll of Science (ND)

Vehicle/Petroleum Products Marketing

Central Comm Coll–Hastings Campus (NE)

Veterinary/Animal Health Technology

Cedar Valley Coll (TX)
Central Florida Comm Coll (FL)
Columbus State Comm Coll (OH)
Lehigh Carbon Comm Coll (PA)
Macomb Comm Coll (MI)
Midland Coll (TX)
Minnesota School of Business–Richfield (MN)
Northampton County Area Comm Coll (PA)
Parkland Coll (IL)
Pima Comm Coll (AZ)
Sussex County Comm Coll (NJ)

Veterinary Sciences

Casper Coll (WY)
Colby Comm Coll (KS)
Highland Comm Coll (KS)
Hinds Comm Coll (MS)
Holmes Comm Coll (MS)
Holyoke Comm Coll (MA)
Isothermal Comm Coll (NC)
Itawamba Comm Coll (MS)
Macomb Comm Coll (MI)
Miami Dade Coll (FL)
Northwest-Shoals Comm Coll (AL)
Pasadena City Coll (CA)
Snow Coll (UT)
State U of NY Coll of Technology at Alfred (NY)
Western Oklahoma State Coll (OK)

Veterinary Technology

Athens Tech Coll (GA)
Bergen Comm Coll (NJ)
Blue Ridge Comm Coll (VA)
Brevard Comm Coll (FL)
Central Carolina Comm Coll (NC)
Colby Comm Coll (KS)
Coll of Southern Idaho (ID)
Colorado Mountn Coll (CO)
Columbia State Comm Coll (TN)
Columbus State Comm Coll (OH)
Comm Coll of Denver (CO)
Comm Coll of Southern Nevada (NV)
Cuyahoga Comm Coll (OH)
Delaware Tech & Comm Coll, Jack F Owens Cmps (DE)
Foothill Coll (CA)
Globe Coll (MN)
Harcum Coll (PA)

Hinds Comm Coll (MS)
Holyoke Comm Coll (MA)
Johnson County Comm Coll (KS)
Lansing Comm Coll (MI)
Maple Woods Comm Coll (MO)
Midland Coll (TX)
Minnesota School of Business–Brooklyn Center (MN)
Minnesota School of Business–Plymouth (MN)
Northern Virginia Comm Coll (VA)
North Shore Comm Coll (MA)
Northwestern Connecticut Comm-Tech Coll (CT)
St. Petersburg Coll (FL)
San Joaquin Valley Coll (CA)
State U of NY Coll of Technology at Canton (NY)
State U of NY Coll of Technology at Delhi (NY)
Tri-County Tech Coll (SC)
Trident Tech Coll (SC)
U of Cincinnati Raymond Walters Coll (OH)
Wayne County Comm Coll District (MI)
Yakima Valley Comm Coll (WA)
Yuba Coll (CA)

Violin, Viola, Guitar and Other Stringed Instruments

Minnesota State Coll–Southeast Tech (MN)

Visual and Performing Arts

Amarillo Coll (TX)
Atlantic Cape Comm Coll (NJ)
Berkshire Comm Coll (MA)
Bristol Comm Coll (MA)
Brookdale Comm Coll (NJ)
Bucks County Comm Coll (PA)
Calhoun Comm Coll (AL)
Citrus Coll (CA)
Holyoke Comm Coll (MA)
Hutchinson Comm Coll and Area Vocational School (KS)
Kingwood Coll (TX)
Laramie County Comm Coll (WY)
Moraine Valley Comm Coll (IL)
Nassau Comm Coll (NY)
Queensborough Comm Coll of City U of NY (NY)
Raritan Valley Comm Coll (NJ)
Western Wyoming Comm Coll (WY)

Visual and Performing Arts Related

The Art Inst of Philadelphia (PA)
Comm Coll of Allegheny County (PA)
Florida Comm Coll at Jacksonville (FL)

Vocational Rehabilitation Counseling

Edmonds Comm Coll (WA)

Voice and Opera

Alvin Comm Coll (TX)
Coastal Bend Coll (TX)
Coffeyville Comm Coll (KS)
Iowa Lakes Comm Coll (IA)
Lansing Comm Coll (MI)
Snow Coll (UT)

Watchmaking and Jewelrymaking

North Seattle Comm Coll (WA)

Water Quality and Wastewater Treatment Management And Recycling Technology
Bay de Noc Comm Coll (MI)
Bristol Comm Coll (MA)
Clackamas Comm Coll (OR)
Collin County Comm Coll District (TX)
Delta Coll (MI)
Florida Comm Coll at Jacksonville (FL)
Green River Comm Coll (WA)
Linn-Benton Comm Coll (OR)
Northwest-Shoals Comm Coll (AL)
St. Cloud Tech Coll (MN)
San Juan Coll (NM)
Trinidad State Jr Coll (CO)

Water Resources Engineering
Bristol Comm Coll (MA)
Dixie State Coll of Utah (UT)

Water, Wetlands, and Marine Resources Management
Iowa Lakes Comm Coll (IA)
Keystone Coll (PA)

Web/Multimedia Management and Webmaster
Academy Coll (MN)
Andover Coll (ME)
Atlantic Cape Comm Coll (NJ)
Black Hawk Coll, Moline (IL)
Cape Cod Comm Coll (MA)
Central Comm Coll–Columbus Campus (NE)
Central Comm Coll–Grand Island Campus (NE)
Central Comm Coll–Hastings Campus (NE)
Clovis Comm Coll (NM)
Columbia-Greene Comm Coll (NY)
Delta Coll (MI)
El Paso Comm Coll (TX)
Fayetteville Tech Comm Coll (NC)
Flathead Valley Comm Coll (MT)
Florida Comm Coll at Jacksonville (FL)
Harrisburg Area Comm Coll (PA)
Hawkeye Comm Coll (IA)
Kennebec Valley Comm Coll (ME)
Laramie County Comm Coll (WY)
Metropolitan Comm Coll-Business & Technology College (MO)
Mid-South Comm Coll (AR)
Milwaukee Area Tech Coll (WI)
Minneapolis Comm and Tech Coll (MN)
Northern Essex Comm Coll (MA)
Northland Comm and Tech Coll–Thief River Falls (MN)
North Seattle Comm Coll (WA)
Olympic Coll (WA)
Pennsylvania Highland Comm Coll (PA)
Pioneer Pacific Coll (OR)
Platt Coll San Diego (CA)
Riverland Comm Coll (MN)
Saint Charles Comm Coll (MO)
St. Petersburg Coll (FL)
St. Philip's Coll (TX)
Sandhills Comm Coll (NC)
Seminole Comm Coll (FL)
Sheridan Coll (WY)
Sinclair Comm Coll (OH)
Southeast Tech Inst (SD)
Springfield Tech Comm Coll (MA)

Stanly Comm Coll (NC)
Trident Tech Coll (SC)
Wake Tech Comm Coll (NC)
Western Wyoming Comm Coll (WY)

Web Page, Digital/Multimedia and Information Resources Design
Academy Coll (MN)
Adirondack Comm Coll (NY)
Alexandria Tech Coll (MN)
Arapahoe Comm Coll (CO)
Berkeley Coll (NJ)
Brevard Comm Coll (FL)
Bunker Hill Comm Coll (MA)
Cape Cod Comm Coll (MA)
Capital Comm Coll (CT)
Central Wyoming Coll (WY)
Cerro Coso Comm Coll (CA)
Clover Park Tech Coll (WA)
Clovis Comm Coll (NM)
Coll of the Mainland (TX)
Collin County Comm Coll District (TX)
Delaware County Comm Coll (PA)
Delta Coll (MI)
Dixie State Coll of Utah (UT)
ECPI Tech Coll, Glen Allen (VA)
ECPI Tech Coll, Richmond (VA)
El Paso Comm Coll (TX)
Erie Business Center, Main (PA)
Fayetteville Tech Comm Coll (NC)
Florida Comm Coll at Jacksonville (FL)
Florida National Coll (FL)
Globe Coll (MN)
Guilford Tech Comm Coll (NC)
Hawaii Business Coll (HI)
Hawkeye Comm Coll (IA)
Heartland Comm Coll (IL)
Hibbing Comm Coll (MN)
Highline Comm Coll (WA)
Kansas City Kansas Comm Coll (KS)
Kennebec Valley Comm Coll (ME)
Laramie County Comm Coll (WY)
Laurel Business Inst (PA)
Mesabi Range Comm and Tech Coll (MN)
Metropolitan Comm Coll-Business & Technology College (MO)
Minneapolis Comm and Tech Coll (MN)
Minnesota School of Business–Brooklyn Center (MN)
Minnesota School of Business–Plymouth (MN)
Minnesota School of Business–Richfield (MN)
Northern Essex Comm Coll (MA)
Northland Comm and Tech Coll–Thief River Falls (MN)
North Seattle Comm Coll (WA)
Palm Beach Comm Coll (FL)
Parkland Coll (IL)
Pasco-Hernando Comm Coll (FL)
Peninsula Coll (WA)
Pennsylvania Inst of Technology (PA)
Platt Coll San Diego (CA)
Richmond Comm Coll (NC)
Riverland Comm Coll (MN)
Salt Lake Comm Coll (UT)
San Antonio Coll (TX)
Seminole Comm Coll (FL)
Sheridan Coll (WY)
Southeastern Tech Coll (GA)
Southeast Tech Inst (SD)
Stanly Comm Coll (NC)
Tacoma Comm Coll (WA)

Thaddeus Stevens Coll of Technology (PA)
Tompkins Cortland Comm Coll (NY)
Trident Tech Coll (SC)
U of Arkansas Comm Coll at Batesville (AR)
Wake Tech Comm Coll (NC)
Western Wyoming Comm Coll (WY)

Welding Technology
Alamance Comm Coll (NC)
Alexandria Tech Coll (MN)
Arizona Western Coll (AZ)
Arkansas Northeastern Coll (AR)
Austin Comm Coll (TX)
Bainbridge Coll (GA)
Beaufort County Comm Coll (NC)
Belmont Tech Coll (OH)
Bevill State Comm Coll (AL)
Big Bend Comm Coll (WA)
Bismarck State Coll (ND)
Black Hawk Coll, Moline (IL)
Bladen Comm Coll (NC)
Brazosport Coll (TX)
Butler County Comm Coll (KS)
Casper Coll (WY)
Cecil Comm Coll (MD)
Central Comm Coll–Columbus Campus (NE)
Central Comm Coll–Grand Island Campus (NE)
Central Comm Coll–Hastings Campus (NE)
Centralia Coll (WA)
Central Oregon Comm Coll (OR)
Central Piedmont Comm Coll (NC)
Central Texas Coll (TX)
Central Wyoming Coll (WY)
Cerro Coso Comm Coll (CA)
Chattanooga State Tech Comm Coll (TN)
Chemeketa Comm Coll (OR)
Clark Coll (WA)
Coastal Bend Coll (TX)
Coffeyville Comm Coll (KS)
Coll of DuPage (IL)
Coll of Southern Idaho (ID)
Coll of the Canyons (CA)
Comm Coll of Allegheny County (PA)
Comm Coll of Southern Nevada (NV)
Compton Comm Coll (CA)
Contra Costa Coll (CA)
Cossatot Comm Coll of the U of Arkansas (AR)
Cowley County Comm Coll and Voc-Tech School (KS)
Danville Area Comm Coll (IL)
Delaware Tech & Comm Coll, Jack F Owens Cmps (DE)
Delta Coll (MI)
Des Moines Area Comm Coll (IA)
Dodge City Comm Coll (KS)
Doña Ana Branch Comm Coll (NM)
East Central Coll (MO)
Eastern Arizona Coll (AZ)
Eastern Idaho Tech Coll (ID)
Eastern Maine Comm Coll (ME)
Elgin Comm Coll (IL)
Everett Comm Coll (WA)
Fayetteville Tech Comm Coll (NC)
Forsyth Tech Comm Coll (NC)
Fort Scott Comm Coll (KS)
Fox Valley Tech Coll (WI)
Frank Phillips Coll (TX)
Front Range Comm Coll (CO)
Garden City Comm Coll (KS)
George Corley Wallace State Comm Coll (AL)

George C. Wallace Comm Coll (AL)
Glendale Comm Coll (CA)
Grand Rapids Comm Coll (MI)
Great Basin Coll (NV)
Green River Comm Coll (WA)
Hawkeye Comm Coll (IA)
Heartland Comm Coll (IL)
Hinds Comm Coll (MS)
Hutchinson Comm Coll and Area Vocational School (KS)
Iowa Central Comm Coll (IA)
Iowa Lakes Comm Coll (IA)
Isothermal Comm Coll (NC)
John A. Logan Coll (IL)
Kalamazoo Valley Comm Coll (MI)
Lane Comm Coll (OR)
Lansing Comm Coll (MI)
Linn-Benton Comm Coll (OR)
Long Beach City Coll (CA)
Lower Columbia Coll (WA)
Macomb Comm Coll (MI)
Manhattan Area Tech Coll (KS)
McDowell Tech Comm Coll (NC)
Metropolitan Comm Coll (NE)
Midland Coll (TX)
Milwaukee Area Tech Coll (WI)
Minnesota State Coll–Southeast Tech (MN)
Moberly Area Comm Coll (MO)
Modesto Jr Coll (CA)
Muskegon Comm Coll (MI)
Napa Valley Coll (CA)
New Hampshire Comm Tech Coll, Manchester/Stratham (NH)
North Central State Coll (OH)
North Dakota State Coll of Science (ND)
Northeast State Tech Comm Coll (TN)
North Idaho Coll (ID)
North Iowa Area Comm Coll (IA)
Northland Comm and Tech Coll–Thief River Falls (MN)
Oakland Comm Coll (MI)
Odessa Coll (TX)
Olympic Coll (WA)
Orange Coast Coll (CA)
Pasadena City Coll (CA)
Phillips Comm Coll of the U of Arkansas (AR)
Pima Comm Coll (AZ)
Pratt Comm Coll and Area Vocational School (KS)
Randolph Comm Coll (NC)
Roanoke-Chowan Comm Coll (NC)
Rock Valley Coll (IL)
Rogue Comm Coll (OR)
St. Cloud Tech Coll (MN)
St. Philip's Coll (TX)
Salt Lake Comm Coll (UT)
San Diego City Coll (CA)
San Juan Coll (NM)
Schoolcraft Coll (MI)
Shawnee Comm Coll (IL)
Shelton State Comm Coll (AL)
Sheridan Coll (WY)
Solano Comm Coll (CA)
Somerset Comm Coll (KY)
Southeast Comm Coll, Lincoln Campus (NE)
Southeast Comm Coll, Milford Campus (NE)
Southwestern Michigan Coll (MI)
Southwestern Oregon Comm Coll (OR)
Southwest Wisconsin Tech Coll (WI)

State U of NY Coll of Technology at Alfred (NY)
State U of NY Coll of Technology at Delhi (NY)
Texas State Tech Coll–Waco/Marshall Campus (TX)
Tri-County Comm Coll (NC)
Trinity Valley Comm Coll (TX)
Truckee Meadows Comm Coll (NV)
Tulsa Welding School (OK)
U of Arkansas Comm Coll at Morrilton (AR)
Walla Walla Comm Coll (WA)
Wayne County Comm Coll District (MI)
Western Nevada Comm Coll (NV)
Western Oklahoma State Coll (OK)
Western Wyoming Comm Coll (WY)
Westmoreland County Comm Coll (PA)
West Virginia U at Parkersburg (WV)
Yuba Coll (CA)

Wildlife and Wildlands Science And Management
Barton County Comm Coll (KS)
Casper Coll (WY)
Chattanooga State Tech Comm Coll (TN)
Comm Coll of Southern Nevada (NV)
Dixie State Coll of Utah (UT)
East Central Coll (MO)
Flathead Valley Comm Coll (MT)
Frederick Comm Coll (MD)
Front Range Comm Coll (CO)
Garrett Coll (MD)
Haywood Comm Coll (NC)
Iowa Lakes Comm Coll (IA)
Itasca Comm Coll (MN)
Keystone Coll (PA)
Laramie County Comm Coll (WY)
North Idaho Coll (ID)
Penn State U DuBois Campus of the Commonwealth Coll (PA)
Pratt Comm Coll and Area Vocational School (KS)
Santa Rosa Jr Coll (CA)
Seward County Comm Coll (KS)
Shawnee Comm Coll (IL)
Snow Coll (UT)
Tacoma Comm Coll (WA)
Western Oklahoma State Coll (OK)
Western Wyoming Comm Coll (WY)

Wildlife Biology
Colby Comm Coll (KS)
Colorado Northwestern Comm Coll (CO)
Dodge City Comm Coll (KS)
Eastern Arizona Coll (AZ)
Ellsworth Comm Coll (IA)
Everett Comm Coll (WA)
Garrett Coll (MD)
Holmes Comm Coll (MS)
Iowa Lakes Comm Coll (IA)
Keystone Coll (PA)
North Idaho Coll (ID)
Pratt Comm Coll and Area Vocational School (KS)
Tacoma Comm Coll (WA)

Wind/Percussion Instruments
Coffeyville Comm Coll (KS)
Iowa Lakes Comm Coll (IA)
Itawamba Comm Coll (MS)

Women'S Studies
Bergen Comm Coll (NJ)
Foothill Coll (CA)

Northern Essex Comm Coll (MA)
Tompkins Cortland Comm Coll (NY)
Yuba Coll (CA)

Wood Science and Wood Products/Pulp And Paper Technology
Allen County Comm Coll (KS)
Bay de Noc Comm Coll (MI)
Copiah-Lincoln Comm Coll (MS)
Cossatot Comm Coll of the U of Arkansas (AR)
Dabney S. Lancaster Comm Coll (VA)
Fox Valley Tech Coll (WI)
Haywood Comm Coll (NC)
Kennebec Valley Comm Coll (ME)
Lower Columbia Coll (WA)
Tacoma Comm Coll (WA)

Woodworking
Bucks County Comm Coll (PA)
Coll of Southern Idaho (ID)
State U of NY Coll of Technology at Delhi (NY)

Woodworking Related
Oakland Comm Coll (MI)

Word Processing
Adirondack Comm Coll (NY)
Baltimore City Comm Coll (MD)
Coastal Bend Coll (TX)
Columbus Tech Coll (GA)
Corning Comm Coll (NY)
Delta Coll (MI)
Eastfield Coll (TX)
Edgecombe Comm Coll (NC)
El Paso Comm Coll (TX)
Fayetteville Tech Comm Coll (NC)
Flathead Valley Comm Coll (MT)
Florida Comm Coll at Jacksonville (FL)
Florida National Coll (FL)
Gateway Comm Coll (CT)
Gogebic Comm Coll (MI)
Hawkeye Comm Coll (IA)
Henderson Comm Coll (KY)
Iowa Lakes Comm Coll (IA)
Iowa Western Comm Coll (IA)
Laurel Business Inst (PA)
Lower Columbia Coll (WA)
Metropolitan Comm Coll-Business & Technology College (MO)
Milwaukee Area Tech Coll (WI)
Modesto Jr Coll (CA)
Mohave Comm Coll (AZ)
Northern Essex Comm Coll (MA)
Northland Comm and Tech Coll–Thief River Falls (MN)
Orange Coast Coll (CA)
Orange County Comm Coll (NY)
Owensboro Comm and Tech Coll (KY)
Palm Beach Comm Coll (FL)
Pratt Comm Coll and Area Vocational School (KS)
Quinebaug Valley Comm Coll (CT)
Richland Comm Coll (IL)
Riverland Comm Coll (MN)
Riverside Comm Coll District (CA)
St. Cloud Tech Coll (MN)
St. Louis Comm Coll at Forest Park (MO)
Salt Lake Comm Coll (UT)
San Antonio Coll (TX)
Seminole Comm Coll (FL)
Sinclair Comm Coll (OH)
Stanly Comm Coll (NC)
Tacoma Comm Coll (WA)

Word Processing

Thaddeus Stevens Coll of
Technology (PA)
Three Rivers Comm Coll
(MO)
Valencia Comm Coll (FL)

Wake Tech Comm Coll (NC)
West Central Tech Coll (GA)
Western Oklahoma State
Coll (OK)

Western Wyoming Comm
Coll (WY)

Yuba Coll (CA)

Zoology/Animal Biology

Casper Coll (WY)
Centralia Coll (WA)
Colby Comm Coll (KS)
Coll of Southern Idaho (ID)

Daytona Beach Comm Coll
(FL)
Dixie State Coll of Utah (UT)
East Central Coll (MO)
Everett Comm Coll (WA)

Frank Phillips Coll (TX)
North Idaho Coll (ID)
Palm Beach Comm Coll (FL)
Snow Coll (UT)
Tacoma Comm Coll (WA)

Associate Degree Programs at Four-Year Colleges

Accounting
Alvernia Coll (PA)
American U of Puerto Rico (PR)
Bacone Coll (OK)
Baker Coll of Allen Park (MI)
Baker Coll of Auburn Hills (MI)
Baker Coll of Cadillac (MI)
Baker Coll of Clinton Township (MI)
Baker Coll of Flint (MI)
Baker Coll of Jackson (MI)
Baker Coll of Muskegon (MI)
Baker Coll of Owosso (MI)
Baker Coll of Port Huron (MI)
Becker Coll (MA)
Bluefield State Coll (WV)
Briarcliffe Coll (NY)
Brigham Young U–Hawaii (HI)
British Columbia Inst of Technology (BC, Canada)
California Coll for Health Sciences (UT)
California U of Pennsylvania (PA)
Calumet Coll of Saint Joseph (IN)
Central Christian Coll of Kansas (KS)
Central Pennsylvania Coll (PA)
Champlain Coll (VT)
Chestnut Hill Coll (PA)
Clayton Coll & State U (GA)
Coll of Mount St. Joseph (OH)
Coll of St. Joseph (VT)
Coll of Saint Mary (NE)
Columbia Union Coll (MD)
Davenport U, Dearborn (MI)
Davenport U, Grand Rapids (MI)
Davenport U, Kalamazoo (MI)
Davenport U, Lansing (MI)
Davenport U, Lapeer (MI)
Davenport U, Warren (MI)
David N. Myers U (OH)
Davis & Elkins Coll (WV)
Evangel U (MO)
Fairmont State U (WV)
Faulkner U (AL)
Ferris State U (MI)
Florida Metropolitan U–Tampa Coll, Brandon (FL)
Florida Metropolitan U–Orlando Coll, North (FL)
Florida Metropolitan U–Orlando Coll, South (FL)
Florida Metropolitan U–Tampa Coll (FL)
Franciscan U of Steubenville (OH)
Franklin U (OH)
Friends U (KS)
Goldey-Beacom Coll (DE)
Gwynedd-Mercy Coll (PA)
Hawai'i Pacific U (HI)
Husson Coll (ME)
Immaculata U (PA)

Indiana Inst of Technology (IN)
Indiana Wesleyan U (IN)
Inter American U of PR, Aguadilla Campus (PR)
Inter American U of PR, Bayamón Campus (PR)
Inter American U of PR, Ponce Campus (PR)
Inter American U of PR, San Germán Campus (PR)
International Coll (FL)
International Coll of the Cayman IslandsCayman Islands)
Johnson & Wales U (FL)
Johnson & Wales U (RI)
Jones Coll, Jacksonville (FL)
Kansas State U (KS)
King's Coll (PA)
Lake Superior State U (MI)
Macon State Coll (GA)
Manchester Coll (IN)
Marian Coll (IN)
Marygrove Coll (MI)
Merrimack Coll (MA)
Methodist Coll (NC)
Midland Lutheran Coll (NE)
Missouri Southern State U (MO)
Mitchell Coll (CT)
Mount Aloysius Coll (PA)
Mount Marty Coll (SD)
Mount Olive Coll (NC)
National American U, Colorado Springs (CO)
National American U, Denver (CO)
National American U, Albuquerque (NM)
National American U, Rapid City (SD)
National American U–Sioux Falls Branch (SD)
Newbury Coll (MA)
Northwood U (MI)
Northwood U, Florida Campus (FL)
Northwood U, Texas Campus (TX)
Oakland City U (IN)
Oklahoma Wesleyan U (OK)
Peirce Coll (PA)
Point Park U (PA)
Post U (CT)
Sacred Heart U (CT)
Saint Francis U (PA)
St. John's U (NY)
Saint Joseph's U (PA)
Shawnee State U (OH)
Siena Heights U (MI)
Southern Adventist U (TN)
Southern Alberta Inst of Technology (AB, Canada)
Southern New Hampshire U (NH)
South U (AL)
South U (GA)
Southwest Baptist U (MO)
State U of NY Coll of A&T at Cobleskill (NY)
Strayer U (DC)
Sullivan U (KY)
Thiel Coll (PA)

Thomas Coll (ME)
Thomas Edison State Coll (NJ)
Thomas More Coll (KY)
Tiffin U (OH)
Tri-State U (IN)
Union Coll (NE)
U of Alaska Anchorage (AK)
U of Charleston (WV)
U of Cincinnati (OH)
U of Dubuque (IA)
The U of Findlay (OH)
U of Mary (ND)
U of Minnesota, Crookston (MN)
U of Rio Grande (OH)
U of the District of Columbia (DC)
U of the Virgin Islands (VI)
The U of Toledo (OH)
The U of West Alabama (AL)
Urbana U (OH)
Utah Valley State Coll (UT)
Villa Julie Coll (MD)
Walsh U (OH)
Washington & Jefferson Coll (PA)
Webber International U (FL)
West Virginia State U (WV)
Wilson Coll (PA)
Youngstown State U (OH)

Accounting and Business/Management
Central Christian Coll of Kansas (KS)
Chestnut Hill Coll (PA)
Mount Aloysius Coll (PA)
National American U, Colorado Springs (CO)
Peirce Coll (PA)

Accounting and Finance
Central Christian Coll of Kansas (KS)
Southern Alberta Inst of Technology (AB, Canada)

Accounting Related
Central Pennsylvania Coll (PA)
Montana State U–Billings (MT)
Park U (MO)
Peirce Coll (PA)

Accounting Technology and Bookkeeping
Baker Coll of Flint (MI)
British Columbia Inst of Technology (BC, Canada)
Cleary U (MI)
Davenport U, Dearborn (MI)
Davenport U, Holland (MI)
Davenport U, Kalamazoo (MI)
Davenport U, Lapeer (MI)
Davenport U, Warren (MI)
Georgia Southwestern State U (GA)
Kent State U (OH)
Lake Superior State U (MI)
Lewis-Clark State Coll (ID)
New York Inst of Technology (NY)
Ohio U (OH)

Peirce Coll (PA)
Pennsylvania Coll of Technology (PA)
Robert Morris Coll (IL)
St. Augustine Coll (IL)
The U of Akron (OH)
U of Alaska Fairbanks (AK)
The U of Montana–Missoula (MT)
U of Rio Grande (OH)
Utah Valley State Coll (UT)
Valdosta State U (GA)
Wright State U (OH)
Youngstown State U (OH)

Acting
Central Christian Coll of Kansas (KS)
New World School of the Arts (FL)

Administrative Assistant and Secretarial Science
Alabama State U (AL)
American U of Puerto Rico (PR)
Arkansas State U (AR)
Atlantic Union Coll (MA)
Bacone Coll (OK)
Baker Coll of Auburn Hills (MI)
Baker Coll of Cadillac (MI)
Baker Coll of Clinton Township (MI)
Baker Coll of Flint (MI)
Baker Coll of Jackson (MI)
Baker Coll of Muskegon (MI)
Baker Coll of Owosso (MI)
Baker Coll of Port Huron (MI)
Ball State U (IN)
Bayamón Central U (PR)
Black Hills State U (SD)
Bluefield State Coll (WV)
Briarcliffe Coll (NY)
British Columbia Inst of Technology (BC, Canada)
Campbellsville U (KY)
Central Missouri State U (MO)
Clayton Coll & State U (GA)
Clearwater Christian Coll (FL)
Columbia Coll, Caguas (PR)
Concordia Coll (NY)
Dakota State U (SD)
Davenport U, Dearborn (MI)
David N. Myers U (OH)
Dickinson State U (ND)
Dordt Coll (IA)
Eastern Kentucky U (KY)
Eastern Oregon U (OR)
Evangel U (MO)
Fairmont State U (WV)
Faith Baptist Bible Coll and Theological Seminary (IA)
Faulkner U (AL)
Fort Hays State U (KS)
Fort Valley State U (GA)
Free Will Baptist Bible Coll (TN)
Georgia Southwestern State U (GA)
God's Bible School and Coll (OH)
Grace Coll (IN)

Henderson State U (AR)
Hobe Sound Bible Coll (FL)
Idaho State U (ID)
Indiana State U (IN)
Inter American U of PR, Aguadilla Campus (PR)
Inter American U of PR, Bayamón Campus (PR)
Inter American U of PR, Ponce Campus (PR)
Inter American U of PR, San Germán Campus (PR)
Johnson & Wales U (RI)
Jones Coll, Jacksonville (FL)
Kent State U (OH)
Lake Superior State U (MI)
Lamar U (TX)
Lancaster Bible Coll (PA)
Lewis-Clark State Coll (ID)
Lincoln Christian Coll (IL)
Lincoln U (MO)
Macon State Coll (GA)
Maranatha Baptist Bible Coll (WI)
Martin Methodist Coll (TN)
Mayville State U (ND)
Mercyhurst Coll (PA)
Mesa State Coll (CO)
Montana State U–Billings (MT)
Montana Tech of The U of Montana (MT)
Mountain State U (WV)
Mount Vernon Nazarene U (OH)
Murray State U (KY)
New York Inst of Technology (NY)
North Central U (MN)
Northern Michigan U (MI)
Northern State U (SD)
Northwestern Coll (IA)
Northwestern State U of Louisiana (LA)
Oakland City U (IN)
Ohio U (OH)
Oklahoma Wesleyan U (OK)
Pennsylvania Coll of Technology (PA)
Pillsbury Baptist Bible Coll (MN)
Pontifical Catholic U of Puerto Rico (PR)
Reformed Bible Coll (MI)
Robert Morris Coll (IL)
St. Augustine Coll (IL)
Southeastern Louisiana U (LA)
Southern Arkansas U–Magnolia (AR)
Southern U at New Orleans (LA)
Southwest Baptist U (MO)
Sullivan U (KY)
Tabor Coll (KS)
Tennessee State U (TN)
Thomas Coll (ME)
Trinity Baptist Coll (FL)
Universidad Adventista de las Antillas (PR)
The U of Akron (OH)
U of Alaska Fairbanks (AK)
U of Alaska Southeast (AK)

U of Arkansas at Fort Smith (AR)
U of Cincinnati (OH)
The U of Findlay (OH)
The U of Montana–Western (MT)
U of Rio Grande (OH)
U of Sioux Falls (SD)
U of the District of Columbia (DC)
U of the Virgin Islands (VI)
The U of Toledo (OH)
Utah State U (UT)
Valdosta State U (GA)
Vermont Tech Coll (VT)
Washburn U (KS)
Weber State U (UT)
West Virginia State U (WV)
Winona State U (MN)
Wright State U (OH)
Youngstown State U (OH)

Adult and Continuing Education Administration
Saint Joseph's Coll of Maine (ME)

Adult Development and Aging
Chestnut Hill Coll (PA)
Madonna U (MI)
Saint Mary-of-the-Woods Coll (IN)
The U of Toledo (OH)

Advertising
Academy of Art U (CA)
The Art Inst of California–San Diego (CA)
Fashion Inst of Technology (NY)
Hussian School of Art (PA)
Johnson & Wales U (RI)
Martin Methodist Coll (TN)
New England School of Communications (ME)
Northwood U (MI)
Northwood U, Florida Campus (FL)
Northwood U, Texas Campus (TX)
Pacific Union Coll (CA)
U of the District of Columbia (DC)
West Virginia State U (WV)
Xavier U (OH)

Aeronautical/Aerospace Engineering Technology
British Columbia Inst of Technology (BC, Canada)
Central Missouri State U (MO)
Pennsylvania Coll of Technology (PA)
Purdue U (IN)
Southern Alberta Inst of Technology (AB, Canada)

Aeronautics/Aviation/Aerospace Science and Technology
Embry-Riddle Aeronautical U, Extended Campus (FL)
Indiana State U (IN)

Purdue U (IN)
Vaughn Coll of Aeronautics and Technology (NY)

Agribusiness
Morehead State U (KY)
Vermont Tech Coll (VT)

Agricultural and Domestic Animals Services Related
Sterling Coll (VT)

Agricultural and Food Products Processing
North Carolina State U (NC)

Agricultural and Horticultural Plant Breeding
Sterling Coll (VT)

Agricultural Animal Breeding
Sterling Coll (VT)

Agricultural/Biological Engineering and Bioengineering
State U of NY Coll of A&T at Cobleskill (NY)

Agricultural Business and Management
Andrews U (MI)
Central Christian Coll of Kansas (KS)
Clayton Coll & State U (GA)
Dickinson State U (ND)
Dordt Coll (IA)
Martin Methodist Coll (TN)
MidAmerica Nazarene U (KS)
Montana State U–Northern (MT)
North Carolina State U (NC)
State U of NY Coll of A&T at Cobleskill (NY)
U of Minnesota, Crookston (MN)
U of New Hampshire (NH)

Agricultural Business and Management Related
Penn State U Abington Coll (PA)
Penn State U Altoona Coll (PA)
Penn State U at Erie, The Behrend Coll (PA)
Penn State U Berks Cmps of Berks-Lehigh Valley Coll (PA)
Penn State U Lehigh Valley Cmps of Berks-Lehigh Valley Coll (PA)
Penn State U Schuylkill Campus of the Capital Coll (PA)
Penn State U Univ Park Campus (PA)

Agricultural Business Technology
U of Alaska Fairbanks (AK)

Agricultural Economics
The U of British Columbia (BC, Canada)

Agricultural Mechanization
Andrews U (MI)
Clayton Coll & State U (GA)
Montana State U–Northern (MT)
State U of NY Coll of A&T at Cobleskill (NY)
Virginia Polytechnic Inst and State U (VA)

Agricultural Production
Western Kentucky U (KY)

Agricultural Production Related
Sterling Coll (VT)

Agricultural Public Services Related
Sterling Coll (VT)

Agriculture
Andrews U (MI)
Clayton Coll & State U (GA)
Dalton State Coll (GA)
Lincoln U (MO)

Lubbock Christian U (TX)
Macon State Coll (GA)
Murray State U (KY)
North Carolina State U (NC)
Oklahoma Panhandle State U (OK)
Purdue U (IN)
South Dakota State U (SD)
Southern Utah U (UT)
State U of NY Coll of A&T at Cobleskill (NY)
Sterling Coll (VT)
U of Delaware (DE)
U of Minnesota, Crookston (MN)

Agriculture and Agriculture Operations Related
Eastern Kentucky U (KY)
Sterling Coll (VT)

Agronomy and Crop Science
Andrews U (MI)
State U of NY Coll of A&T at Cobleskill (NY)
U of Minnesota, Crookston (MN)

Aircraft Powerplant Technology
British Columbia Inst of Technology (BC, Canada)
Embry-Riddle Aeronautical U (FL)
Embry-Riddle Aeronautical U, Extended Campus (FL)
Georgia Southwestern State U (GA)
Idaho State U (ID)
Kansas State U (KS)
Northern Michigan U (MI)
Pennsylvania Coll of Technology (PA)
Thomas Edison State Coll (NJ)

Airframe Mechanics and Aircraft Maintenance Technology
British Columbia Inst of Technology (BC, Canada)
Clayton Coll & State U (GA)
Georgia Southwestern State U (GA)
Kansas State U (KS)
Lewis U (IL)
U of Alaska Anchorage (AK)
U of Alaska Fairbanks (AK)
Utah State U (UT)
Vaughn Coll of Aeronautics and Technology (NY)
Wentworth Inst of Technology (MA)

Airline Flight Attendant
The U of Akron (OH)

Airline Pilot and Flight Crew
Andrews U (MI)
Baker Coll of Flint (MI)
Baker Coll of Muskegon (MI)
Central Christian Coll of Kansas (KS)
Embry-Riddle Aeronautical U (FL)
Kansas State U (KS)
Southern Illinois U Carbondale (IL)
Thomas Edison State Coll (NJ)
U of Alaska Anchorage (AK)
U of Dubuque (IA)
Utah Valley State Coll (UT)
Vaughn Coll of Aeronautics and Technology (NY)
Winona State U (MN)

Air Traffic Control
Thomas Edison State Coll (NJ)
U of Alaska Anchorage (AK)
Valdosta State U (GA)

Allied Health and Medical Assisting Services Related
Bloomsburg U of Pennsylvania (PA)
National American U, Colorado Springs (CO)

Allied Health Diagnostic, Intervention, and Treatment Professions Related
British Columbia Inst of Technology (BC, Canada)
Cameron U (OK)
Gwynedd-Mercy Coll (PA)
Kent State U (OH)
Pennsylvania Coll of Technology (PA)
The U of Akron (OH)

American History
Central Christian Coll of Kansas (KS)
Emmanuel Coll (GA)

American Indian/Native American Studies
Bacone Coll (OK)

American Literature
Haskell Indian Nations U (KS)
Huron U USA in LondonUnited Kingdom)

American Native/Native American Languages
Idaho State U (ID)

American Sign Language (Asl)
Bethel Coll (IN)
Idaho State U (ID)
Madonna U (MI)
North Central U (MN)
Rochester Inst of Technology (NY)

American Studies
Martin Methodist Coll (TN)
Paul Smith's Coll of Arts and Sciences (NY)

Ancient Near Eastern and Biblical Languages
Bethel Coll (IN)
Indiana Wesleyan U (IN)
North Central U (MN)

Anesthesiologist Assistant
Thompson Rivers U (BC, Canada)

Animal Health
Sterling Coll (VT)

Animal/Livestock Husbandry and Production
Saint Mary-of-the-Woods Coll (IN)
Sterling Coll (VT)
Thompson Rivers U (BC, Canada)
U of Connecticut (CT)
U of New Hampshire (NH)

Animal Nutrition
Sterling Coll (VT)

Animal Physiology
Martin Methodist Coll (TN)

Animal Sciences
Andrews U (MI)
Becker Coll (MA)
State U of NY Coll of A&T at Cobleskill (NY)
Sterling Coll (VT)
U of Connecticut (CT)
U of Minnesota, Crookston (MN)
U of New Hampshire (NH)

Animal Sciences Related
Sterling Coll (VT)

Animal Training
Becker Coll (MA)

Animation, Interactive Technology, Video Graphics and Special Effects
Academy of Art U (CA)
Champlain Coll (VT)

Kent State U (OH)
New England School of Communications (ME)

Anthropology
Kwantlen U Coll (BC, Canada)
Richmond, The American International U in LondonUnited Kingdom)
Université Laval (QC, Canada)

Apparel and Accessories Marketing
California Design Coll (CA)
Clayton Coll & State U (GA)
The U of Montana–Missoula (MT)

Apparel and Textiles
Academy of Art U (CA)
Fashion Inst of Technology (NY)

Applied Art
Academy of Art U (CA)
The Art Inst of Fort Lauderdale (FL)
The Art Inst of Houston (TX)
The Art Inst of Pittsburgh (PA)
Friends U (KS)
National American U, Albuquerque (NM)
New World School of the Arts (FL)
Rochester Inst of Technology (NY)
U of Maine at Presque Isle (ME)
The U of Montana–Western (MT)
Villa Julie Coll (MD)

Applied Horticulture
Georgia Southwestern State U (GA)
Kent State U (OH)
Oakland City U (IN)
Sterling Coll (VT)
Temple U (PA)
U of Connecticut (CT)
The U of Maine at Augusta (ME)
Valdosta State U (GA)

Applied Horticulture/ Horticultural Business Services Related
Pennsylvania Coll of Technology (PA)
U of Massachusetts Amherst (MA)

Applied Mathematics
Central Methodist U (MO)
Hawai'i Pacific U (HI)
Rochester Inst of Technology (NY)

Aquaculture
The U of British Columbia (BC, Canada)

Archeology
Weber State U (UT)

Architectural Drafting and Cad/Cadd
Baker Coll of Flint (MI)
Baker Coll of Muskegon (MI)
British Columbia Inst of Technology (BC, Canada)
Indiana State U (IN)
Indiana U–Purdue U Indianapolis (IN)
Montana Tech of The U of Montana (MT)
The U of Toledo (OH)
Western Kentucky U (KY)

Architectural Engineering Technology
Baker Coll of Cadillac (MI)
Baker Coll of Clinton Township (MI)
Baker Coll of Owosso (MI)
Baker Coll of Port Huron (MI)
Bluefield State Coll (WV)

British Columbia Inst of Technology (BC, Canada)
Central Christian Coll of Kansas (KS)
Clayton Coll & State U (GA)
Ferris State U (MI)
Indiana U–Purdue U Fort Wayne (IN)
Northern Kentucky U (KY)
Northern Michigan U (MI)
Pennsylvania Coll of Technology (PA)
Purdue U (IN)
Purdue U Calumet (IN)
Southern Alberta Inst of Technology (AB, Canada)
Thomas Edison State Coll (NJ)
U of Alaska Anchorage (AK)
U of Cincinnati (OH)
U of the District of Columbia (DC)
Vermont Tech Coll (VT)
Wentworth Inst of Technology (MA)
West Virginia State U (WV)

Architectural Technology
Southern Alberta Inst of Technology (AB, Canada)
The U of Maine at Augusta (ME)

Architecture
Central Christian Coll of Kansas (KS)
Coll of Staten Island of the City U of NY (NY)
New York Inst of Technology (NY)

Architecture Related
Abilene Christian U (TX)

Army R.O.T.C./Military Science
Methodist Coll (NC)

Art
Academy of Art U (CA)
Adrian Coll (MI)
The Art Inst of Colorado (CO)
Ashland U (OH)
Bacone Coll (OK)
Carroll Coll (MT)
Central Christian Coll of Kansas (KS)
Clayton Coll & State U (GA)
Coll of Saint Mary (NE)
Defiance Coll (OH)
Eastern New Mexico U (NM)
Fashion Inst of Technology (NY)
Felician Coll (NJ)
Friends U (KS)
Huron U USA in LondonUnited Kingdom)
Idaho State U (ID)
Immaculata U (PA)
Indiana Wesleyan U (IN)
John Brown U (AR)
Lindsey Wilson Coll (KY)
Lourdes Coll (OH)
Macon State Coll (GA)
Madonna U (MI)
Manchester Coll (IN)
Marian Coll (IN)
Martin Methodist Coll (TN)
Mesa State Coll (CO)
Methodist Coll (NC)
Miami International U of Art & Design (FL)
Mount Olive Coll (NC)
North Greenville Coll (SC)
Pontifical Catholic U of Puerto Rico (PR)
Reinhardt Coll (GA)
Richmond, The American International U in LondonUnited Kingdom)
Rivier Coll (NH)
Rochester Inst of Technology (NY)
Sacred Heart U (CT)
St. Gregory's U (OK)
Shawnee State U (OH)
Siena Heights U (MI)

State U of NY Empire State Coll (NY)
Suffolk U (MA)
Union Coll (NE)
U of Rio Grande (OH)
The U of Toledo (OH)
U of Wisconsin–Green Bay (WI)
Villa Julie Coll (MD)
West Virginia State U (WV)

Art History, Criticism and Conservation
Lourdes Coll (OH)
Thomas More Coll (KY)
Université Laval (QC, Canada)

Artificial Intelligence and Robotics
Clayton Coll & State U (GA)
Huron U USA in LondonUnited Kingdom)
Lamar U (TX)
Pacific Union Coll (CA)
Southern Alberta Inst of Technology (AB, Canada)
U of Cincinnati (OH)

Art Teacher Education
Central Christian Coll of Kansas (KS)
Clayton Coll & State U (GA)
Immaculata U (PA)
Martin Methodist Coll (TN)

Athletic Training
Central Christian Coll of Kansas (KS)
Mitchell Coll (CT)

Audio Engineering
The Art Inst of Seattle (WA)
Five Towns Coll (NY)
New England School of Communications (ME)

Audiology and Hearing Sciences
Ohio U (OH)

Autobody/Collision and Repair Technology
British Columbia Inst of Technology (BC, Canada)
Georgia Southwestern State U (GA)
Idaho State U (ID)
Lewis-Clark State Coll (ID)
Montana State U–Billings (MT)
Montana Tech of The U of Montana (MT)
Northern Michigan U (MI)
Pennsylvania Coll of Technology (PA)
Utah Valley State Coll (UT)
Valdosta State U (GA)
Weber State U (UT)

Automobile/Automotive Mechanics Technology
Andrews U (MI)
Arkansas State U (AR)
Baker Coll of Flint (MI)
Boise State U (ID)
British Columbia Inst of Technology (BC, Canada)
Central Missouri State U (MO)
Ferris State U (MI)
Georgia Southwestern State U (GA)
Idaho State U (ID)
Lamar U (TX)
Lewis-Clark State Coll (ID)
McPherson Coll (KS)
Mesa State Coll (CO)
Montana State U–Billings (MT)
Montana State U–Northern (MT)
Montana Tech of The U of Montana (MT)
Northern Michigan U (MI)
Oakland City U (IN)
Pittsburg State U (KS)
Southern Adventist U (TN)

Southern Alberta Inst of
Technology (AB, Canada)
Southern Utah U (UT)
U of Alaska Anchorage (AK)
U of Alaska Southeast (AK)
Utah Valley State Coll (UT)
Valdosta State U (GA)
Walla Walla Coll (WA)
Weber State U (UT)

Automotive Engineering Technology
State U of NY at Farmingdale
(NY)
Pennsylvania Coll of
Technology (PA)
The U of Akron (OH)
Vermont Tech Coll (VT)

Aviation/Airway Management
Clayton Coll & State U (GA)
Everglades U, Boca Raton
(FL)
Fairmont State U (WV)
Mountain State U (WV)
Northern Kentucky U (KY)
Park U (MO)
The U of Akron (OH)
U of Alaska Anchorage (AK)
U of Alaska Fairbanks (AK)
U of Dubuque (IA)
U of Minnesota, Crookston
(MN)
U of the District of Columbia
(DC)

Avionics Maintenance Technology
Andrews U (MI)
Baker Coll of Flint (MI)
British Columbia Inst of
Technology (BC, Canada)
Clayton Coll & State U (GA)
Fairmont State U (WV)
Georgia Southwestern State
U (GA)
Hampton U (VA)
Lewis U (IL)
Mountain State U (WV)
Northern Michigan U (MI)
Pennsylvania Coll of
Technology (PA)
Southern Alberta Inst of
Technology (AB, Canada)
U of Alaska Anchorage (AK)
U of Minnesota, Crookston
(MN)
U of the District of Columbia
(DC)
Vaughn Coll of Aeronautics
and Technology (NY)
Walla Walla Coll (WA)
Wentworth Inst of
Technology (MA)

Baking and Pastry Arts
The Art Inst of California–
San Diego (CA)
The Art Inst of Pittsburgh
(PA)
The Culinary Inst of America
(NY)
Johnson & Wales U (RI)
Kendall Coll (IL)
Pennsylvania Coll of
Technology (PA)
Southern New Hampshire U
(NH)

Banking and Financial Support Services
Globe Inst of Technology
(NY)
Hilbert Coll (NY)
International Coll of the
Cayman IslandsCayman
Islands)
Mountain State U (WV)
Northwood U (MI)
Northwood U, Florida
Campus (FL)
Northwood U, Texas Campus
(TX)
Pennsylvania Coll of
Technology (PA)
The U of Akron (OH)

U of Indianapolis (IN)
Utah Valley State Coll (UT)

Behavioral Sciences
Central Christian Coll of
Kansas (KS)
Circleville Bible Coll (OH)
Coll for Lifelong Learning
(NH)
Felician Coll (NJ)
Lewis-Clark State Coll (ID)
Martin Methodist Coll (TN)
Methodist Coll (NC)
Mount Aloysius Coll (PA)
Oklahoma Wesleyan U (OK)

Biblical Studies
Alaska Bible Coll (AK)
American Baptist Coll of
American Baptist Theol
Sem (TN)
Appalachian Bible Coll (WV)
Barclay Coll (KS)
Bethel Coll (IN)
Beulah Heights Bible Coll
(GA)
Boston Baptist Coll (MA)
California Christian Coll (CA)
Calvary Bible Coll and
Theological Seminary (MO)
Central Bible Coll (MO)
Central Christian Coll of
Kansas (KS)
Central Christian Coll of the
Bible (MO)
Cincinnati Christian U (OH)
Circleville Bible Coll (OH)
Clear Creek Baptist Bible
Coll (KY)
Coll of Biblical Studies–
Houston (TX)
Columbia International U
(SC)
Corban Coll (OR)
Covenant Coll (GA)
Crown Coll (MN)
Dallas Baptist U (TX)
Eastern Mennonite U (VA)
Emmaus Bible Coll (IA)
Faith Baptist Bible Coll and
Theological Seminary (IA)
Faulkner U (AL)
Florida Christian Coll (FL)
Fresno Pacific U (CA)
Geneva Coll (PA)
God's Bible School and Coll
(OH)
Grace Coll (IN)
Grace U (NE)
Heritage Christian U (AL)
Hillsdale Free Will Baptist
Coll (OK)
Hobe Sound Bible Coll (FL)
Houghton Coll (NY)
Howard Payne U (TX)
International Baptist Coll
(AZ)
John Brown U (AR)
Lancaster Bible Coll (PA)
Life Pacific Coll (CA)
Lincoln Christian Coll (IL)
Manhattan Christian Coll
(KS)
Nazarene Bible Coll (CO)
North Central U (MN)
Oak Hills Christian Coll (MN)
Ohio Valley Coll (WV)
Ouachita Baptist U (AR)
Pacific Union Coll (CA)
Reformed Bible Coll (MI)
Roanoke Bible Coll (NC)
Shasta Bible Coll (CA)
Simpson U (CA)
Southeastern Bible Coll (AL)
Southern Methodist Coll
(SC)
Tabor Coll (KS)
Trinity Coll of Florida (FL)
Trinity Lutheran Coll (WA)
Universidad Adventista de
las Antillas (PR)
Valley Forge Christian Coll
(PA)
Warner Pacific Coll (OR)
Washington Bible Coll (MD)

Biochemistry
Saint Joseph's Coll (IN)

Biological and Biomedical Sciences Related
Gwynedd-Mercy Coll (PA)

Biological and Physical Sciences
Bluefield State Coll (WV)
Central Christian Coll of
Kansas (KS)
Clayton Coll & State U (GA)
Crown Coll (MN)
Dalton State Coll (GA)
Heritage U (WA)
Indiana U East (IN)
Madonna U (MI)
Martin Methodist Coll (TN)
Medgar Evers Coll of The City
U of NY (NY)
Mitchell Coll (CT)
Montana Tech of The U of
Montana (MT)
Mount Olive Coll (NC)
Ohio U (WI)
Ohio U–Zanesville (OH)
Penn State U Altoona Coll
(PA)
Penn State U Schuylkill
Campus of the Capital Coll
(PA)
Rochester Coll (MI)
Sacred Heart U (CT)
State U of NY Coll of A&T at
Cobleskill (NY)
State U of NY Empire State
Coll (NY)
Sterling Coll (VT)
Tri-State U (IN)
U of Cincinnati (OH)
Valparaiso U (IN)
Villa Julie Coll (MD)
Washburn U (KS)

Biological Specializations Related
Kent State U (OH)

Biology/Biological Sciences
Adrian Coll (MI)
Brewton-Parker Coll (GA)
Canadian Mennonite U (MB,
Canada)
Central Christian Coll of
Kansas (KS)
Chestnut Hill Coll (PA)
Cleveland Chiropractic
Coll-Los Angeles Campus
(CA)
Crown Coll (MN)
Cumberland U (TN)
Dalton State Coll (GA)
Felician Coll (NJ)
Fresno Pacific U (CA)
Idaho State U (ID)
Indiana U–Purdue U Fort
Wayne (IN)
Indiana U South Bend (IN)
Indiana Wesleyan U (IN)
Lourdes Coll (OH)
Macon State Coll (GA)
Martin Methodist Coll (TN)
Mesa State Coll (CO)
Methodist Coll (NC)
Montana Tech of The U of
Montana (MT)
Mount Olive Coll (NC)
Oklahoma Wesleyan U (OK)
Pennsylvania Coll of
Technology (PA)
Pine Manor Coll (MA)
Reinhardt Coll (GA)
Rochester Inst of Technology
(NY)
Sacred Heart U (CT)
Saint Joseph's U (PA)
Shawnee State U (OH)
Thomas Edison State Coll
(NJ)
Thomas More Coll (KY)
U of Dubuque (IA)
The U of Maine at Augusta
(ME)
U of New Hampshire at
Manchester (NH)
U of Rio Grande (OH)

The U of Tampa (FL)
The U of Toledo (OH)
U of Wisconsin–Green Bay
(WI)
Utah Valley State Coll (UT)
Villa Julie Coll (MD)
Wright State U (OH)
York Coll of Pennsylvania
(PA)

Biology/Biotechnology Laboratory Technician
British Columbia Inst of
Technology (BC, Canada)
Ferris State U (MI)
State U of NY Coll of A&T at
Cobleskill (NY)
U of the District of Columbia
(DC)
Villa Julie Coll (MD)
Weber State U (UT)

Biology Teacher Education
Central Christian Coll of
Kansas (KS)

Biomedical/Medical Engineering
Vermont Tech Coll (VT)

Biomedical Technology
Baker Coll of Flint (MI)
Faulkner U (AL)
Indiana U–Purdue U
Indianapolis (IN)
Pennsylvania Coll of
Technology (PA)
Penn State U Altoona Coll
(PA)
Penn State U at Erie, The
Behrend Coll (PA)
Penn State U Berks Cmps of
Berks-Lehigh Valley Coll
(PA)
Penn State U Schuylkill
Campus of the Capital Coll
(PA)
Thomas Edison State Coll
(NJ)
Wentworth Inst of
Technology (MA)

Biotechnology
British Columbia Inst of
Technology (BC, Canada)
Vermont Tech Coll (VT)

Broadcast Journalism
Cornerstone U (MI)
Evangel U (MO)
Five Towns Coll (NY)
International Coll of the
Cayman IslandsCayman
Islands)
John Brown U (AR)
Manchester Coll (IN)
Martin Methodist Coll (TN)
New England School of
Communications (ME)
North Central U (MN)
Ohio U–Zanesville (OH)
Pennsylvania Coll of
Technology (PA)
Southern Alberta Inst of
Technology (AB, Canada)
Trevecca Nazarene U (TN)

Buddhist Studies
Heritage Bible Coll (NC)

Building/Home/Construction Inspection
Utah Valley State Coll (UT)

Building/Property Maintenance and Management
Park U (MO)
Utah Valley State Coll (UT)
Valdosta State U (GA)

Business Administration and Management
Adrian Coll (MI)
Alabama State U (AL)
Alaska Pacific U (AK)
Alderson-Broaddus Coll
(WV)
Alvernia Coll (PA)

American International Coll
(MA)
The American U in
DubaiUnited Arab
Emirates)
American U of Puerto Rico
(PR)
The American U of
RomeItaly)
Andrews U (MI)
Anna Maria Coll (MA)
Austin Peay State U (TN)
Averett U (VA)
Bacone Coll (OK)
Baker Coll of Allen Park (MI)
Baker Coll of Auburn Hills
(MI)
Baker Coll of Cadillac (MI)
Baker Coll of Clinton
Township (MI)
Baker Coll of Flint (MI)
Baker Coll of Jackson (MI)
Baker Coll of Muskegon (MI)
Baker Coll of Owosso (MI)
Baker Coll of Port Huron (MI)
Ball State U (IN)
Becker Coll (MA)
Benedictine U (IL)
Bentley Coll (MA)
Bethel Coll (IN)
Briarcliffe Coll (NY)
British Columbia Inst of
Technology (BC, Canada)
Bryan Coll (TN)
California U of Pennsylvania
(PA)
Calumet Coll of Saint Joseph
(IN)
Cameron U (OK)
Campbellsville U (KY)
Cardinal Stritch U (WI)
Carroll Coll (MT)
Central Baptist Coll (AR)
Central Christian Coll of
Kansas (KS)
Central Pennsylvania Coll
(PA)
Chaminade U of Honolulu
(HI)
Champlain Coll (VT)
Charleston Southern U (SC)
Chestnut Hill Coll (PA)
Clarion U of Pennsylvania
(PA)
Clayton Coll & State U (GA)
Cleary U (MI)
Coll for Lifelong Learning
(NH)
Coll of Mount St. Joseph
(OH)
Coll of Mount Saint Vincent
(NY)
Coll of St. Joseph (VT)
Coll of Saint Mary (NE)
Coll of Santa Fe (NM)
Columbia Coll (MO)
Columbia Coll, Caguas (PR)
Concordia Coll (NY)
Concordia U (OR)
Concord U (WV)
Corban Coll (OR)
Covenant Coll (GA)
Crown Coll (MN)
Dakota State U (SD)
Dakota Wesleyan U (SD)
Dallas Baptist U (TX)
Dalton State Coll (GA)
Davenport U, Dearborn (MI)
Davenport U, Grand Rapids
(MI)
Davenport U, Kalamazoo
(MI)
Davenport U, Lansing (MI)
Davenport U, Lapeer (MI)
Davenport U, Warren (MI)
David N. Myers U (OH)
Davis & Elkins Coll (WV)
Defiance Coll (OH)
East-West U (IL)
Edinboro U of Pennsylvania
(PA)
Emmanuel Coll (GA)
Excelsior Coll (NY)
Fairmont State U (WV)

State U of NY at Farmingdale
(NY)
Faulkner U (AL)
Felician Coll (NJ)
Five Towns Coll (NY)
Florida Metropolitan
U-Tampa Coll, Brandon
(FL)
Florida Metropolitan
U-Orlando Coll, North (FL)
Florida Metropolitan
U-Orlando Coll, South (FL)
Florida Metropolitan
U-Tampa Coll (FL)
Franciscan U of Steubenville
(OH)
Franklin U (OH)
Free Will Baptist Bible Coll
(TN)
Fresno Pacific U (CA)
Friends U (KS)
Gannon U (PA)
Geneva Coll (PA)
Globe Inst of Technology
(NY)
Goldey-Beacom Coll (DE)
Grace Bible Coll (MI)
Grantham U (LA)
Gwynedd-Mercy Coll (PA)
Haskell Indian Nations U
(KS)
Hawai'i Pacific U (HI)
Heritage U (WA)
Hilbert Coll (NY)
Huron U USA in
LondonUnited Kingdom)
Husson Coll (ME)
Immaculata U (PA)
Indiana Inst of Technology
(IN)
Indiana State U (IN)
Indiana U Northwest (IN)
Indiana U of Pennsylvania
(PA)
Indiana U–Purdue U Fort
Wayne (IN)
Indiana Wesleyan U (IN)
Inter American U of PR,
Aguadilla Campus (PR)
Inter American U of PR,
Bayamón Campus (PR)
Inter American U of PR,
Ponce Campus (PR)
Inter American U of PR, San
Germán Campus (PR)
International Coll (FL)
International Coll of the
Cayman IslandsCayman
Islands)
Johnson & Wales U (CO)
Johnson & Wales U (RI)
Jones Coll, Jacksonville (FL)
Kent State U (OH)
King's Coll (PA)
Lake Superior State U (MI)
Limestone Coll (SC)
Lindsey Wilson Coll (KY)
Long Island U, Brooklyn
Campus (NY)
Lourdes Coll (OH)
Lyndon State Coll (VT)
MacMurray Coll (IL)
Macon State Coll (GA)
Madonna U (MI)
Maine Maritime Academy
(ME)
Manchester Coll (IN)
Marian Coll (IN)
Marietta Coll (OH)
Martin Methodist Coll (TN)
Mayville State U (ND)
Medaille Coll (NY)
Medgar Evers Coll of the City
U of NY (NY)
Mercyhurst Coll (PA)
Merrimack Coll (MA)
Mesa State Coll (CO)
Methodist Coll (NC)
MidAmerica Nazarene U
(KS)
Midway Coll (KY)
Missouri Baptist U (MO)
Missouri Southern State U
(MO)

Missouri Western State Coll (MO)
Mitchell Coll (CT)
Montana State U–Billings (MT)
Montana State U–Northern (MT)
Montreat Coll (NC)
Mountain State U (WV)
Mount Aloysius Coll (PA)
Mount Ida Coll (MA)
Mount Marty Coll (SD)
Mount Olive Coll (NC)
Mount St. Mary's Coll (CA)
National American U, Colorado Springs (CO)
National American U, Denver (CO)
National American U, Albuquerque (NM)
National American U, Rapid City (SD)
National American U–Sioux Falls Branch (SD)
Newbury Coll (MA)
Newman U (KS)
New Mexico Inst of Mining and Technology (NM)
New York Inst of Technology (NY)
Niagara U (NY)
Nichols Coll (MA)
North Central U (MN)
Northern Kentucky U (KY)
Northern Michigan U (MI)
Northern State U (SD)
Northwestern State U of Louisiana (LA)
Northwest U (WA)
Northwood U (MI)
Northwood U, Florida Campus (FL)
Northwood U, Texas Campus (TX)
Notre Dame Coll (OH)
Nyack Coll (NY)
Oakland City U (IN)
Ohio Dominican U (OH)
Ohio U (OH)
Oklahoma Panhandle State U (OK)
Oklahoma Wesleyan U (OK)
Park U (MO)
Paul Smith's Coll of Arts and Sciences (NY)
Peirce Coll (PA)
Pennsylvania Coll of Technology (PA)
Pikeville Coll (KY)
Pine Manor Coll (MA)
Point Park U (PA)
Pontifical Catholic U of Puerto Rico (PR)
Post U (CT)
Providence Coll (RI)
Reinhardt Coll (GA)
Richmond, The American International U in LondonUnited Kingdom)
Rider U (NJ)
Rivier Coll (NH)
Robert Morris Coll (IL)
Rochester Inst of Technology (NY)
Roger Williams U (RI)
Rust Coll (MS)
Sacred Heart U (CT)
Sage Coll of Albany (NY)
St. Augustine Coll (IL)
St. Francis Coll (NY)
Saint Francis U (PA)
St. Gregory's U (OK)
Saint Joseph's U (PA)
Saint Peter's Coll (NJ)
Salem International U (WV)
Salve Regina U (RI)
Schiller International UFrance)
Schiller International USpain)
Shawnee State U (OH)
Shaw U (NC)
Sheldon Jackson Coll (AK)
Shepherd U (WV)
Siena Heights U (MI)

Southeastern U (DC)
Southern Alberta Inst of Technology (AB, Canada)
Southern New Hampshire U (NH)
Southern Vermont Coll (VT)
Southern Wesleyan U (SC)
South U (AL)
South U (GA)
Southwest Baptist U (MO)
Spalding U (KY)
Spring Hill Coll (AL)
State U of NY Coll of A&T at Cobleskill (NY)
State U of NY Empire State Coll (NY)
Stratford U (VA)
Strayer U (DC)
Sullivan U (KY)
Taylor U (IN)
Taylor U Fort Wayne (IN)
Thomas Coll (ME)
Thomas Edison State Coll (NJ)
Tiffin U (OH)
Tri-State U (IN)
Troy U Dothan (AL)
Tulane U (LA)
Union Coll (NE)
Universidad Adventista de las Antillas (PR)
The U of Akron (OH)
U of Alaska Anchorage (AK)
U of Alaska Fairbanks (AK)
U of Alaska Southeast (AK)
U of Bridgeport (CT)
U of Charleston (WV)
U of Cincinnati (OH)
U of Dubuque (IA)
The U of Findlay (OH)
U of Indianapolis (IN)
The U of Maine at Augusta (ME)
U of Maine at Fort Kent (ME)
U of Management and Technology (VA)
U of Mary (ND)
U of Minnesota, Crookston (MN)
The U of Montana–Western (MT)
U of New Hampshire (NH)
U of New Hampshire at Manchester (NH)
U of Regina (SK, Canada)
U of Rio Grande (OH)
U of Saint Francis (IN)
The U of Scranton (PA)
U of Sioux Falls (SD)
U of the Virgin Islands (VI)
The U of Toledo (OH)
U of Wisconsin–Green Bay (WI)
Upper Iowa U (IA)
Urbana U (OH)
Utah Valley State Coll (UT)
Valdosta State U (GA)
Vermont Tech Coll (VT)
Villa Julie Coll (MD)
Walla Walla Coll (WA)
Walsh U (OH)
Washington & Jefferson Coll (PA)
Wayland Baptist U (TX)
Waynesburg Coll (PA)
Webber International U (FL)
Wentworth Inst of Technology (MA)
Wesley Coll (DE)
Western Kentucky U (KY)
West Virginia State U (WV)
Williamson Christian Coll (TN)
Wilson Coll (PA)
York Coll of Pennsylvania (PA)
Youngstown State U (OH)

Business Administration, Management and Operations Related
Briarcliffe Coll (NY)
Coleman Coll, La Mesa (CA)
DeVry U (NJ)

Embry-Riddle Aeronautical U (FL)
Embry-Riddle Aeronautical U, Extended Campus (FL)
Mountain State U (WV)
Peirce Coll (PA)
St. Augustine Coll (IL)
Southern Alberta Inst of Technology (AB, Canada)
U of Management and Technology (VA)

Business and Personal/Financial Services Marketing
Southern New Hampshire U (NH)

Business Automation/Technology/Data Entry
Austin Peay State U (TN)
Baker Coll of Clinton Township (MI)
Central Christian Coll of Kansas (KS)
Kent State U (OH)
Montana State U–Billings (MT)
Montana Tech of The U of Montana (MT)
Pace U (NY)
Pennsylvania Coll of Technology (PA)
The U of Akron (OH)
The U of Montana–Western (MT)
U of Rio Grande (OH)
The U of Toledo (OH)
Utah Valley State Coll (UT)
Youngstown State U (OH)

Business/Commerce
Anderson U (IN)
Atlanta Christian Coll (GA)
Baker Coll of Flint (MI)
Bayamón Central U (PR)
Bluefield State Coll (WV)
Brescia U (KY)
California Coll for Health Sciences (UT)
California U of Pennsylvania (PA)
Castleton State Coll (VT)
Central Christian Coll of Kansas (KS)
Champlain Coll (VT)
Coll of Staten Island of the City U of NY (NY)
Crown Coll (MN)
Cumberland U (TN)
Dalton State Coll (GA)
Delaware Valley Coll (PA)
Gannon U (PA)
Glenville State Coll (WV)
God's Bible School and Coll (OH)
Hillsdale Free Will Baptist Coll (OK)
Idaho State U (ID)
Indiana U East (IN)
Indiana U Kokomo (IN)
Indiana U South Bend (IN)
Indiana U Southeast (IN)
Kent State U (OH)
Limestone Coll (SC)
Macon State Coll (GA)
Marygrove Coll (MI)
Marymount Coll of Fordham U (NY)
Montana State U–Billings (MT)
Mount Vernon Nazarene U (OH)
New Mexico State U (NM)
Nicholls State U (LA)
Northern Kentucky U (KY)
Peirce Coll (PA)
Penn State U Abington Coll (PA)
Penn State U Altoona Coll (PA)
Penn State U at Erie, The Behrend Coll (PA)
Penn State U Berks Cmps of Berks-Lehigh Valley Coll (PA)

Penn State U Harrisburg Campus of the Capital Coll (PA)
Penn State U Lehigh Valley Cmps of Berks-Lehigh Valley Coll (PA)
Penn State U Schuylkill Campus of the Capital Coll (PA)
Penn State U Univ Park Campus (PA)
Southern Nazarene U (OK)
Southern Wesleyan U (SC)
Southwest Baptist U (MO)
Thomas More Coll (KY)
Thomas U (GA)
Troy U Montgomery (AL)
Tulane U (LA)
U of Management and Technology (VA)
The U of Montana–Western (MT)
The U of Toledo (OH)
Utah Valley State Coll (UT)
Webber International U (FL)
Western Governors U (UT)
Xavier U (OH)

Business/Corporate Communications
Central Christian Coll of Kansas (KS)
Chestnut Hill Coll (PA)

Business Machine Repair
Boise State U (ID)
Idaho State U (ID)
Lamar U (TX)
U of Alaska Anchorage (AK)

Business, Management, and Marketing Related
The Art Inst of California–San Francisco (CA)
The U of Akron (OH)
U of Southern Indiana (IN)

Business/Managerial Economics
Central Christian Coll of Kansas (KS)
Hawai'i Pacific U (HI)
Northwood U (MI)
Saint Peter's Coll (NJ)
Urbana U (OH)

Business Operations Support and Secretarial Services Related
The U of Akron (OH)

Business Teacher Education
Central Christian Coll of Kansas (KS)
Clayton Coll & State U (GA)
Faulkner U (AL)
Macon State Coll (GA)
Martin Methodist Coll (TN)
U of the District of Columbia (DC)

Cabinetmaking and Millwork
British Columbia Inst of Technology (BC, Canada)
Pennsylvania Coll of Technology (PA)
Utah Valley State Coll (UT)
Valdosta State U (GA)

Cad/Cadd Drafting/Design Technology
Kent State U (OH)
Shawnee State U (OH)
Southern Alberta Inst of Technology (AB, Canada)

Cardiopulmonary Technology
Bacone Coll (OK)

Cardiovascular Technology
Argosy U/Twin Cities, Eagan (MN)
British Columbia Inst of Technology (BC, Canada)
Gwynedd-Mercy Coll (PA)
Molloy Coll (NY)
Nebraska Methodist Coll (NE)

Thompson Rivers U (BC, Canada)
The U of Toledo (OH)

Carpentry
British Columbia Inst of Technology (BC, Canada)
Idaho State U (ID)
Northern Michigan U (MI)
Pennsylvania Coll of Technology (PA)
Southern Utah U (UT)
Thompson Rivers U (BC, Canada)
Valdosta State U (GA)

Cartography
Northern Michigan U (MI)
Southern Alberta Inst of Technology (AB, Canada)
U of Arkansas at Fort Smith (AR)

Celtic Languages
Sacred Heart U (CT)

Ceramic Arts and Ceramics
Friends U (KS)
Rochester Inst of Technology (NY)

Chemical Engineering
Ball State U (IN)
Excelsior Coll (NY)
Ferris State U (MI)
U of New Haven (CT)
U of the District of Columbia (DC)
West Virginia State U (WV)

Chemical Technology
British Columbia Inst of Technology (BC, Canada)
Indiana U–Purdue U Fort Wayne (IN)
Lawrence Technological U (MI)
Millersville U of Pennsylvania (PA)
Nicholls State U (LA)
Southern Alberta Inst of Technology (AB, Canada)
State U of NY Coll of A&T at Cobleskill (NY)
The U of Akron (OH)
U of New Haven (CT)
The U of Toledo (OH)
Weber State U (UT)

Chemistry
Adrian Coll (MI)
Bethel Coll (IN)
Castleton State Coll (VT)
Central Christian Coll of Kansas (KS)
Central Methodist U (MO)
Chestnut Hill Coll (PA)
Clayton Coll & State U (GA)
Dalton State Coll (GA)
Hannibal-LaGrange Coll (MO)
Idaho State U (ID)
Indiana U South Bend (IN)
Indiana Wesleyan U (IN)
Keene State Coll (NH)
Lake Superior State U (MI)
Lindsey Wilson Coll (KY)
Lourdes Coll (OH)
Macon State Coll (GA)
Madonna U (MI)
Martin Methodist Coll (TN)
Methodist Coll (NC)
Ohio Dominican U (OH)
Oklahoma Wesleyan U (OK)
Rochester Inst of Technology (NY)
Sacred Heart U (CT)
Saint Joseph's U (PA)
Siena Heights U (MI)
Thomas Edison State Coll (NJ)
Thomas More Coll (KY)
U of Indianapolis (IN)
U of Rio Grande (OH)
The U of Tampa (FL)
U of Wisconsin–Green Bay (WI)
Villa Julie Coll (MD)

Wright State U (OH)
York Coll of Pennsylvania (PA)

Chemistry Related
U of the Incarnate Word (TX)

Chemistry Teacher Education
Central Christian Coll of Kansas (KS)

Child Care and Support Services Management
The Baptist Coll of Florida (FL)
Central Missouri State U (MO)
Chestnut Hill Coll (PA)
Eastern New Mexico U (NM)
Henderson State U (AR)
Idaho State U (ID)
Mount Aloysius Coll (PA)
Mount Vernon Nazarene U (OH)
Nicholls State U (LA)
Pennsylvania Coll of Technology (PA)
Post U (CT)
St. Augustine Coll (IL)
Southeast Missouri State U (MO)
Thompson Rivers U (BC, Canada)
U of Central Arkansas (AR)
Weber State U (UT)
Youngstown State U (OH)

Child Care/Guidance
Eastern Kentucky U (KY)

Child Care Provision
Eastern Kentucky U (KY)
Mayville State U (ND)
Mercy Coll (NY)
Murray State U (KY)
Pacific Union Coll (CA)
Pennsylvania Coll of Technology (PA)
Saint Mary-of-the-Woods Coll (IN)
U of Alaska Fairbanks (AK)

Child Care Services Management
Cameron U (OK)
U of Louisiana at Monroe (LA)

Child Development
Alabama State U (AL)
Boise State U (ID)
Central Pennsylvania Coll (PA)
Eastern Kentucky U (KY)
Evangel U (MO)
Fairmont State U (WV)
Ferris State U (MI)
Franciscan U of Steubenville (OH)
Friends U (KS)
Grambling State U (LA)
Lamar U (TX)
Lewis-Clark State Coll (ID)
Madonna U (MI)
Mitchell Coll (CT)
Northern Michigan U (MI)
Ohio U (OH)
Purdue U Calumet (IN)
Reformed Bible Coll (MI)
Southern Utah U (UT)
Southern Vermont Coll (VT)
Trevecca Nazarene U (TN)
U of Cincinnati (OH)
U of the District of Columbia (DC)
Villa Julie Coll (MD)
Washburn U (KS)
Weber State U (UT)
Youngstown State U (OH)

Child Guidance
Siena Heights U (MI)
Thomas Edison State Coll (NJ)

Christian Studies
Coll of Biblical Studies–Houston (TX)

God's Bible School and Coll (OH)
Heritage Bible Coll (NC)
Vennard Coll (IA)
Wayland Baptist U (TX)

Cinematography and Film/Video Production
Academy of Art U (CA)
American InterContinental U, Atlanta (GA)
The Art Inst of Atlanta (GA)
The Art Inst of California–Los Angeles (CA)
The Art Inst of Colorado (CO)
The Art Inst of Fort Lauderdale (FL)
The Art Inst of Pittsburgh (PA)
Five Towns Coll (NY)
Florida Metropolitan U-Orlando Coll, North (FL)
Miami International U of Art & Design (FL)
New England School of Communications (ME)
Rochester Inst of Technology (NY)
Southern Adventist U (TN)

City/Urban, Community and Regional Planning
U of the District of Columbia (DC)

Civil Drafting and Cad/Cadd
British Columbia Inst of Technology (BC, Canada)
Montana Tech of The U of Montana (MT)
Southern Alberta Inst of Technology (AB, Canada)

Civil Engineering
Macon State Coll (GA)

Civil Engineering Technology
Bluefield State Coll (WV)
British Columbia Inst of Technology (BC, Canada)
Fairmont State U (WV)
Ferris State U (MI)
Idaho State U (ID)
Indiana U–Purdue U Fort Wayne (IN)
Indiana U–Purdue U Indianapolis (IN)
Kansas State U (KS)
Michigan Technological U (MI)
Missouri Western State Coll (MO)
Montana State U–Northern (MT)
Murray State U (KY)
Pennsylvania Coll of Technology (PA)
Point Park U (PA)
Purdue U Calumet (IN)
Southern Alberta Inst of Technology (AB, Canada)
Thomas Edison State Coll (NJ)
U of Cincinnati (OH)
U of Massachusetts Lowell (MA)
U of New Hampshire (NH)
U of the District of Columbia (DC)
The U of Toledo (OH)
Vermont Tech Coll (VT)
Wentworth Inst of Technology (MA)
Youngstown State U (OH)

Clinical Laboratory Science/ Medical Technology
Arkansas State U (AR)
Clayton Coll & State U (GA)
Dalton State Coll (GA)
Faulkner U (AL)
Indiana U East (IN)
Northern Michigan U (MI)
The U of Toledo (OH)
Villa Julie Coll (MD)
Weber State U (UT)

Clinical/Medical Laboratory Assistant
Northern Michigan U (MI)
The U of Maine at Augusta (ME)
Youngstown State U (OH)

Clinical/Medical Laboratory Science and Allied Professions Related
The U of Akron (OH)

Clinical/Medical Laboratory Technology
Argosy U/Twin Cities, Eagan (MN)
Baker Coll of Owosso (MI)
British Columbia Inst of Technology (BC, Canada)
City U (WA)
Clayton Coll & State U (GA)
Coll of Staten Island of the City U of NY (NY)
Dakota State U (SD)
Dalton State Coll (GA)
Eastern Kentucky U (KY)
Fairmont State U (WV)
State U of NY at Farmingdale (NY)
Faulkner U (AL)
Felician Coll (NJ)
Ferris State U (MI)
Friends U (KS)
The George Washington U (DC)
Indiana U Northwest (IN)
Macon State Coll (GA)
Madonna U (MI)
Marshall U (WV)
Martin Methodist Coll (TN)
Northern Michigan U (MI)
Our Lady of the Lake Coll (LA)
Penn State U Schuylkill Campus of the Capital Coll (PA)
Shawnee State U (OH)
Southern Alberta Inst of Technology (AB, Canada)
State U of NY Coll of A&T at Cobleskill (NY)
U of Alaska Anchorage (AK)
U of Cincinnati (OH)
U of Maine at Presque Isle (ME)
U of Rio Grande (OH)
U of the District of Columbia (DC)
Villa Julie Coll (MD)
Weber State U (UT)
Youngstown State U (OH)

Clothing/Textiles
The Art Inst of Fort Lauderdale (FL)
Indiana U Bloomington (IN)

Commercial and Advertising Art
Academy of Art U (CA)
Andrews U (MI)
The Art Inst of Atlanta (GA)
The Art Inst of California–Los Angeles (CA)
The Art Inst of California–San Diego (CA)
The Art Inst of California–San Francisco (CA)
The Art Inst of Colorado (CO)
The Art Inst of Dallas (TX)
The Art Inst of Fort Lauderdale (FL)
The Art Inst of Houston (TX)
The Art Inst of Pittsburgh (PA)
The Art Inst of Washington (VA)
The Art Insts International Minnesota (MN)
Baker Coll of Auburn Hills (MI)
Baker Coll of Clinton Township (MI)
Baker Coll of Flint (MI)
Baker Coll of Muskegon (MI)
Baker Coll of Owosso (MI)
Baker Coll of Port Huron (MI)

Becker Coll (MA)
Briarcliffe Coll (NY)
British Columbia Inst of Technology (BC, Canada)
Champlain Coll (VT)
Fairmont State U (WV)
Fashion Inst of Technology (NY)
Felician Coll (NJ)
Ferris State U (MI)
Florida Metropolitan U-Orlando Coll, North (FL)
Florida Metropolitan U-Tampa Coll (FL)
Friends U (KS)
Hussian School of Art (PA)
The Illinois Inst of Art (IL)
Indiana U–Purdue U Fort Wayne (IN)
International Academy of Design & Technology (FL)
International Acad of Merchandising & Design, Ltd (IL)
Mesa State Coll (CO)
Miami International U of Art & Design (FL)
Mitchell Coll (CT)
Montana State U–Northern (MT)
Mount Ida Coll (MA)
Newbury Coll (MA)
Northern Michigan U (MI)
Northern State U (SD)
Pace U (NY)
Pennsylvania Coll of Technology (PA)
Pratt Inst (NY)
Robert Morris Coll (IL)
Sacred Heart U (CT)
Sage Coll of Albany (NY)
Silver Lake Coll (WI)
Suffolk U (MA)
U of Arkansas at Fort Smith (AR)
U of New Haven (CT)
U of Saint Francis (IN)
U of the District of Columbia (DC)
Utah Valley State Coll (UT)
Villa Julie Coll (MD)
Virginia Intermont Coll (VA)
Walla Walla Coll (WA)

Commercial Photography
The Art Inst of Atlanta (GA)
The Art Inst of Pittsburgh (PA)
Harrington Coll of Design (IL)
Paier Coll of Art, Inc. (CT)
The U of Akron (OH)

Communication and Journalism Related
Champlain Coll (VT)
New England School of Communications (ME)
Tulane U (LA)

Communication and Media Related
Champlain Coll (VT)

Communication/Speech Communication and Rhetoric
Baker Coll of Jackson (MI)
Brigham Young U–Hawaii (HI)
Cameron U (OK)
Central Christian Coll of Kansas (KS)
Clearwater Christian Coll (FL)
Coll of Mount St. Joseph (OH)
Idaho State U (ID)
Indiana Wesleyan U (IN)
Lyndon State Coll (VT)
The New England Inst of Art (MA)
Sage Coll of Albany (NY)
Southern Nazarene U (OK)
Thomas More Coll (KY)
Tri-State U (IN)
Tulane U (LA)

The U of Montana–Missoula (MT)
U of New Haven (CT)
U of Rio Grande (OH)
Utah Valley State Coll (UT)
West Virginia State U (WV)
Wright State U (OH)

Communications Systems Installation and Repair Technology
Idaho State U (ID)
Thompson Rivers U (BC, Canada)

Communications Technologies and Support Services Related
New England School of Communications (ME)

Communications Technology
Bluefield State Coll (WV)
East Stroudsburg U of Pennsylvania (PA)
Ferris State U (MI)
Vennard Coll (IA)

Community Health and Preventive Medicine
Utah Valley State Coll (UT)

Community Organization and Advocacy
Alabama State U (AL)
Cazenovia Coll (NY)
Fairmont State U (WV)
Martin Methodist Coll (TN)
Midland Lutheran Coll (NE)
Montana State U–Northern (MT)
Samford U (AL)
State U of NY Empire State Coll (NY)
Thomas Edison State Coll (NJ)
The U of Akron (OH)
The U of Findlay (OH)
U of New Hampshire (NH)
U of New Mexico (NM)

Community Psychology
Kwantlen U Coll (BC, Canada)
Woodbury Coll (VT)

Computer and Information Sciences
Alderson-Broaddus Coll (WV)
Baker Coll of Allen Park (MI)
Black Hills State U (SD)
Bluefield State Coll (WV)
Central Christian Coll of Kansas (KS)
Chaminade U of Honolulu (HI)
Champlain Coll (VT)
Coleman Coll, La Mesa (CA)
Columbia Coll (MO)
Dalton State Coll (GA)
Delaware Valley Coll (PA)
Edinboro U of Pennsylvania (PA)
Florida Metropolitan U-Tampa Coll, Brandon (FL)
Florida Metropolitan U-Orlando Coll, South (FL)
Franklin U (OH)
Georgia Southwestern State U (GA)
Globe Inst of Technology (NY)
Haskell Indian Nations U (KS)
Huron U USA in LondonUnited Kingdom)
Indiana Wesleyan U (IN)
Kentucky State U (KY)
King's Coll (PA)
Lewis-Clark State Coll (ID)
Lyndon State Coll (VT)
Madonna U (MI)
Midway Coll (KY)
Millersville U of Pennsylvania (PA)

Montana State U–Billings (MT)
National American U, Denver (CO)
Oklahoma Panhandle State U (OK)
Pacific Union Coll (CA)
Pennsylvania Coll of Technology (PA)
Penn State U Schuylkill Campus of the Capital Coll (PA)
Sacred Heart U (CT)
Sage Coll of Albany (NY)
St. Augustine Coll (IL)
Southern New Hampshire U (NH)
Spring Hill Coll (AL)
Thomas Coll (ME)
Thomas Edison State Coll (NJ)
Thomas More Coll (KY)
Tri-State U (IN)
Troy U Montgomery (AL)
Tulane U (LA)
U of Alaska Anchorage (AK)
U of Arkansas at Fort Smith (AR)
U of Charleston (WV)
U of Cincinnati (OH)
The U of Maine at Augusta (ME)
The U of Montana–Western (MT)
Utah Valley State Coll (UT)
Villa Julie Coll (MD)
Weber State U (UT)
Youngstown State U (OH)

Computer and Information Sciences And Support Services Related
Becker Coll (MA)
Cleary U (MI)
Florida Metropolitan U-Tampa Coll, Brandon (FL)
Huron U USA in LondonUnited Kingdom)
Montana State U–Billings (MT)
Mountain State U (WV)
Pennsylvania Coll of Technology (PA)
Strayer U (DC)
U of Arkansas at Fort Smith (AR)

Computer and Information Sciences Related
Huron U USA in LondonUnited Kingdom)
Lindsey Wilson Coll (KY)
Madonna U (MI)
National American U, Denver (CO)

Computer and Information Systems Security
Champlain Coll (VT)
Huron U USA in LondonUnited Kingdom)

Computer Engineering
The U of Scranton (PA)

Computer Engineering Related
Thompson Rivers U (BC, Canada)
Western Governors U (UT)

Computer Engineering Technologies Related
Southern Alberta Inst of Technology (AB, Canada)

Computer Engineering Technology
Andrews U (MI)
Baker Coll of Owosso (MI)
Capitol Coll (MD)
Clayton Coll & State U (GA)
Dalton State Coll (GA)
Eastern Kentucky U (KY)
Excelsior Coll (NY)
Grantham U (LA)
Johnson & Wales U (RI)
Kansas State U (KS)

Lake Superior State U (MI)
Madonna U (MI)
National American U, Rapid City (SD)
Oakland City U (IN)
Oregon Inst of Technology (OR)
Peirce Coll (PA)
Purdue U Calumet (IN)
U of Cincinnati (OH)
U of the District of Columbia (DC)
Vermont Tech Coll (VT)
Weber State U (UT)
Wentworth Inst of Technology (MA)

Computer Graphics
Academy of Art U (CA)
The Art Inst of California–Orange County (CA)
The Art Inst of California–San Francisco (CA)
The Art Inst of Colorado (CO)
The Art Inst of Dallas (TX)
The Art Inst of Houston (TX)
The Art Inst of Pittsburgh (PA)
The Art Inst of Washington (VA)
Baker Coll of Cadillac (MI)
Champlain Coll (VT)
Coleman Coll, La Mesa (CA)
Huron U USA in LondonUnited Kingdom)
The Illinois Inst of Art (IL)
International Academy of Design & Technology (FL)
International Acad of Merchandising & Design, Ltd (IL)
Kent State U (OH)
Miami International U of Art & Design (FL)
New England School of Communications (ME)
Southern Alberta Inst of Technology (AB, Canada)
Thompson Rivers U (BC, Canada)
U of Advancing Technology (AZ)
Vaughn Coll of Aeronautics and Technology (NY)
Villa Julie Coll (MD)

Computer Hardware Technology
Inter American U of PR, Aguadilla Campus (PR)

Computer/Information Technology Services Administration Related
Champlain Coll (VT)
Dalton State Coll (GA)
Huron U USA in LondonUnited Kingdom)
Medgar Evers Coll of the City U of NY (NY)
National American U, Denver (CO)
Pennsylvania Coll of Technology (PA)
Southern Alberta Inst of Technology (AB, Canada)
The U of Akron (OH)
Vennard Coll (IA)

Computer Installation and Repair Technology
Dalton State Coll (GA)
Inter American U of PR, Bayamón Campus (PR)
Thompson Rivers U (BC, Canada)

Computer Maintenance Technology
Eastern Kentucky U (KY)

Computer Management
Champlain Coll (VT)
Coll for Lifelong Learning (NH)
Davenport U, Lansing (MI)
Faulkner U (AL)
Five Towns Coll (NY)

Computer Management (continued)
International Coll of the Cayman IslandsCayman Islands)
Life U (GA)
Northwood U (MI)
Northwood U, Florida Campus (FL)
Oakland City U (IN)
Thomas Coll (ME)

Computer Programming
Atlantic Union Coll (MA)
Baker Coll of Flint (MI)
Baker Coll of Muskegon (MI)
Baker Coll of Owosso (MI)
Baker Coll of Port Huron (MI)
Black Hills State U (SD)
Briarcliffe Coll (NY)
California U of Pennsylvania (PA)
Castleton State Coll (VT)
Charleston Southern U (SC)
Coll of Staten Island of the City U of NY (NY)
Dakota State U (SD)
Delaware Valley Coll (PA)
State U of NY at Farmingdale (NY)
Florida Metropolitan U-Orlando Coll, North (FL)
Florida Metropolitan U-Tampa Coll (FL)
Friends U (KS)
Gwynedd-Mercy Coll (PA)
Huron U USA in LondonUnited Kingdom)
Indiana U East (IN)
Johnson & Wales U (RI)
Kansas State U (KS)
Kent State U (OH)
Limestone Coll (SC)
Lindsey Wilson Coll (KY)
Macon State Coll (GA)
Martin Methodist Coll (TN)
Midland Lutheran Coll (NE)
National American U, Denver (CO)
National American U, Rapid City (SD)
National American U–Sioux Falls Branch (SD)
Newbury Coll (MA)
New York U (NY)
Oakland City U (IN)
Oregon Inst of Technology (OR)
Pontifical Catholic U of Puerto Rico (PR)
Purdue U Calumet (IN)
Richmond, The American International U in LondonUnited Kingdom)
Saint Francis U (PA)
State U of NY Coll of A&T at Cobleskill (NY)
Stratford U (VA)
Tiffin U (OH)
U of Advancing Technology (AZ)
U of Cincinnati (OH)
U of Indianapolis (IN)
The U of Toledo (OH)
Utah Valley State Coll (UT)
Villa Julie Coll (MD)
Walla Walla Coll (WA)
West Virginia State U (WV)
York Coll of Pennsylvania (PA)
Youngstown State U (OH)

Computer Programming Related
Central Pennsylvania Coll (PA)
Huron U USA in LondonUnited Kingdom)
National American U, Denver (CO)
Stratford U (VA)

Computer Programming (Specific Applications)
Georgia Southwestern State U (GA)
Huron U USA in LondonUnited Kingdom)

Idaho State U (ID)
Kent State U (OH)
Macon State Coll (GA)
National American U, Denver (CO)
Peirce Coll (PA)
Pennsylvania Coll of Technology (PA)
Robert Morris Coll (IL)
The U of Toledo (OH)

Computer Programming (Vendor/Product Certification)
Huron U USA in LondonUnited Kingdom)

Computer Science
Bacone Coll (OK)
Baker Coll of Allen Park (MI)
Baker Coll of Owosso (MI)
Bayamón Central U (PR)
Bethel Coll (IN)
Black Hills State U (SD)
British Columbia Inst of Technology (BC, Canada)
Calumet Coll of Saint Joseph (IN)
Carroll Coll (MT)
Central Christian Coll of Kansas (KS)
Central Methodist U (MO)
Chestnut Hill Coll (PA)
Clayton Coll & State U (GA)
Columbia Union Coll (MD)
Columbus State U (GA)
Creighton U (NE)
Dalton State Coll (GA)
Davis & Elkins Coll (WV)
Defiance Coll (OH)
East-West U (IL)
Excelsior Coll (NY)
State U of NY at Farmingdale (NY)
Felician Coll (NJ)
Florida Metropolitan U-Tampa Coll (FL)
Friends U (KS)
Grantham U (LA)
Heritage U (WA)
Huron U USA in LondonUnited Kingdom)
Indiana U–Purdue U Fort Wayne (IN)
Indiana U South Bend (IN)
Indiana U Southeast (IN)
Inter American U of PR, Aguadilla Campus (PR)
Inter American U of PR, Bayamón Campus (PR)
Inter American U of PR, Ponce Campus (PR)
Johnson & Wales U (RI)
Keene State Coll (NH)
Limestone Coll (SC)
Lincoln U (MO)
Lyndon State Coll (VT)
Macon State Coll (GA)
Madonna U (MI)
Manchester Coll (IN)
Martin Methodist Coll (TN)
Medgar Evers Coll of the City U of NY (NY)
Merrimack Coll (MA)
Mesa State Coll (CO)
Methodist Coll (NC)
Millersville U of Pennsylvania (PA)
Missouri Southern State U (MO)
Montana Tech of The U of Montana (MT)
Mountain State U (WV)
Mount Aloysius Coll (PA)
Newbury Coll (MA)
Oakland City U (IN)
Park U (MO)
Richmond, The American International U in LondonUnited Kingdom)
Rivier Coll (NH)
Rochester Inst of Technology (NY)
Sacred Heart U (CT)
Saint Joseph's U (PA)

Southeastern U (DC)
Southern Adventist U (TN)
Southern U at New Orleans (LA)
Southwest Baptist U (MO)
State U of NY Coll of A&T at Cobleskill (NY)
Sullivan U (KY)
Tabor Coll (KS)
Thomas Edison State Coll (NJ)
Universidad Adventista de las Antillas (PR)
U of Dubuque (IA)
The U of Findlay (OH)
U of Maine at Fort Kent (ME)
U of New Haven (CT)
U of Rio Grande (OH)
U of the Virgin Islands (VI)
Utah Valley State Coll (UT)
Weber State U (UT)
Wentworth Inst of Technology (MA)
West Virginia State U (WV)

Computer Software and Media Applications Related
Huron U USA in LondonUnited Kingdom)
Indiana U–Purdue U Fort Wayne (IN)
New England School of Communications (ME)

Computer Software Engineering
Grantham U (LA)

Computer Software Technology
U of New Hampshire (NH)

Computer Systems Analysis
Baker Coll of Flint (MI)
British Columbia Inst of Technology (BC, Canada)
Davenport U, Dearborn (MI)
Davenport U, Gaylord (MI)
Davenport U, Grand Rapids (MI)
Davenport U, Holland (MI)
Davenport U, Kalamazoo (MI)
Davenport U, Lansing (MI)
Davenport U, Warren (MI)
Huron U USA in LondonUnited Kingdom)
Kansas State U (KS)
The U of Akron (OH)
The U of Toledo (OH)
Utah Valley State Coll (UT)

Computer Systems Networking and Telecommunications
Baker Coll of Allen Park (MI)
Baker Coll of Flint (MI)
Champlain Coll (VT)
Coleman Coll, La Mesa (CA)
Davenport U, Dearborn (MI)
Davenport U, Gaylord (MI)
Davenport U, Grand Rapids (MI)
Davenport U, Holland (MI)
Davenport U, Kalamazoo (MI)
Davenport U, Lansing (MI)
Davenport U, Warren (MI)
DeVry U (NJ)
Huron U USA in LondonUnited Kingdom)
National American U, Denver (CO)
Pennsylvania Coll of Technology (PA)
Robert Morris Coll (IL)
Sage Coll of Albany (NY)
Stratford U (VA)
Strayer U (DC)
Utah Valley State Coll (UT)
Vermont Tech Coll (VT)

Computer Teacher Education
Baker Coll of Flint (MI)
Central Christian Coll of Kansas (KS)

Computer Technology/Computer Systems Technology
Dalton State Coll (GA)
Eastern Kentucky U (KY)
Kent State U (OH)
Peirce Coll (PA)
Pennsylvania Coll of Technology (PA)
Southeast Missouri State U (MO)
State U of NY Coll of A&T at Cobleskill (NY)
Thompson Rivers U (BC, Canada)

Computer Typography and Composition Equipment Operation
Baker Coll of Auburn Hills (MI)
Baker Coll of Cadillac (MI)
Baker Coll of Clinton Township (MI)
Baker Coll of Flint (MI)
Baker Coll of Jackson (MI)
Calumet Coll of Saint Joseph (IN)
Davis & Elkins Coll (WV)
Faulkner U (AL)
McNeese State U (LA)
Northern Michigan U (MI)
The U of Toledo (OH)

Conducting
Central Christian Coll of Kansas (KS)

Construction Engineering Technology
Baker Coll of Owosso (MI)
British Columbia Inst of Technology (BC, Canada)
Central Missouri State U (MO)
Coll of Staten Island of the City U of NY (NY)
Fairmont State U (WV)
Ferris State U (MI)
Lake Superior State U (MI)
Lawrence Technological U (MI)
Northern Michigan U (MI)
Pennsylvania Coll of Technology (PA)
Purdue U Calumet (IN)
The U of Akron (OH)
U of Alaska Southeast (AK)
U of Cincinnati (OH)
U of New Hampshire (NH)
The U of Toledo (OH)
Vermont Tech Coll (VT)
Wentworth Inst of Technology (MA)
Wright State U (OH)

Construction Management
Baker Coll of Flint (MI)
British Columbia Inst of Technology (BC, Canada)
John Brown U (AR)
Pratt Inst (NY)
U of New Hampshire (NH)
Wentworth Inst of Technology (MA)

Construction Trades
Utah Valley State Coll (UT)

Construction Trades Related
British Columbia Inst of Technology (BC, Canada)

Consumer Merchandising/Retailing Management
Baker Coll of Owosso (MI)
Central Pennsylvania Coll (PA)
Fairmont State U (WV)
Johnson & Wales U (RI)
Madonna U (MI)
Mount Ida Coll (MA)
Newbury Coll (MA)
Sullivan U (KY)
Thomas Edison State Coll (NJ)
The U of Toledo (OH)

Cooking and Related Culinary Arts
The Art Inst of California–Orange County (CA)
The Art Inst of California–San Diego (CA)
The Art Inst of Pittsburgh (PA)
Kendall Coll (IL)
Lexington Coll (IL)

Corrections
Baker Coll of Muskegon (MI)
Bluefield State Coll (WV)
Eastern Kentucky U (KY)
John Jay Coll of Criminal Justice, the City U of NY (NY)
Lake Superior State U (MI)
Lamar U (TX)
Macon State Coll (GA)
Marygrove Coll (MI)
U of Indianapolis (IN)
U of the District of Columbia (DC)
The U of Toledo (OH)
Washburn U (KS)
Weber State U (UT)
Xavier U (OH)
York Coll of Pennsylvania (PA)
Youngstown State U (OH)

Cosmetology
Lamar U (TX)
Valdosta State U (GA)

Counseling Psychology
Central Christian Coll of Kansas (KS)

Counselor Education/School Counseling and Guidance
Central Christian Coll of Kansas (KS)
Martin Methodist Coll (TN)
Our Lady of Holy Cross Coll (LA)

Court Reporting
Johnson & Wales U (RI)
U of Cincinnati (OH)
Villa Julie Coll (MD)

Creative Writing
Bethel Coll (IN)
Haskell Indian Nations U (KS)
Huron U USA in LondonUnited Kingdom)
Manchester Coll (IN)
U of Maine at Presque Isle (ME)
The U of Tampa (FL)

Criminal Justice/Law Enforcement Administration
Adrian Coll (MI)
Anderson U (IN)
Arkansas State U (AR)
Ashland U (OH)
Ball State U (IN)
Becker Coll (MA)
Bemidji State U (MN)
Boise State U (ID)
Calumet Coll of Saint Joseph (IN)
Campbellsville U (KY)
Castleton State Coll (VT)
Central Christian Coll of Kansas (KS)
Central Pennsylvania Coll (PA)
Champlain Coll (VT)
Chestnut Hill Coll (PA)
Clayton Coll & State U (GA)
Columbia Coll (MO)
Columbus State U (GA)
Dakota Wesleyan U (SD)
Dalton State Coll (GA)
Defiance Coll (OH)
Eastern Kentucky U (KY)
State U of NY at Farmingdale (NY)
Faulkner U (AL)
Finlandia U (MI)

Florida Metropolitan U-Tampa Coll (FL)
Fort Valley State U (GA)
Glenville State Coll (WV)
Grambling State U (LA)
Hannibal-LaGrange Coll (MO)
Hilbert Coll (NY)
Indiana U Northwest (IN)
Indiana U South Bend (IN)
Johnson & Wales U (FL)
Johnson & Wales U (RI)
Lake Superior State U (MI)
Lincoln U (MO)
Louisiana Coll (LA)
Lourdes Coll (OH)
MacMurray Coll (IL)
Macon State Coll (GA)
Mansfield U of Pennsylvania (PA)
Martin Methodist Coll (TN)
Mercyhurst Coll (PA)
Mesa State Coll (CO)
Methodist Coll (NC)
Mitchell Coll (CT)
Mount Ida Coll (MA)
Newbury Coll (MA)
Northern Michigan U (MI)
Park U (IN)
Roger Williams U (RI)
St. John's U (NY)
Saint Joseph's U (PA)
Salve Regina U (RI)
Siena Heights U (MI)
Southern Utah U (UT)
Southern Vermont Coll (VT)
Suffolk U (MA)
Thomas Edison State Coll (NJ)
Thomas More Coll (KY)
Thomas U (GA)
Tri-State U (IN)
U of Arkansas at Fort Smith (AR)
U of Cincinnati (OH)
The U of Findlay (OH)
U of Indianapolis (IN)
U of Maine at Fort Kent (ME)
U of Maine at Presque Isle (ME)
U of the District of Columbia (DC)
Urbana U (OH)
Utah Valley State Coll (UT)
Washburn U (KS)
West Virginia State U (WV)
Youngstown State U (OH)

Criminal Justice/Police Science
Arkansas State U (AR)
Becker Coll (MA)
Bluefield State Coll (WV)
Cameron U (OK)
Dalton State Coll (GA)
Defiance Coll (OH)
Eastern Kentucky U (KY)
Edinboro U of Pennsylvania (PA)
Fairmont State U (WV)
Husson Coll (ME)
Idaho State U (ID)
Inter American U of PR, Ponce Campus (PR)
John Jay Coll of Criminal Justice, the City U of NY (NY)
Lake Superior State U (MI)
MacMurray Coll (IL)
Macon State Coll (GA)
Martin Methodist Coll (TN)
Mercyhurst Coll (PA)
Middle Tennessee State U (TN)
Missouri Southern State U (MO)
Nicholls State U (LA)
Northern Kentucky U (KY)
Northern Michigan U (MI)
Northwestern State U of Louisiana (LA)
Ohio U (OH)
Southeastern Louisiana U (LA)

Southern U and A&M Coll (LA)
Tiffin U (OH)
The U of Akron (OH)
U of Arkansas at Pine Bluff (AR)
U of Cincinnati (OH)
U of Louisiana at Monroe (LA)
U of New Haven (CT)
U of the District of Columbia (DC)
U of the Virgin Islands (VI)
The U of Toledo (OH)
U of Wisconsin–Superior (WI)
Washburn U (KS)
Weber State U (UT)
York Coll of Pennsylvania (PA)
Youngstown State U (OH)

Criminal Justice/Safety
Augusta State U (GA)
Bethel Coll (IN)
Cazenovia Coll (NY)
Central Christian Coll of Kansas (KS)
Champlain Coll (VT)
Florida Metropolitan U-Tampa Coll, Brandon (FL)
Florida Metropolitan U-Orlando Coll, North (FL)
Florida Metropolitan U-Orlando Coll, South (FL)
Georgia Southwestern State U (GA)
Husson Coll (ME)
Idaho State U (ID)
Indiana U East (IN)
Indiana U Kokomo (IN)
Indiana U–Purdue U Fort Wayne (IN)
Indiana U–Purdue U Indianapolis (IN)
Indiana Wesleyan U (IN)
International Coll (FL)
Kent State U (OH)
King's Coll (PA)
Madonna U (MI)
Manchester Coll (IN)
Missouri Western State Coll (MO)
Mountain State U (WV)
Mount Aloysius Coll (PA)
Murray State U (KY)
New Mexico State U (NM)
Penn State U Altoona Coll (PA)
Pikeville Coll (KY)
St. Francis Coll (NY)
St. Gregory's U (OK)
Saint Joseph's Coll of Maine (ME)
Shaw U (NC)
Shepherd U (WV)
The U of Maine at Augusta (ME)
The U of Scranton (PA)
Weber State U (UT)
Xavier U (OH)

Criminology
Ball State U (IN)
Chaminade U of Honolulu (HI)
Dalton State Coll (GA)
Faulkner U (AL)
Indiana State U (IN)
Indiana U of Pennsylvania (PA)
Kwantlen U Coll (BC, Canada)
Marquette U (WI)
U of the District of Columbia (DC)

Crop Production
Sterling Coll (VT)
U of Massachusetts Amherst (MA)

Culinary Arts
The Art Inst of Atlanta (GA)
The Art Inst of California–Los Angeles (CA)

The Art Inst of California–San Diego (CA)
The Art Inst of Colorado (CO)
The Art Inst of Dallas (TX)
The Art Inst of Fort Lauderdale (FL)
The Art Inst of Houston (TX)
The Art Inst of Phoenix (AZ)
The Art Inst of Pittsburgh (PA)
The Art Inst of Seattle (WA)
The Art Insts International Minnesota (MN)
Baker Coll of Muskegon (MI)
Boise State U (ID)
The Culinary Inst of America (NY)
Idaho State U (ID)
Johnson & Wales U (CO)
Johnson & Wales U (FL)
Johnson & Wales U (RI)
Kendall Coll (IL)
Lexington Coll (IL)
Mercyhurst Coll (PA)
Mesa State Coll (CO)
Newbury Coll (MA)
Nicholls State U (LA)
Oakland City U (IN)
Paul Smith's Coll of Arts and Sciences (NY)
Pennsylvania Coll of Technology (PA)
Purdue U Calumet (IN)
Robert Morris Coll (IL)
St. Augustine Coll (IL)
Saint Francis U (PA)
Southern New Hampshire U (NH)
State U of NY Coll of A&T at Cobleskill (NY)
Stratford U (VA)
Sullivan U (KY)
The U of Akron (OH)
U of Alaska Anchorage (AK)
U of Alaska Fairbanks (AK)
The U of Montana–Missoula (MT)
U of New Hampshire (NH)
Utah Valley State Coll (UT)
Virginia Intermont Coll (VA)

Culinary Arts Related
The Art Inst of Pittsburgh (PA)
The Culinary Inst of America (NY)
Delaware Valley Coll (PA)
Lexington Coll (IL)
New York Inst of Technology (NY)
Shepherd U (WV)

Cultural Studies
Indiana Wesleyan U (IN)

Customer Service Support/Call Center/Teleservice Operation
Davenport U, Dearborn (MI)
Davenport U, Grand Rapids (MI)
Davenport U, Holland (MI)
Davenport U, Kalamazoo (MI)
Davenport U, Lansing (MI)
Davenport U, Warren (MI)
National American U–Sioux Falls Branch (SD)

Cytotechnology
Indiana U–Purdue U Indianapolis (IN)
Indiana U Southeast (IN)

Dairy Husbandry and Production
Sterling Coll (VT)

Dairy Science
State U of NY Coll of A&T at Cobleskill (NY)
U of New Hampshire (NH)
Vermont Tech Coll (VT)

Dance
New World School of the Arts (FL)
Utah Valley State Coll (UT)

Dance Related
New World School of the Arts (FL)

Data Entry/Microcomputer Applications
Baker Coll of Allen Park (MI)
Huron U USA in LondonUnited Kingdom)
National American U, Denver (CO)

Data Entry/Microcomputer Applications Related
Baker Coll of Allen Park (MI)
Huron U USA in LondonUnited Kingdom)

Data Modeling/Warehousing and Database Administration
Huron U USA in LondonUnited Kingdom)

Data Processing and Data Processing Technology
Baker Coll of Auburn Hills (MI)
Baker Coll of Cadillac (MI)
Baker Coll of Clinton Township (MI)
Baker Coll of Flint (MI)
Baker Coll of Jackson (MI)
Baker Coll of Muskegon (MI)
Baker Coll of Owosso (MI)
Baker Coll of Port Huron (MI)
British Columbia Inst of Technology (BC, Canada)
Campbellsville U (KY)
Clayton Coll & State U (GA)
Davenport U, Kalamazoo (MI)
Dordt Coll (IA)
State U of NY at Farmingdale (NY)
Five Towns Coll (NY)
Florida Metropolitan U-Orlando Coll, North (FL)
Florida Metropolitan U-Tampa Coll (FL)
Hawai'i Pacific U (HI)
Huron U USA in LondonUnited Kingdom)
Lake Superior State U (MI)
Lamar U (TX)
Lincoln U (MO)
Macon State Coll (GA)
Midway Coll (KY)
Missouri Southern State U (MO)
Montana State U–Billings (MT)
Montana Tech of The U of Montana (MT)
New York Inst of Technology (NY)
Northern Michigan U (MI)
Northern State U (SD)
Sacred Heart U (CT)
St. Francis Coll (NY)
Saint Francis U (PA)
St. John's U (NY)
Saint Peter's Coll (NJ)
State U of NY Coll of A&T at Cobleskill (NY)
Thomas More Coll (KY)
The U of Akron (OH)
U of Cincinnati (OH)
The U of Montana–Western (MT)
U of the Virgin Islands (VI)
The U of Toledo (OH)
Utah Valley State Coll (UT)
Western Kentucky U (KY)
Wright State U (OH)
Youngstown State U (OH)

Dental Assisting
Louisiana State U Health Sciences Center (LA)
U of Alaska Anchorage (AK)
The U of Maine at Augusta (ME)
U of Southern Indiana (IN)
Valdosta State U (GA)

Dental Hygiene
Argosy U/Twin Cities, Eagan (MN)
Baker Coll of Port Huron (MI)
Clayton Coll & State U (GA)
Dalton State Coll (GA)
East Tennessee State U (TN)
State U of NY at Farmingdale (NY)
Ferris State U (MI)
Indiana U Northwest (IN)
Indiana U–Purdue U Fort Wayne (IN)
Indiana U–Purdue U Indianapolis (IN)
Indiana U South Bend (IN)
Lamar U (TX)
Louisiana State U Health Sciences Center (LA)
Mass Coll of Pharmacy and Allied Health Sciences (MA)
Minnesota State U Mankato (MN)
Missouri Southern State U (MO)
Montana State U–Billings (MT)
Mount Ida Coll (MA)
New York U (NY)
Pennsylvania Coll of Technology (PA)
Shawnee State U (OH)
Southern Adventist U (TN)
Tennessee State U (TN)
U of Alaska Anchorage (AK)
U of Arkansas at Fort Smith (AR)
U of Bridgeport (CT)
U of Louisville (KY)
The U of Maine at Augusta (ME)
U of New England (ME)
U of New Haven (CT)
U of New Mexico (NM)
The U of South Dakota (SD)
U of Southern Indiana (IN)
Utah Valley State Coll (UT)
Valdosta State U (GA)
Vermont Tech Coll (VT)
Weber State U (UT)
Western Kentucky U (KY)
West Liberty State Coll (WV)
Wichita State U (KS)
Youngstown State U (OH)

Dental Laboratory Technology
Idaho State U (ID)
Indiana U–Purdue U Fort Wayne (IN)
Louisiana State U Health Sciences Center (LA)
Southern Illinois U Carbondale (IL)

Design and Applied Arts Related
The Art Inst of Seattle (WA)

Design and Visual Communications
American InterContinental U, Atlanta (GA)
The American U in DubaiUnited Arab Emirates)
The Art Inst of Pittsburgh (PA)
Champlain Coll (VT)
International Academy of Design & Technology (FL)
Pace U (NY)
Shepherd U (WV)
Wilmington Coll (DE)

Desktop Publishing and Digital Imaging Design
Davenport U, Dearborn (MI)
Davenport U, Holland (MI)
Davenport U, Kalamazoo (MI)
Davenport U, Lansing (MI)
Davenport U, Lapeer (MI)
Davenport U, Warren (MI)
Thompson Rivers U (BC, Canada)

Developmental and Child Psychology
Central Christian Coll of Kansas (KS)
Fresno Pacific U (CA)
Mitchell Coll (CT)
U of Sioux Falls (SD)
Villa Julie Coll (MD)

Diagnostic Medical Sonography and Ultrasound Technology
Argosy U/Twin Cities, Eagan (MN)
Baker Coll of Auburn Hills (MI)
Baker Coll of Owosso (MI)
Baker Coll of Port Huron (MI)
Coll of St. Catherine (MN)
Mountain State U (WV)
Nebraska Methodist Coll (NE)
New York U (NY)
Southern Alberta Inst of Technology (AB, Canada)

Diesel Mechanics Technology
British Columbia Inst of Technology (BC, Canada)
Georgia Southwestern State U (GA)
Idaho State U (ID)
Lewis-Clark State Coll (ID)
Montana State U–Billings (MT)
Pennsylvania Coll of Technology (PA)
U of Alaska Anchorage (AK)
Utah Valley State Coll (UT)
Valdosta State U (GA)
Weber State U (UT)

Dietetics
Ball State U (IN)
Faulkner U (AL)
Loma Linda U (CA)
Purdue U Calumet (IN)
Rochester Inst of Technology (NY)
U of Minnesota, Crookston (MN)
U of New Hampshire (NH)
U of Ottawa (ON, Canada)
Youngstown State U (OH)

Dietetic Technician
U of New Hampshire (NH)

Dietician Assistant
Eastern Kentucky U (KY)

Dietitian Assistant
Pacific Union Coll (CA)
Pennsylvania Coll of Technology (PA)
Penn State U Univ Park Campus (PA)
Youngstown State U (OH)

Digital Communication and Media/Multimedia
Academy of Art U (CA)
The Art Inst of Pittsburgh (PA)
The Art Insts International Minnesota (MN)
Champlain Coll (VT)
Utah Valley State Coll (UT)

Divinity/Ministry
Atlantic Union Coll (MA)
Bethany Coll of the Assemblies of God (CA)
Carson-Newman Coll (TN)
Central Christian Coll of Kansas (KS)
Clear Creek Baptist Bible Coll (KY)
Coll of Biblical Studies–Houston (TX)
Faith Baptist Bible Coll and Theological Seminary (IA)
Faulkner U (AL)
Florida Christian Coll (FL)
International Baptist Coll (AZ)
Manhattan Christian Coll (KS)

MidAmerica Nazarene U (KS)
Mount Olive Coll (NC)
North Central U (MN)
Pacific Union Coll (CA)
Warner Pacific Coll (OR)

Dog/Pet/Animal Grooming
Becker Coll (MA)

Drafting
Eastern Kentucky U (KY)
U of Arkansas at Fort Smith (AR)

Drafting and Design Technology
Baker Coll of Auburn Hills (MI)
Baker Coll of Cadillac (MI)
Baker Coll of Clinton Township (MI)
Baker Coll of Flint (MI)
Baker Coll of Muskegon (MI)
Baker Coll of Owosso (MI)
Baker Coll of Port Huron (MI)
Black Hills State U (SD)
Boise State U (ID)
British Columbia Inst of Technology (BC, Canada)
California U of Pennsylvania (PA)
Central Christian Coll of Kansas (KS)
Central Missouri State U (MO)
Clayton Coll & State U (GA)
Dalton State Coll (GA)
Eastern Kentucky U (KY)
Fairmont State U (WV)
Ferris State U (MI)
Georgia Southwestern State U (GA)
Hamilton Tech Coll (IA)
Idaho State U (ID)
Keene State Coll (NH)
Kentucky State U (KY)
Lake Superior State U (MI)
Lamar U (TX)
LeTourneau U (TX)
Lewis-Clark State Coll (ID)
Lincoln U (MO)
Missouri Southern State U (MO)
Montana State U–Billings (MT)
Montana State U–Northern (MT)
Montana Tech of The U of Montana (MT)
Murray State U (KY)
Northern Michigan U (MI)
Northern State U (SD)
Pennsylvania Coll of Technology (PA)
Saint Francis U (PA)
Southern Utah U (UT)
Thomas Edison State Coll (NJ)
Thompson Rivers U (BC, Canada)
Tri-State U (IN)
The U of Akron (OH)
U of Alaska Anchorage (AK)
U of Cincinnati (OH)
U of Rio Grande (OH)
The U of Toledo (OH)
Utah State U (UT)
Utah Valley State Coll (UT)
Weber State U (UT)
West Virginia State U (WV)
Wright State U (OH)
Youngstown State U (OH)

Drafting/Design Engineering Technologies Related
Idaho State U (ID)
Pennsylvania Coll of Technology (PA)
The U of Akron (OH)

Drama and Dance Teacher Education
Central Christian Coll of Kansas (KS)

Dramatic/Theatre Arts
Adrian Coll (MI)
Bacone Coll (OK)
Brigham Young U–Hawaii (HI)
Central Christian Coll of Kansas (KS)
Clayton Coll & State U (GA)
Five Towns Coll (NY)
Indiana U Bloomington (IN)
Macon State Coll (GA)
Martin Methodist Coll (TN)
Mesa State Coll (CO)
Methodist Coll (NC)
Murray State U (KY)
North Central U (MN)
North Greenville Coll (SC)
Thomas More Coll (KY)
Université Laval (QC, Canada)
U Coll of the Fraser Valley (BC, Canada)
U of Sioux Falls (SD)
U of Wisconsin–Green Bay (WI)
Utah Valley State Coll (UT)
Villa Julie Coll (MD)

Drawing
Academy of Art U (CA)
Central Christian Coll of Kansas (KS)
New World School of the Arts (FL)
Northern Michigan U (MI)
Pratt Inst (NY)
Sacred Heart U (CT)

Early Childhood Education
Baker Coll of Allen Park (MI)
Baker Coll of Jackson (MI)
Bethel Coll (IN)
Champlain Coll (VT)
Coll for Lifelong Learning (NH)
Coll of Saint Mary (NE)
Columbia Union Coll (MD)
Crown Coll (MN)
Indiana U–Purdue U Fort Wayne (IN)
Lancaster Bible Coll (PA)
Lindsey Wilson Coll (KY)
Mercyhurst Coll (PA)
Montana State U–Billings (MT)
Oakland City U (IN)
Point Park U (PA)
St. Augustine Coll (IL)
Thompson Rivers U (BC, Canada)
U of Great Falls (MT)
Utah Valley State Coll (UT)
Wheelock Coll (MA)
Wilmington Coll (DE)
Wilson Coll (PA)

Ecology
Paul Smith's Coll of Arts and Sciences (NY)
Sterling Coll (VT)

E-Commerce
Champlain Coll (VT)

Economics
Adrian Coll (MI)
Central Christian Coll of Kansas (KS)
Clayton Coll & State U (GA)
Dalton State Coll (GA)
Macon State Coll (GA)
Martin Methodist Coll (TN)
Methodist Coll (NC)
Richmond, The American International U in London United Kingdom)
Sacred Heart U (CT)
State U of NY Empire State Coll (NY)
Strayer U (DC)
Thomas More Coll (KY)
U of Sioux Falls (SD)
The U of Tampa (FL)
U of Wisconsin–Green Bay (WI)
Washington & Jefferson Coll (PA)

Education
Alabama State U (AL)
Bacone Coll (OK)
Baker Coll of Auburn Hills (MI)
Baker Coll of Cadillac (MI)
Central Baptist Coll (AR)
Central Christian Coll of Kansas (KS)
Cincinnati Christian U (OH)
Circleville Bible Coll (OH)
Clayton Coll & State U (GA)
Cumberland U (TN)
Dalton State Coll (GA)
Evangel U (MO)
Friends U (KS)
Kent State U (OH)
Lamar U (TX)
Lindsey Wilson Coll (KY)
Macon State Coll (GA)
Martin Methodist Coll (TN)
Medgar Evers Coll of the City U of NY (NY)
Montreat Coll (NC)
Mountain State U (WV)
Pontifical Catholic U of Puerto Rico (PR)
Reinhardt Coll (GA)
Saint Francis U (PA)
Spring Hill Coll (AL)
State U of NY Empire State Coll (NY)
U of Southern Indiana (IN)

Educational/Instructional Media Design
Bayamón Central U (PR)
Ferris State U (MI)
U of Wisconsin–Superior (WI)

Educational Leadership and Administration
Shasta Bible Coll (CA)

Education Related
Kent State U (OH)
The U of Akron (OH)
Wayland Baptist U (TX)

Education (Specific Levels and Methods) Related
Sheldon Jackson Coll (AK)

Education (Specific Subject Areas) Related
Pennsylvania Coll of Technology (PA)

Electrical and Electronic Engineering Technologies Related
Boise State U (ID)
Kent State U (OH)
Lawrence Technological U (MI)
New York Inst of Technology (NY)
Pennsylvania Coll of Technology (PA)
Southern Alberta Inst of Technology (AB, Canada)

Electrical and Power Transmission Installation
British Columbia Inst of Technology (BC, Canada)

Electrical, Electronic and Communications Engineering Technology
Andrews U (MI)
Arkansas State U (AR)
Arkansas Tech U (AR)
Baker Coll of Cadillac (MI)
Baker Coll of Muskegon (MI)
Baker Coll of Owosso (MI)
Bluefield State Coll (WV)
Boise State U (ID)
Briarcliffe Coll (NY)
British Columbia Inst of Technology (BC, Canada)
Cameron U (OK)
Capitol Coll (MD)
Clayton Coll & State U (GA)
Columbia Coll, Caguas (PR)
Dalton State Coll (GA)
DeVry Inst of Technology (NY)

DeVry U, Phoenix (AZ)
DeVry U, Fremont (CA)
DeVry U, Long Beach (CA)
DeVry U, Pomona (CA)
DeVry U, West Hills (CA)
DeVry U, Colorado Springs (CO)
DeVry U, Orlando (FL)
DeVry U, Alpharetta (GA)
DeVry U, Decatur (GA)
DeVry U, Addison (IL)
DeVry U, Chicago (IL)
DeVry U, Tinley Park (IL)
DeVry U, Kansas City (MO)
DeVry U (NJ)
DeVry U, Columbus (OH)
DeVry U, Irving (TX)
DeVry U, Arlington (VA)
DeVry U, Federal Way (WA)
Eastern Kentucky U (KY)
Excelsior Coll (NY)
Fairmont State U (WV)
Fort Valley State U (GA)
Grantham U (LA)
Hamilton Tech Coll (IA)
Idaho State U (ID)
Indiana State U (IN)
Indiana–Purdue U Fort Wayne (IN)
Indiana–Purdue U Indianapolis (IN)
Johnson & Wales U (RI)
Kansas State U (KS)
Keene State Coll (NH)
Kentucky State U (KY)
Lake Superior State U (MI)
Lamar U (TX)
Lawrence Technological U (MI)
Lincoln U (MO)
McNeese State U (LA)
Merrimack Coll (MA)
Mesa State Coll (CO)
Michigan Technological U (MI)
Missouri Western State Coll (MO)
Montana State U–Northern (MT)
Murray State U (KY)
Northern Michigan U (MI)
Northern State U (SD)
Northwestern State U of Louisiana (LA)
Ohio U (OH)
Oregon Inst of Technology (OR)
Pennsylvania Coll of Technology (PA)
Penn State U Altoona Coll (PA)
Penn State U at Erie, The Behrend Coll (PA)
Penn State U Berks Cmps of Berks-Lehigh Valley Coll (PA)
Penn State U Schuylkill Campus of the Capital Coll (PA)
Pittsburg State U (KS)
Point Park U (PA)
Purdue U (IN)
Purdue U Calumet (IN)
Rochester Inst of Technology (NY)
Shepherd U (WV)
Southern Utah U (UT)
Thomas Edison State Coll (NJ)
The U of Akron (OH)
U of Alaska Anchorage (AK)
U of Cincinnati (OH)
U of Massachusetts Lowell (MA)
The U of Montana–Missoula (MT)
U of the District of Columbia (DC)
The U of Toledo (OH)
Utah Valley State Coll (UT)
Vermont Tech Coll (VT)
Washburn U (KS)
Weber State U (UT)

Wentworth Inst of Technology (MA)
West Virginia State U (WV)
Wichita State U (KS)
Wright State U (OH)
Youngstown State U (OH)

Electrical, Electronics and Communications Engineering
Fairfield U (CT)
Macon State Coll (GA)
Thompson Rivers U (BC, Canada)

Electrical/Electronics Drafting and Cad/Cadd
Johnson & Wales U (RI)

Electrical/Electronics Equipment Installation and Repair
Georgia Southwestern State U (GA)
Idaho State U (ID)
Lewis-Clark State Coll (ID)
Thompson Rivers U (BC, Canada)
U of Arkansas at Fort Smith (AR)
Valdosta State U (GA)

Electrician
Georgia Southwestern State U (GA)
Pennsylvania Coll of Technology (PA)
Thompson Rivers U (BC, Canada)
Valdosta State U (GA)

Electromechanical and Instrumentation And Maintenance Technologies Related
Georgia Southwestern State U (GA)
Southern Alberta Inst of Technology (AB, Canada)

Electromechanical Technology
Clayton Coll & State U (GA)
Excelsior Coll (NY)
Idaho State U (ID)
Michigan Technological U (MI)
Northern Michigan U (MI)
Shawnee State U (OH)
Shepherd U (WV)
The U of Akron (OH)
U of the District of Columbia (DC)
Utah Valley State Coll (UT)
Walla Walla Coll (WA)
Wright State U (OH)

Elementary Education
Alaska Pacific U (AK)
Central Christian Coll of Kansas (KS)
Clayton Coll & State U (GA)
Dalton State Coll (GA)
God's Bible School and Coll (OH)
Hillsdale Free Will Baptist Coll (OK)
Macon State Coll (GA)
Mountain State U (WV)
New Mexico Highlands U (NM)
Utah Valley State Coll (UT)
Vennard Coll (IA)
Villa Julie Coll (MD)
Wilson Coll (PA)

Emergency Care Attendant (Emt Ambulance)
Kent State U (OH)
Southern Alberta Inst of Technology (AB, Canada)

Emergency Medical Technology (Emt Paramedic)
Arkansas State U (AR)
Baker Coll of Cadillac (MI)
Baker Coll of Clinton Township (MI)
Baker Coll of Muskegon (MI)

Ball State U (IN)
Clayton Coll & State U (GA)
Creighton U (NE)
Eastern Kentucky U (KY)
Faulkner U (AL)
Hannibal-LaGrange Coll (MO)
Idaho State U (ID)
Indiana U–Purdue U Indianapolis (IN)
Kent State U (OH)
Montana State U–Billings (MT)
Mountain State U (WV)
Nebraska Methodist Coll (NE)
Nicholls State U (LA)
Our Lady of the Lake Coll (LA)
Pennsylvania Coll of Technology (PA)
Saint Francis U (PA)
Shawnee State U (OH)
Shepherd U (WV)
Southwest Baptist U (MO)
U of Alaska Anchorage (AK)
U of Arkansas at Fort Smith (AR)
U of Pittsburgh at Johnstown (PA)
U of Saint Francis (IN)
U of the District of Columbia (DC)
The U of Toledo (OH)
Valdosta State U (GA)
Weber State U (UT)
Western Kentucky U (KY)
Youngstown State U (OH)

Energy Management and Systems Technology
Baker Coll of Flint (MI)
U of Cincinnati (OH)

Engineering
Brescia U (KY)
Briar Cliff U (IA)
Campbell U (NC)
Central Christian Coll of Kansas (KS)
Clayton Coll & State U (GA)
Coll of Staten Island of the City U of NY (NY)
Columbia Union Coll (MD)
Columbus State U (GA)
Faulkner U (AL)
Geneva Coll (PA)
Lake Superior State U (MI)
Macon State Coll (GA)
Mesa State Coll (CO)
Mitchell Coll (CT)
Montana Tech of The U of Montana (MT)
Mountain State U (WV)
Palm Beach Atlantic U (FL)
Robert Morris U (PA)
Southern Adventist U (TN)
Thompson Rivers U (BC, Canada)
Union Coll (NE)
Utah Valley State Coll (UT)
York Coll of Pennsylvania (PA)
Youngstown State U (OH)

Engineering Related
British Columbia Inst of Technology (BC, Canada)
Eastern Kentucky U (KY)
Montana State U–Billings (MT)

Engineering-Related Technologies
Southern Alberta Inst of Technology (AB, Canada)

Engineering Science
Merrimack Coll (MA)
Pennsylvania Coll of Technology (PA)
Rochester Inst of Technology (NY)
U of Cincinnati (OH)

Engineering Technologies Related
Cameron U (OK)
Kent State U (OH)
McNeese State U (LA)
Shepherd U (WV)
The U of Akron (OH)
Western Kentucky U (KY)

Engineering Technology
Andrews U (MI)
Arkansas State U (AR)
Clayton Coll & State U (GA)
Fairmont State U (WV)
John Brown U (AR)
Lake Superior State U (MI)
Macon State Coll (GA)
McNeese State U (LA)
Montana Tech of The U of Montana (MT)
New Mexico State U (NM)
New Mexico State U (NM)
Pacific Union Coll (CA)
Rochester Inst of Technology (NY)
State U of NY Coll of A&T at Cobleskill (NY)
Tri-State U (IN)
U of Alaska Anchorage (AK)
U of the District of Columbia (DC)
Valdosta State U (GA)
Vaughn Coll of Aeronautics and Technology (NY)
Vermont Tech Coll (VT)
Wentworth Inst of Technology (MA)
Youngstown State U (OH)

English
Adrian Coll (MI)
Calumet Coll of Saint Joseph (IN)
Carroll Coll (MT)
Central Christian Coll of Kansas (KS)
Central Methodist U (MO)
Clayton Coll & State U (GA)
Clearwater Christian Coll (FL)
Coll of Santa Fe (NM)
Dalton State Coll (GA)
Felician Coll (NJ)
Fresno Pacific U (CA)
Hannibal-LaGrange Coll (MO)
Hillsdale Free Will Baptist Coll (OK)
Huron U USA in London United Kingdom)
Idaho State U (ID)
Indiana U–Purdue U Fort Wayne (IN)
Indiana Wesleyan U (IN)
Kwantlen U Coll (BC, Canada)
Lourdes Coll (OH)
Macon State Coll (GA)
Madonna U (MI)
Manchester Coll (IN)
Martin Methodist Coll (TN)
Mesa State Coll (CO)
Methodist Coll (NC)
Pine Manor Coll (MA)
Richmond, The American International U in London United Kingdom)
Sacred Heart U (CT)
Siena Heights U (MI)
Thomas More Coll (KY)
Université Laval (QC, Canada)
U of Dubuque (IA)
U of Rio Grande (OH)
The U of Tampa (FL)
U of the District of Columbia (DC)
U of Wisconsin–Green Bay (WI)
Utah Valley State Coll (UT)
Xavier U (OH)

English Composition
Central Christian Coll of Kansas (KS)

Huron U USA in
LondonUnited Kingdom)
Kwantlen U Coll (BC,
Canada)

**English/Language Arts
Teacher Education**
Central Christian Coll of
Kansas (KS)
Lyndon State Coll (VT)

**English Literature (British
and Commonwealth)**
Huron U USA in
LondonUnited Kingdom)

**Entrepreneurial and Small
Business Related**
Haskell Indian Nations U
(KS)

Entrepreneurship
Baker Coll of Flint (MI)
British Columbia Inst of
Technology (BC, Canada)
Davenport U, Dearborn (MI)
Davenport U, Gaylord (MI)
Davenport U, Grand Rapids
(MI)
Davenport U, Warren (MI)
Lyndon State Coll (VT)
Northwood U (MI)
The U of Akron (OH)
U of the District of Columbia
(DC)

**Environmental Control
Technologies Related**
Kent State U (OH)
Pennsylvania Coll of
Technology (PA)

**Environmental Design/
Architecture**
Northern Michigan U (MI)

**Environmental Engineering
Technology**
Baker Coll of Flint (MI)
Baker Coll of Owosso (MI)
Baker Coll of Port Huron (MI)
Kansas State U (KS)
Mesa State Coll (CO)
New York Inst of Technology
(NY)
Ohio U (OH)
Pennsylvania Coll of
Technology (PA)
Southern Alberta Inst of
Technology (AB, Canada)
U of Cincinnati (OH)
U of the District of Columbia
(DC)
The U of Toledo (OH)
Utah Valley State Coll (UT)
Vermont Tech Coll (VT)
Wentworth Inst of
Technology (MA)

**Environmental/
Environmental Health
Engineering**
British Columbia Inst of
Technology (BC, Canada)
Ohio U (OH)

Environmental Health
British Columbia Inst of
Technology (BC, Canada)
The U of Akron (OH)

Environmental Science
Central Christian Coll of
Kansas (KS)
U of Wisconsin–Green Bay
(WI)

Environmental Studies
Central Christian Coll of
Kansas (KS)
Defiance Coll (OH)
Dickinson State U (ND)
Kent State U (OH)
Macon State Coll (GA)
Mountain State U (WV)
Paul Smith's Coll of Arts and
Sciences (NY)
Samford U (AL)
Southern Vermont Coll (VT)
State U of NY Coll of A&T at
Cobleskill (NY)

Sterling Coll (VT)
Thomas Edison State Coll
(NJ)
U of Cincinnati (OH)
U of Dubuque (IA)
The U of Findlay (OH)
U of Ottawa (ON, Canada)
The U of Toledo (OH)
U of Wisconsin–Green Bay
(WI)

Equestrian Studies
Centenary Coll (NJ)
Johnson & Wales U (RI)
Midway Coll (KY)
Murray State U (KY)
Ohio U (OH)
Post U (CT)
Saint Mary-of-the-Woods
Coll (IN)
State U of NY Coll of A&T at
Cobleskill (NY)
The U of Findlay (OH)
U of Massachusetts Amherst
(MA)
U of Minnesota, Crookston
(MN)
The U of Montana–Western
(MT)
U of New Hampshire (NH)

European History
Emmanuel Coll (GA)

European Studies
Richmond, The American
International U in
LondonUnited Kingdom)
Sacred Heart U (CT)

**Executive Assistant/
Executive Secretary**
Baker Coll of Allen Park (MI)
Baker Coll of Flint (MI)
Central Pennsylvania Coll
(PA)
Davenport U, Dearborn (MI)
Davenport U, Holland (MI)
Davenport U, Kalamazoo
(MI)
Davenport U, Lansing (MI)
Davenport U, Lapeer (MI)
Davenport U, Warren (MI)
Kentucky State U (KY)
Montana Tech of The U of
Montana (MT)
Murray State U (KY)
Robert Morris Coll (IL)
Thompson Rivers U (BC,
Canada)
The U of Akron (OH)
The U of Montana–Missoula
(MT)
Utah Valley State Coll (UT)
Western Kentucky U (KY)
Youngstown State U (OH)

**Family and Community
Services**
Baker Coll of Flint (MI)
Central Christian Coll of
Kansas (KS)
State U of NY Coll of A&T at
Cobleskill (NY)

**Family and Consumer
Economics Related**
Dalton State Coll (GA)
Fairmont State U (WV)

**Family and Consumer
Sciences/Human Sciences**
Clayton Coll & State U (GA)
Mount Vernon Nazarene U
(OH)
U of Alaska Anchorage (AK)

**Family and Consumer
Sciences/Human Sciences
Related**
Morehead State U (KY)

**Farm and Ranch
Management**
Idaho State U (ID)
Johnson & Wales U (RI)
Midway Coll (KY)
Oklahoma Panhandle State
U (OK)

Fashion/Apparel Design
Academy of Art U (CA)
American InterContinental U,
Atlanta (GA)
The Art Inst of California–
San Francisco (CA)
The Art Inst of Dallas (TX)
The Art Inst of Fort
Lauderdale (FL)
The Art Inst of Portland (OR)
The Art Inst of Seattle (WA)
California Design Coll (CA)
Cazenovia Coll (NY)
Fashion Inst of Technology
(NY)
The Illinois Inst of Art (IL)
Indiana U Bloomington (IN)
International Academy of
Design & Technology (FL)
International Acad of
Merchandising & Design,
Ltd (IL)
Miami International U of Art &
Design (FL)
Mount Ida Coll (MA)
U of the Incarnate Word (TX)

Fashion Merchandising
Academy of Art U (CA)
American InterContinental U,
Atlanta (GA)
The Art Inst of Seattle (WA)
California Design Coll (CA)
Clayton Coll & State U (GA)
Fairmont State U (WV)
International Acad of
Merchandising & Design,
Ltd (IL)
Johnson & Wales U (FL)
Johnson & Wales U (RI)
Laboratory Inst of
Merchandising (NY)
Lynn U (FL)
Miami International U of Art &
Design (FL)
Mount Ida Coll (MA)
Newbury Coll (MA)
Northwood U (MI)
Northwood U, Texas Campus
(TX)
Shepherd U (WV)
Southern New Hampshire U
(NH)
Thomas Coll (ME)
The U of Akron (OH)
U of Bridgeport (CT)
U of the District of Columbia
(DC)
U of the Incarnate Word (TX)
Weber State U (UT)
West Virginia State U (WV)

**Fiber, Textile and Weaving
Arts**
Academy of Art U (CA)

Film/Cinema Studies
Academy of Art U (CA)
Indiana U South Bend (IN)

**Film/Video and
Photographic Arts Related**
The Art Inst of Pittsburgh
(PA)
The Art Inst of Seattle (WA)
Haskell Indian Nations U
(KS)
New England School of
Communications (ME)

Finance
British Columbia Inst of
Technology (BC, Canada)
California Coll for Health
Sciences (UT)
Central Christian Coll of
Kansas (KS)
Central Pennsylvania Coll
(PA)
Chestnut Hill Coll (PA)
Clayton Coll & State U (GA)
Davenport U, Dearborn (MI)
Davenport U, Grand Rapids
(MI)
Davenport U, Warren (MI)
Fairmont State U (WV)
Hawai'i Pacific U (HI)

Indiana U South Bend (IN)
Indiana Wesleyan U (IN)
International Coll of the
Cayman IslandsCayman
Islands)
Johnson & Wales U (RI)
Marian Coll (IN)
Methodist Coll (NC)
Newbury Coll (MA)
Sacred Heart U (CT)
Saint Joseph's U (PA)
Saint Peter's Coll (NJ)
Southern Alberta Inst of
Technology (AB, Canada)
Thomas Edison State Coll
(NJ)
U of Cincinnati (OH)
Walsh U (OH)
Webber International U (FL)
West Virginia State U (WV)
Youngstown State U (OH)

**Finance and Financial
Management Services
Related**
British Columbia Inst of
Technology (BC, Canada)

**Financial Planning and
Services**
British Columbia Inst of
Technology (BC, Canada)
The U of Maine at Augusta
(ME)

Fine Arts Related
Saint Francis U (PA)
York Coll of Pennsylvania
(PA)

Fine/Studio Arts
Academy of Art U (CA)
Corcoran Coll of Art and
Design (DC)
Manchester Coll (IN)
Pace U (NY)
Pine Manor Coll (MA)
Pratt Inst (NY)
Richmond, The American
International U in
LondonUnited Kingdom)
Rochester Inst of Technology
(NY)
Sage Coll of Albany (NY)
St. Gregory's U (OK)
Thomas More Coll (KY)
The U of Maine at Augusta
(ME)
U of New Hampshire at
Manchester (NH)

**Fire Protection and Safety
Technology**
British Columbia Inst of
Technology (BC, Canada)
Eastern Kentucky U (KY)
Montana State U–Billings
(MT)
Thomas Edison State Coll
(NJ)
The U of Akron (OH)
U of Nebraska–Lincoln (NE)
U of New Haven (CT)
The U of Toledo (OH)

Fire Science
Idaho State U (ID)
Lake Superior State U (MI)
Lamar U (TX)
Lewis-Clark State Coll (ID)
Madonna U (MI)
Mountain State U (WV)
Providence Coll (RI)
U of Alaska Anchorage (AK)
U of Alaska Fairbanks (AK)
U of Cincinnati (OH)
U of the District of Columbia
(DC)
Utah Valley State Coll (UT)

Fish/Game Management
State U of NY Coll of A&T at
Cobleskill (NY)
Winona State U (MN)

**Fishing and Fisheries
Sciences And Management**
Sterling Coll (VT)

Folklore
Université Laval (QC,
Canada)

Food Preparation
The Art Inst of Pittsburgh
(PA)
Lexington Coll (IL)

Food Science
Lamar U (TX)
Macon State Coll (GA)

**Food Service and Dining
Room Management**
Lexington Coll (IL)

Food Services Technology
Purdue U Calumet (IN)
State U of NY Coll of A&T at
Cobleskill (NY)
U of the District of Columbia
(DC)

**Foodservice Systems
Administration**
Murray State U (KY)
U of New Haven (CT)

**Foods, Nutrition, and
Wellness**
Cedar Crest Coll (PA)
Eastern Kentucky U (KY)
Madonna U (MI)
Southern Adventist U (TN)
U of Maine at Presque Isle
(ME)
U of New Hampshire (NH)
U of Ottawa (ON, Canada)

**Foreign Languages and
Literatures**
Dalton State Coll (GA)

Foreign Languages Related
U of Alaska Fairbanks (AK)

**Forensic Science and
Technology**
Arkansas State U (AR)
British Columbia Inst of
Technology (BC, Canada)
U of Arkansas at Fort Smith
(AR)

Forest Engineering
Columbus State U (GA)

**Forest/Forest Resources
Management**
British Columbia Inst of
Technology (BC, Canada)
Sterling Coll (VT)
U of Maine at Presque Isle
(ME)

**Forest Resources
Production and
Management**
Sterling Coll (VT)

Forestry
Clayton Coll & State U (GA)
Columbus State U (GA)
Dalton State Coll (GA)
Paul Smith's Coll of Arts and
Sciences (NY)
Sterling Coll (VT)
Thomas Edison State Coll
(NJ)
U of Maine at Fort Kent (ME)
Winona State U (MN)

Forestry Related
Sterling Coll (VT)

Forestry Technology
British Columbia Inst of
Technology (BC, Canada)
Glenville State Coll (WV)
Michigan Technological U
(MI)
Paul Smith's Coll of Arts and
Sciences (NY)
Pennsylvania Coll of
Technology (PA)
The U of British Columbia
(BC, Canada)
U of Maine at Fort Kent (ME)
U of New Hampshire (NH)

**Forest Sciences and
Biology**
Sterling Coll (VT)

French
Adrian Coll (MI)
Chestnut Hill Coll (PA)
Clayton Coll & State U (GA)
Idaho State U (ID)
Indiana U–Purdue U Fort
Wayne (IN)
Methodist Coll (NC)
Université Laval (QC,
Canada)
U of Wisconsin–Green Bay
(WI)
Xavier U (OH)

**Funeral Service and
Mortuary Science**
Lynn U (FL)
Mount Ida Coll (MA)
Point Park U (PA)

**Furniture Design and
Manufacturing**
Rochester Inst of Technology
(NY)

General Studies
American Public U System
(WV)
Anderson U (IN)
Arkansas State U (AR)
Arkansas Tech U (AR)
Austin Peay State U (TN)
Averett U (VA)
Avila U (MO)
Bacone Coll (OK)
Black Hills State U (SD)
Brewton-Parker Coll (GA)
Calumet Coll of Saint Joseph
(IN)
Cameron U (OK)
Castleton State Coll (VT)
Central Baptist Coll (AR)
Chaminade U of Honolulu
(HI)
City U (WA)
Clearwater Christian Coll
(FL)
Coll for Lifelong Learning
(NH)
Coll of Saint Mary (NE)
Columbia Union Coll (MD)
Concordia Coll (AL)
Concordia U (MI)
Concordia U, St. Paul (MN)
Crown Coll (MN)
Dalton State Coll (GA)
Eastern Connecticut State U
(CT)
Eastern Mennonite U (VA)
Eastern New Mexico U (NM)
Finlandia U (MI)
Franciscan U of Steubenville
(OH)
Hillsdale Free Will Baptist
Coll (OK)
Hope International U (CA)
Huron U USA in
LondonUnited Kingdom)
Idaho State U (ID)
Indiana State U (IN)
Indiana U Bloomington (IN)
Indiana U East (IN)
Indiana U Kokomo (IN)
Indiana U Northwest (IN)
Indiana U of Pennsylvania
(PA)
Indiana U–Purdue U Fort
Wayne (IN)
Indiana U–Purdue U
Indianapolis (IN)
Indiana U South Bend (IN)
Indiana U Southeast (IN)
Indiana Wesleyan U (IN)
Lawrence Technological U
(MI)
Lebanon Valley Coll (PA)
Liberty U (VA)
Louisiana Tech U (LA)
Macon State Coll (GA)
McNeese State U (LA)
Messenger Coll (MO)
Monmouth U (NJ)
Morehead State U (KY)
Mount Aloysius Coll (PA)
Mount Marty Coll (SD)

General Studies

Mount Vernon Nazarene U (OH)
New Mexico State U (NM)
New York U (NY)
Nicholls State U (LA)
Northwestern State U of Louisiana (LA)
Nyack Coll (NY)
Oakland City U (IN)
Ohio Dominican U (OH)
Okanagan U Coll (BC, Canada)
Oklahoma Panhandle State U (OK)
Our Lady of the Lake Coll (LA)
Palm Beach Atlantic U (FL)
Pennsylvania Coll of Technology (PA)
Rider U (NJ)
Rochester Inst of Technology (NY)
St. Augustine Coll (IL)
Saint Joseph's Coll of Maine (ME)
Shawnee State U (OH)
Sheldon Jackson Coll (AK)
Shepherd U (WV)
Siena Heights U (MI)
Silver Lake Coll (WI)
Simpson U (CA)
South Dakota School of Mines and Technology (SD)
Southeastern Louisiana U (LA)
Southern Adventist U (TN)
Southern Arkansas U–Magnolia (AR)
Southwest Baptist U (MO)
Temple U (PA)
Toccoa Falls Coll (GA)
Trevecca Nazarene U (TN)
U of Arkansas at Fort Smith (AR)
U of Central Arkansas (AR)
U of Louisiana at Monroe (LA)
U of Maine at Fort Kent (ME)
U of Mobile (AL)
U of New Haven (CT)
U of North Florida (FL)
U of Phoenix–Hawaii Campus (HI)
U of Phoenix–Louisiana Campus (LA)
U of Phoenix–Phoenix Campus (AZ)
U of Rio Grande (OH)
The U of South Dakota (SD)
The U of Toledo (OH)
Utah State U (UT)
Utah Valley State Coll (UT)
Vennard Coll (IA)
Virginia Intermont Coll (VA)
Warner Southern Coll (FL)
Western Kentucky U (KY)
Wilmington Coll (DE)
Woodbury Coll (VT)

Geography

Dalton State Coll (GA)
Kwantlen U Coll (BC, Canada)
Université Laval (QC, Canada)
The U of Tampa (FL)
Wright State U (OH)

Geological and Earth Sciences/Geosciences Related

Kwantlen U Coll (BC, Canada)

Geology/Earth Science

Adrian Coll (MI)
Clayton Coll & State U (GA)
Dalton State Coll (GA)
Idaho State U (ID)
Indiana U East (IN)
Mesa State Coll (CO)
U of Wisconsin–Green Bay (WI)

Geophysics and Seismology

U of Ottawa (ON, Canada)

German

Adrian Coll (MI)
Idaho State U (ID)
Indiana U–Purdue U Fort Wayne (IN)
Methodist Coll (NC)
Xavier U (OH)

Germanic Languages

U of Wisconsin–Green Bay (WI)

Gerontology

Coll of Mount St. Joseph (OH)
King's Coll (PA)
Madonna U (MI)
Manchester Coll (IN)
Millersville U of Pennsylvania (PA)
Ohio Dominican U (OH)
Pontifical Catholic U of Puerto Rico (PR)
Siena Heights U (MI)
Thomas More Coll (KY)
The U of Toledo (OH)
West Virginia State U (WV)
Winona State U (MN)

Graphic and Printing Equipment Operation/Production

Ball State U (IN)
Chowan Coll (NC)
Fairmont State U (WV)
Ferris State U (MI)
Idaho State U (ID)
Lewis-Clark State Coll (ID)
Murray State U (KY)
Pacific Union Coll (CA)
Pennsylvania Coll of Technology (PA)
U of the District of Columbia (DC)

Graphic Communications

Academy of Art U (CA)
New England School of Communications (ME)

Graphic Communications Related

The Art Insts International Minnesota (MN)

Graphic Design

Academy of Art U (CA)
Art Academy of Cincinnati (OH)
The Art Inst of California–Orange County (CA)
The Art Inst of California–San Diego (CA)
The Art Inst of Pittsburgh (PA)
The Art Inst of Portland (OR)
The Art Inst of Seattle (WA)
The Art Insts International Minnesota (MN)
Becker Coll (MA)
Champlain Coll (VT)
Coll of Mount St. Joseph (OH)
Corcoran Coll of Art and Design (DC)
New World School of the Arts (FL)
Pratt Inst (NY)
Rochester Inst of Technology (NY)
Thompson Rivers U (BC, Canada)
Union Coll (NE)
Utah Valley State Coll (UT)

Graphic/Printing Equipment

Eastern Kentucky U (KY)

Greenhouse Management

Sterling Coll (VT)

Hazardous Materials Information Systems Technology

Ohio U (OH)

Hazardous Materials Management and Waste Technology

Ohio U (OH)

Health and Medical Administrative Services Related

British Columbia Inst of Technology (BC, Canada)
Kent State U (OH)
The U of Akron (OH)

Health and Physical Education

Bethel Coll (IN)
Central Christian Coll of Kansas (KS)
Haskell Indian Nations U (KS)
Mount Vernon Nazarene U (OH)
Robert Morris Coll (IL)
Utah Valley State Coll (UT)

Health and Physical Education Related

Pennsylvania Coll of Technology (PA)

Health/Health Care Administration

Baker Coll of Auburn Hills (MI)
Baker Coll of Flint (MI)
Baker Coll of Muskegon (MI)
British Columbia Inst of Technology (BC, Canada)
Cabarrus Coll of Health Sciences (NC)
Chestnut Hill Coll (PA)
Madonna U (MI)
Martin Methodist Coll (TN)
Methodist Coll (NC)
National American U, Denver (CO)
New York U (NY)
Point Park U (PA)
Saint Joseph's U (PA)
Southeastern U (DC)
The U of Scranton (PA)

Health Information/Medical Records Administration

Baker Coll of Auburn Hills (MI)
Baker Coll of Cadillac (MI)
Baker Coll of Clinton Township (MI)
Baker Coll of Flint (MI)
Baker Coll of Jackson (MI)
Baker Coll of Port Huron (MI)
Boise State U (ID)
California Coll for Health Sciences (UT)
Charles R. Drew U of Medicine and Science (CA)
Clayton Coll & State U (GA)
Coll of Saint Mary (NE)
Dakota State U (SD)
Dalton State Coll (GA)
Davenport U, Kalamazoo (MI)
Davenport U, Warren (MI)
Eastern Kentucky U (KY)
Fairmont State U (WV)
Faulkner U (AL)
Ferris State U (MI)
Gwynedd-Mercy Coll (PA)
Indiana U Northwest (IN)
Inter American U of PR, San Germán Campus (PR)
Montana State U–Billings (MT)
Park U (MO)
Pennsylvania Coll of Technology (PA)
Southern Alberta Inst of Technology (AB, Canada)
Universidad Adventista de las Antillas (PR)
Washburn U (KS)

Health Information/Medical Records Technology

Baker Coll of Flint (MI)
Baker Coll of Jackson (MI)
Coll of St. Catherine (MN)
Davenport U, Dearborn (MI)
Davenport U, Holland (MI)
Davenport U, Lapeer (MI)
Davenport U, Warren (MI)

Eastern Kentucky U (KY)
Gwynedd-Mercy Coll (PA)
Idaho State U (ID)
International Coll (FL)
Louisiana Tech U (LA)
Macon State Coll (GA)
Missouri Western State Coll (MO)
Molloy Coll (NY)
New York U (NY)
Weber State U (UT)
Western Kentucky U (KY)

Health/Medical Preparatory Programs Related

Emmanuel Coll (GA)
Union Coll (NE)

Health Professions Related

British Columbia Inst of Technology (BC, Canada)
East Tennessee State U (TN)
Howard Payne U (TX)
Lock Haven U of Pennsylvania (PA)

Health Science

California Coll for Health Sciences (UT)
Covenant Coll (GA)
Howard Payne U (TX)
Macon State Coll (GA)
Martin Methodist Coll (TN)
Newman U (KS)
Northwest U (WA)
South U (AL)
Union Coll (NE)

Health Services/Allied Health/Health Sciences

Central Christian Coll of Kansas (KS)
Lindsey Wilson Coll (KY)
National American U, Denver (CO)

Health Teacher Education

Central Christian Coll of Kansas (KS)
Clayton Coll & State U (GA)
Martin Methodist Coll (TN)

Heating, Air Conditioning and Refrigeration Technology

Central Missouri State U (MO)
Pennsylvania Coll of Technology (PA)

Heating, Air Conditioning, Ventilation and Refrigeration Maintenance Technology

Boise State U (ID)
British Columbia Inst of Technology (BC, Canada)
Ferris State U (MI)
Georgia Southwestern State U (GA)
Lamar U (TX)
Lewis-Clark State Coll (ID)
Montana State U–Billings (MT)
Northern Michigan U (MI)
Oakland City U (IN)
U of Alaska Anchorage (AK)
U of Cincinnati (OH)
Utah Valley State Coll (UT)
Valdosta State U (GA)

Heavy Equipment Maintenance Technology

British Columbia Inst of Technology (BC, Canada)
Ferris State U (MI)
Georgia Southwestern State U (GA)
Mesa State Coll (CO)
Montana State U–Northern (MT)
Pennsylvania Coll of Technology (PA)
U of Alaska Anchorage (AK)
The U of Montana–Missoula (MT)
Valdosta State U (GA)

Heavy/Industrial Equipment Maintenance Technologies Related

Pennsylvania Coll of Technology (PA)

Hebrew

North Central U (MN)

Histologic Technology/Histotechnologist

Argosy U/Twin Cities, Eagan (MN)

History

Adrian Coll (MI)
Bacone Coll (OK)
Central Christian Coll of Kansas (KS)
Dalton State Coll (GA)
Felician Coll (NJ)
Fresno Pacific U (CA)
Idaho State U (ID)
Indiana U East (IN)
Indiana U–Purdue U Fort Wayne (IN)
Indiana Wesleyan U (IN)
Kwantlen U Coll (BC, Canada)
Lindsey Wilson Coll (KY)
Lourdes Coll (OH)
Macon State Coll (GA)
Marian Coll (IN)
Martin Methodist Coll (TN)
Methodist Coll (NC)
Millersville U of Pennsylvania (PA)
North Central U (MN)
Pine Manor Coll (MA)
Richmond, The American International U in London United Kingdom)
Sacred Heart U (CT)
Saint Joseph's Coll of Maine (ME)
State U of NY Empire State Coll (NY)
Thomas More Coll (KY)
U of Rio Grande (OH)
The U of Tampa (FL)
U of the District of Columbia (DC)
U of Wisconsin–Green Bay (WI)
Villa Julie Coll (MD)
Wright State U (OH)
Xavier U (OH)

History of Philosophy

Martin Methodist Coll (TN)

History Teacher Education

Central Christian Coll of Kansas (KS)

Home Furnishings

Eastern Kentucky U (KY)

Home Furnishings and Equipment Installation

Eastern Kentucky U (KY)

Horticultural Science

Andrews U (MI)
Bacone Coll (OK)
Boise State U (ID)
Eastern Kentucky U (KY)
Murray State U (KY)
State U of NY Coll of A&T at Cobleskill (NY)
Thomas Edison State Coll (NJ)
U of Connecticut (CT)
U of Minnesota, Crookston (MN)
U of New Hampshire (NH)
Vermont Tech Coll (VT)

Hospitality Administration

The Art Inst of Pittsburgh (PA)
Baker Coll of Flint (MI)
Baker Coll of Owosso (MI)
Champlain Coll (VT)
Indiana U–Purdue U Fort Wayne (IN)
Johnson & Wales U (FL)
Kendall Coll (IL)
Lewis-Clark State Coll (ID)
Lexington Coll (IL)

National American U, Albuquerque (NM)
Paul Smith's Coll of Arts and Sciences (NY)
Siena Heights U (MI)
The U of Akron (OH)
U of Alaska Southeast (AK)
U of Minnesota, Crookston (MN)
U of the District of Columbia (DC)
Utah Valley State Coll (UT)
Washburn U (KS)
Youngstown State U (OH)

Hospitality Administration Related

The Art Inst of Pittsburgh (PA)
Champlain Coll (VT)
Lexington Coll (IL)
Mountain State U (WV)
Penn State U Berks Cmps of Berks-Lehigh Valley Coll (PA)
Penn State U Univ Park Campus (PA)
Purdue U (IN)

Hospitality and Recreation Marketing

Champlain Coll (VT)
Thompson Rivers U (BC, Canada)
The U of Akron (OH)

Hotel/Motel Administration

The Art Inst of Pittsburgh (PA)
Baker Coll of Muskegon (MI)
Baker Coll of Owosso (MI)
Baker Coll of Port Huron (MI)
Bluefield State Coll (WV)
Central Pennsylvania Coll (PA)
Champlain Coll (VT)
Indiana U–Purdue U Indianapolis (IN)
International Coll of the Cayman Islands Cayman Islands)
Johnson & Wales U (FL)
Johnson & Wales U (RI)
Kendall Coll (IL)
Lexington Coll (IL)
Mercyhurst Coll (PA)
Mesa State Coll (CO)
Mount Ida Coll (MA)
National American U, Colorado Springs (CO)
National American U, Albuquerque (NM)
Newbury Coll (MA)
Northwood U (MI)
Northwood U, Florida Campus (FL)
Northwood U, Texas Campus (TX)
Paul Smith's Coll of Arts and Sciences (NY)
Purdue U Calumet (IN)
Rochester Inst of Technology (NY)
Southern Alberta Inst of Technology (AB, Canada)
State U of NY Coll of A&T at Cobleskill (NY)
Stratford U (VA)
Sullivan U (KY)
Thomas Edison State Coll (NJ)
Thompson Rivers U (BC, Canada)
The U of Akron (OH)
U of Minnesota, Crookston (MN)
U of the Virgin Islands (VI)
Webber International U (FL)
West Virginia State U (WV)
Youngstown State U (OH)

Human Development and Family Studies

Mitchell Coll (CT)
Penn State U Altoona Coll (PA)

Penn State U Schuylkill Campus of the Capital Coll (PA)
Penn State U Univ Park Campus (PA)
State U of NY Empire State Coll (NY)

Human Development and Family Studies Related
The U of Toledo (OH)
Utah State U (UT)

Human Ecology
Sterling Coll (VT)

Humanities
Bacone Coll (OK)
Central Christian Coll of Kansas (KS)
Faulkner U (AL)
Felician Coll (NJ)
Huron U USA in LondonUnited Kingdom)
Immaculata U (PA)
Macon State Coll (GA)
Martin Methodist Coll (TN)
Mesa State Coll (CO)
Michigan Technological U (MI)
Montana State U–Northern (MT)
Newbury Coll (MA)
Ohio U (OH)
Sage Coll of Albany (NY)
St. Gregory's U (OK)
Saint Peter's Coll (NJ)
Shawnee State U (OH)
State U of NY Empire State Coll (NY)
U of Cincinnati (OH)
The U of Findlay (OH)
U of Sioux Falls (SD)
U of Wisconsin–Green Bay (WI)
Utah Valley State Coll (UT)
Villa Julie Coll (MD)
Washburn U (KS)
Wichita State U (KS)

Human Resources Management
Baker Coll of Owosso (MI)
British Columbia Inst of Technology (BC, Canada)
Central Christian Coll of Kansas (KS)
Chestnut Hill Coll (PA)
King's Coll (PA)
Montana State U–Billings (MT)
Montana Tech of The U of Montana (MT)
Thomas Edison State Coll (NJ)
The U of Findlay (OH)
The U of Montana–Western (MT)
U of Richmond (VA)
Urbana U (OH)

Human Resources Management and Services Related
Becker Coll (MA)
Concordia U Coll of Alberta (AB, Canada)

Human Services
Adrian Coll (MI)
Baker Coll of Clinton Township (MI)
Baker Coll of Flint (MI)
Baker Coll of Muskegon (MI)
Beacon Coll (FL)
Champlain Coll (VT)
Chestnut Hill Coll (PA)
Coll of Saint Mary (NE)
Grace Bible Coll (MI)
Hilbert Coll (NY)
Indiana U East (IN)
Indiana U–Purdue U Fort Wayne (IN)
Kendall Coll (IL)
Kent State U (OH)
Kent State U (OH)
La Sierra U (CA)
Martin Methodist Coll (TN)

Mercy Coll (NY)
Merrimack Coll (MA)
Metropolitan Coll of New York (NY)
Mitchell Coll (CT)
Mount Vernon Nazarene U (OH)
Mount Vernon Nazarene U (OH)
New York U (NY)
Northern Kentucky U (KY)
Ohio U (OH)
Sheldon Jackson Coll (AK)
Southern Vermont Coll (VT)
State U of NY Empire State Coll (NY)
U of Alaska Anchorage (AK)
U of Cincinnati (OH)
U of Great Falls (MT)
The U of Maine at Augusta (ME)
U of Maine at Fort Kent (ME)
U of Saint Francis (IN)
The U of Scranton (PA)
Walsh U (OH)

Hydrology and Water Resources Science
Lake Superior State U (MI)
Montana State U–Northern (MT)
U of the District of Columbia (DC)

Illustration
Academy of Art U (CA)
The Art Inst of Pittsburgh (PA)
Becker Coll (MA)
Pratt Inst (NY)

Industrial Arts
Austin Peay State U (TN)
Dalton State Coll (GA)
Eastern Kentucky U (KY)
U of Cincinnati (OH)
The U of Montana–Missoula (MT)
Weber State U (UT)

Industrial Design
Academy of Art U (CA)
The Art Inst of Pittsburgh (PA)
The Art Inst of Seattle (WA)
Ferris State U (MI)
Northern Michigan U (MI)
Oakland City U (IN)
Rochester Inst of Technology (NY)
Wentworth Inst of Technology (MA)

Industrial Electronics Technology
Dalton State Coll (GA)
Lewis-Clark State Coll (ID)
Pennsylvania Coll of Technology (PA)
Thompson Rivers U (BC, Canada)

Industrial Engineering
The U of Toledo (OH)

Industrial Mechanics and Maintenance Technology
Arkansas Tech U (AR)
British Columbia Inst of Technology (BC, Canada)
Dalton State Coll (GA)
Pennsylvania Coll of Technology (PA)
Valdosta State U (GA)

Industrial Production Technologies Related
Fashion Inst of Technology (NY)
Kent State U (OH)
Pennsylvania Coll of Technology (PA)
U of Nebraska–Lincoln (NE)

Industrial Radiologic Technology
Baker Coll of Owosso (MI)
Ball State U (IN)
Boise State U (ID)
Faulkner U (AL)

Ferris State U (MI)
Fort Hays State U (KS)
The George Washington U (DC)
Inter American U of PR, San Germán Campus (PR)
Lamar U (TX)
Mesa State Coll (CO)
Northern Kentucky U (KY)
Our Lady of the Lake Coll (LA)
U of Cincinnati (OH)
U of the District of Columbia (DC)
Washburn U (KS)
Widener U (PA)

Industrial Technology
Baker Coll of Muskegon (MI)
Ball State U (IN)
British Columbia Inst of Technology (BC, Canada)
Cameron U (OK)
Central Missouri State U (MO)
Dalton State Coll (GA)
Eastern Kentucky U (KY)
Edinboro U of Pennsylvania (PA)
Excelsior Coll (NY)
Fairmont State U (WV)
Ferris State U (MI)
Indiana U–Purdue U Fort Wayne (IN)
Kansas State U (KS)
Keene State Coll (NH)
Kent State U (OH)
Mesa State Coll (CO)
Millersville U of Pennsylvania (PA)
Montana State U–Northern (MT)
Morehead State U (KY)
Murray State U (KY)
Northern Michigan U (MI)
Oklahoma Panhandle State U (OK)
Pennsylvania Coll of Technology (PA)
Purdue U Calumet (IN)
Southeastern Louisiana U (LA)
Southern Alberta Inst of Technology (AB, Canada)
Southern Arkansas U–Magnolia (AR)
Thomas Edison State Coll (NJ)
Tri-State U (IN)
The U of Akron (OH)
U of Alaska Fairbanks (AK)
U of Arkansas at Pine Bluff (AR)
U of Cincinnati (OH)
U of New Haven (CT)
U of Rio Grande (OH)
The U of Toledo (OH)
Weber State U (UT)
Wentworth Inst of Technology (MA)
Wright State U (OH)

Information Science/Studies
Albertus Magnus Coll (CT)
Alvernia Coll (PA)
Arkansas Tech U (AR)
Baker Coll of Cadillac (MI)
Baker Coll of Clinton Township (MI)
Baker Coll of Flint (MI)
Baker Coll of Jackson (MI)
Baker Coll of Muskegon (MI)
Baker Coll of Owosso (MI)
Baker Coll of Port Huron (MI)
Ball State U (IN)
Briarcliffe Coll (NY)
British Columbia Inst of Technology (BC, Canada)
Calumet Coll of Saint Joseph (IN)
Campbellsville U (KY)
Central Pennsylvania Coll (PA)
Champlain Coll (VT)
Clayton Coll & State U (GA)

Coll of St. Joseph (VT)
Dakota State U (SD)
Dalton State Coll (GA)
DeVry U, Colorado Springs (CO)
DeVry U (NJ)
Fairmont State U (WV)
State U of NY at Farmingdale (NY)
Faulkner U (AL)
Goldey-Beacom Coll (DE)
Grantham U (LA)
Huron U USA in LondonUnited Kingdom)
Husson Coll (ME)
Indiana Inst of Technology (IN)
Jones Coll, Jacksonville (FL)
Limestone Coll (SC)
Macon State Coll (GA)
Mansfield U of Pennsylvania (PA)
Missouri Southern State U (MO)
Montana State U–Northern (MT)
Mountain State U (WV)
Mount Olive Coll (NC)
Murray State U (KY)
National American U, Colorado Springs (CO)
National American U, Denver (CO)
National American U, Albuquerque (NM)
National American U, Rapid City (SD)
National American U–Sioux Falls Branch (SD)
Newman U (KS)
Oakland City U (IN)
Oklahoma Panhandle State U (OK)
Oklahoma Wesleyan U (OK)
Pacific Union Coll (CA)
Penn State U Altoona Coll (PA)
Penn State U Berks Cmps of Berks-Lehigh Valley Coll (PA)
Penn State U Lehigh Valley Cmps of Berks-Lehigh Valley Coll (PA)
Penn State U Schuylkill Campus of the Capital Coll (PA)
Richmond, The American International U in LondonUnited Kingdom)
Rivier Coll (NH)
Saint Peter's Coll (NJ)
Shepherd U (WV)
Siena Heights U (MI)
Southeastern U (DC)
Southern New Hampshire U (NH)
Southern Utah U (UT)
South U (AL)
South U (GA)
State U of NY Coll of A&T at Cobleskill (NY)
Strayer U (DC)
Trevecca Nazarene U (TN)
Tulane U (LA)
Union Coll (NE)
U of Alaska Anchorage (AK)
U of Cincinnati (OH)
U of Indianapolis (IN)
U of Minnesota, Crookston (MN)
The U of Montana–Western (MT)
U of Pittsburgh at Bradford (PA)
The U of Scranton (PA)
The U of Tampa (FL)
The U of Toledo (OH)
U of Wisconsin–Green Bay (WI)
Villa Julie Coll (MD)
Washburn U (KS)
Weber State U (UT)
Western Governors U (UT)
Youngstown State U (OH)

Information Technology
Huron U USA in LondonUnited Kingdom)
Indiana Inst of Technology (IN)
International Acad of Merchandising & Design, Ltd (IL)
International Coll (FL)
McNeese State U (LA)
National American U, Denver (CO)
National American U–Sioux Falls Branch (SD)
Pennsylvania Coll of Technology (PA)
Point Park U (PA)
South U (GA)
U of Massachusetts Lowell (MA)
Western Governors U (UT)

Institutional Food Workers
The Art Inst of Pittsburgh (PA)
Fairmont State U (WV)
Kendall Coll (IL)
Lexington Coll (IL)
Pennsylvania Coll of Technology (PA)
State U of NY Coll of A&T at Cobleskill (NY)

Instrumentation Technology
Clayton Coll & State U (GA)
Idaho State U (ID)
McNeese State U (LA)
Pennsylvania Coll of Technology (PA)

Insurance
Mercyhurst Coll (PA)
Thomas Edison State Coll (NJ)
Université Laval (QC, Canada)
U of Cincinnati (OH)

Interdisciplinary Studies
Bluefield State Coll (WV)
Cardinal Stritch U (WI)
Central Methodist U (MO)
Coll of Mount Saint Vincent (NY)
Friends U (KS)
Heritage U (WA)
Hillsdale Free Will Baptist Coll (OK)
Kansas State U (KS)
Montana State U–Northern (MT)
Mountain State U (WV)
North Central U (MN)
Northwest U (WA)
Ohio Dominican U (OH)
State U of NY Empire State Coll (NY)
Suffolk U (MA)
Tabor Coll (KS)
Unity Coll (ME)
The U of Akron (OH)
U of Sioux Falls (SD)
U of Wisconsin–Green Bay (WI)
Villa Julie Coll (MD)

Interior Architecture
Fashion Inst of Technology (NY)
U of New Haven (CT)
Watkins Coll of Art and Design (TN)

Interior Design
Academy of Art U (CA)
American InterContinental U, Atlanta (GA)
The American U in DubaiUnited Arab Emirates)
The Art Inst of Dallas (TX)
The Art Inst of Houston (TX)
The Art Inst of Pittsburgh (PA)
The Art Inst of Portland (OR)
The Art Inst of Seattle (WA)
The Art Insts International Minnesota (MN)

Baker Coll
Baker Coll of Allen Park (MI)
Baker Coll of Auburn Hills (MI)
Baker Coll of Clinton Township (MI)
Baker Coll of Flint (MI)
Baker Coll of Muskegon (MI)
Baker Coll of Owosso (MI)
Baker Coll of Port Huron (MI)
Becker Coll (MA)
British Columbia Inst of Technology (BC, Canada)
Chaminade U of Honolulu (HI)
Coll of Mount St. Joseph (OH)
Corcoran Coll of Art and Design (DC)
Eastern Kentucky U (KY)
Fairmont State U (WV)
Harrington Coll of Design (IL)
The Illinois Inst of Art (IL)
Indiana U–Purdue U Fort Wayne (IN)
International Academy of Design & Technology (FL)
International Acad of Merchandising & Design, Ltd (IL)
Marian Coll (IN)
Martin Methodist Coll (TN)
Miami International U of Art & Design (FL)
Newbury Coll (MA)
New York School of Interior Design (NY)
Robert Morris Coll (IL)
Rochester Inst of Technology (NY)
Sage Coll of Albany (NY)
Southern Utah U (UT)
U of the Incarnate Word (TX)
Watkins Coll of Art and Design (TN)
Weber State U (UT)
Wentworth Inst of Technology (MA)

Intermedia/Multimedia
The Art Inst of Atlanta (GA)
The Art Inst of California–Los Angeles (CA)
The Art Inst of Colorado (CO)
The Art Inst of Houston (TX)
The Art Inst of Pittsburgh (PA)
The Art Inst of Portland (OR)
The Art Inst of Seattle (WA)
The Art Insts International Minnesota (MN)
Champlain Coll (VT)
International Academy of Design & Technology (FL)
International Acad of Merchandising & Design, Ltd (IL)
New England School of Communications (ME)
New World School of the Arts (FL)
Robert Morris Coll (IL)

International Business/Trade/Commerce
The American U of Romeltaly)
British Columbia Inst of Technology (BC, Canada)
Champlain Coll (VT)
Northwood U (MI)
Northwood U, Florida Campus (FL)
Richmond, The American International U in LondonUnited Kingdom)
Saint Peter's Coll (NJ)
Schiller International U (FL)
Schiller International UFrance)
Schiller International UGermany)
Schiller International USpain)
Schiller International UUnited Kingdom)

International Business/Trade/Commerce

Southern New Hampshire U (NH)
State U of NY Coll of A&T at Cobleskill (NY)
Thomas Edison State Coll (NJ)
U of Saint Francis (IN)
Webber International U (FL)

International Relations and Affairs
Richmond, The American International U in London United Kingdom)
Thomas More Coll (KY)

Italian
Immaculata U (PA)

Italian Studies
John Cabot U Italy)

Japanese
Winona State U (MN)

Jazz/Jazz Studies
Five Towns Coll (NY)
Indiana U South Bend (IN)
Southern U and A&M Coll (LA)
Université Laval (QC, Canada)

Journalism
Bacone Coll (OK)
Ball State U (IN)
Bethel Coll (IN)
Central Christian Coll of Kansas (KS)
Clayton Coll & State U (GA)
Creighton U (NE)
Dalton State Coll (GA)
Evangel U (MO)
Indiana U Southeast (IN)
John Brown U (AR)
Macon State Coll (GA)
Madonna U (MI)
Manchester Coll (IN)
North Central U (MN)
Villa Julie Coll (MD)

Kindergarten/Preschool Education
Atlantic Union Coll (MA)
Baker Coll of Clinton Township (MI)
Baker Coll of Muskegon (MI)
Baker Coll of Owosso (MI)
Becker Coll (MA)
Bethany Coll of the Assemblies of God (CA)
Bethel Coll (IN)
California Coll for Health Sciences (UT)
California U of Pennsylvania (PA)
Central Christian Coll of Kansas (KS)
Champlain Coll (VT)
Clayton Coll & State U (GA)
Coll of Mount St. Joseph (OH)
Crown Coll (MN)
Edinboro U of Pennsylvania (PA)
Friends U (KS)
Heritage U (WA)
Hope International U (CA)
Indiana U–Purdue U Indianapolis (IN)
Indiana U South Bend (IN)
Johnson Bible Coll (TN)
Keene State Coll (NH)
Kendall Coll (IL)
Lake Superior State U (MI)
Lourdes Coll (OH)
Lynn U (FL)
Manchester Coll (IN)
Maranatha Baptist Bible Coll (WI)
Marian Coll (IN)
Martin Methodist Coll (TN)
Marygrove Coll (MI)
McNeese State U (LA)
Mesa State Coll (CO)
Midland Lutheran Coll (NE)
Mitchell Coll (CT)
Mount Aloysius Coll (PA)

Mount Ida Coll (MA)
Mount St. Mary's Coll (CA)
Nova Southeastern U (FL)
Pacific Union Coll (CA)
Purdue U Calumet (IN)
Rivier Coll (NH)
Rust Coll (MS)
State U of NY Coll of A&T at Cobleskill (NY)
Taylor U (IN)
Tennessee State U (TN)
U of Alaska Fairbanks (AK)
U of Alaska Southeast (AK)
U of Arkansas at Pine Bluff (AR)
U of Great Falls (MT)
The U of Montana–Western (MT)
U of Rio Grande (OH)
U of Sioux Falls (SD)
Valley Forge Christian Coll (PA)
Villa Julie Coll (MD)
Washburn U (KS)
Western Kentucky U (KY)
Wilmington Coll (DE)

Kinesiology and Exercise Science
Atlantic Union Coll (MA)
Manchester Coll (IN)
Thomas More Coll (KY)

Labor and Industrial Relations
Indiana U Bloomington (IN)
Indiana U Kokomo (IN)
Indiana U Northwest (IN)
Indiana U–Purdue U Indianapolis (IN)
Indiana U South Bend (IN)
Indiana U Southeast (IN)
Providence Coll (RI)
State U of NY Empire State Coll (NY)
Université Laval (QC, Canada)
The U of Akron (OH)
Youngstown State U (OH)

Labor Studies
Indiana U–Purdue U Fort Wayne (IN)

Landscape Architecture
Eastern Kentucky U (KY)
State U of NY Coll of A&T at Cobleskill (NY)
U of New Hampshire (NH)

Landscaping and Groundskeeping
State U of NY at Farmingdale (NY)
North Carolina State U (NC)
State U of NY Coll of A&T at Cobleskill (NY)
U of Massachusetts Amherst (MA)
U of New Hampshire (NH)
Vermont Tech Coll (VT)

Laser and Optical Technology
Capitol Coll (MD)
Excelsior Coll (NY)
Idaho State U (ID)
Indiana U Bloomington (IN)
Pacific Union Coll (CA)
Pennsylvania Coll of Technology (PA)

Latin
Idaho State U (ID)

Latin American Studies
U Coll of the Fraser Valley (BC, Canada)

Legal Administrative Assistant/Secretary
Baker Coll of Auburn Hills (MI)
Baker Coll of Clinton Township (MI)
Baker Coll of Flint (MI)
Baker Coll of Jackson (MI)
Baker Coll of Muskegon (MI)
Baker Coll of Owosso (MI)
Baker Coll of Port Huron (MI)

Ball State U (IN)
Central Pennsylvania Coll (PA)
Clarion U of Pennsylvania (PA)
Clayton Coll & State U (GA)
Davenport U, Dearborn (MI)
Davenport U, Kalamazoo (MI)
David N. Myers U (OH)
Dordt Coll (IA)
Ferris State U (MI)
Johnson & Wales U (RI)
Lamar U (TX)
Lewis-Clark State Coll (ID)
Martin Methodist Coll (TN)
Mesa State Coll (CO)
Midland Lutheran Coll (NE)
Montana State U–Billings (MT)
Montana Tech of The U of Montana (MT)
Mountain State U (WV)
Northern Michigan U (MI)
Pacific Union Coll (CA)
Peirce Coll (PA)
Robert Morris Coll (IL)
Shawnee State U (OH)
Southern Alberta Inst of Technology (AB, Canada)
Sullivan U (KY)
Thomas Coll (ME)
The U of Akron (OH)
U of Cincinnati (OH)
U of Detroit Mercy (MI)
The U of Montana–Missoula (MT)
U of Richmond (VA)
U of Rio Grande (OH)
U of the District of Columbia (DC)
The U of Toledo (OH)
Washburn U (KS)
Wright State U (OH)
Youngstown State U (OH)

Legal Assistant/Paralegal
Anna Maria Coll (MA)
Atlantic Union Coll (MA)
Ball State U (IN)
Becker Coll (MA)
Bluefield State Coll (WV)
Boise State U (ID)
Briarcliffe Coll (NY)
Central Pennsylvania Coll (PA)
Champlain Coll (VT)
Clayton Coll & State U (GA)
Coll of Mount St. Joseph (OH)
Coll of Saint Mary (NE)
Davenport U, Grand Rapids (MI)
Davenport U, Kalamazoo (MI)
David N. Myers U (OH)
Eastern Kentucky U (KY)
Faulkner U (AL)
Ferris State U (MI)
Florida Metropolitan U–Tampa Coll, Brandon (FL)
Florida Metropolitan U–Orlando Coll, North (FL)
Florida Metropolitan U–Orlando Coll, South (FL)
Florida Metropolitan U–Tampa Coll (FL)
Gannon U (PA)
Grambling State U (LA)
Hilbert Coll (NY)
Husson Coll (ME)
Indiana U South Bend (IN)
International Coll (FL)
Johnson & Wales U (RI)
Jones Coll, Jacksonville (FL)
Kent State U (OH)
Lake Superior State U (MI)
Lewis-Clark State Coll (ID)
Madonna U (MI)
Marywood U (PA)
McNeese State U (LA)
Merrimack Coll (MA)
Missouri Western State Coll (MO)

Mountain State U (WV)
Mount Aloysius Coll (PA)
National American U, Rapid City (SD)
National American U–Sioux Falls Branch (SD)
Newbury Coll (MA)
Nicholls State U (LA)
Peirce Coll (PA)
Pennsylvania Coll of Technology (PA)
Post U (CT)
Robert Morris Coll (IL)
Sage Coll of Albany (NY)
St. John's U (NY)
Saint Mary-of-the-Woods Coll (IN)
Shawnee State U (OH)
Shepherd U (WV)
South U (AL)
South U (GA)
Suffolk U (MA)
Sullivan U (KY)
Thomas Coll (ME)
Thomas Edison State Coll (NJ)
Tulane U (LA)
The U of Akron (OH)
U of Alaska Anchorage (AK)
U of Alaska Fairbanks (AK)
U of Alaska Southeast (AK)
U of Arkansas at Fort Smith (AR)
U of Cincinnati (OH)
U of Great Falls (MT)
U of Hartford (CT)
U of Indianapolis (IN)
U of Louisville (KY)
The U of Montana–Missoula (MT)
The U of Toledo (OH)
U of West Florida (FL)
Utah Valley State Coll (UT)
Villa Julie Coll (MD)
Washburn U (KS)
Wesley Coll (DE)
Western Kentucky U (KY)
Wichita State U (KS)
Widener U (PA)
William Woods U (MO)
Woodbury Coll (VT)

Legal Professions and Studies Related
Peirce Coll (PA)

Legal Studies
Becker Coll (MA)
Central Christian Coll of Kansas (KS)
Central Christian Coll of Kansas (KS)
Clayton Coll & State U (GA)
Hilbert Coll (NY)
Lake Superior State U (MI)
Mountain State U (WV)
Ohio Dominican U (OH)
Sage Coll of Albany (NY)
Southeastern U (DC)
U of Detroit Mercy (MI)
The U of Montana–Missoula (MT)
U of New Haven (CT)

Legal Support Services Related
Central Missouri State U (MO)

Liberal Arts and Sciences And Humanities Related
Beacon Coll (FL)
Huron U USA in London United Kingdom)
Pennsylvania Coll of Technology (PA)
Troy U Dothan (AL)
Troy U Montgomery (AL)
The U of Akron (OH)
U of Hartford (CT)

Liberal Arts and Sciences/ Liberal Studies
Adams State Coll (CO)
Adelphi U (NY)
Alabama State U (AL)
Albertus Magnus Coll (CT)

Alderson-Broaddus Coll (WV)
Alvernia Coll (PA)
Alverno Coll (WI)
American International Coll (MA)
American U of Puerto Rico (PR)
The American U of Rome Italy)
Anderson Coll (SC)
Andrews U (MI)
Aquinas Coll (MI)
Aquinas Coll (TN)
Ashland U (OH)
Augusta State U (GA)
Averett U (VA)
Bacone Coll (OK)
Ball State U (IN)
Beacon Coll (FL)
Becker Coll (MA)
Bemidji State U (MN)
Bethany Coll of the Assemblies of God (CA)
Bethany Lutheran Coll (MN)
Bethel Coll (IN)
Bethel U (MN)
Bluefield State Coll (WV)
Boricua Coll (NY)
Brescia U (KY)
Briar Cliff U (IA)
Bryan Coll (TN)
Bryn Athyn Coll of the New Church (PA)
Butler U (IN)
Calumet Coll of Saint Joseph (IN)
Campbell U (NC)
Cardinal Stritch U (WI)
Cazenovia Coll (NY)
Centenary Coll (NJ)
Champlain Coll (VT)
Charleston Southern U (SC)
Charter Oak State Coll (CT)
Chester Coll of New England (NH)
Christendom Coll (VA)
Clarion U of Pennsylvania (PA)
Clarke Coll (IA)
Colby-Sawyer Coll (NH)
Coll for Lifelong Learning (NH)
Coll of St. Catherine (MN)
Coll of St. Joseph (VT)
The Coll of Saint Thomas More (TX)
Coll of Staten Island of the City U of NY (NY)
Colorado Christian U (CO)
Columbia Coll (MO)
Columbus State U (GA)
Concordia Coll (NY)
Concordia U (OR)
Crossroads Coll (MN)
Crown Coll (MN)
Cumberland U (TN)
Dakota State U (SD)
Dakota Wesleyan U (SD)
Dallas Baptist U (TX)
Dickinson State U (ND)
Dominican Coll (NY)
Eastern Connecticut State U (CT)
Eastern U (PA)
East Texas Baptist U (TX)
East-West U (IL)
Edgewood Coll (WI)
Edinboro U of Pennsylvania (PA)
Emmanuel Coll (GA)
Endicott Coll (MA)
Excelsior Coll (NY)
Fairleigh Dickinson U, Teaneck-Metro Campus (NJ)
Fairmont State U (WV)
State U of NY at Farmingdale (NY)
Faulkner U (AL)
Felician Coll (NJ)
Ferris State U (MI)
Five Towns Coll (NY)
Florida A&M U (FL)

Florida Atlantic U (FL)
Florida Coll (FL)
Florida State U (FL)
The Franciscan U of the Prairies (IA)
Franklin Coll Switzerland Switzerland)
Fresno Pacific U (CA)
Gannon U (PA)
Glenville State Coll (WV)
Grace Bible Coll (MI)
Grace U (NE)
Grand View Coll (IA)
Gwynedd-Mercy Coll (PA)
Haskell Indian Nations U (KS)
Heritage U (WA)
Hilbert Coll (NY)
Hillsdale Free Will Baptist Coll (OK)
Huron U USA in London United Kingdom)
Immaculata U (PA)
Indiana State U (IN)
International Coll of the Cayman Islands Cayman Islands)
John Brown U (AR)
John Wesley Coll (NC)
Keene State Coll (NH)
Kent State U (OH)
Kentucky State U (KY)
LaGrange Coll (GA)
Lake Superior State U (MI)
La Salle U (PA)
Lebanon Valley Coll (PA)
Lewis-Clark State Coll (ID)
Limestone Coll (SC)
Long Island U, Brooklyn Campus (NY)
Loras Coll (IA)
Lourdes Coll (OH)
Lyndon State Coll (VT)
Macon State Coll (GA)
Marian Coll (IN)
Marietta Coll (OH)
Martin Methodist Coll (TN)
Marygrove Coll (MI)
Marymount Coll of Fordham U (NY)
Marymount U (VA)
Medaille Coll (NY)
Medgar Evers Coll of the City U of NY (NY)
Mercy Coll (NY)
Mercyhurst Coll (PA)
Merrimack Coll (MA)
Mesa State Coll (CO)
Methodist Coll (NC)
MidAmerica Nazarene U (KS)
Millersville U of Pennsylvania (PA)
Minnesota State U Mankato (MN)
Minnesota State U Moorhead (MN)
Mitchell Coll (CT)
Molloy Coll (NY)
Montana State U–Billings (MT)
Montana Tech of The U of Montana (MT)
Mountain State U (WV)
Mount Aloysius Coll (PA)
Mount Marty Coll (SD)
Mount Olive Coll (NC)
Mount St. Mary's Coll (CA)
Murray State U (KY)
National American U, Rapid City (SD)
National U (CA)
Neumann Coll (PA)
Newman U (KS)
New Mexico Inst of Mining and Technology (NM)
New York U (NY)
Niagara U (NY)
North Central U (MN)
Northern Michigan U (MI)
Northern State U (SD)
North Greenville Coll (SC)
Northwestern Coll (MN)
Northwest U (WA)

Nyack Coll (NY)
Oak Hills Christian Coll (MN)
Oakland City U (IN)
The Ohio State U at Lima (OH)
The Ohio State U at Marion (OH)
The Ohio State U–Mansfield Campus (OH)
The Ohio State U–Newark Campus (OH)
Ohio U (OH)
Ohio U–Zanesville (OH)
Ohio Valley Coll (WV)
Okanagan U Coll (BC, Canada)
Oklahoma Wesleyan U (OK)
Oregon Inst of Technology (OR)
Pace U (NY)
Pacific Union Coll (CA)
Park U (MO)
Paul Smith's Coll of Arts and Sciences (NY)
Pennsylvania Coll of Technology (PA)
Penn State U Abington Coll (PA)
Penn State U Altoona Coll (PA)
Penn State U at Erie, The Behrend Coll (PA)
Penn State U Berks Cmps of Berks-Lehigh Valley Coll (PA)
Penn State U Harrisburg Campus of the Capital Coll (PA)
Penn State U Lehigh Valley Cmps of Berks-Lehigh Valley Coll (PA)
Penn State U Schuylkill Campus of the Capital Coll (PA)
Penn State U Univ Park Campus (PA)
Pine Manor Coll (MA)
Post U (CT)
Providence Coll (RI)
Reformed Bible Coll (MI)
Reinhardt Coll (GA)
Richmond, The American International U in LondonUnited Kingdom)
Rivier Coll (NH)
Rochester Coll (MI)
Rocky Mountain Coll (MT)
Roger Williams U (RI)
Sacred Heart U (CT)
Sage Coll of Albany (NY)
St. Augustine Coll (IL)
St. Cloud State U (MN)
St. Francis Coll (NY)
St. Gregory's U (OK)
St. John's U (NY)
Saint Joseph's U (PA)
Saint Leo U (FL)
Saint Mary-of-the-Woods Coll (IN)
Salem International U (WV)
Salve Regina U (RI)
Schiller International U (FL)
Schiller International UFrance)
Schiller International UGermany)
Schiller International USpain)
Schiller International UUnited Kingdom)
Schiller International U, American Coll of SwitzerlandSwitzerland)
Schreiner U (TX)
Simon's Rock Coll of Bard (MA)
Southern Connecticut State U (CT)
Southern New Hampshire U (NH)
Southern Polytechnic State U (GA)
Southern Vermont Coll (VT)
Spring Arbor U (MI)

State U of NY Coll of A&T at Cobleskill (NY)
Stephens Coll (MO)
Sterling Coll (VT)
Strayer U (DC)
Taylor U Fort Wayne (IN)
Thiel Coll (PA)
Thomas Edison State Coll (NJ)
Thomas More Coll (KY)
Thomas U (GA)
Tri-State U (IN)
The U of Akron (OH)
U of Alaska Fairbanks (AK)
U of Alaska Southeast (AK)
U of Arkansas at Fort Smith (AR)
U of Bridgeport (CT)
U of Central Florida (FL)
U of Cincinnati (OH)
U of Delaware (DE)
U of Hartford (CT)
U of Indianapolis (IN)
U of La Verne (CA)
The U of Maine at Augusta (ME)
U of Maine at Fort Kent (ME)
U of Maine at Presque Isle (ME)
U of New Hampshire (NH)
U of New Hampshire at Manchester (NH)
U of Saint Francis (IN)
U of Saint Mary (KS)
U of South Carolina at Beaufort (SC)
U of South Florida (FL)
The U of Toledo (OH)
U of Wisconsin–Eau Claire (WI)
U of Wisconsin–La Crosse (WI)
U of Wisconsin–Oshkosh (WI)
U of Wisconsin–Platteville (WI)
U of Wisconsin–Stevens Point (WI)
U of Wisconsin–Superior (WI)
U of Wisconsin–Whitewater (WI)
Upper Iowa U (IA)
Urbana U (OH)
Valdosta State U (GA)
Villa Julie Coll (MD)
Villanova U (PA)
Virginia Intermont Coll (VA)
Walsh U (OH)
Washburn U (KS)
Waynesburg Coll (PA)
Weber State U (UT)
Wesley Coll (DE)
Western Connecticut State U (CT)
Western New England Coll (MA)
Western Oregon U (OR)
West Virginia State U (WV)
Wichita State U (KS)
Wilson Coll (PA)
Winona State U (MN)
Xavier U (OH)
York Coll (NE)
York Coll of Pennsylvania (PA)

Library Assistant
Ohio Dominican U (OH)
Southern Alberta Inst of Technology (AB, Canada)
The U of Maine at Augusta (ME)

Library Science
U of the District of Columbia (DC)

Lineworker
Utah Valley State Coll (UT)

Linguistics
Oklahoma Wesleyan U (OK)

Literature
Friends U (KS)
Manchester Coll (IN)

North Central U (MN)
Sacred Heart U (CT)
Université Laval (QC, Canada)

Livestock Management
Sterling Coll (VT)

Logistics and Materials Management
Park U (MO)
The U of Akron (OH)
The U of Toledo (OH)

Machine Shop Technology
Dalton State Coll (GA)
Georgia Southwestern State U (GA)
Pennsylvania Coll of Technology (PA)
Valdosta State U (GA)

Machine Tool Technology
Boise State U (ID)
British Columbia Inst of Technology (BC, Canada)
Fashion Inst of Technology (NY)
Ferris State U (MI)
Georgia Southwestern State U (GA)
Idaho State U (ID)
Lake Superior State U (MI)
Lamar U (TX)
Mesa State Coll (CO)
Missouri Southern State U (MO)
Montana State U–Northern (MT)
Utah Valley State Coll (UT)
Vaughn Coll of Aeronautics and Technology (NY)
Weber State U (UT)

Management Information Systems
Arkansas State U (AR)
Bayamón Central U (PR)
Cameron U (OK)
Coll of Saint Mary (NE)
Colorado Christian U (CO)
Columbia Coll, Caguas (PR)
Davenport U, Dearborn (MI)
Davenport U, Warren (MI)
Globe Inst of Technology (NY)
Hilbert Coll (NY)
Husson Coll (ME)
Inter American U of PR, Bayamón Campus (PR)
Lake Superior State U (MI)
Lindsey Wilson Coll (KY)
Lock Haven U of Pennsylvania (PA)
Morehead State U (KY)
National American U, Albuquerque (NM)
National American U–Sioux Falls Branch (SD)
Northern Michigan U (MI)
Northwood U (MI)
Northwood U, Texas Campus (TX)
Peirce Coll (PA)
Robert Morris Coll (IL)
St. Augustine Coll (IL)
Saint Joseph's Coll (IN)
Saint Joseph's U (PA)
Shawnee State U (OH)
Southeastern U (DC)
Southern Alberta Inst of Technology (AB, Canada)
Taylor U (IN)
Thiel Coll (PA)
The U of Akron (OH)
U of Management and Technology (VA)
U of Wisconsin–Green Bay (WI)
Weber State U (UT)
Wilson Coll (PA)
Wright State U (OH)

Management Information Systems and Services Related
Coll of Mount St. Joseph (OH)

Davis & Elkins Coll (WV)
Purdue U (IN)
U of Southern Indiana (IN)

Management Science
British Columbia Inst of Technology (BC, Canada)

Manufacturing Technology
Kent State U (OH)
Lawrence Technological U (MI)
Lewis-Clark State Coll (ID)
Missouri Western State Coll (MO)
Pennsylvania Coll of Technology (PA)
Penn State U at Erie, The Behrend Coll (PA)
Thompson Rivers U (BC, Canada)
Utah Valley State Coll (UT)

Marine Biology and Biological Oceanography
Mitchell Coll (CT)

Marine Science/Merchant Marine Officer
U of the District of Columbia (DC)

Marine Technology
Thomas Edison State Coll (NJ)
U of Alaska Southeast (AK)

Maritime Science
Maine Maritime Academy (ME)
Martin Methodist Coll (TN)

Marketing/Marketing Management
American InterContinental U, Atlanta (GA)
Baker Coll of Allen Park (MI)
Baker Coll of Auburn Hills (MI)
Baker Coll of Cadillac (MI)
Baker Coll of Clinton Township (MI)
Baker Coll of Flint (MI)
Baker Coll of Jackson (MI)
Baker Coll of Muskegon (MI)
Baker Coll of Owosso (MI)
Baker Coll of Port Huron (MI)
Ball State U (IN)
Bluefield State Coll (WV)
Boise State U (ID)
British Columbia Inst of Technology (BC, Canada)
Central Christian Coll of Kansas (KS)
Central Pennsylvania Coll (PA)
Champlain Coll (VT)
Chestnut Hill Coll (PA)
Clayton Coll & State U (GA)
Dalton State Coll (GA)
Davenport U, Dearborn (MI)
Davenport U, Grand Rapids (MI)
Davenport U, Kalamazoo (MI)
Davenport U, Lansing (MI)
Davenport U, Warren (MI)
David N. Myers U (OH)
Five Towns Coll (NY)
Florida Metropolitan U–Tampa Coll, Brandon (FL)
Florida Metropolitan U–Orlando Coll, North (FL)
Florida Metropolitan U–Tampa Coll (FL)
Hawai'i Pacific U (HI)
Idaho State U (ID)
Johnson & Wales U (CO)
Johnson & Wales U (FL)
Johnson & Wales U (RI)
King's Coll (PA)
Martin Methodist Coll (TN)
Newbury Coll (MA)
New England School of Communications (ME)
Peirce Coll (PA)
Post U (CT)

Sage Coll of Albany (NY)
Saint Joseph's U (PA)
Saint Peter's Coll (NJ)
Siena Heights U (MI)
Southeastern U (DC)
Southern New Hampshire U (NH)
Strayer U (DC)
Sullivan U (KY)
Thomas Edison State Coll (NJ)
Tulane U (LA)
U of Bridgeport (CT)
U of Cincinnati (OH)
U of Management and Technology (VA)
U of Sioux Falls (SD)
U of the District of Columbia (DC)
Urbana U (OH)
Walsh U (OH)
Webber International U (FL)
Weber State U (UT)
West Virginia State U (WV)
Wilson Coll (PA)
Wright State U (OH)
Youngstown State U (OH)

Marketing Related
Southern Alberta Inst of Technology (AB, Canada)

Marriage and Family Therapy/Counseling
Central Christian Coll of Kansas (KS)
Martin Methodist Coll (TN)

Masonry
Pennsylvania Coll of Technology (PA)
Valdosta State U (GA)

Massage Therapy
National American U–Sioux Falls Branch (SD)

Mass Communication/Media
Adrian Coll (MI)
Bacone Coll (OK)
Becker Coll (MA)
Black Hills State U (SD)
Central Christian Coll of Kansas (KS)
Central Pennsylvania Coll (PA)
Champlain Coll (VT)
Clayton Coll & State U (GA)
Cornerstone U (MI)
Evangel U (MI)
Five Towns Coll (NY)
Fresno Pacific U (CA)
Inter American U of PR, Bayamón Campus (PR)
Macon State Coll (GA)
Madonna U (MI)
Martin Methodist Coll (TN)
Methodist Coll (NC)
Newbury Coll (MA)
North Central U (MN)
Pennsylvania Coll of Technology (PA)
Reinhardt Coll (GA)
Richmond, The American International U in LondonUnited Kingdom)
Sacred Heart U (CT)
Salem International U (WV)
U Coll of the Fraser Valley (BC, Canada)
U of Dubuque (IA)
U of Rio Grande (OH)
Villa Julie Coll (MD)
Wilson Coll (PA)

Materials Science
U of New Hampshire (NH)

Mathematics
Bacone Coll (OK)
Central Baptist Coll (AR)
Central Christian Coll of Kansas (KS)
Clayton Coll & State U (GA)
Creighton U (NE)
Dalton State Coll (GA)
Felician Coll (NJ)
Fresno Pacific U (CA)

Sage Coll of Albany (NY)
Heritage U (WA)
Hillsdale Free Will Baptist Coll (OK)
Huron U USA in LondonUnited Kingdom)
Idaho State U (ID)
Indiana U East (IN)
Indiana U–Purdue U Fort Wayne (IN)
Indiana Wesleyan U (IN)
Lindsey Wilson Coll (KY)
Macon State Coll (GA)
Martin Methodist Coll (TN)
Mesa State Coll (CO)
Methodist Coll (NC)
Richmond, The American International U in LondonUnited Kingdom)
Sacred Heart U (CT)
State U of NY Empire State Coll (NY)
Thomas Edison State Coll (NJ)
Thomas More Coll (KY)
Thomas U (GA)
Tri-State U (IN)
U of Great Falls (MT)
U of Rio Grande (OH)
The U of Tampa (FL)
U of Wisconsin–Green Bay (WI)
Utah Valley State Coll (UT)
York Coll of Pennsylvania (PA)

Mathematics Teacher Education
Central Christian Coll of Kansas (KS)

Mechanical Design Technology
Clayton Coll & State U (GA)
Ferris State U (MI)
Lincoln U (MO)

Mechanical Drafting
Cameron U (OK)

Mechanical Drafting and Cad/Cadd
Baker Coll of Flint (MI)
British Columbia Inst of Technology (BC, Canada)
Indiana U–Purdue U Indianapolis (IN)
Montana Tech of The U of Montana (MT)
Purdue U (IN)

Mechanical Engineering
Fairfield U (CT)
Macon State Coll (GA)

Mechanical Engineering/ Mechanical Technology
Andrews U (MI)
Baker Coll of Flint (MI)
Bluefield State Coll (WV)
British Columbia Inst of Technology (BC, Canada)
Excelsior Coll (NY)
Fairmont State U (WV)
State U of NY at Farmingdale (NY)
Ferris State U (MI)
Indiana U–Purdue U Fort Wayne (IN)
Indiana U–Purdue U Indianapolis (IN)
Johnson & Wales U (RI)
Kansas State U (KS)
Kent State U (OH)
Lake Superior State U (MI)
Lawrence Technological U (MI)
Michigan Technological U (MI)
Murray State U (KY)
New York Inst of Technology (NY)
Penn State U Altoona Coll (PA)
Penn State U at Erie, The Behrend Coll (PA)
Penn State U Berks Cmps of Berks-Lehigh Valley Coll (PA)

Point Park U (PA)
Purdue U Calumet (IN)
Rochester Inst of Technology (NY)
Southern Alberta Inst of Technology (AB, Canada)
Thomas Edison State Coll (NJ)
The U of Akron (OH)
U of Cincinnati (OH)
U of Massachusetts Lowell (MA)
U of Rio Grande (OH)
U of the District of Columbia (DC)
The U of Toledo (OH)
Vermont Tech Coll (VT)
Weber State U (UT)
Wentworth Inst of Technology (MA)
Youngstown State U (OH)

Mechanical Engineering Technologies Related
Purdue U (IN)

Mechanic and Repair Technologies Related
Pennsylvania Coll of Technology (PA)

Mechanics and Repair
Idaho State U (ID)
Lewis-Clark State Coll (ID)

Medical Administrative Assistant and Medical Secretary
Baker Coll of Auburn Hills (MI)
Baker Coll of Cadillac (MI)
Baker Coll of Clinton Township (MI)
Baker Coll of Flint (MI)
Baker Coll of Jackson (MI)
Baker Coll of Muskegon (MI)
Baker Coll of Owosso (MI)
Baker Coll of Port Huron (MI)
Boise State U (ID)
British Columbia Inst of Technology (BC, Canada)
Central Pennsylvania Coll (PA)
Davenport U, Dearborn (MI)
Davenport U, Lansing (MI)
Davenport U, Lapeer (MI)
Davenport U, Warren (MI)
Dickinson State U (ND)
Hannibal-LaGrange Coll (MO)
Lamar U (TX)
Martin Methodist Coll (TN)
Mesa State Coll (CO)
Midland Lutheran Coll (NE)
Montana State U–Billings (MT)
Montana Tech of The U of Montana (MT)
Northern Michigan U (MI)
Pacific Union Coll (CA)
Pennsylvania Coll of Technology (PA)
Sullivan U (KY)
Thomas Coll (ME)
Universidad Adventista de las Antillas (PR)
The U of Akron (OH)
U of Cincinnati (OH)
The U of Montana–Missoula (MT)
U of Rio Grande (OH)
Utah Valley State Coll (UT)
Washburn U (KS)
Wright State U (OH)
Youngstown State U (OH)

Medical/Clinical Assistant
Arkansas Tech U (AR)
Baker Coll of Allen Park (MI)
Baker Coll of Auburn Hills (MI)
Baker Coll of Cadillac (MI)
Baker Coll of Clinton Township (MI)
Baker Coll of Flint (MI)
Baker Coll of Jackson (MI)
Baker Coll of Muskegon (MI)

Baker Coll of Owosso (MI)
Baker Coll of Port Huron (MI)
Bluefield State Coll (WV)
Cabarrus Coll of Health Sciences (NC)
Central Pennsylvania Coll (PA)
Clayton Coll & State U (GA)
Davenport U, Lansing (MI)
Eastern Kentucky U (KY)
Faulkner U (AL)
Florida Metropolitan U–Tampa Coll, Brandon (FL)
Florida Metropolitan U–Orlando Coll, North (FL)
Florida Metropolitan U–Orlando Coll, South (FL)
Florida Metropolitan U–Tampa Coll (FL)
Georgia Southwestern State U (GA)
Idaho State U (ID)
International Coll (FL)
Jones Coll, Jacksonville (FL)
Montana State U–Billings (MT)
Mountain State U (WV)
Mount Aloysius Coll (PA)
National American U, Colorado Springs (CO)
National American U, Denver (CO)
National American U–Sioux Falls Branch (SD)
Ohio U (OH)
Palmer Coll of Chiropractic (IA)
Robert Morris Coll (IL)
South U (AL)
South U (GA)
The U of Akron (OH)
U of Alaska Anchorage (AK)
U of Alaska Fairbanks (AK)
The U of Toledo (OH)
Valdosta State U (GA)
West Virginia State U (WV)
Youngstown State U (OH)

Medical/Health Management and Clinical Assistant
Lewis-Clark State Coll (ID)
National American U, Denver (CO)

Medical Illustration
Clayton Coll & State U (GA)

Medical Insurance Coding
Baker Coll of Allen Park (MI)
Davenport U, Dearborn (MI)
Davenport U, Holland (MI)
Davenport U, Kalamazoo (MI)
Davenport U, Lansing (MI)
Davenport U, Lapeer (MI)
Davenport U, Warren (MI)

Medical Insurance/Medical Billing
Baker Coll of Allen Park (MI)
Davenport U, Dearborn (MI)
Davenport U, Holland (MI)
Davenport U, Kalamazoo (MI)
Davenport U, Lansing (MI)
Davenport U, Warren (MI)

Medical Laboratory Technology
Argosy U/Twin Cities, Eagan (MN)
British Columbia Inst of Technology (BC, Canada)
Evangel U (MO)
Villa Julie Coll (MD)

Medical Office Assistant
Lewis-Clark State Coll (ID)
Mercy Coll of Health Sciences (IA)

Medical Office Computer Specialist
Baker Coll of Allen Park (MI)

Medical Office Management
Dalton State Coll (GA)

National American U, Colorado Springs (CO)
The U of Akron (OH)
Youngstown State U (OH)

Medical Radiologic Technology
Argosy U/Twin Cities, Eagan (MN)
Arkansas State U (AR)
Bacone Coll (OK)
Bluefield State Coll (WV)
British Columbia Inst of Technology (BC, Canada)
Coll of St. Catherine (MN)
Fairleigh Dickinson U, Florham (NJ)
Fairleigh Dickinson U, Teaneck-Metro Campus (NJ)
Gannon U (PA)
Idaho State U (ID)
Indiana U Northwest (IN)
Indiana U–Purdue U Indianapolis (IN)
Indiana U South Bend (IN)
Kent State U (OH)
La Roche Coll (PA)
Loma Linda U (CA)
Mercy Coll of Health Sciences (IA)
Missouri Southern State U (MO)
Morehead State U (KY)
Northern Kentucky U (KY)
Pennsylvania Coll of Technology (PA)
Penn State U Schuylkill Campus of the Capital Coll (PA)
Saint Joseph's Coll of Maine (ME)
Shawnee State U (OH)
Southern Adventist U (TN)
Southern Alberta Inst of Technology (AB, Canada)
Thomas Edison State Coll (NJ)
The U of Akron (OH)
U of Arkansas at Fort Smith (AR)
U of New Mexico (NM)
U of Saint Francis (IN)
U of Southern Indiana (IN)
Valdosta State U (GA)
Weber State U (UT)

Medical Transcription
Baker Coll of Flint (MI)
Baker Coll of Jackson (MI)
Dalton State Coll (GA)
Davenport U, Holland (MI)
Davenport U, Lansing (MI)

Mental and Social Health Services And Allied Professions Related
U of Alaska Fairbanks (AK)
The U of Maine at Augusta (ME)

Mental Health/Rehabilitation
Evangel U (MO)
Felician Coll (NJ)
Lake Superior State U (MI)
St. Augustine Coll (IL)
The U of Toledo (OH)
Washburn U (KS)

Merchandising
Clayton Coll & State U (GA)
The U of Akron (OH)

Merchandising, Sales, and Marketing Operations Related (General)
Clayton Coll & State U (GA)

Merchandising, Sales, and Marketing Operations Related (Specialized)
Central Missouri State U (MO)
Clayton Coll & State U (GA)

Metal and Jewelry Arts
Academy of Art U (CA)
Rochester Inst of Technology (NY)

Metallurgical Technology
Montana State U–Northern (MT)
Penn State U Altoona Coll (PA)
Penn State U at Erie, The Behrend Coll (PA)
Penn State U Berks Cmps of Berks-Lehigh Valley Coll (PA)
Penn State U Schuylkill Campus of the Capital Coll (PA)
Purdue U Calumet (IN)

Microbiology
Canadian Mennonite U (MB, Canada)

Middle School Education
Central Christian Coll of Kansas (KS)
Dalton State Coll (GA)
U of Arkansas at Fort Smith (AR)

Military Studies
Hawai'i Pacific U (HI)

Mining Technology
British Columbia Inst of Technology (BC, Canada)

Missionary Studies and Missiology
Central Christian Coll of Kansas (KS)
Circleville Bible Coll (OH)
Faith Baptist Bible Coll and Theological Seminary (IA)
God's Bible School and Coll (OH)
Hillsdale Free Will Baptist Coll (OK)
Hobe Sound Bible Coll (FL)
Hope International U (CA)
Manhattan Christian Coll (KS)
North Central U (MN)
Southern Methodist Coll (SC)

Modern Greek
North Central U (MN)

Modern Languages
Macon State Coll (GA)
North Central U (MN)
Sacred Heart U (CT)
York Coll of Pennsylvania (PA)

Molecular Biochemistry
Sacred Heart U (CT)

Multi-/Interdisciplinary Studies Related
International Coll (FL)
Mountain State U (WV)
Ohio U (OH)
Pennsylvania Coll of Technology (PA)
Shepherd U (WV)
Sterling Coll (VT)
The U of Akron (OH)
U of Alaska Fairbanks (AK)
U of Arkansas at Fort Smith (AR)
The U of Toledo (OH)

Music
Bethel Coll (IN)
Brigham Young U–Hawaii (HI)
Central Baptist Coll (AR)
Central Christian Coll of Kansas (KS)
Chowan Coll (NC)
Clayton Coll & State U (GA)
Crown Coll (MN)
Dallas Baptist U (TX)
Emmanuel Coll (GA)
Five Towns Coll (NY)
Fresno Pacific U (CA)
Grace Bible Coll (MI)
Grace U (NE)
Hillsdale Free Will Baptist Coll (OK)
Indiana Wesleyan U (IN)
John Brown U (AR)

Kwantlen U Coll (BC, Canada)
Lourdes Coll (OH)
Macon State Coll (GA)
Marian Coll (IN)
Martin Methodist Coll (TN)
Mesa State Coll (CO)
Methodist Coll (NC)
Mount Olive Coll (NC)
Mount Vernon Nazarene U (OH)
North Central U (MN)
Reinhardt Coll (GA)
Sacred Heart U (CT)
Shawnee State U (OH)
Thomas More Coll (KY)
The U of Maine at Augusta (ME)
U of Rio Grande (OH)
The U of Tampa (FL)
U of the District of Columbia (DC)
Utah Valley State Coll (UT)
York Coll of Pennsylvania (PA)

Musical Instrument Fabrication and Repair
Indiana U Bloomington (IN)

Music History, Literature, and Theory
Central Christian Coll of Kansas (KS)

Music Management and Merchandising
Central Christian Coll of Kansas (KS)
Chowan Coll (NC)
Five Towns Coll (NY)
Friends U (KS)
The New England Inst of Art (MA)

Music Performance
Central Christian Coll of Kansas (KS)
New World School of the Arts (FL)

Music Related
Alverno Coll (WI)

Music Teacher Education
Central Christian Coll of Kansas (KS)
Martin Methodist Coll (TN)
Union Coll (NE)

Music Theory and Composition
Central Christian Coll of Kansas (KS)
Kwantlen U Coll (BC, Canada)
New World School of the Arts (FL)
North Central U (MN)

Natural Resources and Conservation Related
Sterling Coll (VT)

Natural Resources/ Conservation
Sterling Coll (VT)
U of Minnesota, Crookston (MN)

Natural Resources/ Conservation Related
Sterling Coll (VT)

Natural Resources Management
Sterling Coll (VT)

Natural Resources Management and Policy
Bacone Coll (OK)
Heritage U (WA)
Lake Superior State U (MI)
Sterling Coll (VT)
U of Alaska Fairbanks (AK)
U of Minnesota, Crookston (MN)

Natural Sciences
Alderson-Broaddus Coll (WV)

Central Christian Coll of Kansas (KS)
Charleston Southern U (SC)
Felician Coll (NJ)
Fresno Pacific U (CA)
Haskell Indian Nations U (KS)
Lourdes Coll (OH)
Madonna U (MI)
Medgar Evers Coll of the City U of NY (NY)
Roberts Wesleyan Coll (NY)
Shawnee State U (OH)
Sterling Coll (VT)
Thomas Edison State Coll (NJ)
U of Cincinnati (OH)
The U of Toledo (OH)
Villanova U (PA)

Naval Architecture and Marine Engineering
British Columbia Inst of Technology (BC, Canada)

Non-Profit Management
Davenport U, Dearborn (MI)

Nuclear Engineering
Arkansas Tech U (AR)

Nuclear Engineering Technology
Excelsior Coll (NY)

Nuclear Medical Technology
Ball State U (IN)
British Columbia Inst of Technology (BC, Canada)
Dalton State Coll (GA)
Ferris State U (MI)
The George Washington U (DC)
Kent State U (OH)
Molloy Coll (NY)
Southern Alberta Inst of Technology (AB, Canada)
Thomas Edison State Coll (NJ)
The U of Findlay (OH)
Valdosta State U (GA)
West Virginia State U (WV)

Nuclear/Nuclear Power Technology
Thomas Edison State Coll (NJ)

Nursing Administration
British Columbia Inst of Technology (BC, Canada)

Nursing Assistant/Aide and Patient Care Assistant
Cabarrus Coll of Health Sciences (NC)
Central Christian Coll of Kansas (KS)
Montana Tech of The U of Montana (MT)

Nursing (Licensed Practical/ Vocational Nurse Training)
Central Christian Coll of Kansas (KS)
Davenport U, Dearborn (MI)
Dickinson State U (ND)
Georgia Southwestern State U (GA)
Grace U (NE)
Kent State U (OH)
Lamar U (TX)
Lewis-Clark State Coll (ID)
Medgar Evers Coll of the City U of NY (NY)
Montana State U–Billings (MT)
Northern Michigan U (MI)
Pennsylvania Coll of Technology (PA)
Thompson Rivers U (BC, Canada)
The U of Montana–Missoula (MT)
U of the District of Columbia (DC)
Vermont Tech Coll (VT)

Nursing (Registered Nurse Training)
Alcorn State U (MS)
Alvernia Coll (PA)
Angelo State U (TX)
Aquinas Coll (TN)
Arkansas State U (AR)
Atlantic Union Coll (MA)
Augusta State U (GA)
Bacone Coll (OK)
Baker Coll of Clinton Township (MI)
Baker Coll of Flint (MI)
Baker Coll of Muskegon (MI)
Baker Coll of Owosso (MI)
Ball State U (IN)
Bayamón Central U (PR)
Becker Coll (MA)
Bethel Coll (IN)
Bluefield State Coll (WV)
Boise State U (ID)
British Columbia Inst of Technology (BC, Canada)
Cabarrus Coll of Health Sciences (NC)
Cardinal Stritch U (WI)
Castleton State Coll (VT)
Central Christian Coll of Kansas (KS)
Clarion U of Pennsylvania (PA)
Coll of Saint Mary (NE)
Coll of Staten Island of the City U of NY (NY)
Columbia Coll (MO)
Columbia Coll, Caguas (PR)
Covenant Coll (GA)
Dakota Wesleyan U (SD)
Dalton State Coll (GA)
Davenport U, Dearborn (MI)
Davis & Elkins Coll (WV)
Eastern Kentucky U (KY)
Excelsior Coll (NY)
Fairmont State U (WV)
State U of NY at Farmingdale (NY)
Felician Coll (NJ)
Ferris State U (MI)
Finlandia U (MI)
Gardner-Webb U (NC)
Gwynedd-Mercy Coll (PA)
Hannibal-LaGrange Coll (MO)
Heritage U (WA)
Hillsdale Free Will Baptist Coll (OK)
Houston Baptist U (TX)
Indiana State U (IN)
Indiana U East (IN)
Indiana U Kokomo (IN)
Indiana U Northwest (IN)
Indiana U–Purdue U Fort Wayne (IN)
Indiana U–Purdue U Indianapolis (IN)
Indiana U South Bend (IN)
Inter American U of PR, Ponce Campus (PR)
Kent State U (OH)
Kentucky State U (KY)
Lamar U (TX)
Lincoln U (MO)
Lock Haven U of Pennsylvania (PA)
Loma Linda U (CA)
Louisiana Tech U (LA)
Macon State Coll (GA)
Marshall U (WV)
Marymount U (VA)
McNeese State U (LA)
Mercy Coll of Health Sciences (IA)
Mercyhurst Coll (PA)
Mesa State Coll (CO)
Midway Coll (KY)
Mississippi U for Women (MS)
Montana State U–Northern (MT)
Montana Tech of The U of Montana (MT)
Morehead State U (KY)
Mount Aloysius Coll (PA)
Mount St. Mary's Coll (CA)

Nebraska Methodist Coll (NE)
Newman U (KS)
Nicholls State U (LA)
North Central U (MN)
Northern Kentucky U (KY)
North Georgia Coll & State U (GA)
Northwestern State U of Louisiana (LA)
Ohio U (OH)
Ohio U–Zanesville (OH)
Oklahoma Panhandle State U (OK)
Our Lady of the Lake Coll (LA)
Pacific Union Coll (CA)
Park U (MO)
Pennsylvania Coll of Technology (PA)
Penn State U Altoona Coll (PA)
Pikeville Coll (KY)
Purdue U Calumet (IN)
Regis Coll (MA)
Reinhardt Coll (GA)
Rivier Coll (NH)
Shawnee State U (OH)
Shepherd U (WV)
Southern Adventist U (TN)
Southern Arkansas U–Magnolia (AR)
Southern Vermont Coll (VT)
Southwest Baptist U (MO)
Tennessee State U (TN)
Thomas U (GA)
Troy U (AL)
Universidad Adventista de las Antillas (PR)
U of Alaska Anchorage (AK)
U of Arkansas at Fort Smith (AR)
U of Charleston (WV)
U of Cincinnati (OH)
U of Indianapolis (IN)
The U of Maine at Augusta (ME)
U of Mobile (AL)
U of New England (ME)
U of Pittsburgh at Bradford (PA)
U of Rio Grande (OH)
U of Saint Francis (IN)
U of South Carolina Spartanburg (SC)
The U of South Dakota (SD)
U of Southern Indiana (IN)
U of the District of Columbia (DC)
U of the Sacred Heart (PR)
U of the Virgin Islands (VI)
The U of Toledo (OH)
The U of West Alabama (AL)
Utah Valley State Coll (UT)
Vermont Tech Coll (VT)
Walsh U (OH)
Warner Pacific Coll (OR)
Weber State U (UT)
Western Kentucky U (KY)

Nursing Related
British Columbia Inst of Technology (BC, Canada)
Inter American U of PR, Aguadilla Campus (PR)
Madonna U (MI)

Nursing Science
La Roche Coll (PA)

Occupational Health and Industrial Hygiene
British Columbia Inst of Technology (BC, Canada)

Occupational Safety and Health Technology
Ferris State U (MI)
Indiana U Bloomington (IN)
Lamar U (TX)
Montana Tech of The U of Montana (MT)
Murray State U (KY)
Shepherd U (WV)
Southwest Baptist U (MO)
U of Cincinnati (OH)
U of New Haven (CT)

Washburn U (KS)
Wright State U (OH)

Occupational Therapist Assistant
Baker Coll of Muskegon (MI)
Cabarrus Coll of Health Sciences (NC)
California U of Pennsylvania (PA)
Clarion U of Pennsylvania (PA)
Coll of St. Catherine (MN)
Idaho State U (ID)
Kent State U (OH)
Loma Linda U (CA)
Mountain State U (WV)
Mount Aloysius Coll (PA)
Mount St. Mary's Coll (CA)
Pennsylvania Coll of Technology (PA)
U of Louisiana at Monroe (LA)
U of Saint Francis (IN)
U of Southern Indiana (IN)
Wichita State U (KS)

Occupational Therapy
Clarkson Coll (NE)
Clayton Coll & State U (GA)
Dalton State Coll (GA)
Faulkner U (AL)
Newman U (KS)
Shawnee State U (OH)
Southern Adventist U (TN)

Office Management
Baker Coll of Flint (MI)
Baker Coll of Jackson (MI)
Dalton State Coll (GA)
Emmanuel Coll (GA)
Georgia Southwestern State U (GA)
God's Bible School and Coll (OH)
International Coll of the Cayman IslandsCayman Islands)
Lake Superior State U (MI)
Mercyhurst Coll (PA)
Park U (MO)
Peirce Coll (PA)
Shawnee State U (OH)
Thompson Rivers U (BC, Canada)
Youngstown State U (OH)

Office Occupations and Clerical Services
Georgia Southwestern State U (GA)
Pennsylvania Coll of Technology (PA)
U of Alaska Fairbanks (AK)
Valdosta State U (GA)
Wright State U (OH)
Youngstown State U (OH)

Operations Management
Baker Coll of Flint (MI)
British Columbia Inst of Technology (BC, Canada)
Indiana State U (IN)
Indiana U–Purdue U Fort Wayne (IN)
Indiana U–Purdue U Indianapolis (IN)
Northern Kentucky U (KY)
Purdue U (IN)
Thomas Edison State Coll (NJ)

Ophthalmic Laboratory Technology
Central Pennsylvania Coll (PA)
Indiana U Bloomington (IN)
Rochester Inst of Technology (NY)

Opticianry
The U of Akron (OH)

Optometric Technician
Indiana U Bloomington (IN)

Organizational Communication
Creighton U (NE)

Ornamental Horticulture
State U of NY at Farmingdale (NY)
Ferris State U (MI)
Pennsylvania Coll of Technology (PA)
State U of NY Coll of A&T at Cobleskill (NY)
U of Massachusetts Amherst (MA)
U of New Hampshire (NH)
Utah State U (UT)
Vermont Tech Coll (VT)

Orthotics/Prosthetics
Baker Coll of Flint (MI)

Painting
Academy of Art U (CA)
The Art Inst of Pittsburgh (PA)
Central Christian Coll of Kansas (KS)
New World School of the Arts (FL)
Pratt Inst (NY)

Parks, Recreation and Leisure
Central Christian Coll of Kansas (KS)
Clayton Coll & State U (GA)
Johnson & Wales U (RI)
Mitchell Coll (CT)
Mount Olive Coll (NC)
Oklahoma Panhandle State U (OK)
Thomas Edison State Coll (NJ)
U of Maine at Presque Isle (ME)
U of the District of Columbia (DC)

Parks, Recreation and Leisure Facilities Management
Eastern Kentucky U (KY)
Indiana Inst of Technology (IN)
Johnson & Wales U (RI)
Martin Methodist Coll (TN)
Paul Smith's Coll of Arts and Sciences (NY)
State U of NY Coll of A&T at Cobleskill (NY)

Pastoral Studies/Counseling
Central Christian Coll of Kansas (KS)
Indiana Wesleyan U (IN)
North Central U (MN)
Notre Dame Coll (OH)
Providence Coll (RI)
Spalding U (KY)

Peace Studies and Conflict Resolution
Woodbury Coll (VT)

Pediatric Nursing
British Columbia Inst of Technology (BC, Canada)

Perfusion Technology
Boise State U (ID)
Thompson Rivers U (BC, Canada)

Perioperative/Operating Room and Surgical Nursing
British Columbia Inst of Technology (BC, Canada)

Personal and Culinary Services Related
The Art Inst of Pittsburgh (PA)
Lexington Coll (IL)

Petroleum Technology
British Columbia Inst of Technology (BC, Canada)
McNeese State U (LA)
Montana State U–Billings (MT)
Montana Tech of The U of Montana (MT)
Nicholls State U (LA)
U of Alaska Anchorage (AK)

Pharmacy
Clayton Coll & State U (GA)
Martin Methodist Coll (TN)

Pharmacy, Pharmaceutical Sciences, and Administration Related
Vermont Tech Coll (VT)

Pharmacy Technician
Baker Coll of Flint (MI)
Baker Coll of Jackson (MI)
Baker Coll of Muskegon (MI)
Florida Metropolitan U–Tampa Coll, Brandon (FL)
Idaho State U (ID)
Mount Aloysius Coll (PA)
Valdosta State U (GA)

Philosophy
Clayton Coll & State U (GA)
Dalton State Coll (GA)
Felician Coll (NJ)
Kwantlen U Coll (BC, Canada)
Martin Methodist Coll (TN)
Methodist Coll (NC)
Sacred Heart U (CT)
Thomas More Coll (KY)
Université Laval (QC, Canada)
The U of Tampa (FL)
U of the District of Columbia (DC)
U of Wisconsin–Green Bay (WI)
Utah Valley State Coll (UT)
York Coll of Pennsylvania (PA)

Photographic and Film/Video Technology
New England School of Communications (ME)

Photography
Academy of Art U (CA)
Andrews U (MI)
The Art Inst of Colorado (CO)
The Art Inst of Fort Lauderdale (FL)
The Art Inst of Pittsburgh (PA)
The Art Inst of Seattle (WA)
Cazenovia Coll (NY)
Central Christian Coll of Kansas (KS)
Corcoran Coll of Art and Design (DC)
New World School of the Arts (FL)
Pacific Union Coll (CA)
Paier Coll of Art, Inc. (CT)
Pillsbury Baptist Bible Coll (MN)
Rochester Inst of Technology (NY)
Sage Coll of Albany (NY)
The U of Maine at Augusta (ME)
Villa Julie Coll (MD)

Photojournalism
Southern Alberta Inst of Technology (AB, Canada)

Physical Education Teaching and Coaching
Adrian Coll (MI)
Central Christian Coll of Kansas (KS)
Clayton Coll & State U (GA)
Fresno Pacific U (CA)
Hillsdale Free Will Baptist Coll (OK)
Macon State Coll (GA)
Martin Methodist Coll (TN)
Methodist Coll (NC)
Mitchell Coll (CT)
U of Rio Grande (OH)

Physical Sciences
Bacone Coll (OK)
Central Christian Coll of Kansas (KS)
Faulkner U (AL)
Martin Methodist Coll (TN)
Mitchell Coll (CT)

Pennsylvania Coll of Technology (PA)
Roberts Wesleyan Coll (NY)
U of the District of Columbia (DC)
Utah Valley State Coll (UT)
Villa Julie Coll (MD)

Physical Science Technologies Related
The U of Akron (OH)
Western Kentucky U (KY)

Physical Therapist Assistant
Arkansas State U (AR)
Baker Coll of Flint (MI)
Baker Coll of Muskegon (MI)
Becker Coll (MA)
Central Christian Coll of Kansas (KS)
Central Pennsylvania Coll (PA)
Coll of St. Catherine (MN)
Fairleigh Dickinson U, Florham (NJ)
Finlandia U (MI)
Idaho State U (ID)
Kent State U (OH)
Loma Linda U (CA)
Missouri Western State Coll (MO)
Mountain State U (WV)
Mount Aloysius Coll (PA)
Mount St. Mary's Coll (CA)
New York U (NY)
Our Lady of the Lake Coll (LA)
Southern Illinois U Carbondale (IL)
South U (AL)
South U (GA)
U of Central Arkansas (AR)
U of Evansville (IN)
U of Indianapolis (IN)
U of Saint Francis (IN)
Wichita State U (KS)

Physical Therapy
Alvernia Coll (PA)
Briar Cliff U (IA)
Central Christian Coll of Kansas (KS)
Clarkson Coll (NE)
Clayton Coll & State U (GA)
Dalton State Coll (GA)
Davenport U, Lansing (MI)
Fairmont State U (WV)
Faulkner U (AL)
Lynn U (FL)
Macon State Coll (GA)
Martin Methodist Coll (TN)
Mercyhurst Coll (PA)
Shawnee State U (OH)
Southern Adventist U (TN)
U of Central Arkansas (AR)
U of Cincinnati (OH)
U of Evansville (IN)
Washburn U (KS)

Physician Assistant
Central Christian Coll of Kansas (KS)
Dalton State Coll (GA)
Southern Adventist U (TN)

Physics
Adrian Coll (MI)
Clayton Coll & State U (GA)
Dalton State Coll (GA)
Idaho State U (ID)
Macon State Coll (GA)
Mesa State Coll (CO)
Rochester Inst of Technology (NY)
Thomas Edison State Coll (NJ)
Thomas More Coll (KY)
U of the Virgin Islands (VI)
Utah Valley State Coll (UT)
York Coll of Pennsylvania (PA)

Piano and Organ
Bethel Coll (IN)
Central Christian Coll of Kansas (KS)
John Brown U (AR)

Kwantlen U Coll (BC, Canada)
New World School of the Arts (FL)
Pacific Union Coll (CA)

Pipefitting and Sprinkler Fitting
British Columbia Inst of Technology (BC, Canada)
Thompson Rivers U (BC, Canada)

Plant Nursery Management
Pennsylvania Coll of Technology (PA)
State U of NY Coll of A&T at Cobleskill (NY)

Plant Protection and Integrated Pest Management
North Carolina State U (NC)
Sterling Coll (VT)

Plant Sciences
State U of NY Coll of A&T at Cobleskill (NY)

Plant Sciences Related
Sterling Coll (VT)

Plastics Engineering Technology
British Columbia Inst of Technology (BC, Canada)
Ferris State U (MI)
Kent State U (OH)
Pennsylvania Coll of Technology (PA)
Penn State U at Erie, The Behrend Coll (PA)
Shawnee State U (OH)

Platemaking/Imaging
Pennsylvania Coll of Technology (PA)

Plumbing Technology
Pennsylvania Coll of Technology (PA)
Thompson Rivers U (BC, Canada)
Valdosta State U (GA)

Political Science and Government
Adrian Coll (MI)
Bacone Coll (OK)
Clayton Coll & State U (GA)
Dalton State Coll (GA)
Fresno Pacific U (CA)
Idaho State U (ID)
Indiana U–Purdue U Fort Wayne (IN)
Indiana Wesleyan U (IN)
Kwantlen U Coll (BC, Canada)
Macon State Coll (GA)
Methodist Coll (NC)
Richmond, The American International U in LondonUnited Kingdom)
Sacred Heart U (CT)
Thomas More Coll (KY)
Université Laval (QC, Canada)
The U of Scranton (PA)
The U of Tampa (FL)
The U of Toledo (OH)
U of Wisconsin–Green Bay (WI)
Villa Julie Coll (MD)
Xavier U (OH)
York Coll of Pennsylvania (PA)

Postal Management
Macon State Coll (GA)
Washburn U (KS)

Precision Production Trades
Valdosta State U (GA)

Precision Systems Maintenance and Repair Technologies Related
Arkansas Tech U (AR)
British Columbia Inst of Technology (BC, Canada)

Pre-Dentistry Studies
Central Christian Coll of Kansas (KS)
Concordia U Wisconsin (WI)
Newman U (KS)

Pre-Engineering
Anderson U (IN)
Atlantic Union Coll (MA)
Boise State U (ID)
Brescia U (KY)
Briar Cliff U (IA)
Campbell U (NC)
Charleston Southern U (SC)
Clayton Coll & State U (GA)
Columbus State U (GA)
Covenant Coll (GA)
Eastern Kentucky U (KY)
Edgewood Coll (WI)
Faulkner U (AL)
Ferris State U (MI)
Fort Valley State U (GA)
Friends U (KS)
Hannibal-LaGrange Coll (MO)
Keene State Coll (NH)
LaGrange Coll (GA)
Macon State Coll (GA)
Marian Coll (IN)
Medgar Evers Coll of the City U of NY (NY)
Mesa State Coll (CO)
Methodist Coll (NC)
Minnesota State U Mankato (MN)
Missouri Southern State U (MO)
Montana State U–Billings (MT)
Newman U (KS)
Niagara U (NY)
Northern State U (SD)
Pacific Union Coll (CA)
Richmond, The American International U in LondonUnited Kingdom)
St. Gregory's U (OK)
Schreiner U (TX)
Shawnee State U (OH)
Siena Heights U (MI)
Southern Utah U (UT)
U of New Hampshire (NH)
U of Sioux Falls (SD)
Vaughn Coll of Aeronautics and Technology (NY)
Washburn U (KS)
West Virginia State U (WV)
Winona State U (MN)

Pre-Law Studies
Calumet Coll of Saint Joseph (IN)
Newman U (KS)
Northwest U (WA)
Peirce Coll (PA)
Thomas More Coll (KY)

Pre-Medical Studies
Central Christian Coll of Kansas (KS)
Concordia U Wisconsin (WI)
Newman U (KS)
Schiller International USpain)
Schiller International UUnited Kingdom)
State U of NY Coll of A&T at Cobleskill (NY)
U of Ottawa (ON, Canada)

Pre-Nursing Studies
Central Christian Coll of Kansas (KS)
Concordia U Wisconsin (WI)
Trinity International U (IL)

Pre-Pharmacy Studies
Central Christian Coll of Kansas (KS)
Dalton State Coll (GA)
Emmanuel Coll (GA)
Macon State Coll (GA)
Thompson Rivers U (BC, Canada)

Pre-Theology/Pre-Ministerial Studies
Manchester Coll (IN)
Nazarene Bible Coll (CO)
St. Gregory's U (OK)

Pre-Veterinary Studies
Central Christian Coll of Kansas (KS)
Newman U (KS)
Schiller International USpain)
Schiller International UUnited Kingdom)
Shawnee State U (OH)

Printing Management
Central Missouri State U (MO)
Southern Alberta Inst of Technology (AB, Canada)

Printmaking
Academy of Art U (CA)
New World School of the Arts (FL)

Professional Studies
Ohio Valley Coll (WV)
Thomas Coll (ME)

Psychiatric/Mental Health Services Technology
Lake Superior State U (MI)
Northern Kentucky U (KY)
Pennsylvania Coll of Technology (PA)
The U of Toledo (OH)

Psychology
Adrian Coll (MI)
Bluefield State Coll (WV)
Calumet Coll of Saint Joseph (IN)
Central Christian Coll of Kansas (KS)
Central Methodist U (MO)
Chestnut Hill Coll (PA)
Crown Coll (MN)
Dalton State Coll (GA)
Davis & Elkins Coll (WV)
Eastern New Mexico U (NM)
Felician Coll (NJ)
Fresno Pacific U (CA)
Heritage U (WA)
Hillsdale Free Will Baptist Coll (OK)
Indiana U–Purdue U Fort Wayne (IN)
Kwantlen U Coll (BC, Canada)
Lourdes Coll (OH)
Macon State Coll (GA)
Marian Coll (IN)
Martin Methodist Coll (TN)
Methodist Coll (NC)
Mitchell Coll (CT)
Montana State U–Billings (MT)
Mount Olive Coll (NC)
Newbury Coll (MA)
North Central U (MN)
Richmond, The American International U in LondonUnited Kingdom)
Sacred Heart U (CT)
Salem International U (WV)
Siena Heights U (MI)
Thomas More Coll (KY)
U of Rio Grande (OH)
The U of Tampa (FL)
U of Wisconsin–Green Bay (WI)
Utah Valley State Coll (UT)
Villa Julie Coll (MD)
Wright State U (OH)
Xavier U (OH)

Psychology Teacher Education
Central Christian Coll of Kansas (KS)

Public Administration
Central Methodist U (MO)
David N. Myers U (OH)
Indiana U Bloomington (IN)
Indiana U Northwest (IN)
Indiana U–Purdue U Fort Wayne (IN)

Indiana U–Purdue U Indianapolis (IN)
Indiana U South Bend (IN)
Macon State Coll (GA)
Medgar Evers Coll of the City U of NY (NY)
Point Park U (PA)
Thomas Edison State Coll (NJ)
The U of Maine at Augusta (ME)
U of Regina (SK, Canada)
U of the District of Columbia (DC)

Public Administration and Social Service Professions Related
Indiana U–Purdue U Fort Wayne (IN)
The U of Akron (OH)
U of Saint Francis (IN)

Public Health
Martin Methodist Coll (TN)
U of Alaska Fairbanks (AK)

Public Policy Analysis
Indiana U Bloomington (IN)
Saint Peter's Coll (NJ)

Public Relations, Advertising, and Applied Communication Related
Champlain Coll (VT)
Madonna U (MI)

Public Relations/Image Management
Champlain Coll (VT)
John Brown U (AR)
Johnson & Wales U (RI)
Madonna U (MI)
New England School of Communications (ME)
Xavier U (OH)

Purchasing, Procurement/ Acquisitions and Contracts Management
Mercyhurst Coll (PA)
Saint Joseph's U (PA)
Strayer U (DC)
Thomas Edison State Coll (NJ)
U of Management and Technology (VA)

Quality Control and Safety Technologies Related
Madonna U (MI)

Quality Control Technology
Baker Coll of Cadillac (MI)
Baker Coll of Flint (MI)
Baker Coll of Muskegon (MI)
Eastern Kentucky U (KY)
Pennsylvania Coll of Technology (PA)
U of Cincinnati (OH)

Rabbinical Studies
Université Laval (QC, Canada)

Radio and Television
Academy of Art U (CA)
The Art Inst of Fort Lauderdale (FL)
The Art Inst of Pittsburgh (PA)
Ashland U (OH)
Newbury Coll (MA)
New England School of Communications (ME)
Northwestern Coll (MN)
Ohio U (OH)
Ohio U–Zanesville (OH)
Salem International U (WV)
Southern Alberta Inst of Technology (AB, Canada)
Xavier U (OH)
York Coll of Pennsylvania (PA)

Radio and Television Broadcasting Technology
British Columbia Inst of Technology (BC, Canada)
Lyndon State Coll (VT)
Mountain State U (WV)

The New England Inst of Art (MA)
New England School of Communications (ME)
New York Inst of Technology (NY)
Southern Adventist U (TN)

Radiologic Technology/ Science
Allen Coll (IA)
Baker Coll of Clinton Township (MI)
Baker Coll of Muskegon (MI)
Boise State U (ID)
Champlain Coll (VT)
Clarkson Coll (NE)
Clayton Coll & State U (GA)
Dalton State Coll (GA)
Indiana U Northwest (IN)
Indiana U–Purdue U Fort Wayne (IN)
Lewis-Clark State Coll (ID)
Mansfield U of Pennsylvania (PA)
Mesa State Coll (CO)
Midwestern State U (TX)
Mountain State U (WV)
Mount Aloysius Coll (PA)
Nebraska Methodist Coll (NE)
Newman U (KS)
Washburn U (KS)

Radio, Television, and Digital Communication Related
Southern Alberta Inst of Technology (AB, Canada)

Range Science and Management
Sterling Coll (VT)

Real Estate
British Columbia Inst of Technology (BC, Canada)
Fairmont State U (WV)
Ferris State U (MI)
Kent State U (OH)
Lamar U (TX)
Saint Francis U (PA)
Southern U at New Orleans (LA)
Thomas Edison State Coll (NJ)
U of Cincinnati (OH)

Receptionist
Baker Coll of Allen Park (MI)
The U of Montana–Missoula (MT)

Recording Arts Technology
New England School of Communications (ME)

Religious Education
Aquinas Coll (MI)
The Baptist Coll of Florida (FL)
Calvary Bible Coll and Theological Seminary (MO)
Central Baptist Coll (AR)
Central Bible Coll (MO)
Cincinnati Christian U (OH)
Circleville Bible Coll (OH)
Cornerstone U (MI)
Dallas Baptist U (TX)
Hillsdale Free Will Baptist Coll (OK)
Houghton Coll (NY)
Indiana Wesleyan U (IN)
Manhattan Christian Coll (KS)
Mercyhurst Coll (PA)
Methodist Coll (NC)
MidAmerica Nazarene U (KS)
Nazarene Bible Coll (CO)
Reformed Bible Coll (MI)
Warner Pacific Coll (OR)
Washington Bible Coll (MD)

Religious/Sacred Music
Aquinas Coll (MI)
The Baptist Coll of Florida (FL)
Central Bible Coll (MO)

Cincinnati Christian U (OH)
Circleville Bible Coll (OH)
Clearwater Christian Coll (FL)
Hillsdale Free Will Baptist Coll (OK)
Immaculata U (PA)
Indiana Wesleyan U (IN)
Manhattan Christian Coll (KS)
MidAmerica Nazarene U (KS)
Mount Vernon Nazarene U (OH)
Nazarene Bible Coll (CO)
North Central U (MN)
Saint Joseph's Coll (IN)
Vennard Coll (IA)

Religious Studies
Adrian Coll (MI)
Aquinas Coll (MI)
Atlantic Union Coll (MA)
Brescia U (KY)
Brewton-Parker Coll (GA)
Calumet Coll of Saint Joseph (IN)
Central Christian Coll of Kansas (KS)
Circleville Bible Coll (OH)
Felician Coll (NJ)
Global U of the Assemblies of God (MO)
Grace Bible Coll (MI)
Griggs U (MD)
Holy Apostles Coll and Seminary (CT)
Howard Payne U (TX)
Kentucky Mountain Bible Coll (KY)
Liberty U (VA)
Lourdes Coll (OH)
Madonna U (MI)
Manchester Coll (IN)
Maranatha Baptist Bible Coll (WI)
Martin Methodist Coll (TN)
MidAmerica Nazarene U (KS)
Missouri Baptist U (MO)
Mount Marty Coll (SD)
Mount Olive Coll (NC)
Sacred Heart U (CT)
Shaw U (NC)
Tabor Coll (KS)
Thomas More Coll (KY)
The U of Findlay (OH)
U of Sioux Falls (SD)
Vennard Coll (IA)
Washington Bible Coll (MD)

Religious Studies Related
Lindsey Wilson Coll (KY)

Resort Management
The Art Inst of Pittsburgh (PA)
Rochester Inst of Technology (NY)
Thompson Rivers U (BC, Canada)

Respiratory Care Therapy
Ball State U (IN)
California Coll for Health Sciences (UT)
Columbia Union Coll (MD)
Dakota State U (SD)
Dalton State Coll (GA)
Faulkner U (AL)
Ferris State U (MI)
Gannon U (PA)
Gwynedd-Mercy Coll (PA)
Indiana U Northwest (IN)
Indiana U–Purdue U Indianapolis (IN)
Lamar U (TX)
Loma Linda U (CA)
Macon State Coll (GA)
Mansfield U of Pennsylvania (PA)
Midland Lutheran Coll (NE)
Missouri Southern State U (MO)
Molloy Coll (NY)
Morehead State U (KY)
Mountain State U (WV)

Nebraska Methodist Coll (NE)
Newman U (KS)
Nicholls State U (LA)
Northern Kentucky U (KY)
Our Lady of Holy Cross Coll (LA)
Point Park U (PA)
St. Augustine Coll (IL)
Shawnee State U (OH)
Shenandoah U (VA)
Southern Adventist U (TN)
Southern Illinois U Carbondale (IL)
Thomas Edison State Coll (NJ)
Universidad Adventista de las Antillas (PR)
The U of Akron (OH)
U of Arkansas at Fort Smith (AR)
The U of Montana–Missoula (MT)
U of Pittsburgh at Johnstown (PA)
U of Southern Indiana (IN)
U of the District of Columbia (DC)
The U of Toledo (OH)
Vermont Tech Coll (VT)
Weber State U (UT)
Western Kentucky U (KY)
York Coll of Pennsylvania (PA)
Youngstown State U (OH)

Respiratory Therapy Technician
Thompson Rivers U (BC, Canada)

Restaurant, Culinary, and Catering Management
Johnson & Wales U (RI)
Lexington Coll (IL)
The U of Akron (OH)
U of New Hampshire (NH)

Restaurant/Food Services Management
The Art Inst of Pittsburgh (PA)
Lexington Coll (IL)
Rochester Inst of Technology (NY)
U of New Hampshire (NH)

Retailing
Johnson & Wales U (RI)

Robotics Technology
British Columbia Inst of Technology (BC, Canada)
Indiana U–Purdue U Indianapolis (IN)
Purdue U (IN)
U of Rio Grande (OH)

Safety/Security Technology
John Jay Coll of Criminal Justice, the City U of NY (NY)
Keene State Coll (NH)
Lamar U (TX)
Madonna U (MI)
Ohio U (OH)
U of Cincinnati (OH)

Sales and Marketing/ Marketing And Distribution Teacher Education
Central Christian Coll of Kansas (KS)

Sales, Distribution and Marketing
Baker Coll of Flint (MI)
Baker Coll of Jackson (MI)
Central Pennsylvania Coll (PA)
Champlain Coll (VT)
Dalton State Coll (GA)
Johnson & Wales U (RI)
Thomas Edison State Coll (NJ)
Thompson Rivers U (BC, Canada)
The U of Findlay (OH)

Science Teacher Education
Central Christian Coll of Kansas (KS)
Martin Methodist Coll (TN)
U of Cincinnati (OH)

Science Technologies Related
British Columbia Inst of Technology (BC, Canada)
Madonna U (MI)
Ohio Valley Coll (WV)

Science, Technology and Society
Samford U (AL)

Sculpture
Academy of Art U (CA)
New World School of the Arts (FL)

Secondary Education
Central Christian Coll of Kansas (KS)
Dalton State Coll (GA)
Mountain State U (WV)
Utah Valley State Coll (UT)
Vennard Coll (IA)

Security and Loss Prevention
John Jay Coll of Criminal Justice, the City U of NY (NY)
York Coll of Pennsylvania (PA)
Youngstown State U (OH)

Security and Protective Services Related
Ohio U (OH)

Selling Skills and Sales
The U of Akron (OH)

Sheet Metal Technology
British Columbia Inst of Technology (BC, Canada)
Montana State U–Billings (MT)

Sign Language Interpretation and Translation
Bethel Coll (IN)
Cincinnati Christian U (OH)
Coll of St. Catherine (MN)
Fairmont State U (WV)
Gardner-Webb U (NC)
Mount Aloysius Coll (PA)
North Central U (MN)
Roanoke Bible Coll (NC)
Rochester Inst of Technology (NY)
Tennessee Temple U (TN)
U of Louisville (KY)

Slavic Languages
U of Ottawa (ON, Canada)

Small Business Administration
Central Christian Coll of Kansas (KS)
Lewis-Clark State Coll (ID)

Small Engine Mechanics and Repair Technology
British Columbia Inst of Technology (BC, Canada)
The U of Montana–Missoula (MT)

Social Psychology
Central Christian Coll of Kansas (KS)
Kwantlen U Coll (BC, Canada)
Park U (MO)

Social Sciences
Adrian Coll (MI)
Campbellsville U (KY)
Central Christian Coll of Kansas (KS)
Clayton Coll & State U (GA)
Crown Coll (MN)
Evangel U (MO)
Faulkner U (AL)
Felician Coll (NJ)
Heritage U (WA)
Indiana Wesleyan U (IN)

Kwantlen U Coll (BC, Canada)
Lindsey Wilson Coll (KY)
Long Island U, Brooklyn Campus (NY)
Mesa State Coll (CO)
Montana State U–Northern (MT)
Newbury Coll (MA)
Ohio U (OH)
Ohio U–Zanesville (OH)
Richmond, The American International U in LondonUnited Kingdom)
Sage Coll of Albany (NY)
Saint Peter's Coll (NJ)
Samford U (AL)
Shawnee State U (OH)
State U of NY Empire State Coll (NY)
Tri-State U (IN)
U of Cincinnati (OH)
The U of Findlay (OH)
The U of Maine at Augusta (ME)
U of Sioux Falls (SD)
U of Southern Indiana (IN)
The U of Toledo (OH)
Utah Valley State Coll (UT)
Valparaiso U (IN)
Villa Julie Coll (MD)
Warner Pacific Coll (OR)
Wayland Baptist U (TX)

Social Science Teacher Education
Central Christian Coll of Kansas (KS)

Social Studies Teacher Education
Central Christian Coll of Kansas (KS)

Social Work
Central Christian Coll of Kansas (KS)
Champlain Coll (VT)
Dalton State Coll (GA)
Edinboro U of Pennsylvania (PA)
Haskell Indian Nations U (KS)
Indiana U East (IN)
Martin Methodist Coll (TN)
Methodist Coll (NC)
Northern State U (SD)
Siena Heights U (MI)
Southern U at New Orleans (LA)
Suffolk U (MA)
U of Cincinnati (OH)
U of Rio Grande (OH)
The U of Toledo (OH)
U of Wisconsin–Green Bay (WI)
Wright State U (OH)
Youngstown State U (OH)

Sociology
Adrian Coll (MI)
Bacone Coll (OK)
Central Christian Coll of Kansas (KS)
Clayton Coll & State U (GA)
Dalton State Coll (GA)
Felician Coll (NJ)
Fresno Pacific U (CA)
Friends U (KS)
Grand View Coll (IA)
Kwantlen U Coll (BC, Canada)
Lourdes Coll (OH)
Macon State Coll (GA)
Martin Methodist Coll (TN)
Methodist Coll (NC)
Montana State U–Billings (MT)
Newbury Coll (MA)
Penn State U Univ Park Campus (PA)
Richmond, The American International U in LondonUnited Kingdom)
Sacred Heart U (CT)
Thomas More Coll (KY)
U of Dubuque (IA)

U of Rio Grande (OH)
The U of Scranton (PA)
The U of Tampa (FL)
Villa Julie Coll (MD)
Wright State U (OH)
Xavier U (OH)

Soil Conservation
U of Minnesota, Crookston (MN)

Soil Science and Agronomy
Sterling Coll (VT)

Soil Sciences Related
Sterling Coll (VT)

Solar Energy Technology
Pennsylvania Coll of Technology (PA)

Spanish
Adrian Coll (MI)
Central Christian Coll of Kansas (KS)
Chestnut Hill Coll (PA)
Clayton Coll & State U (GA)
Fresno Pacific U (CA)
Friends U (KS)
Idaho State U (ID)
Indiana U–Purdue U Fort Wayne (IN)
Methodist Coll (NC)
Sacred Heart U (CT)
Thomas More Coll (KY)
The U of Tampa (FL)
U of Wisconsin–Green Bay (WI)
Xavier U (OH)

Spanish Language Teacher Education
Central Christian Coll of Kansas (KS)

Special Education
Edinboro U of Pennsylvania (PA)
Montana State U–Billings (MT)
St. Augustine Coll (IL)

Special Education (Mentally Retarded)
Valdosta State U (GA)

Special Education Related
Minot State U (ND)

Special Education (Speech Or Language Impaired)
U of Nebraska at Omaha (NE)

Special Products Marketing
The Art Inst of Houston (TX)
Ball State U (IN)
Ferris State U (MI)
Johnson & Wales U (FL)
Johnson & Wales U (RI)
Lamar U (TX)
Newbury Coll (MA)
Northern Michigan U (MI)
Purdue U Calumet (IN)
U of Minnesota, Crookston (MN)

Speech and Rhetoric
Clayton Coll & State U (GA)
Dalton State Coll (GA)
Ferris State U (MI)
Macon State Coll (GA)
Madonna U (MI)

Speech-Language Pathology
Baker Coll of Muskegon (MI)
Indiana State U (IN)
Southern Adventist U (TN)

Speech Teacher Education
Central Christian Coll of Kansas (KS)

Sport and Fitness Administration
Central Christian Coll of Kansas (KS)
Lake Superior State U (MI)
Mitchell Coll (CT)
Northwood U (MI)
Northwood U, Texas Campus (TX)

Thompson Rivers U (BC, Canada)
Webber International U (FL)

Statistics
Huron U USA in LondonUnited Kingdom)

Substance Abuse/Addiction Counseling
Bacone Coll (OK)
Calumet Coll of Saint Joseph (IN)
Charles R. Drew U of Medicine and Science (CA)
Indiana Wesleyan U (IN)
Keene State Coll (NH)
Newman U (KS)
St. Augustine Coll (IL)
The U of Akron (OH)
U of Great Falls (MT)
The U of Toledo (OH)

Surgical Technology
Baker Coll of Clinton Township (MI)
Baker Coll of Flint (MI)
Baker Coll of Jackson (MI)
Baker Coll of Muskegon (MI)
Boise State U (ID)
Cabarrus Coll of Health Sciences (NC)
Florida Metropolitan U-Tampa Coll, Brandon (FL)
Loma Linda U (CA)
Mercy Coll of Health Sciences (IA)
Montana State U–Billings (MT)
Mountain State U (WV)
Mount Aloysius Coll (PA)
Our Lady of the Lake Coll (LA)
The U of Akron (OH)
U of Arkansas at Fort Smith (AR)
The U of Montana–Missoula (MT)
U of Pittsburgh at Johnstown (PA)
U of Saint Francis (IN)
Valdosta State U (GA)

Survey Technology
British Columbia Inst of Technology (BC, Canada)
Ferris State U (MI)
Glenville State Coll (WV)
Kansas State U (KS)
Paul Smith's Coll of Arts and Sciences (NY)
Pennsylvania Coll of Technology (PA)
Thomas Edison State Coll (NJ)
The U of Akron (OH)
U of Alaska Anchorage (AK)
U of New Hampshire (NH)

System Administration
Coleman Coll, La Mesa (CA)
DeVry U, Colorado Springs (CO)
Huron U USA in LondonUnited Kingdom)
National American U, Denver (CO)
Thompson Rivers U (BC, Canada)
Western Governors U (UT)

System, Networking, and Lan/Wan Management
Baker Coll of Auburn Hills (MI)
Champlain Coll (VT)
Huron U USA in LondonUnited Kingdom)
National American U, Denver (CO)
Peirce Coll (PA)
Thompson Rivers U (BC, Canada)

Taxation
British Columbia Inst of Technology (BC, Canada)

Teacher Assistant/Aide
Alabama State U (AL)
Alverno Coll (WI)
Boise State U (ID)
Dordt Coll (IA)
Johnson Bible Coll (TN)
Lamar U (TX)
Martin Methodist Coll (TN)
Mount Ida Coll (MA)
New Mexico Highlands U (NM)
New Mexico State U (NM)
Our Lady of Holy Cross Coll (LA)
The U of Akron (OH)
U of New Mexico (NM)

Technical and Business Writing
Ferris State U (MI)
Murray State U (KY)
Paul Smith's Coll of Arts and Sciences (NY)

Technical Teacher Education
Eastern Kentucky U (KY)
New York Inst of Technology (NY)
Northern Kentucky U (KY)
Western Kentucky U (KY)

Technology/Industrial Arts Teacher Education
Arkansas State U (AR)

Telecommunications
Briarcliffe Coll (NY)
Capitol Coll (MD)
Champlain Coll (VT)
Clayton Coll & State U (GA)
Coll of Saint Mary (NE)
Columbia Coll Hollywood (CA)
Inter American U of PR, Bayamón Campus (PR)
Salem International U (WV)
State U of NY Coll of A&T at Cobleskill (NY)
Vermont Tech Coll (VT)

Telecommunications Technology
Penn State U Altoona Coll (PA)
Penn State U at Erie, The Behrend Coll (PA)
Penn State U Berks Cmps of Berks-Lehigh Valley Coll (PA)
Penn State U Schuylkill Campus of the Capital Coll (PA)
Southern Alberta Inst of Technology (AB, Canada)

Theatre Design and Technology
Indiana U Bloomington (IN)
U of Rio Grande (OH)

Theatre/Theatre Arts Management
Haskell Indian Nations U (KS)

Theological and Ministerial Studies Related
Bacone Coll (OK)
Brescia U (KY)
Central Baptist Coll (AR)
Pillsbury Baptist Bible Coll (MN)
U of Saint Francis (IN)

Theology
Appalachian Bible Coll (WV)
The Baptist Coll of Florida (FL)
Briar Cliff U (IA)
Central Christian Coll of Kansas (KS)
Circleville Bible Coll (OH)
Creighton U (NE)
Franciscan U of Steubenville (OH)
Griggs U (MD)
Heritage Bible Coll (NC)
Marian Coll (IN)
Martin Methodist Coll (TN)

Theology

Ohio Dominican U (OH)
Sacred Heart Major
  Seminary (MI)
Université Laval (QC,
  Canada)
Warner Southern Coll (FL)
Washington Bible Coll (MD)
William Jessup U (CA)
Xavier U (OH)

Therapeutic Recreation
Indiana Inst of Technology
  (IN)
Johnson & Wales U (RI)
Mitchell Coll (CT)
U of Southern Maine (ME)

Tool and Die Technology
Pennsylvania Coll of
  Technology (PA)

**Tourism and Travel Services
Management**
Baker Coll of Flint (MI)
Baker Coll of Muskegon (MI)
Black Hills State U (SD)
Brigham Young U–Hawaii
  (HI)
British Columbia Inst of
  Technology (BC, Canada)
Central Pennsylvania Coll
  (PA)
Champlain Coll (VT)
Inter American U of PR,
  Ponce Campus (PR)
International Coll of the
  Cayman IslandsCayman
  Islands)
Johnson & Wales U (FL)
Johnson & Wales U (RI)
Mesa State Coll (CO)
Midland Lutheran Coll (NE)
Mountain State U (WV)
National American U,
  Colorado Springs (CO)
Newbury Coll (MA)
Ohio U (OH)
Paul Smith's Coll of Arts and
  Sciences (NY)
Pennsylvania Coll of
  Technology (PA)
Robert Morris Coll (IL)
Rochester Inst of Technology
  (NY)
Schiller International U (FL)
Southern Alberta Inst of
  Technology (AB, Canada)
Sullivan U (KY)

The U of Akron (OH)
U of Alaska Southeast (AK)
The U of Montana–Western
  (MT)
Webber International U (FL)

**Tourism and Travel Services
Marketing**
Champlain Coll (VT)
Johnson & Wales U (RI)
Ohio U (OH)
Pontifical Catholic U of
  Puerto Rico (PR)
State U of NY Coll of A&T at
  Cobleskill (NY)
The U of Montana–Western
  (MT)

Tourism Promotion
Champlain Coll (VT)
Thompson Rivers U (BC,
  Canada)

**Trade and Industrial Teacher
Education**
British Columbia Inst of
  Technology (BC, Canada)
Cincinnati Christian U (OH)
Indiana State U (IN)
Murray State U (KY)
Purdue U (IN)
Valdosta State U (GA)

**Transportation and Highway
Engineering**
British Columbia Inst of
  Technology (BC, Canada)

**Transportation and
Materials Moving Related**
Southern Alberta Inst of
  Technology (AB, Canada)

Transportation Technology
Baker Coll of Flint (MI)
Maine Maritime Academy
  (ME)
U of Cincinnati (OH)
The U of Toledo (OH)

**Turf and Turfgrass
Management**
North Carolina State U (NC)
Pennsylvania Coll of
  Technology (PA)
State U of NY Coll of A&T at
  Cobleskill (NY)
U of Massachusetts Amherst
  (MA)

Urban Studies/Affairs
Beulah Heights Bible Coll
  (GA)
Clayton Coll & State U (GA)
Mount St. Mary's Coll (CA)
Saint Peter's Coll (NJ)
U of the District of Columbia
  (DC)
U of Wisconsin–Green Bay
  (WI)

**Vehicle and Vehicle Parts
And Accessories Marketing**
Northwood U (MI)
Northwood U, Florida
  Campus (FL)
Northwood U, Texas Campus
  (TX)
Pennsylvania Coll of
  Technology (PA)

**Vehicle/Equipment
Operation**
Baker Coll of Flint (MI)
The U of Montana–Missoula
  (MT)

**Vehicle Maintenance and
Repair Technologies
Related**
British Columbia Inst of
  Technology (BC, Canada)
Pennsylvania Coll of
  Technology (PA)
U of Alaska Fairbanks (AK)

**Veterinary/Animal Health
Technology**
Baker Coll of Cadillac (MI)
Baker Coll of Jackson (MI)
Baker Coll of Muskegon (MI)
Becker Coll (MA)
Medaille Coll (NY)
Morehead State U (KY)
Northwestern State U of
  Louisiana (LA)
Purdue U (IN)
Thompson Rivers U (BC,
  Canada)
The U of Maine at Augusta
  (ME)
Wilson Coll (PA)

Veterinary Sciences
Clayton Coll & State U (GA)
Fort Valley State U (GA)
Martin Methodist Coll (TN)

Veterinary Technology
Argosy U/Twin Cities, Eagan
  (MN)
Becker Coll (MA)
Fairmont State U (WV)
Fort Valley State U (GA)
Medaille Coll (NY)
Mount Ida Coll (MA)
National American U, Rapid
  City (SD)
Vermont Tech Coll (VT)

**Violin, Viola, Guitar and
Other Stringed Instruments**
Five Towns Coll (NY)
Kwantlen U Coll (BC,
  Canada)
New World School of the Arts
  (FL)

Visual and Performing Arts
Briarcliffe Coll (NY)
Indiana U East (IN)
Miami International U of Art &
  Design (FL)
Thomas More Coll (KY)
U of Arkansas at Fort Smith
  (AR)

Voice and Opera
Central Christian Coll of
  Kansas (KS)
Five Towns Coll (NY)
Kwantlen U Coll (BC,
  Canada)
New World School of the Arts
  (FL)

**Watchmaking and
Jewelrymaking**
Fashion Inst of Technology
  (NY)

**Water Quality and
Wastewater Treatment
Management And Recycling
Technology**
Lake Superior State U (MI)
Murray State U (KY)
U of the District of Columbia
  (DC)
Wright State U (OH)

**Web/Multimedia
Management and
Webmaster**
Academy of Art U (CA)
The Art Inst of Pittsburgh
  (PA)

Central Pennsylvania Coll
  (PA)
Champlain Coll (VT)
Davenport U, Dearborn (MI)
Davenport U, Grand Rapids
  (MI)
Davenport U, Holland (MI)
Davenport U, Kalamazoo
  (MI)
Davenport U, Warren (MI)
Huron U USA in
  LondonUnited Kingdom)
Lewis-Clark State Coll (ID)
Limestone Coll (SC)
New England School of
  Communications (ME)

**Web Page, Digital/
Multimedia and Information
Resources Design**
The Art Inst of Atlanta (GA)
The Art Inst of Houston (TX)
The Art Inst of Pittsburgh
  (PA)
The Art Inst of Portland (OR)
The Art Insts International
  Minnesota (MN)
Baker Coll of Allen Park (MI)
Champlain Coll (VT)
Huron U USA in
  LondonUnited Kingdom)
National American U, Denver
  (CO)
New England School of
  Communications (ME)
Pennsylvania Coll of
  Technology (PA)
Robert Morris Coll (IL)
Strayer U (DC)
Thompson Rivers U (BC,
  Canada)
Utah Valley State Coll (UT)

Welding Technology
Boise State U (ID)
British Columbia Inst of
  Technology (BC, Canada)
Excelsior Coll (NY)
Ferris State U (MI)
Georgia Southwestern State
  U (GA)
Idaho State U (ID)
Lamar U (TX)
Lewis-Clark State Coll (ID)
Mesa State Coll (CO)
Montana State U–Northern
  (MT)

Oakland City U (IN)
Pennsylvania Coll of
  Technology (PA)
Southern Alberta Inst of
  Technology (AB, Canada)
U of Alaska Anchorage (AK)
The U of Montana–Missoula
  (MT)
The U of Toledo (OH)
Utah Valley State Coll (UT)
Valdosta State U (GA)

Western Civilization
Central Christian Coll of
  Kansas (KS)

**Wildlife and Wildlands
Science And Management**
British Columbia Inst of
  Technology (BC, Canada)
Martin Methodist Coll (TN)
State U of NY Coll of A&T at
  Cobleskill (NY)
Sterling Coll (VT)
U of Minnesota, Crookston
  (MN)
Winona State U (MN)

Wildlife Biology
Central Christian Coll of
  Kansas (KS)
Martin Methodist Coll (TN)

**Wind/Percussion
Instruments**
Five Towns Coll (NY)
New World School of the Arts
  (FL)

Women'S Studies
Indiana U–Purdue U Fort
  Wayne (IN)
Nazarene Bible Coll (CO)

Woodworking Related
Pennsylvania Coll of
  Technology (PA)

Word Processing
Baker Coll of Allen Park (MI)
Huron U USA in
  LondonUnited Kingdom)

Youth Ministry
Central Christian Coll of
  Kansas (KS)

Zoology/Animal Biology
Central Christian Coll of
  Kansas (KS)
Martin Methodist Coll (TN)

Alphabetical Listing of Two-Year Colleges

In this index, the page locations of profiles are printed in regular type, **Special Messages** in *italics*, and **In-Depth Descriptions** in **bold type**. When there is more than one number in **bold type**, it indicates that the institution has more than one **In-Depth Description;** in most such cases, the first of the series is a general institutional description.

NOTES

NOTES

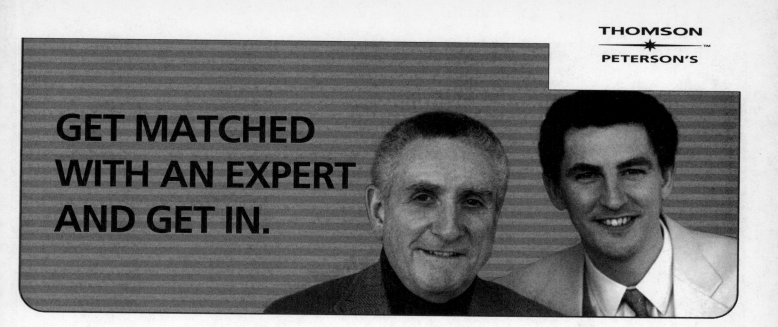